Masterpieces
of the Drama

Alexander W. Allison   Late of The University of Michigan

Arthur J. Carr   Williams College

Arthur M. Eastman   Virginia Polytechnic Institute
and State University

Masterpieces of the Drama

FIFTH EDITION

MACMILLAN PUBLISHING COMPANY
New York

Macmillan Publishing Company
866 Third Avenue, New York, New York 10022

Library of Congress Cataloging-in-Publication Data
Main entry under title:
Masterpieces of the drama.
    1. Drama—Collections.   I. Allison, Alexander W.
II. Carr, Arthur Japheth.
III. Eastman, Arthur M.
PN6112.M38 1986   808.82   85-13600
ISBN 0-02-301970-0

Printing: 4 5 6 7 8   Year: 7 8 9 0 1 2 3 4

ISBN 0-02-301970-0
NB2I

Preface

The fifth edition of *Masterpieces of the Drama* offers thirty plays from across the centuries, the number and variety meeting, we hope, the requirements of a wide range of drama courses. We have not grouped the plays by types, for generic boundaries are notoriously imprecise; nor have we fitted the plays into neat historical categories, although they appear here in the order of their stage presentations, for great literature, if rooted in a particular age and culture, yet branches outward across time. Plays are written to be staged, of course, and the theater is their proper home. Nonetheless, each actor, each director, each staging stamps such a unique image on a play that we have been content to present here the texts with little theatrical commentary. Students of literature and theater will read and render them according to their individual bents.

Excellence has remained the chief criterion for inclusion, although we acknowledge the vagaries of fluctuating tastes and fashions. We keenly regret that our occasional inability to negotiate copyright arrangements has denied the reader certain authors, certain plays; and space, inevitably, has circumscribed our offering.

In response to advices from the field, we have regretfully dropped Webster's *Duchess of Malfi;* we have replaced Shakespeare's *Henry IV, Part I,* with *Othello,* although Falstaff's departure from these pages grieves us; we have abandoned Molière's *Miser* for his *Tartuffe,* not least to gain the benefit of Richard Wilbur's gift as translator; and although Strindberg's *Ghost Sonata* heralded a new kind of drama in its day, that play is good in vain, to paraphrase Dr. Johnson, that is not read: we have replaced it with *Miss Julie.* And we take pleasure in adding Harold Pinter's *The Caretaker* and the brilliant improvization of Athol Fugard, John Kani, and Winston Ntshona, *Sizwe Bansi Is Dead.*

In carrying out our latest revision, we wish to offer particular thanks to the persons who made scores of comments and suggestions that we seriously weighed and often followed, even though not all could be accommodated and reconciled. We hope these many advisors will recognize the evidences of their contributions.

Contents

Introduction   1

Agamemnon   7
Aeschylus

Oedipus Rex   35
Sophocles

Lysistrata   63
Aristophanes

The Bacchae   89
Euripides

The Second Shepherds' Play   119
Anonymous

Othello   135
William Shakespeare

Volpone, or the Fox   193
Ben Jonson

Tartuffe   253
Molière

The Country Wife   287
William Wycherley

Phaedra   341
Jean Racine

The Rivals   367
  Richard Brinsley Sheridan

Miss Julie   411
  August Strindberg

Hedda Gabler   433
  Henrik Ibsen

The Importance
of Being Earnest   479
  Oscar Wilde

The Cherry Orchard   515
  Anton Chekhov

Riders to the Sea   545
  John Millington Synge

Six Characters in Search of
an Author   553
  Luigi Pirandello

Saint Joan   585
  Bernard Shaw

Juno and the Paycock   641
  Sean O'Casey

Desire Under the Elms   677
  Eugene O'Neill

The House
of Bernarda Alba   711
Federico Garcia Lorca

The Good Woman
of Setzuan   737
Bertolt Brecht

The Glass Menagerie   779
Tennessee Williams

Death of a Salesman   815
Arthur Miller

All That Fall
and
Act Without Words I   867
Samuel Beckett

The Caretaker   885
Harold Pinter

Dutchman   917
Imamu Amiri Baraka

Sizwe Bansi Is Dead   929
*Athol Fugard,
John Kani, and
Winston Ntshona*

Equus   951
Peter Shaffer

Introduction

"All the world's a stage,
And all the men and women merely players;
They have their exits and their entrances,
And one man in his time plays many parts. . ."

—Shakespeare, *As You Like It*

In calling the world itself a stage, Shakespeare is uttering more than a striking metaphor. Drama—what may be called unconscious drama—really does underlie a great deal of human experience. Much of what we know we learn by imitation, by acting parts, by practicing what we shall say and do. Children's games of "Let's pretend" significantly prepare for future social roles and activities. The implications of such natural playacting are vast, for good and for ill—for good, because individual and social happiness depends on right acting; for ill, because misrepresentations, deceit, mischief, and falsehood can also be learned by imitation. Hence, the essentials of drama not only inhere in social experience; in basic ways they determine it. In communities of any size and duration, moreover, rituals and ceremonies proliferate, often assuming complex shapes, with performers and spectators, and often with music, dancing, and the reenactment of important deeds and occasions. Such are the materials of drama.

But theater-drama—drama as we recognize it in the history of western culture—has by no means been practiced everywhere and at all times. Written drama, with staged performances presented to audiences by means of acting, has flourished in relatively few epochs of rather short duration, often separated by periods of comparative inactivity, and it has arisen in markedly different historical environments.

The Greek Classics

In ancient Greece, where the record of drama mainly begins, public theatrical performances appear to have grown out of religious celebrations honoring the deeds of gods and heroes. Choral chants and dancing

1

are said to have been converted into drama by the addition (legend says by Thespis, in 534 B.C.) of a single actor who could play more than one role and might enter into dialogue with members of the chorus. Eventually as many as three actors were used. In the fifth century B.C., Athens was the site of annual festivals that witnessed a great succession of tragedies, the work of Aeschylus, Sophocles, and Euripides, as well as the comedies of Aristophanes. Deplorably, most of their plays, totalling perhaps three hundred, are lost, but those that were rediscovered in the Renaissance produced a profound and enduring effect.

The Middle Ages

During most of the medieval period, the Church discouraged or prohibited dramatic entertainments, but by the fifteenth century there had nevertheless developed, notably in England at such centers as York and Coventry, sequences of plays dramatizing for popular audiences the famous Biblical stories. These "mystery plays"—so called because they expounded the mysteries of the Christian faith—were performed at festivals lasting sometimes for several days. No names of individual playwrights have come down to us.

The Elizabethan Drama

In England in the late sixteenth and early seventeenth centuries there was a sustained burst of literary activity, including drama, especially in London, where theaters enjoyed the protection of the Crown under Elizabeth I and James I and the favor of increasingly supportive audiences. This drama, hospitable to a wide variety of subjects from fiction and from Roman and English history, was the creation of such gifted authors as Christopher Marlowe, Ben Jonson, and—supremely—Shakespeare. The publication of Shakespeare's *Comedies, Histories, and Tragedies* ("the First Folio") in 1623 marks the apex of English Renaissance literature.

Neo-Classical French Drama

In France, during the long reign of Louis XIV (1643–1715), the Court and the Parisian upper classes generously supported and yet closely scrutinized the appearance of "neo-classical" dramas that were expected to adhere to the rules and models of the Greek and Roman classics and also to observe the strictest Catholic morality. Under such constraints Pierre Corneille and Jean Racine produced their lofty tragedies and Molière his elegant yet often rambunctious comedies.

The Modern Drama

The next century and a half saw the spread of theaters throughout the important European cities (as well as latterly in America), the acceptance of playgoing as a valued feature of middle- and upper-class urban culture, and—very slowly—the formation of a few small elite audiences in some of the capital cities. These developments prepared the way for the eruption of what has come to be called "the modern drama," itself the creation of Ibsen, Strindberg, Chekhov, Shaw, and Pirandello—to name only the most influential playwrights. Their work dominated the half-century between 1880 and 1930. These dramatists, often breaking sharply with established customs and expectations, first made their impress through relatively small and dedicated acting companies working against odds in experimental and "independent" theaters—free, that is, of official supervision and censorship. Such were the Théâtre Libre in Paris, the Independent Theatre in London, the Moscow Art Theatre, and the Abbey Theatre in Dublin. The effects of this powerful literary movement are still found in much contemporary drama.

Types of Theaters

Each of the important periods of drama has been identified with certain physical and architectural conditions and social conventions that were deeply imprinted on the ways in which the plays of each period were written and received.

The Greek plays in this anthology were performed by daylight in a large outdoor amphitheater and in front of a facade that represented a palace or a temple. The actors entered from central gates or from the sides. They wore elevated boots to increase their stature and masks to accentuate the dominant traits of the characters they portrayed. The focal area of the amphitheater was a large "orchestra" or dancing circle. During the first ode of the drama a chorus of about fifteen men entered the orchestra and remained in view until the end of the performance. Their chants were accompanied by stylized dance steps. At times they divided into semichoruses that chanted and danced responsively. The leader of the chorus might enter into dialogue with the actors. The solemn tragedies were often followed by rowdy comedies, and although the two kinds of drama were sharply differentiated, both were performed for the same audiences on the same festive occasions.

The medieval *Second Shepherd's Play,* one in a series based on Biblical stories, may have been performed on a movable stage, called a "pageant." A procession of such pageants could carry individual plays from one location to another, or for plays composing a cycle on a given subject, such as Noah and the Flood or the Nativity of Jesus, the pageants might be arranged around the sides of a market place or in open fields. Because actors and audiences were not necessarily separated by barriers, there could be by-play and interchange between performers and spectators.

The Elizabethan plays (such as *Othello* and *Volpone*) were usually performed in a theater derived from the plan of an inn that enclosed a sizable courtyard, with a large stage, uncurtained, thrusting well out into the courtyard area. Spectators either sat in the surrounding galleries or stood in the open area around the stage. At the back of the stage there could be two small curtained acting areas, one above the other, the lower perhaps representing an interior, such as Desdemona's bedchamber, the upper perhaps a balcony. Together they might represent the facade of a house fronting on a street. In such theaters there was little use of scenery, but stage effects and costumes were often quite elaborate. Scenes were played in rapid sequence with little interruption. The actors were men and, for women's parts, adolescent boys. Not until after the middle of the seventeenth century did women appear as professional actresses in European theaters.

Most of the remaining plays in this book were designed for proscenium-arch theaters that exhibit three essentials: a stage recessed into the wall under the arch; the use of a full curtain to open and close the stage; and artificial illumination. This basic design lends itself to powerful kinds of illusion. As the curtain rises, the audience gazes through the transparent "fourth wall" of a room or scene and into the lives of characters within. Such a stage can accommodate a variety of effects, ranging from the quite formal groupings required in *Tartuffe* or *The Rivals* to the meticulously realistic decor of *Hedda Gabler* and the panoramic sequences of *The Good Woman of Setzuan.*

Many recent playwrights have veered away from fourth-wall illusionism toward the use of more suggestive, symbolic, and improvisatory staging and design. An uncurtained "arena stage," for example, can imitate some of the features of the Greek or Elizabethan theaters. The introduction of electric lighting capable of an almost endless range of effects, and the development of machines, such as revolving platforms and electronic amplification, have offered the dramatist alluring opportunities for experimentation.

Some Theories of Drama

Dramatic theorizing has more or less followed the changes in kinds of drama and the conditions of theatrical representation. It has seldom been literary theorizing alone but has been mixed with political, religious, and practical interests. Hence it is not surprising that no comprehensive theory of dramatic form and function has won general and lasting assent or is ever likely to do so. Inevitably, theorizing about drama divides in several directions—some aimed at observing actual practice, some at prescribing desirable or even ideal forms and subjects, some at the question of origins, some at harnessing drama to social or religious programs, and some at emancipating it from them. Twentieth-century theorizing has drawn heavily upon anthropology (especially that concerned with the origins of classical mythology), upon Freudian psychoanalysis (for its emphasis upon repressed sexuality and dream-symbolism), and upon Marxist-oriented social theory, with its stress upon the overriding processes of historical development.

Admitting the futility of trying to summarize so rich a variety of theories in brief, a few important ideas may nevertheless be singled out that have exerted a commanding influence on methods of dramatic composition and on standards of criticism. According to a widely accepted view that has received several formulations, a drama, a true drama, a "well-made" play, should achieve a high degree of structural coherence. The details can be spun out at length, but the underlying concept is so simple as to appear practically self-evident. A drama should exhibit a three-part structure. It begins with (1) an *exposition* that imparts essential information and impels (2) the *complication*—a series of events rising to a turning point, after which the plot falls swiftly to (3) a *resolution* (or "denouement" or "unravelling") and its foreordained end. This ideal of efficient structure has sparked hot debates over terminology. (For example, does a "turning point" require a "crisis" or a "climax," or are the terms synonymous?) Despite such uncertainties, it is remarkable how many plays of quite different sorts seem to conform to this tripartite scheme. Or is this an illusion? Cannot almost anything be accommodated to a three-part plan? One consequence of any theory of ideal structure is that plays that do not fit it are deemed deviant and inferior. As a result, this theory has been roundly attacked as reductively "linear" and as intolerant of experiment, creative ambiguity, and artistic liberty.

Another long-prevalent and not unrelated theory of drama insists on the fundamental difference between the genres of tragedy and comedy and—at least by implication—the necessity of keeping them separate. The most coherent and long-enduring statement of tragic theory is set forth in Aristotle's *Poetics*, a philosophic treatise written near the end of the great Athenian age. One of its central formulations follows:

A perfect tragedy . . . should imitate actions which excite pity and fear, this being the distinctive mark of tragic imitation. It follows plainly, in the first place, that the change of fortune presented must not be the spectacle of a virtuous man brought from prosperity to adversity: for this moves neither pity nor fear; it merely shocks us. Nor, again, that of a bad man passing from adversity to prosperity: for nothing can be more alien to the spirit of Tragedy; it possesses no single tragic quality; it neither satisfies the moral sense nor calls forth pity or fear. Nor, again, should the downfall of the utter villain be exhibited. A plot of this kind would, doubtless, satisfy the moral sense, but it would inspire neither pity nor fear; for pity is aroused by unmerited misfortune, fear by the misfortune of a man like ourselves. Such an event, therefore, will be neither pitiful nor terrible. There remains, then, the character between these two extremes,—that of a man who is not eminently good and just, yet whose misfortune is brought about not by vice or depravity, but by some error or frailty. He must be one who is highly renowned and prosperous,—a personage like Oedipus, Thyestes, or other illustrious men of such families.

(*Trans.*, S. H. BUTCHER)

In addition to emphasizing "error or frailty" as the source of tragic events, Aristotle insists on the moral quality of action and on the sense of release ("purgation" or "catharsis") that the audience should experience. Even tragic dramas that are not constructed according to his demanding principles may be illuminated by his insights. For compactness, completeness, and perfection of structure, subject, and effect, Aristotle found his ideal embodied in *Oedipus Rex.*

No theory of comedy has won anything like the favor and prestige of Aristotle on tragedy. (If he finished a treatise on comedy, it is lost to us.) Nor is it self-evident that tragedy and comedy must comprise the only true genres nor that they must never be mingled. Some recent theory finds comedy rooted in ancient rituals of the vernal equinox and the summer solstice—and ascribes tragedy to autumn and winter. Others trace comedy to the spirit of folk festivals. These theories have won some acceptance but are hard to demonstrate. Moreover, modern comedies are not very amenable to such patterns. There exists a measure of agreement that satiric comedy depends upon postulating norms of just and reasonable conduct against which folly or vice may be projected as comic incongruities. Yet comparable norms appear no less essential to the perspective of tragedy. The possibilities of mixing tragic and comic modes have often been explored, especially by modern dramatists such as O'Casey and Beckett, whose plays are not easily categorized.

Critical theory can claim an interest of its own but is most useful when asked to illuminate one feature or another of particular plays. Just which questions of theory will prove relevant, however, can be decided only by experience. For example, seasonal festivals may not have much relevance to *Death of a Salesman,* but Aristotle's idea of the proper tragic character may. Analyzing such starkly contrasting plays as *Riders to the Sea* and *Miss Julie* according to the standards of the well-made play is a legitimate but possibly mechanical exercise, whereas viewing these plays in the light of ancient rituals may be more enlightening. Theory is of necessity secondary to drama itself. It is a noteworthy paradox that the plays of Shakespeare, least theoretical of playwrights, have inspired some of the liveliest and most penetrating critical theorists, from John Dryden in the seventeenth century to Northrop Frye in our own times. Neither theory nor history offers any evidence that the potentials of dramatic form and subject will be exhausted. One of the delights of literary study is the discovery that although great works conform in part to recurrent patterns, each work takes a shape distinctively its own.

Aeschylus

525–456 B.C.

Agamemnon

458 B.C.

Based on Homeric myth yet profoundly imbued with the spirit of fifth-century Athens, *Agamemnon* stands among those "monuments of unageing intellect" celebrated by Yeats. Yet only in retrospect does it appear monumental, massive, and serene. When confronted directly in the text or in the theater, it involves us in a torsion of thought and feeling mounting through a sequence of scenes and choric odes unmatched for eloquence and economy of dramatic means.

One of the oldest known Greek dramas, and the first part of the only surviving complete trilogy—the *Oresteia*—*Agamemnon* is itself a perfected tragedy yet points consistently forward to its sequels. In the second play, *The Libation Bearers,* Orestes and his sister Electra must avenge their father's murder and so in turn claim the life of their mother, Clytemnestra. In the third, *The Eumenides,* Apollo and Athena themselves descend to earth to ajudicate the otherwise unending blood-feud and bless the advent of a society under the benign rule of a court of law dispensing both human and divine justice. The last play concludes with a procession celebrating the founding of Athens.

As usual in Greek tragedy the action on stage is austerely simple, and its significance is repeatedly pondered in choric odes rich in metaphor and cadence. To some degree the chorus functions as an on-stage audience, responding to events that it can neither control nor fully understand. Because the chorus is constantly remembering the dreadful past and hoping to foresee a less dreadful future, it endows the movement of time with special significance. Events do not simply unfold in sequence: they recapitulate and inform the past; they foreordain the future. The sense of deeply contemplated causality springs directly from the interplay between the brief scenes of dialogue and action and the soaring meditations of the odes. In few dramas are we given so keen an impression of being carried through visible and audible surfaces to deeper levels of meaning. Nightmarish scenes and terrifying possibilities of evil are confronted by the humane and fallible chorus, endowed by Aeschylus with aspirations to both wisdom and courage.

The theme of *Agamemnon,* as of the entire trilogy, is the entanglement of justice with injustice and the painful evolution of the ideal of civic justice in human consciousness. *Dikê,* the Greek word that is on the lips and conscience of every character in the play, does not translate readily: it means that which is right, that which is ordained, not to be exceeded or opposed, something enforced obscurely yet adamantly by fates, furies, or *daimons,* by memories and curses. In the mythic time in which these dramas are laid, *dikê* operates without explicit laws, without tribunal, and without appeal. The sacramental founding of an Athenian court— the Areopagus—brings justice out of primeval shadows into the light of Hellenic history.

Aeschylus presents this struggle toward justice against the background of the contention between two "houses"—that of Priam (Troy) just fallen and that of Atreus (representing Greece) apparently triumphant in Agamemnon's victory. Yet the house of Atreus is deeply torn by a series of ancestral crimes perpetuated by the requirements of vengeance. The as-yet unwritten law—*dikê* —broken by one murder demands satisfaction by another, in the interminable and merciless reciprocity of the blood-feud. Crime requires justice; justice requires crime. Hence the ineluctable Aeschylean irony everywhere manifest in *Agamemnon,* in explicit pronouncements and, more significantly, in the dramatic conception of the play as it moves through a single symbolic day. *That* day, "born from the womb" of a ten-year-long night, is signaled by a beacon kindled at the burning of Troy. That day witnesses the return of triumphant Agamemnon to the house and household that he has both avenged and desecrated. In his

train is the enslaved Trojan princess, Cassandra, whose presence as his concubine manifests his victory. Her presence also aggravates the fury of Clytemnestra's determination to sacrifice her husband at the household altar that he had profaned when, on the way to Troy, he sacrificed their daughter, Iphigeneia, to advance the war. This long-awaited day recalls and reenacts the foulest crimes, and Agamemnon's high noon of splendor, as he reenters his house—treading with naked feet tapestries appropriate only for the gods— is the hour of his sacrificial murder.

That hour is the crest of the action and is prolonged almost intolerably. When Agamemnon has solemnly entered his palace, Clytemnestra closes the doors. The scene that follows, a *kommos,* a mixture of choric lament and of dialogue between Cassandra and the chorus of elders, is the crest and—at length—the breaking point. At first in obscure prophetic lamentations, but at last forthrightly, Cassandra evokes the old crimes of the house of Atreus and then the evil about to engulf Agamemnon and herself. The chorus is paralyzed with misgivings and doubts, pity and fear. Cassandra enters the palace and the doors shut again. For yet another minute the crest hangs suspended as the chorus meditates. Then Agamemnon's cries are heard:

ōmoi, peplēgmai kairian plēgēn esō.
("Oh! I am struck a mortal blow—within!")

The crest breaks, and the dark hour of Clytemnestra's victory begins.

Clytemnestra alone of the characters has more than a single scene, and the double meanings of theme and action all center in her. But no character is free of entangling and divided purposes. All seem wound in an ever-lengthening chain of crime and necessary retribution, itself impure. Yet through this darkness shines in each character some nobility of purpose matched by the electric instancy of the dramatic action. Nothing is accidental, nothing tangential or abstract. The "unageing intellect" does not intellectualize. It is present in every pulsation of the action and in the opulent, dense, and enigmatic style that challenges our understanding.

Agamemnon

AESCHYLUS

Translated by Louis MacNeice

CHARACTERS (IN ORDER OF APPEARANCE)

A WATCHMAN
CHORUS OF OLD MEN
CLYTEMNESTRA *the Queen, wife of Agamemnon*
A HERALD
AGAMEMNON *King of Argos and son of Atreus*
CASSANDRA *daughter of Priam, the King of Troy*
AEGISTHUS *son of Thyestes, who was a brother of Atreus*
SOLDIERS OF THE PALACE GUARD

PROLOGUE°

[SCENE. *A space in front of the palace of Agamemnon in Argos. Night. A* WATCHMAN *on the roof of the palace.*]

    WATCHMAN. The gods it is I ask to release me
                      [from this watch   5

Prologue this play consists of a prologue, a párados, five scenes—each accompanied by an ode or a kommos (a dialogue between a character and the chorus in which are mingled lyrical measures of choral lament)—and an éxodos. The **párados** is the ode sung by the chorus as it enters the orchestra, where it remains throughout the play; the **éxodos** is that part of the play that follows the last ode or kommos. The play, then, is composed of a beginning (prologue and parados) in which the situation is defined and explored; a middle (the five scenes with their odes or kommoi) in which the plot develops, with choral commentary, to the catastrophe; and an end (the éxodos) in which the consequences of the catastrophe are explored, and in part, realized.

Reprinted by permission of Faber and Faber Ltd.

A year's length now, spending my nights like a
[dog,
Watching on my elbow on the roof of the sons
[of Atreus°
5 So that I have come to know the assembly of
[the nightly stars
Those which bring storm and those which bring
[summer to men,
The shining Masters riveted in the sky—
10 I know the decline and rising of those stars.
And now I am waiting for the sign of the
[beacon,
The flame of fire that will carry the report from
[Troy,
15 News of her taking. Which task has been
[assigned me
By a woman of sanguine heart but a man's
[mind.
Yet when I take my restless rest in the soaking
20 [dew,
My night not visited with dreams—
For fear stands by me in the place of sleep
That I cannot firmly close my eyes in sleep—
Whenever I think to sing or hum to myself
25 As an antidote to sleep, then every time I groan
And fall to weeping for the fortunes of this
[house
Where not as before are things well ordered
[now.
30 But now may a good chance fall, escape from
[pain,
The good news visible in the midnight fire.
    [*Pause. A light appears, gradually increasing,
    the light of the beacon.*]
35 Ha! I salute you, torch of the night whose light
Is like the day, an earnest of many dances
In the city of Argos, celebration of Peace.
I call to Agamemnon's wife; quickly to rise

sons of Atreus specifically, Agamemnon and Menelaus; but the "house" of Atreus also includes the descendants of Pelops, the father of Atreus, and connotes the acts of fratricide, incest, and childmurder that mark the successive royal generations, particularly the relationship between Atreus and his brother Thyestes. Agamemnon married Clytemnestra, daughter of Tyndareus and Leda; Menelaus married Helen, daughter of Leda and Zeus. Her abduction by Paris incited the ten-year-long Trojan War.

Out of her bed and in the house to raise
Clamor of joy in answer to this torch   40
For the city of Troy is taken—
Such is the evident message of the beckoning
[flame.
And I myself will dance my solo first
For I shall count my master's fortune mine   45
Now that this beacon has thrown me a lucky
[throw.
And may it be when he comes, the master of
[this house,
That I grasp his hand in my hand.   50
As to the rest, I am silent. A great ox, as they
[say,
Stands on my tongue. The house itself, if it
[took voice,
Could tell the case most clearly. But I will only 55
[speak
To those who know. For the others I remember
[nothing.

PÁRADOS

[*Enter* CHORUS OF OLD MEN. *During the following chorus the day begins to dawn.*]   60
    CHORUS. The tenth year it is since Priam's
[high
Adversary, Menelaus the king
And Agamemnon, the double-throned and
[sceptered 65
Yoke of the sons of Atreus
Ruling in fee from God,
From this land gathered an Argive army
On a mission of war a thousand ships,
Their hearts howling in boundless bloodlust   70
In eagles' fashion who in lonely
Grief for nestlings above their homes hang
Turning in cycles
Beating the air with the oars of their wings,
    Now to no purpose   75
    Their love and task of attention.

But above there is One,
Maybe Pan, maybe Zeus or Apollo,
Who hears the harsh cries of the birds
Guests in his kingdom,   80
Wherefore, though late, in requital
He sends the Avenger.

Thus Zeus our master
Guardian of guest and of host
Sent against Paris the sons of Atreus
For a woman of many men,
5 Many the dog-tired wrestlings
Limbs and knees in the dust pressed—
 For both the Greeks and Trojans
 An overture of breaking spears.

Things are where they are, will finish
10 In the manner fated and neither
Fire beneath nor oil above can soothe
The stubborn anger of the unburnt offering.
As for us, our bodies are bankrupt,
The expedition left us behind
15 And we wait supporting on sticks
Our strength—the strength of a child;
For the marrow that leaps in a boy's body
Is no better than that of the old
For the War God is not in his body;
20 While the man who is very old
And his leaf withering away
Goes on the three-foot way°
No better than a boy, and wanders
A dream in the middle of the day.

25 But you, daughter of Tyndareus,
Queen Clytemnestra,
What is the news, what is the truth, what have
      [you learnt,
On the strength of whose word have you thus
30 Sent orders for sacrifice round?
All the gods, the gods of the town,
Of the worlds of Below and Above,
By the door, in the square,
Have their altars ablaze with your gifts,
35 From here, from there, all sides, all corners,
Sky-high leap the flame-jets fed
By gentle and undeceiving
Persuasion of sacred unguent,
Oil from the royal stores.
40 Of these things tell
That which you can, that which you may,
Be healer of this our trouble
Which at times torments with evil
Though at times by propitiations

three-foot way on two legs and a staff

A shining hope repels   45
The insatiable thought upon grief
Which is eating away our hearts.
Of the omen which powerfully speeded
That voyage of strong men, by God's grace
         [even I 50
Can tell, my age can still
Be galvanized to breathe the strength of song,
To tell how the kings of all the youth of Greece
Two-throned but one in mind
Were launched with pike and punitive hand 55
Against the Trojan shore by angry birds.
Kings of the birds to our kings came,
One with a white rump, the other black,
Appearing near the palace on the spear-arm
        [side 60
Where all could see them,
Tearing a pregnant hare with the unborn young
Foiled of their courses.
 Cry, cry upon Death; but may the good
        [prevail. 65

But the diligent prophet of the army seeing the
        [sons
Of Atreus twin in temper knew
That the hare-killing birds were the two
Generals, explained it thus—   70
"In time this expedition sacks the town
Of Troy before whose towers
By Fate's force the public
Wealth will be wasted.
Only let not some spite from the gods benight 75
     [the bulky battalions,
The bridle of Troy,° nor strike them untimely;
For the goddess feels pity, is angry
With the winged dogs of her father
Who killed the cowering hare with her unborn 80
        [young;
Artemis° hates the eagles' feast."

bridle of Troy the Greek army, likened to horse tamers
Artemis sister of Apollo and protectress of flocks and
 young animals; because she favored the Trojans and
 because Agamemnon killed one of her sacred animals, she caused the Greek ships to be bound in
 the harbor of Aulis by adverse winds. To appease her
 Agamemnon sacrificed his daughter Iphigeneia, thus
 continuing the series of crimes blighting the "house"
 of Atreus.

Cry, cry upon Death; but may the good
[prevail.

"But though you are so kind, goddess,
To the little cubs of lions
5 And to all the sucking young of roving beasts
In whom your heart delights,
Fulfil us the signs of these things,
The signs which are good but open to blame,
And I call on Apollo the Healer
10 That his sister raise not against the Greeks
Unremitting gales to balk their ships,
Hurrying on another kind of sacrifice, with no
[feasting,
Barbarous building of hates and disloyalties
15 Grown on the family. For anger grimly returns
Cunningly haunting the house, avenging the
[death of a child, never forgetting its due."
So cried the prophet—evil and good together,
Fate that the birds foretold to the king's house.
20 In tune with this
Cry, cry upon Death; but may the good
[prevail.

Zeus, whoever He is, if this
Be a name acceptable,
25 By this name I will call him.
There is no one comparable
When I reckon all of the case
Excepting Zeus, if ever I am to jettison
The barren care which clogs my heart.

30 Not He who° formerly was great
With brawling pride and mad for broils
Will even be said to have been.
And He° who was next has met
His match and is seen no more,
35 But Zeus is the name to cry in your triumph-
[song
And win the prize for wisdom.

Who setting us on the road
Made this a valid law—
40   "That men must learn by suffering."

Drop by drop in sleep upon the heart
Falls the laborious memory of pain,
Against one's will comes wisdom;
The grace of the gods is forced on us
    Throned inviolably.   45

So at that time the elder
Chief of the Greek ships
Would not blame any prophet
Nor face the flail of fortune;
For unable to sail, the people°   50
Of Greece were heavy with famine,
Waiting in Aulis where the tides
    Flow back, opposite Chalcis.°

But the winds that blew from the Strymon,°
Bringing delay, hunger, evil harborage,   55
Crazing men, rotting ships and cables,
By drawing out the time
Were shredding into nothing the flower of
[Argos,
When the prophet screamed a new   60
Cure for that bitter tempest
And heavier still for the chiefs,
Pleading the anger of Artemis so that the sons
[of Atreus
Beat the ground with their scepters and shed   65
[tears.

Then the elder king found voice and answered:
"Heavy is my fate, not obeying,
And heavy it is if I kill my child, the delight of
[my house, 70
And with a virgin's blood upon the altar
Make foul her father's hands.
Either alternative is evil.
How can I betray the fleet
And fail the allied army?   75
It is right they should passionately cry for the
[winds to be lulled
By the blood of a girl. So be it. May it be well."

But when he had put on the halter of Necessity

He who Uranus, first of the great king-gods
And He Cronos, who dispossessed him and was in
turn overthrown by Zeus

people army
Chalchis . . . Strymon a town and a river in Asia
Minor, across the straits from Aulis where the Greeks
were anchored

Breathing in his heart a veering wind of evil
Unsanctioned, unholy, from that moment
[forward
He changed his counsel, would stop at nothing.
5 For the heart of man is hardened by infatuation,
A faulty adviser, the first link of sorrow.
Whatever the cause, he brought himself to slay
His daughter, an offering to promote the voyage
To a war for a runaway wife.
10 Her prayers and her cries of father,
Her life of a maiden,
Counted for nothing with those militarists;
But her father, having duly prayed, told the
[attendants
15 To lift her, like a goat, above the altar
With her robes falling about her,
To lift her boldly, her spirit fainting,
And hold back with a gag upon her lovely
[mouth
20 By the dumb force of a bridle
The cry which would curse the house.
Then dropping on the ground her saffron dress,
Glancing at each of her appointed
Sacrificers a shaft of pity,
25 Plain as in a picture she wished
To speak to them by name, for often
At her father's table where men feasted
She had sung in celebration for her father
With a pure voice, affectionately, virginally,
30 The hymn for happiness at the third libation.
The sequel to this I saw not and tell not
But the crafts of Calchas gained their object.
To learn by suffering is the equation of Justice;
[the Future
35 Is known when it comes, let it go till then.
To know in advance is to sorrow in advance.
The facts will appear with the shining of the
[dawn.

SCENE I

[*Enter* CLYTEMNESTRA.]
40 But may good, at the least, follow after
As the queen here wishes, who stands
Nearest the throne, the only
Defense of the land of Argos.
    LEADER OF THE CHORUS. I have come,

[Clytemnestra, reverencing your authority. 45
For it is right to honor our master's wife
When the man's own throne is empty.
But you, if you have heard good news for
[certain, or if
You sacrifice on the strength of flattering 50
[hopes,
I would gladly hear. Though I cannot cavil at
[silence.
    CLYTEMNESTRA. Bearing good news, as the
[proverb says, may Dawn 55
Spring from her mother Night.
You will hear something now that was beyond
[your hopes.
The men of Argos have taken Priam's city.
    LEADER. What! I cannot believe it. It escapes 60
[me.
    CLYT. Troy in the hands of the Greeks. Do I
[speak plain?
    LEADER. Joy creeps over me, calling out my
[tears. 65
    CLYT. Yes. Your eyes proclaim your loyalty.
    LEADER. But what are your grounds? Have
[you a proof of it?
    CLYT. There is proof indeed—unless God has
[cheated us. 70
    LEADER. Perhaps you believe the inveigling
[shapes of dreams?
    CLYT. I would not be credited with a dozing
[brain!
    LEADER. Or are you puffed up by Rumor, the 75
[wingless flyer?
    CLYT. You mock my common sense as if I
[were a child.
    LEADER. But at what time was the city given
[to sack? 80
    CLYT. In this very night that gave birth to this
[day.
    LEADER. What messenger could come so fast?
    CLYT. Hephaestus,° launching a fine flame
[from Ida,° 85
Beacon forwarding beacon, despatch-riders of
[fire,

Hephaestus god of fire
Ida a mountain overlooking the Trojan plain and from
    which the gods beheld the battles. The place names
    that follow trace a course that would send a series
    of beacon flares to Argos in peninsular Greece.

Ida relayed to Hermes' cliff in Lemnos
And the great glow from the island was taken
                                        [over third
By the height of Athos that belongs to Zeus,
5   And towering then to straddle over the sea
The might of the running torch joyfully tossed
The gold gleam forward like another sun,
Herald of light to the heights of Mount
                                        [Macistus,
10   And he without delay, nor carelessly by sleep
Encumbered, did not shirk his intermediary
                                        [role,
His farflung ray reached the Euripus' tides
And told Messapion's watchers, who in turn
15   Sent on the message further
Setting a stack of dried-up heather on fire.
And the strapping flame, not yet enfeebled,
                                        [leapt
Over the plain of Asopus like a blazing moon
20   And woke on the crags of Cithaeron
Another relay in the chain of fire.
The light that was sent from far was not
                                        [declined
By the look-out men, who raised a fiercer yet,
25   A light which jumped the water of Gorgopis
And to Mount Aegiplanctus duly come
Urged the reveille of the punctual fire.
So then they kindle it squanderingly and launch
A beard of flame big enough to pass
30   The headland that looks down upon the Saronic
                                        [gulf,
Blazing and bounding till it reached at length
The Arachnaean steep, our neighboring
                                        [heights;
35   And leaps in the latter end on the roof of the
                                        [sons of Atreus
Issue and image of the fire on Ida.
Such was the assignment of my torch-racers,
The task of each fulfilled by his successor,
40   And victor is he who ran both first and last.
Such is the proof I offer you, the sign
My husband sent me out of Troy.
     LEADER. To the gods, queen, I shall give
                                        [thanks presently.
45   But I would like to hear this story further,
To wonder at it in detail from your lips.
     CLYT. The Greeks hold Troy upon this day.
The cries in the town I fancy do not mingle.

Pour oil and vinegar into the same jar,
You would say they stand apart unlovingly;   50
Of those who are captured and those who have
                                        [conquered
Distinct are the sounds of their diverse
                                        [fortunes,
For *these* having flung themselves about the   55
                                        [bodies
Of husbands and brothers, or sons upon the
                                        [bodies
Of aged fathers from a throat no longer
Free, lament the fate of their most loved.   60
But *those* a night's marauding after battle
Sets hungry to what breakfast the town offers
Not billeted duly in any barracks order
But as each man has drawn his lot of luck.
So in the captive homes of Troy already   65
They take their lodging, free of the frosts
And dews of the open. Like happy men
They will sleep all night without sentry.
But if they respect duly the city's gods,
Those of the captured land and the sanctuaries   70
                                        [of the gods,
They need not, having conquered, fear
                                        [reconquest.
But let no lust fall first upon the troops
To plunder what is not right, subdued by gain,   75
For they must still, in order to come home safe,
Get round the second lap of the doubled course.
So if they return without offense to the gods
The grievance of the slain may learn at last
A friendly talk—unless some fresh wrong falls.   80
Such are the thoughts you hear from me, a
                                        [woman.
But may the good prevail for all to see.
We have much good. I only ask to enjoy it.
     LEADER. Woman, you speak with sense like   85
                                        [a prudent man.
I, who have heard your valid proofs, prepare
To give the glory to God.
Fair recompense is brought us for our troubles.
     [CLYTEMNESTRA *goes back into the palace.*]   90

ODE I

CHORUS. O Zeus our king and Night our
                                        [friend
Donor of glories,

Night who cast on the towers of Troy
A close-clinging net so that neither the grown
Nor any of the children can pass
The enslaving and huge
5   Trap of all-taking destruction.
Great Zeus, guardian of host and guest,
I honor who has done his work and taken
A leisured aim at Paris so that neither
Too short nor yet over the stars
10   He might shoot to no purpose.

From Zeus is the blow they can tell of,
This at least can be established,
They have fared according to his ruling. For
[some
15   Deny that the gods deign to consider those
[among men
Who trample on the grace of inviolate things;
It is the impious man says this,
For Ruin is revealed the child
20   Of not to be attempted actions
When men are puffed up unduly
And their houses are stuffed with riches.
Measure is the best. Let danger be distant,
This should suffice a man
25   With a proper part of wisdom.
    For a man has no protection
    Against the drunkenness of riches
    Once he has spurned from his sight
    The high altar of Justice.

30   Somber Persuasion compels him,
Intolerable child of calculating Doom;
All cure is vain, there is no glozing it over
But the mischief shines forth with a deadly light
And like bad coinage
35   By rubbings and frictions
He stands discolored and black
Under the test—like a boy
Who chases a winged bird.
He has branded his city for ever.
40   His prayers are heard by no god.
Who makes such things his practice
The gods destroy him.
    This way came Paris
    To the house of the sons of Atreus
45   And outraged the table of friendship
    Stealing the wife of his host.

Leaving to her countrymen clanging of
Shields and of spears and
Launching of warships
And bringing instead of a dowry destruction to   50
[Troy
Lightly she was gone through the gates daring
Things undared. Many the groans
Of the palace spokesmen on this theme—
"O the house, the house, and its princes,   55
O the bed and the imprint of her limbs;
One can see him crouching in silence
Dishonored and unreviling."
Through desire for her who is overseas, a ghost
Will seem to rule the household.   60
    And now her husband hates
    The grace of shapely statues;
    In the emptiness of their eyes
    All their appeal is departed.

But appearing in dreams persuasive   65
Images come bringing a joy that is vain,
Vain for when in fancy he looks to touch her—
Slipping through his hands the vision
Rapidly is gone
Following on wings the walks of sleep.   70
Such are his griefs in his house on his hearth,
Such as these and worse than these,
But everywhere through the land of Greece
[which men have left
Are mourning women with enduring hearts   75
To be seen in all houses; many
Are the thoughts which stab their hearts;
    For those they sent to war
    They know, but in place of men
    That which comes home to them   80
    Is merely an urn and ashes.

But the money-changer War, changer of bodies,
Holding his balance in the battle
Home from Troy refined by fire
Sends back to friends the dust   85
That is heavy with tears, stowing
A man's worth of ashes
In an easily handled jar.
And they wail speaking well of the men how
[that one   90
Was expert in battle, and one fell well in the
[carnage—

But for another man's wife.
Muffled and muttered words;
And resentful grief creeps up against the sons
Of Atreus and their cause.
5   But others there by the wall
    Entombed in Trojan ground
    Lie, handsome of limb,
    Holding and hidden in enemy soil.

Heavy is the murmur of an angry people
10 Performing the purpose of a public curse;
There is something cowled in the night
That I anxiously wait to hear.
For the gods are not blind to the
Murderers of many and the black
15 Furies in time
When a man prospers in sin
By erosion of life reduce him to darkness,
Who, once among the lost, can no more
Be helped. Over-great glory
20 Is a sore burden. The high peak
Is blasted by the eyes of Zeus.
    I prefer an unenvied fortune,
    Not to be a sacker of cities
    Nor to find myself living at another's
25   Ruling, myself a captive.

AN OLD MAN. From the good news' beacon
                              [a swift
Rumor is gone through the town.
Who knows if it be true
30 Or some deceit of the gods?
    ANOTHER O.M. Who is so childish or broken
                                [in wit
To kindle his heart at a new-fangled message
                               [of flame
35 And then be downcast
At a change of report?
    ANOTHER O.M. It fits the temper of a woman
To give her assent to a story before it is proved.
    ANOTHER O.M. The over-credulous passion
40   [of women expands
In swift conflagration but swiftly declining is
                              [gone
The news that a woman announced.
    LEADER OF THE CHORUS. Soon we shall know
45   [about the illuminant torches,

The beacons and the fiery relays,
Whether they were true or whether like dreams
That pleasant light came here and hoaxed our
                                [wits.
Look: I see, coming from the beach, a herald   50
Shadowed with olive shoots; the dust upon
                                [him,
Mud's thirsty sister and colleague, is my
                              [witness
That he will not give dumb news nor news by   55
                              [lighting
A flame of fire with the smoke of mountain
                              [timber;
In words he will either corroborate our joy—
But the opposite version I reject with horror.   60
To the good appeared so far may good be
                              [added.
    ANOTHER SPEAKER. Whoever makes other
                [prayers for this our city,
May he reap himself the fruits of his wicked   65
                              [heart.

SCENE II

[*Enter the* HERALD, *who kisses the ground before speaking.*]
    HERALD. Earth of my fathers, O the earth of
                            [Argos,   70
In the light of the tenth year I reach you thus
After many shattered hopes achieving one,
For never did I dare to think that here in Argive
                              [land
I should win a grave in the dearest soil of home;   75
But now hail, land, and hail, light of the sun,
And Zeus high above the country and the
                      [Pythian king—°
May he no longer shoot his arrows at us
(Implacable long enough beside Scamander)°   80
But now be savior to us and be healer,
King Apollo. And all the Assembly's gods
I call upon, and him my patron, Hermes,
The dear herald whom all heralds adore,
And the Heroes who sped our voyage, again   95
                            [with favor
Take back the army that has escaped the spear.

Pythian king   Apollo, who favored the Trojan cause
Scamander   river flowing beside Troy

O cherished dwelling, palace of royalty,
O august thrones and gods facing the sun,
If ever before, now with your bright eyes
Gladly receive your king after much time,
5 Who comes bringing light to you in the night
                                                    [time,
And to all these as well—King Agamemnon.
Give him a good welcome as he deserves,
Who with the axe of judgment-awarding God
10 Has smashed Troy and levelled the Trojan
                                                    [land;
The altars are destroyed, the seats of the gods,
And the seed of all the land is perished from it.
Having cast this halter round the neck of Troy
15 The King, the elder son of Atreus, a blessed
                                                    [man,
Comes, the most worthy to have honor of all
Men that are now. Paris nor his guilty city
Can boast that the crime was greater than the
20   [atonement.
Convicted in a suit for rape and robbery
He has lost his stolen goods and with
                                                    [consummate ruin
Mowed down the whole country and his
25   [father's house.
The sons of Priam have paid their account
                                                    [with interest.
LEADER OF THE CHORUS. Hail and be glad,
                                                    [herald of the Greek army.
30 HERALD. Yes. Glad indeed! So glad that at the
                                                    [gods' demand
I should no longer hesitate to die.
LEADER. Were you so harrowed by desire for
                                                    [home?
35 HERALD. Yes. The tears come to my eyes for
                                                    [joy.
LEADER. Sweet then is the fever which afflicts
                                                    [you.
HERALD. What do you mean? Let me learn
40   [your drift.
LEADER. Longing for those whose love came
                                                    [back in echo.
HERALD. Meaning the land was homesick for
                                                    [the army?
45 LEADER. Yes. I would often groan from a
                                                    [darkened heart.
HERALD. This sullen hatred—how did it
                                                    [fasten on you?

LEADER. I cannot say. Silence is my stock
                                                    [prescription. 50
HERALD. What? In your masters' absence
                                                    [were there some you feared?
LEADER. Yes. In your phrase, death would
                                                    [now be a gratification.
HERALD. Yes, for success is ours. These 55
                                                    [things have taken time.
Some of them we could say have fallen well,
While some we blame. Yet who except the gods
Is free from pain the whole duration of life?
If I were to tell of our labors, our hard lodging, 60
The sleeping on crowded decks, the scanty
                                                    [blankets,
Tossing and groaning, rations that never
                                                    [reached us—
And the land too gave matter for more disgust, 65
For our beds lay under the enemy's walls.
Continuous drizzle from the sky, dews from the
                                                    [marshes,
Rotting our clothes, filling our hair with lice.
And if one were to tell of the bird-destroying 70
                                                    [winter
Intolerable from the snows of Ida
Or of the heat when the sea slackens at noon
Waveless and dozing in a depressed calm—
But why make these complaints? The weariness 75
                                                    [is over;
Over indeed for some who never again
Need even trouble to rise.
Why make a computation of the lost?
Why need the living sorrow for the spites of 80
                                                    [fortune?
I wish to say a long goodbye to disasters.
For us, the remnant of the troops of Argos,
The advantage remains, the pain can not
                                                    [outweigh it; 85
So we can make our boast to this sun's light,
Flying on words above the land and sea:
"Having taken Troy the Argive expedition
Has nailed up throughout Greece in every
                                                    [temple 90
These spoils, these ancient trophies."
Those who hear such things must praise the city
And the generals. And the grace of God be
                                                    [honored
Which brought these things about. You have 95
                                                    [the whole story.

LEADER. I confess myself convinced by your
[report.
Old men are always young enough to learn.
[*Enter* CLYTEMNESTRA *from the palace.*]
5 This news belongs by right first to the house
And Clytemnestra—though I am enriched also.
CLYT. Long before this I shouted at joy's
[command
At the coming of the first night-messenger of
10 [fire
Announcing the taking and capsizing of Troy.
And people reproached me saying, "Do mere
[beacons
Persuade you to think that Troy is already
15 [down?
Indeed a woman's heart is easily exalted."
Such comments made me seem to be wandering
[but yet
I began my sacrifices and in the women's
20 [fashion
Throughout the town they raised triumphant
[cries
And in the gods' enclosures
Lulling the fragrant, incense-eating flame.
25 And now what need is there for you to tell me
[more?
From the King himself I shall learn the whole
[story.
But how the best to welcome my honored lord
30 I shall take pains when he comes back—For
[what
Is a kinder light for a woman to see than this,
To open the gates to her man come back from
[war
35 When God has saved him? Tell this to my
[husband,
To come with all speed, the city's darling;
May he returning find a wife as loyal
As when he left her, watchdog of the house,
40 Good to *him* but fierce to the ill-intentioned,
And in all other things as ever, having
[destroyed
No seal or pledge at all in the length of time.
I know no pleasure with another man, no
45 [scandal,
More than I know how to dye metal red.
Such is my boast, bearing a load of truth,

A boast that need not disgrace a noble wife.
[*Exit.*]
LEADER. Thus has she spoken; if you take her 50
[meaning,
Only a specious tale to shrewd interpreters.
But do you, herald, tell me; I ask after Menelaus
Whether he will, returning safe preserved,
Come back with you, our land's loved master. 55
HERALD. I am not able to speak the lovely
[falsehood
To profit you, my friends, for any stretch of
[time.
LEADER. But if only the true tidings could be 60
[also good!
It is hard to hide a division of good and true.
HERALD. The prince is vanished out of the
[Greek fleet,
Himself and ship. I speak no lie. 65
LEADER. Did he put forth first in the sight of
[all from Troy,
Or a storm that troubled all sweep him apart?
HERALD. You have hit the target like a master
[archer, 70
Told succinctly a long tale of sorrow.
LEADER. Did the rumors current among the
[remaining ships
Represent him as alive or dead?
HERALD. No one knows so as to tell for sure 75
Except the sun who nurses the breeds of earth.
LEADER. Tell me how the storm came on the
• [host of ships
Through the divine anger, and how it ended.
HERALD. Day of good news should not be 80
[fouled by tongue
That tells ill news. To each god his season.
When, despair in his face, a messenger brings
[to a town
The hated news of a fallen army— 85
One general wound to the city and many men
Outcast, outcursed, from many homes
By the double whip which War is fond of,
Doom with a bloody spear in either hand,
One carrying such a pack of grief could well 90
Recite this hymn of the Furies at your asking.
But when our cause is saved and a messenger of
[good
Comes to a city glad with festivity,

How am I to mix good news with bad,
          [recounting
The storm that meant God's anger on the
          [Greeks?
5 For they swore together, those inveterate
          [enemies,
Fire and sea, and proved their alliance,
          [destroying
The unhappy troops of Argos.
10 In night arose ill-waved evil,
Ships on each other the blasts from Thrace
Crashed colliding, which butting with horns in
          [the violence
Of big wind and rattle of rain were gone
15 To nothing, whirled all ways by a wicked
          [shepherd.
But when there came up the shining light of
          [the sun
We saw the Aegean sea flowering with corpses
20 Of Greek men and their ships' wreckage.
But for us, our ship was not damaged,
Whether someone snatched it away or begged
          [it off,
Some god, not a man, handling the tiller;
25 And Saving Fortune was willing to sit upon our
          [ship
So that neither at anchor we took the tilt of
          [waves
Nor ran to splinters on the crag-bound coast.
30 But then having thus escaped death on the sea,
In the white day, not trusting our fortune,
We pastured this new trouble upon our
          [thoughts,
The fleet being battered, the sailors weary,
35 And now if any of *them* still draw breath,
They are thinking no doubt of us as being lost
And we are thinking of them as being lost.
May the best happen. As for Menelaus
The first guess and most likely is a disaster.
40 But still—if any ray of sun detects him
Alive, with living eyes, by the plan of Zeus
Not yet resolved to annul the race completely,
There is some hope then that he will return
          [home.
45 So much you have heard. Know that it is the
          [truth.

    [*Exit.*]

ODE II

CHORUS. Who was it named her thus
In all ways appositely
Unless it was Someone whom we do not see,   50
Fore-knowing fate
And plying an accurate tongue?
Helen, bride of spears and conflict's
Focus, who as was befitting
Proved a hell° to ships and men,   55
Hell to her country, sailing
Away from delicately-sumptuous curtains,
Away on the wind of a giant Zephyr,
And shielded hunters mustered many
On the vanished track of the oars,   60
Oars beached on the leafy
Banks of a Trojan river
For the sake of bloody war.

But on Troy was thrust a marring marriage
By the Wrath that working to an end exacts   65
In time a price from guests
Who dishonored their host
And dishonored Zeus of the Hearth,
From those noisy celebrants
Of the wedding hymn which fell   70
To the brothers of Paris
To sing upon that day.
But learning this, unlearning that,
Priam's ancestral city now
Continually mourns, reviling   75
Paris the fatal bridegroom.
The city has had much sorrow,
Much desolation in life,
From the pitiful loss of her people.

So in his house a man might rear   80
A lion's cub caught from the dam
In need of suckling,
In the prelude of its life
Mild, gentle with children,
For old men a playmate,   85
Often held in the arms
Like a new-born child,

hell in Greek the name *Helen* and a verb meaning *to destroy* sound alike

Wheedling the hand,
Fawning at belly's bidding.

But matured by time he showed
The temper of his stock and paid
5 Thanks for his fostering
With disaster of slaughter of sheep
Making an unbidden banquet
And now the house is a shambles,
Irremediable grief to its people,
10 Calamitous carnage:
For the pet they had fostered was sent
By God as a priest of Ruin.

So I would say there came
To the city of Troy
15 A notion of windless calm,
Delicate adornment of riches,
Soft shooting of the eyes and flower
Of desire that stings the fancy.
But swerving aside she achieved
20 A bitter end to her marriage,
Ill guest and ill companion,
Hurled upon Priam's sons, convoyed
By Zeus, patron of guest and host,
Dark angel dowered with tears.

25 Long current among men an old saying
Runs that a man's prosperity
When grown to greatness
Comes to the birth, does not die childless—
His good luck breeds for his house
30 Distress that shall not be appeased.
I only, apart from the others,
Hold that the unrighteous action
Breeds true to its kind,
Leaves its own children behind it.
35 But the lot of a righteous house
Is a fair offspring always.

Ancient self-glory is accustomed
To bear to light in the evil sort of men
A new self-glory and madness,
40 Which sometime or sometime finds
The appointed hour for its birth,
And born therewith is the Spirit, intractable,
                [unholy, irresistible,
The reckless lust that brings black Doom upon
45   [the house,

A child that is like its parents.

But Honest Dealing is clear
Shining in smoky homes,
Honors the god-fearing life.
Mansions gilded by filth of hands she leaves,   50
Turns her eyes elsewhere, visits the innocent
                        [house,
Not respecting the power
Of wealth mis-stamped with approval,
But guides all to the goal.   55

SCENE III

[*Enter* AGAMEMNON *and* CASSANDRA *on char-
iots.*]
    CHORUS. Come then my King, stormer of
                        [Troy,
Offspring of Atreus,   60
How shall I hail you, how give you honor
Neither overshooting nor falling short
    Of the measure of homage?
There are many who honor appearance too
                      [much 65
Passing the bounds that are right.
To condole with the unfortunate man
Each one is ready but the bite of the grief
    Never goes through to the heart.
And they join in rejoicing, affecting to share it, 70
Forcing their face to a smile.
But he who is shrewd to shepherd his sheep
Will fail not to notice the eyes of a man
Which seem to be loyal but lie,
    Fawning with watery friendship.   75
Even you, in my thought, when you marshalled
                    [the troops
For Helen's sake, I will not hide it,
Made a harsh and ugly picture,
Holding badly the tiller of reason,   80
Paying with the death of men
    Ransom for a willing whore.
But now, not unfriendly, not superficially,
I offer my service, well-doers' welcome.
In time you will learn by inquiry   85
Who has done rightly, who transgressed
    In the work of watching the city.
    AGAMEMNON. First to Argos and the country's
                    [gods
My fitting salutations, who have aided me   90

To return and in the justice which I exacted
From Priam's city. Hearing the unspoken case
The gods unanimously had cast their vote
Into the bloody urn for the massacre of Troy;
5 But to the opposite urn
Hope came, dangled her hand, but did no more.
Smoke marks even now the city's capture.
Whirlwinds of doom are alive, the dying ashes
Spread on the air the fat savor of wealth.
10 For these things we must pay some memorable
[return
To Heaven, having exacted enormous
[vengeance
For wife-rape; for a woman
15 The Argive monster ground a city to powder,
Sprung from a wooden horse°, shield-
[wielding folk,
Launching a leap at the setting of the Pleiads,
Jumping the ramparts, a ravening lion,
20 Lapped its fill of the kingly blood.
To the gods I have drawn out this overture
But as for your concerns, I bear them in my
[mind
And say the same, you have me in agreement.
25 To few of men does it belong by nature
To congratulate their friends unenviously,
For a sullen poison fastens on the heart,
Doubling the pain of a man with this disease;
He feels the weight of his own griefs and when
30 He sees another's prosperity he groans.
I speak with knowledge, being well acquainted
With the mirror of comradeship—ghost of a
[shadow
Were those who seemed to be so loyal to me.
35 Only Odysseus, who sailed against his will,
Proved, when yoked with me, a ready
[tracehorse;
I speak of him not knowing if he is alive.
But for what concerns the city and the gods
40 Appointing public debates in full assembly
We shall consult. That which is well already
We shall take steps to ensure it remain well.
But where there is need of medical remedies,
By applying benevolent cautery or surgery
45 We shall try to deflect the dangers of disease.

horse the great wooden horse in which Greek soldiers
hid themselves; when it was conveyed inside the
citadel of Troy, they captured it

But now, entering the halls where stands my
[hearth,
First I shall make salutation to the gods
Who sent me a far journey and have brought
[me back. 50
And may my victory not leave my side.
[*Enter* CLYTEMNESTRA, *followed by women
slaves carrying purple tapestries.*]
CLYT. Men of the city, you the aged of Argos,
I shall feel no shame to describe to you my love 55
Towards my husband. Shyness in all of us
Wears thin with time. Here are the facts first
[hand.
I will tell you of my own unbearable life
I led so long as this man was at Troy. 60
For first that the woman separate from her man
Should sit alone at home is extreme cruelty,
Hearing so many malignant rumors—First
Comes one, and another comes after, bad news
[to worse, 65
Clamor of grief to the house. If Agamemnon
Had had so many wounds as those reported
Which poured home through the pipes of
[hearsay, then—
Then he would be gashed fuller than a net has 70
[holes!
And if only he had died . . . as often as rumor
[told us,
He would be like the giant° in the legend,
Three-bodied. Dying once for every body, 75
He should have by now three blankets of earth
[above him—
All that above him; I care not how deep the
[mattress under!
Such are the malignant rumors thanks to which 80
They have often seized me against my will and
[undone
The loop of a rope° from my neck.
And this is why our son is not standing here,
The guarantee of your pledges and mine, 85
As he should be, Orestes.° Do not wonder;
He is being brought up by a friendly ally and
[host,

giant Geryon, said to have three heads or three
bodies
rope with which, she implies, she tried to hang herself
in despair
Orestes who in the next play of the trilogy returns
and avenges his father

Strophius the Phocian, who warned me in
[advance
Of dubious troubles, both your risks at Troy
And the anarchy of shouting mobs that might
5 Overturn policy, for it is born in men
To kick the man who is down.
This is not a disingenuous excuse.
For me the outrushing wells of weeping are
[dried up,
10 There is no drop left in them.
My eyes are sore from sitting late at nights
Weeping for you and for the baffled beacons,
Never lit up. And, when I slept, in dreams
I have been waked by the thin whizz of a
15 [buzzing
Gnat, seeing more horrors fasten on you
Than could take place in the mere time of my
[dream
Having endured all this, now, with unsorrowed
20 [heart
I would hail this man as the watchdog of the
[farm,
Forestay that saves the ship, pillar that props
The lofty roof, appearance of an only son
25 To a father or of land to sailors past their hope,
The loveliest day to see after the storm,
Gush of well-water for the thirsty traveller.
Such are the metaphors I think befit him,
But envy be absent. Many misfortunes already
30 We have endured. But now, dear head, come
[down
Out of that car, not placing upon the ground
Your foot, O King, the foot that trampled Troy.
Why are you waiting, slaves, to whom the task
35 [is assigned
To spread the pavement of his path with
[tapestries?
At once, at once let his way be strewn with
[purple
40 That Justice lead him toward his unexpected
[home.
The rest a mind, not overcome by sleep
Will arrange rightly, with God's help, as
[destined.
45 AGAM. Daughter of Leda, guardian of my
[house,
You have spoken in proportion to my absence.
You have drawn your speech out long. Duly to
[praise me,
That is a duty to be performed by others.   50
And further—do not by women's methods
[make me
Effeminate nor in barbarian fashion
Gape ground-grovelling acclamations at me
Nor strewing my path with cloths make it   55
[invidious.
It is the gods should be honored in this way.
But being mortal to tread embroidered beauty
For me is no way without fear.
I tell you to honor me as a man, not god.   60
Footcloths are very well—Embroidered stuffs
Are stuff for gossip. And not to think unwisely
Is the greatest gift of God. Call happy only him
Who has ended his life in sweet prosperity.
I have spoken. This thing I could not do with   65
[confidence.
CLYT. Tell me now, according to your
[judgment.
AGAM. I tell you you shall not override my
[judgment.   70
CLYT. Supposing you had feared
[something . . .
Could you have vowed to God to do this thing?
AGAM. Yes. If an expert had prescribed that
[vow.   75
CLYT. And how would Priam have acted in
[your place?
AGAM. He would have trod the cloths, I
[think, for certain.
CLYT. Then do not flinch before the blame of   80
[men.
AGAM. The voice of the multitude is very
[strong.
CLYT. But the man none envy is not enviable.
AGAM. It is not a woman's part to love   85
[disputing.
CLYT. But it is a conqueror's part to yield
[upon occasion.
AGAM. You think such victory worth fighting
[for?   90
CLYT. Give way. Consent to let me have the
[mastery.
AGAM. Well, if such is your wish, let
[someone quickly loose
My vassal sandals, underlings of my feet,   95
And stepping on these sea-purples may no god

Shoot me from far with the envy of his eye.
Great shame it is to ruin my house and spoil
The wealth of costly weavings with my feet.
But of this matter enough. This stranger woman
5   [here
Take in with kindness. The man who is a
                            [gentle master
God looks on from far off complacently.
For no one of his will bears the slave's yoke.
10 This woman, of many riches being the chosen
Flower, gift of the soldiers, has come with me.
But since I have been prevailed on by your
                            [words
I will go to my palace home, treading on
15   [purples.
    [*He dismounts from the chariot and begins
to walk up the tapestried path. During the fol-
lowing speech he enters the palace.*]
    CLYT. There is the sea and who shall drain
20   [it dry? It breeds
Its wealth in silver of plenty of purple gushing
And ever-renewed, the dyeings of our
                            [garments.
The house has its store of these by God's grace,
25   [King.
This house is ignorant of poverty
And I would have vowed a pavement of many
                           [garments
Had the palace oracle enjoined that vow
30 Thereby to contrive a ransom for his life.
For while there is root, foliage comes to the
                            [house
Spreading a tent of shade against the Dog
                            [Star.°
35 So now that you have reached your hearth and
                            [home
You prove a miracle—advent of warmth in
                            [winter;
And further this—even in the time of heat
40 When God is fermenting wine from the bitter
                            [grape,
Even then it is cool in the house if only
Its master walk at home, a grown man, ripe.
O Zeus the Ripener, ripen these my prayers;
45 Your part it is to make the ripe fruit fall.
    [*She enters the palace.*]

Dog Star Sirius, associated with hot summer weather

ODE III

   CHORUS. Why, why at the doors
Of my fore-seeing heart
Does this terror keep beating its wings?
And my song play the prophet   50
Unbidden, unhired—
Which I cannot spit out
Like the enigmas of dreams
Nor plausible confidence
Sit on the throne of my mind?   55
It is long time since
The cables let down from the stern
Were chafed by the sand when the seafaring
                     [army started for Troy.

And I learn with my eyes   60
And witness myself their return;
But the hymn without lyre goes up,
The dirge of the Avenging Fiend,°
In the depths of my self-taught heart
Which has lost its dear   65
Possession of the strength of hope.
But my guts and my heart
Are not idle which seethe with the waves
Of trouble nearing its hour.
But I pray that these thoughts   70
May fall out not as I think
    And not be fulfilled in the end.

Truly when health grows much
It respects not limit; for disease,
Its neighbor in the next door room,   75
Presses upon it.
A man's life, crowding sail,
Strikes on the blind reef:
But if caution in advance
Jettison part of the cargo   80
With the derrick of due proportion,
The whole house does not sink,
Though crammed with a weight of woe
The hull does not go under.
The abundant bounty of God   85

Fiend here, as in later references to "demons,"
"black Spirit," and "Evil Genius," the concept is that
of Furies, or certain *daimons*, or Erinyes, all dark
and fearful divinities who mercilessly punish crimes
against hearth and home

And his gifts from the year's furrows
Drive the famine back.

But when upon the ground there has fallen
[once
5   The black blood of a man's death,
Who shall summon it back by incantations?
Even Asclepius° who had the art
To fetch the dead to life, even to him
Zeus put a provident end.
10   But, if of the heaven-sent fates
One did not check the other,
Cancel the other's advantage,
My heart would outrun my tongue
In pouring out these fears.
15   But now it mutters in the dark,
Embittered, no way hoping
To unravel a scheme in time
     From a burning mind.

SCENE IV

[CLYTEMNESTRA appears in the door of the
20   palace.]
     CLYT. Go in too, you; I speak to you,
[Cassandra,
Since God in his clemency has put you in this
[house
25   To share our holy water, standing with many
[slaves
Beside the altar that protects the house,
Step down from the car there, do not be
[overproud.
30   Heracles° himself they say was once
Sold, and endured to eat the bread of slavery.
But should such a chance inexorably fall,
There is much advantage in masters who have
[long been rich.
35   Those who have reaped a crop they never
[expected

Asclepius   a god of medicine and healing, whom Zeus
    is said to have killed lest he give immortality to
    mortals
Heracles   (or Hercules) the godlike athlete who in a
    spasm of madness killed his friend and was sen-
    tenced by the Delphic Oracle to work three years as
    a servant. In an earlier fit of madness he had mur-
    dered his own children.

Are in all things hard on their slaves and
[overstep the line.
From us you will have the treatment of
[tradition.   40
     LEADER OF CHORUS. You, it is you she has
[addressed, and clearly.
Caught as you are in these predestined toils
Obey her if you can. But should you disobey . . .
     CLYT. If she has more than the gibberish of   45
[the swallow,
An unintelligible barbaric speech,
I hope to read her mind, persuade her reason.
     LEADER. As things now stand for you, she
[says the best.   50
Obey her; leave that car and follow her.
     CLYT. I have no leisure to waste out here,
[outside the door.
Before the hearth in the middle of my house
The victims stand already, wait the knife.   55
You, if you will obey me, waste no time.
But if you cannot understand my language—
     [To CHORUS LEADER.]
You make it plain to her with the brute and
[voiceless hand.   60
     LEADER. The stranger seems to need a clear
[interpreter.
She bears herself like a wild beast newly
[captured.
     CLYT. The fact is she is mad, she listens to evil   65
[thoughts,
Who has come here leaving a city newly
[captured
Without experience how to bear the bridle
So as not to waste her strength in foam and   70
[blood.
I will not spend more words to be ignored.
     [She re-enters the palace.]

KOMMOS I

CHORUS. But I, for I pity her, will not be
[angry.   75
Obey, unhappy woman. Leave this car.
Yield to your fate. Put on the untried yoke.
     CASS. Apollo! Apollo!
     CHORUS. Why do you cry like this upon
[Apollo?   80
He is not the kind of god that calls for dirges.

Cass. Apollo! Apollo!

Chorus. Once more her funereal cries invoke
[the god
Who has no place at the scene of lamentation.

5   Cass. Apollo! Apollo!
God of the Ways! My destroyer!
Destroyed again—and this time utterly!

Chorus. She seems about to predict her own
[misfortunes.

10 The gift of the god endures, even in a slave's
[mind.

Cass. Apollo! Apollo!
God of the Ways! My destroyer!
Where? To what house? Where, where have
[you brought me?

15

Chorus. To the house of the sons of Atreus.
[If you do not know it,
I will tell you so. You will not find it false.

Cass. No, no, but to a god-hated, but to an
[accomplice

20

In much kin-killing, murdering nooses,
Man-shambles, a floor asperged with blood.

Chorus. The stranger seems like a hound
[with a keen scent,

25 Is picking up a trail that leads to murder.

Cass. Clues! I have clues! Look! They are
[these.
These wailing, these children, butchery of
[children;°

30 Roasted flesh, a father sitting to dinner.

Chorus. Of your prophetic fame we have
[heard before
But in this matter prophets are not required.

Cass. What is she doing? What is she
[planning?

35

What is this new great sorrow?
Great crime . . . within here . . . planning
Unendurable to his folk, impossible
Ever to be cured. For help

40   Stands far distant.

Chorus. This reference I cannot catch. But
[the children

children   two brothers of Aegisthus, and sons of Thyestes,
the brother of Atreus. Thyestes committed adultery with
Atreus' wife. In revenge Atreus secretly slaughtered
Thyestes' elder sons and served their flesh to their father
at the banquet described in Aegisthus' first speech
(p. 32, ll. 15–60).

I recognized; that refrain is hackneyed.

Cass. Damned, damned, bringing this work
[to completion—   45
Your husband who shared your bed
To bathe him, to cleanse him, and then—
How shall I tell of the end?
Soon, very soon, it will fall.
The end comes hand over hand   50
Grasping in greed.

Chorus. Not yet do I understand. After her
[former riddles
Now I am baffled by these dim
[pronouncements.   55

Cass. Ah God, the vision! God, God, the
[vision!
A net, is it? Net of Hell!
But herself is the net; shared bed; shares
[murder.   60
O let the pack ever-hungering after the family
Howl for the unholy ritual, howl for the victim.

Chorus. What black Spirit is this you call
[upon the house—
To raise aloft her cries? Your speech does not   65
[lighten me.
Into my heart runs back the blood
Yellow as when for men by the spear fallen
The blood ebbs out with the rays of the setting
[life   70
And death strides quickly.

Cass. Quick! Be on your guard! The bull—
Keep him clear of the cow.
Caught with a trick, the black horn's point,
She strikes. He falls; lies in the water.   75
Murder; a trick in a bath. I tell what I see.

Chorus. I would not claim to be expert in
[oracles
But these, as I deduce, portend disaster.
Do men ever get a good answer from oracles?   80
No. It is only through disaster
That their garrulous craft brings home
The meaning of the prophet's panic.

Cass. And for me also, for me, chance
[ill-destined!   85
My own now I lament, pour into the cup my
[own.
Where is this you have brought me in my
[misery?
Unless to die as well. What else is meant?   90

CHORUS. You are mad, mad, carried away by
[the god,
Raising the dirge, the tuneless
Tune, for yourself. Like the tawny
5 Unsatisfied singer from her luckless heart
Lamenting "Itys, Itys," ° the nightingale
Lamenting a life luxuriant with grief.
    CASS. Oh the lot of the songful nightingale!
The gods enclosed her in a winged body,
10 Gave her a sweet and tearless passing.
But for me remains the two-edged cutting
[blade.
    CHORUS. From whence these rushing and
[God-inflicted
15 Profitless pains?
Why shape with your sinister crying
The piercing hymn—fear-piercing?
How can you know the evil-worded landmarks
    On the prophetic path?
20   CASS. Oh the wedding, the wedding of Paris
[—death to his people!
O river Scamander, water drunk by my fathers!
When I was young, alas, upon your beaches
I was brought up and cared for.
25 But now it is the River of Wailing and the
[banks of Hell
That shall hear my prophecy soon.
    CHORUS. What is this clear speech, too clear?
A child could understand it.
30 I am bitten with fangs that draw blood
By the misery of your cries,
Cries harrowing the heart.
    CASS. Oh trouble on trouble of a city lost,
[lost utterly!
35 My father's sacrifices before the towers,
Much killing of cattle and sheep,
No cure—availed not at all
To prevent the coming of what came to Troy,
And I, my brain on fire, shall soon enter the
40 [trap.
    CHORUS. This speech accords with the
[former.
What god, malicious, over-heavy, persistently
[pressing,

"Itys" the traditional lamenting bird-call of Philomela,
who was transformed by the gods into a nightingale
after she had been raped by her brother-in-law
Tereus. Like Thyestes, Tereus was deceived into
eating the flesh of his son, Itys.

Drives you to chant of these lamentable 45
Griefs with death their burden?
But I cannot see the end.

SCENE V

[CASSANDRA *now steps down from the car*.]
    CASS. The oracle now no longer from behind
[veils 50
Will be peeping forth like a newly-wedded
[bride;
But I can feel it like a fresh wind swoop
And rush in the face of the dawn and, wave-
[like, wash 55
Against the sun a vastly greater grief
Than this one. I shall speak no more
[conundrums.
And bear me witness, pacing me, that I
Am trailing on the scent of ancient wrongs. 60
For this house here a choir never deserts,
Chanting together ill. For they mean ill,
And to puff up their arrogance they have drunk
Men's blood, this band of revellers that haunts
[the house, 65
Hard to be rid of, fiends that attend the family.
Established in its rooms they hymn their hymn
Of that original sin, abhor in turn
The adultery that proved a brother's ruin.
A miss? Or do my arrows hit the mark? 70
Or am I a quack prophet who knocks at doors,
[a babbler?
Give me your oath, confess I have the facts,
The ancient history of this house's crimes.
    LEADER. And how could an oath's assurance, 75
[however finely assured,
Turn out a remedy? I wonder, though, that you
Being brought up overseas, of another tongue,
Should hit on the whole tale as if you had been
[standing by. 80
    CASS. Apollo the prophet set me to prophesy.
    LEADER. Was he, although a god, struck by
[desire?
    CASS. Till now I was ashamed to tell that
[story. 85
    LEADER. Yes. Good fortune keeps us all
[fastidious.
    CASS. He wrestled hard upon me, panting
[love.

LEADER. And did you come, as they do, to
                              [child-getting?
CASS. No. I agreed to him. And I cheated
                              [him.
5   LEADER. Were you already possessed by the
                              [mystic art?
CASS. Already I was telling the townsmen all
                              [their future suffering.
LEADER. Then how did you escape the doom
10   [of Apollo's anger?
CASS. I did not escape. No one ever believed
                              [me.
LEADER. Yet to us your words seem worthy of
                              [belief.
15 CASS. Oh misery, misery!
Again comes on me the terrible labor of true
Prophecy, dizzying prelude; distracts . . .
Do you see these who sit before the house,
Children, like the shapes of dreams?
20 Children who seem to have been killed by their
                              [kinsfolk,
Filling their hands with meat, flesh of
                              [themselves,
Guts and entrails, handfuls of lament—
25 Clear what they hold—the same their father
                              [tasted.
For this I declare someone is plotting
                              [vengeance—
A lion? Lion but coward, that lurks in bed,
30 Good watchdog truly against the lord's
                              [return—
My lord, for I must bear the yoke of serfdom.
Leader of the ships, overturner of Troy,
He does not know what plots the accursed
35   [hound
With the licking tongue and the pricked-up ear
                              [will plan
In the manner of a lurking doom, in an evil
                              [hour.
40 A daring criminal! Female murders male.
What monster could provide her with a title?
An amphisbaena or hag of the sea who dwells
In rocks to ruin sailors—
A raving mother of death who breathes against
45   [her folk
War to the finish. Listen to her shout of
                              [triumph,
Who shirks no horrors, like men in a rout of
                              [battle.

And yet she poses as glad at their return.   50
If you distrust my words, what does it matter?
That which will come will come. You too will
                              [soon stand here
And admit with pity that I spoke too truly.
LEADER. Thyestes' dinner of his children's   55
                              [meat
I understood and shuddered, and fear grips me
To hear the truth, not framed in parables.
But hearing the rest I am thrown out of my
                              [course. 60
CASS. It is Agamemnon's death I tell you you
                              [shall witness.
LEADER. Stop! Provoke no evil. Quiet your
                              [mouth!
CASS. The god who gives me words is here   65
                              [no healer.
LEADER. Not if this shall be so. But may some
                              [chance avert it.
CASS. *You* are praying. But others are busy
                              [with murder. 70
LEADER. What man is he promotes this
                              [terrible thing?
CASS. Indeed you have missed my drift by a
                              [wide margin!
LEADER. But I do not understand the   75
                              [assassin's method.
CASS. And yet too well I know the speech of
                              [Greece!
LEADER. So does Delphi° but the replies are
                              [hard. 80
CASS. Ah what a fire it is! It comes upon me.
Apollo, Wolf-Destroyer, pity, pity . . .
It is the two-foot lioness who beds
Beside a wolf, the noble lion away,
It is she will kill me. Brewing a poisoned cup   85
She will mix my punishment too in the angry
                              [draught
And boasts, sharpening the dagger for her
                              [husband,
To pay back murder for my bringing here.   90
Why then do I wear these mockeries of myself,
The wand and the prophet's garland round my
                              [neck?
My hour is coming—but you shall perish first.
Destruction! Scattered thus you give me my   95
                              [revenge;

Delphi the oracle of Apollo

Go and enrich some other woman with ruin.
See: Apollo himself is stripping me
Of my prophetic gear, who has looked on
When in this dress I have been a laughing-
5   [stock
To friends and foes alike, and to no purpose;
They called me crazy, like a fortune-teller,
A poor starved beggar-woman—and I bore it.
And now the prophet undoing his prophetess
10 Has brought me to this final darkness.
Instead of my father's altar the executioner's
                                  [block
Waits me the victim, red with my hot blood.
But the gods will not ignore me as I die.
15 One will come after to avenge my death,
A matricide, a murdered father's champion.
Exile and tramp and outlaw he will come back
To gable the family house of fatal crime;
His father's outstretched corpse shall lead him
20   [home.
Why need I then lament so pitifully?
For now that I have seen the town of Troy
Treated as she was treated, while her captors
Come to their reckoning thus by the gods'
25   [verdict,
I will go in and have the courage to die.
Look, these gates are the gates of Death. I greet
                                  [them.
And I pray that I may meet a deft and mortal
30   [stroke
So that without a struggle I may close
My eyes and my blood ebb in easy death.
    LEADER. Oh woman very unhappy and very
                                  [wise,
35 Your speech was long. But if in sober truth
You know your fate, why like an ox that the
                                  [gods
Drive, do you walk so bravely to the altar?
    CASS. There is no escape, strangers. No; not
40   [by postponement.
    LEADER. But the last moment has the privilege
                                 [of hope.
    CASS. The day is here. Little should I gain by
                                  [flight.
45   LEADER. This patience of yours comes from a
                                  [brave soul.
    CASS. A happy man is never paid that
                                  [compliment.

    LEADER. But to die with credit graces a mortal
                               [man. 50
    CASS. Oh my father! You and your noble
                                [sons!
[She approaches the door, then suddenly
recoils.]
    LEADER. What is it? What is the fear that   55
                             [drives you back?
    CASS. Faugh.
    LEADER. Why faugh? Or is this some
                             [hallucination?
    CASS. These walls breathe out a death that   60
                             [drips with blood.
    LEADER. Not so. It is only the smell of the
                             [sacrifice.
    CASS. It is like a breath out of a charnel-
                             [house. 65
    LEADER. You think our palace burns odd
                             [incense then!
    CASS. But I will go to lament among the dead
My lot and Agamemnon's. Enough of life!
Strangers,   70
I am not afraid like a bird afraid of a bush
But witness you my words after my death
When a woman dies in return for me a woman
And a man falls for a man with a wicked wife.
I ask this service, being about to die.   75
    LEADER. Alas, I pity you for the death you
                             [have foretold.
    CASS. One more speech I have; I do not wish
                             [to raise
The dirge for my own self. But to the sun I pray   80
In face of his last light that my avengers
May make my murderers pay for this my death,
Death of a woman slave, an easy victim.
    [She enters the palace.]

CHORAL INTERLUDE

    LEADER. Ah the fortunes of men! When they   85
                             [go well
A shadow sketch would match them, and in
                             [ill-fortune
The dab of a wet sponge destroys the drawing.
It is not myself but the life of man I pity.   90
    CHORUS. Prosperity in all men cries
For more prosperity. Even the owner

Of the finger-pointed-at palace never shuts
His door against her, saying "Come no more."
So to our king the blessed gods had granted
To take the town of Priam, and heaven-favored
5 He reaches home. But now if for former
[bloodshed
He must pay blood
And dying for the dead shall cause
Other deaths in atonement
10 What man could boast he was born
Secure, who heard this story?
AGAM. [*within*]. Oh! I am struck a mortal
[blow—within!
LEADER. Silence! Listen. Who calls out,
15 [wounded with a mortal stroke?
AGAM. Again—the second blow—I am
[struck again.
LEADER. You heard the king cry out. I think
[the deed is done.
20 Let us see if we can concert some sound
[proposal.
2ND OLD MAN. Well, I will tell you my
[opinion—
Raise an alarm, summon the folk to the palace.
25 3RD OLD MAN. I say burst in with all speed
[possible,
Convict them of the deed while still the sword
[is wet.
4TH OLD MAN. And I am partner to some
30 [such suggestion.
I am for taking some course. No time to
[dawdle.
5TH OLD MAN. The case is plain. This is but
[the beginning.
35 They are going to set up dictatorship in the
[state.
6TH OLD MAN: We are wasting time. The
[assassins tread to earth
The decencies of delay and give their hands no
40 [sleep.
7TH OLD MAN. I do not know what plan I
[could hit on to propose.
The man who acts is in the position to plan.
8TH OLD MAN. So I think, too, for I am at a
45 [loss
To raise the dead man up again with words.
9TH OLD MAN. Then to stretch out our life
[shall we yield thus

To the rule of these profaners of the house?
10TH OLD MAN. It is not to be endured. To die 50
[is better.
Death is more comfortable than tyranny.
11TH OLD MAN. And are we on the evidence
[of groans
Going to give oracle that the prince is dead? 55
12TH OLD MAN. We must know the facts for
[sure and *then* be angry.
Guesswork is not the same as certain
[knowledge.
LEADER. Then all of you back me and approve 60
[this plan—
To ascertain how it is with Agamemnon.
[*The doors of the palace open, revealing the
bodies of* AGAMEMNON *and* CASSANDRA. CLY-
TEMNESTRA *stands above them.*] 65
CLYT. Much having been said before to fit the
[moment,
To say the opposite now will not outface me.
How else could one serving hate upon the
[hated, 70
Thought to be friends, hang high the nets of
[doom
To preclude all leaping out?
For me I have long been training for this match,
I tried a fall and won—a victory overdue. 75
I stand here where I struck, above my victims;
So I contrived it—this I will not deny—
That he could neither fly nor ward off death;
Inextricable like a net for fishes
I cast about him a vicious wealth of raiment 80
And struck him twice and with two groans he
[loosed
His limbs beneath him, and upon him fallen
I deal him the third blow to the God beneath
[the earth, 85
To the safe keeper of the dead a votive gift,
And with that he spits his life out where he lies
And smartly spouting blood he sprays me with
The somber drizzle of bloody dew and I
Rejoice no less than in God's gift of rain. 90
The crops are glad when the ear of corn gives
[birth.
These things being so, you, elders of Argos,
Rejoice if rejoice you will. Mine is the glory.
And if I could pay this corpse his due libation 95
I should be right to pour it and more than right;

With so many horrors this man mixed and
[filled
The bowl—and, coming home, has drained the
[draught himself.
5   LEADER. Your speech astonishes us. This
[brazen boast
Above the man who was your king and
[husband!
CLYT. You challenge me as a woman without
10   [foresight
But I with unflinching heart to you who know
Speak. And you, whether you will praise or
[blame,
It makes no matter. Here lies Agamemnon,
15   My husband, dead, the work of this right hand,
An honest workman. There you have the facts.

KOMMOS II

CHORUS. Woman, what poisoned
Herb of the earth have you tasted
Or potion of the flowing sea
20   To undertake this killing and the people's
[curses?
You threw down, you cut off—The people will
[cast you out,
Black abomination to the town.
25   CLYT. Now your verdict—in my case—is
[exile
And to have the people's hatred, the public
[curses,
Though then in no way you opposed this man
30   Who carelessly, as if it were a head of sheep
Out of the abundance of his fleecy flocks,
Sacrificed his own daughter, to me the dearest
Fruit of travail, charm for the Thracian winds.
He was the one to have banished from this
35   [land,
Pay off the pollution. But when you hear what I
Have done, you judge severely. But I warn
[you—
Threaten me on the understanding that I am
40   [ready
For two alternatives—Win by force the right
To rule me, but, if God brings about the
[contrary,
Late in time you will have to learn self-
45   [discipline.

CHORUS. You are high in the thoughts,
You speak extravagant things,
After the soiling murder your crazy heart
Fancies your forehead with a smear of blood.
Unhonored, unfriended, you must   50
Pay for a blow with a blow.
CLYT. Listen then to this—the sanction of my
[oaths:
By the Justice totting up my child's atonement,
By the Avenging Doom and Fiend to whom I   55
[killed this man,
For me hope walks not in the rooms of fear
So long as my fire is lit upon my hearth
By Aegisthus, loyal to me as he was before.
The man who outraged me lies here,   60
The darling of each courtesan at Troy,
And here with him is the prisoner clairvoyante,
The fortune-teller that he took to bed,
Who shares his bed as once his bench on
[shipboard,   65
A loyal mistress. Both have their deserts.
He lies so; and she who like a swan
Sang her last dying lament
Lies his lover, and the sight contributes
An appetizer to my own bed's pleasure.   70
CHORUS. Ah would some quick death come
[not overpainful,
Not overlong on the sickbed,
Establishing in us the ever-
Lasting unending sleep now that our guardian   75
Has fallen, the kindest of men,
Who suffering much for a woman
By a woman has lost his life.
O Helen, insane, being one
One to have destroyed so many   80
And many souls under Troy,
Now is your work complete, blossomed not
[for oblivion,
Unfading stain of blood. Here now, if in any
[home,   85
Is Discord, here is a man's deep-rooted ruin.
CLYT. Do not pray for the portion of death
Weighed down by these things, do not turn
Your anger on Helen as destroyer of men,
One woman destroyer of many   90
Lives of Greek men,
A hurt that cannot be healed.
CHORUS. O Evil Spirit, falling on the family,

On the two sons of Atreus and using
Two sisters in heart as your tools,
A power that bites to the heart—
See on the body
5 Perched like a raven he gloats
Harshly croaking his hymn.
    CLYT. Ah, now you have amended your lips'
                [opinion,
Calling upon this family's three times gorged
10 Genius—demon who breeds
Blood-hankering lust in the belly:
Before the old sore heals, new pus collects.
    CHORUS. It is a great spirit—great—
You tell of, harsh in anger,
15 A ghastly tale, alas,
Of unsatisfied disaster
Brought by Zeus, by Zeus,
Cause and worker of all.
For without Zeus what comes to pass among us?
20 Which of these things is outside Providence?
    O my king, my king,
    How shall I pay you in tears,
    Speak my affection in words?
    You lie in that spider's web,
25 In a desecrating death breathe out your life,
Lie ignominiously
Defeated by a crooked death
And the two-edged cleaver's stroke.
    CLYT. You say this is *my* work—mine?
30 Do not cozen yourself that I am Agamemnon's
                [wife.
Masquerading as the wife
Of the corpse there the old sharp-witted Genius
Of Atreus who gave the cruel banquet
35 Has paid with a grown man's life
The due for children dead.
    CHORUS. That you are not guilty of
This murder who will attest?
No, but you may have been abetted
40 By some ancestral Spirit of Revenge.
Wading a millrace of the family's blood
The black Manslayer forces a forward path
To make the requital at last
For the eaten children, the blood-clot cold with
45   [time.
    O my king, my king,
    How shall I pay you in tears,
    Speak my affection in words?

You lie in that spider's web,
In a desecrating death breathe out your life, 50
Lie ignominiously
Defeated by a crooked death
And the two-edged cleaver's stroke.
    CLYT. Did he not, too, contrive a crooked
Horror for the house? My child by him, 55
Shoot that I raised, much-wept-for Iphigeneia,
He treated her like this;
So suffering like this he need not make
Any great brag in Hell having paid with death
Dealt by the sword for work of his own 60
                [beginning.
    CHORUS. I am at a loss for thought, I lack
All nimble counsel as to where
To turn when the house is falling.
I fear the house-collapsing crashing 65
Blizzard of blood—of which these drops are
                [earnest.
Now is Destiny sharpening her justice
On other whetstones for a new infliction.
    O earth, earth, if only you had received me 70
    Before I saw this man lie here as if in bed
      In a bath lined with silver.
Who will bury him? Who will keen him?
Will you, having killed your own husband,
Dare now to lament him 75
And after great wickedness make
    Unamending amends to his ghost?
And who above this godlike hero's grave
Pouring praises and tears
    Will grieve with a genuine heart? 80
    CLYT. It is not your business to attend to that.
By my hand he fell low, lies low and dead,
And I shall bury him low down in the earth,
And his household need not weep him
For Iphigeneia his daughter 85
Tenderly, as is right,
Will meet her father at the rapid ferry of
                [sorrows,
Put her arms round him and kiss him!
    CHORUS. Reproach answers reproach, 90
It is hard to decide,
The catcher is caught, the killer pays for his kill.
But the law abides while Zeus abides enthroned
That the wrongdoer suffers. That is established.
Who could expel from the house the seed of the 95
                [Curse?

The race is soldered in sockets of Doom and
[Vengeance.
CLYT. In this you say what is right and the
[will of God.
5 But for my part I am ready to make a contract
With the Evil Genius of the House of Atreus
To accept what has been till now, hard though
[it is,
But that for the future he shall leave this house
10 And wear away some other stock with deaths
Imposed among themselves. Of my possessions
A small part will suffice if only I
Can rid these walls of the mad exchange of
[murder.

ÉXODOS

15 [Enter AEGISTHUS, followed by soldiers.]
AEG. O welcome light of a justice-dealing
[day!
From now on I will say that the gods, avenging
[men,
20 Look down from above on the crimes of earth,
Seeing as I do in woven robes of the Furies
This man lying here—a sight to warm my
[heart—
Paying for the crooked violence of his father.
25 For his father Atreus, when he ruled the
[country,
Because his power was challenged, hounded
[out
From state and home his own brother Thyestes.
30 My father—let me be plain—was this Thyestes,
Who later came back home a suppliant,
There, miserable, found so much asylum
As not to die on the spot, stain the ancestral
[floor.
35 But to show his hospitality godless Atreus
Gave him an eager if not a loving welcome,
Pretending a day of feasting and rich meats
Served my father with his children's flesh.
The hands and feet, fingers and toes, he hid
40 At the bottom of the dish. My father sitting
[apart
Took unknowing the unrecognizable portion
And ate of a dish that has proved, as you see,
[expensive.

But when he knew he had eaten worse than   45
[poison
He fell back groaning, vomiting their flesh,
And invoking a hopeless doom on the sons of
[Pelops
Kicked over the table to confirm his curse—   50
So may the whole race perish!
Result of this—you see this man lie here.
I stitched this murder together; it was my title.
Me the third son he left, an unweaned infant,
To share the bitterness of my father's exile.   55
But I grew up and Justice brought me back,
I grappled this man while still beyond his door,
Having pieced together the program of his ruin.
So now would even death be beautiful to me
Having seen Agamemnon in the nets of Justice.   60
LEADER. Aegisthus. I cannot respect brutality
[in distress.
You claim that you deliberately killed this
[prince
And that you alone planned this pitiful murder. 65
Be sure that in your turn your head shall not
[escape
The people's volleyed curses mixed with
[stones.
AEG. Do you speak so who sit at the lower   70
[oar
While those on the upper bench control the
[ship?
Old as you are, you will find it is a heavy load
To go to school when old to learn the lesson of 75
[tact.
For old age, too, jail and hunger are fine
Instructors in wisdom, second-sighted doctors.
You have eyes. Cannot you see?
Do not kick against the pricks. The blow will   80
[hurt you.
LEADER. You woman° waiting in the house
[for those who return from battle
While you seduce their wives! Was it you
[devised   85
The death of a master of armies?

woman   whereas Clytemnestra is said to have "a man's
mind" because of her audacity, Aegisthus is here
called "woman" because he skulked at home instead
of going to the war

AEG. And these words, too, prepare the way
[for tears.
Contrast your voice with the voice of Orpheus:
[he
5 Led all things after him bewitched with joy, but
[you
Having stung me with your silly yelps shall be
Led off yourself, to prove more mild when
[mastered.
10 LEADER. Indeed! So you are now to be king
[of Argos,
You who, when you had plotted the king's
[death,
Did not even dare to do that thing yourself!
15 AEG. No. For the trick of it was clearly
[woman's work.
I was suspect, an enemy of old.
But now I shall try with Agamemnon's wealth
To rule the people. Any who is disobedient
20 I will harness in a heavy yoke, no tracehorse
[work for him
Like barley-fed colt, but hateful hunger lodging
Beside him in the dark will see his temper
[soften.
25 LEADER. Why with your cowardly soul did
[you yourself
Not strike this man but left that work to a
[woman
Whose presence pollutes our country and its
30 [gods?
But Orestes—does he somewhere see the light
That he may come back here by favor of
[fortune
And kill this pair and prove the final victor?
35 AEG. [*summoning his guards*]. Well, if such
[is your design in deeds and words, you
[will quickly learn—
Here my friends, here my guards, there is
[work for you at hand.
40 LEADER. Come then, hands on hilts, be each
[and all of us prepared.
[*The old men and the guards threaten each
other.*]
AEG. Very well! I too am ready to meet death
45 [with sword in hand.
LEADER. We are glad you speak of dying. We
[accept your words for luck.

CLYT. No, my dearest, do not so. Add no
[more to the train of wrong.
To reap these many present wrongs is harvest 50
[enough of misery.
Enough of misery. Start no more. Our hands
[are red.
But do you, and you old men, go home and
[yield to fate in time, 55
In time before you suffer. We have acted as we
[had to act.
If only our afflictions now could prove enough,
[we should agree—
We who have been so hardly mauled in the 60
[heavy claws of the evil god.
So stands my word, a woman's, if any man
[thinks fit to hear.
AEG. But to think that these should thus
[pluck the blooms of an idle tongue 65
And should throw out words like these, giving
[the evil god his chance,
And should miss the path of prudence and
[insult their master so!
LEADER. It is not the Argive way to fawn 70
[upon a cowardly man.
AEG. Perhaps. But I in later days will take
[further steps with you.
LEADER. Not if the god who rules the family
[guides Orestes to his home. 75
AEG. Yes. I know that men in exile feed
[themselves on barren hopes.
LEADER. Go on, grow fat defiling justice . . .
[while you have your hour.
AEG. Do not think you will not pay me a 80
[price for your stupidity.
LEADER. Boast on in your self-assurance, like
[a cock beside his hen.
CLYT. Pay no heed, Aegisthus, to these futile
[barkings. 85
You and I,
Masters of this house, from now shall order all
[things well.
[*They enter the palace.*]

Sophocles

496?–406 B.C.

Oedipus Rex

430 B.C.

In *Oedipus Rex* Sophocles endows the figures of a legend with such distinctive yet universal traits that we seem to know them as well as our own acquaintances. We recognize his Oedipus as a mighty and benevolent man who turns rashly tyrannical when crossed, who out of pride and a need for self-assertion imposes his own character on his community, and who from an honesty more compelling than pride destroys himself in a quest for truth. "I am on the brink of dreadful speech!" says the shepherd, and Oedipus replies, "And I of dreadful hearing. Yet I must hear."

Sophocles develops his plot with the same profound fidelity to universal human experience that governs his characterization. From Oedipus' opening assertion of authority to Creon's final rebuff ("Think no longer That you are in command here"), we witness a sequence of events recognizably true in even their smallest elements to the motives, feelings, and temperaments of the characters involved. We understand, for example, why Oedipus responds to Teiresias' silence with irritation mounting to wrath, why Teiresias finally tells his secret, and why Oedipus cannot begin to apprehend it. The importance of plot rendered thus true to human experience is that it gives intelligible form to that experience. As we understand merely one character or another, one act or another, we understand only the accidents of human nature, the unrelated particulars of life. But when we see one act lead naturally to another and that to another, as in Sophocles' linked chain of causation from glorious beginning to hideous end, we have seen through accident to form, through experience to the laws that govern experience.

To understand Oedipus and the laws that govern him, we must understand more than psychology. We must apprehend the world in which he acts and reacts. This world, as the religious festival that gives the play its occasion suggests, is one that the gods govern. And the gods, be it said, are no mere

SOPHOCLES

collection of superstitious oddities. They are the embodiments of a profound conviction that the universe, however mysterious, is governed by an agency that takes moral cognizance of man. The play begins in religious supplication; Teiresias speaks with supernatural authority; the chorus repeatedly prays to the gods; and when Oedipus makes his final discovery, it is that he and his parents, in their desperate efforts to escape the oracles, have lived out, against their own wills, the wills of the gods.

This conflict between Oedipus and the oracles, between the pride of self-sufficient man and the authority of divine law, gives the play its form, which is based on a separation between human will and divine will, a separation rhythmically narrowing with each accession of knowledge until the two merge. The units of rhythm are the individual scenes, each of which shows an Oedipus who is convinced of his own innocence seeking a knowledge that, as he approaches it, turns ironically into an evidence of his own guilt.

The irony of the play deserves particular mention. That it informs the plot is already evident. It also throws its oblique light on every character. Teiresias means to keep his secret but tells it; Iocastê cheers Oedipus with her tale of a false oracle that turns out to be deadly true; the messenger brings good news but finds it most evil. Even the shepherd thought to save a child but committed him to an unspeakable destiny. The irony enters, too, into scores of lines that mean one thing to the speaker, another to the audience. "Poor children," says Oedipus, "I know that you are deathly sick; and yet, Sick as you are, not one is as sick as I." The importance of this pervading irony is that it gives us a dual vision, a view of things as seen by mortal man and a view of the same things under the aspect of eternity. It catches in its duality the play's conflict and the play's theme.

Oedipus and the chorus ultimately discover what the irony keeps making us see—that the individual mind, self-sufficient in its ignorance, responds in fact to control beyond its ken, gives unknown allegiance to a will that unites the infinity of the world's separate wills into a single harmony. Before that greater will man can only do what Creon does—submit himself—and say with the chorus:

Let me be reverent in the ways of right,
Lowly the paths I journey on;
Let all my words and actions keep
The laws of the pure universe
From highest Heaven handed down.

Oedipus Rex

SOPHOCLES

*An English Version
by Dudley Fitts and Robert Fitzgerald*

CHARACTERS

OEDIPUS   *King of Thebes*
A PRIEST
CREON   *brother of Iocastê*
TEIRESIAS   *a blind seer*
IOCASTÊ   *the Queen, wife of Oedipus*
MESSENGER
SHEPHERD OF LAÏOS
SECOND MESSENGER
CHORUS OF THEBAN ELDERS

SCENE. *Before the palace of Oedipus, King of Thebes. A central door and two lateral doors open onto a platform which runs the length of the façade. On the platform, right and left, are*
5 *altars; and three steps lead down into the* orchestra, *or chorus-ground. At the beginning of the action these steps are crowded by suppliants who have brought branches and chaplets of olive leaves and who lie in various attitudes*
10 *of despair.* OEDIPUS *enters.*

PROLOGUE°

OEDIPUS. My children, generations of the
                                                    [living
In the line of Kadmos,° nursed at his ancient
                                                    [hearth:
Why have you strewn yourselves before these   15
                                                    [altars
In supplication, with your boughs and
                                                    [garlands?
The breath of incense rises from the city
With a sound of prayer and lamentation.   20
                                    Children,
I would not have you speak through
                                    [messengers,
And therefore I have come myself to hear
                                            [you—   25
I, Oedipus, who bear the famous name.
    [*To a* PRIEST.]
You, there, since you are eldest in the company,
Speak for them all, tell me what preys upon
                                            [you,   30
Whether you come in dread, or crave some
                                            [blessing:
Tell me, and never doubt that I will help you
In every way I can; I should be heartless
Were I not moved to find you suppliant here.   35
    PRIEST. Great Oedipus, O powerful King of
                                            [Thebes!
You see how all the ages of our people
Cling to your altar steps: here are boys
Who can barely stand alone, and here are   40
                                            [priests
By weight of age, as I am a priest of God,
And young men chosen from those yet
                                            [unmarried;
As for the others, all that multitude,   45
They wait with olive chaplets in the squares,
At the two shrines of Pallas, and where Apollo
Speaks in the glowing embers.
                            Your own eyes
Must tell you: Thebes is in her extremity   50

Prologue   see p. 9. Although it lacks the kommoi and is a scene shorter, *Oedipus Rex* has the same essential structure as *Agamemnon*.
Kadmos   founder of Thebes, great-great-grandfather of Oedipus, Cf. p. 41, ll. 71–72.

And can not lift her head from the surge of
[death.
A rust consumes the buds and fruits of the
[earth;
5 The herds are sick; children die unborn,
And labor is vain. The god of plague and pyre
Raids like detestable lightning through the city,
And all the house of Kadmos is laid waste,
All emptied, and all darkened: Death alone
10 Battens upon the misery of Thebes.

You are not one of the immortal gods, we
[know;
Yet we have come to you to make our prayer
As to the man of all men best in adversity
15 And wisest in the ways of God. You saved us
From the Sphinx,° that flinty singer, and the
[tribute
We paid to her so long; yet you were never
Better informed than we, nor could we teach
20 [you:
It was some god breathed in you to set us free.

Therefore, O mighty King, we turn to you:
Find us our safety, find us a remedy,
Whether by counsel of the gods or men.
25 A king of wisdom tested in the past
Can act in a time of troubles, and act well.
Noblest of men, restore
Life to your city! Think how all men call you
Liberator for your triumph long ago;
30 Ah, when your years of kingship are
[remembered,
Let them not say We rose, but later fell—
Keep the State from going down in the storm!
Once, years ago, with happy augury,
35 You brought us fortune; be the same again!
No man questions your power to rule the land:
But rule over men, not over a dead city!
Ships are only hulls, citadels are nothing,
When no life moves in the empty passageways.

Sphinx monster that settled near Thebes and slew all
passers-by who failed to solve the riddle she asked
of them: "What being has four feet in the morning,
two at noon, and three at night?" Years before the
play's opening Oedipus had rescued Thebes by
solving the riddle ("Man"), whereupon the Sphinx
killed herself, and the Thebans made Oedipus their
king.

OEDIPUS. Poor children! You may be sure I   40
[know
All that you longed for in your coming here.
I know that you are deathly sick; and yet,
Sick as you are, not one is as sick as I.
Each of you suffers in himself alone   45
His anguish, not another's; but my spirit
Groans for the city, for myself, for you.

I was not sleeping, you are not waking me.
No, I have been in tears for a long while
And in my restless thought walked many ways.   50
In all my search, I found one helpful course,
And that I have taken: I have sent Creon,
Son of Menoikeus, brother of the Queen,
To Delphi, Apollo's place of revelation,
To learn there, if he can,   55
What act or pledge of mine may save the city.
I have counted the days, and now, this very
[day,
I am troubled, for he has overstayed his time.
What is he doing? He has been gone too long.   60
Yet whenever he comes back, I should do ill
To scant whatever hint the god may give.
    PRIEST. It is a timely promise. At this instant
They tell me Creon is here.
    OEDIPUS.   O Lord Apollo!   65
May his news be fair as his face is radiant!
    PRIEST. It could not be otherwise: he is
[crowned with bay,°
The chaplet is thick with berries.
    OEDIPUS.   We shall soon know;   70
He is near enough to hear us now.
    [Enter CREON.]
                    O Prince:
Brother: son of Menoikeus:
What answer do you bring us from the god?   75
    CREON. It is favorable. I can tell you, great
[afflictions
Will turn out well, if they are taken well.
    OEDIPUS. What was the oracle? These vague
[words 80
Leave me still hanging between hope and fear.
    CREON. Is it your pleasure to hear me with all
[these
Gathered around us? I am prepared to speak,

bay the laurel, sacred to Apollo and, when worn in
wreaths or crowns, symbolic of victory

But should we not go in?

OEDIPUS.　　　　　Let them all hear it.
It is for them I suffer, more than for myself.

CREON. Then I will tell you what I heard at
　　　　　　　　　　　　　　　　[Delphi.

5

In plain words
The god commands us to expel from the land
　　　　　　　　　　　　　　　[of Thebes
An old defilement that it seems we shelter.

10 It is a deathly thing, beyond expiation.
We must not let it feed upon us longer.

OEDIPUS. What defilement? How shall we rid
　　　　　　　　　　　　　　[ourselves of it?

CREON. By exile or death, blood for blood. It

15　　　　　　　　　　　　　　　　　[was
Murder that brought the plague-wind on the
　　　　　　　　　　　　　　　　　[city.

OEDIPUS. Murder of whom? Surely the god
　　　　　　　　　　　　　　　[has named him?

20 CREON. My lord: long ago Laïos was our
　　　　　　　　　　　　　　　　　[king,
Before you came to govern us.

OEDIPUS.　　　　　　　I know;
I learned of him from others; I never saw him.

25 CREON. He was murdered; and Apollo
　　　　　　　　　　　　　[commands us now
To take revenge upon whoever killed him.

OEDIPUS. Upon whom? Where are they?
　　　　　　　　[Where shall we find a clue

30 To solve that crime, after so many years?

CREON. Here in this land, he said.
　　　　　　　　　　　If we make enquiry,
We may touch things that otherwise escape us.

OEDIPUS. Tell me: Was Laïos murdered in his

35　　　　　　　　　　　　　　　[house,
Or in the fields, or in some foreign country?

CREON. He said he planned to make a
　　　　　　　　　　　　　　　[pilgrimage.
He did not come home again.

40 OEDIPUS.　　　　　And was there no one,
No witness, no companion, to tell what
　　　　　　　　　　　　　　　[happened?

CREON. They were all killed but one, and he
　　　　　　　　　　　　　　　[got away

45 So frightened that he could remember one
　　　　　　　　　　　　　　　[thing only.

OEDIPUS. What was that one thing? One may
　　　　　　　　　　　　　　　[be the key

To everything, if we resolve to use it.

CREON. He said that a band of highwaymen　50
　　　　　　　　　　　　　　[attacked them,
Outnumbered them, and overwhelmed the
　　　　　　　　　　　　　　　　[King.

OEDIPUS. Strange, that a highwayman should
　　　　　　　　　　　　[be so daring—　55
Unless some faction here bribed him to do it.

CREON. We thought of that. But after Laïos'
　　　　　　　　　　　　　　　[death
New troubles arose and we had no avenger.

OEDIPUS. What troubles could prevent your　60
　　　　　　　　　[hunting down the killers?

CREON. The riddling Sphinx's song
Made us deaf to all mysteries but her own.

OEDIPUS. Then once more I must bring what
　　　　　　　　　　　[is dark to light.　65
It is most fitting that Apollo shows,
As you do, this compunction for the dead.
You shall see how I stand by you, as I should,
To avenge the city and the city's god,
And not as though it were for some distant　70
　　　　　　　　　　　　　　　[friend,
But for my own sake, to be rid of evil.
Whoever killed King Laïos might—who
　　　·　　　　　　　　　　　[knows?—
Decide at any moment to kill me as well.　75
By avenging the murdered king I protect
　　　　　　　　　　　　　　　[myself.

Come, then, my children: leave the altar steps,
Lift up your olive boughs!
　　　　　　　　　　One of you go　80
And summon the people of Kadmos to gather
　　　　　　　　　　　　　　　[here.
I will do all that I can; you may tell them that.
[*Exit a* PAGE.]
So, with the help of God,°　85
We shall be saved—or else indeed we are lost.

PRIEST. Let us rise, children. It was for this
　　　　　　　　　　　　　　　[we came,
And now the King has promised it himself.
Phoibos has sent us an oracle; may he descend　90
Himself to save us and drive out the plague.

God Apollo, god of music, archery, healing, light
(**Phoibos,** as he is called at l. 90, means *light* or
pure), and truth. Through his oracle he mediates
between man and the gods.

[*Exeunt* OEDIPUS *and* CREON *into the palace by the central door. The* PRIEST *and the* SUPPLIANTS *disperse R. and L. After a short pause the* CHORUS *enters the orchestra.*]

PÁRODOS

Strophe 1

5 CHORUS. What is the god singing in his
[profound
Delphi of gold and shadow?
What oracle for Thebes, the sunwhipped city?

Fear unjoints me, the roots of my heart tremble.

10 Now I remember, O Healer, your power, and
[wonder:
Will you send doom like a sudden cloud, or
[weave it
Like nightfall of the past?

15 Ah no: be merciful, issue of holy sound:
Dearest to our expectancy: be tender!

Antistrophe 1

Let me pray to Athenê, the immortal daughter
[of Zeus,
And to Artemis her sister
20 Who keeps her famous throne in the market
[ring,
And to Apollo, bowman at the far butts of
[heaven—

O gods, descend! Like three streams leap
25 [against
The fires of our grief, the fires of darkness;
Be swift to bring us rest!

As in the old time from the brilliant house
Of air you stepped to save us, come again!

Strophe 2

30 Now our afflictions have no end.
Now all our stricken host lies down
And no man fights off death with his mind;

The noble plowland bears no grain,
And groaning mothers can not bear—

See, how our lives like birds take wing, 35
Like sparks that fly when a fire soars,
To the shore of the god of evening.

Antistrophe 2

The plague burns on, it is pitiless,
Though pallid children laden with death
Lie unwept in the stony ways, 40

And old gray women by every path
Flock to the strand about the altars

There to strike their breasts and cry
Worship of Zeus in wailing prayers:
Be kind, God's golden child!° 45

Strophe 3

There are no swords in this attack by fire,
No shields, but we are ringed with cries.

Send the besieger plunging from our homes
Into the vast sea-room of the Atlantic
Or into the waves that foam eastward of 50
[Thrace—

For the day ravages what the night spares—

Destroy our enemy, lord of the thunder!
Let him be riven by lightning from heaven!

Antistrophe 3

Phoibos Apollo, stretch the sun's bowstring, 55
That golden cord, until it sing for us,
Flashing arrows in heaven!
                    Artemis, Huntress,
Race with flaring lights upon our mountains!

O scarlet° god, O golden-banded brow, 60
O Theban° Bacchos in a storm of Maenads,
[*Enter* OEDIPUS, *center.*]
Whirl upon Death, that all the Undying hate!
Come with blinding cressets, come in joy!

God's golden child Athena, daughter of Zeus
scarlet flushed with wine
Theban born in Thebes and descended on his mortal side from Kadmos

SCENE I

OEDIPUS. Is this your prayer? It may be
[answered. Come,
Listen to me, act as the crisis demands,
And you shall have relief from all these evils.

5   Until now I was a stranger to this tale,
As I had been a stranger to the crime.
Could I track down the murderer without a
[clue?
But now, friends,
10 As one who became a citizen after the murder,
I make this proclamation to all Thebans:
If any man knows by whose hands Laïos, son of
[Labdakos,
Met his death, I direct that man to tell me
15 [everything,
No matter what he fears for having so long
[withheld it.
Let it stand as promised that no further trouble
Will come to him, but he may leave the land in
20 [safety.

Moreover: If anyone knows the murderer to
[be foreign,
Let him not keep silent: he shall have his
[reward from me.
25 However, if he does conceal it, if any man
Fearing for his friend or for himself disobeys
[this edict,
Hear what I propose to do:

I solemnly forbid the people of this country,
30 Where power and throne are mine, ever to
[receive that man
Or speak to him, no matter who he is, or let
[him
Join in sacrifice, lustration, or in prayer.
35 I decree that he be driven from every house,
Being, as he is, corruption itself to us: the
[Delphic
Voice of Zeus has pronounced this revelation.
Thus I associate myself with the oracle
40 And take the side of the murdered king.

As for the criminal, I pray to God—
Whether it be a lurking thief, or one of a
[number—
I pray that that man's life be consumed in evil
[and wretchedness.   45
And as for me, this curse applies no less
If it should turn out that the culprit is my guest
[here,
Sharing my hearth.
You have heard the penalty.   50
I lay it on you now to attend to this
For my sake, for Apollo's, for the sick
Sterile city that heaven has abandoned.
Suppose the oracle had given you no command:
Should this defilement go uncleansed for ever?   55
You should have found the murderer: your
[king,
A noble king, had been destroyed!
Now I,
Having the power that he held before me,   60
Having his bed, begetting children there
Upon his wife, as he would have, had he
[lived—
Their son would have been my children's
[brother,   65
If Laïos had had luck in fatherhood!
(But surely ill luck rushed upon his reign)—
I say I take the son's part, just as though
I were his son, to press the fight for him
And see it won! I'll find the hand that brought   70
Death to Labdakos' and Polydoros' child,
Heir of Kadmos' and Agenor's line.°
And as for those who fail me,
May the gods deny them the fruit of the earth,
Fruit of the womb, and may they rot utterly!   75
Let them be wretched as we are wretched, and
[worse!

For you, for loyal Thebans, and for all
Who find my actions right, I pray the favor
Of justice, and of all the immortal gods.   80
LEADER OF THE CHORUS. Since I am under
[oath, my lord, I swear
I did not do the murder, I can not name
The murderer. Might not the oracle

Labdakos' . . . line   the child is Laïos, whose male ancestry Oedipus traces back: Laïos-Labdakos-Poly-
doros-Kadmos-Agenor

That has ordained the search tell where to find
[him?
OEDIPUS. An honest question. But no man in
[the world
5   Can make the gods do more than the gods will.
LEADER. There is one last expedient—
OEDIPUS.   Tell me what it is.
Though it seem slight, you must not hold it
[back.
10   LEADER. A lord clairvoyant to the lord Apollo,
As we all know, is the skilled Teiresias.
One might learn much about this from him,
[Oedipus.
OEDIPUS. I am not wasting time:
15   Creon spoke of this and I have sent for him—
Twice, in fact; it is strange that he is not here.
LEADER. The other matter—that old report—
[seems useless.
OEDIPUS. Tell me. I am interested in all
20   [reports.
LEADER. The King was said to have been
[killed by highwaymen.
OEDIPUS. I know. But we have no witnesses
[to that.
25   LEADER. If the killer can feel a particle of
[dread,
Your curse will bring him out of hiding!
OEDIPUS.   No.
The man who dared that act will fear no curse.
30   [Enter the blind seer TEIRESIAS led by a PAGE.]
LEADER. But there is one man who may detect
[the criminal.
This is Teiresias, this is the holy prophet
In whom, alone of all men, truth was born.
35   OEDIPUS. Teiresias: seer: student of
[mysteries,
Of all that's taught and all that no man tells,
Secrets of Heaven and secrets of the earth:
Blind though you are, you know the city lies
40   Sick with plague; and from this plague, my
[lord,
We find that you alone can guard or save us.

Possibly you did not hear the messengers?
Apollo, when we sent to him,
45   Sent us back word that this great pestilence
Would lift, but only if we established clearly
The identity of those who murdered Laïos.

They must be killed or exiled.
                              Can you use
Birdflight or any art of divination   50
To purify yourself, and Thebes, and me
From this contagion? We are in your hands.
There is no fairer duty
Than that of helping others in distress.
TEIRESIAS. How dreadful knowledge of the   55
[truth can be
When there's no help in truth! I knew this well,
But did not act on it: else I should not have
[come.
OEDIPUS. What is troubling you? Why are   60
[your eyes so cold?
TEIRESIAS. Let me go home. Bear your own
[fate, and I'll
Bear mine. It is better so: trust what I say.
OEDIPUS. What you say is ungracious and   65
[unhelpful
To your native country. Do not refuse to speak.
TEIRESIAS. When it comes to speech, your
[own is neither temperate
Nor opportune. I wish to be more prudent.   70
OEDIPUS. In God's name, we all beg you—
TEIRESIAS.   You are all ignorant.
No; I will never tell you what I know.
Now it is my misery; then, it would be yours.
OEDIPUS. What! You do know something,   75
[and will not tell us?
You would betray us all and wreck the State?
TEIRESIAS. I do not intend to torture myself,
[or you.
Why persist in asking? You will not persuade   80
[me.
OEDIPUS. What a wicked old man you are!
[You'd try a stone's
Patience! Out with it! Have you no feeling at
[all?   85
TEIRESIAS. You call me unfeeling. If you
[could only see
The nature of your own feelings . . .
OEDIPUS.   Why,
Who would not feel as I do? Who could endure   90
Your arrogance toward the city?
TEIRESIAS.   What does it matter!
Whether I speak or not, it is bound to come.
OEDIPUS. Then, if "it" is bound to come, you
[are bound to tell me.   95

TEIRESIAS. No, I will not go on. Rage as you
                           [please.
OEDIPUS. Rage? Why not!
               And I'll tell you what I think:
5 You planned it, you had it done, you all but
Killed him with your own hands: if you had
                        [eyes,
I'd say the crime was yours, and yours alone.
TEIRESIAS. So? I charge you, then,
10 Abide by the proclamation you have made:
From this day forth
Never speak again to these men or to me;
You yourself are the pollution of this country.
OEDIPUS. You dare say that! Can you
15   [possibly think you have
Some way of going free, after such insolence?
TEIRESIAS. I have gone free. It is the truth
                  [sustains me.
OEDIPUS. Who taught you shamelessness?
20   [It was not your craft.
TEIRESIAS. You did. You made me speak. I
               [did not want to.
OEDIPUS. Speak what? Let me hear it again
               [more clearly.
25 TEIRESIAS. Was it not clear before? Are you
               [tempting me?
OEDIPUS. I did not understand it. Say it again.
TEIRESIAS. I say that you are the murderer
               [whom you seek.
30 OEDIPUS. Now twice you have spat out
            [infamy. You'll pay for it!
TEIRESIAS. Would you care for more? Do you
            [wish to be really angry?
OEDIPUS. Say what you will. Whatever you
35   [say is worthless.
TEIRESIAS. I say that you live in hideous love
              [with her
Who is nearest you in blood. You are blind to
              [the evil.
40 OEDIPUS. It seems you can go on mouthing
            [like this for ever.
TEIRESIAS. I can, if there is power in truth.
OEDIPUS.   There is:
But not for you, not for you,
45 You sightless, witless, senseless, mad old man!
TEIRESIAS. You are the madman. There is no
             [one here
Who will not curse you soon, as you curse me.

OEDIPUS. You child of endless night! You
            [can not hurt me 50
Or any other man who sees the sun.
   TEIRESIAS. True: it is not from me your fate
               [will come.
That lies within Apollo's competence,
As it is his concern.   55
   OEDIPUS.   Tell me:
Are you speaking for Creon, or for yourself?
   TEIRESIAS. Creon is no threat. You weave
              [your own doom.
   OEDIPUS. Wealth, power, craft of   60
              [statesmanship!
Kingly position, everywhere admired!
What savage envy is stored up against these,
If Creon, who I trusted, Creon my friend,
For this great office which the city once   65
Put in my hands unsought—if for this power
Creon desires in secret to destroy me!

He has bought this decrepit fortune-teller, this
Collector of dirty pennies, this prophet fraud—
Why, he is no more clairvoyant than I am!   70
                         Tell us:
Has your mystic mummery ever approached
               [the truth?
When that hellcat the Sphinx was performing
               [here, 75
What help were you to these people?
Her magic was not for the first man who came
               [along:
It demanded a real exorcist. Your birds—
What good are they? or the gods, for the matter 80
               [of that?
But I came by,
Oedipus, the simple man, who knows
               [nothing—
I thought it out for myself, no birds helped me! 85
And this is the man you think you can destroy,
That you may be close to Creon when he's king!
Well, you and your friend Creon, it seems to me,
Will suffer most. If you were not an old man,
You would have paid already for your plot.   90
   LEADER OF THE CHORUS. We can not see that
            [his words or yours
Have been spoken except in anger, Oedipus,
And of anger we have no need. How can God's
               [will 95

Be accomplished best? That is what most
[concerns us.
TEIRESIAS. You are a king. But where
[argument's concerned
5   I am your man, as much a king as you.
I am not your servant, but Apollo's.
I have no need of Creon to speak for me.

Listen to me. You mock my blindness, do you?
But I say that you, with both your eyes, are
10   [blind:
You can not see the wretchedness of your life,
Nor in whose house you live, no, nor with
[whom.
Who are your father and mother? Can you tell
15   [me?
You do not even know the blind wrongs
That you have done them, on earth and in the
[world below.
But the double lash of your parents' curse will
20   [whip you
Out of this land some day, with only night
Upon your precious eyes.
Your cries then—where will they not be heard?
What fastness of Kithairon° will not echo
25   [them?
And that bridal-descant of yours—you'll know
[it then,
The song they sang when you came here to
[Thebes
30   And found your misguided berthing.
All this, and more, that you can not guess at
[now,
Will bring you to yourself among your
[children.

35   Be angry then. Curse Creon. Curse my words.
I tell you, no man that walks upon the earth
Shall be rooted out more horribly than you.
OEDIPUS. Am I to bear this from him?—
[Damnation
40   Take you! Out of this place! Out of my sight!
TEIRESIAS. I would not have come at all if you
[had not asked me.
OEDIPUS. Could I have told that you'd talk

Kithairon mountain near Thebes where the infant
Oedipus was left to die. Cf. pp. 48–50, ll. 86–2.

[nonsense, that
You'd come here to make a fool of yourself,   45
[and of me?
TEIRESIAS. A fool? Your parents thought me
[sane enough.
OEDIPUS. My parents again!—Wait: who
[were my parents?   50
TEIRESIAS. This day will give you a father,
[and break your heart.
OEDIPUS. Your infantile riddles! Your
[damned abracadabra!
TEIRESIAS. You were a great man once at   55
[solving riddles.
OEDIPUS. Mock me with that if you like; you
[will find it true.
TEIRESIAS. It was true enough. It brought
[about your ruin.   60
OEDIPUS. But if it saved this town?
TEIRESIAS [to the PAGE]. Boy, give me your
[hand.
OEDIPUS. Yes, boy; lead him away.
—While you are here   65
We can do nothing. Go; leave us in peace.
TEIRESIAS. I will go when I have said what I
[have to say.
How can you hurt me? And I tell you again:
The man you have been looking for all this   70
[time,
The damned man, the murderer of Laïos,
That man is in Thebes. To your mind he is
[foreign-born,
But it will soon be shown that he is a Theban,   75
A revelation that will fail to please.
A blind man,
Who has his eyes now; a penniless man, who
[is rich now;
And he will go tapping the strange earth with   80
[his staff.
To the children with whom he lives now he
[will be
Brother and father—the very same; to her
Who bore him, son and husband—the very   85
[same
Who came to his father's bed, wet with his
[father's blood.

Enough. Go think that over.
If later you find error in what I have said,   90

You may say that I have no skill in prophecy.
[*Exit* TEIRESIAS, *led by his* PAGE. OEDIPUS *goes into the palace.*]

ODE I

Strophe 1

CHORUS. The Delphic stone of prophecies°
5 Remembers ancient regicide
And a still bloody hand.
That killer's hour of flight has come.
He must be stronger than riderless
Coursers of untiring wind,
10 For the son of Zeus° armed with his father's
[thunder
Leaps in lightning after him;
And the Furies follow him, the sad Furies.

Antistrophe 1

Holy Parnassos'° peak of snow
15 Flashes and blinds that secret man,
That all shall hunt him down:
Though he may roam the forest shade
Like a bull gone wild from pasture
To rage through glooms of stone.
20 Doom comes down on him; flight will not avail
[him;
For the world's heart calls him desolate,
And the immortal Furies follow, for ever
[follow.

Strophe 2

25 But now a wilder thing is heard
From the old man skilled at hearing Fate in the
[wingbeat of a bird.
Bewildered as a blown bird, my soul hovers and
[can not find
30 Foothold in this debate, or any reason or rest
[of mind.
But no man ever brought—none can bring
Proof of strife between Thebes' royal house,
Labdakos' line, and the son of Polybos;°

Delphic stone of prophecies platform of rock on which
stood the temple of the Delphic oracle
son of Zeus Apollo
Parnassos mountain, sacred to Apollo, on the side of
which Delphi and its oracle stood
son of Polybos Oedipus. Cf. pp. 49–50, ll. 94–1.

And never until now has any man brought   35
[word
Of Laïos' dark death staining Oedipus the
[King.

Antistrophe 2

Divine Zeus and Apollo hold
Perfect intelligence alone of all tales ever told;   40
And well though this diviner works, he works
[in his own night;
No man can judge that rough unknown or trust
[in second sight,
For wisdom changes hands among the wise.   45
Shall I believe my great lord criminal
At a raging word that a blind old man let fall?
I saw him, when the carrion woman faced him
[of old,
Prove his heroic mind! These evil words are   50
[lies.

SCENE II

CREON. Men of Thebes:
I am told that heavy accusations
Have been brought against me by King
[Oedipus.   55

I am not the kind of man to bear this tamely.

If in these present difficulties
He holds me accountable for any harm to him
Through anything I have said or done—why,
[then,   60
I do not value life in this dishonor.
It is not as though this rumor touched upon
Some private indiscretion. The matter is grave.
The fact is that I am being called disloyal
To the State, to my fellow citizens, to my   65
[friends.
LEADER OF THE CHORUS. He may have spoken
[in anger, not from his mind.
CREON. But did you hear him say I was the
[one   70
Who seduced the old prophet into lying?
LEADER. The thing was said; I do not know
[how seriously.
CREON. But you were watching him! Were
[his eyes steady?   75

Did he look like a man in his right mind?
   LEADER.   I do not know.
I can not judge the behavior of great men.
But here is the King himself.
5   [Enter OEDIPUS.]
   OEDIPUS.   So you dared come back.
Why? How brazen of you to come to my house,
You murderer!
               Do you think I do not know
10 That you plotted to kill me, plotted to steal my
                          [throne?
Tell me, in God's name: am I coward, a fool,
That you should dream you could accomplish
                          [this?
15 A fool who could not see your slippery game?
A coward, not to fight back when I saw it?
You are the fool, Creon, are you not? hoping
Without support or friends to get a throne?
Thrones may be won or bought: you could do
20   [neither.
   CREON. Now listen to me. You have talked;
                      [let me talk, too.
You can not judge unless you know the facts.
   OEDIPUS. You speak well: there is one fact;
25   [but I find it hard
To learn from the deadliest enemy I have.
   CREON. That above all I must dispute with
                      [you.
   OEDIPUS. That above all I will not hear you
30   [deny.
   CREON. If you think there is anything good in
                   [being stubborn
Against all reason, then I say you are wrong.
   OEDIPUS. If you think a man can sin against
35   [his own kind
And not be punished for it, I say you are mad.
   CREON. I agree. But tell me: what have I done
                    [to you?
   OEDIPUS. You advised me to send for that
40   [wizard, did you not?
   CREON. I did. I should do it again.
   OEDIPUS.   Very well. Now tell me:
How long has it been since Laïos—
   CREON.   What of Laïos?
45   OEDIPUS. Since he vanished in that onset by
                   [the road?
   CREON. It was long ago, a long time.
   OEDIPUS.   And this prophet,

Was he practicing here then?
   CREON.   He was; and with honor, as now.   50
   OEDIPUS. Did he speak of me at that time?
   CREON.   He never did;
At least, not when I was present.
   OEDIPUS.   But . . . the enquiry?
I suppose you held one?   55
   CREON.   We did, but we learned nothing.
   OEDIPUS. Why did the prophet not speak
                  [against me then?
   CREON. I do not know; and I am the kind of
                  [man   60
Who holds his tongue when he has no facts to
                  [go on.
   OEDIPUS. There's one fact that you know,
                  [and you could tell it.
   CREON. What fact is that? If I know it, you   65
                  [shall have it.
   OEDIPUS. If he were not involved with you,
                  [he could not say
That it was I who murdered Laïos.
   CREON. If he says that, you are the one that   70
                  [knows it?—
But now it is my turn to question you.
   OEDIPUS. Put your questions. I am no
                  [murderer.
   CREON. First, then: You married my sister?   75
   OEDIPUS.   I married your sister.
   CREON. And you rule the kingdom equally
                  [with her?
   OEDIPUS. Everything that she wants she has
                  [from me.   80
   CREON. And I am the third, equal to both of
                  [you?
   OEDIPUS. That is why I call you a bad friend.
   CREON. No. Reason it out, as I have done.
Think of this first: Would any sane man prefer   85
Power, with all a king's anxieties,
To that same power and the grace of sleep?
Certainly not I.
I have never longed for the king's power—only
                  [his rights.   90
Would any wise man differ from me in this?
As matters stand, I have my way in everything
With your consent, and no responsibilities.
If I were king, I should be a slave to policy.

How could I desire a scepter more   95

Than what is now mine—untroubled influence?
No, I have not gone mad; I need no honors,
Except those with the perquisites I have now.
I am welcome everywhere; every man salutes
5   [me,
And those who want your favor seek my ear,
Since I know how to manage what they ask.
Should I exchange this ease for that anxiety?
Besides, no sober mind is treasonable.
10 I hate anarchy
And never would deal with any man who likes
                                     [it.

Test what I have said. Go to the priestess
At Delphi, ask if I quoted her correctly.
15 And as for this other thing: if I am found
Guilty of treason with Teiresias,
Then sentence me to death! You have my word
It is a sentence I should cast my vote for—
But not without evidence!
20   You do wrong
When you take good men for bad, bad men for
                                  [good.
A true friend thrown aside—why, life itself
Is not more precious!
25   In time you will know this well:
For time, and time alone, will show the just
                                  [man,
Though scoundrels are discovered in a day.
    LEADER. This is well said, and a prudent man
30   [would ponder it.
Judgments too quickly formed are dangerous.
    OEDIPUS. But is he not quick in his duplicity?
And shall I not be quick to parry him?
Would you have me stand still, hold my peace,
35   [and let
This man win everything, through my inaction?
    CREON. And you want—what is it, then? To
                              [banish me?
    OEDIPUS. No; not exile. It is your death I
40   [want,
So that all the world may see what treason
                                  [means.
    CREON. You will persist, then? You will not
                            [believe me?
45 OEDIPUS. How can I believe you?
    CREON.   Then you are a fool.
    OEDIPUS. To save myself?

CREON.   In justice, think of me.
OEDIPUS. You are evil incarnate.
CREON.   But suppose that you are wrong?   50
OEDIPUS. Still I must rule.
CREON.   But not if you rule badly.
OEDIPUS. O city, city!
CREON.   It is my city, too!
LEADER. Now, my lords, be still. I see the   55
                              [Queen,
Iocastê, coming from her palace chambers;
And it is time she came, for the sake of you
                                [both.
This dreadful quarrel can be resolved through 60
                                  [her.
    [*Enter* IOCASTÊ.]
IOCASTÊ. Poor foolish men, what wicked din
                              [is this?
With Thebes sick to death, is it not shameful   65
That you should rake some private quarrel up?
    [*To* OEDIPUS.]
Come into the house.
                     —And you, Creon, go now:
Let us have no more of this tumult over   70
                                [nothing.
    CREON. Nothing? No, sister: what your
                        [husband plans for me
Is one of two great evils: exile or death.
    OEDIPUS. He is right.   75
        Why, woman I have caught him squarely
Plotting against my life.
    CREON.   No! Let me die.
Accurst if ever I have wished you harm!
    IOCASTÊ. Ah, believe it, Oedipus!   80
In the name of the gods, respect this oath of his
For my sake, for the sake of these people here!

               Strophe 1
LEADER. Open your mind to her, my lord. Be
                    [ruled by her, I beg you!
OEDIPUS. What would you have me do?   85
LEADER. Respect Creon's word He has never
                    [spoken like a fool,
And now he has sworn an oath.
OEDIPUS.   You know what you ask?
LEADER.   I do.   90
OEDIPUS.   Speak on, then.
LEADER. A friend so sworn should not be
                         [baited so,

In blind malice, and without final proof.
OEDIPUS. You are aware, I hope, that what
                                              [you say
Means death for me, or exile at the least.

Strophe 2

5   LEADER. No, I swear by Helios,° first in
                                              [Heaven!
    May I die friendless and accurst,
    The worst of deaths, if ever I meant that!
    It is the withering fields
10   That hurt my sick heart:
    Must we bear all these ills,
            And now your bad blood as well?
    OEDIPUS. Then let him go. And let me die,
                                              [if I must,
15 Or be driven by him in shame from the land of
                                              [Thebes.
    It is your unhappiness, and not his talk,
    That touches me.
                    As for him—
20 Wherever he is, I will hate him as long as I live.
        CREON. Ugly in yielding, as you were ugly in
                                              [rage!
    Natures like yours chiefly torment themselves.
        OEDIPUS. Can you not go? Can you not leave
25   [me?
        CREON.   I can.
    You do not know me; but the city knows me,
    And in its eyes I am just, if not in yours.
        [*Exit* CREON.]

Antistrophe 1

30 LEADER. Lady Iocastê, did you not ask the
                                              [King to go to his chambers?
    IOCASTÊ. First tell me what has happened.
    LEADER. There was suspicion without
                                              [evidence; yet it rankled
35 As even false charges will.
        IOCASTÊ.   On both sides?
        LEADER.   On both.
        IOCASTÊ.   But what was said?
        LEADER. Oh let it rest, let it be done with!
40 Have we not suffered enough?
        OEDIPUS. You see to what your decency has
                                              [brought you:

Helios the sun-god

You have made difficulties where my heart saw
                                              [none.

Antistrophe 2

LEADER. Oedipus, it is not once only I have   45
                                              [told you—
    You must know I should count myself unwise
    To the point of madness, should I now forsake
                                              [you—
            You, under whose hand,   50
            In the storm of another time,
            Our dear land sailed out free.
                But now stand fast at the helm!
    IOCASTÊ. In God's name, Oedipus, inform
                                              [your wife as well: 55
    Why are you so set in this hard anger?
    OEDIPUS. I will tell you, for none of these
                                              [men deserves
    My confidence as you do. It is Creon's work,
    His treachery, his plotting against me.   60
    IOCASTÊ. Go on, if you can make this clear to
                                              [me.
    OEDIPUS. He charges me with the murder of
                                              [Laïos.
    IOCASTÊ. Has he some knowledge? Or does he 65
                                              [speak from hearsay?
    OEDIPUS. He would not commit himself to
                                              [such a charge,
    But he has brought in that damnable soothsayer
    To tell his story.   70
        IOCASTÊ.   Set your mind at rest.
    If it is a question of soothsayers, I tell you
    That you will find no man whose craft gives
                                              [knowledge
    Of the unknowable.   75
                Here is my proof:

    An oracle was reported to Laïos once
    (I will not say from Phoibos himself, but from
    His appointed ministers, at any rate)
    That his doom would be death at the hands of   80
                                              [his own son—
    His son, born of his flesh and of mine!
    Now, you remember the story: Laïos was killed
    By marauding strangers where three highways
                                              [meet; 85
    But his child had not been three days in this
                                              [world

Before the King had pierced the baby's ankles
And had him left to die on a lonely mountain.

Thus, Apollo never caused that child
To kill his father, and it was not Laïos' fate
5   To die at the hands of his son, as he had feared.
This is what prophets and prophecies are
                                    [worth!
Have no dread of them.
                        It is God himself
10 Who can show us what he wills, in his own
                                    [way.
    OEDIPUS. How strange a shadowy memory
                            [crossed my mind,
Just now while you were speaking; it chilled
15   [my heart.
    IOCASTÊ. What do you mean? What memory
                            [do you speak of?
    OEDIPUS. If I understand you, Laïos was
                                    [killed
20 At a place where three roads meet.
    IOCASTÊ.   So it was said;
We have no later story.
    OEDIPUS.   Where did it happen?
    IOCASTÊ. Phokis, it is called: at a place where
25   [the Theban Way
Divides into the roads toward Delphi and
                                    [Daulia.
    OEDIPUS. When?
    IOCASTÊ.   We had the news not long
30   [before you came
And proved the right to your succession here.
    OEDIPUS. Ah, what net has God been weaving
                                    [for me?
    IOCASTÊ. Oedipus! Why does this trouble
35   [you?
    OEDIPUS.   Do not ask me yet.
First, tell me how Laïos looked, and tell me
How old he was.
    IOCASTÊ.   He was tall, his hair just touched
40 With white; his form was not unlike your own.
    OEDIPUS. I think that I myself may be accurst
By my own ignorant edict.
    IOCASTÊ.   You speak strangely.
It makes me tremble to look at you, my King.
45 OEDIPUS. I am not sure that the blind man can
                                    [not see.
But I should know better if you were to tell

                                    [me—
    IOCASTÊ. Anything—though I dread to hear
                            [you ask it. 50
    OEDIPUS. Was the King lightly escorted, or
                                [did he ride
With a large company, as a ruler should?
    IOCASTÊ. There were five men with him in all:
                            [one was a herald; 55
And a single chariot, which he was driving.
    OEDIPUS. Alas, that makes it plain enough!
                            But who—
Who told you how it happened?
    IOCASTÊ.   A household servant,   60
The only one to escape.
    OEDIPUS.   And is he still
A servant of ours?
    IOCASTÊ.   No; for when he came back at
                                    [last 65
And found you enthroned in the place of the
                                [dead king,
He came to me, touched my hand with his, and
                                [begged
That I would send him away to the frontier   70
                                [district
Where only the shepherds go—
As far away from the city as I could send him.
I granted his prayer; for although the man was
                            [a slave, 75
He had earned more than this favor at my
                                [hands.
    OEDIPUS. Can he be called back quickly?
    IOCASTÊ.   Easily.
But why?   80
    OEDIPUS.   I have taken too much upon
                                [myself
Without enquiry; therefore I wish to consult
                                [him.
    IOCASTÊ. Then he shall come.   85
                    But am I not one also
To whom you might confide these fears of
                                [yours?
    OEDIPUS. That is your right; it will not be
                            [denied you, 90
Now least of all; for I have reached a pitch
Of wild foreboding. Is there anyone
To whom I should sooner speak?

Polybos of Corinth is my father.

SOPHOCLES | Scene II

My mother is a Dorian: Meropê.
I grew up chief among the men of Corinth
Until a strange thing happened—
Not worth my passion, it may be, but strange.

5 At a feast, a drunken man maundering in his
                                              [cups
Cries out that I am not my father's son!

I contained myself that night, though I felt
                                              [anger
10 And a sinking heart. The next day I visited
My father and mother, and questioned them.
                                          [They stormed,
Calling it all the slanderous rant of a fool;
And this relieved me. Yet the suspicion
15 Remained always aching in my mind;
I knew there was talk; I could not rest;
And finally, saying nothing to my parents,
I went to the shrine at Delphi.

The god dismissed my question without reply;
20 He spoke of other things.
                          Some were clear,
Full of wretchedness, dreadful, unbearable:
As, that I should lie with my own mother, breed
Children from whom all men would turn their
25   [eyes;
And that I should be my father's murderer.

I heard all this, and fled. And from that day
Corinth to me was only in the stars
Descending in that quarter of the sky,
30 As I wandered farther and farther on my way
To a land where I should never see the evil
Sung by the oracle. And I came to this country
Where, so you say, King Laïos was killed.

I will tell you all that happened there, my lady.

35 There were three highways
Coming together at a place I passed;
And there a herald came towards me, and a
                                          [chariot
Drawn by horses, with a man such as you
40   [describe
Seated in it. The groom leading the horses
Forced me off the road at his lord's command;

But as this charioteer lurched over towards me
I struck him in my rage. The old man saw me
And brought his double goad down upon my   45
                                          [head
As I came abreast.
                    He was paid back, and more!
Swinging my club in this right hand I knocked
                                          [him 50
Out of his car, and he rolled on the ground.
                                    I killed him.

I killed them all.
Now if that stranger and Laïos were—kin,
Where is a man more miserable than I?   55
More hated by the gods? Citizen and alien alike
Must never shelter me or speak to me—
I must be shunned by all.
                          And I myself
Pronounced this malediction upon myself!   60
Think of it: I have touched you with these
                                          [hands,
These hands that killed your husband. What
                                          [defilement!

Am I all evil, then? It must be so,   65
Since I must flee from Thebes, yet never again
See my own countrymen, my own country,
For fear of joining my mother in marriage
And killing Polybos, my father.
                                Ah,   70
If I was created so, born to this fate,
Who could deny the savagery of God?

O holy majesty of heavenly powers!
May I never see that day! Never!
Rather let me vanish from the race of men   75
Than know the abomination destined me!
    LEADER. We too, my lord, have felt dismay at
                                          [this.
But there is hope: you have yet to hear the
                                      [shepherd. 80
    OEDIPUS. Indeed, I fear no other hope is left
                                          [me.
    IOCASTÊ. What do you hope for him when
                                      [he comes?
    OEDIPUS.   This much: 85
If his account of the murder tallies with yours,
Then I am cleared.

IocastÊ.   What was it that I said
Of such importance?
     Oedipus.   Why, "marauders," you said,
Killed the King, according to this man's story.
5 If he maintains that still, if there were several,
Clearly the guilt is not mine: I was alone.
But if he says one man, singlehanded, did it,
Then the evidence all points to me.
     IocastÊ. You may be sure that he said there
10   [were several;
And can he call back that story now? He can
                                        [not.
The whole city heard it as plainly as I.
But suppose he alters some detail of it:
15 He can not ever show that Laïos' death
Fulfilled the oracle: for Apollo said
My child was doomed to kill him; and my
                                        [child—
Poor baby!—it was my child that died first.
20 No. From now on, where oracles are concerned,
I would not waste a second thought on any.
     Oedipus. You may be right.
                         But come: let someone go
For the shepherd at once. This matter must be
25   [settled.
     IocastÊ. I will send for him.
I would not wish to cross you in anything,
And surely not in this.—Let us go in.
     [*Exeunt into the palace.*]

ODE II

Strophe 1
30 Chorus. Let me be reverent in the ways of
                                        [right,
Lowly the paths I journey on;
Let all my words and actions keep
The laws of the pure universe
35 From highest Heaven handed down.
For Heaven is their bright nurse,
Those generations of the realms of light;
Ah, never of mortal kind were they begot,
Nor are they slaves of memory, lost in sleep:
40 Their Father is greater than Time, and ages not.

Antistrophe 1
The tyrant is a child of Pride
Who drinks from his great sickening cup

Recklessness and vanity,
Until from his high crest headlong
He plummets to the dust of hope.   45
That strong man is not strong.
But let no fair ambition be denied;
May God protect the wrestler for the State
In government, in comely policy,
Who will fear God, and on His ordinance wait. 50

Strophe 2
Haughtiness and the high hand of disdain
Tempt and outrage God's holy law;
And any mortal who dares hold
No immortal Power in awe
Will be caught up in a net of pain: 55
The price for which his levity is sold.
Let each man take due earnings, then,
And keep his hands from holy things,
And from blasphemy stand apart—
Else the crackling blast of heaven   60
Blows on his head, and on his desperate heart;
Though fools will honor impious men,
In their cities no tragic poet sings.

Antistrophe 2
Shall we lose faith in Delphi's obscurities,
We who have heard the world's core   65
Discredited, and the sacred wood
Of Zeus at Elis praised no more?
The deeds and the strange prophecies
Must make a pattern yet to be understood.
Zeus, if indeed you are lord of all,   70
Throned in light over night and day,
Mirror this in your endless mind:
Our masters call the oracle
Words on the wind, and the Delphic vision
                                        [blind! 75
Their hearts no longer know Apollo,
And reverence for the gods has died away.

SCENE III

[*Enter* IocastÊ.]
     IocastÊ. Princes of Thebes, it has occurred to
                                        [me 80
To visit the altars of the gods, bearing
These branches as a suppliant, and this incense.
Our King is not himself: his noble soul

Is overwrought with fantasies of dread,
Else he would consider
The new prophecies in the light of the old.
He will listen to any voice that speaks disaster,
5 And my advice goes for nothing.
    [*She approaches the altar, R.*]
                              To you, then, Apollo,
Lycean lord,° since you are nearest, I turn in
                              [prayer.
10 Receive these offerings, and grant us
                              [deliverance
From defilement. Our hearts are heavy with
                              [fear
When we see our leader distracted, as helpless
15   [sailors
Are terrified by the confusion of their
                              [helmsman.
    [*Enter* MESSENGER.]
MESSENGER. Friends, no doubt you can direct
20   [me:
Where shall I find the house of Oedipus,
Or, better still, where is the King himself?
    LEADER. It is this very place, stranger; he is
                              [inside.
25 This is his wife and mother of his children.
    MESSENGER. I wish her happiness in a happy
                              [house,
Blest in all the fulfillment of her marriage.
    IOCASTÊ. I wish as much for you: your
30   [courtesy
Deserves a like good fortune. But now, tell me:
Why have you come? What have you to say to
                              [us?
    MESSENGER. Good news, my lady, for your
35   [house and your husband.
    IOCASTÊ. What news? Who sent you here?
    MESSENGER.   I am from Corinth.
The news I bring ought to mean joy for you,
Though it may be you will find some grief in it.
40 IOCASTÊ. What is it? How can it touch us in
                              [both ways?
    MESSENGER. The people of Corinth, they say,
Intend to call Oedipus to be their king.
    IOCASTÊ. But old Polybos—is he not reigning
45   [still?
    MESSENGER. No. Death holds him in his

Lycean lord lord of light. Cf. p. 39, l. 85n.

                              [sepulchre.
    IOCASTÊ. What are you saying? Polybos is
                              [dead?
    MESSENGER. If I am not telling the truth, may   50
                              [I die myself.
    IOCASTÊ [*to a* MAID-SERVANT]. Go in, go
                              [quickly; tell this to your master.

O riddlers of God's will, where are you now!
This was the man whom Oedipus, long ago,   55
Feared so, fled so, in dread of destroying him—
But it was another fate by which he died.
    [*Enter* OEDIPUS, *center.*]
    OEDIPUS. Dearest Iocastê, why have you sent
                              [for me?   60
    IOCASTÊ. Listen to what this man says, and
                              [then tell me
What has become of the solemn prophecies.
    OEDIPUS. Who is this man? What is his news
                              [for me?   65
    IOCASTÊ. He has come from Corinth to
                              [announce your father's death!
    OEDIPUS. Is it true, stranger? Tell me in your
                              [own words.
    MESSENGER. I can not say it more clearly: the   70
                              [King is dead.
    OEDIPUS. Was it by treason? Or by an attack
                              [of illness?
    MESSENGER. A little thing brings old men to
                              [their rest.   75
    OEDIPUS. It was sickness, then?
    MESSENGER.   Yes, and his many years.
    OEDIPUS. Ah!
Why should a man respect the Pythian hearth,°
                              [or   80
Give heed to the birds that jangle above his
                              [head?
They prophesied that I should kill Polybos,
Kill my own father; but he is dead and buried,
And I am here—I never touched him, never,   85
Unless he died of grief for my departure,
And thus, in a sense, through me. No. Polybos
Has packed the oracles off with him
                              [underground.
They are empty words.   90

Pythian hearth Delphic oracle, where Apollo slew the
    serpent Python

IOCASTÊ.   Had I not told you so?
OEDIPUS. You had; it was my faint heart that
                              [betrayed me.
IOCASTÊ. From now on never think of those
5   [things again.
OEDIPUS. And yet—must I not fear my
                              [mother's bed?
IOCASTÊ. Why should anyone in this world be
                              [afraid,
10 Since Fate rules us and nothing can be foreseen?
A man should live only for the present day.

Have no more fear of sleeping with your
                              [mother:
How many men, in dreams, have lain with
15   [their mothers!
No reasonable man is troubled by such things.
    OEDIPUS. That is true; only—
If only my mother were not still alive!
But she is alive. I can not help my dread.
20   IOCASTÊ. Yet this news of your father's death
                              [is wonderful.
OEDIPUS. Wonderful. But I fear the living
                              [woman.
MESSENGER. Tell me, who is this woman that
25   [you fear?
OEDIPUS. It is Meropê, man; the wife of King
                              [Polybos.
MESSENGER. Meropê? Why should you be
                              [afraid of her?
30 OEDIPUS. An oracle of the gods, a dreadful
                              [saying.
MESSENGER. Can you tell me about it or are
                              [you sworn to silence?
OEDIPUS. I can tell you, and I will.
35 Apollo said through his prophet that I was the
                              [man
Who should marry his own mother, shed his
                              [father's blood
With his own hands. And so, for all these years
40 I have kept clear of Corinth, and no harm has
                              [come—
Though it would have been sweet to see my
                              [parents again.
MESSENGER. And is this the fear that drove
45   [you out of Corinth?
OEDIPUS. Would you have me kill my father?
MESSENGER.   As for that

You must be reassured by the news I gave you.
    OEDIPUS. If you could reassure me, I would
                              [reward you.   50
MESSENGER. I had that in mind, I will confess:
                              [I thought
I could count on you when you returned to
                              [Corinth.
OEDIPUS. No: I will never go near my parents   55
                              [again.
MESSENGER. Ah, son, you still do not know
                              [what you are doing—
OEDIPUS. What do you mean? In the name of
                              [God tell me!   60
MESSENGER. —If these are your reasons for
                              [not going home.
OEDIPUS. I tell you, I fear the oracle may
                              [come true.
MESSENGER. And guilt may come upon you   65
                              [through your parents?
OEDIPUS. That is the dread that is always in
                              [my heart.
MESSENGER. Can you not see that all your
                              [fears are groundless?   70
OEDIPUS. How can you say that? They are
                              [my parents, surely?
MESSENGER. Polybos was not your father.
OEDIPUS.   Not my father?
MESSENGER. No more your father than the   75
                              [man speaking to you.
OEDIPUS. But you are nothing to me!
MESSENGER.   Neither was he.
OEDIPUS. Then why did he call me son?
MESSENGER.   I will tell you: 80
Long ago he had you from my hands, as a gift.
    OEDIPUS. Then how could he love me so, if I
                              [was not his?
MESSENGER. He had no children, and his heart
                              [turned to you.   85
OEDIPUS. What of you? Did you buy me?
                              [Did you find me by chance?
MESSENGER. I came upon you in the crooked
                              [pass of Kithairon.
OEDIPUS. And what were you doing there?   90
MESSENGER.   Tending my flocks.
OEDIPUS. A wandering shepherd?
MESSENGER.   But your savior, son, that
                              [day.
OEDIPUS. From what did you save me?   95

MESSENGER.   Your ankles should tell you
[that.
OEDIPUS. Ah, stranger, why do you speak of
[that childhood pain?
5   MESSENGER. I cut the bonds that tied your
[ankles together.
OEDIPUS. I have had the mark as long as I
[can remember.
MESSENGER. That was why you were given
10   [the name you bear.°
OEDIPUS. God! Was it my father or my
[mother who did it?
Tell me!
MESSENGER. I do not know. The man who
15   [gave you to me
Can tell you better than I.
OEDIPUS. It was not you that found me, but
[another?
MESSENGER. It was another shepherd gave
20   [you to me.
OEDIPUS. Who was he? Can you tell me who
[he was?
MESSENGER. I think he was said to be one of
[Laïos' people.
25   OEDIPUS. You mean the Laïos who was king
[here years ago?
MESSENGER. Yes; King Laïos, and the man
[was one of his herdsmen.
OEDIPUS. Is he still alive? Can I see him?
30   MESSENGER.   These men here
Know best about such things.
OEDIPUS.   Does anyone here
Know this shepherd that he is talking about?
Have you seen him in the fields, or in the town?
35   If you have, tell me. It is time things were made
[plain.
LEADER. I think the man he means is that
[same shepherd
You have already asked to see. Iocastê perhaps
40   Could tell you something.
OEDIPUS.   Do you know anything
About him, Lady? Is he the man we have
[summoned?
Is that the man this shepherd means?
45   IOCASTÊ.   Why think of him?
Forget this herdsman. Forget it all.
This talk is a waste of time.

the name you bear Oedipus means *swollen-foot*

OEDIPUS.   How can you say that,
When the clues to my true birth are in my
[hands?   50
IOCASTÊ. For God's love, let us have no more
[questioning!
Is your life nothing to you?
My own is pain enough for me to bear.
OEDIPUS. You need not worry. Suppose my   55
[mother a slave,
And born of slaves: no baseness can touch you.
IOCASTÊ. Listen to me, I beg you: do not do
[this thing!
OEDIPUS. I will not listen; the truth must be   60
[made known.
IOCASTÊ. Everything that I say is for your
[own good!
OEDIPUS.   My own good
Snaps my patience, then; I want none of it.   65
IOCASTÊ. You are fatally wrong! May you
[never learn who you are!
OEDIPUS. Go, one of you, and bring the
[shepherd here.
Let us leave this woman to brag of her royal   70
[name.
IOCASTÊ. Ah, miserable!
That is the only word I have for you now.
That is the only word I can ever have.
[*Exit into the palace.*]   75
LEADER. Why has she left us, Oedipus? Why
[has she gone
In such a passion of sorrow? I fear this silence:
Something dreadful may come of it.
OEDIPUS.   Let it come!   80
However base my birth, I must know about it.
The Queen, like a woman, is perhaps ashamed
To think of my low origin. But I
Am a child of Luck; I cannot be dishonored.
Luck is my mother; the passing months, my   85
[brothers,
Have seen me rich and poor.
If this is so,
How could I wish that I were someone else?
How could I not be glad to know my birth?   90

ODE III

Strophe
CHORUS. If ever the coming time were known
To my heart's pondering,

Kithairon, now by Heaven I see the torches
At the festival of the next full moon,
And see the dance, and hear the choir sing
A grace to your gentle shade:
5   Mountain where Oedipus was found,
O mountain guard of a noble race!
May the god who heals us lend his aid,
And let that glory come to pass
For our king's cradling-ground.°

Antistrophe
10 Of the nymphs that flower beyond the years,
Who bore you, royal child,
To Pan of the hills or the timberline Apollo,
Cold in delight where the upland clears,
Or Hermês for whom Kyllenê's° heights are
15   [piled?
Or flushed as evening cloud,
Great Dionysos, roamer of mountains,
He—was it he who found you there,
And caught you up in his own proud
20 Arms from the sweet god-ravisher°
Who laughed by the Muses' fountains?°

SCENE IV

Oedipus. Sirs: though I do not know the man,
I think I see him coming, this shepherd we
                         [want:
25 He is old, like our friend here, and the men
Bringing him seem to be servants of my house.
But you can tell, if you have ever seen him.
   [*Enter* Shepherd *escorted by servants.*]
   Leader. I know him, he was Laïos' man. You
30   [can trust him.
   Oedipus. Tell me first, you from Corinth: is
                   [this the shepherd
We were discussing?
   Messenger.   This is the very man.
35   Oedipus [*to* Shepherd]. Come here. No, look

And let that glory . . . cradling-ground i.e., let this
wonderful thing which I prophesy come true for
Kithairon
Kyllenê highest mountain in the Peloponnesus, sacred
to Hermes
god-ravisher nymph whom the chorus conjecture to
have been Oedipus' mother
Muses' fountains springs of Helicon, sacred to Apollo
and the Muses

                  [at me. You must answer
Everything I ask.—You belonged to Laïos?
   Shepherd. Yes: born his slave, brought up in
                   [his house.
   Oedipus. Tell me: what kind of work did you 40
                   [do for him?
   Shepherd. I was a shepherd of his, most of
                   [my life.
   Oedipus. Where mainly did you go for
                   [pasturage? 45
   Shepherd. Sometimes Kithairon, sometimes
                   [the hills near-by.
   Oedipus. Do you remember ever seeing this
                   [man out there?
   Shepherd. What would he be doing there? 50
                   [This man?
   Oedipus. This man standing here. Have you
                   [ever seen him before?
   Shepherd. No. At least, not to my
                   [recollection. 55
   Messenger. And that is not strange, my
                   [lord. But I'll refresh
His memory: he must remember when we two
Spent three whole seasons together, March to
                 [September, 60
On Kithairon or thereabouts. He had two
                   [flocks;
I had one. Each autumn I'd drive mine home
And he would go back with his to Laïos'
                 [sheepfold.— 65
Is this not true, just as I have described it?
   Shepherd. True, yes; but it was all so long
                 [ago.
   Messenger. Well, then: do you remember,
                 [back in those days, 70
That you gave me a baby boy to bring up as my
                 [own?
   Shepherd. What if I did? What are you
                 [trying to say?
   Messenger. King Oedipus was once that 75
                 [little child.
   Shepherd. Damn you, hold your tongue!
   Oedipus.   No more of that!
It is your tongue needs watching, not this
                 [man's. 80
   Shepherd. My King, my Master, what is it I
                 [have done wrong?
   Oedipus. You have not answered his question
                 [about the boy.

SHEPHERD. He does not know . . . He is only
[making trouble . . .
OEDIPUS. Come, speak plainly, or it will go
[hard with you.
5 SHEPHERD. In God's name, do not torture an
[old man!
OEDIPUS. Come here, one of you; bind his
[arms behind him.
SHEPHERD. Unhappy king! What more do you
10 [wish to learn?
OEDIPUS. Did you give this man the child he
[speaks of?
SHEPHERD. I did.
And I would to God I had died that very day.
15 OEDIPUS. You will die now unless you speak
[the truth.
SHEPHERD. Yet if I speak the truth, I am
[worse than dead.
OEDIPUS. Very well; since you insist upon
20 [delaying—
SHEPHERD. No! I have told you already that I
[gave him the boy.
OEDIPUS. Where did you get him? From your
[house? From somewhere else?
25 SHEPHERD. Not from mine, no. A man gave
[him to me.
OEDIPUS. Is that man here? Do you know
[whose slave he was?
SHEPHERD. For God's love, my King, do not
30 [ask me any more!
OEDIPUS. You are a dead man if I have to
[ask you again.
SHEPHERD. Then . . . Then the child was from
[the palace of Laïos.
35 OEDIPUS. A slave child? or a child of his own
[line?
SHEPHERD. Ah, I am on the brink of dreadful
[speech!
OEDIPUS. And I of dreadful hearing. Yet I
40 [must hear.
SHEPHERD. If you must be told, then . . .
They say it was Laïos' child;
But it is your wife who can tell you about that.
OEDIPUS. My wife!—Did she give it to you?
45 SHEPHERD. My lord, she did.
OEDIPUS. Do you know why?
SHEPHERD. I was told to get rid of it.
OEDIPUS. An unspeakable mother!

SHEPHERD. There had been prophecies . . .
OEDIPUS. Tell me. 50
SHEPHERD. It was said that the boy would
[kill his own father.
OEDIPUS. Then why did you give him over
[to this old man?
SHEPHERD. I pitied the baby, my King, 55
And I thought that this man would take him
[far away
To his own country.
He saved him—but for what a fate!
For if you are what this man says you are, 60
No man living is more wretched than Oedipus.
OEDIPUS. Ah God!
It was true!
All the prophecies!
—Now, 65
O Light, may I look on you for the last time!
I, Oedipus,
Oedipus, damned in his birth, in his marriage
[damned,
Damned in the blood he shed with his own 70
[hand!

[*He rushes into the palace.*]

ODE IV

Strophe 1
CHORUS. Alas for the seed of men.

What measure shall I give these generations
That breathe on the void and are void 75
And exist and do not exist?

Who bears more weight of joy
Than mass of sunlight shifting in images,
Or who shall make his thought stay on
That down time drifts away? 80

Your splendor is all fallen.

O naked brow of wrath and tears,
O change of Oedipus!
I who saw your days call no man blest—
Your great days like ghosts gone. 85

Antistrophe 1
That mind was a strong bow.

Deep, how deep you drew it then, hard archer,
At a dim fearful range,
And brought dear glory down!

You overcame the stranger—
5 The virgin with her hooking lion claws—
And though death sang, stood like a tower
To make pale Thebes take heart.

Fortress against our sorrow!

Divine king, giver of laws,
10 Majestic Oedipus!
No prince in Thebes had ever such renown,
No prince won such grace of power.

Strophe 2
And now of all men ever known
Most pitiful is this man's story:
15 His fortunes are most changed, his state
Fallen to a low slave's
Ground under bitter fate.

O Oedipus, most royal one!
The great door that expelled you to the light
20 Gave at night—ah, gave night to your glory:
As to the father, to the fathering son.

All understood too late.

How could that queen whom Laïos won,
The garden that he harrowed at his height,
25 Be silent when that act was done?

Antistrophe 2
But all eyes fail before time's eye,
All actions come to justice there.
Though never willed, though far down the deep
[past,
30 Your bed, your dread sirings,
Are brought to book at last.

Child by Laïos doomed to die,
Then doomed to lose that fortunate little death,
Would God you never took breath in this air
35 That with my wailing lips I take to cry:

For I weep the world's outcast.

Blind I was, and cannot tell why;
Asleep, for you had given ease of breath;
A fool, while the false years went by.

ÉXODOS

[*Enter, from the palace,* SECOND MESSENGER.]   40
2ND MESSENGER. Elders of Thebes, most
                    [honored in this land,
What horrors are yours to see and hear, what
                    [weight
Of sorrow to be endured, if, true to your birth,   45
You venerate the line of Labdakos!
I think neither Istros nor Phasis,° those great
                    [rivers,
Could purify this place of the corruption
It shelters now, or soon must bring to light—   50
Evil not done unconsciously, but willed.

The greatest griefs are those we cause
                    [ourselves.
    LEADER. Surely, friend, we have grief enough
                    [already;   55
What new sorrow do you mean?
    2ND MESSENGER.   The Queen is dead.
    LEADER. Iocastê? Dead? But at whose hand?
    2ND MESSENGER.   Her own.
The full horror of what happened you cannot   60
                    [know,
For you did not see it: but I, who did, will tell
                    [you
As clearly as I can how she met her death.

When she had left us,   65
In passionate silence, passing through the court,
She ran to her apartment in the house,
Her hair clutched by the fingers of both hands.
She closed the doors behind her; then, by that
                    [bed   70
Where long ago the fatal son was conceived—
That son who should bring about his father's
                    [death—
We heard her call upon Laïos, dead so many
                    [years,   75

Istros . . . Phasis the Danube and the Rion, conventional types of great rivers

And heard her wail for the double fruit of her
[marriage,
A husband by her husband, children by her
[child.
5 Exactly how she died I do not know:
For Oedipus burst in moaning and would not
[let us
Keep vigil to the end: it was by him
As he stormed about the room that our eyes
10 [were caught.
From one to another of us he went, begging a
[sword,
Cursing the wife who was not his wife, the
[mother
15 Whose womb had carried his own children and
[himself.
I do not know: it was none of us aided him,
But surely one of the gods was in control!
For with a dreadful cry
20 He hurled his weight, as though wrenched out
[of himself,
At the twin doors: the bolts gave, and he rushed
[in.
And there we saw her hanging, her body
25 [swaying
From the cruel cord she had noosed about her
[neck.
A great sob broke from him, heartbreaking to
[hear,
30 As he loosed the rope and lowered her to the
[ground.

I would blot out from my mind what happened
[next!
For the King ripped from her gown the golden
35 [brooches
That were her ornament, and raised them, and
[plunged them down
Straight into his own eyeballs, crying, "No
[more,
40 No more shall you look on the misery about
[me,
The horrors of my own doing! Too long you
[have known
The faces of those whom I should never have
45 [seen,
Too long been blind to those for whom I was
[searching!

From this hour, go in darkness!"And as he
[spoke,
He struck at his eyes—not once, but many   50
[times;
And the blood spattered his beard,
Bursting from his ruined sockets like red hail.
So from the unhappiness of two this evil has
[sprung,   55
A curse on the man and woman alike. The old
Happiness of the house of Labdakos
Was happiness enough: where is it today?
It is all wailing and ruin, disgrace, death—all
The misery of mankind that has a name—   60
And it is wholly and for ever theirs.
      LEADER. Is he in agony still? Is there no rest
[for him?
      2ND MESSENGER. He is calling for someone to
[lead him to the gates   65
So that all the children of Kadmos may look
[upon
His father's murderer, his mother's—no,
I can not say it!
            And then he will leave Thebes,   70
Self-exiled, in order that the curse
Which he himself pronounced may depart from
[the house.
He is weak, and there is none to lead him,
So terrible is his suffering.   75
            But you will see:
Look, the doors are opening; in a moment
You will see a thing that would crush a heart
[of stone.
      [*The central door is opened;* OEDIPUS, *blind-*   80
ed, is led in.]
      LEADER. Dreadful indeed for men to see.
Never have my own eyes
Looked on a sight so full of fear.

Oedipus!   85
What madness came upon you, what daemon
Leaped on your life with heavier
Punishment than a mortal man can bear?
No: I cannot even
Look at you, poor ruined one.   90
And I would speak, question, ponder,
If I were able. No.
You make me shudder.
      OEDIPUS. God.   God.

Is there a sorrow greater?
Where shall I find harbor in this world?
My voice is hurled far on a dark wind.
What has God done to me?
5 LEADER. Too terrible to think of, or to see.

Strophe 1

OEDIPUS. O cloud of night,
Never to be turned away: night coming on,
I can not tell how: night like a shroud!

My fair winds brought me here.
10   O God. Again
The pain of the spikes where I had sight,
The flooding pain
Of memory, never to be gouged out.
LEADER. This is not strange.
15 You suffer it all twice over, remorse in pain,
Pain in remorse.

Antistrophe 1

OEDIPUS. Ah dear friend
Are you faithful even yet, you alone?
Are you still standing near me, will you stay
20   [here,
Patient, to care for the blind?
                                             The blind man!
Yet even blind I know who it is attends me,
By the voice's tone—
25 Though my new darkness hide the comforter.
LEADER. Oh fearful act!
What god was it drove you to rake black
Night across your eyes?

Strophe 2

OEDIPUS. Apollo. Apollo. Dear
30 Children, the god was Apollo.
He brought my sick, sick fate upon me.
But the blinding hand was my own!
How could I bear to see
When all my sight was horror everywhere?
35   LEADER. Everywhere; that is true.
OEDIPUS. And now what is left?
Images? Love? A greeting even,
Sweet to the senses? Is there anything?
Ah, no, friends: lead me away.
40 Lead me away from Thebes.
                                             Lead the great wreck

And hell of Oedipus, whom the gods hate.
LEADER. Your fate is clear, you are not blind
                                                             [to that.
Would God you had never found it out!   45

Antistrophe 2

OEDIPUS. Death take the man who unbound
My feet on that hillside
And delivered me from death to life! What life?
If only I had died,
This weight of monstrous doom   50
Could not have dragged me and my darlings
                                                                     [down.
LEADER. I would have wished the same.
OEDIPUS. Oh never to have come here
With my father's blood upon me! Never   55
To have been the man they call his mother's
                                                             [husband!
Oh accurst! Oh child of evil,
To have entered that wretched bed—
                                             the selfsame one! 60
More primal than sin itself, this fell to me.
LEADER. I do not know how I can answer you.
You were better dead than alive and blind.
OEDIPUS. Do not counsel me any more. This
                                                     [punishment 65
That I have laid upon myself is just.
If I had eyes,
I do not know how I could bear the sight
Of my father, when I came to the house of
                                                             [Death, 70
Or my mother: for I have sinned against them
                                                             [both
So vilely that I could not make my peace
By strangling my own life.
                                     Or do you think my children, 75
Born as they were born, would be sweet to my
                                                             [eyes?
Ah never, never! Nor this town with its high
                                                             [walls,
Nor the holy images of the gods.   80
                                     For I,
Thrice miserable!—Oedipus, noblest of all the
                                                             [line
Of Kadmos, have condemned myself to enjoy
These things no more, by my own malediction 85
Expelling that man whom the gods declared
To be a defilement in the house of Laïos.

After exposing the rankness of my own guilt,
How could I look men frankly in the eyes?
No, I swear it,
If I could have stifled my hearing at its source,
5 I would have done it and made all this body
A tight cell of misery, blank to light and sound:
So I should have been safe in a dark agony
Beyond all recollection.
                    Ah Kithairon!
10 Why did you shelter me? When I was cast upon
                                    [you,
Why did I not die? Then I should never
Have shown the world my execrable birth.

Ah Polybos! Corinth, city that I believed
15 The ancient seat of my ancestors: how fair
I seemed, your child! And all the while this evil
Was cancerous within me!
                    For I am sick
In my daily life, sick in my origin.

20 O three roads, dark ravine, woodland and way
Where three roads met: you, drinking my
                        [father's blood,
My own blood, spilled by my own hand: can
                        [you remember
25 The unspeakable things I did there, and the
                        [things
I went on from there to do?
                    O marriage, marriage!
The act that engendered me, and again the act
30 Performed by the son in the same bed—
                        Ah, the net
Of incest, mingling fathers, brothers, sons,
With brides, wives, mothers: the last evil
That can be known by men: no tongue can say
35 How evil!
            No. For the love of God, conceal me
Somewhere far from Thebes; or kill me; or hurl
                            [me
Into the sea, away from men's eyes for ever.

40 Come, lead me. You need not fear to touch me.
Of all men, I alone can bear this guilt.
    [Enter CREON.]
    LEADER. We are not the ones to decide; but
                            [Creon here
45 May fitly judge of what you ask. He only
Is left to protect the city in your place.

OEDIPUS. Alas, how can I speak to him? What
                            [right have I
To beg his courtesy whom I have deeply
                            [wronged? 50
CREON. I have not come to mock you,
                            [Oedipus,
Or to reproach you, either.
    [To ATTENDANTS.]—You, standing there:
If you have lost all respect for man's dignity, 55
At least respect the flame of Lord Helios:
Do not allow this pollution to show itself
Openly here, an affront to the earth
And Heaven's rain and the light of day. No,
                            [take him 60
Into the house as quickly as you can.
For it is proper
That only the close kindred see his grief.
    OEDIPUS. I pray you in God's name, since
                            [your courtesy 65
Ignores my dark expectation, visiting
With mercy this man of all men most execrable:
Give me what I ask—for your good, not for
                            [mine.
    CREON: And what is it that you would have 70
                            [me do?
    OEDIPUS. Drive me out of this country as
                            [quickly as may be
To a place where no human voice can ever
                            [greet me. 75
    CREON. I should have done that before now—
                            [only,
God's will had not been wholly revealed to me.
    OEDIPUS. But his command is plain: the
                            [parricide 80
Must be destroyed. I am that evil man.
    CREON. That is the sense of it, yes; but as
                            [things are,
We had best discover clearly what is to be done.
    OEDIPUS. You would learn more about a man 85
                            [like me?
    CREON. You are ready now to listen to the
                            [god.
    OEDIPUS. I will listen. But it is to you
That I must turn for help. I beg you, hear me. 90

The woman in there—
Give her whatever funeral you think proper:
She is your sister.
                —But let me go, Creon!

Let me purge my father's Thebes of the
[pollution
Of my living here, and go out to the wild hills,
To Kithairon, that has won such fame with me,
5 The tomb my mother and father appointed for
[me,
And let me die there, as they willed I should.
And yet I know
Death will not ever come to me through
10 [sickness
Or in any natural way: I have been preserved
For some unthinkable fate. But let that be.

As for my sons, you need not care for them.
They are men, they will find some way to live.
15 But my poor daughters, who have shared my
[table,
Who never before have been parted from their
[father—
Take care of them, Creon; do this for me.
20 And will you let me touch them with my hands
A last time, and let us weep together?
Be kind, my lord,
Great prince, be kind!
Could I but touch them,
25 They would be mine again, as when I had my
[eyes.
[*Enter* ANTIGONE *and* ISMENE, *attended*.]
Ah, God!
Is it my dearest children I hear weeping?
30 Has Creon pitied me and sent my daughters?
CREON. Yes, Oedipus: I knew that they were
[dear to you
In the old days, and know you must love them
[still.
35 OEDIPUS. May God bless you for this—and
[be a friendlier
Guardian to you than he has been to me!

Children, where are you?
Come quickly to my hands; they are your
40 [brother's—
Hands that have brought your father's once
[clear eyes
To this way of seeing—
Ah dearest ones,
45 I had neither sight nor knowledge then, your
[father
By the woman who was the source of his own

[life!
And I weep for you—having no strength to see
[you—, 50
I weep for you when I think of the bitterness
That men will visit upon you all your lives.
What homes, what festivals can you attend
Without being forced to depart again in tears?
And when you come to marriageable age, 55
Where is the man, my daughters, who would
[dare
Risk the bane that lies on all my children?
Is there any evil wanting? Your father killed
His father; sowed the womb of her who bore 60
[him;
Engendered you at the fount of his own
[existence!

That is what they will say of you.

Then, whom 65
Can you ever marry? There are no bridegrooms
[for you,
And your lives must wither away in sterile
[dreaming.

O Creon, son of Menoikeus! 70
You are the only father my daughters have,
Since we, their parents, are both of us gone for
[ever.
They are your own blood: you will not let them
Fall into beggary and loneliness; 75
You will keep them from the miseries that are
[mine!
Take pity on them; see, they are only children,
Friendless except for you. Promise me this,
Great Prince, and give me your hand in token 80
[of it.

[CREON *clasps his right hand*.]
Children:
I could say much, if you could understand me,
But as it is, I have only this prayer for you: 85
Live where you can, be as happy as you can—
Happier, please God, than God has made your
[father!
CREON. Enough. You have wept enough. Now
[go within. 90
OEDIPUS. I must; but it is hard.
CREON. Time eases all things.
OEDIPUS. But you must promise—

CREON.   Say what you desire.
OEDIPUS. Send me from Thebes!
CREON.   God grant that I may!
OEDIPUS. But since God hates me . . .
5   CREON.   No, he will grant your wish.
OEDIPUS. You promise?
CREON.   I can not speak beyond my
                    [knowledge.
OEDIPUS. Then lead me in.
10   CREON.   Come now, and leave your
                    [children.
OEDIPUS. No! Do not take them from me!
CREON.   Think no longer
That you are in command here, but rather think
15 How, when you were, you served your own
                    [destruction.
[*Exeunt into the house all but the* CHORUS;
the LEADER *chants directly to the audience.*]
LEADER. Men of Thebes: look upon Oedipus.
20 This is the king who solved the famous riddle
And towered up, most powerful of men.
No mortal eyes but looked on him with envy,
Yet in the end ruin swept over him.

Let every man in mankind's frailty
25 Consider his last day; and let none
Presume on his good fortune until he find
Life, at his death, a memory without pain.

Aristophanes

447?–385? B.C.

Lysistrata

411 B.C.

Produced in the twentieth year of the Peloponnesian War, in which Athens at the ultimate sacrifice of her democracy and her sovereignty attempted to dominate the other city-states of Greece, *Lysistrata* is one of the most remarkable peace plays in world literature. It avails itself of neither pathos nor moral indignation, the stocks-in-trade of its genre. It mentions neither material nor spiritual cost. About death it is silent. Instead it deals broadly, explicitly, and always comically with sex—with full breasts, rounded buttocks, frankly admired vulvas (hairless in the high Greek fashion), then increasingly with phalluses monstrously, persistently, and futilely erect. For the women of Greece, all Greece, have joined the energetic and farsighted Lysistrata in a marital strike to end the war. The state of Greece, so runs the unspoken argument, should be one as husbands and wives should be one. If the men in their folly force divisions in the political sphere, then to bring them to their senses women will force divisions in the domestic sphere. In the end there will be reconciliation, and bodies both political and domestic will be reunited.

Lysistrata is a feminist play as well as a pacifist play, treating the masculine establishment with visible derision. On stage the women invariably best the men. Sprightly old women beat their doddering male coevals, the female battalions beat back the magistrate's policemen, and Lysistrata and her followers transform the irascible magistrate first into a woman, then into a corpse.

These feminine conquests, moreover, are as just as they are amusing. From start to finish the men are little better than overgrown adolescents, warring first because they have the money to afford it—as though war were some leisure-class sport—and secondly because they have, like idlers on a street corner, a positive instinct for trouble. ("We go to Sparta when we're sober," an Athenian says, "and look around to stir up trouble. And then we don't hear what they say—and as for what they *don't* say, we have all sorts of suspicions.") They like to dress in armor and visit the marketplace to clank and jangle and frighten the old marketwomen. Listening to the homely analogy in which Lysistrata likens statecraft to washing, carding, and blending a fleece of wool (an analogy comparable in imaginative force to those of the garden in Shakespeare's *Richard II* and of the hive in *Henry V*), they are conscious only of its lowly domesticity, not at all of its cogency. And it is perhaps just to see in their final capitulation a continuation of the frivolity of which the play has indicted them all along: the ambassadors are lured into peace at the sight of the naked statue of the goddess Reconciliation, coveting her anatomical territory as warriors covet geographical territory.

The women, to be sure, are not without frailty. The tipsy Calonice finds it almost impossible to keep the vow of abstinence ("O Lysistrata, I feel so weak in the knees"), and after five days the pact threatens to fall apart as the ladies backslide and desert in increasing numbers. Collectively, however, with Lysistrata's moral force to strengthen them, they hold out long enough for victory.

Structurally the play is remarkably tight, its parts balanced and interlocked, its different veins of comedy counterpointing one another. The plot is symmetrical, with the first part, the rising action that sets in motion the combined marital strike and the women's occupation of the Acropolis (site of the treasury), being about equal in length to the progress toward the conclusion. The play has, furthermore, formal and thematic unity from prologue through éxodos; the interactions between principal characters alternate with lively choral passages, and the whole elides from the tension of the posing of the problem to the calm of its resolution.

Perhaps the most notable aspect of the play is the high and happy religious solemnity of the éxodos. Gone now are the broad humor and the horseplay, the

exposures of masculine and feminine frailty, the divisions within families and states. Now in the mood of reconciliation, Spartans and Athenians, husbands and wives, celebrate their unity, call on the gods to witness "peace and bonds of harmonious love," and leave the stage singing and dancing.

This is how wars and efforts to end wars may in fantasy be concluded. And Aristophanes, that very bawdy and very moral playwright, comes close to demonstrating that this is how they could end in fact.

Lysistrata

ARISTOPHANES

*Translated into English Prose and Verse
by Charles T. Murphy*

CHARACTERS°

LYSISTRATA }
CALONICE   } *Athenian women*
MYRRHINE   }
LAMPITO   *a Spartan woman*
LEADER OF THE CHORUS OF OLD MEN
CHORUS OF OLD MEN
LEADER OF THE CHORUS OF OLD WOMEN
CHORUS OF OLD WOMEN
ATHENIAN MAGISTRATE
THREE ATHENIAN WOMEN
CINESIAS *an Athenian, husband of* MYRRHINE
SPARTAN HERALD
SPARTAN AMBASSADORS
ATHENIAN AMBASSADORS
TWO ATHENIAN CITIZENS
CHORUS OF ATHENIANS
CHORUS OF SPARTANS

characters "As is usual in ancient comedy, the leading characters have significant names. Lysistrata is 'She who disbands the armies'; Myrrhine's name is chosen to suggest *myrton*, a Greek word meaning *pudenda muliebria*; Lampito is a celebrated Spartan name; Cinesias, although a real name in Athens, is chosen to suggest a Greek verb *kinein, to move*, then *to make love, to have intercourse*; and the name of his deme, Paionidai, suggests the verb *paiein*, which has about the same significance." [Translator's note.]

Copyright 1947 by Longmans Green and Company. From Greek Literature in Translation, published by Longmans Green and Co. Reprinted by permission of David McKay Co., Inc. Douglass Parker's footnotes are used by permission of The New American Library, publishers, from The Complete Greek Comedy, *edited by William Arrowsmith.*

SCENE. *In Athens, beneath the Acropolis. In the center of the stage is the Propylaea, or gateway to the Acropolis; to one side is a small grotto, sacred to Pan. The Orchestra represents a slope leading up to the gate-way. It is early in* 5 *the morning.* LYSISTRATA *is pacing impatiently up and down.*

PROLOGUE°

LYS. If they'd been summoned to worship the God of Wine, or Pan, or to visit the Queen of Love, why, you couldn't have pushed your way 10 through the streets for all the timbrels. But now there's not a single woman here—except my neighbor; here she comes. [*Enter* CALONICE.] Good day to you, Calonice.

CAL. And to you, Lysistrata. [*Noticing* LY- 15 SISTRATA's *impatient air.*] But what ails you? Don't scowl, my dear; it's not becoming to you to knit your brows like that.

LYS. [*sadly*]. Ah, Calonice, my heart aches; I'm so annoyed at us women. For among men 20 we have a reputation for sly trickery—

CAL. And rightly too, on my word!

LYS. —but when they were told to meet here to consider a matter of no small importance, they lie abed and don't come. 25

CAL. Oh, they'll come all right, my dear. It's not easy for a woman to get out, you know. One is working on her husband, another is getting up the maid, another has to put the baby to bed, or wash and feed it. 30

LYS. But after all, there are other matters more important than all that.

CAL. My dear Lysistrata, just what is this matter you've summoned us women to consider? What's up? Something big? 35

LYS. Very big.

CAL. [*interested*]. Is it stout, too?

LYS. [*smiling*]. Yes indeed—both big and stout.

prologue the division of the text into its constituent parts—prologue, párodos, scenes, choral episodes, and éxodos—follows Dudley Fitts, *Aristophanes'* Lysistrata: *An English Version*, Harcourt Brace Jovanovich, Inc., 1954, 1962

CAL. What? And the women still haven't come?

LYS. It's not what you suppose; they'd come soon enough for *that*. But I've worked up something, and for many a sleepless night I've turned it this way and that.

CAL. [*in mock disappointment*]. Oh, I guess it's pretty fine and slender, if you've turned it this way and that.

LYS. So fine that the safety of the whole of Greece lies in us women.

CAL. In us women? It depends on a very slender reed then.

LYS. Our country's fortunes are in our hands; and whether the Spartans shall perish—

CAL.: Good! Let them perish, by all means.

LYS. —and the Boeotians shall be completely annihilated.

CAL. Not completely! Please spare the eels.°

LYS. As for Athens, I won't use any such unpleasant words. But you understand what I mean. But if the women will meet here—the Spartans, the Boeotians, and we Athenians— then all together we will save Greece.

CAL. But what could women do that's clever or distinguished? We just sit around all dolled up in silk robes, looking pretty in our sheer gowns and evening slippers.

LYS. These are just the things I hope will save us: these silk robes, perfumes, evening slippers, rouge, and our chiffon blouses.

CAL. How so?

LYS. So never a man alive will lift a spear against the foe—

CAL. I'll get a silk gown at once.

LYS. —or take up his shield—

CAL. I'll put on my sheerest gown!

LYS. —or sword.

CAL. I'll buy a pair of evening slippers.

LYS. Well then, shouldn't the women have come?

CAL. Come? Why, they should have *flown* here.

LYS. Well, my dear, just watch: they'll act in true Athenian fashion—everything too late!

And now there's not a woman here from the shore or from Salamis.

CAL. They're coming, I'm sure; at daybreak they were laying—to their oars to cross the straits.

LYS. And those I expected would be the first to come—the women of Acharnae—they haven't arrived.

CAL. Yet the wife of Theagenes means to come: she consulted Hecate about it. [*Seeing a group of women approaching.*] But look! Here come a few. And there are some more over here. Hurrah! Where do they come from?

LYS. From Anagyra.

CAL. Yes indeed! We've raised up quite a stink from Anagyra° anyway.

[*Enter* MYRRHINE *in haste, followed by several other women.*]

MYR. [*breathlessly*]. Have we come in time, Lysistrata? What do you say? Why so quiet?

LYS. I can't say much for you, Myrrhine, coming at this hour on such important business.

MYR. Why, I had trouble finding my girdle in the dark. But if it's so important, we're here now; tell us.

LYS. No. Let's wait a little for the women from Boeotia and the Peloponnesus.

MYR. That's a much better suggestion. Look! Here comes Lampito now.

[*Enter* LAMPITO *with two other women.*]

LYS. Greetings, my dear Spartan friend. How pretty you look, my dear. What a smooth complexion and well-developed figure. You could throttle an ox.

LAM. Faith, yes, I think I could. I take exercises and kick my heels against my bum. [*She demonstrates with a few steps of the Spartan "bottom-kicking" dance.*]

LYS. And what splendid breasts you have.

LAM. La! You handle me like a prize steer.

LYS. And who is this young lady with you?

LAM. Faith, she's an Ambassadress from Boeotia.

---

eels Boeotia was noted for its seafood, especially its eels

stink from Anagyra a punning reference to a proverbial phrase. The deme or township of Anagyra took its name from an ill-smelling plant, to stir which meant, colloquially, to raise a stink.

Lys. Oh yes, a Boeotian, and blooming like a garden too.

Cal. [*lifting up her skirt*]. My word! How neatly her garden's weeded!°

5 Lys. And who is the other girl?

Lam. Oh, she's a Corinthian swell.

Myr. [*after a rapid examination*]. Yes indeed. She swells very nicely [*pointing*] here and here.

Lam. Who has gathered together this com-
10 pany of women?

Lys. I have.

Lam. Speak up, then. What do you want?

Myr. Yes, my dear, do tell us what this important matter is.

15 Lys. Very well, I'll tell you. But before I speak, let me ask you a little question.

Myr. Anything you like.

Lys. [*earnestly*]. Tell me: don't you yearn for the fathers of your children, who are away at
20 the wars? I know you all have husbands abroad.

Cal. Why, yes; mercy me! my husband's been away for five months in Thrace keeping guard on—Eucrates.°

Myr. And mine for seven whole months in
25 Pylus.

Lam. And mine, as soon as ever he returns from the fray, readjusts his shield and flies out of the house again.

Lys. And as for lovers, there's not even a
30 ghost of one left. Since the Milesians revolted from us,° I've not even seen an eight-inch dingus to be a leather consolation for us widows. Are you willing, if I can find a way, to help me end the war?

35 Myr. Goodness, yes! I'd do it, even if I had to pawn my dress and—get drunk on the spot!

Cal. And I, even if I had to let myself be split in two like a flounder.

Lam. I'd climb up Mt. Taygetus° if I could
40 catch a glimpse of peace.

Lys. I'll tell you, then, in plain and simple

words. My friends, if we are going to force our men to make peace, we must do without—

Myr. Without what? Tell us.

Lys. Will you do it?   45

Myr. We'll do it, if it kills us.

Lys. Well then, we must do without sex altogether. [*General consternation.*] Why do you turn away? Where go you? Why turn so pale? Why those tears? Will you do it or not?   50
What means this hesitation?

Myr. I won't do it! Let the war go on.

Cal. Nor I! Let the war go on.

Lys. So, my little flounder? Didn't you say just now you'd split yourself in half?   55

Cal. Anything else you like. I'm willing, even if I have to walk through fire. Anything rather than sex. There's nothing like it, my dear.

Lys. [*to* Myrrhine]. What about you?   60

Myr. [*sullenly*]. I'm willing to walk through fire, too.

Lys. Oh vile and cursed breed! No wonder they make tragedies about us: we're naught but "love-affairs and bassinets."° But you, my dear   65
Spartan friend, if you alone are with me, our enterprise might yet succeed. Will you vote with me?

Lam. 'Tis cruel hard, by my faith, for a woman to sleep alone without her nooky; but   70
for all that, we certainly do need peace.

Lys. O my dearest friend! You're the only real woman here.

Cal. [*wavering*]. Well, if we do refrain from —[*shuddering*] what you say (God forbid!),   75
would that bring peace?

Lys. My goodness, yes! If we sit at home all rouged and powdered, dressed in our sheerest gowns, and neatly depilated, our men will get excited and want to take us; but if you don't   80
come to them and keep away, they'll soon make a truce.

Lam. Aye; Menelaus caught sight of Helen's

---

weeded i.e., depilated

Eucrates an Athenian general who, according to un-
verified tradition, was mercenary and traitorous

Milesians . . . us Milesia was recognized for its leather
goods among which, apparently, were dildos, the lack
of which Lysistrata here laments

Mt. Taygetus a mountain range looming over Sparta

"love-affairs and bassinets" Lysistrata's point seems
to be that although women have passionate and tender experiences, which are the material of tragedy,
they lack character, resolution, fortitude

naked breast and dropped his sword,° they say.

CAL. What if the men give us up?

LYS. "Flay a skinned dog," as Pherecrates°
5 says.

CAL. Rubbish! These make-shifts are no good. But suppose they grab us and drag us into the bedroom?

LYS. Hold on to the door.

10 CAL. And if they beat us?

LYS. Give in with a bad grace. There's no pleasure in it for them when they have to use violence. And you must torment them in every possible way. They'll give up soon enough; a
15 man gets no joy if he doesn't get along with his wife.

MYR. If this is your opinion, we agree.

LAM. As for our own men, we can persuade them to make a just and fair peace; but what
20 about the Athenian rabble? Who will persuade them not to start any more monkey-shines?

LYS. Don't worry. We guarantee to convince them.

LAM. Not while their ships are rigged so well
25 and they have that mighty treasure in the temple of Athene.

LYS. We've taken good care for that too: we shall seize the Acropolis today. The older women have orders to do this, and while we are
30 making our arrangements, they are to pretend to make a sacrifice and occupy the Acropolis.

LAM. All will be well then. That's a very fine idea.

LYS. Let's ratify this, Lampito, with the most
35 solemn oath.

LAM. Tell us what oath we shall swear.

LYS. All right? Where's our Policewoman? [To a Scythian slave.] What are you gaping at?

Set a shield upside-down here in front of me, and give me the sacred meats. 40

CAL. Lysistrata, what sort of an oath are we to take?

LYS. What oath? I'm going to slaughter a sheep over the shield, as they do in Aeschylus.°

CAL. Don't, Lysistrata! No oaths about peace 45 over a shield.

LYS. What shall the oath be, then?

CAL. How about getting a white horse somewhere and cutting out its entrails for the sacrifice? 50

LYS. White horse indeed!

CAL. Well then, how shall we swear?

MYR. I'll tell you: let's place a large black bowl upside-down and then slaughter—a flask of Thasian wine. And then let's swear—not to 55 pour in a single drop of water.

LAM. Lord! How I like that oath!

LYS. Someone bring out a bowl and a flask.

[A slave brings the utensils for the sacrifice.]

CAL. Look, my friends! What a big jar! Here's 60 a cup that 'twould give me joy to handle. [She picks up the bowl.]

LYS. Set it down and put your hands on our victim. [As CALONICE places her hands on the flask.] O Lady of Persuasion and dear Loving 65 Cup, graciously vouchsafe to receive this sacrifice from us women. [She pours the wine into the bowl.]

CAL. The blood has a good color and spurts out nicely. 70

LAM. Faith, it has a pleasant smell, too.

MYR. Oh, let me be the first to swear, ladies!

CAL. No, by my Lady! Not unless you're alloted the first turn.

LYS. Place all your hands on the cup, and one 75 of you repeat on behalf of all what I say. Then all will swear and ratify the oath. *I will suffer no man, be he husband or lover,*

CAL. *I will suffer no man, be he husband or lover,* 80

LYS. *To approach me all hot and horny.* [As CALONICE hesitates.] Say it!

CAL. [slowly and painfully]. *To approach me*

Menelaus . . . sword in Euripides' *Andromache*, "Menelaus, about to stab his faithless wife, is overcome by her beauty and drops his sword." [Fitts's note.]

Pherecrates a comic writer none of whose work is extant. The quoted phrase seems tantamount to "absurd" or "impossible," but most translators assume that Aristophanes is twisting it ironically. One reads: "We'll have to take things into our own hands"; another: "We'd have to fall back on ourselves."

Aeschylus "In the *Seven against Thebes*." [Translator's note.]

all hot and horny. O Lysistrata, I feel so weak in the knees!

Lys. *I will remain at home unmated,*

Cal. *I will remain at home unmated,*

5 Lys. *Wearing my sheerest gown and carefully adorned,*

Cal. *Wearing my sheerest gown and carefully adorned,*

Lys. *That my husband may burn with desire*
10 *for me.*

Cal. *That my husband may burn with desire for me.*

Lys. *And if he takes me by force against my will,*

15 Cal. *And if he takes me by force against my will,*

Lys. *I shall do it badly and keep from moving.*

Cal. *I shall do it badly and keep from mov-*
20 *ing.*

Lys. *I will not stretch my slippers toward the ceiling,*

Cal. *I will not stretch my slippers toward the ceiling,*

25 Lys. *Nor will I take the posture of the lioness on the knife-handle.*°

Cal. *Nor will I take the posture of the lioness on the knife-handle.*

Lys. *If I keep this oath, may I be permitted to*
30 *drink from this cup,*

Cal. *If I keep this oath, may I be permitted to drink from this cup,*

Lys. *But if I break it, may the cup be filled with water.*

35 Cal. *But if I break it, may the cup be filled with water.*

Lys. Do you all swear to this?

All. I do, so help me!

Lys. Come then, I'll just consummate this
40 offering. [*She takes a long drink from the cup.*]

Cal. [*snatching the cup away*]. Shares, my dear! Let's drink to our continued friendship.

[*A shout is heard from off-stage.*]

Lam. What's that shouting?

45 Lys. That's what I was telling you: the women have just seized the Acropolis. Now, Lampito, go home and arrange matters in Sparta; and leave these two ladies here as hostages. We'll enter the Acropolis to join our friends and help them lock the gates.   50

Cal. Don't you suppose the men will come to attack us?

Lys. Don't worry about them. Neither threats nor fire will suffice to open the gates, except on the terms we've stated.   55

Cal. I should say not! Else we'd belie our reputation as unmanageable pests.

[Lampito *leaves the stage, The other women retire and enter the Acropolis through the Propylaea.*]   60

[*Enter the* Chorus of Old Men, *carrying fire-pots and a load of heavy sticks.*]

PÁRODOS

Leader of Men. Onward, Draces, step by
          [step, though your shoulder's aching.
Cursèd logs of olive-wood, what a load you're   65
          [making!
1st Semi-chorus of Old Men [*singing*].
Aye, many surprises await a man who lives to a
          [ripe old age;
For who could suppose, Strymodorus my lad,   70
          [that the women we've nourished (alas!),
Who sat at home to vex our days,
Would seize the holy image here,
And occupy this sacred shrine.
With bolts and bars, with fell design,   75
To lock the Propylaea?
          Leader. Come with speed, Philourgus, come!
          [to the temple hast'ning.
There we'll heap these logs about in a circle
          [round them,   80
And whoever has conspired, raising this
          [rebellion,
Shall be roasted, scorched, and burnt, all
          [without exception,
Doomed by one unanimous vote—but first the   85
          [wife of Lycon.°

---

posture . . . knife-handle   i.e., on all fours

wife of Lycon Rhodia, the wife of the demagogue, much lampooned for the laxness of her morality

2ND SEMI-CHORUS [*singing*].
No, no! by Demeter, while I'm alive, no woman
[shall mock at me.
Not even the Spartan Cleomenes,° our citadel
5 [first to seize,
Got off unscathed; for all his pride
And haughty Spartan arrogance,
He left his arms and sneaked away,
Stripped to his shirt, unkempt, unshav'd,
10 With six years' filth still on him.
LEADER. I besieged that hero bold, sleeping
[at my station,
Marshalled at these holy gates sixteen deep
[against him.
15 Shall I not these cursèd pests punish for their
[daring,
Burning these Euripides-and-God-detested
[women?
Aye! Or else may Marathon overturn my
20 [trophy.
1ST SEMI-CHORUS [*singing*]. There remains of
[my road
Just this brow of the hill;
There I speed on my way.
25 Drag the logs up the hill, though we've got no
[ass to help.
(God! my shoulder's bruised and sore!)
Onward still must we go.
Blow the fire! Don't let it go out
30 Now we're near the end of our road.
ALL [*blowing on the fire-pots*]. Whew!
[Whew! Drat the smoke!
2ND SEMI-CHORUS [*singing*]. Lord, what
[smoke rushing forth
35 From the pot, like a dog
Running mad, bites my eyes!
This must be Lemnos-fire.° What a sharp and
[stinging smoke!
Rushing onward to the shrine
40 Aid the gods. Once for all

Show your mettle, Laches my boy!
To the rescue hastening all!
ALL [*blowing on the fire-pots*]. Whew!
[Whew! Drat the smoke!
[*The chorus has now reached the edge of the* 45
orchestra nearest the stage, in front of the
Propylaea. They begin laying their logs and
fire-pots on the ground.]
LEADER. Thank heaven, this fire is still alive.
Now let's first put down these logs here and 50
place our torches in the pots to catch; then let's
make a rush for the gates with a battering-
ram. If the women don't unbar the gate at our
summons, we'll have to smoke them out.
Let me put down my load. Ouch! That hurts! 55
[*To the audience.*] Would any of the generals
in Samos° like to lend a hand with this log?
[*Throwing down a log.*] Well, *that* won't break
my back any more, at any rate. [*Turning to his*
fire-pot.] Your job, my little pot, is to keep 60
those coals alive and furnish me shortly with a
red-hot torch.
O mistress Victory, be my ally and grant me
to rout these audacious women in the Acropolis.
[*While the men are busy with their logs and* 65
fires, the CHORUS OF OLD WOMEN *enters, carry-*
ing pitchers of water.]
LEADER OF WOMEN. What's this I see? Smoke
[and flames? Is that a fire ablazing?
Let's rush upon them. Hurry up! They'll find 70
[us women ready.
1ST SEMI-CHORUS OF OLD WOMEN [*singing*].
With wingèd foot onward I fly,
Ere the flames consume Neodice;
Lest Critylla be overwhelmed 75
By a lawless, accurst herd of old men.
I shudder with fear. Am I too late to aid them?
At break of the day filled we our jars with water
Fresh from the spring, pushing our way straight
[through the crowds. Oh, what a din! 80
Mid crockery crashing, jostled by slave-girls,
Sped we to save them, aiding our neighbors,
Bearing this water to put out the flames.
2ND SEMI-CHORUS OF OLD WOMEN [*singing*].
Such news I've heard: doddering fools 85

Cleomenes a Spartan king who occupied the Acropolis for two days (not six years!) almost a hundred
years before the incidents of the play. The men of
the chorus would seem either extraordinarily old or
invested with a communal but unreliable memory.

Lemnos-fire according to Fitts, a bad pun, the Greek
words for Lemnos (an island in the Aegean) and for
sore eyes being similar

Samos an island in the Aegean that was still allied to
Athens

Come with logs, like furnace-attendants,
Loaded down with three hundred pounds
Breathing many a vain, blustering threat,
That all these abhorred sluts will be burnt to
5   [charcoal.
O goddess, I pray never may they be kindled;
Grant them to save Greece and our men;
       [madness and war help them to end.
With this as our purpose, golden-plumed
10   [Maiden,°
Guardian of Athens, seized we thy precinct.
Be my ally, Warrior-maiden,
'Gainst these old men, bearing water with me.
[*The women have now reached their position*
15 *in the orchestra, and their* LEADER *advances*
toward the LEADER OF THE MEN.]
    L. WOM. Hold on there! What's this, you
utter scoundrels? No decent, God-fearing citizens would act like this.
20   L. MEN. Oho! Here's something unexpected:
a swarm of women have come out to attack us.
    L. WOM. What, do we frighten you? Surely
you don't think we're too many for you. And
yet there are ten thousand times more of us
25 whom you haven't even seen.
    L. MEN. What say, Phaedria? Shall we let
these women wag their tongues? Shan't we take
our sticks and break them over their backs?
    L. WOM. Let's set our pitchers on the ground;
30 then if anyone lays a hand on us, they won't
get in our way.
    L. MEN. By God! If someone gave them two
or three smacks on the jaw, like Bupalus,° they
wouldn't talk so much!
35   L. WOM. Go on, hit me, somebody! Here's
my jaw! But no other bitch will bite a piece out
of you before me.
    L. MEN. Silence! or I'll knock out your—
senility!
40   L. WOM. Just lay one finger on Stratyllis, I
dare you!
    L. MEN. Suppose I dust you off with this
fist? What will you do?

golden-plumed Maiden Athene
Bupalus according to the poet Hipponax, Bupalus
    was the recipient, not the bestower, of smacks on the
    jaw

    L. WOM. I'll tear the living guts out of you
with my teeth.   45
    L. MEN. No poet is more clever than Euripe-
des: "There is no beast so shameless as a
woman."
    L. WOM. Let's pick up our jars of water,
Rhodippe.   50
    L. MEN. Why have you come here with water,
you detestable slut?
    L. WOM. And why have you come with fire,
you funeral vault? To cremate yourself?
    L. MEN. To light a fire and singe your friends. 55
    L. WOM. And I've brought water to put out
your fire.
    L. MEN. What? You'll put out my fire?
    L. WOM. Just try and see!
    L. MEN. I wonder: shall I scorch you with 60
this torch of mine?
    L. WOM. If you've got any soap, I'll give you
a bath.
    L. MEN. Give *me* a bath, you stinking hag?
    L. WOM. Yes—a bridal bath!   65
    L. MEN. Just listen to her! What crust!
    L. WOM. Well, I'm a free citizen.
    L. MEN. I'll put an end to your bawling. [*The
men pick up their torches.*]
    L. WOM. You'll never do jury-duty again. 70
[*The women pick up their pitchers.*]
    L. MEN. Singe her hair for her!
    L. WOM. Do your duty, water! [*The women
empty their pitchers on the men.*]
    L. MEN. Ow! Ow! For heaven's sake!   75
    L. WOM. Is it too hot?
    L. MEN. What do you mean "hot"? Stop!
What are you doing?
    L. WOM. I'm watering you, so you'll be fresh
and green.   80
    L. MEN. But I'm all withered up with shaking.
    L. WOM. Well, you've got a fire; why don't
you dry yourself?

SCENE I

[*Enter an Athenian* MAGISTRATE, *accompa-*
nied by four Scythian policemen.]   85
    MAG. Have these wanton women flared up
again with their timbrels and their continual

72

worship of Sabazius?° Is this another Adonis-dirge upon the roof-tops—which we heard not long ago in the Assembly? That confounded Demostratus was urging us to sail to Sicily,
5 and the whirling women shouted, "Woe for Adonis!"° And then Demostratus said we'd best enroll the infantry from Zacynthus, and a tipsy woman on the roof shrieked, "Beat your breasts for Adonis!" And that vile and filthy
10 lunatic forced his measure through. Such license do our women take.

L. MEN. What if you heard of the insolence of these women here? Besides their other violent acts, they threw water all over us, and
15 we have to shake out our clothes just as if we'd leaked in them.

MAG. And rightly too, by God! For we ourselves lead the women astray and teach them to play the wanton; from these roots such notions
20 blossom forth. A man goes into the jeweler's shop and says, "About that necklace you made for my wife, goldsmith: last night, while she was dancing, the fastening-bolt slipped out of the hole. I have to sail over to Salamis today;
25 if you're free, do come around tonight and fit in a new bolt for her." Another goes to the shoe-maker, a strapping young fellow with manly parts, and says, "See here, cobbler, the sandal-strap chafes my wife's little—toe; it's so
30 tender. Come around during the siesta and stretch it a little, so she'll be more comfortable." Now we see the results of such treatment: here I'm a special Councillor and need money to procure oars for the galleys; and I'm locked
35 out of the Treasury by these women.

But this is no time to stand around. Bring up crow-bars there! I'll put an end to their insolence. [To one of the policemen.] What are you gaping at, you wretch? What are you star-
40 ing at? Got an eye out for a tavern, eh? Set your crow-bars here to the gates and force them

open. [Retiring to a safe distance.] I'll help from over here.

[The gates are thrown open and LYSISTRATA comes out followed by several other women.] 45
LYS. Don't force the gates; I'm coming out of my own accord. We don't need crow-bars here; what we need is good sound common-sense.

MAG. Is that so, you strumpet? Where's my 50 policeman? Officer, arrest her and tie her arms behind her back.

LYS. By Artemis, if he lays a finger on me, he'll pay for it, even if he is a public servant.

[The policeman retires in terror.] 55
MAG. You there, are you afraid? Seize her round the waist—and you, too. Tie her up, both of you!

1ST WOMAN [as the second policeman approaches LYSISTRATA]. By Pandrosus,° if you 60 but touch her with your hand, I'll kick the stuffings out of you.

[The second policeman retires in terror.]
MAG. Just listen to that: "kick the stuffings out." Where's another policeman? Tie her up 65 first, for her chatter.

2ND WOMAN. By the Goddess of the Light,° if you lay the tip of your finger on her, you'll soon need a doctor.

[The third policemen retires in terror.] 70
MAG. What's this? Where's my policeman? Seize her too. I'll soon stop your sallies.

3RD WOMAN. By the Goddess of Tauros,° if you go near her, I'll tear out your hair until it shrieks with pain. 75

[The fourth policeman retires in terror.]
MAG. Oh, damn it all! I've run out of policemen. But women must never defeat us. Officers, let's charge them all together. Close up your ranks! 80

Sabazius a Thracian and Phrygian deity whom the Greeks usually identified with Dionysus
Demostratus . . . Adonis Demostratus took a leading part in selling the disastrous Sicilian expedition to the Athenian assembly. Plutarch records the women's dirge for Adonis as among the evil omens precedent to the expedition.

Pandrosus goddess of the dew. Parker wonders if pandrosus (all-bedewing) may not have been another epithet for Artemis, "classical antiquity's best-attested virgin, who is otherwise invoked here in three out of the four instances"—Aristophanes, Lysistrata, Douglass Parker, trans., The Complete Greek Comedy, William Arrowsmith, ed. (Ann Arbor: The University of Michigan Press, 1964).
Goddess of the Light Artemis
Goddess of Tauros Artemis. Tauros is the Crimea.

[*The policemen rally for a mass attack.*]

Lys. By heaven, you'll soon find out that we have four companies of warrior-women, all fully equipped within!

5 Mag. [*advancing*]. Twist their arms off, men!

Lys. [*shouting*]. To the rescue, my valiant women!

O sellers-of-barley-green-stuffs-and-eggs,

O sellers-of-garlic, ye keepers-of-taverns, and

10   [vendors-of-bread,

Grapple! Smite! Smash!

Won't you heap filth on them? Give them a

               [tongue-lashing!

[*The women beat off the policemen.*]

15 Halt! Withdraw! No looting on the field.

Mag. Damn it! My police-force has put up a very poor show.

Lys. What did you expect? Did you think you were attacking slaves? Didn't you know that

20 women are filled with passion?

Mag. Aye, passion enough—for a good

               [strong drink!

L. Men. O chief and leader of this land, why

               [spend your words in vain?

25 Don't argue with these shameless beasts. You

               [know not how we've fared:

A soapless bath they've given us; our clothes

               [are soundly soaked.

L. Wom. Poor fool! You never should attack

30   [or strike a peaceful girl.

But if you do, your eyes must swell. For I am

               [quite content

To sit unmoved, like modest maids, in peace

               [and cause no pain;

35 But let a man stir up my hive, he'll find me

               [like a wasp.

Chorus of Men [*singing*].

O God, whatever shall we do with creatures like

               [Womankind?

40 This can't be endured by any man alive.

               [Question them!

Let us try to find out what this means.

To what end have they seized on this shrine,

This steep and rugged, high and holy,

45 Undefiled Acropolis?

L. Men. Come, put your questions; don't

               [give in, and probe her every statement.

For base and shameful it would be to leave this

               [plot untested.

50 Mag. Well then, first of all I wish to ask her this: for what purpose have you barred us from the Acropolis?

Lys. To keep the treasure safe, so you won't make war on account of it.

55 Mag. What? Do we make war on account of the treasure?

Lys. Yes, and you cause all our other troubles for it, too. Peisander° and those greedy office-seekers keep things stirred up so they can find

60 occasions to steal. Now let them do what they like: they'll never again make off with any of this money.

Mag. What will you do?

Lys. What a question! We'll administer it

65   [ourselves.

Mag. *You* will administer the treasure?

Lys. What's so strange in that? Don't we administer the household money for you?

Mag. That's different.

70 Lys. How is it different?

Mag. We've got to make war with this money.

Lys. But that's the very first thing: you mustn't make war.

75 Mag. How else can we be saved?

Lys. We'll save you.

Mag. *You?*

Lys. Yes, we!

Mag. God forbid!

80 Lys. We'll save you, whether you want it or not.

Mag. Oh! This is terrible!

Lys. You don't like it, but we're going to do it none the less.

85 Mag. Good God! it's illegal!

Lys. We *will* save you, my little man!

Mag. Suppose I don't want you to?

Lys. That's all the more reason.

Mag. What business have you with war and

90 peace?

Peisander "Engineer of the oligarchic revolt which overthrew the Athenian constitution in May 411 and set up the Council of Four Hundred." [Parker's note.]

Lys. I'll explain.

Mag. [*shaking his fist*]. Speak up, or you'll smart for it.

Lys. Just listen, and try to keep your hands
5 still.

Mag. I can't. I'm so mad I can't stop them.

First Woman. Then you'll be the one to smart for it.

Mag. Croak to yourself, old hag! [*To Ly-*
10 *sistrata*.] Now then, speak up.

Lys. Very well. Formerly we endured the war for a good long time with our usual restraint, no matter what you men did. You wouldn't let us say "boo," although nothing you did suited
15 us. But we watched you well, and though we stayed at home we'd often hear of some terribly stupid measure you'd proposed. Then, though grieving at heart, we'd smile sweetly and say, "What was passed in the Assembly
20 today about writing on the treaty-stone?" "What's that to you?" my husband would say. "Hold your tongue!" And I held my tongue.

1st Woman. But I wouldn't have—not I!

Mag. You'd have been soundly smacked, if
25 you hadn't kept still.

Lys. So I kept still at home. Then we'd hear of some plan still worse than the first; we'd say, "Husband, how could you pass such a stupid proposal?" He'd scowl at me and say,
30 "If you don't mind your spinning, your head will be sore for weeks. *War shall be the concern of Men.*"°

Mag. And he was right, upon my word!

Lys. Why right, you confounded fool, when
35 your proposals were so stupid and we weren't allowed to make suggestions?

"There's not a *man* left in the country," says one. "No, not one," says another. Therefore all we women have decided in council to make a
40 common effort to save Greece. How long should we have waited? Now, if you're willing to listen to our excellent proposals and keep silence for us in your turn, we still may save you.

Mag. We men keep silence for you? That's
45 terrible; I won't endure it!

Lys. Silence!

War ... Men Homer, *Iliad* vi. 492. [Translator's note.]

Mag. Silence for *you*, you wench, when you're wearing a snood?° I'd rather die!

Lys. Well, if that's all that bothers you— here! take my snood and tie it round your head. 50 [*During the following words the women dress up the* Magistrate *in women's garments*.] And *now* keep quiet! Here, take this spinning-basket, too, and card your wool with robes tucked up, munching on beans. *War shall be the con-* 55 *cern of Women!*

L. Wom. Arise and leave your pitchers, girls;
                    [no time is this to falter.
We too must aid our loyal friends; our turn has
                    [come for action. 60
Chorus of Women [*singing*].
I'll never tire of aiding them with song and
                    [dance; never may
Faintness keep my legs from moving to and fro
                    [endlessly. 65
For I yearn to do all for my friends;
They have charm, they have wit, they have
                    [grace,
With courage, brains, and best of virtues—
Patriotic sapience. 70
L. Wom. Come, child of manliest ancient
                    [dames, offspring of stinging nettles,
Advance with rage unsoftened; for fair
                    [breezes speed you onward.

Lys. If only sweet Eros and the Cyprian 75 Queen of Love° shed charm over our breasts and limbs and inspire our men with amorous longing and priapic spasms, I think we may soon be called Peacemakers among the Greeks.

Mag. What will you do? 80

Lys. First of all, we'll stop those fellows who run madly about the Marketplace in arms.

1st Wom. Indeed we shall, by the Queen of Paphos.°

snood the Greek word is variously translated *snood*, *fillet*, *wimple*. To the magistrate it signifies female inferiority.
Cyprian ... Love Aphrodite
Queen of Paphos Aphrodite, who was believed to have risen from the sea near Paphos in western Cyprus

LYS. For now they roam about the market, amid the pots and greenstuffs, armed to the teeth like Corybantes.

MAG. That's what manly fellows ought to do!

5 LYS. But it's so silly: a chap with a Gorgon-emblazoned shield buying pickled herring.

1ST WOM. Why, just the other day I saw one of those long-haired dandies who command our cavalry ride up on horseback and pour into his 10 bronze helmet the egg-broth he'd bought from an old dame. And there was a Thracian slinger too, shaking his lance like Tereus; he'd scared the life out of the poor fig-peddler and was gulping down all her ripest fruit.

15 MAG. How can you stop all the confusion in the various states and bring them together?

LYS. Very easily.

MAG. Tell me how.

LYS. Just like a ball of wool, when it's con-20 fused and snarled: we take it thus, and draw out a thread here and a thread there with our spindles; thus we'll unsnarl this war, if no one prevents us, and draw together the various states with embassies here and embassies there.

25 MAG. Do you suppose you can stop this dreadful business with balls of wool and spindles, you nit-wits?

LYS. Why, if *you* had any wits, you'd manage all affairs of state like our wool-working.

30 MAG. How so?

LYS. First you ought to treat the city as we do when we wash the dirt out of a fleece: stretch it out and pluck and thrash out of the city all those prickly scoundrels; aye, and card 35 out those who conspire and stick together to gain office, pulling off their heads. Then card the wool, all of it, into one fair basket of good-will, mingling in the aliens residing here, any loyal foreigners, and anyone who's in debt to 40 the Treasury; and consider that all our colonies lie scattered round about like remnants; from all of these collect the wool and gather it together here, wind up a great ball, and then weave a good stout cloak for the democracy.

45 MAG. Dreadful! Talking about thrashing and winding balls of wool, when you haven't the slightest share in the war!

LYS. Why, you dirty scoundrel, we bear more than twice as much as you. First, we bear children and send off our sons as soldiers. 50

MAG. Hush! Let bygones be bygones!

LYS. Then, when we ought to be happy and enjoy our youth, we sleep alone because of your expeditions abroad. But never mind us married women: I grieve most for the maids 55 who grow old at home unwed.

MAG. Don't men grow old, too?

LYS. For heaven's sake! That's not the same thing. When a man comes home, no matter how grey he is, he soon finds a girl to marry. 60 But woman's bloom is short and fleeting; if she doesn't grasp her chance, no man is willing to marry her and she sits at home a prey to every fortune-teller.

MAG. [*coarsely*]. But if a man can still get 65 it up—

LYS. See here, you: what's the matter? Aren't you dead yet? There's plenty of room for you. Buy yourself a shroud and I'll bake you a honey-cake. [*Handing him a copper coin for* 70 *his passage across the Styx.*] Here's your fare! Now get yourself a wreath.

[*During the following dialogue the women dress up the* MAGISTRATE *as a corpse.*]

1ST WOM. Here, take these fillets. 75

2ND WOM. Here, take this wreath.

LYS. What do you want? What's lacking? Get moving; off to the ferry! Charon is calling you; don't keep him from sailing.

MAG. Am I to endure these insults? By God! 80 I'm going straight to the magistrates to show them how I've been treated.

LYS. Are you grumbling that you haven't been properly laid out? Well, the day after tomorrow we'll send around all the usual offer- 85 ings early in the morning.

[*The* MAGISTRATE *goes out still wearing his funeral decorations.* LYSISTRATA *and the women retire into the Acropolis.*]

CHORAL EPISODE

L. MEN. Wake, ye sons of freedom, wake! 90
           ['Tis no time for sleeping.
Up and at them, like a man! Let us strip for
           [action.

[*The* CHORUS OF MEN *remove their outer cloaks.*]

CHORUS OF MEN [*singing*].
Surely there is something here greater than
5   [meets the eye;
For without a doubt I smell Hippias' tyranny.°
Dreadful fear assails me lest certain bands of
                [Spartan men,
Meeting here with Cleisthenes,° have inspired
10   [through treachery
All these god-detested women secretly to
                [seize
Athens' treasure in the temple, and to stop that
                [pay
15 Whence I live at my ease.°

L. MEN. Now isn't it terrible for them to advise the state and chatter about shields, being mere women?

And they think to reconcile us with the
20 Spartans—men who hold nothing sacred any more than hungry wolves. Surely this is a web of deceit, my friends, to conceal an attempt at tyranny. But they'll never lord it over me; I'll be on my guard and from now on,
25 "The blade I bear   A myrtle spray shall wear."
I'll occupy the market under arms and stand next to Aristogeiton.

Thus I'll stand beside him. [*He strikes the pose of the famous statue of tyrannicides, with*
30 *one arm raised.*] And here's my chance to take this accurst old hag and—[*striking the* LEADER OF WOMEN] smack her on the jaw!

L. WOM. You'll go home in such a state your
                [Ma won't recognize you!
35 Ladies all, upon the ground let us place these
                [garments.

[*The* CHORUS OF WOMEN *remove their outer garments.*]

CHORUS OF WOM. [*singing*]. Citizens of
      [Athens, hear useful words for the state. 40
Rightly; for it nurtured me in my youth
                [royally.
As a child of seven years carried I the sacred
                [box;°
Then I was a Miller-maid, grinding at Athene's 45
                [shrine;
Next I wore the saffron robe and played
                [Brauronia's Bear;
And I walked as Basket-bearer, wearing chains
                [of figs, 50
As a sweet maiden fair.

L. WOM. Therefore, am I not bound to give good advice to the city?

Don't take it ill that I was born a woman, if I contribute something better than our present 55 troubles. I pay my share; for I contribute MEN. But you miserable old fools contribute nothing, and after squandering our ancestral treasure, the fruit of the Persian Wars, you make no contribution in return. And now, all on account of 60 you, we're facing ruin.

What, muttering, are you? If you annoy me, I'll take this hard, rough slipper and—[*striking the* LEADER OF MEN] smack you on the jaw!

CHORUS OF MEN [*singing*]. This is outright 65
      [insolence! Things go from bad to worse.

---

carried . . . box "Since this passage is frequently cited as primary evidence for the *cursus honorum* of a high-born young girl in fifth-century Athens, here are the steps set forth a bit more explicitly: (1) *arrêphoros* ('relic-bearer') to Athene, one of four little girls who carried the Goddess' sacred objects in Her semiannual festival of the *Arréphoria;* (2) *aletris* ('millgirl') to the Founding Mother (doubtless Athene), one of the girls who ground the meal to be made into sacrificial cakes; (3) *arktos* ('she-bear') at the *Brauronia,* a festival of Artemis held every fifth year at Brauron in Attika, centering on a myth which told of the killing of a tame bear sacred to that goddess; and (4) *kanêphoros* ('basket-bearer'), the maiden who bore the sacrificial cake and led the procession at Athens' most important festivals, such as the City Dionysia and the Great Panathenaia." [Parker's note.]

Hippias' tyranny Hippias, the last of the Tyrants of Athens, ruled 527–510 B.C.

Cleisthenes a notorious homosexual, also mentioned unmentionably [Fitts's phrase] at l. 8, p. 82.

stop . . . ease this phrase and l. 70, p. 69. ("You'll never do jury-duty again") make it reasonably clear that the basic source of income for the old men of the chorus is jury duty, for which they received three obols a day. The money, says Parker, "would naturally be stored inside the Citadel in the Treasury."

If you're men with any guts, prepare to meet
[the foe.
Let us strip our tunics off! We need the smell
[of male
5 Vigor. And we cannot fight all swaddled up in
[clothes.
[*They strip off their tunics.*]
Come then, my comrades, on to the battle,
[ye who once to Leipsydrion° came;
10 Then ye were MEN. Now call back your
[youthful vigor.
With light, wingèd footstep advance,
Shaking old age from your frame.

L. MEN. If any of us give these wenches the
15 slightest hold, they'll stop at nothing: such is
their cunning.

They will even build ships and sail against us,
like Artemisia.° Or if they turn to mounting,
I count our Knights as done for: a woman's
20 such a tricky jockey when she gets astraddle,
with a good firm seat for trotting. Just look at
those Amazons that Micon painted, fighting on
horseback against men!

But we must throw them all in the pillory—
25 [*seizing and choking the* LEADER OF WOMEN]
grabbing hold of yonder neck!

CHORUS OF WOM. [*singing*]. 'Ware my anger!
[Like a boar 'twill rush upon you men.
Soon you'll bawl aloud for help, you'll be so
30 [soundly trimmed!
Come, my friends, let's strip with speed, and
[lay aside these robes;
Catch the scent of women's rage. Attack with
[tooth and nail!
35 [*They strip off their tunics.*]
Now then, come near me, you miserable man!
[you'll never eat garlic or black beans again.
And if you utter a single hard word, in rage I

Leipsydrion a mountain slope north of Athens where,
a century before the time of the play, the exiled
Alkmaionids or Patriots for a time fought off the
the forces of the tyrant Hippias
Artemisia "Queen of Halikarnassos, who, as an ally
of the Persian King Xerxes in his invasion of Greece,
fought with particular distinction at the sea battle
of Salamis in 480." [Parker's note.]

[will "nurse" you as once
The beetle requited her foe.°   40

L. WOM. For you don't worry me; no, not so
long as my Lampito lives and our Theban
friend, the noble Ismenia.

You can't do anything, not even if you pass a
dozen—decrees! You miserable fool, all our   45
neighbors hate you. Why, just the other day
when I was holding a festival for Hecate, I invited as a playmate from our neighbors the
Boeotians a charming, well-bred Copaic—eel.
But they refused to send me one on account of   50
your decrees.

And you'll never stop passing decrees until I
grab your foot and—[*tripping up the* LEADER
OF MEN] toss you down and break your neck!

[*Here an interval of five days is supposed to   55
elapse.*]

SCENE II

[LYSISTRATA *comes out from the Acropolis.*]
L. WOM. [*dramatically*]. Empress of this great
[emprise and undertaking,
Why come you forth, I pray, with frowning   60
[brow?

LYS. Ah, these cursèd women! Their deeds
and female notions make me pace up and down
in utter despair.

L. WOM. Ah, what sayest thou?   65
LYS. The truth, alas! the truth.
L. WOM. What dreadful tale hast thou to
tell thy friends?
LYS. 'Tis shame to speak, and not to speak
is hard.   70
L. WOM. Hide not from me whatever woes
we suffer.
LYS. Well then, to put it briefly, we want—
laying!
L. WOM. O Zeus, Zeus!   75
LYS. Why call on Zeus? That's the way things

---

beetle . . . foe Aesop's fable (No. 223), *The Eagle
and the Beetle* [translator's note]. Injured by the
eagle, the beetle retaliated by breaking the eagle's
eggs wherever they were laid—even in the bosom
of Zeus.

are. I can no longer keep them away from the men, and they're all deserting. I caught one wriggling through a hole near the grotto of Pan, another sliding down a rope, another de-
5 serting her post; and yesterday I found one getting on a sparrow's back to fly off to Orsilochus,° and had to pull her back by the hair. They're digging up all sorts of excuses to get home. Look, here comes one of them now. [*A*
10 *woman comes hastily out of the Acropolis.*] Here you! Where are you off to in such a hurry?

1st Wom. I want to go home. My very best wool is being devoured by moths.

Lys. Moths? Nonsense! Go back inside.

15 1st Wom. I'll come back; I swear it. I just want to lay it out on the bed.

Lys. Well, you won't lay it out, and you won't go home, either.

1st Wom. Shall I let my wool be ruined?

20 Lys. If necessary, yes. [*Another woman comes out.*]

2nd Wom. Oh dear! Oh dear! My precious flax! I left it at home all unpeeled.

Lys. Here's another one, going home for her
25 "flax." Come back here!

2nd Wom. But I just want to work it up a little and then I'll be right back.

Lys. No indeed! If you start this, all the other women will want to do the same. [*A third
30 woman comes out.*]

3rd Wom. O Eilithyia, goddess of travail, stop my labor till I come to a lawful spot!

Lys. What's this nonsense?

3rd Wom. I'm going to have a baby—right
35 now!

Lys. But you weren't even pregnant yesterday.

3rd Wom. Well, I am today. O Lysistrata, do send me home to see a midwife, right away.

40 Lys. What are you talking about? [*Putting her hand on her stomach.*] What's this hard lump here?

3rd Wom. A little boy.

Lys. My goodness, what have you got there?
45 It seems hollow; I'll just find out. [*Pulling aside her robe.*] Why, you silly goose, you've got

Orsilochus keeper of a brothel

Athene's sacred helmet there. And you said you were having a baby!

3rd Wom. Well, I *am* having one, I swear!

Lys. Then what's this helmet for? 50

3rd Wom. If the baby starts coming while I'm still in the Acropolis, I'll creep into this like a pigeon and give birth to it there.

Lys. Stuff and nonsense! It's plain enough what you're up to. You just wait here for the 55 christening of this—helmet.

3rd Wom. But I can't sleep in the Acropolis since I saw the sacred snake.

1st Wom. And I'm dying for lack of sleep: the hooting of the owls keeps me awake. 60

Lys. Enough of these shams, you wretched creatures. You want your husbands, I suppose. Well, don't you think they want us? I'm sure they're spending miserable nights. Hold out, my friends, and endure for just a little while. 65 There's an oracle that we shall conquer, if we don't split up. [*Producing a roll of paper.*] Here it is.

1st Wom. Tell us what it says.

Lys. Listen. 70
"When in the length of time the Swallows shall
[gather together,
Fleeing the Hoopoe's amorous flight and the
[Cockatoo shunning,
Then shall your woes be ended and Zeus who 75
[thunders in heaven
Set what's below on top—"

1st Wom. What? Are we going to be on top?

Lys. "But if the Swallows rebel and flutter
[away from the temple, 80
Never a bird in the world shall seem more
[wanton and worthless."

1st Wom. That's clear enough, upon my word!

Lys. By all that's holy, let's not give up the 85 struggle now. Let's go back inside. It would be a shame, my dear friends, to disobey the oracle.

[*The women all retire to the Acropolis again.*]

CHORAL EPISODE

Chorus of Men [*singing*]. I have a tale to tell,
Which I know full well. 90
It was told me

In the nursery.

Once there was a likely lad,
    Melanion they name him;
The thought of marriage made him mad,
5   For which I cannot blame him.

So off he went to mountains fair;
    (No women to upbraid him!)
A mighty hunter of the hare,
    He had a dog to aid him.

10 He never came back home to see
    Detested women's faces.
He showed a shrewd mentality.
    With him I'd fain change places!

ONE OF THE MEN [*to one of the women*].
15 Come here, old dame; give me a kiss.
    WOM. You'll ne'er eat garlic, if you dare!
MAN. I want to kick you—just like this!
    WOM. Oh, there's a leg with bushy hair!
MAN. Myronides and Phormio°
20 Were hairy—and they thrashed the foe.

CHORUS OF WOMEN [*singing*]. I have another
                                    [tale,
With which to assail
    Your contention
25   'Bout Melanion.

Once upon a time a man
    Named Timon left our city,
To live in some deserted land.
    (We thought him rather witty.)

30 He dwelt alone amidst the thorn;
    In solitude he brooded.
From some grim Fury he was born:
    Such hatred he exuded.

He cursed you men, as scoundrels through
35   And through, till life he ended.
He couldn't stand the sight of YOU!
    But women he befriended.

Myronides and Phormio respectively a victorious Athenian general, admiral

WOM. [*to one of the men*]. I'll smash your
                                 [face in, if you like.
MAN. Oh no, please don't! You frighten me.   40
WOM. I'll lift my foot—and thus I'll strike.
MAN. Aha! Look there! What's that I see?
WOM. Whate'er you see, you cannot say
That I'm not neatly trimmed today.

SCENE III

[LYSISTRATA *appears on the wall of the Acrop-*   45
olis.]
    LYS. Hello! Hello! Girls, come here quick!
[*Several women appear beside her.*]
    WOM. What is it? Why are you calling?
    LYS. I see a man coming: he's in a dreadful   50
state. He's mad with passion. O Queen of
Cyprus, Cythera, and Paphos, just keep on
this way!
    WOM. Where is the fellow?
    LYS. There, beside the shrine of Demeter.   55
    WOM. Oh yes, so he is. Who is he?
    LYS. Let's see. Do any of you know him?
    MYR. Yes indeed. That's my husband, Cin-
esias.
    LYS. It's up to you, now: roast him, rack him,   60
fool him, love him—and leave him! Do everything, except what our oath forbids.
    MYR. Don't worry; I'll do it.
    LYS. I'll stay here to tease him and warm him
up a bit. Off with you.   65
    [*The other women retire from the wall. Enter*
CINESIAS *followed by a slave carrying a baby.*
CINESIAS *is obviously in great pain and distress.*]
    CIN. [*groaning*]. Oh-h! Oh-h-h! This is kill-
ing me! O God, what tortures I'm suffering!   70
    LYS. [*from the wall*]. Who's that within our
lines?
    CIN. Me.
    LYS. A *man*?
    CIN. [*pointing*]. A *man*, indeed!   75
    LYS. Well, go away!
    CIN. Who are you to send me away?
    LYS. The captain of the guard.
    CIN. Oh, for heaven's sake, call out Myrrhine
for me.   80
    LYS. Call Myrrhine? Nonsense! Who are
you?

CIN. Her husband, Cinesias of Paionidai.

LYS. [appearing much impressed]. Oh, greetings, friend. Your name is not without honor here among us. Your wife is always talking
5 about you, and whenever she takes an egg or an apple, she says, "Here's to my dear Cinesias!"

CIN. [quivering with excitement]. Oh, ye gods in heaven!

10 LYS. Indeed she does! And whenever our conversations turn to men, your wife immediately says, "All men are mere rubbish compared with Cinesias."

CIN. [groaning]. Oh! Do call her for me.

15 LYS. Why should I? What will you give me?

CIN. Whatever you want. All I have is yours —and you see what I've got!

LYS. Well then, I'll go down and call her. [She descends.]

20 CIN. And hurry up! I've had no joy of life ever since she left home. When I go in the house, I feel awful: everything seems so empty and I can't enjoy my dinner. I'm in such a state all the time!

25 MYR. [from behind the wall]. I do love him so. But he won't let me love him. No, no! Don't ask me to see him!

CIN. O my darling, O Myrrhine honey, why do you do this to me? [MYRRHINE appears on
30 the wall.] Come down here!

MYR. No, I won't come down.

CIN. Won't you come, Myrrhine, when I call you?

MYR. No; you don't want me.

35 CIN. Don't want you? I'm in agony!

MYR. I'm going now.

CIN. Please don't! At least, listen to your baby. [To the baby.] Here you, call your mamma! [Pinching the baby.]

40 BABY. Ma-ma! Ma-ma! Ma-ma!

CIN. [to MYRRHINE]. What's the matter with you? Have you no pity for your child, who hasn't been washed or fed for five whole days?

MYR. Oh, poor child; your father pays no
45 attention to you.

CIN. Come down then, you heartless wretch, for the baby's sake.

MYR. Oh, what it is to be a mother! I've got

to come down, I suppose. [She leaves the wall and shortly reappears at the gate.] 50

CIN. [to himself]. She seems much younger, and she has such a sweet look about her. Oh, the way she teases me! And her pretty, provoking ways make me burn with longing.

MYR. [coming out of the gate and taking the 55 baby]. O my sweet little angel. Naughty papa! Here, let Mummy kiss you, Mamma's little sweetheart! [She fondles the baby lovingly.]

CIN. [in despair]. You heartless creature, why do you do this? Why follow these other women 60 and make both of us suffer so? [He tries to embrace her.]

MYR. Don't touch me!

CIN. You're letting all our things at home go to wrack and ruin. 65

MYR. I don't care.

CIN. You don't care that your wool is being plucked to pieces by the chickens?

MYR. Not in the least.

CIN. And you haven't celebrated the rites of 70 Aphrodite for ever so long. Won't you come home?

MYR. Not on your life, unless you men make a truce and stop the war.

CIN. Well then, if that pleases you, we'll do 75 it.

MYR. Well then, if that pleases you, I'll come home—afterwards! Right now I'm on oath not to.

CIN. Then just lie down here with me for a 80 moment.

MYR. No—[in a teasing voice] and yet, I won't say I don't love you.

CIN. You love me? Oh, do lie down here, Myrrhine dear! 85

MYR. What, you silly fool! in front of the baby?

CIN. [hastily thrusting the baby at the slave]. Of course not. Here—home! Take him, Manes! [The slave goes off with the baby.] See, the 90 baby's out of the way. Now won't you lie down?

MYR. But where, my dear?

CIN. Where? The grotto of Pan's a lovely spot. 95

MYR. How could I purify myself before re-

turning to the shrine?

CIN. Easily: just wash here in the Clepsydra.

MYR. And then, shall I go back on my oath?

CIN. On my head be it! Don't worry about
5 the oath.

MYR. All right, then. Just let me bring out a
bed.

CIN. No, don't. The ground's all right.

MYR. Heavens, no! Bad as you are, I won't
10 let you lie on the bare ground. [*She goes into
the Acropolis.*]

CIN. Why, she really loves me; it's plain to
see.

MYR. [*returning with a bed*]. There! Now
15 hurry up and lie down. I'll just slip off this
dress. But—let's see: oh yes, I must fetch a
mattress.

CIN. Nonsense! No mattress for me.

MYR. Yes indeed! It's not nice on the bare
20 springs.

CIN. Give me a kiss.

MYR. [*giving him a hasty kiss*]. There! [*She
goes.*]

CIN. [*in mingled distress and delight*]. Oh-h!
25 Hurry back!

MYR. [*returning with a mattress*]. Here's the
mattress; lie down on it. I'm taking my things
off now—but—let's see: you have no pillow.

CIN. I don't *want* a pillow!

30 MYR. But I do. [*She goes.*]

CIN. Cheated again, just like Heracles and his
dinner!°

MYR. [*returning with a pillow*]. Here lift your
head. [*To herself, wondering how else to tease
35 him.*] Is that all?

CIN. Surely that's all! Do come here, precious!

MYR. I'm taking off my girdle. But remember: don't go back on your promise about the
40 truce.

CIN. Hope to die, if I do.

MYR. You don't have a blanket.

CIN. [*shouting in exasperation*]. *I don't want*

one! I WANT TO—

MYR. Sh-h! There, there, I'll be back in a 45
minute. [*She goes.*]

CIN. She'll be the death of me with these bed-
clothes.

MYR. [*returning with a blanket*]. Here, get
up. 50

CIN. I've got *this* up!

MYR. Would you like some perfume?

CIN. Good heavens, no! I won't have it!

MYR. Yes, you shall, whether you want it or
not. [*She goes.*] 55

CIN. O lord! Confound all perfumes anyway!

MYR. [*returning with a flask*]. Stretch out
your hand and put some on.

CIN. [*suspiciously*]. By God, I don't much
like this perfume. It smacks of shilly-shallying, 60
and has no scent of the marriage-bed.

MYR. Oh dear! This is Rhodian perfume I've
brought.

CIN. It's quite all right, dear. Never mind.

MYR. Don't be silly! [*She goes out with the 65
flask.*]

CIN. Damn the man who first concocted
perfumes!

MYR. [*returning with another flask*]. Here,
try this flask. 70

CIN. I've got another one all ready for you.
Come, you wretch, lie down and stop bringing
me things.

MYR. All right; I'm taking off my shoes. But,
my dear, see that you vote for peace. 75

CIN. [*absently*]. I'll consider it. [MYRRHINE
runs away to the Acropolis.] I'm ruined! The
wench has skinned me and run away! [*Chanting, in tragic style.*] Alas! Alas! Deceived, deserted by this fairest of women, whom shall I— 80
lay? Ah, my poor child, how shall I nurture
thee? Where's Cynalopex?° I needs must hire
a nurse!

L. MEN. [*chanting*]. Ah, wretched man, in
dreadful wise beguiled, bewrayed, thy soul is 85
sore distressed. I pity thee, alas! alas! What
soul, what loins, what liver could stand this

Heracles . . . dinner "A stock comedy bit wherein the
glutton hero, raving with hunger, is systematically
diddled of his dinner by his hosts." [Parker's note.]

Cynalopex a pimp. The "poor little child" in the preceding line is Cinesias's phallus.

strain? How firm and unyielding he stands,
with naught to aid him of a morning.

CIN. O lord! O Zeus! What tortures I endure!

L. MEN. This is the way she's treated you,
5 that vile and cursèd wanton.

L. WOM. Nay, not vile and cursèd, but sweet
and dear.

L. MEN. Sweet, you say? Nay, hateful, hateful!

10 CIN. Hateful indeed! O Zeus, Zeus!
Seize her and snatch her away,
Like a handful of dust, in a mighty,
Fiery tempest! Whirl her aloft, then let her
[drop
15 Down to the earth, with a crash, as she falls—
On the point of this waiting
Thingummybob! [He goes out.]

SCENE IV

[Enter a Spartan HERALD in an obvious state
of excitement, which he is doing his best to
20 conceal.]

HER. Where can I find the Senate or the
Prytanes?° I've got an important message. [The
Athenian MAGISTRATE enters.]

MAG. Say there, are you a man or Priapus?

25 HER. [in annoyance]. I'm a herald, you lout!
I've come from Sparta about the truce.

MAG. Is that a spear you've got under your
cloak?

HER. No, of course not!

30 MAG. Why do you twist and turn so? Why
hold your cloak in front of you? Did you rupture yourself on the trip?

HER. By gum, the fellow's an old fool.

MAG. [pointing]. Why, you dirty rascal,
35 you're all excited.

HER. Not at all. Stop this tom-foolery.

MAG. Well, what's that I see?

HER. A Spartan message-staff.

MAG. Oh, certainly! That's just the kind of
40 message-staff I've got. But tell me the honest
truth: how are things going in Sparta?

HER. All the land of Sparta is up in arms—
and our allies are up, too. We need Pellene.°

MAG. What brought this trouble on you? A
sudden Panic? 45

HER. No, Lampito started it and then all
the other women in Sparta with one accord
chased their husbands out of their beds.

MAG. How do you feel?

HER. Terrible. We walk around the city bent 50
over like men lighting matches in a wind. For
our women won't let us touch them until we all
agree and make peace throughout Greece.

MAG. This is a general conspiracy of the
women; I see it now. Well, hurry back and tell 55
the Spartans to send ambassadors here with full
powers to arrange a truce. And I'll go tell the
Council to choose ambassadors from here; I've
got a little something here that will persuade
them! 60

HER. I'll fly there; for you've made an excellent suggestion.

[The HERALD and the MAGISTRATE depart on
opposite sides of the stage.]

CHORAL EPISODE

L. MEN. No beast or fire is harder than 65
[womankind to tame,
Nor is the spotted leopard so devoid of shame.

L. WOM. Knowing this, you dare provoke us
[to attack?
I'd be your steady friend, if you'd but take us 70
[back.

L. MEN. I'll never cease my hatred keen of
[womankind.

L. WOM. Just as you will. But now just let
[me help you find 75
That cloak you threw aside. You look so silly
[there
Without your clothes. Here, put it on and don't
[go bare.

Prytanes members of the executive committee of the
Senate

Pellene a petty state allied with Sparta. Commentators
differ as to the point here. Perhaps it's that, after the
string of double entendres, one expects yet another
or the plain truth (they need women) and receives
instead an answer merely military and, given the
relative unimportance of Pellene, comically unsatisfactory.

L. MEN. That's very kind, and shows you're
[not entirely bad.
But I threw off my things when I was good and
[mad.
5   L. WOM. At last you seem a man, and won't
[be mocked, my lad.
If you'd been nice to me, I'd take this little
[gnat
That's in your eye and pluck it out for you,
10   [like that.
L. MEN. So that's what's bothered me and bit
[my eye so long!
Please dig it out for me. I own that I've been
[wrong.
15   L. WOM. I'll do so, though you've been a most
[ill-natured brat.
Ye gods! See here! A huge and monstrous little
[gnat!
L. MEN. Oh, how that helps! For it was
20   [digging wells in me.
And now it's out, my tears are flowing fast and
[free.
L. WOM. Here, let me wipe them off, although
[you're such a knave,
25   And kiss me.
     L. MEN.   No!
     L. WOM.   Whate'er you say, a kiss I'll
[have. [*She kisses him.*]
L. MEN. Oh, confound these women! They've
30   [a coaxing way about them.
He was wise and never spoke a truer word, who
[said,
"We can't live with women, but we cannot live
[without them."
35   Now I'll make a truce with you. We'll fight no
[more; instead
I will not injure you if you do me no wrong.
And now let's join our ranks and then begin
[a song.

40   COMBINED CHORUS [*singing*]. Athenians,
[we're not prepared,
To say a single ugly word
About our fellow-citizens.
Quite the contrary: we desire but to say and to
45   [do
Naught but good. Quite enough are the ills
[now on hand.

Men and women, be advised:
   If anyone requires
Money—minae two or three—,   50
   We've got what he desires.

My purse is yours, on easy terms:
   When Peace shall reappear,
Whate'er you've borrowed will be due.
   So speak up without fear.   55

You needn't pay me back, you see,
If you can get a cent from me!

We're about to entertain
   Some foreign gentlemen;
We've soup and tender, fresh-killed pork.   60
   Come round to dine at ten.

Come early; wash and dress with care,
   And bring the children, too.
Then step right in, no "by your leave."
   We'll be expecting you.   65

Walk in as if you owned the place.
You'll find the door—shut in your face!

SCENE V

[*Enter a group of Spartan* AMBASSADORS;
*they are in the same desperate condition as the
Herald in the previous scene.*]   70
   LEADER OF CHORUS: Here come the envoys
from Sparta, sprouting long beards and looking
for all the world as if they were carrying pig-
pens in front of them.
   Greetings, gentlemen of Sparta. Tell me, in   75
what state have you come?
   SPARTAN. Why waste words? You can plainly
see what state we've come in!
   L. CHO. Wow! You're in a pretty high-strung
condition, and it seems to be getting worse.   80
   SPA. It's indescribable. Won't someone please
arrange a peace for us—in any way you like.
   L. CHO. Here come our own, native ambassadors, crouching like wrestlers and holding
their clothes in front of them; this seems an   85
athletic kind of malady.
   [*Enter several Athenian* AMBASSADORS.]

ATH. Can anyone tell us where Lysistrata is? You see our condition.

L. CHO. Here's another case of the same complaint. Tell me, are the attacks worse in the
5 morning?

ATH. No, we're always afflicted this way. If someone doesn't soon arrange a truce, you'd better not let me get my hands on—Cleisthenes!°

10 L. CHO. If you're smart, you'll arrange your cloaks so none of the fellows who smashed the Hermae° can see you.

ATH. Right you are; a very good suggestion.

SPA. Aye, by all means. Here, let's hitch up
15 our clothes.

ATH. Greetings, Spartan. We've suffered dreadful things.

SPA. My dear fellow, we'd have suffered still worse if one of those fellows had seen us in
20 this condition.

ATH. Well, gentlemen, we must get down to business. What's your errand here?

SPA. We're ambassadors about peace.

ATH. Excellent; so are we. Only Lysistrata
25 can arrange things for us; shall we summon her?

SPA. Aye, and Lysistratus too, if you like.

L. CHO. No need to summon her, it seems. She's coming out of her own accord.

30 [Enter LYSISTRATA accompanied by a statue of a nude female figure, which represents Reconciliation.]

Hail, noblest of women; now must thou be
A judge shrewd and subtle, mild and severe,
35 Be sweet yet majestic: all manners employ.
The leaders of Hellas, caught by thy love-
[charms,
Have come to thy judgment, their charges
[submitting.

40 LYS. This is no difficult task, if one catch them

Cleisthenes cf. I, 9, p. 76, and note
fellows ... Hermae just before the sailing of the Sicilian expedition vandals smashed off the heads and phalluses of the statues of Hermes that served the Athenians as boundary markers and protectors of houses

still in amorous passion, before they've resorted to each other. But I'll soon find out. Where's Reconciliation? Go, first bring the Spartans here, and don't seize them rudely and violently, as our tactless husbands used to do, but as be- 45 fits a woman, like an old, familiar friend; if they won't give you their hands, take them however you can. Then go fetch these Athenians here, taking hold of whatever they offer you. Now then, men of Sparta, stand here beside me, and 50 you Athenians on the other side, and listen to my words.

I am a woman, it is true, but I have a mind; I'm not badly off in native wit, and by listening to my father and my elders, I've had a decent 55 schooling.

Now I intend to give you a scolding which you both deserve. With one common font you worship at the same altars, just like brothers, at Olympia, at Thermopylae, at Delphi—how 60 many more might I name, if time permitted— and the Barbarians stand by waiting with their armies; yet you are destroying the men and towns of Greece.

ATH. Oh, this tension is killing me! 65

LYS. And now, men of Sparta—to turn to you—don't you remember how the Spartan Pericleidas came here once as a suppliant, and sitting at our altar, all pale with fear in his crimson cloak, begged us for an army? For all 70 Messene had attacked you and the god sent an earthquake too? Then Cimon went forth with four thousand hoplites and saved all Lacedaemon. Such was the aid you received from Athens, and now you lay waste the country 75 which once treated you so well.

ATH. [hotly]. They're in the wrong, Lysistrata, upon my word, they are!

SPA. [absently, looking at the statue of Reconciliation]. We're in the wrong. What hips! 80 How lovely they are!

LYS. Don't think I'm going to let you Athenians off. Don't you remember how the Spartans came in arms when you were wearing the rough, sheepskin cloak of slaves and slew 85 the host of Thessalians, the comrades and allies of Hippias? Fighting with you on that day, alone of all the Greeks, they set you free and instead of a sheepskin gave your folk a handsome robe to wear.

SPA. [*looking at* LYSISTRATA]. I've never seen a more distinguished woman.

5 ATH. [*looking at Reconciliation*]. I've never seen a more voluptuous body!

LYS. Why then, with these many noble deeds to think of, do you fight each other? Why don't you stop this villainy? Why not make peace?
10 Tell me, what prevents it?

SPA. [*waving vaguely at Reconciliation*]. We're willing, if you're willing to give up your position on yonder flank.

LYS. What position, my good man?

15 SPA. Pylus; we've been panting for it for ever so long.

ATH. No, by God! You shan't have it!

LYS. Let them have it, my friend.

ATH. Then what shall we have to rouse things
20 up with?

LYS. Ask for another place in exchange.

ATH. Well, let's see: first of all [*pointing to various parts of Reconciliation's anatomy*] give us Echinus here, this Maliac Inlet in back there,
25 and these two Megarian legs.

SPA. No, by heavens! You can't have *everything*, you crazy fool!

LYS. Let it go. Don't fight over a pair of legs.

ATH. [*taking off his cloak*]. I think I'll strip
30 and do a little planting now.

SPA. [*following suit*]. And I'll just do a little fertilizing, by gosh!

LYS. Wait until the truce is concluded. Now if you've decided on this course, hold a con-
35 ference and discuss the matter with your allies.

ATH. Allies? Don't be ridiculous! They're in the same state we are. Won't all our allies want the same thing we do—to jump in bed with their women?

40 SPA. Ours will, I know.

ATH. Especially the Carystians, by God!

LYS. Very well. Now purify yourselves, that your wives may feast and entertain you in the Acropolis; we've provisions by the basketful.
45 Exchange your oaths and pledges there, and then each of you may take his wife and go home.

ATH. Let's go at once.

SPA. Come on, where you will.

ATH. For God's sake, let's hurry! 50
[*They all go into the Acropolis.*]

CHO. [*singing*]. Whate'er I have of coverlets
  And robes of varied hue
And golden trinkets,—without stint
  I offer them to you. 55

Take what you will and bear it home,
  Your children to delight,
Or if your girl's a Basket-maid;
  Just choose whate'er's in sight.

There's naught within so well secured 60
  You cannot break the seal
And bear it off; just help yourselves;
  No hesitation feel.

But you'll see nothing, though you try,
Unless you've sharper eyes than I! 65

If anyone needs bread to feed
  A growing family,
I've lots of wheat and full-grown loaves;
  So just apply to me.

Let every poor man who desires 70
  Come round and bring a sack
To fetch the grain; my slave is there
  To load it on his back.

But don't come near my door, I say:
Beware the dog, and stay away! 75

ÉXODOS

[*An* ATHENIAN *enters carrying a torch; he knocks at the gate.*]

ATH. Open the door! [*To the* CHORUS, *which is clustered around the gate.*] Make way, won't you! What are you hanging around for? Want 80
me to singe you with this torch? [*To himself.*] No; it's a stale trick, I won't do it! [*To the audience.*] Still, if I've got to do it to please *you*, I suppose I'll have to take the trouble.

[*A* SECOND ATHENIAN *comes out of the gate.*] 85
2ND ATH. And I'll help you.

1ST ATH. [*waving his torch at the* CHORUS]. Get out! Go bawl your heads off! Move on there, so the Spartans can leave in peace when the banquet's over.

5   [*They brandish their torches until the* CHO-RUS *leaves the Orchestra.*]

2ND ATH. I've never seen such a pleasant banquet: the Spartans are charming fellows, indeed they are! And we Athenians are very

10 witty in our cups.

1ST ATH. Naturally: for when we're sober we're never at our best. If the Athenians would listen to me, we'd always get a little tipsy on our embassies. As things are now, we go to

15 Sparta when we're sober and look around to stir up trouble. And then we don't hear what they say—and as for what they *don't* say, we have all sorts of suspicions. And then we bring back varying reports about the mission. But

20 this time everything is pleasant; even if a man should sing the Telamon-song when he ought to sing "Cleitagoras," we'd praise him and swear it was excellent.°

   [*The two* CHORUSES *return, as a* CHORUS OF

25 ATHENIANS *and a* CHORUS OF SPARTANS.]

Here they come back again. Go to the devil, you scoundrels!

2ND ATH. Get out, I say! They're coming out from the feast.

30   [*Enter the Spartan and Athenian envoys, fol-lowed by* LYSISTRATA *and all the women.*]

SPA. [*to one of his fellow-envoys*]. My good fellow, take up your pipes; I want to do a fancy two-step and sing a jolly song for the Athe-

35 nians.

ATH. Yes, do take up your pipes, by all means. I'd love to see you dance.

SPA. [*singing and dancing with the* CHORUS OF SPARTANS].

40   These youths inspire
To song and dance, O Memory;
Stir up my Muse, to tell how we
And Athens' men, in our galleys clashing

At Artemisium, 'gainst foemen dashing
   In godlike ire,   45
Conquered the Persian° and set Greece free.

   Leonidas
Led on his valiant warriors
Whetting their teeth like angry boars.
Abundant foam on their lips was flow'ring,   50
A stream of sweat from their limbs was
                     [show'ring.
   The Persian was
Numberless as the sand on the shores.

O Huntress° who slayest the beasts in the   55
                     [glade,
O Virgin divine, hither come to our truce,
Unite us in bonds which all time will not loose.
Grant us to find in this treaty, we pray,
An unfailing source of true friendship today,   60
And all of our days, helping us to refrain
From weaseling tricks which bring war in their
                     [train.
   Then hither, come hither! O huntress maid.

LYS. Come then, since all is fairly done, men   65
of Sparta, lead away your wives, and you, Athe-nians, take yours. Let every man stand beside his wife, and every wife beside her man, and then, to celebrate our fortune, let's dance. And in the future, let's take care to avoid these mis-   70
understandings.

CHORUS OF ATHENIANS [*singing and dancing*].
Lead on the dances, your graces revealing.
Call Artemis hither, call Artemis' twin,
Leader of dances, Apollo the Healing,   75
Kindly God—hither! let's summon him in!

   Nysian° Bacchus call,
Who with his Maenads, his eyes flashing fire,
   Dances, and last of all
Zeus of the thunderbolt flaming, the Sire,   80

---

swear . . . excellent the reference here is to a song-capping game, common at Athenian banquets, and to the gaffe of failing to follow one's cue

Conquered the Persian Xerxes, at the battle of Sala-mis
Huntress Artemis
Nysian Nysa was the mountain on which Bacchus was said to have been reared

And Hera in majesty,
Queen of prosperity.

Come, ye Powers who dwell above
Unforgetting, our witnesses be
5 Of Peace with bonds of harmonious love—
The Peace which Cypris° has wrought for me.
Alleluia! Io Paean!
Leap in joy—hurrah! hurrah!
'Tis victory—hurrah! hurrah!
10 Euoi! Euoi! Euai! Euai!

LYS. [*to the Spartans*]. Come now, sing a
new song to cap ours.

CHORUS OF SPARTANS [*singing and dancing*].
Leaving Taygetus fair and renown'd,
15 Muse of Laconia,° hither come:
Amyclae's god in hymns resound,
Athene of the Brazen Home,
And Castor and Pollux, Tyndareus' sons,
Who sport where Eurotas murmuring runs.

20 On with the dance! Heia! Ho!
All leaping along,
Mantles a-swinging as we go!
Of Sparta our song.
There the holy chorus ever gladdens,
25 There the beat of stamping feet,
As our winsome fillies, lovely maidens,
Dance, beside Eurotas' banks a-skipping,—
Nimbly go to and fro
Hast'ning, leaping feet in measures tripping,
30 Like the Bacchae's revels, hair a-streaming.
Leda's child, divine and mild,
Leads the holy dance, her fair face beaming.
On with the dance! as your hand
Presses the hair
35 Streaming away unconfined.

Leap in the air
Light as the deer; footsteps resound
Aiding our dance, beating the ground.
Praise Athene, Maid divine, unrivalled in her
[might, 40
Dweller in the Brazen Home, unconquered in
[the fight.

[*All go out singing and dancing.*]

Cypris Aphrodite
Laconia the country of which Sparta was the capital.
In the following lines further references to Sparta
appear. Amyclae was a town on the river Eurotas
near to Sparta that had a famous sanctuary and
throne of Apollo. The Brazen Home was a temple on
the Spartan Acropolis. Tyndareus had been a king
of Sparta. His sons, by Leda, were worshipped in
Sparta as the tutelary gods of warlike youth.

Euripides

485?–406? B.C.

The Bacchae

406? B.C.

In a narrow sense, *The Bacchae* is a play about Dionysus' revenge on Thebes for denying his divine paternity and present deity. It is a well-made play and builds unrelentingly to its catastrophe. From the beginning, when Dionysus manifests his identity and purpose, the conclusion is foregone. Pentheus, king of Thebes, *thinks* that he is the hunter, tracking down the stranger to destroy him. We *know,* in a metaphor the play repeats, that the hunter is the hunted, that each step he makes toward the kill is toward his own destruction. We see Pentheus flout Dionysus and plan to destroy the god's converts among the Theban women. We hear, too, that Pentheus' mother, Agauë, one of those who once repudiated the god, has become one of his converts and leads the Theban Bacchae on the side of Mt. Cithaeron. Son and mother, we apprehend with ironic certainty, are moving toward a fatal convergence. And when they come, in their agonies, to the knowledge of what Dionysus has willed for them, they discover indeed that a god insulted does not forgive.

Thus seen, the play has about it the special if chilly gratification that comes from dramas of intrigue, in which the schemer is hoist with his own petard. But Euripides so manipulates the audience's feelings that the promised gratification is not attained. At first we are attracted to Dionysus, the injured deity concerned for his mother's honor and his own. The chorus of Asian women, his devotees who have followed him into this land, compellingly testifies to his power and appeal. Even Cadmus and Teiresias, submitting their withered limbs to the Bacchic dance, add their witness. And Pentheus so fatuously refuses to hear reason, so disgustingly reveals the obscene shape of his own imaginings, that we side with Dionysus and look forward to his revenge. When the god enters Pentheus, however, metamorphosing his blunt masculinity into effeminacy, our pleasure may begin to pall. At length Euripides forces on us the full horror of Pentheus' destruction, the man crying out as his body is torn asunder, "Mother, have mercy; I have sinned, But I am still your own son. Do not take my life!" We are further made to behold Agauë's agony as her eyes clear and she sees what it is that she has held aloft in ecstatic triumph. So terrible is this suffering, so terrible the god ruthlessly exacting it, that our allegiances shift—from the injured god to the more cruelly injured mortals. In their plight we experience our own.

The Bacchae is about Dionysus, not Apollo. No character raises the great questions, as Oedipus does, or arrives at the great answers. We appear to be in a diminished universe where the gods are gods not because they are wise and good, but because they are powerful. Here there is feeling, not thought, and the Dionysian feeling operates with the ambiguity of wine. Wine frees man from what diminishes him and releases his powers. "Without wine," says the herdsman, "neither love nor any other pleasure would be left for us." The god-intoxicated Theban women sing and decorously dance on the mountain side; they feed the animal young and ride joyful children on their shoulders. Dionysus is genial, benign—a savior. But wine liberates in another way; it rids man of what keeps him human, and surrenders him to his lusts. The Bacchae tear the flesh of heifers, bulls, human beings. They glut themselves with blood and triumph in kindless savagery. Dionysus is violent, brutal—a destroyer.

Euripides visits upon us the meaning of the Dionysian spirit, whether the intoxication be that of grape, religious enthusiasm, or political cult. He preaches no lesson of abstinence, certainly, or even of moderation. But, making Dionysus manifest both to the dying eyes of the Theban king and to the living eyes of the audience, he compels us at once to acknowledge and to fear this ambiguous power, demonic or divine.

The Bacchae

EURIPIDES

CHARACTERS

DIONYSUS
CHORUS   *of Oriental women, devotees of Dionysus*
TEIRESIAS   *a blind seer*
CADMUS   *founder of Thebes, and formerly king*
PENTHEUS   *his grandson, now king of Thebes*
A GUARD   *attending Pentheus*
A HERDSMAN
A MESSENGER
AGAUË   *daughter of Cadmus and mother of Pentheus*

SCENE. *Before the palace of Pentheus in Thebes. At one side of the stage is the monument of Semele; above it burns a low flame, and around it are the remains of ruined and blackened masonry.*

5

PROLOGUE°

[DIONYSUS *enters on stage right. He has a crown of ivy, a thyrsus° in his hand, and a fawnskin draped over his body. He has long*

Prologue   see p. 9. Although it lacks the kommoi, *The Bacchae* has essentially the same structure as *Agamemnon*.

thyrsus   a light stick of reed or fennel, with fresh strands of ivy twined round it. It was carried by every devotee of Dionysus, and the action of the play illustrates the supernatural power that was held to reside in it. [Translator's note.]

From The Bacchae and Other Plays, *translated by Phillip Vellacott. Copyright © Phillip Vellacott. Reprinted by permission of Penguin Books Ltd.*

flowing hair and a youthful, almost feminine beauty.]

DIONYSUS. I am Dionysus, son of Zeus. My
[mother was
5 Semele, Cadmus' daughter. From her womb the
[fire
Of a lightning-flash delivered me. I have come
[here
To Thebes and her two rivers, Dirce and
10 [Ismenus,
Veiling my godhead in a mortal shape. I see
Here near the palace my mother's monument,
[that records
Her death by lightning. Here her house stood;
15 [and its ruins
Smoulder with the still living flame of Zeus's
[fire—
The immortal cruelty Hera wreaked upon my
[mother.
20 Cadmus does well to keep this ground
[inviolable,
A precinct consecrated in his daughter's name;
And I have decked it round with sprays of
[young vineleaves.
25 From the fields of Lydia and Phrygia, fertile in
[gold,
I travelled first to the sun-smitten Persian
[plains,
The walled cities of Bactria, the harsh Median
30 [country,
Wealthy Arabia, and the whole tract of the
[Asian coast
Where mingled swarms of Greeks and
[Orientals live
35 In vast magnificent cities; and before reaching
[this,
The first city of Hellas I have visited,
I had already, in all those regions of the east,
Performed my dances and set forth my ritual
40 To make my godhead manifest to mortal men.

The reason why I have chosen Thebes as the
[first place
To raise my Bacchic shout, and clothe all who
[respond
45 In fawnskin habits, and put my thyrsus in their
[hands—
The weapon wreathed with ivy-shoots—my

[reason is this:
My mother's sisters said—what they should
[have been the last 50
To say—that I, Dionysus, was not Zeus's son;
That Semele, being with child—they said—by
[some mortal,
Obeyed her father's prompting, and ascribed to
[Zeus 55
The loss of her virginity; and they loudly
[claimed
That this lie was the sin for which Zeus took
[her life.

Therefore I have driven those same sisters mad, 60
[turned them
All frantic out of doors; their home now is the
[mountain;
Their wits are gone. I have made them bear the
[emblem of 65
My mysteries; the whole female population of
[Thebes,
To the last woman, I have sent raving from
[their homes.
Now, side by side with Cadmus' daughters, 70
[one and all
Sit roofless on the rocks under the silver pines.
For Thebes, albeit reluctantly, must learn in full
This lesson, that my Bacchic worship is a matter
As yet beyond her knowledge and experience; 75
And I must vindicate my mother Semele
By manifesting myself before the human race
As the divine son whom she bore to immortal
[Zeus.

Now Cadmus has made over his throne and 80
[kingly honors
To Pentheus, son of his eldest daughter Agauë.
[He
Is a fighter against gods, defies me, excludes me
[from 85
Libations, never names me in prayers.
[Therefore I will
Demonstrate to him, and to all Thebes, that I
[am a god.

When I have set all in order here, I will pass on 90
To another place, and manifest myself.
[Meanwhile

If Thebes in anger tries to bring the Bacchants
[home
By force from the mountain, I myself will join
[that army
5   Of women possessed and lead them to battle.
[That is why
I have changed my form and taken the likeness
[of a man.
Come, my band of worshippers, women whom
10   [I have brought

From lands of the east, from Tmolus, bastion
[of Lydia,
To be with me and share my travels! Raise the
[music
15 Of your own country, the Phrygian drums
[invented by
Rhea the Great Mother and by me. Fill
[Pentheus' palace
With a noise to make the city of Cadmus turn
20   [and look!
—And I will go to the folds of Mount
[Cithaeron, where
The Bacchants are, and join them in their holy
[dance.
25   [DIONYSUS goes out towards the mountain.
The CHORUS enter where DIONYSUS entered,
from the road by which they have travelled.]

PÁRODOS

Strophe 1
CHORUS. From far-off lands of Asia,
From Tmolus the holy mountain,
30 We run with the god of laughter;
Labor is joy and weariness is sweet,
And our song resounds to Bacchus!

Antistrophe 1
Who stands in our path?
Make way, make way!
35 Who in the house? Close every lip,
Keep holy silence, while we sing
The appointed hymn to Bacchus!

Strophe 2
Blest is the happy man
Who knows the mysteries the gods ordain,

And sanctifies his life,   40
Joins soul with soul in mystic unity,
And, by due ritual made pure,
Enters the ecstasy of mountain solitudes;
Who observes the mystic rites
Made lawful by Cybele the Great Mother;   45
Who crowns his head with ivy,
And shakes aloft his wand in worship of
[Dionysus.

On, on! Run, dance, delirious, possessed!
Dionysus comes to his own;   50
Bring from the Phrygian hills to the broad
[streets of Hellas
The god, child of a god,
Spirit of revel and rapture, Dionysus!

Antistrophe 2
Once, on the womb that held him   55
The fire-bolt flew from the hand of Zeus;
And pains of child-birth bound his mother fast,
And she cast him forth untimely,
And under the lightning's lash relinquished
[life; 60
And Zeus the son of Cronos
Ensconced him instantly in a secret womb
Chambered within his thigh,
And with golden pins closed him from Hera's
[sight. 65

So, when the Fates had made him ripe for birth,
Zeus bore the bull-horned god
And wreathed his head with wreaths of
[writhing snakes;
Which is why the Maenads catch   70
Wild snakes, nurse them and twine them round
[their hair.

Strophe 3
O Thebes, old nurse that cradled Semele,
Be ivy garlanded, burst into flower
With wreaths of lush bright-berried bryony,   75
Bring sprays of fir, green branches torn from
[oaks,
Fill soul and flesh with Bacchus' mystic power;
Fringe and bedeck your dappled fawnskin
[cloaks 80

With wooly tufts and locks of purest white.
There's a brute wildness in the fennel-wands—
Reverence it well. Soon the whole land will
[dance
5 When the god with ecstatic shout
Leads his companies out
To the mountain's mounting height
Swarming with riotous bands
Of Theban women leaving
10 Their spinning and their weaving
Stung with the maddening trance
Of Dionysus!

Antistrophe 3
O secret chamber the Curetes° knew!
O holy cavern in the Cretan glade
15 Where Zeus was cradled, where for our delight
The triple-crested Corybantes drew
Tight the round drum-skin, till its wild beat
[made
Rapturous rhythm to the breathing sweetness
20 Of Phrygian flutes! Then divine Rhea found
The drum could give her Bacchic airs
[completeness;
From her, the Mother of all,
The crazy Satyrs soon,
25 In their dancing festival
When the second year comes round,
Seized on the timbrel's tune
To play the leading part
In feasts that delight the heart
30 Of Dionysus.

Epode
O what delight is in the mountains!
There the celebrant,° wrapped in his sacred
[fawnskin,
Flings himself on the ground surrendered,
35 While the swift-footed company streams on;
There he hunts for blood, and rapturously
Eats the raw flesh of the slaughtered goat,

Curetes demigods who cared for the infant Zeus
celebrant Dionysus and the Chorus comprise the
  typical group of Bacchic worshippers, a male leader
  with a devoted band of women and girls. The leader
  flings himself on the ground in the climax of ecstasy,
  when the power of the god enters into him and he
  becomes possessed. [Translator's note.]

Hurrying on to the Phrygian or Lydian
[mountain heights.
Possessed, ecstatic, he leads their happy cries;   40
The earth flows with milk, flows with wine,
Flows with nectar of bees;
The air is thick with a scent of Syrian myrrh.
The celebrant runs entranced, whirling the
[torch   45
That blazes red from the fennel-wand in his
[grasp,
And with shouts he rouses the scattered bands,
Sets their feet dancing,
As he shakes his delicate locks to the wild wind.   50
And amidst the frenzy of song he shouts like
[thunder:
"On, on! Run, dance, delirious, possessed!
You, the beauty and grace of golden Tmolus,
Sing to the rattle of thunderous drums,   55
Sing for joy,
Praise Dionysus, god of joy!
Shout like Phrygians, sing out the tunes you
[know,
While the sacred pure-toned flute   60
Vibrates the air with holy merriment,
In time with the pulse of the feet that flock
To the mountains, to the mountains!"
And, like a foal with its mother at pasture,
Runs and leaps for joy every daughter of   65
[Bacchus.

SCENE I

[*Enter* TEIRESIAS. *Though blind, he makes
his way unaided to the door, and knocks.*]
  TEIRESIAS. Who keeps the gate? Call Cadmus
[out, Agenor's son,   70
Who came from Sidon here to build these walls
[of Thebes.
Go, someone, say Teiresias is looking for him.
He knows why; I'm an old man, and he's older
[still—   75
But we agreed to equip ourselves with Bacchic
[wands
And fawnskin cloaks, and put on wreaths of
[ivy-shoots.
  [*Enter* CADMUS.]   80
  CADMUS. Dear friend, I knew your voice,
[although I was indoors,

As soon as I heard it—the wise voice of a wise
                                          [man.
I am ready. See, I have all that the god
                                          [prescribes.
5   He is my daughter's son; we must do all we can
To exalt and honor him. Where shall we go to
                                          [dance
And take our stand with others, tossing our
                                          [gray heads?
10   You tell me what to do, Teiresias. We're both
                                          [old,
But you're the expert. [*He stumps about, beat-
ing his thyrsus on the ground.*] I could drum
                                          [the ground all night
15   And all day too, without being tired. What joy
                                          [it is
To forget one's age!
        TEIRESIAS. I feel exactly the same way,
Bursting with youth! I'll try it—I'll dance with
20   [the rest.
        CADMUS. You don't think we should go to the
                                          [mountain in a coach?
        TEIRESIAS. No, no. That would not show the
                                          [god the same respect.
25   CADMUS. I'll take you there myself then—
                                          [old as we both are.
        TEIRESIAS. The god will guide us there, and
                                          [without weariness.
        CADMUS. Are we the only Thebans who will
30   [dance to him?
        TEIRESIAS. We see things clearly; all the
                                          [others are perverse.
        CADMUS. We're wasting time; come, take my
                                          [hand.
35   TEIRESIAS. Here, then; hold tight.
        CADMUS. I don't despise religion. I'm a mortal
                                          [man.
        TEIRESIAS. We have no use for theological
                                          [subtleties.
40   The beliefs we have inherited, as old as time,
Cannot be overthrown by any argument,
Not by the most inventive ingenuity.
It will be said, I lack the dignity of my age,
To wear this ivy-wreath and set off for the
45   [dance.
No so; the god draws no distinction between
                                          [young
And old, to tell us which should dance and

[which should not.
He desires equal worship from all men; his   50
                                          [claim
To glory is universal; no one is exempt.
        CADMUS. Teiresias, I shall be your prophet,
                                          [since you are blind.
Pentheus, to whom I have resigned my rule in   55
                                          [Thebes,
Is hurrying here towards the palace. He appears
Extremely agitated. What news will he bring?
        [*Enter* PENTHEUS. *He addresses the audience,
without at first noticing* CADMUS *and* TEIRESIAS,   60
who stand at the opposite side of the stage.]
        PENTHEUS. I happen to have been away from
                                          [Thebes; reports
Of this astounding scandal have just been
                                          [brought to me.   65
Our women, it seems, have left their homes on
                                          [some pretense
Of Bacchic worship, and now are gadding about
On the wooded mountain-slopes, dancing in
                                          [honor of   70
This upstart god Dionysus, whoever he may be.
Amidst these groups of worshippers, they tell
                                          [me, stand
Bowls full of wine; and our women go creeping
                                          [off   75
This way and that to lonely places and give
                                          [themselves
To lecherous men. They are Maenad
                                          [priestesses, if you please!
Aphrodite supplants Bacchus in their ritual.   80
Well, those I've caught, my guards are keeping
                                          [safe; we've tied
Their hands, and lodged them at state expense.
                                          [Those still at large
On the mountain I am going to hunt out; and   85
                                          [that
Includes my own mother Agauë and her sisters
Ino and Autonoë. Once they're fast in iron
                                          [fetters,
I'll put a stop to this outrageous Bacchism.   90

They tell me, too, some oriental conjurer
Has come from Lydia, a magician with golden
                                          [hair
Flowing in scented ringlets, his face flushed
                                          [with wine,   95

His eyes lit with the charm of Aphrodite; and
                                        [he
Entices young girls with his Bacchic mysteries,
Spends days and nights consorting with them.
                                        [Once let me
5   Get that fellow inside my walls—I'll cut his
                                        [head
From his shoulders, that will stop him
                        [drumming with his thyrsus,
10 Tossing his long hair. *He's the one*—this
                        [foreigner—
Who says Dionysus is a god; who says he was
Sewn up in Zeus's thigh. The truth about
                        [Dionysus
15 Is that he's dead, burnt to a cinder by lightning
Along with his mother, because she said Zeus
                        [lay with her.
Whoever the man may be, is not his arrogance
An outrage? Has he not earned a rope around
20   [his neck?
    [PENTHEUS *turns to go, and sees* CADMUS *and*
TEIRESIAS.]
Why, look! Another miracle! Here's Teiresias
The prophet—in a fawnskin; and my mother's
25   [father—
A Bacchant with a fennel-wand! Well, there's a
                        [sight
For laughter! [*But he is raging, not laughing.*]

Sir, I am ashamed to see two men
30 Of your age with so little sense of decency.
Come, you're my grandfather: throw down that
                        [ivy-wreath,
Get rid of that thyrsus!—*You* persuaded him
                        [to this,
35 Teiresias. By introducing a new god, you hope
To advance your augurer's business, to collect
                        [more fees
For inspecting sacrifices. Listen: your gray hairs
Are your protection; otherwise you'd be sitting
40   [now
In prison with all these crazy females, for
                        [promoting
Pernicious practices. As for women, I tell you
                        [this:
45 Wherever the sparkle of sweet wine adorns
                        [their feast,
No good will follow from such Bacchic

                        [ceremonies.
CHORUS. Have you no reverence, Sir, no
                        [piety? Do you mock   50
Cadmus, who sowed the dragon-seed of
                        [earth-born men?°
Do you, Echion's son, dishonor your own race?
    TEIRESIAS. When a good speaker has a sound
                        [case to present,   55
Then eloquence is no great feat. Your fluent
                        [tongue
Promises wisdom; but the content of your
                        [speech
Is ignorant. Power and eloquence in a   60
                        [headstrong man
Spell folly; such a man is a peril to the state.

This new god, whom you ridicule—no words
                        [of mine
Could well express the ascendency he will   65
                        [achieve
In Hellas. There are two powers, young man,
                        [which are supreme
In human affairs: first, Demeter—the same
                        [goddess   70
Is also Earth; give her which name you please
                        [—and she
Supplies mankind with solid food. After her
                        [came
Dionysus, Semele's son; the blessing he   75
                        [procured
And gave to men is counterpart to that of
                        [bread:
The clear juice of the grape. When mortals
                        [drink their fill   80
Of wine, the sufferings of our unhappy race
Are banished, each day's troubles are forgotten
                        [in sleep.
There is no other cure for sorrow. Dionysus,
Himself a god, is thus poured out in offering   85
To the gods, so that through him come blessings
                        [on mankind.
And do you scorn this legend, that he was sewn
                        [up

earth-born men by Athena's advice Cadmus sowed
the teeth of a dragon he had slain; the harvest was
armed men who fought and slew each other until
only five were left—the ancestors of the Theban
nobility

In Zeus's thigh? I will explain the truth to you.
When Zeus snatched Dionysus from the
[lightning flame
And took the child up to Olympus as a god,
5   Hera resolved to cast him out of heaven. But
[Zeus
Found such means to prevent her as a god will
[find.
He took a fragment of the ether that surrounds
10 The earth, fashioned it like a child, presented it
To Hera as a pledge to sooth her jealousy,
And saved Dionysus from her. Thus, in time,
[because
The ancient words for "pledge" and "thigh"°
15 [are similar,
People confused them, and the "pledge" Zeus
[gave to Hera
Became transformed, as time went on, into the
[tale
20 That Dionysus was sewn up in Zeus's thigh.

And this god is a prophet; the Bacchic ecstasy
And frenzy hold a strong prophetic element.
When he fills irresistibly a human body
He gives those so possessed power to foretell
25 [the future.
In Ares' province too Dionysus has his share;
Sometimes an army, weaponed and drawn up
[for battle,
Has fled in wild panic before a spear was raised.
30 This too is an insanity sent by Dionysus.

Ay, and the day will come when, on the very
[crags
Of Delphi, you shall see him leaping, amidst
[the blaze
35 Of torches, over the twin-peaked ridge, waving
[aloft
And brandishing his Bacchic staff, while all
[Hellas
Exalts him. Pentheus, pay heed to my words.
40 [You rely
On force; but it is not force that governs human

[affairs.
Do not mistake for wisdom that opinion which
May rise from a sick mind. Welcome this god
[to Thebes,   45
Offer libations to him, celebrate his rites,
Put on his garland. Dionysus will not compel
Women to be chaste, since in all matters
[self-control
Resides in our own natures. You should   50
[consider this;
For in the Bacchic ritual, as elsewhere, a woman
Will be safe from corruption if her mind is
[chaste.

Think of this too: when crowds stand at the   55
[city gates
And Thebes extols the name of Pentheus, you
[rejoice;
So too, I think, the god is glad to receive honor.

Well, I at least, and Cadmus, whom you mock,   60
[will wear
The ivy-wreath and join the dancing—we are
[a pair
Of gray heads, but this is our duty; and no
[words   65
Of yours shall lure me into fighting against
[gods.
For a most cruel insanity has warped your
[mind;
While drugs may well have caused it, they can   70
[bring no cure.
CHORUS. What you have said, Teiresias,
[shows no disrespect
To Apollo; at the same time you prove your
[judgment sound   75
In honoring Dionysus as a mighty god.
CADMUS. My dear son, Teiresias has given
[you good advice.
Don't stray beyond pious tradition; live with
[us.   80
Your wits have flown to the winds, your sense
[is foolishness.
Even if, as you say, Dionysus is no god,
Let him have *your* acknowledgment; lie royally,
That Semele may get honor as having borne a   85
[god,
And credit come to us and to all our family.

the ancient words for "pledge" and "thigh" the
translation necessarily expands the original.
Homeros means *pledge*, and *meros thigh* [Trans-
lator's note.]

Remember, too, Actaeon's miserable fate—
Torn and devoured by hounds which he himself
                                    [had bred,
Because he filled the mountains with the boast
5   [that he
Was a more skillful hunter than Artemis
                                    [herself.
Don't share his fate, my son! Come, let me
                                [crown your head
10 With a wreath of ivy; join us in worshipping
                                    [this god.
    PENTHEUS. Keep your hands off! Go to your
                            [Bacchic rites, and don't
Wipe off your crazy folly on me. But I will
15   [punish
This man who has been your instructor in
                                    [lunacy.
Go, someone, quickly to his seat of augury,
Smash it with crowbars, topple the walls,
20   [throw all his things
In wild confusion, turn the whole place upside
                                    [down,
Fling out his holy fripperies to the hurricane
                                    [winds!
25 This sacrilege will sting him more than
                                [anything else.
The rest of you—go, comb the country and
                                [track down
That effeminate foreigner, who plagues our
30   [women with
This new disease, fouls the whole land with
                                    [lechery;
And once you catch him, tie him up and bring
                                [him here
35 To me; I'll deal with him. He shall be stoned to
                                    [death.
He'll wish he'd never brought his Bacchic rites
                                [to Thebes.
    [*Exit* PENTHEUS.]
40   TEIRESIAS. Foolhardy man! You do not know
                            [what you have said.
Before, you were unbalanced; now you are
                                    [insane.
Come, Cadmus; let us go and pray both for
45   [this man,
Brutish as he is, and for our city, and beg the
                                    [god
To show forbearance. Come, now, take your

                                    [ivy staff
And let us go. Try to support me; we will help   50
Each other. It would be scandalous for two old
                                    [men
To fall; still, we must go, and pay our due
                                    [service
To Dionysus, son of Zeus. Cadmus, the name   55
Pentheus means *sorrow*. God grant he may not
                                [bring sorrow
Upon your house. Do not take that as prophecy;
I judge his acts. Such foolish words bespeak a
                                    [fool.   60

[*Exeunt* TEIRESIAS *and* CADMUS.]

ODE I

Strophe 1
CHORUS. Holiness, Queen of heaven,
Holiness, golden-winged ranging the earth,
Do you hear his blasphemy?
Pentheus dares—do you hear?—to revile the   65
                                [god of joy,
The son of Semele, who when the gay-crowned
                                    [feast is set
Is named among gods the chief;
Whose gifts are joy and union of soul in   70
                                    [dancing,
Joy in music of flutes,
Joy when sparkling wine at feasts of the gods
Soothes the sore regret,
Banishes every grief,   75
When the reveller rests, enfolded deep
In the cool shade of ivy-shoots,
On wine's soft pillow of sleep.

Antistrophe 1
The brash, unbridled tongue,
The lawless folly of fools, will end in pain.   80
But the life of wise content
Is blest with quietness, escapes the storm
And keeps its house secure.
Though blessed gods dwell in the distant skies,
They watch the ways of men.   85
To know much is not to be wise.
Pride more than mortal hastens life to its end;
And they who in pride pretend
Beyond man's limit, will lose what lay
Close to their hand and sure.   90

I count it madness, and know no cure can mend
The evil man and his evil way.

Strophe 2

O to set foot on Aphrodite's island,
On Cyprus, haunted by the Loves, who enchant
5 Brief life with sweetness; or in that strange land
Whose fertile river carves a hundred channels
To enrich her rainless sand;
Or where the sacred pastures of Olympus slant
Down to Pieria, where the Muses dwell—
10 Take me, O Bromius,° take me and inspire
Laughter and worship! There our holy spell
And ecstasy are welcome; there the gentle band
Of Graces have their home, and sweet Desire.
Dionysus, son of Zeus, delights in banquets;

Antistrophe 2

15 And his dear love is Peace, giver of wealth,
Savior of young men's lives—a goddess rare!
In wine, his gift that charms all griefs away,
Alike both rich and poor may have their part.
His enemy is the man who has no care
20 To pass his years in happiness and health,
His days in quiet and his nights in joy,
Watchful to keep aloof both mind and heart
From men whose pride claims more than
[mortals may.
25 The life that wins the poor man's common
[voice,
His creed, his practice—this shall be my choice.

SCENE II

[*Some of the guards whom* PENTHEUS *sent to
arrest* DIONYSUS *now enter with their prisoner.*
30 PENTHEUS *enters from the palace.*]
GUARD. Pentheus, we've brought the prey
[you sent us out to catch;
We hunted him, and here he is. But, Sir, we
[found
35 The beast was gentle; made no attempt to run
[away,
Just held his hands out to be tied; didn't turn
[pale,
But kept his florid color, smiling, telling us

Bromius another name for Dionysus

To tie him up and run him in; gave us no   40
[trouble
At all, just waited for us. Naturally I felt
A bit embarrassed. "You'll excuse me, Sir," I
[said,
"I don't want to arrest you; it's the king's   45
[command."

Another thing, sir—those women you rounded
[up
And put in fetters in the prison, those
[Bacchants;   50
Well, they're all gone, turned loose to the glens;
[and there they are,
Frisking about, calling on Bromius their god.
The fetters simply opened and fell off their
[feet;   55
The bolts shot back, untouched by mortal hand;
[the doors
Flew wide. Master, this man has come here
[with a load
Of miracles. Well, what happens next is your   60
[concern.
PENTHEUS. Untie this man's hands. (*The*
[GUARD *does so.*) He's securely in the trap.
He's not so nimble-footed as to escape me now.

Well, friend: your shape is not unhandsome—   65
[for the pursuit
Of women, which is the purpose of your
[presence here.
You are no wrestler, I can tell from these long
[curls   70
Cascading most seductively over your cheek.
Your skin, too, shows a whiteness carefully
[preserved;
You keep away from the sun's heat, walk in
[the shade,   75
So hunting Aphrodite with your lovely face.

Ah, well; first tell me who you are. What is
[your birth?
DIONYSUS. Your question's easily answered,
[it is no secret.   80
Perhaps you have heard of Tmolus, a mountain
[decked with flowers.
PENTHEUS. A range that curves round Sardis?
[Yes, I know of it.

DIONYSUS. That is my home. I am a Lydian by
[birth.
PENTHEUS. How comes it that you bring these
[rituals to Hellas?
5 DIONYSUS. Dionysus, son of Zeus, himself
[instructed me.
PENTHEUS. Is there a Lydian Zeus, then, who
[begets new gods?
DIONYSUS. I speak of Zeus who wedded
10 [Semele here in Thebes.
PENTHEUS. Did he possess you in a dream, or
[visibly?
DIONYSUS. Yes, face to face; he gave these
[mysteries to me.
15 PENTHEUS. These mysteries you speak of:
[what form do they take?
DIONYSUS. To the uninitiated that must not
[be told.
PENTHEUS. And those who worship—what
20 [advantage do they gain?
DIONYSUS. It is not for you to learn; yet it is
[worth knowing.
PENTHEUS. You bait your answer well, to
[arouse my eagerness.
25 DIONYSUS. His rituals abhor a man of impious
[life.
PENTHEUS. You say you saw him face to face:
[what was he like?
DIONYSUS. Such as he chose to be. I had no
30 [say in that.
PENTHEUS. Still you side-track my question
[with an empty phrase.
DIONYSUS. Just so. A prudent speech sleeps
[in a foolish ear.
35 PENTHEUS. Is Thebes the first place where
[you have introduced this god?
DIONYSUS. No; every eastern land dances
[these mysteries.
PENTHEUS. No doubt. Their moral standards
40 [fall far below ours.
DIONYSUS. In this they are superior; but their
[customs differ.
PENTHEUS. Do you perform these mysteries
[by night or day?
45 DIONYSUS. Chiefly by night. Darkness
[promotes religious awe.
PENTHEUS. For women darkness is deceptive
[and impure.

DIONYSUS. Impurity can be pursued by
[daylight too. 50
PENTHEUS. You must be punished for your
[foul and slippery tongue.
DIONYSUS. And you for blindness and impiety
[to the god.
PENTHEUS. How bold this Bacchant is! A 55
[practiced pleader too.
DIONYSUS. Tell me my sentence. What dread
[pain will you inflict?
PENTHEUS. I'll start by cutting off your
[delicate long hair. 60
DIONYSUS. My hair is sacred; I preserve it for
[the god.
PENTHEUS. And next, that thyrsus in your
[hand—give to to me.
DIONYSUS. Take it from me yourself; it is the 65
[god's emblem.
PENTHEUS. I'll lock you up in prison and keep
[you there.
DIONYSUS.   The god
Himself, whenever I desire, will set me free. 70
PENTHEUS. Of course—when you, with all
[your Bacchants, call to him!
DIONYSUS. He is close at hand here, and sees
[what is done to me.
PENTHEUS. Indeed? Where is he, then? Not 75
[visible to my eyes.
DIONYSUS. Beside me. You, being a
[blasphemer, see nothing.
PENTHEUS [*to the* GUARDS]. Get hold of him;
[he's mocking me and the whole city. 80
DIONYSUS [*to the* GUARDS]. Don't bind me,
[I warn you. [*To* PENTHEUS.] I am sane,
[and you are mad.
PENTHEUS. My word overrules yours. (*To the*
GUARDS.) I tell you, bind him fast. 85
DIONYSUS. You know not what you are
[saying, what you do, nor who
You are.
PENTHEUS. Who? Pentheus, son of Echion
[and Agaüe. 90
DIONYSUS. Your name points to calamity. It
[fits you well.
PENTHEUS. Take him away and shut him in
[my stables, where
He can stay staring at darkness.—You can 95
[dance in there!

As for these women you've brought as your
[accomplices,
I'll either send them to the slave-market to be
[sold,
5 Or keep them in my own household to work
[the looms;
And that will stop their fingers drumming on
[tamborines!
DIONYSUS. I'll go. Nothing can touch me that
10 [is not ordained.
But I warn you: Dionysus, who you say is dead,
Will come in swift pursuit to avenge this
[sacrilege.
You are putting *him* in prison when you lay
15 [hands on me.
[GUARDS *take* DIONYSUS *away to the stables;*
PENTHEUS *follows.*]

ODE II

Strophe

CHORUS. Dirce, sweet and holy maid,
Acheloüs' Theban daughter,
20 Once the child of Zeus was made
Welcome in your welling water,
When the lord of earth and sky
Snatched him from the undying flame,
Laid him safe within his thigh,
25 Calling loud the infant's name:
"Twice-born Dithyrambus! Come,
Enter here your father's womb;
Bacchic child, I now proclaim
This in Thebes shall be your name."
30 Now, divine Dirce, when my head is crowned
And my feet dance in Bacchus' revelry—
Now you reject me from your holy ground.
Why should you fear me? By the purple fruit
That glows in glory on Dionysus' tree,
35 His dread name yet shall haunt your memory!

Antistrophe

Oh, what anger lies beneath
Pentheus' voice and sullen face—
Offspring of the dragon's teeth,
And Echion's earth-born race,
40 Brute with bloody jaws agape,
God-defying, gross and grim,
Slander of his human shape!

Soon he'll chain us limb to limb—
Bacchus' servants! Yes, and more:
Even now our comrade lies   45
Deep on his dark prison floor.
Dionysus! Do your eyes
See us? O son of Zeus, the oppressor's rod
Falls on your worshippers; come, mighty god,
Brandish your golden thyrsus and descend   50
From great Olympus; touch this murderous
[man,
And bring his violence to a sudden end!

Epode

Where are you, Dionysus? Leading your
[dancing bands   55
Over the mountain slopes, past many a wild
[beast's lair,
Or on Corycian crags, with the thyrsus in their
[hands?
Or in the wooded coverts, maybe, of Olympus,   60
[where
Orpheus once gathered the trees and mountain
[beasts,
Gathered them with his lyre, and sang an
[enchanting air.   65
Happy vale of Pieria! Bacchus delights in you;
He will cross the flood and foam of the Axius
[river, and there,
He will bring his whirling Maenads, with
[dancing and with feasts,   70
Cross the father of waters, Lydias, generous
[giver
Of wealth and luck, they say, to the land he
[wanders through,
Whose famous horses graze by the rich and   75
[lovely river.

SCENE III

[*Suddenly a shout is heard from inside the
building—the voice of* DIONYSUS.]
DIONYSUS. Io,° Io! Do you know my voice,
[do you hear?   80
Worshippers of Bacchus! Io, Io!
CHORUS. Who is that? Where is he?
The shout of Dionysus is calling us!

Io an ecstatic cry

DIONYSUS. Io, Io! hear me again:
I am the son of Semele, the son of Zeus!
CHORUS. Io, Io, our lord, our lord!
Come, then, come to our company, lord of joy!
5 DIONYSUS. O dreadful earthquake, shake the
                              [floor of the world!
CHORUS [*with a scream of terror*].
Pentheus' palace is falling, crumbling in
                    [pieces! [*They continue severally.*]
10 —Dionysus stands in the palace; bow before
                              [him!
—We bow before him.—See how the roof
                              [and pillars
Plunge to the ground!—Bromius is with us,
15 He shouts from prison the shout of victory!
[*The flame on Semele's tomb grows and*
brightens.]
DIONYSUS. Fan to a blaze the lightning lit;
Kindle the conflagration of Pentheus' palace!
20 CHORUS. Look, look, look!
Do you see, do you see the flame of Semele's
                              [tomb,
The flame that lived when she died of the
                              [lightning-stroke?
25 [*A noise of crashing masonry is heard.*]
Down, trembling Maenads! Hurl yourselves to
                              [the ground.
Your god is wrecking the palace, roof to floor;
He heard our cry—he is coming, the son of
30   [Zeus!
[*The doors open and* DIONYSUS *appears.*]
DIONYSUS. Women of Asia, why do you
                    [cower thus, prostrate and terrified?
Surely you could hear Dionysus shattering
35   [Pentheus' palace? Come,
Lift yourselves up, take good courage, stop this
                    [trembling of your limbs!
CHORUS. We are saved! Oh, what a joy to
                    [hear your Bacchic call ring out!
40 We were all alone, deserted; you have come,
                              [and we rejoice.
DIONYSUS. Were you comfortless,
                    [despondent, when I was escorted in,
Helpless, sentenced to be cast in Pentheus'
45   [murky prison-cell?
CHORUS. Who could help it? What protector
                    [had we, once deprived of you?
Tell us now how you escaped the clutches of
                              [this wicked man.

DIONYSUS. I alone, at once, unaided,   50
                    [effortlessly freed myself.
CHORUS. How could that be? Did not
                    [Pentheus bind your arms with
                    [knotted ropes?
DIONYSUS. There I made a mockery of him.   55
                    [He thought he was binding me;
But he neither held nor touched me, save in his
                    [deluded mind.
Near the mangers where he meant to tie me up,
                    [he found a bull;   60
And he tied his rope round the bull's knees and
                    [hooves, panting with rage,
Dripping sweat, biting his lips; while I sat
                    [quietly by and watched.
It was then that Dionysus shook the building,   65
                    [made the flame
On his mother's tomb flare up. When Pentheus
                    [saw this, he supposed
The whole place was burning. He rushed this
                    [way, that way, calling out   70
To the servants to bring water; every slave
                    [about the place
Was engaged upon this futile task. He left it
                    [presently,
Thinking I had escaped; snatched up his   75
                    [murderous sword, darted indoors.
Thereupon Dionysus—as it seemed to me; I
                    [merely guess—
Made a phantom hover in the courtyard.
                    [Pentheus flew at it,   80
Stabbing at the empty sunlight, thinking he
                    [was killing *me*.
Yet a further humiliation Bacchus next
                    [contrived for him:
He destroyed the stable buildings. Pentheus   85
                    [sees my prison now
Lying there, a heap of rubble; and the picture
                    [grieves his heart.
Now he's dazed and helpless with exhaustion.
                    [He has dropped his sword.   90
He, a man, dared to take arms against a god. I
                    [quietly walked
Out of the palace here to join you, giving
                    [Pentheus not a thought.
But I hear his heavy tread inside the palace.   95
                    [Soon, I think,

He'll be out here in the forecourt. After what
    [has happened now,
What will he have to say? For all his rage, he
    [shall not ruffle *me*.
5 It's a wise man's part to practice a smooth-
    [tempered self-control.
    [*Enter* PENTHEUS.]
PENTHEUS. This is outrageous. He has escaped
    [—that foreigner.
10 Only just now I had him locked up and in
    [chains.
    [*He sees* DIONYSUS *and gives an excited
shout.*]
He's there! Well, what's going on now? How
15   [did you get out?
How dare you show your face here at my very
    [door?
DIONYSUS. Stay where you are. You are
    [angry; now control yourself.
20 PENTHEUS. You were tied up inside there.
    [How did you escape?
DIONYSUS. I said—did you not hear?—that I
    [should be set free—
PENTHEUS. By whom? You're always finding
25   [something new to say.
DIONYSUS. By him who plants for mortals the
    [rich-clustered vine.
PENTHEUS. The god who frees his worshippers
    [from every law.
30 DIONYSUS. Your insult to Dionysus is a
    [compliment.
PENTHEUS [*to attendant* GUARDS]. Go round
    [the walls and tell them to close every gate.
DIONYSUS. And why? Or cannot gods pass
35   [even over walls?
PENTHEUS. Oh, you know everything—save
    [what you ought to know.
DIONYSUS. The things most needful to be
    [known, those things I know.
40 But listen first to what this man has to report;
He comes from the mountain, and he has some
    [news for you.
I will stay here; I promise not to run away.
    [*Enter a* HERDSMAN.]
45 HERDSMAN. Pentheus, great king of Thebes!
    [I come from Mount Cithaeron,
Whose slopes are never free from dazzling
    [shafts of snow.

PENTHEUS. And what comes next? What
    [urgent message do you bring? 50
HERDSMAN. I have seen the holy Bacchae,
    [who like a flight of spears
Went streaming bare-limbed, frantic, out of
    [the city gate.
I have come with the intention of telling you, 55
    [my lord,
And the city, of their strange and terrible
    [doings—things
Beyond all wonder. But first I would learn
    [whether 60
I may speak freely of what is going on there, or
If I should trim my words. I fear your hastiness,
My lord, your anger, your too potent royalty.
PENTHEUS. From me fear nothing. Say all that
    [you have to say; 65
Anger should not grow hot against the
    [innocent.
The more dreadful your story of these Bacchic
    [rites,
The heavier punishment I will inflict upon 70
This man who enticed our women to their evil
    [ways.
HERDSMAN. At dawn today, when first the
    [sun's rays warmed the earth,
My herd of cattle was slowly climbing up 75
    [towards
The high pastures; and there I saw three
    [separate
Companies of women. The leader of one
    [company 80
Was Autonoë, your mother Agauë was at the
    [head
Of the second, Ino of the third; and they all lay
Relaxed and quietly sleeping. Some rested on
    [beds 85
Of pine-needles, others had pillows of oak-
    [leaves.
They lay just as they had thrown themselves
    [down on the ground,
But modestly, not—as you told us—drunk with 90
    [wine
Or flute-music, seeking the solitary woods
For the pursuit of love.
When your mother Agauë
Heard the horned cattle bellowing, she stood 95
    [upright

Among the Bacchae, and called to them to stir
                                    [themselves
From sleep; and they shook off the strong
                                    [sleep from their eyes
5 And leapt to their feet. They were a sight to
                                    [marvel at
For modest comeliness; women both old and
                                    [young,
Girls still unmarried. First they let their hair fall
10   [free
Over their shoulders; some tied up the
                                    [fastenings
Of fawnskins they had loosened; round the
                                    [dappled fur
15 Curled snakes that licked their cheeks. Some
                                    [would have in their arms
A young gazelle, or wild wolf-cubs, to which
                                    [they gave
Their own white milk—those of them who had
20   [left at home
Young children newly born, so that their
                                    [breasts were full.
And they wore wreathes of ivy-leaves, or oak,
                                    [or flowers
25 Of bryony. One would strike her thyrsus on a
                                    [rock,
And from the rock a limpid stream of water
                                    [sprang.
Another dug her wand into the earth, and there
30 The god sent up a fountain of wine. Those who
                                    [desired
Milk had only to scratch the earth with finger-
                                    [tips,
And there was the white stream flowing for
35   [them to drink,
While from the thyrsus a sweet ooze of honey
                                    [dripped.
Oh! if you had been there and seen all this, you
                                    [would
40 Have offered prayers to this god whom you now
                                    [condemn.
We herdsmen, then, and shepherds gathered
                                    [to exchange
Rival reports of these strange and extraordinary
45 Performances; and one, who had knocked about
                                    [the town,
And had a ready tongue, addressed us: "You
                                    [who live

On the holy mountain heights," he said, "shall
                                    [we hunt down 50
Agaüe, Pentheus' mother, and bring her back
                                    [from these
Rituals, and gratify the king? What do you
                                    [say?"
This seemed a good suggestion; so we hid   55
                                    [ourselves
In the leafy bushes, waiting. When the set time
                                    [came,
The women began brandishing their wands,
                                    [preparing 60
To dance, calling in unison on the son of Zeus,
"Iacchus! Bromius!" And with them the whole
                                    [mountain,
And all the creatures there, joined in the mystic
                                    [rite 65
Of Dionysus, and with their motion all things
                                    [moved.

Now, Agaüe as she danced passed close to me;
                                    [and I
At once leapt out from hiding, bent on 70
                                    [capturing her.
But she called out, "Oh, my swift-footed
                                    [hounds, these men
Are hunting us. Come, follow me! Each one of
                                    [you 75
Arm yourself with the holy thyrsus, and
                                    [follow me!"

So we fled, and escaped being torn in pieces by
Those possessed women. But our cattle were
                                    [there, cropping 80
The fresh grass; and the women attacked them,
                                    [with their bare hands.
You could see one take a full-uddered bellowing
                                    [young heifer
And hold it by the legs with her two arms 85
                                    [stretched wide;
Others seized on our cows and tore them limb
                                    [from limb;
You'd see some ribs, or a cleft hoof, tossed high
                                    [and low; 90
And rags of flesh hung from pine-branches,
                                    [dripping blood.
Bulls, which one moment felt proud rage hot
                                    [in their horns,

The next were thrown bodily to the ground,
[dragged down
By hands of girls in thousands; and they
[stripped the flesh
5 From the bodies faster than you could wink
[your royal eyes.

Then, skimming bird-like over the surface of
[the ground,
They scoured the plain which stretches by
10 [Asopus' banks
And yields rich crops for Thebes; and like an
[enemy force
They fell on Hysiae and Erythrae, two villages
On the low slopes of Cithaeron, and ransacked
15 [them both;
Snatched babies out of the houses; any plunder
[which
They carried on their shoulders stayed there
[without straps—
20 Nothing fell to the ground, not bronze or iron;
[they carried
Fire on their heads, and yet their soft hair was
[not burnt.
The villagers, enraged at being so plundered,
25 [armed
Themselves to resist; and then, my lord, an
[amazing sight
Was to be seen. The spears those men were
[throwing drew
30 No blood; but the women, hurling a thyrsus
[like a spear,
Dealt wounds; in short, those women turned
[the men to flight.
There was the power of a god in that. Then
35 [they went back
To the place where they had started from, to
[those fountains
The god had caused to flow for them. And they
[washed off
40 The blood; and snakes licked clean the stains,
[till their cheeks shone.

So, master, whoever this divinity may be,
Receive him in this land. His powers are
[manifold;
45 But chiefly, as I hear, he gave to men the vine

To cure their sorrows; and without wine,
[neither love
Nor any other pleasure would be left for us.
CHORUS. I shrink from speaking freely before
[the king; yet I 50
Will say it: there is no greater god than
[Dionysus.
PENTHEUS. This Bacchic arrogance advances
[on us like
A spreading fire, disgracing us before all Hellas. 55
We must act now. [To the HERDSMAN.] Go
[quickly to the Electran gate;
Tell all my men who carry shields, heavy or
[light,
All riders on fast horses, all my archers with 60
Their twanging bows, to meet me there in
[readiness
For an onslaught on these maniacs. This is
[beyond
All bearing, if we must let women so defy us. 65
DIONYSUS. You refuse, Pentheus, to give heed
[to what I say
Or change your ways. Yet still, despite your
[wrongs to me,
I warn you: stay here quietly; do not take up 70
[arms
Against a god. Dionysus will not tolerate
Attempts to drive his worshippers from their
[holy hills.
PENTHEUS. I'll not have you instruct me. You 75
[have escaped your chains;
Now be content—or must I punish you again?
DIONYSUS. I would control my rage and
[sacrifice to him
If I were you, rather than kick against the goad. 80
Can you, a mortal, measure your strength with
[a god's?
PENTHEUS. I'll sacrifice, yes—blood of women,
[massacred
Wholesale, as they deserve, among Cithaeron's 85
[glens.
DIONYSUS. Your army will be put to flight.
[What a disgrace
For bronze shields to be routed by those
[women's wands! 90
PENTHEUS. How can I deal with this
[impossible foreigner?
In prison or out, nothing will make him hold

[his tongue.

DIONYSUS. My friend, a happy settlement
[may still be found.

PENTHEUS. How? must I be a slave to my own
[slave-women?

DIONYSUS. I will, using no weapons, bring
[those women here.

PENTHEUS. Hear that, for the gods' sake!
[You're playing me some trick.

DIONYSUS. What trick?—if I am ready to save
[you by my skill.

PENTHEUS. You've planned this with them,
[so that the rituals can go on.

DIONYSUS. Indeed I have planned this—not
[with them, but with the god.

PENTHEUS. Bring out my armor, there!—
[That is enough from you.

DIONYSUS [*with an authoritative shout*].
Wait! [*Then quietly.*] Do you want *to see*
Those women, where they sit together, up in
[the hills?

PENTHEUS. Why, yes; for that, I'd give a
[weighty sum of gold.

DIONYSUS. What made you fall into this
[great desire to see?

PENTHEUS. It would cause me distress to see
[them drunk with wine.

DIONYSUS. Yet you would gladly witness this
[distressing sight?

PENTHEUS. Of course—if I could quietly sit
[under the pines.

DIONYSUS. They'll track you down, even if
[you go there secretly.

PENTHEUS. Openly, then. Yes, what you say
[is very true.

DIONYSUS. Then shall I lead you? You will
[undertake to go?

PENTHEUS. Yes, lead me there at once; I am
[impatient.

DIONYSUS. Then,
You must first dress yourself in a fine linen
[gown.

PENTHEUS. Why in a linen gown? Must I
[then change my sex?

DIONYSUS. In case they kill you, if you are
[seen there as a man.

PENTHEUS. Again you are quite right. How
[you think of everything!

DIONYSUS. It was Dionysus who inspired me
[with that thought.

PENTHEUS. Then how can your suggestion
[best be carried out?

DIONYSUS. I'll come indoors with you myself
[and dress you.

PENTHEUS. What?
Dress me? In woman's clothes? But I would be
[ashamed.

DIONYSUS. Do you want to watch the
[Maenads? Are you less eager now?

PENTHEUS. What kind of dress did you say
[you would put on me?

DIONYSUS. First I'll adorn your head with
[locks of flowing hair.

PENTHEUS. And after that? What style of
[costume shall I have?

DIONYSUS. A full-length robe; and on your
[head shall be a snood.

PENTHEUS. Besides these, is there anything
[else you'll put on me?

DIONYSUS. A dappled fawnskin round you,
[a thyrsus in your hand.

PENTHEUS. I could not bear to dress myself
[in woman's clothes.

DIONYSUS. If you join battle with the
[Maenads, blood will flow.

PENTHEUS. You are right; I must first go to
[spy on them.

DIONYSUS. That way
Is better than inviting force by using it.

PENTHEUS. And how shall I get through the
[town without being seen?

DIONYSUS. We'll go by empty streets; I will
[show you the way.

PENTHEUS. The Maenads must not mock me;
[better anything
Than that. Now I'll go in, and think how best
[to act.

DIONYSUS. You may do so. My preparations
[are all made.

PENTHEUS. I'll go in, then; and either I'll set
[forth at the head
Of my armed men—or else I'll follow your
[advice.

[*Exit* PENTHEUS.]

DIONYSUS. Women, this man is walking into
[the net. He will

Visit the Bacchae; and there death shall punish
[him.
Dionysus!—for you are not far distant—all is
[now
5 In your hands. Let us be revenged on him! And
[first
Fill him with wild delusions, drive him out of
[his mind.
While sane, he'll not consent to put on woman's
10   [clothes;
Once free from the curb of reason, he will put
[them on.
I long to set Thebes laughing at him, as he walks
In female garb through all the streets; to
15   [humble him
From the arrogance he showed when first he
[threatened me.
Now I will go, to array Pentheus in the dress
• Which he will take down with him to the house
20   [of Death,
Slaughtered by his own mother's hands. And
[he shall know
Dionysus, son of Zeus, in his full nature God,
Most terrible, although most gentle, to
25   [mankind.
[DIONYSUS follows PENTHEUS into the palace.]

ODE III

Strophe
CHORUS. O for long nights of worship, gay
With the pale gleam of dancing feet,
With head tossed high to the dewy air—
30 Pleasure mysterious and sweet!
O for the joy of a fawn at play
In the fragrant meadow's green delight,
Who has leapt out free from the woven snare,
Away from the terror of chase and flight,
35 And the huntsman's shout, and the straining
[pack,
And skims the sand by the river's brim
With the speed of wind in each aching limb,
To the blessed lonely forest where
40 The soil's unmarked by a human track,
And leaves hang thick and the shades are dim.

Refrain
What prayer should we call wise?

What gift of Heaven should man
Count a more noble prize,
A prayer more prudent, than   45
To stretch a conquering arm
Over the fallen crest
Of those who wished us harm?
And what is noble every heart loves best.

Antistrophe
Slow, yet unfailing, move the Powers   50
Of heaven with the moving hours.
When mind runs mad, dishonors God,
And worships self and senseless pride,
Then Law eternal wields the rod.
Still Heaven hunts down the impious man,   55
Though divine subtlety may hide
Time's creeping foot. No mortal ought
To challenge Time—to overbear
Custom in act, or age in thought.
All men, at little cost, may share   60
The blessing of a pious creed;
Truths more than mortal, which began
In the beginning, and belong
To very nature—these indeed
Reign in our world, are fixed and strong.   65

Refrain
What prayer should we call wise?
What gift of heaven should man
Count a more noble prize,
A prayer more prudent, than
To stretch a conquering arm   70
Over the fallen crest
Of those who wished us harm?
And what is noble every heart loves best.

Epode
Blest is the man who cheats the stormy sea
And safely moors beside the sheltering quay;   75
So, blest is he who triumphs over trial.
One man, by various means, in wealth or
[strength
Outdoes his neighbor; hope in a thousand
[hearts 80
Colors a thousand different dreams; at length
Some find a dear fulfilment, some denial.
But this I say
That he who best

Enjoys each passing day
Is truly blest.

SCENE IV

[*Enter* Dionysus. *He turns to call* Pentheus.]
Dionysus. Come, perverse man, greedy for
5   [sights you should not see,
Eager for deeds you should not do—Pentheus!
                [Come out
Before the palace and show yourself to me,
                [wearing
10 The garb of a frenzied Bacchic woman, and
                [prepared
To spy on your mother and all her Bacchic
                [company.
[*Enter* Pentheus *dressed as a Bacchic devotee.*
15 *He is dazed and entirely subservient to* Diony-
sus.]
You are the very image of one of Cadmus'
                [daughters.
     Pentheus. Why now! I seem to see two suns;
20   [a double Thebes;
Our city's wall with seven gates appears double.
[Dionysus *takes* Pentheus *by the hand and
leads him forward.*]
You are a bull I see leading me forward now;
25 A pair of horns seems to have grown upon your
                [head.
Were you a beast before? You have become a
                [bull.
     Dionysus. The god then did not favor us; he
30   [is with us now,
We have made our peace with him; you see as
                [you should see.
     Pentheus. How do I look? Tell me, is not the
                [way I stand
35 Like the way Ino stands, or like my mother
                [Agauë?
     Dionysus. Looking at you, I think I see them
                [both. Wait, now;
Here is a curl has slipped out of its proper place,
40 Not as I tucked it carefully below your snood.
     Pentheus. Indoors, as I was tossing my head
                [up and down
Like a Bacchic dancer, I dislodged it from its
                [place.
45   Dionysus. Come, then; I am the one who

                [should look after you.
I'll fix it in its place again. There; lift your head.
     Pentheus. You dress me, please; I have put
                [myself in your hands now.
     Dionysus. Your girdle has come loose; and   50
                [now your dress does not
Hang, as it should, in even pleats down to the
                [ankle.
     Pentheus. That's true, I think—at least by
                [the right leg, on this side;   55
But on the other side the gown hangs well to
                [the heel.
     Dionysus. You'll surely count me chief
                [among your friends, when you
Witness the Maenads' unexpected modesty.   60
     Pentheus. Ought I to hold my thyrsus in the
                [right hand—so,
Or in the left, to look more like a Bacchanal?
     Dionysus. In the right hand; and raise it at
                [the same time as   65
Your right foot. I am glad you are so changed
                [in mind.
     Pentheus. Could I lift up on my own
                [shoulders the whole weight
Of Mount Cithaeron, and all the women   70
                [dancing there?
     Dionysus. You could, if you so wished. The
                [mind you had before
Was sickly; now your mind is just as it should
                [be.   75
     Pentheus. Shall we take crowbars? Or shall
                [I put my shoulder under
The rocks, and heave the mountain up with
                [my two arms?
     Dionysus. Oh, come now! Don't destroy the   80
                [dwellings of the nymphs,
And the quiet places where Pan sits to play his
                [pipes.
     Pentheus. You are right. We ought not to
                [use force to overcome   85
Those women. I will hide myself among the
                [pines.
     Dionysus. Hide—yes, you'll hide, and find
                [the proper hiding-place
For one who comes by stealth to spy on Bacchic   90
                [rites.
     Pentheus. Why, yes! I think they are there
                [now in their hidden nests,

Like birds, all clasped close in the sweet prison
[of love.
DIONYSUS. What you are going to watch for
[is this very thing!
5 Perhaps you will catch them—if you are not
[first caught yourself.
PENTHEUS. Now take me through the central
[streets of Thebes; for I
Am the one man among them all that dares do
10 [this.
DIONYSUS. One man alone, you agonize for
[Thebes; therefore
It is your destined ordeal that awaits you now.
Come with me; I will bring you safely to the
15 [place;
Another shall conduct you back.
PENTHEUS. My mother—yes?
DIONYSUS. A sight for all to witness.
PENTHEUS. To this end I go.
20 DIONYSUS. You will return borne high—
PENTHEUS. Royal magnificence!
DIONYSUS. In your own mother's arms.
PENTHEUS. You insist that I be spoiled.
DIONYSUS One kind of spoiling.
25 PENTHEUS. Yet I win what I deserve.
[Exit PENTHEUS.]
DIONYSUS. Pentheus, you are a man to make
[men fear; fearful
Will be your end—an end that shall lift up your
30 [fame
To the height of heaven.
Agauë, and you her sisters, daughters of
[Cadmus,
Stretch out your hands! See, I am bringing this
35 [young man
To his great battle; and I and Bromius shall be
Victors. What more shall happen, the event will
[show.
[Exit DIONYSUS.]

ODE IV

Strophe
40 CHORUS. Hounds of Madness, fly to the
[mountain, fly
Where Cadmus' daughters are dancing in
[ecstasy!
Madden them like a frenzied herd stampeding,

Against the madman hiding in woman's clothes   45
To spy on the Maenads' rapture!
First his mother shall see him craning his neck
Down from a rounded rock or a sharp crag.
And shout to the Maenads, "Who is the man,
[you Bacchae,   50
Who has come to the mountain, come to the
[mountain spying
On the swift wild mountain—dances of
[Cadmus' daughters?
Which of you is his mother?   55
No, that lad never lay in a woman's womb;
A lioness gave him suck, or a Libyan Gorgon!"

Justice, now be revealed! Now let your sword
Thrust—through and through—to sever the
[throat   60
Of the godless, lawless, shameless son of
[Echion,
Who sprang from the womb of Earth!

Antistrophe
See! With contempt of right, with a reckless
[rage   65
To combat your and your mother's mysteries,
[Bacchus,
With maniac fury out he goes, stark mad,
For a trial of strength against *your* invincible
[arm!   70
His proud purposes death shall discipline.
He who unquestioning gives the gods their due,
And knows that his days are as dust, shall live
[untouched.
I have no wish to grudge the wise their wisdom;   75
But the joys I seek are greater, outshine all
[others,
And lead our life to goodness and loveliness:
The joy of the holy heart
That night and day is bent to honor the gods   80
And disown all custom that breaks the bounds
[of right.

Justice, now be revealed! Now let your sword
Thrust—through and through—to sever the
[throat   85
Of the godless, lawless, shameless son of
[Echion,
Who sprang from the womb of Earth!

[*Then with growing excitement, shouting in unison, and dancing to the rhythm of their words.*]

Epode

Come, Dionysus!
5 Come, and appear to us!
Come like a bull or a
Hundred-headed serpent,
Come like a lion snorting
Flame from your nostrils!
10 Swoop down, Bacchus, on the
Hunter of the Bacchae;
Smile at him and snare him;
Then let the stampeding
Herd of the Maenads
15 Throw him and throttle him,
Catch, trip, trample him to death!

SCENE V

[*Enter a* MESSENGER.]

MESSENGER. O house that once shone glorious
[throughout Hellas, home
20 Of the old Sidonian king who planted in this
[soil
The dragon's earth-born harvest! How I weep
[for you!
Slave though I am, I suffer with my master's
25 [fate.
CHORUS. Are you from the mountain, from
[the Bacchic rites? What news?
MESSENGER. Pentheus, son of Echion, is dead.
CHORUS. Bromius, lord! Your divine power is
30 [revealed!
MESSENGER. What, woman? What was that
[you said? Do you exult
When such a cruel fate has overtaken the king?
CHORUS. I am no Greek.
35 I sing my joy in a foreign tune.
Not any more do I cower in terror of prison!
MESSENGER. Do you think Thebes has no
[men left who can take command?
CHORUS. Dionysus commands *me*;
40 Not Thebes, but Dionysus.
MESSENGER. Allowance must be made for
[you; yet, to rejoice
At the accomplishment of horrors, is not right.

CHORUS. Tell us everything, then: this tyrant
[king 45
Bent on cruelty—how did he die?
MESSENGER. When we had left behind the
[outlying parts of Thebes
And crossed the river Asopus, we began to
[climb 50
Toward the uplands of Cithaeron, Pentheus
[and I—
I went as his attendant—and the foreigner
Who was our guide to the spectacle we were to
[see. 55
Well, first we sat down in a grassy glade. We
[kept
Our footsteps and our talk as quiet as possible,
So as to see without being seen. We found
[ourselves 60
In a valley full of streams, with cliffs on either
[side.
There, under the close shade of branching
[pines, the Maenads
Were sitting, their hands busy at their happy 65
[tasks;
Some of them twining a fresh crown of ivy-
[leaves
For a stripped thyrsus; others, gay as fillies
[loosed 70
From painted yokes, were singing holy Bacchic
[songs,
Each answering other. But the ill-fated
[Pentheus saw
None of this; and he said, "My friend, from 75
[where we stand
My eyes cannot make out these so-called
[worshippers;
But if I climb a towering pine-tree on the cliff
I would have a clear view of their shameful 80
[practices."

And then I saw that foreigner do an amazing
[thing.
He took hold of a pine-tree's soaring, topmost
[branch, 85
And dragged it down, down to the dark earth.
[It was bent
In a circle as a bow is bent, as a wheel's curve,
Drawn with a compass, bends the rim to its
[own shape; 90

The foreigner took that mountain-pine in his
[two hands
And bent it down—a thing no mortal man
[could do.
5 Then seating Pentheus on a high branch, he
[began
To let the tree spring upright, slipping it
[through his hands
Steadily, taking care he should not be flung off.
10 The pine-trunk, straightened, soared into the
[soaring sky,
Bearing my master seated astride, so that he
[was
More visible to the Maenads than they were to
[him.
15
He was just coming into view on his high perch,
When out of the sky a voice—Dionysus, I
[suppose;
That foreigner was nowhere to be seen—pealed
20 [forth:
"Women, here is the man who made a mock of
[you,
And me, and of my holy rites. Now punish
[him."
25 And in the very moment the voice spoke, a
[flash
Of dreadful fire stretched between earth and
[high heaven.

The air fell still. The wooded glade held every
30 [leaf
Still. You could hear no cry of any beast. The
[women,
Not having caught distinctly what the voice
[uttered,
35 Stood up and gazed around. Then came a
[second word
Of command. As soon as Cadmus' daughters
[recognized
The clear bidding of Bacchus, with the speed of
40 [doves
They darted forward, and all the Bacchae after
[them.
Through the torrent-filled valley, over the
[rocks, possessed
45 By the very breath of Bacchus they went
[leaping on.
Then, when they saw my master crouched high
[in the pine,

At first they climbed the cliff which towered
[opposite, 50
And violently flung at him pieces of rocks, or
[boughs
Of pine-trees which they hurled as javelins;
[and some
Aimed with the thyrsus; through the high air 55
[all around
Their wretched target missiles flew. Yet every
[aim
Fell short, the tree's height baffled all their
[eagerness; 60
While Pentheus, helpless in this pitiful trap, sat
[there.
Then, with a force like lightning, they tore
[down branches
Of oak, and with these tried to prize up the 65
[tree's roots.
When all their struggles met with no success,
[Agauë
Cried out, "Come, Maenads, stand in a circle
[round the tree 70
And take hold of it. We must catch this
[climbing beast,
Or he'll disclose the secret dances of Dionysus."
They came; a thousand hands gripped on the
[pine and tore it 75
Out of the ground. Then from his high perch
[plunging, crashing
To the earth Pentheus fell, with one incessant
[scream
As he understood what end was near. 80

His mother first,
As priestess, led the rite of death, and fell upon
[him.
He tore the headband from his hair, that his
[wretched mother 85
Might recognize him and not kill him.
"Mother," he cried,
Touching her cheek, "it is I, your own son
[Pentheus, whom
You bore to Echion. Mother, have mercy; I 90
[have sinned,
But I am still your own son. Do not take my
[life!"

Agauë was foaming at the mouth; her rolling
[eyes 95

Were wild; she was not in her right mind, but
                                        [possessed
By Bacchus, and she paid no heed to him. She
                                        [grasped
5 His right arm between wrist and elbow, set her
                                        [foot
Against his ribs, and tore his arm off by the
                                        [shoulder.
It was no strength of hers that did it, but the
10   [god
Filled her, and made it easy. On the other side
Ino was at him, tearing at his flesh; and now
Autonoë joined them, and the whole maniacal
                                        [horde.
15 A single and continuous yell arose—Pentheus
Shrieking as long as life was left in him, the
                                        [women
Howling in triumph. One of them carried off an
                                        [arm,
20 Another a foot, the boot still laced on it. The
                                        [ribs
Were stripped, clawed clean; and women's
                    [hands, thick red with blood,
Were tossing, catching, like a plaything,
25   [Pentheus' flesh.

His body lies—no easy task to find—scattered
Under hard rocks, or in the green woods. His
                                        [poor head—
His mother carries it, fixed on her thyrsus-
30   [point,
Openly over Cithaeron's pastures, thinking it
The head of a young mountain-lion. She has
                                        [left her sisters
Dancing among the Maenads, and herself
35   [comes here
Inside the walls, exulting in her hideous prey,
Shouting to Bacchus, calling him her fellow-
                                        [hunter,
Her partner in the kill, comrade in victory.
40 But Bacchus gives her bitter tears for her
                                        [reward.

Now I will go. I must find some place far away
From this horror, before Agauë returns home.
A sound and humble heart that reverences the
45   [gods
Is man's noblest possession; and the same
                                        [virtue

Is wisest too, I think, for those who practice it.
[*Exit the* MESSENGER.]

ODE V

CHORUS. Let us dance a dance to Bacchus,   50
                                        [shout and sing
For the fall of Pentheus, heir of the dragon's
                                        [seed,
Who hid his beard in a woman's gown,
And sealed his death with the holy sign   55
Of ivy wreathing a fennel-reed,
When bull led man to the ritual slaughter-ring.
Frenzied daughters of Cadmus, what renown
Your victory wins you—such a song
As groans must stifle, tears must drown!   60

Emblem of conquest, brave and fine!—
A mother's hand, defiled
With blood and dripping red
Caresses the torn head
Of her own murdered child!   _   65

But look! I see her—there, running towards the
                                        [palace—
Agauë, Pentheus' mother, her eyes wildly
                                        [rolling.
Come, welcome them—Dionysus' holy   70
                                        [company.

ÉXODOS

AGAUË *appears, frenzied and panting, with*
PENTHEUS' *head held in her hand. The rest of
her band of devotees, whom the* CHORUS *saw
approaching with her, do not enter; but a few*   75
*are seen standing by the entrance, where they
wait until the end of the play.*]
AGAUË. Women of Asia! Worshippers of
                                        [Bacchus!
[AGAUË *tries to show them* PENTHEUS' *head;*   80
they shrink from it.]
CHORUS. Why do you urge me? Oh!
AGAUË. I am bringing home from the
                                        [mountains
A vine-branch freshly cut,   85
For the gods have blessed our hunting.
CHORUS. We see it . . . and welcome you in
                                        [fellowship.

AGAUË. I caught him without a trap,
A lion-cub, young and wild.
Look, you may see him: there!
    CHORUS. Where was it?
5   AGAUË. On Cithareon;
The wild and empty mountain—
    CHORUS. Cithaeron!
AGAUË. . . . spilt his life-blood.
    CHORUS. Who shot him?
10 AGAUË. I was first;
All the women are singing,
"Honor to great Agauë!"
    CHORUS. And then—who next?
    AGAUË. Why, Cadmus' . . .
15 CHORUS. What—Cadmus?
AGAUË. Yes, his daughters—
But after me, after me—
Laid their hands to the kill.
Today was a splendid hunt!
20 Come now, join in the feast!
    CHORUS. What, wretched woman? *Feast?*
    AGAUË [*tenderly stroking the head as she
holds it*]. This calf is young: how thickly
The new-grown hair goes crisping
25 Up to his delicate crest!
    CHORUS. Indeed, his long hair makes him
Look like some wild creature.
    AGAUË. The god is a skilled hunter?
And he poised his hunting women,
30 And hurled them at the quarry.
    CHORUS. True, our god is a hunter.
    AGAUË. Do you praise me?
    CHORUS. Yes, we praise you.
    AGAUË. So will the sons of Cadmus . . .
35 CHORUS. And Pentheus too, Agauë?
    AGAUË. Yes he will praise his mother
For the lion-cub she killed.
    CHORUS. Oh, fearful!
    AGAUË. Ay, fearful!
40 CHORUS. You are happy?
    AGAUË. I am enraptured;
Great in the eyes of the world,
Great are the deeds I've done,
And the hunt that I hunted there!
45   CHORUS. Then show it, poor Agauë—this
               [triumphant spoil
You've brought home; show it to all the citizens
               [of Thebes.
AGAUË. Come, all you Thebans living within
             [these towered walls, 50
Come, see the beast we, Cadmus' daughters,
             [caught and killed;
Caught not with nets or thonged Thessalian
             [javelins,
But with our own bare arms and fingers. After 55
             [this
Should huntsmen glory in their exploits, who
             [must buy
Their needless tools from armorers? We with
             [our hands 60
Hunted and took this beast, then tore it limb
             [from limb.

Where is my father? Let old Cadmus come.
             [And where
Is my son Pentheus? Let him climb a strong 65
             [ladder
And nail up on the cornice of the palace wall
This lion's head that I have hunted and brought
             [home.
    [*Enter* CADMUS *with attendants bearing the* 70
body of PENTHEUS.]
    CADMUS. Come, men, bring your sad burden
             [that was Pentheus. Come,
Set him at his own door. By weary, endless
             [search 75
I found his body's remnants scattered far and
             [wide
About Cithaeron's glens, or hidden in thick
             [woods.
I gathered them and brought them here. 80

I had already
Returned with old Teiresias from the Bacchic
             [dance,
And was inside the walls, when news was
             [brought me of 85
My daughters' terrible deed. I turned straight
             [back; and now
Return, bringing my grandson, whom the
             [Maenads killed.
I saw Autonoë, who bore Actaeon to Aristaeus, 90
And Ino with her, there among the trees, still
             [rapt

In their unhappy frenzy; but I understood
That Agauë had come dancing on her way to
[Thebes—
And there indeed she is, a sight for misery!

5   AGAUË. Father! Now you may boast as
[loudly as you will
That you have sired the noblest daughters of
[this age!
I speak of all three, but myself especially.

10 I have left weaving at the loom for greater
[things,
For hunting wild beasts with my bare hands.
[See this prize,
Here in my arms; I won it, and it shall be hung

15 On your palace wall. There, father, take it in
[your hands.
Be proud of my hunting; call your friends to a
[feast; let them
Bless you and envy you for the splendor of my

20   [deed.
   CADMUS. Oh, misery unmeasured, sight
[intolerable!
Oh, bloody deed enacted by most pitiful hands!
What noble prize is this you lay at the gods'

25   [feet,
Calling the city, and me, to a banquet? Your
[wretchedness
Demands the bitterest tears; but mine is next
[to yours.

30 Dionysus has dealt justly, but pursued justice
Too far; born of my blood, he has destroyed
[my house.
   AGAUË. What an ill-tempered creature an old
[man is! How full

35 Of scowls! I wish my son were a great hunter
[like
His mother, hunting beasts with the young men
[of Thebes;
But *he* can only fight with gods. Father, you

40   [must
Correct him.—Will not someone go and call
[him here
To see me, and to share in my great happiness?
   CADMUS. Alas, my daughters! If you come
[to understand

45 What you have done, how terrible your pain
[will be!

If you remain as you are now, though you could
[not
Be happy, at least you will not feel your   50
[wretchedness.
   AGAUË. Why not happy? What cause have I
[for wretchedness?
   CADMUS. Come here. First turn your eyes
[this way. Look at the sky.   55
   AGAUË. I am looking. Why should you want
[me to look at it?
   CADMUS. Does it appear the same to you, or is
[it changed?
   AGAUË. Yes, it is clearer than before, more   60
[luminous.
   CADMUS. And this disturbance of your
[mind—is it still there?
   AGAUË. I don't know what you mean; but—
[yes, I feel a change;   65
My mind is somehow clearer than it was
[before.
   CADMUS. Could you now listen to me and
[give a clear reply?
   AGAUË. Yes, father. I have forgotten what we   70
[said just now.
   CADMUS. When you were married, whose
[house did you go to then?
   AGAUË. You gave me to Echion, of the sown
[race, they said.   75
   CADMUS. Echion had a son born to him. Who
[was he?
   AGAUË. Pentheus. His father lay with me; I
[bore a son.
   CADMUS. Yes, and whose head is that you are   80
[holding in your arms?
   AGAUË. A lion's—so the women said who
[hunted it.
   CADMUS. Then look straight at it. Come, to
[look is no great task.   85
[AGAUË *looks; and suddenly screams.*]
   AGAUË. What am I looking at? What is this
[in my hands?
   CADMUS. Look at it steadily; come closer to
[the truth.   90
   AGAUË. I see—O gods, what horror! Oh,
[what misery!
   CADMUS. Does this appear to you to be a
[lion's head?

AGAUË. No! I hold Pentheus' head in my
[accursed hand.
CADMUS. It is so. Tears have been shed for
[him, before you knew.
5 AGAUË. But who killed him? How did he
[come into my hands?
CADMUS. O cruel hour, that brings a bitter
[truth to light!
AGAUË. Tell me—my heart is bursting, I
10 [must know the rest.
CADMUS. It was you, Agauë, and your sisters.
[You killed him.
AGAUË. Where was it done? Here in the
[palace? Or where else?
15 CADMUS. Where, long ago, Actaeon was
[devoured by hounds.
AGAUË. Cithaeron. But what evil fate took
[Pentheus there?
CADMUS. He went to mock Dionysus and
20 [your Bacchic rites.
AGAUË. Why were we on Cithaeron? What
[had brought us there.
CADMUS. You were possessed. All Thebes
[was in a Bacchic trance.
25 AGAUË. Dionysus has destroyed us. Now I
[understand.
CADMUS. He was insulted. You refused to call
[him god.
AGAUË. Father, where is the beloved body of
30 [my son?
CADMUS. Here. It was I who brought it, after
[painful search.
AGAUË. And are his limbs now decently
[composed?
35 CADMUS. Not yet.
We came back to the city with all possible
[haste.
AGAUË. How could I touch his body with
[these guilty hands?
40 CADMUS. Your guilt, my daughter, was not
[heavier than his.
AGAUË. What part did Pentheus have, then,
[in my insanity?
CADMUS. He sinned like you, refusing
45 [reverence to a god.
Therefore the god has joined all in one ruin—
[you,
Your sisters, Pentheus—to destroy my house
[and me.

I have no son; and now, my unhappy child, I 50
[see
This son of yours dead by a shameful, hideous
[death.
You were the new hope of our house, its bond
[of strength, 55
Dear grandson. And Thebes feared you; no
[one dared insult
Your old grandfather if he saw you near; you
[would
Teach him his lesson. But now I shall live 60
[exiled,
Dishonored—I, Cadmus the great, who planted
[here,
And reaped, that glorious harvest of the
[Theban race. 65

O dearest son—yes, even in death you shall be
[held
Most dear—you will never touch my beard
[again, and call
Me Grandfather, and put your arm round me 70
[and say,
"Who has wronged you or insulted you? Who
[is unkind,
Or vexes or disturbs you? Tell me, Grandfather,
That I may punish him." Never again. For me 75
All that remains is pain; for you, the pity of
[death;
For your mother, tears; torment for our whole
[family.

If any man derides the unseen world, let him 80
Ponder the death of Pentheus, and believe in
[gods.
CHORUS. I grieve for your fate, Cadmus;
[though your grandson's death
Was justly merited, it falls cruelly on you. 85
AGAUË. Father, you see how one disastrous
[day has shattered
My whole life . . .

[At this point the two MSS on which the
text of this play depends show a lacuna of con- 90
siderable extent; it covers the end of this scene,
in which Agauë mourns over Pentheus' body,
and the appearance of Dionysus manifested as
a god. The MSS resume in the middle of a
speech by Dionysus. A number of quotations by 95

ancient authors, together with less than 20
lines from *Christus Patiens* (an anonymous
fourth century A.D. work consisting largely of
lines adapted from Greek tragedies), make it
5 possible to attempt a guess at the content of
the missing lines. Because this play is often
performed, it seems worthwhile to provide here
a usable text. In the lines that follow, the words
printed in italics are mere conjecture, and have
10 no value except as a credible completion of the
probable sense; while those in Roman type
represent the sources available from *Christus
Patiens* and elsewhere.—Translator's note.]

. . . my whole life, turned my pride to shame,
15 *[my happiness*
To horror, Now my only wish is to compose
My son's body for burial, and lament for him;
And then die. But this is not lawful; for my
[hands
20 *Are filthy with pollution of their own making.*
When I have spilt the blood I bore, and torn the
[flesh
That grew in my own womb, how can I after
[this
25 *Enfold him to my breast, or chant his ritual*
[dirge?
And yet, I beg you, pity me, and let me touch
My son, and say farewell to that dear body
[which
30 *I cherished, and destroyed unknowing. It is*
[right
That you should pity, for your hands are
[innocent.
CADMUS. *My daughter, you and I and our*
35 *[whole house are crushed*
And broken by the anger of this powerful god.
It is not for me to keep you from your son.
[Only
Be resolute, and steel your heart against a sight
40 *Which must be fearful to any eyes, but most*
[of all
To a mother's. [To attendants.] *Men, put down*
[your burden on the ground
Before Agauë, and remove the covering.
45 AGAUË. *Dear child, how cruel, how unnatural*
[are these tears,
Which should have fallen from your eyes on my
[dead face.

Now I shall die with none to mourn me. This is
[just; 50
For in my pride I did not recognize the god,
Nor understand the things I ought to have
[understood.
You too are punished for the same impiety;
But which is the more terrible, your fate or 55
[mine,
I cannot tell. Since you have suffered too, you
[will
Forgive both what I did, not knowing what I
[did, 60
And what I do now, touching you with unholy
[hands—
At once your cruellest enemy and your dearest
[friend.

I place your limbs as they should lie; I kiss the 65
[flesh
That my own body nourished and my own
[care reared
To manhood. Help me, father; lay his poor
[head here. 70
Make all exact and seemly, with what care we
[can.
O dearest face, O young fresh cheek? O kingly
[eyes,
Your light now darkened! O my Son! See, with 75
[this veil
I now cover your head, your torn and
[bloodstained limbs.
Take him up, carry him to burial, a king
Lured to a shameful death by the anger of a 80
[god.
[Enter DIONYSUS.]
CHORUS. *But look! Who is this, rising above*
[the palace door?
It is he—Dionysus comes himself, no more 85
[disguised
As mortal, but in the glory of his divinity!
DIONYSUS. *Behold me, a god great and*
[powerful, Dionysus,
The son whom Theban Semele bore to immortal 90
[Zeus.
I come to the city of seven gates, to famous
[Thebes,
Whose people slighted me, denied my divinity,
Refused my ritual dances. Now they reap the 95
[fruit

Of impious folly. The royal house is
[overthrown;
The city's streets tremble in guilt, as every
[Theban
5 Repents too late his blindness and his
[blasphemy.
Foremost in sin was Pentheus, who not only
[scorned
My claims, but put me in fetters and insulted
10 [me.
Therefore death came to him in the most
[shameful way,
At his own mother's hands. This fate he justly
[earned;
15 No god can see his worship scorned, and hear
[his name
Profaned, and not take vengeance to the utmost
[limit.
Thus men may learn that gods are more
20 [powerful than they.
Agaüe and her sisters must immediately
Depart from Thebes; their exile will be just
[penance
For the pollution which this blood has brought
25 [on them.
Never again shall they enjoy their native land;
That such defilement ever should appear before
The city's altars, is an offense to piety.

Now Cadmus, hear what suffering Fate
30 [appoints for you.

[Here the MSS resume.—Translator's note.]

You shall transmute your nature, and become
[a serpent.
Your wife Harmonia, whom her father Ares
35 [gave
To you, a mortal, likewise shall assume the
[nature
Of beasts, and live a snake. The oracle of Zeus
Foretells that you, at the head of a barbaric
40 [horde,
Shall with your wife drive forth a pair of
[heifers yoked,
And with your countless army destroy many
[cities;

But when they plunder Loxias' oracle, they shall 45
[find
A miserable homecoming. However, Ares shall
At last deliver both you and Harmonia,
And grant you immortal life among the blessed
[gods. 50

I who pronounce these fates am Dionysus,
[begotten
Not by a mortal father, but by Zeus. If you
Had chosen wisdom, when you would not, you
[would have lived 55
In wealth and safety, having the son of Zeus
[your friend.
CADMUS. Have mercy on us, Dionysus. We
[have sinned.
DIONYSUS. You know too late. You did not 60
[know me when you should.
CADMUS. We acknowledge this; but your
[revenge is merciless.
DIONYSUS. And rightly; I am a god, and you
[insulted me. 65
CADMUS. Gods should not be like mortals in
[vindictiveness.
DIONYSUS. All this my father Zeus ordained
[from the beginning.
AGAÜE. No hope, father. Our harsh fate is 70
[decreed: exile.
DIONYSUS. Then why put off a fate which is
[inevitable?
[Exit DIONYSUS.]
CADMUS. Dear child, what misery has 75
[overtaken us all—
You, and your sisters, and your old unhappy
[father!
I must set forth from home and live in
[barbarous lands; 80
Further than that, it is foretold that I shall lead
A mixed barbarian horde to Hellas. And my
[wife,
Harmonia, Ares' daughter, and I too, must take
The brutish form of serpents; and I am to lead 85
[her thus
At the head of an armed force, to desecrate the
[tombs
And temples of our native land. I am to reach
No respite from this curse; I may not even cross 90

The downward stream of Acheron to find peace
                [in death.
  AGAUË. And I in exile, father, shall live far
                [from you.
5 CADMUS. Poor child, why do you cling to me,
                [as the young swan
Clings fondly to the old, helpless and white
                [with age?
  AGAUË. Where can I turn for comfort,
10   [homeless and exiled?
  CADMUS. I do not know. Your father is little
                [help to you.
  AGAUË. Farewell, my home; farewell the land
                [I know.
15 Exiled, accursed and wretched, now I go
Forth from this door where first I came a bride.
  CADMUS. Go, daughter, find some secret place
                [to hide
Your shame and sorrow.
20   AGAUË. Father, I weep for you.
  CADMUS. I for your suffering, and your
                [sisters' too.
  AGAUË. There is strange tyranny in the god
                [who sent
25 Against your house this cruel punishment.
  CADMUS. Not strange: our citizens despised
                [his claim,
And you, and they, put him to open shame.
  AGAUË. Father, farewell.
30 CADMUS. Poor child! I cannot tell
How you can *fare well*; yet I say, Farewell.
  AGAUË. I go to lead my sisters by the hand
To share my wretchedness in a foreign land.
  [*She turns to the Theban women who have*
35 *been waiting at the edge of the stage.*]
Come, see me forth.
Gods, lead me to some place
Where loath'd Cithaeron may not see my face,
Nor I Cithaeron. I have had my fill
40 Of mountain-ecstasy; now take who will
My holy ivy-wreath, my thyrsus-rod,
All that reminds me how I served this god!
  [*Exit, followed by* CADMUS.]
  CHORUS. Gods manifest themselves in many
45   [forms,
Bring many matters to surprising ends;
The things we thought would happen do not
              [happen;
The unexpected God makes possible:
And that is what has happened here today.   50
  [*Exeunt.*]

Anonymous

The Second Shepherds' Play

Late Fourteenth Century

In the late medieval cycles of plays celebrating human history from the Creation through the Incarnation to the Day of Judgment, there was place for a play about the shepherds to whom came an angel with tidings that a savior was born. In the cycle at Wakefield, in Yorkshire, there were two such plays, called simply *The First* and *The Second Shepherds' Plays.* The latter is the crowning achievement of the author, whom we know only as the Wakefield Master, and perhaps of the religious drama of the Middle Ages.

The world of this play, like that of medieval art generally, comprehends, but is not confined by, particularities of time and space. Although Christ is not yet born in the early scenes, the shepherds call upon His Cross and His name and also upon Christian saints, among them St. Nicholas, who lived more than three centuries after Christ. Also, the shepherds seem firmly grounded near Wakefield, inasmuch as the nearby village of Horbury is referred to; yet when the angel sends them to Bethlehem, they go, arriving before dawn and without crossing water. Such literal impossibilities seem not to have concerned artists who, from the perspective of eternity, saw history as synchronous, space as seamless and unitary. And in their art they captured, both realistically and ritualistically, timely and timeless truths.

The liveried retainers who expropriate to their own use the goods of such underlings as Coll; the feckless and procreant among the lower orders, like Mak and Gill, who cog, shuffle, and filch, with imagination if without much success; and the lowly and oppressed herdsmen who scrabble for a living and find little more than song and the brief charitable impulses of their own hearts to rejoice in—these come to us with remarkable particularity from the Wakefield Master's contemporary experience; yet surely they embody as well the nature and condition of such men as, fourteen centuries before, would have journeyed to the town of

Bethlehem or dwelt in the fields nearby, keeping watch over their flocks by night.

Mary and the "little day-star" in her lap, by contrast, are unique as well as typical. To render them vivid as a mother and child, the same kind of particularity that the Wakefield Master had invested in the shepherds was needed. To celebrate them as the transcendent Mother and Child, ritual was called for—in the pageants of communal drama as in the services of the Church. And these modes are handled with a brilliance virtually unexampled.

In the beginning, when the three shepherds lament the political, domestic, and natural causes of their suffering, and when they are joined by the light-fingered and slippery-tongued night-walker Mak, the mode is realistic if anachronistic. Even here, though, we see symbolic elements anticipating the Adoration of the Christ Child. This is the darkness before the dawn, the suffering before the redemption, and the local flood is likened to the Flood of Noah, the antetype of Christ, who preserved a remnant of mankind from destruction and with whom the Lord established an everlasting covenant.

In the play's middle portion realism is again the mode—comic realism now, exploiting the petty irritabilities of the shepherds, the cat-and-dog marriage of Mak and Gill, the theft and discovery of the sheep. Nevertheless, for all the comedy, the symbols gain in intensity. Mak, commending himself to the hands of Pontius Pilate and then casting a spell on the shepherds, looms momentarily as the devil. Gill's device for hiding the sheep is a false nativity, preparing by contrast for the true one to follow. Mak's anticipated meal and his somewhat insistent invitations to the shepherds to eat and drink are clear if oblique reminders of the mass, the eucharistic feast.

In the final scene the realistic detail typifies as before—more powerfully, perhaps; certainly without the former hint of abrasiveness—as the shepherds offer their humble gifts and bestow on the child just such happy affection as men have felt at cradles throughout all ages: "he merries," "he laughs," "darling dear." The element of ritual, anticipated by the earlier symbols, now achieves its fullest expression. No longer allusively but directly the play deals with Mary and her Son. In one of the imposing tableaux of Christian art, the shepherds kneel and are inspired to a litany of grateful praise, uniting worship with natural affection in perfect expression of their faith that God has become man:

Hail, sovereign savior . . .
Hail, little tiny mop!

When they depart, singing, to publish their story, the miracle of spirit made flesh and dwelling among mankind has been fully confirmed as a vision at once contemporary and timeless.

The Second Shepherds' Play

ANONYMOUS

Adapted by Arthur M. Eastman from the modernizations of Clarence Griffin Child and Martial Rose

CHARACTERS

COLL   *the first shepherd*
GIB   *the second shepherd*
DAW   *the third shepherd, a boy*
MAK   *the sheep-stealer*
GILL   *Mak's wife*
ANGEL
MARY   *with the baby Jesus*

SCENE I

[*The open fields.*]
COLL. Lord, but this weather is cold, and I
                    [am ill wrapped,
Near numb, were truth told, so long have I
                    [napped;
5   My legs they fold, my fingers are chapped.
It is not as I would, for I am all lapped
     In sorrow.
In storms and tempest,
10 Now in the east, now in the west,
Woe is him has never rest

Now or tomorrow.

But we simple shepherds that walk on the moor,
In faith, we are near-hands out of the door.°
No wonder, as it stands, if we be poor,   15
For the tilth° of our lands lies as fallow as the
                    [floor,
     As you ken.°
We are so lamed,
Overtaxed and maimed,   20
We are made hand-tamed,
     By these gentry men.

They rob us of our rest, our Lady them harry!
These men that are lord-fast,° they cause the
                    [plow tarry.   25
That, men say, is for the best; we find it
                    [contrary.
Thus are husbandmen oppressed, in point to
                    [miscarry,
     In life.   30
Thus hold they us under,
Thus bring us to blunder;
It were great wonder,
     If ever we should thrive.

Get a man a liveried sleeve or a brooch,   35
                    [nowadays
Woe is him that him grieves, or once him
                    [gainsays!
No blame may he receive, howe'er grasping
                    [his ways;   40
And yet may no man believe one word that he
                    [says—
     Not a letter.
He can seize what he's lacking,
Boastfully and bragging;   45
And all is through the backing
     Of men who are greater.

There shall come a swain, a proud peacock,
                    [you know;
He must borrow my wain, my plough also;   50

near-hands . . . door   nearly homeless
tilth   arable part
ken   know
lord-fast   attached to or retained by lords

Modification of The Second Shepherds' Play *of the Towneley Cycle as translated by Clarence Griffin Child, from* Riverside Literature Series Number 191, *copyright © 1910, 1938 by Houghton Mifflin Company. "The Second Shepherds' Play" from the book* The Wakefield Mystery Plays *edited by Martial Rose. Copyright 1961 by Martial Rose. Reprinted by Doubleday & Company, Inc.*

ANONYMOUS | Scene I

These I am full fain to grant ere he go.
Thus live we in pain, anger and woe
   By night and day.
He must have, if he choose,
5 What I must needs lose;
I were better hanged than refuse,
   Than once say him nay.

It does me good, as I walk thus on my own,
Of this world for to talk, and so make my
10   [moan.
To my sheep will I stalk and harken anon,
There abide on a balk° or sit on a stone
   Full soon.
For I trow, pardie,°
15 True men, if they be,
We get more company
   Ere it be noon.

       [*He steps aside. Gib enters.*]

    GIB. *Benste and Dominus!*° What may this
20   [mean?
The world faring thus, how oft have we seen?
Lord, this weather works through us, and the
                [wind is full keen,
And the frosts so hideous they water mine
25   [een—°
   No lie!
Now in dry, now in wet,
Now in snow, now in sleet,
When my shoes freeze to my feet,
30   It's not at all easy.

But as far as I ken, wherever I go,
We poor wedded men suffer much woe;
We have sorrow ever again—it falls often so.
Silly Copple, our hen, both to and fro
35   She cackles;
But begin she to croak
To groan or to cluck,
For our cock it's no joke

For he is in shackles.

These men that are wed have not all their will; 40
When they're full hard bestead,° they sigh
               [mighty still.
God knows the life they're led is full hard and
               [full ill;
In bower nor in bed may they speak their will. 45
   This tide°
My part have I found,
Learned my lesson sound:
Woe to him who is bound,
   For he must it abide. 50

But now late in our lives—a marvel to me,
That I think my heart rives such wonders to
               [see;
That which destiny drives will come to be—
Some men will have two wives, and some men 55
               [three
   In store.
Some are grieved that have any,
But I'll wager my penny
Woe is him that has many, 60
   For he feels sore!

But, young men, of wooing, for God that you
               [bought,
Beware well of wedding, and hold well in
               [thought, 65
"Had I known" is a thing that serves not a jot.
Much constant mourning has wedding home
               [brought,
   And grief,
With many a sharp shower;° 70
For you may catch in an hour
What shall savor full sour
   As long as you live.

For, as e'er read I Epistle, I have one to my fere°
As sharp as a thistle, as rough as a briar. 75
She is browed like a bristle, with a sour face by
               [her.

---

balk strip of grassland between plowed fields
trow, pardie believe, by God
Benste . . . Dominus bless us (*benste* is a shortened
  form of *benedicite*) and Lord
een eyes

bestead put to it
tide time
shower pain
fere mate

If she once wets her whistle she can sing full
                                                [clear
  Her paternoster.
As great as a whale,
5 She has a gallon of gall.
By him that died for us all,
  I would I'd run till I'd lost her!

    COLL. Gib, look over the row! Full deafly you
                                                [stand.
10 GIB. Yea, the devil in your maw, so tarrying!
Did'st see aught of Daw?
    COLL.   Yea, on the lea-land°
I heard him blow.° He comes near at hand,
  Not far.
15 Stand still.
    GIB.   Why?
    COLL. For he comes, think I.
    GIB. He'll beguile us with a lie
Unless we beware.

20 [*Enter* DAW.]
    DAW. Christ's cross me speed, and Saint
                                                [Nicholas!
Thereof have I need; it is worse than it was.
Who knows should take heed and let the world
25   [pass;
Ill ever it speeds; it's as brittle as glass,
  And drifts.
But the world never fared so,
And marvels greater grow—
30 Now in weal, now in woe—
  And everything shifts.

Was never since Noah's flood such floodings
                                                [seen,
Winds and rains so rude and storms so keen:
35 Some stammered, some stood in doubt,° as I
                                                [ween.
Now God turn all to good! I say as I mean,
  For ponder:
These floods they so drown,
40 Both in fields and in town,
  And bear all down;

And that is a wonder.

We that walk in the nights our cattle to keep,
We see fearful sights when other men sleep.
  [*Catching sight of the others.*]   45
Yet my heart grows light—I see rascals a-peep.
[*Aside.*] You two are tall wights°—I will give
                                                [my sheep
  A turn, below
But full ill have I meant;°   50
As I walk on this bent,°
I may lightly repent,
  If I stub my toe.

Ah, sir, God you save, and master mine!
A drink would I have and somewhat to dine. 55
    COLL. Christ's curse, my knave, you're a lazy
                                                [hind!
    GIB. What, let the boy rave!—Wait till later
                                                [this time.
  We've had our food.   60
Ill luck to your pate!—
Though the knave came late,
Yet he's in a state
  To sup, if he could.

    DAW. Such servants as I, who work and 65
                                                [sweat,
Eat our bread full dry, and that makes me fret.
We're oft wet and weary while our masters
                                                [sleep yet;
But comes full tardy the food that we get— 70
  And less than our due.
Both our dame and our sire,
When we've run in the mire,
Take a nip at our hire—
  And pay us late, too.   75

But hear the truth, master, for the fare that you
                                                [pay
I shall work hereafter—tit for tat is fair play.
I shall do little, sir, but sport as I may,

---

lea-land meadow
blow i.e., his horn
Some . . . doubt i.e., at the time of Noah's flood

tall wights proper creatures; i.e., a fine pair
But . . . meant Daw reproves himself for the disrespect
  he has just expressed toward his elders, then, in the
  following lines, proposes for himself an easy penance
bent field

For ne'er does my supper my stomach dismay
   In fields.
Why should I threap?°
With my staff can I leap;°
5 Men say, "Bargain cheap
   But a poor return yields."

   COLL. You were an ill lad to go a-wooing
With a master that had but little for spending.
   GIB. Peace, I say, lad. No more jangling,
10 Or I'll make you full sad, by heaven's king!
   Your gauds—°
Where are our sheep, boy?—We scorn.
   DAW. Sir, this same day at morn°
I left them in the corn,
15   When they rang Lauds.°

They have pasture good, they cannot go wrong.
   COLL. That is right. By the rood,° these
                    [nights are long!
Ere we go now, I would someone gave us a
20   [song.
   GIB. So I thought as I stood, to cheer us
                     [along.
   DAW.
   I agree.
25   COLL. The tenor I'll try.
   GIB. And I the treble so high.
   DAW. Then the mean° shall be I.
How you chant now, let's see!

   [*They sing. Then* MAK *enters, wearing a*
30 *cloak.*]

   MAK. Now, lord, by thy seven names' spell,
           [that made the stars on high,
Full more than I can tell, thy will for me lack I.
I'm all at odds, naught's well—that oft my
35   [brains doth try.

threap haggle
leap i.e., run away
gauds pranks
morn i.e., after midnight
Lauds matins, the church service held at midnight
  (as here) or dawn
rood cross
mean middle part

Would God I might in heaven dwell, for there
                [no children cry,
  So shrill.
   COLL. Who is it pipes so poor?
   MAK. Would God you knew of me, sure!   40
Lo, a man that walks on the moor,
   And has not all his will.

   GIB. Mak, whither do you speed? What news
               [do you bring?
   DAW. Is he come? Then take heed each one to 45
               [his thing.
   [*He takes* MAK's *cloak from him.*]
   MAK. I be a yeoman, indeed, under the king,
The self and the same. A lord's message I
               [bring— 50
  No lie.
Fie on you! Go hence
Out of my presence!
I must have reverence.
   Why, who be I?   55

   COLL. Why play it so quaint? Mak, you do
                    [wrong.
   GIB. Would you play the saint? For that do
                   [you long?
   DAW. With words he can paint—the devil 60
                [him hang!
   MAK. I'll make a complaint: you'll be flogged
               [ere long,
  At a word,
And wracked without ruth.   65
   COLL. But, Mak, is that truth?
Now take out that southern tooth,°
   And set in a turd.

   GIB. Mak, the devil in your eye! A blow I'd
                [fain give you. 70
   DAW. Mak, know you not me? By God, I
               [could beat you!
   MAK. God keep you all three! Methought I
               [had seen you.
You're a fair company!   75
   COLL.   Now you remember, do you?

southern tooth Mak has been speaking in a southern
  dialect

GIB.
Take heed!
When thus late a man goes,
What will folks suppose?
5   You've a bad name, God knows,
        For stealing of sheep.

MAK. That I am true as steel no men debate,
But a sickness I feel has brought me to this
                                    [state:
10   My belly lacks a meal and suffers ill fate.
        DAW. "Seldom lies the de'il dead by the
                                    [gate."°
MAK.
    Therefore
15   Full sore am I and ill;
    May I turn stone-still
    If I've eaten a morsel
        This month and more.

        COLL. How fares your wife? By my hood,
20   [how fares she?
    MAK. Sprawling, by the rood, at the fire
                                    [she'll be,
    And a house full of brood. With the bottle
                                    [she's free—
25   For else not much good for aught I can see
        Or do.
    Eats as fast as she can,
    And each year that comes to man
    Adds another to our clan—
30   And some years two.

    Now were I richer and full of purse
    I'd be eaten clear out of home and house.
    She's a foul dear, if look you durst!
    There's none can see her, who knows a worse
35   Than know I.
    Would you see what I'd proffer?
    I'd give all in my coffer
    For her soul might I offer
        A prayer for aye.

40   GIB. I know so wearièd none is in this shire;

I'd sleep though I earnèd less for my hire.
    DAW. I'm cold and naked and long for a fire.
    COLL. I'm weary with walk and am covered
                                    [with mire.
    Look to!   45
    GIB. Nay, near shall I lie
For I must sleep soundly.
    DAW. As good a man's son, I,
    As any of you.

[*They lie down.*]   50

But, Mak, come lie here—in between—if you
                                    [please.
    MAK. You'll be hindered, I fear, from talking
                                    [at ease,
    Indeed.   55
    [*He lies among them. They sleep.*]
From my top to my toe,
Manus tuas commendo,
Pontio Pilato.°
    Christ's cross me speed!   60

[*He rises.*]

It is time to strike ere the iron grows cold,
And craftily creep now into the fold,
And nimbly to work, but not be too bold,
For bitter the bargain, if all were told   65
    At the ending.
Time now for haste, truth to tell,
But he needs good counsel
That fain would fare well
    With but little for spending.   70

Put about you a circle as round as the moon,
    [*He draws the circle.*]
Till I have done what I will, until it be noon,
Lie you stone still until I have done
While I summon my skill some magic to croon.   75
    "On high,
Over your heads I raise my hand.
Your sight is lost on sea and land!"
But I must gain much more command

"**Seldom . . . gate**" proverbial: appearances are deceptive

Manus . . . Pilato I commend your hands to Pontius Pilate

To work it right.

Lord, but they sleep hard—as you may all hear.
Never yet was I shepherd, but of that I've no
[fear.
5 If the flock be scared, yet shall I nip near
Hey! Draw hitherward! [*He seizes a sheep.*]
[Now mends our cheer
From sorrow.
A fat sheep, I dare say,
10 A good fleece, dare I lay.
When I can, I'll repay,
But this will I borrow.

[*He departs with the sheep.*]

SCENE II

[Mak's *cottage.*]
15 MAK [*outside*]. Hey, Gill, are you in? Get us
[some light!
GILL [*within*]. Who makes such a din this
[time of the night?
I've sat down to spin; I doubt that I might
20 Rise a penny to win—I curse them on high!
So fares
A housewife that has been
Fretted 'twixt and between.
Here may no work be seen
25 For such small chores.

MAK. Good wife, open this hatch. See you
[not what I bring?
GILL. I'll let you draw the latch (MAK *opens*
[*the door.*) Ah, come in, my sweeting.
30 MAK. You care not a scratch for my long
[standing.
GILL. By your naked neck are you like to be
[hanging.
MAK.
35 Away!
I am worth my meat,
For in a fix can I get
More than they that toil and sweat
All the long day.

40 Thus it fell to my lot, Gill! Such luck came my
[way!

GILL. It were a foul blot to be hanged, as you
[may.
MAK. I've oft 'scaped, Gillot, as risky a play.
GILL. "But so long goes the pot to the water," 45
[men say,
"At last
Comes it home broken."
MAK. Well know I the token,
But let it never be spoken! 50
But come and help fast.

I would he were slain, I want so to eat.
Not this year was I so fain to have some sheep's
[meat.
GILL. If they come ere he's slain and hear the 55
[sheep bleat—
MAK. Then might I be ta'en: that were a cold
[sweat!
Go bar
The outer door. 60
GILL. Yes, Mak,
For if they come at your back—
MAK. Then might I get from the whole pack
The devil, and more.

GILL. A good trick have I spied, since you 65
[think of none:
Here shall we him hide till they be gone.
In my cradle. Abide! Let me alone,
And I shall lie beside, as in childbed, and groan.
MAK. 70
Well said!
And I shall say this night
A boy child saw the light.
GILL. Now bless I that day bright
That saw me born and bred! 75

This is a good device and a far cast.°
Ever a woman's advice helps at the last.
I never know who spies: go you back fast.
MAK. Save I come ere they raise, there'll
[blow a cold blast! 80

I will go sleep.
[*He returns to the shepherds.*]
Still sleeps all this company,
And I shall slip in privily

far cast clever trick

As it had never been I
That carried off their sheep.

SCENE III

[*The open fields.*]
COLL. *Resurrex a mortruus!*° Reach me a
5   [hand!
Judas carnas dominus!° I scarcely can stand:
My foot sleeps, by Jesus; hunger has me
                                                    [unmanned.
I thought that we laid us full nigh to England.
10   GIB. Verily!
Lord, but I have slept well!
As fresh as an eel,
As light I do feel
        As leaf on a tree.

15   DAW [*disoriented.*] A blessing within!
                            [Whatever is shaking
My heart from my skin, my body thus quaking?
Who's making this din that's set my head
                                            [aching?
20 To the door I'll win. Hark, fellows, be waking!
        Four we were—
See you aught of Mak now?
        COLL. We were up ere you.
        GIB. Man, to God I vow,
25   He's yet gone nowhere.

        DAW. Methought he was lapped in a wolf's
                                            [skin.
        COLL. So many are wrapped now—namely
                                            [within.
30   DAW. When we had long napped, methought
                                        [with a gin°
A fat sheep he trapped; but he made no din.
        GIB.
        Be still!
35 Your dream makes you mad;
It's a nightmare you've had.
        COLL. God bring good out of bad,
        If it be his will.

Resurrex a mortruus garbled Latin, referring appar-
    ently to Christ's resurrection from the dead
Judas . . . dominus Judas, lord (in?)carnate
gin snare

GIB. Rise, Mak, for shame! Right long you
                                            [do lie.   40
MAK. Now Christ's holy name be with us for
                                            [aye!
What's this? By Saint James, I can't move when
                                            [I try.
I suppose I'm the same. Aah, my neck's lain   45
                                            [awry
Herein.
[*They help him get up.*]
Many thanks! Since yester-even,
Now by Saint Stephen,   50
I was so flayed by a dream
        My heart jumped from my skin.

I thought Gill began to croak and travail full
                                            [sad;
Well-nigh at the first cock she bore a young lad 55
To add to our flock. Then will I never be glad.
Of cares I've a stock more than ever I had.
        Ah, my head!
A house full of hunger pains—
The devil knock out their brains!   60
Woe is him has many bairns
        And has but little bread.

I must go home, by your leave, to Gill, as I
                                            [thought.
Pray look up my sleeve that I've stolen naught: 65
I am loath you to grieve or from you take
                                            [aught.
[*He goes.*]
DAW. Go forth, ill may you thrive! Now
                            [would I we sought   70
This morn
For the sheep in our care.
        COLL. First I shall fare.
Let us meet.
        GIB.   Where?   75
DAW.
At the crooked thorn.

SCENE IV

[MAK's *cottage.*]
MAK [*outside*]. Undo this door! Who is here?
                            [How long shall I stand?   80

GILL [*within*]. Who makes such a blare?
      [Now walk in the wenyand!°
MAK. Ah, Gill, what cheer? It is I, Mak, your
      [husband.
5 GILL. Then may we see here the devil in a
      [band—°

[*Opening the door.*]
Sir Guile!
Lo, he comes with a croak
10 As though held by the throat.
And I cannot devote
   To my work any while.

MAK. Oh, the fuss that she makes to get an
      [excuse.
15 Naught but pleasure she takes, and curls up
      [her toes.
GILL. Why, who works and who wakes?
      [Who comes, who goes?
Who brews, who bakes? What makes me thus
20   [hoarse?
   And then
It is sad to behold—
Now in hot, now in cold,
Full woeful the household
25   That wants a woman!

But how have you sped with the shepherds,
      [Mak?
MAK. The last word that they said when I
      [turned my back,
30 They would count each head of sheep in their
      [pack.
They'll not be pleased, I'm afraid, when they
      [their sheep lack,
   Pardie!
35 But howe'er the game go,
They'll suspect me, I know,
And raise a great bellow,
   And cry out against me.

But now do as you hight.°
40   GILL.   To that I agree.
I'll swaddle him right in the cradle by me.
Were it a greater sleight, yet could I help be.

wenyand waning of the moon: an unlucky time
band noose
hight promised

I will lie down straight. Come cover me.
   [*She lies down.* MAK *tucks her in.*]
   Behind!   45
Come Coll and his crew,
They'll pry through and through.
   MAK. For help I'll halloo
   The sheep if they find.

GILL. Hark now for their call—they will 50
      [come anon.
Come and make ready all, and sing on your
      [own—
Sing lullay° you shall, for I must groan
And cry out by the wall on Mary and John 55
   Full sore.
Sing lullay quite fast
When you hear them at last.
If my part is miscast,
   Trust me no more.   60

SCENE V

[*The crooked thorn.*]
DAW. Ah, Coll, good morn! Why sleep you
      [not?
COLL. Alas that ever I was born! We have a
      [foul blot— 65
A fat wether have we lorn.°
   DAW.   God forbid, say it not!
GIB. Who should give us this scorn? That's
      [a foul spot.
   COLL.   70
   Some shrew.°
I have searched with my dogs
All Horbury shrogs,°
And with fifteen hogs°
   Found I only the ewe.   75

DAW. Now trust me, if you will, by Saint
      [Thomas of Kent,
Either Mak or Gill had a hand in this event.
   COLL. Peace, man, be still! I saw when he
      [went. 80

lullay a lullaby
lorn lost
shrew rascal
shrogs thickets
hogs young sheep

You slander him ill; you ought to repent
  With good speed.
    GIB. Now as ever I might thrive,
As I hope to keep alive,
5 Only Mak could contrive
  To do that same deed.

    DAW. Then off to his homestead, be brisk on
                    [our feet.
I shall never eat bread till I know all complete.
10   COLL. Nor have drink in my head till with
                    [him I meet.
    GIB. In no place will I bed until I him greet—
My brother!
  One vow will I plight,
15 Till I see him in sight,
  I will ne'er sleep one night
    Where I do another!

SCENE VI

[MAK's *cottage*.]
[MAK, *hearing the shepherds coming, be-*
20 *gins to sing a lullaby at the top of his voice;*
GILL *groans in concert*.]
    DAW. D'you hear how they croak? Our sire
                 [will now croon.
    COLL. Never heard I folk so clean out of tune.
25 Call him.
    GIB.   Mak! Undo your door soon!
    MAK. Who is it that spoke, as if it were noon,
So loud?
Who is it, I say?
30   DAW. Good fellows, were it day!
    MAK. [*as the shepherds enter*]. As far as you
                    [may,
  Speak low

Over a sick woman's head, who is not at her
35   [ease;
I had rather be dead than she suffer unease.
    GILL [*as they approach her*]. Get away from
             [my bed! Let me breathe, if you please.
Each step that you tread from my nose to my
40   [knees
  Goes through me.
    COLL. Tell us, Mak, if you may,
How fare you, I say?
    MAK. Are you in town today?

How fare you three?   45

You have run in the mire, and now are all wet.
I shall make you a fire, if you will sit.
A nurse would I hire—remember you yet
My dream, which entire has fulfilled its threat
  In due season?   50
I have bairns, if you knew,
Far more than a few;
But we must drink as we brew,
  And that is but reason.

I would you'd dine ere you went. Methinks   55
                    [that you sweat.
    GIB. Our mood won't be mended by drink
                    [nor by meat.
    MAK. Is ought then ill sent?
    DAW.   Our loss is great.   60
A sheep stol'n we lament, ta'en while we slept.
    MAK.
  Sirs, drink!
Had I been there
Some should have paid full dear.   65
    COLL. Marry, some trow that you were,
  And that makes us think!

    GIB. Mak, one and another trows it must
                    [have been thee.
    DAW. Either you or your spouse, so say we.   70
    MAK. Now if aught suspicion throws on Gill
                    [or me,
Come and search our house, and then may you
                    [see
Who had her—   75
If I any sheep got,
Either cow or stot—°
And Gill, my wife, rose not,
  Here since she laid her.

As I am true and leal,° to God, here I say   80
That this be the first meal I shall eat this day.
    COLL. Mak, as hope I for weal, advise you, I
                    [say:
"He learned timely to steal that could not say
                    [nay."   85

[*They begin to search.*]

cow or stot female or male
leal loyal, honest

GILL.
My death you've dealt!
Out, thieves, nor come again,
You've come to rob us, that's plain.
5 MAK. Hear you not how she groans amain?
Your hearts should melt!

GILL. Out, thieves, from my bairn. Go not to
            [him near.
MAK. If you knew all she's borne, your hearts
10   [would be sore.
You do wrong, I you warn, thus to come before
A woman that has borne—but I say no more.
GILL.
Oh, my middle—I die!
15 I vow to God so mild,
If e'er I you beguiled,
May I eat this child
    That in this cradle lies!

MAK. Peace, woman, for God's pain, and cry
20   [not so!
You'll burst your brain and fill me with woe.
GIB. I trow our sheep be slain. What find you
            [two, though?
Our work's all in vain. We may as well go.
25 Save clothes and such matters
I can find no flesh
Hard or nesh°
Salt nor fresh,
    Save two empty platters.
30 [Gesturing toward the cradle.] No live stock
    but this, tame or wild,
None, so may I have bliss, as loud as he°
            [smelled.
GILL. No, so God me bless, and give me joy
35   [of my child!
COLL. We have aimed amiss; I hold us
            [beguiled.
GIB.
    Completely, each one!
40 Sir—our Lady him save!—
Is your child a knave?°
    MAK. Any lord might him have,
    This child, for his son.

When he wakes, so he grips, it's a pleasure to
            [see. 45
DAW. Good luck to his hips,° and blessing,
            [say we!
But who were his gossips,° that were so soon
            [ready?
MAK. Blest be their lips— [Hesitates, at a 50
            [loss.]
COLL.   A lie now, hark ye!
MAK.
God give them thanks.
Parkin and Gibbon Waller, I say. 55
And gentle John Horn, in good fay—°
He made such droll display
    With his long shanks.

GIB. Mak, friends will we be, for we are all
            [one. 60
MAK. We? Count not on me, for amends get
            [I none.
Farewell all three! And gladly begone.
[The shepherds leave, speaking outside the
cottage.] 65
DAW. Fair words there may be, but love there
            [is none
This year.
COLL. Gave you the child anything?
GIB. I trow not one farthing. 70
DAW. Fast back will I fling.
Wait for me here.

[He reenters the cottage, COLL and GIB slowly
following.]

DAW. Mak, I trust you'll not grieve, if I come 75
            [to your child.
MAK. Nay, great shame I receive—you have
            [acted full vile.
DAW. Your bairn 'twill not grieve, little day-
            [star so mild. 80
Mak, by your leave, let me give your child
    But sixpence.
[He goes to the cradle and starts to draw
away the cover.]
    MAK. Nay, stop it—he sleeps! 85

nesh soft
he i.e., the stolen sheep
knave boy

to his hips i.e., to him
gossips godparents
fay faith

Daw. Methinks he peeps—
Mak. When he wakens, he weeps.
I pray you go hence.

Daw. Give me leave him to kiss, and lift
5   [up the clout.
[Lifts the cover.]
What the devil is this? He has a long snout!
Coll. He's birth-marked amiss. We waste
                       [time hereabout.
10 Gib. A weft that ill-spun is comes ever foul
                       [out.
Aye—so!
He is like to our sheep!
Daw. Ho, Gib, may I peep?
15 Coll. I trow Nature will creep
Where it may not go.°

Gib. This was a quaint gaud and a far cast.
It was a high fraud.
Daw.   Yea, sirs, that was't.
20 Let's burn this bawd and bind her fast.
A false scold, by the Lord, will hang at the last.
So shalt thou!
Do you see how they swaddle
His four feet in the middle?
25 Saw I never in the cradle
A horned lad ere now.

Mak. Peace, I say! What, let be your blare!
It was I him begot and yon woman him bare.
Coll. What devil's name has he got, Mak?—
30   [Lo, God, Mak's heir!
Gib. Come, joke with him not. Now, God
                 [give him care,
I say!
Gill. A pretty child is he
35 As sits on a woman's knee,
A darling, perdie,
To make a man gay.

Daw. I know him by the ear-mark—that's a
                 [good token.
40 Mak. I tell you, sirs, hark! His nose was
                 [broken.
There told me a clerk he'd been forspoken.°

Coll. You deal falsely and dark; I would
                 [fain be wroken.°
Get a weapon!   45
Gill. He was witched by an elf;
I saw it myself.
When the clock struck twelve,
He was misshapen.

Gib. You two are at one, that's plain, in all   50
             [you've done and said.
Coll. Since their theft they maintain, let's
             [strike them dead.
Mak. If I trespass again, cut off my head.
At your will I remain.   55
Daw.
Sirs, take my counsel instead.
For this trespass
We'll neither curse nor chide,
Fight nor deride,   60
Nor longer bide,
But toss him in canvas.

[They toss Mak *in a blanket.]*

SCENE VII

[The open fields.]
Coll. Lord, but I'm sore, ready to burst!   65
In faith, I may no more; therefore will I rest.
Gib. Like a sheep of seven score he weighed
             [in my fist.
To sleep anywhere I think I'd like best.
Daw.   70
Now I you pray.
On this green let us lie.
Coll. O'er those thieves yet chafe I.
Daw. Let your anger go by.   75
Come do as I say.

[They sleep. An Angel *sings "Gloria in excelsis," then speaks.]*

Angel. Rise, herdsmen gentle, for now is he
             [born
That shall take from the fiend what Adam had 80
             [lorn;
That warlock° to end, this night is he born.

go walk; i.e., the truth will out
clerk, forspoken priest, bewitched

wroken revenged
warlock devil

God is made your friend now on this morn.
　　Leave your flocks:
To Bethlehem go see
Where he lies so free,
5　In a crib full poorly,
　　Between ass and ox.

　　[The ANGEL goes.]

　　COLL. This was a fine voice, even as ever I
　　　　　　　　　　　　　　　　　　[heard.
10　It's a marvel to dream on, thus with dread to be
　　　　　　　　　　　　　　　　　　[stirred.
　　GIB. To God's son from heaven these tidings
　　　　　　　　　　　　　　　　　　[referred.
All the wood with a lightning methought at his
15　　　　　　　　　　　　　　　　　[word
　　Shone fair.
　　DAW. Of a child did he tell,
In Bethlehem, mark well.
　　COLL. Yon star there doth dwell.
20　Let us seek him there.

　　GIB. Say, what was his song—how it went,
　　　　　　　　　　　　　　　　　[did you hear?
Three breves° to a long—
　　DAW.　　　　　　　Marry, yes. To my ear
25　There was no crotchet° wrong, nothing lacked,
　　　　　　　　　　　　　　　　　[and 'twas clear.
　　COLL. To sing it here, us among, as he sang
　　　　　　　　　　　　　　　　　[it, full near,
　　I know how—
30　GIB. Let's see how you croon.
Can you bark at the moon?
　　DAW. Hold your tongues! Have done!
Hark after me now.

　　[They sing.]

35　GIB. To Bethlehem he bade that we should
　　　　　　　　　　　　　　　　　[go;
And sure we be mad to tarry so.
　　DAW. Be merry and not sad, our mirth may
　　　　　　　　　　　　　　　　　[flow.
40　Ever to be glad is the reward we shall know
　　And choose.

breves　short notes
crotchet　note

COLL. Then let us hither hie,
Though we be wet and weary,
To that child and that lady;
　　We have no time to lose.　　　　　　　　45

GIB. We find by the prophecy—let be your
　　　　　　　　　　　　　　　　　[din!—
Of David and Isaiah, and more of their kin—
They prophesied learnedly that in a virgin
Should God come to lie, to atone for our sin,　　50
　　And take it,
Our nature, from woe.
Isaiah said so.
Ecce virgo
　　Concipiet° a child that is naked.　　　　　55

DAW. Full glad may we be if we await the
　　　　　　　　　　　　　　　　　[day,
That sweet sight to see who all power may
　　　　　　　　　　　　　　　　　[sway.
Lord, well were me, now and for aye,　　　　60
Might I kneel on my knee some word for to say
　　To that child.
But the angel said
In a crib was he laid;
He was poorly arrayed,　　　　　　　　　65
　　Both meek and mild.

COLL. Patriarchs that have been and prophets
　　　　　　　　　　　　　　　　　[of yore
Desired to have seen this child that is born.
They are gone full clean—that they have lorn.　70
We shall see him, I ween, ere it be morn,
　　As a token.
When I see him and feel,
I shall know full well,
It is true as steel,　　　　　　　　　　75
　　What prophets have spoken:

To so poor as we are that he would appear
First, and declare by his messenger.
　　GIB. Go we now, let us fare; the place is us
　　　　　　　　　　　　　　　　　[near.　80
　　DAW. I am ready and eager. Let's together
　　　　　　　　　　　　　　　　　[with cheer
　　To that bright one go.

Ecce . . . concipiet　Behold, a virgin shall conceive
(Isaiah vii.14)

Lord, if thy will it be—
We are simple all three—
On thy child grant that we
    May some comfort bestow.

SCENE VIII

5   [*The stable in Bethlehem, the shepherds kneeling before Mary and Jesus.*]
    COLL. Hail, comely and clean! Hail, young
                             [child!
Hail creator, I mean, from a maiden so mild!
10 Thou hast cursed, I ween, the warlock so wild:
The beguiler of men, now goes he beguiled.
    Lo, he merries,
Lo, he laughs, my sweeting!
A happy meeting!
15 Here's my promised greeting:
    Have a bob° of cherries.

    GIB. Hail, sovereign savior, for thou hast us
                             [sought!
Hail, noble food and flower, that all things hast
20   [wrought!
Hail, full of favor, that made all of naught!
Hail! I kneel and I cower. A bird have I brought,
    Bairn that you are.
Hail, little tiny mop!
25 Of our creed thou art top;
I would drink from thy cup,
    Little day-star.

    DAW. Hail, darling dear, full of godhead!
I pray thee be near when that I have need.
30 Hail, sweet is thy cheer!° My heart would bleed
To see thee sit here in so poor a weed
    With no pennies.
Hail! Put forth thy dall.°
I bring thee but a ball:
35 Take it and play withal,
    And go to the tennis.

    MARY. The father of heaven, God
                         [omnipotent,
That made all in days seven—his son has he

                               [sent. 40
My name he namèd, in me alighted ere he
                               [went.
Conceived I him, even through his might, as he
                             [meant;°
    And now is he born.   45
May he keep you from woe!
I shall pray him do so.
Tell of him as you go,
    And remember this morn.

    COLL. Farewell, lady, so fair to behold,   50
With thy child on thy knee.
    GIB.   But he lies full cold.
Lord, well is me! Now back to our fold.
    DAW. Forsooth, already it seems to be told
Full oft.   55
    COLL. What grace we have found!
    GIB. We are won safe and sound!
    DAW. To sing are we bound:
Make it ring then aloft!

[*They depart singing.*]   60

---

bob bunch
cheer countenance
dall hand

meant intended

William Shakespeare

1564–1616

Othello, the Moor of Venice

1604

Among the several radical differences between such a Renaissance tragedy as *Othello* and such classical tragedies as *Agamemnon* or *Oedipus Rex,* one is the degree of complexity of plot. The plot of classical tragedy has a spare linearity; that of the renaissance a rich variety. Around and into his main plot of the love and deaths of Othello and Desdemona, Shakespeare arabesques underplots on kindred themes— Roderigo's love-lust of Desdemona, for example; Iago's jealousy of Emilia; Cassio's intimacy with the courtesan Bianca; and more. The effect is to endow the play's central themes with such a range of resonance that one can only turn to Shakespeare's sonnets for just paraphrase: Sonnet 116 on "the marriage of true minds" and Sonnet 129 on "The expense of spirit in a waste of shame." Even these superlative definitions of love and lust, however— although they may define the poles of *Othello*'s universe—can no more than suggest the rich and tragic harmonies of the play itself.

Another radical difference between classical and Shakespearean tragedy, at least such instances of the latter as *Hamlet, Macbeth,* and *Othello,* lies in the governance of their cosmos. Inevitably the worlds of *Agamemnon* and *Oedipus Rex* are presided over by Zeus and the pantheon of deities we now relegate to mythology. *Othello*'s cosmos, however, is explicitly Christian. Iago likens himself to a devil, serving the "Divinity of hell." "Perdition [damnation] catch my soul,/ But I do love thee!" says Othello "and when I love thee not,/[Primal] Chaos is come again." Finally, standing over Desdemona's corpse and convinced of his own guilt, Othello foresees the Judgment Day foretold in the Book of Revelation:

> when we shall meet at compt,
> This look of thine will hurl my soul from
> [heaven,
> And fiends will snatch at it.

The Christianity of *Othello* offers more, of

course, than spiritual perspective. It provides that radical structure of characters and choice that Shakespeare's theater inherited from the Middle Ages: Everyman wooed by the alternating forces of darkness and light and wavering between them before making his ultimate choice. So Iago, in one sense, incarnates the diabolic, Desdemona the angelic, and between them, drawn to them both, finding both in a sense within himself, wavers Othello. The process of his choosing provides the play its plot.

Othello and the others are, of course, far more than allegorical abstractions. Othello has a history, the glorious romance of which he relates to the Venetian Senate, capturing its admiration as it has captured Desdemona's. He is "an extravagant and erring stranger," an alien, wheeling into the world of Venice as might a comet from the far reaches of the universe. He speaks a special language that critics have called musical, words that provide magnificent extension to his emotions. Consider simply one of his farewells, that to his occupation when, apprehending Desdemona's infidelity, he sees himself divorced from the "Pride, pomp and circumstance of glorious war!"

Othello's speech, his adventures, his profession, his race, culture, and color all distinguish him from the "wealthy curled darlings" who have hitherto wooed Desdemona. And she, "A maiden never bold;/ Of spirit so still and quiet, that her motion/ Blush'd at herself," has seen "Othello's visage in his mind" and has consecrated her soul and fortunes "to his honours and his valiant parts." In her there is something still young and ingenuous, perhaps, a desire for adventure, for escape from Venetian convention. She will become, as Othello calls her, his "fair warrior," and will glory in the role of nurturing wife who advises her spouse on what to wear and eat. Theirs is a marriage of extremes, a union of opposites so all but unimaginable that Brabantio, her father, can only attribute it to magic, so extraordinary that Roderigo and Iago can find its only explanation in depraved lust.

The extremes illuminate the transcendence of this love and the deep damnation of its destruction—by Iago, by Othello.

Iago, the devil's stand-in, has been called many things: a practical joker, an amateur of tragedy in real life, a psychopath, a Machiavellian villain, the figure of Envy, among others. To the extent that he is human, his surface is that of the soldierly type: blunt, bold, able to take care of number one, cynical. His bluntness, of course, is a pose; his boldness genuine if sadistic; his self-sufficiency fully adequate until the end; and his cynicism is that of gutter and crotch. From Iago come the images of an old black ram tupping a white ewe, of Brabantio's daughter covered with a Barbary horse, of "the beast with two backs." And it is Iago, naturally, who hits on sexual jealousy as the means to destroy Othello.

Othello, alas, is destroyed too easily, for every opposition that his marriage has overcome becomes to his faltering faith evidence of Desdemona's infidelity. What the play offers, in its whole and its parts, is Othello's falling from order to disorder, from control to loss of control, from bliss to perdition. Out of the ugly recesses that perhaps all minds contain, the "all in all sufficient" Othello spawns vile imaginings and imposes them on his wife. He is a customer in a brothel, she the whore. Although, when he comes to destroy her, he sees himself as humane minister of the chaste heavens, he completes the deed in murderous fury.

At the play's ending, it may seem that hell, Iago, and the demonic potential in the great warrior's soul have triumphed. Othello in effect condemns himself to everlasting torture in the devil's domain; although Iago will die, it will be only after the completion of his mission; and Desdemona, the innocent and uncomprehending, will have been sacrificed. True. On the other hand, to be Iago is one definition of damnation. Where he is is hell nor can he be out of it. To be Othello, even in his fallen state, is something else, for he now knows what he had only intuited before—and we know with a knowledge all the characters have helped refine by their own engagements with lust, jealousy, loyalty, and love—that Othello's original vision of what love might be was valid. The Desdemona who saw Othello's visage in his mind has confirmed the words of Sonnet 116, that true love alters not even when it alteration finds, "But bears it out even to the edge of doom."

Othello, the Moor of Venice

SHAKESPEARE

CHARACTERS

DUKE OF VENICE
BRABANTIO *a senator*
Other senators
GRATIANO *brother to Brabantio*
LODOVICO *kinsman to Brabantio*
OTHELLO *a noble Moor in the service of the Venetian state*
CASSIO *his lieutenant*
IAGO *his ancient*
RODERIGO *a Venetian gentleman*
MONTANO *Othello's predecessor in the government of Cyprus*
CLOWN *servant to Othello*
DESDEMONA *daughter to Brabantio and wife to Othello*
EMILIA *wife to Iago*
BIANCA *mistress to Cassio*
SAILOR, MESSENGER, HERALD, OFFICERS, GENTLEMEN, MUSICIANS, *and* ATTENDANTS

SCENE: *Venice: a Sea-port in Cyprus*

ACT I

Scene i

[*Enter* RODERIGO *and* IAGO.]
ROD. Tush! never tell me; I take it much
                  [unkindly
That thou, Iago, who hast had my purse

Othello from The Living Shakespeare © *1949. Permission to modernize and edit the notes of Oscar James Campbell obtained from Macmillan Publishing Co. Inc.*

As if the strings were thine, shouldst know of
[this.°
  IAGO. 'Sblood,° but you will not hear me:
If ever I did dream of such a matter,
5 Abhor me.
    ROD. Thou told'st me thou didst hold him
[in thy hate.
  IAGO. Despise me, if I do not. Three great ones
[of the city,
10 In personal suit to make me his lieutenant,
Off-capp'd° to him: and, by the faith of man,
I know my price, I am worth no worse a place:
But he, as loving his own pride and purposes,
Evades them, with a bombast circumstance°
15 Horribly stuff'd with epithets of war;°
And, in conclusion,
Nonsuits° my mediators; for "Certes," says he,
"I have already chose my officer."
And what was he?
20 Forsooth, a great arithmetician,°
One Michael Cassio, a Florentine,
A fellow almost damn'd in a fair wife;°
That never set a squadron in the field,
Nor the division° of a battle knows
25 More than a spinster; unless the bookish
[theoric,°
Wherein the togèd° consuls° can propose°
As masterly as he: mere prattle, without
[practice,
30 Is all his soldiership. But he, sir, had the
[election:
And I, of whom his eyes had seen the proof

At Rhodes, at Cyprus and on other grounds
Christian and heathen, must be be-lee'd° and
[calm'd 35
By debitor and creditor: this counter-caster.°
He, in good time,° must his lieutenant be,
And I—God bless the mark!—his Moorship's
[ancient.°
    ROD. By heaven, I rather would have been his 40
[hangman.
  IAGO. Why, there's no remedy; 'tis the curse
[of service,
Preferment goes by letter° and affection,°
And not by old gradation,° where each second 45
Stood heir to the first. Now, sir, be judge
[yourself,
Whether I in any just term° am affined°
To love the Moor.
    ROD. I would not follow him then. 50
  IAGO. O, sir, content you;°
I follow him to serve my turn upon him:
We cannot all be masters, nor all masters
Cannot be truly follow'd. You shall mark
Many a duteous and knee-crooking knave, 55
That, doting on his own obsequious bondage,
Wears out his time, much like his master's ass,
For nought but provender, and when he's
[old, cashier'd:
Whip me such honest knaves. Others there are 60
Who, trimm'd in forms and visages of duty,
Keep yet their hearts attending on themselves,
And, throwing but shows of service on their
[lords,
Do well thrive by them and when they have 65
[lined their coats
Do themselves homage: these fellows have
[some soul;
And such a one do I profess myself. For, sir,

this Desdemona's elopement
'Sblood by God's blood
Off-capp'd stood with cap in hand (like suppliants)
bombast circumstance high-sounding circumlocution. Bombast is cotton padding
epithets of war military terms
Nonsuits rejects
arithmetician one whose knowledge of military tactics is derived only from books
almost . . . wife unexplained; perhaps merely an expression of Iago's cynicism about women. Cf. II.i.130 ff.
division disposition of troops
theoric theory
togèd wearing the toga, the gown of a civilian officer
consuls here = senators
propose speak

be-lee'd placed in the lee of, i.e., where the wind is kept from his sails
counter-caster bookkeeper
in good time forsooth
ancient ensign, standard bearer
letter i.e., of recommendation
affection personal regard, i.e., favoritism
old gradation the established system of promotion, i.e., seniority
term respect
affined bound
content you don't worry

It is as sure as you are Roderigo,
Were I the Moor, I would not be Iago:
In following him, I follow but myself;
Heaven is my judge, not I for love and duty,
5 But seeming so, for my peculiar° end:
For when my outward action doth demonstrate
The native° act and figure of my heart
In compliment extern,° 'tis not long after
But I will wear my heart upon my sleeve
10 For daws to peck at: I am not what I am.
　Rod. What a full fortune does the thicklips
　　　　　　　　　　　　　　　[owe,°
If he can carry 't thus!
　Iago.　　　　　　　　　Call up her father
15 Rouse him: make after him, poison his delight,
Proclaim him in the streets; incense her
　　　　　　　　　　　　　　　[kinsmen,
And, though he in a fertile climate dwell,
Plague him with flies; though that his joy be
20 　　　　　　　　　　　　　　[joy,
Yet throw such changes of vexation on 't,
As it may lose some colour.
　Rod. Here is her father's house; I'll call aloud.
　Iago. Do, with like timorous° accent and dire
25 　　　　　　　　　　　　　　[yell
As when, by night and negligence,° the fire
Is spied in populous cities.
　Rod. What, ho, Brabantio! Signior
　　　　　　　　　　　　[Brabantio, ho!
30 　Iago. Awake! what, ho, Brabantio! thieves!
　　　　　　　　　　　　　[thieves! thieves!
Look to your house, your daughter and your
　　　　　　　　　　　　　　　[bags!°
Thieves! thieves!
35 [Brabantio *appears above, at a window.*]
　Bra. What is the reason of this terrible
　　　　　　　　　　　　　　[summons?
What is the matter there?
　Rod. Signior, is all your family within?
40 　Iago. Are your doors lock'd?
　Bra. Why, wherefore ask you this?

peculiar personal
native genuine
compliment extern external form
owe own
timorous terrifying
by . . . negligence "at" night and "through" negligence
bags money bags

　Iago. 'Zounds, sir, you're robb'd; for
　　　　　　　　[shame, put on your gown;
Your heart is burst, you have lost half your soul;
Even now, now, very now, an old black ram　45
Is tupping your white ewe. Arise, arise;
Awake the snorting° citizens with the bell,
Or else the devil will make a grandsire of you:
Arise, I say.
　Bra. What, have you lost your wits?　50
　Rod. Most reverend signior, do you know my
　　　　　　　　　　　　　　[voice?
　Bra. Not I: what are you?
　Rod. My name is Roderigo.
　Bra.　　　　　　　The worser welcome:　55
I have charged thee not to haunt about my
　　　　　　　　　　　　　　[doors:
In honest plainness thou hast heard me say
My daughter is not for thee; and now, in
　　　　　　　　　　　　[madness,　60
Being full of supper and distempering°
　　　　　　　　　　　　[draughts,
Upon malicious bravery,° dost thou come
To start° my quiet.
　Rod. Sir, sir, sir,—　65
　Bra.　　　　But thou must needs be sure
My spirits and my place have in them power
To make this bitter to thee.
　Rod.　　　　　　　Patience, good sir.
　Bra. What tell'st thou me of robbing? this is　70
　　　　　　　　　　　　[Venice;
My house is not a grange.°
　Rod.　　　　　　Most grave Brabantio,
In simple and pure soul I come to you.
　Iago. 'Zounds, sir, you are one of those that will　75
not serve God, if the devil bid you. Because we
come to do you service and you think we are ruf-
fians, you'll have your daughter covered with a
Barbary horse; you'll have your nephews° neigh
to you; you'll have coursers for cousins and gen-　80
nets° for germans.°

snorting snoring
distempering intoxicating
bravery bravado
start disturb
grange lonely farmhouse
nephews grandsons
gennets Moorish horses
germans relatives

BRA. What profane wretch art thou?

IAGO. I am one, sir, that comes to tell you your daughter and the Moor are now making the beast with two backs.

5 BRA. Thou art a villain.

IAGO.   You are—a senator.

BRA. This thou shalt answer; I know thee,
                              [Roderigo.

ROD. Sir, I will answer any thing. But, I
10   [beseech you,
If't be your pleasure and most wise consent,
As partly I find it is, that your fair daughter,
At this odd-even° and dull watch o' the night,
Transported, with no worse nor better guard
15 But with a knave of common hire, a gondolier,
To the gross clasps of a lascivious Moor—
If this be known to you and your allowance,
We then have done you bold and saucy wrongs;
But if you know not this, my manners tell me
20 We have your wrong rebuke. Do not believe
That, from° the sense of all civility,
I thus would play and trifle with your
                              [reverence:
Your daughter, if you have not given her leave,
25 I say again, hath made a gross revolt;
Tying her duty, beauty, wit and fortunes
In an extravagant° and wheeling° stranger
Of here and every where. Straight° satisfy
                              [yourself:
30 If she be in her chamber or your house,
Let loose on me the justice of the state
For thus deluding you.

BRA.   Strike on the tinder, ho!
Give me a taper! call up all my people!
35 This accident° is not unlike my dream:
Belief of it oppresses me already.
Light, I say! light!   [Exit above.]

IAGO. Farewell; for I must leave you:
It seems not meet, nor wholesome to my place,
40 To be produced°—as, if I stay, I shall—

Against the Moor: for, I do know, the state,
However this may gall him with some check,°
Cannot with safety cast° him, for he's embark'd
With such loud° reason to the Cyprus wars,
Which even now stand in act,° that, for their   45
                              [souls,
Another of his fathom° they have none,
To lead their business: in which regard,
Though I do hate him as I do hell-pains,
Yet, for necessity of present life,   50
I must show out a flag and sign of love,
Which is indeed but sign. That you shall surely
                              [find him,
Lead to the Sagittary° the raisèd search;
And there will I be with him. So, farewell.   55
                              [Exit.]
[Enter, below, BRABANTIO, and SERVANTS with
torches.]

BRA. It is too true an evil: gone she is;
And what's to come of my despisèd time°   60
Is nought but bitterness. Now, Roderigo,
Where didst thou see her? O unhappy girl!
With the Moor, say'st thou? Who would be a
                              [father!
How didst thou know 'twas she? O, she   65
                              [deceives me
Past thought! What said she to you? Get more
                              [tapers:
Raise all my kindred. Are they married, think
                              [you? 70
ROD. Truly, I think they are.

BRA. O heaven! How got she out? O treason
                              [of the blood!
Fathers, from hence trust not your daughters'
                              [minds 75
By what you see them act. Is there not charms
By which the property° of youth and maidhood
May be abused? Have you not read, Roderigo,
Of some such thing?

ROD.   Yes, sir, I have indeed. 80

---

odd-even about midnight
from contrary to
extravagant vagabond
wheeling wandering
Straight straightway
accident event
produced i.e., as a witness

check rebuke
cast dismiss
loud impressive, emphatic
stand in act are going on
fathom capacity
the Sagittary probably an inn
time remaining life
property nature

BRA. Call up my brother. O, would you had
[had her!
Some one way, some another. Do you know
Where we may apprehend her and the Moor?
5   ROD. I think I can discover him, if you please
To get good guard and go along with me.
    BRA. Pray you, lead on. At every house I'll
[call;
I may command at most. Get weapons, ho!
10 And raise some special officers of night.°
Oh, good Roderigo: I'll deserve your pains.
                          [*Exeunt.*]

Scene ii

[*Enter* OTHELLO, IAGO, *and* ATTENDANTS *with torches.*]

15   IAGO. Though in the trade of war I have slain
[men,
Yet do I hold it very stuff o' the conscience
To do no contrived° murder: I lack iniquity
Sometimes to do me service: nine or ten times
20 I had thought to have yerk'd° him here under
[the ribs.
    OTH. 'Tis better as it is.
    IAGO.   Nay, but he prated,
And spoke such scurvy and provoking terms
25 Against your honour
That, with the little godliness I have,
I did full hard forbear° him. But, I pray you, sir,
Are you fast married? Be assured of this,
That the magnifico° is much beloved,
30 And hath in his effect° a voice potential°
As double° as the duke's: he will divorce you;
Or put upon you what restraint and grievances°
The law, with all his might to enforce it on,
Will give him cable.°
35   OTH.   Let him do his spite;
My services which I have done the signiory°

Shall out-tongue his complaints. 'Tis yet to
[know—
Which, when I know that boasting is an honour,
I shall promulgate—I fetch my life and being 40
From men of royal siege,° and my demerits°
May speak unbonneted° to as proud a fortune
As this that I have reach'd: for know, Iago,
But that I love the gentle Desdemona,
I would not my unhousèd° free condition 45
Put into circumscription° and confine
For the sea's worth.° But, look! what lights
[come yond?
    IAGO. Those are the raisèd father and his
[friends: 50
You were best go in.
    OTH.   Not I; I must be found:
My parts,° my title° and my perfect soul°
Shall manifest me rightly. Is it they?
    IAGO. By Janus, I think no. 55
[*Enter* CASSIO, *and certain* OFFICERS *with torches.*]
    OTH. The servants of the duke, and my
[lieutenant.
The goodness of the night upon you, friends!
What is the news? 60
    CAS. The duke does greet you, general,
And he requires your haste-post-haste
[appearance,
Even on the instant,
    OTH.   What is the matter, think you? 65
    CAS. Something from Cyprus, as I may divine:
It is a business of some heat: the galleys
Have sent a dozen sequent° messengers
This very night at one another's heels,
And many of the consuls, raised and met, 70
Are at the duke's already: you have been
[hotly call'd for;
When, being not at your lodging to be found,
The senate hath sent about three several quests

---

officers of night the night watch
contrived deliberate
yerk'd stabbed
full . . . forbear with great difficulty spared
magnifico Venetian senator
effect influence
potential powerful
As double as effective
grievance punishment
cable scope
signiory Venetian senate

siege rank
demerits deserts
unbonneted with hat off, i.e., courteously
unhousèd undomesticated
circumscription restraint
sea's worth treasures buried in the sea
parts abilities
title reputation
perfect soul unsmirched honor
sequent successive

To search you out.

OTH.   'Tis well I am found by you.
I will but spend a word here in the house,
And go with you.   [*Exit.*]
5   CAS.   Ancient, what makes° he here?
IAGO. 'Faith, he to-night hath boarded a land
                    [carack:°
If it prove lawful prize, he's made for ever.
CAS. I do not understand.
10   IAGO.   He's married.
CAS.   To who?
[*Re-enter* OTHELLO.]
IAGO. Marry, to—Come, captain, will you go?
OTH.   Have with you.
15   CAS. Here comes another troop to seek for
                    [you.
IAGO. It is Brabantio. General, be advised;
He comes to bad intent.
[*Enter* BRABANTIO, RODERIGO, *and* OFFICERS *with*
20 *torches and weapons.*]
OTH.   Holla! stand there!
ROD. Signior, it is the Moor.
BRA.   Down with him, thief!
[*They draw on both sides.*]
25   IAGO. You, Roderigo! come, sir, I am for you.
OTH. Keep up your bright swords, for the
                    [dew will rust them.
Good signior, you shall more command with
                    [years
30   Than with your weapons.
BRA. O thou foul thief, where hast thou
                    [stow'd my daughter?
Damn'd as thou art, thou hast enchanted her;
For I'll refer me to all things of sense°,
35   If she in chains of magic were not bound,
Whether a maid so tender, fair, and happy,
So opposite to marriage that she shunn'd
The wealthy curlèd darlings of our nation,
Would ever have, to incur a general mock,°
40   Run from her guardage to the sooty bosom
Of such a thing as thou, to fear,° not to delight.
Judge me the world, if 'tis not gross in sense°

That thou hast practised on° her with foul
                    [charms,
Abused her delicate youth with drugs or   45
                    [minerals
That weaken motion:° I'll have't disputed on;°
'Tis probable and palpable to thinking.
I therefore apprehend and do attach° thee
For an abuser of the world, a practiser   50
Of arts inhibited° and out of warrant.°
Lay hold upon him: if he do resist,
Subdue him at his peril.
OTH.   Hold your hands,
Both you of my inclining°, and the rest: 55
Were it my cue to fight, I should have known it
Without a prompter. Where will you that I go
To answer this your charge?
BRA.   To prison, till fit time
Of law and course of direct session°   60
Call thee to answer.
OTH.   What if I do obey?
How may the duke be therewith satisfied,
Whose messengers are here about my side,
Upon some present business of the state   65
To bring me to him?
FIRST OFF. 'Tis true, most worthy signior;
The duke's in council, and your noble self,
I am sure, is sent for.
BRA.   How! the duke in council!   70
In this time of the night! Bring him away:
Mine's not an idle cause; the duke himself,
Or any of my brothers of the state,
Cannot but feel this wrong as 'twere their own;
For if such action may have passage free,   75
Bond-slaves and pagans shall our statesmen be.
                    [*Exeunt.*]

Scene iii

[*The* DUKE *and* SENATORS *sitting at a table;*
OFFICERS *attending.*]

---

makes does
carack large merchantman
refer me . . . sense appeal to common sense
mock derision
fear frighten
gross in sense obvious

practised on plotted against
motion the mental faculties
disputed on debated (in court)
attach arrest
inhibited prohibited
out of warrant forbidden
inclining following
course . . . session normal process of law (Ridley)

DUKE. There is no composition° in these news
That gives them credit.°
FIRST SEN. Indeed, they are disproportion'd;
My letters say a hundred and seven galleys.
5 DUKE. And mine, a hundred and forty.
SEC. SEN. And mine, two hundred:
But though they jump° not on a just° account—
As in these cases, where the aim reports,°
'Tis oft with difference—yet do they all confirm
10 A Turkish fleet, and bearing up to Cyprus.
DUKE. Nay, it is possible enough to
                                   [judgement:
I do not so secure me in the error,
But the main article I do approve
15 In fearful sense.°
SAILOR [*Within*]. What, ho! what, ho! what, ho!
FIRST OFF. A messenger from the galleys.
[*Enter a* SAILOR.]
DUKE.   Now, what's the business!
20 SAIL. The Turkish preparation makes for
                                   [Rhodes;
So was I bid report here to the state
By Signior Angelo.   [*Exit Sailor*]
DUKE. How say you by° this change?
25 FIRST SEN.   This cannot be,
By no assay of reason:° 'tis a pageant,°
To keep us in false gaze.° When we consider
The importance of Cyprus to the Turk,
And let ourselves again but understand,
30 That as it more concerns the Turk than Rhodes,
So may he with more facile question bear it,°
For that it stands not in such warlike brace,°
But altogether lacks the abilities
That Rhodes is dress'd in: if we make thought
35   [of this,

We must not think the Turk is so unskilful
To leave that latest which concerns him first,
Neglecting an attempt of ease and gain,
To wake and wage° a danger profitless.
DUKE. Nay, in all confidence, he's not for   40
                                   [Rhodes.
FIRST OFF. Here is more news.
[*Enter a* MESSENGER.]
MESS. The Ottomites,° reverend and gracious,
Steering with due course towards the isle of   45
                                   [Rhodes,
Have there injointed them with an after° fleet.
FIRST SEN. Ay, so I thought. How many, as
                                   [you guess?
MESS. Of thirty sail: and now they do restem   50
Their backward course, bearing with frank
                                   [appearance°
Their purposes toward Cyprus. Signior
                                   [Montano,
Your trusty and most valiant servitor,   55
With his free duty° recommends° you thus
And prays you to believe him
                                   [*Exit* MESSENGER.]
DUKE. 'Tis certain, then, for Cyprus.
Marcus Luccicos, is not he in town?   60
FIRST SEN. He's now in Florence.
DUKE. Write from us to him; post-post-haste.
                                   [Dispatch.
FIRST SEN. Here comes Brabantio and the
                                   [valiant Moor. 65
[*Enter* BRABANTIO, OTHELLO, CASSIO, IAGO, RODER-
IGO, *and* OFFICERS.]
DUKE. Valiant Othello, we must straight
                                   [employ you
Against the general° enemy Ottoman.   70
[*To* BRABANTIO] I did not see you; welcome,
                                   [gentle signior;
We lack'd your counsel and your help tonight.
BRA. So did I yours. Good your grace, pardon
                                   [me; 75
Neither my place not aught I heard of business

composition consistency
gives . . . credit makes them credible
jump agree
just exact
aim reports report is founded on conjecture
I do not . . . sense I do not feel myself so secure because
   of the discrepancy (in these accounts) as not to believe the
   essential and alarming fact
by to
no . . . reason by any reasonable test
pageant show, pretense
in . . . gaze looking the wrong way
more. . . bear it more easily take it by force of arms
brace readiness

wage hazard
Ottomites Turks
after following
with . . . appearance openly
free duty willing deference
recommends advises, informs
general universal

Hath raised me from my bed, nor doth the
                [general care
Take hold on me, for my particular grief
Is of so flood-gate and o'erbearing nature
5 That it engluts and swallows other sorrows
And it is still itself.
     DUKE.   Why, what's the matter?
     BRA. My daughter! O, my daughter!
     DUKE AND SEN.   Dead?
10 BRA.   Ay, to me;
She is abused°, stol'n from me, and corrupted
By spells and medicines bought of mountebanks;
For nature so preposterously to err,
Being not deficient, blind, or lame of sense,
15 Sans° witchcraft could not.
     DUKE. Whoe'er he be that in this foul
                  [proceeding
Hath thus beguiled your daughter of herself
And you of her, the bloody book of law
20 You shall yourself read in the bitter letter
After your own sense, yea, though our proper°
                    [son
Stood in your action.°
     BRA.   Humbly I thank your grace.
25 Here is the man, this Moor, whom now, it
                 [seems,
Your special mandate for the state-affairs
Hath hither brought.
     DUKE AND SEN. We are very sorry for 't.
30 DUKE [*To* OTHELLO] What, in your own part,
                [can you say to this?
     BRA. Nothing, but this is so.
     OTH. Most potent, grave, and reverend
                [signiors,
35 My very noble and approved° good masters,
That I have ta'en away this old man's daughter,
It is most true; true, I have married her:
The very head and front° of my offending
Hath this extent, no more. Rude am I in my
40   [speech,
And little bless'd with the soft phrase of peace;

For since these arms of mine had seven years'
                [pith,°
Till now some nine moons wasted, they have
                [used 45
Their dearest° action in the tented field,
And little of this great world can I speak,
More than pertains to feats of broil and battle,
And therefore little shall I grace my cause
In speaking for myself. Yet, by your gracious 50
                [patience,
I will a round° unvarnish'd tale deliver
Of my whole course of love; what drugs, what
                [charms,
What conjuration and what mighty magic, 55
For such proceeding I am charged withal,
I won his daughter.
     BRA.   A maiden never bold;
Of spirit so still and quiet, that her motion
Blush'd at herself;° and she, in spite of nature, 60
Of years, of country, credit,° every thing,
To fall in love with what she fear'd to look on!
It is a judgement maim'd and most imperfect
That will confess perfection so could err
Against all rules of nature, and must be driven 65
To find out practices° of cunning hell,
Why this should be. I therefore vouch again
That with some mixtures powerful o'er the
                [blood,°
Or with some dram conjured to this effect, 70
He wrought upon her.
     DUKE.   To vouch this, is no proof,
Without more wider and more overt test
Than these thin habits° and poor likelihoods
Of modern seeming° do prefer against him. 75
     FIRST SEN. But, Othello, speak:
Did you by indirect and forced courses
Subdue and poison this young maid's affections?
Or came it by request and such fair question°

abused deceived
Sans without
proper own
stood . . . action were the subject of your accusations
approved proven
front forehead

pith strength
dearest most important
round plain
her motion . . . herself her emotions made her blush
credit i.e., her good name
practices stratagems
blood passion
thin habits superficial appearances
modern seeming slight suspicion
question conversation

As soul to soul affordeth?
OTH.   I do beseech you,
Send for the lady to the Sagittary,
And let her speak of me before her father:
5   If you do find me foul in her report,
The trust, the office I do hold of you,
Not only take away, but let your sentence
Even fall upon my life.
DUKE   Fetch Desdemona hither.
10 OTH. Ancient, conduct them; you best know
                                    [the place.
[*Exeunt* IAGO *and* ATTENDANTS.]
And, till she come, as truly as to heaven
I do confess the vices of my blood,
15 So justly to your grave ears I'll present
How I did thrive in this fair lady's love,
And she in mine.
DUKE. Say it, Othello.
OTH. Her father loved me; oft invited me;
20 Still° question'd me the story of my life,
From year to year, the battles, sieges, fortunes,
That I have pass'd.
I ran it through, even from my boyish days,
To the very moment that he bade me tell it;
25 Wherein I spake of most disastrous chances,°
Of moving accidents by flood and field,
Of hair-breadth scapes i' the imminent° deadly
                                    [breach,
Of being taken by the insolent foe
30 And sold to slavery, of my redemption thence
And portance° in my travels' history:
Wherein of antres° vast and deserts idle,°
Rough quarries, rocks and hills whose heads
                                    [touch heaven,
35 It was my hint to speak—such was my process:
And of the Cannibals that each other eat,
The Anthropophagi° and men whose heads
Do grow beneath their shoulders. This to hear
Would Desdemona seriously incline:
40 But still the house-affairs would draw her
                                    [thence:

Still continually
chances accidents
imminent threatening
portance behavior
antres caves
idle barren
Anthropophagi man-eaters

Which ever as she could with haste dispatch,
She'ld come again, and with a greedy ear
Devour up my discourse: which I observing,
Took once a pliant hour, and found good means   45
To draw from her a prayer of earnest heart
That I would all my pilgrimage dilate,°
Whereof by parcels she had something heard,
But not intentively:° I did consent,
And often did beguile her of her tears,   50
When I did speak of some distressful stroke
That my youth suffer'd. My story being done,
She gave me for my pains a world of sighs:
She swore, in faith, 'twas strange, 'twas passing°
                                    [strange, 55
'Twas pitiful, 'twas wondrous pitiful:
She wish'd she had not heard it, yet she wish'd
That heaven had made her such a man: she
                                    [thank'd me,
And bade me, if I had a friend that loved her,   60
I should but teach him how to tell my story,
And that would woo her. Upon this hint I
                                    [spake:
She loved me for the dangers I had pass'd,
And I loved her that she did pity them.   65
This only is the witchcraft I have used:
Here comes the lady, let her witness it.
[*Enter* DESDEMONA, IAGO, *and* ATTENDANTS.]
DUKE. I think this tale would win my
                                    [daughter too. 70
Good Brabantio,
Take up this mangled matter at the best:°
Men do their broken weapons rather use
Than their bare hands.
BRA. I pray you, hear her speak: 75
If she confess that she was half the wooer,
Destruction on my head, if my bad blame
Light on the man! Come hither, gentle mistress:
Do you perceive in all this noble company
Where most you owe obedience?   80
DES.   My noble father,
I do perceive here a divided duty:
To you I am bound for life and education;
My life and education both do learn° me

dilate tell in detail
intentively attentively
passing exceedingly
Take up ... best make the best of
learn teach

How to respect you; you are the lord of duty;°
I am hitherto your daughter: but here's my
[husband,
And so much duty as my mother show'd
5 To you, preferring you before her father,
So much I challenge° that I may profess
Due to the Moor my lord.
     BRA.   God be wi' you! I have done.
Please it your grace, on to the state-affairs:
10 I had rather to adopt a child than get° it.
Come hither, Moor:
I here do give thee that with all my heart
Which, but thou hast already, with all my heart
I would keep from thee. For your sake,° jewel,
15 I am glad at soul I have no other child;
For thy escape would teach me tyranny,
To hang clogs on them. I have done, my lord.
     DUKE. Let me speak like yourself,° and lay a
[sentence,
20 Which, as a grise° or step, may help these lovers
Into your favour.
When remedies are past, the griefs are ended
By seeing the worst, which° late on hopes
[depended.
25 To mourn a mischief that is past and gone
Is the next° way to draw new mischief on.
What cannot be preserved when fortune takes,
Patience her injury a mockery makes.
The robb'd that smiles steals something from
30   [the thief;
He robs himself that spends a bootless grief.
     BRA. So let the Turk of Cyprus us beguile;
We lose it not, so long as we can smile.
He bears the sentence well that nothing bears
35 But the free comfort which from thence he
[hears,
But he bears both the sentence and the sorrow
That, to pay grief, must of poor patience
[borrow.
40 These sentences, to sugar, or to gall,

lord of duty man to whom I owe duty
challenge claim
get beget
For your sake because of you
like yourself i.e., as you ought
grise a step (in a flight of steps)
which i.e., the griefs
next nearest, surest

Being strong on both sides, are equivocal:
But words are words; I never yet did hear
That the bruised heart was piercèd° through the
[ear.
I humbly beseech you, proceed to the affairs   45
[of state.
     DUKE. The Turk with a most mighty preparation
makes for Cyprus. Othello, the fortitude° of the
place is best known to you; and though we have
there a substitute of most allowed° sufficiency, yet 50
opinion,° a sovereign mistress of effects, throws a
more safer voice on you: you must therefore be
content to slubber° the gloss of your new fortunes
with this more stubborn and boisterous expedi-
tion.   55
     OTH. The tyrant custom, most grave senators.
Hath made the flinty and steel couch of war
My thrice-driven° bed of down: I do agnize°
A natural and prompt alacrity
I find in hardness,° and do undertake   60
These present wars against the Ottomites.
Most humbly therefore bending to your state,°
I crave fit disposition for my wife,
Due reference of place and exhibition,°
With such accommodation and besort°   65
As levels with° her breeding.
     DUKE.   If you please,
Be 't at her father's.
     BRA.   I'll not have it so.
     OTH. Nor I.   70
     DUKE.   Nor I; I would not there reside,
To put my father in impatient thoughts
By being in his eye. Most gracious duke,
To my unfolding° lend your prosperous° ear;
And let me find a charter° in your voice,   75

pierced i.e., reached or healed
fortitude strength
allowed acknowledged
opinion i.e., public opinion
slubber soil
driven winnowed
agnize acknowledge
hardness hardship
state authority
exhibition allowance
besort retinue
levels with suits
unfolding i.e., what I am going to reveal
prosperous favorable
charter guaranty

To assist my simpleness.
    DUKE. What would you. Desdemona?
    DES. That I did love the Moor to live with him,
My downright violence and storm of fortunes°
5 May trumpet to the world: my heart's subdued
Even to the very quality° of my lord:
I saw Othello's visage in his mind,
And to his honours and his valiant parts
Did I my soul and fortunes consecrate.
10 So that, dear lords, if I be left behind,
A moth of peace, and he go to the war,
The rites for which I love him are bereft me,
And I a heavy interim shall support
By his dear absence. Let me go with him.
15   OTH. Let her have your voices.
Vouch with me, heaven, I therefore beg it not,
To please the palate of my appetite,
Nor to comply with heat°—the young affects°
In me defunct—and proper satisfaction.°
20 But to be free and bounteous to her mind:°
And heaven defend° your good souls, that you
                          [think
I will your serious and great business scant
For she is with me: no, when light-wing'd toys
25 Of feather'd Cupid seel° with wanton dullness
My speculative and officed instruments,°
That° my disports° corrupt and taint my
                          [business,
Let housewives make a skillet of my helm,
30 And all indign° and base adversities
Make head° against my estimation!°
    DUKE. Be it as you shall privately determine,
Either for her stay or going: the affair cries
    haste,

And speed must answer it.   35
  FIRST SEN. You must away to-night.
  DES. To-night, my lord?
  DUKE.   This night.
  OTH.   With all my heart.
  DUKE. At nine i' the morning here we'll meet   40
                        [again.
Othello, leave some officer behind,
And he shall our commission bring to you;
With such things else of quality and respect°
As doth import° you.   45
    OTH.   So please your grace, my ancient;
A man he is of honesty and trust:
To his conveyance I assign my wife,
With what else needful your good grace shall
                        [think 50
To be sent after me.
    DUKE.   Let it be so.
Good night to every one. [*To* BRAB.] And, noble
                        [signior,
If virtue no delighted° beauty lack,   55
Your son-in-law is far more fair than black,
  FIRST SEN. Adieu, brave Moor; use
                  [Desdemona well.
  BRA. Look to her, Moor, if thou hast eyes to
                    [see: 60
She has deceived her father, and may thee.
    [*Exeunt* DUKE, SENATORS, OFFICERS.]
  OTH. My life upon her faith! Honest Iago,
My Desdemona must I leave to thee:
I prithee, let thy wife attend on her;   65
And bring them after in the best advantage.°
Come, Desdemona; I have but an hour
Of love, of worldly matters and direction,
To spend with thee: we must obey the time.
    [*Exeunt* OTHELLO *and* DESDEMONA.] 70
  ROD. Iago—
  IAGO. What say'st thou, noble heart?
  ROD. What will I do, thinkest thou?
  IAGO. Why, go to bed, and sleep.
  ROD. I will incontinently° drown myself.   75
  IAGO. If thou dost, I shall never love thee after.
Why, thou silly gentleman!

My ... fortunes the unrestrained impetuosity of taking my
    fortunes by storm
quality nature, profession
heat passion
young affects youthful desires
proper satisfaction i.e., consummation of the marriage
mind i.e., her wish to accompany him
defend forbid
seel sew up
speculative ... instruments visual and active powers
That so that
disports pastimes
indign unworthy
make head raise an armed force
estimation reputation

of quality and respect pertaining to your honored rank
import concern
delighted delightful
in ... advantage at the most favorable opportunity
incontinently immediately

Rod. It is silliness to live when to live is torment; and then have we a prescription to die when death is our physician.

Iago. O villanous! I have looked upon the world
5 for four times seven years; and since I could distinguish betwixt a benefit and an injury, I never found man that knew how to love himself. Ere I would say, I would drown myself for the love of a guinea-hen, I would change my humanity with
10 a baboon.

Rod. What should I do? I confess it is my shame to be so fond; but it is not in my virtue° to amend it.

Iago. Virtue! a fig! 'tis in ourselves that we are
15 thus or thus. Our bodies are our gardens, to the which our wills are gardeners; so that if we will plant nettles, or sow lettuce, set hyssop and weed up thyme, supply it with one gender° of herbs, or distract° it with many, either to have it sterile with
20 idleness or manured with industry, why, the power and corrigible° authority of this lies in our wills. If the balance of our lives had not one scale of reason to poise° another of sensuality, the blood and baseness° of our natures would conduct us to most
25 preposterous conclusions:° but we have reason to cool our raging motions,° our carnal stings, our unbitted° lusts, whereof I take this that you call love to be a sect° or scion.°

Rod. It cannot be.

30 Iago. It is merely a lust of the blood and a permission of the will. Come, be a man. Drown thyself! drown cats and blind puppies. I have professed me thy friend, and I confess me knit to thy deserving with cables of perdurable toughness; I
35 could never better stead° thee than now. Put money in thy purse; follow thou the wars; defeat thy fa-

vor° with an usurped° beard; I say, put money in thy purse. It cannot be that Desdemona should long continue her love to the Moor—put money in thy purse—nor he his to her; it was a violent 40 commencement, and thou shalt see an answerable sequestration°—put but money in thy purse. These Moors are changeable in their wills—fill thy purse with money. The food that to him now is as luscious as locusts,° shall be to him shortly as bitter 45 as coloquintida.° She must change for youth, when she is sated with his body, she will find the error of her choice: she must have change, she must; therefore put money in thy purse. If thou wilt needs damn thyself, do it a more delicate way than 50 drowning. Make all the money thou canst: if sanctimony° and a frail vow betwixt an erring° barbarian and a super-subtle Venetian be not too hard for my wits and all the tribe of hell, thou shalt enjoy her; therefore make money. A pox of 55 drowning thyself! it is clean out of the way; seek thou rather to be hanged in compassing° thy joy than to be drowned and go without her.

Rod. Wilt thou be fast to my hopes, if I depend on the issue? 60

Iago. Thou art sure of me—go, make money— I have told thee often, and I re-tell thee again and again, I hate the Moor: my cause is hearted;° thine hath no less reason. Let us be conjunctive° in our revenge against him; if thou canst cuckold him, 65 thou dost thyself a pleasure, me a sport. There are many events in the womb of time which will be delivered. Traverse!° go, provide thy money. We will have more of this to-morrow. Adieu.

Rod. Where shall we meet i' the morning? 70

Iago. At my lodging.

Rod. I'll be with thee betimes.°

---

virtue manhood
gender kind
distract vary
corrigible corrective
poise counterbalance
blood and baseness base passions
conclusions results
motions sexual appetites
unbitted unbridled
sect cutting
scion shoot
stead help

defeat . . . favor disguise your face
usurped assumed
answerable sequestration corresponding rupture
locusts fruit of the carob tree, an evergreen tree of the Mediterranean region
coloquintida colocynth or bitter apple
sanctimony holy bond
erring vagabond
compassing obtaining
hearted fixed in my heart
conjunctive united
Traverse a military term, "Forward march."
betimes soon

IAGO. Go to, farewell. Do you hear, Roderigo?
ROD. What say you?
IAGO. No more of drowning, do you hear?
ROD. I am changed; I'll go sell all my land.

5   [*Exit.*]

IAGO. Thus do I ever make my fool my purse;
For I mine own gain'd knowledge should
                                        [profane,
If I would time expend with such a snipe°

10   But for my sport and profit. I hate the Moor;
And it is thought abroad, that 'twixt my sheets
He has done my office: I know not if 't be true;
But I, for mere suspicion in that kind,
Will do as if for surety.° He holds me well;

15   The better shall my purpose work on him.
Cassio's a proper° man: let me see now:
To get his place and to plume up° my will
In double knavery—How, how?—Let's see—
After some time, to abuse Othello's ear

20   That he is too familiar with his wife.
He hath a person and a smooth dispose°
To be suspected, framed to make women false.
The Moor is of a free° and open nature,
That thinks men honest that but seem to be so,

25   And will as tenderly be led by the nose
As asses are.
I have 't. It is engender'd. Hell and night
Must bring this monstrous birth to the world's
light.   [*Exit.*]

ACT II

Scene i

30   *Enter* MONTANO *and two* GENTLEMEN.]
MON. What from the cape can you discern
                                        [at sea?
FIRST GENT. Nothing at all: it is a high-
                                        [wrought flood;

35   I cannot, 'twixt the heaven and the main,
Descry a sail.
MON. Methinks the wind hath spoke aloud
                                        [at land;

A fuller blast ne'er shook our battlements:
If it hath ruffian'd so upon the sea,   40
What ribs of oak, when mountains melt on
                                        [them,
Can hold the mortise?° What shall we hear of
                                        [this?
        SEC. GENT. A segregation° of the Turkish fleet: 45
For do but stand upon the foaming shore,
The chidden billow seems to pelt the clouds;
The wind-shaked surge, with high and
                                        [monstrous mane,
Seems to cast water on the burning bear,°   50
And quench the guards° of the ever-fixèd pole:
I never did like molestation view
On the enchafèd flood.
        MON.   If that the Turkish fleet
Be not enshelter'd and embay'd, they are   55
                                        [drown'd;
It is impossible they bear it out.
        [*Enter a third* GENTLEMAN.]
        THIRD GENT. News, lads! our wars are done.
The desperate tempest hath so bang'd the Turks, 60
That their designment° halts:° a noble ship of
                                        [Venice
Hath seen a grievous wreck and sufferance°
On most part of their fleet.
        MON. How! is this true?   65
        THIRD GENT.   The ship is here put in,
A Veronesa;° Michael Cassio,
Lieutenant to the warlike Moor Othello,
Is come on shore: the Moor himself at sea,
And is in full commission here for Cyprus.   70
        MON. I am glad on 't; 'tis a worthy governor.
        THIRD GENT. But this same Cassio, though he
                                        [speaks of comfort
Touching the Turkish loss, yet he looks sadly,
And prays the Moor be safe; for they were   75
                                        [parted

---

snipe a proverbially silly bird
for surety upon a certainty
proper handsome
plume up i.e., put a feather in the cap of, glorify
dispose manner
free i.e., from guile

hold the mortise remain jointed
segregation dispersion
burning bear constellation of Ursa Minor or the Little Dipper
guards two stars in the Little Dipper pointing to the pole or
    North Star
designment enterprise
halts limps
sufferance disaster
Veronesa a ship fitted out by Verona, then subject to Venice

With foul and violent tempest.
   MON.   Pray heavens he be;
For I have served him, and the man commands
Like a full soldier. Let's to the seaside, ho!
5 As well to see the vessel that's come in
As to throw out our eyes for brave Othello,
Even till we make the main and the aerial blue
An indistinct regard.°
   THIRD GENT.   Come, let's do so;
10 For every minute is expectancy
Of more arrivance.
     [*Enter* CASSIO.]
   CAS. Thanks, you the valiant of this warlike
                                [isle,
15 That so approve the Moor! O, let the heavens
Give him defence against the elements,
For I have lost him on a dangerous sea.
   MON. Is he well shipp'd?
   CAS. His bark is stoutly timber'd, and his pilot
20 Of very expert and approved allowance;°
Therefore my hopes, not surfeited to death,
Stand in bold cure.°
     [*A cry within:* "A sail, a sail, a sail!"]
     [*Enter a fourth* GENTLEMAN.]
25 CAS. What noise?
   FOURTH GENT. The town is empty; on the brow
                               [o' the sea
Stand ranks of people, and they cry "A sail!"
   CAS. My hopes do shape him for the
30   governor.   [*Guns heard.*]
   SEC. GENT. They do discharge their shot of
                             [courtesy:
Our friends at least.
   CAS.   I pray you, sir, go forth,
35 And give us truth who 'tis that is arrived.
   SEC. GENT. I shall.   [*Exit.*]
   MON. But, good lieutenant, is your general
                           [wived?
   CAS. Most fortunately: he hath achieved a
40   [maid
That paragons° description and wild fame;°

One that excels the quirks° of blazoning° pens,
And in the essential vesture of creation°
Does tire the ingener.°
     [*Re-enter second* GENTLEMAN.]   45
                   How now! who has put in?
   SEC. GENT. 'Tis one Iago, ancient to the
                           [general.
   CAS. Has had most favourable and happy
                            [speed: 50
Tempests themselves, high seas and howling
                            [winds,
The gutter'd° rocks and congregated sands—
Traitors ensteep'd° to clog the guiltless keel—
As having sense of beauty, do omit°   55
Their mortal° natures, letting go safely by
The divine Desdemona.
   MON.   What is she?
   CAS. She that I spake of, our great captain's
                       [captain, 60
Left in the conduct of the bold Iago,
Whose footing° here anticipates our thoughts
A se'nnight's speed. Great Jove, Othello guard,
And swell his sail with thine own powerful
                           [breath, 65
That he may bless this bay with his tall ship,
Make love's quick pants in Desdemona's arms,
Give renew'd fire to our extincted spirits,
And bring all Cyprus comfort!
     [*Enter* DESDEMONA, EMILIA, IAGO, RODERIGO, and 70
ATTENDANTS.]
                       O, behold,
The riches of the ship is come on shore!
Ye men of Cyprus, let her have your knees.
Hail to thee, lady! and the grace of heaven, 75
Before, behind thee, and on every hand,
Enwheel thee round!
   DES.   I thank you, valiant Cassio.
What tidings can you tell me of my lord?
   CAS. He is not yet arrived: nor know I aught 80
But that he's well and will be shortly here.

regard   view, i.e., until the line between the sea and the sky
   becomes indistinct
approved allowance   acknowledged and tested skill
my hopes . . . bold cure   i.e., my hopes are reasonably temperate and so healthily strong (Ridley)
paragons   surpasses
wild fame   unrestrained reports

quirks   extravagant fancies
blazoning   extolling
essential . . . creation   native endowments
ingener   inventor (of eulogies)
gutter'd   jagged
ensteep'd   submerged
omit   throw off
mortal   deadly, destructive
footing   landing

DES. O, but I fear—How lost you company?
CAS. The great contention of the sea and skies
Parted our fellowship—but, hark! a sail.
[*Within: "A sail, a sail!" Guns heard.*]
5   SEC. GENT. They give their greeting to the
[citadel:
This likewise is a friend.
CAS.   See for the news.
[*Exit* GENTLEMAN.]
10 Good ancient, you are welcome. [*To* EMILIA]
Welcome, mistress:
Let it not gall your patience, good Iago,
That I extend° my manners; 'tis my breeding°
That gives me this bold show of courtesy.
15 [*Kissing her.*]
IAGO. Sir, would she give you so much of
[her lips
As of her tongue she oft bestows on me,
You'ld have enough.
20   DES.   Alas, she has no speech.
IAGO. In faith, too much;
I find it still,° when I have list° to sleep:
Marry, before your ladyship, I grant,
She puts her tongue a little in her heart,
25 And chides with thinking.
EMIL. You have little cause to say so.
IAGO. Come on, come on; you are pictures° out
[of doors,
Bells° in your parlours, wild-cats in your
30   [kitchens,
Saints in your injuries,° devils being offended,
Players° in your housewifery, and housewives°
[in your beds.
DES. O, fie upon thee, slanderer!
35 IAGO. Nay, it is true, or else I am a Turk:
You rise to play and go to bed to work.
EMIL. You shall not write my praise.
IAGO.   No, let me not.

DES. What wouldst thou write of me, if thou
[shouldst praise me? 40
IAGO. O gentle lady, do not put me to 't;
For I am nothing, if not critical.
DES. Come on, assay. There's one gone to the
[harbour?
IAGO. Ay, madam.   45
DES. I am not merry, but I do beguile
The thing I am,° by seeming otherwise.
Come, how wouldst thou praise me?
IAGO. I am about it; but indeed my invention
Comes from my pate as birdlime° does from 50
[frize;°
It plucks out brains and all: but my Muse
[labours,
And thus she is deliver'd.
If she be fair and wise, fairness and wit,   55
The one's for use, the other useth it.
DES. Well praised! How if she be black° and
[witty?
IAGO. If she be black, and thereto have a wit,
She'll find a white° that shall her blackness fit. 60
DES. Worse and worse.
EMIL. How if fair and foolish?
IAGO. She never yet was foolish that was fair;
For even her folly help'd her to an heir.
DES. These are old fond° paradoxes to make fools 65
laugh i' the alehouse. What miserable praise hast
thou for her that's foul° and foolish?
IAGO. There's none so foul and foolish
[thereunto.
But does foul pranks which fair and wise ones 70
[do.
DES. O heavy ignorance! thou praisest the worst
best. But what praise couldst thou bestow on a
deserving woman indeed, one that, in the authority of her merit, did justly put on the vouch° 75
of very malice itself?
IAGO. She that was ever fair and never proud,
Had tongue at will and yet was never loud,

extend show
breeding bringing up, i.e., as a gentleman, which makes it
  proper to me to kiss the wife of a social inferior
still always
list inclination
pictures i.e., painted and speechless
Bells i.e., with tongues going like bell clappers (Kermode)
Saints . . . injuries say insulting things with a sanctimonious
  air
Players triflers
housewives hussies, wanton creatures

thing I am i.e., anxiety
birdlime sticky substance spread on twigs for catching birds
frize coarse woolen cloth
black a brunette
white (1) a fair person (2) a wight (i.e., a person)
fond silly
foul ugly
put . . . vouch challenge the testimony

Never lack'd gold and yet went never gay,°
Fled from her wish and yet said "Now I may,"
She that being anger'd, her revenge being nigh,
Bade her wrong stay and her displeasure fly,
5 She that in wisdom never was so frail
To change the cod's head for the salmon's tail,°
She that could think and ne'er disclose her
[mind,
See suitors following and not look behind,
10 She was a wight, if ever such wight were—
    DES. To do what?
    IAGO. To suckle fools and chronicle small
[beer.°
    DES. O most lame and impotent conclusion! Do
15 not learn of him, Emilia, though he be thy husband. How say you, Cassio? is he not a most profane and liberal° counsellor?
    CAS. He speaks home,° madam: you may relish
him more in the soldier than in the scholar.
20   IAGO. [Aside] He takes her by the palm: ay, well
said,° whisper: with as little a web as this will I
ensnare as great a fly as Cassio. Ay, smile upon
her, do; I will gyve° thee in thine own courtship.°
You say true; 'tis so indeed: if such tricks as these
25 strip you out of your lieutenantry, it had been better you had not kissed your three fingers° so oft,
which now again you are most apt to play the sir°
in. Very good; well kissed! an excellent courtesy!
'tis so, indeed. Yet again your fingers to your lips?
30 would they were clyster-pipes° for your sake!
[Trumpet within.] The Moor! I know his trumpet.
    CAS. 'Tis truly so.
    DES. Let's meet him and receive him.
    CAS. Lo, where he comes!
35   [Enter OTHELLO and ATTENDANTS.]
    OTH. O my fair warrior!
    DES.   My dear Othello!

    OTH. It gives me wonder great as my content°
To see you here before me. O my soul's joy!
If after every tempest come such calms,   40
May the winds blow till they have waken'd
[death!
And let the labouring bark climb hills of seas
Olympus-high and duck again as low
As hell's from heaven! If it were now to die,   45
'Twere now to be most happy; for, I fear,
My soul hath her content so absolute
That not another comfort like to this
Succeeds in unknown fate.
    DES.   The heavens forbid 50
But that our loves and comforts should increase,
Even as our days do grow!
    OTH.   Amen to that, sweet powers!
I cannot speak enough of this content;
It stops me here;° it is too much of joy: 55
And this, and this, the greatest discords be
[Kissing her]
That e'er our hearts shall make!
    IAGO. [Aside] O, you are well tuned now!
But I'll set down the pegs° that make this music, 60
As honest as I am.
    OTH.   Come, let us to the castle.
News, friends; our wars are done, the Turks are
[drown'd.
How does my old acquaintance of this isle?   65
Honey, you shall be well-desired° in Cyprus;
I have found great love amongst them. O my
[sweet,
I prattle out of fashion,° and I dote
In mine own comforts, I prithee, good Iago,   70
Go to the bay and disembark my coffers:
Bring thou the master° to the citadel;
He is a good one, and his worthiness
Does challenge° much respect. Come,
[Desdemona, 75
Once more, well met at Cyprus.
    [Exeunt OTHELLO, DESDEMONA, and ATTENDANTS.]

gay showy, gaudy
To ... tail to exchange a delicacy for refuse
chronicle ... beer keep petty household accounts
liberal licentious
home with utter frankness
well said well done
gyve fetter
courtship courtesy
kissed ... fingers as a piece of gallantry to Desdemona
sir gallant
clyster-pipes tubes used for enemas

content joy
here i.e., in the heart
set ... pegs loosen the pegs and so untune the instrument
well-desired well-loved
out of fashion unconventionally
master ship's master, i.e., captain
challenge demand

IAGO. Do thou meet me presently° at the harbour. Come hither. If thou be'st valiant—as, they say, base men being in love have then a nobility in their natures more than is native to them—list
5 me. The lieutenant tonight watches on the court of guard°—first, I must tell thee this—Desdemona is directly in love with him.

ROD. With him! why, 'tis not possible.

IAGO. Lay thy finger thus,° and let thy soul be
10 instructed. Mark me with what violence she first loved the Moor, but for bragging and telling her fantastical lies: and will she love him still for prating? let not thy discreet heart think it. Her eye must be fed; and what delight shall she have to
15 look on the devil? When the blood° is made dull with the act of sport, there should be, again to inflame it and to give satiety a fresh appetite, loveliness in favour,° sympathy in years, manners and beauties; all which the Moor is defective in: now,
20 for want of these required conveniences,° her delicate tenderness will find itself abused, begin to heave the gorge,° disrelish and abhor the Moor; very nature will instruct her in it and compel her to some second choice. Now, sir, this granted—
25 as it is a most pregnant° and unforced position— who stands so eminent in the degree of this fortune as Cassio does? a knave very voluble; no further conscionable° than in putting on the mere form of civil and humane seeming,° for the better com-
30 passing of his salt° and most hidden loose affection? why, none; why, none: a slipper° and subtle knave, a finder of occasions, that has an eye can stamp° and counterfeit advantages,° though true advantage never present itself; a devilish knave.
35 Besides, the knave is handsome, young, and hath

all those requisites in him that folly and green° minds look after: a pestilent complete knave; and the woman hath found him already.

ROD. I cannot believe that in her; she's full of most blessed condition.°   40

IAGO. Blessed fig's-end! the wine she drinks is made of grapes: if she had been blessed, she would never have loved the Moor. Blessed pudding! Didst thou not see her paddle with the palm of his hand? didst not mark that?   45

ROD. Yes, that I did; but that was but courtesy.

IAGO. Lechery, by this hand; an index° and obscure prologue to the history of lust and foul thoughts. They met so near with their lips that their breaths embraced together. Villanous 50 thoughts, Roderigo! when these mutualities so marshal° the way, hard at hand comes the master and main exercise, the incorporate° conclusion, Pish! But, sir, be you ruled by me: I have brought you from Venice. Watch you to-night; for the com- 55 mand, I'll lay 't upon you. Cassio knows you not, I'll not be far from you: do you find some occasion to anger Cassio, either by speaking too loud, or tainting° his discipline; or from what other course you please, which the time shall more favourably 60 minister.

ROD. Well.

IAGO. Sir, he is rash and very sudden in choler, and haply may strike at you: provoke him, that he may; for even out of that will I cause these of Cy- 65 prus to mutiny; whose qualification° shall come into no true taste° again but by the displanting of Cassio. So shall you have a shorter journey to your desires by the means I shall then have to prefer° them; and the impediment most profitably re- 70 moved, without the which there were no expectation of our prosperity.

ROD. I will do this, if I can bring it to any opportunity.

---

presently immediately
court of guard guardhouse
thus i.e., on your lips (while in silence you listen to me).
blood passion
favour countenance
conveniences compatibilities (Kermode)
heave the gorge be nauseated
pregnant obvious
conscionable bound by conscience
humane seeming the appearance of morality
salt licentious
slipper slippery
stamp coin
advantages favorable occasions

green inexperienced
condition qualities
index then placed at the front of a book
marshal lead
incorporate carnal
tainting disparaging
qualification appeasement
come . . . taste not be made palatable
prefer promote

IAGO. I warrant thee.° Meet me by and by at the citadel: I must fetch his necessaries ashore. Farewell.

ROD. Adieu.   [*Exit.*]

5   IAGO. That Cassio loves her, I do well believe
                                                    [it;
That she loves him, 'tis apt and of great
                                                [credit:°
The Moor, howbeit that I endure him not,
10 Is of a constant, loving, noble nature,
And I dare think he'll prove to Desdemona
A most dear husband. Now, I do love her too;
Not out of absolute lust, though peradventure
I stand accountant for as great a sin,
15 But partly led to diet my revenge,
For that I do suspect the lusty Moor
Hath leap'd into my seat; the thought whereof
Doth, like a poisonous mineral, gnaw my
                                            [inwards;
20 And nothing can or shall content my soul
Till I am even'd with him, wife for wife,
Or failing so, yet that I put the Moor
At least into a jealousy so strong
That judgement cannot cure. Which thing to do,
25 If this poor trash of Venice, whom I trash°
For his quick hunting, stand the putting on,
I'll have our Michael Cassio on the hip,
Abuse him to the Moor in the rank garb°—
For I fear Cassio with my night-cap too—
30 Make the Moor thank me, love me and reward
                                            [me,
For making him egregiously an ass
And practising upon° his peace and quiet
Even to madness. 'Tis here, but yet confused:
35 Knavery's plain face is never seen till used.
    [*Exit.*]

Scene ii

[*Enter a* HERALD *with a proclamation;* PEOPLE *following.*]

HER. It is Othello's pleasure, our noble and val-
40 iant general, that, upon certain tidings now ar-
rived, importing the mere perdition° of the Turkish fleet, every man put himself into triumph; some to dance, some to make bonfires, each man to what sport and revels his addiction leads him: for, besides these beneficial news, it is the celebration of 45 his nuptial. So much was his pleasure should be proclaimed. All offices° are open, and there is full liberty of feasting from this present hour of five till the bell have told eleven. Heaven bless the isle of Cyprus and our noble general Othello! 50
                                    [*Exeunt.*]

Scene iii

[*Enter* OTHELLO, DESDEMONA, CASSIO, *and* ATTENDANTS.]

OTH. Good Michael, look you to the guard
                                    [to-night: 55
Let's teach ourselves that honourable stop,
Not to outsport discretion.
CAS. Iago hath direction what to do;
But, notwithstanding, with my personal eye
Will I look to 't.   60
OTH.   Iago is most honest.
Michael, good night: to-morrow with your
                                        [earliest°
Let me have speech with you. [*To* DESDEMONA]
                            [Come, my dear love, 65
The purchase made, the fruits are to ensue;
That profit's yet to come 'tween me and you.
Good night.
    [*Exeunt* OTHELLO, DESDEMONA, *and* ATTENDANTS.]
    [*Enter* IAGO.]   70
CAS. Welcome, Iago; we must to the watch.
IAGO. Not this hour, lieutenant; 'tis not yet ten o' the clock. Our general cast° us thus early for the love of his Desdemona; who let us not therefore blame: he hath not yet made wanton the night 75 with her; and she is sport for Jove.
CAS. She's a most exquisite lady.
IAGO. And, I'll warrant her, full of game.
CAS. Indeed, she's a most fresh and delicate creature.   80

I warrant thee I guarantee you will
apt . . . credit likely and very credible
trash check, hold back (a hunting term)
rank garb coarse fashion
practising upon plotting against

mere perdition complete loss
offices rooms in which food and drink were prepared and served
with your earliest as early as possible
cast dismissed

IAGO. What an eye she has! methinks it sounds
a parley of provocation.

CAS. An inviting eye; and yet methinks right
modest.

5 IAGO. And when she speaks, is it not an alarum°
to love?

CAS. She is indeed perfection.

IAGO. Well, happiness to their sheets! Come,
lieutenant, I have a stoup° of wine; and here with-
10 out are a brace of Cyprus gallants that would fain
have a measure to the health of black Othello.

CAS. Not to-night, good Iago: I have very poor
and unhappy brains for drinking: I could well wish
courtesy would invent some other custom of en-
15 tertainment.

IAGO. O, they are our friends; but one cup: I'll
drink for you.

CAS. I have drunk but one cup to-night, and that
was craftily qualified° too, and, behold, what in-
20 novation° it makes here:° I am unfortunate in the
infirmity, and dare not task° my weakness with
any more.

IAGO. What, man! 'tis a night of revels: the gallants desire it.

25 CAS. Where are they?

IAGO. Here at the door; I pray you, call them in.

CAS. I'll do 't; but it dislikes me.   [*Exit.*]

IAGO. If I can fasten but one cup upon him,
With that which he hath drunk to-night already,
30 He'll be as full of quarrel and offence
As my young mistress' dog. Now, my sick fool
                                        [Roderigo,
Whom love hath turn'd almost the wrong side
                                        [out,
35 To Desdemona hath to-night caroused
Potations pottle-deep;° and he's to watch:
Three lads of Cyprus, noble swelling° spirits,
That hold their honours in a wary distance,°

The very elements° of this warlike isle,
Have I to-night fluster'd with flowing cups,   40
And they watch° too. Now, 'mongst this flock of
                                        [drunkards,
Am I to put our Cassio in some action
That may offend the isle.—But here they come:
If consequence° do but approve my dream,°   45
My boat sails freely, both with wind and stream.
[*Re-enter* CASSIO; *with him* MONTANO *and* GENTLEMEN;
SERVANTS *following with wine.*]

CAS. 'Fore God, they have given me a rouse°
                                        [already. 50

MON. Good faith, a little one; not past a pint,
                                        [as I am a soldier.

IAGO. Some wine, ho!
[*Sings*] And let me the canakin clink, clink;
          And let me the canakin clink: 55
             A soldier's a man;
             A life's but a span;°
          Why, then, let a soldier drink.
Some wine, boys!

CAS. 'Fore God, an excellent song.   60

IAGO. I learned it in England, where, indeed,
they are most potent in potting: your Dane, your
German, and your swag-bellied° Hollander—Drink,
ho!—are nothing to your English.

CAS. Is your Englishman so expert in his drink- 65
ing?

IAGO. Why, he drinks you, with facility, your
Dane dead drunk; he sweats not to overthrow your
Almain;° he gives your Hollander a vomit, ere the
next pottle° can be filled.   70

CAS. To the health of our general!

MON. I am for it, lieutenant; and I'll do you justice.°

IAGO. O sweet England!
          King Stephen was a worthy peer,   75
             His breeches cost him but a crown;

---

alarum call to arms
stoup a large flagon
craftily qualified slyly diluted (by Cassio)
innovation disturbance
here i.e., in his head
task impose upon
pottle-deep i.e., to the bottom of the pottle or tankard, i.e.,
   "bottoms up"
swelling swaggering
hold . . . distance are very sensitive about their honor

very elements perfect specimens
watch are on guard duty
consequence the result
approve my dream confirm my expectation
rouse drink
span the distance between the little finger and thumb of an
   outstretched hand; hence "small space" or "brief time"
swag-bellied i.e., pot-bellied
Almain German
pottle tankard
I'll . . . justice i.e., I'll drink as much as you

He held them sixpence all too dear,
    With that he call'd the tailor lown.°
He was a wight of high renown,
    And thou art but of low degree:
5   'Tis pride that pulls the country down;
    Then take thine auld cloak about thee.
Some wine, ho!

CAS. Why, this is a more exquisite song than the other.

10 IAGO. Will you hear 't again?

CAS. No; for I hold him to be unworthy of his place that does those things. Well, God's above all; and there be souls must be saved, and there be souls must not be saved.

15 IAGO. It's true, good lieutenant.

CAS. For mine own part—no offence to the general, nor any man of quality°—I hope to be saved.

IAGO. And so do I too, lieutenant.

CAS. Ay, but, by your leave, not before me; the
20 lieutenant is to be saved before the ancient. Let's have no more of this; let's to our affairs.—Forgive us our sins!—Gentlemen, let's look to our business. Do not think, gentlemen, I am drunk: this is my ancient; this is my right hand, and this is
25 my left: I am not drunk now; I can stand well enough, and speak well enough.

ALL. Excellent well.

CAS. Why, very well then; you must not think then that I am drunk.   [Exit.]
30 MON. To the platform, masters; come, let's set the watch.

IAGO. You see this fellow that is gone before;
He is a soldier fit to stand by Caesar
And give direction: and do but see his vice;
35 'Tis to his virtue a just equinox,°
The one as long as the other; 'tis pity of him.
I fear the trust Othello puts him in,
On some odd time of his infirmity,
Will shake this island.
40 MON.   But is he often thus?
IAGO. 'Tis evermore the prologue to his sleep:
He'll watch° the horologe a double set,°

If drink rock not his cradle.
  MON.   It were well
The general were put in mind of it.   45
Perhaps he sees it not; or his good nature
Prizes the virtue that appears in Cassio,
And looks not on his evils: is not this true?
  [Enter RODERIGO.]
IAGO. [Aside to him] How now, Roderigo!   50
I pray you, after the lieutenant; go.
  [Exit RODERIGO.]
MON. And 'tis great pity that the noble Moor
Should hazard such a place as his own second
With one of an ingraft° infirmity: 55
It were an honest action to say
So to the Moor.
  IAGO.   Not I, for this fair island:
I do love Cassio well; and would do much
To cure him of this evil—But, hark! what noise?   60
    [Cry within: "Help! help!"]
  [Re-enter CASSIO, driving in RODERIGO.]
CAS. You rogue! you rascal!
  MON.   What's the matter, lieutenant?
CAS. A knave teach me my duty!   65
I'll beat the knave into a twiggen bottle.°
  ROD. Beat me!
  CAS.   Dost thou prate, rogue?
  [Striking RODERIGO.]
  MON.   Nay, good lieutenant;   70
  [Staying him.]
I pray you, sir, hold your hand.
  CAS.   Let me go, sir,
Or I'll knock you o'er the mazzard.°
  MON. Come, come, you're drunk.   75
  CAS. Drunk!   [They fight.]
IAGO. [Aside to RODERIGO] Away, I say; go out, and cry a mutiny.   [Exit RODERIGO.]
Nay, good lieutenant—alas, gentlemen—
Help, ho!—Lieutenant—sir—Montano—sir—   80
Help, masters!—Here's a goodly watch indeed!
    [Bell rings.]
Who's that which rings the bell?—Diablo,° ho!
The town will rise: God's will, lieutenant, hold!

---

lown lout
quality rank
just equinox exact counterpart
watch keep awake
horologe ... set twice around the clock

ingraft ingrained
twiggen bottle bottle covered with a network of interwoven twigs
mazzard head
Diablo Spanish for "Devil"

You will be shamed for ever.
[*Re-enter* OTHELLO *and* ATTENDANTS.]
OTH.   What is the matter here?
MON. 'Zounds, I bleed still; I am hurt to the
5   death.   [*Faints.*]
OTH. Hold, for your lives!
IAGO. Hold, ho! Lieutenant—sir—
                    [Montano—gentlemen—
Have you forgot all sense of place° and duty?
10 Hold! the general speaks to you; hold, hold,
                                [for shame!
OTH. Why, how now, ho! from whence
                          [ariseth this?
Are we turn'd Turks, and to ourselves do that
15 Which heaven hath forbid the Ottomites?
For Christian shame, put by this barbarous
                                      [brawl:
He that stirs next to carve for° his own rage
Holds his soul light; he dies upon his motion.°
20 Silence that dreadful bell: it frights the isle
From her propriety.° What is the matter,
                                  [masters?
Honest Iago, that look'st dead with grieving,
Speak, who began this? on thy love, I charge
25   [thee.
IAGO. I do not know: friends all but now, even
                                  [now,
In quarter,° and in terms like bride and groom
Devesting them for bed; and then, but now—
30 As if some planet had unwitted men—
Swords out, and tilting one at other's breast,
In opposition bloody. I cannot speak
Any beginning to this peevish odds;°
And would in action glorious I had lost
35 Those legs that brought me to a part of it!
OTH. How comes it, Michael, you are thus
                              [forgot?°
CAS. I pray you, pardon me; I cannot speak.
OTH. Worthy Montano, you were wont be
40   [civil;
The gravity and stillness of your youth

The world hath noted, and your name is great
In mouths of wisest censure:° what's the
                                  [matter,
That you unlace° your reputation thus   45
And spend your rich opinion° for the name
Of a night-brawler? give me answer to it.
MON. Worthy Othello, I am hurt to danger:
Your officer, Iago, can inform you—
While I spare speech, which something now   50
                              [offends° me—
Of all that I do know: nor know I aught
By me that's said or done amiss this night;
Unless self-charity be sometimes a vice,
And to defend ourselves it be a sin   55
When violence assails us.
OTH.   Now, by heaven,
My blood begins my safer guides to rule;
And passion, having my best judgement
                            [collied,° 60
Assays to lead the way: if I once stir,
Or do but lift this arm, the best of you
Shall sink in my rebuke. Give me to know
How this foul rout began, who set it on;
And he that is approved in° this offence,   65
Though he had twinn'd with me, both at a
                                [birth,
Shall lose me. What! in a town of war,
Yet wild, the people's hearts brimful of fear,
To manage° private and domestic quarrel,   70
In night, and on the court and guard° of safety!
'Tis monstrous. Iago, who began 't?
MON. If partially affined,° or leagued in
                              [office,°
Thou dost deliver more or less than truth,   75
Thou art no soldier.
IAGO.   Touch me not so near:
I had rather have this tongue cut from my
                                [mouth

place your position
carve for indulge
upon his motion the moment he moves
From her propriety out of herself
In quarter on good terms
peevish odds childish quarrel
you . . . forgot have thus forgotten yourself

censure judgment
unlace loosen, disgrace
opinion reputation
offends pains
collied blackened, i.e., obscured
approved in proved guilty of
manage conduct
on the court and guard the guarding place, i.e., the guard-
    house
partially affined made partial by nearness of relationship
leagued in office because a fellow officer

Than it should do offence to Michael Cassio;
Yet, I persuade myself, to speak the truth
Shall nothing wrong him. Thus it is, general.
Montano and myself being in speech,
5   There comes a fellow crying out for help;
And Cassio following him with determined
                                        [sword,
To execute upon him. Sir, this gentleman
Steps in to Cassio, and entreats his pause:
10 Myself the crying fellow did pursue,
Lest by his clamour—as it so fell out—
The town might fall in fright: he, swift of foot,
Outran my purpose; and I return'd the rather
For that I heard the clink and fall of swords,
15 And Cassio high in oath; which till to-night
I ne'er might say before. When I came back—
For this was brief—I found them close together,
At blow and thrust; even as again they were
When you yourself did part them.
20 More of this matter cannot I report:
But men are men; the best sometimes forget:
Though Cassio did some little wrong to him,
As men in rage strike those that wish them best,
Yet surely Cassio, I believe, received
25 From him that fled some strange indignity,
Which patience could not pass.°
          OTH.   I know, Iago,
Thy honesty and love doth mince° this matter,
Making it light to Cassio. Cassio, I love thee;
30 But never more be officer of mine.
          [Re-enter DESDEMONA, attended.]
Look, if my gentle love be not raised up!
I'll make thee an example.
          DES.   What's the matter?
35 OTH. All's well now, sweeting; come away
                                        [to bed.
Sir, for your hurts, myself will be your surgeon:
Lead him off. [To MONTANO, who is led off.]
Iago, look with care about the town,
40 And silence those whom this vile brawl
                                        [distracted.
Come, Desdemona: 'tis the soldiers' life
To have their balmy slumbers waked with strife.
                    [Exeunt all but IAGO and CASSIO.]
45 IAGO. What, are you hurt, lieutenant?

pass pass over
mince cut fine, i.e., minimize

CAS. Ay, past all surgery.
IAGO. Marry, heaven forbid!
CAS. Reputation, reputation, reputation! O, I
have lost my reputation! I have lost the immortal
part of myself, and what remains is bestial. My   50
reputation, Iago, my reputation!
IAGO. As I am an honest man, I thought you
had received some bodily wound; there is more
sense° in that than in reputation. Reputation is an
idle and most false imposition;° oft got without   55
merit, and lost without deserving: you have lost
no reputation at all, unless you repute yourself
such a loser. What, man! there are ways to re-
cover° the general again: you are but now cast° in
his mood,° a punishment more in policy than in   60
malice; even so as one would beat his offenceless
dog to affright an imperious lion: sue to him again,
and he's yours.
CAS. I will rather sue to be despised than to
deceive so good a commander with so slight, so   65
drunken, and so indiscreet an officer. Drunk? and
speak parrot° and squabble? swagger? swear? and
discourse fustian° with one's own shadow? O thou
invisible spirit of wine, if thou has no name to be
known by, let us call thee devil!   70
IAGO. What was he that you followed with your
sword? What had he done to you?
CAS. I know not.
IAGO. Is 't possible?
CAS. I remember a mass of things, but nothing   75
distinctly; a quarrel, but nothing wherefore. O God,
that men should put an enemy in their mouths to
steal away their brains! that we should, with joy,
pleasance, revel and applause, transform ourselves into beasts!   80
IAGO. Why, but you are now well enough: how
came you thus recovered?
CAS. It hath pleased the devil drunkenness to
give place to the devil wrath: one unperfectness
shows me another, to make me frankly despise   85
myself.

sense feeling
imposition attribution
recover reconcile
cast dismissed
mood i.e., anger
speak parrot talk nonsense
fustian bombast

IAGO. Come, you are too severe a moraler: as
the time, the place, and the condition of this country stands, I could heartily wish this had not be-
fallen; but, since it is as it is, mend it for your own
5 good.

CAS. I will ask him for my place again; he shall
tell me I am a drunkard! Had I as many mouths
as Hydra,° such an answer would stop them all.
To be now a sensible man, by and by a fool, and
10 presently a beast! O strange! Every inordinate cup
is unblessed and the ingredient is a devil.

IAGO. Come, come, good wine is a good famil-
iar° creature, if it be well used: exclaim no more
against it. And, good lieutenant, I think you think
15 I love you.

CAS. I have well approved° it, sir. I drunk!

IAGO. You or any man living may be drunk at a
time, man. I'll tell you what you shall do. Our
general's wife is now the general: I may say so in
20 this respect, for that° he hath devoted and given
up himself to the contemplation, mark, and de-
notement° of her parts° and graces: confess yourself freely to her; importune her help to put you
in your place again: she is of so free,° so kind, so
25 apt,° so blessed a disposition, she holds it a vice
in her goodness not to do more than she is requested: this broken joint between you and her
husband entreat her to splinter,° and, my fortunes
against any lay° worth naming, this crack of your
30 love shall grow stronger than it was before.

CAS. You advise me well.

IAGO. I protest, in the sincerity of love and honest kindness.

CAS. I think it freely; and betimes° in the morn-
35 ing I will beseech the virtuous Desdemona to un-

dertake for me: I am desperate of my fortunes if
they check me here.°

IAGO. You are in the right. Good night, lieutenant; I must to the watch.

CAS. Good night, honest Iago.   [*Exit.*]   40

IAGO. And what's he then that says I play the
                                              [villain?
When this advice is free I give and honest,
Probal° to thinking and indeed the course
To win the Moor again? For 'tis most easy   45
The inclining° Desdemona to subdue°
In any honest suit: she's framed as fruitful°
As the free elements.° And then for her
To win the Moor—were 't to renounce his
                                              [baptism,   50
All seals and symbols of redeemèd sin,
His soul is so enfetter'd to her love,
That she may make, unmake, do what she list,
Even as her appetite shall play the god
With his weak function.° How am I then a   55
                                              [villain
To counsel Cassio to this parallel° course,
Directly to his good? Divinity of hell!
When devils will the blackest sins put on,°
They do suggest° at first with heavenly shows,   60
As I do now: for whiles this honest fool
Plies Desdemona to repair his fortunes
And she for him pleads strongly to the Moor,
I'll pour this pestilence into his ear,
That she repeals° him for her body's lust;   65
And by how much she strives to do him good,
She shall undo her credit with the Moor.
So will I turn her virtue into pitch,
And out of her own goodness make the net
That shall enmesh them all.   70
          [*Re-enter* RODERIGO.]
                    How now, Roderigo!

Hydra a fabulous monster with nine heads, slain by Hercules
familiar affable
approved proved
for that because
denotement noting
parts qualities
free open, generous
apt kindly disposed
splinter splint
lay wager
betimes early

desperate . . . here I despair of my career if it is stopped
  short at this point
Probal probable
inclining favorably disposed
subdue overcome by persuasion
fruitful bountiful
free elements elements out of which all things are produced
function operation of his mind
parallel i.e., parallel to his wishes
put on instigate
suggest tempt
repeals recalls

Rod. I do follow here in the chase, not like a
hound that hunts, but one that fills up the cry.°
My money is almost spent; I have been to-night
exceedingy well cudgelled; and I think the issue
5 will be, I shall have so much experience for my
pains, and so, with no money at all and a little
more wit, return again to Venice.

Iago. How poor are they that have not
[patience!
10 What wound did ever heal but by degrees?
Thou know'st we work by wit, and not by
[witchcraft;
And wit depends on dilatory time.
Does 't not go well? Cassio hath beaten thee,
15 And thou, by that small hurt, hast cashier'd
[Cassio:
Though other things grow fair against the sun,
Yet fruits that blossom first will first be ripe:
Content thyself awhile. By the mass, 'tis
20 [morning;
Pleasure and action make the hours seem short.
Retire thee; go where thou art billeted:
Away, I say; thou shalt know more hereafter:
Nay, get thee gone. [Exit Roderigo.] Two
25 [things are to be done:
My wife must move for Cassio to her mistress;
I'll set her on;
Myself the while to draw the Moor apart,
And bring him jump° when he may Cassio find
30 Soliciting his wife: ay, that's the way:
Dull not device by coldness and delay. [Exit.]

ACT III

Scene i

[Enter Cassio and some Musicians.]
Cas. Masters, play here; I will content° your
[pains;
35 Something that's brief; and bid "Good morrow,
general." [Music.]
[Enter Clown.]
Clo. Why, masters, have your instruments been

in Naples,° that they speak i' the nose thus?
First Mus. How, sir, how! 40
Clo. Are these, I pray you, wind-instruments?
First Mus. Ay, marry, are they, sir.
Clo. O, thereby hangs a tail.
First Mus. Whereby hangs a tale, sir?
Clo. Marry, sir, by many a wind-instrument that 45
I know. But, masters, here's money for you: and
the general so likes your music, that he desires
you, for love's sake, to make no more noise with
it.
First Mus. Well, sir, we will not. 50
Clo. If you have any music that may not be
heard, to 't again: but, as they say, to hear music
the general does not greatly care.
First Mus. We have none such, sir.
Clo. Then put up your pipes in your bag, for 55
I'll away: go, vanish into air; away!
[Exeunt Musicians.]
Cas. Dost thou hear, my honest friend?
Clo. No, I hear not your honest friend; I hear
you. 60
Cas. Prithee, keep up thy quillets.° There's a
poor piece of gold for thee: if the gentlewoman
that attends the general's wife be stirring, tell her
there's one Cassio entreats her a little favour of
speech: wilt thou do this? 65
Clo. She is stirring, sir: if she will stir hither, I
shall seem to notify unto her.
Cas. Do, good my friend. [Exit Clown.]
[Enter Iago.]
In happy time,° Iago. 70
Iago. You have not been a-bed, then?
Cas. Why, no; the day had broke
Before we parted, I have made bold, Iago,
To send in to your wife: my suit to her
Is, that she will to virtuous Desdemona 75
Procure me some access.
Iago. I'll send her to you presently;°
And I'll devise a mean to draw the Moor
Out of the way, that your converse and business
May be more free. 80

---

in Naples (1) Neapolitans spoke with a nasal drawl (2) syphilis (known in England as the Neapolitan disease) causes
nasal deterioration
keep . . . quillets put your wise-cracks away
In happy time i.e., I am glad to see you
presently at once

cry pack
jump at the precise moment
content reward

CAS. I humbly thank you for 't.   [*Exit* IAGO.]
                                    [I never knew
A Florentine more kind and honest.
     [*Enter* EMILIA.]
5   EMIL. Good morrow, good lieutenant: I am
                                    [sorry
For your displeasure;° but all will sure be well.
The general and his wife are talking of it;
And she speaks for you stoutly: the Moor
10   [replies,
That he you hurt is of great fame in Cyprus
And great affinity° and that in wholesome
                                    [wisdom
He might not but refuse you, but he protests
15   [he loves you
And needs no other suitor but his likings
To take the safest occasion° by the front°
To bring you in again.
     CAS.   Yet, I beseech you,
20   If you think fit, or that it may be done,
Give me advantage of some brief discourse
With Desdemona alone.
     EMIL.   Pray you, come in:
I will bestow° you where you shall have time
25   To speak your bosom freely.°
     CAS.   I am much bound to you. [*Exeunt.*]

Scene ii

[*Enter* OTHELLO, IAGO, *and* GENTLEMEN.]
     OTH. These letters give, Iago, to the pilot;
And by him do my duties° to the senate:
30   That done, I will be walking on the works;°
Repair there to me.
     IAGO.   Well, my good lord, I'll do 't.
     OTH. This fortification, gentlemen, shall we
                                    [see 't?
35   GENT. We'll wait upon your lordship.
                                    [*Exeunt.*]

Scene iii

[*Enter* DESDEMONA, CASSIO, *and* EMILIA.]
     DES. Be thou assured, good Cassio, I will do
All my abilities° in thy behalf.
     EMIL. Good madam, do: I warrant it grieves   40
                                    [my husband,
As if the case were his.
     DES. O, that's an honest fellow. Do not
                                    [doubt, Cassio,
But I will have my lord and you again   45
As friendly as you were.
     CAS.   Bounteous madam,
Whatever shall become of Michael Cassio,
He's never any thing but your true servant.
     DES. I know 't; I thank you. You do love my   50
                                    [lord:
You have known him long; and be you well
                                    [assured
He shall in strangeness° stand no further off
Than in a politic° distance.   55
     CAS.   Ay, but, lady,
That policy may either last so long,
Or feed upon such nice° and waterish diet,
Or breed itself so out of circumstance,°
That, I being absent and my place supplied,   60
My general will forget my love and service.
     DES. Do not doubt° that; before Emilia here
I give thee warrant of thy place: assure thee,
If I do vow a friendship, I'll perform it
To the last article: my lord shall never rest;   65
I'll watch him tame° and talk him out of
                                    [patience;
His bed shall seem a school, his board a shrift;°
I'll intermingle every thing he does
With Cassio's suit: therefore be merry, Cassio;   70
For thy solicitor shall rather die
Than give thy cause away.°

displeasure discomfort
affinity family connections
occasion opportunity
front forelock
bestow put you in a place
speak . . . freely say whatever you wish
do my duties pay my respects
works fortifications

All my abilities all that I am able
strangeness aloofness
politic expedient
nice thin
breed . . . circumstance increase itself so much from mere accidents
doubt suspect
watch him tame tame him by keeping him awake (a method of training falcons)
shrift confessional
away up

[*Enter* OTHELLO *and* IAGO.]

EMIL. Madam, here comes my lord.

CAS. Madam, I'll take my leave.

DES. Why, stay, and hear me speak.

5   CAS. Madam, not now: I am very ill at ease,

Unfit for mine own purposes.

DES. Well, do your discretion.

                        [*Exit* CASSIO.]

IAGO. Ha! I like not that.

10   OTH.   What dost thou say?

IAGO. Nothing, my lord: or if—I know not

                        [what.

OTH. Was not that Cassio parted from my

                        [wife?

15   IAGO. Cassio, my lord! No, sure, I cannot

                        [think it,

That he would steal away so guilty-like,

Seeing you coming.

OTH.   I do believe 'twas he.

20   DES. How now, my lord!

I have been talking with a suitor here,

A man that languishes in your displeasure.

OTH. Who is 't you mean?

DES. Why, your lieutenant, Cassio. Good

25   [my lord,

If I have any grace or power to move you,

His present reconciliation take;

For if he be not one that truly loves you,

That errs in ignorance and not in cunning,°

30   I have no judgement in an honest face:

I prithee, call him back.

OTH.   Went he hence now?

DES. Ay, sooth; so humbled

That he hath left part of his grief with me,

35   To suffer with him. Good love, call him back.

OTH. Not now, sweet Desdemona; some

                    [other time.

DES. But shall 't be shortly?

OTH.   The sooner, sweet, for you.

40   DES. Shall 't be to-night at supper?

OTH.   No, not to-night.

DES. To-morrow dinner, then?

OTH.   I shall not dine at home;

I meet the captains at the citadel.

45   DES. Why, then, to-morrow night; or

                    [Tuesday morn;

On Tuesday noon, or night; on Wednesday

                    [morn:

I prithee, name the time, but let it not

Exceed three days: in faith, he's penitent;   50

And yet his trespass, in our common reason—

Save that, they say, the wars must make

                    [examples

Out of their best—is not almost° a fault

To incur a private check.° When shall he come?   55

Tell me, Othello: I wonder in my soul,

What you would ask me, that I should deny,

Or stand so mammering° on. What! Michael

                    [Cassio,

That came a-wooing with you, and so many a   60

                    [time,

When I have spoke of you dispraisingly,

Hath ta'en your part; to have so much to do

To bring him in! Trust me, I could do much—

OTH. Prithee, no more: let him come when   65

                    [he will;

I will deny thee nothing.

DES.   Why, this is not a boon;

'Tis as I should entreat you wear your gloves.

Or feed on nourishing dishes, or keep you   70

                    [warm,

Or sue to you to do a peculiar° profit

To your own person: nay, when I have a suit

Wherein I mean to touch your love indeed,

It shall be full of poise° and difficult weight   75

And fearful to be granted.

OTH.   I will deny thee nothing:

Whereon, I do beseech thee, grant me this,

To leave me but a little to myself.

DES. Shall I deny you? no: farewell, my lord.   80

OTH. Farewell, my Desdemona: I'll come to

                    [thee straight.

DES. Emilia, come. Be as your fancies teach

                    [you:

Whate'er you be, I am obedient.   85

             [*Exeunt* DESDEMONA *and* EMILIA.]

OTH. Excellent wretch! Perdition catch my

                    [soul,

But I do love thee! and when I love thee not,

in cunning intentionally

not almost hardly
check rebuke
mammering hesitating
peculiar private
poise importance

Chaos is come again.
Iago. My noble lord—
Oth.   What dost thou say, Iago?
Iago. Did Michael Cassio, when you woo'd
5   [my lady,
Know of your love?
Oth. He did, from first to last: why dost
                       [thou ask?
Iago. But for a satisfaction of my thought;
10 No further harm.
Oth.   Why of thy thought, Iago?
Iago. I did not think he had been acquainted
                       [with her.
Oth. O, yes; and went between us very oft.
15 Iago. Indeed!
Oth. Indeed! ay, indeed: discern'st thou
                       [aught in that?
Is he not honest?°
Iago.   Honest, my lord!
20 Oth.   Honest! ay, honest.
Iago. My lord, for aught I know.
Oth. What dost thou think?
Iago.   Think, my lord!
Oth.   Think, my lord!
25 By heaven, he echoes me,
As if there were some monster in his thought
Too hideous to be shown. Thou dost mean
                       [something:
I heard thee say even now, thou likedst not that,
30 When Cassio left my wife: what didst not like?
And when I told thee he was of my counsel°
In my whole course of wooing, thou criedst
                       ["Indeed!"
And didst contract and purse thy brow together,
35 As if thou then hadst shut up in thy brain
Some horrible conceit:° if thou dost love me,
Show me thy thought.
Iago. My lord, you know I love you.
Oth.   I think thou dost;
40 And, for I know thou'rt full of love and
                       [honesty,
And weigh'st thy words before thou givest
                       [them breath,

Therefore these stops° of thine fright me the
                       [more: 45
For such things in a false disloyal knave
Are tricks of custom, but in a man that's just
They are close delations,° working from the
                       [heart
That passion cannot rule.°   50
Iago.   For Michael Cassio,
I dare be sworn I think that he is honest.
Oth. I think so too.
Iago.   Men should be what they seem;
Or those that be not, would they might seem 55
                       [none!
Oth. Certain, men should be what they seem.
Iago. Why, then, I think Cassio's an honest
                       [man.
Oth. Nay, there's more in this: 60
I prithee, speak to me as to thy thinkings,
As thou dost ruminate, and give thy worst of
                       [thoughts
The worst of words.
Iago.   Good my lord, pardon me: 65
Though I am bound to every act of duty,
I am not bound to that all slaves are free to.
Utter my thoughts? Why, say they are vile and
                       [false;
As where's that palace whereinto foul things 70
Sometimes intrude not? who has a breast so
                       [pure,
But some uncleanly apprehensions°
Keep leets° and law-days and in session sit
With meditations lawful?   75
Oth. Thou dost conspire against thy friend,
                       [Iago,
If thou but think'st him wrong'd and makest
                       [his ear
A stranger to thy thoughts.   80
Iago.   I do beseech you—
Though I perchance am vicious in my guess,
As, I confess, it is my nature's plague
To spy into abuses, and oft my jealousy°

honest honorable
of my counsel in my confidence
conceit conception

stops interruptions
close delations secret suspicions
passion . . . rule i.e., that cannot control its indignation
apprehensions suspicions
leets days on which courts are in session
jealousy suspicion

Shapes faults that are not—that your wisdom
                                                    [yet,
From one that so imperfectly conceits,°
Would take no notice, nor build yourself a
5   [trouble
Out of his scattering and unsure observance.
It were not for your quiet nor your good,
Nor for my manhood, honesty, or wisdom,
To let you know my thoughts.
10   OTH.   What dost thou mean?
        IAGO. Good name in man and woman, dear
                                            [my lord,
Is the immediate jewel of their souls:
Who steals my purse steals trash; 'tis something,
15   [nothing;
'Twas mine, 'tis his, and has been slave to
                                        [thousands;
But he that filches from me my good name
Robs me of that which not enriches him
20 And makes me poor indeed.
        OTH. By heaven, I'll know thy thoughts.
        IAGO. You cannot, if my heart were in your
                                            [hand;
Nor shall not, whilst 'tis in my custody.
25   OTH. Ha!
        IAGO.   O, beware, my lord, of jealousy;
It is the green-eyed monster which doth mock
The meat it feeds on:° that cuckold lives in bliss
Who, certain of his fate, loves not his wronger;
30 But, O, what damnèd minutes tells° he o'er
Who dotes, yet doubts, suspects, yet strongly
                                            [loves!
        OTH. O misery!
        IAGO. Poor and content is rich and rich
35   [enough.
But riches fineless° is as poor as winter
To him that ever fears he shall be poor.
Good heaven, the souls of all my tribe defend
From jealousy!
40   OTH.   Why, why is this?
Think'st thou I'ld make a life of jealousy,
To follow still the changes of the moon

With fresh suspicions? No; to be once in doubt
Is once to be resolved: exchange me for a goat,
When I shall turn the business of my soul   45
To such exsufflicate and blown° surmises,
Matching thy inference. 'Tis not to make me
                                            [jealous
To say my wife is fair, feeds well, loves
                                        [company,   50
Is free of speech, sings, plays and dances well;
Where virtue is, these are more virtuous:
Nor from mine own weak merits will I draw
The smallest fear or doubt° of her revolt;°
For she had eyes, and chose me. No, Iago;   55
I'll see before I doubt; when I doubt, prove;°
And on the proof, there is no more but this—
Away at once with love or jealousy!
        IAGO. I am glad of it; for now I shall have
                                            [reason   60
To show the love and duty that I bear you
With franker spirit; therefore, as I am bound,
Receive it from me. I speak not yet of proof.
Look to your wife; observe her well with Cassio;
Wear your eye thus, not jealous nor secure:°   65
I would not have your free and noble nature,
Out of self-bounty,° be abused; look to 't:
I know our country disposition well;
In Venice they do let heaven see the pranks
They dare not show their husbands; their best   70
    conscience
Is not to leave 't undone, but keep 't unknown.
        OTH. Dost thou say so?
        IAGO. She did deceive her father, marrying
                                            [you;   75
And when she seem'd to shake and fear your
                                            [looks,
She loved them most.
        OTH.   And so she did.
        IAGO.   Why, go to then;   80
She that, so young, could give out such a
                                            [seeming,

---

imperfectly conceits has such imperfect ideas
meat . . . on i.e., the heart of the man who suffers it (Kermode)
tells counts
fineless boundless

exsufflicate and blown inflated and blown up (like a bubble)
doubt suspicion
revolt inconstancy
prove test
secure free from suspicion
self-bounty natural generosity

To seel° her father's eyes up close as oak°—
He thought 'twas witchcraft—but I am much
[to blame;
I humbly do beseech you of your pardon
5 For too much loving you.
    OTH.   I am bound to thee for ever.
    IAGO. I see this hath a little dash'd your
      spirits.
    OTH. Not a jot, not a jot.
10   IAGO.   I' faith, I fear it has.
I hope you will consider what is spoke
Comes from my love. But I do see you're
[moved:
I am to pray you not to strain my speech
15 To grosser issues° nor to larger reach
Than to suspicion.
    OTH. I will not.
    IAGO.   Should you do so, my lord,
My speech should fall into such vile success°
20 As my thoughts aim not at. Cassio's my worthy
[friend—
My lord, I see you're moved.
    OTH.   No, not much moved:
I do not think but Desdemona's honest.°
25   IAGO. Long live she so! and long live you to
[think so!
    OTH. And yet, how nature erring from itself—
    IAGO. Ay, there's the point: as—to be bold
[with you—
30 Not to affect° many proposed matches
Of her own clime, complexion, and degree,°
Whereto we see in all things nature tends—
Foh! one may smell in such a will° most rank,
Foul disproportion, thoughts unnatural.
35 But pardon me; I do not in position°
Distinctly speak of her; though I may fear
Her will, recoiling° to her better judgement,

May fall to match° you with her country forms°
And happily° repent.
    OTH.   Farewell, farewell: 40
If more thou dost perceive, let me know more;
Set on thy wife to observe: leave me, Iago.
    IAGO. [*Going*] My lord, I take my leave.
    OTH. Why did I marry? This honest
[creature doubtless 45
Sees and knows more, much more, than he
[unfolds.
    IAGO. [*Returning*] My Lord, I would I might
[entreat your honour
To scan this thing no further; leave it to time: 50
Though it be fit that Cassio have his place,
For, sure, he fills it up with great ability,
Yet, if you please to hold him off awhile,
You shall by that perceive him and his means:°
Note, if your lady strain his entertainment°   55
With any strong or vehement importunity;
Much will be seen in that. In the mean time,
Let me be thought too busy in my fears—
As worthy cause I have to fear I am—
And hold her free,° I do beseech your honour.   60
    OTH. Fear not my government.°
    IAGO. I once more take my leave.   [*Exit.*]
    OTH. This fellow's of exceeding honesty,
And knows all qualities,° with a learned spirit,
Of human dealings. If I do prove her haggard,°   65
Though that her jesses° were my dear
[heartstrings,
I'ld whistle her off and let her down the wind,°
To prey at fortune.° Haply, for° I am black
And have not those soft parts of conversation°   70

fall to match begin to compare
country forms the appearance of her countrymen
happily haply, perhaps
his means i.e., the means he adopts to regain your favor
strain his entertainment over-urge his reinstatement
free innocent
government self-control
qualities kinds
haggard wild, untamed hawk
jesses straps attached to the legs of the hawk by which the
  falconer held her
down the wind i.e., go free; trained hawks flew against the
  wind
at fortune at random
for because
parts of conversation gifts for social intercourse

seel sew up (as the eyes of a falcon)
oak i.e., the grain of an oak
issues conclusions
success consequences
honest chaste
affect like
degree rank
will desire
position formal assertion
recoiling reverting

That chamberers° have, or for I am declined
Into the vale of years—yet that's not much—
She's gone. I am abused; and my relief
Must be to loathe her. O curse of marriage,
5 That we can call these delicate creatures ours,
And not their appetites! I had rather be a toad,
And live upon the vapour of a dungeon,
Than keep a corner in the thing I love
For others' uses. Yet, 'tis the plague of great
10   [ones;
Prerogatived° are they less than the base;
'Tis destiny unshunnable, like death:
Even then this forkèd plague° is fated to us
When we do quicken.° Desdemona comes:
15 [Re-enter DESDEMONA and EMILIA.]
If she be false, O, then heaven mocks itself!
I'll not believe 't.
   DES.   How now, my dear Othello!
Your dinner, and the generous° islanders
20 By you invited, do attend your presence.
   OTH. I am to blame.
   DES.   Why do you speak so faintly?
Are you not well?
   OTH. I have a pain upon my forehead here.
25 DES. 'Faith, that's with watching;° 'twill away
      again:
Let me but bind it hard, within this hour
It will be well.
   OTH.   Your napkin° is too little:
30 [He puts the handkerchief from him; and it drops.]
Let it alone. Come, I'll go in with you.
   DES. I am very sorry that you are not well.
            [Exeunt OTHELLO and DESDEMONA.]
   EMIL. I am glad I have found this napkin:
35 This was her first remembrance from the Moor:
My wayward° husband hath a hundred times
Woo'd me to steal it; but she so loves the token,
For he conjured her she should ever keep it,
That she reserves it evermore about her

To kiss and talk to. I'll have the work ta'en out,° 40
And give 't Iago: what he will do with it
Heaven knows, not I;
I nothing but to please his fantasy.°
   [Re-enter IAGO.]
   IAGO. How now! what do you here alone?   45
   EMIL. Do not you chide; I have a thing for you.
   IAGO. A thing for me? it is a common thing—
   EMIL. Ha!
   IAGO. To have a foolish wife.
   EMIL. O, is that all? What will you give me   50
                                              [now
For that same handkerchief?
   IAGO.   What handkerchief?
   EMIL. What handkerchief!
Why, that the Moor first gave to Desdemona;   55
That which so often you did bid me steal.
   IAGO. Hast stol'n it from her?
   EMIL. No, 'faith; she let it drop by negligence,
And, to the advantage,° I, being here, took 't
                                              [up. 60
Look, here it is.
   IAGO.   A good wench; give it me.
   EMIL. What will you do with 't, that you
                            [have been so earnest
To have me filch it?   65
   IAGO. [Snatching it] Why, what's that to you?
   EMIL. If it be not for some purpose of import,
Give 't me again: poor lady, she'll run mad
When she shall lack° it
   IAGO. Be not acknown on 't;° I have use for it. 70
Go, leave me.   [Exit EMILIA.]
I will in Cassio's lodging lose this napkin,
And let him find it. Trifles light as air
Are to the jealous confirmations strong
As proofs of holy writ: this may do something. 75
The Moor already changes with my poison:
Dangerous conceits° are, in their natures,
                                              [poisons,
Which at the first are scarce found to distaste,

chamberers gallants
prerogatived privileged
forked plague the horns of a cuckold
quicken begin to live
generous noble
watching lying awake
napkin handkerchief
wayward willfull, insistent

work ta'en out embroidery copied
fantasy whim
to the advantage upon the opportunity
lack miss
Be . . . 't do not admit any knowledge of it
conceits conceptions

But with a little act° upon the blood,
Burn like the mines of sulphur. I did say so:
Look, where he comes!
[*Re-enter* OTHELLO.]
5   Not poppy, nor mandragora,°
Nor all the drowsy syrups of the world,
Shall ever medicine thee to that sweet sleep
Which thou owedst° yesterday.
OTH.   Ha! ha! false to me?
10 IAGO. Why, how now, general! no more of
                      [that.
OTH. Avaunt! be gone! thou hast set me on
                    [the rack:
I swear 'tis better to be much abused
15 Than but to know 't a little.
IAGO.   How now, my lord!
OTH. What sense had I of her stol'n hours
                  [of lust?
I saw't not, thought it not, it harm'd not me:
20 I slept the next night well, was free and merry;
I found not Cassio's kisses on her lips:
He that is robb'd, not wanting° what is stol'n,
Let him not know 't, and he's not robb'd at all.
IAGO. I am sorry to hear this.
25 OTH. I had been happy, if the general camp,
Pioners° and all, had tasted her sweet body,
So I had nothing known. O, now, for ever
Farewell the tranquil mind! farewell content!
Farewell the plumèd troop, and the big wars,
30 That make ambition virtue! O, farewell!
Farewell the neighing steed, and the shrill
                  [trump,
The spirit-stirring drum, the ear-piercing fife,
The royal banner, and all quality,
35 Pride, pomp and circumstance° of glorious war!
And, O you mortal engines,° whose rude throats
The immortal Jove's dread clamours counterfeit,°
Farewell! Othello's occupation's gone!
IAGO. Is 't possible, my lord?

OTH. Villain, be sure thou prove my love a   40
                [whore,
Be sure of it; give me the ocular proof;
Or, by the worth of man's eternal soul,
Thou hadst been better have been born a dog
Than answer my waked wrath!   45
IAGO.   Is 't come to this?
OTH. Make me to see 't; or, at the least, so
                [prove it,
That the probation° bear no hinge nor loop
To hang a doubt on; or woe upon thy life!   50
IAGO. My noble lord—
OTH. If thou dost slander her and torture me,
Never pray more; abandon all remorse;
On horror's head horrors accumulate;
Do deeds to make heaven weep, all earth   55
                [amazed;
For nothing canst thou to damnation add
Greater than that.
IAGO.   O grace! O heaven forgive me!
Are you a man? have you a soul or sense?   60
God be wi' you;° take mine office. O wretched
                [fool,
That livest to make thine honesty a vice!
O monstrous world! Take note, take note, O
                [world, 65
To be direct and honest is not safe.
I thank you for this profit;° and from hence
I'll love no friend, sith° love breeds such offence.
OTH. Nay, stay: thou shouldst be honest.
IAGO. I should be wise, for honesty's a fool   70
And loses that it works for.
OTH.   By the world,
I think my wife be honest and think she is not;
I think that thou art just and think thou art not.
I'll have some proof. Her name, that was as   75
                [fresh
As Dian's° visage, is now begrimed and black
As mine own face. If there be cords, or knives,
Poison, or fire, or suffocating streams,
I'll not endure it. Would I were satisfied!   80
IAGO. I see, sir, you are eaten up with passion:
I do repent me that I put it to you.

act action
mandragora mandrake root, an opiate
owedst owned
wanting missing
Pioners the lowest rank in the army
circumstance ceremony
mortal engines deadly cannon
counterfeit imitate

probation proof
God . . . you good-bye
profit profitable lesson
sith since
Dian Diana, goddess of chastity

You would be satisfied?

    OTH.   Would! nay, I will.

    IAGO. And may: but, how? how satisfied, my
                                 [lord?

5 Would you, the supervisor,° grossly gape on—
Behold her topp'd?

    OTH.   Death and damnation! O!

    IAGO. It were a tedious difficulty, I think,
To bring them to that prospect:° damn them

10   [then,
If ever mortal eyes do see them bolster°
More than their own! What then? how then?
What shall I say? Where's satisfaction?
It is impossible you should see this,

15 Were they as prime° as goats, as hot as
                            [monkeys,
As salt° as wolves in pride,° and fools as gross
As ignorance made drunk. But yet, I say,
If imputation and strong circumstances,

20 Which lead directly to the door of truth,
Will give you satisfaction, you may have 't.

    OTH. Give me a living reason she's disloyal.

    IAGO. I do not like the office:
But, sith I am enter'd in this cause so far,

25 Prick'd° to 't by foolish honesty and love,
I will go on. I lay with Cassio lately;
And, being troubled with a raging tooth,
I could not sleep.
There are a kind of men so loose of soul,

30 That in their sleeps will mutter their affairs:
One of this kind is Cassio:
In sleep I heard him say "Sweet Desdemona,
Let us be wary, let us hide our loves;"
And then, sir, would he gripe and wring my

35   [hand,
Cry "O sweet creature!" and then kiss me hard,
As if he pluck'd up kisses by the roots
That grew upon my lips: then laid his leg
Over my thigh, and sigh'd, and kiss'd; and then

40 Cried "Cursed fate that gave thee to the Moor!"

    OTH. O monstrous! monstrous!

    IAGO.   Nay, this was but his dream.

    OTH. But this denoted a foregone conclusion:°
'Tis a shrewd doubt,° though it be but a dream.

    IAGO. And this may help to thicken other   45
                            [proofs
That do demonstrate thinly.

    OTH.   I'll tear her all to pieces.

    IAGO. Nay, but be wise: yet we see nothing
                        [done;   50
She may be honest yet. Tell me but this,
Have you not sometimes seen a handkerchief
Spotted with strawberries in your wife's hand?

    OTH. I gave her such a one; 'twas my first gift.

    IAGO. I know not that: but such a   55
                  [handkerchief—
I am sure it was your wife's—did I to-day
See Cassio wipe his beard with.

    OTH.   If it be that—

    IAGO. If it be that, or any that was hers,   60
It speaks against her with the other proofs.

    OTH. O, that the slave had forty thousand
                        [lives!
One is too poor, too weak for my revenge,
Now do I see 'tis true. Look here, Iago;   65
All my fond love thus do I blow to heaven.
'Tis gone.
Arise, black vengeance, from thy hollow cell!
Yield up, O love, thy crown and hearted° throne
To tyrannous hate! Swell, bosom, with thy   70
                      [fraught,°
For 'tis of aspics'° tongues!

    IAGO.   Yet be content.°

    OTH. O, blood, blood, blood!

    IAGO. Patience, I say; your mind perhaps may   75
                      [change.

    OTH. Never, Iago. Like to the Pontic° sea,
Whose icy current and compulsive course
Ne'er feels retiring ebb, but keeps due on
To the Propontic° and the Hellespont,°   80

supervisor onlooker
prospect exposure
bolster bed together
prime licentious
salt sensual
in pride in heat
prick'd spurred on

foregone conclusion previous experience
shrewd doubt strong ground for suspecting evil
hearted fixed in the heart
fraught freight
aspics' asps'
be content contain yourself
Pontic sea Black Sea
Propontic Sea of Marmora
Hellespont the Dardanelles

Even so my bloody thoughts, with violent pace,
Shall ne'er look back, ne'er ebb to humble love,
Till that a capable° and wide revenge
Swallow them up. [*Kneels*] Now, by yond marble
5   [heaven,
In the due reverence of a sacred vow
I here engage my words.
    IAGO.   Do not rise yet.
[*Kneels*] Witness, you ever-burning lights
10   [above,
You elements that clip° us round about,
Witness that here Iago doth give up°
The execution of his wit,° hands, heart,
To wrong'd Othello's service! Let him command,
15 And to obey shall be in me remorse,°
What bloody business ever.   [*They rise.*]
    OTH.   I greet thy love,
Not with vain thanks, but with acceptance
                               [bounteous,
20 And will upon the instant put thee to 't:°
Within these three days let me hear thee say
That Cassio's not alive.
    IAGO. My friend is dead; 'tis done at your
                                  [request:
25 But let her live.
    OTH. Damn her, lewd minx! O, damn her!
Come, go with me apart; I will withdraw,
To furnish me with some swift means of death
For the fair devil. Now art thou my lieutenant.
30   IAGO. I am your own for ever.   [*Exeunt.*]

Scene iv

[*Enter* DESDEMONA, EMILIA, *and* CLOWN.]
    DES. Do you know, sirrah, where Lieutenant
Cassio lies?°
    CLO. I dare not say he lies any where.
35   DES. Why, man?
    CLO. He's a soldier, and for one to say a soldier
lies, is stabbing.
    DES. Go to: where lodges he?

    CLO. To tell you where he lodges, is to tell you
where I lie.   40
    DES. Can any thing be made of this?
    CLO. I know not where he lodges, and for me
to devise a lodging and say he lies here or he lies
there, were to lie in mine own throat.
    DES. Can you inquire him out, and be edified°   45
by report?
    CLO. I will catechize the world for him; that is,
make questions, and by them answer.
    DES. Seek him, bid him come hither: tell him I
have moved my lord on his behalf, and hope all   50
will be well.
    CLO. To do this is within the compass of man's
wit; and therefore I will attempt the doing it.
                                      [*Exit.*]
    DES. Where should° I lose that handkerchief,   55
                                  [Emilia?
    EMIL. I know not, madam.
    DES. Believe me, I had rather have lost my
                                  [purse
Full of crusadoes:° and, but my noble Moor   60
Is true of mind and made of no such baseness
As jealous creatures are, it were enough
To put him to ill thinking.
    EMIL.   Is he not jealous?
    DES. Who, he? I think the sun where he   65
                                [was born
Drew all such humours from him.
    EMIL.   Look, where he comes.
    DES. I will not leave him now till Cassio
Be call'd to him.   70
    [*Enter* OTHELLO.]
                      How is 't with you, my lord?
    OTH. Well, my good lady. [*Aside*] O,
                      [hardness to dissemble!—
How do you, Desdemona?   75
    DES.   Well, my good lord.
    OTH. Give me your hand: this hand is
                        [moist,° my lady.
    DES. It yet hath felt no age nor known no
                           [sorrow.   80

---

capable comprehensive
clip embrace
give up dedicate
execution . . . wit exercise of his intelligence
remorse pity
put thee to 't give you something to do
lies dwells

edified enlightened
should could
crusadoes Portuguese gold coins stamped with a cross
moist a moist hand was supposed to be a sign of desire

Отн. This argues fruitfulness and liberal°
                                                    [heart:
Hot, hot, and moist: this hand of yours requires
A sequester° from liberty, fasting and prayer,
5   Much castigation, exercise devout;
For here's a young and sweating devil here,
That commonly rebels. 'Tis a good hand,
A frank one.
        Des.   You may, indeed, say so:
10 For 'twas that hand that gave away my heart.
        Отн. A liberal hand: the hearts of old gave
                                                    [hands;
But our new heraldry is hands, not hearts.°
        Des. I cannot speak of this. Come now, your
15   [promise.
        Отн. What promise, chuck?
        Des. I have sent to bid Cassio come speak
                                                    [with you.
        Отн. I have a salt° and sorry rheum° offends
20   [me;
Lend me thy handkerchief.
        Des.   Here, my lord.
        Отн. That which I gave you.
        Des.   I have it not about me.
25   Отн. Not?
        Des.   No, indeed, my lord.
        Отн.   That is a fault.
That handkerchief
Did an Egyptian to my mother give;
30 She was a charmer,° and could almost read
The thoughts of people: she told her, while she
                                                    [kept it,
'Twould make her amiable° and subdue my
                                                    [father
35 Entirely to her love, but if she lost it
Or made a gift of it, my father's eye
Should hold her loathed and his spirits should
                                                    [hunt
After new fancies: she, dying, gave it me;
40 And bid me, when my fate would have me
                                                    [wive,

To give it her, I did so: and take heed on 't;
Make it a darling like your precious eye;
To lose 't or give 't away were such perdition°
As nothing else could match.
        Des.   Is 't possible?   45
        Отн. 'Tis true: there's magic in the web of it:
A sibyl,° that had number'd in the world
The sun to course two hundred compasses,
In her prophetic fury° sew'd the work;
The worms were hallow'd that did breed the   50
                                                    [silk;
And it was dyed in mummy° which the skillful
Conserved° of maidens' hearts.
        Des.   Indeed! is 't true?
        Отн. Most veritable; therefore look to 't well.   55
        Des. Then would to God that I had never
                                                    [seen 't!
        Отн. Ha! wherefore?
        Des. Why do you speak so startingly and
                                                    [rash?°   60
        Отн. Is 't lost? is 't gone? speak, is it out o'
                                                    [the way?
        Des. Heaven bless us!
        Отн. Say you?
        Des. It is not lost; but what an if it were?   65
        Отн. How!
        Des. I say, it is not lost.
        Отн.   Fetch 't, let me see 't.
        Des. Why, so I can, sir, but I will not now.
This is a trick to put me from my suit: 70
Pray you, let Cassio be received again.
        Отн. Fetch me the handkerchief: my mind
                                                    [misgives.
        Des. Come, come;
You'll never meet a more sufficient° man.   75
        Отн. The handkerchief!
        Des.   I pray, talk me of Cassio.
        Отн. The handkerchief!
        Des.   A man that all his time
Hath founded his good fortunes on your love,   80

perdition loss
sibyl prophetess
prophetic fury divinely inspired madness
mummy the embalming fluid that oozed from mummies was
    supposed to be medicinal
conserved prepared
startingly and rash abruptly and violently
sufficient competent

liberal too generous, yielding
sequester separation
hands not hearts i.e., loveless marriages
salt here = watery
sorry rheum painful cold in the head
charmer enchantress
amiable lovable

Shared dangers with you,—

OTH. The handkerchief!

DES. In sooth, you are to blame.

OTH. Away!   [*Exit.*]

5   EMIL. Is not this man jealous?

DES. I ne'er saw this before.

Sure, there's some wonder in this handkerchief:

I am most unhappy in the loss of it.

EMIL. 'Tis not a year or two shows us a man:

10 They are all but stomachs, and we all but

[food;

They eat us hungerly, and when they are full,

They belch us. Look you, Cassio and my

[husband!

15 [*Enter* CASSIO *and* IAGO.]

IAGO. There is no other way; 'tis she must

[do 't:

And, lo, the happiness! go, and importune her.

DES. How now, good Cassio! what's the

20   [news with you?

CAS. Madam, my former suit: I do beseech

[you

That by your virtuous° means I may again

Exist, and be a member of his love

25 Whom I with all the office° of my heart

Entirely honour: I would not be delay'd.

If my offence be of such mortal° kind

That nor my service past, nor present sorrows,

Nor purposed merit in futurity,

30 Can ransom me into his love again,

But to know so must be my benefit;°

So shall I clothe me in a forced content,

And shut myself up in some other course,

To fortune's alms.°

35   DES.   Alas, thrice-gentle Cassio!

My advocation° is not now in tune;

My lord is not my lord; nor should I know him,

Were he in favour° as in humor alter'd.

So help me every spirit sanctified,

40 As I have spoken for you all my best

And stood within the blank° of his displeasure

For my free speech! you must awhile be patient:

What I can do I will; and more I will

Than for myself I dare: let that suffice you.

IAGO. Is my lord angry?   45

EMIL.   He went hence but now,

And certainly in strange unquietness.

IAGO. Can he be angry? I have seen the

[cannon,

When it hath blown his ranks into the air,   50

And, like the devil, from his very arm

Puff'd his own brother:—and can he be angry?

Something of moment then: I will go meet him:

There's matter in't indeed, if he be angry.

DES. I prithee, do so.   [*Exit* IAGO.] 55

Something, sure, of state,

Either from Venice, or some unhatch'd practice°

Made demonstrable here in Cyprus to him,

Hath puddled° his clear spirit; and in such cases

Men's natures wrangle with inferior things,   60

Though great ones are their object. 'Tis even so;

For let our finger ache, and it indues°

Our other healthful members even to that sense

Of pain: nay, we must think men are not gods,

Nor of them look for such observances   65

As fit the bridal. Beshrew me much, Emilia,

I was, unhandsome° warrior as I am,

Arraigning his unkindness with° my soul;

But now I find I had suborn'd the witness,

And he's indicted falsely.   70

EMIL. Pray heaven it be state-matters, as you

[think,

And no conception nor no jealous toy

Concerning you.

DES. Alas the day! I never gave him cause   75

EMIL. But jealous souls will not be answer'd

[so;

They are not ever jealous for the cause,

But jealous for they are jealous: 'tis a monster

Begot upon itself, born on itself.   80

DES. Heaven keep that monster from Othello's

[mind!

---

virtuous effective
office services
mortal deadly
my benefit an act of kindness to me
To fortune's alms to whatever fortune bestows
advocation advocacy
favour face

blank range, literally: the white spot at the center of a target
unhatch'd practice unrevealed plot
puddled muddied
indues induces
unhandsome unfair
with before (the bar of)

EMIL. Lady, amen.

DES. I will go seek him, Cassio, walk here
[about:

If I do find him fit, I'll move your suit
5 And seek to effect it to my uttermost.

CAS. I humbly thank your ladyship.

[Exeunt DESDEMONA and EMILIA.]

[Enter BIANCA.]

BIAN. Save you, friend Cassio!
10 CAS. What make you from home?
How is it with you, my most fair Bianca?
I' faith, sweet love, I was coming to your house.

BIAN. And I was going to your lodging,
[Cassio.

15 What, keep a week away? seven days and
[nights?

Eight score eight hours? and lovers' absent
[hours,

More tedious than the dial eight score times?
20 O weary reckoning!

CAS. Pardon me, Bianca:
I have this while with leaden thoughts been
[press'd;

But I shall, in a more continuate° time,
25 Strike off this score° of absence. Sweet Bianca,

[Giving her DESDEMONA's handkerchief.]

Take me this work out.°

BIAN. O Cassio, whence came this?
This is some token from a newer friend:
30 To the felt absence now I feel a cause:
Is 't come to this? Well, well.

CAS. Go to, woman!
Throw your vile guesses in the devil's teeth,
From whence you have them, You are jealous
35 [now

That this is from some mistress, some
[remembrance:

No, in good troth, Bianca.

BIAN. Why, whose is it?
40 CAS. I know not, sweet: I found it in my
[chamber.

I like the work well: ere it be demanded—
As like enough it will—I'ld have it copied:
Take it, and do 't; and leave me for this time.

BIAN. Leave you! wherefore? 45

CAS. I do attend here on the general;
And think it no addition,° nor my wish,
To have him see me woman'd.

BIAN. Why, I pray you?

CAS. Not that I love you not. 50

BIAN. But that you do not love me.
I pray you, bring° me on the way a little,
And say if I shall see you soon at night.

CAS. 'Tis but a little way that I can bring you;
For I attend here: but I'll see you soon. 55

BIAN. 'Tis very good; I must be
circumstanced.° *[Exeunt.]*

ACT IV

Scene i

[Enter OTHELLO and IAGO.]

IAGO. Will you think so?

OTH. Think so, Iago! 60

IAGO. What,
To kiss in private?

OTH. An unauthorized kiss.

IAGO. Or to be naked with her friend in bed
An hour or more, not meaning any harm? 65

OTH. Naked in bed, Iago, and not mean harm!
It is hypocrisy° against the Devil:
They that mean virtuously, and yet do so,
The Devil their virtue tempts, and they tempt
[heaven. 70

IAGO. So they do nothing, 'tis a venial slip:
But if I give my wife a handkerchief—

OTH. What then?

IAGO. Why, then, 'tis hers, my lord; and,
[being hers, 75

She may, I think, bestow 't on any man.

OTH. She is protectress of her honour too:
May she give that?

IAGO. Her honour is an essence that's not
[seen: 80

They have it very oft that have it not:
But, for the handkerchief—

OTH. By heaven, I would most gladly have
[forgot it.

continuate uninterrupted (by other affairs)
Strike ... score erase this account
Take ... out copy this embroidery for me

addition honor, credit
bring accompany
circumstanced yield to circumstances
hypocrisy i.e., seeming to sin without sinning

Thou said'st—O, it comes o'er my memory,
As doth the raven o'er the infected house,
Boding° to all—he had my handkerchief.
    Iago. Ay, what of that?
5   Oth.   That's not so good now.
    Iago.   What,
If I had said I had seen him do you wrong?
Or heard him say as knaves be such abroad,
Who having, by their own importunate suit,
10 Or voluntary dotage of some mistress,
Convinced or supplied° them, cannot choose
But they must blab—
    Oth.   Hath he said any thing?
    Iago. He hath, my lord; but be you well
15   [assured,
No more than he'll unswear.
    Oth.   What hath he said?
    Iago. 'Faith, that he did—I know not what
                            [he did.
20   Oth. What? what?
    Iago. Lie—
    Oth.   With her?
    Iago.   With her, on her; what you will.
    Oth. Lie with her! lie on her! We say lie on her,
25 when they belie her. Lie with her! that's ful-
some.—Handkerchief—confessions—handkerchief!—To confess, and be hanged for his labour—
first, to be hanged, and then to confess.—I tremble at it. Nature would not invest herself in such
30 shadowing passion without some instruction.° It
is not words that shake me thus. Pish! Noses, ears,
and lips.—Is 't possible?—Confess—handkerchief!—O devil!
    [*Falls in a trance.*]
35   Iago. Work on,
My medicine, work! Thus credulous fools are
                            [caught;
And many worthy and chaste dames even thus,
All guiltless, meet reproach. What, ho! my lord!
40 My lord, I say! Othello!
    [*Enter* Cassio.]
                       How now, Cassio!
    Cas. What's the matter?

    Iago. My lord is fall'n into an epilepsy: This is
his second fit; he had one yesterday,   45
    Cas. Rub him about the temples.
    Iago.   No, forbear;
The lethargy° must have his quiet course;
If not, he foams at mouth and by and by
Breaks out to savage madness. Look, he stirs: 50
Do you withdraw yourself a little while,
He will recover straight: when he is gone,
I would on great occasion° speak with you.
                        [*Exit* Cassio.]
How is it, general? have you not hurt your   55
                                  [head?
    Oth. Dost thou mock me?
    Iago.   I mock you! no, by heaven.
Would you would bear your fortune like a man!
    Oth. A horned man's° a monster and a beast. 60
    Iago. There's many a beast then in a
                            [populous city,
And many a civil° monster.
    Oth. Did he confess it?
    Iago.   Good sir, be a man;   65
Think every bearded fellow that's but yoked°
May draw° with you: there's millions now alive
That nightly lie in those unproper° beds
Which they dare swear peculiar:° your case is
                         [better. 70
O, 'tis the spite of hell, the fiend's arch-mock,
To lip a wanton in a secure° couch,
And to suppose her chaste! No, let me know;
And knowing what I am, I know what she
                         [shall be. 75
    Oth. O, thou art wise; 'tis certain.
    Iago.   Stand you awhile apart;
Confine yourself but in a patient list.°
Whilst you were here o'erwhelmed with your
                         [grief— 80
A passion most unsuiting such a man—

boding foreboding evil
convinced or supplied conquered or satisfied (Kermode)
Nature . . . instruction natural imagination would not arouse
    such darkening (blinding) passions in me unless it were based
    on fact.

lethargy coma
great occasion an urgent matter
horned man i.e., cuckold
civil in civilized life
yoked married
draw i.e., like the horned ox
unproper not their own
peculiar private
secure free from suspicion
in . . . list within the bounds of patience

Cassio came hither: I shifted him away,°
And laid good 'scuse upon your ecstasy,°
Bade him anon return and here speak with me;
The which he promised. Do but encave°
5   [yourself,
And mark the fleers,° the gibes, and notable
                                            [scorns,
That dwell in every region of his face;
For I will make him tell the tale anew,
10   Where, how, how oft, how long ago, and when
He hath, and is again to cope° your wife:
I say, but mark his gesture. Marry, patience;
Or I shall say you are all in all in spleen,°
And nothing of a man.
15   OTH.   Dost thou hear, Iago?
I will be found most cunning in my patience;
But—dost thou hear?—most bloody.
       IAGO.   That's not amiss;
But yet keep time in all. Will you withdraw?
20   [OTHELLO retires.]
Now will I question Cassio of Bianca,
A housewife° that by selling her desires
Buys herself bread and clothes: it is a creature
That dotes on Cassio; as 'tis the strumpet's
25   [plague
To beguile many and be beguiled by one:
He, when he hears of her, cannot refrain
From the excess of laughter. Here he comes:
       [Re-enter CASSIO.]
30   As he shall smile, Othello shall go mad;
And his unbookish° jealousy must construe
Poor Cassio's smiles, gestures and light
                                            [behaviour,
Quite in the wrong. How do you now,
35   [lieutenant?
       CAS. The worser that you give me the
                                            [addition°
Whose want even kills me.
       IAGO. Ply Desdemona well, and you are
40   [sure on 't.

shifted him away managed to get rid of him
ecstasy swoon
encave conceal
fleers sneers
cope encounter
all ... spleen completely the victim of anger
housewife hussy
unbookish ignorant
addition title

[Speaking lower] Now, if this suit lay in
                                          [Bianca's power.
How quickly should you speed!
       CAS.   Alas, poor caitiff!°
OTH. Look, how he laughs already!   45
IAGO. I never knew a woman love man so.
CAS. Alas, poor rogue! I think, i' faith, she
                                          [loves me.
OTH. Now he denies it faintly, and laughs it
                                          [out. 50
IAGO. Do you hear, Cassio?
OTH.   Now he importunes him
To tell it o'er: go to; well said, well said.
IAGO. She gives it out that you shall marry her:
Do you intend it?   55
       CAS. Ha, ha, ha!
       OTH. Do you triumph, Roman?° do you
                                          [triumph?
       CAS. I marry her! what? a customer!° Prithee,
bear some charity to my wit; do not think it so 60
unwholesome. Ha, ha, ha!
       OTH. So, so, so, so: they laugh that win.
       IAGO. 'Faith, the cry° goes that you shall marry
her.
       CAS. Prithee, say true.   65
       IAGO. I am a very villain else.
       OTH. Have you scored° me? Well.
       CAS. This is the monkey's own giving out: she
is persuaded I will marry her, out of her own love
and flattery,° not out of my promise.   70
       OTH. Iago beckons° me; now he begins the story.
       CAS. She was here even now; she haunts me in
every place. I was the other day talking on the
sea-bank with certain Venetians; and thither comes
the bauble,° and, by this hand, she falls me thus 75
about my neck—
       OTH. Crying, "O dear Cassio!" as it were: his
gesture imports it.
       CAS. So hangs, and lolls, and weeps upon me;
so hales, and pulls me; ha, ha, ha!   80

caitiff wretch
Roman suggested by triumph
customer harlot
cry common report
scored beaten, settled my fate
flattery i.e., self-flattery
beckons signals
bauble plaything

OTH. Now he tells how she plucked him to my chamber. O, I see that nose of yours, but not that dog I shall throw it to.

CAS. Well, I must leave her company.

5   IAGO. Before me!° look, where she comes.
[Enter BIANCA.]

CAS. 'Tis such another fitchew!° marry, a perfumed one. What do you mean by this haunting of me?

10   BIAN. Let the devil and his dam haunt you! What did you mean by that same handkerchief you gave me even now? I was a fine fool to take it. I must take out the work?—A likely piece of work, that you should find it in your chamber, and not know

15 who left it there! This is some minx's token, and I must take out the work? There; give it your hobby-horse,° wheresoever you had it, I'll take out no work on 't.

CAS. How now,° my sweet Bianca! how now!

20 how now!

OTH. By heaven, that should be° my handkerchief!

BIAN. An° you'll come to supper to-night, you may; an you will not, come when you are next

25 prepared for.   *[Exit.]*

IAGO. After her, after her.

CAS. 'Faith, I must; she'll rail in the street else.

IAGO. Will you sup there?

CAS. 'Faith, I intend so.

30   IAGO. Well, I may chance to see you; for I would very fain speak with you.

CAS. Prithee, come; will you?

IAGO. Go to; say no more.   *[Exit CASSIO.]*

OTH. *[Advancing]* How shall I murder him, Iago?

35   IAGO. Did you perceive how he laughed at his vice?

OTH. O Iago!

IAGO. And did you see the handkerchief?

OTH. Was that mine?

40   IAGO. Yours, by this hand: and to see how he prizes the foolish woman your wife! she gave it him, and he hath given it his whore.

OTH. I would have him nine years a-killing. A fine woman! a fair woman! a sweet woman!

IAGO. Nay, you must forget that.   45

OTH. Ay, let her rot, and perish, and be damned to-night; for she shall not live: no, my heart is turned to stone; I strike it, and it hurts my hand. O, the world hath not a sweeter creature: she might lie by an emperor's side and command him tasks.   50

IAGO. Nay, that's not your way.

OTH. Hang her! I do but say what she is: so delicate with her needle: an admirable musician: O! she will sing the savageness out of a bear: of so high and plenteous wit and invention°—   55

IAGO. She's the worse for all this.

OTH. O, a thousand thousand times: and then, of so gentle a condition!°

IAGO. Ay, too gentle.

OTH. Nay, that's certain: but yet the pity of it,   60 Iago! O Iago, the pity of it, Iago!

IAGO. If you are so fond over° her iniquity, give her patent° to offend; for, if it touch not you, it comes near nobody.

OTH. I will chop her into messes:° cuckold me!   65

IAGO. O, 'tis foul in her.

OTH. With mine officer!

IAGO. That's fouler.

OTH. Get me some poison, Iago; this night: I'll not expostulate with her, lest her body and beauty   70 unprovide° my mind again: this night, Iago.

IAGO. Do it not with poison, strangle her in her bed, even the bed she hath contaminated.

OTH. Good, good: the justice of it pleases: very good.   75

IAGO. And for Cassio, let me be his undertaker:° you shall hear more by midnight.

OTH. Excellent good. *[A trumpet within.]*
                [What trumpet is that same?

IAGO. Something from Venice, sure, 'tis   80
                    [Lodovico
Come from the duke: and, see, your wife is
                        [with him.

Before me on my life
fitchew polecat
hobby-horse whore
How now What's the matter?
should be must be
An if

invention imagination
condition disposition
fond over foolish about
patent license
messes small pieces of food
unprovide unfit, weaken
let . . . undertaker let me take care of him

[*Enter* LODOVICO, DESDEMONA, *and* ATTENDANTS.]
LOD. Save you, worthy general!
OTH.   With all my heart,° sir.
LOD. The duke and senators of Venice greet
5   you.   [*Gives him a letter.*]
OTH. I kiss the instrument of their pleasures.
                         [*Opens the letter, and reads.*]
DES. And what's the news, good cousin
                                              [Lodovico?
10   IAGO. I am very glad to see you, signior; Wel-
come to Cyprus.
LOD. I thank you. How does Lieutenant
                                              [Cassio?
IAGO. Lives, sir.
15   DES. Cousin, there's fall'n between him and
                                              [my lord
An unkind breach:° but you shall make all well.
OTH. Are you sure of that?
DES. My lord?
20   OTH. [*Reads*] "This fail you not to do, as you
will—"
LOD. He did not call; he's busy in the paper. Is
there division 'twixt my lord and Cassio?
DES. A most unhappy one: I would do much
25   To atone° them, for the love I bear to Cassio.
OTH. Fire and brimstone!
DES.   My lord?
OTH.   Are you wise?
DES. What, is he angry?
30   LOD.   May be the letter moved him;
For, as I think, they do command him home,
Deputing Cassio in his government.
DES. Trust me, I am glad on 't.
OTH.   Indeed!
35   DES.   My lord?
OTH. I am glad to see you mad.
DES.   Why, sweet Othello,
OTH. [*Striking her*] Devil!
DES. I have not deserved this.
40   LOD. My lord, this would not be believed in
                                              [Venice,
Though I should swear I saw 't: 'tis very much:
Make her amends; she weeps.
OTH.   O devil, devil!

If that the earth could teem° with woman's   45
                                              [tears,
Each drop she falls° would prove a crocodile.
Out of my sight!
DES. I will not stay to offend you. [*Going.*]
LOD. Truly, an obedient lady: 50
I do beseech your lordship, call her back.
OTH. Mistress!
DES.   My lord?
OTH.   What would you with her, sir?
LOD. Who, I, my lord?   55
OTH. Ay; you did wish that I would make her
                                              [turn:
Sir, she can turn, and turn, and yet go on,
And turn again; and she can weep, sir, weep;
And she's obedient, as you say, obedient,   60
Very obedient. Proceed you in your tears.
Concerning this, sir—O well-painted passion!—
I am commanded home. Get you away;
I'll send for you anon. Sir, I obey the mandate,
And will return to Venice. Hence, avaunt!   65
                              [*Exit* DESDEMONA.]
Cassio shall have my place. And, sir, to-night,
I do entreat that we may sup together:
You are welcome, sir, to Cyprus.—Goats and
      monkeys!   [*Exit.*]   70
LOD. Is this the noble Moor whom our full
                                              [senate
Call all in all sufficient?° Is this the nature
Whom passion could not shake? whose solid.
                                              [virtue   75
The shot of accident, nor dart of chance,
Could neither graze nor pierce?
IAGO.   He is much changed.
LOD. Are his wits safe?° is he not light of
                                              [brain?   80
IAGO. He's that he is: I may not breathe my
                                              [censure°
What he might be: if what he might he is not,
I would to heaven he were!
LOD.   What, strike his wife!   85
IAGO. 'Faith, that was not so well; yet would I
                                              [knew

teem conceive
falls lets fall
sufficient competent
safe sound
censure opinion

---

with . . . heart i.e., I heartily thank you (Kermode)
unkind breach unnatural rupture
atone reconcile

That stroke would prove the worst!
    Lod.   Is it his use?°
Or did the letters work upon his blood,°
And new-create this fault?
5   Iago.   Alas, alas!
It is not honesty in me to speak
What I have seen and known. You shall observe
                              [him,
And his own courses° will denote him so
10 That I may save my speech: do but go after,
And mark how he continues.
    Lod. I am sorry that I am deceived in him.
                          [Exeunt.]

Scene ii

[*Enter* Othello *and* Emilia.]
15 Oth. You have seen nothing then?
    Emil. Not ever heard, nor ever did suspect.
    Oth. Yes, you have seen Cassio and she
                         [together.
    Emil. But then I saw no harm, and then I
20   [heard
Each syllable that breath made up between
                          [them.
    Oth. What, did they never whisper?
    Emil.   Never, my lord.
25 Oth. Nor send you out o' the way?
    Emil. Never.
    Oth. To fetch her fan, her gloves, her mask,
                    [nor nothing?
    Emil. Never, my lord.
30 Oth. That's strange.
    Emil. I durst, my lord, to wager she is honest,
Lay down my soul at stake:° if you think other,
Remove your thought; it doth abuse your
                      [bosom.
35 If any wretch have put this in your head,
Let heaven requite it with the serpent's curse!°
For, if she be not honest, chaste, and true,
There's no man happy; the purest of their wives
Is foul as slander.
40 Oth.   Bid her come hither: go.

---

use habit
blood passion
courses conduct
at stake as the stake
serpent's curse God's curse on the serpent in the Garden
    of Eden; cf. Genesis III

                          [*Exit* Emilia.]
She says enough; yet she's a simple bawd
That cannot say as much. This is a subtle whore,
A closet lock and key° of villanous secrets:
And yet she'll kneel and pray; I have seen her 45
                        [do 't.
[*Enter* Desdemona *with* Emilia.]
    Des. My lord, what is your will?
    Oth.   Pray, chuck, come hither.
    Des. What is your pleasure? 50
    Oth.   Let me see your eyes;
Look in my face.
    Des.   What horrible fancy 's this?
    Oth. [*To* Emilia] Some of your function,°
                      [mistress; 55
Leave procreants alone and shut the door;
Cough, or cry "hem," if any body come:
Your mystery, your mystery:° nay, dispatch.
                      [*Exit* Emilia.]
    Des. Upon my knees, what doth your speech 60
                      [import?
I understand a fury in your words,
But not the words.
    Oth. Why, what art thou?
    Des.   Your wife, my lord; your true 65
And loyal wife.
    Oth.   Come, swear it, damn thyself;
Lest, being like one of heaven, the devils
                      [themselves
Should fear to seize thee: therefore be double 70
                      [damn'd:
Swear thou art honest.
    Des.   Heaven doth truly know it.
    Oth. Heaven truly knows that thou art false
                      [as hell. 75
    Des. To whom, my lord? with whom? how
                      [am I false?
    Oth. O Desdemona! away! away! away!
    Des. Alas the heavy day! Why do you weep?
Am I the motive° of these tears, my lord? 80
If haply you my father do suspect
An instrument of this your calling back,
Lay not your blame on me: if you have lost him,

---

closet ... key secret storehouse
some ... function perform your duties (of bawd)
mystery trade
motive cause

Why, I have lost him too.
OTH.   Had it pleased heaven
To try me with affliction; had they° rain'd
All kinds of sores and shames on my bare head,
5   Steep'd me in poverty to the very lips,
Given to captivity me and my utmost hopes,
I should have found in some place of my soul
A drop of patience: but, alas, to make me
A fixèd figure° for the time of scorn°
10 To point his slow° unmoving° finger at!
Yet could I bear that too; well, very well:
But there, where I have garner'd up my heart,
Where either I must live, or bear no life;
The fountain from the which my current runs,
15 Or else dries up; to be discarded thence!
Or keep it as a cistern for foul toads
To knot° and gender° in! Turn thy complexion
                                    [there,°
Patience, thou young and rose-lipp'd
20   [cherubin—
Ay, there, look grim as hell!
    DES. I hope my noble lord esteems me honest.
    OTH. O, ay; as summer flies are in the
                                    [shambles,°
25 That quicken even with blowing.° O thou weed,
Who art so lovely fair and smell'st so sweet
That the sense aches at thee, would thou hadst
                                    [ne'er been born!
    DES. Alas, what ignorant sin have I committed?
30 OTH. Was this fair paper, this most goodly
                                    [book,
Made to write "whore" upon? What committed!
Committed! O thou public commoner!°
I should make very forges of my cheeks,
35 That would to cinders burn up modesty,
Did I but speak thy deeds. What committed!

they   i.e., the heavenly powers
fixèd figure   Othello apparently imagines himself set in a pil-
    lory
time of scorn   scornful world
slow   i.e., to change its direction
unmoving   seeming not to move
knot   entangle
gender   engender
Turn . . . there   i.e., turn pale at that
shambles   slaughter-house
quicken . . . blowing   that come to life as soon as the eggs
    are laid (Kermode)
commoner   harlot

Heaven stops the nose at it and the moon
                                    [winks,°
The bawdy wind that kisses all it meets
Is hush'd within the hollow mine of earth,   40
And will not hear it. What committed!
Impudent strumpet!
    DES.   By heaven, you do me wrong.
    OTH. Are not you a strumpet?
    DES.   No, as I am a Christian: 45
If to preserve this vessel for my lord
From any other foul unlawful touch
Be not to be a strumpet, I am none.
    OTH. What, not a whore?
    DES.   No, as I shall be saved.   50
    OTH. Is 't possible?
    DES. O, heaven forgive us!
    OTH.   I cry you mercy,° then:
I took you for that cunning whore of Venice
That married with Othello. [*Raising his voice*]   55
                          [You, mistress,
That have the office opposite to Saint Peter,
And keep the gate of hell!
    [*Re-enter* EMILIA.]
                          You, you, ay, you!   60
We have done our course; there's money for
                          [your pains:
I pray you, turn the key and keep our counsel.
                                    [*Exit.*]
    EMIL. Alas, what does this gentleman   65
                          [conceive?
How do you, madam? how do you, my good
                          [lady?
    DES. 'Faith, half asleep.
    EMIL. Good madam, what's the matter with   70
                          [my lord?
    DES. With who?
    EMIL. Why, with my lord, madam.
    DES. Who is thy lord?
    EMIL.   He that is yours, sweet lady.   75
    DES. I have none: do not talk to me, Emilia;
I cannot weep; nor answer have I none,
But what should go by water.° Prithee, tonight
Lay on my bed my wedding sheets: remember;
And call thy husband hither.   80
    EMIL.   Here's a change indeed! [*Exit.*]

winks   closes its eyes
cry . . . mercy   beg your pardon
go by water   be expressed by tears

DES. 'Tis meet I should be used so, very meet.
How have I been behaved,° that he might stick°
The small'st opinion on my least misuse?°
[*Re-enter* EMILIA *with* IAGO.]

5 IAGO. What is your pleasure, madam? How
[is 't with you?
DES. I cannot tell. Those that do teach young
[babes
Do it with gentle means and easy tasks:
10 He might have chid me so; for, in good faith,
I am a child to chiding.
    IAGO.   What's the matter, lady?
    EMIL. Alas, Iago, my lord hath so bewhored
[her,
15 Thrown such despite° and heavy terms upon
[her,
As true hearts cannot bear.
    DES. Am I that name, Iago?
    IAGO.   What name, fair lady?
20 DES. Such as she says my lord did say I was.
    EMIL. He call'd her whore: a beggar in his
[drink
Could not have laid such terms upon his callet.°
    IAGO. Why did he so?
25 DES. I do not know; I am sure I am none such.
    IAGO. Do not weep, do not weep. Alas the
[day!
    EMIL. Hath she forsook so many noble
[matches,
30 Her father and her country and her friends,
To be call'd whore? would it not make one
[weep?
    DES. It is my wretched fortune.
    IAGO.   Beshrew° him for 't!
35 How comes this trick upon him?
    DES.   Nay, heaven doth know.
    EMIL. I will be hang'd, if some eternal° villain,
Some busy° and insinuating rogue,

Some cogging,° cozening° slave, to get some
[office, 40
Have not devised this slander; I'll be hanged
[else.
    IAGO. Fie, there is no such man; it is
[impossible.
    DES. If any such there be, heaven pardon him! 45
    EMIL. A halter pardon him! and hell gnaw his
[bones!
Why should he call her whore? who keeps her
[company?
What place? what time? what form? what 50
[likelihood?
The Moor's abused by some most villanous
[knave.
Some base notorious knave, some scurvy fellow.
O heaven, that such companions° thou'ldst 55
[unfold,°
And put in every honest hand a whip
To lash the rascals naked through the world
Even from the east to the west!
    IAGO.   Speak within door.° 60
    EMIL. O, fie upon them! Some such squire he
[was
That turn'd your wit the seamy side without,
And made you to suspect me with the Moor.
    IAGO. You are a fool; go to. 65
    DES.   O good Iago,
What shall I do to win my lord again?
Good friend, go to him; for, by this light of
[heaven,
I know not how I lost him. Here I kneel: 70
If e'er my will did trespass 'gainst his love,
Either in discourse° of thought or actual deed,
Or that mine eyes, mine ears, or any sense,
Delighted them in any other form;
Or that I do not yet, and ever did, 75
And ever will—though he do shake me off
To beggarly divorcement—love him dearly,
Comfort forswear me! Unkindness may do
[much;

been behaved, conducted myself
stick attach
small'st . . . misuse the least bit of censure on my slightest
    misconduct
despite contempt
callet whore
Beshrew curse
eternal infernal
busy meddling

cogging deceiving
cozening cheating
companions fellows
unfold expose
Speak . . . door don't talk so loud
discourse range

And his unkindness may defeat° my life,
But never taint my love. I cannot say "whore."
It doth abhor me now I speak the word;
To do the act that might the addition° earn
5 Not the world's mass of vanity could make me.
    IAGO. I pray you, be content; 'tis but his
                                              [humour:
The business of the state does him offence,
And he does chide with you.
10   DES. If 'twere no other—
      IAGO.   'Tis but so, I warrant.
    [Trumpets within.]
Hark how these instruments summon you to
                                          [supper!
15 The messengers of Venice stay the meat:°
Go in, and weep not; all things shall be well.
    [Exeunt DESDEMONA and EMILIA.]
    [Enter RODERIGO.]
How now, Roderigo!
20   ROD. I do not find that thou dealest justly with
    me.
      IAGO. What in the contrary?
      ROD. Every day thou daffest me° with some de-
    vice,° Iago; and rather, as it seems to me now,
25 keepest from me all conveniency° than suppliest
    me with the least advantage of hope. I will indeed
    no longer endure it, nor am I yet persuaded to put
    up in peace° what already I have foolishly suf-
    fered.
30   IAGO. Will you hear me, Roderigo?
      ROD. 'Faith, I have heard too much, for your
    words and performances are no kin together.
      IAGO. You charge me most unjustly.
      ROD. With nought but truth. I have wasted my-
35 self out of my means.° The jewels you have had
    from me to deliver to Desdemona would half have
    corrupted a votarist:° you have told me she hath
    received them and returned me expectations and

comforts of sudden respect° and acquaintance, but
I find none.   40
    IAGO. Well; go to; very well.
    ROD. Very well! go to! I cannot go to, man; nor
'tis not very well: nay, I think it is scurvy, and
begin to find myself fopped° in it.
    IAGO. Very well.   45
    ROD. I tell you 'tis not very well. I will make
myself known to Desdemona: if she will return
me my jewels, I will give over my suit and repent
my unlawful solicitation; if not, assure yourself I
will seek satisfaction of you.   50
    IAGO. You have said now.
    ROD. Ay, and said nothing but what I protest
intendment of doing.
    IAGO. Why, now I see there's mettle in thee, and
even from this instant do build on thee a better   55
opinion than ever before. Give me thy hand, Roderigo: thou hast taken against me a most just exception; but yet, I protest, I have dealt most directly in thy affair.
    ROD. It hath not appeared.   60
    IAGO. I grant indeed it hath not appeared, and
your suspicion is not without wit and judgement.
But, Roderigo, if thou hast that in thee indeed,
which I have greater reason to believe now than
ever, I mean purpose, courage and valour, this   65
night show it: if thou the next night following enjoy not Desdemona, take me from this world with
treachery and devise engines for° my life.
    ROD. Well, what is it? is it within reason and
compass?   70
    IAGO. Sir, there is especial commission come from
Venice to depute Cassio in Othello's place.
    ROD. Is that true? why, then Othello and Des-
demona return again to Venice.
    IAGO. O, no; he goes into Mauritania and takes   75
away with him the fair Desdemona, unless his
abode be lingered here by some accident: wherein
none can be so determinate° as the removing of
Cassio.
    ROD. How do you mean, removing of him?   80

defeat destroy
addition term
stay the meat to dine
daffest me put me off
device deception
conveniency opportunity
put . . . peace submit silently to
wasted . . . means squandered my money
votarist nun

sudden respect immediate attention
fopped duped
engines for plots against
determinate decisive

IAGO. Why, by making him uncapable of
Othello's place; knocking out his brains.

ROD. And that you would have me to do?

IAGO. Ay, if you dare do yourself a profit and a
5 right. He sups to-night with a harlotry,° and thither
will I go to him: he knows not yet of his honourable fortune. If you will watch his going thence,
which I will fashion to fall out between twelve and
one, you may take him at your pleasure: I will be
10 near to second your attempt, and he shall fall between us. Come, stand not amazed at it, but go
along with me; I will show you such a necessity
in his death that you shall think yourself bound
to put it on him. It is now high supper-time,° and
15 the night grows to waste: about it.

ROD. I will hear further reason for this.

IAGO. And you shall be satisfied.

[*Exeunt.*]

Scene iii

[*Enter* OTHELLO, LODOVICO, DESDEMONA, EMILIA,
20 *and* ATTENDANTS.]

LOD. I do beseech you, sir, trouble yourself
[no further.

OTH. O, pardon me; 'twill do me good to
walk.

25 LOD. Madam, good night; I humbly thank
[your ladyship.

DES. Your honour is most welcome.

OTH.   Will you walk, sir?
O—Desdemona—

30 DES. My lord?

OTH. Get you to bed on the instant; I will be
returned forthwith: dismiss your attendant there:
look it be done.

DES. I will, my lord.

35 [*Exeunt* OTHELLO, LODOVICO, *and* ATTENDANTS.]

EMIL. How goes it now? he looks gentler
[than he did.

DES. He says he will return incontinent:°
He hath commanded me to go to bed,
40 And bade me to dismiss you.

EMIL.   Dismiss me!

DES. It was his bidding; therefore, good
[Emilia,

Give me my nightly wearing, and adieu:
We must not now displease him.   45

EMIL. I would you had never seen him!

DES. So would not I: my love doth so approve
[him,
That even his stubbornness,° his checks,° his
[frowns— 50
Prithee, unpin me—have grace and favour in
[them.

EMIL. I have laid those sheets you bade me
[on the bed.

DES. All's one.° Good faith, how foolish are   55
[our minds!
If I do die before thee, prithee, shroud me
In one of those same sheets.

EMIL.   Come, come, you talk.°

DES. My mother had a maid call'd Barbara: 60
She was in love, and he she loved proved mad°
And did forsake her: she had a song of
["willow;"
An old thing 'twas, but it express'd her fortune,
And she died singing it: that song to-night   65
Will not go from my mind; I have much to do,°
But° to go hang my head all at one side,
And sing it like poor Barbara. Prithee, dispatch.

EMIL. Shall I go fetch your night-gown?

DES.   No, unpin me here. 70
This Lodovico is a proper man.

EMIL. A very handsome man.

DES. He speaks well.

EMIL. I know a lady in Venice would have walked
barefoot to Palestine for a touch of his nether lip. 75

DES. [*Singing*] The poor soul sat sighing by a
[sycamore tree,
Sing all a green willow;
Her hand on her bosom, her head on her knee,
Sing willow, willow, willow: 80
The fresh streams ran by her, and murmur'd
[her moans;
Sing willow, willow, willow;
Her salt tears fell from her, and soften'd the
[stones;— 85

harlotry wench
high supper-time high time for supper
incontinent immediately

stubbornness harshness
checks rebukes
All's one no matter
talk i.e., talk nonsense
mad wild, i.e., inconstant
much to do i.e., to make a great effort
But not

Lay by these:—
[*Singing*] Sing willow, willow, willow;
Prithee, hie thee; he'll come anon:—
[*Singing*] Sing all a green willow must be my
5   [garland.
Let nobody blame him; his scorn I approve—
Nay, that's not next.—Hark! who is 't that
                                    [knocks?
EMIL. It's the wind.
10 DES. [*Singing*] I call'd my love false love; but
                                  [what said he then?
   Sing willow, willow, willow:
If I court moe women, you'll couch with
                                  [moe men.—
15 So, get thee gone; good night. Mine eyes do
                                  [itch;
Doth that bode weeping?
EMIL.   'Tis neither here nor there.
DES. I have heard it said so. O, these men,
20   [these men!
Dost thou in conscience° think—tell me,
                                  [Emilia—
That there be women do abuse their husbands
In such gross kind?
25 EMIL.   There be some such, no question.
DES. Wouldst thou do such a deed for all the
                                  [world?
EMIL. Why, would not you?
DES.   No, by this heavenly light!
30 EMIL. Nor I neither by this heavenly light;
I might do 't as well i' the dark.
DES. Wouldst thou do such a deed for all the
                                  [world?
EMIL. The world's a huge thing: it is a great
35   [price
For a small vice.
DES. In troth, I think thou wouldst not.
EMIL. In troth, I think I should; and undo 't when
I had done. Marry, I would not do such a thing
40 for a joint-ring,° nor for measures of lawn,° nor
for gowns, petticoats, nor caps, nor any petty ex-
hibition;° but, for the whole world—why, who
would not make her husband a cuckold to make
him a monarch? I should venture purgatory for 't.

in conscience in your inmost thought
joint-ring a ring made in interlocking halves
lawn fine linen
exhibition gift, payment

DES. Beshrew me, if I would do such a wrong   45
For the whole world.
EMIL. Why, the wrong is but a wrong i' the world;
and having the world for your labour, 'tis a wrong
in your own world, and you might quickly make
it right.   50
DES. I do not think there is any such woman.
EMIL. Yes, a dozen; and as many to the vantage°
as would store the world they played for.
But I do think it is their husbands' faults
If wives do fall: say that they slack their duties,   55
And pour our treasures into foreign laps,
Or else break out in peevish jealousies,
Throwing restraint upon us; or say they strike
                                    [us,
Or scant° our former having° in despite;°   60
Why, we have galls,° and though we have some
                                    [grace,°
Yet have we some revenge. Let husbands know
Their wives have sense° like them: they see and
                                  [smell 65
And have their palates both for sweet and sour,
As husbands have. What is it that they do
When they change us for others? Is it sport?
I think it is: and doth affection breed it?
I think it doth: is 't frailty that thus errs?   70
It is so too: and have not we affections,
Desires for sport, and frailty, as men have?
Then let them use us well: else let them know,
The ills we do, their ills instruct us so.
DES. Good night, good night: heaven me such   75
                                  [uses° send,
   Not to pick bad from bad, but by bad mend!
                                  [*Exeunt.*]

ACT V

Scene i

[*Enter* IAGO *and* RODERIGO.]
IAGO. Here, stand behind this bulk;° straight   80
                                  [will he come:

to the vantage to boot
scant cut down
having allowance
in despite out of malice
galls tempers
grace disposition to forgive
sense feeling
uses practices
bulk projecting shop stall

Wear thy good rapier bare, and put it home:
Quick, quick; fear nothing; I'll be at thy elbow:
It makes us, or it mars us; think on that,
And fix most firm thy resolution.
5   Rod. Be near at hand; I may miscarry in 't.
    Iago. Here, at thy hand: be bold, and take thy
        stand.   [*Retires.*]
    Rod. I have no great devotion to the deed;
And yet he hath given me satisfying reasons:
10 'Tis but a man gone. Forth, my sword: he dies.
    Iago. I have rubb'd this young quat° almost
                    [to the sense,°
And he grows angry. Now, whether he kill
                    [Cassio,
15 Or Cassio him, or each do kill the other,
Every way makes my gain; live Roderigo,
He calls me to a restitution large
Of gold and jewels that I bobb'd° from him,
As gifts to Desdemona;
20 It must not be: if Cassio do remain,
He hath a daily beauty in his life
That makes me ugly; and, besides, the Moor
May unfold me to him; there stand I in much
                    [peril:
25 No, he must die. But so: I hear him coming.
        [*Enter* Cassio.]
    Rod. I know his gait, 'tis he—Villain, thou
        diest!   [*Makes a pass at* Cassio.]
    Cas. That thrust had been mine enemy
30   [indeed,
But that my coat° is better than thou know'st:
I will make proof° of thine.
        [*Draws, and wounds* Roderigo]
    Rod.   O, I am slain!
35 [Iago *from behind wounds* Cassio *in the leg, and
exit.*]
    Cas. I am maim'd for ever. Help, ho! murder!
        murder!   [*Falls.*]
        [*Enter* Othello.]
40 Oth. The voice of Cassio: Iago keeps his
                    [word.
    Rod. O, villain that I am!
    Oth.   It is even so.

Cas. O, help, ho! light! a surgeon!
Oth. 'Tis he—O brave Iago, honest and just.   45
That hast such noble sense of thy friend's
                    [wrong!
Thou teachest me. Minion,° your dear lies dead,
And your unblest fate hies:° strumpet, I come.
Forth of my heart those charms, thine eyes, are 50
                    [blotted;
Thy bed, lust-stain'd, shall with lust's blood be
    spotted.   [*Exit.*]
[*Enter* Lodovico *and* Gratiano.]
Cas. What, ho! no watch?° no passage?°   55
                    [murder! murder!
Gra. 'Tis some mischance; the cry is very
                    [direful.
Cas. O, help!
Lod. Hark!   60
Rod. O wretched villain!
Lod. Two or three groan: it is a heavy° night:
These may be counterfeits: let's think 't unsafe
To come in to the cry without more help.
Rod. Nobody come? then shall I bleed to   65
                    [death.
Lod. Hark!
[*Re-enter* Iago, *with a light.*]
Gra. Here's one comes in his shirt, with light
                    [and weapons. 70
Iago. Who's there? whose noise is this that
                    [cries on° murder?
Lod. We do not know.
Iago.   Did not you hear a cry?
Cas. Here, here! for heaven's sake, help me! 75
Iago.   What's the matter?
Gra. This is Othello's ancient, as I take it.
Lod. The same indeed; a very valiant fellow.
Iago. What are you here that cry so
                    [grievously? 80
Cas. Iago? O, I am spoil'd, undone by villains!
Give me some help.
Iago. O me, lieutenant! what villains have
                    [done this?
Cas. I think that one of them is hereabout,   85
And cannot make away.

Minion darling
hies hurries (toward you)
watch sentry
passage passers-by
heavy thick, cloudy
cries on cries out

quat pimple
sense quick
bobb'd cheated
coat coat or shirt of mail
proof trial

IAGO.   O treacherous villains!
[*To* LODOVICO *and* GRATIANO]
What are you there? come in, and give some
                                        [help.
5   ROD. O, help me here!
    CAS. That's one of them.
    IAGO. O murderous slave! O villain!
    [*Stabs* RODERIGO.]
    ROD. O damn'd Iago! O inhuman dog!
10 IAGO. Kill men i' the dark!—Where be these
                                [bloody thieves?—
How silent is this town!—Ho! murder!
    murder!—
What may you be? are you of good or evil?
15 LOD. As you shall prove us, praise us.
    IAGO. Signior Lodovico?
    LOD. He, sir.
    IAGO. I cry you mercy. Here's Cassio hurt by
villains.
20 GRA. Cassio!
    IAGO. How is 't, brother!
    CAS. My leg is cut in two.
    IAGO.   Marry, heaven forbid!
Light, gentlemen: I'll bind it with my shirt.
25 [*Enter* BIANCA.]
    BIAN. What is the matter, ho? who is 't that
                                        [cried?
    IAGO. Who is 't that cried?
    BIAN. O my dear Cassio! my sweet Cassio!
30 O Cassio, Cassio, Cassio!
    IAGO. O notable strumpet! Cassio, may you
                                    [suspect
Who they should be that have thus mangled
                                        [you?
35 CAS. No.
    GRA. I am sorry to find you thus: I have been
                                    [to seek you.
    IAGO. Lend me a garter. So. O, for a chair,
To bear him easily hence!
40 BIAN. Alas, he faints! O Cassio, Cassio, Cassio!
    IAGO. Gentlemen all, I do suspect this trash°
To be a party in this injury.
Patience awhile, good Cassio. Come, come;
Lend me a light. Know we this face or no?
45 Alas, my friend and my dear countryman
Roderigo! no—yes, sure—O heaven! Roderigo.

trash worthless creature, i.e., Bianca

GRA. What, of Venice?
IAGO. Even he, sir: did you know him?
GRA.   Know him! ay.
IAGO. Signior Gratiano? I cry you gentle   50
                                    [pardon;
These bloody accidents must excuse my
                                    [manners,
That so neglected you.
    GRA.   I am glad to see you.   55
IAGO. How do you, Cassio? O, a chair, a chair!
GRA. Roderigo!
IAGO. He, he, 'tis he. [*A chair brought in.*] O,
                            [that's well said;° the chair.
Some good man bear him carefully from hence; 60
I'll fetch the general's surgeon. [*To* BIANCA] For
                                    [you, mistress,
Save you your labour. He that lies slain here,
                                    [Cassio,
Was my dear friend: what malice was between   65
                                        [you?
    CAS. None in the world; nor do I know the
                                        [man.
IAGO. [*To* BIANCA] What, look you pale? O,
                        [bear him out o' the air.   70
[CASSIO *and* RODERIGO *are borne off.*]
Stay you, good gentlemen. Look you pale,
                                    [mistress?
Do you perceive the gastness° of her eye?
Nay, if you stare, we shall hear more anon.   75
Behold her well; I pray you, look upon her:
Do you see, gentlemen? nay, guiltiness will
                                        [speak,
Though tongues were out of use.
[*Enter* EMILIA.]   80
    EMIL. 'Las, what's the matter? what's the
                                [matter, husband?
IAGO. Cassio hath here been set on in the dark
By Roderigo and fellows that are scaped:
He's almost slain, and Roderigo dead.   85
    EMIL. Alas, good gentleman! alas, good Cassio!
IAGO. This is the fruit of whoring. Prithee,
                                        [Emilia,
Go know of Cassio where he supp'd to-night.
[*To* BIANCA] What, do you shake at that?   90

well said well done
gastness terror

BIAN. He supp'd at my house; but I therefore
                        [shake not.
IAGO. O, did he so? I charge you, go with me.
EMIL. Fie, fie upon thee, strumpet!
5 BIAN. I am no strumpet; but of life as honest
As you that thus abuse me.
    EMIL.   As I! foh! fie upon thee!
    IAGO. Kind gentlemen, let's go see poor Cassio
                        [dress'd.°
10 Come, mistress, you must tell 's another tale.
Emilia, run you to the citadel,
And tell my lord and lady what hath happ'd.
Will you go on? I pray. [*Aside*] This is the night
That either makes me or fordoes° me quite.
15   [*Exeunt.*]

Scene ii

[*Enter* OTHELLO; DESDEMONA *in bed asleep; a light burning.*]

    OTH. It is the cause,° it is the cause, my soul—
Let me not name it to you, you chaste stars!—
20 It is the cause. Yet I'll not shed her blood;
Nor scar that whiter skin of hers than snow,
And smooth as monumental alabaster.
Yet she must die, else she'll betray more men.
Put out the light, and then put out the light:
25 If I quench thee, thou flaming minister,°
I can again thy former light restore,
Should I repent me: but once put out thy light,
Thou cunning'st° pattern of excelling nature,
I know not where is that Promethean heat°
30 That can thy light relume.° When I have pluck'd
                         [the rose,
I cannot give it vital growth again,
It must needs wither: I'll smell it on the tree.
    [*Kissing her.*]
35 Ah, balmy breath, that dost almost persuade
Justice to break her sword! One more, one more.

dress'd bandaged
fordoes undoes
cause the provocation, perhaps with some suggestion of
    "ground for legal action," a meaning which makes Othello
    regard his deed as an act of justice
minister servant
cunning'st most ingeniously contrived
Promethean heat the divine creative fire stolen by Prome-
    theus from heaven
relume rekindle

Be thus when thou art dead, and I will kill thee,
And love thee after. One more, and this the last:
So sweet was ne'er so fatal. I must weep,
But they are cruel tears: this sorrow's heavenly;° 40
It strikes where it doth love. She wakes.
    DES. Who's there? Othello?
    OTH.   Ay, Desdemona.
    DES. Will you come to bed, my lord?
    OTH. Have you pray'd to-night, Desdemona? 45
    DES.   Ay, my lord.
    OTH. If you bethink yourself of any crime
Unreconciled as yet to heaven and grace,
Solicit for it straight.
    DES. Alas, my lord, what do you mean by 50
                      [that?
    OTH. Well, do it, and be brief; I will walk by:
I would not kill thy unprepared spirit;
No; heaven forfend!° I would not kill thy soul.
    DES. Talk you of killing? 55
    OTH.   Ay, I do.
    DES.   Then heaven
Have mercy on me!
    OTH.   Amen, with all my heart!
    DES. If you say so, I hope you will not kill me. 60
    OTH. Hum!
    DES. And yet I fear you; for you are fatal then
When your eyes roll so: why I should fear I
                      [know not,
Since guiltiness I know not; but yet I feel I fear. 65
    OTH. Think on thy sins.
    DES.   They are loves I bear to you.
    OTH. Ay, and for that thou diest.
    DES. That death's unnatural that kills for
                      [loving. 70
Alas, why gnaw you so your nether lip?
Some bloody passion shakes your very frame:
These are portents; but yet I hope, I hope,
They do not point on me.
    OTH.   Peace, and be still! 75
    DES. I will so. What's the matter?
    OTH. That handkerchief which I so loved and
                      [gave thee
Thou gavest to Cassio.
    DES.   No, by my life and soul! 80
Send for the man, and ask him.

sorrow's heavenly "whom the Lord loveth he chasteneth"
forfend forbid

OTH.   Sweet soul, take heed,
Take heed of perjury; thou art on thy deathbed.
  DES. Ay, but not yet to die.
  OTH.   Yes, presently:°
5 Therefore confess thee freely of thy sin;
For to deny each article with oath
Cannot remove nor choke the strong conception°
That I do groan withal. Thou art to die.
  DES. Then Lord have mercy on me!
10 OTH.   I say, amen.
  DES. And have you mercy too! I never did
Offend you in my life; never loved Cassio
But with such general warranty° of heaven
As I might love; I never gave him token.
15 OTH. By heaven, I saw my handkerchief in 's
                              [hand.
O perjured woman! thou dost stone° my heart,
And makest me call what I intend to do
A murder, which I thought a sacrifice:
20 I saw the handkerchief.
  DES.   He found it then;
I never gave it him: send for him, hither;
Let him confess a truth.
  OTH.   He hath confess'd.
25 DES. What, my lord?
  OTH. That he hath used thee.
  DES.   How? unlawfully?
  OTH.   Ay.
  DES. He will not say so.
30 OTH.   No, his mouth is stopp'd;
Honest Iago hath ta'en order° for 't.
  DES. O! my fear interprets: what, is he dead?
  OTH. Had all his hairs been lives, my great
                              [revenge
35 Had stomach° for them all.
  DES. Alas! he is betray'd and I undone.
  OTH. Out, strumpet! weep'st thou for him to
                              [my face?
  DES. O, banish me, my lord, but kill me not!
40 OTH. Down, strumpet!
  DES. Kill me to-morrow: let me live tonight!
  OTH. Nay, if you strive—

  DES. But half an hour!
  OTH.   Being done, there is no pause.
  DES. But while I say one prayer!   45
  OTH.   It is too late. [He smothers her.]
  EMIL. [Within] My lord, my lord! what, ho!
                              [my lord, my lord!
  OTH. What noise is this? Not dead? not yet
                              [quite dead? 50
I that am cruel am yet merciful;
I would not have thee linger in thy pain:
So, so.
  EMIL. [Within] What, ho! my lord, my lord!
  OTH.   Who's there?   55
  EMIL. [Within] O, good my lord, I would
                              [speak a word with you!
  OTH. Yes: 'tis Emilia. By and by. She's dead.
'Tis like she comes to speak of Cassio's death.—
The noise was here. Ha! no more moving?   60
Still as the grave. Shall she come in? were 't
                              [good?—
I think she stirs again—no. What's best to do?
If she come in, she'll sure speak to my wife:
My wife! my wife! what wife? I have no wife.   65
O, insupportable! O heavy hour!
Methinks it should be now a huge eclipse
Of sun and moon, and that the affrighted globe
Should yawn° at alteration.
  EMIL. [Within] I do beseech you   70
That I may speak with you, O, good my lord!
  OTH. I had forgot thee: O, come in, Emilia:
Soft, by and by. Let me the curtains draw.
Where art thou?   [Unlocks the door.]
  [Enter EMILIA.]   75
                    What's the matter with thee now?
  EMIL. O, my good lord, yonder's foul murders
                              [done!
  OTH. What, now?
  EMIL. But now, my lord.   80
  OTH. It is the very error° of the moon;
She comes more nearer earth than she was
                              [wont,
And makes men mad.
  EMIL. Cassio, my lord, hath kill'd a young   85
                              [Venetian

presently at once
conception conviction
warranty sanction
stone turn to stone
ta'en order taken measure
stomach appetite

yawn earthquakes were believed to accompany eclipses of
the sun
error aberration, i.e., departure of the moon from its normal
course

Call'd Roderigo.

OTH.   Roderigo kill'd!
And Cassio kill'd!

EMIL. No, Cassio is not kill'd.

5   OTH. Not Cassio kill'd! then murder's out of
                      [tune,
And sweet revenge grows harsh.

DES. O, falsely, falsely murder'd!

EMIL.   Alas, what cry is that?

10   OTH. That! what?

EMIL. Out, and alas! that was my lady's voice.
Help, help, ho! help! O lady, speak again!
Sweet Desdemona! O sweet mistress, speak!

DES. A guiltless death I die.

15   EMIL. O, who hath done this deed?

DES. Nobody; I myself. Farewell:
Commend me to my kind lord: O, farewell!
                      [*Dies.*]

OTH. Why, how should she° be murder'd?

20   EMIL.   Alas, who knows?

OTH. You heard her say herself, it was not I.

EMIL. She said so: I must needs report the
                      [truth.

OTH. She's like a liar, gone to burning hell:

25   'Twas I that kill'd her.

EMIL.   O, the more angel she,
And you the blacker devil!

OTH. She turn'd to folly, and she was a
                      [whore.

30   EMIL. Thou dost belie her, and thou art a
                      [devil.

OTH. She was false as water.

EMIL.   Thou art rash as fire, to say
That she was false: O, she was heavenly true!

35   OTH. Cassio did top her; ask thy husband else.
O, I were damn'd beneath all depth in hell,
But that I did proceed upon just grounds
To this extremity. Thy husband knew it all.

EMIL. My husband!

40   OTH. Thy husband.

EMIL. That she was false to wedlock?

OTH. Ay, with Cassio. Nay, had she been
                      [true,
If heaven would make me such another world

45   Of one entire and perfect chrysolite,°

I'ld not have sold her for it.

EMIL. My husband!

OTH.   Ay, 'twas he that told me first:
An honest man he is, and hates the slime
That sticks on filthy deeds.   50

EMIL.   My husband!

OTH. What needs this iteration, woman? I say
                      [thy husband.

EMIL. O mistress, villany hath made mocks
                      [with° love! 55
My husband say that she was false!

OTH.   He, woman;
I say thy husband: dost understand the word?
My friend, thy husband, honest, honest Iago.

EMIL. If he say so, may his pernicious soul   60
Rot half a grain a day! he lies to the heart:
She was too fond of her most filthy bargain.

OTH. Ha!

EMIL. Do thy worst:
This deed of thine is no more worthy heaven   65
Than thou wast worthy her.

OTH.   Peace, you were best.°

EMIL. Thou hast not half that power to do me
                      [harm
As I have to be hurt.° O gull! O dolt!   70
As ignorant as dirt! thou has done a deed—
I care not for thy sword; I'll make thee known,
Though I lost twenty lives.—Help! help, ho!
                      [help!
The Moor hath kill'd my mistress! Murder!   75
                      [murder!

[*Enter* MONTANO, GRATIANO, IAGO, *and others.*]

MON. What is the matter? How now, general!

EMIL. O, are you come, Iago? you have done
                      [well, 80
That men must lay their murders on your neck.

GRA. What is the matter?

EMIL. Disprove this villain, if thou be'st a man:
He says thou told'st him that his wife was false:
I know thou didst not, thou'rt not such a villain: 85
Speak, for my heart is full.

IAGO. I told him what I thought, and told no
                      [more

should she can she have been
chrysolite topaz

made . . . with made sport of
Peace . . . best you had better keep still
to be hurt to endure being hurt

Than what he found himself was apt° and true.
   EMIL. But did you ever tell him she was false?
   IAGO. I did.
   EMIL. You told a lie; an odious, damnèd lie;
5 Upon my soul, a lie; a wicked lie.
She false with Cassio!—did you say with Cassio?
   IAGO. With Cassio, mistress. Go to, charm°
                          [your tongue.
   EMIL. I will not charm my tongue; I am
10   [bound to speak:
My mistress here lies murder'd in her bed—
   ALL. O heavens forfend!
   EMIL. And your reports have set the murder
                             [on.
15   OTH. Nay, stare not, masters: it is true, indeed.
   GRA. 'Tis a strange truth.
   MON. O monstrous act!
   EMIL. Villany, villany, villany!
I think upon 't, I think: I smell 't: O villany!—
20 I thought so then°—I'll kill myself for grief—
O villany, villany!
   IAGO. What, are you mad? I charge you, get
                        [you home.
   EMIL. Good gentlemen, let me have leave to
25   [speak:
'Tis proper I obey him, but not now.
Perchance, Iago, I will ne'er go home.
   OTH. O! O! O!   [He falls on the bed.]
   EMIL.   Nay, lay thee down and roar;
30 For thou hast kill'd the sweetest innocent
That e'er did lift up eye.
   OTH. [Rising] O, she was foul!
I scarce did know you, uncle: there lies your
                         [niece,
35 Whose breath, indeed, these hands have newly
                        [stopp'd:
I know this act shows horrible and grim.
   GRA. Poor Desdemona! I am glad thy father's
                        [dead:
40 Thy match was mortal to him, and pure grief
Shore his old thread in twain: did he live now,
This sight would make him do a desperate turn,
Yea, curse his better angel from his side,
And fall to reprobation.°

   OTH. 'Tis pitiful; but yet Iago knows   45
That she with Cassio hath the act of shame
A thousand times committed; Cassio confess'd
                         [it:
And she did gratify his amorous works
With that recognizance° and pledge of love   50
Which I first gave her; I saw it in his hand:
It was a handkerchief, an antique token
My father gave my mother.
   EMIL. O heaven! O heavenly powers!
   IAGO. Come, hold your peace.   55
   EMIL. 'Twill out, 'twill out: I peace!
No, I will speak as liberal as the north:°
Let heaven and men and devils, let them all,
All, all cry shame against me, yet I'll speak.
   IAGO. Be wise, and get you home.   60
   EMIL.   I will not.
[IAGO offers to stab EMILIA.]
   GRA.   Fie!
Your sword upon a woman?
   EMIL. O thou dull Moor! that handkerchief   65
                       [thou speak'st of
I found by fortune and did give my husband;
For often, with a solemn earnestness,
More than indeed belong'd to such a trifle,
He begg'd of me to steal it.   70
   IAGO.   Villanous whore!
   EMIL. She give it Cassio! no, alas! I found it.
And I did give 't my husband.
   IAGO.   Filth, thou liest!
   EMIL: By heaven, I do not; I do not,   75
                       [gentlemen.
O murderous coxcomb!° what should such a fool
Do with so good a woman?
   OTH.   Are there no stones° in heaven
But what serve for the thunder?—Precious   80
   villain.
[He runs at IAGO, is disarmed by MONTANO; IAGO,
from behind, stabs EMILIA, and exit.]
   GRA. The woman falls; sure, he hath kill'd
                       [his wife. 85
   EMIL. Ay, ay: O lay me by my mistress' side.
   GRA. He's gone, but his wife's kill'd.

---

apt likely
charm check as with a charm
then cf. IV, ii, p. 179, lines 37–41.
reprobation damnation

recognizance token
liberal . . . north freely as the north wind
coxcomb fool
stones thunderbolts

MON. 'Tis a notorious villain. Take you this
[weapon,
Which I have here recover'd from the Moor:
Come, guard the door without; let him not
5 [pass,
But kill him rather. I'll after that same villain,
For 'tis a damned slave.
[*Exeunt all but* OTHELLO *and* EMILIA.]
OTH. I am not valiant neither.
10 But every puny whipster° gets my sword:
But why should honour outlive honesty?°
Let it go all.
EMIL. What did thy song bode, lady?
Hark, canst thou hear me? I will play the swan,
15 And die in music. [*Singing*] Willow, willow,
[willow.—
Moor, she was chaste; she loved thee, cruel
[Moor;
So come my soul to bliss, as I speak true;
20 So speaking as I think, I die, I die. [*Dies.*]
OTH. I have another weapon in this chamber;
It is a sword of Spain, the ice-brook's temper—°
O, here it is. Uncle, I must come forth.
GRA. [*Within*] If thou attempt it, it will cost
25 [thee dear:
Thou hast no weapon, and perforce must suffer.
OTH. Look in upon me then and speak with
[me,
Or, naked° as I am, I will assault thee.
30 [*Re-enter* GRATIANO.]
GRA. What is the matter?
OTH. Behold, I have a weapon;
A better never did itself sustain
Upon a soldier's thigh: I have seen the day,
35 That, with this little arm and this good sword,
I have made my way through more impediments
Than twenty times your stop:° but, O vain boast!
Who can control his fate? 'tis not so now.
Be not afraid, though you do see me weapon'd;
40 Here is my journey's end, here is my butt,°

And very sea-mark° of my utmost sail.°
Do you go back dismay'd? 'tis a lost fear;
Man but a rush° against Othello's breast,
And he retires. Where should Othello go?
No, how dost thou look now? O ill-starr'd 45
[wench!
Pale as thy smock! when we shall meet at
[compt,°
This look of thine will hurl my soul from
[heaven, 50
And fiends will snatch at it. Cold, cold, my girl!
Even like thy chastity. O cursèd slave!
Whip me, ye devils,
From the possession of this heavenly sight!
Blow me about in winds! roast me in sulphur! 55
Wash me in steep-down gulfs of liquid fire!
O Desdemona! Desdemona! dead!
Oh! Oh! Oh!
[*Enter* LODOVICO, MONTANO, CASSIO *carried in a*
chair, and OFFICERS *with* IAGO, *prisoner.*] 60
LOD. Where is this rash and most
[unfortunate man?
OTH. That's he that was Othello: here I am.
LOD. Where is that viper? bring the villain
[forth. 65
OTH. I look down towards his feet;° but that's
[a fable.
If that thou be'st a devil, I cannot kill thee.
[*Wounds* IAGO.]
LOD. Wrench his sword from him. 70
IAGO. I bleed, sir; but not kill'd.
OTH. I am not sorry neither: I'ld have thee
live;
For, in my sense, 'tis happiness to die.
LOD. O thou Othello, that wert once so good, 75
Fall'n in the practice° of a damnèd slave,
What shall be said to thee?
OTH. Why, any thing:
An honourable murderer, if you will;
For nought I did in hate, but all in honour. 80
LOD. This wretch hath part confess'd his
[villany:

---

whipster whippersnapper
honour . . . honesty reputation for courage outlive honor
ice-brook's temper tempered in ice-cold water
naked unarmed
stop i.e., power to stop me
butt goal

sea-mark beacon, limit
utmost sail last voyage
man . . . rush do but attack
compt the last reckoning, Judgment Day
feet i.e., to see if they are cloven, like the Devil's
practice plot, snare

Did you and he consent.in Cassio's death?
  OTH. Ay.
  CAS. Dear general, I never gave you cause.
  OTH. I do believe it, and I ask you pardon.
5 Will you, I pray, demand that demi-devil
Why he hath thus ensnared my soul and body?
  IAGO. Demand me nothing: what you know,
                      [you know:
From this time forth I never will speak word.
10 Lod. What, not to pray?
  GRA.   Torments will ope your lips.
  OTH. Well, thou dost best.
  LOD. Sir, you shall understand what hath
                    [befall'n,
15 Which, as I think, you know not. Here is a letter
Found in the pocket of the slain Roderigo;
And here another: the one of them imports
The death of Cassio to be undertook
By Roderigo.
20   OTH. O villain!
  CAS.   Most heathenish and most gross!
  LOD. Now here's another discontented° paper,
Found in his pocket too; and this, it seems,
Roderigo meant to have sent this damnèd
25   villain;
But that belike Iago in the interim
Came in and satisfied him.
  OTH.   O the pernicious caitiff!
How came you, Cassio, by that handkerchief
30 That was my wife's!
  CAS.   I found it in my chamber:
And he himself confess'd but even now
That there he dropp'd it for a special purpose
Which wrought to his desire.°
35   OTH.   O fool! fool! fool!
  CAS. There is besides in Roderigo's letter,
How he upbraids Iago, that he made him
Brave° me upon the watch; whereon it came
That I was cast: and even but now he spake,
40 After long seeming dead, Iago hurt him,
Iago set him on.
  LOD. You must forsake this room, and go with
                 [us:
Your power and your command is taken off,
45 And Cassio rules in Cyprus. For this slave,

discontented expressing dissatisfaction
wrought . . . desire had the effect he desired
Brave defy

If there be any cunning cruelty
That can torment him much and hold him long,
It shall be his. You shall close prisoner rest,
Till that the nature of your fault be known
To the Venetian state. Come, bring him away. 50
  OTH. Soft you; a word or two before you go.
I have done the state some service, and they
                  [know 't.
No more of that. I pray you, in your letters,
When you shall these unlucky deeds relate, 55
Speak of me as I am; nothing extenuate,
Nor set down aught in malice: then must you
                  [speak
Of one that loved not wisely but too well;
Of one not easily jealous, but being wrought° 60
Perplex'd° in the extreme; of one whose hand,
Like the base Indian, threw a pearl away
Richer than all his tribe; of one whose subdued
                  [eyes,
Albeit unusèd to the melting mood, 65
Drop tears as fast as the Arabian trees
Their medicinal gum. Set you down this;
And say besides, that in Aleppo once,
Where a malignant and a turban'd Turk
Beat a Venetian and traduced the state, 70
I took by the throat the circumcised dog,
And smote him, thus.   [*Stabs himself.*]
  LOU. O bloody period!°
  GRA.   All that's spoke is marr'd.
  OTH. I kiss'd thee ere I kill'd thee: no way but 75
                  [this;
Killing myself, to die upon a kiss.
  [*Falls on the bed, and dies.*]
  CAS. This did I fear, but thought he had no
                  [weapon; 80
For he was great of heart.
  LOD.   [*To* IAGO]. O Spartan° dog,
More fell° than anguish, hunger, or the sea!
Look on the tragic loading of this bed;
This is thy work: the object poisons sight; 85
Let it be hid, Gratiano, keep the house,
And seize upon the fortunes of the Moor,

wrought worked upon
Perplex'd distracted
period end
Spartan fierce
fell cruel

For they succeed on you. To you, lord governor,
Remains the censure° of this hellish villain;
The time, the place, the torture: O, enforce it!
Myself will straight aboard; and to the state
5   This heavy act with heavy heart relate.

                                   [Exeunt.]

censure sentencing

Ben Jonson

1573?–1637

Volpone, or the Fox

1606

The theater-goer who saw Ben Jonson's new comedy *Volpone, or the Fox* for the first time may well have been reminded of Shakespeare's recent tragedy, *Othello, the Moor of Venice.* Both plays are set against the background of a city noted alike for its magnificence and its vice. Both present characters of "rare ingenious knavery" (Shakespeare's Iago resembling both Volpone and Mosca). And both exhibit the dramatic inventiveness and varied eloquence of the finest Elizabethan drama. At the center of Jonson's satiric comedy, however, there stands not a heroic Othello but Volpone, a genius in crime, incapable of either generosity or self-knowledge. His fall reveals not the mystery of the human lot but the tendency of vice to overreach itself.

Although the satire is ultimately moral, its immediate perspective is largely social and legal. It traces the features of vice under the masks of respectability, exposing the manipulations of the hypocrites without altogether excusing the imperceptiveness of their victims. Against scoundrels cloaked in propriety and skilled in legal dodging, the mainly passive virtuous characters are practically defenseless. Even the good-natured guardians of the law are dull-witted, and the true innocents, Bonario and Celia, finally get free only because the knaves ensnare themselves in their own subtleties. The laws of the state are vindicated, but only at long last and in tones of slightly hollow self-congratulation.

Despite its consistently satiric purpose, *Volpone* at first appears bewilderingly diverse. A seemingly irrelevant academic skit is enacted by a dwarf, a eunuch, and a hermaphrodite. Disguised as a mountebank, Volpone makes a long-winded spiel aimed as much at burlesquing itinerant quacks as at advancing his designs on Celia. The English travelers play out an almost independent farce of their own. And in the unraveling of the main plot Jonson risks anticlimax by launching, as late as the fifth act, a brilliant new series of complications.

BEN JONSON

Such fertility of dramatic device may well leave an impression of rich disorder.

The play is rich but it is not disordered. Volpone, flanked by the indefatigable Mosca, draws all events and characters into his orbit. Around him circle the lesser predators —a "Vulture," a "Raven," a "Crow"— impelled by avarice and dragging in their train others less guilty, merely foolish, or altogether innocent. Even Sir Politic Would-be, with his little schemes for getting rich, his pretentious misinformation, and his empty suspicions, is in some ways a parody of Volpone and has an equally appropriate comeuppance.

Beyond these adroit elaborations of plot and character a principle of thematic integration is at work. From Volpone's first speech, in idolatry of gold, to the final plainspoken summary of the magistrate, Jonson tirelessly explores the idea of hypocrisy as the mask of lust and of lust as perversion of human nature. Lust in the guise of avarice is thematically developed in references to possessions, possessing, and—at length—being possessed. That lust is perverse and deceptive is expressed by emphasis on tricks and transformations. The themes interlace. Volpone's lust for gold fires his imagination to feats of deception and rhetoric beyond the reach of his victims. Mosca, touched with the same fire, caters to Volpone's lust for Celia, which in turn leads him to impersonate a mountebank, the very emblem of greed and falsehood. Lust for Volpone's possessions makes a husband eager to prostitute his wife and a father to disown his son. In the oddly relevant academic skit the deformed and mutilated servants of Volpone's household make sport of greed, hypocrisy, and perversion to gratify their master's taste.

Throughout the play the figures of speech and the historical and classical allusions embroider these themes of possession and transformation. They concur most explicitly in Volpone's attempt to transform Celia, the object of his lust, into a prize possession.

That is the turning point of his fortunes. Thereafter his brilliance decays as he becomes more and more visibly what he is. In the last three scenes of the play the word *possession,* echoed by almost every character, attains a culminating definition: *possessed by demons.*

The final transformations reveal the truth. Volpone's last stratagem is to remove his last disguise and to pull all the hypocrites down in his own ruin. Virtue is barely saved as the virtuosity of Ben Jonson triumphs.

Volpone, or the Fox

JONSON

CHARACTERS°

VOLPONE   *a magnifico*
MOSCA   *his parasite*
VOLTORE   *an advocate*
CORBACCIO   *an old gentleman*
CORVINO   *a merchant*
BONARIO   *a young gentleman*
POLITIC WOULD-BE   *a knight*
PEREGRINE   *a gentleman traveler*
NANO   *a dwarf*
CASTRONE   *a eunuch*
ANDROGYNO   *a hermaphrodite*
GREGE   *mob*
COMMANDADORI   *officers*
MERCATORI   *three merchants*
AVOCATORI   *four magistrates*
NOTARIO   *the register*
SERVITORE   *a servant*
MADAM WOULD-BE   *the knight's wife*
CELIA   *Corvino's wife*
WOMEN

SCENE. *Venice.*

The Argument

V OLPONE, childless, rich, feigns, sick, despairs,
O ffers his state to hopes of several heirs,
L ies languishing; his parasite receives

Characters: **Mosca** the fly **Voltore** the vulture **Corbaccio** the raven **Corvino** the crow **Bonario** the well-favored man **Politic Would-be** the professed man of the world **Celia** the heavenly one

P resents of all, assures, deludes; then weaves   5
O ther cross plots, which ope themselves, are told.
N ew tricks for safety are sought; they thrive: when, bold,
E ach tempts th' other again, and all are sold.°   10

ACT I

Scene i

[*A room in* VOLPONE'S *house.*]
[*Enter* VOLPONE *and* MOSCA.]
  VOLPONE. Good morning to the day; and next,
            [my gold.
Open the shrine, that I may see my saint.—   15
Hail the world's soul, and mine. More glad
            [than is
The teeming earth to see the long'd-for sun
Peep through the horns of the celestial Ram°,
Am I, to view thy splendor darkening his;   20
That, lying here, amongst my other hoards,
Show'st like a flame by night, or like the day
Struck out of chaos, when all darkness fled
Unto the center.° O thou son of Sol,
But brighter than thy father, let me kiss,   25
With adoration, thee, and every relic
Of sacred treasure in this blessed room.
Well did wise poets, by thy glorious name,
Title that age which they would have the best;
Thou being the best of things, and far   30
            [transcending
All style of joy, in children, parents, friends,
Or any other waking dream on earth.
Thy looks when they to Venus did ascribe,
They should have giv'n her twenty thousand   35
            [Cupids;
Such are thy beauties and our loves! Dear saint,

sold defrauded
Ram zodiacal sign, Aries, which the sun enters in late March
day . . . center the first day of the Creation, when darkness fled to the center of the earth. In this speech Volpone also alludes to the Golden Age (that age), the golden goddess (**Venus**), the adage that Silence is Golden (the dumb god), and the old belief that gold ore was imprisoned sunlight and was plentiful in the soil of hell.

BEN JONSON | Act I, Scene i

Riches, the dumb god, that giv'st all men
[tongues,
That canst do naught, and yet mak'st men do
[all things;
5 The price of souls; even hell, with thee to boot,
Is made worth Heaven. Thou art virtue, fame,
Honor, and all things else! Who can get thee,
He shall be noble, valiant, honest, wise—
  Mosca. And what he will, sir. Riches are in
10 [fortune
A greater good than wisdom is in nature.
  Volpone. True, my beloved Mosca. Yet I
[glory
More in the cunning purchase° of my wealth
15 Than in the glad possession, since I gain
No common way; I use no trade, no venture;
I wound no earth with plowshares, fat no
[beasts
To feed the shambles; have no mills for iron,
20 Oil, corn, or men, to grind 'em into powder;
I blow no subtle glass,° expose no ships
To threat'nings of the furrow-faced sea;
I turn no monies in the public bank,
No usure° private—
25   Mosca.   No, sir, nor devour
Soft prodigals. You shall ha' some will swallow
A melting heir as glibly as your Dutch
Will pills of butter, and ne'er purge for 't;
Tear forth the fathers of poor families
30 Out of their beds, and coffin them alive
In some kind clasping prison, where their bones
May be forthcoming, when the flesh is rotten.
But your sweet nature doth abhor these courses;
You loathe the widow's or the orphan's tears
35 Should wash your pavements, or their piteous
[cries
Ring in your roofs, and beat the air for
[vengeance.
  Volpone. Right, Mosca; I do loathe it.—
40   Mosca.   And, besides, sir,
You are not like the thresher that doth stand
With a huge flail, watching a heap of corn,
And, hungry, dares not taste the smallest grain,
But feeds on mallows, and such bitter herbs;

Nor like the merchant, who hath fill'd his   45
[vaults
With Romagnía, rich and Candian wines,
Yet drinks the lees of Lombard's vinegar.
You will not lie in straw, whilst moths and
[worms 50
Feed on your sumptuous hangings and soft
[beds.
You know the use of riches, and dare give now
From that bright heap, to me, your poor
[observer,° 55
Or to your dwarf, or your hermaphrodite,
Your eunuch, or what other household trifle
Your pleasure allows maintenance.—
  Volpone.   Hold thee, Mosca;
Take of my hand; thou strik'st on truth in all, 60
And they° are envious term thee parasite.
Call forth my dwarf, my eunuch, and my fool,
And let 'em make me sport.
  [Exit Mosca.]
                    What should I do, 65
But cocker up° my genius, and live free
To all delights my fortune calls me to?
I have no wife, no parent, child, ally,
To give my substance to; but whom I make
Must be my heir; and this makes men observe° 70
[me.
This draws new clients daily to my house,
Women and men of every sex and age,
That bring me presents, send me plate, coin,
[jewels, 75
With hope that when I die (which they expect
Each greedy minute) it shall then return
Tenfold upon them; whilst some, covetous
Above the rest, seek to engross me whole,
And counter work the one unto the other, 80
Contend in gifts, as they would seem in love;
All which I suffer, playing with their hopes,
And am content to coin 'em into profit,
And look upon their kindness, and take more,
And look on that; still bearing them in hand, 85
Letting the cherry knock against their lips,
And draw it by their mouths, and back again.—
How now!

purchase acquisition
subtle glass fine Venetian glassware
usure usury

observer servant
they those who
cocker up indulge
observe be attentive to

Scene ii

[*Enter* Mosca *with* Nano, Androgyno, *and*
Castrone.]

Nano. Now, room for fresh gamesters, who
               [do will you to know
5 They do bring you neither play nor university
               [show,
  And therefore do entreat you that whatsoever
               [they rehearse
  May not fare a whit the worse for the false
10   [pace of the verse.
  If you wonder at this, you will wonder more ere
               [we pass;
  For know, here° is enclos'd the soul of
               [Pythagoras,
15 That juggler divine, as hereafter shall follow,
  Which soul, fast and loose, sir, came first from
               [Apollo,
  And was breath'd into Aethalides, Mercurius
               [his son,
20 Where it had the gift to remember all that ever
               [was done.
  From thence it fled forth, and made quick
               [transmigration
  To goldy-lock'd Euphorbus, who was kill'd, in
25   [good fashion,
  At the siege of old Troy, by the cuckold of
               [Sparta.
  Hermotimus was next (I find it in my charta);
  To whom it did pass, where no sooner it was
30   [missing,
  But with one Pyrrhus of Delos it learn'd to go
               [a-fishing;

And thence did it enter the sophist of Greece.
From Pythagore, she went into a beautiful
               [piece, 35
Hight Aspasia, the meretrix; and the next toss
               [of her
Was again of a whore—she became a
               [philosopher,
Crates the cynic, as itself doth relate it. 40
Since, kings, knights, and beggars, knaves,
               [lords, and fools gat it,
Besides ox and ass, camel, mule, goat, and
               [brock,
In all which it hath spoke, as in the cobbler's 45
               [cock.
But I came not here to discourse of that matter,
Or his one, two, or three, or his great oath, "By
               [Quater!"
His musics, his trigon, his golden thigh,° 50
Or his telling how elements shift; but I
Would ask, how of late thou hast suffered
               [translation,
And shifted thy coat in these days of
               [reformation. 55
  Androgyno. Like one of the reformed,° a
               [fool, as you see,
Counting all old doctrine heresy.
  Nano. But not on thine own forbid meats
               [hast thou ventur'd? 60
  Androgyno. On fish, when first a Carthusian
               [I enter'd.
  Nano. Why, then thy dogmatical silence°
               [hath left thee?
  Androgyno. Of that an obstreperous lawyer 65
               [bereft me.
  Nano. O wonderful change! When sir lawyer
               [forsook thee,
For Pythagore's sake, what body then took
               [thee, 70

here in Androgyno, the "man-woman." This scene, in the style of an academic skit, refers especially to Lucian's dialogue between a cobbler who longs for riches and a cock who embodies the soul of the Greek philosopher, Pythagoras. The soul recounts its transmigrations through the lives of men and women famous for the pursuit of wealth (e.g., **Aethalides,** herald of the Argonauts who found the Golden Fleece; **Aspasia,** the noted courtesan, mistress of Pericles) and of philosophers who, it is implied, prostituted their talents. By alluding to the Pythagorean Brotherhood, a mystic society that strictly forbade the eating of flesh and beans and employed an esoteric symbolism of numbers, Jonson also satirizes some of the religious extremists of his time.

Or his . . . thigh or of Pythagorean practices and traditions: the number-symbolism; the oath **By Quater!** on the "triangle of four"; the abstruse theory of musical intervals; the symbolic triangular harp (**trigon**); and the legend that the thigh of Pythagoras was all of gold
reformed extreme Protestants
silence vowed by Pythagoreans as well as, later, by Carthusians, who were members of a rigorous monastic order

ANDROGYNO. A good dull mule.
NANO.   And how! by that means
Thou wert brought to allow of the eating of
    [beans?
5 ANDROGYNO. Yes.
NANO.   But from the mule into whom
    [didst thou pass?
ANDROGYNO. Into a very strange beast, by
    [some writers call'd an ass;
10 By others a precise, pure, illuminate brother°
Of those devour flesh—and sometimes one
    [another;
And will drop you forth a libel, or a sanctifi'd
    [lie,
15 Betwixt every spoonful of a nativity-pie.°
NANO. Now quit thee, 'fore Heaven, of that
    [profane nation;
And gently report thy next transmigration.
ANDROGYNO. To the same that I am.
20 NANO.   A creature of delight,
And, what is more than a fool,° an
    [hermaphrodite!
Now, pray thee, sweet soul, in all thy variation,
Which body wouldst thou choose to take up
25   [thy station?
ANDROGYNO. Troth, this I am in; even here
    [would I tarry.
NANO. 'Cause here the delight of each sex
    [thou canst vary?
30 ANDROGYNO. Alas, those pleasures be stale
    [and forsaken;
No, 'tis your fool wherewith I am so taken,
The only one creature that I can call blessed;
For all other forms I have prov'd most
35   [distressed.
NANO. Spoke true, as thou wert in Pythagoras
    [still.
This learned opinion we celebrate will,
Fellow eunuch, as behoves us, with all our wit
40   [and art,
To dignify that whereof ourselves are so great
    [and special a part.

precise . . . brother hair-splitting, self-righteous Puritan who claims to be divinely enlightened
nativity-pie Christmas pie (another dig at the "precise" Puritan who shrank from saying "Christmas"
to avoid the "Popish" reference to "Christ's Mass")
fool jester, not necessarily a simpleton

VOLPONE. Now, very, very pretty. Mosca,
    [this
Was thy invention?   45
MOSCA.   If it please my patron,
Not else.
VOLPONE.   It doth, good Mosca.
MOSCA.   Then it was, sir.
[Sings.]   50
Fools they are the only nation
Worth men's envy or admiration;
Free from care or sorrow taking,
Selves and others merry making:
All they speak or do is sterling.   55
Your fool he is your great man's dearling,
And your ladies' sport and pleasure;
Tongue and bauble are his treasure.
E'en his face begetteth laughter,
And he speaks truth free from slaughter;°   60
He's the grace of every feast,
And sometimes the chiefest guest;
Hath his trencher and his stool,
When wit waits upon the fool.
    O, who would not be   65
    He, he, he,?
    [One knocks without.]
    VOLPONE. Who's that? Away! Look, Mosca.
MOSCA.   Fool, begone!
[Exeunt NANO, CASTRONE, and ANDROGYNO.]   70
'Tis Signior Voltore, the advocate;
I know him by his knock.
VOLPONE.   Fetch me my gown,
My furs, and nightcaps; say my couch is
    [changing, 75
And let him entertain himself awhile
Without, i' th' gallery. [Exit MOSCA.] Now,
    [now, my clients
Begin their visitation! Vulture, kite,
Raven, and gorcrow, all my birds of prey,   80
That think me turning carcass, now they come;
I am not for 'em yet.
[Reenter MOSCA, with the gown, etc.]
    How now! the news?
MOSCA. A piece of plate,° sir.   85
VOLPONE.   Of what bigness?
MOSCA.   Huge,

slaughter punishment
plate dish of gold or silver

Massy, and antique with your name inscrib'd,
And arms engraven.
  VOLPONE.   Good! and not a fox
Stretch'd on the earth, with fine delusive
          [sleights,
5 Mocking a gaping crow? ha, Mosca?
  MOSCA.   Sharp, sir.
  VOLPONE. Give me my furs—Why dost thou
       [laugh so, man?
10 Mosca. I cannot choose, sir, when I
       [apprehend
What thoughts he has without now, as he
        [walks:
That this might be the last gift he should give,
15 That this would fetch you;° if you died today,
And gave him all, what he should be tomorrow;
What large return would come of all his
        [ventures;
How he should worshipp'd be, and reverenc'd;
20 Ride with his furs and footcloths,° waited on
By herds of fools and clients; have clear way
Made for his mule, as letter'd as himself;
Be call'd the great and learned advocate!
And then concludes there's naught impossible.
25 VOLPONE. Yes, to be learned, Mosca.
  MOSCA. O, no! rich
Implies it. Hood an ass with reverend purple,
So you can hide his two ambitious ears,
And he shall pass for a cathedral doctor.°
30 VOLPONE. My caps, my caps, good Mosca.
       [Fetch him in.
  MOSCA. Stay, sir; your ointment for your
        [eyes.
  VOLPONE. That's true;
35 Dispatch, dispatch; I long to have possession
Of my new present.
  MOSCA.   That, and thousands more,
I hope to see you lord of.
  VOLPONE.   Thanks, kind Mosca.
40 MOSCA. And that, when I am lost in blended
       [dust,
And hundred such as I am, in succession—
  VOLPONE. Nay, that were too much, Mosca.
  MOSCA. You shall live

Still to delude these harpies.   45
  VOLPONE.   Loving Mosca!
'Tis well; my pillow now, and let him enter.
 [*Exit* MOSCA.]
Now, my feign'd cough, my phthisic, and my
       [gout, 50
My apoplexy, palsy, and catarrhs,
Help, with your forced functions this my
       [posture,°
Wherein, this three year, I have milk'd their
       [hopes. 55
He comes; I hear him—Uh, uh, uh, uh!—Oh!

Scene iii

[*Enter* MOSCA *with* VOLTORE.]
 MOSCA. You still are what you were, sir. Only
       [you,
Of all the rest, are he commands his love, 60
And you do wisely to preserve it thus,
With early visitation and kind notes
Of your good meaning to him, which, I know,
Cannot but come most grateful. Patron! sir!
Here's Signior Voltore is come— 65
  VOLPONE.   What say you?
  MOSCA. Sir, Signior Voltore is come this
       [morning
To visit you.
  VOLPONE. I thank him. 70
  MOSCA.   And hath brought
A piece of antique plate, bought of St. Mark,°
With which he here presents you.
  VOLPONE. He is welcome.
Pray him to come more often. 75
  MOSCA.   Yes.
  VOLTORE. What says he?
  MOSCA. He thanks you, and desires you see
       [him often.
  VOLPONE. Mosca. 80
  MOSCA. My patron!
  VOLPONE. Bring him near. Where is he?
I long to feel his hand.
  MOSCA.   The plate is here, sir.
  VOLTORE. How fare you, sir? 85
  VOLPONE. I thank you, Signior Voltore.

fetch you persuade you to make him your heir
footcloths decorative trappings of a horse
cathedral doctor university professor

Help . . . posture help with your simulated actions this my (im)posture
St. Mark St. Mark's Square

Where is the plate? mine eyes are bad.
    VOLTORE.   I'm sorry
To see you still thus weak.
    MOSCA [aside].   That he is not weaker.
5   VOLPONE. You are too munificent.
    VOLTORE.   No, sir; would to Heaven
I could as well give health to you, as that plate.
    VOLPONE. You give, sir, what you can. I
                      [thank you. Your love
10 Hath taste in this, and shall not be unanswer'd.
I pray you see me often.
    VOLTORE.   Yes, I shall, sir.
    VOLPONE. Be not far from me.
    MOSCA.   Do you observe that, sir?
15   VOLPONE. Harken unto me still; it will
                     [concern you.
    MOSCA. You are a happy man, sir; know
                     [your good.
    VOLPONE. I cannot now last long—
20   MOSCA [aside].   You are his heir, sir.
    VOLTORE [aside]. Am I?
    VOLPONE. I feel me going—uh, uh, uh, uh!—
I'm sailing to my port—uh, uh, uh, uh!—
And I am glad I am so near my haven.
25   MOSCA. Alas, kind gentleman; well, we must
                     [all go—
    VOLTORE. But, Mosca—
    MOSCA.   Age will conquer.
    VOLTORE.   'Pray thee, hear me.
30 Am I inscrib'd his heir, for certain?
    MOSCA.   Are you!
I do beseech you, sir, you will vouchsafe
To write me i' your family.° All my hopes
Depend upon your Worship. I am lost
35 Except the rising sun do shine on me.
    VOLTORE. It shall both shine, and warm thee,
                   [Mosca.
    MOSCA.   Sir,
I am a man that hath not done your love
40 All the worst offices; here I wear your keys,
See all your coffers and your caskets lock'd,
Keep the poor inventory of your jewels,
Your plate, and monies; am your steward, sir,
Husband your goods here.
45   VOLTORE.   But am I sole heir?

    MOSCA. Without a partner, sir; confirm'd this
                 [morning;
The wax is warm yet, and the ink scarce dry
Upon the parchment.
    VOLTORE.   Happy, happy me!   50
By what good chance, sweet Mosca?
    MOSCA.   Your desert, sir;
I know no second cause.
    VOLTORE.   Thy modesty
Is loath to know it; well, we shall requite it.   55
    MOSCA. He ever lik'd your course, sir; that
                 [first took him.
I oft have heard him say how he admir'd
Men of your large profession, that could speak
To every cause, and things mere contraries,   60
Till they were hoarse again, yet all be law;
That, with most quick agility, could turn,
And return; make knots, and undo them;
Give forked counsel; take provoking gold°
On either hand, and put it up;° these men,   65
He knew, would thrive with their humility.
And, for his part, he thought he should be blest
To have his heir of such a suffering° spirit,
So wise, so grave, of so perplex'd a tongue,°
And loud withal, that would not wag, nor   70
                    [scarce
Lie still, without a fee; when every word
Your Worship but lets fall, is a cecchine!°
  [Another knocks.]
Who's that? One knocks; I would not have you 75
                   [seen, sir.
And yet—pretend you came and went in haste;
I'll fashion an excuse. And, gentle sir,
When you do come to swim in golden lard,
Up to the arms in honey, that your chin   80
Is borne up stiff with fatness of the flood,
Think on your vassal; but remember me:
I ha' not been your worst of clients.
    VOLTORE.   Mosca—
    MOSCA. When will you have your inventory   85
                 [brought, sir?
Or see a copy of the will?—Anon.—

---

write . . . family regard me as a servant of your household

provoking gold a legal fee
put it up pocket it
suffering tolerant
so . . . tongue such devious utterance
cecchine gold coin

I'll bring 'em to you, sir. Away, begone,
Put business i' your face.
    [*Exit* VOLTORE.]
    VOLPONE.   Excellent Mosca!
5 Come hither, let me kiss thee.
    MOSCA.   Keep you still, sir.
Here is Corbaccio.
    VOLPONE.   Set the plate away.
The vulture's gone, and the old raven's come.

Scene iv

10   [MOSCA *and* VOLPONE *remain.*]
    MOSCA. Betake you to your silence, and your
                             [sleep.—
    [*To the plate.*] Stand there and multiply.—
                [(*Aside.*) Now shall we see
15 A wretch who is indeed more impotent°
Than this can feign to be; yet hopes to hop
Over his grave.—
    [*He admits* CORBACCIO.]
               Signior Corbaccio!
20 You're very welcome, sir.
    CORBACCIO.   How does your patron?
    MOSCA. Troth, as he did, sir; no amends.
    CORBACCIO.   What? mends he?
    MOSCA. No, sir: he is rather worse.
25   CORBACCIO.   That's well. Where is he?
    MOSCA. Upon his couch, sir, newly fall'n
                          [asleep.
    CORBACCIO. Does he sleep well?
    MOSCA.   No wink, sir, all this night,
30 Nor yesterday; but slumbers.°
    CORBACCIO.   Good! he should take
Some counsel of physicians. I have brought
                        [him
An opiate here, from mine own doctor—
35   MOSCA. He will not hear of drugs.
    CORBACCIO.   Why? I myself
Stood by while 'twas made, saw all th'
                       [ingredients,
And know it cannot but most gently work.
40 My life for his, 'tis but to make him sleep.
    VOLPONE [*aside*]. Ay, his last sleep, if he
                     [would take it.
    MOSCA.   Sir,

impotent infirm
slumbers dozes

He has no faith in physic.
    CORBACCIO.   Say you? say you?   45
    MOSCA. He has no faith in physic; he does
                        [think
Most of your doctors are the greater danger,
And worse disease, t' escape. I often have
Heard him protest that your° physician   50
Should never be his heir.
    CORBACCIO.   Not I his heir?
    MOSCA. Not your physician, sir.
    CORBACCIO.   O, no, no, no;   55
I do not mean it.
    MOSCA.   No, sir, nor their fees
He cannot brook; he says they flay a man
Before they kill him.
    CORBACCIO.   Right, I do conceive you.
    MOSCA. And then they do it by experiment;   60
For which the law not only doth absolve 'em,
But gives them great reward; and he is loath
To hire his death so.
    CORBACCIO.   It is true, they kill
With as much license as a judge.   65
    MOSCA.   Nay, more;
For he but kills, sir, where the law condemns,
And these can kill him too.
    CORBACCIO.   Ay, or me,
Or any man. How does his apoplex?   70
Is that strong on him still?
    MOSCA.   Most violent.
His speech is broken, and his eyes are set,
His face drawn longer than 'twas wont—
    CORBACCIO.   How? how?   75
Stronger than he was wont?
    MOSCA.   No, sir; his face
Drawn longer than 'twas wont.
    CORBACCIO.   O good.
    MOSCA.   His mouth   80
Is ever gaping, and his eyelids hang.
    CORBACCIO.   Good.
    MOSCA. A freezing numbness stiffens all his
                         [joints,
And makes the color of his flesh like lead.   85
    CORBACCIO.   'Tis good.
    MOSCA. His pulse beats slow, and dull.
    CORBACCIO.   Good symptoms still.
    MOSCA. And from his brain—

your the

CORBACCIO.   Ha? How? Not from his
                              [brain?
MOSCA. Yes, sir, and from his brain—
CORBACCIO.   I conceive you; good.
5   MOSCA. Flows a cold sweat, with a continual
                              [rheum,
Forth the resolved° corners of his eyes.
      CORBACCIO. Is 't possible? Yet I am better, ha!
How does he with the swimming of his head?
10   MOSCA. O, sir, 'tis past the scotomy;° he now
Hath lost his feeling, and hath left° to snort;
You hardly can perceive him, that he breathes.
      CORBACCIO. Excellent, excellent; sure I shall
                              [outlast him;
15   This makes me young again, a score of years.
      MOSCA. I was a-coming for you, sir.
      CORBACCIO.   Has he made his will?
What has he giv'n me?
      MOSCA.   No, sir.
20   CORBACCIO.   Nothing? ha?
      MOSCA. He has not made his will, sir.
      CORBACCIO.   Oh, oh, oh.
What then did Voltore, the lawyer, here?
      MOSCA. He smelt a carcass, sir, when he but
25   [heard
My master was about his testament;°
As I did urge him to it for your good—
      CORBACCIO. He came unto him, did he? I
                              [thought so.
30   MOSCA. Yes, and presented him this piece of
                              [plate.
      CORBACCIO. To be his heir?
      MOSCA.   I do not know, sir.
      CORBACCIO.   True;
35   I know it too.
      MOSCA [aside]. By your own scale, sir.
      CORBACCIO.   Well,
I shall prevent° him yet. See, Mosca, look,
Here I have brought a bag of bright cecchines,
40   Will quite weigh down his plate.
      MOSCA.   Yea, marry, sir.
This is true physic, this your sacred medicine;
No talk of opiates to this great elixir!

CORBACCIO. 'Tis aurum palpabile, if not
                              [potabile.° 45
MOSCA. It shall be minister'd to him in his
                              [bowl!
CORBACCIO. Ay, do, do, do.
MOSCA.   Most blessed cordial!
This will recover him.°   50
      CORBACCIO.   Yes, do, do, do.
      MOSCA. I think it were not best, sir.
      CORBACCIO.   What?
      MOSCA.   To recover° him.
      CORBACCIO. O, no, no, no; by no means.   55
      MOSCA.   Why, sir, this
Will work some strange effect, if he but feel it.
      CORBACCIO. 'Tis true; therefore forbear. I'll
                              [take my venture;
Give me 't again.   60
      MOSCA.   At no hand;° pardon me,
You shall not do yourself that wrong, sir. I
Will so advise you, you shall have it all.
      CORBACCIO. How?
      MOSCA.   All, sir; 'tis your right, your own; 65
                              [no man
Can claim a part; 'tis yours without a rival,
Decreed by destiny.
      CORBACCIO.   How, how, good Mosca?
      MOSCA. I'll tell you, sir. This fit he shall   70
                              [recover—
      CORBACCIO. I do conceive you.
      MOSCA.   And, on first advantage
Of his gain'd sense, will I re-importune him
Unto the making of his testament,   75
And show him this. [Points to the money.]
      CORBACCIO.   Good, good.
      MOSCA.   'Tis better yet,
If you will hear, sir.
      CORBACCIO.   Yes, with all my heart.   80
      MOSCA. Now would I counsel you, make
                              [home with speed;
There, frame a will; whereto you shall inscribe
My master your sole heir.
      CORBACCIO.   And disinherit   85
My son?

resolved decomposing
scotomy giddiness
left ceased
about his testament planning his will
prevent get ahead of

aurum . . . potabile gold tangible, if not drinkable.
      Elixir of gold was an esteemed restorative.
recover him recover his favor
recover cure
At no hand by no means

MOSCA.   O, sir, the better; for that color°
Shall make it much more taking.
  CORBACCIO.   O, but color?
  MOSCA. This will, sir, you shall send it unto
5   [me.
Now, when I come to enforce, as I will do,
Your cares, your watchings, and your many
                              [prayers,
Your more than many gifts, your this day's
10   [present,
And last, produce your will; where (without
                            [thought
Or least regard unto your proper issue,
A son so brave, and highly meriting)
15 The stream of your diverted love hath thrown
                            [you
Upon my master, and made him your heir;
He cannot be so stupid or stone-dead,
But, out of conscience and mere gratitude—
20   CORBACCIO. He must pronounce me his?
  MOSCA.   'Tis true.
  CORBACCIO.   This plot
Did I think on before.
  MOSCA.   I do believe it.
25   CORBACCIO. Do you not believe it?
  MOSCA.   Yes, sir.
  CORBACCIO.   Mine own project.
  MOSCA. Which, when he hath done, sir—
  CORBACCIO.   Publish'd me his heir?
30   MOSCA. And you so certain to survive him—
  CORBACCIO.   Ay.
  MOSCA. Being so lusty a man—
  CORBACCIO.   'Tis true.
  MOSCA.   Yes, sir—
35   CORBACCIO. I thought on that too. See, how
                          [he should be°
The very organ to express my thoughts!
  MOSCA. You have not only done yourself a
                           [good—
40   CORBACCIO. But multiplied it on my son!
  MOSCA. 'Tis right, sir.
  CORBACCIO. Still, my invention.
  MOSCA.   'Las, sir! Heaven knows,
It hath been all my study, all my care,
45 (I e'en grow gray withal) how to work things—

color pretense
he should be Mosca is

CORBACCIO. I do conceive, sweet Mosca.
  MOSCA.   You are he
For whom I labor here.
  CORBACCIO.   Ay, do, do, do.
I'll straight about it.   50
  MOSCA *[aside]*. Rook go with you, raven.
  CORBACCIO. I know thee honest.
  MOSCA.   You do lie, sir—
  CORBACCIO.   And—
  MOSCA. Your knowledge is no better than   55
                          [your ears, sir.
  CORBACCIO. I do not doubt to be a father to
                            [thee.
  MOSCA. Nor I to gull my brother of his
                         [blessing.   60
  CORBACCIO. I may ha' my youth restor'd to
                        [me, why not?
  MOSCA. Your Worship is a precious ass—
  CORBACCIO.   What say'st thou?
  MOSCA. I do desire your Worship to make   65
                        [haste,° sir.
  CORBACCIO. 'Tis done, 'tis done; I go.
[*Exit.*]
  VOLPONE [*leaping from his couch*]. Oh, I shall
                        [burst!   70
Let out my sides, let out my sides—
  MOSCA.   Contain
Your flux of laughter, sir; you know this hope
Is such a bait, it covers any hook.
  VOLPONE. O, but thy working, and thy   75
                       [placing it!
I cannot hold; good rascal, let me kiss thee;
I never knew thee in so rare a humor.
  MOSCA. Alas, sir, I but do as I am taught;
Follow your grave instructions, give 'em words,   80
Pour oil into their ears, and send them hence.
  VOLPONE. 'Tis true, 'tis true. What a rare
                       [punishment
Is avarice to itself!
  MOSCA.   Ay, with our help, sir.   85
  VOLPONE. So many cares, so many maladies,
So many fears attending on old age.
Yea, death so often call'd on, as no wish
Can be more frequent with 'em, their limbs
                       [faint,   90
Their senses dull, their seeing, hearing, going,

haste pronounced hasst

All dead before them; yea, their very teeth,
Their instruments of eating, failing them.
Yet this is reckon'd life! Nay, here was one,
Is now gone home, that wishes to live longer!
5 Feels not his gout, nor palsy; feigns himself
Younger by scores of years, flatters his age
With confident belying it, hopes he may
With charms like Aeson° have his youth
[restor'd;
10 And with these thoughts so battens, as if fate
Would be as easily cheated on as he;
And all turns air! Who's that there, now? a
[third?

[*Another knocks.*]

15 MOSCA. Close; to your couch again; I hear
[his voice.
It is Corvino, our spruce merchant.
VOLPONE [*lying down*].   Dead.
MOSCA. Another bout, sir, with your eyes.
20   [(*Anointing them.*)—Who's there?

Scene v

[*Enter* CORVINO.]
Signior Corvino! come most wish'd for! Oh,
How happy were you, if you knew it, now!
CORVINO. Why? what? wherein?
25 MOSCA.   The tardy hour is come, sir.
CORVINO. He is not dead?
MOSCA.   Not dead, sir, but as
[good;
He knows no man.
30 CORVINO.   How shall I do then?
MOSCA.   Why, sir?
CORVINO. I have brought him here a pearl.
MOSCA.   Perhaps he has
So much rembrance left as to know you, sir.
35 He still calls on you; nothing but your name
Is in his mouth. Is your pearl orient, sir?
CORVINO. Venice was never owner of the like.
VOLPONE. Signior Corvino!
MOSCA.   Hark!
40 VOLPONE.   Signior Corvino.
MOSCA. He calls you; step and give it him.—
[H' is here, sir.
And he has brought you a rich pearl.
CORVINO.   How do you do, sir?—
45 Tell him it doubles the twelfth carat.

Aeson a legendary Greek king

MOSCA.   Sir,
He cannot understand: his hearing's gone;
And yet it comforts him to see you—
CORVINO.   Say
I have a diamond for him, too.   50
MOSCA.   Best show 't, sir;
Put it into his hand; 'tis only there
He apprehends; he has his feeling yet.
See, how he grasps it!
CORVINO.   'Las, good gentleman!   55
How pitiful the sight is!
MOSCA.   Tut, forget, sir.
The weeping of an heir should still be laughter
Under a visor.
CORVINO.   Why, am I his heir?   60
MOSCA. Sir, I am sworn, I may not show the
[will
Till he be dead. But here has been Corbaccio,
Here has been Voltore, here were others too—
I cannot number 'em, they were so many—   65
All gaping here for legacies; but I,
Taking the vantage of his naming you,
"Signior Corvino, Signior Corvino," took
Paper, and pen, and ink, and there I ask'd him
Whom he would have his heir! "Corvino."   70
[Who
Should be executor? "Corvino." And
To any question he was silent to,
I still interpreted the nods he made,
Through weakness, for consent; and sent home 75
[th' others,
Nothing bequeath'd them, but to cry and
[curse.
CORVINO. Oh, my dear Mosca. (*They*
[*embrace.*) Does he not perceive us?   80
MOSCA. No more than a blind harper. He
[knows no man,
No face of friend, nor name of any servant,
Who 'twas that fed him last, or gave him drink;
Not those he hath begotten, or brought up,   85
Can he remember.
CORVINO.   Has he children?
MOSCA.   Bastards,
Some dozen, or more, that he begot on beggars,
Gypsies, and Jews, and black-moors, when he   90
[was drunk.
Knew you not that, sir? 'Tis the common fable.
The dwarf, the fool, the eunuch, are all his;
H' is the true father of his family,

In all save me. But he has giv'n 'em nothing.
    CORVINO. That's well, that's well. Art sure
                   [he does not hear us?
    MOSCA. Sure, sir! Why, look you, credit your
5   [own sense. (*Shouts in* VOLPONE's *ear.*)
The pox approach, and add to your diseases,
If it would send you hence the sooner, sir;
For your incontinence it hath deserv'd it
Throughly and throughly, and the plague to
10   [boot!—
You may come near, sir.—Would you would
                   [once close
Those filthy eyes of yours, that flow with slime
Like two frog-pits; and those same hanging
15   [cheeks,
Cover'd with hide instead of skin—Nay, help,
                   [sir—
That look like frozen dishclouts set on end.
    CORVINO. Or like an old smok'd wall, on
20   [which the rain
Ran down in streaks.
    MOSCA.   Excellent, sir! speak out;
You may be louder yet; a culverin
Discharged in his ear would hardly bore it.
25   CORVINO. His nose is like a common sewer,
                 [still running.
    MOSCA. 'Tis good! And what his mouth?
    CORVINO.   A very draught.
    MOSCA. O, stop it up—
30   CORVINO.   By no means.
    MOSCA.   Pray you, let me;
Faith, I could stifle him rarely° with a pillow
As well as any woman that should keep° him.
    CORVINO. Do as you will; but I'll be gone.
35   MOSCA.   Be so;
It is your presence makes him last so long.
    CORVINO. I pray you use no violence.
    MOSCA.   No, sir? why?
Why should you be thus scrupulous, 'pray you,
40   [sir?
    CORVINO. Nay, at your discretion.
    MOSCA.   Well, good sir, begone.
    CORVINO. I will not trouble him now to take
                [my pearl?
45   MOSCA. Pooh, nor your diamond. What a
                [needless care

rarely exceedingly well
keep attend

Is this afflicts you? Is not all here yours?
Am not I here, whom you have made, your
                   [creature,
That owe my being to you?   50
    CORVINO.   Grateful Mosca!
Thou art my friend, my fellow, my companion,
My partner, and shalt share in all my fortunes.
    MOSCA. Excepting one.
    CORVINO.   What's that?   55
    MOSCA.   Your gallant wife, sir.
    [*Exit* CORVINO.]
Now is he gone; we had no other means
To shoot him hence but this.
    VOLPONE.   My divine Mosca! 60
Thou hast today outgone thyself. Who's there?
    [*Another knocks.*]
I will be troubled with no more. Prepare
Me music, dances, banquets, all delights;
The Turk is not more sensual in his pleasures 65
Than will Volpone. [*Exit* MOSCA.] Let me see;
               [a pearl!
A diamond! plate! *cecchines*! Good morning's
               [purchase.
Why, this is better than rob churches, yet; 70
Or fat, by eating, once a month, a man—
    [*Re-enter* MOSCA.]
Who is 't?
    MOSCA.   The beauteous Lady Would-be,
               [sir. 75
Wife to the English knight, Sir Politic Would-
               [be—
This is the style, sir, is directed me—
Hath sent to know how you have slept tonight,
And if you would be visited.   80
    VOLPONE.   Not now.
Some three hours hence—
    MOSCA.   I told the squire so much.
    VOLPONE. When I am high with mirth and
             [wine; then, then. 85
'Fore Heaven, I wonder at the desperate valor
Of the bold English, that they dare let loose
Their wives to all encounters!
    MOSCA.   Sir, this knight
Had not his name for nothing: he is politic,° 90
And knows, howe'er his wife affect strange
             [airs,
She hath not yet the face to be dishonest.

politic worldly wise, devious and urbane

But had she Signior Corvino's wife's face—
   VOLPONE. Hath she so rare a face?
   MOSCA.   O, sir, the wonder,
The blazing star of Italy! a wench
5 Of the first year! a beauty ripe as harvest!
Whose skin is whiter than a swan, all over!
Than silver, snow, or lilies! a soft lip,
Would tempt you to eternity of kissing!
And flesh that melteth in the touch to blood!
10 Bright as your gold! and lovely as your gold!
   VOLPONE. Why had not I known this before?
   MOSCA.   Alas, sir,
Myself but yesterday discover'd it.
   VOLPONE. How might I see her?
15   MOSCA.   Oh, not possible;
She's kept as warily as is your gold;
Never does come abroad, never takes air
But at a window. All her looks are sweet,
As the first grapes or cherries, and are watch'd
20 As near as they are.
   VOLPONE.   I must see her—
   MOSCA.   Sir,
There is a guard of ten spies thick upon her,
All his whole household; each of which is set
25 Upon his fellow, and have all their charge,
When he goes out, when he comes in, examin'd.
   VOLPONE. I will go see her, though but at her
            [window.
   MOSCA. In some disguise then.
30   VOLPONE.   That is true; I must
Maintain mine own shape still the same; we'll
           [think.
    [Exeunt.]

ACT II

Scene i

[Before CORVINO's house in St. Mark's
35 Square.]
   [Enter SIR POLITIC WOULD-BE and PEREGRINE.]
   POLITIC. Sir, to a wise man, all the world's his
           [soil:
It is not Italy, nor France, nor Europe,
40 That must bound me, if my fates call me forth.
Yet I protest, it is no salt desire
Of seeing countries, shifting a religion,
Nor any disaffection to the state
Where I was bred, and unto which I owe

My dearest plots, hath brought me out; much 45
           [less
That idle, antic, stale, gray-headed project
Of knowing men's minds and manners, with
           [Ulysses!
But a peculiar humor of my wife's 50
Laid for° this height of° Venice, to observe,
To quote,° to learn the language, and so forth—
I hope you travel, sir, with license?°
   PEREGRINE.   Yes.
   POLITIC. I dare the safelier converse.—How 55
           [long, sir,
Since you left England?
   PEREGRINE.   Seven weeks.
   POLITIC.   So lately!
You ha' not been with my Lord Ambassador? 60
   PEREGRINE.   Not yet, sir.
   POLITIC. Pray you, what news, sir, vents our
           [climate?
I heard last night a most strange thing reported
By some of my Lord's followers, and I long 65
To hear how 'twill be seconded!
   PEREGRINE.   What was 't, sir?
   POLITIC. Marry, sir, of a raven° that should
           [build
In a ship royal of the king's. 70
   PEREGRINE [aside].   This fellow,
Does he gull me, trow? or is gull'd?—Your
           [name, sir?
   POLITIC. My name is Politic Would-be.
   PEREGRINE [aside].   O, that speaks him.— 75
A knight, sir?
   POLITIC.   A poor knight, sir.
   PEREGRINE.   Your lady
Lies here in Venice, for intelligence
Of tires and fashions and behavior, 80
Among the courtesans? The fine Lady Would-
           [be?

Laid for headed for   **height of** highly fashionable
quote note
license government authorization
raven this reference, like the following ones to lion's
   whelps, the new star (a famous nova, of 1604), porpoises, and a whale, indicates both the ready
   credulity of Sir Politic and the widespread interest in
   omens associated with the wars and negotiations
   between the Protestants (of Great Britain and the
   Low Countries) and the Catholics (of Austria, Italy,
   and Spain)

POLITIC. Yes, sir; the spider and the bee
                                        [ofttimes
Suck from one flower.
    PEREGRINE.   Good Sir Politic!
5   I cry you mercy; I have heard much of you.
'Tis true, sir, of your raven.
    POLITIC.   On your knowledge?
    PEREGRINE. Yes, and your lion's whelping in
                                        [the Tower.
10 POLITIC. Another whelp!
    PEREGRINE.   Another, sir.
    POLITIC.   Now Heaven!
What prodigies be these? The fires° at Berwick!
And the new star! These things concurring,
15   [strange!
And full of omen! Saw you those meteors?
    PEREGRINE. I did, sir.
    POLITIC.   Fearful! Pray you, sir,
                                        [confirm me,
20 Were there three porpoises seen, above the
                                        [Bridge,
As they give out?
    PEREGRINE.   Six, and a sturgeon, sir.
    POLITIC. I am astonish'd!
25 PEREGRINE.   Nay, sir, be not so;
I'll tell you a greater prodigy than these—
    POLITIC. What should these things portend?
    PEREGRINE.   The very day,
Let me be sure, that I put forth from London,
30 There was a whale discover'd in the river,
As high as Woolwich, that had waited there,
Few know how many months, for the
                                        [subversion
Of the Stode fleet.°
35 POLITIC.   Is 't possible? Believe it,
'Twas either sent from Spain, or the
                                        [Archdukes!°
Spinola's° whale, upon my life, my credit!
Will they not leave these projects? Worthy sir,

fires meteors
Stode fleet vessels of the English Merchant Adven-
    turers, a trading company with a base at Stade, near
    Hamburg, Germany
Archdukes Archduke Albert of Austria and his wife,
    the Spanish Infanta Isabella, jointly the governors
    of the Netherlands and titled "the Archdukes"
Spinola commander of Spanish forces in the Nether-
    lands

Some other news.   40
    PEREGRINE.   Faith, Stone, the fool, is dead,
And they do lack a tavern fool extremely.
    POLITIC. Is Mas' Stone dead?
    PEREGRINE.   He's dead, sir; why, I hope
You thought him not immortal?—[*Aside.*] Oh, 45
                                        [this knight,
Were he well known, would be a precious
                                        [thing
To fit our English stage. He that should write
But such a fellow, should be thought to feign 50
Extremely, if not maliciously.
    POLITIC.   Stone dead!
    PEREGRINE. Dead.—Lord! how deeply, sir,
                                        [you apprehend it!
He was no kinsman to you?   55
    POLITIC.   That I know of.
Well! that same fellow was an unknown° fool.
    PEREGRINE. And yet you knew him, it seems?
    POLITIC.   I did so. Sir,
I knew him one of the most dangerous heads   60
Living within the state, and so I held him.
    PEREGRINE. Indeed, sir?
    POLITIC.   While he liv'd, in action,
He has receiv'd weekly intelligence,
Upon my knowledge, out of the Low Countries; 65
For all parts of the world, in cabbages;
And those dispens'd again to ambassadors.
In oranges, muskmelons, apricots,
Lemons, pome-citrons, and such like;
                                        [sometimes 70
In Colchester oysters, and your Selsey cockles.
    PEREGRINE. You make me wonder!
    POLITIC.   Sir, upon my knowledge.
Nay, I have observ'd him, at your public
                                        [ordinary,° 75
Take his advertisement° from a traveller
(A conceal'd statesman) in a trencher of meat;
And instantly, before the meal was done,
Convey an answer in a toothpick.
    PEREGRINE.   Strange!   80
How could this be, sir?
    POLITIC.   Why, the meat was cut
So like his character, and so laid as he

unknown unrecognized
ordinary tavern
advertisement information

208

Must easily read the cipher.
PEREGRINE.   I have heard
He could not read, sir.
POLITIC.   So 'twas given out,
5 In polity,° by those that did employ him;
But he could read, and had your languages,
And to 't, as sound a noddle—
PEREGRINE.   I have heard, sir,
That your baboons were spies, and that they
10   [were
A kind of subtle nation near to China.
POLITIC. Ay, ay, your Mamaluchi.° Faith,
                              [they had
Their hand in a French plot or two; but they
15 Were so extremely given to women, as
They made discovery of all: yet I
Had my advices here, on Wednesday last,
From one of their own coat, they were return'd,
Made their relations, as the fashion is,
20 And now stand fair for fresh employment.
PEREGRINE [aside].   Heart!
This Sir Pol will be ignorant of nothing.—
It seems, sir, you know all.
POLITIC.   Not all, sir. But
25 I have some general notions. I do love
To note and to observe. Though I live out,
Free from the active torrent, yet I'd mark
The currents and the passages of things
For mine own private use; and know the ebbs
30 And flows of state.
PEREGRINE.   Believe it, sir, I hold
Myself in no small tie unto my fortunes,
For casting me thus luckily upon you,
Whose knowledge, if your bounty equal it,
35 May do me great assistance, in instruction
For my behavior, and my bearing, which
Is yet so rude and raw—
POLITIC.   Why? came you forth
Empty of rules for travel?
40 PEREGRINE.   Faith, I had
Some common ones, from out that vulgar
                              [grammar,
Which he that cri'd Italian to me, taught me.
POLITIC. Why, this it is that spoils all our

                              [brave bloods, 45
Trusting our hopeful gentry unto pedants,
Fellows of outside, and mere bark. You seem
To be a gentleman of ingenuous race.—
I not profess it, but my fate hath been
To be where I have been consulted with,   50
In this high kind, touching some great men's
                              [sons,
Persons of blood and honor.—
PEREGRINE.   Who be these, sir?

Scene ii

[Enter MOSCA and NANO disguised, with 55
workmen who erect a stage.]
MOSCA. Under that window, there 't must be.
                              [The same.
POLITIC. Fellows to mount a bank!° Did your
                              [instructor 60
In the dear tongues never discourse to you
Of the Italian mountebanks?
PEREGRINE.   Yes, sir.
POLITIC.   Why,
Here shall you see one.   65
PEREGRINE.   They are quacksalvers,
Fellows that live by venting° oils and drugs!
POLITIC. Was that the character he gave you
                              [of them?
PEREGRINE. As I remember.   70
POLITIC.   Pity his ignorance.
They are the only knowing men of Europe!
Great general scholars, excellent physicians,
Most admir'd statesmen, profess'd favorites
And cabinet counsellors to the greatest princes! 75
The only languag'd men of all the world!
PEREGRINE. And, I have heard, they are most
                              [lewd° impostors;
Made all of terms and shreds; no less beliers
Of great men's favors, than their own vile 80
                              [med'cines;
Which they will utter° upon monstrous oaths;
Selling that drug for twopence, ere they part,
Which they have valu'd at twelve crowns
                              [before. 85

In polity for political reasons
Mamaluchi Mamelukes, a powerful group of Moham-
    medan white slaves, noted for their machinations
bank a small platform
venting vending
lewd ignorant
utter dispense

POLITIC. Sir, calumnies are answer'd best with [silence.
Yourself shall judge.—Who is it mounts, my [friends?

5 MOSCA. Scoto of Mantua, sir.

POLITIC. Is 't he? Nay, then
I'll proudly promise, sir, you shall behold
Another man than has been phant'sied° to you.
I wonder yet, that he should mount his bank
10 Here in this nook, that has been wont t' appear
In face of the Piazza! Here he comes.

[*Enter* VOLPONE, *disguised as a mountebank doctor, and followed by a crowd of people.*]

VOLPONE [*to* NANO]. Mount, zany.

15 GREGE. Follow, follow, follow, follow, follow.

POLITIC. See how the people follow him! he's [a man
May write ten thousand crowns in bank here. [Note,
20 Mark but his gesture—I do use to observe
The state he keeps in getting up!

PEREGRINE. 'Tis worth it, sir.

VOLPONE. Most noble gentlemen, and my worthy patrons, it may seem strange that I,
25 your Scoto Mantuano, who was ever wont to fix my bank in the face of the public Piazza, near the shelter of the portico to the Procuratia, should now, after eight months' absence from this illustrious city of Venice, humbly retire
30 myself into an obscure nook of the Piazza.

POLITIC. Did not I now object the same?

PEREGRINE. Peace, sir.

VOLPONE. Let me tell you: I am not, as your Lombard proverb saith, cold on my feet; or
35 content to part with my commodities at a cheaper rate than I accustomed—look not for it. Nor that the calumnious reports of that impudent detractor, and shame to our profession (Alessandro Buttone, I mean), who gave out, in public, I was condemn'd *a' sforzato*° to the
40 galleys, for poisoning the Cardinal Bembo's cook, hath at all attached, much less dejected me. No, no, worthy gentlemen; to tell you true, I cannot endure to see the rabble of these

ground *ciarlitani*° that spread their cloaks on 45
the pavement, as if they meant to do feats of activity, and then come in lamely, with their mouldy tales of Boccaccio, like stale Tabarin, the fabulist; some of them discoursing their travels, and of their tedious captivity in the 50
Turk's galleys, when, indeed, were the truth° known, they were the Christian's galleys, where very temperately they ate bread, and drunk water, as a wholesome penance, enjoin'd them by their confessors, for base pilferies. 55

POLITIC. Note but his bearing, and contempt of these.

VOLPONE. These turdy-facy-nasty-paty-lousy-fartical rogues, with one poor groat's-worth of unprepar'd antimony, finely wrapp'd 60
up in several *scartoccios*,° are able, very well, to kill their twenty a week, and play; yet these meager, starv'd spirits, who have half stopp'd the organs of their minds with earthy oppilations,° want not their favorers among your 65
shrivell'd salad-eating artisans, who are over-joy'd that they may have their half-pe'rth° of physic; though it purge 'em into another world, 't makes no matter.

POLITIC. Excellent! ha' you heard better lan- 70
guage, sir?

VOLPONE. Well, let 'em go. And, gentlemen, know that for this time our bank, being thus remov'd from the clamors of the *canaglia*,° shall be the scene of pleasure and delight; for I have 75
nothing to sell, little or nothing to sell.

POLITIC. I told you, sir, his end.

PEREGRINE. You did so, sir.

VOLPONE. I protest I and my six servants are not able to make of this precious liquor so fast 80
as it is fetch'd away from my lodging by gentle-men of your city, strangers of the terra-firma, worshipful merchants, ay, and senators, too, who, ever since my arrival, have detained me to

---

ground ciarlitani cheap entertainers
the truth i.e., that they were criminals being properly punished rather than slaves of the Turkish infidels
scartoccios twists of paper
oppilations obstructions
half-pe'rth halfpenny's worth
canaglia rabble

phant'sied represented
a' sforzato to hard labor

their uses, by their splendidous liberalities. And
worthily. For what avails your rich man to have
his magazines° stuff'd with *moscadelli,*° or of
the purest grape, when his physicians prescribe
5   him, on pain of death, to drink nothing but
water cocted with aniseeds? O health! health!
the blessing of the rich! the riches of the poor!
who can buy thee at too dear a rate, since
there is no enjoying this world without thee?
10 Be not then so sparing of your purses, honorable gentlemen, as to abridge the natural course
of life—
    PEREGRINE. You see his end.
    POLITIC.   Ay, is 't not good?
15 VOLPONE. For, when a humid flux, or catarrh,
by the mutability of air, falls from your head
into an arm or shoulder, or any other part, take
you a ducat, or your *cecchine* of gold, and apply
to the place affected; see what good effect it
20 can work. No, no; 'tis this blessed *unguento,*
this rare extraction, that hath only power to
disperse all malignant humors° that proceed
either of hot, cold, moist, or windy causes—
    PEREGRINE. I would he had put in dry too.
25 POLITIC.   'Pray you, observe.
    VOLPONE. To fortify the most indigest and
crude stomach, ay, were it of one that, through
extreme weakness, vomited blood, applying
only a warm napkin to the place, after the unc-
30 tion and fricace;°—for the *vertigine* in the
head, putting but a drop into your nostrils, likewise behind the ears, a most sovereign and
approv'd remedy; the *mal caduco,* cramps, convulsions, paralyses, epilepsies, *tremor cordia,*
35 retir'd nerves, ill vapors of the spleen, stoppings
of the liver, the stone, the strangury, *hernia
ventosa, iliaca passio;* stops a *dysenteria* immediately; easeth the torsion of the small guts;
and cures *melancholia hypochondriaca,* being
40 taken and applied according to my printed re-

ceipt. [*Pointing to his bill and his glass.*] For
this is the physician, this the medicine; this
counsels, this cures; this gives direction, this
works the effect; and, in sum, both together
may be term'd an abstract of the theoric and   45
practic in the Aesculapian art. 'Twill cost you
eight crowns.—And, Zan Fritada, pray thee
sing a verse, extempore, in honor of it.
    POLITIC. How do you like him, sir?
    PEREGRINE.   Most strangely, I!   50
    POLITIC. Is not his language rare?
    PEREGRINE.   But° alchemy,
I never heard the like, or Broughton's° books.
    NANO [*sings*]. Had old Hippocrates, or Galen,
That to their books put med'cines all in,   55
But known this secret, they had never
(Of which they will be guilty ever)
Been murderers of so much paper,
Or wasted many a hurtless taper;
No Indian drug had e'er been famed,   60
Tobacco, sassafras, not named;
Ne yet of guacum one small stick, sir,
Nor Raymund Lully's great elixir.°
Ne had been known the Danish Gonswart,
Or Paracelsus, with his long-sword.   65
    PEREGRINE. All this, yet, will not do; eight
crowns is high.
    VOLPONE. No more.—Gentlemen, if I had but
time to discourse to you the miraculous effects
of this my oil, surnamed *oglio del Scoto,* with   70
the countless catalogue of those I have cured
of th' aforesaid, and many more diseases; the
patents and privileges of all the princes and
commonwealths of Christendom; or but the
depositions of those that appear'd on my part,   75
before the signiory of the Sanitâ° and most
learned College of Physicians; where I was
authorized, upon notice taken of the admirable
virtues of my medicaments, and mine own ex-
cellency in matter of rare and unknown secrets,   80
not only to disperse them publicly in this famous city, but in all the territories that happily
joy under the government of the most pious and

---

magazines storage vaults   **moscadelli** muscatel
humors in medieval physiology, the four kinds of
    body-fluid, corresponding to the traditional four
    elements, that determined both health and temper-
    ament
unction and fricace ointment and massage. In the rest
    of this speech Volpone makes a flourish of medical
    terminology not to inform but to impress.

But except for
Broughton an eccentric English theologian
great elixir of youth
signiory . . . Sanitâ governors of the hospital

magnificent states of Italy. But may some other gallant fellow say, "Oh, there be divers that make profession to have as good, and as experimented receipts as yours." Indeed, very 5 many have assay'd, like apes, in imitation of that which is really and essentially in me, to make of this oil; bestow'd great cost in furnaces, stills, alembics, continual fires, and preparation of the ingredients (as indeed there 10 goes to it six hundred several simples, besides some quantity of human fat, for the conglutination, which we buy of the anatomists); but when these practitioners come to the last decoction—blow, blow, puff, puff, and all flies in 15 fumo. Ha, ha, ha! Poor wretches! I rather pity their folly and indiscretion, than their loss of time and money; for those may be recovered by industry; but to be a fool born, is a disease incurable. For myself, I always from my youth 20 have endeavor'd to get the rarest secrets, and book them, either in exchange or for money; I spared nor cost nor labor where anything was worthy to be learned. And, gentlemen, honorable gentlemen, I will undertake, by virtue of 25 chemical art, out of the honorable hat that covers your head, to extract the four elements; that is to say, the fire, air, water, and earth, and return you your felt without burn or stain. For, whilst others have been at the *balloo*° I have 30 been at my book; and am now past the craggy paths of study, and come to the flow'ry plains of honor and reputation.

POLITIC. I do assure you, sir, that is his aim.

VOLPONE. But, to our price.

35 PEREGRINE.   And that withal, Sir Pol.

VOLPONE. You all know, honorable gentlemen, I never valu'd this *ampulla*, or vial, at less than eight crowns; but for this time, I am content to be depriv'd of it for six; six crowns is 40 the price, and less in courtesy I know you cannot offer me; take it or leave it, howsoever, both it and I am at your service. I ask you not as the value of the thing, for then I should demand of you a thousand crowns; so the Cardinals Mon-45 talto, Fernese, the great Duke of Tuscany, my

gossip,° with divers other princes, have given me; but I despise money. Only to show my affection to you, honorable gentlemen, and your illustrious state here, I have neglected the messages of these princes, mine own offices, fram'd 50 my journey hither, only to present you with the fruits of my travels.—Tune your voices once more to the touch of your instruments, and give the honorable assembly some delightful recreation. 55

PEREGRINE. What monstrous and most pain-
[ful circumstance
Is here, to get some three or four gazets,°
Some threepence i' the whole! for that 'twill
[come to. 60

NANO [*sings*]. You that would last long, list
[to my song;
Make no more coil, but buy of this oil.
Would you be ever fair, and young?
Stout of teeth, and strong of tongue? 65
Tart of palate? quick of ear?
Sharp of sight? of nostril clear?
Moist of hand? and light of foot?
Or (I will come nearer to 't)
Would you live free from all diseases? 70
Do the act your mistress pleases,
Yet fright all aches from your bones?
Here's a med'cine for the nones.°

VOLPONE. Well, I am in humor, at this time, to make a present of the small quantity my coffer 75 contains; to the rich in courtesy, and to the poor for God's sake. Wherefore now mark: I ask'd you six crowns; and six crowns, at other times, you have paid me; you shall not give me six crowns, nor five, nor four, nor three, nor 80 two, nor one; nor half a ducat; no, nor a *moccinigo*.° Sixpence it will cost you, or six hundred pound—expect no lower price, for, by the banner of my front,° I will not bate a bagatine,°— that I will have, only, a pledge of your loves, 85 to carry something from amongst you, to show I am not contemn'd by you. Therefore, now,

---

gossip   close friend
gazets   small coins
nones   purpose
moccinigo   small Venetian coin
banner of my front   flag of my profession
bagatine   trivial coin

balloo   a game of ball

toss your handkerchiefs, cheerfully, cheerfully;
and be advertised, that the first heroic spirit
that deigns to grace me with a handkerchief, I
will give it a little remembrance of something
5 beside, shall please it better than if I had presented it with a double pistolet.°
    PEREGRINE. Will you be that heroic spark, Sir
Pol?
    [CELIA, *at the window, throws down her*
10 *handkerchief.*]
O, see! the window has prevented you.
    VOLPONE. Lady, I kiss your bounty; and, for
this timely grace you have done your poor Scoto
of Mantua, I will return you, over and above
15 my oil, a secret of that high and inestimable
nature, shall make you for ever enamor'd on
that minute wherein your eye first descended
on so mean, yet not altogether to be despis'd an
object. Here is a powder conceal'd in this paper,
20 of which, if I should speak to the worth, nine
thousand volumes were but as one page, that
page as a line, that line as a word; so short is
this pilgrimage of man, which some call life, to
the expressing of it. Would I reflect on the
25 price? Why, the whole world is but as an
empire, that empire as a province, that province
as a bank, that bank as a private purse, to the
purchase of it. I will only tell you: it is the powder that made Venus a goddess, given her by
30 Apollo, that kept her perpetually young, clear'd
her wrinkles, firm'd her gums, fill'd her skin,
color'd her hair; from her deriv'd to Helen, and
at the sack of Troy unfortunately lost; till now,
in this our age, it was as happily recover'd, by a
35 studious antiquary, out of some ruins of Asia,
who sent a moiety of it to the court of France
(but much sophisticated), wherewith the ladies
there now color their hair. The rest, at this present, remains with me, extracted to a quintes-
40 sence; so that, wherever it but touches, in youth
it perpetually preserves, in age restores the
complexion; seats your teeth, did they dance
like virginal jacks,° firm as a wall; makes them
white as ivory, that were black as—

pistolet gold coin
virginal jacks activating levers, or keys, of a small
   harpsichord

Scene iii

[*Enter* CORVINO.]   45
CORVINO. Spite o' the devil, and my shame!
              [Come down here;
Come down!—No house but mine to make your
              [scene?
Signior Flaminio,° will you down, sir? down? 50
What, is my wife your Franciscina,° sir?
No windows on the whole piazza, here,
To make your properties, but mine? but mine?
    [*He beats away the mountebank, etc.*]
Heart! ere tomorrow I shall be new christen'd, 55
And called the *Pantalone di Bisognosi*°
About the town.
    PEREGRINE.   What should this mean, Sir
             [Pol?
    POLITIC. Some trick of state, believe it; I will 60
             [home.
    PEREGRINE. It may be some design on you.
    POLITIC.   I know not.
I'll stand upon my guard.
    PEREGRINE.   It is your best, sir. 65
    POLITIC. This three weeks, all my advices, all
             [my letters,
They have been intercepted.
    PEREGRINE.   Indeed, sir?
Best have a care.   70
    POLITIC.   Nay, so I will.
    PEREGRINE [*aside*].   This knight.
I may not lose him, for my mirth, till night.
    [*Exeunt.*]

Scene iv

[*A room in* VOLPONE's *house.*]   75
[*Enter* VOLPONE *and* MOSCA.]
VOLPONE. O, I am wounded.
    MOSCA.   Where, sir?
    VOLPONE.   Not without;
Those blows were nothing; I could bear them 80
             [ever.
But angry Cupid, bolting from her eyes,

Signior Flaminio "Mr. Leading Actor"
Franciscina cute little maidservant (a type in the
   Italian popular plays)
Pantalone di Bisognosi the doting old fool (another
   such type)

Hath shot himself into me like a flame;
Where now he flings about his burning heat,
As in a furnace some ambitious fire
Whose vent is stopp'd. The fight is all within
5   [me.
I cannot live, except thou help me, Mosca;
My liver melts, and I, without the hope
Of some soft air from her refreshing breath,
Am but a heap of cinders.
10   MOSCA.   'Las, good sir,
Would you had never seen her.
     VOLPONE.   Nay, would thou
Hadst never told me of her.
     MOSCA.   Sir, 'tis true;
15 I do confess I was unfortunate,
And you unhappy; but I am bound in
                               [conscience,
No less than duty, to effect my best
To your release of torment, and I will, sir.
20   VOLPONE. Dear Mosca, shall I hope?
     MOSCA.   Sir, more than dear,
I will not bid you to despair of aught
Within a human compass.
     VOLPONE.   O, there spoke
25 My better angel. Mosca, take my keys,
Gold, plate, and jewels, all 's at thy devotion;
Employ them how thou wilt—nay, coin me
                               [too—
So thou in this but crown my longings, Mosca!
30   MOSCA. Use but your patience.
     VOLPONE.   So I have.
     MOSCA.   I doubt not
To bring success to your desires.
     VOLPONE.   Nay, then,
35 I not repent me of my late disguise.
     MOSCA. If you can horn° him, sir, you need
                               [not.
     VOLPONE.   True.
Besides, I never meant him for my heir.
40 Is not the color o' my beard and eyebrows
To make me known?
     MOSCA.   No jot.
     VOLPONE.   I did it well.
     MOSCA. So well, would I could follow you in
45   [mine,

With half the happiness; and yet I would
Escape your epilogue.
     VOLPONE.   But were they gull'd
With a belief that I was Scoto?
     MOSCA.   Sir,   50
Scoto himself could hardly have distinguish'd!
I have not time to flatter you now; we'll part,
And as I prosper, so applaud my art.
     [*Exeunt.*]

Scene v

[*A room in* CORVINO'S *house.*]   55
[*Enter* CORVINO, *with his sword in his hand,
dragging in* CELIA.]
     CORVINO. Death of mine honor, with the
                               [city's fool!
A juggling, tooth-drawing, prating   60
                               [mountebank!
And at a public window! where, whilst he,
With his strain'd action, and his dole of faces,
To his drug-lecture draws your itching ears,
A crew of old, unmarried, noted lechers,   65
Stood leering up like satyrs, and you smile
Most graciously! and fan your favors forth,
To give your hot spectators satisfaction!
What, was your mountebank their call? their
                               [whistle? 70
Or were you enamor'd on his copper rings,
His saffron jewel, with the toad-stone in 't,
Or his embroid'red suit, with the cope-stitch,
Made of a hearse cloth, or his old tilt-feather,
Or his starch'd beard? Well! you shall have   75
                               [him, yes.
He shall come home, and minister unto you
The fricace for the mother.° Or, let me see,
I think you'd rather mount! Would you not
                               [mount? 80
Why, if you'll mount, you may; yes, truly, you
                               [may.
And so you may be seen, down to th' foot.
Get you a cittern, Lady Vanity,°
And be a dealer with the virtuous man;   85
Make one. I'll but protest myself a cuckold,
And save your dowry. I am a Dutchman, I!

---

horn cuckold. Folk tradition had it that a deceived
  husband grew horns.

fricace . . . mother literally, massage to cure hysteria
Lady Vanity character representing worldly pleasure
  in the old morality plays

For if you thought me an Italian,
You would be damn'd ere you did this, you
                  [whore.
Thou 'dst tremble to imagine that the murder
5 Of father, mother, brother, all thy race,
Should follow, as the subject of my justice!
    CELIA. Good sir, have patience!
    CORVINO.   What couldst thou propose
Less to thyself, than in this heat of wrath,
10 And stung with my dishonor, I should strike
This steel into thee, with as many stabs
As thou wert gaz'd upon with goatish eyes?
    CELIA. Alas, sir, be appeas'd! I could not
                  [think
15 My being at the window should more now
Move your impatience than at other times.
    CORVINO. No? not to seek and entertain a
                  [parley
With a known knave? before a multitude?
20 You were an actor with your handkerchief!
Which he most sweetly kiss'd in the receipt,
And might, no doubt, return it with a letter
And 'point the place where you might meet;
                [your sister's,
25 Your mother's, or your aunt's might serve the
                  [turn.
    CELIA. Why, dear sir, when do I make these
                [excuses,
Or ever stir abroad, but to the church?
30 And that so seldom—
    CORVINO.   Well, it shall be less;
And thy restraint before was liberty,
To what I now decree; and therefore mark me.
First, I will have this bawdy light° damm'd up;
35 And till 't be done, some two or three yards off
I'll chalk a line; o'er which if thou but chance
To set thy desp'rate foot, more hell, more
                [horror,
More wild remorseless rage shall seize on thee
40 Than on a conjuror that had heedless left
His circle's safety ere his devil was laid.
Then here's a lock which I will hang upon thee,
And, now I think on 't, I will keep thee
              [backwards;°
45 Thy lodging shall be backwards, thy walks

light window
backwards in the back rooms of the house

                [backwards,
Thy prospect—all be backwards, and no
                [pleasure,
That thou shalt know but backwards. Nay,
             [since you force 50
My honest nature, know it is your own
Being too open, makes me use you thus.
Since you will not contain your subtle nostrils
In a sweet room, but they must snuff the air
Of rank and sweaty passengers°—(knock 55
           [within) one knocks.
Away, and be not seen, pain of thy life;
Nor look toward the window; if thou dost—
Nay, stay, hear this—let me not prosper,
               [whore, 60
But I will make thee an anatomy,
Dissect thee mine own self, and read a lecture
Upon thee to the city, and in public.
Away!—
    [*Exit* CELIA.]   65
    [*Enter* SERVITORE.]
        Who's there?
    SERVITORE.   'Tis Signior Mosca, sir.

Scene vi

[CORVINO *and* SERVITORE *remain.*]
    CORVINO. Let him come in. [*Exit* SERVITORE.] 70
           [—His master's dead!
There's yet
Some good to help the bad.—[*Enter* MOSCA.]
           [My Mosca, welcome;
I guess your news.   75
    MOSCA.   I fear you cannot, sir.
    CORVINO. Is 't not his death?
    MOSCA.   Rather the contrary.
    CORVINO. Not his recovery?
    MOSCA.   Yes, sir.   80
    CORVINO.   I am curs'd;
I am bewitch'd; my crosses meet to vex me.
How? how? how? how?
    MOSCA.   Why, sir, with Scoto's oil!
Corbaccio and Voltore brought of it,   85
Whilst I was busy in an inner room—
    CORVINO. Death! that damn'd mountebank!
           [but for the law,
Now, I could kill the rascal. 'T cannot be

passengers passers-by

His oil should have that virtue. Ha' not I
Known him a common rogue, come fiddling in
To th' *osteria*,° with a tumbling whore,
And, when he has done all his forc'd tricks,
5   [been glad
Of a poor spoonful of dead wine, with flies
                          [in 't?
It cannot be. All his ingredients
Are a sheep's gall, a roasted bitch's marrow,
10 Some few sod earwigs, pounded caterpillars,
A little capon's grease, and fasting spittle:
I know 'em to a dram.
    MOSCA.   I know not, sir;
But some on 't, there, they pour'd into his ears,
15 Some in his nostrils, and recover'd him;
Applying but the fricace.
    CORVINO.   Pox° o' that fricace.
    MOSCA. And, since, to seem the more officious
And flatt'ring of his health, there, they have
20   [had,
At extreme fees, the college of physicians
Consulting on him, how they might restore
                         [him;
Where one would have a cataplasm of spices,
25 Another a flay'd ape clapp'd to his breast,
A third would ha' it a dog, a fourth an oil,
With wildcats' skins. At last, they all resolv'd
That, to preserve him, was no other means
But some young woman must be straight
30   [sought out,
Lusty, and full of juice, to sleep by him;
And to this service most unhappily,
And most unwillingly, am I now employ'd,
Which here I thought to pre-acquaint you with,
35 For your advice, since it concerns you most;
Because I would not do that thing might cross
Your ends, on whom I have my whole
                        [dependence, sir.
Yet, if I do not they may relate
40 My slackness to my patron, work me out
Of his opinion; and there all your hopes,
Ventures, or whatsoever, are all frustrate.
I do but tell you, sir. Besides, they are all
Now striving who shall first present him.
45   [Therefore—

I could entreat you, briefly, conclude somewhat:
Prevent 'em if you can.
    CORVINO.   Death to my hopes!
This is my villainous fortune! Best to hire
Some common courtesan!   50
    MOSCA.   Ay, I thought on that, sir;
But they are all so subtle, full of art—
And age again doting and flexible,
So as—I cannot tell—we may, perchance,
Light on a quean may cheat us all.   55
    CORVINO.   'Tis true.
    MOSCA. No, no; it must be one that has no
                        [tricks, sir,
Some simple thing, a creature made unto it;
Some wench you may command. Ha' you no   60
                        [kinswoman?
Gods so°—Think, think, think, think, think,
                        [think, think, sir.
One o' the doctors offer'd there his daughter.
    CORVINO. How!   65
    MOSCA.   Yes, Signior Lupo, the physician.
    CORVINO. His daughter!
    MOSCA.   And a virgin, sir. Why, alas,
He knows the state of 's body, what it is:
That naught can warm his blood, sir, but a   70
                        [fever,
Nor any incantation raise his spirit;
A long forgetfulness hath seiz'd that part.
Besides, sir, who shall know it? Some one or
                     [two— 75
    CORVINO. I pray thee give me leave.—
            [(*Stepping aside*.) If any man
But I had had this luck—The thing in 't self,
I know, is nothing.—Wherefore should not I
As well command my blood and my affections 80
As this dull doctor? In the point of honor,
The cases are all one of wife and daughter.
    MOSCA [*aside*]. I hear him coming.
    CORVINO [*aside*].   She shall do 't; 'tis
                     [done. 85
'Slight!° if this doctor, who is not engag'd,
Unless 't be for his counsel, which is nothing,
Offer his daughter, what should I, that am
So deeply in? I will prevent him. Wretch!
Covetous wretch!—Mosca, I have determin'd. 90

osteria hostelry
Pox a plague

Gods so on God's oath
'Slight by God's light

MOSCA. How sir?

CORVINO.   We'll make all sure. The party
                                    [you wot of
Shall be mine own wife, Mosca.

5   MOSCA.   Sir, the thing,
But that I would not seem to counsel you,
I should have motion'd to you, at the first;
And make your count, you have cut all their
                                    [throats.

10   Why! 'tis directly taking a possession!
And in his next fit, we may let him go.
'Tis but to pull the pillow from his head,
And he is throttled; it had been done before
But for your scrupulous doubts.

15   CORVINO.   Ay, a plague on 't;
My conscience fools my wit! Well, I'll be brief,
And so be thou, lest they should be before us.
Go home; prepare him; tell him with what zeal
And willingness I do it. Swear it was

20   On the first hearing, as thou mayst do, truly,
Mine own free motion.

     MOSCA.   Sir, I warrant you,
I'll so possess him with it, that the rest
Of his starv'd clients shall be banish'd all;

25   And only you receiv'd. But come not, sir,
Until I send, for I have something else
To ripen for your good—you must not know 't.

     CORVINO. But do not you forget to send, now.

     MOSCA.   Fear not.

30   [Exit.]

Scene vii

[CORVINO remains.]

CORVINO. Where are you, wife? My Celia!
                                    [Wife!

[Enter CELIA.]

35   —What, blubbering?
Come, dry those tears. I think you thought'st
                                    [me in earnest;
Ha? By this light I talk'd so but to try thee.
Methinks, the lightness of the occasion

40   Should ha' confirmed thee. Come, I am not
                                    [jealous.

     CELIA. No?

     CORVINO. Faith I am not, I, nor never was;
It is a poor, unprofitable humor.

45   Do not I know, if women have a will,
They'll do 'gainst all the watches o' the world,

And that the fiercest spies are tam'd with gold?
Tut, I am confident in thee, thou shalt see 't;
And see I'll give thee cause, too, to believe it.
Come, kiss me.—Go, and make thee ready   50
                                    [straight,
In all thy best attire, thy choicest jewels,
Put 'em all on, and, with 'em, thy best looks:
We are invited to a solemn feast,
At old Volpone's, where it shall appear   55
How far I am free from jealousy or fear.

     [Exeunt.]

ACT III

Scene i

[A street.]

[Enter MOSCA.]

     MOSCA. I fear I shall begin to grow in love   60
With my dear self and my most prosp'rous
                                    [parts;°
They do so spring and burgeon. I can feel
A whimsy i' my blood—I know not how—
Success hath made me wanton. I could skip   65
Out of my skin now, like a subtle snake.
I am so limber. Oh! your parasite
Is a most precious thing, dropp'd from above,
Not bred 'mongst clods and clotpolls,° here on
                                    [earth.   70
I muse the mystery° was not made a science,
It is so liberally profess'd! Almost
All the wise world is little else, in nature,
But parasites or sub-parasites. And yet
I mean not those that have your bare town-art,   75
To know who's fit to feed 'em; have no house,
No family, no care, and therefore mold
Tales for men's ears, to bait that sense; or get
Kitchen-invention, and some stale receipts
To please the belly, and the groin; nor those,   80
With their court dog-tricks, that can fawn and
                                    [fleer,
Make their revenue out of legs and faces,°
Echo my Lord, and lick away a moth:
But your fine, elegant rascal, that can rise   85

---

parts abilities
clotpolls blockheads
muse the mystery wonder that the trade
legs and faces bows and smiles

And stoop, almost together, like an arrow;
Shoot through the air as nimbly as a star;
Turn short as doth a swallow; and be here,
And there, and here, and yonder, all at once;
5   Present to any humor, all occasion;
And change a visor° swifter than a thought!
This is the creature had the art born with him;
Toils not to learn it, but doth practise it
Out of most excellent nature; and such sparks
10   Are the true parasites, others but their zanies.

Scene ii

[*Enter* BONARIO.]
MOSCA. Who's this? Bonario, old Corbaccio's
[son?
The person I was bound to seek. Fair sir,
15   You are happ'ly met.
BONARIO.   That cannot be by thee.
MOSCA. Why, sir?
BONARIO.   Nay, 'pray thee know thy way,
[and leave me.
20   I would be loath to interchange discourse
With such a mate as thou art.
MOSCA.   Courteous sir,
Scorn not my poverty.
BONARIO.   Not I, by Heaven;
25   But thou shalt give me leave to hate thy
[baseness.
MOSCA. Baseness!
BONARIO.   Ay; answer me, is not thy sloth
Sufficient argument? thy flattery?
30   Thy means of feeding?
MOSCA.   Heaven be good to me.
These imputations are too common, sir,
And eas'ly stuck on virtue, when she's poor.
You are unequal° to me, and howe'er
35   Your sentence may be righteous, yet you are
[not,
That, ere you know me, thus proceed in
[censure.
St. Mark bear witness 'gainst you, 'tis inhuman.
40   [*Weeps.*]
BONARIO [*aside*]. What! does he weep? the
[sign is soft and good!
I do repent me that I was so harsh.

MOSCA. 'Tis true, that, sway'd by strong
[necessity,   45
I am enforc'd to eat my careful bread
With too much obsequy;° 'tis true, beside,
That I am fain to spin mine own poor raiment
Out of my mere observance, being not born
To a free fortune; but that I have done   50
Base offices, in rending friends asunder,
Dividing families, betraying counsels,
Whispering false lies, or mining° men with
[praises,
Train'd their credulity with perjuries,   55
Corrupted chastity, or am in love
With mine own tender ease, but would not
[rather
Prove the most rugged and laborious course,
That might redeem my present estimation,   60
Let me here perish, in all hopes of goodness.
BONARIO [*aside*]. This cannot be a
[personated passion!—
I was to blame, so to mistake thy nature;
'Pray thee forgive me; and speak out thy   65
[bus'ness.
MOSCA. Sir, it concerns you; and though I
[may seem
At first to make a main offence in manners,
And in my gratitude unto my master,   70
Yet for the pure love which I bear all right,
And hatred of the wrong, I must reveal it.
This very hour your father is in purpose
To disinherit you—
BONARIO.   How!   75
MOSCA.   And thrust you forth,
As a mere stranger to his blood; 'tis true, sir.
The work no way engageth me, but as
I claim an interest in the general state
Of goodness and true virtue, which I hear   80
T' abound in you; and for which mere respect,
Without a second aim, sir, I have done it.
BONARIO. This tale hath lost thee much of the
[late trust
Thou hadst with me; it is impossible.   85
I know not how to lend it any thought
My father should be so unnatural.
MOSCA. It is a confidence that well becomes

---

a visor his expression
unequal (1) of superior rank (2) unjust

obsequy obsequiousness
mining undermining

Your piety;° and form'd, no doubt, it is
From your own simple innocence; which makes
Your wrong more monstrous and abhorr'd. But,
                                            [sir,
5 I now will tell you more. This very minute,
It is, or will be doing; and if you
Shall be put pleas'd to go with me, I'll bring
                                            [you,
I dare not say where you shall be, but where
10 Your ear shall be a witness of the deed;
Hear yourself written bastard, and profess'd
The common issue of the earth.
     BONARIO.   I'm maz'd!
     MOSCA. Sir, if I do it not, draw your just
                                            [sword,
15 And score your vengeance on my front° and
                                            [face;
Mark me your villain. You have too much
                                            [wrong,
20 And I do suffer for you, sir. My heart
Weeps blood in anguish—
     BONARIO.   Lead. I follow thee.
     [Exeunt.]

Scene iii

[A room in VOLPONE's house.]
25 [Enter VOLPONE, NANO, ANDROGYNO, and
CASTRONE.]
     VOLPONE. Mosca stays long, methinks.—
                         [Bring forth your sports,
And help to make the wretched time more
30   [sweet.
     NANO. Dwarf, fool, and eunuch, well met
                                    [here we be.
A question it were now, whether of us three,
Being all the known delicates of a rich man,
35 In pleasing him, claim the precedency can?
     CASTRONE. I claim for myself.
     ANDROGYNO.   And so doth the fool.
     NANO. 'Tis foolish indeed; let me set you
                              [both to school.
40 First for your dwarf, he's little and witty,
And everything, as it is little, is pretty;
Else why do men say to a creature of my shape,
So soon as they see him, "It's a pretty little

piety filial loyalty
front brow

                                          [ape"?
And why a pretty ape, but for pleasing   45
                                      [imitation
Of greater men's action, in a ridiculous fashion?
Beside, this feat body of mine doth not crave
Half the meat, drink, and cloth, one of your
                                 [bulks will have. 50
Admit your fool's face be the mother of
                                      [laughter,
Yet, for his brain, it must always come after;
And though that do feed him, it's a pitiful case,
His body is beholding to such a bad face.   55
     [One knocks.]
     VOLPONE. Who's there? My couch: away!
                         [Look, Nano, see.—
     [Exeunt ANDROGYNO and CASTRONE.]
Give me my caps first—go, inquire. (Exit   60
                         [NANO.) Now, Cupid
Send it be Mosca, and with fair return.
     [Re-enter NANO.]
     NANO. It is the beauteous Madam—
     VOLPONE.   Would-be—is it?   65
     NANO. The same.
     VOLPONE.   Now torment on me! Squire
                                      [her in;
For she will enter, or dwell here for ever.
Nay, quickly. (Exit NANO; VOLPONE retires to his   70
               [couch.)—That my fit were past! I fear
A second hell too, that my loathing this
Will quite expel my appetite to the other.
Would she were taking now her tedious leave.
Lord, how it threats me what I am to suffer!   75

Scene iv

[Enter NANO and LADY POLITIC WOULD-BE.]
     LADY. I thank you, good sir. Pray you signify
Unto your patron I am here.—This band
Shows not my neck enough.—I trouble you,
                                      [sir;   80
Let me request you bid one of my women
Come hither to me. [Exit NANO.]—In good
                         [faith, I am dress'd
Most favorably today; it is no matter;
'Tis well enough.   85
     [Re-enter NANO with a WAITING WOMAN.]
               Look, see, these petulant things!
How they have done this!
     VOLPONE [aside].   I do feel the fever

Ent'ring in at mine ears; oh, for a charm
To fright it hence.
    LADY.   Come nearer. Is this curl
In his right place? or this? Why is this higher
5 Than all the rest? You ha' not wash'd your
                    [eyes yet?
Or do they not stand even i' your head?
Where's your fellow? call her.
    [*Exit* WOMAN.]
10   NANO [*aside.*]   Now, St. Mark
Deliver us! anon she'll beat her women,
Because her nose is red.
    [*Re-enter* WOMAN *with another.*]
    LADY.   I pray you view
15 This tire, forsooth. Are all things apt, or no?
    WOMAN. One hair a little here sticks out,
                    [forsooth.
    LADY. Does 't so, forsooth! and where was
                  [your dear sight,
20 When it did so, forsooth? What now! bird-
                    [ey'd?
And you, too? 'Pray you, both approach and
                  [mend it.
Now, by that light I muse you're not asham'd!
25 I, that have preach'd these things so oft unto
                    [you,
Read you the principles, argu'd all the grounds,
Disputed every fitness, every grace,
Call'd you to counsel of so frequent dressings—
30   NANO [*aside*]. More carefully than of your
                  [fame or honor.
    LADY. Made you acquainted what an ample
                  [dowry
The knowledge of these things would be unto
35   [you,
Able alone to get you noble husbands
At your return; and you thus to neglect it!
Besides, you seeing what a curious° nation
Th' Italians are, what will they say of me?
40 "The English lady cannot dress herself."
Here's a fine imputation to our country!
Well, go your ways, and stay i' the next room.
This fucus° was too coarse too; it's no
                  [matter.—
45 Good sir, you'll give 'em entertainment?

curious fastidious
fucus rouge

[*Exeunt* NANO *and* WAITING WOMEN.]
VOLPONE [*aside*]. The storm comes toward
                  [me.
    LADY [*going to the couch*].   How does my
                  [Volpone? 50
    VOLPONE. Troubled with noise; I cannot
                  [sleep. I dreamt
That a strange Fury ent'red now my house,
And, with the dreadful tempest of her breath,
Did cleave my roof asunder.   55
    LADY.   Believe me, and I
Had the most fearful dream, could I
                [remember 't—
    VOLPONE [*aside*]. Out on my fate! I ha' giv'n
                [her the occasion 60
How to torment me: she will tell me hers.
    LADY. Methought the golden mediocrity,°
Polite, and delicate—
    VOLPONE.   O, if you do love me,
No more; I sweat, and suffer, at the mention 65
Of any dream. Feel how I tremble yet.
    LADY. Alas, good soul! the passion of the
                [heart.°
Seed-pearl were good now, boil'd with syrup of
                [apples, 70
Tincture of gold, and coral, citron-pills,
Your elecampane root, myrobalans—
    VOLPONE [*aside*]. Ay me, I have ta'en a
                [grasshopper by the wing!
    LADY. Burnt silk and amber. You have 75
                [muscadel
Good i' the house—
    VOLPONE.   You will not drink, and part?
    LADY. No, fear not that. I doubt we shall not
                [get 80
Some English saffron—half a dram would
                [serve;
Your sixteen cloves, a little musk, dried mints,
Bugloss, and barley meal—
    VOLPONE [*aside*].   She's in again; 85
Before I feign'd diseases—now I have one.
    LADY. And these appli'd with a right scarlet
                [cloth—

the . . . mediocrity a personification of the Golden
  Mean
passion . . . heart a symptom of love-melancholy. A
  catalogue of supposed remedies follows.

VOLPONE [*aside*]. Another flood of words! a
                                  [very torrent!
LADY. Shall I, sir, make you a poultice?
VOLPONE.   No, no, no.
5 I am very well; you need prescribe no more.
     LADY. I have studied physic; but now
I'm all for music, save i' the forenoons,
An hour or two for painting. I would have
A lady, indeed, t' have all letters and arts,
10 Be able to discourse, to write, to paint;
But principal, as Plato holds, your music
(And so does wise Pythagoras, I take it)
Is your true rapture, when there is consent°
In face, in voice, and clothes, and is, indeed,
15 Our sex's chiefest ornament.
     VOLPONE.   The poet
As old in time as Plato, and as knowing,
Says that your highest female grace is silence.
     LADY. Which o' your poets? Petrarch, or
20   [Tasso, or Dante?
Guarini? Ariosto? Aretine?
Cieco di Hadria? I have read them all.
     VOLPONE [*aside*]. Is everything a cause to my
                              [destruction?
25 LADY. I think I ha' two or three of 'em about
                              [me.
     VOLPONE [*aside*]. The sun, the sea, will
                              [sooner both stand still
Than her eternal tongue! Nothing can 'scape it.
30 LADY. Here's *Pastor Fido*°—
     VOLPONE [*aside*].   Profess obstinate
                              [silence;
That's now my safest.
     LADY.   All our English writers,
35 I mean such as are happy in th' Italian,
Will deign to steal out of this author, mainly;
Almost as much as from Montagnié:°
He has so modern and facile a vein,
Fitting the time, and catching the court-ear.
40 Your Petrarch is more passionate, yet he,
In days of sonneting, trusted 'em with much.°
Dante is hard, and few can understand him.

consent harmony
Pastor Fido Guarini's *Faithful Shepherd*, a pastoral
tragicomedy then much in vogue as a model of elegant style and sentiment
Montagnié Montaigne
trusted 'em with much was much copied by English
sonnet writers

But for a desperate° wit, there's Aretine!°
Only, his pictures are a little obscene—
You mark me not!   45
     VOLPONE.   Alas, my mind's perturb'd.
     LADY. Why, in such cases, we must cure
                              [ourselves,
Make use of our philosophy—
     VOLPONE.   Oh, ay me!   50
     LADY. And as we find our passions do rebel,
Encounter 'em with reason, or divert 'em,
By giving scope unto some other humor
Of lesser danger; as, in politic bodies,
There's nothing more doth overwhelm the   55
                              [judgment,
And clouds the understanding, than too much
Settling and fixing, and, as 'twere, subsiding
Upon one object. For the incorporating
Of these same outward things into that part   60
Which we call mental, leaves some certain
                              [faeces
That stop the organs, and, as Plato says,
Assassinates our knowledge.
     VOLPONE [*aside*].   Now, the spirit   65
Of patience help me.
     LADY.   Come, in faith, I must
Visit you more, a' days, and make you well—
Laugh and be lusty.
     VOLPONE [*aside*]. My good angel save   70
                              [me!
     LADY. There was but one sole man in all the
                              [world
With whom I e'er could sympathize; and he
Would lie you, often, three, four hours together 75
To hear me speak; and be sometimes so rapt,
As he would answer me quite from the purpose,
Like you, and you are like him, just. I'll
                              [discourse,
An't be but only, sir, to bring you asleep,   80
How we did spend our time and loves together,
For some six years.
     VOLPONE.   Oh, oh, oh, oh, oh, oh!
     LADY. For we were coaetanei,° and brought
                              [up— 85
     VOLPONE [*aside*]. Some power, some fate,
                              [some fortune rescue me!

desperate extraordinary   **Aretine** Pietro Aretino,
author of sonnets based on obscene drawings by
Giulio Romano
coaetanei of the same age

Scene v

[*Enter* MOSCA.]

MOSCA. God save you, madam.

LADY.   Good sir.

VOLPONE.   Mosca! welcome—

5 [*aside*]. Welcome to my redemption.

MOSCA [*aside*].   Why, sir?

VOLPONE [*aside*].   Oh,
Rid me of this my torture, quickly, there;
My madam with the everlasting voice.
10 The bells,° in time of pestilence, ne'er made
Like noise, or were in that perpetual motion—
The cockpit comes not near it. All my house,
But now, steam'd like a bath with her thick
                              [breath,
15 A lawyer could not have been heard; nor scarce
Another woman, such a hail of words
She has let fall. For hell's sake, rid her hence.

    MOSCA. Has she presented?°

VOLPONE.   Oh, I do not care:
20 I'll take her absence upon any price,
With any loss.

    MOSCA.   Madam—

    LADY.   I ha' brought your patron·
A toy, a cap here, of mine own work—

25   MOSCA.   'Tis well.
I had forgot to tell you I saw your knight
Where you'd little think it—

    LADY.   Where?

    MOSCA.   Marry,°

30 Where yet, if you make haste, you may
                    [apprehend him,
Rowing upon the water in a gondola,
With the most cunning courtesan of Venice.

    LADY. Is 't true?

35   MOSCA.   Pursue 'em, and believe your
                    [eyes;
Leave me to make your gift. [*Exit* LADY.]—I
                    [knew 'twould take;
For, lightly, they that use themselves most
40   [license,°
Are still most jealous.

---

bells which, in time of plague, were tolled almost
    continuously for the dead and dying
presented given a present
Marry indeed
lightly . . . license generally, those who allow them-
    selves most leeway

VOLPONE.   Mosca, hearty thanks
For thy quick fiction, and delivery of me.
Now to my hopes, what say'st thou?

    [*Re-enter* LADY.]   45

    LADY.   But do you hear, sir?—

    VOLPONE [*aside*]. Again! I fear a paroxysm.

    LADY.   Which way
Row'd they together?

    MOSCA.   Toward the Rialto.   50

    LADY. I pray you lend me your dwarf.

    MOSCA.   I pray you take him.

    [*Exit* LADY.]
Your hopes, sir, are like happy blossoms, fair,
And promise timely fruit, if you will stay   55
But the maturing. Keep you at your couch;
Corbaccio will arrive straight, with the will;
When he is gone, I'll tell you more.

    [*Exit.*]

    VOLPONE.   My blood,   60
My spirits are return'd; I am alive;
And, like your wanton gamester at primero,°
Whose thought had whisper'd to him, not go
                    [less,
Methinks I lie, and draw—for an encounter.   65

Scene vi

[*Enter* MOSCA *and* BONARIO.]

MOSCA. Sir, here conceal'd [*opening a door*]
                    [you may hear all. But, pray you,
Have patience, sir; [*one knocks*] the same 's
                    [your father knocks.   70
I am compell'd to leave you.

    [*Exit.*]

    BONARIO.   Do so.—Yet
Cannot my thought imagine this a truth.

    [*Goes in.*]   75

Scene vii

[*Enter* MOSCA, CORVINO, *and* CELIA.]

MOSCA. Death on me! You are come too
                    [soon, What meant you?
Did not I say I would send?

    CORVINO.   Yes, but I fear'd   80
You might forget it, and then they prevent us.

    MOSCA. Prevent!—[*Aside.*] Did e'er man
                    [haste so for his horns?

---

primero a kind of poker, on the terms of which Vol-
    pone puns as he draws the curtain of his bed

A courtier would not ply it so for a place.—°
Well, now there is no helping it, stay here;
I'll presently return.
[*Exit.*]
5 CORVINO.   Where are you, Celia?
You know not wherefore I have brought you
[hither?
CELIA. Not well, except you told me.
CORVINO.   Now I will.
10 Hark hither. [*They retire to one side.*]
[*Re-enter* MOSCA.]
MOSCA [*to* BONARIO]. Sir, your father hath
[sent word
It will be half an hour ere he come;
15 And therefore, if you please to walk the while
Into the gallery—at the upper end,
There are some books to entertain the time;
And I'll take care no man shall come unto you,
[sir.
20 BONARIO. Yes, I will stay there.—[*Aside.*] I
[do doubt this fellow.
[*Exit.*]
MOSCA [*looking after him*]. There; he is far
[enough; he can hear nothing.
25 And for his father, I can keep him off.
CORVINO [*advancing with* CELIA]. Nay, now,
[there is no starting back, and therefore,
Resolve upon it; I have so decreed.
It must be done. Nor would I move 't afore,°
30 Because I would avoid all shifts and tricks,
That might deny me.
CELIA.   Sir, let me beseech you,
Affect not these strange trials; if you doubt
My chastity, why, lock me up for ever;
35 Make me the heir of darkness. Let me live
Where I may please your fears, if not your
[trust.
CORVINO. Believe it, I have no such humor, I.
All that I speak I mean; yet I am not mad;
40 Not horn-mad, see you? Go to, show yourself
Obedient, and a wife.
CELIA.   O Heaven!
CORVINO.   I say it,
Do so.
45 CELIA.   Was this the train?°

CORVINO.   I have told you reasons;
What the physicians have set down; how much
It may concern me; what my engagements are;
My means, and the necessity of those means
For my recovery. Wherefore, if you be   50
Loyal, and mine, be won; respect my venture.
CELIA. Before your honor?
CORVINO.   Honor! tut, a breath.
There's no such thing in nature; a mere term
Invented to awe fools. What is my gold   55
The worse for touching, clothes for being
[look'd on?
Why, this 's no more. An old decrepit wretch,
That has no sense, no sinew; takes his meat
With others' fingers; only knows to gape   60
When you do scald his gums; a voice, a
[shadow;
And what can this man hurt you?
CELIA [*aside*].   Lord! what spirit
Is this hath ent'red him?   65
CORVINO.   And for your fame,°
That's such a jig;° as if I would go tell it,
Cry it on the Piazza! Who shall know it
But he that cannot speak it, and this fellow,
Whose lips are i' my pocket? Save yourself—   70
If you'll proclaim 't, you may,—I know no
[other
Should come to know it.
CELIA.   Are Heaven and saints then
[nothing?   75
Will they be blind or stupid?
CORVINO.   How?
CELIA.   Good sir,
Be jealous still, emulate them; and think
What hate they burn with toward every sin.   80
CORVINO. I grant you; if I thought it were a
[sin
I would not urge you. Should I offer this
To some young Frenchman, or hot Tuscan
[blood 85
That had read Aretine, conn'd all his prints,
Knew every quirk within lust's labyrinth,
And were profess'd critic in lechery;
And I would look upon him, and applaud him;
This were a sin: but here, 'tis contrary,   90
A pious work, mere charity, for physic,

---

ply . . . place try so hard to wangle an official position
move 't afore propose it before now
train trick

fame reputation
jig jest

And honest polity, to assure mine own.
CELIA. O Heaven! canst thou suffer such a
                                   [change?
VOLPONE [*aside*]. Thou art mine honor,
5   [Mosca, and my pride,
My joy, my tickling, my delight! Go bring 'em.
MOSCA. Please you draw near, sir.
CORVINO.   Come on, what—
You will not be rebellious? By that light—
MOSCA. Sir, Signior Corvino, here, is come to
10   [see you.
VOLPONE. Oh.
MOSCA.   And hearing of the consultation
                                   [had,
15 So lately, for your health, is come to offer,
Or rather, sir, to prostitute—
CORVINO.   Thanks, sweet Mosca.
MOSCA. Freely, unask'd, or unentreated—
CORVINO.   Well.
20 MOSCA. As the true fervent instance of his
                                   [love,
His own most fair and proper wife, the beauty
Only of price° in Venice—
CORVINO.   'Tis well urg'd.
25 MOSCA. To be your comfortress, and to
                              [preserve you.
VOLPONE. Alas, I am past, already! 'Pray you,
                              [thank him
For his good care and promptness; but for that,
30 'Tis a vain labor e'en to fight 'gainst Heaven;
Applying fire to a stone—uh, uh, uh, uh!—
Making a dead leaf grow again. I take
His wishes gently, though; and you may tell
                                   [him
35 What I have done for him; marry, my state is
                                   [hopeless!
Will him to pray for me; and t' use his fortune
With reverence when he comes to 't.
MOSCA.   Do you hear, sir?
40 Go to him with your wife.
CORVINO.   Heart of my father!
Wilt thou persist thus? Come, I pray thee, come.
Thou seest 'tis nothing, Celia. By this hand,
I shall grow violent. Come, do 't, I say.
45 CELIA. Sir, kill me, rather. I will take down
                                   [poison,
Eat burning coals, do anything—

Only of price peerless

CORVINO.   Be damn'd!
Heart, I will drag thee hence home by the hair;
Cry thee a strumpet through the streets; rip up   50
Thy mouth unto thine ears; and slit thy nose,
Like a raw rochet°—Do not tempt me, come;
Yield; I am loath—Death! I will buy some
                                   [slave
Whom I will kill, and bind thee to him alive,   55
And at my window hang you forth, devising
Some monstrous crime, which I, in capital
                                   [letters,
Will eat into thy flesh with aqua fortis,
And burning cor'sives,° on this stubborn breast.   60
Now, by the blood thou hast incens'd, I'll do it!
CELIA. Sir, what you please, you may; I am
                              [your martyr.
CORVINO. Be not thus obstinate; I ha' not
                              [deserv'd it.   65
Think who it is entreats you. 'Pray thee, sweet;
Good faith, thou shalt have jewels, gowns,
                                   [attires,
What thou wilt think, and ask. Do but go kiss
                                   [him.   70
Or touch him but. For my sake. At my suit.°
This once. No? not? I shall remember this.
Will you disgrace me thus? Do you thirst my
                                   [undoing?
MOSCA. Nay, gentle lady, be advis'd.   75
CORVINO.   No, no.
She has watch'd her time. God's precious,° this
                              [is scurvy,
'Tis very scurvy; and you are—
MOSCA.   Nay, good sir.   80
CORVINO. An errant locust—by heaven, a
                         [locust!—Whore,
Crocodile, that hast thy tears prepar'd,
Expecting how thou'lt bid 'em flow.
MOSCA.   Nay, 'pray you, sir!   85
She will consider.
CELIA.   Would my life would serve
To satisfy—
CORVINO.   'Sdeath!° if she would but
                         [speak to him,   90

rochet large-headed fish
cor'sives corrosives
suit plea
God's precious a truncated oath, short for "God's
  precious body" or "bones" or "wounds," etc.
'Sdeath by God's death (the Crucifixion)

And save my reputation, 'twere somewhat;
But spitefully to affect my utter ruin!
    Mosca [*aside to* CORVINO]. Ay, now you have
        [put your fortune in her hands.
5 Why, i' faith, it is her modesty. I must quit°
        [her.
If you were absent, she would be more coming;
I know it, and dare undertake for her.
What woman can before her husband? 'Pray
10   [you,
Let us depart and leave her here.
    CORVINO.   Sweet Celia,
Thou mayst redeem all yet; I'll say no more.
If not, esteem yourself as lost.—Nay, stay
15   [there.
    [*Exit with* MOSCA.]
    CELIA. O God, and his good angels! whither,
        [whither,
Is shame fled human breasts? that with such
20   [ease,
Men dare put off your honors, and their own?
Is that which ever was a cause of life°
Now plac'd beneath the basest circumstance,
And modesty an exile made, for money?
25   VOLPONE. Ay, in Corvino, and such earth-fed
        [minds,
    [*He leaps off from his couch.*]
That never tasted the true heav'n of love.
Assure thee, Celia, he that would sell thee,
30 Only for hope of gain, and that uncertain,
He would have sold his part of Paradise
For ready money, had he met a copeman.°
Why art thou maz'd to see me thus reviv'd?
Rather applaud thy beauty's miracle;
35 'Tis thy great work, that hath, not now alone,
But sundry times, rais'd me, in several shapes,
And, but this morning, like a mountebank,
To see thee at thy window; ay, before
I would have left my practice° for thy love,
40 In varying figures I would have contended
With the blue Proteus, or the horned flood.°

---

quit acquit
cause of life principle to be defended with life itself
copeman dealer
left . . . practice left off my stratagems
contended . . . flood rivaled the Old Man of the Sea or
    even Acheloüs, Greek legendary figures adept at
    transforming themselves

Now art thou welcome.
    CELIA.   Sir!
    VOLPONE.   Nay, fly me not,
Nor let thy false imagination   45
That I was bedrid, make thee think I am so—
Thou shalt not find it. I am now as fresh,
As hot, as high, and in as jovial plight
As when, in that so celebrated scene,
At recitation of our comedy,   50
For entertainment of the great Valois,°
I acted young Antinoüs,° and attracted
The eyes and ears of all the ladies present,
T' admire each graceful gesture, note, and
        [footing.   55
    [*Sings.*]
Come, my Celia, let us prove,
While we can, the sports of love.
Time will not be ours for ever,
He, at length, our good will sever.   60
Spend not then his gifts in vain.
Suns that set may rise again;
But if once we lose this light,
'Tis with us perpetual night.
Why should we defer our joys?   65
Fame and rumor are but toys.
Cannot we delude the eyes
Of a few poor household spies?
Or his easier ears beguile,
Thus removed by our wile?   70
'Tis no sin love's fruits to steal,
But the sweet thefts to reveal;
To be taken, to be seen,
These have crimes accounted been.

    CELIA. Some serene° blast me, or dire   75
        [lightning strike
This my offending face.
    VOLPONE.   Why droops my Celia?
Thou hast, in place of a base husband, found
A worthy lover; use thy fortune well,   80
With secrecy and pleasure. See, behold,
What thou art queen of; not in expectation,
As I feed others, but possess'd and crown'd.

Valois Henry III of France, who visited Venice in 1574
Antinoüs a handsome boy beloved by the Roman
    emperor Hadrian
serene baneful night mist

See, here, a rope of pearl; and each more orient
Than that the brave Egyptian queen carous'd.°
Dissolve and drink 'em. See, a carbuncle,
May put out both the eyes of our St. Mark;°
5 A diamond would have bought Lollia Paulina,°
When she came in like starlight, hid with jewels
That were the spoils of provinces; take these,
And wear and lose 'em; yet remains an earring
To purchase them again, and this whole state.
10 A gem but worth a private patrimony
Is nothing; we will eat such at a meal.
The heads of parrots, tongues of nightingales,
The brains of peacocks and of estriches,
Shall be our food; and, could we get the
15   [phoenix,
Though nature lost her kind, she were our dish.
      CELIA. Good sir, these things might move a
                                          [mind affected
With such delights; but I, whose innocence
20 Is all I can think wealthy, or worth th' enjoying,
And which, once lost, I have naught to lose
                                                   [beyond it,
Cannot be taken with these sensual baits.
If you have conscience—
25   VOLPONE.   'Tis the beggar's virtue;
If thou hast wisdom, hear me, Celia.
Thy baths shall be the juice of July-flowers,°
Spirit of roses and of violets,
The milk of unicorns, and panthers' breath
30 Gather'd in bags and mix'd with Cretan wines.
Our drink shall be prepared gold and amber,
Which we will take until my roof whirl round
With the vertigo; and my dwarf shall dance,
My eunuch sing, my fool make up the antic,
35 Whilst we, in changed shapes, act Ovid's
                                                   [tales:°
Thou like Europa now, and I like Jove;

Then I like Mars, and thou like Erycine;
So of the rest, till we have quite run through
And wearied all the fables of the gods.   40
Then will I have thee in more modern forms,
Attired like some sprightly dame of France,
Brave Tuscan lady, or proud Spanish beauty;
Sometimes unto the Persian sophy's° wife,
Or the Grand Signior's° mistress; and, for   45
                                                   [change,
To one of our most artful courtesans,
Or some quick Negro, or cold Russian;
And I will meet thee in as many shapes,
Where we may so transfuse our wand'ring   50
                                                   [souls
Out at our lips, and score up sums of pleasures,

That the curious shall not know
How to tell them as they flow;
And the envious, when they find   55
What their number is, be pin'd.

      CELIA. If you have ears that will be pierc'd—
                                                   [or eyes
That can be open'd—a heart, may be touch'd—
Or any part that yet sounds man about you—   60
If you have touch of holy saints, or Heaven,
Do me the grace to let me 'scape. If not,
Be bountiful and kill me. You do know
I am a creature hither ill betray'd
By one whose shame I would forget it were;   65
If you will deign me neither of these graces,
Yet feed your wrath, sir, rather than your lust,
(It is a vice comes nearer manliness)
And punish that unhappy crime of nature,
Which you miscall my beauty; flay my face,   70
Or poison it with ointments for seducing
Your blood to this rebellion. Rub these hands
With what may cause an eating leprosy,
E'en to my bones and marrow, anything
That may disfavor me, save in my honor.   75
And I will kneel to you, pray for you, pay down
A thousand hourly vows, sir, for your health;
Report, and think you virtuous—
      VOLPONE.   Think me cold,
Frozen, and impotent, and so report me!   80

that . . . carous'd the pearl that Cleopatra drank in
   a cup of wine (an example of great luxury)
put . . . Mark outshine the jewels in the treasury of
   St. Mark's cathedral
Lollia Paulina a notorious Roman beauty whom the
   emperor Caligula married and divorced
July-flowers gillyflowers
Ovid's tales his *Metamorphoses* ("Transformations")
   relating such stories as that of Europa, a maiden
   abducted by Jove in the shape of a bull, and the
   love-affair of Venus (**Erycine**) and **Mars**

sophy's king's
Grand Signior's Sultan of Turkey's

That I had Nestor's° hernia, thou wouldst
[think.
I do degenerate, and abuse my nation,
To play with opportunity thus long;
5   I should have done the act, and then have
[parley'd.
Yield, or I'll force thee.
CELIA.   O! just God!
VOLPONE.   In vain—
10   BONARIO [*leaps out from where* MOSCA *had
placed him*]. Forbear, foul ravisher, libidinous
[swine;
Free the forc'd lady, or thou di'st, impostor.
But that I am loath to snatch thy punishment
15   Out of the hand of justice, thou shouldst yet
Be made the timely sacrifice of vengeance,
Before this altar and this dross, thy idol.—
Lady, let's quit the place; it is the den
Of villainy; fear naught: you have a guard;
20   And he ere long shall meet his just reward.
[*Exeunt* BONARIO *and* CELIA.]
VOLPONE. Fall on me, roof, and bury me in
[ruin;
Become my grave, that wert my shelter. Oh!
25   I am unmask'd, unspirited, undone,
Betray'd to beggary, to infamy—

Scene viii

[*Enter* MOSCA.]
MOSCA. Where shall I run, most wretched
[shame of men,
30   To beat out my unlucky brains?
VOLPONE.   Here, here.
What! dost thou bleed?
MOSCA.   O, that his well-driv'n sword
Had been so courteous to have cleft me down
35   Unto the navel, ere I liv'd to see
My life, my hopes, my spirits, my patron, all
Thus desperately engaged, by my error.
VOLPONE. Woe on thy fortune.
MOSCA.   And my follies, sir.
40   VOLPONE. Th' hast made me miserable.
MOSCA.   And myself, sir.
Who would have thought he would have
[harken'd so?
VOLPONE. What shall we do?
45   MOSCA.   I know not; if my heart

Nestor's the aged Homeric hero's

Could expiate the mischance, I'd pluck it out.
Will you be pleas'd to hang me, or cut my
[throat?
And I'll requite you, sir. Let's die like Romans,°
Since we have liv'd like Grecians.°   50
[*They knock without.*]
VOLPONE.   Hark! who's there?
I hear some footing; officers, the saffi,°
Come to apprehend us! I do feel the brand
Hissing already at my forehead; now   55
Mine ears are boring.°
MOSCA.   To your couch, sir, you;
Make that place good, however.
[VOLPONE *lies down as before.*]
—[*Aside.*] Guilty men   60
Suspect what they deserve still.—Signior
[Corbaccio!

Scene ix

[*Enter* CORBACCIO.]
CORBACCIO. Why, how now, Mosca?
MOSCA.   O, undone, amaz'd, sir.   65
Your son, I know not by what accident,
Acquainted with your purpose to my patron,
Touching your will and making him your heir,
Ent'red our house with violence, his sword
[drawn, 70
Sought for you, call'd you wretch, unnatural,
Vow'd he would kill you.
CORBACCIO.   Me?
MOSCA.   Yes, and my patron.
CORBACCIO. This act shall disinherit him   75
[indeed.
Here is the will.
MOSCA.   'Tis well, sir.
CORBACCIO.   Right and well:
Be you as careful now for me.   80
[*Enter* VOLTORE *behind.*]
MOSCA.   My life, sir,
Is not more tender'd;° I am only yours.
CORBACCIO. How does he? Will he die shortly,
[think'st thou? 85
MOSCA.   I fear

like Romans by suicide, as if honorably
like Grecians for pleasure
saffi police
boring being pierced (as punishment)
tender'd cared for

He'll outlast May.

CORBACCIO.   Today?

MOSCA.   No, last out May, sir.

CORBACCIO. Couldst thou not gi' him a dram?

5   MOSCA.   Oh, by no means, sir.

CORBACCIO. Nay, I'll not bid you.

VOLTORE [*coming forward*].   This is a
        [knave, I see.

MOSCA [*aside*]. How! Signior Voltore! did he
10   [hear me?

VOLTORE.   Parasite!

MOSCA. Who's that?—Oh, sir, most timely
        [welcome—

VOLTORE.   Scarce,

15 To the discovery of your tricks, I fear.

You are his, only? and mine also, are you not?

        MOSCA. Who? I, sir!

VOLTORE.   You, sir. What device is this

About a will?

20   MOSCA.   A plot for you, sir.

VOLTORE.   Come,

Put not your foists° upon me; I shall scent 'em.

        MOSCA. Did you not hear it?

VOLTORE.   Yes, I hear Corbaccio

25 Hath made your patron there his heir.

        MOSCA.   'Tis true,

By my device, drawn to it by my plot,

With hope—

VOLTORE.   Your patron should
30   [reciprocate?

And you have promis'd?

        MOSCA.   For your good I did, sir.

Nay, more, I told his son, brought, hid him
        [here,

35 Where he might hear his father pass the deed;

Being persuaded to it by this thought, sir,

That the unnaturalness, first, of the act,

And then his father's oft disclaiming in him

(Which I did mean t' help on), would sure
40   [enrage him

To do some violence upon his parent,

On which the law should take sufficient hold,

And you be stated in a double hope.

Truth be my comfort, and my conscience,

45 My only aim was to dig you a fortune

Out of these two rotten sepulchres—

        VOLTORE. I cry thee mercy, Mosca.

MOSCA.   Worth your patience,

And your great merit, sir. And see the change!

VOLTORE. Why, what success?   50

MOSCA.   Most hapless! You must help,
        [sir.

Whilst we expected th' old raven, in comes

Corvino's wife, sent hither by her husband—

        VOLTORE. What, with a present?   55

        MOSCA.   No, sir, on visitation

(I'll tell you how anon); and, staying long,

The youth he grows impatient, rushes forth,

Seizeth the lady, wounds me, makes me swear

(Or he would murder her—that was his vow)   60

T' affirm my patron to have done her rape;

Which how unlike it is, you see! and hence,

With that pretext he's gone, t' accuse his father,

Defame my patron, defeat you—

        VOLTORE.   Where's her husband?   65

Let him be sent for straight.

        MOSCA.   Sir, I'll go fetch him.

        VOLTORE. Bring him to the Scrutineo.°

        MOSCA.   Sir, I will.

VOLTORE. This must be stopp'd.   70

        MOSCA.   Oh, you do nobly, sir.

Alas, 'twas labor'd all, sir, for your good;

Nor was there want of counsel in the plot

But Fortune can, at any time, o'erthrow

The projects of a hundred learned clerks, sir.   75

        CORBACCIO [*listening*]. What's that?

        VOLTORE.   Wilt please you, sir, to go
        [along?

[*Exit* CORBACCIO *followed by* VOLTORE.]

        MOSCA. Patron, go in, and pray for our   80
        [success.

VOLTORE. Need makes devotion; Heaven
        [your labor bless!

[*Exeunt.*]

ACT IV

Scene i

[*A street.*]   85

[*Enter* SIR POLITIC WOULD-BE *and* PEREGRINE.]

        POLITIC. I told you, sir, it was a plot; you see

What observation is. You mention'd° me

For some instructions; I will tell you, sir,

Put . . . foists do not try your deceits

Scrutineo Senate House
mention'd applied to

(Since we are met here in this height of Venice)
Some few particulars I have set down,
Only for this meridian, fit to be known
Of your crude traveller; and they are these.
5 I will not touch, sir, at your phrase, or clothes,
For they are old.°
    PEREGRINE.   Sir, I have better.
    POLITIC.   Pardon,
I meant, as they are themes.
10   PEREGRINE.   Oh, sir, proceed;
I'll slander you no more of wit, good sir.
    POLITIC. First, for your garb,° it must be
                [grave and serious,
Very reserv'd and lock'd; not tell a secret
15 On any terms, not to your father; scarce
A fable, but with caution, make sure choice
Both of your company and discourse; beware
You never speak a truth—
    PEREGRINE.   How!
20   POLITIC.   Not to strangers,
For those be they you must converse with most;
Others I would not know, sir, but at distance
So as I still might be a saver in° 'em—
You shall have tricks else pass'd upon you,
25   [hourly.
And then, for your religion, profess none,
But wonder at the diversity of all;
And, for your part, protest, were there no other
But simply the laws o' th' land, you could
30   [content you.
Nic. Machiavel and Monsieur Bodin,° both
Were of this mind. Then must you learn the use
And handling of your silver fork at meals,
The metal of your glass° (these are main
35   [matters
With your Italian); and to know the hour
When you must eat your melons and your figs.
    PEREGRINE. Is that a point of state too?
    POLITIC.   Here, it is;
40 For your Venetian, if he see a man
Preposterous in the least, he has him straight;
He has; he strips him. I'll acquaint you, sir,

I now have liv'd here, 'tis some fourteen
             [months.
Within the first week of my landing here,   45
All took me for a citizen of Venice,
I knew the forms so well—
    PEREGRINE [aside].   And nothing else.
    POLITIC. I had read Contarene, took me a
             [house, 50
Dealt with my Jews to furnish it with
             [movables—°
Well, if I could but find one man, one man,
To mine own heart, whom I durst trust, I
            [would— 55
    PEREGRINE. What? what, sir?
    POLITIC.   Make him rich; make him a
            [fortune:
He should not think again. I would command it.
    PEREGRINE. As how?   60
    POLITIC.   With certain projects that I have,
Which I may not discover.
    PEREGRINE [aside].   If I had
But one to wager with, I would lay odds now,
He tells me instantly.   65
    POLITIC.   One is (and that
I care not greatly who knows) to serve the state
Of Venice with red herrings for three years,
And at a certain rate, from Rotterdam,
Where I have correspondence. There's a letter,   70
Sent me from one o' th' states,° and to that
            [purpose;
He cannot write his name, but that's his mark.
    PEREGRINE. He is a chandler?°
    POLITIC.   No, a cheesemonger.   75
There are some other too with whom I treat
About the same negotiation;
And I will undertake it; for 'tis thus:
I'll do 't with ease; I have cast it all. Your hoy°
Carries but three men in her, and a boy;   80
And she shall make me three returns° a year:
So if there come but one of three, I save;°
If two, I can defalk.° But this is now,

---

old trite
garb demeanor
be . . . in play it safe with
Bodin a writer on statecraft, like **Contarene** (l. 49)
metal . . . glass fine distinctions in glassware

movables household goods
states Dutchmen of high rank
chandler candlemaker (the paper being so greasy)
hoy small coastal vessel
returns round trips
I save I'm safe
defalk make a profit

If my main project fail.

PEREGRINE.   Then you have others?

POLITIC. I should be loath to draw the subtle
                                                          [air
5   Of such a place without my thousand aims.
I'll not dissemble, sir: where'er I come,
I love to be considerative; and 'tis true,
I have at my free hours thought upon
Some certain goods unto the state of Venice,
10 Which I do call my cautions; and, sir, which
I mean, in hope of pension, to propound
To the Great Council, then unto the Forty,
So to the Ten.° My means are made already—

PEREGRINE. By whom?

15 POLITIC.   Sir, one that though his place
                                                          [b'obscure
Yet he can sway, and they will hear him. He's
A *commandadore*.°

PEREGRINE.   What, a common serjeant?

20 POLITIC. Sir, such as they are, put it in their
                                                          [mouths,
What they should say, sometimes; as well as
                                                          [greater.
I think I have my notes to show you—
25   [(*searching his pockets*)

PEREGRINE.   Good, sir.

POLITIC. But you shall swear unto me, on
                                                   [your gentry,°
Not to anticipate—

30 PEREGRINE.   I, sir?

POLITIC.   Nor reveal
A circumstance—my paper is not with me.

PEREGRINE. O, but you can remember, sir.

POLITIC.   My first is
35 Concerning tinder boxes. You must know,
No family is here without its box.
Now, sir, it being so portable a thing,
Put case that you or I were ill affected
Unto the state, sir; with it in our pockets,
40 Might not I go into the Arsenal,
Or you come out again, and none the wiser?

PEREGRINE. Except yourself, sir.

POLITIC.   Go to, then. I therefore

Advertise to the state, how fit it were
That none but such as were known patriots,   45
Sound lovers of their country, should be
                                                          [suffer'd
T' enjoy them in their houses; and even those
Seal'd° at some office, and at such a bigness
As might not lurk in pockets.   50

PEREGRINE.   Admirable!

POLITIC. My next is, how t' inquire, and be
                                                          [resolv'd
By present demonstration, whether a ship,
Newly arriv'd from Syria, or from   55
Any suspected part of all the Levant,
Be guilty of the plague; and where they use
To lie out forty, fifty days, sometimes,
About the Lazaretto,° for their trial,
I'll save that charge and loss unto the merchant, 60
And in an hour clear the doubt.

PEREGRINE.   Indeed, sir?

POLITIC. Or—I will lose my labor.

PEREGRINE.   'My faith, that's much.

POLITIC. Nay, sir, conceive me. 'Twill cost me   65
                                                       [in onions,
Some thirty livres—

PEREGRINE.   ₊Which is one pound sterling.

POLITIC. Beside my waterworks. For this I do,
                                                       [sir: 70
First, I bring in your ship 'twixt two brick
                                                       [walls—
But those the state shall venture.° On the one
I strain me a fair tarpaulin, and in that
I stick my onions, cut in halves; the other   75
Is full of loopholes, out at which I thrust
The noses of my bellows; and those bellows
I keep, with waterworks, in perpetual motion
(Which is the easi'st matter of a hundred).
Now, sir, your onion, which doth naturally   80
Attract th' infection, and your bellows blowing
The air upon him, will show, instantly,
By his chang'd color, if there be contagion;
Or else remain as fair as at the first.
Now 'tis known, 'tis nothing.   85

PEREGRINE.   You are right, sir.

POLITIC. I would I had my note.

Great . . . Ten governing bodies of the Venetian Republic

commandadore sergeant-at-arms, a minor officer of the law courts

gentry honor as a gentleman

Seal'd registered

About . . . Lazaretto in quarantine

venture invest in

PEREGRINE.   'Faith, so would I;
But you ha' done well for once, sir.
    POLITIC.   Were I false,
Or would be made so, I could show you reasons
5   How I could sell this state now to the Turk,
Spite of their° galleys, or their—(*examining his*
                                    [*papers*)
    PEREGRINE.   Pray you, Sir Pol.
    POLITIC. I have 'em not about me.
10 PEREGRINE.   That I fear'd.
They are there, sir?
    POLITIC.   No, this is my diary,
Wherein I note my actions of the day.
    PEREGRINE. 'Pray you let's see, sir.—What is
15   [here? "*Notandum*,°
A rat had gnawn my spur-leathers;
                            [notwithstanding,
I put on new, and did go forth; but first
I threw three beans over the threshold. *Item*,
20 I went and bought two toothpicks, whereof one
I burst immediately, in a discourse
With a Dutch merchant, 'bout *ragion' del*
                                    [*stato*.°
From him I went and paid a *moccinigo*
25 For piecing my silk stockings; by the way
I cheapen'd° sprats; and at St. Mark's I
                            [urin'd."—
'Faith these are politic notes!
    POLITIC.   Sir, I do slip
30 No action of my life, thus but I quote it.
    PEREGRINE. Believe me, it is wise!
    POLITIC.   Nay, sir, read forth.

Scene ii

[*Enter, at a distance,* LADY POLITIC WOULD-
BE, NANO, *and the two* WAITING WOMEN.]
35 LADY. Where should this loose knight be,
                        [trow? Sure h' is hous'd.
NANO. Why, then he's fast.
LADY.   Ay, he plays both with me.
I pray you stay. This heat will do more harm
40 To my complexion than his heart is worth.
(I do not care to hinder, but to take him.)

How it comes off!
    [*Rubs her cheeks.*]
WOMAN.   My master's yonder.
LADY.   Where?   45
WOMAN. With a young gentleman.
LADY.   That same's the party!
In man's apparel.—'Pray you, sir, jog° my
                                [knight.
I will be tender to his reputation,   50
However he demerit.
    POLITIC.   My lady!
    PEREGRINE.   Where?
    POLITIC. 'Tis she indeed, sir; you shall know
                        [her. She is,   55
Were she not mine, a lady of that merit,
For fashion and behavior, and for beauty,
I durst compare—
    PEREGRINE.   It seems you are not jealous,
That dare commend her.   60
    POLITIC.   Nay, and for
                                [discourse—
    PEREGRINE. Being your wife, she cannot miss
                                [that.
    POLITIC.   Madam,   65
Here is a gentleman, 'pray you use him fairly;
He seems a youth, but he is—
    LADY.   None?
    POLITIC.   Yes, one
Has put his face as soon into the world—   70
    LADY. You mean, as early? But° today?
    POLITIC.   How's this!
    LADY. Why, in this habit,° sir; you apprehend
                                [me.
Well, Master Would-be, this doth not become   75
                                [you;
I had thought the odor, sir, of your good name
Had been more precious to you; that you would
                                [not
Have done this dire massacre on your honor;   80
One of your gravity, and rank besides!
But knights, I see, care little for the oath
They make to ladies—chiefly their own ladies.
    POLITIC. Now, by my spurs, the symbol of my
                            [knighthood—   85

---

their the Venetians'
Notandum for the record
ragion' del stato matters of state
cheapen'd priced

jog nudge
But only
this habit male attire

PEREGRINE [*aside*]. Lord, how his brain is
            [humbled° for an oath.
POLITIC. I reach you not.
LADY.   Right, sir: your polity
5 May bear it through thus.—[*To* PEREGRINE.]
              [Sir, a word with you.
I would be loath to contest publicly
With any gentlewoman, or to seem
Froward, or violent, as the courtier says;
10 It comes too near rusticity in a lady,
Which I would shun by all means; and however
I may deserve from Master Would-be, yet
'T have one fair gentlewoman thus be made
Th' unkind instrument to wrong another,
15 And one she knows not, ay, and to persever;
In my poor judgment, is not warranted
From being a solecism° in our sex,
If not in manners.
    PEREGRINE.   How is this!
20 POLITIC.   Sweet madam,
Come nearer to your aim.
    LADY.   Marry, and will, sir.
Since you provoke me with your impudence,
And laughter of your light land-siren here,
25 Your Sporus,° your hermaphrodite—
    PEREGRINE.   What's here?
Poetic fury and historic storms!
    POLITIC. The gentleman, believe it, is of worth
And of our nation.
30   LADY.   Ay, your Whitefriars nation?°
Come, I blush for you, Master Would-be, I;
And am asham'd you should ha' no more
                [forehead°
Than thus to be the patron, or St. George,°
35 To a lewd harlot, a base fricatrice,°
A female devil, in a male outside.
    POLITIC.   Nay,
An you be such a one! I must bid adieu

To your delights. The case appears too liquid.°
    [*Exit.*]   40
    LADY. Ay, you may carry 't clear, with your
              [state-face!—
But for your carnival concupiscence,
Who here is fled for liberty of conscience,
From furious persecution of the marshal,   45
Her will I disc'ple.°
    PEREGRINE.   This is fine, i' faith!
And do you use° this often? Is this part
Of your wit's exercise, 'gainst you have
              [occasion? 50
Madam—
    LADY.   Go to, sir.
    PEREGRINE.   Do you hear me, lady?
Why, if your knight have set you to beg shirts,
Or to invite me home, you might have done it 55
A nearer way by far.
    LADY.   This cannot work you
Out of my snare.
    PEREGRINE.   Why, am I in it, then?
Indeed your husband told me you were fair, 60
And so you are; only your nose inclines,
That side that's next the sun, to the queen-
              [apple.°
    LADY. This cannot be endur'd by any
              [patience. 65

Scene iii

[*Enter* MOSCA.]
MOSCA. What's the matter, madam?
LADY.   If the Senate
Right not my quest in this, I will protest 'em
To all the world no aristocracy.   70
    MOSCA. What is the injury, lady?
    LADY.   Why, the callet°
You told me of, here I have ta'en disguis'd.
    MOSCA. Who? this? what means your
             [Ladyship? The creature 75
I mention'd to you is apprehended now,
Before the Senate; you shall see her—
    LADY.   Where?

---

humbled brought low, i.e., to his heels
solecism impropriety
Sporus Roman eunuch, a notorious victim of the
    emperor Nero's perversions
Whitefriars nation criminals (Whitefriars being a dis-
    trict in London where lawbreakers were safe from
    arrest)
forehead self-respect
St. George the patron saint of England
fricatrice prostitute

liquid transparent
disc'ple punish
use do
queen-apple red-cheeked apple
callet wench

MOSCA. I'll bring you to her. This young
                                    [gentleman,
I saw him land this morning at the port.
        LADY. Is 't possible? How has my judgment
5   [wander'd!
Sir, I must, blushing, say to you, I have err'd;
And plead your pardon.
        PEREGRINE.   What! more changes yet?
        LADY. I hope you've not the malice to
10   [remember
A gentlewoman's passion. If you stay
In Venice here, please you to use me, sir—
        MOSCA. Will you go, madam?
        LADY.   'Pray you, sir, use me; in faith,
15   The more you see me the more I shall conceive
You have forgot our quarrel.
        [Exeunt LADY WOULD-BE, MOSCA, NANO, and
WAITING WOMEN.]
        PEREGRINE.   This is rare!
20   Sir Politic Would-be? No, Sir Politic Bawd!
To bring me thus acquainted with his wife!
Well, wise Sir Pol, since you have practis'd thus
Upon my freshmanship, I'll try your salthead,°
What proof it is against a counterplot.
25   [Exit.]

Scene iv

[The Senate House.]

[Enter VOLTORE, CORBACCIO, CORVINO, and
MOSCA.]
        VOLTORE. Well, now you know the carriage°
30   [of the business,
Your constancy is all that is requir'd
Unto the safety of it.
        [He stands aside.]
        MOSCA.   Is the lie
35   Safely convey'd amongst us? Is that sure?
Knows every man his burden?°
        CORVINO.   Yes.
        MOSCA.   Then shrink not.
        CORVINO. But knows the advocate° the truth?
40   MOSCA.   Oh, sir,

By no means; I devis'd a formal tale,
That salv'd your reputation. But be valiant, sir.
        CORVINO. I fear no one but him, that this his
                                    [pleading
Should make him stand for a co-heir—   45
        MOSCA.   Co-halter!
Hang him; we will but use his tongue, his noise,
As we do croaker's° here.
        CORVINO.   Ay, what shall he do?
        MOSCA. When we ha' done, you mean?   50
        CORVINO.   Yes.
        MOSCA.   Why, we'll think;
Sell him for mummia:° he's half dust already.—
[To VOLTORE.] Do you not smile, to see this
                                    [buffalo,°   55
How he doth sport it with his head?—[Aside.]
                                    [I should,
If all were well and past.—[To CORBACCIO.] Sir,
                                    [only you
Are he that shall enjoy the crop of all,   60
And these not know for whom they toil.
        CORBACCIO.   Ay, peace.
        MOSCA [to CORVINO]. But you shall eat it.—
        [Aside.] Much!—[Then to VOLTORE again.]
                                    [Worshipful sir,   65
Mercury° sit upon your thund'ring tongue,
Or the French Hercules,° and make your
                                    [language
As conquering as his club, to beat along,
As with a tempest, flat, our adversaries;   70
But much more yours, sir.
        VOLTORE.   Here they come; ha' done.
        MOSCA. I have another witness, if you need,
                                    [sir,
I can produce.   75
        VOLTORE.   Who is it?
        MOSCA.   Sir, I have her.

Scene v

[Enter four AVOCATORI, BONARIO, CELIA,
NOTARIO, COMMANDADORI, SAFFI, and other
OFFICERS OF JUSTICE.]   80

---

salthead seniority or "seasoned" experience, also
   connoting lechery
carriage setup
burden part
the advocate Voltore

croaker's Corbaccio's
mummia a drug made from mummies
buffalo cuckold (Corvino)
Mercury god of eloquence, perjury, and commerce
French Hercules Ogmius, a legendary spellbinder

1ST AVOCATORE. The like of this the Senate
[never heard of.
2ND AVOCATORE. 'Twill come most strange to
[them when we report it.
5 4TH AVOCATORE. The gentlewoman has been
[ever held
Of unreproved name.
3RD AVOCATORE. So, the young man.
4TH AVOCATORE. The more unnatural part
10   [that of his father.
2ND AVOCATORE. More of the husband.
1ST AVOCATORE. I not know to give
His act a name, it is so monstrous!
4TH AVOCATORE. But the impostor, he is a
15   [thing created
T' exceed example!
1ST AVOCATORE. And all after-times!
2ND AVOCATORE. I never heard a true
[voluptuary
20 Describ'd but him.
3RD AVOCATORE. Appear yet those were
[cited?
NOTARIO. All but the old magnifico, Volpone.
1ST AVOCATORE. Why is not he here?
25 MOSCA. Please your Fatherhoods.
Here is his advocate. Himself's so weak,
So feeble—
4TH AVOCATORE. What are you?
BONARIO. His parasite,
30 His knave, his pander. I beseech the court
He may be forc'd to come, that your grave eyes
May bear strong witness of his strange
[impostures.
VOLTORE. Upon my faith and credit with your
35   [Virtues,
He is not able to endure the air.
2ND AVOCATORE. Bring him, however.
3RD AVOCATORE. We will see him.
4TH AVOCATORE. Fetch him.
40 VOLTORE. Your Fatherhoods' fit pleasures be
[obey'd;
[*Exeunt* OFFICERS.]
But sure, the sight will rather move your pities
Than indignation. May it please the court,
45 In the meantime, he may be heard in me.
I know this place most void of prejudice,
And therefore crave it, since we have no reason
To fear our truth should hurt our cause.

3RD AVOCATORE. Speak free.
VOLTORE. Then know, most honor'd fathers, 50
[I must now
Discover to your strangely abused ears,
The most prodigious and most frontless° piece
Of solid impudence and treachery
That ever vicious nature yet brought forth 55
To shame the state of Venice. This lewd
[woman,
That wants no artificial looks or tears
To help the visor she has now put on,
Hath long been known a close° adultress 60
To that lascivious youth there; not suspected,
I say, but known, and taken in the act
With him; and by this man, the easy husband,
Pardon'd; whose timeless° bounty makes him
[now 65
Stand here, the most unhappy, innocent person
That ever man's own goodness made accus'd.
For these, not knowing how to owe a gift
Of that dear grace, but with their shame, being
[plac'd 70
So above all powers of their gratitude,
Began to hate the benefit, and, in place
Of thanks, devise t' extirp° the memory
Of such an act. Wherein I pray your
[Fatherhoods 75
To observe the malice, yea, the rage of creatures
Discover'd in their evils; and what heart
Such take, ev'n from their crimes. But that anon
Will more appear. This gentleman, the father,
Hearing of this foul fact, with many others, 80
Which daily struck at his too tender ears,
And griev'd in nothing more than that he
[could not
Preserve himself a parent (his son's ills
Growing to that strange flood), at last decreed 85
To disinherit him.
1ST AVOCATORE. These be strange turns!
2ND AVOCATORE. The young man's fame was
[ever fair and honest.
VOLTORE. So much more full of danger is his 90
[vice,

frontless shameless
close secret
timeless untimely
extirp extirpate

That can beguile so, under shade of virtue.
But, as I said, my honor'd sires, his father
Having this settled purpose, by what means
To him betray'd, we know not, and this day
5   Appointed for the deed; that parricide
I cannot style him better, by confederacy
Preparing this his paramour to be there,
Ent'red Volpone's house (who was the man,
Your Fatherhoods must understand, design'd
10 For the inheritance), there sought his father:—
But with what purpose sought he him, my
                    [Lords?
I tremble to pronounce it, that a son
Unto a father, and to such a father,
15 Should have so foul, felonious intent—
It was to murder him; when, being prevented
By his more happy absence, what then did he?
Not check his wicked thoughts; no, now new
                    [deeds
20 (Mischief doth ever end where it begins)—
An act of horror, fathers! He dragg'd forth
The aged gentleman that had there lain bedrid
Three years and more, out off his innocent
                    [couch,
25 Naked upon the floor; there left him; wounded
His servant in the face, and with this strumpet,
The stale° to his forg'd practice, who was glad
To be so active,—I shall here desire
Your Fatherhoods to note but my collections,°
30 As most remarkable,—thought at once to stop
His father's ends, discredit his free choice
In the old gentleman,° redeem themselves,
By laying infamy upon this man,°
To whom, with blushing, they should owe their
35   [lives.
    1st Avocatore. What proofs have you of
                    [this?
    Bonario.   Most honor'd fathers,
I humbly crave there be no credit given
40 To this man's mercenary tongue.
      2nd Avocatore.   Forbear.
    Bonario. His soul moves in his fee.
      3rd Avocatore.   O, sir.

    Bonario.   This fellow,
For six sols more would plead against his   45
                    [Maker.
    1st Avocatore. You do forget yourself.
    Voltore.   Nay, nay, grave fathers,
Let him have scope! Can any man imagine
That he will spare his accuser, that would not   50
Have spar'd his parent?
    1st Avocatore.   Well, produce your
                    [proofs.
    Celia. I would I could forget I were a
                    [creature. 55
    Voltore. Signior Corbaccio.
    4th Avocatore.   What is he?
    Voltore.   The father.
    2nd Avocatore. Has he had an oath?
    Notario.   Yes.   60
    Corbaccio.   What must I do now?
    Notario. Your testimony's crav'd.
    Corbaccio.   Speak to the knave?
I'll ha' my mouth first stopp'd with earth; my
                    [heart 65
Abhors his knowledge: I disclaim in him.
    1st Avocatore. But for what cause?
    Corbaccio.   The mere portent of nature.°
He is an utter stranger to my loins.
    Bonario. Have they made° you to this!   70
    Corbaccio.   I will not hear thee,
Monster of men, swine, goat, wolf, parricide;
Speak not, thou viper.
    Bonario.   Sir, I will sit down,
And rather wish my innocence should suffer   75
Than I resist the authority of a father.
    Voltore. Signior Corvino.
    2nd Avocatore.   This is strange!
    1st Avocatore.   Who's this?
    Notario. The husband.   80
    4th Avocatore.   Is he sworn?
    Notario.   He is.
    3rd Avocatore.   Speak then.
    Corvino. This woman, please your
             [Fatherhoods, is a whore, 85
Of most hot exercise, more than a partridge,
Upon record—

---

stale decoy
collections conclusions, summary
gentleman Volpone
this man Corvino

The . . . nature the direct evidence of his unnatural behavior
made brought

1ST AVOCATORE.   No more.
CORVINO.   Neighs like a jennet.
NOTARIO. Preserve the honor of the court.
CORVINO.   I shall,
5 And modesty of your most reverend ears.
And yet I hope that I may say these eyes
Have seen her glu'd unto that piece of cedar,
That fine well-timber'd gallant; and that here°
The letters may be read, thorough the horn,°
10 That make the story perfect.
     MOSCA [*aside to* CORVINO].   Excellent, sir!
     CORVINO [*aside to* MOSCA]. There is no shame
                              [in this now, is there?
     MOSCA [*aside to* CORVINO].   None.
15   CORVINO. Or if I said, I hop'd that she were
                              [onward
To her damnation, if there be a hell
Greater than whore and woman, a good
                              [Catholic
20 May make the doubt.°
     3RD AVOCATORE.   His grief hath made him
                              [frantic.
     1ST AVOCATORE. Remove him hence.
     2ND AVOCATORE.   Look to the woman.
25   [*She swoons.*]
     CORVINO.   Rare!
Prettily feign'd! again!
     4TH AVOCATORE.   Stand from about her.
     1ST AVOCATORE. Give her the air.
30   3RD AVOCATORE [*to* MOSCA].   What can
                              [you say?
     MOSCA.   My wound,
May 't please your Wisdoms, speaks for me,
                              [receiv'd
35 In aid of my good patron, when he miss'd
His sought-for father, when that well-taught
                              [dame
Had her cue giv'n her to cry out, "A rape!"
     BONARIO. O most laid° impudence! Fathers—
40   3RD AVOCATORE.   Sir, be silent;

---

here on my forehead
horn of a cuckold; also the sheet of transparent horn
   used to protect the page of a child's reader
Or . . . doubt or if I were to say I hoped that she
   were going to hell, an orthodox Catholic might still
   doubt whether there is a hell worse than being a
   whore and woman
laid contrived

You had your hearing free, so must they theirs.
     2ND AVOCATORE. I do begin to doubt th'
                              [imposture here.
     4TH AVOCATORE. This woman has too many
                              [moods. 45
     VOLTORE.   Grave fathers,
She is a creature of a most profess'd
And prostituted lewdness.
     CORVINO.   Most impetuous!
Unsatisfied, grave fathers!   50
     VOLTORE.   May her feignings
Not take your wisdoms. But this day she baited
A stranger, a grave knight, with her loose eyes
And more lascivious kisses. This man saw 'em
Together on the water, in a gondola.   55
     MOSCA. Here is the lady herself, that saw
                              ['em too,
Without; who then had in the open streets
Pursu'd them, but for saving her knight's
                              [honor. 60
     1ST AVOCATORE. Produce that lady.
     2ND AVOCATORE.   Let her come.
     [*Exit* MOSCA.]
     4TH AVOCATORE.   These things,
They strike with wonder!   65
     3RD AVOCATORE.   I am turn'd a stone!

Scene vi

[*Re-enter* MOSCA *with* LADY WOULD-BE.]
MOSCA. Be resolute, madam.
LADY.   Ay, this same is she.—
Out, thou chameleon harlot! now thine eyes   70
Vie tears with the hyena. Dar'st thou look
Upon my wronged face?—I cry your pardons.
I fear I have forgettingly transgress'd
Against the dignity of the court—
     2ND AVOCATORE.   No, madam.   75
LADY. And been exorbitant—
     2ND ADVOCATORE.   You have not, lady.
     4TH AVOCATORE. These proofs are strong.
     LADY.   Surely, I had no purpose
To scandalize your honors, or my sex's.   80
     3RD AVOCATURE. We do believe it.
     LADY.   Surely you may believe it.
     2ND AVOCATORE. Madam, we do.
     LADY.   Indeed you may; my breeding
Is not so coarse—   85
     4TH AVOCATORE.   We know it.

LADY.   To offend
With pertinacy—
3RD AVOCATORE.   Lady—
LADY.   Such a presence;
5 No, surely.
1ST AVOCATORE.   We will think it.
LADY.   You may think it.
1ST AVOCATORE. Let her o'ercome—What
                    [witnesses have you,
10 To make good your report?
BONARIO.   Our consciences.
CELIA. And Heaven, that never fails the
                    [innocent.
1ST AVOCATORE. These are no testimonies.
15 BONARIO.   Not in your courts,
Where multitude and clamor overcomes.
1ST AVOCATORE. Nay, then you do wax
                    [insolent.
[VOLPONE is brought in, as impotent.]
20 VOLTORE.   Here, here,
The testimony comes that will convince,
And put to utter dumbness their bold tongues.
See here, grave fathers, here's the ravisher,
The rider on men's wives, the great impostor,
25 The grand voluptuary! Do you not think
These limbs should affect venery? or these eyes
Covet a concubine? Pray you mark these hands.
Are they not fit to stroke a lady's breasts?
Perhaps he doth dissemble!
30 BONARIO.   So he does.
VOLTORE. Would you ha' him tortur'd?
BONARIO.   I would have him prov'd.
VOLTORE. Best try him then with goads, or
                    [burning irons;
35 Put him to the strappado; I have heard
The rack hath cur'd the gout; faith, give it him,
And help him of a malady; be courteous.
I'll undertake, before these honor'd fathers,
He shall have yet as many left diseases,
40 As she has known adulterers, or thou
                    [strumpets.
O, my most equal° hearers, if these deeds,
Acts of this bold and most exorbitant strain,
May pass with sufferance, what one citizen
45 But owes the forfeit of his life, yea, fame,
To him that dares traduce him? Which of you

equal equitable

Are safe, my honor'd fathers? I would ask,
With leave of your grave Fatherhoods, if their
                    [plot
Have any face or color like to truth?   50
Or if, unto the dullest nostril here,
It smell not rank, and most abhorred slander?
I crave your care of this good gentleman,
Whose life is much endanger'd by their fable;
And as for them, I will conclude with this: 55
That vicious persons, when they are hot, and
                    [flesh'd°
In impious acts, their constancy abounds:
Damn'd deeds are done with greatest
                    [confidence. 60
1ST AVOCATORE. Take 'em to custody, and
                    [sever them.
2ND AVOCATORE. 'Tis pity two such prodigies
                    [should live.
1ST AVOCATORE. Let the old gentleman be   65
                    [return'd with care.
[Exeunt OFFICERS with VOLPONE.]
I am sorry our credulity wrong'd him.
4TH AVOCATORE. These are two creatures!
3RD AVOCATORE.   I have an earthquake in 70
                    [me!
2ND AVOCATORE. Their shame, even in their
                    [cradles, fled their faces.
4TH AVOCATORE. You have done a worthy
                    [service to the state, sir, 75
In their discovery.
1ST AVOCATORE.   You shall hear, ere
                    [night,
What punishment the court decrees upon 'em.
[Exeunt AVOCATORI, NOTARIO, and OFFICERS 80
with BONARIO and CELIA.]
VOLTORE. We thank your Fatherhoods.—
                    [How like you it?
MOSCA.   Rare.
I'd ha' your tongue, sir, tipp'd with gold for 85
                    [this;
I'd ha' you be the heir to the whole city;
The earth I'd have want men ere you want
                    [living:
They are bound to erect your statue in St.   90
                    [Mark's.—
Signior Corvino, I would have you go

flesh'd plunged

And show yourself that you have conquer'd.

CORVINO.   Yes.

MOSCA. It was much better that you should
[profess

5 Yourself a cuckold thus, than that the other
Should have been prov'd.

CORVINO.   Nay, I consider'd that;
Now it is her fault.

MOSCA.   Then, it had been yours.

10 CORVINO. True.—[*Aside to* MOSCA.] I do
[doubt this advocate still.

MOSCA [*aside*].   I' faith,
You need not; I dare ease you of that care.

CORVINO [*aside*]. I trust thee, Mosca.

15 MOSCA [*aside*].   As your own soul, sir.
[*Exit* CORVINO.]

CORBACCIO.   Mosca!

MOSCA. Now for your business, sir.

CORBACCIO.   How? ha' you business?

20 MOSCA. Yes, yours, sir.

CORBACCIO.   O, none else?

MOSCA.   None else, not I.

CORBACCIO. Be careful then.

MOSCA.   Rest you with both your eyes,°

25   [sir.

CORBACCIO. Dispatch it.

MOSCA.   Instantly.

CORBACCIO.   And look that all,
Whatever, be put in, jewels, plate, monies,

30 Household stuff, bedding, curtains.

MOSCA.   Curtain-rings, sir;
Only, the advocate's fee must be deducted.

CORBACCIO. I'll pay him now; you'll be too
[prodigal.

35 MOSCA. Sir, I must tender it.

CORBACCIO.   Two *cecchines* is well.

MOSCA. No, six, sir.

CORBACCIO.   'Tis too much.

MOSCA.   He talk'd a great while;

40 You must consider that, sir.

CORBACCIO.   Well, there's three—

MOSCA. I'll give it him.

CORBACCIO.   Do so, and there's for thee.
[*Exit.*]

45 MOSCA [*aside*]. Bountiful bones! What horrid
[strange offence

Did he commit 'gainst nature, in his youth,
Worthy this age?—[*Aside to* VOLTORE.] You
[see, sir, how I work
Unto your ends; take you no notice.   50

VOLTORE.   No,
I'll leave you.

MOSCA [*aside*]. All is yours, the devil and all,
Good advocate.—Madam, I'll bring you home.

LADY. No, I'll go see your patron.   55

MOSCA.   That you shall not;
I'll tell you why. My purpose is to urge
My patron to reform his will, and for
The zeal you have shown today, whereas before
You were but third or fourth, you shall be now   60
Put in the first; which would appear as begg'd
If you were present. Therefore—

LADY.   You shall sway me.
[*Exeunt.*]

ACT V

Scene i

[*A room in* VOLPONE'S *house.*]   65
[*Enter* VOLPONE.]

VOLPONE. Well, I am here, and all this brunt
[is past.
I ne'er was in dislike with my disguise
Till this fled moment: here 'twas good, in   70
[private;
But in the your public, *cave,*° whilst I breathe.
'Fore God, my left leg 'gan to have the cramp.
And I apprehended straight some power had
[struck me   75
With a dead palsy. Well, I must be merry,
And shake it off. A many of these fears
Would put me into some villainous disease,
Should they come thick upon me. I'll prevent
['em.   80
Give me a bowl of lusty wine, to fright
This humor from my heart.—[*He drinks.*] Hum,
[hum, hum!—
'Tis almost gone already; I shall conquer.
Any device now of rare ingenious knavery,   85
That would possess me with a violent laughter,
Would make me up again!—[*Drinks again.*] So,
[so, so, so!—

Rest . . . eyes   don't lose a wink of sleep

cave   beware

This heat is life; 'tis blood by this time.—
                                [Mosca!

Scene ii

[*Enter* MOSCA.]
MOSCA. How now, sir? Does the day look
5   [clear again?
Are we recover'd, and wrought out of error,
Into our way, to see our path before us?
Is our trade free once more?
      VOLPONE.   Exquisite Mosca!
10   MOSCA. Was it not carri'd learnedly?
      VOLPONE.   And stoutly:
Good wits are greatest in extremities.
      MOSCA. It were folly beyond thought to trust
Any grand act unto a cowardly spirit.
15   You are not taken with it enough, methinks.
      VOLPONE. Oh, more than if I had enjoy'd the
                                [wench;
The pleasure of all womankind's not like it.
      MOSCA. Why, now you speak, sir. We must
20   [here be fix'd;
Here we must rest;° this is our masterpiece;
We cannot think to go beyond this.
      VOLPONE.   True,
Thou hast play'd thy prize, my precious Mosca.
25   MOSCA.   Nay, sir,
To gull the court—
      VOLPONE.   And quite divert the torrent
Upon the innocent.
      MOSCA.   Yes, and to make
30   So rare a music out of discords—
      VOLPONE.   Right.
That yet to me's the strangest! how th' hast
                                [borne it!
That these, being so divided 'mongst
35   [themselves,
Should not scent somewhat, or in me or thee,
Or doubt their own side.
      MOSCA.   True, they will not see' t.
Too much light blinds 'em, I think. Each of 'em
40   Is so possess'd and stuff'd with his own hopes
That anything unto the contrary,
Never so true, or never so apparent,
Never so palpable, they will resist it—
      VOLPONE. Like a temptation of the Devil.

rest stop

MOSCA.   Right, sir.   45
Merchants may talk of trade, and your great
                                [signiors
Of land that yields well; but if Italy
Have any glebe more fruitful than these
                                [fellows, 50
I am deceiv'd. Did not your advocate rare?°
      VOLPONE. Oh—"My most honor'd fathers,
                                [my grave fathers,
Under correction of your Fatherhoods,
What face of truth is here? If these strange   55
                                [deeds
May pass, most honor'd fathers"—I had much
                                [ado
To forbear laughing.
      MOSCA.   'T seem'd to me you sweat, sir. 60
      VOLPONE. In troth, I did a little.
      MOSCA.   But confess, sir,
Were you not daunted?
      VOLPONE.   In good faith, I was
A little in a mist, but not dejected;   65
Never, but still myself.
      MOSCA.   I think it, sir.
Now, so truth help me, I must needs say this,
                                [sir,
And out of conscience for your advocate,   70
He has taken pains, in faith, sir, and deserv'd
In my poor judgment, I speak it under favor,
Not to contrary you, sir, very richly—
Well—to be cozen'd.°
      VOLPONE.   Troth, and I think so too, 75
By that I heard him in the latter end.
      MOSCA. O, but before, sir: had you heard him
                                [first
Draw it to certain heads, then aggravate,
Then use his vehement figures°—I look'd still 80
When he would shift° a shirt; and doing this
Out of pure love, no hope of gain—
      VOLPONE.   'Tis right.
I cannot answer him, Mosca, as I would,
Not yet; but for thy sake, at thy entreaty,   85
I will begin, ev'n now—to vex 'em all,
This very instant.

rare excellently
cozen'd cheated
figures of speech and gesture
shift change (because of his violent exertions)

MOSCA.   Good, sir.
VOLPONE.   Call the dwarf
And eunuch forth.
MOSCA.   Castrone, Nano!
5 [*Enter* CASTRONE *and* NANO.]
NANO.   Here.
VOLPONE. Shall we have a jig now?
MOSCA.   What you please, sir.
VOLPONE.   Go,
10 Straight give out about the streets, you two,
That I am dead; do it with constancy,
Sadly, do you hear? Impute it to the grief
Of this late slander.
   [*Exeunt* CASTRONE *and* NANO.]
15 MOSCA.   What do you mean, sir?
VOLPONE.   Oh,
I shall have instantly my Vulture, Crow,
Raven, come flying hither, on the news,
To peck for carrion, my she-wolf, and all,
20 Greedy, and full of expectation—
MOSCA. And then to have it ravish'd from their
                              [mouths?
VOLPONE. 'Tis true. I will ha' thee put on a
                              [gown,°
25 And take upon thee, as thou wert mine heir;
Show 'em a will. Open that chest, and reach
Forth one of those that has the blanks. I'll
                              [straight
Put in thy name.
30 MOSCA.   It will be rare, sir.
VOLPONE.   Ay,
When they e'en gape, and find themselves
                              [deluded—
MOSCA. Yes.
35 VOLPONE.   And thou use them scurvily.
                              [Dispatch;
Get on thy gown.
MOSCA.   But what, sir, if they ask
After the body?
40 VOLPONE.   Say it was corrupted.
MOSCA. I'll say it stunk, sir; and was fain
                              [t' have it
Coffin'd up instantly, and sent away.
VOLPONE. Anything; what thou wilt.—Hold,
45   [here's my will.
Get thee a cap, a count-book, pen and ink,

gown a gentleman's attire

Papers afore thee; sit as thou wert taking
An inventory of parcels. I'll get up
Behind the curtain, on a stool, and harken;
Sometime peep over, see how they do look,   50
With what degrees their blood doth leave their
                              [faces!
O, 'twill afford me a rare meal of laughter.
   MOSCA. Your advocate will turn stark dull
                              [upon it. 55
VOLPONE. It will take off his oratory's edge.
   MOSCA. But your clarissimo,° old roundback,
                              [he
Will crump you° like a hog-louse, with the
                              [touch. 60
VOLPONE. And what Corvino?
   MOSCA.   O, sir, look for him,
Tomorrow morning, with a rope and a dagger,
To visit all the streets; he must run mad.
My Lady too, that came into the court,   65
To bear false witness for your Worship—
   VOLPONE.   Yes.
And kiss'd me 'fore the fathers, when my face
Flow'd all with oils—
   MOSCA.   And sweat, sir. Why, your gold 70
Is such another med'cine, it dries up
All those offensive savors. It transforms
The most deformed, and restores 'em lovely,
As 'twere the strange poetical girdle.° Jove
Could not invent t' himself a shroud more   75
                              [subtle
To pass Acrisius'° guards. It is the thing
Makes all the world her grace, her youth, her
                              [beauty.
   VOLPONE. I think she loves me.   80
   MOSCA.   Who? the lady, sir?
She's jealous of you.
   VOLPONE.   Dost thou say so?
[*Knocking within.*]
   MOSCA.   Hark. 85
There's some already.
   VOLPONE.   Look.
   MOSCA.   It is the Vulture;

clarissimo grandee (Corbaccio)
crump you crumple you up
girdle of Venus
Acrisius whose daughter, Danae, was seduced by
   Jove disguised in a shower of gold

He has the quickest scent.
VOLPONE.   I'll to my place,
Thou to thy posture.
          [*Goes behind the curtain.*]
5   MOSCA.   I am set.
     VOLPONE.   But, Mosca,
Play the artificer now; torture 'em rarely.

Scene iii

          [*Enter* VOLTORE.]
     VOLTORE. How now, my Mosca?
10   MOSCA [*writing*].   Turkey carpets, nine—
     VOLTORE. Taking an inventory! that is well.
     MOSCA. Two suits of bedding, tissue—
     VOLTORE.   Where's the will?
Let me read that the while.
15   [*Enter* SERVANTS *with* CORBACCIO *in a chair.*]
     CORBACCIO.   So, set me down,
And get you home.
          [*Exeunt* SERVANTS.]
     VOLTORE.   Is he come now, to trouble us?
20   MOSCA. Of cloth of gold, two more—
     CORBACCIO.   Is it done, Mosca?
     MOSCA. Of several velvets, eight—
     VOLTORE.   I like his care.
     CORBACCIO. Dost thou not hear?
25   [*Enter* CORVINO.]
     CORVINO.   Ha! is the hour come, Mosca?
     VOLPONE [*aside*]. Ay, now they muster.
          [*Peeps from behind a traverse.*°]
     CORVINO.   What does the advocate here?
30 Or this Corbaccio?
     CORBACCIO.   What do these here?
          [*Enter* LADY WOULD-BE.]
     LADY.   Mosca!
Is his thread° spun?
35   MOSCA.   Eight chests of linen—
     VOLPONE [*aside*].   Oh,
My fine Dame Would-be, too!
     CORVINO.   Mosca, the will,
That I may show it these, and rid 'em hence.
40   MOSCA. Six chests of diaper, four of damask
                                        [—there.
          [*Gives the will.*]
     CORBACCIO. Is that the will?

traverse curtain
thread of life

MOSCA [*writing*].   Down-beds, and
                              [bolsters— 45
     VOLPONE [*aside*].   Rare!
Be busy still. Now they begin to flutter;
They never think of me. Look, see, see, see!
How their swift eyes run over the long deed,
Unto the name, and to the legacies,   50
What is bequeath'd them there—
     MOSCA.   Ten suits of hangings—
     VOLPONE [*aside*]. Ay, in their garters, Mosca.
                              [Now their hopes
Are at the gasp.   55
     VOLTORE.   Mosca the heir!
     CORBACCIO.   What's that?
     VOLPONE [*aside*]. My advocate is dumb; look
                              [to my merchant—°
He has heard of some strange storm; a ship is 60
                              [lost—
He faints. My Lady will swoon. Old glazen-
                              [eyes,
He hath not reach'd his despair yet.
     CORBACCIO.   All these 65
Are out of hope; I am, sure, the man.
          [*Takes the will.*]
     CORVINO.   But, Mosca—
     MOSCA. Two cabinets—
     CORVINO.   Is this in earnest? 70
     MOSCA.   One
Of ebony—
     CORVINO.   Or do you but delude me?
     MOSCA. The other, mother-of-pearl—I am
                              [very busy. 75
Good faith, it is a fortune thrown upon me—
Item, one salt° of agate—not my seeking.
     LADY. Do you hear, sir?
     MOSCA.   A perfum'd box—'pray you
                              [forbear; 80
You see I am troubled—made of an onyx—
     LADY.   How!
     MOSCA. Tomorrow or next day, I shall be at
                              [leisure
To talk with you all.   85
     CORVINO.   Is this my large hope's issue?
     LADY. Sir, I must have a fairer answer.
     MOSCA.   Madam!

merchant Corvino
salt salt-dish

Marry, and shall: 'pray you, fairly quit my
[house.
Nay, raise no tempest with your looks; but hark
[you,
5 Remember what your Ladyship off'red me
To put you in, an heir; go to; think on it.
And what you said e'en your best madams did
For maintentance, and why not you? Enough.
Go home, and use the poor Sir Pol, your knight,
10 [well,
For fear I tell some riddles; go, be melancholic.
    [*Exit* LADY WOULD-BE.]
    VOLPONE [*aside*]. Oh, my fine devil!
    CORVINO.   Mosca, pray you a word.
15 MOSCA. Lord! will not you take your dispatch
[hence yet?
Methinks, of all, you should have been th'
[example.
Why should you stay here? with what thought,
20 [what promise?
    Hear you; do not you know, I know you an ass,
And that you would most fain have been a
[wittol
If fortune would have let you? that you are
25 A declar'd cuckold, on good terms? This pearl,
You'll say, was yours? right; this diamond?
I'll not deny 't, but thank you. Much here else?
It may be so. Why, think that these good works
May help to hide your bad. I'll not betray you;
30 Although you be but extraordinary,°
And have it only in title, it sufficeth:
Go home; be melancholic too, or mad.
    [*Exit* CORVINO.]
    VOLPONE [*aside*]. Rare Mosca! how his
35 [villainy becomes him!
    VOLTORE [*aside*]. Certain he doth delude all
[these for me.
    CORBACCIO. Mosca the heir?
    VOLPONE [*aside*].   O, his four eyes have
40 [found it!
    CORBACCIO. I am cozen'd, cheated, by a
[parasite-slave;
Harlot, th' hast gull'd me.
    MOSCA.   Yes, sir. Stop your mouth,
45 Or I shall draw the only tooth is left.
Are not you he, that filthy covetous wretch,

but extraordinary a cuckold only in a special sense

With the three legs, that here, in hope of prey,
Have, any time this three year, snuff'd about,
With your most grov'ling nose, and would
[have hir'd 50
Me to the pois'ning of my patron, sir?
Are not you he that have today in court
Profess'd the disinheriting of your son?
Perjur'd yourself? Go home, and die, and stink;
If you but croak a syllable, all comes out: 55
Away, and call your porters! [*Exit* CORBACCIO.]
[Go, go, stink.
    VOLPONE [*aside*]. Excellent varlet!°
    VOLTORE.   Now, my faithful Mosca,
I find thy constancy— 60
    MOSCA.   Sir!
    VOLTORE.   Sincere.
    MOSCA [*writing*].   A table
Of porphyry—I mar'l you'll be thus
[troublesome. 65
    VOLTORE. Nay, leave off now, they are gone.
    MOSCA.   Why, who are you?
What! who did send for you? Oh, cry you
[mercy,
Reverend sir! Good faith, I am griev'd for you, 70
That any chance of mine should thus defeat
Your (I must needs say) most deserving
[travails;
But I protest, sir, it was cast upon me,
And I could almost wish to be without it, 75
But that the will o' the' dead must be observ'd.
Marry, my joy is that you need it not;
You have a gift, sir, (thank your education)
Will never let you want, while there are men,
And malice, to breed causes.° Would I had 80
But half the like, for all my fortune, sir.
If I have any suits, as I do hope,
Things being so easy and direct, I shall not,
I will make bold with your obstreperous° aid
(Conceive me) for your fee, sir. In meantime, 85
You that have so much law, I know ha' the
[conscience
Not to be covetous of what is mine.
Good sir, I thank you for my plate; 'twill help
To set up a young man. Good faith, you look 90

varlet servant
causes law cases
obstreperous clamorous

As you were costive; best go home and purge,
[sir.
[*Exit* VOLTORE.]
VOLPONE [*coming from behind the curtain*].
5   Bid him eat lettuce well. My witty mischief,
Let me embrace thee. O that I could now
Transform thee to a Venus!—Mosca, go,
Straight take my habit of clarissimo.°
And walk the streets; be seen, torment 'em
10   [more;
We must pursue, as well as plot. Who would
Have lost this feast?
    MOSCA.   I doubt° it will lose them.
    VOLPONE. O, my recovery shall recover all.
15 That I could now but think on some disguise
To meet 'em in, and ask 'em questions.
How I would vex 'em still at every turn!
    MOSCA. Sir, I can fit you.
    VOLPONE.   Canst thou?
20 MOSCA.   Yes, I know
One o' the commandadori, sir; so like you,
Him will I straight make drunk, and bring you
                                          [his habit.
    VOLPONE. A rare disguise, and answering thy
25   [brain!
O, I will be a sharp disease unto 'em.
    MOSCA. Sir, you must look for curses—
    VOLPONE.   Till they burst;
The Fox fares ever best when he is curs'd.
30 [*Exeunt.*]

Scene iv

[*A hall in* SIR POLITIC'S *house.*]
[*Enter* PEREGRINE *disguised and three* MER-
CATORI.]
    PEREGRINE. Am I enough disguis'd?
35 1ST MERCATORE.   I warrant you.
    PEREGRINE. All my ambition is to fright him
                                          [only.
    2ND MERCATORE. If you could ship him away,
                                          ['twere excellent.
40 3RD MERCATORE. To Zant, or to Aleppo!
    PEREGRINE.   Yes, and ha' his
Adventures put i' th' Book of Voyages,°

And his gull'd story regist'red for truth!
Well, gentlemen, when I am in awhile,
And that you think us warm in our discourse,   45
Know your approaches.
    1ST MERCATORE.   Trust it to our care.
[*Exeunt* MERCATORI.]
[*Enter* WAITING WOMAN.]
    PEREGRINE. Save you, fair lady! Is Sir Pol   50
                                          [within?
    WOMAN. I do not know, sir.
    PEREGRINE.   'Pray you say unto him
Here is a merchant, upon earnest business,
Desires to speak with him.   55
    WOMAN.   I will see, sir.
[*Exit.*]
    PEREGRINE.   'Pray you.
I see the family is all female here.
[*Re-enter* WAITING WOMAN.]   60
    WOMAN. He says, sir, he has weighty affairs
                                          [of state,
That now require him whole; some other time
You may possess him.
    PEREGRINE.   'Pray you say again,   65
If those require him whole, these will exact°
                                          [him,
Whereof I bring him tidings. [*Exit* WOMAN.]
                                          [What might be
His grave affair of state now! How to make   70
Bolognian sausages here in Venice, sparing
One o' th' ingredients?
    [*Re-enter* WAITING WOMAN.]
    WOMAN.   Sir, he says he knows
By your word "tidings,"° that you are no   75
                                          [statesman,
And therefore wills you stay.
    PEREGRINE.   Sweet, 'pray you return him
I have not read so many proclamations,
And studied them for words, as he has done—   80
    But—here he deigns to come.
    [*Exit* WOMAN.]
    [*Enter* SIR POLITIC.]
    POLITIC.   Sir, I must crave
Your courteous pardon. There hath chanc'd   85
                                          [today

---

habit of clarissimo   robes of state
doubt   fear
Book of Voyages   travel narratives, of which Richard
    Hakluyt's *Principal Navigations, Voyages and Dis-
    coveries* was the type

exact   draw out; as opposed to *require*, which literally
    means *call back*. Peregrine is matching Sir Politic's
    Latinisms.
"tidings"   (a plain English word)

Unkind disaster 'twixt my lady and me;
And I was penning my apology,
To give her satisfaction, as you came now.
    PEREGRINE. Sir, I am griev'd I bring you worse
                          [disaster.
  5
The gentleman you met at th' port today,
That told you he was newly arriv'd—
    POLITIC.   Ay, was
A fugitive punk?°
  10   PEREGRINE.   No, sir, a spy set on you;
And he has made relation to the Senate,
That you profess'd to him to have a plot
To sell the state of Venice to the Turk.
    POLITIC. O me!
  15   PEREGRINE.   For which warrants are sign'd
                         [by this time,
To apprehend you, and to search your study
For papers—
    POLITIC.   Alas, sir, I have none, but notes
  20 Drawn out of play-books—
    PEREGRINE.   .All the better, sir.
    POLITIC. And some essays. What shall I do?
    PEREGRINE.   Sir, best
Convey yourself into a sugar-chest;
  25 Or, if you could lie round, a frail were rare;°
And I could send you abroad.
    POLITIC.   Sir, I but talk'd so.
For discourse sake merely.
    [*They knock without.*]
  30   PEREGRINE.   Hark! they are there.
    POLITIC. I am a wretch, a wretch!
    PEREGRINE.   What will you do, sir?
Have you ne'er a currant-butt° to leap into?
They'll put you to the rack; you must be
  35   [sudden.
    POLITIC. Sir, I have an ingine—°
    3RD MERCATORE [*within*].   Sir Politic
                         [Would-be!
    2ND MERCATORE [*within*]. Where is he?
  40   POLITIC.   That I've thought upon, before
                        [time.
    PEREGRINE. What is it?
    POLITIC.   I shall ne'er endure the
                        [torture.—

punk prostitute
frail . . . rare basket would be fine
currant-butt wine cask
ingine invention

Marry, it is, sir, of a tortoise shell,   45
Fitted for these extremities; 'pray you, sir, help
                          [me.
Here I have a place, sir, to put back my legs,
Please you to lay it on, sir [*lies down while*
PEREGRINE *places the shell upon him*], with this 50
                          [cap,
And my black gloves. I'll lie, sir, like a tortoise,
Till they are gone.
    PEREGRINE.   And call you this an ingine?
    POLITIC. Mine own device.—Good sir, bid my 55
                        [wife's women
To burn my papers.
    [*Exit* PEREGRINE.]
    [*The three* MERCATORI *rush in.*]
    1ST MERCATORE. Where's he hid?   60
    3RD MERCATORE.   We must,
And will, sure, find him.
    2ND MERCATORE.   Which is his study?
    [*Re-enter* PEREGRINE.]
    1ST MERCATORE.   What   65
Are you, sir?
    PEREGRINE.   I am a merchant, that came
                         [here
To look upon this tortoise.
    3RD MERCATORE.   How?   70
    1ST MERCATORE.   St. Mark!
What beast is this?
    PEREGRINE.   It is a fish.
    2ND MERCATORE.   Come out here!
    PEREGRINE. Nay, you may strike him, sir, and 75
                      [tread upon him;
He'll bear a cart.
    1ST MERCATORE.   What, to run over him?
    PEREGRINE.   Yes, sir.
    3RD MERCATORE. Let's jump upon him.   80
    2ND MERCATORE.   Can he not go?
    PEREGRINE.   He creeps, sir.
    1ST MERCATORE. Let's see him creep.
    PEREGRINE.   No, good sir, you will hurt
                       [him. 85
    2ND MERCATORE. Heart, I'll see him creep, or
                    [prick his guts.
    3RD MERCATORE. Come out here.
    PEREGRINE.   'Pray you, sir!—(*Aside to* SIR
                [POLITIC.) Creep a little. 90
    1ST MERCATORE.   Forth.
    2ND MERCATORE. Yet further.
    PEREGRINE.   Good sir!—[*Aside.*] Creep!

2ND MERCATORE.   We'll see his legs.
[*They pull off the shell and discover him.*]
3RD MERCATORE. Gods so, he has garters!
1ST MERCATORE.   Ay, and gloves!
5   2ND MERCATORE.   Is this
Your fearful tortoise?
       PEREGRINE [*discovering himself*]. Now, Sir
                              [Pol, we are even;
For your next project I shall be prepar'd;
10   I am sorry for the funeral of your notes, sir.
       1ST MERCATORE. 'Twere a rare motion° to be
                              [seen in Fleet Street.
       2ND MERCATORE. Ay, i' the term.°
       1ST MERCATORE.   Or Smithfield,° in the
15   [fair.
       3RD MERCATORE. Methinks 'tis but a
                              [melancholic sight!
       PEREGRINE. Farewell, most politic tortoise.
       [*Exeunt* PEREGRINE *and* MERCATORI.]
20   [*Re-enter* WAITING WOMAN.]
       POLITIC.   Where's my Lady?
Knows she of this?
       WOMAN.   I know not, sir.
       POLITIC.   Inquire.—
25   Oh, I shall be the fable of all feasts,
The freight of the gazetti,° ship-boys' tale;
And, which is worst, even talk for ordinaries.
       WOMAN. My Lady's come most melancholic
                              [home,
30   And says, sir, she will straight to sea, for
                              [physic.
       POLITIC. And I, to shun this place and clime
                              [for ever,
Creeping with house on back, and think it well
35   To shrink my poor head in my politic shell.
       [*Exeunt.*]

Scene v

[*A room in* VOLPONE's *house.*]
[*Enter* VOLPONE *and* MOSCA, *the first in the
habit of a commandadore, the other of a claris-*
40   *simo.*]

VOLPONE. Am I then like him?
MOSCA.   O, sir, you are he;
No man can sever you.
VOLPONE.   Good.
MOSCA.   But what am I?   45
VOLPONE. 'Fore Heav'n, a brave clarissimo;
                              [thou becom'st it!
Pity thou wert not born one.
       MOSCA.   If I hold
My made one, 'twill be well.   50
       VOLPONE.   I'll go and see
What news first at the court.
[*Exit.*]
MOSCA.   Do so.—My Fox
Is out on his hole, and ere he shall re-enter,   55
I'll make him languish in his borrow'd case,°
Except he come to composition° with me.—
Androgyno, Castrone, Nano!
       [*Enter* ANDROGYNO, CASTRONE, *and* NANO.]
ALL.   Here.   60
MOSCA. Go, recreate yourselves abroad; go,
                              [sport.—
[*Exeunt all but* MOSCA.]
So, now I have the keys, and am possess'd.
Since he will needs be dead afore his time,   65
I'll bury him, or gain by him. I am his heir,
And so will keep me, till he share, at least.
To cozen him of all, were but a cheat
Well plac'd; no man would construe it a sin;
Let his sport pay for 't. This is call'd the Fox- 70
                              [trap.
       [*Exit.*]

Scene vi

[*A street.*]
[*Enter* CORBACCIO *and* CORVINO.]
CORBACCIO. They say the court is set.   75
CORVINO.   We must maintain
Our first tale good, for both our reputations.
       CORBACCIO. Why, mine's no tale, my son
                              [would there have kill'd me.
       CORVINO. That's true; I had forgot;—[*aside*] 80
                              [mine is, I am sure.—
But for your will, sir.
       CORBACCIO.   Ay, I'll come upon him

---

motion show
term when prisoners from the Fleet prison were led
   to trial
Smithfield London market, site of the great annual fair
The . . . gazetti grist for the gossip-sheets

case skin
composition terms

For that hereafter, now his patron's dead.
[*Enter* VOLPONE *disguised.*]
VOLPONE. Signior Corvino! and Corbaccio!
[sir,
5 Much joy unto you.
CORVINO.   Of what?
VOLPONE.   The sudden good
Dropp'd down upon you—
CORBACCIO.   Where?
10 VOLPONE.   And none knows how—
From old Volpone, sir.
CORBACCIO.   Out, errant knave!
VOLPONE. Let not your too much wealth, sir,
[make you furious.
15 CORBACCIO. Away, thou varlet.
VOLPONE.   Why, sir?
CORBACCIO.   Dost thou mock me?
VOLPONE. You mock the world, sir; did you
[not change wills?
20 CORBACCIO. Out, harlot.
VOLPONE.   O! belike you are the man,
Signior Corvino? Faith, you carry it well;
You grow not mad withal; I love your spirit.
You are not overleaven'd with your fortune.
25 You should ha' some would swell now like a
[wine-vat,
With such an autumn.—Did he gi' you all, sir?
CORVINO. Avoid, you rascal.
VOLPONE.   Troth, your wife has shown
30 Herself a very woman; but you are well,
You need not care, you have a good estate,
To bear it out, sir, better by this chance—
Except Corbaccio have a share.
CORBACCIO.   Hence, varlet.
35 VOLPONE. You will not be acknown, sir; why,
['tis wise.
Thus do all gamesters, at all games, dissemble:
No man will seem to win.
[*Exeunt* CORVINO *and* CORBACCIO.]
40   Here comes my vulture,
Heaving his beak up i' the air, and snuffing.

Scene vii

[*Enter* VOLTORE.]
VOLTORE. Outstripp'd thus, by a parasite! a
[slave!
45 Would run on errands, and make legs for
[crumbs!

Well, what I'll do—
VOLPONE.   The court stays for your
[Worship.
I e'en rejoice, sir, at your Worship's happiness, 50
And that it fell into so learned hands,
That understand the fingering—
VOLTORE.   What do you mean?
VOLPONE. I mean to be a suitor to your
[Worship, 55
For the small tenement, out of reparations,
That at the end of your long row of houses,
By the Piscaria;° it was, in Volpone's time,
Your predecessor, ere he grew diseas'd,
A handsome, pretty, custom'd° bawdyhouse 60
As any was in Venice, none disprais'd;
But fell with him: his body and that house
Decay'd together.
VOLTORE.   Come, sir, leave your prating.
VOLPONE. Why, if your Worship give me but 65
[your hand
That I may ha' the refusal,° I have done.
'Tis a mere toy to you, sir, candle-rents;°
As your learn'd Worship knows—
VOLTORE.   What do I know? 70
VOLPONE. Marry, no end of your wrath, sir;
[God decrease it!
VOLTORE. Mistaking knave! what, mock'st
[thou my misfortune?
[*Exit.*] 75
VOLPONE. His blessing on your heart, sir;
[would 'twere more!—
Now to my first again, at the next corner.
[*Exit.*]

Scene viii

[*Another corner of the street.*] 80
[*Enter* CORBACCIO *and* CORVINO, MOSCA *passant.*]
CORBACCIO. See, in our habit! see the
[impudent varlet!
CORVINO. That I could shoot mine eyes at 85
[him, like gun-stones.°

Piscaria fishmarket
custom'd well patronized
refusal option
candle-rents small change
gun-stones cannon balls

246

[*Enter* VOLPONE.]
VOLPONE. But is this true, sir, of the parasite?
CORBACCIO. Again, t' afflict us? monster!
VOLPONE.   In good faith, sir,
5 I am heartily griev'd, a beard of your grave
                                        [length
Should be so overreach'd. I never brook'd
That parasite's hair; methought his nose should
                                        [cozen:
10 There still was somewhat in his look, did
                                        [promise
The bane of a clarissimo.
     CORBACCIO.   Knave—
     VOLPONE.   Methinks
15 Yet you, that are so traded i' the world,
A witty merchant, the fine bird, Corvino,
That have such moral emblems on your name,
Should not have sung° your shame, and
                              [dropp'd your cheese,
20 To let the Fox laugh at your emptiness.
     CORVINO. Sirrah, you think the privilege of
                                        [the place,
And your red saucy cap, that seems to me
Nail'd to your jolt-head° with those two
25   [cecchines,°
Can warrant your abuses; come you hither;
You shall perceive, sir, I dare beat you;
                                        [approach.
     VOLPONE. No haste, sir, I do know your valor
30   [well,
Since you durst publish what you are, sir.
     CORVINO.   Tarry,
I'd speak with you.
     VOLPONE.   Sir, sir, another time—
35 CORVINO. Nay, now.
     VOLPONE.   O God, sir! I were a wise man,
Would stand the fury of a distracted cuckold.
     [MOSCA *walks by 'em.*]
     CORBACCIO. What, come again!
40 VOLPONE.   Upon 'em, Mosca; save me.
     CORBACCIO. The air's infected where he
                                        [breathes.
     CORVINO.   Let's fly him.
     [*Exeunt* CORVINO *and* CORBACCIO.]

VOLPONE. Excellent basilisk!° turn upon the   45
                                        [Vulture.

Scene ix

[*Enter* VOLTORE.]
VOLTORE. Well, flesh-fly, it is summer with
                                        [you now;
Your winter will come on.   50
     MOSCA.   Good advocate,
'Pray thee not rail, nor threaten out of place
                                        [thus;
Thou 'lt make a solecism, as Madam says.
Get you a biggin more;° your brain breaks   55
                                        [loose.
     [*Exit.*]
     VOLTORE. Well, sir.
     VOLPONE.   Would you ha' me beat the
                                   [insolvent slave? 60
Throw dirt upon his first good clothes?
     VOLTORE.   This same
Is doubtless some familiar!°
     VOLPONE.   Sir, the court,
In troth, stays for you. I am mad, a mule   65
That never read Justinian should get up
And ride an advocate. Had you no quirk
To avoid gullage, sir, by such a creature?
I hope you do but jest; he has not done 't;
This 's but confederacy to blind the rest.   70
You are the heir?
     VOLTORE.   A strange, officious,
Troublesome knave! Thou dost torment me.
     VOLPONE.   I know—
It cannot be, sir, that you should be cozen'd;   75
'Tis not within the wit of man to do it;
You are so wise, so prudent; and 'tis fit
That wealth and wisdom still should go
                                        [together.
     [*Exeunt.*]   80

Scene x

[*The Senate House.*]
[*Enter four* AVOCATORI, NOTARIO, BONARIO,
CELIA, CORBACCIO, CORVINO, COMMANDADORI,

---

sung like the crow whom the fox flattered in Aesop's
fable
jolt-head blockhead   **cecchines** gold buttons

basilisk mythical serpent whose breath or look could
kill
biggin more larger cap
familiar demon to tempt me

Saffi, *etc.*]

1st Avocatore. Are all the parties here?

Notario.   All but the advocate.

2nd Avocatore. And here he comes.

5   [*Enter* Voltore *and* Volpone.]

1st Avocatore.   Then bring 'em forth to
[sentence.

Voltore. O, my most honor'd fathers, let
[your mercy

10 Once win upon your justice, to forgive—
I am distracted—

Volpone [*aside*].   What will he do now?

Voltore.   Oh,
I know not which t' address myself to first;

15 Whether your Fatherhoods, or these
[innocents—

Corvino [*aside*]. Will he betray himself?

Voltore.   Whom equally
I have abus'd, out of most covetous ends—

20 Corvino. The man is mad!

Corbaccio.   What's that?

Corvino.   He is possess'd.°

Voltore. For which, now struck in
[conscience, here I prostrate

25 Myself at your offended feet, for pardon.

1st, 2nd Avocatori. Arise.

Celia.   O Heav'n, how just thou art!

Volpone.   I am caught
I' mine own noose—

30 Corvino [*to* Corbaccio]. Be constant, sir;
[naught now
Can help but impudence.°

1st Avocatore.   Speak forward.

Commandadore.   Silence!

35 Voltore. It is not passion in me, reverend
[fathers,
But only conscience, conscience, my good sires,
That makes me now tell truth. That parasite,
That knave, hath been the instrument of all.

40 1st Avocatore. Where is that knave? Fetch
[him.

Volpone.   I go.
[*Exit.*]

Corvino.   Grave fathers,

45 This man's distracted; he confess'd it now:

For, hoping to be old Volpone's heir,
Who now is dead—

3rd Avocatore.   How?

2nd Avocatore.   Is Volpone dead?

Corvino. Dead since, grave fathers.   50

Bonario.   O sure vengeance!

1st Avocatore.   Stay;
Then he was no deceiver?

Voltore.   Oh, no, none.
This parasite, grave fathers—   55

Corvino.   He does speak
Out of mere envy, 'cause the servant's made
The thing he gap'd for. Please your
[Fatherhoods,
This is the truth, though I'll not justify   60
The other, but he may be somedeal faulty.°

Voltore. Ay, to your hopes, as well as mine,
[Corvino;
But I'll use modesty.° Pleaseth your Wisdoms
To view these certain notes, and but confer°   65
[them;
As I hope favor, they shall speak clear truth.

Corvino. The Devil has ent'red him!

Bonario.   Or bides in you.

4th Avocatore. We have done ill, by a   70
[public officer
To send for him, if he be heir.

2nd Avocatore.   For whom?

4th Avocatore. Him that they call the
[parasite. 75

3rd Avocatore.   'Tis true,
He is a man of great estate, now left.

4th Avocatore. Go you, and learn his
[name, and say the court
Entreats his presence here, but to the clearing   80
Of some few doubts.
[*Exit* Notario.]

2nd Avocatore.   This same's a labyrinth!

1st Avocatore. Stand you unto your first
[report? 85

Corvino.   My state,
My life, my fame—

Bonario.   Where is 't?

---

justify . . . faulty guarantee that Mosca is not somewhat deceitful
modesty moderation
confer compare

possess'd i.e., by a demon
impudence sheer audacity

CORVINO.   Are at the stake.
1ST AVOCATORE. Is yours so too?
CORBACCIO.   The advocate's a knave,
And has a forked tongue—
5   2ND AVOCATORE.   Speak to the point.
CORBACCIO. So is the parasite too.
1ST AVOCATORE.   This is confusion.
VOLTORE. I do beseech your Fatherhoods,
                              [read but those—
10   [*Giving them papers.*]
CORVINO. And credit nothing the false spirit
                              [hath writ:
It cannot be but he's possess'd, grave fathers.
[*The scene closes.*]

Scene xi

15   [*A street.*]
[*Enter* VOLPONE.]
VOLPONE. To make a snare for mine own
                              [neck, and run
My head into it, wilfully! with laughter!
20   When I had newly 'scap'd, was free and clear!
Out of mere wantonness! Oh, the dull devil
Was in this brain of mine when I devis'd it,
And Mosca gave it second; he must now
Help to sear up this vein, or we bleed dead.
25   [*Enter* NANO, ANDROGYNO, *and* CASTRONE.]
How now! Who let you loose? Whither go you
                              [now?
What, to buy gingerbread, or to drown kitlings?
NANO. Sir, Master Mosca call'd us out of
30   [doors,
And bid us all go play, and took the keys.
ANDROGYNO. Yes.
VOLPONE. Did Master Mosca take the keys?
                              [Why so!
35   I'm farther in. These are my fine conceits!°
I must be merry, with a mischief to me!
What a vile wretch was I, that could not bear
My fortune soberly? I must° ha' my crotchets,°
And my conundrums!—Well, go you, and seek
40   [him;
His meaning may be truer than my fear.
Bid him he straight come to me to the court;

conceits   fancy devices
must   had to
crotchets   little eccentricities

Thither will I, and, if 't be possible,
Unscrew my advocate, upon new hopes.
When I provok'd him, then I lost myself.   45
[*Exeunt.*]

Scene xii

[*The Senate House.*]
[AVOCATORI, *etc., are discovered, as before.*]
1ST AVOCATORE. These things can ne'er be
                              [reconcil'd. He here   50
[*Shows the papers.*]
Professeth that the gentleman was wrong'd,
And that the gentlewoman was brought thither,
Forc'd by her husband, and there left.
VOLTORE.   Most true.   55
CELIA. How ready is Heav'n to those that
                              [pray!
1ST AVOCATORE.   But that
Volpone would have ravish'd her, he holds
Utterly false, knowing his impotence.   60
CORVINO. Grave fathers, he is possess'd;
                              [again, I say,
Possess'd; nay, if there be possession,
And obsession, he has both.
3RD AVOCATORE.   Here comes our officer.   65
[*Enter* VOLPONE.]
VOLPONE. The parasite will straight be here,
                              [grave fathers.
4TH AVOCATORE. You might invent some
                              [other name, Sir Varlet.   70
3RD AVOCATORE. Did not the notary meet
                              [him?
VOLPONE.   Not that I know.
4TH AVOCATORE. His coming will clear all.
2ND AVOCATORE.   Yet it is misty.   75
VOLTORE. May 't please your Fatherhoods—
VOLPONE [*whispers to the* ADVOCATE]. Sir, the
                              [parasite
Will'd me to tell you that his master lives;
That you are still the man; your hopes the   80
                              [same;
And this was only a jest—
VOLTORE.   How?
VOLPONE.   Sir, to try
If you were firm, and how you stood affected.   85
VOLTORE. Art sure he lives?
VOLPONE.   Do I live, sir?
VOLTORE.   O me!

I was too violent.

VOLPONE.   Sir, you may redeem it.
They said you were possess'd; fall down, and
                                    [seem so:
5 I'll help to make it good. [VOLTORE *falls*.] God
                                    [bless the man!—
[*Aside to* VOLTORE.] Stop your wind hard, and
                                    [swell.—See, see, see, see!
He vomits crooked pins!° His eyes are set,
10 Like a dead hare's hung in a poulter's shop!
His mouth's running away! Do you see,
                                    [signior?
Now it is in his belly.

CORVINO.   Ay, the devil!

15 VOLPONE. Now in his throat.

CORVINO.   Ay, I perceive it plain.

VOLPONE. 'Twill out, 'twill out! stand clear.
                                    [See where it flies!
In shape of a blue toad, with a bat's wings!
20 Do not you see it, sir?

CORBACCIO.   What? I think I do.

CORVINO. 'Tis too manifest.

VOLPONE.   Look! he comes t' himself!

VOLTORE. Where am I?

25 VOLPONE.   Take good heart, the worst is
                                    [past, sir.
You're dispossess'd.

1ST AVOCATORE. What accident is this?

2ND AVOCATORE. Sudden and full of wonder!

30 3RD AVOCATORE.   If he were
Possess'd, as it appears, all this is nothing.

CORVINO. He has been often subject to these
                                    [fits.

1ST AVOCATORE. Show him that writing:—do
35   [you know it, sir?

VOLPONE [*aside to* VOLTORE]. Deny it, sir,
                                    [forswear it; know it not.

VOLTORE. Yes, I do know it well: it is my
                                    [hand;
40 But all that it contains is false.

BONARIO.   O practice!

2ND AVOCATORE. What maze is this!

1ST AVOCATORE.   Is he not guilty then,
Whom you there name the parasite?
45 VOLTORE.   Grave fathers,
No more than his good patron, old Volpone.

crooked pins indicating demonic possession

4TH AVOCATORE. Why, he is dead.

VOLTORE.   O no, my honor'd fathers.
He lives—

1ST AVOCATORE.   How! lives?   50

VOLTORE.   Lives.

2ND AVOCATORE.   This is subtler yet!

3RD AVOCATORE. You said he was dead!

VOLTORE.   Never.

3RD AVOCATORE.   You said so!   55

CORVINO.   I heard so.

4TH AVOCATORE. Here comes the gentleman;
                                    [make him way.

[*Enter* MOSCA.]

3RD AVOCATORE.   A stool.   60

4TH AVOCATORE [*aside*]. A proper man! and,
                                    [Volpone dead,
A fit match for my daughter.

3RD AVOCATORE.   Give him way.

VOLPONE [*aside to* MOSCA]. Mosca, I was   65
                                    [a'most lost: the advocate
Had betray'd all; but now it is recover'd;
All's on the hinge again—say I am living.

MOSCA. What busy knave is this?—Most
                                    [reverend fathers,   70
I sooner had attended your grave pleasures,
But that my order for the funeral
Of my dear patron did require me—

VOLPONE [*aside*].   Mosca!

MOSCA. Whom I intend to bury like a   75
                                    [gentleman.

VOLPONE [*aside*]. Ay, quick, and cozen me of
                                    [all.

2ND AVOCATORE.   Still stranger!
More intricate!   80

1ST AVOCATORE.   And come about again!

4TH AVOCATORE [*aside*]. It is a match; my
                                    [daughter is bestow'd.

MOSCA [*aside to* VOLPONE]. Will you gi' me
                                    [half? 85

VOLPONE [*aside*].   First I'll be hanged.

MOSCA [*aside*]. I know
Your voice is good; cry not so loud.

1ST AVOCATORE.   Demand
The advocate.—Sir, did not you affirm   90
Volpone was alive?

VOLPONE.   Yes, and he is;
This gent'man told me so.—[*Aside to* MOSCA.]
                                    [Thou shalt have half.

MOSCA. Whose drunkard is this same? Speak,
             [some that know him;
I never saw his face.—[*Aside to* VOLPONE.] I
                         [cannot now
5   Afford it you so cheap.
       VOLPONE [*aside*].   No?
       1ST AVOCATORE.   What say you?
       VOLTORE. The officer told me.
       VOLPONE.   I did, grave fathers,
10 And will maintain he lives, with mine own life,
    And that this creature [*pointing to* MOSCA] told
                     [me.—(*Aside.*) I was born
    With all good stars my enemies.
       MOSCA.   Most grave fathers,
15 If such an insolence as this must pass
    Upon me, I am silent; 'twas not this
    For which you sent, I hope.
       2ND AVOCATORE.   Take him away.
       VOLPONE. Mosca!
20   3RD AVOCATORE. Let him be whipp'd.
       VOLPONE [*aside to* MOSCA].   Wilt thou
                         [betray me?
    Cozen me?
       3RD AVOCATORE.   And taught to bear
25   [himself
    Toward a person of his rank.
       4TH AVOCATORE.   Away.
       MOSCA. I humbly thank your Fatherhoods.
       VOLPONE.   Soft, soft;—[*aside*] whipp'd!
30 And lose all that I have! If I confess,
    It cannot be much more.
       4TH AVOCATORE.   Sir, are you married?
       VOLPONE. They'll be alli'd anon; I must be
                         [resolute;
35 The Fox shall here uncase. (*He puts off his
                         [disguise.*)
       MOSCA [*aside*].   Patron!
       VOLPONE.   Nay, now
    My ruins shall not come alone; your match
40 I'll hinder sure; my substance shall not glue
                         [you,
    Nor screw you into a family.
       MOSCA [*aside*].   Why, patron!
       VOLPONE. I am Volpone, and this (*pointing
45   [to* MOSCA) is my knave;
    This [*to* VOLTORE], his own knave; this (*to
                     [*CORBACCIO), avarice's fool;
    This [*to* CORVINO], a chimaera of wittol, fool,

                         [and knave:
    And, reverend fathers, since we all can hope   50
    Naught but a sentence, let's not now despair it.
    You hear me brief.
       CORVINO.   May it please your
                         [Fatherhoods—
       COMMANDADORE.   Silence.   55
       1ST AVOCATORE. The knot is now undone, by
                         [miracle!
       2ND AVOCATORE. Nothing can be more clear.
       3RD AVOCATORE.   Or can more prove
    These innocent.   60
       1ST AVOCATORE.   Give 'em their liberty.
       BONARIO. Heaven could not long let such
                         [gross crimes be hid.
       2ND AVOCATORE. If this be held the highway
                         [to get riches, 65
    May I be poor.
       3RD AVOCATORE. This 's not the gain, but
                         [torment.
       1ST AVOCATORE. These possess wealth, as sick
                         [men possess fevers, 70
    Which trulier may be said to possess them.
       2ND AVOCATORE. Disrobe that parasite.
       CORVINO and MOSCA.   Most honor'd
                         [fathers—
       1ST AVOCATORE. Can you plead aught to stay 75
                         [the course of justice?
    If you can, speak.
       CORVINO and VOLTORE. We beg favor.
       CELIA.   And mercy.
       1ST AVOCATORE. You hurt your innocence,   80
                         [suing for the guilty.
    Stand forth; and, first, the parasite. You appear
    T' have been the chiefest minister, if not plotter,
    In all these lewd impostures, and now, lastly,
    Have with your impudence abus'd the court,   85
    And habit of a gentleman of Venice,
    Being a fellow of no birth or blood;
    For which our sentence is, first, thou be
                         [whipp'd;
    Then live perpetual prisoner in our galleys.   90
       VOLPONE. I thank you for him.
       MOSCA.   Bane to thy wolfish nature!
       1ST AVOCATORE. Deliver him to the saffi.—
                         [Thou, Volpone,
    By blood and rank a gentleman, canst not fall   95
    Under like censure; but our judgment on thee

Is that thy substance all be straight confiscate
To the hospital of the Incurabili.
And since the most was gotten by imposture,
By feigning lame, gout, palsy, and such
5   [diseases,
Thou art to lie in prison, cramp'd with irons,
Till thou be'st sick and lame indeed.—Remove
                     [him.
    VOLPONE. This is called mortifying of a Fox.
10   1ST AVOCATORE. Thou, Voltore, to take away
                     [the scandal
Thou hast giv'n all worthy men of thy
                     [profession,
Art banish'd from their fellowship, and our
15   [state.—
Corbaccio!—Bring him near.—We here possess
Thy son of all thy state, and confine thee
To the monastery of San' Spirito;
Where, since thou knew'st not how to live well
20   [here,
Thou shalt be learn'd to die well.
    CORBACCIO   Ha! what said he?
    COMMANDADORE. You shall know anon, sir.
    1ST AVOCATORE.   Thou, Corvino, shalt
25 Be straight embark'd from thine own house,
                   [and row'd
Round about Venice, through the Grand Canal,
Wearing a cap, with fair long ass's ears,
Instead of horns; and so to mount, a paper
30 Pinn'd on thy breast, to the Berlina.°
    CORVINO.   Yes,
And mine eyes beat out with stinking fish,
Bruis'd fruit, and rotten eggs—'tis well. I am
                   [glad
35 I shall not see my shame yet.
    1ST AVOCATORE.   And to expiate
Thy wrongs done to thy wife, thou are to send
                   [her
Home to her father, with her dowry trebled;
40 And these are all your judgments.°
    ALL.   Honor'd fathers—
    1ST AVOCATORE. Which may not be revok'd.
                 [Now you begin,
When crimes are done and past, and to be
45   [punish'd,

To think what your crimes are.—Away with
                   [them!
Let all that see these vices thus rewarded,
Take heart, and love to study 'em. Mischiefs
                 [feed 50
Like beasts, till they be fat, and then they bleed.
  [*Exeunt.*]
              VOLPONE
The seasoning of a play is the applause.
Now, though the Fox be punish'd by the laws,   55
He yet doth hope, there is no suff'ring due,
For any fact which he hath done 'gainst you;
If there be, censure him; here he doubtful
                 [stands.
If not, fare jovially, and clap your hands.   60
  [*Exit.*]

Berlina pillory
judgments sentences

Molière

(Jean-Baptiste Poquelin)

1622–1673

Tartuffe

1669

The close alliance between the French classical drama and the French monarchy in the middle decades of the seventeenth century was far from accidental. Louis XIV (styled "The Sun King") was personally and symbolically the center of a court that meant to be, and meant to be seen to be, the apex of political, financial, intellectual, and religious culture in all of Europe, especially of Catholic Europe. It was the ambition of that monarchy to strike an equilibrium between upholding the highest Christian standards of morality and promoting worldly pomp and power on a scale unrivalled at least since the days of Augustan Rome. That ambition eventually was embodied in the extravagant ostentation of Versailles. A consequence of this concern was an enormous preoccupation with propriety and every detail of deportment. With its pageants and processions, its grand spectacles and gorgeous rituals, the court of Louis presented itself as a theater in which were enacted the great events of national life. Decorum, the principle of imperturbable dignity, applied to every detail of public—and, presumably, also of private—conduct, and it governed the officially sponsored drama of the day.

By some high religious authorities all theatrical entertainments were regarded as inherently deceitful and as invitations to vanity and sinful pleasures. Yet the court, for all its respectful deference to religion, sponsored drama on a generous scale. The tragedies of Corneille and, rather later, of Racine offered grandeur of design, moral eloquence, and immense dignity of poetic style. As such they would hardly seem open to charges of impropriety. Yet Racine himself would eventually forsake the court and the secular theater as incompatible with his Catholic conscience.

The comedy favored by the court—and this meant essentially the comedy of Molière—was more susceptible to moral criticism. Are not absurdity, folly, indecorum, and vice the very stuff of comedy? Satirical comedy, in particular, can scarcely ridicule wrong or wicked conduct without exhibiting it in action. No matter how plausible the claim that such comedy is really the enemy of vice, still it thrives on deceptions, disguises, calculated role-playing and trickery, and even upon the naked exposure of down-to-earth facts. How can such things be squared with the principle of decorum? To make matters worse, is not the principle of decorum itself all too exposed to the suspicion of hypocrisy?

In making Tartuffe, plainly labeled "a hypocrite," the focus of his satire, Molière incurred the charge of venturing disrespectfully near the sanctities of church and state. It made little difference that the disorders that beset the household of Orgon, in the play, are remedied by the god-like intervention of an all-wise and forgiving monarch, none other than Louis himself. For years powerful influences tried to prevent its performance and publication. No doubt Molière did not mean to tread on such perilous ground, and no doubt the fact that his play at length won the royal favor served to demonstrate that no low suspicion could touch the throne. (Yet even the royal gesture might be read as a higher refinement of hypocrisy.)

In *Tartuffe* Molière presents not only the malign face of hypocrisy but its counterfoil as well. This last springs from a benign sense of the word that goes back to its Greek origin: *hypocrisy,* the art of the stage, the art of the actor. Clearly the black-frocked Tartuffe is a malignant double-dealer and spoiler. His effective opponents are not Cléante, Damis, and Dorine, all of whom see through his pretenses and can ridicule him but cannot expose and undo him. His effective opponent is Elmire, a benign hypocrite—in the basic sense. Ingenious, poised, and genuinely virtuous, she risks her cunning in the cause of right. In a justly famous scene she pretends (with her husband as a concealed audience) to fall in with Tartuffe's scheme of adultery, and she thus unmasks his roguery. For this she— and of course Molière—were tasked with indecorum: "No really nice woman or chaste

wife could ever lower herself," etc. To which she makes her answer, and Molière's: "My taste is for good-natured rectitude." That is, without "good nature," without the benign medicine of the comic imagination, righteousness itself is perhaps wanting in virtue. The remote monarch of the play's end can repair the fortunes of the Orgon family. But the victory over malign hypocrisy is won by means of the art of comedy.

Molière's comedies are usually more light-hearted than *Tartuffe,* and in a way they established a decorum of their own that has had lasting influence on later playwrights, as witness Wycherley, Sheridan, and Wilde. For the most part his plays conform to principles that his contemporaries regarded as classical, consistent with rules believed to derive from Greek and Roman practice. His plot designs, though sometimes complicated by incidental developments, are straightforward and drive steadily toward a decisive resolution. Scene opens upon scene with apparent inevitability in linked episodes that somewhat resemble a series of musical pieces. His characters are often memorable, not as unique individuals but rather as strikingly recognizable social types. They are not abundantly developed but only sufficiently. His style, whether in prose or verse, seldom calls attention to itself; it serves in many varied ways the needs at hand. In all, there are principles of modesty and balance. Molière himself was an expert of the theater, a celebrated actor as well as director and producer. What his comedies require and what they amply reward is not elaborate theatrical mounting or effect but, and above all, accomplished acting.

Tartuffe

A Comedy in Five Acts

MOLIÈRE

Translated by Richard Wilbur

CHARACTERS

MME PERNELLE   *Orgon's mother*
ORGON   *Elmire's husband*
ELMIRE   *Orgon's wife*
DAMIS   *Orgon's son, Elmire's stepson*
MARIANE   *Orgon's daughter, Elmire's*
  stepdaughter, in love with Valère
VALÈRE   *in love with Mariane*
CLÉANTE   *Orgon's brother-in-law*
TARTUFFE   *a hypocrite*
DORINE   *Mariane's lady's-maid*
M. LOYAL   *a bailiff*
A POLICE OFFICER
FLIPOTE   *Mme Pernelle's maid*

  The scene throughout: Orgon's house in Paris

Moliere's Tartuffe *translated by Richard Wilbur, copyright
© 1961, 1962, 1963 by Richard Wilbur. Reprinted by permission of Harcourt Brace Jovanovich, Inc.*
  *Caution: Professionals and amateurs are hereby warned
that this translation, being fully protected under the copyright laws of the United States of America, the British
Empire, including the Dominion of Canada, and all other
countries which are signatories to the Universal Copyright
Convention and International Copyright Union, is subject
to royalty. All rights, including professional, amateur, motion picture, recitation, lecturing, public reading, radio
broadcasting, and television are strictly reserved. Inquiries
on professional and amateur rights should be addressed to
Mr. Gilbert Parker, Curtis Brown Ltd., 575 Madison Avenue, New York, New York 10022. Inquiries on translation
rights should be addressed to Harcourt Brace Jovanovich,
Inc., Orlando, Florida 32887.*

ACT I

Scene i

MADAME PERNELLE *and* FLIPOTE, *her maid,* ELMIRE,
MARIANE, DORINE, DAMIS, CLÉANTE
  MADAME PERNELLE. Come, come, Flipote; it's
                    [time I left this place.
  ELMIRE. I can't keep up, you walk at such a   5
                    [pace.
  MADAME PERNELLE. Don't trouble, child; no
                    [need to show me out.
It's not your manners I'm concerned about.
  ELMIRE. We merely pay you the respect we   10
                    [owe.
But, Mother, why this hurry? Must you go?
  MADAME PERNELLE. I must. This house appals
                    [me. No one in it
Will pay attention for a single minute.   15
Children, I take my leave much vexed in spirit.
I offer good advice, but you won't hear it.
You all break in and chatter on and on.
It's like a madhouse with the keeper gone.
  DORINE. If . . .   20
  MADAME PERNELLE.   Girl, you talk too much,
                    [and I'm afraid
You're far too saucy for a lady s-maid.
You push in everywhere and have your say.
  DAMIS. But . . .   25
  MADAME PERNELLE.   You, boy, grow more
                    [foolish every day.
To think my grandson should be such a dunce!
I've said a hundred times, if I've said it once,
That if you keep the course on which you've   30
                    [started,
You'll leave your worthy father broken-hearted.
  MARIANE. I think . . .
  MADAME PERNELLE.   And you, his sister,
                    [seem so pure,   35
So shy, so innocent, and so demure,
But you know what they say about still waters.
I pity parents with secretive daughters.
  ELMIRE. Now, Mother . . .
  MADAME PERNELLE.   And as for you, child,   40
                    [let me add
That your behavior is extremely bad,
And a poor example for these children, too.
Their dear, dead mother did far better than you.

You're much too free with money, and I'm
                                    [distressed
To see you so elaborately dressed.
When it's one's husband that one aims to
5   [please,
One has no need of costly fripperies.
        CLÉANTE. Oh, Madam, really . . .
        MADAME PERNELLE.   You are her brother, Sir,
And I respect and love you; yet if I were
10 My son, this lady's good and pious spouse,
I wouldn't make you welcome in my house.
You're full of worldly counsels which, I fear,
Aren't suitable for decent folk to hear.
I've spoken bluntly, Sir; but it behooves us
15 Not to mince words when righteous fervor
                                    [moves us.
        DAMIS. Your man Tartuffe is full of holy
                                    [speeches . . .
        MADAME PERNELLE. And practises precisely
20   [what he preaches.
He's a fine man, and should be listened to.
I will not hear him mocked by fools like you.
        DAMIS. Good God! Do you expect me to
                                    [submit
25 To the tyranny of that carping hypocrite?
Must we forgo all joys and satisfactions
Because that bigot censures all our actions?
        DORINE. To hear him talk—and he talks all the
                                    [time—
30 There's nothing one can do that's not a crime.
He rails at everything, your dear Tartuffe.
        MADAME PERNELLE. Whatever he reproves
                                    [deserves reproof.
He's out to save your souls, and all of you
35 Must love him, as my son would have you do.
        DAMIS. Ah no, Grandmother, I could never
                                    [take
To such a rascal, even for my father's sake.
That's how I feel, and I shall not dissemble.
40 His every action makes me seethe and tremble
With helpless anger, and I have no doubt
That he and I will shortly have it out.
        DORINE. Surely it is a shame and a disgrace
To see this man usurp the master's place—
45 To see this beggar who, when first he came,
Had not a shoe or shoestring to his name
So far forget himself that he behaves
As if the house were his, and we his slaves.

        MADAME PERNELLE. Well, mark my words, your
                                    [souls would fare far better 50
If you obeyed his precepts to the letter.
        DORINE. You see him as a saint. I'm far less
                                    [awed;
In fact, I see right through him. He's a fraud.
        MADAME PERNELLE. Nonsense!   55
        DORINE.   His man Laurent's the same, or
                                    [worse;
I'd not trust either with a penny purse.
        MADAME PERNELLE. I can't say what his
                                    [servant's morals may be; 60
His own great goodness I can guarantee.
You all regard him with distaste and fear
Because he tells you what you're loath to hear,
Condemns your sins, points out your moral
                                    [flaws, 65
And humbly strives to further Heaven's cause.
        DORINE. If sin is all that bothers him, why is it
He's so upset when folk drop in to visit?
Is Heaven so outraged by a social call
That he must prophesy against us all?   70
I'll tell you what I think: if you ask me,
He's jealous of my mistress' company.
        MADAME PERNELLE. Rubbish! [To ELMIRE] He's
                                    [not alone, child, in complaining
Of all your promiscuous entertaining.   75
Why, the whole neighborhood's upset, I know,
By all these carriages that come and go,
With crowds of guests parading in and out
And noisy servants loitering about.
In all of this, I'm sure there's nothing vicious; 80
But why give people cause to be suspicious?
        CLÉANTE. They need no cause; they'll talk in
                                    [any case.
Madam, this world would be a joyless place
If, fearing what malicious tongues might say, 85
We locked our doors and turned our friends
                                    [away.
And even if one did so dreary a thing,
D'you think those tongues would cease their
                                    [chattering? 90
One can't fight slander; it's a losing battle;
Let us instead ignore their tittle-tattle.
Let's strive to live by conscience' clear decrees,
And let the gossips gossip as they please.
        DORINE. If there is talk against us, I know the 95
                                    [source:

It's Daphne and her little husband, of course.
Those who have greatest cause for guilt and
[shame
Are quickest to besmirch a neighbor's name.
5 When there's a chance for libel, they never miss
[it;
When something can be made to seem illicit
They're off at once to spread the joyous news,
Adding to fact what fantasies they choose.
10 By talking up their neighbor's indiscretions
They seek to camouflage their own
[transgressions,
Hoping that others' innocent affairs
Will lend a hue of innocence to theirs,
15 Or that their own black guilt will come to seem
Part of a general shady color-scheme.
    MADAME PERNELLE. All that is quite irrelevant. I
[doubt
That anyone's more virtuous and devout
20 Than dear Orante; and I'm informed that she
Condemns your mode of life most vehemently.
    DORINE. Oh, yes, she's strict, devout, and has
[no taint
Of worldliness; in short, she seems a saint.
25 But it was time which taught her that disguise;
She's thus because she can't be otherwise.
So long as her attractions could enthrall,
She flounced and flirted and enjoyed it all,
But now that they're no longer what they were
30 She quits a world which fast is quitting her,
And wears a veil of virtue to conceal
Her bankrupt beauty and her lost appeal.
That's what becomes of old coquettes today:
Distressed when all their lovers fall away,
35 They see no recourse but to play the prude,
And so confer a style on solitude.
Thereafter, they're severe with everyone,
Condemning all our actions, pardoning none,
And claiming to be pure, austere, and zealous
40 When, if the truth were known, they're merely
[jealous,
And cannot bear to see another know
The pleasures time has forced them to forgo.
    MADAME PERNELLE [*Initially to* ELMIRE]. That sort
45   [of talk is what you like to hear;
Therefore you'd have us all keep still, my dear,
While Madam rattles on the livelong day.
Nevertheless, I mean to have my say.

I tell you that you're blest to have Tartuffe
Dwelling, as my son's guest, beneath this roof;   50
That Heaven has sent him to forestall its wrath
By leading you, once more, to the true path;
That all he reprehends is reprehensible,
And that you'd better heed him, and be
[sensible,   55
These visits, balls, and parties in which you
[revel
Are nothing but inventions of the Devil.
One never hears a word that's edifying:
Nothing but chaff and foolishness and lying,   60
As well as vicious gossip in which one's
[neighbor
Is cut to bits with epee, foil, and saber.
People of sense are driven half-insane
At such affairs, where noise and folly reign   65
And reputations perish thick and fast.
As a wise preacher said on Sunday last,
Parties are Towers of Babylon, because
The guests all babble on with never a pause;
And then he told a story which, I think . . .   70
    [*To* CLÉANTE]
I heard that laugh, Sir, and I saw that wink!
Go find your silly friends and laugh some more!
Enough; I'm going; don't show me to the door.
I leave this household much dismayed and   75
[vexed;
I cannot say when I shall see you next.
    [*Slapping* FLIPOTE]
Wake up, don't stand there gaping into space!
I'll slap some sense into that stupid face.   80
Move, move, you slut.

Scene ii

CLÉANTE, DORINE
CLÉANTE I think I'll stay behind;
I want no further pieces of her mind.
How that old lady. . .   85
    DORINE.   Oh, what wouldn't she say
If she could hear you speak of her that way!
She'd thank you for the *lady*, but I'm sure
She'd find the *old* a little premature.
    CLÉANTE. My, what a scene she made, and   90
[what a din!
And how this man Tartuffe has taken her in!
    DORINE. Yes, but her son is even worse
[deceived;

His folly must be seen to be believed.
In the late troubles, he played an able part
And served his king with wise and loyal heart,
But he's quite lost his senses since he fell
5   Beneath Tartuffe's infatuating spell.
He calls him brother, and loves him as his life,
Preferring him to mother, child, or wife.
In him and him alone will he confide;
He's made him his confessor and his guide;
10 He pets and pampers him with love more tender
Than any pretty mistress could engender,
Gives him the place of honor when they dine,
Delights to see him gorging like a swine,
Stuffs him with dainties till his guts distend,
15 And when he belches, cries "God bless you,
                                          [friend!"
In short, he's mad; he worships him; he dotes;
His deeds he marvels at, his words he quotes,
Thinking each act a miracle, each word
20 Oracular as those that Moses heard.
Tartuffe, much pleased to find so easy a victim,
Has in a hundred ways beguiled and tricked
                                          [him,
Milked him of money, and with his permission
25 Established here a sort of Inquisition.
Even Laurent, his lackey, dares to give
Us arrogant advice on how to live;
He sermonizes us in thundering tones
And confiscates our ribbons and colognes.
30 Last week he tore a kerchief into pieces
Because he found it pressed in a *Life of Jesus:*
He said it was a sin to juxtapose
Unholy vanities and holy prose.

Scene iii

ELMIRE, MARIANE, DAMIS, CLÉANTE, DORINE
35 ELMIRE [*To* CLÉANTE]. You did well not to
                          [follow; she stood in the door
And said *verbatim* all she'd said before.
I saw my husband coming, I think I'd best
Go upstairs now, and take a little rest.
40   CLÉANTE. I'll wait and greet him here; then I
                                          [must go.
I've really only time to say hello.
      DAMIS. Sound him about my sister's wedding,
                                          [please.
45 I think Tartuffe's against it, and that he's
Been urging Father to withdraw his blessing.

As you well know, I'd find that most
                                          [distressing.
Unless my sister and Valère can marry,
My hopes to wed *his* sister will miscarry,   50
And I'm determined . . .
DORINE.   He's coming.

Scene iv

ORGON, CLÉANTE, DORINE
ORGON.   Ah, Brother, good-day.
CLÉANTE. Well, welcome back. I'm sorry I can't   55
                                          [stay.
How was the country? Blooming, I trust, and
                                          [green?
      ORGON. Excuse me, Brother; just one moment.
[*To* DORINE]   60
Dorine . . .
[*To* CLÉANTE]
To put my mind at rest, I always learn
The household news the moment I return.
[*To* DORINE]   65
Has all been well, these two days I've been
                                          [gone?
How are the family? What's been going on?
      DORINE. Your wife, two days ago, had a bad
                                          [fever, 70
And a fierce headache which refused to leave
                                          [her.
      ORGON. Ah. And Tartuffe?
      DORINE.   Tartuffe? Why, he's round and
                                          [red, 75
Bursting with health, and excellently fed.
      ORGON. Poor fellow!
      DORINE.   That night, the mistress was
                                          [unable
To take a single bite at the dinner-table.   80
Her headache-pains, she said, were simply
                                          [hellish.
      ORGON. Ah. And Tartuffe?
      DORINE.   He ate his meal with relish,
And zealously devoured in her presence   85
A leg of mutton and a brace of pheasants.
      ORGON. Poor fellow!
      DORINE.   Well, the pains continued strong,
And so she tossed and tossed the whole night
                                          [long, 90
Now icy-cold, now burning like a flame.
We sat beside her bed till morning came.

ORGON. Ah. And Tartuffe?

DORINE.   Why, having eaten, he rose
And sought his room, already in a doze,
Got into his warm bed, and snored away
5 In perfect peace until the break of day.

ORGON. Poor fellow!

DORINE.   After much ado, we talked her
Into dispatching someone for the doctor.
He bled her, and the fever quickly fell.
10 ORGON. Ah. And Tartuffe?

DORINE.   He bore it very well.
To keep his cheerfulness at any cost,
And make up for the blood *Madame* had lost,
He drank, at lunch, four beakers full of port.
15 ORGON. Poor fellow!

DORINE.   Both are doing well, in short.
I'll go and tell *Madame* that you've expressed
Keen sympathy and anxious interest.

Scene v

ORGON, CLÉANTE

20 CLÉANTE. That girl was laughing in your face,
                     [and though
I've no wish to offend you, even so
I'm bound to say that she had some excuse.
How can you possibly be such a goose?
25 Are you so dazed by this man's hocus-pocus
That all the world, save him, is out of focus?
You've given him clothing, shelter, food, and
                      [care;
Why must you also . . .

30 ORGON.   Brother, stop right there.
You do not know the man of whom you speak.

CLÉANTE. I grant you that. But my judgment's
                    [not so weak
That I can't tell, by his effect on others . . .
35 ORGON. Ah, when you meet him, you two will
                    [be like brothers!
There's been no loftier soul since time began.
He is a man who . . . a man who . . . an
                  [excellent man.
40 To keep his precepts is to be reborn,
And view this dunghill of a world with scorn.
Yes, thanks to him I'm a changed man indeed.
Under his tutelage my soul's been freed
From earthly loves, and every human tie:
45 My mother, children, brother, and wife could
                  [die,

And I'd not feel a single moment's pain.

CLÉANTE. That's a fine sentiment, Brother;
                  [most humane.

ORGON. Oh, had you seen Tartuffe as I first   50
                  [knew him,
Your heart, like mine, would have surrendered
                  [to him.
He used to come into our church each day
And humbly kneel nearby, and start to pray.   55
He'd draw the eyes of everybody there
By the deep fervor of his heartfelt prayer;
He'd sigh and weep, and sometimes with a
                  [sound
Of rapture he would bend and kiss the ground;   60
And when I rose to go, he'd run before
To offer me holy-water at the door.
His serving-man, no less devout than he,
Informed me of his master's poverty;
I gave him gifts, but in his humbleness   65
He'd beg me every time to give him less,
"Oh, that's too much," he'd cry, "too much by
                  [twice!
I don't deserve it. The half, Sir, would suffice."
And when I wouldn't take it back, he'd share   70
Half of it with the poor, right then and there.
At length, Heaven prompted me to take him in
To dwell with us, and free our souls from sin.
He guides our lives, and to protect my honor
Stays by my wife, and keeps an eye upon her;   75
He tells me whom she sees, and all she does,
And seems more jealous than I ever was!
And how austere he is! Why, he can detect
A mortal sin where you would least suspect;
In smallest trifles, he's extremely strict.   80
Last week, his conscience was severely pricked
Because, while praying, he had caught a flea
And killed it, so he felt, too wrathfully.

CLÉANTE. Good God, man! Have you lost your
                [common sense—   85
Or is this all some joke at my expense?
How can you stand there and in all sobriety . . .

ORGON. Brother, your language savors of
                [impiety.
Too much free-thinking's made your faith   90
                [unsteady,
And as I've warned you many times already,
'Twill get you into trouble before you're
                [through.

CLÉANTE. So I've been told before by dupes
             [like you:
Being blind, you'd have all others blind as well;
The clear-eyed man you call an infidel,
5 And he who sees through humbug and pretense
Is charged, by you, with want of reverence,
Spare me your warnings, Brother; I have no fear
Of speaking out, for you and Heaven to hear,
Against affected zeal and pious knavery.
10 There's true and false in piety, as in bravery,
And just as those whose courage shines the
             [most
In battle, are the least inclined to boast,
So those whose hearts are truly pure and lowly
15 Don't make a flashy show of being holy.
There's a vast difference, so it seems to me,
Between true piety and hypocrisy:
How do you fail to see it, may I ask?
Is not a face quite different from a mask?
20 Cannot sincerity and cunning art,
Reality and semblance, be told apart?
Are scarecrows just like men, and do you hold
That a false coin is just as good as gold?
Ah, Brother, man's a strangely fashioned
25   [creature
Who seldom is content to follow Nature,
But recklessly pursues his inclination
Beyond the narrow bounds of moderation,
And often, by transgressing Reason's laws,
30 Perverts a lofty aim or noble cause.
A passing observation, but it applies.
    ORGON. I see, dear Brother, that you're
            [profoundly wise;
You harbor all the insight of the age.
35 You are our one clear mind, our only sage,
The era's oracle, its Cato° too,
And all mankind are fools compared to you.
    CLÉANTE. Brother, I don't pretend to be a sage,
Nor have I all the wisdom of the age.
40 There's just one insight I would dare to claim:
I know that true and false are not the same;
And just as there is nothing I more revere
Than a soul whose faith is steadfast and sincere,
Nothing that I more cherish and admire

Than honest zeal and true religious fire,   45
So there is nothing that I find more base
Than specious piety's dishonest face—
Than these bold mountebanks, these histrios
Whose impious mummeries and hollow shows
Exploit our love of Heaven, and make a jest   50
Of all that men think holiest and best;
These calculating souls who offer prayers
Not to their Maker, but as public wares,
And seek to buy respect and reputation
With lifted eyes and sighs of exaltation;   55
These charlatans, I say, whose pilgrim souls
Proceed, by way of Heaven, toward earthly
            [goals,
Who weep and pray and swindle and extort,
Who preach the monkish life, but haunt the   60
            [court,
Who make their zeal the partner of their vice—
Such men are vengeful, sly, and cold as ice,
And when there is an enemy to defame
They cloak their spite in fair religion's name,   65
Their private spleen and malice being made
To seem a high and virtuous crusade,
Until, to mankind's reverent applause,
They crucify their foe in Heaven's cause.
Such knaves are all too common; yet, for the   70
            [wise,
True piety isn't hard to recognize,
And, happily, these present times provide us
With bright examples to instruct and guide us.
Consider Ariston and Périandre;   75
Look at Oronte, Alcidamas, Clitandre;°
Their virtue is acknowledged, who could doubt
            [it?
But you won't hear them beat the drum about it.
They're never ostentatious, never vain,   80
And their religion's moderate and humane;
It's not their way to criticize and chide:
They think censoriousness a mark of pride,
And therefore, letting others preach and rave,
They show, by deeds, how Christians should   85
            [behave.
They think no evil of their fellow man,
But judge of him as kindly as they can.

Cato Marcus Porcius Cato (234–149 B.C.), "the Censor," a Roman statesman who severely condemned private and public corruption

Ariston . . . Clitandre fictitious names, men of moderation and good sense

They don't intrigue and wangle and conspire;
To lead a good life is their one desire;
The sinner wakes no rancorous hate in them;
It is the sin alone which they condemn;
5 Nor do they try to show a fiercer zeal
For Heaven's cause than Heaven itself could
[feel.
These men I honor, these men I advocate
As models for us all to emulate.
10 Your man is not their sort at all, I fear:
And, while your praise of him is quite sincere,
I think that you've been dreadfully deluded.
ORGON. Now then, dear Brother, is your
[speech concluded?
15 CLÉANTE. Why yes.
ORGON.   Your servant, Sir. [*He turns to go.*]
CLÉANTE.   No, Brother, wait.
There's one more matter. You agreed of late
That young Valère might have your daughter's
20   [hand.
ORGON. I did.
CLÉANTE.   And set the date, I understand.
ORGON. Quite so.
CLÉANTE.   You've now postponed it; is that
25   [true?
ORGON. No doubt.
CLÉANTE.   The match no longer pleases you?
ORGON. Who knows?
CLÉANTE.   D'you mean to go back, on your
30   [word?
ORGON. I won't say that.
CLÉANTE.   Has anything occurred
Which might entitle you to break your pledge?
ORGON. Perhaps.
35 CLÉANTE.   Why must you hem, and haw,
[and hedge?
The boy asked me to sound you in this affair . . .
ORGON. It's been a pleasure.
CLÉANTE.   But what shall I tell Valère?
40 ORGON. Whatever you like.
CLÉANTE.   But what have you decided?
What are your plans?
ORGON.   I plan, Sir, to be guided
By Heaven's will.
45 CLÉANTE.   Come, Brother, don't talk rot.
You've given Valère your word; will you keep it,
[or not?
ORGON. Good day.

CLÉANTE.   This looks like poor Valère's
[undoing, 50
I'll go and warn him that there's trouble
[brewing.

ACT II

Scene i

ORGON, MARIANE
ORGON. Mariane.
MARIANE.   Yes, Father?   55
ORGON.   A word with you, come here.
MARIANE. What are you looking for?
ORGON [*Peering into a small closet*].
                    [Eavesdroppers, dear.
I'm making sure we shan't be overheard.   60
Someone in there could catch our every word.
Ah, good, we're safe. Now, Mariane, my child,
You're a sweet girl who's traceable and mild,
Whom I hold dear, and think most highly of.
MARIANE. I'm deeply grateful, Father, for your 65
[love.
ORGON. That's well said, Daughter; and you
[can repay me
If, in all things, you'll cheerfully obey me.
MARIANE. To please you, Sir, is what delights   70
[me best.
ORGON. Good, good. Now, what d'you think
[of Tartuffe, our guest?
MARIANE. I, Sir?
ORGON.   Yes. Weigh your answer; think it   75
[through.
MARIANE. Oh, dear. I'll say whatever you wish
[me to.
ORGON. That's wisely said, my Daughter. Say
[of him, then, 80
That he's the very worthiest of men,
And that you're fond of him, and would rejoice
In being his wife, if that should be my choice.
Well?
MARIANE. What?   85
ORGON.   What's that?
MARIANE. I . . .
ORGON.   Well?
MARIANE.   Forgive me, pray.
ORGON. Did you not hear me?   90
MARIANE.   Of *whom*, Sir, must I say
That I am fond of him, and would rejoice

In being his wife, if that should be your choice?
ORGON. Why, of Tartuffe.
MARIANE.   But, Father, that's false, you
[know.
5 Why would you have me say what isn't so?
ORGON. Because I am resolved it shall be true.
That it's my wish should be enough for you.
MARIANE. You can't mean, Father . . .
ORGON.   Yes, Tartuffe shall be
10 Allied by marriage to this family,
And he's to be your husband, is that clear?
It's a father's privilege . . .

Scene ii

DORINE, ORGON, MARIANE
ORGON [To DORINE].   What are you doing in
15   [here?
Is curiosity so fierce a passion
With you, that you must eavesdrop in this
[fashion?
DORINE. There's lately been a rumor going
20   [about—
Based on some hunch or chance remark, no
[doubt—
That you mean Mariane to wed Tartuffe.
I've laughed it off, of course, as just a spoof.
25 ORGON. You find it so incredible?
DORINE.   Yes, I do.
I won't accept that story, even from you.
ORGON. Well, you'll believe it when the thing
[is done.
30 DORINE. Yes, yes, of course. Go on and have
[your fun.
ORGON. I've never been more serious in my
[life.
DORINE. Ha!
35 ORGON.   Daughter, I mean it; you're to be
[his wife.
DORINE. No, don't believe your father; it's all
[a hoax.
ORGON. See here, young woman . . .
40 DORINE.   Come, Sir, no more jokes;
You can't fool us.
ORGON.   How dare you talk that way?
DORINE. All right, then: we believe you, sad to
[say.
45 But how a man like you, who looks so wise

And wears a moustache of such splendid size,
Can be so foolish as to . . .
ORGON.   Silence, please!
My girl, you take too many liberties.
I'm master here, as you must not forget.   50
DORINE. Do let's discuss this calmly; don't be
[upset.
You can't be serious, Sir, about this plan.
What should that bigot want with Mariane?
Praying and fasting ought to keep him busy.   55
And then, in terms of wealth and rank, what is
[he?
Why should a man of property like you
Pick out a beggar son-in-law?
ORGON.   That will do.   60
Speak of his poverty with reverence.
His is a pure and saintly indigence
Which far transcends all worldly pride and pelf.
He lost his fortune, as he says himself,
Because he cared for Heaven alone, and so   65
Was careless of his interests here below.
I mean to get him out of his present straits
And help him to recover his estates—
Which, in his part of the world, have no small
[fame.   70
Poor though he is, he's a gentleman just the
[same.
DORINE. Yes, so he tells us; and, Sir, it seems
[to me
Such pride goes very ill with piety.   75
A man whose spirit spurns this dungy earth
Ought not to brag of lands and noble birth;
Such worldly arrogance will hardly square
With meek devotion and the life of prayer.
. . . But this approach, I see, has drawn a blank;   80
Let's speak, then, of his person, not his rank.
Doesn't it seem to you a trifle grim
To give a girl like her to a man like him?
When two are so ill-suited, can't you see
What the sad consequence is bound to be?   85
A young girl's virtue is imperilled, Sir,
When such a marriage is imposed on her;
For if one's bridegroom isn't to one's taste,
It's hardly an inducement to be chaste,
And many a man with horns upon his brow   90
Has made his wife the thing that she is now.
It's hard to be a faithful wife, in short,
To certain husbands of a certain sort,

And he who gives his daughter to a man she
[hates
Must answer for her sins at Heaven's gates.
Think, Sir, before you play so risky a role.
5   ORGON. This servant-girl presumes to save my
[soul!
DORINE. You would do well to ponder what
[I've said.
ORGON. Daughter, we'll disregard this
10   [dunderhead.
Just trust your father's judgment. Oh, I'm aware
That I once promised you to young Valère;
But now I hear he gambles, which greatly
[shocks me;
15   What's more, I've doubts about his orthodoxy.
His visits to church, I note, are very few.
      DORINE. Would you have him go at the same
[hours as you,
And kneel nearby, to be sure of being seen?
20   ORGON. I can dispense with such remarks,
[Dorine.

      [*To* MARIANE]
Tartuffe, however, is sure of Heaven's blessing,
And that's the only treasure worth possessing.
25   This match will bring you joys beyond all
[measure;
Your cup will overflow with every pleasure;
You two will interchange your faithful loves
Like two sweet cherubs, or two turtle-doves.
30   No harsh word shall be heard, no frown be
[seen,
And he shall make you happy as a queen.
      DORINE. And she'll make him a cuckold, just
[wait and see.
35   ORGON. What language!
      DORINE.   Oh, he's a man of destiny;
He's *made* for horns, and what the stars demand
Your daughter's virtue surely can't withstand.
      ORGON. Don't interrupt me further. Why can't
40   [you learn
That certain things are none of your concern?
      DORINE. It's for your own sake that I interfere.
      [*She repeatedly interrupts* ORGON *just as he is turning to speak to his daughter:*]
45   ORGON. Most kind of you. Now, hold your
[tongue, d'you hear?
      DORINE. If I didn't love you . . .
      ORGON.   Spare me your affection.

DORINE. I'll love you, Sir, in spite of your
[objection.   50
ORGON. Blast!
DORINE.   I can't bear, Sir, for your honor's
[sake,
To let you make this ludicrous mistake.
ORGON. You mean to go on talking?   55
DORINE.   If I didn't protest
This sinful marriage, my conscience couldn't
[rest.
ORGON. If you don't hold your tongue, you
[little shrew . . .   60
DORINE. What, lost your temper? A pious man
[like you?
ORGON. Yes! Yes! You talk and talk. I'm
[maddened by it.
Once and for all, I tell you to be quiet.   65
      DORINE. Well, I'll be quiet. But I'll be thinking
[hard.
      ORGON. Think all you like, but you had better
[guard
That saucy tongue of yours, or I'll . . .   70
      [*Turning back to* MARIANE]
      Now, child,
I've weighted this matter fully.
      DORINE [*Aside*].   It drives me wild
That I can't speak.   75
      [ORGON *turns his head, and she is silent.*]
ORGON.   Tartuffe is no young dandy,
But, still, his person . . .
      DORINE [*Aside*].   Is as sweet as candy.
      ORGON. Is such that, even if you shouldn't   80
[care
For his other merits . . .
      [*He turns and stands facing* DORINE, *arms crossed.*]
      DORINE [*Aside*].   They'll make a lovely pair.
If I were she, no man would marry me   85
Against my inclination, and go scot-free.
He'd learn, before the wedding-day was over,
How readily a wife can find a lover.
      ORGON [*To* DORINE]. It seems you treat my
[orders as a joke.   90
      DORINE. Why, what's the matter? 'Twas not to
[you I spoke.
      ORGON. What *were* you doing?
      DORINE.   Talking to myself, that's all.
      ORGON. Ah! [*Aside*] One more bit of   95
[impudence and gall,

And I shall give her a good slap in the face.
[*He puts himself in position to slap her;* DORINE,
whenever he glances at her, stands immobile and silent.]
Daughter, you shall accept, and with good
5   [grace,
The husband I've selected . . . Your wedding-
                        [day . . .
[*To* DORINE]
Why don't you talk to yourself?
10 DORINE.   I've nothing to say.
ORGON. Come, just one word.
DORINE.   No thank you, Sir. I pass.
ORGON. Come, speak; I'm waiting.
DORINE.   I'd not be such an ass.
15 ORGON [*Turning to* MARIANE]. In short, dear
              [Daughter, I mean to be obeyed,
And you must bow to the sound choice I've
                     [made.
DORINE [*Moving away*]. I'd not wed such a
20   [monster, even in jest.
[ORGON *attempts to slap her, but misses.*]
ORGON. Daughter, that maid of yours is a
                  [thorough pest;
She makes me sinfully annoyed and nettled.
25 I can't speak further; my nerves are too
                   [unsettled.
She's so upset me by her insolent talk,
I'll calm myself by going for a walk.

Scene iii

DORINE, MARIANE

30 DORINE [*Returning*]. Well, have you lost your
              [tongue, girl? Must I play
Your part, and say the lines you ought to say?
Faced with a fate so hideous and absurd,
Can you not utter one dissenting word?
35 MARIANE. What good would it do? A father's
              [power is great.
DORINE. Resist him now, or it will be too late.
MARIANE. But . . .
DORINE.   Tell him one cannot love at a
40   [father's whim;
That you shall marry for yourself, not him;
That since it's you who are to be the bride,
It's you, not he, who must be satisfied;
And that if his Tartuffe is so sublime,
45 He's free to marry him at any time.

MARIANE. I've bowed so long to Father's strict
              [control,
I couldn't oppose him now, to save my soul.
DORINE. Come, come, Mariane. Do listen to
            [reason, won't you? 50
Valère had asked your hand. Do you love him,
            [or don't you?
MARIANE. Oh, how unjust of you! What can
            [you mean
By asking such a question, dear Dorine? 55
You know the depth of my affection for him;
I've told you a hundred times how I adore him.
DORINE. I don't believe in everything I hear;
Who knows if your professions were sincere?
MARIANE. They were, Dorine, and you do me 60
            [wrong to doubt it;
Heaven knows that I've been all too frank about
            [it.
DORINE. You love him, then?
MARIANE.   Oh, more than I can express. 65
DORINE. And he, I take it, cares for you no
            [less?
MARIANE. I think so.
DORINE.   And you both, with equal fire,
Burn to be married? 70
MARIANE.   That is our one desire.
DORINE. What of Tartuffe, then? What of your
            [father's plan?
MARIANE. I'll kill myself, if I'm forced to wed
            [that man. 75
DORINE. I hadn't thought of that recourse.
            [How splendid!
Just die, and all your troubles will be ended!
A fine solution. Oh, it maddens me
To hear you talk in that self-pitying key. 80
MARIANE. Dorine, how harsh you are! It's most
            [unfair.
You have no sympathy for my despair.
DORINE. I've none at all for people who talk
            [drivel 85
And, faced with difficulties, whine and snivel.
MARIANE. No doubt I'm timid, but it would be
            [wrong . . .
DORINE. True love requires a heart that's firm
            [and strong. 90
MARIANE. I'm strong in my affection for Valère,
But coping with my father is his affair.
DORINE. But if your father's brain has grown so
            [cracked

Over his dear Tartuffe that he can retract
His blessing, though your wedding-day was
[named,
It's surely not Valère who's to be blamed.
5   MARIANE. If I defied my father, as you suggest,
Would it not seem unmaidenly, at best?
Shall I defend my love at the expense
Of brazenness and disobedience?
Shall I parade my heart's desires, and flaunt . . .
10   DORINE. No, I ask nothing of you. Clearly you
[want
To be Madame Tartuffe, and I feel bound
Not to oppose a wish so very sound.
What right have I to criticize the match?
15   Indeed, my dear, the man's a brilliant catch.
Monsieur Tartuffe! Now, there's a man of
[weight!
Yes, yes, Monsieur Tartuffe, I'm bound to state,
Is quite a person; that's not to be denied;
20   'Twill be no little thing to be his bride.
The world already rings with his renown;
He's a great noble—in his native town;
His ears are red, he has a pink complexion,
And all in all, he'll suit you to perfection.
25   MARIANE. Dear God!
     DORINE.   Oh, how triumphant you will feel
At having caught a husband so ideal!
     MARIANE. Oh, do stop teasing, and use your
[cleverness
30   To get me out of this appalling mess.
Advise me, and I'll do whatever you say.
     DORINE. Ah no, a dutiful daughter must obey
Her father, even if he weds her to an ape.
You've a bright future; why struggle to escape?
35   Tartuffe will take you back where his family
[lives,
To a small town a-swarm with relatives—
Uncles and cousins whom you'll be charmed to
[meet.
40   You'll be received at once by the elite,
Calling upon the bailiff's wife, no less—
Even, perhaps, upon the mayoress,
Who'll sit you down in the *best* kitchen chair.
Then, once a year, you'll dance at the village fair
45   To the drone of bagpipes—two of them, in
[fact—
And see a puppet-show, or an animal act.
Your husband . . .
     MARIANE.   Oh, you turn my blood to ice!

Stop torturing me, and give me your advice.   50
     DORINE [*Threatening to go*]. Your servant,
[Madam.
     MARIANE.   Dorine, I beg of you . . .
DORINE. No, you deserve it; this marriage must
[go through.   55
     MARIANE. Dorine!
DORINE.   No.
     MARIANE.   Not Tartuffe! You know I think
[him . . .
DORINE. Tartuffe's your cup of tea, and you   60
[shall drink him.
     MARIANE. I've always told you everything, and
[relied . . .
DORINE. No. You deserve to be tartuffified.°
     MARIANE. Well, since you mock me and refuse   65
[to care,
I'll henceforth seek my solace in despair:
Despair shall be my counsellor and friend,
And help me bring my sorrows to an end.
     [*She starts to leave.*]   70
     DORINE. There now, come back; my anger has
[subsided.
You do deserve some pity, I've decided.
     MARIANE. Dorine, if Father makes me undergo
This dreadful martyrdom, I'll die, I know.   75
     DORINE. Don't fret; it won't be difficult to
[discover
Some plan of action . . . But here's Valère, your
[lover.

Scene iv

VALÈRE, MARIANE, DORINE   80
VALÈRE. Madam, I've just received some
[wondrous news
Regarding which I'd like to hear your views.
     MARIANE. What news?
VALÈRE.   You're marrying Tartuffe.   85
     MARIANE.   I find
That Father does have such a match in mind.
     VALÈRE. Your father, Madam . . .
     MARIANE.   . . . has just this minute said
That it's Tartuffe he wishes me to wed.   90
     VALÈRE. Can he be serious?
     MARIANE.   Oh, indeed he can;
He's clearly set his heart upon the plan.

tartuffified   a word of Dorine's invention; in French a *tartuffe*
now means a hypocrite.

VALÈRE. And what position do you propose to
[take,
Madam?
MARIANE. Why—I don't know.
5   VALÈRE.   For heaven's sake—
You don't know?
MARIANE.   No.
VALÈRE.   Well, well!
MARIANE.   Advise me, do.
10   VALÈRE. Marry the man. That's my advice to
[you.
MARIANE. That's your advice?
VALÈRE.   Yes.
MARIANE. Truly?
15   VALÈRE. Oh, absolutely.
You couldn't choose more wisely, more astutely.
MARIANE. Thanks for this counsel; I'll follow it,
[of course.
VALÈRE. Do, do; I'm sure 'twill cost you no
20   [remorse.
MARIANE. To give it didn't cause your heart to
[break.
VALÈRE. I gave it, Madam, only for your sake.
MARIANE. And it's for your sake that I take it,
25   [Sir.
DORINE [Withdrawing to the rear of the stage].
[Let's see which fool will prove the
[stubborner.
VALÈRE. So! I am nothing to you, and it was
30   [flat
Deception when you . . .
MARIANE.   Please, enough of that.
You've told me plainly that I should agree
To wed the man my father's chosen for me,
35   And since you've deigned to counsel me so
[wisely,
I promise, Sir, to do as you advise me.
VALÈRE. Ah, no, 'twas not by me that you
[were swayed.
40   No, your decision was already made;
Though, now, to save appearances, you protest
That you're betraying me at my behest.
MARIANE. Just as you say.
VALÈRE.   Quite so, And I now see
45   That you were never truly in love with me.
MARIANE. Alas, you're free to think so if you
[choose.
VALÈRE. I choose to think so, and here's a bit
[of news:

You've spurned my hand, but I know where to   50
[turn
For kinder treatment, as you shall quickly learn.
MARIANE. I'm sure you do. Your noble qualities
Inspire affection . . .
VALÈRE.   Forget my qualities, please.   55
They don't inspire you overmuch, I find.
But there's another lady I have in mind
Whose sweet and generous nature will not
[scorn
To compensate me for the loss I've borne.   60
MARIANE. I'm no great loss, and I'm sure that
[you'll transfer
Your heart quite painlessly from me to her.
VALÈRE. I'll do my best to take it in my stride.
The pain I feel at being cast aside.   65
Time and forgetfulness may put an end to.
Or if I can't forget, I shall pretend to.
No self-respecting person is expected
To go on loving once he's been rejected.
MARIANE. Now, that's a fine, high-minded   70
[sentiment.
VALÈRE. One to which any sane man would
[assent.
Would you prefer it if I pined away
In hopeless passion till my dying day?   75
Am I to yield you to a rival's arms
And not console myself with other charms?
MARIANE. Go then: console yourself; don't
[hesitate.
I wish you to; indeed, I cannot wait.   80
VALÈRE. You wish me to?
MARIANE.   Yes.
VALÈRE.   That's the final straw.
Madam, farewell. Your wish shall be my law.
[He starts to leave, and then returns: this repeatedly.]   85
MARIANE. Splendid.
VALÈRE. [Coming back again].   This breach,
[remember, is of your making;
It's you who've driven me to the step I'm
[taking.   90
MARIANE. Of course.
VALÈRE. [Coming back again].   Remember,
[too, that I am merely
Following your example.
MARIANE.   I see that clearly.   95
VALÈRE. Enough. I'll go and do your bidding,
[then.
MARIANE. Good.

VALÈRE. [*Coming back again*].   You shall
[never see my face again.
MARIANE. Excellent.
VALÈRE. [*Walking to the door, then turning about*].
5   Yes?
MARIANE.   What?
VALÈRE.   What's that? What did you say?
MARIANE. Nothing. You're dreaming.
VALÈRE.   Ah. Well, I'm on my way.
10 Farewell, *Madame*.
[*He moves slowly away.*]
MARIANE.   Farewell.
DORINE [*To* MARIANE].   If you ask me,
Both of you are as mad as mad can be.
15 Do stop this nonsense, now. I've only let you
Squabble so long to see where it would get you.
Whoa there, Monsieure Valère!
[*She goes and seizes* VALÈRE *by the arm; he makes
a great show of resistance.*]
20   VALÈRE.   What's this, Dorine?
DORINE. Come here.
VALÈRE.   No, no, my heart's too full of
[spleen.
Don't hold me back; her wish must be obeyed.
25   DORINE. Stop!
VALÈRE.   It's too late now, my decision's
[made.
DORINE. Oh, pooh!
MARIANE [*Aside*].   He hates the sight of me,
30   [that's plain.
I'll go, and so deliver him from pain.
DORINE [*Leaving* VALÈRE, *running after* MARIANE].
And now *you* run away! Come back.
MARIANE.   No, no.
35 Nothing you say will keep me here. Let go!
VALÈRE. [*Aside*]. She cannot bear my presence,
[I perceive.
To spare her further torment, I shall leave.
DORINE [*Leaving* MARIANE, *running after* VALÈRE].
40 Again! You'll not escape, Sir; don't you try it.
Come here, you two. Stop fussing, and be quiet.
[*She takes Valère by the hand, then Mariane, and
draws them together.*]
VALÈRE. [*To* DORINE]. What do you want of me?
45   MARIANE. [*To* DORINE]. What is the point of
[this?
DORINE. We're going to have a little armistice.
[*To* VALÈRE]
Now, weren't you silly to get so overheated?

VALÈRE. Didn't you see how badly I was   50
[treated?
DORINE [*To* MARIANE]. Aren't you a simpleton,
[to have lost your head?
MARIANE. Didn't you hear the hateful things he
[said?   55
DORINE [*To* VALÈRE]. You're both great fools.
[Her sole desire, Valère,
Is to be yours in marriage. To that I'll swear.
[*To* MARIANE]
He loves you only, and he wants no wife   60
But you, Mariane. On that I'll stake my life.
MARIANE [*To* VALÈRE]. Then why you advised
[me so, I cannot see.
VALÈRE [*To* MARIANE]. On such a question, why
[ask advice of *me*?   65
DORINE. Oh, you're impossible. Give me your
[hands, you two.
[*To* VALÈRE]
Yours first.
VALÈRE [*Giving* DORINE *his hand*].   But why?   70
DORINE [*To* MARIANE].   And now a hand
[from you.
MARIANE [*Also giving* DORINE *her hand*].
[What are you doing?
DORINE.   There: a perfect fit.   75
You suit each other better than you'll admit.
[VALÈRE *and* MARIANE *hold hands for some time with-
out looking at each other.*]
VALÈRE. [*Turning toward* MARIANE]. Ah, come,
[don't be so haughty. Give a man   80
A look of kindness, won't you, Mariane?
[MARIANE *turns toward* VALÈRE *and smiles.*]
DORINE. I tell you, lovers are completely mad!
VALÈRE [*To* MARIANE]. Now come, confess that
[you were very bad   85
To hurt my feelings as you did just now.
I have a just complaint, you must allow.
MARIANE. *You* must allow that you were most
[unpleasant . . .
DORINE. Let's table that discussion for the   90
[present;
Your father has a plan which must be
[stopped.
MARIANE. Advise us, then; what means must
[we adopt?   95
DORINE. We'll use all manner of means, and all
[at once.
[*To* MARIANE]

Your father's addled; he's acting like a dunce.
Therefore you'd better humor the old fossil.
Pretend to yield to him, be sweet and docile,
And then postpone, as often as necessary,
5 The day on which you have agreed to marry.
You'll thus gain time, and time will turn the
                                            [trick.
Sometimes, for instance, you'll be taken sick,
And that will seem good reason for delay;
10 Or some bad omen will make you change the
                                            [day—
You'll dream of muddy water, or you'll pass
A dead man's hearse, or break a looking-glass.
If all else fails, no man can marry you
15 Unless you take his ring and say "I do."
But now, let's separate. If they should find
Us talking here, our plot might be divined.
        [To VALÈRE]
Go to your friends, and tell them what's
20   [occurred,
And have them urge her father to keep his
                                            [word.
Meanwhile, we'll stir her brother into action,
And get Elmire, as well, to join our faction.
25 Good-bye.
    VALÈRE [To MARIANE].   Though each of us will
                                          [do his best,
It's your true heart on which my hopes shall rest.
        MARIANE [To VALÈRE]. Regardless of what
30   [Father may decide,
None but Valère shall claim me as his bride.
        VALÈRE. Oh, how those words content me!
                                    [Come what will . . .
    DORINE. Oh, lovers, lovers! Their tongues are
35   [never still.
Be off, now.
    VALÈRE [Turning to go, then turning back].
                One last word . . .
    DORINE.   No time to chat:
40 You leave by this door; and you leave by that.
        [DORINE pushes them, by the shoulders, toward op-
        posing doors.]

ACT III

Scene i

DAMIS, DORINE
DAMIS. May lightning strike me even as I
45   [speak,

May all men call me cowardly and weak,
If any fear or scruple holds me back
From settling things, at once, with that great
                                            [quack!
    DORINE. Now, don't give way to violent 50
                                          [emotion.
Your father's merely talked about this notion,
And words and deeds are far from being one.
Much that is talked about is left undone.
    DAMIS. No, I must stop that scoundrel's 55
                                      [machinations;
I'll go and tell him off; I'm out of patience.
    DORINE. Do calm down and be practical. I had
                                          [rather
My mistress dealt with him—and with your 60
                                          [father.
She has some influence with Tartuffe, I've
                                          [noted.
He hangs upon her words, seems most devoted,
And may, indeed, be smitten by her charm. 65
Pray Heaven it's true! 'Twould do our cause no
                                          [harm.
She sent for him, just now, to sound him out
On this affair you're so incensed about;
She'll find out where he stands, and tell him, 70
                                          [too,
What dreadful strife and trouble will ensue
If he lends countenance to your father's plan.
I couldn't get in to see him, but his man
Says that he's almost finished with his prayers. 75
Go, now. I'll catch him when he comes
                                        [downstairs.
    DAMIS. I want to hear this conference, and I
                                            [will.
    DORINE. No, they must be alone. 80
    DAMIS.   Oh, I'll keep still.
    DORINE. Not you. I know your temper. You'd
                                      [start a brawl,
And shout and stamp your foot and spoil it all.
Go on. 85
    DAMIS.   I won't; I have a perfect right. . .
    DORINE. Lord, you're a nuisance! He's coming;
                                    [get out of sight.
        [DAMIS conceals himself in a closet at the rear of the
        stage.] 90

Scene ii

TARTUFFE, DORINE
TARTUFFE [Observing DORINE, and calling to his

manservant offstage). Hang up my hair-shirt°,
       [put my scourge° in place,
And pray, Laurent, for Heaven's perpetual
       [grace.
5 I'm going to the prison now, to share
My last few coins with the poor wretches there.
    DORINE [*Aside*]. Dear God, what affectation!
       [What a fake!
    TARTUFFE. You wished to see me?
10 DORINE.   Yes . . .
    TARTUFFE [*Taking a handkerchief from his pocket*].
       For mercy's sake,
Please take this handkerchief, before you speak.
    DORINE. What?
15 TARTUFFE.   Cover that bosom, girl. The flesh
       [is weak,
And unclean thoughts are difficult to control.
Such sights as that can undermine the soul.
    DORINE. Your soul, it seems, has very poor
20   [defenses,
And flesh makes quite an impact on your
       [senses.
It's strange that you're so easily excited;
My own desires are not so soon ignited,
25 And if I saw you naked as a beast,
Not all your hide would tempt me in the least.
    TARTUFFE. Girl, speak more modestly; unless
       [you do,
I shall be forced to take my leave of you.
30   DORINE. Oh, no, it's I who must be on my
       [way;
I've just one little message to convey.
Madame is coming down, and begs you, Sir,
To wait and have a word or two with her.
35   TARTUFFE. Gladly.
    DORINE [*Aside*].   *That* had a softening effect!
I think my guess about him was correct.
    TARTUFFE. Will she be long?
    DORINE.   No: that's her step I hear.
40 Ah, here she is, and I shall disappear.

Scene iii

ELMIRE, TARTUFFE
TARTUFFE. May Heaven, whose infinite
       [goodness we adore,

hair-shirt an uncomfortable undershirt made of animal hair,
    worn as a penance
scourge a whip used for the same purpose—to "mortify" the
    flesh

Preserve your body and soul forevermore,
And bless your days, and answer thus the plea   45
Of one who is its humblest votary.
    ELMIRE. I thank you for that pious wish. But
       [please,
Do take a chair and let's be more at ease.
    [*They sit down.*]   50
    TARTUFFE. I trust that you are once more well
       [and strong?
    ELMIRE. Oh, yes: the fever didn't last for long.
    TARTUFFE. My prayers are too unworthy, I am
       [sure,   55
To have gained from Heaven this most gracious
       [cure;
But lately, Madam, my every supplication
Has had for object your recuperation.
    ELMIRE. You shouldn't have troubled so. I   60
       [don't deserve it.
    TARTUFFE. Your health is priceless, Madam,
       [and to preserve it
I'd gladly give my own, in all sincerity.
    ELMIRE. Sir, you outdo us all in Christian   65
       [charity.
You've been most kind. I count myself your
       [debtor.
    TARTUFFE. 'Twas nothing, Madam. I long to
       [serve you better.   70
    ELMIRE. There's a private matter I'm anxious to
       [discuss.
I'm glad there's no one here to hinder us.
    TARTUFFE. I too am glad; it floods my heart
       [with bliss 75
To find myself alone with you like this.
For just this chance I've prayed with all my
       [power—
But prayed in vain, until this happy hour.
    ELMIRE. This won't take long, Sir, and I hope   80
       [you'll be
Entirely frank and unconstrained with me.
    TARTUFFE. Indeed, there's nothing I had rather
       [do
Than bare my inmost heart and soul to you.   85
First, let me say that what remarks I've made
About the constant visits you are paid
Were prompted not by any mean emotion,
But rather by a pure and deep devotion,
A fervent zeal . . .   90
    ELMIRE.   No need for explanation.
Your sole concern, I'm sure, was my salvation.

TARTUFFE (*Taking* ELMIRE's *hand and pressing her* [*fingertips*). Quite so; and such great fervor
                                              [do I feel . . .
    ELMIRE. Ooh! Please! You're pinching!
5   TARTUFFE.   'Twas from excess of zeal.
I never meant to cause you pain, I swear.
I'd rather . . .
    [*He places his hand on Elmire's knee.*]
    ELMIRE.   What can your hand be doing
10   [there?
    TARTUFFE. Feeling your gown; what soft, fine-
                                  [woven stuff!
    ELMIRE. Please, I'm extremely ticklish. That's
                                  [enough.
15   [*She draws her chair away;* TARTUFFE *pulls his after her.*]
    TARTUFFE (*Fondling the lace collar of her gown*).
        [My, my, what lovely lacework on your
                                 [dress!
20 The workmanship's miraculous, no less.
I've not seen anything to equal it.
    ELMIRE. Yes, quite. But let's talk business for a
                                  [bit.
They say my husband means to break his word
25 And give his daughter to you, Sir. Had you
                                  [heard!
    TARTUFFE. He did once mention it. But I
                                  [confess
I dream of quite a different happiness.
30 It's elsewhere, Madam, that my eyes discern
The promise of that bliss for which I yearn.
    ELMIRE. I see: you care for nothing here below.
    TARTUFFE. Ah, well—my heart's not made of
                                 [stone, you know.
35   ELMIRE. All your desires mount heavenward,
                                 [I'm sure,
In scorn of all that's earthly and impure.
    TARTUFFE. A love of heavenly beauty does not
                                 [preclude
40 A proper love for earthly pulchritude;
Our senses are quite rightly captivated
By perfect works our Maker has created.
Some glory clings to all that Heaven has made;
In you, all Heaven's marvels are displayed.
45 On that fair face, such beauties have been
                                 [lavished,
The eyes are dazzled and the heart is ravished;
How could I look on you, O flawless creature,

And not adore the Author of all Nature,
Feeling a love both passionate and pure   50
For you, his triumph of self-portraiture?
At first, I trembled lest that love should be
A subtle snare that Hell had laid for me;
I vowed to flee the sight of you, eschewing
A rapture that might prove my soul's undoing;   55
But soon, fair being, I became aware
That my deep passion could be made to square
With rectitude, and with my bounden duty.
I thereupon surrendered to your beauty.
It is, I know, presumptuous on my part   60
To bring you this poor offering of my heart,
And it is not my merit, Heaven knows,
But your compassion on which my hopes
                                 [repose.
You are my peace, my solace, my salvation;   65
On you depends my bliss—or desolation;
I bide your judgment and, as you think best,
I shall be either miserable or blest.
    ELMIRE. Your declaration is most gallant. Sir,
But don't you think it's out of character?   70
You'd have done better to restrain your passion
And think before you spoke in such a fashion.
It ill becomes a pious man like you . . .
    TARTUFFE. I may be pious, but I'm human too:
With your celestial charms before his eyes,   75
A man has not the power to be wise.
I know such words sound strangely, coming
                                 [from me,
But I'm no angel, nor was meant to be,
And if you blame my passion, you must needs   80
Reproach as well the charms on which it feeds.
Your loveliness I had no sooner seen
Than you became my soul's unrivalled queen;
Before your seraph glance, divinely sweet,
My heart's defenses crumbled in defeat,   85
And nothing fasting, prayer, or tears might do
Could stay my spirit from adoring you.
My eyes, my sighs have told you in the past
What now my lips make bold to say at last,
And if, in your great goodness, you will deign   90
To look upon your slave, and ease his pain,—
If, in compassion for my soul's distress,
You'll stoop to comfort my unworthiness,
I'll raise to you, in thanks for that sweet manna,
An endless hymn, an infinite hosanna.   95
With me, of course, there need be no anxiety,

No fear of scandal or of notoriety.
These young court gallants, whom all the ladies
[fancy,
Are vain in speech, in action rash and chancy;
5   When they succeed in love, the world soon
[knows it;
No favor's granted them but they disclose it
And by the looseness of their tongues profane
The very altar where their hearts have lain.
10 Men of my sort, however, love discreetly,
And one may trust our reticence completely.
My keen concern for my good name insures
The absolute security of yours;
In short, I offer you, my dear Elmire,
15 Love without scandal, pleasure without fear.
    ELMIRE. I've heard your well-turned speeches
[to the end,
And what you urge I clearly apprehend.
Aren't you afraid that I may take a notion
20 To tell my husband of your warm devotion,
And that, supposing he were duly told,
His feelings toward you might grow rather cold?
    TARTUFFE. I know, dear lady, that your
[exceeding charity
25 Will lead your heart to pardon my temerity;
That you'll excuse my violent affection
As human weakness, human imperfection;
And that—O fairest!—you will bear in mind
That I'm but flesh and blood, and am not blind.
30 ELMIRE. Some women might do otherwise,
[perhaps,
But I shall be discreet about your lapse;
I'll tell my husband nothing of what's occurred
If, in return, you'll give your solemn word
35 To advocate as forcefully as you can
The marriage of Valère and Mariane,
Renouncing all desire to dispossess
Another of his rightful happiness,
And . . .

Scene iv

40 DAMIS, ELMIRE, TARTUFFE
    DAMIS (*Emerging from the closet where he has been
[hiding*).   No! We'll not hush up this vile
[affair;
I heard it all inside that closet there,
45 Where Heaven, in order to confound the pride
Of this great rascal, prompted me to hide.

Ah, now I have my long-awaited chance
To punish his deceit and arrogance,
And give my father clear and shocking proof
Of the black character of his dear Tartuffe.   50
    ELMIRE. Ah no, Damis; I'll be content if he
Will study to deserve my leniency.
I've promised silence—don't make me break my
[word;
To make a scandal would be too absurd.   55
Good wives laugh off such trifles, and forget
[them;
Why should they tell their husbands, and upset
[them?
    DAMIS. You have your reasons for taking such   60
[a course,
And I have reasons, too, of equal force.
To spare him now would be insanely wrong.
I've swallowed my just wrath for far too long
And watched this insolent bigot bringing strife   65
And bitterness into our family life.
Too long he's meddled in my father's affairs,
Thwarting my marriage-hopes, and poor
[Valère's.
It's high time that my father was undeceived,   70
And now I've proof that can't be disbelieved—
Proof that was furnished me by Heaven above.
It's too good not to take advantage of.
This is my chance, and I deserve to lose it
If, for one moment, I hesitate to use it.   75
    ELMIRE. Damis . . .
    DAMIS.   No, I must do what I think right.
Madam, my heart is bursting with delight,
And, say whatever you will, I'll not consent
To lose the sweet revenge on which I'm bent.   80
I'll settle matters without more ado;
And here, most opportunely, is my cue.

Scene v

ORGON, DAMIS, TARTUFFE, ELMIRE
DAMIS. Father, I'm glad you've joined us. Let
[us advise you   85
Of some fresh news which doubtless will
[surprise you.
You've just now been repaid with interest
For all your loving-kindness to our guest.
He's proved his warm and grateful feelings   90
[toward you;
It's with a pair of horns he would reward you.

Yes, I surprised him with your wife, and heard
His whole adulterous offer, every word.
She, with her all too gentle disposition,
Would not have told you of his proposition;
5 But I shall not make terms with brazen lechery,
And feel that not to tell you would be treachery.

   ELMIRE. And I hold that one's husband's peace
                            [of mind
Should not be spoilt by tattle of this kind.
10 One's honor doesn't require it: to be proficient
In keeping men at bay is quite sufficient.
These are my sentiments, and I wish, Damis,
That you had heeded me and held your peace.

Scene vi

ORGON, DAMIS, TARTUFFE

15 ORGON. Can it be true, this dreadful thing I
                                  [hear?

   TARTUFFE. Yes, Brother, I'm a wicked man, I
                                  [fear:
A wretched sinner, all depraved and twisted,
20 The greatest villain that has ever existed.
My life's one heap of crimes, which grows each
                                  [minute;
There's naught but foulness and corruption in it;
And I perceive that Heaven, outraged by me,
25 Has chosen this occasion to mortify me.
Charge me with any deed you wish to name;
I'll not defend myself, but take the blame.
Believe what you are told, and drive Tartuffe
Like some base criminal from beneath your roof;
30 Yes, drive me hence, and with a parting curse:
I shan't protest, for I deserve far worse.

   ORGON [To DAMIS]. Ah, you deceitful boy, how
                               [dare you try
To stain his purity with so foul a lie?
35   DAMIS. What! Are you taken in by such a
                               [bluff?
Did you not hear . . .?

     ORGON.   Enough, you rogue, enough!

   TARTUFFE. Ah, Brother, let him speak: you're
40   [being unjust.
Believe his story; the boy deserves your trust.
Why, after all, should you have faith in me?
How can you know what I might do, or be?
Is it on my good actions that you base
45 Your favor? Do you trust my pious face?

Ah, no, don't be deceived by hollow shows;
I'm far, alas, from being what men suppose;
Though the world takes me for a man of worth,
I'm truly the most worthless man on earth.

   [To DAMIS]   50
Yes, my dear son, speak out now, call me the
                                [chief
Of sinners, a wretch, a murderer, a thief;
Load me with all the names men most abhor;
I'll not complain; I've earned them all, and more; 55
I'll kneel here while you pour them on my head
As a just punishment for the life I've led.

   ORGON [To TARTUFFE]. This is too much, dear
                                [Brother.

   [To DAMIS]   Have you no heart?   60

   DAMIS. Are you so hoodwinked by this rascal's
                                [art . . .?

   ORGON. Be still, you monster.

   [To TARTUFFE]
Brother, I pray you, rise.   65

   [To DAMIS]
Villain!

   DAMIS.   But . . .

   ORGON.   Silence!

   DAMIS.   Can't you realize . . . ?   70

   ORGON. Just one word more, and I'll tear you
                                [limb from limb.

   TARTUFFE. In God's name, Brother, don't be
                                [harsh with him.
I'd rather far be tortured at the stake   75
Than see him bear one scratch for my poor sake.

   ORGON [To DAMIS]. Ingrate!

   TARTUFFE.   If I must beg you, on bended
                                [knee,
To pardon him . . .   80

   ORGON [Falling to his knees, addressing TARTUFFE].
                              [Such goodness cannot be!
Now, *there's* true charity!

   DAMIS.   What, you . . . ?

   ORGON.   Villain, be still!   85
I know your motives; I know you wish him ill:
Yes, all of you—wife, children, servants, all—
Conspire against him and desire his fall,
Employing every shameful trick you can
To alienate me from this saintly man.   90
Ah, but the more you seek to drive him away,
The more I'll do to keep him. Without delay,
I'll spite this household and confound its pride

By giving him my daughter as his bride.
   Damis. You're going to force her to accept his
                       [hand?
   Orgon. Yes, and this very night, d'you
5   [understand?
I shall defy you all, and make it clear
That I'm the one who gives the orders here.
Come, wretch, kneel down and clasp his blessed
                       [feet,
10 And ask his pardon for your black deceit.
   Damis. I ask that swindler's pardon? Why, I'd
                      [rather . . .
   Orgon. So! You insult him, and defy your
                      [father!
15 A stick! A stick! [*To* Tartuffe] No, no—release
                      [me, do.
   [*To* Damis]
Out of my house this minute! Be off with you,
And never dare set foot in it again.
20   Damis. Well, I shall go, but . . .
   Orgon.   Well, go quickly, then.
I disinherit you; an empty purse
Is all you'll get from me—except my curse!

Scene vii

Orgon, Tartuffe
25   Orgon. How he blasphemed your goodness!
                      [What a son!
   Tartuffe. Forgive him, Lord, as I've already
                      [done.
   [*To* Orgon]
30 You can't know how it hurts when someone
                      [tries
To blacken me in my dear Brother's eyes.
   Orgon. Ahh!
   Tartuffe.   The mere thought of such
35   [ingratitude
Plunges my soul into so dark a mood . . .
Such horror grips my heart . . . I gasp for
                      [breath,
And cannot speak, and feel myself near death.
40   Orgon. [*He runs, in tears, to the door through
which he has just driven his son.*]
You blackguard! Why did I spare you? Why did
                      [I not
Break you in little pieces on the spot?

Compose yourself, and don't be hurt, dear friend. 45
   Tartuffe. These scenes, these dreadful
                  [quarrels, have got to end.
I've much upset your household, and I perceive
That the best thing will be for me to leave.
   Orgon. What are you saying!   50
   Tartuffe.   They're all against me here:
They'd have you think me false and insincere.
   Orgon. Ah, what of that? Have I ceased
                  [believing in you?
   Tartuffe. Their adverse talk will certainly   55
                  [continue,
And charges which you now repudiate
You may find credible at a later date.
   Orgon. No, Brother, never.
   Tartuffe.   Brother, a wife can sway   60
Her husband's mind in many a subtle way.
   Orgon. No, no.
   Tartuffe.   To leave at once is the solution;
Thus only can I end their persecution.
   Orgon. No, no, I'll not allow it; you shall   65
                  [remain.
   Tartuffe Ah, well; 'twill mean much
                [martyrdom and pain,
But if you wish it . . .
   Orgon.   Ah!   70
   Tartuffe.   Enough; so be it.
But one thing must be settled, as I see it.
For your dear honor, and for our friendship's
                  [sake,
There's one precaution I feel bound to take.   75
I shall avoid your wife, and keep away . . .
   Orgon. No, you shall not, whatever they may
                  [say.
It pleases me to vex them, and for spite
I'd have them see you with her day and night.   80
What's more, I'm going to drive them to despair
By making you my only son and heir;
This very day, I'll give to you alone
Clear deed and title to everything I own.
A dear, good friend and son-in-law-to-be   85
Is more than wife, or child, or kin to me.
Will you accept my offer, dearest son?
   Tartuffe. In all things, let the will of Heaven
                [be done.
   Orgon. Poor fellow! Come, we'll go draw up   90
                [the deed.
Then let them burst with disappointed greed!

ACT IV

Scene i

CLÉANTE, TARTUFFE

CLÉANTE. Yes, all the town's discussing it, and
[truly,
Their comments do not flatter you unduly.
5 I'm glad we've met, Sir, and I'll give my view
Of this sad matter in a word or two.
As for who's guilty, that I shan't discuss;
Let's say it was Damis who caused the fuss;
Assuming then, that you have been ill-used
10 By young Damis, and groundlessly accused,
Ought not a Christian to forgive, and ought
He not to stifle every vengeful thought?
Should you stand by and watch a father make
His only son an exile for your sake?
15 Again I tell you frankly, be advised:
The whole town, high and low, is scandalized;
This quarrel must be mended, and my advice is
Not to push matters to a further crisis.
No, sacrifice your wrath to God above,
20 And help Damis regain his father's love.
    TARTUFFE. Alas, for my part I should take great
[joy
In doing so, I've nothing against the boy.
I pardon all, I harbor no resentment;
25 To serve him would afford me much
[contentment.
But Heaven's interest will not have it so:
If he comes back, then I shall have to go.
After his conduct—so extreme, so vicious—
30 Our further intercourse would look suspicious.
God knows what people would think! Why,
[they'd describe
My goodness to him as a sort of bribe;
They'd say that out of guilt I made pretense
35 Of loving-kindness and benevolence—
That, fearing my accuser's tongue, I strove
To buy his silence with a show of love.
    CLÉANTE. Your reasoning is badly warped and
[stretched,
40 And these excuses, Sir, are most far-fetched.
Why put yourself in charge of Heaven's cause?
Does Heaven need our help to enforce its laws?
Leave vengeance to the Lord, Sir; while we live,
Our duty's not to punish, but forgive;

And what the Lord commands, we should obey   45
Without regard to what the world may say.
What! Shall the fear of being misunderstood
Prevent our doing what is right and good?
No, no; let's simply do what Heaven ordains,
And let no other thoughts perplex our brains.   50
    TARTUFFE. Again, Sir, let me say that I've
[forgiven
Damis, and thus obeyed the laws of Heaven;
But I am not commanded by the Bible
To live with one who smears my name with   55
[libel.
    CLÉANTE. Were you commanded, Sir, to
[indulge the whim
Of poor Orgon, and to encourage him
In suddenly transferring to your name   60
A large estate to which you have no claim?
    TARTUFFE. 'Twould never occur to those who
[know me best
To think I acted from self-interest.
The treasures of this world I quite despise;   65
Their specious glitter does not charm my eyes;
And if I have resigned myself to taking
The gift which my dear Brother insists on
[making,
I do so only, as he well understands,   70
Lest so much wealth fall into wicked hands,
Lest those to whom it might descend in time
Turn it to purposes of sin and crime,
And not, as I shall do, make use of it
For heaven's glory and mankind's benefit.   75
    CLÉANTE. Forget these trumped-up fears. Your
[argument
Is one the rightful heir might well resent;
It *is* a moral burden to inherit
Such wealth, but give Damis a chance to bear it.   80
And would it not be worse to be accused
Of swindling, than to see that wealth misused?
I'm shocked that you allowed Orgon to broach
This matter, and that you feel no self-reproach;
Does true religion teach that lawful heirs   85
May freely be deprived of what is theirs?
And if the Lord has told you in your heart
That you and young Damis must dwell apart,
Would it not be the decent thing to beat
A generous and honorable retreat,   90
Rather than let the son of the house be sent,
For your convenience, into banishment?

Sir, if you wish to prove the honesty
Of your intentions . . .
   TARTUFFE.   Sir, it is half-past three.
I've certain pious duties to attend to,
5 And hope my prompt departure won't offend
                   [you.
   CLÉANTE [*Alone*]. Damn.

Scene ii

ELMIRE, MARIANE, CLÉANTE, DORINE
   DORINE.   Stay, Sir, and help Mariane, for
10   [Heaven's sake!
She's suffering so, I fear her heart will break.
Her father's plan to marry her off tonight
Has put the poor child in a desperate plight.
I hear him coming. Let's stand together, now,
15 And see if we can't change his mind, somehow,
About this match we all deplore and fear.

Scene iii

ORGON, ELMIRE, MARIANE, CLÉANTE, DORINE
   ORGON. Hah! Glad to find you all assembled
                  [here.
20 [*To* MARIANE]
This contract, child, contains your happiness,
And what it says I think your heart can guess.
   MARIANE [*Falling to her knees*]. Sir, by that
        [Heaven which sees me here distressed,
25 And by whatever else can move your breast,
Do not employ a father's power, I pray you,
To crush my heart and force it to obey you,
Nor by your harsh commands oppress me so
That I'll begrudge the duty which I owe—
30 And do not so embitter and enslave me
That I shall hate the very life you gave me.
If my sweet hopes must perish, if you refuse
To give me to the one I've dared to choose,
Spare me at least—I beg you, I implore—
35 The pain of wedding one whom I abhor;
And do not, by a heartless use of force,
Drive me to contemplate some desperate course.
   ORGON [*Feeling himself touched by her*].
Be firm, my soul. No human weakness, now.
40   MARIANE. I don't resent your love for him.
                 [Allow
Your heart free rein, Sir; give him your property,
And if that's not enough, take mine from me;
He's welcome to my money, take it, do,

But don't, I pray, include my person too. 45
Spare me, I beg you; and let me end the tale
Of my sad days behind a convent veil.
   ORGON. A convent! Hah! When crossed in
         [their amours,
All lovesick girls have the same thoughts as 50
         [yours.
Get up! The more you loathe the man, and
         [dread him,
The more ennobling it will be to wed him.
Marry Tartuffe, and mortify your flesh! 55
Enough; don't start that whimpering afresh.
   DORINE. But why . . . ?
   ORGON.   Be still, there. Speak when you're
         [spoken to.
Not one more bit of impudence out of you. 60
   CLÉANTE. If I may offer a word of counsel
         [here . . .
   ORGON. Brother, in counseling you have no
         [peer;
All your advice is forceful, sound, and clever; 65
I don't propose to follow it, however.
   ELMIRE [*To* ORGON]. I am amazed, and don't
        [know what to say;
Your blindness simply takes my breath away.
You are indeed bewitched, to take no warning 70
From our account of what occurred this
         [morning.
   ORGON. Madam, I know a few plain facts, and
         [one
Is that you're partial to my rascal son; 75
Hence, when he sought to make Tartuffe the
         [victim
Of a base lie, you dared not contradict him.
Ah, but you underplayed your part, my pet;
You should have looked more angry, more 80
         [upset.
   ELMIRE. When men make overtures, must we
        [reply
With righteous anger and a battle-cry?
Must we turn back their amorous advances 85
With sharp reproaches and with fiery glances?
Myself, I find such offers merely amusing,
And make no scenes and fusses in refusing;
My taste is for good-natured rectitude,
And I dislike the savage sort of prude 90
Who guards her virtue with her teeth and claws,
And tears men's eyes out for the slightest cause:

The Lord preserve me from such honor as that,
Which bites and scratches like an alley-cat!
I've found that a polite and cool rebuff
Discourages a lover quite enough.
5   ORGON. I know the facts, and I shall not be
                              [shaken.
     ELMIRE. I marvel at your power to be mistaken.
Would it, I wonder, carry weight with you
If I could *show* you that our tale was true?
10   ORGON. Show me?
     ELMIRE.   Yes.
                    Rot.
     ELMIRE.   Come, what if I found a way
To make you see the facts as plain as day?
15   ORGON. Nonsense.
     ELMIRE.   Do answer me; don't be absurd.
I'm not now asking you to trust our word.
Suppose that from some hiding-place in here
You learned the whole sad truth by eye and
20   [ear—
What would you say of your good friend, after
                              [that?
     ORGON. Why, I'd say . . . nothing, by
                    [Jehoshaphat!°
25 It can't be true.
     ELMIRE.   You've been too long deceived,
And I'm quite tired of being disbelieved.
Come now: let's put my statements to the test,
And you shall see the truth made manifest.
30   ORGON. I'll take that challenge. Now do your
                              [uttermost.
We'll see how you make good your empty
                              [boast.
     ELMIRE [*To* DORINE]. Send him to me.
35   DORINE.   He's crafty; it may be hard
To catch the cunning scoundrel off his guard.
     ELMIRE. No, amorous men are gullible. Their
                              [conceit
So blinds them that they're never hard to cheat.
40 Have him come down [*To* CLÉANTE & MARIANE]
                    [Please leave us, for a bit.

Scene iv

ELMIRE, ORGON
ELMIRE. Pull up this table, and get under it.

Jehoshaphat!   name of a Biblical king, here used as a mild
oath.

ORGON. What?
ELMIRE.   It's essential that you be well-   45
                              [hidden.
ORGON. Why there?
ELMIRE.   Oh, Heavens! Just do as you are
                              [bidden.
I have my plans; we'll soon see how they fare.   50
Under the table, now; and once you're there,
Take care that you are neither seen nor heard.
     ORGON. Well, I'll indulge you, since I gave my
                              [word
To see you through this infantile charade.   55
     ELMIRE. Once it is over, you'll be glad we
                              [played.

[*To her husband, who is now under the table*]
I'm going to act quite strangely, now, and you
Must not be shocked at anything I do.   60
Whatever I may say, you must excuse
As part of that deceit I'm forced to use.
I shall employ sweet speeches in the task
Of making that imposter drop his mask;
I'll give encouragement to his bold desires,   65
And furnish fuel to his amorous fires.
Since it's for your sake, and for his destruction,
That I shall seem to yield to his seduction,
I'll gladly stop whenever you decide
That all your doubts are fully satisfied.   70
I'll count on you, as soon as you have seen
What sort of man he is, to intervene,
And not expose me to his odious lust
One moment longer than you feel you must.
Remember: you're to save me from my plight   75
Whenever . . . He's coming! Hush! Keep out of
                              [sight!

Scene v

TARTUFFE, ELMIRE, ORGON
TARTUFFE. You wish to have a word with me,
                              [I'm told.   80
     ELMIRE. Yes, I've a little secret to unfold.
Before I speak, however, it would be wise
To close that door, and look about for spies.
     [TARTUFFE *goes to the door, closes it, and returns.*]
The very last thing that must happen now   85
Is a repetition of this morning's row.
I've never been so badly caught off guard.
Oh, how I feared for you! You saw how hard
I tried to make this troublesome Damis

Control his dreadful temper, and hold his peace.
In my confusion, I didn't have the sense
Simply to contradict his evidence;
But as it happened, that was for the best,
5   And all has worked out in our interest.
This storm has only bettered your position;
My husband doesn't have the least suspicion,
And now, in mockery of those who do,
He bids me be continually with you.
10 And that is why, quite fearless of reproof,
I now can be alone with my Tartuffe,
And why my heart—perhaps too quick to
[yield—
Feels free to let its passion be revealed.
15 TARTUFFE. Madam, your words confuse me.
[Not long ago,
You spoke in quite a different style, you know.
ELMIRE. Ah, Sir, if that refusal made you smart,
It's little that you know of woman's heart,
20 Or what that heart is trying to convey
When it resists in such a feeble way!
Always, at first, our modesty prevents
The frank avowal of tender sentiments;
However high the passion which inflames us,
25 Still, to confess its power somehow shames us.
Thus we reluct, at first, yet in a tone
Which tells you that our heart is overthrown,
That what our lips deny, our pulse confesses,
And that, in time, all noes will turn to yesses.
30 I fear my words are all too frank and free,
And a poor proof of woman's modesty;
But since I'm started, tell me, if you will—
Would I have tried to make Damis be still,
Would I have listened, calm and unoffended,
35 Until your lengthy offer of love was ended,
And been so very mild in my reaction,
Had your sweet words not given me
[satisfaction?
And when I tried to force you to undo
40 The marriage-plans my husband has in view,
What did my urgent pleading signify
If not that I admired you, and that I
Deplored the thought that someone else might
[own
45 Part of a heart I wished for mine alone?
TARTUFFE. Madam, no happiness is so complete
As when, from lips we love, come words so
[sweet;

Their nectar floods my every sense, and drains
In honeyed rivulets through all my veins.   50
To please you is my joy, my only goal;
Your love is the restorer of my soul;
And yet I must beg leave, now, to confess
Some lingering doubts as to my happiness.
Might this not be a trick? Might not the catch   55
Be that you wish me to break off the match
With Mariane, and so have feigned to love me?
I shan't quite trust your fond opinion of me
Until the feelings you've expressed so sweetly
Are demonstrated somewhat more concretely,   60
And you have shown, by certain kind
[concessions,
That I may put my faith in your professions.
ELMIRE [*She coughs, to warn her husband*]. Why
[be in such a hurry? Must my heart   65
Exhaust its bounty at the very start?
To make that sweet admission cost me dear,
But you'll not be content, it would appear,
Unless my store of favors is disbursed
To the last farthing, and at the very first.   70
TARTUFFE. The less we merit, the less we dare
[to hope,
And with our doubts, mere words can never
[cope.
We trust no promised bliss till we receive it;   75
Not till a joy is ours can we believe it.
I, who so little merit your esteem,
Can't credit this fulfillment of my dream,
And shan't believe it, Madam, until I savor
Some palpable assurance of your favor.   80
ELMIRE. My, how tyrannical your love can be,
And how it flusters and perplexes me!
How furiously you take one's heart in hand,
And make your every wish a fierce command!
Come, must you hound and harry me to death?   85
Will you not give me time to catch my breath?
Can it be right to press me with such force,
Give me no quarter, show me no remorse,
And take advantage, by your stern insistence,
Of the fond feelings which weaken my   90
[resistance?
TARTUFFE. Well, if you look with favor upon
[my love,
Why, then, begrudge me some clear proof
[thereof?   95
ELMIRE. But how can I consent without offense

To Heaven, toward which you feel such
                                        [reverence?
TARTUFFE. If Heaven is all that holds you back,
                                        [don't worry.
5 I can remove that hindrance in a hurry.
Nothing of that sort need obstruct our path.
        ELMIRE. Must one not be afraid of Heaven's
                                        [wrath?
        TARTUFFE. Madam, forget such fears, and be
10   [my pupil,
And I shall teach you how to conquer scruple.
Some joys, it's true, are wrong in Heaven's eyes;
Yet Heaven is not averse to compromise;
There is a science, lately formulated,
15 Whereby one's conscience may be liberated,
And any wrongful act you care to mention
May be redeemed by purity of intention.°
I'll teach you, Madam, the secrets of that
                                        [science;
20 Meanwhile, just place on me your full reliance.
Assuage my keen desires, and feel no dread:
The sin, if any, shall be on my head.
        [ELMIRE coughs, this time more loudly.]
You've a bad cough.
25   ELMIRE.   Yes, yes. It's bad indeed.
        TARTUFFE [Producing a little paper bag]. A bit of
                                        [licorice may be what you need.
        ELMIRE. No, I've a stubborn cold, it seems. I'm
                                        [sure it
30 Will take much more than licorice to cure it.
        TARTUFFE. How aggravating.
        ELMIRE.   Oh, more than I can say.
        TARTUFFE. If you're still troubled, think of
                                        [things this way:
35 No one shall know our joys, save us alone,
And there's no evil till the act is known;
It's scandal, Madam, which makes it an offense,
And it's no sin to sin in confidence.
        ELMIRE [Having coughed once more]. Well, clearly
40   [I must do as you require,
And yield to your importunate desire.
It is apparent, now, that nothing less
Will satisfy you, and so I acquiesce.
To go so far is much against my will;

Yet . . . intention a passage especially attacked by Molière's
critics because it was thought to ridicule a teaching of the
Jesuits

I'm vexed that it should come to this; but still,   45
Since you are so determined on it, since you
Will not allow mere language to convince you,
And since you ask for concrete evidence, I
See nothing for it, now, but to comply.
If this is sinful, if I'm wrong to do it,   50
So much the worse for him who drove me to it.
The fault can surely not be charged to me.
        TARTUFFE. Madam, the fault is mine, if fault
                                        [there be,
And . . .   55
        ELMIRE.   Open the door a little, and peek
                                        [out;
I wouldn't want my husband poking about.
        TARTUFFE. Why worry about the man? Each
                                        [day he grows 60
More gullible; one can lead him by the nose.
To find us here would fill him with delight,
And if he saw the worst, he'd doubt his sight.
        ELMIRE. Nevertheless, do step out for a minute
Into the hall, and see that no one's in it.   65

Scene vi

ORGON, ELMIRE

ORGON [Coming out from under the table]. That
                                        [man's a perfect monster, I must admit!
I'm simply stunned. I can't get over it.
        ELMIRE. What, coming out so soon? How   70
                                        [premature!
Get back in hiding, and wait until you're sure.
Stay till the end, and be convinced completely;
We mustn't stop till things are proved
                                        [concretely.   75
        ORGON. Hell never harbored anything so
                                        [vicious!
        ELMIRE. Tut, don't be hasty. Try to be
                                        [judicious.
Wait, and be certain that there's no mistake.   80
No jumping to conclusions, for Heaven's sake!
        [She places ORGON behind her, as TARTUFFE re-enters.]

Scene vii

TARTUFFE, ELMIRE, ORGON

TARTUFFE [Not seeing ORGON]. Madam, all things
                                        [have worked out to perfection; 85
I've given the neighboring rooms a full
                                        [inspection;
No one's about; and now I may at last . . .

ORGON [*Intercepting him*]. Hold on, my
                              [passionate fellow, not so fast!
I should advise a little more restraint.
Well, so you thought you'd fool me, my dear
5   [saint!
How soon you wearied of the saintly life—
Wedding my daughter, and coveting my wife!
I've long suspected you, and had a feeling
That soon I'd catch you at your double-dealing.
10 Just now, you've given me evidence galore;
It's quite enough; I have no wish for more.
    ELMIRE [*To* TARTUFFE]. I'm sorry to have treated
                              [you so slyly,
But circumstances forced me to be wily.
15   TARTUFFE. Brother, you can't think . . .
    ORGON.   No more talk from you;
Just leave this household, without more ado.
    TARTUFFE. What I intended . . .
    ORGON.   That seems fairly clear.
20 Spare me your falsehoods and get out of here.
    TARTUFFE. No, I'm the master, and you're the
                              [one to go!
This house belongs to me, I'll have you know,
And I shall show you that you can't hurt *me*
25 By this contemptible conspiracy,
That those who cross me know not what they
                              [do,
And that I've means to expose and punish you,
Avenge offended Heaven, and make you grieve
30 That ever you dared order me to leave.

Scene viii

ELMIRE, ORGON
ELMIRE. What was the point of all that angry
                              [chatter?
ORGON. Dear God, I'm worried. This is no
35   [laughing matter.
ELMIRE. How so!
ORGON.   I fear I understood his drift.
I'm much disturbed about that deed of gift.
ELMIRE. You gave him . . . ?
40 ORGON.   Yes, it's all been drawn and
                              [signed.
But one thing more is weighing on my mind.
ELMIRE. What's that?
ORGON.   I'll tell you; but first let's see if
45   [there's
A certain strong-box in his room upstairs.

ACT V

Scene i

ORGON, CLÉANTE
CLÉANTE. Where are you going so fast?
ORGON.   God knows!
CLÉANTE.   Then wait;   50
Let's have a conference, and deliberate
On how this situation's to be met.
    ORGON. That strong-box has me utterly upset;
This is the worst of many, many shocks.
    CLÉANTE. Is there some fearful mystery in that 55
                              [box?
    ORGON. My poor friend Argas brought that
                              [box to me
With his own hands, in utmost secrecy;
'Twas on the very morning of his flight.   60
It's full of papers which, if they came to light,
Would ruin him—or such is my impression.
    CLÉANTE. Then why did you let it out of your
                              [possession?
    ORGON. Those papers vexed my conscience, 65
                              [and it seemed best
To ask the counsel of my pious guest,
The cunning scoundrel got me to agree
To leave the strong-box in his custody,
So that, in case of an investigation,   70
I could employ a slight equivocation
And swear I didn't have it, and thereby,
At no expense to conscience, tell a lie.
    CLÉANTE. It looks to me as if you're out on a
                              [limb. 75
Trusting him with that box, and offering him
That deed of gift, were actions of a kind
Which scarcely indicate a prudent mind.
With two such weapons, he has the upper hand,
And since you're vulnerable, as matters stand, 80
You erred once more in bringing him to bay.
You should have acted in some subtler way.
    ORGON. Just think of it: behind that fervent
                              [face,
A heart so wicked, and a soul so base!   85
I took him in, a hungry beggar, and then . . .
Enough, by God! I'm through with pious men:
Henceforth I'll hate the whole false brotherhood,
And persecute them worse than Satan could.
    CLÉANTE. Ah, there you go—extravagant as   90
                              [ever!

Why can you not be rational? You never
Manage to take the middle course, it seems,
But jump, instead, between absurd extremes.
You've recognized your recent grave mistake
5 In falling victim to a pious fake;
Now, to correct that error, must you embrace
An even greater error in its place,
And judge our worthy neighbors as a whole
By what you've learned of one corrupted soul?
10 Come, just because one rascal made you
[swallow
A show of zeal which turned out to be hollow,
Shall you conclude that all men are deceivers,
And that, today, there are no true believers?
15 Let atheists make that foolish inference;
Learn to distinguish virtue from pretense,
Be cautious in bestowing admiration,
And cultivate a sober moderation.
Don't humor fraud, but also don't asperse
20 True piety; the latter fault is worse,
And it is best to err, if err one must,
As you have done, upon the side of trust.

Scene ii

DAMIS, ORGON, CLÉANTE
DAMIS. Father, I hear that scoundrel's uttered
25 [threats
Against you; that he pridefully forgets
How, in his need, he was befriended by you,
And means to use your gifts to crucify you.
ORGON. It's true, my boy. I'm too distressed
30 [for tears.
DAMIS. Leave it to me, Sir; let me trim his ears.
Faced with such insolence, we must not waver.
I shall rejoice in doing you the favor
Of cutting short his life, and your distress.
35 CLÉANTE. What a display of young
[hotheadedness!
Do learn to moderate your fits of rage.
In this just kingdom, this enlightened age,
One does not settle things by violence.

Scene iii

40 MADAME PERNELLE, MARIANE, ELMIRE, DORINE,
DAMIS, ORGON, CLÉANTE
MADAME PERNELLE. I hear strange tales of very
[strange events.

ORGON. Yes, strange events which these two
[eyes beheld. 45
The man's ingratitude is unparalleled.
I save a wretched pauper from starvation,
House him, and treat him like a blood relation,
Shower him every day with my largesse,
Give him my daughter, and all that I possess; 50
And meanwhile the unconscionable knave
Tries to induce my wife to misbehave;
And not content with such extreme rascality,
Now threatens me with my own liberality,
And aims, by taking base advantage of 55
The gifts I gave him out of Christian love,
To drive me from my house, a ruined man,
And make me end a pauper, as he began.
DORINE. Poor fellow!
MADAME PERNELLE.   No, my son, I'll never 60
[bring
Myself to think him guilty of such a thing.
ORGON. How's that?
MADAME PERNELLE.   The righteous always
[were maligned. 65
ORGON. Speak clearly, Mother. Say what's on
[your mind.
MADAME PERNELLE.   I mean that I can smell a
[rat, my dear.
You know how everybody hates him, here. 70
ORGON. That has no bearing on the case at all.
MADAME PERNELLE. I told you a hundred times,
[when you were small.
That virtue in this world is hated ever;
Malicious men may die, but malice never. 75
ORGON. No doubt that's true, but how does it
[apply?
MADAME PERNELLE. They've turned you against
[him by a clever lie.
ORGON. I've told you, I was there and saw it 80
[done.
MADAME PERNELLE. Ah, slanderers will stop at
[nothing, Son.
ORGON. Mother, I'll lose my temper . . . For
[the last time, 85
I tell you I was witness to the crime.
MADAME PERNELLE. The tongues of spite are
[busy night and noon,
And to their venom no man is immune.
ORGON. You're talking nonsense. Can't you 90
[realize

I saw it; saw it; saw it with my eyes?
Saw, do you understand me? Must I shout it
Into your ears before you'll cease to doubt it?
  MADAME PERNELLE. Appearances can deceive,
5   [my son. Dear me,
We cannot always judge by what we see.
  ORGON. Drat! Drat!
  MADAME PERNELLE.   One often interprets
                [things awry;
10 Good can seem evil to a suspicious eye.
  ORGON. Was I to see his pawing at Elmire
As an act of charity?
  MADAME PERNELLE. Till his guilt is clear,
A man deserves the benefit of the doubt.
15 You should have waited, to see how things
                [turned out.
  ORGON. Great God in Heaven, what more
                [proof did I need?
Was I to sit there, watching, until he'd . . .
20 You drive me to the brink of impropriety.
  MADAME PERNELLE. No, no, a man of such
                [surpassing piety
Could not do such a thing. You cannot shake
                [me.
25 I don't believe it, and you shall not make me.
  ORGON. You vex me so that, if you weren't my
                [mother,
I'd say to you . . . some dreadful thing or other.
  DORINE. It's your turn now, Sir, not to be
30   [listened to;
You'd not trust us, and now she won't trust
                [you.
  CLÉANTE. My friends, we're wasting time
             [which should be spent
35 In facing up to our predicament.
I fear that scoundrel's threats weren't made in
                [sport.
  DAMIS. Do you think he'd have the nerve to go
                [to court?
40 ELMIRE. I'm sure he won't: they'd find it all too
                [crude
A case of swindling and ingratitude.
  CLÉANTE. Don't be too sure. He won't be at a
                [loss
45 To give his claims a high and righteous gloss;
And clever rogues with far less valid cause
Have trapped their victims in a web of laws.
I say again that to antagonize

A man so strongly armed was most unwise.
  ORGON. I know it; but the man's appalling   50
                [cheek
Outraged me so, I couldn't control my pique.
  CLÉANTE. I wish to Heaven that we could
                [devise
Some truce between you, or some compromise. 55
  ELMIRE. If I had known what cards he held, I'd
                [not
Have roused his anger by my little plot.
  ORGON [*To* DORINE, *as* M. LOYAL *enters*]. What is
           [that fellow looking for? Who is he? 60
Go talk to him—and tell him that I'm busy.

Scene iv

MONSIEUR LOYAL, MADAME PERNELLE, ORGON, DAMIS, MARIANE, DORINE, ELMIRE, CLÉANTE
  MONSIEUR LOYAL. Good day, dear sister, Kindly
                [let me see 65
Your master.
  DORINE.   He's involved with company,
And cannot be disturbed just now, I fear.
  MONSIEUR LOYAL. I hate to intrude; but what
               [has brought me here 70
Will not disturb your master, in any event.
Indeed, my news will make him most content.
  DORINE. Your name?
  MONSIEUR LOYAL.   Just say that I bring
                [greetings from 75
Monsieur Tartuffe, on whose behalf I've come.
  DORINE [*To* ORGON]. Sir, he's a very gracious
                [man, and bears
A message from Tartuffe, which, he declares,
Will make you most content.   80
  CLÉANTE.   Upon my word,
I think this man had best be seen, and heard.
  ORGON. Perhaps he has some settlement to
                [suggest.
How shall I treat him? What manner would be 85
                [best?
  CLÉANTE. Control your anger, and if he should
                [mention
Some fair adjustment, give him your full
                [attention. 90
  MONSIEUR LOYAL. Good health to you, good
                [Sir. May Heaven confound
Your enemies, and may your joys abound.

ORGON [*Aside, to* CLÉANTE]. A gentle salutation:
[it confirms
My guess that he is here to offer terms.
MONSIEUR LOYAL. I've always held your family
5 [most dear;
I served your father, Sir, for many a year.
ORGON. Sir, I must ask your pardon; to my
[shame,
I cannot now recall your face or name.
10 MONSIEUR LOYAL. Loyal's my name; I come
[from Normandy,
And I'm a bailiff, in all modesty.
For forty years, praise God, it's been my boast
To serve with honor in that vital post,
15 And I am here, Sir, if you will permit
The liberty, to serve you with this writ . . .
ORGON. To—*what*?
MONSIEUR LOYAL. Now, please, Sir, let us
[have no friction:
20 It's nothing but an order of eviction.
You are to move your goods and family out
And make way for new occupants, without
Deferment or delay, and give the keys . . .
ORGON. I? Leave this house?
25 MONSIEUR LOYAL. Why yes, Sir, if you
[please.
This house, Sir, from the cellar to the roof,
Belongs now to the good Monsieur Tartuffe,
And he is lord and master of your estate
30 By virtue of a deed of present date,
Drawn in due form, with clearest legal
[phrasing . . .
DAMIS. Your insolence is utterly amazing!
MONSIEUR LOYAL. Young man, my business
35 [here is not with you,
But with your wise and temperate father, who,
Like every worthy citizen, stands in awe
Of justice, and would never obstruct the law.
ORGON. But . . .
40 MONSIEUR LOYAL. Not for a million, Sir,
[would you rebel
Against authority, I know that well.
You'll not make trouble, Sir, or interfere
With the execution of my duties here.
45 DAMIS. Someone may execute a smart tattoo
On that black jacket of yours, before you're
[through.
MONSIEUR LOYAL. Sir, bid your son be silent.
[I'd much regret

Having to mention such a nasty threat 50
Of violence, in writing my report.
DORINE [*Aside*]. This man Loyal's a most
[disloyal sort!
MONSIEUR LOYAL. I love all men of upright
[character, 55
And when I agreed to serve these papers, Sir,
It was your feelings that I had in mind.
I couldn't bear to see the case assigned
To someone else, who might esteem you less
And so subject you to unpleasantness. 60
ORGON. What's more unpleasant than telling a
[man to leave
His house and home?
MONSIEUR LOYAL. You'd like a short
[reprieve? 65
If you desire it, Sir, I shall not press you,
But wait until tomorrow to dispossess you.
Splendid. I'll come and spend the night here,
[then,
Most quietly, with half a score of men. 70
For form's sake, you might bring me, just before
You go to bed, the keys to the front door.
My men, I promise, will be on their best
Behavior, and will not disturb your rest.
But bright and early, Sir, you must be quick 75
And move out all your furniture, every stick:
The men I've chosen are both young and strong,
And with their help it shouldn't take you long.
In short, I'll make things pleasant and
[convenient, 80
And since I'm being so extremely lenient,
Please show me, Sir, a like consideration,
And give me your entire cooperation.
ORGON [*Aside*]. I may be all but bankrupt, but I
[vow 85
I'd give a hundred louis, here and now,
Just for the pleasure of landing one good clout
Right on the end of that complacent snout.
CLÉANTE. Careful; don't make things worse.
DAMIS. My bootsole itches 90
To give that beggar a good kick in the
[breeches.
DORINE. Monsieur Loyal, I'd love to hear the
[whack
Of a stout stick across your fine broad back. 95
MONSIEUR LOYAL. Take care: a woman too may
[go to jail if
She uses threatening language to a bailiff.

CLÉANTE. Enough, enough, Sir. This must not
[go on.
Give me that paper, please, and then begone.
    MONSIEUR LOYAL. Well, *au revoir*. God give you
5   [all good cheer!
    ORGON. May God confound you, and him who
[sent you here!

Scene v

ORGON, CLÉANTE, MARIANE, ELMIRE, MADAME
PERNELLE, DORINE, DAMIS
10   ORGON. Now, Mother, was I right or not? This
[writ
Should change your notion of Tartuffe a bit.
Do you perceive his villainy at last?
    MADAME PERNELLE. I'm thunderstruck. I'm
15   [utterly aghast.
    DORINE. Oh, come, be fair. You mustn't take
[offense
At this new proof of his benevolence.
He's acting out of selfless love, I know.
20 Material things enslave the soul, and so
He kindly has arranged your liberation
From all that might endanger your salvation.
    ORGON. Will you not ever hold your tongue,
[you dunce?
25   CLÉANTE. Come, you must take some action,
[and at once.
    ELMIRE. Go tell the world of the low trick he's
[tried.
The deed of gift is surely nullified
30 By such behavior, and public rage will not
Permit the wretch to carry out his plot.

Scene vi

VALÈRE, ORGON, CLÉANTE, ELMIRE, MARIANE,
MADAME PERNELLE, DAMIS, DORINE
    VALÈRE. Sir, though I hate to bring you more
35   [bad news,
Such is the danger that I cannot choose.
A friend who is extremely close to me
And knows my interest in your family
Has, for my sake, presumed to violate
40 The secrecy that's due to things of state,
And sends me word that you are in a plight
From which your one salvation lies in flight.
That scoundrel who's imposed upon you so
Denounced you to the King an hour ago
45 And, as supporting evidence, displayed

The strong-box of a certain renegade
Whose secret papers, so he testified,
You had disloyally agreed to hide.
I don't know just what charges may be pressed,
But there's a warrant out for your arrest;   50
Tartuffe has been instructed, furthermore,
To guide the arresting officer to your door.
    CLÉANTE. He's clearly done this to facilitate
His seizure of your house and your estate.
    ORGON. That man, I must say, is a vicious   55
[beast!
    VALÈRE. Quick, Sir, you mustn't tarry in the
[least.
My carriage is outside, to take you hence;
This thousand louis should cover all expense.   60
Let's lose no time, or you shall be undone;
The sole defense, in this case, is to run.
I shall go with you all the way, and place you
In a safe refuge to which they'll never trace you.
    ORGON. Alas, dear boy, I wish that I could   65
[show you
My gratitude for everything I owe you.
But now is not the time; I pray the Lord
That I may live to give you your reward.
Farewell, my dears; be careful . . .   70
    CLÉANTE.   Brother, hurry.
We shall take care of things; you needn't worry.

Scene vii

THE OFFICER, TARTUFFE, VALÈRE, ORGON, ELMIRE,
MARIANE, MADAME PERNELLE, DORINE, CLÉANTE, DAMIS
    TARTUFFE. Gentle, Sir, gently; stay right where   75
[you are.
No need for haste; your lodging isn't far.
You're off to prison, by order of the Prince.
    ORGON. This is the crowning blow, you
[wretch; and since 80
It means my total ruin and defeat,
Your villainy is now at last complete.
    TARTUFFE. You needn't try to provoke me; it's
[no use.
Those who serve Heaven must expect abuse.   85
    CLÉANTE. You are indeed most patient, sweet,
[and blameless.
    DORINE. How he exploits the name of Heaven!
[It's shameless.
    TARTUFFE. Your taunts and mockeries are all for   90
[naught;
To do my duty is my only thought.

MARIANE. Your love of duty is most
[meritorious,
And what you've done is little short of glorious.
TARTUFFE. All deeds are glorious, Madam,
5 [which obey
The sovereign prince who sent me here today.
ORGON. I rescued you when you were
[destitute;
Have you forgotten that, you thankless brute?
10 TARTUFFE. No, no, I well remember everything;
But my first duty is to serve my King.
That obligation is so paramount
That other claims, beside it, do not count;
And for it I would sacrifice my wife,
15 My family, my friend, or my own life.
ELMIRE. Hypocrite!
DORINE. All that we most revere, he uses
To cloak his plots and camouflage his ruses.
CLÉANTE. If it is true that you are animated
20 By pure and loyal zeal, as you have stated,
Why was this zeal not roused until you'd sought
To make Orgon a cuckold, and been caught?
Why weren't you moved to give your evidence
Until your outraged host had driven you hence?
25 I shan't say that the gift of all his treasure
Ought to have damped your zeal in any
[measure;
But if he is a traitor, as you declare,
How could you condescend to be his heir?
30 TARTUFFE [To the OFFICER]. Sir, spare me all this
[clamor; it's growing shrill.
Please carry out your orders, if you will.
OFFICER. Yes, I've delayed too long, Sir. Thank
[you kindly.
35 You're just the proper person to remind me.
Come, you are off to join the other boarders
In the King's prison, according to his orders.
TARTUFFE. Who? I, Sir?
OFFICER. Yes.
40 TARTUFFE. To prison? This can't be true!
OFFICER. I owe an explanation, but not to you.
[To ORGON]
Sir, all is well; rest easy, and be grateful.
We serve a Prince to whom all sham is hateful,
45 A Prince who sees into our inmost hearts,
And can't be fooled by any trickster's arts.
His royal soul, though generous and human,
Views all things with discernment and acumen;

His sovereign reason is not lightly swayed,
And all his judgments are discreetly weighed. 50
He honors righteous men of every kind,
And yet his zeal for virtue is not blind,
Nor does his love of piety numb his wits
And make him tolerant of hypocrites.
'Twas hardly likely that this man could cozen 55
A King who's foiled such liars by the dozen.
With one keen glance, the King perceived the
[whole
Perverseness and corruption of his soul,
And thus high Heaven's justice was displayed: 60
Betraying you, the rogue stood self-betrayed.
The King soon recognized Tartuffe as one
Notorious by another name, who'd done
So many vicious crimes that one could fill
Ten volumes with them, and be writing still. 65
But to be brief: our sovereign was appalled
By this man's treachery toward you, which he
[called
The last, worst villainy of a vile career,
And bade me follow the impostor here 70
To see how gross his impudence could be,
And force him to restore your property.
Your private papers, by the King's command,
I hereby seize and give into your hand.
The King, by royal order, invalidates 75
The deed which gave this rascal your estates,
And pardons, furthermore, your grave offense
In harboring an exile's documents.
By these decrees, our Prince rewards you for
Your loyal deeds in the late civil war, 80
And shows how heartfelt is his satisfaction
In recompensing any worthy action,
How much he prizes merit, and how he makes
More of men's virtues than of their mistakes.
DORINE. Heaven be praised! 85
MADAME PERNELLE. I breathe again, at last.
ELMIRE. We're safe.
MARIANE. I can't believe the danger's past.
ORGON. [To TARTUFFE]. Well traitor, now you
[see . . . 90
CLÉANTE. Ah, Brother, please,
Let's not descend to such indignities.
Leave the poor wretch to his unhappy fate,
And don't say anything to aggravate
His present woes; but rather hope that he 95
Will soon embrace an honest piety,

And mend his ways, and by a true repentance
Move our just King to moderate his sentence.
Meanwhile, go kneel before your sovereign's
                                    [throne
5 And thank him for the mercies he has shown.
    ORGON. Well said: let's go at once and, gladly
                                    [kneeling,
Express the gratitude which all are feeling.
Then, when that first great duty has been done,
10 We'll turn with pleasure to a second one,
And give Valère, whose love has proven so true,
The wedded happiness which is his due.

William Wycherley

1640–1715

The Country Wife

1675

The characters in *The Country Wife* appear to have stepped directly out of the fashionable drawing rooms of seventeenth-century London. More accurately, they have walked straight into a highly stylized stage-game governed by a few simple axioms: first, that a gentleman and a lady will freely copulate if left together in private—unless they are man and wife; second, that husbands exist to be cuckolded and their wives to be willingly seduced; third, that pretenders to respectability and virtue ("honor") are almost invariably hypocrites, fools, or villains. Such axioms hardly offer a steady and comprehensive view of social life, but neither are they altogether fictitious. Some readers have been so repelled by them as to regard this as "the most bestial" of all plays. Others have found it a superlative satire against marital jealousy, still others merely an audacious fantasy, and some an early prophecy of the revolution that would eventually overturn the old European aristocratic order itself. It is easy to exaggerate this last possibility, although sexual liberty—"free love"—has more than once been enlisted to "raise consciousness" in the wider cause of political liberty and equality.

What *The Country Wife* is is a first-class comedy directly in the tradition of Molière. This means that it is not in the ordinary sense realistic, that its moral perspectives are ironic, never absolute, and that the energy of the dialogue is both high and exquisitely controlled. But Wycherley's was a more skeptical intelligence than Molière's. He was, in seventeenth-century parlance, a "libertine" or freethinker, which is to say that he tended to regard social institutions and ethical ideals as justified only insofar as they serve the interests of pleasure and convenience; otherwise they are nuisances —or worse. In his view abstract principles all too readily serve tyranny, the outward tyranny of social repression as well as the inward tyranny of repressive conscience. Specifically, *The Country Wife,* like many other comedies of its kind and time, sees matrimony as only a legal form of bondage and prostitution from which anyone in his or her right mind would seek escape, either deviously (by "hypocrisy") or openly, by defying convention. Violations of such bondage can be regarded, then, as striking a blow for personal liberty, especially if the defiance is enlightened.

In such a perspective of liberty, both Mr. Horner and Margery Pinchwife honor the promptings of natural impulse as primary. Both are in revolt—the one consciously, the other instinctively—against conventional inhibitions. Hence their unabashed search for sexual gratification may be read as a sincere impulse toward personal freedom. This is particularly true of Margery, who is not cynically motivated, whereas Horner is. Her virtue, in contrast to that of Lady Fidget and her friends—who also seek pleasure but uphold the tyranny of convention—is to see straight through the pretentions and try to evade them. Horner, not dissimilarly, is a necessary and benevolent predator in a society operating by the axioms already stated. His pretending impotence to gratify his appetite is only a mirror image of his "victims' " counterfeiting honor. His virtue is sophisticated wit, a lucid and clever intelligence unencumbered with principles. He and Margery Pinchwife naturally gravitate to each other from mutually attractive poles of sophistication and naiveté. A stage tradition established at the first performances is worth noting. Horner is to be played by an actor of magnetic charm and virility, Margery by an actress having a figure bewitchingly attractive in the silk stockings and tight *culottes* that she dons in her disguise as a youth. Their animal endowments are for Wycherley the badges of native worth.

If we grant Wycherley the rules of his game, he pays back with a series of richly comic entertainments, scenes increasingly risqué and absurd, as first one husband then another complacently or ignorantly yields his wife to Horner's ministrations. The climax, of course, is a near miss, as the all-too-honest Margery begins to blurt out the plain truth of Horner's proven potency. For an instant the whole fabric of deceit and polite tyranny seems ready to collapse, but the scene ends in a kind of seven-voice chorus ironically acquiescing in things as they are. Yet there is no disguising the fact that Horner is still sitting pretty and that Margery has set foot on the crooked path to freedom.

The vocal effects throughout the play are remarkable, for their cadenced emphasis and the execution of skillful variations on a single word and theme—virtuoso passages difficult to illustrate except in performance. Examples are the famous or infamous "china scene" in Act IV, the drinking party in Act V —building elaborate chords on the notes of "virtue" and "honor"—and, above all, the fifth act finale beginning with Alithea's "There's doctrine for all husbands, Mr. Harcourt."

To anyone who does not concede Wycherley's denial of principles higher than pleasure and convenience, he allows the possible exception of Harcourt and Alithea, who are neither ignorant, unfashionable, cynical, nor dishonest—just comparatively pallid and no source of inspiration to their author. The focal plane of his sympathies is not deep, but what it lacks in depth it makes good in sharpness of observation capable of making his audience wince. For he enrolls us in complicity, like it or not. To understand his notorious and recurrent double entendres is to acknowledge, no matter how uneasily, that we are capable of being his accomplices in ribald skepticism. Harcourt and Alithea are all very well as conciliating gestures toward decorum, but they do not prevent Horner and Margery from soliciting not so much our respect as an involuntary warmth of approval, however guilty or reluctant. Judged as moral or immoral, or neither, *The Country Wife* will not let its audience easily off the hook of a difficult moral choice.

The Country Wife

WYCHERLEY

CHARACTERS

Mr. Horner
Mr. Harcourt
Mr. Dorilant
Mr. Pinchwife
Mr. Sparkish
Sir Jasper Fidget
Mrs. Margery Pinchwife
Mrs. Alithea
Lady Fidget
Mrs. Dainty Fidget
Mrs. Squeamish
Old Lady Squeamish
Lucy *Alithea's maid*
Waiters, Servants, and Attendants
A Boy
A Quack

scene. *London.*

ACT I

[Horner's *lodging.*]

[*Enter* Horner, *and* Quack *following him at a distance.*]

Horner [*aside*]. A quack is as fit for° a pimp
5 as a midwife for a bawd; they are still but in
their way both helpers of nature.—[*Aloud.*]
Well, my dear Doctor, hast thou done what I
desired?

Quack. I have undone you for ever with the
10 women, and reported you throughout the whole
town as bad as an eunuch, with as much trouble
as if I had made you one in earnest.

Horner. But have you told all the midwives
you know, the orange-wenches° at the playhouses, the city husbands, and old fumbling 15
keepers of this end of the town, for they'll be
the readiest to report it?

Quack. I have told all the chambermaids,
waiting-women, tire-women, and old women
of my acquaintance; nay, and whispered it as a 20
secret to 'em, and to the whisperers of Whitehall;° so that you need not doubt 'twill spread,
and you will be as odious to the handsome
young women as—

Horner. As the small-pox. Well— 25

Quack. And to the married women of this
end of the town, as—

Horner. As the great ones;° nay, as their
own husbands.

Quack. And to the city dames, as aniseed 30
Robin,° of filthy and contemptible memory;
and they will frighten their children with your
name, especially their females.

Horner. And cry, Horner's coming to carry
you away. I am only afraid 'twill not be be- 35
lieved. You told 'em 'twas by an English-French
disaster, and an English-French chirurgeon,°
who has given me at once not only a cure, but
an antidote for the future against that damned
malady, and that worse distemper, love, and all 40
other women's evils?

Quack. Your late journey into France has
made it the more credible, and your being here
a fortnight before you appeared in public looks
as if you apprehended the shame, which I won- 45
der you do not. Well, I have been hired by
young gallants to belie 'em t'other way, but you
are the first would be thought a man unfit for
women.

Horner. Dear Mr. Doctor, let vain rogues 50

---

for to be

orange-wenches girls who sold fruit in the theater. Many were prostitutes.
Whitehall the royal palace, a center of rumor and gossip
great ones venereal diseases
aniseed Robin a London street character supposed to be a hermaphrodite. Why he was nicknamed "aniseed" is not known.
English-French chirurgeon surgeon who treats venereal diseases (such as had presumably deprived Horner of his potency)

be contented only to be thought abler men than they are; generally 'tis all the pleasure they have, but mine lies another way.

QUACK. You take, methinks, a very prepos-
5 terous way to it, and as ridiculous as if we operators in physic should put forth bills° to disparage our medicaments, with hopes to gain customers.

HORNER. Doctor, there are quacks in love
10 as well as physic, who get but the fewer and worse patients for their boasting; a good name is seldom got by giving it one's self; and women no more than honor are compassed by bragging. Come, come, Doctor, the wisest lawyer never
15 discovers the merits of his cause till the trial; the wealthiest man conceals his riches, and the cunning gamester his play. Shy husbands and keepers, like old rooks, are not to be cheated but by a new unpractised trick: false friend-
20 ship will pass now no more than false dice upon 'em; no, not in the city.

[Enter BOY.]

BOY. There are two ladies and a gentleman coming up.

25 [Exit.]

HORNER. A pox! some unbelieving sisters of my former acquaintance, who, I am afraid, expect their sense should be satisfied of the falsity of the report. No—this formal fool and
30 women!

[Enter SIR JASPER FIDGET, LADY FIDGET, and MRS. DAINTY FIDGET.]

QUACK. His wife and sister.

SIR JASPER FIDGET. My coach breaking just
35 now before your door, sir, I look upon as an occasional reprimand to me, sir, for not kissing your hands,° sir, since your coming out of France, sir; and so my disaster, sir, has been my good fortune, sir; and this is my wife and
40 sister, sir.

HORNER. What then, sir?

SIR JASPER FIDGET. My lady, and sister, sir.— Wife, this is Master Horner.

LADY FIDGET. Master Horner, husband!

45 SIR JASPER FIDGET. My lady, my Lady Fidget,

sir.

HORNER. So, sir.

SIR JASPER FIDGET. Won't you be acquainted with her, sir?—[Aside.] So, the report is true, I find, by his coldness or aversion to the sex; 50 but I'll play the wag with him.—Pray salute my wife, my lady, sir.

HORNER. I will kiss no man's wife, sir, for him, sir; I have taken my eternal leave, sir, of the sex already, sir. 55

SIR JASPER FIDGET [aside]. Ha! ha! ha! I'll plague him yet.—Not know my wife, sir?

HORNER. I do know your wife, sir; she's a woman, sir, and consequently a monster, sir, a greater monster than a husband, sir. 60

SIR JASPER FIDGET. A husband! how, sir?

HORNER. So, sir; but I make no more cuck-olds, sir. [Makes horns.]

SIR JASPER FIDGET. Ha! ha! ha! Mercury! Mercury!° 65

LADY FIDGET. Pray, Sir Jasper, let us be gone from this rude fellow.

MRS. DAINTY FIDGET. Who, by his breeding, would think he had ever been in France?

LADY FIDGET. Foh! he's but too much a French 70 fellow, such as hate women of quality and virtue for their love to their husbands, Sir Jas-per; a woman is hated by 'em as much for loving her husband as for loving their money. But pray, let's be gone. 75

HORNER. You do well, madam, for I have nothing that you came for; I have brought over not so much as a bawdy picture, new postures,° nor the second part of the Escole des Filles;° nor— 80

QUACK [apart to HORNER]. Hold, for shame sir! what d'ye mean? You'll ruin yourself for ever with the sex—

SIR JASPER FIDGET. Ha! ha! ha! he hates wom-en perfectly, I find. 85

MRS. DAINTY FIDGET. What pity 'tis he should!

---

bills handbills
kissing your hands paying a formal visit

Mercury Sir Jasper implies that an overdose of mer-cury, used in treating syphilis, rendered Horner impotent.
postures depictions of postures for copulation
Escole des Filles School for Whores, a pornographic book

LADY FIDGET. Ay, he's a base rude fellow for't. But affectation makes not a woman more odious to them than virtue.

HORNER. Because your virtue is your greatest
5 affectation, madam.

LADY FIDGET. How, you saucy fellow! would you wrong my honor?

HORNER. If I could.

LADY FIDGET. How d'ye mean, sir?

10 SIR JASPER FIDGET. Ha! ha! ha! no, he can't wrong your Ladyship's honor, upon my honor; he, poor man—hark you in your ear—a mere eunuch.

LADY FIDGET. O filthy French beast! foh! foh!
15 why do we stay? let's be gone. I can't endure the sight of him.

SIR JASPER FIDGET. Stay but till the chairs° come; they'll be here presently.

LADY FIDGET. No, no.

20 SIR JASPER FIDGET. Nor can I stay longer. 'Tis —let me see, a quarter and a half quarter of a minute past eleven. The council° will be sat; I must away. Business must be preferred always before love and ceremony with the wise, Mr.
25 Horner.

HORNER. And the impotent, Sir Jasper.

SIR JASPER FIDGET. Ay, ay, the impotent, Master Horner; ha! ha! ha!

LADY FIDGET. What, leave us with a filthy man
30 alone in his lodgings?

SIR JASPER FIDGET. He's an innocent man now, you know. Pray stay, I'll hasten the chairs to you.—Mr. Horner, your servant; I should be glad to see you at my house. Pray come and
35 dine with me, and play at cards with my wife after dinner; you are fit for women at that game yet, ha! ha!—[*Aside.*] 'Tis as much a husband's prudence to provide innocent diversion for a wife as to hinder her unlawful plea-
40 sures; and he had better employ her than let her employ herself.—Farewell.

HORNER. Your servant, Sir Jasper.

[*Exit* SIR JASPER.]

LADY FIDGET. I will not stay with him, foh!—

HORNER. Nay, madam, I beseech you stay, 45 if it be but to see I can be as civil to ladies yet as they would desire.

LADY FIDGET. No, no, foh! you cannot be civil to ladies.

MRS. DAINTY FIDGET. You as civil as ladies 50 would desire?

LADY FIDGET. No, no, no, foh! foh! foh!

[*Exeunt* LADY FIDGET *and* MRS. DAINTY FIDGET.]

QUACK. Now, I think I, or you yourself, 55 rather, have done your business with the women.

HORNER. Thou art an ass. Don't you see already, upon the report and my carriage,° this grave man of business leaves his wife in my 60 lodgings, invites me to his house and wife, who before would not be acquainted with me out of jealousy?

QUACK. Nay, by this means you may be the more acquainted with the husbands, but the 65 less with the wives.

HORNER. Let me alone; if I can but abuse the husbands, I'll soon disabuse the wives. Stay— I'll reckon you up the advantages I am like to have by my stratagem. First, I shall be rid of 70 all my old acquaintances, the most insatiable sorts of duns, that invade our lodgings in a morning; and next to the pleasure of making a new mistress is that of being rid of an old one, and of all old debts. Love, when it comes to be 75 so, is paid the most unwillingly.

QUACK. Well, you may be so rid of your old acquaintances; but how will you get any new ones?

HORNER. Doctor, thou wilt never make a good 80 chemist,° thou art so incredulous and impatient. Ask but all the young fellows of the town if they do not lose more time, like huntsmen, in starting the game, than in running it down. One knows not where to find 'em, who will or will 85 not. Women of quality are so civil you can hardly distinguish love from good breeding,

---

chairs sedan chairs, sent for because the carriage broke down
council the King's Privy Council, of which Sir Jasper is a member

carriage behavior (in avoiding the society of ladies)
a good chemist chemists, like alchemists before them, were expected to be men of exemplary virtue

and a man is often mistaken; but now I can be sure she that shows an aversion to me loves the sport, as those women that are gone, whom I warrant to be right. And then the next thing
5 is, your women of honor, as you call 'em, are only chary of their reputations, not their persons; and 'tis scandal they would avoid, not men. Now may I have, by the reputation of an eunuch, the privileges of one, and be seen in
10 a lady's chamber in a morning as early as her husband; kiss virgins before their parents or lovers; and may be, in short, the *passe-partout*° of the town. Now, Doctor.

QUACK. Nay, now you shall be the doctor,
15 and your process is so new that we do not know but it may succeed.

HORNER. Not so new neither; *probatum est,*° Doctor.

QUACK. Well, I wish you luck and many
20 patients, whilst I go to mine.

[*Exit.*]

[*Enter* HARCOURT *and* DORILANT.]

HARCOURT. Come, your appearance at the play yesterday has, I hope, hardened you for
25 the future against the women's contempt and the men's raillery; and now you'll abroad as you were wont.

HORNER. Did I not bear it bravely?

DORILANT. With a most theatrical impudence,
30 nay, more than the orange-wenches show there, or a drunken vizard-mask,° or a greatbellied° actress; nay, or the most impudent of creatures, an ill poet; or what is yet more impudent, a second-hand critic.

35 HORNER. But what say the ladies? have they no pity?

HARCOURT. What ladies? The vizard-masks, you know, never pity a man when all's gone, though in their service.

40 DORILANT. And for the women in the boxes, you'd never pity them when 'twas in your power.

HARCOURT. They say 'tis pity but all that deal with common women should be served so.

DORILANT. Nay, I dare swear they won't 45 admit you to play at cards with them, go to plays with 'em, or do the little duties which other shadows of men are wont to do for 'em.

HORNER. Who do you call shadows of men?

DORILANT. Half-men. 50

HORNER. What, boys?

DORILANT. Ay, your old boys, old *beaux garçons,*° who, like superannuated stallions, are suffered to run, feed, and whinny with the mares as long as they live, though they can do 55 nothing else.

HORNER. Well, a pox on love and wenching! Women serve but to keep a man from better company. Though I can't enjoy them, I shall you the more. Good fellowship and friendship 60 are lasting, rational, and manly pleasures.

HARCOURT. For all that, give me some of those pleasures you call effeminate too; they help to relish one another.

HORNER. They disturb one another. 65

HARCOURT. No, mistresses are like books. If you pore upon them too much, they doze you, and make you unfit for company; but if used discreetly, you are the fitter for conversation by 'em. 70

DORILANT. A mistress should be like a little country retreat near the town; not to dwell in constantly, but only for a night and away, to taste the town the better when a man returns.

HORNER. I tell you, 'tis as hard to be a good 75 fellow, a good friend, and a lover of women, as 'tis to be a good fellow, a good friend, and a lover of money. You cannot follow both, then choose your side. Wine gives you liberty, love takes it away. 80

DORILANT. Gad, he's in the right on't.

HORNER. Wine gives you joy; love, grief and tortures, besides the chirurgeon's. Wine makes us witty; love, only sots. Wine makes us sleep; love breaks it. 85

DORILANT. By the world, he has reason, Harcourt.

HORNER. Wine makes—

---

passe-partout   master key
probatum est   "it has been put to the test," as previously in the classical comedy *The Eunuch* by the Roman dramatist Terence
vizard-mask   a fashionable prostitute
great-bellied   obviously pregnant

beaux garçons   dandies; men-about-town

DORILANT. Ay, wine makes us—makes us princes; love makes us beggars, poor rogues, egad—and wine—

HORNER. So, there's one converted.—No, no, love and wine, oil and vinegar.

HARCOURT. I grant it; love will still be uppermost.

HORNER. Come, for my part, I will have only those glorious manly pleasures of being very drunk and very slovenly.

[*Enter* BOY.]

BOY. Mr. Sparkish is below, sir.

[*Exit.*]

HARCOURT. What, my dear friend! a rogue that is fond of me, only I think, for abusing him.

DORILANT. No, he can no more think the men laugh at him than that women jilt him, his opinion of himself is so good.

HORNER. Well, there's another pleasure by drinking I thought not of—I shall lose his acquaintance, because he cannot drink; and you know 'tis a very hard thing to be rid of him, for he's one of those nauseous offerers at wit, who, like the worst fiddlers, run themselves into all companies.

HARCOURT. One that, by being in the company of men of sense, would pass for one.

HORNER. And may so to the short-sighted world, as a false jewel amongst true ones is not discerned at a distance. His company is as troublesome to us as a cuckold's when you have a mind to his wife's.

HARCOURT. No, the rogue will not let us enjoy one another, but ravishes our conversation, though he signifies no more to't than Sir Martin Mar-all's° gaping, and awkward thrumming upon the lute, does to his man's voice and music.

DORILANT. And to pass for a wit in town shows himself a fool every night to us, that are guilty of the plot.

HORNER. Such wits as he are, to a company of reasonable men, like rooks to the gamesters, who only fill a room at the table, but are so far from contributing to the play, that they only serve to spoil the fancy of those that do.

DORILANT. Nay, they are used like rooks too, snubbed, checked, and abused; yet the rogues will hang on.

HORNER. A pox on 'em, and all that force nature, and would be still what she forbids 'em! Affectation is her greatest monster.

HARCOURT. Most men are the contraries to that they would seem. Your bully, you see, is a coward with a long sword; the little humbly fawning physician, with his ebony cane, is he that destroys men.

DORILANT. The usurer, a poor rogue, possessed of mouldy bonds and mortgages; and we they call spendthrifts are only wealthy who lay out his money upon daily new purchases of pleasure.

HORNER. Ay, your arrantest cheat is your trustee or executor, your jealous man, the greatest cuckold, your churchman the greatest atheist, and your noisy pert rogue of a wit, the greatest fop, dullest ass, and worst company, as you shall see; for here he comes.

[*Enter* SPARKISH.]

SPARKISH. How is't, sparks?° how is't? Well, faith, Harry, I must rally thee a little, ha! ha! ha! upon the report in town of thee, ha! ha! ha! I can't hold i'faith; shall I speak?

HORNER. Yes; but you'll be so bitter then.

SPARKISH. Honest Dick and Frank here shall answer for me, I will not be extreme bitter, by the universe.

HARCOURT. We will be bound in ten-thousand-pound bond, he shall not be bitter at all.

DORILANT. Nor sharp, nor sweet.

HORNER. What, not downright insipid?

SPARKISH. Nay then, since you are so brisk, and provoke me, take what follows. You must know, I was discoursing and rallying with some ladies yesterday, and they happened to talk of the fine new signs in town.

HORNER. Very fine ladies, I believe.

SPARKISH. Said I, I know where the best new sign is.—Where? says one of the ladies.—In

---

Martin Mar-all in a comedy by Dryden a character who serenades his mistress in pantomime while his servant actually makes the music

sparks witty gentlemen

Covent Garden, I replied.—Said another, In what street?—In Russell Street, answered I.—Lord, says another, I'm sure there was ne'er a fine new sign there yesterday.—Yes, but there
5 was, said I again, and it came out of France, and has been there a fortnight.

DORILANT. A pox! I can hear no more, prithee.

HORNER. No, hear him out; let him tune his crowd° a while.

10 HARCOURT. The worst music, the greatest preparation.

SPARKISH. Nay, faith, I'll make you laugh.—It cannot be, says a third lady.—Yes, yes, quoth I again.—Says a fourth lady—

15 HORNER. Look to't, we'll have no more ladies.

SPARKISH. No—then mark, mark, now. Said I to the fourth, Did you never see Mr. Horner? he lodges in Russell Street, and he's a sign° of a man, you know, since he came out of France;
20 ha! ha! ha!

HORNER. But the devil take me if thine be the sign of a jest.

SPARKISH. With that they all fell a-laughing, till they bepissed themselves. What, but it does
25 not move you, methinks? Well, I see one had as good go to law without a witness, as break a jest without a laugher on one's side.—Come, come, sparks, but where do we dine? I have left at Whitehall an earl to dine with you.

30 DORILANT. Why, I thought thou hadst loved a man with a title better than a suit with a French trimming to't.

HARCOURT. Go to him again.

SPARKISH. No, sir, a wit to me is the greatest
35 title in the world.

HORNER. But go dine with your earl, sir; he may be exceptious.° We are your friends, and will not take it ill to be left, I do assure you.

HARCOURT. Nay, faith, he shall go to him.

40 SPARKISH. Nay, pray, gentlemen.

DORILANT. We'll thrust you out, if you won't; what, disappoint anybody for us?

SPARKISH. Nay, dear gentlemen, hear me.

HORNER. No, no, sir, by no means; pray go, sir.   45

SPARKISH. Why, dear rogues—

DORILANT. No, no.

[*They all thrust him out of the room.*]

ALL. Ha! ha! ha!

[SPARKISH *returns.*]   50

SPARKISH. But, sparks, pray hear me. What, d'ye think I'll eat then with gay shallow fops and silent coxcombs? I think wit as necessary at dinner as a glass of good wine, and that's the reason I never have any stomach when I eat   55
alone.—Come, but where do we dine?

HORNER. Even where you will.

SPARKISH. At Chateline's?

DORILANT. Yes, if you will.

SPARKISH. Or at the Cock?   60

DORILANT. Yes, if you please.

SPARKISH. Or at the Dog and Partridge?

HORNER. Ay, if you have a mind to't; for we shall dine at neither.

SPARKISH. Pshaw! with your fooling we shall   65
lose the new play; and I would no more miss seeing a new play the first day, than I would miss sitting in the wits' row. Therefore I'll go fetch my mistress,° and away.

[*Exit.*]   70

[HORNER, HARCOURT, DORILANT *remain; enter* MR. PINCHWIFE.]

HORNER. Who have we here? Pinchwife?

PINCHWIFE. Gentlemen, your humble servant.

HORNER. Well, Jack, by thy long absence from   75
the town, the grumness of thy countenance, and the slovenliness of thy habit, I should give thee joy, should I not, of marriage?

PINCHWIFE [*aside*]. Death! does he know I'm married too? I thought to have concealed it from   80
him at least.—My long stay in the country will excuse my dress; and I have a suit of law that brings me up to town, that puts me out of humor. Besides, I must give Sparkish tomorrow five thousand pound to lie with my sister.   85

HORNER. Nay, you country gentlemen, rather than not purchase, will buy anything; and he is

---

crowd fiddle
sign mere representation
exceptious take exception to your breaking an engagement

mistress in the seventeenth century this term was a title of courtesy or endearment for a lady, either married or unmarried

a cracked title,° if we may quibble. Well, but am I to give thee joy? I heard thou wert married.

PINCHWIFE. What then?

HORNER. Why, the next thing that is to be heard is, thou'rt a cuckold.

PINCHWIFE [*aside*]. Insupportable name!

HORNER. But I did not expect marriage from such a whoremaster as you, one that knew the town so much, and women so well.

PINCHWIFE. Why, I have married no London wife.

HORNER. Pshaw! that's all one. That grave circumspection in marrying a country wife is like refusing a deceitful pampered Smithfield jade° to go and be cheated by a friend in the country.

PINCHWIFE [*aside*]. A pox on him and his simile!—At least we are a little surer of the breed there, know what her keeping has been, whether foiled° or unsound.

HORNER. Come, come, I have known a clap gotten in Wales; and there are cousins, justices' clerks, and chaplains in the country, I won't say coachmen. But she's handsome and young?

PINCHWIFE [*aside*]. I'll answer as I should do. —No, no; she has no beauty but her youth, no attraction but her modesty; wholesome, homely, and huswifely; that's all.

DORILANT. He talks as like a grazier° as he looks.

PINCHWIFE. She's too awkward, ill-favored, and silly to bring to town.

HARCOURT. Then methinks you should bring her to be taught breeding.

PINCHWIFE. To be taught! no, sir, I thank you. Good wives and private soldiers should be ignorant. [*Aside.*] I'll keep her from your instructions, I warrant you.

HARCOURT [*aside*]. The rogue is as jealous as if his wife were not ignorant.

HORNER. Why, if she be ill-favored, there will be less danger here for you than by leaving her in the country. We have such variety of dainties that we are seldom hungry.

DORILANT. But they have always coarse, constant, swingeing° stomachs in the country.

HARCOURT. Foul feeders indeed!

DORILANT. And your hospitality is great there.

HARCOURT. Open house; every man's welcome.

PINCHWIFE. So, so, gentlemen.

HORNER. But prithee, why wouldst thou marry her? If she be ugly, ill-bred, and silly, she must be rich then.

PINCHWIFE. As rich as if she brought me twenty thousand pound out of this town; for she'll be as sure not to spend her moderate portion as a London baggage would be to spend hers, let it be what it would: so 'tis all one. Then, because she's ugly, she's the likelier to be my own; and being ill-bred, she'll hate conversation; and since silly and innocent, will not know the difference betwixt a man of one-and-twenty and one of forty.

HORNER. Nine—to my knowledge. But if she be silly, she'll expect as much from a man of forty-nine, as from him of one-and-twenty. But methinks wit is more necessary than beauty; and I think no young woman ugly, that has it, and no handsome woman agreeable without it.

PINCHWIFE. 'Tis my maxim, he's a fool that marries; but he's a greater that does not marry a fool. What is wit in a wife good for, but to make a man a cuckold?

HORNER. Yes, to keep it from his knowledge.

PINCHWIFE. A fool cannot contrive to make her husband a cuckold.

HORNER. No; but she'll club° with a man that can and what is worse, if she cannot make her husband a cuckold, she'll make him jealous and pass for one; and then 'tis all one.

PINCHWIFE. Well, well, I'll take care for one. My wife shall make me no cuckold, though she had your help, Mr. Horner. I understand the town, sir.

---

cracked title bad bargain
Smithfield jade a mare sold at a London horse market
  where cheating was common
foiled of a horse, lamed; of a woman, deflowered
grazier cattle herder

swingeing whopping
club associate

DORILANT [*aside*]. His help!

HARCOURT [*aside*]. He's come newly to town, it seems, and has not heard how things are with him.

5 HORNER. But tell me, has marriage cured thee of whoring, which it seldom does?

HARCOURT. 'Tis more than age can do.

HORNER. No, the word is, I'll marry and live honest; but a marriage vow is like a penitent
10 gamester's oath, and entering into bonds and penalties to stint himself to such a particular small sum at play for the future, which makes him but the more eager; and not being able to hold out, loses his money again, and his forfeit
15 to boot.

DORILANT. Ay, ay, a gamester will be a gamester whilst his money lasts, and a whoremaster whilst his vigor.

HARCOURT. Nay, I have known 'em, when
20 they are broke, and can lose no more, keep a-fumbling with the box in their hands to fool with only, and hinder other gamesters.

DORILANT. That had wherewithal to make lusty stakes.

25 PINCHWIFE. Well, gentlemen, you may laugh at me; but you shall never lie with my wife; I know the town.

HORNER. But prithee, was not the way you were in better? is not keeping° better than
30 marriage?

PINCHWIFE. A pox on't! the jades would jilt me, I could never keep a whore to myself.

HORNER. So, then, you only married to keep a whore to yourself. Well, but let me tell you,
35 women, as you say, are like soldiers, made constant and loyal by good pay, rather than by oaths and covenants. Therefore I'd advise my friends to keep rather than marry, since too I find, by your example, it does not serve one's
40 turn; for I saw you yesterday in the eighteen-penny place° with a pretty country wench.

PINCHWIFE [*aside*]. How the devil! did he see my wife then? I sat there that she might not be seen. But she shall never go to a play again.

45 HORNER. What! dost thou blush at nine-and-forty for having been seen with a wench?

DORILANT. No, faith, I warrant 'twas his wife, which he seated there out of sight; for he's a cunning rogue, and understands the town.

HARCOURT. He blushes. Then 'twas his wife; 50 for men are now more ashamed to be seen with them in public than with a wench.

PINCHWIFE [*aside*]. Hell and damnation! I'm undone, since Horner has seen her, and they know 'twas she. 55

HORNER. But prithee, was it thy wife? She was exceedingly pretty; I was in love with her at that distance.

PINCHWIFE. You are like never to be nearer to her. Your servant, gentlemen. [*Offers to go.*] 60

HORNER. Nay, prithee stay.

PINCHWIFE. I cannot; I will not.

HORNER. Come, you shall dine with us.

PINCHWIFE. I have dined already.

HORNER. Come, I know thou hast not. I'll 65 treat thee, dear rogue; thou shalt spend none of thy Hampshire money today.

PINCHWIFE [*aside*]. Treat me! So, he uses me already like his cuckold.

HORNER. Nay, you shall not go. 70

PINCHWIFE. I must; I have business at home. [*Exit.*]

HARCOURT. To beat his wife. He's as jealous of her as a Cheapside husband of a Covent Garden wife.° 75

HORNER. Why, 'tis as hard to find an old whoremaster without jealousy and the gout, as a young one without fear or the pox.

As gout in age from pox in youth proceeds, So wenching past, then jealousy succeeds, 80 The worst disease that love and wenching
                                             [breeds.

[*Exeunt.*]

ACT II

[*A room in* PINCHWIFE's *house.*]

[MRS. MARGERY PINCHWIFE *and* ALITHEA. 85 PINCHWIFE *peeping behind at the door.*]

MRS. PINCHWIFE. Pray, sister, where are the best fields and woods to walk in, in London?

---

keeping keeping a prostitute
eighteen-penny place cheap, inconspicuous seats in a theater

Cheapside . . . Covent Garden wife as a merchant who has married into a newly rich family

ALITHEA. A pretty question! Why, sister, Mulberry Garden and St. James's Park; and, for close walks, the New Exchange.

MRS. PINCHWIFE. Pray, sister, tell me why my
5 husband looks so grum here in town, and keeps me up so close, and will not let me go a-walking, nor let me wear my best gown yesterday.

ALITHEA. Oh, he's jealous, sister.

MRS. PINCHWIFE. Jealous! what's that?

10 ALITHEA. He's afraid you should love another man.

MRS. PINCHWIFE. How should he be afraid of my loving another man, when he will not let me see any but himself?

15 ALITHEA. Did he not carry you yesterday to a play?

MRS. PINCHWIFE. Ay; but we sat amongst ugly people. He would not let me come near the gentry, who sat under us, so that I could not
20 see 'em. He told me none but naughty women sat there, whom they toused and moused. But I would have ventured, for all that.

ALITHEA. But how did you like the play?

MRS. PINCHWIFE. Indeed I was a-weary of the
25 play, but I liked hugeously the actors. They are the goodliest, properest men, sister!

ALITHEA. Oh, but you must not like the actors, sister.

MRS. PINCHWIFE. Ay, how should I help it,
30 sister? Pray, sister, when my husband comes in, will you ask leave for me to go a-walking?

ALITHEA [*aside*]. A-walking! ha! ha! Lord, a country-gentlewoman's pleasure is the drudgery of a footpost;° and she requires as much
35 airing as her husband's horses.—But here comes your husband. I'll ask, though I'm sure he'll not grant it.

MRS. PINCHWIFE. He says he won't let me go abroad for fear of catching the pox.

40 ALITHEA. Fy! the small-pox you should say.

[*Enter* PINCHWIFE.]

MRS. PINCHWIFE. O my dear, dear bud,° welcome home! Why dost thou look so fropish?

Who has nangered° thee?

PINCHWIFE. You're a fool. 45

[MRS. PINCHWIFE *goes aside, and cries.*]

ALITHEA. Faith, so she is, for crying for no fault, poor tender creature!

PINCHWIFE. What, you would have her as impudent as yourself, as arrant a jillflirt,° a gad- 50 der, a magpie; and to say all, a mere notorious town-woman?

ALITHEA. Brother, you are my only censurer; and the honor of your family shall sooner suffer in your wife there than in me, though I take the 55 innocent liberty of the town.

PINCHWIFE. Hark you, mistress, do not talk so before my wife.—The innocent liberty of the town!

ALITHEA. Why, pray, who boasts of any in- 60 trigue with me? what lampoon has made my name notorious? what ill women frequent my lodgings? I keep no company with any women of scandalous reputations.

PINCHWIFE. No, you keep the men of scan- 65 dalous reputations company.

ALITHEA. Where? would you not have me civil? answer 'em in a box at the plays, in the drawing-room at Whitehall, in St. James's Park, Mulberry Garden, or— 70

PINCHWIFE. Hold, hold! Do not teach my wife where the men are to be found; I believe she's the worse for your town-documents° already. I bid you keep her in ignorance, as I do.

MRS. PINCHWIFE. Indeed, be not angry with 75 her, bud, she will tell me nothing of the town, though I ask her a thousand times a day.

PINCHWIFE. Then you are very inquisitive to know, I find?

MRS. PINCHWIFE. Not I indeed, dear; I hate 80 London. Our place-house in the country is worth a thousand of't; would I were there again!

PINCHWIFE. So you shall, I warrant. But were you not talking of plays and players when I 85 came in? [*To* ALITHEA.] You are her encourager in such discourses.

MRS. PINCHWIFE. No, indeed, dear; she chid

---

footpost someone who goes errands on foot, who cannot afford to ride

bud a rustic term of endearment; but also meaning a yearling calf that has not yet grown horns (hence with the usual allusion to a cuckold's horns)

fropish...nangered peevish, angered
jillflirt giddy girl
town-documents information about London social life

me just now for liking the playermen.

PINCHWIFE [*aside*]. Nay, if she be so innocent as to own to me her liking them, there is no hurt in't.—Come, my poor rogue, but thou 5 lik'st none better than me?

MRS. PINCHWIFE. Yes, indeed, but I do. The playermen are finer folks.

PINCHWIFE. But you love none better than me?

10 MRS. PINCHWIFE. You are mine own dear bud, and I know you. I hate a stranger.

PINCHWIFE. Ay, my dear, you must love me only, and not be like the naughty town-women, who only hate their husbands, and love every 15 man else; love plays, visits, fine coaches, fine clothes, fiddles, balls, treats, and so lead a wicked town-life.

MRS. PINCHWIFE. Nay, if to enjoy all these things be a town-life, London is not so bad a 20 place, dear.

PINCHWIFE. How! if you love me, you must hate London.

ALITHEA [*aside*]. The fool has forbid me discovering to her the pleasures of the town, and 25 he is now setting her agog upon them himself.

MRS. PINCHWIFE. But, husband, do the town-women love the playermen too?

PINCHWIFE. Yes, I warrant you.

MRS. PINCHWIFE. Ay, I warrant you.

30 PINCHWIFE. Why, you do not, I hope?

MRS. PINCHWIFE. No, no, bud. But why have we no playermen in the country?

PINCHWIFE. Ha!—Mrs. Minx, ask me no more to go to a play.

35 MRS. PINCHWIFE. Nay, why love? I did not care for going; but when you forbid me, you make me, as 'twere, desire it.

ALITHEA [*aside*]. So 'twill be in other things, I warrant.

40 MRS. PINCHWIFE. Pray let me go to a play, dear.

PINCHWIFE. Hold your peace, I wo' not.

MRS. PINCHWIFE. Why, love?

PINCHWIFE. Why, I'll tell you.

45 ALITHEA [*aside*]. Nay, if he'll tell her, she'll give him more cause to forbid her that place.

MRS. PINCHWIFE. Pray why, dear?

PINCHWIFE. First, you like the actors; and the gallants may like you.

MRS. PINCHWIFE. What, a homely country 50 girl! No, bud, nobody will like me.

PINCHWIFE. I tell you yes, they may.

MRS. PINCHWIFE. No, no, you jest—I won't believe; I will go.

PINCHWIFE. I tell you then, that one of the 55 lewdest fellows in town, who saw you there, told me he was in love with you.

MRS. PINCHWIFE. Indeed! who, who, pray who was't?

PINCHWIFE [*aside*]. I've gone too far, and 60 slipped before I was aware; how overjoyed she is!

MRS. PINCHWIFE. Was it any Hampshire gallant, any of our neighbors? I promise you, I am beholden to him. 65

PINCHWIFE. I promise you, you lie; for he would but ruin you, as he has done hundreds. He has no other love for women but that; such as he look upon women, like basilisks,° but to destroy 'em. 70

MRS. PINCHWIFE. Ay, but if he loves me, why should he ruin me? answer me to that. Methinks he should not, I would do him no harm.

ALITHEA. Ha! ha! ha!

PINCHWIFE. 'Tis very well; but I'll keep him 75 from doing you any harm, or me either. But here comes company; get you in, get you in.

MRS. PINCHWIFE. But, pray, husband, is he a pretty gentleman that loves me?

PINCHWIFE. In, baggage, in. [*Thrusts her in,* 80 *shuts the door.*]

[*Enter* SPARKISH *and* HARCOURT.]

What, all the lewd libertines of the town brought to my lodging by this easy coxcomb! 'Sdeath, I'll not suffer it. 85

SPARKISH. Here, Harcourt, do you approve my choice?—Dear little rogue. I told you I'd bring you acquainted with all my friends, the wits and—[HARCOURT *salutes her.*]

PINCHWIFE. Ay, they shall know her, as well 90 as you yourself will, I warrant you.

SPARKISH. This is one of those, my pretty rogue, that are to dance at your wedding to-

basilisks legendary reptiles whose very glance was fatal

morrow; and him you must bid welcome ever, to what you and I have.

PINCHWIFE [*aside*]. Monstrous!

SPARKISH. Harcourt, how dost thou like her, faith? Nay, dear, do not look down; I should hate to have a wife of mine out of countenance at anything.

PINCHWIFE [*aside*]. Wonderful!

SPARKISH. Tell me, I say, Harcourt, how dost thou like her? Thou hast stared upon her enough to resolve me.

HARCOURT. So infinitely well, that I could wish I had a mistress too, that might differ from her in nothing but her love and engagement to you.

ALITHEA. Sir, Master Sparkish has often told me that his acquaintance were all wits and railleurs, and now I find it.

SPARKISH. No, by the universe, madam, he does not rally now; you may believe him, I do assure you, he is the honestest, worthiest, true-hearted gentleman—a man of such perfect honor, he would say nothing to a lady he does not mean.

PINCHWIFE [*aside*]. Praising another man to his mistress!

HARCOURT. Sir, you are so beyond expectation obliging, that—

SPARKISH. Nay, egad, I am sure you do admire her extremely; I see't in your eyes.—He does admire you, madam.—By the world, don't you?

HARCOURT. Yes, above the world, or the most glorious part of it, her whole sex; and till now I never thought I should have envied you or any man about to marry, but you have the best excuse for marriage I ever knew.

ALITHEA. Nay, now, sir, I'm satisfied you are of the society of the wits and railleurs, since you cannot spare your friend, even when he is but too civil to you; but the surest sign is, since you are an enemy to marriage, for that I hear you hate as much as business or bad wine.

HARCOURT. Truly, madam, I never was an enemy to marriage till now, because marriage was never an enemy to me before.

ALITHEA. But why, sir, is marriage an enemy to you now? Because it robs you of your friend here? for you look upon a friend married as one gone into a monastery, that is, dead to the world.

HARCOURT. 'Tis indeed, because you marry him; I see, madam, you can guess my meaning. I do confess heartily and openly I wish it were in my power to break the match; by Heavens I would.

SPARKISH. Poor Frank!

ALITHEA. Would you be so unkind to me?

HARCOURT. No, no, 'tis not because I would be unkind to you.

SPARKISH. Poor Frank! no gad, 'tis only his kindness to me.

PINCHWIFE [*aside*]. Great kindness to you indeed! Insensible fop, let a man make love to his wife to his face!

SPARKISH. Come, dear Frank, for all my wife there, that shall be, thou shalt enjoy me sometimes, dear rogue. By my honor, we men of wit condole for our deceased brother in marriage, as much as for one dead in earnest; I think that was prettily said of me, ha, Harcourt?—But come, Frank, be not melancholy for me.

HARCOURT. No, I assure you, I am not melancholy for you.

SPARKISH. Prithee, Frank, dost think my wife that shall be there, a fine person?

HARCOURT. I could gaze upon her till I became as blind as you are.

SPARKISH. How as I am? how?

HARCOURT. Because you are a lover, and true lovers are blind, struck blind.

SPARKISH. True, true; but by the world, she has wit too, as well as beauty. Go, go with her into a corner, and try if she has wit; talk to her anything; she's bashful before me.

HARCOURT. Indeed if a woman wants wit in a corner, she has it nowhere.

ALITHEA [*aside to* SPARKISH]. Sir, you dispose of me a little before your time—

SPARKISH. Nay, nay, madam, let me have an earnest of your obedience, or—go, go, madam—[HARCOURT *courts* ALITHEA *aside*].

PINCHWIFE. How, sir! if you are not concerned for the honor of a wife, I am for that of a sister; he shall not debauch her. Be a pander to your own wife! bring men to her! let 'em make love before your face! thrust 'em into a corner together, then leave 'em in private! is this your town wit and conduct?

SPARKISH. Ha! ha! ha! a silly wise rogue would make one laugh more than a stark fool, ha! ha! I shall burst. Nay, you shall not disturb 'em; I'll vex thee, by the world.

[*Struggles with* PINCHWIFE *to keep him from* HARCOURT *and* ALITHEA.]

ALITHEA. The writings are drawn, sir, settlements made; 'tis too late, sir, and past all revocation.

HARCOURT. Then so is my death.

ALITHEA. I would not be unjust to him.

HARCOURT. Then why to me so?

ALITHEA. I have no obligation to you.

HARCOURT. My love.

ALITHEA. I had his before.

HARCOURT. You never had it; he wants, you see, jealousy, the only infallible sign of it.

ALITHEA. Love proceeds from esteem; he cannot distrust my virtue; besides, he loves me, or he would not marry me.

HARCOURT. Marrying you is no more sign of his love than bribing your woman, that he may marry you, is a sign of his generosity. Marriage is rather a sign of interest than love; and he that marries a fortune covets a mistress, not loves her. But if you take marriage for a sign of love, take it from me immediately.

ALITHEA. No, now you have put a scruple in my head; but in short, sir, to end our dispute, I must marry him; my reputation would suffer in the world else.

HARCOURT. No; if you do marry him, with your pardon, madam, your reputation suffers in the world, and you would be thought in necessity for a cloak.

ALITHEA. Nay, now you are rude, sir.—Mr Sparkish, pray come hither, your friend here is very troublesome, and very loving.

HARCOURT [*aside to* ALITHEA]. Hold! hold!—

PINCHWIFE. D'ye hear that?

SPARKISH. Why, d'ye think I'll seem to be jealous, like a country bumpkin?

PINCHWIFE. No, rather be a cuckold, like a credulous cit.

HARCOURT. Madam, you would not have been so little generous as to have told him.

ALITHEA. Yes, since you could be so little generous as to wrong him.

HARCOURT. Wrong him! no man can do't, he's beneath an injury; a bubble,° a coward, a senseless idiot, a wretch so contemptible to all the world but you, that—

ALITHEA. Hold, do not rail at him, for since he is like to be my husband, I am resolved to like him; nay, I think I am obliged to tell him you are not his friend.—Master Sparkish, Master Sparkish!

SPARKISH. What, what?—Now, dear rogue, has not she wit?

HARCOURT [*speaks surlily*]. Not as much as I thought, and hoped she had.

ALITHEA. Mr. Sparkish, do you bring people to rail at you?

HARCOURT. Madam—

SPARKISH. How! no; but if he does rail at me, 'tis but in jest, I warrant; what we wits do for one another, and never take any notice of it.

ALITHEA. He spoke so scurrilously of you, I had no patience to hear him; besides, he has been making love to me.

HARCOURT [*aside*]. True, damned tell-tale woman!

SPARKISH. Pshaw! to show his parts—we wits rail and make love often, but to show our parts; as we have no affections, so we have no malice, we—

ALITHEA. He said you were a wretch below an injury—

SPARKISH. Pshaw!

HARCOURT [*aside*]. Damned, senseless, impudent, virtuous jade! Well, since she won't let me have her, she'll do as good, she'll make me hate her.

ALITHEA. A common bubble—

SPARKISH. Pshaw!

ALITHEA. A coward—

SPARKISH. Pshaw, pshaw!

ALITHEA. A senseless, drivelling idiot—

SPARKISH. How! did he disparage my parts? Nay, then, my honor's concerned, I can't put up that, sir, by the world—brother, help me to kill him—[*aside*] I may draw now, since we

bubble nitwit

have the odds of him—'tis a good occasion, too, before my mistress—[*offers to draw*].

ALITHEA. Hold, hold!

SPARKISH. What, what?

5 ALITHEA [*aside*]. I must not let 'em kill the gentleman neither, for his kindness to me. I am so far from hating him, that I wish my gallant had his person and understanding. Nay, if my honor—

10 SPARKISH. I'll be thy death.

ALITHEA. Hold, hold! Indeed, to tell the truth, the gentleman said after all, that what he spoke was but out of friendship to you.

SPARKISH. How! say I am—I am a fool, that 15 is no wit, out of friendship to me?

ALITHEA. Yes, to try whether I was concerned enough for you; and made love to me only to be satisfied of my virtue, for your sake.

HARCOURT [*aside*]. Kind, however.°

20 SPARKISH. Nay, if it were so, my dear rogue, I ask thee pardon; but why would not you tell me so, faith?

HARCOURT. Because I did not think on't, faith.

SPARKISH. Come, Horner does not come; Har- 25 court, let's be gone to the new play.—Come, madam.

ALITHEA. I will not go if you intend to leave me alone in the box and run into the pit,° as you use to do.

30 SPARKISH. Pshaw! I'll leave Harcourt with you in the box to entertain you, and that's as good; if I sat in the box, I should be thought no judge but of trimmings.°—Come away, Harcourt, lead her down.

35 [*Exeunt* SPARKISH, HARCOURT, *and* ALITHEA.]

PINCHWIFE. Well, go thy ways, for the flower of the true town fops, such as spend their estates before they come to 'em, and are cuckolds before they're married. But let me go back 40 to my own freehold.—How!

[*Enter* LADY FIDGET, MRS. DAINTY FIDGET, *and* MRS. SQUEAMISH.]

Kind, however because Alithea has put Harcourt's conduct in a good light
pit where ladies of dubious character showed themselves conspicuously
trimmings of ladies' dresses (rather than of the ladies themselves)

LADY FIDGET. Your servant, sir; where is your lady? We are come to wait upon her to the new play. 45

PINCHWIFE. New play!

LADY FIDGET. And my husband will wait upon you presently.

PINCHWIFE [*aside*]. Damn your civility.— Madam, by no means; I will not see Sir Jasper 50 here till I have waited upon him at home; nor shall my wife see you till she has waited upon your ladyship at your lodgings.

LADY FIDGET. Now we are here, sir?

PINCHWIFE. No, madam. 55

MRS. DAINTY FIDGET. Pray, let us see her.

MRS. SQUEAMISH. We will not stir till we see her.

PINCHWIFE [*aside*]. A pox on you all!—[*Goes to the door, and returns.*] She has locked the 60 door, and is gone abroad.

LADY FIDGET. No, you have locked the door, and she's within.

MRS. DAINTY FIDGET. They told us below she was here. 65

PINCHWIFE [*aside*]. Will nothing do?—Well, it must out then. To tell you the truth, ladies, which I was afraid to let you know before, lest it might endanger your lives, my wife has just now the small-pox come out upon her; do not 70 be frightened, but pray be gone, ladies; you shall not stay here in danger of your lives; pray get you gone, ladies.

LADY FIDGET. No, no, we have all had 'em.

MRS. SQUEAMISH. Alack, alack! 75

MRS. DAINTY FIDGET. Come, come, we must see how it goes with her; I understand the disease.

LADY FIDGET. Come!

PINCHWIFE [*aside*]. Well, there is no being too 80 hard for women at their own weapon, lying, therefore I'll quit the field.

[*Exit.*]

MRS. SQUEAMISH. Here's an example of jealousy! 85

LADY FIDGET. Indeed, as the world goes, I wonder there are no more jealous, since wives are so neglected.

MRS. DAINTY FIDGET. Pshaw! as the world goes, to what end should they be jealous? 90

LADY FIDGET. Foh! 'tis a nasty world.

MRS. SQUEAMISH. That men of parts, great acquaintance, and quality, should take up with and spend themselves and fortunes in keeping
5 little playhouse creatures, foh!

LADY FIDGET. Nay, that women of understanding, great acquaintance, and good quality, should fall a-keeping too of little creatures, foh!

MRS. SQUEAMISH. Why, 'tis the men of qual-
10 ity's fault; they never visit women of honor and reputation as they used to do; and have not so much as common civility for ladies of our rank, but use us with the same indifferency and ill-breeding as if we were all married to 'em.

15 LADY FIDGET. She says true; 'tis an arrant shame women of quality should be so slighted; methinks birth—birth should go for something; I have known men admired, courted, and followed for their titles only.

20 MRS. SQUEAMISH. Ay, one would think men of honor should not love, no more than marry, out of their own rank.

MRS. DAINTY FIDGET. Fy, fy, upon 'em! they are come to think cross breeding for themselves
25 best, as well as for their dogs and horses.

LADY FIDGET. They are dogs and horses for't.

MRS. SQUEAMISH. One would think, if not for love, for vanity a little.

MRS. DAINTY FIDGET. Nay, they do satisfy
30 their vanity upon us sometimes; and are kind to us in their report, tell all the world they lie with us.

LADY FIDGET. Damned rascals, that we should be only wronged by 'em! To report a man has
35 had a person, when he has not had a person, is the greatest wrong in the whole world that can be done to a person.

MRS. SQUEAMISH. Well, 'tis an arrant shame noble persons should be so wronged and ne-
40 glected.

LADY FIDGET. But still 'tis an arranter shame for a noble person to neglect her own honor, and defame her own noble person with little inconsiderable fellows, foh!

45 MRS. DAINTY FIDGET. I suppose the crime against our honor is the same with a man of quality as with another.

LADY FIDGET. How! no, sure, the man of

quality is likest one's husband, and therefore the fault should be the less. 50

MRS. DAINTY FIDGET. But then the pleasure should be the less.

LADY FIDGET. Fy, fy, fy, for shame, sister! whither shall we ramble? Be continent in your discourse, or I shall hate you. 55

MRS. DAINTY FIDGET. Besides, an intrigue is so much the more notorious for the man's quality.

MRS. SQUEAMISH. 'Tis true, nobody takes notice of a private man,° and therefore with him 60 'tis more secret; and the crime's the less when 'tis not known.

LADY FIDGET. You say true; i' faith, I think you are in the right on't; 'tis not an injury to a husband till it be an injury to our honors; so 65 that a woman of honor loses no honor with a private person; and to say truth—

MRS. DAINTY FIDGET [apart to MRS. SQUEAMISH]. So, the little fellow is grown a private person—with her— 70

LADY FIDGET. But still my dear, dear honor—

[Enter SIR JASPER, HORNER, and DORILANT.]

SIR JASPER FIDGET. Ay, my dear, dear of honor, thou hast still so much honor in thy mouth— 75

HORNER [aside]. That she has none elsewhere.

LADY FIDGET. Oh, what d'ye mean to bring in these upon us?

MRS. DAINTY FIDGET. Foh! these are as bad 80 as wits.

MRS. SQUEAMISH. Foh!

LADY FIDGET. Let us leave the room.

SIR JASPER FIDGET. Stay, stay; faith, to tell you the naked truth— 85

LADY FIDGET. Fy, Sir Jasper! do not use that word naked.

SIR JASPER FIDGET. Well, well, in short I have business at Whitehall, and cannot go to the play with you, therefore would have you go— 90

LADY FIDGET. With those two to a play?

SIR JASPER FIDGET. No, not with t'other, but with Mr. Horner; there can be no more scandal

private man not a person in public life and the public eye to go with him than with Mr. Tattle, or Master Limberham.°

LADY FIDGET. With that nasty fellow! no—no.

SIR JASPER FIDGET. Nay, prithee, dear, hear me. [*Whispers to* LADY FIDGET.]

HORNER. Ladies—

[HORNER, DORILANT *drawing near* MRS. SQUEAMISH *and* MRS. DAINTY FIDGET.]

MRS. DAINTY FIDGET. Stand off.

MRS. SQUEAMISH. Do not approach us.

MRS. DAINTY FIDGET. You herd with the wits, you are obscenity all over.

MRS. SQUEAMISH. And I would as soon look upon a picture of Adam and Eve without fig-leaves as any of you, if I could help it; therefore keep off, and do not make us sick.

DORILANT. What a devil are these?

HORNER. Why, these are pretenders to honor, as critics to wit, only by censuring others; and as every raw, peevish, out-of-humored, affected, dull, tea-drinking, arithmetical fop, sets up for a wit by railing at men of sense, so these for honor, by railing at the court, and ladies of as great honor as quality.

SIR JASPER FIDGET. Come, Mr. Horner, I must desire you to go with these ladies to the play, sir.

HORNER. I, sir?

SIR JASPER FIDGET. Ay, ay, come, sir.

HORNER. I must beg your pardon, sir, and theirs; I will not be seen in women's company in public again for the world.

SIR JASPER FIDGET. Ha, ha, strange aversion!

MRS. SQUEAMISH. No, he's for women's company in private.

SIR JASPER FIDGET. He—poor man—he—ha! ha! ha!

MRS. DAINTY FIDGET. 'Tis a greater shame amongst lewd fellows to be seen in virtuous women's company, than for the women to be seen with them.

HORNER. Indeed, madam, the time was I only hated virtuous women, but now I hate the other too; I beg your pardon, ladies.

LADY FIDGET. You are very obliging, sir, because we would not be troubled with you.

SIR JASPER FIDGET. In sober sadness, he shall go.

DORILANT. Nay, if he wo' not, I am ready to wait upon the ladies, and I think I am the fitter man.

SIR JASPER FIDGET. You, sir! no, I thank you for that. Master Horner is a privileged man amongst the virtuous ladies, 'twill be a great while before you are so; he! he! he! he's my wife's gallant; he! he! he! No, pray withdraw, sir, for as I take it, the virtuous ladies have no business with you.

DORILANT. And I am sure he can have none with them. 'Tis strange a man can't come amongst virtuous women now, but upon the same terms as men are admitted into the Great Turk's seraglio.° But heavens keep me from being an ombre° player with 'em!—But where is Pinchwife?

[*Exit.*]

SIR JASPER FIDGET. Come, come, man; what, avoid the sweet society of womankind? that sweet, soft, gentle, tame, noble creature, woman, made for man's companion—

HORNER. So is that soft, gentle, tame, and more noble creature a spaniel, and has all their tricks; can fawn, lie down, suffer beating, and fawn the more; barks at your friends when they come to see you, makes your bed hard, gives you fleas, and the mange sometimes. And all the difference is, the spaniel's the more faithful animal, and fawns but upon one master.

SIR JASPER FIDGET. He! he! he!

MRS. SQUEAMISH. Oh, the rude beast!

MRS. DAINTY FIDGET. Insolent brute!

LADY FIDGET. Brute! stinking, mortified, rotten French wether,° to dare—

SIR JASPER FIDGET. Hold, an't please your ladyship.—For shame, Master Horner! your

Tattle . . . Limberham by implication, silly old gentlemen who are capable only of bearing gossip or of "bending a leg" (a limber ham) in flattery

Great Turk's seraglio harem of the Sultan of Turkey. The only men permitted there as guards or servants were eunuchs.
ombre a fashionable card game
French wether a castrated ram; a eunuch

mother was a woman.—[*Aside.*] Now shall I never reconcile 'em.—[*Aside to* LADY FIDGET.] Hark you, madam, take my advice in your anger. You know you often want one to make
5   up your drolling pack of ombre players, and you may cheat him easily; for he's an ill game-ster, and consequently loves play. Besides, you know you have but two old civil gentlemen° (with stinking breaths too) to wait upon you
10 abroad; take in the third into your service. The others are but crazy;° and a lady should have a supernumerary gentleman-usher° as a super-numerary coach-horse, lest sometimes you should be forced to stay at home.
15   LADY FIDGET. But are you sure he loves play and has money?
        SIR JASPER FIDGET. He loves play as much as you, and has money as much as I.
        LADY FIDGET. Then I am contented to make
20 him pay for his scurrility. [*Aside.*] Money makes up in a measure all other wants in men. Those whom we cannot make hold for gal-lants, we make fine.°
        SIR JASPER FIDGET [*aside*]. So, so; now to mol-
25 lify, to wheedle him.—[*Aside to* HORNER.] Mas-ter Horner, will you never keep civil company? Methinks 'tis time now, since you are only fit for them. Come, come, man, you must e'en fall to visiting our wives, eating at our tables, drink-
30 ing tea with our virtuous relations after dinner, dealing cards to 'em, reading plays and gazettes to 'em, picking fleas out of their shocks° for 'em, collecting receipts, new songs, women, pages, and footmen for em.
35   HORNER. I hope they'll afford me better em-ployment, sir.
        SIR JASPER FIDGET. He! he! he! 'tis fit you know your work before you come into your place. And since you are unprovided of a lady
40 to flatter, and a good house to eat at, pray fre-quent mine, and call my wife mistress, and she shall call you gallant, according to the custom.
        HORNER. Who, I?
        SIR JASPER FIDGET. Faith, thou shalt for my sake; come, for my sake only.   45
        HORNER. For your sake—
        SIR JASPER FIDGET [*to* LADY FIDGET]. Come, come, here's a gamester for you; let him be a little familiar sometimes; nay, what if a little rude? Gamesters may be rude with ladies, you   50 know.
        LADY FIDGET. Yes; losing gamesters have a privilege with women.
        HORNER. I always thought the contrary, that the winning gamester had most privilege with   55 women; for when you have lost your money to a man, you'll lose anything you have—all you have, they say—and he may use you as he pleases.
        SIR JASPER FIDGET. He! he! he! well, win or   60 lose, you shall have your liberty with her.
        LADY FIDGET. As he behaves himself, and for your sake I'll give him admittance and freedom.
        HORNER. All sorts of freedom, madam?
        SIR JASPER FIDGET. Ay, ay, ay, all sorts of   65 freedom thou canst take. And so go to her, be-gin thy new employment; wheedle her, jest with her, and be better acquainted one with another.
        HORNER [*aside*]. I think I know her already;   70 therefore may venture with her my secret for hers. [HORNER *and* LADY FIDGET *whisper.*]
        SIR JASPER FIDGET. Sister, cuz,° I have pro-vided an innocent playfellow for you there.
        MRS. DAINTY FIDGET. Who, he?   75
        MRS. SQUEAMISH. There's a playfellow, in-deed!
        SIR JASPER FIDGET. Yes, sure. What, he is good enough to play at cards, blindman's-buff, or the fool with, sometimes!   80
        MRS. SQUEAMISH. Foh! we'll have no such playfellows.
        MRS. DAINTY FIDGET. No, sir; you shan't choose playfellows for us, we thank you.
        SIR JASPER FIDGET. Nay, pray hear me. [*Whis-*   85 *pering to them.*]

civil gentlemen Mr. Tattle and Mr. Limberham, already
    mentioned
crazy ailing; shaky
gentleman-usher a servant to tend the door and per-
    form small personal services, as Sir Jasper explains
    in a moment
fine pay
shocks lap dogs

cuz (or **coz**) *cousin*, a merely friendly endearment

LADY FIDGET. But, poor gentleman, could you be so generous, so truly a man of honor, as for the sakes of us women of honor, to cause yourself to be reported no man? No man! and to suffer yourself the greatest shame that could fall upon a man, that none might fall upon us women by your conversation? But, indeed, sir, as perfectly, perfectly the same man as before your going into France, sir? as perfectly, perfectly, sir?

HORNER. As perfectly, perfectly, madam. Nay, I scorn you should take my word; I desire to be tried only, madam.

LADY FIDGET. Well, that's spoken again like a man of honor: all men of honor desire to come to the test. But, indeed, generally you men report such things of yourselves, one does not know how or whom to believe; and it is come to that pass we dare not take your words no more than your tailor's, without some staid servant of yours be bound with you. But I have so strong a faith in your honor, dear, dear, noble sir, that I'd forfeit mine for yours, at any time, dear sir.

HORNER. No, madam, you should not need to forfeit it for me; I have given you security already to have you harmless, my late reputation being so well known in the world, madam.

LADY FIDGET. But if upon any future falling-out, or upon a suspicion of my taking the trust out of your hands to employ some other, you yourself should betray your trust, dear sir? I mean, if you'll give me leave to speak obscenely, you might tell, dear sir.

HORNER. If I did, nobody would believe me. The reputation of impotency is as hardly recovered again in the world as that of cowardice, dear madam.

LADY FIDGET. Nay, then, as one may say, you may do your worst, dear, dear sir.

SIR JASPER FIDGET. Come, is your ladyship reconciled to him yet? have you agreed on matters? For I must be gone to Whitehall.

LADY FIDGET. Why, indeed, Sir Jasper, Master Horner is a thousand, thousand times a better man than I thought him. Cousin Squeamish, sister Dainty, I can name him now. Truly, not long ago, you know, I thought his very name obscenity; and I would as soon have lain with him as have named him.

SIR JASPER FIDGET. Very likely, poor madam.

MRS. DAINTY FIDGET. I believe it.

MRS. SQUEAMISH. No doubt on't.

SIR JASPER FIDGET. Well, well—that your ladyship is as virtuous as any she, I know, and him all the town knows—he! he! he! Therefore, now you like him, get you gone to your business together; go, go to your business, I say, pleasure; whilst I go to my pleasure, business.

LADY FIDGET. Come, then, dear gallant.

HORNER. Come away, my dearest mistress.

SIR JASPER FIDGET. So, so; why, 'tis as I'd have it.

[*Exit.*]

HORNER. And as I'd have it.

LADY FIDGET.
Who for his business from his wife will run,
Takes the best care to have her business
                                    [done.

[*Exeunt omnes.*]

ACT III

Scene i

[*A room in* PINCHWIFE'S *house.*]

[*Enter* ALITHEA *and* MRS. PINCHWIFE.]

ALITHEA. Sister, what ails you? You are grown melancholy.

MRS. PINCHWIFE. Would it not make any one melancholy to see you go every day fluttering abroad, whilst I must stay at home like a poor lonely sullen bird in a cage?

ALITHEA. Ay, sister, but you came young, and just from the nest to your cage, so that I thought you liked it, and could be as cheerful in't as others that took their flight themselves early, and are hopping abroad in the open air.

MRS. PINCHWIFE. Nay, I confess I was quiet enough till my husband told me what pure° lives the London ladies live abroad, with their dancing, meetings, and junketings, and dressed every day in their best gowns; and I warrant you, play at nine-pins every day of the week, so they do.

pure flourishing

[*Enter* PINCHWIFE.]

PINCHWIFE. Come, what's here to do? You are putting the town-pleasures in her head, and setting her a-longing.

ALITHEA. Yes, after nine-pins. You suffer none to give her those longings you mean but yourself.

PINCHWIFE. I tell her of the vanities of the town like a confessor.

ALITHEA. A confessor! just such a confessor as he that, by forbidding a silly ostler to grease the horse's teeth,° taught him to do't.

PINCHWIFE. Come, Mistress Flippant, good precepts are lost when bad examples are still before us; the liberty you take abroad makes her hanker after it, and out of humor at home. Poor wretch! she desired not to come to London; I would bring her.

ALITHEA. Very well.

PINCHWIFE. She has been this week in town, and never desired till this afternoon to go abroad.

ALITHEA. Was she not at a play yesterday?

PINCHWIFE. Yes, but she ne'er asked me; I was myself the cause of her going.

ALITHEA. Then if she ask you again, you are the cause of her asking, and not my example.

PINCHWIFE. Well, tomorrow night I shall be rid of you; and the next day, before 'tis light, she and I'll be rid of the town, and my dreadful apprehensions.—Come, be not melancholy; for thou shalt go into the country after to-morrow, dearest.

ALITHEA. Great comfort!

MRS. PINCHWIFE. Pish! what d'ye tell me of the country for?

PINCHWIFE. How's this! what, pish at the country?

MRS. PINCHWIFE. Let me alone; I am not well.

PINCHWIFE. Oh, if that be all—what ails my dearest?

MRS. PINCHWIFE. Truly, I don't know; but I have not been well since you told me there was a gallant at the play in love with me.

PINCHWIFE. Ha!—

ALITHEA. That's by my example too!

PINCHWIFE. Nay, if you are not well, but are so concerned because a lewd fellow chanced to lie, and say he liked you, you'll make me sick too.

MRS. PINCHWIFE. Of what sickness?

PINCHWIFE. Oh, of that which is worse than the plague, jealousy.

MRS. PINCHWIFE. Pish, you jeer! I'm sure there's no such disease in our receipt-book at home.

PINCHWIFE. No, thou never met'st with it, poor innocent.—[*Aside.*] Well, if thou cuckold me, 'twill be my own fault—for cuckolds and bastards are generally makers of their own fortune.

MRS. PINCHWIFE. Well, but pray, bud, let's go to a play tonight.

PINCHWIFE. 'Tis just done, she comes from it. But why are you so eager to see a play?

MRS. PINCHWIFE. Faith, dear, not that I care one pin for their talk there; but I like to look upon the playermen, and would see, if I could, the gallant you say loves me; that's all, dear bud.

PINCHWIFE. Is that all, dear bud?

ALITHEA. This proceeds from my example!

MRS. PINCHWIFE. But if the play be done, let's go abroad, however, dear bud.

PINCHWIFE. Come, have a little patience and thou shalt go into the country on Friday.

MRS. PINCHWIFE. Therefore I would see first some sights to tell my neighbors of. Nay, I will go abroad, that's once.

ALITHEA. I'm the cause of this desire, too!

PINCHWIFE. But now I think on't, who, who was the cause of Horner's coming to my lodgings today? That was you.

ALITHEA. No, you, because you would not let him see your handsome wife out of your lodging.

MRS. PINCHWIFE. Why, O Lord! did the gentleman come hither to see me indeed?

PINCHWIFE. No, no. You are not cause of that damned question too, Mistress Alithea?— [*Aside.*] Well, she's in the right of it. He is in love with my wife—and comes after her—'tis

---

to grease . . . teeth hence, to put the horse off his feed, a trick of dishonest hostlers to economize on provender

so—but I'll nip his love in the bud, lest he should follow us into the country, and break his chariot-wheel near our house, on purpose for an excuse to come to't. But I think I know the town.

5 MRS. PINCHWIFE. Come, pray, bud, let's go abroad before 'tis late; for I will go, that's flat and plain.

PINCHWIFE [*aside*]. So! the obstinacy already

10 of a town-wife; and I must, whilst she's here, humor her like one.—Sister, how shall we do, that she may not be seen or known?

ALITHEA. Let her put on her mask.

PINCHWIFE. Pshaw! a mask makes people but

15 the more inquisitive, and is as ridiculous a disguise as a stage-beard; her shape, stature, habit will be known. And if we should meet with Horner, he would be sure to take acquaintance with us, must wish her joy, kiss her, talk to

20 her, leer upon her, and the devil and all. No, I'll not use her to a mask; 'tis dangerous, for masks have made more cuckolds than the best faces that ever were known.

ALITHEA. How will you do then?

25 MRS. PINCHWIFE. Nay, shall we go? The Exchange° will be shut, and I have a mind to see that.

PINCHWIFE. So—I have it—I'll dress her up in the suit we are to carry down to her brother,

30 little Sir James; nay, I understand the town-tricks. Come, let's go dress her. A mask! no—a woman masked, like a covered dish, gives a man curiosity and appetite; when, it may be, uncovered, 'twould turn his stomach; no, no.

35 ALITHEA. Indeed your comparison is something a greasy one: but I had a gentle gallant used to say, "A beauty masked, like the sun in eclipse, gathers together more gazers than if it shined out."

40 [*Exeunt.*]

Scene ii

[*The scene changes to the New Exchange, with* CLASP, *a book-seller, in his stall.*]

[*Enter* HORNER, HARCOURT, *and* DORILANT.]

DORILANT. Engaged to women, and not sup

45 with us!

HORNER. Ay, a pox on 'em all!

HARCOURT. You were much a more reasonable man in the morning, and had as noble resolutions against 'em as a widower of a week's

50 liberty.

DORILANT. Did I ever think to see you keep company with women in vain?

HORNER. In vain! no—'tis since I can't love 'em, to be revenged on 'em.

55 HARCOURT. Now your sting is gone, you looked in the box amongst all those women like a drone in the hive; all upon you, shoved and ill-used by 'em all, and thrust from one side to t'other.

60 DORILANT. Yet he must be buzzing amongst 'em still, like other old beetle-headed liquorish° drones. Avoid 'em, and hate 'em, as they hate you.

HORNER. Because I do hate 'em, and would

65 hate 'em yet more, I'll frequent 'em. You may see by marriage, nothing makes a man hate a woman more than her constant conversation. In short, I converse with 'em as you do with rich fools, to laugh at 'em and use 'em ill.

70 DORILANT. But I would no more sup with women unless I could lie with 'em than sup with a rich coxcomb unless I could cheat him.

HORNER. Yes, I have known thee sup with a fool for his drinking; if he could set out your

75 hand° that way only, you were satisfied, and if he were a wine-swallowing mouth, 'twas enough.

HARCOURT. Yes, a man drinks often with a fool, as he tosses with a marker,° only to keep

80 his hand in ure.° But do the ladies drink?

HORNER. Yes, sir; and I shall have the pleasure at least of laying 'em flat with a bottle, and bring as much scandal that way upon 'em as formerly t'other.

85 HARCOURT. Perhaps you may prove as weak

The Exchange an arcade of fashionable shops and stalls, fine for strolling, "window-shopping," and meeting acquaintances

liquorish greedy; lecherous
set ... hand provide free drinks
marker scorekeeper at dice; not one of the gamblers
in ure in practice

a brother amongst 'em that way as t'other.

DORILANT. Foh! drinking with women is as unnatural as scolding with 'em. But 'tis a pleasure of decayed fornicators, and the basest way
5 of quenching love.

HARCOURT. Nay, 'tis drowning love, instead of quenching it. But leave us for civil women too!

DORILANT. Ay, when he can't be the better
10 for 'em. We hardly pardon a man that leaves his friend for a wench, and that's a pretty lawful call.

HORNER. Faith, I would not leave you for 'em, if they would not drink.

15 DORILANT. Who would disappoint his company at Lewis's° for a gossiping?

HARCOURT. Foh! Wine and women, good apart, together as nauseous as sack and sugar. But hark you, sir, before you go, a little of your
20 advice; an old maimed general, when unfit for action, is fittest for counsel. I have other designs upon women than eating and drinking with them; I am in love with Sparkish's mistress, whom he is to marry tomorrow. Now how shall
25 I get her?

[*Enter* SPARKISH, *looking about.*]

HORNER. Why, here comes one will help you to her.

HARCOURT. He! he, I tell you, is my rival, and
30 will hinder my love.

HORNER. No; a foolish rival and a jealous husband assist their rival's designs, for they are sure to make their women hate them, which is the first step to their love for another man.

35 HARCOURT. But I cannot come near his mistress but in his company.

HORNER. Still the better for you; for fools are most easily cheated when they themselves are accessories, and he is to be bubbled° of his mis-
40 tress as of his money, the common mistress, by keeping him company.

SPARKISH. Who is that that is to be bubbled? Faith, let me snack;° I han't met with a bubble

since Christmas. 'Gad, I think bubbles are like
their brother woodcocks,° go out with the cold 45
weather.

HARCOURT [*apart to* HORNER]. A pox! he did
not hear all, I hope.

SPARKISH. Come, you bubbling rogues you,
where do we sup?—Oh, Harcourt, my mistress 50
tells me you have been making fierce love to
her all the play long: ha! ha! But I—

HARCOURT. I make love to her!

SPARKISH. Nay, I forgive thee, for I think
I know thee, and I know her; but I am sure I 55
know myself.

HARCOURT. Did she tell you so? I see all
women are like these of the Exchange; who, to
enhance the price of their commodities, report
to their fond customers offers which were never 60
made 'em.

HORNER. Ay, women are as apt to tell before
the intrigue, as men after it, and so show themselves the vainer sex. But hast thou a mistress,
Sparkish? 'Tis as hard for me to believe it as 65
that thou ever hadst a bubble, as you bragged
just now.

SPARKISH. Oh, your servant, sir; are you at
your raillery, sir? But we were some of us beforehand with you today at the play. The wits 70
were something bold with you, sir; did you not
hear us laugh?

HORNER. Yes; but I thought you had gone to
plays to laugh at the poet's wit, not at your
own. 75

SPARKISH. Your servant, sir; no, I thank you.
'Gad, I go to a play as to a country treat; I carry
my own wine to one, and my own wit to t'other,
or else I'm sure I should not be merry at either.
And the reason why we are so often louder 80
than the players is because we think we speak
more wit, and so become the poet's rivals in his
audience; for to tell you the truth, we hate the
silly rogues, nay, so much that we find fault
even with their bawdy upon the stage, whilst 85
we talk nothing else in the pit as loud.

HORNER. But why shouldst thou hate the silly

Lewis's   unknown; presumably a tavern
bubbled   swindled
snack   have a share in it

woodcocks   game birds in season in the fall; anyone
readily deceived

poets? Thou hast too much wit to be one; and
they, like whores, are only hated by each other;
and thou dost scorn writing, I'm sure.

SPARKISH. Yes; I'd have you to know I scorn
5 writing; but women, women, that make men do
all foolish things, make 'em write songs too.
Everybody does it. 'Tis even as common with
lovers as playing with fans; and you can no
more help rhyming to your Phyllis, than drink-
10 ing to your Phyllis.

HARCOURT. Nay, poetry in love is no more to
be avoided than jealousy.

DORILANT. But the poets damned your songs,
did they?

15 SPARKISH. Damn the poets! they turned 'em
into burlesque, as they call it. That burlesque is
a hocus-pocus trick they have got, which, by
the virtue of *Hictius doctius, topsy turvy*,° they
make a wise and witty man in the world, a fool
20 upon the stage, you know not how; and 'tis
therefore I hate 'em too, for I know not but it
may be my own case; for they'll put a man into
a play for looking asquint. Their predecessors
were contented to make serving-men only their
25 stage-fools; but these rogues must have gentlemen with a pox to 'em, nay, knights; and, indeed, you shall hardly see a fool upon the stage
but he's a knight. And to tell you the truth,
they have kept me these six years from being
30 a knight in earnest, for fear of being knighted
in a play, and dubbed a fool.

DORILANT. Blame 'em not, they must follow
their copy, the age.

HARCOURT. But why shouldst thou be afraid
35 of being in a play, who expose yourself every
day in the playhouses, and at public places?

HORNER. 'Tis but being on the stage, instead
of standing on a bench in the pit.

DORILANT. Don't you give money to painters
40 to draw you like? and are you afraid of your
pictures at length in a playhouse, where all your
mistresses may see you?

SPARKISH. A pox! painters don't draw the
small-pox or pimples in one's face. Come, damn

all your silly authors whatever, all books and 45
booksellers, by the world, and all readers, courteous or uncourteous!

HARCOURT. But who comes here, Sparkish?
[*Enter* MR. PINCHWIFE *and his wife in man's
clothes*, ALITHEA, LUCY *her maid*.] 50

SPARKISH. Oh, hide me! There's my mistress
too. [SPARKISH *hides himself behind* HARCOURT.]

HARCOURT. She sees you.

SPARKISH. But I will not see her. 'Tis time to
go to Whitehall, and I must not fail the draw- 55
ing-room.

HARCOURT. Pray, first carry me, and reconcile
me to her.

SPARKISH. Another time. Faith, the king will
have supped. 60

HARCOURT. Not with the worse stomach for
thy absence. Thou art one of those fools that
think their attendance at the king's meals as
necessary as his physicians', when you are
more troublesome to him than his doctors or 65
his dogs.

SPARKISH. Pshaw! I know my interest, sir.
Prithee hide me.

HORNER. Your servant, Pinchwife.—What,
he knows us not! 70

PINCHWIFE [*to his wife aside*]. Come along.

MRS. PINCHWIFE. Pray, have you any ballads? give me sixpenny worth.

CLASP. We have no ballads.

MRS. PINCHWIFE. Then give me "Covent Gar- 75
den Drollery,"° and a play or two.—Oh, here's
"Tarugo's Wiles," and "The Slighted Maiden";
I'll have them.

PINCHWIFE [*apart to her*]. No; plays are not
for your reading. Come along; will you discover 80
yourself?

HORNER. Who is that pretty youth with him,
Sparkish?

SPARKISH. I believe his wife's brother, because he's something like her; but I never saw 85
her but once.

HORNER. Extremely handsome; I have seen a
face like it too. Let us follow 'em.

Hictius doctius, topsy turvy nonsense formulas for
performing sleight-of-hand

"Covent Garden Drollery," etc. popular ballads and
plays of the time

[*Exeunt* PINCHWIFE, MRS. PINCHWIFE, ALITHEA, LUCY, HORNER, DORILANT *following them.*]

HARCOURT. Come, Sparkish, your mistress saw you, and will be angry you go not to her. Besides, I would fain be reconciled to her, which
5 none but you can do, dear friend.

SPARKISH. Well, that's a better reason, dear friend. I would not go near her now for hers or my own sake; but I can deny you nothing;
10 for though I have known thee a great while, never go, if I do not love thee as well as a new acquaintance.

HARCOURT. I am obliged to you indeed, dear friend. I would be well with her, only to be
15 well with thee still; for these ties to wives usually dissolve all ties to friends. I would be contented she should enjoy you a-nights, but I would have you to myself a-days as I have had, dear friend.

20 SPARKISH. And thou shalt enjoy me a-days, dear, dear friend, never stir; and I'll be divorced from her, sooner than from thee. Come along.

HARCOURT [*aside*]. So, we are hard put to't,
25 when we make our rival our procurer; but neither she nor her brother would let me come near her now. When all's done, a rival is the best cloak to steal to a mistress under, without suspicion; and when we have once got to her
30 as we desire, we throw him off like other cloaks.

[*Exit* SPARKISH, *and* HARCOURT *following him.*]

[*Re-enter* PINCHWIFE, MRS. PINCHWIFE *in*
35 *man's clothes.*]

PINCHWIFE [*to* ALITHEA]. Sister, if you will not go, we must leave you.—[*Aside.*] The fool her gallant and she will muster up all the young saunterers of this place, and they will leave their
40 dear seamstresses° to follow us. What a swarm of cuckolds and cuckold-makers are here!— Come, let's be gone, Mistress Margery.

MRS. PINCHWIFE. Don't you believe that; I han't half my bellyfull of sights yet.

45 PINCHWIFE. Then walk this way.

MRS. PINCHWIFE. Lord, what a power of brave signs are here! stay—the Bull's-Head, the Ram's-Head, and the Stag's-Head, dear—

PINCHWIFE. Nay, if every husband's proper sign here were visible, they would be all alike. 50

MRS. PINCHWIFE. What d'ye mean by that, bud?

PINCHWIFE. 'Tis no matter—no matter, bud.

MRS. PINCHWIFE. Pray tell me: nay, I will know. 55

PINCHWIFE. They would be all Bulls',° Stags', and Rams'-heads.

[*Exeunt* MR. PINCHWIFE *and* MRS. PINCHWIFE.]

[*Re-enter* SPARKISH, HARCOURT, ALITHEA, LUCY, *at the other door.*] 60

SPARKISH. Come, dear madam, for my sake you shall be reconciled to him.

ALITHEA. For your sake I hate him.

HARCOURT. That's something too cruel, madam, to hate me for his sake. 65

SPARKISH. Ay indeed, madam, too, too cruel to me, to hate my friend for my sake.

ALITHEA. I hate him because he is your enemy; and you ought to hate him too, for making love to me, if you love me. 70

SPARKISH. That's a good one! I hate a man for loving you! If he did love you, 'tis but what he can't help; and 'tis your fault, not his, if he admires you; I hate a man for being of my opinion? I'll ne'er do't, by the world! 75

ALITHEA. Is it for your honor, or mine, to suffer a man to make love to me, who am to marry you tomorrow?

SPARKISH. Is it for your honor, or mine, to have me jealous? That he makes love to you, is 80 a sign you are handsome; and that I am not jealous, is a sign you are virtuous. That I think is for your honor.

ALITHEA. But 'tis your honor too I am concerned for. 85

HARCOURT. But why, dearest madam, will you be more concerned for his honor than he is himself? Let his honor alone, for my sake and his. He! he has no honor—

SPARKISH. How's that? 90

HARCOURT. But what my dear friend can guard himself.

SPARKISH. Oh ho—that's right again.

HARCOURT. Your care of his honor argues his

---

seamstresses dressmakers, often also prostitutes

Bulls', etc. with the usual allusion to cuckold's horns neglect of it, which is no honor to my dear friend here. Therefore once more, let his honor go which way it will, dear madam.

SPARKISH. Ay, ay; were it for my honor to
5 marry a woman whose virtue I suspected, and could not trust her in a friend's hands?

ALITHEA. Are you not afraid to lose me?

HARCOURT. He afraid to lose you, madam! No, no—you may see how the most estimable
10 and most glorious creature in the world is valued by him. Will you not see it?

SPARKISH. Right, honest Frank, I have that noble value for her that I cannot be jealous of her.

15 ALITHEA. You mistake him. He means, you care not for me, nor who has me.

SPARKISH. Lord, madam, I see you are jealous. Will you wrest a poor man's meaning from his words?

20 ALITHEA. You astonish me, sir, with your want of jealousy.

SPARKISH. And you make me giddy, madam, with your jealousy and fears, and virtue and honor. 'Gad, I see virtue makes a woman as
25 troublesome as a little reading or learning.

ALITHEA. Monstrous!

LUCY [behind]. Well, to see what easy husbands these women of quality can meet with! A poor chambermaid can never have such lady-
30 like luck. Besides, he's thrown away upon her. She'll make no use of her fortune, her blessing, none to a gentleman, for a pure cuckold, for it requires good breeding to be a cuckold.

ALITHEA. I tell you then plainly, he pursues
35 me to marry me.

SPARKISH. Pshaw.

HARCOURT. Come, madam, you see you strive in vain to make him jealous of me. My dear friend is the kindest creature in the world to
40 me.

SPARKISH. Poor fellow.

HARCOURT. But his kindness only is not enough for me, without your favor, your good opinion, dear madam: 'tis that must perfect
45 my happiness. Good gentleman, he believes all I say; would you would do so. Jealous of me! I would not wrong him nor you for the world.

SPARKISH. Look you there. Hear him, hear him, and do not walk away so. [ALITHEA walks 50 carelessly to and fro.]

HARCOURT. I love you, madam, so—

SPARKISH. How's that? Nay, now you begin to go too far indeed.

HARCOURT. So much, I confess, I say, I love 55 you, that I would not have you miserable, and cast yourself away upon so unworthy and inconsiderable a thing as what you see here. [Clapping his hand on his breast, points at SPARKISH.] 60

SPARKISH. No, faith, I believe thou wouldst not; now his meaning is plain; but I knew before thou wouldst not wrong me, nor her.

HARCOURT. No, no, Heavens forbid the glory of her sex should fall so low, as into the em- 65 braces of such a contemptible wretch, the last of mankind—my dear friend here—I injure him! [Embracing SPARKISH.]

ALITHEA. Very well.

SPARKISH. No, no, dear friend, I knew it.— 70 Madam, you see he will rather wrong himself than me, in giving himself such names.

ALITHEA. Do you not understand him yet?

SPARKISH. Yes, how modestly he speaks of himself, poor fellow! 75

ALITHEA. Methinks he speaks impudently of yourself, since—before yourself too; insomuch that I can no longer suffer his scurrilous abusiveness to you, no more than his love to me. [Offers to go.] 80

SPARKISH. Nay, nay, madam, pray stay—his love to you! Lord, madam, has he not spoke yet plain enough?

ALITHEA. Yes, indeed, I should think so.

SPARKISH. Well then, by the world, a man 85 can't speak civilly to a woman now, but presently she says he makes love to her. Nay, madam, you shall stay, with your pardon, since you have not yet understood him, till he has made an *éclaircissement*° of his love to you, 90 that is, what kind of love it is. Answer to thy catechism, friend; do you love my mistress here?

HARCOURT. Yes, I wish she would not doubt it.

SPARKISH. But how do you love her? 95

HARCOURT. With all my soul.

éclaircissement disclosure (a faddish French word)

ALITHEA. I thank him, methinks he speaks plain enough now.

SPARKISH [to ALITHEA]. You are out still.—But with what kind of love, Harcourt?

5 HARCOURT. With the best and truest love in the world.

SPARKISH. Look you there then, that is with no matrimonial love, I'm sure.

ALITHEA. How's that? do you say matrimonial
10 love is not best?

SPARKISH. 'Gad, I went too far ere I was aware. But speak for thyself, Harcourt, you said you would not wrong me nor her.

HARCOURT. No, no, madam, e'en take him for
15 Heaven's sake—

SPARKISH. Look you there, madam.

HARCOURT. Who should in all justice be yours, he that loves you most. [Claps his hand on his breast.]

20 ALITHEA. Look you there, Mr. Sparkish, who's that?

SPARKISH. Who should it be?—Go on, Harcourt.

HARCOURT. Who loves you more than women
25 titles, or fortune fools. [Points at SPARKISH.]

SPARKISH. Look you there, he means me still, for he points at me.

ALITHEA. Ridiculous!

HARCOURT. Who can only match your faith
30 and constancy in love.

SPARKISH. Ay.

HARCOURT. Who knows, if it be possible, how to value so much beauty and virtue.

SPARKISH. Ay.

35 HARCOURT. Whose love can no more be equalled in the world, than that heavenly form of yours.

SPARKISH. No.

HARCOURT. Who could no more suffer a rival
40 than your absence, and yet could no more suspect your virtue than his own constancy in his love to you.

SPARKISH. No.

HARCOURT. Who, in fine, loves you better
45 than his eyes, that first made him love you.

SPARKISH. Ay—Nay, madam, faith, you shan't go till—

ALITHEA. Have a care, lest you make me stay too long.

SPARKISH. But till he has saluted you; that I 50 may be assured you are friends, after his honest advice and declaration. Come, pray, madam, be friends with him.

[Enter PINCHWIFE, MRS. PINCHWIFE.]

ALITHEA. You must pardon me, sir, that I 55 am not yet so obedient to you.

PINCHWIFE. What, invite your wife to kiss men? Monstrous! Are you not ashamed? I will never forgive you.

SPARKISH. Are you not ashamed that I should 60 have more confidence in the chastity of your family than you have? You must not teach me; I am a man of honor, sir, though I am frank and free; I am frank, sir—

PINCHWIFE. Very frank, sir, to share your 65 wife with your friends.

SPARKISH. He is an humble, menial friend, such as reconciles the differences of the marriage bed; you know man and wife do not always agree; I design him for that use, there- 70 fore would have him well with my wife.

PINCHWIFE. A menial friend!—you will get a great many menial friends, by showing your wife as you do.

SPARKISH. What then? It may be I have a 75 pleasure in't, as I have to show fine clothes at a playhouse the first day, and count money before poor rogues.

PINCHWIFE. He that shows his wife or money will be in danger of having them borrowed 80 sometimes.

SPARKISH. I love to be envied, and would not marry a wife that I alone could love; loving alone is as dull as eating alone. Is it not a frank age? and I am a frank person; and to tell you 85 the truth, it may be I love to have rivals in a wife; they make her seem to a man still but as a kept mistress; and so good night, for I must to Whitehall.—Madam, I hope you are now reconciled to my friend; and so I wish you a 90 good night, madam, and sleep if you can; for tomorrow you know I must visit you early with a canonical gentleman.° Good night, dear Harcourt.

canonical gentleman clergyman

[*Exit* SPARKISH.]

HARCOURT. Madam, I hope you will not refuse my visit tomorrow, if it should be earlier with a canonical gentleman than Mr. Sparkish's.

PINCHWIFE. This gentlewoman is yet under my care, therefore you must yet forbear your freedom with her, sir. [*Coming between* ALITHEA *and* HARCOURT.]

HARCOURT. Must, sir?

PINCHWIFE. Yes, sir, she is my sister.

HARCOURT. 'Tis well she is, sir—for I must be her servant, sir.—Madam—

PINCHWIFE. Come away, sister, we had been gone if it had not been for you, and so avoided these lewd rake-hells, who seem to haunt us.

[*Enter* HORNER, DORILANT.]

HORNER. How now, Pinchwife!

PINCHWIFE. Your servant.

HORNER. What! I see a little time in the country makes a man turn wild and unsociable, and only fit to converse with his horses, dogs, and his herds.

PINCHWIFE. I have business, sir, and must mind it; your business is pleasure; therefore you and I must go different ways.

HORNER. Well, you may go on, but this pretty young gentleman—[*takes hold of* MRS. PINCHWIFE].

HARCOURT. The lady—

DORILANT. And the maid—

HORNER. Shall stay with us; for I suppose their business is the same with ours, pleasure.

PINCHWIFE [*aside*]. 'Sdeath, he knows her, she carries it so sillily! Yet if he does not, I should be more silly to discover it first.

ALITHEA. Pray, let us go, sir.

PINCHWIFE. Come, come—

HORNER [*to* MRS. PINCHWIFE]. Had you not rather stay with us?—Prithee, Pinchwife, who is this pretty young gentleman?

PINCHWIFE. One to whom I'm a guardian.— [*Aside*.] I wish I could keep her out of your hands.

HORNER. Who is he? I never saw anything so pretty in all my life.

PINCHWIFE. Pshaw! do not look upon him so much, he's a poor bashful youth; you'll put him out of countenance.—Come away, brother. [*Offers to take her away*.]

HORNER. Oh, your brother!

PINCHWIFE. Yes, my wife's brother.—Come, come, she'll stay supper for us.

HORNER. I thought so, for he is very like her I saw you at the play with, whom I told you I was in love with.

MRS. PINCHWIFE [*aside*]. O jeminy! is this he that was in love with me? I am glad on't, I vow, for he's a curious fine gentleman, and I love him already, too.—[*To* PINCHWIFE.] Is this he, bud?

PINCHWIFE [*to his wife*]. Come away, come away.

HORNER. Why, what haste are you in? Why won't you let me walk with him?

PINCHWIFE. Because you'll debauch him: he's yet young and innocent, and I would not have him debauched for anything in the world.— [*Aside*.] How she gazes on him! the devil!

HORNER. Harcourt, Dorilant, look you here, this is the likeness of that dowdy he told us of, his wife; did you ever see a lovelier creature? The rogue has reason to be jealous of his wife, since she is like him, for she would make all that see her in love with her.

HARCOURT. And, as I remember now, she is as like him here as can be.

DORILANT. She is indeed very pretty, if she be like him.

HORNER. Very pretty? a very pretty condemnation!—she is a glorious creature, beautiful beyond all things I ever beheld.

PINCHWIFE. So, so.

HARCOURT. More beautiful than a poet's first mistress of imagination.

HORNER. Or another man's last mistress of flesh and blood.

MRS. PINCHWIFE. Nay, now you jeer, sir; pray don't jeer me.

PINCHWIFE. Come, come.—[*Aside*.] By Heavens, she'll discover herself!

HORNER. I speak of your sister, sir.

PINCHWIFE. Ay, but saying she was handsome, if like him, made him blush.—[*Aside*.] I am upon a rack!

HORNER. Methinks he is so handsome he should not be a man.

PINCHWIFE [*aside*]. Oh, there 'tis out! he has discovered her! I am not able to suffer any longer.—[*To his wife.*] Come, come away, I say.

5 HORNER. Nay, by your leave, sir, he shall not go yet. [*Aside to them.*] Harcourt, Dorilant, let us torment this jealous rogue a little.

HARCOURT. } How?
DORILANT. }

10 HORNER. I'll show you.

PINCHWIFE. Come, pray let him go, I cannot stay fooling any longer; I tell you his sister stays supper for us.

HORNER. Does she? Come then, we'll all go 15 sup with her and thee.

PINCHWIFE. No, now I think on't, having stayed so long for us, I warrant she's gone to bed.—[*Aside.*] I wish she and I were well out of their hands.—Come, I must rise early tomor-20 row, come.

HORNER. Well then, if she be gone to bed, I wish her and you a good night. But pray, young gentleman, present my humble service to her.

MRS. PINCHWIFE. Thank you heartily, sir.

25 PINCHWIFE [*aside*]. 'Sdeath she will discover herself yet in spite of me.—He is something more civil to you, for your kindness to his sister, than I am, it seems.

HORNER. Tell her, dear sweet little gentle-30 man, for all your brother there, that you have revived the love I had for her at first sight in the playhouse.

MRS. PINCHWIFE. But did you love her indeed, and indeed?

35 PINCHWIFE [*aside*]. So, so.--Away, I say.

HORNER. Nay, stay.—Yes, indeed, and indeed, pray do you tell her so, and give her this kiss from me. [*Kisses her.*]

PINCHWIFE [*aside*]. O Heavens! what do I 40 suffer? Now 'tis too plain he knows her, and yet—

HORNER. And this, and this—[*kisses her again*].

MRS. PINCHWIFE. What do you kiss me for? 45 I am no woman.

PINCHWIFE [*aside*]. So, there, 'tis out.—Come, I cannot, nor will stay any longer.

HORNER. Nay, they shall send your lady a kiss too. Here, Harcourt, Dorilant, will you not? [*They kiss her.*] 50

PINCHWIFE [*aside*]. How! do I suffer this? Was I not accusing another just now for this rascally patience, in permitting his wife to be kissed before his face? Ten thousand ulcers gnaw away their lips.—Come, come. 55

HORNER. Good night, dear little gentleman; madam, good night; farewell, Pinchwife.— [*Apart to* HARCOURT *and* DORILANT.] Did not I tell you I would raise his jealous gall?

[*Exeunt* HORNER, HARCOURT, *and* DORILANT.] 60

PINCHWIFE. So, they are gone at last; stay, let me see first if the coach be at this door.

[*Exit.*]

[HORNER. HARCOURT, DORILANT *return.*]

HORNER. What, not gone yet? Will you be 65 sure to do as I desired you, sweet sir?

MRS. PINCHWIFE. Sweet sir, but what will you give me then?

HORNER. Anything. Come away into the next walk. 70

[*Exit, haling away* MRS. PINCHWIFE.]

ALITHEA. Hold! hold! what d'ye do?

LUCY. Stay, stay, hold—

HARCOURT. Hold, madam, hold, let him present him—he'll come presently; nay, I will 75 never let you go till you answer my question. [ALITHEA, LUCY, *struggling with* HARCOURT *and* DORILANT.]

LUCY. For God's sake, sir, I must follow 'em.

DORILANT. No, I have something to present 80 you with too, you shan't follow them.

[PINCHWIFE *returns.*]

PINCHWIFE. Where?—how—what's become of?—gone!—whither?

LUCY. He's only gone with the gentleman, 85 who will give him something, an't please your worship.

PINCHWIFE. Something!—give him something, with a pox!—where are they?

ALITHEA. In the next walk only, brother. 90

PINCHWIFE. Only, only! where, where?

[*Exit* PINCHWIFE *and returns presently, then goes out again.*]

HARCOURT. What's the matter with him?

Why so much concerned? But, dearest madam—

ALITHEA. Pray let me go, sir; I have said and suffered enough already.

HARCOURT. Then you will not look upon, nor
5 pity, my sufferings?

ALITHEA. To look upon 'em, when I cannot help 'em, were cruelty, not pity; therefore, I will never see you more.

HARCOURT. Let me then, madam, have my
10 privilege of a banished lover, complaining or railing, and giving you but a farewell reason why, if you cannot condescend to marry me, you should not take that wretch, my rival.

ALITHEA. He only, not you, since my honor
15 is engaged so far to him, can give me a reason why I should not marry him; but if he be true, and what I think him to me; I must be so to him. Your servant, sir.

HARCOURT. Have women only constancy
20 when 'tis a vice, and, like Fortune, only true to fools?

DORILANT [*to* LUCY, *who struggles to get from him.*] Thou shalt not stir, thou robust creature; you see, I can deal with you, therefore you
25 should stay the rather, and be kind.

[*Enter* PINCHWIFE.]

PINCHWIFE. Gone, gone, not to be found! quite gone! ten thousand plagues go with 'em! which way went they?

30 ALITHEA. But into t'other walk, brother.

LUCY. Their business will be done presently sure, an't please your worship; it can't be long in doing, I'm sure on't.

ALITHEA. Are they not there?

35 PINCHWIFE. No, you know where they are, you infamous wretch, eternal shame of your family, which you do not dishonor enough yourself, you think, but you must help her to do it too, thou legion of bawds!

40 ALITHEA. Good brother—

PINCHWIFE. Damned, damned sister!

ALITHEA. Look you here, she's coming.

[*Enter* MRS. PINCHWIFE *in man's clothes, running, with her hat under her arm, full of
45 oranges and dried fruit,* HORNER *following.*]

MRS. PINCHWIFE. O dear bud, look you here what I have got, see!

PINCHWIFE [*aside, rubbing his forehead*]. And what I have got here too, which you can't
50 see.

MRS. PINCHWIFE. The fine gentleman has given me better things yet.

PINCHWIFE. Has he so?—[*Aside.*] Out of breath and colored!°—I must hold yet.

55 HORNER. I have only given your little brother an orange, sir.

PINCHWIFE [*to* HORNER]. Thank you, sir.— [*Aside.*] You have only squeezed my orange, I suppose, and given it me again; yet I must
60 have a city patience.—[*To his wife.*] Come, come away.

MRS. PINCHWIFE. Stay, till I have put up my fine things, bud.

[*Enter* SIR JASPER FIDGET.]

65 SIR JASPER FIDGET. O, Master Horner, come, come, the ladies stay for you; your mistress, my wife, wonders you make not more haste to her.

HORNER. I have stayed this half hour for
70 you here, and 'tis your fault I am not now with your wife.

SIR JASPER FIDGET. But, pray, don't let her know so much; the truth on't is, I was advancing a certain project to his majesty—
75 about—I'll tell you.

HORNER. No, let's go, and hear it at your house.—Good night, sweet little gentleman; one kiss more, you'll remember me now, I hope. [*Kisses her.*]

80 DORILANT. What, Sir Jasper, will you separate friends? He promised to sup with us, and if you take him to your house, you'll be in danger of our company too.

SIR JASPER FIDGET. Alas! gentlemen, my
85 house is not fit for you; there are none but civil women there, which are not for your turn. He, you know, can bear with the society of civil women now, ha! ha! ha! besides, he's one of my family—he's—he! he! he!

90 DORILANT. What is he?

SIR JASPER FIDGET. Faith, my eunuch, since you'll have it; he! he! he!

colored blushing

[*Exeunt* SIR JASPER FIDGET *and* HORNER.]

DORILANT. I rather wish thou wert his or my cuckold. Harcourt, what a good cuckold is lost there for want of a man to make him one!
5 Thee and I cannot have Horner's privilege, who can make use of it.

HARCOURT. Ay, to poor Horner 'tis like coming to an estate at three-score, when a man can't be the better for't.

10 PINCHWIFE. Come.

MRS. PINCHWIFE. Presently, bud.

DORILANT. Come, let us go too.—[*To* ALITHEA.] Madam, your servant.—[*To* LUCY.] Good night, strapper.

15 HARCOURT. Madam, though you will not let me have a good day or night, I wish you one; but dare not name the other half of my wish.

ALITHEA. Good night, sir, for ever.

MRS. PINCHWIFE. I don't know where to put
20 this here, dear bud, you shall eat it; nay, you shall have part of the fine gentleman's good things, or treat, as you call it, when we come home.

PINCHWIFE. Indeed, I deserve it, since I fur-
25 nished the best part of it. [*Strikes away the orange.*]

The gallant treats presents, and gives the ball,

But 'tis the absent cuckold pays for all.

ACT IV

Scene i

30 [PINCHWIFE'S *house in the morning.*]

[*Enter* LUCY, ALITHEA *dressed in new clothes.*]

LUCY. Well, madam, now have I dressed you, and set you out with so many ornaments, and
35 spent upon you ounces of essence and pul-villio;° and all this for no other purpose but as people adorn and perfume a corpse for a stinking second-hand grave; such, or as bad, I think Master Sparkish's bed.

40 ALITHEA. Hold your peace.

LUCY. Nay, madam, I will ask you the reason why you should banish poor Master Harcourt for ever from your sight; how could you be so

hard-hearted?

ALITHEA. 'Twas because I was not hard-   45
hearted.

LUCY. No, no; 'twas stark love and kindness, I warrant.

ALITHEA. It was so; I would see him no more because I love him.   50

LUCY. Hey day, a very pretty reason!

ALITHEA. You do not understand me.

LUCY. I wish you may yourself.

ALITHEA. I was engaged to marry, you see, another man, whom my justice will not suffer   55
me to deceive or injure.

LUCY. Can there be a greater cheat or wrong done to a man than to give him your person without your heart? I should make a con-science of it.   60

ALITHEA. I'll retrieve it for him after I am married a while.

LUCY. The woman that marries to love better will be as much mistaken as the wencher that marries to live better. No,   65
madam, marrying to increase love is like gaming to become rich; alas! you only lose what little stock you had before.

ALITHEA. I find by your rhetoric you have been bribed to betray me.   70

LUCY. Only by his merit, that has bribed your heart, you see, against your word and rigid honor. But what a devil is this honor! 'tis sure a disease in the head, like the megrim or falling-sickness,° that always hurries people   75
away to do themselves mischief. Men lose their lives by it; women, what's dearer to 'em, their love, the life of life.

ALITHEA. Come, pray talk you no more of honor, nor Master Harcourt; I wish the other   80
would come to secure my fidelity to him and his right in me.

LUCY. You will marry him then?

ALITHEA. Certainly; I have given him already my word, and will my hand too, to   85
make it good, when he comes.

LUCY. Well, I wish I may never stick pin more, if he be not an arrant natural to° t'other fine gentleman.

---

pulvillio scented powder

megrim or falling-sickness dizziness or epilepsy
natural to fool as compared with

ALITHEA. I own he wants the wit of Harcourt, which I will dispense withal for another want he has, which is want of jealousy, which men of wit seldom want.

5 LUCY. Lord, madam, what should you do with a fool to your husband? You intend to be honest, don't you? Then that husbandly virtue, credulity, is thrown away upon you.

ALITHEA. He only that could suspect my
10 virtue should have cause to do it; 'tis Sparkish's confidence in my truth that obliges me to be so faithful to him.

LUCY. You are not sure his opinion may last.

ALITHEA. I am satisfied 'tis impossible for
15 him to be jealous after the proofs I have had of him. Jealousy in a husband—Heaven defend me from it! it begets a thousand plagues to a poor woman, the loss of her honor, her quiet, and her—

20 LUCY. And her pleasure.

ALITHEA. What d'ye mean, impertinent?

LUCY. Liberty is a great pleasure, madam.

ALITHEA. I say, loss of her honor, her quiet, nay, her life sometimes; and what's as bad
25 almost, the loss of this town; that is, she is sent into the country, which is the last ill-usage of a husband to a wife, I think.

LUCY [*aside*]. Oh, does the wind lie there?— Then of necessity, madam, you think a man
30 must carry his wife into the country, if he be wise. The country is as terrible, I find, to our young English ladies, as a monastery to those abroad; and, on my virginity, I think they would rather marry a London jailer than a
35 high sheriff of a county, since neither can stir from his employment. Formerly women of wit married fools for a great estate, a fine seat,° or the like; but now 'tis for a pretty seat only in Lincoln's Inn Fields,° St. James's Fields, or the
40 Pall Mall.

[*Enter* SPARKISH, *and* HARCOURT, *dressed like a parson.*]

SPARKISH. Madam, your humble servant, a happy day to you, and to us all.

45 HARCOURT. Amen.

ALITHEA. Who have we here?

SPARKISH. My Chaplain, faith—O madam, poor Harcourt remembers his humble service to you; and, in obedience to your last commands, refrains coming into your sight. 50

ALITHEA. Is not that he?

SPARKISH. No, fy, no; but to show that he ne'er intended to hinder our match, has sent his brother here to join our hands. When I get me a wife, I must get her a chaplain, according 55 to the custom; this is his brother, and my chaplain.

ALITHEA. His brother!

LUCY. [*aside*]. And your chaplain, to preach in your pulpit then— 60

ALITHEA. His brother!

SPARKISH. Nay, I knew you would not believe it.—I told you, sir, she would take you for your brother Frank.

ALITHEA. Believe it! 65

LUCY [*aside*]. His brother! ha! ha! ha! He has a trick left still, it seems.

SPARKISH. Come, my dearest, pray let us go to church before the canonical hour° is past.

ALITHEA. For shame, you are abused still. 70

SPARKISH. By the world, 'tis strange now you are so incredulous.

ALITHEA. 'Tis strange you are so credulous.

SPARKISH. Dearest of my life, hear me. I tell you this is Ned Harcourt of Cambridge, by the 75 world; you see he has a sneaking college look. 'Tis true he's something like his brother Frank; and they differ from each other no more than in their age, for they were twins.

LUCY. Ha! ha! he! 80

ALITHEA. Your servant, sir; I cannot be so deceived, though you are. But come, let's hear, how do you know what you affirm so confidently?

SPARKISH. Why, I'll tell you all. Frank Har- 85 court coming to me this morning to wish me joy, and present his service to you, I asked him if he could help me to a parson. Whereupon he told me he had a brother in town who was in orders; and he went straight away, and sent 90 him, you see there, to me.

---

fine seat well-situated country house
Lincoln's Inn Fields, etc. fashionable places for promenades

canonical hour noon. Weddings were required to be performed in the morning.

ALITHEA. Yes, Frank goes and puts on a black coat, then tells you he is Ned; that's all you have for't.

SPARKISH. Pshaw! pshaw! I tell you, by the
5 same token, the midwife put her garter about Frank's neck, to know 'em asunder, they were so like.

ALITHEA. Frank tells you this too?

SPARKISH. Ay, and Ned there too; nay, they
10 are both in a story.

ALITHEA. So, so; very foolish.

SPARKISH. Lord, if you won't believe one, you had best try him by your chambermaid there; for chambermaids must needs know
15 chaplains from other men, they are so used to 'em.

LUCY. Let's see; nay, I'll be sworn he has the canonical smirk, and the filthy clammy palm of a chaplain.

20 ALITHEA. Well, most reverend doctor, pray let us make an end of this fooling.

HARCOURT. With all my soul, divine heavenly creature, when you please.

ALITHEA. He speaks like a chaplain indeed.

25 SPARKISH. Why, was there not soul, divine, heavenly, in what he said?

ALITHEA. Once more, most impertinent black coat, cease your persecution, and let us have a conclusion of this ridiculous love.

30 HARCOURT [aside]. I had forgot; I must suit my style to my coat, or I wear it in vain.

ALITHEA. I have no more patience left; let us make once an end of this troublesome love, I say.

35 HARCOURT. So be it, seraphic lady, when your honor shall think it meet and convenient so to do.

SPARKISH. 'Gad, I'm sure none but a chaplain could speak so, I think.

40 ALITHEA. Let me tell you, sir, this dull trick will not serve your turn; though you delay our marriage, you shall not hinder it.

HARCOURT. Far be it from me, munificent patroness, to delay your marriage; I desire
45 nothing more than to marry you presently, which I might do, if you yourself would; for my noble, good-natured, and thrice generous patron here would not hinder it.

SPARKISH. No, poor man, not I, faith.

HARCOURT. And now, madam, let me tell 50 you plainly nobody else shall marry you. By Heavens! I'll die first, for I'm sure I should die after it.

LUCY. How his love has made him forget his function, as I have seen it in real parsons! 55

ALITHEA. That was spoken like a chaplain too? Now you understand him, I hope.

SPARKISH. Poor man, he takes it heinously to be refused; I can't blame him, 'tis putting an indignity upon him, not to be suffered; but 60 you'll pardon me, madam, it shan't be; he shall marry us; come away, pray, madam.

LUCY. Ha! ha! he! more ado! 'tis late.

ALITHEA. Invincible stupidity! I tell you, he would marry me as your rival, not as your 65 chaplain.

SPARKISH. Come, come, madam. [Pulling her away.]

LUCY. I pray, madam, do not refuse this reverend divine the honor and satisfaction of 70 marrying you; for I dare say he has set his heart upon't, good doctor.

ALITHEA. What can you hope or design by this?

HARCOURT [aside]. I could answer her, a 75 reprieve for a day only, often revokes a hasty doom. At worst, if she will not take mercy on me, and let me marry her, I have at least the lover's second pleasure, hindering my rival's enjoyment, though but for a time. 80

SPARKISH. Come, madam, t'is e'en twelve o'clock, and my mother charged me never to be married out of the canonical hours. Come, come; Lord, here's such a deal of modesty, I warrant, the first day. 85

LUCY. Yes, an't please your worship, married women show all their modesty the first day, because married men show all their love the first day.

[Exeunt SPARKISH, ALITHEA, HARCOURT, and 90 LUCY.]

Scene ii

[The scene changes to a bedchamber, where appear PINCHWIFE and MRS. PINCHWIFE.]

PINCHWIFE. Come, tell me, I say.

MRS. PINCHWIFE. Lord! han't I told it an hundred times over?

PINCHWIFE [*aside*]. I would try, if in the repetition of the ungrateful tale, I could find her altering it in the least circumstance; for if her story be false, she is so too.—Come, how was't, baggage?

MRS. PINCHWIFE. Lord, what pleasure you take to hear it, sure!

PINCHWIFE. No, you take more in telling it, I find; but speak, how was't?

MRS. PINCHWIFE. He carried me up into the house next to the Exchange.

PINCHWIFE. So, and you two were only in the room!

MRS. PINCHWIFE. Yes, for he sent away a youth that was there, for some dried fruits and China orange.

PINCHWIFE. Did he so? Damn him for it—and for—

MRS. PINCHWIFE. But presently came up the gentlewoman of the house.

PINCHWIFE. Oh, 'twas well she did; but what did he do whilst the fruit came?

MRS. PINCHWIFE. He kissed me an hundred times, and told me he fancied he kissed my fine sister, meaning me, you know, whom he said he loved with all his soul, and bid me be sure to tell her so, and to desire her to be at her window, by eleven of the clock this morning, and he would walk under at that time.

PINCHWIFE [*aside*]. And he was as good as his word, very punctual; a pox reward him for't.

MRS. PINCHWIFE. Well, and he said if you were not within, he would come up to her, meaning me, you know, bud, still.

PINCHWIFE [*aside*]. So—he knew her certainly; but for this confession, I am obliged to her simplicity.—But what, you stood very still when he kissed you?

MRS. PINCHWIFE. Yes, I warrant you; would you have had me discover myself?

PINCHWIFE. But you told me he did some beastliness to you, as you call it; what was't?

MRS. PINCHWIFE. Why, he put—

PINCHWIFE. What?

MRS. PINCHWIFE. Why, he put the tip of his tongue between my lips, and so mousled me—and I said, I'd bite it.

PINCHWIFE. An eternal canker seize it, for a dog!

MRS. PINCHWIFE. Nay, you need not be so angry with him neither, for to say truth, he has the sweetest breath I ever knew.

PINCHWIFE. The devil! you were satisfied with it then, and would do it again?

MRS. PINCHWIFE. Not unless he should force me.

PINCHWIFE. Force you, changeling!° I tell you, no woman can be forced.

MRS. PINCHWIFE. Yes, but she may sure, by such a one as he, for he's a proper, goodly, strong man; 'tis hard, let me tell you, to resist him.

PINCHWIFE. [*aside*]. So, 'tis plain she loves him, yet she has not love enough to make her conceal it from me; but the sight of him will increase her aversion for me and love for him, and that love instruct her how to deceive me and satisfy him, all idiot as she is. Love! 'twas he gave women first their craft, their art of deluding. Out of Nature's hands they came plain, open, silly, and fit for slaves, as she and Heaven intended 'em; but damned Love—well—I must strangle that little monster whilst I can deal with him.—Go fetch pen, ink, and paper out of the next room.

MRS. PINCHWIFE. Yes, bud.

PINCHWIFE. Why should women have more invention in love than men? It can only be because they have more desires, more soliciting passions, more lust, and more of the devil.

[MRS. PINCHWIFE *returns.*]
Come, minx, sit down and write.

MRS. PINCHWIFE. Ay, dear bud, but I can't do't very well.

PINCHWIFE. I wish you could not at all.

MRS. PINCHWIFE. But what should I write for?

PINCHWIFE. I'll have you write a letter to your lover.

MRS. PINCHWIFE. O Lord, to the fine gentleman a letter!

changeling idiot

PINCHWIFE. Yes, to the fine gentleman.

MRS. PINCHWIFE. Lord, you do but jeer; sure you jest.

PINCHWIFE. I am not so merry; come, write as I bid you.

MRS. PINCHWIFE. What, do you think I am a fool?

PINCHWIFE [aside]. She's afraid I would not dictate any love to him, therefore she's unwilling.—But you had best begin.

MRS. PINCHWIFE. Indeed, and indeed, but I won't, so I won't.

PINCHWIFE. Why?

MRS. PINCHWIFE. Because he's in town; you may send for him if you will.

PINCHWIFE. Very well, you would have him brought to you; is it come to this? I say, take the pen and write, or you'll provoke me.

MRS. PINCHWIFE. Lord, what d'ye make a fool of me for? Don't I know that letters are never writ but from the country to London, and from London into the country? Now he's in town, and I am in town too; therefore I can't write to him, you know.

PINCHWIFE [aside]. So, I am glad it is no worse; she is innocent enough yet.—Yes, you may, when your husband bids you, write letters to people that are in town.

MRS. PINCHWIFE. Oh, may I so? then I'm satisfied.

PINCHWIFE. Come, begin [dictates]—"Sir"—

MRS. PINCHWIFE. Shan't I say, "Dear Sir"? You know one says always something more than bare "Sir."

PINCHWIFE. Write as I bid you, or I will write whore with this penknife in your face.

MRS. PINCHWIFE. Nay, good bud [she writes] —"Sir"—

PINCHWIFE. "Though I suffered last night your nauseous, loathed kisses and embraces" —Write!

MRS. PINCHWFE. Nay, why should I say so? You know I told you he had a sweet breath.

PINCHWIFE. Write!

MRS. PINCHWIFE. Let me but put out "loathed."

PINCHWIFE. Write, I say!

MRS. PINCHWIFE. Well then. [Writes.]

PINCHWIFE. Let's see, what have you writ?— [Takes the paper and reads.] "Though I suffered last night your kisses and embraces"— Thou impudent creature! where is "nauseous" and "loathed"?

MRS. PINCHWIFE. I can't abide to write such filthy words.

PINCHWIFE. Once more write as I'd have you, and question it not, or I will spoil thy writing with this. I will stab out those eyes that cause my mischief. [Holds up the penknife.]

MRS. PINCHWIFE. O Lord! I will.

PINCHWIFE. So—so—let's see now.—[Reads.] "Though I suffered last night your nauseous, loathed kisses and embraces"—go on—"yet I would not have you presume that you shall ever repeat them"—so—.[She writes.]

MRS. PINCHWIFE. I have writ it.

PINCHWIFE. On, then—"I then concealed myself from your knowledge, to avoid your insolencies."—[She writes.]

MRS. PINCHWIFE. So—

PINCHWIFE. "The same reason, now I am out of your hands"—.[She writes.]

MRS. PINCHWIFE. So—

PINCHWIFE. "Makes me own to you my unfortunate, though innocent frolic, of being in man's clothes"—.[She writes.]

MRS. PINCHWIFE. So—

PINCHWIFE. "That you may for evermore cease to pursue her, who hates and detests you" —.[She writes on.]

MRS. PINCHWIFE. So-h—[sighs].

PINCHWIFE. What, do you sigh?—"detests you—as much as she loves her husband and her honor."

MRS. PINCHWIFE. I vow, husband, he'll ne'er believe I should write such a letter.

PINCHWIFE. What, he'd expect a kinder from you? Come, now your name only.

MRS. PINCHWIFE. What, shan't I say "Your most faithful humble servant till death"?

PINCHWIFE. No, tormenting fiend!—[Aside.] Her style, I find, would be very soft.—Come, wrap it up now, whilst I go fetch wax and a candle; and write on the backside, "For Mr. Horner."

[Exit PINCHWIFE.]

MRS. PINCHWIFE. "For Mr. Horner."—So, I am glad he has told me his name. Dear Mr. Horner! But why should I send thee such a letter that will vex thee, and make thee angry
5 with me?—Well, I will not send it.—Ay, but then my husband will kill me—for I see plainly he won't let me love Mr. Horner—but what care I for my husband? I won't, so I won't, send poor Mr. Horner such a letter.—
10 But then my husband—but oh, what if I writ at bottom my husband made me write it?—Ay, but then my husband would see't.—Can one have no shift?° Ah, a London woman would have had a hundred presently. Stay—
15 what if I should write a letter, and wrap it up like this, and write upon't too? Ay, but then my husband would see't—I don't know what to do.—But yet evads° I'll try, so I will—for I will not send this letter to poor Mr. Horner,
20 come what will on't.

"Dear, sweet Mr. Horner"—[*she writes and repeats what she hath writ*]—so—"my husband would have me send you a base, rude, unmannerly letter; but I won't"—so—"and
25 would have me forbid you loving me; but I won't"—so—"and would have me say to you, I hate you, poor Mr. Horner; but I won't tell a lie for him"—there—"for I'm sure if you and I were in the country at cards together"—
30 so—"I could not help treading on your toe under the table"—so—"or rubbing knees with you, and staring in your face, till you saw me" —very well—"and then looking down, and blushing for an hour together"—so—"but I
35 must make haste before my husband come; and now he has taught me to write letters, you shall have longer ones from me, who am, dear, dear, poor, dear Mr. Horner, your most humble friend, and servant to command till
40 death.—Margery Pinchwife."

Stay, I must give him a hint at bottom—so —now wrap it up just like t'other—so—now write "For Mr. Horner"—But oh now, what shall I do with it? for here comes my husband.
45 [*Enter* PINCHWIFE.]

PINCHWIFE [*aside*]. I have been detained by a sparkish coxcomb, who pretended a visit to me; but I fear 'twas to my wife.—What, have you done?

MRS. PINCHWIFE. Ay, ay, bud, just now.   50

PINCHWIFE. Let's see't; what d'ye tremble for? what, you would not have it go?

MRS. PINCHWIFE. Here.—[*Aside.*] No, I must not give him that; so I had been served if I had given him this. [*He opens and reads the*   55
first letter.]

PINCHWIFE. Come, where's the wax and seal?

MRS. PINCHWIFE [*aside*]. Lord, what shall I do now? Nay, then I have it.—Pray let me see't. Lord, you think me so arrant a fool I   60
cannot seal a letter; I will do't, so I will. [*Snatches the letter from him, changes it for the other, seals it, and delivers it to him.*]

PINCHWIFE. Nay, I believe you will learn that, and other things too, which I would not   65
have you.

MRS. PINCHWIFE. So, han't I done it curiously?°—[*Aside.*] I think I have; there's my letter going to Mr. Horner, since he'll needs have me send letters to folks.   70

PINCHWIFE. 'Tis very well; but I warrant you would not have it go now?

MRS. PINCHWIFE. Yes, indeed, but I would, bud, now.

PINCHWIFE. Well, you are a good girl then.   75
Come, let me lock you up in your chamber till I come back; and be sure you come not within three strides of the window when I am gone, for I have a spy in the street.—[*Exit* MRS. PINCHWIFE. PINCHWIFE *locks the door.*] At least,   80
'tis fit she think so. If we do not cheat women, they'll cheat us, and fraud may be justly used with secret enemies, of which a wife is the most dangerous; and he that has a handsome one to keep, and a frontier town, must provide   85
against treachery, rather than open force. Now I have secured all within, I'll deal with the foe without, with false intelligence. [*Holds up the letter.*]

[*Exit.*]   90

---

shift method of evasion
evads in faith

curiously nicely

Scene iii

[*The scene changes to* HORNER's *lodging.*]
[*Enter* QUACK *and* HORNER.]

QUACK. Well, sir, how fadges° the new design? Have you not the luck of all your
5 brother projectors, to deceive only yourself at last?

HORNER. No, good domine° doctor, I deceive you, it seems, and others too; for the grave matrons, and old, rigid husbands think me as
10 unfit for love as they are; but their wives, sisters, and daughters know, some of 'em, better things already.

QUACK. Already!

HORNER. Already, I say. Last night I was
15 drunk with half-a-dozen of your civil persons, as you call 'em, and people of honor, and so was made free of their society and dressing-rooms for ever hereafter; and am already come to the privileges of sleeping upon their pallets,
20 warming smocks, tying shoes and garters, and the like, doctor, already, already, doctor.

QUACK. You have made use of your time, sir.

HORNER. I tell thee, I am now no more interruption to 'em when they sing, or talk,
25 bawdy, than a little squab° French page who speaks no English.

QUACK. But do civil persons and women of honor drink, and sing bawdy songs?

HORNER. Oh, amongst friends, amongst
30 friends. For your bigots in honor are just like those in religion; they fear the eye of the world more than the eye of Heaven, and think there is no virtue but railing at vice, and no sin but giving scandal. They rail at a poor
35 little kept player, and keep themselves some young modest pulpit comedian° to be privy to their sins in their closets,° not to tell 'em of them in their chapels.

QUACK. Nay, the truth on't is, priests,

fadges prospers
domine master
squab plump
comedian who cuts a ridiculous figure in a show of piety
in their closets in private

amongst the women now, have quite got the 40 better of us lay-confessors, physicians.

HORNER. And they are rather their patients; but—

[*Enter* LADY FIDGET, *looking about her.*]
Now we talk of women of honor, here comes 45 one. Step behind the screen there, and but observe if I have not particular privileges with the women of reputation already, doctor, already.

[QUACK *retires.*] 50

LADY FIDGET. Well, Horner, am not I a woman of honor? You see, I'm as good as my word.

HORNER. And you shall see, madam, I'll not be behindhand with you in honor; and I'll be 55 as good as my word too, if you please but to withdraw into the next room.

LADY FIDGET. But first, my dear sir, you must promise to have a care of my dear honor.

HORNER. If you talk a word more of your 60 honor, you'll make me incapable to wrong it. To talk of honor in the mysteries of love, is like talking of Heaven or the Diety in an operation of witchcraft just when you are employing the devil; it makes the charm 65 impotent.

LADY FIDGET. Nay, fy! let us not be smutty. But you talk of mysteries and bewitching to me; I don't understand you.

HORNER. I tell you, madam, the word money 70 in a mistress's mouth, at such a nick of time, is not a more disheartening sound to a younger brother, than that of honor to an eager lover like myself.

LADY FIDGET. But you can't blame a lady of 75 my reputation to be chary.

HORNER. Chary! I have been chary of it already, by the report I have caused of myself.

LADY FIDGET. Ay, but if you should ever let other women know that dear secret, it would 80 come out. Nay, you must have a great care of your conduct; for my acquaintance are so censorious (oh, 'tis a wicked, censorious world, Mr. Horner!), I say, are so censorious and detracting that perhaps they'll talk to the pre- 85 judice of my honor, though you should not let them know the dear secret.

HORNER. Nay, madam, rather than they shall prejudice your honor, I'll prejudice theirs; and, to serve you, I'll lie with 'em all, make the secret their own, and then they'll keep it. I am a Machiavel in love, madam.

LADY FIDGET. Oh, no, sir, not that way.

HORNER. Nay, the devil take me if censorious women are to be silenced any other way.

LADY FIDGET. A secret is better kept, I hope, by a single person than a multitude; therefore pray do not trust anybody else with it, dear, dear Mr. Horner. [*Embracing him.*]

[*Enter* SIR JASPER FIDGET.]

SIR JASPER FIDGET. How now!

LADY FIDGET [*aside*]. Oh my husband!—prevented—and what's almost as bad, found with my arms about another man—that will appear too much—what shall I say?—Sir Jasper, come hither. I am trying if Mr. Horner were ticklish, and he's as ticklish as can be. I love to torment the confounded toad; let you and I tickle him.

SIR JASPER FIDGET. No, your ladyship will tickle him better without me, I suppose. But is this your buying china? I thought you had been at the china-house.

HORNER [*aside*]. China-house; that's my cue, I must take it.—A pox! can't you keep your impertinent wives at home? Some men are troubled with the husbands, but I with the wives; but I'd have you to know, since I cannot be your journeyman by night, I will not be your drudge by day, to squire your wife about, and be your man of straw, or scarecrow only to pies and jays,° that would be nibbling at your forbidden fruit; I shall be shortly the hackney° gentleman-usher of the town.

SIR JASPER FIDGET [*aside*]. He! he! he! poor fellow, he's in the right on't, faith. To squire women about for other folks is as ungrateful an employment as to tell money for other folks. —He! he! he! be'n't angry, Horner.

LADY FIDGET. No, 'tis I have more reason to be angry, who am left by you to go abroad indecently alone; or, what is more indecent, to

pin myself upon such ill-bred people of your acquaintance as this is.

SIR JASPER FIDGET. Nay, prithee, what has he done?

LADY FIDGET. Nay, he has done nothing.

SIR JASPER FIDGET. But what d'ye take ill, if he has done nothing?

LADY FIDGET. Ha! ha! ha! faith, I can't but laugh, however; why, d'ye think the unmannerly toad would come down to me to the coach? I was fain to come up to fetch him, or go without him, which I was resolved not to do; for he knows china very well, and has himself very good, but will not let me see it lest I should beg some; but I will find it out, and have what I came for yet.

[*Exit* LADY FIDGET, *followed by* HORNER *to the door.*]

HORNER [*apart to* LADY FIDGET]. Lock the door, madam. So, she has got into my chamber and locked me out. Oh the impertinency of womankind! Well, Sir Jasper, plain-dealing is a jewel; if ever you suffer your wife to trouble me again here she shall carry you home a pair of horns, by my lord mayor she shall; though I cannot furnish you myself, you are sure, yet I'll find a way.

SIR JASPER FIDGET. Ha! ha! he!—[*Aside.*] At my first coming in, and finding her arms about him, tickling him it seems, I was half jealous, but now I see my folly.—He! he! he! poor Horner.

HORNER. Nay, though you laugh now, 'twill be my turn ere long. Oh, women, more impertinent, more cunning, and more mischievous than their monkeys, and to me almost as ugly! —Now is she throwing my things about and rifling all I have; but I'll get in to her the back way, and so rifle her for it.

SIR JASPER FIDGET. Ha! ha! ha! poor angry Horner.

HORNER. Stay here a little, I'll ferret her out to you presently, I warrant.

[*Exit at the other door.*]

[SIR JASPER *calls through the door to his wife; she answers from within.*]

SIR JASPER FIDGET. Wife! my Lady Fidget! wife! he is coming in to you the back way.

pies and jays tattlers and dandies
the hackney commonest available

LADY FIDGET. Let him come and welcome, which way he will.

SIR JASPER FIDGET. He'll catch you, and use you roughly, and be too strong for you.

5 LADY FIDGET. Don't you trouble yourself, let him if he can.

QUACK [behind]. This indeed I could not have believed from him, nor any but my own eyes.

10 [Enter MRS. SQUEAMISH.]

MRS. SQUEAMISH. Where's this woman-hater, this toad, this ugly, greasy, dirty sloven?

SIR JASPER FIDGET [aside]. So, the women all will have him ugly; methinks he is a comely 15 person, but his wants make his form contemptible to 'em; and 'tis e'en as my wife said yesterday, talking of him, that a proper handsome eunuch was as ridiculous a thing as a gigantic coward.

20 MRS. SQUEAMISH. Sir Jasper, your servant. Where is the odious beast?

SIR JASPER FIDGET. He's within in his chamber, with my wife; she's playing the wag with him.

25 MRS. SQUEAMISH. Is she so? and he's a clownish beast, he'll give her no quarter, he'll play the wag with her again, let me tell you. Come, let's go help her.—What, the door's locked?

30 SIR JASPER FIDGET. Ay, my wife locked it.

MRS. SQUEAMISH. Did she so? Let us break it open then.

SIR JASPER FIDGET. No, no; he'll do her no hurt.

35 MRS. SQUEAMISH. No.—[Aside]. But is there no other way to get in to 'em? Whither goes this? I will disturb 'em.

[Exit MRS. SQUEAMISH at another door.]

[Enter OLD LADY SQUEAMISH.]

40 OLD LADY SQUEAMISH. Where is this harlotry, this impudent baggage, this rambling tomrigg?° O Sir Jasper, I'm glad to see you here; did you not see my vile grandchild come in hither just now?

45 SIR JASPER FIDGET. Yes.

OLD LADY SQUEAMISH. Ay, but where is she then? where is she? Lord, Sir Jasper, I have e'en rattled myself to pieces in pursuit of her. But can you tell what she makes here? They say below, no woman lodges here. 50

SIR JASPER FIDGET. No.

OLD LADY SQUEAMISH. No! what does she here then? Say, if it be not a woman's lodging, what makes she here? But are you sure no woman lodges here? 55

SIR JASPER FIDGET. No, nor no man neither; this is Mr. Horner's lodging.

OLD LADY SQUEAMISH. Is it so, are you sure?

SIR JASPER FIDGET. Yes, yes.

OLD LADY SQUEAMISH. So; then there's no 60 hurt in't, I hope. But where is he?

SIR JASPER FIDGET. He's in the next room with my wife.

OLD LADY SQUEAMISH. Nay, if you trust him with your wife, I may with my Biddy. They say 65 he's a merry harmless man now, e'en as harmless a man as ever come out of Italy with a good voice,° and as pretty, harmless company for a lady as a snake without his teeth.

SIR JASPER FIDGET. Ay, ay, poor man. 70

[Enter MRS. SQUEAMISH.]

MRS. SQUEAMISH. I can't find 'em.—Oh, are you here, grandmother? I followed, you must know, my Lady Fidget hither; 'tis the prettiest lodging, and I have been staring on the prettiest 75 pictures—

[Enter LADY FIDGET with a piece of china in her hand, and HORNER following.]

LADY FIDGET. And I have been toiling and moiling for the prettiest piece of china, my dear. 80

HORNER. Nay, she has been too hard for me, do what I could.

MRS. SQUEAMISH. O Lord, I'll have some china too. Good Mr. Horner, don't think to give other people china, and me none; come in 85 with me too.

HORNER. Upon my honor, I have none left now.

MRS. SQUEAMISH. Nay, nay, I have known you deny your china before now, but you shan't 90 put me off so. Come.

HORNER. This lady had the last there.

LADY FIDGET. Yes, indeed, madam, to my certain knowledge, he has no more left.

---

tomrigg tomboy; immodest woman

with a good voice i.e., a male soprano, a eunuch

MRS. SQUEAMISH. Oh, but it may be he may have some you could not find.

LADY FIDGET. What, d'ye think if he had had any left, I would not have had it too? for we
5 women of quality never think we have china enough.

HORNER. Do not take it ill, I cannot make china for you all, but I will have a roll-waggon° for you too, another time.

10 MRS. SQUEAMISH. Thank you, dear toad.

LADY FIDGET [*to* HORNER *aside*]. What do you mean by that promise?

HORNER [*apart to* LADY FIDGET]. Alas, she has an innocent, literal understanding.

15 OLD LADY SQUEAMISH. Poor Mr. Horner! he has enough to do to please you all, I see.

HORNER. Ay, madam, you see how they use me.

OLD LADY SQUEAMISH. Poor gentleman, I pity
20 you.

HORNER. I thank you, madam. I could never find pity but from such reverend ladies as you are; the young ones will never spare a man.

MRS. SQUEAMISH. Come, come, beast, and go
25 dine with us; for we shall want a man at ombre after dinner.

HORNER. That's all their use of me, madam, you see.

MRS. SQUEAMISH. Come, sloven, I'll lead you,
30 to be sure of you. [*Pulls him by the cravat.*]

OLD LADY SQUEAMISH. Alas, poor man, how she tugs him! Kiss, kiss her; that's the way to make such women quiet.

HORNER. No, madam, that remedy is worse
35 than the torment; they know I dare suffer anything rather than do it.

OLD LADY SQUEAMISH. Prithee kiss her, and I'll give you her picture in little, that you admired so last night; prithee do.

40 HORNER. Well, nothing but that could bribe me. I love a woman only in effigy and good painting, as much as I hate them. I'll do't, for I could adore the devil well painted. [*Kisses* MRS. SQUEAMISH.]

45 MRS. SQUEAMISH. Foh, you filthy toad! nay,

---

roll-waggon (etymology uncertain) a tall, cylindrical blue-and-white china vase

now I've done jesting.

OLD LADY SQUEAMISH. Ha! ha! ha! I told you so.

MRS. SQUEAMISH. Foh! a kiss of his—

SIR JASPER FIDGET. Has no more hurt in't than 50 one of my spaniel's.

MRS. SQUEAMISH. Nor no more good neither.

QUACK [*behind*]. I will now believe anything he tells me.

[*Enter* PINCHWIFE.] 55

LADY FIDGET. O Lord, here's a man! Sir Jasper, my mask, my mask! I would not be seen here for the world.

SIR JASPER FIDGET. What, not when I am with you? 60

LADY FIDGET. No, no, my honor—let's be gone.

MRS. SQUEAMISH. O grandmother, let us be gone; make haste, make haste, I know not how he may censure us. 65

LADY FIDGET. Be found in the lodging of anything like a man!—Away.

[*Exeunt* SIR JASPER FIDGET, LADY FIDGET, OLD LADY SQUEAMISH, MRS. SQUEAMISH.]

QUACK [*behind*]. What's here? another 70 cuckold? he looks like one, and none else sure have any business with him.

HORNER. Well, what brings my dear friend hither?

PINCHWIFE. Your impertinency. 75

HORNER. My impertinency!—Why, you gentlemen that have got handsome wives think you have a privilege of saying anything to your friends, and are as brutish as if you were our creditors. 80

PINCHWIFE. No, sir, I'll ne'er trust you any way.

HORNER. But why not, dear Jack? Why diffide° in me thou know'st so well?

PINCHWIFE. Because I do know you so well. 85

HORNER. Han't I been always thy friend, honest Jack, always ready to serve thee, in love or battle, before thou wert married, and am so still?

PINCHWIFE. I believe so; you would be my 90 second now, indeed.

HORNER. Well then, dear Jack, why so

---

diffide not trust

unkind, so grum, so strange to me? Come, prithee, kiss me, dear rogue. Gad, I was always, I say, and am still as much thy servant as—

PINCHWIFE. As I am yours, sir. What, you
5 would send a kiss to my wife, is that it?

HORNER. So, there 'tis—a man can't show his friendship to a married man, but presently he talks of his wife to you. Prithee, let thy wife alone, and let thee and I be all one, as we were
10 wont. What, thou art as shy of my kindness as a Lombard Street alderman° of a courtier's civility at Locket's!°

PINCHWIFE. But you are overkind to me, as kind as if I were your cuckold already; yet I
15 must confess you ought to be kind and civil to me, since I am so kind, so civil to you, as to bring you this. Look you there, sir. [*Delivers him a letter.*]

HORNER. What is't?
20 PINCHWIFE. Only a love letter, sir.

HORNER. From whom?—how! this is from your wife—hum—and hum—[*reads*].

PINCHWIFE. Even from my wife, sir; am I not wondrous kind and civil to you now too?—
25 [*Aside.*] But you'll not think her so.

HORNER [*aside*]. Ha! is this a trick of his or hers?

PINCHWIFE. The gentleman's surprised I find. —What, you expected a kinder letter?
30 HORNER. No faith, not I, how could I?

PINCHWIFE. Yes, yes, I'm sure you did. A man so well made as you are must needs be disappointed if the women declare not their passion at first sight or opportunity.
35 HORNER [*aside*]. But what should this mean? Stay, the postscript.—[*Reads aside.*] "Be sure you love me, whatsoever my husband says to the contrary, and let him not see this, lest he should come home and pinch me, or kill my
40 squirrel."—It seems he knows not what the letter contains.

PINCHWIFE. Come, ne'er wonder at it so much.

HORNER. Faith, I can't help it.

as a Lombard Street alderman as a moneylender being flattered by stone-broke gentlemen looking for credit
Locket's a fashionable tavern

PINCHWIFE. Now, I think I have deserved 45 your infinite friendship and kindness, and have showed myself sufficiently an obliging kind friend and husband; am I not so, to bring a letter from my wife to her gallant?

HORNER. Ay, the devil take me, art thou, the 50 most obliging, kind friend and husband in the world, ha! ha!

PINCHWIFE. Well, you may be merry, sir; but in short I must tell you, sir, my honor will suffer no jesting. 55

HORNER. What dost thou mean?

PINCHWIFE. Does the letter want a comment? Then, know, sir, though I have been so civil a husband as to bring you a letter from my wife, to let you kiss and court her to my face, I will 60 not be a cuckold, sir, I will not.

HORNER. Thou art mad with jealousy. I never saw thy wife in my life but at the play yesterday, and I know not if it were she or no. I court her, kiss her! 65

PINCHWIFE. I will not be a cuckold, I say; there will be danger in making me a cuckold.

HORNER. Why, wert thou not well cured of thy last clap?

PINCHWIFE. I wear a sword. 70

HORNER. It should be taken from thee, lest thou shouldst do thyself a mischief with it; thou art mad, man.

PINCHWIFE. As mad as I am, and as merry as you are, I must have more reason from you ere 75 we part. I say again, though you kissed and courted last night my wife in man's clothes, as she confesses in her letter—

HORNER [*aside*]. Ha!

PINCHWIFE. Both she and I say you must not 80 design it again, for you have mistaken your woman, as you have done your man.

HORNER [*aside*]. Oh—I understand something now.—Was that thy wife? Why wouldst thou not tell me 'twas she? Faith, my freedom 85 with her was your fault, not mine.

PINCHWIFE [*aside*]. Faith, so 'twas.

HORNER. Fy! I'd never do't to a woman before her husband's face, sure.

PINCHWIFE. But I had rather you should do't 90 to my wife before my face, than behind my back; and that you shall never do.

HORNER. No—you will hinder me.

PINCHWIFE. If I would not hinder you, you see by her letter she would.

HORNER. Well, I must acquiesce then, and be contented with what she writes.

5 PINCHWIFE. I'll assure you 'twas voluntarily writ; I had no hand in't, you may believe me.

HORNER. I do believe thee, faith.

PINCHWIFE. And believe her too, for she's an innocent creature, has no dissembling in her;
10 and so fare you well, sir.

HORNER. Pray, however, present my humble service to her, and tell her I will obey her letter to a tittle, and fulfill her desires, be what they will, or with what difficulty soever I do't; and
15 you shall be no more jealous of me, I warrant her, and you.

PINCHWIFE. Well then, fare you well; and play with any man's honor but mine, kiss any man's wife but mine, and welcome.

20 [*Exit.*]

HORNER. Ha! ha! ha!—Doctor.

QUACK. It seems he has not heard the report of you, or does not believe it.

HORNER. Ha! ha!—now, doctor, what think
25 you?

QUACK. Pray let's see the letter—hum— [*reads the letter*]—"for—dear—love you—"

HORNER. I wonder how she could contrive it! What say'st thou to't? 'Tis an original.°

30 QUACK. So are your cuckolds, too, originals, for they are like no other common cuckolds, and I will henceforth believe it not impossible for you to cuckold the Grand Signior° amidst his guards of eunuchs, that I say.

35 HORNER. And I say for the letter, 'tis the first love letter that ever was without flames, darts, fates, destinies, lying and dissembling in't.

[*Enter* SPARKISH *pulling in* MR. PINCHWIFE.]

SPARKISH. Come back, you are a pretty
40 brother-in-law, neither go to church nor to dinner with your sister bride!

PINCHWIFE. My sister denies her marriage, and you see is gone away from you dissatisfied.

SPARKISH. Pshaw! upon a foolish scruple that
45 our parson was not in lawful orders, and did not say all the common prayer; but 'tis her

modesty only I believe. But let women be never so modest the first day, they'll be sure to come to themselves by night, and I shall have enough of her then. In the meantime, Harry Horner, 50 you must dine with me. I keep my wedding at my aunt's in the Piazza.°

HORNER. Thy wedding! What stale maid has lived to despair of a husband, or what young one of a gallant? 55

SPARKISH. Oh, your servant, sir—this gentleman's sister then,—no stale maid.

HORNER. I'm sorry for't.

PINCHWIFE [*aside*]. How comes he so concerned for her? 60

SPARKISH. You sorry for't? Why, do you know any ill by her?

HORNER. No, I know none but by thee; 'tis for her sake, not yours, and another man's sake that might have hoped, I thought. 65

SPARKISH. Another man! another man! What is his name?

HORNER. Nay, since 'tis past, he shall be nameless.—[*Aside.*] Poor Harcourt! I am sorry thou hast missed her. 70

PINCHWIFE [*aside*]. He seems to be much troubled at the match.

SPARKISH. Prithee, tell me—Nay, you shan't go, brother.

PINCHWIFE. I must of necessity, but I'll come 75 to you to dinner.

[*Exit.*]

SPARKISH. But, Harry, what, have I a rival in my wife already? But with all my heart, for he may be of use to me hereafter; for though my 80 hunger is now my sauce, and I can fall on heartily without, the time will come when a rival will be as good sauce for a married man to a wife, as an orange to veal.

HORNER. O thou damned rogue! thou hast set 85 my teeth on edge with thy orange.

SPARKISH. Then let's to dinner—there I was with you again. Come.

HORNER. But who dines with thee?

SPARKISH. My friends and relations, my 90 brother Pinchwife, you see, of your acquaintance.

HORNER. And his wife?

an original most extraordinary
Grand Signior the Sultan of Turkey

Piazza The square of Covent Garden

SPARKISH. No, 'gad, he'll ne'er let her come amongst us good fellows; your stingy country coxcomb keeps his wife from his friends, as he does his little firkin of ale for his own drinking,
5 and a gentleman can't get a smack on't; but his servants, when his back is turned, broach it at their pleasures, and dust it away, ha! ha! ha!—'Gad, I'm witty, I think, considering I was married today, by the world; but come—

10 HORNER. No, I will not dine with you, unless you can fetch her too.

SPARKISH. Pshaw! what pleasure canst thou have with women now, Harry?

HORNER. My eyes are not gone; I love a good
15 prospect yet, and will not dine with you unless she does too; go fetch her, therefore, but do not tell her husband 'tis for my sake.

SPARKISH. Well, I'll go try what I can do; in the meantime, come away to my aunt's lodging;
20 'tis in the way to Pinchwife's.

HORNER. The poor woman has called for aid, and stretched forth her hand, doctor; I cannot but help her over the pale° out of the briars.

[Exeunt SPARKISH, HORNER, QUACK.]

Scene iv

25 [The scene changes to PINCHWIFE's house.]

[Mrs. PINCHWIFE alone, leaning on her elbow. A table, pen, ink, and paper.]

MRS. PINCHWIFE. Well, 'tis e'en so, I have got the London disease they call love; I am sick of
30 my husband, and for my gallant. I have heard this distemper called a fever, but methinks 'tis liker an ague; for when I think of my husband, I tremble, and am in a cold sweat, and have inclinations to vomit; but when I think of my
35 gallant, dear Mr. Horner, my hot fit comes, and I am all in a fever indeed; and, as in other fevers, my own chamber is tedious to me, and I would fain be removed to his, and then methinks I should be well. Ah, poor Mr. Horner!
40 Well, I cannot, will not stay here; therefore I'll make an end of my letter to him, which shall be a finer letter than my last, because I have studied it like anything. Oh, sick, sick! [Takes the pen and writes.]

pale fence

[Enter PINCHWIFE, who, seeing her writing, 45 steals softly behind her, and, looking over her shoulder, snatches the paper from her.]

PINCHWIFE. What, writing more letters?

MRS. PINCHWIFE. O Lord, bud, why d'ye fright me so? [She offers to run out; he stops 50 her, and reads.]

PINCHWIFE. How's this? nay, you shall not stir, madam;—"Dear, dear, dear Mr. Horner"—very well—I have taught you to write letters to good purpose—but let's see't. "First, I am to 55 beg your pardon for my boldness in writing to you, which I'd have you to know I would not have done, had you not said first you loved me so extremely, which if you do, you will never suffer me to lie in the arms of another man 60 whom I loathe, nauseate, and detest."—Now you can write these filthy words. But what follows?—"Therefore, I hope you will speedily find some way to free me from this unfortunate match, which was never, I assure you, of my 65 choice, but I'm afraid 'tis already too far gone; however, if you love me, as I do you, you will try what you can do; but you must help me away before tomorrow, or else, alas! I shall be for ever out of your reach, for I can defer no 70 longer our—our—"[the letter concludes] what is to follow "our"?—speak, what? Our journey into the country I suppose.—Oh woman, damned woman! and Love, damned Love, their old tempter! for this is one of his miracles; in a 75 moment he can make those blind that could see, and those see that were blind, those dumb that could speak, and those prattle who were dumb before; nay, what is more than all, make these dough-baked, senseless, indocile animals, 80 women, too hard for us, their politic lords and rulers, in a moment. But make an end of your letter, and then I'll make an end of you thus, and all my plagues together. [Draws his sword.] 85

MRS. PINCHWIFE. O Lord, O Lord, you are such a passionate man, bud!

[Enter SPARKISH.]

SPARKISH. How now, what's here to do?

PINCHWIFE. This fool here now! 90

SPARKISH. What, drawn upon your wife? You should never do that, but at night in the dark,

when you can't hurt her. This is my sister-in-
law, is it not? ay, faith, e'en our country Margery [*pulls aside her handkerchief*]; one may
know her. Come, she and you must go dine
5 with me; dinner's ready, come. But where's my
wife? Is she not come home yet? Where is she?

PINCHWIFE. Making you a cuckold; 'tis that
they all do, as soon as they can.

SPARKISH. What, the wedding-day? No, a
10 wife that designs to make a cully° of her husband will be sure to let him win the first stake
of love, by the world. But come, they stay
dinner for us; come, I'll lead down our Margery.

15 MRS. PINCHWIFE. No.—Sir, go, we'll follow
you.

SPARKISH. I will not wag without you.

PINCHWIFE [*aside*]. This coxcomb is a sensible
torment to me amidst the greatest in the world.

20 SPARKISH. Come, come, Madam Margery.

PINCHWIFE. No; I'll lead her my way: what,
would you treat your friends with mine, for
want of your own wife?—[*Leads her to the
other door, and locks her in and returns.*] I am
25 contented my rage should take breath—

SPARKISH [*aside*]. I told Horner this.

PINCHWIFE. Come now.

SPARKISH. Lord, how shy you are of your wife!
But let me tell you, brother, we men of wit have
30 amongst us a saying that cuckolding, like the
small-pox, comes with a fear; and you may
keep your wife as much as you will out of
danger of infection, but if her constitution
incline her to't, she'll have it sooner or later, by
35 the world, say they.

PINCHWIFE [*aside*]. What a thing is a cuckold,
that every fool can make him ridiculous!—
Well, sir—but let me advise you, now you are
come to be concerned, because you suspect the
40 danger, not to neglect the means to prevent it,
especially when the greatest share of the
malady will light upon your own head, for
Hows'e'er the kind wife's belly comes to
[swell,
45 The husband breeds for her, and first is ill.

cully dupe

ACT V

Scene i

[MR. PINCHWIFE'S *house.*]
[*Enter* MR. PINCHWIFE *and* MRS. PINCHWIFE.
A table and candle.]

PINCHWIFE. Come, take the pen and make an
end of the letter, just as you intended; if you 50
are false in a tittle, I shall soon perceive it, and
punish you with this as you deserve.—[*Lays
his hand on his sword.*] Write what was to
follow—let's see—"You must make haste, and
help me away before tomorrow, or else I shall 55
be for ever out of your reach, for I can defer no
longer our"—what follows "our"?

MRS. PINCHWIFE. Must all out, then, bud?—
Look you there, then. [MRS. PINCHWIFE *takes
the pen and writes.*] 60

PINCHWIFE. Let's see—"For I can defer no
longer our—wedding—Your slighted Alithea."
—What's the meaning of this? My sister's
name to't? Speak, unriddle.

MRS. PINCHWIFE. Yes, indeed, bud. 65

PINCHWIFE. But why her name to't? Speak—
speak, I say.

MRS. PINCHWIFE. Ay, but you'll tell her then
again. If you would not tell her again—

PINCHWIFE. I will not—I am stunned, my 70
head turns round.—Speak.

MRS. PINCHWIFE. Won't you tell her, indeed,
and indeed?

PINCHWIFE. No; speak, I say.

MRS. PINCHWIFE. She'll be angry with me; 75
but I had rather she should be angry with me
than you, bud; and, to tell you the truth, 'twas
she made me write the letter, and taught me
what I should write.

PINCHWIFE [*aside*]. Ha! I thought the style 80
was somewhat better than her own.—But how
could she come to you to teach you, since I had
locked you up alone?

MRS. PINCHWIFE. Oh, through the keyhole,
bud. 85

PINCHWIFE. But why should she make you
write a letter for her to him, since she can write
herself?

MRS. PINCHWIFE. Why, she said because—for
I was unwilling to do it— 90

PINCHWIFE. Because what—because?

MRS. PINCHWIFE. Because, lest Mr. Horner should be cruel, and refuse her; or vain afterwards, and show the letter, she might disown it, the hand not being hers.

PINCHWIFE [aside]. How's this? Ha!—then I think I shall come to myself again. This changeling could not invent this lie, but if she could, why should she? she might think I should soon discover it.—Stay—now I think on't too, Horner said he was sorry she had married Sparkish; and her disowning her marriage to me makes me think she has evaded it for Horner's sake. Yet why should she take this course? But men in love are fools; women may well be so.—But hark you, madam, your sister went out in the morning, and I have not seen her within since.

MRS. PINCHWIFE. Alack-a-day, she has been crying all day above, it seems, in a corner.

PINCHWIFE. Where is she? Let me speak with her.

MRS. PINCHWIFE [aside]. O Lord, then he'll discover all!—Pray hold, bud; what, d'ye mean to discover me? She'll know I have told you then. Pray, bud, let me talk with her first.

PINCHWIFE. I must speak with her, to know whether Horner ever made her any promise, and whether she be married to Sparkish or no.

MRS. PINCHWIFE. Pray, dear bud, don't, till I have spoken with her, and told her that I have told you all; for she'll kill me else.

PINCHWIFE. Go then, and bid her come out to me.

MRS. PINCHWIFE. Yes, yes, bud.

PINCHWIFE. Let me see—

MRS. PINCHWIFE [aside]. I'll go, but she is not within to come to him. I have just got time to know of Lucy, her maid, who first set me on work, what lie I shall tell next; for I am e'en at my wit's end.

[Exit.]

PINCHWIFE. Well, I resolve it, Horner shall have her. I'd rather give him my sister than lend him my wife; and such an alliance will prevent his pretensions to my wife, sure. I'll make him of kin to her, and then he won't care for her.

[MRS. PINCHWIFE returns.]

MRS. PINCHWIFE. O Lord, bud! I told you what anger you would make me with my sister.

PINCHWIFE. Won't she come hither?

MRS. PINCHWIFE. No, no. Alack-a-day, she's ashamed to look you in the face, and she says, if you go in to her, she'll run away downstairs, and shamefully go herself to Mr. Horner, who has promised her marriage, she says; and she will have no other, so she won't.

PINCHWIFE. Did he so?—promise her marriage!—then she shall have no other. Go tell her so; and if she will come and discourse with me a little concerning the means, I will about it immediately. Go.—[Exit MRS. PINCHWIFE.] His estate is equal to Sparkish's, and his extraction as much better than his as his parts are; but my chief reason is I'd rather be akin to him by the name of brother-in-law than that of cuckold.

[Enter MRS. PINCHWIFE.]

Well, what says she now?

MRS. PINCHWIFE. Why, she says she would only have you lead her to Horner's lodging; with whom she first will discourse the matter before she talks with you, which yet she cannot do; for alack, poor creature, she says she can't so much as look you in the face, therefore she'll come to you in a mask. And you must excuse her if she make you no answer to any question of yours, till you have brought her to Mr. Horner; and if you will not chide her, nor question her, she'll come out to you immediately.

PINCHWIFE. Let her come. I will not speak a word to her, nor require a word from her.

MRS. PINCHWIFE. Oh, I forgot; besides, she says she cannot look you in the face, though through a mask; therefore would desire you to put out the candle.

PINCHWIFE. I agree to all. Let her make haste. —There, 'tis out.—[Puts out the candle. Exit MRS. PINCHWIFE.] My case is something better; I'd rather fight with Horner for not lying with my sister, than for lying with my wife; and of the two, I had rather find my sister too forward than my wife. I expected no other from her free education, as she calls it, and her passion for the town. Well, wife and sister are names which make us expect love and duty, pleasure and comfort; but we find 'em plagues and torments, and are equally, though differently, troublesome to their keeper, for we have as much ado to get people to lie with our sisters as to keep 'em from lying with our wives.

[*Enter* MRS. PINCHWIFE *masked, and in hoods and scarfs, and a night-gown and petticoat° of* ALITHEA's, *in the dark.*]

What, are you come, sister? let us go then.— But first let me lock up my wife. Mrs. Margery, where are you?

MRS. PINCHWIFE. Here, bud.

PINCHWIFE. Come hither, that I may lock you up; get you in.—[*Locks the door.*] Come, sister, where are you now?

[MRS. PINCHWIFE *gives him her hand; but when he lets her go, she steals softly on the other side of him, and is led away by him for his sister,* ALITHEA.]

Scene ii

[*The scene changes to* HORNER's *lodging.*]
[QUACK, HORNER.]

QUACK. What, all alone? not so much as one of your cuckolds here, nor one of their wives! They use to take their turns with you, as if they were to watch you.

HORNER. Yes, it often happens that a cuckold is but his wife's spy, and is more upon family duty when he is with her gallant abroad, hindering his pleasure, than when he is at home with her playing the gallant. But the hardest duty a married woman imposes upon a lover is keeping her husband company always.

QUACK. And his fondness wearies you almost as soon as hers.

HORNER. A pox! keeping a cuckold company, after you have had his wife, is as tiresome as the company of a country squire to a witty fellow of the town, when he has got all his money.

QUACK. And as at first a man makes a friend of the husband to get the wife, so at last you

are fain to fall out with the wife to be rid of the husband.

HORNER. Ay, most cuckold-makers are true courtiers, when once a poor man has cracked his credit for 'em, they can't abide to come near him.

QUACK. But at first, to draw him in, are so sweet, so kind, so dear! just as you are to Pinchwife. But what becomes of that intrigue with his wife?

HORNER. A pox! he's as surly as an alderman that has been bit; and since he's so coy, his wife's kindness is in vain, for she's a silly innocent.

QUACK. Did she not send you a letter by him?

HORNER. Yes; but that's a riddle I have not yet solved. Allow the poor creature to be willing, she is silly too, and he keeps her up so close—

QUACK. Yes, so close, that he makes her but the more willing, and adds but revenge to her love; which two, when met, seldom fail of satisfying each other one way or other.

HORNER. What! here's the man we are talking of, I think.

[*Enter* MR. PINCHWIFE, *leading in his wife masked, muffled, and in her sister's gown.*]
Pshaw!

QUACK. Bringing his wife to you is the next thing to bringing a love letter from her.

HORNER. What means this?

PINCHWIFE. The last time, you know, sir, I brought you a letter; now, you see, a mistress; I think you'll say I am a civil man to you.

HORNER. Ay, the devil take me, will I say thou art the civilest man I ever met with; and I have known some. I fancy I understand thee now better than I did the letter. But, hark thee, in thy ear—

PINCHWIFE. What?

HORNER. Nothing but the usual question, man: is she sound, on thy word?

PINCHWIFE. What, you take her for a wench, and me for a pimp?

HORNER. Pshaw! wench and pimp, paw° words; I know thou art an honest fellow, and

---

night-gown and petticoat loose cloak for evening wear and a fancy skirt

paw improper

hast a great acquaintance among the ladies, and perhaps hast made love for me, rather than let me make love to thy wife.

PINCHWIFE. Come, sir, in short, I am for no fooling.

HORNER. Nor I neither; therefore prithee, let's see her face presently. Make her show, man; art thou sure I don't know her?

PINCHWIFE. I am sure you do know her.

HORNER. A pox! why dost thou bring her to me then?

PINCHWIFE. Because she's a relation of mine—

HORNER. Is she, faith, man? then thou art still more civil and obliging, dear rogue.

PINCHWIFE. Who desired me to bring her to you.

HORNER. Then she is obliging, dear rogue.

PINCHWIFE. You'll make her welcome for my sake, I hope.

HORNER. I hope she is handsome enough to make herself welcome. Prithee, let her unmask.

PINCHWIFE. Do you speak to her; she would never be ruled by me.

HORNER. Madam—[Mrs. PINCHWIFE *whispers to* HORNER]. She says she must speak with me in private. Withdraw, prithee.

PINCHWIFE. [*aside*]. She's unwilling, it seems, I should know all her undecent conduct in this business.—Well then, I'll leave you together, and hope when I am gone, you'll agree; if not, you and I shan't agree, sir.

HORNER. What means the fool? if she and I agree 'tis no matter what you and I do. [*Whispers to* MRS. PINCHWIFE, *who makes signs with her hand for* PINCHWIFE *to be gone.*]

PINCHWIFE. In the meantime I'll fetch a parson, and find out Sparkish and disabuse him. You would have me fetch a parson, would you not? Well then—now I think I am rid of her, and shall have no more trouble with her. Our sisters and daughters, like usurers' money, are safest when put out; but our wives, like their writings, never safe but in our closets under lock and key.

[*Exit.*]
[*Enter* BOY.]

BOY. Sir Jasper Fidget, sir, is coming up.

[*Exit.*]

HORNER. Here's the trouble of a cuckold now we are talking of. A pox on him! has he not enough to do to hinder his wife's sport, but he must other women's too?—Step in here, madam.

[*Exit* MRS. PINCHWIFE.]
[*Enter* SIR JASPER FIDGET.]

SIR JASPER FIDGET. My best and dearest friend.

HORNER [*aside to* QUACK]. The old style, doctor.—Well, be short, for I am busy. What would your impertinent wife have now?

SIR JASPER FIDGET. Well guessed, i'faith; for I do come from her.

HORNER. To invite me to supper! Tell her, I can't come; go.

SIR JASPER FIDGET. Nay, now you are out, faith; for my lady, and the whole knot of the virtuous gang, as they call themselves, are resolved upon a frolic of coming to you tonight in masquerade, and are all dressed already.

HORNER. I shan't be at home.

SIR JASPER FIDGET [*aside*]. Lord, how churlish he is to women!—Nay, prithee don't disappoint 'em; they'll think 'tis my fault; prithee don't. I'll send in the banquet and the fiddles. But make no noise on't; for the poor virtuous rogues would not have it known, for the world, that they go a-masquerading; and they would come to no man's ball but yours.

HORNER. Well, well—get you gone; and tell 'em, if they come, 'twill be at the peril of their honor and yours.

SIR JASPER FIDGET. He! he! he!—We'll trust you for that; farewell.

[*Exit.*]

HORNER.
Doctor, anon you too shall be my guest,
But now I'm going to a private feast.
[*Exeunt.*]

Scene iii

[*The scene changes to the piazza of Covent Garden.*]

[SPARKISH, PINCHWIFE.]

SPARKISH [*with the letter in his hand*]. But who would have thought a woman could have been false to me? By the world, I could not have thought it.

PINCHWIFE. You were for giving and taking liberty; she has taken it only, sir, now you find in that letter. You are a frank person, and so is she, you see there.

SPARKISH. Nay, if this be her hand—for I never saw it.

PINCHWIFE. 'Tis no matter whether that be her hand or no; I am sure this hand, at her desire, led her to Mr. Horner, with whom I left her just now, to go fetch a parson to 'em at their desire too, to deprive you of her for ever; for it seems yours was but a mock marriage.

SPARKISH. Indeed, she would needs have it that 'twas Harcourt himself, in a parson's habit, that married us; but I'm sure he told me 'twas his brother Ned.

PINCHWIFE. Oh, there 'tis out; and you were deceived, not she; for you are such a frank person. But I must be gone.—You'll find her at Mr. Horner's. Go, and believe your eyes.

[*Exit.*]

SPARKISH. Nay, I'll to her, and call her as many crocodiles, sirens, harpies, and other heathenish names as a poet would do a mistress who had refused to hear his suit, nay more, his verses on her.—But stay, is not that she following a torch at t'other end of the piazza? and from Horner's certainly—'tis so.

[*Enter* ALITHEA *following a torch, and* LUCY *behind.*]

You are well met, madam, though you don't think so. What, you have made a short visit to Mr. Horner. But I suppose you'll return to him presently; by that time the parson can be with him.

ALITHEA. Mr. Horner and the parson, sir!

SPARKISH. Come, madam, no more dissembling, no more jilting; for I am no more a frank person.

ALITHEA. How's this?

LUCY [*aside*]. So, 'twill work, I see.

SPARKISH. Could you find out no easy country fool to abuse? none but me, a gentleman of wit and pleasure about the town? But it was your pride to be too hard for a man of parts, unworthy false woman! false as a friend that lends a man money to lose; false as dice, who undo those that trust all they have to 'em.

LUCY [*aside*]. He has been a great bubble, by his similes, as they say.

ALITHEA. You have been too merry, sir, at your wedding-dinner, sure.

SPARKISH. What, d'ye mock me too?

ALITHEA. Or you have been deluded.

SPARKISH. By you.

ALITHEA. Let me understand you.

SPARKISH. Have you the confidence—I should call it something else, since you know your guilt—to stand my just reproaches? You did not write an impudent letter to Mr. Horner? who I find now has clubbed with you in deluding me with his aversion for women, that I might not, forsooth, suspect him for my rival.

LUCY [*aside*]. D'ye think the gentleman can be jealous now, madam?

ALITHEA. I write a letter to Mr. Horner!

SPARKISH. Nay, madam, do not deny it. Your brother showed it me just now; and told me likewise, he left you at Horner's lodging to fetch a parson to marry you to him, and I wish you joy, madam, joy, joy; and to him, too, much joy; and to myself more joy, for not marrying you.

ALITHEA [*aside*]. So, I find my brother would break off the match; and I can consent to't, since I see this gentleman can be made jealous. —O Lucy, by his rude usage and jealousy, he makes me almost afraid I am married to him. Art thou sure 'twas Harcourt himself, and no parson, that married us?

SPARKISH. No, madam, I thank you. I suppose that was a contrivance too of Mr. Horner's and yours, to make Harcourt play the parson; but I would as little as you have him one now, no, not for the world. For shall I tell you another truth? I never had any passion for you till now, for now I hate you. 'Tis true, I might have married your portion,° as other men of parts of the town do sometimes; and so, your servant. And to show my unconcernedness, I'll come to your wedding, and resign you with as much joy as I would a stale wench to a new cully; nay, with

portion dowry

as much joy as I would after the first night, if I had been married to you. There's for you; and so your servant, servant.

[*Exit.*]

5 ALITHEA. How was I deceived in a man!

LUCY. You'll believe then a fool may be made jealous now? For that easiness in him that suffers him to be led by a wife, will likewise permit him to be persuaded against her by 10 others.

ALITHEA. But marry Mr. Horner! my brother does not intend it, sure; if I thought he did, I would take thy advice, and Mr. Harcourt for my husband. And now I wish that if there be 15 any overwise woman of the town, who, like me, would marry a fool for fortune, liberty, or title, first, that her husband may love play, and be a cully to all the town but her, and suffer none but Fortune to be mistress of his purse; 20 then, if for liberty, that he may send her into the country under the conduct of some huswifely mother-in-law; and if for title, may the world give 'em none but that of cuckold.

LUCY. And for her greater curse, madam, 25 may he not deserve it.

ALITHEA. Away, impertinent! Is not this my old Lady Lanterlu's?

LUCY. Yes, madam.—[*Aside.*] And here I hope we shall find Mr. Harcourt.

30 [*Exeunt.*]

Scene iv

[*The scene changes again to* HORNER'S *lodging. A table, banquet, and bottles.*]

[*Enter* HORNER, LADY FIDGET, MRS. DAINTY FIDGET, MRS. SQUEAMISH.]

35 HORNER. [*aside*]. A pox! they are come too soon—before I have sent back my new mistress. All I have now to do is to lock her in, that they may not see her.

LADY FIDGET. That we may be sure of our 40 welcome, we have brought our entertainment with us, and are resolved to treat thee, dear toad.

MRS. DAINTY FIDGET. And that we may be merry to purpose, have left Sir Jasper and my 45 old Lady Squeamish quarreling at home at backgammon.

MRS. SQUEAMISH. Therefore let us make use of our time, lest they should chance to interrupt us.

LADY FIDGET. Let us sit then. 50

HORNER. First, that you may be private, let me lock this door and that, and I'll wait upon you presently.

LADY FIDGET. No, sir, shut 'em only, and your lips for ever; for we must trust you as much as 55 our women.

HORNER. You know all vanity's killed in me; I have no occasion for talking.

LADY FIDGET. Now, ladies, supposing we had drank each of us our two bottles, let us speak 60 the truth of our hearts.

MRS. DAINTY FIDGET *and* MRS. SQUEAMISH. Agreed.

LADY FIDGET. By this brimmer,° for truth is nowhere else to be found.—[*Aside to* HORNER.] 65 Not in thy heart, false man!

HORNER [*aside to* LADY FIDGET]. You have found me a true man, I'm sure.

LADY FIDGET [*aside to* HORNER]. Not every way.—But let us sit and be merry. [LADY 70 FIDGET *sings.*]

1

Why should our damned tyrants oblige us to
[live
On the pittance of pleasure which they only
[give? 75
We must not rejoice
With wine and with noise;
In vain we must wake in a dull bed alone,
Whilst to our warm rival, the bottle, they're
[gone. 80
Then lay aside charms,
And take up these arms.

2

'Tis wine only gives 'em their courage and
[wit;
Because we live sober, to men we submit. 85
If for beauties you'd pass,
Take a lick of the glass,

brimmer wine glass

'Twill mend your complexions, and when
[they are gone,
The best red we have is the red of the grape.
Then, sisters, lay't on,
5   And damn a good shape.

MRS. DAINTY FIDGET. Dear brimmer! Well, in
token of our openness and plain-dealing, let us
throw our masks over our heads.

HORNER. So, 'twill come to the glasses anon.

10 MRS. SQUEAMISH. Lovely brimmer! let me
enjoy him first.

LADY FIDGET. No, I never part with a gallant
till I've tried him. Dear brimmer! that makest
our husbands short-sighted.

15 MRS. DAINTY FIDGET. And our bashful gallants bold.

MRS. SQUEAMISH. And, for want of a gallant,
the butler lovely in our eyes.—Drink, eunuch.

LADY FIDGET. Drink, thou representative of a
20 husband.—Damn a husband!

MRS. DAINTY FIDGET. And, as it were a husband, an old keeper.°

MRS. SQUEAMISH. And an old grandmother.

HORNER. And an English bawd, and a French
25 chirurgeon.

LADY FIDGET. Ay, we have all reason to curse
'em.

HORNER. For my sake, ladies?

LADY FIDGET. No, for our own; for the first
30 spoils all young gallants' industry.

MRS. DAINTY FIDGET. And the other's art
makes 'em bold only with common women.

MRS. SQUEAMISH. And rather run the hazard
of the vile distemper amongst them, than of a
35 denial amongst us.

MRS. DAINTY FIDGET. The filthy toads choose
mistresses now as they do stuffs, for having
been fancied and worn by others.

MRS. SQUEAMISH. For being common and
40 cheap.

LADY FIDGET. Whilst women of quality, like
the richest stuffs, lie untumbled, and unasked
for.

HORNER. Ay, neat, and cheap, and new, often
45 they think best.

MRS. DAINTY FIDGET. No, sir, the beasts will
be known by a mistress longer than by a suit.

MRS. SQUEAMISH. And 'tis not for cheapness
neither.

LADY FIDGET. No; for the vain fops will take   50
up druggets° and embroider 'em. But I wonder
at the depraved appetites of witty men; they
use to be out of the common road, and hate
imitation. Pray tell me, beast, when you were a
man, why you rather chose to club with a   55
multitude in a common house for an entertainment than to be the only guest at a good table.

HORNER. Why, faith, ceremony and expectation are unsufferable to those that are
sharp bent.° People always eat with the best   60
stomach at an ordinary,° where every man is
snatching for the best bit.

LADY FIDGET. Though he get a cut over the
fingers.—But I have heard people eat most
heartily of another man's meat, that is, what   65
they do not pay for.

HORNER. When they are sure of their welcome and freedom; for ceremony in love and
eating is as ridiculous as in fighting; falling on
briskly is all should be done on those occasions.   70

LADY FIDGET. Well then, let me tell you, sir,
there is nowhere more freedom than in our
houses; and we take freedom from a young
person as a sign of good breeding; and a person
may be as free as he pleases with us, as frolic,   75
as gamesome, as wild as he will.

HORNER. Han't I heard you all declaim
against wild men?

LADY FIDGET. Yes; but for all that, we think
wildness in a man as desirable a quality as in a   80
duck or rabbit; a tame man! foh!

HORNER. I know not, but your reputations
frightened me as much as your faces invited
me.

LADY FIDGET. Our reputation! Lord, why   85
should you not think that we women made use
of our reputation, as you men of yours, only to
deceive the world with less suspicion? Our
virtue is like the statesman's religion, the

keeper of a prostitute

druggets coarse fabrics of mixed weave
sharp bent with a keen appetite
ordinary public eating house

Quaker's word, the gamester's oath, and the great man's honor—but to cheat those that trust us.

MRS. SQUEAMISH. And that demureness, coyness, and modesty that you see in our faces in the boxes at plays, is as much a sign of a kind woman, as a vizard-mask in the pit.

MRS. DAINTY FIDGET. For, I assure you, women are least masked when they have the velvet vizard on.

LADY FIDGET. You would have found us modest women in our denials only.

MRS. SQUEAMISH. Our bashfulness is only the reflection of the men's.

MRS. DAINTY FIDGET. We blush when they are shamefaced.

HORNER. I beg your pardon, ladies, I was deceived in you devilishly. But why that mighty pretense to honor?

LADY FIDGET. We have told you; but sometimes 'twas for the same reason you men pretend business often, to avoid ill company, to enjoy the better and more privately those you love.

HORNER. But why would you ne'er give a friend a wink then?

LADY FIDGET. Faith, your reputation frightened us as much as ours did you, you were so notoriously lewd.

HORNER. And you so seemingly honest.

LADY FIDGET. Was that all that deterred you?

HORNER. And so expensive—you allow freedom, you say—

LADY FIDGET. Ay, ay.

HORNER. That I was afraid of losing my little money, as well as my little time, both which my other pleasures required.

LADY FIDGET. Money! foh! you talk like a little fellow now; do such as we expect money?

HORNER. I beg your pardon, madam, I must confess, I have heard that great ladies, like great merchants, set but the higher prices upon what they have, because they are not in necessity of taking the first offer.

MRS. DAINTY FIDGET. Such as we make sale of our hearts?

MRS. SQUEAMISH. We bribed for our love? foh!

HORNER. With your pardon, ladies, I know, like great men in offices, you seem to exact flattery and attendance only from your followers; but you have receivers° about you, and such fees to pay a man is afraid to pass your grants.° Besides, we must let you win at cards, or we lose your hearts; and if you make an assignation, 'tis at a goldsmith's, jeweller's, or china-house, where for your honor you deposit to him, he must pawn his to the punctual cit,° and so paying for what you take up, pays for what he takes up.

MRS. DAINTY FIDGET. Would you not have us assured of our gallants' love?

MRS. SQUEAMISH. For love is better known by liberality than by jealousy.

LADY FIDGET. For one may be dissembled, the other not.—[Aside.] But my jealousy can be no longer dissembled, and they are telling ripe.—Come, here's to our gallants in waiting, whom we must name, and I'll begin. This is my false rogue. [Claps him on the back.]

MRS. SQUEAMISH. How!

HORNER. So, all will out now.

MRS. SQUEAMISH [aside to HORNER]. Did you not tell me 'twas for my sake only you reported yourself no man?

MRS. DAINTY FIDGET [aside to HORNER]. Oh, wretch! did you not swear to me, 'twas for my love and honor you passed for that thing you do?

HORNER. So, so.

LADY FIDGET. Come, speak, ladies, this is my false villain.

MRS. SQUEAMISH. And mine too.

MRS. DAINTY FIDGET. And mine.

HORNER. Well then, you are all three my false rogues too, and there's an end on't.

LADY FIDGET. Well then, there's no remedy; sister sharers, let us not fall out, but have a care of our honor. Though we get no presents, no jewels of him, we are savers of our honor, the jewel of most value and use, which shines yet to the world unsuspected, though it be counterfeit.

HORNER. Nay, and is e'en as good as if it were

---

receivers   servants to be bribed
pass your grants   cross your threshold
punctual cit   tradesman demanding prompt payment

true, provided the world think so; for honor, like beauty now, only depends on the opinion of others.

LADY FIDGET. Well, Harry Common, I hope you can be true to three. Swear; but 'tis to no purpose to require your oath, for you are as often forsworn as you swear to new women.

HORNER. Come, faith, madam, let us e'en pardon one another; for all the difference I find betwixt we men and you women, we forswear ourselves at the beginning of an amour; you as long as it lasts.

[*Enter* SIR JASPER FIDGET *and* OLD LADY SQUEAMISH.]

SIR JASPER FIDGET. Oh, my Lady Fidget, was this your cunning, to come to Mr. Horner without me? But you have been nowhere else, I hope.

LADY FIDGET. No, Sir Jasper.

OLD LADY SQUEAMISH. And you came straight hither, Biddy?

MRS. SQUEAMISH. Yes, indeed, lady grandmother.

SIR JASPER FIDGET. 'Tis well, 'tis well; I knew when once they were thoroughly acquainted with poor Horner, they'd ne'er be from him. You may let her masquerade it with my wife and Horner, and I warrant her reputation safe.

[*Enter* BOY.]

BOY. O sir, here's the gentleman come, whom you bid me not suffer to come up without giving you notice, with a lady too, and other gentlemen.

HORNER. Do you all go in there, whilst I send em away; and, boy, do you desire 'em to stay below till I come, which shall be immediately.

[*Exeunt* SIR JASPER, OLD LADY SQUEAMISH, LADY FIDGET, MRS. DAINTY, MRS. SQUEAMISH.]

BOY. Yes, sir.

[*Exit.*]

[*Exit* HORNER *at the other door, and returns with* MRS. PINCHWIFE.]

HORNER. You would not take my advice, to be gone home before your husband came back; he'll now discover all. Yet pray, my dearest, be persuaded to go home, and leave the rest to my management; I'll let you down the back way.

MRS. PINCHWIFE. I don't know the way home, so I don't.

HORNER. My man shall wait upon you.

MRS. PINCHWIFE. No, don't you believe that I'll go at all; what, are you weary of me already?

HORNER. No, my life, 'tis that I may love you long, 'tis to secure my love, and your reputation with your husband; he'll never receive you again else.

MRS. PINCHWIFE. What care I? d'ye think to frighten me with that? I don't intend to go to him again; you shall be my husband now.

HORNER. I cannot be your husband, dearest, since you are married to him.

MRS. PINCHWIFE. Oh, would you make me believe that? Don't I see every day, at London here, women leave their first husbands, and go and live with other men as their wives? Pish, pshaw! you'd make me angry, but that I love you so mainly.

HORNER. So, they are coming up.—In again, in, I hear 'em.—[*Exit* MRS. PINCHWIFE.] Well, a silly mistress is like a weak place, soon got, soon lost, a man has scarce time for plunder; she betrays her husband first to her gallant, and then her gallant to her husband.

[*Enter* PINCHWIFE, ALITHEA, HARCOURT, SPARKISH, LUCY *and a* PARSON.]

PINCHWIFE. Come, madam, 'tis not the sudden change of your dress, the confidence of your asseverations, and your false witness there, shall persuade me I did not bring you hither just now; here's my witness, who cannot deny it, since you must be confronted.—Mr. Horner, did not I bring this lady to you just now?

HORNER [*aside*]. Now must I wrong one woman for another's sake—but that's no new thing with me, for in these cases I am still on the criminal's side against the innocent.

ALITHEA. Pray speak, sir.

HORNER [*aside*]. It must be so. I must be impudent, and try my luck; impudence uses to be too hard for truth.

PINCHWIFE. What, are you studying an evasion or excuse for her! Speak, sir.

HORNER. No, faith, I am something backward only to speak in women's affairs or disputes.

PINCHWIFE. She bids you speak.

ALITHEA. Ah, pray, sir, do, pray satisfy him.

HORNER. Then truly, you did bring that lady to me just now.

PINCHWIFE. Oh ho!

ALITHEA. How, sir?

5 HARCOURT. How, Horner?

ALITHEA. What mean you, sir? I always took you for a man of honor.

HORNER [aside]. Ay, so much a man of honor, that I must save my mistress, I thank you, come
10 what will on't.

SPARKISH. So, if I had had her, she'd have made me believe the moon had been made of a Christmas pie.

LUCY [aside]. Now could I speak, if I durst,
15 and solve the riddle, who am the author of it.

ALITHEA. O unfortunate woman! A combination against my honor! which most concerns me now, because you share in my disgrace, sir, and it is your censure, which I
20 must now suffer, that troubles me, not theirs.

HARCOURT. Madam, then have no trouble, you shall now see 'tis possible for me to love too, without being jealous; I will not only believe your innocence myself, but make all the
25 world believe it.—[Apart to HORNER.] Horner, I must now be concerned for this lady's honor.

HORNER. And I must be concerned for a lady's honor too.

HARCOURT. This lady has her honor, and I
30 will protect it.

HORNER. My lady has not her honor, but has given it me to keep, and I will preserve it.

HARCOURT. I understand you not.

HORNER. I would not have you.

35 MRS. PINCHWIFE [peeping in behind]. What's the matter with 'em all?

PINCHWIFE. Come, come, Mr. Horner, no more disputing; here's the parson, I brought him not in vain.

40 HARCOURT. No, sir, I'll employ him, if this lady please.

PINCHWIFE. How! what d'ye mean?

SPARKISH. Ay, what does he mean?

HORNER. Why, I have resigned your sister to
45 him; he has my consent.

PINCHWIFE. But he has not mine, sir; a woman's injured honor, no more than a man's, can be repaired or satisfied by any but him that first wronged it; and you shall marry her presently, or—[lays his hand on his sword]. 50

[Enter MRS. PINCHWIFE.]

MRS. PINCHWIFE [aside]. O Lord, they'll kill poor Mr. Horner! Besides, he shan't marry her whilst I stand by and look on; I'll not lose my second husband so. 55

PINCHWIFE. What do I see?

ALITHEA. My sister in my clothes!

SPARKISH. Ha!

MRS. PINCHWIFE [to MR. PINCHWIFE]. Nay, pray now don't quarrel about finding work for 60 the parson; he shall marry me to Mr. Horner; for now, I believe, you have enough of me.

HORNER [aside]. Damned, damned loving changeling!

MRS. PINCHWIFE. Pray, sister, pardon me for 65 telling so many lies of you.

HORNER. I suppose the riddle is plain now.

LUCY. No, that must be my work.—Good sir, hear me. [Kneels to MR. PINCHWIFE, who stands doggedly with his hat over his eyes.] 70

PINCHWIFE. I will never hear women again, but make 'em all silent thus—[offers to draw upon his wife].

HORNER. No, that must not be.

PINCHWIFE. You then shall go first, 'tis all one 75 to me. [Offers to draw on HORNER, stopped by HARCOURT.]

HARCOURT. Hold!

[Enter SIR JASPER FIDGET, LADY FIDGET, OLD LADY SQUEAMISH, MRS. DAINTY FIDGET, MRS. 80 SQUEAMISH.]

SIR JASPER FIDGET. What's the matter? what's the matter? pray, what's the matter, sir? I beseech you communicate, sir.

PINCHWIFE. Why, my wife has communicated, 85 sir, as your wife may have done too, sir, if she knows him, sir.

SIR JASPER FIDGET. Pshaw, with him! ha! ha! he!

PINCHWIFE. D'ye mock me, sir? A cuckold is 90 a kind of a wild beast; have a care, sir.

SIR JASPER FIDGET. No, sure, you mock me, sir. He cuckold you! it can't be, ha! ha! he! why, I'll tell you, sir—[offers to whisper].

PINCHWIFE. I tell you again, he has whored 95 my wife, and yours too, if he knows her, and all the women he comes near; 'tis not his dissembling, his hypocrisy, can wheedle me.

SIR JASPER FIDGET. How! does he dissemble? is he a hypocrite? Nay, then—how—wife—
5 sister, is he a hypocrite?

OLD LADY SQUEAMISH. A hypocrite! a dissembler! Speak, young harlotry, speak, how?

SIR JASPER FIDGET. Nay, then.—Oh my head too!—Oh thou libidinous lady!

10 OLD LADY SQUEAMISH. Oh thou harloting harlotry! hast thou done't then?

SIR JASPER FIDGET. Speak, good Horner, art thou a dissembler, a rogue? hast thou—

HORNER. Soh!

15 LUCY [*apart to* HORNER]. I'll fetch you off, and her too, if she will but hold her tongue.

HORNER [*apart to* LUCY]. Can'st thou? I'll give thee—

LUCY [*to* MR. PINCHWIFE]. Pray have but
20 patience to hear me, sir, who am the unfortunate cause of all this confusion. Your wife is innocent, I only culpable; for I put her upon telling you all these lies concerning my mistress, in order to the breaking off the match
25 between Mr. Sparkish and her, to make way for Mr. Harcourt.

SPARKISH. Did you so, eternal rotten tooth? Then, it seems, my mistress was not false to me, I was only deceived by you. Brother, that
30 should have been, now man of conduct, who is a frank person now, to bring your wife to her lover, ha?

LUCY. I assure you, sir, she came not to Mr. Horner out of love, for she loves him no
35 more—

MRS. PINCHWIFE. Hold, I told lies for you, but you shall tell none for me, for I do love Mr. Horner with all my soul, and nobody shall say me nay; pray, don't you go to make poor Mr.
40 Horner believe to the contrary; 'tis spitefully done of you, I'm sure.

HORNER [*aside to* MRS. PINCHWIFE]. Peace, dear idiot.

MRS. PINCHWIFE. Nay, I will not peace.

45 PINCHWIFE. Not till I make you.

[*Enter* DORILANT, QUACK.]

DORILANT. Horner, your servant; I am the doctor's guest, he must excuse our intrusion.

QUACK. But what's the matter, gentlemen?
for Heaven's sake, what's the matter? 50

HORNER. Oh, 'tis well you are come. 'Tis a censorious world we live in; you may have brought me a reprieve, or else I had died for a crime I never committed, and these innocent ladies had suffered with me; therefore, pray 55 satisfy these worthy, honorable, jealous gentlemen—that—[*whispers*].

QUACK. Oh, I understand you; is that all?—Sir Jasper, by Heavens, and upon the word of a physician, sir—[*whispers to* SIR JASPER]. 60

SIR JASPER FIDGET. Nay, I do believe you truly.—Pardon me, my virtuous lady, and dear of honor.

OLD LADY SQUEAMISH. What, then all's right again? 65

SIR JASPER FIDGET. Ay, ay, and now let us satisfy him too. [*They whisper with* MR. PINCHWIFE.]

PINCHWIFE. An eunuch! Pray, no fooling with me. 70

QUACK. I'll bring half the chirurgeons in town to swear it.

PINCHWIFE. They!—they'll swear a man that bled to death through his wounds died of an apoplexy. 75

QUACK. Pray, hear me, sir—why, all the town has heard the report of him.

PINCHWIFE. But does all the town believe it?

QUACK. Pray, inquire a little, and first of all these. 80

PINCHWIFE. I'm sure when I left the town, he was the lewdest fellow in't.

QUACK. I tell you, sir, he has been in France since; pray, ask but these ladies and gentlemen, your friend Mr. Dorilant. Gentlemen and ladies, 85 han't you all heard the late sad report of poor Mr. Horner?

ALL THE LADIES. Ay, ay, ay.

DORILANT. Why, thou jealous fool, dost thou doubt it? he's an arrant French capon. 90

MRS. PINCHWIFE. 'Tis false, sir, you shall not disparage poor Mr. Horner, for to my certain knowledge—

LUCY. Oh, hold!

MRS. SQUEAMISH [*aside to* LUCY]. Stop her 95 mouth!

LADY FIDGET [*to* PINCHWIFE]. Upon my honor, sir, 'tis as true

MRS. DAINTY FIDGET. D'ye think we would have been seen in his company?

5 MRS. SQUEAMISH. Trust our unspotted reputations with him?

LADY FIDGET [*aside to* HORNER]. This you get, and we too, by trusting your secret to a fool.

HORNER. Peace, madam.—[*Aside to* QUACK.]
10 Well, doctor, is not this a good design, that carries a man on unsuspected, and brings him off safe?

PINCHWIFE [*aside*]. Well, if this were true— but my wife—

15 [DORILANT *whispers with* MRS. PINCHWIFE.]

ALITHEA. Come, brother, your wife is yet innocent, you see; but have a care of too strong an imagination, lest, like an over-concerned timorous gamester, by fancying an unlucky
20 cast, it should come. Women and fortune are truest still to those that trust 'em.

LUCY. And any wild thing grows but the more fierce and hungry for being kept up, and more dangerous to the keeper.

25 ALITHEA. There's doctrine for all husbands, Mr. Harcourt.

HARCOURT. I edify, madam, so much, that I am impatient till I am one.

DORILANT. And I edify so much by example,
30 I will never be one.

SPARKISH. And because I will not disparage my parts, I'll ne'er be one.

HORNER. And I, alas! can't be one.

PINCHWIFE. But I must be one—against my
35 will to a country wife, with a country murrain° to me!

MRS. PINCHWIFE [*aside*]. And I must be a country wife still too, I find; for I can't, like a city one, be rid of my musty husband, and do
40 what I list.

HORNER. Now, sir, I must pronounce your wife innocent, though I blush whilst I do it; and I am the only man by her now exposed to shame, which I will straight drown in wine, as
45 you shall your suspicion; and the ladies'

troubles we'll divert with a ballet.—Doctor, where are your maskers?

LUCY. Indeed, she's innocent, sir, I am her witness; and her end of coming out was but to see her sister's wedding; and what she has said 50
to your face of her love to Mr. Horner was but the usual innocent revenge on a husband's jealousy—was it not, madam, speak?

MRS. PINCHWIFE [*aside to* LUCY *and* HORNER]. Since you'll have me tell more lies.—Yes, 55
indeed, bud.

PINCHWIFE.
For my own sake fain I would all believe;
Cuckolds, like lovers, should themselves
                                            [deceive. 60
But—[*sighs.*] his honor is least safe (too late
                                            [I find)
Who trusts it with a foolish wife or friend.
[*A dance of cuckolds.*]
HORNER.   65
Vain fops but court and dress, and keep a
                                            [pother,
To pass for women's men with one another;
But he who aims by woman to be prized,
First by the men, you see, must be despised. 70

---

murrain plague

Jean Racine

1639–1699

Phaedra

1677

Sobriety of plot design, rigorous intellectual clarity, and refinement of language—these are the acknowledged virtues of Racine, master of the French classical theater. Why, then, do they arouse in many modern readers and playgoers only perfunctory appreciation? Because Racine's real power lies in the philosophical anguish and the undeviating intellectual sincerity of which these virtues are only manifestations. Moreover, Racine is not readily understandable apart from the French language, French poetics, and the intellectual preoccupations of the court of Louis XIV. *Phaedra,* which Racine called "the clearest and most close-knit play I have written," is immediately related to those preoccupations, with the efforts of seventeenth-century European thought to preserve or salvage its classical and Christian heritage. Racine knew that he lived in a center of intellectual crisis. *Phaedra* is directly derived from the *Hippolytus* of Euripides, himself a philosophical skeptic, and, although remaining a period-piece in its way, it deals with some intellectual issues that still reverberate today.

The seventeenth-century climate of theology and philosophy was tempestuous. (It was the era of Descartes, Hobbes, Pascal, and Spinoza.) And it had heavy implications for the future of the Christian faith. To propose that the Greek—that is, "pagan"—myths might convey serious ethical and psychological truths raised a spectre. By analogy might the supernatural beings and the miracles of Christianity turn out to be as fictitious as the Greek mythology and if true at all be true only in human terms? Racine does not articulate this question, but it was, so to speak, trembling in the air.

Racine correctly renamed his version of the tragedy *Phaedra.* It is not an antiquarian piece of Greek theater revived. In the world of Euripides, sacred genealogies and invocations of the gods still seemed authentic. In Racine's world, the authenticity

342

JEAN RACINE

of all such invocations is in question. Even Theseus' all-too-instantly granted prayer that the god Neptune redeem an old pledge only serves to reveal "Neptune" as a mindless expression of infantile rage. The metaphors of destiny and of ethical value are, so to speak, within quotation marks, with the result that Phaedra comes to represent the human psyche facing the tortuous question of its identity, and so she is at the center of the play.

Phaedra is an audacious, although conditional, attempt to translate mythological and theological concepts into their psychological equivalents. The ideas at issue are those of fate and free will, the paradox of a soul that intuitively feels itself free yet is constrained or driven by irresistible forces. Growing out of Phaedra's intense passion for Hippolytus and her equally intense loathing of her passion, the tragic events are almost entirely internalized, almost exclusively psychic. Contrast Phaedra with Iocastê, the mother of Oedipus. Iocastê unknowingly commits the act of incest that Phaedra has only imagined. Iocastê is ruined, but she is not in her heart at fault. Whatever guilt she must accept is an imposition of the gods. Phaedra accepts her guilt as her own, with great anguish of spirit, and recognizes that her suffering is grounded in her very identity. Phaedra finds herself at the center of a labyrinth into which no rescuer can come.

What causes this suffering—self-conscious, involuntary, self-motivating, self-condemned? Some external imposition or internal compulsion? They can scarcely be differentiated, although they can be given different names. For Phaedra, in a moment of vision, the cause is "Venus":

C'est Vénus toute entière á sa proie attachée

Yet this "Venus"—"altogether devouring her prey"—is only another name for Phaedra's obsession, and the obsession itself is only a headless, primal drive violently at odds with the judgment of her conscious mind. Venus and her prey are one and the same. What had once been represented as fate or a divinity is here being converted into an aspect of the psyche itself.

A similar process of interpretation is discernible in Hippolytus' celebrated line characterizing Phaedra as "the daughter of Minos and of Pasiphaë." This line, defiant of poetic translation, explains Phaedra's plight as the result of a family curse descending through generations. In Racine this explanation is in question. What does such an explanation mean? To be the daughter of these parents is to be the incarnation of a father (Minos) so righteous in judgment that he will sentence Phaedra even from Hades, and equally of a mother (Pasiphaë) whose name is a synonym for sexual depravity. It means, in terms that might have seemed already outmoded to Racine, that man is at the mercy of divine justice and the prey of demonic forces, or, in terms more current, that man is divided at the intersection of reason and nature.

Racine tends to treat abstractions, or at least parables—and in view of their implications for orthodox Christian doctrine, they are perilous ones. Although the play focuses on the confrontation of character with character, in scenes advancing with measured inevitability, it is as if behind each face there were another centuries-old countenance, anxiously contemplating human solitude in a world gradually losing faith in the reign of providence.

Racine had received a stern Catholic education in the theology of predestination, and after writing *Phaedra* he returned to a life of severe piety. It is scarcely accidental that in *Phaedra* he had boldly—and some thought amorally—called into thinly veiled question the viability of religious explanations for human motivation and the governance of states.

Phaedra

RACINE

Translated by John Cairncross

CHARACTERS

THESEUS   *son of Aegeus, King of Athens*
PHAEDRA   *wife of Theseus, daughter of Minos
   and Pasiphaë*
HIPPOLYTUS   *son of Theseus and Antiope,
   Queen of the Amazons*
ARICIA   *princess of the blood royal of Athens*
THERAMENES   *Hippolytus's governor*
OENONE   *Phaedra's nurse and confidante*
ISMENE   *Aricia's confidante*
PANOPE   *a woman of Phaedra's retinue*

SCENE. *Troezen, a town in the Peloponnesus.*

ACT I

Scene i

[HIPPOLYTUS, THERAMENES.]
HIPPOLYTUS. It is resolved, Theramenes. I go.
I will depart from Troezen's pleasant land.
5   Torn by uncertainty about the King,
I am ashamed of standing idly by.
For over half a year I have not heard
Of my dear father Theseus'° destiny

Theseus   one of the legendary Greek heroes, famed
as hunter, traveler, seducer of women, companion of
Hercules and Jason, conqueror of the Amazonian
queen, Hippolyta, by whom he fathered Hippolytus.
With the assistance of Ariadne he entered the labyrinth and slew the Minotaur; he brought Phaedra
to Athens. He restored his father, Aegus, to the
throne of Athens, from which he had been expelled

From Phaedra and Other Plays, *translated by John
Cairncross. Copyright © John Cairncross, 1963, 1970.
Reprinted by permission of Penguin Books Ltd.*

Nor even by what far sky he is concealed.
THERAMENES. And where, my lord, would you   10
                    [make search for him?
Already, to allay your proper fears,
I have scoured both the seas that Corinth joins;
I have sought news of Theseus on the shores
Of Acheron, the river of the dead;   15
Elis I searched, then sailed past Tenaros
On to the sea where Icarus came down.
What makes you hope that you may find his
                    [trace
In some more favored region of the world?   20
Who knows indeed if it is his desire
To have the secret of his absence known?
And whether, as we tremble for his life,
He is not tasting all the joys of love,
And soon the outraged victim of his wiles. . . .   25
HIPPOLYTUS. No more of this, Theramenes.
                    [The King
Has seen the errors of his amorous youth.
He is above unworthy dalliance,
And, stronger than his old inconstancy,   30
Phaedra has in his heart long reigned alone.
But, to be brief, I must make search for him
Far from this city where I dare not stay.
THERAMENES. Since when do you, my lord,
                    [fear to frequent   35
These peaceful haunts you cherished as a boy,
Which I have seen you many a time prefer
To the loud pomp of Athens and the court?
What peril, or what trouble, drives you hence?
HIPPOLYTUS. Those happy days are gone, and   40
                    [all is changed,
Since to these shores the mighty gods have sent
The child of Minos° and Pasiphaë°

---

by descendants of Pallas and Erectheus, earlier
kings. As the play opens, Theseus is absent on a
legendary expedition that was to take him to Hades,
in an attempt to rescue Proserpine from her ab-
ductor, the god Pluto. (In Act III, Scene v., Racine's
Theseus gives a less mythical version of his journey.)

Minos   legendary king of Crete, a son of Zeus (Jove)
and father of Phaedra and of her sister Ariadne; after
his death appointed one of the supreme judges in
Hades

Pasiphaë   his wife, a daughter of Helios, the sun. By
copulating with a bull she conceived the Minotaur,
half man and half bull, who was kept in a labyrinth.
He yearly devoured seven youths and seven maidens
surrendered by Athens as tributes to Minos.

THERAMENES. I understand. The cause of your
[distress
Is known. The sight of Phaedra vexes you.
Theseus' new wife had scarcely seen you than
5   Your exile gave the measure of her power.
But now her hate that never let you be
Has vanished or is greatly on the wane.
Besides what perils threaten you from her—
A woman dying or who seeks to die?
10 Racked by a malady she will not name,
Tired of herself and of the light of day,
Phaedra has not the strength to do you ill.
    HIPPOLYTUS. I do not fear her vain hostility.
If I go hence, I flee, let me confess,
15 Another enemy . . . Aricia,
Last of a line that plotted Theseus' death.
    THERAMENES. What! Would you stoop to
[persecute her too?
Though she is sprung of Pallas' cruel race,
20 She never joined in her false brothers' schemes.
Why hate her then if she is innocent?
    HIPPOLYTUS. I would not flee her if I hated
[her.
    THERAMENES. My lord, may I explain your
25   [sudden flight?
Are you no more the man that once you were,
Relentless foe of all the laws of love
And of a yoke Theseus himself has borne?
Will Venus whom you haughtily disdained
30 Vindicate Theseus after all these years
By forcing you to worship with the throng
Of ordinary mortals at her shrine?
Are you in love?
    HIPPOLYTUS.   My friend, what have you
35   [said?
You who have known me since I first drew
[breath,
You ask me shamefully to disavow
The feelings of a proud disdainful heart?
40 The Amazon, my mother, with her milk
Suckled me on that pride you wonder at.
And I myself, on reaching man's estate,
Approved my nature when I knew myself.
Serving me with unfeignéd loyalty,
45 You would relate my father's history.
You know how, as I hung upon your words,
My heart would glow at tales of his exploits

When you portrayed Theseus, that demi-god,
Consoling mortals for Alcides'° loss,
Monsters suppressed and brigands brought to 50
[book—
Procrustes, Sciron, Sinis, Cercyon;
The giants' bones in Epidaurus strewn
And Crete red with the slaughtered Minotaur.
But, when you told me of less glorious deeds, 55
His word pledged and believed in countless
[lands:
Helen in Sparta ravished from her home,
Salamis, scene of Periboea's tears;
Others whose very names he has forgot, 60
Too trusting spirits all deceived by him;
Wronged Ariadne crying to the winds;
Phaedra abducted, though for lawful ends;
You know how, loath to hear this sorry tale,
I often urged you quickly to conclude, 65
Happy could I have kept the shameful half
Of these adventures from posterity.
And am I to be vanquished in my turn?
And can the gods have humbled me so far?
In base defeat the more despicable 70
Since countless exploits plead on his behalf,
Whereas no monsters overcome by me
Have given me the right to err like him.
And, even if I were fated to succumb,
Should I have chosen to love Aricia? 75
Should not my wayward feelings have recalled
That she is barred from me eternally?
King Theseus frowns upon her and decrees
That she shall not prolong her brothers' line:
He fears this guilty stock will blossom forth, 80
And, to ensure her name shall end with her,
Condemns her to be single till she dies—
No marriage torch shall ever blaze for her.
Should I espouse her cause and brave his wrath?
Set an example to foolhardiness? 85
And, on a foolish passion launched, my
[youth . . .
    THERAMENES. Ah! when your hour has once
[but struck, my lord,

Alcides Hercules. Theseus set out to rival Hercules'
famed "labors." Hippolytus here differentiates between his father's heroic feats and his amatory exploits, of which no Racinian hero could approve.

Heaven of our reasons takes but little heed.
Theseus opens your eyes despite yourself.
His hatred of Aricia has fanned
Your passion and has lent her added grace.
5 Besides, my lord, why fear a worthy love?
If it is sweet, will you not dare to taste?
Will you be always ruled by modesty?
Can you go wrong where Hercules has trod?
What hearts has Venus' power not subdued?
10 Where would you be yourself, who fight her
[now,
If, combating her love, Antiope
Had never been consumed for Theseus?
However, what avails this haughty tone?
15 Confess it, all is changed; for some days past
You are less often seen, aloof and proud,
Speeding your chariot along the shore,
Or, skillful in the seagod Neptune's art,
Bending an untamed courser to the curb.
20 The woods less often to your cries resound;
Your eyes grow heavier with secret fire.
There is no doubt, you are consumed with love.
You perish from a malady you hide.
Has fair Aricia enraptured you?
25   HIPPOLYTUS. Theramenes, I go to seek the
[King.
    THERAMENES. And will you see Phaedra
[before you leave,
My lord?
30   HIPPOLYTUS.   I mean to. You may tell her
[so.
See her I must, since duty so commands.
But what new burden weighs Oenone down?

Scene ii

[HIPPOLYTUS, OENONE, THERAMENES.]
35   OENONE. Alas, my lord, what cares can equal
[mine?
The Queen is almost at her destined end.
In vain I watch over her night and day.
She's dying from a hidden malady;
40 Eternal discord reigns within her mind.
Her restless anguish tears her from her bed.
She longs to see the light, and yet, distraught
With pain, she bids me banish everyone . . .
But here she comes.
45   HIPPOLYTUS.   Enough. I'll take my leave

And will not show her my detested face.

Scene iii

[PHAEDRA, OENONE.]
PHAEDRA. No further. Here, Oenone, let us
[stay.
I faint, I fall; my strength abandons me.   50
My eyes are dazzled by the daylight's glare,
And my knees, trembling, give beneath my
[weight.
Alas!
OENONE.   May our tears move you,   55
[mighty gods!
PHAEDRA. How these vain jewels, these veils
[weigh on me!
What meddling hand has sought to re-arrange
My hair, by braiding it across my brow?   60
All things contrive to grieve and thwart me, all.
    OENONE. How all her wishes war among
[themselves!
Yourself, condemning your unlawful plans,
A moment past, bade us adorn your brow;   65
Yourself, summoning up your former strength,
Wished to come forth and see the light again.
Scarce have you seen it than you long to hide,
You hate the daylight you came forth to see.
    PHAEDRA. O shining founder° of an ill-   70
[starred line,
You, whom my mother dared to boast her sire,
Who blush perhaps to see me thus distraught,
Sungod, for the last time, I look on you.
    OENONE. What? you will not give up this fell   75
[desire?
And will you, always saying no to life,
Make mournful preparation for your death?
    PHAEDRA. Would I were seated in the forest's
[shade!   80
When can I follow through the swirling dust
The lordly chariot's flight along the course?
    OENONE. What?
    PHAEDRA.   Madness! Where am I, what
[have I said?   85
Whither have my desires, my reason strayed?
Lost, lost, the gods have carried it away.
Oenone, blushes sweep across my face;

founder Helios, father of Pasiphaë

My grievous shame stands all too clear
                                    [revealed,
And tears despite me fill my aching eyes.
     OENONE. If you must blush, blush for your
5   [silence, for
It but inflames the fury of your ills.
Deaf to our wild entreaties, pitiless,
Will you allow yourself to perish thus?
What madness cuts you off in mid career?
10 What spell, what poison, has dried up the
                                    [source?
Thrice have the shades of night darkened the
                                    [skies
Since sleep last made its entry to your eyes,
15 And thrice the day has driven forth dim night
Since last your fainting lips took nourishment.
What dark temptation lures you to your doom?
What right have you to plot to end your life?
In this you wrong the gods from whom you
20   [spring,
You are unfaithful to your wedded lord;
Unfaithful also to your hapless sons,
Whom you would thrust beneath a heavy yoke.
Remember, that same day their mother dies,
25 Hope for the alien woman's son revives,
For that fierce enemy of you and yours,
That youth whose mother was an Amazon,
Hippolytus . . .
     PHAEDRA.   God!
30   OENONE.   *That* reproach struck home.
     PHAEDRA. Ah! wretched woman, what name
                                    [crossed your lips?
     OENONE. Your anger now bursts forth, and
                                    [rightly so.
35 I love to see you shudder at the name.
Live then. Let love and duty spur you on.
Live on. Do not allow a Scythian's son°
To lord it with his harsh and odious rule
Over the pride of Greece and of the gods.
40 Do not delay! for every moment kills.
Haste to replenish your enfeebled strength
While yet the fires of life, though all but spent,
Are burning and can still flame bright again.
     PHAEDRA. I have prolonged my guilty days

Scythian's son Hippolytus. As the son of an Amazon
he was regarded as an alien unfit to rule in Athens.

                                    [too far. 45
     OENONE. What, are you harried by some keen
                                    [remorse?
What crime could ever bring you to this pass?
Your hands were never stained with guiltless
                                    [blood. 50
     PHAEDRA. Thanks be to Heaven, my hands
                                    [have done no wrong.
Would God my heart were innocent as they!
     OENONE. What fearful project then have you
                                    [conceived 55
Which strikes such terror deep into my heart?
     PHAEDRA. I have revealed enough. Spare me
                                    [the rest.
I die, and my grim secret dies with me.
     OENONE. Keep silence then, inhuman one, 60
                                    [and die;
But seek some other hand to close your eyes.
Although the candle of your life burns low,
I will go down before you to the dead.
Thither a thousand different roads converge, 65
My misery will choose the shortest one.
When have I ever failed you, cruel one?
Remember, you were born into my arms.
For you I have lost country, children, all.
Is this how you reward fidelity? 70
     PHAEDRA. What do you hope to gain by
                                    [violence?
If I should speak, you would be thunderstruck.
     OENONE. And what, ye gods, could be more
                                    [terrible 75
Than seeing you expire before my eyes?
     PHAEDRA. Even when you know my crime
                                    [and cruel fate,
I yet will die, and die the guiltier.
     OENONE. By all the tears that I have shed for 80
                                    [you,
And by your faltering knees I hold entwined,
Deliver me from dire uncertainty.
     PHAEDRA. You wish it. Rise.
     OENONE.   Speak. I await your words. 85
     PHAEDRA. What shall I say to her and where
                                    [begin?
     OENONE. Wound me no longer by such vain
                                    [affrights!
     PHAEDRA. Oh hate of Venus! Anger-laden 90
                                    [doom!

Into what dark abyss love hurled my mother!
   OENONE. Ah, Queen, forget; and for all time
                          [to come
Eternal silence seal this memory.
5   PHAEDRA. Oh sister Ariadne, from what love
You died deserted on a barren shore!
   OENONE. What ails you, and what mortal
                          [agony
Drives you to fury against all your race?
10   PHAEDRA. Since Venus wills it, of this unblest
                          [line
I perish, I, the last and wretchedest.
   OENONE. You are in love?
   PHAEDRA.   Love's furies rage in me.
15 OENONE. For whom?
   PHAEDRA.   Prepare to hear the crowning
                        [woe.
I love . . . I tremble, shudder at the name;
I love . . .
20 [OENONE *leans forward.*]
   PHAEDRA.   You know that prince whom I
                        [myself
So long oppressed, son of the Amazon?
   OENONE. Hippolytus?
25 PHAEDRA.   *You* have pronounced his
                        [name.
   OENONE. Merciful heavens! My blood chills
                        [in my veins.
O grief! O crime! O lamentable race!
30 Ill-fated journey and thrice ill-starred coast!
Would we had never neared your dangerous
                        [shores!
   PHAEDRA. My malady goes further back. I
                        [scarce
35 Was bound by marriage to Aegeus' son;
My peace of mind, my happiness seemed sure—
Athens revealed to me my haughty foe.
As I beheld, I reddened, I turned pale.
A tempest raged in my distracted mind.
40 My eyes no longer saw. I could not speak.
I felt my body freezing, burning; knew
Venus was on me with her dreaded flames,
The fatal torments of a race she loathes.
By sleepless vows, I thought to ward her off.
45 I built a temple to her, rich and fair.
No hour went by but I made sacrifice,
Seeking my reason in the victims' flanks.

Weak remedies for love incurable!
In vain my hand burned incense on the shrine.
Even when my lips invoked the goddess' name,   50
I worshipped *him*. His image followed me.
Even on the altar's steps, my offerings
Were only to the god I dared not name.
I shunned him everywhere. O crowning woe!
I found him mirrored in his father's face!   55
Against myself at last I dared revolt.
I spurred my feelings on to harass him.
To banish my adoréd enemy,
I feigned a spite against this stepson, kept
Urging his exile, and my ceaseless cries   60
Wrested him from a father's loving arms.
I breathed more freely since I knew him gone.
The days flowed by, untroubled, innocent.
Faithful to Theseus, hiding my distress,
I nursed the issue of our ill-starred bed.   65
Ah vain precautions! Cruel destiny!
Brought by my lord himself to Troezen's
                        [shores,
I saw once more the foe I had expelled.
My open wound at once poured blood again.   70
The fire no longer slumbers in the veins.
All Venus' might has fastened on her prey.
I have a fitting horror for my crime;
I hate this passion and I loathe my life.
Dying, I could have kept my name unstained,   75
And my dark passion from the light of day;
Your tears, your pleas have forced me to
                        [confess,
And I will not regret what I have done,
If you, respecting the approach of death,   80
Will cease to vex me with reproaches, and
Your vain assistance will not try to fan
The last faint flicker still alight in me.

Scene iv

[PHAEDRA, OENONE, PANOPE.]
   PANOPE. Would I could hide from you the   85
                        [grievous news,
My lady, but I cannot hold it back.
Death has abducted your unconquered lord
And this mischance is known to all but you.
   OENONE. What, Panope?   90
   PANOPE.   The Queen in vain, alas!
Importunes heaven for Theseus' safe return,

For, from the vessels just arrived in port,
Hippolytus, his son, has learned his death.
    PHAEDRA. God!
    PANOPE.   Athens is divided in its choice
5 Of master. Some favor the prince, your son,
Others, forgetful of the State's decrees,°
Dare to support the foreign woman's son.
Rumor even has it that a bold intrigue
Wishes to give Aricia the throne.
10 I deemed it right to warn you of this threat.
Hippolytus is ready to set sail,
And in this turmoil it is to be feared
He may win fickle Athens to his cause.
    OENONE. Panope, cease! You may be sure the
15   [Queen
Will give due heed to this important news.

Scene v

[PHAEDRA, OENONE.]
    OENONE. Ah Queen, I had relinquished you
                                  [to death
20 And thought to follow you down to the tomb.
I had no longer words to turn you back;
But this news bids you steer another course.
Now all is changed, and fortune smiles on you.
The King is dead, and you must take his place.
25 He leaves a son with whom your duty lies:
A slave without you; if you live, a king.
On whom in his misfortune can he lean?
If you are dead, no hand will dry his tears;
And his fond cries, borne upwards to the gods,
30 Will bring his forebears' anger down on you.
Live then, no longer tortured by reproach.
Your love becomes like any other love.
Theseus, in dying, has dissolved the bonds
Which made your love a crime to be abhorred.
35 You need no longer dread Hippolytus,
And you may see him and be guiltless still.
Perhaps, convinced of your hostility,
He is prepared to captain the revolt.
Quick, undeceive him; bend him to your will.
40 King of these fertile shores, Troezen is his.
But well he knows the laws assign your son
The soaring ramparts that Minerva° built.

---

decrees forbidding the throne to anyone not wholly
   of Greek parentage
Minerva or Athena, patron goddess of Athens

Both of you have a common enemy.
Join forces then against Aricia.
    PHAEDRA. Then be it so. Your counsels have   45
                                 [prevailed.
I'll live, if I can be recalled to life,
And if the love I bear my son can still
In this grim hour revive my failing strength.

ACT II

Scene i

[ARICIA, ISMENE.]   50
    ARICIA. Hippolytus has asked to see me here?
Hippolytus wishes to say farewell?
Ismene, are you not mistaken?
    ISMENE.   No.
This is the first result of Theseus' death.   55
Make ready to receive from every side
Allegiances that Theseus filched from you.
Aricia is mistress of her fate,
And soon all Greece will bow the knee to her.
    ARICIA. This was no rumor then, Ismene.   60
                                  [Now
My enemy, my tyrant is no more.
    ISMENE. Indeed. The gods no longer frown on
                               [you,
And Theseus wanders with your brothers'   65
                                  [shades.
    ARICIA. By what adventure did he meet his
                                  [end?
    ISMENE. The tales told of his death are past
                                 [belief.   70
They say that in some amorous escapade
The waters closed over his faithless head.
The thousand tongues of rumor even assert
That with Pirithous he went down to Hell,
Beheld Cocytus and the somber shores,   75
Showed himself living to the shades below,
But that he could not, from the house of death,
Recross the river whence is no return.
    ARICIA. Can mortal man, before he breathes
                              [his last,   80
Descend into the kingdom of the dead?
What magic lured him to that dreaded shore?
    ISMENE. You alone doubt it. Theseus is no
                                 [more.
Athens is stricken; Troezen knows the news,   85
And now pays tribute to Hippolytus.

Here in this palace, trembling for her son,
Phaedra takes counsel with her anxious friends.
    ARICIA. But will Hippolytus be kinder than
His father was to me, loosen my chains,
5 And pity my mishaps?
      ISMENE.   I think he will.
    ARICIA. Do you not know severe Hippolytus?
How can you hope that he will pity me,
Honoring in me alone a sex he spurns?
10 How constantly he has avoided us,
Haunting those places which he knows we
                      [shun!
    ISMENE. I know the tales of his unfeelingness;
But I have seen him in your presence, and
15 The legend of Hippolytus' reserve
Doubled my curiosity in him.
His aspect did not tally with his fame;
At the first glance from you he grew confused.
His eyes, seeking in vain to shun your gaze,
20 Brimming with languor, took their fill of you.
Although the name of lover wounds his pride,
He has a lover's eye, if not his tongue.
    ARICIA. How avidly, Ismene, does my heart,
Drink in these words, baseless though they
25   [may be!
Oh you who know me, can it be believed
That the sad plaything of a ruthless fate,
A heart that always fed on bitterness,
Should ever know the frenzied pangs of love?
30 Last of the issue of Earth's royal son,°
I only have escaped the scourge of war.
I lost, all in their springtime's flowering,
Six brothers, pride of an illustrious line.
The sword swept all away and drenched the
35   [earth,
Which drank, unwillingly, Erechtheus' blood.
You know that, since their death, a cruel law
Forbids all Greeks to seek me as their wife,
Since it was feared my offspring might one day
40 Kindle my brothers' ashes into life.
But you recall with what disdain I viewed
These moves of a suspicious conqueror,
For, as a lifelong enemy of love,
I rendered thanks to Theseus' tyranny,
45 Which merely helped to keep me fancy free.
My eyes had not yet lighted on his son.

royal son Erectheus, the father of Aricia

Not that my eyes alone yield to the charm
Of his much vaunted grace, his handsomeness,
Bestowed by nature, but which he disdains,
And seems not even to realize he owns.   50
I love and prize in him far nobler gifts,
His father's virtues, not his weaknesses.
I love, let me confess, that manly pride,
Which never yet has bowed beneath love's
                      [yoke. 55
Phaedra in vain gloried in Theseus' sighs.
I am more proud, and spurn the easy prize
Of homage to a thousand others paid
And of a heart accessible to all.
But to bring an unbending spirit down,   60
To cause an aching where no feeling was,
To stun a conqueror with his defeat,
In vain revolt against a yoke he loves.
That rouses my ambition, my desire.
Even Hercules was easier to disarm.   65
Vanquished more often than Hippolytus,
He yielded a less glorious victory.
But, dear Ismene, what rash hopes are these?
For his resistance will be all too strong.
You yet may hear me, humble in my grief   70
Bewail the very pride I now admire.
Hippolytus in love? By what excess
Of fortune could I . . .
    ISMENE.   You yourself will hear.
Hither he comes.   75

Scene ii

[HIPPOLYTUS, ARICIA, ISMENE.]
    HIPPOLYTUS. Princess, before I go
I deemed it right to let you know your fate.
My father is no more. My fears divined
The secret of his lengthy absence. Death,   80
Death only, ending his illustrious deeds,
Could hide him from the universe so long.
The gods at last deliver to the Fates
Alcides' friend, companion, and his heir.
I feel that, silencing your hate, even you   85
Hear in good part the honors due to him.
One hope alone tempers my mortal grief.
I can release you from a stern control,
Revoking laws whose harshness I deplore.
Yourself, your heart, do with them what you   90
                      [will;
And in this Troezen, now assigned to me

As my sage grandsire Pittheus'° heritage,
Which with a single voice proclaimed me king,
I leave you free as I am; nay, more free.
    ARICIA. Limit your boundless generosity.
5 By honoring me, despite adversity,
My lord, you place me, more than you believe,
Beneath those laws from which you set me free.
    HIPPOLYTUS. Athens, uncertain whom to
                [choose as heir,
10 Talks of yourself, of me, and the Queen's son.
    ARICIA. Me?
    HIPPOLYTUS. I would not wish to deceive
                [myself.
My claim appears to be annulled by law
15 Because my mother was an Amazon.
But, if my only rival for the throne
Were Phaedra's son, my stepbrother, I could
Protect my rights against the law's caprice.
If I do not assert my claim, it is
20 To hand, or rather to return, to you
A scepter given to your ancestors°
By that great mortal whom the earth begot.
Adoption placed it in Aegeus' hands.
Theseus, his son, defended and enlarged
25 The bounds of Athens, which proclaimed him
                [king
And left your brothers in oblivion.
Athens recalls you now within her walls.
Too long has she deplored this endless feud;
30 Too long your noble kinsmen's blood has
                [flown,
Drenching the very fields from which it sprang.
If Troezen falls to me, the lands of Crete
Offer a rich domain to Phaedra's son.
35 But Attica is yours. And I go hence
To unify our votes on your behalf.
    ARICIA. At all I hear, astounded and amazed,
I almost fear a dream deceives my ears.
Am I awake? Is it to be believed?
40 What god, my lord, inspired you with the
                [thought?
How rightly is your glory spread abroad!
And how the truth surpasses your renown!
You in my favor will renounce your claim?

Pittheus grandfather of Theseus, who assigned his
  royal rights in Troezen to Hippolytus
ancestors Aricia's royal forebears

Surely it was enough to keep your heart 45
So long free from that hatred of my line,
That enmity . . .
    HIPPOLYTUS. *I* hate you, Princess? No.
However my aloofness be decried,
Do you believe a monster gave me birth? 50
What churlish breeding, what unbending hate
Would not have melted at the sight of you?
Could I resist the soft beguiling spell . . .
    ARICIA. What! My lord . . .
    HIPPOLYTUS.   No, I cannot now draw 55
                [back!
Reason, I see, gives way to violence.
And, since I have begun to speak my mind,
Princess, I must go on: I must reveal
A secret that my heart cannot conceal. 60
Before you stands a pitiable prince,
Signal example of rash arrogance.
I who, in proud rebellion against love,
Have long mocked other captives' sufferings,
Who, pitying the shipwrecks of the weak, 65
Had thought to watch them always from the
                [shore,
Am now, in bondage to the common law,
Cut from my moorings by a surging swell.
A single blow has quelled my recklessness: 70
My haughty spirit is at last in thrall.
For six long months ashamed and in despair,
Pierced by the shaft implanted in my side,
I battle with myself, with you, in vain.
Present I flee you; absent, you are near. 75
Deep in the woods, your image follows me.
The light of day, the shadows of the night,
Everything conjures up the charms I flee.
Each single thing delivers up my heart.
And, sole reward for all my fruitless care, 80
I seek but cannot find myself again,
Bow, chariot, javelins, all importune me;
The lessons Neptune taught me are forgot.
My idle steeds no longer know my voice,
And only to my cries the woods resound. 85
Perhaps the tale of so uncouth a love
Brings as you listen, blushes to your face.
What words with which to offer you a heart!
How strange a conquest for so fair a maid!
But you should prize the offering the more. 90
Remember that I speak an unknown tongue,
And do not scorn my clumsy gallantry,

Which, but for you, I never would have shown.

Scene iii

[HIPPOLYTUS, ARICIA, THERAMENES, ISMENE.]
THERAMENES. The Queen is coming, Prince.
                              [She looks for you.
5   HIPPOLYTUS. For me?
    THERAMENES.   I do not know what she
                              [intends.
You have been sent for by her messenger.
Before you leave, Phaedra would speak with
10   [you.
    HIPPOLYTUS. What can I say? And what can
                              [she expect . . .
    ARICIA. Consent at least, my lord, to hear
                              [her speak.
15 Although she was your bitter enemy,
You owe some shade of pity to her tears.
    HIPPOLYTUS. Meanwhile you go. I leave, and
                              [am in doubt
Whether I have offended my beloved,
20 Or if my heart that I commit to you . . .
    ARICIA. Go, Prince. Pursue your generous
                              [designs.
Make Athens' State pay homage to me. All
The gifts you offer to me I accept.
25 But Athens' empire, glorious though it be,
Is not your most endearing offering.

Scene iv

[HIPPOLYTUS, THERAMENES.]
HIPPOLYTUS. Are you all ready? But here
                              [comes the Queen.
30 Let everyone prepare with all dispatch
To sail. Go, give the signal; hasten back,
And free me from a tedious interview.

Scene v

[PHAEDRA, HIPPOLYTUS, OENONE.]
    PHAEDRA [*to* OENONE *at the back of the*
35 *stage*]. He comes . . . My blood sweeps back into
                              [my heart.
Forgotten are the words I had prepared.
    OENONE. Think of your son, who hopes in
                              [you alone.
40 PHAEDRA. They say that you are leaving us at
                              [once,
My lord. I come to join my tears to yours.

I come to tell you of a mother's fears.
My son is fatherless, and soon, too soon,
He must behold my death as well. Even now,   45
Numberless enemies beset his youth.
You, only you, can see to his defense.
But I am harried by remorse within.
I fear lest you refuse to hear his cries.
I tremble lest you visit on a son   50
Your righteous anger at a mother's crimes.
    HIPPOLYTUS. How could I ever be so
                              [infamous?
    PHAEDRA. If you should hate me, I would not
                              [complain, 55
For I appeared resolved to do you ill.
Deep in my inmost heart you could not read.
I drew upon myself your enmity,
And where I dwelt, I would not suffer you.
With unrelenting hate, I sought to be   60
Divided from you by a waste of seas.
I even ordained by an express decree
That in my presence none should speak your
                              [name.
But, if the punishment should fit the crime,   65
If hate alone could bring on me your hate,
Never did woman merit pity more
And less, my lord, deserve your enmity.
    HIPPOLYTUS. A mother jealous of her
                              [children's rights 70
Rarely forgives another woman's son,
I realize; and from a second bed
Awkward suspicion all too often springs.
Another would have taken like offense,
And at her hands I might have suffered more.   75
    PHAEDRA. Ah! My lord, heaven, I dare here
                              [attest,
Has quite dispensed me from the common rule.
Far other is the care that weighs on me.
    HIPPOLYTUS. Lady, it is too early yet to   80
                              [grieve.
Who knows, your husband may be still alive.
Heaven may vouchsafe him to your tears again.
Protected by the seagod, not in vain
Will Theseus call on mighty Neptune's aid.   85
    PHAEDRA. No mortal visits twice the house of
                              [death.
Since Theseus has beheld the somber shores,
In vain you hope a god will send him back,
And hungry Acheron holds fast his prey.   90

But no, he is not dead; he lives, in you.
Always I think I see my husband's face.
I see him, speak to him, and my fond heart . . .
My frenzied love bursts forth in spite of me.
5   HIPPOLYTUS. In this I see the wonder of your
                                          [love.
Dead as he is, Theseus still lives for you.
Still does his memory inflame your heart.
      PHAEDRA. Yes, Prince, I pine, I am on fire for
10   [him.
I love King Theseus, not as once he was,
The fickle worshipper at countless shrines,
Dishonoring the couch of Hades' god;°
But constant, proud, and even a little shy;
15   Enchanting, young, the darling of all hearts,
Fair as the gods; or fair as you are now.
He had your eyes, your bearing, and your
                                          [speech.
His face flushed with your noble modesty.
When towards my native Crete he cleft the
20   [waves,
Well might the hearts of Minos' daughters
                                          [burn!
What were you doing then? Why without you
25   Did he assemble all the flower of Greece?
Why could you not, too young, alas, have fared
Forth with the ship that brought him to our
                                          [shores?
You would have slain the monstrous Cretan
30   [bull
Despite the windings of his endless lair.
My sister would have armed you with the
                                          [thread
To lead you through the dark entangled maze—
35   No. I would have forestalled her. For my love
Would instantly have fired me with the
                                          [thought.
I, only I, would have revealed to you
The subtle windings of the labyrinth.
40   What care I would have lavished on your head!
A thread would not have reassured my fears.
Affronting danger side by side with you,
I would myself have wished to lead the way,
And Phaedra, with you in the labyrinth,
45   Would have returned with you or met her
                                          [doom.

Hades' god Pluto

HIPPOLYTUS. What do I hear? Have you
                                          [forgotten that
King Theseus is my father, you his wife?
      PHAEDRA. What makes you think, my lord, I   50
                                          [have forgot,
Or am no longer mindful of my name?
      HIPPOLYTUS. Forgive me. Blushing, I confess
                                          [your words
Were innocent, and I misunderstood.   55
For very shame I cannot bear your gaze.
I go . . .
      PHAEDRA.   Ah, cruel, you have understood
Only too well. I have revealed enough.
Know Phaedra then, and all her wild desires.   60
I burn with love. Yet, even as I speak,
Do not imagine I feel innocent,
Nor think that my complacency has fed
The poison of the love that clouds my mind.
The hapless victim of heaven's vengeances,   65
I loathe myself more deeply than you do.
The gods are witness, they who in my breast
Have lit the fire fatal to all my line.
Those gods whose cruel glory it has been
To lead astray a feeble mortal's heart.   70
Yourself recall to mind the past, and how
I shunned you, cruel one, nay, drove you forth.
I strove to seem to you inhuman, vile;
The better to resist, I sought your hate.
But what availed my needless sufferings?   75
You hated me the more, I loved not less.
Even your misfortunes lent you added charms.
I pined, I drooped, in torments and in tears.
Your eyes alone could see that it is so,
If for a moment they could look at me.   80
Nay, this confession to you, ah! the shame,
Think you I made it of my own free will?
I meant to beg you, trembling, not to hate
My helpless children, whom I dared not fail.
My foolish heart, alas, too full of you,   85
Could talk to you of nothing but yourself.
Take vengeance. Punish me for loving you.
Come, prove yourself your father's worthy son,
And rid the world of a monstrosity.
I, Theseus' widow, dare to love his son!   90
This frightful monster must not now escape.
Here is my heart. Here must your blow strike
                                          [home.
Impatient to atone for its offense,

I feel it strain to meet your mighty arm.
Strike. Or if it's unworthy of your blows,
Or such a death too mild for my deserts,
Or if you deem my blood too vile to stain
5   Your hand, lend me, if not your arm, your
                                    [sword.
Give me it!
    OENONE.   Ah! What are you doing? God!
Someone is coming. You must not be seen.
10 Come, let's go in, quick, to avoid disgrace.

Scene vi

[HIPPOLYTUS, THERAMENES.]
THERAMENES. Can that be Phaedra who was
                            [dragged away?
Why, my lord, why this sudden, sharp dismay?
15 I find you without sword, aghast and pale.
    HIPPOLYTUS. Flee, flee, Theramenes. I
                                [cannot speak,
Nor without horror look upon myself.
Phaedra. . . . No, mighty gods, let us consign
20 This shameful secret to oblivion.
    THERAMENES. If you will leave, the sails are
                                [all unfurled.
But Athens has already made her choice.
Her chieftains have consulted all the tribes.
25 Your brother° rules; and Phaedra wins the day.
    HIPPOLYTUS. Phaedra?
    THERAMENES.   A herald speaking Athens'
                                    [will
Into her hands conveyed the reins of state.
30 Her son is king, my lord.
    HIPPOLYTUS.   Oh God, who knows
Her heart, is it her virtue you reward?
    THERAMENES. Meanwhile, vague rumors say
                            [the King still lives,
35 And even that in Epirus he was seen.
But I, who sought him there, my lord, I
                                [know . . .
    HIPPOLYTUS. No matter. Let us study every
                                    [clue.
40 Have this new rumor traced back to its source.
But, if it does not then prove credible,
Let us depart and, at whatever cost,
Replace the scepter in more worthy hands.

brother half-brother, a son of Theseus and Phaedra

ACT III

Scene i

[PHAEDRA, OENONE.]
    PHAEDRA. Ah, take away those royal honors.   45
                                    [How
Can you importune me to show myself?
And why seek to beguile my grieving heart?
Rather conceal me. I have said too much.
My frantic passion has revealed itself.   50
I have said what should never have been heard.
God! how he listened to me. By what shifts
He long pretended not to understand.
How his whole being hankered to be gone.
And how his blushes added to my shame.   55
Why did you ever thwart my baneful plan?
Ah! when his sword was pointed at my breast,
Did he turn pale for me, or did he wrench
It from me? I had but to touch it once
To make it horrible for him, and for   60
The wretched sword to soil his cruel hands.
    OENONE. Thus your misfortunes breed self-
                                [pity, and
Only inflame a fire you ought to quench.
Daughter of Minos, should you not aspire   65
To seek your peace of mind in nobler cares?
Resort to flight from an ungrateful youth,
Reign, and assume the guidance of the State?
    PHAEDRA. *I* reign? *I* bring a State beneath my
                                    [rule, 70
When reason reigns no longer over me;
When I have lost my self-dominion; when
Beneath a shameful sway I scarcely breathe;
When I am dying?
    OENONE.   Flee.   75
    PHAEDRA.   I cannot go.
    OENONE. You sent him into exile. Shun him
                                    [now.
    PHAEDRA. Too late, too late. He knows my
                            [mad desires. 80
I have transgressed the bounds of modesty.
I to Hippolytus have bared my shame,
And hope, despite me, has seduced my heart,
You yourself, rallying my failing strength
When on my lips my soul was hovering,   85
By guileful counsels brought me back to life.
You gave me glimpses of a sinless love.
    OENONE. Alas! guilty or no of your mishaps,

What would I not have done to save your life?
But, if by insults you were ever stung,
Can you forget a haughty youth's disdain?
God! with what cruel, stern, unfeeling heart
5 He left you well-nigh prostrate at his feet!
How hateful was his virtuous haughtiness!
Why did not Phaedra see him with my eyes?
    PHAEDRA. He may discard this pride that
                        [angers you.
10 Bred in the forests, he is wild like them.
Hardened by rude upbringing, he perhaps
For the first time listens to words of love.
Perhaps his silence mirrors his surprise,
And our reproaches are too violent.
15   OENONE. An Amazon, forget not, gave him
                        [birth.
    PHAEDRA. Though a barbarian, yet did she
                        [love.
    OENONE. He hates all women with a deadly
20   [hate.
    PHAEDRA. No rival, then, will triumph over
                        [me.
In short, the time for good advice is past.
Serve my wild heart, Oenone, not my head.
25 If he is inaccessible to love,
Let us attack him at some weaker point.
He seemed attracted by an empire's rule.
He could not hide it; Athens beckoned him.
Thither his vessels' prows were headed, and
30 The white sails fluttered, streaming in the wind.
Oenone, play on his ambition. Go,
Dazzle him with the glitter of the crown.
Let him assume the sacred diadem.
Myself to bind it on is all I ask,
35 Yielding to him the power I cannot hold.
He will instruct my son how to command;
Perhaps he will be father to the boy.
Mother and son I will commit to him.
In short, try every means to win him round.
40 Your words will find a readier ear than mine.
Urge! Weep! Paint Phaedra at death's door.
You may assume a supplicating tone.
I will endorse it, whatsoe'er you do.
Go. Upon your success depends my fate.

Scene ii

45   PHAEDRA. O you who see the depths of this
                        [my shame,
Relentless Venus, is my fall complete?

Your cruelty could go no further. Now
You triumph. All your arrows have struck
                        [home. 50
O cruel goddess! if you seek new fame,
Attack a more rebellious enemy.
Frigid Hippolytus, flouting your wrath,
Has at your altars never bowed the knee.
Your name seems to offend his haughty ear. 55
Goddess, avenge yourself. Our cause is one.
Make him love . . . but Oenone, you are back.
Did he not listen? Does he loathe me still?

Scene iii

[PHAEDRA, OENONE.]
    OENONE. Your love is vain and you must stifle 60
                        [it,
O Queen, and summon up your former
                        [strength.
The King we thought was dead will soon be
                        [here; 65
Theseus is come; Theseus is on his way.
Headlong, the crowd rushes to welcome him.
I had gone out to seek Hippolytus
When, swelling to the heavens, a thousand
                        [cries . . . 70
    PHAEDRA. My husband lives. Oenone, say no
                        [more.
I have confessed a love that soils his name.
He is alive, and more I will not know.
    OENONE. What? 75
    PHAEDRA.   I foretold it but you would not
                        [hear.
Your tears prevailed over my keen remorse.
I died this morning worthy to be mourned;
I took your counsel and dishonored die. 80
    OENONE. You mean to die?
    PHAEDRA.   Great God, what have I done?
My husband and his son are on their way.
I will behold the witness of my guilt
Observe me as I dare approach the King, 85
My heart heavy with sighs he heard unmoved,
My eyes wet with the tears the wretch
                        [disdained.
Mindful of Theseus' honor, as he is,
Will he conceal from him my fierce desires? 90
Will he be false to father and to king,
Restrain the horror that he feels for me?
His silence would be vain, Oenone, for
I know my baseness, and do not belong

To those bold wretches who with brazen front
Can revel in their crimes unblushingly.
I know my transports and recall them all.
Even now I feel these very walls, these vaults,

5 Will soon give tongue and, with accusing voice,
Await my husband to reveal the truth.
Then, death, come free me from so many woes.
Is it so terrible to cease to live?
Death holds no terrors for the wretched. No.

10 I fear only the name I leave behind,
For my poor children what a heritage.
The blood of Jove° should make their spirit
[swell;
But, whatsoever pride that blood inspires,

15 A mother's crime lies heavy on her sons.
I tremble lest reports, alas, too true,
One day upbraid them with a mother's guilt.
I tremble lest, crushed by this odious weight,
Neither will ever dare hold up his head.

20   OENONE. Ah! do not doubt it. Pity both of
[them.
Never was fear more justified than yours.
But why expose them to such base affronts?
And why bear witness now against yourself?

25 That way lies ruin. Phaedra, they will say,
Fled from the dreaded aspect of her lord.
Hippolytus is fortunate indeed.
By laying down your life, you prove him right.
How can I answer your accuser's charge?

30 I will be all too easy to confound.
I will behold his hideous triumph as
He tells your shame to all who care to hear.
Ah! sooner let the flames of heaven fall.
But tell me truly do you love him still?

35 What do you feel for this audacious prince?
    PHAEDRA. He is a fearful monster in my eyes.
    OENONE. Then why concede him such a
[victory?
You fear him. Dare then to accuse him first

40 Of the offense he soon may charge you with.
Nothing is in his favor; all is yours—
His sword, left by good fortune in your hands,
Your present agitation, your past grief,
His father, turned against him by your cries,

45 And, last, his exile you yourself obtained.
    PHAEDRA. Should I oppress and blacken

---

blood of Jove because Minos, Phaedra's father, was
a son of Jove

[innocence?
    OENONE. All I need is your silence to succeed.
Like you I tremble and I feel remorse.
Sooner would I affront a thousand deaths, 50
But, since without this remedy you die,
For me your life must come before all else.
Therefore I'll speak. Despite his wrath, the King
Will do naught to his son but banish him.
A father when he punishes is still 55
A father, and his judgment will be mild.
But, even if guiltless blood must still be shed,
What does your threatened honor not demand?
It is too precious to be compromised.
Its dictates, all of them, must be obeyed. 60
And, to safeguard your honor, everything,
Yes, even virtue, must be sacrificed.
But who comes here? Theseus!
    PHAEDRA.   Hippolytus!
In his bold gaze my ruin is writ large. 65
Do as you will. My fate is in your hands.
My whirling mind has left me powerless.

Scene iv

[THESEUS, HIPPOLYTUS, PHAEDRA, OENONE,
THERAMENES.]
    THESEUS. Fortune at last ceases to frown on 70
[me,
O Queen, and in your arms again . . .
    PHAEDRA.   No more.
Do not profane your transports of delight.
No more do I deserve this tenderness. 75
You have been outraged. Jealous fortune's
[blows
During your absence have not spared your wife.
I am unworthy to approach you, and
Henceforth my only thought must be to hide. 80

Scene v

[THESEUS, HIPPOLYTUS, THERAMENES.]
    THESEUS. Why this cold welcome to your
[father?
    HIPPOLYTUS.   Sire,
Phaedra alone can solve this mystery. 85
But, if my ardent wish can move you still,
Allow me never to set eyes on her.
Suffer your trembling son to disappear
For ever from the place where Phaedra dwells.
    THESEUS. You, my son, leave me? 90
    HIPPOLYTUS.   Yes. It was not I

Who sought her. You, my lord, you brought
                                    [her here.
For you, on leaving, brought Aricia
And your Queen, Phaedra, here to Troezen's
5   [shore.
You even committed them into my care.
But, since your safe return, why should I stay?
Long have I squandered in the woods of Greece
My manhood's skill on paltry enemies.
10   Should not I, fleeing shameful idleness,
Redden my javelins in more glorious blood?
Before you had attained my present years,
More than one tyrant, one ferocious beast,
Had felt the might of your unconquered arm;
15   Even then, you were the scourge of insolence.
You had cleared all the shores of both the seas.
The traveller now fares freely through the land.
Hercules, resting on his laurels' fame,
Already for his labors looked to you.
20   And I, a glorious father's unknown son,
Lag far behind even my mother's deeds.
Let me at least show you my mettle and,
If some fell monster has escaped your sword,
Place at your feet its honorable spoils.
25   Or let the memory of a glorious death,
Engraving in eternity my life,
Prove to the universe I was your son.
        THESEUS. What do I see? What horror spread
                                    [around
30   Drives back from me, distraught, my family?
If I return, so feared, so undesired,
Oh heaven! why did you free me from my jail?
I had one friend° alone. He rashly tried
To seize the consort of Epirus' King.
35   I served his amorous plan reluctantly;
But fate in anger blinded both of us.
The tyrant took me by surprise unarmed.
I saw Pirithous, a woeful sight,
Thrown to fierce monsters by the barbarous
40   [king,
Who fed them on the blood of helpless men.
Myself in somber caverns he enchained

---

friend Pirithous, Theseus' friend and his companion
   in many adventures. Legend reported that Pirithous
   accompanied Theseus to Hades and was imprisoned
   there by Pluto, although Theseus was rescued by
   Hercules; again, Racine's Theseus gives a less mythical account of their misfortunes.

Beside the shadowy kingdom of the dead.
The gods at last relented towards me and
Allowed me to outwit my guardian.   45
I purged the world of a perfidious knave
And his own monsters battened on his flesh.
But when I joyfully prepared to meet
My dearest ones, all that the gods have spared,
Nay, when my soul, that is its own again,   50
Would feast itself upon so dear a sight,
Only with shudders am I welcomed home;
Everyone flees, rejecting my embrace.
Myself, filled with the horror I inspire,
Would I were prisoner in Epirus still.   55
Speak! Phaedra tells of outrage done to me.
Who played me false? Why am I unavenged?
Has Greece, so often guarded by my arm,
Afforded shelter to the criminal?
You do not answer. Is my son, my own   60
Dear son, in league, then, with my enemies?
Let us go in and end this grim suspense.
Let us discover criminal and crime,
And Phaedra tell us why she is distraught.

Scene vi

[HIPPOLYTUS, THERAMENES.]   65
HIPPOLYTUS. What meant these words that
                            [made my blood run cold?
Will Phaedra, still in her delirium,
Denounce herself, bring ruin on her head?
O God! What will the King say then? How love 70
Has spread its baleful poison through the
                                        [house!
Myself, full of a passion he condemns,
As once he knew me, so he finds me still.
Gloomy forebodings terrify my soul.   75
But innocence has surely naught to fear.
Come, let me with some new and happier
Approach revive my father's tenderness,
And tell him of a love he may oppose
But which it is not in his power to change.   80

ACT IV

Scene i

[THESEUS, OENONE.]
THESEUS. What do I hear? A reckless libertine
Conceived this outrage on his father's name?
How harshly you pursue me, destiny.

I know not where I am, whither I go.
O son! O ill-rewarded tenderness!
Daring the scheme, detestable the thought.
To gain his lustful and nefarious ends,
5 The shameless villain had resort to force.
I recognized the sword he drew on her,
That sword I gave him for a nobler use.
Could all the ties of blood not hold him back?
Phaedra was slow in bringing him to book?
10 In keeping silent, Phaedra spared the knave?
    OENONE. Rather did Phaedra spare a father's
                        [tears.
Ashamed of a distracted lover's suit,
And of the vicious passion she had caused,
15 Phaedra, my lord, was dying and her hand
Was on the point of cutting short her days.
I saw her raise her arm, I ran to her.
I, only I, preserved her for your love,
And, pitying her distress and your alarm,
20 Reluctantly I lent her tears a voice.
    THESEUS. The criminal! He blanched despite
                        [himself.
As I drew near, I saw him start with fear.
I was astonished by his joyless mien;
25 His cold embraces froze my tenderness
But had this guilty love that eats him up
Already, even in Athens, shown itself?
    OENONE. My lord, recall how oft the Queen
                        [complained.
30 Infamous love gave rise to all her hate.
    THESEUS. And here in Troezen this flamed up
                        [again?
    OENONE. My lord, I have related all I know.
The grieving Queen too long remains alone;
35 Allow me to withdraw and go to her.

Scene ii

[THESEUS, HIPPOLYTUS.]
    THESEUS. Ah, it is he. Great gods! what eye
                        [would not
Be duped like mine by such nobility?
40 Must needs the brow of an adulterer
Be bright with virtue's sacred character?
And ought we not by fixed and certain signs
To see into perfidious mortals' hearts?
    HIPPOLYTUS. May I inquire of you what
45   [baleful cloud
Has overcast, my lord, your regal brow?

Will you not venture to confide in me?
    THESEUS. Villain! How dare you come before
                        [me now?
Monster, the thunderbolt too long has spared! 50
Last of the brigands whom I swept away!
After the frenzy of your wicked lust
Has driven you to assault your father's bed,
You dare to show your hateful face to me,
Here in this place full of your infamy, 55
And seek not out, under an unknown sky,
Countries to which your fame has never spread.
Flee, villain, flee. Brave not my hatred here
Nor tempt my anger that I scarce restrain.
I have my portion of eternal shame 60
To have begot so criminal a son,
Without his death, disgrace to my renown,
Soiling the glory of my labors past.
Flee, and if you desire not to be joined
To all the villains fallen by my hand, 65
Take care that never does the shining sun
Behold you in these palaces again.
Flee then, and never more return;
And of your hideous presence purge my realm.
And, Neptune, in time past if my strong hand 70
Of infamous assassins cleared your shores,
Remember that, to recompense my deeds,
You swore to grant the first of my desires.
In the long hardships of a cruel jail
I did not call on your immortal power; 75
With miser's care I put aside your aid,
Holding it in reserve for greater needs.
I call upon you now. Revenge my wrong.
I give this villain over to your wrath;
Drown in his blood his shameless foul desires. 80
Your favors will be measured by your rage.
    HIPPOLYTUS. Phaedra accuses me of sinful
                        [love?
So infinite a horror numbs my soul.
So many unforeseen and heavy blows 85
Rain down upon me that I cannot speak.
    THESEUS. Villain, you thought that Phaedra
                        [would conceal
In craven silence your vile insolence.
You should not, as you fled, have dropped the 90
                        [sword
That, in her hands, establishes your guilt.
Rather should you have crowned your perfidy
And at one stroke robbed her of speech and life.

HIPPOLYTUS. Rightly indignant at so black a
[lie,
I ought, my lord, to let the truth speak out,
But I will not resolve this mystery
5 Out of the deep respect that seals my lips.
And, if you will not deepen your distress,
Look at my life; remember who I am.
Some little crimes lead up to greater crimes.
Whoever goes beyond the bounds of law
10 Can in the end flout the most sacred rules.
No less than virtue, crime has its degrees,
And innocence has never yet been known
To swing at once to license's extreme.
A single day cannot change virtuous men
15 To craven and incestuous murderers.
Reared by a virtuous Amazon from birth,
I never have belied my mother's blood.
Pittheus, esteemed the wisest far of men,
Instructed me after I left her hands.
20 I do not seek to paint myself too fair;
But, if one virtue is my birthright, that
Is above all, my lord, as I have shown,
Hate of the crime that they accuse me of.
That is what I am famous for in Greece.
25 I carried virtue to the sternest lengths,
My obdurate austerity is known;
The daylight is not purer than my heart.
Yet I, they say, fired by unholy love . . .
    THESEUS. Yes, by that very pride you stand
30   [condemned.
The reason why you were so cold is clear;
Phaedra alone entranced your lustful eyes.
And, by all other charms unmoved, your heart
Disdained to glow with innocent desire.
35   HIPPOLYTUS. No, father, for this may not be
                                      [concealed,
I have not scorned to glow with virtuous love,
And at your feet confess my real offense.
I am in love; in love despite your ban.
40 Aricia is mistress of my heart
And Pallas' daughter has subdued your son.
I worship her and, flouting your command,
For her alone I pine, I am consumed.
    THESEUS. You love her? God! The ruse is
45   [gross indeed!
You feign to err to justify yourself.
    HIPPOLYTUS. For half a year I have been deep
                                      [in love.

Trembling, I came to tell you so myself.
What! Can no word of mine unseal your eyes?   50
What fearful oath, to move you, must I swear?
May heaven and earth and everything that
                                      [is . . .
    THESEUS. Foulness goes hand in hand with
                                    [perjury.   55
Cease! Spare me an importunate harangue,
If your false virtue has no other stay.
    HIPPOLYTUS. To you I may seem false and full
                                      [of guile.
Phaedra does justice to me in her heart.   60
    THESEUS. Ah! how my wrath grows at your
                                 [shamelessness.
    HIPPOLYTUS. What time and what the place of
                                   [banishment?
    THESEUS. Were you beyond Alcides' pillars,°   65
                                          [still
Would I believe your villainy too near.
    HIPPOLYTUS. Crushed by the crime that you
                               [suspect me of,
If you desert me who will pity me?   70
    THESEUS. Go seek out friends who in their
                                 [viciousness
Applaud adultery and incest. These
Villains and ingrates, lawless, honorless,
Will shelter evildoers such as you.   75
    HIPPOLYTUS. You harp on incest and adultery.
I will say naught; but Phaedra, as you know,
My lord, is of a mother, of a line,
Richer in all these horrors than my own.
    THESEUS. What! are there no bounds to your   80
                                 [frantic rage?
For the last time, begone from out my sight.
Go, libertine, before a father's wrath
Has you with ignominy torn from hence.

Scene iii

[THESEUS alone.]   85
    THESEUS. Unhappy youth! Haste to your
                                 [certain doom.
By the stream dreaded even of the gods
Neptune has given and will fulfil his word.
A god of vengeance follows hard on you.   90
I loved you and, in spite of your offense,
My heart is stirred for you forebodingly.

Alcides' pillars   the Pillars of Hercules; i.e., Gibraltar

But you have forced me to pronounce your
        [doom.
Was ever wretched father outraged so?
O God who see my overwhelming grief,
5 How could I have begot so foul a child?

Scene iv

[PHAEDRA, THESEUS.]
PHAEDRA. My Lord, I come stricken with
        [terror, for
Your dreaded voice has reached me and I fear
10 Your menace may be given prompt effect.
If it is not too late, then spare your son.
Respect your flesh and blood, I beg of you,
And save me from the horror of his cries.
Do not lay up for me the endless grief
15 Of causing bloodshed by a father's hand.
      THESEUS. No, Queen, my hand has not bathed
        [in his blood,
But still the villain will not now escape.
Immortal hands are with his ruin charged.
20 This Neptune owes me. You will be avenged.
      PHAEDRA. This Neptune owes you. What?
        [Your anger calls ...
      THESEUS. How! You already fear I may be
        [heard?
25 Rather unite your wishes with my own.
In all their heinousness depict his crimes;
Stir up my sluggish cold resentment, for
You do not know the measure of his crimes.
His fury showers affronts upon your name.
30 Your mouth, he says, speaks nothing but
        [deceit;
He swears Aricia has won his heart,
And that he loves her.
      PHAEDRA.   What!
35   THESEUS.   Those were his words.
But I am not the dupe of vain pretense.
Let us expect swift justice from the god.
I will myself to Neptune's altars go
To urge fulfilment of immortal oaths.

Scene v

40 [PHAEDRA *alone.*]
    PHAEDRA. He's gone. What tidings have
        [assailed my ears!
What smoldering fire awakens in my heart!
God! What a thunderbolt! What baleful news!

Flying with but one thought to aid his son,   45
I tore myself from pale Oenone's arms,
Yielding to the remorse that tortured me.
Who knows how far repentance would have
        [gone?
Perhaps I might even have accused myself?   50
Perhaps, had not my voice died in my throat,
The frightful truth would have escaped my lips.
Hippolytus can love but loves not me.
Aricia has won his heart, his troth.
Ah! when, inexorable to my pleas,   55
Hippolytus put on a front of steel,
I thought his heart for ever closed to love,
And against women all alike was armed.
Another none the less has conquered him.
She has found favor in his cruel eyes.   60
Perhaps he has a heart easy to move.
Alone of women me he cannot bear.
And I was hastening to his defense!

Scene vi

[PHAEDRA, OENONE.]
PHAEDRA. Oenone, do you know what I have   65
        [heard?
    OENONE. No, but I still am trembling, to be
        [frank.
As you rushed forth, I blanched at your intent.
I was afraid you would destroy yourself.   70
    PHAEDRA. Who would have thought it? There
        [was someone else.
    OENONE. What!
    PHAEDRA.   Yes. Hippolytus is deep in love.
This shy, invincible antagonist,   75
Whom my respect displeased, my tears
        [annoyed,
Whom I could never speak to unafraid,
Submissive, tamed, proclaims his own defeat.
Aricia is mistress of his heart.   80
    OENONE. Aricia?
    PHAEDRA.   Ah! unplumbed depths of woe!
For what new torments have I spared myself?
All I have suffered, jealous torments, fears,
Raging desire, the horror of remorse,   85
A cruel, harsh, intolerable slight,
Were a mere foretaste of my torments now.
They love each other. By what spell did they
Deceive me? How, where did they meet, since
        [when?   90

You knew. Why did you let me be misled?
Why did you keep from me their stealthy love?
Were they seen oft exchanging looks and
[words?
5 Deep in the forests were they wont to hide?
Alas! They had the utmost liberty.
Heaven smiled upon their innocent desires.
They followed where love led them, conscience
[free.
10 For them the dawn rose shining and serene.
And I, rejected by all living things,
I hid myself from day, I shunned the light;
Death was the only god I dared invoke.
I waited for the moment of my end,
15 Feeding on gall and drinking deep of tears.
Too closely watched, I did not even dare
Give myself up in freedom to my grief.
Trembling, this baleful pleasure I enjoyed
And, cloaking with a feignéd calm my woes,
20 Was often driven to forego my tears.
    OENONE. What good will their love do them?
[Never will
They meet again.
    PHAEDRA.   Their love will always live.
25 Even as I speak, ah cruel, deadly thought!
They flout the fury of my insane rage.
Despite this exile which will sever them
They swear a thousand oaths never to part.
No. No. Their happiness is gall to me.
30 Oenone, pity my wild jealousy.
Aricia must perish, and the King
Be stirred to wrath against her odious race.
No trifling retribution will suffice.
The sister has outdone her brothers' crime.
35 I will implore him in my jealous rage.
What am I doing? I have lost my mind!
I, jealous? and 'tis Theseus I implore!
My husband is alive and yet I pine.
For whom? Whose heart have I been coveting?
40 At every word my hair stands up on end.
Henceforth the measure of my crimes is full.
I reek with foulest incest and deceit.
My hands, that strain for murder and revenge,
Burn with desire to plunge in guiltless blood.
45 Wretch! and I live and can endure the gaze
Of the most sacred sun from which I spring.
My grandsire is the lord of all the gods;

My forebears fill the sky, the universe.
Where can I hide? In dark infernal night?
No, there my father holds the urn of doom.   50
Destiny placed it in his ruthless hands.
Minos judges in hell the trembling dead.
Ah! how his horror-stricken shade will start
To see before him his own daughter stand,
Forced to admit to such a host of sins   55
And some, perhaps, unknown even in hell!
What, father, will you say to that dread sight?
I see your hand slip from the fateful urn;
I see you searching for new punishments,
Yourself your own kin's executioner.   60
Forgive me. Venus' wrath has doomed your
[race.
Your daughter's frenzy shows that vengeance
[forth.
Alas, my sad heart never has enjoyed   65
The fruits of crimes whose dark shame follows
[me.
Dogged by misfortune to my dying breath,
I end upon the rack a life of pain.
    OENONE. Ah, Queen! dismiss these   70
[unbecoming fears,
And of your error take a different view.
You are in love. We cannot change our fate.
By destined magic you were swept along.
Is that so strange or so miraculous?   75
Has love then triumphed only over you?
Frailty is human and but natural.
Mortal, you must a mortal's lot endure.
This thraldom was imposed long, long ago.
The gods themselves that in Olympus dwell,   80
Who smite the evildoer with their bolt,
Have sometimes felt unlawful passions' fire.
    PHAEDRA. Great gods! What counsels dare
[you offer me?
Even to the last you seek to poison me.   85
Wretch! Thus it is that you have caused my
[doom.
You, when I fled from life, you called me back;
At your entreaties duty was forgot;
It was *you* made me see Hippolytus.   90
You meddling fool. Why did your impious lips,
Falsely accusing him, besmirch his life?
You may have killed him, if the gods have
[heard

A maddened father's sacrilegious wish.
I'll hear no more. Hence, loathsome monster,
[hence.
Go, leave me to my pitiable fate.
5 May the just heavens reward you fittingly,
And may your punishment forever fright
All who, as you have done, by base deceit,
Pander to ill-starred princes' weaknesses,
Urging them on to yield to their desires,
10 And dare to smooth the path of crime for them,
Vile flatterers, the most ill-fated boon
The anger of the gods can make to kings!
    OENONE. Ah God! to save her what have I
[not done,
15 But this is the reward I have deserved.

ACT V

Scene i

[HIPPOLYTUS, ARICIA.]
    ARICIA. What, in this peril you refuse to
[speak?
You leave a loving father undeceived?
20 Cruel one, can you, by my tears unmoved,
Consent without a sigh to part from me?
Go hence and leave me to my grieving heart.
But, if you go, at least preserve your life.
Defend your honor from a foul reproach
25 And force your father to revoke your doom.
There still is time. Wherefore, from what
[caprice,
Will you let Phaedra's slander hold the field?
Tell Theseus all.
30   HIPPOLYTUS. Ah, what have I not said?
Should I make known the outrage to his bed
And by an all too frank relation bring
Over my father's brow a blush of shame?
This odious secret you alone have pierced.
35 My sole confidants are the gods and you.
Judge of my love, I have not hid from you
All I desired to hide even from myself.
But, since you have been sworn to secrecy,
Forget, if it be possible, my words.
40 And never may your pure unsullied lips
Recount the details of this horrid scene.
Let's trust the justice of the gods above.
Their interest lies in vindicating me.

Sooner or later Phaedra will be brought
To book and meet an ignominious doom.   45
That is the only boon I ask of you.
My anger takes all other liberties.
Reject the bondage under which you pine;
Dare to accompany me in my flight.
Tear yourself free from an unhallowed spot   50
Where virtue breathes a foul, polluted air.
Let us to cover our escape exploit
The wild confusion that my downfall spreads.
I can provide you with the means for flight.
The only guards controlling you are mine.   55
Mighty defenders will take up our cause.
Argos awaits us; Sparta summons us.
Let's bear our grievance to our new allies.
Phaedra must never profit from our fall
And drive us both from off my father's throne,   60
Making her son the heir to our estates.
Now is our chance. We must lay hands on it.
What holds you back? You seem to hesitate.
Only your interest thus emboldens me.
When I am ardent, why are you so cold?   65
Are you afraid to share an exile's lot?
    ARICIA. Alas! How pleasant to be banished
[thus!
With what delight, linking my fate with yours,
By all the world forgotten I would live!   70
But, since we are not joined by that sweet bond,
Could I in honor flee from here with you?
I know that, even by the strictest code,
I may throw off your father's tutelage.
No bond of home or parents holds me back,   75
And flight from tyrants is permissible.
You love me, though, my lord, and my good
[name . . .
    HIPPOLYTUS. No. No. Your honor is too dear
[to me.   80
I come before you with a nobler plan.
Flee from my foes. Flee as my wedded wife.
Alone in exile, since heaven wills it so,
We need no man's consent to pledge our faith.
Not always torches blaze for Hymen's rites.   85
Not far from Troezen's gates, among these
[tombs,
My princely forebears' ancient burial place,
There stands a shrine dreaded of perjurers.
There mortals never swear an oath in vain.   90

Who breaks his word is punished instantly,
And men forsworn, afraid of certain death,
Are held in check by this most dreaded threat.
There, if you trust me, we will ratify
5 By solemn oath our everlasting love,
Taking to witness this old temple's god.
We'll pray him to be father to us both.
I'll call to witness the most sacred gods,
And chaste Diana, Juno the august,
10 And all the gods, witnesses of my love,
Will lend their blessing to my holy vows.
    ARICIA. The King is coming. Flee, make haste.
                          [To cloak
My own departure, I will stay awhile.
15 Go now, but leave me someone I can trust
To lead my steps to the appointed place.

Scene ii

[THESEUS, ARICIA, ISMENE.]
    THESEUS. O God! lighten the darkness of my
                              [mind.
20 Show me the truth that I am searching for.
    ARICIA. Make ready, dear Ismene, for our
                              [flight.

Scene iii

[THESEUS, ARICIA.]
    THESEUS. Your color changes and you seem
25   [aghast,
Lady. What was the young prince doing here?
    ARICIA. My lord, he took eternal leave of me.
    THESEUS. You have subdued that proud
                        [rebellious heart,
30 And his first raptures were inspired by you.
    ARICIA. My lord, I cannot well deny the truth.
Your unjust hatred is not shared by him.
He did not treat me like a criminal.
    THESEUS. I know. He swore eternal love to
35   [you.
Do not rely on that inconstant heart,
For he to others swore the selfsame oaths.
    ARICIA. He, Sire?
    THESEUS.   You ought to have restrained
40   [him. How
Could you endure to share his fickle heart?
    ARICIA. And how could you allow such
                         [calumny
To tarnish the bright glory of his life?

Have you so little knowledge of his heart?   45
Can you not tell baseness from innocence?
Must from your eyes alone an odious cloud
Conceal his virtues which shine bright to all?
I cannot let him further be maligned.
Stop and repent of your assassin's prayer.   50
Fear, my lord, fear lest the unbending heavens
Hate you enough to grant you your desire.
Oft in their wrath they take our sacrifice.
Often their gifts are sent to scourge our sins.
    THESEUS. In vain you seek to cover his   55
                          [offense.
Your passion blinds you to his faults. But I
Have faith in sure, trustworthy witnesses.
I have seen tears which surely were not feigned.
    ARICIA. Take care, my lord. Invincible, your   60
                          [hands
Have freed the world from monsters
                          [numberless;
But all are not destroyed. You still let live
One . . . But your son forbids me to proceed.   65
Knowing his wishes, I respect you still.
I would but grieve him if I dared to speak.
Following his restraint, I will withdraw
Rather than let the truth escape my lips.

Scene iv

[THESEUS alone.]   70
    THESEUS. What does she mean, and what do
                        [these words hide,
Begun and broken off, begun again?
Is it their aim to trick me by a feint?
Are they in league to put me on the rack?   75
But I myself, despite my stern resolve,
What plaintive voice cries in my inmost heart?
A lurking burst of pity harrows me.
I'll have Oenone questioned once again;
I must have more light thrown upon the crime.   80
Guards, bring Oenone out to me alone.

Scene v

[THESEUS, PANOPE.]
    PANOPE. I do not know what the Queen
                        [purposes,
But her distraction is a fearful sight.   85
Mortal despair cries from her haggard face,
And death has laid its paleness on her cheeks.
Oenone, driven out with shame, has plunged

Already into the unsounded sea.
We do not know what led her to this death;
The waves have closed for ever over her.
    THESEUS. What?
5   PANOPE.   This dark action did not calm
                         [the Queen.
Distraction grows in her storm-ridden heart.
Sometimes, to soothe her secret sufferings,
She takes her children, bathes them in her tears;
10 Then, suddenly, renouncing mother's love,
Shuddering with horror, will have none of
                          [them.
This way and that, she wanders aimlessly;
Wildly she looks at us, but knows us not.
15 She thrice has written, then has changed her
                          [mind,
And thrice torn up the letter she began.
See her, we beg you. We implore your help.
    THESEUS. Oenone's dead, and Phaedra seeks
20   [to die.
Call back my son, let him defend himself
And speak to me! I'll lend a willing ear.
[*Alone.*] Do not be overhasty with your gifts,
Neptune! I wish my prayer may not be heard.
25 Perhaps I have believed false witnesses,
Lifting too soon my cruel hand to you.
Ah! if you act, what will be my despair!

Scene vi

[THESEUS, THERAMENES.]
    THESEUS. What have you done with him,
30   [Theramenes?
I put him as a boy into your hands.
But why the tears that trickle down your
                         [cheeks?
What of my son?
35   THERAMENES. O tardy vain concern!
O unavailing love! Your son's no more.
    THESEUS. God!
    THERAMENES. I have seen the best of mortals
                          [die,
40 And the most innocent, I dare to add.
    THESEUS. Dead? When I open wide my arms
                         [to him,
The gods, impatient, hasten on his death?
What blow, what thunderbolt snatched him
45   [away?
    THERAMENES. Scarce were we issuing from

[Troezen's gates;
He drove his chariot; round about him ranged,
Copying his silence, were his cheerless guards.
Pensive, he followed the Mycenae road,   50
And let the reins hang loose upon his steeds.
These haughty steeds, that once upon a time,
Noble, high-spirited, obeyed his voice,
Now dull of eye and with dejected air
Seemed to conform to his despondent thoughts. 55
A ghastly cry from out the water's depths
That moment rent the quiet of the air.
From the earth's entrails then a fearful voice
Made answer with a groan to that dread cry.
Deep in our hearts the horror froze our blood.   60
The coursers' manes, on hearing, stood erect.
And now, there rose upon the liquid plain
A watery mountain seething furiously.
The surge drew near, dissolved and vomited
A raging monster from among the foam.   65
His forehead huge was armed with fearsome
                        [horns
And his whole body sheathed in yellow scales,
Half bull, half dragon, wild, impetuous.
His crupper curved in many a winding fold.   70
The shore quaked with his long-drawn
                        [bellowings.
The heavens beheld the monster, horror-struck;
It poisoned all the air; it rocked the earth.
The wave that brought it in recoiled aghast.   75
Everyone, throwing courage to the winds,
Took refuge in the temple near at hand.
Hippolytus alone, undaunted, stayed,
Reined in his steeds and seized his javelins,
Had at the monster and, with sure-flung dart,   80
Dealt him a gaping wound deep in his flank.
With rage and pain the monster, starting up,
Collapsed and, falling at the horses' feet,
Rolled over, opening wide his flaming jaws,
And covered them with smoke and blood and 85
                        [fire.
Carried away by terror, deaf, the steeds
No more responded to his curb or voice.
Their master spent his efforts all in vain.
They stained the bridle with their bloody foam. 90
In this wild tumult, it is even said,
A god appeared, goading their dusty flanks.
Over the rocks fear drove them headlong on;
The axle groaned and broke. Hippolytus

Saw his whole chariot shattered into bits.
He fell at last, entangled in the reins.
Forgive my grief. For me this picture spells
Eternal sorrow and perpetual tears.
5 I have beheld, my lord, your ill-starred son
Dragged by the horses that his hand had fed.
His voice that called them merely frightened
                                          [them.
Onward they flew—his body one whole wound.
10 The plain resounded with our cries of woe.
At last they slackened their impetuous course.
They halted near the old ancestral tombs
Where all his royal forebears lie in state.
I and his guards hastened to him in tears.
15 The traces of his blood showed us the way.
The rocks were stained with it, the cruel thorns
Dripped with the bleeding remnants of his hair.
I saw him, called him; giving me his hand,
He opened, then that moment closed, his eyes.
20 "Heaven takes my life, though innocent," he
                                          [cried.
"When I am dead, protect Aricia.
Friend, if my father ever learns the truth,
And pities the misfortunes of his son,
25 And would appease me in the life to come,
Tell him to show that princess clemency,
To give her back...." And then he passed
                                          [away,
And in my arms lay a disfigured corpse,
30 A tribute to the anger of the gods
That even his father would not recognize.
    THESEUS. My son, fond hope I have myself
                                          [destroyed!
Inexorable, all too helpful gods!
35 What keen remorse will haunt me all my life!
    THERAMENES. Aricia then came upon the
                                          [scene.
She came, my lord, fleeing your royal wrath,
Before the gods to pledge her faith to him.
40 As she drew near, she saw the reeking grass.
She saw, a grim sight for a lover's eyes,
Hippolytus, disfigured, deadly pale.
A while she tried to doubt her evil fate.
She sees the body of Hippolytus,
45 Yet still pursues the quest for her beloved.
But, in the end, only too sure 'tis he,
With one sad look, accusing heaven's spite,
Cold, moaning, and well nigh inanimate,

She falls, unconscious, at her sweetheart's feet.
Ismene, bending over her, in tears,   50
Summons her back to life, a life of pain.
And I have come, my lord, hating the world,
To tell you of Hippolytus' last wish
And to discharge the bitter embassy
Which he entrusted to me as he died.   55
But hither comes his deadly enemy.

Scene vii

[THESEUS, PHAEDRA, THERAMENES, PANOPE,
GUARDS.]
    THESEUS. Well, then, you triumph and my
                                          [son's no more. 60
What grounds I have for fear! What cruel doubt
Gnaws at my heart, pleading his innocence!
But he is dead. Accept your victim. Joy
In his undoing, justified or no,
For I am willing to deceive myself.   65
Since you accuse him, I accept his guilt.
His death will make my tears flow fast enough
Without my seeking for enlightenment
Which could not ever bring him back to me
And might perhaps but sharpen my distress.   70
Let me flee, far from you and from these shores,
The bloody vision of my mangled son.
Stunned and pursued by this grim memory,
Would I were in another universe!
Everything seems to brand my wicked wrath.   75
My very name increases my despair.
Less known of mortals, I could hide myself.
I hate even the favors of the gods.
And now I must bewail their murderous gifts,
No longer tiring them with fruitless prayers.   80
Whatever they have done for me, their aid
Cannot give back what they have robbed me of.
    PHAEDRA. No, Theseus. No, I must at last
                                          [speak out.
I must redress the wrong I did your son,   85
For he was innocent.
    THESEUS.   Wretch that I am!
If I condemned him, it was on your word.
Cruel one, do you hope to be forgiven...
    PHAEDRA. Each moment's precious. Listen.   90
                                          [It was I,
Theseus, who on your virtuous, filial son
Made bold to cast a lewd, incestuous eye.
Heaven in my heart lit an ill-omened fire.

Detestable Oenone did the rest.
She feared your son, knowing my frenzy, might
Reveal a guilty passion he abhorred.
The wretch, exploiting my enfeebled state,
5   Rushed to denounce Hippolytus to you.
She has exacted justice on herself
And found beneath the waves too mild a death.
By now I would have perished by the sword,
But first I wished to clear my victim's name.
10 I wished, revealing my remorse to you,
To choose a slower road down to the dead.
I have instilled into my burning veins
A poison that Medea brought to Greece.
Already it has reached my heart and spread
15 A strange chill through my body. Even now
Only as through a cloud I see the bright
Heaven and the husband whom I still defile.
But death, robbing my eyes of light, will give
Back to the sun its tarnished purity.
20   PANOPE. Ah! she is dying.
        THESEUS.   Would the memory
Of her appalling misdeeds die with her!
Let us, now that my error's all too clear,
Go out and mourn over my ill-starred son.
25 Let us embrace my cherished son's remains
And expiate my mad atrocious wish,
Rendering him the honors he deserves,
And, to appease the anger of his shade,
Let his beloved, despite her brothers' crime,
30 Be as a daughter to me from this day.

Richard Brinsley Sheridan

1751–1816

The Rivals

1775

The author of *The Rivals* was an ebullient young man of twenty-four, and one can argue that the only really apt comment on his play is pure and exuberant laughter. Unless there is laughter, at least, all comment is fruitless. When Mrs. Malaprop, with her customary misapplication of a word, writes, "Female punctuation forbids me to say more," or when Bob Acres' valet, to express admiration for his master's new clothes, says, "There a'nt a dog in the house but would bark," one is first of all amused; if he is not amused, there is no basis for discussing things further. But laughter is not likely to fail *The Rivals* now. It has brought merriment in both theater and study throughout its long history.

Sheridan's humor is of several kinds, and often of several kinds at once. The play can be sheerly witty; some of its quips—those of Captain Absolute's man Fag, for instance—could stand alone in collections of clever sayings. Sometimes it comments on prevailing mores and so moves toward "comedy of manners"; Lydia Languish and Faulkland, although differing from each other, are both parodies of fashionable sentimentality. And sometimes it puts personal eccentricities on display and so moves toward "comedy of humors"—a type already exemplified in this collection in parts of *Volpone* and *The Miser*. Inasmuch as Mrs. Malaprop has proved the most memorable person in the play, and inasmuch as she and her fellow eccentrics tend to upstage the hero and heroine in theatrical performances, humors comedy is perhaps the most vital of the three strains. But the real genius of the play lies in its simultaneous realization of more than one comic possibility. Sir Lucius O'Trigger, for example, intent on a duel, says to his puzzled adversary, "Pray, Sir, be easy: the quarrel is a very pretty quarrel as it stands—we should only spoil it by trying to explain it." The expression is at once so deft, and the penchant for bloodshed so extreme, that one cannot separate the wit from Sir Lucius's quarrelsome "humor."

367

Such a classification of things laughed at, however, if allowed to stand alone, would suggest fallaciously that comedy has no other task than to find matter for mirth. Comedy becomes disorderly and raucous unless it also satisfies our minds and consciences that it is provoking laughter at things that deserve ridicule. *The Rivals* is good comedy not only because it is lavish of humor but also because its sense of the absurd is both reasonable and moral. It quite frankly evaluates human relationships, especially between men and women, and postulates an ideal relationship based on a combination of good sense and genuine feeling. In their departures from this ideal, Sheridan's characters form that arabesque of follies at which we laugh.

Among the characters who err in their romantic relationships, Lydia Languish is deficient in both sense and feeling; until the last act she is more enamored of her own role as romantic lover than she is in love with Absolute. Faulkland, too, is more concerned with himself than with his affianced. Sir Lucius is fantastically willing to fight for a mistress; Bob Acres, ludicrously unwilling. And Mrs. Malaprop's weakness for Sir Lucius is mere wishful thinking, empty alike of reason and true passion.

In the midst of this company, Captain Absolute, although falling far short of personal perfection, represents the ideal, the "absolute" man. He is really in love. For the meltingly lovely Lydia he is willing to make extreme sacrifices. Yet he has not sacrificed his good sense to his sentiment. He does not love Lydia's faults. And he knows, as she does not, that, other things being equal, it is better to be young and in love on a substantial income than on a pitifully small one. It is this concept of the passionate yet reasonable man that gives the play its ethical center.

Without such an ethical center, *The Rivals* would fragment into a gallery of fantastics. Without its humor, it might embody the most admirable of lessons, but no audience would remain to admire.

The Rivals

SHERIDAN

CHARACTERS

Captain Absolute
Lydia Languish
Sir Anthony Absolute   *father of Captain Absolute*
Mrs. Malaprop   *aunt of Lydia Languish*
Faulkland
Julia Melville   *cousin of Lydia Languish*
Bob Acres
Sir Lucius O'Trigger
Fag   *valet of Captain Absolute*
Lucy   *lady's maid of Lydia Languish*
David   *valet of Bob Acres*
Coachman
Maid
Boy
Servants

scene. *Bath.*°
time of action. *Within one day.*

ACT I

Scene i

[*A street in Bath.*]
[Coachman *crosses the stage.—Enter* Fag, *looking after him.*]   5
    Fag. What!—Thomas! Sure, 'tis he?—What!—Thomas!—Thomas!

Bath a fashionable health and pleasure resort in southwest England. Places in Bath referred to include the **Pump Room,** where the fashionable assembled to drink the mineral waters; **Gyde's Porch,** an entranceway to some older ballrooms (?); the **North** and **South Parades,** or promenades; the **New Room(s),** ballroom(s) opened in 1771; **King's-Mead-Fields** in the outskirts of town; and **Spring Gardens,** a riverside picnic ground.

COACHMAN. Hey! Odd's life!°—Mr. Fag!—give us your hand, my old fellow-servant.

FAG. Excuse my glove, Thomas:—I'm dev'-lish glad to see you, my lad: why, my prince
5 of charioteers, you look as hearty!—but who the deuce thought of seeing you in Bath!

COACHMAN. Sure, Master, Madam Julia, Harry, Mrs. Kate, and the postilion be all come!

FAG. Indeed!

10 COACHMAN. Aye! Master thought another fit of the gout was coming to make him a visit: so he'd a mind to gi't the slip, and whip! we were all off at an hour's warning.

FAG. Aye, aye! hasty in everything, or it
15 would not be Sir Anthony Absolute!

COACHMAN. But tell us, Mr. Fag, how does young master? Odd! Sir Anthony will stare to see the Captain here!

FAG. I do not serve Captain Absolute now.

20 COACHMAN. Why sure!

FAG. At present I am employed by Ensign Beverley.

COACHMAN. I doubt, Mr. Fag, you ha'n't changed for the better.

25 FAG. I have not changed, Thomas.

COACHMAN. No! why, didn't you say you had left young master?

FAG. No.—Well, honest Thomas, I must puzzle you no farther: briefly then—Captain
30 Absolute and Ensign Beverley are one and the same person.

COACHMAN. The devil they are!

FAG. So it is indeed, Thomas; and the *Ensign*-

half of my master being on guard at present—the *Captain* has nothing to do with me. 35

COACHMAN. So, so!—What, this is some freak, I warrant!—Do tell us, Mr. Fag, the meaning o't—you know I ha' trusted you.

FAG. You'll be secret, Thomas?

COACHMAN. As a coach-horse. 40

FAG. Why then the cause of all this is—LOVE—Love, Thomas, who (as you may get read to you) has been a masquerader ever since the days of Jupiter.

COACHMAN. Aye, aye;—I guessed there was 45 a lady in the case: but pray, why does your master pass only for *Ensign*? Now if he had shammed *General*, indeed—

FAG. Ah! Thomas, there lies the mystery o' the matter. Hark'ee, Thomas, my master is in 50 love with a lady of a very singular taste: a lady who likes him better as a *half-pay Ensign* than if she knew he was son and heir to Sir Anthony Absolute, a baronet of three thousand a year!

COACHMAN. That is an odd taste indeed!— 55 but has she got the stuff, Mr. Fag? is she rich, hey?

FAG. Rich!—why, I believe she owns half the stocks—Z——ds! Thomas, she could pay the national debt as easily as I could my washer- 60 woman! She has a lap-dog that eats out of gold—she feeds her parrot with small pearls—and all her thread-papers° are made of bank-notes!

COACHMAN. Bravo!—Faith!—Odd! I warrant she has a set of thousands° at least. But does 65 she draw kindly with the Captain?

FAG. As fond as pigeons.

COACHMAN. May one hear her name?

FAG. Miss Lydia Languish. But there is an old tough aunt in the way; though, by the bye, she 70 has never seen my master, for he got acquainted with Miss while on a visit in Gloucestershire.

COACHMAN. Well—I wish they were once harnessed together in matrimony.—But pray, Mr. Fag, what kind of a place is this Bath? I ha' 75 heard a deal of it—here's a mort o' merry-making, hey?

FAG. Pretty well, Thomas, pretty well—'tis

Odd's life the first of a number of minced oaths. These are profane expressions that have been mis-pronounced at some time in the past, either euphe-mistically or in the natural course of repetition, and that, as their origins have been forgotten, have pass-ed into general slang. Modern examples are "Gosh!" "Darn!" "Goldern it!" "Golly Ned!" The less familiar minced oaths in *The Rivals*, together with the words they mince, include **Lud** Lord; **Odd** God; **Odd's life** God's life; **Odd rabbit it** (variant of "Odd rat it") God rot it; **Odd so** God's oath; **Oons** (variant of "Zounds") God's wounds, an oath on the wounds of Christ; **'Sdeath** God's death, an oath on the death of Christ; **Zooks** (variant of "Gadzooks") God's hooks, an oath on the nails of the cross; and **Zounds** God's wounds (see "Oons" above). Bob Acres' "ref-erential oaths" put together the form "Odds" with terms from the context of his thought.

thread-papers papers on which thread is wound
set of thousands six-horse team worth thousands of pounds

a good lounge.° In the morning we go to the Pump-room (though neither my master nor I drink the waters); after breakfast we saunter on the Parades, or play a game at billiards; at
5 night we dance: but d——n the place, I'm tired of it: their regular hours stupefy me—not a fiddle nor a card after eleven! However, Mr. Faulkland's gentleman and I keep it up a little in private parties—I'll introduce you there,
10 Thomas: you'll like him much.

COACHMAN. Sure I know Mr. Du-Peigne— you know his master is to marry Madam Julia.

FAG. I had forgot.—But Thomas, you must polish a little—indeed you must. Here now—
15 this wig! what the devil do you do with a *wig*, Thomas?—none of the London whips of any degree of *ton* wear *wigs* now.

COACHMAN. More's the pity! more's the pity, I say—Odd's life! when I heard how the law-
20 yers and doctors had took to their own hair, I thought how 'twould go next:—Odd rabbit it! when the fashion had got foot on the Bar, I guessed 'twould mount to the Box!° But 'tis all out of character, believe me, Mr. Fag: and
25 look'ee, I'll never gi' up mine—the lawyers and doctors may do as they will.

FAG. Well, Thomas, we'll not quarrel about that.

COACHMAN. Why, bless you, the gentlemen
30 of the professions ben't all of a mind—for in our village now, tho'ff *Jack Gauge*, the *excise-man*, has ta'en to his carrots, there's little Dick, the farrier, swears he'll never forsake his *bob*, tho' all the college should appear with their
35 own heads!°

FAG. Indeed! well said, Dick! But hold— mark! mark! Thomas.

COACHMAN. Zooks! 'tis the Captain!—Is that the lady with him?
40 FAG. No! no! that is Madam Lucy—my master's mistress's maid. They lodge at that

house—but I must after him to tell him the news.

COACHMAN. Odd! he's giving her money!— Well, Mr. Fag— 45

FAG. Good-bye, Thomas.—I have an appointment in Gyde's Porch this evening at eight; meet me there, and we'll make a little party.

[*Exeunt severally.*]

Scene ii

[*A dressing-room in* MRS. MALAPROP's *lodg-* 50 *ings.*]

[LYDIA *sitting on a sofa, with a book in her hand.* LUCY, *as just returned from a message.*]

LUCY. Indeed, Ma'am, I traversed half the town in search of it: I don't believe there's a 55 circulating library in Bath I ha'n't been at.

LYDIA. And could not you get *The Reward of Constancy?*

LUCY. No, indeed, Ma'am.

LYDIA. Nor *The Fatal Connection?* 60

LUCY. No, indeed, Ma'am.

LYDIA. Nor *The Mistakes of the Heart?*

LUCY. Ma'am, as ill-luck would have it, Mr. Bull said Miss Sukey Saunter had just fetched it away. 65

LYDIA. Heigh-ho! Did you inquire for *The Delicate Distress?*

LUCY. Or *The Memoirs of Lady Woodford?* Yes, indeed, Ma'am. I asked everywhere for it; and I might have brought it from Mr. Fred- 70 erick's, but Lady Slattern Lounger, who had just sent it home, had so soiled and dog's-eared it, it wa'n't fit for a Christian to read.

LYDIA. Heigh-ho!—Yes, I always know when Lady Slattern has been before me. She has a 75 most observing thumb; and I believe cherishes her nails for the convenience of making mar-ginal notes.—Well, child, what *have* you brought me?

LUCY. Oh! here, Ma'am. [*Taking books from* 80 *under her cloak, and from her pockets.*] This is *The Gordian Knot*, and this *Peregrine Pickle.* Here are *The Tears of Sensibility* and *Humphry Clinker.* This is *The Memoirs of a Lady of Quality, written by herself,* and here the second 85 volume of *The Sentimental Journey.*

LYDIA. Heigh-ho!—What are those books by the glass?

---

lounge place to spend leisure time
had got foot . . . Box i.e., had caught on among lawyers, I guessed it would then catch on among coachmen
has ta'en . . . heads has begun to wear his natural red hair, there's little Dick, the farrier, swears he'll never forsake his wig, though all his professional associates should appear wearing their own hair

LUCY. The great one is only *The Whole Duty of Man*—where I press a few blonds,° Ma'am.

LYDIA. Very well—give me the *sal volatile*.

LUCY. Is it in a blue cover, Ma'am?

5 LYDIA. My smelling bottle, you simpleton!

LUCY. Oh, the drops!—Here, Ma'am.

LYDIA. Hold!—here's some one coming—quick! see who it is.

[*Exit* LUCY.]

10 Surely I heard my cousin Julia's voice!

[*Re-enter* LUCY.]

LUCY. Lud! Ma'am, here is Miss Melville.

LYDIA. Is it possible!—

[*Enter* JULIA.]

15 My dearest Julia, how delighted am I!—[*Embrace.*] How unexpected was this happiness!

JULIA. True, Lydia—and our pleasure is the greater; but what has been the matter?—you were denied to me at first!

20 LYDIA. Ah! Julia, I have a thousand things to tell you! But first inform me what has conjured you to Bath? Is Sir Anthony here?

JULIA. He is—we are arrived within this hour, and I suppose he will be here to wait on 25 Mrs. Malaprop as soon as he is dressed.

LYDIA. Then, before we are interrupted, let me impart to you some of my distress! I know your gentle nature will sympathize with me, though your prudence may condemn me! My 30 letters have informed you of my whole connexion with Beverley—but I have lost him, Julia! My aunt has discovered our intercourse by a note she intercepted, and has confined me ever since! Yet, would you believe it? she has 35 fallen absolutely in love with a tall Irish baronet she met one night since we. have been here, at Lady Macshuffle's rout.°

JULIA. You jest, Lydia!

LYDIA. No, upon my word. She really carries 40 on a kind of correspondence with him, under a feigned name though, till she chooses to be known to him; but it is a *Delia* or a *Celia,* I assure you.

JULIA. Then surely she is now more indulgent 45 to her niece.

LYDIA. Quite the contrary. Since she has dis-covered her own frailty she is become more suspicious of mine. Then I must inform you of another plague! That odious Acres is to be in Bath to-day; so that I protest I shall be teased 50 out of all spirits!

JULIA. Come, come, Lydia, hope the best. Sir Anthony shall use his interest with Mrs. Malaprop.

LYDIA. But you have not heard the worst. 55 Unfortunately I had quarreled with my poor Beverley just before my aunt made the discovery, and I have not seen him since to make it up.

JULIA. What was his offence? 60

LYDIA. Nothing at all! But, I don't know how it was, as often as we had been together we had never had a quarrel! And, somehow, I was afraid he would never give me an opportunity. So last Thursday I wrote a letter to my- 65 self to inform myself that Beverley was at that time paying his addresses to another woman. I signed it *your friend unknown,* showed it to Beverley, charged him with his falsehood, put myself in a violent passion, and vowed I'd 70 never see him more.

JULIA. And you let him depart so, and have not seen him since?

LYDIA. 'Twas the next day my aunt found the matter out. I intended only to have teased 75 him three days and a half, and now I've lost him forever!

JULIA. If he is as deserving and sincere as you have represented him to me, he will never give you up so. Yet consider, Lydia, you tell me he 80 is but an ensign, and you have thirty thousand pounds!

LYDIA. But you know I lose most of my fortune if I marry without my aunt's consent, till of age; and that is what I have determined 85 to do ever since I knew the penalty. Nor could I love the man who would wish to wait a day for the alternative.

JULIA. Nay, this is caprice!

LYDIA. What, does Julia tax me with caprice? 90 I thought her lover Faulkland had enured her to it.

JULIA. I do not love even *his* faults.

LYDIA. But a-propos—you have sent to him, I suppose?

blonds silk laces
rout evening party

JULIA. Not yet, upon my word, nor has he the least idea of my being in Bath. Sir Anthony's resolution was so sudden I could not inform him of it.

5 LYDIA. Well, Julia, you are your own mistress (though under the protection of Sir Anthony), yet have you for this long year been a slave to the caprice, the whim, the jealousy of this ungrateful Faulkland, who will ever delay assuming the right of a husband, while you suffer him to be equally imperious as a lover.

JULIA. Nay, you are wrong entirely. We were contracted before my father's death. That, and some consequent embarrassments, have delayed what I know to be my Faulkland's most ardent wish. He is too generous to trifle on such a point. And for his character, you wrong him there too. No, Lydia, he is too proud, too noble to be jealous: if he is captious, 'tis without dissembling; if fretful, without rudeness. Unused to the fopperies of love, he is negligent of the little duties expected from a lover—but being unhackneyed in the passion, his affection is ardent and sincere; and as it engrosses his whole soul, he expects every thought and emotion of his mistress to move in unison with his. Yet, though his pride calls for this full return, his humility makes him undervalue those qualities in him which would entitle him to it; and not feeling why he should be loved to the degree he wishes, he still suspects that he is not loved enough. This temper, I must own, has cost me many unhappy hours; but I have learned to think myself his debtor for those imperfections which arise from the ardour of his attachment.

LYDIA. Well, I cannot blame you for defending him. But tell me candidly, Julia, had he never saved your life, do you think you should have been attached to him as you are? Believe me, the rude blast that overset your boat was a prosperous gale of love to him.

JULIA. Gratitude may have strengthened my attachment to Mr. Faulkland, but I loved him before he had preserved me; yet surely that alone were an obligation sufficient—

LYDIA. Obligation! Why, a water-spaniel would have done as much! Well, I should never think of giving my heart to a man because he could swim! 50

JULIA. Come, Lydia, you are too inconsiderate.

LYDIA. Nay, I do but jest.—What's here?

[*Enter* LUCY *in a hurry.*]

LUCY. O Ma'am, here is Sir Anthony Absolute just come home with your aunt. 55

LYDIA. They'll not come here.—Lucy, do you watch.

[*Exit* LUCY.]

JULIA. Yet I must go. Sir Anthony does not 60 know I am here, and if we meet, he'll detain me, to show me the town. I'll take another opportunity of paying my respects to Mrs. Malaprop, when she shall treat me, as long as she chooses, with her select words so ingeniously 65 *misapplied*, without being *mispronounced*.

[*Re-enter* LUCY.]

LUCY. O lud! Ma'am, they are both coming upstairs.

LYDIA. Well, I'll not detain you, coz. Adieu, 70 my dear Julia. I'm sure you are in haste to send to Faulkland. There—through my room you'll find another stair-case.

JULIA. Adieu.—[*Embrace.*]

[*Exit* JULIA.] 75

LYDIA. Here, my dear Lucy, hide these books. Quick, quick! Fling *Peregrine Pickle* under the toilet—throw *Roderick Random* into the closet —put *The Innocent Adultery* into *The Whole Duty of Man*—thrust *Lord Aimworth* under 80 the sofa—cram *Ovid* behind the bolster—there —put *The Man of Feeling* into your pocket— so, so,—now lay *Mrs. Chapone* in sight, and leave *Fordyce's Sermons* open on the table.

LUCY. Oh burn it, Ma'am! the hair-dresser 85 has torn away as far as *Proper Pride*.

LYDIA. Never mind—open at *Sobriety.*— Fling me *Lord Chesterfield's Letters.*—Now for 'em.

[*Enter* MRS. MALAPROP, *and* SIR ANTHONY 90 ABSOLUTE.]

MRS. MALAPROP. There, Sir Anthony, there sits the deliberate simpleton who wants to disgrace her family, and lavish herself on a fellow not worth a shilling! 95

LYDIA. Madam, I thought you once—

MRS. MALAPROP. You thought, Miss! I don't know any business you have to think at all. Thought does not become a young woman. But the point we would request of you is, that you will promise to forget this fellow—to illiterate him, I say, quite from your memory.

LYDIA. Ah! Madam! our memories are independent of our wills. It is not so easy to forget.

MRS. MALAPROP. But I say it is, Miss; there is nothing on earth so easy as to *forget*, if a person chooses to set about it. I'm sure I have as much forgot your poor dear uncle as if he had never existed—and I thought it my duty so to do; and let me tell you, Lydia, these violent memories don't become a young woman.

SIR ANTHONY. Why sure she won't pretend to remember what she's ordered not!—aye, this comes of her reading!

LYDIA. What crime, Madam, have I committed to be treated thus?

MRS. MALAPROP. Now don't attempt to extirpate yourself from the matter; you know I have proof controvertible of it. But tell me, will you promise to do as you're bid? Will you take a husband of your friend's choosing?

LYDIA. Madam, I must tell you plainly, that had I no preference for anyone else, the choice you have made would be my aversion.

MRS. MALAPROP. What business have you, Miss, with *preference* and *aversion*? They don't become a young woman; and you ought to know, that as both always wear off, 'tis safest in matrimony to begin with a little *aversion*. I am sure I hated your poor dear uncle before marriage as if he'd been a blackamoor—and yet, Miss, you are sensible what a wife I made!—and when it pleased heaven to release me from him, 'tis unknown what tears I shed! But suppose we were going to give you another choice, will you promise us to give up this Beverley?

LYDIA. Could I belie my thoughts so far as to give that promise, my actions would certainly as far belie my words.

MRS. MALAPROP. Take yourself to your room. You are fit company for nothing but your own ill-humours.

LYDIA. Willingly, Ma'am—I cannot change for the worse.

[*Exit* LYDIA.]

MRS. MALAPROP. There's a little intricate hussy for you!

SIR ANTHONY. It is not to be wondered at, Ma'am—all this is the natural consequence of teaching girls to read. Had I a thousand daughters, by heaven! I'd as soon have them taught the black art as their alphabet!

MRS. MALAPROP. Nay, nay, Sir Anthony, you are an absolute misanthropy.

SIR ANTHONY. In my way hither, Mrs. Malaprop, I observed your niece's maid coming forth from a circulating library! She had a book in each hand—they were half-bound volumes, with marble covers! From that moment I guessed how full of duty I should see her mistress!

MRS. MALAPROP. Those are vile places, indeed!

SIR ANTHONY. Madam, a circulating library in a town is as an evergreen tree of diabolical knowledge! It blossoms through the year! And depend on it, Mrs. Malaprop, that they who are so fond of handling the leaves, will long for the fruit at last.

MRS. MALAPROP. Fie, fie, Sir Anthony, you surely speak laconically!

SIR ANTHONY. Why, Mrs. Malaprop, in moderation, now, what would you have a woman know?

MRS. MALAPROP. Observe me, Sir Anthony. I would by no means wish a daughter of mine to be a progeny of learning; I don't think so much learning becomes a young woman; for instance—I would never let her meddle with Greek, or Hebrew, or Algebra, or Simony, or Fluxions, or Paradoxes, or such inflammatory branches of learning—neither would it be necessary for her to handle any of your mathematical, astronomical, diabolical instruments; —but, Sir Anthony, I would send her, at nine years old, to a boarding-school, in order to learn a little ingenuity and artifice. Then, Sir, she should have a supercilious knowledge in accounts—and as she grew up, I would have her instructed in geometry, that she might know something of the contagious countries—but above all, Sir Anthony, she should be mistress of orthodoxy, that she might not misspell, and mispronounce words so shamefully as girls usually do; and likewise that she might reprehend the true meaning of what she is saying. This, Sir Anthony, is what I would have a woman know—and I don't think there is a superstitious article in it.

SIR ANTHONY. Well, well, Mrs. Malaprop, I will dispute the point no further with you; though I must confess that you are a truly moderate and polite arguer, for almost every third word you say is on my side of the question. But, Mrs. Malaprop, to the more important point in debate—you say you have no objection to my proposal.

MRS. MALAPROP. None, I assure you. I am under no positive engagement with Mr. Acres, and as Lydia is so obstinate against him, perhaps your son may have better success.

SIR ANTHONY. Well, Madam, I will write for the boy directly. He knows not a syllable of this yet, though I have for some time had the proposal in my head. He is at present with his regiment.

MRS. MALAPROP. We have never seen your son, Sir Anthony; but I hope no objection on his side.

SIR ANTHONY. Objection!—let him object if he dare! No, No, Mrs. Malaprop, Jack knows that the least demur puts me in a frenzy directly. My process was always very simple—in their young days, 'twas "Jack do this";—if he demurred—I knocked him down—and if he grumbled at that—I always sent him out of the room.

MRS. MALAPROP. Aye, and the properest way, o' my conscience!—nothing is so conciliating to young people as severity. Well, Sir Anthony, I shall give Mr. Acres his discharge, and prepare Lydia to receive your son's invocations; and I hope you will represent *her* to the Captain as an object not altogether illegible.

SIR ANTHONY. Madam, I will handle the subject prudently. Well, I must leave you—and let me beg you, Mrs. Malaprop, to enforce this matter roundly to the girl; take my advice—keep a tight hand; if she rejects this proposal—clap her under lock and key—and if you were just to let the servants forget to bring her dinner for three or four days, you can't conceive how she'd come about!

[*Exit* SIR ANTHONY.]

MRS. MALAPROP. Well, at any rate I shall be glad to get her from under my intuition. She has somehow discovered my partiality for Sir Lucius O'Trigger—sure, Lucy can't have betrayed me! No, the girl is such a simpleton, I should have made her confess it.—[*Calls.*] Lucy!—Lucy—Had she been one of your artificial ones, I should never have trusted her.

[*Enter* LUCY.]

LUCY. Did you call, Ma'am?

MRS. MALAPROP. Yes, girl. Did you see Sir Lucius while you was out?

LUCY. No, indeed, Ma'am, not a glimpse of him.

MRS. MALAPROP. You are sure, Lucy, that you never mentioned—

LUCY. O Gemini! I'd sooner cut my tongue out.

MRS. MALAPROP. Well, don't let your simplicity be imposed on.

LUCY. No, Ma'am.

MRS. MALAPROP. So, come to me presently, and I'll give you another letter to Sir Lucius; but mind, Lucy—if ever you betray what you are intrusted with (unless it be other people's secret to me) you forfeit my malevolence forever, and your being a simpleton shall be no excuse for your locality.

[*Exit* MRS. MALAPROP.]

LUCY. Ha! ha! ha!—So, my dear *simplicity*, let me give you a little respite—[*altering her manner*]—let girls in my station be as fond as they please of appearing expert, and knowing in their trusts—commend me to a mask of *silliness*, and a pair of sharp eyes for my own interest under it! Let me see to what account have I turned my *simplicity* lately—[*looks at a paper*]. For *abetting Miss Lydia Languish in a design of running away with an Ensign!—in money—sundry times—twelve pound twelve—gowns, five—hats, ruffles, caps, &c., &c.—numberless! From the said Ensign, within this last month, six guineas and a half.—About a*

quarter's pay!—Item, *from Mrs. Malaprop, for
betraying the young people to her*—when I
found matters were likely to be discovered—
two guineas, and a black paduasoy.—Item,
5 *from Mr. Acres, for carrying divers letters*—
which I never delivered—*two guineas, and a
pair of buckles.*—Item, *from Sir Lucius O'Trigger—three crowns—two gold pocket-pieces—
and a silver snuff-box!*—Well done, *simplicity!*
10 —Yet I was forced to make my Hibernian believe that he was corresponding, not with the
aunt, but with the *niece*: for, though not over-
rich, I found he had too much pride and
delicacy to sacrifice the feelings of a gentleman
15 to the necessities of his fortune.
[*Exit.*]

ACT II

Scene i

[CAPTAIN ABSOLUTE's *lodgings.*]
[CAPTAIN ABSOLUTE *and* FAG.]
FAG. Sir, while I was there Sir Anthony came
20 in: I told him you had sent me to inquire after
his health, and to know if he was at leisure
to see you.
ABSOLUTE. And what did he say on hearing I
was at Bath?
25 FAG. Sir, in my life I never saw an elderly
gentleman more astonished! He started back
two or three paces, rapped out a dozen inter-
jectoral oaths, and asked what the devil had
brought you here!
30 ABSOLUTE. Well, Sir, and what did you say?
FAG. Oh, I lied, Sir— I forget the precise lie;
but you may depend on't, he got no truth from
me. Yet, with submission, for fear of blunders
in future, I should be glad to fix what *has*
35 brought us to Bath, in order that we may lie a
little consistently. Sir Anthony's servants were
curious, Sir, very curious indeed.
ABSOLUTE. You have said nothing to them?
FAG. Oh, not a word, Sir—not a word. Mr.
40 Thomas, indeed, the coachman (whom I take
to be the discreetest of whips)—
ABSOLUTE. 'Sdeath!—you rascal! you have
not trusted him!
FAG. Oh, *no*, Sir!—no—no—not a syllable,
45 upon my veracity! He was, indeed, a little in-

quisitive; but I was sly, Sir—devilish sly!—
My master (said I), honest Thomas (you know,
Sir, one says *honest* to one's inferiors), is come
to Bath to *recruit*—yes, Sir—I said, *to recruit*—
and whether for men, money, or constitution, 50
you know, Sir, is nothing to him, nor anyone
else.
ABSOLUTE. Well—*recruit* will do—let it be
so—
FAG. Oh, Sir, recruit will do surprisingly— 55
indeed, to give the thing an air, I told Thomas
that your Honour had already enlisted five
disbanded chairmen, seven minority waiters,
and thirteen billiard markers.°
ABSOLUTE. You blockhead, never say more 60
than is necessary.
FAG. I beg pardon, Sir—I beg pardon.—But
with submission, a lie is nothing unless one
supports it. Sir, whenever I draw on my invention for a good current lie, I always forge 65
indorsements, as well as the bill.
ABSOLUTE. Well, take care you don't hurt
your credit by offering too much security. Is
Mr. Faulkland returned?
FAG. He is above, Sir, changing his dress. 70
ABSOLUTE. Can you tell whether he has been
informed of Sir Anthony's and Miss Melville's
arrival?
FAG. I fancy not, Sir; he has seen no one
since he came in but his gentleman, who was 75
with him at Bristol.—I think, Sir, I hear Mr.
Faulkland coming down—
ABSOLUTE. Go tell him I am here.
FAG. Yes, Sir [*going*]. I beg pardon, Sir, but
should Sir Anthony call, you will do me the 80
favor to remember that we are *recruiting*, if you
please.
ABSOLUTE. Well, well.
FAG. And in tenderness to my character, if
your Honour could bring in the chairmen and 85
waiters, I shall esteem it as an obligation; for
though I never scruple a lie to serve my
master, yet it hurts one's conscience to be
found out.
[*Exit.*] 90

five . . . markers five sedan chair bearers who have
been dismissed, seven unemployed waiters, and
thirteen men who chalk up scores in billiard rooms

ABSOLUTE. Now for my whimsical friend—if he does not know that his mistress is here, I'll tease him a little before I tell him—

[*Enter* FAULKLAND.]

5 Faulkland, you're welcome to Bath again; you are punctual in your return.

FAULKLAND. Yes; I had nothing to detain me when I had finished the business I went on. Well, what news since I left you? How stand
10 matters between you and Lydia?

ABSOLUTE. Faith, much as they were; I have not seen her since our quarrel; however, I expect to be recalled every hour.

FAULKLAND. Why don't you persuade her to
15 go off with you at once?

ABSOLUTE. What, and lose two-thirds of her fortune? You forget that, my friend. No, no, I could have brought her to that long ago.

FAULKLAND. Nay then, you trifle too long—
20 if you are sure of *her*, propose to the aunt *in your own character*, and write to Sir Anthony for his consent.

ABSOLUTE. Softly, softly, for though I am convinced my little Lydia would elope with me
25 as Ensign Beverley, yet am I by no means certain that she would take me with the impediment of our friend's consent, a regular humdrum wedding, and the reversion of° a good fortune on my side; no, no, I must pre-
30 pare her gradually for the discovery, and make myself necessary to her, before I risk it.— Well, but Faulkland, you'll dine with us to-day at the hotel?

FAULKLAND. Indeed, I cannot: I am not in
35 spirits to be of such a party.

ABSOLUTE. By heavens! I shall forswear your company. You are the most teasing, captious, incorrigible lover! Do love like a man!

FAULKLAND. I own I am unfit for company.
40 ABSOLUTE. Am not *I* a lover; aye, and a romantic one too? Yet do I carry everywhere with me such a confounded farrago of doubts, fears, hopes, wishes, and all the flimsy furniture of a country miss's brain!

45 FAULKLAND. Ah! Jack, your heart and soul are not, like mine, fixed immutably on one only

reversion of prospect of inheriting

object. You throw for a large stake, but losing —you could stake, and throw again. But I have set my sum of happiness on this cast, and not to succeed were to be stripped of all.   50

ABSOLUTE. But, for heaven's sake! what grounds for apprehension can your whimsical brain conjure up at present?

FAULKLAND. What grounds for apprehension did you say? Heavens! are there not a thou- 55 sand! I fear for her spirits—her health—her life. My absence may fret her; her anxiety for my return, her fears for me, may oppress her gentle temper. And for her health—does not every hour bring me cause to be alarmed? If it 60 rains, some shower may even then have chilled her delicate frame! If the wind be keen, some rude blast may have affected her! The heat of noon, the dews of the evening, may endanger the life of her, for whom only I value mine. O! 65 Jack, when delicate and feeling souls are separated, there is not a feature in the sky, not a movement of the elements, not an aspiration of the breeze, but hints some cause for a lover's apprehension!   70

ABSOLUTE. Aye, but we may choose whether we will take the hint or not. So then, Faulkland, if you were convinced that Julia were well and in spirits, you would be entirely content?

FAULKLAND. I should be happy beyond 75 measure—I am anxious only for that.

ABSOLUTE. Then to cure your anxiety at once —Miss Melville is in perfect health, and is at this moment in Bath!

FAULKLAND. Nay, Jack—don't trifle with me. 80

ABSOLUTE. She is arrived here with my father within this hour.

FAULKLAND. Can you be serious?

ABSOLUTE. I thought you knew Sir Anthony better than to be surprised at a sudden whim 85 of this kind. Seriously then, it is as I tell you— upon my honour.

FAULKLAND. My dear friend!—Hollo, Du-Peigne! my hat—my dear Jack—now nothing on earth can give me a moment's uneasiness. 90

[*Enter* FAG.]

FAG. Sir, Mr. Acres just arrived is below.

ABSOLUTE. Stay, Faulkland, this Acres lives within a mile of Sir Anthony, and he shall tell you how your mistress has been ever since you left her.—Fag, show the gentleman up.

[*Exit* FAG.]

FAULKLAND. What, is he much acquainted in
5 the family?

ABSOLUTE. Oh, very intimate. I insist on your not going: besides, his character will divert you.

FAULKLAND. Well, I should like to ask him a
10 few questions.

ABSOLUTE. He is likewise a rival of mine—that is of my *other self's,* for he does not think his friend Captain Absolute ever saw the lady in question; and it is ridiculous enough to hear
15 him complain to me of *one Beverley,* a concealed skulking rival, who—

FAULKLAND. Hush! He's here.

[*Enter* ACRES.]

ACRES. Hah! my dear friend, noble captain,
20 and honest Jack, how dost thou? Just arrived, faith, as you see. Sir, your humble servant. Warm work on the roads, Jack!—Odds whips and wheels! I've travelled like a comet, with a tail of dust all the way as long as the Mall.°

25 ABSOLUTE. Ah! Bob, you are indeed an eccentric planet, but we know your attraction hither. Give me leave to introduce Mr. Faulkland to you; Mr. Faulkland, Mr. Acres.

ACRES. Sir, I am most heartily glad to see
30 you: Sir, I solicit your connexions.—Hey, Jack —what—this is Mr. Faulkland, who—?

ABSOLUTE. Aye, Bob, Miss Melville's Mr. Faulkland.

ACRES. Odd so! she and your father can be
35 but just arrived before me—I suppose you have seen them. Ah! Mr. Faulkland, you are indeed a happy man.

FAULKLAND. I have not seen Miss Melville yet, Sir. I hope she enjoyed full health and
40 spirits in Devonshire?

ACRES. Never knew her better in my life, Sir—never better. Odds blushes and blooms! she has been as healthy as the German Spa.°

the Mall   the promenade in St. James's Park in London
the German spa   the original health resort itself. Reference is to a long-established watering place in Belgium.

FAULKLAND. Indeed! I did hear that she had been a little indisposed.   45

ACRES. False, false, Sir—only said to vex you: quite the reverse, I assure you.

FAULKLAND. There, Jack, you see she has the advantage of me; I had almost fretted myself ill.   50

ABSOLUTE. Now are you angry with your mistress for not having been sick.

FAULKLAND. No, no, you misunderstand me: yet surely a little trifling indisposition is not an unnatural consequence of absence from   55 those we love. Now confess—isn't there something unkind in this violent, robust, unfeeling health?

ABSOLUTE. Oh, it was very unkind of her to be well in your absence, to be sure!   60

ACRES. Good apartments, Jack.

FAULKLAND. Well, Sir, but you were saying that Miss Melville has been so *exceedingly* well —what, then she has been merry and gay, I suppose? Always in spirits—hey?   65

ACRES. Merry! Odds crickets! she has been the belle and spirit of the company wherever she has been—so lively and entertaining! so full of wit and humour!

FAULKLAND. There, Jack, there! Oh, by my   70 soul! there is an innate levity in woman, that nothing can overcome. What! happy, and I away!

ABSOLUTE. Have done—how foolish this is! Just now you were only apprehensive for your   75 mistress's *spirits.*

FAULKLAND. Why, Jack, have I been the joy and spirit of the company?

ABSOLUTE. No, indeed, you have not.

FAULKLAND. Have I been lively and enter-   80 taining?

ABSOLUTE. Oh, upon my word, I acquit you.

FAULKLAND. Have I been full of wit and humour?

ABSOLUTE. No, faith; to do you justice, you   85 have been confoundedly stupid indeed.

ACRES. What's the matter with the gentleman?

ABSOLUTE. He is only expressing his great satisfaction at hearing that Julia has been so   90 well and happy—that's all—hey, Faulkland?

FAULKLAND. Oh! I am rejoiced to hear it—yes, yes, she has a *happy* disposition!

ACRES. That she has indeed. Then she is so accomplished—so sweet a voice—so expert at her harpsichord—such a mistress of flat and sharp, squallante, rumblante, and quiverante!° There was this time month—Odds minims and crotchets!° how she did chirrup at Mrs. Piano's concert!

FAUKLAND. There again, what say you to this? You see she has been all mirth and song—not a thought of me!

ABSOLUTE. Pho! man, is not music the food of love?

FAULKLAND. Well, well, it may be so.—Pray, Mr.—— what's his d——d name? Do you remember what songs Miss Melville sung?

ACRES. Not I, indeed.

ABSOLUTE. Stay now, they were some pretty, melancholy, purling-stream airs, I warrant; perhaps you may recollect; did she sing "When absent from my soul's delight"?

ACRES. No, that wa'nt it.

ABSOLUTE. Or "Go, gentle gales"?—"Go, gentle gales!" [Sings.]

ACRES. Oh no! nothing like it. Odds! now I recollect one of them—"My heart's my own, my will is free." [Sings.]

FAULKLAND. Fool! fool that I am! to fix all my happiness on such a trifler! 'Sdeath! to make herself the pipe° and ballad-monger of a circle! to soothe her light heart with catches and glees!° What can you say to this, Sir?

ABSOLUTE. Why, that I should be glad to hear my mistress had been so merry, Sir.

FAULKLAND. Nay, nay, nay—I am not sorry that she has been happy—no, no, I am glad of that—I would not have had her sad or sick—yet surely a sympathetic heart would have shown itself even in the choice of a song: she might have been temperately healthy, and, somehow, plaintively gay; but she has been dancing too, I doubt not!

ACRES. What does the gentleman say about dancing?

ABSOLUTE. He says the lady we speak of dances as well as she sings.

ACRES. Aye, truly, does she—there was at our last race-ball—

FAULKLAND. Hell and the devil! There! there! —I told you so! I told you so! Oh! she thrives in my absence! Dancing! But her whole feelings have been in opposition with mine! I have been anxious, silent, pensive, sedentary—my days have been hours of care, my nights of watchfulness. She has been all Health! Spirit! Laugh! Song! Dance! Oh! d——n'd, d——n'd levity!

ABSOLUTE. For heaven's sake! Faulkland, don't expose yourself so. Suppose she has danced, what then? Does not the ceremony of society often oblige—

FAULKLAND. Well, well, I'll contain myself. Perhaps, as you say, for form sake. What, Mr. Acres, you were praising Miss Melville's manner of dancing a *minuet*—hey?

ACRES. Oh I dare insure her for that—but what I was going to speak of was her *country dancing*. Odds swimmings! she has such an air with her!

FAULKLAND. Now disappointment on her! Defend this, Absolute, why don't you defend this? Country-dances! jigs, and reels! Am I to blame now? A minuet I could have forgiven—I should not have minded that—I say I should not have regarded a minuet—but *country-dances*! Z——ds! had she made one in a cotillion—I believe I could have forgiven even that—but to be monkey-led for a night! to run the gauntlet through a string of amorous palming puppies! to show paces like a managed filly! O Jack, there never can be but *one* man in the world whom a truly modest and delicate woman ought to pair with in a *country-dance*; and even then, the rest of the couples should be her great uncles and aunts!

ABSOLUTE. Aye, to be sure!—grandfathers and grandmothers!

FAULKLAND. If there be but one vicious mind in the Set, 'twill spread like a contagion—the action of their pulse beats to the lascivious movement of the jig—their quivering, warm-

---

squallante . . . quiverante fictitious musical terms
minims and crotchets half-notes and quarter-notes
pipe piper
catches and glees humorous rounds and other part-
songs

breathed sighs impregnate the very air—the atmosphere becomes electrical to love, and each amorous spark darts through every link of the chain! I must leave you—I own I am somewhat
5 flurried—and that confounded looby° has perceived it. [*Going.*]

ABSOLUTE. Nay, but stay, Faulkland, and thank Mr. Acres for his good news.

FAULKLAND. D——n his news!
10 [*Exit* FAULKLAND.]

ABSOLUTE. Ha! ha! ha! Poor Faulkland! Five minutes since—"nothing on earth could give him a moment's uneasiness!"

ACRES. The gentleman wa'n't angry at my
15 praising his mistress, was he?

ABSOLUTE. A little jealous, I believe, Bob.

ACRES. You don't say so? Ha! ha! jealous of me?—that's a good joke.

ABSOLUTE. There's nothing strange in that,
20 Bob: let me tell you, that sprightly grace and insinuating manner of yours will do some mischief among the girls here.

ACRES. Ah! you joke—ha! ha!—mischief—ha! ha! But you know I am not my own
25 property; my dear Lydia has forestalled me. She could never abide me in the country, because I used to dress so badly—but odds frogs and tambours!° I shan't take matters so here—now ancient madam has no voice in it. I'll make
30 my old clothes know who's master. I shall straightway cashier the hunting-frock, and render my leather breeches incapable. My hair has been in training some time.

ABSOLUTE. Indeed!
35 ACRES. Aye—and tho'ff the side-curls are a little restive, my hindpart takes to it very kindly.

ABSOLUTE. O, you'll polish, I doubt not.

ACRES. Absolutely, I propose so. Then if I
40 find out this Ensign Beverley, odds triggers and flints! I'll make him know the difference o't.

ABSOLUTE. Spoke like a man—but pray, Bob, I observe you have got an odd kind of a new method of swearing—
45 ACRES. Ha! ha! you've taken notice of it?

looby oaf
frogs and tambours ornamental loop fastenings and the embroidery on them

'Tis genteel, isn't it? I didn't invent it myself, though; but a commander in our militia—a great scholar, I assure you—says that there is no meaning in the common oaths, and that
50 nothing but their antiquity makes them respectable, because, he says, the ancients would never stick to an oath or two, but would say, by Jove! or by Bacchus! or by Mars! or by Venus! or by Pallas! according to the sent-
55 iment; so that to swear with propriety, says my little major, the "oath should be an echo to the sense"; and this we call the *oath referential*, or *sentimental swearing*—ha! ha! ha! 'tis genteel, isn't it?
60 ABSOLUTE. Very genteel, and very new, indeed—and I dare say will supplant all other figures of imprecation.

ACRES. Aye, aye, the best terms will grow obsolete. Damns have had their day.
65 [*Enter* FAG.]

FAG. Sir, there is a gentleman below desires to see you. Shall I show him into the parlour?

ABSOLUTE. Aye—you may.

ACRES. Well, I must be gone—
70 ABSOLUTE. Stay; who is it, Fag?

FAG. Your father, Sir.

ABSOLUTE. You puppy, why didn't you show him up directly?

[*Exit* FAG.]
75 ACRES. You have business with Sir Anthony. I expect a message from Mrs. Malaprop at my lodgings. I have sent also to my dear friend, Sir Lucius O'Trigger. Adieu, Jack! We must meet at night, when you shall give me a dozen
80 bumpers to little Lydia.

ABSOLUTE. That I will, with all my heart.

[*Exit* ACRES.]

Now for a parental lecture. I hope he has heard nothing of the business that has brought me
85 here. I wish the gout had held him fast in Devonshire, with all my soul!

[*Enter* SIR ANTHONY.]

Sir, I am delighted to see you here; and looking so well! Your sudden arrival at Bath made
90 me apprehensive for your health.

SIR ANTHONY. Very apprehensive, I dare say, Jack. What, you are recruiting here, hey?

ABSOLUTE. Yes, Sir, I am on duty.

SIR ANTHONY. Well, Jack, I am glad to see

you, though I did not expect it, for I was going to write to you on a little matter of business. Jack, I have been considering that I grow old and infirm, and shall probably not trouble

5 you long.

ABSOLUTE. Pardon me, Sir, I never saw you look more strong and hearty; and I pray frequently that you may continue so.

SIR ANTHONY. I hope your prayers may be

10 heard with all my heart. Well then, Jack, I have been considering that I am so strong and hearty, I may continue to plague you a long time. Now, Jack, I am sensible that the income of your commission, and what I have hitherto

15 allowed you, is but a small pittance for a lad of your spirit.

ABSOLUTE. Sir, you are very good.

SIR ANTHONY. And it is my wish, while yet I live, to have my boy make some figure in the

20 world. I have resolved, therefore, to fix you at once in a noble independence.

ABSOLUTE. Sir, your kindness overpowers me—such generosity makes the gratitude of reason more lively than the sensations even

25 of filial affection.

SIR ANTHONY. I am glad you are so sensible of my attention—and you shall be master of a large estate in a few weeks.

ABSOLUTE. Let my future life, Sir, speak my

30 gratitude: I cannot express the sense I have of your munificence. Yet, Sir, I presume you would not wish me to quit the army?

SIR ANTHONY. Oh, that shall be as your wife chooses.

35 ABSOLUTE. My wife, Sir!

SIR ANTHONY. Aye, aye—settle that between you—settle that between you.

ABSOLUTE. A *wife*, Sir, did you say?

SIR ANTHONY. Aye, a wife—why; did not I

40 mention her before?

ABSOLUTE. Not a word of her, Sir.

SIR ANTHONY. Odd so!—I mus'n't forget *her*, though. Yes, Jack, the independence I was talking of is by a marriage—the fortune is

45 saddled with a wife—but I suppose that makes no difference.

ABSOLUTE. Sir! Sir!—you amaze me!

SIR ANTHONY. Why, what the devil's the matter with the fool? Just now you were all gratitude and duty.

ABSOLUTE. I was, Sir—you talked to me of independence and a fortune, but not a word of a wife. 50

SIR ANTHONY. Why—what difference does that make? Odd's life, Sir! if you have the estate, you must take it with the live stock on it, as it stands.

ABSOLUTE. If my happiness is to be the price, 55 I must beg leave to decline the purchase. Pray, Sir, who is the lady?

SIR ANTHONY. What's that to you, Sir? Come, give me your promise to love, and to marry her directly. 60

ABSOLUTE. Sure, Sir, this is not very reasonable, to summon my affections for a lady I know nothing of!

SIR ANTHONY. I am sure, Sir, 'tis more unreasonable in you to *object* to a lady you know 65 nothing of.

ABSOLUTE. Then, Sir, I must tell you plainly that my inclinations are fixed on another— my heart is engaged to an angel.

SIR ANTHONY. Then pray let it send an 70 excuse. It is very sorry—but *business* prevents its waiting on her.

ABSOLUTE. But my vows are pledged to her.

SIR ANTHONY. Let her foreclose, Jack; let her foreclose; they are not worth redeeming: be- 75 sides, you have the angel's vows in exchange, I suppose; so there can be no loss there.

ABSOLUTE. You must excuse me, Sir, if I tell you, once for all, that in this point I cannot obey you. 80

SIR ANTHONY. Hark'ee, Jack: I have heard you for some time with patience—I have been cool—quite cool; but take care—you know I am compliance itself when I am not thwarted —no one more easily led when I have my own 85 way; but don't put me in a frenzy.

ABSOLUTE. Sir, I must repeat it—in this I cannot obey you.

SIR ANTHONY. Now, d——n me! if ever I call you *Jack* again while I live! 90

ABSOLUTE. Nay, Sir, but hear me.

SIR ANTHONY. Sir, I won't hear a word—not a word! not one word! so give me your promise by a nod—and I'll tell you what, Jack—I mean, you dog—if you don't, by—

ABSOLUTE. What, Sir, promise to link myself to some mass of ugliness! to—

5 SIR ANTHONY. Z——ds! Sirrah! the lady shall be as ugly as I choose: she shall have a hump on each shoulder; she shall be as crooked as the Crescent; her one eye shall roll like the Bull's in Cox's Museum°—she shall have a
10 skin like a mummy, and the beard of a Jew— she shall be all this, Sirrah!—yet I'll make you ogle her all day, and sit up all night to write sonnets on her beauty.

ABSOLUTE. This is reason and moderation
15 indeed!

SIR ANTHONY. None of your sneering, puppy! no grinning, jackanapes!

ABSOLUTE. Indeed, Sir, I never was in a worse humour for mirth in my life.

20 SIR ANTHONY. 'Tis false, Sir! I know you are laughing in your sleeve; I know you'll grin when I am gone, Sirrah!

ABSOLUTE. Sir, I hope I know my duty better.

SIR ANTHONY. None of your passion, Sir!
25 none of your violence! if you please. It won't do with me, I promise you.

ABSOLUTE. Indeed, Sir, I never was cooler in my life.

SIR ANTHONY. 'Tis a confounded lie!—I
30 know you are in a passion in your heart; I know you are, you hypocritical young dog! But it won't do.

ABSOLUTE. Nay, Sir, upon my word.

SIR ANTHONY. So you will fly out! Can't you
35 be cool, like me? What the devil good can *passion* do! *Passion* is of no service, you impudent, insolent, overbearing reprobate!—There you sneer again! don't provoke me! But you rely upon the mildness of my temper—you do, you
40 dog! you play upon the meekness of my disposition! Yet take care—the patience of a saint may be overcome at last!—but mark! I give you six hours and a half to consider of this: if you then agree, without any condition, to do
45 everything on earth that I choose, why—con-

found you! I may in time forgive you. If not, z——ds! don't enter the same hemisphere with me! don't dare to breathe the same air, or use the same light with me; but get an atmosphere
50 and a sun of your own! I'll strip you of your commission; I'll lodge a five-and-threepence in the hands of trustees,° and you shall live on the interest. I'll disown you, I'll disinherit you, I'll unget you! and—d——n me, if ever I call you
55 Jack again!

[*Exit* SIR ANTHONY.]

[ABSOLUTE *solus.*]

ABSOLUTE. Mild, gentle, considerate Father— I kiss your hands. What a tender method of giving his opinion in these matters Sir Anthony
60 has! I dare not trust him with the truth. I wonder what old wealthy hag it is that he wants to bestow on me! Yet he married himself for love! and was in his youth a bold intriguer, and a gay companion!
65

[*Enter* FAG.]

FAG. Assuredly, Sir, our father is wrath to a degree; he comes downstairs eight or ten steps at a time—muttering, growling, and thumping
70 the bannisters all the way: I, and the cook's dog, stand bowing at the door—rap! he gives me a stroke on the head with his cane; bids me carry that to my master; then kicking the poor turnspit into the area,° d——ns us all for
75 a puppy triumvirate! Upon my credit, Sir, were I in your place, and found my father such very bad company, I should certainly drop his acquaintance.

ABSOLUTE. Cease your impertinence, Sir, at present. Did you come in for nothing more?
80 Stand out of the way!

[*Pushes him aside, and exit.*]

[FAG *solus.*]

FAG. Soh! Sir Anthony trims° my master. He is afraid to reply to his father—then vents his
85 spleen on poor Fag! When one is vexed by one person, to revenge one's self on another who happens to come in the way is the vilest

---

the Bull's . . . Museum a toy bull, a mechanical marvel of the time

lodge . . . trustees deposit five shillings and three-pence (a quarter-guinea) in the hands of executors
area sunken space before the basement door
trims abuses

injustice. Ah! it shows the worst temper—the basest—

[*Enter* ERRAND BOY.]

BOY. Mr. Fag! Mr. Fag! your master calls
5 you.

FAG. Well, you little dirty puppy, you need not bawl so!—The meanest disposition! the—

BOY. Quick, quick, Mr. Fag!

FAG. *Quick, quick,* you impudent jackanapes!
10 am I to be commanded by you too? you little, impertinent, insolent, kitchen-bred—

[*Exit, kicking and beating him.*]

Scene ii

[*The North Parade.*]

[*Enter* LUCY.]

15 LUCY. So—I shall have another rival to add to my mistress's list—Captain Absolute. However, I shall not enter his name till my purse has received notice in form. Poor Acres is dismissed! Well, I have done him a last friendly
20 office in letting him know that Beverley was here before him. Sir Lucius is generally more punctual when he expects to hear from his *dear Dalia,* as he calls her: I wonder he's not here! I have a little scruple of conscience from
25 this deceit; though I should not be paid so well, if my hero knew that *Delia* was near fifty, and her own mistress.

[*Enter* SIR LUCIUS O'TRIGGER.]

SIR LUCIUS. Hah! my little embassadress—
30 upon my conscience, I have been looking for you; I have been on the South Parade this half-hour.

LUCY [*speaking simply*]. O Gemini! and I have been waiting for your worship here on
35 the North.

SIR LUCIUS. Faith!—maybe that was the reason we did not meet; and it is very comical, too, how you could go out and I not see you—for I was only taking a nap at the Parade
40 Coffee-house, and I chose the *window* on purpose that I might not miss you.

LUCY. My stars! Now I'd wager a sixpence I went by while you were asleep.

SIR LUCIUS. Sure enough it must have been
45 so—and I never dreamt it was so late, till I waked. Well, but my little girl, have you got nothing for me?

LUCY. Yes, but I have: I've got a letter for you in my pocket.

SIR LUCIUS. Oh faith! I guessed you weren't 50 come empty-handed—well—let me see what the dear creature says.

LUCY. There, Sir Lucius. [*Gives him a letter.*]

SIR LUCIUS [*reads*]. *Sir—there is often a sudden incentive impulse in love, that has a* 55 *greater induction than years of domestic combination: such was the commotion I felt at the first superfluous view of Sir Lucius O'Trigger.* —Very pretty, upon my word.—*Female punctuation forbids me to say more; yet let me add,* 60 *that it will give me joy infallible to find Sir Lucius worthy the last criterion of my affections.* DELIA. Upon my conscience! Lucy, your lady is a great mistress of language. Faith, she's quite the queen of the dictionary!—for 65 the devil a word dare refuse coming at her call—though one would think it was quite out of hearing.

LUCY. Aye, Sir, a lady of her experience—

SIR LUCIUS. Experience! what, at seventeen? 70

LUCY. O true, Sir—but then she reads so— my stars! how she will read off-hand!

SIR LUCIUS. Faith, she must be very deep read to write this way—though she is rather an arbitrary writer too—for here are a great 75 many poor words pressed into the service of this note, that would get their *habeas corpus* from any court in Christendom.

LUCY. Ah! Sir Lucius, if you were to hear how she talks of you! 80

SIR LUCIUS. Oh tell her I'll make her the best husband in the world, and Lady O'Trigger into the bargain! But we must get the old gentlewoman's consent—and do everything fairly.

LUCY. Nay, Sir Lucius, I thought you wa'n't 85 rich enough to be so nice!°

SIR LUCIUS. Upon my word, young woman, you have hit it: I am so poor that I can't afford to do a dirty action. If I did not want money I'd steal your mistress and her fortune with a 90 great deal of pleasure. However, my pretty girl [*gives her money*], here's a little something to buy you a ribband; and meet me in the evening, and I'll give you an answer to this. So,

nice scrupulous

hussy, take a kiss beforehand to put you in mind. [*Kisses her.*]

Lucy. O lud! Sir Lucius—I never seed such a gemman! My lady won't like you if you're so impudent.

Sir Lucius. Faith she will, Lucy—That same —pho! what's the name of it?—*Modesty!*—is a quality in a lover more praised by the women than liked; so, if your mistress asks you whether Sir Lucius ever gave you a kiss, tell her *fifty*—my dear.

Lucy. What, would you have me tell her a lie?

Sir Lucius. Ah, then, you baggage! I'll make it a truth presently.

Lucy. For shame now; here is someone coming.

Sir Lucius. Oh faith, I'll quiet your conscience.

[*Sees* Fag.—*Exit, humming a tune.*]

[*Enter* Fag.]

Fag. So, so, Ma'am. I humbly beg pardon.

Lucy. O lud!—now, Mr. Fag, you flurry one so.

Fag. Come, come, Lucy, here's no one by— so a little less simplicity, with a grain or two more sincerity, if you please. You play false with us, Madam. I saw you give the baronet a letter. My master shall know this, and if he don't call him out—I will.

Lucy. Ha! ha! ha! you gentlemen's gentlemen are so hasty. That letter was from Mrs. Malaprop, simpleton. She is taken with Sir Lucius's address.

Fag. How! what tastes some people have! Why, I suppose I have walked by her window an hundred times. But what says our young lady? Any message to my master?

Lucy. Sad news, Mr. Fag! A worse rival than Acres! Sir Anthony Absolute has proposed his son.

Fag. What, Captain Absolute?

Lucy. Even so. I overheard it all.

Fag. Ha! ha! ha!—very good, faith. Goodbye, Lucy, I must away with this news.

Lucy. Well—you may laugh, but it is true, I assure you. [*Going.*] But—Mr. Fag—tell your master not to be cast down by this.

Fag. Oh, he'll be so disconsolate!

Lucy. And charge him not to think of quarrelling with young Absolute.

Fag. Never fear!—never fear!

Lucy: Be sure—bid him keep up his spirits.

Fag. We will—we will.

[*Exeunt severally.*]

ACT III

Scene i

[*The North Parade.*]

[*Enter* Absolute.]

Absolute. 'Tis just as Fag told me, indeed. Whimsical enough, faith! My father wants to *force* me to marry the very girl I am plotting to run away with! He must not know of my connexion with her yet awhile. He has too summary a method of proceeding in these matters. However, I'll read my recantation instantly. My conversion is something sudden, indeed, but I can assure him it is very *sincere.* —So, so—here he comes. He looks plaguy gruff. [*Steps aside.*]

[*Enter* Sir Anthony.]

Sir Anthony. No—I'll die sooner than forgive him. *Die,* did I say? I'll live these fifty years to plague him. At our last meeting, his impudence had almost put me out of temper. An obstinate, passionate, self-willed boy! Who can he take after? This is my return for getting him before all his brothers and sisters!— for putting him, at twelve years old, into a marching regiment, and allowing him fifty pounds a year, beside his pay ever since! But I have done with him; he's anybody's son for me. I never will see him more—never—never —never—never!

Absolute. Now for a penitential face.

Sir Anthony. Fellow, get out of my way.

Absolute. Sir, you see a penitent before you.

Sir Anthony. I see an impudent scoundrel before me.

Absolute. A sincere penitent. I am come, Sir, to acknowledge my error, and to submit entirely to your will.

Sir Anthony. What's that?

Absolute. I have been revolving, and reflecting, and considering on your past goodness, and kindness, and condescension to me.

Sir Anthony. Well, Sir?

Absolute. I have been likewise weighing and balancing what you were pleased to mention concerning duty, and obedience, and authority.

5 Sir Anthony. Well, puppy?

Absolute. Why, then, Sir, the result of my reflections is—a resolution to sacrifice every inclination of my own to your satisfaction.

Sir Anthony. Why, now you talk sense—
10 absolute sense—I never heard anything more sensible in my life. Confound you, you shall be *Jack* again!

Absolute. I am happy in the appellation.

Sir Anthony. Why then, Jack, my dear Jack,
15 I will now inform you who the lady really is. Nothing but your passion and violence, you silly fellow, prevented my telling you at first. Prepare, Jack, for wonder and rapture! prepare! What think you of Miss Lydia Languish?

20 Absolute. Languish! What, the Languishes of Worcestershire?

Sir Anthony. Worcestershire! No. Did you never meet Mrs. Malaprop and her niece, Miss Languish, who came into our country just be-
25 fore you were last ordered to your regiment?

Absolute. Malaprop! Languish! I don't remember ever to have heard the names before. Yet, stay—I think I do recollect something.—*Languish! Languish!* She squints, don't she?
30 A little, red-haired girl?

Sir Anthony. Squints? A red-haired girl! Z——ds, no!

Absolute. Then I must have forgot; it can't be the same person.

35 Sir Anthony. Jack! Jack! what think you of blooming, love-breathing seventeen?

Absolute. As to that, Sir, I am quite indifferent. If I can please you in the matter, 'tis all I desire.

40 Sir Anthony. Nay, but Jack, such eyes! such eyes! so innocently wild! so bashfully irresolute! Not a glance but speaks and kindles some thought of love! Then, Jack, her cheeks! her cheeks, Jack! so deeply blushing at the in-
45 sinuations of her tell-tale eyes! Then, Jack, her lips!—O Jack, lips smiling at their own discretion; and if not smiling, more sweetly pouting, more lovely in sullenness!

Absolute. [*aside*]. That's she, indeed. Well done, old gentleman!

Sir Anthony. Then, Jack, her neck!—O Jack! Jack!

Absolute. And which is to be mine, Sir, the 50 niece or the aunt?

Sir Anthony. Why, you unfeeling, insensible puppy, I despise you! When I was of your age, such a description would have made me fly like a rocket! The *aunt*, indeed! Odd's life! 55 when I ran away with your mother, I would not have touched anything old or ugly to gain an empire.

Absolute. Not to please your father, Sir?

Sir Anthony. To please my father! Z——ds! 60 not to please—Oh, my father!—Odd so!—yes —yes!—if my father, indeed, had desired— that's quite another matter. Though he wa'n't the indulgent father that I am, Jack.

Absolute. I dare say not, Sir. 65

Sir Anthony. But, Jack, you are not sorry to find your mistress is so beautiful?

Absolute. Sir, I repeat it; if I please you in this affair, 'tis all I desire. Not that I think a woman the worse for being handsome; but, 70 Sir, if you please to recollect, you before hinted something about a hump or two, one eye, and a few more graces of that kind. Now, without being very nice, I own I should rather choose a wife of mine to have the usual number of 75 limbs, and a limited quantity of back: and though *one* eye may be very agreeable, yet as the prejudice has always run in favor of *two*, I would not wish to affect a singularity in that article. 80

Sir Anthony. What a phlegmatic sot it is! Why, Sirrah, you're an anchorite! a vile, insensible stock. You a soldier! you're a walking block, fit only to dust the company's regimentals on! Odd's life! I've a great mind to 85 marry the girl myself!

Absolute. I am entirely at your disposal, Sir; if you should think of addressing Miss Languish yourself, I suppose you would have me marry the *aunt*; or if you should change your 90 mind, and take the old lady—'tis the same to me—I'll marry the *niece*.

Sir Anthony. Upon my word, Jack, thou'rt

either a very great hypocrite, or—But come, I
know your indifference on such a subject must
be all a lie—I'm sure it must—come, now—
damn your demure face!—come, confess, Jack
5 —you have been lying—ha'n't you? you have
been playing the hypocrite, hey?—I'll never
forgive you if you ha'n't been lying and playing the hypocrite.

ABSOLUTE. I'm sorry, Sir, that the respect and
10 duty which I bear to you should be so mistaken.

SIR ANTHONY. Hang your respect and duty!
But come along with me, I'll write a note to
Mrs. Malaprop, and you shall visit the lady
15 directly. Her eyes shall be the Promethean
torch to you°—come along. I'll never forgive
you if you don't come back stark mad with
rapture and impatience. If you don't, egad, I'll
marry the girl myself!
20 [*Exeunt.*]

Scene ii

[JULIA'S *dressing-room.*]
[FAULKLAND *solus.*]
FAULKLAND. They told me Julia would return
directly; I wonder she is not yet come! How
25 mean does this captious, unsatisfied temper
of mine appear to my cooler judgment! Yet I
know not that I indulge it in any other point:
but on this one subject, and to this one subject,
whom I think I love beyond my life, I am ever
30 ungenerously fretful, and madly capricious! I
am conscious of it—yet I cannot correct myself! What tender, honest joy sparkled in her
eyes when we met! How delicate was the
warmth of her expressions! I was ashamed to
35 appear less happy, though I had come resolved
to wear a face of coolness and upbraiding. Sir
Anthony's presence prevented my proposed
expostulations, yet I must be satisfied that she
has not been so *very* happy in my absence. She
40 is coming! Yes! I know the nimbleness of her
tread when she thinks her impatient Faulkland
counts the moments of her stay.
[*Enter* JULIA.]

be . . . you kindle a fire in you as Prometheus' torch,
lit on Olympus, first kindled fires on earth

JULIA. I had not hoped to see you again so
soon. 45
FAULKLAND. Could I, Julia, be contented with
my first welcome—restrained as we were by
the presence of a third person?
JULIA. O Faulkland, when your kindness can
make me thus happy, let me not think that I 50
discovered something of coldness in your first
salutation.
FAULKLAND. 'Twas but your fancy, Julia. I
was rejoiced to see you—to see you in such
health. Sure I had no cause for coldness? 55
JULIA. Nay then, I see you have taken something ill. You must not conceal from me what
it is.
FAULKLAND. Well then—shall I own to you—
that my joy at hearing of your health and ar- 60
rival here, by your neighbour Acres, was somewhat damped by his dwelling much on the high
spirits you had enjoyed in Devonshire—on
your mirth, your singing, dancing, and I know
not what! For such is my temper, Julia, that I 65
should regard every mirthful moment in your
absence as a treason to constancy. The mutual
tear that steals down the cheek of parting
lovers is a compact that no smile shall live
there till they meet again. 70
JULIA. Must I never cease to tax my Faulkland with this teasing minute caprice? Can the
idle reports of a silly boor weigh in your breast
against my tried affection?
FAULKLAND. They have no weight with me, 75
Julia: no, no—I am happy if you have been so
—yet only say that you did not sing with *mirth*
—say that you *thought* of Faulkland in the
dance.
JULIA. I never can be happy in your absence. 80
If I wear a countenance of content, it is to show
that my mind holds no doubt of my Faulkland's truth. If I seemed sad, it were to make
malice triumph, and say that I had fixed my
heart on one who left me to lament his roving, 85
and my own credulity. Believe me, Faulkland, I
mean not to upbraid you when I say that I have
often dressed sorrow in smiles, lest my friends
should guess whose unkindness had caused my
tears. 90
FAULKLAND. You were ever all goodness to

me. Oh, I am a brute when I but admit a doubt of your true constancy!

JULIA. If ever, without such cause from you, as I will not suppose possible, you find my affections veering but a point, may I become a proverbial scoff for levity and base ingratitude.

FAULKLAND. Ah! Julia, that last word is grating to me. I would I had no title to your *gratitude*! Search your heart, Julia; perhaps what you have mistaken for love, is but the warm effusion of a too thankful heart!

JULIA. For what quality must I love you?

FAULKLAND. For no quality! To regard me for any quality of mind or understanding were only to *esteem* me. And for person—I have often wished myself deformed, to be convinced that I owed no obligation *there* for any part of your affection.

JULIA. Where Nature has bestowed a show of nice attention in the features of a man, he should laugh at it as misplaced. I have seen men who in *this* vain article perhaps might rank above you; but my heart has never asked my eyes if it were so or not.

FAULKLAND. Now this is not well from *you*, Julia. I despise person in a man. Yet if you loved me as I wish, though I were an Æthiop, you'd think none so fair.

JULIA. I see you are determined to be unkind. The *contract* which my poor father bound us in gives you more than a lover's privilege.

FAULKLAND. Again, Julia, you raise ideas that feed and justify my doubts. I would not have been more free—no—I am proud of my restraint. Yet—yet—perhaps your high respect alone for this solemn compact has fettered your inclinations, which else had made a worthier choice. How shall I be sure, had you remained unbound in thought and promise, that I should still have been the object of your persevering love?

JULIA. Then try me now. Let us be free as strangers as to what is past: *my* heart will not feel more liberty!

FAULKLAND. There now! so hasty, Julia! so anxious to be free! If your love for me were fixed and ardent, you would not loose your hold, even though I wished it!

JULIA. Oh, you torture me to the heart! I cannot bear it.

FAULKLAND. I do not mean to distress you. If I loved you less I should never give you an uneasy moment. But hear me. All my fretful doubts arise from this: women are not used to weigh, and separate the motives of their affections; the cold dictates of prudence, gratitude, or filial duty, may sometimes be mistaken for the pleadings of the heart. I would not boast—yet let me say that I have neither age, person, or character to found dislike on; my fortune such as few ladies could be charged with *indiscretion* in the match. O Julia! when *Love* receives such countenance from *Prudence*, nice minds will be suspicious of its birth.

JULIA. I know not whither your insinuations would tend, but as they seem pressing to insult me, I will spare you the regret of having done so. I have given you no cause for this!

[*Exit in tears.*]

FAULKLAND. In tears! Stay, Julia: stay but for a moment.—The door is fastened! Julia—my soul—but for one moment. I hear her sobbing! 'Sdeath! what a brute am I to use her thus! Yet stay!—Aye—she is coming now. How little resolution there is in woman! How a few soft words can turn them!—No, faith!—she is *not* coming either! Why, Julia—my love—say but that you forgive me—come but to tell me that. Now, this is being *too* resentful.—Stay! she *is* coming too—I thought she would—no *steadiness* in anything! her going away must have been a mere trick then. She sha'n't see that I was hurt by it. I'll affect indifference. [*Hums a tune: then listens.*]—No—Z——ds! she's *not* coming!—nor don't intend it, I suppose. This is not *steadiness*, but *obstinacy*! Yet I deserve it. What, after so long an absence to quarrel with her tenderness!—'twas barbarous and unmanly! I should be ashamed to see her now. I'll wait till her just resentment is abated —and when I distress her so again, may I lose her forever, and be linked instead to some antique virago, whose gnawing passions, and long-hoarded spleen shall make me curse my folly half the day, and all the night!

[*Exit.*]

Scene iii

[Mrs. Malaprop's *lodgings.*]

Mrs. Malaprop, *with a letter in her hand, and* Captain Absolute.]

Mrs. Malaprop. Your being Sir Anthony's son, Captain, would itself be a sufficient accommodation; but from the ingenuity of your appearance, I am convinced you deserve the character here given of you.

Absolute. Permit me to say, Madam, that as I never yet have had the pleasure of seeing Miss Languish, my principal inducement in this affair at present is the honour of being allied to Mrs. Malaprop; of whose intellectual accomplishments, elegant manners, and unaffected learning, no tongue is silent.

Mrs. Malaprop. Sir, you do me infinite honour! I beg, Captain, you'll be seated. [*Sit.*] Ah! few gentlemen now-a-days know how to value the ineffectual qualities in a woman! few think how a little knowledge becomes a gentlewoman! Men have no sense now but for the worthless flower of beauty!

Absolute. It is but too true, indeed, Ma'am. Yet I fear our ladies should share the blame—they think our admiration of *beauty* so great, that *knowledge* in *them* would be superfluous. Thus, like garden-trees, they seldom show fruit till time has robbed them of the more specious blossom. Few, like Mrs. Malaprop and the orange-tree, are rich in both at once!

Mrs. Malaprop. Sir—you overpower me with good-breeding. [*Aside.*] He is the very pineapple of politeness!—You are not ignorant, Captain, that this giddy girl has somehow contrived to fix her affections on a beggarly, strolling, eaves-dropping Ensign, whom none of us have seen, and nobody knows anything of.

Absolute. Oh, I have heard the silly affair before. I'm not at all prejudiced against her on *that* account.

Mrs. Malaprop. You are very good, and very considerate, Captain. I am sure I have done everything in my power since I exploded the affair! Long ago I laid my positive conjunctions on her never to think on the fellow again; I have since laid Sir Anthony's preposition before her; but, I'm sorry to say, she seems resolved to decline every particle that I enjoin her.

Absolute. It must be very distressing, indeed, Ma'am.

Mrs. Malaprop. Oh! it gives me the hydrostatics to such a degree! I thought she had persisted from corresponding with him; but behold this very day I have interceded another letter from the fellow! I believe I have it in my pocket.

Absolute [*aside*]. Oh the devil! my last note.

Mrs. Malaprop. Aye, here it is.

Absolute [*aside*]. Aye, my note, indeed! Oh the little traitress Lucy!

Mrs. Malaprop. There, perhaps you may know the writing. [*Gives him the letter.*]

Absolute. I think I have seen the hand before—yes, I certainly must have seen this hand before—

Mrs. Malaprop. Nay, but read it, Captain.

Absolute [*reads*]. "*My soul's idol, my adored Lydia!*"—Very tender, indeed!

Mrs. Malaprop. Tender! aye, and profane, too, o' my conscience!

Absolute. "*I am excessively alarmed at the intelligence you send me, the more so as my new rival*"—

Mrs. Malaprop. That's *you*, Sir.

Absolute. "*Has universally the character of being an accomplished gentleman, and a man of honour.*"—Well, that's handsome enough.

Mrs. Malaprop. Oh, the fellow had some design in writing so.

Absolute. That he had, I'll answer for him, Ma'am.

Mrs. Malaprop. But go on, Sir—you'll see presently.

Absolute. "*As for the old weather-beaten she-dragon who guards you*"—Who can he mean by that?

MRS. MALAPROP. Me! Sir—*me!*—he means *me!* There—what do you think now? But go on a little further.

ABSOLUTE. Impudent scoundrel!—*"it shall go hard but I will elude her vigilance, as I am told that the same ridiculous vanity which makes her dress up her coarse features, and deck her dull chat with hard words which she don't understand"*—

MRS. MALAPROP. There, Sir! an attack upon my language! What do you think of that?—an aspersion upon my parts of speech! Was ever such a brute! Sure if I reprehend anything in this world, it is the use of my oracular tongue, and a nice derangement of epitaphs!

ABSOLUTE. He deserves to be hanged and quartered! Let me see—*"same ridiculous vanity"*—

MRS. MALAPROP. You need not read it again, Sir.

ABSOLUTE. I beg pardon, Ma'am—*"does also lay her open to the grossest deceptions from flattery and pretended admiration"*—an impudent coxcomb!—*"so that I have a scheme to see you shortly with the old harridan's consent, and even to make her a go-between in our interviews."*—Was ever such assurance!

MRS. MALAPROP. Did you ever hear anything like it? He'll elude my vigilance, will he? Yes, yes! ha! ha! He's very likely to enter these doors! We'll try who can plot best!

ABSOLUTE. So we will, Ma'am—so we will. Ha! ha! ha! A conceited puppy, ha! ha! ha! Well, but Mrs. Malaprop, as the girl seems so infatuated by this fellow, suppose you were to wink at her corresponding with him for a little time—let her even plot an elopement with him—then do you connive at her escape—while *I*, just in the nick, will have the fellow laid by the heels, and fairly contrive to carry her off in his stead.

MRS. MALAPROP. I am delighted with the scheme; never was anything better perpetrated!

ABSOLUTE. But, pray, could not I see the lady for a few minutes now? I should like to try her temper a little.

MRS. MALAPROP. Why, I don't know—I doubt° she is not prepared for a visit of this kind. There is a decorum in these matters.

ABSOLUTE. O Lord! she won't mind *me*—only tell her Beverley—

MRS. MALAPROP. Sir!—

ABSOLUTE [*aside*]. Gently, good tongue.

MRS. MALAPROP. What did you say of Beverley?

ABSOLUTE. Oh, I was going to propose that you should tell her, by way of jest, that it was Beverley who was below—she'd come down fast enough then—ha! ha! ha!

MRS. MALAPROP. 'Twould be a trick she well deserves. Besides, you know the fellow tells her he'll get my consent to see her—ha! ha! Let him if he can, I say again. [*Calling.*] Lydia, come down here!—He'll make me a *go-between in their interviews!*—ha! ha! ha!—Come down, I say, Lydia!—I don't wonder at your laughing, ha! ha! ha!—his impudence is truly ridiculous.

ABSOLUTE. 'Tis very ridiculous, upon my soul, Ma'am, ha! ha! ha!

MRS. MALAPROP. The little hussy won't hear. Well, I'll go and tell her at once who it is. She shall know that Captain Absolute is come to wait on her. And I'll make her behave as becomes a young woman.

ABSOLUTE. As you please, Ma'am.

MRS. MALAPROP. For the present, Captain, your servant. Ah! you've not done laughing yet, I see—*elude my vigilance!*—yes, yes, ha! ha! ha!

[*Exit.*]

ABSOLUTE. Ha! ha! ha! one would think now that I might throw off all disguise at once, and seize my prize with security—but such is Lydia's caprice that to undeceive were probably to lose her. I'll see whether she knows me. [*Walks aside, and seems engaged in looking at the pictures.*]

[*Enter* LYDIA.]

LYDIA. What a scene am I now to go through! Surely nothing can be more dreadful than to be obliged to listen to the loathsome addresses of a stranger to one's heart. I have

doubt fear

heard of girls persecuted as I am, who have appealed in behalf of their favoured lover to the generosity of his rival: suppose I were to try it. There stands the hated rival—an officer,
5 too!—but oh, how unlike my Beverley! I wonder he don't begin. Truly he seems a very negligent wooer! Quite at his ease, upon my word! I'll speak first. [*Aloud.*] Mr. Absolute.

ABSOLUTE. Madam. [*Turns around.*]
10 LYDIA. O heavens! Beverley!

ABSOLUTE. Hush!—hush, my life! Softly! Be not surprised.

LYDIA. I am so astonished! and so terrified! and so overjoyed! For heaven's sake! how
15 came you here?

ABSOLUTE. Briefly—I have deceived your aunt. I was informed that my new rival was to visit here this evening, and contriving to have him kept away, have passed myself on
20 her for Captain Absolute.

LYDIA. Oh, charming! And she really takes you for young Absolute?

ABSOLUTE. Oh, she's convinced of it.

LYDIA. Ha! ha! ha! I can't forbear laughing
25 to think how her sagacity is overreached!

ABSOLUTE. But we trifle with our precious moments. Such another opportunity may not occur. Then let me now conjure my kind, my condescending angel, to fix the time when I
30 may rescue her from undeserved persecution, and with a licensed warmth plead for my reward.

LYDIA. Will you then, Beverley, consent to forfeit that portion of my paltry wealth? that
35 burden on the wings of love?

ABSOLUTE. Oh, come to me—rich only thus —in loveliness. Bring no portion to me but thy love—'twill be generous in you, Lydia—for well you know, it is the only dower your poor
40 Beverley can repay.

LYDIA. How persuasive are his words! How charming will poverty be with him!

ABSOLUTE. Ah! my soul, what a life will we then live! Love shall be our idol and support!
45 We will worship him with a monastic strictness; abjuring all worldly toys, to center every thought and action there. Proud of calamity, we will enjoy the wreck of wealth; while the surrounding gloom of adversity shall make the flame of our pure love show doubly bright. By
50 heavens! I would fling all goods of fortune from me with a prodigal hand to enjoy the scene where I might clasp my Lydia to my bosom, and say, the world affords no smile to me—but here. [*Embracing her.*]—[*Aside.*] If
55 she holds out now the devil is in it!

LYDIA [*aside*]. Now could I fly with him to the Antipodes! but my persecution is not yet come to a crisis.

[*Enter* MRS. MALAPROP, *listening.*]
60 MRS. MALAPROP [*aside*]. I am impatient to know how the little hussy deports herself.

ABSOLUTE. So pensive, Lydia!—is then your warmth abated?

MRS. MALAPROP [*aside*]. *Warmth abated!*
65 So! she has been in a passion, I suppose.

LYDIA. No—nor ever can while I have life.

MRS. MALAPROP [*aside*]. An ill-tempered little devil! She'll be *in a passion all her life*—will she?
70 LYDIA. Think not the idle threats of my ridiculous aunt can ever have any weight with me.

MRS. MALAPROP [*aside*]. Very dutiful, upon
75 my word!

LYDIA. Let her choice be Captain Absolute, but Beverley is mine.

MRS. MALAPROP [*aside*]. I am astonished at her assurance!—to his face—this is to his face!

ABSOLUTE. Thus then let me enforce my suit.
80 [*Kneeling.*]

MRS. MALAPROP [*aside*]. Aye—poor young man! down on his knees entreating for pity! I can contain no longer.—[*Aloud.*] Why, thou vixen! I have overheard you.
85 ABSOLUTE [*aside*]. Oh, confound her vigilance!

MRS. MALAPROP. Captain Absolute—I know not how to apologize for her shocking rudeness.
90 ABSOLUTE [*aside*]. So—all's safe, I find.— [*Aloud.*] I have hopes, Madam, that time will bring the young lady—

MRS. MALAPROP. Oh, there's nothing to be hoped for from her! She's as headstrong as an
95 allegory on the banks of Nile.

LYDIA. Nay, Madam, what do you charge me with now?

MRS. MALAPROP. Why, thou unblushing rebel—didn't you tell this gentleman to his
5 face that you loved another better?—didn't you say you never would be his?

LYDIA. No, Madam—I did not.

MRS. MALAPROP. Good heavens! what assurance! Lydia, Lydia, you ought to know that
10 lying don't become a young woman! Didn't you boast that Beverley—that stroller Beverley—possessed your heart? Tell me that, I say.

LYDIA. 'Tis true, Ma'am, and none but Beverley—

15 MRS. MALAPROP. Hold—hold, Assurance! you shall not be so rude.

ABSOLUTE. Nay, pray Mrs. Malaprop, don't stop the young lady's speech: she's very welcome to talk thus—it does not hurt *me* in the
20 least, I assure you.

MRS. MALAPROP. You are *too* good, Captain —*too* amiably patient—but come with me, Miss. Let us see you again soon, Captain. Remember what we have fixed.

25 ABSOLUTE. I shall, Ma'am.

MRS. MALAPROP. Come, take a graceful leave of the gentleman.

LYDIA. May every blessing wait on my Beverley, my loved Bev—

30 MRS. MALAPROP. Hussy! I'll choke the word in your throat!—come along—come along.

[*Exeunt severally,* ABSOLUTE *kissing his hand to* LYDIA—MRS. MALAPROP *stopping her from speaking.*]

Scene iv

35 [ACRES's *lodgings.*]

[ACRES *and* DAVID, ACRES *as just dressed.*]

ACRES. Indeed, David—do you think I become it so?

DAVID. You are quite another creature, be-
40 lieve me, master, by the Mass! an' we've any luck we shall see the Devon monkeyrony in all the print-shops° in Bath!

ACRES. Dress *does* make a difference, David.

DAVID. 'Tis all in all, I think. Difference!
45 why, an' you were to go now to Clod-Hall, I am certain the old lady wouldn't know you: Master Butler wouldn't believe his own eyes, and Mrs. Pickle would cry, "Lard presarve me!"—our dairy-maid would come giggling to
50 the door, and I warrant Dolly Tester, your Honour's favourite, would blush like my waistcoat. Oons! I'll hold a gallon, there a'n't a dog in the house but would bark, and I question whether *Phillis* would wag a hair of her tail!

55 ACRES. Aye, David, there's nothing like polishing.

DAVID. So I says of your Honour's boots; but the boy never heeds me!

ACRES. But, David, has Mr. De-la-Grace
60 been here? I must rub up my balancing, and chasing, and boring.°

DAVID. I'll call again, Sir.

ACRES. Do—and see if there are any letters for me at the post office.

65 DAVID. I will. By the Mass, I can't help looking at your head! If I hadn't been by at the cooking, I wish I may die if I should have known the dish again myself!

[*Exit.*]

70 [ACRES *comes forward, practising a dancing step.*]

ACRES. Sink, slide—coupee! Confound the first inventor of cotillions! say I—they are as bad as algebra to us country gentlemen. I can
75 walk a minuet easy enough when I'm forced! and I have been accounted a good stick in a country-dance. Odds jigs and tabours! I never valued your cross-over to couple—figure in— right and left—and I'd foot it with e'er a cap-
80 tain in the county! But these outlandish heathen allemandes and cotillions are quite beyond me! I shall never prosper at 'em, that's sure. Mine are true-born English legs—they don't understand their curst French lingo! their
85 *pas* this, and *pas* that, and *pas* t'other! D——n me! my feet dont' like to be called paws! No,

---

an' . . . print-shops if we've any luck, we shall see pictures of you, the Devonshire dandy, in all the print-shops

balancing . . . boring anglicized French dancing terms. Acres continues to use such terms and to corrupt some of them.

'tis certain I have most anti-Gallican toes!

[*Enter* SERVANT.]

SERVANT. Here is Sir Lucius O'Trigger to wait on you, Sir.

5 ACRES. Show him in.

[*Enter* SIR LUCIUS.]

SIR LUCIUS. Mr. Acres, I am delighted to embrace you.

ACRES. My dear Sir Lucius, I kiss your 10 hands.

SIR LUCIUS. Pray, my friend, what has brought you so suddenly to Bath?

ACRES. Faith! I have followed Cupid's Jack-a-Lantern, and find myself in a quagmire at 15 last. In short, I have been very ill-used, Sir Lucius. I don't choose to mention names, but look on me as on a very ill-used gentleman.

SIR LUCIUS. Pray, what is the case? I ask no names.

20 ACRES. Mark me, Sir Lucius, I fall as deep as need be in love with a young lady—her friends take my part—I follow her to Bath—send word of my arrival, and receive answer that the lady is to be otherwise disposed of. 25 This, Sir Lucius, I call being ill-used.

SIR LUCIUS. Very ill, upon my conscience. Pray, can you divine the cause of it?

ACRES. Why, there's the matter: she has another lover, one Beverley, who, I am told, is 30 now in Bath. Odds slanders and lies! he must be at the bottom of it.

SIR LUCIUS. A rival in the case, is there? And you think he has supplanted you unfairly?

ACRES. Unfairly!—to be sure he has. He 35 never could have done it fairly.

SIR LUCIUS. Then sure you know what is to be done!

ACRES. Not I, upon my soul!

SIR LUCIUS. We wear no swords here, but 40 you understand me.

ACRES. What! fight him?

SIR LUCIUS. Aye, to be sure: what can I mean else?

ACRES. But he has given me no provocation.

45 SIR LUCIUS. Now, I think he has given you the greatest provocation in the world. Can a man commit a more heinous offence against another than to fall in love with the same woman? Oh, by my soul, it is the most unpardonable breach of friendship! 50

ACRES. Breach of friendship! Aye, aye; but I have no acquaintance with this man. I never saw him in my life.

SIR LUCIUS. That's no argument at all—he has the less right then to take such a liberty. 55

ACRES. 'Gad, that's true. I grow full of anger, Sir Lucius! I fire apace! Odds hilts and blades! I find a man may have a deal of valour in him and not know it! But couldn't I contrive to have a little right of my side? 60

SIR LUCIUS. What the devil signifies *right* when your *honour* is concerned? Do you think Achilles, or my little Alexander the Great ever inquired where the right lay? No, by my soul, they drew their broadswords, and left the lazy 65 sons of peace to settle the justice of it.

ACRES. Your words are a grenadier's march to my heart! I believe courage must be catching! I certainly do feel a kind of valour rising, as it were—a kind of courage, as I may say. 70 Odds flints, pans, and triggers! I'll challenge him directly.

SIR LUCIUS. Ah, my little friend! if we had Blunderbuss-Hall here—I could show you a range of ancestry, in the O'Trigger line, that 75 would furnish the New Room, every one of whom had killed his man! For though the mansion-house and dirty acres have slipped through my fingers, I thank heaven our honour, and the family-pictures, are as fresh 80 as ever.

ACRES. O Sir Lucius! I have had ancestors too! every man of 'em colonel or captain in the militia! Odds balls and barrels! say no more—I'm braced for it. The thunder of your words 85 has soured the milk of human kindness in my breast! Z——ds! as the man in the play says, "I could do such deeds!"

SIR LUCIUS. Come, come, there must be no passion at all in the case—these things should 90 always be done civilly.

ACRES. I must be in a passion, Sir Lucius—I must be in a rage. Dear Sir Lucius, let me be in a rage, if you love me. Come, here's pen and paper. [*Sits down to write.*] I would the ink 95 were red! Indite, I say, indite! How shall I

begin? Odds bullets and blades! I'll write a
good bold hand, however.

SIR LUCIUS. Pray compose yourself.

ACRES. Come now, shall I begin with an
5 oath? Do, Sir Lucius, let me begin with a
damme.

SIR LUCIUS. Pho! pho! do the thing decently
and like a Christian. Begin now—"Sir"—

ACRES. That's too civil by half.

10 SIR LUCIUS. "To prevent the confusion that
might arise"—

ACRES. Well—

SIR LUCIUS. "From our both addressing the
same lady"—

15 ACRES. Aye—there's the reason—"same
lady"—Well—

SIR LUCIUS. "I shall expect the honour of
your company"—

ACRES. Z——ds! I'm not asking him to
20 dinner.

SIR LUCIUS. Pray be easy.

ACRES. Well then—"honour of your company"—

SIR LUCIUS. "To settle our pretensions"—

25 ACRES. Well—

SIR LUCIUS. Let me see—aye, King's-Mead-
Fields will do—"In King's-Mead-Fields."

ACRES. So that's done.—Well, I'll fold it up
presently; my own crest—a hand and dagger
30 shall be the seal.

SIR LUCIUS. You see now, this little explanation will put a stop at once to all confusion or
misunderstanding that might arise between
you.

35 ACRES. Aye, we fight to prevent any misunderstanding.

SIR LUCIUS. Now, I'll leave you to fix your
own time. Take my advice, and you'll decide it
this evening if you can; then let the worst
40 come of it, 'twill be off your mind to-morrow.

ACRES. Very true.

SIR LUCIUS. So I shall see nothing more of
you, unless it be by letter, till the evening. I
would do myself the honour to carry your
45 message; but, to tell you a secret, I believe I
shall have just another affair on my own
hands. There is a gay captain here who put a
jest on me lately at the expense of my country,

and I only want to fall in with the gentleman
to call him out. 50

ACRES. By my valour, I should like to see
you fight first! Odd's life! I should like to see
you kill him, if it was only to get a little lesson.

SIR LUCIUS. I shall be very proud of instruct-
ing you. Well for the present—but remember 55
now, when you meet your antagonist, do
everything in a mild and agreeable manner.
Let your courage be as keen, but at the same
time as polished, as your sword.

[Exeunt severally.] 60

ACT IV

Scene i

[ACRES's lodgings.]
[ACRES and DAVID.]

DAVID. Then, by the Mass, Sir! I would do
no such thing—ne'er a Sir Lucius O'Trigger in
the kingdom should make me fight, when I 65
wa'n't so minded. Oons! what will the old lady
say when she hears o't!

ACRES. Ah! David, if you had heard Sir
Lucius! Odds sparks and flames! he would
have roused your valour. 70

DAVID. Not he, indeed. I hates such bloodthirsty cormorants. Look'ee, master, if you'd
wanted a bout at boxing, quarterstaff, or
shortstaff, I should never be the man to bid
you cry off: but for your curst sharps and 75
snaps,° I never knew any good come of 'em.

ACRES. But my honour, David, my honour!
I must be very careful of my honour.

DAVID. Aye, by the Mass! and I would be
very careful of it; and I think in return my 80
honour couldn't do less than to be very careful
of me.

ACRES. Odds blades! David, no gentleman
will ever risk the loss of his honour!

DAVID. I say then, it would be but civil in 85
honour never to risk the loss of a gentleman.
Look'ee, master, this honour seems to me to
be a marvellous false friend; aye, truly, a very
courtier-like servant. Put the case, I was a

sharps and snaps swords and pistols

gentleman (which, thank God, no one can say of me); well—my honour makes me quarrel with another gentleman of my acquaintance. So—we fight. (Pleasant enough that.) Boh!—I kill him (the more's my luck). Now, pray who gets the profit of it? Why, my *honour*. But put the case that he kills me!—by the Mass! I go to the worms, and my honour whips over to my enemy!

ACRES. No, David—in that case—odds crowns and laurels!—your honour follows you to the grave.

DAVID. Now, that's just the place where I could make a shift to do without it.

ACRES. Z——ds, David, you're a coward! It doesn't become my valour to listen to you. What, shall I disgrace my ancestors? Think of that, David—think what it would be to disgrace my ancestors!

DAVID. Under favour, the surest way of not disgracing them is to keep as long as you can out of their company. Look'ee now, master, to go to them in such haste—with an ounce of lead in your brains—I should think might as well be let alone. Our ancestors are very good kind of folks; but they are the last people I should choose to have a visiting acquaintance with.

ACRES. But David, now, you don't think there is such very, very, *very* great danger, hey? Odds life! people often fight without any mischief done!

DAVID. By the Mass, I think 'tis ten to one against you! Oons! here to meet some lion-headed fellow, I warrant, with his d——n'd double-barrelled swords, and cut-and-thrust pistols! Lord bless us! it makes me tremble to think o't. Those be such desperate bloody-minded weapons! Well, I never could abide 'em! from a child I never could fancy 'em! I suppose there a'n't so merciless a beast in the world as your loaded pistol!

ACRES. Z——ds! I *won't* be afraid! Odds fire and fury! you sha'n't make me afraid! Here is the challenge, and I have sent for my dear friend Jack Absolute to carry it for me.

DAVID. Aye, i' the name of mischief, let *him* be the messenger. For my part, I wouldn't lend a hand to it for the best horse in your stable. By the Mass! it don't look like another letter! It is, as I may say, a designing and malicious-looking letter! and I warrant smells of gunpowder, like a soldier's pouch! Oons! I wouldn't swear it mayn't go off!

ACRES. Out, you poltroon! You ha'n't the valour of a grasshopper.

DAVID. Well, I say no more—'twill be sad news, to be sure, at Clod-Hall!—but I ha' done. How Phillis will howl when she hears of it! Aye, poor bitch, she little thinks what shooting her master's going after! And I warrant old Crop, who has carried your Honour, field and road, these ten years, will curse the hour he was born. [*Whimpering.*]

ACRES. It won't do, David—I am determined to fight—so get along, you coward, while I'm in the mind.

[*Enter* SERVANT.]

SERVANT. Captain Absolute, Sir.

ACRES. Oh! show him up.

[*Exit* SERVANT.]

DAVID. Well, heaven send we be all alive this time to-morrow.

ACRES. What's that! Don't provoke me, David!

DAVID. Good-bye, master. [*Whimpering.*]

ACRES. Get along, you cowardly, dastardly, croaking raven.

[*Exit* DAVID.]

[*Enter* ABSOLUTE.]

ABSOLUTE. What's the matter, Bob?

ACRES. A vile, sheep-hearted blockhead! If I hadn't the valour of St. George and the dragon to boot—

ABSOLUTE. But what did you want with me, Bob?

ACRES. Oh! There—[*gives him the challenge*].

ABSOLUTE. "*To Ensign Beverley.*" [*Aside.*] So—what's going on now? [*Aloud.*] Well, what's this?

ACRES. A challenge!

ABSOLUTE. Indeed! Why, you won't fight him, will you, Bob?

ACRES. 'Egad, but I will, Jack. Sir Lucius has wrought me to it. He has left me full of rage, and I'll fight this evening, that so much good passion mayn't be wasted.

ABSOLUTE. But what have I to do with this?

ACRES. Why, as I think you know something of this fellow, I want you to find him out for me, and give him this mortal defiance.

ABSOLUTE. Well, give it to me, and trust me he gets it.

ACRES. Thank you, my dear friend, my dear Jack; but it is giving you a great deal of trouble.

ABSOLUTE. Not in the least—I beg you won't mention it. No trouble in the world, I assure you.

ACRES. You are very kind. What it is to have a friend! You couldn't be my second—could you, Jack?

ABSOLUTE. Why no, Bob—not in *this* affair. It would not be quite so proper.

ACRES. Well then, I must get my friend Sir Lucius. I shall have your good wishes, however, Jack.

ABSOLUTE. Whenever he meets you, believe me.

[*Enter* SERVANT.]

SERVANT. Sir Anthony Absolute is below, inquiring for the Captain.

ABSOLUTE. I'll come instantly. Well, my little hero, success attend you. [*Going.*]

ACRES. Stay—stay, Jack. If Beverley should ask you what kind of a man your friend Acres is, do tell him I am a devil of a fellow—will you, Jack?

ABSOLUTE. To be sure I shall. I'll say you are a determined dog—hey, Bob?

ACRES. Aye, do, do—and if that frightens him, 'egad, perhaps he mayn't come. So tell him I generally kill a man a week—will you, Jack?

ABSOLUTE. I will, I will; I'll say you are called in the country "*Fighting Bob!*"

ACRES. Right, right—'tis all to prevent mischief; for I don't want to take his life if I clear my honour.

ABSOLUTE. No!—that's very kind of you.

ACRES. Why, you don't wish me to kill him —do you, Jack?

ABSOLUTE. No, upon my soul, I do not. But

a devil of a fellow, hey? [*Going.*]

ACRES. True, true—but stay—stay, Jack. You may add that you never saw me in such a rage before—a most devouring rage!

ABSOLUTE. I will, I will.

ACRES. Remember, Jack—a determined dog!

ABSOLUTE. Aye, aye, "*Fighting Bob!*"

[*Exeunt severally.*]

Scene ii

[MRS. MALAPROP's *lodgings.*]

[MRS. MALAPROP *and* LYDIA.]

MRS. MALAPROP. Why, thou perverse one! tell me what you can object to him? Isn't he a handsome man? tell me that. A genteel man? a pretty figure of a man?

LYDIA [*aside*]. She little thinks whom she is praising!—[*Aloud.*] So is Beverley, Ma'am.

MRS. MALAPROP. No caparisons, Miss, if you please! Caparisons don't become a young woman. No! Captain Absolute is indeed a fine gentleman!

LYDIA [*aside*]. Aye, the Captain Absolute *you* have seen.

MRS. MALAPROP. Then he's *so* well bred; *so* full of alacrity, and adulation! and has *so much* to say for himself—in such good language, too! His physiognomy so grammatical! Then his presence is so noble! I protest, when I saw him, I thought of what Hamlet says° in the play: "Hesperian curls!—the front of *Job* himself! An eye, like *March*, to threaten at command—a station, like Harry Mercury, new"—something about kissing on a hill— however, the similitude struck me directly.

LYDIA [*aside*]. How enraged she'll be presently when she discovers her mistake!

[*Enter* SERVANT.]

SERVANT. Sir Anthony and Captain Absolute are below, Ma'am.

MRS. MALAPROP. Show them up here.

[*Exit* SERVANT.]

---

what Hamlet says cf. Hamlet, III.iv, 56–59: "Hyperion's curls, the front of Jove himself, An eye like Mars, to threaten and command; A station like the herald Mercury New-lighted on a heaven-kissing hill."

Now, Lydia, I insist on your behaving as becomes a young woman. Show your good breeding at least, though you have forgot your duty.

LYDIA. Madam, I have told you my resolution; I shall not only give him no encouragement, but I won't even speak to, or look at him. [*Flings herself into a chair with her face from the door.*]

[*Enter* SIR ANTHONY *and* ABSOLUTE.]

SIR ANTHONY. Here we are, Mrs. Malaprop, come to mitigate the frowns of unrelenting beauty—and difficulty enough I had to bring this fellow. I don't know what's the matter; but if I hadn't held him by force, he'd have given me the slip.

MRS. MALAPROP. You have infinite trouble, Sir Anthony, in the affair. I am ashamed for the cause!—[*Aside to her.*] Lydia, Lydia, rise, I beseech you!—pay your respects!

SIR ANTHONY. I hope, Madam, that Miss Languish has reflected on the worth of this gentleman, and the regard due to her aunt's choice, and my alliance.—[*Aside to him.*] Now, Jack, speak to her!

ABSOLUTE [*aside*]. What the devil shall I do! —[*Aloud.*] You see, Sir, she won't even look at me whilst you are here. I knew she wouldn't! I told you so. Let me entreat you, Sir, to leave us together!

[ABSOLUTE *seems to expostulate with his father.*]

LYDIA [*aside*]. I wonder I ha'n't heard my aunt exclaim yet! Sure she can't have looked at him! Perhaps their regimentals are alike, and she is something blind.

SIR ANTHONY. I say, Sir, I won't stir a foot yet!

MRS. MALAPROP. I am sorry to say, Sir Anthony, that my affluence over my niece is very small.—[*Aside to her.*] Turn round, Lydia; I blush for you!

SIR ANTHONY. May I not flatter myself that Miss Languish will assign what cause of dislike she can have to my son! Why don't you begin, Jack?—[*Aside to him.*] Speak, you puppy—speak!

MRS. MALAPROP. It is impossible, Sir Anthony, she can have any. She will not *say* she has.—[*Aside to her.*] Answer, hussy! why don't you answer?

SIR ANTHONY. Then, Madam, I trust that a childish and hasty predilection will be no bar to Jack's happiness.—[*Aside to him.*] Z——ds! Sirrah! why don't you speak?

LYDIA [*aside*]. I think my lover seems as little inclined to conversation as myself. How strangely blind my aunt must be!

ABSOLUTE. Hem! hem!—Madam—hem!— [ABSOLUTE *attempts to speak, then returns to* SIR ANTHONY.]—Faith! Sir, I am so confounded! and so—so—confused! I told you I should be so, Sir, I knew it. The—the—tremor of my passion entirely takes away my presence of mind.

SIR ANTHONY. But it don't take away your voice, fool, does it? Go up, and speak to her directly!

[ABSOLUTE *makes signs to* MRS. MALAPROP *to leave them together.*]

MRS. MALAPROP. Sir Anthony, shall we leave them together?—[*Aside to her.*] Ah! you stubborn little vixen!

SIR ANTHONY. Not yet, Ma'am, not yet!— [*Aside to him.*] What the devil are you at? Unlock your jaws, Sirrah, or—

[ABSOLUTE *draws near* LYDIA.]

ABSOLUTE [*aside*]. Now heaven send she may be too sullen to look round! I must disguise my voice.—[*Speaks in a low hoarse tone.*] Will not Miss Languish lend an ear to the mild accents of true love? Will not—

SIR ANTHONY. What the devil ails the fellow? Why don't you speak out?—not stand croaking like a frog in a quinsy!

ABSOLUTE. The—the—excess of my awe, and my—my—my modesty quite choke me!

SIR ANTHONY. Ah! your *modesty* again! I'll tell you what, Jack, if you don't speak out directly, and glibly, too, I shall be in such a rage! Mrs. Malaprop, I wish the lady would favour us with something more than a sidefront!

[MRS. MALAPROP *seems to chide* LYDIA.]

ABSOLUTE. So! All will out I see! [*Goes up to* LYDIA, *speaks softly.*] Be not surprised, my Lydia; suppress all surprise at present.

LYDIA [aside]. Heavens! 'tis Beverley's voice! Sure he can't have imposed on Sir Anthony, too!—[Looks round by degrees, then starts up.] Is this possible—my Beverley!—how can this be?—my Beverley?

ABSOLUTE [aside]. Ah! 'tis all over.

SIR ANTHONY. Beverley!—the devil!—Beverley! What can the girl mean? This is my son, Jack Absolute!

MRS. MALAPROP. For shame, hussy! for shame! your head runs so on that fellow that you have him always in your eyes! Beg Captain Absolute's pardon directly.

LYDIA. I see no Captain Absolute, but my loved Beverley!

SIR ANTHONY. Z——ds! the girl's mad!—her brain's turned by reading!

MRS. MALAPROP. O' my conscience, I believe so! What do you mean by Beverley, hussy? You saw Captain Absolute before to-day; there he is—your husband that shall be.

LYDIA. With all my soul, Ma'am. When I refuse my Beverley—

SIR ANTHONY. Oh! she's as mad as Bedlam! Or has this fellow been playing us a rogue's trick! Come here, Sirrah!—who the devil are you?

ABSOLUTE. Faith, Sir, I am not quite clear myself, but I'll endeavour to recollect.

SIR ANTHONY. Are you my son, or not? Answer for your mother, you dog, if you won't for me.

MRS. MALAPROP. Aye, Sir, who are you? Oh mercy! I begin to suspect!—

ABSOLUTE [aside]. Ye Powers of Impudence befriend me!—[Aloud.] Sir Anthony, most assuredly I am your wife's son; and that I sincerely believe myself to be yours also, I hope my duty has always shown.—Mrs. Malaprop, I am your most respectful admirer—and shall be proud to add affectionate nephew. —I need not tell my Lydia, that she sees her faithful Beverley, who, knowing the singular generosity of her temper, assumed that name, and a station which has proved a test of the most disinterested love, which he now hopes to enjoy in a more elevated character.

LYDIA [sullenly]. So!—there will be no elopement after all!

SIR ANTHONY. Upon my soul, Jack, thou art a very impudent fellow! to do you justice, I think I never saw a piece of more consummate assurance!

ABSOLUTE. Oh you flatter me, Sir—you compliment—'tis my modesty you know, Sir—my modesty that has stood in my way.

SIR ANTHONY. Well, I am glad you are not the dull, insensible varlet you pretended to be, however! I'm glad you have made a fool of your father, you dog—I am. So this was your penitence, your duty, and obedience! I thought it was d——d sudden! You never heard their names before, not you! What! The Languishes of Worcestershire, hey?—if you could please me in the affair, 'twas all you desired!—Ah! you dissembling villain! What!—[pointing to LYDIA] she squints, don't she?—a little red-haired girl!—hey? Why, you hypocritical young rascal! I wonder you a'n't ashamed to hold up your head!

ABSOLUTE. 'Tis with difficulty, Sir. I am confused—very much confused, as you must perceive.

MRS. MALAPROP. O lud! Sir Anthony!—a new light breaks in upon me! Hey! how! what! Captain, did you write the letters then? What! —am I to thank you for the elegant compilation of "an old weather-beaten she-dragon"— hey? O mercy! was it you that reflected on my parts of speech?

ABSOLUTE. Dear Sir! my modesty will be overpowered at last, if you don't assist me. I shall certainly not be able to stand it!

SIR ANTHONY. Come, come, Mrs. Malaprop, we must forget and forgive. Odd's life! matters have taken so clever a turn all of a sudden, that I could find in my heart to be so good-humoured! and so gallant!—hey! Mrs. Malaprop!

MRS. MALAPROP. Well, Sir Anthony, since you desire it, we will not anticipate the past; so mind, young people: our retrospection will now be all to the future.

SIR ANTHONY. Come, we must leave them together; Mrs. Malaprop, they long to fly into each other's arms, I warrant!—[Aside.] Jack— isn't the cheek as I said, hey?—and the eye, you rogue!—and the lip—hey? Come, Mrs.

Malaprop, we'll not disturb their tenderness—theirs is the time of life for happiness!—[*Sings.*] "Youth's the season made for joy"—hey! Odd's life! I'm in such spirits, I don't

5 know what I couldn't do! Permit me, Ma'am.—[*Gives his hand to* Mrs. MALAPROP. *Sings.*] Tol-de-rol!—'gad, I should like a little fooling myself. Tol-de-rol! de-rol! [*Exit singing, and handing* Mrs. MALAPROP.]

10 [LYDIA *sits sullenly in her chair.*]

ABSOLUTE [*aside*]. So much thought bodes me no good.—[*Aloud.*] So grave, Lydia!

LYDIA. Sir!

ABSOLUTE [*aside*]. So!—egad! I thought as
15 much! That d——d monosyllable has froze me!—[*Aloud.*] What, Lydia, now that we are as happy in our friends' consent, as in our mutual vows—

LYDIA [*peevishly*]. Friends' consent, indeed!

20 ABSOLUTE. Come, come, we must lay aside some of our romance—a little *wealth* and *comfort* may be endured after all. And for your fortune, the lawyers shall make such settlements as—

25 LYDIA. *Lawyers! I hate* lawyers!

ABSOLUTE. Nay then, we will not wait for their lingering forms but instantly procure the licence, and—

LYDIA. The *licence! I hate* license!

30 ABSOLUTE. O my love! be not so unkind! Thus let me intreat—[*kneeling*].

LYDIA. Pshaw! what signifies kneeling when you know I *must* have you?

ABSOLUTE [*rising*]. Nay, Madam, there shall
35 be no constraint upon your inclinations, I promise you. If I have lost your heart, I resign the rest.—[*Aside.*] 'Gad, I must try what a little *spirit* will do.

LYDIA [*rising*]. Then, Sir, let me tell you, the
40 interest you had there was acquired by a mean, unmanly imposition, and deserves the punishment of fraud. What, you have been treating *me* like a child!—humouring my romance! and laughing, I suppose, at your success!

45 ABSOLUTE. You wrong me, Lydia, you wrong me. Only hear—

LYDIA. So, while *I* fondly imagined we were deceiving my relations, and flattered myself that I should outwit and incense them all—be-

hold! my hopes are to be crushed at once, by 50 my aunt's consent and approbation!—and *I* am myself the only dupe at last! [*Walking about in heat.*] But here, Sir, here is the picture —Beverley's picture! [*taking a miniature from her bosom*] which I have worn, night and day, 55 in spite of threats and entreaties! There, Sir [*flings it to him*]—and be assured I throw the original from my heart as easily.

ABSOLUTE. Nay, nay, Ma'am, we will not differ as to that. Here [*taking out a picture*], 60 here is Miss Lydia Languish. What a difference! Aye, *there* is the heavenly assenting smile that first gave soul and spirit to my hopes!—those are the lips which sealed a vow, as yet scarce dry in Cupid's calendar!—and 65 *there*, the half resentful blush that *would* have checked the ardour of my thanks. Well, all that's past—all over indeed! There, Madam, in beauty, that copy is not equal to you, but in my mind its merit over the original, in being still 70 the same, is such—that—I cannot find in my heart to part with it. [*Puts it up again.*]

LYDIA [*softening*]. 'Tis *your own* doing, Sir. I—I—I suppose you are perfectly satisfied.

ABSOLUTE. Oh, most certainly. Sure now this 75 is much better than being in love! Ha! ha! ha! —there's some spirit in *this*! What signifies breaking some scores of solemn promises, half an hundred vows, under one's hand, with the marks of a dozen or two angels to witness!— 80 all that's of no consequence, you know. To be sure, people will say that Miss didn't know her own mind—but never mind that: or perhaps they may be ill-natured enough to hint that the gentleman grew tired of the lady and forsook 85 her—but don't let that fret you.

LYDIA. There's no bearing his insolence. [*Bursts into tears.*]

[*Enter* Mrs. MALAPROP *and* SIR ANTHONY.]

MRS. MALAPROP [*entering*]. Come, we must 90 interrupt your billing and cooing a while.

LYDIA. This is worse than your treachery and deceit, you base ingrate! [*Sobbing.*]

SIR ANTHONY. What the devil's the matter now! Z——ds! Mrs. Malaprop, this is the *odd-* 95 *est billing* and *cooing* I ever heard! But what the deuce is the meaning of it? I'm quite astonished!

ABSOLUTE. Ask the lady, Sir.

MRS. MALAPROP. Oh mercy! I'm quite analysed, for my part! Why, Lydia, what is the reason of this?

5 LYDIA. Ask the *gentleman*, Ma'am.

SIR ANTHONY. Z——ds! I shall be in a frenzy!—Why, Jack, you are not come out to be anyone else, are you?

MRS. MALAPROP. Aye, Sir, there's no more 10 *trick*, is there? You are not like Cerberus, *three* gentlemen at once, are you?

ABSOLUTE. You'll not let me speak. I say the lady can account for this much better than I can.

15 LYDIA. Ma'am, you once commanded me never to think of Beverley again. There is the man—I now obey you:—for, from this moment I renounce him forever.

[*Exit* LYDIA.]

20 MRS. MALAPROP. Oh mercy! and miracles! what a turn here is! Why, sure, Captain, you haven't behaved disrespectfully to my niece?

SIR ANTHONY. Ha! ha! ha!—ha! ha! ha!— now I see it—ha! ha! ha!—now I see it—you 25 have been too lively, Jack.

ABSOLUTE. Nay, Sir, upon my word—

SIR ANTHONY. Come, no lying, Jack—I'm sure 'twas so.

MRS. MALAPROP. O lud! Sir Anthony! Oh fie, 30 Captain!

ABSOLUTE. Upon my soul, Ma'am—

SIR ANTHONY. Come, no excuses, Jack; why, your father, you rogue, was so before you: the blood of the Absolutes was always impatient. 35 Ha! ha! ha! poor little Lydia!—why, you've frightened her, you dog, you have.

ABSOLUTE. By all that's good, Sir—

SIR ANTHONY. Z——ds! say no more, I tell you. Mrs. Malaprop shall make your peace.— 40 You must make his peace, Mrs. Malaprop; you must tell her 'tis Jack's way—tell her 'tis all our ways—it runs in the blood of our family! Come, away, Jack—ha! ha! ha! Mrs. Malaprop —a young villain! [*Pushes him out.*]

45 MRS. MALAPROP. Oh, Sir Anthony! Oh fie, Captain!

[*Exeunt severally.*]

Scene iii

[*The North Parade.*]

[*Enter* SIR LUCIUS O'TRIGGER.]

SIR LUCIUS. I wonder where this Captain 50 Absolute hides himself. Upon my conscience! these officers are always in one's way in love-affairs. I remember I might have married Lady Dorothy Carmine, if it had not been for a little rogue of a major, who ran away with her before 55 she could get a sight of me! And I wonder too what it is the ladies can see in them to be so fond of them—unless it be a touch of the old serpent in 'em, that makes the little creatures be caught, like vipers, with a bit of red cloth.— 60 Hah!—isn't this the Captain coming?—faith it is! There is a probability of succeeding about that fellow that is mighty provoking! Who the devil is he talking to? [*Steps aside.*]

[*Enter* CAPTAIN ABSOLUTE.] 65

ABSOLUTE. To what fine purpose I have been plotting! A noble reward for all my schemes, upon my soul! A little gypsy! I did not think her romance could have made her so d——d absurd either. 'Sdeath, I never was in a worse 70 humour in my life! I could cut my own throat, or any other person's, with the greatest pleasure in the world!

SIR LUCIUS. Oh, faith! I'm in the luck of it— I never could have found him in a sweeter tem- 75 per for my purpose—to be sure I'm just come in the nick! Now to enter into conversation with him, and so quarrel genteelly. [SIR LUCIUS *goes up to* ABSOLUTE.]—With regard to that matter, Captain, I must beg leave to differ in 80 opinion with you.

ABSOLUTE. Upon my word then, you must be a very subtle disputant, because, Sir, I happened just then to be giving no opinion at all.

SIR LUCIUS. That's no reason. For give me 85 leave to tell you, a man may *think* an untruth as well as *speak* one.

ABSOLUTE. Very true, Sir, but if a man never utters his thoughts I should think they might stand a chance of escaping controversy. 90

SIR LUCIUS. Then, Sir, you differ in opinion with me, which amounts to the same thing.

ABSOLUTE. Hark'ee, Sir Lucius—if I had not before known you to be a gentleman, upon my soul, I should not have discovered it at this interview, for what you can drive at, unless 5 you mean to quarrel with me, I cannot conceive!

SIR LUCIUS. I humbly thank you, Sir, for the quickness of your apprehension. [*Bowing.*] You have named the very thing I would be at.

10 ABSOLUTE. Very well, Sir—I shall certainly not balk your inclinations—but I should be glad you would please to explain your motives.

SIR LUCIUS. Pray, Sir, be easy: the quarrel is a very pretty quarrel as it stands—we should 15 only spoil it by trying to explain it. However, your memory is very short or you could not have forgot an affront you passed on me within this week. So no more, but name your time and place.

20 ABSOLUTE. Well, Sir, since you are so bent on it, the sooner the better; let it be this evening —here, by the Spring-Gardens. We shall scarcely be interrupted.

SIR LUCIUS. Faith! that same interruption in 25 affairs of this nature shows very great ill-breeding. I don't know what's the reason, but in England, if a thing of this kind gets wind, people make such a pother that a gentleman can never fight in peace and quietness. How-30 ever, if it's the same to you, Captain, I should take it as a particular kindness if you'd let us meet in King's-Mead-Fields, as a little business will call me there about six o'clock, and I may dispatch both matters at once.

35 ABSOLUTE. 'Tis the same to me exactly. A little after six, then, we will discuss this matter more seriously.

SIR LUCIUS. If you please, Sir, there will be very pretty small-sword light, though it won't 40 do for a long shot. So that matter's settled! and my mind's at ease!

[*Exit* SIR LUCIUS.]

[*Enter* FAULKLAND, *meeting* ABSOLUTE.]

ABSOLUTE. Well met. I was going to look for 45 you. O Faulkland! all the daemons of spite and disappointment have conspired against me! I'm so vexed that if I had not the prospect of a resource in being knocked o' the head by and by, I should scarce have spirits to tell you the cause. 50

FAULKLAND. What can you mean? Has Lydia changed her mind? I should have thought her duty and inclination would now have pointed to the same object.

ABSOLUTE. Aye, just as the eyes do of a per-55 son who squints: when her love-eye was fixed on me—t'other—her eye of duty, was finely obliqued:—but when duty bid her point that the same way—off t'other turned on a swivel, and secured its retreat with a frown! 60

FAULKLAND. But what's the resource you—

ABSOLUTE. Oh, to wind up the whole, a good-natured Irishman here has [*mimicking* SIR LUCIUS] begged leave to have the pleasure of cutting my throat, and I mean to indulge him 65 —that's all.

FAULKLAND. Prithee, be serious.

ABSOLUTE. 'Tis fact, upon my soul. Sir Lucius O'Trigger—you know him by sight—for some affront, which I am sure I never intended, has 70 obliged me to meet him this evening at six o'clock: 'tis on that account I wished to see you —you must go with me.

FAULKLAND. Nay, there must be some mistake, sure. Sir Lucius shall explain himself— 75 and I dare say matters may be accommodated. But this evening, did you say? I wish it had been any other time.

ABSOLUTE. Why? there will be light enough. There will (as Sir Lucius says) "be very pretty 80 small-sword light, though it won't do for a long shot." Confound his long shots!

FAULKLAND. But I am myself a good deal ruffled by a difference I have had with Julia. My vile tormenting temper has made me treat 85 her so cruelly that I shall not be myself till we are reconciled.

ABSOLUTE. By heavens, Faulkland, you don't deserve her.

[*Enter* SERVANT, *gives* FAULKLAND *a letter.*] 90

FAULKLAND. O Jack! this is from Julia. I dread to open it. I fear it may be to take a last leave—perhaps to bid me return her letters and restore—Oh! how I suffer for my folly!

ABSOLUTE. Here—let me see. [*Takes the letter and opens it.*] Aye, a final sentence indeed! —'tis all over with you, faith!

FAULKLAND. Nay, Jack—don't keep me in 5 suspense.

ABSOLUTE. Hear then.—"*As I am convinced that my dear* FAULKLAND's *own reflections have already upbraided him for his last unkindness to me, I will not add a word on the subject. I* 10 *wish to speak with you as soon as possible.— Yours ever and truly,* JULIA."—There's stubbornness and resentment for you! [*Gives him the letter.*] Why, man, you don't seem one whit happier at this.

15 FAULKLAND. Oh, yes, I am—but—but—

ABSOLUTE. Confound your *buts.* You never hear anything that would make another man bless himself, but you immediately d——n it with a *but.*

20 FAULKLAND. Now, Jack, as you are my friend, own honestly—don't you think there is something forward, something indelicate, in this haste to forgive? Women should never sue for reconciliation: that should always come from 25 us. They should retain their coldness till *wooed* to kindness—and their *pardon,* like their *love,* should "not unsought be won."

ABSOLUTE. I have not patience to listen to you—thou'rt incorrigible!—so say no more on 30 the subject. I must go to settle a few matters. Let me see you before six—remember—at my lodgings. A poor industrious devil like me, who have toiled, and drudged, and plotted to gain my ends, and am at last disappointed by other 35 people's folly, may in pity be allowed to swear and grumble a little; but a captious sceptic in love, a slave to fretfulness and whim, who has no difficulties but of his own creating, is a subject more fit for ridicule than compassion!

40 [*Exit* ABSOLUTE.]

FAULKLAND. I feel his reproaches, yet I would not change this too exquisite nicety for the gross content with which *he* tramples on the thorns of love. His engaging me in this duel 45 has started an idea in my head, which I will instantly pursue. I'll use it as the touchstone of Julia's sincerity and disinterestedness. If her love prove pure and sterling ore, my name will rest on it with honour!—and once I've stamped it there, I lay aside my doubts forever—; but 50 if the dross of selfishness, the alloy of pride predominate, 'twill be best to leave her as a toy for some less cautious fool to sigh for.

[*Exit* FAULKLAND.]

ACT V

Scene i

[JULIA's *dressing-room.*] 55

[JULIA *sola.*]

JULIA. How this message has alarmed me! What dreadful accident can he mean? why such charge to be alone? O Faulkland! how many unhappy moments, how many tears, 60 have you cost me!

[*Enter* FAULKLAND.]

JULIA. What means this?—why this caution, Faulkland?

FAULKLAND. Alas! Julia, I am come to take a 65 long farewell.

JULIA. Heavens! what do you mean?

FAULKLAND. You see before you a wretch whose life is forfeited. Nay, start not! the infirmity of my temper has drawn all this misery 70 on me. I left you fretful and passionate—an untoward accident drew me into a quarrel—the event is that I must fly this kingdom instantly. O Julia, had I been so fortunate as to have called you mine entirely before this mischance 75 had fallen on me, I should not so deeply dread my banishment!

JULIA. My soul is oppressed with sorrow at the nature of your misfortune: had these adverse circumstances arisen from a less fatal 80 cause, I should have felt strong comfort in the thought that I could now chase from your bosom every doubt of the warm sincerity of my love. My heart has long known no other guardian. I now entrust my person to your 85 honour—we will fly together. When safe from pursuit, my father's will may be fulfilled, and I receive a legal claim to be the partner of your sorrows, and tenderest comforter. Then on the bosom of your wedded Julia, you may lull your 90 keen regret to slumbering; while virtuous love, with a cherub's hand, shall smooth the brow of upbraiding thought, and pluck the thorn from compunction.

FAULKLAND. O Julia! I am bankrupt in gratitude! But the time is so pressing, it calls on you for so hasty a resolution—would you not wish some hours to weigh the advantages you forego, and what little compensation poor Faulkland can make you beside his solitary love?

JULIA. I ask not a moment. No, Faulkland, I have loved you for yourself: and if I now, more than ever, prize the solemn engagement which so long has pledged us to each other, it is because it leaves no room for hard aspersions on my fame, and puts the seal of duty to an act of love.—But let us not linger. Perhaps this delay—

FAULKLAND. 'Twill be better I should not venture out again till dark. Yet am I grieved to think what numberless distresses will press heavy on your gentle disposition!

JULIA. Perhaps your fortune may be forfeited by this unhappy act. I know not whether 'tis so, but sure that alone can never make us unhappy. The little I have will be sufficient to support us; and exile never should be splendid.

FAULKLAND. Aye, but in such an abject state of life, my wounded pride perhaps may increase the natural fretfulness of my temper, till I become a rude, morose companion, beyond your patience to endure. Perhaps the recollection of a deed my conscience cannot justify may haunt me in such gloomy and unsocial fits that I shall hate the tenderness that would relieve me, break from your arms, and quarrel with your fondness!

JULIA. If your thoughts should assume so unhappy a bent, you will the more want some mild and affectionate spirit to watch over and console you, one who, by bearing *your* infirmities with gentleness and resignation, may teach you *so* to bear the evils of your fortune.

FAULKLAND. Julia, I have proved you to the quick! and with this useless device I throw away all my doubts. How shall I plead to be forgiven this last unworthy effect of my restless, unsatisfied disposition?

JULIA. Has no such disaster happened as you related?

FAULKLAND. I am ashamed to own that it was all pretended; yet in pity, Julia, do not kill me with resenting a fault which never can be repeated, but sealing, this once, my pardon, let me to-morrow, in the face of heaven, receive my future guide and monitress, and expiate my past folly by years of tender adoration.

JULIA. Hold, Faulkland! That you are free from a crime which I before feared to name, heaven knows how sincerely I rejoice! These are tears of thankfulness for that! But that your cruel doubts should have urged you to an imposition that has wrung my heart, gives me now a pang more keen than I can express!

FAULKLAND. By heavens! Julia—

JULIA. Yet hear me. My father loved you, Faulkland! and you preserved the life that tender parent gave me; in his presence I pledged my hand—joyfully pledged it—where before I had given my heart. When, soon after, I lost that parent, it seemed to me that Providence had, in Faulkland, shown me whither to transfer without a pause my grateful duty, as well as my affection: hence I have been content to bear from you what pride and delicacy would have forbid me from another. I will not upbraid you by repeating how you have trifled with my sincerity.

FAULKLAND. I confess it all! yet hear—

JULIA. After such a year of trial, I might have flattered myself that I should not have been insulted with a new probation of my sincerity, as cruel as unnecessary! I now see it is not in your nature to be content or confident in love. With this conviction, I never will be yours. While I had hopes that my persevering attention and unreproaching kindness might in time reform your temper, I should have been happy to have gained a dearer influence over you; but I will not furnish you with a licensed power to keep alive an incorrigible fault, at the expense of one who never would contend with you.

FAULKLAND. Nay, but Julia, by my soul and honour, if after this—

JULIA. But one word more. As my faith has once been given to you, I never will barter it with another. I shall pray for your happiness with the truest sincerity; and the dearest bles-
5 sing I can ask of heaven to send you will be to charm you from that unhappy temper which alone has prevented the performance of our solemn engagement. All I request of *you* is that you will yourself reflect upon this
10 infirmity, and when you number up the many true delights it has deprived you of, let it not be your *least* regret that it lost you the love of one, who would have followed you in beggary through the world!

15 [*Exit.*]

FAULKLAND. She's gone!—forever! There was an awful resolution in her manner, that riveted me to my place. O fool!—dolt!—barbarian! Curst as I am with more imperfections
20 than my fellow-wretches, kind Fortune sent a heaven-gifted cherub to my aid, and, like a ruffian, I have driven her from my side! I must now haste to my appointment. Well, my mind is tuned for such a scene. I shall wish
25 only to become a principal in it, and reverse the tale my cursed folly put me upon forging here. O love!—tormentor!—fiend! whose influence, like the moon's, acting on men of dull souls, makes idiots of them, but meeting
30 subtler spirits, betrays their course, and urges sensibility to madness!

[*Exit.*]

[*Enter* MAID *and* LYDIA.]

MAID. My mistress, Ma'am, I know, was
35 here just now—perhaps she is only in the next room.

[*Exit* MAID.]

LYDIA. Heigh-ho! Though he has used me so, this fellow runs strangely in my head. I
40 believe one lecture from my grave cousin will make me recall him.

[*Enter* JULIA.]

LYDIA. O Julia, I am come to you with such an appetite for consolation.—Lud! child,
45 what's the matter with you? You have been crying! I'll be hanged if that Faulkland has not been tormenting you!

JULIA. You mistake the cause of my uneasi-

ness. Something *has* flurried me a little. Nothing that you can guess at.—[*Aside.*] I would 50 not accuse Faulkland to a sister!

LYDIA. Ah! whatever vexations you may have, I can assure you mine surpass them.— You know who Beverley proves to be?

JULIA. I will now own to you, Lydia, that 55 Mr. Faulkland had before informed me of the whole affair. Had young Absolute been the person you took him for, I should not have accepted your confidence on the subject without a serious endeavour to counteract your 60 caprice.

LYDIA. So, then, I see I have been deceived by everyone! But I don't care—I'll never have him.

JULIA. Nay, Lydia— 65

LYDIA. Why, is it not provoking? when I thought we were coming to the prettiest distress imaginable, to find myself made a mere Smithfield bargain° of at last! There had I projected one of the most sentimental elopements! 70 so becoming a disguise! so amiable a ladder of ropes! Conscious moon—four horses—Scotch parson—with such surprise to Mrs. Malaprop, and such paragraphs in the newspapers! Oh, I shall die with disappointment! 75

JULIA. I don't wonder at it!

LYDIA. Now—sad reverse!—what have I to expect, but, after a deal of flimsy preparation, with a bishop's licence, and my aunt's blessing, to go simpering up to the altar; or perhaps be 80 cried three times in a country-church, and have an unmannerly fat clerk ask the consent of every butcher in the parish to join John Absolute and Lydia Languish, Spinster! Oh, that I should live to hear myself called Spinster! 85

JULIA. Melancholy, indeed!

LYDIA. How mortifying to remember the dear delicious shifts I used to be put to, to gain half a minute's conversation with this fellow! How often have I stole forth in the coldest 90 night in January, and found him in the garden, stuck like a dripping statue! There would he kneel to me in the snow, and sneeze and

Smithfield bargain article of trade. Smithfield was a London market

cough so pathetically! he shivering with cold, and I with apprehension! and while the freezing blast numbed our joints, how warmly would he press me to pity his flame, and glow with mutual ardour! Ah, Julia, that was something like being in love!

JULIA. If I were in spirits, Lydia, I should chide you only by laughing heartily at you: but it suits more the situation of my mind, at present, earnestly to entreat you not to let a man, who loves you with sincerity, suffer that unhappiness from your caprice, which I know too well caprice can inflict.

LYDIA. O lud! what has brought my aunt here?

[*Enter* MRS. MALAPROP, FAG, *and* DAVID.]

MRS. MALAPROP. So! so! here's fine work!— here's fine suicide, parricide, and simulation going on in the fields! and Sir Anthony not to be found to prevent the antistrophe!

JULIA. For heaven's sake, Madam, what's the meaning of this?

MRS. MALAPROP. That gentleman can tell you—'twas he enveloped the affair to me.

LYDIA [*to* FAG]. Do, Sir, will you, inform us.

FAG. Ma'am, I should hold myself very deficient in every requisite that forms the man of breeding if I delayed a moment to give all the information in my power to a lady so deeply interested in the affair as you are.

LYDIA. But quick! quick, Sir!

FAG. True, Ma'am, as you say, one should be quick in divulging matters of this nature; for should we be tedious, perhaps while we are flourishing on the subject, two or three lives may be lost!

LYDIA. O patience! Do, Ma'am, for heaven's sake! tell us what is the matter!

MRS. MALAPROP. Why, murder's the matter! slaughter's the matter! killing's the matter! But he can tell you the perpendiculars.

LYDIA. Then, prithee, Sir, be brief.

FAG. Why then, Ma'am—as to murder, I cannot take upon me to say—and as to slaughter, or manslaughter, that will be as the jury finds it.

LYDIA. But who, Sir—who are engaged in this?

FAG. Faith, Ma'am, one is a young gentleman whom I should be very sorry anything was to happen to—a very pretty behaved gentleman! We have lived much together, and always on terms.

LYDIA. But who is this? who! who! who!

FAG. My master, Ma'am, my master—I speak of my master.

LYDIA. Heavens! What, Captain Absolute!

MRS. MALAPROP. Oh, to be sure, you are frightened now!

JULIA. But who are with him, Sir?

FAG. As to the rest, Ma'am, this gentleman can inform you better than I.

JULIA [*to* DAVID]. Do speak, friend.

DAVID. Look'ee, my lady—by the Mass! there's mischief going on. Folks don't use to meet for amusement with fire-arms, fire-locks, fire-engines, fire-screens, fire-office,° and the devil knows what other crackers° beside! This, my lady, I say, has an angry favour.

JULIA. But who is there beside Captain Absolute, friend?

DAVID. My poor master—under favour, for mentioning him first. You know me, my lady —I am David, and my master, of course, is, or *was*, Squire Acres. Then comes Squire Faulkland.

JULIA. Do, Ma'am, let us instantly endeavour to prevent mischief.

MRS. MALAPROP. Oh fie—it would be very inelegant in us: we should only participate things.

DAVID. Ah! do, Mrs. Aunt, save a few lives. They are desperately given, believe me. Above all, there is that bloodthirsty Philistine, Sir Lucius O'Trigger.

MRS. MALAPROP. Sir Lucius O'Trigger! O mercy! have they drawn poor little dear Sir Lucius into the scrape? Why, how you stand, girl! you have no more feeling than one of the Derbyshire putrefactions!°

LYDIA. What are we to do, Madam?

---

fire-office office of a fire-insurance company
crackers explosives
putrefactions petrifactions, the rock formations for
  which Derbyshire is well known

MRS. MALAPROP. Why, fly with the utmost felicity, to be sure, to prevent mischief. Here, friend—you can show us the place?

FAG. If you please, Ma'am, I will conduct 5 you.—David, do you look for Sir Anthony.

[*Exit* DAVID.]

MRS. MALAPROP. Come, girls!—this gentleman will exhort us.—Come, Sir, you're our envoy—lead the way, and we'll precede.

10 FAG. Not a step before the ladies for the world!

MRS. MALAPROP. You're sure you know the spot?

FAG. I think I can find it, Ma'am; and one 15 good thing is we shall hear the report of the pistols as we draw near, so we can't well miss them; never fear, Ma'am, never fear.

[*Exeunt, he talking.*]

Scene ii

[*South Parade.*]

20 [*Enter* ABSOLUTE, *putting his sword under his greatcoat.*]

ABSOLUTE. A sword seen in the streets of Bath would raise as great an alarm as a mad dog. How provoking this is in Faulkland! never 25 punctual! I shall be obliged to go without him at last. Oh, the devil! here's Sir Anthony! How shall I escape him? [*Muffles up his face, and takes a circle to go off.*]

[*Enter* SIR ANTHONY.]

30 SIR ANTHONY. How one may be deceived at a little distance! Only that I see he don't know me, I could have sworn that was Jack!—Hey! 'Gad's life! it is. Why, Jack!—what are you afraid of, hey!—Sure I'm right.—Why, Jack! 35 —Jack Absolute! [*Goes up to him.*]

ABSOLUTE. Really, Sir, you have the advantage of me: I don't remember ever to have had the honour. My name is Saunderson, at your service.

40 SIR ANTHONY. Sir, I beg your pardon—I took you—hey!—why, z——ds! it is—stay—[*looks up to his face*]. So, so—your humble servant, Mr. Saunderson! Why, you scoundrel, what tricks are you after now?

45 ABSOLUTE. Oh! a joke, Sir, a joke! I came here on purpose to look for you, Sir.

SIR ANTHONY. You did! Well, I am glad you were so lucky. But what are you muffled up so for? What's this for?—hey?

ABSOLUTE. 'Tis cool, Sir; isn't it?—rather 50 chilly, somehow. But I shall be late—I have a particular engagement.

SIR ANTHONY. Stay. Why, I thought you were looking for me? Pray, Jack, where is't you are going? 55

ABSOLUTE. Going, Sir!

SIR ANTHONY. Aye—where are you going?

ABSOLUTE. Where am I going?

SIR ANTHONY. You unmannerly puppy!

ABSOLUTE. I was going, Sir, to—to—to—to 60 Lydia—Sir, to Lydia, to make matters up if I could; and I was looking for you, Sir, to—to—

SIR ANTHONY. To go with you, I suppose. Well, come along.

ABSOLUTE. Oh! z——ds! no, Sir, not for the 65 world! I wished to meet with you, Sir—to—to —to—. You find it cool, I'm sure, Sir—you'd better not stay out.

SIR ANTHONY. Cool!—not at all. Well, Jack —and what will you say to Lydia? 70

ABSOLUTE. O, Sir, beg her pardon, humour her, promise and vow. But I detain you, Sir— consider the cold air on your gout.

SIR ANTHONY. Oh, not at all!—not at all! I'm in no hurry. Ah! Jack, you youngsters, 75 when once you are wounded here—[*putting his hand to* ABSOLUTE'S *breast*]. Hey! what the deuce have you got here?

ABSOLUTE. Nothing, Sir—nothing.

SIR ANTHONY. What's this? here's something 80 d——d hard!

ABSOLUTE. Oh, trinkets, Sir! trinkets—a bauble for Lydia!

SIR ANTHONY. Nay, let me see your taste. [*Pulls his coat open, the sword falls.*] Trinkets! 85 —a bauble for Lydia! Z——ds! Sirrah, you are not going to cut her throat, are you?

ABSOLUTE. Ha! ha! ha! I thought it would divert you, Sir; though I didn't mean to tell you till afterwards. 90

SIR ANTHONY. You didn't? Yes, this is a very diverting trinket, truly!

ABSOLUTE. Sir, I'll explain to you. You know, Sir, Lydia is romantic, dev'lish romantic, and very absurd of course. Now, Sir, I intend, if she refuses to forgive me, to unsheathe this
5 sword and swear I'll fall upon its point, and expire at her feet!

SIR ANTHONY. Fall upon a fiddle-stick's end! Why, I suppose it is the very thing that would please her. Get along, you fool.

10 ABSOLUTE. Well, Sir, you shall hear of my success—you shall hear. "O Lydia!—forgive me, or this pointed steel"—says I.

SIR ANTHONY. "O, booby! stab away and welcome"—says she. Get along!—and d———n
15 your trinkets!

[*Exit* ABSOLUTE.]

[*Enter* DAVID, *running.*]

DAVID. Stop him! Stop him! Murder! Thief! Fire! Stop fire! Stop fire! O! Sir Anthony—
20 call! call! bid 'em stop! Murder! Fire!

SIR ANTHONY. Fire! Murder! Where?

DAVID. Oons! he's out of sight! and I'm out of breath, for my part! O, Sir Anthony, why didn't you stop him? why didn't you stop him?

25 SIR ANTHONY. Z———ds! the fellow's mad! Stop whom? Stop Jack?

DAVID. Aye, the Captain, Sir! there's murder and slaughter—

SIR ANTHONY. Murder!

30 DAVID. Aye, please you, Sir Anthony, there's all kinds of murder, all sorts of slaughter to be seen in the fields: there's fighting going on, Sir—bloody sword-and-gun fighting!

SIR ANTHONY. Who are going to fight,
35 dunce?

DAVID. Everybody that I know of, Sir Anthony—everybody is going to fight; my poor master, Sir Lucius O'Trigger, your son, the Captain—

40 SIR ANTHONY. Oh, the dog! I see his tricks. —Do you know the place?

DAVID. King's-Mead-Fields.

SIR ANTHONY. You know the way?

DAVID. Not an inch; but I'll call the mayor—
45 aldermen — constables—church-wardens—and beadles—we can't be too many to part them.

SIR ANTHONY. Come along—give me your shoulder! we'll get assistance as we go. The lying villain! Well, I shall be in such a frenzy! So—this was the history of his trinkets! I'll
50 bauble him!

[*Exeunt.*]

Scene iii

[*King's-Mead-Fields.*]

[SIR LUCIUS *and* ACRES, *with pistols.*]

ACRES. By my valour! then, Sir Lucius, forty
55 yards is a good distance. Odds levels and aims! I say it is a good distance.

SIR LUCIUS. Is it for muskets or small field-pieces? Upon my conscience, Mr. Acres, you must leave those things to me. Stay now—I'll
60 show you. [*Measures paces along the stage.*] There now, that is a very pretty distance—a pretty gentleman's distance.

ACRES. Z———ds! we might as well fight in a sentry-box! I tell you, Sir Lucius, the farther
65 he is off, the cooler I shall take my aim.

SIR LUCIUS. Faith! then I suppose you would aim at him best of all if he was out of sight!

ACRES. No, Sir Lucius, but I should think forty, or eight and thirty yards—
70

SIR LUCIUS. Pho! pho! nonsense! Three or four feet between the mouths of your pistols is as good as a mile.

ACRES. Odds bullets, no! By my valour! there is no merit in killing him so near: do,
75 my dear Sir Lucius, let me bring him down at a long shot—a long shot, Sir Lucius, if you love me!

SIR LUCIUS. Well—the gentleman's friend and I must settle that. But tell me now, Mr.
80 Acres, in case of an accident, is there any little will or commission I could execute for you?

ACRES. I am much obliged to you, Sir Lucius, but I don't understand—

SIR LUCIUS. Why, you may think there's no
85 being shot at without a little risk, and if an unlucky bullet should carry a *quietus* with it —I say it will be no time then to be bothering you about family matters.

ACRES. A *quietus*!
90

SIR LUCIUS. For instance, now—if that should be the case—would you choose to be pickled and sent home? or would it be the same to you to lie here in the Abbey? I'm told there is very snug lying in the Abbey.

ACRES. Pickled! Snug lying in the Abbey! Odds tremors! Sir Lucius, don't talk so!

SIR LUCIUS. I suppose, Mr. Acres, you never were engaged in an affair of this kind before?

ACRES. No, Sir Lucius, never before.

SIR LUCIUS. Ah! that's a pity! there's nothing like being used to a thing. Pray now, how would you receive the gentleman's shot?

ACRES. Odds files! I've practiced that. There, Sir Lucius—there [*puts himself in an attitude*] —a side-front, hey? Odd! I'll make myself small enough: I'll stand edge-ways.

SIR LUCIUS. Now—you're quite out, for if you stand so when I take my aim—[*levelling at him*].

ACRES. Z——ds! Sir Lucius—are you sure it is not cocked?

SIR LUCIUS. Never fear.

ACRES. But—but—you don't know—it may go off of its own head!

SIR LUCIUS. Pho! be easy. Well, now if I hit you in the body, my bullet has a double chance, for if it misses a vital part on your right side, 'twill be very hard if it don't succeed on the left!

ACRES. A vital part!

SIR LUCIUS. But, there—fix yourself so. [*Placing him.*] Let him see the broad side of your full front—there—now a ball or two may pass clean through your body, and never do any harm at all.

ACRES. Clean through me! a ball or two clean through me!

SIR LUCIUS. Aye, may they; and it is much the genteelest attitude into the bargain.

ACRES. Look'ee! Sir Lucius—I'd just as lieve be shot in an awkward posture as a genteel one —so, by my valour! I will stand edge-ways.

SIR LUCIUS [*looking at his watch*]. Sure they don't mean to disappoint us. Hah? No, faith— I think I see them coming.

ACRES. Hey! what!—coming!—

SIR LUCIUS. Aye. Who are those yonder getting over the stile?

ACRES. There are two of them indeed! Well —let them come—hey, Sir Lucius? We—we— we—we—won't run.

SIR LUCIUS. Run!

ACRES. No—I say—we *won't* run, by my valour!

SIR LUCIUS. What the devil's the matter with you?

ACRES. Nothing—nothing—my dear friend —my dear Sir Lucius—but—I—I—I don't feel quite so bold, somehow—as I did.

SIR LUCIUS. Oh fie! consider your honour.

ACRES. Aye—true—my honour. Do, Sir Lucius, edge in a word or two every now and then about my honour.

SIR LUCIUS [*looking*]. Well, here they're coming.

ACRES. Sir Lucius—if I wa'n't with you, I should almost think I was afraid. If my valour should leave me! Valour will come and go.

SIR LUCIUS. Then, pray, keep it fast while you have it.

ACRES. Sir Lucius—I doubt it is going—yes —my valour is certainly going! it is sneaking off! I feel it oozing out as it were at the palms of my hands!

SIR LUCIUS. Your honour—your honour. Here they are.

ACRES. Oh mercy! now that I were safe at Clod-Hall! or could be shot before I was aware!

[*Enter* FAULKLAND *and* ABSOLUTE.]

SIR LUCIUS. Gentlemen, your most obedient —hah!—what—Captain Absolute! So, I suppose, Sir, you are come here, just like myself— to do a kind office, first for your friend—then to proceed to business on your own account.

ACRES. What, Jack! my dear Jack! my dear friend!

ABSOLUTE. Hark'ee, Bob, Beverley's at hand.

SIR LUCIUS. Well, Mr. Acres, I don't blame your saluting the gentleman civilly. So, Mr. Beverley [*to* FAULKLAND], if you'll choose your weapons, the Captain and I will measure the ground.

FAULKLAND. *My* weapons, Sir!

ACRES. Odd's life! Sir Lucius, I'm not going to fight Mr. Faulkland; these are my particular friends.

SIR LUCIUS. What, Sir, did not you come here to fight Mr. Acres?

FAULKLAND. Not I, upon my word, Sir.

SIR LUCIUS. Well, now, that's mighty provoking! But I hope, Mr. Faulkland, as there are three of us come on purpose for the game, you won't be so cantankerous as to spoil the party by sitting out.

ABSOLUTE. Oh pray, Faulkland, fight to oblige Sir Lucius.

FAULKLAND. Nay, if Mr. Acres is so bent on the matter—

ACRES. No, no, Mr. Faulkland—I'll bear my disappointment like a Christian. Look'ee, Sir Lucius, there's no occasion at all for me to fight; and if it is the same to you, I'd as lieve let it alone.

SIR LUCIUS. Observe me, Mr. Acres—I must not be trifled with. You have certainly challenged somebody, and you came here to fight him. Now, if that gentleman is willing to represent him, I can't see, for my soul, why it isn't just the same thing.

ACRES. Why no, Sir Lucius—I tell you, 'tis one Beverley I've challenged—a fellow you see, that dare not show his face! If *he* were here, I'd make him give up his pretensions directly!

ABSOLUTE. Hold, Bob—let me set you right. There is no such man as Beverley in the case. The person who assumed that name is before you; and as his pretensions are the same in both characters, he is ready to support them in whatever way you please.

SIR LUCIUS. Well, this is lucky! Now you have an opportunity—

ACRES. What, quarrel with my dear friend Jack Absolute? Not if he were fifty Beverleys! Z——ds! Sir Lucius, you would not have me be so unnatural.

SIR LUCIUS. Upon my conscience, Mr. Acres, your valour has *oozed* away with a vengeance!

ACRES. Not in the least! Odds backs and abettors! I'll be your second with all my heart, and if you should get a *quietus*, you may command me entirely. I'll get you *snug lying* in the Abbey here; or *pickle* you, and send you over to Blunderbuss-Hall, or anything of the kind, with the greatest pleasure.

SIR LUCIUS. Pho! pho! you are little better than a coward.

ACRES. Mind, gentlemen, he calls me a coward; coward was the word, by my valour!

SIR LUCIUS. Well, Sir?

ACRES. Look'ee, Sir Lucius, 'tisn't that I mind the word coward—*coward* may be said in joke. But if you had called me a *poltroon*, odds daggers and balls!—

SIR LUCIUS. Well, Sir?

ACRES. —I should have thought you a very ill-bred man.

SIR LUCIUS. Pho! you are beneath my notice.

ABSOLUTE. Nay, Sir Lucius, you can't have a better second than my friend Acres. He is a most *determined dog*, called in the country, *Fighting Bob*. He generally *kills a man a week*; don't you, Bob?

ACRES. Aye—at home!

SIR LUCIUS. Well then, Captain, 'tis we must begin. So come out, my little counsellor [*draws his sword*], and ask the gentleman whether he will resign the lady without forcing you to proceed against him.

ABSOLUTE. Come on then, Sir [*draws*]; since you won't let it be an amicable suit, here's my reply.

[*Enter* SIR ANTHONY, DAVID, *and the Women*.]

DAVID. Knock 'em all down, sweet Sir Anthony; knock down my master in particular, and bind his hands over to their good behaviour!

SIR ANTHONY. Put up, Jack, put up, or I shall be in a frenzy. How came you in a duel, Sir?

ABSOLUTE. Faith, Sir, that gentleman can tell you better than I; 'twas he called on me, and you know, Sir, I serve his Majesty.

SIR ANTHONY. Here's a pretty fellow! I catch him going to cut a man's throat, and he tells me he serves his Majesty! Z——ds! Sirrah, then how durst you draw the King's sword against one of his subjects?

ABSOLUTE. Sir, I tell you! That gentleman called me out, without explaining his reasons.

SIR ANTHONY. Gad! Sir, how came you to call my son out, without explaining your reasons?

SIR LUCIUS. Your son, Sir, insulted me in a manner which my honour could not brook.

SIR ANTHONY. Z——ds! Jack, how durst you insult the gentleman in a manner which his
5 honour could not brook?

MRS. MALAPROP. Come, come, let's have no honour before ladies. Captain Absolute, come here. How could you intimidate us so? Here's Lydia has been terrified to death for you.

10 ABSOLUTE. For fear I should be killed, or escape, Ma'am?

MRS. MALAPROP. Nay, no delusions to the past. Lydia is convinced; speak, child.

SIR LUCIUS. With your leave, Ma'am, I must
15 put in a word here. I believe I could interpret the young lady's silence. Now mark—

LYDIA. What is it you mean, Sir?

SIR LUCIUS. Come, come, Delia, we must be serious now—this is no time for trifling.

20 LYDIA. 'Tis true, Sir; and your reproof bids me offer this gentleman my hand, and solicit the return of his affections.

ABSOLUTE. O! my little angel, say you so? Sir Lucius, I perceive there must be some mis-
25 take here. With regard to the affront which you affirm I have given you, I can only say that it could not have been intentional. And as you must be convinced that I should not fear to support a real injury, you shall now see that
30 I am not ashamed to atone for an inadvertency. I ask your pardon. But for this lady, while honoured with her approbation, I will support my claim against any man whatever.

SIR ANTHONY. Well said, Jack! and I'll stand
35 by you, my boy.

ACRES. Mind, I give up all my claim—I make no pretensions to anything in the world—and if I can't get a wife without fighting for her, by my valour! I'll live a bachelor.

40 SIR LUCIUS. Captain, give me your hand— an affront handsomely acknowledged becomes an obligation—and as for the lady, if she chooses to deny her own handwriting here— [takes out letters].

45 MRS. MALAPROP. Oh, he will dissolve my mystery! Sir Lucius, perhaps there's some mis- take—perhaps, I can illuminate—

SIR LUCIUS. Pray, old gentlewoman, don't interfere where you have no business. Miss Languish, are you my Delia, or not? 50

LYDIA. Indeed, Sir Lucius, I am not.

[LYDIA and ABSOLUTE walk aside.]

MRS. MALAPROP. Sir Lucius O'Trigger, un- grateful as you are, I own the soft impeach- ment—pardon my blushes, I am Delia. 55

SIR LUCIUS. You Delia!—pho! pho! be easy.

MRS. MALAPROP. Why, thou barbarous Vandyke!—those letters are mine. When you are more sensible of your benignity, perhaps I may be brought to encourage your addresses. 60

SIR LUCIUS. Mrs. Malaprop, I am extremely sensible of your condescension; and whether you or Lucy have put this trick upon me, I am equally beholden to you. And to show you I'm not ungrateful—Captain Absolute! since you 65 have taken that lady from me, I'll give you my Delia into the bargain.

ABSOLUTE. I am much obliged to you, Sir Lucius; but here's our friend, Fighting Bob, unprovided for. 70

SIR LUCIUS. Hah! little Valour—here, will you make your fourtune?

ACRES. Odds wrinkles! No. But give me your hand, Sir Lucius; forget and forgive; but if ever I give you a chance of *pickling* me again, 75 say Bob Acres is a dunce, that's all.

SIR ANTHONY. Come, Mrs. Malaprop, don't be cast down—you are in your bloom yet.

MRS. MALAPROP. O Sir Anthony!—men are all barbarians— 80

[*All retire but* JULIA *and* FAULKLAND.]

JULIA [*aside*]. He seems dejected and un- happy—not sullen. There was some founda- tion, however, for the tale he told me. O woman! how true should be your judgment, 85 when your resolution is so weak!

FAULKLAND. Julia! how can I sue for what I so little deserve? I dare not presume—yet Hope is the child of Penitence.

JULIA. Oh! Faulkland, you have not been 90 more faulty in your unkind treatment of me than I am now in wanting inclination to resent it. As my heart honestly bids me place my weakness to the account of love, I should be ungenerous not to admit the same plea for 95 yours.

FAULKLAND. Now I shall be blest indeed!

[SIR ANTHONY *comes forward.*]

SIR ANTHONY. What's going on here? So you
have been quarrelling too, I warrant. Come,
5 Julia, I never interfered before; but let me have
a hand in the matter at last. All the faults I
have ever seen in my friend Faulkland seemed
to proceed from what he calls the *delicacy* and
warmth of his affection for you. There, marry
10 him directly, Julia; you'll find he'll mend surprisingly!

[*The rest come forward.*]

SIR LUCIUS. Come now, I hope there is no
dissatisfied person but what is content; for as
15 I have been disappointed myself, it will be very
hard if I have not the satisfaction of seeing
other people succeed better—

ACRES. You are right, Sir Lucius. So, Jack, I
wish you joy—Mr. Faulkland the same.—
20 Ladies,—come now, to show you I'm neither
vexed nor angry, odds tabours and pipes! I'll
order the fiddles in half an hour to the New
Rooms, and I insist on your all meeting me
there.

25 SIR ANTHONY. Gad! Sir, I like your spirit;
and at night we single lads will drink a health
to the young couples, and a husband to Mrs.
Malaprop.

FAULKLAND. Our partners are stolen from us,
30 Jack—I hope to be congratulated by each other
—*yours* for having checked in time the errors
of an ill-directed imagination, which might
have betrayed an innocent heart; and *mine*,
for having, by her gentleness and candour,
35 reformed the unhappy temper of one who by it
made wretched whom he loved most, and tortured the heart he ought to have adored.

ABSOLUTE. Well, Faulkland, we have both
tasted the bitters, as well as the sweets, of love
40 —with this difference only, that *you* always
prepared the bitter cup for yourself, while *I*—

LYDIA. Was always obliged to *me* for it, hey!
Mr. Modesty?—But come, no more of that:
our happiness is now as unalloyed as general.

45 JULIA. Then let us study to preserve it so;
and while Hope pictures to us a flattering scene
of future Bliss, let us deny its pencil those
colors which are too bright to be lasting. When
Hearts deserving Happiness would unite their
fortunes, Virtue would crown them with an 50
unfading garland of modest, hurtless flowers;
but ill-judging Passion will force the gaudier
Rose into the wreath, whose thorn offends
them, when its leaves are dropt!

[*Exeunt omnes.*] 55

August Strindberg

1849–1912

Miss Julie

1888

To open *Miss Julie* is to find oneself squarely in the world of what we now call the modern drama. It is that extraordinary outburst of dramatic creativity marked by the achievements of such masters as Ibsen, Chekhov, Shaw, Pirandello and—later in America—Eugene O'Neill. It spans the years from the 1880s to the 1920s (and in some respects continues down to the present). Strindberg in his prodigious and varied productions represents almost the whole spectrum of that unprecedented international movement. Not that the modern drama is defined only or even mainly by historical chronology. One can turn from *The Rivals* (1775) to *The Importance of Being Earnest* (1895) with no sense of discontinuity whatsoever because Wilde adhered to the proprieties of subject, form, and style that Sheridan observed. But to turn from *The Rivals* to *Miss Julie* is to experience a violent transition.

One way to define that transition is to mark Strindberg's intenser realism, both social and psychological. Another is to take note of his expressionism or symbolism. Although *Miss Julie* is relatively one of his more realistic dramas, expressionistic elements are also active, and both are among the hallmarks of the modern drama.

Strindberg's realism lies both on and beneath the surface. On the surface it appears in the setting, a workaday kitchen (not a drawing room or garden); in references to matters thitherto prohibited in the theater—to menstruation, for example, to dogs in heat, to a man's shaving himself in sight of the audience, to an act of sadism (the butchering of a pet songbird). Such violations of theater decorum are meant to be unsettling and also to assert the author's claim to freedom of subject matter; they are not trivial or accidental. At a deeper level Strindberg demonstrates his refusal—made explicit in the famous preface—to depict "simple theatrical characters," that is, "automatons." Instead, he writes, "my souls (characters) are conglomerates of past and present cultural phases, bits from books and newspapers, scraps of humanity . . . patched together as is the human soul." In particular he will motivate Miss Julie's "tragic fate" by showing a confluence of circumstances: "her father's absence, her monthly indisposition, her preoccupation with animals, the provocative effect of the dancing, the magical midsummer twilight, the powerful aphrodisiac influence of flowers. . . ." Indeed, he asserts, "Every event in life—and this is rather a new discovery!—is ordinarily the result of a whole series of more or less deep-lying motives." (Such a declaration is absolutely characteristic of the modern dramatist.) The deep motives are set forward as contraries, even as contradictions, that defeat any expectation of superficial consistency and at the same time reinforce the impression of psychological penetration and, hence, of realism.

In light of this principle of contraries, Strindberg can say of Jean, the valet, that "he is an aristocrat because of his masculine strength, his more keenly developed senses . . ." and still assert that "His slave mentality expresses itself in the fearful respect he has for the Count (the boots) and his religious superstition." Similarly Jean can be made to depict his adolescent crush on Julie as taking place in a "Garden of Eden" and yet confess that he had "the same dirty thoughts all boys have." So too Strindberg can call Julie "a modern character"—"a half-woman . . . who pushes her way ahead, selling herself nowadays for power, decorations, honors, and diplomas." (Strindberg was the reverse of a pro-feminist.) Yet he can also find in her "a relic of the old warrior nobility." His realism of character springs largely from such contraries. The resulting dissonance is intensified in *Miss Julie* by making the play run as "a single, long coherent act" without interruption, allowing the audience no reprieve from sustained attention.

The expressionistic or symbolic dimensions of the play are perhaps less noticeable and not so readily categorized. Unlike the realistic details they do not specify but rather suggest, underscoring tonalities of feeling that are difficult to convey except by indirection, and they are highly characteristic of Strindberg's turbulent imagination, always uneasy with totally rational explanation. The most evident symbolic dimension appears in the dual time-setting, which is described both as Midsummer Eve and as the eve of St. John's Day, commemorating John the Baptist. Midsummer Eve, with its traditional all-night merrymaking and its vestiges of ancient fertility rites, provides a ripe occasion for the swift sexual encounter. On the other hand, the several allusions to John the Baptist, who was beheaded at the instigation of the dancer Salome, counterpoint the ironic and even weird tragedy that is being performed. Some of these allusions are direct—as when the kitchen maid tells Jean (that is, "John") that the text in church that day will be "the beheading of John the Baptist"—or less overt, as when Julie exclaims, "I'd like to see your blood and your brains on a chopping block." Others are marginal. How far the parallels and the ironic contrasts ought to be pursued may not be perfectly clear, yet they are insistently to be reckoned with. Although neither realism nor expressionism explains all that is modern in the modern drama, they are among the essentials, and both are vividly present in *Miss Julie*.

Miss Julie

STRINDBERG

Translated by Harry G. Carlson

CHARACTERS

MISS JULIE   *25 years old*
JEAN   *her father's valet, 30 years old*
KRISTINE   *her father's cook, 35 years old*

[*The action takes place in the count's kitchen on midsummer eve.*°]

Setting

[*A large kitchen, the ceiling and side walls of which are hidden by draperies. The rear wall runs diagonally from down left to up right. On the wall down left are two shelves with copper, iron, and pewter*
5   *utensils; the shelves are lined with scalloped paper. Visible to the right is most of a set of large, arched glass doors, through which can be seen a fountain with a statue of Cupid, lilac bushes in bloom, and the tops of some Lombardy poplars. At down left is*
10   *the corner of a large tiled stove; a portion of its hood is showing. At right, one end of the servants' white pine dining table juts out; several chairs stand around it. The stove is decorated with birch branches; juniper twigs are strewn on the floor. On the end of the table*
15   *stands a large Japanese spice jar, filled with lilac blossoms. An ice-box, a sink, and a washstand. Above the door is an old-fashioned bell on a spring; to the left of the door, the mouthpiece of a speaking tube is visible.*
20   [KRISTINE *is frying something on the stove. She is*

midsummer eve   the night of June 23, the traditional celebration of the summer solstice, often observed by all-night merrymaking; also, the eve of St. John's Day, dedicated to John the Baptist.

wearing a light-colored cotton dress and an apron. JEAN *enters. He is wearing livery and carries a pair of high riding-boots with spurs, which he puts down on the floor where they can be seen by the audience.*]

JEAN. Miss Julie's crazy again tonight; absolutely   25
crazy!

KRISTINE. So you finally came back?

JEAN. I took the Count to the station and when I returned past the barn I stopped in for a dance. Who do I see but Miss Julie leading off the dance   30
with the gamekeeper! But as soon as she saw me she rushed over to ask me for the next waltz. And she's been waltzing ever since—I've never seen anything like it. She's crazy!

KRISTINE. She always has been, but never as bad   35
as the last two weeks since her engagement was broken off.

JEAN. Yes, I wonder what the real story was there. He was a gentleman, even if he wasn't rich. Ah! These people have such romantic ideas. [*sits at the*   40
end of the table] Still, it's strange, isn't it? I mean that she'd rather stay home with the servants on midsummer eve instead of going with her father to visit relatives?

KRISTINE. She's probably embarrassed after that   45
row with her fiancé.

JEAN. Probably! He gave a good account of himself, though. Do you know how it happened, Kristine? I saw it, you know, though I didn't let on I had.   50

KRISTINE. No! You saw it?

JEAN. Yes, I did.—— That evening they were out near the stable, and she was "training" him—as she called it. Do you know what she did? She made him jump over her riding crop, the way you'd   55
teach a dog to jump. He jumped twice and she hit him each time. But the third time he grabbed the crop out of her hand, hit her with it across the cheek, and broke it in pieces. Then he left.

KRISTINE. So, that's what happened! I can't be-   60
lieve it!

JEAN. Yes, that's the way it went!——What have you got for me that's tasty, Kristine?

KRISTINE [*serving him from the pan*]. Oh, it's only a piece of kidney I cut from the veal roast.   65

JEAN [*smelling the food*]. Beautiful! That's my favorite *délice.* [*feeling the plate*] But you could have warmed the plate!

KRISTINE. You're fussier than the Count himself, once you start! [*She pulls his hair affectionately.*]

JEAN [*angry*]. Stop it, leave my hair alone! You know I'm touchy about that.

5 KRISTINE. Now, now, it's only love, you know that. [JEAN *eats.* KRISTINE *opens a bottle of beer.*]

JEAN. Beer? On midsummer eve? No thank you! I can do better than that. [*opens a drawer in the table and takes out a bottle of red wine with yellow sealing*
10 *wax*] See that? Yellow seal! Give me a glass! A wine glass! I'm drinking this *pur*.

KRISTINE [*returns to the stove and puts on a small saucepan*]. God help the woman who gets you for a husband! What a fussbudget.

15 JEAN. Nonsense! You'd be damned lucky to get a man like me. It certainly hasn't done you any harm to have people call me your sweetheart. [*tastes the wine*] Good! Very good! Just needs a little warming. [*warms the glass between his hands*] We bought this
20 in Dijon. Four francs a liter, not counting the cost of the bottle, or the customs duty.——What are you cooking now? It stinks like hell!

KRISTINE. Oh, some slop Miss Julie wants to give Diana.

25 JEAN. Watch your language, Kristine. But why should you have to cook for that damn mutt on midsummer eve? Is she sick?

KRISTINE. Yes, she's sick! She sneaked out with the gatekeeper's dog—and now there's hell to pay.
30 Miss Julie won't have it!

JEAN. Miss Julie has too much pride about some things and not enough about others, just like her mother was. The Countess was most at home in the kitchen and the cowsheds, but a *one*-horse car-
35 riage wasn't elegant enough for her. The cuffs of her blouse were dirty, but she had to have her coat of arms on her cufflinks.——And Miss Julie won't take proper care of herself either. If you ask me, she just isn't refined. Just now, when she was
40 dancing in the barn, she pulled the gamekeeper away from Anna and made him dance with her. We wouldn't behave like that, but that's what happens when aristocrats pretend they're common people—they get *common*!——But she is quite
45 a woman! Magnificent! What shoulders, and what—et cetera!

KRISTINE. Oh, don't overdo it! I've heard what Clara says, and she dresses her.

JEAN. Ha, Clara! You're all jealous of each other! I've been out riding with her . . . And the way she 50 dances!

KRISTINE. Listen, Jean! You're going to dance with me, when I'm finished here, aren't you?

JEAN. Of course I will.

KRISTINE. Promise? 55

JEAN. Promise? When I say I'll do something, I do it! By the way, the kidney was very good. [*corks the bottle*]

JULIE [*in the doorway to someone outside*]. I'll be right back! You go ahead for now! [JEAN *sneaks the* 60 *bottle back into the table drawer and gets up respectfully.* MISS JULIE *enters and crosses to* KRISTINE *by the stove.*] Well? Is it ready? [KRISTINE *indicates that* JEAN *is present.*]

JEAN [*gallantly*]. Are you ladies up to something 65 secret?

JULIE [*flicking her handkerchief in his face*]. None of your business!

JEAN. Hmm! I like the smell of violets!

JULIE [*coquettishly*]. Shame on you! So you know 70 about perfumes, too? You certainly know how to dance. Ah, ah! No peeking! Go away.

JEAN [*boldly but respectfully*]. Are you brewing up a magic potion for midsummer eve? Something to prophesy by under a lucky star, so you'll catch a 75 glimpse of your future husband!

JULIE [*caustically*]. You'd need sharp eyes to see him! [*to* KRISTINE] Pour out half a bottle and cork it well.—— Come and dance a schottische with me, Jean . . . 80

JEAN [*hesitating*]. I don't want to be impolite to anyone, and I've already promised this dance to Kristine . . .

JULIE. Oh, she can have another one—can't you Kristine? Won't you lend me Jean? 85

KRISTINE. It's not up to me, ma'am. [*to* JEAN] If the mistress is so generous, it wouldn't do for you to say no. Go on, Jean, and thank her for the honor.

JEAN. To be honest, and no offense intended, I wonder whether it's wise for you to dance twice 90 running with the same partner, especially since these people are quick to jump to conclusions . . .

JULIE [*flaring up*]. What's that? What sort of conclusions? What do you mean?

JEAN [*submissively*]. If you don't understand, 95 ma'am, I must speak more plainly. It doesn't look good to play favorites with your servants. . . .

JULIE. Play favorites! What an idea! I'm aston-ished! As mistress of the house, I honor your dance with my presence. And when I dance, I want to dance with someone who can lead, so I won't look ridiculous.

JEAN. As you order, ma'am! I'm at your service!

JULIE [*gently*]. Don't take it as an order! On a night like this we're all just ordinary people hav-ing fun, so we'll forget about rank. Now, take my arm!——Don't worry, Kristine! I won't steal your sweetheart! [JEAN *offers his arm and leads* MISS JULIE *out.*]

Mime

[*The following should be played as if the actress playing* KRISTINE *were really alone. When she has to, she turns her back to the audience. She does not look toward them, nor does she hurry as if she were afraid they would grow impatient. Schottische music played on a fiddle sounds in the distance.* KRISTINE *hums along with the music. She clears the table, washes the dishes, dries them, and puts them away. She takes off her apron. From a table drawer she removes a small mirror and leans it against the bowl of lilacs on the table. She lights a candle, heats a hairpin over the flame, and uses it to set a curl on her forehead. She crosses the door and listens, then returns to the table. She finds the handkerchief* MISS JULIE *left behind, picks it up, and smells it. Then, preoccupied, she spreads it out, stretches it, smoothes out the wrinkles, and folds it into quarters, and so forth.*]

JEAN [*enters alone*]. God, she really *is* crazy! What a way to dance! Everybody's laughing at her be-hind her back. What do you make of it, Kristine?

KRISTINE. Ah! It's that time of the month for her, and she always gets peculiar like that. Are you going to dance with me now?

JEAN. You're not mad at me, are you, for leav-ing . . . ?

KRISTINE. Of course not!——Why should I be, for a little thing like that? Besides, I know my place . . .

JEAN [*puts his arm around her waist*]. You're a sensible girl, Kristine, and you'd make a good wife . . .

JULIE [*entering; uncomfortably surprised; with forced good humor*]. What a charming escort—running away from his partner.

JEAN. On the contrary, Miss Julie. Don't you see how I rushed back to the partner I abandoned!

JULIE [*changing her tone*]. You know, you're a su-perb dancer!——But why are you wearing livery on a holiday? Take it off at once!

JEAN. Then I must ask you to go outside for a moment. You see, my black coat is hanging over there . . . [*gestures and crosses right*]

JULIE. Are you embarrassed about changing your coat in front of me? Well, go in your room then. Either that or stay and I'll turn my back.

JEAN. With your permission, ma'am [*He crosses right. His arm is visible as he changes his jacket.*]

JULIE [*to* KRISTINE]. Tell me, Kristine—you two are so close—. Is Jean your fiancé?

KRISTINE. Fiancé? Yes, if you wish. We can call him that.

JULIE. What do you mean?

KRISTINE. You had a fiancé yourself, didn't you? So . . .

JULIE. Well, we were properly engaged . . .

KRISTINE. But nothing came of it, did it? [JEAN *returns dressed in a frock coat and bowler hat.*]

JULIE. *Très gentil, monsieur Jean! Très gentil!*

JEAN. *Vous voulez plaisanter, madame!*

JULIE. *Et vous voulez parler français!°* Where did you learn that?

JEAN. In Switzerland, when I was wine steward in one of the biggest hotels in Lucerne!

JULIE. You look like a real gentleman in that coat! *Charmant!* [*sits at the table*]

JEAN. Oh, you're flattering me!

JULIE [*offended*]. Flattering you?

JEAN. My natural modesty forbids me to believe that you would really compliment someone like me, and so I took the liberty of assuming that you were exaggerating, which polite people call flat-tering.

JULIE. Where did you learn to talk like that? You must have been to the theater often.

JEAN. Of course, And I've done a lot of travel-ing.

Julie.   Very fine, monsieur Jean! Very fine indeed!
Jean.   You are making fun of me, Madame.
Julie.   And just to think, You can speak French as well!

JULIE. But you come from here, don't you?

JEAN. My father was a farm hand on the district attorney's estate nearby. I used to see you when you were little, but you never noticed me.

5 JULIE. No! Really?

JEAN. Sure. I remember one time especially . . . but I can't talk about that.

JULIE. Oh, come now! Why not? Just this once!

JEAN. No, I really couldn't, not now. Some other
10 time, perhaps.

JULIE. Why some other time? What's so dangerous about now?

JEAN. It's not dangerous, but there are obstacles.——Her, for example. [indicating KRISTINE, who
15 has fallen asleep in a chair by the stove]

JULIE. What a pleasant wife she'll make! She probably snores, too.

JEAN. No, she doesn't, but she talks in her sleep.

JULIE [cynically]. How do you know?

20 JEAN [audaciously]. I've heard her! [pause, during which they stare at each other]

JULIE. Why don't you sit down?

JEAN. I couldn't do that in your presence.

JULIE. But if I order you to?

25 JEAN. Then I'd obey.

JULIE. Sit down, then.——No, wait. Can you get me something to drink first?

JEAN. I don't know what we have in the ice box. I think there's only beer.

30 JULIE. Why do you say "only"? My tastes are so simple I prefer beer to wine. [JEAN takes a bottle of beer from the ice box and opens it. He looks for a glass and a plate in the cupboard and serves her.]

JEAN. Here you are, ma'am.

35 JULIE. Thank you. Won't you have something yourself?

JEAN. I'm not partial to beer, but if it's an order . . .

JULIE. An order?——Surely a gentleman can keep
40 his lady company.

JEAN. You're right, of course. [opens a bottle and gets a glass]

JULIE. Now, drink to my health! [He hesitates.] What? A man of the world—and shy?

45 JEAN [In mock romantic fashion, he kneels and raises his glass.]. Skål to my mistress!

JULIE. Bravo!——Now kiss my shoe, to finish it properly. [JEAN hesitates, then boldly seizes her foot and kisses it lightly.] Perfect! You should have been
50 an actor.

JEAN [rising]. That's enough now, Miss Julie! Someone might come in and see us.

JULIE. What of it?

JEAN. People talk, that's what! If you knew how their tongues were wagging just now at the dance,
55 you'd . . .

JULIE. What were they saying? Tell me!——Sit down!

JEAN [sits]. I don't want to hurt you, but they were sayings things——suggestive things, that, that
60 . . . well, you can figure it out for yourself! You're not a child. If a woman is seen drinking alone with a man—let alone a servant—at night—then . . .

JULIE. Then what? Besides, we're not alone. Kristine is here.
65

JEAN. Asleep!

JULIE. Then I'll wake her up. [rising] Kristine! Are you asleep? [KRISTINE mumbles in her sleep.]

JULIE. Kristine!——She certainly can sleep!

KRISTINE [in her sleep]. The Count's boots are
70 brushed—put the coffee on—right away, right away—uh, huh—oh!

JULIE [grabbing KRISTINE's nose]. Will you wake up!

JEAN [severely]. Leave her alone—let her sleep!

JULIE [sharply]. What?
75

JEAN. Someone who's been standing over a stove all day has a right to be tired by now. Sleep should be respected . . .

JULIE [changing her tone]. What a considerate thought—it does you credit—thank you! [offering
80 her hand] Come outside and pick some lilacs for me! [During the following, KRISTINE awakens and shambles sleepily off right to bed.]

JEAN. Go with you?

JULIE. With me!
85

JEAN. We couldn't do that! Absolutely not!

JULIE. I don't understand. Surely you don't imagine . . .

JEAN. No I don't, but the others might.

JULIE. What? That I've fallen in love with a ser-
90 vant?

JEAN. I'm not a conceited man, but such things happen—and for these people, nothing is sacred.

JULIE. I do believe you're an aristocrat!

JEAN. Yes, I am.
95

JULIE. And I'm stepping down . . .

JEAN. Don't step down, Miss Julie, take my advice. No one'll believe you stepped down voluntarily. People will always say you fell.

JULIE. I have a higher opinion of people than you. Come and see!——Come! [*She stares at him broodingly.*]

JEAN. You're very strange, do you know that?

JULIE. Perhaps! But so are you!——For that matter, everything is strange. Life, people, everything. Like floating scum, drifting on and on across the water, until it sinks down and down! That reminds me of a dream I have now and then. I've climbed up on top of a pillar. I sit there and see no way of getting down. I get dizzy when I look down, and I must get down, but I don't have the courage to jump. I can't hold on firmly, and I long to be able to fall, but I don't fall. And yet I'll have no peace until I get down, no rest unless I get down, down on the ground! And if I did get down to the ground, I'd want to be under the earth . . . Have you ever felt anything like that?

JEAN. No. I dream that I'm lying under a high tree in a dark forest. I want to get up, up on top, and look out over the bright landscape, where the sun is shining, and plunder the bird's nest up there, where the golden eggs lie. And I climb and climb, but the trunk's so thick and smooth, and it's so far to the first branch. But I know if I just reached the first branch, I'd go right to the top, like up a ladder. I haven't reached it yet, but I will, even if it's only a dream!

JULIE. Here I am chattering with you about dreams. Come, let's go out! Just into the park! [*She offers him her arm, and they start to leave.*]

JEAN. We'll have to sleep on nine midsummer flowers, Miss Julie, to make our dreams come true! [*They turn at the door.* JEAN *puts his hand to his eye.*]

JULIE. Did you get something in your eye?

JEAN. It's nothing—just a speck—it'll be gone in a minute.

JULIE. My sleeve must have brushed against you. Sit down and let me help you. [*She takes him by the arm and seats him. She tilts his head back and with the tip of a handkerchief tries to remove the speck.*] Sit still, absolutely still! [*She slaps his hand.*] Didn't you hear me?——Why, you're trembling; the big, strong man is trembling! [*feels his biceps*] What muscles you have!

JEAN [*warning*]. Miss Julie!

JULIE. Yes, *monsieur* Jean. 50

JEAN. *Attention! Je ne suis qu'un homme!°*

JULIE. Will you sit still!——There! Now it's gone! Kiss my hand and thank me.

JEAN [*rising*]. Miss Julie, listen to me!——Kristine has gone to bed!——Will you listen to me! 55

JULIE. Kiss my hand first!

JEAN. Listen to me!

JULIE. Kiss my hand first!

JEAN. All right, but you've only yourself to blame!

JULIE. For what? 60

JEAN. For what? Are you still a child at twenty-five? Don't you know that it's dangerous to play with fire?

JULIE. Not for me. I'm insured.

JEAN [*boldly*]. No, you're not! But even if you 65 were, there's combustible material close by.

JULIE. Meaning you?

JEAN. Yes! Not because it's me, but because I'm young——

JULIE. And handsome—what incredible conceit! 70 A Don Juan perhaps! Or a Joseph.° Yes, that's it, I do believe you're a Joseph!

JEAN. Do you?

JULIE. I'm almost afraid so. [JEAN *boldly tries to put his arm around her waist and kiss her. She slaps* 75 *his face.*] How dare you?

JEAN. Are you serious or joking?

JULIE. Serious.

JEAN. Then so was what just happened. You play games too seriously, and that's dangerous. Well, 80 I'm tired of games. You'll excuse me if I get back to work. I haven't done the Count's boots yet and it's long past midnight.

JULIE. Put the boots down!

JEAN. No! It's the work I have to do. I never 85 agreed to be your playmate, and never will. It's beneath me.

JULIE. You're proud.

JEAN. In certain ways, but not in others.

JULIE. Have you ever been in love? 90

JEAN. We don't use that word, but I've been fond

Jean. Watch out! I am only a man!

Joseph the young Israelite servant who is accused by Potiphar's wife of trying to rape her; in fact, it was she who made the advances. See Genesis 39:7–21

of many girls, and once I was sick because I couldn't have the one I wanted. That's right, sick, like those princes in the Arabian Nights—who couldn't eat or drink because of love.

5 JULIE. Who was she? [JEAN *is silent.*] Who was she?

JEAN. You can't force me to tell you that.

JULIE. But if I ask you as an equal, as a—friend! Who was she?

10 JEAN. You!

JULIE. [*sits*]. How amusing . . .

JEAN. Yes, if you like! It was ridiculous!——You see, that was the story I didn't want to tell you earlier. Maybe I will now. Do you know how the

15 world looks from down below?——Of course you don't. Neither do hawks and falcons, whose backs we can't see because they're usually soaring up there above us. I grew up in a shack with seven brothers and sisters and a pig, in the middle of a

20 wasteland, where there wasn't a single tree. But from our window I could see the tops of apple trees above the wall of your father's garden. This was the Garden of Eden, guarded by angry angels with flaming swords. All the same, the other boys

25 and I managed to find our way to the Tree of Life. ——Now you think I'm contemptible, I suppose.

JULIE. Oh, all boys steal apples.

JEAN. You say that, but you think I'm contemptible anyway. Oh well! One day I went into the

30 Garden of Eden with my mother, to weed the onion beds. Near the vegetable garden was a small Turkish pavilion in the shadow of jasmine bushes and overgrown with honeysuckle. I had no idea what it was used for, but I'd never seen such a

35 beautiful building. People went in and came out again, and one day the door was left open. I sneaked close and saw walls covered with pictures of kings and emperors, and red curtains with fringes at the windows—now you know the place

40 I mean. I——[*breaks off a sprig of lilac and holds it in front of* MISS JULIE's *nose*]——I'd never been inside the manor house, never seen anything except the church—but this was more beautiful. From then on, no matter where my thoughts wandered, they

45 returned—there. And gradually I got a longing to experience, just once, the full pleasure of—*enfin*, I sneaked in, saw, and marveled! But then I heard someone coming! There was only one exit for la-

dies and gentlemen, but for me there was another, and I had no choice but to take it! [MISS JULIE, *who* 50 *has taken the lilac sprig, lets it fall on the table.*] Afterwards, I started running, I crashed through a raspberry bush, flew over a strawberry patch, and came up onto the rose terrace. There I caught sight of a pink dress and a pair of white stockings—it was 55 you. I crawled under a pile of weeds, and I mean under—under thistles that pricked me and wet dirt that stank. And I looked at you as you walked among the roses, and I thought: if it's true that a thief can enter heaven and be with the angels, 60 then why can't a farmhand's son here on God's earth enter the manor house garden and play with the Count's daughter?

JULIE [*romantically*]. Do you think all poor children would have thought the way you did? 65

JEAN [*at first hesitant, then with conviction*]. If *all* poor—yes—of course. Of course!

JULIE. It must be terrible to be poor!

JEAN [*with exaggerated suffering*]. Oh, Miss Julie! Oh!——A dog can lie on the Countess's sofa, a 70 horse can have his nose patted by a young lady's hand, but a servant——[*changing his tone*]——oh, I know—now and then you find one with enough stuff in him to get ahead in the world, but how often?——Anyhow, do you know what I did 75 then?——I jumped in the millstream with my clothes on, was pulled out, and got a beating. But the following Sunday, when my father and all the others went to my grandmother's, I arranged to stay home. I scrubbed myself with soap and water, 80 put on my best clothes, and went to church so that I could see you! I saw you and returned home, determined to die. But I wanted to die beautifully and pleasantly, without pain. And then I remembered that it was dangerous to sleep under an elder 85 bush. We had a big one, and it was in full flower. I plundered its treasures and bedded down under them in the oat bin. Have you ever noticed how smooth oats are?—and soft to the touch, like human skin . . . ! Well, I shut the lid and closed my 90 eyes. I fell asleep and woke up feeling very sick. But I didn't die, as you can see. What was I after? ——I don't know. There was no hope of winning you, of course.——You were a symbol of the hopelessness of ever rising out of the class in which 95 I was born.

JULIE. You're a charming storyteller. Did you ever go to school?

JEAN. A bit, but I've read lots of novels and been to the theater often. And then I've listened to peo-
5 ple like you talk—that's where I learned most.

JULIE. Do you listen to what we say?

JEAN. Naturally! And I've heard plenty, too, driving the carriage or rowing the boat. Once I heard you and a friend . . .

10 JULIE. Oh?——What did you hear?

JEAN. I'd better not say. But I was surprised a little. I couldn't imagine where you learned such words. Maybe at bottom there isn't such a great difference between people as we think.

15 JULIE. Shame on you! We don't act like you when we're engaged.

JEAN [*staring at her*]. Is that true?——You don't have to play innocent with me, Miss . . .

JULIE. The man I gave my love to was a swine.

20 JEAN. That's what you all say—afterwards.

JULIE. All?

JEAN. I think so. I know I've heard that phrase before, on similar occasions.

JULIE. What occasions?

25 JEAN. Like the one I'm talking about. The last time . . .

JULIE [*rising*]. Quiet! I don't want to hear any more!

JEAN. That's interesting—that's what *she* said,
30 too. Well, if you'll excuse me, I'm going to bed.

JULIE [*gently*]. To bed? On midsummer eve?

JEAN. Yes! Dancing with the rabble out there doesn't amuse me much.

JULIE. Get the key to the boat and row me out
35 on the lake. I want to see the sun come up.

JEAN. Is that wise?

JULIE. Are you worried about your reputation?

JEAN. Why not? Why should I risk looking ri-diculous and getting fired without a reference, just
40 when I'm trying to establish myself. Besides, I think I owe something to Kristine.

JULIE. So, now it's Kristine . . .

JEAN. Yes, but you, too.——Take my advice, go up and go to bed!

45 JULIE. Am I to obey you?

JEAN. Just this once—for your own good! Please! It's very late. Drowsiness makes people giddy and liable to lose their heads! Go to bed! Besides—

unless I'm mistaken—I hear the others coming to look for me. And if they find us together, you'll 50 be lost!

[*The* CHORUS *approaches, singing:*]
The swineherd found his true love
a pretty girl so fair,
The swineherd found his true love 55
but let the girl beware.

For then he saw the princess
the princess on the golden hill,
but then saw the princess,
so much fairer still. 60

So the swineherd and the princess
they danced the whole night through,
and he forgot his first love,
to her he was untrue.

And when the long night ended, 65
and in the light of day, of day,
the dancing too was ended,
and the princess could not stay.

Then the swineherd lost his true love,
and the princess grieves him still, 70
and never more she'll wander
from atop the golden hill.

JULIE. I know all these people and I love them, just as they love me. Let them come in and you'll see. 75

JEAN. No, Miss Julie, they don't love you. They take your food, but they spit on it! Believe me! Listen to them, listen to what they're singing! ——No, don't listen to them!

JULIE [*listening*]. What are they singing? 80

JEAN. It's a dirty song! About you and me!

JULIE. Disgusting! Oh! How deceitful!——

JEAN. The rabble is always cowardly! And in a battle like this, you don't fight; you can only run away! 85

JULIE. Run away? But where? We can't go out— or into Kristine's room.

JEAN. True. But there's my room. Necessity knows no rules. Besides, you can trust me. I'm your friend and I respect you. 90

JULIE. But suppose—suppose they look for you in there?

JEAN. I'll bolt the door, and if anyone tries to break in, I'll shoot!——Come! [*on his knees*] Come!

JULIE [*urgently*]. Promise me . . . ? 95

AUGUST STRINDBERG

JEAN. I swear! [MISS JULIE *runs off right.* JEAN *hastens after her.*]

Ballet

[*Led by a fiddler, the servants and farm people enter, dressed festively, with flowers in their hats.*
5 *On the table they place a small barrel of beer and a keg of schnapps, both garlanded. Glasses are brought out, and the drinking starts. A dance circle is formed and "The Swineherd and the Princess" is sung. When the dance is finished, everyone leaves, singing.*]

10 [MISS JULIE *enters alone. She notices the mess in the kitchen, wrings her hands, then takes out her powder puff and powders her nose.*]

JEAN [*enters, agitated*]. There, you see? And you heard them. We can't possibly stay here now, you
15 know that.

JULIE. Yes, I know. But what can we do?

JEAN. Leave, travel, far away from here.

JULIE. Travel? Yes, but where?

JEAN. To Switzerland, to the Italian lakes. Have
20 you ever been there?

JULIE. No. Is it beautiful?

JEAN. Oh, an eternal summer—oranges growing everywhere, laurel trees, always green . . .

JULIE. But what'll we do there?

25 JEAN. I'll open a hotel—with first-class service for first-class people.

JULIE. Hotel?

JEAN. That's the life, you know. Always new faces, new languages. No time to worry or be
30 nervous. No hunting for something to do—there's always work to be done; bells ringing night and day, train whistles blowing, carriages coming and going, and all the while gold rolling into the till! That's the life!

35 JULIE. Yes, it sounds wonderful. But what'll I do?

JEAN. You'll be mistress of the house: the jewel in our crown! With your looks . . . and your manner—oh—success is guaranteed! It'll be wonder-
40 ful! You'll sit in your office like a queen and push an electric button to set your slaves in motion. The guests will file past your throne and timidly lay their treasures before you.——You have no idea how people tremble when they get their bill.——
45 I'll salt the bills and you'll sweeten them with your prettiest smile.——Let's get away from here——

[*takes a timetable out of his pocket*]——Right away, on the next train!——We'll be in Malmö six-thirty tomorrow morning, Hamburg at eight-forty; from Frankfort to Basel will take a day, then on to Como 50 by way of the St. Gotthard Tunnel, in, let's see, three days. Three days!

JULIE. That's all very well! But Jean—you must give me courage! Tell me you love me! Put your arms around me! 55

JEAN [*hesitating*]. I want to—but I don't dare. Not in this house, not again. I love you—never doubt that—you don't doubt it, do you, Miss Julie?

JULIE [*shy; very feminine*]. "Miss!"——Call me Julie! There are no barriers between us any more. 60 Call me Julie!

JEAN [*tormented*]. I can't! There'll always be barriers between us as long as we stay in this house.
——There's the past and there's the Count. I've never met anyone I had such respect for.——When 65 I see his gloves lying on a chair, I feel small.——
When I hear that bell up there ring, I jump like a skittish horse.——And when I look at his boots standing there so stiff and proud, I feel like bowing! [*kicking the boots*] Superstitions and prejudices 70 we learned as children—but they can easily be forgotten. If I can just get to another country, a republic, people will bow and scrape when they see my livery—*they'll* bow and scrape, you hear, not me! I wasn't born to cringe. I've got stuff in me, 75 I've got character, and if I can only grab onto that first branch, you watch me climb! I'm a servant today, but next year I'll own my own hotel. In ten years I'll have enough to retire. Then I'll go to Rumania and be decorated. I could—mind you I 80 said *could*—end up a count!

JULIE. Wonderful, wonderful!

JEAN. Ah, in Rumania you just buy your title, and so you'll be a countess after all. My countess!

JULIE. But I don't care about that—that's what 85 I'm putting behind me! Show me you love me, otherwise—otherwise, what am I?

JEAN. I'll show you a thousand times—afterwards! Not here! And whatever you do, no emotional outbursts, or we'll both be lost! We must 90 think this through coolly, like sensible people. [*He takes out a cigar, snips the end, and lights it.*] You sit there, and I'll sit here. We'll talk as if nothing happened.

JULIE [*desperately*]. Oh, my God! Have you no feelings?

JEAN. Me? No one has more feelings than I do, but I know how to control them.

5   JULIE. A little while ago you could kiss my shoe— and now!

JEAN [*harshly*]. Yes, but that was before. Now we have other things to think about.

JULIE. Don't speak harshly to me!

10   JEAN. I'm not—just sensibly! We've already done one foolish thing, let's not have any more. The Count could return any minute, and by then we've got to decide what to do with our lives. What do you think of my plans for the future? Do you ap-

15 prove?

JULIE. They sound reasonable enough. I have only one question: for such a big undertaking you need capital—do you have it?

JEAN [*chewing on the cigar*]. Me? Certainly! I have

20 my professional expertise, my wide experience, and my knowledge of languages. That's capital enough, I should think!

JULIE. But all that won't even buy a train ticket.

JEAN. That's true. That's why I'm looking for a

25 partner to advance me the money.

JULIE. Where will you find one quickly enough?

JEAN. That's up to you, if you want to come with me.

JULIE. But I can't; I have no money of my own.

30 [*pause*]

JEAN. Then it's all off . . .

JULIE. And . . .

JEAN. Things stay as they are.

JULIE. Do you think I'm going to stay in this

35 house as your lover? With all the servants pointing their fingers at me? Do you imagine I can face my father after this? No! Take me away from here, away from shame and dishonor——Oh, what have I done! My God, my God! [*She cries.*]

40   JEAN. Now, don't start that old song!——What have you done? The same as many others before you.

JULIE [*screaming convulsively*]. And now you think I'm contemptible!——I'm falling, I'm falling!

45   JEAN. Fall down to my level and I'll lift you up again.

JULIE. What terrible power drew me to you? The attraction of the weak to the strong? The falling to the rising? Or was it love? Was this love? Do you know what love is?   50

JEAN. Me? What do you take me for? You don't think this was my first time, do you?

JULIE. The things you say, the thoughts you think!

JEAN. That's the way I was taught, and that's the way I am! Now don't get excited and don't   55 play the grand lady, because we're in the same boat now!——Come on, Julie, I'll pour you a glass of something special! [*He opens a drawer in the table, takes out a wine bottle, and fills two glasses already used.*]   60

JULIE. Where did you get that wine?

JEAN. From the cellar.

JULIE. My father's burgundy!

JEAN. That'll do for his son-in-law, won't it?

JULIE. And I drink beer! Beer!   65

JEAN. That only shows I have better taste.

JULIE. Thief.

JEAN. Planning to tell?

JULIE. Oh, oh! Accomplice of a common thief! Was I drunk? Have I been walking in a dream the   70 whole evening? Midsummer eve! A time of innocent fun!

JEAN. Innocent, eh?

JULIE [*pacing back and forth*]. Is there anyone on earth more miserable than I am at this moment?   75

JEAN. Why should you be? After such a conquest? Think of Kristine in there. Don't you think she has feelings, too?

JULIE. I thought so awhile ago, but not any more. No, a servant is a servant . . .   80

JEAN. And a whore is a whore!

JULIE [*on her knees, her hands clasped*]. Oh, God in Heaven, end my wretched life! Take me away from the filth I'm sinking into! Save me! Save me!

JEAN. I can't deny I feel sorry for you. When I   85 lay in that onion bed and saw you in the rose garden, well . . . I'll be frank . . . I had the same dirty thoughts all boys have.

JULIE. And you wanted to die for me!

JEAN. In the oat bin? That was just talk.   90

JULIE. A lie, in other words!

JEAN [*beginning to feel sleepy*]. More or less! I got the idea from a newspaper story about a chimney sweep who curled up in a firewood bin full of lilacs because he got a summons for not support-   95 ing his illegitimate child . . .

AUGUST STRINDBERG

JULIE. So, that's what you're like . . .

JEAN. I had to think of something. And that's the kind of story women always go for.

JULIE. Swine!

5 JEAN. *Merde!°*

JULIE. And now you've seen the hawk's back . . .

JEAN. Not exactly its *back* . . .

JULIE. And I was to be the first branch . . .

JEAN. But the branch was rotten . . .

10 JULIE. I was to be the sign on the hotel . . .

JEAN. And I the hotel . . .

JULIE. Sit at your desk, entice your customers, pad their bills . . .

JEAN. That I'd do myself . . .

15 JULIE. How can anyone be so thoroughly filthy?

JEAN. Better clean up then!

JULIE. You lackey, you menial, stand up, when I speak to you!

JEAN. Menial's strumpet, lackey's whore, shut
20 up and get out of here! Who are you to lecture me on coarseness? None of my kind is ever as coarse as you were tonight. Do you think one of your maids would throw herself at a man the way you did? Have you ever seen any girl of my class offer
25 herself like that? I've only seen it among animals and streetwalkers.

JULIE [*crushed*]. You're right. Hit me, trample on me. I don't deserve any better. I'm worthless. But help me! If you see any way out of this, help me,
30 Jean, please!

JEAN [*more gently*]. I'd be lying if I didn't admit to a sense of triumph in all this, but do you think that a person like me would have dared even to look at someone like you if you hadn't invited it?
35 I'm still amazed . . .

JULIE. And proud . . .

JEAN. Why not? Though I must say it was too easy to be really exciting.

JULIE. Go on, hit me, hit me harder!

40 JEAN [*rising*]. No! Forgive me for what I've said! I don't hit a man when he's down, let alone a woman. I can't deny though, that I'm pleased to find out that what looked so dazzling to us from below was only tinsel, that the hawk's back was
45 only gray, after all, that the lovely complexion was only powder, that those polished fingernails

Jean. Filth!

had black edges, and that a dirty handkerchief is still dirty, even if it smells of perfume . . . ! On the other hand, it hurts me to find out that what I was striving for wasn't finer, more substantial. 50 It hurts me to see you sunk so low that you're inferior to your own cook. It hurts like watching flowers beaten down by autumn rains and turned into mud.

JULIE. You talk as if you were already above me. 55

JEAN. I am. You see, I could make you a countess, but you could never make me a count.

JULIE. But I'm the child of a count—something you could never be!

JEAN. That's true. But I could be the father of 60 counts—if . . .

JULIE. But you're a thief. I'm not.

JEAN. There are worse things than being a thief! Besides, when I'm working in a house, I consider myself sort of a member of the family, like one of 65 the children. And you don't call it stealing when a child snatches a berry off a full bush. [*His passion is aroused again.*] Miss Julie, you're a glorious woman, much too good for someone like me! You were drinking and you lost your head. Now you 70 want to cover up your mistake by telling yourself that you love me! You don't. Maybe there was a physical attraction—but then your love is no better than mine.——I could never be satisfied to be no more than an animal to you, and I could never 75 arouse real love in you.

JULIE. Are you sure of that?

JEAN. You're suggesting it's possible——Oh, I could fall in love with you, no doubt about it. You're beautiful, you're refined——[*approaching and tak-* 80 *ing her hand*]——cultured, lovable when you want to be, and once you start a fire in a man, it never goes out. [*putting his arm around her waist*] You're like hot, spicy wine, and one kiss from you . . . [*He tries to lead her out, but she slowly frees* 85 *herself.*]

JULIE. Let me go!?——You'll never win me like that.

JEAN. *How* then?——Not like that? Not with caresses and pretty speeches. Not with plans about 90 the future or rescue from disgrace! *How* then?

JULIE. How? How? I don't know!——I have no idea!——I detest you as I detest rats, but I can't escape from you.

JEAN. Escape with me!

JULIE. [*pulling herself together*]. Escape? Yes, we must escape!——But I'm so tired. Give me a glass of wine? [JEAN *pours the wine. She looks at her watch.*] But we must talk first. We still have a little time. [*She drains the glass, then holds it out for more.*]

JEAN. Don't drink so fast. It'll go to your head.

JULIE. What does it matter?

JEAN. What does it matter? It's vulgar to get drunk! What did you want to tell me?

JULIE. We must escape! But first we must talk, I mean I must talk. You've done all the talking up to now. You told about your life, now I want to tell about mine, so we'll know all about each other before we go off together.

JEAN. Just a minute! Forgive me! If you don't want to regret it afterwards, you'd better think twice before revealing any secrets about yourself.

JULIE. Aren't you my friend?

JEAN. Yes, sometimes! But don't rely on me.

JULIE. You're only saying that.——Besides, everyone already knows my secrets.——You see, my mother was a commoner—very humble background. She was brought up believing in social equality, women's rights, and all that. The idea of marriage repelled her. So, when my father proposed, she replied that she would never become his wife, but he could be her lover. He insisted that he didn't want the woman he loved to be less respected than he. But his passion ruled him, and when she explained that the world's respect meant nothing to her, he accepted her conditions.

But now his friends avoided him and his life was restricted to taking care of the estate, which couldn't satisfy him. I came into the world—against my mother's wishes, as far as I can understand. She wanted to bring me up as a child of nature, and, what's more, to learn everything a boy had to learn, so that I might be an example of how a woman can be as good as a man. I had to wear boy's clothes and learn to take care of horses, but I was never allowed in the cowshed. I had to groom and harness the horses and go hunting—and even had to watch them slaughter animals—that was disgusting! On the estate men were put on women's jobs and women on men's jobs—with the result that the property became run down and we became the laughing stock of the district. Finally, my father must have awakened from his trance because he rebelled and changed everything his way. My parents were then married quietly. Mother became ill—I don't know what illness it was—but she often had convulsions, hid in the attic and in the garden, and sometimes stayed out all night. Then came the great fire, which you've heard about. The house, the stables, and the cowshed all burned down, under very curious circumstances, suggesting arson, because the accident happened the day after the insurance had expired. The quarterly premium my father sent in was delayed because of a messenger's carelessness and didn't arrive in time. [*She fills her glass and drinks.*]

JEAN. Don't drink any more!

JULIE. Oh, what does it matter.——We were left penniless and had to sleep in the carriages. My father had no idea where to find money to rebuild the house because he had so slighted his old friends that they had forgotten him. Then my mother suggested that he borrow from a childhood friend of hers, a brick manufacturer who lived nearby. Father got the loan without having to pay interest, which surprised him. And that's how the estate was rebuilt.——[*drinks again*] Do you know who started the fire?

JEAN. The Countess, your mother.

JULIE. Do you know who the brick manufacturer was?

JEAN. Your mother's lover?

JULIE. Do you know whose money it was?

JEAN. Wait a moment—no, I don't.

JULIE. It was my mother's.

JEAN. You mean the Count's, unless they didn't sign an agreement when they were married.

JULIE. They didn't.——My mother had a small inheritance which she didn't want under my father's control, so she entrusted it to her—friend.

JEAN. Who stole it!

JULIE. Exactly! He kept it.——All this my father found out, but he couldn't bring it to court, couldn't repay his wife's lover, couldn't prove it was his wife's money! It was my mother's revenge for being forced into marriage against her will. It nearly drove him to suicide—there was a rumor that he tried with a pistol, but failed. So, he managed to live through it and my mother had to suffer for what she'd done. You can imagine that those were a

terrible five years for me. I loved my father, but I sided with my mother because I didn't know the circumstances. I learned from her to hate men—you've heard how she hated the whole male sex—
5   and I swore to her I'd never be a slave to any man.

JEAN. But you got engaged to that lawyer.

JULIE. In order to make him my slave.

JEAN. And he wasn't willing.

JULIE. He was willing, all right, but I wouldn't
10   let him. I got tired of him.

JEAN. I saw it—out near the stable.

JULIE. What did you see?

JEAN. I saw—how he broke off the engagement.

JULIE. That's a lie! I was the one who broke it
15   off. Has he said that he did? That swine . . .

JEAN. He was no swine, I'm sure. So, you hate men, Miss Julie?

JULIE. Yes!——Most of the time! But sometimes—when the weakness comes, when passion
20   burns! Oh, God, will the fire never die out?

JEAN. Do you hate me, too?

JULIE. Immeasurably! I'd like to have you put to death, like an animal . . .

JEAN. I see—the penalty for bestiality°—the
25   woman gets two years at hard labor and the animal is put to death. Right?

JULIE. Exactly!

JEAN. But there's no prosecutor here—and no animal. So, what'll we do?
30   JULIE. Go away!

JEAN. To torment each other to death?

JULIE. No! To be happy for—two days, a week, as long as we can be happy, and then—die . . .

JEAN. Die? That's stupid! It's better to open a
35   hotel!

JULIE [without listening].——on the shore of Lake Como, where the sun always shines, where the laurels are green at Christmas and the oranges glow.
40   JEAN. Lake Como is a rainy hole, and I never saw any oranges outside the stores. But tourists are attracted there because there are plenty of villas to be rented out to lovers, and that's a profitable business.——Do you know why? Because they
45   sign a lease for six months—and then leave after three weeks!

bestiality   copulating with an animal

JULIE [naively]. Why after three weeks?

JEAN. They quarrel, of course! But they still have to pay the rent in full! And so you rent the villas out again. And that's the way it goes, time after
50   time. There's never a shortage of love—even if it doesn't last long!

JULIE. You don't want to die with me?

JEAN. I don't want to die at all! For one thing, I like living, and for another, I think suicide is a
55   crime against the Providence which gave us life.

JULIE. You believe in God? *You?*

JEAN. Of course I do. And I go to church every other Sunday.——To be honest, I'm tired of all this, and I'm going to bed.
60   JULIE. Are you? And do you think I can let it go at that? A man owes something to the woman he's shamed.

JEAN [taking out his purse and throwing a silver coin on the table]. Here! I don't like owing anything to
65   anybody.

JULIE [pretending not to notice the insult]. Do you know what the law states . . .

JEAN. Unfortunately the law doesn't state any punishment for the woman who seduces a man!
70   JULIE [as before]. Do you see any way out but to leave, get married, and then separate?

JEAN. Suppose I refuse such a *mésalliance?°*

JULIE. *Mésalliance* . . .

JEAN. Yes, for me! You see, I come from better
75   stock than you. There's no arsonist in my family.

JULIE. How do you know?

JEAN. You can't prove otherwise. We don't keep charts on our ancestors—there's just the police records! But I've read about your family. Do you
80   know who the founder was? He was a miller who let the king sleep with his wife one night during the Danish War. I don't have any noble ancestors like that. I don't have any noble ancestors at all, but I could become one myself.
85   JULIE. This is what I get for opening my heart to someone unworthy, for giving my family's honor . . .

JEAN. Dishonor!——Well, I told you so: when people drink, they talk, and talk is dangerous!
90   JULIE. Oh, how I regret it!——How I regret it!——If you at least loved me.

mésalliance   marriage with a social inferior

JEAN. For the last time—what do you want? Shall I cry; shall I jump over your riding crop? Shall I kiss you and lure you off to Lake Como for three weeks, and then God knows what . . . ? What shall
5 I do? What do you want? This is getting painfully embarrassing! But that's what happens when you stick your nose in women's business. Miss Julie! I see that you're unhappy. I know you're suffering, but I can't understand you. We don't have such
10 romantic ideas; there's not this kind of hate between us. Love is a game we play when we get time off from work, but we don't have all day and night, like you. I think you're sick, really sick. Your mother was crazy, and her ideas have poisoned
15 your life.

JULIE. Be kind to me. At least now you're talking like a human being.

JEAN. Be human yourself, then. You spit on me, and you won't let me wipe myself off——

20 JULIE. Help me! Help me! Just tell me what to do, where to go!

JEAN. In God's name, if I only knew myself!

JULIE. I've been crazy, out of my mind, but isn't there any way out?

25 JEAN. Stay here and keep calm! No one knows anything!

JULIE. Impossible! The others know and Kristine knows.

JEAN. No they don't, and they'd never believe a
30 thing like that!

JULIE [*hesitantly*]. But—it could happen again!

JEAN. That's true!

JULIE. And then?

JEAN [*frightened*]. Then?——Why didn't I think
35 about that? Yes, there is only one thing to do—get away from here! Right away! I can't come with you, then we'd be finished, so you'll have to go alone—away—anywhere!

JULIE. Alone?——Where?——I can't do that!

40 JEAN. You must! And before the Count gets back! If you stay, you know what'll happen. Once you make a mistake like this, you want to continue because the damage has already been done . . . Then you get bolder and bolder—until finally you're
45 caught! So leave! Later you can write to the Count and confess everything—except that it was me! He'll never guess who it was, and he's not going to be eager to find out, anyway.

JULIE. I'll go if you come with me.

JEAN. Are you out of your head? Miss Julie runs 50 away with her servant! In two days it would be in the newspapers, and that's something your father would never live through.

JULIE. I can't go and I can't stay! Help me! I'm so tired, so terribly tired.——Order me! Set me in 55 motion!—I can't think or act on my own . . .

JEAN. What miserable creatures you people are! You strut around with your noses in the air as if you were the lords of creation! All right, I'll order you. Go upstairs and get dressed! Get some money 60 for the trip, and then come back down!

JULIE [*in a half-whisper*]. Come up with me!

JEAN. To your room?——Now you're crazy again! [*hesitates for a moment*] No! Go, at once! [*takes her hand to lead her out*] 65

JULIE [*as she leaves*]. Speak kindly to me, Jean!

JEAN. An order always sounds unkind—now you know how it feels. [JEAN, *alone, sighs with relief. He sits at the table, takes out a notebook and pencil, and begins adding up figures, counting aloud as he works.* 70 *He continues in dumb show until* KRISTINE *enters, dressed for church. She is carrying a white tie and shirt front.*]

KRISTINE. Lord Jesus, what a mess! What have you been up to?

JEAN. Oh, Miss Julie dragged everybody in here. 75 You mean you didn't hear anything? You must have been sleeping soundly.

KRISTINE. Like a log.

JEAN. And dressed for church already?

KRISTINE. Of course! You remember you prom- 80 ised to come with me to communion today!

JEAN. Oh, yes, that's right.——And you brought my things. Come on, then! [*He sits down.* KRISTINE *starts to put on his shirt front and tie. Pause.* JEAN *begins sleepily*] What's the gospel text for today? 85

KRISTINE. On St. John's Day?—the beheading of John the Baptist,° I should think!

JEAN. Ah, that'll be a long one, for sure.—— Hey, you're choking me!——Oh, I'm sleepy, so sleepy! 90

KRISTINE. Yes, what have you been doing, up all night? Your face is absolutely green.

John the Baptist See Mark 6:17–29, where it is told how Salome danced before King Herod Antipas and claimed the head of John the Baptist as her reward. (In fact, the appointed gospel reading for the day relates the birth of John.)

JEAN. I've been sitting here gabbing with Miss Julie.

KRISTINE. She has no idea what's proper, that one! [*pause*]

5 JEAN. You know, Kristine . . .

KRISTINE. What?

JEAN. It's really strange when you think about it.——Her!

KRISTINE. What's so strange?

10 JEAN. Everything! [*pause*]

KRISTINE [*looking at the half-empty glasses standing on the table*]. Have you been drinking together, too?

JEAN. Yes.

KRISTINE. Shame on you!——Look me in the eye!

15 JEAN. Well?

KRISTINE. Is it possible? Is it possible?

JEAN [*thinking it over for a moment*]. Yes, it is.

KRISTINE. Ugh! I never would have believed it! No, shame on you, shame!

20 JEAN. You're not jealous of her, are you?

KRISTINE. No, not of her! If it had been Clara or Sofie I'd have scratched your eyes out!——I don't know why, but that's the way I feel.——Oh, it's disgusting!

25 JEAN. Are you angry at her, then?

KRISTINE. No, at you! That was an awful thing to do, awful! Poor girl!——No, I don't care who knows it—I won't stay in a house where we can't respect the people we work for.

30 JEAN. Why should we respect them?

KRISTINE. You're so clever, you tell me! Do you want to wait on people who can't behave decently? Do you? You disgrace yourself that way, if you ask me.

35 JEAN. But it's a comfort to know they aren't any better than us.

KRISTINE. Not for me. If they're no better, what do we have to strive for to better ourselves.—— And think of the Count! Think of him! As if he hasn't had enough misery in his life! Lord Jesus!

40 No, I won't stay in this house any longer!——And it had to be with someone like you! If it had been that lawyer, if it had been a real gentleman . . .

JEAN. What do you mean?

45 KRISTINE. Oh, you're all right for what you are, but there are men and gentlemen, after all!—— No, this business with Miss Julie I can never forget. She was so proud, so arrogant with men, you wouldn't have believed she could just go and give herself—and to someone like you! And she was 50 going to have poor Diana shot for running after the gatekeepers' mutt!——Yes, I'm giving my notice, I mean it—I won't stay here any longer. On the twenty-fourth of October, I leave!

JEAN. And then? 55

KRISTINE. Well, since the subject has come up, it's about time you looked around for something since we're going to get married, in any case.

JEAN. Where am I going to look? I couldn't find a job like this if I was married. 60

KRISTINE. No, that's true. But you can find work as a porter or as a caretaker in some government office. The state doesn't pay much, I know, but it's secure, and there's a pension for the wife and children . . . 65

JEAN [*grimacing*]. That's all very well, but it's a bit early for me to think about dying for a wife and children. My ambitions are a little higher than that.

KRISTINE. Your ambitions, yes! Well, you have 70 obligations, too! Think about them!

JEAN. Don't start nagging me about obligations, I know what I have to do! [*listening for something outside*] Besides, this is something we have plenty of time to think over. Go and get ready for church. 75

KRISTINE. Who's that walking around up there?

JEAN. I don't know, unless it's Clara.

KRISTINE [*going*]. You don't suppose it's the Count, who came home without us hearing him?

JEAN [*frightened*]. The Count? No, I don't think 80 so. He'd have rung.

KRISTINE [*going*]. Well, God help us! I've never seen anything like this before. [*The sun has risen and shines through the treetops in the park. The light shifts gradually until it slants in through the windows.* 85 JEAN *goes to the door and signals.* MISS JULIE *enters, dressed in travel clothes and carrying a small birdcage, covered with a cloth, which she places on a chair.*]

JULIE. I'm ready now.

JEAN. Shh! Kristine is awake. 90

JULIE [*very nervous during the following*]. Does she suspect something?

JEAN. She doesn't know anything. But my God, you look awful!

JULIE. Why? How do I look?

JEAN. You're pale as a ghost and—excuse me, but your face is dirty.

JULIE. Let me wash up then.——[*She goes to the* 5 *basin and washes her hands and face.*] Give me a towel!——Oh—the sun's coming up.

JEAN. Then the goblins will disappear.

JULIE. Yes, there must have been goblins out last night!——Jean, listen, come with me! I have some 10 money now.

JEAN [*hesitantly*]. Enough?

JULIE. Enough to start with. Come with me! I just can't travel alone on a day like this—midsummer day on a stuffy train—jammed in among 15 crowds of people staring at me. Eternal delays at every station, while I'd wish I had wings. No, I can't, I can't! And then there'll be memories, memories of midsummer days when I was little. The church—decorated with birch leaves and li- 20 lacs; dinner at the big table with relatives and friends; the afternoons in the park, dancing, music, flowers, and games. Oh, no matter how far we travel, the memories will follow in the baggage car, with remorse and guilt!

25 JEAN. I'll go with you—but right away, before it's too late. Right this minute!

JULIE. Get dressed, then! [*picking up the bird cage*]

JEAN. But no baggage! It would give us away!

JULIE. No, nothing! Only what we can have in 30 the compartment with us.

JEAN [*has taken his hat*]. What've you got there? What is it?

JULIE. It's only my greenfinch. I couldn't leave her behind.

35 JEAN. What? Bring a birdcage with us? You're out of your head! Put it down!

JULIE. It's the only thing I'm taking from my home —the only living being that loves me, since Diana was unfaithful. Don't be cruel! Let me take her!

40 JEAN. Put the cage down, I said!——And don't talk so loudly—Kristine will hear us!

JULIE. No, I won't leave her in the hands of strangers! I'd rather you killed her.

JEAN. Bring the thing here, then, I'll cut its head 45 off!

JULIE. Oh! But don't hurt her! Don't . . . no, I can't.

JEAN. Bring it here! I can!

JULIE [*taking the bird out of the cage and kissing it*]. Oh, my little Serena, must you die and leave your 50 mistress?

JEAN. Please don't make a scene! Your whole future is at stake! Hurry up! [*He snatches the bird from her, carries it over to the chopping block, and picks up a meat cleaver. Miss Julie turns away.*] You should 55 have learned how to slaughter chickens instead of how to fire pistols. [*He chops off the bird's head.*] Then you wouldn't feel faint at the sight of blood.

JULIE [*screaming*]. Kill me, too! Kill me! You, who can slaughter an innocent animal without blinking 60 an eye! Oh, how I hate, how I detest you! There's blood between us now! I curse the moment I set eyes on you! I curse the moment I was conceived in my mother's womb!

JEAN. What good does cursing do? Let's go! 65

JULIE [*approaching the chopping block, as if drawn against her will*]. No, I don't want to go yet. I can't . . . until I see . . . Shh! I hear a carriage——[*She listens, but her eyes never leave the cleaver and the chopping block.*] Do you think I can't stand the sight 70 of blood? You think I'm so weak . . . Oh—I'd like to see your blood and your brains on a chopping block!——I'd like to see your whole sex swimming in a sea of blood, like my little bird . . . I think I could drink from your skull! I'd like to bathe my 75 feet in your open chest and eat your heart roasted whole!——You think I'm weak. You think I love you because my womb craved your seed. You think I want to carry your spawn under my heart and nourish it with my blood—bear your child and 80 take your name! By the way, what is your family name? I've never heard it.——Do you have one? I was to be Mrs. Bootblack—or Madame Pigsty. ——You dog, who wears my collar, you lackey, who bears my coat of arms on your buttons—do 85 I have to share you with my cook, compete with my own servant? Oh! Oh! Oh!——You think I'm a coward who wants to run away! No, now I'm staying—and let the storm break! My father will come home . . . to find his desk broken open . . . 90 and his money gone! Then he'll ring—that bell . . . twice for his valet—and then he'll send for the police . . . and then I'll tell everything! Everything! Oh, what a relief it'll be to have it all end—if only

it will end!——And then he'll have a stroke and die . . . That'll be the end of all of us—and there'll be peace . . . quiet . . . eternal rest!——And then our coat of arms will be broken against his coffin—
5 the family title extinct—but the valet's line will go on in an orphanage . . . win laurels in the gutter, and end in jail!

JEAN. There's the blue blood talking! Very good, Miss Julie! Just don't let that miller out of the closet!
10 [KRISTINE enters, dressed for church, with a psalmbook in her hand.]

JULIE [rushing to KRISTINE and falling into her arms, as if seeking protection]. Help me Kristine! Help me against this man!
15 KRISTINE [unmoved and cold]. What a fine way to behave on a Sunday morning! [sees the chopping block] And look at this mess!——What does all this mean? Why all this screaming and carrying on?

JULIE. Kristine! You're a woman and my friend!
20 Beware of this swine!

JEAN [uncomfortable]. While you ladies discuss this, I'll go in and shave. [slips off right]

JULIE. You must listen to me so you'll understand!
25 KRISTINE. No, I could never understand such disgusting behavior! Where are you off to in your traveling clothes?——And he had his hat on.—— Well?——Well?——

JULIE. Listen to me, Kristine! Listen, and I'll tell
30 you everything——

KRISTINE. I don't want to hear it . . .

JULIE. But you must listen to me . . .

KRISTINE. What about? If it's about silliness with Jean, I'm not interested, because it's none of my
35 business. But if you're thinking of tricking him into running out, we'll soon put a stop to that!

JULIE [extremely nervous]. Try to be calm now, Kristine, and listen to me! I can't stay here, and neither can Jean—so we must go away . . .
40 KRISTINE. Hm, hm!

JULIE [brightening]. You see, I just had an idea ——What if all three of us go—abroad—to Switzerland and start a hotel together?——I have money, you see—and Jean and I could run it—
45 and I thought you, you could take care of the kitchen . . . Wouldn't that be wonderful?——Say yes! And come with us, and then everything will

be settled!——Oh, do say yes! [embracing KRISTINE and patting her warmly]

KRISTINE [coolly, thoughtfully]. Hm, hm! 50

JULIE [presto tempo].° You've never traveled, Kristine.——You must get out and see the world. You can't imagine how much fun it is to travel by train— always new faces—new countries.——And when we get to Hamburg, we'll stop off at the zoo— 55 you'll like that.——and then we'll go to the theater and the opera—and when we get to Munich, dear, there we have museums, with Rubens and Raphael, the great painters, as you know.——You've heard of Munich, where King Ludwig lived—the 60 king who went mad.——And then we'll see his castles—they're still there and they're like castles in fairy tales.——And from there it isn't far to Switzerland—and the Alps.——Imagine—the Alps have snow on them even in the middle of sum- 65 mer!——And oranges grow there and laurel trees that are green all year round——[JEAN can be seen in the wings right, sharpening his razor on a strop which he holds with his teeth and his left hand. He listens to the conversation with satisfaction, nodding now and then 70 in approval. MISS JULIE continues tempo prestissimo.]° And then we'll start a hotel—and I'll be at the desk, while Jean greets the guests . . . does the shopping . . . writes letters.——You have no idea what a life it'll be—the train whistles blowing and 75 the carriages arriving and the bells ringing in the rooms and down in the restaurant.——And I'll make out the bills—and I know how to salt them! . . . You'll never believe how timid travelers are when they have to pay their bills!——And you— 80 you'll be in charge of the kitchen.——Naturally, you won't have to stand over the stove yourself. ——And since you're going to be seen by people, you'll have to wear beautiful clothes.——And you, with your looks—no, I'm not flatter- 85 ing you—one fine day you'll grab yourself a husband!——You'll see!——A rich Englishman—they're so easy to——[slowing down]—— catch—and then we'll get rich—and build ourselves a villa on Lake Como.——It's true it rains 90

presto tempo   in rapid rhythm
tempo prestissimo   faster and faster

there a little now and then, but——[*dully*]——
the sun has to shine sometimes—although it
looks dark—and then . . . of course we could
always come back home again——[*pause*]——
5 here—or somewhere else——

KRISTINE. Listen, Miss Julie, do you believe all
this?

JULIE [*crushed*]. Do I believe it?

KRISTINE. Yes!

10 JULIE [*wearily*]. I don't know. I don't believe in
anything any more. [*She sinks down on the bench
and cradles her head in her arms on the table.*] Nothing!
Nothing at all!

KRISTINE [*turning right to where* JEAN *is standing*].
15 So, you thought you'd run out!

JEAN [*embarrassed; puts the razor on the table*]. Run
out? That's no way to put it. You hear Miss Julie's
plan, and even if she is tired after being up all
night, it's still a practical plan.

20 KRISTINE. Now you listen to me! Did you think
I'd work as a cook for that . . .

JEAN [*sharply*]. You watch what you say in front
of your mistress! Do you understand?

KRISTINE. Mistress!

25 JEAN. Yes!

KRISTINE. Listen to him! Listen to him!

JEAN. Yes, you listen! It'd do you good to listen
more and talk less! Miss Julie is your mistress. If
you despise her, you have to despise yourself for
30 the same reason!

KRISTINE. I've always had enough self-
respect——

JEAN.——to be able to despise other people!

KRISTINE.——to stop me from doing anything
35 that's beneath me. You can't say that the Count's
cook has been up to something with the groom or
the swineherd! Can you?

JEAN. No, you were lucky enough to get hold of
a gentleman!

40 KRISTINE. Yes, a gentleman who sells the Count's
oats from the stable.

JEAN. You should talk—taking a commission from
the grocer and bribes from the butcher.

KRISTINE. What?

45 JEAN. And you say you can't respect your employers any longer. You, you, you!

KRISTINE. Are you coming to church with me,
now? You could use a good sermon after your fine
deed!

50 JEAN. No, I'm not going to church today. You'll
have to go alone and confess what you've been
up to.

KRISTINE. Yes, I'll do that, and I'll bring back
enough forgiveness for you, too. The Savior suf-
55 fered and died on the Cross for all our sins, and
if we go to Him with faith and a penitent heart,
He takes all our sins on Himself.

JEAN. Even grocery sins?

JULIE. And do you believe that, Kristine?

60 KRISTINE. It's my living faith, as sure as I stand
here. It's the faith I learned as a child, Miss Julie,
and kept ever since. "Where sin abounded, grace
did much more abound!"°

JULIE. Oh, if I only had your faith. If only . . .

65 KRISTINE. Well, you see, we can't have it without
God's special grace, and that isn't given to everyone——

JULIE. Who is it given to then?

KRISTINE. That's the great secret of the workings
70 of grace, Miss Julie, and God is no respecter of
persons, for the last shall be the first . . .

JULIE. Then He does respect the last.

KRISTINE [*continuing*]. . . . and it is easier for a
camel to go through the eye of a needle, than for
75 a rich man to enter the Kingdom of God. That's
how it is, Miss Julie! Anyhow, I'm going now—
alone, and on the way I'm going to tell the groom
not to let any horses out, in case anyone wants to
leave before the Count gets back!——Goodbye!
80 [*leaves*]

JEAN. What a witch!——And all this because of
a greenfinch!——

JULIE [*dully*]. Never mind the greenfinch!——Can
you see any way out of this? Any end to it?

85 JEAN [*thinking*]. No!

JULIE. What would you do in my place?

JEAN. In your place? Let's see—as a person of
position, as a woman who had—fallen. I don't
know—wait, now I know.

90 JULIE [*taking the razor and making a gesture*]. You
mean like this?

"Where . . . abound!" from Paul's epistle to the Romans,
5:20–21

JEAN. Yes! But—understand—*I* wouldn't do it! That's the difference between us!

JULIE. Because you're a man and I'm a woman? What sort of difference is that?

5   JEAN. The usual difference—between a man and a woman.

JULIE [*with the razor in her hand*]. I want to, but I can't!——My father couldn't either, the time he should have done it.

10   JEAN. No, he shouldn't have! He had to revenge himself first.

JULIE. And now my mother is revenged again, through me.

JEAN. Didn't you ever love your father, Miss Julie?

15   JULIE. Oh yes, deeply, but I've hated him, too. I must have done so without realizing it! It was he who brought me up to despise my own sex, making me half woman, half man. Whose fault is what's happened? My father's, my mother's, my

20   own? My own? I don't have anything that's my own. I don't have a single thought that I didn't get from my father, not an emotion that I didn't get from my mother, and this last idea—that all people are equal—I got that from my fiancé.——

25   That's why I called him a swine! How can it be my fault? Shall I let Jesus take on the blame, the way Kristine does?——No, I'm too proud to do that and too sensible—thanks to my father's teachings.——And as for someone rich not going

30   to heaven, that's a lie. But Kristine won't get in—how will she explain the money she has in the savings bank? Whose fault is it?——What does it matter whose fault it is? I'm still the one who has to bear the blame, face the consequences . . .

35   JEAN. Yes, but . . . [*the bell rings sharply twice. Miss Julie jumps up. Jean changes his coat.*] The Count is back! Do you suppose Kristine—[*He goes to the speaking tube, taps the lid, and listens.*]

JULIE. He's been to his desk!

40   JEAN. It's Jean, sir! [*listening; the audience cannot hear the Count's voice.*] Yes, sir! [*listening*] Yes, sir! Right away! [*listening*] At once, sir! [*listening*] I see, in half an hour!

JULIE [*desperately frightened*]. What did he say?

45   Dear Lord, what did he say?

JEAN. He wants his boots and his coffee in half an hour.

JULIE. So, in half an hour! Oh, I'm so tired. I'm not able to do anything. I can't repent, can't run away, can't stay, can't live—can't die! Help me

50   now! Order me, and I'll obey like a dog! Do me this last service, save my honor, save his name! You know what I *should* do, but don't have the will to . . . You will it, you order me to do it!

JEAN. I don't know why——but now I can't

55   either——I don't understand.——It's as if this coat made it impossible for me to order you to do anything.——And now, since the Count spoke to me—I—I can't really explain it—but—ah, it's the damn lackey in me!——I think if the Count came down

60   here now—and ordered me to cut my throat, I'd do it on the spot.

JULIE. Then pretend you're he, and I'm you!——You gave such a good performance before when you knelt at my feet.——You were a real

65   nobleman.——Or—have you ever seen a hypnotist in the theatre? [JEAN *nods.*] He says to his subject: "Take the broom," and he takes it. He says: "Sweep," and he sweeps——

JEAN. But the subject has to be asleep.

70   JULIE [*ecstatically*]. I'm already asleep.——The whole room is like smoke around me . . . and you look like an iron stove . . . shaped like a man in black, with a tall hat—and your eyes glow like coals when the fire is dying—and your face is a

75   white patch, like ashes——[*The sunlight has reached the floor and now shines on* JEAN.]——it's so warm and good——[*She rubs her hands as if warming them before a fire.*]——and bright—and so peaceful!

JEAN [*taking the razor and putting it in her hand*].

80   Here's the broom! Go now while it's bright—out to the barn—and . . . [*whispers in her ear*]

JULIE [*awake*]. Thank you. I'm going now to rest! But just tell me—that those who are first can also receive the gift of grace. Say it, even if you don't

85   believe it.

JEAN. The first? No, I can't!——But wait—Miss Julie—now I know! You're no longer among the first—you're now among—the last!

JULIE. That's true.——I'm among the very last.

90   I'm the last one of all! Oh!——But now I can't go!——Tell me once more to go!

JEAN. No, now I can't either! I can't!

JULIE. And the first shall be the last!

JEAN. Don't think, don't think! You're taking all

95   my strength from me, making me a coward.——

What was that? I thought the bell moved!——No!
Shall we stuff paper in it?——To be so afraid of a
bell!——But it isn't just a bell.——There's someone behind it—a hand sets it in motion—and
5 something else sets the hand in motion.——Maybe
if you cover your ears—cover your ears! But then
it rings even louder! rings until someone answers.——And then it's too late! And then the
police come—and—then——[*The bell rings twice*
10 *loudly.* JEAN *flinches, then straightens up.*] It's horrible! But there's no other way!——Go! [MISS JULIE
walks firmly out through the door.]

Henrik Ibsen

1828–1906

Hedda Gabler

1890

Ibsen has long been regarded as a special critic of Norwegian society in the 1870's and 1880's and hence as somewhat exclusively of his own time. Perhaps, however, the view of Ibsen as passé is now itself passé. He never was primarily a social critic, he was primarily dramatic craftsman and moralist. And his mature plays are still virtually unique in the firmness of their dramaturgy and of their moral conviction. With Strindberg and Chekhov he is one of the founders of the modern drama.

Hedda Gabler, the fruit of forty years of theatrical experience, represents his craftsmanship at its most assured. It is an almost perfectly artistic play—concentrated, coherent, symmetrical; and its structure is an almost perfect reflection of the nature of its leading character.

The central motive in the play is Hedda's desire to mold a human destiny. She conceives this destiny as a triumph of the Dionysian spirit, for she would know vicariously an abandon that she cannot know in her own person; and she selects a man as her deputy because, having rejected her own womanhood, she identifies herself with the dominant male role. The play rises naturally to crisis when she sends Lövborg out, so she imagines, to an evening of exultant revel. But the collapse of her venture is inherent in the spirit in which she conceived it. What she calls her "craving for life" is not a natural appetite; her will to dominate men incorporates also her will to destroy them; she has inevitably selected a weakling to do her living for her. When the third-act curtain rises on the gray weariness of the morning after, the play has turned as inevitably toward her catastrophe as before this it turned toward her illusory triumph. Her own character is a fate as unrelenting as any the Delphic Oracle could have pronounced. Hence the spare and classic structure of the play.

If *Hedda Gabler* is like the classic drama in its deft ordering of plot, it resembles it too in its multitude of ironies. But as its plot is spun not by divine agency but by human character, so also its ironies are derived not from a metaphysical perspective but from an ethical one.

Enough of these ironies tend toward comedy to lighten the whole with a genuine if sometimes grim humor. There is, for example, Aunt Julia's utterly devoted, utterly damning admiration for a nephew whom "no one can beat" at "collecting and arranging things." There is Tesman's own perfectly daft accession of wonder when Hedda burns the manuscript ("I wonder, now, whether this sort of thing is usual in young wives? Eh?"). There is the descent from Hedda's breathless memory of "something beautiful, something fascinating—something daring" to the bathos of the thing remembered: the prurient girl, hiding behind an illustrated paper and listening to her young man talk about sex.

As these instances make clear, however, the disparities that such irony calls attention to are ethically revealing as well as sometimes amusing. Ibsen often invites a double perspective of this sort when he is most deeply earnest. When he wants to emphasize the difference between a superficial social view of people and a profoundly ethical view, he so orders his play that characters who are in sharp ethical contrast are placed in ironic juxtaposition.

Hedda herself is high fashion. She has style and wit, and a kind of verve. But from a moral perspective, the attributes for which she is so generally admired are inconsequential. To contrast with her, Ibsen introduces good people and right actions through the back and side doors, so to speak, in humble and almost ridiculous guise. Lovingkindness enters in the person of a garrulous maiden aunt bearing an old pair of embroidered morning slippers. Rectitude glimmers, goes out, then glimmers again in her dull and pedantic nephew. But the most exact foil to Hedda is the fragile young woman from the provinces, "dressed not quite in the latest fashion," who reveals little by little the fullness of womanly courage and passion. Through these lesser characters, Ibsen would show us that human goodness characteristically reveals itself in those whom complacency would overlook and pride disdain.

Hedda Gabler

IBSEN

*Translated by William Archer and
Sir Edmund Gosse*

CHARACTERS°

GEORGE TESMAN
HEDDA TESMAN *his wife*
MISS JULIANA TESMAN *his aunt*
MRS. ELVSTED
JUDGE BRACK
EILERT LÖVBORG
BERTA *servant at the Tesman's*

SCENE. *Tesman's villa, in the west end of
Christiania.*

ACT I

[*A spacious, handsome and tastefully furnished drawing-room, decorated in dark colors.
In the back, a wide doorway with curtains
drawn back, leading into a smaller room dec-*

Characters: Judge Brack In Norway during the
1880's official position was a general determinant
of social standing, and official titles were in frequent
use. The titles that may prove obscure or misleading
in this translation are those of "Judge" Brack, an
assessor, or associate judge; "Secretary" Falk, a
cabinet minister; and "Sheriff" Elvsted, a district
magistrate. Tesman, as holder of a scholarship in
his field, has an officially conferred status though
he is called by no title.

From The Collected Works of Henrik Ibsen,
*Volume X, entirely revised and edited by William
Archer, copyright 1907 by Charles Scribner's Sons,
New York, 1935 by Frank Archer. Reprinted by
permission of the publishers.*

*orated in the same style as the drawing-room.
In the right-hand wall of the front room, a
folding door leading out to the hall. In the
opposite wall, on the left, a glass door, also
with curtains drawn back. Through the panes
can be seen part of a verandah outside, and
trees covered with autumn foliage. An oval
table, with a cover on it, and surrounded by
chairs, stands well forward. In front, by the
wall on the right, a wide stove of dark por-
celain, a high-backed arm-chair, a cushioned
foot-rest, and two foot-stools. A settee, with a
small round table in front of it, fills the upper
right-hand corner. In front, on the left, a little
way from the wall, a sofa. Farther back than
the glass door, a piano. On either side of the
doorway at the back a whatnot with terra-cotta
and majolica ornaments.—Against the back
wall of the inner room a sofa, with a table, and
one or two chairs. Over the sofa hangs the
portrait of a handsome elderly man in a General's uniform. Over the table a hanging lamp,
with an opal glass shade.—A number of bouquets are arranged about the drawing-room,
in vases and glasses. Others lie upon the tables.
The floors in both rooms are covered with thick
carpets.—Morning light. The sun shines in
through the glass door.*

MISS JULIANA TESMAN, *with her bonnet on
and carrying a parasol, comes in from the hall,
followed by* BERTA, *who carries a bouquet
wrapped in paper.* MISS TESMAN *is a comely
and pleasant-looking lady of about sixty-five.
She is nicely but simply dressed in a gray
walking-costume.* BERTA *is a middle-aged
woman of plain and rather countrified appearance.*]

MISS TESMAN [*stops close to the door, listens,
and says softly*]. Upon my word, I don't believe they are stirring yet!

BERTA [*also softly*]. I told you so, Miss. Remember how late the steamboat got in last
night. And then, when they got home!—good
Lord, what a lot the young mistress had to un-
pack before she could get to bed.

MISS TESMAN. Well, well—let them have
their sleep out. But let us see that they get a

[10]
[15]
[20]
[25]
[30]
[35]
[40]
[45]
[50]

good breath of the fresh morning air when they do appear. [*She goes to the glass door and throws it open.*]

BERTA [*beside the table, at a loss what to do with the bouquet in her hand*]. I declare there isn't a bit of room left. I think I'll put it down here, Miss. [*She places it on the piano.*]

MISS TESMAN. So you've got a new mistress now, my dear Berta. Heaven knows it was a wrench to me to part with you.

BERTA [*on the point of weeping*]. And do you think it wasn't hard for me too, Miss? After all the blessed years I've been with you and Miss Rina.

MISS TESMAN. We must make the best of it, Berta. There was nothing else to be done. George can't do without you, you see—he absolutely can't. He has had you to look after him ever since he was a little boy.

BERTA. Ah, but, Miss Julia, I can't help thinking of Miss Rina lying helpless at home there, poor thing. And with only that new girl, too! She'll never learn to take proper care of an invalid.

MISS TESMAN. Oh, I shall manage to train her. And of course, you know, I shall take most of it upon myself. You needn't be uneasy about my poor sister, my dear Berta.

BERTA. Well, but there's another thing, Miss. I'm so mortally afraid I shan't be able to suit the young mistress.

MISS TESMAN. Oh, well—just at first there may be one or two things—

BERTA. Most like she'll be terrible grand in her ways.

MISS TESMAN. Well, you can't wonder at that —General Gabler's daughter! Think of the sort of life she was accustomed to in her father's time. Don't you remember how we used to see her riding down the road along with the General? In that long black habit—and with feathers in her hat?

BERTA. Yes, indeed—I remember well enough—! But good Lord, I should never have dreamt in those days that she and Master George would make a match of it.

MISS TESMAN. Nor I.—But, by-the-bye, Berta —while I think of it: in future you mustn't say Master George. You must say Dr. Tesman.

BERTA. Yes, the young mistress spoke of that too—last night—the moment they set foot in the house. Is it true, then, Miss?

MISS TESMAN. Yes, indeed it is. Only think, Berta—some foreign university has made him a doctor—while he has been abroad, you understand. I hadn't heard a word about it, until he told me himself upon the pier.

BERTA. Well, well, he's clever enough for anything, he is. But I didn't think he'd have gone in for doctoring people too.

MISS TESMAN. No, no, it's not that sort of doctor he is. [*Nods significantly.*] But let me tell you, we may have to call him something still grander before long.

BERTA. You don't say so! What can that be, Miss?

MISS TESMAN [*smiling*]. H'm—wouldn't you like to know! [*With emotion.*] Ah, dear, dear —if my poor brother could only look up from his grave now, and see what his little boy has grown into! [*Looks around.*] But bless me, Berta—why have you done this? Taken the chintz covers off all the furniture?

BERTA. The mistress told me to. She can't abide covers on the chairs, she says.

MISS TESMAN. Are they going to make this their everyday sitting-room then?

BERTA. Yes, that's what I understood—from the mistress. Master George—the doctor—he said nothing.

[GEORGE TESMAN *comes from the right into the inner room, humming to himself, and carrying an unstrapped empty portmanteau. He is a middle-sized, young-looking man of thirty-three, rather stout, with a round, open, cheerful face, fair hair and beard. He wears spectacles, and is somewhat carelessly dressed in comfortable indoor clothes.*]

MISS TESMAN. Good morning, good morning, George.

TESMAN [*in the doorway between the rooms*]. Aunt Julia! Dear Aunt Julia! [*Goes up to her and shakes hands warmly.*] Come all this way—so early! Eh?

MISS TESMAN. Why of course I had to come and see how you were getting on.

TESMAN. In spite of your having had no proper night's rest?

MISS TESMAN. Oh, that makes no difference to me.

5 TESMAN. Well, I suppose you got home all right from the pier? Eh?

MISS TESMAN. Yes, quite safely, thank goodness. Judge Brack was good enough to see me right to my door.

10 TESMAN. We were so sorry we couldn't give you a seat in the carriage. But you saw what a pile of boxes Hedda had to bring with her.

MISS TESMAN. Yes, she had certainly plenty of boxes.

15 BERTA [*to* TESMAN]. Shall I go in and see if there's anything I can do for the mistress?

TESMAN. No thank you, Berta—you needn't. She said she would ring if she wanted anything.

20 BERTA [*going towards the right*]. Very well.

TESMAN. But look here—take this portmanteau with you.

BERTA [*taking it*]. I'll put it in the attic.

[*She goes out by the hall door.*]

25 TESMAN. Fancy, Auntie—I had the whole of that portmanteau chock full of copies of documents. You wouldn't believe how much I have picked up from all the archives I have been examining—curious old details that no
30 one has had any idea of—

MISS TESMAN. Yes, you don't seem to have wasted your time on your wedding trip, George.

TESMAN. No, that I haven't. But do take off
35 your bonnet, Auntie. Look here! Let me untie the strings—eh?

MISS TESMAN [*while he does so*]. Well, well —this is just as if you were still at home with us.

40 TESMAN [*with the bonnet in his hand, looks at it from all sides*]. Why, what a gorgeous bonnet you've been investing in!

MISS TESMAN. I bought it on Hedda's account.

45 TESMAN. On Hedda's account? Eh?

MISS TESMAN. Yes, so that Hedda needn't be ashamed of me if we happened to go out together.

TESMAN [*patting her cheek*]. You always think of everything, Aunt Julia. [*Lays the bon-
50 net on a chair beside the table.*] And now, look here—suppose we sit comfortably on the sofa and have a little chat, till Hedda comes.

[*They seat themselves. She places her parasol in the corner of the sofa.*]
55
MISS TESMAN [*takes both his hands and looks at him*]. What a delight it is to have you again, as large as life, before my very eyes, George! My George—my poor brother's own boy!
60
TESMAN. And it's a delight for me, too, to see you again, Aunt Julia! You, who have been father and mother in one to me.

MISS TESMAN. Oh, yes, I know you will always keep a place in your heart for your old
65 aunts.

TESMAN. And what about Aunt Rina? No improvement—eh?

MISS TESMAN. Oh, no—we can scarcely look for any improvement in her case, poor thing.
70 There she lies, helpless, as she has lain for all these years. But heaven grant I may not lose her yet awhile! For if I did, I don't know what I should make of my life, George—especially now that I haven't you to look after any more.
75
TESMAN [*patting her back*]. There, there, there—!

MISS TESMAN [*suddenly changing her tone*]. And to think that here you are a married man, George!—And that you should be the one to
80 carry off Hedda Gabler, the beautiful Hedda Gabler! Only think of it—she, that was so beset with admirers!

TESMAN [*hums a little and smiles complacently*]. Yes, I fancy I have several good
85 friends about town who would like to stand in my shoes—eh?

MISS TESMAN. And then this fine long wedding-tour you have had! More than five— nearly six months—
90
TESMAN. Well, for me it has been a sort of tour of research as well. I have had to do so much grubbing among old records—and to read no end of books too, Auntie.

MISS TESMAN. Oh, yes, I suppose so. [*More
95 confidentially, and lowering her voice a little.*]

But listen now, George—have you nothing—nothing special to tell me?

TESMAN. As to our journey?

MISS TESMAN. Yes.

5   TESMAN. No, I don't know of anything except what I have told you in my letters. I had a doctor's degree conferred on me—but that I told you yesterday.

MISS TESMAN. Yes, yes, you did. But what I
10   mean is—haven't you any—any—expectations—?

TESMAN. Expectations?

MISS TESMAN. Why, you know, George—I'm your old auntie!

15   TESMAN. Why, of course I have expectations.

MISS TESMAN. Ah!

TESMAN. I have every expectation of being a professor one of these days.

MISS TESMAN. Oh, yes, a professor—

20   TESMAN. Indeed, I may say I am certain of it. But my dear Auntie—you know all about that already!

MISS TESMAN [laughing to herself]. Yes, of course I do. You are quite right there. [Chang-
25   ing the subject.] But we were talking about your journey. It must have cost a great deal of money, George?

TESMAN. Well, you see—my handsome traveling-scholarship went a good way.

30   MISS TESMAN. But I can't understand how you can have made it go far enough for two.

TESMAN. No, that's not so easy to understand—eh?

MISS TESMAN. And especially traveling with
35   a lady—they tell me that makes it ever so much more expensive.

TESMAN. Yes, of course—it makes it a little more expensive. But Hedda had to have this trip, Auntie! She really had to. Nothing else
40   would have done.

MISS TESMAN. No, no, I suppose not. A wedding-tour seems to be quite indispensable nowadays.—But tell me now—have you gone thoroughly over the house yet?

45   TESMAN. Yes, you may be sure I have. I have been afoot ever since daylight.

MISS TESMAN. And what do you think of it all?

TESMAN. I'm delighted! Quite delighted!

Only I can't think what we are to do with the   50
two empty rooms between this inner parlor and Hedda's bedroom.

MISS TESMAN [laughing]. Oh, my dear George, I dare say you may find some use for them—in the course of time.   55

TESMAN. Why of course you are quite right, Aunt Julia! You mean as my library increases—eh?

MISS TESMAN. Yes, quite so, my dear boy. It was your library I was thinking of.   60

TESMAN. I am specially pleased on Hedda's account. Often and often, before we were engaged, she said that she would never care to live anywhere but in Secretary Falk's villa.

MISS TESMAN. Yes, it was lucky that this   65
very house should come into the market, just after you had started.

TESMAN. Yes, Aunt Julia, the luck was on our side, wasn't it—eh?

MISS TESMAN. But the expense, my dear   70
George! You will find it very expensive, all this.

TESMAN [looks at her, a little cast down]. Yes, I suppose I shall, Aunt!

MISS TESMAN. Oh, frightfully!   75

TESMAN. How much do you think? In round numbers?—Eh?

MISS TESMAN. Oh, I can't even guess until all the accounts come in.

TESMAN. Well, fortunately, Judge Brack has   80
secured the most favourable terms for me,—so he said in a letter to Hedda.

MISS TESSMAN. Yes, don't be uneasy, my dear boy.—Besides, I have given security for the furniture and all the carpets.   85

TESMAN. Security? You? My dear Aunt Julia—what sort of security could you give?

MISS TESMAN. I have given a mortgage on our annuity.

TESMAN [jumps up]. What! On your—and   90
Aunt Rina's annuity!

MISS TESMAN. Yes, I knew of no other plan, you see.

TESMAN [placing himself before her]. Have you gone out of your senses, Auntie! Your   95
annuity—it's all that you and Aunt Rina have to live upon.

MISS TESMAN. Well, well, don't get so excited about it. It's only a matter of form you know—Judge Brack assured me of that. It was he that was kind enough to arrange the whole affair for me. A mere matter of form, he said.

TESMAN. Yes, that may be all very well. But nevertheless—

MISS TESMAN. You will have your own salary to depend upon now. And, good heavens, even if we did have to pay up a little—! To eke things out a bit at the start—! Why, it would be nothing but a pleasure to us.

TESMAN. Oh, Auntie—will you never be tired of making sacrifices for me!

MISS TESMAN [*rises and lays her hands on his shoulders*]. Have I had any other happiness in this world except to smooth your way for you, my dear boy? You, who have had neither father nor mother to depend on. And now we have reached the goal, George! Things have looked black enough for us, sometimes; but, thank heaven, now you have nothing to fear.

TESMAN. Yes, it is really marvelous how everything has turned out for the best.

MISS TESMAN. And the people who opposed you—who wanted to bar the way for you— now you have them at your feet. They have fallen, George. Your most dangerous rival—his fall was the worst.—And now he has to lie on the bed he has made for himself—poor misguided creature.

TESMAN. Have you heard anything of Eilert? Since I went away, I mean.

MISS TESMAN. Only that he is said to have published a new book.

TESMAN. What! Eilert Lövborg! Recently— eh?

MISS TESMAN. Yes, so they say. Heaven knows whether it can be worth anything! Ah, when your new book appears—that will be another story, George! What is it to be about?

TESMAN. It will deal with the domestic industries of Brabant during the Middle Ages.

MISS TESMAN. Fancy—to be able to write on such a subject as that!

TESMAN. However, it may be some time before the book is ready. I have all these collections to arrange first, you see.

MISS TESMAN. Yes, collecting and arranging —no one can beat you at that. There you are

my poor brother's own son.

TESMAN. I am looking forward eagerly to setting to work at it; especially now that I have my own delightful home to work in.

MISS TESMAN. And, most of all, now that you have got the wife of your heart, my dear George.

TESMAN [*embracing her*]. Oh, yes, yes, Aunt Julia. Hedda—she is the best part of all! [*Looks towards the doorway.*] I believe I hear her coming—eh?

[HEDDA *enters from the left through the inner room. She is a woman of nine-and-twenty. Her face and figure show refinement and distinction. Her complexion is pale and opaque. Her steel-gray eyes express a cold, unruffled repose. Her hair is of an agreeable medium brown, but not particularly abundant. She is dressed in a tasteful, somewhat loose-fitting morning-gown.*]

MISS TESMAN [*going to meet* HEDDA]. Good morning, my dear Hedda! Good morning, and a hearty welcome.

HEDDA [*holds out her hand*]. Good morning, dear Miss Tesman! So early a call! This is kind of you.

MISS TESMAN [*with some embarrassment*]. Well—has the bride slept well in her new home?

HEDDA. Oh yes, thanks. Passably.

TESMAN [*laughing*]. Passably! Come, that's good, Hedda! You were sleeping like a stone when I got up.

HEDDA. Fortunately. Of course one has always to accustom one's self to new surroundings, Miss Tesman—little by little. [*Looking towards the left.*] Oh—there the servant has gone and opened the verandah door, and let in a whole flood of sunshine.

MISS TESMAN [*going towards the door*]. Well, then, we will shut it.

HEDDA. No, no, not that! Tesman, please draw the curtains. That will give a softer light.

TESMAN [*at the door*]. All right—all right. There now, Hedda, now you have both shade and fresh air.

HEDDA. Yes, fresh air we certainly must have, with all these stacks of flowers— But— won't you sit down, Miss Tesman?

MISS TESMAN. No, thank you. Now that I have seen that everything is all right here—thank heaven!—I must be getting home again. My sister is lying longing for me, poor thing.

5 TESMAN. Give her my very best love, Auntie; and say I shall look in and see her later in the day.

MISS TESMAN. Yes, yes, I'll be sure to tell her. But by-the-bye, George—[*feeling in her* 10 *dress pocket*]—I have almost forgotten—I have something for you here.

TESMAN. What is it, Auntie? Eh?

MISS TESMAN [*produces a flat parcel wrapped in newspaper and hands it to him*]. Look here, 15 my dear boy.

TESMAN [*opening the parcel*]. Well, I declare! Have you really saved them for me, Aunt Julia! Hedda, isn't this touching—eh?

HEDDA [*beside the whatnot on the right*]. 20 Well, what is it?

TESMAN. My old morning-shoes! My slippers.

HEDDA. Indeed. I remember you often spoke of them while we were abroad.

25 TESMAN. Yes, I missed them terribly. [*Goes up to her.*] Now you shall see them, Hedda!

HEDDA [*going towards the stove*]. Thanks, I really don't care about it.

TESMAN [*following her*]. Only think—ill as 30 she was, Aunt Rina embroidered these for me. Oh you can't think how many associations cling to them.

HEDDA [*at the table*]. Scarcely for me.

MISS TESMAN. Of course not for Hedda, 35 George.

TESMAN. Well, but now that she belongs to the family, I thought—

HEDDA [*interrupting*]. We shall never get on with this servant, Tesman.

40 MISS TESMAN. Not get on with Berta?

TESMAN. Why, dear, what puts that in your head? Eh?

HEDDA [*pointing*]. Look there! She has left her old bonnet lying about on a chair.

45 TESMAN [*in consternation, drops the slippers on the floor*]. Why, Hedda—

HEDDA. Just fancy, if any one should come in and see it.

TESMAN. But Hedda—that's Aunt Julia's bonnet. 50

HEDDA. Is it!

MISS TESMAN [*taking up the bonnet*]. Yes, indeed it's mine. And what's more, it's not old, Madame Hedda.

HEDDA. I really did not look closely at it, 55 Miss Tesman.

MISS TESMAN [*trying on the bonnet*]. Let me tell you it's the first time I have worn it—the very first time.

TESMAN. And a very nice bonnet it is too— 60 quite a beauty!

MISS TESMAN. Oh, it's no such great thing, George. [*Looks around her.*] My parasol—? Ah, here. [*Takes it.*] For this is mine too—[*mutters*]—not Berta's. 65

TESMAN. A new bonnet and a new parasol! Only think, Hedda!

HEDDA. Very handsome indeed.

TESMAN. Yes, isn't it? But Auntie, take a good look at Hedda before you go! See how 70 handsome she is!

MISS TESMAN. Oh, my dear boy, there's nothing new in that. Hedda was always lovely. [*She nods and goes towards the right.*]

TESMAN [*following*]. Yes, but have you 75 noticed what splendid condition she is in? How she has filled out on the journey?

HEDDA [*crossing the room*]. Oh, do be quiet—!

MISS TESMAN [*who has stopped and turned*]. 80 Filled out?

TESMAN. Of course you don't notice it so much now that she has that dress on. But I, who can see—

HEDDA [*at the glass door, impatiently*]. Oh, 85 you can't see anything.

TESMAN. It must be the mountain air in the Tyrol—

HEDDA [*curtly, interrupting*]. I am exactly as I was when I started. 90

TESMAN. So you insist; but I'm quite certain you are not. Don't you agree with me, Auntie?

MISS TESMAN [*who has been gazing at her with folded hands*]. Hedda is lovely—lovely—lovely. [*Goes up to her, takes her head between* 95 *both hands, draws it downwards, and kisses*

her hair]. God bless and preserve Hedda Tesman—for George's sake.

HEDDA [*gently freeing herself*]. Oh—! Let
me go.

5 MISS TESMAN [*in quiet emotion*]. I shall not
let a day pass without coming to see you.

TESMAN. No you won't, will you, Auntie?
Eh?

MISS TESMAN. Good-bye—good-bye!

10 [*She goes out by the hall door.* TESMAN *ac-
companies her. The door remains half open.*
TESMAN *can be heard repeating his message to
Aunt Rina and his thanks for the slippers.*

In the meantime, HEDDA *walks about the
15 room raising her arms and clenching her hands
as if in desperation. Then she flings back the
curtains from the glass door, and stands there
looking out.*

Presently TESMAN *returns and closes the
20 door behind him.*]

TESMAN [*picks up the slippers from the
floor*]. What are you looking at, Hedda?

HEDDA [*once more calm and mistress of herself*]. I am only looking at the leaves. They are
25 so yellow—so withered.

TESMAN [*wraps up the slippers and lays
them on the table*]. Well you see, we are well
into September now.

HEDDA [*again restless*]. Yes, to think of it!
30 —Already in—in September.

TESMAN. Don't you think Aunt Julia's manner was strange, dear? Almost solemn? Can
you imagine what was the matter with her?
Eh?

35 HEDDA. I scarcely know her, you see. Is she
often like that?

TESMAN. No, not as she was today.

HEDDA [*leaving the glass door*]. Do you
think she was annoyed about the bonnet?

40 TESMAN. Oh, scarcely at all. Perhaps a little,
just at the moment—

HEDDA. But what an idea, to pitch her bonnet about in the drawing-room! No one does
that sort of thing.

45 TESMAN. Well you may be sure Aunt Julia
won't do it again.

HEDDA. In any case, I shall manage to make
my peace with her.

TESMAN. Yes, my dear, good Hedda, if you
only would.   50

HEDDA. When you call this afternoon, you
might invite her to spend the evening here.

TESMAN. Yes, that I will. And there's one
thing more you could do that would delight
her heart.   55

HEDDA. What is it?

TESMAN. If you could only prevail on yourself to say *du*° to her. For my sake, Hedda?
Eh?

HEDDA. No, no, Tesman—you really mustn't   60
ask that of me. I have told you so already. I
shall try to call her "Aunt"; and you must be
satisfied with that.

TESMAN. Well, well. Only I think now that
you belong to the family, you—   65

HEDDA. H'm—I can't in the least see why—
[*She goes up towards the middle doorway.*]

TESMAN [*after a pause*]. Is there anything
the matter with you, Hedda? Eh?

HEDDA. I'm only looking at my old piano. It   70
doesn't go at all well with all the other things.

TESMAN. The first time I draw my salary,
we'll see about exchanging it.

HEDDA. No, no—nó exchanging. I don't
want to part with it. Suppose we put it there   75
in the inner room, and then get another here
in its place. When it's convenient, I mean.

TESMAN [*a little taken aback*]. Yes—of
course we could do that.

HEDDA [*takes up the bouquet from the*   80
piano]. These flowers were not here last night
when we arrived.

TESMAN. Aunt Julia must have brought them
for you.

HEDDA [*examining the bouquet*]. A visiting-   85
card. [*Takes it out and reads.*] "Shall return
later in the day." Can you guess whose card it
is?

TESMAN. No. Whose? Eh?

HEDDA. The name is "Mrs. Elvsted."   90

---

du thou. Norwegian, like French and German, has a
familiar second-person pronoun *du* ("thou") which is
sharply distinguished from the formal or neutral *de*
("you"). The most significant occurrences of both
pronouns are called attention to in footnotes.

TESMAN. Is it really? Sheriff Elvsted's wife? Miss Rysing that was.

HEDDA. Exactly. The girl with the irritating hair, that she was always showing off. An old 5 flame of yours, I've been told.

TESMAN [laughing]. Oh, that didn't last long; and it was before I knew you, Hedda. But fancy her being in town!

HEDDA. It's odd that she should call upon us. 10 I have scarcely seen her since we left school.

TESMAN. I haven't seen her either for— heaven knows how long. I wonder how she can endure to live in such an out-of-the-way hole —eh?

15 HEDDA [after a moment's thought says suddenly]. Tell me, Tesman—isn't it somewhere near there that he—that—Eilert Lövborg is living?

TESMAN. Yes, he is somewhere in that part 20 of the country.

[BERTA enters by the hall door.]

BERTA. That lady, ma'am, that brought some flowers a little while ago, is here again. [Pointing.] The flowers you have in your hand, 25 ma'am.

HEDDA. Ah, is she? Well, please show her in.

[BERTA opens the door for MRS. ELVSTED, and goes out herself.—MRS. ELVSTED is a woman of fragile figure, with pretty, soft features. Her 30 eyes are light blue, large, round, and somewhat prominent, with a startled, inquiring expression. Her hair is remarkably light, almost flaxen, and unusually abundant and wavy. She is a couple of years younger than HEDDA. She 35 wears a dark visiting dress, tasteful, but not quite in the latest fashion.]

HEDDA [receives her warmly]. How do you do, my dear Mrs. Elvsted? It's delightful to see you again.

40 MRS. ELVSTED [nervously, struggling for self-control]. Yes, it's a very long time since we met.

TESMAN [gives her his hand]. And we too— eh?

45 HEDDA. Thanks for your lovely flowers—

MRS. ELVSTED. Oh, not at all— I would have come straight here yesterday afternoon; but I heard that you were away—

TESMAN. Have you just come to town? Eh?

MRS. ELVSTED. I arrived yesterday, about 50 midday. Oh, I was quite in despair when I heard that you were not at home.

HEDDA. In despair! How so?

TESMAN. Why, my dear Mrs. Rysing—I mean Mrs. Elvsted— 55

HEDDA. I hope that you are not in any trouble?

MRS. ELVSTED. Yes, I am. And I don't know another living creature here that I can turn to.

HEDDA [laying the bouquet on the table]. 60 Come—let us sit here on the sofa—

MRS. ELVSTED. Oh, I am too restless to sit down.

HEDDA. Oh no, you're not. Come here. [She draws MRS. ELVSTED down upon the sofa and 65 sits at her side.]

TESMAN. Well? What is it, Mrs. Elvsted?

HEDDA. Has anything particular happened to you at home?

MRS. ELVSTED. Yes—and no. Oh—I am so 70 anxious you should not misunderstand me—

HEDDA. Then your best plan is to tell us the whole story, Mrs. Elvsted.

TESMAN. I suppose that's what you have come for—eh? 75

MRS. ELVSTED. Yes, yes—of course it is. Well then, I must tell you—if you don't already know—that Eilert Lövborg is in town, too.

HEDDA. Lövborg—!

TESMAN. What! Has Eilert Lövborg come 80 back? Fancy that, Hedda!

HEDDA. Well, well—I hear it.

MRS. ELVSTED. He has been here a week already. Just fancy—a whole week! In this terrible town, alone! With so many temptations 85 on all sides.

HEDDA. But my dear Mrs. Elvsted—how does he concern you so much?

MRS. ELVSTED [looks at her with a startled air, and says rapidly]. He was the children's 90 tutor.

HEDDA. Your children's?

MRS. ELVSTED. My husband's. I have none.

HEDDA. Your step-children's, then?

MRS. ELVSTED. Yes. 95

TESMAN [somewhat hesitatingly]. Then was

he—I don't know how to express it—was he—regular enough in his habits to be fit for the post? Eh?

MRS. ELVSTED. For the last two years his con-
5 duct has been irreproachable.

TESMAN. Has it indeed? Fancy that, Hedda!

HEDDA. I hear it.

MRS. ELVSTED. Perfectly irreproachable, I assure you! In every respect. But all the same
10 —now that I know he is here—in this great town—and with a large sum of money in his hands—I can't help being in mortal fear for him.

TESMAN. Why did he not remain where he was? With you and your husband? Eh?
15 MRS. ELVSTED. After his book was published he was too restless and unsettled to remain with us.

TESMAN. Yes, by-the-bye, Aunt Julia told me he had published a new book.
20 MRS. ELVSTED. Yes, a big book, dealing with the march of civilization—in broad outline, as it were. It came out about a fortnight ago. And since it has sold so well, and been so much read—and made such a sensation—
25 TESMAN. Has it indeed? It must be something he has had lying by since his better days.

MRS. ELVSTED. Long ago, you mean?

TESMAN. Yes.

MRS. ELVSTED. No, he has written it all since
30 he has been with us—within the last year.

TESMAN. Isn't that good news, Hedda? Think of that.

MRS. ELVSTED. Ah, yes, if only it would last!

HEDDA. Have you seen him here in town?
35 MRS. ELVSTED. No, not yet. I have had the greatest difficulty in finding out his address. But this morning I discovered it at last.

HEDDA [*looks searchingly at her*]. Do you know, it seems to me a little odd of your hus-
40 band—h'm—

MRS. ELVSTED [*starting nervously*]. Of my husband! What?

HEDDA. That he should send you to town on such an errand—that he does not come himself
45 and look after his friend.

MRS. ELVSTED. Oh, no, no—my husband has no time. And besides, I—I had some shopping to do.

HEDDA [*with a slight smile*]. Ah, that is a different matter. 50

MRS. ELVSTED [*rising quickly and uneasily*]. And now I beg and implore you, Mr. Tesman—receive Eilert Lövborg kindly if he comes to you! And that he is sure to do. You see you were such great friends in the old days. And 55 then you are interested in the same studies—the same branch of science—so far as I can understand.

TESMAN. We used to be, at any rate.

MRS. ELVSTED. That is why I beg so earnestly 60 that you—you too—will keep a sharp eye upon him. Oh, you will promise me that, Mr. Tesman—won't you?

TESMAN. With the greatest of pleasure, Mrs. Rysing— 65

HEDDA. Elvsted.

TESMAN. I assure you I shall do all I possibly can for Eilert. You may rely upon me.

MRS. ELVSTED. Oh, how very, very kind of you! [*Presses his hands.*] Thanks, thanks, 70 thanks! [*Frightened.*] You see, my husband is very fond of him!

HEDDA [*rising*]. You ought to write to him, Tesman. Perhaps he may not care to come to you of his own accord. 75

TESMAN. Well, perhaps it would be the right thing to do, Hedda? Eh?

HEDDA. And the sooner the better. Why not at once?

MRS. ELVSTED [*imploringly*]. Oh, if you only 80 would!

TESMAN. I'll write this moment. Have you his address, Mrs.—Mrs. Elvsted?

MRS. ELVSTED. Yes. [*Takes a slip of paper from her pocket, and hands it to him.*] Here it is. 85

TESMAN. Good, good. Then I'll go in—[*Looks about him.*] By-the-bye,—my slippers? Oh, here. [*Takes the packet, and is about to go.*]

HEDDA. Be sure you write him a cordial, 90 friendly letter. And a good long one too.

TESMAN. Yes, I will.

MRS. ELVSTED. But please, please don't say a word to show that I have suggested it.

TESMAN. No, how could you think I would? 95 Eh?

[*He goes out to the right, through the inner room.*]

HEDDA [*goes up to* MRS. ELVSTED, *smiles, and says in a low voice*]. There. We have killed two birds with one stone.

MRS. ELVSTED. What do you mean?

HEDDA. Could you not see that I wanted him to go?

MRS. ELVSTED. Yes, to write the letter—

HEDDA. And that I might speak to you alone.

MRS. ELVSTED [*confused*]. About the same thing?

HEDDA. Precisely.

MRS. ELVSTED [*apprehensively*]. But there is nothing more, Mrs. Tesman! Absolutely nothing!

HEDDA. Oh, yes, but there is. There is a great deal more—I can see that. Sit here—and we'll have a cosy, confidential chat. [*She forces* MRS. ELVSTED *to sit in the easy-chair beside the stove, and seats herself on one of the footstools.*]

MRS. ELVSTED [*anxiously, looking at her watch*]. But, my dear Mrs. Tesman—I was really on the point of going.

HEDDA. Oh, you can't be in such a hurry.— Well? Now tell me something about your life at home.

MRS. ELVSTED. Oh, that is just what I care least to speak about.

HEDDA. But to me, dear—? Why, weren't we school-fellows?

MRS. ELVSTED. Yes, but you were in the class above me. Oh, how dreadfully afraid of you I was then!

HEDDA. Afraid of me?

MRS. ELVSTED. Yes, dreadfully. For when we met on the stairs you used always to pull my hair.

HEDDA. Did I, really?

MRS. ELVSTED. Yes, and once you said you would burn it off my head.

HEDDA. Oh, that was all nonsense, of course.

MRS. ELVSTED. Yes, but I was so silly in those days.—And since then, too—we have drifted so far—far apart from each other. Our circles have been so entirely different.

HEDDA. Well then, we must try to drift together again. Now listen! At school we said *du* to each other; and we called each other by our Christian names—

MRS. ELVSTED. No, I am sure you must be mistaken.

HEDDA. No, not at all! I can remember quite distinctly. So now we are going to renew our old friendship. [*Draws the foot-stool closer to* MRS. ELVSTED.] There now! [*Kisses her cheek.*] You must say *du* to me and call me Hedda.

MRS. ELVSTED [*presses and pats her hands*]. Oh, how good and kind you are! I am not used to such kindness.

HEDDA. There, there, there! And I shall say *du* to you, as in the old days, and call you my dear Thora.

MRS. ELVSTED. My name is Thea.

HEDDA. Why, of course! I meant Thea. [*Looks at her compassionately.*] So you are not accustomed to goodness and kindness, Thea? Not in your own home?

MRS. ELVSTED. Oh, if I only had a home! But I haven't any; I have never had a home.

HEDDA [*looks at her for a moment*]. I almost suspected as much.

MRS. ELVSTED [*gazing helplessly before her*]. Yes—yes—yes.

HEDDA. I don't quite remember—was it not as housekeeper that you first went to Mr. Elvsted's?

MRS. ELVSTED. I really went as governess. But his wife—his late wife—was an invalid, —and rarely left her room. So I had to look after the housekeeping as well.

HEDDA. And then—at last—you became mistress of the house.

MRS. ELVSTED [*sadly*]. Yes, I did.

HEDDA. Let me see—about how long ago was that?

MRS. ELVSTED. My marriage?

HEDDA. Yes.

MRS ELVSTED. Five years ago.

HEDDA. To be sure; it must be that.

MRS. ELVSTED. Oh, those five years—! Or at all events the last two or three of them! Oh, if you could only imagine—

HEDDA [*giving her a little slap on the hand*]. *De*? Fie, Thea!

MRS. ELVSTED. Yes, yes, I will try— Well if —you could only imagine and understand—

HEDDA [*lightly*]. Eilert Lövborg has been in your neighborhood about three years, hasn't he?

MRS. ELVSTED [*looks at her doubtfully*]. Eilert Lövborg? Yes—he has.

HEDDA. Had you known him before, in town here?

MRS. ELVSTED. Scarcely at all. I mean—I knew him by name of course.

HEDDA. But you saw a good deal of him in the country?

MRS. ELVSTED. Yes, he came to us every day. You see, he gave the children lessons; for in the long run I couldn't manage it all myself.

HEDDA. No, that's clear.—And your husband—? I suppose he is often away from home?

MRS. ELVSTED. Yes. Being Sheriff, you know, he has to travel about a good deal in his district.

HEDDA [*leaning against the arm of the chair*]. Thea—my poor, sweet Thea—now you must tell me everything—exactly as it stands.

MRS. ELVSTED. Well then, you must question me.

HEDDA. What sort of a man is your husband, Thea? I mean—you know—in everyday life. Is he kind to you?

MRS. ELVSTED [*evasively*]. I am sure he means well in everything.

HEDDA. I should think he must be altogether too old for you. There is at least twenty years' difference between you, is there not?

MRS. ELVSTED [*irritably*]. Yes, that is true, too. Everything about him is repellent to me! We have not a thought in common. We have no single point of sympathy—he and I.

HEDDA. But is he not fond of you all the same? In his own way?

MRS. ELVSTED. Oh, I really don't know. I think he regards me simply as a useful property. And then it doesn't cost much to keep me. I am not expensive.

HEDDA. That is stupid of you.

MRS. ELVSTED [*shakes her head*]. It cannot be otherwise—not with him. I don't think he really cares for any one but himself—and perhaps a little for the children.

HEDDA. And for Eilert Lövborg, Thea.

MRS. ELVSTED [*looking at her*]. For Eilert Lövborg? What puts that into your head?

HEDDA. Well, my dear—I should say, when he sends you after him all the way to town— [*smiling almost imperceptibly*]. And besides, you said so yourself, to Tesman.

MRS. ELVSTED [*with a little nervous twitch*]. Did I? Yes, I suppose I did. [*Vehemently, but not loudly.*] No—I may just as well make a clean breast of it at once! For it must all come out in any case.

HEDDA. Why, my dear Thea—?

MRS. ELVSTED. Well, to make a long story short: My husband did not know that I was coming.

HEDDA. What! Your husband didn't know it!

MRS. ELVSTED. No, of course not. For that matter, he was away from home himself—he was traveling. Oh, I could bear it no longer, Hedda! I couldn't indeed—so utterly alone as I should have been in future.

HEDDA. Well? And then?

MRS. ELVSTED. So I put together some of my things—what I needed most—as quietly as possible. And then I left the house.

HEDDA. Without a word?

MRS. ELVSTED. Yes—and took the train straight to town.

HEDDA. Why, my dear, good Thea—to think of you daring to do it!

MRS. ELVSTED [*rises and moves about the room*]. What else could I possibly do?

HEDDA. But what do you think your husband will say when you go home again?

MRS. ELVSTED [*at the table, looks at her*]. Back to him?

HEDDA. Of course.

MRS. ELVSTED. I shall never go back to him again.

HEDDA [*rising and going towards her*]. Then you have left your home—for good and all?

MRS. ELVSTED. Yes. There was nothing else to be done.

HEDDA. But then—to take flight so openly.

MRS. ELVSTED. Oh, it's impossible to keep things of that sort secret.

HEDDA. But what do you think people will say of you, Thea?

5 MRS. ELVSTED. They may say what they like for aught I care. [Seats herself wearily and sadly on the sofa.] I have done nothing but what I had to do.

HEDDA [after a short silence]. And what are
10 your plans now? What do you think of doing?

MRS. ELVSTED. I don't know yet. I only know this, that I must live here, where Eilert Lövborg is—if I am to live at all.

HEDDA [takes a chair from the table, seats
15 herself beside her, and strokes her hands]. My dear Thea—how did this—this friendship—between you and Eilert Lövborg come about?

MRS. ELVSTED. Oh, it grew up gradually. I gained a sort of influence over him.

20 HEDDA. Indeed?

MRS. ELVSTED. He gave up his old habits. Not because I asked him to, for I never dared do that. But of course he saw how repulsive they were to me; and so he dropped them.

25 HEDDA [concealing an involuntary smile of scorn]. Then you have reclaimed him—as the saying goes—my little Thea.

MRS. ELVSTED. So he says himself, at any rate. And he, on his side, has made a real
30 human being of me—taught me to think, and to understand so many things.

HEDDA. Did he give you lessons too, then?

MRS. ELVSTED. No, not exactly lessons. But he talked to me—talked about such an infinity
35 of things. And then came the lovely, happy time when I began to share in his work—when he allowed me to help him!

HEDDA. Oh, he did, did he?

MRS. ELVSTED. Yes! He never wrote anything
40 without my assistance.

HEDDA. You were two good comrades, in fact?

MRS. ELVSTED [eagerly]. Comrades! Yes, fancy, Hedda—that is the very word he used!
45 —Oh, I ought to feel perfectly happy; and yet I cannot; for I don't know how long it will last.

HEDDA. Are you no surer of him than that?

MRS. ELVSTED [gloomily]. A woman's shadow stands between Eilert Lövborg and me.

HEDDA [looks at her anxiously]. Who can 50 that be?

MRS. ELVSTED. I don't know. Some one he knew in his—in his past. Some one he has never been able wholly to forget.

HEDDA. What has he told you—about this? 55

MRS. ELVSTED. He has only once—quite vaguely—alluded to it.

HEDDA. Well! And what did he say?

MRS. ELVSTED. He said that when they parted, she threatened to shoot him with a 60 pistol.

HEDDA [with cold composure]. Oh, nonsense! No one does that sort of thing here.

MRS. ELVSTED. No. And that is why I think it must have been that red-haired singing 65 woman whom he once—

HEDDA. Yes, very likely.

MRS. ELVSTED. For I remember they used to say of her that she carried loaded firearms.

HEDDA. Oh—then of course it must have 70 been she.

MRS. ELVSTED [wringing her hands]. And now just fancy, Hedda—I hear that this singing-woman—that she is in town again! Oh, I don't know what to do— 75

HEDDA [glancing towards the inner room]. Hush! Here comes Tesman. [Rises and whispers.] Thea—all this must remain between you and me.

MRS. ELVSTED [springing up]. Oh, yes, yes! 80 for heaven's sake—!

[GEORGE TESMAN, with a letter in his hand, comes from the right through the inner room.]

TESMAN. There now—the epistle is finished.

HEDDA. That's right. And now Mrs. Elvsted 85 is just going. Wait a moment—I'll go with you to the garden gate.

TESMAN. Do you think Berta could post the letter, Hedda dear?

HEDDA [takes it]. I will tell her to. 90

[BERTA enters from the hall.]

BERTA. Judge Brack wishes to know if Mrs. Tesman will receive him.

HEDDA. Yes, ask Judge Brack to come in. And look here—put this letter in the post. 95

BERTA [taking the letter]. Yes, ma'am.

[*She opens the door for* JUDGE BRACK *and goes out herself.* BRACK *is a man of forty-five; thick-set, but well-built and elastic in his movements. His face is roundish with an aristocratic profile. His hair is short, still almost black, and carefully dressed. His eyes are lively and sparkling. His eyebrows thick. His moustaches are also thick, with short-cut ends. He wears a well-cut walking-suit, a little too youthful for his age. He uses an eye-glass, which he now and then lets drop.*]

JUDGE BRACK [*with his hat in his hand, bowing*]. May one venture to call so early in the day?

HEDDA. Of course one may.

TESMAN [*presses his hand*]. You are welcome at any time. [*Introducing him.*] Judge Brack— Miss Rysing—

HEDDA. Oh—!

BRACK [*bowing*]. Ah—delighted—

HEDDA [*looks at him and laughs*]. It's nice to have a look at you by daylight, Judge!

BRACK. Do you find me—altered?

HEDDA. A little younger, I think.

BRACK. Thank you so much.

TESMAN. But what do you think of Hedda— eh? Doesn't she look flourishing? She has actually—

HEDDA. Oh, do leave me alone. You haven't thanked Judge Brack for all the trouble he has taken—

BRACK. Oh, nonsense—it was a pleasure to me—

HEDDA. Yes, you are a friend indeed. But here stands Thea all impatience to be off—so *au revoir*, Judge. I shall be back again presently. [*Mutual salutations.* MRS. ELVSTED *and* HEDDA *go out by the hall door.*]

BRACK. Well,—is your wife tolerably satisfied—

TESMAN. Yes, we can't thank you sufficiently. Of course she talks of a little re-arrangement here and there; and one or two things are still wanting. We shall have to buy some additional trifles.

BRACK. Indeed!

TESMAN. But we won't trouble you about these things. Hedda says she herself will look after what is wanting.—Shan't we sit down? Eh?

BRACK. Thanks, for a moment. [*Seats himself beside the table.*] There is something I wanted to speak to you about, my dear Tesman.

TESMAN. Indeed? Ah, I understand! [*Seating himself.*] I suppose it's the serious part of the frolic that is coming now. Eh?

BRACK. Oh, the money question is not so very pressing; though, for that matter, I wish we had gone a little more economically to work.

TESMAN. But that would never have done, you know! Think of Hedda, my dear fellow! You, who know her so well—. I couldn't possibly ask her to put up with a shabby style of living!

BRACK. No, no—that is just the difficulty.

TESMAN. And then—fortunately—it can't be long before I receive my appointment.

BRACK. Well, you see—such things are often apt to hang fire for a time.

TESMAN. Have you heard anything definite? Eh?

BRACK. Nothing exactly definite—[*interrupting himself*]. But, by-the-bye—I have one piece of news for you.

TESMAN. Well?

BRACK. Your old friend, Eilert Lövborg, has returned to town.

TESMAN. I know that already.

BRACK. Indeed! How did you learn it?

TESMAN. From that lady who went out with Hedda.

BRACK. Really? What was her name? I didn't quite catch it.

TESMAN. Mrs. Elvsted.

BRACK. Aha—Sheriff Elvsted's wife? Of course—he has been living up in their regions.

TESMAN. And fancy—I'm delighted to hear that he is quite a reformed character!

BRACK. So they say.

TESMAN. And then he has published a new book—eh?

BRACK. Yes, indeed he has.

TESMAN. And I hear it has made some sensation!

BRACK. Quite an unusual sensation.

TESMAN. Fancy—isn't that good news! A man of such extraordinary talents— I felt so grieved to think that he had gone irretrievably to ruin.

BRACK. That was what everybody thought.

TESMAN. But I cannot imagine what he will take to now! How in the world will he be able to make his living? Eh?

[*During the last words,* HEDDA *has entered by the hall door.*]

HEDDA [*to* BRACK, *laughing with a touch of scorn*]. Tesman is forever worrying about how people are to make their living.

TESMAN. Well, you see, dear—we were talking about poor Eilert Lövborg.

HEDDA [*glancing at him rapidly*]. Oh, indeed? [*Seats herself in the arm-chair beside the stove and asks indifferently.*] What is the matter with him?

TESMAN. Well—no doubt he has run through all his property long ago; and he can scarcely write a new book every year—eh? So I really can't see what is to become of him.

BRACK. Perhaps I can give you some information on that point.

TESMAN. Indeed!

BRACK. You must remember that his relations have a good deal of influence.

TESMAN. Oh, his relations, unfortunately have entirely washed their hands of him.

BRACK. At one time they called him the hope of the family.

TESMAN. At one time, yes! But he has put an end to all that.

HEDDA. Who knows? [*With a slight smile.*] I hear they have reclaimed him up at Sheriff Elvsted's—

BRACK. And then this book that he has published—

TESMAN. Well, well, I hope to goodness they may find something for him to do. I have just written to him. I asked him to come and see us this evening, Hedda dear.

BRACK. But, my dear fellow, you are booked for my bachelors' party this evening. You promised on the pier last night.

HEDDA. Had you forgotten, Tesman?

TESMAN. Yes, I had utterly forgotten.

BRACK. But it doesn't matter, for you may be sure he won't come.

TESMAN. What makes you think that? Eh?

BRACK [*with a little hesitation, rising and resting his hands on the back of his chair*]. My dear Tesman—and you too, Mrs. Tesman—I think I ought not to keep you in the dark about something that—that—

TESMAN. That concerns Eilert—?

BRACK. Both you and him.

TESMAN. Well, my dear Judge, out with it.

BRACK. You must be prepared to find your appointment deferred longer than you desired or expected.

TESMAN [*jumping up uneasily*]. Is there some hitch about it? Eh?

BRACK. The nomination may perhaps be made conditional on the result of a competition—

TESMAN. Competition! Think of that, Hedda!

HEDDA [*leans farther back in the chair*]. Aha—aha!

TESMAN. But who can my competitor be? Surely not—?

BRACK. Yes, precisely—Eilert Lövborg.

TESMAN [*clasping his hands*]. No, no—it's quite inconceivable! Quite impossible! Eh?

BRACK. H'm—that is what it may come to, all the same.

TESMAN. Well but, Judge Brack—it would show the most incredible lack of consideration for me. [*Gesticulates with his arms.*] For—just think—I'm a married man. We have been married on the strength of these prospects, Hedda and I; and run deep into debt; and borrowed money from Aunt Julia too. Good heavens, they had as good as promised me the appointment. Eh?

BRACK. Well, well, well—no doubt you will get it in the end; only after a contest.

HEDDA [*immovable in her arm-chair*]. Fancy, Tesman, there will be a sort of sporting interest in that.

TESMAN. Why, my dearest Hedda, how can you be so indifferent about it?

HEDDA [*as before*]. I am not at all indifferent. I am most eager to see who wins.

BRACK. In any case, Mrs. Tesman, it is best that you should know how matters stand. I mean—before you set about the little purchases I hear you are threatening.

5 HEDDA. This can make no difference.

BRACK. Indeed! Then I have no more to say. Good-bye! [*To* TESMAN.] I shall look in on my way back from my afternoon walk, and take you home with me.

10 TESMAN. Oh yes, yes—your news has quite upset me.

HEDDA [*reclining, holds out her hand*]. Good-bye, Judge; and be sure you call in the afternoon.

15 BRACK. Many thanks. Good-bye, good-bye!

TESMAN [*accompanying him to the door*]. Good-bye, my dear Judge! You must really excuse me—

[JUDGE BRACK *goes out by the hall door.*]

20 TESMAN [*crosses the room*]. Oh, Hedda— one should never rush into adventures. Eh?

HEDDA [*looks at him, smiling*]. Do you do that?

TESMAN. Yes, dear—there is no denying—it 25 was adventurous to go and marry and set up house upon mere expectations.

HEDDA. Perhaps you are right there.

TESMAN. Well—at all events, we have our delightful home, Hedda! Fancy, the home we 30 both dreamed of—the home we were in love with, I may almost say. Eh?

HEDDA [*rising slowly and wearily*]. It was part of our compact that we were to go into society—to keep open house.

35 TESMAN. Yes, if you only knew how I had been looking forward to it! Fancy—to see you as hostess—in a select circle? Eh? Well, well, well—for the present we shall have to get on without society, Hedda—only to invite Aunt 40 Julia now and then.—Oh, I intended you to lead such an utterly different life, dear—!

HEDDA. Of course I cannot have my man in livery just yet.

TESMAN. Oh no, unfortunately. It would be 45 out of the question for us to keep a footman, you know.

HEDDA. And the saddle-horse I was to have had—

TESMAN [*aghast*]. The saddle-horse!

HEDDA. —I suppose I must not think of that 50 now.

TESMAN. Good heavens, no!—that's as clear as daylight.

HEDDA [*goes up the room*]. Well, I shall have one thing at least to kill time with in the 55 meanwhile.

TESMAN [*beaming*]. Oh, thank heaven for that! What is it, Hedda? Eh?

HEDDA [*in the middle doorway, looks at him with covert scorn*]. My pistols, George. 60

TESMAN [*in alarm*]. Your pistols!

HEDDA [*with cold eyes*]. General Gabler's pistols.

[*She goes out through the inner room, to the left.*] 65

TESMAN [*rushes up to the middle doorway and calls after her*]. No, for heaven's sake, Hedda darling—don't touch those dangerous things! For my sake, Hedda! Eh?

ACT II

[*The room at the* TESMANS' *as in the first act,* 70 *except that the piano has been removed, and an elegant little writing-table with bookshelves put in its place. A smaller table stands near the sofa at the left. Most of the bouquets have been taken away.* MRS. ELVSTED's *bouquet is* 75 *upon the large table in front.—It is afternoon.*]

HEDDA, *dressed to receive callers, is alone in the room. She stands by the open glass door, loading a revolver. The fellow to it lies in an open pistol-case on the writing-table.*] 80

HEDDA [*looks down the garden, and calls*]. So you are here again, Judge!

BRACK [*is heard calling from a distance*]. As you see, Mrs. Tesman!

HEDDA [*raises the pistol and points*]. Now 85 I'll shoot you, Judge Brack!

BRACK [*calling unseen*]. No, no, no! Don't stand aiming at me!

HEDDA. This is what comes of sneaking in by the back way. [*She fires.*] 90

BRACK [*nearer*]. Are you out of your senses—!

HEDDA. Dear me—did I happen to hit you?

BRACK [*still outside*]. I wish you would let these pranks alone!

HEDDA. Come in then, Judge.

[JUDGE BRACK, *dressed as though for a men's party, enters by the glass door. He carries a light overcoat over his arm.*]

BRACK. What the deuce—haven't you tired of that sport, yet? What are you shooting at?

HEDDA. Oh, I am only firing in the air.

BRACK [*gently takes the pistol out of her hand*]. Allow me, madam! [*Looks at it.*] Ah—I know this pistol well! [*Looks around.*] Where is the case? Ah, here it is. [*Lays the pistol in it, and shuts it.*] Now we won't play at that game any more today.

HEDDA. Then what in heaven's name would you have me do with myself?

BRACK. Have you had no visitors?

HEDDA [*closing the glass door*]. Not one. I suppose all our set are still out of town.

BRACK. And is Tesman not at home either?

HEDDA [*at the writing-table, putting the pistol-case in a drawer which she shuts*]. No. He rushed off to his aunt's directly after lunch; he didn't expect you so early.

BRACK. H'm—how stupid of me not to have thought of that!

HEDDA [*turning her head to look at him*]. Why stupid?

BRACK. Because if I had thought of it I should have come a little—earlier.

HEDDA [*crossing the room*]. Then you would have found no one to receive you; for I have been in my room changing my dress ever since lunch.

BRACK. And is there no sort of little chink that we could hold a parley through?

HEDDA. You have forgotten to arrange one.

BRACK. That was another piece of stupidity.

HEDDA. Well, we must just settle down here —and wait. Tesman is not likely to be back for some time yet.

BRACK. Never mind; I shall not be impatient.

[HEDDA *seats herself in the corner of the sofa.* BRACK *lays his overcoat over the back of the nearest chair, and sits down, but keeps his hat in his hand. A short silence. They look at each other.*]

HEDDA. Well?

BRACK [*in the same tone*]. Well?

HEDDA. I spoke first.

BRACK [*bending a little forward*]. Come, let us have a cosy little chat, Mrs. Hedda.

HEDDA [*leaning further back in the sofa*]. Does it not seem like a whole eternity since our last talk? Of course I don't count those few words yesterday evening and this morning.

BRACK. You mean since our last confidential talk? Our last *tête-à-tête*?

HEDDA. Well, yes—since you put it so.

BRACK. Not a day has passed but I have wished that you were home again.

HEDDA. And I have done nothing but wish the same thing.

BRACK. You? Really, Mrs. Hedda? And I thought you had been enjoying your tour so much!

HEDDA. Oh, yes, you may be sure of that!

BRACK. But Tesman's letters spoke of nothing but happiness.

HEDDA. Oh, Tesman! You see, he thinks nothing so delightful as grubbing in libraries and making copies of old parchments, or whatever you call them.

BRACK [*with a spice of malice*]. Well, that is his vocation in life—or part of it at any rate.

HEDDA. Yes, of course; and no doubt when it's your vocation— But I! Oh, my dear Mr. Brack, how mortally bored I have been.

BRACK [*sympathetically*]. Do you really say so? In downright earnest?

HEDDA. Yes, you can surely understand it—! To go for six whole months without meeting a soul that knew anything of our circle, or could talk about the things we are interested in.

BRACK. Yes, yes—I too should feel that a deprivation.

HEDDA. And then, what I found most intolerable of all—

BRACK. Well?

HEDDA. —was being everlastingly in the company of—one and the same person—

BRACK [*with a nod of assent*]. Morning, noon, and night, yes—at all possible times and seasons.

HEDDA. I said "everlastingly."

BRACK. Just so. But I should have thought, with our excellent Tesman, one could—

HEDDA. Tesman is—a specialist, my dear Judge.

5   BRACK. Undeniably.

HEDDA. And specialists are not at all amusing to travel with. Not in the long run at any rate.

BRACK. Not even—the specialist one happens 10   to love?

HEDDA. Faugh—don't use that sickening word!

BRACK [*taken aback*]. What do you say, Mrs. Hedda? ·

15   HEDDA [*half laughing, half irritated*]. You should just try it! To hear of nothing but the history of civilization, morning, noon, and night—

BRACK. Everlastingly.

20   HEDDA. Yes, yes, yes! And then all this about the domestic industry of the middle ages—! That's the most disgusting part of it!

BRACK [*looks searchingly at her*]. But tell me —in that case, how am I to understand your 25   —? H'm—

HEDDA. My accepting George Tesman, you mean?

BRACK. Well, let us put it so.

HEDDA. Good heavens, do you see anything 30   so wonderful in that?

BRACK. Yes and no—Mrs. Hedda.

HEDDA. I had positively danced myself tired, my dear Judge. My day was done— [*With a slight shudder.*] Oh no—I won't say that; nor 35   think it either!

BRACK. You have assuredly no reason to.

HEDDA. Oh, reasons— [*Watching him closely.*] And George Tesman—after all, you must admit that he is correctness itself.

40   BRACK. His correctness and respectability are beyond all question.

HEDDA. And I don't see anything absolutely ridiculous about him.—Do you?

BRACK. Ridiculous? N—no—I shouldn't 45   exactly say so—

HEDDA. Well—and his powers of research, at all events, are untiring.—I see no reason why he should not one day come to the front, after all.

BRACK [*looks at her hesitatingly*]. I thought that you, like every one else, expected him to 50   attain the highest distinction.

HEDDA [*with an expression of fatigue*]. Yes, so I did.—And then, since he was bent, at all hazards, on being allowed to provide for me— I really don't know why I should not have 55   accepted his offer?

BRACK. No—if you look at it in that light—

HEDDA. It was more than my other adorers were prepared to do for me, my dear Judge.

BRACK [*laughing*]. Well, I can't answer for 60   all the rest; but as for myself, you know quite well that I have always entertained a—a certain respect for the marriage tie—for marriage as an institution, Mrs. Hedda.

HEDDA [*jestingly*]. Oh, I assure you I have 65   never cherished any hopes with respect to you.

BRACK. All I require is a pleasant and intimate interior, where I can make myself useful in every way, and am free to come and go as— a trusted friend—   70

HEDDA. Of the master of the house, do you mean?

BRACK [*bowing*]. Frankly—of the mistress first of all; but of course of the master, too, in the second place. Such a triangular friendship 75   —if I may call it so—is really a great convenience for all parties, let me tell you.

HEDDA. Yes, I have many a time longed for some one to make a third on our travels. Oh —those railway-carriage *tête-à-têtes*—!   80

BRACK. Fortunately your wedding journey is over now.

HEDDA [*shaking her head*]. Not by a long— long way. I have only arrived at a station on the line.   85

BRACK. Well, then the passengers jump out and move about a little, Mrs. Hedda.

HEDDA. I never jump out.

BRACK. Really?

HEDDA. No—because there is always some 90   one standing by to—

BRACK [*laughing*]. To look at your ankles, do you mean?

HEDDA. Precisely.

BRACK. Well but, dear me—   95

HEDDA [*with a gesture of repulsion*]. I won't

have it. I would rather keep my seat where I happen to be—and continue the *tête-à-tête*.

BRACK. But suppose a third person were to jump in and join the couple.

HEDDA. Ah—that is quite another matter!

BRACK. A trusted, sympathetic friend—

HEDDA. —with a fund of conversation on all sorts of lively topics—

BRACK. —and not the least bit of a specialist!

HEDDA [*with an audible sigh*]. Yes, that would be a relief indeed.

BRACK [*hears the front door open, and glances in that direction*]. The triangle is completed.

HEDDA [*half aloud*]. And on goes the train.

[GEORGE TESMAN, *in a gray walking-suit, with a soft felt hat, enters from the hall. He has a number of unbound books under his arm and in his pockets.*]

TESMAN [*goes up to the table beside the corner settee*]. Ouf—what a load for a warm day—all these books. [*Lays them on the table.*] I'm positively perspiring, Hedda. Hallo—are you there already, my dear Judge? Eh? Berta didn't tell me.

BRACK [*rising*]. I came in through the garden.

HEDDA. What books have you got there?

TESMAN [*stands looking them through*]. Some new books on my special subjects—quite indispensable to me.

HEDDA. Your special subjects?

BRACK. Yes, books on his special subjects, Mrs. Tesman. [BRACK *and* HEDDA *exchange a confidential smile.*]

HEDDA. Do you need still more books on your special subjects?

TESMAN. Yes, my dear Hedda, one can never have too many of them. Of course one must keep up with all that is written and published.

HEDDA. Yes, I suppose one must.

TESMAN [*searching among his books*]. And look here—I have got hold of Eilert Lövborg's new book too. [*Offering it to her.*] Perhaps you would like to glance through it, Hedda? Eh?

HEDDA. No, thank you. Or rather—afterwards perhaps.

TESMAN. I looked into it a little on the way home.

BRACK. Well, what do you think of it—as a specialist?

TESMAN. I think it shows quite remarkable soundness of judgment. He never wrote like that before. [*Putting the books together.*] Now I shall take all these into my study. I'm longing to cut the leaves—! And then I must change my clothes. [*To* BRACK.] I suppose we needn't start just yet? Eh?

BRACK. Oh, dear no—there is not the slightest hurry.

TESMAN. Well then, I will take my time. [*Is going with his books, but stops in the doorway and turns.*] By-the-bye, Hedda—Aunt Julia is not coming this evening.

HEDDA. Not coming? Is it that affair of the bonnet that keeps her away?

TESMAN. Oh, not at all. How could you think such a thing of Aunt Julia? Just fancy—! The fact is, Aunt Rina is very ill.

HEDDA. She always is.

TESMAN. Yes, but today she is much worse than usual, poor dear.

HEDDA. Oh, then it's only natural that her sister should remain with her. I must bear my disappointment.

TESMAN. And you can't imagine, dear, how delighted Aunt Julia seemed to be—because you had come home looking so flourishing!

HEDDA [*half aloud, rising*]. Oh, those everlasting aunts!

TESMAN. What?

HEDDA [*going to the glass door*]. Nothing.

TESMAN. Oh, all right.

[*He goes through the inner room, out to the right.*]

BRACK. What bonnet were you talking about?

HEDDA. Oh, it was a little episode with Miss Tesman this morning. She had laid down her bonnet on the chair there—[*looks at him and smiles.*]—And I pretended to think it was the servant's.

BRACK [*shaking his head*]. Now my dear Mrs. Hedda, how could you do such a thing? To that excellent old lady, too!

HEDDA [*nervously crossing the room*]. Well,

you see—these impulses come over me all of a sudden; and I cannot resist them. [*Throws herself down in the easy-chair by the stove.*] Oh, I don't know how to explain it.

BRACK [*behind the easy-chair*]. You are not really happy—that is at the bottom of it.

HEDDA [*looking straight before her*]. I know of no reason why I should be—happy. Perhaps you can give me one?

BRACK. Well—amongst other things, because you have got exactly the home you had set your heart on.

HEDDA [*looks up at him and laughs*]. Do you too believe in that legend?

BRACK. Is there nothing in it, then?

HEDDA. Oh, yes, there is something in it.

BRACK. Well?

HEDDA. There is this in it, that I made use of Tesman to see me home from evening parties last summer—

BRACK. I, unfortunately, had to go quite a different way.

HEDDA. That's true. I know you were going a different way last summer.

BRACK [*laughing*]. Oh fie, Mrs. Hedda! Well, then—you and Tesman—?

HEDDA. Well, we happened to pass here one evening; Tesman, poor fellow, was writhing in the agony of having to find conversation; so I took pity on the learned man—

BRACK [*smiles doubtfully*]. You took pity? H'm—

HEDDA. Yes, I really did. And so—to help him out of his torment—I happened to say, in pure thoughtlessness, that I should like to live in this villa.

BRACK. No more than that?

HEDDA. Not that evening.

BRACK. But afterwards?

HEDDA. Yes, my thoughtlessness had consequences, my dear Judge.

BRACK. Unfortunately that too often happens, Mrs. Hedda.

HEDDA. Thanks! So you see it was this enthusiasm for Secretary Falk's villa that first constituted a bond of sympathy between George Tesman and me. From that came our engagement and our marriage, and our wedding journey, and all the rest of it. Well, well, my dear Judge—as you make your bed so you must lie, I could almost say.

BRACK. This is exquisite! And you really cared not a rap about it all the time?

HEDDA. No, heaven knows I didn't.

BRACK. But now? Now that we have made it so homelike for you?

HEDDA. Uh—the rooms all seem to smell of lavender and dried rose-leaves.—But perhaps it's Aunt Julia that has brought that scent with her.

BRACK [*laughing*]. No, I think it must be a legacy from the late Mrs. Secretary Falk.

HEDDA. Yes, there is an odor of mortality about it. It reminds me of a bouquet—the day after the ball. [*Clasps her hands behind her head, leans back in her chair and looks at him.*] Oh, my dear Judge—you cannot imagine how horribly I shall bore myself here.

BRACK. Why should not you, too, find some sort of vocation in life, Mrs. Hedda?

HEDDA. A vocation—that should attract me?

BRACK. If possible, of course.

HEDDA. Heaven knows what sort of a vocation that could be. I often wonder whether—[*breaking off*]. But that would never do either.

BRACK. Who can tell? Let me hear what it is.

HEDDA. Whether I might not get Tesman to go into politics, I mean.

BRACK [*laughing*]. Tesman? No, really now, political life is not the thing for him—not at all in his line.

HEDDA. No, I daresay not.—But if I could get him into it all the same?

BRACK. Why—what satisfaction could you find in that? If he is not fitted for that sort of thing, why should you want to drive him into it?

HEDDA. Because I am bored, I tell you! [*After a pause.*] So you think it quite out of the question that Tesman should ever get into the ministry?

BRACK. H'm—you see, my dear Mrs. Hedda—to get into the ministry, he would have to be a tolerably rich man.

HEDDA [*rising impatiently*]. Yes, there we have it! It is this genteel poverty I have managed to drop into—! [*Crosses the room.*] That is what makes life so pitiable! So utterly ludicrous!—For that's what it is.

BRACK. Now *I* should say the fault lay else-5 where.

HEDDA. Where, then?

BRACK. You have never gone through any really stimulating experience.

HEDDA. Anything serious, you mean?

10 BRACK. Yes, you may call it so. But now you may perhaps have one in store.

HEDDA [*tossing her head*]. Oh, you're thinking of the annoyances about this wretched professorship! But that must be Tesman's own 15 affair. I assure you I shall not waste a thought upon it.

BRACK. No, no. I daresay not. But suppose now that what people call—in elegant language—a solemn responsibility were to come 20 upon you? [*Smiling.*] A new responsibility, Mrs. Hedda?

HEDDA [*angrily*]. Be quiet! Nothing of that sort will ever happen!

BRACK [*warily*]. We will speak of this again 25 a year hence—at the very outside.

HEDDA [*curtly*]. I have no turn for anything of the sort, Judge Brack. No responsibilities for me!

BRACK. Are you so unlike the generality of 30 women as to have no turn for duties which—?

HEDDA [*beside the glass door*]. Oh, be quiet, I tell you!—I often think there is only one thing in the world I have any turn for.

BRACK [*drawing near to her*]. And what is 35 that, if I may ask?

HEDDA [*stands looking out*]. Boring myself to death. Now you know it. [*Turns, looks towards the inner room, and laughs.*] Yes, as I thought! Here comes the Professor.

40 BRACK [*softly, in a tone of warning*]. Come, come, come, Mrs. Hedda!

[GEORGE TESMAN, *dressed for the party, with his gloves and hat in his hand, enters from the right through the inner room.*]

45 TESMAN. Hedda, has no message come from Eilert Lövborg? Eh?

HEDDA. No.

TESMAN. Then you'll see he'll be here presently.

BRACK. Do you really think he will come? 50

TESMAN. Yes, I am almost sure of it. For what you were telling us this morning must have been a mere floating rumor.

BRACK. You think so?

TESMAN. At any rate, Aunt Julia said she did 55 not believe for a moment that he would ever stand in my way again. Fancy that!

BRACK. Well then, that's all right.

TESMAN [*placing his hat and gloves on a chair on the right*]. Yes, but you must really 60 let me wait for him as long as possible.

BRACK. We have plenty of time yet. None of my guests will arrive before seven or half-past.

TESMAN. Then meanwhile we can keep Hedda company, and see what happens. Eh? 65

HEDDA [*placing* BRACK'S *hat and overcoat upon the corner settee*]. And at the worst Mr. Lövborg can remain here with me.

BRACK [*offering to take his things*]. Oh, allow me, Mrs. Tesman!—What do you mean 70 by "At the worst"?

HEDDA. If he won't go with you and Tesman.

TESMAN [*looks dubiously at her*]. But, Hedda dear—do you think it would quite do 75 for him to remain with you? Eh? Remember, Aunt Julia can't come.

HEDDA. No, but Mrs. Elvsted is coming. We three can have a cup of tea together.

TESMAN. Oh, yes, that will be all right. 80

BRACK [*smiling*]. And that would perhaps be the safest plan for him.

HEDDA. Why so?

BRACK. Well, you know, Mrs. Tesman, how you used to gird at my little bachelor parties. 85 You declared they were adapted only for men of the strictest principles.

HEDDA. But no doubt Mr. Lövborg's principles are strict enough now. A converted sinner— 90

[BERTA *appears at the hall door.*]

BERTA. There's a gentleman asking if you are at home, ma'am—

HEDDA. Well, show him in.

TESMAN [*softly*]. I'm sure it is he! Fancy 95 that!

[EILERT LÖVBORG *enters from the hall. He is slim and lean; of the same age as* TESMAN, *but*

*looks older and somewhat worn-out. His hair
and beard are of a blackish brown, his face
long and pale, but with patches of color on the
cheek-bones. He is dressed in a well-cut black
visiting suit, quite new. He has dark gloves and
a silk hat. He stops near the door, and makes a
rapid bow, seeming somewhat embarrassed.]*

TESMAN [*goes up to him and shakes him
warmly by the hand*]. Well, my dear Eilert—
so at last we meet again!

EILERT LÖVBORG [*speaks in a subdued voice*].
Thanks for your letter, Tesman. [*Approaching
HEDDA.*] Will you too shake hands with me,
Mrs. Tesman?

HEDDA [*taking his hand*]. I am glad to see
you, Mr. Lövborg. [*With a motion of her
hand.*] I don't know whether you two gentlemen—?

LÖVBORG [*bowing slightly*]. Judge Brack, I
think.

BRACK [*doing likewise*]. Oh, yes,—in the old
days—

TESMAN [*to LÖVBORG, with his hands on his
shoulders*]. And now you must make yourself
entirely at home, Eilert! Mustn't he, Hedda?—
For I hear you are going to settle in town
again? Eh?

LÖVBORG. Yes, I am.

TESMAN. Quite right, quite right. Let me tell
you, I have got hold of your new book; but I
haven't had time to read it yet.

LÖVBORG. You may spare yourself the
trouble.

TESMAN. Why so?

LÖVBORG. Because there is very little in it.

TESMAN. Just fancy—how can you say so?

BRACK. But it has been very much praised, I
hear.

LÖVBORG. That was what I wanted; so I put
nothing into the book but what every one
would agree with.

BRACK. Very wise of you.

TESMAN. Well but, my dear Eilert—!

LÖVBORG. For now I mean to win myself a
position again—to make a fresh start.

TESMAN [*a little embarrassed*]. Ah, that is
what you wish to do? Eh?

LÖVBORG [*smiling, lays down his hat, and
draws a packet, wrapped in paper, from his
coat pocket*]. But when this one appears,
George Tesman, you will have to read it. For
this is the real book—the book I have put my
true self into.

TESMAN. Indeed? And what is it?

LÖVBORG. It is the continuation.

TESMAN. The continuation? Of what?

LÖVBORG. Of the book.

TESMAN. Of the new book?

LÖVBORG. Of course.

TESMAN. Why, my dear Eilert—does it not
come down to our own days?

LÖVBORG. Yes, it does; and this one deals
with the future.

TESMAN. With the future! But, good heavens,
we know nothing of the future!

LÖVBORG. No; but there is a thing or two to
be said about it all the same. [*Opens the
packet.*] Look here—

TESMAN. Why, that's not your handwriting.

LÖVBORG. I dictated it. [*Turning over the
pages.*] It falls into two sections. The first deals
with the civilizing forces of the future. And
here is the second—[*running through the pages
towards the end*]—forecasting the probable
line of development.

TESMAN. How odd now! I should never have
thought of writing anything of that sort.

HEDDA [*at the glass door, drumming on the
pane*]. H'm—I daresay not.

LÖVBORG [*replacing the manuscript in its
paper and laying the packet on the table*]. I
brought it, thinking I might read you a little of
it this evening.

TESMAN. That was very good of you, Eilert.
But this evening—? [*Looking at BRACK.*] I
don't quite see how we can manage it—

LÖVBORG. Well then, some other time. There
is no hurry.

BRACK. I must tell you, Mr. Lövborg—there
is a little gathering at my house this evening
—mainly in honor of Tesman, you know—

LÖVBORG [*looking for his hat*]. Oh—then I
won't detain you—

BRACK. No, but listen—will you not do me
the favor of joining us?

LÖVBORG [*curtly and decidedly*]. No, I can't
—thank you very much.

BRACK. Oh, nonsense—do! We shall be quite

a select little circle. And I assure you we shall have a "lively time," as Mrs. Hed—as Mrs. Tesman says.

LÖVBORG. I have no doubt of it. But never-
5 theless—

BRACK. And then you might bring your manuscript with you, and read it to Tesman at my house. I could give you a room to your-selves.

10 TESMAN. Yes, think of that, Eilert,—why shouldn't you? Eh?

HEDDA [*interposing*]. But, Tesman, if Mr. Lövborg would really rather not! I am sure Mr. Lövborg is much more inclined to remain here
15 and have supper with me.

LÖVBORG [*looking at her*]. With you, Mrs. Tesman?

HEDDA. And with Mrs. Elvsted.

LÖVBORG. Ah— [*Lightly.*] I saw her for a
20 moment this morning.

HEDDA. Did you? Well, she is coming this evening. So you see you are almost bound to remain, Mr. Lövborg, or she will have no one to see her home.

25 LÖVBORG. That's true. Many thanks, Mrs. Tesman—in that case I will remain.

HEDDA. Then I have one or two orders to give the servant—

[*She goes to the hall door and rings.* BERTA
30 *enters.* HEDDA *talks to her in a whisper, and points towards the inner room.* BERTA *nods and goes out again.*]

TESMAN [*at the same time, to* LÖVBORG]. Tell me, Eilert—is it this new subject—the future
35 —that you are going to lecture about?

LÖVBORG. Yes.

TESMAN. They told me at the bookseller's, that you are going to deliver a course of lec-tures this autumn.

40 LÖVBORG. That is my intention. I hope you won't take it ill, Tesman.

TESMAN. Oh no, not in the least! But—?

LÖVBORG. I can quite understand that it must be disagreeable to you.

45 TESMAN [*cast down*]. Oh, I can't expect you, out of consideration for me, to—

LÖVBORG. But I shall wait till you have re-ceived your appointment.

TESMAN. Will you wait? Yes, but—yes, but—
are you not going to compete with me? Eh? 50

LÖVBORG. No; it is only the moral victory I care for.

TESMAN. Why, bless me—then Aunt Julia was right after all! Oh yes—I knew it! Hedda! Just fancy—Eilert Lövborg is not going to 55 stand in our way!

HEDDA [*curtly*]. Our way? Pray leave me out of the question.

[*She goes up towards the inner room, where* BERTA *is placing a tray with decanters and* 60 *glasses on the table.* HEDDA *nods approval, and comes forward again.* BERTA *goes out.*]

TESMAN [*at the same time*]. And you, Judge Brack—what do you say to this? Eh?

BRACK. Well, I say that a moral victory— 65 h'm—may be all very fine—

TESMAN. Yes, certainly. But all the same—

HEDDA [*looking at* TESMAN *with a cold smile*]. You stand there looking as if you were thunderstruck— 70

TESMAN. Yes—so I am—I almost think—

BRACK. Don't you see, Mrs. Tesman, a thunderstorm has just passed over?

HEDDA [*pointing towards the inner room*]. Will you not take a glass of cold punch, gentle- 75 men?

BRACK [*looking at his watch*]. A stirrup-cup? Yes, it wouldn't come amiss.

TESMAN. A capital idea, Hedda! Just the thing! Now that the weight has been taken off 80 my mind—

HEDDA. Will you not join them, Mr. Löv-borg?

LÖVBORG [*with a gesture of refusal*]. No, thank you. Nothing for me. 85

BRACK. Why, bless me—cold punch is surely not poison.

LÖVBORG. Perhaps not for every one.

HEDDA. I will keep Mr. Lövborg company in the meantime. 90

TESMAN. Yes, yes, Hedda dear, do.

[*He and* BRACK *go into the inner room, seat themselves, drink punch, smoke cigarettes, and carry on a lively conversation during what follows.* EILERT LÖVBORG *remains beside the* 95 *stove.* HEDDA *goes to the writing-table.*]

HEDDA [*raising her voice a little*]. Do you care to look at some photographs, Mr. Lövborg? You know Tesman and I made a tour in the Tyrol on our way home?

5 [*She takes up an album, and places it on the table beside the sofa, in the further corner of which she seats herself.* EILERT LÖVBORG *approaches, stops, and looks at her. Then he takes a chair and seats himself at her left, with*
10 *his back towards the inner room.*]

HEDDA [*opening the album*]. Do you see this range of mountains, Mr. Lövborg? It's the Ortler group. Tesman has written the name underneath. Here it is: "The Ortler group near
15 Meran."

LÖVBORG [*who has never taken his eyes off her, says softly and slowly*]. Hedda—Gabler!

HEDDA [*glancing hastily at him*]. Ah! Hush!

LÖVBORG [*repeats softly*]. Hedda Gabler!

20 HEDDA [*looking at the album*]. That was my name in the old days—when we two knew each other.

LÖVBORG. And I must teach myself never to say Hedda Gabler again—never, as long as I
25 live.

HEDDA [*still turning over the pages*]. Yes, you must. And I think you ought to practice in time. The sooner the better, I should say.

LÖVBORG [*in a tone of indignation*]. Hedda
30 Gabler married? And married to—George Tesman!

HEDDA. Yes—so the world goes.

LÖVBORG. Oh, Hedda, Hedda—how could you° throw yourself away!

35 HEDDA [*looks sharply at him*]. What? I can't allow this!

LÖVBORG. What do you mean? [TESMAN *comes into the room and goes towards the sofa.*]

40 HEDDA [*hears him coming and says in an indifferent tone*]. And this is a view from the Val d'Ampezzo, Mr. Lövborg. Just look at these peaks! [*Looks affectionately up at* TESMAN.] What's the name of these curious peaks,
45 dear?

TESMAN. Let me see? Oh, those are the Dolomites.

HEDDA. Yes, that's it!—Those are the Dolomites, Mr. Lövborg.

TESMAN. Hedda dear,—I only wanted to ask 50 whether I shouldn't bring you a little punch after all? For yourself at any rate—eh?

HEDDA. Yes, do, please; and perhaps a few biscuits.

TESMAN. No cigarettes? 55

HEDDA. No.

TESMAN. Very well.

[*He goes into the inner room and out to the right.* BRACK *sits in the inner room, and keeps an eye from time to time on* HEDDA *and* LÖV- 60 BORG.]

LÖVBORG [*softly, as before*]. Answer me, Hedda—how could you go and do this?

HEDDA [*apparently absorbed in the album*]. If you continue to say *du* to me I won't talk to 65 you.

LÖVBORG. May I not say *du* when we are alone?

HEDDA. No. You may think it; but you mustn't say it. 70

LÖVBORG. Ah, I understand. It is an offense against George Tesman, whom you°—love.

HEDDA [*glances at him and smiles*]. Love? What an idea!

LÖVBORG. You don't love him then! 75

HEDDA. But I won't hear of any sort of unfaithfulness! Remember that.

LÖVBORG. Hedda—answer me one thing—

HEDDA. Hush!

[TESMAN *enters with a small tray from the* 80 *inner room.*]

TESMAN. Here you are! Isn't this tempting? [*He puts the tray on the table.*]

HEDDA. Why do you bring it yourself?

TESMAN [*filling the glasses*]. Because I think 85 it's such fun to wait upon you, Hedda.

HEDDA. But you have poured out two glasses. Mr. Lövborg said he wouldn't have any—

TESMAN. No, but Mrs. Elvsted will soon be here, won't she? 90

---

you *du*

you *de.* After this Lövborg reverts to the formal pronoun, which Hedda uses throughout.

HEDDA. Yes, by-the-bye—Mrs. Elvsted—

TESMAN. Had you forgotten her? Eh?

HEDDA. We were so absorbed in these photographs. [*Shows him a picture.*] Do you remem-
5 ber this little village?

TESMAN. Oh, it's that one just below the Brenner Pass. It was there we passed the night—

HEDDA. —and met that lively party of
10 tourists.

TESMAN. Yes, that was the place. Fancy—if we could only have had you with us, Eilert! Eh? [*He returns to the inner room and sits beside* BRACK.]

15 LÖVBORG. Answer me this one thing, Hedda—

HEDDA. Well?

LÖVBORG. Was there no love in your friendship for me either? Not a spark—not a tinge of
20 love in it?

HEDDA. I wonder if there was? To me it seems as though we were two good comrades —two thoroughly intimate friends. [*Smilingly.*] You especially were frankness itself.

25 LÖVBORG. It was you that made me so.

HEDDA. As I look back upon it all, I think there was really something beautiful, something fascinating—something daring—in—in that secret intimacy—that comradeship which
30 no living creature so much as dreamed of.

LÖVBORG. Yes, yes, Hedda! Was there not?— When I used to come to your father's in the afternoon—and the General sat over at the window reading his papers—with his back
35 towards us—

HEDDA. And we two on the corner sofa—

LÖVBORG. Always with the same illustrated paper before us—

HEDDA. For want of an album, yes.

40 LÖVBORG. Yes, Hedda, and when I made my confessions to you—told you about myself, things that at that time no one else knew! There I would sit and tell you of my escapades —my days and nights of devilment. Oh, Hedda
45 —what was the power in you that forced me to confess these things?

HEDDA. Do you think it was any power in me?

LÖVBORG. How else can I explain it? And all those—those roundabout questions you used 50 to put to me—

HEDDA. Which you understood so particularly well—

LÖVBORG. How could you sit and question me like that? Question me quite frankly— 55

HEDDA. In roundabout terms, please observe.

LÖVBORG. Yes, but frankly nevertheless. Cross-question me about—all that sort of thing?

HEDDA. And how could you answer, Mr. 60 Lövborg?

LÖVBORG. Yes, that is just what I can't understand—in looking back upon it. But tell me now, Hedda—was there not love at the bottom of our friendship? On your side, did you not 65 feel as though you might purge my stains away if I made you my confessor? Was it not so?

HEDDA. No, not quite.

LÖVBORG. What was your motive, then? 70

HEDDA. Do you think it quite incomprehensible that a young girl—when it can be done— without any one knowing—

LÖVBORG. Well?

HEDDA. —should be glad to have a peep, 75 now and then, into a world which—

LÖVBORG. Which—?

HEDDA. —which she is forbidden to know anything about?

LÖVBORG. So that was it? 80

HEDDA. Partly. Partly—I almost think.

LÖVBORG. Comradeship in the thirst for life. But why should not that, at any rate, have continued?

HEDDA. The fault was yours. 85

LÖVBORG. It was you that broke with me.

HEDDA. Yes, when our friendship threatened to develop into something more serious. Shame upon you, Eilert Lövborg! How could you think of wronging your—your frank comrade? 90

LÖVBORG [*clenching his hands*]. Oh, why did you not carry out your threat? Why did you not shoot me down?

HEDDA. Because I have such a dread of scandal. 95

LÖVBORG. Yes, Hedda, you are a coward at heart.

HEDDA. A terrible coward. [*Changing her*

tone.] But it was a lucky thing for you. And now you have found ample consolation at the Elvsteds'.

LÖVBORG. I know what Thea has confided to
5 you.

HEDDA. And perhaps you have confided to her something about us?

LÖVBORG. Not a word. She is too stupid to understand anything of that sort.

10 HEDDA. Stupid?

LÖVBORG. She is stupid about matters of that sort.

HEDDA. And I am cowardly. [*Bends over towards him, without looking him in the face,*
15 *and says more softly—*] But now I will confide something to you.

LÖVBORG [*eagerly*]. Well?

HEDDA. The fact that I dared not shoot you down—

20 LÖVBORG. Yes!

HEDDA. —that was not my most arrant cowardice—that evening.

LÖVBORG [*looks at her a moment, understands, and whispers passionately*]. Oh,
25 Hedda! Hedda Gabler! Now I begin to see a hidden reason beneath our comradeship! You° and I—! After all, then, it was your craving for life—

HEDDA [*softly, with a sharp glance*]. Take
30 care! Believe nothing of the sort!

[*Twilight has begun to fall. The hall door is opened from without by* BERTA.]

HEDDA [*closes the album with a bang and calls smilingly*]. Ah, at last! My darling Thea,
35 —come along!

[MRS. ELVSTED *enters from the hall. She is in evening dress. The door is closed behind her.*]

HEDDA [*on the sofa, stretches out her arms towards her*]. My sweet Thea—you can't think
40 how I have been longing for you!

[MRS. ELVSTED, *in passing, exchanges slight salutations with the gentlemen in the inner room, then goes up to the table and gives* HEDDA *her hands.* EILERT LÖVBERG *has risen.*
45 *He and* MRS. ELVSTED *greet each other with a silent nod.*]

you *du*

MRS. ELVSTED. Ought I to go in and talk to your husband for a moment?

HEDDA. Oh, not at all. Leave those two alone. They will soon be going.   50

MRS. ELVSTED. Are they going out?

HEDDA. Yes, to a supper-party.

MRS. ELVSTED [*quickly, to* LÖVBORG]. Not you?

LÖVBORG. No.   55

HEDDA. Mr. Lövborg remains with us.

MRS. ELVSTED [*takes a chair and is about to seat herself at his side*]. Oh, how nice it is here!

HEDDA. No, thank you, my little Thea! Not 60
there! You'll be good enough to come over here to me. I will sit between you.

MRS. ELVSTED. Yes, just as you please.

[*She goes round the table and seats herself on the sofa on* HEDDA's *right.* LÖVBORG *re-seats* 65
himself on his chair.]

LÖVBORG [*after a short pause, to* HEDDA]. Is not she lovely to look at?

HEDDA [*lightly stroking her hair*]. Only to look at?   70

LÖVBORG. Yes. For we two—she and I—we are two real comrades. We have absolute faith in each other; so we can sit and talk with perfect frankness—

HEDDA. Not roundabout, Mr. Lövborg?   75

LÖVBORG. Well—

MRS. ELVSTED [*softly, clinging close to* HEDDA]. Oh, how happy I am, Hedda; for, only think, he says I have inspired him too.

HEDDA [*looks at her with a smile*]. Ah! Does 80
he say that, dear?

LÖVBORG. And then she is so brave, Mrs. Tesman!

MRS. ELVSTED. Good heavens—am I brave?

LÖVBORG. Exceedingly—where your comrade 85
is concerned.

HEDDA. Ah, yes—courage! If one only had that!

LÖVBORG. What then? What do you mean?

HEDDA. Then life would perhaps be liveable, 90
after all. [*With a sudden change of tone.*] But now, my dearest Thea, you really must have a glass of cold punch.

MRS. ELVSTED. No, thanks—I never take anything of that kind.   95

HEDDA. Well then, you, Mr. Lövborg.

LÖVBORG. Nor I, thank you.

MRS. ELVSTED. No, he doesn't either.

HEDDA [looks fixedly at him]. But if I say

5 you shall?

LÖVBORG. It would be no use.

HEDDA [laughing]. Then I, poor creature, have no sort of power over you?

LÖVBORG. Not in that respect.

10 HEDDA. But seriously, I think you ought to —for your own sake.

MRS. ELVSTED. Why, Hedda—!

LÖVBORG. How so?

HEDDA. Or rather on account of other people.

15 LÖVBORG. Indeed?

HEDDA. Otherwise people might be apt to suspect that—in your heart of hearts—you did not feel quite secure—quite confident of yourself.

20 MRS. ELVSTED [softly]. Oh please, Hedda—

LÖVBORG. People may suspect what they like —for the present.

MRS. ELVSTED [joyfully]. Yes, let them!

HEDDA. I saw it plainly in Judge Brack's face

25 a moment ago.

LÖVBORG. What did you see?

HEDDA. His contemptuous smile, when you dared not go with them into the inner room.

LÖVBORG. Dared not? Of course I preferred

30 to stop here and talk to you.

MRS. ELVSTED. What could be more natural, Hedda?

HEDDA. But the Judge could not guess that. And I saw, too, the way he smiled and glanced

35 at Tesman when you dared not accept his invitation to this wretched little supper-party of his.

LÖVBORG. Dared not! Do you say I dared not?

HEDDA. I don't say so. But that was how

40 Judge Brack understood it.

LÖVBORG. Well, let him.

HEDDA. Then you are not going with them?

LÖVBORG. I will stay here with you and Thea.

MRS. ELVSTED. Yes, Hedda—how can you

45 doubt that?

HEDDA [smiles and nods approvingly to LÖVBORG]. Firm as a rock! Faithful to your principles, now and forever! Ah, that is how a man should be! [Turns to MRS. ELVSTED and

caresses her.] Well now, what did I tell you, 50 when you came to us this morning in such a state of distraction—

LÖVBORG [surprised]. Distraction!

MRS. ELVSTED [terrified]. Hedda—oh Hedda—! 55

HEDDA. You can see for yourself; you haven't the slightest reason to be in such mortal terror —[interrupting herself]. There! Now we can all three enjoy ourselves!

LÖVBORG [who has given a start]. Ah—what 60 is all this, Mrs. Tesman?

MRS. ELVSTED. Oh my God, Hedda! What are you saying? What are you doing?

HEDDA. Don't get excited! That horrid Judge Brack is sitting watching you. 65

LÖVBORG. So she was in mortal terror! On my account!

MRS. ELVSTED [softly and piteously]. Oh, Hedda—now you have ruined everything!

LÖVBORG [looks fixedly at her for a moment. 70 His face is distorted]. So that was my comrade's frank confidence in me?

MRS. ELVSTED [imploringly]. Oh, my dearest friend—only let me tell you—

LÖVBORG [takes one of the glasses of punch, 75 raises it to his lips, and says in a low, husky voice]. Your health, Thea!

[He empties the glass, puts it down, and takes the second.]

MRS. ELVSTED [softly]. Oh, Hedda, Hedda— 80 how could you do this?

HEDDA. I do it? I? Are you crazy?

LÖVBORG. Here's your health, too, Mrs. Tesman. Thanks for the truth. Hurrah for the truth! [He empties the glass and is about to 85 re-fill it.]

HEDDA [lays her hand on his arm]. Come, come—no more for the present. Remember you are going out to supper.

MRS. ELVSTED. No, no, no! 90

HEDDA. Hush! They are sitting watching you.

LÖVBORG [putting down the glass]. Now. Thea—tell me the truth—

MRS. ELVSTED. Yes.

LÖVBORG. Did your husband know that you 95 had come after me?

MRS. ELVSTED [wringing her hands]. Oh, Hedda—do you hear what he is asking?

LÖVBORG. Was it arranged between you and him that you were to come to town and look after me? Perhaps it was the Sheriff himself that urged you to come? Aha, my dear—no doubt he wanted my help in his office! Or was it at the card-table that he missed me?

MRS. ELVSTED [*softly, in agony*]. Oh, Lövborg, Lövborg—!

LÖVBORG [*seizes a glass and is on the point of filling it*]. Here's a glass for the old Sheriff too!

HEDDA [*preventing him*]. No more just now. Remember, you have to read your manuscript to Tesman.

LÖVBORG [*calmly, putting down the glass*]. It was stupid of me all this, Thea—to take it in this way, I mean. Don't be angry with me, my dear, dear comrade. You shall see—both of you and the others—that if I was fallen once—now I have risen again! Thanks to you, Thea.

MRS. ELVSTED [*radiant with joy*]. Oh, heaven be praised—!

[BRACK *has in the meantime looked at his watch. He and* TESMAN *rise and come into the drawing-room.*]

BRACK [*takes his hat and overcoat*]. Well, Mrs. Tesman, our time has come.

HEDDA. I suppose it has.

LÖVBORG [*rising*]. Mine too, Judge Brack.

MRS. ELVSTED [*softly and imploringly*]. Oh, Lövborg, don't do it!

HEDDA [*pinching her arm*]. They can hear you!

MRS. ELVSTED [*with a suppressed shriek*]. Ow!

LÖVBORG [*to* BRACK]. You were good enough to invite me.

BRACK. Well, are you coming after all?

LÖVBORG. Yes, many thanks.

BRACK. I'm delighted—

LÖVBORG [*to* TESMAN, *putting the parcel of MS. in his pocket*]. I should like to show you one or two things before I send it to the printer's.

TESMAN. Fancy—that will be delightful. But, Hedda dear, how is Mrs. Elvsted to get home? Eh?

HEDDA. Oh, that can be managed somehow.

LÖVBORG [*looking towards the ladies*]. Mrs. Elvsted? Of course, I'll come again and fetch her. [*Approaching.*] At ten or thereabouts, Mrs. Tesman? Will that do?

HEDDA. Certainly. That will do capitally.

TESMAN. Well, then, that's all right. But you must not expect me so early, Hedda.

HEDDA. Oh, you may stop as long—as long as ever you please.

MRS. ELVSTED [*trying to conceal her anxiety*]. Well then, Mr. Lövborg—I shall remain here until you come.

LÖVBORG [*with his hat in his hand*]. Pray do, Mrs. Elvsted.

BRACK. And now off goes the excursion train, gentlemen! I hope we shall have a lively time, as a certain fair lady puts it.

HEDDA. Ah, if only the fair lady could be present unseen—!

BRACK. Why unseen?

HEDDA. In order to hear a little of your liveliness at first hand, Judge Brack.

BRACK [*laughing*]. I should not advise the fair lady to try it.

TESMAN [*also laughing*]. Come, you're a nice one, Hedda! Fancy that!

BRACK. Well, good-bye, good-bye, ladies.

LÖVBORG [*bowing*]. About ten o'clock, then.

[BRACK, LÖVBORG, *and* TESMAN *go out by the hall door. At the same time* BERTA *enters from the inner room with a lighted lamp, which she places on the dining-room table; she goes out by the way she came.*]

MRS. ELVSTED [*who has risen and is wandering restlessly about the room*]. Hedda—Hedda —what will come of all this?

HEDDA. At ten o'clock—he will be here. I can see him already—with vine-leaves° in his hair—flushed and fearless—

MRS. ELVSTED. Oh, I hope he may.

HEDDA. And then, you see—then he will have regained control over himself. Then he will be a free man for all his days.

MRS. ELVSTED. Oh God!—if he would only come as you see him now!

HEDDA. He will come as I see him—so, and

vine-leaves the garland of Dionysus, symbol of divine intoxication

not otherwise! [*Rises and approaches* THEA.] You may doubt him as long as you please; I believe in him. And now we will try—

MRS. ELVSTED. You have some hidden motive in this, Hedda!

HEDDA. Yes, I have. I want for once in my life to have power to mold a human destiny.

MRS. ELVSTED. Have you not the power?

HEDDA. I have not—and have never had it.

MRS. ELVSTED. Not your husband's?

HEDDA. Do you think that is worth the trouble? Oh, if you could only understand how poor I am. And fate has made you so rich! [*Clasps her passionately in her arms.*] I think I must burn your hair off, after all.

MRS. ELVSTED. Let me go! Let me go! I am afraid of you, Hedda!

BERTA [*in the middle doorway*]. Tea is laid in the dining-room, ma'am.

HEDDA. Very well. We are coming.

MRS. ELVSTED. No, no, no! I would rather go home alone! At once.

HEDDA. Nonsense! First you shall have a cup of tea, you little stupid. And then—at ten o'clock—Eilert Lövborg will be here—with vine-leaves in his hair. [*She drags* MRS. ELVSTED *almost by force towards the middle doorway.*]

ACT III

[*The room at the* TESMANS'. *The curtains are drawn over the middle doorway, and also over the glass door. The lamp, half turned down, and with a shade over it, is burning on the table. In the stove, the door of which stands open, there has been a fire, which is now nearly burnt out.*

MRS. ELVSTED, *wrapped in a large shawl, and with her feet upon a foot-rest, sits close to the stove, sunk back in the arm-chair.* HEDDA, *fully dressed, lies sleeping upon the sofa, with a sofa-blanket over her.*]

MRS. ELVSTED [*after a pause, suddenly sits up in her chair, and listens eagerly. Then she sinks back again wearily, moaning to herself*]. Not yet!—Oh God—oh God—not yet!

[BERTA *slips in by the hall door. She has a letter in her hand.*]

MRS. ELVSTED [*turns and whispers eagerly*]. Well—has any one come?

BERTA [*softly*]. Yes, a girl has brought this letter.

MRS. ELVSTED [*quickly, holding out her hand*]. A letter! Give it to me!

BERTA. No, it's for Dr. Tesman, ma'am.

MRS. ELVSTED. Oh, indeed.

BERTA. It was Miss Tesman's servant that brought it. I'll lay it here on the table.

MRS. ELVSTED. Yes, do.

BERTA [*laying down the letter*]. I think I had better put out the lamp. It's smoking.

MRS. ELVSTED. Yes, put it out. It must soon be daylight now.

BERTA [*putting out the lamp*]. It is daylight already, ma'am.

MRS. ELVSTED. Yes, broad day! And no one come back yet—!

BERTA. Lord bless you, ma'am! I guessed how it would be.

MRS. ELVSTED. You guessed?

BERTA. Yes, when I saw that a certain person had come back to town—and that he went off with them. For we've heard enough about that gentleman before now.

MRS. ELVSTED. Don't speak so loud. You will waken Mrs. Tesman.

BERTA [*looks towards the sofa and sighs*]. No, no—let her sleep, poor thing. Shan't I put some wood on the fire?

MRS. ELVSTED. Thanks, not for me.

BERTA. Oh, very well. [*She goes softly out by the hall door.*]

HEDDA [*is awakened by the shutting of the door, and looks up*]. What's that—?

MRS. ELVSTED. It was only the servant—

HEDDA [*looking about her*]. Oh, we're here—! Yes, now I remember. [*Sits erect upon the sofa, stretches herself, and rubs her eyes.*] What o'clock is it, Thea?

MRS. ELVSTED [*looks at her watch*]. It's past seven.

HEDDA. When did Tesman come home?

MRS. ELVSTED. He has not come.

HEDDA. Not come home yet?

MRS. ELVSTED [*rising*]. No one has come.

HEDDA. Think of our watching and waiting here till four in the morning—

5 MRS. ELVSTED [*wringing her hands*]. And how I watched and waited for him!

HEDDA [*yawns, and says with her hand before her mouth*]. Well, well—we might have spared ourselves the trouble.

10 MRS. ELVSTED. Did you get a little sleep?

HEDDA. Oh yes; I believe I have slept pretty well. Have you not?

MRS. ELVSTED. Not for a moment. I couldn't, Hedda!—not to save my life.

15 HEDDA [*rises and goes towards her*]. There, there, there! There's nothing to be so alarmed about. I understand quite well what has happened.

MRS. ELVSTED. Well, what do you think? 20 Won't you tell me?

HEDDA. Why, of course it has been a very late affair at Judge Brack's—

MRS. ELVSTED. Yes, yes, that is clear enough. But all the same—

25 HEDDA. And then, you see, Tesman hasn't cared to come home and ring us up in the middle of the night. [*Laughing.*] Perhaps he wasn't inclined to show himself either—immediately after a jollification.

30 MRS. ELVSTED. But in that case—where can he have gone?

HEDDA. Of course he has gone to his aunts' and slept there. They have his old room ready for him.

35 MRS. ELVSTED. No, he can't be with them; for a letter has just come for him from Miss Tesman. There it lies.

HEDDA. Indeed? [*Looks at the address.*] Why yes, it's addressed in Aunt Julia's own hand. 40 Well then, he has remained at Judge Brack's. And as for Eilert Lövborg—he is sitting, with vine-leaves in his hair, reading his manuscript.

MRS. ELVSTED. Oh Hedda, you are just saying things you don't believe a bit.

45 HEDDA. You really are a little blockhead, Thea.

MRS. ELVSTED. Oh yes, I suppose I am.

HEDDA. And how mortally tired you look.

MRS. ELVSTED. Yes, I am mortally tired.

HEDDA. Well then, you must do as I tell you. 50 You must go into my room and lie down for a little while.

MRS. ELVSTED. Oh no, no—I shouldn't be able to sleep.

HEDDA. I am sure you would. 55

MRS. ELVSTED. Well, but your husband is certain to come soon now; and then I want to know at once—

HEDDA. I shall take care to let you know when he comes. 60

MRS. ELVSTED. Do you promise me, Hedda?

HEDDA. Yes, rely upon me. Just you go in and have a sleep in the meantime.

MRS. ELVSTED. Thanks; then I'll try to. [*She goes off through the inner room.*] 65

[HEDDA *goes up to the glass door and draws back the curtains. The broad daylight streams into the room. Then she takes a little hand-glass from the writing-table, looks at herself in it, and arranges her hair. Next she goes to the* 70 *hall door and presses the bell-button.* BERTA *presently appears at the hall door.*]

BERTA. Did you want anything, ma'am?

HEDDA. Yes; you must put some more wood in the stove. I am shivering. 75

BERTA. Bless me—I'll make up the fire at once. [*She rakes the embers together and lays a piece of wood upon them; then stops and listens.*] That was a ring at the front door, ma'am. 80

HEDDA. Then go to the door. I will look after the fire.

BERTA. It'll soon burn up. [*She goes out by the hall door.*]

[HEDDA *kneels on the foot-rest and lays* 85 *some more pieces of wood in the stove. After a short pause,* GEORGE TESMAN *enters from the hall. He looks tired and rather serious. He steals on tiptoe towards the middle doorway and is about to slip through the curtains.*] 90

HEDDA [*at the stove, without looking up.*] Good morning.

TESMAN [*turns*]. Hedda! [*Approaching her.*] Good heavens—are you up so early? Eh?

HEDDA. Yes, I am up very early this morning.

TESMAN. And I never doubted you were still sound asleep! Fancy that, Hedda!

5 HEDDA. Don't speak so loud. Mrs. Elvsted is resting in my room.

TESMAN. Has Mrs. Elvsted been here all night?

HEDDA. Yes, since no one came to fetch her.

10 TESMAN. Ah, to be sure.

HEDDA [closes the door of the stove and rises]. Well, did you enjoy yourself at Judge Brack's?

TESMAN. Have you been anxious about me?

15 Eh?

HEDDA. No, I should never think of being anxious. But I asked if you had enjoyed yourself.

TESMAN. Oh yes,—for once in a way. Espe-
20 cially the beginning of the evening; for then Eilert read me part of his book. We arrived more than an hour too early—fancy that! And Brack had all sorts of arrangements to make —so Eilert read to me.

25 HEDDA [seating herself by the table on the right]. Well? Tell me, then—

TESMAN [sitting on a foot-stool near the stove]. Oh Hedda, you can't conceive what a book that is going to be! I believe it is one of
30 the most remarkable things that have ever been written. Fancy that!

HEDDA. Yes, yes; I don't care about that—

TESMAN. I must make a confession to you, Hedda. When he had finished reading—a hor-
35 rid feeling came over me.

HEDDA. A horrid feeling?

TESMAN. I felt jealous of Eilert for having had it in him to write such a book. Only think, Hedda!

40 HEDDA. Yes, yes, I am thinking!

TESMAN. And then how pitiful to think that he—with all his gifts—should be irreclaimable after all.

HEDDA. I suppose you mean that he has
45 more courage than the rest?

TESMAN. No, not at all—I mean that he is incapable of taking his pleasures in moderation.

HEDDA. And what came of it all—in the end?

TESMAN. Well, to tell the truth, I think it might best be described as an orgy, Hedda. 50

HEDDA. Had he vine-leaves in his hair?

TESMAN. Vine-leaves? No, I saw nothing of the sort. But he made a long, rambling speech in honor of the woman who had inspired him in his work—that was the phrase he used. 55

HEDDA. Did he name her?

TESMAN. No, he didn't; but I can't help thinking he meant Mrs. Elvsted. You may be sure he did.

HEDDA. Well—where did you part from him? 60

TESMAN. On the way to town. We broke up —the last of us at any rate—all together; and Brack came with us to get a breath of fresh air. And then, you see, we agreed to take Eilert home; for he had had far more than was good 65 for him.

HEDDA. I daresay.

TESMAN. But now comes the strange part of it, Hedda; or, I should rather say, the melancholy part of it. I declare I am almost ashamed 70 —on Eilert's account—to tell you—

HEDDA. Oh, go on—!

TESMAN. Well, as we were getting near town, you see, I happened to drop a little behind the others. Only for a minute or two—fancy that! 75

HEDDA. Yes, yes, yes, but—?

TESMAN. And then, as I hurried after them —what do you think I found by the wayside? Eh?

HEDDA. Oh, how should I know! 80

TESMAN. You mustn't speak of it to a soul, Hedda! Do you hear! Promise me, for Eilert's sake. [Draws a parcel, wrapped in paper, from his coat pocket.] Fancy, dear—I found this.

HEDDA. Is not that the parcel he had with 85 him yesterday?

TESMAN. Yes, it is the whole of his precious, irreplaceable manuscript! And he had gone and lost it, and knew nothing about it. Only fancy, Hedda! So deplorably— 90

HEDDA. But why did you not give him back the parcel at once?

TESMAN. I didn't dare to—in the state he was then in—

HEDDA. Did you not tell any of the others 95 that you had found it?

TESMAN. Oh, far from it! You can surely understand that, for Eilert's sake, I wouldn't do that.

HEDDA. So no one knows that Eilert Lövborg's manuscript is in your possession?

TESMAN. No. And no one must know it.

HEDDA. Then what did you say to him afterwards?

TESMAN. I didn't talk to him again at all; for when we got in among the streets, he and two or three of the others gave us the slip and disappeared. Fancy that!

HEDDA. Indeed! They must have taken him home then.

TESMAN. Yes, so it would appear. And Brack, too, left us.

HEDDA. And what have you been doing with yourself since?

TESMAN. Well, I and some of the others went home with one of the party, a jolly fellow, and took our morning coffee with him; or perhaps I should rather call it our night coffee—eh? But now, when I have rested a little, and given Eilert, poor fellow, time to have his sleep out, I must take this back to him.

HEDDA [*holds out her hand for the packet*]. No—don't give it to him! Not in such a hurry, I mean. Let me read it first.

TESMAN. No, my dearest Hedda, I mustn't, I really mustn't.

HEDDA. You must not?

TESMAN. No—for you can imagine what a state of despair he will be in when he awakens and misses the manuscript. He has no copy of it, you must know! He told me so.

HEDDA [*looking searchingly at him*]. Can such a thing not be reproduced? Written over again?

TESMAN. No, I don't think that would be possible. For the inspiration, you see—

HEDDA. Yes, yes—I suppose it depends on that. [*Lightly.*] But, by-the-bye—here is a letter for you.

TESMAN. Fancy—!

HEDDA [*handing it to him*]. It came early this morning.

TESMAN. It's from Aunt Julia! What can it be? [*He lays the packet on the other foot-stool, opens the letter, runs his eye through it, and jumps up.*] Oh, Hedda—she says that poor Aunt Rina is dying!

HEDDA. Well, we were prepared for that.

TESMAN. And that if I want to see her again, I must make haste. I'll run in to them at once.

HEDDA [*suppressing a smile*]. Will you run?

TESMAN. Oh, dearest Hedda—if you could only make up your mind to come with me! Just think!

HEDDA [*rises and says wearily, repelling the idea*]. No, no, don't ask me. I will not look upon sickness and death. I loathe all sorts of ugliness.

TESMAN. Well, well, then—! [*Bustling around.*] My hat—My overcoat—? Oh, in the hall—I do hope I mayn't come too late, Hedda! Eh?

HEDDA. Oh, if you run—

[BERTA *appears at the hall door.*]

BERTA. Judge Brack is at the door, and wishes to know if he may come in.

TESMAN. At this time! No, I can't possibly see him.

HEDDA. But I can. [*To* BERTA.] Ask Judge Brack to come in.

[BERTA *goes out.*]

HEDDA [*quickly whispering*]. The parcel, Tesman! [*She snatches it up from the stool.*]

TESMAN. Yes, give it to me!

HEDDA. No, no, I will keep it till you come back.

[*She goes to the writing-table and places it in the book-case.* TESMAN *stands in a flurry of haste, and cannot get his gloves on.* JUDGE BRACK *enters from the hall.*]

HEDDA [*nodding to him*]. You are an early bird, I must say.

BRACK. Yes, don't you think so? [*To* TESMAN.] Are you on the move, too?

TESMAN. Yes, I must rush off to my aunts'. Fancy—the invalid one is lying at death's door, poor creature.

BRACK. Dear me, is she indeed? Then on no account let me detain you. At such a critical moment—

TESMAN. Yes, I must really rush—Good-bye! Good-bye!

[*He hastens out by the hall door.*]

HEDDA [*approaching.*] You seem to have made a particularly lively night of it at your rooms, Judge Brack.

5   BRACK. I assure you I have not had my clothes off, Mrs. Hedda.

HEDDA. Not you, either?

BRACK. No, as you may see. But what has Tesman been telling you of the night's adven-
10 tures?

HEDDA. Oh, some tiresome story. Only that they went and had coffee somewhere or other.

BRACK. I have heard about that coffee-party already. Eilert Lövborg was not with them, I
15 fancy?

HEDDA. No, they had taken him home before that.

BRACK. Tesman, too?

HEDDA. No, but some of the others, he said.
20   BRACK [*smiling*]. George Tesman is really an ingenuous creature, Mrs. Hedda.

HEDDA. Yes, heaven knows he is. Then is there something behind all this?

BRACK. Yes, perhaps there may be.
25   HEDDA. Well then, sit down, my dear Judge, and tell your story in comfort.

[*She seats herself to the left of the table.* BRACK *sits near her, at the long side of the table.*]
30   HEDDA. Now then?

BRACK. I had special reasons for keeping track of my guests—or rather of some of my guests—last night.

HEDDA. Of Eilert Lövborg among the rest,
35 perhaps?

BRACK. Frankly, yes.

HEDDA. Now you make me really curious—

BRACK. Do you know where he and one or two of the others finished the night, Mrs.
40 Hedda?

HEDDA. If it is not quite unmentionable, tell me.

BRACK. Oh no, it's not at all unmentionable. Well, they put in an appearance at a particu-
45 larly animated soirée.

HEDDA. Of the lively kind?

BRACK. Of the very liveliest—

HEDDA. Tell me more of this, Judge Brack—

BRACK. Lövborg, as well as the others, had been invited in advance. I knew all about it. 50 But he had declined the invitation; for now, as you know, he has become a new man.

HEDDA. Up at the Elvsteds', yes. But he went after all, then?

BRACK. Well, you see, Mrs. Hedda—unhap- 55 pily the spirit moved him at my rooms last evening—

HEDDA. Yes, I hear he found inspiration.

BRACK. Pretty violent inspiration. Well, I fancy, that altered his purpose; for we men 60 folk are unfortunately not always so firm in our principles as we ought to be.

HEDDA. Oh, I am sure you are an exception, Judge Brack. But as to Lövborg—?

BRACK. To make a long story short—he 65 landed at last in Mademoiselle Diana's rooms.

HEDDA. Mademoiselle Diana's?

BRACK. It was Mademoiselle Diana that was giving the soirée, to a select circle of her admirers and her lady friends. 70

HEDDA. Is she a red-haired woman?

BRACK. Precisely.

HEDDA. A sort of a—singer?

BRACK. Oh yes—in her leisure moments. And moreover a mighty huntress—of men— 75 Mrs. Hedda. You have no doubt heard of her. Eilert Lövborg was one of her most enthusiastic protectors—in the days of his glory.

HEDDA. And how did all this end?

BRACK. Far from amicably, it appears. After 80 a most tender meeting, they seem to have come to blows—

HEDDA. Lövborg and she?

BRACK. Yes. He accused her or her friends of having robbed him. He declared that his 85 pocket-book had disappeared—and other things as well. In short, he seems to have made a furious disturbance.

HEDDA. And what came of it all?

BRACK. It came to a general scrimmage, in 90 which the ladies as well as the gentlemen took part. Fortunately the police at last appeared on the scene.

HEDDA. The police too?

BRACK. Yes. I fancy it will prove a costly frolic for Eilert Lövborg, crazy being that he is.

HEDDA. How so?

5 BRACK. He seems to have made a violent resistance—to have hit one of the constables on the head and torn the coat off his back. So they had to march him off to the police-station with the rest.

10 HEDDA. How have you learnt all this?

BRACK. From the police themselves.

HEDDA [*gazing straight before her*]. So that is what happened. Then he had no vine-leaves in his hair.

15 BRACK. Vine-leaves, Mrs. Hedda?

HEDDA [*changing her tone*]. But tell me now, Judge—what is your real reason for tracking out Eilert Lövborg's movements so carefully?

BRACK. In the first place, it could not be en-
20 tirely indifferent to me if it should appear in the police-court that he came straight from my house.

HEDDA. Will the matter come into court, then?

25 BRACK. Of course. However, I should scarcely have troubled so much about that. But I thought that, as a friend of the family, it was my duty to supply you and Tesman with a full account of his nocturnal exploits.

30 HEDDA. Why so, Judge Brack?

BRACK. Why, because I have a shrewd suspicion that he intends to use you as a sort of blind.

HEDDA. Oh, how can you think such a
35 thing!

BRACK. Good heavens, Mrs. Hedda—we have eyes in our head. Mark my words! This Mrs. Elvsted will be in no hurry to leave town again.

40 HEDDA. Well, even if there should be anything between them, I suppose there are plenty of other places where they could meet.

BRACK. Not a single home. Henceforth, as before, every respectable house will be closed
45 against Eilert Lövborg.

HEDDA. And so ought mine to be, you mean?

BRACK. Yes. I confess it would be more than painful to me if this personage were to be made free of your house. How superfluous, how intrusive, he would be, if he were to force 50 his way into—

HEDDA. —into the triangle?

BRACK. Precisely. It would simply mean that I should find myself homeless.

HEDDA [*looks at him with a smile*]. So you 55 want to be the one cock in the basket—that is your aim.

BRACK [*nods slowly and lowers his voice*]. Yes, that is my aim. And for that I will fight— with every weapon I can command. 60

HEDDA [*her smile vanishing*]. I see you are a dangerous person—when it comes to the point.

BRACK. Do you think so?

HEDDA. I am beginning to think so. And I 65 am exceedingly glad to think—that you have no sort of hold over me.

BRACK [*laughing equivocally*]. Well, well, Mrs. Hedda—perhaps you are right there. If I had, who knows what I might be capable of? 70

HEDDA. Come, come now, Judge Brack. That sounds almost like a threat.

BRACK [*rising*]. Oh, not at all! The triangle, you know, ought, if possible, to be spontaneously constructed. 75

HEDDA. There I agree with you.

BRACK. Well, now I have said all I had to say; and I had better be getting back to town. Good-bye, Mrs. Hedda. [*He goes towards the glass door.*] 80

HEDDA [*rising*]. Are you going through the garden?

BRACK. Yes, it's a short cut for me.

HEDDA. And then it is the back way, too.

BRACK. Quite so. I have no objection to back 85 ways. They may be piquant enough at times.

HEDDA. When there is ball practice going on, you mean?

BRACK [*in the doorway, laughing to her*]. Oh, people don't shoot their tame poultry, I 90 fancy.

HEDDA [*also laughing*]. Oh no, when there is only one cock in the basket—

[*They exchange laughing nods of farewell.*

He goes. She closes the door behind him.
HEDDA, *who has become quite serious, stands for a moment looking out. Presently she goes and peeps through the curtain over the middle*
5 *doorway. Then she goes to the writing-table, takes* LÖVBORG's *packet out of the book-case, and is on the point of looking through its contents.* BERTA *is heard speaking loudly in the hall.* HEDDA *turns and listens. Then she hastily*
10 *locks up the packet in the drawer, and lays the key on the inkstand.* EILERT LÖVBORG, *with his great coat on and his hat in his hand, tears open the hall door. He looks somewhat confused and irritated.*]

15 LÖVBORG [*looking towards the hall*]. And I tell you I must and will come in! There!

[*He closes the door, turns and sees* HEDDA, *at once regains his self-control, and bows.*]

HEDDA [*at the writing-table*]. Well, Mr. Löv-
20 borg, this is rather a late hour to call for Thea.

LÖVBORG. You mean rather an early hour to call on you. Pray pardon me.

HEDDA. How do you know that she is still here?

25 LÖVBORG. They told me at her lodgings that she had been out all night.

HEDDA [*going to the oval table*]. Did you notice anything about the people of the house when they said that?

30 LÖVBORG [*looks inquiringly at her*]. Notice anything about them?

HEDDA. I mean, did they seem to think it odd?

LÖVBORG [*suddenly understanding*]. Oh yes,
35 of course! I am dragging her down with me! However, I didn't notice anything.—I suppose Tesman is not up yet?

HEDDA. No—I think not—

LÖVBORG. When did he come home?

40 HEDDA. Very late.

LÖVBORG. Did he tell you anything?

HEDDA. Yes, I gathered that you had had an exceedingly jolly evening at Judge Brack's.

LÖVBORG. Nothing more?

45 HEDDA. I don't think so. However, I was so dreadfully sleepy—

[MRS. ELVSTED *enters through the curtains of the middle doorway.*]

MRS. ELVSTED [*going towards him*]. Ah,
Lövborg! At last—!   50

LÖVBORG. Yes, at last. And too late!

MRS. ELVSTED [*looks anxiously at him*]. What is too late?

LÖVBORG. Everything is too late now. It is all over with me.   55

MRS. ELVSTED. Oh no, no—don't say that!

LÖVBORG. You will say the same when you hear—

MRS. ELVSTED. I won't hear anything!

HEDDA. Perhaps you would prefer to talk to   60
her alone! If so, I will leave you.

LÖVBORG. No, stay—you too. I beg you to stay.

MRS. ELVSTED. Yes, but I won't hear anything, I tell you.   65

LÖVBORG. It is not last night's adventures that I want to talk about.

MRS. ELVSTED. What is it then—?

LÖVBORG. I want to say that now our ways must part.   70

MRS. ELVSTED. Part!

HEDDA [*involuntarily*]. I knew it!

LÖVBORG. You can be of no more service to me, Thea.

MRS. ELVSTED. How can you stand there and   75
say that! No more service to you! Am I not to help you now, as before? Are we not to go on working together?

LÖVBORG. Henceforward I shall do no work.

MRS. ELVSTED [*despairingly*]. Then what am   80
I to do with my life?

LÖVBORG. You must try to live your life as if you had never known me.

MRS. ELVSTED. But you know I cannot do that!   85

LÖVBORG. Try if you cannot, Thea. You must go home again—

MRS. ELVSTED [*in vehement protest*]. Never in this world! Where you are, there will I be also! I will not let myself be driven away like   90
this! I will remain here! I will be with you when the book appears.

HEDDA [*half aloud, in suspense*]. Ah yes—
the book!

LÖVBORG [*looks at her*]. My book and   95
Thea's; for that is what it is.

MRS. ELVSTED. Yes, I feel that it is. And that is why I have a right to be with you when it appears! I will see with my own eyes how respect and honor pour in upon you afresh. And
5 the happiness—the happiness—oh, I must share it with you!

LÖVBORG. Thea—our book will never appear.

HEDDA. Ah!

10 MRS. ELVSTED. Never appear!

LÖVBORG. Can never appear.

MRS. ELVSTED [*in agonized foreboding*]. Lövborg—what have you done with the manuscript?

15 HEDDA [*looks anxiously at him*]. Yes, the manuscript—?

MRS. ELVSTED. Where is it?

LÖVBORG. Oh Thea—don't ask me about it!

MRS. ELVSTED. Yes, yes, I will know. I de-
20 mand to be told at once.

LÖVBORG. The manuscript—Well then—I have torn the manuscript into a thousand pieces.

MRS. ELVSTED [*shrieks*]. Oh no, no—!

25 HEDDA [*involuntarily*]. But that's not—

LÖVBORG [*looks at her*]. Not true, you think?

HEDDA [*collecting herself*]. Oh well, of course—since you say so. But it sounded so improbable—

30 LÖVBORG. It is true, all the same.

MRS. ELVSTED [*wringing her hands*]. Oh God—oh God, Hedda—torn his own work to pieces!

LÖVBORG. I have torn my own life to pieces.
35 So why should I not tear my life-work too—?

MRS. ELVSTED. And you did this last night?

LÖVBORG. Yes, I tell you! Tore it into a thousand pieces and scattered them on the fiord—far out. There there is cool sea-water at
40 any rate—let them drift upon it—drift with the current and the wind. And then presently they will sink—deeper and deeper—as I shall, Thea.

MRS. ELVSTED. Do you know, Lövborg, that what you have done with the book—I shall
45 think of it to my dying day as though you had killed a little child.

LÖVBORG. Yes, you are right. It is a sort of child-murder.

MRS. ELVSTED. How could you, then—! Did not the child belong to me too?
50

HEDDA [*almost inaudibly*]. Ah, the child—

MRS. ELVSTED [*breathing heavily*]. It is all over then. Well, well, now I will go, Hedda.

HEDDA. But you are not going away from town?
55

MRS. ELVSTED. Oh, I don't know what I shall do. I see nothing but darkness before me. [*She goes out by the hall door.*]

HEDDA [*stands waiting for a moment*]. So you are not going to see her home, Mr. 60 Lövborg?

LÖVBORG. I? Through the streets? Would you have people see her walking with me?

HEDDA. Of course I don't know what else may have happened last night. But is it so 65 utterly irretrievable?

LÖVBORG. It will not end with last night—I know that perfectly well. And the thing is that now I have no taste for that sort of life either. I won't begin it anew. She has broken my 70 courage and my power of braving life out.

HEDDA [*looking straight before her*]. So that pretty little fool has had her fingers in a man's destiny. [*Looks at him.*] But all the same, how could you treat her so heartlessly? 75

LÖVBORG. Oh, don't say that it was heartless!

HEDDA. To go and destroy what has filled her whole soul for months and years. You do not call that heartless!

LÖVBORG. To you I can tell the truth, Hedda. 80

HEDDA. The truth?

LÖVBORG. First promise me—give me your word—that what I now confide to you Thea shall never know.

HEDDA. I give you my word. 85

LÖVBORG. Good. Then let me tell you that what I said just now was untrue.

HEDDA. About the manuscript?

LÖVBORG. Yes. I have not torn it to pieces—nor thrown it into the fiord. 90

HEDDA. No, no—But—where is it then?

LÖVBORG. I have destroyed it none the less—utterly destroyed it, Hedda!

HEDDA. I don't understand.

LÖVBORG. Thea said that what I had done 95 seemed to her like a child-murder.

HEDDA. Yes, so she said.

LÖVBORG. But to kill his child—that is not the worst thing a father can do to it.

HEDDA. Not the worst?

5 LÖVBORG. No. I wanted to spare Thea from hearing the worst.

HEDDA. Then what is the worst?

LÖVBORG. Suppose now, Hedda, that a man —in the small hours of the morning—came 10 home to his child's mother after a night of riot and debauchery, and said: "Listen—I have been here and there—in this place and in that. And I have taken our child with me—to this place and to that. And I have lost the child— 15 utterly lost it. The devil knows into what hands it may have fallen—who may have had their clutches on it."

HEDDA. Well—but when all is said and done, you know—that was only a book—

20 LÖVBORG. Thea's pure soul was in that book.

HEDDA. Yes, so I understand.

LÖVBORG. And you can understand, too, that for her and me together no future is possible.

HEDDA. What path do you mean to take 25 then?

LÖVBORG. None. I will only try to make an end of it all—the sooner the better.

HEDDA [a step nearer to him]. Eilert Lövborg —listen to me. Will you not try to—to do it 30 beautifully?

LÖVBORG. Beautifully? [Smiling.] With vine-leaves in my hair, as you used to dream in the old days—?

HEDDA. No, no. I have lost my faith in the 35 vine-leaves. But beautifully, nevertheless! For once in a way!—Good-bye! You must go now —and do not come here any more.

LÖVBORG. Good-bye, Mrs. Tesman. And give George Tesman my love. [He is on the point of 40 going.]

HEDDA. No, wait! I must give you a memento to take with you.

[She goes to the writing-table and opens the drawer and the pistol-case; then returns to 45 LÖVBORG with one of the pistols.]

LÖVBORG [looks at her]. This? Is this the memento?

HEDDA [nodding slowly]. Do you recognize it? It was aimed at you once.

LÖVBORG. You should have used it then. 50

HEDDA. Take it—and do you use it now.

LÖVBORG [puts the pistol in his breast pocket]. Thanks!

HEDDA. And beautifully, Eilert Lövborg. Promise me that! 55

LÖVBORG. Good-bye, Hedda Gabler. [He goes out by the hall door.]

[HEDDA listens for a moment at the door. Then she goes up to the writing-table, takes out the packet of manuscript, peeps under the 60 cover, draws a few of the sheets half out, and looks at them. Next she goes over and seats herself in the arm-chair beside the stove, with the packet in her lap. Presently she opens the stove door, and then the packet.] 65

HEDDA [throws one of the quires into the fire and whispers to herself]. Now I am burning your child, Thea!—Burning it, curly-locks! [Throwing one or two more quires into the stove.] Your child and Eilert Lövborg's. 70 [Throws the rest in.] I am burning—I am burning your child.

ACT IV

[The same rooms at the TESMANS'. It is evening. The drawing-room is in darkness. The back room is lighted by the hanging lamp over 75 the table. The curtains over the glass door are drawn close.

HEDDA, dressed in black, walks to and fro in the dark room. Then she goes into the back room and disappears for a moment to the left. 80 She is heard to strike a few chords on the piano. Presently she comes in sight again, and returns to the drawing-room. BERTA enters from the right, through the inner room, with a lighted lamp, which she places on the table 85 in front of the corner settee in the drawing-room. Her eyes are red with weeping, and she has black ribbons in her cap. She goes quietly and circumspectly out to the right. HEDDA goes up to the glass door, lifts the cur- 90 tain a little aside, and looks out into the darkness. Shortly afterwards, MISS TESMAN, in mourning, with a bonnet and veil on, comes in from the hall. HEDDA goes towards her and holds out her hand.] 95

MISS TESMAN. Yes, Hedda, here I am, in mourning and forlorn; for now my poor sister has at last found peace.

HEDDA. I have heard the news already, as you see. Tesman sent me a card.

MISS TESMAN. Yes, he promised me he would. But nevertheless I thought that to Hedda—here in the house of life—I ought myself to bring the tidings of death.

HEDDA. That was very kind of you.

MISS TESMAN. Ah, Rina ought not to have left us just now. This is not the time for Hedda's house to be a house of mourning.

HEDDA [*changing the subject*]. She died quite peacefully, did she not, Miss Tesman?

MISS TESMAN. Oh, her end was so calm, so beautiful. And then she had the unspeakable happiness of seeing George once more—and bidding him good-bye.—Has he come home yet?

HEDDA. No. He wrote that he might be detained. But won't you sit down?

MISS TESMAN. No thank you, my dear, dear Hedda. I should like to, but I have so much to do. I must prepare my dear one for her rest as well as I can. She shall go to her grave looking her best.

HEDDA. Can I not help you in any way?

MISS TESMAN. Oh, you must not think of it! Hedda Tesman must have no hand in such mournful work. Nor let her thoughts dwell on it either—not at this time.

HEDDA. One is not always mistress of one's thoughts—

MISS TESMAN [*continuing*]. Ah yes, it is the way of the world. At home we shall be sewing a shroud; and here there will soon be sewing too, I suppose—but of another sort, thank God!

[GEORGE TESMAN *enters by the hall door.*]

HEDDA. Ah, you have come at last!

TESMAN. You here, Aunt Julia? With Hedda? Fancy that!

MISS TESMAN. I was just going, my dear boy. Well, have you done all you promised?

TESMAN. No; I'm really afraid I have forgotten half of it. I must come to you again tomorrow. Today my brain is all in a whirl. I can't keep my thoughts together.

MISS TESMAN. Why, my dear George, you mustn't take it in this way.

TESMAN. Mustn't—? How do you mean?

MISS TESMAN. Even in your sorrow you must rejoice, as I do—rejoice that she is at rest.

TESMAN. Oh yes, yes—you are thinking of Aunt Rina.

HEDDA. You will feel lonely now, Miss Tesman.

MISS TESMAN. Just at first, yes. But that will not last very long, I hope. I daresay I shall soon find an occupant for poor Rina's little room.

TESMAN. Indeed? Who do you think will take it? Eh?

MISS TESMAN. Oh, there's always some poor invalid or other in want of nursing, unfortunately.

HEDDA. Would you really take such a burden upon you again?

MISS TESMAN. A burden! Heaven forgive you, child—it has been no burden to me.

HEDDA. But suppose you had a total stranger on your hands—

MISS TESMAN. Oh, one soon makes friends with sick folk; and it's such an absolute necessity for me to have some one to live for. Well, heaven be praised, there may soon be something in this house, too, to keep an old aunt busy.

HEDDA. Oh, don't trouble about anything here.

TESMAN. Yes, just fancy what a nice time we three might have together, if—?

HEDDA. If—?

TESMAN [*uneasily*]. Oh, nothing. It will all come right. Let us hope so—eh?

MISS TESMAN. Well, well, I daresay you two want to talk to each other. [*Smiling.*] And perhaps Hedda may have something to tell you too, George. Good-bye! I must go home to Rina. [*Turning at the door.*] How strange it is to think that now Rina is with me and with my poor brother as well!

TESMAN. Yes, fancy that, Aunt Julia! Eh?

[MISS TESMAN *goes out by the hall door.*]

HEDDA [*follows* TESMAN *coldly and searchingly with her eyes*]. I almost believe your Aunt Rina's death affects you more than it does your Aunt Julia.

TESMAN. Oh, it's not that alone. It's Eilert I am so terribly uneasy about.

HEDDA [*quickly*]. Is there anything new about him?

5   TESMAN. I looked in at his rooms this afternoon, intending to tell him the manuscript was in safe keeping.

HEDDA. Well, did you not find him?

TESMAN. No. He wasn't at home. But afterwards I met Mrs. Elvsted, and she told me he had been here early this morning.

10

HEDDA. Yes, directly after you had gone.

TESMAN. And he said that he had torn his manuscript to pieces—eh?

15   HEDDA. Yes, so he declared.

TESMAN. Why, good heavens, he must have been completely out of his mind! And I suppose you thought it best not to give it back to him, Hedda?

20   HEDDA. No, he did not get it.

TESMAN. But of course you told him that we had it?

HEDDA. No. [*Quickly.*] Did you tell Mrs. Elvsted?

25   TESMAN. No; I thought I had better not. But you ought to have told him. Fancy, if, in desperation, he should go and do himself some injury! Let me have the manuscript, Hedda! I will take it to him at once. Where is it?

30   HEDDA [*cold and immovable, leaning on the arm-chair*]. I have not got it.

TESMAN. Have not got it? What in the world do you mean?

HEDDA. I have burnt it—every line of it.

35   TESMAN [*with a violent movement of terror*]. Burnt! Burnt Eilert's manuscript!

HEDDA. Don't scream so. The servant might hear you.

TESMAN. Burnt! Why, good God—! No, no, no! It's impossible!

40

HEDDA. It is so, nevertheless.

TESMAN. Do you know what you have done, Hedda? It's unlawful appropriation of lost property. Fancy that! Just ask Judge Brack, and he'll tell you what it is.

45

HEDDA. I advise you not to speak of it—either to Judge Brack, or to any one else.

TESMAN. But how could you do anything so unheard-of? What put it into your head? What possessed you? Answer me that—eh?   50

HEDDA [*suppressing an almost imperceptible smile*]. I did it for your sake, George.

TESMAN. For my sake!

HEDDA. This morning, when you told me about what he had read to you—   55

TESMAN. Yes, yes—what then?

HEDDA. You acknowledged that you envied his work.

TESMAN. Oh, of course I didn't mean that literally.   60

HEDDA. No matter—I could not bear the idea that any one should throw you into the shade.

TESMAN. [*in an outburst of mingled doubt and joy*]. Hedda! Oh, is this true? But—but—I never knew you to show your love like that   65 before. Fancy that!

HEDDA. Well, I may as well tell you that—just at this time—[*impatiently, breaking off*]. No, no; you can ask Aunt Julia. She will tell you, fast enough.   70

TESMAN. Oh, I almost think I understand you, Hedda! [*Clasps his hands together.*] Great heavens! do you really mean it! Eh?

HEDDA. Don't shout so. The servant might hear.   75

TESMAN [*laughing in irrepressible glee*]. The servant! Why, how absurd you are, Hedda. It's only my old Berta! Why, I'll tell Berta myself.

HEDDA [*clenching her hands together in desperation*]. Oh, it is killing me,—it is killing me,   80 all this!

TESMAN. What is, Hedda? Eh?

HEDDA [*coldly, controlling herself*]. All this —absurdity—George.

TESMAN. Absurdity! Do you see anything   85 absurd in my being overjoyed at the news! But after all perhaps I had better not say anything to Berta.

HEDDA. Oh—why not that too?

TESMAN. No, no, not yet! But I must certainly tell Aunt Julia. And then that you have   90 begun to call me George too! Fancy that! Oh, Aunt Julia will be so happy—so happy.

HEDDA. When she hears that I have burnt Eilert Lövborg's manuscript—for your sake?   95

TESMAN. No, by-the-bye—that affair of the

manuscript—of course nobody must know about that. But that you love me° so much, Hedda—Aunt Julia must really share my joy in that! I wonder, now, whether this sort of thing is usual in young wives? Eh?

HEDDA. I think you had better ask Aunt Julia that question too.

TESMAN. I will indeed, some time or other. [*Looks uneasy and downcast again.*] And yet the manuscript—the manuscript! Good God! it is terrible to think what will become of poor Eilert now.

[MRS. ELVSTED, *dressed as in the first act, with hat and cloak, enters by the hall door.*]

MRS. ELVSTED [*greets them hurriedly, and says in evident agitation*]. Oh, dear Hedda, forgive my coming again.

HEDDA. What is the matter with you, Thea?

TESMAN. Something about Eilert Lövborg again—eh?

MRS. ELVSTED. Yes! I am dreadfully afraid some misfortune has happened to him.

HEDDA [*seizes her arm*]. Ah,—do you think so?

TESMAN. Why, good Lord—what makes you think that, Mrs. Elvsted?

MRS. ELVSTED. I heard them talking of him at my boarding-house—just as I came in. Oh, the most incredible rumors are afloat about him today.

TESMAN. Yes, fancy, so I heard too! And I can bear witness that he went straight home to bed last night. Fancy that!

HEDDA. Well, what did they say at the boarding-house?

MRS. ELVSTED. Oh, I couldn't make out anything clearly. Either they knew nothing definite, or else— They stopped talking when they saw me; and I did not dare to ask.

TESMAN [*moving about uneasily*]. We must hope—we must hope that you misunderstood them, Mrs. Elvsted.

MRS. ELVSTED. No, no; I am sure it was of him they were talking. And I heard something about the hospital or—

TESMAN. The hospital?

love me "burn for me" in the Norwegian

HEDDA. No—surely that cannot be!

MRS. ELVSTED. Oh, I was in such mortal terror! I went to his lodgings and asked for him there.

HEDDA. You could make up your mind to that, Thea!

MRS. ELVSTED. What else could I do? I really could bear the suspense no longer.

TESMAN. But you didn't find him either—eh?

MRS. ELVSTED. No. And the people knew nothing about him. He hadn't been home since yesterday afternoon, they said.

TESMAN. Yesterday! Fancy, how could they say that?

MRS. ELVSTED. Oh, I am sure something terrible must have happened to him.

TESMAN. Hedda dear—how would it be if I were to go and make inquiries—?

HEDDA. No, no—don't you mix yourself up in this affair.

[JUDGE BRACK, *with his hat in his hand, enters by the hall door, which* BERTA *opens, and closes behind him. He looks grave and bows in silence.*]

TESMAN. Oh, is that you, my dear Judge? Eh?

BRACK. Yes. It was imperative I should see you this evening.

TESMAN. I can see you have heard the news about Aunt Rina.

BRACK. Yes, that among other things.

TESMAN. Isn't it sad—eh?

BRACK. Well, my dear Tesman, that depends on how you look at it.

TESMAN [*looks doubtfully at him*]. Has anything else happened?

BRACK. Yes.

HEDDA [*in suspense*]. Anything sad, Judge Brack?

BRACK. That, too, depends on how you look at it, Mrs. Tesman.

MRS. ELVSTED [*unable to restrain her anxiety*]. Oh! it is something about Eilert Lövborg!

BRACK [*with a glance at her*]. What makes you think that, Madam? Perhaps you have already heard something—?

MRS. ELVSTED [*in confusion*]. No, nothing at all, but—

TESMAN. Oh, for heaven's sake, tell us!

BRACK [*shrugging his shoulders*]. Well, I regret to say Eilert Lövborg has been taken to the hospital. He is lying at the point of death.

MRS. ELVSTED [*shrieks*]. Oh God! Oh God—

5 TESMAN. To the hospital! And at the point of death.

HEDDA [*involuntarily*]. So soon then—

MRS. ELVSTED [*wailing*]. And we parted in anger, Hedda!

10 HEDDA [*whispers*]. Thea—Thea—be careful!

MRS. ELVSTED [*not heeding her*]. I must go to him! I must see him alive!

BRACK. It is useless, Madam. No one will be 15 admitted.

MRS. ELVSTED. Oh, at least tell me what has happened to him? What is it?

TESMAN. You don't mean to say that he has himself— Eh?

20 HEDDA. Yes, I am sure he has.

TESMAN. Hedda, how can you—?

BRACK [*keeping his eyes fixed upon her*]. Unfortunately you have guessed quite correctly, Mrs. Tesman.

25 MRS. ELVSTED. Oh, how horrible!

TESMAN. Himself, then! Fancy that!

HEDDA. Shot himself!

BRACK. Rightly guessed again, Mrs. Tesman.

MRS. ELVSTED [*with an effort at self-control*].
30 When did it happen, Mr. Brack?

BRACK. This afternoon—between three and four.

TESMAN. But, good Lord, where did he do it? Eh?

35 BRACK [*with some hesitation*]. Where? Well —I suppose at his lodgings.

MRS. ELVSTED. No, that cannot be; for I was there between six and seven.

BRACK. Well, then, somewhere else. I don't 40 know exactly. I only know that he was found—. He had shot himself—in the breast.

MRS. ELVSTED. Oh, how terrible! That he should die like that!

HEDDA [*to* BRACK]. Was it in the breast?
45 BRACK. Yes—as I told you.

HEDDA. Not in the temple?

BRACK. In the breast, Mrs. Tesman.

HEDDA. Well, well—the breast is a good place, too.

BRACK. How do you mean, Mrs. Tesman? 50

HEDDA [*evasively*]. Oh, nothing—nothing.

TESMAN. And the wound is dangerous, you say—eh?

BRACK. Absolutely mortal. The end has probably come by this time. 55

MRS. ELVSTED. Yes, yes, I feel it. The end! The end! Oh, Hedda—!

TESMAN. But tell me, how have you learnt all this?

BRACK [*curtly*]. Through one of the police. A 60 man I had some business with.

HEDDA [*in a clear voice*]. At last a deed worth doing!

TESMAN [*terrified*]. Good heavens, Hedda! what are you saying? 65

HEDDA. I say there is beauty in this.

BRACK. H'm, Mrs. Tesman—

TESMAN. Beauty! Fancy that!

MRS. ELVSTED. Oh, Hedda, how can you talk of beauty in such an act! 70

HEDDA. Eilert Lövborg has himself made up his account with life. He has had the courage to do—the one right thing.

MRS. ELVSTED. No, you must never think that was how it happened! It must have been in 75 delirium that he did it.

TESMAN. In despair!

HEDDA. That he did not. I am certain of that.

MRS. ELVSTED. Yes, yes! In delirium! Just as when he tore up our manuscript. 80

BRACK [*starting*]. The manuscript? Has he torn that up?

MRS. ELVSTED. Yes, last night.

TESMAN [*whispers softly*]. Oh, Hedda, we shall never get over this. 85

BRACK. H'm, very extraordinary.

TESMAN [*moving about the room*]. To think of Eilert going out of the world in this way! And not leaving behind him the book that would have immortalized his name— 90

MRS. ELVSTED. Oh, if only it could be put together again!

TESMAN. Yes, if it only could! I don't know what I would not give—

Mrs. Elvsted. Perhaps it can, Mr. Tesman.

Tesman. What do you mean?

Mrs. Elvsted [*searches in the pocket of her dress*]. Look here. I have kept all the loose notes he used to dictate from.

Hedda [*a step forward*]. Ah—!

Tesman. You have kept them, Mrs. Elvsted! Eh?

Mrs. Elvsted. Yes, I have them here. I put them in my pocket when I left home. Here they still are—

Tesman. Oh, do let me see them!

Mrs. Elvsted [*hands him a bundle of papers*]. But they are in such disorder—all mixed up.

Tesman. Fancy, if we could make something out of them, after all! Perhaps if we two put our heads together—

Mrs. Elvsted. Oh, yes, at least let us try—

Tesman. We will manage it! We must! I will dedicate my life to this task.

Hedda. You, George? Your life?

Tesman. Yes, or rather all the time I can spare. My own collections must wait in the meantime. Hedda—you understand, eh? I owe this to Eilert's memory.

Hedda. Perhaps.

Tesman. And so, my dear Mrs. Elvsted, we will give our whole minds to it. There is no use in brooding over what can't be undone—eh? We must try to control our grief as much as possible, and—

Mrs. Elvsted. Yes, yes, Mr. Tesman, I will do the best I can.

Tesman. Well then, come here. I can't rest until we have looked through the notes. Where shall we sit? Here? No, in there, in the back room. Excuse me, my dear Judge. Come with me, Mrs. Elvsted.

Mrs. Elvsted. Oh, if only it were possible!

[Tesman *and* Mrs. Elvsted *go into the back room. She takes off her hat and cloak. They both sit at the table under the hanging lamp, and are soon deep in an eager examination of the papers.* Hedda *crosses to the stove and sits in the arm-chair. Presently* Brack *goes up to her.*]

Hedda [*in a low voice*]. Oh, what a sense of freedom it gives one, this act of Eilert Lövborg's.

Brack. Freedom, Mrs. Hedda? Well, of course, it is a release for him—

Hedda. I mean for me. It gives me a sense of freedom to know that a deed of deliberate courage is still possible in this world,—a deed of spontaneous beauty.

Brack [*smiling*]. H'm—my dear Mrs. Hedda—

Hedda. Oh, I know what you are going to say. For you are a kind of a specialist too, like —you know!

Brack [*looking hard at her*]. Eilert Lövborg was more to you than perhaps you are willing to admit to yourself. Am I wrong?

Hedda. I don't answer such questions. I only know Eilert Lövborg has had the courage to live his life after his own fashion. And then—the last great act, with its beauty! Ah! that he should have the will and the strength to turn away from the banquet of life—so early.

Brack. I am sorry, Mrs. Hedda,—but I fear I must dispel an amiable illusion.

Hedda. Illusion?

Brack. Which could not have lasted long in any case.

Hedda. What do you mean?

Brack. Eilert Lövborg did not shoot himself voluntarily.

Hedda. Not voluntarily?

Brack. No. The thing did not happen exactly as I told it.

Hedda [*in suspense*]. Have you concealed something? What is it?

Brack. For poor Mrs. Elvsted's sake I idealized the facts a little.

Hedda. What are the facts?

Brack. First, that he is already dead.

Hedda. At the hospital?

Brack. Yes—without regaining consciousness.

Hedda. What more have you concealed?

Brack. This—the event did not happen at his lodgings.

Hedda. Oh, that can make no difference.

BRACK. Perhaps it may. For I must tell you—Eilert Lövborg was found shot in—in Mademoiselle Diana's boudoir.

HEDDA [*makes a motion as if to rise, but sinks back again*]. That is impossible, Judge Brack! He cannot have been there again today.

BRACK. He was there this afternoon. He went there, he said, to demand the return of something which they had taken from him. Talked wildly about a lost child—

HEDDA. Ah—so that was why—

BRACK. I thought probably he meant his manuscript; but now I hear he destroyed that himself. So I suppose it must have been his pocket-book.

HEDDA. Yes, no doubt. And there—there he was found?

BRACK. Yes, there. With a pistol in his breast-pocket, discharged. The ball had lodged in a vital part.

HEDDA. In the breast—yes.

BRACK. No—in the bowels.

HEDDA [*looks up at him with an expression of loathing*]. That too! Oh, what curse is it that makes everything I touch turn ludicrous and mean?

BRACK. There is one point more, Mrs. Hedda—another disagreeable feature in the affair.

HEDDA. And what is that?

BRACK. The pistol he carried—

HEDDA [*breathless*]. Well? What of it?

BRACK. He must have stolen it.

HEDDA [*leaps up*]. Stolen it! That is not true! He did not steal it!

BRACK. No other explanation is possible. He must have stolen it— Hush!

[TESMAN *and* MRS. ELVSTED *have risen from the table in the back room, and come into the drawing-room.*]

TESMAN [*with the papers in both his hands*]. Hedda dear, it is almost impossible to see under that lamp. Think of that!

HEDDA. Yes, I am thinking.

TESMAN. Would you mind our sitting at your writing-table—eh?

HEDDA. If you like. [*Quickly.*] No, wait! Let me clear it first!

TESMAN. Oh, you needn't trouble, Hedda. There is plenty of room.

HEDDA. No, no; let me clear it, I say! I will take these things in and put them on the piano. There! [*She has drawn out an object, covered with sheet music, from under the book-case, places several other pieces of music upon it, and carries the whole into the inner room, to the left.* TESMAN *lays the scraps of paper on the writing-table, and moves the lamp there from the corner table.* HEDDA *returns.*]

HEDDA [*behind* MRS. ELVSTED'S *chair, gently ruffling her hair*]. Well, my sweet Thea,—how goes it with Eilert Lövborg's monument?

MRS. ELVSTED [*looks dispiritedly up at her*]. Oh, it will be terribly hard to put in order.

TESMAN. We must manage it. I am determined. And arranging other people's papers is just the work for me.

[HEDDA *goes over to the stove, and seats herself on one of the foot-stools.* BRACK *stands over her, leaning on the arm-chair.*]

HEDDA [*whispers*]. What did you say about the pistol?

BRACK [*softly*]. That he must have stolen it.

HEDDA. Why stolen it?

BRACK. Because every other explanation ought to be impossible, Mrs. Hedda.

HEDDA. Indeed?

BRACK [*glances at her*]. Of course Eilert Lövborg was here this morning. Was he not?

HEDDA. Yes.

BRACK. Were you alone with him?

HEDDA. Part of the time.

BRACK. Did you not leave the room whilst he was here?

HEDDA. No.

BRACK. Try to recollect. Were you not out of the room a moment?

HEDDA. Yes, perhaps just a moment—out in the hall.

BRACK. And where was your pistol-case during that time?

HEDDA. I had it locked up in—

BRACK. Well, Mrs. Hedda?

HEDDA. The case stood there on the writing-table.

BRACK. Have you looked since, to see whether both the pistols are there?

HEDDA. No.

BRACK. Well, you need not. I saw the pistol
5 found in Lövborg's pocket, and I knew it at once as the one I had seen yesterday—and before, too.

HEDDA. Have you it with you?

BRACK. No; the police have it.

10 HEDDA. What will the police do with it?

BRACK. Search till they find the owner.

HEDDA. Do you think they will succeed?

BRACK [*bends over her and whispers*]. No, Hedda Gabler—not so long as I say nothing.

15 HEDDA [*looks frightened at him*]. And if you do not say nothing,—what then?

BRACK [*shrugs his shoulders*]. There is always the possibility that the pistol was stolen.

HEDDA [*firmly*]. Death rather than that.

20 BRACK [*smiling*]. People say such things— but they don't do them.

HEDDA [*without replying*]. And supposing the pistol was stolen, and the owner is discovered? What then?

25 BRACK. Well, Hedda—then comes the scandal.

HEDDA. The scandal!

BRACK. Yes, the scandal—of which you are mortally afraid. You will, of course, be brought
30 before the court—both you and Mademoiselle Diana. She will have to explain how the thing happened—whether it was an accidental shot or murder. Did the pistol go off as he was trying to take it out of his pocket, to threaten
35 her with? Or did she tear the pistol out of his hand, shoot him, and push it back into his pocket? That would be quite like her; for she is an able-bodied young person, this same Mademoiselle Diana.

40 HEDDA. But *I* have nothing to do with all this repulsive business.

BRACK. No. But you will have to answer the question: Why did you give Eilert Lövborg the pistol? And what conclusions will people
45 draw from the fact that you did give it to him?

HEDDA [*lets her head sink*]. That is true. I did not think of that.

BRACK. Well, fortunately, there is no danger, so long as I say nothing.

HEDDA [*looks up at him*]. So I am in your 50 power, Judge Brack. You have me at your beck and call, from this time forward.

BRACK [*whispers softly*]. Dearest Hedda— believe me—I shall not abuse my advantage.

HEDDA. I am in your power none the less. 55 Subject to your will and your demands. A slave, a slave then! [*Rises impetuously.*] No, I cannot endure the thought of that! Never!

BRACK [*looks half-mockingly at her*]. People generally get used to the inevitable. 60

HEDDA [*returns his look*]. Yes, perhaps. [*She crosses to the writing-table. Suppressing an involuntary smile, she imitates* TESMAN's *intonations.*] Well? Are you getting on, George? Eh? 65

TESMAN. Heaven knows, dear. In any case it will be the work of months.

HEDDA [*as before*]. Fancy that! [*Passes her hands softly through* MRS. ELVSTED's *hair.*] Doesn't it seem strange to you, Thea? Here are 70 you sitting with Tesman—just as you used to sit with Eilert Lövborg?

MRS. ELVSTED. Ah, if I could only inspire your husband in the same way.

HEDDA. Oh, that will come too—in time. 75

TESMAN. Yes, do you know, Hedda—I really think I begin to feel something of the sort. But won't you go and sit with Brack again?

HEDDA. Is there nothing I can do to help you two? 80

TESMAN. No, nothing in the world. [*Turning his head.*] I trust to you to keep Hedda company, my dear Brack.

BRACK [*with a glance at* HEDDA]. With the very greatest of pleasure. 85

HEDDA. Thanks. But I am tired this evening. I will go in and lie down a little on the sofa.

TESMAN. Yes, do dear—eh?

[HEDDA *goes into the back room and draws the curtains. A short pause. Suddenly she is* 90 *heard playing a wild dance on the piano.*]

MRS. ELVSTED [*starts from her chair*]. Oh— what is that?

TESMAN [*runs to the doorway*]. Why, my

dearest Hedda—don't play dance music to-
night! Just think of Aunt Rina! And of Eilert
too!

HEDDA [*puts her head out between the cur-*
5 *tains*]. And of Aunt Julia. And of all the rest
of them.—After this, I will be quiet. [*Closes the
curtains again.*]

TESMAN [*at the writing-table*]. It's not good
for her to see us at this distressing work. I'll
10 tell you what, Mrs. Elvsted,—you shall take
the empty room at Aunt Julia's, and then I will
come over in the evenings, and we can sit and
work there—eh?

HEDDA [*in the inner room*]. I hear what you
15 are saying, Tesman. But how am *I* to get
through the evenings out here?

TESMAN [*turning over the papers*]. Oh, I
daresay Judge Brack will be so kind as to look
in now and then, even though I am out.

20 BRACK [*in the arm-chair, calls out gaily*].
Every blessed evening, with all the pleasure in
life, Mrs. Tesman! We shall get on capitally
together, we two!

HEDDA [*speaking loud and clear*]. Yes, don't
25 you flatter yourself we will, Judge Brack? Now
that you are the one cock in the basket—

[*A shot is heard within.* TESMAN, MRS. ELV-
STED, *and* BRACK *leap to their feet.*]

TESMAN. Oh, now she is playing with those
30 pistols again.

[*He throws back the curtains and runs in,
followed by* MRS. ELVSTED. HEDDA *lies stretched
on the sofa, lifeless. Confusion and cries.*
BERTA *enters in alarm from the right.*]

35 TESMAN [*shrieks to* BRACK]. Shot herself!
Shot herself in the temple! Fancy that!

BRACK [*half-fainting in the arm-chair*]. Good
God!—people don't do such things.

Oscar Wilde

1854–1900

The Importance of Being Earnest

1895

"The Importance of Being Earnest . . . imitates nothing, represents nothing, means nothing, is nothing, except a sort of *rondo capriccioso,* in which the artist's fingers run with crisp irresponsibility up and down the keyboard of life."

—William Archer, 1895

Wilde tauntingly subtitled it, "a trivial play for serious people." From the first it inspired pronounced responses, mainly admiring, though sometimes qualified with bafflement. It has been awarded a place of honor in the line of Wycherley and Sheridan. It surely owes something, in the farcical revelation of Jack Worthing's actual parentage, to Gilbert and Sullivan. It seems a mere bubble, translucent yet opaque; flimsy—but only as a cobweb woven of steel filaments might be flimsy. Abounding in paradoxes, it is itself a paradox. A tissue of theater clichés, it glitters with originality. As the viewer's perspective shifts, this chameleon of a play changes hues. Consider some possible perspectives.

I. It seems less "an imitation of an action" (in the classic phrase) than an imitation of play-acting itself. Its plot, strictly ordered, parodies one of the persistent dramatic plots for both tragedy and comedy from *Oedipus Rex* down to the present: the search for and revelation of concealed or lost identity, with a climactic "recognition scene." Wilde pursues this formula with all the vigor of Jonson designing the sudden overthrow of Volpone, but in the end it is merely absurd. As for characters in the usual sense, who are they? Hardly more than names, charming masks with no "real" faces behind them. Even the formidable Lady Bracknell is the caricature of a she-dragon. Ostensibly concerned with serious matters of courtship and romance, they seem passionate only about cucumber sandwiches and muffins. What the actors are required to display is not convincing characterization but the art of acting itself, combined with the ability to show off expensive and stylish clothes and, above all, to speak the bouts of quip and repartee with the perfect timing, intonation, and super-elegant diction that are to this day a distinction of the English stage— as well as a source of envy or aversion to Americans. The interest of the play is systematically displaced from the usual dramatic centers to surfaces, to the theater itself. All is said and done as if in earnest but with the strongest underscoring, of *as if.* It is a play consisting entirely of play, playing with roles, playing with words and ideas. It is truly about nothing at all, all style and no content, all form and no substance. In Wilde's favorite phrase, "That is all."

II. But as Algernon observes, "The truth is rarely pure and never simple." Not absolutely pure and simple is the "Bunburying"—those subterfuges and fictions that symbolize almost every character's impulse to get away from the triviality of pressing social engagements, the nagging exactions of etiquette, the tyranny of high fashion, and the domination of Lady Bracknell. She alone is immune to the impulse, for she personifies voracious triviality itself. It is this theme that brings the play to what Eric Bentley calls "the frontier of satire," a frontier reached but perhaps not crossed. The Bunburyists only Bunbury off to whence they came: Algernon from West End flat to country estate; Jack from country estate to West End flat. From the intricately structured realm of high society, depicted just barely short of caricature, there is really no escape.

If this idea is nowhere directly uttered it still manages to permeate a play that only seems to be nothing but play. Elsewhere, in *The Soul of Man Under Socialism,* Wilde had explicitly declared that the existing social order, tolerating extremes of wealth and poverty, and exalting a supremely privileged upper class, impoverished the expression of "Individuality" at every level. From this viewpoint "Bunburying," even in its feeblest manifestation, protests against the empty tedium behind the social mask. The implied satire is aimed against not "nothing" but nothingness. Like the endless and at last boring scintillation of talk, the feeble little fiction resists what Byron termed "the awful yawn that sleep cannot abate," the sapping of personal vitality. From this viewpoint, the farcical happy ending is also total catastrophe. Everyone capitulates to Lady Bracknell.

III. "And certainly once a man begins to neglect his domestic duties he becomes painfully effeminate, does he not? And I don't like that. It makes men so very attractive." In Gwendolen's remark (and in several other places) Wilde knew as he wrote the words that he was planting a little time-bomb, sure to go off. It applied factually to himself — "effeminate" being a code-word for "homosexual" — as many of his audience knew full well, especially those most nearly depicted in the play. They also knew that homosexuality was fairly prevalent and secretly tolerated, but absolutely not acknowledged. The run of the play was abruptly halted by the outbreak of a scandal in which Wilde was the not altogether unwilling protagonist. His own version of "Bunburying" took the form of ill-concealed forays into the homosexual underworld and led to a criminal action against him. "Feasting with panthers," he called these forays, a phrase referring to the irresistible thrill of danger he derived from flouting the severest taboo of the very class represented in his play, the very class that applauded it. When the opportunity arose, they struck him down without compunction. In a way, he consented — provoked his trial, submitted to avoidable arrest, underwent two years at hard labor, and suffered total ruin. This story is also a drama but a tragic one. It is the dark root from which this comedy flowered.

For those "in the know" — and that must now mean all informed readers — this play, so light-hearted, so unoffending, contains the echo of tormented laughter. The self-destructive suggestions can be ignored. Wilde provided for that. But once they are entertained, the play has an altered look. **From the first perspective, it appears to be the last and most delicate hybrid flower of seventeenth- and eighteenth-century comic satire. From the second and third perspectives, it is almost secretly subversive of the society that it ostensibly flatters.**

The Importance of Being Earnest

WILDE

CHARACTERS

JOHN WORTHING, J.P.°
ALGERNON MONCRIEFF
REV. CANON CHASUBLE, D.D.°
MERRIMAN *butler*
LANE *manservant*
LADY BRACKNELL
HON. GWENDOLEN FAIRFAX°
CECILY CARDEW
MISS PRISM *governess*

THE SCENES OF THE PLAY

ACT I. *Algernon Moncrieff's Flat in Half-Moon Street, W.°*

ACT II. *The Garden at the Manor House, Woolton.*

ACT III. *Drawing-Room of the Manor House, Woolton.*

TIME. *The Present.*

PLACE. *London.*

J.P. justice of the peace; here, indicating a country gentleman with extensive property
Rev. Canon Chasuble, D.D. rector of an English country parish; holder of an honorary position (Canon) in a cathedral; a "chasuble" (a priest's vestment) identifies him as "high church" or Anglo-Catholic; and doctor of divinity, a degree in theology
Hon. Gwendolen Fairfax her father is a peer and carries a title of nobility, "Bracknell"; the family surname is Fairfax
Half-Moon Street, W in the fashionable West End of London; this like other addresses mentioned — the Albany, Willis's restaurant, Belgrave and Grosvenor squares — signifies wealth and social standing

ACT I

SCENE. *Morning-room in* ALGERNON'S *flat in Half-Moon Street. The room is luxuriously and artistically furnished. The sound of a piano is heard in the adjoining room.*

LANE *is arranging afternoon tea on the table,* 5
and after the music has ceased, ALGERNON *enters.*

ALGERNON. Did you hear what I was playing, Lane?

LANE. I didn't think it polite to listen, sir.

ALGERNON. I'm sorry for that, for your sake. I 10 don't play accurately—anyone can play accurately—but I play with wonderful expression. As far as the piano is concerned, sentiment is my forte. I keep science for Life.

LANE. Yes, sir. 15

ALGERNON. And, speaking of the science of Life, have you got the cucumber sandwiches cut for Lady Bracknell?

LANE. Yes, sir.

[*Hands them on a salver.*] 20

ALGERNON [*Inspects them, takes two, and sits down on the sofa*]. Oh! . . . by the way, Lane, I see from your book° that on Thursday night, when Lord Shoreman and Mr. Worthing were dining with me, eight bottles of champagne 25 are entered as having been consumed.

LANE. Yes, sir; eight bottles and a pint.

ALGERNON. Why is it that at a bachelor's establishment the servants invariably drink the champagne? I ask merely for information. 30

LANE. I attribute it to the superior quality of the wine, sir. I have often observed that in married households the champagne is rarely of a first-rate brand.

ALGERNON. Good Heavens! Is marriage so 35 demoralizing as that?

LANE. I believe it *is* a very pleasant state, sir. I have had very little experience of it myself up to the present. I have only been married once. That was in consequence of a misunder- 40 standing between myself and a young person.

ALGERNON [*Languidly*]. I don't know that I am much interested in your family life, Lane.

book housekeeping accounts ledger

LANE. No, sir; it is not a very interesting subject. I never think of it myself.

ALGERNON. Very natural, I am sure. That will do, Lane, thank you.

5 LANE. Thank you, sir. [LANE *goes out.*]

ALGERNON. Lane's views on marriage seem somewhat lax. Really, if the lower orders don't set us a good example, what on earth is the use of them? They seem, as a class, to have abso-
10 lutely no sense of moral responsibility. [*Enter* LANE.]

LANE. Mr. Ernest Worthing.

[*Enter* JACK. LANE *goes out.*]

ALGERNON. How are you, my dear Ernest?
15 What brings you up to town?

JACK. Oh, pleasure, pleasure! What else should bring one anywhere? Eating as usual, I see, Algy!

ALGERNON [*Stiffly*]. I believe it is customary
20 in good society to take some slight refreshment at five o'clock. Where have you been since last Thursday?

JACK [*Sitting down on the sofa*]. In the country.

25 ALGERNON. What on earth do you do there?

JACK [*Pulling off his gloves*]. When one is in town one amuses oneself. When one is in the country one amuses other people. It is excessively boring.

30 ALGERNON. And who are the people you amuse?

JACK [*Airily*]. Oh, neighbours, neighbours.

ALGERNON. Got nice neighbours in your part of Shropshire?

35 JACK. Perfectly horrid! Never speak to one of them.

ALGERNON. How immensely you must amuse them! [*Goes over and takes sandwich.*] By the way, Shropshire° is your county, is it
40 not?

JACK. Eh? Shropshire? Yes, of course. Hallo! Why all these cups? Why cucumber sandwiches? Why such reckless extravagance in one so young? Who is coming to tea?

45 ALGERNON. Oh! merely Aunt Augusta and Gwendolen.

Shropshire a county far from London

JACK. How perfectly delightful!

ALGERNON. Yes, that is all very well; but I am afraid Aunt Augusta won't quite approve of your being here. 50

JACK. May I ask why?

ALGERNON. My dear fellow, the way you flirt with Gwendolen is perfectly disgraceful. It is almost as bad as the way Gwendolen flirts with you. 55

JACK. I am in love with Gwendolen. I have come up to town expressly to propose to her.

ALGERNON. I thought you had come up for pleasure? . . . I call that business.

JACK. How utterly unromantic you are! 60

ALGERNON. I really don't see anything romantic in proposing. It is very romantic to be in love. But there is nothing romantic about a definite proposal. Why, one may be accepted. One usually is, I believe. Then the excitement 65 is all over. The very essence of romance is uncertainty. If ever I get married, I'll certainly try to forget the fact.

JACK. I have no doubt about that, dear Algy. The Divorce Court was specially invented for 70 people whose memories are so curiously constituted.

ALGERNON. Oh! there is no use speculating on that subject. Divorces are made in Heaven ——[JACK *puts out his hand to take a sandwich.* 75 ALGERNON *at once interferes.*] Please don't touch the cucumber sandwiches. They are ordered specially for Aunt Augusta. [*Takes one and eats it.*]

JACK. Well, you have been eating them all 80 the time.

ALGERNON. That is quite a different matter. She is my aunt. [*Takes plate from below.*] Have some bread and butter. The bread and butter is for Gwendolen. Gwendolen is devoted to 85 bread and butter.

JACK [*Advancing to table and helping himself*]. And very good bread and butter it is too.

ALGERNON. Well, my dear fellow, you need not eat as if you were going to eat it all. You 90 behave as if you were married to her already. You are not married to her already, and I don't think you ever will be.

JACK. Why on earth do you say that?

ALGERNON. Well, in the first place girls never 95

marry the men they flirt with. Girls don't think it right.

JACK. Oh, that is nonsense!

ALGERNON. It isn't. It is a great truth. It accounts for the extraordinary number of bachelors that one sees all over the place. In the second place, I don't give my consent.

JACK. Your consent!

ALGERNON. My dear fellow, Gwendolen is my first cousin. And before I allow you to marry her, you will have to clear up the whole question of Cecily. [*Rings bell.*]

JACK. Cecily! What on earth do you mean? What do you mean, Algy, by Cecily? I don't know anyone of the name of Cecily.

[*Enter LANE.*]

ALGERNON. Bring me that cigarette case° Mr. Worthing left in the smoking-room the last time he dined here.

LANE. Yes, sir. [LANE *goes out.*]

JACK. Do you mean to say you have had my cigarette case all this time? I wish to goodness you had let me know. I have been writing frantic letters to Scotland Yard about it. I was very nearly offering a large reward.

ALGERNON. Well, I wish you would offer one. I happen to be more than usually hard up.

JACK. There is no good offering a large reward now that the thing is found. [*Enter LANE with the cigarette case on a salver. ALGERNON takes it at once. LANE goes out.*]

ALGERNON. I think that is rather mean of you, Ernest, I must say. [*Opens case and examines it.*] However, it makes no matter, for, now that I look at the inscription inside, I find that the thing isn't yours after all.

JACK. Of course it's mine. [*Moving to him.*] You have seen me with it a hundred times, and you have no right whatsoever to read what is written inside. It is a very ungentlemanly thing to read a private cigarette case.

ALGERNON. Oh! it is absurd to have a hard-and-fast rule about what one should read and what one shouldn't. More than half of modern culture depends on what one shouldn't read.

JACK. I am quite aware of the fact, and I don't propose to discuss modern culture. It isn't the sort of thing one should talk of in private. I simply want my cigarette case back.

ALGERNON. Yes; but this isn't your cigarette case. This cigarette case is a present from someone of the name of Cecily, and you said you didn't know anyone of that name.

JACK. Well, if you want to know, Cecily happens to be my aunt.

ALGERNON. Your aunt!

JACK. Yes. Charming old lady she is, too. Lives at Tunbridge Wells. Just give it back to me, Algy.

ALGERNON [*Retreating to back of sofa*]. But why does she call herself little Cecily if she is your aunt and lives at Tunbridge Wells? [*Reading*]. 'From little Cecily with her fondest love.'

JACK [*Moving to sofa and kneeling upon it*]. My dear fellow, what on earth is there in that? Some aunts are tall, some aunts are not tall. That is a matter that surely an aunt may be allowed to decide for herself. You seem to think that every aunt should be exactly like your aunt! That is absurd! For Heaven's sake give me back my cigarette case. [*Follows AL-GERNON round the room.*]

ALGERNON. Yes. But why does your aunt call you her uncle? 'From little Cecily, with her fondest love to her dear Uncle Jack.' There is no objection, I admit, to an aunt being a small aunt, but why an aunt, no matter what her size may be, should call her own nephew her uncle, I can't quite make out. Besides, your name isn't Jack at all; it is Ernest.

JACK. It isn't Ernest; it's Jack.

ALGERNON. You have always told me it was Ernest. I have introduced you to everyone as Ernest. You answer to the name of Ernest. You look as if your name was Ernest. You are the most earnest looking person I ever saw in my life. It is perfectly absurd your saying that your name isn't Ernest. It's on your cards.° Here is one of them [*Taking it from case.*] 'Mr. Ernest

---

cigarette case a gold or silver item of high fashion; imported cigarettes were coming into vogue for men but were not to be smoked in the company of ladies; hence Algernon's allusion to the "smoking room," another touch of luxury

cards small and neatly engraved, sent or left according to exacting rules of etiquette

Worthing, B 4, The Albany.' I'll keep this as a proof your name is Ernest if ever you attempt to deny it to me, or to Gwendolen, or to anyone else. [*Puts the card in his pocket.*]

5 JACK. Well, my name is Ernest in town and Jack in the country, and the cigarette case was given to me in the country.

ALGERNON. Yes, but that does not account for the fact that your small Aunt Cecily, who 10 lives at Tunbridge Wells, calls you her dear uncle. Come, old boy, you had much better have the thing out at once.

JACK. My dear Algy, you talk exactly as if you were a dentist. It is very vulgar to talk like a 15 dentist when one isn't a dentist. It produces a false impression.

ALGERNON. Well, that is exactly what dentists always do. Now, go on! Tell me the whole thing. I may mention that I have always sus- 20 pected you of being a confirmed and secret Bunburyist; and I am quite sure of it now.

JACK. Bunburyist? What on earth do you mean by a Bunburyist?

ALGERNON. I'll reveal to you the meaning of 25 that incomparable expression as soon as you are kind enough to inform me why you are Ernest in town and Jack in the country.

JACK. Well, produce my cigarette case first.

ALGERNON. Here it is. [*Hands cigarette case.*] 30 Now produce your explanation, and pray make it improbable. [*Sits on sofa.*]

JACK. My dear fellow, there is nothing improbable about my explanation at all. In fact it's perfectly ordinary. Old Mr. Thomas 35 Cardew, who adopted me when I was a little boy, made me in his will guardian to his grand-daughter, Miss Cecily Cardew. Cecily, who addresses me as her uncle from motives of respect that you could not possibly appre- 40 ciate, lives at my place in the country under the charge of her admirable governess, Miss Prism.

ALGERNON. Where is that place in the country, by the way?

45 JACK. That is nothing to you, dear boy. You are not going to be invited. . . . I may tell you candidly that the place is not in Shropshire.

ALGERNON. I suspected that, my dear fellow! I have Bunburyed all over Shropshire on two separate occasions. Now, go on. Why are you 50 Ernest in town and Jack in the country?

JACK. My dear Algy, I don't know whether you will be able to understand my real motives. You are hardly serious enough. When one is placed in the position of guardian, one has to 55 adopt a very high moral tone on all subjects. It's one's duty to do so. And as a high moral tone can hardly be said to conduce very much to either one's health or one's happiness, in order to get up to town I have always pre- 60 tended to have a younger brother of the name of Ernest, who lives in the Albany, and gets into the most dreadful scrapes. That, my dear Algy, is the whole truth pure and simple.

ALGERNON. The truth is rarely pure and 65 never simple. Modern life would be very tedious if it were either, and modern literature a complete impossibility!

JACK. That wouldn't be at all a bad thing.

ALGERNON. Literary criticism is not your 70 forte, my dear fellow. Don't try it. You should leave that to people who haven't been at a University. They do it so well in the daily papers. What you really are is a Bunburyist. I was quite right in saying you were a Bun- 75 buryist. You are one of the most advanced Bunburyists I know.

JACK. What on earth do you mean?

ALGERNON. You have invented a very useful younger brother called Ernest, in order that 80 you may be able to come up to town as often as you like. I have invented an invaluable permanent invalid called Bunbury, in order that I may be able to go down into the country whenever I choose. Bunbury is perfectly in- 85 valuable. If it wasn't for Bunbury's extraordinary bad health, for instance, I wouldn't be able to dine with you at Willis's to-night, for I have been really engaged to Aunt Augusta for more than a week. 90

JACK. I haven't asked you to dine with me anywhere to-night.

ALGERNON. I know. You are absurdly careless about sending out invitations. It is very foolish of you. Nothing annoys people so much 95 as not receiving invitations.

JACK. You had much better dine with your Aunt Augusta.

ALGERNON. I haven't the smallest intention of doing anything of the kind. To begin with, I dined there on Monday, and once a week is quite enough to dine with one's own relations.
5 In the second place, whenever I do dine there I am always treated as a member of the family, and sent down with either no woman at all, or two. In the third place, I know perfectly well whom she will place me next to, to-night.
10 She will place me next Mary Farquhar, who always flirts with her own husband across the dinner-table. That is not very pleasant. Indeed, it is not even decent . . . and that sort of thing is enormously on the increase. The
15 amount of women in London who flirt with their own husbands is perfectly scandalous. It looks so bad. It is simply washing one's clean linen in public. Besides, now that I know you to be a confirmed Bunburyist I naturally want
20 to talk to you about Bunburying. I want to tell you the rules.

JACK. I'm not a Bunburyist at all. If Gwendolen accepts me, I am going to kill my brother, indeed I think I'll kill him in any case. Cecily
25 is a little too much interested in him. It is rather a bore. So I am going to get rid of Ernest. And I strongly advise you to do the same with Mr. . . . with your invalid friend who has the absurd name.
30 ALGERNON. Nothing will induce me to part with Bunbury, and if you ever get married, which seems to me extremely problematic, you will be very glad to know Bunbury. A man who marries without knowing Bunbury has a very
35 tedious time of it.

JACK. That is nonsense. If I marry a charming girl like Gwendolen, and she is the only girl I ever saw in my life that I would marry, I certainly won't want to know Bunbury.
40 ALGERNON. Then your wife will. You don't seem to realize, that in married life three is company and two is none.

JACK [*Sententiously*]. That, my dear young friend, is the theory that the corrupt French
45 Drama° has been propounding for the last fifty years.

ALGERNON. Yes; and that the happy English home has proved in half the time.

JACK. For heaven's sake, don't try to be cynical. It's perfectly easy to be cynical. 50

ALGERNON. My dear fellow, it isn't easy to be anything now-a-days. There's such a lot of beastly competition about. [*The sound of an electric bell is heard.*] Ah! that must be Aunt Augusta. Only relatives, or creditors, ever ring 55 in that Wagnerian° manner. Now, if I get her out of the way for ten minutes, so that you can have an opportunity for proposing to Gwendolen, may I dine with you to-night at Willis's?

JACK. I suppose so, if you want to. 60

ALGERNON. Yes, but you must be serious about it. I hate people who are not serious about meals. It is so shallow of them.

[*Enter* LANE.]

LANE. Lady Bracknell and Miss Fairfax. 65

[ALGERNON *goes forward to meet them. Enter* LADY BRACKNELL *and* GWENDOLEN.]

LADY BRACKNELL. Good afternoon, dear Algernon, I hope you are behaving very well.

ALGERNON. I'm feeling very well, Aunt 70 Augusta.

LADY BRACKNELL. That's not quite the same thing. In fact the two things rarely go together. [*Sees* JACK *and bows to him with icy coldness.*]

ALGERNON [*To* GWENDOLEN]. Dear me, you 75 are smart!°

GWENDOLEN. I am always smart! Aren't I, Mr. Worthing?

JACK. You're quite perfect, Miss Fairfax.

GWENDOLEN. Oh! I hope I am not that. It 80 would leave no room for developments, and I intend to develop in many directions. [GWENDOLEN *and* JACK *sit down together in the corner.*]

LADY BRACKNELL. I'm sorry if we are a little late, Algernon, but I was obliged to call on dear 85 Lady Harbury. I hadn't been there since her poor husband's death. I never saw a woman so altered; she looks quite twenty years younger. And now I'll have a cup of tea, and one of those nice cucumber sandwiches you promised me. 90

ALGERNON. Certainly, Aunt Augusta. [*Goes over to tea-table.*]

---

corrupt French Drama Paris was far more hospitable to plays dealing with sexual misconduct than London, where censorship was in force

Wagnerian after the manner of the operas of Richard Wagner (1813–1883); here, imperious, dramatic
smart very stylish

LADY BRACKNELL. Won't you come and sit here, Gwendolen?

GWENDOLEN. Thanks, mamma, I'm quite comfortable where I am.

5 ALGERNON [*Picking up empty plate in horror*]. Good heavens! Lane! Why are there no cucumber sandwiches? I ordered them specially.

LANE [*Gravely*]. There were no cucumbers in the market this morning, sir. I went down 10 twice.

ALGERNON. No cucumbers!

LANE. No, sir. Not even for ready money.°

ALGERNON. That will do, Lane, thank you.

LANE. Thank you, sir. [*Goes out.*]

15 ALGERNON. I am greatly distressed, Aunt Augusta, about there being no cucumbers, not even for ready money.

LADY BRACKNELL. It really makes no matter, Algernon. I had some crumpets with Lady 20 Harbury, who seems to me to be living entirely for pleasure now.

ALGERNON. I hear her hair has turned quite gold from grief.

LADY BRACKNELL. It certainly has changed 25 its colour. From what cause I, of course, cannot say. [ALGERNON *crosses and hands tea.*] Thank you. I've quite a treat for you to-night, Algernon. I am going to send you down° with Mary Farquhar. She is such a nice woman, and 30 so attentive to her husband. It's delightful to watch them.

ALGERNON. I am afraid, Aunt Augusta, I shall have to give up the pleasure of dining with you to-night after all.

35 LADY BRACKNELL [*Frowning*]. I hope not, Algernon. It would put my table completely out.° Your uncle would have to dine upstairs. Fortunately he is accustomed to that.

ALGERNON. It is a great bore, and, I need 40 hardly say, a terrible disappointment to me, but the fact is I have just had a telegram to say that my poor friend Bunbury is very ill again.

---

for ready money cash payment on the spot; evidently Algernon tends to run up bills
send you down ask you to escort
out making an uneven number of men and women at table

[*Exchanges glances with* JACK.] They seem to think I should be with him.

LADY BRACKNELL. It is very strange. This 45 Mr. Bunbury seems to suffer from curiously bad health.

ALGERNON. Yes; poor Bunbury is a dreadful invalid.

LADY BRACKNELL. Well, I must say, Alger- 50 non, that I think it is high time that Mr. Bunbury made up his mind whether he was going to live or to die. This shilly-shallying with the question is absurd. Nor do I in any way approve of the modern sympathy with invalids. 55 I consider it morbid. Illness of any kind is hardly a thing to be encouraged in others. Health is the primary duty of life. I am always telling that to your poor uncle, but he never seems to take much notice . . . as far as any 60 improvement in his ailments goes. I should be much obliged if you would ask Mr. Bunbury, from me, to be kind enough not to have a relapse on Saturday, for I rely on you to arrange my music for me. It is my last reception and 65 one wants something that will encourage conversation, particularly at the end of the season when everyone has practically said whatever they had to say, which, in most cases, was probably not much. 70

ALGERNON. I'll speak to Bunbury, Aunt Augusta, if he is still conscious, and I think I can promise you he'll be all right by Saturday. Of course the music is a great difficulty. You see, if one plays good music, people don't listen, 75 and if one plays bad music people don't talk. But I'll run over the programme I've drawn out, if you will kindly come into the next room for a moment.

LADY BRACKNELL. Thank you, Algernon. It 80 is very thoughtful of you. [*Rising, and following* ALGERNON.] I'm sure the programme will be delightful, after a few expurgations. French songs I cannot possibly allow. People always seem to think that they are improper, and 85 either look shocked, which is vulgar, or laugh, which is worse. But German sounds a thoroughly respectable language, and indeed, I believe is so. Gwendolen, you will accompany me. 90

GWENDOLEN. Certainly, mamma.

[LADY BRACKNELL *and* ALGERNON *go into the music room,* GWENDOLEN *remains behind.*]

JACK. Charming day it has been, Miss Fairfax.

GWENDOLEN. Pray don't talk to me about the weather, Mr. Worthing. Whenever people talk to me about the weather, I always feel quite certain that they mean something else. And that makes me so nervous.

JACK. I do mean something else.

GWENDOLEN. I thought so. In fact, I am never wrong.

JACK. And I would like to be allowed to take advantage of Lady Bracknell's temporary absence . . .

GWENDOLEN. I would certainly advise you to do so. Mamma has a way of coming back suddenly into a room that I have often had to speak to her about.

JACK [*Nervously*]. Miss Fairfax, ever since I met you I have admired you more than any girl . . . I have ever met since . . . I met you.

GWENDOLEN. Yes, I am quite aware of the fact. And I often wish that in public, at any rate, you had been more demonstrative. For me you have always had an irresistible fascination. Even before I met you I was far from indifferent to you. [JACK *looks at her in amazement.*] We live, as I hope you know, Mr. Worthing, in an age of ideals. The fact is constantly mentioned in the more expensive monthly magazines, and has reached the provincial pulpits I am told: and my ideal has always been to love some one of the name of Ernest. There is something in that name that inspires absolute confidence. The moment Algernon first mentioned to me that he had a friend called Ernest, I knew I was destined to love you.

JACK. You really love me, Gwendolen?

GWENDOLEN. Passionately!

JACK. Darling! You don't know how happy you've made me.

GWENDOLEN. My own Ernest!

JACK. But you don't really mean to say that you couldn't love me if my name wasn't Ernest?

GWENDOLEN. But your name is Ernest.

JACK. Yes, I know it is. But supposing it was something else? Do you mean to say you couldn't love me then?

GWENDOLEN [*Glibly*]. Ah! that is clearly a metaphysical speculation, and like most metaphysical speculations has very little reference at all to the actual facts of real life, as we know them.

JACK. Personally, darling, to speak quite candidly, I don't much care about the name of Ernest . . . I don't think the name suits me at all.

GWENDOLEN. It suits you perfectly. It is a divine name. It has a music of its own. It produces vibrations.

JACK. Well, really, Gwendolen, I must say that I think there are lots of other much nicer names. I think Jack, for instance, a charming name.

GWENDOLEN. Jack? . . . No, there is very little music in the name Jack, if any at all, indeed. It does not thrill. It produces absolutely no vibrations. . . . I have known several Jacks, and they all, without exception, were more than usually plain. Besides, Jack is a notorious domesticity° for John! And I pity any woman who is married to a man called John. She would probably never be allowed to know the entrancing pleasure of a single moment's solitude. The only really safe name is Ernest.

JACK. Gwendolen, I must get christened at once—I mean we must get married at once. There is no time to be lost.

GWENDOLEN. Married, Mr. Worthing?

JACK [*Astounded*]. Well . . . surely. You know that I love you, and you led me to believe, Miss Fairfax, that you were not absolutely indifferent to me.

GWENDOLEN. I adore you. But you haven't proposed to me yet. Nothing has been said at all about marriage. The subject has not even been touched on.

JACK. Well . . . may I propose to you now?

GWENDOLEN. I think it would be an ad-

domesticity family nickname

mirable opportunity. And to spare you any possible disappointment, Mr. Worthing, I think it only fair to tell you quite frankly beforehand that I am fully determined to accept
5 you.

JACK. Gwendolen!

GWENDOLEN. Yes, Mr. Worthing, what have you got to say to me?

JACK. You know what I have got to say to
10 you.

GWENDOLEN. Yes, but you don't say it.

JACK. Gwendolen, will you marry me? [*Goes on his knees.*]

GWENDOLEN. Of course I will, darling. How
15 long you have been about it! I am afraid you have had very little experience in how to propose.

JACK. My own one, I have never loved anyone in the world but you.

20 GWENDOLEN. Yes, but men often propose for practice. I know my brother Gerald does. All my girl-friends tell me so. What wonderfully blue eyes you have, Ernest! They are quite, quite, blue. I hope you will always look at
25 me just like that, especially when there are other people present. [*Enter* LADY BRACKNELL.]

LADY BRACKNELL. Mr. Worthing! Rise, sir, from this semi-recumbent posture. It is most indecorous.

30 GWENDOLEN. Mamma! [*He tries to rise; she restrains him.*] I must beg you to retire. This is no place for you. Besides, Mr. Worthing has not quite finished yet.

LADY BRACKNELL. Finished what, may I ask?

35 GWENDOLEN. I am engaged to Mr. Worthing, mamma. [*They rise together.*]

LADY BRACKNELL. Pardon me, you are not engaged to anyone. When you do become engaged to some one, I, or your father, should
40 his health permit him, will inform you of the fact. An engagement should come on a young girl as a surprise, pleasant or unpleasant, as the case may be. It is hardly a matter that she could be allowed to arrange for herself. . . .
45 And now I have a few questions to put to you, Mr. Worthing. While I am making these inquiries, you, Gwendolen, will wait for me below in the carriage.

GWENDOLEN [*Reproachfully*]. Mamma!

LADY BRACKNELL. In the carriage, Gwen- 50
dolen!

[GWENDOLEN *goes to the door. She and* JACK *blow kisses to each other behind* LADY BRACK-NELL'S *back.* LADY BRACKNELL *looks vaguely about as if she could not understand what the* 55
noise was. Finally turns round.] Gwendolen, the carriage!

GWENDOLEN. Yes, mamma. [*Goes out, looking back at* JACK.]

LADY BRACKNELL [*Sitting down*]. You can 60
take a seat, Mr. Worthing. [*Looks in her pocket for note-book and pencil*]

JACK. Thank you, Lady Bracknell, I prefer standing.

LADY BRACKNELL [*Pencil and note-book in* 65
hand]. I feel bound to tell you that you are not down on my list of eligible young men, although I have the same list as the dear Duchess of Bolton has. We work together, in fact. However, I am quite ready to enter your name, 70
should your answers be what a really affectionate mother requires. Do you smoke?

JACK. Well, yes, I must admit I smoke.

LADY BRACKNELL. I am glad to hear it. A man should always have an occupation of some 75
kind. There are far too many idle men in London as it is. How old are you?

JACK. Twenty-nine.

LADY BRACKNELL. A very good age to be married at. I have always been of opinion 80
that a man who desires to get married should know either everything or nothing. Which do you know?

JACK [*After some hesitation*]. I know nothing, Lady Bracknell. 85

LADY BRACKNELL. I am pleased to hear it. I do not approve of anything that tampers with natural ignorance. Ignorance is like a delicate exotic fruit; touch it and the bloom is gone. The whole theory of modern education is 90
radically unsound. Fortunately in England, at any rate, education produces no effect whatsoever. If it did, it would prove a serious danger to the upper classes, and probably lead to acts of violence in Grosvenor Square. 95
What is your income?

JACK. Between seven and eight thousand a year.

LADY BRACKNELL [*Makes a note in her book*]. In land, or in investments?

JACK. In investments, chiefly.

LADY BRACKNELL. That is satisfactory. What between the duties expected of one during one's lifetime, and the duties° exacted from one after one's death, land has ceased to be either a profit or a pleasure. It gives one position, and prevents one from keeping it up. That's all that can be said about land.

JACK. I have a country house with some land, of course, attached to it, about fifteen hundred acres, I believe; but I don't depend on that for my real income. In fact, as far as I can make out, the poachers° are the only people who make anything out of it.

LADY BRACKNELL. A country house! How many bedrooms? Well, that point can be cleared up afterwards. You have a town house, I hope? A girl with a simple, unspoiled nature, like Gwendolen, could hardly be expected to reside in the country.

JACK. Well, I own a house in Belgrave Square, but it is let by the year to Lady Bloxham. Of course, I can get it back whenever I like, at six months' notice.

LADY BRACKNELL. Lady Bloxham? I don't know her.

JACK. Oh, she goes about very little. She is a lady considerably advanced in years.

LADY BRACKNELL. Ah, now-a-days that is no guarantee of respectability of character. What number in Belgrave Square?

JACK. 149.

LADY BRACKNELL [*Shaking her head*]. The unfashionable side. I thought there was something. However, that could easily be altered.

JACK. Do you mean the fashion, or the side?

LADY BRACKNELL [*Sternly*]. Both, if necessary, I presume. What are your politics?

JACK. Well, I am afraid I really have none.

I am a Liberal Unionist.°

LADY BRACKNELL. Oh, they count as Tories. They dine with us. Or come in the evening, at any rate. Now to minor matters. Are your parents living?

JACK. I have lost both my parents.

LADY BRACKNELL. Both? . . . That seems like carelessness. Who was your father? He was evidently a man of some wealth. Was he born in what the Radical papers call the purple of commerce, or did he rise from the ranks of the aristocracy?

JACK. I am afraid I really don't know. The fact is, Lady Bracknell, I said I had lost my parents. It would be nearer the truth to say that my parents seem to have lost me . . . I don't actually know who I am by birth. I was . . . well, I was found.

LADY BRACKNELL. Found!

JACK. The late Mr. Thomas Cardew, an old gentleman of a very charitable and kindly disposition, found me, and gave me the name of Worthing, because he happened to have a first-class ticket for Worthing in his pocket at the time. Worthing is a place in Sussex. It is a seaside resort.

LADY BRACKNELL. Where did the charitable gentleman who had a first-class ticket for this seaside resort find you?

JACK [*Gravely*]. In a hand-bag.°

LADY BRACKNELL. A hand-bag?

JACK [*Very seriously*]. Yes, Lady Bracknell. I was in a hand-bag—a somewhat large, black leather hand-bag, with handles to it—an ordinary hand-bag in fact.

LADY BRACKNELL. In what locality did this Mr. James, or Thomas, Cardew come across this ordinary hand-bag?

JACK. In the cloak-room at Victoria Station. It was given to him in mistake for his own.

LADY BRACKNELL. The cloak-room at Victoria Station?

duties "death duties," estate taxes
poachers trespassers who steal wild game; much complained of by landowners

Liberal Unionist a member of the Liberal Party who opposed its leader, Gladstone, on his advocacy of Home Rule for Ireland and on most other policies as well; hence, acceptable to the opposition party, the Tories
hand-bag not a lady's purse but a medium-size travelling bag

JACK. Yes. The Brighton line.

LADY BRACKNELL. The line is immaterial. Mr. Worthing, I confess I feel somewhat bewildered by what you have just told me. To
5 be born, or at any rate bred, in a hand-bag, whether it had handles or not, seems to me to display a contempt for the ordinary decencies of family life that remind one of the worst excesses of the French Revolution. And
10 I presume you know what that unfortunate movement led to? As for the particular locality in which the hand-bag was found, a cloak-room at a railway station might serve to conceal a social indiscretion—has probably, in-
15 deed, been used for that purpose before now— but it could hardly be regarded as an assured basis for a recognized position in good society.

JACK. May I ask you then what you would advise me to do? I need hardly say I would do
20 anything in the world to ensure Gwendolen's happiness.

LADY BRACKNELL. I would strongly advise you, Mr. Worthing, to try and acquire some relations as soon as possible, and to make a
25 definite effort to produce at any rate one parent, of either sex, before the season is quite over.

JACK. Well, I don't see how I could possibly manage to do that. I can produce the hand-bag
30 at any moment. It is in my dressing-room at home. I really think that should satisfy you, Lady Bracknell.

LADY BRACKNELL. Me, sir! What has it to do with me? You can hardly imagine that I and
35 Lord Bracknell would dream of allowing our only daughter—a girl brought up with the utmost care—to marry into a cloak-room, and form an alliance with a parcel? Good morning, Mr. Worthing!
40 [LADY BRACKNELL sweeps out in majestic indignation.]

JACK. Good morning! [ALGERNON, from the other room, strikes up the Wedding March. JACK looks perfectly furious, and goes to the door.] For
45 goodness' sake don't play that ghastly tune, Algy! How idiotic you are!

[The music stops, and ALGERNON enters cheerily.]

ALGERNON. Didn't it go off all right, old boy? You don't mean to say Gwendolen refused 50 you? I know it is a way she has. She is always refusing people. I think it is most ill-natured of her.

JACK. Oh, Gwendolen is as right as a trivet.° As far as she is concerned, we are engaged. 55 Her mother is perfectly unbearable. Never met such a Gorgon . . .° I don't really know what a Gorgon is like, but I am quite sure that Lady Bracknell is one. In any case, she is a monster, without being a myth, which is rather un- 60 fair. . . . I beg your pardon, Algy, I suppose I shouldn't talk about your own aunt in that way before you.

ALGERNON. My dear boy, I love hearing my relations abused. It is the only thing that makes 65 me put up with them at all. Relations are simply a tedious pack of people, who haven't got the remotest knowledge of how to live, nor the smallest instinct about when to die.

JACK. Oh, that is nonsense! 70

ALGERNON. It isn't!

JACK. Well, I won't argue about the matter. You always want to argue about things.

ALGERNON. That is exactly what things were originally made for. 75

JACK. Upon my word, if I thought that, I'd shoot myself . . . [A pause.] You don't think there is any chance of Gwendolen becoming like her mother in about a hundred and fifty years, do you Algy? 80

ALGERNON. All women become like their mothers. That is their tragedy. No man does. That's his.

JACK. Is that clever?

ALGERNON. It is perfectly phrased! and quite 85 as true as any observation in civilized life should be.

JACK. I am sick to death of cleverness. Everybody is clever now-a-days. You can't go anywhere without meeting clever people. The 90 thing has become an absolute public nuisance. I wish to goodness we had a few fools left.

right as a trivet perfectly fine
Gorgon in Greek mythology, any one of three sisters so hideous that the mere sight of any of them turned men into stone

ALGERNON. We have.

JACK. I should extremely like to meet them. What do they talk about?

ALGERNON. The fools? Oh! about the clever
5 people, of course.

JACK. What fools!

ALGERNON. By the way, did you tell Gwendolen the truth about your being Ernest in town, and Jack in the country?

10 JACK [*In a very patronising manner*]. My dear fellow, the truth isn't quite the sort of thing one tells to a nice, sweet, refined girl. What extraordinary ideas you have about the way to behave to a woman!

15 ALGERNON. The only way to behave to a woman is to make love to her, if she is pretty, and to someone else if she is plain.

JACK. Oh, that is nonsense.

ALGERNON. What about your brother? What
20 about the profligate Ernest?

JACK. Oh, before the end of the week I shall have got rid of him. I'll say he died in Paris of apoplexy. Lots of people die of apoplexy, quite suddenly, don't they?

25 ALGERNON. Yes, but it's hereditary, my dear fellow. It's a sort of thing that runs in families. You had much better say a severe chill.

JACK. You are sure a severe chill isn't hereditary, or anything of that kind?

30 ALGERNON. Of course it isn't!

JACK. Very well, then. My poor brother Ernest is carried off suddenly in Paris, by a severe chill. That gets rid of him.

ALGERNON. But I thought you said that . . .
35 Miss Cardew was a little too much interested in your poor brother Ernest? Won't she feel his loss a good deal?

JACK. Oh, that is all right. Cecily is not a silly, romantic girl, I am glad to say. She has got a
40 capital appetite, goes long walks, and pays no attention at all to her lessons.

ALGERNON. I would rather like to see Cecily.

JACK. I will take very good care you never do. She is excessively pretty, and she is only
45 just eighteen.

ALGERNON. Have you told Gwendolen yet that you have an excessively pretty ward who is only just eighteen?

JACK. Oh! One doesn't blurt these things out to people. Cecily and Gwendolen are perfectly 50 certain to be extremely great friends. I'll bet you anything you like that half an hour after they have met, they will be calling each other sister.

ALGERNON. Women only do that when they 55 have called each other a lot of other things first. Now, my dear boy, if we want to get a good table at Willis's, we really must go and dress. Do you know it is nearly seven?

JACK [*Irritably*]. Oh! it always is nearly 60 seven.

ALGERNON. Well, I'm hungry.

JACK. I never knew you when you weren't. . . .

ALGERNON. What shall we do after dinner? Go to a theatre? 65

JACK. Oh no! I loathe listening.

ALGERNON. Well, let us go to the Club?

JACK. Oh, no! I hate talking.

ALGERNON. Well, we might trot round to the Empire° at ten? 70

JACK. Oh, no! I can't bear looking at things. It is so silly.

ALGERNON. Well, what shall we do?

JACK. Nothing!

ALGERNON. It is awfully hard work doing 75 nothing. However, I don't mind hard work where there is no definite object of any kind.

[*Enter* LANE.]

LANE. Miss Fairfax.

[*Enter* GWENDOLEN. LANE *goes out.*] 80

ALGERNON. Gwendolen, upon my word!

GWENDOLEN. Algy, kindly turn your back. I have something very particular to say to Mr. Worthing.

ALGERNON. Really, Gwendolen, I don't think 85 I can allow this at all.

GWENDOLEN. Algy, you always adopt a strictly immoral attitude towards life. You are not quite old enough to do that. [ALGERNON *retires to the fireplace.*] 90

JACK. My own darling!

GWENDOLEN. Ernest, we may never be married. From the expression on mamma's face I fear we never shall. Few parents now-a-days

Empire theater for popular music and farce

pay any regard to what their children say to them. The old-fashioned respect for the young is fast dying out. Whatever influence I ever had over mamma, I lost at the age of three. But

5 although she may prevent us from becoming man and wife, and I may marry someone else, and marry often, nothing that she can possibly do can alter my eternal devotion to you.

JACK. Dear Gwendolen!

10 GWENDOLEN. The story of your romantic origin, as related to me by mamma, with unpleasing comments, has naturally stirred the deeper fibres of my nature. Your Christian name° has an irresistible fascination. The sim-

15 plicity of your character makes you exquisitely incomprehensible to me. Your town address at the Albany I have. What is your address in the country?

JACK. The Manor House, Woolton, Hert-

20 fordshire.°

[ALGERNON, *who has been carefully listening, smiles to himself, and writes the address on his shirt-cuff. Then picks up the Railway Guide.*]

GWENDOLEN. There is a good postal service,

25 I suppose? It may be necessary to do something desperate. That, of course, will require serious consideration. I will communicate with you daily.

JACK. My own one!

30 GWENDOLEN. How long do you remain in town?

JACK. Till Monday.

GWENDOLEN. Good! Algy, you may turn round now.

35 ALGERNON. Thanks, I've turned round already.

GWENDOLEN. You may also ring the bell.

JACK. You will let me see you to your carriage, my own darling?

40 GWENDOLEN. Certainly.

JACK [*To LANE, who now enters*]. I will see Miss Fairfax out.

LANE. Yes, sir. [*JACK and GWENDOLEN go off.*]

Christian name the first name given in the sacrament of baptism (christening); in the English Church ordinarily conferred on infants and to be received once only
Hertfordshire a county near London

LANE *presents several letters on a salver to* ALGERNON. *It is to be surmised that they are bills,* 45 *as* ALGERNON *after looking at the envelopes, tears them up.*]

ALGERNON. A glass of sherry, Lane.

LANE. Yes, sir.

ALGERNON. To-morrow, Lane, I'm going 50 Bunburying.

LANE. Yes, sir.

ALGERNON. I shall probably not be back till Monday. You can put up my dress clothes, my smoking jacket, and all the Bunbury suits . . . 55

LANE. Yes, sir. [*Handing sherry.*]

ALGERNON. I hope to-morrow will be a fine day, Lane.

LANE. It never is, sir.

ALGERNON. Lane, you're a perfect pessimist. 60

LANE. I do my best to give satisfaction, sir. [*Enter JACK. LANE goes off.*]

JACK. There's a sensible, intellectual girl! the only girl I ever cared for in my life. [ALGERNON *is laughing immoderately.*] What on earth are 65 you so amused at?

ALGERNON. Oh, I'm a little anxious about poor Bunbury, that is all.

JACK. If you don't take care, your friend Bunbury will get you into a serious scrape some 70 day.

ALGERNON. I love scrapes. They are the only things that are never serious.

JACK. Oh, that's nonsense, Algy. You never talk anything but nonsense. 75

ALGERNON. Nobody ever does.

[JACK *looks indignantly at him, and leaves the room.* ALGERNON *lights a cigarette, reads his shirt-cuff, and smiles.*]

Act-drop 80

ACT II

SCENE. *Garden at the Manor House. A flight of gray stone steps leads up to the house. The garden, an old-fashioned one, full of roses. Time of year, July. Basket chairs, and a table covered with books, are set under a large yew tree.* 85

MISS PRISM *discovered seated at the table.* CECILY *is at the back watering flowers.*

MISS PRISM [*Calling*]. Cecily, Cecily! Surely such a utilitarian occupation as the watering of flowers is rather Moulton's duty than yours? Especially at a moment when intellectual pleasures await you. Your German grammar is on the table. Pray open it at page fifteen. We will repeat yesterday's lesson.

CECILY [*Coming over very slowly*]. But I don't like German. It isn't at all a becoming language. I know perfectly well that I look quite plain after my German lesson.

MISS PRISM. Child, you know how anxious your guardian is that you should improve yourself in every way. He laid particular stress on your German, as he was leaving for town yesterday. Indeed, he always lays stress on your German when he is leaving for town.

CECILY. Dear Uncle Jack is so very serious! Sometimes he is so serious that I think he cannot be quite well.

MISS PRISM [*Drawing herself up*]. Your guardian enjoys the best of health, and his gravity of demeanour is especially to be commended in one so comparatively young as he is. I know no one who has a higher sense of duty and responsibility.

CECILY. I suppose that is why he often looks a little bored when we three are together.

MISS PRISM. Cecily! I am surprised at you. Mr. Worthing has many troubles in his life. Idle merriment and triviality would be out of place in his conversation. You must remember his constant anxiety about that unfortunate young man, his brother.

CECILY. I wish Uncle Jack would allow that unfortunate young man, his brother, to come down here sometimes. We might have a good influence over him, Miss Prism. I am sure you certainly would. You know German, and geology, and things of that kind influence a man very much. [CECILY *begins to write in her diary.*]

MISS PRISM [*Shaking her head*]. I do not think that even I could produce any effect on a character that according to his own brother's admission is irretrievably weak and vacillating. Indeed I am not sure that I would desire to reclaim him. I am not in favour of this modern mania for turning bad people into good people

at a moment's notice. As a man sows so let him reap. You must put away your diary, Cecily. I really don't see why you should keep a diary at all.

CECILY. I keep a diary in order to enter the wonderful secrets of my life. If I didn't write them down I should probably forget all about them.

MISS PRISM. Memory, my dear Cecily, is the diary that we all carry about with us.

CECILY. Yes, but it usually chronicles the things that have never happened, and couldn't possibly have happened. I believe that Memory is responsible for nearly all the three-volume novels that Mudie° sends us.

MISS PRISM. Do not speak slightingly of the three-volume novel, Cecily. I wrote one myself in earlier days.

CECILY. Did you really, Miss Prism? How wonderfully clever you are! I hope it did not end happily? I don't like novels that end happily. They depress me so much.

MISS PRISM. The good ended happily, and the bad unhappily. That is what Fiction means.

CECILY. I suppose so. But it seems very unfair. And was your novel ever published?

MISS PRISM. Alas! no. The manuscript unfortunately was abandoned. I use the word in the sense of lost or mislaid. To your work, child, these speculations are profitless.

CECILY [*Smiling*]. But I see dear Dr. Chasuble coming up through the garden.

MISS PRISM [*Rising and advancing*]. Dr. Chasuble! This is indeed a pleasure.

[*Enter* CANON CHASUBLE.]

CHASUBLE. And how are we this morning? Miss Prism, you are, I trust, well?

CECILY. Miss Prism has just been complaining of a slight headache. I think it would do her so much good to have a short stroll with you in the park,° Dr. Chasuble.

MISS PRISM. Cecily, I have not mentioned anything about a headache.

CECILY. No, dear Miss Prism, I know that, but I felt instinctively that you had a head-

Mudie a popular lending-library service
park private grounds of an estate

ache. Indeed I was thinking about that, and not about my German lesson, when the Rector came in.

CHASUBLE. I hope, Cecily, you are not in-
5 attentive.

CECILY. Oh, I am afraid I am.

CHASUBLE. That is strange. Were I fortunate enough to be Miss Prism's pupil, I would hang upon her lips. [MISS PRISM glares.] I spoke
10 metaphorically.—My metaphor was drawn from bees. Ahem! Mr. Worthing, I suppose, has not returned from town yet?

MISS PRISM. We do not expect him till Monday afternoon.

15 CHASUBLE. Ah yes, he usually likes to spend his Sunday in London. He is not one of those whose sole aim is enjoyment, as, by all accounts, that unfortunate young man, his brother, seems to be. But I must not disturb
20 Egeria° and her pupil any longer.

MISS PRISM. Egeria? My name is Lætitia, Doctor.

CHASUBLE [Bowing]. A classical allusion merely, drawn from the Pagan authors. I shall
25 see you both no doubt at Evensong.

MISS PRISM. I think, dear Doctor, I will have a stroll with you. I find I have a headache after all, and a walk might do it good.

CHASUBLE. With pleasure, Miss Prism, with
30 pleasure. We might go as far as the schools and back.

MISS PRISM. That would be delightful. Cecily, you will read your Political Economy in my absence. The chapter on the Fall of the
35 Rupee you may omit. It is somewhat too sensational. Even these metallic problems have their melodramatic side.

[Goes down the garden with DR. CHASUBLE.]

CECILY [Picks up books and throws them back
40 on table.] Horrid Political Economy! Horrid Geography! Horrid, horrid German!

[Enter MERRIMAN with a card on a salver.]

MERRIMAN. Mr. Ernest Worthing has just driven over from the station. He has brought

Egeria in Roman legend, a water-nymph who revealed religious mysteries to Numa Pompilius, the second king of Rome; guardian-spirit of child-bearing

his luggage with him.   45

CECILY [Takes the card and reads it]. 'Mr. Ernest Worthing, B 4, The Albany, W.' Uncle Jack's brother! Did you tell him Mr. Worthing was in town?

MERRIMAN. Yes, Miss. He seemed very much 50 disappointed. I mentioned that you and Miss Prism were in the garden. He said he was anxious to speak to you privately for a moment.

CECILY. Ask Mr. Ernest Worthing to come here. I suppose you had better talk to the 55 housekeeper about a room for him.

MERRIMAN. Yes, Miss.

[MERRIMAN goes off.]

CECILY. I have never met any really wicked person before. I feel rather frightened. I am so 60 afraid he will look just like everyone else.

[Enter ALGERNON, very gay and debonair.]
He does!

ALGERNON [Raising his hat]. You are my little cousin Cecily, I'm sure.   65

CECILY. You are under some strange mistake. I am not little. In fact, I believe I am more than usually tall for my age. [ALGERNON is rather taken aback.] But I am your cousin Cecily. You, I see from your card, are Uncle Jack's brother, 70 my cousin Ernest, my wicked cousin Ernest.

ALGERNON. Oh! I am not really wicked at all, cousin Cecily. You musn't think that I am wicked.

CECILY. If you are not, then you have cer- 75 tainly been deceiving us all in a very inexcusable manner. I hope you have not been leading a double life, pretending to be wicked and being really good all the time. That would be hypocrisy.   80

ALGERNON [Looks at her in amazement]. Oh! of course I have been rather reckless.

CECILY. I am glad to hear it.

ALGERNON. In fact, now you mention the subject, I have been very bad in my own small 85 way.

CECILY. I don't think you should be so proud of that, though I am sure it must have been very pleasant.

ALGERNON. It is much pleasanter being here 90 with you.

CECILY. I can't understand how you are here

at all. Uncle Jack won't be back till Monday afternoon.

ALGERNON. That is a great disappointment. I am obliged to go up by the first train on
5 Monday morning. I have a business appointment that I am anxious . . . to miss.

CECILY. Couldn't you miss it anywhere but in London?

ALGERNON. No: the appointment is in
10 London.

CECILY. Well, I know, of course, how important it is not to keep a business engagement, if one wants to retain any sense of the beauty of life, but still I think you had better
15 wait till Uncle Jack arrives. I know he wants to speak to you about your emigrating.

ALGERNON. About my what?

CECILY. Your emigrating. He has gone up to buy your outfit.

20 ALGERNON. I certainly wouldn't let Jack buy my outfit. He has no taste in neckties at all.

CECILY. I don't think you will require neckties. Uncle Jack is sending you to Australia.

ALGERNON. Australia! I'd sooner die.

25 CECILY. Well, he said at dinner on Wednesday night, that you would have to choose between this world, the next world, and Australia.

ALGERNON. Oh, well! The accounts I have
30 received of Australia and the next world, are not particularly encouraging. This world is good enough for me, cousin Cecily.

CECILY. Yes, but are you good enough for it?

ALGERNON. I'm afraid I'm not that. That is
35 why I want you to reform me. You might make that your mission, if you don't mind, cousin Cecily.

CECILY. I'm afraid I've no time, this afternoon.

40 ALGERNON. Well, would you mind my reforming myself this afternoon?

CECILY. It is rather Quixotic of you. But I think you should try.

ALGERNON. I will. I feel better already.

45 CECILY. You are looking a little worse.

ALGERNON. That is because I am hungry.

CECILY. How thoughtless of me. I should have remembered that when one is going to

lead an entirely new life, one requires regular and wholesome meals. Won't you come in? 50

ALGERNON. Thank you. Might I have a buttonhole first? I never have any appetite unless I have a buttonhole° first.

CECILY. A Maréchal Niel?° [*Picks up scissors.*] 55

ALGERNON. No, I'd sooner have a pink rose.

CECILY. Why? [*Cuts a flower.*]

ALGERNON. Because you are like a pink rose, cousin Cecily.

CECILY. I don't think it can be right for you 60
to talk to me like that. Miss Prism never says such things to me.

ALGERNON. Then Miss Prism is a short-sighted old lady. [CECILY *puts the rose in his buttonhole.*] You are the prettiest girl I ever 65
saw.

CECILY. Miss Prism says that all good looks are a snare.

ALGERNON. They are a snare that every sensible man would like to be caught in. 70

CECILY. Oh! I don't think I would care to catch a sensible man. I shouldn't know what to talk to him about.

[*They pass into the house.* MISS PRISM *and* DR. CHASUBLE *return.*] 75

MISS PRISM. You are too much alone, dear Dr. Chasuble. You should get married. A misanthrope I can understand—a womanthrope,° never!

CHASUBLE [*With a scholar's shudder*]. Be- 80
lieve me, I do not deserve so neologistic a phrase. The precept as well as the practice of the Primitive Church was distinctly against matrimony.

MISS PRISM [*Sententiously*]. That is obvi- 85
ously the reason why the Primitive Church has not lasted up to the present day. And you do not seem to realize, dear Doctor, that by persistently remaining single, a man converts himself into a permanent public temptation. 90

buttonhole flower to wear in the lapel
Maréchal Niel a pale yellow rose named in honor of a
  French general
womanthrope a word of Miss Prism's invention (a
  "neologism") meaning "a despiser of women," as
  against *misanthrope*, a despiser of mankind as a whole

Men should be more careful; this very celibacy leads weaker vessels astray.

CHASUBLE. But is a man not equally attractive when married?

5 MISS PRISM. No married man is ever attractive except to his wife.

CHASUBLE. And often, I've been told, not even to her.

MISS PRISM. That depends on the intellectual
10 sympathies of the woman. Maturity can always be depended on. Ripeness can be trusted. Young women are green. [DR. CHASUBLE starts.] I spoke horticulturally. My metaphor was drawn from fruits. But where is Cecily?

15 CHASUBLE. Perhaps she followed us to the schools.

[Enter JACK slowly from the back of the garden. He is dressed in the deepest mourning,° with crape hat-band and black gloves.]

20 MISS PRISM. Mr. Worthing!

CHASUBLE. Mr. Worthing?

MISS PRISM. This is indeed a surprise. We did not look for you till Monday afternoon.

JACK [Shakes MISS PRISM's hand in a tragic
25 manner]. I have returned sooner than I expected. Dr. Chasuble, I hope you are well?

CHASUBLE. Dear Mr. Worthing, I trust this garb of woe does not betoken some terrible calamity?

30 JACK. My brother.

MISS PRISM. More shameful debts and extravagance?

CHASUBLE. Still leading his life of pleasure?

JACK [Shaking his head]. Dead!

35 CHASUBLE. Your brother Ernest dead?

JACK. Quite dead.

MISS PRISM. What a lesson for him! I trust he will profit by it.

CHASUBLE. Mr. Worthing, I offer you my
40 sincere condolence. You have at least the consolation of knowing that you were always the most generous and forgiving of brothers.

JACK. Poor Ernest! He had many faults, but it is a sad, sad blow.

45 CHASUBLE. Very sad indeed. Were you with him at the end?

deepest mourning severely formal black outfit, including top hat banded with wide silk ribbon ("crape")

JACK. No. He died abroad; in Paris, in fact. I had a telegram last night from the manager of the Grand Hotel.

CHASUBLE. Was the cause of death men- 50 tioned?

JACK. A severe chill, it seems.

MISS PRISM. As a man sows, so shall he reap.

CHASUBLE [Raising his hand]. Charity, dear Miss Prism, charity! None of us are perfect. 55 I myself am peculiarly susceptible to draughts. Will the interment take place here?

JACK. No. He seemed to have expressed a desire to be buried in Paris.

CHASUBLE. In Paris! [Shakes his head.] I fear 60 that hardly points to any very serious state of mind at the last. You would no doubt wish me to make some slight allusion to this tragic domestic affliction next Sunday. [JACK presses his hand convulsively.] My sermon on the 65 meaning of the manna° in the wilderness can be adapted to almost any occasion, joyful, or, as in the present case, distressing. [All sigh.] I have preached it at harvest celebrations, christenings, confirmations, on days of hu- 70 miliation and festal days. The last time I delivered it was in the Cathedral, as a charity sermon on behalf of the Society for the Prevention of Discontent among the Upper Orders. The Bishop, who was present, was 75 much struck by some of the analogies I drew.

JACK. Ah! that reminds me, you mentioned christenings I think, Dr. Chasuble? I suppose you know how to christen all right? [DR. CHASUBLE looks astounded.] I mean, of course, 80 you are continually christening, aren't you?

MISS PRISM. It is, I regret to say, one of the Rector's most constant duties in this parish. I have often spoken to the poorer classes on the subject. But they don't seem to know what 85 thrift is.

CHASUBLE. But is there any particular infant in whom you are interested, Mr. Worthing? Your brother was, I believe, unmarried, was he not? 90

JACK. Oh, yes.

manna the miraculous "bread from heaven" provided the Israelites in the wilderness (Exod. 16)

MISS PRISM [*Bitterly*]. People who live entirely for pleasure usually are.

JACK. But it is not for any child, dear Doctor. I am very fond of children. No! the fact is, I
5 would like to be christened myself, this afternoon, if you have nothing better to do.

CHASUBLE. But surely, Mr. Worthing, you have been christened already?

JACK. I don't remember anything about it.
10 CHASUBLE. But have you any grave doubts on the subject?

JACK. I certainly intend to have. Of course, I don't know if the thing would bother you in any way, or if you think I am a little too old
15 now.

CHASUBLE. Not at all. The sprinkling, and, indeed, the immersion of adults is a perfectly canonical practice.

JACK. Immersion!
20 CHASUBLE. You need have no apprehensions. Sprinkling is all that is necessary, or indeed I think advisable. Our weather is so changeable. At what hour would you wish the ceremony performed?
25 JACK. Oh, I might trot round about five if that would suit you.

CHASUBLE. Perfectly, perfectly! In fact I have two similar ceremonies to perform at that time. A case of twins that occurred re-
30 cently in one of the outlying cottages on your own estate. Poor Jenkins the carter, a most hard-working man.

JACK. Oh! I don't see much fun in being christened along with other babies. It would
35 be childish. Would half-past five do?

CHASUBLE. Admirably! Admirably! [*Takes out watch.*] And now, dear Mr. Worthing, I will not intrude any longer into a house of sorrow. I would merely beg you not to be too
40 much bowed down by grief. What seem to us bitter trials are often blessings in disguise.

MISS PRISM. This seems to me a blessing of an extremely obvious kind.

[*Enter CECILY from the house.*]
45 CECILY. Uncle Jack! Oh, I am pleased to see you back. But what horrid clothes you have got on! Do go and change them.

MISS PRISM. Cecily!

CHASUBLE. My child! my child!

[*CECILY goes towards JACK; he kisses her* 50 *brow in a melancholy manner.*]

CECILY. What is the matter, Uncle Jack? Do look happy! You look as if you had toothache, and I have got a surprise for you. Who do you think is in the dining-room? Your brother! 55

JACK. Who?

CECILY. Your brother Ernest. He arrived about half an hour ago.

JACK. What nonsense! I haven't got a brother.

CECILY. Oh, don't say that. However badly 60 he may have behaved to you in the past, he is still your brother. You couldn't be so heartless as to disown him. I'll tell him to come out. And you will shake hands with him, won't you, Uncle Jack? [*Runs back into the house.*] 65

CHASUBLE. These are very joyful tidings.

MISS PRISM. After we had all been resigned to his loss, his sudden return seems to me peculiarly distressing.

JACK. My brother is in the dining-room? I 70 don't know what it all means. I think it is perfectly absurd.

[*Enter ALGERNON and CECILY hand in hand. They come slowly up to JACK.*]

JACK. Good Heavens! [*Motions ALGERNON* 75 *away.*]

ALGERNON. Brother John, I have come down from town to tell you that I am very sorry for all the trouble I have given you, and that I intend to lead a better life in the future. [*JACK* 80 *glares at him and does not take his hand.*]

CECILY. Uncle Jack, you are not going to refuse your own brother's hand?

JACK. Nothing will induce me to take his hand. I think his coming down here disgrace- 85 ful. He knows perfectly well why.

CECILY. Uncle Jack, do be nice. There is some good in everyone. Ernest has just been telling me about his poor invalid friend Mr. Bunbury, whom he goes to visit so often. And 90 surely there must be much good in one who is kind to an invalid, and leaves the pleasures of London to sit by a bed of pain.

JACK. Oh! he has been talking about Bunbury, has he? 95

CECILY. Yes, he has told me all about poor

Mr. Bunbury, and his terrible state of health.

JACK. Bunbury! Well, I won't have him talk to you about Bunbury or about anything else. It is enough to drive one perfectly frantic.

5   ALGERNON. Of course I admit that the faults were all on my side. But I must say that I think that brother John's coldness to me is peculiarly painful. I expected a more en-thusiastic welcome, especially considering it

10   is the first time I have come here.

CECILY. Uncle Jack, if you don't shake hands with Ernest I will never forgive you.

JACK. Never forgive me?

CECILY. Never, never, never!

15   JACK. Well, this is the last time I shall ever do it. [Shakes hands with ALGERNON and glares.]

CHASUBLE. It's pleasant, is it not, to see so perfect a reconciliation? I think we might leave the two brothers together.

20   MISS PRISM. Cecily, you will come with us.

CECILY. Certainly, Miss Prism. My little task of reconciliation is over.

CHASUBLE. You have done a beautiful action to-day, dear child.

25   MISS PRISM. We must not be premature in our judgments.

CECILY. I feel very happy. [They all go off.]

JACK. You young scoundrel, Algy, you must get out of this place as soon as possible. I

30   don't allow any Bunburying here.

[Enter MERRIMAN.]

MERRIMAN. I have put Mr. Ernest's things in the room next to yours, sir. I suppose that is all right?

35   JACK. What?

MERRIMAN. Mr. Ernest's luggage, sir. I have unpacked it and put it in the room next to your own.

JACK. His luggage?

40   MERRIMAN. Yes, sir. Three portmanteaus, a dressing-case, two hat-boxes, and a large luncheon-basket.

ALGERNON. I am afraid I can't stay more than a week this time.

45   JACK. Merriman, order the dog-cart° at once.

dog-cart small, horse-drawn open carriage

Mr. Ernest has been suddenly called back to town.

MERRIMAN. Yes, sir. [Goes back into the house.]

ALGERNON. What a fearful liar you are, Jack.   50
I have not been called back to town at all.

JACK. Yes, you have.

ALGERNON. I haven't heard anyone call me.

JACK. Your duty as a gentleman calls you back.   55

ALGERNON. My duty as a gentleman has never interfered with my pleasures in the smallest degree.

JACK. I can quite understand that.

ALGERNON. Well, Cecily is a darling.   60

JACK. You are not to talk of Miss Cardew like that. I don't like it.

ALGERNON. Well, I don't like your clothes. You look perfectly ridiculous in them. Why on earth don't you go up and change? It is per-   65
fectly childish to be in deep mourning for a man who is actually staying for a whole week with you in your house as a guest. I call it grotesque.

JACK. You are certainly not staying with me   70
for a whole week as a guest or anything else. You have got to leave . . . by the four-five train.

ALGERNON. I certainly won't leave you so long as you are in mourning. It would be most unfriendly. If I were in mourning you would   75
stay with me, I suppose. I should think it very unkind if you didn't.

JACK. Well, will you go if I change my clothes?

ALGERNON. Yes, if you are not too long. I   80
never saw anybody take so long to dress, and with such little result.

JACK. Well, at any rate, that is better than being always over-dressed as you are.

ALGERNON. If I am occasionally a little over-   85
dressed, I make up for it by being always immensely over-educated.

JACK. Your vanity is ridiculous, your conduct an outrage, and your presence in my garden utterly absurd. However, you have got to   90
catch the four-five, and I hope you will have a pleasant journey back to town. This Bun-burying, as you call it, has not been a great

success for you.

[*Goes into the house.*]

ALGERNON. I think it has been a great success. I'm in love with Cecily, and that is everything.

[*Enter* CECILY *at the back of the garden. She picks up the can and begins to water the flowers.*] But I must see her before I go, and make arrangements for another Bunbury. Ah, there she is.

CECILY. Oh, I merely came back to water the roses. I thought you were with Uncle Jack.

ALGERNON. He's gone to order the dog-cart for me.

CECILY. Oh, is he going to take you for a nice drive?

ALGERNON. He's going to send me away.

CECILY. Then have we got to part?

ALGERNON. I am afraid so. It's a very painful parting.

CECILY. It is always painful to part from people whom one has known for a very brief space of time. The absence of old friends one can endure with equanimity. But even a momentary separation from anyone to whom one has just been introduced is almost unbearable.

ALGERNON. Thank you.

[*Enter* MERRIMAN.]

MERRIMAN. The dog-cart is at the door, sir. [ALGERNON *looks appealingly at* CECILY.]

CECILY. It can wait, Merriman . . . for . . . five minutes.

MERRIMAN. Yes, Miss. [*Exit* MERRIMAN.]

ALGERNON. I hope, Cecily, I shall not offend you if I state quite frankly and openly that you seem to me to be in every way the visible personification of absolute perfection.

CECILY. I think your frankness does you great credit, Ernest. If you will allow me I will copy your remarks into my diary. [*Goes over to table and begins writing in diary.*]

ALGERNON. Do you really keep a diary? I'd give anything to look at it. May I?

CECILY. Oh, no. [*Puts her hand over it.*] You see, it is simply a very young girl's record of her own thoughts and impressions, and consequently meant for publication. When it appears in volume form I hope you will order a copy. But pray, Ernest, don't stop. I delight in taking down from dictation. I have reached 'absolute perfection.' You can go on. I am quite ready for more.

ALGERNON [*Somewhat taken aback*]. Ahem! Ahem!

CECILY. Oh, don't cough, Ernest. When one is dictating one should speak fluently and not cough. Besides, I don't know how to spell a cough. [*Writes as* ALGERNON *speaks.*]

ALGERNON [*Speaking very rapidly*]. Cecily, ever since I first looked upon your wonderful and incomparable beauty, I have dared to love you wildly, passionately, devotedly, hopelessly.

CECILY. I don't think that you should tell me that you love me wildly, passionately, devotedly, hopelessly. Hopelessly doesn't seem to make much sense, does it?

ALGERNON. Cecily!

[*Enter* MERRIMAN.]

MERRIMAN. The dog-cart is waiting, sir.

ALGERNON. Tell it to come round next week, at the same hour.

MERRIMAN [*Looks at* CECILY, *who makes no sign*]. Yes, sir. [MERRIMAN *retires.*]

CECILY. Uncle Jack would be very much annoyed if he knew you were staying on till next week, at the same hour.

ALGERNON. Oh, I don't care about Jack. I don't care for anybody in the whole world but you. I love you, Cecily. You will marry me, won't you?

CECILY. You silly boy! Of course. Why, we have been engaged for the last three months.

ALGERNON. For the last three months?

CECILY. Yes, it will be exactly three months on Thursday.

ALGERNON. But how did we become engaged?

CECILY. Well, ever since dear Uncle Jack first confessed to us that he had a younger brother who was very wicked and bad, you of course have formed the chief topic of conversation between myself and Miss Prism. And of course a man who is much talked about is always very attractive. One feels there must be something in him after all. I daresay it was foolish of me, but I fell in love with you, Ernest.

ALGERNON. Darling! And when was the engagement actually settled?

5   CECILY. On the 4th of February last. Worn out by your entire ignorance of my existence, I determined to end the matter one way or the other, and after a long struggle with myself I accepted you under this dear old tree here.
10 The next day I bought this little ring in your name, and this is the little bangle with the true lovers' knot I promised you always to wear.

ALGERNON. Did I give you this? It's very
15 pretty, isn't it?

CECILY. Yes, you've wonderfully good taste, Ernest. It's the excuse I've always given for your leading such a bad life. And this is the box in which I keep all your dear letters. [*Kneels*
20 *at table, opens box, and produces letters tied up with blue ribbon.*]

ALGERNON. My letters! But my own sweet Cecily, I have never written you any letters.

CECILY. You need hardly remind me of that,
25 Ernest. I remember only too well that I was forced to write your letters for you. I wrote always three times a week, and sometimes oftener.

ALGERNON. Oh, do let me read them, Cecily?
30   CECILY. Oh, I couldn't possibly. They would make you far too conceited. [*Replaces box.*] The three you wrote me after I had broken off the engagement are so beautiful, and so badly spelled, that even now I can hardly read them
35 without crying a little.

ALGERNON. But was our engagement ever broken off?

CECILY. Of course it was. On the 22nd of last March. You can see the entry if you like.
40 [*Shows diary.*] 'To-day I broke off my engagement with Ernest. I feel it is better to do so. The weather still continues charming.'

ALGERNON. But why on earth did you break it off? What had I done? I had done nothing
45 at all. Cecily, I am very much hurt indeed to hear you broke it off. Particularly when the weather was so charming.

CECILY. It would hardly have been a really serious engagement if it hadn't been broken off at least once. But I forgave you before the 50 week was out.

ALGERNON [*Crossing to her, and kneeling*]. What a perfect angel you are, Cecily.

CECILY. You dear romantic boy. [*He kisses her, she puts her fingers through his hair.*] I hope 55 your hair curls naturally, does it?

ALGERNON. Yes, darling, with a little help from others.

CECILY. I am so glad.

ALGERNON. You'll never break off our en- 60 gagement again, Cecily?

CECILY. I don't think I could break it off now that I have actually met you. Besides, of course, there is the question of your name.

ALGERNON. Yes, of course. [*Nervously.*] 65

CECILY. You must not laugh at me, darling, but it had always been a girlish dream of mine to love some one whose name was Ernest. [ALGERNON *rises*, CECILY *also.*] There is something in that name that seems to inspire 70 absolute confidence. I pity any poor married woman whose husband is not called Ernest.

ALGERNON. But, my dear child, do you mean to say you could not love me if I had some other name? 75

CECILY. But what name?

ALGERNON. Oh, any name you like — Algernon — for instance . . .

CECILY. But I don't like the name of Algernon.

ALGERNON. Well, my own dear, sweet, lov- 80 ing little darling, I really can't see why you should object to the name of Algernon. It is not at all a bad name. In fact, it is rather an aristocratic name. Half of the chaps° who get into the Bankruptcy Court are called Algernon. 85 But seriously, Cecily . . . [*Moving to her*] . . . if my name was Algy, couldn't you love me?

CECILY [*Rising*]. I might respect you, Ernest, I might admire your character, but I fear that I should not be able to give you my undivided 90 attention.

ALGERNON. Ahem! Cecily! [*Picking up hat.*] Your Rector here is, I suppose, thoroughly

---

Half of the chaps upper-class young men who have rapidly squandered their fortunes

experienced in the practice of all the rites and ceremonials of the Church?

CECILY. Oh yes. Dr. Chasuble is a most learned man. He has never written a single book, so you can imagine how much he knows.

ALGERNON. I must see him at once on a most important christening—I mean on most important business.

CECILY. Oh!

ALGERNON. I shan't be away more than half an hour.

CECILY. Considering that we have been engaged since February the 14th, and that I only met you to-day for the first time, I think it is rather hard that you should leave me for so long a period as half an hour. Couldn't you make it twenty minutes?

ALGERNON. I'll be back in no time.

[*Kisses her and rushes down the garden.*]

CECILY. What an impetuous boy he is! I like his hair so much. I must enter his proposal in my diary.

[*Enter* MERRIMAN.]

MERRIMAN. A Miss Fairfax has just called to see Mr. Worthing. On very important business Miss Fairfax states.

CECILY. Isn't Mr. Worthing in his library?

MERRIMAN. Mr. Worthing went over in the direction of the Rectory some time ago.

CECILY. Pray ask the lady to come out here; Mr. Worthing is sure to be back soon. And you can bring tea.

MERRIMAN. Yes, Miss. [*Goes out.*]

CECILY. Miss Fairfax! I suppose one of the many good elderly women who are associated with Uncle Jack in some of his philanthropic work in London. I don't quite like women who are interested in philanthropic work. I think it is so forward of them.

[*Enter* MERRIMAN.]

MERRIMAN. Miss Fairfax.

[*Enter* GWENDOLEN. *Exit* MERRIMAN.]

CECILY [*Advancing to meet her*]. Pray let me introduce myself to you. My name is Cecily Cardew.

GWENDOLEN. Cecily Cardew? [*Moving to her and shaking hands*]. What a very sweet name! Something tells me that we are going to be great friends. I like you already more than I can say. My first impressions of people are never wrong.

CECILY. How nice of you to like me so much after we have known each other such a comparatively short time. Pray sit down.

GWENDOLEN [*Still standing up*]. I may call you Cecily, may I not?

CECILY. With pleasure!

GWENDOLEN. And you will always call me Gwendolen, won't you.

CECILY. If you wish.

GWENDOLEN. Then that is all quite settled, is it not?

CECILY. I hope so. [*A pause. They both sit down together.*]

GWENDOLEN. Perhaps this might be a favorable opportunity for my mentioning who I am. My father is Lord Bracknell. You have never heard of papa, I suppose?

CECILY. I don't think so.

GWENDOLEN. Outside the family circle, papa, I am glad to say, is entirely unknown. I think that is quite as it should be. The home seems to me to be the proper sphere for the man. And certainly once a man begins to neglect his domestic duties he becomes painfully effeminate, does he not? And I don't like that. It makes men so very attractive. Cecily, mamma, whose views on education are remarkably strict, has brought me up to be extremely short-sighted; it is part of her system; so do you mind my looking at you through my glasses?

CECILY. Oh! not at all, Gwendolen. I am very fond of being looked at.

GWENDOLEN [*After examining* CECILY *carefully through a lornette°*]. You are here on a short visit I suppose.

CECILY. Oh no! I live here.

GWENDOLEN [*Severely*]. Really? Your mother, no doubt, or some female relative of advanced years, resides here also?

CECILY. Oh no! I have no mother, nor, in fact, any relations.

lorgnette eye-glasses or opera glasses mounted on an ornate handle; its use a sign of supercilious condescension

GWENDOLEN. Indeed?

CECILY. My dear guardian, with the assist-ance of Miss Prism, has the arduous task of looking after me.

5 GWENDOLEN. Your guardian?

CECILY. Yes, I am Mr. Worthing's ward.

GWENDOLEN. Oh! It is strange he never mentioned to me that he had a ward. How secretive of him! He grows more interesting 10 hourly. I am not sure, however, that the news inspires me with feelings of unmixed delight. [*Rising and going to her.*] I am very fond of you, Cecily; I have liked you ever since I met you! But I am bound to state that now that I know 15 that you are Mr. Worthing's ward, I cannot help expressing a wish you were — well just a little older than you seem to be — and not quite so very alluring in appearance. In fact, if I may speak candidly —

20 CECILY. Pray do! I think that whenever one has anything unpleasant to say, one should always be quite candid.

GWENDOLEN. Well, to speak with perfect candour, Cecily, I wish that you were fully 25 forty-two, and more than usually plain for your age. Ernest has a strong upright nature. He is the very soul of truth and honour. Dis-loyalty would be as impossible to him as de-ception. But even men of the noblest possible 30 moral character are extremely susceptible to the influence of the physical charms of others. Modern, no less than Ancient History, supplies us with many most painful examples of what I refer to. If it were not so, indeed, History 35 would be quite unreadable.

CECILY. I beg your pardon, Gwendolen, did you say Ernest?

GWENDOLEN. Yes.

CECILY. Oh, but it is not Mr. Ernest Worth-40 ing who is my guardian. It is his brother — his elder brother.

GWENDOLEN [*Sitting down again*]. Ernest never mentioned to me that he had a brother.

CECILY. I am sorry to say they have not been 45 on good terms for a long time.

GWENDOLEN. Ah! that accounts for it. And now that I think of it I have never heard any man mention his brother. The subject seems distasteful to most men. Cecily, you have

lifted a load from my mind. I was growing 50 almost anxious. It would have been terrible if any cloud had come across a friendship like ours, would it not? Of course you are quite, quite sure that it is not Mr. Ernest Worthing who is your guardian? 55

CECILY. Quite sure. [*A pause.*] In fact, I am going to be his.

GWENDOLEN [*Enquiringly*]. I beg your par-don?

CECILY [*Rather shy and confidingly*]. Dearest 60 Gwendolen, there is no reason why I should make a secret of it to you. Our little county newspaper is sure to chronicle the fact next week. Mr. Ernest Worthing and I are engaged to be married. 65

GWENDOLEN [*Quite politely, rising*]. My darling Cecily, I think there must be some slight error. Mr. Ernest Worthing is engaged to me. The announcement will appear in the 'Morning Post' on Saturday at the latest. 70

CECILY [*Very politely, rising*]. I am afraid you must be under some misconception. Ernest proposed to me exactly ten minutes ago. [*Shows diary.*]

GWENDOLEN [*Examines diary through her* 75 *lorgnette carefully*]. It is certainly very curious, for he asked me to be his wife yesterday after-noon at 5:30. If you would care to verify the incident, pray do so. [*Produces diary of her own.*] I never travel without my diary. One 80 should always have something sensational to read in the train. I am so sorry, dear Cecily, if it is any disappointment to you, but I am afraid *I* have the prior claim.

CECILY. It would distress me more than I can 85 tell you, dear Gwendolen, if it caused you any mental or physical anguish, but I feel bound to point out that since Ernest proposed to you he clearly has changed his mind.

GWENDOLEN [*Meditatively*]. If the poor 90 fellow has been entrapped into any foolish promise I shall consider it my duty to rescue him at once, and with a firm hand.

CECILY [*Thoughtfully and sadly*]. Whatever unfortunate entanglement my dear boy may 95 have got into, I will never reproach him with it after we are married.

GWENDOLEN. Do you allude to me, Miss

Cardew, as an entanglement? You are presumptuous. On an occasion of this kind it becomes more than a moral duty to speak one's mind. It becomes a pleasure.

5 CECILY. Do you suggest, Miss Fairfax, that I entrapped Ernest into an engagement? How dare you? This is no time for wearing the shallow mask of manners. When I see a spade I call it a spade.

10 GWENDOLEN [*Satirically*]. I am glad to say that I have never seen a spade. It is obvious that our social spheres have been widely different.

[*Enter* MERRIMAN, *followed by the footman.*
15 *He carries a salver, table cloth, and plate stand.* CECILY *is about to retort. The presence of the servants exercises a restraining influence, under which both girls chafe.*]

MERRIMAN. Shall I lay tea here as usual,
20 Miss?

CECILY [*Sternly, in a calm voice*]. Yes, as usual. [MERRIMAN *begins to clear and lay cloth. A long pause.* CECILY *and* GWENDOLEN *glare at each other.*]

25 GWENDOLEN. Are there many interesting walks in the vicinity, Miss Cardew?

CECILY. Oh! yes! a great many. From the top of one of the hills quite close one can see five counties.

30 GWENDOLEN. Five counties! I don't think I should like that. I hate crowds.

CECILY [*Sweetly*]. I suppose that is why you live in town? [GWENDOLEN *bites her lip, and beats her foot nervously with her parasol.*]

35 GWENDOLEN [*Looking round*]. Quite a well-kept garden this is, Miss Cardew.

CECILY. So glad you like it, Miss Fairfax.

GWENDOLEN. I had no idea there were any flowers in the country.

40 CECILY. Oh, flowers are as common° here, Miss Fairfax, as people are in London.

GWENDOLEN. Personally I cannot understand how anybody manages to exist in the country, if anybody who is anybody does. The country
45 always bores me to death.

CECILY. Ah! This is what the newspapers

---

common abundant, with pun on "commonplace" or "vulgar"

call agricultural depression, is it not? I believe the aristocracy are suffering very much from it just at present. It is almost an epidemic amongst them, I have been told. May I offer 50 you some tea, Miss Fairfax?

GWENDOLEN [*With elaborate politeness*]. Thank you. [*Aside*] Detestable girl! But I require tea!

CECILY [*Sweetly*]. Sugar? 55

GWENDOLEN [*Superciliously*]. No, thank you. Sugar is not fashionable any more. [CECILY *looks angrily at her, takes up the tongs and puts four lumps of sugar into the cup.*]

CECILY [*Severely*]. Cake or bread and butter? 60

GWENDOLEN [*In a bored manner*]. Bread and butter, please. Cake is rarely seen at the best houses nowadays.

CECILY [*Cuts a very large slice of cake, and puts it on the tray*]. Hand that to Miss Fairfax. 65

[MERRIMAN *does so, and goes out with footman.* GWENDOLEN *drinks the tea and makes a grimace. Puts down cup at once, reaches out her hand to the bread and butter, looks at it, and finds it is cake. Rises in indignation.*] 70

GWENDOLEN. You have filled my tea with lumps of sugar, and though I asked most distinctly for bread and butter, you have given me cake. I am known for the gentleness of my disposition, and the extraordinary sweetness 75 of my nature, but I warn you, Miss Cardew, you may go too far.

CECILY [*Rising*]. To save my poor, innocent, trusting boy from the machinations of any other girl there are no lengths to which I would 80 not go.

GWENDOLEN. From the moment I saw you I distrusted you. I felt that you were false and deceitful. I am never deceived in such matters. My first impressions of people are invariably 85 right.

CECILY. It seems to me, Miss Fairfax, that I am trespassing on your valuable time. No doubt you have many other calls of a similar character to make in the neighbourhood. 90

[*Enter* JACK.]

GWENDOLEN [*Catching sight of him*]. Ernest! My own Ernest!

JACK. Gwendolen! Darling! [*Offers to kiss her.*] 95

GWENDOLEN [*Drawing back*]. A moment! May I ask if you are engaged to be married to this young lady? [*Points to* CECILY.]

JACK [*Laughing*]. To dear little Cecily! Of course not! What could have put such an idea into your pretty little head?

GWENDOLEN. Thank you. You may. [*Offers her cheek.*]

CECILY [*Very sweetly*]. I knew there must be some misunderstanding, Miss Fairfax. The gentleman whose arm is at present around your waist is my dear guardian, Mr. John Worthing.

GWENDOLEN. I beg your pardon?

CECILY. This is Uncle Jack.

GWENDOLEN [*Receding*]. Jack! Oh!

[*Enter* ALGERNON.]

CECILY. Here is Ernest.

ALGERNON [*Goes straight over to* CECILY *without noticing anyone else*]. My own love! [*Offers to kiss her.*]

CECILY [*Drawing back*]. A moment, Ernest! May I ask you—are you engaged to be married to this young lady?

ALGERNON [*Looking around*]. To what young lady? Good heavens! Gwendolen!

CECILY. Yes! to good heavens, Gwendolen, I mean to Gwendolen.

ALGERNON [*Laughing*]. Of course not! What could have put such an idea into your pretty little head?

CECILY. Thank you. [*Presenting her cheek to be kissed.*] You may. [ALGERNON *kisses her.*]

GWENDOLEN. I felt there was some slight error, Miss Cardew. The gentleman who is now embracing you is my cousin, Mr. Algernon Moncrieff.

CECILY [*Breaking away from* ALGERNON]. Algernon Moncrieff! Oh! [*The two girls move towards each other and put their arms round each other's waist as if for protection.*]

CECILY. Are you called Algernon?

ALGERNON. I cannot deny it.

CECILY. Oh!

GWENDOLEN. Is your name really John?

JACK [*Standing rather proudly*]. I could deny it if I liked. I could deny anything if I liked. But my name certainly is John. It has been John for years.

CECILY [*To* GWENDOLEN]. A gross deception has been practised on both of us.

GWENDOLEN. My poor wounded Cecily!

CECILY. My sweet wronged Gwendolen!

GWENDOLEN [*Slowly and seriously*]. You will call me sister, will you not? [*They embrace.* JACK *and* ALGERNON *groan and walk up and down.*]

CECILY [*Rather brightly*]. There is just one question I would like to be allowed to ask my guardian.

GWENDOLEN. An admirable idea! Mr. Worthing, there is just one question I would like to be permitted to put to you. Where is your brother Ernest? We are both engaged to be married to your brother Ernest, so it is a matter of some importance to us to know where your brother Ernest is at present.

JACK [*Slowly and hesitatingly*]. Gwendolen—Cecily—it is very painful for me to be forced to speak the truth. It is the first time in my life that I have ever been reduced to such a painful position, and I am really quite inexperienced in doing anything of the kind. However, I will tell you quite frankly that I have no brother Ernest. I have no brother at all. I never had a brother in my life, and I certainly have not the smallest intention of ever having one in the future.

CECILY [*Surprised*]. No brother at all?

JACK [*Cheerily*]. None!

GWENDOLEN [*Severely*]. Had you never a brother of any kind?

JACK [*Pleasantly*]. Never. Not even of any kind.

GWENDOLEN. I am afraid it is quite clear, Cecily, that neither of us is engaged to be married to anyone.

CECILY. It is not a very pleasant position for a young girl suddenly to find herself in. Is it?

GWENDOLEN. Let us go into the house. They will hardly venture to come after us there.

CECILY. No, men are so cowardly, aren't they?

[*They retire into the house with scornful looks.*]

JACK. This ghastly state of things is what you call Bunburying, I suppose?

ALGERNON. Yes, and a perfectly wonderful Bunbury it is. The most wonderful Bunbury I have ever had in my life.

JACK. Well, you've no right whatsoever to Bunbury here.

ALGERNON. That is absurd. One has a right to Bunbury anywhere one chooses. Every serious Bunburyist knows that.

JACK. Serious Bunburyist! Good heavens!

ALGERNON. Well, one must be serious about something, if one wants to have any amusement in life. I happen to be serious about Bunburying. What on earth you are serious about I haven't got the remotest idea. About everything, I should fancy. You have such an absolutely trivial nature.

JACK. Well, the only small satisfaction I have in the whole of this wretched business is that your friend Bunbury is quite exploded. You won't be able to run down to the country quite so often as you used to do, dear Algy. And a very good thing too.

ALGERNON. Your brother is a little off colour, isn't he, dear Jack? You won't be able to disappear to London quite so frequently as your wicked custom was. And not a bad thing either.

JACK. As for your conduct towards Miss Cardew, I must say that your taking in a sweet, simple, innocent girl like that is quite inexcusable. To say nothing of the fact that she is my ward.

ALGERNON. I can see no possible defence at all for your deceiving a brilliant, clever, thoroughly experienced young lady like Miss Fairfax. To say nothing of the fact that she is my cousin.

JACK. I wanted to be engaged to Gwendolen, that is all. I love her.

ALGERNON. Well, I simply wanted to be engaged to Cecily. I adore her.

JACK. There is certainly no chance of your marrying Miss Cardew.

ALGERNON. I don't think there is much likelihood, Jack, of you and Miss Fairfax being united.

JACK. Well, that is no business of yours.

ALGERNON. If it was my business, I wouldn't talk about it. [*Begins to eat muffins.*] It is very vulgar to talk about one's business. Only people like stockbrokers do that, and then merely at dinner parties.

JACK. How can you sit there, calmly eating muffins when we are in this horrible trouble, I can't make out. You seem to me to be perfectly heartless.

ALGERNON. Well, I can't eat muffins in an agitated manner. The butter would probably get on my cuffs. One should always eat muffins quite calmly. It is the only way to eat them.

JACK. I say it's perfectly heartless your eating muffins at all, under the circumstances.

ALGERNON. When I am in trouble, eating is the only thing that consoles me. Indeed, when I am in really great trouble, as anyone who knows me intimately will tell you, I refuse everything except food and drink. At the present moment I am eating muffins because I am unhappy. Besides, I am particularly fond of muffins. [*Rising.*]

JACK [*Rising*]. Well, that is no reason why you should eat them all in that greedy way. [*Takes muffins from* ALGERNON.]

ALGERNON [*Offering tea-cake*]. I wish you would have tea-cake instead. I don't like tea-cake.

JACK. Good heavens! I suppose a man may eat his own muffins in his own garden.

ALGERNON. But you have just said it was perfectly heartless to eat muffins.

JACK. I said it was perfectly heartless of you, under the circumstances. That is a very different thing.

ALGERNON. That may be. But the muffins are the same. [*He seizes the muffin-dish from* JACK.]

JACK. Algy, I wish to goodness you would go.

ALGERNON. You can't possibly ask me to go without having some dinner. It's absurd. I never go without my dinner. No one ever does, except vegetarians and people like that. Besides I have just made arrangements with Dr. Chasuble to be christened at a quarter to six under the name of Ernest.

JACK. My dear fellow, the sooner you give up that nonsense the better. I made arrangements this morning with Dr. Chasuble to be christened myself at 5.30, and I naturally will take the name of Ernest. Gwendolen would wish it.

We can't both be christened Ernest. It's absurd. Besides, I have a perfect right to be christened if I like. There is no evidence at all that I ever have been christened by anybody. I should think it extremely probable I never was, and so does Dr. Chasuble. It is entirely different in your case. You have been christened already.

ALGERNON. Yes, but I have not been christened for years.

JACK. Yes, but you have been christened. That is the important thing.

ALGERNON. Quite so. So I know my constitution can stand it. If you are not quite sure about your ever having been christened, I must say I think it rather dangerous your venturing on it now. It might make you very unwell. You can hardly have forgotten that someone very closely connected with you was very nearly carried off this week in Paris by a severe chill.

JACK. Yes, but you said yourself that a severe chill was not hereditary.

ALGERNON. It usen't to be, I know — but I daresay it is now. Science is always making wonderful improvements in things.

JACK [*Picking up the muffin-dish*]. Oh, that is nonsense; you are always talking nonsense.

ALGERNON. Jack, you are at the muffins again! I wish you wouldn't. There are only two left. [*Takes them.*] I told you I was particularly fond of muffins.

JACK. But I hate tea-cake.

ALGERNON. Why on earth then do you allow tea-cake to be served up for your guests? What ideas you have of hospitality!

JACK. Algernon! I have already told you to go. I don't want you here. Why don't you go!

ALGERNON. I haven't quite finished my tea yet! and there is still one muffin left. [JACK *groans, and sinks into a chair.* ALGERNON *continues eating.*]

Act-Drop

ACT III

SCENE. *Morning-room at the Manor House.*

GWENDOLEN *and* CECILY *are at the window, looking out into the garden.*

GWENDOLEN. The fact that they did not follow us at once into the house, as anyone else would have done, seems to me to show that they have some sense of shame left.

CECILY. They have been eating muffins. That looks like repentance.

GWENDOLEN [*After a pause*]. They don't seem to notice us at all. Couldn't you cough?

CECILY. But I haven't a cough.

GWENDOLEN. They're looking at us. What effrontery!

CECILY. They're approaching. That's very forward of them.

GWENDOLEN. Let us preserve a dignified silence.

CECILY. Certainly. It's the only thing to do now.

[*Enter* JACK *followed by* ALGERNON. *They whistle some dreadful popular air from a British Opera.*]

GWENDOLEN. This dignified silence seems to produce an unpleasant effect.

CECILY. A most distasteful one.

GWENDOLEN. But we will not be the first to speak.

CECILY. Certainly not.

GWENDOLEN. Mr. Worthing, I have something very particular to ask you. Much depends on your reply.

CECILY. Gwendolen, your common sense is invaluable. Mr. Moncrieff, kindly answer me the following question: Why did you pretend to be my guardian's brother?

ALGERNON. In order that I might have an opportunity of meeting you.

CECILY [*To* GWENDOLEN]. That certainly seems a satisfactory explanation, does it not?

GWENDOLEN. Yes, dear, if you can believe him.

CECILY. I don't. But that does not affect the wonderful beauty of his answer.

GWENDOLEN. True. In matters of grave importance, style, not sincerity is the vital thing. Mr. Worthing, what explanation can you offer to me for pretending to have a brother? Was it in order that you might have an opportunity of coming up to town to see me as often as possible?

JACK. Can you doubt it, Miss Fairfax?

GWENDOLEN. I have the gravest doubts upon the subject. But I intend to crush them. This is not the moment for German scepticism.° [*Moving to* CECILY.] Their explanations appear to be quite satisfactory, especially Mr. Worthing's. That seems to me to have the stamp of truth upon it.

CECILY. I am more than content with what Mr. Moncrieff said. His voice alone inspires one with absolute credulity.

GWENDOLEN. Then you think we should forgive them?

CECILY. Yes. I mean no.

GWENDOLEN. True! I had forgotten. There are principles at stake that one cannot surrender. Which of us should tell them? The task is not a pleasant one.

CECILY. Could we not both speak at the same time?

GWENDOLEN. An excellent idea! I nearly always speak at the same time as other people. Will you take the time from me?

CECILY. Certainly. [GWENDOLEN *beats time with uplifted finger.*]

GWENDOLEN and CECILY [*Speaking together*]. Your Christian names are still an insuperable barrier. That is all!

JACK and ALGERNON [*Speaking together*]. Our Christian names! Is that all? But we are going to be christened this afternoon.

GWENDOLEN [*To* JACK]. For my sake you are prepared to do this terrible thing?

JACK. I am.

CECILY [*To* ALGERNON]. To please me you are ready to face this fearful ordeal?

ALGERNON. I am!

GWENDOLEN. How absurd to talk of the equality of the sexes! Where questions of self-sacrifice are concerned, men are infinitely beyond us.

JACK. We are. [*Clasps hands with* ALGERNON.]

CECILY. They have moments of physical courage of which we women know absolutely nothing.

German scepticism movements in nineteenth-century German philosophy calling first principles of religion and ethics into question

GWENDOLEN [*To* JACK]. Darling!

ALGERNON [*To* CECILY]. Darling! [*They fall into each other's arms.*]

[*Enter* MERRIMAN. *When he enters he coughs loudly, seeing the situation.*]

MERRIMAN. Ahem! Ahem! Lady Bracknell!

JACK. Good heavens!

[*Enter* LADY BRACKNELL. *The couples separate in alarm. Exit* MERRIMAN.]

LADY BRACKNELL. Gwendolen! What does this mean?

GWENDOLEN. Merely that I am engaged to be married to Mr. Worthing, mamma.

LADY BRACKNELL. Come here. Sit down. Sit down immediately. Hesitation of any kind is a sign of mental decay in the young, of physical weakness in the old. [*Turns to* JACK.] Apprised, sir, of my daughter's sudden flight by her trusty maid, whose confidence I purchased by means of a small coin, I followed her at once by a luggage train. Her unhappy father is, I am glad to say, under the impression that she is attending a more than usually lengthy lecture by the University Extension Scheme on the Influence of a permanent income on Thought. I do not propose to undeceive him. Indeed I have never undeceived him on any question. I would consider it wrong. But of course, you will clearly understand that all communication between yourself and my daughter must cease immediately from this moment. On this point, as indeed on all points, I am firm.

JACK. I am engaged to be married to Gwendolen, Lady Bracknell!

LADY BRACKNELL. You are nothing of the kind, sir. And now, as regards Algernon! . . . Algernon!

ALGERNON. Yes, Aunt Augusta.

LADY BRACKNELL. May I ask if it is in this house that your invalid friend Mr. Bunbury resides?

ALGERNON [*Stammering*]. Oh! No! Bunbury doesn't live here. Bunbury is somewhere else at present. In fact, Bunbury is dead.

LADY BRACKNELL. Dead! When did Mr. Bunbury die? His death must have been extremely sudden.

ALGERNON [*Airily*]. Oh! I killed Bunbury this afternoon. I mean poor Bunbury died this afternoon.

LADY BRACKNELL. What did he die of?

5   ALGERNON. Bunbury? Oh, he was quite exploded.

LADY BRACKNELL. Exploded! Was he the victim of a revolutionary outrage? I was not aware that Mr. Bunbury was interested in
10   social legislation. If so, he is well punished for his morbidity.

ALGERNON. My dear Aunt Augusta, I mean he was found out! The doctors found out that Bunbury could not live, that is what I mean—
15   so Bunbury died.

LADY BRACKNELL. He seems to have had great confidence in the opinion of his physicians. I am glad, however, that he made up his mind at the last to some definite course of
20   action, and acted under proper medical advice. And now that we have finally got rid of this Mr. Bunbury, may I ask, Mr. Worthing, who is that young person whose hand my nephew Algernon is now holding in what
25   seems to me a peculiarly unnecessary manner?

JACK. That lady is Miss Cecily Cardew, my ward. [LADY BRACKNELL *bows coldly to* CECILY.]

ALGERNON. I am engaged to be married to Cecily, Aunt Augusta.

30   LADY BRACKNELL. I beg your pardon?

CECILY. Mr. Moncrieff and I are engaged to be married, Lady Bracknell.

LADY BRACKNELL [*With a shiver, crossing to the sofa and sitting down*]. I do not know
35   whether there is anything peculiarly exciting in the air of this particular part of Hertfordshire, but the number of engagements that go on seems to me considerably above the proper average that statistics have laid down for our
40   guidance. I think some preliminary enquiry on my part would not be out of place. Mr. Worthing, is Miss Cardew at all connected with any of the larger railway stations in London? I merely desire information. Until yesterday I
45   had no idea that there were any families or persons whose origin was a Terminus. [JACK *looks perfectly furious, but restrains himself.*]

JACK [*In a clear, cold voice*]. Miss Cardew is the granddaughter of the late Mr. Thomas Cardew of 149, Belgrave Square, S.W.; Gervase   50 Park, Dorking, Surrey; and the Sporran, Fifeshire, N.B.°

LADY BRACKNELL. That sounds not unsatisfactory. Three addresses always inspire confidence, even in tradesmen. But what proof   55 have I of their authenticity?

JACK. I have carefully preserved the Court Guides of the period. They are open to your inspection, Lady Bracknell.

LADY BRACKNELL [*Grimly*]. I have known   60 strange errors in that publication.

JACK. Miss Cardew's family solicitors are Messrs. Markby, Markby, and Markby.

LADY BRACKNELL. Markby, Markby, and Markby! A firm of the very highest position   65 in their profession. Indeed I am told that one of the Mr. Markbys is occasionally to be seen at dinner parties. So far I am satisfied.

JACK [*Very irritably*]. How extremely kind of you, Lady Bracknell! I have also in my pos-   70 session, you will be pleased to hear, certificates of Miss Cardew's birth, baptism, whooping cough, registration, vaccination, confirmation, and the measles; both the German and the English variety.   75

LADY BRACKNELL. Ah! A life crowded with incident, I see; though perhaps somewhat too exciting for a young girl. I am not myself in favour of premature experiences. [*Rises, looks at her watch.*] Gwendolen! the time approaches   80 for our departure. We have not a moment to lose. As a matter of form, Mr. Worthing, I had better ask you if Miss Cardew has any little fortune?

JACK. Oh! about a hundred and thirty thou-   85 sand pounds in the Funds.° That is all. Goodbye, Lady Bracknell. So pleased to have seen you.

LADY BRACKNELL [*Sitting down again*]. A moment, Mr. Worthing. A hundred and thirty   90 thousand pounds! And in the Funds! Miss

N.B. North Britain, a snobbish English term for Scotland
a hundred and thirty thousand pounds in the Funds the present-day equivalent of a million dollars or so, in government securities, regarded as a most prudent investment

Cardew seems to me a most attractive young lady, now that I look at her. Few girls of the present day have any really solid qualities, any of the qualities that last, and improve with time. We live, I regret to say, in an age of surfaces. [*To* CECILY.] Come over here, dear. [CECILY *goes across.*] Pretty child! your dress is sadly simple, and your hair seems almost as Nature might have left it. But we can soon alter all that. A thoroughly experienced French maid produces a really marvellous result in a very brief space of time. I remember recommending one to young Lady Lancing, and after three months her own husband did not know her.

JACK [*Aside*]. And after six months nobody knew her.°

LADY BRACKNELL [*Glares at* JACK *for a few moments. Then bends, with a practised smile, to* CECILY]. Kindly turn round, sweet child. [CECILY *turns completely round.*] No, the side view is what I want. [CECILY *presents her profile.*] Yes, quite as I expected. There are distinct social possibilities in your profile. The two weak points in our age are its want of principle and its want of profile. The chin a little higher, dear. Style largely depends on the way the chin is worn. They are worn very high, just at present. Algernon!

ALGERNON. Yes, Aunt Augusta!

LADY BRACKNELL. There are distinct social possibilities in Miss Cardew's profile.

ALGERNON. Cecily is the sweetest, dearest, prettiest girl in the whole world. And I don't care twopence about social possibilities.

LADY BRACKNELL. Never speak disrespectfully of Society, Algernon. Only people who can't get into it do that. [*To* CECILY.] Dear child, of course you know that Algernon has nothing but his debts to depend upon. But I do not approve of mercenary marriages. When I married Lord Bracknell I had no fortune of any kind. But I never dreamed for a moment of allowing that to stand in my way. Well, I suppose I must give my consent.

ALGERNON. Thank you, Aunt Augusta.

LADY BRACKNELL. Cecily, you may kiss me!

CECILY [*Kisses her*]. Thank you, Lady Bracknell.

LADY BRACKNELL. You may also address me as Aunt Augusta for the future.

CECILY. Thank you, Aunt Augusta.

LADY BRACKNELL. The marriage, I think, had better take place quite soon.

ALGERNON. Thank you, Aunt Augusta.

CECILY. Thank you, Aunt Augusta.

LADY BRACKNELL. To speak frankly, I am not in favour of long engagements. They give people the opportunity of finding out each other's character before marriage, which I think is never advisable.

JACK. I beg your pardon for interrupting you, Lady Bracknell, but this engagement is quite out of the question. I am Miss Cardew's guardian, and she cannot marry without my consent until she comes of age. That consent I absolutely decline to give.

LADY BRACKNELL. Upon what grounds, may I ask? Algernon is an extremely, I may almost say an ostentatiously, eligible young man. He has nothing, but he looks everything. What more can one desire?

JACK. It pains me very much to have to speak frankly to you, Lady Bracknell, about your nephew, but the fact is that I do not approve at all of his moral character. I suspect him of being untruthful. [ALGERNON *and* CECILY *look at him in indignant amazement.*]

LADY BRACKNELL. Untruthful! My nephew Algernon? Impossible! He is an Oxonian.°

JACK. I fear there can be no possible doubt about the matter. This afternoon, during my temporary absence in London on an important question of romance, he obtained admission to my house by means of the false pretence of being my brother. Under an assumed name he drank, I've just been informed by my butler, an entire pint bottle of my Perrier-Jouet, Brut, '89; a wine I was specially reserving for myself. Continuing his disgraceful deception, he succeeded in the course of the afternoon in alienating the affections of my only ward. He

knew her would acknowledge her acquaintance

Oxonian graduate of Oxford; without fault or flaw, presumably

subsequently stayed to tea, and devoured every single muffin. And what makes his conduct all the more heartless is, that he was perfectly well aware from the first that I have
5 no brother, that I never had a brother, and that I don't intend to have a brother, not even of any kind. I distinctly told him so myself yesterday afternoon.

LADY BRACKNELL. Ahem! Mr. Worthing, after
10 careful consideration I have decided entirely to overlook my nephew's conduct to you.

JACK. That is very generous of you, Lady Bracknell. My own decision, however, is unalterable. I decline to give my consent.

15 LADY BRACKNELL. [To CECILY]. Come here, sweet child. [CECILY goes over.] How old are you, dear?

CECILY. Well, I am really only eighteen, but I always admit to twenty when I go to evening
20 parties.

LADY BRACKNELL. You are perfectly right in making some slight alteration. Indeed, no woman should ever be quite accurate about her age. It looks so calculating. . . . [In a medita-
25 tive manner.] Eighteen, but admitting to twenty at evening parties. Well, it will not be very long before you are of age and free from the restraints of tutelage. So I don't think your guardian's consent is, after all, a matter of
30 any importance.

JACK. Pray excuse me, Lady Bracknell, for interrupting you again, but it is only fair to tell you that according to the terms of her grandfather's will Miss Cardew does not
35 come legally of age till she is thirty-five.

LADY BRACKNELL. That does not seem to me to be a grave objection. Thirty-five is a very attractive age. London society is full of women of the very highest birth who have, of their
40 own free choice, remained thirty-five for years. Lady Dumbleton is an instance in point. To my own knowledge she has been thirty-five ever since she arrived at the age of forty, which was many years ago now. I see no reason why
45 our dear Cecily should not be even still more attractive at the age you mention than she is at present. There will be a large accumulation of property.

CECILY. Algy, could you wait for me till I was thirty-five? 50

ALGERNON. Of course I could, Cecily. You know I could.

CECILY. Yes, I felt it instinctively, but I couldn't wait all that time. I hate waiting even five minutes for anybody. It always makes 55 me rather cross. I am not punctual myself, I know, but I do like punctuality in others, and waiting, even to be married, is quite out of the question.

ALGERNON. Then what is to be done, Cecily? 60

CECILY. I don't know, Mr. Moncrieff.

LADY BRACKNELL. My dear Mr. Worthing, as Miss Cardew states positively that she cannot wait till she is thirty-five — a remark which I am bound to say seems to me to show a some- 65 what impatient nature — I would beg of you to reconsider your decision.

JACK. But my dear Lady Bracknell, the matter is entirely in your own hands. The moment you consent to my marriage with Gwendolen, 70 I will most gladly allow your nephew to form an alliance with my ward.

• LADY BRACKNELL [Rising and drawing herself up]. You must be quite aware that what you propose is out of the question. 75

JACK. Then a passionate celibacy is all that any of us can look forward to.

LADY BRACKNELL. That is not the destiny I propose for Gwendolen. Algernon, of course, can choose for himself. [Pulls out her watch.] 80 Come dear; [GWENDOLEN rises.] we have already missed five, if not six, trains. To miss any more might expose us to comment on the platform.

[Enter DR. CHASUBLE.] 85

CHASUBLE. Everything is quite ready for the christenings.

LADY BRACKNELL. The christenings, sir! Is not that somewhat premature?

CHASUBLE [Looking rather puzzled, and point- 90 ing to JACK and ALGERNON]. Both these gentlemen have expressed a desire for immediate baptism.

LADY BRACKNELL. At their age? The idea is grotesque and irreligious! Algernon, I forbid 95 you to be baptised. I will not hear of such excesses. Lord Bracknell would be highly displeased if he learned that that was the way in which you wasted your time and money.

CHASUBLE. Am I to understand then that there are to be no christenings at all this afternoon?

JACK. I don't think that, as things are now, it would be of much practical value to either of us, Dr. Chasuble.

CHASUBLE. I am grieved to hear such sentiments from you, Mr. Worthing. They savour of the heretical views of the Anabaptists,° views that I have completely refuted in four of my unpublished sermons. However, as your present mood seems to be one peculiarly secular, I will return to the church at once. Indeed, I have just been informed by the pew-opener that for the last hour and a half Miss Prism has been waiting for me in the vestry.

LADY BRACKNELL [*Starting*]. Miss Prism! Did I hear you mention a Miss Prism?

CHASUBLE. Yes, Lady Bracknell. I am on my way to join her.

LADY BRACKNELL. Pray allow me to detain you for a moment. This matter may prove to be one of vital importance to Lord Bracknell and myself. Is this Miss Prism a female of repellent aspect, remotely connected with education?

CHASUBLE [*Somewhat indignantly*]. She is the most cultivated of ladies, and the very picture of respectability.

LADY BRACKNELL. It is obviously the same person. May I ask what position she holds in your household?

CHASUBLE [*Severely*]. I am a celibate, madam.

JACK [*Interposing*]. Miss Prism, Lady Bracknell, has been for the last three years Miss Cardew's esteemed governess and valued companion.

LADY BRACKNELL. In spite of what I hear of her, I must see her at once. Let her be sent for.

CHASUBLE [*Looking off*]. She approaches; she is nigh.

[*Enter* MISS PRISM *hurriedly.*]

Anabaptists a sect advocating adult baptism, and re-baptism if it had been conferred in infancy

MISS PRISM. I was told you expected me in the vestry, dear Canon. I have been waiting for you there for an hour and three-quarters. [*Catches sight of* LADY BRACKNELL, *who has fixed her with a stony glare.* MISS PRISM *grows pale and quails. She looks anxiously round as if desirous to escape.*]

LADY BRACKNELL [*In a severe, judicial voice*]. Prism! [MISS PRISM *bows her head in shame.*] Come here, Prism! [MISS PRISM *approaches in a humble manner.*] Prism! Where is that baby? [*General consternation. The Canon starts back in horror.* ALGERNON *and* JACK *pretend to be anxious to shield* CECILY *and* GWENDOLEN *from hearing the details of a terrible public scandal.*] Twenty-eight years ago, Prism, you left Lord Bracknell's house, Number 104, Upper Grosvenor Street, in charge of a perambulator that contained a baby, of the male sex. You never returned. A few weeks later, through the elaborate investigations of the Metropolitan police, the perambulator was discovered at midnight, standing by itself in a remote corner of Bayswater. It contained the manuscript of a three-volume novel of more than usually revolting sentimentality. [MISS PRISM *starts in involuntary indignation*]. But the baby was not there! [*Everyone looks at* MISS PRISM.] Prism: Where is that baby? [*A pause.*]

MISS PRISM. Lady Bracknell, I admit with shame that I do not know. I only wish I did. The plain facts of the case are these. On the morning of the day you mention, a day that is for ever branded on my memory, I prepared as usual to take the baby out in its perambulator. I had also with me a somewhat old, but capacious hand-bag in which I had intended to place the manuscript of a work of fiction that I had written during my few unoccupied hours. In a moment of mental abstraction, for which I never can forgive myself, I deposited the manuscript in the bassinette, and placed the baby in the hand-bag.

JACK [*Who has been listening attentively*]. But where did you deposit the hand-bag?

MISS PRISM. Do not ask me, Mr. Worthing.

JACK. Miss Prism, this is a matter of no small importance to me. I insist on knowing where you deposited the hand-bag that contained that infant.

MISS PRISM. I left it in the cloak room of one of the larger railway stations in London.

5   JACK. What railway station?

MISS PRISM [*Quite crushed*]. Victoria. The Brighton line. [*Sinks into a chair.*]

JACK. I must retire to my room for a moment. Gwendolen, wait here for me.

10   GWENDOLEN. If you are not too long, I will wait here for you all my life.

[*Exit* JACK *in great excitement.*]

CHASUBLE. What do you think this means, Lady Bracknell?

15   LADY BRACKNELL. I dare not even suspect, Dr. Chasuble. I need hardly tell you that in families of high position strange coincidences are not supposed to occur. They are hardly considered the thing.

20   [*Noises heard overhead as if someone was throwing trunks about. Everyone looks up.*]

CECILY. Uncle Jack seems strangely agitated.

CHASUBLE. Your guardian has a very emotional nature.

25   LADY BRACKNELL. This noise is extremely unpleasant. It sounds as if he was having an argument. I dislike arguments of any kind. They are always vulgar, and often convincing.

CHASUBLE [*Looking up*]. It has stopped now.

30   [*The noise is redoubled.*]

LADY BRACKNELL. I wish he would arrive at some conclusion.

GWENDOLEN. This suspense is terrible. I hope it will last.

35   [*Enter* JACK *with a hand-bag of black leather in his hand.*]

JACK [*Rushing over to* MISS PRISM]. Is this the hand-bag, Miss Prism? Examine it carefully before you speak. The happiness of more

40   than one life depends on your answer.

MISS PRISM [*Calmly*]. It seems to be mine. Yes, here is the injury it received through the upsetting of a Gower Street omnibus in younger and happier days. Here is the stain

45   on the lining caused by the explosion of a temperance beverage, an incident that occurred at Leamington. And here, on the lock, are my initials. I had forgotten that in an ex-

travagant mood I had had them placed there. The bag is undoubtedly mine. I am delighted 50 to have it so unexpectedly restored to me. It has been a great inconvenience being without it all these years.

JACK [*In a pathetic voice*]. Miss Prism, more is restored to you than this hand-bag. I was 55 the baby you placed in it.

MISS PRISM [*Amazed*]. You?

JACK [*Embracing her*]. Yes . . . mother!

MISS PRISM [*Recoiling in indignant astonishment*]. Mr. Worthing! I am unmarried! 60

JACK. Unmarried! I do not deny that is a serious blow. But after all, who has the right to cast a stone against one who has suffered? Cannot repentance wipe out an act of folly? Why should there be one law for men, and 65 another for women? Mother, I forgive you. [*Tries to embrace her again.*]

MISS PRISM [*Still more indignant*]. Mr. Worthing, there is some error. [*Pointing to* LADY BRACKNELL.] There is the lady who can tell 70 you who you really are.

JACK [*After a pause*]. Lady Bracknell, I hate to seem inquisitive, but would you kindly inform me who I am?

LADY BRACKNELL. I am afraid that the news 75 I have to give you will not altogether please you. You are the son of my poor sister, Mrs. Moncrieff, and consequently Algernon's elder brother.

JACK. Algy's elder brother? Then I have a 80 brother after all. I knew I had a brother! I always said I had a brother! Cecily,—how could you have ever doubted that I had a brother. [*Seizes hold of* ALGERNON.] Dr. Chasuble, my unfortunate brother. Miss Prism, 85 my unfortunate brother. Gwendolen, my unfortunate brother. Algy, you young scoundrel, you will have to treat me with more respect in the future. You have never behaved to me like a brother in all your life. 90

ALGERNON. Well, not till to-day, old boy, I admit. I did my best, however, though I was out of practice. [*Shakes hands.*]

GWENDOLEN [*To* JACK]. My own! But what own are you? What is your Christian name, 95 now that you have become someone else?

JACK. Good heavens! . . . I had quite forgotten that point. Your decision on the subject of my name is irrevocable, I suppose?

GWENDOLEN. I never change, except in my affections.

CECILY. What a noble nature you have, Gwendolen!

JACK. Then the question had better be cleared up at once. Aunt Augusta, a moment. At the time when Miss Prism left me in the hand-bag, had I been christened already?

LADY BRACKNELL. Every luxury that money could buy, including christening, had been lavished on you by your fond and doting parents.

JACK. Then I was christened! That is settled. Now, what name was I given? Let me know the worst.

LADY BRACKNELL. Being the eldest son you were naturally christened after your father.

JACK [*Irritably*]. Yes, but what was my father's Christian name?

LADY BRACKNELL [*Meditatively*]. I cannot at the present moment recall what the General's Christian name was. But I have no doubt he had one. He was eccentric, I admit. But only in later years. And that was the result of the Indian climate, and marriage, and indigestion, and other things of that kind.

JACK. Algy! Can't you recollect what our father's Christian name was?

ALGERNON. My dear boy, we were never even on speaking terms. He died before I was a year old.

JACK. His name would appear in the Army Lists of the period, I suppose, Aunt Augusta?

LADY BRACKNELL. The General was essentially a man of peace, except in his domestic life. But I have no doubt his name would appear in any military directory.

JACK. The Army Lists of the last forty years are here. These delightful records should have been my constant study [*Rushes to bookcase and tears the books out*]. M. Generals . . . Mallam, Maxbohm, Magley, what ghastly names they have—Markby, Migsby, Moss, Moncrieff! Lieutenant 1840, Captain, Lieutenant-Colonel, Colonel, General 1869, Christian names, Er-nest John [*Puts book very quietly down and speaks quite calmly*]. I always told you, Gwendolen, my name was Ernest, didn't I? Well, it is Ernest after all. I mean it naturally is Ernest.

LADY BRACKNELL. Yes, I remember that the General was called Ernest. I knew I had some particular reason for disliking the name.

GWENDOLEN. Ernest! My own Ernest! I felt from the first that you could have no other name!

JACK. Gwendolen, it is a terrible thing for a man to find out suddenly that all his life he has been speaking nothing but the truth. Can you forgive me?

GWENDOLEN. I can. For I feel that you are sure to change.

JACK. My own one!

CHASUBLE [*To* MISS PRISM]. Lætitia! [*Embraces her.*]

MISS PRISM [*Enthusiastically*]. Frederick! At last!

ALGERNON. Cecily! [*Embraces her*]. At last!

JACK. Gwendolen! [*Embraces her*]. At last!

LADY BRACKNELL. My nephew, you seem to be displaying signs of triviality.

JACK. On the contrary, Aunt Augusta, I've now realized for the first time in my life the vital Importance of Being Earnest.

TABLEAU°

Curtain

tableau all "freeze" into rigid postures, an old theatrical device in farce

Anton Chekhov

1860–1904

The Cherry Orchard

1904

There are ranges of significance in almost every detail of *The Cherry Orchard,* which give the playgoer a sense, sometimes rather mysterious, that a great many meaningful things are going on all the while and make the play delightful to read and reread closely. In Lyubov's first-act entrance, for example, we at once take in a number of significant impresssions, which, when dwelt on, we find to comprise all the major components of the play. In this scene Lyubov is preceded by the hobbling figure of the old house-servant Firs and followed by a chaotic assembly of family, friends, and servants. "Joyfully through her tears," she greets the room as her one-time nursery. "And here I am," she adds, "like a little child." But the other characters interrupt at once, one with an idle complaint about the train's not running on time, and another with a comment on the appetite of her pet dog. We perceive immediately that Lyubov's entrance is anticipated by a discordant happening and is shortly swallowed up in confusion. And if we dwell on the source of these impressions—Firs crossing the stage, Lyubov's reaction to the nursery, the idle interruptions—we see also a fuller metaphoric meaning: the order of things to which she would return is moribund now, although her feeling for it remains; and misrule or the absence of any intelligible rule has succeeded it.

In making every detail tell in this way, Chekhov inevitably states his major ideas over and over again. Their recurrence is not obtrusive, because they receive a different coloration every time they appear: as they are embodied in particular speeches they take on both the emotions and attitudes of the speaker and ours toward him. But they do recognizably recur, and we find them interacting with one another from the beginning of the play to the end. In other words, they are formal elements. Chekhov has used ideas somewhat as a composer uses melodic phrases. His play is a quasi-musical interweaving of memories of a past order of things with the fact of present chaos.

The cherry orchard itself, a relic of the past order, is the most significant embodiment of idea in the work, and a simple catalogue of references to the orchard illustrates Chekhov's manner of developing and varying his themes. The first stage direction mentions the orchard: "The cherry trees are in flower." In Act I Lopahin says, "The cherry orchard must be cut down." And later in the act Lyubov exclaims, "Oh, my childhood, my innocence! . . . Oh, my orchard! . . . you are young again and full of happiness." Trofimov says in Act II that "Your orchard is a fearful thing . . . dreaming of centuries gone by and tortured by fearful visions. . . . We must first expiate our past." When Lopahin gains the estate in Act III he shouts, "Come, all of you, and look how Yermolay Lopahin will take his axe to the cherry orchard!" In Act IV Lyubov again addresses the orchard: "Oh, my orchard, my sweet beautiful orchard! my life, my youth, my happiness, good-bye!" And the last stage direction reads: "All is still again, and there is nothing heard but the strokes of the axe far away in the orchard." For the successful orchestration of such fine details of characterization and sequences of apparently quite casual activity, Chekhov called on the resources of the newly organized Moscow Art Theatre, which was bringing ensemble acting to an unprecedented perfection.

Such is the form of *The Cherry Orchard* and such, in part, its meaning. It perhaps should be added that any discussion of the play, including this one, tends to take its tone too largely from the play's general import, which is sad and dark. Chekhov understands very well the over-all haplessness of the scene upon which he looks. But seeing the people in this scene clearly and steadily, he finds them in equal parts pitiful and absurd, and presents them with humor and compassion in delicate balance—so that the subtitle, *A Comedy in Four Acts,* is apt.

The Cherry Orchard

A Comedy in Four Acts

CHEKHOV

Translated by Constance Garnett

CHARACTERS°

MADAME RANEVSKY (LYUBOV ANDREYEVNA)
  the owner of the Cherry Orchard
ANYA *her daughter, aged 17*
VARYA *her adopted daughter, aged 24*
GAEV (LEONID ANDREYEVITCH) *brother of Madame Ranevsky*
LOPAHIN (YERMOLAY ALEXEYEVITCH)
  a merchant
TROFIMOV (PYOTR SERGEYEVITCH) *a student*
SEMYONOV-PISHTCHIK *a landowner*
CHARLOTTA IVANOVNA *a governess*
EPIHODOV (SEMYON PANTALEYEVITCH) *a clerk*
DUNYASHA *a maid*
FIRS *an old valet, aged 87*
YASHA *a young valet*
A VAGRANT
THE STATION MASTER

Characters: Russians have three names: a given name (Lyubov), a patronymic (Andreyevna = daughter of Andrey), and a surname (Ranevsky). In the Russia of Chekhov's day, decorum prescribed title and surname (Madame Ranevsky) for formal relationships; given name and patronymic (Lyubov Andreyevna) for relationships somewhat less formal; given name alone for familiarity; and a diminutive of the given name (Lyuba for Lyubov) to indicate affection or condescension.

A POST-OFFICE CLERK
VISITORS, SERVANTS

SCENE. *The estate of* MADAME RANEVSKY.

ACT I

[*A room, which has always been called the nursery. One of the doors leads into* ANYA'*s room. Dawn, sun rises during the scene. May, the cherry trees in flower, but it is cold in the garden° with the frost of early morning. Windows closed.*

Enter DUNYASHA *with a candle and* LOPAHIN *with a book in his hand.*]

LOPAHIN. The train's in, thank God. What time is it?

DUNYASHA. Nearly two o'clock. [*Puts out the candle.*] It's daylight already.

LOPAHIN. The train's late! Two hours, at least. [*Yawns and stretches.*] I'm a pretty one; what a fool I've been. Came here on purpose to meet them at the station and dropped asleep. . . . Dozed off as I sat in the chair. It's annoying. . . . You might have waked me.

DUNYASHA. I thought you had gone. [*Listens.*] There, I do believe they're coming!

LOPAHIN [*listens*]. No, what with the luggage and one thing and another. [*A pause.*] Lyubov Andreyevna has been abroad five years; I don't know what she is like now. . . . She's a splendid woman. A good-natured, kind-hearted woman. I remember when I was a lad of fifteen, my poor father—he used to keep a little shop here in the village in those days—gave me a punch in the face with his fist and made my nose bleed. We were in the yard here, I forget what we'd come about—he had had a drop. Lyubov Andreyevna—I can see her now—she was a slim young girl then—took me to wash my face, and then brought me into this very room, into the nursery. "Don't cry, little peasant," says she, "it will be well in time for your wedding day." . . . [*A pause.*] Little peasant. . . . My father was a peasant, it's true, but

here am I in a white waistcoat and brown shoes, like a pig in a bun shop. Yes, I'm a rich man, but for all my money, come to think, a peasant I was, and a peasant I am. [*Turns over the pages of the book.*] I've been reading this book and I can't make head or tail of it. I fell asleep over it. [*A pause.*]

DUNYASHA. The dogs have been awake all night, they feel that the mistress is coming.

LOPAHIN. Why, what's the matter with you, Dunyasha?

DUNYASHA. My hands are all of a tremble. I feel as though I should faint.

LOPAHIN. You're a spoilt soft creature, Dunyasha. And dressed like a lady too, and your hair done up. That's not the thing. One must know one's place.

[*Enter* EPIHODOV *with a nosegay; he wears a pea-jacket and highly polished creaking top-boots; he drops the nosegay as he comes in.*]

EPIHODOV [*picking up the nosegay.*] Here! the gardener's sent this, says you're to put it in the dining-room. [*Gives* DUNYASHA *the nosegay.*]

LOPAHIN. And bring me some kvass.

DUNYASHA. I will.

[*Goes out.*]

EPIHODOV. It's chilly this morning, three degrees of frost, though the cherries are all in flower. I can't say much for our climate [*sighs*]. I can't. Our climate is not often propitious to the occasion. Yermolay Alexeyevitch, permit me to call your attention to the fact that I purchased myself a pair of boots the day before yesterday, and they creak, I venture to assure you, so that there's no tolerating them. What ought I to grease them with?

LOPAHIN. Oh, shut up! Don't bother me.

EPIHODOV. Every day some misfortune befalls me. I don't complain, I'm used to it, and I wear a smiling face.

[DUNYASHA *comes in, hands* LOPAHIN *the kvass.*]

EPIHODOV. I am going. [*Stumbles against a chair, which falls over.*] There! [*As though triumphant.*] There you see now, excuse the expression, an accident like that among others . . . It's positively remarkable.

---

garden orchard. The Russian word *sad*, which appears here and in the title, means both garden and orchard.

[*Goes out.*]

DUNYASHA. Do you know, Yermolay Alexeyevitch, I must confess, Epihodov has made me a proposal.

5   LOPAHIN. Ah!

DUNYASHA. I'm sure I don't know. . . . He's a harmless fellow, but sometimes when he begins talking, there's no making anything of it. It's all very fine and expressive, only there's

10 no understanding it. I've a sort of liking for him too. He loves me to distraction. He's an unfortunate man; every day there's something. They tease him about it—two and twenty misfortunes they call him.

15 LOPAHIN [*listening*]. There! I do believe they're coming.

DUNYASHA. They are coming! What's the matter with me? . . . I'm cold all over.

LOPAHIN. They really are coming. Let's go

20 and meet them. Will she know me? It's five years since I saw her.

DUNYASHA [*in a flutter*]. I shall drop this very minute. . . . Ah, I shall drop.

[*There is a sound of two carriages driving

25 up to the house. LOPAHIN and DUNYASHA go out quickly. The stage is left empty. A noise is heard in the adjoining rooms. FIRS, who has driven to meet MADAME RANEVSKY, crosses the stage hurriedly leaning on a stick. He is wear-

30 ing old-fashioned livery and a high hat. He says something to himself, but not a word can be distinguished. The noise behind the scene goes on increasing. A voice: "Come, let's go in here." Enter LYUBOV ANDREYEVNA, ANYA, and

35 CHARLOTTA IVANOVNA with a pet dog on a chain, all in travelling dresses. VARYA in an out-door coat with a kerchief over her head, GAEV, SEMYONOV-PISHTCHIK, LOPAHIN, DUNY-ASHA with bag and parasol, servants with other

40 articles. All walk across the room.*]

ANYA. Let's come in here. Do you remember what room this is, mamma?

LYUBOV [*joyfully, through her tears*]. The nursery!

45 VARYA. How cold it is, my hands are numb. [*To LYUBOV ANDREYEVNA.*] Your rooms, the white room and the lavender one, are just the same as ever, mamma.

LYUBOV. My nursery, dear delightful room. . . . I used to sleep here when I was little. . . .   50
[*Cries.*] And here I am, like a little child. . . . [*Kisses her brother and VARYA, and then her brother again.*] Varya's just the same as ever, like a nun. And I knew Dunyasha. [*Kisses DUNYASHA.*]   55

GAEV. The train was two hours late. What do you think of that? Is that the way to do things?

CHARLOTTA [*to PISHTCHIK*]. My dog eats nuts, too.   60

PISHTCHIK [*wonderingly*]. Fancy that!

[*They all go out except ANYA and DUNY-ASHA.*]

DUNYASHA. We've been expecting you so long. [*Takes ANYA's hat and coat.*]   65

ANYA. I haven't slept for four nights on the journey. I feel dreadfully cold.

DUNYASHA. You set out in Lent, there was snow and frost, and now? My darling! [*Laughs and kisses her.*] I *have* missed you, my   70
precious, my joy. I must tell you . . . I can't put it off a minute. . . .

ANYA [*wearily*]. What now?

DUNYASHA. Epihodov, the clerk, made me a proposal just after Easter.   75

ANYA. It's always the same thing with you. . . . [*Straightening her hair.*] I've lost all my hairpins. . . . [*She is staggering from exhaustion.*]

DUNYASHA. I don't know what to think,   80
really. He does love me, he does love me so!

ANYA [*looking towards her door, tenderly*]. My own room, my windows just as though I had never gone away. I'm home! Tomorrow morning I shall get up and run into the garden.   85
. . . Oh, if I could get to sleep! I haven't slept all the journey, I was so anxious and worried.

DUNYASHA. Pyotr Sergeyevitch came the day before yesterday.

ANYA [*joyfully*]. Petya!   90

DUNYASHA. He's asleep in the bath house, he has settled in there. I'm afraid of being in their way, says he. [*Glancing at her watch.*] I was to have waked him, but Varvara Mihalovna told me not to. Don't you wake him,   95
says she.

[*Enter* VARYA *with a bunch of keys at her waist.*]

VARYA. Dunyasha, coffee and make haste. . . . Mamma's asking for coffee.

5 DUNYASHA. This very minute.

[*Goes out.*]

VARYA. Well, thank God, you've come. You're home again. [*Petting her.*] My little darling has come back! My precious beauty

10 has come back again!

ANYA. I have had a time of it!

VARYA. I can fancy.

ANYA. We set off in Holy Week—it was so cold then, and all the way Charlotta would

15 talk and show off her tricks. What did you want to burden me with Charlotta for?

VARYA. You couldn't have travelled all alone, darling. At seventeen!

ANYA. We got to Paris at last, it was cold

20 there—snow. I speak French shockingly. Mamma lives on the fifth floor, I went up to her and there were a lot of French people, ladies, an old priest with a book. The place smelt of tobacco and so comfortless. I felt

25 sorry, oh! so sorry for mamma all at once, I put my arms round her neck, and hugged her and wouldn't let her go. Mamma was as kind as she could be, and she cried. . . .

VARYA [*through her tears*]. Don't speak of it,

30 don't speak of it!

ANYA. She had sold her villa at Mentone, she had nothing left, nothing. I hadn't a farthing left either, we only just had enough to get here. And mamma doesn't understand!

35 When we had dinner at the stations, she always ordered the most expensive things and gave the waiters a whole rouble. Charlotta's just the same. Yasha too must have the same as we do; it's simply awful. You know Yasha

40 is mamma's valet now, we brought him here with us.

VARYA. Yes, I've seen the young rascal.

ANYA. Well, tell me—have you paid the arrears on the mortgage?

45 VARYA. How could we get the money?

ANYA. Oh, dear! Oh, dear!

VARYA. In August the place will be sold.

ANYA. My goodness!

LOPAHIN [*peeps in at the door and moos like a cow*]. Moo! [*Disappears.*] 50

VARYA [*weeping*]. There, that's what I could do to him. [*Shakes her fist.*]

ANYA [*embracing* VARYA, *softly*]. Varya, has he made you an offer? [VARYA *shakes her head.*] Why, but he loves you. Why is it you 55 don't come to an understanding? What are you waiting for?

VARYA. I believe that there never will be anything between us. He has a lot to do, he has no time for me . . . and takes no notice of 60 me. Bless the man, it makes me miserable to see him. . . . Everyone's talking of our being married, everyone's congratulating me, and all the while there's really nothing in it; it's all like a dream! [*In another tone.*] You have 65 a new brooch like a bee.

ANYA [*mournfully*]. Mamma bought it. [*Goes into her own room and in a light-hearted childish tone:*] And you know, in Paris I went up in a balloon! 70

VARYA. My darling's home again! My pretty is home again!

[DUNYASHA *returns with the coffee-pot and is making the coffee.*]

VARYA [*standing at the door*]. All day long, 75 darling, as I go about looking after the house, I keep dreaming all the time. If only we could marry you to a rich man, then I should feel more at rest. Then I would go off by myself on a pilgrimage to Kiev, to Moscow . . . and 80 so I would spend my life going from one place to another. . . . I would go on and on. . . . What bliss!

ANYA. The birds are singing in the garden. What time is it? 85

VARYA. It must be nearly three. It's time you were asleep, darling. [*Going into* ANYA'S *room.*] What bliss!

[YASHA *enters with a rug and a travelling bag.*] 90

YASHA [*crosses the stage, mincingly*]. May one come in here, pray?

DUNYASHA. I shouldn't have known you, Yasha. How you have changed abroad.

YASHA. H'm! . . . And who are you? 95

DUNYASHA. When you went away, I was that

high. [*Shows distance from floor.*] Dunyasha, Fyodor's daughter. . . . You don't remember me!

YASHA. H'm! . . . You're a peach! [*Looks round and embraces her: she shrieks and drops a saucer. YASHA goes out hastily.*]

VARYA [*in the doorway, in a tone of vexation*]. What now?

DUNYASHA [*through her tears*]. I have broken a saucer.

VARYA. Well, that brings good luck.

ANYA [*coming out of her room*]. We ought to prepare mamma: Petya is here.

VARYA. I told them not to wake him.

ANYA [*dreamily*]. It's six years since father died. Then only a month later little brother Grisha was drowned in the river, such a pretty boy he was, only seven. It was more than mamma could bear, so she went away, went away without looking back. [*Shuddering.*] . . . How well I understand her, if only she knew! [*A pause.*] And Petya Trofimov was Grisha's tutor, he may remind her.

[*Enter FIRS: he is wearing a pea-jacket and a white waistcoat.*]

FIRS [*goes up to the coffee-pot, anxiously*]. The mistress will be served here. [*Puts on white gloves.*] Is the coffee ready? [*Sternly to DUNYASHA.*] Girl! Where's the cream?

DUNYASHA Ah, mercy on us!

[*Goes out quickly.*]

FIRS [*fussing round the coffee-pot*]. Ech! you good-for-nothing! [*Muttering to himself.*] Come back from Paris. And the old master used to go to Paris too . . . horses all the way. [*Laughs.*]

VARYA. What is it, Firs?

FIRS. What is your pleasure? [*Gleefully.*] My lady has come home! I have lived to see her again! Now I can die. [*Weeps with joy.*]

[*Enter LYUBOV ANDREYEVNA, GAEV, LOPAHIN, and SEMYONOV-PISHTCHIK; the latter is in a short-waisted full coat of fine cloth, and full trousers. GAEV, as he comes in, makes a gesture with his arms and his whole body, as though he were playing billiards.*]

LYUBOV. How does it go? Let me remember. Cannon off the red!

GAEV. That's it—in off the white! Why, once, sister, we used to sleep together in this very room, and now I'm fifty-one, strange as it seems.

LOPAHIN. Yes, time flies.

GAEV. What do you say?

LOPAHIN. Time, I say, flies.

GAEV. What a smell of patchouli!

ANYA. I'm going to bed. Good-night, mamma. [*Kisses her mother.*]

LYUBOV. My precious darling. [*Kisses her hands.*] Are you glad to be home? I can't believe it.

ANYA. Good-night, uncle.

GAEV [*kissing her face and hands*]. God bless you! How like you are to your mother! [*To his sister.*] At her age you were just the same, Lyuba.

[*ANYA shakes hands with LOPAHIN and PISHTCHIK, then goes out, shutting the door after her.*]

LYUBOV. She's quite worn out.

PISHTCHIK. Aye, it's a long journey, to be sure.

VARYA [*to LOPAHIN and PISHTCHIK*]. Well, gentlemen? It's three o'clock and time to say good-bye.

LYUBOV [*laughs*]. You're just the same as ever, Varya. [*Draws her to her and kisses her.*] I'll just drink my coffee and then we will all go and rest. [*FIRS puts a cushion under her feet.*] Thanks, friend. I am so fond of coffee, I drink it day and night. Thanks, dear old man. [*Kisses FIRS.*]

VARYA. I'll just see whether all the things have been brought in.

[*Goes out.*]

LYUBOV. Can it really be me sitting here? [*Laughs.*] I want to dance about and clap my hands. [*Covers her face with her hands.*] And I could drop asleep in a moment! God knows I love my country, I love it tenderly; I couldn't look out of the window in the train, I kept crying so. [*Through her tears.*] But I must drink my coffee, though. Thank you, Firs, thanks, dear old man. I'm so glad to find you still alive.

FIRS. The day before yesterday.

GAEV. He's rather deaf.

LOPAHIN. I have to set off for Harkov directly, at five o'clock. . . . It is annoying! I wanted to have a look at you, and a little talk. . . . You are just as splendid as ever.

PISHTCHIK [*breathing heavily*]. Handsomer, indeed. . . . Dressed in Parisian style . . . completely bowled me over.

LOPAHIN. Your brother, Leonid Andreyevitch here, is always saying that I'm a low-born knave, that I'm a money-grubber, but I don't care one straw for that. Let him talk. Only I do want you to believe in me as you used to. I do want your wonderful tender eyes to look at me as they used to in the old days. Merciful God! My father was a serf of your father and of your grandfather, but you—you—did so much for me once, that I've forgotten all that; I love you as though you were my kin . . . more than my kin.

LYUBOV. I can't sit still, I simply can't. . . . [*Jumps up and walks about in violent agitation.*] This happiness is too much for me. . . . You may laugh at me, I know I'm silly. . . . My own bookcase. [*Kisses the bookcase.*] My little table.

GAEV. Nurse died while you were away.

LYUBOV [*sits down and drinks coffee*]. Yes, the Kingdom of Heaven be hers! You wrote me of her death.

GAEV. And Anastasy is dead. Squinting Petruchka has left me and is in service now with the police captain in the town. [*Takes a box of caramels out of his pocket and sucks one.*]

PISHTCHIK. My daughter, Dashenka, wishes to be remembered to you.

LOPAHIN. I want to tell you something very pleasant and cheering. [*Glancing at his watch.*] I'm going directly . . . there's no time to say much . . . well, I can say it in a couple of words. I needn't tell you your cherry orchard is to be sold to pay your debts; the 22nd of August is the date fixed for the sale; but don't you worry, dearest lady, you may sleep in peace, there is a way of saving it. . . . This is what I propose. I beg your attention! Your estate is not twenty miles from the town, the railway runs close by it, and if the cherry orchard and the land along the river bank were cut up into building plots and then let on lease for summer villas, you would make an income of at least 25,000 roubles a year out of it.

GAEV. That's all rot, if you'll excuse me.

LYUBOV. I don't quite understand you, Yermolay Alexeyevitch.

LOPAHIN. You will get a rent of at least 25 roubles a year for a three-acre plot from summer visitors, and if you say the word now, I'll bet you what you like there won't be one square foot of ground vacant by the autumn, all the plots will be taken up. I congratulate you; in fact, you are saved. It's a perfect situation with that deep river. Only, of course, it must be cleared—all the old buildings, for example, must be removed, this house too, which is really good for nothing, and the old cherry orchard must be cut down.

LYUBOV. Cut down? My dear fellow, forgive me, but you don't know what you are talking about. If there is one thing interesting—remarkable indeed—in the whole province, it's our cherry orchard.

LOPAHIN. The only thing remarkable about the orchard is that it's a very large one. There's a crop of cherries every alternate year, and then there's nothing to be done with them, no one buys them.

GAEV. This orchard is mentioned in the "Encyclopaedia."

LOPAHIN [*glancing at his watch*]. If we don't decide on something and don't take some steps, on the 22nd of August the cherry orchard and the whole estate too will be sold by auction. Make up your minds! There is no other way of saving it, I'll take my oath on that. No, No!

FIRS. In the old days, forty or fifty years ago, they used to dry the cherries, soak them, pickle them, make jam too, and they used . . .

GAEV. Be quiet, Firs.

FIRS. And they used to send the preserved cherries to Moscow and to Harkov by the wagon-load. That brought the money in! And the preserved cherries in those days were soft and juicy, sweet and fragrant. . . . They knew the way to do them then. . . .

LYUBOV. And where is the recipe now?

FIRS. It's forgotten. Nobody remembers it.

PISHTCHIK [to LYUBOV ANDREYEVNA]. What's it like in Paris? Did you eat frogs there?

5 LYUBOV. Oh, I ate crocodiles.

PISHTCHIK. Fancy that now!

LOPAHIN. There used to be only the gentlefolks and the peasants in the country, but now there are these summer visitors. All the towns, 10 even the small ones, are surrounded nowadays by these summer villas. And one may say for sure, that in another twenty years there'll be many more of these people and that they'll be everywhere. At present the summer visitor 15 only drinks tea in his verandah, but maybe he'll take to working his bit of land too, and then your cherry orchard would become happy, rich and prosperous. . . .

GAEV [indignant]. What rot!

20 [Enter VARYA and YASHA.]

VARYA. There are two telegrams for you, mamma. [Takes out keys and opens an old-fashioned bookcase with a loud crack.] Here they are.

25 LYUBOV. From Paris. [Tears the telegrams, without reading them.] I have done with Paris.

GAEV. Do you know, Lyuba, how old that bookcase is? Last week I pulled out the bottom 30 drawer and there I found the date branded on it. The bookcase was made just a hundred years ago. What do you say to that? We might have celebrated its jubilee. Though it's an inanimate object, still it is a book case.

35 PISHTCHIK [amazed]. A hundred years! Fancy that now.

GAEV. Yes. . . . It is a thing . . . [feeling the bookcase]. Dear, honored bookcase! Hail to thee who for more than a hundred years hast 40 served the pure ideals of good and justice; thy silent call to fruitful labor has never flagged in those hundred years, maintaining [in tears] in the generations of man, courage and faith in a brighter future and fostering in us ideals of 45 good and social consciousness [a pause].

LOPAHIN. Yes. . . .

LYUBOV. You are just the same as ever, Leonid.

GAEV [a little embarrassed]. Cannon off the right into the pocket! 50

LOPAHIN [looking at his watch]. Well, it's time I was off.

YASHA [handing LYUBOV ANDREYEVNA medicine]. Perhaps you will take your pills now.

PISHTCHIK. You shouldn't take medicines, my 55 dear madam . . . they do no harm and no good. Give them here . . . honored lady. [Takes the pill-box, pours the pills into the hollow of his hand, blows on them, puts them in his mouth and drinks off some kvass.] There! 60

LYUBOV [in alarm]. Why, you must be out of your mind!

PISHTCHIK. I have taken all the pills.

LOPAHIN. What a glutton! [All laugh.]

FIRS. His honor stayed with us in Easter 65 week, ate a gallon and a half of cucumbers . . . [mutters].

LYUBOV. What is he saying?

VARYA. He has taken to muttering like that for the last three years. We are used to it. 70

YASHA. His declining years!

[CHARLOTTA IVANOVNA, a very thin, lanky figure in a white dress with a lorgnette in her belt, walks across the stage.]

LOPAHIN. I beg your pardon, Charlotta Ivan- 75 ovna, I have not had time to greet you. [Tries to kiss her hand.]

CHARLOTTA [pulling away her hand]. If I let you kiss my hand, you'll be wanting to kiss my elbow, and then my shoulder. 80

LOPAHIN. I've no luck today! [All laugh.] Charlotta Ivanovna, show us some tricks!

LYUBOV. Charlotta, do show us some tricks!

CHARLOTTA. I don't want to. I'm sleepy. [Goes out.] 85

LOPAHIN. In three weeks' time we shall meet again. [Kisses LYUBOV ANDREYEVNA's hand.] Good-bye till then—I must go. [To GAEV.] Good-bye. [Kisses PISHTCHIK.] Good-bye. [Gives his hand to VARYA, then to FIRS and 90 YASHA.] I don't want to go. [To LYUBOV ANDRE-YEVNA.] If you think over my plan for the villas and make up your mind, then let me know; I will lend you 50,000 roubles. Think of it seriously. 95

VARYA [angrily]. Well, do go, for goodness' sake.

LOPAHIN. I'm going, I'm going.

[*Goes out.*]

GAEV. Low-born knave! I beg pardon, though . . . Varya is going to marry him, he's Varya's fiancé.

VARYA. Don't talk nonsense, uncle.

LYUBOV. Well, Varya, I shall be delighted. He's a good man.

PISHTCHIK. He is, one must acknowledge, a most worthy man. And my Dashenka . . . says too that . . . she says . . . various things. [*Snores, but at once wakes up.*] But all the same, honored lady, could you oblige me . . . with a loan of 240 roubles . . . to pay the interest on my mortgage tomorrow?

VARYA [*dismayed*]. No, no.

LYUBOV. I really haven't any money.

PISHTCHIK. It will turn up. [*Laughs.*] I never lose hope. I thought everything was over, I was a ruined man, and lo and behold—the railway passed through my land and . . . they paid me for it. And something else will turn up again, if not today, then tomorrow . . . Dashenka'll win two hundred thousand . . . she's got a lottery ticket.

LYUBOV. Well, we've finished our coffee, we can go to bed.

FIRS [*brushes GAEV, reprovingly*]. You have got on the wrong trousers again! What am I to do with you?

VARYA [*softly*]. Anya's asleep. [*Softly opens the window.*] Now the sun's risen, it's not a bit cold. Look, mamma, what exquisite trees! My goodness! And the air! The starlings are singing!

GAEV [*opens another window*]. The orchard is all white. You've not forgotten it, Lyuba? That long avenue that runs straight, straight as an arrow, how it shines on a moonlight night. You remember? You've not forgotten?

LYUBOV [*looking out of the window into the garden*]. Oh, my childhood, my innocence! It was in this nursery I used to sleep, from here I looked out into the orchard, happiness waked with me every morning and in those days the orchard was just the same, nothing has changed. [*Laughs with delight.*] All, all white! Oh, my orchard! After the dark gloomy autumn, and the cold winter; you are young again, and full of happiness, the heavenly angels have never left you. . . . If I could cast off the burden that weighs on my heart, if I could forget the past!

GAEV. H'm! and the orchard will be sold to pay our debts; it seems strange. . . .

LYUBOV. See, our mother walking . . . all in white, down the avenue! [*Laughs with delight.*] It is she!

GAEV. Where?

VARYA. Oh, don't, mamma!

LYUBOV. There is no one. It was my fancy. On the right there, by the path to the arbor, there is a white tree bending like a woman. . . .

[*Enter TROFIMOV wearing a shabby student's uniform and spectacles.*]

LYUBOV. What a ravishing orchard! White masses of blossoms, blue sky. . . .

TROFIMOV. Lyubov Andreyevna! [*She looks round at him.*] I will just pay my respects to you and then leave you at once. [*Kisses her hand warmly.*] I was told to wait until morning, but I hadn't the patience to wait any longer. . . .

[*LYUBOV ANDREYEVNA looks at him in perplexity.*]

VARYA [*through her tears*]. This is Petya Trofimov.

TROFIMOV. Petya Trofimov, who was your Grisha's tutor. . . . Can I have changed so much?

[*LYUBOV ANDREYEVNA embraces him and weeps quietly.*]

GAEV [*in confusion*]. There, there, Lyuba.

VARYA [*crying*]. I told you, Petya, to wait till tomorrow.

LYUBOV. My Grisha . . . my boy . . . Grisha . . . my son!

VARYA. We can't help it, mamma, it is God's will.

TROFIMOV [*softly through his tears*]. There . . . there.

LYUBOV [*weeping quietly*]. My boy was lost . . . drowned. Why? Oh, why, dear Petya? [*More quietly.*] Anya is asleep in there, and I'm talking loudly . . . making this noise. . . . But, Petya? Why have you grown so ugly? Why do you look so old?

TROFIMOV. A peasant-woman in the train called me a mangy-looking gentleman.

Lyubov. You were quite a boy then, a pretty little student, and now your hair's thin—and spectacles. Are you really a student still?

[*Goes towards the door.*]

5 Trofimov. I seem likely to be a perpetual student.

Lyubov [*kisses her brother, then* Varya]. Well, go to bed. . . . You are older too, Leonid.

Pishtchik [*follows her*]. I suppose it's time 10 we were asleep. . . . Ugh! my gout. I'm staying the night! Lyubov Andreyevna, my dear soul, if you could . . . tomorrow morning . . . 240 roubles.

Gaev. That's always his story.

15 Pishtchik. 240 roubles . . . to pay the interest on my mortgage.

Lyubov. My dear man, I have no money.

Pishtchik. I'll pay it back, my dear . . . a trifling sum.

20 Lyubov. Oh, well, Leonid will give it you . . . You give him the money, Leonid.

Gaev. Me give it him! Let him wait till he gets it!

Lyubov. It can't be helped, give it him. He 25 needs it. He'll pay it back.

[Lyubov Andreyevna, Trofimov, Pishtchik, *and* Firs *go out.* Gaev, Varya, *and* Yasha *remain.*]

Gaev. Sister hasn't got out of the habit of 30 flinging away her money. [*To* Yasha.] Get away, my good fellow, you smell of the hen-house.

Yasha [*with a grin*]. And you, Leonid Andreyevitch, are just the same as ever.

35 Gaev. What's that? [*To* Varya.] What did he say?

Varya [*to* Yasha]. Your mother has come from the village; she has been sitting in the servants' room since yesterday, waiting to see 40 you.

Yasha. Oh, bother her!

Varya. For shame!

Yasha. What's the hurry? She might just as well have come tomorrow.

45 [*Goes out.*]

Varya. Mamma's just the same as ever, she hasn't changed a bit. If she had her own way, she'd give away everything.

Gaev. Yes. [*A pause.*] If a great many reme-

dies are suggested for some disease, it means 50 that the disease is incurable. I keep thinking and racking my brains; I have many schemes, a great many, and that really means none. If we could only come in for a legacy from somebody, or marry our Anya to a very rich man, 55 or we might go to Yaroslavl and try our luck with our old aunt, the Countess. She's very, very rich, you know.

Varya [*weeps*]. If God would help us.

Gaev. Don't blubber. Aunt's very rich, but 60 she doesn't like us. First, sister married a lawyer instead of a nobleman. . . .

[Anya *appears in the doorway.*]

Gaev. And then her conduct, one can't call it virtuous. She is good, and kind, and nice, 65 and I love her, but, however one allows for extenuating circumstances, there's no denying that she's an immoral woman. One feels it in her slightest gesture.

Varya [*in a whisper*]. Anya's in the door- 70 way.

Gaev. What do you say? [*A pause.*] It's queer, there seems to be something wrong with my right eye. I don't see as well as I did. And on Thursday when I was in the district 75 Court . . .

[*Enter* Anya.]

Varya. Why aren't you asleep, Anya?

Anya. I can't get to sleep.

Gaev. My pet. [*Kisses* Anya's *face and* 80 *hands.*] My child. [*Weeps.*] You are not my niece, you are my angel, you are everything to me. Believe me, believe . . .

Anya. I believe you, uncle. Everyone loves you and respects you . . . but, uncle dear, you 85 must be silent . . . simply be silent. What were you saying just now about my mother, about your own sister? What made you say that?

Gaev. Yes, yes . . . [*puts his hand over his* *face*]. Really, that was awful! My God, save 90 me! And today I made a speech to the bookcase . . . so stupid! And only when I had finished, I saw how stupid it was.

Varya. It's true, uncle, you ought to keep quiet. Don't talk, that's all. 95

Anya. If you could keep from talking, it would make things easier for you, too.

Gaev. I won't speak. [*Kisses* Anya's *and*

VARYA's *hands.*] I'll be silent. Only this is about business. On Thursday I was in the district Court; well, there was a large party of us there and we began talking of one thing and another, and this and that, and do you know, I believe that it will be possible to raise a loan on an I.O.U. to pay the arrears on the mortgage.

VARYA. If the Lord would help us!

GAEV. I'm going on Tuesday; I'll talk of it again. [*To* VARYA.] Don't blubber. [*To* ANYA.] Your mamma will talk to Lopahin; of course, he won't refuse her. And as soon as you're rested you shall go to Yaroslavl to the Countess, your great-aunt. So we shall all set to work in three directions at once, and the business is done. We shall pay off arrears, I'm convinced of it. [*Puts a caramel in his mouth.*] I swear on my honor, I swear by anything you like, the estate shan't be sold. [*Excitedly.*] By my own happiness, I swear it! Here's my hand on it, call me the basest, vilest of men, if I let it come to an auction! Upon my soul I swear it!

ANYA [*her equanimity has returned, she is quite happy*]. How good you are, uncle, and how clever! [*Embraces her uncle.*] I'm at peace now! Quite at peace! I'm happy!

[*Enter* FIRS.]

FIRS [*reproachfully*]. Leonid Andreyevitch, have you no fear of God? When are you going to bed?

GAEV. Directly, directly. You can go, Firs. I'll . . . yes, I will undress myself. Come, children, bye-bye. We'll go into details tomorrow, but now go to bed. [*Kisses* ANYA *and* VARYA.] I'm a man of the 'eighties.° They run down that period, but still I can say I have had to suffer not a little for my convictions in my life. It's not for nothing that the peasant loves me. One must know the peasant! One must know how . . .

ANYA. At it again, uncle!

'eighties a period of political reaction in Russia. The 'sixties saw major political and social reforms; the 'seventies (l.65, p. 527) saw those reforms undermined; the 'eighties saw a return to repressive oligarchy. Gaev thinks of his reactionary leanings as devotion to old-fashioned ideals.

VARYA. Uncle dear, you'd better be quiet!

FIRS [*angrily*]. Leonid Andreyevitch!

GAEV. I'm coming. I'm coming. Go to bed. Potted the shot—there's a shot for you! A beauty!

[*Goes out,* FIRS *hobbling after him.*]

ANYA. My mind's at rest now. I don't want to go to Yaroslavl, I don't like my great-aunt, but still my mind's at rest. Thanks to uncle. [*Sits down.*]

VARYA. We must go to bed. I'm going. Something unpleasant happened while you were away. In the old servants' quarters there are only the old servants, as you know—Efimyushka, Polya and Yevstigney—and Karp too. They began letting stray people in to spend the night—I said nothing. But all at once I heard they had been spreading a report that I gave them nothing but pease pudding to eat. Out of stinginess, you know. . . . And it was all Yevstigney's doing. . . . Very well, I said to myself. . . . If that's how it is, I thought, wait a bit. I sent for Yevstigney. . . . [*Yawns.*] He comes. . . . "How's this, Yevstigney," I said, "you could be such a fool as to? . . ." [*Looking at* ANYA.] Anitchka! [*A pause.*] She's asleep. [*Puts her arm round* ANYA.] Come to bed . . . come along! [*Leads her.*] My darling has fallen asleep! Come . . .

[*They go.*]

[*Far away beyond the orchard a shepherd plays on a pipe.* TROFIMOV *crosses the stage and, seeing* VARYA *and* ANYA, *stands still.*]

VARYA. Sh! asleep, asleep. Come, my own.

ANYA [*softly, half asleep*]. I'm so tired. Still those bells. Uncle . . . dear . . . mamma and uncle. . . .

VARYA. Come, my own, come along.

[*They go into* ANYA's *room.*]

TROFIMOV [*tenderly*]. My sunshine! My spring.

The Curtain Falls

ACT II

[*The open country. An old shrine, long abandoned and fallen out of the perpendicular; near it a well, large stones that have apparently once been tombstones, and an old garden seat.*

The road to GAEV's *house is seen. On one side rise dark poplars; and there the cherry orchard begins. In the distance a row of telegraph poles and far, far away on the horizon there is*
5 *faintly outlined a great town, only visible in very fine clear weather. It is near sunset.* CHARLOTTA, YASHA *and* DUNYASHA *are sitting on the seat.* EPIHODOV *is standing near, playing something mournful on a guitar. All sit*
10 *plunged in thought.* CHARLOTTA *wears an old forage cap; she has taken a gun from her shoulder and is tightening the buckle on the strap.*]

CHARLOTTA [*musingly*]. I haven't a real pass-
15 port of my own, and I don't know how old I am, and I always feel that I'm a young thing. When I was a little girl, my father and mother used to travel about to fairs and give performances—very good ones. And I used to dance
20 *salto-mortale*° and all sorts of things. And when papa and mamma died, a German lady took me and had me educated. And so I grew up and became a governess. But where I came from, and who I am, I don't know. . . . Who
25 my parents were, very likely they weren't married . . . I don't know. [*Takes a cucumber out of her pocket and eats.*] I know nothing at all. [*A pause.*] One wants to talk and has no one to talk to . . . I have nobody.
30 EPIHODOV [*plays on the guitar and sings*]. "What care I for the noisy world! What care I for friends or foes!" How agreeable it is to play on the mandolin!

DUNYASHA. That's a guitar, not a mandolin.
35 [*Looks in a hand-mirror and powders herself.*]

EPIHODOV. To a man mad with love, it's a mandolin. [*Sings.*] "Were her heart but aglow with love's mutual flame." [YASHA *joins in.*]

CHARLOTTA. How shockingly these people
40 sing! Foo! Like jackals!

DUNYASHA [*to* YASHA]. What happiness, though, to visit foreign lands.

YASHA. Ah, yes! I rather agree with you there. [*Yawns, then lights a cigar.*]
45 EPIHODOV. That's comprehensible. In foreign lands everything has long since reached full

complexion.

YASHA. That's so, of course.

EPIHODOV. I'm a cultivated man, I read re-
markable books of all sorts, but I can never 50 make out the tendency I am myself precisely inclined for, whether to live or to shoot myself, speaking precisely, but nevertheless I always carry a revolver. Here it is . . . [*shows revolver*]. 55

CHARLOTTA. I've had enough, and now I'm going. [*Puts on the gun.*] Epihodov, you're a very clever fellow, and a very terrible one too, all the women must be wild about you. Br-r-r! [*Goes.*] These clever fellows are all so stupid; 60 there's not a creature for me to speak to. . . . Always alone, alone, nobody belonging to me . . . and who I am, and why I'm on earth, I don't know.

[*Walks away slowly.*] 65

EPIHODOV. Speaking precisely, not touching upon other subjects, I'm bound to admit about myself, that destiny behaves mercilessly to me, as a storm to a little boat. If, let us suppose, I am mistaken, then why did I wake up this 70 morning, to quote an example, and look round, and there on my chest was a spider of fearful magnitude . . . like this. [*Shows with both hands.*] And then I take up a jug of kvass, to quench my thirst, and in it there is something 75 in the highest degree unseemly of the nature of a cockroach. [*A pause.*] Have you read Buckle?° [*A pause.*] I am desirous of troubling you, Dunyasha, with a couple of words.

DUNYASHA. Well, speak. 80

EPIHODOV. I should be desirous to speak with you alone. [*Sighs.*]

DUNYASHA [*embarrassed*]. Well—only bring me my mantle first. It's by the cupboard. It's rather damp here. 85

EPIHODOV. Certainly. I will fetch it. Now I know what I must do with my revolver.

[*Takes guitar and goes off playing on it.*]

YASHA. Two and twenty misfortunes! Between ourselves, he's a fool. [*Yawns.*] 90

DUNYASHA. God grant he doesn't shoot himself! [*A pause.*] I am so nervous, I'm always in

---

salto-mortale the "leap of death," a standing somer-
sault in which only the feet touch the ground

Buckle nineteenth-century English historian, highly
regarded in Russia as an advanced thinker

a flutter. I was a little girl when I was taken into our lady's house, and now I have quite grown out of peasant ways, and my hands are white, as white as a lady's. I'm such a delicate, sensitive creature, I'm afraid of everything. I'm so frightened. And if you deceive me, Yasha, I don't know what will become of my nerves.

YASHA [*kisses her*]. You're a peach! Of course a girl must never forget herself; what I dislike more than anything is a girl being flighty in her behavior.

DUNYASHA. I'm passionately in love with you, Yasha; you are a man of culture—you can give your opinion about anything. [*A pause.*]

YASHA [*yawns*]. Yes, that's so. My opinion is this: if a girl loves anyone, that means that she has no principles. [*A pause.*] It's pleasant smoking a cigar in the open air. [*Listens.*] Someone's coming this way . . . it's the gentle-folk. [DUNYASHA *embraces him impulsively.*] Go home, as though you had been to the river to bathe; go by that path, or else they'll meet you and suppose I have made an appointment with you here. That I can't endure.

DUNYASHA [*coughing softly*]. The cigar has made my head ache. . . .

[*Goes off.*]

[YASHA *remains sitting near the shrine. Enter* LYUBOV ANDREYEVNA, GAEV, *and* LOPAHIN.]

LOPAHIN. You must make up your mind once for all—there's no time to lose. It's quite a simple question, you know. Will you consent to letting the land for building or not? One word in answer: Yes or no? Only one word!

LYUBOV. Who is smoking such horrible cigars here? [*Sits down.*]

GAEV. Now the railway line has been brought near, it's made things very convenient. [*Sits down.*] Here we have been over and lunched in town. Cannon off the white! I should like to go home and have a game.

LYUBOV. You have plenty of time.

LOPAHIN. Only one word! [*Beseechingly.*] Give me an answer!

GAEV [*yawning*]. What do you say?

LYUBOV [*looks in her purse*]. I had quite a lot of money here yesterday, and there's scarcely any left today. My poor Varya feeds us all on milk soup for the sake of economy; the old folks in the kitchen get nothing but pease pudding, while I waste my money in a senseless way. [*Drops purse, scattering gold pieces.*] There, they have all fallen out! [*Annoyed.*]

YASHA. Allow me, I'll soon pick them up. [*Collects the coins.*]

LYUBOV. Pray do, Yasha. And what did I go off to the town to lunch for? Your restaurant's a wretched place with its music and the table-cloth smelling of soap. . . . Why drink so much, Leonid? And eat so much? And talk so much? Today you talked a great deal again in the restaurant, and all so inappropriately. About the era of the 'seventies, about the decadents. And to whom? Talking to waiters about decadents!°

LOPAHIN. Yes.

GAEV [*waving his hand*]. I'm incorrigible; that's evident. [*Irritably to* YASHA.] Why is it you keep fidgeting about in front of us!

YASHA [*laughs*]. I can't help laughing when I hear your voice.

GAEV [*to his sister*]. Either I or he . . .

LYUBOV. Get along! Go away, Yasha.

YASHA [*gives* LYUBOV ANDREYEVNA *her purse*]. Directly. [*Hardly able to suppress his laughter.*] This minute . . .

[*Goes off.*]

LOPAHIN. Deriganov, the millionaire, means to buy your estate. They say he is coming to the sale himself.

LYUBOV. Where did you hear that?

LOPAHIN. That's what they say in town.

GAEV. Our aunt in Yaroslavl has promised to send help; but when, and how much she will send, we don't know.

LOPAHIN. How much will she send? A hundred thousand? Two hundred?

LYUBOV. Oh, well! . . . Ten or fifteen thousand, and we must be thankful to get that.

LOPAHIN. Forgive me, but such reckless people as you are—such queer, unbusiness-like people—I never met in my life. One tells you

---

decadents artists and thinkers of the 1890's whose pursuit of novelty in art and politics was widely stigmatized as corrupt

in plain Russian your estate is going to be sold, and you seem not to understand it.

LYUBOV. What are we to do? Tell us what to do.

5 LOPAHIN. I do tell you every day. Every day I say the same thing. You absolutely must let the cherry orchard and the land on building leases; and do it at once, as quick as may be—the auction's close upon us! Do understand! Once 10 make up your mind to build villas, and you can raise as much money as you like, and then you are saved.

LYUBOV. Villas and summer visitors—forgive me saying so—it's so vulgar.

15 GAEV. There I perfectly agree with you.

LOPAHIN. I shall sob, or scream, or fall into a fit. I can't stand it! You drive me mad! [To GAEV.] You're an old woman!

GAEV. What do you say?

20 LOPAHIN. An old woman! [Gets up to go.]

LYUBOV [in dismay]. No, don't go! Do stay, my dear friend! Perhaps we shall think of something.

LOPAHIN. What is there to think of?

25 LYUBOV. Don't go, I entreat you! With you here it's more cheerful, anyway. [A pause.] I keep expecting something, as though the house were going to fall about our ears.

GAEV [in profound dejection]. Potted the 30 white! It fails—a kiss.

LYUBOV. We have been great sinners. . . .

LOPAHIN. You have no sins to repent of.

GAEV [puts a caramel in his mouth]. They say I've eaten up my property in caramels. 35 [Laughs.]

LYUBOV. Oh, my sins! I've always thrown my money away recklessly like a lunatic. I married a man who made nothing but debts. My husband died of champagne—he drank dread- 40 fully. To my misery I loved another man, and immediately—it was my first punishment—the blow fell upon me, here, in the river . . . my boy was drowned and I went abroad—went away for ever, never to return, not to see that 45 river again . . . I shut my eyes, and fled, distracted, and he after me . . . pitilessly, brutally. I bought a villa at Mentone, for he fell ill there, and for three years I had no rest day or

night. His illness wore me out, my soul was dried up. And last year, when my villa was sold 50 to pay my debts, I went to Paris and there he robbed me of everything and abandoned me for another woman; and I tried to poison myself. . . . So stupid, so shameful! . . . And suddenly I felt a yearning for Russia, for my 55 country, for my little girl . . . [dries her tears]. Lord, Lord, be merciful! Forgive my sins! Do not chastise me more! [Takes a telegram out of her pocket.] I got this today from Paris. He implores forgiveness, entreats me to return. 60 [Tears up the telegram.] I fancy there is music somewhere. [Listens.]

GAEV. That's our famous Jewish orchestra. You remember, four violins, a flute and a double bass. 65

LYUBOV. That still in existence? We ought to send for them one evening, and give a dance.

LOPAHIN [listens]. I can't hear. . . . [Hums softly.] "For money the Germans will turn a Russian into a Frenchman."° [Laughs.] I did 70 see such a piece at the theatre yesterday! It was funny!

LYUBOV. And most likely there was nothing funny in it. You shouldn't look at plays, you should look at yourselves a little oftener. How 75 grey your lives are! How much nonsense you talk.

LOPAHIN. That's true. One may say honestly, we live a fool's life. [Pause.] My father was a peasant, an idiot; he knew nothing and taught 80 me nothing, only beat me when he was drunk, and always with his stick. In reality I am just such another blockhead and idiot. I've learnt nothing properly. I write a wretched hand. I write so that I feel ashamed before folks, like a 85 pig.

LYUBOV. You ought to get married, my dear fellow.

LOPAHIN. Yes . . . that's true.

LYUBOV. You should marry our Varya, she's 90 a good girl.

"For money the Germans . . . Frenchman" i.e. for money the Germans (numbers of whom had settled in Russia as "experts" in various fields) will turn the barbarian into a model of elegance

LOPAHIN. Yes.

LYUBOV. She's a good-natured girl, she's busy all day long, and what's more, she loves you. And you have liked her for ever so long.

5 LOPAHIN. Well? I'm not against it. . . . She's a good girl. [*Pause.*]

GAEV. I've been offered a place in the bank: 6,000 roubles a year. Did you know?

LYUBOV. You would never do for that! You 10 must stay as you are.

[*Enter* FIRS *with overcoat.*]

FIRS. Put it on, sir, it's damp.

GAEV [*putting it on*]. You bother me, old fellow.

15 FIRS. You can't go on like this. You went away in the morning without leaving word. [*Looks him over.*]

LYUBOV. You look older, Firs!

FIRS. What is your pleasure?

20 LOPAHIN. You look older, she said.

FIRS. I've had a long life. They were arranging my wedding before your papa was born. . . . [*Laughs.*] I was the head footman before the emancipation° came. I wouldn't con-25 sent to be set free then; I stayed on with the old master. . . . [*A pause.*] I remember what rejoicings they made and didn't know themselves what they were rejoicing over.

LOPAHIN. Those were fine old times. There 30 was flogging anyway.

FIRS [*not hearing*]. To be sure! The peasants knew their place, and the masters knew theirs; but now they're all at sixes and sevens, there's no making it out.

35 GAEV. Hold your tongue, Firs. I must go to town tomorrow. I have been promised an introduction to a general, who might let us have a loan.

LOPAHIN. You won't bring that off. And you 40 won't pay your arrears, you may rest assured of that.

LYUBOV. That's all his nonsense. There is no such general.

[*Enter* TROFIMOV, ANYA, *and* VARYA.]

45 GAEV. Here come our girls.

ANYA. There's mamma on the seat.

the emancipation of the serfs in 1861

LYUBOV [*tenderly*]. Come here, come along. My darlings! [*Embraces* ANYA *and* VARYA.] If you only knew how I love you both. Sit beside me, there, like that. [*All sit down.*] 50

LOPAHIN. Our perpetual student is always with the young ladies.

TROFIMOV. That's not your business.

LOPAHIN. He'll soon be fifty, and he's still a student. 55

TROFIMOV. Drop your idiotic jokes.

LOPAHIN. Why are you so cross, you queer fish?

TROFIMOV. Oh, don't persist!

LOPAHIN [*laughs*]. Allow me to ask you 60 what's your idea of me?

TROFIMOV. I'll tell you my idea of you, Yermolay Alexeyevitch: you are a rich man, you'll soon be a millionaire. Well, just as in the economy of nature a wild beast is of use, who 65 devours everything that comes in his way, so you too have your use. [*All laugh.*]

VARYA. Better tell us something about the planets, Petya.

LYUBOV. No, let us go on with the conversa-70 tion we had yesterday.

TROFIMOV. What was it about?

GAEV. About pride.

TROFIMOV. We had a long conversation yesterday, but we came to no conclusion. In 75 pride, in your sense of it, there is something mystical. Perhaps you are right from your point of view; but if one looks at it simply, without subtlety, what sort of pride can there be, what sense is there in it, if man in his 80 physiological formation is very imperfect, if in the immense majority of cases he is coarse, dull-witted, profoundly unhappy? One must give up glorification of self. One should work, and nothing else. 85

GAEV. One must die in any case.

TROFIMOV. Who knows? And what does it mean—dying? Perhaps man has a hundred senses, and only the five we know are lost at death, while the other ninety-five remain alive. 90

LYUBOV. How clever you are, Petya!

LOPAHIN [*ironically*]. Fearfully clever!

TROFIMOV. Humanity progresses, perfecting its powers. Everything that is beyond its ken now will one day become familiar and comprehensible; only we must work, we must with all our powers aid the seeker after truth. Here among us in Russia the workers are few in number as yet. The vast majority of the intellectual people I know, seek nothing, do nothing, are not fit as yet for work of any kind. They call themselves intellectual, but they treat their servants as inferiors, behave to the peasants as though they were animals, learn little, read nothing seriously, do practically nothing, only talk about science and know very little about art. They are all serious people, they all have severe faces, they all talk of weighty matters and air their theories, and yet the vast majority of us—ninety-nine per cent—live like savages, at the least thing fly to blows and abuse, eat piggishly, sleep in filth and stuffiness, bugs everywhere, stench and damp and moral impurity. And it's clear all our fine talk is only to divert our attention and other people's. Show me where to find the crèches° there's so much talk about, and the reading-rooms? They only exist in novels: in real life there are none of them. There is nothing but filth and vulgarity and Asiatic apathy. I fear and dislike very serious faces. I'm afraid of serious conversations. We should do better to be silent.

LOPAHIN. You know, I get up at five o'clock in the morning, and I work from morning to night; and I've money, my own and other people's, always passing through my hands, and I see what people are made of all round me. One has only to begin to do anything to see how few honest, decent people there are. Sometimes when I lie awake at night, I think: "Oh! Lord, thou hast given us immense forests, boundless plains, the widest horizons, and living here we ourselves ought really to be giants."

LYUBOV. You ask for giants! They are no good except in story-books; in real life they frighten us.

[EPIHODOV *advances in the background, playing on the guitar.*]

LYUBOV [*dreamily*]. There goes Epihodov.
ANYA [*dreamily*]. There goes Epihodov.

crèches day nurseries

GAEV. The sun has set, my friends.
TROFIMOV. Yes.
GAEV [*not loudly, but, as it were, declaiming*]. O nature, divine nature, thou art bright with eternal luster, beautiful and indifferent! Thou, whom we call mother, thou dost unite within thee life and death! Thou dost give life and dost destroy!
VARYA [*in a tone of supplication*]. Uncle!
ANYA. Uncle, you are at it again!
TROFIMOV. You'd much better be cannoning off the red!
GAEV. I'll hold my tongue, I will.
[*All sit plunged in thought. Perfect stillness. The only thing audible is the muttering of* FIRS. *Suddenly there is a sound in the distance, as it were from the sky—the sound of a breaking harp-string, mournfully dying away.*]
LYUBOV. What is that?
LOPAHIN. I don't know. Somewhere far away a bucket fallen and broken in the pits. But somewhere very far away.
GAEV. It might be a bird of some sort—such as a heron.
TROFIMOV. Or an owl.
LYUBOV [*shudders*]. I don't know why, but it's horrid. [*A pause.*]
FIRS. It was the same before the calamity—the owl hooted and the samovar hissed all the time.
GAEV. Before what calamity?
FIRS. Before the emancipation. [*A pause.*]
LYUBOV. Come, my friends, let us be going; evening is falling. [*To* ANYA.] There are tears in your eyes. What is it, darling? [*Embraces her.*]
ANYA. Nothing, mamma; it's nothing.
TROFIMOV. There is somebody coming.
[THE WAYFARER *appears in a shabby white forage cap and an overcoat; he is slightly drunk.*]
WAYFARER. Allow me to inquire, can I get to the station this way?
GAEV. Yes. Go along that road.
WAYFARER. I thank you most feelingly. [*Coughing.*] The weather is superb. [*Declaims.*] My brother, my suffering brother! . . . Come out to the Volga! Whose groan do you hear? . . .

[*To* VARYA.] Mademoiselle, vouchsafe a hungry Russian thirty kopeks.

[VARYA *utters a shriek of alarm.*]

LOPAHIN [*angrily*]. There's a right and a
5 wrong way of doing everything!

LYUBOV [*hurriedly*]. Here, take this. [*Looks in her purse.*] I've no silver. No matter—here's gold for you.

WAYFARER. I thank you most feelingly!

10 [*Goes off.*]

[*Laughter.*]

VARYA [*frightened*]. I'm going home—I'm going. . . . Oh, mamma, the servants have nothing to eat, and you gave him gold!

15 LYUBOV. There's no doing anything with me. I'm so silly! When we get home, I'll give you all I possess. Yermolay Alexeyevitch, you will lend me some more . . . !

LOPAHIN. I will.

20 LYUBOV. Come, friends, it's time to be going. And Varya, we have made a match of it for you. I congratulate you.

VARYA [*through her tears*]. Mamma, that's not a joking matter.

25 LOPAHIN. "Ophelia, get thee to a nunnery!"

GAEV. My hands are trembling; it's a long while since I had a game of billiards.

LOPAHIN. "Ophelia! Nymph, in thy orisons be all my sins remember'd."

30 LYUBOV. Come, it will soon be supper-time.

VARYA. How he frightened me! My heart's simply throbbing.

LOPAHIN. Let me remind you, ladies and gentlemen: on the 22nd of August the cherry
35 orchard will be sold. Think about that! Think about it!

[*All go off, except* TROFIMOV *and* ANYA.]

ANYA [*laughing*]. I'm grateful to the wayfarer! He frightened Varya and we are left
40 alone.

TROFIMOV. Varya's afraid we shall fall in love with each other, and for days together she won't leave us. With her narrow brain she can't grasp that we are above love. To eliminate
45 the petty and transitory which hinders us from being free and happy—that is the aim and meaning of our life. Forward! We go forward irresistibly towards the bright star that shines yonder in the distance. Forward! Do not lag behind, friends.
50

ANYA [*claps her hands*]. How well you speak! [*A pause.*] It is divine here today.

TROFIMOV. Yes, it's glorious weather.

ANYA. Somehow, Petya, you've made me so that I don't love the cherry orchard as I used 55 to. I used to love it so dearly. I used to think that there was no spot on earth like our garden.

TROFIMOV. All Russia is our garden. The earth is great and beautiful—there are many beautiful places in it. [*A pause.*] Think only, 60 Anya, your grandfather, and great-grandfather, and all your ancestors were slave-owners—the owners of living souls—and from every cherry in the orchard, from every leaf, from every trunk there are human creatures looking at you. 65 Cannot you hear their voices? Oh, it is awful! Your orchard is a fearful thing, and when in the evening or at night one walks about the orchard, the old bark on the trees glimmers dimly in the dusk, and the old cherry trees seem to be 70 dreaming of centuries gone by and tortured by fearful visions. Yes! We are at least two hundred years behind, we have really gained nothing yet, we have no definite attitude to the past, we do nothing but theorize or complain 75 of depression or drink vodka. It is clear that to begin to live in the present we must first expiate our past, we must break with it; and we can expiate it only by suffering, by extraordinary unceasing labor. Understand that, 80 Anya.

ANYA. The house we live in has long ceased to be our own, and I shall leave it, I give you my word.

TROFIMOV. If you have the house keys, fling 85 them into the well and go away. Be free as the wind.

ANYA [*in ecstasy*]. How beautifully you said that!

TROFIMOV. Believe me, Anya, believe me! I 90 am not thirty yet, I am young, I am still a student, but I have gone through so much already! As soon as winter comes, I am hungry, sick, careworn, poor as a beggar, and what ups and downs of fortune have I not known! And my 95 soul was always, every minute, day and night,

full of inexplicable forebodings. I have a foreboding of happiness, Anya. I see glimpses of it
already.

ANYA [*pensively*]. The moon is rising.

5 [EPIHODOV *is heard playing still the same
mournful song on the guitar. The moon rises.
Somewhere near the poplars* VARYA *is looking
for* ANYA *and calling "Anya! Where are you?"*]

TROFIMOV. Yes, the moon is rising. [*A
10 pause.*] Here is happiness—here it comes! It is
coming nearer and nearer; already I can hear its
footsteps. And if we never see it—if we may
never know it—what does it matter? Others
will see it after us.

15 VARYA'S VOICE. Anya! Where are you?

TROFIMOV. That Varya again! [*Angrily.*] It's
revolting!

ANYA. Well, let's go down to the river. It's
lovely there.

20 TROFIMOV. Yes, let's go.

[*They go.*]

VARYA'S VOICE. Anya! Anya!

The Curtain Falls

ACT III

[*A drawing-room divided by an arch from a
larger drawing-room. A chandelier burning.*
25 *The Jewish orchestra, the same that was mentioned in Act II, is heard playing in the ante-
room. It is evening. In the larger drawing-room
they are dancing the grand chain. The voice of*
SEMYONOV-PISHTCHIK: *"Promenade à une
30 paire!" Then enter the drawing-room in couples
first* PISHTCHIK *and* CHARLOTTA IVANOVNA, *then*
TROFIMOV *and* LYUBOV ANDREYEVNA, *thirdly*
ANYA *with* the POST-OFFICE CLERK, *fourthly*
VARYA *with the* STATION MASTER, *and other
35 guests.* VARYA *is quietly weeping and wiping
away her tears as she dances. In the last couple
is* DUNYASHA. *They move across the drawing-
room.* PISHTCHIK *shouts:* "Grand rond, balan-
cez!" *and* "Les Cavaliers à genou et remerciez
40 vos dames." FIRS *in a swallow-tail coat brings
in seltzer water on a tray.* PISHTCHIK *and*
TROFIMOV *enter the drawing-room.*]

PISHTCHIK. I am a full-blooded man; I have
already had two strokes. Dancing's hard work

for me, but as they say, if you're in the pack, 45
you must bark with the rest. I'm as strong, I
may say, as a horse. My parent, who would
have his joke—may the Kingdom of Heaven
be his!—used to say about our origin that the
ancient stock of the Semyonov-Pishtchiks was 50
derived from the very horse that Caligula made
a member of the senate. [*Sits down.*] But I've
no money, that's where the mischief is. A hungry dog believes in nothing but meat. . . .
[*Snores, but at once wakes up.*] That's like 55
me . . . I can think of nothing but money.

TROFIMOV. There really is something horsy
about your appearance.

PISHTCHIK. Well . . . a horse is a fine beast . . .
a horse can be sold. 60

[*There is the sound of billiards being played
in an adjoining room.* VARYA *appears in the
arch leading to the larger drawing-room.*]

TROFIMOV [*teasing*]. Madame Lopahin!
Madame Lopahin! 65

VARYA [*angrily*]. Mangy-looking gentleman!

TROFIMOV. Yes, I am a mangy-looking
gentleman, and I'm proud of it!

VARYA [*pondering bitterly*]. Here we have
hired musicians and nothing to pay them! 70

[*Goes out.*]

TROFIMOV [*to* PISHTCHIK]. If the energy you
have wasted during your lifetime in trying to
find the money to pay your interest, had gone
to something else, you might in the end have 75
turned the world upside down.

PISHTCHIK. Nietzsche, the philosopher, a very
great and celebrated man . . . of enormous
intellect . . . says in his works, that one can
make° forged bank-notes. 80

TROFIMOV. Why, have you read Nietzsche?

PISHTCHIK. What next . . . Dashenka told me.
. . . And now I am in such a position, I might
just as well forge bank-notes. The day after
tomorrow I must pay 310 roubles—130 I have 85
procured. [*Feels in his pockets, in alarm.*] The
money's gone! I have lost my money! [*Through
his tears.*] Where's the money? [*Gleefully.*]
Why, here it is behind the lining. . . . It has
made me hot all over. 90

one can make it is ethical to make

[*Enter* LYUBOV ANDREYEVNA *and* CHARLOTTA IVANOVNA.]

LYUBOV [*hums the Lezginka°*]. Why is Leonid so long? What can he be doing in town?
5 [*To* DUNYASHA.] Offer the musicians some tea.

TROFIMOV. The sale hasn't taken place, most likely.

LYUBOV. It's the wrong time to have the orchestra, and the wrong time to give a dance.
10 Well, never mind. [*Sits down and hums softly.*]

CHARLOTTA [*gives* PISHTCHIK *a pack of cards*]. Here's a pack of cards. Think of any card you like.

PISHTCHIK. I've thought of one.

15 CHARLOTTA. Shuffle the pack now. That's right. Give it here, my dear Mr. Pishtchik. Ein, zwei, drei—now look, it's in your breast pocket.

PISHTCHIK [*taking a card out of his breast pocket*]. The eight of spades! Perfectly right!
20 [*Wonderingly.*] Fancy that now!

CHARLOTTA [*holding pack of cards in her hands, to* TROFIMOV]. Tell me quickly which is the top card.

TROFIMOV. Well, the queen of spades.

25 CHARLOTTA. It is! [*To* PISHTCHIK.] Well, which card is uppermost?

PISHTCHIK. The ace of hearts.

CHARLOTTA. It is! [*Claps her hands, pack of cards disappears.*]
30 Ah! what lovely weather it is today!

[*A mysterious feminine voice which seems coming out of the floor answers her.* "Oh, yes, it's magnificent weather, madam."]

CHARLOTTA. You are my perfect ideal.

35 VOICE. And I greatly admire you too, madam.

STATION MASTER [*applauding*]. The lady ventriloquist—bravo!

PISHTCHIK [*wonderingly*]. Fancy that now! Most enchanting Charlotta Ivanovna, I'm
40 simply in love with you.

CHARLOTTA. In love? [*Shrugging shoulders.*] What do you know of love, guter Mensch, aber schlechter Musikant.°

TROFIMOV [*pats* PISHTCHIK *on the shoulder*].

You dear old horse. . . . 45

CHARLOTTA. Attention, please! Another trick! [*Takes a travelling rug from the chair.*] Here's a very good rug; I want to sell it. [*Shaking it out.*] Doesn't anyone want to buy it?

PISHTCHIK [*wonderingly*]. Fancy that! 50

CHARLOTTA. Ein, zwei, drei! [*Quickly picks up rug she has dropped; behind the rug stands* ANYA; *she makes a curtsey, runs to her mother, embraces her and runs back into the larger drawing-room amidst general enthusiasm.*] 55

LYUBOV [*applauds*]. Bravo! Bravo!

CHARLOTTA. Now again! Ein, zwei, drei! [*Lifts up the rug; behind the rug stands* VARYA, *bowing.*]

PISHTCHIK [*wonderingly*]. Fancy that now! 60

CHARLOTTA. That's the end. [*Throws the rug at* PISHTCHIK, *makes a curtsey, runs into the larger drawing-room.*]

PISHTCHIK [*hurries after her*]. Mischievous creature! Fancy! 65
[*Goes out.*]

LYUBOV. And still Leonid doesn't come. I can't understand what he's doing in the town so long! Why, everything must be over by now. The estate is sold, or the sale has not taken 70 place. Why keep us so long in suspense?

VARYA [*trying to console her*]. Uncle's bought it. I feel sure of that.

TROFIMOV [*ironically*]. Oh, yes!

VARYA. Great-aunt sent him an authorization 75 to buy it in her name, and transfer the debt. She's doing it for Anya's sake, and I'm sure God will be merciful. Uncle will buy it.

LYUBOV. My aunt in Yaroslavl sent fifteen thousand to buy the estate in her name, she 80 doesn't trust us—but that's not enough even to pay the arrears. [*Hides her face in her hands.*] My fate is being sealed today, my fate . . .

TROFIMOV [*teasing* VARYA]. Madame Lopa- 85 hin.

VARYA [*angrily*]. Perpetual student! Twice already you've been sent down° from the University.

LYUBOV. Why are you angry, Varya? He's 90

---

the Lezginka a sprightly Caucasian dance tune
guter Mensch . . . Musikant "a good man but a bad musician"

sent down expelled

teasing you about Lopahin. Well, what of that? Marry Lopahin if you like, he's a good man, and interesting; if you don't want to, don't! Nobody compels you, darling.

5 VARYA. I must tell you plainly, mamma, I look at the matter seriously; he's a good man, I like him.

LYUBOV. Well, marry him. I can't see what you're waiting for.

10 VARYA. Mamma, I can't make him an offer myself. For the last two years, everyone's been talking to me about him. Everyone talks; but he says nothing or else makes a joke. I see what it means. He's growing rich, he's absorbed in 15 business, he has no thoughts for me. If I had money, were it ever so little, if I had only a hundred roubles, I'd throw everything up and go far away. I would go into a nunnery.

TROFIMOV. What bliss!

20 VARYA [to TROFIMOV]. A student ought to have sense! [In a soft tone with tears.] How ugly you've grown, Petya! How old you look! [To LYUBOV ANDREYEVNA, no longer crying.] But I can't do without work, mamma; I must 25 have something to do every minute.

[Enter YASHA.]

YASHA [hardly restraining his laughter]. Epihodov has broken a billiard cue!

[Goes out.]

30 VARYA. What is Epihodov doing here? Who gave him leave to play billiards? I can't make these people out.

[Goes out.]

LYUBOV. Don't tease her, Petya. You see she 35 has grief enough without that.

TROFIMOV. She is so very officious, meddling in what's not her business. All the summer she's given Anya and me no peace. She's afraid of a love affair between us. What's it to do with 40 her? Besides, I have given no grounds for it. Such triviality is not in my line. We are above love!

LYUBOV. And I suppose I am beneath love. [Very uneasily.] Why is it Leonid's not here? 45 If only I could know whether the estate is sold or not! It seems such an incredible calamity that I really don't know what to think. I am distracted . . . I shall scream in a minute . . . I shall do something stupid. Save me, Petya, tell me something, talk to me! 50

TROFIMOV. What does it matter whether the estate is sold today or not? That's all done with long ago. There's no turning back, the path is overgrown. Don't worry yourself, dear Lyubov Andreyevna. You mustn't deceive yourself; for 55 once in your life you must face the truth!

LYUBOV. What truth? You see where the truth lies, but I seem to have lost my sight, I see nothing. You settle every great problem so boldly, but tell me, my dear boy, isn't it be- 60 cause you're young—because you haven't yet understood one of your problems through suffering? You look forward boldly, and isn't it that you don't see and don't expect anything dreadful because life is still hidden from your 65 young eyes? You're bolder, more honest, deeper than we are, but think, be just a little magnanimous, have pity on me. I was born here, you know, my father and mother lived here, my grandfather lived here, I love this house. I 70 can't conceive of life without the cherry orchard, and if it really must be sold, then sell me with the orchard. [Embraces TROFIMOV, kisses him on the forehead.] My boy was drowned here. [Weeps.] Pity me, my dear kind 75 fellow.

TROFIMOV. You know I feel for you with all my heart.

LYUBOV. But that should have been said differently, so differently. [Takes out her 80 handkerchief, telegram falls on the floor.] My heart is so heavy today. It's so noisy here, my soul is quivering at every sound, I'm shuddering all over, but I can't go away; I'm afraid to be quiet and alone. Don't be hard on me, 85 Petya . . . I love you as though you were one of ourselves. I would gladly let you marry Anya—I swear I would—only, my dear boy, you must take your degree, you do nothing— you're simply tossed by fate from place to 90 place. That's so strange. It is, isn't it? And you must do something with your beard to make it grow somehow. [Laughs.] You look so funny!

TROFIMOV [picks up the telegram]. I've no wish to be a beauty. 95

LYUBOV. That's a telegram from Paris. I get

one every day. One yesterday and one today. That savage creature is ill again, he's in trouble again. He begs forgiveness, beseeches me to go, and really I ought to go to Paris to see him. You
5 look shocked, Petya. What am I to do, my dear boy, what am I to do? He is ill, he is alone and unhappy, and who'll look after him, who'll keep him from doing the wrong thing, who'll give him his medicine at the right time? And
10 why hide it or be silent? I love him, that's clear. I love him! I love him! He's a millstone about my neck, I'm going to the bottom with him, but I love that stone and can't live without it. [*Presses* TROFIMOV's *hand.*] Don't think ill of
15 me, Petya, don't tell me anything, don't tell me . . .
TROFIMOV [*through his tears*]. For God's sake forgive my frankness: why, he robbed you!
LYUBOV. No! No! No! You mustn't speak like
20 that. [*Covers her ears.*]
TROFIMOV. He is a wretch! You're the only person that doesn't know it! He's a worthless creature! A despicable wretch!
LYUBOV [*getting angry, but speaking with*
25 *restraint*]. You're twenty-six or twenty-seven years old, but you're still a schoolboy.
TROFIMOV. Possibly.
LYUBOV. You should be a man at your age! You should understand what love means! And
30 you ought to be in love yourself. You ought to fall in love! [*Angrily.*] Yes, yes, and it's not purity in you, you're simply a prude, a comic fool, a freak.
TROFIMOV [*in horror*]. The things she's say-
35 ing!
LYUBOV. I am above love! You're not above love, but simply as our Firs here says, "You are a good-for-nothing." At your age not to have a mistress!
40 TROFIMOV [*in horror*]. This is awful! The things she is saying! [*Goes rapidly into the larger drawing-room clutching his head.*] This is awful! I can't stand it! I'm going. [*Goes off, but at once returns.*] All is over between us!
45 [*Goes off into the ante-room.*]
LYUBOV [*shouts after him*]. Petya! Wait a minute! You funny creature! I was joking! Petya!

[*There is a sound of somebody running quickly downstairs and suddenly falling with a*
50 *crash.* ANYA *and* VARYA *scream, but there is a sound of laughter at once.*]
LYUBOV. What has happened?
[ANYA *runs in.*]
ANYA [*laughing*]. Petya's fallen downstairs!
55 [*Runs out.*]
LYUBOV. What a queer fellow that Petya is!
[*The* STATION MASTER *stands in the middle of the larger room and reads "The Magda-lene,"° by Alexey Tolstoy. They listen to him,*
60 *but before he has recited many lines strains of a waltz are heard from the ante-room and the reading is broken off. All dance.* TROFIMOV, ANYA, VARYA, *and* LYUBOV ANDREYEVNA *come in from the ante-room.*]
65 LYUBOV. Come, Petya—come, pure heart! I beg your pardon. Let's have a dance! [*Dances with* PETYA.]
[ANYA *and* VARYA *dance.* FIRS *comes in, puts his stick down near the side-door.* YASHA *also*
70 *comes into the drawing-room and looks on at the dancing.*]
YASHA. What is it, old man?
FIRS. I don't feel well. In old days we used to have generals, barons and admirals dancing at
75 our balls, and now we send for the post-office clerk and the station master and even they're not overanxious to come. I am getting feeble. The old master, the grandfather, used to give sealing-wax for all complaints. I have been
80

The Magdalene a poem which celebrates Christ's sudden appearance at a banquet of dazzling magnificence. Its opening lines follow:

The crowd seethes—merrymaking, laughter,
The sound of lutes and clash of cymbals;
All around are greenness, flowers,
And between the columns at the entrance of the
[house
Sections of heavy brocade
Are raised in patterned ribbons.
The chambers are richly furnished,
Crystal and gold burn everywhere;
The courtyard is filled with drivers and horses.
Crowding at the huge banquet table
The noisy chorus of guests celebrates;
Their criss-cross conversation
Goes on, fusing with the music.
(Trans. Horace W. Dewey)

taking sealing-wax for twenty years or more. Perhaps that's what's kept me alive.

YASHA. You bore me, old man! [*Yawns.*] It's time you were done with.

5 FIRS. Ach, you're a good-for-nothing! [*Mutters.*]

[TROFIMOV *and* LYUBOV ANDREYEVNA *dance in larger room and then on to the stage.*]

LYUBOV. Merci. I'll sit down a little. [*Sits*
10 *down.*] I'm tired.

[*Enter* ANYA.]

ANYA [*excitedly*]. There's a man in the kitchen has been saying that the cherry orchard's been sold today.

15 LYUBOV. Sold to whom?

ANYA. He didn't say to whom. He's gone away.

[*She dances with* TROFIMOV, *and they go off into the larger room.*]

20 YASHA. There was an old man gossiping there, a stranger.

FIRS. Leonid Andreyevitch isn't here yet, he hasn't come back. He has his light overcoat on, *demi-saison*, he'll catch cold for sure. Ach!
25 Foolish young things!

LYUBOV. I feel as though I should die. Go, Yasha, find out to whom it has been sold.

YASHA. But he went away long ago, the old chap. [*Laughs.*]

30 LYUBOV [*with slight vexation*]. What are you laughing at? What are you pleased at?

YASHA. Epihodov is so funny. He's a silly fellow, two and twenty misfortunes.

LYUBOV. Firs, if the estate is sold, where will
35 you go?

FIRS. Where you bid me, there I'll go.

LYUBOV. Why do you look like that? Are you ill? You ought to be in bed.

FIRS. Yes. [*Ironically.*] Me go to bed and
40 who's to wait here? Who's to see to things without me? I'm the only one in all the house.

YASHA [*to* LYUBOV ANDREYEVNA]. Lyubov Andreyevna, permit me to make a request of you; if you go back to Paris again, be so kind
45 as to take me with you. It's positively impossible for me to stay here. [*Looking about him; in an undertone.*] There's no need to say it, you

see for yourself—an uncivilized. country, the people have no morals, and then the dullness! The food in the kitchen's abominable, and then
50 Firs runs after one muttering all sorts of unsuitable words. Take me with you, please do!

[*Enter* PISHTCHIK.]

PISHTCHIK. Allow me to ask you for a waltz, my dear lady. [LYUBOV ANDREYEVNA *goes with*
55 *him.*] Enchanting lady, I really must borrow of you just 180 roubles [*dances*], only 180 roubles.

[*They pass into the larger room.*]

YASHA [*hums softly*]. "Knowest thou my
60 soul's emotion."

[*In the larger drawing-room, a figure in a gray top hat and in check trousers is gesticulating and jumping about. Shouts of "Bravo, Charlotta Ivanovna."*]
65

DUNYASHA [*she has stopped to powder herself*]. My young lady tells me to dance. There are plenty of gentlemen, and too few ladies, but dancing makes me giddy and makes my heart beat. Firs, the post-office clerk said something
70 to me just now that quite took my breath away.

[*Music becomes more subdued.*]

FIRS. What did he say to you?

DUNYASHA. He said I was like a flower.

YASHA [*yawns*]. What ignorance!
75

[*Goes out.*]

DUNYASHA. Like a flower. I am a girl of such delicate feelings, I am awfully fond of soft speeches.

FIRS. Your head's being turned.
80

[*Enter* EPIHODOV.]

EPIHODOV. You have no desire to see me, Dunyasha. I must be an insect. [*Sighs.*] Ah! life!

DUNYASHA. What is it you want?
85

EPIHODOV. Undoubtedly you may be right. [*Sighs.*] But of course, if one looks at it from that point of view, if I may so express myself, you have, excuse my plain speaking, reduced me to a complete state of mind. I know my
90 destiny. Every day some misfortune befalls me and I have long ago grown accustomed to it, so that I look upon my fate with a smile. You gave me your word, and though I . . .

DUNYASHA. Let us have a talk later, I entreat you, but now leave me in peace, for I am lost in reverie. [*Plays with her fan.*]

EPIHODOV. I have a misfortune every day, and if I may venture to express myself, I merely smile at it, I even laugh.

[VARYA *enters from the larger drawing-room.*]

VARYA. You still have not gone, Epihodov. What a disrespectful creature you are, really! [*To* DUNYASHA.] Go along, Dunyasha! [*To* EPIHODOV.] First you play billiards and break the cue, then you go wandering about the drawing-room like a visitor!

EPIHODOV. You really cannot, if I may so express myself, call me to account like this.

VARYA. I'm not calling you to account, I'm speaking to you: You do nothing but wander from place to place and don't do your work. We keep you as a counting-house clerk, but what use you are I can't say.

EPIHODOV [*offended*]. Whether I work or whether I walk, whether I eat or whether I play billiards, is a matter to be judged by persons of understanding and my elders.

VARYA. You dare to tell me that! [*Firing up.*] You dare! You mean to say I've no understanding. Begone from here! This minute!

EPIHODOV [*intimidated*]. I beg you to express yourself with delicacy.

VARYA [*beside herself with anger*]. This moment! get out! away! [*He goes towards the door, she following him.*] Two and twenty misfortunes! Take yourself off! Don't let me set eyes on you! [EPIHODOV *has gone out, behind the door his voice,* "I shall lodge a complaint against you."] What! You're coming back? [*Snatches up the stick* FIRS *has put down near the door.*] Come! Come! Come! I'll show you! What! you're coming? Then take that! [*She swings the stick, at the very moment that* LOPAHIN *comes in.*]

LOPAHIN. Very much obliged to you!

VARYA [*angrily and ironically*]. I beg your pardon!

LOPAHIN. Not at all! I humbly thank you for your kind reception!

VARYA. No need of thanks for it. [*Moves away, then looks round and asks softly:*] I haven't hurt you?

LOPAHIN. Oh, no! Not at all! There's an immense bump coming up, though!

VOICES FROM LARGER ROOM. Lopahin has come! Yermolay Alexeyevitch!

PISHTCHIK. What do I see and hear? [*Kisses* LOPAHIN.] There's a whiff of cognac about you, my dear soul, and we're making merry here too!

[*Enter* LYUBOV ANDREYEVNA.]

LYUBOV. Is it you, Yermolay Alexeyevitch? Why have you been so long? Where's Leonid?

LOPAHIN. Leonid Andreyevitch arrived with me. He is coming.

LYUBOV [*in agitation*]. Well! Well! Was there a sale? Speak!

LOPAHIN [*embarrassed, afraid of betraying his joy*]. The sale was over at four o'clock. We missed our train—had to wait till half-past nine. [*Sighing heavily.*] Ugh! I feel a little giddy.

[*Enter* GAEV. *In his right hand he has purchases, with his left hand he is wiping away his tears.*]

LYUBOV. Well, Leonid? What news? [*Impatiently, with tears.*] Make haste, for God's sake!

GAEV [*makes her no answer, simply waves his hand. To* FIRS, *weeping*]. Here, take them; there's anchovies, Kertch herrings. I have eaten nothing all day. What I have been through! [*Door into the billiard room is open. There is heard a knocking of balls and the voice of* YASHA *saying "Eighty-seven."* GAEV's *expression changes, he leaves off weeping.*] I am fearfully tired. Firs, come and help me change my things.

[*Goes to his own room across the larger drawing-room.*]

PISHTCHIK. How about the sale? Tell us, do!

LYUBOV. Is the cherry orchard sold?

LOPAHIN. It is sold.

LYUBOV. Who has bought it?

LOPAHIN. I have bought it.

[*A pause.* LYUBOV *is crushed; she would fall*

down if she were not standing near a chair and table. VARYA *takes keys from her waistband, flings them on the floor in middle of drawing-room and goes out.*]

5 LOPAHIN. I have bought it! Wait a bit, ladies and gentlemen, pray. My head's a bit muddled, I can't speak. [*Laughs.*] We came to the auction. Deriganov was there already. Leonid Andreyevitch only had 15,000 and Deriganov bid 10 30,000, besides the arrears, straight off. I saw how the land lay. I bid against him. I bid 40,000, he bid 45,000, I said 55, and so he went on, adding 5 thousands and I adding 10. Well . . . So it ended. I bid 90, and it was knocked 15 down to me. Now the cherry orchard's mine! Mine! [*Chuckles.*] My God, the cherry orchard's mine! Tell me that I'm drunk, that I'm out of my mind, that it's all a dream. [*Stamps with his feet.*] Don't laugh at me! If my father 20 and my grandfather could rise from their graves and see all that has happened! How their Yermolay, ignorant, beaten Yermolay, who used to run about barefoot in winter, how that very Yermolay has bought the finest estate in the 25 world! I have bought the estate where my father and grandfather were slaves, where they weren't even admitted into the kitchen. I am asleep, I am dreaming! It is all fancy, it is the work of your imagination plunged in the dark-30 ness of ignorance. [*Picks up keys, smiling fondly.*] She threw away the keys; she means to show she's not the housewife now. [*Jingles the keys.*] Well, no matter. [*The orchestra is heard tuning up.*] Hey, musicians! Play! I want 35 to hear you. Come, all of you, and look how Yermolay Lopahin will take the axe to the cherry orchard, how the trees will fall to the ground! We will build houses on it and our grandsons and great-grandsons will see a new 40 life springing up there. Music! Play up!

[*Music begins to play.* LYUBOV ANDREYEVNA *has sunk into a chair and is weeping bitterly.*]

LOPAHIN [*reproachfully*]. Why, why didn't you listen to me? My poor friend! Dear lady, 45 there's no turning back now. [*With tears.*] Oh, if all this could be over, oh, if our miserable disjointed life could somehow soon be changed!

PISHTCHIK [*takes him by the arm; in an undertone*]. She's weeping, let us go and leave her alone. Come. 50

[*Takes him by the arm and leads him into the larger drawing-room.*]

LOPAHIN. What's that? Musicians, play up! All must be as I wish it. [*With irony.*] Here comes the new master, the owner of the cherry 55 orchard! [*Accidentally tips over a little table, almost upsetting the candelabra.*] I can pay for everything!

[*Goes out with* PISHTCHIK. *No one remains on the stage or in the larger drawing-room except* 60 LYUBOV, *who sits huddled up, weeping bitterly. The music plays softly.* ANYA *and* TROFIMOV *come in quickly.* ANYA *goes up to her mother and falls on her knees before her.* TROFIMOV *stands at the entrance to the larger drawing-* 65 *room.*]

ANYA. Mamma! Mamma, you're crying, dear, kind, good mamma! My precious! I love you! I bless you! The cherry orchard is sold, it is gone, that's true, that's true! But don't weep, 70 mamma! Life is still before you, you have still your good, pure heart! Let us go, let us go, darling, away from here! We will make a new garden, more splendid than this one; you will see it, you will understand. And joy, quiet, deep 75 joy, will sink into your soul like the sun at evening! And you will smile, mamma! Come, darling, let us go!

The Curtain Falls

ACT IV

[SCENE: *Same as in Act I. There are neither curtains on the windows nor pictures on the* 80 *walls: only a little furniture remains piled up in a corner as if for sale. There is a sense of desolation; near the outer door and in the background of the scene are packed trunks, travelling bags, etc. On the left the door is open,* 85 *and from here the voices of* VARYA *and* ANYA *are audible.* LOPAHIN *is standing waiting.* YASHA *is holding a tray with glasses full of champagne. In front of the stage* EPIHODOV *is tying up a box. In the background behind the scene a hum* 90 *of talk from the peasants who have come to say goodbye. The voice of* GAEV: "Thanks, brothers, thanks!"]

YASHA. The peasants have come to say good-bye. In my opinion, Yermolay Alexeyevitch, the peasants are good-natured, but they don't know much about things.

[*The hum of talk dies away. Enter across front of stage* LYUBOV ANDREYEVNA *and* GAEV. *She is not weeping, but is pale; her face is quivering—she cannot speak.*]

GAEV. You gave them your purse, Lyuba. That won't do—that won't do!

LYUBOV. I couldn't help it! I couldn't help it!

[*Both go out.*]

LOPAHIN [*in the doorway, calls after them*]. You will take a glass at parting? Please do. I didn't think to bring any from the town, and at the station I could only get one bottle. Please take a glass. [*A pause.*] What? You don't care for any? [*Comes away from the door.*] If I'd known, I wouldn't have bought it. Well, and I'm not going to drink it. [YASHA *carefully sets the tray down on a chair.*] You have a glass, Yasha, anyway.

YASHA. Good luck to the travellers, and luck to those that stay behind! [*Drinks.*] This champagne isn't the real thing, I can assure you.

LOPAHIN. It cost eight roubles the bottle. [*A pause.*] It's devilish cold here.

YASHA. They haven't heated the stove today—it's all the same since we're going. [*Laughs.*]

LOPAHIN. What are you laughing for?

YASHA. For pleasure.

LOPAHIN. Though it's October, it's as still and sunny as though it were summer. It's just right for building! [*Looks at his watch; says in doorway:*] Take note, ladies and gentlemen, the train goes in forty-seven minutes: so you ought to start for the station in twenty minutes. You must hurry up!

[TROFIMOV *comes in from out of doors wearing a great-coat.*]

TROFIMOV. I think it must be time to start, the horses are ready. The devil only knows what's become of my goloshes; they're lost. [*In the doorway.*] Anya! My goloshes aren't here. I can't find them.

LOPAHIN. And I'm getting off to Harkov. I am going in the same train with you. I'm spending all the winter at Harkov. I've been wasting all my time gossiping with you and fretting with no work to do. I can't get on without work. I don't know what to do with my hands, they flap about so queerly, as if they didn't belong to me.

TROFIMOV. Well, we're just going away, and you will take up your profitable labors again.

LOPAHIN. Do take a glass.

TROFIMOV. No, thanks.

LOPAHIN. Then you're going to Moscow now?

TROFIMOV. Yes. I shall see them as far as the town, and tomorrow I shall go on to Moscow.

LOPAHIN. Yes, I daresay, the professors aren't giving any lectures, they're waiting for your arrival.

TROFIMOV. That's not your business.

LOPAHIN. How many years have you been at the University?

TROFIMOV. Do think of something newer than that—that's stale and flat. [*Hunts for goloshes.*] You know we shall most likely never see each other again, so let me give you one piece of advice at parting: don't wave your arms about—get out of the habit. And another thing, building villas, reckoning up that the summer visitors will in time become independent farmers—reckoning like that, that's not the thing to do either. After all, I am fond of you: you have fine delicate fingers like an artist, you've a fine delicate soul.

LOPAHIN [*embraces him*]. Good-bye, my dear fellow. Thanks for everything. Let me give you money for the journey, if you need it.

TROFIMOV. What for? I don't need it.

LOPAHIN. Why, you haven't got a halfpenny.

TROFIMOV. Yes, I have, thank you. I got some money for a translation. Here it is in my pocket. [*Anxiously.*] But where can my goloshes be!

VARYA [*from the next room*]. Take the nasty things! [*Flings a pair of goloshes onto the stage.*]

TROFIMOV. Why are you so cross, Varya? h'm! . . . but those aren't my goloshes.

LOPAHIN. I sowed three thousand acres with poppies in the spring, and now I have cleared
5 forty thousand profit. And when my poppies were in flower, wasn't it a picture! So here, as I say, I made forty thousand, and I'm offering you a loan because I can afford to. Why turn up your nose? I am a peasant—I speak bluntly.

10 TROFIMOV. Your father was a peasant, mine was a chemist—and that proves absolutely nothing whatever. [LOPAHIN *takes out his pocketbook.*] Stop that—stop that. If you were to offer me two hundred thousand I wouldn't
15 take it. I am an independent man, and everything that all of you, rich and poor alike, prize so highly and hold so dear, hasn't the slightest power over me—it's like so much fluff fluttering in the air. I can get on without you. I can
20 pass by you. I am strong and proud. Humanity is advancing towards the highest truth, the highest happiness which is possible on earth, and I am in the front ranks.

LOPAHIN. Will you get there?

25 TROFIMOV. I shall get there. [*A pause.*] I shall get there, or I shall show others the way to get there.

[*In the distance is heard the stroke of an axe on a tree.*]

30 LOPAHIN. Good-bye, my dear fellow; it's time to be off. We turn up our noses at one another, but life is passing all the while. When I am working hard without resting, then my mind is more at ease, and it seems to me as though
35 I too know what I exist for; but how many people there are in Russia, my dear boy, who exist, one doesn't know what for. Well, it doesn't matter. That's not what keeps things spinning. They tell me Leonid Andreyevitch
40 has taken a situation. He is going to be a clerk at the bank—6,000 roubles a year. Only, of course, he won't stick to, it—he's too lazy.

ANYA [*in doorway*]. Mamma begs you not to let them chop down the orchard until she's
45 gone.

TROFIMOV. Yes, really, you might have the tact.

[*Walks out across the front of the stage.*]

LOPAHIN. I'll see to it! I'll see to it! Stupid fellows! 50

[*Goes out after him.*]

ANYA. Has Firs been taken to the hospital?

YASHA. I told them this morning. No doubt they have taken him.

ANYA [*to* EPIHODOV, *who passes across the* 55 *drawing-room*]. Semyon Pantaleyevitch, inquire, please, if Firs has been taken to the hospital.

YASHA [*in a tone of offense*]. I told Yegor this morning—why ask a dozen times? 60

EPIHODOV. Firs is advanced in years. It's my conclusive opinion no treatment would do him good; it's time he was gathered to his fathers. And I can only envy him. [*Puts a trunk down on a cardboard hat-box and crushes it.*] There 65 now, of course—I knew it would be so.

YASHA [*jeeringly*]. Two and twenty misfortunes!

VARYA [*through the door*]. Has Firs been taken to the hospital? 70

ANYA. Yes.

VARYA. Why wasn't the note for the doctor taken too?

ANYA. Oh, then, we must send it after them. [*Goes out.*] 75

VARYA [*from the adjoining room*]. Where's Yasha? Tell him his mother's come to say good-bye to him.

YASHA [*waves his hand*]. They put me out of all patience! 80

[DUNYASHA *has all this time been busy about the luggage. Now, when* YASHA *is left alone, she goes up to him.*]

DUNYASHA. You might just give me one look, Yasha. You're going away. You're leaving me. 85 [*Weeps and throws herself on his neck.*]

YASHA. What are you crying for? [*Drinks the champagne.*] In six days I shall be in Paris again. Tomorrow we shall get into the express train and roll away in a flash. I can scarcely 90 believe it! *Vive la France!* It doesn't suit me here—it's not the life for me; there's no doing anything. I have seen enough of the ignorance here. I have had enough of it. [*Drinks champagne.*] What are you crying for? Behave your- 95 self properly, and then you won't cry.

DUNYASHA [*powders her face, looking in a pocket-mirror*]. Do send me a letter from Paris. You know how I loved you, Yasha—how I loved you! I am a tender creature, Yasha.

YASHA. Here they are coming!.

[*Busies himself about the trunks, humming softly. Enter* LYUBOV ANDREYEVNA, GAEV, ANYA, *and* CHARLOTTA IVANOVNA.]

GAEV. We ought to be off. There's not much time now. [*Looking at* YASHA.] What a smell of herrings!

LYUBOV. In ten minutes we must get into the carriage. [*Casts a look about the room.*] Farewell, dear house, dear old home of our fathers! Winter will pass and spring will come, and then you will be no more; they will tear you down! How much those walls have seen! [*Kisses her daughter passionately.*] My treasure, how bright you look! Your eyes are sparkling like diamonds! Are you glad? Very glad?

ANYA. Very glad! A new life is beginning, mamma.

GAEV. Yes, really, everything is all right now. Before the cherry orchard was sold, we were all worried and wretched, but afterwards, when once the question was settled conclusively, irrevocably, we all felt calm and even cheerful. I am a bank clerk now—I am a financier—cannon off the red. And you, Lyuba, after all, you are looking better; there's no question of that.

LYUBOV. Yes. My nerves are better, that's true. [*Her hat and coat are handed to her.*] I'm sleeping well. Carry out my things, Yasha. It's time. [*To* ANYA.] My darling, we shall soon see each other again. I am going to Paris. I can live there on the money your Yaroslavl auntie sent us to buy the estate with—hurrah for auntie—but that money won't last long.

ANYA. You'll come back soon, mamma, won't you? I'll be working up for my examination in the high school, and when I have passed that, I shall set to work and be a help to you. We will read all sorts of things together, mamma, won't we? [*Kisses her mother's hands.*] We will read in the autumn evenings. We'll read lots of books, and a new wonderful world will open out before us. [*Dreamily.*]

Mamma, come soon.

LYUBOV. I shall come, my precious treasure. [*Embraces her.*]

[*Enter* LOPAHIN. CHARLOTTA *softly hums a song.*]

GAEV. Charlotta's happy; she's singing!

CHARLOTTA [*picks up a bundle like a swaddled baby*]. Bye, bye, my baby. [*A baby is heard crying: "Ooah! ooah!"*] Hush, hush, my pretty boy! [*Ooah! ooah!*] Poor little thing! [*Throws the bundle back.*] You must please find me a situation. I can't go on like this.

LOPAHIN. We'll find you one, Charlotta Ivanovna. Don't you worry yourself.

GAEV. Everyone's leaving us. Varya's going away. We have become of no use all at once.

CHARLOTTA. There's nowhere for me to be in the town. I must go away. [*Hums.*] What care I . . .

[*Enter* PISHTCHIK.]

LOPAHIN. The freak of nature!

PISHTCHIK [*gasping*]. Oh! . . . let me get my breath. . . . I'm worn out . . . my most honored . . . give me some water.

GAEV. Want some money, I suppose? Your humble servant! I'll go out of the way of temptation.

[*Goes out.*]

PISHTCHIK. It's a long while since I have been to see you . . . dearest lady. [*To* LOPAHIN.] You are here . . . glad to see you . . . a man of immense intellect . . . take . . . here [*gives* LOPAHIN] 400 roubles. That leaves me owing 840.

LOPAHIN [*shrugging his shoulders in amazement*]. It's like a dream. Where did you get it?

PISHTCHIK. Wait a bit . . . I'm hot . . . a most extraordinary occurrence! Some Englishmen came along and found in my land some sort of white clay. [*To* LYUBOV ANDREYEVNA.] And 400 for you . . . most lovely . . . wonderful. [*Gives money.*] The rest later. [*Sips water.*] A young man in the train was telling me just now that a great philosopher advises jumping off a housetop. "Jump!" says he; "the whole gist of the problem lies in that." [*Wonderingly.*] Fancy that, now! Water, please!

LOPAHIN. What Englishmen?

PISHTCHIK. I have made over to them the rights to dig the clay for twenty-four years . . . and now, excuse me . . . I can't stay . . . I must be trotting on. I'm going to Znoikovo . . . to Kardamanovo. . . . I'm in debt all round. [*Sips.*] . . . To your very good health! . . . I'll come in on Thursday.

LYUBOV. We are just off to the town, and to-morrow I start for abroad.

PISHTCHIK. What! [*In agitation.*] Why to the town? Oh, I see the furniture . . . the boxes. No matter . . . [*through his tears*] . . . no matter . . . men of enormous intellect . . . these English-men. . . . Never mind . . . be happy. God will succor you . . . no matter . . . everything in this world must have an end. [*Kisses* LYUBOV ANDREYEVNA's *hand.*] If the rumor reaches you that my end has come, think of this . . . old horse, and say: "There once was such a man in the world . . . Semyonov-Pishtchik . . . the Kingdom of Heaven be his!" . . . most extra-ordinary weather . . . yes. [*Goes out in violent agitation, but at once returns and says in the doorway:*] Dashenka wishes to be remembered to you.

[*Goes out.*]

LYUBOV. Now we can start. I leave with two cares in my heart. The first is leaving Firs ill. [*Looking at her watch.*] We still have five minutes.

ANYA. Mamma, Firs has been taken to the hospital. Yasha sent him off this morning.

LYUBOV. My other anxiety is Varya. She is used to getting up early and working; and now, without work, she's like a fish out of water. She is thin and pale, and she's crying, poor dear! [*A pause.*] You are well aware, Yermolay Alexeyevitch, I dreamed of marrying her to you, and everything seemed to show that you would get married. [*Whispers to* ANYA *and motions to* CHARLOTTA *and both go out.*] She loves you—she suits you. And I don't know—I don't know why it is you seem, as it were, to avoid each other. I can't understand it!

LOPAHIN. I don't understand it myself, I con-fess. It's queer somehow, altogether. If there's still time, I'm ready now at once. Let's settle it straight off, and go ahead; but without you, I feel I shan't make her an offer.

LYUBOV. That's excellent. Why, a single moment's all that's necessary. I'll call her at once.

LOPAHIN. And there's champagne all ready too. [*Looking into the glasses.*] Empty! Some-one's emptied them already. [YASHA *coughs.*] I call that greedy.

LYUBOV [*eagerly*]. Capital! We will go out. Yasha, *allez!* I'll call her in. [*At the door.*] Varya, leave all that; come here. Come along!

[*Goes out with* YASHA.]

LOPAHIN [*looking at his watch*]. Yes.

[*A pause. Behind the door, smothered laughter and whispering, and, at last, enter* VARYA.]

VARYA [*looking a long while over the things*]. It is strange, I can't find it anywhere.

LOPAHIN. What are you looking for?

VARYA. I packed it myself, and I can't re-member. [*A pause.*]

LOPAHIN. Where are you going now, Varvara Mihailova?

VARYA. I? To the Ragulins. I have arranged to go to them to look after the house—as a housekeeper.

LOPAHIN. That's in Yashnovo? It'll be seventy miles away. [*A pause.*] So this is the end of life in this house!

VARYA [*looking among the things*]. Where is it? Perhaps I put it in the trunk. Yes, life in this house is over—there will be no more of it.

LOPAHIN. And I'm just off to Harkov—by this next train. I've a lot of business there. I'm leaving Epihodov here, and I've taken him on.

VARYA. Really!

LOPAHIN. This time last year we had snow already, if you remember; but now it's so fine and sunny. Though it's cold, to be sure—three degrees of frost.

VARYA. I haven't looked. [*A pause.*] And besides, our thermometer's broken. [*A pause.*]

[*Voice at the door from the yard:* "Yermolay Alexeyevitch!"]

LOPAHIN [*as though he had long been ex-pecting this summons*]. This minute!

[LOPAHIN *goes out quickly.* VARYA *sitting on the floor and laying her head on a bag full of*

clothes, sobs quietly. The door opens. Lyubov
Andreyevna *comes in cautiously.*]

Lyubov. Well? [*A pause.*] We must be going.

Varya [*has wiped her eyes and is no longer
crying*]. Yes, mamma, it's time to start. I shall
have time to get to the Ragulins today, if only
you're not late for the train.

Lyubov [*in the doorway*]. Anya, put your
things on.

[*Enter* Anya, *then* Gaev *and* Charlotta
Ivanovna. Gaev *has on a warm coat with a
hood. Servants and cabmen come in.* Epihodov
bustles about the luggage.]

Lyubov. Now we can start on our travels.

Anya [*joyfully*]. On our travels!

Gaev. My friends—my dear, my precious
friends! Leaving this house for ever, can I be
silent? Can I refrain from giving utterance at
leave-taking to those emotions which now flood
all my being?

Anya [*supplicatingly*]. Uncle!

Varya. Uncle, you mustn't!

Gaev [*dejectedly*]. Cannon and into the
pocket . . . I'll be quiet. . . .

[*Enter* Trofimov *and afterwards* Lopahin.]

Trofimov. Well, ladies and gentlemen, we
must start.

Lopahin. Epihodov, my coat!

Lyubov. I'll stay just one minute. It seems
as though I have never seen before what the
walls, what the ceilings in this house were
like, and now I look at them with greediness,
with such tender love.

Gaev. I remember when I was six years old
sitting in that window on Trinity Day watching my father going to church.

Lyubov. Have all the things been taken?

Lopahin. I think all. [*Putting on overcoat, to
Epihodov.*] You, Epihodov, mind you see everything is right.

Epihodov [*in a husky voice*]. Don't you
trouble, Yermolay Alexeyevitch.

Lopahin. Why, what's wrong with your
voice?

Epihodov. I've just had a drink of water, and
I choked over something.

Yasha [*contemptuously*]. The ignorance!

Lyubov. We are going—and not a soul will

be left here.

Lopahin. Not till the spring.

Varya [*pulls a parasol out of a bundle, as
though about to hit someone with it.* Lopahin
makes a gesture as though alarmed]. What is
it? I didn't mean anything.

Trofimov. Ladies and gentlemen, let us get
into the carriage. It's time. The train will be in
directly.

Varya. Petya, here they are, your goloshes,
by that box. [*With tears.*] And what dirty old
things they are!

Trofimov [*putting on his goloshes*]. Let us
go, friends!

Gaev [*greatly agitated, afraid of weeping*].
The train—the station! Double baulk, ah!

Lyubov. Let us go!

Lopahin. Are we all here? [*Locks the side-
door on left.*] The things are all here. We must
lock up. Let us go!

Anya. Good-bye, home! Good-bye to the
old life!

Trofimov. Welcome to the new life!

[Trofimov *goes out with* Anya. Varya *looks
round the room and goes out slowly.* Yasha
and Charlotta Ivanovna, *with her dog, go
out.*]

Lopahin. Till the spring, then! Come, friends,
till we meet!

[*Goes out.*]

[Lyubov Andreyevna *and* Gaev *remain
alone. As though they had been waiting for
this, they throw themselves on each other's
necks, and break into subdued smothered sobbing, afraid of being overheard.*]

Gaev [*in despair*]. Sister, my sister!

Lyubov. Oh, my orchard!—my sweet,
beautiful orchard! My life, my youth, my happiness, good-bye! good-bye!

Voice of Anya [*calling gaily*]. Mamma!

Voice of Trofimov [*gaily, excitedly*]. Aa—
oo!

Lyubov. One last look at the walls, at the
windows. My dear mother loved to walk about
this room.

Gaev. Sister, sister!

Voice of Anya. Mamma!

Voice of Trofimov. Aa—oo!

LYUBOV. We are coming.

[*They go out.*]

[*The stage is empty. There is the sound of the doors being locked up, then of the carriages*
5 *driving away. There is silence. In the stillness there is the dull stroke of an axe in a tree, clanging with a mournful lonely sound. Footsteps are heard.* FIRS *appears in the doorway on the right. He is dressed as always—in a pea-*
10 *jacket and white waistcoat, with slippers on his feet. He is ill.*]

FIRS [*goes up to the doors, and tries the handles*]. Locked! They have gone. . . . [*Sits down on sofa.*] They have forgotten me. . . .
15 Never mind . . . I'll sit here a bit. . . . I'll be bound Leonid Andreyevitch hasn't put his fur coat on and has gone off in his thin overcoat. [*Sighs anxiously.*] I didn't see after him. . . . These young people . . . [*mutters something*
20 *that can't be distinguished*]. Life has slipped by as though I hadn't lived. [*Lies down.*] I'll lie down a bit. . . . There's no strength in you, nothing left you—all gone! Ech! I'm good for nothing. [*Lies motionless.*]
25 [*A sound is heard that seems to come from the sky, like a breaking harp-string, dying away mournfully. All is still again, and there is heard nothing but the strokes of the axe far away in the orchard.*]

The Curtain Falls

John Millington Synge

1871–1909

Riders
to the Sea

1904

The story of *Riders to the Sea* is a mere moment in the lives of a few characters, but it holds within it the meaning of what they and millions like them have done and suffered. They have struggled for survival; they have gone down to defeat before the indifferent forces of wind and sea. Out of fatalism touched with faith and out of a supreme weariness, they resign themselves to defeat and in that resignation find release.

Synge captures this moment in the vivid dialect of the islanders. The images are sharp-edged and simple, held in the rise and fall of a speech as naturally cadenced as breathing. The rope is "on a nail by the white boards. I hung it up this morning, for the pig with the black feet was eating it." "There were two men . . . and they rowing round with poteen before the cocks crowed, and the oar of one of them caught the body, and they passing the black cliffs of the north." The images are held, too, in a larger, more complex rhythmic pattern. From start to finish the play is filled with its own echoes. We hear again and again of the pig, the boards, the pony until we begin to realize that such recurrence is itself an image of the lives portrayed—ever changing, ever the same. At the play's end Maurya lives over the deaths of her sons: "I was sitting here with Bartley, and he a baby, lying on my two knees, and I seen two women, and three women, and four women coming in, and they crossing themselves, and not saying a word . . . and there were men coming in after them, and they holding a thing in the half of a red sail." Then comes the stage direction: "She pauses again with her hand stretched out toward the door. It opens softly and old women begin to come in, crossing themselves." And later, "Then men carry in the body of Bartley, laid on a plank, with a bit of a sail over it." Present echoes past, past enters present in a moment that in the perfection of its presentation becomes an image of unchanging human experience.

JOHN MILLINGTON SYNGE

Riders to the Sea

SYNGE

(

CHARACTERS

MAURYA   *an old woman*
BARTLEY   *her son*
CATHLEEN   *her daughter*
NORA   *a younger daughter*
MEN AND WOMEN

SCENE. *An Island off the West of Ireland.*

[*Cottage kitchen, with nets, oil-skins, spin-ning-wheel, some new boards standing by the wall, etc.* CATHLEEN, *a girl of about twenty,*
5   *finishes kneading cake, and puts it down in the pot-oven° by the fire; then wipes her hands, and begins to spin at the wheel.* NORA, *a young girl, puts her head in at the door.*]

NORA [*in a low voice*]. Where is she?
10   CATHLEEN. She's lying down, God help her, and may be sleeping, if she's able.

[NORA *comes in softly, and takes a bundle from under her shawl.*]

CATHLEEN [*spinning the wheel rapidly*]. What
15   is it you have?

NORA. The young priest is after bringing them. It's a shirt and a plain stocking were got off a drowned man in Donegal.

[CATHLEEN *stops her wheel with a sudden*
20   *movement, and leans out to listen.*]

NORA. We're to find out if it's Michael's they are, some time herself will be down looking by the sea.

CATHLEEN. How would they be Michael's,
25   Nora? How would he go the length of that way to the far north?

NORA. The young priest says he's known the like of it. "If it's Michael's they are," says he,

"you can tell herself he's got a clean burial by the grace of God, and if they're not his, let no   30
one say a word about them, for she'll be get-ting her death," says he, "with crying and lamenting."

[*The door which* NORA *half closed is blown open by a gust of wind.*]   35

CATHLEEN [*looking out anxiously*]. Did you ask him would he stop Bartley going this day with the horses to the Galway fair?

NORA. "I won't stop him," says he, "but let you not be afraid. Herself does be saying   40
prayers half through the night, and the Al-mighty God won't leave her destitute," says he, "with no son living."

CATHLEEN. Is the sea bad by the white rocks, Nora?   45

NORA. Middling bad, God help us. There's a great roaring in the west, and it's worse it'll be getting when the tide's turned to the wind. [*She goes over to the table with the bundle.*] Shall I open it now?   50

CATHLEEN. Maybe she'd wake up on us, and come in before we'd done. [*Coming to the table.*] It's a long time we'll be, and the two of us crying.

NORA [*goes to the inner door and listens*].   55
She's moving about on the bed. She'll be com-ing in a minute.

CATHLEEN. Give me the ladder, and I'll put them up in the turf-loft, the way° she won't know of them at all, and maybe when the tide   60
turns she'll be going down to see would he be floating from the east.

[*They put the ladder against the gable of the chimney;* CATHLEEN *goes up a few steps and hides the bundle in the turf-loft.* MAURYA *comes*   65
from the inner room.]

MAURYA [*looking up at* CATHLEEN *and speak-ing querulously*]. Isn't it turf enough you have for this day and evening?

CATHLEEN. There's a cake baking at the fire   70
for a short space [*throwing down the turf*] and Bartley will want it when the tide turns if he goes to Connemara.

[NORA *picks up the turf and puts it round the pot-oven.*]   75

---

pot-oven heated iron plate covered by a pot

the way so that

MAURYA [*sitting down on a stool at the fire*]. He won't go this day with the wind rising from the south and west. He won't go this day, for the young priest will stop him surely.

5 NORA. He'll not stop him, mother, and I heard Eamon Simon and Stephen Pheety and Colum Shawn saying he would go.

MAURYA. Where is he itself?

NORA. He went down to see would there be 10 another boat sailing in the week, and I'm thinking it won't be long till he's here now, for the tide's turning at the green head,° and the hooker's tacking from the east.

CATHLEEN. I hear some one passing the big 15 stones.

NORA [*looking out*]. He's coming now, and he in a hurry.

BARTLEY [*comes in and looks round the room. Speaking sadly and quietly*]. Where is the bit 20 of new rope, Cathleen, was bought in Connemara?

CATHLEEN [*coming down*]. Give it to him, Nora; it's on a nail by the white boards. I hung it up this morning, for the pig with the black 25 feet was eating it.

NORA [*giving him a rope*]. Is that it, Bartley?

MAURYA. You'd do right to leave that rope, Bartley, hanging by the board. [BARTLEY *takes the rope.*] It will be wanting in this place, I'm 30 telling you, if Michael is washed up to-morrow morning, or the next morning, or any morning in the week, for it's a deep grave we'll make him by the grace of God.

BARTLEY [*beginning to work with the rope*]. 35 I've no halter the way I can ride down on the mare, and I must go now quickly. This is the one boat going for two weeks or beyond it, and the fair will be a good fair for horses I heard them saying below.

40 MAURYA. It's a hard thing they'll be saying below if the body is washed up and there's no man in it° to make the coffin, and I after giving a big price for the finest white boards you'd find in Connemara. [*She looks round at the* 45 *boards.*]

BARTLEY. How would it be washed up, and

we after looking each day for nine days, and a strong wind blowing a while back from the west and south?

50 MAURYA. If it wasn't found itself, that wind is raising the sea, and there was a star up against the moon, and it rising in the night. If it was a hundred horses, or a thousand horses you had itself, what is the price of a thousand 55 horses against a son where there is one son only?

BARTLEY [*working at the halter, to* CATHLEEN]. Let you go down each day, and see the sheep aren't jumping in on the rye, and if the 60 jobber comes you can sell the pig with the black feet if there is a good price going.

MAURYA. How would the like of her get a good price for a pig?

BARTLEY [*to* CATHLEEN]. If the west wind 65 holds with the last bit of the moon let you and Nora get up weed enough for another cock for the kelp.° It's hard set° we'll be from this day with no one in it but one man to work.

MAURYA. It's hard set we'll be surely the 70 day you're drownd'd with the rest. What way will I live and the girls with me, and I an old woman looking for the grave?

[BARTLEY *lays down the halter, takes off his old coat, and puts on a newer one of the same* 75 *flannel.*]

BARTLEY [*to* NORA]. Is she coming to the pier?

NORA [*looking out*]. She's passing the green head and letting fall her sails.

80 BARTLEY [*getting his purse and tobacco*]. I'll have half an hour to go down, and you'll see me coming again in two days, or in three days, or maybe in four if the wind is bad.

MAURYA [*turning round to the fire, and put-* 85 *ing her shawl over her head*]. Isn't it a hard and cruel man won't hear a word from an old woman, and she holding him from the sea?

CATHLEEN. It's the life of a young man to be going on the sea, and who would listen to an 90 old woman with one thing and she saying it over?

---

head headland, promontory
in it there

kelp ash of various seaweeds, used as a source for iodine. Bartley's request means: get seaweed enough to make another pile to be burned to ash.
set put to it

BARTLEY [*taking the halter*]. I must go now quickly. I'll ride down on the red mare, and the gray pony'll run behind me. . . . The blessing of God on you.

5 [*He goes out.*]

MAURYA [*crying out as he is in the door*]. He's gone now, God spare us, and we'll not see him again. He's gone now, and when the black night is falling I'll have no son left in the 10 world.

CATHLEEN. Why wouldn't you give him your blessing and he looking round in the door? Isn't it sorrow enough is on every one in this house without your sending him out with an 15 unlucky word behind him, and a hard word in his ear?

[MAURYA *takes up the tongs and begins raking the fire aimlessly without looking round.*]

20 NORA [*turning towards her*]. You're taking away the turf from the cake.

CATHLEEN [*crying out*]. The Son of God forgive us, Nora, we're after forgetting his bit of bread.

25 [*She comes over to the fire.*]

NORA. And it's destroyed he'll be going till dark night, and he after eating nothing since the sun went up.

CATHLEEN [*turning the cake out of the oven*]. 30 It's destroyed he'll be, surely. There's no sense left on any person in a house where an old woman will be talking for ever.

[MAURYA *sways on her stool.*]

CATHLEEN [*cutting off some of the bread and* 35 *rolling it in a cloth; to* MAURYA]. Let you go down now to the spring well and give him this and he passing. You'll see him then and the dark word will be broken, and you can say "God speed you," the way he'll be easy in his 40 mind.

MAURYA [*taking the bread*]. Will I be in it as soon as himself?

CATHLEEN. If you go now quickly.

MAURYA [*standing up unsteadily*]. It's hard 45 set I am to walk.

CATHLEEN [*looking at her anxiously*]. Give her the stick, Nora, or maybe she'll slip on the big stones.

NORA. What stick?

CATHLEEN. The stick Michael brought from 50 Connemara.

MAURYA [*taking a stick* NORA *gives her*]. In the big world the old people do be leaving things after them for their sons and children, but in this place it is the young men do be 55 leaving things behind for them that do be old.

[*She goes out slowly.* NORA *goes over to the ladder.*]

CATHLEEN. Wait, Nora, maybe she'd turn back quickly. She's that sorry,° God help her, 60 you wouldn't know the thing she'd do.

NORA. Is she gone round by the bush?

CATHLEEN [*looking out*]. She's gone now. Throw it down quickly, for the Lord knows when she'll be out of it again. 65

NORA [*getting the bundle from the loft*]. The young priest said he'd be passing to-morrow, and we might go down and speak to him below if it's Michael's they are surely.

CATHLEEN [*taking the bundle*]. Did he say 70 what way they were found?

NORA [*coming down*]. "There were two men," says he, "and they rowing round with poteen before the cocks crowed, and the oar of one of them caught the body, and they pass- 75 ing the black cliffs of the north."

CATHLEEN [*trying to open the bundle*]. Give me a knife, Nora, the string's perished° with the salt water, and there's a black knot on it you wouldn't loosen in a week. 80

NORA [*giving her a knife*]. I've heard tell it was a long way to Donegal.

CATHLEEN [*cutting the string*]. It is surely. There was a man in here a while ago—the man sold us that knife—and he said if you set off 85 walking from the rocks beyond, it would be seven days you'd be in Donegal.

NORA. And what time would a man take, and he floating?

[CATHLEEN *opens the bundle and takes out* 90 *a bit of stocking. They look at them eagerly.*]

CATHLEEN [*in a low voice*]. The Lord spare

---

sorry wretched
perished stiffened

us, Nora! isn't it a queer hard thing to say if it's his they are surely?

NORA. I'll get his shirt off the hook the way we can put the one flannel on the other. [*She looks through some clothes hanging in the corner*]. It's not with them, Cathleen, and where will it be?

CATHLEEN. I'm thinking Bartley put it on him in the morning, for his own shirt was heavy with the salt in it. [*Pointing to the corner.*] There's a bit of a sleeve was of the same stuff. Give me that and it will do.

[NORA *brings it to her and they compare the flannel.*]

CATHLEEN. It's the same stuff, Nora; but if it is itself aren't there great rolls of it in the shops of Galway, and isn't it many another man may have a shirt of it as well as Michael himself?

NORA [*who has taken up the stocking and counted the stitches, crying out*]. It's Michael, Cathleen, it's Michael; God spare his soul, and what will herself say when she hears this story, and Bartley on the sea?

CATHLEEN [*taking the stocking*]. It's a plain stocking.

NORA. It's the second one of the third pair I knitted, and I put up three score stitches, and I dropped four of them.

CATHLEEN [*counts the stitches*]. It's that number is in it. [*Crying out.*] Ah, Nora, isn't it a bitter thing to think of him floating that way to the far north, and no one to keen him but the black hags that do be flying on the sea?

NORA [*swinging herself round, and throwing out her arms on the clothes*]. And isn't it a pitiful thing when there is nothing left of a man who was a great rower and fisher, but a bit of an old shirt and a plain stocking?

CATHLEEN [*after an instant*]. Tell me is herself coming, Nora? I hear a little sound on the path.

NORA [*looking out*]. She is, Cathleen. She's coming up to the door.

CATHLEEN. Put these things away before she'll come in. Maybe it's easier she'll be after giving her blessing to Bartley, and we won't let on we've heard anything the time he's on the sea.

NORA [*helping* CATHLEEN *to close the bundle*]. We'll put them here in the corner.

[*They put them into a hole in the chimney corner.* CATHLEEN *goes back to the spinning-wheel.*]

NORA. Will she see it was crying I was?

CATHLEEN. Keep your back to the door the way the light'll not be on you.

[NORA *sits down at the chimney corner, with her back to the door.* MAURYA *comes in very slowly, without looking at the girls, and goes over to her stool at the other side of the fire. The cloth with the bread is still in her hand. The girls look at each other, and* NORA *points to the bundle of bread.*]

CATHLEEN [*after spinning for a moment*]. You didn't give him his bit of bread?

[MAURYA *begins to keen softly, without turning round.*]

CATHLEEN. Did you see him riding down?

[MAURYA *goes on keening.*]

CATHLEEN [*a little impatiently*]. God forgive you; isn't it a better thing to raise your voice and tell what you seen, than to be making lamentation for a thing that's done? Did you see Bartley, I'm saying to you.

MAURYA [*with a weak voice*]. My heart's broken from this day.

CATHLEEN [*as before*]. Did you see Bartley?

MAURYA. I seen the fearfulest thing.

CATHLEEN [*leaves her wheel and looks out*]. God forgive you; he's riding the mare now over the green head, and the gray pony behind him.

MAURYA [*starts, so that her shawl falls back from her head and shows her white tossed hair. With a frightened voice.*] The gray pony behind him.

CATHLEEN [*coming to the fire*]. What is it ails you, at all?

MAURYA [*speaking very slowly*]. I've seen the fearfulest thing any person has seen, since the day Bride Dara seen the dead man with the child in his arms.

CATHLEEN and NORA. Uah.

[*They crouch down in front of the old woman at the fire.*]

NORA. Tell us what it is you seen.

MAURYA. I went down to the spring well, and I stood there saying a prayer to myself. Then Bartley came along, and he riding on the red mare with the gray pony behind him. [*She puts up her hands, as if to hide something from her eyes.*] The Son of God spare us, Nora!

CATHLEEN. What is it you seen?

MAURYA. I seen Michael himself.

CATHLEEN [*speaking softly*]. You did not, mother; it wasn't Michael you seen, for his body is after being found in the far north, and he's got a clean burial by the grace of God.

MAURYA [*a little defiantly*]. I'm after seeing him this day, and he riding and galloping. Bartley came first on the red mare; and I tried to say "God speed you," but something choked the words in my throat. He went by quickly; and "the blessing of God on you," says he, and I could say nothing. I looked up then, and I crying, at the gray pony, and there was Michael upon it—with fine clothes on him, and new shoes on his feet.

CATHLEEN [*begins to keen*]. It's destroyed we are from this day. It's destroyed, surely.

NORA. Didn't the young priest say the Almighty God wouldn't leave her destitute with no son living?

MAURYA [*in a low voice, but clearly*]. It's little the like of him knows of the sea. . . . Bartley will be lost now, and let you call in Eamon and make me a good coffin out of the white boards, for I won't live after them. I've had a husband, and a husband's father, and six sons in this house—six fine men, though it was a hard birth I had with every one of them and they coming to the world—and some of them were found and some of them were not found, but they're gone now the lot of them. . . . There were Stephen, and Shawn, were lost in the great wind, and found after in the Bay of Gregory of the Golden Mouth, and carried up the two of them on the one plank, and in by that door.

[*She pauses for a moment, the girls start as if they heard something through the door that is half open behind them.*]

NORA [*in a whisper*]. Did you hear that, Cathleen? Did you hear a noise in the northeast?

CATHLEEN [*in a whisper*]. There's some one after crying out by the seashore.

MAURYA [*continues without hearing anything*]. There was Sheamus and his father, and his own father again, were lost in a dark night, and not a stick or sign was seen of them when the sun went up. There was Patch after was drowned out of a curragh that turned over. I was sitting here with Bartley, and he a baby, lying on my two knees, and I seen two women, and three women, and four women coming in, and they crossing themselves, and not saying a word. I looked out then, and there were men coming after them, and they holding a thing in the half of a red sail, and water dripping out of it—it was a dry day, Nora—and leaving a track to the door.

[*She pauses again with her hand stretched out towards the door. It opens softly and old women begin to come in, crossing themselves on the threshold, and kneeling down in front of the stage with red petticoats over their heads.*]

MAURYA [*half in a dream, to* CATHLEEN]. Is it Patch, or Michael, or what is it at all?

CATHLEEN. Michael is after being found in the far north, and when he is found there how could he be here in this place?

MAURYA. There does be a power of young men floating round in the sea, and what way would they know if it was Michael they had, or another man like him, for when a man is nine days in the sea, and the wind blowing, it's hard set his own mother would be to say what man was it.

CATHLEEN. It's Michael, God spare him, for they're after sending us a bit of his clothes from the far north.

[*She reaches out and hands* MAURYA *the clothes that belonged to Michael.* MAURYA *stands up slowly and takes them in her hands.* NORA *looks out.*]

NORA. They're carrying a thing among them and there's water dripping out of it and leaving a track by the big stones.

CATHLEEN [*in a whisper to the women who have come in*]. Is it Bartley it is?

ONE OF THE WOMEN. It is surely, God rest his soul.

[*Two younger women come in and pull out the table. Then men carry in the body of Bartley, laid on a plank, with a bit of a sail over it, and lay it on the table.*]

CATHLEEN [*to the women, as they are doing so*]. What way was he drowned?

ONE OF THE WOMEN. The gray pony knocked him into the sea, and he was washed out where there is a great surf on the white rocks.

[MAURYA *has gone over and knelt down at the head of the table. The women are keening softly and swaying themselves with a slow movement.* CATHLEEN *and* NORA *kneel at the other end of the table. The men kneel near the door.*]

MAURYA [*raising her head and speaking as if she did not see the people around her*]. They're all gone now, and there isn't anything more the sea can do to me. . . . I'll have no call now to be up crying and praying when the wind breaks from the south, and you can hear the surf is in the east, and the surf is in the west, making a great stir with the two noises, and they hitting one on the other. I'll have no call now to be going down and getting Holy Water in the dark nights after Samhain,° and I won't care what way the sea is when the other women will be keening. [*To* NORA.] Give me the Holy Water, Nora, there's a small sup still on the dresser.

[NORA *gives it to her.*]

MAURYA [*drops Michael's clothes across Bartley's feet, and sprinkles the Holy Water over him*]. It isn't that I haven't prayed for you, Bartley, to the Almighty God. It isn't that I haven't said prayers in the dark night till you wouldn't know what I'd be saying; but it's a great rest I'll have now, and it's time surely. It's a great rest I'll have now, and great sleeping in the long nights after Samhain, if it's only a bit of wet flour we do have to eat, and maybe a fish that would be stinking.

[*She kneels down again, crossing herself, and saying prayers under her breath.*]

CATHLEEN [*to an old man*]. Maybe yourself and Eamon would make a coffin when the sun

rises. We have fine white boards herself bought, God help her, thinking Michael would be found, and I have a new cake you can eat while you'll be working.

THE OLD MAN [*looking at the boards*]. Are there nails with them?

CATHLEEN. There are not, Colum; we didn't think of the nails.

ANOTHER MAN. It's a great wonder she wouldn't think of the nails, and all the coffins she's seen made already.

CATHLEEN. It's getting old she is, and broken.

[MAURYA *stands up again very slowly and spreads out the pieces of Michael's clothes beside the body, sprinkling them with the last of the Holy Water.*]

NORA [*in a whisper to* CATHLEEN.] She's quiet now and easy; but the day Michael was drowned you could hear her crying out from this to the spring well. It's fonder she was of Michael, and would any one have thought that?

CATHLEEN [*slowly and clearly*]. An old woman will be soon tired with anything she will do, and isn't it nine days herself is after crying and keening, and making great sorrow in the house?

MAURYA [*puts the empty cup mouth downwards on the table, and lays her hands together on Bartley's feet*]. They're all together this time, and the end is come. May the Almighty God have mercy on Bartley's soul, and on Michael's soul, and on the souls of Sheamus and Patch, and Stephen and Shawn; [*bending her head*] and may He have mercy on my soul, Nora, and on the soul of every one is left living in the world.

[*She pauses, and the keen rises a little more loudly from the women, then sinks away.*]

MAURYA [*continuing*]. Michael has a clean burial in the far north, by the grace of the Almighty God. Bartley will have a fine coffin out of the white boards, and a deep grave surely. What more can we want than that? No man at all can be living for ever, and we must be satisfied.

[*She kneels down again and the curtain falls slowly.*]

° **Samhain** November 1, the beginning of the Celtic winter half year.

Luigi Pirandello

1867–1936

Six Characters in Search of an Author

1921

As Pirandello's title indicates, one should check his accustomed expectations with his coat before he enters the theater. The play is about *characters,* which are not the same as *actors,* although actors play them, and not the same as *people,* although they bleed when pricked, laugh when tickled, and die—after a fashion—when drowned or shot.

The ostensive topic of the play, then, is the theater. Its world is the boards, lights, and props; the actors, managers, and prompters; the books, plots, and characters. And its integrating motive is, as the critic Francis Fergusson says, " 'to take the stage'—with all that this suggestive phrase implies." In Fergusson's apt summary, "The real actors and the director want to take it for the realistic purposes—vain or (with the box-office in mind) venal—of their rehearsal. Each of the characters wants to take it for the rationalized myth which is, or would be, his very being."

As the characters vie with the actors for the stage, the play brilliantly exploits the paradoxes implicit in its central metaphor. The astonished spectator is asked to consider competing approximations of reality: the immutable world of the dramatist's creation, the ordered but conventionalized world of the theater, and the evanescent and disordered world of his own personal experience. Is he himself more significantly alive than the perennial if stereotypical roles of an acting company? Or than the intensely realized and proverbially immortal figments of the artistic imaginations? What is truth? the play demands. And, having teased us with its paradoxes, it leaves the question unanswered.

Except for the Manager, who keeps bumping into these paradoxes—now manfully seeking to surmount them, now impatiently brushing them aside—the acting troupe is thinly drawn. The actors are shallow, vain, and pedestrian in their responses. Yet they occupy the stage from

LUIGI PIRANDELLO

first to last, along with the characters, and serve a multitude of functions. They support the Manager's skeptical and pragmatic opinion, urging him toward a popular and commonsense point of view. With him they provide moments of amusement, raising their noses at the characters, indulging in fits of jealousy, and themselves becoming, for splendid moments, the butt of the Father's and the Step-Daughter's laughter. More significantly, as they seek to render the drama before them banal and conventional, they both intensify its horror and lend it esthetic distance, setting it off for our own clearer vision.

The horror we experience derives immediately from the deeds and interrelations of the six characters: the stillbirth of the original marriage, the revolting intimacy of Father and Step-Daughter in the bordello, the emotional incapacitation of the Son, the agony of the Mother unable to commune with him, and the deaths of the little children by drowning and suicide. These are nevertheless only the stuff of melodrama. Our emotion goes deeper than that.

The characters are trapped by self-isolation. Whatever they say to one another, they are unable to escape from or mitigate the egocentricity that each brings to the common doom. The Father may express his sentiments for the Mother, but he cannot influence her feelings. The son may be told again and again how he is destroying Mother and children, but he cannot desist. Each is locked in the prison of self—fulfilling thereby one theological and literary definition of damnation.

They are really not in this world but in a kind of hell. In the world of our personal experience, the shames and agonies yield little by little to the ministry of time. We simply forget. Or, by reliving our failures and embarrassments in dreams and memories and conversations, we wear them down. It is not so for these characters. For them there is no rest from pain, because they are *characters*. For them, to die is not to sleep, because they are immortal: death is only a point on the circumference of an endless circle; the final gunshot only presages recurrences of the same agony. Furthermore, the characters are forever self-conscious. In every moment until the end of time they will rationalize their dilemmas, extenuate their faults, and struggle to shift from their shoulders the burden of shame. They will never know where they really stand. For all of them—as also, ultimately, for the Manager and the actors— the quality and texture and even the actuality of their existence will always be evasive. The only constants are that each will remain alone and that each will suffer.

Six Characters so blends its grimness, its banality, and its philosophical play that to focus on any one at the expense of the others is to miss the richness of Pirandello's evocation. But there is a question of how, ideally, one ought to respond to the ambivalence of this theater piece. Pirandello himself ultimately chose to stand apart from his characters rather than with them. More the contemplative spectator than the empathic witness, closer to Shaw than to Ibsen, he somewhat curiously subtitled his play "A *Comedy* in the Making" (italics added).

Six Characters in Search of an Author

A Comedy in the Making   (

PIRANDELLO

CHARACTERS OF THE COMEDY IN THE MAKING

THE FATHER
THE MOTHER
THE STEP-DAUGHTER
THE SON
THE BOY
THE CHILD
(The last two do not speak)
MADAME PACE

ACTORS OF THE COMPANY

THE MANAGER
LEADING LADY
LEADING MAN
SECOND LADY LEAD
L'INGÉNUE
JUVENILE LEAD
OTHER ACTORS AND ACTRESSES
PROPERTY MAN
PROMPTER
MACHINIST
MANAGER'S SECRETARY
DOOR-KEEPER

From the book Naked Masks *by Luigi Pirandello. Edited by Eric Bentley. Copyright, 1922, 1952 by E. P. Dutton & Co., Inc. Renewal, 1950 in the names of Stefano, Fausto, and Lietta Pirandello and 1978 by Eric Bentley. Reprinted by permission of the publisher, E. P. Dutton, a division of New American Library.*

SCENE-SHIFTERS
STAGE HANDS

Daytime. The Stage of a Theatre

N.B. *The Comedy is without acts or scenes. The performance is interrupted once, without the curtain being lowered, when the manager and the chief characters withdraw to arrange* 5 *the scenario. A second interruption of the action takes place when, by mistake, the stage hands let the curtain down.*

ACT I

[*The spectators will find the curtain raised and the stage as it usually is during the day* 10 *time. It will be half dark, and empty, so that from the beginning the public may have the impression of an impromptu performance.*

Prompter's box and a small table and chair for the MANAGER. 15

Two other small tables and several chairs scattered about as during rehearsals.

The ACTORS *and* ACTRESSES *of the company enter from the back of the stage: first one, then another, then two together; nine* 20 *or ten in all. They are about to rehearse a Pirandello play: "Mixing It Up". Some of the company move off towards their dressing rooms. The* PROMPTER *who has the "book" under his arm, is waiting for the* MANAGER *in* 25 *order to begin the rehearsal.*

The ACTORS *and* ACTRESSES, *some standing, some sitting, chat and smoke. One perhaps reads a paper; another cons his part.*

Finally, the MANAGER *enters and goes to the* 30 *table prepared for him. His* SECRETARY *brings him his mail, through which he glances. The* PROMPTER *takes his seat, turns on a light, and opens the "book."*]

THE MANAGER [*throwing a letter down on* 35 *the table*]. I can't see. [*To* PROPERTY MAN.] Let's have a little light, please!

PROPERTY MAN. Yes sir, yes, at once. [*A light comes down on to the stage.*]

THE MANAGER [*clapping his hands*]. Come 40 along! Come along! Second act of "Mixing It Up." [*Sits down.*]

[*The* ACTORS *and* ACTRESSES *go from the front of the stage to the wings, all except the three who are to begin the rehearsal.*]

THE PROMPTER [*reading the "book"*]. "Leo
5 Gala's house. A curious room serving as dining-room and study."

THE MANAGER [*to* PROPERTY MAN]. Fix up the old red room.

PROPERTY MAN [*noting it down*]. Red set.
10 All right!

THE PROMPTER [*continuing to read from the "book"*]. "Table already laid and writing desk with books and papers. Book-shelves. Exit rear to Leo's bedroom. Exit left to kitchen. Principal
15 exit to right."

THE MANAGER [*energetically*]. Well, you understand: The principal exit over there; here, the kitchen. [*Turning to* ACTOR *who is to play the part of* SOCRATES.] You make your en-
20 trances and exits here. [*To* PROPERTY MAN.] The baize doors at the rear, and curtains.

PROPERTY MAN [*noting it down*]. Right!

PROMPTER [*reading as before*]. "When the curtain rises, Leo Gala, dressed in cook's cap
25 and apron is busy beating an egg in a cup. Philip, also dressed as a cook, is beating another egg. Guido Venanzi is seated and listening."

LEADING MAN [*to* MANAGER]. Excuse me,
30 but must I absolutely wear a cook's cap?

THE MANAGER [*annoyed*]. I imagine so. It says so there anyway. [*Pointing to the "book."*]

LEADING MAN. But it's ridiculous!

35 THE MANAGER [*jumping up in a rage*]. Ridiculous? Ridiculous? Is it my fault if France won't send us any more good comedies, and we are reduced to putting on Pirandello's works, where nobody understands anything,
40 and where the author plays the fool with us all? [*The* ACTORS *grin. The* MANAGER *goes to* LEADING MAN *and shouts.*] Yes sir, you put on the cook's cap and beat eggs. Do you suppose that with all this egg-beating business you are
45 on an ordinary stage? Get that out of your head. You represent the shell of the eggs you are beating! [*Laughter and comments among*

the ACTORS.] Silence! and listen to my explanations, please! [*To* LEADING MAN.] "The empty form of reason without the fullness of 50 instinct, which is blind."—You stand for reason, your wife is instinct. It's a mixing up of the parts, according to which you who act your own part become the puppet of yourself. Do you understand? 55

LEADING MAN. I'm hanged if I do.

THE MANAGER. Neither do I. But let's get on with it. It's sure to be a glorious failure anyway. [*Confidentially.*] But I say, please face three-quarters. Otherwise, what with the 60 abstruseness of the dialogue, and the public that won't be able to hear you, the whole thing will go to hell. Come on! come on!

PROMPTER. Pardon sir, may I get into my box? There's a bit of a draft. 65

THE MANAGER. Yes, yes, of course!

[*At this point, the* DOOR-KEEPER *has entered from the stage door and advances towards the* MANAGER'S *table, taking off his braided cap. During this maneuver, the* SIX CHARACTERS 70 *enter, and stop by the door at back of stage, so that when the* DOOR-KEEPER *is about to announce their coming to the* MANAGER, *they are already on the stage. A tenuous light surrounds them, almost as if irradiated by them* 75 *—the faint breath of their fantastic reality.*

This light will disappear when they come forward towards the actors. They preserve, however, something of the dream lightness in which they seem almost suspended; but this 80 *does not detract from the essential reality of their forms and expressions.*

He who is known as the FATHER *is a man of about 50: hair, reddish in color, thin at the temples; he is not bald, however; thick* 85 *moustaches, falling over his still fresh mouth, which often opens in an empty and uncertain smile. He is fattish, pale; with an especially wide forehead. He has blue, oval-shaped eyes, very clear and piercing. Wears light trousers* 90 *and a dark jacket. He is alternatively mellifluous and violent in his manner.*

The MOTHER *seems crushed and terrified as if by an intolerable weight of shame and abasement. She is dressed in modest black and wears a thick widow's veil of crêpe. When she lifts this, she reveals a wax-like face. She always keeps her eyes downcast.*

The STEP-DAUGHTER is dashing, almost impudent, beautiful. She wears mourning too, but with great elegance. She shows contempt for the timid half-frightened manner of the wretched BOY (14 years old, and also dressed in black); on the other hand, she displays a lively tenderness for her little sister, the CHILD (about four), who is dressed in white, with a black silk sash at the waist.

The SON (22) tall, severe in his attitude of contempt for the FATHER, supercilious and indifferent to the MOTHER. He looks as if he had come on the stage against his will.]

DOOR-KEEPER [*cap in hand*]. Excuse me, sir . . .

THE MANAGER [*rudely*]. Eh? What is it?

DOOR-KEEPER [*timidly*]. These people are asking for you, sir.

THE MANAGER [*furious*]. I am rehearsing, and you know perfectly well no one's allowed to come in during rehearsals! [*Turning to the* CHARACTERS.] Who are you, please? What do you want?

THE FATHER [*coming forward a little, followed by the others who seem embarrassed*]. As a matter of fact . . . we have come here in search of an author . . .

THE MANAGER [*half angry, half amazed*]. An author? What author?

THE FATHER. Any author, sir.

THE MANAGER. But there's no author here. We are not rehearsing a new piece.

THE STEP-DAUGHTER [*vivaciously*]. So much the better, so much the better! We can be your new piece.

AN ACTOR [*coming forward from the others*]. Oh, do you hear that?

THE FATHER [*to* STEP-DAUGHTER]. Yes, but if the author isn't here . . . [*to* MANAGER] unless you would be willing . . .

THE MANAGER. You are trying to be funny.

THE FATHER. No, for Heaven's sake, what are you saying? We bring you a drama, sir.

THE STEP-DAUGHTER. We may be your fortune.

THE MANAGER. Will you oblige me by going away? We haven't time to waste with mad people.

THE FATHER [*mellifluously*]. Oh sir, you know well that life is full of infinite absurdities, which, strangely enough, do not even need to appear plausible, since they are true.

THE MANAGER. What the devil is he talking about?

THE FATHER. I say that to reverse the ordinary process may well be considered a madness: that is, to create credible situations, in order that they may appear true. But permit me to observe that if this be madness, it is the sole *raison d'être* of your profession, gentlemen. [*The* ACTORS *look hurt and perplexed.*]

THE MANAGER [*getting up and looking at him*]. So our profession seems to you one worthy of madmen then?

THE FATHER. Well, to make seem true that which isn't true . . . without any need . . . for a joke as it were. . . . Isn't that your mission, gentlemen: to give life to fantastic characters on the stage?

THE MANAGER [*interpreting the rising anger of the* COMPANY]. But I would beg you to believe, my dear sir, that the profession of the comedian is a noble one. If today, as things go, the playwrights give us stupid comedies to play and puppets to represent instead of men, remember we are proud to have given life to immortal works here on these very boards! [*The* ACTORS, *satisfied, applaud their* MANAGER.]

THE FATHER [*interrupting furiously*]. Exactly, perfectly, to living beings more alive than those who breathe and wear clothes: beings less real perhaps, but truer! I agree with you entirely. [*The* ACTORS *look at one another in amazement.*]

THE MANAGER. But what do you mean? Before, you said . . .

THE FATHER. No, excuse me, I meant it for you, sir, who were crying out that you had no time to lose with madmen, while no one better than yourself knows that nature uses the instrument of human fantasy in order to pursue her creative purpose.

THE MANAGER. Very well,—but where does all this take us?

5 THE FATHER. Nowhere! It is merely to show you that one is born to life in many forms, in many shapes, as tree, or as stone, as water, as butterfly, or as woman. So one may also be born a character in a play.

10 THE MANAGER [*with feigned comic dismay*]. So you and these other friends of yours have been born characters?

THE FATHER. Exactly, and alive as you see! [MANAGER *and* ACTORS *burst out laughing.*]

15 THE FATHER [*hurt*]. I am sorry you laugh, because we carry in us a drama, as you can guess from this woman here veiled in black.

THE MANAGER [*losing patience at last and almost indignant*]. Oh, chuck it! Get away

20 please! Clear out of here! [*To* PROPERTY MAN.] For Heaven's sake, turn them out!

THE FATHER [*resisting*]. No, no, look here, we . . .

THE MANAGER [*roaring*]. We come here to

25 work, you know.

LEADING ACTOR. One cannot let oneself be made such a fool of.

THE FATHER [*determined, coming forward*]. I marvel at your incredulity, gentlemen. Are

30 you not accustomed to see the characters created by an author spring to life in yourselves and face each other? Just because there is no "book" [*pointing to the* PROMPTER'S *box*] which contains us, you refuse to believe . . .

35 THE STEP-DAUGHTER [*advances towards* MANAGER, *smiling and coquettish*]. Believe me, we are really six most interesting characters, sir; side-tracked however.

THE FATHER. Yes, that is the word! [*To*

40 MANAGER *all at once.*] In the sense, that is, that the author who created us alive no longer wished, or was no longer able, materially to put us into a work of art. And this was a real crime, sir; because he who has had the luck

45 to be born a character can laugh even at death. He cannot die. The man, the writer, the instrument of the creation will die, but his creation does not die. And to live for ever, it does not need to have extraordinary gifts or to be able to work wonders. Who was Sancho Panza? 50 Who was Don Abbondio?° Yet they live eternally because—live germs as they were— they had the fortune to find a fecundating matrix, a fantasy which could raise and nourish them: make them live for ever! 55

THE MANAGER. That is quite all right. But what do you want here, all of you?

THE FATHER. We want to live.

THE MANAGER [*ironically*]. For Eternity?

THE FATHER. No, sir, only for a moment . . . 60 in you.

AN ACTOR. Just listen to him!

LEADING LADY. They want to live, in us . . . !

JUVENILE LEAD [*pointing to the* STEP-DAUGHTER]. I've no objection, as far as that one is 65 concerned!

THE FATHER. Look here! look here! The comedy has to be made. [*To the* MANAGER.] But if you and your actors are willing, we can soon concert it among ourselves. 70

THE MANAGER [*annoyed*]. But what do you want to concert? We don't go in for concerts here. Here we play dramas and comedies!

THE FATHER. Exactly! That is just why we have come to you. 75

THE MANAGER. And where is the "book"?

THE FATHER. It is in us! [*The* ACTORS *laugh.*] The drama is in us, and we are the drama. We are impatient to play it. Our inner passion drives us on to this. 80

THE STEP-DAUGHTER [*disdainful, alluring, treacherous, full of impudence*]. My passion, sir! Ah, if you only knew! My passion for him! [*Points to the* FATHER *and makes a pretense of embracing him. Then she breaks out* 85 *into a loud laugh.*]

THE FATHER [*angrily*]. Behave yourself! And please don't laugh in that fashion.

THE STEP-DAUGHTER. With your permission, gentlemen, I, who am a two months' orphan, 90 will show you how I can dance and sing.

Don Abbondio the parish priest in Manzoni's *The Betrothed* (*I Promessi Sposi*, 1825-1826)

[*Sings and then dances* Prenez garde à Tchou-Tchin-Tchou.°]

Les chinois sont un peuple malin,
De Shangaî à Pekin,
5 Ils ont mis des écriteaux partout:
Prenez garde à Tchou-Tchin-Tchou.

ACTORS AND ACTRESSES. Bravo! Well done! Tip-top!

THE MANAGER. Silence! This isn't a café
10 concert, you know! [*Turning to the* FATHER *in consternation.*] Is she mad?

THE FATHER. Mad? No, she's worse than mad.

THE STEP-DAUGHTER [*to* MANAGER]. Worse?
15 Worse? Listen! Stage this drama for us at once! Then you will see that at a certain moment I . . . when this little darling here . . . [*takes the* CHILD *by the hand and leads her to the* MANAGER]. Isn't she a dear? [*Takes her up
20 and kisses her.*] Darling! Darling! [*Puts her down again and adds feelingly.*] Well, when God suddenly takes this dear little child away from that poor mother there; and this imbecile here [*seizing hold of the* BOY *roughly and push-
25 ing him forward*] does the stupidest things, like the fool he is, you will see me run away. Yes, gentlemen, I shall be off. But the moment hasn't arrived yet. After what has taken place between him and me [*indicates the* FATHER
30 *with a horrible wink*] I can't remain any longer in this society, to have to witness the anguish of this mother here for that fool . . . [*indicates the* SON]. Look at him! Look at him! See how indifferent, how frigid he is, because he is the
35 legitimate son. He despises me, despises him [*pointing to the* BOY], despises this baby here; because . . . we are bastards. [*Goes to the* MOTHER *and embraces her.*] And he doesn't

---

Prenez . . . Tchou-Tchin-Tchou "beware of Chu-Chin-Chow," a French version of "Chu-Chin-Chow," a lyric from the *Ziegfeld Follies of 1917* celebrating the current success on Broadway of the musical revue *Chu Chin Chow*, book by Oscar Asche, music by Frederic Norton. The first stanza of the French version follows: "The Chinese are a cunning folk, From Shanghai to Peking, They've put up posters everywhere: Beware of Chu-Chin Chow."

---

want to recognize her as his mother—she who
is the common mother of us all. He looks 40
down upon her as if she were only the mother
of us three bastards. Wretch! [*She says all
this very rapidly, excitedly. At the word
"bastards" she raises her voice, and almost
spits out the final "Wretch!"*] 45

THE MOTHER [*to the* MANAGER, *in anguish*].
In the name of these two little children, I beg
you . . . [*she grows faint and is about to fall*].
Oh God!

THE FATHER [*coming forward to support her* 50
as do some of the ACTORS]. Quick, a chair, a
chair for this poor widow!

THE ACTORS. Is it true? Has she really
fainted?

THE MANAGER. Quick, a chair! Here! 55

[*One of the* ACTORS *brings a chair, the
OTHERS proffer assistance. The* MOTHER *tries
to prevent the* FATHER *from lifting the veil
which covers her face.*]

THE FATHER. Look at her! Look at her! 60

THE MOTHER. No, no; stop it please!

THE FATHER [*raising her veil*]. Let them see
you!

THE MOTHER [*rising and covering her face
with her hands, in desperation*]. I beg you, sir, 65
to prevent this man from carrying out his plan
which is loathsome to me.

THE MANAGER [*dumbfounded*]. I don't understand at all. What is the situation? Is this
lady your wife? [*To the* FATHER.] 70

THE FATHER. Yes, gentlemen: my wife!

THE MANAGER. But how can she be a widow
if you are alive? [*The* ACTORS *find relief for
their astonishment in a loud laugh.*]

THE FATHER. Don't laugh! Don't laugh like 75
that, for Heaven's sake. Her drama lies just
here in this: she has had a lover, a man who
ought to be here.

THE MOTHER [*with a cry*]. No! No!

THE STEP-DAUGHTER. Fortunately for her, he 80
is dead. Two months ago as I said. We are
in mourning, as you see.

THE FATHER. He isn't here you see, not
because he is dead. He isn't here—look at her
a moment and you will understand—because 85

her drama isn't a drama of the love of two men for whom she was incapable of feeling anything except possibly a little gratitude—gratitude not for me but for the other. She isn't a
5 woman, she is a mother, and her drama—powerful sir, I assure you—lies, as a matter of fact, all in these four children she has had by two men.

THE MOTHER. I had them? Have you got the
10 courage to say that I wanted them? [*To the* COMPANY.] It was his doing. It was he who gave me that other man, who forced me to go away with him.

THE STEP-DAUGHTER. It isn't true.

15 THE MOTHER [*startled*]. Not true, isn't it?

THE STEP-DAUGHTER. No, it isn't true, it just isn't true.

THE MOTHER. And what can you know about it?

20 THE STEP-DAUGHTER. It isn't true. Don't believe it. [*To* MANAGER.] Do you know why she says so? For that fellow there. [*Indicates the* SON.] She tortures herself, destroys herself on account of the neglect of that son there;
25 and she wants him to believe that if she abandoned him when he was only two years old, it was because he [*indicates the* FATHER] made her do so.

THE MOTHER [*vigorously*]. He forced me to
30 it, and I call God to witness it. [*To the* MANAGER.] Ask him [*indicates* HUSBAND] if it isn't true. Let him speak. You [*to* DAUGHTER] are not in a position to know anything about it.

THE STEP-DAUGHTER. I know you lived in
35 peace and happiness with my father while he lived. Can you deny it?

THE MOTHER. No, I don't deny it . . .

THE STEP-DAUGHTER. He was always full of affection and kindness for you. [*To the* BOY,
40 *angrily*.] It's true, isn't it? Tell them! Why don't you speak, you little fool?

THE MOTHER. Leave the poor boy alone. Why do you want to make me appear ungrateful, daughter? I don't want to offend your father.
45 I have answered him that I didn't abandon my house and my son through any fault of mine, nor from any wilful passion.

THE FATHER. It is true. It was my doing.

LEADING MAN [*to the* COMPANY]. What a spectacle!
50
LEADING LADY. We are the audience this time.

JUVENILE LEAD. For once, in a way.

THE MANAGER [*beginning to get really interested*]. Let's hear them out. Listen!

THE SON. Oh yes, you're going to hear a
55 fine bit now. He will talk to you of the Demon of Experiment.

THE FATHER. You are a cynical imbecile. I've told you so already a hundred times. [*To the* MANAGER.] He tries to make fun of me on
60 account of this expression which I have found to excuse myself with.

THE SON [*with disgust*]. Yes, phrases! phrases!

THE FATHER. Phrases! Isn't everyone con-
65 soled when faced with a trouble or fact he doesn't understand, by a word, some simple word, which tells us nothing and yet calms us?

THE STEP-DAUGHTER. Even in the case of remorse. In fact, especially then.
70
THE FATHER. Remorse? No, that isn't true. I've done more than use words to quiet the remorse in me.

THE STEP-DAUGHTER. Yes, there was a bit of money too. Yes, yes, a bit of money. There
75 were the hundred lire he was about to offer me in payment, gentlemen . . .

[*Sensation of horror among the* ACTORS.]

THE SON [*to the* STEP-DAUGHTER]. This is vile.
80
THE STEP-DAUGHTER. Vile? There they were in a pale blue envelope on a little mahogany table in the back of Madame Pace's shop. You know Madame Pace—one of those ladies who attract poor girls of good family into their
85 ateliers, under the pretext of their selling *robes et manteaux*.°

THE SON. And he thinks he has bought the right to tyrannize over us all with those hundred lire he was going to pay; but which,
90 fortunately—note this, gentlemen—he had no chance of paying.

THE STEP-DAUGHTER. It was a near thing, though, you know! [*Laughs ironically*.]

robes et manteaux dresses and cloaks.

THE MOTHER [*protesting*]. Shame, my daughter, shame!

THE STEP-DAUGHTER. Shame indeed! This is my revenge! I am dying to live that scene . . .

5 The room . . . I see it . . . Here is the window with the mantles exposed, there the divan, the looking-glass, a screen, there in front of the window the little mahogany table with the blue envelope containing one hundred lire. I

10 see it. I see it. I could take hold of it . . . But you, gentlemen, you ought to turn your backs now: I am almost nude, you know. But I don't blush: I leave that to him. [*Indicating* FATHER.]

THE MANAGER. I don't understand this at all.

15 THE FATHER. Naturally enough. I would ask you, sir, to exercise your authority a little here, and let me speak before you believe all she is trying to blame me with. Let me explain.

THE STEP-DAUGHTER. Ah yes, explain it in

20 your own way.

THE FATHER. But don't you see that the whole trouble lies here. In words, words. Each one of us has within him a whole world of things, each man of us his own special world. And

25 how can we ever come to an understanding if I put in the words I utter the sense and value of things as I see them; while you who listen to me must inevitably translate them according to the conception of things each one of you

30 has within himself. We think we understand each other, but we never really do. Look here! This woman [*indicating the* MOTHER] takes all my pity for her as a specially ferocious form of cruelty.

35 THE MOTHER. But you drove me away.

THE FATHER. Do you hear her? I drove her away! She believes I really sent her away.

THE MOTHER. You know how to talk, and I don't; but, believe me, sir [*to* MANAGER], after

40 he had married me . . . who knows why? . . . I was a poor insignificant woman . . .

THE FATHER. But, good Heavens! it was just for your humility that I married you. I loved this simplicity in you. [*He stops when he sees*

45 *she makes signs to contradict him, opens his arms wide in sign of desperation, seeing how hopeless it is to make himself understood.*] You see she denies it. Her mental deafness,

believe me, is phenomenal, the limit: [*touches his forehead*] deaf, deaf, mentally deaf! She 50 has plenty of feeling. Oh yes, a good heart for the children; but the brain—deaf, to the point of desperation—!

THE STEP-DAUGHTER. Yes, but ask him how his intelligence has helped us. 55

THE FATHER. If we could see all the evil that may spring from good, what should we do? [*At this point the* LEADING LADY *who is biting her lips with rage at seeing the* LEADING MAN *flirting with the* STEP-DAUGHTER, *comes for-* 60 *ward and says to the* MANAGER:]

LEADING LADY. Excuse me, but are we going to rehearse today?

MANAGER. Of course, of course; but let's hear them out. 65

JUVENILE LEAD. This is something quite new.

L'INGÉNUE. Most interesting!

LEADING LADY. Yes, for the people who like that kind of thing. [*Casts a glance at* LEADING MAN.] 70

THE MANAGER [*to* FATHER]. You must please explain yourself quite clearly. [*Sits down.*]

THE FATHER. Very well then: listen! I had in my service a poor man, a clerk, a secretary of mine, full of devotion, who became friends 75 with her. [*Indicating the* MOTHER.] They understood one another, were kindred souls in fact, without, however, the least suspicion of any evil existing. They were incapable even of thinking of it. 80

THE STEP-DAUGHTER. So he thought of it— for them!

THE FATHER. That's not true. I meant to do good to them—and to myself, I confess, at the same time. Things had come to the point 85 that I could not say a word to either of them without their making a mute appeal, one to the other, with their eyes. I could see them silently asking each other how I was to be kept in countenance, how I was to be kept 90 quiet. And this, believe me, was just about enough of itself to keep me in a constant rage, to exasperate me beyond measure.

THE MANAGER. And why didn't you send him away then—this secretary of yours? 95

THE FATHER. Precisely what I did, sir. And

then I had to watch this poor woman drifting forlornly about the house like an animal without a master, like an animal one has taken in out of pity.

5 THE MOTHER. Ah yes . . . !

THE FATHER [*suddenly turning to the* MOTHER]. It's true about the son anyway, isn't it?

THE MOTHER. He took my son away from 10 me first of all.

THE FATHER. But not from cruelty. I did it so that he should grow up healthy and strong by living in the country.

THE STEP-DAUGHTER [*pointing to him iron-* 15 *ically*]. As one can see.

THE FATHER [*quickly*]. Is it my fault if he has grown up like this? I sent him to a wet nurse in the country, a peasant, as *she* did not seem to me strong enough, though she is of 20 humble origin. That was, anyway, the reason I married her. Unpleasant all this may be, but how can it be helped? My mistake possibly, but there we are! All my life I have had these confounded aspirations towards a certain moral 25 sanity. [*At this point the* STEP-DAUGHTER *bursts into a noisy laugh.*] Oh, stop it! Stop it! I can't stand it.

THE MANAGER. Yes, please stop it, for Heaven's sake.

30 THE STEP-DAUGHTER. But imagine moral sanity from him, if you please—the client of certain ateliers like that of Madame Pace!

THE FATHER. Fool! That is the proof that I am a man! This seeming contradiction, gentle-35 men, is the strongest proof that I stand here a live man before you. Why, it is just for this very incongruity in my nature that I have had to suffer what I have. I could not live by the side of that woman [*indicating the* MOTHER] 40 any longer; but not so much for the boredom she inspired me with as for the pity I felt for her.

THE MOTHER. And so he turned me out—

THE FATHER. —well provided for! Yes, I sent 45 her to that man, gentlemen . . . to let her go free of me.

THE MOTHER. And to free himself.

THE FATHER. Yes, I admit it. It was also a liberation for me. But great evil has come of it. I meant well when I did it; and I did it more 50 for her sake than mine. I swear it. [*Crosses his arms on his chest; then turns suddenly to the* MOTHER.] Did I ever lose sight of you until that other man carried you off to another town, like the angry fool he was? And on account 55 of my pure interest in you . . . my pure interest, I repeat, that had no base motive in it . . . I watched with the tenderest concern the new family that grew up around her. She can bear witness to this. [*Points to the* STEP-DAUGHTER.] 60

THE STEP-DAUGHTER. Oh yes, that's true enough. When I was a kiddie, so so high, you know, with plaits over my shoulders and knickers longer than my skirts, I used to see him waiting outside the school for me to come 65 out. He came to see how I was growing up.

THE FATHER. This is infamous, shameful!

THE STEP-DAUGHTER. No. Why?

THE FATHER. Infamous! infamous! [*Then excitedly to* MANAGER *explaining.*] After she 70 [*indicating* MOTHER] went away, my house seemed suddenly empty. She was my incubus, but she filled my house. I was like a dazed fly alone in the empty rooms. This boy here [*indicating the* SON] was educated away from 75 home, and when he came back, he seemed to me to be no more mine. With no mother to stand between him and me, he grew up entirely for himself, on his own, apart, with no tie of intellect or affection binding him to me. And 80 then—strange but true—I was driven, by curiosity at first and then by some tender sentiment, towards her family, which had come into being through my will. The thought of her began gradually to fill up the emptiness 85 I felt all around me. I wanted to know if she were happy in living out the simple daily duties of life. I wanted to think of her as fortunate and happy because far away from the complicated torments of my spirit. And so, 90 to have proof of this, I used to watch that child coming out of school.

THE STEP-DAUGHTER. Yes, yes. True. He used to follow me in the street and smiled at me, waved his hand, like this. I would look at him 95 with interest, wondering who he might be. I

told my mother, who guessed at once. [*The* MOTHER *agrees with a nod.*] Then she didn't want to send me to school for some days; and when I finally went back, there he was again
5 —looking so ridiculous—with a paper parcel in his hands. He came close to me, caressed me, and drew out a fine straw hat from the parcel, with a bouquet of flowers—all for me!

THE MANAGER. A bit discursive this, you
10 know!

THE SON [*contemptuously*]. Literature! Literature!

THE FATHER. Literature indeed! This is life, this is passion!

15 THE MANAGER. It may be, but it won't act.

THE FATHER. I agree. This is only the part leading up. I don't suggest this should be staged. She [*pointing to the* STEP-DAUGHTER], as you see, is no longer the flapper with plaits
20 down her back—.

THE STEP-DAUGHTER. —and the knickers showing below the skirt!

THE FATHER. The drama is coming now, sir; something new, complex, most interesting.

25 THE STEP-DAUGHTER. As soon as my father died . . .

THE FATHER. —there was absolute misery for them. They came back here, unknown to me. Through her stupidity! [*Pointing to the*
30 MOTHER.] It is true she can barely write her own name; but she could anyhow have got her daughter to write to me that they were in need . . .

THE MOTHER. And how was I to divine
35 all this sentiment in him?

THE FATHER. That is exactly your mistake, never to have guessed any of my sentiments.

THE MOTHER. After so many years apart, and all that had happened . . .

40 THE FATHER. Was it my fault if that fellow carried you away? It happened quite suddenly; for after he had obtained some job or other, I could find no trace of them; and so, not unnaturally, my interest in them dwindled. But
45 the drama culminated unforeseen and violent on their return, when I was impelled by my miserable flesh that still lives. . . . Ah! what misery, what wretchedness is that of the man who is alone and disdains debasing *liaisons!*
50 Not old enough to do without women, and not young enough to go and look for one without shame. Misery? It's worse than misery; it's a horror; for no woman can any longer give him love; and when a man feels this. . . .
55 One ought to do without, you say? Yes, yes, I know. Each of us when he appears before his fellows is clothed in a certain dignity. But every man knows what unconfessable things pass within the secrecy of his own heart. One
60 gives way to the temptation, only to rise from it again, afterwards, with a great eagerness to re-establish one's dignity, as if it were a tombstone to place on the grave of one's shame, and a monument to hide and sign the memory of
65 our weaknesses. Everybody's in the same case. Some folks haven't the courage to say certain things, that's all!

THE STEP-DAUGHTER. All appear to have the courage to do them though.

70 THE FATHER. Yes, but in secret. Therefore, you want more courage to say these things. Let a man but speak these things out, and folks at once label him a cynic. But it isn't true. He is like all the others, better indeed,
75 because he isn't afraid to reveal with the light of the intelligence the red shame of human bestiality on which most men close their eyes so as not to see it.

Woman—for example, look at her case! She
80 turns tantalizing inviting glances on you. You seize her. No sooner does she feel herself in your grasp than she closes her eyes. It is the sign of her mission, the sign by which she says to man: "Blind yourself, for I am blind."

85 THE STEP-DAUGHTER. Sometimes she can close them no more: when she no longer feels the need of hiding her shame to herself, but dry-eyed and dispassionately, sees only that of the man who has blinded himself without
90 love. Oh, all these intellectual complications make me sick, disgust me—all this philosophy that uncovers the beast in man, and then seeks to save him, excuse him . . . I can't stand it, sir. When a man seeks to "simplify" life
95 bestially, throwing aside every relic of humanity, every chaste aspiration, every pure feeling,

all sense of ideality, duty, modesty, shame . . .
then nothing is more revolting and nauseous
than a certain kind of remorse—crocodiles'
tears, that's what it is.

5 THE MANAGER. Let's come to the point. This
is only discussion.

THE FATHER. Very good, sir! But a fact is
like a sack which won't stand up when it is
empty. In order that it may stand up, one has
10 to put into it the reason and sentiment which
have caused it to exist. I couldn't possibly
know that after the death of that man, they
had decided to return here, that they were in
misery, and that she [pointing to the MOTHER]
15 had gone to work as a modiste, and at a shop
of the type of that of Madame Pace.

THE STEP-DAUGHTER. A real high-class
modiste, you must know, gentlemen. In appearance, she works for the leaders of the best
20 society; but she arranges matters so that these
elegant ladies serve her purpose . . . without
prejudice to other ladies who are . . . well . . .
only so so.

THE MOTHER. You will believe me, gentle-
25 men, that it never entered my mind that the
old hag offered me work because she had her
eye on my daughter.

THE STEP-DAUGHTER. Poor mamma! Do you
know, sir, what that woman did when I
30 brought her back the work my mother had
finished? She would point out to me that I
had torn one of my frocks, and she would give
it back to my mother to mend. It was I who
paid for it, always I; while this poor creature
35 here believed she was sacrificing herself for me
and these two children here, sitting up at night
sewing Madame Pace's robes.

THE MANAGER. And one day you met there
. . .

40 THE STEP-DAUGHTER. Him, him. Yes sir, an
old client. There's a scene for you to play!
Superb!

THE FATHER. She, the Mother arrived just
then . . .

45 THE STEP-DAUGHTER [treacherously]. Almost
in time!

THE FATHER [crying out]. No, in time! in

time! Fortunately I recognized her . . . in time.
And I took them back home with me to my
house. You can imagine now her position and 50
mine; she, as you see her; and I who cannot
look her in the face.

THE STEP-DAUGHTER. Absurd! How can I
possibly be expected—after that—to be a
modest young miss, a fit person to go with his 55
confounded aspirations for "a solid moral
sanity"?

THE FATHER. For the drama lies all in this—
in the conscience that I have, that each one of
us has. We believe this conscience to be a 60
single thing, but it is many-sided. There is one
for this person, and another for that. Diverse
consciences. So we have this illusion of being
one person for all, of having a personality that
is unique in all our acts. But it isn't true. We 65
perceive this when, tragically perhaps, in something we do, we are as it were, suspended,
caught up in the air on a kind of hook. Then
we perceive that all of us was not in that act,
and that it would be an atrocious injustice to 70
judge us by that action alone, as if all our
existence were summed up in that one deed.
Now do you understand the perfidy of this
girl? She surprised me in a place, where she
ought not to have known me, just as I could 75
not exist for her; and she now seeks to attach
to me a reality such as I could never suppose
I should have to assume for her in a shameful
and fleeting moment of my life. I feel this
above all else. And the drama, you will see, 80
acquires a tremendous value from this point.
Then there is the position of the others . . . his
. . . [indicating the SON].

THE SON [shrugging his shoulders scorn-
fully]. Leave me alone! I don't come into this. 85

THE FATHER. What? You don't come into
this?

THE SON. I've got nothing to do with it, and
don't want to have; because you know well
enough I wasn't made to be mixed up in all 90
this with the rest of you.

THE STEP-DAUGHTER. We are only vulgar
folk! He is the fine gentleman. You may have
noticed, Mr. Manager, that I fix him now and

again with a look of scorn while he lowers his eyes—for he knows the evil he has done me.

THE SON [*scarcely looking at her*]. I?

THE STEP-DAUGHTER. You! you! I owe my life on the streets to you. Did you or did you not deny us, with your behavior, I won't say the intimacy of home, but even that mere hospitality which makes guests feel at their ease? We were intruders who had come to disturb the kingdom of your legitimacy. I should like to have you witness, Mr. Manager, certain scenes between him and me. He says I have tyrannized over everyone. But it was just his behavior which made me insist on the reason for which I had come into the house,— this reason he calls "vile"—into his house, with my mother who is his mother too. And I came as mistress of the house.

THE SON. It's easy for them to put me always in the wrong. But imagine, gentlemen, the position of a son, whose fate it is to see arrive one day at his home a young woman of impudent bearing, a young woman who inquires for his father, with whom who knows what business she has. This young man has then to witness her return bolder than ever, accompanied by that child there. He is obliged to watch her treat his father in an equivocal and confidential manner. She asks money of him in a way that lets one suppose he must give it her, *must*, do you understand, because he has every obligation to do so.

THE FATHER. But I have, as a matter of fact, this obligation. I owe it to your mother.

THE SON. How should I know? When had I ever seen or heard of her? One day there arrive with her [*indicating* STEP-DAUGHTER] that lad and this baby here. I am told: "This is *your* mother too, you know." I divine from her manner [*indicating* STEP-DAUGHTER *again*] why it is they have come home. I had rather not say what I feel and think about it. I shouldn't even care to confess to myself. No action can therefore be hoped for from me in this affair. Believe me, Mr. Manager, I am an "unrealized" character, dramatically speaking; and I find myself not at all at ease in their company. Leave me out of it, I beg you.

THE FATHER. What? It is just because you are so that . . .

THE SON. How do you know what I am like? When did you ever bother your head about me?

THE FATHER. I admit it. I admit it. But isn't that a situation in itself? This aloofness of yours which is so cruel to me and to your mother, who returns home and sees you almost for the first time grown up, who doesn't recognize you but knows you are her son . . . [*pointing out the* MOTHER *to the* MANAGER]. See, she's crying!

THE STEP-DAUGHTER [*angrily, stamping her foot*]. Like a fool!

THE FATHER [*indicating* STEP-DAUGHTER]. She can't stand him you know. [*Then referring again to the* SON.] He says he doesn't come into the affair, whereas he is really the hinge of the whole action. Look at that lad who is always clinging to his mother, frightened and humiliated. It is on account of this fellow here. Possibly his situation is the most painful of all. He feels himself a stranger more than the others. The poor little chap feels mortified, humiliated at being brought into a home out of charity as it were. [*In confidence.*] He is the image of 'his father. Hardly talks at all. Humble and quiet.

THE MANAGER. Oh, we'll cut him out. You've no notion what a nuisance boys are on the stage . . .

THE FATHER. He disappears soon, you know. And the baby too. She is the first to vanish from the scene. The drama consists finally in this: when that mother re-enters my house, her family—born outside of it, and shall we say superimposed on the original—ends with the death of the little girl, the tragedy of the boy and the flight of the elder daughter. It cannot go on, because it is foreign to its surroundings. So after much torment, we three remain: I, the mother, that son. Then, owing to the disappearance of that extraneous family, we too find ourselves strange to one another. We find

we are living in an atmosphere of mortal desolation which is the revenge, as he [*indicating* Son] scornfully said of the Demon of Experiment, that unfortunately hides in me.
5 Thus, sir, you see when faith is lacking, it becomes impossible to create certain states of happiness, for we lack the necessary humility. Vaingloriously, we try to substitute ourselves for this faith, creating thus for the rest of the
10 world a reality which we believe after their fashion, while, actually, it doesn't exist. For each one of us has his own reality to be respected before God, even when it is harmful to one's very self.

15 THE MANAGER. There is something in what you say. I assure you all this interests me very much. I begin to think there's the stuff for a drama in all this, and not a bad drama either.

THE STEP-DAUGHTER [*coming forward*].
20 When you've got a character like me.

THE FATHER [*shutting her up, all excited to learn the decision of the* MANAGER]. You be quiet!

THE MANAGER [*reflecting, heedless of inter-*
25 *ruption*]. It's new . . . hem . . . yes . . .

THE FATHER. Absolutely new!

THE MANAGER. You've got a nerve though, I must say, to come here and fling it at me like this . . .

30 THE FATHER. You will understand, sir, born as we are for the stage . . .

THE MANAGER. Are you amateur actors then?

THE FATHER. No. I say born for the stage, because . . .

35 THE MANAGER. Oh, nonsense. You're an old hand, you know.

THE FATHER. No sir, no. We act that rôle for which we have been cast, that rôle which we are given in life. And in my own case, passion
40 itself, as usually happens, becomes a trifle theatrical when it is exalted.

THE MANAGER. Well, well, that will do. But you see, without an author . . . I could give you the address of an author if you like . . .

45 THE FATHER. No, no. Look here! You must be the author.

THE MANAGER. I? What are you talking about?

THE FATHER. Yes, you, you! Why not?

THE MANAGER. Because I have never been 50 an author: that's why.

THE FATHER. Then why not turn author now? Everybody does it. You don't want any special qualities. Your task is made much easier by the fact that we are all here alive before you . . . 55

THE MANAGER. It won't do.

THE FATHER. What? When you see us live our drama . . .

THE MANAGER. Yes, that's all right. But you want someone to write it. 60

THE FATHER. No, no. Someone to take it down, possibly, while we play it, scene by scene! It will be enough to sketch it out at first, and then try it over.

THE MANAGER. Well . . . I am almost tempted. 65 It's a bit of an idea. One might have a shot at it.

THE FATHER. Of course. You'll see what scenes will come out of it. I can give you one, at once . . . 70

THE MANAGER. By Jove, it tempts me. I'd like to have a go at it. Let's try it out. Come with me to my office. [*Turning to the* ACTORS.] You are at liberty for a bit, but don't step out of the theatre for long. In a quarter of an 75 hour, twenty minutes, all back here again! [*To the* FATHER.] We'll see what can be done. Who knows if we don't get something really extraordinary out of it?

THE FATHER. There's no doubt about it. They 80 [*indicating the* CHARACTERS] had better come with us too, hadn't they?

THE MANAGER. Yes, yes. Come on! come on! [*Moves away and then turning to the* ACTORS.] Be punctual, please! [MANAGER *and the* SIX 85 CHARACTERS *cross the stage and go off. The other* ACTORS *remain, looking at one another in astonishment.*]

LEADING MAN. Is he serious? What the devil does he want to do? 90

JUVENILE LEAD. This is rank madness.

THIRD ACTOR. Does he expect to knock up a drama in five minutes?

JUVENILE LEAD. Like the improvisers!

LEADING LADY. If he thinks I'm going to take 95 part in a joke like this . . .

JUVENILE LEAD. I'm out of it anyway.

FOURTH ACTOR. I should like to know who they are. [*Alludes to* CHARACTERS.]

THIRD ACTOR. What do you suppose? Madmen or rascals!

JUVENILE LEAD. And he takes them seriously!

L'INGÉNUE. Vanity! He fancies himself as an author now.

LEADING MAN. It's absolutely unheard of. If the stage has come to this . . . well I'm . . .

FIFTH ACTOR. It's rather a joke.

THIRD ACTOR. Well, we'll see what's going to happen next.

[*Thus talking, the* ACTORS *leave the stage; some going out by the little door at the back; others retiring to their dressing-rooms.*

The curtain remains up.

The action of the play is suspended for twenty minutes.]

ACT II

[*The stage call-bells ring to warn the company that the play is about to begin again.*

The STEP-DAUGHTER *comes out of the* MANAGER's *office along with the* CHILD *and the* BOY. *As she comes out of the office, she cries:*—

Nonsense! nonsense! Do it yourselves! I'm not going to mix myself up in this mess. [*Turning to the* CHILD *and coming quickly with her on to the stage.*] Come on, Rosetta, let's run!

[*The* BOY *follows them slowly, remaining a little behind and seeming perplexed.*]

THE STEP-DAUGHTER [*stops, bends over the* CHILD *and takes the latter's face between her hands*]. My little darling! You're frightened, aren't you? You don't know where we are, do you? [*Pretending to reply to a question of the* CHILD.] What is the stage? It's a place, baby, you know, where people play at being serious, a place where they act comedies. We've got to act a comedy now, dead serious, you know; and you're in it also, little one. [*Embraces her, pressing the little head to her breast, and rocking the* CHILD *for a moment.*] Oh darling, darling, what a horrid comedy you've got to play! What a wretched part they've found for you! A garden . . . a fountain . . . look . . . just suppose, kiddie, it's here. Where, you say? Why, right here in the middle. It's all pretense you know. That's the trouble, my pet: it's all make-believe here. It's better to imagine it though, because if they fix it up for you, it'll only be painted cardboard, painted cardboard for the rockery, the water, the plants. . . . Ah, but I think a baby like this one would sooner have a make-believe fountain than a real one, so she could play with it. What a joke it'll be for the others! But for you, alas! not quite such a joke: you who are real, baby dear, and really play by a real fountain that is big and green and beautiful, with ever so many bamboos around it that are reflected in the water, and a whole lot of little ducks swimming about. . . . No, Rosetta, no, your mother doesn't bother about you on account of that wretch of a son there. I'm in the devil of a temper, and as for that lad . . . [*seizes* BOY *by the arm to force him to take one of his hands out of his pockets*]. What have you got there? What are you hiding? [*Pulls his hand out of his pocket, looks into it and catches the glint of a revolver.*] Ah! where did you get this? [*The* BOY, *very pale in the face, looks at her, but does not answer.*] Idiot! If I'd been in your place, instead of killing myself, I'd have shot one of those two, or both of them: father and son.

[*The* FATHER *enters from the office, all excited from his work. The* MANAGER *follows him.*]

THE FATHER. Come on, come on dear! Come here for a minute! We've arranged everything. It's all fixed up.

THE MANAGER [*also excited*]. If you please, young lady, there are one or two points to settle still. Will you come along?

THE STEP-DAUGHTER [*following him towards the office*]. Ouff! what's the good, if you've arranged everything.

[*The* FATHER, MANAGER, *and* STEP-DAUGHTER *go back into the office again (off) for a moment. At the same time, the* SON *followed by the* MOTHER *comes out.*]

THE SON [*looking at the three entering office*]. Oh this is fine, fine! And to think I can't even get away!

[*The* MOTHER *attempts to look at him, but lowers her eyes immediately when he turns away from her. She then sits down. The* BOY *and the* CHILD *approach her. She casts a glance again at the* SON, *and speaks with humble tones, trying to draw him into conversation.*]

THE MOTHER. And isn't my punishment the worst of all? [*Then seeing from the* SON'S *manner that he will not bother himself about her.*] My God! Why are you so cruel? Isn't it enough for one person to support all this torment? Must you then insist on others seeing it also?

THE SON [*half to himself, meaning the* MOTHER *to hear, however*]. And they want to put it on the stage! If there was at least a reason for it! He thinks he has got at the meaning of it all. Just as if each one of us in every circumstance of life couldn't find his own explanation of it! [*Pauses.*] He complains he was discovered in a place where he ought not to have been seen, in a moment of his life which ought to have remained hidden and kept out of the reach of that convention which he has to maintain for other people. And what about my case? Haven't I had to reveal what no son ought ever to reveal: how father and mother live and are man and wife for themselves quite apart from that idea of father and mother which we give them? When this idea is revealed, our life is then linked at one point only to that man and that woman; and as such it should shame them, shouldn't it?

[*The* MOTHER *hides her face in her hands. From the dressing-rooms and the little door at the back of the stage the* ACTORS *and* STAGE MANAGER *return, followed by the* PROPERTY MAN, *and the* PROMPTER. *At the same moment, the* MANAGER *comes out of his office, accompanied by the* FATHER *and the* STEP-DAUGHTER.]

THE MANAGER. Come on, come on, ladies and gentlemen! Heh! you there, machinist!

MACHINIST. Yes sir?

THE MANAGER. Fix up the white parlor with the floral decorations. Two wings and a drop with a door will do. Hurry up!

[*The* MACHINIST *runs off at once to prepare the scene, and arranges it while the* MANAGER *talks with the* STAGE MANAGER, *the* PROPERTY MAN, *and the* PROMPTER *on matters of detail.*]

THE MANAGER [*to* PROPERTY MAN]. Just have a look, and see if there isn't a sofa or divan in the wardrobe . . .

PROPERTY MAN. There's the green one.

THE STEP-DAUGHTER. No no! Green won't do. It was yellow, ornamented with flowers—very large! and most comfortable!

PROPERTY MAN. There isn't one like that.

THE MANAGER. It doesn't matter. Use the one we've got.

THE STEP-DAUGHTER. Doesn't matter? It's most important!

THE MANAGER. We're only trying it now. Please don't interfere. [*To* PROPERTY MAN.] See if we've got a shop window—long and narrowish.

THE STEP-DAUGHTER. And the little table! The little mahogany table for the pale blue envelope!

PROPERTY MAN [*to* MANAGER]. There's that little gilt one.

THE MANAGER. That'll do fine.

THE FATHER. A mirror.

THE STEP-DAUGHTER. And the screen! We must have a screen. Otherwise how can I manage?

PROPERTY MAN. That's all right, Miss. We've got any amount of them.

THE MANAGER [*to the* STEP-DAUGHTER]. We want some clothes pegs too, don't we?

THE STEP-DAUGHTER. Yes, several, several!

THE MANAGER. See how many we've got and bring them all.

PROPERTY MAN. All right!

[*The* PROPERTY MAN *hurries off to obey his orders. While he is putting the things in their places, the* MANAGER *talks to the* PROMPTER *and then with the* CHARACTERS *and the* ACTORS.]

THE MANAGER [*to* PROMPTER]. Take your seat. Look here: this is the outline of the scenes, act by act. [*Hands him some sheets of paper.*] And now I'm going to ask you to do something out of the ordinary.

PROMPTER. Take it down in shorthand?

THE MANAGER [*pleasantly surprised*]. Exactly! Can you do shorthand?

PROMPTER. Yes, a little.

THE MANAGER. Good! [*Turning to a* STAGE HAND.] Go and get some paper from my office, plenty, as much as you can find.

[*The* STAGE HAND *goes off, and soon returns with a handful of paper which he gives to the* PROMPTER.]

THE MANAGER [*to* PROMPTER]. You follow the scenes as we play them, and try and get the points down, at any rate the most important ones. [*Then addressing the* ACTORS.] Clear the stage, ladies and gentlemen! Come over here [*pointing to the left*] and listen attentively.

LEADING LADY. But, excuse me, we . . .

THE MANAGER [*guessing her thought*]. Don't worry! You won't have to improvise.

LEADING MAN. What have we to do then?

THE MANAGER. Nothing. For the moment you just watch and listen. Everybody will get his part written out afterwards. At present we're going to try the thing as best we can. They're going to act now.

THE FATHER [*as if fallen from the clouds into the confusion of the stage*]. We? What do you mean, if you please, by a rehearsal?

THE MANAGER. A rehearsal for them. [*Points to the* ACTORS.]

THE FATHER. But since we are the characters . . .

THE MANAGER. All right: "characters" then, if you insist on calling yourselves such. But here, my dear sir, the characters don't act. Here the actors do the acting. The characters are there, in the "book" [*pointing towards* PROMPTER's *box*]—when there is a "book"!

THE FATHER. I won't contradict you; but excuse me, the actors aren't the characters. They want to be, they pretend to be, don't they? Now if these gentlemen here are fortunate enough to have us alive before them . . .

THE MANAGER. Oh this is grand! You want to come before the public yourselves then?

THE FATHER. As we are . . .

THE MANAGER. I can assure you it would be a magnificent spectacle!

LEADING MAN. What's the use of us here anyway then?

THE MANAGER. You're not going to pretend that you can act? It makes me laugh! [*The* ACTORS *laugh*.] There, you see, they are laughing at the notion. But, by the way, I must cast the parts. That won't be difficult. They cast themselves. [*To the* SECOND LADY LEAD.] You play the Mother. [*To the* FATHER.] We must find her a name.

THE FATHER. Amalia, sir.

THE MANAGER. But that is the real name of your wife. We don't want to call her by her real name.

THE FATHER. Why ever not, if it is her name? . . . Still, perhaps, if that lady must . . . [*makes a slight motion of the hand to indicate the* SECOND LADY LEAD]. I see this woman here [*means the* MOTHER] as Amalia. But do as you like. [*Gets more and more confused.*] I don't know what to say to you. Already, I begin to hear my own words ring false, as if they had another sound . . .

THE MANAGER. Don't you worry about it. It'll be our job to find the right tones. And as for her name, if you want her Amalia, Amalia it shall be; and if you don't like it, we'll find another! For the moment though, we'll call the characters in this way: [*To* JUVENILE LEAD.] You are the Son. [*To the* LEADING LADY.] You naturally are the Step-Daughter . . .

THE STEP-DAUGHTER [*excitedly*]. What? what? I, that woman there? [*Bursts out laughing.*]

THE MANAGER [*angry*]. What is there to laugh at?

LEADING LADY [*indignant*]. Nobody has ever dared to laugh at me. I insist on being treated with respect; otherwise I go away.

THE STEP-DAUGHTER. No, no, excuse me . . . I am not laughing at you . . .

THE MANAGER [*to* STEP-DAUGHTER]. You ought to feel honored to be played by . . .

LEADING LADY [*at once, contemptuously*]. "That woman there" . . .

THE STEP-DAUGHTER. But I wasn't speaking of you, you know. I was speaking of myself—whom I can't see at all in you! That is all. I don't know . . . but . . . you . . . aren't in the least like me . . .

THE FATHER. True. Here's the point. Look here, sir, our temperaments, our souls . . .

THE MANAGER. Temperament, soul, be hanged! Do you suppose the spirit of the piece is in you? Nothing of the kind!

THE FATHER. What, haven't we our own temperaments, our own souls?

THE MANAGER. Not at all. Your soul or whatever you like to call it takes shape here. The actors give body and form to it, voice and gesture. And my actors—I may tell you—have given expression to much more lofty material than this little drama of yours, which may or may not hold up on the stage. But if it does, the merit of it, believe me, will be due to my actors.

THE FATHER. I don't dare contradict you, sir; but, believe me, it is a terrible suffering for us who are as we are, with these bodies of ours, these features to see . . .

THE MANAGER [cutting him short and out of patience]. Good heavens! The make-up will remedy all that, man, the make-up . . .

THE FATHER. Maybe. But the voice, the gestures . . .

THE MANAGER. Now, look here! On the stage, you as yourself, cannot exist. The actor here acts you, and that's an end to it!

THE FATHER. I understand. And now I think I see why our author who conceived us as we are, all alive, didn't want to put us on the stage after all. I haven't the least desire to offend your actors. Far from it! But when I think that I am to be acted by . . . I don't know by whom . . .

LEADING MAN [on his dignity]. By me, if you've no objection!

THE FATHER [humbly, mellifluously]. Honored, I assure you, sir. [Bows.] Still, I must say that try as this gentleman may, with all his good will and wonderful art, to absorb me into himself . . .

LEADING MAN. Oh, chuck it! "Wonderful art!" Withdraw that, please!

THE FATHER. The performance he will give, even doing his best with make-up to look like me . . .

LEADING MAN. It will certainly be a bit difficult! [The ACTORS laugh.]

THE FATHER. Exactly! It will be difficult to act me as I really am. The effect will be rather—apart from the make-up—according as to how he supposes I am, as he senses me—if he does sense me—and not as I inside of myself feel myself to be. It seems to me then that account should be taken of this by everyone whose duty it may become to criticize us . . .

THE MANAGER. Heavens! The man's starting to think about the critics now! Let them say what they like. It's up to us to put on the play if we can. [Looking around.] Come on! come on! Is the stage set? [To the ACTORS and CHARACTERS.] Stand back—stand back! Let me see, and don't let's lose any more time! [To the STEP-DAUGHTER.] Is it all right as it is now?

THE STEP-DAUGHTER. Well, to tell the truth, I don't recognize the scene.

THE MANAGER. My dear lady, you can't possibly suppose that we can construct that shop of Madame Pace piece by piece here? [To the FATHER.] You said a white room with flowered wall paper, didn't you?

THE FATHER. Yes.

THE MANAGER. Well then. We've got the furniture right more or less. Bring that little table a bit further forward. [The STAGE HANDS obey the order. To PROPERTY MAN.] You go and find an envelope, if possible, a pale blue one; and give it to that gentleman. [Indicates FATHER.]

PROPERTY MAN. An ordinary envelope?

MANAGER AND FATHER. Yes, yes, an ordinary envelope.

PROPERTY MAN. At once, sir. [Exit.]

THE MANAGER. Ready, everyone! First scene—the Young Lady. [The LEADING LADY comes forward.] No, no, you must wait. I meant her [indicating the STEP-DAUGHTER]. You just watch—

THE STEP-DAUGHTER [adding at once]. How I shall play it, how I shall live it! . . .

LEADING LADY [offended]. I shall live it also, you may be sure, as soon as I begin!

THE MANAGER [*with his hands to his head*]. Ladies and gentlemen, if you please! No more useless discussions! Scene I: the young lady with Madame Pace: Oh! [*Looks around as if lost.*] And this Madame Pace, where is she?

THE FATHER. She isn't with us, sir.

THE MANAGER. Then what the devil's to be done?

THE FATHER. But she is alive too.

THE MANAGER. Yes, but where is she?

THE FATHER. One minute. Let me speak! [*Turning to the* ACTRESSES.] If these ladies would be so good as to give me their hats for a moment . . .

THE ACTRESSES [*half surprised, half laughing, in chorus*]. What?

Why?

Our hats?

What does he say?

THE MANAGER. What are you going to do with the ladies' hats? [*The* ACTORS *laugh.*]

THE FATHER. Oh nothing. I just want to put them on these pegs for a moment. And one of the ladies will be so kind as to take off her mantle . . .

THE ACTORS. Oh, what d'you think of that?

Only the mantle?

He must be mad.

SOME ACTRESSES. But why?

Mantles as well?

THE FATHER. To hang them up here for a moment. Please be so kind, will you?

THE ACTRESSES [*taking off their hats, one or two also their cloaks, and going to hang them on the racks*]. After all, why not?

There you are!

This is really funny.

We've got to put them on show.

THE FATHER. Exactly; just like that, on show.

THE MANAGER. May we know why?

THE FATHER. I'll tell you. Who knows if, by arranging the stage for her, she does not come here herself, attracted by the very articles of her trade? [*Inviting the* ACTORS *to look towards the exit at back of stage.*] Look! Look!

[*The door at the back of stage opens and* MADAME PACE *enters and takes a few steps forward. She is a fat, oldish woman with puffy oxygenated hair. She is rouged and powdered, dressed with a comical elegance in black silk. Round her waist is a long silver chain from which hangs a pair of scissors. The* STEP-DAUGHTER *runs over to her at once amid the stupor of the* ACTORS.]

THE STEP-DAUGHTER [*turning towards her*]. There she is! There she is!

THE FATHER [*radiant*]. It's she! I said so, didn't I? There she is!

THE MANAGER [*conquering his surprise, and then becoming indignant*]. What sort of a trick is this?

LEADING MAN [*almost at the same time*]. What's going to happen next?

JUVENILE LEAD. Where does *she* come from?

L'INGÉNUE. They've been holding her in reserve, I guess.

LEADING LADY. A vulgar trick!

THE FATHER [*dominating the protests*]. Excuse me, all of you! Why are you so anxious to destroy in the name of a vulgar, commonplace sense of truth, this reality which comes to birth attracted and formed by the magic of the stage itself, which has indeed more right to live here than you, since it is much truer than you—if you don't mind my saying so? Which is the actress among you who is to play Madame Pace? Well, here is Madame Pace herself. And you will allow, I fancy, that the actress who acts her will be less true than this woman here, who is herself in person. You see my daughter recognized her and went over to her at once. Now you're going to witness the scene!

[*But the scene between the* STEP-DAUGHTER *and* MADAME PACE *has already begun despite the protest of the actors and the reply of the* FATHER. *It has begun quietly, naturally, in a manner impossible for the stage. So when the* ACTORS, *called to attention by the* FATHER, *turn round and see* MADAME PACE, *who has placed one hand under the* STEP-DAUGHTER'S *chin to raise her head, they observe her at first with great attention, but hearing her speak in an unintelligible manner their interest begins to wane.*]

THE MANAGER. Well? well?

LEADING MAN. What does she say?

LEADING LADY. One can't hear a word.

JUVENILE LEAD. Louder! Louder please!

5 THE STEP-DAUGHTER [*leaving* MADAME PACE, *who smiles a Sphinx-like smile, and advancing towards the* ACTORS]. Louder? Louder? What are you talking about? These aren't matters which can be shouted at the top of one's voice. If 10 I have spoken them out loud, it was to shame him and have my revenge. [*Indicates* FATHER.] But for Madame it's quite a different matter.

THE MANAGER. Indeed? indeed? But here, you know, people have got to make themselves 15 heard, my dear. Even we who are on the stage can't hear you. What will it be when the public's in the theatre? And anyway, you can very well speak up now among yourselves, since we shan't be present to listen to you as 20 we are now. You've got to pretend to be alone in a room at the back of a shop where no one can hear you.

[*The* STEP-DAUGHTER *coquettishly and with a touch of malice makes a sign of disagreement* 25 *two or three times with her finger*.]

THE MANAGER. What do you mean by no?

THE STEP-DAUGHTER [*sotto voce, mysteriously*]. There's someone who will hear us if she [*indicating* MADAME PACE] speaks out 30 loud.

THE MANAGER [*in consternation*]. What? Have you got someone else to spring on us now? [*The* ACTORS *burst out laughing*.]

THE FATHER. No, no sir. She is alluding to 35 me. I've got to be here—there behind that door, in waiting; and Madame Pace knows it. In fact, if you will allow me, I'll go there at once, so I can be quite ready. [*Moves away*.]

THE MANAGER [*stopping him*]. No! Wait! 40 wait! We must observe the conventions of the theatre. Before you are ready . . .

THE STEP-DAUGHTER [*interrupting him*]. No, get on with it at once! I'm just dying, I tell you, to act this scene. If he's ready, I'm more than 45 ready.

THE MANAGER [*shouting*]. But, my dear young lady, first of all, we must have the scene between you and this lady . . . [*indicates* MADAME PACE]. Do you understand? . . .

THE STEP-DAUGHTER. Good Heavens! She's 50 been telling me what you know already: that mamma's work is badly done again, that the material's ruined; and that if I want her to continue to help us in our misery I must be patient . . . 55

MADAME PACE [*coming forward with an air of great importance*]. Yes indeed, sir, I no wanta take advantage of her, I no wanta be hard . . .

[*Note*. MADAME PACE *is supposed to talk in* 60 *a jargon half Italian, half English*.]

THE MANAGER [*alarmed*]. What? What? She talks like that? [*The* ACTORS *burst out laughing again*.]

THE STEP-DAUGHTER [*also laughing*]. Yes 65 yes, that's the way she talks, half English, half Italian! Most comical it is!

MADAME PACE. Itta seem not verra polite gentlemen laugha atta me eef I trya best speaka English. 70

THE MANAGER. *Diamine!* Of course! Of course! Let her talk like that! Just what we want. Talk just like that, Madame, if you please! The effect will be certain. Exactly what was wanted to put a little comic relief into 75 the crudity of the situation. Of course she talks like that! Magnificent!

THE STEP-DAUGHTER. Magnificent? Certainly! When certain suggestions are made to one in language of that kind, the effect is certain, 80 since it seems almost a joke. One feels inclined to laugh when one hears her talk about an "old signore" "who wanta talka nicely with you." Nice old signore, eh, Madame?

MADAME PACE. Not so old my dear, not so 85 old! And even if you no lika him, he won't make any scandal!

THE MOTHER [*jumping up amid the amazement and consternation of the* ACTORS *who had not been noticing her. They move to restrain* 90 *her*]. You old devil! You murderess!

THE STEP-DAUGHTER [*running over to calm her* MOTHER]. Calm yourself, Mother, calm yourself! Please don't . . .

THE FATHER [*going to her also at the same time*]. Calm yourself! Don't get excited! Sit down now!

THE MOTHER. Well then, take that woman away out of my sight!

THE STEP-DAUGHTER [*to* MANAGER]. It is impossible for my mother to remain here.

THE FATHER [*to* MANAGER]. They can't be here together. And for this reason, you see: that woman there was not with us when we came . . . If they are on together, the whole thing is given away inevitably, as you see.

THE MANAGER. It doesn't matter. This is only a first rough sketch—just to get an idea of the various points of the scene, even confusedly . . . [*turning to the* MOTHER *and leading her to her chair*]. Come along, my dear lady, sit down now, and let's get on with the scene . . .

[*Meanwhile, the* STEP-DAUGHTER, *coming forward again, turns to* MADAME PACE.]

THE STEP-DAUGHTER. Come on, Madame, come on!

MADAME PACE [*offended*]. No, no, *grazie*. I not do anything witha your mother present.

THE STEP-DAUGHTER. Nonsense! Introduce this "old signore" who wants to talk nicely to me. [*Addressing the* COMPANY *imperiously*.] We've got to do this scene one way or another, haven't we? Come on! [*To* MADAME PACE.] You can go!

MADAME PACE. Ah yes! I go'way! I go'way! Certainly! [*Exits furious.*]

THE STEP-DAUGHTER [*to the* FATHER]. Now you make your entry. No, you needn't go over here. Come here. Let's suppose you've already come in. Like that, yes! I'm here with bowed head, modest like. Come on! Out with your voice! Say "Good morning, Miss" in that peculiar tone, that special tone . . .

THE MANAGER. Excuse me, but are you the Manager, or am I? [*To the* FATHER, *who looks undecided and perplexed*.] Get on with it, man! Go down there to the back of the stage. You needn't go off. Then come right forward here.

[*The* FATHER *does as he is told, looking troubled and perplexed at first. But as soon as he begins to move, the reality of the action affects him, and he begins to smile and to be more natural. The* ACTORS *watch intently*.]

THE MANAGER [*sotto voce, quickly to the* PROMPTER *in his box*]. Ready! ready? Get ready to write now.

THE FATHER [*coming forward and speaking in a different tone*]. Good afternoon, Miss!

THE STEP-DAUGHTER [*head bowed down slightly, with restrained disgust*]. Good afternoon!

THE FATHER [*looks under her hat which partly covers her face. Perceiving she is very young, he makes an exclamation, partly of surprise, partly of fear lest he compromise himself in a risky adventure*]. Ah . . . but . . . ah . . . I say . . . this is not the first time that you have come here, is it?

THE STEP-DAUGHTER [*modestly*]. No sir.

THE FATHER. You've been here before, eh? [*Then seeing her nod agreement*.] More than once? [*Waits for her to answer, looks under her hat, smiles, and then says*.] Well then, there's no need to be so shy, is there? May I take off your hat?

THE STEP-DAUGHTER [*anticipating him and with veiled disgust*]. No sir . . . I'll do it myself. [*Takes it off quickly*.]

[*The* MOTHER, *who watches the progress of the scene with the* SON *and the other two children who cling to her, is on thorns; and follows with varying expressions of sorrow, indignation, anxiety, and horror the words and actions of the other two. From time to time she hides her face in her hands and sobs*.]

THE MOTHER. Oh, my God, my God!

THE FATHER [*playing his part with a touch of gallantry*]. Give it to me! I'll put it down. [*Takes hat from her hands*.] But a dear little head like yours ought to have a smarter hat. Come and help me choose one from the stock, won't you?

L'INGÉNUE [*interrupting*]. I say . . . those are our hats you know.

THE MANAGER [*furious*]. Silence! silence! Don't try and be funny, if you please . . .we're playing the scene now I'd have you notice. [*To the* STEP-DAUGHTER.] Begin again, please!

THE STEP-DAUGHTER [*continuing*]. No thank you, sir.

5 THE FATHER. Oh, come now. Don't talk like that. You must take it. I shall be upset if you don't. There are some lovely little hats here; and then—Madame will be pleased. She expects it, anyway, you know.

10 THE STEP-DAUGHTER. No, no! I couldn't wear it!

THE FATHER. Oh, you're thinking about what they'd say at home if they saw you come in with a new hat? My dear girl, there's always 15 a way round these little matters, you know.

THE STEP-DAUGHTER [*all keyed up*]. No, it's not that. I couldn't wear it because I am . . . as you see . . . you might have noticed . . . [*showing her black dress*].

20 THE FATHER. . . . in mourning! Of course: I beg your pardon: I'm frightfully sorry . . .

THE STEP-DAUGHTER [*forcing herself to conquer her indignation and nausea*]. Stop! Stop! It's I who must thank you. There's no 25 need for you to feel mortified or specially sorry. Don't think any more of what I've said. [*Tries to smile.*] I must forget that I am dressed so . . .

THE MANAGER [*interrupting and turning to* 30 *the* PROMPTER]. Stop a minute! Stop! Don't write that down. Cut out that last bit. [*Then to the* FATHER *and* STEP-DAUGHTER.] Fine! it's going fine! [*To the* FATHER *only.*] And now you can go on as we arranged. [*To the* ACTORS.] 35 Pretty good that scene, where he offers her the hat, eh?

THE STEP-DAUGHTER. The best's coming now. Why can't we go on?

THE MANAGER. Have a little patience! [*To* 40 *the* ACTORS.] Of course, it must be treated rather lightly.

LEADING MAN. Still, with a bit of go in it!

LEADING LADY. Of course! It's easy enough! [*To* LEADING MAN.] Shall you and I try it now?

45 LEADING MAN. Why, yes! I'll prepare my entrance. [*Exit in order to make his entrance.*]

THE MANAGER [*to* LEADING LADY]. See here! The scene between you and Madame Pace is finished. I'll have it written out properly after. You remain here . . . oh, where are you going? 50

LEADING LADY. One minute. I want to put my hat on again. [*Goes over to hat-rack and puts her hat on her head.*]

THE MANAGER. Good! You stay here with your head bowed down a bit. 55

THE STEP-DAUGHTER. But she isn't dressed in black.

LEADING LADY. But I shall be, and much more effectively than you.

THE MANAGER [*to* STEP-DAUGHTER]. Be quiet 60 please, and watch! You'll be able to learn something. [*Clapping his hands.*] Come on! come on! Entrance, please!

[*The door at rear of stage opens, and the* LEADING MAN *enters with the lively manner* 65 *of an old gallant. The rendering of the scene by the* ACTORS *from the very first words is seen to be quite a different thing, though it has not in any way the air of a parody. Naturally, the* STEP-DAUGHTER *and the* FATHER, *not being able* 70 *to recognize themselves in the* LEADING LADY *and the* LEADING MAN, *who deliver their words in different tones and with a different psychology, express, sometimes with smiles, sometimes with gestures, the impression they* 75 *receive.*]

LEADING MAN. Good afternoon, Miss . . .

THE FATHER [*at once unable to contain himself*]. No! no!

[*The* STEP-DAUGHTER *noticing the way the* 80 LEADING MAN *enters, bursts out laughing.*]

THE MANAGER [*furious*]. Silence! And you please just stop that laughing. If we go on like this, we shall never finish.

THE STEP-DAUGHTER. Forgive me, sir, but it's 85 natural enough. This lady [*indicating* LEADING LADY] stands there still; but if she is supposed to be me, I can assure you that if I heard anyone say "Good afternoon" in that manner and in that tone, I should burst out laughing as I 90 did.

THE FATHER. Yes, yes, the manner, the tone . . .

THE MANAGER. Nonsense! Rubbish! Stand aside and let me see the action. 95

LEADING MAN. If I've got to represent an old

fellow who's coming into a house of an equivocal character . . .

THE MANAGER. Don't listen to them, for Heaven's sake! Do it again! It goes fine. [*Waiting for the* ACTORS *to begin again.*] Well?

LEADING MAN. Good afternoon, Miss.

LEADING LADY. Good afternoon.

LEADING MAN [*imitating the gesture of the* FATHER *when he looked under the hat, and then expressing quite clearly first satisfaction and then fear*]. Ah, but . . . I say . . . this is not the first time that you have come here, is it?

THE MANAGER. Good, but not quite so heavily. Like this. [*Acts himself.*] "This isn't the first time that you have come here" . . . [*To* LEADING LADY.] And you say: "No, sir."

LEADING LADY. No, sir.

LEADING MAN. You've been here before, more than once.

THE MANAGER. No, no, stop! Let her nod "yes" first. "You've been here before, eh?" [*The* LEADING LADY *lifts up her head slightly and closes her eyes as though in disgust. Then she inclines her head twice.*]

THE STEP-DAUGHTER [*unable to contain herself*]. Oh my God! [*Puts a hand to her mouth to prevent herself from laughing.*]

THE MANAGER [*turning round*]. What's the matter?

THE STEP-DAUGHTER. Nothing, nothing!

THE MANAGER [*to* LEADING MAN]. Go on!

LEADING MAN. You've been here before, eh? Well then, there's no need to be so shy, is there? May I take off your hat?

[*The* LEADING MAN *says this last speech in such a tone and with such gestures that the* STEP-DAUGHTER, *though she has her hand to her mouth, cannot keep from laughing.*]

LEADING LADY [*indignant*]. I'm not going to stop here to be made a fool of by that woman there.

LEADING MAN. Neither am I! I'm through with it!

THE MANAGER [*shouting to* STEP-DAUGHTER]. Silence! for once and all, I tell you!

THE STEP-DAUGHTER. Forgive me! forgive me!

THE MANAGER. You haven't any manners: that's what it is! You go too far.

THE FATHER [*endeavoring to intervene*]. Yes, it's true, but excuse her . . .

THE MANAGER. Excuse what? It's absolutely disgusting.

THE FATHER. Yes, sir, but believe me, it has such a strange effect when . . .

THE MANAGER. Strange? Why strange? Where is it strange?

THE FATHER. No sir; I admire your actors—this gentleman here, this lady; but they are certainly not us!

THE MANAGER. I should hope not. Evidently they cannot be you, if they are actors.

THE FATHER. Just so: actors! Both of them act our parts exceedingly well. But, believe me, it produces quite a different effect on us. They want to be us, but they aren't, all the same.

THE MANAGER. What is it then anyway?

THE FATHER. Something that is . . . that is theirs—and no longer ours . . .

THE MANAGER. But naturally, inevitably. I've told you so already.

THE FATHER. Yes, I understand . . . I understand . . .

THE MANAGER. Well then, let's have no more of it! [*Turning to the* ACTORS.] We'll have the rehearsals by ourselves, afterwards, in the ordinary way. I never could stand rehearsing with the author present. He's never satisfied! [*Turning to* FATHER *and* STEP-DAUGHTER.] Come on! Let's get on with it again; and try and see if you can't keep from laughing.

THE STEP-DAUGHTER. Oh, I shan't laugh any more. There's a nice little bit coming for me now: you'll see.

THE MANAGER. Well then: when she says "Don't think any more of what I've said. I must forget, etc.," you [*addressing the* FATHER] come in sharp with "I understand, I understand"; and then you ask her . . .

THE STEP-DAUGHTER [*interrupting*]. What?

THE MANAGER. Why she is in mourning.

THE STEP-DAUGHTER. Not at all! See here: when I told him that it was useless for me to be thinking about my wearing mourning, do you know how he answered me? "Ah well," he said, "then let's take off this little frock."

THE MANAGER. Great! Just what we want, to make a riot in the theatre!

THE STEP-DAUGHTER. But it's the truth!

THE MANAGER. What does that matter?
5 Acting is our business here. Truth up to a certain point, but no further.

THE STEP-DAUGHTER. What do you want to do then?

THE MANAGER. You'll see, you'll see! Leave
10 it to me.

THE STEP-DAUGHTER. No sir! What you want to do is to piece together a little romantic sentimental scene out of my disgust, out of all the reasons, each more cruel and viler than the
15 other, why I am what I am. He is to ask me why I'm in mourning; and I'm to answer with tears in my eyes, that it is just two months since papa died. No sir, no! He's got to say to me; as he did say: "Well let's take off this
20 little dress at once." And I; with my two months' mourning in my heart, went there behind that screen, and with these fingers tingling with shame . . .

THE MANAGER [running his hands through
25 his hair]. For Heaven's sake! What are you saying?

THE STEP-DAUGHTER [crying out excitedly]. The truth! The truth!

THE MANAGER. It may be. I don't deny it, and
30 I can understand all your horror; but you must surely see that you can't have this kind of thing on the stage. It won't go.

THE STEP-DAUGHTER. Not possible, eh? Very well! I'm much obliged to you—but I'm off!

35 THE MANAGER. Now be reasonable! Don't lose your temper!

THE STEP-DAUGHTER. I won't stop here! I won't! I can see you've fixed it all up with him in your office. All this talk about what is pos-
40 sible for the stage . . . I understand! He wants to get at his complicated "cerebral drama," to have his famous remorses and torments acted; but I want to act my part, my part!

THE MANAGER [annoyed, shaking his shoul-
45 ders]. Ah! Just your part! But, if you will pardon me, there are other parts than yours: His [indicating the FATHER] and hers! [Indicating the MOTHER.] On the stage you can't have a character becoming too prominent and over-shadowing all the others. The thing is to pack 50 them all into a neat little framework and then act what is actable. I am aware of the fact that everyone has his own interior life which he wants very much to put forward. But the difficulty lies in this fact: to set out just so much as 55 is necessary for the stage, taking the other characters into consideration, and at the same time hint at the unrevealed interior life of each. I am willing to admit, my dear young lady, that from your point of view it would be a fine 60 idea if each character could tell the public all his troubles in a nice monologue or a regular one hour lecture. [Good humoredly.] You must restrain yourself, my dear, and in your own interest, too; because this fury of yours, this 65 exaggerated disgust you show, may make a bad impression, you know. After you have confessed to me that there were others before him at Madame Pace's and more than once . . .

THE STEP-DAUGHTER [bowing her head, im- 70 pressed]. It's true. But remember those others mean him for me all the same.

THE MANAGER [not understanding]. What? The others? What do you mean?

THE STEP-DAUGHTER. For one who has gone 75 wrong, sir, he who was responsible for the first fault is responsible for all that follow. He is responsible for my faults, was, even before I was born. Look at him, and see if it isn't true!

THE MANAGER. Well, well! And does the 80 weight of so much responsibility seem nothing to you? Give him a chance to act it, to get it over!

THE STEP-DAUGHTER. How? How can he act all his "noble remorses," all his "moral tor- 85 ments," if you want to spare him the horror of being discovered one day—after he had asked her what he did ask her—in the arms of her, that already fallen woman, that child, sir, that child he used to watch come out of school? 90 [She is moved.]

[THE MOTHER at this point is overcome with emotion, and breaks out into a fit of crying. All are touched. A long pause.]

THE STEP-DAUGHTER [as soon as the MOTHER 95 becomes a little quieter, adds resolutely and

gravely]. At present, we are unknown to the public. Tomorrow, you will act us as you wish, treating us in your own manner. But do you really want to see drama, do you want to see
5 it flash out as it really did?

THE MANAGER. Of course! That's just what I do want, so I can use as much of it as is possible.

THE STEP-DAUGHTER. Well then, ask that
10 Mother there to leave us.

THE MOTHER [*changing her low plaint into a sharp cry*]. No! No! Don't permit it, sir, don't permit it!

THE MANAGER. But it's only to try it.
15   THE MOTHER. I can't bear it. I can't.

THE MANAGER. But since it has happened already . . . I don't understand!

THE MOTHER. It's taking place now. It happens all the time. My torment isn't a pretended
20 one. I live and feel every minute of my torture. Those two children there—have you heard them speak? They can't speak any more. They cling to me to keep up my torment actual and vivid for me. But for themselves, they do not
25 exist, they aren't any more. And she [*indicating the* STEP-DAUGHTER] has run away, she has left me, and is lost. If I now see her here before me, it is only to renew for me the tortures I have suffered for her too.

30   THE FATHER. The eternal moment! She [*indicating the* STEP-DAUGHTER] is here to catch me, fix me, and hold me eternally in the stocks for that one fleeting and shameful moment of my life. She can't give it up! And you sir, can-
35 not either fairly spare me it.

THE MANAGER. I never said I didn't want to act it. It will form, as a matter of fact, the nucleus of the whole first act right up to her surprise. [*Indicates the* MOTHER.]

40   THE FATHER. Just so! This is my punishment: the passion in all of us that must culminate in her final cry.

THE STEP-DAUGHTER. I can hear it still in my ears. It's driven me mad, that cry!—You can
45 put me on as you like; it doesn't matter. Fully dressed, if you like—provided I have at least the arm bare; because, standing like this [*she goes close to the* FATHER *and leans her head on*

his breast] with my head so, and my arms round his neck, I saw a vein pulsing in my 50 arm here; and then, as if that live vein had awakened disgust in me, I closed my eyes like this, and let my head sink on his breast. [*Turning to the* MOTHER.] Cry out mother! Cry out! [*Buries head in* FATHER's *breast, and with her* 55 *shoulders raised as if to prevent her hearing the cry, adds in tones of intense emotion.*] Cry out as you did then!

THE MOTHER [*coming forward to separate them*]. No! My daughter, my daughter! [*And* 60 *after having pulled her away from him.*] You brute! you brute! She is my daughter! Don't you see she's my daughter?

THE MANAGER [*walking backwards towards footlights*]. Fine! fine! Damned good! And 65 then, of course—curtain!

THE FATHER [*going towards him excitedly*]. Yes, of course, because that's the way it really happened.

THE MANAGER [*convinced and pleased*]. Oh, 70 yes, no doubt about it. Curtain here, curtain!

[*At the reiterated cry of the* MANAGER, *the* MACHINIST *lets the curtain down, leaving the* MANAGER *and the* FATHER *in front of it before the footlights.*] 75

THE MANAGER. The darned idiot! I said "curtain" to show the act should end there, and he goes and lets it down in earnest. [*To the* FATHER, *while he pulls the curtain back to go on to the stage again.*] Yes, yes, it's all right. 80 Effect certain! That's the right ending. I'll guarantee the first act at any rate.

ACT III

[*When the curtain goes up again, it is seen that the* STAGE HANDS *have shifted the bit of* 85 *scenery used in the last part, and have rigged up instead at the back of the stage a drop, with some trees, and one or two wings. A portion of a fountain basin is visible. The* MOTHER *is sitting on the right with the two children by* 90 *her side. The* SON *is on the same side, but away from the others. He seems bored, angry, and full of shame. The* FATHER *and the* STEP-DAUGHTER *are also seated towards the right front. On the other side (left) are the* ACTORS, *much in the positions they occupied before the curtain was lowered. Only the* MANAGER *is standing up in the middle of the stage, with his hand closed over his mouth in the act of meditating.*]

THE MANAGER [*shaking his shoulders after a brief pause*]. Ah yes: the second act! Leave it to me, leave it all to me as we arranged, and you'll see! It'll go fine!

THE STEP-DAUGHTER. Our entry into his house [*indicates* FATHER] in spite of him . . . [*indicates the* SON].

THE MANAGER [*out of patience*]. Leave it to me, I tell you!

THE STEP-DAUGHTER. Do let it be clear, at any rate, that it is in spite of my wishes.

THE MOTHER [*from her corner, shaking her head*]. For all the good that's come of it . . .

THE STEP-DAUGHTER [*turning towards her quickly*]. It doesn't matter. The more harm done us, the more remorse for him.

THE MANAGER [*impatiently*]. I understand! Good Heavens! I understand! I'm taking it into account.

THE MOTHER [*supplicatingly*]. I beg you, sir, to let it appear quite plain that for conscience' sake I did try in every way . . .

THE STEP-DAUGHTER [*interrupting indignantly and continuing for the* MOTHER]. . . . . to pacify me, to dissuade me from spiting him. [*To* MANAGER.] Do as she wants: satisfy her, because it is true! I enjoy it immensely. Anyhow, as you can see, the meeker she is, the more she tries to get at his heart, the more distant and aloof does he become.

THE MANAGER. Are we going to begin this second act or not?

THE STEP-DAUGHTER. I'm not going to talk any more now. But I must tell you this: you can't have the whole action take place in the garden, as you suggest. It isn't possible!

THE MANAGER. Why not?

THE STEP-DAUGHTER. Because he [*indicates the* SON *again*] is always shut up alone in his room. And then there's all the part of that poor dazed-looking boy there which takes place indoors.

THE MANAGER. Maybe! On the other hand, you will understand—we can't change scenes three or four times in one act.

THE LEADING MAN. They used to once.

THE MANAGER. Yes, when the public was up to the level of that child there.

THE LEADING LADY. It makes the illusion easier.

THE FATHER [*irritated*]. The illusion! For Heaven's sake, don't say illusion. Please don't use that word, which is particularly painful for us.

THE MANAGER [*astounded*]. And why, if you please?

THE FATHER. It's painful, cruel, really cruel; and you ought to understand that.

THE MANAGER. But why? What ought we to say then? The illusion, I tell you, sir, which we've got to create for the audience . . .

THE LEADING MAN. With our acting.

THE MANAGER. The illusion of a reality.

THE FATHER. I understand; but you, perhaps, do not understand us. Forgive me! You see . . . here for you and your actors, the thing is only —and rightly so . . . a kind of game . . .

THE LEADING LADY [*interrupting indignantly*]. A game! We're not children here, if you please! We are serious actors.

THE FATHER. I don't deny it. What I mean is the game, or play, of your art, which has to give, as the gentleman says, a perfect illusion of reality.

THE MANAGER. Precisely—!

THE FATHER. Now, if you consider the fact that we [*indicates himself and the other five* CHARACTERS], as we are, have no other reality outside of this illusion . . .

THE MANAGER [*astonished, looking at his* ACTORS, *who are also amazed*]. And what does that mean?

THE FATHER [*after watching them for a moment with a wan smile*]. As I say, sir, that which is a game of art for you is our sole reality. [*Brief pause. He goes a step or two nearer the* MANAGER *and adds.*] But not only for us, you know, by the way. Just you think it over well. [*Looks him in the eyes.*] Can you tell me who you are?

THE MANAGER [*perplexed, half smiling*]. What? Who am I? I am myself.

THE FATHER. And if I were to tell you that that isn't true, because you and I . . . ?

5 THE MANAGER. I should say you were mad—! [*The* ACTORS *laugh.*]

THE FATHER. You're quite right to laugh: because we are all making believe here. [*To* MANAGER.] And you can therefore object that

10 it's only for a joke that that gentleman there [*indicates the* LEADING MAN], who naturally is himself, has to be me, who am on the contrary myself—this thing you see here. You see I've caught you in a trap! [*The* ACTORS *laugh.*]

15 THE MANAGER [*annoyed*]. But we've had all this over once before. Do you want to begin again?

THE FATHER. No, no! That wasn't my meaning! In fact, I should like to request you

20 to abandon this game of art [*looking at the* LEADING LADY *as if anticipating her*] which you are accustomed to play here with your actors, and to ask you seriously once again: who are you?

25 THE MANAGER [*astonished and irritated, turning to his* ACTORS]. If this fellow here hasn't got a nerve! A man who calls himself a character comes and asks me who I am!

THE FATHER [*with dignity, but not offended*].

30 A character, sir, may always ask a man who he is. Because a character has really a life of his own, marked with his especial characteristics; for which reason he is always "somebody." But a man—I'm not speaking of you now—

35 may very well be "nobody."

THE MANAGER. Yes, but you are asking these questions of me, the boss, the manager! Do you understand?

THE FATHER. But only in order to know if

40 you, as you really are now, see yourself as you once were with all the illusions that were yours then, with all the things both inside and outside of you as they seemed to you—as they were then indeed for you. Well, sir, if you think of

45 all those illusions that mean nothing to you now, of all those things which don't even *seem* to you to exist any more, while once they *were* for you, don't you feel that—I won't say these

boards—but the very earth under your feet is sinking away from you when you reflect that 50 in the same way this *you* as you feel it today— all this present reality of yours—is fated to seem a mere illusion to you tomorrow?

THE MANAGER [*without having understood much, but astonished by the specious argu-* 55 *ment*]. Well, well! And where does all this take us anyway?

THE FATHER. Oh, nowhere! It's only to show you that if we [*indicating the* CHARACTERS] have no other reality beyond the illusion, you 60 too must not count overmuch on your reality as you feel it today, since, like that of yester- day, it may prove an illusion for you tomor- row.

THE MANAGER [*determining to make fun of* 65 *him*]. Ah, excellent! Then you'll be saying next that you, with this comedy of yours that you brought here to act, are truer and more real than I am.

THE FATHER [*with the greatest seriousness*]. 70 But of course; without doubt!

THE MANAGER. Ah, really?

THE FATHER. Why, I thought you'd under- stand that from the beginning.

THE MANAGER. More real than I? 75

THE FATHER. If your reality can change from one day to another . . .

THE MANAGER. But everyone knows it can change. It is always changing, the same as anyone else's. 80

THE FATHER [*with a cry*]. No, sir, not ours! Look here! That is the very difference! Our reality doesn't change: it can't change! It can't be other than what it is, because it is already fixed for ever. It's terrible. Ours is an immu- 85 table reality which should make you shudder when you approach us if you are really con- scious of the fact that your reality is a mere transitory and fleeting illusion, taking this form today and that tomorrow, according to 90 the conditions, according to your will, your sentiments, which in turn are controlled by an intellect that shows them to you today in one manner and tomorrow . . . who knows how? . . . Illusions of reality represented in this 95 fatuous comedy of life that never ends, nor can

ever end! Because if tomorrow it were to end
. . . then why, all would be finished.

THE MANAGER. Oh for God's sake, will you
at least finish with this philosophizing and let
5 us try and shape this comedy which you yourself have brought me here? You argue and
philosophize a bit too much, my dear sir. You
know you seem to me almost, almost . . .
[*stops and looks him over from head to foot*].
10 Ah, by the way, I think you introduced yourself to me as a—what shall . . . we say—a
"character," created by an author who did not
afterward care to make a drama of his own
creations.

15 THE FATHER. It is the simple truth, sir.

THE MANAGER. Nonsense! Cut that out,
please! None of us believes it, because it isn't a
thing, as you must recognize yourself, which
one can believe seriously. If you want to know,
20 it seems to me you are trying to imitate the
manner of a certain author whom I heartily
detest—I warn you—although I have unfortunately bound myself to put on one of his
works. As a matter of fact, I was just starting
25 to rehearse it, when you arrived. [*Turning to
the* ACTORS.] And this is what we've gained—
out of the frying-pan into the fire!

THE FATHER. I don't know to what author
you may be alluding, but believe me I feel
30 what I think; and I seem to be philosophizing
only for those who do not think what they
feel, because they blind themselves with their
own sentiment. I know that for many people
this self-blinding seems much more "human";
35 but the contrary is really true. For man never
reasons so much and becomes so introspective
as when he suffers; since he is anxious to get
at the cause of his sufferings, to learn who has
produced them, and whether it is just or unjust
40 that he should have to bear them. On the other
hand, when he is happy, he takes his happiness as it comes and doesn't analyze it, just as
if happiness were his right. The animals suffer
without reasoning about their sufferings. But
45 take the case of a man who suffers and begins
to reason about it. Oh no! it can't be allowed!
Let him suffer like an animal, and then—ah
yet, he is "human"!

THE MANAGER. Look here! Look here! You're
off again, philosophizing worse than ever.   50

THE FATHER. Because I suffer, sir! I'm not
philosophizing: I'm crying aloud the reason of
my sufferings.

THE MANAGER [*makes brusque movement
as he is taken with a new idea*]. I should like   55
to know if anyone has ever heard of a character who gets right out of his part and perorates
and speechifies as you do. Have you ever heard
of a case? I haven't.

THE FATHER. You have never met such a   60
case, sir, because authors, as a rule, hide the
labor of their creations. When the characters
are really alive before their author, the latter
does nothing but follow them in their action,
in their words, in the situations which they   65
suggest to him; and he has to will them the
way they will themselves—for there's trouble
if he doesn't. When a character is born, he
acquires at once such an independence, even
of his own author, that he can be imagined by   70
everybody even in many other situations
where the author never dreamed of placing
him; and so he acquires for himself a meaning
which the author never thought of giving him.

THE MANAGER. Yes, yes, I know this.   75

THE FATHER. What is there then to marvel at
in us? Imagine such a misfortune for characters
as I have described to you: to be born of an
author's fantasy, and be denied life by him;
and then answer me if these characters left   80
alive, and yet without life, weren't right in
doing what they did do and are doing now,
after they have attempted everything in their
power to persuade him to give them their stage
life. We've all tried him in turn, I, she [*in-   85
dicating the* STEP-DAUGHTER] and she [*indicating the* MOTHER].

THE STEP-DAUGHTER. It's true. I too have
sought to tempt him, many, many times, when
he has been sitting at his writing table, feeling   90
a bit melancholy, at the twilight hour. He
would sit in his armchair too lazy to switch
on the light, and all the shadows that crept
into his room were full of our presence coming to tempt him. [*As if she saw herself still   95
there by the writing table, and was annoyed*

by the presence of the ACTORS.] Oh, if you would only go away, go away and leave us alone—mother here with that son of hers—I with that Child—that Boy there always alone
5 —and then I with him [*just hints at the* FATHER]—and then I alone, alone . . . in those shadows! [*Makes a sudden movement as if in the vision she has of herself illuminating those shadows she wanted to seize hold of herself.*]
10 Ah! my life! my life! Oh, what scenes we proposed to him—and I tempted him more than any of the others!

THE FATHER. Maybe. But perhaps it was your fault that he refused to give us life: because
15 you were too insistent, too troublesome.

THE STEP-DAUGHTER. . . . Nonsense! Didn't he make me so himself? [*Goes close to the* MANAGER *to tell him as if in confidence.*] In my opinion he abandoned us in a fit of de-
20 pression, of disgust for the ordinary theatre as the public knows it and likes it.

THE SON. Exactly what it was, sir; exactly that!

THE FATHER. Not at all! Don't believe it for
25 a minute. Listen to me! You'll be doing quite right to modify, as you suggest, the excesses both of this girl here, who wants to do too much, and of this young man, who won't do anything at all.
30 THE SON. No, nothing!

THE MANAGER. You too get over the mark occasionally, my dear sir, if I may say so.

THE FATHER. I? When? Where?

THE MANAGER. Always! Continuously! Then
35 there's this insistence of yours in trying to make us believe you are a character. And then too, you must really argue and philosophize less, you know, much less.

THE FATHER. Well, if you want to take away
40 from me the possibility of representing the torment of my spirit which never gives me peace, you will be suppressing me: that's all. Every true man, sir, who is a little above the level of the beasts and plants does not live for
45 the sake of living, without knowing how to live; but he lives so as to give a meaning and a value of his own to life. For me this is *everything*. I cannot give up this, just to represent a mere fact as she [*indicating the* STEP-DAUGHTER] wants. It's all very well for her,
50 since her "vendetta" lies in the "fact." I'm not going to do it. It destroys my *raison d'être*.

THE MANAGER. Your *raison d'être*! Oh, we're going ahead fine! First she starts off, and then you jump in. At this rate, we'll never finish.
55 THE FATHER. Now, don't be offended! Have it your own way—provided, however, that within the limits of the parts you assign us each one's sacrifice isn't too great.

THE MANAGER. You've got to understand
60 that you can't go on arguing at your own pleasure. Drama is action, sir, action and not confounded philosophy.

THE FATHER. All right, I'll do just as much arguing and philosophizing as everybody does
65 when he is considering his own torments.

THE MANAGER. If the drama permits! But for Heaven's sake, man, let's get along and come to the scene.

THE STEP-DAUGHTER. It seems to me we've
70 got too much action with our coming into his house. [*Indicating* FATHER.] You said, before, you couldn't change the scene every five minutes.

THE MANAGER. Of course not. What we've
75 got to do is to combine and group up all the facts in one simultaneous, close-knit, action. We can't have it as you want, with your little brother wandering like a ghost from room to room, hiding behind doors and meditating a
80 project which—what did you say it did to him?

THE STEP-DAUGHTER. Consumes him, sir, wastes him away!

THE MANAGER. Well, it may be. And then at the same time, you want the little girl there to
85 be playing in the garden . . . one in the house, and the other in the garden: isn't that it?

THE STEP-DAUGHTER. Yes, in the sun, in the sun! That is my only pleasure: to see her happy and careless in the garden after the
90 misery and squalor of the horrible room where we all four slept together. And I had to sleep with her—I, do you understand?—with my vile contaminated body next to hers; with her folding me fast in her loving little arms. In the
95 garden, whenever she spied me, she would run

to take me by the hand. She didn't care for the big flowers, only the little ones; and she loved to show me them and pet me.

THE MANAGER. Well then, we'll have it in the garden. Everything shall happen in the garden; and we'll group the other scenes there. [*Calls a* STAGE HAND.] Here, a backcloth with trees and something to do as a fountain basin. [*Turning round to look at the back of the stage.*] Ah, you've fixed it up. Good! [*To* STEP-DAUGHTER.] This is just to give an idea, of course. The Boy, instead of hiding behind the doors, will wander about here in the garden, hiding behind the trees. But it's going to be rather difficult to find a child to do that scene with you where she shows you the flowers. [*Turning to the* BOY.] Come forward a little, will you please? Let's try it now! Come along! come along! [*Then seeing him come shyly forward, full of fear and looking lost.*] It's a nice business, this lad here. What's the matter with him? We'll have to give him a word or two to say. [*Goes close to him, puts a hand on his shoulders, and leads him behind one of the trees.*] Come on! come on! Let me see you a little! Hide here . . . yes, like that. Try and show your head just a little as if you were looking for someone. . . . [*Goes back to observe the effect, when the* BOY *at once goes through the action.*] Excellent! fine! [*Turning to* STEP-DAUGHTER.] Suppose the little girl there were to surprise him as he looks round, and run over to him, so we could give him a word or two to say?

THE STEP-DAUGHTER. It's useless to hope he will speak, as long as that fellow there is here . . . [*indicates the* SON]. You must send him away first.

THE SON [*jumping up*]. Delighted! Delighted! I don't ask for anything better. [*Begins to move away.*]

THE MANAGER [*at once stopping him*]. No! No! Where are you going? Wait a bit!

[*The* MOTHER *gets up alarmed and terrified at the thought that he is really about to go away. Instinctively she lifts her arms to prevent him, without, however, leaving her seat.*]

THE SON [*to* MANAGER *who stops him*]. I've got nothing to do with this affair. Let me go please! Let me go!

THE MANAGER. What do you mean by saying you've got nothing to do with this?

THE STEP-DAUGHTER [*calmly, with irony*]. Don't bother to stop him: he won't go away.

THE FATHER. He has to act the terrible scene in the garden with his mother.

THE SON [*suddenly resolute and with dignity*]. I shall act nothing at all. I've said so from the very beginning. [*To the* MANAGER.] Let me go!

THE STEP-DAUGHTER [*going over to the* MANAGER]. Allow me? [*Puts down the* MANAGER'S *arm which is restraining the* SON.] Well, go away then, if you want to! [*The* SON *looks at her with contempt and hatred. She laughs and says.*] You see, he can't, he can't go away! He is obliged to stay here, indissolubly bound to the chain. If I, who fly off when that happens which has to happen, because I can't bear him—if I am still here and support that face and expression of his, you can well imagine that he is unable to move. He has to remain here, has to stop with that nice father of his, and that mother whose only son he is. [*Turning to the* MOTHER.] Come on, mother, come along! [*Turning to* MANAGER *to indicate her.*] You see, she was getting up to keep him back. [*To the* MOTHER, *beckoning her with her hand.*] Come on! come on! [*Then to* MANAGER.] You can imagine how little she wants to show these actors of yours what she really feels; but so eager is she to get near him that. . . . There, you see? She is willing to act her part. [*And in fact, the* MOTHER *approaches him; and as soon as the* STEP-DAUGHTER *has finished speaking, opens her arms to signify that she consents.*]

THE SON [*suddenly*]. No! no! If I can't go away, then I'll stop here; but I repeat: I act nothing!

THE FATHER [*to* MANAGER *excitedly*]. You can force him, sir.

THE SON. Nobody can force me.

THE FATHER. I can.

THE STEP-DAUGHTER. Wait a minute, wait. . . . First of all, the baby has to go to the fountain . . . [*runs to take the* CHILD *and leads her to the fountain*].

THE MANAGER. Yes, yes of course; that's it. Both at the same time.

[*The* SECOND LADY LEAD *and the* JUVENILE LEAD *at this point separate themselves from the group of* ACTORS. *One watches the* MOTHER *attentively; the other moves about studying the movements and manner of the* SON *whom he will have to act.*]

THE SON [*to* MANAGER]. What do you mean by both at the same time? It isn't right. There was no scene between me and her. [*Indicates the* MOTHER.] Ask her how it was!

THE MOTHER. Yes, it's true. I had come into his room . . .

THE SON. Into my room, do you understand? Nothing to do with the garden.

THE MANAGER. It doesn't matter. Haven't I told you we've got to group the action?

THE SON [*observing the* JUVENILE LEAD *studying him*]. What do you want?

THE JUVENILE LEAD. Nothing! I was just looking at you.

THE SON [*turning towards the* SECOND LADY LEAD]. Ah! she's at it too: to re-act her part! [*Indicating the* MOTHER.]

THE MANAGER. Exactly! And it seems to me that you ought to be grateful to them for their interest.

THE SON. Yes, but haven't you yet perceived that it isn't possible to live in front of a mirror which not only freezes us with the image of ourselves, but throws our likeness back at us with a horrible grimace?

THE FATHER. That is true, absolutely true. You must see that.

THE MANAGER [*to* SECOND LADY LEAD *and* JUVENILE LEAD]. He's right! Move away from them!

THE SON. Do as you like. I'm out of this!

THE MANAGER. Be quiet, you, will you? And let me hear your mother! [*To* MOTHER.] You were saying you had entered . . .

THE MOTHER. Yes, into his room, because I couldn't stand it any longer. I went to empty my heart to him of all the anguish that tortures me . . . . But as soon as he saw me come in . . .

THE SON. Nothing happened! There was no scene. I went away, that's all! I don't care for scenes!

THE MOTHER. It's true, true. That's how it was.

THE MANAGER. Well now, we've got to do this bit between you and him. It's indispensable.

THE MOTHER. I'm ready . . . when you are ready. If you could only find a chance for me to tell him what I feel here in my heart.

THE FATHER [*going to* SON *in a great rage*]. You'll do this for your mother, for your mother, do you understand?

THE SON [*quite determined*]. I do nothing!

THE FATHER [*taking hold of him and shaking him*]. For God's sake, do as I tell you! Don't you hear your mother asking you for a favor? Haven't you even got the guts to be a son?

THE SON [*taking hold of the* FATHER]. No! No! And for God's sake stop it, or else . . . [*General agitation. The* MOTHER, *frightened, tries to separate them*].

THE MOTHER [*pleading*]. Please! Please!

THE FATHER [*not leaving hold of the* SON]. You've got to obey, do you hear?

THE SON [*almost crying from rage*]. What does it mean, this madness you've got? [*They separate.*] Have you no decency, that you insist on showing everyone our shame? I won't do it! I won't! And I stand for the will of our author in this. He didn't want to put us on the stage, after all!

THE MANAGER. Man alive! You came here . . .

THE SON [*indicating* FATHER]. *He* did! I didn't!

THE MANAGER. Aren't you here now?

THE SON. It was his wish, and he dragged us along with him. He's told you not only the things that did happen, but also things that have never happened at all.

THE MANAGER. Well, tell me then what did happen. You went out of your room without saying a word?

THE SON. Without a word, so as to avoid a scene!

THE MANAGER. And then what did you do?

THE SON. Nothing . . . walking in the garden . . . [hesitates for a moment with expression of gloom].

5 THE MANAGER [coming closer to him, interested by his extraordinary reserve]. Well, well . . . Walking in the garden . . .

THE SON [exasperated]. Why on earth do you insist? It's horrible! [The MOTHER trembles,
10 sobs, and looks towards the fountain.]

THE MANAGER [slowly observing the glance and turning towards the SON with increasing apprehension]. The baby?

THE SON. There in the fountain . . .

15 THE FATHER [pointing with tender pity to the MOTHER]. She was following him at the moment . . .

THE MANAGER [to the SON anxiously]. And then you . . .

20 THE SON. I ran over to her; I was jumping in to drag her out when I saw something that froze my blood . . . the boy standing stock still, with eyes like a madman's, watching his little drowned sister, in the fountain! [The STEP-
25 DAUGHTER bends over the fountain to hide the CHILD. She sobs.] Then . . . [a revolver shot rings out behind the trees where the BOY is hidden].

THE MOTHER [with a cry of terror runs over
30 in that direction together with several of the ACTORS amid general confusion]. My son! My son! [Then amid the cries and exclamations one hears her voice.] Help! Help!

THE MANAGER [pushing the ACTORS aside
35 while they lift up the BOY and carry him off]. Is he really wounded?

SOME ACTORS. He's dead! dead!

OTHER ACTORS. No, no, it's only make believe, it's only pretense!

THE FATHER [with a terrible cry]. Pretense?
40 Reality, sir, reality!

THE MANAGER. Pretense? Reality? To hell with it all! Never in my life has such a thing happened to me. I've lost a whole day over
45 these people, a whole day!

Curtain

Bernard Shaw

1856–1950

Saint Joan

1923

Shaw called his play not *The Maid of Orleans,* nor *Joan of Arc,* but *Saint Joan,* with emphasis on the *Saint.* The term is to be understood in his sense, not the usual one. In a lengthy and argumentative preface he calls her "the first Protestant martyr," and this is paradoxical, because in Joan's lifetime (1412–1431) there were as yet no Protestant churches. Shaw means that his saint personifies the rights of private conscience. "What other judgment can I judge by but my own?" she exclaims at the critical moment of her trial, deeply shocking the judges who officially embody a contrary view. She was also, says Shaw, "one of the first apostles of Nationalism." Again, a paradox, because as yet there were no modern nation-states. In other words, Shaw's Joan exemplifies Shaw's theory of history: history is progressive, and progress comes through the often quite spontaneous and unself-conscious actions of men and women of genius. They are the agents of some vital force or spirit that guides the advance of civilization. Joan's sainthood is conferred on her by this spirit, in which Shaw believed as devoutly as a good Catholic believes in Providence.

Although Shaw at least pretends that his idea of sainthood is quite as Catholic as the Pope's, it would indeed be a trial of catholicity to suppose that religious truths can be so liberally rewritten. Clearly, Shaw does not believe in Heaven, even less in Hell, and his idea of Providence has less in common with Saint Paul than with Darwin. Shaw subtitles his play a "chronicle," and he does in fact incorporate some of the actual records of Joan's trial for heresy and witchcraft. But the chronicle is modernized to suit Shaw's theory. Her judges, in his view, are not scoundrels and bigots but merely prisoners of medieval ideas that are in process of being superseded by Joan's "Protestantism" and "Nationalism," ideas that Shaw is prepared to grant would be superseded in their turn. Nevertheless, for all the modernizing, these scenes from the

GEORGE BERNARD SHAW

life of Saint Joan—ranging from country to court, from court to battlefield, and onward to her martyrdom and her elevation to sainthood—are not at all unlike a traditional "saint's life," and they convey a consistent sense of the miraculous, from the homely miracle of the laying hens upward to the miraculous "radiance" that gathers on her head at the final moment. Even while he insists on an altogether human explanation for the miracles, Shaw does not cast away the emotions of surprise and joy.

In his preface Shaw also makes a large point of his pro-feminism in portraying Joan as a forerunner of the emancipated woman. This is perfectly just. Joan's short hair and masculine garb—even more, her bluff humor and down-to-earth good sense—are very much at odds with the delicacy of Victorian female types, very much at odds with the starchy piety of conventional feminine sainthood. Shaw's Joan shows no susceptibility to a romance of the heart. Still, in her wit and self-reliance she has more in common with Rosalind in *As You Like It* and Viola in *Twelfth Night* than with present-day liberationists. What Joan wins is the allegiance of men's hearts—an extremely old-fashioned achievement.

Shaw's play is not only a chronicle and a tract setting forth his own idea of history, it is also, properly speaking, a comedy, with more than a dash of melodrama in the scene describing Joan's martyrdom. It is a comedy not only because the situations are frequently funny and because it is populated with characters who say and do amusing things, both wittingly and not. It is comic also because whatever trace it has of tragic experience passes away in the renewed peacefulness and benignity of the conclusion. Hence, the epilogue, which has been unfavorably criticized, is appropriate even if not strictly necessary. It reasserts the geniality of the early scenes and the optimism of the postulates on which the play is based.

On some occasions Shaw himself was prepared to entertain the possibility that such postulates—all those witty but sometimes tedious debates over State and Church—are not the heart of the matter. A work of art, he felt, cannot fly except on the wings of its author's deeply held convictions, and (as he says in the preface to *Man and Superman*) "Effectiveness of assertion is the Alpha and Omega of style." Then he adds this significant sentence: "All the assertions get disproved sooner or later; and so we find the world full of a magnificent débris of artistic fossils, with the matter-of-fact credibility gone clean out of them, but the form still splendid." That "splendid form" in *Saint Joan* is to be perceived in the expert modulations of emotional tone, from scene to scene, and in the long crescendo of sympathy that climaxes with the reentrance of the Chaplain after Joan's death.

The esthetic achievement is even more evident in the evolution of Joan as a character, with her own speech and gesture, her own range of feeling, her individualistic style of thought, so that at length she stands forth as "real"—one of those persons whom we "know" through fiction or drama more convincingly than we might in real life. Shaw's Saint Joan may no more resemble the historical figure, now almost entirely obscured from us, than Shakespeare's immortal Cleopatra does the Egyptian queen of history. What is thus created through the dramatists' "splendid form" Shaw would have willingly pronounced a "miracle"—and this of a kind that he never presumed to explain.

Saint Joan

SHAW

CHARACTERS°
(In the order of their appearance)

ROBERT DE BAUDRICOURT *Commander of the Castle of Vaucouleurs*
STEWARD *de Baudricourt's servant*
JOAN *a country girl from Domrémy*
BERTRAND DE POULENGEY *a garrison officer*
LA TRÉMOUILLE *Lord Chamberlain to the King*
THE ARCHBISHOP OF RHEIMS *Councillor to the King*
GILLES DE RAIS ("BLUEBEARD") *a courtier*
LA HIRE *a military commander*
CHARLES VII (THE DAUPHIN) *King of France*
DUCHESS DE LA TRÉMOUILLE *wife of the Lord Chamberlain*
DUNOIS ("THE BASTARD") *Commander of the French army*
RICHARD DE BEAUCHAMP, EARL OF WARWICK *Commander of the English forces*
JOHN DE STOGUMBER *Warwick's chaplain*
CAUCHON *Bishop of Beauvais*
BROTHER JOHN LEMAITRE *The Inquisitor*
CANON JOHN D'ESTIVET ⎫
CANON DE COURCELLES ⎬ *Members of the ecclesiastical court*
BROTHER MARTIN LADVENU ⎭

Characters Because Shaw took great care to introduce each character as the play progressed, he pointedly omitted a preliminary list. Nevertheless, a cast of characters is here provided for convenient reference.

THE EXECUTIONER
AN ENGLISH SOLDIER
A CLERICAL GENTLEMAN FROM THE VATICAN

SCENE I

[*A fine spring morning on the river Meuse, between Lorraine and Champagne, in the year 1429 A.D., in the castle of Vaucouleurs.*

CAPTAIN ROBERT DE BAUDRICOURT, *a military squire, handsome and physically energetic, but* 5 *with no will of his own, is disguising that defect in his usual fashion by storming terribly at his* STEWARD, *a trodden worm, scanty of flesh, scanty of hair, who might be any age from 18 to 55, being the sort of man whom age cannot* 10 *wither because he has never bloomed.*

The two are in a sunny stone chamber on the first floor of the castle. At a plain strong oak table, seated in chair to match, the captain presents his left profile. The STEWARD *stands* 15 *facing him at the other side of the table, if so deprecatory a stance as his can be called standing. The mullioned thirteenth-century window is open behind him. Near it in the corner is a turret with a narrow arched doorway leading* 20 *to a winding stair which descends to the courtyard. There is a stout fourlegged stool under the table, and a wooden chest under the window.*]

ROBERT. No eggs! No eggs!! Thousand 25 thunders, man, what do you mean by no eggs?

STEWARD. Sir: it is not my fault. It is the act of God.

ROBERT. Blasphemy. You tell me there are no eggs; and you blame your Maker for it. 30

STEWARD. Sir: what can I do? I cannot lay eggs.

ROBERT [*sarcastic*]. Ha! You jest about it.

STEWARD. No, sir, God knows. We all have to go without eggs just as you have, sir. The 35 hens will not lay.

ROBERT. Indeed! [*Rising.*] Now listen to me, you.

STEWARD [*humbly*]. Yes, sir.

ROBERT. What am I? 40

STEWARD. What are you, sir?

ROBERT [*coming at him*]. Yes: what am I?

Am I Robert, squire of Baudricourt and captain of this castle of Vaucouleurs; or am I a cowboy?

STEWARD. Oh, sir, you know you are a greater man here than the king himself.

ROBERT. Precisely. And now, do you know what you are?

STEWARD. I am nobody, sir, except that I have the honor to be your steward.

ROBERT [driving him to the wall, adjective by adjective]. You have not only the honor of being my steward, but the privilege of being the worst, most incompetent, drivelling snivelling jibbering jabbering idiot of a steward in France. [He strides back to the table.]

STEWARD [cowering on the chest]. Yes, sir: to a great man like you I must seem like that.

ROBERT [turning]. My fault, I suppose. Eh?

STEWARD [coming to him deprecatingly]. Oh, sir: you always give my most innocent words such a turn!

ROBERT. I will give your neck a turn if you dare tell me, when I ask you how many eggs there are, that you cannot lay any.

STEWARD [protesting]. Oh sir, oh sir—

ROBERT. No: not oh sir, oh sir, but no sir, no sir. My three Barbary hens and the black are the best layers in Champagne. And you come and tell me that there are no eggs! Who stole them? Tell me that, before I kick you out through the castle gate for a liar and a seller of my goods to thieves. The milk was short yesterday, too: do not forget that.

STEWARD [desperate]. I know, sir. I know only too well. There is no milk: there are no eggs: tomorrow there will be nothing.

ROBERT. Nothing! You will steal the lot: eh?

STEWARD. No, sir: nobody will steal anything. But there is a spell on us: we are bewitched.

ROBERT. That story is not good enough for me. Robert de Baudricourt burns witches and hangs thieves. Go. Bring me four dozen eggs and two gallons of milk here in this room before noon, or Heaven have mercy on your bones! I will teach you to make a fool of me. [He resumes his seat with an air of finality.]

STEWARD. Sir: I tell you there are no eggs. There will be none—not if you were to kill me for it—as long as The Maid is at the door.

ROBERT. The Maid! What maid? What are you talking about?

STEWARD. The girl from Lorraine, sir. From Domrémy.

ROBERT [rising in fearful wrath]. Thirty thousand thunders! Fifty thousand devils! Do you mean to say that that girl, who had the impudence to ask to see me two days ago, and whom I told you to send back to her father with my orders that he was to give her a good hiding, is here still?

STEWARD. I have told her to go, sir. She wont.

ROBERT. I did not tell you to tell her to go: I told you to throw her out. You have fifty men-at-arms and a dozen lumps of ablebodied servants to carry out my orders. Are they afraid of her?

STEWARD. She is so positive, sir.

ROBERT [seizing him by the scruff of the neck]. Positive! Now see here. I am going to throw you downstairs.

STEWARD. No, sir. Please.

ROBERT. Well, stop me by being positive. It's quite easy: any slut of a girl can do it.

STEWARD [hanging limp in his hands]. Sir, sir: you cannot get rid of her by throwing me out. [ROBERT has to let him drop. He squats on his knees on the floor, contemplating his master resignedly.] You see, sir, you are much more positive than I am. But so is she.

ROBERT. I am stronger than you are, you fool.

STEWARD. No, sir: it isnt that: it's your strong character, sir. She is weaker than we are: she is only a slip of a girl; but we cannot make her go.

ROBERT. You parcel of curs: you are afraid of her.

STEWARD [rising cautiously]. No, sir: we are afraid of you; but she puts courage into us. She really doesnt seem to be afraid of anything. Perhaps you could frighten her, sir.

ROBERT [grimly]. Perhaps. Where is she now?

STEWARD. Down in the courtyard, sir, talking

to the soldiers as usual. She is always talking
to the soldiers except when she is praying.

ROBERT. Praying! Ha! You believe she prays,
you idiot. I know the sort of girl that is always
5 talking to soldiers. She shall talk to me a bit.
[*He goes to the window and shouts fiercely
through it.*] Hallo, you there!

A GIRL'S VOICE [*bright, strong and rough*].
Is it me, sir?

10 ROBERT. Yes, you.

THE VOICE. Be you captain?

ROBERT. Yes, damn your impudence, I be
captain. Come up here. [*To the soldiers in the
yard.*] Shew her the way, you. And shove her
15 along quick. [*He leaves the window, and returns to his place at the table, where he sits
magisterially.*]

STEWARD [*whispering*]. She wants to go and
be a soldier herself. She wants you to give her
20 soldier's clothes. Armor, sir! And a sword!
Actually! [*He steals behind* ROBERT.]

[JOAN *appears in the turret doorway. She is
an ablebodied country girl of 17 or 18, respectably dressed in red, with an uncommon face:
25 eyes very wide apart and bulging as they often
do in very imaginative people, a long well-
shaped nose with wide nostrils, a short upper
lip, resolute but full-lipped mouth, and handsome fighting chin. She comes eagerly to the
30 table, delighted at having penetrated to
* BAUDRICOURT'S *presence at last, and full of
hope as to the result. His scowl does not check
or frighten her in the least. Her voice is
normally a hearty coaxing voice, very confi-
35 dent, very appealing, very hard to resist.*]

JOAN [*bobbing a curtsey*]. Good morning,
captain squire. Captain: you are to give me a
horse and armor and some soldiers, and send
me to the Dauphin. Those are your orders
40 from my Lord.

ROBERT [*outraged*]. Orders from your lord!
And who the devil may your lord be? Go back
to him, and tell him that I am neither duke
nor peer at his orders: I am squire of Bau-
45 dricourt; and I take no orders except from the
king.

JOAN [*reassuringly*]. Yes, squire: that is all

right. My Lord is the King of Heaven.

ROBERT. Why, the girl's mad. [*To the
STEWARD.*] Why didnt you tell me so, you 50
blockhead?

STEWARD. Sir: do not anger her: give her
what she wants.

JOAN [*impatient, but friendly*]. They all say
I am mad until I talk to them, squire. But you 55
see that it is the will of God that you are to
do what He has put into my mind.

ROBERT. It is the will of God that I shall
send you back to your father with orders to
put you under lock and key and thrash the 60
madness out of you. What have you to say
to that?

JOAN. You think you will, squire; but you
will find it all coming quite different. You said
you would not see me; but here I am. 65

STEWARD [*appealing*]. Yes, sir. You see, sir.

ROBERT. Hold your tongue, you.

STEWARD [*abjectly*]. Yes, sir.

ROBERT [*to* JOAN, *with a sour loss of confidence*]. So you are presuming on my seeing 70
you, are you?

JOAN [*sweetly*]. Yes, squire.

ROBERT [*feeling that he has lost ground,
brings down his two fists squarely on the table,
and inflates his chest imposingly to cure the 75
unwelcome and only too familiar sensation*].
Now listen to me. I am going to assert myself.

JOAN [*busily*]. Please do, squire. The horse
will cost sixteen francs. It is a good deal of
money; but I can save it on the armor. I can 80
find a soldier's armor that will fit me well
enough: I am very hardy; and I do not need
beautiful armor made to my measure like you
wear. I shall not want many soldiers: the
Dauphin will give me all I need to raise the 85
siege of Orleans.

ROBERT [*flabbergasted*]. To raise the siege
of Orleans!

JOAN [*simply*]. Yes, squire: that is what God
is sending me to do. Three men will be enough 90
for you to send with me if they are good men
and gentle to me. They have promised to come
with me. Polly and Jack and—

ROBERT. Polly!! You impudent baggage, do

you dare call squire Bertrand de Poulengey Polly to my face?

JOAN. His friends call him so, squire: I did not know he had any other name. Jack—

5 ROBERT. That is Monsieur John of Metz, I suppose?

JOAN. Yes, squire. Jack will come willingly: he is a very kind gentleman, and gives me money to give to the poor. I think John God-
10 save will come, and Dick the Archer, and their servants John of Honecourt and Julian. There will be no trouble for you, squire: I have arranged it all: you have only to give the order.

15 ROBERT [contemplating her in a stupor of amazement]. Well, I am damned!

JOAN [with unruffled sweetness]. No, squire: God is very merciful; and the blessed saints Catherine and Margaret, who speak to me
20 every day [he gapes], will intercede for you. You will go to paradise; and your name will be remembered for ever as my first helper.

RORERT [to the STEWARD, still much bothered, but changing his tone as he pursues a new
25 clue]. Is this true about Monsieur de Poulengey?

STEWARD [eagerly]. Yes, sir, and about Monsieur de Metz too. They both want to go with her.

30 ROBERT [thoughtful]. Mf! [He goes to the window, and shouts into the courtyard.] Hallo! You there: send Monsieur de Poulengey to me, will you? [He turns to JOAN.] Get out; and wait in the yard.

35 JOAN [smiling brightly at him]. Right, squire. [She goes out.]

ROBERT [to the STEWARD]. Go with her, you, you dithering imbecile. Stay within call; and keep your eye on her. I shall have her up here
40 again.

STEWARD. Do so in God's name, sir. Think of those hens, the best layers in Champagne; and—

ROBERT. Think of my boot; and take your
45 backside out of reach of it.

[The STEWARD retreats hastily and finds himself confronted in the doorway by BERTRAND DE POULENGEY, a lymphatic French gentleman-at-arms, aged 36 or thereabout, employed in the department of the provost-marshal, 50 dreamily absent-minded, seldom speaking unless spoken to, and then slow and obstinate in reply: altogether in contrast to the self-assertive, loud-mouthed, superficially energetic, fundamentally will-less ROBERT. The STEWARD 55 makes way for him, and vanishes.]

[POULENGEY salutes, and stands awaiting orders.]

ROBERT [genially]. It isnt service, Polly. A friendly talk. Sit down. [He hooks the stool 60 from under the table with his instep.]

[POULENGEY relaxing, comes into the room; places the stool between the table and the window; and sits down ruminatively. ROBERT, half sitting on the end of the table, begins the 65 friendly talk.]

ROBERT. Now listen to me, Polly. I must talk to you like a father.

[POULENGEY looks up at him gravely for a moment, but says nothing.] 70

ROBERT. It's about this girl you are interested in. Now, I have seen her. I have talked to her. First, she's mad. That doesnt matter. Second, she's not a farm wench. She's a bourgeoise. That matters a good deal. I know her class 75 exactly. Her father came here last year to represent his village in a lawsuit: he is one of their notables. A farmer. Not a gentleman farmer: he makes money by it, and lives by it. Still, not a laborer. Not a mechanic. He 80 might have a cousin a lawyer, or in the Church. People of this sort may be of no account socially; but they can give a lot of bother to the authorities. That is to say, to me. Now no doubt it seems to you a very simple thing to 85 take this girl away, humbugging her into the belief that you are taking her to the Dauphin. But if you get her into trouble, you may get me into no end of a mess, as I am her father's lord, and responsible for her protection. So 90 friends or no friends, Polly, hands off her.

POULENGEY [with deliberate impressiveness]. I should as soon think of the Blessed Virgin herself in that way, as of this girl.

ROBERT [coming off the table]. But she says 95 you and Jack and Dick have offered to go with her. What for? You are not going to tell me that you take her crazy notion of going to the Dauphin seriously, are you?

POULENGEY [*slowly*]. There is something about her. They are pretty foulmouthed and foulminded down there in the guardroom, some of them. But there hasnt been a word that has anything to do with her being a woman. They have stopped swearing before her. There is something. Something. It may be worth trying.

ROBERT. Oh, come, Polly! pull yourself together. Commonsense was never your strong point; but this is a little too much. [*He retreats disgustedly.*]

POULENGEY [*unmoved*]. What is the good of commonsense? If we had any commonsense we should join the Duke of Burgundy and the English king. They hold half the country, right down to the Loire. They have Paris. They have this castle: you know very well that we had to surrender it to the Duke of Bedford, and that you are only holding it on parole. The Dauphin is in Chinon, like a rat in a corner, except that he wont fight. We dont even know that he is the Dauphin: his mother says he isnt; and she ought to know. Think of that! the queen denying the legitimacy of her own son!

ROBERT. Well, she married her daughter to the English king. Can you blame the woman?

POULENGEY. I blame nobody. But thanks to her, the Dauphin is down and out; and we may as well face it. The English will take Orleans: the Bastard will not be able to stop them.

ROBERT. He beat the English the year before last at Montargis. I was with him.

POULENGEY. No matter: his men are cowed now; and he cant work miracles. And I tell you that nothing can save our side now but a miracle.

ROBERT. Miracles are all right, Polly. The only difficulty about them is that they dont happen nowadays.

POULENGEY. I used to think so. I am not so sure now. [*Rising, and moving ruminatively towards the window.*] At all events this is not a time to leave any stone unturned. There is something about the girl.

ROBERT. Oh! You think the girl can work miracles, do you?

POULENGEY. I think the girl herself is a bit of a miracle. Anyhow, she is the last card left in our hand. Better play her than throw up the game. [*He wanders to the turret.*]

ROBERT [*wavering*]. You really think that?

POULENGEY [*turning*]. Is there anything else left for us to think?

ROBERT [*going to him*]. Look here, Polly. If you were in my place would you let a girl like that do you out of sixteen francs for a horse?

POULENGEY. I will pay for the horse.

ROBERT. You will!

POULENGEY. Yes: I will back my opinion.

ROBERT. You will really gamble on a forlorn hope to the tune of sixteen francs?

POULENGEY. It is not a gamble.

ROBERT. What else is it?

POULENGEY. It is a certainty. Her words and her ardent faith in God have put fire into me.

ROBERT [*giving him up*]. Whew! You are as mad as she is.

POULENGEY [*obstinately*]. We want a few mad people now. See where the sane ones have landed us!

ROBERT [*his irresoluteness now openly swamping his affected decisiveness*]. I shall feel like a precious fool. Still, if you feel sure—?

POULENGEY. I feel sure enough to take her to Chinon—unless you stop me.

ROBERT. This is not fair. You are putting the responsibility on me.

POULENGEY. It is on you whichever way you decide.

ROBERT. Yes: thats just it. Which way am I to decide? You dont see how awkward this is for me. [*Snatching at a dilatory step with an unconscious hope that* JOAN *will make up his mind for him.*] Do you think I ought to have another talk to her?

POULENGEY [*rising*]. Yes. [*He goes to the window and calls.*] Joan!

JOAN'S VOICE. Will he let us go, Poily?

POULENGEY. Come up. Come in. [*Turning to* ROBERT.] Shall I leave you with her?

ROBERT. No: stay here; and back me up.

[POULENGEY *sits down on the chest.* ROBERT *goes back to his magisterial chair, but remains standing to inflate himself more imposingly.*
5 JOAN *comes in, full of good news.*]

JOAN. Jack will go halves for the horse.

ROBERT. Well!! [*He sits, deflated.*]

POULENGEY [*gravely*]. Sit down, Joan.

JOAN [*checked a little, and looking to*
10 ROBERT]. May I?

ROBERT. Do what you are told.

[JOAN *curtsies and sits down on the stool between them.* ROBERT *outfaces his perplexity with his most peremptory air.*]

15 ROBERT. What is your name?

JOAN [*chattily*]. They always call me Jenny in Lorraine. Here in France I am Joan. The soldiers call me The Maid.

ROBERT. What is your surname?

20 JOAN. Surname? What is that? My father sometimes calls himself d'Arc; but I know nothing about it. You met my father. He—

ROBERT. Yes, yes: I remember. You come from Domrémy in Lorraine, I think.

25 JOAN. Yes; but what does it matter? we all speak French.

ROBERT. Dont ask questions: answer them. How old are you?

JOAN. Seventeen: so they tell me. It might
30 be nineteen. I dont remember.

ROBERT. What did you mean when you said that St Catherine and St Margaret talked to you every day?

JOAN. They do.

35 ROBERT. What are they like?

JOAN [*suddenly obstinate*]. I will tell you nothing about that: they have not given me leave.

ROBERT. But you actually see them; and they
40 talk to you just as I am talking to you?

JOAN. No: it is quite different. I cannot tell you: you must not talk to me about my voices.

ROBERT. How do you mean? voices?

JOAN. I hear voices telling me what to do.
45 They come from God.

ROBERT. They come from your imagination.

JOAN. Of course. That is how the messages of God come to us.

POULENGEY. Checkmate.

ROBERT. No fear! [*To* JOAN.] So God says 50
you are to raise the siege of Orleans?

JOAN. And to crown the Dauphin in Rheims Cathedral.

ROBERT [*gasping*]. Crown the D———!
Gosh! 55

JOAN. And to make the English leave France.

ROBERT [*sarcastic*]. Anything else?

JOAN [*charming*]. Not just at present, thank you, squire.

ROBERT. I suppose you think raising a siege 60
is as easy as chasing a cow out of a meadow. You think soldiering is anybody's job?

JOAN. I do not think it can be very difficult if God is on your side, and you are willing to put your life in His hand. But many soldiers 65
are very simple.

ROBERT [*grimly*]. Simple! Did you ever see English soldiers fighting?

JOAN. They are only men. God made them just like us; but He gave them their own 70
country and their own language; and it is not His will that they should come into our country and try to speak our language.

ROBERT. Who has been putting such non-sense into your head? Dont you know that 75
soldiers are subject to their feudal lord, and that it is nothing to them or to you whether he is the duke of Burgundy or the king of England or the king of France? What has their language to do with it? 80

JOAN. I do not understand that a bit. We are all subject to the King of Heaven; and He gave us our countries and our languages, and meant us to keep to them. If it were not so it would be murder to kill an Englishman in 85
battle; and you, squire, would be in great danger of hell fire. You must not think about your duty to your feudal lord, but about your duty to God.

POULENGEY. It's no use, Robert: she can 90
choke you like that every time.

ROBERT. Can she, by Saint Dennis! We shall see. [*To* JOAN.] We are not talking about God: we are talking about practical affairs. I ask you again, girl, have you ever seen English 95
soldiers fighting? Have you ever seen them

plundering, burning, turning the countryside into a desert? Have you heard no tales of their Black Prince who was blacker than the devil himself, or of the English king's father?

5 JOAN. You must not be afraid, Robert—

ROBERT. Damn you, I am not afraid. And who gave you leave to call me Robert?

JOAN. You were called so in church in the name of our Lord. All the other names are your 10 father's or your brother's or anybody's.

ROBERT. Tcha!

JOAN. Listen to me, squire. At Domrémy we had to fly to the next village to escape from the English soldiers. Three of them were left 15 behind, wounded. I came to know these three poor goddams quite well. They had not half my strength.

ROBERT. Do you know why they are called goddams?

20 JOAN. No. Everyone calls them goddams.

ROBERT. It is because they are always calling on their God to condemn their souls to perdition. That is what goddam means in their language. How do you like it?

25 JOAN. God will be merciful to them; and they will act like His good children when they go back to the country He made for them, and made them for. I have heard the tales of the Black Prince. The moment he touched the soil 30 of our country the devil entered into him and made him a black fiend. But at home, in the place made for him by God, he was good. It is always so. If I went into England against the will of God to conquer England, and tried to 35 live there and speak its language, the devil would enter into me; and when I was old I should shudder to remember the wickednesses I did.

ROBERT. Perhaps. But the more devil you 40 were the better you might fight. That is why the goddams will take Orleans. And you cannot stop them, nor ten thousand like you.

JOAN. One thousand like me can stop them. Ten like me can stop them with God on our side. 45 [*She rises impetuously, and goes at him, unable to sit quiet any longer.*] You do not understand, squire. Our soldiers are always beaten because they are fighting only to save

their skins; and the shortest way to save your skin is to run away. Our knights are thinking 50 only of the money they will make in ransoms: it is not kill or be killed with them, but pay or be paid. But I will teach them all to fight that the will of God may be done in France; and then they will drive the poor goddams before 55 them like sheep. You and Polly will live to see the day when there will not be an English soldier on the soil of France; and there will be but one king there: not the feudal English king, but God's French one. 60

ROBERT [*to* POULENGEY]. This may be all rot, Polly; but the troops might swallow it, though nothing that we can say seems able to put any fight into them. Even the Dauphin might swallow it. And if she can put fight into him, 65 she can put it into anybody.

POULENGEY. I can see no harm in trying. Can you? And there is something about the girl—

ROBERT [*turning to* JOAN]. Now listen you to me; and [*desperately*] dont cut in before I 70 have time to think.

JOAN [*plumping down on the stool again, like an obedient schoolgirl*]. Yes, squire.

ROBERT. Your orders are, that you are to go to Chinon under the escort of this gentleman 75 and three of his friends.

JOAN [*radiant, clasping her hands*]. Oh, squire! Your head is all circled with light, like a saint's.

POULENGEY. How is she to get into the royal 80 presence?

ROBERT [*who has looked up for his halo rather apprehensively*]. I dont know: how did she get into my presence? If the Dauphin can keep her out he is a better man than I take 85 him for. [*Rising.*] I will send her to Chinon; and she can say I sent her. Then let come what may: I can do no more.

JOAN. And the dress? I may have a soldier's dress, maynt I, squire? 90

ROBERT. Have what you please. I wash my hands of it.

JOAN [*wildly excited by her success*]. Come, Polly. [*She dashes out.*]

ROBERT [*shaking* POULENGEY'S *hand*]. Good- 95 bye, old man, I am taking a big chance. Few other men would have done it. But as you say, there is something about her.

POULENGEY. Yes: there is something about her. Goodbye. [*He goes out.*]

5 [ROBERT, *still very doubtful whether he has not been made a fool of by a crazy female, and a social inferior to boot, scratches his head and slowly comes back from the door.*]

[*The* STEWARD *runs in with a basket.*]

10 STEWARD. Sir, sir—

ROBERT. What now?

STEWARD. The hens are laying like mad, sir. Five dozen eggs!

ROBERT [*stiffens convulsively; crosses him-*
15 *self; and forms with his pale lips the words*]. Christ in heaven! [*Aloud but breathless.*] She did come from God.

SCENE II

[*Chinon, in Touraine. An end of the throne-room in the castle, curtained off to make an*
20 *antechamber. The* ARCHBISHOP OF RHEIMS, *close on 50, a full-fed political prelate with nothing of the ecclesiastic about him except his imposing bearing, and the* LORD CHAMBER-LAIN, MONSEIGNEUR DE LA TRÉMOUILLE, *a*
25 *monstrous arrogant wineskin of a man, are waiting for the* DAUPHIN. *There is a door in the wall to the right of the two men. It is late in the afternoon on the 8th of March, 1429. The* ARCHBISHOP *stands with dignity whilst the*
30 CHAMBERLAIN, *on his left, fumes about in the worst of tempers.*]

LA TRÉMOUILLE. What the devil does the Dauphin mean by keeping us waiting like this? I dont know how you have the patience
35 to stand there like a stone idol.

THE ARCHBISHOP. You see, I am an arch-bishop; and an archbishop is a sort of idol. At any rate he has to learn to keep still and suffer fools patiently. Besides, my dear Lord Cham-
40 berlain, it is the Dauphin's royal privilege to keep you waiting, is it not?

LA TRÉMOUILLE. Dauphin be damned! saving your reverence. Do you know how much money he owes me?

THE ARCHBISHOP. Much more than he owes 45 me, I have no doubt, because you are a much richer man. But I take it he owes you all you could afford to lend him. That is what he owes me.

LA TRÉMOUILLE. Twentyseven thousand: that 50 was his last haul. A cool twentyseven thousand!

THE ARCHBISHOP. What becomes of it all? He never has a suit of clothes that I would throw to a curate. 55

LA TRÉMOUILLE. He dines on a chicken or a scrap of mutton. He borrows my last penny; and there is nothing to shew for it. [*A* PAGE *appears in the doorway.*] At last!

THE PAGE. No, my lord: it is not His Majesty. 60 Monsieur de Rais is approaching.

LA TRÉMOUILLE. Young Bluebeard! Why announce him?

THE PAGE. Captain La Hire is with him. Something has happened, I think. 65

[GILLES DE RAIS, *a young man of 25, very smart and self-possessed, and sporting the extravagance of a little curled beard dyed blue at a clean-shaven court, comes in. He is deter-mined to make himself agreeable, but lacks* 70 *natural joyousness, and is not really pleasant. In fact when he defies the Church some eleven years later he is accused of trying to extract pleasure from horrible cruelties, and hanged. So far, however, there is no shadow of the* 75 *gallows on him. He advances gaily to the* ARCHBISHOP. *The* PAGE *withdraws.*]

BLUEBEARD. Your faithful lamb, Archbishop. Good day, my lord. Do you know what has happened to La Hire? 80

LA TRÉMOUILLE. He has sworn himself into a fit, perhaps.

BLUEBEARD. No: just the opposite. Foul Mouthed Frank, the only man in Touraine who could beat him at swearing, was told by a 85 soldier that he shouldnt use such language when he was at the point of death.

THE ARCHBISHOP. Nor at any other point. But was Foul Mouthed Frank on the point of death?

BLUEBEARD. Yes: he has just fallen into a well 90

and been drowned. La Hire is frightened out of his wits.

[CAPTAIN LA HIRE *comes in: a war dog with no court manners and pronounced camp ones.*]

BLUEBEARD. I have just been telling the Chamberlain and the Archbishop. The Archbishop says you are a lost man.

LA HIRE [*striding past* BLUEBEARD, *and planting himself between the* ARCHBISHOP *and* LA TRÉMOUILLE]. This is nothing to joke about. It is worse than we thought. It was not a soldier, but an angel dressed as a soldier.

THE ARCHBISHOP
THE CHAMBERLAIN } [*exclaiming all together*]. An angel!
BLUEBEARD

LA HIRE. Yes, an angel. She has made her way from Champagne with half a dozen men through the thick of everything: Burgundians, goddams, deserters, robbers, and Lord knows who; and they never met a soul except the country folk. I know one of them: de Poulengey. He says she's an angel. If ever I utter an oath again may my soul be blasted to eternal damnation!

THE ARCHBISHOP. A very pious beginning, Captain.

[BLUEBEARD *and* LA TRÉMOUILLE *laugh at him. The* PAGE *returns.*]

THE PAGE. His Majesty.

[*They stand perfunctorily at court attention. The* DAUPHIN, *aged 26, really* KING CHARLES THE SEVENTH *since the death of his father, but as yet uncrowned, comes in through the curtains with a paper in his hands. He is a poor creature physically; and the current fashion of shaving closely, and hiding every scrap of hair under the head-covering or headdress, both by women and men, makes the worst of his appearance. He has little narrow eyes, near together, a long pendulous nose that droops over his thick short upper lip, and the expression of a young dog accustomed to be kicked, yet incorrigible and irrepressible. But he is neither vulgar nor stupid; and he has a cheeky humor which enables him to hold his own in conversation. Just at present he is excited, like a child with a new toy. He comes to the* ARCH-

BISHOP's *left hand.* BLUEBEARD *and* LA HIRE *retire towards the curtains.*]

CHARLES. Oh, Archbishop, do you know what Robert de Baudricourt is sending me from Vaucouleurs?

THE ARCHBISHOP [*contemptuously*]. I am not interested in the newest toys.

CHARLES [*indignantly*]. It isnt a toy. [*Sulkily.*] However, I can get on very well without your interest.

THE ARCHBISHOP. Your Highness is taking offence very unnecessarily.

CHARLES. Thank you. You are always ready with a lecture, arnt you?

LA TRÉMOUILLE [*roughly*]. Enough grumbling. What have you got there?

CHARLES. What is that to you?

LA TRÉMOUILLE. It is my business to know what is passing between you and the garrison at Vaucouleurs. [*He snatches the paper from the* DAUPHIN's *hand, and begins reading it with some difficulty, following the words with his finger and spelling them out syllable by syllable.*]

CHARLES [*mortified*]. You all think you can treat me as you please because I owe you money, and because I am no good at fighting. But I have the blood royal in my veins.

THE ARCHBISHOP. Even that has been questioned, your Highness. One hardly recognizes in you the grandson of Charles the Wise.

CHARLES. I want to hear no more of my grandfather. He was so wise that he used up the whole family stock of wisdom for five generations, and left me the poor fool I am, bullied and insulted by all of you.

THE ARCHBISHOP. Control yourself, sir. These outbursts of petulance are not seemly.

CHARLES. Another lecture! Thank you. What a pity it is that though you are an archbishop saints and angels dont come to see you!

THE ARCHBISHOP. What do you mean?

CHARLES. Aha! Ask that bully there [*pointing to* LA TRÉMOUILLE].

LA TRÉMOUILLE [*furious*]. Hold your tongue. Do you hear?

CHARLES. Oh, I hear. You neednt shout. The whole castle can hear. Why dont you go and shout at the English, and beat them for me?

LA TRÉMOUILLE [*raising his fist*]. You young—

CHARLES [*running behind the* ARCHBISHOP]. Dont you raise your hand to me. It's high treason.

LA HIRE. Steady, Duke! Steady!

THE ARCHBISHOP [*resolutely*]. Come, come! this will not do. My lord Chamberlain: please! please! we must keep some sort of order. [*To the* DAUPHIN.] And you, sir: if you cannot rule your kingdom, at least try to rule yourself.

CHARLES. Another lecture! Thank you.

LA TRÉMOUILLE [*handing the paper to the* ARCHBISHOP]. Here: read the accursed thing for me. He has sent the blood boiling into my head: I cant distinguish the letters.

CHARLES [*coming back and peering round* LA TRÉMOUILLE'S *left shoulder*]. I will read it for you if you like. I can read, you know.

LA TRÉMOUILLE [*with intense contempt, not at all stung by the taunt*]. Yes: reading is about all you are fit for. Can you make it out, Archbishop?

THE ARCHBISHOP. I should have expected more commonsense from De Baudricourt. He is sending some cracked country lass here—

CHARLES [*interrupting*]. No: he is sending a saint: an angel. And she is coming to me: to me, the king, and not to you, Archbishop, holy as you are. She knows the blood royal if you dont. [*He struts up to the curtains between* BLUEBEARD *and* LA HIRE.]

THE ARCHBISHOP. You cannot be allowed to see this crazy wench.

CHARLES [*turning*]. But I am the king; and I will.

LA TRÉMOUILLE [*brutally*]. Then she cannot be allowed to see you. Now!

CHARLES. I tell you I will. I am going to put my foot down—

BLUEBEARD [*laughing at him*]. Naughty! What would your wise grandfather say?

CHARLES. That just shews your ignorance, Bluebeard. My grandfather had a saint who used to float in the air when she was praying, and told him everything he wanted to know. My poor father had two saints, Marie de Maillé and the Gasque of Avignon. It is in our family; and I dont care what you say: I will have my saint too.

THE ARCHBISHOP. This creature is not a saint. She is not even a respectable woman. She does not wear women's clothes. She is dressed like a soldier, and rides round the country with soldiers. Do you suppose such a person can be admitted to your Highness's court?

LA HIRE. Stop. [*Going to the* ARCHBISHOP.] Did you say a girl in armor, like a soldier?

THE ARCHBISHOP. So De Baudricourt describes her.

LA HIRE. But by all the devils in hell—Oh, God forgive me, what am I saying?—by Our Lady and all the saints, this must be the angel that struck Foul Mouthed Frank dead for swearing.

CHARLES [*triumphantly*]. You see! A miracle!

LA HIRE. She may strike the lot of us dead if we cross her. For Heaven's sake, Archbishop, be careful what you are doing.

THE ARCHBISHOP [*severely*]. Rubbish! Nobody has been struck dead. A drunken blackguard who has been rebuked a hundred times for swearing has fallen into a well, and been drowned. A mere coincidence.

LA HIRE. I do not know what a coincidence is. I do know that the man is dead, and that she told him he was going to die.

THE ARCHBISHOP. We are all going to die, Captain.

LA HIRE [*crossing himself*]. I hope not. [*He backs out of the conversation.*]

BLUEBEARD. We can easily find out whether she is an angel or not. Let us arrange when she comes that I shall be the Dauphin, and see whether she will find me out.

CHARLES. Yes: I agree to that. If she cannot find the blood royal I will have nothing to do with her.

THE ARCHBISHOP. It is for the Church to make saints: let De Baudricourt mind his own business, and not dare usurp the function of his priest. I say the girl shall not be admitted.

BLUEBEARD. But, Archbishop—

THE ARCHBISHOP [*sternly*]. I speak in the Church's name. [*To the* DAUPHIN.] Do you dare say she shall?

CHARLES [*intimidated but sulky*]. Oh, if you make it an excommunication matter, I have nothing more to say, of course. But you havnt read the end of the letter. De Baudricourt says she will raise the siege of Orleans, and beat the English for us.

LA TRÉMOUILLE. Rot!

CHARLES. Well, will you save Orleans for us, with all your bullying?

LA TRÉMOUILLE [*savagely*]. Do not throw that in my face again: do you hear? I have done more fighting than you ever did or ever will. But I cannot be everywhere.

THE DAUPHIN. Well, thats something.

BLUEBEARD [*coming between the* ARCHBISHOP *and* CHARLES]. You have Jack Dunois at the head of your troops in Orleans: the brave Dunois, the handsome Dunois, the wonderful invincible Dunois, the darling of all the ladies, the beautiful bastard. Is it likely that the country lass can do what he cannot do?

CHARLES. Why doesnt he raise the siege, then?

LA HIRE. The wind is against him.

BLUEBEARD. How can the wind hurt him at Orleans? It is not on the Channel.

LA HIRE. It is on the river Loire; and the English hold the bridgehead. He must ship his men across the river and upstream, if he is to take them in the rear. Well, he cannot, because there is a devil of a wind blowing the other way. He is tired of paying the priests to pray for a west wind. What he needs is a miracle. You tell me that what the girl did to Foul Mouthed Frank was no miracle. No matter: it finished Frank. If she changes the wind for Dunois, that may not be a miracle either; but it may finish the English. What harm is there in trying?

THE ARCHBISHOP. [*who has read the end of the letter and become more thoughtful*]. It is true that De Baudricourt seems extraordinarily impressed.

LA HIRE. De Baudricourt is a blazing ass; but he is a soldier; and if he thinks she can beat the English, all the rest of the army will think so too.

LA TRÉMOUILLE [*to the* ARCHBISHOP, *who is hesitating*]. Oh, let them have their way. Dunois' men will give up the town in spite of him if somebody does not put some fresh spunk into them.

THE ARCHBISHOP. The Church must examine the girl before anything decisive is done about her. However, since his Highness desires it, let her attend the Court.

LA HIRE. I will find her and tell her. [*He goes out.*]

CHARLES. Come with me, Bluebeard; and let us arrange so that she will not know who I am. You will pretend to be me. [*He goes out through the curtains.*]

BLUEBEARD. Pretend to be that thing! Holy Michael! [*He follows the* DAUPHIN.]

LA TRÉMOUILLE. I wonder will she pick him out!

THE ARCHBISHOP. Of course she will.

LA TRÉMOUILLE. Why? How is she to know?

THE ARCHBISHOP. She will know what everybody in Chinon knows: that the Dauphin is the meanest-looking and worst-dressed figure in the Court, and that the man with the blue beard is Gilles de Rais.

LA TRÉMOUILLE. I never thought of that.

THE ARCHBISHOP. You are not so accustomed to miracles as I am. It is part of my profession.

LA TRÉMOUILLE [*puzzled and a little scandalized*]. But that would not be a miracle at all.

THE ARCHBISHOP [*calmly*]. Why not?

LA TRÉMOUILLE. Well, come! what is a miracle?

THE ARCHBISHOP. A miracle, my friend, is an event which creates faith. That is the purpose and nature of miracles. They may seem very wonderful to the people who witness them, and very simple to those who perform them. That does not matter: if they confirm or create faith they are true miracles.

LA TRÉMOUILLE. Even when they are frauds, do you mean?

THE ARCHBISHOP. Frauds deceive. An event which creates faith does not deceive: therefore it is not a fraud, but a miracle.

LA TRÉMOUILLE [*scratching his neck in his perplexity*]. Well, I suppose as you are an archbishop you must be right. It seems a bit fishy to me. But I am no churchman, and dont
5 understand these matters.

THE ARCHBISHOP. You are not a churchman; but you are a diplomatist and a soldier. Could you make our citizens pay war taxes, or our soldiers sacrifice their lives, if they knew what
10 is really happening instead of what seems to them to be happening?

LA TRÉMOUILLE. No, by Saint Dennis: the fat would be in the fire before sundown.

THE ARCHBISHOP. Would it not be quite easy
15 to tell them the truth?

LA TRÉMOUILLE. Man alive, they wouldnt believe it.

THE ARCHBISHOP. Just so. Well, the Church has to rule men for the good of their souls as
20 you have to rule them for the good of their bodies. To do that, the Church must do as you do: nourish their faith by poetry.

LA TRÉMOUILLE. Poetry! I should call it humbug.

25 THE ARCHBISHOP. You would be wrong, my friend. Parables are not lies because they describe events that have never happened. Miracles are not frauds because they are often —I do not say always—very simple and inno-
30 cent contrivances by which the priest fortifies the faith of his flock. When this girl picks out the Dauphin among his courtiers, it will not be a miracle for me, because I shall know how it has been done, and my faith will not be
35 increased. But as for the others, if they feel the thrill of the supernatural, and forget their sinful clay in a sudden sense of the glory of God, it will be a miracle and a blessed one. And you will find that the girl herself will be
40 more affected than anyone else. She will forget how she really picked him out. So, perhaps, will you.

LA TRÉMOUILLE. Well, I wish I were clever enough to know how much of you is God's
45 archbishop and how much the most artful fox in Touraine. Come on, or we shall be late for the fun; and I want to see it, miracle or no miracle.

THE ARCHBISHOP [*detaining him a moment*]. Do not think that I am a lover of crooked 50 ways. There is a new spirit rising in men: we are at the dawning of a wider epoch. If I were a simple monk, and had not to rule men, I should seek peace for my spirit with Aristotle and Pythagoras rather than with the saints 55 and their miracles.

LA TRÉMOUILLE. And who the deuce was Pythagoras?

THE ARCHBISHOP. A sage who held that the earth is round, and that it moves round the sun. 60

LA TRÉMOUILLE. What an utter fool! Couldnt he use his eyes?

[*They go out together through the curtains, which are presently withdrawn, revealing the full depth of the throne-room with the* COURT 65 *assembled. On the right are two Chairs of State on a dais.* BLUEBEARD *is standing theatrically on the dais, playing the king, and, like the courtiers, enjoying the joke rather obviously. There is a curtained arch in the wall behind* 70 *the dais; but the main door, guarded by* MEN-AT-ARMS, *is at the other side of the room; and a clear path across is kept and lined by the courtiers.* CHARLES *is in this path in the middle of the room.* LA HIRE *is on his right. The* 75 ARCHBISHOP, *on his left, has taken his place by the dais:* LA TRÉMOUILLE *at the other side of it. The* DUCHESS DE LA TRÉMOUILLE, *pretending to be the Queen, sits in the Consort's chair, with a group of ladies in waiting close by, behind* 80 *the* ARCHBISHOP.

The chatter of the COURTIERS *makes such a noise that nobody notices the appearance of the* PAGE *at the door.*]

THE PAGE. The Duke of—[*Nobody listens.*] 85 The Duke of—[*The chatter continues. Indignant at his failure to command a hearing, he snatches the halberd of the nearest* MAN-AT-ARMS, *and thumps the floor with it. The chatter ceases; and everybody looks at him in silence.*] 90 Attention! [*He restores the halberd to the* MAN-AT-ARMS.] The Duke of Vendôme presents Joan the Maid to his Majesty.

CHARLES [*putting his finger on his lip*]. Ssh! [*He hides behind the nearest courtier, peering* 95 *out to see what happens.*]

BLUEBEARD [*majestically*]. Let her approach the throne.

[JOAN, *dressed as a soldier, with her hair bobbed and hanging thickly round her face, is led in by a bashful and speechless* NOBLEMAN, *from whom she detaches herself to stop and look round eagerly for the* DAUPHIN.]

THE DUCHESS [*to the nearest lady in waiting*]. My dear! Her hair!

[*All the ladies explode in uncontrollable laughter.*]

BLUEBEARD [*trying not to laugh, waving his hand in deprecation of their merriment*]. Ssh—ssh! Ladies! Ladies!!

JOAN [*not at all embarrassed*]. I wear it like this because I am a soldier. Where be Dauphin?

[*A titter runs through the* COURT *as she walks to the dais.*]

BLUEBEARD [*condescendingly*]. You are in the presence of the Dauphin.

[JOAN *looks at him sceptically for a moment, scanning him hard up and down to make sure. Dead silence, all watching her. Fun dawns in her face.*]

JOAN. Coom, Bluebeard! Thou canst not fool me. Where be Dauphin?

[*A roar of laughter breaks out as* GILLES, *with a gesture of surrender, joins in the laugh, and jumps down from the dais beside* LA TRÉMOUILLE. JOAN, *also on the broad grin, turns back, searching along the row of courtiers, and presently makes a dive, and drags out* CHARLES *by the arm.*]

JOAN [*releasing him and bobbing him a little curtsey*]. Gentle little Dauphin, I am sent to you to drive the English away from Orleans and from France, and to crown you king in the cathedral at Rheims, where all true kings of France are crowned.

CHARLES [*triumphant, to the* COURT]. You see, all of you: she knew the blood royal. Who dare say now that I am not my father's son? [*To* JOAN.] But if you want me to be crowned at Rheims you must talk to the Archbishop, not to me. There he is [*he is standing behind her*]!

JOAN [*turning quickly, overwhelmed with emotion*]. Oh, my lord! [*She falls on both knees before him, with bowed head, not daring to look up.*] My lord: I am only a poor country girl; and you are filled with the blessedness and glory of God Himself; but you will touch me with your hands, and give me your blessing, wont you?

BLUEBEARD [*whispering to* LA TRÉMOUILLE]. The old fox blushes.

LA TRÉMOUILLE. Another miracle!

THE ARCHBISHOP [*touched, putting his hand on her head*]. Child: you are in love with religion.

JOAN [*startled: looking up at him*]. Am I? I never thought of that. Is there any harm in it?

THE ARCHBISHOP. There is no harm in it, my child. But there is danger.

JOAN [*rising, with sunflush of reckless happiness irradiating her face*]. There is always danger, except in heaven. Oh, my lord, you have given me such strength, such courage. It must be a most wonderful thing to be Archbishop.

[*The* COURT *smiles broadly: even titters a little.*]

THE ARCHBISHOP [*drawing himself up sensitively*]. Gentlemen: your levity is rebuked by this maid's faith. I am, God help me, all unworthy; but your mirth is a deadly sin.

[*Their faces fall. Dead silence.*]

BLUEBEARD. My lord: we were laughing at her, not at you.

THE ARCHBISHOP. What? Not at my unworthiness but at her faith! Gilles de Rais: this maid prophesied that the blasphemer should be drowned in his sin—

JOAN [*distressed*]. No!

THE ARCHBISHOP [*silencing her by a gesture*]. I prophesy now that you will be hanged in yours if you do not learn when to laugh and when to pray.

BLUEBEARD. My lord: I stand rebuked. I am sorry: I can say no more. But if you prophesy that I shall be hanged, I shall never be able to resist temptation, because I shall always be telling myself that I may as well be hanged for a sheep as a lamb.

[*The* COURTIERS *take heart at this. There is more tittering.*]

JOAN [*scandalized*]. You are an idle fellow, Bluebeard; and you have great impudence to answer the Archbishop.

LA HIRE [*with a huge chuckle*]. Well said, 5 lass! Well said!

JOAN [*impatiently to the* ARCHBISHOP]. Oh, my lord, will you send all these silly folks away so that I may speak to the Dauphin alone?

10 LA HIRE [*goodhumoredly*]. I can take a hint. [*He salutes; turns on his heel; and goes out.*]

THE ARCHBISHOP. Come, gentlemen. The Maid comes with God's blessing, and must be obeyed.

15 [*The* COURTIERS *withdraw, some through the arch, others at the opposite side. The* ARCH-BISHOP *marches across to the door, followed by the* DUCHESS *and* LA TRÉMOUILLE. *As the* ARCH-BISHOP *passes* JOAN, *she falls on her knees, and*
20 *kisses the hem of his robe fervently. He shakes his head in instinctive remonstrance; gathers the robe from her; and goes out. She is left kneeling directly in the* DUCHESS'S *way.*]

THE DUCHESS [*coldly*]. Will you allow me
25 to pass, please?

JOAN [*hastily rising, and standing back*]. Beg pardon, maam, I am sure.

[*The* DUCHESS *passes on.* JOAN *stares after her; then whispers to the* DAUPHIN.]

30 JOAN. Be that Queen?

CHARLES. No. She thinks she is.

JOAN [*again staring after the* DUCHESS]. Oo-oo-ooh! [*Her awestruck amazement at the figure cut by the magnificently dressed lady is*
35 *not wholly complimentary.*]

LA TRÉMOUILLE [*very surly*]. I'll trouble your Highness not to gibe at my wife. [*He goes out. The others have already gone.*]

JOAN [*to the* DAUPHIN]. Who be old Gruff-
40 and-Grum?

CHARLES. He is the Duke de la Trémouille.

JOAN. What be his job?

CHARLES. He pretends to command the army. And whenever I find a friend I can care for,
45 he kills him.

JOAN. Why dost let him?

CHARLES [*petulantly moving to the throne side of the room to escape from her magnetic field*]. How can I prevent him? He bullies me. They all bully me. 50

JOAN. Art afraid?

CHARLES. Yes: I am afraid. It's no use preaching to me about it. It's all very well for these big men with their armor that is too heavy for me, and their swords that I can 55 hardly lift, and their muscle and their shouting and their bad tempers. They like fighting: most of them are making fools of themselves all the time they are not fighting; but I am quiet and sensible; and I dont want to kill people: I only 60 want to be left alone to enjoy myself in my own way. I never asked to be a king: it was pushed on me. So if you are going to say "Son of St Louis: gird on the sword of your ances-tors, and lead us to victory" you may spare 65 your breath to cool your porridge; for I can-not do it. I am not built that way; and there is an end of it.

JOAN [*trenchant and masterful*]. Blethers! We are all like that to begin with. I shall put 70 courage into thee.

CHARLES. But I dont want to have courage put into me. I want to sleep in a comfortable bed, and not live in continual terror of being killed or wounded. Put courage into the others, 75 and let them have their bellyful of fighting; but let me alone.

JOAN. It's no use, Charlie: thou must face what God puts on thee. If thou fail to make thyself king, thoult be a beggar: what else art 80 fit for? Come! Let me see thee sitting on the throne. I have looked forward to that.

CHARLES. What is the good of sitting on the throne when the other fellows give all the orders? However! [*he sits enthroned, a piteous* 85 *figure*] here is the king for you! Look your fill at the poor devil.

JOAN. Thourt not king yet, lad: thourt but Dauphin. Be not led away by them around thee. Dressing up dont fill empty noddle. I 90 know the people: the real people that make thy bread for thee; and I tell thee they count no man king of France until the holy oil has been poured on his hair, and himself consecrated and crowned in Rheims Cathedral. And thou needs new clothes, Charlie. Why does not Queen look after thee properly?

CHARLES. We're too poor. She wants all the money we can spare to put on her own back. Besides, I like to see her beautifully dressed; and I dont care what I wear myself: I should look ugly anyhow.

JOAN. There is some good in thee, Charlie; but it is not yet a king's good.

CHARLES. We shall see. I am not such a fool as I look. I have my eyes open; and I can tell you that one good treaty is worth ten good fights. These fighting fellows lose all on the treaties that they gain on the fights. If we can only have a treaty, the English are sure to have the worst of it, because they are better at fighting than at thinking.

JOAN. If the English win, it is they that will make the treaty; and then God help poor France! Thou must fight, Charlie, whether thou will or no. I will go first to hearten thee. We must take our courage in both hands: aye, and pray for it with both hands too.

CHARLES [*descending from his throne and again crossing the room to escape from her dominating urgency*]. Oh do stop talking about God and praying. I cant bear people who are always praying. Isnt it bad enough to have to do it at the proper times?

JOAN [*pitying him*]. Thou poor child, thou hast never prayed in thy life. I must teach thee from the beginning.

CHARLES. I am not a child: I am a grown man and a father; and I will not be taught any more.

JOAN. Aye, you have a little son. He that will be Louis the Eleventh when you die. Would you not fight for him?

CHARLES. No: a horrid boy. He hates me. He hates everybody, selfish little beast! I dont want to be bothered with children. I dont want to be a father; and I dont want to be a son: especially a son of St Louis. I dont want to be any of these fine things you all have your heads full of: I want to be just what I am. Why cant you mind your own business, and let me mind mine?

JOAN [*again contemptuous*]. Minding your own business is like minding your own body: it's the shortest way to make yourself sick. What is my business? Helping mother at home. What is thine? Petting lapdogs and sucking sugarsticks. I call that muck. I tell thee it is God's business we are here to do: not our own. I have a message to thee from God; and thou must listen to it, though thy heart break with the terror of it.

CHARLES. I dont want a message; but can you tell me any secrets? Can you do any cures? Can you turn lead into gold, or anything of that sort?

JOAN. I can turn thee into a king, in Rheims Cathedral; and that is a miracle that will take some doing, it seems.

CHARLES. If we go to Rheims, and have a coronation, Anne will want new dresses. We cant afford them. I am all right as I am.

JOAN. As you are! And what is that? Less than my father's poorest shepherd. Thourt not lawful owner of thy own land of France till thou be consecrated.

CHARLES. But I shall not be lawful owner of my own land anyhow. Will the consecration pay off my mortgages? I have pledged my last acre to the Archbishop and that fat bully. I owe money even to Bluebeard.

JOAN [*earnestly*]. Charlie: I come from the land, and have gotten my strength working on the land; and I tell thee that the land is thine to rule righteously and keep God's peace in, and not to pledge at the pawnshop as a drunken woman pledges her children's clothes. And I come from God to tell thee to kneel in the cathedral and solemnly give thy kingdom to Him for ever and ever, and become the greatest king in the world as His steward and His bailiff, His soldier and His servant. The very clay of France will become holy: her soldiers will be the soldiers of God: the rebel dukes will be rebels against God: the English will fall on their knees and beg thee let them return to their lawful homes in peace. Wilt be a poor little Judas, and betray me and Him that sent me?

CHARLES [*tempted at last*]. Oh, if I only dare!

JOAN. I shall dare, dare, and dare again, in God's name! Art for or against me?

5 CHARLES [*excited*]. I'll risk it. I warn you I shant be able to keep it up; but I'll risk it. You shall see. [*Running to the main door and shouting.*] Hallo! Come back, everybody. [*To* JOAN, *as he runs back to the arch opposite.*]
10 Mind you stand by and dont let me be bullied. [*Through the arch.*] Come along, will you: the whole Court. [*He sits down in the royal chair as they all hurry in to their former places, chattering and wondering.*] Now I'm in for it; but
15 no matter: here goes! [*To the* PAGE.] Call for silence, you little beast, will you?

THE PAGE [*snatching a halberd as before and thumping with it repeatedly*]. Silence for His Majesty the King. The King speaks. [*Peremp-*
20 *torily.*] Will you be silent there? [*Silence.*]

CHARLES [*rising*]. I have given the command of the army to The Maid. The Maid is to do as she likes with it. [*He descends from the dais.*]

25 [*General amazement.* LA HIRE, *delighted, slaps his steel thigh-piece with his gauntlet.*]

LA TRÉMOUILLE [*turning threateningly towards* CHARLES]. What is this? I command the army.

30 [JOAN *quickly puts her hand on* CHARLES'S *shoulder as he instinctively recoils.* CHARLES, *with a grotesque effort culminating in an extravagant gesture, snaps his fingers in the* CHAMBERLAIN'S *face.*]

35 JOAN. Thourt answered, old Gruff-and-Grum. [*Suddenly flashing out her sword as she divines that her moment has come.*] Who is for God and His Maid? Who is for Orleans with me?

40 LA HIRE [*carried away, drawing also*]. For God and His Maid! To Orleans!

ALL THE KNIGHTS [*following his lead with enthusiasm*]. To Orleans!

[JOAN, *radiant, falls on her knees in thanks-*
45 *giving to God. They all kneel, except the* ARCHBISHOP, *who gives his benediction with a sign, and* LA TRÉMOUILLE, *who collapses, cursing.*]

SCENE III

[*Orleans, May 29th, 1429.* DUNOIS, *aged 26, is pacing up and down a patch of ground on* 50 *the south bank of the silver Loire, commanding a long view of the river in both directions. He has had his lance stuck up with a pennon, which streams in a strong east wind. His shield with its bend sinister° lies beside it. He has his* 55 *commander's baton in his hand. He is well built, carrying his armor easily. His broad brow and pointed chin give him an equilaterally triangular face, already marked by active service and responsibility, with the expression of* 60 *a goodnatured and capable man who has no affectations and no foolish illusions. His* PAGE *is sitting on the ground, elbows on knees, cheeks on fists, idly watching the water. It is evening; and both man and boy are affected* 65 *by the loveliness of the Loire.*]

DUNOIS [*halting for a moment to glance up at the streaming pennon and shake his head wearily before he resumes his pacing*]. West wind, west wind, west wind. Strumpet: stead- 70 fast when you should be wanton, wanton when you should be steadfast. West wind on the silver Loire: what rhymes to Loire? [*He looks again at the pennon, and shakes his fist at it.*] Change, curse you, change, English harlot of 75 a wind, change. West, west, I tell you. [*With a growl he resumes his march in silence, but soon begins again.*] West wind, wanton wind, wilful wind, womanish wind, false wind from over the water, will you never blow again? 80

THE PAGE [*bounding to his feet*]. See! There! There she goes!

DUNOIS [*startled from his reverie: eagerly*]. Where? Who? The Maid?

THE PAGE. No: the kingfisher. Like blue 85 lightning. She went into that bush.

DUNOIS [*furiously disappointed*]. Is that all? You infernal young idiot: I have a mind to pitch you into the river.

THE PAGE [*not afraid, knowing his man*]. It 90

___

bend sinister a heraldic pattern denoting an illegitimate child, usually a descendant "on the left hand" of royalty, as was true of Dunois

looked frightfully jolly, that flash of blue. Look! There goes the other!

DUNOIS [*running eagerly to the river brim*]. Where? Where?

5   THE PAGE [*pointing*]. Passing the reeds.

DUNOIS [*delighted*]. I see.

[*They follow the flight till the bird takes cover.*]

THE PAGE. You blew me up because you
10 were not in time to see them yesterday.

DUNOIS. You knew I was expecting The Maid when you set up your yelping. I will give you something to yelp for next time.

THE PAGE. Arnt they lovely? I wish I could
15 catch them.

DUNOIS. Let me catch you trying to trap them, and I will put you in the iron cage for a month to teach you what a cage feels like. You are an abominable boy.

20 THE PAGE [*laughs, and squats down as before*]!

DUNOIS [*pacing*]. Blue bird, blue bird, since I am friend to thee, change thou the wind for me. No: it does not rhyme. He who has sinned
25 for thee: thats better. No sense in it, though. [*He finds himself close to the* PAGE.] You abominable boy! [*He turns away from him.*] Mary in the blue snood, kingfisher color: will you grudge me a west wind?

30 A SENTRY'S VOICE WESTWARD. Halt! Who goes there?

JOAN'S VOICE. The Maid.

DUNOIS. Let her pass. Hither, Maid! To me! [*Joan, in splendid armor, rushes in in a
35 blazing rage. The wind drops; and the pennon flaps idly down the lance; but* DUNOIS *is too much occupied with* JOAN *to notice it.*]

JOAN [*bluntly*]. Be you Bastard of Orleans?

DUNOIS [*cool and stern, pointing to his
40 shield*]. You see the bend sinister. Are you Joan the Maid?

JOAN. Sure.

DUNOIS. Where are your troops?

JOAN. Miles behind. They have cheated me.
45 They have brought me to the wrong side of the river.

DUNOIS. I told them to.

JOAN. Why did you? The English are on the other side!

DUNOIS. The English are on both sides.   50

JOAN. But Orleans is on the other side. We must fight the English there. How can we cross the river?

DUNOIS [*grimly*]. There is a bridge.

JOAN. In God's name, then, let us cross the   55
bridge, and fall on them.

DUNOIS. It seems simple; but it cannot be done.

JOAN. Who says so?

DUNOIS. I say so; and older and wiser heads   60
than mine are of the same opinion.

JOAN [*roundly*]. Then your older and wiser heads are fatheads: they have made a fool of you; and now they want to make a fool of me too, bringing me to the wrong side of the river.   65
Do you not know that I bring you better help than ever came to any general or any town?

DUNOIS [*smiling patiently*]. Your own?

JOAN. No: the help and counsel of the King of Heaven. Which is the way to the bridge?   70

DUNOIS. You are impatient, Maid.

JOAN. Is this a time for patience? Our enemy is at our gates; and here we stand doing nothing. Oh, why are you not fighting? Listen to me: I will deliver you from fear. I—   75

DUNOIS [*laughing heartily, and waving her off*]. No, no, my girl: if you delivered me from fear I should be a good knight for a story book, but a very bad commander of the army. Come! let me begin to make a soldier of you. [*He   80
takes her to the water's edge.*] Do you see those two forts at this end of the bridge? the big ones?

JOAN. Yes. Are they ours or the goddams'?

DUNOIS. Be quiet, and listen to me. If I   85
were in either of those forts with only ten men I could hold it against an army. The English have more than ten times ten goddams in those forts to hold them against us.

JOAN. They cannot hold them against God.   90
God did not give them the land under those forts: they stole it from Him. He gave it to us. I will take those forts.

DUNOIS. Single-handed?

JOAN. Our men will take them. I will lead   95
them.

DUNOIS. Not a man will follow you.

JOAN. I will not look back to see whether anyone is following me.

DUNOIS [recognizing her mettle, and clapping
5 her heartily on the shoulder]. Good. You have the makings of a soldier in you. You are in love with war.

JOAN [startled]. Oh! And the Archbishop said I was in love with religion.

10 DUNOIS. I, God forgive me, am a little in love with war myself, the ugly devil! I am like a man with two wives. Do you want to be like a woman with two husbands?

JOAN [matter-of-fact]. I will never take a
15 husband. A man in Toul took an action against me for breach of promise; but I never promised him. I am a soldier: I do not want to be thought of as a woman. I will not dress as a woman. I do not care for the things women
20 care for. They dream of lovers, and of money. I dream of leading a charge, and of placing the big guns. You soldiers do not know how to use the big guns: you think you can win battles with a great noise and smoke.

25 DUNOIS [with a shrug]. True. Half the time the artillery is more trouble than it is worth.

JOAN. Aye, lad; but you cannot fight stone walls with horses: you must have guns, and much bigger guns too.

30 DUNOIS [grinning at her familiarity, and echoing it]. Aye, lass; but a good heart and a stout ladder will get over the stoniest wall.

JOAN. I will be first up the ladder when we reach the fort, Bastard. I dare you to follow
35 me.

DUNOIS. You must not dare a staff officer, Joan: only company officers are allowed to indulge in displays of personal courage. Besides, you must know that I welcome you
40 as a saint, not as a soldier. I have daredevils enough at my call, if they could help me.

JOAN. I am not a daredevil: I am a servant of God. My sword is sacred: I found it behind the altar in the church of St Catherine, where
45 God hid it for me; and I may not strike a blow with it. My heart is full of courage, not of anger. I will lead; and your men will follow:

that is all I can do. But I must do it: you shall not stop me.

DUNOIS. All in good time. Our men cannot 50 take those forts by a sally across the bridge. They must come by water, and take the English in the rear on this side.

JOAN [her military sense asserting itself]. Then make rafts and put big guns on them; 55 and let your men cross to us.

DUNOIS. The rafts are ready; and the men are embarked. But they must wait for God.

JOAN. What do you mean? God is waiting for them. 60

DUNOIS. Let Him send us a wind then. My boats are downstream: they cannot come up against both wind and current. We must wait until God changes the wind. Come: let me take you to the church. 65

JOAN. No. I love church; but the English will not yield to prayers: they understand nothing but hard knocks and slashes. I will not go to church until we have beaten them.

DUNOIS. You must: I have business for you 70 there.

JOAN. What business?

DUNOIS. To pray for a west wind. I have prayed; and I have given two silver candlesticks; but my prayers are not answered. Yours 75 may be: you are young and innocent.

JOAN. Oh yes: you are right. I will pray: I will tell St Catherine: she will make God give me a west wind. Quick: shew me the way to the church. 80

THE PAGE [sneezes violently]. At-cha!!!

JOAN. God bless you, child! Coom, Bastard.

[They go out. The PAGE rises to follow. He picks up the shield, and is taking the spear as well when he notices the pennon, which is now 85 streaming eastward.]

THE PAGE [dropping the shield and calling excitedly after them]. Seigneur! Seigneur! Mademoiselle!

DUNOIS [running back]. What is it? The 90 kingfisher? [He looks eagerly for it up the river.]

JOAN [joining them]. Oh, a kingfisher! Where?

THE PAGE. No: the wind, the wind, the wind [*pointing to the pennon*]: that is what made me sneeze.

DUNOIS [*looking at the pennon*]. The wind has changed. [*He crosses himself.*] God has spoken. [*Kneeling and handing his baton to* JOAN.] You command the king's army. I am your soldier.

THE PAGE [*looking down the river*]. The boats have put off. They are ripping upstream like anything.

DUNOIS [*rising*]. Now for the forts. You dared me to follow. Dare you lead?

JOAN [*bursting into tears and flinging her arms round* DUNOIS, *kissing him on both cheeks*]. Dunois, dear comrade in arms, help me. My eyes are blinded with tears. Set my foot on the ladder, and say "Up, Joan."

DUNOIS [*dragging her out*]. Never mind the tears: make for the flash of the guns.

JOAN [*in a blaze of courage*]. Ah!

DUNOIS [*dragging her along with him*]. For God and Saint Dennis!

THE PAGE [*shrilly*]. The Maid! The Maid! God and The Maid! Hurray-ay-ay! [*He snatches up the shield and lance, and capers out after them, mad with excitement.*]

SCENE IV

[*A tent in the English camp. A bullnecked* ENGLISH CHAPLAIN *of 50 is sitting on a stool at a table, hard at work writing. At the other side of the table an imposing* NOBLEMAN, *aged 46, is seated in a handsome chair turning over the leaves of an illuminated Book of Hours. The* NOBLEMAN *is enjoying himself: the* CHAPLAIN *is struggling with suppressed wrath. There is an unoccupied leather stool on the* NOBLEMAN'S *left. The table is on his right.*]

THE NOBLEMAN. Now this is what I call workmanship. There is nothing on earth more exquisite than a bonny book, with well-placed columns of rich black writing in beautiful borders, and illuminated pictures cunningly inset. But nowadays, instead of looking at books, people read them. A book might as well be one of those orders for bacon and bran that you are scribbling.

THE CHAPLAIN. I must say, my lord, you take our situation very coolly. Very coolly indeed.

THE NOBLEMAN [*supercilious*]. What is the matter?

THE CHAPLAIN. The matter, my lord, is that we English have been defeated.

THE NOBLEMAN. That happens, you know. It is only in history books and ballads that the enemy is always defeated.

THE CHAPLAIN. But we are being defeated over and over again. First, Orleans—

THE NOBLEMAN [*poohpoohing*]. Oh, Orleans!

THE CHAPLAIN. I know what you are going to say, my lord: that was a clear case of witchcraft and sorcery. But we are still being defeated. Jargeau, Meung, Beaugency, just like Orleans. And now we have been butchered at Patay, and Sir John Talbot taken prisoner. [*He throws down his pen, almost in tears.*] I feel it, my lord: I feel it very deeply. I cannot bear to see my countrymen defeated by a parcel of foreigners.

THE NOBLEMAN. Oh! you are an Englishman, are you?

THE CHAPLAIN. Certainly not, my lord: I am a gentleman. Still, like your lordship, I was born in England; and it makes a difference.

THE NOBLEMAN. You are attached to the soil, eh?

THE CHAPLAIN. It pleases your lordship to be satirical at my expense: your greatness privileges you to be so with impunity. But your lordship knows very well that I am not attached to the soil in a vulgar manner, like a serf. Still, I have a feeling about it; [*with growing agitation*] and I am not ashamed of it; and [*rising wildly*] by God, if this goes on any longer I will fling my cassock to the devil, and take arms myself, and strangle the accursed witch with my own hands.

THE NOBLEMAN [*laughing at him goodnaturedly*]. So you shall, chaplain: so you shall, if we can do nothing better. But not yet, not quite yet.

[*The* CHAPLAIN *resumes his seat very sulkily.*]

THE NOBLEMAN [*airily*]. I should not care

very much about the witch—you see, I have made my pilgrimage to the Holy Land; and the Heavenly Powers, for their own credit, can hardly allow me to be worsted by a village 5 sorceress—but the Bastard of Orleans is a harder nut to crack; and as he has been to the Holy Land too, honors are easy between us as far as that goes.

THE CHAPLAIN. He is only a Frenchman, my 10 lord.

THE NOBLEMAN. A Frenchman! Where did you pick up that expression? Are these Burgundians and Bretons and Picards and Gascons beginning to call themselves Frenchmen, just 15 as our fellows are beginning to call themselves Englishmen? They actually talk of France and England as their countries. Theirs, if you please! What is to become of me and you if that way of thinking comes into fashion?

20 THE CHAPLAIN. Why, my lord? Can it hurt us?

THE NOBLEMAN. Men cannot serve two masters. If this cant of serving their country once takes hold of them, goodbye to the authority 25 of their feudal lords, and goodbye to the authority of the Church. That is, goodbye to you and me.

THE CHAPLAIN. I hope I am a faithful servant of the Church; and there are only six cousins 30 between me and the barony of Stogumber, which was created by the Conqueror. But is that any reason why I should stand by and see Englishmen beaten by a French bastard and a witch from Lousy Champagne?

35 THE NOBLEMAN. Easy, man, easy: we shall burn the witch and beat the bastard all in good time. Indeed I am waiting at present for the Bishop of Beauvais, to arrange the burning with him. He has been turned out of his diocese 40 by her faction.

THE CHAPLAIN. You have first to catch her, my lord.

THE NOBLEMAN. Or buy her. I will offer a king's ransom.

45 THE CHAPLAIN. A king's ransom! For that slut!

THE NOBLEMAN. One has to leave a margin.

Some of Charles's people will sell her to the Burgundians; the Burgundians will sell her to us; and there will probably be three or four 50 middlemen who will expect their little commissions.

THE CHAPLAIN. Monstrous. It is all those scoundrels of Jews: they get in every time money changes hands. I would not leave a 55 Jew alive in Christendom if I had my way.

THE NOBLEMAN. Why not? The Jews generally give value. They make you pay; but they deliver the goods. In my experience the men who ·want something for nothing are invariably 60 Christians.

[A PAGE appears.]

THE PAGE. The Right Reverend the Bishop of Beauvais: Monseigneur Cauchon.

[CAUCHON, aged about 60, comes in. The 65 PAGE withdraws. The two Englishmen rise.]

THE NOBLEMAN [with effusive courtesy]. My dear Bishop, how good of you to come! Allow me to introduce myself: Richard de Beauchamp, Earl of Warwick, at your service. 70

CAUCHON. Your lordship's fame is well known to me.

WARWICK. This reverend cleric is Master John de Stogumber.

THE CHAPLAIN [glibly]. John Bowyer Spenser 75 Neville de Stogumber, at your service, my lord: Bachelor of Theology, and Keeper of the Private Seal to His Eminence the Cardinal of Winchester.

WARWICK [to CAUCHON]. You call him the 80 Cardinal of England, I believe. Our king's uncle.

CAUCHON. Messire John de Stogumber: I am always the very good friend of His Eminence. [He extends his hand to the CHAPLAIN, who 85 kisses his ring.]

WARWICK. Do me the honor to be seated. [He gives CAUCHON his chair, placing it at the head of the table.]

[CAUCHON accepts the place of honor with a 90 grave inclination. WARWICK fetches the leather stool carelessly, and sits in his former place. The CHAPLAIN goes back to his chair.

Though WARWICK has taken second place

in calculated deference to the BISHOP, *he assumes the lead in opening the proceedings as a matter of course. He is still cordial and expansive; but there is a new note in his voice which means that he is coming to business.*]

WARWICK. Well, my Lord Bishop, you find us in one of our unlucky moments. Charles is to be crowned at Rheims, practically by the young woman from Lorraine; and—I must not deceive you, nor flatter your hopes—we cannot prevent it. I suppose it will make a great difference to Charles's position.

CAUCHON. Undoubtedly. It is a masterstroke of The Maid's.

THE CHAPLAIN [*again agitated*]. We were not fairly beaten, my lord. No Englishman is ever fairly beaten.

[CAUCHON *raises his eyebrow slightly, then quickly composes his face.*]

WARWICK. Our friend here takes the view that the young woman is a sorceress. It would, I presume, be the duty of your reverend lordship to denounce her to the Inquisition, and have her burnt for that offence.

CAUCHON. If she were captured in my diocese: yes.

WARWICK [*feeling that they are getting on capitally*]. Just so. Now I suppose there can be no reasonable doubt that she is a sorceress.

THE CHAPLAIN. Not the least. An arrant witch.

WARWICK [*gently reproving the interruption*]. We are asking for the Bishop's opinion, Messire John.

CAUCHON. We shall have to consider not merely our own opinions here, but the opinions —the prejudices, if you like—of a French court.

WARWICK [*correcting*]. A Catholic court, my lord.

CAUCHON. Catholic courts are composed of mortal men, like other courts, however sacred their function and inspiration may be. And if the men are Frenchmen, as the modern fashion calls them, I am afraid the bare fact that an English army has been defeated by a French one will not convince them that there is any sorcery in the matter.

THE CHAPLAIN. What! Not when the famous Sir John Talbot himself has been defeated and actually taken prisoner by a drab from the ditches of Lorraine!

CAUCHON. Sir John Talbot, we all know, is a fierce and formidable soldier, Messire; but I have yet to learn that he is an able general. And though it pleases you to say that he has been defeated by this girl, some of us may be disposed to give a little of the credit to Dunois.

THE CHAPLAIN [*contemptuously*]. The Bastard of Orleans!

CAUCHON. Let me remind—

WARWICK [*interposing*]. I know what you are going to say, my lord. Dunois defeated me at Montargis.

CAUCHON [*bowing*]. I take that as evidence that the Seigneur Dunois is a very able commander indeed.

WARWICK. Your lordship is the flower of courtesy. I admit, on our side, that Talbot is a mere fighting animal, and that it probably served him right to be taken at Patay.

THE CHAPLAIN [*chafing*]. My lord: at Orleans this woman had her throat pierced by an English arrow, and was seen to cry like a child from the pain of it. It was a death wound; yet she fought all day; and when our men had repulsed all her attacks like true Englishmen, she walked alone to the wall of our fort with a white banner in her hand; and our men were paralyzed, and could neither shoot nor strike whilst the French fell on them and drove them on to the bridge, which immediately burst into flames and crumbled under them, letting them down into the river, where they were drowned in heaps. Was this your bastard's generalship? or were those flames the flames of hell, conjured up by witchcraft?

WARWICK. You will forgive Messire John's vehemence, my lord; but he has put our case. Dunois is a great captain, we admit; but why could he do nothing until the witch came?

CAUCHON. I do not say that there were no supernatural powers on her side. But the names on that white banner were not the names of Satan and Beelzebub, but the blessed names of our Lord and His holy mother. And your commander who was drowned—Clahz-da I think you call him—

WARWICK. Glasdale. Sir William Glasdale.

5 CAUCHON. Glass-dell, thank you. He was no saint; and many of our people think that he was drowned for his blasphemies against The Maid.

WARWICK [beginning to look very dubious]. 10 Well, what are we to infer from all this, my lord? Has The Maid converted you?

CAUCHON. If she had, my lord, I should have known better than to have trusted myself here within your grasp.

15 WARWICK [blandly deprecating]. Oh! oh! My lord!

CAUCHON. If the devil is making use of this girl—and I believe he is—

WARWICK [reassured]. Ah! You hear, Mes- 20 sire John? I knew your lordship would not fail us. Pardon my interruption. Proceed.

CAUCHON. If it be so, the devil has longer views than you give him credit for.

WARWICK. Indeed? In what way? Listen to 25 this, Messire John.

CAUCHON. If the devil wanted to damn a country girl, do you think so easy a task would cost him the winning of half a dozen battles? No, my lord: any trumpery imp could do that 30 much if the girl could be damned at all. The Prince of Darkness does not condescend to such cheap drudgery. When he strikes, he strikes at the Catholic Church, whose realm is the whole spiritual world. When he damns, he damns the 35 souls of the entire human race. Against that dreadful design The Church stands ever on guard. And it is as one of the instruments of that design that I see this girl. She is inspired, but diabolically inspired.

40 THE CHAPLAIN. I told you she was a witch.

CAUCHON [fiercely]. She is not a witch. She is a heretic.

THE CHAPLAIN. What difference does that make?

45 CAUCHON. You, a priest, ask me that! You English are strangely blunt in the mind. All these things that you call witchcraft are capable of a natural explanation. The woman's miracles would not impose on a rabbit: she does not claim them as miracles herself. What do her 50 victories prove but that she has a better head on her shoulders than your swearing Glass-dells and mad bull Talbots, and that the courage of faith, even though it be a false faith, will always outstay the courage of wrath? 55

THE CHAPLAIN [hardly able to believe his ears]. Does your lordship compare Sir John Talbot, three times Governor of Ireland, to a mad bull?!!!

WARWICK. It would not be seemly for you to 60 do so, Messire John, as you are still six removes from a barony. But as I am an earl, and Talbot is only a knight, I may make bold to accept the comparison. [To the BISHOP.] My lord: I wipe the slate as far as the witchcraft goes. None 65 the less, we must burn the woman.

CAUCHON. I cannot burn her. The Church cannot take life. And my first duty is to seek this girl's salvation.

WARWICK. No doubt. But you do burn people 70 occasionally.

CAUCHON. No. When The Church cuts off an obstinate heretic as a dead branch from the tree of life, the heretic is handed over to the secular arm. The Church has no part in what 75 the secular arm may see fit to do.

WARWICK. Precisely. And I shall be the sec-ular arm in this case. Well, my lord, hand over your dead branch; and I will see that the fire is ready for it. If you will answer for The 80 Church's part, I will answer for the secular part.

CAUCHON [with smouldering anger]. I can answer for nothing. You great lords are too prone to treat The Church as a mere political convenience. 85

WARWICK [smiling and propitiatory]. Not in England, I assure you.

CAUCHON. In England more than anywhere else. No, my lord: the soul of this village girl is of equal value with yours or your king's 90 before the throne of God; and my first duty is to save it. I will not suffer your lordship to smile at me as if I were repeating a meaning-less form of words, and it were well understood between us that I should betray the girl to you. 95 I am no mere political bishop: my faith is to me what your honor is to you; and if there be a loophole through which this baptized child of God can creep to her salvation, I shall guide her to it.

5 THE CHAPLAIN [*rising in a fury*]. You are a traitor.

CAUCHON [*springing up*]. You lie, priest. [*Trembling with rage.*] If you dare do what this woman has done—set your country above the 10 holy Catholic Church—you shall go to the fire with her.

THE CHAPLAIN. My lord: I—I went too far. I— [*He sits down with a submissive gesture.*]

WARWICK [*who has risen apprehensively*]. 15 My lord: I apologize to you for the word used by Messire John de Stogumber. It does not mean in England what it does in France. In your language traitor means betrayer: one who is perfidious, treacherous, unfaithful, disloyal. 20 In our country it means simply one who is not wholly devoted to our English interests.

CAUCHON. I am sorry: I did not understand. [*He subsides into his chair with dignity.*]

WARWICK [*resuming his seat, much relieved*]. 25 I must apologize on my own account if I have seemed to take the burning of this poor girl too lightly. When one has seen whole country-sides burnt over and over again as mere items in military routine, one has to grow a very thick 30 skin. Otherwise one might go mad: at all events, I should. May I venture to assume that your lordship also, having to see so many heretics burned from time to time, is compelled to take —shall I say a professional view of what would 35 otherwise be a very horrible incident?

CAUCHON. Yes: it is a painful duty: even, as you say, a horrible one. But in comparison with the horror of heresy it is less than nothing. I am not thinking of this girl's body, which will suf- 40 fer for a few moments only, and which must in any event die in some more or less painful man-ner, but of her soul, which may suffer to all eternity.

WARWICK. Just so; and God grant that her 45 soul may be saved! But the practical problem would seem to be how to save her soul with-out saving her body. For we must face it, my lord: if this cult of The Maid goes on, our

cause is lost.

THE CHAPLAIN [*his voice broken like that of* 50 *a man who has been crying*]. May I speak, my lord?

WARWICK. Really, Messire John, I had rather you did not, unless you can keep your temper.

THE CHAPLAIN. It is only this. I speak under 55 correction; but The Maid is full of deceit: she pretends to be devout. Her prayers and con-fessions are endless. How can she be accused of heresy when she neglects no observance of a faithful daughter of The Church? 60

CAUCHON [*flaming up*]. A faithful daughter of The Church! The Pope himself at his proudest dare not presume as this woman pre-sumes. She acts as if she herself were The Church. She brings the message of God to 65 Charles; and The Church must stand aside. She will crown him in the cathedral of Rheims: she, not The Church! She sends letters to the king of England giving him God's command through her to return to his island on pain of 70 God's vengeance, which she will execute. Let me tell you that the writing of such letters was the practice of the accursed Mahomet, the anti-Christ. Has she ever in all her utterances said one word of The Church? Never. It is 75 always God and herself.

WARWICK. What can you expect? A beggar on horseback! Her head is turned.

CAUCHON. Who has turned it? The devil. And for a mighty purpose. He is spreading 80 this heresy everywhere. The man Hus,° burnt only thirteen years ago at Constance, infected all Bohemia with it. A man named WcLeef,° himself an anointed priest, spread the pesti-lence in England; and to your shame you let 85 him die in his bed. We have such people here in France too: I know the breed. It is can-cerous: if it be not cut out, stamped out, burnt

Hus John Huss (1369-1415), Czech religious refor-mer and national leader; tried for heresy and burned at the stake

WcLeef John Wycliff (1328-1384), English religious reformer and popular preacher, early translator of the Bible into English; condemned for heresy but not executed; influenced Huss and, later, Martin Luther

out, it will not stop until it has brought the whole body of human society into sin and corruption, into waste and ruin. By it an Arab camel driver drove Christ and His Church out of Jerusalem, and ravaged his way west like a wild beast until at last there stood only the Pyrenees and God's mercy between France and damnation. Yet what did the camel driver do at the beginning more than this shepherd girl is doing? He had his voices from the angel Gabriel: she has her voices from St Catherine and St Margaret and the Blessed Michael. He declared himself the messenger of God, and wrote in God's name to the kings of the earth. Her letters to them are going forth daily. It is not the Mother of God now to whom we must look for intercession, but to Joan the Maid. What will the world be like when The Church's accumulated wisdom and knowledge and experience, its councils of learned, venerable pious men, are thrust into the kennel by every ignorant laborer or dairymaid whom the devil can puff up with the monstrous self-conceit of being directly inspired from heaven? It will be a world of blood, of fury, of devastation, of each man striving for his own hand: in the end a world wrecked back into barbarism. For now you have only Mahomet and his dupes, and the Maid and her dupes; but what will it be when every girl thinks herself a Joan and every man a Mahomet? I shudder to the very marrow of my bones when I think of it. I have fought it all my life; and I will fight it to the end. Let all this woman's sins be forgiven her except only this sin; for it is the sin against the Holy Ghost; and if she does not recant in the dust before the world, and submit herself to the last inch of her soul to her Church, to the fire she shall go if she once falls into my hand.

WARWICK [unimpressed]. You feel strongly about it, naturally.

CAUCHON. Do not you?

WARWICK. I am a soldier, not a churchman. As a pilgrim I saw something of the Mahometans. They were not so illbred as I had been led to believe. In some respects their conduct compared favorably with ours.

CAUCHON [displeased]. I have noticed this before. Men go to the East to convert the infidels. And the infidels pervert them. The Crusader comes back more than half a Saracen. Not to mention that all Englishmen are born heretics.

THE CHAPLAIN. Englishmen heretics!!! [Appealing to WARWICK.] My lord: must we endure this? His lordship is beside himself. How can what an Englishman believes be heresy? It is a contradiction in terms.

CAUCHON. I absolve you, Messire de Stogumber, on the ground of invincible ignorance. The thick air of your country does not breed theologians.

WARWICK. You would not say so if you heard us quarrelling about religion, my lord! I am sorry you think I must be either a heretic or a blockhead because, as a travelled man, I know that the followers of Mahomet profess great respect for our Lord, and are more ready to forgive St Peter for being a fisherman than your lordship is to forgive Mahomet for being a camel driver. But at least we can proceed in this matter without bigotry.

CAUCHON. When men call the zeal of the Christian Church bigotry I know what to think.

WARWICK. They are only east and west views of the same thing.

CAUCHON [bitterly ironical]. Only east and west! Only!!

WARWICK. Oh, my Lord Bishop, I am not gainsaying you. You will carry The Church with you; but you have to carry the nobles also. To my mind there is a stronger case against The Maid than the one you have so forcibly put. Frankly, I am not afraid of this girl becoming another Mahomet, and superseding The Church by a great heresy. I think you exaggerate that risk. But have you noticed that in these letters of hers, she proposes to all the kings of Europe, as she has already pressed on Charles, a transaction which would wreck the whole social structure of Christendom?

CAUCHON. Wreck The Church. I tell you so.

WARWICK [whose patience is wearing out]. My lord: pray get The Church out of your head for a moment; and remember that there are temporal institutions in the world as well as spiritual ones. I and my peers represent the feudal aristocracy as you represent The Church. We are the temporal power. Well, do you not see how this girl's idea strikes at us?

CAUCHON. How does her idea strike at you, except as it strikes at all of us, through The Church?

WARWICK. Her idea is that the kings should give their realms to God, and then reign as God's bailiffs.

CAUCHON [*not interested*]. Quite sound theologically, my lord. But the king will hardly care, provided he reign. It is an abstract idea: a mere form of words.

WARWICK. By no means. It is a cunning device to supersede the aristocracy, and make the king sole and absolute autocrat. Instead of the king being merely the first among his peers, he becomes their master. That we cannot suffer: we call no man master. Nominally we hold our lands and dignities from the king, because there must be a keystone to the arch of human society; but we hold our lands in our own hands, and defend them with our own swords and those of our own tenants. Now by The Maid's doctrine the king will take our lands—our lands!—and make them a present to God; and God will then vest them wholly in the king.

CAUCHON. Need you fear that? You are the makers of kings after all. York or Lancaster in England, Lancaster or Valois in France: they reign according to your pleasure.

WARWICK. Yes; but only as long as the people follow their feudal lords, and know the king only as a travelling show, owning nothing but the highway that belongs to everybody. If the people's thoughts and hearts were turned to the king, and their lords became only the king's servants in their eyes, the king could break us across his knee one by one; and then what should we be but liveried courtiers in his halls?

CAUCHON. Still you need not fear, my lord. Some men are born kings; and some are born statesmen. The two are seldom the same.

Where would the king find counsellors to plan and carry out such a policy for him?

WARWICK [*with a not too friendly smile*]. Perhaps in the Church, my lord.

[CAUCHON, *with an equally sour smile, shrugs his shoulders, and does not contradict him.*]

WARWICK. Strike down the barons; and the cardinals will have it all their own way.

CAUCHON [*conciliatory, dropping his polemical tone*]. My lord: we shall not defeat The Maid if we strive against one another. I know well that there is a Will to Power in the world. I know that while it lasts there will be a struggle between the Emperor and the Pope, between the dukes and the political cardinals, between the barons and the kings. The devil divides us and governs. I see you are no friend to The Church: you are an earl first and last, as I am a churchman first and last. But can we not sink our differences in the face of a common enemy? I see now that what is in your mind is not that this girl has never once mentioned The Church, and thinks only of God and herself, but that she has never once mentioned the peerage, and thinks only of the king and herself.

WARWICK. Quite so. These two ideas of hers are the same idea at bottom. It goes deep, my lord. It is the protest of the individual soul against the interference of priest or peer between the private man and his God. I should call it Protestantism if I had to find a name for it.

CAUCHON [*looking hard at him*]. You understand it wonderfully well, my lord. Scratch an Englishman, and find a Protestant.

WARWICK [*playing the pink of courtesy*]. I think you are not entirely void of sympathy with The Maid's secular heresy, my lord. I leave you to find a name for it.

CAUCHON. You mistake me, my lord. I have no sympathy with her political presumptions. But as a priest I have gained a knowledge of the minds of the common people; and there you will find yet another most dangerous idea. I can express it only by such phrases as France for the French, England for the English, Italy

for the Italians, Spain for the Spanish, and so forth. It is sometimes so narrow and bitter in country folk that it surprises me that this country girl can rise above the idea of her
5 village for its villagers. But she can. She does. When she threatens to drive the English from the soil of France she is undoubtedly thinking of the whole extent of country in which French is spoken. To her the French-speaking people
10 are what the Holy Scriptures describe as a nation. Call this side of her heresy Nationalism if you will: I can find you no better name for it. I can only tell you that it is essentially anti-Catholic and anti-Christian; for the Catholic
15 Church knows only one realm, and that is the realm of Christ's kingdom. Divide that kingdom into nations, and you dethrone Christ. Dethrone Christ, and who will stand between our throats and the sword? The world will
20 perish in a welter of war.

WARWICK. Well, if you will burn the Protestant, I will burn the Nationalist, though perhaps I shall not carry Messire John with me there. England for the English will appeal to
25 him.

THE CHAPLAIN. Certainly England for the English goes without saying: it is the simple law of nature. But this woman denies to England her legitimate conquests, given her by
30 God because of her peculiar fitness to rule over less civilized races for their own good. I do not understand what your lordships mean by Protestant and Nationalist: you are too learned and subtle for a poor clerk like myself.
35 But I know as a matter of plain commonsense that the woman is a rebel; and that is enough for me. She rebels against Nature by wearing man's clothes, and fighting. She rebels against The Church by usurping the divine authority
40 of the Pope. She rebels against God by her damnable league with Satan and his evil spirits against our army. And all these rebellions are only excuses for her great rebellion against England. That is not to be endured. Let her
45 perish. Let her burn. Let her not infect the whole flock. It is expedient that one woman die for the people.

WARWICK [rising]. My lord: we seem to be agreed.

CAUCHON [rising also, but in protest]. I will 50 not imperil my soul. I will uphold the justice of The Church. I will strive to the utmost for this woman's salvation.

WARWICK. I am sorry for the poor girl. I hate these severities. I will spare her if I can. 55

THE CHAPLAIN [implacably]. I would burn her with my own hands.

CAUCHON [blessing him]. Sancta simplicitas!°

SCENE V

[The ambulatory in the cathedral of Rheims, near the door of the vestry. A pillar bears one 60 of the stations of the cross. The organ is playing the people out of the nave after the coronation. JOAN is kneeling in prayer before the station. She is beautifully dressed, but still in male attire. The organ ceases as DUNOIS, also 65 splendidly arrayed, comes into the ambulatory from the vestry.]

DUNOIS. Come, Joan! you have had enough praying. After that fit of crying you will catch a chill if you stay here any longer. It is all 70 over: the cathedral is empty; and the streets are full. They are calling for The Maid. We have told them you are staying here alone to pray; but they want to see you again.

JOAN. No: let the king have all the glory. 75

DUNOIS. He only spoils the show, poor devil. No, Joan: you have crowned him; and you must go through with it.

JOAN [shakes her head reluctantly].

DUNOIS [raising her]. Come come! it will be 80 over in a couple of hours. It's better than the bridge at Orleans: eh?

JOAN. Oh, dear Dunois, how I wish it were the bridge at Orleans again! We lived at that bridge. 85

DUNOIS. Yes, faith, and died too: some of us.

Sancta simplicitas! Blessed simplicity! Huss was rumored so to have blessed an old woman even as she added fuel to the fire in which he was burned; Cauchon speaks sarcastically.

JOAN. Isnt it strange, Jack? I am such a coward: I am frightened beyond words before a battle; but it is so dull afterwards when there is no danger: oh, so dull! dull! dull!

5 DUNOIS. You must learn to be abstemious in war, just as you are in your food and drink, my little saint.

JOAN. Dear Jack: I think you like me as a soldier likes his comrade.

10 DUNOIS. You need it, poor innocent child of God. You have not many friends at court.

JOAN. Why do all these courtiers and knights and churchmen hate me? What have I done to them? I have asked nothing for myself except 15 that my village shall not be taxed; for we cannot afford war taxes. I have brought them luck and victory: I have set them right when they were doing all sorts of stupid things: I have crowned Charles and made him a real king; 20 and all the honors he is handing out have gone to them. Then why do they not love me?

DUNOIS [*rallying her*]. Sim-ple-ton! Do you expect stupid people to love you for shewing them up? Do blundering old military dug-outs° 25 love the successful young captains who supersede them? Do ambitious politicians love the climbers who take the front seats from them? Do archbishops enjoy being played off their own altars, even by saints? Why, I should be 30 jealous of you myself if I were ambitious enough.

JOAN. You are the pick of the basket here, Jack: the only friend I have among all these nobles. I'll wager your mother was from the 35 country. I will go back to the farm when I have taken Paris.

DUNOIS. I am not so sure that they will let you take Paris.

JOAN [*startled*]. What!

40 DUNOIS. I should have taken it myself before this if they had all been sound about it. Some of them would rather Paris took you, I think. So take care.

JOAN. Jack: the world is too wicked for me.

dug-outs retired officers recalled to military service in an emergency

If the goddams and the Burgundians do not 45 make an end of me, the French will. Only for my voices I should lose all heart. That is why I had to steal away to pray here alone after the coronation. I'll tell you something, Jack. It is in the bells I hear my voices. Not to-day, when 50 they all rang: that was nothing but jangling. But here in this corner, where the bells come down from heaven, and the echoes linger, or in the fields, where they come from a distance through the quiet of the countryside, my voices 55 are in them. [*The cathedral clock chimes the quarter.*] Hark! [*She becomes rapt.*] Do you hear? "Dear-child-of-God": just what you said. At the half-hour they will say "Be-brave-go-on." At the three-quarters they will say "I-am- 60 thy-Help." But it is at the hour, when the great bell goes after "God-will-save-France": it is then that St Margaret and St Catherine and sometimes even the blessed Michael will say things that I cannot tell beforehand. Then, oh 65 then—

DUNOIS [*interrupting her kindly but not sympathetically*]. Then, Joan, we shall hear whatever we fancy in the booming of the bell. You make me uneasy when you talk about 70 your voices: I should think you were a bit cracked if I hadnt noticed that you give me very sensible reasons for what you do, though I hear you telling others you are only obeying Madame Saint Catherine. 75

JOAN [*crossly*]. Well, I have to find reasons for you, because you do not believe in my voices. But the voices come first; and I find the reasons after: whatever you may choose to believe. 80

DUNOIS. Are you angry, Joan?

JOAN. Yes. [*Smiling.*] No: not with you. I wish you were one of the village babies.

DUNOIS. Why?

JOAN. I could nurse you for awhile. 85

DUNOIS. You are a bit of a woman after all.

JOAN. No: not a bit: I am a soldier and nothing else. Soldiers always nurse children when they get a chance.

DUNOIS. That is true. [*He laughs.*] 90

[KING CHARLES, *with* BLUEBEARD *on his left*

and LA HIRE *on his right, comes from the vestry, where he has been disrobing.* JOAN *shrinks away behind the pillar.* DUNOIS *is left between* CHARLES *and* LA HIRE.]

5 DUNOIS. Well, your Majesty is an anointed king at last. How do you like it?

CHARLES. I would not go through it again to be emperor of the sun and moon. The weight of those robes! I thought I should have dropped
10 when they loaded that crown on to me. And the famous holy oil they talked so much about was rancid: phew! The Archbishop must be nearly dead: his robes must have weighed a ton: they are stripping him still in the vestry.

15 DUNOIS [*drily*]. Your majesty should wear armor oftener. That would accustom you to heavy dressing.

CHARLES. Yes: the old jibe! Well, I am not going to wear armor: fighting is not my job.
20 Where is The Maid?

JOAN [*coming forward between* CHARLES *and* BLUEBEARD, *and falling on her knee*]. Sire: I have made you king: my work is done. I am going back to my father's farm.

25 CHARLES [*surprised, but relieved*]. Oh, are you? Well, that will be very nice.

[JOAN *rises, deeply discouraged.*]

CHARLES [*continuing heedlessly*]. A healthy life, you know.

30 DUNOIS. But a dull one.

BLUEBEARD. You will find the petticoats tripping you up after leaving them off for so long.

LA HIRE. You will miss the fighting. It's a bad habit, but a grand one, and the hardest of
35 all to break yourself of.

CHARLES [*anxiously*]. Still, we dont want you to stay if you would really rather go home.

JOAN [*bitterly*]. I know well that none of you will be sorry to see me go. [*She turns her
40 shoulder to* CHARLES *and walks past him to the more congenial neighborhood of* DUNOIS *and* LA HIRE.]

LA HIRE. Well, I shall be able to swear when I want to. But I shall miss you at times.

45 JOAN. La Hire: in spite of all your sins and swears we shall meet in heaven; for I love you as I love Pitou, my old sheep dog. Pitou could kill a wolf. You will kill the English wolves until they go back to their country and become good dogs of God, will you not? 50

LA HIRE. You and I together: yes.

JOAN. No: I shall last only a year from the beginning.

ALL THE OTHERS. What!

JOAN. I know it somehow. 55

DUNOIS. Nonsense!

JOAN. Jack: do you think you will be able to drive them out?

DUNOIS [*with quiet conviction*]. Yes: I shall drive them out. They beat us because we 60 thought battles were tournaments and ransom markets. We played the fool while the goddams took war seriously. But I have learnt my lesson, and taken their measure. They have no roots here. I have beaten them before; and 65 I shall beat them again.

JOAN. You will not be cruel to them, Jack?

DUNOIS. The goddams will not yield to tender handling. We did not begin it.

JOAN [*suddenly*]. Jack: before I go home, let 70 us take Paris.

CHARLES [*terrified*]. Oh no no. We shall lose everything we have gained. Oh dont let us have any more fighting. We can make a very good treaty with the Duke of Burgundy. 75

JOAN. Treaty! [*She stamps with impatience.*]

CHARLES. Well, why not, now that I am crowned and anointed? Oh, that oil!

[*The* ARCHBISHOP *comes from the vestry, and joins the group between* CHARLES *and* BLUE- 80 BEARD.]

CHARLES. Archbishop: The Maid wants to start fighting again.

THE ARCHBISHOP. Have we ceased fighting, then? Are we at peace? 85

CHARLES. No: I suppose not; but let us be content with what we have done. Let us make a treaty. Our luck is too good to last; and now is our chance to stop before it turns.

JOAN. Luck! God has fought for us; and 90 you call it luck! And you would stop while there are still Englishmen on this holy earth of dear France!

THE ARCHBISHOP [*sternly*]. Maid: the king addressed himself to me, not to you. You forget 95 yourself. You very often forget yourself.

JOAN [*unabashed, and rather roughly*]. Then speak, you; and tell him that it is not God's will that he should take his hand from the plough.

THE ARCHBISHOP. If I am not so glib with the name of God as you are, it is because I interpret His will with the authority of The Church and of my sacred office. When you first came you respected it, and would not have dared to speak as you are now speaking. You came clothed with the virtue of humility; and because God blessed your enterprises accordingly, you have stained yourself with the sin of pride. The old Greek tragedy is rising among us. It is the chastisement of hubris.

CHARLES. Yes: she thinks she knows better than everyone else.

JOAN [*distressed, but naïvely incapable of seeing the effect she is producing*]. But I do know better than any of you seem to. And I am not proud: I never speak unless I know I am right.

BLUEBEARD ⎱ [*exclaiming* ⎰ Ha ha!
CHARLES ⎰ *together*]. ⎱ Just so.

THE ARCHBISHOP. How do you know you are right?

JOAN. I always know. My voices—

CHARLES. Oh, your voices, your voices. Why dont the voices come to me? I am king, not you.

JOAN. They do come to you; but you do not hear them. You have not sat in the field in the evening listening for them. When the angelus rings you cross yourself and have done with it; but if you prayed from your heart, and listened to the thrilling of the bells in the air after they stop ringing, you would hear the voices as well as I do. [*Turning brusquely from him.*] But what voices do you need to tell you what the blacksmith can tell you: that you must strike while the iron is hot? I tell you we must make a dash at Compiègne and relieve it as we relieved Orleans. Then Paris will open its gates; or if not, we will break through them. What is your crown worth without your capital?

LA HIRE. That is what I say too. We shall go through them like a red hot shot through a pound of butter. What do you say, Bastard?

DUNOIS. If our cannon balls were all as hot as your head, and we had enough of them, we should conquer the earth, no doubt. Pluck and impetuosity are good servants in war, but bad masters: they have delivered us into the hands of the English every time we have trusted to them. We never know when we are beaten: that is our great fault.

JOAN. You never know when you are victorious: that is a worse fault. I shall have to make you carry looking-glasses in battle to convince you that the English have not cut off all your noses. You would have been besieged in Orleans still, you and your councils of war, if I had not made you attack. You should always attack; and if you only hold on long enough the enemy will stop first. You dont know how to begin a battle; and you dont know how to use your cannons. And I do.

[*She squats down on the flags with crossed ankles, pouting.*]

DUNOIS. I know what you think of us, General Joan.

JOAN. Never mind that, Jack. Tell them what you think of me.

DUNOIS. I think that God was on your side; for I have not forgotten how the wind changed, and how our hearts changed when you came; and by my faith I shall never deny that it was in your sign that we conquered. But I tell you as a soldier that God is no man's daily drudge, and no maid's either. If you are worthy of it he will sometimes snatch you out of the jaws of death and set you on your feet again; but that is all: once on your feet you must fight with all your might and all your craft. For he has to be fair to your enemy too: dont forget that. Well, he set us on our feet through you at Orleans; and the glory of it has carried us through a few good battles here to the coronation. But if we presume on it further, and trust to God to do the work we should do ourselves, we shall be defeated; and serve us right!

JOAN. But—

DUNOIS. Sh! I have not finished. Do not think, any of you, that these victories of ours were won without generalship. King Charles: you have said no word in your proclamations

of my part in this campaign; and I make no complaint of that; for the people will run after The Maid and her miracles and not after the Bastard's hard work finding troops for her and
5 feeding them. But I know exactly how much God did for us through The Maid, and how much He left me to do by my own wits; and I tell you that your little hour of miracles is over, and that from this time on he who plays
10 the war game best will win—if the luck is on his side.

JOAN. Ah! if, if, if, if! If ifs and ans were pots and pans there'd be no need of tinkers. [*Rising impetuously.*] I tell you, Bastard, your
15 art of war is no use, because your knights are no good for real fighting. War is only a game to them, like tennis and all their other games: they make rules as to what is fair and what is not fair, and heap armor on themselves and on
20 their poor horses to keep out the arrows; and when they fall they cant get up, and have to wait for their squires to come and lift them to arrange about the ransom with the man that has poked them off their horse. Cant you see
25 that all the like of that is gone by and done with? What use is armor against gunpowder? And if it was, do you think men that are fighting for France and for God will stop to bargain about ransoms, as half your knights live by
30 doing? No: they will fight to win; and they will give up their lives out of their own hand into the hand of God when they go into battle, as I do. Common folks understand this. They cannot afford armor and cannot pay ransoms;
35 but they follow me half naked into the moat and up the ladder and over the wall. With them it is my life or thine, and God defend the right! You may shake your head, Jack; and Bluebeard may twirl his billygoat's beard
40 and cock his nose at me; but remember the day your knights and captains refused to follow me to attack the English at Orleans! You locked the gates to keep me in; and it was the townsfolk and the common people that fol-
45 lowed me, and forced the gate, and shewed you the way to fight in earnest.

BLUEBEARD [*offended*]. Not content with

being Pope Joan, you must be Caesar and Alexander as well.

THE ARCHBISHOP. Pride will have a fall, Joan. 50

JOAN. Oh, never mind whether it is pride or not: is it true? is it commonsense?

LA HIRE. It is true. Half of us are afraid of having our handsome noses broken; and the other half are out for paying off their mort- 55 gages. Let her have her way, Dunois: she does not know everything; but she has got hold of the right end of the stick. Fighting is not what it was; and those who know least about it often make the best job of it. 60

DUNOIS. I know all that. I do not fight in the old way: I have learnt the lesson of Agincourt, of Poitiers and Crecy.° I know how many lives any move of mine will cost; and if the move is worth the cost I make it and pay the cost. 65 But Joan never counts the cost at all: she goes ahead and trusts to God: she thinks she has God in her pocket. Up to now she has had the numbers on her side; and she has won. But I know Joan; and I see that some day she will 70 go ahead when she has only ten men to do the work of a hundred. And then she will find that God is on the side of the big battalions. She will be taken by the enemy. And the lucky man that makes the capture will receive sixteen 75 thousand pounds from the Earl of Ouareek.°

JOAN [*flattered*]. Sixteen thousand pounds! Eh, laddie, have they offered that for me? There cannot be so much money in the world.

DUNOIS. There is, in England. And now tell 80 me, all of you, which of you will lift a finger to save Joan once the English have got her? I speak first, for the army. The day after she has been dragged from her horse by a goddam or a Burgundian, and he is not struck dead: the 85 day after she is locked in a dungeon, and the bars and bolts do not fly open at the touch of St Peter's angel: the day when the enemy finds

Agincourt, Poitiers, Crécy in the mid-fourteenth and early fifteenth centuries, battles in which the English defeated largely superior French forces and brought an end to old-fashioned chivalric tactics, which, Dunois says, were not sufficiently realistic
Ouareek French pronunciation of *Warwick*

out that she is as vulnerable as I am and not a bit more invincible, she will not be worth the life of a single soldier to us; and I will not risk that life, much as I cherish her as a companion-in-arms.

JOAN. I dont blame you, Jack: you are right. I am not worth one soldier's life if God lets me be beaten; but France may think me worth my ransom after what God has done for her through me.

CHARLES. I tell you I have no money; and this coronation, which is all your fault, has cost me the last farthing I can borrow.

JOAN. The Church is richer than you. I put my trust in The Church.

THE ARCHBISHOP. Woman: they will drag you through the streets, and burn you as a witch.

JOAN [*running to him*]. Oh, my lord, do not say that. It is impossible. I a witch!

THE ARCHBISHOP. Peter Cauchon knows his business. The University of Paris has burnt a woman for saying that what you have done was well done, and according to God.

JOAN [*bewildered*]. But why? What sense is there in it? What I have done is according to God. They could not burn a woman for speaking the truth.

THE ARCHBISHOP. They did.

JOAN. But you know that she was speaking the truth. You would not let them burn me.

THE ARCHBISHOP. How could I prevent them?

JOAN. You would speak in the name of The Church. You are a great prince of The Church. I would go anywhere with your blessing to protect me.

THE ARCHBISHOP. I have no blessing for you while you are proud and disobedient.

JOAN. Oh, why will you go on saying things like that? I am not proud and disobedient. I am a poor girl, and so ignorant that I do not know A from B. How could I be proud? And how can you say that I am disobedient when I always obey my voices, because they come from God.

THE ARCHBISHOP. The voice of God on earth is the voice of the Church Militant; and all the voices that come to you are the echoes of your own wilfulness.

JOAN. It is not true.

THE ARCHBISHOP [*flushing angrily*]. You tell the Archbishop in his cathedral that he lies; and yet you say you are not proud and disobedient.

JOAN. I never said you lied. It was you that as good as said my voices lied. When have they ever lied? If you will not believe in them: even if they are only the echoes of my own commonsense, are they not always right? and are not your earthly counsels always wrong?

THE ARCHBISHOP [*indignantly*]. It is waste of time admonishing you.

CHARLES. It always comes back to the same thing. She is right; and everyone else is wrong.

THE ARCHBISHOP. Take this as your last warning. If you perish through setting your private judgment above the instructions of your spiritual directors, The Church disowns you, and leaves you to whatever fate' your presumption may bring upon you. The Bastard has told you that if you persist in setting up your military conceit above the counsels of your commanders—

DUNOIS [*interposing*]. To put it quite exactly, if you attempt to relieve the garrison in Compiègne without the same superiority in numbers you had at Orleans—

THE ARCHBISHOP. The army will disown you, and will not rescue you. And His Majesty the King has told you that the throne has not the means of ransoming you.

CHARLES. Not a penny.

THE ARCHBISHOP. You stand alone: absolutely alone, trusting to your own conceit, your own ignorance, your own headstrong presumption, your own impiety in hiding all these sins under the cloak of a trust in God. When you pass through these doors into the sunlight, the crowd will cheer you. They will bring you their little children and their invalids to heal: they will kiss your hands and feet, and do what they can, poor simple souls, to turn your head, and madden you with the self-confidence that is leading you to your destruction. But you will be none the less alone: they cannot save you.

We and we only can stand between you and the stake at which our enemies have burnt that wretched woman in Paris.

JOAN [*her eyes skyward*]. I have better
5 friends and better counsel than yours.

THE ARCHBISHOP. I see that I am speaking in vain to a hardened heart. You reject our protection, and are determined to turn us all against you. In future, then, fend for yourself;
10 and if you fail, God have mercy on your soul.

DUNOIS. That is the truth, Joan. Heed it.

JOAN. Where would you all have been now if I had heeded that sort of truth? There is no help, no counsel, in any of you. Yes: I am
15 alone on earth: I have always been alone. My father told my brothers to drown me if I would not stay to mind his sheep while France was bleeding to death: France might perish if only our lambs were safe. I thought France would
20 have friends at the court of the king of France; and I find only wolves fighting for pieces of her poor torn body. I thought God would have friends everywhere, because He is the friend of everyone; and in my innocence I believed
25 that you who now cast me out would be like strong towers to keep harm from me. But I am wiser now; and nobody is any the worse for being wiser. Do not think you can frighten me by telling me that I am alone. France is
30 alone; and God is alone; and what is my loneliness before the loneliness of my country and my God? I see now that the loneliness of God is His strength: what would He be if He listened to your jealous little counsels? Well,
35 my loneliness shall be my strength too: it is better to be alone with God: His friendship will not fail me, nor His counsel, nor His love. In His strength I will dare, and dare, and dare, until I die. I will go out now to the common
40 people, and let the love in their eyes comfort me for the hate in yours. You will all be glad to see me burnt; but if I go through the fire I shall go through it to their hearts for ever and ever. And so, God, be with me!

45 [*She goes from them. They stare after her in glum silence for a moment. Then* GILLES DE RAIS *twirls his beard.*]

BLUEBEARD. You know, the woman is quite impossible. I dont dislike her, really; but what are you to do with such a character?   50

DUNOIS. As God is my judge, if she fell into the Loire I would jump in in full armor to fish her out. But if she plays the fool at Compiègne, and gets caught, I must leave her to her doom.

LA HIRE. Then you had better chain me up;   55 for I could follow her to hell when the spirit rises in her like that.

THE ARCHBISHOP. She disturbs my judgment too: there is a dangerous power in her outbursts. But the pit is open at her feet; and for 60 good or evil we cannot turn her from it.

CHARLES. If only she would keep quiet, or go home!

[*They follow her dispiritedly.*]

SCENE VI

[*Rouen, 30th May 1431. A great stone hall*   65 *in the castle, arranged for a trial-at-law, but not a trial-by-jury, the court being the* BISHOP's *court with the Inquisition participating: hence there are two raised chairs side by side for the* BISHOP *and the* INQUISITOR° *as judges. Rows of* 70 *chairs radiating from them at an obtuse angle are for the* CANONS, *the doctors of law and theology, and the* DOMINICAN MONKS, *who act as assessors. In the angle is a table for the scribes, with stools. There is also a heavy* 75 *rough wooden stool for the prisoner. All these are at the inner end of the hall. The further end is open to the courtyard through a row of arches. The court is shielded from the weather by screens and curtains.*   80

Looking down the great hall from the middle of the inner end, the judicial chairs and scribes' table are to the right. The prisoner's stool is to the left. There are arched doors right and left. It is a fine sunshiny May morning.   85

WARWICK *comes in through the arched doorway on the judges' side, followed by his* PAGE.]

THE PAGE [*pertly*]. I suppose your lordship

Inquisitor a representative of the "Holy Office," charged directly by the papacy to inquire into heresy; an expert in theological questions and in court procedures

is aware that we have no business here. This is an ecclesiastical court; and we are only the secular arm.

WARWICK. I am aware of that fact. Will it please your impudence to find the Bishop of Beauvais for me, and give him a hint that he can have a word with me here before the trial, if he wishes?

THE PAGE [*going*]. Yes, my lord.

WARWICK. And mind you behave yourself. Do not address him as Pious Peter.

THE PAGE. No, my lord. I shall be kind to him, because, when The Maid is brought in, Pious Peter will have to pick a peck of pickled pepper.

[CAUCHON *enters through the same door with a* DOMINICAN MONK *and a* CANON, *the latter carrying a brief.*]

THE PAGE. The Right Reverend his lordship the Bishop of Beauvais. And two other reverend gentlemen.

WARWICK. Get out; and see that we are not interrupted.

THE PAGE. Right, my lord. [*He vanishes airily.*]

CAUCHON. I wish your lordship good-morrow.

WARWICK. Good-morrow to your lordship. Have I had the pleasure of meeting your friends before? I think not.

CAUCHON [*introducing the* MONK, *who is on his right*]. This, my lord, is Brother John Lemaître, of the order of St Dominic. He is acting as deputy for the Chief Inquisitor into the evil of heresy in France. Brother John: the Earl of Warwick.

WARWICK. Your Reverence is most welcome. We have no Inquisitor in England, unfortunately; though we miss him greatly, especially on occasions like the present.

[*The* INQUISITOR *smiles patiently, and bows. He is a mild elderly gentleman, but has evident reserves of authority and firmness.*]

CAUCHON [*introducing the* CANON, *who is on his left*]. This gentleman is Canon John D'Estivet, of the Chapter of Bayeux. He is acting as Promoter.

WARWICK. Promoter?

CAUCHON. Prosecutor, you would call him in civil law.

WARWICK. Ah! prosecutor. Quite, quite. I am very glad to make your acquaintance, Canon D'Estivet.

[D'ESTIVET *bows. (He is on the young side of middle age, well mannered, but vulpine beneath his veneer.)*]

WARWICK. May I ask what stage the proceedings have reached? It is now more than nine months since The Maid was captured at Compiègne by the Burgundians. It is fully four months since I bought her from the Burgundians for a very handsome sum, solely that she might be brought to justice. It is very nearly three months since I delivered her up to you, my Lord Bishop, as a person suspected of heresy. May I suggest that you are taking a rather unconscionable time to make up your minds about a very plain case? Is this trial never going to end?

THE INQUISITOR [*smiling*]. It has not yet begun, my lord.

WARWICK. Not yet begun! Why, you have been at it eleven weeks!

CAUCHON. We have not been idle, my lord. We have held fifteen examinations of The Maid: six public and nine private.

THE INQUISITOR [*always patiently smiling*]. You see, my lord, I have been present at only two of these examinations. They were proceedings of the Bishop's court solely, and not of the Holy Office. I have only just decided to associate myself—that is, to associate the Holy Inquisition—with the Bishop's court. I did not at first think that this was a case of heresy at all. I regarded it as a political case, and The Maid as a prisoner of war. But having now been present at two of the examinations, I must admit that this seems to be one of the gravest cases of heresy within my experience. Therefore everything is now in order; and we proceed to trial this morning. [*He moves towards the judicial chairs.*]

CAUCHON. This moment, if your lordship's convenience allows.

WARWICK [*graciously*]. Well, that is good news, gentlemen. I will not attempt to conceal from you that our patience was becoming strained.

CAUCHON. So I gathered from the threats of your soldiers to drown those of our people who favor The Maid.

WARWICK. Dear me! At all events their intentions were friendly to you, my lord.

CAUCHON [sternly]. I hope not. I am determined that the woman shall have a fair hearing. The justice of The Church is not a mockery, my lord.

THE INQUISITOR [returning]. Never has there been a fairer examination within my experience, my lord. The Maid needs no lawyers to take her part: she will be tried by her most faithful friends, all ardently desirous to save her soul from perdition.

D'ESTIVET. Sir: I am the Promoter; and it has been my painful duty to present the case against the girl; but believe me, I would throw up my case today and hasten to her defence if I did not know that men far my superiors in learning and piety, in eloquence and persuasiveness, have been sent to reason with her, to explain to her the danger she is running, and the ease with which she may avoid it. [Suddenly bursting into forensic eloquence, to the disgust of CAUCHON and the INQUISITOR, who have listened to him so far with patronizing approval.] Men have dared to say that we are acting from hate; but God is our witness that they lie. Have we tortured her? No. Have we ceased to exhort her; to implore her to have pity on herself; to come to the bosom of her Church as an erring but beloved child? Have we—

CAUCHON [interrupting drily]. Take care, Canon. All that you say is true; but if you make his lordship believe it I will not answer for your life, and hardly for my own.

WARWICK [deprecating, but by no means denying]. Oh, my lord, you are very hard on us poor English. But we certainly do not share your pious desire to save The Maid: in fact I tell you now plainly that her death is a political necessity which I regret but cannot help. If The Church lets her go—

CAUCHON [with fierce and menacing pride].

If The Church lets her go, woe to the man, were he the Emperor himself, who dares lay a finger on her! The Church is not subject to political necessity, my lord.

THE INQUISITOR [interposing smoothly]. You need have no anxiety about the result, my lord. You have an invincible ally in the matter: one who is far more determined than you that she shall burn.

WARWICK. And who is this very convenient partisan, may I ask?

THE INQUISITOR. The Maid herself. Unless you put a gag in her mouth you cannot prevent her from convicting herself ten times over every time she opens it.

D'ESTIVET. That is perfectly true, my lord. My hair bristles on my head when I hear so young a creature utter such blasphemies.

WARWICK. Well, by all means do your best for her if you are quite sure it will be of no avail. [Looking hard at CAUCHON.] I should be sorry to have to act without the blessing of The Church.

CAUCHON [with a mixture of cynical admiration and contempt]. And yet they say Englishmen are hypocrites! You play for your side, my lord, even at the peril of your soul. I cannot but admire such devotion; but I dare not go so far myself. I fear damnation.

WARWICK. If we feared anything we could never govern England, my lord. Shall I send your people in to you?

CAUCHON. Yes: it will be very good of your lordship to withdraw and allow the court to assemble.

[WARWICK turns on his heel, and goes out through the courtyard. CAUCHON takes one of the judicial seats: and D'ESTIVET sits at the scribes' table, studying his brief.]

CAUCHON [casually, as he makes himself comfortable]. What scoundrels these English nobles are!

THE INQUISITOR [taking the other judicial chair on CAUCHON's left]. All secular power makes men scoundrels. They are not trained for the work; and they have not the Apostolic Succession. Our own nobles are just as bad.

[The BISHOP'S ASSESSORS hurry into the hall,

headed by CHAPLAIN DE STOGUMBER *and* CANON DE COURCELLES, *a young priest of* 30. *The scribes sit at the table, leaving a chair vacant opposite* D'ESTIVET. *Some of the* ASSESSORS *take their seats: others stand chatting, waiting for the proceedings to begin formally.* DE STOGUMBER, *aggrieved and obstinate, will not take his seat: neither will the* CANON, *who stands on his right.*]

CAUCHON. Good morning, Master de Stogumber. [*To the* INQUISITOR.] Chaplain to the Cardinal of England.

THE CHAPLAIN [*correcting him*]. Of Winchester, my lord. I have to make a protest, my lord.

CAUCHON. You make a great many.

THE CHAPLAIN. I am not without support, my lord. Here is Master de Courcelles, Canon of Paris, who associates himself with me in my protest.

CAUCHON. Well, what is the matter?

THE CHAPLAIN [*sulkily*]. Speak you, Master de Courcelles, since I do not seem to enjoy his lordship's confidence. [*He sits down in dudgeon next to* CAUCHON, *on his right.*]

COURCELLES. My lord: we have been at great pains to draw up an indictment of The Maid on sixtyfour counts. We are now told that they have been reduced, without consulting us.

THE INQUISITOR. Master de Courcelles: I am the culprit. I am overwhelmed with admiration for the zeal displayed in your sixtyfour counts; but in accusing a heretic, as in other things, enough is enough. Also you must remember that all the members of the court are not so subtle and profound as you, and that some of your very great learning might appear to them to be very great nonsense. Therefore I have thought it well to have your sixtyfour articles cut down to twelve—

COURCELLES [*thunderstruck*]. Twelve! ! !

THE INQUISITOR. Twelve will, believe me, be quite enough for your purpose.

THE CHAPLAIN. But some of the most important points have been reduced almost to nothing. For instance, The Maid has actually declared that the blessed saints Margaret and Catherine, and the holy Archangel Michael, spoke to her in French. That is a vital point.

THE INQUISITOR. You think, doubtless, that they should have spoken in Latin?

CAUCHON. No: he thinks they should have spoken in English.

THE CHAPLAIN. Naturally, my lord.

THE INQUISITOR. Well, as we are here agreed, I think, that these voices of The Maid are the voices of evil spirits tempting her to her damnation, it would not be very courteous to you, Master de Stogumber, or to the King of England, to assume that English is the devil's native language. So let it pass. The matter is not wholly omitted from the twelve articles. Pray take your places, gentlemen; and let us proceed to business.

[*All who have not taken their seats, do so.*]

THE CHAPLAIN. Well, I protest. That is all.

COURCELLES. I think it hard that all our work should go for nothing. It is only another example of the diabolical influence which this woman exercises over the court. [*He takes his chair, which is on the* CHAPLAIN's *right.*]

CAUCHON. Do you suggest that I am under diabolical influence?

COURCELLES. I suggest nothing, my lord. But it seems to me that there is a conspiracy here to hush up the fact that The Maid stole the Bishop of Senlis's horse.

CAUCHON [*keeping his temper with difficulty*]. This is not a police court. Are we to waste our time on such rubbish?

COURCELLES [*rising, shocked*]. My lord: do you call the Bishop's horse rubbish?

THE INQUISITOR [*blandly*]. Master de Courcelles: The Maid alleges that she paid handsomely for the Bishop's horse, and that if he did not get the money the fault was not hers. As that may be true, the point is one on which The Maid may well be acquitted.

COURCELLES. Yes, if it were an ordinary horse. But the Bishop's horse! how can she be acquitted for that? [*He sits down again, bewildered and discouraged.*]

THE INQUISITOR. I submit to you, with great respect, that if we persist in trying The Maid on trumpery issues on which we may have to declare her innocent, she may escape us on the great main issue of heresy, on which she seems so far to insist on her own guilt. I will ask you, therefore, to say nothing, when The Maid is brought before us, of these stealings of horses, and dancings round fairy trees with the village 5 children, and prayings at haunted wells, and a dozen other things which you were diligently inquiring into until my arrival. There is not a village girl in France against whom you could not prove such things: they all dance round 10 haunted trees, and pray at magic wells. Some of them would steal the Pope's horse if they got the chance. Heresy, gentlemen, heresy is the charge we have to try. The detection and suppression of heresy is my peculiar business: 15 I am here as an inquisitor, not as an ordinary magistrate. Stick to the heresy, gentlemen; and leave the other matters alone.

CAUCHON. I may say that we have sent to the girl's village to make inquiries about her; 20 and there is practically nothing serious against her.

THE CHAPLAIN *[rising and* COURCELLES *clamoring together].* Nothing serious, my lord—What! The fairy tree 25 not—

CAUCHON [*out of patience*]. Be silent, gentlemen; or speak one at a time.

[COURCELLES *collapses into his chair intimidated.*]

30 THE CHAPLAIN [*sulkily resuming his seat*]. That is what The Maid said to us last Friday.

CAUCHON. I wish you had followed her counsel, sir. When I say nothing serious, I mean nothing that men of sufficiently large mind to 35 conduct an inquiry like this would consider serious. I agree with my colleague the Inquisitor that it is on the count of heresy that we must proceed.

LADVENU [*a young but ascetically fine-drawn* 40 *Dominican who is sitting next* COURCELLES, *on his right*]. But is there any great harm in the girl's heresy? Is it not merely her simplicity? Many saints have said as much as Joan.

THE INQUISITOR [*dropping his blandness and* 45 *speaking very gravely*]. Brother Martin: if you had seen what I have seen of heresy, you would not think it a light thing even in its most apparently harmless and even lovable and pious origins. Heresy begins with people who are to all appearance better than their neigh- 50 bors. A gentle and pious girl, or a young man who has obeyed the command of our Lord by giving all his riches to the poor, and putting on the garb of poverty, the life of austerity, and the rule of humility and charity, may be 55 the founder of a heresy that will wreck both Church and Empire if not ruthlessly stamped out in time. The records of the holy Inquisition are full of histories we dare not give to the world, because they are beyond the belief of 60 honest men and innocent women; yet they all began with saintly simpletons. I have seen this again and again. Mark what I say: the woman who quarrels with her clothes, and puts on the dress of a man, is like the man who throws 65 off his fur gown and dresses like John the Baptist: they are followed, as surely as the night follows the day, by bands of wild women and men who refuse to wear any clothes at all. When maids will neither marry nor take regular 70 vows, and men reject marriage and exalt their lusts into divine inspirations, then, as surely as the summer follows the spring, they begin with polygamy, and end by incest. Heresy at first seems innocent and even laudable; but it 75 ends in such a monstrous horror of unnatural wickedness that the most tender-hearted among you, if you saw it at work as I have seen it, would clamor against the mercy of The Church in dealing with it. For two hundred years the 80 Holy Office has striven with these diabolical madnesses; and it knows that they begin always by vain and ignorant persons setting up their own judgment against The Church, and taking it upon themselves to be the interpreters 85 of God's will. You must not fall into the common error of mistaking these simpletons for liars and hypocrites. They believe honestly and sincerely that their diabolical inspiration is divine. Therefore you must be on your guard 90 against your natural compassion. You are all, I hope, merciful men: how else could you have devoted your lives to the service of our gentle Savior? You are going to see before you a young girl, pious and chaste; for I must tell 95 you, gentlemen, that the things said of her by our English friends are supported by no evidence, whilst there is abundant testimony that her excesses have been excesses of religion and charity and not of worldliness and wantonness. This girl is not one of those whose hard features are the sign of hard hearts, and whose brazen looks and lewd demeanor condemn them before they are accused. The devilish pride that has led her into her present peril has left no mark on her countenance. Strange as it may seem to you, it has even left no mark on her character outside those special matters in which she is proud; so that you will see a diabolical pride and a natural humility seated side by side in the selfsame soul. Therefore be on your guard. God forbid that I should tell you to harden your hearts; for her punishment if we condemn her will be so cruel that we should forfeit our own hope of divine mercy were there one grain of malice against her in our hearts. But if you hate cruelty—and if any man here does not hate it I command him on his soul's salvation to quit this holy court— I say, if you hate cruelty, remember that nothing is so cruel in its consequences as the toleration of heresy. Remember also that no court of law can be so cruel as the common people are to those whom they suspect of heresy. The heretic in the hands of the Holy Office is safe from violence, is assured of a fair trial, and cannot suffer death, even when guilty, if repentance follows sin. Innumerable lives of heretics have been saved because the Holy Office has taken them out of the hands of the people, and because the people have yielded them up, knowing that the Holy Office would deal with them. Before the Holy Inquisition existed, and even now when its officers are not within reach, the unfortunate wretch suspected of heresy, perhaps quite ignorantly and unjustly, is stoned, torn in pieces, drowned, burned in his house with all his innocent children, without a trial, unshriven, unburied save as a dog is buried: all of them deeds hateful to God and most cruel to man. Gentlemen: I am compassionate by nature as well as by my profession; and though the work I have to do may seem cruel to those who do not know

how much more cruel it would be to leave it undone, I would go to the stake myself sooner than do it if I did not know its righteousness, its necessity, its essential mercy. I ask you to address yourself to this trial in that conviction. Anger is a bad counsellor: cast out anger. Pity is sometimes worse: cast out pity. But do not cast out mercy. Remember only that justice comes first. Have you anything to say, my lord, before we proceed to trial?

CAUCHON. You have spoken for me, and spoken better than I could. I do not see how any sane man could disagree with a word that has fallen from you. But this I will add. The crude heresies of which you have told us are horrible; but their horror is like that of the black death: they rage for a while and then die out, because sound and sensible men will not under any incitement be reconciled to nakedness and incest and polygamy and the like. But we are confronted today throughout Europe with a heresy that is spreading among men not weak in mind nor diseased in brain: nay, the stronger the mind, the more obstinate the heretic. It is neither discredited by fantastic extremes nor corrupted by the common lusts of the flesh; but it, too, sets up the private judgment of the single erring mortal against the considered wisdom and experience of The Church. The mighty structure of Catholic Christendom will never be shaken by naked madmen or by the sins of Moab and Ammon. But it may be betrayed from within, and brought to barbarous ruin and desolation, by this arch heresy which the English Commander calls Protestantism.

THE ASSESSORS [*whispering*]. Protestantism! What was that? What does the Bishop mean? Is it a new heresy? The English Commander, he said. Did you ever hear of Protestantism? etc., etc.

CAUCHON [*continuing*]. And that reminds me. What provision has the Earl of Warwick made for the defence of the secular arm should The Maid prove obdurate, and the people be moved to pity her?

THE CHAPLAIN. Have no fear on that score, my lord. The noble earl has eight hundred men-at-arms at the gates. She will not slip through our English fingers even if the whole city be on her side.

CAUCHON [revolted]. Will you not add, God
5 grant that she repent and purge her sin?

THE CHAPLAIN. That does not seem to me to be consistent; but of course I agree with your lordship.

CAUCHON [giving him up with a shrug of
10 contempt]. The court sits.

THE INQUISITOR. Let the accused be brought in.

LADVENU [calling]. The accused. Let her be brought in.

15 [JOAN, chained by the ankles, is brought in through the arched door behind the prisoner's stool by a guard of ENGLISH SOLDIERS. With them is the EXECUTIONER and his ASSISTANTS. They lead her to the prisoner's stool, and place
20 themselves behind it after taking off her chain. She wears a page's black suit. Her long imprisonment and the strain of the examinations which have preceded the trial have left their mark on her; but her vitality still holds: she
25 confronts the court unabashed, without a trace of the awe which their formal solemnity seems to require for the complete success of its impressiveness.]

THE INQUISITOR [kindly]. Sit down, Joan.
30 [She sits on the prisoner's stool.] You look very pale today. Are you not well?

JOAN. Thank you kindly: I am well enough. But the Bishop sent me some carp; and it made me ill.

35 CAUCHON. I am sorry. I told them to see that it was fresh.

JOAN. You meant to be good to me, I know; but it is a fish that does not agree with me. The English thought you were trying to poison
40 me—

CAUCHON ⎱ [together]. ⎰ What!
THE CHAPLAIN ⎰   ⎱ No, my lord.

JOAN [continuing]. They are determined that I shall be burnt as a witch; and they sent their
45 doctor to cure me; but he was forbidden to bleed me because the silly people believe that a witch's witchery leaves her if she is bled; so

he only called me filthy names. Why do you leave me in the hands of the English? I should be in the hands of The Church. And why must 50
I be chained by the feet to a log of wood? Are you afraid I will fly away?

D'ESTIVET [harshly]. Woman: it is not for you to question the court: it is for us to question you. 55

COURCELLES. When you were left unchained, did you not try to escape by jumping from a tower sixty feet high? If you cannot fly like a witch, how is it that you are still alive?

JOAN. I suppose because the tower was not 60
so high then. It has grown higher every day since you began asking me questions about it.

D'ESTIVET. Why did you jump from the tower?

JOAN. How do you know that I jumped? 65

D'ESTIVET. You were found lying in the moat. Why did you leave the tower?

JOAN. Why would anybody leave a prison if they could get out?

D'ESTIVET. You tried to escape? 70

JOAN. Of course I did; and not for the first time either. If you leave the door of the cage open the bird will fly out.

D'ESTIVET [rising]. That is a confession of heresy. I call the attention of the court to it. 75

JOAN. Heresy, he calls it! Am I a heretic because I try to escape from prison?

D'ESTIVET. Assuredly, if you are in the hands of The Church, and you wilfully take yourself out of its hands, you are deserting The Church; 80
and that is heresy.

JOAN. It is great nonsense. Nobody could be such a fool as to think that.

D'ESTIVET. You hear, my lord, how I am reviled in the execution of my duty by this 85
woman. [He sits down indignantly.]

CAUCHON. I have warned you before, Joan, that you are doing yourself no good by these pert answers.

JOAN. But you will not talk sense to me. I am 90
reasonable if you will be reasonable.

THE INQUISITOR [interposing]. This is not yet in order. You forget, Master Promoter, that the proceedings have not been formally opened. The time for questions is after she has sworn on the Gospels to tell us the whole truth.

JOAN. You say this to me every time. I have said again and again that I will tell you all that concerns this trial. But I cannot tell you the whole truth: God does not allow the whole truth to be told. You do not understand it when I tell it. It is an old saying that he who tells too much truth is sure to be hanged. I am weary of this argument: we have been over it nine times already. I have sworn as much as I will swear; and I will swear no more.

COURCELLES. My lord: she should be put to the torture.

THE INQUISITOR. You hear, Joan? That is what happens to the obdurate. Think before you answer. Has she been shewn the instruments?

THE EXECUTIONER. They are ready, my lord. She has seen them.

JOAN. If you tear me limb from limb until you separate my soul from my body you will get nothing out of me beyond what I have told you. What more is there to tell that you could understand? Besides, I cannot bear to be hurt; and if you hurt me I will say anything you like to stop the pain. But I will take it all back afterwards; so what is the use of it?

LADVENU. There is much in that. We should proceed mercifully.

COURCELLES. But the torture is customary.

THE INQUISITOR. It must not be applied wantonly. If the accused will confess voluntarily, then its use cannot be justified.

COURCELLES. But this is unusual and irregular. She refuses to take the oath.

LADVENU [*disgusted*]. Do you want to torture the girl for the mere pleasure of it?

COURCELLES [*bewildered*]. But it is not a pleasure. It is the law. It is customary. It is always done.

THE INQUISITOR. That is not so, Master, except when the inquiries are carried on by people who do not know their legal business.

COURCELLES. But the woman is a heretic. I assure you it is always done.

CAUCHON [*decisively*]. It will not be done today if it is not necessary. Let there be an end of this. I will not have it said that we proceeded on forced confessions. We have sent our best preachers and doctors to this woman to exhort and implore her to save her soul and body from the fire: we shall not now send the executioner to thrust her into it.

COURCELLES. Your lordship is merciful, of course. But it is a great responsibility to depart from the usual practice.

JOAN. Thou art a rare noodle, Master. Do what was done last time is thy rule, eh?

COURCELLES [*rising*]. Thou wanton: dost thou dare call me noodle?

THE INQUISITOR. Patience, Master, patience: I fear you will soon be only too terribly avenged.

COURCELLES [*mutters*]. Noodle indeed! [*He sits down, much discontented.*]

THE INQUISITOR. Meanwhile, let us not be moved by the rough side of a shepherd lass's tongue.

JOAN. Nay: I am no shepherd lass, though I have helped with the sheep like anyone else. I will do a lady's work in the house—spin or weave—against any woman in Rouen.

THE INQUISITOR. This is not a time for vanity, Joan. You stand in great peril.

JOAN. I know it: have I not been punished for my vanity? If I had not worn my cloth of gold surcoat in battle like a fool, that Burgundian soldier would never have pulled me backwards off my horse; and I should not have been here.

THE CHAPLAIN. If you are so clever at woman's work why do you not stay at home and do it?

JOAN. There are plenty of other women to do it; but there is nobody to do my work.

CAUCHON. Come! we are wasting time on trifles. Joan: I am going to put a most solemn question to you. Take care how you answer; for your life and salvation are at stake on it. Will you for all you have said and done, be it good or bad, accept the judgment of God's Church on earth? More especially as to the acts and words that are imputed to you in this trial by the Promoter here, will you submit your case to the inspired interpretation of the Church Militant?

JOAN. I am a faithful child of The Church. I
5 will obey The Church—

CAUCHON [hopefully leaning forward]. You will?

JOAN. —provided it does not command anything impossible.

10 [CAUCHON sinks back in his chair with a heavy sigh. The INQUISITOR purses his lips and frowns. LADVENU shakes his head pitifully.]

D'ESTIVET. She imputes to The Church the error and folly of commanding the impossible.

15 JOAN. If you command me to declare that all I have done and said, and all the visions and revelations I have had, were not from God, then that is impossible: I will not declare it for anything in the world. What God made me do
20 I will never go back on; and what He has commanded or shall command I will not fail to do in spite of any man alive. That is what I mean by impossible. And in case The Church should bid me do anything contrary to the
25 command I have from God, I will not consent to it, no matter what it may be.

THE ASSESSORS [shocked and indignant]. Oh! The Church contrary to God! What do you say now? Flat heresy. This is beyond every-
30 thing, etc., etc.

D'ESTIVET [throwing down his brief]. My lord: do you need anything more than this?

CAUCHON. Woman: you have said enough to burn ten heretics. Will you not be warned?
35 Will you not understand?

THE INQUISITOR. If the Church Militant tells you that your revelations and visions are sent by the devil to tempt you to your damnation, will you not believe that The Church is wiser
40 than you?

JOAN. I believe that God is wiser than I; and it is His commands that I will do. All the things that you call my crimes have come to me by the command of God. I say that I have done
45 them by the order of God: it is impossible for me to say anything else. If any Churchman says the contrary I shall not mind him: I shall mind God alone, whose command I always follow.

LADVENU [pleading with her urgently]. You 50 do not know what you are saying, child. Do you want to kill yourself? Listen. Do you not believe that you are subject to the Church of God on earth?

JOAN. Yes. When have I ever denied it? 55

LADVENU. Good. That means, does it not, that you are subject to our Lord the Pope, to the cardinals, the archbishops, and the bishops for whom his lordship stands here today?

JOAN. God must be served first. 60

D'ESTIVET. Then your voices command you not to submit yourself to the Church Militant?

JOAN. My voices do not tell me to disobey The Church; but God must be served first.

CAUCHON. And you, and not The Church, 65 are to be the judge?

JOAN. What other judgment can I judge by but my own?

THE ASSESSORS [scandalized]. Oh! [They cannot find words.] 70

CAUCHON. Out of your own mouth you have condemned yourself. We have striven for your salvation to the verge of sinning ourselves: we have opened the door to you again and again; and you have shut it in our faces and in the 75 face of God. Dare you pretend, after what you have said, that you are in a state of grace?

JOAN. If I am not, may God bring me to it: if I am, may God keep me in it!

LADVENU. That is a very good reply, my lord. 80

COURCELLES. Were you in a state of grace when you stole the Bishop's horse?

CAUCHON [rising in a fury]. Oh, devil take the Bishop's horse and you too! We are here to try a case of heresy; and no sooner do we 85 come to the root of the matter than we are thrown back by idiots who understand nothing but horses. [Trembling with rage, he forces himself to sit down.]

THE INQUISITOR. Gentlemen, gentlemen: in 90 clinging to these small issues you are The Maid's best advocates. I am not surprised that his lordship has lost patience with you. What does the Promoter say? Does he press these trumpery matters? 95

D'ESTIVET. I am bound by my office to press everything; but when the woman confesses a heresy that must bring upon her the doom of

excommunication, of what consequence is it that she has been guilty also of offences which expose her to minor penances? I share the impatience of his lordship as to these minor
5 charges. Only, with great respect, I must emphasize the gravity of two very horrible and blasphemous crimes which she does not deny. First, she has intercourse with evil spirits, and is therefore a sorceress. Second, she wears
10 men's clothes, which is indecent, unnatural, and abominable; and in spite of our most earnest remonstrances and entreaties, she will not change them even to receive the sacrament.

JOAN. Is the blessed St Catherine an evil
15 spirit? Is St Margaret? Is Michael the Archangel?

COURCELLES. How do you know that the spirit which appears to you is an archangel? Does he not appear to you as a naked man?
20 JOAN. Do you think God cannot afford clothes for him?

[*The* ASSESSORS *cannot help smiling, especially as the joke is against* COURCELLES.]

LADVENU. Well answered, Joan.
25 THE INQUISITOR. It is, in effect, well answered. But no evil spirit would be so simple as to appear to a young girl in a guise that would scandalize her when he meant her to take him for a messenger from the Most High. Joan:
30 The Church instructs you that these apparitions are demons seeking your soul's perdition. Do you accept the instruction of The Church?

JOAN. I accept the messenger of God. How could any faithful believer in The Church
35 refuse him?

CAUCHON. Wretched woman: again I ask you, do you know what you are saying?

THE INQUISITOR. You wrestle in vain with the devil for her soul, my lord: she will not
40 be saved. Now as to this matter of the man's dress. For the last time, will you put off that impudent attire, and dress as becomes your sex?

JOAN. I will not.
45 D'ESTIVET [*pouncing*]. The sin of disobedience, my lord.

JOAN [*distressed*]. But my voices tell me I must dress as a soldier.

LADVENU. Joan, Joan: does not that prove to

you that the voices are the voices of evil spirits? 50
Can you suggest to us one good reason why an angel of God should give you such shameless advice?

JOAN. Why, yes: what can be plainer commonsense? I was a soldier living among 55
soldiers. I am a prisoner guarded by soldiers. If I were to dress as a woman they would think of me as a woman; and then what would become of me? If I dress as a soldier they think of me as a soldier, and I can live with them as 60
I do at home with my brothers. That is why St Catherine tells me I must not dress as a woman until she gives me leave.

COURCELLES. When will she give you leave?

JOAN. When you take me out of the hands 65
of the English soldiers. I have told you that I should be in the hands of The Church, and not left night and day with four soldiers of the Earl of Warwick. Do you want me to live with them in petticoats? 70

LADVENU. My lord: what she says is, God knows, very wrong and shocking; but there is a grain of worldly sense in it such as might impose on a simple village maiden.

JOAN. If we were as simple in the village as 75
you are in your courts and palaces, there would soon be no wheat to make bread for you.

CAUCHON. That is the thanks you get for trying to save her, Brother Martin.

LADVENU. Joan: we are all trying to save 80
you. His lordship is trying to save you. The Inquisitor could not be more just to you if you were his own daughter. But you are blinded by a terrible pride and self-sufficiency.

JOAN. Why do you say that? I have said 85
nothing wrong. I cannot understand.

THE INQUISITOR. The blessed St Athanasius has laid it down in his creed that those who cannot understand are damned. It is not enough to be simple. It is not enough even to be what 90
simple people call good. The simplicity of a darkened mind is no better than the simplicity of a beast.

JOAN. There is great wisdom in the simplicity of a beast, let me tell you; and sometimes great 95
foolishness in the wisdom of scholars.

LADVENU. We know that, Joan: we are not so foolish as you think us. Try to resist the temptation to make pert replies to us. Do you see that man who stands behind you [*he indicates the* EXECUTIONER]?

JOAN [*turning and looking at the man*]. Your
5 torturer? But the Bishop said I was not to be tortured.

LADVENU. You are not to be tortured because you have confessed everything that is necessary to your condemnation. That man is not only
10 the torturer: he is also the Executioner. Executioner: let The Maid hear your answers to my questions. Are you prepared for the burning of a heretic this day?

THE EXECUTIONER. Yes, Master.
15 LADVENU. Is the stake ready?

THE EXECUTIONER. It is. In the market-place. The English have built it too high for me to get near her and make the death easier. It will be a cruel death.
20 JOAN [*horrified*]. But you are not going to burn me now?

THE INQUISITOR. You realize it at last.

LADVENU. There are eight hundred English soldiers waiting to take you to the market-
25 place the moment the sentence of excommunication has passed the lips of your judges. You are within a few short moments of that doom.

JOAN [*looking round desperately for rescue*]. Oh God!
30 LADVENU. Do not despair, Joan. The Church is merciful. You can save yourself.

JOAN [*hopefully*]. Yes: my voices promised me I should not be burnt. St Catherine bade me be bold.
35 CAUCHON. Woman: are you quite mad? Do you not yet see that your voices have deceived you?

JOAN. Oh no: that is impossible.

CAUCHON. Impossible! They have led you
40 straight to your excommunication, and to the stake which is there waiting for you.

LADVENU [*pressing the point hard*]. Have they kept a single promise to you since you were taken at Compiègne? The devil has be-
45 trayed you. The Church holds out its arms to you.

JOAN [*despairing*]. Oh, it is true: it is true: my voices have deceived me. I have been

mocked by devils: my faith is broken. I have dared and dared; but only a fool will walk into 50
a fire: God, who gave me my commonsense, cannot will me to do that.

LADVENU. Now God be praised that He has saved you at the eleventh hour! [*He hurries to the vacant seat at the scribes' table, and* 55
snatches a sheet of paper, on which he sets to work writing eagerly.]

CAUCHON. Amen!

JOAN. What must I do?

CAUCHON. You must sign a solemn recanta- 60
tion of your heresy.

JOAN. Sign? That means to write my name. I cannot write.

CAUCHON. You have signed many letters before. 65

JOAN. Yes; but someone held my hand and guided the pen. I can make my mark.

THE CHAPLAIN [*who has been listening with growing alarm and indignation*]. My lord: do you mean that you are going to allow this 70
woman to escape us?

THE INQUISITOR. The law must take its course, Master de Stogumber. And you know the law.

THE CHAPLAIN [*rising, purple with fury*]. I 75
know that there is no faith in a Frenchman. [*Tumult, which he shouts down.*] I know what my lord the Cardinal of Winchester will say when he hears of this. I know what the Earl of Warwick will do when he learns that you 80
intend to betray him. There are eight hundred men at the gate who will see that this abominable witch is burnt in spite of your teeth.

THE ASSESSORS [*meanwhile*]. What is this? What did he say? He accuses us of treachery! 85
This is past bearing. No faith in a Frenchman! Did you hear that? This is an intolerable fellow. Who is he? Is this what English Churchmen are like? He must be mad or drunk, etc., etc. 90

THE INQUISITOR [*rising*]. Silence, pray! Gentlemen: pray silence! Master Chaplain: bethink you a moment of your holy office: of what you are, and where you are. I direct you to sit down. 95

THE CHAPLAIN [*folding his arms doggedly,*

his face working convulsively]. I will NOT sit down.

CAUCHON. Master Inquisitor: this man has called me a traitor to my face before now.

THE CHAPLAIN. So you are a traitor. You are all traitors. You have been doing nothing but begging this damnable witch on your knees to recant all through this trial.

THE INQUISITOR [*placidly resuming his seat*]. If you will not sit, you must stand: that is all.

THE CHAPLAIN. I will NOT stand. [*He flings himself back into his chair.*]

LADVENU [*rising with the paper in his hand*]. My lord: here is the form of recantation for The Maid to sign.

CAUCHON. Read it to her.

JOAN. Do not trouble. I will sign it.

THE INQUISITOR. Woman: you must know what you are putting your hand to. Read it to her, Brother Martin. And let all be silent.

LADVENU [*reading quietly*]. "I, Joan, commonly called The Maid, a miserable sinner, do confess that I have most grievously sinned in the following articles. I have pretended to have revelations from God and the angels and the blessed saints, and perversely rejected The Church's warnings that these were temptations by demons. I have blasphemed abominably by wearing an immodest dress, contrary to the Holy Scripture and the canons of The Church. Also I have clipped my hair in the style of a man, and, against all the duties which have made my sex specially acceptable in heaven, have taken up the sword, even to the shedding of human blood, inciting men to slay each other, invoking evil spirits to delude them, and stubbornly and most blasphemously imputing these sins to Almighty God. I confess to the sin of sedition, to the sin of idolatry, to the sin of disobedience, to the sin of pride, and to the sin of heresy. All of which sins I now renounce and abjure and depart from, humbly thanking you Doctors and Masters who have brought me back to the truth and into the grace of our Lord. And I will never return to my errors, but will remain in communion with our Holy Church and in obedience to our Holy Father the Pope of Rome. All this I swear by God

Almighty and the Holy Gospels, in witness whereto I sign my name to this recantation."

THE INQUISITOR. You understand this, Joan?

JOAN [*listless*]. It is plain enough, sir.

THE INQUISITOR. And it is true?

JOAN. It may be true. If it were not true, the fire would not be ready for me in the marketplace.

LADVENU [*taking up his pen and a book, and going to her quickly lest she should compromise herself again*]. Come, child: let me guide your hand. Take the pen. [*She does so; and they begin to write, using the book as a desk.*] J.E.H.A.N.E. So. Now make your mark by yourself.

JOAN [*makes her mark, and gives him back the pen, tormented by the rebellion of her soul against her mind and body*]. There!

LADVENU [*replacing the pen on the table, and handing the recantation to CAUCHON with a reverence*]. Praise be to God, my brothers, the lamb has returned to the flock; and the shepherd rejoices in her more than in ninety and nine just persons. [*He returns to his seat.*]

THE INQUISITOR [*taking the paper from CAUCHON*]. We declare thee by this act set free from the danger of excommunication in which thou stoodest. [*He throws the paper down to the table.*]

JOAN. I thank you.

THE INQUISITOR. But because thou hast sinned most presumptuously against God and the Holy Church, and that thou mayst repent thy errors in solitary contemplation, and be shielded from all temptation to return to them, we, for the good of thy soul, and for a penance that may wipe out thy sins and bring thee finally unspotted to the throne of grace, do condemn thee to eat the bread of sorrow and drink the water of affliction to the end of thy earthly days in perpetual imprisonment.

JOAN [*rising in consternation and terrible anger*]. Perpetual imprisonment! Am I not then to be set free?

LADVENU [*mildly shocked*]. Set free, child, after such wickedness as yours! What are you dreaming of?

JOAN. Give me that writing. [*She rushes to*

the table; *snatches up the paper; and tears it
into fragments.*] Light your fire: do you think
I dread it as much as the life of a rat in a hole?
My voices were right.

5   LADVENU. Joan! Joan!

JOAN. Yes: they told me you were fools [*the
word gives great offence*], and that I was not
to listen to your fine words nor trust to your
charity. You promised me my life; but you lied
10   [*indignant exclamations*]. You think that life
is nothing but not being stone dead. It is not
the bread and water I fear: I can live on bread:
when have I asked for more? It is no hardship
to drink water if the water be clean. Bread has
15   no sorrow for me, and water no affliction. But
to shut me from the light of the sky and the
sight of the fields and flowers; to chain my
feet so that I can never again ride with the
soldiers nor climb the hills; to make me breathe
20   foul damp darkness, and keep from me everything that brings me back to the love of God
when your wickedness and foolishness tempt
me to hate Him: all this is worse than the
furnace in the Bible that was heated seven
25   times. I could do without my warhorse; I
could drag about in a skirt; I could let the
banners and the trumpets and the knights and
soldiers pass me and leave me behind as they
leave the other women, if only I could still hear
30   the wind in the trees, the larks in the sunshine,
the young lambs crying through the healthy
frost, and the blessed blessed church bells that
send my angel voices floating to me on the
wind. But without these things I cannot live;
35   and by your wanting to take them away from
me, or from any human creature, I know that
your counsel is of the devil, and that mine is
of God.

THE ASSESSORS [*in great commotion*]. Blas-
40   phemy! blasphemy! She is possessed. She said
our counsel was of the devil. And hers of God.
Monstrous! The devil is in our midst, etc., etc.

D'ESTIVET [*shouting above the din*]. She is
a relapsed heretic, obstinate, incorrigible, and
45   altogether unworthy of the mercy we have
shewn her. I call for her excommunication.

THE CHAPLAIN [*to the* EXECUTIONER]. Light
your fire, man. To the stake with her.

[*The* EXECUTIONER *and his* ASSISTANTS *hurry
out through the courtyard.*]   50

LADVENU. You wicked girl: if your counsel
were of God would He not deliver you?

JOAN. His ways are not your ways. He wills
that I go through the fire to His bosom; for I
am His child, and you are not fit that I should   55
live among you. That is my last word to you.

[*The* SOLDIERS *seize her.*]

CAUCHON [*rising*]. Not yet.

[*They wait. There is a dead silence.* CAUCHON
turns to the INQUISITOR *with an inquiring look.*   60
The INQUISITOR *nods affirmatively. They rise
solemnly, and intone the sentence antiphon-
ally.*]

CAUCHON. We decree that thou art a relapsed
heretic.   65

THE INQUISITOR. Cast out from the unity of
the Church.

CAUCHON. Sundered from her body.

THE INQUISITOR. Infected with the leprosy
of heresy.   70

CAUCHON. A member of Satan.

THE INQUISITOR. We declare that thou must
be excommunicate.

CAUCHON. And now we do cast thee out,
segregate thee, and abandon thee to the secular   75
power.

THE INQUISITOR. Admonishing the same
secular power that it moderate its judgment of
thee in respect of death and division of the
limbs. [*He resumes his seat.*]   80

CAUCHON. And if any true sign of penitence
appear in thee, to permit our Brother Martin
to administer to thee the sacrament of penance.

THE CHAPLAIN. Into the fire with the witch.
[*He rushes at her, and helps the* SOLDIERS *to*   85
push her out.]

[JOAN *is taken away through the courtyard.
The* ASSESSORS *rise in disorder, and follow the*
SOLDIERS, *except* LADVENU, *who has hidden his
face in his hands.*]   90

CAUCHON [*rising again in the act of sitting
down*]. No, no: this is irregular. The representative of the secular arm should be here to
receive her from us.

THE INQUISITOR [*also on his feet again*]. That   95
man is an incorrigible fool.

CAUCHON. Brother Martin: see that everything is done in order.

LADVENU. My place is at her side, my lord. You must exercise your own authority. [*He hurries out.*]

CAUCHON. These English are impossible: they will thrust her straight into the fire. Look!

[*He points to the courtyard, in which the glow and flicker of fire can now be seen reddening the May daylight. Only the* BISHOP *and the* INQUISITOR *are left in the court.*]

CAUCHON [*turning to go*]. We must stop that.

THE INQUISITOR [*calmly*]. Yes; but not too fast, my lord.

CAUCHON [*halting*]. But there is not a moment to lose.

THE INQUISITOR. We have proceeded in perfect order. If the English choose to put themselves in the wrong, it is not our business to put them in the right. A flaw in the procedure may be useful later on: one never knows. And the sooner it is over, the better for that poor girl.

CAUCHON [*relaxing*]. That is true. But I suppose we must see this dreadful thing through.

THE INQUISITOR. One gets used to it. Habit is everything. I am accustomed to the fire: it is soon over. But it is a terrible thing to see a young and innocent creature crushed between these mighty forces, The Church and the Law.

CAUCHON. You call her innocent!

THE INQUISITOR. Oh, quite innocent. What does she know of The Church and the Law? She did not understand a word we were saying. It is the ignorant who suffer. Come, or we shall be late for the end.

CAUCHON [*going with him*]. I shall not be sorry if we are: I am not so accustomed as you.

[*They are going out when* WARWICK *comes in, meeting them.*]

WARWICK. Oh, I am intruding. I thought it was all over. [*He makes a feint of retiring.*]

CAUCHON. Do not go, my lord. It is all over.

THE INQUISITOR. The execution is not in our hands, my lord; but it is desirable that we should witness the end. So by your leave— [*He bows, and goes out through the courtyard.*]

CAUCHON. There is some doubt whether your people have observed the forms of law, my lord.

WARWICK. I am told that there is some doubt whether your authority runs in this city, my lord. It is not in your diocese. However, if you will answer for that I will answer for the rest.

CAUCHON. It is to God that we both must answer. Good morning, my lord.

WARWICK. My lord: good morning.

[*They look at one another for a moment with unconcealed hostility. Then* CAUCHON *follows the* INQUISITOR *out.* WARWICK *looks round. Finding himself alone, he calls for attendance.*]

WARWICK. Hallo: some attendance here! [*Silence.*] Hallo, there! [*Silence.*] Hallo! Brian, you young blackguard, where are you? [*Silence.*] Guard! [*Silence.*] They have all gone to see the burning: even that child.

[*The silence is broken by someone frantically howling and sobbing.*]

WARWICK. What in the devil's name—?

[*The* CHAPLAIN *staggers in from the courtyard like a demented creature, his face streaming with tears, making the piteous sounds that* WARWICK *has heard. He stumbles to the prisoner's stool, and throws himself upon it with heartrending sobs.*]

WARWICK [*going to him and patting him on the shoulder*]. What is it, Master John? What is the matter?

THE CHAPLAIN [*clutching at his hands*]. My lord, my lord: for Christ's sake pray for my wretched guilty soul.

WARWICK [*soothing him*]. Yes, yes: of course I will. Calmly, gently—

THE CHAPLAIN [*blubbering miserably*]. I am not a bad man, my lord.

WARWICK. No, no: not at all.

THE CHAPLAIN. I meant no harm. I did not know what it would be like.

WARWICK [*hardening*]. Oh! You saw it, then?

THE CHAPLAIN. I did not know what I was doing. I am a hotheaded fool; and I shall be damned to all eternity for it.

WARWICK. Nonsense! Very distressing, no doubt; but it was not your doing.

THE CHAPLAIN [*lamentably*]. I let them do it.

If I had known, I would have torn her from
their hands. You dont know: you havnt seen:
it is so easy to talk when you dont know. You
madden yourself with words: you damn your-
5 self because it feels grand to throw oil on the
flaming hell of your own temper. But when
it is brought home to you; when you see the
thing you have done; when it is blinding your
eyes, stifling your nostrils, tearing your heart,
10 then—then— [Falling on his knees.] O God,
take away this sight from me; O Christ, deliver
me from this fire that is consuming me! She
cried to Thee in the midst of it: Jesus! Jesus!
Jesus! She is in Thy bosom; and I am in hell
15 for evermore.

WARWICK [summarily hauling him to his
feet]. Come come, man! you must pull yourself
together. We shall have the whole town talking
of this. [He throws him not too gently into a
20 chair at the table.] If you have not the nerve
to see these things, why do you not do as I do,
and stay away?

THE CHAPLAIN [bewildered and submissive].
She asked for a cross. A soldier gave her two
25 sticks tied together. Thank God he was an
Englishman! I might have done it; but I did
not: I am a coward, a mad dog, a fool. But he
was an Englishman too.

WARWICK. The fool! they will burn him too
30 if the priests get hold of him.

THE CHAPLAIN [shaken with a convulsion].
Some of the people laughed at her. They would
have laughed at Christ. They were French
people, my lord: I know they were French.

35 WARWICK. Hush! someone is coming. Control yourself.

[LADVENU comes back through the courtyard
to WARWICK's right hand, carrying a bishop's
cross which he has taken from a church. He is
40 very grave and composed.]

WARWICK. I am informed that it is all over,
Brother Martin.

LADVENU [enigmatically]. We do not know,
my lord. It may have only just begun.

45 WARWICK. What does that mean, exactly?

LADVENU. I took this cross from the church
for her that she might see it to the last: she
had only two sticks that she put into her
bosom. When the fire crept round us, and she
saw that if I held the cross before her I should 50
be burnt myself, she warned me to get down
and save myself. My lord: a girl who could
think of another's danger in such a moment
was not inspired by the devil. When I had to
snatch the cross from her sight, she looked up 55
to heaven. And I do not believe that the
heavens were empty. I firmly believe that her
Savior appeared to her then in His tenderest
glory. She called to Him and died. This is not
the end for her, but the beginning. 60

WARWICK. I am afraid it will have a bad
effect on the people.

LADVENU. It had, my lord, on some of them.
I heard laughter. Forgive me for saying that
I hope and believe it was English laughter. 65

THE CHAPLAIN [rising frantically]. No: it
was not. There was only one Englishman there
that disgraced his country; and that was the
mad dog, de Stogumber. [He rushes wildly out,
shrieking.] Let them torture him. Let them 70
burn him. I will go pray among her ashes. I
am no better than Judas: I will hang myself.

WARWICK. Quick, Brother Martin: follow
him: he will do himself some mischief. After
him, quick. 75

[LADVENU hurries out, WARWICK urging him.
The EXECUTIONER comes in by the door behind
the judges' chairs; and WARWICK, returning,
finds himself face to face with him.]

WARWICK. Well, fellow: who are you? 80

THE EXECUTIONER [with dignity]. I am not
addressed as fellow, my lord. I am the Master
Executioner of Rouen: it is a highly skilled
mystery. I am come to tell your lordship that
your orders have been obeyed. 85

WARWICK. I crave your pardon, Master Executioner; and I will see that you lose nothing
by having no relics to sell. I have your word,
have I, that nothing remains, not a bone, not
a nail, not a hair? 90

THE EXECUTIONER. Her heart would not burn,
my lord; but everything that was left is at the
bottom of the river. You have heard the last
of her.

WARWICK [*with a wry smile, thinking of what* LADVENU *said*]. The last of her? Hm! I wonder!

EPILOGUE

[*A restless fitfully windy night in June 1456, full of summer lightning after many days of heat.* KING CHARLES THE SEVENTH OF FRANCE, *formerly Joan's Dauphin, now Charles the Victorious, aged 51, is in bed in one of his royal chateaux. The bed, raised on a dais of two steps, is towards the side of the room so as to avoid blocking a tall lancet window in the middle. Its canopy bears the royal arms in embroidery. Except for the canopy and the huge down pillows there is nothing to distinguish it from a broad settee with bed-clothes and a valance. Thus its occupant is in full view from the foot.*

CHARLES *is not asleep: he is reading in bed, or rather looking at the pictures in Fouquet's Boccaccio with his knees doubled up to make a reading desk. Beside the bed on his left is a little table with a picture of the Virgin, lighted by candles of painted wax. The walls are hung from ceiling to floor with painted curtains which stir at times in the draughts. At first glance the prevailing yellow and red in these hanging pictures is somewhat flamelike when the folds breathe in the wind.*

The door is on CHARLES's *left, but in front of him close to the corner farthest from him. A large watchman's rattle, handsomely designed and gaily painted, is in the bed under his hand.*

CHARLES *turns a leaf. A distant clock strikes the half-hour softly.* CHARLES *shuts the book with a clap; throws it aside; snatches up the rattle; and whirls it energetically, making a deafening clatter.* LADVENU *enters, 25 years older, strange and stark in bearing, and still carrying the cross from Rouen.* CHARLES *evidently does not expect him; for he springs out of bed on the farther side from the door.*]

CHARLES. Who are you? Where is my gentleman of the bedchamber? What do you want?

LADVENU [*solemnly*]. I bring you glad tidings of great joy. Rejoice, O king; for the taint is removed from your blood, and the stain from your crown. Justice, long delayed, is at last triumphant.

CHARLES. What are you talking about? Who are you?

LADVENU. I am Brother Martin.

CHARLES. And who, saving your reverence, may Brother Martin be?

LADVENU. I held this cross when The Maid perished in the fire. Twenty-five years have passed since then: nearly ten thousand days. And on every one of those days I have prayed God to justify His daughter on earth as she is justified in heaven.

CHARLES [*reassured, sitting down on the foot of the bed*]. Oh, I remember now. I have heard of you. You have a bee in your bonnet about The Maid. Have you been at the inquiry?

LADVENU. I have given my testimony.

CHARLES. Is it over?

LADVENU. It is over.

CHARLES. Satisfactorily?

LADVENU. The ways of God are very strange.

CHARLES. How so?

LADVENU. At the trial which sent a saint to the stake as a heretic and a sorceress, the truth was told; the law was upheld; mercy was shewn beyond all custom; no wrong was done but the final and dreadful wrong of the lying sentence and the pitiless fire. At this inquiry from which I have just come, there was shameless perjury, courtly corruption, calumny of the dead who did their duty according to their lights, cowardly evasion of the issue, testimony made of idle tales that could not impose on a ploughboy. Yet out of this insult to justice, this defamation of The Church, this orgy of lying and foolishness, the truth is set in the noonday sun on the hilltop; the white robe of innocence is cleansed from the smirch of the burning faggots; the holy life is sanctified; the true heart that lived through the flame is consecrated; a great lie is silenced for ever; and a great wrong is set right before all men.

CHARLES. My friend: provided they can no longer say that I was crowned by a witch and a heretic, I shall not fuss about how the trick has been done. Joan would not have fussed about it if it came all right in the end: she was not that sort: I knew her. Is her rehabilitation 5 complete? I made it pretty clear that there was to be no nonsense about it.

LADVENU. It is solemnly declared that her judges were full of corruption, cozenage, fraud, and malice. Four falsehoods.

10 CHARLES. Never mind the falsehoods: her judges are dead.

LADVENU. The sentence on her is broken, annulled, annihilated, set aside as non-existent, without value or effect.

15 CHARLES. Good. Nobody can challenge my consecration now, can they?

LADVENU. Not Charlemagne nor King David himself was more sacredly crowned.

CHARLES [rising]. Excellent. Think of what 20 that means to me!

LADVENU. I think of what it means to her!

CHARLES. You cannot. None of us ever knew what anything meant to her. She was like nobody else; and she must take care of herself 25 wherever she is; for I cannot take care of her; and neither can you, whatever you may think: you are not big enough. But I will tell you this about her. If you could bring her back to life, they would burn her again within six months, 30 for all their present adoration of her. And you would hold up the cross, too, just the same. So [crossing himself] let her rest; and let you and I mind our own business, and not meddle with hers.

35 LADVENU. God forbid that I should have no share in her, nor she in me! [He turns and strides out as he came, saying:] Henceforth my path will not lie through palaces, nor my conversation be with kings.

40 CHARLES [following him towards the door, and shouting after him]. Much good may it do you, holy man! [He returns to the middle of the chamber, where he halts, and says quizzically to himself.] That was a funny chap. How 45 did he get in? Where are my people? [He goes impatiently to the bed, and swings the rattle. A rush of wind through the open door sets the walls swaying agitatedly. The candles go out. He calls in the darkness.] Hallo! Someone come and shut the windows: everything is 50 being blown all over the place. [A flash of summer lightning shews up the lancet window. A figure is seen in silhouette against it.] Who is there? Who is that? Help! Murder! [Thunder. He jumps into bed, and hides under the 55 clothes.]

JOAN'S VOICE. Easy, Charlie, easy. What art making all that noise for? No one can hear thee. Thourt asleep. [She is dimly seen in a pallid greenish light by the bedside.] 60

CHARLES [peeping out]. Joan! Are you a ghost, Joan?

JOAN. Hardly even that, lad. Can a poor burnt-up lass have a ghost? I am but a dream that thourt dreaming. [The light increases: they 65 become plainly visible as he sits up.] Thou looks older, lad.

CHARLES. I am older. Am I really asleep?

JOAN. Fallen asleep over thy silly book.

CHARLES. That's funny. 70

JOAN. Not so funny as that I am dead, is it?

CHARLES. Are you really dead?

JOAN. As dead as anybody ever is, laddie. I am out of the body.

CHARLES. Just fancy! Did it hurt much? 75

JOAN. Did what hurt much?

CHARLES. Being burnt.

JOAN. Oh, that! I cannot remember very well. I think it did at first; but then it all got mixed up; and I was not in my right mind until I 80 was free of the body. But do not thou go handling fire and thinking it will not hurt thee. How hast been ever since?

CHARLES. Oh, not so bad. Do you know, I actually lead my army out and win battles? 85 Down into the moat up to my waist in mud and blood. Up the ladders with the stones and hot pitch raining down. Like you.

JOAN. No! Did I make a man of thee after all, Charlie? 90

CHARLES. I am Charles the Victorious now. I had to be brave because you were. Agnes put a little pluck into me too.

JOAN. Agnes! Who was Agnes?

CHARLES. Agnes Sorel. A woman I fell in love with. I dream of her often. I never dreamed of you before.

JOAN. Is she dead, like me?

5 CHARLES. Yes. But she was not like you. She was very beautiful.

JOAN [*laughing heartily*]. Ha ha! I was no beauty: I was always a rough one: a regular soldier. I might almost as well have been a

10 man. Pity I wasn't: I should not have bothered you all so much then. But my head was in the skies; and the glory of God was upon me; and, man or woman, I should have bothered you as long as your noses were in the mud. Now tell

15 me what has happened since you wise men knew no better than to make a heap of cinders of me?

CHARLES. Your mother and brothers have sued the courts to have your case tried over

20 again. And the courts have declared that your judges were full of corruption and cozenage, fraud and malice.

JOAN. Not they. They were as honest a lot of poor fools as ever burned their betters.

25 CHARLES. The sentence on you is broken, annihilated, annulled: null, non-existent, without value or effect.

JOAN. I was burned, all the same. Can they unburn me?

30 CHARLES. If they could, they would think twice before they did it. But they have decreed that a beautiful cross be placed where the stake stood, for your perpetual memory and for your salvation.

35 JOAN. It is the memory and the salvation that sanctify the cross, not the cross that sanctifies the memory and the salvation. [*She turns away, forgetting him.*] I shall outlast that cross. I shall be remembered when men will

40 have forgotten where Rouen stood.

CHARLES. There you go with your self-conceit, the same as ever! I think you might say a word of thanks to me for having had justice done at last.

45 CAUCHON [*appearing at the window between them*]. Liar!

CHARLES. Thank you.

JOAN. Why, if it isnt Peter Cauchon! How are you, Peter? What luck have you had since you burned me? 50

CAUCHON. None. I arraign the justice of Man. It is not the justice of God.

JOAN. Still dreaming of justice, Peter? See what justice came to with me! But what has happened to thee? Art dead or alive? 55

CAUCHON. Dead. Dishonored. They pursued me beyond the grave. They excommunicated my dead body: they dug it up and flung it into the common sewer.

JOAN. Your dead body did not feel the spade 60 and the sewer as my live body felt the fire.

CAUCHON. But this thing that they have done against me hurts justice; destroys faith; saps the foundation of the Church. The solid earth sways like the treacherous sea beneath the feet 65 of men and spirits alike when the innocent are slain in the name of law, and their wrongs are undone by slandering the pure of heart.

JOAN. Well, well, Peter, I hope men will be the better for remembering me; and they 70 would not remember me so well if you had not burned me.

CAUCHON. They will be the worse for remembering me: they will see in me evil triumphing over good, falsehood over truth, 75 cruelty over mercy, hell over heaven. Their courage will rise as they think of you, only to faint as they think of me. Yet God is my witness I was just: I was merciful: I was faithful to my light: I could do no other than I did. 80

CHARLES [*scrambling out of the sheets and enthroning himself on the side of the bed*]. Yes: it is always you good men that do the big mischiefs. Look at me! I am not Charles the Good, nor Charles the Wise, nor Charles the 85 Bold. Joan's worshippers may even call me Charles the Coward because I did not pull her out of the fire. But I have done less harm than any of you. You people with your heads in the sky spend all your time trying to turn the 90 world upside down; but I take the world as it is, and say that top-side-up is right-side-up; and I keep my nose pretty close to the ground. And I ask you, what king of France has done better, or been a better fellow in his little way?

JOAN. Art really king of France, Charlie? Be the English gone?

DUNOIS [*coming through the tapestry on*
5 JOAN's *left, the candles relighting themselves at the same moment, and illuminating his armour and surcoat cheerfully*]. I have kept my word: the English are gone.

JOAN. Praised be God! now is fair France a
10 province in heaven. Tell me all about the fighting, Jack. Was it thou that led them? Wert thou God's captain to thy death?

DUNOIS. I am not dead. My body is very comfortably asleep in my bed at Chateaudun;
15 but my spirit is called here by yours.

JOAN. And you fought them my way, Jack: eh? Not the old way, chaffering for ransoms; but The Maid's way: staking life against death, with the heart high and humble and void of
20 malice, and nothing counting under God but France free and French. Was it my way, Jack?

DUNOIS. Faith, it was any way that would win. But the way that won was always your way. I give you best, lassie. I wrote a fine letter
25 to set you right at the new trial. Perhaps I should never have let the priests burn you; but I was busy fighting; and it was The Church's business, not mine. There was no use in both of us being burned, was there?

30 CAUCHON. Ay! put the blame on the priests. But I, who am beyond praise and blame, tell you that the world is saved neither by its priests nor its soldiers, but by God and His Saints. The Church Militant sent this woman
35 to the fire; but even as she burned, the flames whitened into the radiance of the Church Triumphant.

[*The clock strikes the third quarter. A rough male voice is heard trolling an improvised*
40 *tune.*]

Rum tum trumpledum,
Bacon fat and rumpledum,

Old Saint mumpledum,
Pull his tail and stumpledum
O my Ma—ry Ann! 45

[*A ruffianly* ENGLISH SOLDIER *comes through the curtains and marches between* DUNOIS *and* JOAN.]

DUNOIS. What villainous troubadour taught you that doggrel? 50

THE SOLDIER. No troubadour. We made it up ourselves as we marched. We were not gentlefolks and troubadours. Music straight out of the heart of the people, as you might say. Rum tum trumpledum, Bacon fat and rumpledum, 55 Old Saint mumpledum, Pull his tail and stumpledum: that dont mean anything, you know; but it keeps you marching. Your servant, ladies and gentlemen. Who asked for a saint? 60

JOAN. Be you a saint?

THE SOLDIER. Yes, lady, straight from hell.

DUNOIS. A saint, and from hell!

THE SOLDIER. Yes, noble captain: I have a day off. Every year, you know. Thats my al- 65 lowance for my one good action.

CAUCHON. Wretch! In all the years of your life did you do only one good action?

THE SOLDIER. I never thought about it: it came natural like. But they scored it up for me. 70

CHARLES. What was it?

THE SOLDIER. Why, the silliest thing you ever heard of. I—

JOAN [*interrupting him by strolling across to the bed, where she sits beside* CHARLES]. He 75 tied two sticks together, and gave them to a poor lass that was going to be burned.

THE SOLDIER. Right. Who told you that?

JOAN. Never mind. Would you know her if you saw her again? 80

THE SOLDIER. Not I. There are so many girls! and they all expect you to remember them as if there was only one in the world. This one

must have been a prime sort; for I have a day off every year for her; and so, until twelve o'clock punctually, I am a saint, at your service, noble lords and lovely ladies.

CHARLES. And after twelve?

THE SOLDIER. After twelve, back to the only place fit for the likes of me.

JOAN [*rising*]. Back there! You! that gave the lass the cross!

THE SOLDIER [*excusing his unsoldierly conduct*]. Well, she asked for it; and they were going to burn her. She had as good a right to a cross as they had; and they had dozens of them. It was her funeral, not theirs. Where was the harm in it?

JOAN. Man: I am not reproaching you. But I cannot bear to think of you in torment.

THE SOLDIER [*cheerfully*]. No great torment, lady. You see I was used to worse.

CHARLES. What! worse than hell?

THE SOLDIER. Fifteen years' service in the French wars. Hell was a treat after that.

[JOAN *throws up her arms, and takes refuge from despair of humanity before the picture of the Virgin.*]

THE SOLDIER [*continuing*].—Suits me somehow. The day off was dull at first, like a wet Sunday. I dont mind it so much now. They tell me I can have as many as I like as soon as I want them.

CHARLES. What is hell like?

THE SOLDIER. You wont find it so bad, sir. Jolly. Like as if you were always drunk without the trouble and expense of drinking. Tip top company too: emperors and popes and kings and all sorts. They chip me about giving that young judy the cross; but I dont care: I stand up to them proper, and tell them that if she hadnt a better right to it than they, she'd be where they are. That dumbfounds them, that does. All they can do is gnash their teeth, hell fashion; and I just laugh, and go off singing the old chanty: Rum tum trumple—Hullo! Who's that knocking at the door?

[*They listen. A long gentle knocking is heard.*]

CHARLES. Come in.

[*The door opens; and an old* PRIEST, *white-haired, bent, with a silly but benevolent smile, comes in and trots over to* JOAN.]

THE NEWCOMER. Excuse me, gentle lords and ladies. Do not let me disturb you. Only a poor old harmless English rector. Formerly chaplain to the cardinal: to my lord of Winchester. John de Stogumber, at your service. [*He looks at them inquiringly.*] Did you say anything? I am a little deaf, unfortunately. Also a little— well, not always in my right mind, perhaps; but still, it is a small village with a few simple people. I suffice: I suffice: they love me there; and I am able to do a little good. I am well connected, you see; and they indulge me.

JOAN. Poor old John! What brought thee to this state?

DE STOGUMBER. I tell my folks they must be very careful. I say to them, "If you only saw what you think about you would think quite differently about it. It would give you a great shock. Oh, a great shock." And they all say "Yes, parson: we all know you are a kind man, and would not harm a fly." That is a great comfort to me. For I am not cruel by nature, you know.

THE SOLDIER. Who said you were?

DE STOGUMBER. Well, you see, I did a very cruel thing once because I did not know what cruelty was like. I had not seen it, you know. That is the great thing: you must see it. And then you are redeemed and saved.

CAUCHON. Were not the sufferings of our Lord Christ enough for you?

DE STOGUMBER. No. Oh no: not at all. I had seen them in pictures, and read of them in books, and been greatly moved by them, as I thought. But it was no use: it was not our Lord that redeemed me, but a young woman whom I saw actually burned to death. It was dreadful: oh, most dreadful. But it saved me. I have been a different man ever since, though a little astray in my wits sometimes.

CAUCHON. Must then a Christ perish in torment in every age to save those that have no imagination?

JOAN. Well, if I saved all those he would have been cruel to if he had not been cruel to me, I was not burnt for nothing, was I?

DE STOGUMBER. Oh no; it was not you. My sight is bad: I cannot distinguish your features: but you are not she: Oh no: she was burned to a cinder: dead and gone, dead and
5 gone.

THE EXECUTIONER [*stepping from behind the bed curtains on* CHARLES'S *right, the bed being between them*]. She is more alive than you, old man. Her heart would not burn; and it would
10 not drown. I was a master at my craft: better than the master of Paris, better than the master of Toulouse; but I could not kill The Maid. She is up and alive everywhere.

THE EARL OF WARWICK [*sallying from the*
15 *bed curtains on the other side, and coming to* JOAN's *left hand*]. Madam: my congratulations on your rehabilitation. I feel that I owe you an apology.

JOAN. Oh, please dont mention it.
20 WARWICK [*pleasantly*]. The burning was purely political. There was no personal feeling against you, I assure you.

JOAN. I bear no malice, my lord.

WARWICK. Just so. Very kind of you to meet
25 me in that way: a touch of true breeding. But I must insist on apologizing very amply. The truth is, these political necessities sometimes turn out to be political mistakes; and this one was a veritable howler; for your spirit con-
30 quered us, madam, in spite of our faggots. History will remember me for your sake, though the incidents of the connection were perhaps a little unfortunate.

JOAN. Ay, perhaps just a little, you funny
35 man.

WARWICK. Still, when they make you a saint, you will owe your halo to me, just as this lucky monarch owes his crown to you.

JOAN [*turning from him*]. I shall owe noth-
40 ing to any man: I owe everything to the spirit of God that was within me. But fancy me a saint! What would St Catherine and St Margaret say if the farm girl was cocked up beside them!

45 [*A clerical-looking* GENTLEMAN *in black frockcoat and trousers, and tall hat, in the fashion of the year* 1920, *suddenly appears before them in the corner on their right. They*

all stare at him. Then they burst into uncontrollable laughter.]
50 THE GENTLEMAN. Why this mirth, gentlemen?

WARWICK. I congratulate you on having invented a most extraordinarily comic dress.

THE GENTLEMAN. I do not understand. You
55 are all in fancy dress: I am properly dressed.

DUNOIS. All dress is fancy dress, is it not, except our natural skins?

THE GENTLEMAN. Pardon me: I am here on serious business, and cannot engage in friv-
60 olous discussions. [*He takes out a paper, and assumes a dry official manner.*] I am sent to announce to you that Joan of Arc, formerly known as The Maid, having been the subject of an inquiry instituted by the Bishop of
65 Orleans—

JOAN [*interrupting*]. Ah! They remember me still in Orleans.

THE GENTLEMAN [*emphatically to mark his indignation at the interruption*].—by the
70 Bishop of Orleans into the claim of the said Joan of Arc to be canonized as a saint—

JOAN [*again interrupting*]. But I never made any such claim.

THE GENTLEMAN [*as before*]. —The Church
75 has examined the claim exhaustively in the usual course, and, having admitted the said Joan successively to the ranks of Venerable and Blessed,—

JOAN [*chuckling*]. Me venerable!
80 THE GENTLEMAN. —has finally declared her to have been endowed with heroic virtues and favored with private revelations, and calls the said Venerable and Blessed Joan to the communion of the Church Triumphant as Saint
85 Joan.

JOAN [*rapt*]. Saint Joan!

THE GENTLEMAN. On every thirtieth day of May, being the anniversary of the death of the said most blessed daughter of God, there shall
90 in every Catholic church to the end of time be celebrated a special office in commemoration of her; and it shall be lawful to dedicate a special chapel to her, and to place her image on its altar in every such church. And it shall
95 be lawful and laudable for the faithful to kneel

and address their prayers through her to the Mercy Seat.

JOAN. Oh no. It is for the saint to kneel. [*She falls on her knees, still rapt.*]

5 THE GENTLEMAN [*putting up his paper, and retiring beside the* EXECUTIONER]. In Basilica Vaticana, the sixteenth day of May, nineteen hundred and twenty.

DUNOIS [*raising Joan*]. Half an hour to burn 10 you, dear Saint; and four centuries to find out the truth about you!

DE STOGUMBER. Sir: I was chaplain to the Cardinal of Winchester once. They always would call him the Cardinal of England. It 15 would be a great comfort to me and to my master to see a fair statue to The Maid in Winchester Cathedral. Will they put one there, do you think?

THE GENTLEMAN. As the building is tem- 20 porarily in the hands of the Anglican heresy, I cannot answer for that.

[*A vision of the statue in Winchester Cathedral is seen through the window.*]

DE STOGUMBER. Oh look! look! that is Win- 25 chester.

JOAN. Is that meant to be me? I was stiffer on my feet.

[*The vision fades.*]

THE GENTLEMAN. I have been requested by 30 the temporal authorities of France to mention that the multiplication of public statues to The Maid threatens to become an obstruction to traffic. I do so as a matter of courtesy to the said authorities, but must point out on behalf 35 of The Church that The Maid's horse is no greater obstruction to traffic than any other horse.

JOAN. Eh! I am glad they have not forgotten my horse.

40 [*A vision of the statue before Rheims Cathedral appears.*]

JOAN. Is that funny little thing me too?

CHARLES. That is Rheims Cathedral where you had me crowned. It must be you.

45 JOAN. Who has broken my sword? My sword was never broken. It is the sword of France.

DUNOIS. Never mind. Swords can be mended. Your soul is unbroken; and you are the soul of France.

[*The vision fades. The* ARCHBISHOP *and the* 50 INQUISITOR *are now seen on the right and left of* CAUCHON.]

JOAN. My sword shall conquer yet: the sword that never struck a blow. Though men destroyed my body, yet in my soul I have seen 55 God.

CAUCHON [*kneeling to her*]. The girls in the field praise thee; for thou hast raised their eyes; and they see that there is nothing between them and heaven. 60

DUNOIS [*kneeling to her*]. The dying soldiers praise thee, because thou art a shield of glory between them and the judgment.

THE ARCHBISHOP [*kneeling to her*]. The princes of The Church praise thee, because 65 thou hast redeemed the faith their worldlinesses have dragged through the mire.

WARWICK [*kneeling to her*]. The cunning counsellors praise thee, because thou hast cut the knots in which they have tied their own 70 souls.

DE STOGUMBER [*kneeling to her*]. The foolish old men on their deathbeds praise thee, because their sins against thee are turned into blessings. 75

THE INQUISITOR [*kneeling to her*]. The judges in the blindness and bondage of the law praise thee, because thou hast vindicated the vision and the freedom of the living soul.

THE SOLDIER [*kneeling to her*]. The wicked 80 out of hell praise thee, because thou hast shewn them that the fire that is not quenched is a holy fire.

THE EXECUTIONER [*kneeling to her*]. The tormentors and executioners praise thee, because 85 thou hast shewn that their hands are guiltless of the death of the soul.

CHARLES [*kneeling to her*]. The unpretending praise thee, because thou hast taken upon thyself the heroic burdens that are too heavy 90 for them.

JOAN. Woe unto me when all men praise me! I bid you remember that I am a saint, and that saints can work miracles. And now tell me: shall I rise from the dead, and come back to 95 you a living woman?

[*A sudden darkness blots out the walls of the room as they all spring to their feet in consternation. Only the figures and the bed remain visible.*]

JOAN. What! Must I burn again? Are none of you ready to receive me?

CAUCHON. The heretic is always better dead. And mortal eyes cannot distinguish the saint from the heretic. Spare them. [*He goes out as he came.*]

DUNOIS. Forgive us, Joan: we are not yet good enough for you. I shall go back to my bed. [*He also goes.*]

WARWICK. We sincerely regret our little mistake; but political necessities, though occasionally erroneous, are still imperative; so if you will be good enough to excuse me— [*He steals discreetly away.*]

THE ARCHBISHOP. Your return would not make me the man you once thought me. The utmost I can say is that though I dare not bless you, I hope I may one day enter into your blessedness. Meanwhile, however— [*He goes.*]

THE INQUISITOR. I who am of the dead, testified that day that you were innocent. But I do not see how The Inquisition could possibly be dispensed with under existing circumstances. Therefore— [*He goes.*]

DE STOGUMBER. Oh, do not come back: you must not come back. I must die in peace. Give us peace in our time, O Lord! [*He goes.*]

THE GENTLEMAN. The possibility of your resurrection was not contemplated in the recent proceedings for your canonization. I must return to Rome for fresh instructions. [*He bows formally, and withdraws.*]

THE EXECUTIONER. As a master in my profession I have to consider its interests. And, after all, my first duty is to my wife and children. I must have time to think over this. [*He goes.*]

CHARLES. Poor old Joan! They have all run away from you except this blackguard who has to go back to hell at twelve o'clock. And what can I do but follow Jack Dunois' example, and go back to bed too? [*He does so.*]

JOAN [*sadly*]. Goodnight, Charlie.

CHARLES [*mumbling in his pillows*]. Goo ni.

[*He sleeps. The darkness envelops the bed.*]

JOAN [*to the soldier*] And you, my one faithful? What comfort have you for Saint Joan?

THE SOLDIER. Well, what do they all amount to, these kings and captains and bishops and lawyers and such like? They just leave you in the ditch to bleed to death; and the next thing is, you meet them down there, for all the airs they give themselves. What I say is, you have as good a right to your notions as they have to theirs, and perhaps better. [*Settling himself for a lecture on the subject.*] You see, it's like this. If— [*the first stroke of midnight is heard softly from a distant bell.*] Excuse me: a pressing appointment— [*He goes on tiptoe.*]

[*The last remaining rays of light gather into a white radiance descending on* JOAN. *The hour continues to strike.*]

JOAN. O God that madest this beautiful earth, when will it be ready to receive Thy saints? How long, O Lord, how long?

The End

Sean O'Casey

1884–1964

Juno and the Paycock

1924

To an unusual degree *Juno and the Paycock* draws partly antagonistic dramatic elements together. At any given moment the distinctive focus of the play is located about midway between certain recognizable limits. The more obvious of these is matter-of-fact emphasis on details of Irish tenement life, personal misfortunes, and political strife. The other lies in the region of symbolism and is mainly discernible through a sad and often lyric undertone. Sometimes nostalgic, sometimes solemn, it gives the commonplace a touch of grandeur. Between these limits the play evokes an awareness of potential tragedy.

Rising and subsiding, but always developing, this awareness permits the fusion of otherwise conflicting moods. Thus, in the comic scenes between Joxer, the Captain, and Juno, the audience is led to perceive that their lives are fixed in social and personal misery that they cannot master and can hardly comprehend. This perception links what they say and do to a circumference of meaning that is felt rather than described.

How opposed moods shape the development of a scene and also clarify the focus of the entire play is impressively apparent in the second act. The jollification in honor of Captain Boyle's prospective inheritance contrasts ironically with the poverty of the setting and the growing foreboding that the prospects are empty. The comic spirit of the party, with its boasts and old songs, has an undertone of longing. It is suddenly broken by Johnny's scream that he has seen the ghost of the murdered Robbie Tancred. For a melodramatic instant the party feels the chill of supernatural fear. The celebrating resumes, again to be suspended by the entrance of Mrs. Tancred on her way to the funeral of her son. A last effort at comfortable cheer droops and perishes in the passing-by of the funeral and the distant murmur of the *Ave Maria.* Each contrasting development has its own integrity; at the same time the alternating moods bracket ever more narrowly the central area of awareness.

As O'Casey interweaves contrasting moods, he also merges different kinds of characterization. The effect is simultaneously to widen and particularize the tragic significance. Each of the main characters appears to some extent as both theatrical stereotype and distinct individual. Mary in her role of the ruined maiden is a somewhat melodramatic figure, and Joxer is identifiable as a "parasite" out of the old Roman comedy. Yet through vigorous touches of realism each character acquires a measure of individual pathos. Mary has read her Ibsen and reaches after a way of life less mean and ignorant than her environment allows; even Joxer keeps a wisp of dignity and a fleeting awareness of his own suffering. ·

In Juno, with her queen-goddess name and her cheerless personal destiny, the various modes and the central perception of the play are most fully defined. Under the aspect of comedy she is something of a Xanthippe, uselessly harrying her inadequate spouse. Under that of melodrama she is the long-suffering mother, hard-working and indestructible. In the realm of symbolism, which the play never wholly enters, she is a heroic and pathetic figure, a legendary queen of sorrows. But this symbolic undertone is subdued. Nothing vague is permitted. Yet mere uncompromising realism is lifted above itself, and well-worn stereotypes and reversals are renewed in vigor.

The two-pronged ending of the play epitomizes its method and its meaning. First comes the exit of Juno and Mary, without positive hope but without despair: "Sacred heart o' Jesus, take away our hearts o' stone, and give us hearts o' flesh!" As a curtain line, the sentiment would underscore the theme of suffering, but the tone is perhaps too poignant. "There is a pause," says the stage direction. Then Boyle and Joxer enter, "both of them very drunk." The maudlin stammering of the two cast-aways, as ignorant of their fate as they are helpless to alter it, is in counterpoint to Juno's words. The two endings partly fuse in an image of the old rivalry between creation and chaos.

Juno and the Paycock

O'CASEY

CHARACTERS°

"Captain" Jack Boyle
Juno Boyle   *his wife*
Johnny Boyle ⎫
Mary Boyle   ⎬ *their children*
"Joxer" Daly
Mrs. Maisie Madigan
"Needle" Nugent   *a tailor*
Mrs. Tancred
Jerry Devine
Charlie Bentham   *a school teacher*
An Irregular Mobilizer
Two Irregulars
A Coal-Block Vendor
A Sewing Machine Man
Two Furniture Removal Men
Two Neighbours

⎱ *Residents in the Tenement*

SCENE. *The living apartment of a two-room tenancy of the Boyle family, in a tenement house in Dublin.*

A few days elapse between Acts I and II, 5 *and two months between Acts II and III.*

During Act III the curtain is lowered for a few minutes to denote the lapse of one hour. Period of the play, 1922.°

Characters: "Captain" Jack Boyle is the "paycock" (peacock), long a symbol of empty ostentation or exhibitionism.

Reprinted by permission of Macmillan & Co., Ltd.

ACT I

[*The living room of a two-room tenancy occupied by the* Boyle *family in a tenement* 10 *house in Dublin. Left, a door leading to another part of the house; left of door a window looking into the street; at back a dresser; farther to right at back, a window looking into the back of the house. Between the window and the* 15 *dresser is a picture of the Virgin; below the picture, on a bracket, is a crimson bowl in which a floating votive light is burning. Farther to the right is a small bed partly concealed by cretonne hangings strung on a twine. To the* 20 *right is the fireplace; near the fireplace is a door leading to the other room. Beside the fireplace is a box containing coal. On the mantelshelf is an alarm clock lying on its face. In a corner near the window looking into the back is a* 25 *galvanized bath. A table and some chairs. On the table are breakfast things for one. A teapot is on the hob and a frying-pan stands inside the fender. There are a few books on the dresser and one on the table. Leaning against the* 30 *dresser is a long-handled shovel—the kind invariably used by labourers when turning concrete or mixing mortar.* Johnny Boyle *is sitting crouched beside the fire.* Mary *with her jumper off—it is lying on the back of a chair* 35 *—is arranging her hair before a tiny mirror perched on the table. Beside the mirror is stretched out the morning paper, which she looks at when she isn't gazing into the mirror. She is a well-made and good-looking girl of* 40

1922 a year in which the newly formed **Irish Free State,** made up of the southern and chiefly Catholic counties of Ireland, was torn by bitter dissension between **Staters,** who would accept the gains already won, and the **Die-hards and Republicans,** who insisted on full independence and a union including Northern Ireland, even at the price of renewed civil war. Although the Irish Republican Army was being replaced by an unarmed **Civic Guard,** some detachments of **Irregulars** were still agitating by terrorism for independence and union.

twenty-two. *Two forces are working in her*
mind—one, through the circumstances of her
life, pulling her back; the other, through the
influence of books she has read, pushing her
5 *forward. The opposing forces are apparent in*
her speech and her manners, both of which are
degraded by her environment, and improved
by her acquaintance—slight though it be—
with literature. The time is early forenoon.]
10   MARY [*looking at the paper*]. On a little bye-
road, out beyant Finglas, he was found.

    [MRS. BOYLE *enters by door on right; she has*
been shopping and carries a small parcel in her
hand. She is forty-five years of age, and twenty
15 *years ago she must have been a pretty woman;*
but her face has now assumed that look which
ultimately settles down upon the faces of the
women of the working-class; a look of listless
monotony and harassed anxiety, blending with
20 *an expression of mechanical resistance. Were*
circumstances favourable, she would probably
be a handsome, active and clever woman.]

    MRS. BOYLE. Isn't he come in yet?

    MARY. No, mother.

25   MRS. BOYLE. Oh, he'll come in when he
likes; struttin' about the town like a paycock
with Joxer, I suppose. I hear all about Mrs.
Tancred's son is in this mornin's paper.

    MARY. The full details are in it this mornin';
30 seven wounds he had—one entherin' the neck,
with an exit wound beneath the left shoulder-
blade; another in the left breast penethratin'
the heart, an' . . .

    JOHNNY [*springing up from the fire*]. Oh,
35 quit that readin', for God's sake! Are yous
losin' all your feelin's? It'll soon be that none
of yous'll read anythin' that's not about
butcherin'!

    [*He goes quickly into the room on left.*]
40   MARY. He's gettin' very sensitive, all of a
sudden!

    MRS. BOYLE. I'll read it myself, Mary, by
an' by, when I come home. Everybody's sayin'
that he was a die-hard—thanks be to God that
45 Johnny had nothin' to do with him this long
time. . . . [*Opening the parcel and taking out*
some sausages, which she places on a plate.]
Ah, then, if that father o' yours doesn't come

in soon for his breakfast, he may go without
any; I'll not wait much longer for him.   50

    MARY. Can't you let him get it himself when
he comes in?

    MRS. BOYLE. Yes, an' let him bring in Joxer
Daly along with him? Ay, that's what he'd
like, an' that's what he's waitin' for—till he   55
thinks I'm gone to work, an' then sail in with
the boul'° Joxer, to burn all the coal an' dhrink
all the tea in the place, to show them what a
good Samaritan he is! But I'll stop here till he
comes in, if I have to wait till tomorrow   60
mornin'.

    VOICE OF JOHNNY INSIDE. Mother!

    MRS. BOYLE. Yis?

    VOICE OF JOHNNY. Bring us in a dhrink o'
wather.   65

    MRS. BOYLE. Bring in that fella a dhrink o'
wather, for God's sake, Mary.

    MARY. Isn't he big an' able enough to come
out an' get it himself?

    MRS. BOYLE. If you weren't well yourself   70
you'd like somebody to bring you in a dhrink
o' wather. [*She brings in drink and returns.*]

    MRS. BOYLE. Isn't it terrible to have to be
waitin' this way! You'd think he was bringin
twenty poun's a week into the house the way   75
he's goin' on. He wore out the Health Insurance
long ago, he's afther wearin' out the unemploy-
ment dole, an', now, he's thryin' to wear out
me! An' constantly singin', no less, when he
ought always to be on his knees offerin' up a   80
Novena for a job!

    MARY [*tying a ribbon fillet-wise around her*
head]. I don't like this ribbon, ma; I think I'll
wear the green—it looks betther than the blue.

    MRS. BOYLE. Ah, wear whatever ribbon you   85
like, girl, only don't be botherin' me. I don't
know what a girl on strike wants to be wearin'
a ribbon round her head for or silk stockin's
on her legs either; it's wearin' them things that
make the employers think they're givin' yous   90
too much money.

    MARY. The hour is past now when we'll ask
the employers' permission to wear what we
like.

boul' bold

MRS. BOYLE. I don't know why you wanted to walk out for Jennie Claffey; up to this you never had a good word for her.

MARY. What's the use of belongin' to a Trades Union if you won't stand up for your principles? Why did they sack her? It was a clear case of victimization. We couldn't let her walk the streets, could we?

MRS. BOYLE. No, of course yous couldn't— yous wanted to keep her company. Wan victim wasn't enough. When the employers sacrifice wan victim, the Trades Unions go wan betther be sacrificin' a hundred.

MARY. It doesn't matther what you say, ma —a principle's a principle.

MRS. BOYLE. Yis; an' when I go into oul' Murphy's tomorrow, an' he gets to know that, instead o' payin' all, I'm goin' to borry more, what'll he say when I tell him a principle's a principle? What'll we do if he refuses to give us any more on tick?

MARY. He daren't refuse—if he does, can't you tell him he's paid?

MRS. BOYLE. It's lookin' as if he was paid, whether he refuses or no.

[JOHNNY *appears at the door on left. He can be plainly seen now; he is a thin delicate fellow, something younger than* MARY. *He has evidently gone through a rough time. His face is pale and drawn; there is a tremulous look of indefinite fear in his eyes. The left sleeve of his coat is empty, and he walks with a slight halt.*]

JOHNNY. I was lyin' down: I thought yous were gone. Oul' Simon Mackay is thrampin' about like a horse over me head, an' I can't sleep with him—they're like thunder-claps in me brain! The curse o'—God forgive me for goin' to curse!

MRS. BOYLE. There, now; go back an' lie down agan, an' I'll bring you in a nice cup o' tay.

JOHNNY. Tay, tay, tay! You're always thinkin' o' tay. If a man was dyin', you'd thry to make him swally a cup o' tay!

[*He goes back.*]

MRS. BOYLE. I don't know what's goin' to be done with him. The bullet he got in the hip in Easter Week° was bad enough, but the bomb that shatthered his arm in the fight in O'Connell Street put the finishin' touch on him. I knew he was makin' a fool of himself. God knows I went down on me bended knees to him not to go agen the Free State.

MARY. He stuck to his principles, an', no matther how you may argue, ma, a principle's a principle.

VOICE OF JOHNNY. Is Mary goin' to stay here?

MARY. No, I'm not goin' to stay here; you can't expect me to be always at your beck an' call, can you?

VOICE OF JOHNNY. I won't stop here be meself!

MRS. BOYLE. Amn't I nicely handicapped with the whole o' yous! I don't know what any o' yous ud do without your ma. [*To* JOHNNY.] Your father'll be here in a minute, an' if you want anythin', he'll get it for you.

JOHNNY. I hate assin' him for anythin'. . . . He hates to be assed to stir. . . . Is the light lightin' before the picture o' the Virgin?

MRS. BOYLE. Yis, yis! The wan inside to St. Anthony isn't enough, but he must have another wan to the Virgin here!

[JERRY DEVINE *enters hastily. He is about twenty-five, well set, active and earnest. He is a type, becoming very common now in the Labour Movement, of a mind knowing enough to make the mass of his associates, who know less, a power, and too little to broaden that power for the benefit of all.* MARY *seizes her jumper and runs hastily into room left.*]

JERRY [*breathless*]. Where's the Captain, Mrs. Boyle, where's the Captain?

MRS. BOYLE. You may well ass a body that: he's wherever Joxer Daly is—dhrinkin' in some snug or another.

JERRY. Father Farrell is just afther stoppin' to tell me to run up an' get him to go to the new job that's goin' on in Rathmines; his cousin is foreman o' the job, an' Father Farrell was speakin' to him about poor Johnny an' his father bein' idle so long, an' the foreman told

Easter Week of April 1916, when bloody street-fighting broke out in Dublin

Father Farrell to send the Captain up an' he'd give him a start—I wondher where I'd find him?

MRS. BOYLE. You'll find he's ayther in Ryan's or Foley's.

JERRY. I'll run round to Ryan's—I know it's a great house o' Joxer's.

[*He rushes out.*]

MRS. BOYLE [*piteously*]. There now, he'll miss that job, or I know for what! If he gets win' o' the word, he'll not come back till evenin', so that it'll be too late. There'll never be any good got out o' him so long as he goes with that shouldher-shruggin' Joxer. I killin' meself workin', an' he sthruttin' about from mornin' till night like a paycock!

[*The steps of two persons are heard coming up a flight of stairs. They are the footsteps of* CAPTAIN BOYLE *and* JOXER. CAPTAIN BOYLE *is singing in a deep, sonorous, self-honouring voice.*]

THE CAPTAIN. Sweet Spirit, hear me prayer! Hear . . . oh . . . hear . . . me prayer . . . hear, oh, hear . . . Oh, he . . . ar . . . oh, he . . . ar . . . me . . . pray . . . er!

JOXER [*outside*]. Ah, that's a darlin' song, a daaarlin' song!

MRS. BOYLE [*viciously*]. Sweet spirit hear his prayer! Oh, then, I'll take me solemn affey-davey, it's not for a job he's prayin'!

[*She sits down on the bed so that the cre-tonne hangings hide her from the view of those entering.* THE CAPTAIN *comes slowly in. He is a man of about sixty; stout, grey-haired and stocky. His neck is short, and his head looks like a stone ball that one sometimes sees on top of a gate-post. His cheeks, reddish-purple, are puffed out, as if he were always repressing an almost irrepressible ejaculation. On his upper lip is a crisp, tightly cropped moustache; he carries himself with the upper part of his body slightly thrown back, and his stomach slightly thrust forward. His walk is a slow, conse-quential strut. His clothes are dingy, and he wears a faded seaman's cap with a glazed peak.*]

BOYLE [*to* JOXER, *who is still outside*]. Come on, come on in, Joxer; she's gone out long ago, man. If there's nothing else to be got, we'll furrage out a cup o' tay, anyway. It's the only bit I get in comfort when she's away. 'Tisn't Juno should be her pet name at all, but Deirdre of the Sorras,° for she's always grousin'.

[JOXER *steps cautiously into the room. He may be younger than* THE CAPTAIN *but he looks a lot older. His face is like a bundle of crinkled paper; his eyes have a cunning twinkle; he is spare and loosely built; he has a habit of constantly shrugging his shoulders with a peculiar twitching movement, meant to be ingratiating. His face is invariably ornamented with a grin.*]

JOXER. It's a terrible thing to be tied to a woman that's always grousin'. I don't know how you stick it—it ud put years on me. It's a good job she has to be so often away, for [*with a shrug*] when the cat's away, the mice can play!

BOYLE [*with a commanding and complacent gesture*]. Pull over to the fire, Joxer, an' we'll have a cup o' tay in a minute.

JOXER. Ah, a cup o' tay's a darlin' thing, a daaarlin' thing—the cup that cheers but doesn't . . .

[JOXER'S *rhapsody is cut short by the sight of* JUNO *coming forward and confronting the two cronies. Both are stupefied.*]

MRS. BOYLE [*with sweet irony—poking the fire, and turning her head to glare at* JOXER]. Pull over to the fire, Joxer Daly, an' we'll have a cup o' tay in a minute! Are you sure, now, you wouldn't like an egg?

JOXER. I can't stop, Mrs. Boyle; I'm in a desperate hurry, a desperate hurry.

MRS. BOYLE. Pull over to the fire, Joxer Daly; people is always far more comfortabler here than they are in their own place.

[JOXER *makes hastily for the door.*]

BOYLE [*stirs to follow him; thinks of something to relieve the situation—stops, and says suddenly*]. Joxer!

JOXER [*at door ready to bolt*]. Yis?

Deirdre of the Sorras a tragic heroine of Irish legend

BOYLE. You know the foreman o' that job that's goin' on down in Killesther, don't you, Joxer?

JOXER [*puzzled*]. Foreman—Killesther? . . . .

BOYLE [*with a meaning look*]. He's a butty o' yours, isn't he?

JOXER [*the truth dawning on him*]. The foreman at Killesther—oh, yis, yis. He's an oul' butty o' mine—oh, he's a darlin' man, a daarlin' man.

BOYLE. Oh, then, it's a sure thing. It's a pity we didn't go down at breakfast first thing this mornin'—we might ha' been working now; but you didn't know it then.

JOXER [*with a shrug*]. It's betther late than never.

BOYLE. It's nearly time we got a start, anyhow; I'm fed up knockin' round, doin' nothin'. He promised you—gave you the straight tip?

JOXER. Yis. "Come down on the blow o' dinner," says he, "an' I'll start you, an' any friend you like to brin' with you." Ah, says I, you're a darlin' man, a daaarlin' man.

BOYLE. Well, it couldn't come at a better time—we're a long time waitin' for it.

JOXER Indeed we were; but it's a long lane that has no turnin'.

BOYLE. The blow up for dinner is at one—wait till I see what time it 'tis. [*He goes over to the mantelpiece, and gingerly lifts the clock.*]

MRS. BOYLE. Min' now, how you go on fiddlin' with that clock—you know the least little thing sets it asthray.

BOYLE. The job couldn't come at a betther time; I'm feelin' in great fettle, Joxer. I'd hardly believe I ever had a pain in me legs, an' last week I was nearly crippled with them.

JOXER. That's betther and betther; ah, God never shut wan door but he opened another!

BOYLE. It's only eleven o'clock; we've lashins o' time. I'll slip on me oul' moleskins afther breakfast, an' we can saunther down at our ayse. [*Putting his hand on the shovel.*] I think, Joxer, we'd betther bring our shovels?

JOXER. Yis, Captain, yis; it's better to go fully prepared an' ready for all eventualities. You bring your long-tailed shovel, an' I'll bring me navvy.° We mighten' want them, an', then agen, we might: for want of a nail the shoe was lost, for want of a shoe the horse was lost, an' for want of a horse the man was lost—aw, that's a darlin' proverb, a daarlin' . . .

[*As* JOXER *is finishing his sentence,* MRS. BOYLE *approaches the door and* JOXER *retreats hurriedly. She shuts the door with a bang.*]

BOYLE [*suggestively*]. We won't be long pullin' ourselves together agen when I'm working for a few weeks.

[MRS. BOYLE *takes no notice.*]

BOYLE. The foreman on the job is an oul' butty o' Joxer's; I have an idea that I know him meself. [*Silence.*] . . . There's a button off the back o' me moleskin trousers. . . . If you leave out a needle an' thread I'll sew it on meself. . . . Thanks be to God, the pains in me legs is gone, anyhow!

MRS. BOYLE [*with a burst*]. Look here. Mr. Jacky Boyle, them yarns won't go down with Juno. I know you an' Joxer Daly of an oul' date, an', if you think you're able to come it over me with them fairy tales, you're in the wrong shop.

BOYLE. [*coughing subduedly to relieve the tenseness of the situation*]. U-u-u-ugh.

MRS. BOYLE. Butty o' Joxer's! Oh, you'll do a lot o' good as long as you continue to be a butty o' Joxer's!

BOYLE. U-u-u-ugh.

MRS. BOYLE. Shovel! Ah, then, me boyo, you'd do far more work with a knife an' fork than ever you'll do with a shovel! If there was e'er a genuine job goin' you'd be dh'other way about—not able to lift your arms with the pains in your legs! Your poor wife slavin' to keep the bit° in your mouth, an' you gallivantin' about all the day like a paycock!

BOYLE. It ud be betther for a man to be dead, betther for a man to be dead.

MRS. BOYLE [*ignoring the interruption*]. Everybody callin' you "Captain," an' you only wanst on the wather, in an oul' collier from

navvy pick or shovel
the bit a bite to eat

here to Liverpool, when anybody, to listen or
look at you, ud take you for a second Christo
For Columbus!

BOYLE. Are you never goin' to give us a rest?

5 MRS. BOYLE. Oh, you're never tired o' lookin'
for a rest.

BOYLE. D'ye want to dhrive me out o' the
house?

MRS. BOYLE. It ud be easier to dhrive you
10 out o' the house than to dhrive you into a job.
Here, sit down an' take your breakfast—it
may be the last you'll get, for I don't know
where the next is goin' to come from.

BOYLE. If I get this job we'll be all right.

15 MRS. BOYLE. Did ye see Jerry Devine?

BOYLE [testily]. No, I didn't see him.

MRS. BOYLE. No, but you seen Joxer. Well,
he was here lookin' for you.

BOYLE. Well, let him look!

20 MRS. BOYLE. Oh, indeed, he may well look,
for it ud be hard for him to see you, an' you
stuck in Ryan's snug.

BOYLE. I wasn't in Ryan's snug—I don't go
into Ryan's.

25 MRS. BOYLE. Oh, is there a mad dog there?
Well, if you weren't in Ryan's you were in
Foley's.

BOYLE. I'm telling you for the last three
weeks I haven't tasted a dhrop of intoxicatin'
30 liquor. I wasn't in ayther wan snug or dh'other
—I could swear that on a prayer-book—I'm as
innocent as the child unborn!

MRS. BOYLE. Well, if you'd been in for your
breakfast you'd ha' seen him.

35 BOYLE [suspiciously]. What does he want me
for?

MRS. BOYLE. He'll be back any minute an'
then you'll soon know.

BOYLE. I'll dhrop out an' see if I can meet
40 him.

MRS. BOYLE. You'll sit down an' take your
breakfast, an' let me go to me work, for I'm
an hour late already waitin' for you.

BOYLE. You needn't ha' waited, for I'll take
45 no breakfast—I've a little spirit left in me still!

MRS. BOYLE. Are you goin' to have your
breakfast—yes or no?

BOYLE [too proud to yield]. I'll have no
breakfast—yous can keep your breakfast.

[Plaintively.] I'll knock out a bit somewhere, 50
never fear.

MRS. BOYLE. Nobody's goin' to coax you—
don't think that. [She vigorously replaces the
pan and the sausages in the press.]

BOYLE. I've a little spirit left in me still. 55

[JERRY DEVINE enters hastily.]

JERRY. Oh, here you are at last! I've been
searchin' for you everywhere. The foreman in
Foley's told me you hadn't left the snug with
Joxer ten minutes before I went in. 60

MRS. BOYLE. An' he swearin' on the holy
prayer-book that he wasn't in no snug!

BOYLE [to JERRY]. What business is it o'
yours whether I was in a snug or no? What do
you want to be gallopin' about afther me for? 65
Is a man not to be allowed to leave his house
for a minute without havin' a pack o' spies,
pimps an' informers cantherin' at his heels?

JERRY. Oh, you're takin' a wrong view of it,
Mr. Boyle; I simply was anxious to do you a 70
good turn. I have a message for you from
Father Farrell: he says that if you go to the
job that's on in Rathmines, an' ask for Foreman Mangan, you'll get a start.

BOYLE. That's all right, but I don't want the 75
motions of me body to be watched the way an
asthronomer ud watch a star. If you're folleyin'
Mary aself, you've no pereeogative to be fol-
leyin' me. [Suddenly catching his thigh.] U-
ugh, I'm afther gettin' a terrible twinge in me 80
right leg!

MRS. BOYLE. Oh, it won't be very long now
till it travels into your left wan. It's miraculous
that whenever he scents a job in front of him,
his legs begin to fail him! Then, me bucko, if 85
you lose this chance, you may go an' furrage
for yourself!

JERRY. This job'll last for some time, too,
Captain, an' as soon as the foundations are in,
it'll be cushy enough. 90

BOYLE. Won't it be a climbin' job? How d'ye
expect me to be able to go up a ladder with
these legs? An', if I get up aself, how am I
goin' to get down agen?

MRS. BOYLE [viciously]. Get wan o' the 95
labourers to carry you down in a hod! You
can't climb a laddher, but you can skip like a
goat into a snug!

JERRY. I wouldn't let myself be let down that easy, Mr. Boyle; a little exercise, now, might do you all the good in the world.

BOYLE. It's a docthor you should have been, Devine—maybe you know more about the pains in me legs than meself that has them?

JERRY [*irritated*]. Oh, I know nothin' about the pains in your legs; I've brought the message that Father Farrell gave me, an' that's all I can do.

MRS. BOYLE. Here, sit down an' take your breakfast, an' go an' get ready; an' don't be actin' as if you couldn't pull a wing out of a dead bee.

BOYLE. I want no breakfast, I tell you; it ud choke me after all that's been said. I've a little spirit left in me still.

MRS. BOYLE. Well, let's see your spirit, then, an' go in at wanst an' put on your moleskin trousers!

BOYLE [*moving towards the door on left*]. It ud be betther for a man to be dead! U-ugh! There's another twinge in me other leg! Nobody but meself knows the sufferin' I'm goin' through with the pains in these legs o' mine! [*He goes into the room on left as* MARY *comes out with her hat in her hand.*]

MRS. BOYLE. I'll have to push off now, for I'm terrible late already, but I was determined to stay an' hunt that Joxer this time.

[*She goes off.*]

JERRY. Are you going out, Mary?

MARY. It looks like it when I'm putting on my hat, doesn't it?

JERRY. The bitther word agen, Mary.

MARY. You won't allow me to be friendly with you; if I thry, you deliberately misundherstand it.

JERRY. I didn't always misundherstand it; you were often delighted to have the arms of Jerry around you.

MARY. If you go on talkin' like this, Jerry Devine, you'll make me hate you!

JERRY. Well, let it be either a weddin' or a wake! Listen, Mary, I'm standin' for the Secretaryship of our Union. There's only one opposin' me; I'm popular with all the men, an' a good speaker—all are sayin' that I'll get elected.

MARY. Well?

JERRY. The job's worth three hundred an' fifty pounds a year, Mary. You an' I could live nice an' cosily on that; it would lift you out o' this place an' . . .

MARY. I haven't time to listen to you now —I have to go. [*She is going out when* JERRY *bars the way.*]

JERRY [*appealingly*]. Mary, what's come over you with me for the last few weeks? You hardly speak to me, an' then only a word with a face o' bitherness on it. Have you forgotten, Mary, all the happy evenin's that were as sweet as the scented hawthorn that sheltered the sides o' the road as we sauntered through the country?

MARY. That's all over now. When you get your new job, Jerry, you won't be long findin' a girl far betther than I am for your sweetheart.

JERRY. Never, never, Mary! No matther what happens you'll always be the same to me.

MARY. I must be off; please let me go, Jerry.

JERRY. I'll go a bit o' the way with you.

MARY. You needn't, thanks; I want to be by meself.

JERRY [*catching her arm*]. You're goin' to meet another fella; you've clicked with some one else, me lady!

MARY. That's no concern o' yours, Jerry Devine; let me go!

JERRY. I saw yous comin' out o' the Cornflower Dance Class, an' you hangin' on his arm—a thin, lanky strip of a Micky Dazzler, with a walkin' stick an' gloves!

VOICE OF JOHNNY [*loudly*]. What are you doin' there—pullin' about everything!

VOICE OF BOYLE [*loudly and viciously*]. I'm puttin' on me moleskin trousers!

MARY. You're hurtin' me arm! Let me go, or I'll scream, an' then you'll have the oul' fella out on top of us!

JERRY. Don't be so hard on a fella, Mary, don't be so hard.

BOYLE [*appearing at the door*]. What's the meanin' of all this hillabaloo?

MARY. Let me go, let me go!

BOYLE. D'ye hear me—what's all this hillabaloo about?

JERRY [*plaintively*]. Will you not give us one kind word, one kind word, Mary?

BOYLE. D'ye hear me talkin' to yous? What's all this hillabaloo for?

5 JERRY. Let me kiss your hand, your little, tiny, white hand!

BOYLE. Your little, tiny, white hand—are you takin' leave o' your senses, man?

[MARY *breaks away and rushes out.*]

10 BOYLE. This is nice goin's on in front of her father!

JERRY. Ah, dhry up, for God's sake!

[*He follows* MARY.]

BOYLE. Chiselurs° don't care a damn now
15 about their parents, they're bringin' their fathers' grey hairs down with sorra to the grave, an' laughin' at it, laughin' at it. Ah, I suppose it's just the same everywhere—the whole worl's in a state o' chassis!° [*He sits by*
20 *the fire.*] Breakfast! Well, they can keep their breakfast for me. Not if they went down on their bended knees would I take it—I'll show them I've a little spirit left in me still! [*He goes over to the press, takes out a plate and looks*
25 *at it.*] Sassige! Well, let her keep her sassige. [*He returns to the fire, takes up the teapot and gives it a gentle shake.*] The tay's wet right enough. [*A pause; he rises, goes to the press, takes out the sausage, puts it on the pan, and*
30 *puts both on the fire. He attends the sausage with a fork.*]

BOYLE [*singing*].
When the robins nest agen,
And the flowers are in bloom,
35 When the Springtime's sunny smile seems
[to banish all sorrow an' gloom;
Then me bonny blue-ey'd lad, if me heart
[be true till then—
He's promised he'll come back to me,
40 When the robins nest agen!

[*He lifts his head at the high note, and then drops his eyes to the pan.*]

BOYLE [*singing*].
When the . . .

Chiselurs children
chassis Boyle's way of saying *chaos*

[*Steps are heard approaching; he whips the* 45 *pan off the fire and puts it under the bed, then sits down at the fire. The door opens and a bearded man looking in says:*]
You don't happen to want a sewin' machine?

BOYLE [*furiously*]. No, I don't want e'er a 50 sewin' machine! [*He returns the pan to the fire, and commences to sing again.*]

BOYLE [*singing*].
When the robins nest agen,
And the flowers they are in bloom, 55
He's . . .

[*A thundering knock is heard at the street door.*]

BOYLE. There's a terrible tatheraraa—that's a stranger—that's nobody belongin' to the 60 house. [*Another loud knock.*]

JOXER [*sticking his head in at the door*]. Did ye hear them tatherarahs?

BOYLE. Well, Joxer, I'm not deaf.

JOHNNY [*appearing in his shirt and trousers* 65 *at the door on left; his face is anxious and his voice is tremulous*]. Who's that at the door; who's that at the door? Who gave that knock —d' yous hear me—are yous deaf or dhrunk or what? 70

BOYLE [*to* JOHNNY]. How the hell do I know who 'tis? Joxer, stick your head out o' the window an' see.

JOXER. An' mebbe get a bullet in the kisser? Ah, none o' them thricks for Joxer! It's betther 75 to be a coward than a corpse!

BOYLE [*looking cautiously out of the window*]. It's a fella in a thrench coat.

JOHNNY. Holy Mary, Mother o' God, I . . .

BOYLE. He's goin' away—he must ha' got 80 tired knockin'.

[JOHNNY *returns to the room on left.*]

BOYLE. Sit down an' have a cup o' tay, Joxer.

JOXER. I'm afraid the missus ud pop in on us agen before we'd know where we are. Some- 85 thin's tellin' me to go at wanst.

BOYLE. Don't be superstitious, man; we're Dublin men, an' not boyos that's only afther comin' up from the bog o' Allen—though if she did come in, right enough, we'd be caught 90 like rats in a thrap.

JOXER. An you know the sort she is—she wouldn't listen to reason—an' wanse bitten twice shy.

BOYLE [*going over to the window at back*]. If the worst came to the worst, you could dart out here, Joxer; it's only a dhrop of a few feet to the roof of the return room, an' the first minute she goes into dh'other room, I'll give you the bend, an' you can slip in an' away.

JOXER [*yielding to the temptation*]. Ah, I won't stop very long anyhow. [*Picking up a book from the table.*] Whose is the buk?

BOYLE. Aw, one o' Mary's; she's always readin' lately—nothin' but thrash, too. There's one I was lookin' at dh'other day: three stories, *The Doll's House, Ghosts*, an' *The Wild Duck*—buks only fit for chiselurs!

JOXER. Didja ever rade *Elizabeth, or Th' Exile o' Sibayria* . . . ah, it's a darlin' story, a daarlin' story!

BOYLE. You eat your sassige, an' never min' *Th' Exile o' Sibayria*.

[*Both sit down;* BOYLE *fills out tea, pours gravy on* JOXER's *plate, and keeps the sausage for himself.*]

JOXER. What are you wearin' your moleskin trousers for?

BOYLE. I have to go to a job, Joxer. Just afther you'd gone, Devine kem runnin' in to tell us that Father Farrell said if I went down to the job that's goin' on in Rathmines I'd get a start.

JOXER. Be the holy, that's good news!

BOYLE. How is it good news? I wonder if you were in my condition, would you call it good news?

JOXER. I thought . . .

BOYLE. You thought! You think too sudden sometimes, Joxer. D'ye know, I'm hardly able to crawl with the pains in me legs!

JOXER. Yis, yis; I forgot the pains in your legs. I know you can do nothin' while they're at you.

BOYLE. You forgot; I don't think any of yous realize the state I'm in with the pains in me legs. What ud happen if I had to carry a bag o' cement?

JOXER. Ah, any man havin' the like of them pains id be down an' out, down an' out.

BOYLE. I wouldn't mind if he had said it to meself; but, no, oh no, he rushes in an' shouts it out in front o' Juno, an' you know what Juno is, Joxer. We all know Devine knows a little more than the rest of us, but he doesn't act as if he did; he's a good boy, sober, able to talk an' all that, but still . . .

JOXER. Oh, ay; able to argufy, but still . . .

BOYLE. If he's runnin' afther Mary, aself, he's not goin' to be runnin' after me. Captain Boyle's able to take care of himself. After all, I'm not gettin' brought up on Virol. I never heard him usin' a curse; I don't believe he was ever dhrunk in his life—sure he's not like a Christian at all!

JOXER. You're afther takin' the word out o' me mouth—afther all, a Christian's natural, but he's unnatural.

BOYLE. His oul' fella was just the same—a Wicklow man.

JOXER. A Wicklow man! That explains the whole thing. I've met many a Wicklow man in me time, but I never met wan that was any good.

BOYLE. "Father Farrell," says he, "sent me down to tell you." Father Farrell! . . . D'ye know, Joxer, I never like to be beholden to any o' the clergy.

JOXER. It's dangerous, right enough.

BOYLE. If they do anything for you, they'd want you to be livin' in the Chapel. . . . I'm goin' to tell you somethin', Joxer, that I wouldn't tell to anybody else—the clergy always had too much power over the people in this unfortunate country.

JOXER. You could sing that if you had an air to it!

BOYLE [*becoming enthusiastic*]. Didn't they prevent the people in '47° from seizin' the corn, an' they starvin'; didn't they down Parnell;° didn't they say that hell wasn't hot

'47   1847, a year of the potato famine
Parnell   Charles Stewart Parnell (1847–1891), who led the fight in the British Parliament for Irish home rule. Upon being involved in a divorce scandal, he was opposed by many of his former supporters, including many of the Irish clergy.

enough nor eternity long enough to punish the Fenians?° We don't forget, we don't forget them things, Joxer. If they've taken everything else from us, Joxer, they've left us our memory.

5 JOXER [emotionally]. For mem'ry's the only friend that grief can call its own, that grief . . . can . . . call . . . its own!

BOYLE. Father Farrell's beginnin' to take a great intherest in Captain Boyle; because of
10 what Johnny did for his country, says he to me wan day. It's a curious way to reward Johnny be makin' his poor oul' father work. But, that's what the clergy want, Joxer—work, work, work for me an' you; havin' us mulin'
15 from mornin' till night, so that they may be in bether fettle when they come hoppin' round for their dues! Job! Well, let him give his job to wan of his hymn-singin', prayer-spoutin', craw-thumpin' Confraternity men!°
20 [The voice of a COAL-BLOCK VENDOR is heard chanting in the street.]

VOICE OF COAL VENDOR. Blocks . . . coal-blocks! Blocks . . . coal-blocks!

JOXER. God be with the young days when
25 you were steppin' the deck of a manly ship, with the win' blowin' a hurricane through the masts, an' the only sound you'd hear was, "Port your helm!" an' the only answer, "Port it is, sir!"
30 BOYLE. Them was days, Joxer, them was days. Nothin' was too hot or too heavy for me then. Sailin' from the Gulf o' Mexico to the Antarctic Ocean. I seen things, I seen things, Joxer, that no mortal man should speak about
35 that knows his Catechism. Ofen, an' ofen, when I was fixed to the wheel with a marlin-spike, an' the win's blowin' fierce an' the waves lashin' an' lashin', till you'd think every minute was goin' to be your last, an' it blowed, an'
40 blowed—blew is the right word, Joxer, but blowed is what the sailors use. . . .

JOXER. Aw, it's a darlin' word, a daarlin' word.

Fenians members of the Sinn Fein, an underground organization that aimed at Irish independence. Some Irishmen regarded them as troublemakers.
Confraternity men members of a religious and charitable association

BOYLE. An', as it blowed an' blowed, I ofen looked up at the sky an' assed meself the 45 question—what is the stars, what is the stars?

VOICE OF COAL VENDOR. Any blocks, coal-blocks; blocks, coal-blocks!

JOXER. Ah, that's the question, that's the question—what is the stars? 50

BOYLE. An' then, I'd have another look, an' I'd ass meself—what is the moon?

JOXER. Ah, that's the question—what is the moon, what is the moon?

[Rapid steps are heard coming towards the 55 door. BOYLE makes desperate efforts to hide everything; JOXER rushes to the window in a frantic effort to get out; BOYLE begins to innocently lilt—"Oh, me darlin' Jennie, I will be thrue to thee," when the door is opened, and 60 the black face of the COAL VENDOR appears.]

THE COAL VENDOR. D'yes want any blocks?

BOYLE [with a roar]. No, we don't want any blocks!

JOXER [coming back with a sigh of relief]. 65 That's afther puttin' the heart across me—I could ha' sworn it was Juno. I'd bether be goin', Captain; you couldn't tell the minute Juno'd hop in on us.

BOYLE. Let her hop in; we may as well have 70 it out first as at last. I've made up me mind—I'm not goin' to do only what she damn well likes.

JOXER. Them sentiments does you credit, Captain; I don't like to say anything as between 75 man an' wife, but I say as a butty, as a butty, Captain, that you've stuck it too long, an' that it's about time you showed a little spunk.

How can a man die bether than facin'
[fearful odds, 80
For th' ashes of his fathers an' the temples
[of his gods.

BOYLE. She has her rights—there's no one denyin' it, but haven't I me rights too?

JOXER. Of course you have—the sacred rights 85 o' man!

BOYLE. Today, Joxer, there's goin' to be issued a proclamation be me, establishin' an independent Republic, an' Juno'll have to take an oath of allegiance. 90

JOXER. Be firm, be firm, Captain; the first few

minutes'll be the worst:—if you gently touch a
nettle it'll sting you for your pains; grasp it
like a lad of mettle, an't as soft as silk remains!

VOICE OF JUNO OUTSIDE. Can't stop, Mrs.
5 Madigan—I haven't a minute!

JOXER [*flying out of the window*]. Holy God,
here she is!

BOYLE [*packing the things away with a rush
in the press*]. I knew that fella ud stop till she
10 was in on top of us! [*He sits down by the fire.*]

[JUNO *enters hastily; she is flurried and
excited.*]

JUNO. Oh, you're in—you must have been
only afther comin' in?

15 BOYLE. No, I never went out.

JUNO. It's curious, then, you never heard the
knockin'. [*She puts her coat and hat on bed.*]

BOYLE. Knockin'? Of course I heard the
knockin'.

20 JUNO. An' why didn't you open the door,
then? I suppose you were so busy with Joxer
that you hadn't time.

BOYLE. I haven't seen Joxer since I seen him
before. Joxer! What ud bring Joxer here?

25 JUNO. D'ye mean to tell me that the pair of
yous wasn't collogin' together here when me
back was turned?

BOYLE. What ud we be collogin' together
about? I have somethin' else to think of besides
30 collogin' with Joxer. I can swear on all the holy
prayer-books . . .

MRS. BOYLE. That you weren't in no snug!
Go on in at wanst now, an' take off that moleskin trousers o' yours, an' put on a collar an'
35 tie to smarten yourself up a bit. There's a
visitor comin' with Mary in a minute, an he
has great news for you.

BOYLE. A job, I suppose; let us get wan first
before we start lookin' for another.

40 MRS. BOYLE. That's the thing that's able to
put the win' up you. Well, it's no job, but
news that'll give you the chance o' your life.

BOYLE. What's all the mystery about?

MRS. BOYLE. G'win an' take off the moleskin
45 trousers when you're told!

[BOYLE *goes into room on left.* MRS. BOYLE
*tidies up the room, puts the shovel under the
bed, and goes to the press.*]

MRS. BOYLE. Oh, God bless us, looka the
way everythin's thrun about! Oh, Joxer was 50
here, Joxer was here!

[MARY *enters with* CHARLIE BENTHAM; *he is
a young man of twenty-five, tall, good-looking,
with a very high opinion of himself generally.
He is dressed in a brown coat, brown knee-* 55
*breeches, grey stockings, a brown sweater, with
a deep blue tie; he carries gloves and a walking-
stick.*]

MRS. BOYLE [*fussing round*]. Come in, Mr.
Bentham; sit down, Mr. Bentham, in this chair; 60
it's more comfortabler than that, Mr. Bentham.
Himself'll be here in a minute; he's just takin'
off his trousers.

MARY. Mother!

BENTHAM. Please don't put yourself to any 65
trouble, Mrs. Boyle—I'm quite all right here,
thank you.

MRS. BOYLE. An' to think of you knowin'
Mary, an' she knowin' the news you had for
us, an' wouldn't let on; but it's all the more 70
welcomer now, for we were on our last lap!

VOICE OF JOHNNY INSIDE. What are you
kickin' up all the racket for?

BOYLE [*roughly*]. I'm takin' off me moleskin
trousers! 75

JOHNNY. Can't you do it, then, without lettin'
th' whole house know you're takin' off your
trousers? What d'ye want puttin' them on an'
takin' them off again?

BOYLE. Will you let me alone, will you let 80
me alone? Am I never goin' to be done thryin'
to please th' whole o' yous?

MRS. BOYLE [*to* BENTHAM]. You must excuse
th' state o' th' place, Mr. Bentham; th' minute
I turn me back that man o' mine always makes 85
a litther o' th' place, a litther o' th' place.

BENTHAM. Don't worry, Mrs. Boyle; it's all
right, I assure . . .

BOYLE [*inside*]. Where's me braces; where in
th' name o' God did I leave me braces. . . . Ay, 90
did you see where I put me braces?

JOHNNY [*inside, calling out*]. Ma, will you
come in here an' take da away ou' o' this or
he'll dhrive me mad.

MRS. BOYLE [*going towards door*]. Dear, 95
dear, dear, that man'll be lookin' for somethin'

on th' day o' Judgement. [*Looking into room and calling to* BOYLE.] Look at your braces, man, hangin' round your neck!

BOYLE [*inside*]. Aw, Holy God!

5 MRS. BOYLE [*calling*]. Johnny, Johnny, come out here for a minute.

JOHNNY. Oh, leave Johnny alone, an' don't be annoyin' him!

MRS. BOYLE. Come on, Johnny, till I intro-
10 duce you to Mr. Bentham. [*To* BENTHAM.] Me son, Mr. Bentham; he's afther goin' through the mill. He was only a chiselur of a Boy Scout in Easter Week, when he got hit in the hip; and his arm was blew off in the fight in O'Con-
15 nell Street. [JOHNNY *comes in*.] Here he is, Mr. Bentham; Mr. Bentham, Johnny. None can deny he done his bit for Irelan', if that's going to do him any good.

JOHNNY [*boastfully*]. I'd do it agen, ma, I'd
20 do it agen; for a principle's a principle.

MRS. BOYLE. Ah, you lost your best principle, me boy, when you lost your arm; them's the only sort o' principles that's any good to a workin' man.

25 JOHNNY. Ireland only half free'll never be at peace while she has a son left to pull a trigger.

MRS. BOYLE. To be sure, to be sure—no bread's a lot betther than half a loaf. [*Calling loudly in to* BOYLE.] Will you hurry up there?

30 [BOYLE *enters in his best trousers, which aren't too good, and looks very uncomfortable in his collar and tie.*]

MRS. BOYLE. This is me husband; Mr. Boyle, Mr. Bentham.

35 BENTHAM. Ah, very glad to know you, Mr. Boyle. How are you?

BOYLE. Ah, I'm not too well at all; I suffer terrible with pains in me legs. Juno can tell you there what . . .

40 MRS. BOYLE. You won't have many pains in your legs when you hear what Mr. Bentham has to tell you.

BENTHAM. Juno! What an interesting name! It reminds one of Homer's glorious story of
45 ancient gods and heroes.

BOYLE. Yis, doesn't it? You see, Juno was born an' christened in June; I met her in June; we were married in June, an' Johnny was born in June, so wan day I says to her, "You should

ha' been called Juno," an' the name stuck to 50 her ever since.

MRS. BOYLE. Here we can talk o' them things agen; let Mr. Bentham say what he has to say now.

BENTHAM. Well, Mr. Boyle, I suppose you'll 55 remember a Mr. Ellison of Santry—he's a relative of yours, I think.

BOYLE [*viciously*]. Is it that prognosticator an' procrastinator! Of course I remember him.

BENTHAM. Well, he's dead, Mr. Boyle . . . 60

BOYLE. Sorra many'll° go into mournin' for him.

MRS. BOYLE. Wait till you hear what Mr. Bentham has to say, an' then, maybe, you'll change your opinion. 65

BENTHAM. A week before he died he sent for me to write his will for him. He told me that there were two only that he wished to leave his property to; his second cousin Michael Finnegan of Santry, and John Boyle, his first 70 cousin of Dublin.

BOYLE [*excitedly*]. Me, is it me, me? . . . . . .

BENTHAM. You, Mr. Boyle; I'll read a copy of the will that I have here with me, which has been duly filed in the Court of Probate. [*He* 75 *takes a paper from his pocket and reads:*]

6th February, 1922.

This is the last Will and Testament of William Ellison, of Santry, in the County of Dublin. I hereby order and wish my property 80 to be sold and divided as follows:—

£20 to the St. Vincent De Paul Society.

£60 for Masses for the repose of my soul (5s. for Each Mass).

The rest of my property to be divided be- 85 tween my first and second cousins.

I hereby appoint Timothy Buckly, of Santry, and Hugh Brierly, of Coolock, to be my Executors.

(*Signed*) WILLIAM ELLISON. 90
HUGH BRIERLY.
TIMOTHY BUCKLY.
CHARLES BENTHAM, N.T.

BOYLE [*eagerly*]. An' how much'll be comin' out of it, Mr. Bentham? 95

BENTHAM. The Executors told me that half

Sorra many very few

of the property would be anything between
£1500 and £2000.

MARY. A fortune, father, a fortune!

JOHNNY. We'll be able to get out o' this place
5 now, an' go somewhere we're not known.

MRS. BOYLE. You won't have to trouble about
a job for a while, Jack.

BOYLE [*fervently*]. I'll never doubt the goodness o' God agen.

10 BENTHAM. I congratulate you, Mr. Boyle.
[*They shake hands.*]

BOYLE. An' now, Mr. Bentham, you'll have
to have a wet.

BENTHAM. A wet?

15 BOYLE. A wet—a jar—a boul!

MRS. BOYLE. Jack, you're speakin' to Mr.
Bentham, an' not to Joxer.

BOYLE [*solemnly*]. Juno . . . Mary . . . Johnny
. . . we'll have to go into mournin' at wanst.
20 . . . I never expected that poor Bill ud die so
sudden. . . . Well, we all have to die some day
. . . you, Juno, today . . . an' me, maybe, tomorrow. . . . It's sad, but it can't be helped. . . .
Requiescat in pace . . . or, usin' our oul' tongue
25 like St. Patrick or St. Briget, Guh sayeree jeea
ayera!

MARY. Oh, father, that's not Rest in Peace;
that's God save Ireland.

BOYLE. U-u-ugh, it's all the same—isn't it a
30 prayer? . . . Juno, I'm done with Joxer; he's
nothin' but a prognosticator an' a . . .

JOXER [*climbing angrily through the window
and bounding into the room*]. You're done with
Joxer, are you? Maybe you thought I'd stop on
35 the roof all the night for you! Joxer out on the
roof with the win' blowin' through him was
nothin' to you an' your friend with the collar
an' tie!

MRS. BOYLE. What in the name o' God
40 brought you out on the roof; what were you
doin' there?

JOXER [*ironically*]. I was dhreamin' I was
standin' on the bridge of a ship, an' she sailin'
the Antarctic Ocean, an' it blowed, an' blowed,
45 an' I lookin' up at the sky an' sayin', what is
the stars, what is the stars?

MRS. BOYLE [*opening the door and standing
at it*]. Here, get ou' o' this, Joxer Daly; I was
always thinkin' you had a slate off.

JOXER [*moving to the door*]. I have to laugh 50
every time I look at the deep sea sailor; an' a
row on a river ud make him sea-sick!

BOYLE. Get ou' o' this before I take the law
into me own hands!

JOXER [*going out*]. Say aw rewaeawr,° but 55
not good-bye. Lookin' for work, an' prayin' to
God he won't get it!
[*He goes.*]

MRS. BOYLE. I'm tired tellin' you what Joxer
was; maybe now you see yourself the kind he 60
is.

BOYLE. He'll never blow the froth off a pint
o' mine agen, that's a sure thing. Johnny . . .
Mary . . . you're to keep yourselves to your-
selves for the future. Juno, I'm done with Joxer. 65
. . . I'm a new man from this out. . . . [*Clasping
JUNO's hand, and singing emotionally.*]

Oh, me darlin' Juno, I will be thrue to thee;
Me own, me darlin' Juno, you're all the
[world to me. 70

The Curtain Falls

ACT II

[SCENE. *The same, but the furniture is more
plentiful, and of a vulgar nature. A glaringly
upholstered arm-chair and lounge; cheap
pictures and photos everywhere. Every available spot is ornamented with huge vases filled* 75
*with artificial flowers. Crossed festoons of
coloured paper chains stretch from end to end
of ceiling. On the table is an old attaché case.
It is about six in the evening, and two days
after Act I.* BOYLE, *in his shirt sleeves, is* 80
*voluptuously stretched on the sofa; he is
smoking a clay pipe. He is half asleep. A lamp
is lighting on the table. After a few moments'
pause the voice of* JOXER *is heard singing softly
outside at the door—"Me pipe I'll smoke, as I* 85
*dhrive me moke°—are you there, Mor . . . ee
. . . ar . . . i . . . teee!"*]

BOYLE [*leaping up, takes a pen in his hand
and busies himself with papers*]. Come along,
Joxer, me son, come along. 90

aw rewaeawr *au revoir*
moke *donkey*

JOXER [*putting his head in*]. Are you be yourself?

BOYLE. Come on, come on; that doesn't matther; I'm masther now, an' I'm goin' to remain masther.

[JOXER *comes in.*]

JOXER. How d'ye feel now, as a man o' money?

BOYLE [*solemnly*]. It's a responsibility, Joxer, a great responsibility.

JOXER. I suppose 'tis now, though you wouldn't think it.

BOYLE. Joxer, han' me over that attackey case on the table there. [JOXER *hands the case.*] Ever since the Will was passed I've run hundhreds o' dockyments through me han's—I tell you, you have to keep your wits about you. [*He busies himself with papers.*]

JOXER. Well, I won't disturb you; I'll dhrop in when . . .

BOYLE [*hastily*]. It's all right, Joxer, this is the last one to be signed today. [*He signs a paper, puts it into the case, which he shuts with a snap, and sits back pompously in the chair.*] Now, Joxer, you want to see me; I'm at your service—what can I do for you, me man?

JOXER. I've just dhropped in with the £3:5s. that Mrs. Madigan riz on the blankets an' table for you, and she says you're to be in no hurry payin' it back.

BOYLE. She won't be long without it; I expect the first cheque for a couple o' hundhred any day. There's the five bob for yourself—go on, take it, man; it'll not be the last you'll get from the Captain. Now an' agen we have our differ, but we're there together all the time.

JOXER. Me for you, an' you for me, like the two Musketeers.

BOYLE. Father Farrell stopped me today an' tole me how glad he was I fell in for the money.

JOXER. He'll be stoppin' you ofen enough now; I suppose it was "Mr." Boyle with him?

BOYLE. He shuk me be the han'. . . .

JOXER [*ironically*]. I met with Napper Tandy, an' he shuk me be the han'!

BOYLE. You're seldom asthray, Joxer, but you're wrong shipped this time. What you're sayin' of Father Farrell is very near to blasfeemey. I don't like any one to talk disrespectful of Father Farrell.

JOXER. You're takin' me up wrong, Captain; I wouldn't let a word be said agen Father Farrell—the heart o' the rowl, that's what he is; I always said he was a darlin' man, a daarlin' man.

BOYLE. Comin' up the stairs who did I meet but that bummer, Nugent. "I seen you talkin' to Father Farrell," says he, with a grin on him. "He'll be folleyin' you," says he, "like a Guardian Angel from this out"—all the time the oul' grin on him, Joxer.

JOXER. I never seen him yet but he had that oul' grin on him!

BOYLE. "Mr. Nugent," says I, "Father Farrell is a man o' the people, an', as far as I know the History of me country, the priests was always in the van of the fight for Irelan's freedom."

JOXER [*fervently*].
Who was it led the van, Soggart Aroon?°
Since the fight first began, Soggart Aroon?

BOYLE. "Who are you tellin'?" says he. "Didn't they let down the Fenians, an' didn't they do in Parnell? An' now . . . " "You ought to be ashamed o' yourself," says I, interruptin' him, "not to know the History o' your country." An' I left him gawkin' where he was.

JOXER. Where ignorance 's bliss 'tis folly to be wise; I wondher did he ever read the Story o' Irelan'.

BOYLE. Be J. L. Sullivan? Don't you know he didn't?

JOXER. Ah, it's a darlin' buk, a daarlin' buk!

BOYLE. You'd betther be goin', now, Joxer, his Majesty, Bentham, 'll be here any minute, now.

JOXER. Be the way things is lookin', it'll be a match between him an' Mary. She's thrun over Jerry altogether. Well, I hope it will, for he's a darlin' man.

Soggart Aroon Gaelic for "priest beloved," a term referring to one of the leaders of an Irish rebellion in the eighteenth century

BOYLE. I'm glad you think so—I don't. [*Irritably.*] What's darlin' about him?

JOXER [*nonplussed*]. I only seen him twiced; if you want to know me, come an' live with me.

BOYLE. He's too ignified for me—to hear him talk you'd think he knew as much as a Boney's Oraculum.° He's given up his job as teacher, an' is goin' to become a solicitor in Dublin— he's been studyin' law. I suppose he thinks I'll set him up, but he's wrong shipped. An' th' other fella—Jerry's as bad. The two o' them ud give you a pain in your face, listenin' to them; Jerry believin' in nothin', an' Bentham believin' in everythin'. One that says all is God an' no man; an' th' other that says all is man an' no God!

JOXER. Well, I'll be off now.

BOYLE. Don't forget to dhrop down afther a while; we'll have a quiet jar, an' a song or two.

JOXER. Never fear.

BOYLE. An' tell Mrs. Madigan that I hope we'll have the pleasure of her organization at our little enthertainment.

JOXER. Righto; we'll come down together.

[*He goes out.*]

[JOHNNY *comes from room on left, and sits down moodily at the fire.* BOYLE *looks at him for a few moments, and shakes his head. He fills his pipe.*]

VOICE OF JUNO AT THE DOOR. Open the door, Jack; this thing has me nearly kilt with the weight.

[BOYLE *opens the door.* JUNO *enters carrying the box of a gramophone, followed by* MARY *carrying the horn, and some parcels.* JUNO *leaves the box on the table and flops into a chair.*]

JUNO. Carryin' that from Henry Street was no joke.

BOYLE. U-u-ugh, that's a grand lookin' insthrument—how much was it?

JUNO. Pound down, an' five to be paid at two shillin's a week.

BOYLE. That's reasonable enough.

JUNO. I'm afraid we're runnin' into too much debt; first the furniture, an' now this.

BOYLE. The whole lot won't be much out of £2000.

MARY. I don't know what you wanted a gramophone for—I know Charlie hates them; he says they're destructive of real music.

BOYLE. Desthructive of music—that fella ud give you a pain in your face. All a gramophone wants is to be properly played; it's thrue wondher is only felt when everythin's quiet— what a gramophone wants is dead silence!

MARY. But, father, Jerry says the same; afther all, you can only appreciate music when your ear is properly trained.

BOYLE. That's another fella ud give you a pain in your face. Properly thrained! I suppose you couldn't appreciate football unless your fut was properly thrained.

MRS. BOYLE [*to* MARY]. Go on in ower that° an' dress, or Charlie 'll be in on you, an' tay nor nothin' 'll be ready.

[MARY *goes into room left.*]

MRS. BOYLE [*arranging table for tea*]. You didn't look at our new gramophone, Johnny?

JOHNNY. 'Tisn't gramophones I'm thinking of.

MRS. BOYLE. An' what is it you're thinkin' of, allana?°

JOHNNY. Nothin', nothin', nothin'.

MRS. BOYLE. Sure, you must be thinkin' of somethin'; it's yourself that has yourself the way y'are; sleepin' wan night in me sisther's, an' the nex' in your father's brother's—you'll get no rest goin' on that way.

JOHNNY. I can rest nowhere, nowhere, nowhere.

MRS. BOYLE. Sure, you're not thryin' to rest anywhere.

JOHNNY. Let me alone, let me alone, let me alone, for God's sake.

[*A knock at street door.*]

MRS. BOYLE [*in a flutter*]. Here he is; here's Mr. Bentham!

Boney's Oraculum Napoleon Bonaparte's *Oraculum,* or *Book of Fate,* or *Lucky Dream Book,* a widely popular compendium of occult lore that Napoleon ("Boney") was supposed to have used to read the future

ower that right away
allana dear one

BOYLE. Well, there's room for him; it's a pity there's not a brass band to play him in.

MRS. BOYLE. We'll han' the tay around, an' not be clusthered round the table, as if we
5 never seen nothin'.

[*Steps are heard approaching, and* JUNO, *opening the door, allows* BENTHAM *to enter.*]

JUNO. Give your hat an' stick to Jack, there . . . sit down, Mr. Bentham . . . no, not there
10 . . . in th' easy chair be the fire . . . there, that's betther. Mary'll be out to you in a minute.

BOYLE [*solemnly*]. I seen be the paper this mornin' that Consols° was down half per cent. That's serious, min' you, an' shows the whole
15 counthry's in a state o' chassis.

MRS. BOYLE. What's Consols, Jack?

BOYLE. Consols? Oh, Consols is—oh, there's no use tellin' women what Consols is—th' wouldn't undherstand.

20 BENTHAM. It's just as you were saying, Mr. Boyle . . .

[MARY *enters charmingly dressed.*]

BENTHAM. Oh, good evening, Mary; how pretty you're looking!

25 MARY [*archly*]. Am I?

BOYLE. We were just talkin' when you kem in, Mary, I was tellin' Mr. Bentham that the whole counthry's in a state o' chassis.

MARY [*to* BENTHAM]. Would you prefer the
30 green or the blue ribbon round me hair, Charlie?

MRS. BOYLE. Mary, your father's speakin'.

BOYLE [*rapidly*]. I was jus' tellin' Mr. Bentham that the whole counthry's in a state o'
35 chassis.

MARY. I'm sure you're frettin', da, whether it is or no.

MRS. BOYLE. With all our churches an' religions, the worl's not a bit the betther.

40 BOYLE [*with a commanding gesture*]. Tay!

[MARY *and* MRS. BOYLE *dispense the tea.*]

MRS. BOYLE. An' Irelan's takin' a leaf out o' the worl's buk; when we got the makin' of our own laws I thought we'd never stop to look
45 behind us, but instead of that we never stopped

to look before us! If the people ud folly up their religion betther there'd be a betther chance for us—what do you think, Mr. Bentham?

50 BENTHAM. I'm afraid I can't venture to express an opinion on that point, Mrs. Boyle; dogma has no attraction for me.

MRS. BOYLE. I forgot you didn't hold with us; what's this you said you were?

55 BENTHAM. A Theosophist, Mrs. Boyle.

MRS. BOYLE. An' what in the name o' God's a Theosophist?

BOYLE. A Theosophist, Juno, 's a—tell her, Mr. Bentham, tell her.

60 BENTHAM. It's hard to explain in a few words: Theosophy's founded on The Vedas, the religious books of the East. Its central theme is the existence of an all-pervading Spirit—the Life-Breath. Nothing really exists but this one
65 Universal Life-Breath. And whatever even seems to exist separately from this Life-Breath, doesn't really exist at all. It is all vital force in man, in all animals, and in all vegetation. This Life-Breath is called the Prawna.

70 MRS. BOYLE. The Prawna! What a comical name!

BOYLE. Prawna; yis, the Prawna. [*Blowing gently through his lips.*] That's the Prawna!

MRS. BOYLE. Whist, whist, Jack.

75 BENTHAM. The happiness of man depends upon his sympathy with this Spirit. Men who have reached a high state of excellence are called Yogi. Some men become Yogi in a short time, it may take others millions of years.

80 BOYLE. Yogi! I seen hundhreds of them in the streets o' San Francisco.

BENTHAM. It is said by these Yogi that if we practise certain mental exercises that we would have powers denied to others—for instance,
85 the faculty of seeing things that happen miles and miles away.

MRS. BOYLE. I wouldn't care to meddle with that sort o' belief; it's a very curious religion, altogether.

90 BOYLE. What's curious about it? Isn't all religions curious? If they weren't, you wouldn't get any one to believe them. But religions is passin' away—they've had their day like every-

thing else. Take the real Dublin people, f'rinstance: they know more about Charlie Chaplin an' Tommy Mix than they do about SS. Peter an' Paul!

5 MRS. BOYLE. You don't believe in ghosts, Mr. Bentham?

MARY. Don't you know he doesn't, mother?

BENTHAM. I don't know that, Mary. Scientists are beginning to think that what we call ghosts
10 are something seen by persons of a certain nature. They say that sensational actions, such as the killing of a person, demand great energy, and that that energy lingers in the place where the action occurred. People may live in the
15 place and see nothing, when some one may come along whose personality has some peculiar connection with the energy of the place, and, in a flash, the person sees the whole affair.

JOHNNY [*rising swiftly, pale and affected*].
20 What sort o' talk is this to be goin' on with? Is there nothin' better to be talkin' about but the killin' o' people? My God, isn't it bad enough for these things to happen without talkin' about them!

25 [*He hurriedly goes into the room on left.*]

BENTHAM. Oh, I'm very sorry, Mrs. Boyle; I never thought . . .

MRS. BOYLE [*apologetically*]. Never mind, Mr. Bentham, he's very touchy.

30 [*A frightened scream is heard from* JOHNNY *inside.*]

MRS. BOYLE. Mother of God! What's that?

[*He rushes out again, his face pale, his lips twitching, his limbs trembling.*]

35 JOHNNY. Shut the door, shut the door, quick, for God's sake! Great God, have mercy on me! Blessed Mother o' God, shelter me, shelter your son!

MRS. BOYLE [*catching him in her arms*].
40 What's wrong with you? What ails you? Sit down, sit down, here, on the bed . . . there now . . . there now.

MARY. Johnny, Johnny, what ails you?

JOHNNY. I seen him, I seen him . . . kneelin'
45 in front o' the statue . . . merciful Jesus, have pity on me!

MRS. BOYLE [*to* BOYLE]. Get him a glass o' whisky . . . quick, man, an' don't stand gawkin'.

[BOYLE *gets the whisky.*]

JOHNNY. Sit here, sit here, mother . . . be- 50 tween me an' the door.

MRS. BOYLE. I'll sit beside you as long as you like, only tell me what was it came across you at all?

JOHNNY [*after taking some drink*]. I seen him. 55 . . . I seen Robbie Tancred kneelin' down before the statue . . . an' the red light shinin' on him . . . an' when I went in . . . he turned an' looked at me . . . an' I seen the woun's bleedin' in his breast. . . . Oh, why did he look at me like that 60 . . . it wasn't my fault that he was done in . . . Mother o' God, keep him away from me!

MRS. BOYLE. There, there, child, you've imagined it all. There was nothin' there at all —it was the red light you seen, an' the talk we 65 had put all the rest into your head. Here, dhrink more o' this—it'll do you good. . . . An', now, stretch yourself down on the bed for a little. [*To* BOYLE.] Go in, Jack, an' show him it was only in his own head it was. 70

BOYLE [*making no move*]. E-e-e-e-eh; it's all nonsense; it was only a shadda he saw.

MARY. Mother o' God, he made me heart lep!

BENTHAM. It was simply due to an overwrought imagination—we all get that way at 75 times.

MRS. BOYLE. There, dear, lie down in the bed, an' I'll put the quilt across you . . . e-e-e-eh, that's it . . . you'll be as right as the mail in a few minutes. 80

JOHNNY. Mother, go into the room an' see if the light's lightin' before the statue.

MRS. BOYLE [*to* BOYLE]. Jack, run in, an' see if the light's lightin' before the statue.

BOYLE [*to* MARY]. Mary, slip in an' see if the 85 light's lightin' before the statue.

[MARY *hesitates to go in.*]

BENTHAM. It's all right; Mary, I'll go.

[*He goes into the room; remains for a few moments, and returns.*] 90

BENTHAM. Everything's just as it was—the light burning bravely before the statue.

BOYLE. Of course; I knew it was all nonsense. [*A knock at the door.*]

BOYLE [*going to open the door*]. E-e-e-e-eh. 95 [*He opens it, and* JOXER, *followed by* MRS.

MADIGAN, *enters.* MRS. MADIGAN *is a strong, dapper little woman of about forty-five; her face is almost always a wide-spread smile of complacency. She is a woman who, in a manner*
5 *at least, can mourn with them that mourn, and rejoice with them that do rejoice. When she is feeling comfortable, she is inclined to be reminiscent; when others say anything, or following a statement made by herself, she has a*
10 *habit of putting her head a little to one side, and nodding it rapidly several times in succession, like a bird pecking at a hard berry. Indeed, she has a good deal of the bird in her, but the bird instinct is by no means a melodious one.*
15 *She is ignorant, vulgar and forward, but her heart is generous withal. For instance, she would help a neighbour's sick child; she would probably kill the child, but her intentions would be to cure it; she would be more*
20 *at home helping a drayman to lift a fallen horse. She is dressed in a rather soiled grey dress and a vivid purple blouse; in her hair is a huge comb, ornamented with huge coloured beads. She enters with a gliding step, beam-*
25 *ing smile and nodding head.* BOYLE *receives them effusively.*]

BOYLE. Come on in, Mrs. Madigan; come on in; I was afraid you weren't comin'. . . . . [*Slyly.*] There's some people able to dhress, ay, Joxer?

30 JOXER. Fair as the blossoms that bloom in the May, an' sweet as the scent of the new mown hay. . . . Ah, well she may wear them.

MRS. MADIGAN [*looking at* MARY]. I know some as are as sweet as the blossoms in the
35 May—oh, no names, no pack dhrill!°

BOYLE. An', now, I'll inthroduce the pair o' yous to Mary's intended: Mr. Bentham, this is Mrs. Madigan, an oul' back-parlour neighbour, that, if she could help it at all, ud never
40 see a body shuk!

BENTHAM [*rising, and tentatively shaking the hand of* MRS. MADIGAN]. I'm sure, it's a great pleasure to know you, Mrs. Madigan.

MRS. MADIGAN. An' I'm goin' to tell you,
45 Mr. Bentham, you're goin' to get as nice a bit o' skirt in Mary, there, as ever you seen in

your puff. Not like some of the dhressed up dolls that's knockin' about lookin' for men when it's a skelpin'° they want. I remember as
50 well as I remember yestherday, the day she was born—of a Tuesday, the 25th o' June, in the year 1901, at thirty-three minutes past wan in the day be Foley's clock, the pub at the corner o' the street. A cowld day it was too,
55 for the season o' the year, an' I remember sayin' to Joxer, there, who I met comin' up th' stairs, that the new arrival in Boyle's ud grow up a hardy chiselur if it lived, an' that she'd be somethin' one o' these days that nobody sus-
60 pected, an' so signs on it, here she is today, goin' to be married to a young man lookin' as if he'd be fit to commensurate in any position in life it ud please God to call him!

BOYLE [*effusively*]. Sit down, Mrs. Madigan, sit down, me oul' sport. [*To* BENTHAM.] This is
65 Joxer Daly, Past Chief Ranger of the Dear Little Shamrock Branch of the Irish National Foresters, an oul' front-top neighbour, that never despaired, even in the darkest days of Ireland's sorra.
70

JOXER. Nil desperandum, Captain, nil desperandum.

BOYLE. Sit down, Joxer, sit down. The two of us was often in a tight corner.

MRS. BOYLE. Ay, in Foley's snug!
75

JOXER. An' we kem out of it flyin', we kem out of it flyin', Captain.

BOYLE. An', now, for a dhrink—I know yous won't refuse an oul' friend.

MRS. MADIGAN [*to* JUNO]. Is Johnny not
80 well, Mrs. . . .

MRS. BOYLE [*warningly*]. S-s-s-sh.

MRS. MADIGAN. Oh, the poor darlin'.

BOYLE. Well, Mrs. Madigan, is it tay or what?

MRS. MADIGAN. Well, speakin' for meself, I
85 jus' had me tay a minute ago, an' I'm afraid to dhrink any more—I'm never the same when I dhrink too much tay. Thanks, all the same, Mr. Boyle.

BOYLE. Well, what about a bottle o' stout or
90 a dhrop o' whisky?

MRS. MADIGAN. A bottle o' stout ud be a

---

pack dhrill formality

skelpin' spanking

little too heavy for me stummock afther me tay. . . . A-a-ah, I'll thry the ball o' malt.

[BOYLE *prepares the whisky*.]

MRS. MADIGAN. There's nothin' like a ball o' malt occasional like—too much of it isn't good. [*To* BOYLE, *who is adding water*.] Ah, God, Johnny, don't put too much wather on it! [*She drinks*.] I suppose yous'll be lavin' this place.

BOYLE. I'm looking for a place near the sea; I'd like the place that you might say was me cradle, to be me grave as well. The sea is always callin' me.

JOXER. She is callin', callin', callin', in the win', an' on the sea.

BOYLE. Another dhrop o' whisky, Mrs. Madigan?

MRS. MADIGAN. Well, now, it ud be hard to refuse seein' the suspicious times that's in it.°

BOYLE [*with a commanding gesture*]. Song! . . . Juno . . . Mary . . . "Home to Our Mount'-ins"!

MRS. MADIGAN [*enthusiastically*]. Hear, hear!

JOXER. Oh, tha's a darlin song, a daarlin' song!

MARY [*bashfully*]. Ah, no, da; I'm not in a singin' humour.

MRS. MADIGAN. Gawn with you, child, an' you only goin' to be marrid; I remember as well as I remember yesherday,—it was on a lovely August evenin', exactly, accordin' to date, fifteen years ago, come the Tuesday fol-leyin' the nex' that's comin' on, when me own man (the Lord be good to him) an' me was sittin' shy together in a doty° little nook on a counthry road, adjacent to The Stiles. "That'll scratch your lovely, little white neck," says he, ketchin' hould of a danglin' bramble branch, holdin' clusters of the loveliest flowers you ever seen, an' breakin' it off, so that his arm fell, accidental like, roun' me waist, an' as I felt it tightenin', an' tightenin', an tightenin', I thought me buzzum was every minute goin' to burst out into a roystherin' song about

The little green leaves that were shakin'
[on the threes,
The gallivantin' butterflies, an' buzzin'
[o' the bees!

BOYLE. Ordher for the song!

JUNO. Come on, Mary—we'll do our best.

[JUNO *and* MARY *stand up, and choosing a suitable position, sing simply "Home to Our Mountains."*]

[*They bow to company, and return to their places.*]

BOYLE [*emotionally, at the end of the song*]. Lull . . . me . . . to . . . rest!

JOXER [*clapping his hands*]. Bravo, bravo! Darlin' girulls, darlin' girulls!

MRS. MADIGAN. Juno, I never seen you in better form.

BENTHAM. Very nicely rendered indeed.

MRS. MADIGAN. A noble call, a noble call!

MRS. BOYLE. What about yourself, Mrs. Madigan? [*After some coaxing*, MRS. MADIGAN *rises, and in a quavering voice sings the following verse.*]

If I were a blackbird I'd whistle and sing;
I'd follow the ship that my thrue love was in;
An' on the top riggin', I'd there build
[me nest,
An' at night I would sleep on me Willie's
[white breast!

[*Becoming husky, amid applause, she sits down.*]

MRS. MADIGAN. Ah, me voice is too husky now, Juno; though I remember the time when Maisie Madigan could sign like a nightingale at matin' time. I remember as well as I remem-ber yesherday, at a party given to celebrate the comin' of the first chiselur to Annie an' Benny Jimeson—who was the barber, yous may remember, in Henrietta Street, that, afther Easter Week, hung out a green, white an' orange° pole, an', then, when the Tans° started their Jazz dancin', whipped it in agen, an'

green, white an' orange the Irish national colors
Tans or Black-and-Tans, the English troops that at-tempted to police Dublin and other parts of Ireland during the civil war. The reprisals with which the English countered Irish terrorism made the "Tans" both dreaded and detested.

that's in it that we live in
doty cosy

stuck out a red, white an' blue° wan instead,
givin' as an excuse that a barber's pole was
strictly non-political—singin' "An You'll Remember Me," with the top notes quiverin' in
5   a dead hush of pethrified attention, folleyed
by a clappin' o' han's that shuk the tumblers
on the table, an' capped be Jimeson, the barber, sayin' that it was the best rendherin' of
"You'll Remember Me" he ever heard in his
10 natural!
        BOYLE [peremptorily]. Ordher for Joxer's
song!
        JOXER. Ah, no, I couldn't; don't ass me,
Captain.
15   BOYLE. Joxer's song, Joxer's song—give us
wan of your shut-eyed wans. [JOXER settles
himself in his chair; takes a drink; clears his
throat; solemnly closes his eyes, and begins to
sing in a very querulous voice.]
20 She is far from the lan' where her
                                [young hero sleeps,
An' lovers around her are sighing.
[He hesitates.]
An' lovers around her are sighin'
25   [. . . sighin' . . . sighin' . . .
[A pause.]
BOYLE [imitating JOXER].
And lovers around her are sighing!
What's the use of you thryin' to sing the song
30 if you don't know it?
        MARY. Thry another one, Mr. Daly—maybe
you'd be more fortunate.
        MRS. MADIGAN. Gawn, Joxer, thry another
wan.
35   JOXER [starting again].
I have heard the mavis singin' his love
                                [song to the morn;
I have seen the dew-dhrop clingin' to the
                                [rose jus' newly born;
40   but . . . but . . . [frantically] to the rose jus'
                        [newly born . . . newly born . . . born.
        JOHNNY. Mother, put on the gramophone,
for God's sake, an' stop Joxer's bawlin'.
        BOYLE [commandingly]. Gramophone! . . . I
45 hate to see fellas thryin' to do what they're not
able to do. [BOYLE arranges the gramophone,

red, white an' blue   the English colors

and is about to start it, when voices are heard
of persons descending the stairs.]
        MRS. BOYLE [warningly]. Whisht, Jack, don't
put it on, don't put it on yet; this must be   50
poor Mrs. Tancred comin' down to go to the
hospital—I forgot all about them bringin' the
body to the church tonight. Open the door,
Mary, an' give them a bit o' light.
        [MARY opens the door, and MRS. TANCRED—   55
a very old woman, obviously shaken by the
death of her son—appears, accompanied by
several NEIGHBOURS. The first few phrases are
spoken before they appear.]
        FIRST NEIGHBOUR. It's a sad journey we're   60
goin' on, but God's good, an' the Republicans
won't be always down.
        MRS. TANCRED. Ah, what good is that to me
now? Whether they're up or down—it won't
bring me darlin' boy from the grave.   65
        MRS. BOYLE. Come in an' have a hot cup o'
tay, Mrs. Tancred, before you go.
        MRS. TANCRED. Ah, I can take nothin' now,
Mrs. Boyle—I won't be long afther him.
        FIRST NEIGHBOUR. Still an' all, he died a noble   70
death, an' we'll bury him like a king.
        MRS. TANCRED. An' I'll go on livin' like a
pauper. Ah, what's the pains I suffered bringin'
him into the world to carry him to his cradle,
to the pains I'm sufferin' now, carryin' him out   75
o' the world to bring him to his grave!
        MARY. It would be better for you not to go
at all, Mrs. Tancred, but to stay at home beside
the fire with some o' the neighbours.
        MRS. TANCRED. I seen the first of him, an' I'll   80
see the last of him.
        MRS. BOYLE. You'd want a shawl, Mrs. Tan-
cred; it's a cowld night, an' the win's blowin'
sharp.
        MRS. MADIGAN [rushing out]. I've a shawl   85
above.
        MRS. TANCRED. Me home is gone, now; he
was me only child, an' to think that he was
lyin' for a whole night stretched out on the
side of a lonely country lane, with his head,   90
his darlin' head, that I ofen kissed an' fondled,
half hidden in the wather of a runnin' brook.
An' I'm told he was the leadher of the ambush
where me nex' door neighbour, Mrs. Mannin',

lost her Free State soldier son. An' now here's the two of us oul' women, standin' one on each side of a scales o' sorra, balanced be the bodies of our two dead darlin' sons. [MRS. MADIGAN
5 *returns, and wraps a shawl around her.*] God bless you, Mrs. Madigan. . . . [*She moves slowly towards the door.*] Mother o' God, Mother o' God, have pity on the pair of us! . . . O Blessed Virgin, where were you when me
10 darlin' son was riddled with bullets, when me darlin' son was riddled with bullets! . . . Sacred Heart of the Crucified Jesus, take away our hearts o' stone . . . an' give us hearts o' flesh! . . . Take away this murdherin' hate . . . an'
15 give us Thine own eternal love!

[*They pass out of the room.*]

MRS. BOYLE [*explanatorily to* BENTHAM]. That was Mrs. Tancred of the two-pair back; her son was found, e'er yestherday, lyin' out
20 beyant Finglas riddled with bullets. A die-hard he was, be all accounts. He was a nice quiet boy, but lattherly he went to hell, with his Republic first, an' Republic last an' Republic over all. He ofen took tay with us here, in the
25 oul' days, an' Johnny, there, an' him used to be always together.

JOHNNY. Am I always to be havin' to tell you that he was no friend o' mine? I never cared for him, an' he could never stick me. It's not
30 because he was Commandant of the Battalion that I was Quarther-Masther of, that we were friends.

MRS. BOYLE. He's gone, now—the Lord be good to him! God help his poor oul' creature
35 of a mother, for no matther whose friend or enemy he was, he was her poor son.

BENTHAM. The whole thing is terrible, Mrs. Boyle; but the only way to deal with a mad dog is to destroy him.

40 MRS. BOYLE. An' to think of me forgettin' about him bein' brought to the church tonight, an' we singin' an' all, but it was well we hadn't the gramophone goin', anyhow.

BOYLE. Even if we had aself. We've nothin'
45 to do with these things, one way or t'other. That's the Government's business, an' let them do what we're payin' them for doin'.

MRS. BOYLE. I'd like to know how a body's not to mind these things; look at the way
50 they're afther leavin' the people in this very house. Hasn't the whole house, nearly, been massacreed? There's young Mrs. Dougherty's husband with his leg off; Mrs. Travers that had her son blew up be a mine in Inchegeela,
55 in Co. Cork; Mrs. Mannin' that lost wan of her sons in an ambush a few weeks ago, an' now, poor Mrs. Tancred's only child gone West with his body made a collandher of. Sure, if it's not our business, I don't know whose business it is.

60 BOYLE. Here, there, that's enough about them things; they don't affect us, an' we needn't give a damn. If they want a wake, well, let them have a wake. When I was a sailor, I was always resigned to meet with a watery
65 grave; an', if they want to be soldiers, well, there's no use o' them squealin' when they meet a soldier's fate.

JOXER. Let me like a soldier fall—me breast expandin' to th' ball!

70 MRS. BOYLE. In wan way, she deserves all she got; for lately, she let th' die-hards make an open house of th' place; an' for th' last couple of months, either when th' sun was risin', or when th' sun was settin', you had
75 C.I.D. men° burstin' into your room, assin' you where were you born, where were you christened, where were you married, an' where would you be buried!

JOHNNY. For God's sake, let us have no more
80 o' this talk.

MRS. MADIGAN. What about Mr. Boyle's song before we start th' gramophone?

MARY [*getting her hat, and putting it on*]. Mother, Charlie and I are goin' out for a little
85 sthroll.

MRS. BOYLE. All right, darlin'.

BENTHAM [*going out with* MARY]. We won't be long away, Mrs. Boyle.

MRS. MADIGAN. Gwan, Captain, gwan.

90 BOYLE. E-e-e-e-eh, I'd want to have a few more jars in me, before I'd be in fettle for singin'.

C.I.D. men from the Criminal Investigation Department of Scotland Yard; later, Free State police agents on the trail of the die-hards

JOXER. Give us that poem you writ t'other day. [*To the rest.*] Aw, it's a darlin' poem, a daarlin' poem.

MRS. BOYLE. God bless us, is he startin' to
5 write poetry!

BOYLE [*rising to his feet*]. E-e-e-e-eh. [*He recites in an emotional, consequential manner the following verses.*]

Shawn an' I were friends, sir, to me he was
10   [all in all.
His work was very heavy and his wages
                   [were very small.
None betther on th' beach as Docker, I'll
                   [go bail,
15 'Tis now I'm feelin' lonely, for today he
                   [lies in jail.
He was not what some call pious—seldom
                   [at church or prayer;
For the greatest scoundrels I know, sir, goes
20   [every Sunday there.
Fond of his pint—well, rather, but hated
                   [the Boss by creed
But never refused a copper to comfort a pal
                   [in need.

25 E-e-e-e-eh. [*He sits down.*]

MRS. MADIGAN. Grand, grand; you should folley that up, you should folley that up.

JOXER. It's a daarlin' poem!

BOYLE [*delightedly*]. E-e-e-e-eh.

30 JOHNNY. Are yous goin' to put on th' gramophone tonight, or are yous not?

MRS. BOYLE. Gwan, Jack, put on a record.

MRS. MADIGAN. Gwan, Captain, gwan.

BOYLE. Well, yous'll want to keep a dead
35 silence.

[*He sets a record, starts the machine, and it begins to play "If you're Irish, come into the Parlour." As the tune is in full blare, the door is suddenly opened by a brisk, little bald-
40 headed man, dressed circumspectly in a black suit; he glares fiercely at all in the room; he is "*NEEDLE NUGENT*," a tailor. He carries his hat in his hands.*]

NUGENT [*loudly, above the noise of the
45 gramophone*]. Are yous goin' to have that thing bawlin' an' the funeral of Mrs. Tancred's son passin' the house? Have none of yous any respect for the Irish people's National regard for the dead?

[*BOYLE stops the gramophone.*] 50

MRS. BOYLE. Maybe, Needle Nugent, it's nearly time we had a little less respect for the dead, an' a little more regard for the livin'.

MRS. MADIGAN. We don't want you, Mr. Nugent, to teach us what we learned at our 55 mother's knee. You don't look yourself as if you were dyin' of grief; if y'ass Maisie Madigan anything, I'd call you a real thrue die-hard an' live-soft Republican, attendin' Republican funerals in the day, an' stoppin' up half the 60 night makin' suits for the Civic Guards!

[*Persons are heard running down to the street, some saying, "Here it is, here it is."* NUGENT *withdraws, and the rest, except* JOHNNY, *go to the window looking into the* 65 *street, and look out. Sounds of a crowd coming nearer are heard; a portion are singing.*]

To Jesus' Heart all burning
With fervent love for men,
My heart with fondest yearning 70
Shall raise its joyful strain.
While ages course along,
Blest be with loudest song,
The Sacred Heart of Jesus
By every heart and tongue. 75

MRS. BOYLE. Here's the hearse, here's the hearse!

BOYLE. There's t'oul' mother walkin' behin' the coffin.

MRS. MADIGAN. You can hardly see the 80 coffin with the wreaths.

JOXER. Oh, it's a darlin' funeral, a daarlin' funeral!

MRS. MADIGAN. We'd have a betther view from the street. 85

BOYLE. Yes—this place ud give you a crick in your neck.

[*They leave the room, and go down.* JOHNNY *sits moodily by the fire.*]

[*A young man enters; he looks at* JOHNNY 90 *for a moment.*]

THE YOUNG MAN. Quarter-Master Boyle.

JOHNNY [*with a start*]. The Mobilizer!

THE YOUNG MAN. You're not at the funeral?

JOHNNY. I'm not well. 95

THE YOUNG MAN. I'm glad I've found you; you were stoppin' at your aunt's; I called there but you'd gone. I've to give you an ordher to attend a Battalion Staff meetin' the night afther tomorrow.

JOHNNY. Where?

THE YOUNG MAN. I don't know; you're to
5 meet me at the Pillar at eight o'clock; then we're to go to a place I'll be told of tonight; there we'll meet a mothor that'll bring us to the meeting. They think you might be able to know somethin' about them that gave the bend
10 where Commandant Tancred was shelterin'.

JOHNNY. I'm not goin', then. I know nothing about Tancred.

THE YOUNG MAN [*at the door*]. You'd betther come for your own sake—remember your oath.
15 JOHNNY [*passionately*]. I won't go! Haven't I done enough for Ireland! I've lost me arm, an' me hip's desthroyed so that I'll never be able to walk right agen! Good God, haven't I done enough for Ireland?
20 THE YOUNG MAN. Boyle, no man can do enough for Ireland!

[*He goes.*]

[*Faintly in the distance the crowd is heard saying:*]
25 Hail, Mary, full of grace, the Lord is with
[Thee;
Blessed art Thou amongst women, and
[blessed, etc.

The Curtain Falls

ACT III

[SCENE. *The same as Act II. It is about half-*
30 *past six on a November evening; a bright fire is burning in the grate;* MARY, *dressed to go out, is sitting on a chair by the fire, leaning forward, her hands under her chin, her elbows on her knees. A look of dejection, mingled with*
35 *uncertain anxiety, is on her face. A lamp, turned low, is lighting on the table. The votive light under the picture of the Virgin gleams more redly than ever.* MRS BOYLE *is putting on her hat and coat. It is two months later.*]
40 MRS. BOYLE. An' has Bentham never even written to you since—not one line for the past month?

MARY [*tonelessly*]. Not even a line, mother.

MRS BOYLE. That's very curious. . . . What
45 came between the two of yous at all? To leave you so sudden, an' yous so great together. . . . To go away t' England, an' not to even leave you his address. . . . The way he was always bringin' you to dances, I thought he was mad afther you. Are you sure you said nothin' to 50 him?

MARY. No, mother—at least nothing that could possibly explain his givin' me up.

MRS. BOYLE. You know you're a bit hasty at times, Mary, an' say things you shouldn't say. 55

MARY. I never said to him what I shouldn't say, I'm sure of that.

MRS. BOYLE. How are you sure of it?

MARY. Because I love him with all my heart and soul, mother. Why, I don't know; I often 60 thought to myself that he wasn't the man poor Jerry was, but I couldn't help loving him, all the same.

MRS. BOYLE. But you shouldn't be frettin' the way you are; when a woman loses a man, 65 she never knows what she's afther losin', to be sure, but, then, she never knows what she's afther gainin', either. You're not the one girl of a month ago—you look like one pinin' away. It's long ago I had a right to bring you to the 70 doctor, instead of waitin' till tonight.

MARY. There's no necessity, really, mother, to go to the doctor; nothing serious is wrong with me—I'm run down and disappointed, that's all. 75

MRS BOYLE. I'll not wait another minute; I don't like the look of you at all. . . . I'm afraid we made a mistake in throwin' over poor Jerry. . . . He'd have been betther for you than that Bentham. 80

MARY. Mother, the best man for a woman is the one for whom she has the most love, and Charlie had it all.

MRS. BOYLE. Well, there's one thing to be said for him—he couldn't have been thinkin' 85 of the money, or he wouldn't ha' left you. . . . It must ha' been somethin' else.

MARY [*wearily*]. I don't know . . . I don't know, mother . . . only I think . . .

MRS. BOYLE. What d'ye think? 90

MARY. I imagine . . . he thought . . . we weren't . . . good enough for him.

MRS. BOYLE. An' what was he himself, only a school teacher? Though I don't blame him

for fightin' shy of people like that Joxer fella
an' that oul' Madigan wan—nice sort o' people
for your father to inthroduce to a man like Mr.
Bentham. You might have told me all about
5 this before now, Mary; I don't know why you
like to hide everything from your mother; you
knew Bentham, an' I'd ha' known nothin'
about it if it hadn't bin for the Will; an' it was
only today, afther long coaxin', that you let
10 out that he'd left you.

MARY. It would have been useless to tell
you—you wouldn't understand.

MRS. BOYLE [hurt]. Maybe not. . . . Maybe I
wouldn't understand. . . . Well, we'll be off
15 now. [She goes over to the door left, and
speaks to BOYLE inside.]

MRS. BOYLE. We're goin' now to the doctor's.
Are you goin' to get up this evenin'?

BOYLE [from inside]. The pain in me legs is
20 terrible! It's me should be poppin' off to the
doctor instead o' Mary, the way I feel.

MRS BOYLE. Sorra mend you! A nice way you
were in last night—carried in in a frog's
march,° dead to the world. If that's the way
25 you'll go on when you get the money it'll be
the grave for you, an asylum for me and the
Poorhouse for Johnny.

BOYLE. I thought you were goin'?

MRS. BOYLE. That's what has you as you are
30 —you can't bear to be spoken to. Knowin' the
way we are, up to our ears in debt, it's a
wondher you wouldn't ha' got up to go to th'
solicitor's an' see if we could ha' gettin' a little
o' the money even.

35 BOYLE [shouting]. I can't be goin' up there
night, noon an' mornin', can I? He can't give
the money till he gets it, can he? I can't get
blood out of a turnip, can I?

MRS. BOYLE. It's nearly two months since we
40 heard of the Will, an' the money seems as far
off as ever. . . . I suppose you know we owe
twenty poun's to oul' Murphy?

BOYLE. I've a faint recollection of you tellin'
me that before.

45 MRS. BOYLE. Well, you'll go over to the shop
yourself for the things in future—I'll face him
no more.

BOYLE. I thought you said you were goin'?
MRS. BOYLE. I'm goin' now; come on, Mary.
BOYLE. Ey, Juno, ey! 50
MRS. BOYLE. Well, what d'ye want now?
BOYLE. Is there e'er a bottle o' stout left?
MRS. BOYLE. There's two o' them here still.
BOYLE. Show us in one o' them an' leave
t'other there till I get up. An' throw us in the 55
paper that's on the table, an' the bottle o'
Sloan's Liniment that's in th' drawer.

MRS. BOYLE [getting the liniment and the
stout]. What paper is it you want—the Messenger? 60

BOYLE. Messenger! The News o' the World!

[MRS. BOYLE brings in the things asked for
and comes out again.]

MRS. BOYLE [at door]. Mind the candle, now,
an' don't burn the house over our heads. I left 65
t'other bottle o' stout on the table.

[She puts bottle of stout on table. She goes
out with MARY. A cork is heard popping inside. A pause; then outside the door is heard
the voice of JOXER lilting softly: "Me pipe I'll 70
smoke, as I dhrive me moke . . . are you . . .
there . . . More . . . aar . . . i . . . tee!" A gentle
knock is heard and, after a pause, the door
opens, and JOXER, followed by NUGENT, enters.]

JOXER. Be God, they must all be out; I was 75
thinkin' there was somethin' up when he didn't
answer the signal. We seen Juno an' Mary
goin', but I didn't see him, an' it's very seldom
he escapes me.

NUGENT. He's not goin' to escape me—he's 80
not goin' to be let go to the fair altogether.

JOXER. Sure, the house couldn't hould them
lately; an' he goin' about like a mastherpiece
of the Free State counthry; forgettin' their
friends; forgettin' God—wouldn't even lift his 85
hat passin' a chapel! Sure they were bound to
get a dhrop! An' you really think there's no
money comin' to him afther all?

NUGENT. Not as much as a red rex,° man;
I've been a bit anxious this long time over me 90
money, an' I went up to the solicitor's to find
out all I could—ah, man, they were goin' to
throw me down the stairs. They toul' me that
the oul' cock himself had the stairs worn away

---

in a frog's march sprawled prone

rex cent

comin' up afther it, an' they black in the face tellin' him he'd get nothing'. Some way or another that the Will is writ he won't be entitled to get as much as a make!°

5   JOXER. Ah, I thought there was somethin' curious about the whole thing; I've bin havin' sthrange dreams for the last couple o' weeks. An' I notice that that Bentham fella doesn't be comin' here now—there must be somethin' on
10   the mat° there too. Anyhow, who, in the name o' God, ud leave anythin' to that oul' bummer? Sure it ud be unnatural. An' the way Juno an' him's been throwin' their weight about for the last few months! Ah him that goes a borrowin'
15   goes a sorrowin'!

NUGENT. Well, he's not goin' to throw his weight about in the suit I made for him much longer. I'm tellin' you seven poun's aren't to be found growin' on the bushes these days.

20   JOXER. An' there isn't hardly a neighbour in the whole street that hasn't lent him money on the strength of what he was goin' to get, but they're after backing the wrong horse. Wasn't it a mercy o' God that I'd nothin' to give
25   him! The softy I am, you know, I'd ha' lent him me last juice! I must have had somebody's good prayers. Ah, afther all, an honest man's the noblest work o' God! [BOYLE *coughs inside.*] Whisht, damn it, he must be inside in bed.

30   NUGENT. Inside o' bed or outside of it he's goin' to pay me for that suit, or give it back— he'll not climb up my back as easily as he thinks.

JOXER. Gwan in at wanst, man, an' get it off
35   him, an' don't be a fool.

NUGENT [*going to the door left, opening it and looking in*]. Ah, don't disturb yourself, Mr. Boyle; I hope you're not sick?

BOYLE. Th' oul' legs, Mr. Nugent, the oul'
40   legs.

NUGENT. I just called over to see if you could let me have anything off the suit?

BOYLE. E-e-e-eh, how much is this it is?

NUGENT. It's the same as it was at the start—
45   seven poun's.

BOYLE. I'm glad you kem, Mr. Nugent; I want a good heavy topcoat—Irish frieze, if you have it. How much would a top-coat like that be now?

NUGENT. About six poun's.   50

BOYLE. Six poun's—six an' seven, six an' seven is thirteen—that'll be thirteen poun's I'll owe you.

[JOXER *slips the bottle of stout that is on the table into his pocket.* NUGENT *rushes into the*   55
room, and returns with the suit on his arm; he pauses at the door.]

NUGENT. You'll owe me no thirteen poun's. Maybe you think you're betther able to owe it than pay it!   60

BOYLE [*frantically*]. Here, come back to hell ower that—where're you goin' with them clothes o' mine?

NUGENT. Where am I goin' with them clothes o' yours? Well, I like your damn cheek!   65

BOYLE. Here, what am I going to dhress meself in when I'm goin' out?

NUGENT. What do I care what you dhress yourself in? You can put yourself in a bolsther cover, if you like.   70

[*He goes towards the other door, followed by* JOXER.]

JOXER. What'll he dhress himself in! Gentleman Jack an' his frieze coat!

[*They go out.*]   75

BOYLE [*inside*]. Ey, Nugent, ey, Mr. Nugent, Mr. Nugent!

[*After a pause* BOYLE *enters hastily, buttoning the braces of his moleskin trousers; his coat and vest are on his arm; he throws these*   80
on a chair and hurries to the door on right.]

BOYLE. Ey, Mr. Nugent, Mr. Nugent!

JOXER [*meeting him at the door*]. What's up, what's wrong, Captain?

BOYLE. Nugent's been here an' took away   85
me suit—the only things I had to go out in!

JOXER. Tuk your suit—for God's sake! An' what were you doin' while he was takin' them?

BOYLE. I was in bed when he stole in like a thief in the night, an' before I knew even what   90
he was thinkin' of, he whipped them from the chair, an' was off like a redshank!°

---

make halfpenny
on the mat the matter

redshank backcountryman, proverbially fast and elusive

JOXER. An' what, in the name o' God, did he do that for?

BOYLE. What did he do it for? How the hell do I know what he done it for? Jealousy an'
5 spite, I suppose.

JOXER. Did he not say what he done it for?

BOYLE. Amn't I afther tellin' you that he had them whipped up an' was gone before I could open me mouth?

10 JOXER. That was a very sudden thing to do; there mus' be somethin' behin' it. Did he hear anythin', I wondher?

BOYLE. Did he hear anythin'?—you talk very queer, Joxer—what could he hear?

15 JOXER. About you not gettin' the money, in some way or t'other?

BOYLE. An' what ud prevent me from gettin' th' money?

JOXER. That's jus' what I was thinkin'—what
20 ud prevent you from gettin' the money—nothin', as far as I can see.

BOYLE [looking round for bottle of stout with an exclamation]. Aw, holy God!

JOXER. What's up, Jack?

25 BOYLE. He must have afther lifted the bottle o' stout that Juno left on the table!

JOXER [horrified]. Ah, no, ah, no! He wouldn't be afther doin' that, now.

BOYLE. An' who done it then? Juno left a
30 bottle o' stout here, an' it's gone—it didn't walk, did it?

JOXER. Oh, that's shockin'; ah, man's inhumanity to man makes countless thousands mourn!

35 MRS. MADIGAN [appearing at the door]. I hope I'm not disturbin' you in any discussion on your forthcomin' legacy—if I may use the word—an' that you'll let me have a barny° for a minute or two with you, Mr. Boyle.

40 BOYLE. [uneasily]. To be sure, Mrs. Madigan —an oul' friends always welcome.

JOXER. Come in the evenin', come in th' mornin'; come when you're assed, or come without warnin', Mrs. Madigan.

45 BOYLE. Sit down, Mrs. Madigan.

barny argument

MRS. MADIGAN [ominously]. Th' few words I have to say can be said standin'. Puttin' aside all formularies, I suppose you remember me lendin' you some time ago three poun's that I raised on blankets an' furniture in me 50 uncle's?

BOYLE. I remember it well. I have it recorded in me book—three poun's five shillin's from Maisie Madigan, raised on articles pawned; an', item: fourpence, given to make up the 55 price of a pint, on th' principle that no bird ever flew on wan wing; all to be repaid at par, when the ship comes home.

MRS. MADIGAN. Well, ever since I shoved in the blankets I've been perishing with th' 60 cowld, an' I've decided, if I'll be too hot in th' nex' world aself, I'm not goin' to be too cowld in this wan; an' consequently, I want me three poun's, if you please.

BOYLE. This is a very sudden demand, Mrs. 65 Madigan, an' can't be met; but I'm willin' to give you a receipt in full, in full.

MRS. MADIGAN. Come on, out with th' money, an' don't be jack-actin'.

BOYLE. You can't get blood out of a turnip, 70 can you?

MRS. MADIGAN [rushing over and shaking him]. Gimme me money, y'oul' reprobate, or I'll shake the worth of it out of you!

BOYLE. Ey, houl' on, there; houl' on, there! 75 You'll wait for your money now, me lassie!

MRS. MADIGAN [looking around the room and seeing the gramophone]. I'll wait for it, will I? Well, I'll not wait long; if I can't get th' cash, I'll get th' worth of it. [She catches 80 up the gramophone.]

BOYLE. Ey, ey, there, where'r you goin' with that?

MRS. MADIGAN. I'm goin' to th' pawn to get me three quid five shillin's; I'll bring you th' 85 ticket, an' then you can do what you like, me bucko.

BOYLE. You can't touch that, you can't touch that! It's not my property, an' it's not ped for yet! 90

MRS. MADIGAN. So much th' better. It'll be an ayse to me conscience, for I'm takin' what doesn't belong to you. You're not goin' to be swankin' it like a paycock with Maisie Madigan's money—I'll pull some o' the gorgeous feathers out o' your tail!

5 [*She goes off with the gramophone.*]

BOYLE. What's th' world comin' to at all? I ass you, Joxer Daly, is there any morality left anywhere?

JOXER. I wouldn't ha' believed it, only I seen 10 it with me own two eyes. I didn't think Maisie Madigan was that sort of a woman; she has either a sup taken, or she's heard somethin'.

BOYLE. Heard somethin'—about what, if it's not any harm to ass you?

15 JOXER. She must ha' heard some rumour or other that you weren't goin' to get th' money.

BOYLE. Who says I'm not goin' to get th' money?

JOXER. Sure, I know—I was only sayin'.

20 BOYLE. Only sayin' what?

JOXER. Nothin'.

BOYLE. You were goin' to say somethin', don't be a twisther.°

JOXER [*angrily*]. Who's a twisther?

25 BOYLE. Why don't you speak your mind, then?

JOXER. You never twisted yourself—no, you wouldn't know how!

BOYLE. Did you ever know me to twist; did 30 you ever know me to twist?

JOXER [*fiercely*]. Did you ever do anythin' else! Sure, you can't believe a word that comes out o' your mouth.

BOYLE. Here, get out, ower o' this; I always 35 knew you were a prognosticator an' a procrastinator!

JOXER [*going out as* JOHNNY *comes in*]. The anchor's weighed, farewell, re . . . mem . . . ber . . . me. Jacky Boyle, Esquire, infernal rogue 40 an' damned liar!

JOHNNY. Joxer an' you at it agen?—when are you goin' to have a little respect for yourself, an' not be always makin' a show of us all?

BOYLE. Are you goin' to lecture me now?

45 JOHNNY. Is mother back from the doctor yet,

---

twisther liar

---

with Mary?

[MRS. BOYLE *enters; it is apparent from the serious look on her face that something has happened. She takes off her hat and coat without a word and puts them by. She then sits* 50 *down near the fire, and there is a few moments' pause.*]

BOYLE. Well, what did the doctor say about Mary?

MRS. BOYLE [*in an earnest manner and with* 55 *suppressed agitation*]. Sit down here, Jack; I've something to say to you . . . about Mary.

BOYLE [*awed by her manner*]. About . . . Mary?

MRS. BOYLE. Close that door there and sit 60 down here.

BOYLE [*closing the door*]. More throuble in our native land, is it? [*He sits down.*] Well, what is it?

MRS. BOYLE. It's about Mary. 65

BOYLE. Well, what about Mary—there's nothin' wrong with her, is there?

MRS. BOYLE. I'm sorry to say there's a gradle wrong with her.

BOYLE. A gradle wrong with her! [*Peevishly.*] 70 First Johnny an' now Mary; is the whole house goin' to become an hospital! It's not consumption, is it?

MRS. BOYLE. No . . . it's not consumption . . . it's worse. 75

JOHNNY. Worse! Well, we'll have to get her into some place ower this, there's no one here to mind her.

MRS. BOYLE. We'll all have to mind her now. You might as well know now, Johnny, as an- 80 other time. [*To* BOYLE.] D'ye you know what the doctor said to me about her, Jack?

BOYLE. How ud I know—I wasn't there, was I?

MRS. BOYLE. He told me to get her married 85 at wanst.

BOYLE. Married at wanst! An' why did he say the like o' that?

MRS. BOYLE. Because Mary's goin' to have a baby in a short time. 90

BOYLE. Goin' to have a baby!—my God, what'll Bentham say when he hears that?

MRS. BOYLE. Are you blind, man, that you can't see that it was Bentham that has done this wrong to her?

BOYLE [*passionately*]. Then he'll marry her, he'll have to marry her!

MRS. BOYLE. You know he's gone to England, an' God knows where he is now.

BOYLE. I'll folley him, I'll folley him, an' bring him back, an' make him do her justice. The scoundrel, I might ha' known what he was, with his yogees an' his prawna!

MRS. BOYLE. We'll have to keep it quiet till we see what we can do.

BOYLE. Oh, isn't this a nice thing to come on top o' me, an' the state I'm in! A pretty show I'll be to Joxer an' to that oul' wan, Madigan! Amn't I afther goin' through enough without havin' to go through this!

MRS. BOYLE. What you an' I'll have to go through'll be nothin to what poor Mary'll have to go through; for you an' me is middlin' old, an' most of our years is spent; but Mary'll have maybe forty years to face an' handle, an' every wan of them'll be tainted with a bitther memory.

BOYLE. Where is she? Where is she till I tell her off? I'm tellin' you when I'm done with her she'll be a sorry girl!

MRS. BOYLE. I left her in me sisther's till I came to speak to you. You'll say nothin' to her, Jack; ever since she left school she's earned her livin', an' your fatherly care never throubled the poor girl.

BOYLE. Gwan, take her part agen her father! But I'll let you see whether I'll say nothin' to her or no! Her an' her readin'! That's more o' th' blasted nonsense that has the house fallin' down on top of us! What did th' likes of her, born in a tenement house, want with readin'? Her readin's afther bringin' her to a nice pass —oh, it's madnin', madnin', madnin'!

MRS. BOYLE. When she comes back say nothin' to her, Jack, or she'll leave this place.

BOYLE. Leave this place! Ay, she'll leave this place, an' quick too!

MRS. BOYLE. If Mary goes, I'll go with her.

BOYLE. Well, go with her! Well, go, th' pair o' yous! I lived before I seen yous, an' I can live when yous are gone. Isn't this a nice thing to come rollin' in on top o' me afther all your prayin' to St. Anthony an' The Little Flower. An' she's a child o' Mary, too—I wonder what'll the nuns think of her now? An it'll be bellows'd all over th' disthrict before you could say Jack Robinson; an' whenever I'm seen they'll whisper, "That's th' father of Mary Boyle that had th' kid be th' swank she used to go with; d'ye know, d'ye know?" To be sure they'll know—more about it than I will meself!

JOHNNY. She should be dhriven out o' th' house she's brought disgrace on!

MRS. BOYLE. Hush, you, Johnny. We needn't let it be bellows'd all over the place; all we've got to do is to leave this place quietly an' go somewhere where we're not known, an' nobody'll be the wiser.

BOYLE. You're talkin' like a two-year-oul', woman. Where'll we get a place ou' o' this?— places aren't that easily got.

MRS. BOYLE. But, Jack, when we get the money . . .

BOYLE. Money—what money?

MRS. BOYLE. Why, oul' Ellison's money, of course.

BOYLE. There's no money comin' from oul' Ellison, or any one else. Since you heard of wan trouble, you might as well hear of another. There's no money comin' to us at all— the Will's a wash out!

MRS. BOYLE. What are you sayin', man—no money?

JOHNNY. How could it be a wash out?

BOYLE. The boyo that's afther doin' it to Mary done it to me as well. The thick made out the Will wrong; he said in th' Will, only first cousin an' second cousin, instead of mentionin' our names, an' now any one that thinks he's a first cousin or second cousin t'oul' Ellison can claim the money as well as me, an' they're springin' up in hundreds, an' comin' from America an' Australia, thinkin' to get their whack out of it, while all the time the lawyers is gobblin' it up, till there's not as much as ud buy a stockin' for your lovely daughter's baby!

MRS. BOYLE. I don't believe it, I don't believe it, I don't believe it!

JOHNNY. Why did you nothin' about this before?

5 MRS. BOYLE. You're not serious, Jack; you're not serious!

BOYLE. I'm tellin' you the scholar, Bentham, made a banjax° o' th' Will; instead o' sayin', "th' rest o' me property to be divided between 10 me first cousin, Jack Boyle, an' me second cousin, Mick Finnegan, o' Santhry," he writ down only, "me first an' second cousins," an' the world an' his wife are afther th' property now.

15 MRS. BOYLE. Now, I know why Bentham left poor Mary in th' lurch; I can see it all now— oh, is there not even a middlin' honest man left in th' world?

JOHNNY [*to* BOYLE]. An' you let us run into 20 debt, an' you borreyed money from everybody to fill yourself with beer! An' now, you tell us the whole thing's a wash out! Oh, if it's thrue, I'm done with you, for you're worse than me sisther Mary!

25 BOYLE. You hole your tongue, d'ye hear? I'll not take any lip from you. Go an' get Bentham if you want satisfaction for all that's afther happenin' us.

JOHNNY. I won't hole me tongue, I won't hole 30 me tongue! I'll tell you what I think of you, father an' all as you are . . . you . . .

MRS. BOYLE. Johnny, Johnny, Johnny, for God's sake, be quiet!

JOHNNY. I'll not be quiet, I'll not be quiet; 35 he's a nice father, isn't he? Is it any wondher Mary went asthray, when . . .

MRS. BOYLE. Johnny, Johnny, for my sake be quiet—for your mother's sake!

BOYLE. I'm goin' out now to have a few 40 dhrinks with th' last few makes I have, an' tell that lassie o' yours not to be here when I come back; for if I lay me eyes on her, I'll lay me han's on her, an' if I lay me han's on her, I won't be accountable for me actions!

45 JOHNNY. Take care somebody doesn't lay his

banjax hodgepodge

han's on you—y'oul' . . .

MRS. BOYLE. Johnny, Johnny!

BOYLE [*at door, about to go out*]. Oh, a nice son, an' a nicer daughter, I have. [*Calling loudly upstairs.*] Joxer, Joxer, are you there? 50

JOXER [*from a distance*]. I'm here, More . . . ee . . . aar . . . i . . . tee!

BOYLE. I'm goin' down to Foley's—are you comin'?

JOXER. Come with you? With that sweet call 55 me heart is stirred; I'm only waiting for the word, an' I'll be with you, like a bird!

[BOYLE *and* JOXER *pass the door going out.*]

JOHNNY [*throwing himself on the bed*]. I've a nice sisther, an' a nice father, there's no 60 bettin' on it. I wish to God a bullet or a bomb had whipped me ou' o' this long ago! Not one o' yous, not one o' yous, have any thought for me!

MRS. BOYLE [*with passionate remonstrance*]. 65 If you don't whisht, Johnny, you'll drive me mad. Who has kep' th' home together for the past few years—only me. An' who'll have to bear th' biggest part o' this throuble but me— but whinin' an' whingin' isn't going to do any 70 good.

JOHNNY. You're to blame yourself for a gradle of it—givin' him his own way in everything, an' never assin' to check him, no matther what he done. Why didn't you look 75 afther th' money? why . . .

[*There is a knock at the door;* MRS. BOYLE *opens it;* JOHNNY *rises on his elbow to look and listen; two men enter.*]

FIRST MAN. We've been sent up be th' 80 Manager of the Hibernian Furnishing Co., Mrs. Boyle, to take back the furniture that was got a while ago.

MRS. BOYLE. Yous'll touch nothin' here— how do I know who yous are? 85

FIRST MAN [*showing a paper*]. There's the ordher, ma'am. [*Reading.*] A chest o' drawers, a table, wan easy an' two ordinary chairs; wan mirror; wan chestherfield divan, an' a wardrobe an' two vases. [*To his comrade.*] Come 90 on, Bill, it's afther knockin' off time already.

JOHNNY. For God's sake, mother, run down

to Foley's an' bring father back, or we'll be left without a stick.

[*The men carry out the table.*]

MRS. BOYLE. What good would it be? You
5 heard what he said before he went out.

JOHNNY. Can't you thry? He ought to be here, an' the like of this goin' on.

[MRS. BOYLE *puts a shawl around her, as* MARY *enters.*]

10 MARY. What's up, mother? I met men carryin' away the table, an' everybody's talking about us not gettin' the money after all.

MRS. BOYLE. Everythin's gone wrong, Mary, everythin'. We're not gettin' a penny out o'
15 the Will, not a penny—I'll tell you all when I come back; I'm goin' for your father.

[*She runs out.*]

JOHNNY [*to* MARY, *who has sat down by the fire*]. It's a wondher you're not ashamed to
20 show your face here, afther what has happened.

[JERRY *enters slowly; there is a look of earnest hope on his face. He looks at* MARY *for a few moments.*]

25 JERRY [*softly*]. Mary! [MARY *does not answer.*] Mary, I want to speak to you for a few moments, may I?

[MARY *remains silent;* JOHNNY *goes slowly into room on left.*]

30 JERRY. Your mother has told me everything, Mary, and I have come to you. . . . I have come to tell you, Mary, that my love for you is greater and deeper than ever. . . .

MARY [*with a sob*]. Oh, Jerry, Jerry, say no
35 more; all that is over now; anything like that is impossible now!

JERRY. Impossible? Why do you talk like that, Mary?

MARY. After all that has happened.

40 JERRY. What does it matter what has happened? We are young enough to be able to forget all those things. [*He catches her hand.*] Mary, Mary, I am pleading for your love. With Labour, Mary, humanity is above everything;
45 we are the Leaders in the fight for a new life. I want to forget Bentham, I want to forget that you left me—even for a while.

MARY. Oh, Jerry, Jerry, you haven't the bitter word of scorn for me after all.

JERRY [*passionately*]. Scorn! I love you, love 50 you, Mary!

MARY [*rising, and looking him in the eyes*]. Even though . . .

JERRY. Even though you threw me over for another man; even though you gave me many 55 a bitter word!

MARY. Yes, yes, I know; but you love me, even though . . . even though . . . I'm . . . goin' . . . goin' . . . . [*He looks at her questioningly, and fear gathers in his eyes.*] Ah, I was 60 thinkin' so. . . . You don't know everything!

JERRY [*poignantly*]. Surely to God, Mary, you don't mean that . . . that . . . that . . .

MARY. Now you know all, Jerry; now you know all! 65

JERRY. My God, Mary, have you fallen as low as that?

MARY. Yes, Jerry, as you say, I have fallen as low as that.

JERRY. I didn't mean it that way, Mary . . . 70 it came on me so sudden, that I didn't mind what I was sayin'. . . . I never expected this— your mother never told me. . . . I'm sorry . . . God knows, I'm sorry for you, Mary.

MARY. Let us say no more, Jerry; I don't 75 blame you for thinkin' it's terrible. . . . I suppose it is. . . . Everybody'll think the same. . . . It's only as I expected—your humanity is just as narrow as the humanity of the others.

JERRY. I'm sorry, all the same. . . . I shouldn't 80 have troubled you. . . . I wouldn't if I'd known . . . if I can do anything for you . . . Mary . . . I will.

[*He turns to go, and halts at the door.*]

MARY. Do you remember, Jerry, the verses 85 you read when you gave the lecture in the Socialist Rooms some time ago, on Humanity's Strife with Nature?

JERRY. The verses—no; I don't remember them. 90

MARY. I do. They're runnin' in me head now—

An' we felt the power that fashion'd
All the lovely things we saw,
That created all the murmur
Of an everlasting law, 95
Was a hand of force an' beauty,
With an eagle's tearin' claw.

Then we saw our globe of beauty
Was an ugly thing as well,
A hymn divine whose chorus
Was an agonizin' yell;
5   Like the story of a demon,
That an angel had to tell.

Like a glowin' picture by a
Hand unsteady, brought to ruin;
Like her craters, if their deadness
10   Could give life unto the moon;
Like the agonizing horror
Of a violin out of tune.

[*There is a pause, and* DEVINE *goes slowly
out.*]
15   JOHNNY [*returning*]. Is he gone?
MARY. Yes.
[*The two men re-enter.*]
FIRST MAN. We can't wait any longer for
t'oul' fella—sorry, Miss, but we have to live
20   as well as th' nex' man.
[*They carry out some things.*]
JOHNNY. Oh, isn't this terrible! . . . I suppose
you told him everything . . . couldn't you have
waited for a few days . . . he'd have stopped
25   th' takin' of the things, if you'd kep' your
mouth shut. Are you burnin' to tell every one
of the shame you've brought on us?
MARY [*snatching up her hat and coat*]. Oh,
this is unbearable!
30   [*She rushes out.*]
FIRST MAN [*re-entering*]. We'll take the chest
o' drawers next—it's the heaviest.
[*The votive light flickers for a moment, and
goes out.*]
35   JOHNNY [*in a cry of fear*]. Mother o' God,
the light's afther goin' out!
FIRST MAN. You put the win' up me the way
you bawled that time. The oil's all gone, that's
all.
40   JOHNNY [*with an agonizing cry*]. Mother o'
God, there's a shot I'm afther gettin'!
FIRST MAN. What's wrong with you, man?
Is it a fit you're takin'?
JOHNNY. I'm afther feelin' a pain in me
45   breast, like the tearin' by of a bullet!
FIRST MAN. He's goin' mad—it's a wondher
they'd leave a chap like that here be himself.

[*Two* IRREGULARS *enter swiftly; they carry
revolvers; one goes over to* JOHNNY; *the other
covers the two furniture men.*]   50
FIRST IRREGULAR [*to the men, quietly and
incisively*]. Who are you—what are yous doin'
here—quick!
FIRST MAN. Removin' furniture that's not
paid for.   55
FIRST IRREGULAR. Get over to the other end
of the room an' turn your faces to the wall—
quick.
[*The two men turn their faces to the wall,
with their hands up.*]   60
SECOND IRREGULAR [*to* JOHNNY]. Come on,
Sean° Boyle, you're wanted; some of us have
a word to say to you.
JOHNNY. I'm sick, I can't—what do you want
with me?   65
SECOND IRREGULAR. Come on, come on; we've
a distance to go, an' haven't much time—come
on.
JOHNNY. I'm an oul' comrade—yous wouldn't
shoot an oul' comrade.   70
SECOND IRREGULAR. Poor Tancred was an oul'
comrade o' yours, but you didn't think o' that
when you gave him away to the gang that
sent him to his grave. But we've no time to
waste; come on—here, Dermot, ketch his arm.   75
[*To* JOHNNY.] Have you your beads?°
JOHNNY. Me beads! Why do you ass me
that, why do you ass me that?
SECOND IRREGULAR. Go on, go on, march!
JOHNNY. Are yous goin' to do in a comrade—   80
look at me arm, I lost it for Ireland.
SECOND IRREGULAR. Commandant Tancred
lost his life for Ireland.
JOHNNY. Sacred Heart of Jesus, have mercy
on me! Mother o' God, pray for me—be with   85
me now in the agonies o' death! . . . Hail, Mary,
full o' grace . . . the Lord is . . . with Thee.
[*They drag out* JOHNNY BOYLE, *and the curtain falls. When it rises again the most of the
furniture is gone.* MARY *and* MRS. BOYLE, *one*   90
*on each side, are sitting in a darkened room,
by the fire; it is an hour later.*]

Sean John. The nationalistic Irregulars prefer the
  Gaelic form of the name.
beads Rosary

MRS. BOYLE. I'll not wait much longer . . . what did they bring him away in the mothor for? Nugent says he thinks they had guns . . . is me throubles never goin' to be over? . . . If anything ud happen to poor Johnny, I think I'd lose me mind . . . I'll go to the Police Station, surely they ought to be able to do somethin'.

[*Below is heard the sound of voices.*]

MRS. BOYLE. Whisht, is that something? Maybe, it's your father, though when I left him in Foley's he was hardly able to lift his head. Whisht!

[*A knock at the door, and the voice of* MRS. MADIGAN, *speaking very softly:* Mrs. Boyle, Mrs. Boyle. MRS. BOYLE *opens the door.*]

MRS. MADIGAN. Oh, Mrs. Boyle, God an' His Blessed Mother be with you this night!

MRS. BOYLE [*calmly*]. What is it, Mrs. Madigan? It's Johnny—something about Johnny.

MRS. MADIGAN. God send it's not. God send it's not Johnny!

MRS. BOYLE. Don't keep me waitin', Mrs. Madigan; I've gone through so much lately that I feel able for anything.

MRS. MADIGAN. Two polismen below wantin' you.

MRS. BOYLE. Wantin' me; an' why do they want me?

MRS. MADIGAN. Some poor fella's been found, an' they think it's, it's . . .

MRS. BOYLE. Johnny, Johnny!

MARY [*with her arms round her mother*]. Oh, mother, mother, me poor, darlin' mother.

MRS. BOYLE. Hush, hush, darlin'; you'll shortly have your own throuble to bear. [*To* MRS. MADIGAN.] An' why do the polis think it's Johnny, Mrs. Madigan?

MRS. MADIGAN. Because one o' the doctors knew him when he was attendin' with his poor arm.

MRS. BOYLE. Oh, it's thrue, then; it's Johnny, it's me son, me own son!

MARY. Oh, it's thrue, it's thrue what Jerry Devine says—there isn't a God, there isn't a God; if there was He wouldn't let these things happen!

MRS. BOYLE. Mary, Mary, you mustn't say them things. We'll want all the help we can get from God an' His Blessed Mother now! These things have nothin' to do with the Will o' God. Ah, what can God do agen the stupidity o' men!

MRS. MADIGAN. The polis want you to go with them to the hospital to see the poor body —they're waitin' below.

MRS. BOYLE. We'll go. Come, Mary, an' we'll never come back here agen. Let your father furrage for himself now; I've done all I could an' it was all no use—he'll be hopeless till the end of his days. I've got a little room in me sisther's where we'll stop till your throuble is over, an' then we'll work together for the sake of the baby.

MARY. My poor little child that'll have no father!

MRS. BOYLE. It'll have what's far betther— it'll have two mothers.

[*A rough voice shouting from below.*]

Are yous goin' to keep us waitin' for yous all night?

MRS. MADIGAN [*going to the door, and shouting down*]. Take your hour, there, take your hour! If yous are in such a hurry, skip off, then, for nobody wants you here—if they did yous wouldn't be found. For you're the same as yous were undher the British Government—never where yous are wanted! As far as I can see, the Polis as Polis, in this city, is Null an' Void!

MRS. BOYLE. We'll go, Mary, we'll go; you to see your poor dead brother, an' me to see me poor dead son!

MARY. I dhread it, mother, I dhread it!

MRS. BOYLE. I forgot, Mary, I forgot; your poor oul' selfish mother was only thinkin' of herself. No, no, you mustn't come—it wouldn't be good for you. You go on to me sisther's an' I'll face th' ordeal meself. Maybe I didn't feel sorry enough for Mrs. Tancred when her poor son was found as Johnny's been found now— because he was a Die-hard! Ah, why didn't I remember that then he wasn't a Die-hard or a Stater, but only a poor dead son! It's well I remember all that she said—an' it's my turn to say it now: What was the pain I suffered,

Johnny, bringin' you into the world to carry
you to your cradle to the pains I'll suffer carryin' you out o' the world to bring you to your
grave! Mother o' God, Mother o' God, have
5 pity on us all! Blessed Virgin, where were you
when me darlin' son was riddled with bullets,
when me darlin' son was riddled with bullets?
Sacred Heart o' Jesus, take away our hearts o'
stone, and give us hearts o' flesh! Take away
10 this murdherin' hate, an' give us Thine own
eternal love!

   [*They all go slowly out. There is a pause;
then a sound of shuffling steps on the stairs
outside. The door opens and* BOYLE *and* JOXER,
15 *both of them very drunk, enter.*]

   BOYLE. I'm able to go no farther. . . . Two
polis, ey . . . what were they doin' here, I
wondher? . . . Up to no good, anyhow . . . an'
Juno an' that lovely daughter o' mine with
20 them. [*Taking a sixpence from his pocket and
looking at it.*] Wan single, solithary tanner
left out of all I borreyed. . . . [*He lets it fall.*]
The last o' the Mohicans. . . . The blinds is
down, Joxer, the blinds is down!

25   JOXER [*walking unsteadily across the room,
and anchoring at the bed*]. Put all . . . your
throubles . . . in your oul' kit bag . . . an' smile
. . . smile . . . smile!

   BOYLE. The counthry'll have to steady itself
30 . . . it's goin' . . . to hell. . . . Where'r all . . . the
chairs . . . gone to . . . steady itself, Joxer. . . .
Chairs'll . . . have to . . . steady themselves. . . .
No matther . . . what any one may . . . say . . .
Irelan's sober . . . is Irelan' . . . free.

35   JOXER [*stretching himself on the bed*]. Chains
. . . an' . . . slaveree . . . that's a darlin' motto
. . . a daaarlin' . . . motto!

   BOYLE. If th' worst comes . . . to th' worse . . .
I can join a . . . flyin' . . . column.° . . . I done
40 . . . me bit . . . in Easther Week . . . had no
business . . . to . . . be . . . there . . . but Captain
Boyle's Captain Boyle!

   JOXER. Breathes there a man with soul . . . so
. . . de . . . ad . . . this . . . me . . . o . . . wn, me
45 nat . . . ive l . . . an'!

   BOYLE [*subsiding into a sitting posture on the
floor*]. Commandant Kelly died . . . in them . . .
arms . . . Joxer. . . . Tell me Volunteer Butties
. . . says he . . . that . . . I died for . . . Irelan'!

   JOXER. D'jever rade Willie . . . Reilly . . . an' 50
his . . . own . . . Colleen . . . Bawn? It's a darlin'
story, a daarlin' story!

   BOYLE. I'm telling you . . . Joxer . . . th' whole
worl's . . . in a terr . . . ible state o' . . . chassis!

The Curtain Falls

---

flyin' column detachment of Irregulars

Eugene O'Neill

1888–1953

Desire Under the Elms

1924

O'Neill's play is not tragedy on the grand scale of *Oedipus, Othello,* or *Phaedra.* It is local tragedy, good—if the events were actually to occur—for a few inches of newspaper copy. The characters are lowly figures, significant only to themselves: a hardscrabble farmer, his hired hand of a son, his orphaned and impoverished wife. Their vocabularies are as meager as the soil of the farm, and their emotions, although powerful, are essentially primitive. If, like their tragic forebears, they engage the supernatural in their own consciousnesses, their gods and spirits lack objective reality. The hard Old Testament deity with whom Cabot communes is the projection of his own craggy nature. The spirit of Eben's mother, hovering like the elms over Eben and Abbie, is the expression of their own vulnerability and passion.

Like *Phaedra, Desire Under the Elms* concerns a father, son, and stepmother. However, whereas in Racine these characters profoundly revere the family union, in O'Neill they honor it not at all: for them the family is at best a cold, contractual relationship; at worst, it is a prison. Eben's incestuous passion, unlike Phaedra's, is self-endorsed, reciprocated, and consummated. It expresses oedipal hatred of the father and love of the mother—the morally uninhibited, psychologically unelaborated drives that energize the play's essentially external conflicts. These conflicts are reducible to the opposition between the desires of the father on the one hand and of the son and the stepmother on the other.

The desire over which the elms initially preside is lust for the land and the house. This is primarily the desire of Cabot, a hard old man, proud of his hardness and contemptuous of anything "soft." Cabot wishes either that his property could vanish with him at his death or that he could have a new son, a reincarnation of himself, to extend his possession into the future. His son Eben, whose mother had owned the farm, counters old Cabot's claim. Abbie, too,

677

EUGENE O'NEILL

taught by deprivation to value property, claims the house as her own: "It's purty—purty! I can't b'lieve it's r'ally mine."

Inevitably the elms come to preside over a second desire—the physical attraction of Eben and Abbie to each other. To this desire they yield in due course, after oscillating between attraction and antagonism. An inexorable conflict thence arises, for the child that is the product of their union is heir, in law, not to Abbie and Eben but to Abbie and Cabot. Old Cabot uses the fact against Eben: "The farm's her'n!" he cries. "An' the dust o' the road—that's your'n!" Considering himself betrayed, Eben pronounces a vengeance on Cabot, Abbie, and the child as well. "I wish he never was born. I wish he'd die this minit." And acting on this cue, Abbie precipitates the catastrophe that brings the play to its close.

Ideally the two desires—for fruitful land and for generative love—are united to provide identity, home, a way to flourish. But in *Desire Under the Elms* the two are irreconcilable alternatives. The curtain goes down with the father still cherishing his land, the stepmother cherishing her love, and the son—perhaps, in O'Neill's conception, doomed by an oedipal choice— aligned against his father and with his father's wife. For each, in the divisive scheme of the play, the basic desire is fulfilled, but the fulfillment entails isolation and death.

As critics, we may question the validity and depth of O'Neill's vision. To some it has seemed pessimistic if not cynical compared to the older, more heroic view of the American frontier. The house, the land, the overarching elms themselves are images from a nobler landscape. And the twisted and destructive passions here are inversions of the pioneer virtues of labor, self-discipline, and taciturn forebearance. In O'Neill the visions of Emerson, Thoreau, and Whitman seem blasted, although not utterly forgotten. To others O'Neill's vision has seemed both romantic and sentimental—Cabot, like Antaeus, gaining from the land a perennial vigor and apocalyptic grandeur, Eben and Abbie deriving from their passion, however infanticidal, a self-vindication at which reason demurs. But O'Neill's intensity and virtually unrivaled sense of theater make it hard for us, while reading or viewing his play, not to succumb. Whatever our objections, *Desire Under the Elms* retains a primal and compelling power.

Desire Under the Elms

O'NEILL

CHARACTERS

EPHRAIM CABOT
SIMEON ⎫
PETER ⎬ *His sons*
EBEN   ⎭
ABBIE PUTNAM

Young Girl, Two Farmers, The Fiddler, A Sheriff, and other folk from the neighboring farms.

The action of the entire play takes place in, and immediately outside of, the Cabot farmhouse in New England, in the year 1850. The south end of the house faces front to a stone
5 wall with a wooden gate at center opening on a country road. The house is in good condition but in need of paint. Its walls are a sickly grayish, the green of the shutters faded. Two enormous elms are on each side of the house.
10 They bend their trailing branches down over the roof. They appear to protect and at the same time subdue. There is a sinister maternity in their aspect, a crushing, jealous absorption. They have developed from the intimate con-
15 tact with the life of man in the house an appalling humaneness. They brood oppressively over the house. They are like exhausted women resting their sagging breasts and hands and hair on its roof, and when it rains their tears
20 trickle down monotonously and rot on the shingles.

There is a path running from the gate around the right corner of the house to the front door. A narrow porch is on this side. The end wall facing us has two windows in its 25 upper story, two larger ones on the floor below. The two upper are those of the father's bedroom and that of the brothers. On the left, ground floor, is the kitchen—on the right, the parlor, the shades of which are always drawn 30 down.

PART I

Scene i

[*Exterior of the farmhouse. It is sunset of a day at the beginning of summer in the year 1850. There is no wind and everything is still. The sky above the roof is suffused with deep 35 colors, the green of the elms glows, but the house is in shadows, seeming pale and washed out by contrast.*

A door opens and EBEN CABOT *comes to the end of the porch and stands looking down the 40 road to the right. He has a large bell in his hand and this he swings mechanically, awakening a deafening clangor. Then he puts his hands on his hips and stares up at the sky. He sighs with a puzzled awe and blurts out with 45 halting appreciation.*]

EBEN. God! Purty! [*His eyes fall and he stares about him frowningly. He is twenty-five, tall and sinewy. His face is well-formed, good-looking, but its expression is resentful and 50 defensive. His defiant, dark eyes remind one of a wild animal's in captivity. Each day is a cage in which he finds himself trapped but inwardy unsubdued. There is a fierce repressed vitality about him. He has black hair, mus- 55 tache, a thin curly trace of beard. He is dressed in rough farm clothes.*

He spits on the ground with intense disgust, turns and goes back into the house.

SIMEON *and* PETER *come in from their work 60 in the fields. They are tall men, much older than their half-brother [*SIMEON *is thirty-nine and* PETER *thirty-seven], built on a squarer, simpler model, fleshier in body, more bovine and homelier in face, shrewder and more prac- 65 tical. *Their shoulders stoop a bit from years of farm work. They clump heavily along in their clumsy thick-soled boots caked with earth. Their clothes, their faces, hands, bare arms*

5 *and throats are earth-stained. They smell of earth. They stand together for a moment in front of the house and, as if with the one impulse, stare dumbly at the sky, leaning on their hoes. Their faces have a compressed, unre-*

10 *signed expression. As they look upward, this softens.]*

SIMEON [*grudgingly*]. Purty.

PETER. Ay-eh.

SIMEON [*suddenly*]. Eighteen years ago.

15 PETER. What?

SIMEON. Jenn. My woman. She died.

PETER. I'd fergot.

SIMEON. I rec'lect—now an' agin. Makes it lonesome. She'd hair long's a hoss' tail—and

20 yaller like gold!

PETER. Waal—she's gone. [*This with indifferent finality—then after a pause.*] They's gold in the West, Sim.

SIMEON [*still under the influence of sunset—*

25 *vaguely*]. In the sky!

PETER. Waal—in a manner o' speakin'—thar's the promise. [*Growing excited.*] Gold in the sky—in the West—Golden Gate—Californi-a!—Golden West!—fields o' gold!

30 SIMEON [*excited in his turn*]. Fortunes layin' just atop o' the ground waitin' t' be picked! Solomon's mines, they says! [*For a moment they continue looking up at the sky—then their eyes drop.*]

35 PETER [*with sardonic bitterness*]. Here—it's stones atop o' the ground—stones atop o' stones—makin' stone walls—year atop o' year—him 'n' yew 'n' me 'n' then Eben—makin' stone walls fur him to fence us in!

40 SIMEON. We've wuked. Give our strength. Give our years. Plowed 'em under in the ground,—[*he stamps rebelliously*]—rottin'—makin' soil for his crops! [*A pause.*] Waal—the farm pays good for hereabouts.

45 PETER. If we plowed in Californi-a, they'd be lumps o' gold in the furrow!

SIMEON. Californi-a's t'other side o' earth, a'most. We got t' calc'late—

PETER [*after a pause*]. 'Twould be hard fur me, too, to give up what we've 'arned here by 50 our sweat. [*A pause, EBEN sticks his head out of the dining-room window, listening.*]

SIMEON. Ay-eh. [*A pause.*] Mebbe—he'll die soon.

PETER [*doubtfully*]. Mebbe. 55

SIMEON. Mebbe—fur all we knows—he's dead now.

PETER. Ye'd need proof.

SIMEON. He's been gone two months—with no word. 60

PETER. Left us in the fields an evenin' like this. Hitched up an' druv off into the West. That's plum onnateral. He hain't never been off this farm 'ceptin' t' the village in thirty year or more, not since he married Eben's maw. [*A* 65 *pause. Shrewdly.*] I calc'late we might git him declared crazy by the court.

SIMEON. He skinned 'em too slick. He got the best o' all on 'em. They'd never b'lieve him crazy. [*A pause.*] We got t' wait—till he's 70 under ground.

EBEN [*with a sardonic chuckle*]. Honor thy father! [*They turn, startled, and stare at him. He grins, then scowls.*] I pray he's died. [*They stare at him. He continues matter-of-factly.*] 75 Supper's ready.

SIMEON *and* PETER [*together*]. Ay-eh.

EBEN [*gazing up at the sky*]. Sun's downin' purty.

SIMEON *and* PETER [*together*]. Ay-eh. They's 80 gold in the West.

EBEN. Ay-eh. [*Pointing.*] Yonder atop o' the hill pasture, ye mean?

SIMEON *and* PETER [*together*]. In Californi-a!

EBEN. Hunh? [*Stares at them indifferently for* 85 *a second, then drawls.*] Waal—supper's gittin' cold. [*He turns back into kitchen.*]

SIMEON [*startled—smacks his lips*]. I air hungry!

PETER [*sniffing*]. I smells bacon! 90

SIMEON [*with hungry appreciation*]. Bacon's good!

PETER [*in same tone*]. Bacon's bacon! [*They turn, shouldering each other, their bodies bumping and rubbing together as they hurry* 95 *clumsily to their food, like two friendly oxen toward their evening meal. They disappear around the right corner of house and can be heard entering the door.*]

Curtain

Scene ii

[*The color fades from the sky. Twilight be-
5 gins. The interior of the kitchen is now visible.
A pine table is at center, a cook-stove in the
right rear corner, four rough wooden chairs, a
tallow candle on the table. In the middle of the
rear wall is fastened a big advertising poster
10 with a ship in full sail and the word "California" in big letters. Kitchen utensils hang from
nails. Everything is neat and in order but the
atmosphere is of a men's camp kitchen rather
than that of a home.*

15 *Places for three are laid.* EBEN *takes boiled
potatoes and bacon from the stove and puts
them on the table, also a loaf of bread and a
crock of water.* SIMEON *and* PETER *shoulder in,
slump down in their chairs without a word.*
20 EBEN *joins them. The three eat in silence for a
moment; the two elder as naturally unrestrained as beasts of the field,* EBEN *picking at
his food without appetite, glancing at them
with a tolerant dislike.*]

25 SIMEON [*suddenly turns to* EBEN]. Looky
here! Ye'd oughtn't t' said that, Eben.

PETER. 'Twa'n't righteous.

EBEN. What?

SIMEON. Ye prayed he'd died.

30 EBEN. Waal—don't yew pray it? [*A pause.*]

PETER. He's our Paw.

EBEN [*violently*]. Not mine!

SIMEON [*dryly*]. Ye'd not let no one else say
that about yer Maw! Ha! [*He gives one abrupt
35 sardonic guffaw.* PETER *grins.*]

EBEN [*very pale*]. I meant—I hain't his'n—
I hain't like him—he hain't me!

PETER [*dryly*]. Wait till ye've growed his age!

EBEN [*intensely*]. I'm Maw—every drop o'
40 blood! [*A pause. They stare at him with indifferent curiosity.*]

PETER [*reminiscently*]. She was good t' Sim
'n' me. A good step-maw's scurse.

SIMEON. She was good t' everyone.

45 EBEN [*greatly moved, gets to his feet and
makes an awkward bow to each of them—
stammering*]. I be thankful t' ye. I'm her—her
heir. [*He sits down in confusion.*]

PETER [*after a pause—judicially*]. She was
good even t' him.   50

EBEN [*fiercely*]. An' fur thanks he killed
her!

SIMEON [*after a pause*]. No one never kills
nobody. It's allus somethin'. That's the mur-
derer.   55

EBEN. Didn't he slave Maw t' death?

PETER. He's slaved himself t' death. He's
slaved Sim 'n' me 'n' yew t' death—on'y none
o' us hain't died—yit.

SIMEON. It's somethin'—drivin' him—t' drive   60
us!

EBEN [*vengefully*]. Waal—I hold him t'
jedgment! [*Then scornfully.*] Somethin'!
What's somethin'?

SIMEON. Dunno.   65

EBEN [*sardonically*]. What's drivin' yew to
Californi-a, mebbe? [*They look at him in surprise.*] Oh, I've heerd ye! [*Then, after a
pause.*] But ye'll never go t' the gold fields!

PETER [*assertively*]. Mebbe!   70

EBEN. Whar'll ye git the money?

PETER. We kin walk. It's an a'mighty ways—
Californi-a—but if yew was t' put all the steps
we've walked on this farm end t' end we'd be
in the moon!   75

EBEN. The Injuns skulp ye on the plains.

SIMEON [*with grim humor*]. We'll mebbe
make 'em pay a hair fur a hair!

EBEN [*decisively*]. But t'aint that. Ye won't
never go because ye'll wait here fur yer share   80
o' the farm, thinkin' allus he'll die soon.

SIMEON [*after a pause*]. We've a right.

PETER. Two-thirds belong t' us.

EBEN [*jumping to his feet*]. Ye've no right!
She wa'nt yewr Maw! It was her farm! Didn't   85
he steal it from her? She's dead. It's my farm.

SIMEON [*sardonically*]. Tell that t' Paw—
when he comes! I'll bet ye a dollar he'll laugh
—fur once in his life. Ha! [*He laughs himself
in one single mirthless bark.*]   90

PETER [*amused in turn, echoes his brother*].
Ha!

SIMEON [*after a pause*]. What've ye got held

agin us, Eben? Year arter year it's skulked in yer eye—somethin'.

PETER. Ay-eh.

EBEN. Ay-eh. They's somethin'. [*Suddenly*
5 *exploding.*] Why didn't ye never stand between him 'n' my Maw when he was slavin' her to her grave—t' pay her back fur the kindness she done t' yew? [*There is a long pause. They stare at him in surprise.*]

10 SIMEON. Waal—the stock's got t' be watered.

PETER. 'R they was woodin' t' do.

SIMEON. 'R plowin'.

PETER. 'R hayin'.

SIMEON. 'R spreadin' manure.

15 PETER. 'R weedin'.

SIMEON. 'R prunin'.

PETER. 'R milkin'.

EBEN [*breaking in harshly*]. An' makin' walls—stone atop o' stone—makin' walls till
20 yer heart's a stone ye heft up out o' the way o' growth onto a stone wall t' wall in yer heart!

SIMEON [*matter-of-factly*]. We never had no time t' meddle.

PETER [*to* EBEN]. Yew was fifteen afore yer
25 Maw died—an' big fur yer age. Why didn't ye never do nothin'?

EBEN [*harshly*]. They was chores t' do, wa'n't they? [*A pause—then slowly.*] It was on'y arter she died I come to think o' it. Me
30 cookin'—doin' her work—that made me know her, suffer her sufferin'—she'd come back t' help—come back t' bile potatoes—come back t' fry bacon—come back t' bake biscuits— come back all cramped up t' shake the fire, an'
35 carry ashes, her eyes weepin' an' bloody with smoke an' cinders same's they used t' be. She still comes back—stands by the stove thar in the evenin'—she can't find it nateral sleepin' an' restin' in peace. She can't git used t' bein'
40 free—even in her grave.

SIMEON. She never complained none.

EBEN. She'd got too tired. She'd got too used t' bein' too tired. That was what he done. [*With vengeful passion.*] An' sooner'r later,
45 I'll meddle. I'll say the thin's I didn't say then t' him! I'll yell 'em at the top o' my lungs. I'll see t' it my Maw gits some rest an' sleep in her grave! [*He sits down again, relapsing into a brooding silence. They look at him with a queer indifferent curiosity.*]
50 PETER [*after a pause*]. Whar in tarnation d'ye s'pose he went, Sim?

SIMEON. Dunno. He druv off in the buggy, all spick an' span, with the mare all breshed an' shiny, druv off clackin' his tongue an' wav-
55 in' his whip. I remember it right well. I was finishin' plowin', it was spring an' May an' sunset, an' gold in the West, an' he druv off into it. I yells "Whar ye goin', Paw?" an' he hauls up by the stone wall a jiffy. His old
60 snake's eyes was glitterin' in the sun like he'd been drinkin' a jugful an' he says with a mule's grin: "Don't ye run away till I come back!"

PETER. Wonder if he knowed we was wantin' fur Californi-a?
65 SIMEON. Mebbe. I didn't say nothin' and he says, lookin' kinder queer an' sick: "I been hearin' the hens cluckin' an' the roosters crowin' all the durn day. I been listenin' t' the cows lowin' an' everythin' else kickin' up till I
70 can't stand it no more. It's spring an' I'm feelin' damned," he says. "Damned like an old bare hickory tree fit on'y fur burnin'," he says. An' then I calc'late I must've looked a mite hopeful, fur he adds real spry and vicious: "But
75 don't git no fool idee I'm dead. I've sworn t' live a hundred an' I'll do it, if on'y t' spite yer sinful greed! An' now I'm ridin' out t' learn God's message t' me in the spring, like the prophets done. An' yew git back t' yer plow-
80 in'," he says. An' he druv off singin' a hymn. I thought he was drunk—'r I'd stopped him goin'.

EBEN [*scornfully*]. No, ye wouldn't! Ye're scared o' him. He's stronger—inside—than
85 both o' ye put together!

PETER [*sardonically*]. An' yew—be yew Samson?

EBEN. I'm gittin' stronger. I kin feel it growin' in me—growin' an' growin'—till it'll bust
90 out—! [*He gets up and puts on his coat and a hat. They watch him, gradually breaking into grins.* EBEN *avoids their eyes sheepishly.*] I'm goin' out for a spell—up the road.

PETER. T' the village?

SIMEON. T' see Minnie?

EBEN [*defiantly*]. Ay-eh!

PETER [*jeeringly*]. The Scarlet Woman!

5 SIMEON. Lust—that's what's growin' in ye!

EBEN. Waal—she's purty!

PETER. She's been purty fur twenty year!

SIMEON. A new coat o' paint'll make a heifer out of forty.

10 EBEN. She hain't forty!

PETER. If she hain't, she's teeterin' on the edge.

EBEN [*desperately*]. What d'yew know—

PETER. All they is . . . Sim knew her—an'

15 then me arter—

SIMEON. An' Paw kin tell yew somethin' too! He was fust!

EBEN. D'ye mean t' say he . . . ?

SIMEON [*with a grin*]. Ay-eh! We air his

20 heirs in everythin'!

EBEN [*intensely*]. That's more to it! That grows on it! It'll bust soon! [*Then violently.*] I'll go smash my fist in her face! [*He pulls open the door in rear violently.*]

25 SIMEON [*with a wink at* PETER—*drawlingly*]. Mebbe—but the night's wa'm—purty—by the time ye git thar mebbe ye'll kiss her instead!

PETER. Sart'n he will! [*They both roar with coarse laughter.* EBEN *rushes out and slams the

30 door—then the outside front door—comes around the corner of the house and stands still by the gate, staring up at the sky.*]

SIMEON [*looking after him*]. Like his Paw.

PETER. Dead spit an' image!

35 SIMEON. Dog'll eat dog!

PETER. Ay-eh. [*Pause. With yearning.*] Mebbe a year from now we'll be in Californi-a.

SIMEON. Ay-eh. [*A pause. Both yawn.*] Let's git t' bed. [*He blows out the candle. They go

40 out door in rear.* EBEN *stretches his arms up to the sky—rebelliously.*]

EBEN. Waal—thar's a star, an' somewhar's they's him, an' here's me, an' thar's Min up the road—in the same night. What if I does

45 kiss her? She's like t'night, she's soft 'n' wa'm, her eyes kin wink like a star, her mouth's wa'm, her arms're wa'm, she smells like a wa'm

plowed field, she's purty. . . . Ay-eh! By God A'mighty she's purty, an' I don't give a damn how many sins she's sinned afore mine or who 50 she's sinned 'em with, my sin's as purty as any one of 'em! [*He strides off down the road to the left.*]

Curtain

Scene iii

[*It is the pitch darkness just before dawn.* EBEN *comes in from the left and goes around to* 55 *the porch, feeling his way, chuckling bitterly and cursing half-aloud to himself.*]

EBEN. The cussed old miser! [*He can be heard going in the front door. There is a pause as he goes upstairs, then a loud knock on the* 60 *bedroom door of the brothers.*] Wake up!

SIMEON [*startledly*]. Who's thar?

EBEN [*pushing open the door and coming in, a lighted candle in his hand. The bedroom of the brothers is revealed. Its ceiling is the slop-* 65 *ing roof. They can stand upright only close to the center dividing wall of the upstairs.* SIMEON *and* PETER *are in a double bed, front.* EBEN's *cot is to the rear.* EBEN *has a mixture of silly grin and vicious scowl on his face*]. I be! 70

PETER [*angrily*]. What in hell's-fire . . . ?

EBEN. I got news fur ye! Ha! [*He gives one abrupt sardonic guffaw.*]

SIMEON [*angrily*]. Couldn't ye hold it 'til we'd got our sleep? 75

EBEN. It's nigh sunup. [*Then explosively.*] He's gone an' married agen!

SIMEON *and* PETER [*explosively*]. Paw?

EBEN. Got himself hitched to a female 'bout thirty-five—an' purty, they says. . . . 80

SIMEON [*aghast*]. It's a durn lie!

PETER. Who says?

SIMEON. They been stringin' ye!

EBEN. Think I'm a dunce, do ye? The hull village says. The preacher from New Dover, 85 he brung the news—told it t' our preacher— New Dover, that's whar the old loon got himself hitched—that's whar the woman lived—

PETER [*no longer doubting—stunned*]. Waal . . . ! 90

SIMEON [*the same*]. Waal . . . !

EBEN [*sitting down on a bed—with vicious hatred*]. Ain't he a devil out o' hell? It's jest t' spite us—the damned old mule!

PETER [*after a pause*]. Everythin'll go t' her now.

SIMEON. Ay-eh. [*A pause—dully.*] Waal—if it's done—

PETER. It's done us. [*Pause—then persuasively.*] They's gold in the fields o' Californi-a, Sim. No good a-stayin' here now.

SIMEON. Jest what I was a-thinkin'. [*Then with decision.*] S'well fust's last! Let's light out and git this mornin'.

PETER. Suits me.

EBEN. Ye must like walkin'.

SIMEON [*sardonically*]. If ye'd grow wings on us we'd fly thar!

EBEN. Ye'd like ridin' better—on a boat, wouldn't ye? [*Fumbles in his pocket and takes out a crumpled sheet of foolscap.*] Waal, if ye sign this ye kin ride on a boat. I've had it writ out an' ready in case ye'd ever go. It says fur three hundred dollars t' each ye agree yewr shares o' the farm is sold t' me. [*They look suspiciously at the paper. A pause.*]

SIMEON [*wonderingly*]. But if he's hitched agen—

PETER. An' whar'd yew git that sum of money, anyways?

EBEN [*cunningly*]. I know whar it's hid. I been waitin'—Maw told me. She knew whar it lay fur years, but she was waitin'. . . . It's her'n—the money he hoarded from her farm an' hid from Maw. It's my money by rights now.

PETER. Whar's it hid?

EBEN [*cunningly*]. Whar yew won't never find it without me. Maw spied on him—'r she'd never knowed. [*A pause. They look at him suspiciously, and he at them.*] Waal, is it fa'r trade?

SIMEON. Dunno.

PETER. Dunno.

SIMEON [*looking at window*]. Sky's grayin'.

PETER. Ye better start the fire, Eben.

SIMEON. An' fix some vittles.

EBEN. Ay-eh. [*Then with a forced jocular heartiness.*] I'll git ye a good one. If ye're startin' t' hoof it t' Californi-a ye'll need somethin' that'll stick t' yer ribs. [*He turns to the door, adding meaningly.*] But ye kin ride on a boat if ye'll swap. [*He stops at the door and pauses. They stare at him.*]

SIMEON [*suspiciously*]. Whar was ye all night?

EBEN [*defiantly*]. Up t' Min's. [*Then slowly.*] Walkin' thar, fust I felt 's if I'd kiss her; then I got a-thinkin' o' what ye'd said o' him an' her an' I says, I'll bust her nose fur that! Then I got t' the village an' heerd the news an' I got madder'n hell an' run all the way t' Min's not knowin' what to do— [*He pauses—then sheepishly but more defiantly.*] Waal—when I seen her, I didn't hit her—nor I didn't kiss her nuther —I begun t' beller like a calf an' cuss at the same time, I was so durn mad—an' she got scared—an' I jest grabbed holt an' tuk her! [*Proudly.*] Yes, siree! I tuk her. She may've been his'n—an' yourn', too—but she's mine now!

SIMEON [*dryly*]. In love, air yew?

EBEN [*with lofty scorn*]. Love! I don't take no stock in sech slop!

PETER [*winking at* SIMEON]. Mebbe Eben's aimin' t' marry, too.

SIMEON. Min'd make a true faithful he'p-meet! [*They snicker.*]

EBEN. What do I care fur her—'ceptin' she's round an' wa'm? The p'int is she was his'n— an' now she b'longs t' me! [*He goes to the door —then turns—rebelliously.*] An' Min hain't sech a bad un. They's worse'n Min in the world, I'll bet ye! Wait'll we see this cow the Old Man's hitched t'! She'll beat Min, I got a notion! [*He starts to go out.*]

SIMEON [*suddenly*]. Mebbe ye'll try t' make her your'n, too?

PETER. Ha! [*He gives a sardonic laugh of relish at this idea.*]

EBEN [*spitting with disgust*]. Her—here— sleepin' with him—stealin' my Maw's farm! I'd as soon pet a skunk 'r kiss a snake! [*He goes out. The two stare after him suspiciously. A pause. They listen to his steps receding.*]

PETER. He's startin' the fire.

SIMEON. I'd like t' ride t' Californi-a—but—

PETER. Min might o' put some scheme in his head.

SIMEON. Mebbe it's all a lie 'bout Paw marryin'. We'd best wait an' see the bride.

5 PETER. An' don't sign nothin' till we does!

SIMEON. Nor till we've tested it's good money! [*Then with a grin.*] But if Paw's hitched we'd be sellin' Eben somethin' we'd never git nohow!

10 PETER. We'll wait an' see. [*Then with sudden vindictive. anger.*] An' till he comes, let's yew 'n' me not wuk a lick, let Eben tend to thin's if he's a mind t', let's us jest sleep an' eat an' drink likker an' let the hull damned farm go
15 t' blazes!

SIMEON [*excitedly*]. By God, we've 'arned a rest! We'll play rich fur a change. I hain't a-going to stir outa bed till breakfast's ready.

PETER. An' on the table!

20 SIMEON [*after a pause—thoughtfully*]. What d'ye calc'late she'll be like—our new Maw? Like Eben thinks?

PETER. More'n likely.

SIMEON [*vindictively*]. Waal—I hope she's a
25 she-devil that'll make him wish he was dead an' livin' in the pit o' hell fur comfort!

PETER [*fervently*]. Amen!

SIMEON [*imitating his father's voice*]. "I'm ridin' out t' learn God's message t' me in the
30 spring like the prophets done," he says. I'll bet right then an' thar he knew plumb well he was goin' whorin', the stinkin' old hypocrite!

Curtain

Scene iv

[*Same as Scene ii—shows the interior of the kitchen with a lighted candle on table. It is
35 gray dawn outside. SIMEON and PETER are just finishing their breakfast. EBEN sits before his plate of untouched food, brooding frowningly.*]

PETER [*glancing at him rather irritably*].
40 Lookin' glum don't help none.

SIMEON [*sarcastically*]. Sorrowin' over his lust o' the flesh!

PETER [*with a grin*]. Was she yer fust?

EBEN [*angrily*]. None o' yer business. [*A
45 pause.*] I was thinkin' o' him. I got a notion he's gittin' near—I kin feel him comin' on like yew kin feel malaria chill afore it takes ye.

PETER. It's too early yet.

SIMEON. Dunno. He'd like t' catch us nappin'
—jest t' have somethin' t' hoss us 'round over. 50

PETER [*mechanically gets to his feet. SIMEON does the same*]. Waal—let's git t' wuk. [*They both plod mechanically toward the door before they realize. Then they stop short.*]

SIMEON [*grinning*]. Ye're a cussed fool, Pete 55
—and I be wuss! Let him see we hain't wukin'! We don't give a durn!

PETER [*as they go back to the table*]. Not a damned durn! It'll serve t' show him we're done with him. [*They sit down again. EBEN 60 stares from one to the other with surprise.*]

SIMEON [*grins at him*]. We're aimin' t' start bein' lilies o' the field.

PETER. Nary a toil 'r spin 'r lick o' wuk do we put in! 65

SIMEON. Ye're sole owner—till he comes—that's what ye wanted. Waal, ye got t' be sole hand, too.

PETER. The cows air bellerin'. Ye better hustle at the milkin'. 70

EBEN [*with excited joy*]. Ye mean ye'll sign the paper?

SIMEON [*dryly*]. Mebbe.

PETER. Mebbe.

SIMEON. We're considerin'. [*Peremptorily.*] 75 Ye better git t' wuk.

EBEN [*with queer excitement*]. It's Maw's farm agen! It's my farm! Them's my cows! I'll milk my durn fingers off fur cows o' mine! [*He goes out door in rear, they stare after him 80 indifferently.*]

SIMEON. Like his Paw.

PETER. Dead spit 'n' image!

SIMEON. Waal—let dog eat dog! [*EBEN comes out of front door and around the corner of the 85 house. The sky is beginning to grow flushed with sunrise. EBEN stops by the gate and stares around him with glowing, possessive eyes. He takes in the whole farm with his embracing glance of desire.*] 90

EBEN. It's purty! It's damned purty! It's mine! [*He suddenly throws his head back boldly and glares with hard, defiant eyes at the sky.*] Mine, d'ye hear? Mine! [*He turns and walks quickly off left, rear, toward the barn. The two brothers light their pipes.*]

5 SIMEON [*putting his muddy boots up on the table, tilting back his chair, and puffing defiantly*]. Waal—this air solid comfort—fur once.

PETER. Ay-eh. [*He follows suit. A pause. Unconsciously they both sigh.*]

10 SIMEON [*suddenly*]. He never was much o' a hand at milkin', Eben wa'n't.

PETER [*with a snort*]. His hands air like hoofs! [*A pause.*]

SIMEON. Reach down the jug thar! Let's take
15 a swaller. I'm feelin' kind o' low.

PETER. Good idee! [*He does so—gets two glasses—they pour out drinks of whisky.*] Here's t' the gold in Californi-a!

SIMEON. An' luck t' find it! [*They drink—*
20 *puff resolutely—sigh—take their feet down from the table.*]

PETER. Likker don't 'pear t' sot right.

SIMEON. We hain't used t' it this early. [*A pause. They become very restless.*]

25 PETER. Gittin' close in this kitchen.

SIMEON [*with immense relief*]. Let's git a breath o' air. [*They arise briskly and go out rear—appear around house and stop by the gate. They stare up at the sky with a numbed
30 appreciation.*]

PETER. Purty!

SIMEON. Ay-eh. Gold's t' the East now.

PETER. Sun's startin' with us fur the Golden West.

35 SIMEON [*staring around the farm, his compressed face tightened, unable to conceal his emotion*]. Waal—it's our last mornin'—mebbe.

PETER [*the same*]. Ay-eh.

SIMEON [*stamps his foot on the earth and
40 addresses it desperately*]. Waal—ye've thirty year o' me buried in ye—spread out over ye—blood an' bone an' sweat—rotted away—fertilizin' ye—richin' yer soul—prime manure, by God, that's what I been t' ye!

45 PETER. Ay-eh! An' me!

SIMEON. An' yew, Peter. [*He sighs—then spits.*] Waal—no use'n cryin' over spilt milk.

PETER. They's gold in the West—an' free-

dom, mebbe. We been slaves t' stone walls here.   50

SIMEON [*defiantly*]. We hain't nobody's slaves from this out—nor no thin's slaves nuther. [*A pause—restlessly.*] Speakin' o' milk, wonder how Eben's managin'?

PETER. I s'pose he's managin'.   55

SIMEON. Mebbe we'd ought t' help—this once.

PETER. Mebbe. The cows knows us.

SIMEON. An' likes us. They don't know him much.   60

PETER. An' the hosses, an' pigs, an' chickens. They don't know him much.

SIMEON. They knows us like brothers—an' likes us! [*Proudly.*] Hain't we raised 'em t' be fust-rate, number one prize stock?   65

PETER. We hain't—not no more.

SIMEON [*dully*]. I was fergettin'. [*Then resignedly.*] Waal, let's go help Eben a spell an' git waked up.

PETER. Suits me. [*They are starting off down   70
left, rear, for the barn when* EBEN *appears from there hurrying toward them, his face excited.*]

EBEN [*breathlessly*]. Waal—thar they be! The old mule an' the bride! I seen 'em from the barn down below at the turnin'.   75

PETER. How could ye tell that far?

EBEN. Hain't I as far-sight as he's near-sight? Don't I know the mare 'n' buggy, an' two people settin' in it? Who else . . . ? An' I tell ye I kin feel 'em a-comin', too! [*He squirms   80
as if he had the itch.*]

PETER [*beginning to be angry*]. Waal—let him do his own unhitchin'!

SIMEON [*angry in his turn*]. Let's hustle in an' git our bundles an' be a-goin' as he's a-   85
comin'. I don't want never t' step inside the door agen arter he's back. [*They both start back around the corner of the house.* EBEN *follows them.*]

EBEN [*anxiously*]. Will ye sign it afore ye   90
go?

PETER. Let's see the color o' the old skinflint's money an' we'll sign. [*They disappear left. The two brothers clump upstairs to get their bundles.* EBEN *appears in the kitchen, runs to   95
window, peers out, comes back and pulls up*

a strip of flooring in under stove, takes out a
canvas bag and puts it on table, then sets the
floorboard back in place. The two brothers ap-
pear a moment after. They carry old carpet-
5 *bags.]*

EBEN [*puts his hand on bag guardingly*].
Have ye signed?

SIMEON [*shows paper in his hand*]. Ay-eh.
[*Greedily.*] Be that the money?

10 EBEN [*opens bag and pours out pile of*
twenty-dollar gold pieces]. Twenty-dollar
pieces—thirty of 'em. Count 'em. [PETER *does*
so, arranging them in stacks of five, biting one
or two to test them.]

15 PETER. Six hundred. [*He puts them in bag*
and puts it inside his shirt carefully.]

SIMEON [*handing paper to* EBEN]. Har ye be.

EBEN [*after a glance, folds it carefully and*
hides it under his shirt—gratefully]. Thank
20 yew.

PETER. Thank yew fur the ride.

SIMEON. We'll send ye a lump o' gold fur
Christmas. [*A pause.* EBEN *stares at them and*
they at him.]

25 PETER [*awkwardly*]. Waal—we're a-goin'.

SIMEON. Comin' out t' the yard?

EBEN. No. I'm waitin' in here a spell.
[*Another silence. The brothers edge awkwardly*
to door in rear—then turn and stand.]

30 SIMEON. Waal—good-by.

PETER. Good-by.

EBEN. Good-by. [*They go out. He sits down*
at the table, faces the stove and pulls out the
paper. He looks from it to the stove. His face,
35 *lighted up by the shaft of sunlight from the*
window, has an expression of trance. His lips
move. The two brothers come out to the gate.]

PETER [*looking off toward barn*]. Thar he be
—unhitchin'.

40 SIMEON [*with a chuckle*]. I'll bet ye he's
riled!

PETER. An' thar she be.

SIMEON. Let's wait 'n' see what our new Maw
looks like.

45 PETER [*with a grin*]. An' give him our part-
in' cuss!

SIMEON [*grinning*]. I feel like raisin' fun. I
feel light in my head an' feet.

PETER. Me, too. I feel like laffin' till I'd split
up the middle. 50

SIMEON. Reckon it's the likker?

PETER. No. My feet feel itchin' t' walk an'
walk—an' jump high over thin's—an'. . . .

SIMEON. Dance? [*A pause.*]

PETER [*puzzled*]. It's plumb onnateral. 55

SIMEON [*a light coming over his face*]. I
calc'late it's 'cause school's out. It's holiday.
Fur once we're free!

PETER [*dazedly*]. Free?

SIMEON. The halter's broke—the harness is 60
busted—the fence bars is down—the stone
walls air crumblin' an' tumblin'! We'll be
kickin' up an' tearin' away down the road!

PETER [*drawing a deep breath—oratorically*].
Anybody that wants this stinkin' old rock-pile 65
of a farm kin hev it. T'aint our'n, no sirree!

SIMEON [*takes the gate off its hinges and puts*
it under his arm]. We harby 'bolishes shet
gates, an' open gates, an' all gates, by thunder!

PETER. We'll take it with us fur luck an' let 70
'er sail free down some river.

SIMEON [*as a sound of voices comes from*
left, rear]. Har they comes! [*The two brothers*
congeal into two stiff, grim-visaged statues.
EPHRAIM CABOT *and* ABBIE PUTNAM *come in.* 75
CABOT *is seventy-five, tall and gaunt, with*
great, wiry, concentrated power, but stoop-
shouldered from toil. His face is as hard as if
it were hewn out of a boulder, yet there is a
weakness in it, a petty pride in its own nar- 80
row strength. His eyes are small, close to-
gether, and extremely near-sighted, blinking
continually in the effort to focus on objects,
their stare having a straining, ingrowing
quality. He is dressed in his dismal black Sun- 85
day suit. ABBIE *is thirty-five, buxom, full of*
vitality. Her round face is pretty but marred
by its rather gross sensuality. There is strength
and obstinacy in her jaw, a hard determination
in her eyes, and about her whole personality 90
the same unsettled, untamed, desperate quality
which is so apparent in EBEN.]

CABOT [*as they enter—a queer strangled*
emotion in his dry cracking voice]. Har we be
t' hum, Abbie. 95

ABBIE [*with lust for the word*]. Hum! [*Her*

eyes gloating on the house without seeming to see the two stiff figures at the gate.] It's purty—purty! I can't b'lieve it's r'ally mine.

CABOT [sharply]. Yewr'n? Mine! [He stares 5 at her penetratingly, she stares back. He adds relentingly.] Our'n—mebbe! It was lonesome too long. I was growin' old in the spring. A hum's got t' hev a woman.

ABBIE [her voice taking possession]. A 10 woman's got t' hev a hum!

CABOT [nodding uncertainly]. Ay-eh. [Then irritably.] Whar be they? Ain't thar nobody about—'r wukin'—'r nothin'?

ABBIE [sees the brothers. She returns their 15 stare of cold appraising contempt with interest —slowly]. Thar's two men loafin' at the gate an' starin' at me like a couple o' strayed hogs.

CABOT [straining his eyes]. I kin see 'em—but I can't make out. . . .

20 SIMEON. It's Simeon.

PETER. It's Peter.

CABOT [exploding]. Why hain't ye wukin'?

SIMEON [dryly]. We're waitin' to welcome ye hum—yew an' the bride!

25 CABOT [confusedly]. Huh? Waal—this be yer new Maw, boys.

[She stares at them and they at her.]

SIMEON [turns away and spits contemptuously]. I see her!

30 PETER [spits also]. An' I see her!

ABBIE [with the conqueror's conscious superiority]. I'll go in an' look at my house. [She goes slowly around to porch.]

SIMEON [with a snort]. Her house!

35 PETER [calls after her]. Ye'll find Eben inside. Ye better not tell him it's yewr house.

ABBIE [mouthing the name]. Eben. [Then quietly.] I'll tell Eben.

CABOT [with a contemptuous sneer]. Ye 40 needn't heed Eben. Eben's a dumb fool—like his Maw—soft an' simple!

SIMEON [with his sardonic burst of laughter]. Ha! Eben's a chip o' yew—spit 'n' image—hard 'n' bitter's a hickory tree! Dog'll eat dog! He'll 45 eat ye yet, old man!

CABOT [commandingly]. Ye git t' wuk!

SIMEON [as ABBIE disappears in house—winks at PETER and says tauntingly]. So that

thar's our new Maw, be it? Whar in hell did ye dig her up? [He and PETER laugh.] 50

PETER. Ha! Ye'd better turn her in the pen with the other sows. [They laugh uproariously, slapping their thighs.]

CABOT [so amazed at their effrontery that he stutters in confusion]. Simeon! Peter! What's 55 come over ye? Air ye drunk?

SIMEON. We're free, old man—free o' yew an' the hull damned farm! [They grow more and more hilarious and excited.]

PETER. An' we're startin' out fur the gold 60 field o' Californi-a!

SIMEON. Ye kin take this place an' burn it!

PETER. An' bury it—fur all we cares!

SIMEON. We're free, old man! [He cuts a caper.] 65

PETER. Free! [He gives a kick in the air.]

SIMEON [in a frenzy]. Whoop!

PETER. Whoop! [They do an absurd Indian war dance about the old man who is petrified between rage and the fear that they are insane.] 70

SIMEON. We're free as Injuns! Lucky we don't skulp ye!

PETER. An' burn yer barn an' kill the stock!

SIMEON. An' rape yer new woman! Whoop! [He and PETER stop their dance, holding their 75 sides, rocking with wild laughter.]

CABOT [edging away]. Lust fur gold—fur the sinful, easy gold o' Californi-a! It's made ye mad!

SIMEON [tauntingly]. Wouldn't yer like us to 80 send ye back some sinful gold, ye old sinner?

PETER. They's gold besides what's in Californi-a! [He retreats back beyond the vision of the old man and takes the bag of money and flaunts it in the air above his head, laughing.] 85

SIMEON. And sinfuller, too!

PETER. We'll be voyagin' on the sea! Whoop! [He leaps up and down.]

SIMEON. Livin' free! Whoop! [He leaps in turn.] 90

CABOT [suddenly roaring with rage]. My cuss on ye!

SIMEON. Take our'n in trade fur it! Whoop!

CABOT. I'll hev ye both chained up in the asylum! 95

PETER. Ye old skinflint! Good-by!

SIMEON. Ye old blood sucker! Good-by!

CABOT. Go afore I . . . !

PETER. Whoop! [*He picks a stone from the road.* SIMEON *does the same.*]

SIMEON. Maw'll be in the parlor.

PETER. Ay-eh! One! Two!

CABOT [*frightened*]. What air ye . . . ?

PETER. Three! [*They both throw, the stones hitting the parlor window with a crash of glass, tearing the shade.*]

SIMEON. Whoop!

PETER. Whoop!

CABOT [*in a fury now, rushing toward them*]. If I kin lay hands on ye—I'll break yer bones fur ye! [*But they beat a capering retreat before him,* SIMEON *with the gate still under his arm.* CABOT *comes back, panting with impotent rage. Their voices as they go off take up the song of the gold-seekers to the old tune of "Oh, Susannah!"*]

"I jumped aboard the Liza ship,
And traveled on the sea.
And every time I thought of home
I wished it wasn't me!

Oh! Californi-a,
That's the land fur me!
I'm off to Californi-a!
With my wash bowl on my knee."

[*In the meantime, the window of the upper bedroom on right is raised and* ABBIE *sticks her head out. She looks down at* CABOT—*with a sigh of relief.*]

ABBIE. Waal—that's the last o' them two, hain't it? [*He doesn't answer. Then in possessive tones.*] This here's a nice bedroom, Ephraim. It's a r'al nice bed. Is it my room, Ephraim?

CABOT [*grimly—without looking up*]. Our'n! [*She cannot control a grimace of aversion and pulls back her head slowly and shuts the window. A sudden horrible thought seems to enter* CABOT'S *head.*] They been up to somethin'! Mebbe—mebbe they've pizened the stock—'r somethin'! [*He almost runs off down toward the barn. A moment later the kitchen door is slowly pushed open and* ABBIE *enters. For a moment she stands looking at* EBEN. *He does not notice her at first. Her eyes take him in penetratingly with a calculating appraisal of his strength as against hers. But under this her desire is dimly awakened by his youth and good looks. Suddenly he becomes conscious of her presence and looks up. Their eyes meet. He leaps to his feet, glowering at her speechlessly.*]

ABBIE [*in her most seductive tones which she uses all through this scene*]. Be you—Eben? I'm Abbie— [*She laughs.*] I mean, I'm yer new Maw.

EBEN [*viciously*]. No, damn ye!

ABBIE [*as if she hadn't heard—with a queer smile*]. Yer Paw's spoke a lot o' yew. . . .

EBEN. Ha!

ABBIE. Ye mustn't mind him. He's an old man. [*A long pause. They stare at each other.*] I don't want t' pretend playin' Maw t' ye, Eben. [*Admiringly.*] Ye're too big an' too strong fur that. I want t' be frens with ye. Mebbe with me fur a fren ye'd find ye'd like livin' here better. I kin make it easy fur ye with him, mebbe. [*With a scornful sense of power.*] I calc'late I kin git him t' do most anythin' fur me.

EBEN [*with bitter scorn*]. Ha! [*They stare again,* EBEN *obscurely moved, physically attracted to her—in forced stilted tones.*] Yew kin go t' the devil!

ABBIE [*calmly*]. If cussin' me does ye good, cuss all ye've a mind t'. I'm all prepared t' have ye agin me—at fust. I don't blame ye nuther. I'd feel the same at any stranger comin' t' take my Maw's place. [*He shudders. She is watching him carefully.*] Yew must've cared a lot fur yewr Maw, didn't ye? My Maw died afore I'd growed. I don't remember her none. [*A pause.*] But yew won't hate me long, Eben. I'm not the wust in the world—an' yew an' me've got a lot in common. I kin tell that by lookin' at ye. Waal—I've had a hard life, too—oceans o' trouble an' nuthin' but wuk fur reward. I was a orphan early an' had t' wuk fur others in other folks' hums. Then I married an' he turned out a drunken spreer an' so he had to wuk for others an' me too agen in other folks' hums, an' the baby died, an' my husband got sick an' died too, an' I was glad sayin' now I'm free fur once, on'y I diskivered right away all

I was free fur was t' wuk agen in other folks' hums, doin' other folks' wuk till I'd most give up hope o' ever doin' my own wuk in my own hum, an' then your Paw come. . . . [CABOT

5 *appears returning from the barn. He comes to the gate and looks down the road the brothers have gone. A faint strain of their retreating voices is heard: "Oh, Californi-a! That's the place for me." He stands glowering, his fist*

10 *clenched, his face grim with rage.*]

EBEN [*fighting against his growing attraction and sympathy—harshly*]. An' bought yew— like a harlot! [*She is stung and flushes angrily. She has been sincerely moved by the recital of*

15 *her troubles. He adds furiously.*] An' the price he's payin' ye—this farm—was my Maw's, damn ye!—an' mine now!

ABBIE [*with a cool laugh of confidence*]. Yewr'n? We'll see 'bout that! [*Then strongly.*]

20 Waal—what if I did need a hum? What else'd I marry an old man like him fur?

EBEN [*maliciously*]. I'll tell him ye said that!

ABBIE [*smiling*]. I'll say ye're lyin' a-purpose —an' he'll drive ye off the place!

25 EBEN. Ye devil!

ABBIE [*defying him*]. This be my farm—this be my hum—this be my kitchen—!

EBEN [*furiously, as if he were going to attack her.*] Shut up, damn ye!

30 ABBIE [*walks up to him—a queer coarse expression of desire in her face and body— slowly*]. An' upstairs—that be my bedroom— an' my bed! [*He stares into her eyes, terribly confused and torn. She adds softly.*] I hain't

35 bad nor mean—'ceptin' fur an enemy—but I got t' fight fur what's due me out o' life, if I ever 'spect t' git it. [*Then putting her hand on his arm—seductively.*] Let's yew 'n' me be frens, Eben.

40 EBEN [*stupidly—as if hypnotized*]. Ay-eh. [*Then furiously flinging off her arm.*] No, ye durned old witch! I hate ye! [*He rushes out the door.*]

ABBIE [*looks after him smiling satisfiedly—

45 then half to herself, mouthing the word*]. Eben's nice. [*She looks at the table, proudly.*] I'll wash up *my* dishes now. [EBEN *appears*

outside, slamming the door behind him. He comes around corner, stops on seeing his father, and stands staring at him with hate.]

50 CABOT [*raising his arms to heaven in the fury he can no longer control*]. Lord God o' Hosts, smite the undutiful sons with Thy wust cuss!

EBEN [*breaking in violently*]. Yew 'n' yewr

55 God! Allus cussin' folks—allus naggin' 'em!

CABOT [*oblivious to him—summoningly*]. God o' the old! God o' the lonesome!

EBEN [*mockingly*]. Naggin' His sheep t' sin! T' hell with yewr God! [CABOT *turns. He and*

60 EBEN *glower at each other.*]

CABOT [*harshly*]. So it's yew. I might've knowed it. [*Shaking his finger threateningly at him.*] Blasphemin' fool! [*Then quickly.*] Why hain't ye t' wuk?

65 EBEN. Why hain't yew? They've went. I can't wuk it all alone.

CABOT [*contemptuously*]. Nor noways! I'm wuth ten o' ye yit, old's I be! Ye'll never be more'n half a man! [*Then, matter-of-factly.*]

70 Waal—let's git t' the barn. [*They go. A last faint note of the "Californi-a" song is heard from the distance.* ABBIE *is washing her dishes.*]

Curtain

PART II

Scene i

[*The exterior of the farmhouse, as in Part I

75 —a hot Sunday afternoon two months later.* ABBIE, *dressed in her best, is discovered sitting in a rocker at the end of the porch. She rocks listlessly, enervated by the heat, staring in front of her with bored, half-closed eyes.*

80 EBEN *sticks his head out of his bedroom window. He looks around furtively and tries to see —or hear—if anyone is on the porch, but although he has been careful to make no noise,* ABBIE *has sensed his movement. She stops*

85 *rocking, her face grows animated and eager, she waits attentively.* EBEN *seems to feel her presence, he scowls back his thoughts of her and spits with exaggerated disdain—then with-*

draws back into the room. ABBIE *waits, holding her breath as she listens with passionate eagerness for every sound within the house.*

EBEN *comes out. Their eyes meet; his falter.*
5 *He is confused, he turns away and slams the door resentfully. At this gesture,* ABBIE *laughs tantalizingly, amused but at the same time piqued and irritated. He scowls, strides off the porch to the path and starts to walk past her*
10 *to the road with a grand swagger of ignoring her existence. He is dressed in his store suit, spruced up, his face shines from soap and water.* ABBIE *leans forward on her chair, her eyes hard and angry now, and, as he passes*
15 *her, gives a sneering, taunting chuckle.*]

EBEN [*stung—turns on her furiously*]. What air yew cacklin' 'bout?

ABBIE [*triumphant*]. Yew!

EBEN. What about me?

20 ABBIE. Ye look all slicked up like a prize bull.

EBEN [*with a sneer*]. Waal—ye hain't so durned purty yerself, be ye? [*They stare into each other's eyes, his held by hers in spite of himself, hers glowingly possessive. Their phys-*
25 *ical attraction becomes a palpable force quivering in the hot air.*]

ABBIE [*softly*]. Ye don't mean that, Eben. Ye may think ye mean it, mebbe, but ye don't. Ye can't. It's agin nature, Eben. Ye been
30 fightin' yer nature ever since the day I come —tryin' t' tell yerself I hain't purty t'ye. [*She laughs a low humid laugh without taking her eyes from his. A pause—her body squirms desirously—she murmurs languorously.*] Hain't
35 the sun strong an' hot? Ye kin feel it burnin' into the earth—Nature—makin' thin's grow —bigger 'n' bigger—burnin' inside ye—makin' ye want t' grow—into somethin' else—till ye're jined with it—an' it's your'n—but it
40 owns ye, too—an' makes ye grow bigger— like a tree—like them elums— [*She laughs again softly, holding his eyes. He takes a step toward her, compelled against his will.*] Nature'll beat ye, Eben. Ye might's well own
45 up t' it fust 's last.

EBEN [*trying to break from her spell—confusedly*]. If Paw'd hear ye goin' on .... [*Re-*

sentfully.] But ye've made such a damned idjit out o' the old devil . . . ! [ABBIE *laughs.*]

ABBIE. Waal—hain't it easier fur yew with 50 him changed softer?

EBEN [*defiantly*]. No. I'm fightin' him— fightin' yew—fightin' fur Maw's rights t' her hum! [*This breaks her spell for him. He glowers at her.*] An' I'm onto ye. Ye hain't 55 foolin' me a mite. Ye're aimin' t' swaller up everythin' an' make it your'n. Waal, you'll find I'm a heap sight bigger hunk nor yew kin chew! [*He turns from her with a sneer.*]

ABBIE [*trying to regain her ascendancy—* 60 *seductively*]. Eben!

EBEN. Leave me be! [*He starts to walk away.*]

ABBIE [*more commandingly*]. Eben!

EBEN [*stops resentfully*]. What d'ye want?

ABBIE [*trying to conceal a growing excite-* 65 *ment*]. Whar air ye goin'?

EBEN [*with malicious nonchalance*]. Oh—up the road a spell.

ABBIE. T' the village?

EBEN [*airily*]. Mebbe. 70

ABBIE [*excitedly*]. T' see that Min, I s'pose?

EBEN. Mebbe.

ABBIE [*weakly*]. What d'ye want t' waste time on her fur?

EBEN [*revenging himself now—grinning at* 75 *her*]. Ye can't beat Nature, didn't ye say? [*He laughs and again starts to walk away.*]

ABBIE [*bursting out*]. An ugly old hake!

EBEN [*with a tantalizing sneer*]. She's purtier'n yew be! 80

ABBIE. That every wuthless drunk in the country has . . . .

EBEN [*tauntingly*]. Mebbe—but she's better'n yew. She owns up fa'r 'n' squar' t' her doin's. 85

ABBIE [*furiously*]. Don't ye dare compare . . . .

EBEN. She don't go sneakin' an' stealin'— what's mine.

ABBIE [*savagely seizing on his weak point*]. 90 Your'n? Yew mean—my farm?

EBEN. I mean the farm yew sold yerself fur like any other old whore—my farm!

ABBIE [*stung—fiercely*]. Ye'll never live t' see

the day when even a stinkin' weed on it 'll belong t' ye! [*Then in a scream.*] Git out o' my sight! Go on t' yer slut—disgracin' yer Paw' 'n' me! I'll git yer Paw t' horsewhip ye
5 off the place if I want t'! Ye're only livin' here 'cause I tolerate ye! Git along! I hate the sight o' ye! [*She stops panting and glaring at him.*]

EBEN [*returning her glance in kind*]. An' I hate the sight o' yew! [*He turns and strides
10 off up the road. She follows his retreating figure with concentrated hate. Old* CABOT *appears coming up from the barn. The hard, grim expression of his face has changed. He seems in some queer way softened, mellowed.
15 His eyes have taken on a strange, incongruous dreamy quality. Yet there is no hint of physical weakness about him—rather he looks more robust and younger.* ABBIE *sees him and turns away quickly with unconcealed aversion.
20 He comes slowly up to her.*]

CABOT [*mildly*]. War yew an' Eben quarrelin' agen?

ABBIE [*shortly*]. No.

CABOT. Ye was talkin' a'mighty loud. [*He
25 sits down on the edge of porch.*]

ABBIE [*snappishly*]. If ye heerd us they hain't no need askin' questions.

CABOT. I didn't hear what ye said.

ABBIE [*relieved*]. Waal—it wa'n't nothin' t'
30 speak on.

CABOT [*after a pause*]. Eben's queer.

ABBIE [*bitterly*]. He's the dead spit 'n' image o' yew!

CABOT [*queerly interested*]. D'ye think so,
35 Abbie? [*After a pause, ruminatingly.*] Me 'n' Eben's allus fit 'n' fit. I never could b'ar him noways. He's so thunderin' soft—like his Maw.

ABBIE [*scornfully*]. Ay-eh! 'Bout as soft as yew be!

40 CABOT [*as if he hadn't heard*]. Mebbe I been too hard on him.

ABBIE [*jeeringly*]. Waal—ye're gittin' soft now—soft as slop! That's what Eben was sayin'.

45 CABOT [*his face instantly grim and ominous*]. Eben was sayin'? Waal, he'd best not do nothin' t' try me 'r he'll soon diskiver. . . . [*A pause. She keeps her face turned away. His

gradually softens. He stares up at the sky.*] Purty, hain't it? 50

ABBIE [*crossly*]. I don't see nothin' purty.

CABOT. The sky. Feels like a wa'm field up thar.

ABBIE [*sarcastically*]. Air yew aimin' t' buy up over the farm too? [*She snickers contemp-* 55 *tuously.*]

CABOT [*strangely*]. I'd like t' own my own place up thar. [*A pause.*] I'm gittin' old, Abbie. I'm gittin' ripe on the bough. [*A pause. She stares at him mystified. He goes on.*] It's allus 60 lonesome cold in the house—even when it's bilin' hot outside. Hain't yew noticed?

ABBIE. No.

CABOT. It's wa'm down t' the barn—nice smellin' an' warm—with the cows. [*A pause.*] 65 Cows is queer.

ABBIE. Like yew?

CABOT. Like Eben. [*A pause.*] I'm gittin' t' feel resigned t' Eben—jest as I got t' feel 'bout his Maw. I'm gittin' t' learn to b'ar his soft- 70 ness—jest like her'n. I calc'late I c'd a'most take t' him—if he wa'n't sech a dumb fool! [*A pause.*] I s'pose it's old age a-creepin' in my bones.

ABBIE [*indifferently*]. Waal—ye hain't dead 75 yet.

CABOT [*roused*]. No, I hain't, yew bet—not by a hell of a sight—I'm sound 'n' tough as hickory! [*Then moodily.*] But arter three score and ten the Lord warns ye t' prepare. [*A 80 pause.*] That's why Eben's come in my head. Now that his cussed sinful brothers is gone their path t' hell, they's no one left but Eben.

ABBIE [*resentfully*]. They's me, hain't they? [*Agitatedly.*] What's all this sudden likin' ye've 85 tuk to Eben? Why don't ye say nothin' 'bout me? Hain't I yer lawful wife?

CABOT [*simply*]. Ay-eh. Ye be. [*A pause— he stares at her desirously—his eyes grow avid—then with a sudden movement he seizes 90 her hands and squeezes them, declaiming in a queer camp-meeting preacher's tempo.*] Yew air my Rose o' Sharon! Behold, yew air fair; yer eyes air doves; yer lips air like scarlet; yer two breasts air like two fawns; yer navel be 95 like a round goblet; yer belly be like a heap o' wheat. . . . [*He covers her hand with kisses She does not seem to notice. She stares before her with hard angry eyes.*]

ABBIE [*jerking her hands away—harshly*]. So ye're plannin' t' leave the farm t' Eben, air ye?

CABOT [*dazedly*]. Leave . . . ? [*Then with resentful obstinacy.*] I hain't a-givin' it t' no one!

ABBIE [*remorselessly*]. Ye can't take it with ye.

CABOT [*thinks a moment—then reluctantly*]. No, I calc'late not. [*After a pause—with a strange passion.*] But if I could, I would, by the Etarnal! 'R if I could, in my dyin' hour, I'd set it afire an' watch it burn—this house an' every ear o' corn an' every tree down t' the last blade o' hay! I'd sit an' know it was all a-dyin' with me an' no one else'd ever own what was mine, what I'd made out o' nothin' with my own sweat 'n' blood! [*A pause—then he adds with a queer affection.*] 'Ceptin' the cows. Them I'd turn free.

ABBIE [*harshly*]. An' me?

CABOT [*with a queer smile*]. Ye'd be turned free, too.

ABBIE [*furiously*]. So that's the thanks I git fur marryin' ye—t' have ye change kind to Eben who hates ye, an' talk o' turnin' me out in the road.

CABOT [*hastily*]. Abbie! Ye know I wa'n't. . . .

ABBIE [*vengefully*]. Just let me tell ye a thing or two 'bout Eben! Whar's he gone? T' see that harlot, Min! I tried fur t' stop him. Disgracin' yew an' me—on the Sabbath, too!

CABOT [*rather guiltily*]. He's a sinner—nateral-born. It's lust eatin' his heart.

ABBIE [*enraged beyond endurance—wildly vindictive*]. An' his lust fur me! Kin ye find excuses fur that?

CABOT [*stares at her—after a dead pause*]. Lust—fur yew?

ABBIE [*defiantly*]. He was tryin' t' make love t' me—when ye heerd us quarrelin'.

CABOT [*stares at her—then a terrible expression of rage comes over his face—he springs to his feet shaking all over*]. By the A'mighty God—I'll end him!

ABBIE [*frightened now for* EBEN]. No! Don't ye!

CABOT [*violently*]. I'll git the shotgun an' blow his soft brains t' the top of them elums!

ABBIE [*throwing her arms around him*]. No, Ephraim!

CABOT [*pushing her away violently*]. I will, by God!

ABBIE [*in a quieting tone*]. Listen, Ephraim. 'Twa'n't nothin' bad—on'y a boy's foolin'— 'twa'n't meant serious—jest jokin' an' teasin'. . . .

CABOT. Then why did ye say—lust?

ABBIE. It must hev sounded wusser'n I meant. An' I was mad at thinkin'—ye'd leave him the farm.

CABOT [*quieter but still grim and cruel*]. Waal then, I'll horsewhip him off the place if that much'll content ye.

ABBIE [*reaching out and taking his hand*]. No. Don't think o' me! Ye mustn't drive him off. 'Tain't sensible. Who'll ye get to help ye on the farm? They's no one hereabouts.

CABOT [*considers this—then nodding his appreciation*]. Ye got a head on ye. [*Then irritably.*] Waal, let him stay. [*He sits down on the edge of the porch. She sits beside him. He murmurs contemptuously.*] I oughtn't t' git riled so—at that 'ere fool calf. [*A pause.*] But har's the p'int. What son o' mine'll keep on here t' the farm—when the Lord does call me? Simeon an' Peter air gone t' hell—an' Eben's follerin' 'em.

ABBIE. They's me.

CABOT. Ye're on'y a woman.

ABBIE. I'm yewr wife.

CABOT. That hain't me. A son is me—my blood—mine. Mine ought t' git mine. An' then it's still mine—even though I be six foot under. D'ye see?

ABBIE [*giving him a look of hatred*]. Ay-eh. I see. [*She becomes very thoughtful, her face growing shrewd, her eyes studying* CABOT *craftily.*]

CABOT. I'm gittin' old—ripe on the bough. [*Then with a sudden forced reassurance.*] Not but what I hain't a hard nut t' crack even yet

—an' fur many a year t' come! By the Etarnal, I kin break most o' the young fellers' backs at any kind o' work any day o' the year!

ABBIE [*suddenly*]. Mebbe the Lord'll give *us* a son.

CABOT [*turns and stares at her eagerly*]. Ye mean—a son—t' me 'n' yew?

ABBIE [*with a cajoling smile*]. Ye're a strong man yet, hain't ye? 'Tain't noways impossible, be it? We know that. Why d'ye stare so? Hain't ye never thought o' that afore? I been thinkin' o' it all along. Ay-eh—an' I been prayin' it'd happen, too.

CABOT [*his face growing full of joyous pride and a sort of religious ecstasy*]. Ye been prayin', Abbie?—fur a son?—t' us?

ABBIE. Ay-eh. [*With a grim resolution.*] I want a son now.

CABOT [*excitedly clutching both of her hands in his*]. It'd be the blessin' o' God, Abbie —the blessin' o' God A'mighty on me—in my old age—in my lonesomeness! They hain't nothin' I wouldn't do fur ye then, Abbie. Ye'd hev on'y t' ask it—anythin' ye'd a mind t'!

ABBIE [*interrupting*]. Would ye will the farm t' me then—t' me an' it . . . ?

CABOT [*vehemently*]. I'd do anythin' ye axed, I tell ye! I swar it! May I be everlastin' damned t' hell if I wouldn't! [*He sinks to his knees pulling her down with him. He trembles all over with the fervor of his hopes.*] Pray t' the Lord agen, Abbie. It's the Sabbath! I'll jine ye! Two prayers air better nor one. "An' God hearkened unto Rachel"! An' God hearkened unto Abbie! Pray, Abbie! Pray fur him to hearken! [*He bows his head, mumbling. She pretends to do likewise but gives him a side glance of scorn and triumph.*]

Curtain

Scene ii

[*About eight in the evening. The interior of the two bedrooms on the top floor is shown. EBEN is sitting on the side of his bed in the room on the left. On account of the heat he has taken off everything but his undershirt and pants. His feet are bare. He faces front, brooding moodily, his chin propped on his hands, a desperate expression on his face.*

In the other room CABOT and ABBIE are sitting side by side on the edge of their bed, an old four-poster with feather mattress. He is in his night shirt, she in her nightdress. He is still in the queer, excited mood into which the notion of a son has thrown him. Both rooms are lighted dimly and flickeringly by tallow candles.]

CABOT. The farm needs a son.

ABBIE. I need a son.

CABOT. Ay-eh. Sometimes ye air the farm an' sometimes the farm be yew. That's why I clove t' ye in my lonesomeness. [*A pause. He pounds his knee with his fist.*] Me an' the farm has got t' beget a son!

ABBIE. Ye'd best go t' sleep. Ye're gittin' thin's all mixed.

CABOT [*with an impatient gesture*]. No, I hain't. My mind's clear's a well. Ye don't know me, that's it. [*He stares hopelessly at the floor.*]

ABBIE [*indifferently*]. Mebbe. [*In the next room EBEN gets up and paces up and down distractedly. ABBIE hears him. Her eyes fasten on the intervening wall with concentrated attention. EBEN stops and stares. Their hot glances seem to meet through the wall. Unconsciously he stretches out his arms for her and she half rises. Then aware, he mutters a curse at himself and flings himself face downward on the bed, his clenched fists above his head, his face buried in the pillow. ABBIE relaxes with a faint sigh but her eyes remain fixed on the wall; she listens with all her attention for some movement from EBEN.*]

CABOT [*suddenly raises his head and looks at her—scornfully*]. Will ye ever know me—'r will any man 'r woman? [*Shaking his head.*] No. I calc'late 't wa'n't t' be. [*He turns away. ABBIE looks at the wall. Then, evidently unable to keep silent about his thoughts without looking at his wife, he puts out his hand and clutches her knee. She starts violently, looks at him, sees he is not watching her, concentrates again on the wall and pays no attention to what he says.*] Listen, Abbie. When I come here fifty odd year ago—I was jest twenty an' the strongest an' hardest ye ever seen—ten times

as strong an' fifty times as hard as Eben. Waal —this place was nothin' but fields o' stones. Folks laughed when I tuk it. They couldn't know what I knowed. When ye kin make corn
5 sprout out o' stones, God's livin' in yew! They wa'n't strong enuf fur that! They reckoned God was easy. They laughed. They don't laugh no more. Some died hereabouts. Some went West an' died. They're all under ground—fur
10 follerin' arter an easy God. God hain't easy. [*He shakes his head slowly.*] An' I growed hard. Folks kept allus sayin' he's a hard man like 'twas sinful t' be hard, so's at last I said back at 'em: Waal then, by thunder, ye'll git
15 me hard an' see how ye like it! [*Then suddenly.*] But I give in t' weakness once. 'Twas arter I'd been here two year. I got weak—despairful—they was so many stones. They was a party leavin', givin' up, goin' West. I jined
20 'em. We tracked on 'n' on. We come t' broad medders, plains, whar the soil was black an' rich as gold. Nary a stone. Easy. Ye'd on'y to plow an' sow an' then set an' smoke yer pipe an' watch thin's grow. I could o' been a rich
25 man—but somethin' in me fit me an' fit me— the voice o' God sayin': "This hain't wuth nothin' t' Me. Git ye back t' hum!" I got afeerd o' that voice an' I lit out back t' hum here, leavin' my claim an' crops t' whoever'd a mind
30 t' take 'em. Ay-eh. I actoolly give up what was rightful mine! God's hard, not easy! God's in the stones! Build my church on a rock—out o' stones an' I'll be in them! That's what He meant t' Peter! [*He sighs heavily—a pause.*]
35 Stones. I picked 'em up an' piled 'em into walls. Ye kin read the years o' my life in them walls, every day a hefted stone, climbin' over the hills up and down, fencin' in the fields that was mine, whar I'd made thin's grow out o' nothin'
40 —like the will o' God, like the servant o' His hand. It wa'n't easy. It was hard an' He made me hard fur it. [*He pauses.*] All the time I kept gittin' lonesomer. I tuk a wife. She bore Simeon an' Peter. She was a good woman. She wuked
45 hard. We was married twenty year. She never knowed me. She helped but she never knowed what she was helpin'. I was allus lonesome. She died. After that it wa'n't so lonesome fur a spell. [*A pause.*] I lost count o' the years. I had no time t' fool away countin' 'em. Sim an'
50 Peter helped. The farm growed. It was all mine! When I thought o' that I didn't feel lonesome. [*A pause.*] But ye can't hitch yer mind t' one thin' day an' night. I tuk another wife—Eben's Maw. Her folks was contestin' me at law over
55 my deeds t' the farm—my farm! That's why Eben keeps a-talkin' his fool talk o' this bein' his Maw's farm. She bore Eben. She was purty —but soft. She tried t' be hard. She couldn't. She never knowed me nor nothin'. It was lone-
60 somer 'n hell with her. After a matter o' sixteen odd years, she died. [*A pause.*] I lived with the boys. They hated me 'cause I was hard. I hated them 'cause they was soft. They coveted the farm without knowin' what it meant. It made
65 me bitter 'n wormwood. It aged me—them coveting what I'd made fur mine. Then this spring the call come—the voice o' God cryin' in my wilderness, in my lonesomeness—t' go out an' seek an' find! [*Turning to her with
70 strange passion.*] I sought ye an' I found ye! Yew air my Rose o' Sharon! Yer eyes air like. . . . [*She has turned a blank face, resentful eyes to his. He stares at her for a moment— then harshly.*] Air ye any the wiser fur all I've
75 told ye?

ABBIE [*confusedly*]. Mebbe.

CABOT [*pushing her away from him angrily*]. Ye don't know nothin'—nor never will. If ye don't hev a son t' redeem ye. . . . [*This is a tone
80 of cold threat.*]

ABBIE [*resentfully*]. I've prayed, hain't I?

CABOT [*bitterly*]. Pray agen—fur understandin'!

ABBIE [*a veiled threat in her tone*]. Ye'll have
85 a son out o' me, I promise ye.

CABOT. How kin ye promise?

ABBIE. I got second-sight mebbe. I kin foretell. [*She gives a queer smile.*]

CABOT. I believe ye have. Ye give me the
90 chills sometimes. [*He shivers.*] It's cold in this house. It's oneasy. They's thin's pokin' about in the dark—in the corner. [*He pulls on his trousers, tucking in his night shirt, and pulls on his boots.*]
95

ABBIE [*surprised*]. Whar air ye goin'?

CABOT [*queerly*]. Down whar it's restful—whar it's warm down t' the barn. [*Bitterly.*] I kin talk t' the cows. They know. They know the farm an' me. They'll give me peace. [*He turns to go out the door.*]

ABBIE [*a bit frightenedly*]. Air ye ailin' tonight, Ephraim?

CABOT. Growin'. Growin' ripe on the bough. [*He turns and goes, his boots clumping down the stairs.* EBEN *sits up with a start, listening.* ABBIE *is conscious of his movement and stares at the wall.* CABOT *comes out of the house around the corner and stands by the gate, blinking at the sky. He stretches up his hands in a tortured gesture.*] God A'mighty, call from the dark! [*He listens as if expecting an answer. Then his arms drop, he shakes his head and plods off toward the barn.* EBEN *and* ABBIE *stare at each other through the wall.* EBEN *sighs heavily and* ABBIE *echoes it. Both become terribly nervous, uneasy. Finally* ABBIE *gets up and listens, her ear to the wall. He acts as if he saw every move she was making, he becomes resolutely still. She seems driven into a decision—goes out the door in rear determinedly. His eyes follow her. Then as the door of his room is opened softly, he turns away, waits in an attitude of strained fixity.* ABBIE *stands for a second staring at him, her eyes burning with desire. Then with a little cry she runs over and throws her arms about his neck, she pulls his head back and covers his mouth with kisses. At first, he submits dumbly; then he puts his arms about her neck and returns her kisses, but finally, suddenly aware of his hatred, he hurls her away from him, springing to his feet. They stand speechless and breathless, panting like two animals.*]

ABBIE [*at last—painfully*]. Ye shouldn't, Eben—ye shouldn't—I'd make ye happy!

EBEN [*harshly*]. I don't want t' be happy—from yew!

ABBIE [*helplessly*]. Ye do, Eben! Ye do! Why d'ye lie?

EBEN [*viciously*]. I don't take t'ye, I tell ye! I hate the sight o' ye!

ABBIE [*with an uncertain troubled laugh*].

Waal, I kissed ye anyways—an' ye kissed back—yer lips was burnin'—ye can't lie 'bout that! [*Intensely.*] If ye don't care, why did ye kiss me back—why was yer lips burnin'?

EBEN [*wiping his mouth*]. It was like pizen on 'em. [*Then tauntingly.*] When I kissed ye back, mebbe I thought 'twas someone else.

ABBIE [*wildly*]. Min?

EBEN. Mebbe.

ABBIE [*torturedly*]. Did ye go t' see her? Did ye r'ally go? I thought ye mightn't. Is that why ye throwed me off jest now?

EBEN [*sneeringly*]. What if it be?

ABBIE [*raging*]. Then ye're a dog, Eben Cabot!

EBEN [*threateningly*]. Ye can't talk that way t' me!

ABBIE [*with a shrill laugh*]. Can't I? Did ye think I was in love with ye—a weak thin' like yew? Not much! I on'y wanted ye fur a purpose o' my own—an' I'll hev ye fur it yet 'cause I'm stronger'n yew be!

EBEN [*resentfully*]. I knowed well it was on'y part o' yer plan t' swaller everythin'!

ABBIE [*tauntingly*]. Mebbe!

EBEN [*furious*]. Git out o' my room!

ABBIE. This air my room an' ye're on'y hired help!

EBEN [*threateningly*]. Git out afore I murder ye!

ABBIE [*quite confident now*]. I hain't a mite afeerd. Ye want me, don't ye? Yes, ye do! An' yer Paw's son'll never kill what he wants! Look at yer eyes! They's lust fur me in 'em, burnin' 'em up! Look at yer lips now! They're tremblin' an' longin' t' kiss me, an' yer teeth t' bite! [*He is watching her now with a horrible fascination. She laughs a crazy triumphant laugh.*] I'm a-goin' t' make all o' this hum my hum! They's one room hain't mine yet, but it's a-goin t' be tonight. I'm a-goin' down now an' light up! [*She makes him a mocking bow.*] Won't ye come courtin' me in the best parlor, Mister Cabot?

EBEN [*staring at her—horribly confused—dully*]. Don't ye dare! It hain't been opened since Maw died an' was laid out thar! Don't

ye . . . ! [*But her eyes are fixed on his so burn-*
ingly that his will seems to wither before hers.
He stands swaying toward her helplessly.]

ABBIE [*holding his eyes and putting all her*
5 *will into her words as she backs out the door*].
I'll expect ye afore long, Eben.

EBEN [*stares after her for a while, walking*
toward the door. A light appears in the parlor
window. He murmurs]. In the parlor? [*This*
10 *seems to arouse connotations for he comes back*
and puts on his white shirt, collar, half ties the
tie mechanically, puts on coat, takes his hat,
stands barefooted looking about him in be-
wilderment, mutters wonderingly.] Maw!
15 Whar air yew? [*Then goes slowly toward the*
door in rear.]

Curtain

Scene iii

[*A few minutes later. The interior of the par-*
lor is shown. A grim, repressed room like a
tomb in which the family has been interred
20 *alive.* ABBIE *sits on the edge of the horsehair*
sofa. She has lighted all the candles and the
room is revealed in all its preserved ugliness.
A change has come over the woman. She
looks awed and frightened now, ready to run
25 *away.*

The door is opened and EBEN *appears. His*
face wears an expression of obsessed confu-
sion. He stands staring at her, his arms hang-
ing disjointedly from his shoulders, his feet
30 *bare, his hat in his hand.*]

ABBIE [*after a pause—with a nervous, for-*
mal politeness]. Won't ye set?

EBEN [*dully*]. Ay-eh. [*Mechanically he places*
his hat carefully on the floor near the door and
35 *sits stiffly beside her on the edge of the sofa. A*
pause. They both remain rigid, looking straight
ahead with eyes full of fear.]

ABBIE. When I fust come in—in the dark—
they seemed somethin' here.

40 EBEN [*simply*]. Maw.

ABBIE. I kin still feel—somethin'. . . .

EBEN. It's Maw.

ABBIE. At fust I was feered o' it. I wanted t'
yell an' run. Now—since yew come—seems

like it's growin' soft an' kind t' me. [*Address-* 45
ing the air—queerly.] Thank yew.

EBEN. Maw allus loved me.

ABBIE. Mebbe it knows I love yew, too.
Mebbe that makes it kind t' me.

EBEN [*dully*]. I dunno. I should think she'd 50
hate ye.

ABBIE [*with certainty*]. No. I kin feel it don't
—not no more.

EBEN. Hate ye fur stealin' her place—here in
her hum—settin' in her parlor whar she was 55
laid— [*He suddenly stops, staring stupidly*
before him.]

ABBIE. What is it, Eben?

EBEN [*in a whisper*]. Seems like Maw didn't
want me t' remind ye. 60

ABBIE [*excitedly*]. I knowed, Eben! It's kind
t' me! It don't b'ar me no grudges fur what I
never knowed an' couldn't help!

EBEN. Maw b'ars him a grudge.

ABBIE. Waal, so does all o' us. 65

EBEN. Ay-eh. [*With passion.*] I does, by
God!

ABBIE [*taking one of his hands in hers and*
patting it]. Thar! Don't git riled thinkin' o'
him. Think o' yer Maw who's kind t' us. Tell 70
me about yer Maw, Eben.

EBEN. They hain't nothin' much. She was
kind. She was good.

ABBIE [*putting one arm over his shoulder.*
He does not seem to notice—passionately]. I'll 75
be kind and good t' ye!

EBEN. Sometimes she used t' sing fur me.

ABBIE. I'll sing fur ye!

EBEN. This was her hum. This was her farm.

ABBIE. This is my hum! This is my farm! 80

EBEN. He married her t' steal 'em. She was
soft an' easy. He couldn't 'preciate her.

ABBIE. He can't 'preciate me!

EBEN. He murdered her with his hardness.

ABBIE. He's murderin' me! 85

EBEN. She died. [*A pause.*] Sometimes she
used to sing fur me. [*He bursts into a fit of*
sobbing.]

ABBIE [*both her arms around him—with*
wild passion.] I'll sing fur ye! I'll die fur ye! 90
[*In spite of her overwhelming desire for him,*

there is a sincere maternal love in her manner and voice—a horribly frank mixture of lust and mother love.] Don't cry, Eben! I'll take yer Maw's place! I'll be everythin' she was t' ye!
5 Let me kiss ye, Eben! *[She pulls his head around. He makes a bewildered pretense of resistance. She is tender.]* Don't be afeered! I'll kiss ye pure, Eben—same 's if I was a Maw t' ye—an' ye kin kiss me back 's if yew was my
10 son—my boy—sayin' good-night t' me! Kiss me, Eben. *[They kiss in restrained fashion. Then suddenly wild passion overcomes her. She kisses him lustfully again and again and he flings his arms about her and returns her*
15 *kisses. Suddenly, as in the bedroom, he frees himself from her violently and springs to his feet. He is trembling all over, in a strange state of terror. ABBIE strains her arms toward him with fierce pleading.]* Don't ye leave me, Eben!
20 Can't ye see it hain't enuf—lovin' ye like a Maw—can't ye see it's got t' be that an' more —much more—a hundred times more—fur me t' be happy—fur yew t' be happy?

EBEN *[to the presence he feels in the room].*
25 Maw! Maw! What d'ye want? What air ye tellin' me?

ABBIE. She's tellin' ye t' love me. She knows I love ye an' I'll be good t' ye. Can't ye feel it? Don't ye know? She's tellin' ye t' love me,
30 Eben!

EBEN. Ay-eh. I feel—mebbe she—but—I can't figger out—why—when ye've stole her place —here in her hum—in the parlor whar she was—

35 ABBIE *[fiercely].* She knows I love ye!

EBEN *[his face suddenly lighting up with a fierce, triumphant grin].* I see it! I see why. It's her vengeance on him—so's she kin rest quiet in her grave!

40 ABBIE *[wildly].* Vengeance o' God on the hull o' us! What d' we give a durn? I love ye, Eben! God knows I love ye! *[She stretches out her arms for him.]*

EBEN *[throws himself on his knees beside the*
45 *sofa and grabs her in his arms—releasing all his pent-up passion].* An' I love yew, Abbie!— now I kin say it! I been dyin' fur want o' ye—

every hour since ye come! I love ye! *[Their lips meet in a fierce, bruising kiss.]*

Curtain

Scene iv

[Exterior of the farmhouse. It is just dawn. 50 *The front door at right is opened and EBEN comes out and walks around to the gate. He is dressed in his working clothes. He seems changed. His face wears a bold and confident expression, he is grinning to himself with* 55 *evident satisfaction. As he gets near the gate, the window of the parlor is heard opening and the shutters are flung back and ABBIE sticks her head out. Her hair tumbles over her shoulders in disarray, her face is flushed, she* 60 *looks at EBEN with tender, languorous eyes and calls softly.]*

ABBIE. Eben. *[As he turns—playfully.]* Jest one more kiss afore ye go. I'm goin' to miss ye fearful all day. 65

EBEN. An' me yew, ye kin bet! *[He goes to her. They kiss several times. He draws away, laughingly.]* Thar. That's enuf, hain't it? Ye won't hev none left fur next time.

ABBIE. I got a million o' 'em left fur yew! 70 *[Then a bit anxiously.]* D'ye r'ally love me, Eben?

EBEN *[emphatically].* I like ye better'n any gal I ever knowed! That's gospel!

ABBIE. Likin' hain't lovin'. 75

EBEN. Waal then—I love ye. Now air yew satisfied?

ABBIE. Ay-eh, I be. *[She smiles at him adoringly.]*

EBEN. I better git t' the barn. The old critter's 80 liable t' suspicion an' come sneakin' up.

ABBIE *[with a confident laugh].* Let him! I kin allus pull the wool over his eyes. I'm goin' t' leave the shutters open and let in the sun 'n' air. This room's been dead long enuf. Now it's 85 goin' t' be my room!

EBEN *[frowning].* Ay-eh.

ABBIE *[hastily].* I meant—our room.

EBEN. Ay-eh.

ABBIE. We made it our'n last night, didn't 90 we? We give it life—our lovin' did. *[A pause.]*

EBEN [*with a strange look*]. Maw's gone back t' her grave. She kin sleep now.

ABBIE. May she rest in peace! [*Then tenderly rebuking.*] Ye oughtn't t' talk o' sad 5 thin's—this mornin'.

EBEN. It jest come up in my mind o' itself.

ABBIE. Don't let it. [*He doesn't answer. She yawns.*] Waal, I'm a-goin' t' steal a wink o' sleep. I'll tell the Old Man I hain't feelin' pert. 10 Let him git his own vittles.

EBEN. I see him comin' from the barn. Ye better look smart an' git upstairs.

ABBIE. Ay-eh. Good-by. Don't ferget me. [*She throws him a kiss. He grins—then squares* 15 *his shoulders and awaits his father confidently.* CABOT *walks slowly up from the left, staring up at the sky with a vague face.*]

EBEN [*jovially*]. Mornin', Paw. Star-gazin' in daylight?

20 CABOT. Purty, hain't it?

EBEN [*looking around him possessively*]. It's a durned purty farm.

CABOT. I mean the sky.

EBEN [*grinning*]. How d'ye know? Them eyes 25 o' your'n can't see that fur. [*This tickles his humor and he slaps his thigh and laughs.*] Ho-ho! That's a good un!

CABOT [*grimly sarcastic*]. Ye're feelin' right chipper, hain't ye? Whar'd ye steal the likker? 30 EBEN [*good-naturedly*]. 'Tain't likker. Jest life. [*Suddenly holding out his hand—soberly.*] Yew 'n' me is quits. Let's shake hands.

CABOT [*suspiciously*]. What's come over ye?

EBEN. Then don't. Mebbe it's jest as well. 35 [*A moment's pause.*] What's come over me? [*Queerly.*] Didn't ye feel her passin'—goin' back t' her grave?

CABOT [*dully*]. Who?

EBEN. Maw. She kin rest now an' sleep con-40 tent. She's quit with ye.

CABOT [*confusedly*]. I rested. I slept good—down with the cows. They know how t' sleep. They're teachin' me.

EBEN [*suddenly jovial again*]. Good fur the 45 cows! Waal—ye better git t' work.

CABOT [*grimly amused*]. Air ye bossin' me, ye calf?

EBEN [*beginning to laugh*]. Ay-eh! I'm bossin' yew! Ha-ha-ha! See how ye like it! Ha-ha-ha! I'm the prize rooster o' this roost. Ha- 50 ha-ha! [*He goes off toward the barn laughing.*]

CABOT [*looks after him with scornful pity*]. Soft-headed. Like his Maw. Dead spit 'n' image. No hope in him! [*He spits with contemptuous disgust.*] A born fool! [*Then mat-* 55 *ter-of-factly.*] Waal—I'm gittin' peckish. [*He goes toward door.*]

Curtain

PART III

Scene i

[*A night in late spring the following year. The kitchen and the two bedrooms upstairs are shown. The two bedrooms are dimly lighted* 60 *by a tallow candle in each.* EBEN *is sitting on the side of the bed in his room, his chin propped on his fists, his face a study of the struggle he is making to understand his conflicting emotions. The noisy laughter and music from* 65 *below where a kitchen dance is in progress annoy and distract him. He scowls at the floor.*

In the next room a cradle stands beside the double bed.

In the kitchen all is festivity. The stove has 70 *been taken down to give more room to the dancers. The chairs, with wooden benches added, have been pushed back against the walls. On these are seated, squeezed in tight against one another, farmers and their wives* 75 *and their young folks of both sexes from the neighboring farms. They are all chattering and laughing loudly. They evidently have some secret joke in common. There is no end of winking, of nudging, of meaning nods of the* 80 *head toward* CABOT *who, in a state of extreme hilarious excitement increased by the amount he has drunk, is standing near the rear door where there is a small keg of whisky and serving drinks to all the men. In the left corner,* 85 *front, dividing the attention with her husband,* ABBIE *is sitting in a rocking chair, a shawl wrapped about her shoulders. She is very pale, her face is thin and drawn, her eyes are fixed anxiously on the open door in rear as if waiting for someone.*

The musician is tuning up his fiddle, seated in the far right corner. He is a lanky young
5 *fellow with a long, weak face. His pale eyes blink incessantly and he grins about him shyly with a greedy malice.*]

ABBIE [*suddenly turning to a young girl on her right*]. Whar's Eben?

10 YOUNG GIRL [*eyeing her scornfully*]. I dunno, Mrs. Cabot. I hain't seen Eben in ages. [*Meaningly.*] Seems like he's spent most o' his time t' hum since yew come.

ABBIE [*vaguely*]. I tuk his Maw's place.

15 YOUNG GIRL. Ay-eh. So I've heerd. [*She turns away to retail this bit of gossip to her mother sitting next to her. ABBIE turns to her left to a big stoutish middle-aged man whose flushed face and starting eyes show the amount*
20 *of "likker" he has consumed.*]

ABBIE. Ye hain't seen Eben, hev ye?

MAN. No, I hain't. [*Then he adds with a wink.*] If yew hain't, who would?

ABBIE. He's the best dancer in the county.
25 He'd ought t' come an' dance.

MAN [*with a wink*]. Mebbe he's doin' the dutiful an' walkin' the kid t' sleep. It's a boy, hain't it?

ABBIE [*nodding vaguely*]. Ay-eh—born two
30 weeks back—purty's a picter.

MAN. They all is—t' their Maws. [*Then in a whisper, with a nudge and a leer.*] Listen, Abbie—if ye ever git tired o' Eben, remember me! Don't fergit now! [*He looks at her un-*
35 *comprehending face for a second—then grunts disgustedly.*] Waal—guess I'll likker agin.[*He goes over and joins CABOT who is arguing noisily with an old farmer over cows. They all drink.*]

40 ABBIE [*this time appealing to nobody in particular*]. Wonder what Eben's a-doin'? [*Her remark is repeated down the line with many a guffaw and titter until it reaches the fiddler. He fastens his blinking eyes on ABBIE.*]

45 FIDDLER [*raising his voice*]. Bet I kin tell ye, Abbie, what Eben's doin'! He's down t' the church offerin' up prayers o' thanksgivin'. [*They all titter expectantly.*]

A MAN. What fur? [*Another titter.*]

FIDDLER. 'Cause unto him a— [*He hesitates* 50
just long enough.] brother is born! [*A roar of laughter. They all look from ABBIE to CABOT. She is oblivious, staring at the door. CABOT, although he hasn't heard the words, is irritated by the laughter and steps forward, glaring* 55
about him. There is an immediate silence.]

CABOT. What're ye all bleatin' about—like a flock o' goats? Why don't ye dance, damn ye? I axed ye here t' dance—t' eat, drink an' be merry—an' thar ye set cacklin' like a lot o' 60
wet hens with the pip! Ye've swilled my likker an' guzzled my vittles like hogs, hain't ye? Then dance fur me, can't ye? That's fa'r an' squar', hain't it? [*A grumble of resentment goes around but they are all evidently in too* 65
much awe of him to express it openly.]

FIDDLER [*slyly*]. We're waitin' fur Eben. [*A suppressed laugh.*]

CABOT [*with a fierce exultation*]. T' hell with Eben! Eben's done fur now! I got a new son! 70
[*His mood switching with drunken sudden-ness.*] But ye needn't t' laugh at Eben, none o' ye! He's my blood, if he be a dumb fóol. He's better nor any o' yew! He kin do a day's work a'most up t' what I kin—an' that'd put any o' 75
yew pore critters t' shame!

FIDDLER. An' he kin do a good night's work too! [*A roar of laughter.*]

CABOT. Laugh, ye damn fools! Ye're right jist the same, Fiddler. He kin work day an' 80
night too, like I kin, if need be!

OLD FARMER [*from behind the keg where he is weaving drunkenly back and forth—with great simplicity*]. They hain't many t' touch ye, Ephraim—a son at seventy-six. That's a 85
hard man fur ye! I be on'y sixty-eight an' I couldn't do it. [*A roar of laughter in which CABOT joins uproariously.*]

CABOT [*slapping him on the back*]. I'm sorry fur ye, Hi. I'd never suspicion sech weakness 90
from a boy like yew!

OLD FARMER. An' I never reckoned yew had it in ye nuther, Ephraim. [*There is another laugh.*]

CABOT [*suddenly grim*]. I got a lot in me— 95
a hell of a lot—folks don't know on. [*Turning to THE FIDDLER.*] Fiddle 'er up, durn ye! Give 'em somethin' t' dance t'! What air ye, an orna-

ment? Hain't this a celebration? Then grease yer elbow an' go it!

FIDDLER [*seizes a drink which the* OLD FARMER *holds out to him and downs it*]. Here goes! [*He starts to fiddle "Lady of the Lake." Four young fellows and four girls form in two lines and dance a square dance. The* FIDDLER *shouts directions for the different movements, keeping his words in the rhythm of the music and interspersing them with jocular personal remarks to the dancers themselves. The people seated along the walls stamp their feet and clap their hands in unison.* CABOT *is especially active in this respect. Only* ABBIE *remains apathetic, staring at the door as if she were alone in a silent room.*]

FIDDLER. Swing your partner t' the right! That's it, Jim! Give her a b'ar hug! Her Maw hain't lookin'. [*Laughter.*] Change partners! That suits ye, don't it, Essie, now ye got Reub afore ye? Look at her redden up, will ye? Waal, life is short an' so's love, as the feller says. [*Laughter.*]

CABOT [*excitedly, stamping his foot*]. Go it, boys! Go it, gals!

FIDDLER [*with a wink at the others*]. Ye're the spryest seventy-six ever I sees, Ephraim! Now if ye'd on'y good eyesight . . . ! [*Suppressed laughter. He gives* CABOT *no chance to retort but roars.*] Promenade! Ye're walkin' like a bride down the aisle, Sarah! Waal, while they's life they's allus hope, I've heerd tell. Swing your partner to the left! Gosh A'mighty, look at Johnny Cook high-steppin'! They hain't goin' t' be much strength left fur howin' in the corn lot t'morrow. [*Laughter.*]

CABOT. Go it! Go it! [*Then suddenly, unable to restrain himself any longer, he prances into the midst of the dancers, scattering them, waving his arms about wildly.*] Ye're all hoofs! Git out o' my road! Give me room! I'll show ye dancin'. Ye're all too soft! [*He pushes them roughly away. They crowd back toward the walls, muttering, looking at him resentfully.*]

FIDDLER [*jeeringly*]. Go it, Ephraim! Go it! [*He starts "Pop Goes the Weasel," increasing the tempo with every verse until at the end he is fiddling crazily as fast as he can go.*]

CABOT [*starts to dance, which he does very well and with tremendous vigor. Then he begins to improvise, cuts incredibly grotesque capers, leaping up and cracking his heels together, prancing around in a circle with body bent in an Indian war dance, then suddenly straightening up and kicking as high as he can with both legs. He is like a monkey on a string. And all the while he intersperses his antics with shouts and derisive comments*]. Whoop! Here's dancin' fur ye! Whoop! See that! Seventy-six, if I'm a day! Hard as iron yet! Beatin' the young 'uns like I allus done! Look at me! I'd invite ye t' dance on my hundredth birthday on'y ye'll all be dead by then. Ye're a sickly generation! Yer hearts air pink, not red! Yer veins is full o' mud an' water! I be the on'y man in the county! Whoop! See that! I'm a Injun! I've killed Injuns in the West afore ye was born—an' skulped 'em too! They's a arrer wound on my backside I c'd show ye! The hull tribe chased me. I outrun 'em all—with the arrer stuck in me! An' I tuk vengeance on 'em. Ten eyes fur an eye, that was my motter! Whoop! Look at me! I kin kick the ceilin' off the room! Whoop!

FIDDLER [*stops playing—exhaustedly*]. God A'mighty, I got enuf. Ye got the devil's strength in ye.

CABOT [*delightedly*]. Did I beat yew, too? Wa'al, ye played smart. Hev a swig. [*He pours whisky for himself and* FIDDLER. *They drink. The others watch* CABOT *silently with cold, hostile eyes. There is a dead pause.* THE FIDDLER *rests.* CABOT *leans against the keg, panting, glaring around him confusedly. In the room above,* EBEN *gets to his feet and tiptoes out the door in rear, appearing a moment later in the other bedroom. He moves silently, even frightenedly, toward the cradle and stands there looking down at the baby. His face is as vague as his reactions are confused, but there is a trace of tenderness, of interested discovery. At the same moment that he reaches the cradle,* ABBIE *seems to sense something. She gets up weakly and goes to* CABOT.]

ABBIE. I'm going up t' the baby.

CABOT [*with real solicitation*]. Air ye able fur the stairs? D'ye want me t' help ye, Abbie?

ABBIE. No. I'm able. I'll be down agen soon.

CABOT. Don't ye get wore out! He needs ye, remember—our son does! [*He grins affectionately, patting her on the back. She shrinks* 5 *from his touch.*]

ABBIE [*dully*]. Don't—tech me. I'm goin'— up. [*She goes.* CABOT *looks after her. A whisper goes around the room.* CABOT *turns. It ceases. He wipes his forehead streaming with sweat.* 10 *He is breathing pantingly.*]

CABOT. I'm a-goin' out t' git fresh air. I'm feelin' a mite dizzy. Fiddle up thar! Dance, all o' ye! Here's likker fur them as wants it. Enjoy yerselves. I'll be back. [*He goes, closing the* 15 *door behind him.*]

FIDDLER [*sarcastically*]. Don't hurry none on our account! [*A suppressed laugh. He imitates* ABBIE.] Whar's Eben? [*More laughter.*]

A WOMAN [*loudly*]. What's happened in this 20 house is plain as the nose on yer face! [ABBIE *appears in the doorway upstairs and stands looking in surprise and adoration at* EBEN *who does not see her.*]

A MAN. Ssshh! He's li-ble t' be listenin' at 25 the door. That'd be like him. [*Their voices die to an intensive whispering. Their faces are concentrated on this gossip. A noise as of dead leaves in the wind comes from the room.* CABOT *has come out from the porch and stands* 30 *by the gate, leaning on it, staring at the sky blinkingly.* ABBIE *comes across the room silently.* EBEN *does not notice her until quite near.*]

EBEN [*starting*]. Abbie!

ABBIE. Ssshh! [*She throws her arms around* 35 *him. They kiss—then bend over the cradle together.*] Ain't he purty?—dead spit 'n' image o' yew!

EBEN [*pleased*]. Air he? I can't tell none.

ABBIE. E-zactly like!

40 EBEN [*frowningly*]. I don't like this. I don't like lettin' on what's mine's his'n. I been doin' that all my life. I'm gittin t' the end o' b'arin' it!

ABBIE [*putting her finger on his lips*]. We're 45 doin' the best we kin. We got t' wait. Somethin's bound t' happen. [*She puts her arms around him.*] I got t' go back.

EBEN. I'm going out. I can't b'ar it with the fiddle playin' an' the laughin'.

ABBIE. Don't git feelin' low. I love ye, Eben. 50 Kiss me. [*He kisses her. They remain in each other's arms.*]

CABOT [*at the gate, confusedly*]. Even the music can't drive it out—somethin'. Ye kin feel it droppin' off the elums, climbin' up the 55 roof, sneakin' down the chimney, pokin' in the corners! They's no peace in houses, they's no rest livin' with folks. Somethin's always livin' with ye. [*With a deep sigh.*] I'll go t' the barn an' rest a spell. [*He goes wearily toward the* 60 *barn.*]

FIDDLER [*tuning up*]. Let's celebrate the old skunk gittin' fooled! We kin have some fun now he's went. [*He starts to fiddle "Turkey in the Straw." There is real merriment now. The* 65 *young folks get up to dance.*]

Curtain

Scene ii

[*A half-hour later—Exterior—*EBEN *is standing by the gate looking up at the sky, an expression of dumb pain bewildered by itself on his face.* CABOT *appears, returning from the* 70 *barn, walking wearily, his eyes on the ground. He sees* EBEN *and his whole mood immediately changes. He becomes excited, a cruel, triumphant grin comes to his lips, he strides up and slaps* EBEN *on the back. From within comes the* 75 *whining of the fiddle and the noise of stamping feet and laughing voices.*]

CABOT. So har ye be!

EBEN [*startled, stares at him with hatred for a moment—then dully*]. Ay-eh. 80

CABOT [*surveying him jeeringly*]. Why hain't ye been in t' dance? They was all axin' fur ye.

EBEN. Let 'em ax!

CABOT. They's a hull passel o' purty gals.

EBEN. T' hell with 'em! 85

CABOT. Ye'd ought t' be marryin' one o' 'em soon.

EBEN. I hain't marryin' no one.

CABOT. Ye might 'arn a share o' a farm that way. 90

EBEN [*with a sneer*]. Like yew did, ye mean? I hain't that kind.

CABOT [*stung*]. Ye lie! 'Twas yer Maw's folks aimed t' steal my farm from me.

EBEN. Other folks don't say so. [*After a* 95

pause—defiantly.] An' I got a farm, anyways!

CABOT [*derisively*]. Whar?

EBEN [*stamps a foot on the ground*]. Har!

CABOT [*throws his head back and laughs
5 coarsely*]. Ho-ho! Ye hev, hev ye? Waal, that's
a good un!

EBEN [*controlling himself—grimly*]. Ye'll
see!

CABOT [*stares at him suspiciously, trying to
10 make him out—a pause—then with scornful
confidence*]. Ay-eh. I'll see. So'll ye. It's ye
that's blind—blind as a mole underground.
[EBEN *suddenly laughs, one short sardonic
bark: "Ha." A pause.* CABOT *peers at him with
15 renewed suspicion.*] Whar air ye hawin' 'bout?
[EBEN *turns away without answering.* CABOT
grows angry.] God A'mighty, yew air a dumb
dunce! They's nothin' in that thick skull o'
your'n but noise—like a empty keg it be!
20 [EBEN *doesn't seem to hear.* CABOT'S *rage
grows.*] Yewr farm! God A'mighty! If ye wa'n't
a born donkey ye'd know ye'll never own stick
nor stone on it, specially now arter him bein'
born. It's his'n, I tell ye—his'n arter I die—but
25 I'll live a hundred jest t' fool ye all—an' he'll
be growed then—yewr age a'most! [EBEN
laughs again his sardonic "Ha." This drives
CABOT *into a fury.*] Ha? Ye think ye kin git
'round that someways, do ye? Waal, it'll be
30 her'n, too—Abbie's—ye won't git 'round her
—she knows yer tricks—she'll be too much
fur ye—she wants the farm her'n—she was
afeerd o' ye—she told me ye was sneakin'
'round tryin' t' make love t' her t' git her on
35 yer side . . . ye . . . ye mad fool, ye! [*He raises
his clenched fists threateningly.*]

EBEN [*is confronting him choking with rage*].
Ye lie, ye old skunk! Abbie never said no sech
thing!

40 CABOT [*suddenly triumphant when he sees
how shaken* EBEN *is*]. She did. An' I says, I'll
blow his brains t' the top o' them elums—an'
she says no, that hain't sense, who'll ye git
t'help ye on the farm in his place—an' then
45 she says yew'n me ought t' have a son—I
know we kin, she says—an' I says, if we do,
ye kin have anythin' I've got ye've a mind t'.
An' she says, I wants Eben cut off so's this
farm'll be mine when ye die! [*With terrible

gloating.] An' that's what's happened, hain't 50
it? An' the farm's her'n! An' the dust o' the
road—that's your'n! Ha! Now who's hawin'?

EBEN [*has been listening, petrified with grief
and rage—suddenly laughs wildly and brokenly*]. Ha-ha-ha! So that's her sneakin' game— 55
all along!—like I suspicioned at fust—t' swaller it all—an' me, too . . . ! [*Madly.*] I'll murder
her! [*He springs toward the porch but* CABOT
is quicker and gets in between.]

CABOT. No, ye don't! 60

EBEN. Git out o' my road! [*He tries to throw*
CABOT *aside. They grapple in what becomes
immediately a murderous struggle. The old
man's concentrated strength is too much for*
EBEN. CABOT *gets one hand on his throat and* 65
*presses him back across the stone well. At the
same moment,* ABBIE *comes out on the porch.
With a stifled cry she runs toward them.*]

ABBIE. Eben! Ephraim! [*She tugs at the hand
on* EBEN'S *throat.*] Let go, Ephraim! Ye're 70
chokin' him!

CABOT [*removes his hand and flings* EBEN
*sideways full length on the grass, gasping and
choking. With a cry,* ABBIE *kneels beside him,
trying to take his head on her lap, but he* 75
pushes her away. CABOT *stands looking down
with fierce triumph*]. Ye needn't t've fret, Abbie,
I wa'n't aimin' t' kill him. He hain't wuth
hangin' fur—not by a hell of a sight! [*More
and more triumphantly.*] Seventy-six an' him 80
not thirty yit—an' look whar he be fur thinkin'
his Paw was easy! No, by God, I hain't easy!
An' him upstairs, I'll raise him t' be like me!
[*He turns to leave them.*] I'm goin' in an' dance!
—sing an' celebrate! [*He walks to the porch— 85
then turns with a great grin.*] I don't calc'late
it's left in him, but if he gits pesky, Abbie, ye
jest sing out. I'll come a-runnin' an' by the
Eternal, I'll put him across my knee an' birch
him! Ha-ha-ha! [*He goes into the house laugh- 90
ing. A moment later his loud "whoop" is
heard.*]

ABBIE [*tenderly*]. Eben. Air ye hurt? [*She
tries to kiss him but he pushes her violently
away and struggles to a sitting position.*] 95

EBEN [*gaspingly*]. T' hell—with ye!

ABBIE [*not believing her ears*]. It's me, Eben
—Abbie—don't ye know me?

EBEN [*glowering at her with hatred*]. Ay-eh —I know ye—now! [*He suddenly breaks down, sobbing weakly.*]

5 ABBIE [*fearfully*]. Eben—what's happened t' ye—why did ye look at me 's if ye hated me?

EBEN [*violently, between sobs and gasps*]. I do hate ye! Ye're a whore—a damn trickin' whore!

ABBIE [*shrinking back horrified*]. Eben! Ye 10 don't know what ye're sayin'!

EBEN [*scrambling to his feet and following her—accusingly*]. Ye're nothin' but a stinkin' passel o' lies! Ye've been lyin' t' me every word ye spoke, day an' night, since we fust—done 15 it. Ye've kept sayin' ye loved me. . . .

ABBIE [*frantically*]. I do love ye! [*She takes his hand but he flings hers away.*]

EBEN [*unheeding*]. Ye've made a fool o' me —a sick, dumb fool—a-purpose! Ye've been on'y 20 playin' yer sneakin', stealin' game all along— gittin' me t' lie with ye so's ye'd hev a son he'd think was his'n, an' makin' him promise he'd give ye the farm and let me eat dust, if ye did git him a son! [*Staring at her with anguished,* 25 *bewildered eyes.*] They must be a devil livin' in ye! T'ain't human t' be as bad as that be!

ABBIE [*stunned—dully*]. He told yew . . . ?

EBEN. Hain't it true? It hain't no good in yew lyin'.

30 ABBIE [*pleadingly*]. Eben, listen—ye must listen—it was long ago—afore we done nothin' —yew was scornin' me—goin' t' see Min— when I was lovin' ye—an' I said it t' him t' git vengeance on ye!

35 EBEN [*unheedingly. With tortured passion*]. I wish ye was dead! I wish I was dead along with ye afore this come! [*Ragingly.*] But I'll git my vengeance too! I'll pray Maw t' come back t' help me—t' put her cuss on yew an' 40 him!

ABBIE [*brokenly*]. Don't ye, Eben! Don't ye! [*She throws herself on her knees before him, weeping.*] I didn't mean t' do bad t' ye! Fergive me, won't ye?

45 EBEN [*not seeming to hear her—fiercely*]. I'll git squar' with the old skunk—an' yew! I'll tell him the truth 'bout the son he's so proud o'! Then I'll leave ye here t' pizen each other —with Maw comin' out o' her grave at nights —an' I'll go t' the gold fields o' Californi-a 50 whar Sim an' Peter be!

ABBIE [*terrified*]. Ye won't—leave me? Ye can't!

EBEN [*with fierce determination*]. I'm a-goin', I tell ye! I'll git rich thar an' come back an' 55 fight him fur the farm he stole—an' I'll kick ye both out in the road—t' beg an' sleep in the woods—an' yer son along with ye—t' starve an' die! [*He is hysterical at the end.*]

ABBIE [*with a shudder—humbly*]. He's yewr 60 son, too, Eben.

EBEN [*torturedly*]. I wish he never was born! I wish he'd die this minit! I wish I'd never sot eyes on him! It's him—yew havin' him—a- purpose t' steal—that's changed everythin'! 65

ABBIE [*gently*]. Did ye believe I loved ye— afore he come?

EBEN. Ay-eh—like a dumb ox!

ABBIE. An' ye don't believe no more?

EBEN. B'lieve a lyin' thief! Ha! 70

ABBIE [*shudders—then humbly*]. An' did ye r'ally love me afore?

EBEN [*brokenly*]. Ay-eh—an' ye was trickin' me!

ABBIE. An' ye don't love me now! 75

EBEN [*violently*]. I hate ye, I tell ye!

ABBIE. An' ye're truly goin' West—goin' t' leave me—all account o' him being born?

EBEN. I'm a-goin' in the mornin'—or may God strike me t' hell! 80

ABBIE [*after a pause—with a dreadful cold intensity—slowly*]. If that's what his comin' 's done t' me—killin' yewr love—takin' yew away—my on'y joy—the on'y joy I ever knowed—like heaven t' me—purtier'n heaven 85 —then I hate him, too, even if I be his Maw!

EBEN [*bitterly*]. Lies! Ye love him! He'll steal the farm fur ye! [*Brokenly.*] But t'ain't the farm so much—not no more—it's yew foolin' me—gittin' me t' love ye—lyin' yew loved me 90 —jest t' git a son t' steal!

ABBIE [*distractedly*]. He won't steal! I'd kill him fust! I do love ye! I'll prove t' ye . . . !

EBEN [*harshly*]. T'ain't no use lyin' no more. I'm deaf t' ye! [*He turns away.*] I hain't seein' 95 ye agen. Good-by!

ABBIE [*pale with anguish*]. Hain't ye even goin' t' kiss me—not once—arter all we loved?

EBEN [*in a hard voice*]. I hain't wantin' t' kiss ye never agen! I'm wantin' t' forget I ever sot eyes on ye!

ABBIE. Eben!—ye mustn't—wait a spell—I want t' tell ye . . . .

EBEN. I'm a-goin' in t' git drunk. I'm a-goin' t' dance.

ABBIE [*clinging to his arm—with passionate earnestness*]. If I could make it—'s if he'd never come up between us—if I could prove t' ye I wa'n't schemin' t' steal from ye—so's everythin' could be jest the same with us, lovin' each other jest the same, kissin' an' happy the same's we've been happy afore he come—if I could do it—ye'd love me agen, wouldn't ye? Ye'd kiss me agen? Ye wouldn't never leave me, would ye?

EBEN [*moved*]. I calc'late not. [*Then shaking her hand off his arm—with a bitter smile.*] But ye hain't God, be ye?

ABBIE [*exultantly*]. Remember ye've promised! [*Then with strange intensity.*] Mebbe I kin take back one thin' God does!

EBEN [*peering at her*]. Ye're gittin' cracked, hain't ye? [*Then going towards door.*] I'm a-goin' t' dance.

ABBIE [*calls after him intensely*]. I'll prove t' ye! I'll prove I love ye better'n . . . . [*He goes in the door, not seeming to hear. She remains standing where she is, looking after him—then she finishes desperately.*] Better'n everythin' else in the world!

Curtain

Scene iii

[*Just before dawn in the morning—shows the kitchen and* CABOT's *bedroom. In the kitchen, by the light of a tallow candle on the table,* EBEN *is sitting, his chin propped on his hands, his drawn face blank and expressionless. His carpetbag is on the floor beside him. In the bedroom, dimly lighted by a small whale-oil lamp,* CABOT *lies asleep.* ABBIE *is bending over the cradle, listening, her face full of terror yet with an under-current of desperate triumph. Suddenly, she breaks down and sobs,*

appears about to throw herself on her knees beside the cradle; but the old man turns restlessly, groaning in his sleep, and she controls herself, and, shrinking away from the cradle with a gesture of horror, backs swiftly toward the door in rear and goes out. A moment later she comes into the kitchen and, running to EBEN, *flings her arms about his neck and kisses him wildly. He hardens himself, he remains unmoved and cold, he keeps his eyes straight ahead.*]

ABBIE [*hysterically*]. I done it, Eben! I told ye I'd do it! I've proved I love ye—better'n everythin'—so's ye can't never doubt me no more!

EBEN [*dully*]. Whatever ye done, it hain't no good now.

ABBIE [*wildly*]. Don't ye say that! Kiss me, Eben, won't ye? I need ye t' kiss me arter what I done! I need ye t' say ye love me!

EBEN [*kisses her without emotion—dully*]. That's fur goodby. I'm a-goin' soon.

ABBIE. No! No! Ye won't go—not now!

EBEN [*going on with his own thoughts*]. I been a-thinkin'—an' I hain't goin' t' tell Paw nothin'. I'll leave Maw t' take vengeance on ye. If I told him, the old skunk'd jest be stinkin' mean enuf to take it out on that baby. [*His voice showing emotion in spite of him.*] An' I don't want nothin' bad t' happen t' him. He hain't t' blame fur yew. [*He adds with a certain queer pride.*] An' he looks like me! An' by God, he's mine! An' some day I'll be a-comin' back an' . . . !

ABBIE [*too absorbed in her own thoughts to listen to him—pleadingly*]. They's no cause fur ye t' go now—they's no sense—it's all the same's it was—they's nothin' come b'tween us now—arter what I done!

EBEN [*something in her voice arouses him. He stares at her a bit frightenedly*]. Ye look mad, Abbie. What did ye do?

ABBIE. I—I killed him, Eben.

EBEN [*amazed*]. Ye killed him?

ABBIE [*dully*]. Ay-eh.

EBEN [*recovering from his astonishment—savagely*]. An' serves him right! But we got t' do somethin' quick t' make it look 's if the old

skunk'd killed himself when he was drunk.
We kin prove by 'em all how drunk he got.

ABBIE [wildly]. No! No! Not him! [Laughing distractedly.] But that's what I ought t'
5 done, hain't it? I oughter killed him instead!
Why didn't ye tell me?

EBEN [appalled]. Instead? What d'ye mean?

ABBIE. Not him.

EBEN [his face grown ghastly]. Not—not
10 that baby!

ABBIE [dully]. Ay-eh!

EBEN [falls to his knees as if he'd been struck
—his voice trembling with horror]. Oh, God
A'mighty! A'mighty God! Maw, whar was ye,
15 why didn't ye stop her?

ABBIE [simply]. She went back t' her grave
that night we fust done it, remember? I hain't
felt her about since. [A pause. EBEN hides his
head in his hands, trembling all over as if he
20 had the ague. She goes on dully.] I left the
piller over his little face. Then he killed himself. He stopped breathin'. [She begins to weep
softly.]

EBEN [rage beginning to mingle with grief].
25 He looked like me. He was mine, damn ye!

ABBIE [slowly and brokenly]. I didn't want
t' do it. I hated myself fur doin' it. I loved him.
He was so purty—dead spit 'n' image o' yew.
But I loved yew more—an' yew was goin'
30 away—far off whar I'd never see ye agen,
never kiss ye, never feel ye pressed agin me
agen—an' ye said ye hated me fur havin' him
—ye said ye hated him an' wished he was
dead—ye said if it hadn't been fur him comin'
35 it'd be the same's afore between us.

EBEN [unable to endure this, springs to his
feet in a fury, threatening her, his twitching
fingers seeming to reach out for her throat].
Ye lie! I never said—I never dreamed ye'd—
40 I'd cut off my head afore I'd hurt his finger!

ABBIE [piteously, sinking on her knees].
Eben, don't ye look at me like that—hatin' me
—not after what I done fur ye—fur us—so's
we could be happy agen—

45 EBEN [furiously now]. Shut up, or I'll kill ye!
I see yer game now—the same old sneakin'
trick—ye're aimin' t' blame me fur the murder
ye done!

ABBIE [moaning—putting her hands over
her ears]. Don't ye, Eben! Don't ye! [She 50
grasps his legs.]

EBEN [his mood suddenly changing to horror,
shrinks away from her]. Don't ye tech me!
Ye're pizen! How could ye—t' murder a pore
little critter— Ye must've swapped yer soul t' 55
hell! [Suddenly raging.] Ha! I kin see why ye
done it! Not the lies ye jest told—but 'cause ye
wanted t' steal agen—steal the last thin' ye'd
left me—my part o' him—no, the hull o' him—
ye saw he looked like me—ye knowed he was 60
all mine—an' ye couldn't b'ar it—I know ye!
Ye killed him fur bein' mine! [All this has
driven him almost insane. He makes a rush
past her for the door—then turns—shaking
both fists at her, violently.] But I'll take ven- 65
geance now! I'll git the Sheriff! I'll tell him
everythin'! Then I'll sing "I'm off to California!" an' go—gold—Golden Gate—gold sun—
fields o' gold in the West! [This last he half
shouts, half croons incoherently, suddenly 70
breaking off passionately.] I'm a-goin' fur the
Sheriff t' come an' git ye! I want ye tuk away,
locked up from me! I can't stand t' luk at ye!
Murderer an' thief 'r not, ye still tempt me!
I'll give ye up t' the Sheriff. [He turns and runs 75
out, around the corner of house, panting and
sobbing, and breaks into a swerving sprint
down the road.]

ABBIE [struggling to her feet, runs to the
door, calling after him]. I love ye, Eben! I love 80
ye! [She stops at the door weakly, swaying,
about to fall.] I don't care what ye do—if ye'll
on'y love me agen— [She falls limply to the
floor in a faint.]

Curtain

Scene iv

[About an hour later. Same as Scene iii. 85
Shows the kitchen and CABOT's bedroom. It is
after dawn. The sky is brilliant with the sunrise. In the kitchen, ABBIE sits at the table, her
body limp and exhausted, her head bowed
down over her arms, her face hidden. Upstairs, 90
CABOT is still asleep but awakens with a start.
He looks toward the window and gives a snort
of surprise and irritation—throws back the

covers and begins hurriedly pulling on his clothes. Without looking behind him, he begins talking to ABBIE *whom he supposes beside him.*]

5 CABOT. Thunder 'n' lightin', Abbie! I hain't slept this late in fifty year! Looks 's if the sun was full riz a'most. Must've been the dancin' an' likker. Must be gittin' old. I hope Eben's t' wuk. Ye might've tuk the trouble t' rouse

10 me, Abbie. [*He turns—sees no one there—surprised.*] Waal—whar air she? Gittin' vittles, I calc'late. [*He tiptoes to the cradle and peers down—proudly.*] Mornin', sonny. Purty's a picture! Sleepin' sound. He don't beller all

15 night like most o' 'em. [*He goes quietly out the door in rear—a few moments later enters kitchen—sees* ABBIE—*with satisfaction.*] So thar ye be. Ye got any vittles cooked?

ABBIE. [*without moving*]. No.

20 CABOT [*coming to her, almost sympathetically*]. Ye feelin' sick?

ABBIE. No.

CABOT [*pats her on shoulder. She shudders*]. Ye'd best lie down a spell. [*Half jocularly.*]

25 Yer son'll be needin' ye soon. He'd ought t' wake up with a gnashin' appetite, the sound way he's sleepin'.

ABBIE [*shudders—then in a dead voice*]. He hain't never goin' t' wake up.

30 CABOT [*jokingly*]. Takes after me this mornin'. I hain't slept so late in. . . .

ABBIE. He's dead.

CABOT [*stares at her—bewilderedly*]. What. . . .

35 ABBIE. I killed him.

CABOT [*stepping back from her—aghast*]. Air ye drunk—'r crazy—'r . . . !

ABBIE [*suddenly lifts her head and turns on him—wildly*]. I killed him, I tell ye! I smoth-

40 ered him. Go up an' see if ye don't b'lieve me! [CABOT *stares at her a second, then bolts out the rear door—can be heard bounding up the stairs—and rushes into the bedroom and over to the cradle.* ABBIE *has sunk back lifelessly*

45 *into her former position.* CABOT *puts his hand down on the body in the crib. An expression of fear and horror comes over his face.*]

CABOT [*shrinking away—trembling*]. God

A'mighty! God A'mighty. [*He stumbles out the door—in a short while returns to the* 50 *kitchen—comes to* ABBIE, *the stunned expression still on his face—hoarsely.*] Why did ye do it? Why? [*As she doesn't answer, he grabs her violently by the shoulder and shakes her.*] I ax ye why ye done it! Ye'd better tell 55 me 'r . . . !

ABBIE [*gives him a furious push which sends him staggering back and springs to her feet— with wild rage and hatred*]. Don't ye dare tech me! What right hev ye t' question me 'bout 60 him? He wa'n't yewr son! Think I'd have a son by yew? I'd die fust! I hate the sight o' ye an' allus did! It's yew I should've murdered, if I'd had good sense! I hate ye! I love Eben. I did from the fust. An' he was Eben's son—mine 65 an' Eben's—not your'n!

CABOT [*stands looking at her dazedly—a pause—finding his words with an effort—dully*]. That was it—what I felt—pokin' round the corners—while ye lied—holdin' yerself from 70 me—sayin' ye'd a'ready conceived— [*He lapses into crushed silence—then with a strange emotion.*] He's dead, sart'n. I felt his heart. Pore little critter! [*He blinks back one tear, wiping his sleeve across his nose.*] 75

ABBIE [*hysterically*]. Don't ye! Don't ye! [*She sobs unrestrainedly.*]

CABOT [*with a concentrated effort that stiffens his body into a rigid line and hardens his face into a stony mask—through his teeth to* 80 *himself*]. I got t' be—like a stone—a rock o' jedgment! [*A pause. He gets complete control over himself—harshly.*] If he was Eben's, I be glad he air gone! An' mebbe I suspicioned it all along. I felt they was somethin' onnateral 85 —somewhars—the house got so lonesome— an' cold—drivin' me down t' the barn—t' the beasts o' the field. . . . Ay-eh. I must've suspicioned—somethin'. Ye didn't fool me—not altogether, leastways—I'm too old a bird— 90 growin' ripe on the bough. . . . [*He becomes aware he is wandering, straightens again, looks at* ABBIE *with a cruel grin.*] So ye'd like t' hev murdered me 'stead o' him, would ye? Waal, I'll live to a hundred! I'll live t' see ye hung! 95 I'll deliver ye up t' the jedgment o' God an' the law! I'll git the Sheriff now. [*Starts for the door.*]

ABBE [*dully*]. Ye needn't. Eben's gone fur him.

5   CABOT [*amazed*]. Eben—gone fur the Sheriff?

ABBIE. Ay-eh.

CABOT. T' inform agen ye?

ABBIE. Ay-eh.

10   CABOT [*considers this—a pause—then in a hard voice*]. Waal, I'm thankful fur him savin' me the trouble. I'll git t' wuk. [*He goes to the door—then turns—in a voice full of strange emotion.*] He'd ought t' been my son, Abbie.

15 Ye'd ought t' loved me. I'm a man. If ye'd loved me, I'd never told no Sheriff on ye no matter what ye did, if they was t' brile me alive!

ABBIE [*defensively*]. They's more to it nor

20 yew know, makes him tell.

CABOT [*dryly*]. Fur yewr sake, I hope they be. [*He goes out—comes around to the gate—stares up at the sky. His control relaxes. For a moment he is old and weary. He murmurs des-*

25 *pairingly.*] God A'mighty, I be lonesomer'n ever! [*He hears running footsteps from the left, immediately is himself again. EBEN runs in, panting exhaustedly, wild-eyed and mad look-ing. He lurches through the gate. CABOT grabs*

30 *him by the shoulder. EBEN stares at him dumbly.*] Did ye tell the Sheriff?

EBEN [*nodding stupidly*]. Ay-eh.

CABOT [*gives him a push away that sends him sprawling—laughing with withering con-*

35 *tempt*]. Good fur ye! A prime chip o' yer Maw ye be! [*He goes toward the barn, laughing harshly. EBEN scrambles to his feet. Suddenly CABOT turns—grimly threatening.*] Git off this farm when the Sheriff takes her—or, by God,

40 he'll have t' come back an' git me fur murder, too! [*He stalks off. EBEN does not appear to have heard him. He runs to the door and comes into the kitchen. ABBIE looks up with a cry of anguished joy. EBEN stumbles over and throws*

45 *himself on his knees beside her—sobbing brokenly.*]

EBEN. Fergive me!

ABBIE [*happily*]. Eben! [*She kisses him and pulls his head over against her breast.*]

EBEN. I love ye! Fergive me!   50

ABBIE [*ecstatically*]. I'd fergive ye all the sins in hell fur sayin' that! [*She kisses his head, pressing it to her with a fierce passion of pos-session.*]

EBEN [*brokenly*]. But I told the Sheriff. He's 55 comin' fur ye!

ABBIE. I kin b'ar what happens t' me—now!

EBEN. I woke him up. I told him. He says, wait 'til I git dressed. I was waiting. I got to thinkin' o' yew. I got to thinkin' how I'd loved 60 ye. It hurt like somethin' was bustin' in my chest an' head. I got t' cryin'. I knowed sudden I loved ye yet, an' allus would love ye!

ABBIE [*caressing his hair—tenderly*]. My boy, hain't ye?   65

EBEN. I begun t' run back. I cut across the fields an' through the woods. I thought ye might have time t' run away—with me—an' . . . .

ABBIE [*shaking her head*]. I got t' take my 70 punishment—t' pay fur my sin.

EBEN. Then I want t' share it with ye.

ABBIE. Ye didn't do nothin'.

EBEN. I put it in yer head. I wisht he was dead! I as much as urged ye t' do it!   75

ABBIE. No. It was me alone!

EBEN. I'm as guilty as yew be! He was the child o' our sin.

ABBIE [*lifting her head as if defying God*]. I don't repent that sin! I hain't askin' God t' 80 fergive that!

EBEN. Nor me—but it led up t' the other—an' the murder ye did, ye did 'count o' me—an' it's my murder, too, I'll tell the Sheriff—an' if ye deny it, I'll say we planned it t'gether 85 —an' they'll all b'lieve me, fur they suspicion everythin' we've done, an' it'll seem likely an' true to 'em. An' it is true—way down. I did help ye—somehow.

ABBIE [*laying her head on his—sobbing*]. 90 No! I don't want yew t' suffer!

EBEN. I got t' pay fur my part o' the sin! An' I'd suffer wust leavin' ye, goin' West, thinkin' o' ye day an' night, bein' out when yew was in— [*lowering his voice*] 'r bein' alive when yew was dead. [*A pause.*] I want t' share with ye, Abbie—prison 'r death 'r hell 'r anythin'! [*He looks into her eyes and forces a trembling* 5 *smile.*] If I'm sharin' with ye, I won't feel lonesome, leastways.

ABBIE [*weakly*]. Eben! I won't let ye! I can't let ye!

EBEN [*kissing her—tenderly*]. Ye can't he'p 10 yerself. I got ye beat fur once!

ABBIE [*forcing a smile—adoringly*]. I hain't beat—s'long's I got ye!

EBEN [*hears the sound of feet outside*]. Ssshh! Listen! They've come t' take us!

15 ABBIE. No, it's him. Don't give him no chance to fight ye, Eben. Don't say nothin'— no matter what he says. An' I won't neither. [*It is* CABOT. *He comes up from the barn in a great state of excitement and strides into the* 20 *house and then into the kitchen.* EBEN *is kneeling beside* ABBIE, *his arm around her, hers around him. They stare straight ahead.*]

CABOT [*stares at them, his face hard. A long pause—vindictively*]. Ye make a slick pair o' 25 murderin' turtle doves! Ye'd ought t' be both hung on the same limb an' left thar t' swing in the breeze an' rot—a warnin' t' old fools like me t' b'ar their lonesomeness alone—an' fur young fools like ye t' hobble their lust. [*A* 30 *pause. The excitement returns to his face, his eyes snap, he looks a bit crazy.*] I couldn't work today. I couldn't take no interest. T' hell with the farm! I'm leavin' it! I've turned the cows an' other stock loose! I've druv 'em into the 35 woods whar they kin be free! By freein' 'em, I'm freein' myself! I'm quittin' here today! I'll set fire t' house an' barn an' watch 'em burn, an' I'll leave yer Maw t' haunt the ashes, an' I'll will the fields back t' God, so that nothin' 40 human kin never touch 'em! I'll be a-goin' to Californi-a—t' jine Simeon an' Peter—true sons o' mine if they be dumb fools—an' the Cabots'll find Solomon's Mines t'gether! [*He suddenly cuts a mad caper.*] Whoop! What 45 was the song they sung? "Oh, Californi-a! That's the land fur me." [*He sings this—then gets on his knees by the floor-board under*

which the money was hid.] An' I'll sail thar on one o' the finest clippers I kin find! I've got the money! Pity ye didn't know whar this was hid- 50 den so's ye could steal. . . . [*He has pulled up the board. He stares—feels—stares again. A pause of dead silence. He slowly turns, slumping into a sitting position on the floor, his eyes like those of a dead fish, his face the sickly* 55 *green of an attack of nausea. He swallows painfully several times—forces a weak smile at last.*] So—ye did steal it!

EBEN [*emotionlessly*]. I swapped it t' Sim an' Peter fur their share o' the farm—t' pay their 60 passage t' Californi-a.

CABOT [*with one sardonic*] Ha! [*He begins to recover. Gets slowly to his feet—strangely.*] I calc'late God give it to 'em—not yew! God's hard, not easy! Mebbe they's easy gold in the 65 West but it hain't God's gold. It hain't fur me. I kin hear His voice warnin' me agen t' be hard an' stay on my farm. I kin see his hand usin' Eben t' steal t' keep me from weakness. I kin feel I be in the palm o' His hand, His fingers 70 guidin' me. [*A pause—then he mutters sadly.*] It's a-goin' t' be lonesomer now than ever it war afore—an' I'm gettin' old, Lord—ripe on the bough. . . . [*Then stiffening.*] Waal—what d'ye want? God's lonesome, hain't He? God's 75 hard an' lonesome! [*A pause. The* SHERIFF *with two men comes up the road from the left. They move cautiously to the door. The* SHERIFF *knocks on it with the butt of his pistol.*]

SHERIFF. Open in the name o' the law! [*They* 80 *start.*]

CABOT. They've come fur ye. [*He goes to the rear door.*] Come in, Jim! [*The three men enter.* CABOT *meets them in doorway.*] Jest a minit, Jim. I got 'em safe here. [*The Sheriff nods. He* 85 *and his companions remain in the doorway.*]

EBEN [*suddenly calls*]. I lied this mornin', Jim. I helped her to do it. Ye kin take me, too.

ABBIE [*brokenly*]. No!

CABOT. Take 'em both. [*He comes forward—* 90 *stares at* EBEN *with a trace of grudging admiration.*] Purty good—fur yew! Waal, I got t' round up the stock. Good-by.

EBEN. Good-by.

ABBIE. Good-by. [CABOT *turns and strides past the men—comes out and around the corner of the house, his shoulders squared, his face stony, and stalks grimly toward the barn.* 5 *In the meantime the Sheriff and men have come into the room.*]

SHERIFF [*embarrassedly*]. Waal—we'd best start.

ABBIE. Wait. [*Turns to* EBEN.] I love ye, 10 Eben.

EBEN. I love ye, Abbie. [*They kiss. The three men grin and shuffle embarrassedly.* EBEN *takes* ABBIE's *hand. They go out the door in rear, the men following, and come from the house,* 15 *walking hand in hand to the gate.* EBEN *stops there and points to the sunrise sky.*] Sun's a-rizin'. Purty, hain't it?

ABBIE. Ay-eh. [*They both stand for a moment looking up raptly in attitudes* 20 *strangely aloof and devout.*]

SHERIFF [*looking around at the farm enviously—to his companions*]. It's a jim-dandy farm, no denyin'. Wished I owned it!

Curtain

Federico García Lorca

1898–1936

The House of Bernarda Alba

1936

Lorca's matriarch stands consciously for social order, for the tradition that gives a community its foundation, and for the unwritten codes in which a society incorporates its values. Such codes govern the lives of men and women everywhere, restraining their anarchic impulses and guiding them toward reconciliation of personal and social needs. They regulate the parents' duties, the child's freedom, the attitudes held toward education, authority, and justice. Perhaps most significantly, they control the relations between the sexes, channeling into courtship, marriage, and the creation of the family an urge that might spend itself in promiscuity.

When Bernarda arranges Angustias' marriage, she obeys and enforces the code of her community as she does in rebuffing Martirio's suitor and in restraining Adela. Something, however, has gone wrong. The code no longer suits the needs that gave it being. It has turned hollow, external. "I don't pry into anyone's heart," says Bernarda, "but I want to put up a good front." A good front may well be the perversion of a good life, and Bernarda herself has turned pathologically rigid. With her husband's death she assumes a man's place and becomes governor of her family—but less governor than tyrant. No longer does she strive to accommodate her children's desires to the needs of society; she opposes the desires themselves. She hates the flesh for the rebellious will within it, hates her daughters for their hunger. "Hot coals in the place where she sinned!" she screams at the end of Act II, and in that cry her negation is proclaimed. She would literally burn out the source of life.

The home, which should be a miniature of a well-ordered society, turns under Bernarda's tyranny into a prison, its white walls gleaming down in ironic purity on the dying souls within. For eight years of unfelt mourning they will desperately embroider their hope-chest linens, tasting the truth of

FEDERICO GARCÍA LORCA

Amelia's conviction that "to be born a woman's the worst punishment." They will torment one another out of sisterly affection corroded to jealousy. Each in her own fashion will seize at any promise of redemption. Angustias, the power of love withering within her, reaches doubtfully toward a face that "seems to fade away." In the desperation of fantasy fulfillment, Martirio steals Pepe's picture. And Adela, who has "seen death under this roof" and who feels the fire of life, resolves to find freedom though she wear "the crown of thorns that belongs to the mistress of a married man."

What one finds in this prison, one finds in the village—in all the villages, Lorca implies, of Spain—for when the code becomes tyrannical, the inhibited will turns corrupt. Hence the prostitution to which Poncia's mother surrendered and the venomous hypocrisy with which Poncia inflames the prurience of the daughters. Hence the rape of Paca la Roseta, which the men discuss with superb impropriety at the funeral of Bernarda's husband. Every whisper sifting through the prison bars tells of flesh escaping into license or succumbing to mortification. Adelaida's "sweetheart doesn't let her go out even to the front doorstep. Before, she was gay. Now, not even powder on her face." And whether the flesh escapes or succumbs, the end is the denial of life. Act II ends with infanticide, Act III with suicide.

In the background the reapers sing their lyric of love, the stallion's hooves explode against his prison walls, and the mad grandmother croons her lullaby, "Little lamb, child of mine, Let's go to the shore of the sea .... Let's go to the palms at Bethlehem's gate." But maternal love is dead. The sea is far from the hot plains of the riverless village. And the gate of Bethlehem is farther yet. The Church, its representative, is indeed near, as its bells proclaim, but it seems not to enter in any redemptive way into the lives of the villagers.

The House of Bernarda Alba

A Drama About Women in the Villages of Spain

LORCA

Translated by James Graham-Lujan and Richard L. O'Connell

CHARACTERS

BERNARDA   *age 60*
MARIA JOSEFA   *Bernarda's mother, age 80*
ANGUSTIAS   *Bernarda's daughter, age 39*
MAGDALENA   *Bernarda's daughter, age 30*
AMELIA   *Bernarda's daughter, age 27*
MARTIRIO   *Bernarda's daughter, age 24*
ADELA   *Bernarda's daughter, age 20*
A MAID   *age 50*
LA PONCIA   *a maid, age 60*
PRUDENCIA   *age 50*
WOMEN IN MOURNING

The writer states that these Three Acts are

Federico García Lorca, Three Tragedies, *translated by James Graham-Lujan and Richard L. O'Connell. Copyright 1947, 1955 by New Directions Publishing Corporation.* Caution: *All persons are hereby warned that these plays are published in translations authorized by the García Lorca Estate, being fully protected under the copyright laws of the United States of America, the Universal Copyright Convention, the Berne and Pan-American Copyright Conventions, and all countries of the world belonging to these conventions, are subject to royalty. They are also warned that the original Spanish works from which they are translated are also copyrighted throughout the world. All rights, including professional, amateur, motion picture, recitation, public reading, radio and television broadcasting, recording on tape or by any means,*

intended as a photographic document.

ACT I

[*A very white room in* BERNARDA ALBA'S *house. The walls are white. There are arched doorways with jute curtains tied back with tassels and ruffles. Wicker chairs. On the walls,* 5 *pictures of unlikely landscapes full of nymphs or legendary kings.*

It is summer. A great brooding silence fills the stage. It is empty when the curtain rises. Bells can be heard tolling outside.]

10 FIRST SERVANT [*entering*]. The tolling of those bells hits me right between the eyes.

PONCIA [*she enters, eating bread and sausage*]. More than two hours of mumbo jumbo. Priests are here from all the towns. The church 15 looks beautiful. At the first responsory for the dead, Magdalena fainted.

FIRST SERVANT. She's the one who's left most alone.

PONCIA. She's the only one who loved her 20 father. Ay! Thank God we're alone for a little. I came over to eat.

FIRST SERVANT. If Bernarda sees you . . . !

PONCIA. She's not eating today so she'd just as soon we'd all die of hunger! Domineering 25 old tyrant! But she'll be fooled! I opened the sausage crock.

FIRST SERVANT [*with an anxious sadness*]. Couldn't you give me some for my little girl, Poncia?

PONCIA. Go ahead! And take a fistful of 30 peas too. She won't know the difference today.

VOICE [*within*]. Bernarda!

PONCIA. There's the grandmother! Isn't she locked up tight?

FIRST SERVANT. Two turns of the key. 35

PONCIA. You'd better put the cross-bar up too. She's got the fingers of a lock-picker!

VOICE [*within*]. Bernarda!

PONCIA [*shouting*]. She's coming! [*To* THE SERVANT.] Clean everything up good. If Bernar- 40 da doesn't find things shining, she'll pull out the few hairs I have left.

SERVANT. What a woman!

PONCIA. Tyrant over everyone around her. She's perfectly capable of sitting on your heart 45 and watching you die for a whole year without turning off that cold little smile she wears on her wicked face. Scrub, scrub those dishes!

SERVANT. I've got blood on my hands from so much polishing of everything. 50

PONCIA. She's the cleanest, she's the decentest, she's the highest everything! A good rest her poor husband's earned!

[*The bells stop.*]

SERVANT. Did all the relatives come? 55

PONCIA. Just hers. His people hate her. They came to see him dead and make the sign of the cross over him; that's all.

SERVANT. Are there enough chairs?

PONCIA. More than enough. Let them sit on 60 the floor. When Bernarda's father died people stopped coming under his roof. She doesn't want them to see her in her "domain." Curse her!

SERVANT. She's been good to you.

PONCIA. Thirty years washing her sheets. 65 Thirty years eating her leftovers. Nights of watching when she had a cough. Whole days peeking through a crack in the shutters to spy on the neighbors and carry her the tale. Life without secrets one from the other. But in spite 70 of that—curse her! May the "pain of the piercing nail"° strike her in the eyes.

"pain of the piercing nail" translators' quotation marks seem designed to point out that Lorca's word for "nail" is the word commonly used for the nails of the cross

SERVANT. Poncia!

PONCIA. But I'm a good watchdog! I bark when I'm told and bite beggars' heels when she sics me on 'em. My sons work in her fields
5 —both of them already married, but one of these days I'll have enough.

SERVANT. And then . . . ?

PONCIA. Then I'll lock myself up in a room with her and spit in her face—a whole year.
10 "Bernarda, here's for this, that and the other!" Till I leave her—just like a lizard the boys have squashed. For that's what she is—she and her whole family! Not that I envy her her life. Five girls are left her, five ugly daughters—not
15 counting Angustias the eldest, by her first husband, who has money—the rest of them, plenty of eyelets to embroider, plenty of linen petticoats, but bread and grapes when it comes to inheritance.°
20 SERVANT. Well, *I'd* like to have what they've got!

PONCIA. All we have is our hands and a hole in God's earth.

SERVANT. And that's the only earth they'll
25 ever leave to us—to us who have nothing!

PONCIA [*at the cupboard*]. This glass has some specks.

SERVANT. Neither soap nor rag will take them off.
30 [*The bells toll.*]

PONCIA. The last prayer! I'm going over and listen. I certainly like the way our priest sings. In the Pater Noster his voice went up, and up —like a pitcher filling with water little by little.
35 Of course, at the end his voice cracked, but it's glorious to hear it. No, there never was anybody like the old Sacristan—Tronchapinos. At my mother's Mass, may she rest in peace, he sang. The walls shook—and when he said
40 "Amen," it was as if a wolf had come into the church. [*Imitating him.*] A-a-a-a-men! [*She starts coughing.*]

SERVANT. Watch out—you'll strain your windpipe!
45 PONCIA. I'd rather strain something else!

[*Goes out laughing.*]

daughters . . . inheritance i.e., of the five daughters only Angustias has a dowry

[THE SERVANT *scrubs. The bells toll.*]

SERVANT [*imitating the bells*]. Dong, dong, dong. Dong, dong, dong. May God forgive him! 50

BEGGAR WOMAN [*at the door, with a little girl*]. Bléssed be God!

SERVANT. Dong, dong, dong. I hope he waits many years for us! Dong, dong, dong.

BEGGAR [*loudly, a little annoyed*]. Bléssed be 55 God!

SERVANT [*annoyed*]. Forever and ever!

BEGGAR. I came for the scraps.

[*The bells stop tolling.*]

SERVANT. You can go right out the way you 60 came in. Today's scraps are for me.

BEGGAR. But you have somebody to take care of you—and my little girl and I are all alone!

SERVANT. Dogs are alone too, and they live. 65

BEGGAR. They always give them to me.

SERVANT. Get out of here! Who let you in anyway? You've already tracked up the place. [THE BEGGAR WOMAN *and* LITTLE GIRL *leave.* THE SERVANT *goes on scrubbing.*] Floors finish- 70 ed with oil, cupboards, pedestals, iron beds— but us servants, we can suffer in silence—and live in mud huts with a plate and a spoon. I hope someday not a one will be left to tell it. [*The bells sound again.*] Yes, yes—ring away. 75 Let them put you in a coffin with gold inlay and brocade to carry it on—you're no less dead than I'll be, so take what's coming to you, Antonio María Benavides—stiff in your broad- cloth suit and your high boots—take what's 80 coming to you! You'll never again lift my skirts behind the corral door!

[*From the rear door, two by two, women in mourning with large shawls and black skirts and fans begin to enter. They come in slowly* 85 *until the stage is full.*]

SERVANT [*breaking into a wail*]. Oh, Antonio María Benavides, now you'll never see these walls, nor break bread in this house again! I'm the one who loved you most of all your 90 servants. [*Pulling her hair.*] *Must* I live on after you've gone? Must I go on living?

[*The women finish coming in, and* BERNARDA *and her five daughters enter.* BERNARDA *leans on a cane.*] 95

BERNARDA [*to* THE SERVANT]. Silence!

SERVANT [*weeping*]. Bernarda!

BERNARDA. Less shrieking and more work. You should have had all this cleaner for the wake. Get out. This isn't your place.

[THE SERVANT *goes off crying.*]

The poor are like animals—they seem to be made of different stuff.

FIRST WOMAN. The poor feel their sorrows too.

BERNARDA. But they forget them in front of a plateful of peas.

FIRST GIRL [*timidly*]. Eating is necessary for living.

BERNARDA. At your age one doesn't talk in front of older people.

WOMAN. Be quiet, child.

BERNARDA. I've never taken lessons from anyone. Sit down. Magdalena, don't cry. If you want to cry, get under your bed. Do you hear me?

SECOND WOMAN [*to* BERNARDA]. Have you started to work the fields?

BERNARDA. Yesterday.

THIRD WOMAN. The sun comes down like lead.

FIRST WOMAN. I haven't known heat like this for years.

[*Pause. They all fan themselves.*]

BERNARDA. Is the lemonade ready?

PONCIA. Yes, Bernarda.

[*She brings in a large tray full of little white jars which she distributes.*]

BERNARDA. Give the men some.

PONCIA. They're already drinking in the patio.

BERNARDA. Let them get out the way they came in. I don't want them walking through here.

A GIRL [*to* ANGUSTIAS]. Pepe el Romano was with the men during the service.

ANGUSTIAS. There he was.

BERNARDA. His mother was there. She saw his mother. Neither she nor I saw Pepe . . .

GIRL. I thought . . .

BERNARDA. The one who *was* there was Darajalí, the widower. Very close to your Aunt. We all of us saw him.

SECOND WOMAN [*aside, in a low voice*]. Wicked, worse than wicked woman!

THIRD WOMAN. A tongue like a knife!

BERNARDA. Women in church shouldn't look at any man but the priest—and him only because he wears skirts. To turn your head is to be looking for the warmth of corduroy.

FIRST WOMAN. Sanctimonious old snake!

PONCIA [*between her teeth*]. Itching for a man's warmth.

BERNARDA [*beating with her cane on the floor*]. Blesséd be God!°

ALL [*crossing themselves*]. Forever blesséd and praised.

BERNARDA. Rest in peace with holy company at your head.

ALL. Rest in peace!

BERNARDA. With the Angel Saint Michael, and his sword of justice.

ALL. Rest in peace!

BERNARDA. With the key that opens, and the hand that locks.

ALL. Rest in peace!

BERNARDA. With the most blesséd, and the little lights of the field.

ALL. Rest in peace!

BERNARDA. With our holy charity, and all souls on land and sea.

ALL. Rest in peace!

BERNARDA. Grant rest to your servant, Antonio María Benavides, and give him the crown of your blesséd glory.

ALL. Amen.

BERNARDA. [*She rises and chants.*] Requiem aeternam donat eis domine.

ALL [*standing and chanting in the Gregorian fashion*]. Et lux perpetua luce ab eis.°

[*They cross themselves.*]

FIRST WOMAN. May you have health to pray for his soul.

[*They start filing out.*]

THIRD WOMAN. You won't lack loaves of hot bread.

Blesséd be God! the following passage is a pastiche of ritual and folk phrases

Requiem . . . luce ab eis Bernarda and her visitors garble a refrain from the Offices for the Dead. The original means, "Grant them eternal rest, O Lord. And let the everlasting light shine upon them."

SECOND WOMAN. Nor a roof for your daughters.

[*They are all filing in front of* BERNARDA *and going out.* ANGUSTIAS *leaves by the door to the patio.*]

FOURTH WOMAN. May you go on enjoying your wedding wheat.

PONCIA. [*She enters, carrying a money bag.*] From the men—this bag of money for Masses.

BERNARDA. Thank them—and let them have a glass of brandy.

GIRL [*to* MAGDALENA]. Magdalena . . .

BERNARDA [*to* MAGDALENA, *who is starting to cry*]. Sh-h-h-h! [*She beats with her cane on the floor.*]

[*All the women have gone out.*]

BERNARDA [*to the women who have just left*]. Go back to your houses and criticize everything you've seen! I hope it'll be many years before you pass under the archway of my door again.

PONCIA. You've nothing to complain about. The whole town came.

BERNARDA. Yes, to fill my house with the sweat from their wraps and the poison of their tongues.

AMELIA. Mother, don't talk like that.

BERNARDA. What other way is there to talk about this curséd village with no river—this village full of wells where you drink water always fearful it's been poisoned?

PONCIA. Look what they've done to the floor!

BERNARDA. As though a herd of goats had passed through. [PONCIA *cleans the floor.*] Adela, give me a fan.

ADELA. Take this one. [*She gives her a round fan with green and red flowers.*]

BERNARDA [*throwing the fan on the floor*]. Is that the fan to give to a widow? Give me a black one and learn to respect your father's memory.

MARTIRIO. Take mine.

BERNARDA. And you?

MARTIRIO. I'm not hot.

BERNARDA. Well, look for another, because you'll need it. For the eight years of mourning, not a breath of air will get in this house from the street. We'll act as if we'd sealed up doors and windows with bricks. That's what happened in my father's house—and in my grandfather's house. Meantime, you can all start embroidering your hope-chest linens. I have twenty bolts of linen in the chest from which to cut sheets and coverlets. Magdalena can embroider them.

MAGDALENA. It's all the same to me.

ADELA [*sourly*]. If you don't want to embroider them—they can go without. That way yours will look better.

MAGDALENA. Neither mine nor yours. I know I'm not going to marry. I'd rather carry sacks to the mill. Anything except sit here day after day in this dark room.

BERNARDA. That's what a woman is for.

MAGDALENA. Cursed be all women.

BERNARDA. In this house you'll do what I order. You can't run with the story to your father any more. Needle and thread for women. Whiplash and mules for men. That's the way it has to be for people who have certain obligations.

[ADELA *goes out.*]

VOICE. Bernarda! Let me out!

BERNARDA [*calling*]. Let her out now!

[THE FIRST SERVANT *enters.*]

FIRST SERVANT. I had a hard time holding her. In spite of her eighty years, your mother's strong as an oak.

BERNARDA. It runs in the family. My grandfather was the same way.

SERVANT. Several times during the wake I had to cover her mouth with an empty sack because she wanted to shout out to you to give her dishwater to drink at least, and some dogmeat, which is what she says you feed her.

MARTIRIO. She's mean!

BERNARDA [*to* SERVANT]. Let her get some fresh air in the patio.

SERVANT. She took her rings and the amethyst earrings out of the box, put them on, and told me she wants to get married.

[*The daughters laugh.*]

BERNARDA. Go with her and be careful she doesn't get near the well.

SERVANT. You don't need to be afraid she'll jump in.

BERNARDA. It's not that—but the neighbors can see her there from their windows.

5 [THE SERVANT *leaves.*]

MARTIRIO. We'll go change our clothes.

BERNARDA. Yes, but don't take the 'kerchiefs from your heads.

[ADELA *enters.*]

10 And Angustias?

ADELA [*meaningfully*]. I saw her looking out through the cracks of the back door. The men had just gone.

BERNARDA. And you, what were *you* doing

15 at the door?

ADELA. I went there to see if the hens had laid.

BERNARDA. But the men had already gone!

ADELA [*meaningfully*]. A group of them

20 were still standing outside.

BERNARDA [*furiously*]. Angustias! Angustias!

ANGUSTIAS [*entering*]. Did you want something?

BERNARDA. For what—and at whom—were

25 you looking?

ANGUSTIAS. Nobody.

BERNARDA. Is it decent for a woman of your class to be running after a man the day of her father's funeral? Answer me! Whom were you

30 looking at?

[*Pause.*]

ANGUSTIAS. I . . .

BERNARDA. Yes, you!

ANGUSTIAS. Nobody.

35 BERNARDA. Soft! Honeytongue! [*She strikes her.*]

PONCIA [*running to her*]. Bernarda, calm down! [*She holds her.* ANGUSTIAS *weeps.*]

BERNARDA. Get out of here, all of you!

40 [*They all go out.*]

PONCIA. She did it not realizing what she was doing—although it's bad, of course. It really disgusted me to see her sneak along to the patio. Then she stood at the window listening

45 to the men's talk which, as usual, was not the sort one should listen to.

BERNARDA. That's what they come to funerals for. [*With curiosity.*] What were they talking about?

50 PONCIA. They were talking about Paca la Roseta. Last night they tied her husband up in a stall, stuck her on a horse behind the saddle, and carried her away to the depths of the olive grove.

55 BERNARDA. And what did she do?

PONCIA. She? She was just as happy—they say her breasts were exposed and Maximiliano held on to her as if he were playing a guitar. Terrible!

60 BERNARDA. And what happened?

PONCIA. What had to happen. They came back almost at daybreak. Paca la Roseta with her hair loose and a wreath of flowers on her head.

65 BERNARDA. She's the only bad woman we have in the village.

PONCIA. Because she's not from here. She's from far away. And those who went with her are the sons of outsiders too. The men from

70 here aren't up to a thing like that.

BERNARDA. No, but they like to see it, and talk about it, and suck their fingers over it.

PONCIA. They were saying a lot more things.

BERNARDA [*looking from side to side with a certain fear*]. What things?

75 PONCIA. I'm ashamed to talk about them.

BERNARDA. And my daughter heard them?

PONCIA. Of course!

BERNARDA. That one takes after her Aunts:

80 white and mealy-mouthed and casting sheep's eyes at any little barber's compliment. Oh, what one has to go through and put up with so people will be decent and not too wild!

PONCIA. It's just that your daughters are of

85 an age when they ought to have husbands. Mighty little trouble they give you. Angustias must be much more than thirty now.

BERNARDA. Exactly thirty-nine.

PONCIA. Imagine. And she's never had a

90 beau . . .

BERNARDA [*furiously*]. None of them has ever had a beau and they've never needed one! They get along very well.

PONCIA. I didn't mean to offend you.

718

FEDERICO GARCÍA LORCA | Act I

BERNARDA. For a hundred miles around there's no one good enough to come near them. The men in this town are not of their class. Do you want me to turn them over to the first shepherd?

PONCIA. You should have moved to another town.

BERNARDA. That's it. To sell them!

PONCIA. No, Bernarda, to change. . . . Of course, any place else, they'd be the poor ones.

BERNARDA. Hold your tormenting tongue!

PONCIA. One can't even talk to you. Do we, or do we not share secrets?

BERNARDA. We do not. You're a servant and I pay you. Nothing more.

PONCIA. But . . .

SERVANT [entering]. Don Arturo's here. He's come to see about dividing the inheritance.

BERNARDA. Let's go. [To THE SERVANT.] You start whitewashing the patio. [To LA PONCIA.] And you start putting all the dead man's clothes away in the chest.

PONCIA. We could give away some of the things.

BERNARDA. Nothing—not a button even! Not even the cloth we covered his face with.

[She goes out slowly, leaning on her cane. At the door she turns to look at the two servants. They go out. She leaves.]

[AMELIA and MARTIRIO enter.]

AMELIA. Did you take the medicine?

MARTIRIO. For all the good it'll do me.

AMELIA. But you took it?

MARTIRIO. I do things without any faith, but like clockwork.

AMELIA. Since the new doctor came you look livelier.

MARTIRIO. I feel the same.

AMELIA. Did you notice? Adelaida wasn't at the funeral.

MARTIRIO. I know. Her sweetheart doesn't let her go out even to the front doorstep. Before, she was gay. Now, not even powder on her face.

AMELIA. These days a girl doesn't know whether to have a beau or not.

MARTIRIO. It's all the same.

AMELIA. The whole trouble is all these wagging tongues that won't let us live. Adelaida has probably had a bad time.

MARTIRIO. She's afraid of our mother. Mother is the only one who knows the story of Adelaida's father and where he got his lands. Everytime she comes here, Mother twists the knife in the wound. Her father killed his first wife's husband in Cuba so he could marry her himself. Then he left her there and went off with another woman who already had one daughter, and then he took up with this other girl, Adelaida's mother, and married her after his second wife died insane.

AMELIA. But why isn't a man like that put in jail?

MARTIRIO. Because men help each other cover up things like that and no one's able to tell on them.

AMELIA. But Adelaida's not to blame for any of that.

MARTIRIO. No. But history repeats itself. I can see that everything is a terrible repetition. And she'll have the same fate as her mother and grandmother—both of them wife to the man who fathered her.

AMELIA. What an awful thing!

MARTIRIO. It's better never to look at a man. I've been afraid of them since I was a little girl. I'd see them in the yard, yoking the oxen and lifting grain sacks, shouting and stamping, and I was always afraid to grow up for fear one of them would suddenly take me in his arms. God has made me weak and ugly and has definitely put such things away from me.

AMELIA. Don't say that! Enrique Humanas was after you and he liked you.

MARTIRIO. That was just people's ideas! One time I stood in my nightgown at the window until daybreak because he let me know through his shepherd's little girl that he was going to come, and he didn't. It was all just talk. Then he married someone else who had more money than I.

AMELIA. And ugly as the devil.

MARTIRIO. What do men care about ugliness? All they care about is lands, yokes of oxen, and a submissive bitch who'll feed them.

AMELIA. Ay!

[MAGDALENA *enters.*]

MAGDALENA. What are you doing?

MARTIRIO. Just here.

5 AMELIA. And you?

MAGDALENA. I've been going through all the rooms. Just to walk a little, and look at Grandmother's needlepoint pictures—the little woolen dog, and the black man wrestling with the
10 lion—which we liked so much when we were children. Those were happier times. A wedding lasted ten days and evil tongues weren't in style. Today people are more refined. Brides wear white veils, just as in the cities, and we
15 drink bottled wine, but we rot inside because of what people might say.

MARTIRIO. Lord knows what went on then!

AMELIA [*to* MAGDALENA]. One of your shoelaces has come untied.

20 MAGDALENA. What of it?

AMELIA. You'll step on it and fall.

MAGDALENA. One less!

MARTIRIO. And Adela?

MAGDALENA. Ah! She put on the green dress
25 she made to wear for her birthday, went out to the yard, and began shouting: "Chickens! Chickens, look at me!" I had to laugh.

AMELIA. If Mother had only seen her!

MAGDALENA. Poor little thing! She's the
30 youngest one of us and still has her illusions. I'd give something to see her happy.

[*Pause.* ANGUSTIAS *crosses the stage, carrying some towels.*]

ANGUSTIAS. What time is it?

35 MAGDALENA. It must be twelve.

ANGUSTIAS. So late?

AMELIA. It's about to strike.

[ANGUSTIAS *goes out.*]

MAGDALENA [*meaningfully*]. Do you know
40 what? [*Pointing after* ANGUSTIAS.]

AMELIA. No.

MAGDALENA. Come on!

MARTIRIO. I don't know what you're talking about!

45 MAGDALENA. Both of you know it better than I do, always with your heads together, like two little sheep, but not letting anybody else in on it. I mean about Pepe el Romano!

MARTIRIO. Ah!

MAGDALENA [*mocking her*]. Ah! The whole
50 town's talking about it. Pepe el Romano is coming to marry Angustias. Last night he was walking around the house and I think he's going to send a declaration soon.

MARTIRIO. I'm glad. He's a good man.
55 AMELIA. Me too. Angustias is well off.

MAGDALENA. Neither one of you is glad.

MARTIRIO. Magdalena! What do you mean?

MAGDALENA. If he were coming because of Angustias' looks, for Angustias as a woman,
60 I'd be glad too, but he's coming for her money. Even though Angustias is our sister, we're her family here and we know she's old and sickly, and always has been the least attractive one of us! Because if she looked like a dressed-up
65 stick at twenty, what can she look like now, now that she's forty?

MARTIRIO. Don't talk like that. Luck comes to the one who least expects it.

AMELIA. But Magdalena's right after all!
70 Angustias has all her father's money; she's the only rich one in the house and that's why, now that Father's dead and the money will be divided, they're coming for her.

MAGDALENA. Pepe el Romano is twenty-five
75 years old and the best looking man around here. The natural thing would be for him to be after you, Amelia, or our Adela, who's twenty —not looking for the least likely one in this house, a woman who, like her father, talks
80 through her nose.

MARTIRIO. Maybe he likes that!

MAGDALENA. I've never been able to bear your hypocrisy.

MARTIRIO. Heavens!
85 [ADELA *enters.*]

MAGDALENA. Did the chickens see you?

ADELA. What did you want me to do?

AMELIA. If Mother sees you, she'll drag you by your hair!
90 ADELA. I had a lot of illusions about this dress. I'd planned to put it on the day we were going to eat watermelons at the well. There wouldn't have been another like it.

MARTIRIO. It's a lovely dress.
95 ADELA. And one that looks very good on

me. It's the best thing Magdalena's ever cut.

MAGDALENA. And the chickens, what did they say to you?

ADELA. They presented me with a few fleas
5 that riddled my legs.

[*They laugh.*]

MARTIRIO. What you can do is dye it black.

MAGDALENA. The best thing you can do is give it to Angustias for her wedding with Pepe
10 el Romano.

ADELA [*with hidden emotion*]. But Pepe el Romano . . .

AMELIA. Haven't you heard about it?

ADELA. No.

15 MAGDALENA. Well, now you know!

ADELA. But it can't be!

MAGDALENA. Money can do anything.

ADELA. Is that why she went out after the funeral and stood looking through the door?
20 [*Pause.*] And that man would . . .

MAGDALENA. Would do anything.

[*Pause.*]

MARTIRIO. What are you thinking, Adela?

ADELA. I'm thinking that this mourning has
25 caught me at the worst moment of my life for me to bear it.

MAGDALENA. You'll get used to it.

ADELA [*bursting out, crying with rage*]. I will not get used to it! I can't be locked up. I don't
30 want my skin to look like yours. I don't want my skin's whiteness lost in these rooms. To-morrow I'm going to put on my green dress and go walking in the streets. I want to go out!

[*The First Servant enters.*]

35 MAGDALENA [*in a tone of authority*]. Adela!

SERVANT. The poor thing! How she misses her father. . . .

[*She goes out.*]

MARTIRIO. Hush!

40 AMELIA. What happens to one will happen to all of us.

[*Adela grows calm.*]

MAGDALENA. The servant almost heard you.

SERVANT [*entering*]. Pepe el Romano is com-
45 ing along at the end of the street.

[*Amelia, Martirio, and Magdalena run hurriedly.*]

MAGDALENA. Let's go see him!

[*They leave rapidly.*]

SERVANT [*to Adela*]. Aren't you going? 50

ADELA. It's nothing to me.

SERVANT. Since he has to turn the corner, you'll see him better from the window of your room.

[*The Servant goes out. Adela is left on the* 55 *stage, standing doubtfully; after a moment, she also leaves rapidly, going toward her room.* BERNARDA *and* LA PONCIA *come in.*]

BERNARDA. Damned portions and shares.

PONCIA. What a lot of money is left to 60 Angustias!

BERNARDA. Yes.

PONCIA. And for the others, considerably less.

BERNARDA. You've told me that three times now, when you know I don't want it men- 65 tioned! Considerably less; a lot less! Don't remind me any more.

[*Angustias comes in, her face heavily made up.*]

Angustias! 70

ANGUSTIAS. Mother.

BERNARDA. Have you dared to powder your face? Have you dared to wash your face on the day of your father's death?

ANGUSTIAS. He wasn't my father. Mine died 75 a long time ago. Have you forgotten that already?

BERNARDA. You owe more to this man, father of your sisters, than to your own. Thanks to him, your fortune is intact. 80

ANGUSTIAS. We'll have to see about that first!

BERNARDA. Even out of decency! Out of respect!

ANGUSTIAS. Let me go out, Mother!

BERNARDA. Let you go out? After I've taken 85 that powder off your face, I will. Spineless! Painted hussy! Just like your Aunts! [*She removes the powder violently with her handkerchief.*] Now get out!

PONCIA. Bernarda, don't be so hateful! 90

BERNARDA. Even though my mother is crazy, I still have my five senses and I know what I'm doing.

[*They all enter.*]

MAGDALENA. What's going on here? 95

BERNARDA. Nothing's "going on here"!

MAGDALENA [*to* ANGUSTIAS]. If you're fighting over the inheritance, you're the richest one
and can hang on to it all.

ANGUSTIAS. Keep your tongue in your pocket-
5 book!

BERNARDA [*beating on the floor*]. Don't fool
yourselves into thinking you'll sway me. Until
I go out of this house feet first I'll give the
orders for myself and for you!

10 [*Voices are heard and* MARIA JOSEFA, BER-
NARDA'S *mother, enters. She is very old and has
decked out her head and breast with flowers.*]

MARIA JOSEFA. Bernarda, where is my man-
tilla? Nothing, nothing of what I own will be
15 for any of you. Not my rings nor my black
moiré dress. Because not a one of you is going
to marry—not a one. Bernarda, give me my
necklace of pearls.

BERNARDA [*to* THE SERVANT]. Why did you
20 let her get in here?

SERVANT [*trembling*]. She got away from me!

MARIA JOSEFA. I ran away because I want to
marry—I want to get married to a beautiful
manly man from the shore of the sea. Because
25 here the men run from women.

BERNARDA. Hush, hush, Mother!

MARIA JOSEFA. No, no—I won't hush. I don't
want to see these single women, longing for
marriage, turning their hearts to dust; and I
30 want to go to my home town. Bernarda, I
want a man to get married to and be happy
with!

BERNARDA. Lock her up!

MARIA JOSEFA. Let me go out, Bernarda!

35 [THE SERVANT *seizes* MARIA JOSEFA.]

BERNARDA. Help her, all of you!

[*They all grab the old woman.*]

MARIA JOSEFA. I want to get away from here!
Bernarda! To get married by the shore of the
40 sea—by the shore of the sea!

Quick Curtain

ACT II

[*A white room in* BERNARDA'S *house. The
doors on the left lead to the bedrooms.*]

BERNARDA'S *daughters are seated on low
chairs, sewing.* MAGDALENA *is embroidering.*

La PONCIA *is with them.*]   45

ANGUSTIAS. I've cut the third sheet.

MARTIRIO. That one goes to Amelia.

MAGDALENA. Angustias, shall I put Pepe's
initials here too?

ANGUSTIAS [*dryly*]. No.   50

MAGDALENA [*calling*]. Adela, aren't you coming?

AMELIA. She's probably stretched out on the
bed.

PONCIA. Something's wrong with that one.   55
I find her restless, trembling, frightened—as
if a lizard were between her breasts.

MARTIRIO. There's nothing, more or less,
wrong with her than there is with all of us.

MAGDALENA. All of us except Angustias.   60

ANGUSTIAS. I feel fine, and anybody who
doesn't like it can pop.

MAGDALENA. We all have to admit the nicest
things about you are your figure and your tact.

ANGUSTIAS. Fortunately, I'll soon be out of   65
this hell.

MAGDALENA. Maybe you won't get out!

MARTIRIO. Stop this talk!

ANGUSTIAS. Besides, a good dowry is better
than dark eyes in one's face!   70

MAGDALENA. All you say just goes in one ear
and out the other.

AMELIA [*to* La PONCIA]. Open the patio door
and see if we can get a bit of a breeze.

[La PONCIA *opens the door.*]   75

MARTIRIO. Last night I couldn't sleep because
of the heat.

AMELIA. Neither could I.

MAGDALENA. I got up for a bit of air. There
was a black storm cloud and a few drops even   80
fell.

PONCIA. It was one in the morning and the
earth seemed to give off fire. I got up too.
Angustias was still at the window with Pepe.

MAGDALENA [*with irony*]. That late? What   85
time did he leave?

ANGUSTIAS. Why do you ask, if you saw him?

AMELIA. He must have left about one-thirty.

ANGUSTIAS. Yes. How did you know?

AMELIA. I heard him cough and heard his   90
mare's hoofbeats.

PONCIA. But I heard him leave around four.

ANGUSTIAS. It must have been someone else!

PONCIA. No, I'm sure of it!

AMELIA. That's what it seemed to me, too.

MAGDALENA. That's very strange!

5 [*Pause.*]

PONCIA. Listen, Angustias, what did he say to you the first time he came by your window?

ANGUSTIAS. Nothing. What should he say? Just talked.

10 MARTIRIO. It's certainly strange that two people who never knew each other should suddenly meet at a window and be engaged.

ANGUSTIAS. Well, I didn't mind.

AMELIA. I'd have felt very strange about it.

15 ANGUSTIAS. No, because when a man comes to a window he knows, from all the busybodies who come and go and fetch and carry, that he's going to be told "yes."

MARTIRIO. All right, but he'd have to ask

20 you.

ANGUSTIAS. Of course!

AMELIA [*inquisitively*]. And how did he ask you?

ANGUSTIAS. Why, no way:—"You know I'm

25 after you. I need a good, well brought up woman, and that's you—if it's agreeable."

AMELIA. These things embarrass me!

ANGUSTIAS. They embarrass me too, but one has to go through it!

30 PONCIA. And did he say anything more?

ANGUSTIAS. Yes, he did all the talking.

MARTIRIO. And you?

ANGUSTIAS. I couldn't have said a word. My heart was almost coming out of my mouth. It

35 was the first time I'd ever been alone at night with a man.

MAGDALENA. And such a handsome man.

ANGUSTIAS. He's not bad looking.

PONCIA. Those things happen among people

40 who have an idea how to do things, who talk and say and move their hand. The first time my husband, Evaristo the Short-tailed, came to my window . . . Ha! Ha! Ha!

AMELIA. What happened?

45 PONCIA. It was very dark. I saw him coming along and as he went by he said, "Good evening," "Good evening," I said. Then we were both silent for more than half an hour. The sweat poured down my body. Then Evaristo got nearer and nearer as if he wanted to 50 squeeze in through the bars and said in a very low voice—"Come here and let me feel you!"

[*They all laugh.* AMELIA *gets up, runs, and looks through the door.*]

AMELIA. Ay, I thought Mother was coming! 55

MAGDALENA. What she'd have done to us!

[*They go on laughing.*]

AMELIA. Sh-h-h! She'll hear us.

PONCIA. Then he acted very decently. Instead of getting some other idea, he went to raising 60 birds, until he died. You aren't married but it's good for you to know, anyway, that two weeks after the wedding a man gives up the bed for the table, then the table for the tavern, and the woman who doesn't like it can just rot, weep- 65 ing in a corner.

AMELIA. You liked it.

PONCIA. I learned how to handle him!

MARTIRIO. Is it true that you sometimes hit him? 70

PONCIA. Yes, and once I almost poked out one of his eyes!

MAGDALENA. All women ought to be like that!

PONCIA. I'm one of your mother's school. 75 One time I don't know what he said to me, and then I killed all his birds—with the pestle!

[*They laugh.*]

MAGDALENA. Adela, child! Don't miss this.

AMELIA. Adela! 80

[*Pause.*]

MAGDALENA. I'll go see!

[*She goes out.*]

PONCIA. That child is sick!

MARTIRIO. Of course. She hardly sleeps! 85

PONCIA. What *does* she do, then?

MARTIRIO. How do I know what she does?

PONCIA. You probably know better than we do, since you sleep with just a wall between you. 90

ANGUSTIAS. Envy gnaws on people.

AMELIA. Don't exaggerate.

ANGUSTIAS. I can tell it in her eyes. She's getting the look of a crazy woman.

MARTIRIO. Don't talk about crazy women. This is one place you're not allowed to say that word.

[MAGDALENA *and* ADELA *enter*.]

5 MAGDALENA. Didn't you say she was asleep?

ADELA. My body aches.

MARTIRIO [*with a hidden meaning*]. Didn't you sleep well last night?

ADELA. Yes.

10 MARTIRIO. Then?

ADELA [*loudly*]. Leave me alone. Awake or asleep, it's no affair of yours. I'll do whatever I want to with my body.

MARTIRIO. I was just concerned about you!

15 ADELA. Concerned?—curious! Weren't you sewing? Well, continue! I wish I were invisible so I could pass through a room without being asked where I was going!

SERVANT [*entering*]. Bernarda is calling you.

20 The man with the laces is here.

[*All but* ADELA *and* LA PONCIA *go out, and as* MARTIRIO *leaves, she looks fixedly at* ADELA.]

ADELA. Don't look at me like that! If you want, I'll give you my eyes, for they're younger,

25 and my back to improve that hump you have, but look the other way when I go by.

PONCIA. Adela, she's your sister, and the one who most loves you besides!

ADELA. She follows me everywhere. Some-

30 times she looks in my room to see if I'm sleeping. She won't let me breathe, and always, "Too bad about that face!" "Too bad about that body! It's going to waste!" But I won't let that happen. My body will be for whom-

35 ever I choose.

PONCIA [*insinuatingly, in a low voice*]. For Pepe el Romano, no?

ADELA [*frightened*]. What do you mean?

PONCIA. What I said, Adela!

40 ADELA. Shut up!

PONCIA [*loudly*]. Don't you think I've noticed?

ADELA. Lower your voice!

PONCIA. Then forget what you're thinking

45 about!

ADELA. What do you know?

PONCIA. We old ones can see through walls.

Where do you go when you get up at night?

ADELA. I wish you were blind!

PONCIA. But my head and hands are full of 50 eyes, where something like this is concerned. I couldn't possibly guess your intentions. Why did you sit almost naked at your window, and with the light on and the window open, when Pepe passed by the second night he came to 55 talk with your sister?

ADELA. That's not true!

PONCIA. Don't be a child! Leave your sister alone. And if you like Pepe el Romano, keep it to yourself. [ADELA *weeps*.] Besides, who 60 says you can't marry him? Your sister Angustias is sickly. She'll die with her first child. Narrow waisted, old—and out of my experience I can tell you she'll die. Then Pepe will do what all widowers do in these parts: he'll 65 marry the youngest and most beautiful, and that's you. Live on that hope, forget him, anything; but don't go against God's law.

ADELA. Hush!

PONCIA. I won't hush! 70

ADELA. Mind your own business. Snooper, traitor!

PONCIA. I'm going to stick to you like a shadow!

ADELA. Instead of cleaning the house and 75 then going to bed and praying for the dead, you root around like an old sow about goings on between men and women—so you can drool over them.

PONCIA. I keep watch; so people won't spit 80 when they pass our door.

ADELA. What a tremendous affection you've suddenly conceived for my sister.

PONCIA. I don't have any affection for any of you. I want to live in a decent house. I don't 85 want to be dirtied in my old age!

ADELA. Save your advice. It's already too late. For I'd leap not over you, just a servant, but over my mother to put out this fire I feel in my legs and my mouth. What can you 90 possibly say about me? That I lock myself in my room and will not open the door? That I don't sleep? I'm smarter than you! See if you can catch the hare with your hands.

724

FEDERICO GARCÍA LORCA │ Act II

PONCIA. Don't defy me, Adela, don't defy me! Because I can shout, light lamps, and make bells ring.

ADELA. Bring four thousand yellow flares
5 and set them about the walls of the yard. No one can stop what has to happen.

PONCIA. You like him that much?

ADELA. That much! Looking in his eyes I seem to drink his blood in slowly.

10 PONCIA. I won't listen to you.

ADELA. Well, you'll have to! I've been afraid of you. But now I'm stronger than you!

[ANGUSTIAS enters.]

ANGUSTIAS. Always arguing!

15 PONCIA. Certainly. She insists that in all this heat I have to go bring her I don't know what from the store.

ANGUSTIAS. Did you buy me the bottle of perfume?

20 PONCIA. The most expensive one. And the face powder. I put them on the table in your room.

[ANGUSTIAS goes out.]

ADELA. And be quiet!

25 PONCIA. We'll see!

[MARTIRIO and AMELIA enter.]

MARTIRIO [to ADELA]. Did you see the laces?

AMELIA. Angustias', for her wedding sheets, are beautiful.

30 ADELA [to MARTIRIO, who is carrying some lace]. And these?

MARTIRIO. They're for me. For a nightgown.

ADELA [with sarcasm]. One needs a sense of humor around here!

35 MARTIRIO [meaningfully]. But only for me to look at. I don't have to exhibit myself before anybody.

PONCIA. No one ever sees us in our nightgowns.

40 MARTIRIO [meaningfully, looking at ADELA]. Sometimes they don't! But I love nice underwear. If I were rich, I'd have it made of Holland Cloth. It's one of the few tastes I've left.

PONCIA. These laces are beautiful for babies'
45 caps and christening gowns. I could never afford them for my own. Now let's see if Angustias will use them for hers. Once she starts having children, they'll keep her running night and day.

MAGDALENA. I don't intend to sew a stitch on 50 them.

AMELIA. And much less bring up some stranger's children. Look how our neighbors across the road are—making sacrifices for four brats. 55

PONCIA. They're better off than you. There at least they laugh and you can hear them fight.

MARTIRIO. Well, you go work for them, then.

PONCIA. No, fate has sent me to this nunnery! 60

[Tiny bells are heard distantly as though through several thicknesses of wall.]

MAGDALENA. It's the men going back to work.

PONCIA. It was three o'clock a minute ago.

MARTIRIO. With this sun! 65

ADELA [sitting down]. Ay! If only we could go out in the fields too!

MAGDALENA [sitting down]. Each class does what it has to!

MARTIRIO [sitting down]. That's it! 70

AMELIA [sitting down]. Ay!

PONCIA. There's no happiness like that in the fields right at this time of year. Yesterday morning the reapers arrived. Forty or fifty handsome young men. 75

MAGDALENA. Where are they from this year?

PONCIA. From far, far away. They came from the mountains! Happy! Like weathered trees! Shouting and throwing stones! Last night a woman who dresses in sequins and dances, 80 with an accordion, arrived, and fifteen of them made a deal with her to take her to the olive grove. I saw them from far away. The one who talked with her was a boy with green eyes— tight knit as a sheaf of wheat. 85

AMELIA. Really?

ADELA. Are you sure?

PONCIA. Years ago another one of those women came here, and I myself gave my eldest son some money so he could go. Men need 90 things like that.

ADELA. Everything's forgiven them.

AMELIA. To be born a woman's the worst possible punishment.

MAGDALENA. Even our eyes aren't our own.

[*A distant song is heard, coming nearer.*]

PONCIA. There they are. They have a beautiful song.

5 AMELIA. They're going out to reap now.

CHORUS.

The reapers have set out
Looking for ripe wheat;
They'll carry off the hearts
10 Of any girls they meet.

[*Tambourines and carrañacas° are heard. Pause. They all listen in the silence cut by the sun.*]

AMELIA. And they don't mind the sun!

15 MARTIRIO. They reap through flames.

ADELA. How I'd like to be a reaper so I could come and go as I pleased. Then we could forget what's eating us all.

MARTIRIO. What do you have to forget?

20 ADELA. Each one of us has something.

MARTIRIO [*intensely*]. Each one!

PONCIA. Quiet! Quiet!

CHORUS [*very distantly*].

Throw wide your doors and windows,
25 You girls who live in the town.
The reaper asks you for roses
With which to deck his crown.

PONCIA. What a song!

MARTIRIO [*with nostalgia*].

30 Throw wide your doors and windows,
You girls who live in the town.

ADELA [*passionately*].

The reaper asks you for roses
With which to deck his crown.

35 [*The song grows more distant.*]

PONCIA. Now they're turning the corner.

ADELA. Let's watch them from the window of my room.

PONCIA. Be careful not to open the shutters
40 too much because they're likely to give them a push to see who's looking.

[*The three leave.* MARTIRIO *is left sitting on the low chair with her head between her hands.*]

45 AMELIA [*drawing near her*]. What's wrong

carrañacas noise-makers(?)

with you?

MARTIRIO. The heat makes me feel ill.

AMELIA. And it's no more than that?

MARTIRIO. I was wishing it were November, the rainy days, the frost—anything except this 50 unending summertime.

AMELIA. It'll pass and come again.

MARTIRIO. Naturally. [*Pause.*] What time did you go to sleep last night?

AMELIA. I don't know. I sleep like a log. 55 Why?

MARTIRIO. Nothing. Only I thought I heard someone in the yard.

AMELIA. Yes?

MARTIRIO. Very late. 60

AMELIA. And weren't you afraid?

MARTIRIO. No. I've heard it other nights.

AMELIA. We'd better watch out! Couldn't it have been the shepherds?

MARTIRIO. The shepherds come at six. 65

AMELIA. Maybe a young, unbroken mule?

MARTIRIO [*to herself, with double meaning*]. That's it! That's it. An unbroken little mule.

AMELIA. We'll have to set a watch.

MARTIRIO. No. No. Don't say anything. It 70 may be I've just imagined it.

AMELIA. Maybe.

[*Pause.* AMELIA *starts to go.*]

MARTIRIO. Amelia!

AMELIA [*at the door*]. What? 75

[*Pause.*]

MARTIRIO. Nothing.

[*Pause.*]

AMELIA. Why did you call me?

[*Pause.*] 80

MARTIRIO. It just came out. I didn't mean to.

[*Pause.*]

AMELIA. Lie down for a little.

ANGUSTIAS. [*She bursts in furiously, in a manner that makes a great contrast with pre-* 85 *vious silence.*] Where's that picture of Pepe I had under my pillow? Which one of you has it?

MARTIRIO. No one.

AMELIA. You'd think he was a silver St. Bartholomew. 90

ANGUSTIAS. Where's the picture?

[PONCIA, MAGDALENA, *and* ADELA *enter.*]

ADELA. What picture?

ANGUSTIAS. One of you has hidden it on me.

MAGDALENA. Do you have the effrontery to say that?

5 ANGUSTIAS. I had it in my room, and now it isn't there.

MARTIRIO. But couldn't it have jumped out into the yard at midnight? Pepe likes to walk around in the moonlight.

10 ANGUSTIAS. Don't joke with me! When he comes I'll tell him.

PONCIA. Don't do that! Because it'll turn up. [Looking at ADELA.]

ANGUSTIAS. I'd like to know which one of 15 you has it.

ADELA [looking at MARTIRIO]. Somebody has it! But not me!

MARTIRIO [with meaning]. Of course not you!

20 BERNARDA [entering, with her cane]. What scandal is this in my house in the heat's heavy silence? The neighbors must have their ears glued to the walls.

ANGUSTIAS. They've stolen my sweetheart's 25 picture!

BERNARDA [fiercely]. Who? Who?

ANGUSTIAS. They have!

BERNARDA. Which one of you? [Silence.] Answer me! [Silence.] [To LA PONCIA.] Search 30 their rooms! Look in their beds.° This comes of not tying you up with shorter leashes. But I'll teach you now! [To ANGUSTIAS.] Are you sure?

ANGUSTIAS. Yes.

35 BERNARDA. Did you look everywhere?

ANGUSTIAS. Yes, Mother.

[They all stand in an embarrassed silence.]

BERNARDA. At the end of my life—to make me drink the bitterest poison a mother knows.

40 [To PONCIA.] Did you find it?

PONCIA. Here it is.

BERNARDA. Where did you find it?

PONCIA. It was . . .

BERNARDA. Say it! Don't be afraid.

Look in their beds Poncia goes out, and reenters at l. 40

PONCIA [wonderingly]. Between the sheets 45 in Martirio's bed.

BERNARDA [to MARTIRIO]. Is that true?

MARTIRIO. It's true.

BERNARDA [advancing on her, beating her with her cane]. You'll come to a bad end yet, 50 you hypocrite! Trouble maker!

MARTIRIO [fiercely]. Don't hit me, Mother!

BERNARDA. All I want to!

MARTIRIO. If I let you! You hear me? Get back! 55

PONCIA. Don't be disrespectful to your mother!

ANGUSTIAS [holding BERNARDA]. Let her go, please!

BERNARDA. Not even tears in your eyes. 60

MARTIRIO. I'm not going to cry just to please you.

BERNARDA. Why did you take the picture?

MARTIRIO. Can't I play a joke on my sister? What else would I want it for? 65

ADELA [leaping forward, full of jealousy]. It wasn't a joke! You never like to play jokes. It was something else bursting in her breast— trying to come out. Admit it openly now.

MARTIRIO. Hush, and don't make me speak; 70 for if I should speak the walls would close together one against the other with shame.

ADELA. An evil tongue never stops inventing lies.

BERNARDA. Adela! 75

MAGDALENA. You're crazy.

AMELIA. And you stone us all with your evil suspicions.

MARTIRIO. But some others do things more wicked! 80

ADELA. Until all at once they stand forth stark naked and the river carries them along.

BERNARDA. Spiteful!

ANGUSTIAS. It's not my fault Pepe el Romano chose me! 85

ADELA. For your money.

ANGUSTIAS. Mother!

BERNARDA. Silence!

MARTIRIO. For your fields and your orchards.

MAGDALENA. That's only fair. 90

BERNARDA. Silence, I say! I saw the storm

coming but I didn't think it'd burst so soon. Oh, what an avalanche of hate you've thrown on my heart! But I'm not old yet—I have five chains for you, and this house my father built, so not even the weeds will know of my desolation. Out of here!

[*They go out.* BERNARDA *sits down desolately.* LA PONCIA *is standing close to the wall.* BERNARDA *recovers herself, and beats on the floor.*]

I'll have to let them feel the weight of my hand! Bernarda, remember your duty!

PONCIA. May I speak?

BERNARDA. Speak. I'm sorry you heard. A stranger is always out of place in a family.

PONCIA. What I've seen, I've seen.

BERNARDA. Angustias must get married right away.

PONCIA. Certainly. We'll have to get her away from here.

BERNARDA. Not her, him!

PONCIA. Of course. He's the one to get away from here. You've thought it all out.

BERNARDA. I'm not thinking. There are things that shouldn't and can't be thought out. I give orders.

PONCIA. And you think he'll be satisfied to go away?

BERNARDA [*rising*]. What are you imagining now?

PONCIA. He will, of course, marry Angustias.

BERNARDA. Speak up! I know you well enough to see that your knife's out for me.

PONCIA. I never knew a warning could be called murder.

BERNARDA. Have you some "warning" for me?

PONCIA. I'm not making any accusations, Bernarda. I'm only telling you to open your eyes and you'll see.

BERNARDA. See what?

PONCIA. You've always been smart, Bernarda. You've seen other people's sins a hundred miles away. Many times I've thought you could read minds. But, your children are your children, and now you're blind.

BERNARDA. Are you talking about Martirio?

PONCIA. Well, yes—about Martirio . . . [*With curiosity.*] I wonder why she hid the picture?

BERNARDA [*shielding her daughter*]. After all, she says it was a joke. What else could it be?

PONCIA [*scornfully*]. Do you believe that?

BERNARDA [*sternly*]. I don't merely believe it. It's so!

PONCIA. Enough of this. We're talking about your family. But if we were talking about your neighbor across the way, what would it be?

BERNARDA. Now you're beginning to pull the point of the knife out.

PONCIA [*always cruelly*]. No, Bernarda. Something very grave is happening here. I don't want to put the blame on your shoulders, but you've never given your daughters any freedom. Martirio is lovesick, I don't care what you say. Why didn't you let her marry Enrique Humanas? Why, on the very day he was coming to her window, did you send him a message not to come?

BERNARDA [*loudly*]. I'd do it a thousand times over! My blood won't mingle with the Humanas' while I live! His father was a shepherd.

PONCIA. And you see now what's happening to you with these airs!

BERNARDA. I have them because I can afford to. And you don't have them because you know where you came from!

PONCIA [*with hate*]. Don't remind me! I'm old now. I've always been grateful for your protection.

BERNARDA [*emboldened*]. You don't seem so!

PONCIA [*with hate, behind softness*]. Martirio will forget this.

BERNARDA. And if she doesn't—the worse for her. I don't believe this is that "very grave thing" that's happening here. Nothing's happening here. It's just that you wish it would! And if it should happen one day, you can be sure it won't go beyond these walls.

PONCIA. I'm not so sure of that! There are people in town who can also read hidden thoughts, from afar.

BERNARDA. How you'd like to see me and my daughters on our way to a whorehouse!

PONCIA. No one knows her own destiny!

BERNARDA. I know my destiny! And my daughters! The whorehouse was for a certain woman, already dead. . . .

5 PONCIA [*fiercely*]. Bernarda, respect the memory of my mother!

BERNARDA. Then don't plague me with your evil thoughts!

[*Pause.*]

10 PONCIA. I'd better stay out of everything.

BERNARDA. That's what you ought to do. Work and keep your mouth shut. The duty of all who work for a living.

PONCIA. But we can't do that. Don't you
15 think it'd be better for Pepe to marry Martirio or . . . yes! : . . Adela?

BERNARDA. No, I don't think so.

PONCIA [*with meaning*]. Adela! She's Romano's real sweetheart!

20 BERNARDA. Things are never the way we want them!

PONCIA. But it's hard work to turn them from their destined course. For Pepe to be with Angustias seems wrong to me—and to other
25 people—and even to the wind. Who knows if they'll get what they want?

BERNARDA. There you go again! Sneaking up on me—giving me bad dreams. But I won't listen to you, because if all you say should
30 come to pass—I'd scratch your face.

PONCIA. Frighten someone else with that.

BERNARDA. Fortunately, my daughters respect me and have never gone against my will!

PONCIA. That's right! But, as soon as they
35 break loose they'll fly to the rooftops!

BERNARDA. And I'll bring them down with stones!

PONCIA. Oh, yes! You were always the bravest one!

40 BERNARDA. I've always enjoyed a good fight!

PONCIA. But aren't people strange. You should see Angustias' enthusiasm for her lover, at her age! And he seems very smitten too. Yesterday my oldest son told me that when
45 he passed by with the oxen at four-thirty in the morning they were still talking.

BERNARDA. At four-thirty?

ANGUSTIAS [*entering*]. That's a lie!

PONCIA. That's what he told me.

BERNARDA [*to* ANGUSTIAS]. Speak up! 50

ANGUSTIAS. For more than a week Pepe has been leaving at one. May God strike me dead if I'm lying.

MARTIRIO [*entering*]. I heard him leave at four too. 55

BERNARDA. But did you see him with your eyes?

MARTIRIO. I didn't want to look out. Don't you talk now through the side window?

ANGUSTIAS. We talk through my bedroom 60
window.

[ADELA *appears at the door.*]

MARTIRIO. Then . . .

BERNARDA. What's going on here?

PONCIA. If you're not careful, you'll find out! 65
At least Pepe was at *one* of your windows— and at four in the morning too!

BERNARDA. Are you sure of that?

PONCIA. You can't be sure of anything in this life! 70

ADELA. Mother, don't listen to someone who wants us to lose everything we have.

BERNARDA. I know how to take care of myself! If the townspeople want to come bearing false witness against me, they'll run into a 75
stone wall! Don't any of you talk about this! Sometimes other people try to stir up a wave of filth to drown us.

MARTIRIO. I don't like to lie.

PONCIA. So there must be something. 80

BERNARDA. There won't be anything. I was born to have my eyes always open. Now I'll watch without closing them 'til I die.

ANGUSTIAS. I have the right to know.

BERNARDA. You don't have any right except 85
to obey. No one's going to fetch and carry for me. [*To* LA PONCIA.] And don't meddle in our affairs. No one will take a step without my knowing it.

SERVANT [*entering*]. There's a big crowd at 90
the top of the street, and all the neighbors are at their doors!

BERNARDA [*to* PONCIA]. Run see what's happening!

[*The girls are about to run out.*] 95
Where are you going? I always knew you for

window-watching women and breakers of your mourning. All of you, to the patio!

[*They go out.* BERNARDA *leaves. Distant shouts are heard.* MARTIRIO *and* ADELA *enter and listen, not daring to step farther than the front door.*]

MARTIRIO. You can be thankful I didn't happen to open my mouth.

ADELA. I would have spoken too.

MARTIRIO. And what were you going to say? Wanting isn't doing!

ADELA. I do what I can and what happens to suit me. You've wanted to, but haven't been able.

MARTIRIO. You won't go on very long.

ADELA. I'll have everything!

MARTIRIO. I'll tear you out of his arms!

ADELA [*pleadingly*]. Martirio, let me be!

MARTIRIO. None of us will have him!

ADELA. He wants me for his house!

MARTIRIO. I saw how he embraced you!

ADELA. I didn't want him to. It's as if I were dragged by a rope.

MARTIRIO. I'll see you dead first!

[MAGDALENA *and* ANGUSTIAS *look in. The tumult is increasing.* THE SERVANT *enters with* BERNARDA. PONCIA *also enters from another door.*]

PONCIA. Bernarda!

BERNARDA. What's happening?

PONCIA. Librada's daughter, the unmarried one, had a child and no one knows whose it is!

ADELA. A child?

PONCIA. And to hide her shame she killed it and hid it under the rocks, but the dogs, with more heart than most Christians, dug it out and, as though directed by the hand of God, left it at her door. Now they want to kill her. They're dragging her through the streets—and down the paths and across the olive groves the men are coming, shouting so the fields shake.

BERNARDA. Yes, let them all come with olive whips and hoe handles—let them all come and kill her!

ADELA. No, not to kill her!

MARTIRIO. Yes—and let us go out too!

BERNARDA. And let whoever loses her de-cency pay for it!

[*Outside a woman's shriek and a great clamor is heard.*]

ADELA. Let her escape! Don't you go out!

MARTIRIO [*looking at* ADELA]. Let her pay what she owes!

BERNARDA [*at the archway*]. Finish her before the guards come! Hot coals in the place where she sinned!

ADELA [*holding her belly*]. No! No!

BERNARDA. Kill her! Kill her!

Curtain

ACT III

[*Four white walls, lightly washed in blue, of the interior patio of* BERNARDA ALBA's *house. The doorways, illumined by the lights inside the rooms, give a tenuous glow to the stage.*

At the center there is a table with a shaded oil lamp about which BERNARDA *and her daughters are eating.* LA PONCIA *serves them.* PRUDENCIA *sits apart. When the curtain rises, there is a great silence interrupted only by the noise of plates and silverware.*]

PRUDENCIA. I'm going. I've made you a long visit. [*She rises.*]

BERNARDA. But wait, Prudencia. We never see one another.

PRUDENCIA. Have they sounded the last call to rosary?

PONCIA. Not yet.

[PRUDENCIA *sits down again.*]

BERNARDA. And your husband, how's he getting on?

PRUDENCIA. The same.

BERNARDA. We never see him either.

PRUDENCIA. You know how he is. Since he quarrelled with his brothers over the inheritance, he hasn't used the front door. He takes a ladder and climbs over the back wall.

BERNARDA. He's a real man! And your daughter?

PRUDENCIA. He's never forgiven her.

BERNARDA. He's right.

PRUDENCIA. I don't know what he told you. I suffer because of it.

BERNARDA. A daughter who's disobedient stops being a daughter and becomes an enemy.

PRUDENCIA. I let water run. The only consolation I've left is to take refuge in the church, but, since I'm losing my sight, I'll have to stop coming so the children won't make fun of me.

[*A heavy blow is heard against the walls.*] What's that?

BERNARDA. The stallion. He's locked in the stall and he kicks against the wall of the house. [*Shouting.*] Tether him and take him out in the yard! [*In a lower voice.*] He must be too hot.

PRUDENCIA. Are you going to put the new mares to him?

BERNARDA. At daybreak.

PRUDENCIA. You've known how to increase your stock.

BERNARDA. By dint of money and struggling.

PONCIA [*interrupting*]. And she has the best herd in these parts. It's a shame that prices are low.

BERNARDA. Do you want a little cheese and honey?

PRUDENCIA. I have no appetite.

[*The blow is heard again.*]

PONCIA. My God!

PRUDENCIA. It quivered in my chest!

BERNARDA [*rising, furiously*]. Do I have to say things twice? Let him out to roll on the straw. [*Pause. Then, as though speaking to the stableman.*] Well, then lock the mares in the corral, but let him run free or he may kick down the walls. [*She returns to the table and sits again.*] Ay, what a life!

PRUDENCIA. You have to fight like a man.

BERNARDA. That's it.

[*ADELA gets up from the table.*]

Where are you going?

ADELA. For a drink of water.

BERNARDA [*raising her voice*]. Bring a pitcher of cool water. [*To ADELA.*] You can sit down.

[*ADELA sits down.*]

PRUDENCIA. And Angustias, when will she get married?

BERNARDA. They're coming to ask for her within three days.

PRUDENCIA. You must be happy.

ANGUSTIAS. Naturally!

AMELIA [*to* MAGDALENA]. You've spilled the salt!

MAGDALENA. You can't possibly have worse luck than you're having.

AMELIA. It always brings bad luck.

BERNARDA. That's enough!

PRUDENCIA [*to* ANGUSTIAS]. Has he given you the ring yet?

ANGUSTIAS. Look at it. [*She holds it out.*]

PRUDENCIA. It's beautiful. Three pearls. In my day, pearls signified tears.

ANGUSTIAS. But things have changed now.

ADELA. I don't think so. Things go on meaning the same. Engagement rings should be diamonds.

PONCIA. The most appropriate.

BERNARDA. With pearls or without them, things are as one proposes.

MARTIRIO. Or as God disposes.

PRUDENCIA. I've been told your furniture is beautiful.

BERNARDA. It cost sixteen thousand *reales*.

PONCIA [*interrupting*]. The best is the wardrobe with the mirror.

PRUDENCIA. I never saw a piece like that.

BERNARDA. We had chests.

PRUDENCIA. The important thing is that everything be for the best.

ADELA. And that you never know.

BERNARDA. There's no reason why it shouldn't be.

[*Bells are heard very distantly.*]

PRUDENCIA. The last call. [*To* ANGUSTIAS.] I'll be coming back to have you show me your clothes.

ANGUSTIAS. Whenever you like.

PRUDENCIA. Good evening—God bless you!

BERNARDA. Good-bye, Prudencia.

ALL FIVE DAUGHTERS [*at the same time*]. God go with you!

[*Pause.* PRUDENCIA *goes out.*]

BERNARDA. Well, we've eaten.

[*They rise.*]

ADELA. I'm going to walk as far as the gate to stretch my legs and get a bit of fresh air.

[MAGDALENA *sits down in a low chair and leans against the wall.*]

AMELIA. I'll go with you.

MARTIRIO. I too.

ADELA [*with contained hate*]. I'm not going to get lost!

AMELIA. One needs company at night.

[*They go out.* BERNARDA *sits down.* ANGUST-IAS *is clearing the table.*]

BERNARDA. I've told you once already! I want you to talk to your sister Martirio. What happened about the picture was a joke and you must forget it.

ANGUSTIAS. You know she doesn't like me.

BERNARDA. Each one knows what she thinks inside. I don't pry into anyone's heart, but I want to put up a good front and have family harmony. You understand?

ANGUSTIAS. Yes.

BERNARDA. Then that's settled.

MAGDALENA. [*She is almost asleep.*] Besides, you'll be gone in no time. [*She falls asleep.*]

ANGUSTIAS. Not soon enough for me.

BERNARDA. What time did you stop talking last night?

ANGUSTIAS. Twelve-thirty.

BERNARDA. What does Pepe talk about?

ANGUSTIAS. I find him absent-minded. He always talks to me as though he were thinking of something else. If I ask him what's the matter, he answers—"We men have our worries."

BERNARDA. You shouldn't ask him. And when you're married, even less. Speak if he speaks, and look at him when he looks at you. That way you'll get along.

ANGUSTIAS. But, Mother, I think he's hiding things from me.

BERNARDA. Don't try to find out. Don't ask him, and above all, never let him see you cry.

ANGUSTIAS. I should be happy, but I'm not.

BERNARDA. It's all the same.

ANGUSTIAS. Many nights I watch Pepe very closely through the window bars and he seems to fade away—as though he were hidden in a cloud of dust like those raised by the flocks.

BERNARDA. That's just because you're not strong.

ANGUSTIAS. I hope so!

BERNARDA. Is he coming tonight?

ANGUSTIAS. No, he went into town with his mother.

BERNARDA. Good, we'll get to bed early. Magdalena!

ANGUSTIAS. She's asleep.

[ADELA, MARTIRIO, *and* AMELIA *enter.*]

AMELIA. What a dark night!

ADELA. You can't see two steps in front of you.

MARTIRIO. A good night for robbers, for anyone who needs to hide.

ADELA. The stallion was in the middle of the corral. White. Twice as large. Filling all the darkness.

AMELIA. It's true. It was frightening. Like a ghost.

ADELA. The sky has stars as big as fists.

MARTIRIO. This one stared at them till she almost cracked her neck.

ADELA. Don't you like them up there?

MARTIRIO. What goes on over the roof doesn't mean a thing to me. I have my hands full with what happens under it.

ADELA. Well, that's the way it goes with you!

BERNARDA. And it goes the same for you as for her.

ANGUSTIAS. Good night.

ADELA. Are you going to bed now?

ANGUSTIAS. Yes, Pepe isn't coming tonight. [*She goes out.*]

ADELA. Mother, why, when a star falls or lightning flashes, does one say:

Holy Barbara, blessed on high
May your name be in the sky
With holy water written high?

BERNARDA. The old people know many things we've forgotten.

AMELIA. I close my eyes so I won't see them.

ADELA. Not I. I like to see what's quiet and been quiet for years on end, running with fire.

MARTIRIO. But all that has nothing to do with us.

BERNARDA. And it's better not to think about it.

ADELA. What a beautiful night! I'd like to stay up till very late and enjoy the breeze from the fields.

BERNARDA. But we have to go to bed. Magdalena!

AMELIA. She's just dropped off.

BERNARDA. Magdalena!

MAGDALENA [*annoyed*]. Leave me alone!

BERNARDA. To bed!

MAGDALENA [rising, in a bad humor]. You don't give anyone a moment's peace!

[She goes off grumbling.]

5 AMELIA. Good night!

[She goes out.]

BERNARDA. You two get along, too.

MARTIRIO. How is it Angustias' sweetheart isn't coming tonight?

10 BERNARDA. He went on a trip.

MARTIRIO [looking at ADELA]. Ah!

ADELA. I'll see you in the morning!

[She goes out. MARTIRIO drinks some water and goes out slowly, looking at the door to the
15 yard. LA PONCIA enters.]

PONCIA. Are you still here?

BERNARDA. Enjoying this quiet and not seeing anywhere the "very grave thing" that's happening here—according to you.

20 PONCIA. Bernarda, let's not go any further with this.

BERNARDA. In this house there's no question of a yes or a no. My watchfulness can take care of anything.

25 PONCIA. Nothing's happening outside. That's true, all right. Your daughters act and are as though stuck in a cupboard. But neither you nor anyone else can keep watch inside a person's heart.

30 BERNARDA. My daughters breathe calmly enough.

PONCIA. That's your business, since you're their mother. I have enough to do just with serving you.

35 BERNARDA. Yes, you've turned quiet now.

PONCIA. I keep my place—that's all.

BERNARDA. The trouble is you've nothing to talk about. If there were grass in this house, you'd make it your business to put the neigh-
40 bors' sheep to pasture here.

PONCIA. I hide more than you think.

BERNARDA. Do your sons still see Pepe at four in the morning? Are they still repeating this house's evil litany?

45 PONCIA. They say nothing.

BERNARDA. Because they can't. Because there's nothing for them to sink their teeth in. And all because my eyes keep constant watch!

PONCIA. Bernarda! I don't want to talk about this because I'm afraid of what you'll do. But 50
don't you feel so safe.

BERNARDA. Very safe!

PONCIA. Who knows, lightning might strike suddenly. Who knows but what all of a sudden, in a rush of blood, your heart might stop. 55

BERNARDA. Nothing will happen here. I'm on guard now against all your suspicions.

PONCIA. All the better for you.

BERNARDA. Certainly, all the better!

SERVANT [entering]. I've just finished with 60
the dishes. Is there anything else, Bernarda?

BERNARDA [rising]. Nothing. I'm going to get some rest.

PONCIA. What time do you want me to call you? 65

BERNARDA. No time. Tonight I intend to sleep well.

[She goes out.]

PONCIA. When you're powerless against the sea, it's easier to turn your back on it and not 70
look at it.

SERVANT. She's so proud! She herself pulls the blindfold over her eyes.

PONCIA. I can do nothing. I tried to head things off, but now they frighten me too much. 75
You feel this silence?—in each room there's a thunderstorm—and the day it breaks, it'll sweep all of us along with it. But I've said what I had to say.

SERVANT. Bernarda thinks nothing can stand 80
against her, yet she doesn't know the strength a man has among women alone.

PONCIA. It's not all the fault of Pepe el Romano. It's true last year he was running after Adela; and she was crazy about him— 85
but she ought to keep her place and not lead him on. A man's a man.

SERVANT. And some there are who believe he didn't have to talk many times with Adela.

PONCIA. That's true. [In a low voice.] And 90
some other things.

SERVANT. I don't know what's going to happen here.

PONCIA. How I'd like to sail across the sea and leave this house, this battleground, behind! 95

SERVANT. Bernarda's hurrying the wedding and it's possible nothing will happen.

PONCIA. Things have gone much too far already. Adela is set° no matter what comes, and the rest of them watch without rest.

SERVANT. Martirio too . . . ?

PONCIA. That one's the worst. She's a pool
5 of poison. She sees El Romano is not for her, and she'd sink the world if it were in her hand to do so.

SERVANT. How bad they all are!

PONCIA. They're women without men, that's
10 all. And in such matters even blood is forgotten. Sh-h-h-h! [*She listens.*]

SERVANT. What's the matter?

PONCIA. [*She rises.*] The dogs are barking.

SERVANT. Someone must have passed by the
15 back door.

[ADELA *enters wearing a white petticoat and corselet.*]

PONCIA. Aren't you in bed yet?

ADELA. I want a drink of water. [*She drinks
20 from a glass on the table.*]

PONCIA. I imagined you were asleep.

ADELA. I got thirsty and woke up. Aren't you two going to get some rest?

SERVANT. Soon now.

25 [ADELA *goes out.*]

PONCIA. Let's go.

SERVANT. We've certainly earned some sleep. Bernarda doesn't let me rest the whole day.

PONCIA. Take the light.

30 SERVANT. The dogs are going mad.

PONCIA. They're not going to let us sleep.

[*They go out. The stage is left almost dark. MARIA JOSEFA enters with a lamb in her arms.*]

MARIA JOSEFA [*singing*].

35 Little lamb, child of mine,
Let's go to the shore of the sea,
The tiny ant will be at his doorway,
I'll nurse you and give you your bread.
Bernarda, old leopard-face,
40 And Magdalena, hyena-face,
Little lamb . . .
Rock, rock-a-bye,
Let's go to the palms at Bethlehem's gate.
[*She laughs.*]
45 Neither you nor I would want to sleep
The door will open by itself
And on the beach we'll go and hide

is set. i.e., has made up her mind

In a little coral cabin.
Bernarda, old leopard-face,
And Magdalena, hyena-face, 50
Little lamb . . .
Rock, rock-a-bye,
Let's go to the palms at Bethlehem's gate.
[*She goes off singing.*]
[ADELA *enters. She looks about cautiously* 55 *and disappears out the door leading to the corral.* MARTIRIO *enters by another door and stands in anguished watchfulness near the center of the stage. She also is in petticoats. She covers herself with a small black scarf.* 60 MARIA JOSEFA *crosses before her.*]

MARTIRIO. Grandmother, where are you going?

MARIA JOSEFA. You are going to open the door for me? Who are you? 65

MARTIRIO. How did you get out here?

MARIA JOSEFA. I escaped. You, who are you?

MARTIRIO. Go back to bed.

MARIA JOSEFA. You're Martirio. Now I see you. Martirio, face of a martyr. And when are 70 you going to have a baby? I've had this one.

MARTIRIO. Where did you get that lamb?

MARIA JOSEFA. I know it's a lamb. But can't a lamb be a baby? It's better to have a lamb than not to have anything. Old Bernarda, 75 leopard-face, and Magdalena, hyena-face!

MARTIRIO. Don't shout.

MARIA JOSEFA. It's true. Everything's very dark. Just because I have white hair you think I can't have babies, but I can—babies and 80 babies and babies. This baby will have white hair, and I'd have *this* baby, and another, and this *one* other; and with all of us with snow white hair we'll be like the waves—one, then another, and another. Then we'll all sit down 85 and all of us will have white heads, and we'll be seafoam. Why isn't there any seafoam here? Nothing but mourning shrouds here.

MARTIRIO. Hush, hush.

MARIA JOSEFA. When my neighbor had a 90 baby, I'd carry her some chocolate and later she'd bring me some, and so on—always and always and always. You'll have white hair, but your neighbors won't come. Now I have to go away, but I'm afraid the dogs will bite 95 me. Won't you come with me as far as the

fields? I don't like fields. I like houses, but open houses, and the neighbor women asleep in their beds with their little tiny tots, and the men outside sitting in their chairs. Pepe el
5 Romano is a giant. All of you love him. But he's going to devour you because you're grains of wheat. No, not grains of wheat. Frogs with no tongues!

MARTIRIO [*angrily*]. Come, off to bed with
10 you. [*She pushes her.*]

MARIA JOSEFA. Yes, but then you'll open the door for me, won't you?

MARTIRIO. Of course.

MARIA JOSEFA [*weeping*].
15   Little lamb, child of mine,
      Let's go to the shore of the sea,
      The tiny ant will be at his doorway,
      I'll nurse you and give you your bread.

[MARTIRIO *locks the door through which*
20 MARIA JOSEFA *came out and goes to the yard door. There she hesitates, but goes two steps farther.*]

MARTIRIO [*in a low voice*]. Adela! [*Pause. She advances to the door. Then, calling.*]
25 Adela!

[ADELA *enters. Her hair is disarranged.*]

ADELA. And what are you looking for me for?

MARTIRIO. Keep away from him.
30 ADELA. Who are you to tell me that?

MARTIRIO. That's no place for a decent woman.

ADELA. How you wish *you'd* been there!

MARTIRIO [*shouting*]. This is the moment for
35 me to speak. This can't go on.

ADELA. This is just the beginning. I've had strength enough to push myself forward—the spirit and looks you lack. I've seen death under this roof, and gone out to look for what was
40 mine, what belonged to me.

MARTIRIO. That soulless man came for another woman. You pushed yourself in front of him.

ADELA. He came for the money, but his eyes
45 were always on me.

MARTIRIO. I won't allow you to snatch him away. He'll marry Angustias.

ADELA. You know better than I he doesn't

love her.

MARTIRIO. I know.   50

ADELA. You know because you've seen— he loves me, me!

MARTIRIO [*desperately*]. Yes.

ADELA [*close before her*]. He loves me, *me!* He loves me, *me!*   55

MARTIRIO. Stick me with a knife if you like, but don't tell me that again.

ADELA. That's why you're trying to fix it so I won't go away with him. It makes no dif- ference to you if he puts his arms around a 60 woman he doesn't love. Nor does it to me. He could be a hundred years with Angustias, but for him to have his arms around me seems terrible to you—because you too love him! You love him!   65

MARTIRIO [*dramatically*]. Yes! Let me say it without hiding my head. Yes! My breast's bit- ter, bursting like a pomegranate. I love him!

ADELA [*impulsively, hugging her*]. Martirio, Martirio, I'm not to blame!   70

MARTIRIO. Don't put your arms around me! Don't try to smooth it over. My blood's no longer yours, and even though I try to think of you as a sister, I see you as just another woman. [*She pushes her away.*]   75

ADELA. There's no way out here. Whoever has to drown—let her drown. Pepe is mine. He'll carry me to the rushes along the river bank. . . .

MARTIRIO. He won't!   80

ADELA. I can't stand this horrible house after the taste of his mouth. I'll be what he wants me to·be. Everybody in the village against me, burning me with their fiery fingers; pursued by those who claim they're decent, and I'll 85 wear, before them all, the crown of thorns that belongs to the mistress of a married man.

MARTIRIO. Hush!

ADELA. Yes, yes. [*In a low voice.*] Let's go to bed. Let's let him marry Angustias. I don't 90 care any more, but I'll go off alone to a little house where he'll come to see me whenever he wants, whenever he feels like it.

MARTIRIO. That'll never happen! Not while I have a drop of blood left in my body.   95

ADELA. Not just weak you, but a wild horse

I could force to his knees with just the strength of my little finger.

MARTIRIO. Don't raise that voice of yours to me. It irritates me. I have a heart full of a
5 force so evil that, without my wanting to be, I'm drowned by it.

ADELA. You show us the way to love our sisters. God must have meant to leave me alone in the midst of darkness, because I can
10 see you as I've never seen you before.

[*A whistle is heard and* ADELA *runs toward the door, but* MARTIRIO *gets in front of her.*]

MARTIRIO. Where are you going?

ADELA. Get away from that door!
15 MARTIRIO. Get by me if you can!

ADELA. Get away!

[*They struggle.*]

MARTIRIO [*shouts*]. Mother! Mother!

ADELA. Let me go!
20 [BERNARDA *enters. She wears petticoats and a black shawl.*]

BERNARDA. Quiet! Quiet! How poor I am without even a man to help me!

MARTIRIO [*pointing to* ADELA]. She was with
25 him. Look at those skirts covered with straw!

BERNARDA [*going furiously toward* ADELA]. That's the bed of a bad woman!

ADELA [*facing her*]. There'll be an end to prison voices here!
30 [ADELA *snatches away her mother's cane and breaks it in two.*]

This is what I do with the tyrant's cane. Not another step. No one but Pepe commands me!

[MAGDALENA *enters.*]
35 MAGDALENA. Adela!

[LA PONCIA *and* ANGUSTIAS *enter.*]

ADELA. I'm his. [*To* ANGUSTIAS.] Know that —and go out in the yard and tell him. He'll be master in this house.
40 ANGUSTIAS. My God!

BERNARDA. The gun! Where's the gun?

[*She rushes out,* MARTIRIO *following.* AMELIA *enters and looks on frightened, leaning her head against the wall.*]
45 ADELA. No one can hold me back! [*She tries to go out.*]

ANGUSTIAS [*holding her*]. You're not getting out of here with your body's triumph! Thief! Disgrace of this house!

MAGDALENA. Let her go where we'll never 50 see her again!

[*A shot is heard.*]

BERNARDA [*entering*]. Just try looking for him now!

MARTIRIO [*entering*]. That does away with 55 Pepe el Romano.

ADELA. Pepe! My God! Pepe!

[*She runs out.*]

PONCIA. Did you kill him?

MARTIRIO. No. He raced away on his mare! 60

BERNARDA. It was my fault. A woman can't aim.

MAGDALENA. Then, why did you say . . . ?

MARTIRIO. For her! I'd like to pour a river of blood over her head!

PONCIA. Curse you! 65

MAGDALENA. Devil!

BERNARDA. Although it's better this way!

[*A thud is heard.*]

Adela! Adela!

PONCIA [*at her door*]. Open this door! 70

BERNARDA. Open! Don't think the walls will hide your shame!

SERVANT [*entering*]. All the neighbors are up!

BERNARDA [*in a low voice, but like a roar*]. Open! Or I'll knock the door down! [*Pause.* 75 *Everything is silent.*] Adela! [*She walks away from the door.*] A hammer!

[LA PONCIA *throws herself against the door. It opens and she goes in. As she enters, she screams and backs out.*] 80

What is it?

PONCIA. [*She puts her hand to her throat.*] May we never die like that!

[THE SISTERS *fall back.* THE SERVANT *crosses herself.* BERNARDA *screams and goes forward.*] 85

Don't go in!

BERNARDA. No, not I! Pepe, you're running now, alive, in the darkness, under the trees, but another day you'll fall. Cut her down! My daughter died a virgin. Take her to another 90 room and dress her as though she were a virgin. No one will say anything about this! She died a virgin. Tell them, so that at dawn, the bells will ring twice.

MARTIRIO. A thousand times happy she, who 95 had him.

BERNARDA. And I want no weeping. Death must be looked at face to face. Silence! [*To one daughter.*] Be still, I said! [*To another daughter.*] Tears when you're alone! We'll 5 drown ourselves in a sea of mourning. She, the youngest daughter of Bernarda Alba, died a virgin. Did you hear me? Silence, silence, I said. Silence!

Curtain

Bertolt Brecht

1898–1956

The Good Woman of Setzuan

1943

Among the legends entering thematically into *The Good Woman of Setzuan* are those of humble folk who have entertained gods or angels (like Baucis and Philemon, the old Greek couple who offered hospitality to Zeus and Hermes in disguise), and those of cities or countries preserved by the presence in them of a remnant of righteous men ("And the Lord said, If I find in Sodom fifty righteous within the city, then I will spare all the place for their sakes." Genesis 18:26.). For Brecht is raising time-honored ethical questions. Where indeed are piety and virtue to be found? And how can they prove generally redemptive, or even survive, in the welter of human stupidity and selfishness?

Having set up these grand resonances, Brecht follows the personal and commercial fortunes of his heroine Shen Te, the Good Woman of the title, who receives as a reward for her hospitality to the gods a gift enabling her to set up a tobacco shop. Shen Te had earlier been selling herself for her livelihood: she is a version of the spiritually unsoiled prostitute, a minor stereotype of romantic literature. As she is by turns coldly efficient and freely charitable in managing her new business, her fortunes wax and wane with a stylized regularity—as in stories where good and bad fairies are alternately in the ascendant. Her sudden turnabouts, meanwhile, ring changes on the theme of the antithetical counterpart: of self and antiself, Dr. Jekyll and Mr. Hyde. Interwoven with her commercial vicissitudes, finally, are the changes of a simple and primal love story: Shen Te meets and falls in love with an aspiring airman—her fitting complement in his skyward yearnings although not in his conduct otherwise.

These conventional patterns—although giving the wry twist that is Brecht's trademark—affirm the simple and familiar quality of the action. And the dramaturgy consistently supports our impression that a fable or parable is unfolding rather than a chapter of "life." The setting is a fancifully

737

remote Chinese province. The players break the illusion by addressing the audience directly. And the characters are developed to the point where we experience quick starts of sympathy for them but no steady empathy; in Brecht's opinion, any "identification" with the persons of a drama produces a mindlessly emotional response. He had a didactic conception of his art— therein resembling G. B. Shaw, whose *Saint Joan* has both thematic and technical affinities with *The Good Woman.*

The message of this play is presented with clarity and animation. Brecht is aware, with realists of every age, that virtue can fail to procure instant and visible rewards. And he goes on to propose—as if in answer to the moralism that crime does not pay—that virtue does not pay either: it is exploited and in a manner punished. Leaving his heroine in anguish, her dilemma conspicuously unresolved, he twits his audience with a cynical proposition: "That virtue to which you so respectably subscribe is in itself ineffectual; to preserve what you hold dear, you must possess yourselves of the instruments of power and wield them unashamedly."

The stoic's answer to such apparent cynicism is that we are to follow virtue for its own sake, whatever the consequences. But this is too close to the view of Brecht's ridiculous and discredited gods. Not moral doctrine but human sympathy is the wellspring of his own Good Woman's goodness. "The charm of Miss Shen Te derives from the goodness of her heart." Kindly affections spring unbidden here and there throughout the play, deriving sometimes from physical attraction, sometimes from spontaneous impulses to succor and befriend. They spring, even, although without sustained energy, in the soiled and selfish soul of Shen Te's beloved Yang Sun. Brecht, who is unabashedly sardonic when he exhibits human baseness, is freely sentimental when he exhibits love and good will. Surrendering neither his critical sense nor his good nature, he weaves a thematic whole that is at once bracing in its honesty and heartwarming in its benevolence.

Brecht, although a Marxist, evidently doubted that an ideal human condition could be programmed. He asserts his independence of any limiting orthodoxy, whether political or literary. He affirms (opposing the absurdists) that we can contemplate the unaccountable and arbitrary aspects of life without surrendering our own minds to irrationality. In contrast to the existentialists—those, at least, who are most preoccupied with human solitude—he presents a balanced view of men as social beings. And in contrast to all dramatists both bourgeois and proletarian who would see in the failure of humble protagonists the stuff of tragedy, Brecht delightfully and delightedly descants on the perennial comic theme: "What fools these mortals be!"

There has hardly been in the modern theater a saner or more engaging playwright than Bertolt Brecht.

The Good Woman of Setzuan

BRECHT

Translated by Eric Bentley

CHARACTERS

WONG, *a water seller*
THREE GODS
SHEN TE, *a prostitute, later a shopkeeper*
MRS. SHIN, *former owner of Shen Te's shop*
A FAMILY OF EIGHT (*husband, wife, brother, sister-in-law, grandfather, nephew, niece, boy*)
AN UNEMPLOYED MAN
A CARPENTER
MRS. MI TZU, *Shen Te's landlady*
YANG SUN, *an unemployed pilot, later a factory manager*
AN OLD WHORE
A POLICEMAN
AN OLD MAN
AN OLD WOMAN, *his wife*
MR. SHU FU, *a barber*
MRS. YANG, *mother of Yang Sun*
GENTLEMEN, VOICES, CHILDREN (3), etc.

PROLOGUE

[*At the gates of the half-westernized city of*

Bertolt Brecht, "The Good Woman of Setzuan" from Parables for the Theater: Two plays by Bertolt Brecht, *translated by Eric Bentley. University of Minnesota Press, Minneapolis. Copyright 1948 by Eric Bentley.*

Setzuan.° Evening. WONG *the Water Seller introduces himself to the audience.*]

WONG. I sell water here in the city of Setzuan. It isn't easy. When water is scarce, I 5 have long distances to go in search of it, and when it is plentiful, I have no income. But in our part of the world there is nothing unusual about poverty. Many people think only the gods can save the situation. And I hear from 10 a cattle merchant—who travels a lot—that some of the highest gods are on their way here at this very moment. Informed sources have it that heaven is quite disturbed at all the complaining. I've been coming out here to 15 the city gates for three days now to bid these gods welcome. I want to be the first to greet them. What about those fellows over there? No, no, they *work*. And that one there has ink on his fingers, he's no god, he must be a 20 clerk from the cement factory. *Those* two are another story. They look as though they'd like to beat you. But gods don't need to beat you, do they? [Enter THREE GODS.] What about those three? Old-fashioned clothes— 25 dust on their feet—they *must* be gods! [*He throws himself at their feet.*] Do with me what you will, illustrious ones!

FIRST GOD [*with an ear trumpet*]. Ah! [*He is pleased.*] So we were expected? 30

WONG [*giving them water*]. Oh, yes. And I *knew* you'd come.

FIRST GOD. We need somewhere to stay the night. You know of a place?

WONG. The whole town is at your service, 35 illustrious ones! What sort of a place would you like?

[*The* GODS *eye each other.*]

FIRST GOD. Just try the first house you come to, my son. 40

WONG. That would be Mr. Fo's place.

FIRST GOD. Mr. Fo.

---

city of Setzuan there is no such city, of course, although there is a Chinese province usually spelled Szechwan. The locale is "half-Westernized" to divorce it from national particularity.

WONG. One moment! [*He knocks at the first house.*]

VOICE FROM MR. FO'S. No!

[WONG *returns a little nervously.*]

WONG. It's too bad. Mr. Fo isn't in. And his servants don't dare do a thing without his consent. He'll have a fit when he finds out who they turned away, won't he?

FIRST GOD [*smiling*]. He will, won't he?

WONG. One moment! The next house is Mr. Cheng's. Won't he be thrilled?

FIRST GOD. Mr. Cheng.

[WONG *knocks.*]

VOICE FROM MR. CHENG'S. Keep your gods. We have our own troubles!

WONG [*back with the GODS*]. Mr. Cheng is very sorry, but he has a houseful of relations. I think some of them are a bad lot, and naturally, he wouldn't like you to see them.

THIRD GOD. Are we so terrible?

WONG. Well, only with bad people, of course. Everyone knows the province of Kwan is always having floods.

SECOND GOD. Really? How's *that*?

WONG. Why, because they're so irreligious.

SECOND GOD. Rubbish. It's because they neglected the dam.

FIRST GOD [*to* SECOND]. Sh! [*To* WONG.] You're still in hopes, aren't you, my son?

WONG. Certainly. All Setzuan is competing for the honor! What happened up to now is pure coincidence. I'll be back. [*He walks away, but then stands undecided.*]

SECOND GOD. What did I tell you?

THIRD GOD. It *could* be pure coincidence.

SECOND GOD. The same coincidence in Shun, Kwan, and Setzuan? People just aren't religious any more, let's face the fact. Our mission has failed!

FIRST GOD. Oh come, we might run into a good person any minute.

THIRD GOD. How did the resolution read? [*Unrolling a scroll and reading from it.*] "The world can stay as it is if enough people are found living lives worthy of human beings." Good people, that is. Well, what about this Water Seller himself? *He's* good, or I'm very much mistaken.

SECOND GOD. You're very much mistaken. When he gave us a drink, I had the impression there was something odd about the cup. Well, look! [*He shows the cup to the* FIRST GOD.]

FIRST GOD. A false bottom!

SECOND GOD. The man is a swindler.

FIRST GOD. Very well, count *him* out. That's one man among millions. And as a matter of fact, we only need one on *our* side. These atheists are saying, "The world must be changed because no one can *be* good and *stay* good." No one, eh? I say: let us find one—just one—and we have those fellows where we want them!

THIRD GOD [*to* WONG]. Water Seller, is it so hard to find a place to stay?

WONG. Nothing could be easier. It's just me. I don't go about it right.

THIRD GOD. Really? [*He returns to the others. A* GENTLEMAN *passes by.*]

WONG. Oh dear, they're catching on. [*He accosts the* GENTLEMAN.] Excuse the intrusion, dear sir, but three gods have just turned up. Three of the very highest. They need a place for the night. Seize this rare opportunity—to have real gods as your guests!

GENTLEMAN [*laughing*]. A new way of finding free rooms for a gang of crooks.

[*Exit* GENTLEMAN.]

WONG [*shouting at him*]. Godless rascal! Have you no religion, gentlemen of Setzuan? [*Pause.*] Patience, illustrious ones! [*Pause.*] There's only one person left. Shen Te, the prostitute. She *can't* say no. [*Calls up to a window.*] Shen Te!

[SHEN TE *opens the shutters and looks out.*]

WONG. *They're* here, and nobody wants them. Will you take them?

SHEN TE. Oh, no, Wong, I'm expecting a gentleman.

WONG. Can't you forget about him for tonight?

SHEN TE. The rent has to be paid by tomorrow or I'll be out on the street.

WONG. This is no time for calculation, Shen Te.

SHEN TE. Stomachs rumble even on the Emperor's birthday, Wong.

WONG. Setzuan is one big dung hill!

SHEN TE. Oh, very well! I'll hide till my gentleman has come and gone. Then I'll take them. [*She disappears.*]

5 WONG. They mustn't see her gentleman or they'll know what she is.

FIRST GOD [*who hasn't heard any of this*]. I think it's hopeless.

[*They approach* WONG.]

10 WONG [*jumping, as he finds them behind him*]. A room has been found, illustrious ones! [*He wipes sweat off his brow.*]

SECOND GOD. Oh, good.

THIRD GOD. Let's see it.

15 WONG [*nervously*]. Just a minute. It has to be tidied up a bit.

THIRD GOD. Then we'll sit down here and wait.

WONG [*still more nervous*]. No, no! [*Hold-*
20 *ing himself back.*] Too much traffic, you know.

THIRD GOD [*with a smile*]. Of course, if you *want* us to move.

[*They retire a little. They sit on a doorstep.* WONG *sits on the ground.*]

25 WONG [*after a deep breath*]. You'll be staying with a single girl—the finest human being in Setzuan!

THIRD GOD. That's nice.

WONG [*to the audience*]. They gave me such
30 a look when I picked up my cup just now.

THIRD GOD. You're worn out, Wong.

WONG. A little, maybe.

FIRST GOD. Do people here have a hard time of it?

35 WONG. The good ones do.

FIRST GOD. What about yourself?

WONG. You mean I'm not good. That's true. And I don't have an easy time either!

[*During this dialogue, a* GENTLEMAN *has*
40 *turned up in front of* SHEN TE's *house, and has whistled several times. Each time* WONG *has given a start.*]

THIRD GOD [*to* WONG, *softly*]. Psst! I think he's gone now.

45 WONG [*confused and surprised*]. Ye-e-es.

[*The* GENTLEMAN *has left now, and* SHEN TE *has come down to the street.*]

SHEN TE [*softly*]. Wong!

[*Getting no answer, she goes off down the street.* WONG *arrives just too late, forgetting* 50 *his carrying pole.*]

WONG [*softly*]. Shen Te! Shen Te! [*To himself.*] So she's gone off to earn the rent. Oh dear, I can't go to the gods *again* with no room to offer them. Having failed in the service of 55 the gods, I shall run to my den in the sewer pipe down by the river and hide from their sight!

[*He rushes off.* SHEN TE *returns, looking for him, but finding the gods. She stops in con-* 60 *fusion.*]

SHEN TE. You are the illustrious ones? My name is Shen Te. It would please me very much if my simple room could be of use to you.

THIRD GOD. Where is the Water Seller, Miss 65 . . . Shen Te?

SHEN TE. I missed him, somehow.

FIRST GOD. Oh, he probably thought you weren't coming, and was afraid of telling us.

THIRD GOD [*picking up the carrying pole*]. 70 We'll leave this with you. He'll be needing it.

[*Led by* SHEN TE, *they go into the house. It grows dark, then light. Dawn. Again escorted by* SHEN TE, *who leads them through the half-light with a little lamp, the* GODS *take their* 75 *leave.*]

FIRST GOD. Thank you, thank you, dear Shen Te, for your elegant hospitality! We shall not forget! And give our thanks to the Water Seller —he showed us a good human being. 80

SHEN TE. Oh, *I'm* not good. Let me tell you something: when Wong asked me to put you up, I hesitated.

FIRST GOD. It's all right to hesitate if you then go ahead! And in giving us that room you 85 did much more than you knew. You proved that good people still exist, a point that has been disputed of late—even in heaven. Farewell!

SECOND GOD. Farewell! 90

THIRD GOD. Farewell!

SHEN TE. Stop, illustrious ones! I'm not sure you're right. I'd like to be good, it's true, but there's the rent to pay. And that's not all: I sell myself for a living. Even so I can't make 95 ends meet, there's too much competition. I'd like to honor my father and mother and speak nothing but the truth and not covet my neighbor's house. I should love to stay with one man. But how? How is it done? Even breaking 5 only a *few* of your commandments, I can hardly manage.

FIRST GOD [*clearing his throat*]. These thoughts are but, um, the misgivings of an unusually good woman!

10 THIRD GOD. Goodbye, Shen Te! Give our regards to the Water Seller!

SECOND GOD. And above all: be good! Farewell!

FIRST GOD. Farewell!

15 THIRD GOD. Farewell!

[*They start to wave goodbye.*]

SHEN TE. But everything is so expensive, I don't feel sure I can do it!

SECOND GOD. That's not in our sphere. We 20 never meddle with economics.

THIRD GOD. One moment.

[*They stop.*]

Isn't it true she might do better if she had more money?

25 SECOND GOD. Come, come! How could we ever account for it Up Above?

FIRST GOD. Oh, there are ways.

[*They put their heads together and confer in dumb show. To* SHEN TE, *with embarrass-* 30 *ment.*] As you say you can't pay your rent, well, um, we're not paupers, so of course we *insist* on paying for our room. [*Awkwardly thrusting money into her hands.*] There! [*Quickly.*] But don't tell anyone! The incident 35 is open to misinterpretation.

SECOND GOD. It certainly is!

FIRST GOD [*defensively*]. But there's no law against it! It was never decreed that a god mustn't pay hotel bills!

40 [*The* GODS *leave.*]

SCENE I

[*A small tobacco shop. The shop is not as yet completely furnished and hasn't started doing business.*]

SHEN TE [*to the audience*]. It's three days since the gods left. When they said they 45 wanted to pay for the room, I looked down at my hand, and there was more than a thousand silver dollars! I bought a tobacco shop with the money, and moved in yesterday. I don't own the building, of course, but I can pay the rent, 50 and I hope to do a lot of good here. Beginning with Mrs. Shin, who's just coming across the square with her pot. She had the shop before me, and yesterday she dropped in to ask for rice for her children. 55

[*Enter* MRS. SHIN. *Both women bow.*]

How do you do, Mrs. Shin.

MRS. SHIN. How do you do, Miss Shen Te. You like your new home?

SHEN TE. Indeed, yes. Did your children 60 have a good night?

MRS. SHIN. In that hovel? The youngest is coughing already.

SHEN TE. Oh, dear!

MRS. SHIN. You're going to learn a thing or 65 two in these slums.

SHEN TE. Slums? That's not what you said when you sold me the shop!

MRS. SHIN. Now don't start nagging! Robbing me and my innocent children of their 70 home and then calling it a slum! That's the limit! [*She weeps.*]

SHEN TE [*tactfully*]. I'll get your rice.

MRS. SHIN. And a little cash while you're at it. 75

SHEN TE. I'm afraid I haven't sold anything yet.

MRS. SHIN [*screeching*]. I've got to have it. Strip the clothes from my back and then cut my throat, will you? I know what I'll do: I'll 80 leave my children on your doorstep! [*She snatches the pot out of* SHEN TE'S *hands.*]

SHEN TE. Please don't be angry. You'll spill the rice.

[*Enter an elderly* HUSBAND *and* WIFE *with* 85 *their shabbily-dressed* NEPHEW.]

WIFE. Shen Te, dear! You've come into money, they tell me. And we haven't a roof over our heads! A tobacco shop. We had one too. But it's gone. Could we spend the night 90 here, do you think?

NEPHEW [*appraising the shop*]. Not bad!

WIFE. He's our nephew. We're inseparable!

MRS. SHIN. And who are these . . . ladies and gentlemen?

5 SHEN TE. They put me up when I first came in from the country. [*To the audience.*] Of course, when my small purse was empty, they put me out on the street, and they may be afraid I'll do the same to them. [*To the new-*
10 *comers, kindly.*] Come in, and welcome, though I've only one little room for you—it's behind the shop.

HUSBAND. That'll do. Don't worry.

WIFE [*bringing* SHEN TE *some tea*]. We'll
15 stay over here, so we won't be in your way. Did you make it a tobacco shop in memory of your first real home? We can certainly give you a hint or two! That's one reason we came.

MRS. SHIN [*to* SHEN TE]. Very nice! As long
20 as you have a few customers too!

HUSBAND. Sh! A customer!

[*Enter an* UNEMPLOYED MAN, *in rags.*]

UNEMPLOYED MAN. Excuse me. I'm unemployed.

25 [MRS. SHIN *laughs.*]

SHEN TE. Can I help you?

UNEMPLOYED MAN. Have you any damaged cigarettes? I thought there might be some damage when you're unpacking.

30 WIFE. What nerve, begging for tobacco! [*Rhetorically.*] Why don't they ask for bread?

UNEMPLOYED MAN. Bread is expensive. One cigarette butt and I'll be a new man.

SHEN TE [*giving him cigarettes*]. That's very
35 important—to be a new man. You'll be my first customer and bring me luck.

[*The* UNEMPLOYED MAN *quickly lights a cigarette, inhales, and goes off, coughing.*]

WIFE. Was that right, Shen Te, dear?

40 MRS. SHIN. If this is the opening of a shop, you can hold the closing at the end of the week.

HUSBAND. I bet he had money on him.

SHEN TE. Oh, no, he said he hadn't!

45 NEPHEW. How d'you know he wasn't lying?

SHEN TE [*angrily*]. How do you know he was?

WIFE [*wagging her head*]. You're too good, Shen Te, dear. If you're going to keep this shop, you'll have to learn to say No. 50

HUSBAND. Tell them the place isn't yours to dispose of. Belongs to . . . some relative who insists on all accounts being strictly in order . . .

MRS. SHIN. That's right! What do you think 55 you are—a philanthropist?

SHEN TE [*laughing*]. Very well, suppose I ask you for my rice back, Mrs. Shin?

WIFE [*combatively, at* MRS. SHIN]. So that's her rice? 60

[*Enter the* CARPENTER, *a small man.*]

MRS. SHIN [*who, at the sight of him, starts to hurry away*]. See you tomorrow, Miss Shen Te! [*Exit* MRS. SHIN.]

CARPENTER. Mrs. Shin, it's you I want! 65

WIFE [*to* SHEN TE]. Has she some claim on you?

SHEN TE. She's hungry. That's a claim.

CARPENTER. Are you the new tenant? And filling up the shelves already? Well, they're 70 not yours, till they're paid for, ma'am. I'm the carpenter, so I should know.

SHEN TE. I took the shop "furnishings included."

CARPENTER. You're in league with that Mrs. 75 Shin, of course. All right: I demand my hundred silver dollars.

SHEN TE. I'm afraid I haven't got a hundred silver dollars.

CARPENTER. Then you'll find it. Or I'll have 80 you arrested.

WIFE [*whispering to* SHEN TE]. That relative: make it a cousin.

SHEN TE. Can't it wait till next month?

CARPENTER. No! 85

SHEN TE. Be a little patient, Mr. Carpenter, I can't settle all claims at once.

CARPENTER. Who's patient with me? [*He grabs a shelf from the wall.*] Pay up—or I take the shelves back! 90

WIFE. Shen Te! Dear! Why don't you let your . . . cousin settle this affair? [*To* CARPENTER.] Put your claim in writing. Shen Te's cousin will see you get paid.

CARPENTER [*derisively*]. Cousin, eh?

HUSBAND. Cousin, yes.

CARPENTER. I know these cousins!

NEPHEW. Don't be silly. He's a personal
5 friend of mine.

HUSBAND. What a man! Sharp as a razor!

CARPENTER. All right. I'll put my claim in
writing. [*Puts shelf on floor, sits on it, writes
out bill.*]

10 WIFE [*to* SHEN TE]. He'd tear the dress off
your back to get his shelves. Never recognize a
claim! That's my motto.

SHEN TE. He's done a job, and wants something in return. It's shameful that I can't give
15 it to him. What will the gods say?

HUSBAND. You did your bit when you took
us in.

[*Enter the* BROTHER, *limping, and the* SISTER-
IN-LAW, *pregnant.*]

20 BROTHER [*to* HUSBAND *and* WIFE]. So this is
where you're hiding out! There's family feeling
for you! Leaving us on the corner!

WIFE [*embarrassed, to* SHEN TE]. It's my
brother and his wife. [*To them.*] Now stop
25 grumbling, and sit quietly in that corner. [*To*
SHEN TE.] It can't be helped. She's in her fifth
month.

SHEN TE. Oh yes. Welcome!

WIFE [*to the couple*]. Say thank you.

30 [*They mutter something.*]

The cups are here. [*To* SHEN TE.] Lucky you
bought this shop when you did!

SHEN TE [*laughing and bringing tea*]. Lucky
indeed!

35 [*Enter* MRS. MI TZU, *the landlady.*]

MRS. MI TZU. Miss Shen Te? I am Mrs. Mi
Tzu, your landlady. I hope our relationship
will be a happy one? I like to think I give my
tenants modern, personalized service. Here is
40 your lease. [*To the others, as* SHEN TE *reads
the lease.*] There's nothing like the opening of
a little shop, is there? A moment of true
beauty! [*She is looking around.*] Not very
much on the shelves, of course. But everything
45 in the gods' good time! Where are your
references, Miss Shen Te?

SHEN TE. Do I *have* to have references?

MRS. MI TZU. After all, I haven't a notion
who you are!

HUSBAND. Oh, *we'd* be glad to vouch for 50
Miss Shen Te! We'd go through fire for her!

MRS. MI TZU. And who may *you* be?

HUSBAND [*stammering*]. Ma Fu, tobacco
dealer.

MRS. MI TZU. Where is your shop, Mr. . . . 55
Ma Fu?

HUSBAND. Well, um, I haven't a shop—I've
just sold it.

MRS. MI TZU. I see. [*To* SHEN TE.] Is there
no one else that knows you? 60

WIFE [*whispering to* SHEN TE]. Your cousin!
Your cousin!

MRS. MI TZU. This is a respectable house,
Miss Shen Te. I never sign a lease without
certain assurances. 65

SHEN TE [*slowly, her eyes downcast*]. I have
. . . a cousin.

MRS. MI TZU. On the square? Let's go over
and see him. What does he do?

SHEN TE [*as before*]. He lives . . . in another 70
city.

WIFE [*prompting*]. Didn't you say he was in
Shung?

SHEN TE. That's right. Shung.

HUSBAND [*prompting*]. I had his name on the 75
tip of my tongue. Mr. . . .

SHEN TE [*with an effort*]. Mr. . . . Shui . . .
Ta.

HUSBAND. That's it! Tall, skinny fellow!

SHEN TE. Shui Ta! 80

NEPHEW [*to* CARPENTER]. *You* were in touch
with him, weren't you? About the shelves?

CARPENTER [*surlily*]. Give him this bill. [*He
hands it over.*] I'll be back in the morning.
[*Exit* CARPENTER.] 85

NEPHEW [*calling after him, but with his eyes
on* MRS. MI TZU]. Don't worry! Mr. Shui Ta
pays on the nail!

MRS. MI TZU [*looking closely at* SHEN TE].
I'll be happy to make his acquaintance, Miss 90
Shen Te. [*Exit* MRS. MI TZU.]

[*Pause.*]

WIFE. By tomorrow morning she'll know
more about you than you do yourself.

SISTER-IN-LAW [*to* NEPHEW]. This thing isn't built to last.

[*Enter* GRANDFATHER.]

WIFE. It's Grandfather! [*To* SHEN TE.] Such
5 a good old soul!

[*The* BOY *enters*.]

BOY [*over his shoulder*]. Here they are!

WIFE. And the boy, how he's grown! But he always could eat enough for ten.

10 [*Enter the* NIECE.]

WIFE [*to* SHEN TE]. Our little niece from the country. There are more of us now than in your time. The less we had, the more there were of us; the more there were of us, the less we
15 had. Give me the key. We must protect ourselves from unwanted guests. [*She takes the key and locks the door*.] Just make yourself at home. I'll light the little lamp.

NEPHEW [*a big joke*]. I hope her cousin
20 doesn't drop in tonight! The strict Mr. Shui Ta!

[SISTER-IN-LAW *laughs*.]

BROTHER [*reaching for a cigarette*]. One cigarette more or less . . .

25 HUSBAND. One cigarette more or less.

[*They pile into the cigarettes. The* BROTHER *hands a jug of wine round*.]

NEPHEW. Mr. Shui Ta'll pay for it!

GRANDFATHER [*gravely, to* SHEN TE]. How
30 do you do?

[SHEN TE, *a little taken aback by the belatedness of the greeting, bows. She has the* CARPENTER's *bill in one hand, the landlady's lease in the other*.]

35 WIFE. How about a bit of a song? To keep Shen Te's spirits up?

NEPHEW. Good idea. Grandfather: you start!

Song of the Smoke

GRANDFATHER.
40 I used to think (before old age beset me)
    That brains could fill the pantry of the
                                    [poor.
    But where did all my cerebration get me?
    I'm just as hungry as I was before.
45   So what's the use?

    See the smoke float free
    Into ever colder coldness!
        It's the same with me.

HUSBAND.
    The straight and narrow path leads to   50
                                    [disaster
    And so the crooked path I tried to tread.
    That got me to disaster even faster.
    (They say we shall be happy when we're
                                    [dead.)   55
            So what's the use, etc.

NIECE.
    You older people, full of expectation,
        At any moment now you'll walk the
                                    [plank!   60
    The future's for the younger generation!
        Yes, even if that future is a blank.
            So what's the use, etc.

NEPHEW [*to the* BROTHER]. Where'd you get that wine?   65

SISTER-IN-LAW [*answering for the* BROTHER]. He pawned the sack of tobacco.

HUSBAND [*stepping in*]. What? That tobacco was all we had to fall back on! You pig!

BROTHER. You'd call a man a pig because   70
your wife was frigid! Did you refuse to drink it?

[*They fight. The shelves fall over*.]

SHEN TE [*imploringly*]. Oh, don't! Don't break everything! Take it, take it all, but don't   75
destroy a gift from the gods!

WIFE [*disparagingly*]. This shop isn't big enough. I should never have mentioned it to Uncle and the others. When *they* arrive, it's going to be disgustingly overcrowded.   80

SISTER-IN-LAW. And did you hear our gracious hostess? She cools off quick!

[*Voices outside. Knocking at the door*.]

UNCLE's VOICE. Open the door!

WIFE. Uncle? Is that you, Uncle?   85

UNCLE's VOICE. Certainly, it's me. Auntie says to tell you she'll have the children here in ten minutes.

WIFE [*to* SHEN TE]. I'll have to let him in.

SHEN TE [*who scarcely hears her*].   90
The little lifeboat is swiftly sent down

Too many men too greedily
Hold on to it as they drown.

SCENE I A

[WONG's *den in a sewer pipe.*]

5 WONG [*crouching there*]. All quiet! It's four days now since I left the city. The gods passed this way on the second day. I heard their steps on the bridge over there. They must be a long way off by this time, so I'm safe.

[*Breathing a sigh of relief, he curls up and* 10 *goes to sleep. In his dream the pipe becomes transparent, and the* GODS *appear.*]

[*Raising an arm, as if in self-defense.*] I know, I know, illustrious ones! I found no one to give you a room—not in all Setzuan! There, 15 it's out. Please continue on your way!

FIRST GOD [*mildly*]. But you did find someone. Someone who took us in for the night, watched over us in our sleep, and in the early morning lighted us down to the street with a 20 lamp.

WONG. It was . . . Shen Te, that took you in?

THIRD GOD. Who else?

WONG. And I ran away! "She isn't coming," I thought, "she just can't afford it."

25 GODS [*singing*].

O you feeble, well-intentioned, and yet
[feeble chap!
Where there's need the fellow thinks there
[is no goodness!
When there's danger he thinks courage
30 [starts to ebb away!
Some people only see the seamy side!
What hasty judgment! What premature
[desperation!

35 WONG. I'm *very* ashamed, illustrious ones.

FIRST GOD. Do us a favor, Water Seller. Go back to Setzuan. Find Shen Te, and give us a report on her. We hear that she's come into a little money. Show interest in her goodness— 40 for no one can be good for long if goodness is not in demand. Meanwhile we shall continue the search, and find other good people. After which, the idle chatter about the impossibility of goodness will stop!

45 [*The* GODS *vanish.*]

SCENE II

[*A knocking.*]

WIFE. Shen Te! Someone at the door. Where is she anyway?

NEPHEW. She must be getting the breakfast. Mr. Shui Ta will pay for it. 50

[*The* WIFE *laughs and shuffles to the door. Enter* MR. SHUI TA *and the* CARPENTER.]

WIFE. Who is it?

SHUI TA. I am Miss Shen Te's cousin.

WIFE. What? 55

SHUI TA. My name is Shui Ta.

WIFE. Her cousin?

NEPHEW. Her cousin?

NIECE. But that was a joke. She hasn't got a cousin. 60

HUSBAND. So early in the morning?

BROTHER. What's all the noise?

SISTER-IN-LAW. This fellow says he's her cousin.

BROTHER. Tell him to prove it. 65

NEPHEW. Right. If you're Shen Te's cousin, prove it by getting the breakfast.

SHUI TA [*whose regime begins as he puts out the lamp to save oil. Loudly, to all present, asleep or awake*]. Would you all please get 70 dressed! Customers will be coming! I wish to open my shop!

HUSBAND. *Your* shop? Doesn't it belong to our good friend Shen Te?

[SHUI TA *shakes his head.*] 75

SISTER-IN-LAW. So we've been cheated. Where *is* the little liar?

SHUI TA. Miss Shen Te has been delayed. She wishes me to tell you there will be nothing she can do—now I am here. 80

WIFE [*bowled over*]. I thought she was *good!*

NEPHEW. Do you have to believe *him?*

HUSBAND. *I* don't.

NEPHEW. Then do something.

HUSBAND. Certainly! I'll send out a search 85 party at once. You, you, you, and you, go out and look for Shen Te.

[*As the* GRANDFATHER *rises and makes for the door.*]

Not you, Grandfather, you and I will hold 90 the fort.

SHUI TA. You won't find Miss Shen Te. She has suspended her hospitable activity for an unlimited period. There are too many of you. She asked me to say: this is a tobacco shop, not a gold mine.

HUSBAND. Shen Te never said a thing like that. Boy, food! There's a bakery on the corner. Stuff your shirt full when they're not looking!

SISTER-IN-LAW. Don't overlook the raspberry tarts.

HUSBAND. And don't let the policeman see you.

[*The* BOY *leaves.*]

SHUI TA. Don't you depend on this shop now? Then why give it a bad name, by stealing from the bakery?

NEPHEW. Don't listen to him. Let's find Shen Te. She'll give him a piece of her mind.

SISTER-IN-LAW. Don't forget to leave us some breakfast.

[BROTHER, SISTER-IN-LAW, *and* NEPHEW *leave.*]

SHUI TA [*to the* CARPENTER]. You see, Mr. Carpenter, nothing has changed since the poet, eleven hundred years ago, penned these lines:

A governor was asked what was needed
To save the freezing people in the city.

He replied:

"A blanket ten thousand feet long
To cover the city and all its suburbs."

[*He starts to tidy up the shop.*]

CARPENTER. Your cousin owes me money. I've got witnesses. For the shelves.

SHUI TA. Yes, I have your bill. [*He takes it out of his pocket.*] Isn't a hundred silver dollars rather a lot?

CARPENTER. No deductions! I have a wife and children.

SHUI TA. How many children?

CARPENTER. Three.

SHUI TA. I'll make you an offer. Twenty silver dollars.

[*The* HUSBAND *laughs.*]

CARPENTER. You're crazy. Those shelves are real walnut.

SHUI TA. Very well. Take them away.

CARPENTER. What?

SHUI TA. They cost too much. Please take them away. 50

WIFE. Not bad! [*And she, too, is laughing.*]

CARPENTER [*a little bewildered*]. Call Shen Te, someone! [*To* SHUI TA.] She's good!

SHUI TA. Certainly. She's ruined.

CARPENTER [*provoked into taking some of the shelves*]. All right, you can keep your tobacco on the floor. 55

SHUI TA [*to the* HUSBAND]. Help him with the shelves.

HUSBAND [*grins and carries one shelf over to the door where the* CARPENTER *now is*]. Goodbye, shelves! 60

CARPENTER [*to the* HUSBAND]. You dog! You want my family to starve?

SHUI TA. I repeat my offer. I have no desire to keep my tobacco on the floor. Twenty silver dollars. 65

CARPENTER [*with desperate aggressiveness*]. One hundred!

[SHUI TA *shows indifference, looks through the window. The* HUSBAND *picks up several shelves.*] 70

[*To* HUSBAND.] You needn't smash them against the doorpost, you idiot! [*To* SHUI TA.] These shelves were made to measure. They're no use anywhere else! 75

SHUI TA. Precisely.

[*The* WIFE *squeals with pleasure.*]

CARPENTER [*giving up, sullenly*]. Take the shelves. Pay what you want to pay. 80

SHUI TA [*smoothly*]. Twenty silver dollars.

[*He places two large coins on the table. The* CARPENTER *picks them up.*]

HUSBAND [*brings the shelves back in*]. And quite enough too! 85

CARPENTER [*slinking off*]. Quite enough to get drunk on.

HUSBAND [*happily*]. Well, we got rid of *him!*

WIFE [*weeping with fun, gives a rendition of the dialogue just spoken*]. "Real walnut," says he. "Very well, take them away," says his lordship. "I have children," says he. "Twenty silver dollars," says his lordship. "They're no use anywhere else," says he. "Precisely," said his lordship! [*She dissolves into shrieks of merriment.*] 90 95

SHUI TA. And now: go!

HUSBAND. What's that?

SHUI TA. You're thieves, parasites. I'm giving you this chance. Go!

5 HUSBAND [*summoning all his ancestral dignity*]. That sort deserves no answer. Besides, one should never shout on an empty stomach.

WIFE. Where's that boy?

SHUI TA. Exactly. The boy. I want no stolen

10 goods in this shop. [*Very loudly.*] I strongly advise you to leave! [*But they remain seated, noses in the air. Quietly.*] As you wish.

[SHUI TA *goes to the door. A* POLICEMAN *appears.* SHUI TA *bows.*]

15 I am addressing the officer in charge of this precinct?

POLICEMAN. That's right, Mr., um . . . what was the name, sir?

SHUI TA. Mr. Shui Ta.

20 POLICEMAN. Yes, of course, sir.

[*They exchange a smile.*]

SHUI TA. Nice weather we're having.

POLICEMAN. A little on the warm side, sir.

SHUI TA. Oh, a little on the warm side.

25 HUSBAND [*whispering to the* WIFE]. If he keeps it up till the boy's back, we're done for. [*Tries to signal* SHUI TA.]

SHUI TA [*ignoring the signal*]. Weather, of course, is one thing indoors, another out on

30 the dusty street!

POLICEMAN. Oh, quite another, sir!

WIFE [*to the* HUSBAND]. It's all right as long as he's standing in the doorway—the boy will see him.

35 SHUI TA. Step inside for a moment! It's quite cool indoors. My cousin and I have just opened the place. And we attach the greatest importance to being on good terms with the, um, authorities.

40 POLICEMAN [*entering*]. Thank you, Mr. Shui Ta. It *is* cool!

HUSBAND [*whispering to the* WIFE]. And now the boy *won't* see him.

SHUI TA [*showing* HUSBAND *and* WIFE *to the*

45 POLICEMAN]. Visitors, I think my cousin knows them. They were just leaving.

HUSBAND [*defeated*]. Ye-e-es, we were . . .

just leaving.

SHUI TA. I'll tell my cousin you couldn't wait. 50

[*Noise from the street. Shouts of "Stop, thief!"*]

POLICEMAN. What's that?

[*The* BOY *is in the doorway with cakes and buns and rolls spilling out of his shirt. The* 55 WIFE *signals desperately to him to leave. He gets the idea.*]

No, you don't! [*He grabs the* BOY *by the collar.*] Where's all this from?

BOY [*vaguely pointing*]. Down the street. 60

POLICEMAN [*grimly*]. So that's it. [*Prepares to arrest the* BOY.]

WIFE [*stepping in*]. And *we* knew nothing about it. [*To the* BOY.] Nasty little thief!

POLICEMAN [*dryly*]. Can you clarify the 65 situation, Mr. Shui Ta?

[SHUI TA *is silent.*]

POLICEMAN [*who understands silence*]. Aha. You're all coming with me—to the station.

SHUI TA. I can hardly say how sorry I am 70 that *my* establishment . . .

WIFE. Oh, he saw the boy leave not ten minutes ago!

SHUI TA. And to conceal the theft asked a policeman in? 75

POLICEMAN. Don't listen to her, Mr. Shui Ta, I'll be happy to relieve you of their presence one and all! [*To all three.*] Out! [*He drives them before him.*]

GRANDFATHER [*leaving last. Gravely*]. Good 80 morning!

POLICEMAN. Good morning!

[SHUI TA, *left alone, continues to tidy up.* MRS. MI TZU *breezes in.*]

MRS. MI TZU. You're her cousin, are you? 85 Then have the goodness to explain what all this means—police dragging people from a respectable house! By what right does your Miss Shen Te turn my property into a house of assignation?—Well, as you see, I know all! 90

SHUI TA. Yes. My cousin has the worst possible reputation: that of being poor.

MRS. MI TZU. No sentimental rubbish, Mr. Shui Ta. Your cousin was a common . . .

SHUI TA. Pauper. Let's use the uglier word.

MRS. MI TZU. I'm speaking of her conduct, not her earnings. But there must have *been* earnings, or how did she buy all this? Several elderly gentlemen took care of it, I suppose. I repeat: this is a respectable house! I have tenants who prefer not to live under the same roof with such a person.

SHUI TA [*quietly*]. How much do you want?

MRS. MI TZU [*he is ahead of her now*]. I beg your pardon.

SHUI TA. To reassure yourself. To reassure your tenants. How much will it cost?

MRS. MI TZU. You're a cool customer.

SHUI TA [*picking up the lease*]. The rent is high. [*He reads on.*] I assume it's payable by the month?

MRS. MI TZU. Not in her case.

SHUI TA [*looking up*]. What?

MRS. MI TZU. Six months' rent payable in advance. Two hundred silver dollars.

SHUI TA. Six . . . ! Sheer usury! And where am I to find it?

MRS. MI TZU. You should have thought of that before.

SHUI TA. Have you no heart, Mrs. Mi Tzu? It's true Shen Te acted foolishly, being kind to all those people, but she'll improve with time. I'll see to it she does. She'll work her fingers to the bone to pay her rent, and all the time be as quiet as a mouse, as humble as a fly.

MRS. MI TZU. Her social background . . .

SHUI TA. Out of the depths! She came out of the depths! And before she'll go back there, she'll work, sacrifice, shrink from nothing. . . . Such a tenant is worth her weight in gold, Mrs. Mi Tzu.

MRS. MI TZU. It's silver we were talking about, Mr. Shui Ta. Two hundred silver dollars or . . .

[*Enter the* POLICEMAN.]

POLICEMAN. Am I intruding, Mr. Shui Ta?

MRS. MI TZU. This tobacco shop is well-known to the police, I see.

POLICEMAN. Mr. Shui Ta has done us a service, Mrs. Mi Tzu. I am here to present our official felicitations!

MRS. MI TZU. That means less than nothing to me, sir. Mr. Shui Ta, all I can say is: I hope your cousin will find my terms acceptable. Good day, gentlemen. [*Exit.*]

SHUI TA. Good day, ma'am.

[*Pause.*]

POLICEMAN. Mrs. Mi Tzu a bit of a stumbling block, sir?

SHUI TA. She wants six months' rent in advance.

POLICEMAN. And you haven't got it, eh?

[SHUI TA *is silent.*]

But surely you can get it, sir? A man like you?

SHUI TA. What about a woman like Shen Te?

POLICEMAN. You're not staying, sir?

SHUI TA. No, and I won't be back. Do you smoke?

POLICEMAN [*taking two cigars, and placing them both in his pocket*]. Thank you, sir—I see your point. Miss Shen Te—let's mince no words—Miss Shen Te lived by selling herself. "What else could she have done?" you ask. "How else was she to pay the rent?" True. But the fact remains, Mr. Shui Ta, it is not respectable. Why not? A very deep question. But, in the first place, love—love isn't bought and sold like cigars, Mr. Shui Ta. In the second place, it isn't respectable to go waltzing off with someone that's paying his way, so to speak—it must be for love! Thirdly and lastly, as the proverb has it: not for a handful of rice but for love! [*Pause. He is thinking hard.*] "Well," you may say, "and what good is all this wisdom if the milk's already spilt?" Miss Shen Te is what she is. Is *where* she is. We have to face the fact that if she doesn't get hold of six months' rent pronto, she'll be back on the streets. The question then as I see it—everything in this world is a matter of opinion—the question as I see it is: *how* is she to get hold of this rent? How? Mr. Shui Ta: I don't know. [*Pause.*] I take that back, sir. It's just come to me. A husband. We must find her a husband!

[*Enter a little* OLD WOMAN.]

OLD WOMAN. A good cheap cigar for my

husband, we'll have been married forty years tomorrow and we're having a little celebration.

SHUI TA. Forty years? And you still want to celebrate?

5 OLD WOMAN. As much as we can afford to. We have the carpet shop across the square. We'll be good neighbors, I hope?

SHUI TA. I hope so too.

POLICEMAN [who keeps making discoveries]. 10 Mr. Shui Ta, you know what we need? We need capital. And how do we acquire capital? We get married.

SHUI TA [to OLD WOMAN]. I'm afraid I've been pestering this gentleman with my per-15 sonal worries.

POLICEMAN [lyrically]. We can't pay six months' rent, so what do we do? We marry money.

SHUI TA. That might not be easy.

20 POLICEMAN. Oh, I don't know. She's a good match. Has a nice, growing business. [To the OLD WOMAN.] What do you think?

OLD WOMAN [undecided]. Well—

POLICEMAN. Should she put an ad in the 25 paper?

OLD WOMAN [not eager to commit herself]. Well, if she agrees—

POLICEMAN. I'll write it for her. You lend us a hand, and we write an ad for you! [He 30 chuckles away to himself, takes out his notebook, wets the stump of a pencil between his lips, and writes away.]

SHUI TA [slowly]. Not a bad idea.

POLICEMAN. "What . . . respectable . . . man 35 . . . with small capital . . . widower . . . not excluded . . . desires . . . marriage . . . into flourishing . . . tobacco shop?" And now let's add: "am . . . pretty . . . " No! . . . "Prepossessing appearance."

40 SHUI TA. If you don't think that's an exaggeration?

OLD WOMAN. Oh, not a bit. I've seen her.

[The POLICEMAN tears the page out of his notebook, and hands it over to SHUI TA.]

45 SHUI TA [with horror in his voice]. How much luck we need to keep our heads above water! How many ideas! How many friends! [To the POLICEMAN.] Thank you, sir. I think I see my way clear.

SCENE III

[Evening in the municipal park. Noise of a 50 plane overhead. YANG SUN, a young man in rags, is following the plane with his eyes: one can tell that the machine is describing a curve above the park. YANG SUN then takes a rope out of his pocket, looking anxiously about him 55 as he does so. He moves toward a large willow. Enter TWO PROSTITUTES, one old, the other the NIECE whom we have already met.]

NIECE. Hello. Coming with me?

YANG SUN [taken aback]. If you'd like to buy 60 me a dinner.

OLD WHORE. Buy you a dinner! [To the NIECE.] Oh, we know him—it's the unemployed pilot. Waste no time on him!

NIECE. But he's the only man left in the park. 65 And it's going to rain.

OLD WHORE. Oh, how do you know?

[And they pass by. YANG SUN again looks about him, again takes his rope, and this time throws it round a branch of the willow tree. 70 Again he is interrupted. It is the TWO PROSTITUTES returning—and in such a hurry they don't notice him.]

NIECE. It's going to pour!

[Enter SHEN TE.] 75

OLD WHORE. There's that gorgon Shen Te! That drove your family out into the cold!

NIECE. It wasn't her. It was that cousin of hers. She offered to pay for the cakes. I've nothing against her. 80

OLD WHORE. I have, though. [So that SHEN TE can hear.] Now where could the little lady be off to? She may be rich now but that won't stop her snatching our young men, will it?

SHEN TE. I'm going to the tearoom by the pond. 85

NIECE. Is it true what they say? You're marrying a widower—with three children?

SHEN TE. Yes. I'm just going to see him.

YANG SUN [his patience at breaking point]. Move on there! This is a park, not a whore-90 house!

OLD WHORE. Shut your mouth!

[But the TWO PROSTITUTES leave.]

YANG SUN. Even in the farthest corner of the park, even when it's raining, you can't get rid 95 of them! [He spits.]

SHEN TE [*overhearing this*]. And what right have you to scold them? [*But at this point she sees the rope.*] Oh!

YANG SUN. Well, what are you staring at?

5 SHEN TE. That rope. What is it for?

YANG SUN. Think! Think! I haven't a penny. Even if I had, I wouldn't spend it on you. I'd buy a drink of water.

[*The rain starts.*]

10 SHEN TE [*still looking at the rope*]. What is the rope for? You mustn't!

YANG SUN. What's it to you? Clear out!

SHEN TE [*irrelevantly*]. It's raining.

YANG SUN. Well, don't try to come under

15 this tree.

SHEN TE. Oh, no. [*She stays in the rain.*]

YANG SUN. Now go away. [*Pause.*] For one thing, I don't like your looks, you're bow-legged.

20 SHEN TE [*indignantly*]. That's not true!

YANG SUN. Well, don't show 'em to me. Look, it's raining. You better come under this tree.

[*Slowly, she takes shelter under the tree.*]

25 SHEN TE. Why did you want to do it?

YANG SUN. You really want to know? [*Pause.*] To get rid of you! [*Pause.*] You know what a flyer is?

SHEN TE. Oh yes, I've met a lot of pilots. At

30 the tearoom.

YANG SUN. You call *them* flyers? Think they know what a machine *is*? Just 'cause they have leather helmets? They gave the airfield director a bribe, that's the way *those* fellows got up in

35 the air! Try one of them out sometime. "Go up to two thousand feet," tell him, "then let it fall, then pick it up again with a flick of the wrist at the last moment." Know what he'll say to that? "It's not in my contract." Then again,

40 there's the landing problem. It's like landing on your own backside. It's no different, planes are human. Those fools don't understand. [*Pause.*] And I'm the biggest fool for reading the book on flying in the Peking school and

45 skipping the page where it says: "we've got enough flyers and we don't need you." I'm a mail pilot and no mail. You understand that?

SHEN TE [*shyly*]. Yes. I do.

YANG SUN. No, you don't. You'd never

50 understand that.

SHEN TE. When we were little we had a crane with a broken wing. He made friends with us and was very good-natured about our jokes. He would strut along behind us and call out

55 to stop us going too fast for him. But every spring and autumn when the cranes flew over the villages in great swarms, he got quite restless. [*Pause.*] I understood that. [*She bursts out crying.*]

60 YANG SUN. Don't!

SHEN TE [*quieting down*]. No.

YANG SUN. It's bad for the complexion.

SHEN TE [*sniffing*]. I've stopped.

[*She dries her tears on her big sleeve. Lean-

65 ing against the tree, but not looking at her, he reaches for her face.*]

YANG SUN. You can't even wipe your own face. [*He is wiping it for her with his handkerchief. Pause.*]

70 SHEN TE [*still sobbing*]. I don't know anything!

YANG SUN. You interrupted me! What for?

SHEN TE. It's such a rainy day. You only wanted to do . . . *that* because it's such a rainy

75 day.

[*To the audience.*]

In our country

The evenings should never be somber

High bridges over rivers

80 The gray hour between night and morning

And the long, long winter:

Such things are dangerous

For, with all the misery,

A very little is enough

85 And men throw away an unbearable life.

[*Pause.*]

YANG SUN. Talk about yourself for a change.

SHEN TE. What about me? I have a shop.

YANG SUN [*incredulous*]. You have a shop,

90 do you? Never thought of walking the streets?

SHEN TE. I *did* walk the streets. Now I have a shop.

YANG SUN [*ironically*]. A gift of the gods, I suppose!

95 SHEN TE. How did you know?

YANG SUN [*even more ironical*]. One fine evening the gods turned up saying: here's some money!

SHEN TE [*quickly*]. One fine morning.

YANG SUN [*fed up*]. This isn't much of an entertainment.

[*Pause.*]

5 SHEN TE. I can play the zither a little. [*Pause.*] And I can mimic men. [*Pause.*] I got the shop, so the first thing I did was to give my zither away. I can be as stupid as a fish now, I said to myself, and it won't matter.

10 I'm rich now, I said
I walk alone, I sleep alone
For a whole year, I said
I'll have nothing to do with a man.

YANG SUN. And now you're marrying one!

15 The one at the tearoom by the pond?

[SHEN TE *is silent.*]

YANG SUN. What do you know about love?

SHEN TE. Everything.

YANG SUN. Nothing. [*Pause.*] Or d'you just

20 mean you enjoyed it?

SHEN TE. No.

YANG SUN [*again without turning to look at her, he strokes her cheek with his hand*]. You like that?

25 SHEN TE. Yes.

YANG SUN [*breaking off*]. You're easily satisfied, I must say. [*Pause.*] What a town!

SHEN TE. You have no friends?

YANG SUN [*defensively*]. Yes, I have!

30 [*Change of tone.*] But they don't want to hear I'm still unemployed. "What?" they ask. "Is there still water in the sea?" You have friends?

SHEN TE [*hesitating*]. Just a . . . cousin.

YANG SUN. Watch him carefully.

35 SHEN TE. He only came once. Then he went away. He won't be back.

[YANG SUN *is looking away.*]

But to be without hope, they say, is to be without goodness!

40 [*Pause.*]

YANG SUN. Go on talking. A voice is a voice.

SHEN TE. Once, when I was a little girl, I fell, with a load of brushwood. An old man picked me up. He gave me a penny too. Isn't

45 it funny how people who don't have very much like to give some of it away? They must like to show what they can do, and how could they show it better than by being kind? Being wicked is just like being clumsy. When we

sing a song, or build a machine, or plant some 50 rice, we're being kind. You're kind.

YANG SUN. You make it sound easy.

SHEN TE. Oh, no. [*Little pause.*] Oh! A drop of rain!

YANG SUN. Where'd you feel it? 55

SHEN TE. Between the eyes.

YANG SUN. Near the right eye? Or the left?

SHEN TE. Near the left eye.

YANG SUN. Oh, good. [*He is getting sleepy.*] So you're through with men, eh? 60

SHEN TE [*with a smile*]. But I'm not bow-legged.

YANG SUN. Perhaps not.

SHEN TE. Definitely not.

[*Pause.*] 65

YANG SUN [*leaning wearily against the willow*]. I haven't had a drop to drink all day, I haven't eaten anything for *two* days. I couldn't love you if I tried.

[*Pause.*] 70

SHEN TE. I like it in the rain.

[*Enter* WONG *the Water Seller, singing.*]

The Song of the Water Seller in the Rain

"Buy my water," I am yelling
And my fury restraining
For no water I'm selling 75
'Cause it's raining, 'cause it's raining!
    I keep yelling: "Buy my water!"
    But no one's buying
    Athirst and dying
    And drinking and paying! 80
Buy water!
Buy water, you dogs!

Nice to dream of lovely weather!
Think of all the consternation
Were there no precipitation 85
Half a dozen years together!
Can't you hear them shrieking: "Water!"
Pretending they adore me!
They all would go down on their knees
            [before me! 90
Down on your knees!
Go down on your knees, you dogs!

What are lawns and hedges thinking?
What are fields and forests saying?

"At the cloud's breast we are drinking!
And we've no idea who's paying!"
    I keep yelling: "Buy my water!"
But no one's buying
Athirst and dying
And drinking and paying!
Buy water!
Buy water, you dogs!

[*The rain has stopped now.* SHEN TE *sees* WONG *and runs toward him.*]

SHEN TE. Wong! You're back! Your carrying pole's at the shop.

WONG. Oh, thank you, Shen Te. And how is life treating *you*?

SHEN TE. I've just met a brave and clever man. And I want to buy him a cup of your water.

WONG [*bitterly*]. Throw back your head and open your mouth and you'll have all the water you need—

SHEN TE [*tenderly*].
    I want *your* water, Wong
    The water that has tired you so
    The water that you carried all this
                     [way
    The water that is hard to sell because
                  it's been raining
    I need it for the young man over there
                 [—he's a flyer!
    A flyer is a bold man:
    Braving the storms
    In company with the clouds
    He crosses the heavens
    And brings to friends in far-away
                    [lands
    The friendly mail!

[*She pays* WONG, *and runs over to* YANG SUN *with the cup. But* YANG SUN *is fast asleep.*]

[*Calling to* WONG, *with a laugh.*] He's fallen asleep! Despair and rain and I have worn him out!

SCENE III A

[WONG'S *den. The sewer pipe is transparent, and the* GODS *again appear to* WONG *in a dream.*]

WONG [*radiant*]. I've seen her, illustrious ones! And she hasn't changed!

FIRST GOD. That's good to hear.

WONG. She loves someone.

FIRST GOD. Let's hope the experience gives her the strength to stay good!

WONG. It does. She's doing good deeds all the time.

FIRST GOD. Ah? What sort? What sort of good deeds, Wong?

WONG. Well, she has a kind word for everybody.

FIRST GOD [*eagerly*]. And then?

WONG. Hardly anyone leaves her shop without tobacco in his pocket—even if he can't pay for it.

FIRST GOD. Not bad at all. Next?

WONG. She's putting up a family of eight.

FIRST GOD [*gleefully, to the* SECOND GOD]. Eight! [*To* WONG.] And that's not all, of course!

WONG. She bought a cup of water from me even though it was raining.

FIRST GOD. Yes, yes, yes, all these smaller good deeds!

WONG. Even they run into money. A little tobacco shop doesn't make so much.

FIRST GOD [*sententiously*]. A prudent gardener works miracles on the smallest plot.

WONG. She hands out rice every morning. That eats up half her earnings.

FIRST GOD [*a little disappointed*]. Well, as a beginning . . .

WONG. They call her the Angel of the Slums —whatever the Carpenter may say!

FIRST GOD. What's this? A carpenter speaks ill of her?

WONG. Oh, he only says her shelves weren't paid for in full.

SECOND GOD [*who has a bad cold and can't pronounce his n's and m's*]. What's this? Not paying a carpenter? Why was that?

WONG. I suppose she didn't have the money.

SECOND GOD [*severely*]. One pays what one owes, that's in our book of rules! First the letter of the law, then the spirit!

WONG. But it wasn't Shen Te, illustrious ones, it was her cousin. She called *him* in to help.

SECOND GOD. Then her cousin must never darken her threshold again!

WONG. Very well, illustrious ones! But in fairness to Shen Te, let me say that her cousin is a businessman.

FIRST GOD. Perhaps we should inquire what

5 is customary? I find business quite unintelligible. But everybody's doing it. Business! Did the Seven Good Kings do business? Did Kung the Just sell fish?

SECOND GOD. In any case, such a thing must

10 not occur again!

[The GODS start to leave.]

THIRD GOD. Forgive us for taking this tone with you. Wong, we haven't been getting enough sleep. The rich recommended us to the

15 poor, and the poor tell us they haven't enough room.

SECOND GOD. Feeble, feeble, the best of them!

FIRST GOD. No great deeds! No heroic

20 daring!

THIRD GOD. On such a *small* scale!

SECOND GOD. Sincere, yes, but what is actually *achieved*?

[One can no longer hear them.]

25 WONG [calling after them]. I've thought of something, illustrious ones: Perhaps you shouldn't ask—too—much—all—at—once!

SCENE IV

[The square in front of SHEN TE's tobacco shop. Beside SHEN TE's place, two other shops

30 are seen: the carpet shop and a barber's. Morning. Outside SHEN TE's the GRANDFATHER, the SISTER-IN-LAW, the UNEMPLOYED MAN, and MRS. SHIN stand waiting.]

SISTER-IN-LAW. She's been out all night

35 again.

MRS. SHIN. No sooner did we get rid of that crazy cousin of hers than Shen Te herself starts carrying on! Maybe she does give us an ounce of rice now and then, but can you de-

40 pend on her? Can you depend on her?

[Loud voices from the Barber's.]

VOICE OF SHU FU. What are you doing in my shop? Get out—at once!

VOICE OF WONG. But sir. They all let me

45 sell . . .

[WONG comes staggering out of the barber's

shop pursued by MR. SHU FU, the barber, a fat man carrying a heavy curling iron.]

SHU FU. Get out, I said! Pestering my cus-

50 tomers with your slimy old water! Get out! Take your cup!

[He holds out the cup. WONG reaches out for it. MR. SHU FU strikes his hand with the curling iron, which is hot. WONG howls.]

You had it coming, my man! 55

[Puffing, he returns to his shop. The UNEMPLOYED MAN picks up the cup and gives it to WONG.]

UNEMPLOYED MAN. You can report that to the police. 60

WONG. My hand! It's smashed up!

UNEMPLOYED MAN. Any bones broken?

WONG. I can't move my fingers.

UNEMPLOYED MAN. Sit down. I'll put some water on it. 65

[WONG sits.]

MRS. SHIN. The water won't cost you anything.

SISTER-IN-LAW. You might have got a bandage from Miss Shen Te till she took to stay- 70 ing out all night. It's a scandal.

MRS. SHIN [despondently]. If you ask me, she's forgotten we ever existed!

[Enter SHEN TE down the street, with a dish of rice.] 75

SHEN TE [to the audience]. How wonderful to see Setzuan in the early morning! I always used to stay in bed with my dirty blanket over my head afraid to wake up. This morning I saw the newspapers being delivered by little 80 boys, the streets being washed by strong men, and fresh vegetables coming in from the country on ox carts. It's a long walk from where Yang Sun lives, but I feel lighter at every step. They say you walk on air when 85 you're in love, but it's even better walking on the rough earth, on the hard cement. In the early morning, the old city looks like a great rubbish heap. Nice, though—with all its little lights. And the sky, so pink, so transparent, 90 before the dust comes and muddies it! What a lot you miss if you never see your city rising from its slumbers like an honest old craftsman pumping his lungs full of air and reaching for his tools, as the poet says! [Cheerfully, to her 95 *waiting guests.*] Good morning, everyone, here's your rice! [*Distributing the rice, she comes upon* WONG.] Good morning, Wong, I'm quite lightheaded today. On my way over, I looked at myself in all the shop windows. I'd love to be beautiful.

[*She slips into the carpet shop.* MR. SHU FU *has just emerged from his shop.*]

SHU FU [*to the audience*]. It surprises me how beautiful Miss Shen Te is looking today! I never gave her a passing thought before. But now I've been gazing upon her comely form for exactly three minutes! I begin to suspect I am in love with her. She is overpoweringly attractive! [*Crossly, to* WONG.] Be off with you, rascal!

[*He returns to his shop.* SHEN TE *comes back out of the carpet shop with the* OLD MAN *its proprietor and his wife—whom we have already met—the* OLD WOMAN. SHEN TE *is wearing a shawl. The* OLD MAN *is holding up a looking glass for her.*]

OLD WOMAN. Isn't it lovely? We'll give you a reduction because there's a little hole in it.

SHEN TE [*looking at another shawl on the* OLD WOMAN'S *arm*]. The other one's nice too.

OLD WOMAN [*smiling*]. Too bad there's no hole in that!

SHEN TE. That's right. My shop doesn't make very much.

OLD WOMAN. And your good deeds eat it all up! Be more careful, my dear . . .

SHEN TE [*trying on the shawl with the hole*]. Just now, I'm light-headed! Does the color suit me?

OLD WOMAN. You'd better ask a man.

SHEN TE [*to the* OLD MAN]. Does the color suit me?

OLD MAN. You'd better ask your young friend.

SHEN TE. I'd like to have your opinion.

OLD MAN. It suits you, very well. But wear it this way: the dull side out.

[SHEN TE *pays up.*]

OLD WOMAN. If you decide you don't like it, you can exchange it. [*She pulls* SHEN TE *to one side.*] Has he got money?

SHEN TE [*with a laugh*]. Yang Sun? Oh, no.

OLD WOMAN. Then how're you going to pay your rent?

SHEN TE. I'd forgotten about that.

OLD WOMAN. And next Monday is the first of the month! Miss Shen Te, I've got something to say to you. After we [*indicating her husband*] got to know you, we had our doubts about that marriage ad. We thought it would be better if you'd let *us* help you. Out of our savings. We reckon we could lend you two hundred silver dollars. We don't need anything in writing—you could pledge us your tobacco stock.

SHEN TE. You're prepared to lend money to a person like me?

OLD WOMAN. It's folks like you that need it. We'd think twice about lending anything to your cousin.

OLD MAN [*coming up*]. All settled, my dear?

SHEN TE. I wish the gods could have heard what your wife was just saying, Mr. Ma. They're looking for good people who're happy —and helping me makes you happy because you know it was love that got me into difficulties!

[*The old couple smile knowingly at each other.*]

OLD MAN. And here's the money, Miss Shen Te.

[*He hands her an envelope.* SHEN TE *takes it. She bows. They bow back. They return to their shop.*]

SHEN TE [*holding up her envelope*]. Look, Wong, here's six months' rent! Don't you believe in miracles now? And how do you like my new shawl?

WONG. For the young fellow I saw you with in the park?

[SHEN TE *nods.*]

MRS. SHIN. Never mind all that. It's time you took a look at his hand!

SHEN TE. Have you hurt your hand?

MRS. SHIN. That barber smashed it with his hot curling iron. Right in front of our eyes.

SHEN TE [*shocked at herself*]. And I never noticed! We must get you to a doctor this minute or who knows what will happen?

UNEMPLOYED MAN. It's not a doctor he should see, it's a judge. He can ask for compensation. The barber's filthy rich.

WONG. You think I have a chance?

MRS. SHIN [with relish]. If it's really good and smashed. But is it?

WONG. I think so. It's very swollen. Could
5 I get a pension?

MRS. SHIN. You'd need a witness.

WONG. Well, you all saw it. You could all testify.

[He looks round. The UNEMPLOYED MAN,
10 the GRANDFATHER, and the SISTER-IN-LAW are all sitting against the wall of the shop eating rice. Their concentration on eating is complete.]

SHEN TE [to MRS. SHIN]. You saw it yourself.
15 MRS. SHIN. I want nothin' to do with the police. It's against my principles.

SHEN TE [to SISTER-IN-LAW]. What about you?

SISTER-IN-LAW. Me? I wasn't looking.
20 SHEN TE [to the GRANDFATHER, coaxingly]. Grandfather, you'll testify, won't you?

SISTER-IN-LAW. And a lot of good that will do. He's simple-minded.

SHEN TE [to the UNEMPLOYED MAN]. You
25 seem to be the only witness left.

UNEMPLOYED MAN. My testimony would only hurt him. I've been picked up twice for begging.

SHEN TE. Your brother is assaulted, and you
30 shut your eyes?

He is hit, cries out in pain, and you are
                                        [silent?

The beast prowls, chooses and seizes his
                                [victim, and you say:
35 "Because we showed no displeasure, he has
                                        [spared us."

If no one present will be a witness, I will. I'll say I saw it.

MRS. SHIN [solemnly]. The name for that is
40 perjury.

WONG. I don't know if I can accept that. Though maybe I'll have to. [Looking at his hand.] Is it swollen enough, do you think? The swelling's not going down?
45 UNEMPLOYED MAN. No, no, the swelling's holding up well.

WONG. Yes. It's more swollen if anything. Maybe my wrist is broken after all. I'd better see a judge at once.

[Holding his hand very carefully, and fixing
50 his eyes on it, he runs off. MRS. SHIN goes quickly into the barber's shop.]

UNEMPLOYED MAN [seeing her]. She is getting on the right side of Mr. Shu Fu.

SISTER-IN-LAW. You and I can't change the
55 world, Shen Te.

SHEN TE. Go away! Go away all of you!

[The UNEMPLOYED MAN, the SISTER-IN-LAW, and the GRANDFATHER stalk off, eating and sulking.]
60

[To the audience.]
They've stopped answering
They stay put
They do as they're told
They don't care   65
Nothing can make them look up
But the smell of food.

[Enter MRS. YANG, YANG SUN's mother, out of breath.]

MRS. YANG. Miss Shen Te. My son has told
70 me everything. I am Mrs. Yang, Sun's mother. Just think. He's got an offer. Of a job as a pilot. A letter has just come. From the director of the airfield in Peking!

SHEN TE. So he can fly again? Isn't that won-
75 derful!

MRS. YANG [less breathlessly all the time]. They won't give him the job for nothing. They want five hundred silver dollars.

SHEN TE. We can't let money stand in his
80 way, Mrs. Yang!

MRS. YANG. If only you could help him out!

SHEN TE. I have the shop. I can try! [She embraces MRS. YANG.] I happen to have two hundred with me now. Take it. [She gives her
85 the old couple's money.] It was a loan but they said I could repay it with my tobacco stock.

MRS. YANG. And they were calling Sun the Dead Pilot of Setzuan! A friend in need!

SHEN TE. We must find another three hun-
90 dred.

MRS. YANG. How?

SHEN TE. Let me think. [Slowly.] I know someone who can help. I didn't want to call

on his services again, he's hard and cunning.
But a flyer must fly. And I'll make this the
last time.

[*Distant sound of a plane.*]

5   MRS. YANG. If the man you mentioned can
do it. . . . Oh, look, there's the morning mail
plane, heading for Peking!

SHEN TE. The pilot can see us, let's wave!

[*They wave. The noise of the engine is*
10 *louder.*]

MRS. YANG. You know that pilot up there?

SHEN TE. Wave, Mrs. Yang! I know the pilot
who *will* be up there. He gave up hope. But
he'll do it now. One man to raise himself above
15 the misery, above us all.

[*To the audience.*]

Yang Sun, my lover:
Braving the storms
In company with the clouds
20 Crossing the heavens
And bringing to friends in far-away lands
The friendly mail!

SCENE IV A

[*In front of the inner curtain. Enter* SHEN TE,
carrying SHUI TA'S *mask. She sings.*]

The Song of Defenselessness

25 In our country
A useful man needs luck
Only if he finds strong backers can he prove
[himself useful
The good can't defend themselves and
30 Even the gods are defenseless.

Oh, why don't the gods have their own
[ammunition
And launch against badness their own
[expedition
35 Enthroning the good and preventing sedition
And bringing the world to a peaceful
[condition?

Oh, why don't the gods do the buying and
[selling
40 Injustice forbidding, starvation dispelling

Give bread to each city and joy to each
[dwelling?
Oh, why don't the gods do the buying and
[selling?

[*She puts on* SHUI TA'S *mask and sings in* 45
his voice.]

You can only help one of your luckless
[brothers
By trampling down a dozen others

Why is it the gods do not feel indignation   50
And come down in fury to end exploitation
Defeat all defeat and forbid desperation
Refusing to tolerate such toleration?

Why is it?

SCENE V

[SHEN TE'S *tobacco shop. Behind the counter,* 55
MR. SHUI TA, *reading the paper.* MRS. SHIN *is*
cleaning up. She talks and he takes no notice.]

MRS. SHIN. And when certain rumors get
about, what *happens* to a little place like this?
It goes to pot. *I* know. So, if you want my ad- 60
vice, Mr. Shui Ta, find out just what exactly
has been going on between Miss Shen Te and
that Yang Sun from Yellow Street. And remember: a certain interest in Miss Shen Te
has been expressed by the barber next door, a 65
man with twelve houses and only one wife,
who, for that matter, is likely to drop off at
any time. A certain interest has been expressed. [*She relishes the phrase.*] He was even
inquiring about her means and, if *that* doesn't 70
prove a man is getting serious, what would?
[*Still getting no response, she leaves with her*
bucket.]

YANG SUN'S VOICE. Is that Miss Shen Te's
tobacco shop?   75

MRS. SHIN'S VOICE. Yes, it is, but it's Mr.
Shui Ta who's here today.

[SHUI TA *runs to the looking glass with the*
short, light steps of SHEN TE, *and is just about*
to start primping, when he realizes his mistake, 80

and turns away, with a short laugh. Enter
YANG SUN. MRS. SHIN *enters behind him and*
slips into the back room to eavesdrop.]

YANG SUN. I am Yang Sun.

5 [SHUI TA *bows.*]

Is Miss Shen Te in?

SHUI TA. No.

YANG SUN. I guess you know our relationship? [*He is inspecting the stock.*] Quite a
10 place! And I thought she was just talking big.
I'll be flying again, all right. [*He takes a cigar,
solicits and receives a light from* SHUI TA.] You
think we can squeeze the other three hundred
out of the tobacco stock?

15 SHUI TA. May I ask if it is your intention to
sell at once?

YANG SUN. It was decent of her to come out
with the two hundred but they aren't much use
with the other three hundred still missing.

20 SHUI TA. Shen Te was overhasty promising
so much. She might have to sell the shop itself
to raise it. Haste, they say, is the wind that
blows the house down.

YANG SUN. Oh, she isn't a girl to keep a man
25 waiting. For one thing or the other, if you take
my meaning.

SHUI TA. I take your meaning.

YANG SUN [*leering*]. Uh, huh.

SHUI TA. Would you explain what the five
30 hundred silver dollars are for?

YANG SUN. Trying to sound me out? Very
well. The director of the Peking airfield is a
friend of mine from flying school. I give him
five hundred: he gets me the job.

35 SHUI TA. The price is high.

YANG SUN. Not as these things go. He'll
have to fire one of the present pilots—for
negligence. Only the man he has in mind isn't
negligent. Not easy, you understand. You
40 needn't mention that part of it to Shen Te.

SHUI TA [*looking intently at* YANG SUN].
Mr. Yang Sun, you are asking my cousin to
give up her possessions, leave her friends, and
place her entire fate in your hands. I presume
45 you intend to marry her?

YANG SUN. I'd be prepared to.

[*Slight pause.*]

SHUI TA. Those two hundred silver dollars

would pay the rent here for six months. If you
were Shen Te wouldn't you be tempted to con- 50
tinue in business?

YANG SUN. What? Can you imagine Yang
Sun the Flyer behind a counter? [*In an oily
voice.*] "A strong cigar or a mild one, worthy
sir?" Not in this century! 55

SHUI TA. My cousin wishes to follow the
promptings of her heart, and, from her own
point of view, she may even have what is
called the right to love. Accordingly, she has
commissioned me to help you to this post. 60
There is nothing here that I am not empowered
to turn immediately into cash. Mrs. Mi Tzu,
the landlady, will advise me about the sale.

[*Enter* MRS. MI TZU.]

MRS. MI TZU. Good morning, Mr. Shui Ta, 65
you wish to see me about the rent? As you
know it falls due the day after tomorrow.

SHUI TA. Circumstances have changed, Mrs.
Mi Tzu: my cousin is getting married. Her
future husband here, Mr. Yang Sun, will be 70
taking her to Peking. I am interested in selling
the tobacco stock.

MRS MI TZU. How much are you asking, Mr.
Shui Ta?

YANG SUN. Three hundred sil— 75

SHUI TA. Five hundred silver dollars.

MRS. MI TZU. How much did she pay for it,
Mr. Shui Ta?

SHUI TA. A thousand. And very little has
been sold. 80

MRS. MI TZU. She was robbed. But I'll make
you a special offer if you'll promise to be out
by the day after tomorrow. Three hundred
silver dollars.

YANG SUN [*shrugging*]. Take it, man, take it. 85

SHUI TA. It is not enough.

YANG SUN. Why not? Why not? Certainly,
it's enough.

SHUI TA. Five hundred silver dollars.

YANG SUN. But why? We only need three! 90

SHUI TA [*to* MRS. MI TZU]. Excuse me.
[*Takes* YANG SUN *on one side.*] The tobacco
stock is pledged to the old couple who gave
my cousin the two hundred.

YANG SUN. Is it in writing? 95

SHUI TA. No.

YANG SUN [*to* MRS. MI TZU]. Three hundred will do.

MRS. MI TZU. Of course, I need an assurance that Miss Shen Te is not in debt.

5 YANG SUN. Mr. Shui Ta?

SHUI TA. She is not in debt.

YANG SUN. When can you let us have the money?

MRS. MI TZU. The day after tomorrow. And
10 remember: I'm doing this because I have a soft spot in my heart for young lovers! [*Exit.*]

YANG SUN [*calling after her*]. Boxes, jars and sacks—three hundred for the lot and the pain's over! [*To* SHUI TA.] Where else can we raise
15 money by the day after tomorrow?

SHUI TA. Nowhere. Haven't you enough for the trip and the first few weeks?

YANG SUN. Oh, certainly.

SHUI TA. How much, exactly?

20 YANG SUN. Oh, I'll dig it up, if I have to steal it.

SHUI TA. I see.

YANG SUN. Well, don't fall off the roof. I'll get to Peking somehow.

25 SHUI TA. Two people can't travel for nothing.

YANG SUN [*not giving* SHUI TA *a chance to answer*]. I'm leaving *her* behind. No millstones round *my* neck!

30 SHUI TA. Oh.

YANG SUN. Don't look at me like that!

SHUI TA. How precisely is my cousin to live?

YANG SUN. Oh, you'll think of something.

SHUI TA. A small request, Mr. Yang Sun.
35 Leave the two hundred silver dollars here until you can show me two tickets for Peking.

YANG SUN. You learn to mind your own business, Mr. Shui Ta.

SHUI TA. I'm afraid Miss Shen Te may not
40 wish to sell the shop when she discovers that . . .

YANG SUN. You don't know women. She'll want to. Even then.

SHUI TA [*a slight outburst*]. She is a human
45 being, sir! And not devoid of common sense!

YANG SUN. Shen Te is a woman: she *is* devoid of common sense. I only have to lay my hand on her shoulder, and church bells ring.

SHUI TA [*with difficulty*]. Mr. Yang Sun!

YANG SUN. Mr. Shui Whatever-it-is! 50

SHUI TA. My cousin is devoted to you . . . because . . .

YANG SUN. Because I have my hands on her breasts. Give me a cigar. [*He takes one for himself, stuffs a few more in his pocket, then* 55 *changes his mind and takes the whole box.*] Tell her I'll marry her, then bring me the three hundred. Or let her bring it. One or the other. [*Exit.*]

MRS. SHIN [*sticking her head out of the back* 60 *room*]. Well, he has your cousin under his thumb, and doesn't care if all Yellow Street knows it!

SHUI TA [*crying out*]. I've lost my shop! And he doesn't love me! [*He runs berserk* 65 *through the room, repeating these lines incoherently. Then stops suddenly, and addresses* MRS. SHIN.] Mrs. Shin, you grew up in the gutter, like me. Are we lacking in hardness? I doubt it. If you steal a penny from me, 70 I'll take you by the throat till you spit it out! You'd do the same to me. The times are bad, this city is hell, but we're like ants, we keep coming, up and up the walls, however smooth! Till bad luck comes. Being in love, for instance. 75 *One* weakness is enough, and love is the deadliest.

MRS. SHIN [*emerging from the back room*]. You should have a little talk with Mr. Shu Fu the Barber. He's a real gentleman and just the 80 thing for your cousin. [*She runs off.*]

SHUI TA.
A caress becomes a stranglehold
A sigh of love turns to a cry of fear
Why are there vultures circling in the air? 85
A girl is going to meet her lover.
[SHUI TA *sits down and* MR. SHU FU *enters with* MRS SHIN.]
Mr. Shu Fu?

SHU FU. Mr. Shui Ta. 90
[*They both bow.*]

SHUI TA. I am told that you have expressed a certain interest in my cousin Shen Te. Let me set aside all propriety and confess: she is at this moment in grave danger. 95

SHU FU. Oh, dear!

SHUI TA. She has lost her shop, Mr. Shu Fu.

SHU FU. The charm of Miss Shen Te, Mr. Shui Ta, derives from the goodness, not of her shop, but of her heart. Men call her the Angel of the Slums.

SHUI TA. Yet her goodness has cost her two hundred silver dollars in a single day: we must put a stop to it.

SHU FU. Permit me to differ, Mr. Shui Ta. Let us rather, open wide the gates to such goodness! Every morning, with pleasure tinged by affection, I watch her charitable ministrations. For they are hungry, and she giveth them to eat! Four of them, to be precise. Why only four? I ask. Why not four hundred? I hear she has been seeking shelter for the homeless. What about my humble cabins behind the cattle run? They are at her disposal. And so forth. And so on. Mr. Shui Ta, do you think Miss Shen Te could be persuaded to listen to certain ideas of mine? Ideas like these?

SHUI TA. Mr. Shu Fu, she would be honored.

[Enter WONG and the POLICEMAN. MR. SHU FU turns abruptly away and studies the shelves.]

WONG. Is Miss Shen Te here?

SHUI TA. No.

WONG. I am Wong the Water Seller. You are Mr. Shui Ta?

SHUI TA. I am.

WONG. I am a friend of Shen Te's.

SHUI TA. An intimate friend, I hear.

WONG [to the POLICEMAN]. You see? [To SHUI TA.] It's because of my hand.

POLICEMAN. He hurt his hand, sir, that's a fact.

SHUI TA [quickly]. You need a sling, I see. [He takes a shawl from the back room, and throws it to WONG.]

WONG. But that's her new shawl!

SHUI TA. She has no more use for it.

WONG. But she bought it to please someone!

SHUI TA. It happens to be no longer necessary.

WONG [making the sling]. She is my only witness.

POLICEMAN. Mr. Shui Ta, your cousin is supposed to have seen the Barber hit the Water Seller with a curling iron.

SHUI TA. I'm afraid my cousin was not present at the time.

WONG. But she was, sir! Just ask her! Isn't she in?

SHUI TA [gravely]. Mr. Wong, my cousin has her own troubles. You wouldn't wish her to add to them by committing perjury?

WONG. But it was she that told me to go to the judge!

SHUI TA. Was the judge supposed to heal your hand?

[MR. SHU FU turns quickly around. SHUI TA bows to SHU FU, and vice versa.]

WONG [taking the sling off, and putting it back]. I see how it is.

POLICEMAN. Well, I'll be on my way. [To WONG.] And you be careful. If Mr. Shu Fu wasn't a man who tempers justice with mercy, as the saying is, you'd be in jail for libel. Be off with you!

[Exit WONG, followed by POLICEMAN.]

SHUI TA. Profound apologies, Mr. Shu Fu.

SHU FU. Not at all, Mr. Shui Ta. [Pointing to the shawl.] The episode is over?

SHUI TA. It may take her time to recover. There are some fresh wounds.

SHU FU. We shall be discreet. Delicate. A short vacation could be arranged . . .

SHUI TA. First, of course, you and she would have to talk things over.

SHU FU. At a small supper in a small, but high-class, restaurant.

SHUI TA. I'll go and find her. [Exit into back room.]

MRS. SHIN [sticking her head in again]. Time for congratulations, Mr. Shu Fu?

SHU FU. Ah, Mrs. Shin! Please inform Miss Shen Te's guests they may take shelter in the cabins behind the cattle run!

[MRS. SHIN nods, grinning.]

[To the audience.] Well? What do you think of me, ladies and gentlemen? What could a man do more? Could he be less selfish? More farsighted? A small supper in a small but . . . Does that bring rather vulgar and clumsy thoughts into your mind? Ts, ts, ts. Nothing of the sort will occur. She won't even be

touched. Not even accidentally while passing the salt. An exchange of ideas only. Over the flowers on the table—white chrysanthemums, by the way [*he writes down a note of this*]—
5 yes, over the white chrysanthemums, two young souls will . . . shall I say "find each other"? We shall NOT exploit the misfortune of others. Understanding? Yes. An offer of assistance? Certainly. But quietly. Almost in-
10 audibly. Perhaps with a single glance. A glance that could also—mean more.

MRS. SHIN [*coming forward*]. Everything under control, Mr. Shu Fu?

SHU FU. Oh, Mrs. Shin, what do you know
15 about this worthless rascal Yang Sun?

MRS. SHIN. Why, he's the most worthless rascal . . .

SHU FU. Is he really? You're sure? [*As she opens her mouth.*] From now on, he doesn't
20 exist! Can't be found anywhere!

[*Enter* YANG SUN.]

YANG SUN. What's been going on here?

MRS. SHIN. Shall I call Mr. Shui Ta, Mr. Shu Fu? He wouldn't want strangers in here!

25 SHU FU. Mr. Shui Ta is in conference with Miss Shen Te. Not to be disturbed!

YANG SUN. Shen Te here? I didn't see her come in. What kind of conference?

SHU FU [*not letting him enter the back
30 room*]. Patience, dear sir! And if by chance I have an inkling who you are, pray take note that Miss Shen Te and I are about to announce our engagement.

YANG SUN. What?

35 MRS. SHIN. You didn't expect that, did you?

[YANG SUN *is trying to push past the barber into the back room when* SHEN TE *comes out.*]

SHU FU. My dear Shen Te, ten thousand apologies! Perhaps you . . .

40 YANG SUN. What is it, Shen Te? Have you gone crazy?

SHEN TE [*breathless*]. My cousin and Mr. Shu Fu have come to an understanding. They wish me to hear Mr. Shu Fu's plans for helping
45 the poor.

YANG SUN. Your cousin wants to part us.

SHEN TE. Yes.

YANG SUN. And you've agreed to it?

SHEN TE. Yes.

YANG SUN. They told you I was bad. 50

[SHEN TE *is silent.*]

And suppose I am. Does that make me need you less? I'm low. Shen Te, I have no money, I don't do the right thing but at least I put up a fight! [*He is near her now, and speaks in an 55
undertone.*] Have you no eyes? Look at him. Have you forgotten already?

SHEN TE. No.

YANG SUN. How it was raining?

SHEN TE. No. 60

YANG SUN. How you cut me down from the willow tree? Bought me water? Promised me money to fly with?

SHEN TE [*shakily*]. Yang Sun, what do you want? 65

YANG SUN. I want you to come with me.

SHEN TE [*in a small voice*]. Forgive me, Mr. Shu Fu, I want to go with Mr. Yang Sun.

YANG SUN. We're lovers you know. Give me the key to the shop. 70

[SHEN TE *takes the key from around her neck.* YANG SUN *puts it on the counter. To* MRS. SHIN.]

Leave it under the mat when you're through. Let's go, Shen Te. 75

SHU FU. But this is rape! Mr. Shui Ta!!

YANG SUN [*to* SHEN TE]. Tell him not to shout.

SHEN TE. Please don't shout for my cousin, Mr. Shu Fu. He doesn't agree with me, I know, 80
but he's wrong. [*To the audience.*]

I want to go with the man I love
I don't want to count the cost
I don't want to consider if it's wise
I don't want to know if he loves me 85
I want to go with the man I love.

YANG SUN. That's the spirit.

[*And the couple leave.*]

SCENE V A

[*In front of the inner curtain.* SHEN TE *in her wedding clothes, on the way to her wed- 90
ding.*]

SHEN TE. Something terrible has happened. As I left the shop with Yang Sun, I found the

old carpet dealer's wife waiting in the street, trembling all over. She told me her husband has taken to his bed—sick with all the worry and excitement over the two hundred silver
5 dollars they lent me. She said it would be best if I gave it back now. Of course, I had to say I would. She said she couldn't quite trust my cousin Shui Ta or even my fiancé Yang Sun. There were tears in her eyes. With my emo-
10 tions in an uproar, I threw myself into Yang Sun's arms, I couldn't resist him. The things he'd said to Shui Ta had taught Shen Te nothing. Sinking into his arms, I said to my-self:

15   To let no one perish, not even oneself
       To fill everyone with happiness, even oneself
       Is so good

How could I have forgotten those two old people? Yang Sun swept me away like a small
20 hurricane. But he's not a bad man, and he loves me. He'd rather work in the cement factory than owe his flying to a crime. Though, of course, flying *is* a great passion with Sun. Now, on the way to my wedding, I waver be-
25 tween fear and joy.

SCENE VI

[*The "private dining room" on the upper floor of a cheap restaurant in a poor section of town. With* SHEN TE: *the* GRANDFATHER, *the* SISTER-IN-LAW, *the* NIECE, MRS. SHIN, *the* UN-
30 EMPLOYED MAN. *In a corner, alone, a* PRIEST. *A* WAITER *pouring wine. Downstage,* YANG SUN *talking to his mother. He wears a dinner jacket.*]

YANG SUN. Bad news, Mamma. She came
35 right out and told me she can't sell the shop for me. Some idiot is bringing a claim because he lent her the two hundred she gave you.

MRS. YANG. What did *you* say? Of course, you can't marry her now.

40 YANG SUN. It's no use saying anything to *her.* I've sent for her cousin, Mr. Shui Ta. He said there was nothing in writing.

MRS. YANG. Good idea. I'll go out and look for him. Keep an eye on things.

[*Exit* MRS. YANG. SHEN TE *has been pouring* 45
wine.]

SHEN TE [*to the audience, pitcher in hand*]. I wasn't mistaken in him. He's bearing up well. Though it must have been an awful blow—giving up flying. I do love him so. [*Calling* 50
across the room to him.] Sun, you haven't drunk a toast with the bride!

YANG SUN. What do we drink to?

SHEN TE. Why, to the future!

YANG SUN. When the bridegroom's dinner 55
jacket won't be a hired one!

SHEN TE. But when the bride's dress will still get rained on sometimes!

YANG SUN. To everything we ever wished for! 60

SHEN TE. May all our dreams come true!

[*They drink.*]

YANG SUN [*with loud conviviality*]. And now, friends, before the wedding gets under way, I have to ask the bride a few questions. 65
I've no idea what kind of a wife she'll make, and it worries me. [*Wheeling on* SHEN TE.] For example. Can you make five cups of tea with three tea leaves?

SHEN TE. No. 70

YANG SUN. So I won't be getting very much tea. Can you sleep on a straw mattress the size of that book? [*He points to the large volume the* PRIEST *is reading.*]

SHEN TE. The two of us? 75

YANG SUN. The one of you.

SHEN TE. In that case, no.

YANG SUN. What a wife! I'm shocked!

[*While the audience is laughing, his mother returns. With a shrug of her shoulders, she* 80
tells YANG SUN *the expected guest hasn't ar-rived. The* PRIEST *shuts the book with a bang, and makes for the door.*]

MRS. YANG. Where are *you* off to? It's only a matter of minutes. 85

PRIEST [*watch in hand*]. Time goes on, Mrs. Yang, and I've another wedding to attend to. Also a funeral.

MRS. YANG [*irately*]. D'you think we plan-ned it this way? I was hoping to manage with 90
one pitcher of wine, and we've run through

two already. [*Points to empty pitcher. Loudly.*] My dear Shen Te, I don't know where your cousin can be keeping himself!

SHEN TE. My cousin?

5 MRS. YANG. Certainly. I'm old fashioned enough to think such a close relative should attend the wedding.

SHEN TE. Oh, Sun, is it the three hundred silver dollars?

10 YANG SUN [*not looking her in the eye*]. Are you deaf? Mother says she's old fashioned. And I say I'm considerate. We'll wait another fifteen minutes.

HUSBAND. Another fifteen minutes.

15 MRS. YANG [*addressing the company*]. Now you all know, don't you, that my son is getting a job as a mail pilot?

SISTER-IN-LAW. In Peking, too, isn't it?

MRS. YANG. In Peking, too! The two of us

20 are moving to Peking!

SHEN TE. Sun, tell your mother Peking is out of the question now.

YANG SUN. Your cousin'll tell her. If he agrees. I don't agree.

25 SHEN TE [*amazed, and dismayed*]. Sun!

YANG SUN. I hate this godforsaken Setzuan. What people! Know what they look like when I half close my eyes? Horses! Whinnying, fretting, stamping, screwing their necks up!

30 [*Loudly.*] And what is it the thunder says? They are su-per-flu-ous! [*He hammers out the syllables.*] They've run their last race! They can go trample themselves to death! [*Pause.*] I've got to get out of here.

35 SHEN TE. But I've promised the money to the old couple.

YANG SUN. And since you always do the wrong thing, it's lucky your cousin's coming. Have another drink.

40 SHEN TE [*quietly*]. My cousin can't be coming.

YANG SUN. How d'you mean?

SHEN TE. My cousin can't be where I am.

YANG SUN. Quite a conundrum!

45 SHEN TE [*desperately*]. Sun, I'm the one that loves you. Not my cousin. He was thinking of the job in Peking when he promised you the

old couple's money—

YANG SUN. Right. And that's why he's bringing the three hundred silver dollars. Here 50 —to my wedding.

SHEN TE. He is not bringing the three hundred silver dollars.

YANG SUN. Huh? What makes you think that? 55

SHEN TE [*looking into his eyes*]. He says you only bought one ticket to Peking.

[*Short pause.*]

YANG SUN. That was yesterday. [*He pulls two tickets part way out of his inside pocket,* 60 *making her look under his coat.*] Two tickets. I don't want Mother to know. She'll get left behind. I sold her furniture to buy these tickets, so you see . . .

SHEN TE. But what's to become of the old 65 couple?

YANG SUN. What's to become of me? Have another drink. Or do you believe in moderation? If I drink, I fly again. And if you drink, you may learn to understand me. 70

SHEN TE. You want to fly. But I can't help you.

YANG SUN. "Here's a plane, my darling— but it's only got one wing!"

[*The WAITER enters.*] 75

WAITER. Mrs. Yang! Mrs. Yang!

MRS. YANG. Yes?

WAITER. Another pitcher of wine, ma'am?

MRS. YANG. We have enough, thanks. Drinking makes me sweat. 80

WAITER. Would you mind paying, ma'am?

MRS. YANG [*to everyone*]. Just be patient a few moments longer, everyone, Mr. Shui Ta is on his way over! [*To the WAITER.*] Don't be a spoilsport. 85

WAITER. I can't let you leave till you've paid your bill, ma'am.

MRS. YANG. But they know me here!

WAITER. That's just it.

PRIEST [*ponderously getting up*]. I humbly 90 take my leave. [*And he does.*]

MRS. YANG [*to the others, desperately*]. Stay where you are, everybody! The priest says he'll be back in two minutes!

YANG SUN. It's no good, Mamma. Ladies and gentlemen, Mr. Shui Ta still hasn't arrived and the priest has gone home. We won't detain you any longer.

5 [*They are leaving now.*]

GRANDFATHER [*in the doorway, having forgotten to put his glass down*]. To the bride! [*He drinks, puts down the glass, and follows the others.*]

10 [*Pause.*]

SHEN TE. Shall I go too?

YANG SUN. You? Aren't you the bride? Isn't this your wedding? [*He drags her across the room, tearing her wedding dress.*] If we can 15 wait, you can wait. Mother calls me her falcon. She wants to see me in the clouds. But I think it may be St. Nevercome's Day before she'll go to the door and see my plane thunder by. [*Pause. He pretends the guests are still 20 present.*] Why such a lull in the conversation, ladies and gentlemen? Don't you like it here? The ceremony is only slightly postponed—because an important guest is expected at any moment. Also because the bride doesn't know 25 what love is. While we're waiting, the bridegroom will sing a little song. [*He does so.*]

The Song of St. Nevercome's Day

On a certain day, as is generally known,
    One and all will be shouting: Hooray,
                                    [hooray!
30 For the beggar maid's son has a solid-gold
                                    [throne
    And the day is St. Nevercome's Day
On St. Nevercome's, Nevercome's,
                            [Nevercome's Day
35 He'll sit on his solid-gold throne

Oh, hooray, hooray! That day goodness
                            [will pay!
    That day badness will cost you your head!
And merit and money will smile and be
40   [funny
    While exchanging salt and bread
On St. Nevercome's, Nevercome's,
                            [Nevercome's Day
    While exchanging salt and bread

And the grass, oh, the grass will look down   45
                            [at the sky
    And the pebbles will roll up the stream
And all men will be good without batting
                            [an eye
    They will make of our earth a dream   50
On St. Nevercome's, Nevercome's,
                            [Nevercome's Day
    They will make of our earth a dream

And as for me, that's the day I shall be
    A flyer and one of the best   55
Unemployed man, you will have work to do
    Washerwoman, you'll get your rest
On St. Nevercome's, Nevercome's,
                            [Nevercome's Day
    Washerwoman, you'll get your rest.   60

MRS. YANG. It looks like he's not coming.
[*The three of them sit looking at the door.*]

SCENE VI A

[WONG's *den. The sewer pipe is again transparent and again the* GODS *appear to* WONG *in a dream.*]   65

WONG. I'm so glad you've come, illustrious ones. It's Shen Te. She's in great trouble from following the rule about loving thy neighbor. Perhaps she's *too* good for this world!

FIRST GOD. Nonsense! You are eaten up by   70
lice and doubts!

WONG. Forgive me, illustrious one, I only meant you might deign to intervene.

FIRST GOD. Out of the question! My colleague here intervened in some squabble or   75
other only yesterday. [*He points to the* THIRD GOD *who has a black eye.*] The results are before us!

WONG. She had to call on her cousin again. But not even he could help. I'm afraid the shop   80
is done for.

THIRD GOD [*a little concerned*]. Perhaps we should help after all?

FIRST GOD. The gods help those that help themselves.   85

WONG. What if we *can't* help ourselves, illustrious ones?

[*Slight pause.*]

SECOND GOD. Try, anyway! Suffering ennobles!

FIRST GOD. Our faith in Shen Te is unshaken!

THIRD GOD. We certainly haven't found any *other* good people. You can see where we spend our nights from the straw on our clothes.

WONG. You might help her find her way by—

FIRST GOD. The good man finds his own way here below!

SECOND GOD. The good woman too.

FIRST GOD. The heavier the burden, the greater her strength!

THIRD GOD. We're only onlookers, you know.

FIRST GOD. And everything will be all right in the end, O ye of little faith!

[*They are gradually disappearing through these last lines.*]

SCENE VII

[*The yard behind* SHEN TE'S *shop. A few articles of furniture on a cart.* SHEN TE *and* MRS. SHIN *are taking the washing off the line.*]

MRS. SHIN. If you ask me, you should fight tooth and nail to keep the shop.

SHEN TE. How can I? I have to sell the tobacco to pay back the two hundred silver dollars today.

MRS. SHIN. No husband, no tobacco, no house and home! What are you going to live on?

SHEN TE. I can work. I can sort tobacco.

MRS. SHIN. Hey, look, Mr. Shui Ta's trousers! He must have left here stark naked!

SHEN TE. Oh, he may have another pair, Mrs. Shin.

MRS. SHIN. But if he's gone for good as you say, why has he left his pants behind?

SHEN TE. Maybe he's thrown them away.

MRS. SHIN. Can I take them?

SHEN TE. Oh, no.

[*Enter* MR. SHU FU, *running.*]

SHU FU. Not a word! Total silence! I know all. You have sacrificed your own love and happiness so as not to hurt a dear old couple who had put their trust in you! Not in vain does this district—for all its malevolent tongues!—call you the Angel of the Slums! That young man couldn't rise to your level, so you left him. And now, when I see you closing up the little shop, that veritable haven of rest for the multitude, well, I cannot, I cannot let it pass. Morning after morning I have stood watching in the doorway not unmoved—while you graciously handed out rice to the wretched. Is that never to happen again? Is the good woman of Setzuan to disappear? If only you would allow *me* to assist you! Now don't say anything! No assurances, no exclamations of gratitude! [*He has taken out his check book.*] Here! A blank check. [*He places it on the cart.*] Just my signature. Fill it out as you wish. Any sum in the world. I herewith retire from the scene, quietly, unobtrusively, making no claims, on tiptoe, full of veneration, absolutely selflessly . . . [*He has gone.*]

MRS. SHIN. Well! You're saved. There's always some idiot of a man . . . Now hurry! Put down a thousand silver dollars and let me fly to the bank before he comes to his senses.

SHEN TE. I can pay you for the washing without any check.

MRS. SHIN. What? You're not going to cash it just because you might have to marry him? Are you crazy? Men like him *want* to be led by the nose! Are you still thinking of that flyer? All Yellow Street knows how he treated you!

SHEN TE.

When I heard his cunning laugh, I was [afraid

But when I saw the holes in his shoes, I loved [him dearly.

MRS. SHIN. Defending that good for nothing after all that's happened!

SHEN TE [*staggering as she holds some of the washing*]. Oh!

MRS. SHIN [*taking the washing from her,*

dryly]. So you feel dizzy when you stretch and bend? There couldn't be a little visitor on the way? If that's it, you can forget Mr. Shu Fu's blank check: it wasn't meant for a christening
5 present!

[*She goes to the back with a basket. SHEN TE's eyes follow MRS. SHIN for a moment. Then she looks down at her own body, feels her stomach, and a great joy comes into her eyes.*]

10 SHEN TE. O joy! A new human being is on the way. The world awaits him. In the cities the people say: he's got to be reckoned with, · this new human being! [*She imagines a little boy to be present, and introduces him to the*
15 *audience.*]

This is my son, the well-known flyer!
Say: Welcome
To the conqueror of unknown mountains
[and unreachable regions
20 Who brings us our mail across the
[impassable deserts!
[*She leads him up and down by the hand.*]
Take a look at the world, my son. That's a tree. Tree, yes. Say: "Hello, tree!" And bow. Like
25 this. [*She bows.*] Now you know each other. And, look, here comes the Water Seller. He's a friend, give him your hand. A cup of fresh water for my little son, please. Yes, it *is* a warm day. [*Handing the cup.*] Oh dear, a policeman,
30 we'll have to make a circle round *him.* Perhaps we can pick a few cherries over there in the rich Mr. Pung's garden. But we mustn't be seen. You want cherries? Just like children with fathers. No, no, you can't go straight at
35 them like that. Don't pull. We must learn to be reasonable. Well, have it your own way. [*She has let him make for the cherries.*] Can you reach? Where to put them? Your mouth is the best place. [*She tries one herself.*] Mmm,
40 they're good. But the policeman, we must run! [*They run.*] Yes, back to the street. Calm now, so no one will notice us. [*Walking the street with her child, she sings.*]

Once a plum—'twas in Japan—
45 Made a conquest of a man
But the man's turn soon did come
For he gobbled up the plum

[*Enter WONG, with a CHILD by the hand. He coughs.*]

SHEN TE. Wong! 50
WONG. It's about the Carpenter, Shen Te. He's lost his shop, and he's been drinking. His children are on the streets. This is one. Can you help?
SHEN TE [*to the child*]. Come here, little man. 55
[*Takes him down to the footlights. To the audience.*]

You there! A man is asking you for shelter!
A man of tomorrow says: what about today?
His friend the conqueror, whom you know, 60
Is his advocate!
[*To WONG.*] He can live in Mr. Shu Fu's cabin. I may have to go there myself. I'm going to have a baby. That's a secret—don't tell Yang Sun—we'd only be in his way. Can you 65
find the Carpenter for me?
WONG. I knew you'd think of something. [*To the CHILD.*] Goodbye, son, I'm going for your father.
SHEN TE. What about your hand, Wong? I 70
wanted to help, but my cousin . . .
WONG. Oh, I can get along with one hand, don't worry. [*He shows how he can handle his pole with his left hand alone.*]
SHEN TE. But your right hand! Look, take 75
this cart, sell everything that's on it, and go to the doctor with the money . . .
WONG. She's still good. But first I'll bring the Carpenter. I'll pick up the cart when I get back. [*Exit WONG.*] 80
SHEN TE [*to the CHILD*]. Sit down over here, son, till your father comes.
[*The CHILD sits crosslegged on the ground. Enter the HUSBAND and WIFE, each dragging a large, full sack.*] 85
WIFE [*furtively*]. You're alone, Shen Te, dear?
[*SHEN TE nods. The WIFE beckons to the NEPHEW offstage. He comes on with another sack.*] 90
Your cousin's away?
[*SHEN TE nods.*]
He's not coming back?
SHEN TE. No. I'm giving up the shop.

WIFE. That's why we're here. We want to know if we can leave these things in your new home. Will you do us this favor?

SHEN TE. Why, yes, I'd be glad to.

HUSBAND [*cryptically*]. And if anyone asks about them, say they're yours.

SHEN TE. Would anyone ask?

WIFE [*with a glance back at her* HUSBAND]. Oh, someone might. The police, for instance. They don't seem to like us. Where can we put it?

SHEN TE. Well, I'd rather not get in any more trouble . . .

WIFE. Listen to her! The good woman of Setzuan!

[SHEN TE *is silent*.]

HUSBAND. There's enough tobacco in those sacks to give us a new start in life. We could have our own tobacco factory!

SHEN TE [*slowly*]. You'll have to put them in the back room.

[*The sacks are taken offstage, while the* CHILD *is left alone. Shyly glancing about him, he goes to the garbage can, starts playing with the contents, and eating some of the scraps. The others return.*]

WIFE. We're counting on you, Shen Te!

SHEN TE. Yes. [*She sees the* CHILD *and is shocked.*]

HUSBAND. We'll see you in Mr. Shu Fu's cabins.

NEPHEW. The day after tomorrow.

SHEN TE. Yes. Now, go. Go! I'm not feeling well.

[*Exeunt all three, virtually pushed off.*]
He is eating the refuse in the garbage can!
Only look at his little gray mouth!
[*Pause. Music.*]
As this is the world *my* son will enter
I will study to defend him.
To be good to you, my son,
I shall be a tigress to all others
If I have to.
And I shall have to.
[*She starts to go.*] One more time, then. I hope really the last.
[*Exit* SHEN TE, *taking* SHUI TA'S *trousers.*

MRS. SHIN *enters and watches her with marked interest. Enter the* SISTER-IN-LAW *and the* GRANDFATHER.]

SISTER-IN-LAW. So it's true, the shop has closed down. And the furniture's in the back yard. It's the end of the road!

MRS. SHIN [*pompously*]. The fruit of high living, selfishness, and sensuality! Down the primrose path to Mr. Shu Fu's cabins—with you!

SISTER-IN-LAW. Cabins? Rat holes! He gave them to us because his soap supplies only went mouldy there!

[*Enter the* UNEMPLOYED MAN.]

UNEMPLOYED MAN. Shen Te is moving?

SISTER-IN-LAW. Yes. She was sneaking away.

MRS. SHIN. She's ashamed of herself, and no wonder!

UNEMPLOYED MAN. Tell her to call Mr. Shui Ta or she's done for this time!

SISTER-IN-LAW. Tell her to call Mr. Shui Ta or *we're* done for this time!

[*Enter* WONG *and* CARPENTER, *the latter with a* CHILD *on each hand.*]

CARPENTER. So we'll have a roof over our heads for a change!

MRS. SHIN. Roof? Whose roof?

CARPENTER. Mr. Shu Fu's cabins. And we have little Feng to thank for it. [FENG, *we find, is the name of the child already there; his* FATHER *now takes him. To the other two.*] Bow to your little brother, you two! [*The* CARPENTER *and the two new arrivals bow to* FENG.]

[*Enter* SHUI TA.]

UNEMPLOYED MAN. Sst! Mr. Shui Ta!

[*Pause.*]

SHUI TA. And what is this crowd here for, may I ask?

WONG. How do you do, Mr. Shui Ta? This is the Carpenter. Miss Shen Te promised him space in Mr. Shu Fu's cabins.

SHUI TA. That will not be possible.

CARPENTER. We can't go there after all?

SHUI TA. All the space is needed for other purposes.

SISTER-IN-LAW. You mean we have to get out? But we've got nowhere to go.

SHUI TA. Miss Shen Te finds it possible to provide employment. If the proposition interests you, you may stay in the cabins.

SISTER-IN-LAW [with distaste]. You mean work? Work for Miss Shen Te?

SHUI TA. Making tobacco, yes. There are three bales here already. Would you like to get them?

SISTER-IN-LAW [trying to bluster]. We have our own tobacco! We were in the tobacco business before you were born!

SHUI TA [to the CARPENTER and the UNEMPLOYED MAN]. You don't have your own tobacco. What about you?

[The CARPENTER and the UNEMPLOYED MAN get the point, and go for the sacks. Enter MRS. MI TZU.]

MRS. MI TZU. Mr. Shui Ta? I've brought you your three hundred silver dollars.

SHUI TA. I'll sign your lease instead. I've decided not to sell.

MRS. MI TZU. What? You don't need the money for that flyer?

SHUI TA. No.

MRS. MI TZU. And you can pay six months' rent?

SHUI TA [takes the barber's blank check from the cart and fills it out]. Here is a check for ten thousand silver dollars. On Mr. Shu Fu's account. Look! [He shows her the signature on the check.] Your six months' rent will be in your hands by seven this evening. And now, if you'll excuse me.

MRS. MI TZU. So it's Mr. Shu Fu now. The flyer has been given his walking papers. These modern girls! In my day they'd have said she was flighty. That poor, deserted Mr. Yang Sun!

[Exit MRS. MI TZU. The CARPENTER and the UNEMPLOYED MAN drag the three sacks back on the stage.]

CARPENTER [to SHUI TA]. I don't know why I'm doing this for you.

SHUI TA. Perhaps your children want to eat, Mr. Carpenter.

SISTER-IN-LAW [catching sight of the sacks]. Was my brother-in-law here?

MRS. SHIN. Yes, he was.

SISTER-IN-LAW. I thought as much. I know those sacks! That's our tobacco!

SHUI TA. Really? I thought it came from my back room? Shall we consult the police on the point?

SISTER-IN-LAW [defeated]. No.

SHUI TA. Perhaps you will show me the way to Mr. Shu Fu's cabins?

[SHUI TA goes off, followed by the CARPENTER and his two older children, the SISTER-IN-LAW, the GRANDFATHER, and the UNEMPLOYED MAN. Each of the last three drags a sack. Enter OLD MAN and OLD WOMAN.]

MRS. SHIN. A pair of pants—missing from the clothes line one minute—and next minute on the honorable backside of Mr. Shui Ta!

OLD WOMAN. We thought Miss Shen Te was here.

MRS. SHIN [preoccupied]. Well, she's not.

OLD MAN. There was something she was going to give us.

WONG. She was going to help me too. [Looking at his hand.] It'll be too late soon. But she'll be back. This cousin has never stayed long.

MRS. SHIN [approaching a conclusion]. No, he hasn't, has he?

SCENE VII A

[The sewer pipe. WONG asleep. In his dream, he tells the GODS his fears. The GODS seem tired from all their travels. They stop for a moment and look over their shoulders at the Water Seller.]

WONG. Illustrious ones, I've been having a bad dream. Our beloved Shen Te was in great distress in the rushes down by the river—the spot where the bodies of suicides are washed up. She kept staggering and holding her head down as if she was carrying something and it was dragging her down into the mud. When I called out to her, she said she had to take your Book of Rules to the other side, and not get it wet, or the ink would all come off. You had talked to her about the virtues, you know, the time she gave you shelter in Setzuan.

THIRD GOD. Well, but what do you suggest, my dear Wong?

WONG. Maybe a little relaxation of the rules, Benevolent One, in view of the bad times.

THIRD GOD. As for instance?

WONG. Well, um, good-will, for instance, might do instead of love?

THIRD GOD. I'm afraid that would create new problems.

WONG. Or, instead of justice, good sportsmanship?

THIRD GOD. That would only mean more work.

WONG. Instead of honor, outward propriety?

THIRD GOD. Still more work! No, no! The rules will have to stand, my dear Wong!

[*Wearily shaking their heads, all three journey on.*]

SCENE VIII

[SHUI TA's *tobacco factory in* SHU FU's *cabins. Huddled together behind bars, several families, mostly women and children. Among these people the* SISTER-IN-LAW, *the* GRANDFATHER, *the* CARPENTER, *and his three children. Enter* MRS. YANG *followed by* YANG SUN.]

MRS. YANG [*to the audience*]. There's something I just *have* to tell you: strength and wisdom are wonderful things. The strong and wise Mr. Shui Ta has transformed my son from a dissipated good-for-nothing into a model citizen. As you may have heard, Mr. Shui Ta opened a small tobacco factory near the cattle runs. It flourished. Three months ago—I shall never forget it—I asked for an appointment, and Mr. Shui Ta agreed to see us—me and my son. I can see him now as he came through the door to meet us . . .

[*Enter* SHUI TA, *from a door.*]

SHUI TA. What can I do for you, Mrs. Yang?

MRS. YANG. This morning the police came to the house. We find you've brought an action for breach of promise of marriage. In the name of Shen Te. You also claim that Sun came by two hundred silver dollars by improper means.

SHUI TA. That is correct.

MRS. YANG. Mr. Shui Ta, the money's all gone. When the Peking job didn't materialize, he ran through it all in three days. I know he's a good-for-nothing. He sold my furniture. He was moving to Peking without me. Miss Shen Te thought highly of him at one time.

SHUI TA. What do *you* say, Mr. Yang Sun?

YANG SUN. The money's gone.

SHUI TA [*to* MRS. YANG]. Mrs. Yang, in consideration of my cousin's incomprehensible weakness for your son, I am prepared to give him another chance. He can have a job—here. The two hundred silver dollars will be taken out of his wages.

YANG SUN. So it's the factory or jail?

SHUI TA. Take your choice.

YANG SUN. May I speak with Shen Te?

SHUI TA. You may not.

[*Pause.*]

YANG SUN [*sullenly*]. Show me where to go.

MRS. YANG. Mr. Shui Ta, you are kindness itself: the gods will reward you! [*To* YANG SUN.] And honest work will make a man of you, my boy.

[YANG SUN *follows* SHUI TA *into the factory.* MRS. YANG *comes down again to the footlights.*]

Actually, honest work didn't agree with him—at first. And he got no opportunity to distinguish himself till—in the third week—when the wages were being paid. . . .

[SHUI TA *has a bag of money. Standing next to his foreman—the former* UNEMPLOYED MAN —*he counts out the wages. It is* YANG SUN's *turn.*]

UNEMPLOYED MAN [*reading*]. Carpenter, six silver dollars. Yang Sun, six silver dollars.

YANG SUN [*quietly*]. Excuse me, sir. I don't think it can be more than five. May I see? [*He takes the foreman's list.*] It says six working days. But that's a mistake, sir. I took a day off for court business. And I won't take what I haven't earned, however miserable the pay is!

UNEMPLOYED MAN. Yang Sun. Five silver dollars. [*To* SHUI TA.] A rare case, Mr. Shui Ta!

SHUI TA. How is it the book says six when it should say five?

UNEMPLOYED MAN. I must've made a mistake, Mr. Shui Ta. [*With a look at* YANG SUN.] It won't happen again.

SHUI TA [*taking* YANG SUN *aside*]. You don't hold back, do you? You give your all to the firm. You're even honest. Do the foreman's mistakes always favor the workers?

YANG SUN. He does have . . . friends.

SHUI TA. Thank you. May I offer you any little recompense?

YANG SUN. Give me a trial period of one week, and I'll prove my intelligence is worth more to you than my strength.

MRS. YANG SUN [*still down at the footlights*]. Fighting words, fighting words! That evening, I said to Sun: "If you're a flyer, then fly, my falcon! Rise in the world!" And he got to be foreman. Yes, in Mr. Shui Ta's tobacco factory, he worked real miracles.

[*We see* YANG SUN *with his legs apart standing behind the workers who are handing along a basket of raw tobacco above their heads.*]

YANG SUN. Faster! Faster! You, there, d'you think you can just stand around now you're not foreman any more? It'll be your job to lead us in song. Sing!

[UNEMPLOYED MAN *starts singing. The others join in the refrain.*]

Song of the Eighth Elephant

Chang had seven elephants—all much the
[same—
But then there was Little Brother
The seven, they were wild, Little Brother,
[he was tame
And to guard them Chang chose Little
[Brother
  Run faster!
  Mr. Chang has a forest park
  Which must be cleared before tonight
  And already it's growing dark!

When the seven elephants cleared that
[forest park
Mr. Chang rode high on Little Brother
While the seven toiled and moiled till dark
On his big behind sat Little Brother
  Dig faster!
  Mr. Chang has a forest park
  Which must be cleared before tonight
  And already it's growing dark!

And the seven elephants worked many an
[hour
Till none of them could work another
Old Chang, he looked sour, on the seven,
[he did glower

But gave a pound of rice to Little Brother
  What was that?
  Mr. Chang has a forest park
  Which must be cleared before tonight
  And already it's growing dark!

And the seven elephants hadn't any tusks
The one that had the tusks was Little
[Brother!
Seven are no match for one, if the one has
[a gun!
How old Chang did laugh at Little
[Brother!
  Keep on digging!
  Mr. Chang has a forest park
  Which must be cleared before tonight
  And already it's growing dark!

[*Smoking a cigar,* SHUI TA *strolls by.* YANG SUN, *laughing, has joined in the refrain of the third stanza and speeded up the tempo of the last stanza by clapping his hands.*]

MRS. YANG. And that's why I say: strength and wisdom are wonderful things. It took the strong and wise Mr. Shui Ta to bring out the best in Yang Sun. A real superior man is like a bell. If you ring it, it rings, and if you don't, it don't, as the saying is.

SCENE IX

[SHEN TE's *shop, now an office with club chairs and fine carpets. It is raining.* SHUI TA, *now fat, is just dismissing the* OLD MAN *and* OLD WOMAN. MRS. SHIN, *in obviously new clothes, looks on, smirking.*]

SHUI TA. No! I can NOT tell you when we expect her back.

OLD WOMAN. The two hundred silver dollars came today. In an envelope. There was no letter, but it must be from Shen Te. We want to write and thank her. May we have her address?

SHUI TA. I'm afraid I haven't got it.

OLD MAN [*pulling* OLD WOMAN's *sleeve*]. Let's be going.

OLD WOMAN. She's got to come back some time! [*They move off, uncertainly, worried.* SHUI TA *bows.*]

MRS. SHIN. They lost the carpet shop because they couldn't pay their taxes. The money arrived too late.

SHUI TA. They could have come to me.

MRS. SHIN. People don't like coming to you.

SHUI TA [*sits suddenly, one hand to his head*]. I'm dizzy.

MRS. SHIN. After all, you *are* in your seventh month. But old Mrs. Shin will be there in your hour of trial! [*She cackles feebly.*]

SHUI TA [*in a satisfied voice*]. Can I count on that?

MRS. SHIN. We all have our price, and mine won't be too high for the great Mr. Shui Ta! [*She opens* SHUI TA's *collar.*].

SHUI TA. It's for the child's sake. All of this.

MRS. SHIN. "All for the child," of course.

SHUI TA. I'm so fat. People must notice.

MRS. SHIN. Oh no, they think it's 'cause you're rich.

SHUI TA [*more feelingly*]. What will happen to the child?

MRS. SHIN. You ask that nine times a day. Why, it'll have the best that money can buy!

SHUI TA. He must never see Shui Ta.

MRS. SHIN. Oh, no. Always Shen Te.

SHUI TA. What about the neighbors? There are rumors, aren't there?

MRS. SHIN. As long as Mr. Shu Fu doesn't find out, there's nothing to worry about. Drink this.

[*Enter* YANG SUN *in a smart business suit, and carrying a businessman's brief case.* SHUI TA *is more or less in* MRS. SHIN's *arms.*]

YANG SUN [*surprised*]. I seem to be in the way.

SHUI TA [*ignoring this, rises with an effort*]. Till tomorrow, Mrs. Shin.

[MRS. SHIN *leaves with a smile, putting her new gloves on.*]

YANG SUN. Gloves now! She couldn't be fleecing you? And since when did *you* have a private life? [*Taking a paper from the brief case.*] You haven't been at your best lately, and things are getting out of hand. The police want to close us down. They say that at the most they can only permit twice the lawful number of workers.

SHUI TA [*evasively*]. The cabins are quite good enough.

YANG SUN. For the workers maybe, not for the tobacco. They're too damp. We must take over some of Mrs. Mi Tzu's buildings.

SHUI TA. Her price is double what I can pay.

YANG SUN. Not unconditionally. If she has me to stroke her knees she'll come down.

SHUI TA. I'll never agree to that.

YANG SUN. What's wrong? Is it the rain? You get so irritable whenever it rains.

SHUI TA. Never! I will never . . .

YANG SUN. Mrs. Mi Tzu'll be here in five minutes. *You* fix it. And Shu Fu will be with her. . . . What's all that noise?

[*During the above dialogue,* WONG *is heard off stage calling:* "The good Shen Te, where is she? Which of you has seen Shen Te, good people? Where is Shen Te?" *A knock. Enter* WONG.]

WONG. Mr. Shui Ta, I've come to ask when Miss Shen Te will be back, it's six months now . . . There are rumors. People say something's happened to her.

SHUI TA. I'm busy. Come back next week.

WONG [*excited*]. In the morning there was always rice on her doorstep—for the needy. It's been there again lately!

SHUI TA. And what do people conclude from this?

WONG. That Shen Te is still in Setzuan! She's been . . . [*He breaks off.*]

SHUI TA. She's been what? Mr. Wong, if you're Shen Te's friend, talk a little less about her, that's my advice to you.

WONG. I don't want your advice! Before she disappeared, Miss Shen Te told me something very important—she's pregnant!

YANG SUN. What? What was that?

SHUI TA [*quickly*]. The man is lying.

WONG. A good woman isn't so easily forgotten, Mr. Shui Ta.

[*He leaves.* SHUI TA *goes quickly into the back room.*]

YANG SUN [*to the audience*]. Shen Te pregnant? So that's why. Her cousin sent her away, so I wouldn't get wind of it. I have a son, a Yang appears on the scene, and what happens? Mother and child vanish into thin air! That scoundrel, that unspeakable . . . [*The sound*

of sobbing is heard from the back room.] What
was that? Someone sobbing? Who was it?
Mr. Shui Ta the Tobacco King doesn't weep his
heart out. And where does the rice come from
5 that's on the doorstep in the morning?

[SHUI TA returns. He goes to the door and
looks out into the rain.]

Where is she?

SHUI TA. Sh! It's nine o'clock. But the rain's
10 so heavy, you can't hear a thing.

YANG SUN. What do you want to hear?

SHUI TA. The mail plane.

YANG SUN. What?

SHUI TA. I've been told you wanted to fly
15 at one time. Is that all forgotten?

YANG SUN. Flying mail is night work. I prefer the daytime. And the firm is very dear to
me—after all it belongs to my ex-fiancée, even
if she's not around. And she's not, is she?

20 SHUI TA. What do you mean by that?

YANG SUN. Oh, well, let's say I haven't altogether—lost interest.

SHUI TA. My cousin might like to know that.

YANG SUN. I might not be indifferent—if I
25 found she was being kept under lock and key.

SHUI TA. By whom?

YANG SUN. By you.

SHUI TA. What could you do about it?

YANG SUN. I could submit for discussion—
30 my position in the firm.

SHUI TA. You are now my Manager. In return for a more appropriate position, you
might agree to drop the enquiry into your ex-
fiancée's whereabouts?

35 YANG SUN. I might.

SHUI TA. What position would be more appropriate?

YANG SUN. The one at the top.

SHUI TA. My own? [Silence.] And if I pre-
40 ferred to throw you out on your neck?

YANG SUN. I'd come back on my feet. With
suitable escort.

SHUI TA. The police?

YANG SUN. The police.

45 SHUI TA. And when the police found no
one?

YANG SUN. I might ask them not to overlook
the back room. [Ending the pretense.] In short,

Mr. Shui Ta, my interest in this young woman
has not been officially terminated. I should like 50
to see more of her. [Into SHUI TA's face.] Besides, she's pregnant and needs a friend. [He
moves to the door.] I shall talk about it with
the Water Seller. [Exit.]

[SHUI TA is rigid for a moment, then he 55
quickly goes into the back room. He returns
with SHEN TE's belongings: underwear, etc.
He takes a long look at the shawl of the previous scene. He then wraps the things in a
bundle which, upon hearing a noise, he hides 60
under the table. Enter MRS. MI TZU and MR.
SHU FU. They put away their umbrellas and
galoshes.]

MRS. MI TZU. I thought your manager was
here, Mr. Shui Ta. He combines charm with 65
business in a way that can only be to the advantage of all of us.

SHU FU. You sent for us, Mr. Shui Ta?

SHUI TA. The factory is in trouble.

SHU FU. It always is. 70

SHUI TA. The police are threatening to close
us down unless I can show that the extension
of our facilities is imminent.

SHU FU. Mr. Shui Ta, I'm sick and tired of
your constantly expanding projects. I place 75
cabins at your cousin's disposal; you make a
factory of them. I hand your cousin a check;
you present it. Your cousin disappears and you
find the cabins too small and talk of yet
more . . . 80

SHUI TA. Mr. Shu Fu, I'm authorized to inform you that Miss Shen Te's return is now
imminent.

SHU FU. Imminent? It's becoming his favorite
word. 85

MRS. MI TZU. Yes, what does it mean?

SHUI TA. Mrs. Mi Tzu, I can pay you exactly
half what you asked for your buildings. Are
you ready to inform the police that I am taking
them over? 90

MRS. MI TZU. Certainly, if I can take over
your manager.

SHU FU. What?

MRS. MI TZU. He's so efficient.

SHUI TA. I'm afraid I need Mr. Yang Sun.

MRS. MI TZU. So do I.

SHUI TA. He will call on you tomorrow.

SHU FU. So much the better. With Shen Te likely to turn up at any moment, the presence of that young man is hardly in good taste.

SHUI TA. So we have reached a settlement. In what was once the good Shen Te's little shop we are laying the foundations for the great Mr. Shui Ta's twelve magnificent super tobacco markets. You will bear in mind that though they call me the Tobacco King of Setzuan, it is my cousin's interests that have been served . . .

VOICES [*off*]. The police, the police! Going to the tobacco shop! Something must have happened! [*Etc.*]

[*Enter* YANG SUN, WONG, *and the* POLICEMAN.]

POLICEMAN. Quiet there, quiet, quiet! [*They quiet down.*] I'm sorry, Mr. Shui Ta, but there's a report that you've been depriving Miss Shen Te of her freedom. Not that I believe all I hear, but the whole city's in an uproar.

SHUI TA. That's a lie.

POLICEMAN. Mr. Yang Sun has testified that he heard someone sobbing in the back room.

SHU FU. Mrs. Mi Tzu and myself will testify that no one here has been sobbing.

MRS. MI TZU. We have been quietly smoking our cigars.

POLICEMAN. Mr. Shui Ta, I'm afraid I shall have to take a look at that room. [*He does so. The room is empty.*] No one there, of course, sir.

YANG SUN. But I heard sobbing. What's that? [*He finds the clothes.*]

WONG. Those are Shen Te's things. [*To crowd.*] Shen Te's clothes are here!

VOICES [*Off. In sequence*]. Shen Te's clothes! They've been found under the table! Body of murdered girl still missing! Tobacco King suspected!

POLICEMAN. Mr. Shui Ta, unless you can tell us where the girl is, I'll have to ask you to come along.

SHUI TA. I do not know.

POLICEMAN. I can't say how sorry I am, Mr. Shui Ta. [*He shows him the door.*]

SHUI TA. Everything will be cleared up in no time. There are still judges in Setzuan.

YANG SUN. I heard sobbing!

SCENE IX A

[WONG's *den. For the last time, the* GODS *appear to the Water Seller in his dream. They have changed and show signs of a long journey, extreme fatigue, and plenty of mishaps. The* FIRST *no longer has a hat; the* THIRD *has lost a leg; all* THREE *are barefoot.*]

WONG. Illustrious ones, at last you're here. Shen Te's been gone for months and today her cousin's been arrested. They think he murdered her to get the shop. But I had a dream and in this dream Shen Te said her cousin was keeping her prisoner. You must find her for us, illustrious ones!

FIRST GOD. We've found very few good people anywhere, and even they didn't keep it up. Shen Te is still the only one that stayed good.

SECOND GOD. If she *has* stayed good.

WONG. Certainly she has. But she's vanished.

FIRST GOD. That's the last straw. All is lost!

SECOND GOD. A little moderation, dear colleague!

FIRST GOD [*plaintively*]. What's the good of moderation now? If she can't be found, we'll have to resign! The world is a terrible place! Nothing but misery, vulgarity, and waste! Even the countryside isn't what it used to be. The trees are getting their heads chopped off by telephone wires, and there's such a noise from all the gunfire, and I can't stand those heavy clouds of smoke, and—

THIRD GOD. The place is absolutely unlivable! Good intentions bring people to the brink of the abyss, and good deeds push them over the edge. I'm afraid our book of rules is destined for the scrap heap—

SECOND GOD. It's people! They're a worthless lot!

THIRD GOD. The world is too cold!

SECOND GOD. It's people! They are too weak!

FIRST GOD. Dignity, dear colleagues, dignity! Never despair! As for this world, didn't we agree that we only have to find one human being who can stand the place? Well, we found her. True, we lost her again. We must find her again, that's all! And at once!

[*They disappear.*]

SCENE X

[*Courtroom. Groups:* SHU FU *and* MRS. MI TZU; YANG SUN *and* MRS. YANG; WONG, *the* CARPENTER, *the* GRANDFATHER, *the* NIECE, *the* OLD MAN, *the* OLD WOMAN; MRS. SHIN, *the* POLICEMAN; *the* UNEMPLOYED MAN, *the* SISTER-IN-LAW.]

OLD MAN. So much power isn't good for one man.

UNEMPLOYED MAN. And he's going to open twelve super tobacco markets!

WIFE. One of the judges is a friend of Mr. Shu Fu's.

SISTER-IN-LAW. Another one accepted a present from Mr. Shui Ta only last night. A great fat goose.

OLD WOMAN [*to* WONG]. And Shen Te is nowhere to be found.

WONG. Only the gods will ever know the truth.

POLICEMAN. Order in the court! My lords the judges!

[*Enter the* THREE GODS *in judges' robes. We overhear their conversation as they pass along the footlights to their bench.*]

THIRD GOD. We'll never get away with it, our certificates were so badly forged.

SECOND GOD. My predecessor's "sudden indigestion" will certainly cause comment.

FIRST GOD. But he *had* just eaten a whole goose.

UNEMPLOYED MAN. Look at that! *New* judges!

WONG. New judges. And what good ones!

[*The* THIRD GOD *hears this, and turns to smile at* WONG. *The* GODS *sit. The* FIRST GOD *beats on the bench with his gavel. The* POLICEMAN *brings in* SHUI TA *who walks with lordly steps. He is whistled at.*]

POLICEMAN [*to* SHUI TA]. Be prepared for a surprise. The judges have been changed.

[SHUI TA *turns quickly round, looks at them, and staggers.*]

NIECE. What's the matter now?

WIFE. The great Tobacco King nearly fainted.

HUSBAND. Yes, as soon as he saw the new judges.

WONG. Does *he* know who they are?

[SHUI TA *picks himself up, and the proceedings open.*]

FIRST GOD. Defendant Shui Ta, you are accused of doing away with your cousin Shen Te in order to take possession of her business. Do you plead guilty or not guilty?

SHUI TA. Not guilty, my lord.

FIRST GOD [*thumbing through the documents of the case*]. The first witness is the Policeman. I shall ask him to tell us something of the respective reputations of Miss Shen Te and Mr. Shui Ta.

POLICEMAN. Miss Shen Te was a young lady who aimed to please, my lord. She liked to live and let live, as the saying goes. Mr. Shui Ta, on the other hand, is a man of principle. Though the generosity of Miss Shen Te forced him at times to abandon half measures, unlike the girl, he was always on the side of the law, my lord. One time, he even unmasked a gang of thieves to whom his too trustful cousin had given shelter. The evidence, in short, my lord, proves that Mr. Shui Ta was *incapable* of the crime of which he stands accused!

FIRST GOD. I see. And are there others who could testify along, shall we say, the same lines?

[SHU FU *rises.*]

POLICEMAN [*whispering to* GODS]. Mr. Shu Fu—a very important person.

FIRST GOD [*inviting him to speak*]. Mr. Shu Fu!

SHU FU. Mr. Shui Ta is a businessman, my lord. Need I say more?

FIRST GOD. Yes.

SHU FU. Very well, I will. He is Vice President of the Council of Commerce and is about to be elected a Justice of the Peace. [*He returns to his seat.*]

WONG. Elected! *He gave him the job!*

[*With a gesture the* FIRST GOD *asks who* MRS. MI TZU *is.*]

POLICEMAN. Another very important person. Mrs. Mi Tzu.

FIRST GOD [*inviting her to speak*]. Mrs. Mi Tzu!

MRS. MI TZU. My lord, as Chairman of the Committee on Social Work, I wish to call attention to just a couple of eloquent facts: Mr. Shui Ta not only has erected a model factory with model housing in our city, he is a regular contributor to our home for the disabled. [*She returns to her seat.*]

POLICEMAN [*whispering*]. And she's a great friend of the judge that ate the goose!

FIRST GOD [*to the* POLICEMAN]. Oh, thank you. What next? [*To the Court, genially.*] Oh, yes. We should find out if any of the evidence is less favorable to the Defendant.

[WONG, *the* CARPENTER, *the* OLD MAN, *the* OLD WOMAN, *the* UNEMPLOYED MAN, *the* SISTER-IN-LAW, *and the* NIECE *come forward.*]

POLICEMAN [*whispering*]. Just the riff raff, my lord.

FIRST GOD [*addressing the "riff raff"*]. Well, um, riff raff—do you know anything of the Defendant, Mr. Shui Ta?

WONG. Too much, my lord.

UNEMPLOYED MAN. What don't we know, my lord?

CARPENTER. He ruined us.

SISTER-IN-LAW. He's a cheat.

NIECE. Liar.

WIFE. Thief.

BOY. Blackmailer.

BROTHER. Murderer.

FIRST GOD. Thank you. We should now let the Defendant state his point of view.

SHUI TA. I only came on the scene when Shen Te was in danger of losing what I had understood was a gift from the gods. Because I did the filthy jobs which someone had to do, they hate me. My activities were held down to the minimum, my lord.

SISTER-IN-LAW. He had us arrested!

SHUI TA. Certainly. You stole from the bakery!

SISTER-IN-LAW. Such concern for the bakery! You didn't want the shop for yourself, I suppose!

SHUI TA. I didn't want the shop overrun with parasites.

SISTER-IN-LAW. We had nowhere else to go.

SHUI TA. There were too many of you.

WONG. What about this old couple. Were *they* parasites?

OLD MAN. We lost our shop because of you!

OLD WOMAN. And we gave your cousin money!

SHUI TA. My cousin's fiancé was a flyer. The money had to go to *him*.

WONG. Did you care whether he flew or not? Did you care whether she married him or not? You wanted her to marry someone else! [*He points at* SHU FU.]

SHUI TA. The flyer unexpectedly turned out to be a scoundrel.

YANG SUN [*jumping up*]. Which was the reason you made him your Manager?

SHUI TA. Later on he improved.

WONG. And when he improved, you sold him to her? [*He points out* MRS. MI TZU.]

SHUI TA. She wouldn't let me have her premises unless she had him to stroke her knees!

MRS. MI TZU. What? The man's a pathological liar. [*To him.*] Don't mention my property to me as long as you live! Murderer! [*She rustles off, in high dudgeon.*]

YANG SUN [*pushing in*]. My lord, I wish to speak for the Defendant.

SISTER-IN-LAW. Naturally. He's your employer.

UNEMPLOYED MAN. And the worst slave driver in the country.

MRS. YANG. That's a lie! My lord, Mr. Shui Ta is a great man. He . . .

YANG SUN. He's this and he's that, but he is not a murderer, my lord. Just fifteen minutes before his arrest I heard Shen Te's voice in his own back room.

FIRST GOD. Oh? Tell us more!

YANG SUN. I heard sobbing, my lord!

FIRST GOD. But lots of women sob, we've been finding.

YANG SUN. Could I fail to recognize her voice?

SHU FU. No, you made her sob so often yourself, young man!

YANG SUN. Yes. But I also made her happy. Till he [pointing at SHUI TA] decided to sell her to you!

SHUI TA. Because you didn't love her.

WONG. Oh, no: it was for the money, my lord!

SHUI TA. And what was the money for, my lord? For the poor! And for Shen Te so she could go on being good!

WONG. For the poor? That he sent to his sweatshops? And why didn't you let Shen Te be good when you signed the big check?

SHUI TA. For the child's sake, my lord.

CARPENTER. What about *my* children? What did he do about them?

[SHUI TA *is silent.*]

WONG. The shop was to be a fountain of goodness. That was the gods' idea. You came and spoiled it!

SHUI TA. If I hadn't, it would have run dry!

MRS. SHIN. There's a lot in that, my lord.

WONG. What have you done with the good Shen Te, bad man? She *was* good, my lords, she was, I swear it! [He raises his hand in an oath.]

THIRD GOD. What's happened to your hand, Water Seller?

WONG [pointing to SHUI TA]. It's all his fault, my lord, *she* was going to send me to a doctor— [To SHUI TA.] You were her worst enemy!

SHUI TA. I was her only friend!

WONG. Where is she then? Tell us where your good friend is!

[The excitement of this exchange has run through the whole crowd.]

ALL. Yes, where is she? Where is Shen Te? [Etc.]

SHUI TA. Shen Te had to go.

WONG. Where? Where to?

SHUI TA. I cannot tell you! I cannot tell you!

ALL. Why? Why did she have to go away? [Etc.]

WONG [into the din with the first words, but talking on beyond the others]. Why not, why not? Why did she have to go away?

SHUI TA [shouting]. Because you'd all have torn her to shreds, that's why! My lords, I have a request. Clear the court! When only the judges remain, I will make a confession.

ALL [except WONG, who is silent, struck by the new turn of events]. So he's guilty? He's confessing! [Etc.]

FIRST GOD [using the gavel]. Clear the court!

POLICEMAN. Clear the court!

WONG. Mr. Shui Ta has met his match this time.

MRS. SHIN [with a gesture toward the judges]. You're in for a little surprise.

[The court is cleared. Silence.]

SHUI TA. Illustrious ones!

[The GODS look at each other, not quite believing their ears.]

SHUI TA. Yes, I recognize you!

SECOND GOD [taking matters in hand, sternly]. What have you done with our good woman of Setzuan?

SHUI TA. I have a terrible confession to make: I am she! [He takes off his mask, and tears away his clothes. SHEN TE stands there.]

SECOND GOD. Shen Te!

SHEN TE. Shen Te, yes. Shui Ta *and* Shen Te. Both.

Your injunction
To be good and yet to live
Was a thunderbolt:
It has torn me in two
I can't tell how it was
But to be good to others
And myself at the same time
I could not do it
Your world is not an easy one, illustrious
[ones!
When we extend our hand to a beggar, he
[tears it off for us
When we help the lost, we are lost ourselves.
And so

Since not to eat is to die
Who can long refuse to be bad?
As I lay prostrate beneath the weight of
[good intentions
5 Ruin stared me in the face
It was when I was unjust that I ate good
[meat
And hobnobbed with the mighty
Why?
10 Why are bad deeds rewarded?
Good ones punished?
I enjoy giving
I truly wished to be the Angel of the Slums
But washed by a foster-mother in the water
15 [of the gutter
I developed a sharp eye
The time came when pity was a thorn in my
[side
And, later, when kind words turned to ashes
20 [in my mouth
And anger took over
I became a wolf
Find me guilty, then, illustrious ones,
But know:
25 All that I have done I did
To help my neighbor
To love my lover
And to keep my little one from want
For your great, godly deeds, I was too poor,
30 [too small.
[*Pause.*]

FIRST GOD [*shocked*]. Don't go on making yourself miserable, Shen Te! We're overjoyed to have found you!

35 SHEN TE. I'm telling you I'm the bad man who committed all those crimes!

FIRST GOD [*using—or failing to use—his ear trumpet*]. The good woman who did all those good deeds?

40 SHEN TE. Yes, but the bad man too!

FIRST GOD [*as if something had dawned*]. Unfortunate coincidences! Heartless neighbors!

THIRD GOD [*shouting in his ear*]. But how is
45 she to continue?

FIRST GOD. Continue? Well, she's a strong, healthy girl . . .

SECOND GOD. You didn't hear what she said!

FIRST GOD. I heard every word! She is con- 50 fused, that's all! [*He begins to bluster.*] And what about this book of rules—we can't renounce our rules, can we? [*More quietly.*] Should the world be changed? How? By whom? The world should *not* be changed! [*At a sign* 55 *from him, the lights turn pink, and music plays.*] ·
And now the hour of parting is at hand.
Dost thou behold, Shen Te, yon fleecy
[cloud? 60
It is our chariot. At a sign from me
'Twill come and take us back to whence
[we came
Above the azure vault and silver stars . . .

SHEN TE. No! Don't go, illustrious ones! 65
FIRST GOD.
Our cloud has landed now in yonder field
From whence it will transport us back to
[heaven.
Farewell, Shen Te, let not thy courage fail 70
[thee . . .
[*Exeunt* GODS.]

SHEN TE. What about the old couple? They've lost their shop! What about the Water Seller and his hand? And I've got to defend 75 myself against the barber, because I don't love him! And against Sun, because I do love him! How? How?

[SHEN TE's *eyes follow the* GODS *as they are imagined to step into a cloud which rises and* 80 *moves forward over the orchestra and up beyond the balcony.*]

FIRST GOD [*from on high*]. We have faith in you, Shen Te!

SHEN TE. There'll be a child. And he'll have 85 to be fed. I can't stay here. Where shall I go?

FIRST GOD. Continue to be good, good woman of Setzuan!

SHEN TE. I need my bad cousin!

FIRST GOD. But not very often! 90

SHEN TE. Once a week at least!

FIRST GOD. Once a month will be quite enough!

SHEN TE [*shrieking*]. No, no! Help!

778

[*But the cloud continues to recede as the* GODS *sing.*]

Valedictory Hymn

What rapture, oh, it is to know
    A good thing when you see it
5   And having seen a good thing, oh,
       What rapture 'tis to flee it

Be good, sweet maid of Setzuan
    Let Shui Ta be clever
Departing, we forget the man
10   Remember your endeavor

Because through all the length of days
    Her goodness faileth never
Sing hallelujah! May Shen Te's
    Good name live on forever!

15   SHEN TE. Help!

Tennessee Williams

1914–

The Glass Menagerie

1945

In studying a play we habitually isolate such constituents of drama as plot, character, setting, and theme, whereas in attending a play we tend to become, as we say, "involved." Williams' Production Notes emphasize not the constituents so much as the unfolding performance in a theater, and his plentiful stage directions are a reminder that what Aristotle called "spectacle" need not be regarded as the mere addition of theatrical effects, but rather the encompassing and progressing action upon the stage.

In this "memory play" Williams borrows from the medium of cinema, especially from silent film, to present the interrupted continuity of Tom Wingfield's stream of thought, which bears his story. The scenes are offered as "flashbacks," punctuated by the slightly nostalgic and self-mocking subtitles. Tom holds in hand a movie script and from time to time waves in a musical sound track providing bittersweet commentary. He is successively author, narrator, director, and actor. All unreels as on the screen of his memories. The combination of the constituents of the play with the mode of cinema creates the effect of discontinuous subjectivity which is the essence of this particular work. The theater in which *The Glass Menagerie* is performed becomes the theater of the mind.

The Glass Menagerie

WILLIAMS

The Author's Production Notes

Being a "memory play," *The Glass Menagerie* can be presented with unusual freedom of convention. Because of its considerably delicate or tenuous material, atmospheric touches and subtleties of direction play a particularly important part. Expressionism and all other unconventional techniques in drama have only one valid aim, and that is a closer approach to truth. When a play employs unconventional techniques, it is not, or certainly shouldn't be, trying to escape its responsibility of dealing with reality, or interpreting experience, but is actually or should be attempting to find a closer approach, a more penetrating and vivid expression of things as they are. The straight realistic play with its genuine frigidaire and authentic ice-cubes, its characters that speak exactly as its audience speaks, corresponds to the academic landscape and has the same

The Glass Menagerie, *by Tennessee Williams. Copyright 1945 by Tennessee Williams and Edwina D. Williams and renewed 1973 by Tennessee Williams. Reprinted by permission of Random House, Inc.*
Caution: *Professionals and amateurs are hereby warned that* The Glass Menagerie, *being fully protected under the copyright laws of the United States of America, the British Empire including the Dominion of Canada, and all other countries of the copyright union, is subject to royalty. All rights, including professional, amateur, motion picture, recitation, lecturing, public reading, radio broadcasting, and the rights of translation into foreign languages, are strictly reserved. Particular emphasis is laid on the question of readings, permission for which must be secured from the author's agent in writing. All inquiries should be addressed to the author's agent, Liebling-Wood, 551 Fifth Avenue, New York City.*

virtue of a photographic likeness. Everyone should know nowadays the unimportance of the photographic in art: that truth, life, or reality is an organic thing which the poetic imagination can represent or suggest, in essence, only through transformation, through changing into other forms than those which were merely present in appearance.

These remarks are not meant as a preface only to this particular play. They have to do with a conception of a new, plastic theatre which must take the place of the exhausted theatre of realistic conventions if the theatre is to resume vitality as a part of our culture.

THE SCREEN DEVICE. There is *only one important difference between the original and acting version of the play* and that is the *omission* in the latter of the device which I tentatively included in my *original* script. This device was the use of a screen on which were projected magic-lantern slides bearing images or titles. I do not regret the omission of this device from the present Broadway production. The extraordinary power of Miss Taylor's performance made it suitable to have the utmost simplicity in the physical production. But I think it may be interesting to some readers to see how this device was conceived. So I am putting it into the published manuscript. These images and legends, projected from behind, were cast on a section of wall between the front-room and dining-room areas, which should be indistinguishable from the rest when not in use.

The purpose of this will probably be apparent. It is to give accent to certain values in each scene. Each scene contains a particular point (or several) which is structurally the most important. In an episodic play, such as this, the basic structure or narrative line may be obscured from the audience; the effect may seem fragmentary rather than architectural. This may not be the fault of the play so much as a lack of attention in the audience. The legend or image upon the screen will strengthen the effect of what is merely allusion in the writing and allow the primary point to be made more simply and lightly than if the entire responsibility were on the spoken lines. Aside from this structural value, I think the screen will have a definite emotional appeal, less definable but just as important. An imaginative producer or director may invent many other uses for this device than those indicated in the present script. In fact the possibilities of the device seem much larger to me than the instance of this play can possibly utilize.

THE MUSIC. Another extra-literary accent in this play is provided by the use of music. A single recurring tune, "The Glass Menagerie," is used to give emotional emphasis to suitable passages. This tune is like circus music, not when you are on the grounds or in the immediate vicinity of the parade, but when you are at some distance and very likely thinking of something else. It seems under those circumstances to continue almost interminably and it weaves in and out of your preoccupied consciousness; then it is the lightest, most delicate music in the world and perhaps the saddest. It expresses the surface vivacity of life with the underlying strain of immutable and inexpressible sorrow. When you look at a piece of delicately spun glass you think of two things: how beautiful it is and how easily it can be broken. Both of those ideas should be woven into the recurring tune, which dips in and out of the play as if it were carried on a wind that changes. It serves as a thread of connection and allusion between the narrator with his separate point in time and space and the subject of his story. Between each episode it returns as reference to the emotion, nostalgia, which is the first condition of the play. It is primarily Laura's music and therefore comes out most clearly when the play focuses upon her and the lovely fragility of glass which is her image.

THE LIGHTING. The lighting in the play is not realistic. In keeping with the atmosphere of memory, the stage is dim. Shafts of light are focused on selected areas or actors, sometimes in contradistinction to what is the apparent center. For instance, in the quarrel scene between Tom and Amanda, in which Laura has no active part, the clearest pool of light is on her figure. This is also true of the supper scene, when her silent figure on the sofa should remain the visual center. The light upon Laura should be distinct from the others, having a peculiar pristine clarity such as light used in early religious portraits of female saints or madonnas. A certain correspondence to light in religious paintings, such as El Greco's, where the figures are radiant in atmosphere that is relatively dusky, could be effectively used throughout the play. (It will also permit a more effective use of the screen.) A free, imaginative use of light can be of enormous value in giving a mobile, plastic quality to plays of a more or less static nature.

THE CHARACTERS

AMANDA WINGFIELD   *the mother. A little woman of great but confused vitality clinging frantically to another time and place. Her characterization must be carefully created, not copied from type. She is not paranoiac, but her life is paranoia. There is much to admire in Amanda, and as much to love and pity as there is to laugh at. Certainly she has endurance and a kind of heroism, and though her foolishness makes her unwittingly cruel at times, there is tenderness in her slight person.*

LAURA WINGFIELD   *her daughter. Amanda, having failed to establish contact with reality, continues to live vitally in her illusions, but Laura's situation is even graver. A childhood illness has left her crippled, one leg slightly shorter than the other, and held in a brace. This defect need not be more than suggested on the stage. Stemming from this, Laura's separation increases till she is like a piece of her own glass collection, too exquisitely fragile to move from the shelf.*

TOM WINGFIELD   *her son. And the narrator of the play. A poet with a job in a warehouse. His nature is not remorseless, but to escape from a trap he has to act without pity.*

JIM O'CONNOR   *the gentleman caller. A nice, ordinary, young man.*

SCENE. *An alley in St. Louis.*
PART I. *Preparation for a Gentleman Caller.*
PART II. *The Gentleman calls.*
TIME:° *Now and the Past.*

SCENE I.

5   *The Wingfield apartment is in the rear of the
building, one of those vast hive-like conglomera-
tions of cellular living-units that flower as warty
growths in overcrowded urban centers of lower
middle-class population and are symptomatic of
10 the impulse of this largest and fundamentally
enslaved section of American society to avoid
fluidity and differentiation and to exist and function as one interfused mass of automatism.*

*The apartment faces an alley and is entered by a
15 fire-escape, a structure whose name is a touch of
accidental poetic truth, for all of these huge
buildings are always burning with the slow and
implacable fires of human desperation. The fire-
escape is included in the set—that is, the landing
20 of it and steps descending from it.*

*The scene is memory and is therefore non-
realistic. Memory takes a lot of poetic license. It
omits some details; others are exaggerated, according to the emotional value of the articles it
25 touches, for memory is seated predominantly in
the heart. The interior is therefore rather dim and
poetic.*

*At the rise of the curtain, the audience is faced
with the dark, grim rear wall of the Wingfield tene-
30 ment. This building, which runs parallel to the
footlights, is flanked on both sides by dark, narrow
alleys which run into murky canyons of tangled
clotheslines, garbage cans and the sinister lattice-
work of neighboring fire-escapes. It is up and
35 down these side alleys that exterior entrances and
exits are made, during the play. At the end of
TOM'S opening commentary, the dark tenement
wall slowly reveals (by means of a transparency)
the interior of the ground floor Wingfield apart-
40 ment.*

*Downstage is the living room, which also serves
as a sleeping room for* LAURA, *the sofa unfolding*

*to make her bed. Upstage, center, and divided by a
wide arch or second proscenium, with transparent
faded portieres (or second curtain), is the dining* 45
*room. In an old-fashioned what-not in the living
room are seen scores of transparent glass animals.
A blown-up photograph of the father hangs on
the wall of the living room, facing the audience,
to the left of the archway. It is the face of a very* 50
*handsome young man in a doughboy's First World
War cap. He is gallantly smiling, ineluctably
smiling, as if to say, "I will be smiling forever."*

*The audience hears and sees the opening scene
in the dining room through both the transparent* 55
*fourth wall of the building and the transparent
gauze portieres of the dining-room arch. It is
during this revealing scene that the fourth wall
slowly ascends, out of sight. This transparent
exterior wall is not brought down again until* 60
the very end of the play, during TOM'S *final
speech.*

*The narrator is an undisguised convention of
the play. He takes whatever license with dramatic
convention as is convenient to his purposes.* 65

TOM *enters dressed as a merchant sailor from
alley, stage left, and strolls across the front of the
stage to the fire-escape. There he stops and lights
a cigarette. He addresses the audience.*

TOM. Yes, I have tricks in my pocket, I have 70
things up my sleeve. But I am the opposite of
a stage magician. He gives you illusion that
has the appearance of truth. I give you truth
in the pleasant disguise of illusion.

To begin with, I turn back time. I reverse it 75
to that quaint period, the thirties, when the
huge middle class of America was matriculat-
ing in a school for the blind. Their eyes had
failed them, or they had failed their eyes, and
so they were having their fingers pressed 80
forcibly down on the fiery Braille alphabet of
a dissolving economy.

In Spain there was revolution. Here there
was only shouting and confusion.

In Spain there was Guernica.° Here there 85
were disturbances of labor, sometimes pretty

Time Tom narrates his memories at about the time of the
outbreak of World War II (1939–1945)

Guernica a town in northern Spain, heavily bombarded
by German aircraft in 1937 during the Spanish Civil War

violent, in otherwise peaceful cities such as Chicago, Cleveland, Saint Louis . . .

This is the social background of the play.

[Music]

5 The play is memory.

Being a memory play, it is dimly lighted, it is sentimental, it is not realistic.

In memory everything seems to happen to music. That explains the fiddle in the wings.

10 I am the narrator of the play, and also a character in it.

The other characters are my mother, Amanda, my sister, Laura, and a gentleman caller who appears in the final scenes.

15 He is the most realistic character in the play, being an emissary from a world of reality that we were somehow set apart from.

But since I have a poet's weakness for symbols, I am using this character also as a symbol;

20 he is the long delayed but always expected something that we live for.

There is a fifth character in the play who doesn't appear except in this larger-than-life-size photograph over the mantel.

25 This is our father who left us a long time ago.

He was a telephone man who fell in love with long distances; he gave up his job with the telephone company and skipped the light fantastic out of town . . .

30 The last we heard of him was a picture postcard from Mazatlan, on the Pacific coast of Mexico, containing a message of two words— "Hello—Good-bye!" and no address.

I think the rest of the play will explain it-

35 self. . . .

[Amanda's *voice becomes audible through the portieres.*]

[legend on screen: "où sont les neiges."]°

He divides the portieres and enters the upstage

40 *area. Amanda and Laura are seated at a drop-leaf table. Eating is indicated by gestures without food or utensils. Amanda faces the audience. Tom and Laura are seated in profile. The in-*

Legend on Screen a caption in the style of "titles" (comment or dialogue) in silent movies; here a line from the French poet Francois Villon (1431–1463?), "Where are the snows of yesteryear?"

terior has lit up softly and through the scrim we see Amanda and Laura seated at the table 45 *in the upstage area.*

Amanda [*Calling*]. Tom?

Tom. Yes, Mother.

Amanda. We can't say grace until you come to the table! 50

Tom. Coming, Mother. [*He bows slightly and withdraws, reappearing a few moments later in his place at the table.*]

Amanda [*To her son*]. Honey, don't *push* with your *fingers.* If you have to push with 55 something, the thing to push with is a crust of bread. And chew—chew! Animals have sections in their stomachs which enable them to digest food without mastication, but human beings are supposed to chew their food before 60 they swallow it down. Eat food leisurely, son, and really enjoy it. A well-cooked meal has lots of delicate flavors that have to be held in the mouth for appreciation. So chew your food and give your salivary glands a chance to function! 65

[Tom *deliberately lays his imaginary fork down and pushes his chair back from the table.*]

Tom. I haven't enjoyed one bite of this dinner because of your constant directions on how to eat it. It's you that make me rush through 70 meals with your hawk-like attention to every bite I take. Sickening—spoils my appetite—all this discussion of—animals' secretion—salivary glands—mastication!

Amanda [*Lightly*]. Temperament like a 75 Metropolitan star! [*He rises and crosses downstage*]. You're not excused from the table.

Tom. I'm getting a cigarette.

Amanda. You smoke too much. [Laura rises.] 80

Laura. I'll bring in the blanc mange. [*He remains standing with his cigarette by the portieres during the following.*]

Amanda [*Rising*]. No, sister, no, sister—you be the lady this time and I'll be the darky. 85

Laura. I'm already up.

Amanda. Resume your seat, little sister—I want you to stay fresh and pretty—for gentlemen callers!

Laura. I'm not expecting any gentlemen 90 callers.

AMANDA [*Crossing out to kitchenette. Airily*]. Sometimes they come when they are least expected! Why, I remember one Sunday afternoon in Blue Mountain—[*Enters kitchenette.*]

5 TOM. I know what's coming!

LAURA. Yes. But let her tell it.

TOM. Again?

LAURA. She loves to tell it.

[AMANDA *returns with bowl of dessert.*]

10 AMANDA. One Sunday afternoon in Blue Mountain—your mother received—*seventeen*—gentlemen callers! Why, sometimes there weren't chairs enough to accommodate them all. We had to send the nigger over to bring in

15 folding chairs from the parish house.

TOM [*Remaining at portieres*]. How did you entertain those gentlemen callers?

AMANDA. I understood the art of conversation!

20 TOM. I bet you could talk.

AMANDA. Girls in those days *knew* how to talk, I can tell you.

TOM. Yes?

[IMAGE: AMANDA AS A GIRL ON A PORCH,

25 GREETING CALLERS.]

AMANDA. They knew how to entertain their gentlemen callers. It wasn't enough for a girl to be possessed of a pretty face and a graceful figure—although I wasn't slighted in either

30 respect. She also needed to have a nimble wit and a tongue to meet all occasions.

TOM. What did you talk about?

AMANDA. Things of importance going on in the world! Never anything coarse or common

35 or vulgar. [*She addresses* TOM *as though he were seated in the vacant chair at the table though he remains by portieres. He plays this scene as though he held the book*].° My callers were gentlemen—all! Among my callers were

40 some of the most prominent young planters of the Mississippi Delta—planters and sons of planters!

[TOM *motions for music and a spot of light on* AMANDA. *Her eyes lift, her face glows, her voice*

45 *becomes rich and elegiac.*]

book script of the play

[SCREEN LEGEND: "OÙ SONT LES NEIGES."]

There was young Champ Laughlin who later became vice-president of the Delta Planters Bank.

Hadley Stevenson who was drowned in 50 Moon Lake and left his widow one hundred and fifty thousand in Government bonds.

There were the Cutrere brothers, Wesley and Bates. Bates was one of my bright particular beaux! He got in a quarrel with that wild 55 Wainwright boy. They shot it out on the floor of Moon Lake Casino. Bates was shot through the stomach. Died in the ambulance on his way to Memphis. His widow was also well-provided for, came into eight or ten thousand 60 acres, that's all. She married him on the rebound—never loved her—carried my picture on him the night he died!

And there was that boy that every girl in the Delta had set her cap for! That beautiful, 65 brilliant young Fitzhugh boy from Greene County!

TOM. What did he leave his widow?

AMANDA. He never married! Gracious, you talk as though all of my old admirers had 70 turned up their toes to the daisies!

TOM. Isn't this the first you've mentioned that still survives?

AMANDA. That Fitzhugh boy went North and made a fortune—came to be known as the 75 Wolf of Wall Street! He had the Midas touch, whatever he touched turned to gold!

And I could have been Mrs. Duncan J. Fitzhugh, mind you! But—I picked your *father!*

LAURA [*Rising*]. Mother, let me clear the 80 table.

AMANDA. No, dear, you go in front and study your typewriter chart. Or practice your shorthand a little. Stay fresh and pretty!—It's almost time for our gentlemen callers to start 85 arriving. [*She flounces girlishly toward the kitchenette*] How many do you suppose we're going to entertain this afternoon?

[TOM *throws down the paper and jumps up with a groan.*] 90

LAURA [*Alone in the dining room*]. I don't believe we're going to receive any, Mother.

AMANDA [*Reappearing, airily*]. What? No

one—not one? You must be joking! [LAURA *nervously echoes her laugh. She slips in a fugitive manner through the half-open portieres and draws them gently behind her. A shaft of very clear light*
5 *is thrown on her face against the faded tapestry of the curtains.* MUSIC:° "THE GLASS MENAGERIE" UNDER FAINTLY. *Lightly*]. Not one gentleman caller? It can't be true! There must be a flood, there must have been a tornado!
0   LAURA. It isn't a flood, it's not a tornado, Mother. I'm just not popular like you were in Blue Mountain. . . . [TOM *utters another groan.* LAURA *glances at him with a faint, apologetic smile. Her voice catching a little*]. Mother's
5 afraid I'm going to be an old maid.

The Scene Dims Out With "Glass Menagerie" Music

SCENE II.

"Laura, Haven't You Ever Liked Some Boy?"
On the dark stage the screen is lighted with the
0 *image of blue roses. Gradually* LAURA'S *figure becomes apparent and the screen goes out. The music subsides.*

LAURA *is seated in the delicate ivory chair at the small clawfoot table. She wears a dress of soft*
5 *violet material for a kimono—her hair tied back from her forehead with a ribbon. She is washing and polishing her collection of glass.*

AMANDA *appears on the fire-escape steps. At the sound of her ascent,* LAURA *catches her*
0 *breath, thrusts the bowl of ornaments away and seats herself stiffly before the diagram of the typewriter keyboard as though it held her spellbound. Something has happened to* AMANDA. *It is written in her face as she climbs to the landing:*
5 *a look that is grim and hopeless and a little absurd. She has on one of those cheap or imitation velvety-looking cloth coats with imitation fur collar. Her hat is five or six years old, one of those dreadful cloche hats that were worn in the late*
0 *twenties and she is clasping an enormous black patent-leather pocketbook with nickel clasps and initials. This is her full-dress outfit, the one*

she usually wears to the D.A.R.° Before entering she looks through the door. She purses her lips, opens her eyes very wide, rolls them upward and 45 *shakes her head. Then she slowly lets herself in the door. Seeing her mother's expression* LAURA *touches her lips with a nervous gesture.*

LAURA. Hello, Mother, I was— [*She makes a nervous gesture toward the chart on the wall.* 50 AMANDA *leans against the shut door and stares at* LAURA *with a martyred look.*]
AMANDA. Deception? Deception? [*She slowly removes her hat and gloves, continuing the sweet suffering stare. She lets the hat and gloves fall* 55 *on the floor—a bit of acting.*]
LAURA [*Shakily*]. How was the D.A.R. meeting? [AMANDA *slowly opens her purse and removes a dainty white handkerchief which she shakes out delicately and delicately touches to* 60 *her lips and nostrils*]. Didn't you go to the D.A.R. meeting, Mother?
AMANDA [*Faintly, almost inaudibly*]—No.— No. [*Then more forcibly*]. I did not have the strength—to go to the D.A.R. In fact, I did not 65 have the courage! I wanted to find a hole in the ground and hide myself in it forever! [*She crosses slowly to the wall and removes the diagram of the typewriter keyboard. She holds it in front of her for a second, staring at it sweetly* 70 *and sorrowfully—then bites her lips and tears it in two pieces.*]
LAURA [*Faintly*]. Why did you do that, Mother? [AMANDA *repeats the same procedure with the chart of the Gregg Alphabet*]. Why are 75 you—
AMANDA. Why? Why? How old are you, Laura?
LAURA. Mother, you know my age.
AMANDA. I thought you were an adult; it 80 seems that I was mistaken. [*She crosses slowly to the sofa and sinks down and stares at* LAURA.]
LAURA: Please don't stare at me, Mother.
[AMANDA *closes her eyes and lowers her head. Count ten.*] 85

D.A.R. Daughters of the American Revolution, a patriotic society of ladies who trace their descent from ancestors who assisted in the Revolutionary War

Music especially composed for this play by Paul Bowles

AMANDA. What are we going to do, what is going to become of us, what is the future? [*Count ten*]

LAURA. Has something happened, Mother?

5 [AMANDA *draws a long breath and takes out the handkerchief again. Dabbing process*]. Mother, has—something happened?

AMANDA. I'll be all right in a minute, I'm just bewildered—[*Count five*]—by life. . . .

10 LAURA. Mother, I wish that you would tell me what's happened!

AMANDA. As you know, I was supposed to be inducted into my office at the D.A.R. this afternoon. [IMAGE: A SWARM OF TYPEWRITERS].

15 But I stopped off at Rubicam's Business College to speak to your teachers about your having a cold and ask them what progress they thought you were making down there.

LAURA. Oh. . . .

20 AMANDA. I went to the typing instructor and introduced myself as your mother. She didn't know who you were. "Wingfield," she said. "We don't have any such student enrolled at the school!"

25 I assured her she did, that you have been going to classes since early in January.

"I wonder," she said, "if you could be talking about that terribly shy little girl who dropped out of school after only a few days'

30 attendance?"

"No," I said, "Laura, my daughter, has been going to school every day for the past six weeks!"

"Excuse me," she said. She took the at-

35 tendance book out and there was your name, unmistakably printed, and all the dates you were absent until they decided that you had dropped out of school.

I still said, "No, there must have been some

40 mistake! There must have been some mix-up in the records!"

And she said, "No—I remember her perfectly now. Her hands shook so that she couldn't hit the right keys! The first time we

45 gave a speed-test, she broke down completely—was sick at the stomach and almost had to be carried into the wash-room! After that morning she never showed up any more.

We phoned the house but never got any answer"—While I was working at Famous and 50 Barr,° I suppose, demonstrating those—Oh! I felt so weak I could barely keep on my feet! I had to sit down while they got me a glass of water!

Fifty dollars' tuition, all of our plans—my 55 hopes and ambitions for you—just gone up the spout, just gone up the spout like that. [LAURA *draws a long breath and gets awkwardly to her feet. She crosses to the victrola and winds it up*]. What are you doing? 60

LAURA. Oh! [*She releases the handle and returns to her seat.*]

AMANDA. Laura, where have you been going when you've gone out pretending that you were going to business college? 65

LAURA. I've just been going out walking.

AMANDA. That's not true.

LAURA. It is. I just went walking.

AMANDA. Walking? Walking? In winter? Deliberately courting pneumonia in that light 70 coat? Where did you walk to, Laura?

LAURA. All sorts of places—mostly in the park.

AMANDA. Even after you'd starting catching that cold? 75

LAURA. It was the lesser of two evils, Mother. [IMAGE: WINTER SCENE IN PARK]. I couldn't go back up. I—threw up—on the floor!

AMANDA. From half past seven till after five every day you mean to tell me you walked 80 around in the park, because you wanted to make me think that you were still going to Rubicam's Business College?

LAURA. It wasn't as bad as it sounds. I went inside places to get warmed up. 85

AMANDA. Inside where?

LAURA. I went in the art museum and the birdhouses at the Zoo. I visited the penguins every day! Sometimes I did without lunch and went to the movies. Lately I've been spending 90 most of my afternoons in the Jewel-box, that big glass house where they raise the tropical flowers.

Famous and Barr a large department store in St. Louis

AMANDA. You did all this to deceive me, just for deception? [LAURA *looks down.*] Why?

LAURA. Mother, when you're disappointed, you get that awful suffering look on your face, like the picture of Jesus' mother in the museum!

AMANDA. Hush!

LAURA. I couldn't face it.

[*Pause. A whisper of strings.*]

[LEGEND: "THE CRUST OF HUMILITY"]

AMANDA [*Hopelessly fingering the huge pocketbook*]. So what are we going to do the rest of our lives? Stay home and watch the parades go by? Amuse ourselves with the glass menagerie, darling? Eternally play those worn-out phonograph records your father left as a painful reminder of him?

We won't have a business career—we've given that up because it gave us nervous indigestion! [*Laughs wearily.*] What is there left but dependency all our lives? I know so well what becomes of unmarried women who aren't prepared to occupy a position. I've seen such pitiful cases in the South—barely tolerated spinsters living upon the grudging patronage of sister's husband or brother's wife!—stuck away in some little mouse-trap of a room—encouraged by one in-law to visit another—little birdlike women without any nest—eating the crust of humility all their life!

Is that the future that we've mapped out for ourselves?

I swear it's the only alternative I can think of!

It isn't a very pleasant alternative, is it?

Of course—some girls *do marry.*

[LAURA *twists her hands nervously.*]

Haven't you ever liked some boy?

LAURA. Yes. I liked one once. [*Rises*]. I came across his picture a while ago.

AMANDA [*With some interest*]. He gave you his picture?

LAURA. No, it's in the year-book.

AMANDA [*Disappointed*]. Oh—a high-school boy.

[SCREEN IMAGE: JIM AS HIGH-SCHOOL HERO BEARING A SILVER CUP.]

LAURA. Yes. His name was Jim. [LAURA *lifts the heavy annual from the claw-foot table.*] Here he is in *The Pirates of Penzance.*

AMANDA [*Absently*]. The what?

LAURA. The operetta the senior class put on. He had a wonderful voice and we sat across the aisle from each other Mondays, Wednesdays and Fridays in the Aud. Here he is with the silver cup for debating! See his grin?

AMANDA [*Absently*]. He must have had a jolly disposition.

LAURA. He used to call me—Blue Roses.

[IMAGE: BLUE ROSES.]

AMANDA. Why did he call you such a name as that?

LAURA. When I had that attack of pleurosis° —he asked me what was the matter when I came back. I said pleurosis—he thought that I said Blue Roses! So that's what he always called me after that. Whenever he saw me, he'd holler, "Hello, Blue Roses!" I didn't care for the girl that he went out with. Emily Meisenbach. Emily was the best-dressed girl at Soldan. She never struck me, though, as being sincere . . . It says in the Personal Section—they're engaged. That's—six years ago! They must be married by now.

AMANDA. Girls that aren't cut out for business careers usually wind up married to some nice man. [*Gets up with a spark of revival.*] Sister, that's what you'll do!

[LAURA *utters a startled, doubtful laugh. She reaches quickly for a piece of glass.*]

LAURA. But, Mother—

AMANDA. Yes? [*Crossing to photograph.*]

LAURA [*In a tone of frightened apology*]. I'm— crippled!

[IMAGE: SCREEN.]

AMANDA. Nonsense! Laura, I've told you never, never to use that word. Why, you're not crippled, you just have a little defect—hardly noticeable, even! When people have some slight disadvantage like that, they cultivate other things to make up for it—develop charm —and vivacity—and—*charm!* That's all you have to do! [*She turns again to the photograph.*] One thing your father had *plenty of*—was *charm!*

pleurosis lung inflammation

[TOM *motions to the fiddle in the wings.*]
The Scene Fades Out With Music

SCENE III

LEGEND ON SCREEN: "AFTER THE FIASCO—"
TOM *speaks from the fire-escape landing.*

5   TOM. After the fiasco at Rubicam's Business
College, the idea of getting a gentleman caller
for Laura began to play a more and more important part in Mother's calculations.

It became an obsession. Like some archetype
10 of the universal unconscious, the image of the
gentleman caller haunted our small apartment. . . .

[IMAGE: YOUNG MAN AT DOOR WITH FLOWERS.]

An evening at home rarely passed without
15 some allusion to this image, this spectre, this
hope. . . .

Even when he wasn't mentioned, his presence hung in Mother's preoccupied look and
in my sister's frightened, apologetic manner—
20 hung like a sentence passed upon the Wing-
fields!

Mother was a woman of action as well as
words.

She began to take logical steps in the planned
25 direction.

Late that winter and in the early spring—
realizing that extra money would be needed to
properly feather the nest and plume the bird—
she conducted a vigorous campaign on the
30 telephone, roping in subscribers to one of
those magazines for matrons called *The Home-
maker's Companion,* the type of journal that
features the serialized sublimations of ladies of
letters who think in terms of delicate cup-like
35 breasts, slim, tapering waists, rich, creamy
thighs, eyes like wood-smoke in autumn,
fingers that soothe and caress like strains of
music, bodies as powerful as Etruscan sculp-
ture.

40   [SCREEN IMAGE: GLAMOR MAGAZINE COVER.]

[AMANDA *enters with phone on long extension
cord. She is spotted in the dim stage.*]

AMANDA. Ida Scott? This is Amanda Wingfield! We *missed* you at the D.A.R. last Monday!

I said to myself: She's probably suffering   45
with that sinus condition! How is that sinus
condition?

Horrors! Heaven have mercy!—You're a
Christian martyr, yes, that's what you are, a
Christian martyr!   50

Well, I just now happened to notice that
your subscription to the *Companion's* about to
expire! Yes, it expires with the next issue,
honey!—just when that wonderful new serial
by Bessie Mae Hopper is getting off to such an 55
exciting start. Oh, honey, it's something that
you can't miss! You remember how *Gone With
the Wind* took everybody by storm? You simply
couldn't go out if you hadn't read it. All everybody *talked* was Scarlett O'Hara. Well, this is a 60
book that critics already compare to *Gone With
the Wind.* It's the *Gone With the Wind* of the
post-World War generation!—What?—Burning?—Oh, honey, don't let them burn, go take
a look in the oven and I'll hold the wire!   65
Heavens—I think she's hung up!

DIM OUT

[LEGEND ON SCREEN: "YOU THINK I'M IN
LOVE WITH CONTINENTAL SHOEMAKERS?"]

[*Before the stage is lighted, the violent voices* 70
of TOM *and* AMANDA *are heard. They are quarreling behind the portieres. In front of them stands*
LAURA *with clenched hands and panicky expression. A clear pool of light on her figure throughout
this scene.*]   75

TOM. What in Christ's name am I—

AMANDA [*Shrilly*]. Don't you use that—

TOM. Supposed to do!

AMANDA. Expression! Not in my—

TOM. Ohhh!   80

AMANDA. Presence! Have you gone out of
your senses?

TOM. I have, that's true, *driven* out!

AMANDA. What is the matter with you, you
—big—big—IDIOT!   85

TOM. Look!—I've got *no thing,* no single
thing—

AMANDA. Lower your voice!

TOM. In my life here that I can call my OWN!
Everything is—   90

AMANDA. Stop that shouting!

TOM. Yesterday you confiscated my books!

You had the nerve to—

AMANDA. I took that horrible novel back to
the library—yes! That hideous book by that
insane Mr. Lawrence.° [TOM *laughs wildly.*]
I cannot control the output of diseased minds
or people who cater to them— [TOM *laughs
still more wildly.*] BUT I WON'T ALLOW SUCH
FILTH BROUGHT INTO MY HOUSE! No, no, no,
no, no!

TOM. House, house! Who pays rent on it,
who makes a slave of himself to—

AMANDA [*Fairly screeching*]. Don't you
DARE to—

TOM. No, no, I mustn't say things! *I've* got
to just—

AMANDA. Let me tell you—

TOM. I don't want to hear any more! [*He tears
the portieres open. The upstage area is lit with a
turgid smoky red glow.*]

[AMANDA's *hair is in metal curlers and she
wears a very old bathrobe, much too large for her
slight figure, a relic of the faithless Mr. Wingfield. An upright typewriter and a wild disarray
of manuscripts is on the drop-leaf table. The
quarrel was probably precipitated by* AMANDA's
*interruption of his creative labor. A chair lying
overthrown on the floor. Their gesticulating
shadows are cast on the ceiling by the fiery glow.*]

AMANDA. You *will* hear more, you—

TOM. No, I won't hear more, I'm going out!

AMANDA. You come right back in—

TOM. Out, out, out! Because I'm—

AMANDA. Come back here, Tom Wingfield!
I'm not through talking to you!

TOM. Oh, go—

LAURA. [*Desperately*].—Tom!

AMANDA. You're going to listen, and no
more insolence from you! I'm at the end of my
patience!

[*He comes back toward her.*]

TOM. What do you think I'm at? Aren't I
supposed to have any patience to reach the
end of, Mother? I know, I know. It seems unimportant to you, what I'm *doing*—what I *want*

Lawrence D. H. Lawrence, English novelist, poet, and
critic (1885–1930), some of whose works were assailed
for sexual indecency

to do—having a little *difference* between them!
You don't think that—

AMANDA. I think you've been doing things
that you're ashamed of. That's why you act like
this. I don't believe that you go every night to
the movies. Nobody goes to the movies night
after night. Nobody in their right minds goes
to the movies as often as you pretend to.
People don't go to the movies at nearly midnight, and movies don't let out at two A.M.
Come in stumbling. Muttering to yourself like
a maniac! You get three hours' sleep and then
go to work. Oh, I can picture the way you're
doing down there. Moping, doping, because
you're in no condition.

TOM [*Wildly*]. No, I'm in no condition!

AMANDA. What right have you got to jeopardize your job? Jeopardize the security of us
all? How do you think we'd manage if you
were—

TOM. Listen! You think I'm crazy *about* the
warehouse? [*He bends fiercely toward her slight
figure.*] You think I'm in love with the Continental Shoemakers? You think I want to
spend fifty-five *years* down there in that—
celotex interior! with—*fluorescent—tubes!* Look!
I'd rather somebody picked up a crowbar and
battered out my brains—than go back mornings! I *go!* Every time you come in yelling that
God damn "*Rise and Shine!*" "*Rise and Shine!*"
I say to myself, "How *lucky dead* people are!"
But I get up. I *go!* For sixty-five dollars a month
I give up all that I dream of doing and being
ever! And you say self—*self's* all I ever think
of. Why, listen, if self is what I thought of,
Mother, I'd be where he is—GONE! [*Pointing
to father's picture.*] As far as the system of trans-
portation reaches! [*He starts past her. She grabs
his arm.*] Don't grab at me, Mother!

AMANDA. Where are you going?

TOM. I'm going to the *movies!*

AMANDA. I don't believe that lie!

TOM [*Crouching toward her, overtowering
her tiny figure. She backs away, gasping*]. I'm
going to opium dens! Yes, opium dens, dens
of vice and criminals' hang-outs, Mother. I've
joined the Hogan gang, I'm a hired assassin,
I carry a tommy-gun in a violin case! I run a

string of cat-houses in the Valley! They call me Killer, Killer Wingfield, I'm leading a double-life, a simple, honest warehouse worker by day, by night a dynamic *czar* of the *under-*
5 *world*, Mother. I go to gambling casinos, I spin away fortunes on the roulette table! I wear a patch over one eye and a false mustache, sometimes I put on green whiskers. On those occasions they call me—El Diablo!° Oh, I could
10 tell you things to make you sleepless! My enemies plan to dynamite this place. They're going to blow us all sky-high some night! I'll be glad, very happy, and so will you! You'll go up, up on a broomstick, over Blue Mountain
15 with seventeen gentlemen callers! You ugly —babbling old—*witch*. . . . [*He goes through a series of violent, clumsy movements, seizing his overcoat, lunging to the door, pulling it fiercely open. The women watch him, aghast. His arm*
20 *catches in the sleeve of the coat as he struggles to pull it on. For a moment he is pinioned by the bulky garment. With an outraged groan he tears the coat off again, splitting the shoulder of it, and hurls it across the room. It strikes against the shelf*
25 *of* LAURA's *glass collection, there is a tinkle of shattering glass.* LAURA *cries out as if wounded.*]
   [MUSIC. LEGEND: "THE GLASS MENAGERIE"]
   LAURA [*Shrilly*]. My glass!—menagerie. . . .
   [*She covers her face and turns away.*]
30   [*But* AMANDA *is still stunned and stupefied by the "ugly witch" so that she barely notices this occurrence. Now she recovers her speech.*]
   AMANDA [*In an awful voice*]. I won't speak to you—until you apologize! [*She crosses*
35 *through portieres and draws them together behind her.* TOM *is left with* LAURA. LAURA *clings weakly to the mantel with her face averted.* TOM *stares at her stupidly for a moment. Then he crosses to shelf. Drops awkwardly on his knees*
40 *to collect the fallen glass, glancing at* LAURA *as if he would speak but couldn't.*]
   "The Glass Menagerie" steals in as

      The Scene Dims Out

SCENE IV

   The interior is dark. Faint light in the alley. A
45 *deep-voiced bell in a church is tolling the hour of*

El Diablo Spanish: The Devil

five as the scene commences.
   TOM *appears at the top of the alley. After each solemn boom of the bell in the tower, he shakes a little noise-maker or rattle as if to express the tiny spasm of man in contrast to the sustained power* 50 *and dignity of the Almighty. This and the un-steadiness of his advance make it evident that he has been drinking. As he climbs the few steps to the fire-escape landing light steals up inside.* LAURA *appears in night-dress, observing* TOM's 55 *empty bed in the front room.* TOM *fishes in his pockets for door-key, removing a motley assortment of articles in the search, including a perfect shower of movie-ticket stubs and an empty bottle. At last he finds the key, but just as he is about to* 60 *insert it, it slips from his fingers. He strikes a match and crouches below the door.*

   TOM [*Bitterly*]. One crack—and it falls through!
   [LAURA *opens the door.*]   65
   LAURA. Tom! Tom, what are you doing?
   TOM. Looking for a door-key.
   LAURA. Where have you been all this time?
   TOM. I have been to the movies.
   LAURA. All this time at the movies?   70
   TOM. There was a very long program. There was a Garbo picture and a Mickey Mouse and a travelogue and a newsreel and a preview of coming attractions. And there was an organ solo and a collection for the milk-fund—simul- 75 taneously—which ended up in a terrible fight between a fat lady and an usher!
   LAURA [*Innocently*]. Did you have to stay through everything?
   TOM. Of course! And, oh, I forgot! There was 80 a big stage show! The headliner on this stage show was Malvolio the Magician. He performed wonderful tricks, many of them, such as pouring water back and forth between pitchers. First it turned to wine and then it 85 turned to beer and then it turned to whiskey. I know it was whiskey it finally turned into because he needed somebody to come up out of the audience to help him, and I came up—both shows! It was Kentucky Straight Bourbon. 90 A very generous fellow, he gave souvenirs. [*He pulls from his back pocket a shimmering rainbow-colored scarf.*] He gave me this. This

is his magic scarf. You can have it, Laura. You wave it over a canary cage and you get a bowl of gold-fish. You wave it over the gold-fish bowl and they fly away canaries. . . . But the
5 wonderfullest trick of all was the coffin trick. We nailed him into a coffin and he got out of the coffin without removing one nail. [*He has come inside.*] There is a trick that would come in handy for me—get me out of this 2 by 4
10 situation. [*Flops onto bed and starts removing shoes.*]

LAURA. Tom—Shhh!

TOM. What're you shushing me for?

LAURA. You'll wake up Mother.

15 TOM. Goody, goody! Pay 'er back for all those "Rise an' Shines." [*Lies down, groaning.*] You know it don't take much intelligence to get yourself into a nailed-up coffin, Laura. But who in hell ever got himself out of one without
20 removing one nail?

[*As if in answer, the father's grinning photograph lights up.*]

Scene Dims Out

[*Immediately following: The church bell is
25 heard striking six. At the sixth stroke the alarm clock goes off in* AMANDA'S *room, and after a few moments we hear her calling: "Rise and Shine! Rise and Shine! Laura, go tell your brother to rise and shine!"*]

30 TOM [*Sitting up slowly*]. I'll rise—but I won't shine.

[*The light increases.*]

AMANDA. Laura, tell your brother his coffee is ready.

35 [LAURA *slips into front room.*]

LAURA. Tom!—It's nearly seven. Don't make Mother nervous. [*He stares at her stupidly. Beseechingly.*] Tom, speak to Mother this morning. Make up with her, apologize, speak to
40 her!

TOM. She won't to me. It's her that started not speaking.

LAURA. If you just say you're sorry she'll start speaking.

45 TOM. Her not speaking—is that such a tragedy?

LAURA. Please—please!

AMANDA [*Calling from kitchenette*]. Laura, are you going to do what I asked you to do, or do I have to get dressed and go out myself?
50 LAURA. Going, going—soon as I get on my coat! [*She pulls on a shapeless felt hat with nervous, jerky movement, pleadingly glancing at* TOM. *Rushes awkwardly for coat. The coat is one of* AMANDA'S, *inaccurately made-over, the
55 sleeves too short for* LAURA]. Butter and what else?

AMANDA [*Entering upstage*]. Just butter. Tell them to charge it.

LAURA. Mother, they make such faces when
60 I do that.

AMANDA. Sticks and stones can break our bones, but the expression on Mr. Garfinkel's face won't harm us! Tell your brother his coffee is getting cold.
65 LAURA [*At door*]. Do what I asked you, will you, will you, Tom?

[*He looks sullenly away.*]

AMANDA. Laura, go now or just don't go at all!
70 LAURA [*Rushing out*]. Going—going! [*A second later she cries out.* TOM *springs up and crosses to door.* AMANDA *rushes anxiously in.* TOM *opens the door.*]

TOM. Laura?
75 LAURA. I'm all right. I slipped, but I'm all right.

AMANDA [*Peering anxiously after her*]. If anyone breaks a leg on those fire-escape steps, the landlord ought to be sued for every cent
80 he possesses! [*She shuts door. Remembers she isn't speaking and returns to other room.*]

[*As* TOM *enters listlessly for his coffee, she turns her back to him and stands rigidly facing the window on the gloomy gray vault of the
85 areaway. Its light on her face with its aged but childish features is cruelly sharp, satirical as a Daumier print.*]

[MUSIC UNDER: "AVE MARIA."]

[TOM *glances sheepishly but sullenly at her
90 averted figure and slumps at the table. The coffee is scalding hot; he sips it and gasps and spits it back in the cup. At his gasp,* AMANDA *catches her breath and half turns. Then catches herself and turns back to the window.* TOM *blows on his
95 coffee, glancing sidewise at his mother. She clears her throat.* TOM *clears his. He starts to rise. Sinks back down again, scratches his head, clears his*

throat again. AMANDA *coughs.* TOM *raises his cup in both hands to blow on it, his eyes staring over the rim of it at his mother for several moments. Then he slowly sets the cup down and* 5 *awkwardly and hesitantly rises from the chair.*]

TOM [*Hoarsely*]. Mother. I—I apologize, Mother. [AMANDA *draws a quick, shuddering breath. Her face works grotesquely. She breaks into childlike tears.*] I'm sorry for what I said, 10 for everything that I said, I didn't mean it.

AMANDA [*Sobbingly*]. My devotion has made me a witch and so I make myself hateful to my children!

TOM. *No, you don't.*

15 AMANDA. I worry so much, don't sleep, it makes me nervous!

TOM [*Gently*]. I understand that.

AMANDA. I've had to put up a solitary battle all these years. But you're my right-hand 20 bower!° Don't fall down, don't fail!

TOM [*Gently*]. I try, Mother.

AMANDA [*With great enthusiasm*]. Try and you will SUCCEED! [*The notion makes her breathless.*] Why, you—you're just *full* of natural 25 endowments! Both of my children—they're *unusual* children! Don't you think I know it? I'm so—*proud!* Happy and—feel I've—so much to be thankful for but—Promise me one thing, Son!

30 TOM. What, Mother?

AMANDA. Promise, son, you'll—never be a drunkard!

TOM [*Turns to her grinning*]. I will never be a drunkard, Mother.

35 AMANDA. That's what frightened me so, that you'd be drinking! Eat a bowl of Purina!

TOM. Just coffee, Mother.

AMANDA. Shredded wheat biscuit?

TOM. No. No, Mother, just coffee.

40 AMANDA. You can't put in a day's work on an empty stomach. You've got ten minutes—don't gulp! Drinking too-hot liquids makes cancer of the stomach. . . . Put cream in.

TOM. No, thank you.

45 AMANDA. To cool it.

TOM. No! No, thank you, I want it black.

right-hand bower trump card

AMANDA. I know, but it's not good for you. We have to do all that we can to build ourselves up. In these trying times we live in, all that we have to cling to is—each other. . . . 50 That's why it's so important to—Tom, I—I sent out your sister so I could discuss something with you. If you hadn't spoken I would have spoken to you. [*Sits down.*]

TOM [*Gently*]. What is it, Mother, that you 55 want to discuss?

AMANDA. *Laura!*

[TOM *puts his cup down slowly.*]

[LEGEND ON SCREEN: "LAURA."]

[MUSIC: "THE GLASS MENAGERIE."] 60

TOM. —Oh.—Laura . . .

AMANDA [*Touching his sleeve*]. You know how Laura is. So quiet but—still water runs deep! She notices things and I think she— broods about them. [TOM *looks up.*] A few days 65 ago I came in and she was crying.

TOM. What about?

AMANDA. You.

TOM. Me?

AMANDA. She has an idea that you're not 70 happy here.

TOM. What gave her that idea?

AMANDA. What gives her any idea? However, you do act strangely. I—I'm not criticizing, understand *that!* I know your ambitions 75 do not lie in the warehouse, that like everybody in the whole wide world—you've had to—make sacrifices, but—Tom—Tom—life's not easy, it calls for—Spartan endurance! There's so many things in my heart that I 80 cannot describe to you! I've never told you but I—*loved* your father. . . .

TOM [*Gently*]. I know that, Mother.

AMANDA. And you—when I see you taking after his ways! Staying out late—and—well, 85 you *had* been drinking the night you were in that—terrifying condition! Laura says that you hate the apartment and that you go out nights to get away from it! Is that true, Tom?

TOM. No. You say there's so much in your 90 heart that you can't describe to me. That's true of me, too. There's so much in my heart that I can't describe to *you!* So let's respect each other's—

AMANDA. But, why — *why*, Tom — are you always so *restless?* Where do you *go* to, nights?

TOM. I — go to the movies.

AMANDA. Why do you go to the movies so
5 much, Tom?

TOM. I go to the movies because — I like adventure. Adventure is something I don't have much of at work, so I go to the movies.

AMANDA. But, Tom, you go to the movies
10 *entirely too much!*

TOM. I like a lot of adventure.

[AMANDA *looks baffled, then hurt. As the familiar inquisition resumes he becomes hard and impatient again.* AMANDA *slips back into her*
15 *querulous attitude toward him.*]

[IMAGE ON SCREEN: SAILING VESSEL° WITH
JOLLY ROGER.]

AMANDA. Most young men find adventure in their careers.

20 TOM. Then most young men are not employed in a warehouse.

AMANDA. The world is full of young men employed in warehouses and offices and factories.

25 TOM. Do all of them find adventure in their careers?

AMANDA. They do or they do without it! Not everybody has a craze for adventure.

TOM. Man is by instinct a lover, a hunter, a
30 fighter, and none of those instincts are given much play at the warehouse!

AMANDA. Man is by instinct! Don't quote instinct to me! Instinct is something that people have got away from! It belongs to
35 animals! Christian adults don't want it!

TOM. What do Christian adults want, then, Mother?

AMANDA. Superior things! Things of the mind and spirit! Only animals have to satisfy
40 instincts! Surely your aims are somewhat higher than theirs! Than monkeys — pigs —

TOM. I reckon they're not.

AMANDA. You're joking. However, that isn't what I wanted to discuss.

45 TOM [*Rising*]. I haven't much time.

---

sailing vessel pirate ship flying the traditional skull-
and-crossbones flag

AMANDA [*Pushing his shoulders*]. Sit down.

TOM. You want me to punch in red° at the warehouse, Mother?

AMANDA. You have five minutes. I want to
talk about Laura. 50

[LEGEND: "PLANS AND PROVISIONS."]

TOM. All right! What about Laura?

AMANDA. We have to be making some plans and provisions for her. She's older than you, two years, and nothing has happened. She just 55 drifts along doing nothing. It frightens me terribly how she just drifts along.

TOM. I guess she's the type that people call home girls.

AMANDA. There's no such type, and if there 60 is, it's a pity! That is unless the home is hers, with a husband!

TOM. What?

AMANDA. Oh, I can see the handwriting on the wall as plain as I see the nose in front of my 65 face! It's terrifying! More and more you remind me of your father! He was out all hours without explanation! — Then *left! Good-bye!* And me with the bag to hold. I saw that letter you got from the Merchant Marine. I know what you're 70 dreaming of. I'm not standing here blindfolded. Very well, then. Then *do* it! But not till there's somebody to take your place.

TOM. What do you mean?

AMANDA. I mean that as soon as Laura has 75 got somebody to take care of her, married, a home of her own, independent — why, then you'll be free to go wherever you please, on land, on sea, whichever way the wind blows you! But until that time you've got to look out 80 for your sister. I don't say me because I'm old and don't matter! I say for your sister because she's young and dependent. I put her in business college — a dismal failure! Frightened her so it made her sick at the stomach. I took her 85 over to the Young People's League at the church. Another fiasco. She spoke to nobody, nobody spoke to her. Now all she does is fool with those pieces of glass and play those worn-out records. What kind of a life is that for a girl 90 to lead?

---

punch in red be late in "punching" the time-clock, and
so lose pay

Tom. What can I do about it?

Amanda. Overcome selfishness! Self, self, self is all that you ever think of! [Tom *springs up and crosses to get his coat. It is ugly and bulky.*
5 *He pulls on a cap with earmuffs.*] Where is your muffler? Put your wool muffler on! [*He snatches is angrily from the closet and tosses it around his neck and pulls both ends tight.*] Tom! I haven't said what I had in mind to ask you.

10 Tom. I'm too late to—

Amanda [*Catching his arm—very importunately. Then shyly*]. Down at the warehouse, aren't there some—nice young men?

Tom. No!

15 Amanda. There *must* be—*some* . . .

Tom. Mother— [*Gesture.*]

Amanda. Find out one that's clean-living— doesn't drink and—ask him out for sister!

Tom. What?

20 Amanda. For *sister! To meet! Get acquainted!*

Tom [*Stamping to door*]. Oh, my go-oosh!

Amanda. Will you? [*He opens door. Imploringly.*] Will you? [*He starts down*]. Will you? *Will you, dear?*

25 Tom [*Calling back*]. YES!

[Amanda *closes the door hesitantly and with a troubled but faintly hopeful expression.*]

[SCREEN IMAGE: GLAMOR MAGAZINE COVER.]

[*Spot* Amanda *at phone.*]

30 Amanda. Ella Cartwright? This is Amanda Wingfield! How are you, honey? How is that kidney condition? [*Count five.*] Horrors! [*Count five.*] You're a Christian martyr, yes, honey, that's what you are, a Christian martyr! Well,
35 I just now happened to notice in my little red book that your subscription to the *Companion* has just run out! I knew that you wouldn't want to miss out on the wonderful serial starting in this new issue. It's by Bessie Mae
40 Hopper, the first thing she's written since *Honeymoon for Three.* Wasn't that a strange and interesting story? Well, this one is even lovelier, I believe. It has a sophisticated, society background. It's all about the horsey set on Long
45 Island!

Fade Out

SCENE V

LEGEND ON SCREEN: "ANNUNCIATION." *Fade with music.*

It is early dusk of a spring evening. Supper has just been finished in the Wingfield apartment. 50 Amanda *and* Laura *in light-colored dresses are removing dishes from the table, in the upstage area, which is shadowy, their movements formalized almost as a dance or ritual, their moving forms as pale and silent as moths.* Tom, *in white* 55 *shirt and trousers, rises from the table and crosses toward the fire-escape.*

Amanda [*As he passes her*]. Son, will you do me a favor?

Tom. What? 60

Amanda. Comb your hair! You look so pretty when your hair is combed! [Tom *slouches on sofa with evening paper. Enormous caption "Franco° Triumphs."*] There is only one respect in which I would like you to emulate 65 your father.

Tom. What respect is that?

Amanda. The care he always took of his appearance. He never allowed himself to look untidy. [*He throws down the paper and crosses* 70 *to fire-escape.*] Where are you going?

Tom. I'm going out to smoke.

Amanda. You smoke too much. A pack a day at fifteen cents a pack. How much would that amount to in a month? Thirty times fifteen is 75 how much, Tom? Figure it out and you will be astounded at what you could save. Enough to give you a night-school course in accounting at Washington U! Just think what a wonderful thing that would be for you, Son! 80

[Tom *is unmoved by the thought.*]

Tom. I'd rather smoke. [*He steps out on landing, letting the screen door slam.*]

Amanda [*Sharply*]. I know! That's the tragedy of it. . . . [*Alone, she turns to look at her* 85 *husband's picture.*]

[DANCE MUSIC: "ALL THE WORLD IS WAITING FOR THE SUNRISE!"]

Tom [*To the audience*]. Across the alley from us was the Paradise Dance Hall. On evenings 90 in spring the windows and doors were open and the music came outdoors. Sometimes the lights were turned out except for a large glass

Franco General Francisco Franco, leader of the forces that, with aid from Mussolini and Hitler, finally overthrew the Spanish Republican government in March 1939

sphere that hung from the ceiling. It would turn slowly about and filter the dusk with delicate rainbow colors. Then the orchestra played a waltz or a tango, something that had a slow and sensuous rhythm. Couples would come outside, to the relative privacy of the alley. You could see them kissing behind ash-pits and telephone poles. This was the compensation for lives that passed like mine, without any change or adventure. Adventure and change were imminent in this year. They were waiting around the corner for all these kids. Suspended in the mist over Berchtesgaden,° caught in the folds of Chamberlain's umbrella°—In Spain there was Guernica! But here there was only hot swing music and liquor, dance halls, bars, and movies, and sex that hung in the gloom like a chandelier and flooded the world with brief, deceptive rainbows. . . . All the world was waiting for bombardments!

[AMANDA *turns from the picture and comes outside.*]

AMANDA [*Sighing*]. A fire-escape landing's a poor excuse for a porch. [*She spreads a newspaper on a step and sits down, gracefully and demurely as if she were settling into a swing on a Mississippi veranda.*] What are you looking at?

TOM. The moon.

AMANDA. Is there a moon this evening?

TOM. It's rising over Garfinkel's Delicatessen.

AMANDA. So it is! A little silver slipper of a moon. Have you made a wish on it yet?

TOM. Um-hum.

AMANDA. What did you wish for?

TOM. That's a secret.

AMANDA. A secret, huh? Well, I won't tell mine either. I will be just as mysterious as you.

TOM. I bet I can guess what yours is.

AMANDA. Is my head so transparent?

TOM. You're not a sphinx.

AMANDA. No, I don't have secrets. I'll tell

Berchtesgaden Hitler's favorite resort in the German Alps

Chamberlain's umbrella Neville Chamberlain, British prime minister, 1937–40; often caricatured with his umbrella, he symbolized efforts to satisfy Hitler's ambitions by "appeasement"

you what I wished for on the moon. Success and happiness for my precious children! I wish for that whenever there's a moon, and when there isn't a moon, I wish for it, too.

TOM. I thought perhaps you wished for a gentleman caller.

AMANDA. Why do you say that?

TOM. Don't you remember asking me to fetch one?

AMANDA. I remember suggesting that it would be nice for your sister if you brought home some nice young man from the warehouse. I think that I've made that suggestion more than once.

TOM. Yes, you have made it repeatedly.

AMANDA. Well?

TOM. We are going to have one.

AMANDA. *What?*

TOM. A gentleman caller!

[THE ANNUNCIATION IS CELEBRATED WITH MUSIC.]

[AMANDA *rises.*]

[IMAGE ON SCREEN: CALLER WITH BOUQUET.]

AMANDA. You mean you have asked some nice young man to come over?

TOM. Yep. I've asked him to dinner.

AMANDA. You really did?

TOM. I did!

AMANDA. You did, and did he—*accept?*

TOM. He did!

AMANDA. Well, well—well, well! That's—lovely!

TOM. I thought that you would be pleased.

AMANDA. It's definite, then?

TOM. Very definite.

AMANDA. Soon?

TOM. Very soon.

AMANDA. For heaven's sake, stop putting on and tell me some things, will you?

TOM. What things do you want me to tell you?

AMANDA. *Naturally* I would like to know when he's *coming!*

TOM. He's coming tomorrow.

AMANDA. *Tomorrow?*

TOM. Yep. Tomorrow.

AMANDA. But, Tom!

TOM. Yes, Mother?

AMANDA. Tomorrow gives me no time!

Tom. Time for what?

Amanda. Preparations! Why didn't you phone me at once, as soon as you asked him, the minute that he accepted? Then, don't you
5 see, I could have been getting ready!

Tom. You don't have to make any fuss.

Amanda. Oh, Tom, Tom, Tom, of course I have to make a fuss! I want things nice, not sloppy! Not thrown together. I'll certainly have
10 to do some fast thinking, won't I?

Tom. I don't see why you have to think at all.

Amanda. You just don't know. We can't have a gentleman caller in a pig-sty. All my wedding silver has to be polished, the mono-
15 grammed table linen ought to be laundered! The windows have to be washed and fresh curtains put up. And how about clothes? We have to *wear* something, don't we?

Tom. Mother, this boy is no one to make a
20 fuss over!

Amanda. Do you realize he's the first young man we've introduced to your sister? It's terrible, dreadful, disgraceful that poor little sister has never received a single gentleman
25 caller! Tom, come inside! [*She opens the screen door.*]

Tom. What for?

Amanda. I want to ask you some things.

Tom. If you're going to make such a fuss, I'll
30 call it off, I'll tell him not to come!

Amanda. You certainly won't do anything of the kind. Nothing offends people worse than broken engagements. It simply means I'll have to work like a Turk! We won't be brilliant,
35 but we will pass inspection. Come on inside. [Tom *follows, groaning.*] Sit down.

Tom. Any particular place you would like me to sit?

Amanda. Thank heavens I've got that new
40 sofa! I'm also making payments on a floor lamp I'll have sent out! And put the chintz covers on, they'll brighten things up! Of course I'd hoped to have these walls re-papered. . . . What is the young man's name?
45 Tom. His name is O'Connor.

Amanda. That, of course, means fish°—

means fish   assuming that he is an Irish Catholic and will
observe the then usual rule against eating meat on
Fridays

tomorrow is Friday! I'll have that salmon loaf —with Durkee's dressing! What does he do? He works at the warehouse?

Tom. Of course! How else would I—   50

Amanda. Tom, he—doesn't drink?

Tom. Why do you ask me that?

Amanda. Your father *did!*

Tom. Don't get started on that!

Amanda. He *does* drink, then?   55

Tom. Not that I know of!

Amanda. Make sure, be certain! The last thing I want for my daughter's a boy who drinks!

Tom. Aren't you being a little bit prema-   60
ture? Mr. O'Connor has not yet appeared on the scene!

Amanda. But will tomorrow. To meet your sister, and what do I know about his character? Nothing! Old maids are better off than wives   65
of drunkards!

Tom. Oh, my God!

Amanda. Be still!

Tom [*Leaning forward to whisper*]. Lots of fellows meet girls whom they don't marry!   70

Amanda. Oh, talk sensibly, Tom—and don't be sarcastic! [*She has gotten a hairbrush.*]

Tom. What are you doing?

Amanda. I'm brushing that cow-lick down! What is this young man's position at the ware-   75
house?

Tom [*Submitting grimly to the brush and the interrogation*]. This young man's position is that of a shipping clerk, Mother.

Amanda. Sounds to me like a fairly re-   80
sponsible job, the sort of a job *you* would be in if you just had more *get-up.*

What is his salary? Have you any idea?

Tom. I would judge it to be approximately eighty-five dollars a month.   85

Amanda. Well—not princely, but—

Tom. Twenty more than I make.

Amanda. Yes, how well I know! But for a family man, eighty-five dollars a month is not much more than you can just get by on. . . .   90

Tom. Yes, but Mr. O'Connor is not a family man.

Amanda. He might be, mightn't he? Some time in the future?

Tom. I see. Plans and provisions.   95

AMANDA. You are the only young man that I know of who ignores the fact that the future becomes the present, the present the past, and the past turns into everlasting regret if you don't plan for it!

TOM. I will think that over and see what I can make of it.

AMANDA. Don't be supercilious with your mother! Tell me some more about this—what do you call him?

TOM. James D. O'Connor. The D. is for Delaney.

AMANDA. Irish on *both* sides! *Gracious!* And doesn't drink?

TOM. Shall I call him up and ask him right this minute?

AMANDA. The only way to find out about those things is to make discreet inquiries at the proper moment. When I was a girl in Blue Mountain and it was suspected that a young man drank, the girl whose attentions he had been receiving, if any girl *was*, would sometimes speak to the minister of his church, or rather her father would if her father was living, and sort of feel him out on the young man's character. That is the way such things are discreetly handled to keep a young woman from making a tragic mistake!

TOM. Then how did you happen to make a tragic mistake?

AMANDA. That innocent look of your father's had everyone fooled! He *smiled*—the world was *enchanted!* No girl can do worse than put herself at the mercy of a handsome appearance! I hope that Mr. O'Connor is not too good-looking.

TOM. No, he's not too good-looking. He's covered with freckles and hasn't too much of a nose.

AMANDA. He's not right-down homely, though?

TOM. Not right-down homely. Just medium homely, I'd say.

AMANDA. Character's what to look for in a man.

TOM. That's what I've always said, Mother.

AMANDA. You've never said anything of the kind and I suspect you would never give it a thought.

TOM. Don't be so suspicious of me.

AMANDA. At least I hope he's the type that's up and coming.

TOM. I think he really goes in for self-improvement.

AMANDA. What reason have you to think so?

TOM. He goes to night school.

AMANDA [*Beaming*]. Splendid! What does he do, I mean study?

TOM. Radio engineering and public speaking!

AMANDA. Then he has visions of being advanced in the world! Any young man who studies public speaking is aiming to have an executive job some day! And radio engineering? A thing for the future! Both of these facts are very illuminating. Those are the sort of things that a mother should know concerning any young man who comes to call on her daughter. Seriously or—not.

TOM. One little warning. He doesn't know about Laura. I didn't let on that we had dark ulterior motives. I just said, why don't you come and have dinner with us? He said okay and that was the whole conversation.

AMANDA. I bet it was! You're eloquent as an oyster. However, he'll know about Laura when he gets here. When he sees how lovely and sweet and pretty she is, he'll thank his lucky stars he was asked to dinner.

TOM. Mother, you mustn't expect too much of Laura.

AMANDA. What do you mean?

TOM. Laura seems all those things to you and me because she's ours and we love her. We don't even notice she's crippled any more.

AMANDA. Don't say crippled. You know that I never allow that word to be used!

TOM. But face facts, Mother. She is and—that's not all—

AMANDA. What do you mean "not all"?

TOM. Laura is very different from other girls.

AMANDA. I think the difference is all to her advantage.

TOM. Not quite all—in the eyes of others—strangers—she's terribly shy and lives in a world of her own and those things make her seem a little peculiar to people outside the house.

AMANDA. Don't say peculiar.

TOM. Face the facts. She is.

[THE DANCE-HALL MUSIC CHANGES TO A
TANGO THAT HAS A MINOR AND SOMEWHAT
5 OMINOUS TONE.]

AMANDA. In what way is she peculiar—may
I ask?

TOM [Gently]. She lives in a world of her
own—a world of—little glass ornaments,
10 Mother. . . . [Gets up. AMANDA remains holding
brush, looking at him, troubled.] She plays old
phonograph records and—that's about all—
[He glances at himself in the mirror and crosses
to door.]

15 AMANDA [Sharply]. Where are you going?

TOM. I'm going to the movies. [Out screen
door.]

AMANDA. Not to the movies, every night to
the movies! [Follows quickly to screen door.] I
20 don't believe you always go to the movies! [He
is gone. AMANDA looks worriedly after him for a
moment. Then vitality and optimism return and
she turns from the door. Crossing to portieres.]
Laura! Laura! [LAURA answers from kitchenette.]
25 LAURA. Yes, Mother.

AMANDA. Let those dishes go and come in
front! [LAURA appears with dish towel. Gaily.]
Laura, come here and make a wish on the
moon!

30 [SCREEN IMAGE: MOON.]

LAURA [Entering]. Moon—moon?

AMANDA. A little silver slipper of a moon.
Look over your left shoulder, Laura, and make
a wish! [LAURA looks faintly puzzled as if called
35 out of sleep. AMANDA seizes her shoulders and
turns her at an angle by the door.] Now! Now,
darling, wish!

LAURA. What shall I wish for, Mother?

AMANDA [Her voice trembling and her eyes
40 suddenly filling with tears]. Happiness, Good
fortune!

[The violin rises and the stage dims out.]

Curtain

SCENE VI

[IMAGE: HIGH SCHOOL HERO.]

45 TOM. And so the following evening I brought
Jim home to dinner. I had known Jim slightly
in high school. In high school Jim was a hero.
He had tremendous Irish good nature and
vitality with the scrubbed and polished look of
white chinaware. He seemed to move in a con- 50
tinual spotlight. He was a star in basketball,
captain of the debating club, president of the
senior class and the glee club and he sang the
male lead in the annual light operas. He was always running or bounding, never just walking. 55
He seemed always at the point of defeating the
law of gravity. He was shooting with such
velocity through his adolescence that you
would logically expect him to arrive at nothing
short of the White House by the time he was 60
thirty. But Jim apparently ran into more interference after his graduation from Soldan. His
speed had definitely slowed. Six years after
he left high school he was holding a job that
wasn't much better than mine. 65

[IMAGE: CLERK.]

He was the only one at the warehouse with
whom I was on friendly terms. I was valuable
to him as someone who could remember his
former glory, who had seen him win basket- 70
ball games and the silver cup in debating. He
knew of my secret practice of retiring to a
cabinet of the wash-room to work on poems
when business was slack in the warehouse.
He called me Shakespeare. And while the other 75
boys in the warehouse regarded me with suspicious hostility, Jim took a humorous attitude
toward me. Gradually his attitude affected the
others, their hostility wore off and they also
began to smile at me as people smile at an 80
oddly fashioned dog who trots across their
path at some distance.

I knew that Jim and Laura had known each
other at Soldan, and I had heard Laura speak
admiringly of his voice. I didn't know if Jim 85
remembered her or not. In high school Laura
had been as unobtrusive as Jim had been
astonishing. If he did remember Laura, it was
not as my sister, for when I asked him to dinner, he grinned and said, "You know, Shake- 90
speare, I never thought of you as having folks!"

He was about to discover that I did. . . .

[Light up stage.]

[LEGEND ON SCREEN: "THE ACCENT OF A COMING FOOT."]°

Friday evening. It is about five o'clock of a late spring evening which comes "scattering poems in the sky."° *A delicate lemony light is in the Wingfield apartment.* AMANDA *has worked like a Turk in preparation for the gentleman caller. The results are astonishing. The new floor lamp with its rose-silk shade is in place, a colored paper lantern conceals the broken light-fixture in the ceiling, new billowing white curtains are at the windows, chintz covers are on chairs and sofa, a pair of new sofa pillows make their initial appearance. Open boxes and tissue paper are* scattered on the floor. LAURA *stands in the middle with lifted arms while* AMANDA *crouches before her, adjusting the hem of the new dress, devout and ritualistic. The dress is colored and designed by memory. The arrangement of* LAURA'S *hair is* changed; *it is softer and more becoming. A fragile, unearthly prettiness has come out in* LAURA: *she is like a piece of translucent glass touched by light, given a momentary radiance, not actual, not lasting.*

AMANDA [*Impatiently*]. Why are you trembling?

LAURA. Mother, you've made me so nervous!

AMANDA. How have I made you nervous?

LAURA. By all this fuss! You make it seem so important!

AMANDA. I don't understand you, Laura. You couldn't be satisfied with just sitting home, and yet whenever I try to arrange something for you, you seem to resist it. [*She gets*

"**The accent of a coming foot**" from a poem by Emily Dickinson (1830–1886):

Elysium is as far as to
The very nearest room,
If in that room a friend await
Felicity or doom.

What fortitude the soul contains
That it can so endure
The accent of a coming foot,
The opening of a door!

"**scattering poems in the sky**" partly quoted from a poem by E. E. Cummings (1894–1962), "Impressions, IV"

---

up.] Now take a look at yourself. No, wait! Wait just a moment—I have an idea!

LAURA. What is it now?

[AMANDA *produces two powder puffs which she wraps in handerchiefs and stuffs in* LAURA'S *bosom.*]

LAURA. Mother, what are you doing?

AMANDA. They call them "Gay Deceivers"!

LAURA. I won't wear them!

AMANDA. You will!

LAURA. Why should I?

AMANDA. Because, to be painfully honest, your chest is flat.

LAURA. You make it seem like we were setting a trap.

AMANDA. All pretty girls are a trap, a pretty trap, and men expect them to be. [LEGEND: "A PRETTY TRAP".] Now look at yourself, young lady. This is the prettiest you will ever be! I've got to fix myself now! You're going to be surprised by your mother's appearance! [*She crosses through portieres, humming gaily.* LAURA *moves slowly to the long mirror and stares solemnly at herself. A wind blows the white curtains inward in a slow, graceful motion and with a faint, sorrowful sighing.*]

AMANDA [*Off stage*]. It isn't dark enough yet. [*She turns slowly before the mirror with a troubled look.*]

[LEGEND ON SCREEN: "THIS IS MY SISTER: CELEBRATE HER WITH STRINGS!" MUSIC.]

AMANDA [*Laughing, off*]. I'm going to show you something. I'm going to make a spectacular appearance!

LAURA. What is it, Mother?

AMANDA. Possess your soul in patience— you will see! Something I've resurrected from that old trunk! Styles haven't changed so terribly much after all. . . . [*She parts the portieres.*] Now just look at your mother! [*She wears a girlish frock of yellowed voile with a blue silk sash. She carries a bunch of jonquils—the legend of her youth is nearly revived. Feverishly.*] This is the dress in which I led the cotillion. Won the cakewalk twice at Sunset Hill, wore one spring to the Governor's ball in Jackson! See how I sashayed around the ballroom, Laura? [*She raises her skirt and does a mincing*

step around the room.] I wore it on Sundays for my gentlemen callers! I had it on the day I met your father—I had malaria fever all that spring. The change of climate from East Tennessee to
5 the Delta—weakened resistance—I had a little temperature all the time—not enough to be serious—just enough to make me restless and giddy!—Invitations poured in—parties all over the Delta!—"Stay in bed," said Mother,
10 "you have fever!"—but I just wouldn't.—I took quinine but kept on going, going!— Evenings, dances!—Afternoons, long, long rides! Picnics—lovely!—So lovely, that country in May.—All lacy with dogwood, literally
15 flooded with jonquils!—That was the spring I had the craze for jonquils. Jonquils became an absolute obsession. Mother said "Honey, there's no more room for jonquils." And still I kept on bringing in more jonquils. When-
20 ever, wherever I saw them, I'd say, "Stop! Stop! I see jonquils!" I made the young men help me gather the jonquils! It was a joke, Amanda and her jonquils! Finally there were no more vases to hold them, every available
25 space was filled with jonquils. No vases to hold them? All right, I'll hold them myself! And then I—[*She stops in front of the picture.* MUSIC] met your father! Malaria fever and jonquils and then—this—boy. . . . [*She switches on the rose-*
30 *colored lamp.*] I hope they get here before it starts to rain. [*She crosses upstage and places the jonquils in bowl on table.*] I gave your brother a little extra change so he and Mr. O'Connor could take the service car home.
35 LAURA [*With altered look*]. What did you say his name was?

AMANDA. O'Connor.

LAURA. What is his first name?

AMANDA. I don't remember. Oh, yes, I do.
40 It was—Jim!

[LAURA *sways slightly and catches hold of a chair.*]

[LEGEND ON SCREEN: "NOT JIM!"]

LAURA [*Faintly*]. Not—Jim!

45 AMANDA. Yes, that was it, it was Jim! I've never known a Jim that wasn't nice!

[MUSIC: OMINOUS.]

LAURA. Are you sure his name is Jim O'Connor?

AMANDA. Yes. Why? 50

LAURA. Is he the one that Tom used to know in high school?

AMANDA. He didn't say so. I think he just got to know him at the warehouse.

LAURA. There was a Jim O'Connor we both 55 knew in high school—[*Then, with effort.*] If that is the one that Tom is bringing to dinner— you'll have to excuse me, I won't come to the table.

AMANDA. What sort of nonsense is this? 60

LAURA. You asked me once if I'd ever liked a boy. Don't you remember I showed you this boy's picture?

AMANDA. You mean the boy you showed me in the year book? 65

LAURA. Yes, that boy.

AMANDA. Laura, Laura, were you in love with that boy?

LAURA. I don't know, Mother. All I know is I couldn't sit at the table if it was him! 70

AMANDA. It won't be him! It isn't the least bit likely. But whether it is or not, you will come to the table. You will not be excused.

LAURA. I'll have to be, Mother.

AMANDA. I don't intend to humor your 75 silliness, Laura. I've had too much from you and your brother, both! So just sit down and compose yourself till they come. Tom has forgotten his key so you'll have to let them in, when they arrive. 80

LAURA [*Panicky*]. Oh, Mother—*you* answer the door!

AMANDA [*Lightly*]. I'll be in the kitchen— busy!

LAURA. Oh, Mother, please answer the door, 85 don't make me do it!

AMANDA [*Crossing into kitchenette*]. I've got to fix the dressing for the salmon. Fuss, fuss— silliness!—over a gentleman caller!

[*Door swings shut.* LAURA *is left alone.*] 90

[LEGEND: "TERROR!"]

[*She utters a low moan and turns off the lamp— sits stiffly on the edge of the sofa, knotting her fingers together.*]

[LEGEND ON SCREEN: "THE OPENING OF A DOOR!"]°

[TOM *and* JIM *appear on the fire-escape steps and climb to landing. Hearing their approach,*
5 LAURA *rises with a panicky gesture. She retreats to the portieres. The doorbell.* LAURA *catches her breath and touches her throat. Low drums.*]

AMANDA [*Calling*]. Laura, sweetheart! The door! [LAURA *stares at it without moving.*]

10 JIM. I think we just beat the rain.

TOM. Uh-huh. [*He rings again, nervously.* JIM *whistles and fishes for a cigarette.*]

AMANDA [*Very, very gaily*]. Laura, that is your brother and Mr. O'Connor! Will you let
15 them in, darling?

[LAURA *crosses toward kitchenette door.*]

LAURA [*Breathlessly*]. Mother—you go to the door!

[AMANDA *steps out of kitchenette and stares*
20 *furiously at* LAURA. *She points imperiously at the door.*]

LAURA. Please, please!

AMANDA [*In a fierce whisper*]. What is the matter with you, you silly thing?

25 LAURA [*Desperately*]. Please, you answer it, *please!*

AMANDA. I told you I wasn't going to humor you, Laura. Why have you chosen this moment to lose your mind?

30 LAURA. Please, please, please, you go!

AMANDA. You'll have to go to the door because I can't!

LAURA [*Despairingly*]. I can't either!

AMANDA. *Why?*

35 LAURA. I'm *sick!*

AMANDA. I'm sick, too—of your nonsense! Why can't you and your brother be normal people? Fantastic whims and behavior! [TOM *gives a long ring.*] Preposterous goings on! Can
40 you give me one reason— [*Calls out lyrically.*] Coming! Just one second!—why you should be afraid to open a door? Now you answer it, Laura!

LAURA. Oh, oh, oh . . . [*She returns through

the portieres. Darts to the victrola and winds it* 45 *frantically and turns it on.*]

AMANDA. Laura Wingfield, you march right to that door!

LAURA. Yes—yes, Mother!

[*A faraway, scratchy rendition of "Dardanella"*° 50 *softens the air and gives her strength to move through it. She slips to the door and draws it cautiously open.* TOM *enters with the caller,* JIM O'CONNOR.]

TOM. Laura, this is Jim. Jim, this is my sister, 55 Laura.

JIM [*Stepping inside*]. I didn't know that Shakespeare had a sister!

LAURA [*Retreating stiff and trembling from the door*]. How—how do you do? 60

JIM [*Heartily extending his hand*]. Okay! [LAURA *touches it hesitantly with hers.*]

Your hand's *cold*, Laura!

LAURA. Yes, well—I've been playing the victrola. . . . 65

JIM. Must have been playing classical music on it! You ought to play a little hot swing music to warm you up!

LAURA. Excuse me—I haven't finished playing the victrola. . . . [*She turns awkwardly and* 70 *hurries into the front room. She pauses a second by the victrola. Then catches her breath and darts through the portieres like a frightened deer.*]

JIM [*Grinning*]. What was the matter?

TOM. Oh—with Laura? Laura is—terribly 75 shy.

JIM. Shy, huh? It's unusual to meet a shy girl nowadays. I don't believe you ever mentioned you had a sister.

TOM. Well, now you know. I have one. Here 80 is the *Post Dispatch.* You want a piece of it?

JIM. Uh-huh.

TOM. What piece? The comics?

JIM. Sports! [*Glances at it.*] Ole Dizzy Dean° is on his bad behavior. 85

TOM [*Disinterest*]. Yeah? [*Lights cigarette and crosses back to fire-escape door.*]

"Dardenella" like Laura's other old records, a dance tune from about the period of her parents' courtship
Dean famous pitcher for the St. Louis Cardinals

"Opening of a door" see poem by Emily Dickinson

JIM. Where are *you* going?

TOM. I'm going out on the terrace.

JIM [*Goes after him*]. You know, Shakespeare —I'm going to sell you a bill of goods!

5 TOM. What goods?

JIM. A course I'm taking.

TOM. Huh?

JIM. In public speaking! You and me, we're not the warehouse type.

10 TOM. Thanks—that's good news. But what has public speaking got to do with it?

JIM. It fits you for—executive positions!

TOM. Awww.

JIM. I tell you it's done a helluva lot for me.

15 [IMAGE: EXECUTIVE AT DESK.]

TOM. In what respect?

JIM. In every! Ask yourself what is the difference between you an' me and men in the office down front? Brains?—No!—Ability?—

20 No! Then what? Just one little thing—

TOM. What is that one little thing?

JIM. Primarily it amounts to—social poise! Being able to square up to people and hold your own on any social level!

25 AMANDA [*Off stage*]. Tom?

TOM. Yes, Mother?

AMANDA. Is that you and Mr. O'Connor?

TOM. Yes, Mother.

AMANDA. Well, you just make yourselves

30 comfortable in there.

TOM. Yes, Mother.

AMANDA. Ask Mr. O'Conner if he would like to wash his hands.

JIM. Aw, no—no—thank you—I took care of

35 that at the warehouse. Tom—

TOM. Yes?

JIM. Mr. Mendoza was speaking to me about you.

TOM. Favorably?

40 JIM. What do you think?

TOM. Well—

JIM. You're going to be out of a job if you don't wake up.

TOM. I am waking up—

45 JIM. You show no signs.

TOM. The signs are interior.

[IMAGE ON SCREEN: THE SAILING VESSEL WITH JOLLY ROGER AGAIN.] ·

TOM. I'm planning to change. [*He leans over

the rail speaking with quiet exhilaration. The* 50 *incandescent marquees and signs of the first-run movie houses light his face from across the alley. He looks like a voyager.*] I'm right at the point of committing myself to a future that doesn't include the warehouse and Mr. Mendoza or 55 even a night-school course in public speaking.

JIM. What are you gassing about?

TOM. I'm tired of the movies.

JIM. Movies!

TOM. Yes, movies! Look at them—[*A wave* 60 *toward the marvels of Grand Avenue.*] All of those glamorous people—having adventures—hogging it all, gobbling the whole thing up! You know what happens? People go to the *movies* instead of *moving!* Hollywood charac- 65 ters are supposed to have all the adventures for everybody in America, while everybody in America sits in a dark room and watches them have them! Yes, until there's a war. That's when adventure becomes available to the 70 masses! *Everyone's* dish, not only Gable's! Then the people in the dark room come out of the dark room to have some adventures them-selves—Goody, goody!—It's our turn now, to go to the South Sea Island—to make a safari— 75 to be exotic, far-off!—but I'm not patient. I don't want to wait till then. I'm tired of the *movies* and I am *about* to *move!*

JIM [*Incredulously*]. Move?

TOM. Yes. 80

JIM. When?

TOM. Soon!

JIM. Where? Where?

[*Theme three music seems to answer the question, while* TOM *thinks it over. He searches among* 85 *his pockets.*]

TOM. I'm starting to boil inside. I know I seem dreamy, but inside—well, I'm boiling!—Whenever I pick up a shoe, I shudder a little thinking how short life is and what I am doing! 90 —Whatever that means. I know it doesn't mean shoes—except as something to wear on a traveler's feet! [*Finds paper.*] Look—

JIM. What?

TOM. I'm a member. 95

JIM [*Reading*]. The Union of Merchant Seamen.

TOM. I paid my dues this month, instead of

the light bill.

JIM. You will regret it when they turn the lights off.

TOM. I won't be here.

JIM. How about your mother?

TOM. I'm like my father. The bastard son of a bastard! See how he grins? And he's been absent going on sixteen years!

JIM. You're just talking, you drip. How does your mother feel about it?

TOM. Shhh!—Here comes Mother! Mother is not acquainted with my plans!

AMANDA [*Enters portieres*]. Where are you all?

TOM. On the terrace, Mother.

[*They start inside. She advances to them. TOM is distinctly shocked at her appearance. Even JIM blinks a little. He is making his first contact with girlish Southern vivacity and in spite of the night-school course in public speaking is somewhat thrown off the beam by the unexpected outlay of social charm. Certain responses are attempted by JIM but are swept aside by AMANDA's gay laughter and chatter. TOM is embarrassed but after the first shock JIM reacts very warmly. Grins and chuckles, is altogether won over.*]

[IMAGE: AMANDA AS A GIRL.]

AMANDA [*Coyly smiling, shaking her girlish ringlets*]. Well, well, well, so this is Mr. O'Connor. Introductions entirely unnecessary. I've heard so much about you from my boy. I finally said to him, Tom—good gracious!— why don't you bring this paragon to supper? I'd like to meet this nice young man at the warehouse!—Instead of just hearing him sing your praises so much!

I don't know why my son is so stand-offish —that's not Southern behavior!

Let's sit down and—I think we could stand a little more air in here! Tom, leave the door open. I felt a nice fresh breeze a moment ago. Where has it gone to?

Mmm, so warm already! And not quite summer, even. We're going to burn up when summer really gets started.

However, we're having—we're having a very light supper. I think light things are better fo' this time of year. The same as light clothes are.

Light clothes an' light food are what warm weather calls fo'. You know our blood gets so thick during th' winter—it takes a while fo' us to *adjust* ou'selves!—when the season changes . . .

It's come so quick this year. I wasn't prepared. All of a sudden—heavens! Already summer!—I ran to the trunk an' pulled out this light dress—Terribly old! Historical almost! But feels so good—so good an' co-ol, y'know. . . .

TOM. Mother—

AMANDA. Yes, honey?

TOM. How about—supper?

AMANDA. Honey, you go ask Sister if supper is ready! You know that Sister is in full charge of supper!

Tell her you hungry boys are waiting for it. [*To JIM.*] Have you met Laura?

JIM. She—

AMANDA. Let you in? Oh, good, you've met already! It's rare for a girl as sweet an' pretty as Laura to be domestic! But Laura is, thank heavens, not only pretty but also very domestic. I'm not at all. I never was a bit. I never could make a thing but angel-food cake. Well, in the South we had so many servants. Gone, gone, gone. All vestige of gracious living! Gone completely! I wasn't prepared for what the future brought me. All of my gentlemen callers were sons of planters and so of course I assumed that I would be married to one and raise my family on a large piece of land with plenty of servants. But man proposes —and woman accepts° the proposal!—To vary that old, old saying a little bit—I married no planter! I married a man who worked for the telephone company!—That gallantly smiling gentleman over there! [*Points to the picture.*] A telephone man who—fell in love with long-distance!—Now he travels and I don't even know where!—But what am I going on for about my tribulations? Tell me yours—I hope you don't have any! Tom?

TOM [*Returning*]. Yes, Mother?

AMANDA. Is supper nearly ready?

and woman accepts her version of the proverb, "Man proposes, God disposes" (that is, "decides")

Tom. It looks to me like supper is on the table.

Amanda. Let me look— [*She rises prettily and looks through portieres.*] Oh, lovely!—But
5 where is Sister?

Tom. Laura is not feeling well and she says that she thinks she'd better not come to the table.

Amanda. What?—Nonsense!—Laura? Oh,
10 Laura!

Laura. [*Off stage, faintly.*] Yes, Mother.

Amanda. You really must come to the table. We won't be seated until you come to the table! Come in, Mr. O'Connor. You sit over
15 there, and I'll—Laura? Laura Wingfield! You're keeping us waiting, honey! We can't say grace until you come to the table!

[*The back door is pushed weakly open and* Laura *comes in. She is obviously quite faint, her*
20 *lips trembling, her eyes wide and staring. She moves unsteadily toward the table.*]

[LEGEND: "TERROR!"]

[*Outside a summer storm is coming abruptly. The white curtains billow inward at the windows*
25 *and there is a sorrowful murmur and deep blue dusk.* Laura *suddenly stumbles—she catches at a chair with a faint moan.*]

Tom. Laura!

Amanda. Laura!
30 [*There is a clap of thunder.*]

[LEGEND: "AH!"]

[*Despairingly.*]

Why, Laura, you *are* sick, darling! Tom, help your sister into the living room, dear! Sit in the
35 living room, Laura—rest on the sofa. Well! [*To the gentleman caller*] Standing over the hot stove made her ill!—I told her that it was just too warm this evening, but— [Tom *comes back in.* Laura *is on the sofa.*] Is Laura all right now?
40 Tom. Yes.

Amanda. What *is* that? Rain? A nice cool rain has come up! [*She gives the gentleman caller a frightened look*] I think we may—have grace—now . . . [Tom *looks at her stupidly.*]
45 Tom, honey—you say grace!

Tom. Oh . . . "For these and all thy mercies—"

[*They bow their heads,* Amanda *stealing a nervous glance at* Jim. *In the living room* Laura, stretched on the sofa, clenches her hand to her
50 lips, to hold back a shuddering sob.*] "God's Holy Name be praised"—

The Scene Dims Out

SCENE VII

A Souvenir.

Half an hour later. Dinner is just being finished
55 *in the upstage area which is concealed by the drawn portieres. As the curtain rises* Laura *is still huddled upon the sofa, her feet drawn under her, her head resting on a pale blue pillow, her eyes wide and mysteriously watchful. The new floor*
60 *lamp with its shade of rose-colored silk gives a soft, becoming light to her face, bringing out the fragile, unearthly prettiness which usually escapes attention. There is a steady murmur of rain, but it is slackening and stops soon after the*
65 *scene begins; the air outside becomes pale and luminous as the moon breaks out. A moment after the curtain rises, the lights in both rooms flicker and go out.*

Jim. Hey, there, Mr. Light Bulb! 70
[Amanda *laughs nervously.*]

[LEGEND. "SUSPENSION OF A PUBLIC SERVICE."]

Amanda. Where was Moses when the lights went out? Ha-ha. Do you know the answer to 75 that one, Mr. O'Connor?

Jim. No, Ma'am, what's the answer?

Amanda. In the dark! [Jim *laughs appreciatively.*]

Everybody sit still. I'll light the candles. Isn't 80 it lucky we have them on the table? Where's a match? Which of you gentlemen can provide a match?

Jim. Here.

Amanda. Thank you, sir. 85

Jim. Not at all, Ma'am!

Amanda. I guess the fuse has burnt out. Mr. O'Connor, can you tell a burnt-out fuse? I know I can't and Tom is a total loss when it comes to mechanics. 90

[*Sound: Getting up: Voices recede a little to kitchenette.*]

Oh, be careful you don't bump into something. We don't want our gentleman caller to break his neck. Now wouldn't that be a fine howdy-do?

JIM. Ha-ha! Where is the fuse-box?

AMANDA. Right here next to the stove. Can you see anything?

JIM. Just a minute.

AMANDA. Isn't electricity a mysterious thing? Wasn't it Benjamin Franklin who tied a key to a kite? We live in such a mysterious universe, don't we? Some people say that science clears up all the mysteries for us. In my opinion it only creates more!

Have you found it yet?

JIM. No, Ma'am. All these fuses look okay to me.

AMANDA. Tom!

TOM. Yes, Mother?

AMANDA. That light bill I gave you several days ago. The one I told you we got the notices about?

[LEGEND: "HA!"]

TOM. Oh.—Yeah.

AMANDA. You didn't neglect to pay it by any chance?

TOM. Why, I—

AMANDA. Didn't! I might have known it!

JIM. Shakespeare probably wrote a poem on that light bill, Mrs. Wingfield.

AMANDA. I might have known better than to trust him with it! There's such a high price for negligence in this world!

JIM. Maybe the poem will win a ten-dollar prize.

AMANDA. We'll just have to spend the remainder of the evening in the nineteenth century, before Mr. Edison made the Mazda lamp!

JIM. Candlelight is my favorite kind of light.

AMANDA. That shows you're romantic! But that's no excuse for Tom. Well, we got through dinner. Very considerate of them to let us get through dinner before they plunged us into everlasting darkness, wasn't it, Mr. O'Connor?

JIM. Ha-ha!

AMANDA. Tom, as a penalty for your carelessness you can help me with the dishes.

JIM. Let me give you a hand.

AMANDA. Indeed you will not!

JIM. I ought to be good for something.

AMANDA. Good for something? [*Her tone is rhapsodic.*] You? Why, Mr. O'Connor, nobody, *nobody's* given me this much entertainment in years—as you have!

JIM. Aw, now, Mrs. Wingfield!

AMANDA. I'm not exaggerating, not one bit! But Sister is all by her lonesome. You go keep her company in the parlor!

I'll give you this lovely old candelabrum that used to be on the altar at the church of the Heavenly Rest. It was melted a little out of shape when the church burnt down. Lightning struck it one spring. Gypsy Jones was holding a revival at the time and he intimated that the church was destroyed because the Episcopalians gave card parties.

JIM. Ha-ha.

AMANDA. And how about you coaxing Sister to drink a little wine? I think it would be good for her! Can you carry both at once?

JIM. Sure. I'm Superman!

AMANDA. Now, Thomas, get into this apron!

[*The door of the kitchenette swings closed on* AMANDA's *gay laughter; the flickering light approaches the portieres.* LAURA *sits up nervously as he enters. Her speech at first is low and breathless from the almost intolerable strain of being alone with a stranger.*]

[THE LEGEND: "I DON'T SUPPOSE YOU REMEMBER ME AT ALL!"]

[*In her first speeches in this scene, before* JIM's *warmth overcomes her paralyzing shyness,* LAURA's *voice is thin and breathless as though she has just run up a steep flight of stairs.* JIM's *attitude is gently humorous. In playing this scene it should be stressed that while the incident is apparently unimportant, it is to* LAURA *the climax of her secret life.*]

JIM. Hello, there, Laura.

LAURA [*Faintly*]. Hello. [*She clears her throat.*]

JIM. How are you feeling now? Better?

LAURA. Yes. Yes, thank you.

JIM. This is for you. A little dandelion wine.

[*He extends it toward her with extravagant gallantry.*]

LAURA. Thank you.

JIM. Drink it—but don't get drunk! [*He
5 laughs heartily.* LAURA *takes the glass uncertainly; laughs shyly.*] Where shall I set the candles?

LAURA. Oh—oh, anywhere . . .

JIM. How about here on the floor? Any
10 objections?

LAURA. No.

JIM. I'll spread a newspaper under to catch the drippings. I like to sit on the floor. Mind if I do?

15 LAURA. Oh, no.

JIM. Give me a pillow?

LAURA. What?

JIM. A pillow!

LAURA. Oh . . . [*Hands him one quickly.*]
20 JIM. How about you? Don't you like to sit on the floor?

LAURA. Oh—yes.

JIM. Why don't you then?

LAURA. I—will.

25 JIM. Take a pillow! [LAURA *does. Sits on the other side of the candelabrum.* JIM *crosses his legs and smiles engagingly at her.*] I can't hardly see you sitting way over there.

LAURA. I can—see you.

30 JIM. I know, but that's not fair, I'm in the lime-light. [LAURA *moves her pillow closer.*] Good! Now I can see you! Comfortable?

LAURA. Yes.

JIM. So am I. Comfortable as a cow! Will you
35 have some gum?

LAURA. No, thank you.

JIM. I think that I will indulge, with your permission. [*Musingly unwraps it and holds it up.*] Think of the fortune made by the guy that in-
40 vented the first piece of chewing gum. Amazing, huh? The Wrigley Building is one of the sights of Chicago.—I saw it summer before last when I went up to the Century of Progress.° Did you take in the Century of Progress?

45 LAURA. No, I didn't.

Century of Progress at Chicago, 1933–1934; among its
wonders a demonstration of closed-circuit television

JIM. Well, it was quite a wonderful exposition. What impressed me most was the Hall of Science. Gives you an idea of what the future will be in America, even more wonderful than the present time is! [*Pause. Smiling* 50
at her.] Your brother tells me you're shy. Is that right, Laura?

LAURA. I—don't know.

JIM. I judge you to be an old-fashioned type of girl. Well, I think that's a pretty good type 55
to be. Hope you don't think I'm being too personal—do you?

LAURA [*Hastily, out of embarrassment*]. I believe I *will* take a piece of gum, if you—don't mind. [*Clearing her throat.*] Mr. O'Connor, 60
have you—kept up with your singing?

JIM. Singing? Me?

LAURA. Yes. I remember what a beautiful voice you had.

JIM. When did you hear me sing? 65
[VOICE OFF STAGE IN THE PAUSE.]

VOICE [*Off stage.*]

O blow, ye winds, heigh-ho,
A-roving I will go! 70
  I'm off to my love
  With a boxing glove—
Ten thousand miles away!

JIM. You say you've heard me sing?

LAURA. Oh, yes! Yes, very often . . . I—don't 75
suppose—you remember me—at all?

JIM [*Smiling doubtfully*]. You know I have an idea I've seen you before. I had that idea as soon as you opened the door. It seemed almost like I was about to remember your 80
name. But the name I started to call you—wasn't a name! And so I stopped myself before I said it.

LAURA. Wasn't it—Blue Roses?

JIM [*Springs up. Grinning*]. Blue Roses!—My 85
gosh, yes—Blue Roses! That's what I had on my tongue when you opened the door! Isn't it funny what tricks your memory plays? I didn't connect you with high school somehow or other. But that's where it was; it was high 90
school. I didn't even know you were Shakespeare's sister! Gosh, I'm sorry.

LAURA. I didn't expect you to. You—barely knew me!

JIM. But we did have a speaking acquaintance, huh?

5 LAURA. Yes, we—spoke to each other.

JIM. When did you recognize me?

LAURA. Oh, right away!

JIM. Soon as I came in the door?

LAURA. When I heard your name I thought
10 it was probably you. I knew that Tom used to know you a little in high school. So when you came in the door—Well, then I was—sure.

JIM. Why didn't you *say* something, then?

LAURA [*Breathlessly*]. I didn't know what to
15 say, I was—too surprised!

JIM. For goodness' sakes! You know, this sure is funny!

LAURA. Yes! Yes, isn't it, though . . .

JIM. Didn't we have a class in something
20 together?

LAURA. Yes, we did.

JIM. What class was that?

LAURA. It was—singing—Chorus!

JIM. Aw!

25 LAURA. I sat across the aisle from you in the Aud.

JIM. Aw.

LAURA. Mondays, Wednesdays and Fridays.

JIM. Now I remember—you always came in
30 late.

LAURA. Yes, it was so hard for me, getting upstairs. I had that brace on my leg—it clumped so loud!

JIM. I never heard any clumping.

35 LAURA [*Wincing at the recollection*]. To me it sounded like—thunder!

JIM. Well, well, well, I never even noticed.

LAURA. And everybody was seated before I came in. I had to walk in front of all those
40 people. My seat was in the back row. I had to go clumping all the way up the aisle with everyone watching!

JIM. You shouldn't have been self-conscious.

LAURA. I know, but I was. It was always such
45 a relief when the singing started.

JIM. Aw, yes, I've placed you now! I used to call you Blue Roses. How was it that I got started calling you that?

LAURA. I was out of school a little while with
50 pleurosis. When I came back you asked me what was the matter. I said I had pleurosis—you thought I said Blue Roses. That's what you always called me after that!

JIM. I hope you didn't mind.

55 LAURA. Oh, no—I liked it. You see, I wasn't acquainted with many—people. . . .

JIM. As I remember you sort of stuck by yourself.

LAURA. I—I—never have had much luck at
60 —making friends.

JIM. I don't see why you wouldn't.

LAURA. Well, I—started out badly.

JIM. You mean being—

LAURA. Yes, it sort of—stood between me—

65 JIM. You shouldn't have let it!

LAURA. I know, but it did, and—

JIM. You were shy with people!

LAURA. I tried not to be but never could—

JIM. Overcome it?

70 LAURA. No, I—I never could!

JIM. I guess being shy is something you have to work out of kind of gradually.

LAURA [*Sorrowfully*]. Yes—I guess it—

JIM. Takes time!

75 LAURA. Yes—

JIM. People are not so dreadful when you know them. That's what you have to remember! And everybody has problems, not just you, but practically everybody has got some
80 problems. You think of yourself as having the only problems, as being the only one who is disappointed. But just look around you and you will see lots of people as disappointed as you are. For instance, I hoped when I was
85 going to high school that I would be further along at this time, six years later, than I am now—You remember that wonderful write-up I had in *The Torch*?

LAURA. Yes! [*She rises and crosses to table.*]

90 JIM. It said I was bound to succeed in anything I went into! [LAURA *returns with the annual.*] Holy Jeez! *The Torch!* [*He accepts it reverently. They smile across it with mutual wonder.* LAURA *crouches beside him and they*
95 *begin to turn through it.* LAURA'S *shyness is dissolving in his warmth.*]

LAURA. Here you are in *The Pirates of Penzance!*

JIM [*Wistfully*]. I sang the baritone lead in that operetta.

5 LAURA [*Raptly*]. So — *beautifully!*

JIM [*Protesting*]. Aw —

LAURA. Yes, yes — beautifully — beautifully!

JIM. You heard me?

LAURA. All three times!

10 JIM. No!

LAURA. Yes!

JIM. All three performances?

LAURA [*Looking down*]. Yes.

JIM. Why?

15 LAURA. I — wanted to ask you to — autograph my program.

JIM. Why didn't you ask me to?

LAURA. You were always surrounded by your own friends so much that I never had a

20 chance to.

JIM. You should have just —

LAURA. Well, I — thought you might think I was —

JIM. Thought I might think you was — what?

25 LAURA. Oh —

JIM [*With reflective relish*]. I was beleaguered by females in those days.

LAURA. You were terribly popular!

JIM. Yeah —

30 LAURA. You had such a — friendly way —

JIM. I was spoiled in high school.

LAURA. Everybody — liked you!

JIM. Including you?

LAURA. I — yes, I — I did, too — [*She gently*

35 *closes the book in her lap.*]

JIM. Well, well, well! — Give me that program, Laura. [*She hands it to him. He signs it with a flourish.*] There you are — better late than never!

40 LAURA. Oh, I — what a — surprise!

JIM. My signature isn't worth very much right now. But some day — maybe — it will increase in value! Being disappointed is one thing and being discouraged is something

45 else. I am disappointed but I am not discouraged. I'm twenty-three years old. How old are you?

LAURA. I'll be twenty-four in June.

JIM. That's not old age!

LAURA. No, but — 50

JIM. You finished high school?

LAURA [*With difficulty*]. I didn't go back.

JIM. You mean you dropped out?

LAURA. I made bad grades in my final examinations. [*She rises and replaces the book and* 55 *the program. Her voice strained.*] How is — Emily Meisenbach getting along?

JIM. Oh, that kraut-head!

LAURA. Why do you call her that?

JIM. That's what she was. 60

LAURA. You're not still — going with her?

JIM. I never see her.

LAURA. It said in the Personal Section that you were — engaged!

JIM. I know, but I wasn't impressed by that 65 — propaganda!

LAURA. It wasn't — the truth?

JIM. Only in Emily's optimistic opinion!

LAURA. Oh —

[LEGEND: "WHAT HAVE YOU DONE SINCE HIGH 70 SCHOOL?"]

[JIM *lights a cigarette and leans indolently back on his elbows smiling at* LAURA *with a warmth and charm which lights her inwardly with altar candles. She remains by the table and turns in her* 75 *hands a piece of glass to cover her tumult.*]

JIM. [*After several reflective puffs on a cigarette*]. What have you done since high school? [*She seems not to hear him.*] Huh? [*Laura looks up.*] I said what have you done since high 80 school, Laura?

LAURA. Nothing much.

JIM. You must have been doing something these six long years.

LAURA. Yes. 85

JIM. Well, then, such as what?

LAURA. I took a business course at business college —

JIM. How did that work out?

LAURA. Well, not very — well — I had to drop 90 out, it gave me — indigestion —

[JIM *laughs gently.*]

JIM. What are you doing now?

LAURA. I don't do anything — much. Oh, please don't think I sit around doing nothing! 95 My glass collection takes up a good deal of time. Glass is something you have to take good care of.

JIM. What did you say—about glass?

LAURA. Collection I said—I have one— [*She clears her throat and turns away again, acutely shy.*]

JIM [*Abruptly*]. You know what I judge to be the trouble with you? Inferiority complex! Know what that is? That's what they call it when someone low-rates himself! I understand it because I had it, too. Although my case was not so aggravated as yours seems to be. I had it until I took up public speaking, developed my voice, and learned that I had an aptitude for science. Before that time I never thought of myself as being outstanding in any way whatsoever! Now I've never made a regular study of it, but I have a friend who says I can analyze people better than doctors that make a profession of it. I don't claim that to be necessarily true, but I can sure guess a person's psychology, Laura! [*Takes out his gum.*] Excuse me, Laura. I always take it out when the flavor is gone. I'll use this scrap of paper to wrap it in. I know how it is to get it stuck on a shoe. Yep—that's what I judge to be your principal trouble. A lack of confidence in yourself as a person. You don't have the proper amount of faith in yourself. I'm basing that fact on a number of your remarks and also on certain observations I've made. For instance that clumping you thought was so awful in high school. You say you even dreaded to walk into class. You see what you did? You dropped out of school, you gave up an education because of a clump, which as far as I know was practically non-existent! A little physical defect is what you have. Hardly noticeable even! Magnified thousands of times by imagination! You know what my strong advice to you is? Think of yourself as *superior* in some way!

LAURA. In what way would I think?

JIM. Why, man alive, Laura! Just look about you a little. What do you see? A world full of common people! All of 'em born and all of 'em going to die! Which of them has one-tenth of your good points! Or mine! Or anyone else's, as far as that goes—Gosh! Everybody excels in some one thing. Some in many! [*Unconsciously glances at himself in the mirror.*] All you've got to do is discover in *what*! Take me, for instance. [*He adjusts his tie at the mirror.*] My interest happens to lie in electro-dynamics. I'm taking a course in radio engineering at night school, Laura, on top of a fairly responsible job at the warehouse. I'm taking that course and studying public speaking.

LAURA. Ohhhh.

JIM. Because I believe in the future of television! [*Turning back to her.*] I wish to be ready to go up right along with it. Therefore I'm planning to get in on the ground floor. In fact I've already made the right connections and all that remains is for the industry to get under way! Full steam— [*His eyes are starry.*] Knowledge—Zzzzzp! Money—Zzzzzp!—Power! That's the cycle democracy is built on! [*His attitude is convincingly dynamic.* LAURA *stares at him, even her shyness eclipsed in her absolute wonder. He suddenly grins.*] I guess you think I think a lot of myself!

LAURA. No—o-o-o, I—

JIM. Now how about you? Isn't there something you take more interest in than anything else?

LAURA. Well, I do—as I said—have my—glass collection—

[*A peal of girlish laughter from the kitchen.*]

JIM. I'm not right sure I know what you're talking about. What kind of glass is it?

LAURA. Little articles of it, they're ornaments mostly! Most of them are little animals made out of glass, the tiniest little animals in the world. Mother calls them a glass menagerie! Here's an example of one, if you'd like to see it! This is one of the oldest. It's nearly thirteen.

[*Music: "The Glass Menagerie."*]

[*He stretches out his hand.*]

Oh, be careful—if you breathe, it breaks!

JIM. I'd better not take it. I'm pretty clumsy with things.

LAURA. Go on, I trust you with him! [*Places it in his palm.*] There now—you're holding him gently! Hold him over the light, he loves the light! You see how the light shines through him?

JIM. It sure does shine!

LAURA. I shouldn't be partial, but he is my favorite one.

JIM. What kind of a thing is this one sup-
5 posed to be?

LAURA. Haven't you noticed the single horn on his forehead?

JIM. A unicorn, huh?

LAURA. Mmm-hmmm!

10 JIM. Unicorns, aren't they extinct in the modern world?

LAURA. I know!

JIM. Poor little fellow, he must feel sort of lonesome.

15 LAURA [Smiling]. Well, if he does he doesn't complain about it. He stays on a shelf with some horses that don't have horns and all of them seem to get along nicely together.

JIM. How do you know?

20 LAURA [Lightly]. I haven't heard any argu-ments among them!

JIM [Grinning]. No arguments, huh? Well, that's a pretty good sign! Where shall I set him!

LAURA. Put him on the table. They all like a
25 change of scenery once in a while!

JIM [Stretching]. Well, well, well, well—Look how big my shadow is when I stretch!

LAURA. Oh, oh, yes—it stretches across the ceiling!

30 JIM [Crossing to door]. I think it's stopped raining. [Opens fire-escape door.] Where does the music come from?

LAURA. From the Paradise Dance Hall across the alley.

35 JIM. How about cutting the rug a little, Miss Wingfield?

LAURA. Oh, I—

JIM. Or is your program filled up? Let me have a look at it. [Grasps imaginary card] Why,
40 every dance is taken! I'll just have to scratch some out. [Waltz music: "La Golondrina."] Ahhh, a waltz! [He executes some sweeping turns by himself then holds his arms toward LAURA.]

45 LAURA [Breathlessly]. I—can't dance!

JIM. There you go, that inferiority stuff!

LAURA. I've never danced in my life!

JIM. Come on, try!

LAURA. Oh, but I'd step on you!

JIM. I'm not made out of glass. 50

LAURA. How—how—how do we start?

JIM. Just leave it to me. You hold your arms out a little.

LAURA. Like this?

JIM. A little bit higher. Right. Now don't 55
tighten up, that's the main thing about it— relax.

LAURA [Laughing breathlessly]. It's hard not to.

JIM. Okay. 60

LAURA. I'm afraid you can't budge me.

JIM. What do you bet I can't? [He swings her into motion.]

LAURA. Goodness, yes, you can!

JIM. Let yourself go, now, Laura, just let 65
yourself go.

LAURA. I'm—

JIM. Come on!

LAURA. Trying!

JIM. Not so stiff—Easy does it! 70

LAURA. I know but I'm—

JIM. Loosen th' backbone! There now, that's a lot better.

LAURA. Am I?

JIM. Lots, lots better! [He moves her about the 75
room in a clumsy waltz.]

LAURA. Oh, my!

JIM. Ha-ha!

LAURA. Oh, my goodness!

JIM. Ha-ha-ha! [They suddenly bump into the 80
table. JIM stops.] What did we hit on?

LAURA. Table.

JIM. Did something fall off it? I think—

LAURA. Yes.

JIM. I hope that it wasn't the little glass horse 85
with the horn!

LAURA. Yes.

JIM. Aw, aw, aw. Is it broken?

LAURA. Now it is just like all the other horses.

JIM. It's lost its— 90

LAURA. Horn! It doesn't matter. Maybe it's a blessing in disguise.

JIM. You'll never forgive me. I bet that that was your favorite piece of glass.

LAURA. I don't have favorites much. It's no 95
tragedy, Freckles. Glass breaks so easily. No

matter how careful you are. The traffic jars the shelves and things fall off them.

JIM. Still I'm awfully sorry that I was the cause

LAURA [*Smiling*]. I'll just imagine he had an operation. The horn was removed to make him feel less—freakish! [*They both laugh.*] Now he will feel more at home with the other horses, the ones that don't have horns . . .

JIM. Ha-ha, that's very funny! [*Suddenly serious.*] I'm glad to see that you have a sense of humor.

You know—you're—well—very different! Surprisingly different from anyone else I know! [*His voice becomes soft and hesitant with a genuine feeling*]. Do you mind me telling you that? [LAURA *is abashed beyond speech.*] I mean it in a nice way . . . [LAURA *nods shyly, looking away.*] You make me feel sort of—I don't know how to put it! I'm usually pretty good at expressing things, but—This is something that I don't know how to say! [LAURA *touches her throat and clears it—turns the broken unicorn in her hands. Even softer*]. Has anyone ever told you that you were pretty?

[PAUSE: MUSIC.]

[LAURA *looks up slowly, with wonder, and shakes her head.*]

Well, you are! In a very different way from anyone else. And all the nicer because of the difference too. [*His voice becomes low and husky.* LAURA *turns away, nearly faint with the novelty of her emotions*]. I wish that you were my sister. I'd teach you to have some confidence in yourself. The different people are not like other people, but being different is nothing to be ashamed of. Because other people are not such wonderful people. They're one hundred times one thousand. You're one times one! They walk all over the earth. You just stay here. They're common as—weeds, but —you—well, you're—*Blue Roses!*

[IMAGE ON SCREEN: BLUE ROSES.]
[MUSIC CHANGES.]

LAURA. But blue is wrong for—roses . . .

JIM. It's right for you!—You're—pretty!

LAURA. In what respect am I pretty?

JIM. In all respects—believe me! Your eyes—

your hair—are pretty! Your hands are pretty! [*He catches hold of her hand.*] You think I'm making this up because I'm invited to dinner and have to be nice. Oh, I could do that! I could put on an act for you, Laura, and say lots of things without being very sincere. But this time I am. I'm talking to you sincerely. I happened to notice you had this inferiority complex that keeps you from feeling comfortable with people. Somebody needs to build your confidence up and make you proud instead of shy and turning away and—blushing—Somebody—ought to—ought to—*kiss* you, Laura! [*His hand slips slowly up her arm to her shoulder.*]

[MUSIC SWELLS TUMULTUOUSLY.]

[*He suddenly turns her about and kisses her on the lips. When he releases her,* LAURA *sinks on the sofa with a bright, dazed look.* JIM *backs away and fishes in his pocket for a cigarette.*]

[LEGEND ON SCREEN: "SOUVENIR."]

Stumble-john! [*He lights the cigarette, avoiding her look. There is a peal of girlish laughter from* AMANDA *in the kitchen.* LAURA *slowly raises and opens her hand. It still contains the little broken glass animal. She looks at it with a tender, bewildered expression.*] Stumble-john! I shouldn't have done that—That was way off the beam. You don't smoke, do you? [*She looks up, smiling, not hearing the question. He sits beside her a little gingerly. She looks at him speechlessly—waiting. He coughs decorously and moves a little farther aside as he considers the situation and senses her feelings, dimly, with perturbation. Gently.*] Would you—care for a —mint? [*She doesn't seem to hear him but her look grows brighter even.*] Peppermint—Life-Saver? My pocket's a regular drug store— wherever I go . . . [*He pops a mint in his mouth. Then gulps and decides to make a clean breast of it. He speaks slowly and gingerly.*] Laura, you know, if I had a sister like you, I'd do the same thing as Tom. I'd bring out fellows and—introduce her to them. The right type of boys of a type to—appreciate her. Only —well—he made a mistake about me. Maybe I've got no call to be saying this. That may not have been the idea in having me over. But what if it was? There's nothing wrong about that. The only trouble is that in my case—I'm not in a situation to—do the right thing.

I can't take down your number and say I'll phone. I can't call up next week and—ask for a date. I thought I had better explain the situation in case you—misunderstood it and—hurt your feelings. . . .

[*Pause. Slowly, very slowly,* LAURA's *look changes, her eyes returning slowly from his to the ornament in her palm.* AMANDA *utters another gay laugh in the kitchen.*]

LAURA [*Faintly*]. You—won't—call again?

JIM. No, Laura, I can't. [*He rises from the sofa.*] As I was just explaining, I've—got strings on me. Laura, I've—been going steady! I go out all of the time with a girl named Betty. She's a home-girl like you, and Catholic, and Irish, and in a great many ways we—get along fine. I met her last summer on a moonlight boat trip up the river to Alton, on the *Majestic.* Well—right away from the start it was—love!

[LEGEND: LOVE!]

[LAURA *sways slightly forward and grips the arm of the sofa. He fails to notice, now enrapt in his own comfortable being.*]

Being in love has made a new man of me! [*Leaning stiffly forward, clutching the arm of the sofa,* LAURA *struggles visibly with her storm. But* JIM *is oblivious, she is a long way off.*] The power of love is really pretty tremendous! Love is something that—changes the whole world, Laura! [*The storm abates a little and* LAURA *leans back. He notices her again.*] It happened that Betty's aunt took sick, she got a wire and had to go to Centralia. So Tom—when he asked me to dinner—I naturally just accepted the invitation, not knowing that you—that he—that I— [*He stops awkwardly.*] Huh—I'm a stumble-john! [*He flops back on the sofa. The holy candles in the altar of* LAURA's *face have been snuffed out. There is a look of almost infinite desolation.* JIM *glances at her uneasily.*] I wish that you would—say something. [*She bites her lip which was trembling and then bravely smiles. She opens her hand again on the broken glass ornament. Then she gently takes his hand and raises it level with her*

own. She carefully places the unicorn in the palm of his hand, then pushes his fingers closed upon it.] What are you—doing that for? You want me to have him?—Laura? [*She nods.*] What for?

LAURA. A—souvenir . . . [*She rises unsteadily and crouches beside the victrola to wind it up.*]

[LEGEND ON SCREEN: "THINGS HAVE A WAY OF TURNING OUT SO BADLY!"]

[OR IMAGE: "GENTLEMAN CALLER WAVING GOOD-BYE!—GAILY."]

[*At this moment* AMANDA *rushes brightly back in the front room. She bears a pitcher of fruit punch in an old-fashioned cut-glass pitcher and a plate of macaroons. The plate has a gold border and poppies painted on it.*]

AMANDA. Well, well, well! Isn't the air delightful after the shower? I've made you children a little liquid refreshment. [*Turns gaily to the gentleman caller.*] Jim, do you know that song about lemonade?

"Lemonade, lemonade
Made in the shade and stirred with a spade—
Good enough for any old maid!"

JIM [*Uneasily*]. Ha-ha! No—I never heard it.

AMANDA. Why, Laura! You look so serious!

JIM. We were having a serious conversation.

AMANDA. Good! Now you're better acquainted!

JIM [*Uncertainly*]. Ha-ha! Yes.

AMANDA. You modern young people are much more serious-minded than my generation. I was so gay as a girl!

JIM. You haven't changed, Mrs. Wingfield.

AMANDA. Tonight I'm rejuvenated! The gaiety of the occasion, Mr. O'Connor! [*She tosses her head with a peal of laughter. Spills lemonade.*] Oooo! I'm baptizing myself!

JIM. Here—let me—

AMANDA [*Setting the pitcher down*]. There now. I discovered we had some maraschino cherries. I dumped them in, juice and all!

JIM. You shouldn't have gone to that trouble, Mrs. Wingfield.

AMANDA. Trouble, trouble? Why, it was loads of fun! Didn't you hear me cutting up in the kitchen? I bet your ears were burning! I told Tom how outdone with him I was for keeping you to himself so long a time! He should have brought you over much, much sooner! Well, now that you've found your way, I want you to be a very frequent caller! Not just occasional but all the time. Oh, we're going to have a lot of gay times together! I see them coming! Mmmm, just breathe that air! So fresh, and the moon's so pretty! I'll skip back out—I know where my place is when young folks are having a—serious conversation!

JIM. Oh, don't go out, Mrs. Wingfield. The fact of the matter is I've got to be going.

AMANDA. Going, now? You're joking! Why, it's only the shank of the evening, Mr. O'Connor!

JIM. Well, you know how it is.

AMANDA. You mean you're a young workingman and have to keep workingmen's hours. We'll let you off early tonight. But only on the condition that next time you stay later. What's the best night for you? Isn't Saturday night the best night for you workingmen?

JIM. I have a couple of time-clocks to punch, Mrs. Wingfield. One at morning, another one at night!

AMANDA. My, but you *are* ambitious! You work at night, too?

JIM. No, Ma'am, not work but—Betty! [*He crosses deliberately to pick up his hat. The band at the Paradise Dance Hall goes into a tender waltz.*]

AMANDA. Betty? Betty? Who's—Betty! [*There is an ominous cracking sound in the sky.*]

JIM. Oh, just a girl! The girl I go steady with! [*He smiles charmingly. The sky falls.*]

[LEGEND: "THE SKY FALLS."]

AMANDA [*A long-drawn exhalation*]. Ohhhh ... Is it a serious romance, Mr. O'Connor?

JIM. We're going to be married the second Sunday in June.

AMANDA. Ohhhh—how nice! Tom didn't mention that you were engaged to be married.

JIM. The cat's not out of the bag at the warehouse yet. You know how they are. They call you Romeo and stuff like that. [*He stops at the oval mirror to put on his hat. He carefully shapes*

the brim and the crown to give a discreetly dashing effect.*] It's been a wonderful evening, Mrs. Wingfield. I guess this is what they mean by Southern hospitality.

AMANDA. It really wasn't anything at all.

JIM. I hope it don't seem like I'm rushing off. But I promised Betty I'd pick her up at the Wabash depot, an' by the time I get my jalopy down there her train'll be in. Some women are pretty upset if you keep 'em waiting.

AMANDA. Yes, I know—The tyranny of women! [*Extends her hand.*] Good-bye, Mr. O'Connor. I wish you luck—and happiness—and success! All three of them, and so does Laura!—Don't you, Laura?

LAURA. Yes!

JIM [*Taking her hand*]. Good-bye, Laura. I'm certainly going to treasure that souvenir. And don't you forget the good advice I gave you. [*Raises his voice to a cheery shout.*] So long, Shakespeare! Thanks again, ladies—Good night! [*He grins and ducks jauntily out. Still bravely grimacing, AMANDA closes the door on the gentleman caller. Then she turns back to the room with a puzzled expression. She and LAURA don't dare to face each other. LAURA crouches beside the victrola to wind it.*]

AMANDA [*Faintly*]. Things have a way of turning out so badly. I don't believe that I would play the victrola. Well, well—well—Our gentleman caller was engaged to be married! Tom!

TOM [*From back*]. Yes, Mother?

AMANDA. Come in here a minute. I want to tell you something awfully funny.

TOM [*Enters with macaroon and a glass of the lemonade*]. Has the gentleman caller gotten away already?

AMANDA. The gentleman caller has made an early departure. What a wonderful joke you played on us!

TOM. How do you mean?

AMANDA. You didn't mention that he was engaged to be married.

TOM. Jim? Engaged?

AMANDA. That's what he just informed us.

TOM. I'll be jiggered! I didn't know about that.

AMANDA. That seems very peculiar.

TOM. What's peculiar about it?

AMANDA. Didn't you call him your best friend down at the warehouse?

5   TOM. He is, but how did I know?

AMANDA. It seems extremely peculiar that you wouldn't know your best friend was going to be married!

TOM. The warehouse is where I work, not
10 where I know things about people!

AMANDA. You don't know things anywhere! You live in a dream; you manufacture illusions! [He crosses to door.] Where are you going?

TOM. I'm going to the movies.

15 AMANDA. That's right, now that you've had us make such fools of ourselves. The effort, the preparations, all the expense! The new floor lamp, the rug, the clothes for Laura! All for what? To entertain some other girl's
20 fiancé! Go to the movies, go! Don't think about us, a mother deserted, an unmarried sister who's crippled and has no job! Don't let anything interfere with your selfish pleasure! Just go, go, go—to the movies!

25 TOM. All right, I will! The more you shout about my selfishness to me the quicker I'll go, and I won't go to the movies!

AMANDA. Go, then! Then go to the moon— you selfish dreamer!

30 [TOM smashes his glass on the floor. He plunges out on the fire-escape, slamming the door. LAURA screams—cut by door. Dance-hall music up. TOM goes to the rail and grips it desperately, lifting his face in the chill white moonlight pene-
35 trating the narrow abyss of the alley.]

[LEGEND ON SCREEN: "AND SO GOOD-BYE . . ."]

[TOM's closing speech is timed with the interior pantomime. The interior scene is played
40 as though viewed through soundproof glass. AMANDA appears to be making a comforting speech to LAURA who is huddled upon the sofa. Now that we cannot hear the mother's speech, her silliness is gone and she has dignity and
45 tragic beauty. LAURA's dark hair hides her face until at the end of the speech she lifts it to smile at her mother. AMANDA's gestures are slow and graceful, almost dance-like, as she comforts the daughter. At the end of her speech she glances a
50 moment at the father's picture—then withdraws through the portieres. At close of TOM's speech, LAURA blows out the candles, ending the play.]

TOM. I didn't go to the moon, I went much further—for time is the longest distance be-
55 tween two places—Not long after that I was fired for writing a poem on the lid of a shoe-box. I left Saint Louis. I descended the steps of this fire-escape for a last time and followed, from then on, in my father's footsteps, attempt-
60 ing to find in motion what was lost in space—I traveled around a great deal. The cities swept about me like dead leaves, leaves that were brightly colored but torn away from the branches. I would have stopped, but I was
65 pursued by something. It always came upon me unawares, taking me altogether by surprise. Perhaps it was a familiar bit of music. Perhaps it was only a piece of transparent glass—Perhaps I am walking along a street at
70 night, in some strange city, before I have found companions. I pass the lighted window of a shop where perfume is sold. The window is filled with pieces of colored glass, tiny transparent bottles in delicate colors, like bits of a
75 shattered rainbow. Then all at once my sister touches my shoulder. I turn around and look into her eyes . . . Oh, Laura. Laura, I tried to leave you behind me, but I am more faithful than I intended to be! I reach for a cigarette,
80 I cross the street, I run into the movies or a bar, I buy a drink, I speak to the nearest stranger—anything that can blow your candles out! [LAURA bends over the candles.]—for now-adays the world is lit by lightning! Blow out
85 your candles, Laura—and so good-bye. . . .
[She blows the candles out.]

The Scene Dissolves

Arthur Miller

1915–

Death of a Salesman

1949

"New York and Boston of today," the settings that Arthur Miller specifies, do not in fact comprise the whole imaginative territory of *Death of a Salesman.* It includes, as well, memories of a former era, the 1920's and 1930's, the period of the great "Boom" and the succeeding Great Depression that overwhelms Willy Loman, the Salesman, during the last days of his life. The times and places are totally American and middle class, scenes of inflated hopes and later of deflated dreams. For Willy, America was "full of beautiful towns and fine, upstanding people," a land of "success" symbolized by such "self-made" tycoons as Thomas Edison and B. F. Goodrich, who thrived in a time of almost unchecked capitalist expansion and officially proclaimed "prosperity" ("In 1928 I had a big year").

As a salesman, Willy is a superb symbol for an era of contradictions. He is specifically a "road man," one of the now-diminished tribe of "drummers" who peddled their wares and spread the gospel of success and profits up and down the land. Equipped with sample cases and ribald anecdotes, full of glad-handing, back-thumping, first-name-dropping optimism ("the sky's the limit"), their existence was at once gregarious and oddly solitary. Their livelihood was hazardous, subject to the vagaries of sales-commission earnings, their confident air of bluff heartiness often contrasting with the regular loneliness of cheap hotels and the pinching anxiety stemming from unrelieved competitiveness, called "playing the game," the rules of which the salesman was powerless to set or alter or even to criticize, at least out loud. His world was staunchly and narrowly masculine, much wanting in human kindness, not altogether ungenerous, but suspicious of love. This world, depicted in *Death of a Salesman,* is an indictment out of American Marxism of the 1930's. "You end up," Willy confesses, "more dead than alive." Where *Desire Under the Elms* would demolish the American

ARTHUR MILLER

agrarian pastoral, *Death of a Salesman* undermines the idyll of "suburbia."

Yet *Death of a Salesman* is not only a social tract. It is, explicitly, the tragedy of a man who has some noble traits, no matter how inarticulately expressed. As his wife Linda insists, "Attention, attention must be finally paid to such a person." In this aging nobody there are rudiments of promethean restlessness. In his struggle to define his aspirations, he searches far less for riches than for love. His life oscillates between confidence and despair: "personality always wins the day"; "I'm always in a race with the junkyard." His final yearning for a meaningful death recapitulates and reassesses his life.

As theater, the play is in the modernist tradition, deriving much in theme and technique from Chekhov and O'Neill. It is a chronicle and an elegy, although with elements of bleak satire. It is also, formally, a tragedy that centers accurately on Willy Loman. All other characters have their being essentially in relation to his and are the persons in a dream that he tries to relive and reinterpret. All the characters address the question of Willy's destiny.

The setting of the play is an interpenetration of times and of levels of Willy's consciousness. In the present, the last days of his life, the physical boundaries are observed; in scenes from the past the boundaries soften and are passed through as if by magic. This past is not merely recollected, it is reenacted in Willy's last agitated striving to understand a father whom he scarcely knew and sons whom he involuntarily betrayed.

In the final scenes the play reaches a mythic dimension emphasized by intermingling of symbolic times and places. Willy, "the son of a great and very wild-hearted man," tries again to plant seeds in the ruined garden, and his brother Ben, now more than ever a potent figure of mystery, reappears to promise a final success that will redeem the failures of a life of tawdry dreams and stunted affections. "It's dark there," Ben warns, speaking of the death toward which he beckons, "but full of diamonds." That is a last deception, consonant with the unfulfillment of the past, but Willy accepts it as inviting to a heroism not altogether discredited by the lure of romantic illusions. Although Willy's death, like the conditions of his life as a salesman, "came with the territory," that territory is not so much America of the 1930's as the realm of unrealized aspirations. He dies, by choice, the death appointed and makes it, no less truly than an Othello or an Antony, his own.

Death of a Salesman

Certain Private Conversations
in Two Acts and a Requiem

MILLER

CHARACTERS

WILLY LOMAN	CHARLEY
LINDA	UNCLE BEN
BIFF	HOWARD WAGNER
HAPPY	JENNY
BERNARD	STANLEY
THE WOMAN	MISS FORSYTHE
LETTA	WAITER

SCENE. *The action takes place in Willy Loman's house and yard and in various places he visits in the New York and Boston of today.*

ACT I

[*A melody is heard, played upon a flute. It is small and fine, telling of grass and trees and the horizon. The curtain rises.*

Before us is the SALESMAN's *house. We are aware of towering, angular shapes behind it, surrounding it on all sides. Only the blue light*

Death of a Salesman *by Arthur Miller. Copyright 1949, renewed © 1977 by Arthur Miller. All rights reserved. Reprinted by permission of The Viking Penguin, Inc.*

of the sky falls upon the house and forestage; the surrounding area shows an angry glow of orange. As more light appears we see a solid vault of apartment houses around the small, fragile-seeming home. An air of the dream clings to the place, a dream rising out of reality. The kitchen at center seems actual enough, for there is a kitchen table with three chairs, and a refrigerator. But no other fixtures are seen. At the back of the kitchen there is a draped entrance, which leads to the living-room. To the right of the kitchen, on a level raised two feet, is a bedroom furnished only with a brass bedstead and a straight chair. On a shelf over the bed a silver athletic trophy stands. A window opens on to the apartment house at the side.

Behind the kitchen, on a level raised six and a half feet, is the boys' bedroom, at present barely visible. Two beds are dimly seen, and at the back of the room a dormer window. (This bedroom is above the unseen living-room.) At the left a stairway curves up to it from the kitchen.

The entire setting is wholly or, in some places, partially transparent. The roof-line of the house is one-dimensional; under and over it we see the apartment buildings. Before the house lies an apron, curving beyond the fore-stage into the orchestra. This forward area serves as the back yard as well as the locale of all Willy's imaginings and of his city scenes. Whenever the action is in the present the actors observe the imaginary wall-lines, entering the house only through its door at the left. But in the scenes of the past these boundaries are broken, and characters enter or leave a room by stepping "through" a wall on to the forestage.]

[*From the right,* WILLY LOMAN, *the Salesman, enters, carrying two large sample cases. The flute plays on. He hears but is not aware of it. He is past sixty years of age, dressed quietly. Even as he crosses the stage to the doorway of the house, his exhaustion is apparent. He unlocks the door, comes into the kitchen, and thankfully lets his burden down, feeling the soreness of his palms. A word-sigh*

escapes his lips—it might be "Oh, boy, oh, boy." He closes the door, then carries his cases out into the living-room, through the draped kitchen doorway. LINDA, *his wife, has stirred*
5 *in her bed at the right. She gets out and puts on a robe, listening. Most often jovial, she has developed an iron repression of her exceptions to* WILLY's *behavior—she more than loves him, she admires him, as though his mercurial*
10 *nature, his temper, his massive dreams and little cruelties, served her only as sharp reminders of the turbulent longings within him, longings which she shares but lacks the temperament to utter and follow to their end.*]

15 LINDA [*hearing* WILLY *outside the bedroom, calls with some trepidation*]. Willy!

WILLY. It's all right. I came back.

LINDA. Why? What happened? [*Slight pause.*] Did something happen, Willy?

20 WILLY. No, nothing happened.

LINDA. You didn't smash the car, did you?

WILLY [*with casual irritation*]. I said nothing happened. Didn't you hear me?

LINDA. Don't you feel well?

25 WILLY. I'm tired to the death. [*The flute has faded away. He sits on the bed beside her, a little numb.*] I couldn't make it. I just couldn't make it, Linda.

LINDA [*very carefully, delicately*]. Where
30 were you all day? You look terrible.

WILLY. I got as far as a little above Yonkers. I stopped for a cup of coffee. Maybe it was the coffee.

LINDA. What?

35 WILLY [*after a pause*]. I suddenly couldn't drive any more. The car kept going off on to the shoulder, y'know?

LINDA [*helpfully*]. Oh. Maybe it was the steering again. I don't think Angelo knows the
40 Studebaker.

WILLY. No, it's me. Suddenly I realize I'm goin' sixty miles an hour and I don't remember the last five minutes. I'm—I can't seem to—keep my mind to it.

45 LINDA. Maybe it's your glasses. You never went for your new glasses.

WILLY. No, I see everything. I came back ten miles an hour. It took me nearly four hours from Yonkers.

LINDA [*resigned*]. Well, you'll just have to 50 take a rest, Willy, you can't continue this way.

WILLY. I just got back from Florida.

LINDA. But you didn't rest your mind. Your mind is over-active, and the mind is what counts, dear. 55

WILLY. I'll start out in the morning. Maybe I'll feel better in the morning. [*She is taking off his shoes.*] These goddam arch supports are killing me.

LINDA. Take an aspirin. Should I get you an 60 aspirin? It'll soothe you.

WILLY [*with wonder*]. I was driving along, you understand? And I was fine. I was even observing the scenery. You can imagine, me looking at scenery, on the road every week of 65 my life. But it's so beautiful up there, Linda, the trees are so thick, and the sun is warm. I opened the windshield and just let the warm air bathe over me. And then all of a sudden I'm goin' off the road! I'm tellin' ya, I absolutely 70 forgot I was driving. If I'd've gone the other way over the white line I might've killed somebody. So I went on again—and five minutes later I'm dreamin' again, and I nearly —[*He presses two fingers against his eyes.*] I 75 have such thoughts, I have such strange thoughts.

LINDA. Willy, dear. Talk to them again. There's no reason why you can't work in New York. 80

WILLY. They don't need me in New York. I'm the New England man. I'm vital in New England.

LINDA. But you're sixty years old. They can't expect you to keep travelling every week. 85

WILLY. I'll have to send a wire to Portland. I'm supposed to see Brown and Morrison tomorrow morning at ten o'clock to show the line. Goddammit, I could sell them! [*He starts putting on his jacket.*] 90

LINDA [*taking the jacket from him*]. Why don't you go down to the place tomorrow and tell Howard you've simply got to work in New York? You're too accommodating, dear.

WILLY. If old man Wagner was alive I'd a 95 been in charge of New York now! That man was a prince, he was a masterful man. But that boy of his, that Howard, he don't appreciate. When I went north the first time, the Wagner Company didn't know where New England was!

LINDA. Why don't you tell those things to Howard, dear?

WILLY [*encouraged*]. I will, I definitely will. Is there any cheese?

LINDA. I'll make you a sandwich.

WILLY. No, go to sleep. I'll take some milk. I'll be up right away. The boys in?

LINDA. They're sleeping. Happy took Biff on a date tonight.

WILLY [*interested*]. That so?

LINDA. It was so nice to see them shaving together, one behind the other, in the bathroom. And going out together. You notice? The whole house smells of shaving lotion.

WILLY. Figure it out. Work a lifetime to pay off a house. You finally own it, and there's nobody to live in it.

LINDA. Well, dear, life is a casting off. It's always that way.

WILLY. No, no, some people—some people accomplish something. Did Biff say anything after I went this morning?

LINDA. You shouldn't have criticized him, Willy, especially after he just got off the train. You mustn't lose your temper with him.

WILLY. When the hell did I lose my temper? I simply asked him if he was making any money. Is that a criticism?

LINDA. But, dear, how could he make any money?

WILLY [*worried and angered*]. There's such an undercurrent in him. He became a moody man. Did he apologize when I left this morning?

LINDA. He was crestfallen, Willy. You know how he admires you. I think if he finds himself, then you'll both be happier and not fight any more.

WILLY. How can he find himself on a farm? Is that a life? A farmhand? In the beginning, when he was young, I thought, well, a young man, it's good for him to tramp around, take a lot of different jobs. But it's more than ten years now and he has yet to make thirty-five dollars a week!

LINDA. He's finding himself, Willy.

WILLY. Not finding yourself at the age of thirty-four is a disgrace!

LINDA. Shh!

WILLY. The trouble is he's lazy, goddammit!

LINDA. Willy, please!

WILLY. Biff is a lazy bum!

LINDA. They're sleeping. Get something to eat. Go on down.

WILLY. Why did he come home? I would like to know what brought him home.

LINDA. I don't know. I think he's still lost, Willy. I think he's very lost.

WILLY. Biff Loman is lost. In the greatest country in the world a young man with such —personal attractiveness, gets lost. And such a hard worker. There's one thing about Biff— he's not lazy.

LINDA. Never.

WILLY [*with pity and resolve*]. I'll see him in the morning; I'll have a nice talk with him. I'll get him a job selling. He could be big in no time. My God! Remember how they used to follow him around in high school? When he smiled at one of them their faces lit up. When he walked down the street. . . . [*He loses himself in reminiscences.*]

LINDA [*trying to bring him out of it*]. Willy, dear, I got a new kind of American-type cheese today. It's whipped.

WILLY. Why do you get American when I like Swiss?

LINDA. I just thought you'd like a change—

WILLY. I don't want a change! I want Swiss cheese. Why am I always being contradicted?

LINDA [*with a covering laugh*]. I thought it would be a surprise.

WILLY. Why don't you open a window in here, for God's sake?

LINDA [*with infinite patience*]. They're all open, dear.

WILLY. The way they boxed us in here. Bricks and windows, windows and bricks.

LINDA. We should've bought the land next door.

WILLY. The street is lined with cars. There's

not a breath of fresh air in the neighborhood. The grass don't grow any more, you can't raise a carrot in the backyard. They should've had a law against apartment houses. Remem-
5 ber those two beautiful elm trees out there? When I and Biff hung the swing between them?

LINDA. Yeah, like being a million miles from the city.

10 WILLY. They should've arrested the builder for cutting those down. They massacred the neighborhood. [Lost.] More and more I think of those days, Linda. This time of year it was lilac and wistaria. And then the peonies would
15 come out, and the daffodils. What a fragrance in this room!

LINDA. Well, after all, people had to move somewhere.

WILLY. No, there's more people now.

20 LINDA. I don't think there's more people, I think—

WILLY. There's more people! That's what's ruining this country! Population is getting out of control. The competition is maddening!
25 Smell the stink from that apartment house! And another one on the other side. . . . How can they whip cheese?

[On WILLY's last line, BIFF and HAPPY raise themselves up in their beds, listening.]

30 LINDA. Go down, try it. And be quiet.

WILLY [turning to LINDA, guiltily]. You're not worried about me, are you, sweetheart?

BIFF. What's the matter?

HAPPY. Listen!

35 LINDA. You've got too much on the ball to worry about.

WILLY. You're my foundation and my support, Linda.

LINDA. Just try to relax, dear. You make
40 mountains out of molehills.

WILLY. I won't fight with him any more. If he wants to go back to Texas, let him go.

LINDA. He'll find his way.

WILLY. Sure. Certain men just don't get
45 started till later in life. Like Thomas Edison, I think. Or B. F. Goodrich. One of them was deaf. [He starts for the bedroom doorway.] I'll put my money on Biff.

LINDA. And Willy—if it's warm Sunday we'll drive in the country. And we'll open the wind- 50 shield, and take lunch.

WILLY. No, the windshields don't open on the new cars.

LINDA. But you opened it today.

WILLY. Me? I didn't. [He stops.] Now isn't 55 that peculiar! Isn't that remarkable—[He breaks off in amazement and fright as the flute is heard distantly.]

LINDA. What, darling?

WILLY. That is the most remarkable thing. 60

LINDA. What, dear?

WILLY. I was thinking of the Chevvy. [Slight pause.] Nineteen twenty-eight . . . when I had that red Chevvy—[Breaks off.] That funny? I coulda sworn I was driving that Chevvy today. 65

LINDA. Well, that's nothing. Something must've reminded you.

WILLY. Remarkable. Ts. Remember those days? The way Biff used to simonize that car? The dealer refused to believe there was eighty 70 thousand miles on it. [He shakes his head.] Heh! [To LINDA.] Close your eyes, I'll be right up. [He walks out of the bedroom.]

HAPPY [to BIFF]. Jesus, maybe he smashed up the car again! 75

LINDA [calling after WILLY]. Be careful on the stairs, dear! The cheese is on the middle shelf! [She turns, goes over to the bed, takes his jacket, and goes out of the bedroom.]

[Light has risen on the boys' room. Unseen, 80 WILLY is heard talking to himself, "Eighty thousand miles," and a little laugh. BIFF gets out of bed, comes downstage a bit, and stands attentively. BIFF is two years older than his brother HAPPY, well built, but in these days 85 bears a worn air and seems less self-assured. He has succeeded less, and his dreams are stronger and less acceptable than HAPPY's. HAPPY is tall, powerfully made. Sexuality is like a visible color on him, or a scent that many 90 women have discovered. He, like his brother, is lost, but in a different way, for he has never allowed himself to turn his face toward defeat and is thus more confused and hard-skinned, although seemingly more content.] 95

HAPPY [getting out of bed]. He's going to

get his license taken away if he keeps that up. I'm getting nervous about him, y'know, Biff?

BIFF. His eyes are going.

HAPPY. No, I've driven with him. He sees all right. He just doesn't keep his mind on it. I drove into the city with him last week. He stops at a green light and then it turns red and he goes. [*He laughs.*]

BIFF. Maybe he's color-blind.

HAPPY: Pop? Why, he's got the finest eye for color in the business. You know that.

BIFF [*sitting down on his bed*]. I'm going to sleep.

HAPPY. You're not still sour on Dad, are you, Biff?

BIFF. He's all right, I guess.

WILLY [*underneath them in the living-room*]. Yes, sir, eighty thousand miles—eighty-two thousand!

BIFF. You smoking?

HAPPY [*holding out a pack of cigarettes*]. Want one?

BIFF [*taking a cigarette*]. I can never sleep when I smell it.

WILLY. What a simonizing job, heh!

HAPPY [*with deep sentiment*]. Funny, Biff, y'know? Us sleeping in here again? The old beds. [*He pats his bed affectionately.*] All the talk that went across those two beds, huh? Our whole lives.

BIFF. Yeah. Lotta dreams and plans.

HAPPY [*with a deep and masculine laugh*]. About five hundred women would like to know what was said in this room.

[*They share a soft laugh.*]

BIFF. Remember that big Betsy something—what the hell was her name—over on Bushwick Avenue?

HAPPY [*combing his hair*]. With the collie dog!

BIFF. That's the one. I got you in there, remember?

HAPPY. Yeah, that was my first time—I think. Boy, there was a pig! [*They laugh, almost crudely.*] You taught me everything I know about women. Don't forget that.

BIFF. I bet you forgot how bashful you used to be. Especially with girls.

HAPPY. Oh, I still am, Biff.

BIFF. Oh, go on.

HAPPY. I just control it, that's all. I think I got less bashful and you got more so. What happened, Biff? Where's the old humor, the old confidence? [*He shakes* BIFF's *knee.* BIFF *gets up and moves restlessly about the room.*] What's the matter?

BIFF. Why does Dad mock me all the time?

HAPPY. He's not mocking you, he—

BIFF. Everything I say there's a twist of mockery on his face. I can't get near him.

HAPPY. He just wants you to make good, that's all. I wanted to talk to you about Dad for a long time, Biff. Something's—happening to him. He—talks to himself.

BIFF. I noticed that this morning. But he always mumbled.

HAPPY. But not so noticeable. It got so embarrassing I sent him to Florida. And you know something? Most of the time he's talking to you.

BIFF. What's he say about me?

HAPPY. I can't make it out.

BIFF. What's he say about me?

HAPPY. I think the fact that you're not settled, that you're still kind of up in the air . . .

BIFF. There's one or two other things depressing him, Happy.

HAPPY. What do you mean?

BIFF. Never mind. Just don't lay it all to me.

HAPPY. But I think if you got started—I mean—is there any future for you out there?

BIFF. I tell ya, Hap, I don't know what the future is. I don't know—what I'm supposed to want.

HAPPY. What do you mean?

BIFF. Well, I spent six or seven years after high school trying to work myself up. Shipping clerk, salesman, business of one kind or another. And it's a measly manner of existence. To get on that subway on the hot mornings in summer. To devote your whole life to keeping stock, or making phone calls, or selling or buying. To suffer fifty weeks of the year for the sake of a two-week vacation, when all you really desire is to be outdoors, with your shirt off. And always to have to get ahead of the next fella. And still—that's how you build a future.

HAPPY. Well, you really enjoy it on a farm? Are you content out there?

5   BIFF [*with rising agitation*]. Hap, I've had twenty or thirty different kinds of job since I left home before the war, and it always turns out the same. I just realized it lately. In Nebraska when I herded cattle, and the Dakotas,
10 and Arizona, and now in Texas. It's why I came home now, I guess, because I realized it. This farm I work on, it's spring there now, see? And they've got about fifteen new colts. There's nothing more inspiring or—beautiful
15 than the sight of a mare and a new colt. And it's cool there now, see? Texas is cool now, and it's spring. And whenever spring comes to where I am, I suddenly get the feeling, my God, I'm not gettin' anywhere. What the hell
20 am I doing, playing around with horses, twenty-eight dollars a week! I'm thirty-four years old, I oughta be makin' my future. That's when I come running home. And now, I get here, and I don't know what to do with my-
25 self. [*After a pause.*] I've always made a point of not wasting my life, and everytime I come back here I know that all I've done is to waste my life.

HAPPY. You're a poet, you know that, Biff?
30 You're a—you're an idealist!

BIFF. No, I'm mixed up very bad. Maybe I oughta get married. Maybe I oughta get stuck into something. Maybe that's my trouble. I'm like a boy. I'm not married, I'm not in business,
35 I just—I'm like a boy. Are you content, Hap? You're a success, aren't you? Are you content?

HAPPY. Hell, no!

BIFF. Why? You're making money, aren't you?
40 HAPPY [*moving about with energy, expressiveness*]. All I can do now is wait for the merchandise manager to die. And suppose I get to be merchandise manager? He's a good friend of mine, and he just built a terrific estate on
45 Long Island. And he lived there about two months and sold it, and now he's building another one. He can't enjoy it once it's finished. And I know that's just what I would do. I don't

know what the hell I'm workin' for. Sometimes I sit in my apartment—all alone. And I think   50 of the rent I'm paying. And it's crazy. But then, it's what I always wanted. My own apartment, a car, and plenty of women. And still, goddammit, I'm lonely.

BIFF [*with enthusiasm*]. Listen, why don't   55 you come out West with me?

HAPPY. You and I, heh?

BIFF. Sure, maybe we could buy a ranch. Raise cattle, use our muscles. Men built like we are should be working out in the open.   60

HAPPY [*avidly*]. The Loman Brothers, heh?

BIFF [*with vast affection*]. Sure, we'd be known all over the counties!

HAPPY [*enthralled*]. That's what I dream about, Biff. Sometimes I want to just rip my   65 clothes off in the middle of the store and outbox that goddam merchandise manager. I mean I can outbox, outrun, and outlift anybody in that store, and I have to take orders from those common, petty sons-of-bitches till   70 I can't stand it any more.

BIFF. I'm tellin' you, kid, if you were with me I'd be happy out there.

HAPPY [*enthused*]. See, Biff, everybody around me is so false that I'm constantly   75 lowering my ideals . . .

BIFF. Baby, together we'd stand up for one another, we'd have someone to trust.

HAPPY. If I were around you—

BIFF. Hap, the trouble is we weren't brought   80 up to grub for money. I don't know how to do it.

HAPPY. Neither can I!

BIFF. Then let's go!

HAPPY. The only thing is—what can you   85 make out there?

BIFF. But look at your friend. Builds an estate and then hasn't the peace of mind to live in it.

HAPPY. Yeah, but when he walks into the   90 store the waves part in front of him. That's fifty-two thousand dollars a year coming through the revolving door, and I got more in my pinky finger than he's got in his head.

BIFF. Yeah, but you just said—   95

HAPPY. I gotta show some of those pompous,

self-important executives over there that Hap
Loman can make the grade. I want to walk
into the store the way he walks in. Then I'll
go with you, Biff. We'll be together yet, I
5 swear. But take those two we had tonight. Now
weren't they gorgeous creatures?

BIFF. Yeah, yeah, most gorgeous I've had in
years.

HAPPY. I get that any time I want, Biff.
10 Whenever I feel disgusted. The only trouble
is, it gets like bowling or something. I just
keep knockin' them over and it doesn't mean
anything. You still run around a lot?

BIFF. Naa. I'd like to find a girl—steady,
15 somebody with substance.

HAPPY. That's what I long for.

BIFF. Go on! You'd never come home.

HAPPY. I would! Somebody with character,
with resistance! Like Mom, y'know? You're
20 gonna call me a bastard when I tell you this.
That girl Charlotte I was with tonight is engaged to be married in five weeks. [*He tries
on his new hat.*]

BIFF. No kiddin'!

25 HAPPY. Sure, the guy's in line for the vice-
presidency of the store. I don't know what
gets into me, maybe I just have an over-
developed sense of competition or something,
but I went and ruined her, and furthermore I
30 can't get rid of her. And he's the third executive I've done that to. Isn't that a crummy
characteristic? And to top it all, I go to their
weddings! [*Indignantly, but laughing.*] Like
I'm not supposed to take bribes. Manufacturers
35 offer me a hundred-dollar bill now and then
to throw an order their way. You know how
honest I am, but it's like this girl, see. I hate
myself for it. Because I don't want the girl,
and, still, I take it and—I love it!

40 BIFF. Let's go to sleep.

HAPPY. I guess we didn't settle anything, heh?

BIFF. I just got one idea that I think I'm
going to try.

HAPPY. What's that?

45 BIFF. Remember Bill Oliver?

HAPPY. Sure, Oliver is very big now. You
want to work for him again?

BIFF. No, but when I quit he said something

to me. He put his arm on my shoulder, and he
said, "Biff, if you ever need anything, come to 50
me."

HAPPY. I remember that. That sounds good.

BIFF. I think I'll go to see him. If I could
get ten thousand or even seven or eight thousand dollars I could buy a beautiful ranch. 55

HAPPY. I bet he'd back you. 'Cause he
thought highly of you, Biff. I mean, they all
do. You're well liked, Biff. That's why I say to
come back here, and we both have the apartment. And I'm tellin' you, Biff, any babe you 60
want . . .

BIFF. No, with a ranch I could do the work
I like and still be something. I just wonder
though. I wonder if Oliver still thinks I stole
that carton of basketballs. 65

HAPPY. Oh, he probably forgot that long
ago. It's almost ten years. You're too sensitive.
Anyway, he didn't really fire you.

BIFF. Well, I think he was going to. I think
that's why I quit. I was never sure whether he 70
knew or not. I know he thought the world of
me, though. I was the only one he'd let lock
up the place.

WILLY [*below*]. You gonna wash the engine,
Biff? 75

HAPPY. Shh!

[BIFF *looks at* HAPPY, *who is gazing down,
listening.* WILLY *is mumbling in the parlor.*]

HAPPY. You hear that?

[*They listen.* WILLY *laughs warmly.*] 80

BIFF [*growing angry*]. Doesn't he know
Mom can hear that?

WILLY. Don't get your sweater dirty, Biff!

[*A look of pain crosses* BIFF's *face.*]

HAPPY. Isn't that terrible? Don't leave again, 85
will you? You'll find a job here. You gotta
stick around. I don't know what to do about
him, it's getting embarrassing.

WILLY. What a simonizing job!

BIFF. Mom's hearing that! 90

WILLY. No kiddin', Biff, you got a date?
Wonderful!

HAPPY. Go on to sleep. But talk to him in the
morning, will you?

BIFF [*reluctantly getting into bed*]. With her 95
in the house. Brother!

HAPPY [*getting into bed*]. I wish you'd have a good talk with him.

[*The light on their room begins to fade.*]

BIFF [*to himself in bed*]. That selfish, stupid . . .

HAPPY. Sh . . . Sleep, Biff.

[*Their light is out. Well before they have finished speaking, WILLY's form is dimly seen below in the darkened kitchen. He opens the refrigerator, searches in there, and takes out a bottle of milk. The apartment houses are fading out, and the entire house and surroundings become covered with leaves. Music insinuates itself as the leaves appear.*]

WILLY. Just wanna be careful with those girls, Biff, that's all. Don't make any promises. No promises of any kind. Because a girl, y'know, they always believe what you tell 'em, and you're very young, Biff, you're too young to be talking seriously to girls.

[*Light rises on the kitchen. WILLY, talking, shuts the refrigerator door and comes downstage to the kitchen table. He pours milk into a glass. He is totally immersed in himself, smiling faintly.*]

WILLY. Too young entirely, Biff. You want to watch your schooling first. Then when you're all set, there'll be plenty of girls for a boy like you. [*He smiles broadly at a kitchen chair.*] That so? The girls pay for you? [*He laughs.*] Boy, you must really be makin' a hit.

[*WILLY is gradually addressing—physically—a point off-stage, speaking through the wall of the kitchen, and his voice has been rising in volume to that of a normal conversation.*]

WILLY. I been wondering why you polish the car so careful. Ha! Don't leave the hubcaps, boys. Get the chamois to the hubcaps. Happy, use newspaper on the windows, it's the easiest thing. Show him how to do it, Biff! You see, Happy? Pad it up, use it like a pad. That's it, that's it, good work. You're doin' all right, Hap. [*He pauses, then nods in approbation for a few seconds, then looks upward.*] Biff, first thing we gotta do when we get time is clip that big branch over the house. Afraid it's gonna fall in a storm and hit the roof. Tell you what. We get a rope and sling her around, and then we climb up there with a couple of saws and take her down. Soon as you finish the car, boys, I wanna see ya. I got a surprise for you, boys.

BIFF [*offstage*]. Whatta ya got, Dad?

WILLY. No, you finish first. Never leave a job till you're finished—remember that. [*Looking toward the "big trees."*] Biff, up in Albany I saw a beautiful hammock. I think I'll buy it next trip, and we'll hang it right between those two elms. Wouldn't that be something? Just swingin' there under those branches. Boy, that would be . . .

[YOUNG BIFF *and* YOUNG HAPPY *appear from the direction* WILLY *was addressing.* HAPPY *carries rags and a pail of water.* BIFF, *wearing a sweater with a block "S," carries a football.*]

BIFF [*pointing in the direction of the car offstage*]. How's that, Pop, professional?

WILLY. Terrific. Terrific job, boys. Good work, Biff.

HAPPY. Where's the surprise, Pop?

WILLY. In the back seat of the car.

HAPPY. Boy! [*He runs off.*]

BIFF. What is it, Dad? Tell me, what'd you buy?

WILLY [*laughing, cuffs him*]. Never mind, something I want you to have.

BIFF [*turns and starts off*]. What is it, Hap?

HAPPY [*offstage*]. It's a punching bag!

BIFF. Oh, Pop!

WILLY. It's got Gene Tunney's signature on it! [HAPPY *runs onstage with a punching bag.*]

BIFF. Gee, how'd you know we wanted a punching bag?

WILLY. Well, it's the finest thing for the timing.

HAPPY [*lies down on his back and pedals with his feet*]. I'm losing weight, you notice, Pop?

WILLY [*to* HAPPY]. Jumping rope is good too.

BIFF. Did you see the new football I got?

WILLY [*examining the ball*]. Where'd you get a new ball?

BIFF. The coach told me to practice my passing.

WILLY. That so? And he gave you the ball, heh?

BIFF. Well, I borrowed it from the locker room. [*He laughs confidentially.*]

WILLY [*laughing with him at the theft*]. I want you to return that.

5 HAPPY. I told you he wouldn't like it!

BIFF [*angrily*]. Well, I'm bringing it back!

WILLY [*stopping the incipient argument, to* HAPPY]. Sure, he's gotta practice with a regulation ball, doesn't he? [*To* BIFF.] Coach'll 10 probably congratulate you on your initiative!

BIFF. Oh, he keeps congratulating my initiative all the time, Pop.

WILLY. That's because he likes you. If somebody else took that ball there'd be an uproar. 15 So what's the report, boys, what's the report?

BIFF. Where'd you go this time, Dad? Gee we were lonesome for you.

WILLY [*pleased, puts an arm around each boy and they come down to the apron*]. Lone-20 some, heh?

BIFF. Missed you every minute.

WILLY. Don't say? Tell you a secret, boys. Don't breathe it to a soul. Someday I'll have my own business, and I'll never have to leave 25 home any more.

HAPPY. Like Uncle Charley, heh?

WILLY. Bigger than Uncle Charley! Because Charley is not—liked. He's liked, but he's not —well liked.

30 BIFF. Where'd you go this time, Dad?

WILLY. Well, I got on the road, and I went north to Providence. Met the Mayor.

BIFF. The Mayor of Providence!

WILLY. He was sitting in the hotel lobby.

35 BIFF. What'd he say?

WILLY. He said, "Morning!" And I said, "You got a fine city here, Mayor." And then he had coffee with me. And then I went to Waterbury. Waterbury is a fine city. Big clock 40 city, the famous Waterbury clock. Sold a nice bill there. And then Boston—Boston is the cradle of the Revolution. A fine city. And a couple of other towns in Mass., and on to Portland and Bangor and straight home!

45 BIFF. Gee, I'd love to go with you sometime, Dad.

WILLY. Soon as summer comes.

HAPPY. Promise?

WILLY. You and Hap and I, and I'll show you all the towns. America is full of beautiful 50 towns and fine, upstanding people. And they know me, boys, they know me up and down New England. The finest people. And when I bring you fellas up, there'll be open sesame for all of us, 'cause one thing, boys: I have friends. 55 I can park my car in any street in New England, and the cops protect it like their own. This summer, heh?

BIFF and HAPPY [*together*]. Yeah! You bet!

WILLY. We'll take our bathing-suits. 60

HAPPY. We'll carry your bags, Pop!

WILLY. Oh, won't that be something! Me comin' into the Boston stores with you boys carryin' my bags. What a sensation!

[BIFF *is prancing around, practicing passing* 65 *the ball.*]

WILLY. You nervous, Biff, about the game?

BIFF. Not if you're gonna be there.

WILLY. What do they say about you in school, now that they made you captain? 70

HAPPY. There's a crowd of girls behind him every time the classes change.

BIFF [*taking* WILLY's *hand*]. This Saturday, Pop, this Saturday—just for you, I'm going to break through for a touchdown. 75

HAPPY. You're supposed to pass.

BIFF. I'm takin' one play for Pop. You watch me, Pop, and when I take off my helmet, that means I'm breakin' out. Then watch me crash through that line! 80

WILLY [*kisses* BIFF]. Oh, wait'll I tell this in Boston!

[BERNARD *enters in knickers. He is younger than* BIFF, *earnest and loyal, a worried boy.*]

BERNARD. Biff, where are you? You're sup-85 posed to study with me today.

WILLY. Hey, looka Bernard. What're you lookin' so anemic about, Bernard?

BERNARD. He's gotta study, Uncle Willy. He's got Regents next week. 90

HAPPY [*tauntingly, spinning* BERNARD *around*]. Let's box, Bernard!

BERNARD. Biff! [*He gets away from* HAPPY.] Listen, Biff, I heard Mr. Birnbaum say that if you don't start studyin' math he's gonna flunk 95 you, and you won't graduate. I heard him!

WILLY. You better study with him, Biff. Go ahead now.

BERNARD. I heard him!

BIFF. Oh, Pop, you didn't see my sneakers!

5 [*He holds up a foot for* WILLY *to look at.*]

WILLY. Hey, that's a beautiful job of printing!

BERNARD [*wiping his glasses*]. Just because he printed University of Virginia on his

10 sneakers doesn't mean they've got to graduate him, Uncle Willy!

WILLY [*angrily*]. What're you talking about? With scholarships to three universities they're gonna flunk him?

15 BERNARD. But I heard Mr. Birnbaum say—

WILLY. Don't be a pest, Bernard! [*To his boys.*] What an anemic!

BERNARD. Okay, I'm waiting for you in my house, Biff.

20 [BERNARD *goes off. The* LOMANS *laugh.*]

WILLY. Bernard is not well liked, is he?

BIFF. He's liked, but he's not well liked.

HAPPY. That's right, Pop.

WILLY. That's just what I mean. Bernard can

25 get the best marks in school, y'understand, but when he gets out in the business world, y'understand, you are going to be five times ahead of him. That's why I thank Almighty God you're both built like Adonises. Because

30 the man who makes an appearance in the business world, the man who creates personal interest, is the man who gets ahead. Be liked and you will never want. You take me, for instance. I never have to wait in line to see

35 a buyer. "Willy Loman is here!" That's all they have to know, and I go right through.

BIFF. Did you knock them dead, Pop?

WILLY. Knocked 'em cold in Providence, slaughtered 'em in Boston.

40 HAPPY [*on his back, pedaling again*]. I'm losing weight, you notice, Pop?

[LINDA *enters, as of old, a ribbon in her hair, carrying a basket of washing.*]

LINDA [*with youthful energy*]. Hello, dear!

45 WILLY. Sweetheart!

LINDA. How'd the Chevvy run?

WILLY. Chevrolet, Linda, is the greatest car ever built. [*To the boys.*] Since when did you let your mother carry wash up the stairs?

BIFF. Grab hold there, boy! 50

HAPPY. Where to, Mom?

LINDA. Hang them up on the line. And you better go down to your friends, Biff. The cellar is full of boys. They don't know what to do with themselves. 55

BIFF. Ah, when Pop comes home they can wait!

WILLY [*laughs appreciatively*]. You better go down and tell them what to do, Biff.

BIFF. I think I'll have them sweep out the 60 furnace room.

WILLY. Good work, Biff.

BIFF [*goes through wall-line of kitchen to doorway at back and calls down*]. Fellas! Everybody sweep out the furnace room! I'll 65 be right down!

VOICES. All right! Okay, Biff.

BIFF. George and Sam and Frank, come out back! We're hangin' up the wash! Come on, Hap, on the double! [*He and* HAPPY *carry out* 70 *the basket.*]

LINDA. The way they obey him!

WILLY. Well, that's training, the training. I'm tellin' you, I was sellin' thousands and thousands, but I had to come home. 75

LINDA. Oh, the whole block'll be at that game. Did you sell anything?

WILLY. I did five hundred gross in Providence and seven hundred gross in Boston.

LINDA. No! Wait a minute, I've got a pencil. 80 [*She pulls pencil and paper out of her apron pocket.*] That makes your commission. . . . Two hundred—my God! Two hundred and twelve dollars!

WILLY. Well, I didn't figure it yet, but . . . 85

LINDA. How much did you do?

WILLY. Well, I—I did—about a hundred and eighty gross in Providence. Well, no—it came to—roughly two hundred gross on the whole trip. 90

LINDA [*without hesitation*]. Two hundred gross. That's . . . [*She figures.*]

WILLY. The trouble was that three of the stores were half-closed for inventory in Boston. Otherwise I woulda broke records. 95

LINDA. Well, it makes seventy dollars and some pennies. That's very good.

WILLY. What do we owe?

LINDA. Well, on the first there's sixteen dollars on the refrigerator—

WILLY. Why sixteen?

LINDA. Well, the fan belt broke, so it was a
5 dollar eighty.

WILLY. But it's brand new.

LINDA. Well, the man said that's the way it is. Till they work themselves in, y'know.

[*They move through the wall-line into the*
10 *kitchen.*]

WILLY. I hope we didn't get stuck on that machine.

LINDA. They got the biggest ads of any of them!

15 WILLY. I know, it's a fine machine. What else?

LINDA. Well, there's nine-sixty for the washing-machine. And for the vacuum cleaner there's three and a half due on the fifteenth.
20 Then the roof, you got twenty-one dollars remaining.

WILLY. It don't leak, does it?

LINDA. No, they did a wonderful job. Then you owe Frank for the carburetor.

25 WILLY. I'm not going to pay that man! That goddam Chevrolet, they ought to prohibit the manufacture of that car!

LINDA. Well, you owe him three and a half. And odds and ends, comes to around a hun-
30 dred and twenty dollars by the fifteenth.

WILLY. A hundred and twenty dollars! My God, if business don't pick up I don't know what I'm gonna do!

LINDA. Well, next week you'll do better.

35 WILLY. Oh, I'll knock 'em dead next week. I'll go to Hartford. I'm very well liked in Hartford. You know, the trouble is, Linda, people don't seem to take to me.

[*They move on to the forestage.*]

40 LINDA. Oh, don't be foolish.

WILLY. I know it when I walk in. They seem to laugh at me.

LINDA. Why? Why would they laugh at you? Don't talk that way, Willy.

45 [WILLY *moves to the edge of the stage.* LINDA *goes into the kitchen and starts to darn stockings.*]

WILLY. I don't know the reason for it, but they just pass me by. I'm not noticed.

LINDA. But you're doing wonderful, dear.
50 You're making seventy to a hundred dollars a week.

WILLY. But I gotta be at it ten, twelve hours a day. Other men—I don't know—they do it easier. I don't know why—I can't stop myself
55 —I talk too much. A man oughta come in with a few words. One thing about Charley. He's a man of few words, and they respect him.

LINDA. You don't talk too much, you're just lively.
60

WILLY [*smiling*]. Well, I figure, what the hell, life is short, a couple of jokes. [*To himself.*] I joke too much! [*The smile goes.*]

LINDA. Why? You're—

WILLY. I'm fat. I'm—very foolish to look at,
65 Linda. I didn't tell you, but Christmas-time I happened to be calling on F. H. Stewarts, and a salesman I know, as I was going in to see the buyer I heard him say something about—walrus. And I—I cracked him right across the
70 face. I won't take that. I simply will not take that. But they laugh at me. I know that.

LINDA. Darling . . .

WILLY. I gotta overcome it. I know I gotta overcome it. I'm not dressing to advantage,
75 maybe.

LINDA. Willy, darling, you're the handsomest man in the world—

WILLY. Oh, no, Linda.

LINDA. To me you are. [*Slight pause.*] The
80 handsomest.

[*From the darkness is heard the laughter of a woman.* WILLY *doesn't turn to it, but it continues through* LINDA'S *lines.*]

LINDA. And the boys, Willy. Few men are
85 idolized by their children the way you are.

[*Music is heard as behind a scrim, to the left of the house, the* WOMAN, *dimly seen, is dressing.*]

WILLY [*with great feeling*]. You're the best
90 there is, Linda, you're a pal, you know that? On the road—on the road I want to grab you sometimes and just kiss the life outa you.

[*The laughter is loud now, and he moves into a brightening area at the left, where the*
95 WOMAN *has come from behind the scrim and is standing, putting on her hat, looking into a "mirror," and laughing.*]

WILLY. 'Cause I get so lonely—especially when business is bad and there's nobody to talk to. I get the feeling that I'll never sell anything again, that I won't make a living for you, or a business, a business for the boys. [*He talks through the* WOMAN's *subsiding laughter. The* WOMAN *primps at the "mirror."*] There's so much I want to make for—

THE WOMAN. Me? You didn't make me, Willy. I picked you.

WILLY [*pleased*]. You picked me?

THE WOMAN [*who is quite proper-looking, Willy's age*]. I did. I've been sitting at that desk watching all the salesmen go by, day in, day out. But you've got such a sense of humor, and we do have such a good time together, don't we?

WILLY. Sure, sure. [*He takes her in his arms.*] Why do you have to go now?

THE WOMAN. It's two o'clock . . .

WILLY. No, come on in! [*He pulls her.*]

THE WOMAN. . . . my sisters'll be scandalized. When'll you be back?

WILLY. Oh, two weeks about. Will you come up again?

THE WOMAN. Sure thing. You do make me laugh. It's good for me. [*She squeezes his arm, kisses him.*] And I think you're a wonderful man.

WILLY. You picked me, heh?

THE WOMAN. Sure. Because you're so sweet. And such a kidder.

WILLY. Well, I'll see you next time I'm in Boston.

THE WOMAN. I'll put you right through to the buyers.

WILLY [*slapping her bottom*]. Right. Well, bottoms up!

THE WOMAN [*slaps him gently and laughs*]. You just kill me, Willy. [*He suddenly grabs her and kisses her roughly.*] You kill me. And thanks for the stockings. I love a lot of stockings. Well, good night.

WILLY. Good night. And keep your pores open!

THE WOMAN. Oh, Willy!

[*The* WOMAN *bursts out laughing, and* LINDA's *laughter blends in* The WOMAN *disappears into the dark. Now the area at the kitchen table brightens.* LINDA *is sitting where she was at the kitchen table, but now is mending a pair of her silk stockings.*]

LINDA. You are, Willy. The handsomest man. You've got no reason to feel that—

WILLY [*coming out of the* WOMAN's *dimming area and going over to* LINDA]. I'll make it all up to you, Linda, I'll—

LINDA. There's nothing to make up, dear. You're doing fine, better than—

WILLY [*noticing her mending*]. What's that?

LINDA. Just mending my stockings. They're so expensive—

WILLY [*angrily taking them from her*]. I won't have you mending stockings in this house! Now throw them out!

[LINDA *puts the stockings in her pocket.*]

BERNARD [*entering on the run*]. Where is he? If he doesn't study!

WILLY [*moving to the forestage, with great agitation*]. You'll give him the answers!

BERNARD. I do, but I can't on a Regents! That's a state exam! They're liable to arrest me!

WILLY. Where is he? I'll whip him, I'll whip him!

LINDA. And he'd better give back that football, Willy, it's not nice.

WILLY. Biff! Where is he? Why is he taking everything?

LINDA. He's too rough with the girls, Willy. All the mothers are afraid of him!

WILLY. I'll whip him!

BERNARD. He's driving the car without a license!

[*The* WOMAN's *laugh is heard.*]

WILLY. Shut up!

LINDA. All the mothers—

WILLY. Shut up!

BERNARD [*backing quietly away and out*]. Mr. Birnbaum says he's stuck up.

WILLY. Get outa here!

BERNARD. If he doesn't buckle down he'll flunk math! [*He goes off.*]

LINDA. He's right, Willy, you've gotta—

WILLY [*exploding at her*]. There's nothing the matter with him! You want him to be a worm like Bernard? He's got spirit, personality . . .

[*As he speaks* LINDA, *almost in tears, exits into the livingroom.* WILLY *is alone in the kitchen, writing and staring. The leaves are gone. It is night again, and the apartment houses look down from behind.*]

WILLY. Loaded with it. Loaded! What is he stealing? He's giving it back, isn't he? Why is he stealing? What did I tell him? I never in my life told him anything but decent things.

[HAPPY *in pajamas has come down the stairs;* WILLY *suddenly becomes aware of* HAPPY'S *presence.*]

HAPPY. Let's go now, come on.

WILLY [*sitting down at the kitchen table*]. Huh! Why did she have to wax the floors herself? Everytime she waxes the floors she keels over. She knows that!

HAPPY. Shh! Take it easy. What brought you back tonight?

WILLY. I got an awful scare. Nearly hit a kid in Yonkers. God! Why didn't I go to Alaska with my brother Ben that time! Ben! That man was a genius, that man was success incarnate! What a mistake! He begged me to go.

HAPPY. Well, there's no use in—

WILLY. You guys! There was a man started with the clothes on his back and ended up with diamond mines!

HAPPY. Boy, someday I'd like to know how he did it.

WILLY. What's the mystery? The man knew what he wanted and went out and got it! Walked into a jungle, and comes out, the age of twenty-one, and he's rich! The world is an oyster, but you don't crack it open on a mattress!

HAPPY. Pop, I told you I'm gonna retire you for life.

WILLY. You'll retire me for life on seventy goddam dollars a week? And your women and your car and your apartment, and you'll retire me for life! Christ's sake, I couldn't get past Yonkers today! Where are you guys, where are you? The woods are burning! I can't drive a car!

[CHARLEY *has appeared in the doorway. He is a large man, slow of speech, laconic, immovable. In all he says, despite what he says, there is pity, and now, trepidation. He has a robe over pajamas, slippers on his feet. He enters the kitchen.*]

CHARLEY. Everything all right?

HAPPY. Yeah, Charley, everything's . . .

WILLY. What's the matter?

CHARLEY. I heard some noise. I thought something happened. Can't we do something about the walls? You sneeze in here, and in my house hats blow off.

HAPPY. Let's go to bed, Dad. Come on.

[CHARLEY *signals to* HAPPY *to go.*]

WILLY. You go ahead, I'm not tired at the moment.

HAPPY [*to* WILLY]. Take it easy, huh? [*He exits.*]

WILLY. What are you doin' up?

CHARLEY [*sitting down at the kitchen table opposite* WILLY]. Couldn't sleep good. I had a heartburn.

WILLY. Well, you don't know how to eat.

CHARLEY. I eat with my mouth.

WILLY. No, you're ignorant. You gotta know about vitamins and things like that.

CHARLEY. Come on, let's shoot. Tire you out a little.

WILLY [*hesitantly*]. All right. You got cards?

CHARLEY [*taking a deck from his pocket*]. Yeah, I got them. Someplace. What is it with those vitamins?

WILLY [*dealing*]. They build up your bones. Chemistry.

CHARLEY. Yeah, but there's no bones in a heartburn.

WILLY. What are you talkin' about? Do you know the first thing about it?

CHARLEY. Don't get insulted.

WILLY. Don't talk about something you don't know anything about.

[*They are playing. Pause.*]

CHARLEY. What're you doin' home?

WILLY. A little trouble with the car.

CHARLEY. Oh. [*Pause.*] I'd like to take a trip to California.

WILLY. Don't say.

CHARLEY. You want a job?

WILLY. I got a job, I told you that. [*After a slight pause.*] What the hell are you offering me a job for?

CHARLEY. Don't get insulted.

5   WILLY. Don't insult me.

CHARLEY. I don't see no sense in it. You don't have to go on this way.

WILLY. I got a good job. [*Slight pause.*] What do you keep comin' in here for?

10   CHARLEY. You want me to go?

WILLY [*after a pause, withering*]. I can't understand it. He's going back to Texas again. What the hell is that?

CHARLEY. Let him go.

15   WILLY. I got nothin' to give him, Charley, I'm clean, I'm clean.

CHARLEY. He won't starve. None of them starve. Forget about him.

WILLY. Then what have I got to remember?

20   CHARLEY. You take it too hard. To hell with it. When a deposit bottle is broken you don't get your nickel back.

WILLY. That's easy enough for you to say.

CHARLEY. That ain't easy for me to say.

25   WILLY. Did you see the ceiling I put up in the living room?

CHARLEY. Yeah, that's a piece of work. To put up a ceiling is a mystery to me. How do you do it?

30   WILLY. What's the difference?

CHARLEY. Well, talk about it.

WILLY. You gonna put up a ceiling?

CHARLEY. How could I put up a ceiling?

WILLY. Then what the hell are you bother-

35   ing me for?

CHARLEY. You're insulted again.

WILLY. A man who can't handle tools is not a man. You're disgusting.

CHARLEY. Don't call me disgusting, Willy.

40   [UNCLE BEN, *carrying a valise and an umbrella, enters the forestage from around the right corner of the house. He is a stolid man, in his sixties, with a mustache and an authoritative air. He is utterly certain of his destiny,*

45   *and there is an aura of far places about him. He enters exactly as* WILLY *speaks.*]

WILLY. I'm getting awfully tired, Ben.

[BEN's *music is heard.* BEN *looks around at everything.*]

CHARLEY. Good, keep playing; you'll sleep   50
better. Did you call me Ben?

[BEN *looks at his watch.*]

WILLY. That's funny. For a second there you reminded me of my brother Ben.

BEN. I only have a few minutes. [*He strolls,*   55
inspecting the place. WILLY *and* CHARLEY *continue playing.*]

CHARLEY. You never heard from him again, heh? Since that time?

WILLY. Didn't Linda tell you? Couple of   60
weeks ago we got a letter from his wife in Africa. He died.

CHARLEY. That so.

BEN [*chuckling*]. So this is Brooklyn, eh?

CHARLEY. Maybe you're in for some of his   65
money.

WILLY. Naa, he had seven sons. There's just one opportunity I had with that man . . .

BEN. I must take a train, William. There are several properties I'm looking at in Alaska.   70

WILLY. Sure, sure! If I'd gone with him to Alaska that time, everything would've been totally different.

CHARLEY. Go on, you'd froze to death up there.   75

WILLY. What're you talking about?

BEN. Opportunity is tremendous in Alaska, William. Surprised you're not up there.

WILLY. Sure, tremendous.

CHARLEY. Heh?   80

WILLY. There was the only man I ever met who knew the answers.

CHARLEY. Who?

BEN. How are you all?

WILLY [*taking a pot, smiling*]. Fine, fine.   85

CHARLEY. Pretty sharp tonight.

BEN. Is Mother living with you?

WILLY. No, she died a long time ago.

CHARLEY. Who?

BEN. That's too bad. Fine specimen of a lady,   90
Mother.

WILLY [*to* CHARLEY]. Heh?

BEN. I'd hoped to see the old girl.

CHARLEY. Who died?

BEN. Heard anything from Father, have you?

WILLY [*unnerved*]. What do you mean, who died?

CHARLEY [*taking a pot*]. What're you talkin' about?

BEN [*looking at his watch*]. William, it's half past eight!

WILLY [*as though to dispel his confusion he angrily stops* CHARLEY's *hand*]. That's my build!

CHARLEY. I put the ace—

WILLY. If you don't know how to play the game I'm not gonna throw my money away on you!

CHARLEY [*rising*]. It was my ace, for God's sake!

WILLY. I'm through, I'm through!

BEN. When did Mother die?

WILLY. Long ago. Since the beginning you never knew how to play cards.

CHARLEY [*picks up the cards and goes to the door*]. All right! Next time I'll bring a deck with five aces.

WILLY. I don't play that kind of game!

CHARLEY [*turning to him*]. You ought to be ashamed of yourself!

WILLY. Yeah?

CHARLEY. Yeah! [*He goes out.*]

WILLY [*slamming the door after him*]. Ignoramus!

BEN [*as* WILLY *comes toward him through the wall-line of the kitchen*]. So you're William.

WILLY [*shaking* BEN's *hand*]. Ben! I've been waiting for you so long! What's the answer? How did you do it?

BEN. Oh, there's a story in that.

[LINDA *enters the forestage, as of old, carrying the wash basket.*]

LINDA. Is this Ben?

BEN [*gallantly*]. How do you do, my dear?

LINDA. Where've you been all these years? Willy's always wondered why you—

WILLY [*pulling* BEN *away from her impatiently*]. Where is Dad? Didn't you follow him? How did you get started?

BEN. Well, I don't know how much you remember.

WILLY. Well, I was just a baby, of course, only three or four years old—

BEN. Three years and eleven months.

WILLY. What a memory, Ben!

BEN. I have many enterprises, William, and I have never kept books.

WILLY. I remember I was sitting under the wagon in—was it Nebraska?

BEN. It was South Dakota, and I gave you a bunch of wild flowers.

WILLY. I remember you walking away down some open road.

BEN [*laughing*]. I was going to find Father in Alaska.

WILLY. Where is he?

BEN. At that age I had a very faulty view of geography, William. I discovered after a few days that I was heading due south, so instead of Alaska, I ended up in Africa.

LINDA. Africa!

WILLY. The Gold Coast!

BEN. Principally diamond mines.

LINDA. Diamond mines!

BEN. Yes, my dear. But I've only a few minutes—

WILLY. No! Boys! Boys! [YOUNG BIFF *and* HAPPY *appear.*] Listen to this. This is your Uncle Ben, a great man! Tell my boys, Ben!

BEN. Why boys, when I was seventeen I walked into the jungle, and when I was twenty-one I walked out. [*He laughs.*] And by God I was rich.

WILLY [*to the boys*]. You see what I been talking about? The greatest things can happen!

BEN [*glancing at his watch*]. I have an appointment in Ketchikan Tuesday week.

WILLY. No, Ben! Please tell about Dad. I want my boys to hear. I want them to know the kind of stock they spring from. All I remember is a man with a big beard, and I was in Mamma's lap, sitting around a fire, and some kind of high music.

BEN. His flute. He played the flute.

WILLY. Sure, the flute, that's right!

[*New music is heard, a high, rollicking tune.*]

BEN. Father was a very great and a very

wild-hearted man. We would start in Boston, and he'd toss the whole family into the wagon, and then he'd drive the team right across the country; through Ohio, and Indiana, Michigan,
5 Illinois, and all the Western states. And we'd stop in the towns and sell the flutes that he'd made on the way. Great inventor, Father. With one gadget he made more in a week than a man like you could make in a lifetime.

10 WILLY. That's just the way I'm bringing them up, Ben—rugged, well liked, all-around.

BEN. Yeah? [To BIFF.] Hit that, boy—hard as you can. [He pounds his stomach.]

BIFF. Oh, no, sir!

15 BEN [taking boxing stance]. Come on, get to me! [He laughs.]

WILLY. Go to it, Biff! Go ahead, show him!

BIFF. Okay! [He cocks his fists and starts in.]

20 LINDA [to WILLY]. Why must he fight, dear?

BEN [sparring with BIFF]. Good boy! Good boy!

WILLY. How's that, Ben, heh?

HAPPY. Give him the left, Biff!

25 LINDA. Why are you fighting?

BEN. Good boy! [Suddenly comes in, trips BIFF, and stands over him, the point of his umbrella poised over BIFF's eye.]

LINDA. Look out, Biff!

30 BIFF. Gee!

BEN [patting BIFF's knee]. Never fight fair with a stranger, boy. You'll never get out of the jungle that way. [Taking LINDA's hand and bowing.] It was an honor and a pleasure to
35 meet you, Linda.

LINDA [withdrawing her hand coldly, frightened]. Have a nice—trip.

BEN [to WILLY]. And good luck with your— what do you do?

40 WILLY. Selling.

BEN. Yes. Well . . . [He raises his hand in farewell to all.]

WILLY. No, Ben, I don't want you to think . . . [He takes BEN's arm to show him.] It's
45 Brooklyn, I know, but we hunt too.

BEN. Really, now.

WILLY. Oh, sure, there's snakes and rabbits

and—that's why I moved out here. Why, Biff can fell any one of these trees in no time! Boys!
Go right over to where they're building the 50 apartment house and get some sand. We're gonna rebuild the entire front stoop right now! Watch this, Ben!

BIFF. Yes, sir! On the double, Hap!

HAPPY [as he and BIFF run off]. I lost weight, 55 Pop, you notice?

[CHARLEY enters in knickers, even before the boys are gone.]

CHARLEY. Listen, if they steal any more from that building the watchman'll put the cops on 60 them!

LINDA [to WILLY]. Don't let Biff . . .

[BEN laughs lustily.]

WILLY. You shoulda seen the lumber they brought home last week. At least a dozen six- 65 by-tens worth all kinds a money.

CHARLEY. Listen, if that watchman—

WILLY. I gave them hell, understand. But I got a couple of fearless characters there.

CHARLEY. Willy, the jails are full of fearless 70 characters.

BEN [clapping WILLY on the back, with a laugh at CHARLEY]. And the stock exchange, friend!

WILLY [joining in BEN's laughter]. Where 75 are the rest of your pants?

CHARLEY. My wife bought them.

WILLY. Now all you need is a golf club and you can go upstairs and go to sleep. [To BEN.] Great athlete! Between him and his son Ber- 80 nard they can't hammer a nail!

BERNARD [rushing in]. The watchman's chasing Biff!

WILLY [angrily]. Shut up! He's not stealing anything! 85

LINDA [alarmed, hurrying off left]. Where is he? Biff, dear!

[She exits.]

WILLY [moving toward the left, away from BEN]. There's nothing wrong. What's the mat- 90 ter with you?

BEN. Nervy boy. Good!

WILLY [laughing]. Oh, nerves of iron, that Biff!

CHARLEY. Don't know what it is. My New England man comes back and he's bleedin', they murdered him up there.

WILLY. It's contacts, Charley, I got impor-5 tant contacts!

CHARLEY [*sarcastically*]. Glad to hear it, Willy. Come in later, we'll shoot a little casino. I'll take some of your Portland money. [*He laughs at* WILLY *and exits.*]

10 WILLY [*turning to* BEN]. Business is bad, it's murderous. But not for me, of course.

BEN. I'll stop by on my way back to Africa.

WILLY [*longingly*]. Can't you stay a few days? You're just what I need, Ben, because I 15 —I have a fine position here, but I—well, Dad left when I was such a baby and I never had a chance to talk to him and I still feel—kind of temporary about myself.

BEN. I'll be late for my train.

20 [*They are at opposite ends of the stage.*]

WILLY. Ben, my boys—can't we talk? They'd go into the jaws of hell for me, see, but I—

BEN. William, you're being first-rate with your boys. Outstanding, manly chaps!

25 WILLY [*hanging on to his words*]. Oh, Ben, that's good to hear! Because sometimes I'm afraid that I'm not teaching them the right kind of—Ben, how should I teach them?

BEN [*giving great weight to each word, and* 30 *with a certain vicious audacity*]. William, when I walked into the jungle, I was seventeen. When I walked out I was twenty-one. And, by God, I was rich! [*He goes off into darkness around the right corner of the house.*]

35 WILLY. . . . was rich! That's just the spirit I want to imbue them with! To walk into a jungle! I was right! I was right! I was right!

[BEN *is gone, but* WILLY *is still speaking to him as* LINDA, *in nightgown and robe, enters* 40 *the kitchen, glances around for* WILLY, *then goes to the door of the house, looks out and sees him. Comes down to his left. He looks at her.*]

LINDA. Willy, dear? Willy?

45 WILLY. I was right!

LINDA. Did you have some cheese? [*He can't answer.*] It's very late, darling. Come to bed, heh?

WILLY [*looking straight up*]. Gotta break your neck to see a star in this yard.

LINDA. You coming in? 50

WILLY. Whatever happened to that diamond watch fob? Remember? When Ben came back from Africa that time? Didn't he give me a watch fob with a diamond in it?

LINDA. You pawned it, dear. Twelve, thir-55 teen years ago. For Biff's radio correspondence course.

WILLY. Gee, that was a beautiful thing. I'll take a walk.

LINDA. But you're in your slippers. 60

WILLY [*starting to go around the house at the left*]. I was right! I was! [*Half to* LINDA, *as he goes, shaking his head.*] What a man! There was a man worth talking to. I was right!

LINDA [*calling after* WILLY]. But your slip-65 pers, Willy!

[WILLY *is almost gone when* BIFF, *in his pajamas, comes down the stairs and enters the kitchen.*]

BIFF. What is he doing out there? 70

LINDA. Sh!

BIFF. God Almighty, Mom, how long has he been doing this?

LINDA. Don't, he'll hear you.

BIFF. What the hell is the matter with him? 75

LINDA. It'll pass by morning.

BIFF. Shouldn't we do anything?

LINDA. Oh, my dear, you should do a lot of things, but there's nothing to do, so go to sleep. 80

[HAPPY *comes down the stairs and sits on the steps.*]

HAPPY. I never heard him so loud, Mom.

LINDA. Well, come around more often; you'll hear him. 85

[*She sits down at the table and mends the lining of* WILLY'S *jacket.*]

BIFF. Why didn't you ever write me about this, Mom?

LINDA. How would I write to you? For over 90 three months you had no address.

BIFF. I was on the move. But you know I thought of you all the time. You know that, don't you, pal?

LINDA. I know, dear, I know. But he likes to have a letter. Just to know that there's still a possibility for better things.

BIFF. He's not like this all the time, is he?

LINDA. It's when you come home he's always the worst.

BIFF. When I come home?

LINDA. When you write you're coming, he's all smiles, and talks about the future, and— he's just wonderful. And then the closer you seem to come, the more shaky he gets, and then, by the time you get here, he's arguing, and he seems angry at you. I think it's just that maybe he can't bring himself to—to open up to you. Why are you so hateful to each other? Why is that?

BIFF [evasively]. I'm not hateful, Mom.

LINDA. But you no sooner come in the door than you're fighting!

BIFF. I don't know why, I mean to change. I'm tryin', Mom; you understand?

LINDA. Are you home to stay now?

BIFF. I don't know. I want to look around, see what's doin'.

LINDA. Biff, you can't look around all your life, can you?

BIFF. I just can't take hold, Mom. I can't take hold of some kind of a life.

LINDA. Biff, a man is not a bird, to come and go with the springtime.

BIFF. Your hair. . . [He touches her hair.] Your hair got so gray.

LINDA. Oh, it's been gray since you were in high school. I just stopped dyeing it, that's all.

BIFF. Dye it again, will ya? I don't want my pal looking old. [He smiles.]

LINDA. You're such a boy! You think you can go away for a year and. . . . You've got to get it into your head now that one day you'll knock on this door and there'll be strange people here—

BIFF. What are you talking about? You're not even sixty, Mom.

LINDA. But what about your father?

BIFF [lamely]. Well, I meant him too.

HAPPY. He admires Pop.

LINDA. Biff, dear, if you don't have any feel-ing for him, then you can't have any feeling for me.

BIFF. Sure I can, Mom.

LINDA. No. You can't just come to see me, because I love him. [With a threat, but only a threat, of tears.] He's the dearest man in the world to me, and I won't have anyone making him feel unwanted and low and blue. You've got to make up your mind now, darling, there's no leeway any more. Either he's your father and you pay him that respect, or else you're not to come here. I know he's not easy to get along with—nobody knows that better than me—but . . .

WILLY [from the left, with a laugh]. Hey, hey, Biffo!

BIFF [starting to go out after WILLY]. What the hell is the matter with him? [HAPPY stops him.]

LINDA. Don't—don't go near him!

BIFF. Stop making excuses for him! He always, always wiped the floor with you. Never had an ounce of respect for you.

HAPPY. He's always had respect for—

BIFF. What the hell do you know about it?

HAPPY [surlily]. Just don't call him crazy!

BIFF. He's got no character—Charley wouldn't do this. Not in his own house— spewing out that vomit from his mind.

HAPPY. Charley never had to cope with what he's got to.

BIFF. People are worse off than Willy Loman. Believe me, I've seen them!

LINDA. Then make Charley your father, Biff. You can't do that, can you? I don't say he's a great man. Willy Loman never made a lot of money. His name was never in the paper. He's not the finest character that ever lived. But he's a human being, and a terrible thing is happening to him. So attention must be paid. He's not to be allowed to fall into his grave like an old dog. Attention, attention must be finally paid to such a person. You called him crazy—

BIFF. I didn't mean—

LINDA. No, a lot of people think he's lost his —balance. But you don't have to be very smart to know what his trouble is. The man is exhausted.

HAPPY. Sure!

LINDA. A small man can be just as exhausted as a great man. He works for a company thirty-six years this March, opens up unheard-of territories to their trademark, and now in his old age they take his salary away.

HAPPY [*indignantly*]. I didn't know that, Mom.

LINDA. You never asked, my dear! Now that you get your spending money someplace else you don't trouble your mind with him.

HAPPY. But I gave you money last—

LINDA. Christmas-time, fifty dollars! To fix the hot water it cost ninety-seven fifty! For five weeks he's been on straight commission, like a beginner, an unknown!

BIFF. Those ungrateful bastards!

LINDA. Are they any worse than his sons? When he brought them business, when he was young, they were glad to see him. But now his old friends, the old buyers that loved him so and always found some order to hand him in a pinch—they're all dead, retired. He used to be able to make six, seven calls a day in Boston. Now he takes his valises out of the car and puts them back and takes them out again and he's exhausted. Instead of walking he talks now. He drives seven hundred miles, and when he gets there no one knows him any more, no one welcomes him. And what goes through a man's mind, driving seven hundred miles home without having earned a cent? Why shouldn't he talk to himself? Why? When he has to go to Charley and borrow fifty dollars a week and pretend to me that it's his pay? How long can that go on? How long? You see what I'm sitting here and waiting for? And you tell me he has no character? The man who never worked a day but for your benefit? When does he get the medal for that? Is this his reward—to turn around at the age of sixty-three and find his sons, who he loved better than his life, one a philandering bum—

HAPPY. Mom!

LINDA. That's all you are, my baby! [*To* BIFF.] And you! What happened to the love you had for him? You were such pals! How you used to talk to him on the phone every night! How lonely he was till he could come home to you!

BIFF. All right, Mom. I'll live here in my room, and I'll get a job. I'll keep away from him, that's all.

LINDA. No, Biff. You can't stay here and fight all the time.

BIFF. He threw me out of this house, remember that.

LINDA. Why did he do that? I never knew why.

BIFF. Because I know he's a fake and he doesn't like anybody around who knows!

LINDA. Why a fake? In what way? What do you mean?

BIFF. Just don't lay it all at my feet. It's between me and him—that's all I have to say. I'll chip in from now on. He'll settle for half my pay check. He'll be all right. I'm going to bed. [*He starts for the stairs.*]

LINDA. He won't be all right.

BIFF [*turning on the stairs, furiously*]. I hate this city and I'll stay here. Now what do you want?

LINDA. He's dying, Biff.

[HAPPY *turns quickly to her, shocked.*]

BIFF [*after a pause*]. Why is he dying?

LINDA. He's been trying to kill himself.

BIFF [*with great horror*]. How?

LINDA. I live from day to day.

BIFF. What're you talking about?

LINDA. Remember I wrote you that he smashed up the car again? In February?

BIFF. Well?

LINDA. The insurance inspector came. He said that they have evidence. That all these accidents in the last year—weren't—weren't—accidents.

HAPPY. How can they tell that? That's a lie.

LINDA. It seems there's a woman . . . [*she takes a breath as*]

BIFF [*sharply but contained*]. What woman?

LINDA [*simultaneously*]. . . . and this woman . . .

LINDA. What?

BIFF. Nothing. Go ahead.

LINDA. What did you say?

BIFF. Nothing. I just said what woman?

HAPPY. What about her?

LINDA. Well, it seems she was walking down the road and saw his car. She says that he
5 wasn't driving fast at all, and that he didn't skid. She says he came to that little bridge, and then deliberately smashed into the railing, and it was only the shallowness of the water that saved him.

10 BIFF. Oh, no, he probably just fell asleep again.

LINDA. I don't think he fell asleep.

BIFF. Why not?

LINDA. Last month. . . . [*With great difficulty.*] Oh, boys, it's so hard to say a thing like
15 this! He's just a big stupid man to you, but I tell you there's more good in him than in many other people. [*She chokes, wipes her eyes.*] I was looking for a fuse. The lights blew out,
20 and I went down the cellar. And behind the fuse-box—it happened to fall out—was a length of rubber pipe—just short.

HAPPY. No kidding?

LINDA. There's a little attachment on the end
25 of it. I knew right away. And sure enough, on the bottom of the water heater there's a new little nipple on the gas pipe.

HAPPY [*angrily*]. That—jerk.

BIFF. Did you have it taken off?

30 LINDA. I'm—I'm ashamed to. How can I mention it to him? Every day I go down and take away that little rubber pipe. But, when he comes home, I put it back where it was. How can I insult him that way? I don't know
35 what to do. I live from day to day, boys. I tell you, I know every thought in his mind. It sounds so old-fashioned and silly, but I tell you he put his whole life into you and you've turned your backs on him. [*She is bent over in
40 the chair, weeping, her face in her hands.*] Biff, I swear to God! Biff, his life is in your hands!

HAPPY [*to* BIFF]. How do you like that damned fool!

BIFF [*kissing her*]. All right, pal, all right.
45 It's all settled now. I've been remiss. I know that, Mom. But now I'll stay, and I swear to you, I'll apply myself. [*Kneeling in front of her, in a fever of self-reproach.*] It's just—you see, Mom, I don't fit in business. Not that I

won't try. I'll try, and I'll make good. 50

HAPPY. Sure you will. The trouble with you in business was you never tried to please people.

BIFF. I know, I—

HAPPY. Like when you worked for Har- 55 rison's. Bob Harrison said you were tops, and then you go and do some damn fool thing like whistling whole songs in the elevator like a comedian.

BIFF [*against* HAPPY]. So what? I like to 60 whistle sometimes.

HAPPY. You don't raise a guy to a responsible job who whistles in the elevator!

LINDA. Well, don't argue about it now.

HAPPY. Like when you'd go off and swim in 65 the middle of the day instead of taking the line around.

BIFF [*his resentment rising*]. Well, don't you run off? You take off sometimes, don't you? On a nice summer day? 70

HAPPY. Yeah, but I cover myself!

LINDA. Boys!

HAPPY. If I'm going to take a fade the boss can call any number where I'm supposed to be and they'll swear to him that I just left. I'll tell 75 you something that I hate to say, Biff, but in the business world some of them think you're crazy.

BIFF [*angered*]. Screw the business world!

HAPPY. All right, screw it! Great, but cover 80 yourself!

LINDA: Hap, Hap!

BIFF. I don't care what they think! They've laughed at Dad for years, and you know why? Because we don't belong in this nuthouse of a 85 city! We should be mixing cement on some open plain, or—or carpenters. A carpenter is allowed to whistle!

[WILLY *walks in from the entrance of the house, at left.*] 90

WILLY. Even your grandfather was better than a carpenter.

[*Pause. They watch him.*] You never grew up. Bernard does not whistle in the elevator, I assure you. 95

BIFF [*as though to laugh* WILLY *out of it*]. Yeah, but you do, Pop.

WILLY. I never in my life whistled in an

elevator! And who in the business world thinks I'm crazy?

BIFF. I didn't mean it like that, Pop. Now don't make a whole thing out of it, will ya?

5 WILLY. Go back to the West! Be a carpenter, a cowboy, enjoy yourself!

LINDA. Willy, he was just saying—

WILLY. I heard what he said!

HAPPY [*trying to quiet* WILLY]. Hey, Pop, 10 come on now . . .

WILLY [*continuing over* HAPPY's *line*]. They laugh at me, heh? Go to Filene's, go to the Hub, go to Slattery's, Boston. Call out the name Willy Loman and see what happens! 15 Big shot!

BIFF. All right, Pop.

WILLY. Big!

BIFF. All right!

WILLY. Why do you always insult me?

20 BIFF. I didn't say a word. [*To* LINDA.] Did I say a word?

LINDA. He didn't say anything, Willy.

WILLY [*going to the doorway of the living-room*]. All right, good night, good night.

25 LINDA. Willy, dear, he just decided . . .

WILLY [*to* BIFF]. If you get tired hanging around tomorrow, paint the ceiling I put up in the living-room.

BIFF. I'm leaving early tomorrow.

30 HAPPY. He's going to see Bill Oliver, Pop.

WILLY [*interestedly*]. Oliver? For what?

BIFF [*with reserve, but trying, trying*]. He always said he'd stake me. I'd like to go into business, so maybe I can take him up on it.

35 LINDA. Isn't that wonderful?

WILLY. Don't interrupt. What's wonderful about it? There's fifty men in the City of New York who'd stake him. [*To* BIFF.] Sporting goods?

40 BIFF. I guess so. I know something about it and—

WILLY. He knows something about it! You know sporting goods better than Spalding, for God's sake! How much is he giving you?

45 BIFF. I don't know. I didn't even see him yet, but—

WILLY. Then what're you talkin' about?

BIFF [*getting angry*]. Well, all I said was I'm gonna see him, that's all!

WILLY [*turning away*]. Ah, you're counting 50 your chickens again.

BIFF [*starting left for the stairs*]. Oh, Jesus, I'm going to sleep!

WILLY [*calling after him*]. Don't curse in this house! 55

BIFF [*turning*]. Since when did you get so clean?

HAPPY [*trying to stop them*]. Wait a . . .

WILLY. Don't use that language to me! I won't have it! 60

HAPPY [*grabbing* BIFF, *shouts*]. Wait a minute! I got an idea. I got a feasible idea. Come here, Biff, let's talk this over now, let's talk some sense here. When I was down in Florida last time, I thought of a great idea to 65 sell sporting goods. It just came back to me. You and I, Biff—we have a line, the Loman Line. We train a couple of weeks, and put on a couple of exhibitions, see?

WILLY. That's an idea! 70

HAPPY. Wait! We form two basketball teams, see? Two water-polo teams. We play each other. It's a million dollars' worth of publicity. Two brothers, see? The Loman Brothers. Displays in the Royal Palms—all the 75 hotels. And banners over the ring and the basketball court: "Loman Brothers." Baby, we could sell sporting goods!

WILLY. That is a one-million-dollar idea!

LINDA. Marvellous! 80

BIFF. I'm in great shape as far as that's concerned.

HAPPY. And the beauty of it is, Biff, it wouldn't be like a business. We'd be out playin' ball again . . . 85

BIFF [*enthused*]. Yeah, that's . . .

WILLY. Million-dollar . . .

HAPPY. And you wouldn't get fed up with it, Biff. It'd be the family again. There'd be the old honor, and comradeship, and if you 90 wanted to go off for a swim or somethin'— well you'd do it! Without some smart cooky gettin' up ahead of you!

WILLY. Lick the world! You guys together could absolutely lick the civilized world. 95

BIFF. I'll see Oliver tomorrow. Hap, if we could work that out . . .

LINDA. Maybe things are beginning to—

WILLY [*wildly enthused, to* LINDA]. Stop interrupting! [*To* BIFF.] But don't wear sports jacket and slacks when you see Oliver.

BIFF. No, I'll—

5 WILLY. A business suit, and talk as little as possible, and don't crack any jokes.

BIFF. He did like me. Always liked me.

LINDA. He loved you!

WILLY [*to* LINDA]. Will you stop! [*To* BIFF.]
10 Walk in very serious. You are not applying for a boy's job. Money is to pass. Be quiet, fine, and serious. Everybody likes a kidder, but nobody lends him money.

HAPPY. I'll try to get some myself, Biff. I'm
15 sure I can.

WILLY. I see great things for you kids, I think your troubles are over. But remember, start big and you'll end big. Ask for fifteen. How much you gonna ask for?

20 BIFF. Gee, I don't know—

WILLY. And don't say "Gee." "Gee" is a boy's word. A man walking in for fifteen thousand dollars does not say "Gee"!

BIFF. Ten, I think, would be top though.

25 WILLY. Don't be so modest. You always started too low. Walk in with a big laugh. Don't look worried. Start off with a couple of your good stories to lighten things up. It's not what you say, it's how you say it—because
30 personality always wins the day.

LINDA. Oliver always thought the highest of him—

WILLY. Will you let me talk?

BIFF. Don't yell at her, Pop, will ya?

35 WILLY [*angrily*]. I was talking, wasn't I?

BIFF. I don't like you yelling at her all the time, and I'm tellin' you, that's all.

WILLY. What're you, takin' over this house?

LINDA. Willy—

40 WILLY [*turning on her*]. Don't take his side all the time, goddammit!

BIFF [*furiously*]. Stop yelling at her!

WILLY [*suddenly pulling on his cheek, beaten down, guilt ridden*]. Give my best to
45 Bill Oliver—he may remember me. [*He exits through the living-room doorway.*]

LINDA [*her voice subdued*]. What'd you have to start that for? [BIFF *turns away.*] You see how sweet he was as soon as you talked hope-

fully? [*She goes over to* BIFF.] Come up and
50 say good night to him. Don't let him go to bed that way.

HAPPY. Come on, Biff, let's buck him up.

LINDA. Please, dear. Just say good night. It takes so little to make him happy. Come. [*She
55 goes through the living-room doorway, calling upstairs from within the living-room.*] Your pajamas are hanging in the bathroom, Willy!

HAPPY [*looking toward where* LINDA *went out*]. What a woman! They broke the mold
60 when they made her. You know that, Biff?

BIFF. He's off salary. My God, working on commission!

HAPPY. Well, let's face it: he's no hot-shot selling man. Except that sometimes, you have
65 to admit, he's a sweet personality.

BIFF [*deciding*]. Lend me ten bucks, will ya? I want to buy some new ties.

HAPPY. I'll take you to a place I know. Beautiful stuff. Wear one of my striped shirts to-
70 morrow.

BIFF. She got gray. Mom got awful old. Gee. I'm gonna go in to Oliver tomorrow and knock him for a—

HAPPY. Come on up. Tell that to Dad. Let's
75 give him a whirl. Come on.

BIFF [*steamed up*]. You know, with ten thousand bucks, boy!

HAPPY [*as they go into the living-room*]. That's the talk, Biff, that's the first time I've
80 heard the old confidence out of you! [*From within the living-room, fading off.*] You're gonna live with me, kid, and any babe you want just say the word. . . . [*The last lines are hardly heard. They are mounting the stairs to
85 their parents' bedroom.*]

LINDA [*entering her bedroom and addressing* WILLY, *who is in the bathroom. She is straightening the bed for him*]. Can you do anything about the shower? It drips.

90

WILLY [*from the bathroom*]. All of a sudden everything falls to pieces! Goddam plumbing, oughta be sued, those people. I hardly finished putting it in and the thing. . . . [*His words rumble off.*]

95

LINDA. I'm just wondering if Oliver will remember him. You think he might?

WILLY [*coming out of the bathroom in his

pajamas]. Remember him? What's the matter with you, you crazy? If he'd've stayed with Oliver he'd be on top by now! Wait'll Oliver gets a look at him. You don't know the average
5 caliber any more. The average young man today—[*he is getting into bed*]—is got a caliber of zero. Greatest thing in the world for him was to bum around.

[BIFF *and* HAPPY *enter the bedroom. Slight*
10 *pause.*]

WILLY [*stops short, looking at* BIFF]. Glad to hear it, boy.

HAPPY. He wanted to say goodnight to you, sport.

15 WILLY [*to* BIFF]. Yeah. Knock him dead, boy. What'd you want to tell me?

BIFF. Just take it easy, Pop. Good night. [*He turns to go.*]

WILLY [*unable to resist*]. And if anything
20 falls off the desk while you're talking to him —like a package or something—don't you pick it up. They have office boys for that.

LINDA. I'll make a big breakfast—

WILLY. Will you let me finish? [*To* BIFF.]
25 Tell him you were in the business in the West. Not farm work.

BIFF. All right, Dad.

LINDA. I think everything—

WILLY [*going right through her speech*].
30 And don't undersell yourself. No less than fifteen thousand dollars.

BIFF [*unable to bear him*]. Okay. Good night, Mom. [*He starts moving.*]

WILLY. Because you got a greatness in you,
35 Biff, remember that. You got all kinds a greatness. . . . [*He lies back, exhausted.* BIFF *walks out.*]

LINDA [*calling after* BIFF]. Sleep well, darling!

40 HAPPY. I'm gonna get married, Mom. I wanted to tell you.

LINDA. Go to sleep, dear.

HAPPY [*going*]. I just wanted to tell you.

WILLY. Keep up the good work. [HAPPY
45 *exits.*] God . . . remember that Ebbets Field°

Ebbets Field   a well-known sports stadium in Brooklyn named after Charles Hercules Ebbets (1859-1925). It was dismantled in 1960.

game? The championship of the city?

LINDA. Just rest. Should I sing to you?

WILLY. Yeah. Sing to me. [LINDA *hums a soft lullaby.*] When that team came out—he was
50 the tallest, remember?

LINDA. Oh, yes. And in gold.

[BIFF *enters the darkened kitchen, takes a cigarette, and leaves the house. He comes downstage into a golden pool of light. He*
55 *smokes, staring at the night.*]

WILLY. Like a young god. Hercules—something like that. And the sun, the sun all around him. Remember how he waved to me? Right up from the field, with the representatives of three colleges standing by? And the buyers I
60 brought, and the cheers when he came out— Loman, Loman, Loman! God Almighty, he'll be great yet. A star like that, magnificent, can never really fade away!

[*The light on* WILLY *is fading. The gas*
65 *heater begins to glow through the kitchen wall, near the stairs, a blue flame beneath red coils.*]

LINDA [*timidly*]. Willy dear, what has he got against you?
70

WILLY. I'm so tired. Don't talk any more.

[BIFF *slowly returns to the kitchen. He stops, stares toward the heater.*]

LINDA. Will you ask Howard to let you work in New York?
75

WILLY. First thing in the morning. Everything'll be all right.

[BIFF *reaches behind the heater and draws out a length of rubber tubing. He is horrified and turns his head toward* WILLY's *room, still*
80 *dimly lit, from which the strains of* LINDA's *desperate but monotonous humming rise.*]

WILLY [*staring through the window into the moonlight*]. Gee, look at the moon moving between the buildings!
85

[BIFF *wraps the tubing around his hand and quickly goes up the stairs.*]

Curtain

ACT II

[*Music is heard, gay and bright. The curtain rises as the music fades away.*]

[WILLY, *in his shirt sleeves, is sitting at the*
90

kitchen table, sipping coffee, his hat in his lap.
LINDA *is filling his cup when she can.*]

WILLY. Wonderful coffee. Meal in itself.

LINDA. Can I make you some eggs?

5   WILLY. No. Take a breath.

LINDA. You look so rested, dear.

WILLY. I slept like a dead one. First time in months. Imagine, sleeping till ten on a Tuesday morning. Boys left nice and early, heh?

10   LINDA. They were out of here by eight o'clock.

WILLY. Good work!

LINDA. It was so thrilling to see them leaving together. I can't get over the shaving lotion in

15   this house!

WILLY [*smiling*]. Mmm—

LINDA. Biff was very changed this morning. His whole attitude seemed to be hopeful. He couldn't wait to get downtown to see Oliver.

20   WILLY. He's heading for a change. There's no question, there simply are certain men that take longer to get—solidified. How did he dress?

LINDA. His blue suit. He's so handsome in

25   that suit! He could be a—anything in that suit!

[WILLY *gets up from the table.* LINDA *holds his jacket for him.*]

WILLY. There's no question, no question at

30   all. Gee, on the way home tonight I'd like to buy some seeds.

LINDA [*laughing*]. That'd be wonderful. But not enough sun gets back there. Nothing'll grow any more.

35   WILLY. You wait, kid, before it's all over we're gonna get a little place out in the country, and I'll raise some vegetables, a couple of chickens . . .

LINDA. You'll do it yet, dear.

40   [WILLY *walks out with his jacket.* LINDA *follows him.*]

WILLY. And they'll get married, and come for a weekend. I'd build a little guest house. 'Cause I got so many fine tools, all I'd need

45   would be a little lumber and some peace of mind.

LINDA [*joyfully*]. I sewed the lining . . .

WILLY. I could build two guest houses, so they'd both come. Did he decide how much he's going to ask Oliver for?   50

LINDA [*getting him into the jacket*]. He didn't mention it, but I imagine ten or fifteen thousand. You going to talk to Howard today?

WILLY. Yeah. I'll put it to him straight and simple. He'll just have to take me off the road.   55

LINDA. And Willy, don't forget to ask for a little advance, because we've got the insurance premium. It's the grace period now.

WILLY. That's a hundred . . .?

LINDA. A hundred and eight, sixty-eight.   60
Because we're a little short again.

WILLY. Why are we short?

LINDA. Well, you had the motor job on the car . . .

WILLY. That goddam Studebaker!   65

LINDA. And you got one more payment on the refrigerator . . .

WILLY. But it just broke again!

LINDA. Well, it's old, dear.

WILLY. I told you we should've bought a   70
well-advertised machine. Charley bought a General Electric and it's twenty years old and it's still good, that son-of-a-bitch.

LINDA. But, Willy—

WILLY. Whoever heard of a Hastings re-   75
frigerator? Once in my life I would like to own something outright before it's broken! I'm always in a race with the junkyard! I just finished paying for the car and it's on its last legs. The refrigerator consumes belts like a   80
goddam maniac. They time those things. They time them so when you finally paid for them, they're used up.

LINDA [*buttoning up his jacket as he unbuttons it*]. All told, about two hundred dollars   85
would carry us, dear. But that includes the last payment on the mortgage. After this payment, Willy, the house belongs to us.

WILLY. It's twenty-five years!

LINDA. Biff was nine years old when we   90
bought it.

WILLY. Well, that's a great thing. To weather a twenty-five-year mortgage is—

LINDA. It's an accomplishment.

WILLY. All the cement, the lumber, the reconstruction I put in this house! There ain't a crack to be found in it any more.

LINDA. Well, it served its purpose.

WILLY. What purpose? Some stranger'll come along, move in, and that's that. If only Biff would take this house, and raise a family. . . . [*He starts to go.*] Good-bye, I'm late.

LINDA [*suddenly remembering*]. Oh, I forgot! You're supposed to meet them for dinner.

WILLY. Me?

LINDA. At Frank's Chop House on Forty-eighth near Sixth Avenue.

WILLY. Is that so! How about you?

LINDA. No, just the three of you. They're gonna blow you to a big meal!

WILLY. Don't say! Who thought of that?

LINDA. Biff came to me this morning, Willy, and he said, "Tell Dad, we want to blow him to a big meal." Be there six o'clock. You and your two boys are going to have dinner.

WILLY. Gee whiz! That's really somethin'. I'm gonna knock Howard for a loop, kid. I'll get an advance, and I'll come home with a New York job. Goddammit, now I'm gonna do it!

LINDA. Oh, that's the spirit, Willy!

WILLY. I will never get behind a wheel the rest of my life!

LINDA. It's changing, Willy, I can feel it changing!

WILLY. Beyond a question. G'bye, I'm late. [*He starts to go again.*]

LINDA [*calling after him as she runs to the kitchen table for a handkerchief*]. You got your glasses?

WILLY [*feels for them, then comes back in*]. Yeah, yeah, got my glasses.

LINDA [*giving him the handkerchief*]. And a handkerchief.

WILLY. Yeah, handkerchief.

LINDA. And your saccharine?

WILLY. Yeah, my saccharine.

LINDA. Be careful on the subway stairs.

[*She kisses him, and a silk stocking is seen hanging from her hand.* WILLY *notices it.*]

WILLY. Will you stop mending stockings? At least while I'm in the house. It gets me nervous. I can't tell you. Please.

[LINDA *hides the stocking in her hand as she follows* WILLY *across the forestage in front of the house.*]

LINDA. Remember, Frank's Chop House.

WILLY [*passing the apron*]. Maybe beets would grow out there.

LINDA [*laughing*]. But you tried so many times.

WILLY. Yeah. Well, don't work hard today. [*He disappears around the right corner of the house.*]

LINDA. Be careful!

[*As* WILLY *vanishes,* LINDA *waves to him. Suddenly the phone rings. She runs across the stage and into the kitchen and lifts it.*]

LINDA. Hello? Oh, Biff! I'm so glad you called, I just. . . . Yes, sure, I just told him. Yes, he'll be there for dinner at six o'clock, I didn't forget. Listen, I was just dying to tell you. You know that little rubber pipe I told you about? That he connected to the gas heater? I finally decided to go down the cellar this morning and take it away and destroy it. But it's gone! Imagine! He took it away himself, it isn't there! [*She listens.*] When? Oh, then you took it. Oh—nothing, it's just that I'd hoped he'd taken it away himself. Oh, I'm not worried, darling, because this morning he left in such high spirits, it was like the old days! I'm not afraid any more. Did Mr. Oliver see you? . . . Well, you wait there then. And make a nice impression on him, darling. Just don't perspire too much before you see him. And have a nice time with Dad. He may have big news too! . . . That's right, a New York job. And be sweet to him tonight, dear. Be loving to him. Because he's only a little boat looking for a harbor. [*She is trembling with sorrow and joy.*] Oh, that's wonderful, Biff, you'll save his life. Thanks, darling. Just put your arms around him when he comes into the restaurant. Give him a smile. That's the boy. . . . Good-bye, dear. . . . You got your comb? . . . That's fine. Good-bye, Biff dear.

[*In the middle of her speech,* HOWARD WAG-

NER, *thirty-six, wheels in a small typewriter table on which is a wire-recording machine and proceeds to plug it in. This is on the left forestage. Light slowly fades on* LINDA *as it rises*
5 *on* HOWARD. HOWARD *is intent on threading the machine and only glances over his shoulder as* WILLY *appears.*]

WILLY. Pst! Pst!

HOWARD. Hello, Willy, come in.

10 WILLY. Like to have a talk with you, Howard.

HOWARD. Sorry to keep you waiting. I'll be with you in a minute.

WILLY. What's that, Howard?

15 HOWARD. Didn't you ever see one of these? Wire recorder.

WILLY. Oh. Can we talk a minute?

HOWARD. Records things. Just got delivery yesterday. Been driving me crazy, the most
20 terrific machine I ever saw in my life. I was up all night with it.

WILLY. What do you do with it?

HOWARD. I bought it for dictation, but you can do anything with it. Listen to this. I had it
25 home last night. Listen to what I picked up. The first one is my daughter. Get this. [*He flicks the switch and "Roll out the Barrel" is heard being whistled.*] Listen to that kid whistle.

30 WILLY. That is lifelike, isn't it?

HOWARD. Seven years old. Get that tone.

WILLY. Ts, ts. Like to ask a little favor if you . . .

[*The whistling breaks off, and the voice of*
35 HOWARD'S *daughter is heard.*]

HIS DAUGHTER. "Now you, Daddy."

HOWARD. She's crazy for me! [*Again the same song is whistled.*] That's me! Ha! [*He winks.*]

40 WILLY. You're very good!

[*The whistling breaks off again. The machine runs silent for a moment.*]

HOWARD. Sh! Get this now, this is my son.

HIS SON. "The capital of Alabama is Mont-
45 gomery; the capital of Arizona is Phoenix; the capital of Arkansas is Little Rock; the capital of California is Sacramento . . ." [*and on, and*

on.]

HOWARD [*holding up five fingers*]. Five years old, Willy! 50

WILLY. He'll make an announcer some day!

HIS SON [*continuing*]. "The capital . . ."

HOWARD. Get that—alphabetical order! [*The machine breaks off suddenly.*] Wait a minute. The maid kicked the plug out. 55

WILLY. It certainly is a—

HOWARD. Sh, for God's sake!

HIS SON. "It's nine o'clock, Bulova watch time. So I have to go to sleep."

WILLY. That really is— 60

HOWARD. Wait a minute! The next is my wife.

[*They wait.*]

HOWARD'S VOICE. "Go on, say something." [*Pause.*] "Well, you gonna talk?" 65

HIS WIFE. "I can't think of anything."

HOWARD'S VOICE. "Well, talk—it's turning."

HIS WIFE [*shyly, beaten*]. "Hello." [*Silence.*] "Oh, Howard, I can't talk into this . . ."

HOWARD [*snapping the machine off*]. That 70 was my wife.

WILLY. That is a wonderful machine. Can we—

HOWARD. I tell you, Willy, I'm gonna take my camera, and my bandsaw, and all my 75 hobbies, and out they go. This is the most fascinating relaxation I ever found.

WILLY. I think I'll get one myself.

HOWARD. Sure, they're only a hundred and a half. You can't do without it. Supposing you 80 wanna hear Jack Benny, see? But you can't be at home at that hour. So you tell the maid to turn the radio on when Jack Benny comes on, and this automatically goes on with the radio . . . 85

WILLY. And when you come home you . . .

HOWARD. You can come home twelve o'clock, one o'clock, any time you like, and you get yourself a Coke and sit yourself down, throw the switch, and there's Jack Benny's 90 program in the middle of the night!

WILLY. I'm definitely going to get one. Because lots of time I'm on the road, and I think to myself, what I must be missing on the radio!

HOWARD. Don't you have a radio in the car?

WILLY. Well, yeah, but who ever thinks of turning it on?

HOWARD. Say, aren't you supposed to be in
5 Boston?

WILLY. That's what I want to talk to you about, Howard. You got a minute? [*He draws a chair in from the wing.*]

HOWARD. What happened? What're you do-
10 ing here?

WILLY. Well . . .

HOWARD. You didn't crack up again, did you?

WILLY. Oh, no. No . . .

15 HOWARD. Geez, you had me worried there for a minute. What's the trouble?

WILLY. Well, tell you the truth, Howard. I've come to the decision that I'd rather not travel any more.

20 HOWARD. Not travel! Well, what'll you do?

WILLY. Remember, Christmas-time, when you had the party here? You said you'd try to think of some spot for me here in town.

HOWARD. With us?

25 WILLY. Well, sure.

HOWARD. Oh, yeah, yeah. I remember. Well, I couldn't think of anything for you, Willy.

WILLY. I tell ya, Howard. The kids are grown up, y'know. I don't need much any more. If I
30 could take home—well, sixty-five dollars a week, I could swing it.

HOWARD. Yeah, but Willy, see I—

WILLY. I tell ya why, Howard. Speaking frankly and between the two of us, y'know—
35 I'm just a little tired.

HOWARD. Oh, I could understand that, Willy. But you're a road man, Willy, and we do a road business. We've only got a half-dozen salesmen on the floor here.

40 WILLY. God knows, Howard, I never asked a favor of any man. But I was with the firm when your father used to carry you in here in his arms.

HOWARD. I know that, Willy, but—

45 WILLY. Your father came to me the day you were born and asked me what I thought of the name of Howard, may he rest in peace.

HOWARD. I appreciate that, Willy, but there is no spot here for you. If I had a spot I'd slam you right in, but I just don't have a single 50 solitary spot.

[*He looks for his lighter. WILLY has picked it up and gives it to him. Pause.*]

WILLY [*with increasing anger*]. Howard, all I need to set my table is fifty dollars a week. 55

HOWARD. But where am I going to put you, kid?

WILLY. Look, it isn't a question of whether I can sell merchandise, is it?

HOWARD. No, but it's a business, kid, and 60 everybody's gotta pull his own weight.

WILLY [*desperately*]. Just let me tell you a story, Howard—

HOWARD. 'Cause you gotta admit, business is business. 65

WILLY [*angrily*]. Business is definitely business, but just listen for a minute. You don't understand this. When I was a boy—eighteen, nineteen—I was already on the road. And there was a question in my mind as to whether sell- 70 ing had a future for me. Because in those days I had a yearning to go to Alaska. See, there were three gold strikes in one month in Alaska, and I felt like going out. Just for the ride, you might say. 75

HOWARD [*barely interested*]. Don't say.

WILLY. Oh, yeah, my father lived many years in Alaska. He was an adventurous man. We've got quite a little streak of self-reliance in our family. I thought I'd go out with my 80 older brother and try to locate him, and maybe settle in the North with the old man. And I was almost decided to go, when I met a salesman in the Parker House. His name was Dave Singleman. And he was eighty-four years old, 85 and he'd drummed merchandise in thirty-one states. And old Dave, he'd go up to his room, y'understand, put on his green velvet slippers —I'll never forget—and pick up his phone and call the buyers, and without ever leaving his 90 room, at the age of eighty-four, he made his living. And when I saw that, I realized that selling was the greatest career a man could want. 'Cause what could be more satisfying

than to be able to go, at the age of eighty-four, into twenty or thirty different cities, and pick up a phone, and be remembered and loved and helped by so many different people? Do you
5 know? when he died—and by the way he died the death of a salesman, in his green velvet slippers in the smoker of the New York, New Haven, and Hartford, going into Boston—when he died, hundreds of salesmen and buyers were
10 at his funeral. Things were said on a lotta trains for months after that. [*He stands up. Howard has not looked at him.*] In those days there was personality in it, Howard. There was respect, and comradeship, and gratitude in it.
15 Today, it's all cut and dried, and there's no chance for bringing friendship to bear—or personality. You see what I mean? They don't know me any more.

HOWARD [*moving away, toward the right*].
20 That's just the thing, Willy.

WILLY. If I had forty dollars a week—that's all I'd need. Forty dollars, Howard.

HOWARD. Kid, I can't take blood from a stone, I—
25 WILLY [*desperation is on him now*]. Howard, the year Al Smith° was nominated, your father came to me and—

HOWARD [*starting to go off*]. I've got to see some people, kid.
30 WILLY [*stopping him*]. I'm talking about your father! There were promises made across this desk! You mustn't tell me you've got people to see—I put thirty-four years into this firm, Howard, and now I can't pay my in-
35 surance! You can't eat the orange and throw the peel away—a man is not a piece of fruit! [*After a pause.*] Now pay attention. Your father—in 1928 I had a big year. I averaged a hundred and seventy dollars a week in com-
40 missions.

HOWARD [*impatiently*]. Now, Willy, you never averaged—

WILLY [*banging his hand on the desk*]. I averaged a hundred and seventy dollars a week

Al Smith Alfred E. Smith (1873–1944), the Democratic nominee for President in 1928, was defeated by Herbert Hoover

in the year of 1928! And your father came to 45
me—or rather, I was in the office here—it was right over this desk—and he put his hand on my shoulder—

HOWARD [*getting up*]. You'll have to excuse me, Willy, I gotta see some people. Pull your- 50
self together. [*Going out.*] I'll be back in a little while.

[*On* HOWARD's *exit, the light on his chair grows very bright and strange.*]

WILLY. Pull myself together! What the hell 55
did I say to him? My God, I was yelling at him! How could I! [WILLY *breaks off, staring at the light, which occupies the chair, animating it. He approaches this chair, standing across the desk from it.*] Frank, Frank, don't you remem- 60
ber what you told me that time? How you put your hand on my shoulder, and Frank. . . . [*He leans on the desk and as he speaks the dead man's name he accidentally switches on the recorder, and instantly—*] 65

HOWARD'S SON. ". . . of New York is Albany. The capital of Ohio is Cincinnati, the capital of Rhode Island is . . ." [*the recitation continues.*]

WILLY [*leaping away with fright, shouting*]. 70
Ha! Howard! Howard! Howard!

HOWARD [*rushing in*]. What happened?

WILLY [*pointing at the machine, which continues nasally, childishly, with capital cities*]. Shut it off! Shut it off! 75

HOWARD [*pulling the plug out*]. Look, Willy . . .

WILLY [*pressing his hands to his eyes*]. I gotta get myself some coffee. I'll get some coffee . . . 80

[WILLY *starts to walk out.* HOWARD *stops him.*]

HOWARD [*rolling up the cord*]. Willy, look . . .

WILLY. I'll go to Boston. 85

HOWARD. Willy, you can't go to Boston for us.

WILLY. Why can't I go?

HOWARD. I don't want you to represent us. I've been meaning to tell you for a long time 90
now.

WILLY. Howard, are you firing me?

HOWARD. I think you need a good long rest, Willy.

WILLY. Howard—

HOWARD. And when you feel better, come back, and we'll see if we can work something out.

WILLY. But I gotta earn money, Howard. I'm in no position to—

HOWARD. Where are your sons? Why don't your sons give you a hand?

WILLY. They're working on a very big deal.

HOWARD. This is no time for false pride, Willy. You go to your sons and you tell them that you're tired. You've got two great boys, haven't you?

WILLY. Oh, no question, no question, but in the meantime . . .

HOWARD. Then that's that, heh?

WILLY. All right, I'll go to Boston tomorrow.

HOWARD. No, no.

WILLY. I can't throw myself on my sons. I'm not a cripple!

HOWARD. Look, kid, I'm busy this morning.

WILLY [*grasping* HOWARD's *arm*]. Howard, you've got to let me go to Boston!

HOWARD [*hard, keeping himself under control*]. I've got a line of people to see this morning. Sit down, take five minutes, and pull yourself together, and then go home, will ya? I need the office, Willy. [*He starts to go, turns, remembering the recorder, starts to push off the table holding the recorder.*] Oh, yeah. Whenever you can this week, stop by and drop off the samples. You'll feel better, Willy, and then come back and we'll talk. Pull yourself together, kid, there's people outside.

[HOWARD *exits, pushing the table off left.* WILLY *stares into space, exhausted. Now the music is heard*—BEN's *music—first distantly, then closer, closer. As* WILLY *speaks,* BEN *enters from the right. He carries valise and umbrella.*]

WILLY. Oh, Ben, how did you do it? What is the answer? Did you wind up the Alaska deal already?

BEN. Doesn't take much time if you know what you're doing. Just a short business trip. Boarding ship in an hour. Wanted to say goodbye.

WILLY. Ben, I've got to talk to you.

BEN [*glancing at his watch*]. Haven't the time, William.

WILLY [*crossing the apron to* BEN]. Ben, nothing's working out. I don't know what to do.

BEN. Now, look here, William. I've bought timberland in Alaska and I need a man to look after things for me.

WILLY. God, timberland! Me and my boys in those grand outdoors!

BEN. You've a new continent at your doorstep, William. Get out of these cities, they're full of talk and time payments and courts of law. Screw on your fists and you can fight for a fortune up there.

WILLY. Yes, yes! Linda, Linda!

[LINDA *enters as of old, with the wash.*]

LINDA. Oh, you're back?

BEN. I haven't much time.

WILLY. No, wait! Linda, he's got a proposition for me in Alaska.

LINDA. But you've got— [*To* BEN.] He's got a beautiful job here.

WILLY. But in Alaska, kid, I could—

LINDA. You're doing well enough, Willy!

BEN [*to* LINDA]. Enough for what, my dear?

LINDA [*frightened of* BEN *and angry at him*]. Don't say those things to him! Enough to be happy right here, right now. [*To* WILLY, *while* BEN *laughs.*] Why must everybody conquer the world? You're well liked, and the boys love you, and someday—[*to* BEN]—why, old man Wagner told him just the other day that if he keeps it up he'll be a member of the firm, didn't he, Willy?

WILLY. Sure, sure. I am building something with this firm, Ben, and if a man is building something he must be on the right track, mustn't he?

BEN. What are you building? Lay your hand on it. Where is it?

WILLY [*hesitantly*]. That's true, Linda, there's nothing.

LINDA. Why? [*To* BEN.] There's a man eighty-four years old—

WILLY. That's right, Ben, that's right. When I look at that man I say, what is there to worry about?

BEN. Bah!

WILLY. It's true, Ben. All he has to do is go into any city, pick up the phone, and he's making his living and you know why?

5 BEN [*picking up his valise*]. I've got to go.

WILLY [*holding* BEN *back*]. Look at this boy!

[BIFF, *in his high-school sweater, enters carrying suitcase.* HAPPY *carries* BIFF's *shoulder guards, gold helmet, and football pants.*]

10 WILLY. Without a penny to his name, three great universities are begging for him, and from there the sky's the limit, because it's not what you do, Ben. It's who you know and the smile on your face! It's contacts, Ben, contacts!

15 The whole wealth of Alaska passes over the lunch table at the Commodore Hotel, and that's the wonder, the wonder of this country, that a man can end with diamonds here on the basis of being liked! [*He turns to* BIFF.] And that's

20 why when you get out on that field today it's important. Because thousands of people will be rooting for you and loving you. [*To* BEN, *who has again begun to leave.*] And Ben! when he walks into a business office his name will

25 sound out like a bell and all the doors will open to him! I've seen it, Ben, I've seen it a thousand times! You can't feel it with your hand like timber, but it's there!

BEN. Good-bye, William.

30 WILLY. Ben, am I right? Don't you think I'm right? I value your advice.

BEN. There's a new continent at your doorstep, William. You could walk out rich. Rich! [*He is gone.*]

35 WILLY. We'll do it here, Ben! You hear me? We're gonna do it here!

[*Young* BERNARD *rushes in. The gay music of the boys is heard.*]

BERNARD. Oh, gee, I was afraid you left

40 already!

WILLY. Why? What time is it?

BERNARD. It's half past one!

WILLY. Well, come on, everybody! Ebbets Field next stop! Where's the pennants? [*He*

45 *rushes through the wall-line of the kitchen and out into the living room.*]

LINDA [*to* BIFF]. Did you pack fresh underwear?

BIFF [*who has been limbering up*]. I want

to go! 50

BERNARD. Biff, I'm carrying your helmet, ain't I?

HAPPY. No, I'm carrying the helmet.

BERNARD. Oh, Biff, you promised me.

HAPPY. I'm carrying the helmet. 55

BERNARD. How am I going to get in the locker room?

LINDA. Let him carry the shoulder guards. [*She puts her coat and hat on in the kitchen.*]

BERNARD. Can I, Biff? 'Cause I told every- 60 body I'm going to be in the locker room.

HAPPY. In Ebbets Field it's the clubhouse.

BERNARD. I meant the clubhouse. Biff!

HAPPY. Biff!

BIFF [*grandly, after a slight pause*]. Let him 65 carry the shoulder guards.

HAPPY [*as he gives* BERNARD *the shoulder guards*]. Stay close to us now.

[WILLY *rushes in with the pennants.*]

WILLY [*handing them out*]. Everybody wave 70 when Biff comes out on the field. [HAPPY *and* BERNARD *run off.*] You set now, boys?

[*The music has died away.*]

BIFF. Ready to go, Pop. Every muscle is ready. 75

WILLY [*at the edge of the apron*]. You realize what this means?

BIFF. That's right, Pop.

WILLY [*feeling* BIFF's *muscles*]. You're coming home this afternoon captain of the All- 80 Scholastic Championship Team of the City of New York.

BIFF. I got it, Pop. And remember, pal, when I take off my helmet, that touchdown is for you. 85

WILLY. Let's go! [*He is starting out, with his arm around* BIFF, *when* CHARLEY *enters, as of old, in knickers.*] I got no room for you, Charley.

CHARLEY. Room? For what? 90

WILLY. In the car.

CHARLEY. You goin' for a ride? I wanted to shoot some casino.

WILLY [*furiously*]. Casino! [*Incredulously.*] Don't you realize what today is? 95

LINDA. Oh, he knows, Willy. He's just kidding you.

WILLY. That's nothing to kid about!

CHARLEY. No, Linda, what's goin' on?

LINDA. He's playing in Ebbets Field.

CHARLEY. Baseball in this weather?

WILLY. Don't talk to him. Come on, come
5 on! [*He is pushing them out.*]

CHARLEY. Wait a minute, didn't you hear
the news?

WILLY. What?

CHARLEY. Don't you listen to the radio?
10 Ebbets Field just blew up.

WILLY. You go to hell! [CHARLEY *laughs.
Pushing them out.*] Come on, come on! We're
late.

CHARLEY [*as they go*]. Knock a homer, Biff,
15 knock a homer!

WILLY [*the last to leave, turning to* CHAR-
LEY]. I don't think that was funny, Charley.
This is the greatest day of his life.

CHARLEY. Willy, when are you going to grow
20 up?

WILLY. Yeah, heh? When this game is over,
Charley, you'll be laughing out of the other
side of your face. They'll be calling him
another Red Grange.° Twenty-five thousand a
25 year.

CHARLEY [*kidding*]. Is that so?

WILLY. Yeah, that's so.

CHARLEY. Well, then, I'm sorry, Willy. But
tell me something.
30 WILLY. What?

CHARLEY. Who is Red Grange?

WILLY. Put up your hands. Goddam you, put
up your hands!

[CHARLEY, *chuckling, shakes his head and
35 walks away, around the left corner of the
stage.* WILLY *follows him. The music rises to a
mocking frenzy.*]

WILLY. Who the hell do you think you are,
better than everybody else? You don't know
40 everything, you big, ignorant, stupid. . . . Put
up your hands!

[*Light rises, on the right side of the forestage, on a small table in the reception room of*
CHARLEY'S *office. Traffic sounds are heard.*

Red Grange Harold Edward Grange, University of
Illinois All-American halfback and quarterback, 1923-
1925

BERNARD, *now mature, sits whistling to him-
45 self. A pair of tennis rackets and an overnight
bag are on the floor beside him.*]

WILLY [*offstage*]. What are you walking
away for? Don't walk away! If you're going
50 to say something say it to my face! I know you
laugh at me behind my back. You'll laugh out
of the other side of your goddam face after
this game. Touchdown! Touchdown! Eighty
thousand people! Touchdown! Right between
55 the goal posts.

[BERNARD *is a quiet, earnest, but self-assured
young man.* WILLY'S *voice is coming from
right upstage now.* BERNARD *lowers his feet off
the table and listens.* JENNY, *his father's secre-
60 tary, enters.*]

JENNY [*distressed*]. Say, Bernard, will you go
out in the hall?

BERNARD. What is that noise? Who is it?

JENNY. Mr. Loman. He just got off the ele-
65 vator.

BERNARD [*getting up*]. Who's he arguing
with?

JENNY. Nobody. There's nobody with him. I
can't deal with him any more, and your father
70 gets all upset everytime he comes. I've got a
lot of typing to do, and your father's waiting
to sign it. Will you see him?

WILLY [*entering*]. Touchdown! Touch— [*He
sees* JENNY.] Jenny, Jenny, good to see you.
75 How're ya? Workin'? Or still honest?

JENNY. Fine. How've you been feeling?

WILLY. Not much any more, Jenny. Ha, ha!
[*He is surprised to see the rackets.*]

BERNARD. Hello, Uncle Willy.

WILLY [*almost shocked*]. Bernard! Well,
80 look who's here!

[*He comes quickly, guiltily, to* BERNARD *and
warmly shakes his hand.*]

BERNARD. How are you? Good to see you.

WILLY. What are you doing here?
85 BERNARD. Oh, just stopped by to see Pop.
Get off my feet till my train leaves. I'm going
to Washington in a few minutes.

WILLY. Is he in?

BERNARD. Yes, he's in his office with the
90 accountant. Sit down.

WILLY [*sitting down*]. What're you going to
do in Washington?

BERNARD. Oh, just a case I've got there, Willy.

WILLY. That so? [*Indicating the rackets.*] You going to play tennis there?

5 BERNARD. I'm staying with a friend who's got a court.

WILLY. Don't say. His own tennis court. Must be fine people I bet.

BERNARD. They are, very nice. Dad tells me
10 Biff's in town.

WILLY [*with a big smile*]. Yeah, Biff's in. Working on a very big deal, Bernard.

BERNARD. What's Biff doing?

WILLY. Well, he's doing very big things in
15 the West. But he decided to establish himself here. Very big. We're having dinner. Did I hear your wife had a boy?

BERNARD. That's right. Our second.

WILLY. Two boys! What do you know!

20 BERNARD. What kind of deal has Biff got?

WILLY. Well, Bill Oliver—very big sporting-goods man—he wants Biff very badly. Called him in from the West. Long distance, *carte blanche*, special deliveries. Your friends have
25 their own private tennis court?

BERNARD. You still with the old firm, Willy?

WILLY [*after a pause*]. I'm—I'm overjoyed to see how you made the grade, Bernard, overjoyed. It's an encouraging thing to see a young
30 man really—really— Looks very good for Biff —very— [*He breaks off, then*] Bernard— [*He is so full of emotion, he breaks off again.*]

BERNARD. What is it, Willy?

WILLY [*small and alone*]. What—what's the
35 secret?

BERNARD. What secret?

WILLY. How—how did you? Why didn't he ever catch on?

BERNARD. I wouldn't know that, Willy.

40 WILLY [*confidentially, desperately*]. You were his friend, his boyhood friend. There's something I don't understand about it. His life ended after that Ebbets Field game. From the age of seventeen nothing good ever happened
45 to him.

BERNARD. He never trained himself for anything.

WILLY. But he did, he did. After high school

he took so many correspondence courses. Radio mechanics; television; God knows what, and 50 never made the slightest mark.

BERNARD [*taking off his glasses*]. Willy, do you want to talk candidly?

WILLY [*rising, faces* BERNARD]. I regard you as a very brilliant man, Bernard. I value your 55 advice.

BERNARD. Oh, the hell with the advice, Willy. I couldn't advise you. There's just one thing I've always wanted to ask you. When he was supposed to graduate, and the math teacher 60 flunked him—

WILLY. Oh, that son-of-a-bitch ruined his life.

BERNARD. Yeah, but, Willy, all he had to do was to go to summer school and make up that 65 subject.

WILLY. That's right, that's right.

BERNARD. Did you tell him not to go to summer school?

WILLY. Me? I begged him to go. I ordered 70 him to go!

BERNARD. Then why wouldn't he go?

WILLY. Why? Why? Bernard, that question has been trailing me like a ghost for the last fifteen years. He flunked the subject, and laid 75 down and died like a hammer hit him!

BERNARD. Take it easy, kid.

WILLY. Let me talk to you—I got nobody to talk to. Bernard, Bernard, was it my fault? Y'see? It keeps going around in my mind, 80 maybe I did something to him. I got nothing to give him.

BERNARD. Don't take it so hard.

WILLY. Why did he lay down? What is the story there? You were his friend! 85

BERNARD. Willy, I remember, it was June, and our grades came out. And he'd flunked math.

WILLY. That son-of-a-bitch!

BERNARD. No, it wasn't right then. Biff just 90 got very angry, I remember, and he was ready to enroll in summer school.

WILLY [*surprised*]. He was?

BERNARD. He wasn't beaten by it at all. But then, Willy, he disappeared from the block for 95 almost a month. And I got the idea that he'd gone up to New England to see you. Did he have a talk with you then?

[WILLY *stares in silence.*]

BERNARD. Willy?

WILLY [*with a strong edge of resentment in his voice*]. Yeah, he came to Boston. What about it?

BERNARD. Well, just that when he came back —I'll never forget this, it always mystifies me. Because I'd thought so well of Biff, even though he'd always taken advantage of me. I loved him, Willy, y'know? And he came back after that month and took his sneakers—remember those sneakers with "University of Virginia" printed on them? He was so proud of those, wore them every day. And he took them down in the cellar, and burned them up in the furnace. We had a fist fight. It lasted at least half an hour. Just the two of us, punching each other down the cellar, and crying right through it. I've often thought of how strange it was that I knew he'd given up his life. What happened in Boston, Willy?

[WILLY *looks at him as at an intruder.*]

BERNARD. I just bring it up because you asked me.

WILLY [*angrily*]. Nothing. What do you mean, "What happened?" What's that got to do with anything?

BERNARD. Well, don't get sore.

WILLY. What are you trying to do, blame it on me? If a boy lays down is that my fault?

BERNARD. Now, Willy, don't get—

WILLY. Well, don't—don't talk to me that way! What does that mean, "What happened?"

[CHARLEY *enters. He is in his vest, and he carries a bottle of bourbon.*]

CHARLEY. Hey, you're going to miss that train. [*He waves the bottle.*]

BERNARD. Yeah, I'm going. [*He takes the bottle.*] Thanks, Pop. [*He picks up his rackets and bag.*] Good-bye, Willy, and don't worry about it. You know, "if at first you don't succeed . . ."

WILLY. Yes, I believe in that.

BERNARD. But sometimes, Willy, it's better for a man just to walk away.

WILLY. Walk away?

BERNARD. That's right.

WILLY. But if you can't walk away?

BERNARD [*after a slight pause*]. I guess that's when it's tough. [*Extending his hand.*] Good-bye, Willy.

WILLY [*shaking BERNARD's hand*]. Good-bye, boy.

CHARLEY [*an arm on BERNARD's shoulder*]. How do you like this kid? Gonna argue a case in front of the Supreme Court.

BERNARD [*protesting*]. Pop!

WILLY [*genuinely shocked, pained, and happy*]. No! The Supreme Court!

BERNARD. I gotta run. 'Bye, Dad!

CHARLEY. Knock 'em dead, Bernard!

[BERNARD *goes off.*]

WILLY [*as CHARLEY takes out his wallet*]. The Supreme Court! And he didn't even mention it!

CHARLEY [*counting out money on the desk*]. He don't have to—he's gonna do it.

WILLY. And you never told him what to do, did you? You never took any interest in him.

CHARLEY. My salvation is that I never took any interest in anything. There's some money —fifty dollars. I got an accountant inside.

WILLY. Charley, look. . . . [*With difficulty.*] I got my insurance to pay. If you can manage it—I need a hundred and ten dollars.

[CHARLEY *doesn't reply for a moment, merely stops moving.*]

WILLY. I'd draw it from my bank but Linda would know, and I . . .

CHARLEY. Sit down, Willy.

WILLY [*moving toward the chair*]. I'm keeping an account of everything, remember. I'll pay every penny back. [*He sits.*]

CHARLEY. Now listen to me, Willy.

WILLY. I want you to know I appreciate . . .

CHARLEY [*sitting down on the table*]. Willy, what're you doin'? What the hell is goin' on in your head?

WILLY. Why? I'm simply . . .

CHARLEY. I offered you a job. You can make fifty dollars a week. And I won't send you on the road.

WILLY. I've got a job.

CHARLEY. Without pay? What kind of a job is a job without pay? [*He rises.*] Now, look, kid, enough is enough. I'm no genius but I know when I'm being insulted.

5 WILLY. Insulted?

CHARLEY. Why don't you want to work for me?

WILLY. What's the matter with you? I've got a job.

10 CHARLEY. Then what're you walkin' in here every week for?

WILLY [*getting up*]. Well, if you don't want me to walk in here—

CHARLEY. I am offering you a job.

15 WILLY. I don't want your goddam job!

CHARLEY. When the hell are you going to grow up?

WILLY [*furiously*]. You big ignoramus, if you say that to me again I'll rap you one! I

20 don't care how big you are! [*He's ready to fight.*]

[*Pause.*]

CHARLEY [*kindly, going to him*]. How much do you need, Willy?

25 WILLY. Charley, I'm strapped, I'm strapped. I don't know what to do. I was just fired.

CHARLEY. Howard fired you?

WILLY. That snotnose. Imagine that? I named him. I named him Howard.

30 CHARLEY. Willy, when're you gonna realize that them things don't mean anything? You named him Howard, but you can't sell that. The only thing you got in this world is what you can sell. And the funny thing is that you're

35 a salesman, and you don't know that.

WILLY. I've always tried to think otherwise, I guess. I always felt that if a man was impressive, and well liked, that nothing—

CHARLEY. Why must everybody like you?

40 Who liked J. P. Morgan?° Was he impressive? In a Turkish bath he'd look like a butcher. But with his pockets on he was very well liked. Now listen, Willy, I know you don't like me, and nobody can say I'm in love with you, but

45 I'll give you a job because—just for the hell

J. P. Morgan John Pierpont Morgan (1887-1943), famous New York banker and financier

of it, put it that way. Now what do you say?

WILLY. I—I just can't work for you, Charley.

CHARLEY. What're you, jealous of me?

WILLY. I can't work for you, that's all, don't

50 ask me why.

CHARLEY [*angered, takes out more bills*]. You been jealous of me all your life, you damned fool! Here, pay your insurance. [*He puts the money in* WILLY's *hand.*]

55 WILLY. I'm keeping strict accounts.

CHARLEY. I've got some work to do. Take care of yourself. And pay your insurance.

WILLY [*moving to the right*]. Funny, y'know? After all the highways, and the trains

60 and the appointments, and the years, you end up worth more dead than alive.

CHARLEY. Willy, nobody's worth nothin' dead. [*After a slight pause.*] Did you hear what I said?

65 [WILLY *stands still, dreaming.*]

CHARLEY. Willy!

WILLY. Apologize to Bernard for me when you see him. I didn't mean to argue with him. He's a fine boy. They're all fine boys, and

70 they'll end up big—all of them. Someday they'll all play tennis together. Wish me luck, Charley. He saw Bill Oliver today.

CHARLEY. Good luck.

WILLY [*on the verge of tears*]. Charley,

75 you're the only friend I got. Isn't that a remarkable thing? [*He goes out.*]

CHARLEY. Jesus!

[CHARLEY *stares after him a moment and follows. All light blacks out. Suddenly raucous

80 music is heard, and a red glow rises behind the screen at right.* STANLEY, *a young waiter, appears, carrying a table, followed by* HAPPY, *who is carrying two chairs.*]

STANLEY [*putting the table down*]. That's all

85 right, Mr. Loman, I can handle it myself. [*He turns and takes the chairs from* HAPPY *and places them at the table.*]

HAPPY [*glancing around*]. Oh, this is better.

STANLEY. Sure, in the front there you're in

90 the middle of all kinds a noise. Whenever you got a party, Mr. Loman, you just tell me and I'll put you back here. Y'know, there's a lotta people they don't like it private, because when

they go out they like to see a lotta action around them because they're sick and tired to stay in the house by theirself. But I know you, you ain't from Hackensack. You know what I mean?

5 HAPPY [*sitting down*]. So how's it coming, Stanley?

STANLEY. Ah, it's a dog's life. I only wish during the war they'd took me in the Army.
10 I coulda been dead by now.

HAPPY. My brother's back, Stanley.

STANLEY. Oh, he come back, heh? From the Far West.

HAPPY. Yeah, big cattle man, my brother, so
15 treat him right. And my father's coming too.

STANLEY. Oh, your father too!

HAPPY. You got a couple of nice lobsters?

STANLEY. Hundred per cent, big.

HAPPY. I want them with the claws.

20 STANLEY. Don't worry, I don't give you no mice. [HAPPY *laughs.*] How about some wine? It'll put a head on the meal.

HAPPY. No. You remember, Stanley, that recipe I brought you from overseas? With the
25 champagne in it?

STANLEY. Oh, yeah, sure. I still got it tacked up yet in the kitchen. But that'll have to cost a buck apiece anyways.

HAPPY. That's all right.

30 STANLEY. What'd you, hit a number or somethin'?

HAPPY. No, it's a little celebration. My brother is—I think he pulled off a big deal today. I think we're going into business to-
35 gether.

STANLEY. Great! That's the best for you. Because a family business, you know what I mean?—that's the best.

HAPPY. That's what I think.

40 STANLEY. 'Cause what's the difference? Somebody steals? It's in the family. Know what I mean? [*Sotto voce.*] Like this bartender here. The boss is goin' crazy what kinda leak he's got in the cash register. You put it in but
45 it don't come out.

HAPPY [*raising his head*]. Sh!

STANLEY. What?

HAPPY. You notice I wasn't lookin' right or

left, was I?

STANLEY. No. 50

HAPPY. And my eyes are closed.

STANLEY. So what's the—?

HAPPY. Strudel's comin'.

STANLEY [*catching on, looks around*]. Ah, no, there's no— 55

[*He breaks off as a furred, lavishly dressed girl enters and sits at the next table. Both follow her with their eyes.*]

STANLEY. Geez, how'd ya know?

HAPPY. I got radar or something. [*Staring* 60 *directly at her profile.*] Oooooooo . . . Stanley.

STANLEY. I think that's for you, Mr. Loman.

HAPPY. Look at that mouth. Oh, God. And the binoculars.

STANLEY. Geez, you got a life, Mr. Loman. 65

HAPPY. Wait on her.

STANLEY [*going to the girl's table*]. Would you like a menu, ma'am?

GIRL. I'm expecting someone, but I'd like a—

HAPPY. Why don't you bring her—excuse 70 me, miss, do you mind? I sell champagne, and I'd like you to try my brand. Bring her a champagne, Stanley.

GIRL. That's awfully nice of you.

HAPPY. Don't mention it. It's all company 75 money. [*He laughs.*]

GIRL. That's a charming product to be selling, isn't it?

HAPPY. Oh, gets to be like everything else. Selling is selling, y'know. 80

GIRL. I suppose.

HAPPY. You don't happen to sell, do you?

GIRL. No, I don't sell.

HAPPY. Would you object to a compliment from a stranger? You ought to be on a mag- 85 azine cover.

GIRL [*looking at him a little archly*]. I have been.

[STANLEY *comes in with a glass of champagne.*] 90

HAPPY. What'd I say before, Stanley? You see? She's a cover girl.

STANLEY. Oh, I could see, I could see.

HAPPY [*to the* GIRL]. What magazine?

GIRL. Oh, a lot of them. [*She takes the* 95 *drink.*] Thank you.

HAPPY. You know what they say in France, don't you? "Champagne is the drink of the complexion"—Hya, Biff!

[BIFF *has entered and sits with* HAPPY.]

5 BIFF. Hello, kid. Sorry I'm late.

HAPPY. I just got here. Uh, Miss—?

GIRL. Forsythe.

HAPPY. Miss Forsythe, this is my brother.

BIFF. Is Dad here?

10 HAPPY. His name is Biff. You might've heard of him. Great football player.

GIRL. Really? What team?

HAPPY. Are you familiar with football?

GIRL. No, I'm afraid I'm not.

15 HAPPY. Biff is quarterback with the New York Giants.

GIRL. Well, that is nice, isn't it? [*She drinks.*]

HAPPY. Good health.

20 GIRL. I'm happy to meet you.

HAPPY. That's my name. Hap. It's really Harold, but at West Point they called me Happy.

GIRL [*now really impressed*]. Oh, I see. How 25 do you do? [*She turns her profile.*]

BIFF. Isn't Dad coming?

HAPPY. You want her?

BIFF. Oh, I could never make that.

HAPPY. I remember the time that idea would 30 never come into your head. Where's the old confidence, Biff?

BIFF. I just saw Oliver—

HAPPY. Wait a minute. I've got to see that old confidence again. Do you want her? She's 35 on call.

BIFF. Oh, no. [*He turns to look at the* GIRL.]

HAPPY. I'm telling you. Watch this. [*Turning to the* GIRL.] Honey? [*She turns to him.*] Are you busy?

40 GIRL. Well, I am . . . but I could make a phone call.

HAPPY. Do that, will you, honey? And see if you can get a friend. We'll be here for a while. Biff is one of the greatest football players in 45 the country.

GIRL [*standing up*]. Well, I'm certainly happy to meet you.

HAPPY. Come back soon.

GIRL. I'll try.

HAPPY. Don't try, honey, try hard. 50

[*The* GIRL *exits.* STANLEY *follows, shaking his head in bewildered admiration.*]

HAPPY. Isn't that a shame now? A beautiful girl like that? That's why I can't get married. There's not a good woman in a thousand. New 55 York is loaded with them, kid!

BIFF. Hap, look—

HAPPY. I told you she was on call!

BIFF [*strangely unnerved*]. Cut it out, will ya? I want to say something to you. 60

HAPPY. Did you see Oliver?

BIFF. I saw him all right. Now look, I want to tell Dad a couple of things and I want you to help me.

HAPPY. What? Is he going to back you? 65

BIFF. Are you crazy? You're out of your goddam head, you know that?

HAPPY. Why? What happened?

BIFF [*breathlessly*]. I did a terrible thing today, Hap. It's been the strangest day I ever 70 went through. I'm all numb, I swear.

HAPPY. You mean he wouldn't see you?

BIFF. Well, I waited six hours for him, see? All day. Kept sending my name in. Even tried to date his secretary so she'd get me to him, 75 but no soap.

HAPPY. Because you're not showin' the old confidence, Biff. He remembered you, didn't he?

BIFF [*stopping* HAPPY *with a gesture*]. 80 Finally, about five o'clock, he comes out. Didn't remember who I was or anything. I felt like such an idiot, Hap.

HAPPY. Did you tell him my Florida idea?

BIFF. He walked away. I saw him for one 85 minute. I got so mad I could've torn the walls down! How the hell did I ever get the idea I was a salesmen there? I even believed myself that I'd been a salesman for him! And then he gave me one look and—I realized what a 90 ridiculous lie my whole life has been. We've been talking in a dream for fifteen years. I was a shipping clerk.

HAPPY. What'd you do?

BIFF [*with great tension and wonder*]. Well, 95 he left, see. And the secretary went out. I was

all alone in the waiting-room. I don't know what came over me, Hap. The next thing I know I'm in his office—panelled walls, everything. I can't explain it. I—Hap, I took his
5 fountain pen.

HAPPY. Geez, did he catch you?

BIFF. I ran out. I ran down all eleven flights. I ran and ran and ran.

HAPPY. That was an awful dumb—what'd
10 you do that for?

BIFF [*agonized*]. I don't know, I just—wanted to take something, I don't know. You gotta help me, Hap, I'm gonna tell Pop.

HAPPY. You crazy? What for?
15 BIFF. Hap, he's got to understand that I'm not the man somebody lends that kind of money to. He thinks I've been spiting him all these years and it's eating him up.

HAPPY. That's just it. You tell him something
20 nice.

BIFF. I can't.

HAPPY. Say you got a lunch date with Oliver tomorrow.

BIFF. So what do I do tomorrow?
25 HAPPY. You leave the house tomorrow and come back at night and say Oliver is thinking it over. And he thinks it over for a couple of weeks, and gradually it fades away and nobody's the worse.
30 BIFF. But it'll go on for ever!

HAPPY. Dad is never so happy as when he's looking forward to something!

[WILLY *enters.*]

HAPPY. Hello, scout!
35 WILLY. Gee, I haven't been here in years!

[STANLEY *has followed* WILLY *in and sets a chair for him.* STANLEY *starts off, but* HAPPY *stops him.*]

HAPPY. Stanley!
40 [STANLEY *stands by, waiting for an order.*]

BIFF [*going to* WILLY *with guilt, as to an invalid*]. Sit down, Pop. You want a drink?

WILLY. Sure, I don't mind.

BIFF. Let's get a load on.
45 WILLY. You look worried.

BIFF. N-no. [*To* STANLEY.] Scotch all around. Make it doubles.

STANLEY. Doubles, right. [*He goes.*]

WILLY. You had a couple already, didn't
50 you?

BIFF. Just a couple, yeah.

WILLY. Well, what happened, boy? [*Nodding affirmatively, with a smile.*] Everything go all right?
55 BIFF [*takes a breath, then reaches out and grasps* WILLY's *hand*]. Pal . . . [*he is smiling bravely, and* WILLY *is smiling too*] I had an experience today.

HAPPY. Terrific, Pop.

WILLY. That so? What happened?
60 BIFF [*high, slightly alcoholic, above the earth*]. I'm going to tell you everything from first to last. It's been a strange day. [*Silence. He looks around, composes himself as best he
65 can, but his breath keeps breaking the rhythm of his voice.*] I had to wait quite a while for him, and—

WILLY. Oliver?

BIFF. Yeah, Oliver. All day, as a matter of
70 cold fact. And a lot of—instances—facts, Pop, facts about my life came back to me. Who was it, Pop? Who ever said I was a salesman with Oliver?

WILLY. Well, you were.
75 BIFF. No, Dad, I was a shipping clerk.

WILLY. But you were practically—

BIFF [*with determination*]. Dad, I don't know who said it first, but I was never a salesman for Bill Oliver.

WILLY. What're you talking about?
80 BIFF. Let's hold on to the facts tonight, Pop. We're not going to get anywhere bullin' around. I was a shipping clerk.

WILLY [*angrily*]. All right, now listen to
85 me—

BIFF. Why don't you let me finish?

WILLY. I'm not interested in stories about the past or any crap of that kind because the woods are burning, boys, you understand?
90 There's a big blaze going on all around. I was fired today.

BIFF [*shocked*]. How could you be?

WILLY. I was fired, and I'm looking for a little good news to tell your mother, because the
95 woman has waited and the woman has suffered. The gist of it is that I haven't got a

story left in my head, Biff. So don't give me a lecture about facts and aspects. I am not interested. Now what've you got to say to me?

[STANLEY *enters with three drinks. They wait until he leaves.*]

5

WILLY. Did you see Oliver?

BIFF. Jesus, Dad!

WILLY. You mean you didn't go up there?

HAPPY. Sure he went up there.

10

BIFF. I did. I—saw him. How could they fire you?

WILLY [*on the edge of his chair*]. What kind of a welcome did he give you?

BIFF. He won't even let you work on commission?

15

WILLY. I'm out! [*Driving.*] So tell me, he gave you a warm welcome?

HAPPY. Sure, Pop, sure!

BIFF [*driven*]. Well, it was kind of—

20

WILLY. I was wondering if he'd remember you. [*To* HAPPY.] Imagine, man doesn't see him for ten, twelve years and gives him that kind of a welcome!

HAPPY. Damn right!

25

BIFF [*trying to return to the offensive.*] Pop, look—

WILLY. You know why he remembered you, don't you? Because you impressed him in those days.

30

BIFF. Let's talk quietly and get this down to the facts, huh?

WILLY [*as though* BIFF *had been interrupting*]. Well, what happened? It's great news, Biff. Did he take you into his office or'd you talk in the waiting-room?

35

BIFF. Well, he came in, see, and—

WILLY [*with a big smile*]. What'd he say? Betcha he threw his arm around you.

BIFF. Well, he kinda—

40

WILLY. He's a fine man. [*To* HAPPY.] Very hard man to see, y'know.

HAPPY [*agreeing*]. Oh, I know.

WILLY [*to* BIFF]. Is that where you had the drinks?

45

BIFF. Yeah, he gave me a couple of—no, no!

HAPPY [*cutting in*]. He told him my Florida idea.

WILLY. Don't interrupt. [*To* BIFF.] How'd he react to the Florida idea?

BIFF. Dad, will you give me a minute to explain?

50

WILLY. I've been waiting for you to explain since I sat down here! What happened? He took you into his office and what?

BIFF. Well—I talked. And—and he listened, see.

55

WILLY. Famous for the way he listens, y'know. What was his answer?

BIFF. His answer was— [*He breaks off, suddenly angry.*] Dad, you're not letting me tell you what I want to tell you!

60

WILLY [*accusing, angered*]. You didn't see him, did you?

BIFF. I did see him!

WILLY. What'd you insult him or something? You insulted him, didn't you?

65

BIFF. Listen, will you let me out of it, will you just let me out of it!

HAPPY. What the hell!

WILLY. Tell me what happened!

70

BIFF [*to* HAPPY]. I can't talk to him!

[*A single trumpet note jars the ear. The light of green leaves stains the house, which holds the air of night and a dream.* YOUNG BERNARD *enters and knocks on the door of the house.*]

75

YOUNG BERNARD [*frantically*]. Mrs. Loman, Mrs. Loman!

HAPPY. Tell him what happened!

BIFF [*to* HAPPY]. Shut up and leave me alone!

80

WILLY. No, no! You had to go and flunk math!

BIFF. What math? What're you talking about?

85

YOUNG BERNARD. Mrs. Loman, Mrs. Loman!

[LINDA *appears in the house, as of old.*]

WILLY [*wildly*]. Math, math, math!

BIFF. Take it easy, Pop!

YOUNG BERNARD. Mrs. Loman!

90

WILLY [*furiously*]. If you hadn't flunked you'd've been set by now!

BIFF. Now look, I'm gonna tell you what happened, and you're going to listen to me.

YOUNG BERNARD. Mrs. Loman!

95

BIFF. I waited six hours—

HAPPY. What the hell are you saying?

BIFF. I kept sending in my name but he wouldn't see me. So finally he. . . . [*He continues unheard as light fades low on the restaurant.*]

YOUNG BERNARD. Biff flunked math!

LINDA. No!

YOUNG BERNARD. Birnbaum flunked him! They won't graduate him!

LINDA. But they have to. He's gotta go to the university. Where is he? Biff! Biff!

YOUNG BERNARD. No, he left. He went to Grand Central.

LINDA. Grand— You mean he went to Boston!

YOUNG BERNARD. Is Uncle Willy in Boston?

LINDA. Oh, maybe Willy can talk to the teacher. Oh, the poor, poor boy!

[*Light on house area snaps out.*]

BIFF [*at the table, now audible, holding up a gold fountain pen*]. . . . so I'm washed up with Oliver, you understand? Are you listening to me?

WILLY [*at a loss*]. Yeah, sure. If you hadn't flunked—

BIFF. Flunked what? What're you talking about?

WILLY. Don't blame everything on me! I didn't flunk math—you did! What pen?

HAPPY. That was awful dumb, Biff, a pen like that is worth—

WILLY [*seeing the pen for the first time*]. You took Oliver's pen?

BIFF [*weakening*]. Dad, I just explained it to you.

WILLY. You stole Bill Oliver's fountain pen!

BIFF. I didn't exactly steal it! That's just what I've been explaining to you!

HAPPY. He had it in his hand and just then Oliver walked in, so he got nervous and stuck it in his pocket!

WILLY. My God, Biff!

BIFF. I never intended to do it, Dad!

OPERATOR'S VOICE. Standish Arms, good evening!

WILLY [*shouting*]. I'm not in my room!

BIFF [*frightened*]. Dad, what's the matter? [*He and HAPPY stand up.*]

OPERATOR. Ringing Mr. Loman for you!

WILLY. I'm not there, stop it!

BIFF [*horrified, gets down on one knee before WILLY*]. Dad, I'll make good, I'll make good. [*WILLY tries to get to his feet. BIFF holds him down.*] Sit down now.

WILLY. No, you're no good, you're no good for anything.

BIFF. I am, Dad, I'll find something else, you understand? Now don't worry about anything. [*He holds up WILLY's face.*] Talk to me, Dad.

OPERATOR. Mr. Loman does not answer. Shall I page him?

WILLY [*attempting to stand, as though to rush and silence the OPERATOR*]. No, no, no!

HAPPY. He'll strike something, Pop.

WILLY. No, no . . .

BIFF [*desperately, standing over WILLY*]. Pop, listen! Listen to me! I'm telling you something good. Oliver talked to his partner about the Florida idea. You listening? He—he talked to his partner, and he came to me . . . I'm going to be all right, you hear? Dad, listen to me, he said it was just a question of the amount!

WILLY. Then you . . . got it?

HAPPY. He's gonna be terrific, Pop!

WILLY [*trying to stand*]. Then you got it, haven't you? You got it! You got it!

BIFF [*agonized, holds WILLY down*]. No, no. Look, Pop. I'm supposed to have lunch with them tomorrow. I'm just telling you this so you'll know that I can still make an impression, Pop. And I'll make good somewhere, but I can't go tomorrow, see?

WILLY. Why not? You simply—

BIFF. But the pen, Pop!

WILLY. You give it to him and tell him it was an oversight!

HAPPY. Sure, have lunch tomorrow!

BIFF. I can't say that—

WILLY. You were doing a crossword puzzle and accidentally used his pen!

BIFF. Listen, kid, I took those balls years ago, now I walk in with his fountain pen? That clinches it, don't you see? I can't face him like that! I'll try elsewhere.

PAGE'S VOICE. Paging Mr. Loman!

WILLY. Don't you want to be anything?

BIFF. Pop, how can I go back?

WILLY. You don't want to be anything, is that what's behind it?

BIFF [now angry at WILLY for not crediting his sympathy]. Don't take it that way! You think it was easy walking into that office after what I'd done to him? A team of horses couldn't have dragged me back to Bill Oliver!

WILLY. Then why'd you go?

BIFF. Why did I go? Why did I go? Look at you! Look at what's become of you!

[Off left, the WOMAN laughs.]

WILLY. Biff, you're going to go to that lunch tomorrow, or—

BIFF. I can't go. I've got no appointment!

HAPPY. Biff, for . . . !

WILLY. Are you spiting me?

BIFF. Don't take it that way! Goddammit!

WILLY [strikes BIFF and falters away from the table]. You rotten little louse! Are you spiting me?

THE WOMAN. Someone's at the door, Willy!

BIFF. I'm no good, can't you see what I am?

HAPPY [separating them]. Hey, you're in a restaurant! Now cut it out, both of you! [The girls enter.] Hello, girls, sit down.

[The WOMAN laughs, off left.]

MISS FORSYTHE. I guess we might as well. This is Letta.

THE WOMAN. Willy, are you going to wake up?

BIFF [ignoring WILLY]. How're ya, miss, sit down. What do you drink?

MISS FORSYTHE. Letta might not be able to stay long.

LETTA. I gotta get up very early tomorrow. I got jury duty. I'm so excited! Were you fellows ever on a jury?

BIFF. No, but I been in front of them! [The girls laugh.] This is my father.

LETTA. Isn't he cute? Sit down with us, Pop.

HAPPY. Sit him down, Biff!

BIFF [going to him]. Come on, slugger, drink us under the table. To hell with it! Come on, sit down, pal.

[On BIFF's last insistence, WILLY is about to sit.]

THE WOMAN [now urgently]. Willy, are you going to answer the door!

[The WOMAN's call pulls WILLY back. He starts right, befuddled.]

BIFF. Hey, where are you going?

WILLY. Open the door.

BIFF. The door?

WILLY. The washroom . . . the door . . . where's the door?

BIFF [leading WILLY to the left]. Just go straight down.

[WILLY moves left.]

THE WOMAN. Willy, Willy, are you going to get up, get up, get up, get up?

[WILLY exits left.]

LETTA. I think it's sweet you bring your daddy along.

MISS FORSYTHE. Oh, he isn't really your father!

BIFF [at left, turning to her resentfully]. Miss Forsythe, you've just seen a prince walk by. A fine, troubled prince. A hardworking, unappreciated prince. A pal, you understand? A good companion. Always for his boys.

LETTA. That's so sweet.

HAPPY. Well, girls, what's the program? We're wasting time. Come on, Biff. Gather round. Where would you like to go?

BIFF. Why don't you do something for him?

HAPPY. Me!

BIFF. Don't you give a damn for him, Hap?

HAPPY. What're you talking about? I'm the one who—

BIFF. I sense it, you don't give a good goddam about him.

[He takes the rolled-up hose from his pocket and puts it on the table in front of HAPPY.] Look what I found in the cellar, for Christ's sake. How can you bear to let it go on?

HAPPY. Me? Who goes away? Who runs off and—

BIFF. Yeah, but he doesn't mean anything to you. You could help him—I can't. Don't you understand what I'm talking about? He's going to kill himself, don't you know that?

HAPPY. Don't I know it! Me!

BIFF. Hap, help him! Jesus . . . help him. . . . Help me, help me, I can't bear to look at his face! [*Ready to weep, he hurries out, up right.*]

HAPPY [*starting after him*]. Where are you going?

MISS FORSYTHE. What's he so mad about?

5 HAPPY. Come on, girls, we'll catch up with him.

MISS FORSYTHE [*as* HAPPY *pushes her out*]. Say, I don't like that temper of his!

HAPPY. He's just a little overstrung, he'll be
10 all right!

WILLY [*off left, as the* WOMAN *laughs*]. Don't answer! Don't answer!

LETTA. Don't you want to tell your father—

HAPPY. No, that's not my father. He's just a
15 guy. Come on, we'll catch Biff, and honey, we're going to paint this town! Stanley, where's the check! Hey, Stanley!

[*They exit.* STANLEY *looks toward left.*]

STANLEY [*calling to* HAPPY *indignantly*]. Mr.
20 Loman! Mr. Loman!

[STANLEY *picks up a chair and follows them off. Knocking is heard off left. The* WOMAN *enters, laughing.* WILLY *follows her. She is in a black slip; he is buttoning his shirt. Raw,*
25 *sensuous music accompanies their speech.*]

WILLY. Will you stop laughing? Will you stop?

THE WOMAN. Aren't you going to answer the door? He'll wake the whole hotel.

30 WILLY. I'm not expecting anybody.

THE WOMAN. Whyn't you have another drink, honey, and stop being so damn self-centered?

WILLY. I'm so lonely.

35 THE WOMAN. You know you ruined me, Willy? From now on, whenever you come to the office, I'll see that you go right through to the buyers. No waiting at my desk any more, Willy. You ruined me.

40 WILLY. That's nice of you to say that.

THE WOMAN. Gee, you are self-centered! Why so sad? You are the saddest, self-centeredest soul I ever did see-saw. [*She laughs. He kisses her.*] Come on inside, drum-
45 mer boy. It's silly to be dressing in the middle of the night. [*As knocking is heard.*] Aren't you going to answer the door?

WILLY. They're knocking on the wrong door.

THE WOMAN. But I felt the knocking. And
50 he heard us talking in here. Maybe the hotel's on fire!

WILLY [*his terror rising*]. It's a mistake.

THE WOMAN. Then tell him to go away!

WILLY. There's nobody there.
55
THE WOMAN. It's getting on my nerves, Willy. There's somebody standing out there and it's getting on my nerves!

WILLY [*pushing her away from him*]. All right, stay in the bathroom here, and don't
60 come out. I think there's a law in Massachusetts about it, so don't come out. It may be that new room clerk. He looked very mean. So don't come out. It's a mistake, there's no fire.
65
[*The knocking is heard again. He takes a few steps away from her, and she vanishes into the wing. The light follows him, and now he is facing* YOUNG BIFF, *who carries a suit-case.* BIFF *steps toward him. The music is
70 gone.*]

BIFF. Why didn't you answer?

WILLY. Biff! What are you doing in Boston?

BIFF. Why didn't you answer! I've been knocking for five minutes, I called you on the
75 phone—

WILLY. I just heard you. I was in the bathroom and had the door shut. Did anything happen home?

BIFF. Dad—I let you down.
80
WILLY. What do you mean?

BIFF. Dad . . .

WILLY. Biffo, what's this about? [*Putting his arm around* BIFF.] Come on, let's go downstairs and get you a malted.
85
BIFF. Dad, I flunked math.

WILLY. Not for the term?

BIFF. The term. I haven't got enough credits to graduate.

WILLY. You mean to say Bernard wouldn't
90 give you the answers?

BIFF. He did, he tried, but I only got a sixty-one.

WILLY. And they wouldn't give you four points?
95
BIFF. Birnbaum refused absolutely. I begged

him, Pop, but he won't give me those points. You gotta talk to him before they close the school. Because if he saw the kind of man you are, and you just talked to him in your way, I'm sure he'd come through for me. The class came right before practice, see, and I didn't go enough. Would you talk to him? He'd like you, Pop. You know the way you could talk.

WILLY. You're on. We'll drive right back.

BIFF. Oh, Dad, good work! I'm sure he'll change it for you!

WILLY. Go downstairs and tell the clerk I'm checkin' out. Go right down.

BIFF. Yes, sir! See, the reason he hates me, Pop—one day he was late for class so I got up at the blackboard and imitated him. I crossed my eyes and talked with a lithp.

WILLY [laughing]. You did? The kids like it?

BIFF. They nearly died laughing!

WILLY. Yeah? What'd you do?

BIFF. The thquare root of thixthy twee is . . . [WILLY bursts out laughing; BIFF joins him]. And in the middle of it he walked in!

[WILLY laughs and the WOMAN joins in offstage.]

WILLY [without hesitation]. Hurry downstairs and—

BIFF. Somebody in there?

WILLY. No, that was next door.

[The WOMAN laughs offstage.]

BIFF. Somebody got in your bathroom!

WILLY. No, it's the next room, there's a party—

THE WOMAN [enters, laughing. She lisps this]. Can I come in? There's something in the bathtub, Willy, and it's moving!

[WILLY looks at BIFF, who is staring openmouthed and horrified at the WOMAN.]

WILLY. Ah—you better go back to your room. They must be finished painting by now. They're painting her room so I let her take a shower here. Go back, go back. . . . [He pushes her.]

THE WOMAN [resisting]. But I've got to get dressed, Willy, I can't—

WILLY. Get out of here! Go back, go back. . . . [Suddenly striving for the ordinary.] This is Miss Francis, Biff, she's a buyer. They're painting her room. Go back, Miss Francis, go back . . .

THE WOMAN. But my clothes, I can't go out naked in the hall!

WILLY [pushing her offstage]. Get outa here! Go back, go back!

[BIFF slowly sits down on his suitcase as the argument continues offstage.]

THE WOMAN. Where's my stockings? You promised me stockings, Willy!

WILLY. I have no stockings here!

THE WOMAN. You had two boxes of size nine sheers for me, and I want them!

WILLY. Here, for God's sake, will you get outa here!

THE WOMAN [enters holding a box of stockings]. I just hope there's nobody in the hall. That's all I hope. [To BIFF.] Are you football or baseball?

BIFF. Football.

THE WOMAN [angry, humiliated]. That's me too. G'night.

[She snatches her clothes from WILLY and walks out.]

WILLY [after a pause]. Well, better get going. I want to get to the school first thing in the morning. Get my suits out of the closet. I'll get my valise. [BIFF doesn't move.] What's the matter? [BIFF remains motionless, tears falling.] She's a buyer. Buys for J. H. Simmons. She lives down the hall—they're painting. You don't imagine— [He breaks off. After a pause.] Now listen, pal, she's just a buyer. She sees merchandise in her room and they have to keep it looking just so. . . . [Pause. Assuming command.] All right, get my suits. [BIFF doesn't move.] Now stop crying and do as I say. I gave you an order. Biff, I gave you an order! Is that what you do when I give you an order? How dare you cry? [Putting his arm around BIFF.] Now look, Biff, when you grow up you'll understand about these things. You mustn't—you mustn't over-emphasize a thing like this. I'll see Birnbaum first thing in the morning.

BIFF. Never mind.

WILLY [getting down beside BIFF]. Never

mind! He's going to give you those points. I'll see to it.

BIFF. He wouldn't listen to you.

WILLY. He certainly will listen to me. You
5 need those points for the U. of Virginia.

BIFF. I'm not going there.

WILLY. Heh? If I can't get him to change that mark you'll make it up in summer school. You've got all summer to—

10 BIFF [*his weeping breaking from him*]. Dad . . .

WILLY [*infected by it*]. Oh, my boy . . .

BIFF. Dad . . .

WILLY. She's nothing to me, Biff. I was
15 lonely, I was terribly lonely.

BIFF. You—you gave her Mama's stockings! [*His tears break through and he rises to go.*]

WILLY [*grabbing for* BIFF]. I gave you an order!

20 BIFF. Don't touch me, you—liar!

WILLY. Apologize for that!

BIFF. You fake! You phony little fake! You fake! [*Overcome he turns quickly and weeping fully goes out with his suitcase.* WILLY *is left
25 on the floor on his knees.*]

WILLY. I gave you an order! Biff, come back here or I'll beat you! Come back here! I'll whip you!

[STANLEY *comes quickly in from the right
30 and stands in front of* WILLY.]

WILLY [*shouts at* STANLEY]. I gave you an order . . .

STANLEY. Hey, let's pick it up, pick it up, Mr. Loman. [*He helps* WILLY *to his feet.*] Your
35 boys left with the chippies. They said they'll see you home.

[*A second waiter watches some distance away.*]

WILLY. But we were supposed to have din-
40 ner together.

[*Music is heard,* WILLY's *theme.*]

STANLEY. Can you make it?

WILLY. I'll—sure, I can make it. [*Suddenly concerned about his clothes.*] Do I—I look
45 all right?

STANLEY. Sure, you look all right. [*He flicks a speck off* WILLY's *lapel.*]

WILLY. Here—here's a dollar.

STANLEY. Oh, your son paid me. It's all right.

WILLY [*putting it in* STANLEY's *hand*]. No, 50
take it. You're a good boy.

STANLEY. Oh, no, you don't have to . . .

WILLY. Here—here's some more. I don't need it any more. [*After a slight pause.*] Tell me— is there a seed store in the neighborhood? 55

STANLEY. Seeds? You mean like to plant?

[*As* WILLY *turns,* STANLEY *slips the money back into his jacket pocket.*]

WILLY. Yes. Carrots, peas . . .

STANLEY. Well, there's hardware stores on 60
Sixth Avenue, but it may be too late now.

WILLY [*anxiously*]. Oh, I'd better hurry. I've got to get some seeds. [*He starts off to the right.*] I've got to get some seeds, right away. Nothing's planted. I don't have a thing in the 65
ground.

[WILLY *hurries out as the light goes down.* STANLEY *moves over to the right after him, watches him off. The other waiter has been staring at* WILLY.] 70

STANLEY [*to the waiter*]. Well, whatta you looking at?

[*The waiter picks up the chairs and moves off right.* STANLEY *takes the table and follows him. The light fades on this area. There is a 75
long pause, the sound of the flute coming over. The light gradually rises on the kitchen, which is empty.* HAPPY *appears at the door of the house, followed by* BIFF. HAPPY *is carrying a large bunch of long-stemmed roses. He enters 80
the kitchen, looks around for* LINDA. *Not seeing her, he turns to* BIFF, *who is just outside the house door, and makes a gesture with his hands, indicating "Not here, I guess." He looks into the living-room and freezes. Inside,* LINDA, 85
unseen, is seated, WILLY's *coat on her lap. She rises ominously and quietly and moves toward* HAPPY, *who backs up into the kitchen, afraid.*]

HAPPY. Hey, what're you doing up? [LINDA *says nothing but moves toward him im- 90
placably.*] Where's Pop? [*He keeps backing to the right, and now* LINDA *is in full view in the doorway to the living-room.*] Is he sleeping?

LINDA. Where were you?

HAPPY [*trying to laugh it off*]. We met two 95
girls, Mom, very fine types. Here, we brought

you some flowers. [*Offering them to her.*] Put them in your room, Ma.

[*She knocks them to the floor at* BIFF's *feet. He has now come inside and closed the door* 5 *behind him. She stares at* BIFF, *silent.*]

HAPPY. Now what'd you do that for? Mom, I want you to have some flowers—

LINDA [*cutting* HAPPY *off, violently to* BIFF]. Don't you care whether he lives or dies?

10 HAPPY [*going to the stairs*]. Come upstairs, Biff.

BIFF [*with a flare of disgust, to* HAPPY]. Go away from me! [*To* LINDA.] What do you mean, lives or dies? Nobody's dying around 15 here, pal.

LINDA. Get out of my sight! Get out of here!

BIFF. I wanna see the boss.

LINDA. You're not going near him!

BIFF. Where is he? [*He moves into the living-* 20 *room and* LINDA *follows.*]

LINDA [*shouting after* BIFF]. You invite him to dinner. He looks forward to it all day— [BIFF *appears in his parents' bedroom, looks around, and exits*]—and then you desert him 25 there. There's no stranger you'd do that to!

HAPPY. Why? He had a swell time with us. Listen, when I—[LINDA *comes back into the kitchen*]—desert him I hope I don't outlive the day!

30 LINDA. Get out of here!

HAPPY. Now look, Mom . . .

LINDA. Did you have to go to women to-night? You and your lousy rotten whores!

[BIFF *re-enters the kitchen.*]

35 HAPPY. Mom, all we did was follow Biff around trying to cheer him up! [*To* BIFF.] Boy, what a night you gave me!

LINDA. Get out of here, both of you, and don't come back! I don't want you tormenting 40 him any more. Go on now, get your things together! [*To* BIFF.] You can sleep in his apartment. [*She starts to pick up the flowers and stops herself.*] Pick up this stuff, I'm not your maid any more. Pick it up, you bum, you!

45 [HAPPY *turns his back to her in refusal.* BIFF *slowly moves over and gets down on his knees, picking up the flowers.*]

LINDA. You're a pair of animals! Not one, not another living soul would have had the cruelty to walk out on that man in a restaur- 50 ant!

BIFF [*not looking at her*]. Is that what he said?

LINDA. He didn't have to say anything. He was so humiliated he nearly limped when he 55 came in.

HAPPY. But, Mom, he had a great time with us—

BIFF [*cutting him off violently*]. Shut up!

[*Without another word,* HAPPY *goes up-* 60 *stairs.*]

LINDA. You! You didn't even go in to see if he was all right!

BIFF [*still on the floor in front of* LINDA, *the flowers in his hand; with self-loathing*]. No. 65 Didn't. Didn't do a damned thing. How do you like that, heh? Left him babbling in a toilet.

LINDA. You louse. You . . .

BIFF. Now you hit it on the nose! [*He gets up, throws the flowers in the wastebasket.*] 70 The scum of the earth, and you're looking at him!

LINDA. Get out of here!

BIFF. I gotta talk to the boss, Mom. Where is he? 75

LINDA. You're not going near him. Get out of this house!

BIFF [*with absolute assurance, determin-ation*]. No. We're gonna have an abrupt con-versation, him and me. 80

LINDA. You're not talking to him!

[*Hammering is heard from outside the house, off right.* BIFF *turns toward the noise.*]

LINDA [*suddenly pleading*]. Will you please leave him alone? 85

BIFF. What's he doing out there?

LINDA. He's planting the garden!

BIFF [*quietly*]. Now? Oh, my God!

[BIFF *moves outside,* LINDA *following. The light dies down on them and comes up on the* 90 *center of the apron as* WILLY *walks into it. He is carrying a flashlight, a hoe, and a handful of seed packets. He raps the top of the hoe sharply to fix it firmly, and then moves to the left, measuring off the distance with his foot. He holds the flashlight to look at the seed packets, reading off the instructions. He is in the blue of night.*]

5 WILLY. Carrots . . . quarter-inch apart. Rows . . . one-foot rows. [*He measures it off.*] One foot. [*He puts down a package and measures off.*] Beets. [*He puts down another package and measures again.*] Lettuce. [*He reads the*
10 *package, puts it down.*] One foot— [*He breaks off as* BEN *appears at the right and moves slowly down to him.*] What a proposition, ts, ts. Terrific, terrific. 'Cause she's suffered, Ben, the woman has suffered. You understand me?
15 A man can't go out the way he came in, Ben, a man has got to add up to something. You can't, you can't— [BEN *moves toward him as though to interrupt.*] You gotta consider, now. Don't answer so quick. Remember, it's a
20 guaranteed twenty-thousand-dollar proposition. Now look, Ben, I want you to go through the ins and outs of this thing with me. I've got nobody to talk to, Ben, and the woman has suffered, you hear me?
25 BEN [*standing still, considering*]. What's the proposition?

WILLY. It's twenty thousand dollars on the barrelhead. Guaranteed, gilt-edged, you understand?
30 BEN. You don't want to make a fool of yourself. They might not honor the policy.

WILLY. How can they dare refuse? Didn't I work like a coolie to meet every premium on the nose? And now they don't pay off! Impos-
35 sible!

BEN. It's called a cowardly thing, William.

WILLY. Why? Does it take more guts to stand here the rest of my life ringing up a zero?
40 BEN [*yielding*]. That's a point, William. [*He moves, thinking, turns.*] And twenty thousand —that *is* something one can feel with the hand, it is there.

WILLY [*now assured, with rising power*]. Oh,
45 Ben, that's the whole beauty of it! I see it like a diamond, shining in the dark, hard and rough, that I can pick up and touch in my

hand. Not like—like an appointment! This would not be another damned-fool appoint-
50 ment, Ben, and it changes all the aspects. Because he thinks I'm nothing, see, and so he spites me. But the funeral— [*Straightening up.*] Ben, that funeral will be massive! They'll come from Maine, Massachusetts, Vermont,
55 New Hampshire! All the old-timers with the strange license plates—that boy will be thunderstruck, Ben, because he never realized—I am known! Rhode Island, New York, New Jersey—I am known, Ben, and he'll see it with
60 his eyes once and for all. He'll see what I am, Ben! He's in for a shock, that boy!

BEN [*coming down to the edge of the garden*]. He'll call you a coward.

WILLY [*suddenly fearful*]. No, that would be terrible.
65
BEN. Yes. And a damned fool.

WILLY. No, no, he mustn't, I won't have that! [*He is broken and desperate.*]

BEN. He'll hate you, William.

[*The gay music of the boys is heard.*]
70
WILLY. Oh, Ben, how do we get back to all the great times? Used to be so full of light, and comradeship, the sleigh-riding in winter, and the ruddiness on his cheeks. And always
75 some kind of good news coming up, always something nice coming up ahead. And never even let me carry the valises in the house, and simonizing, simonizing that little red car! Why, can't I give him something and not have him
80 hate me?

BEN. Let me think about it. [*He glances at his watch.*] I still have a little time. Remarkable proposition, but you've got to be sure you're not making a fool of yourself.

[BEN *drifts off upstage and goes out of sight.*
85 BIFF *comes down from the left.*]

WILLY [*suddenly conscious of* BIFF, *turns and looks up at him, then begins picking up the packages of seeds in confusion*]. Where the hell is that seed? [*Indignantly.*] You can't
90 see nothing out here! They boxed in the whole goddam neighborhood!

BIFF. There are people all around here. Don't you realize that?

WILLY. I'm busy. Don't bother me.

BIFF [taking the hoe from WILLY]. I'm saying good-bye to you, Pop. [WILLY looks at him, silent, unable to move.] I'm not coming back any more.

WILLY. You're not going to see Oliver tomorrow?

BIFF. I've got no appointment, Dad.

WILLY. He put his arm around you, and you've got no appointment?

BIFF. Pop, get this now, will you? Everytime I've left it's been a fight that sent me out of here. Today I realized something about myself and I tried to explain it to you and I— I think I'm just not smart enough to make any sense out of it for you. To hell with whose fault it is or anything like that. [He takes WILLY's arm.] Let's just wrap it up, heh? Come on in, we'll tell Mom. [He gently tries to pull WILLY to left.]

WILLY [frozen, immobile, with guilt in his voice]. No, I don't want to see her.

BIFF. Come on! [He pulls again, and WILLY tries to pull away.]

WILLY [highly nervous]. No, no, I don't want to see her.

BIFF [tries to look into WILLY's face, as if to find the answer there]. Why don't you want to see her?

WILLY [more harshly now]. Don't bother me, will you?

BIFF. What do you mean, you don't want to see her? You don't want them calling you yellow, do you? This isn't your fault; it's me, I'm a bum. Now come inside! [WILLY strains to get away.] Did you hear what I said to you?

[WILLY pulls away and quickly goes by himself into the house. BIFF follows.]

LINDA [to WILLY]. Did you plant, dear?

BIFF [at the door, to LINDA]. All right, we had it out. I'm going and I'm not writing any more.

LINDA [going to WILLY in the kitchen]. I think that's the best way, dear. 'Cause there's no use drawing it out, you'll just never get along.

[WILLY doesn't respond.]

BIFF. People ask where I am and what I'm doing, you don't know, and you don't care. That way it'll be off your mind and you can start brightening up again. All right? That clears it, doesn't it? [WILLY is silent, and BIFF goes to him.] You gonna wish me luck, scout! [He extends his hand.] What do you say?

LINDA. Shake his hand, Willy.

WILLY [turning to her, seething with hurt]. There's no necessity to mention the pen at all, y'know.

BIFF [gently]. I've got no appointment, Dad.

WILLY [erupting fiercely]. He put his arm around . . .?

BIFF. Dad, you're never going to see what I am, so what's the use of arguing? If I strike oil I'll send you a check. Meantime forget I'm alive.

WILLY [to LINDA]. Spite, see?

BIFF. Shake hands, Dad.

WILLY. Not my hand.

BIFF. I was hoping not to go this way.

WILLY. Well, this is the way you're going. Good-bye.

[BIFF looks at him a moment, then turns sharply and goes to the stairs.]

WILLY [stops him with]. May you rot in hell if you leave this house!

BIFF [turning]. Exactly what is it that you want from me?

WILLY. I want you to know, on the train, in the mountains, in the valleys, wherever you go, that you cut down your life for spite!

BIFF. No, no.

WILLY. Spite, spite, is the word of your undoing! And when you're down and out, remember what did it. When you're rotting somewhere beside the railroad tracks, remember, and don't you dare blame it on me!

BIFF. I'm not blaming it on you!

WILLY. I won't take the rap for this, you hear?

[HAPPY comes down the stairs and stands on the bottom step, watching.]

BIFF. That's just what I'm telling you!

WILLY [sinking into a chair at the table, with full accusation]. You're trying to put a knife in

me—don't think I don't know what you're
doing!

BIFF. All right, phony! Then let's lay it on
the line. [*He whips the rubber tube out of his*
5 *pocket and puts it on the table.*]

HAPPY. You crazy—

LINDA. Biff! [*She moves to grab the hose,
but* BIFF *holds it down with his hand.*]

BIFF. Leave it there! Don't move it!

10 WILLY [*not looking at it*]. What is that?

BIFF. You know goddam well what that is.

WILLY [*caged, wanting to escape*]. I never
saw that.

BIFF. You saw it. The mice didn't bring it
15 into the cellar! What is this supposed to do,
make a hero out of you? This supposed to
make me sorry for you?

WILLY. Never heard of it.

BIFF. There'll be no pity for you, you hear
20 it? No pity!

WILLY [*to* LINDA]. You hear the spite!

BIFF. No, you're going to hear the truth—
what you are and what I am!

LINDA. Stop it!

25 WILLY. Spite!

HAPPY [*coming down toward* BIFF]. You cut
it now!

BIFF [*to* HAPPY]. The man don't know who
we are! The man is gonna know! [*To* WILLY.]
30 We never told the truth for ten minutes in
this house!

HAPPY. We always told the truth!

BIFF [*turning on him*]. You big blow, are
you the assistant buyer? You're one of the two
35 assistants to the assistant, aren't you?

HAPPY. Well, I'm practically—

BIFF. You're practically full of it! We all are!
And I'm through with it. [*To* WILLY.] Now
hear this, Willy, this is me.

40 WILLY. I know you!

BIFF. You know why I had no address for
three months? I stole a suit in Kansas City and
I was in jail. [*To* LINDA, *who is sobbing.*] Stop
crying. I'm through with it.

45 [LINDA *turns away from them, her hands
covering her face.*]

WILLY. I suppose that's my fault!

BIFF. I stole myself out of every good job
since high school!

WILLY. And whose fault is that? 50

BIFF. And I never got anywhere because
you blew me so full of hot air I could never
stand taking orders from anybody! That's
whose fault it is!

WILLY. I hear that! 55

LINDA. Don't, Biff!

BIFF. It's goddam time you heard that! I had
to be boss big shot in two weeks, and I'm
through with it!

WILLY. Then hang yourself! For spite, hang 60
yourself!

BIFF. No! Nobody's hanging himself, Willy!
I ran down eleven flights with a pen in my
hand today. And suddenly I stopped, you hear
me? And in the middle of that office building, 65
do you hear this? I stopped in the middle of
that building and I saw—the sky. I saw the
things that I love in this world. The work and
the food and time to sit and smoke. And I
looked at the pen and said to myself, what 70
the hell am I grabbing this for? Why am I
trying to become what I don't want to be?
What am I doing in an office, making a contemptuous, begging fool of myself, when all I
want is out there, waiting for me the minute 75
I say I know who I am! Why can't I say that,
Willy? [*He tries to make* WILLY *face him, but*
WILLY *pulls away and moves to the left.*]

WILLY [*with hatred, threateningly*]. The
door of your life is wide open! 80

BIFF. Pop! I'm a dime a dozen, and so are
you!

WILLY [*turning on him now in an uncon-
trolled outburst*]. I am not a dime a dozen! I
am Willy Loman, and you are Biff Loman! 85

[BIFF *starts for* WILLY, *but is blocked by*
HAPPY. *In his fury,* BIFF *seems on the verge
of attacking his father.*]

BIFF. I am not a leader of men, Willy, and
neither are you. You were never anything but 90
a hard-working drummer who landed in the
ash-can like all the rest of them! I'm one dollar
an hour, Willy! I tried seven states and
couldn't raise it. A buck an hour! Do you

gather my meaning? I'm not bringing home any prizes any more, and you're going to stop waiting for me to bring them home!

WILLY [*directly to* BIFF]. You vengeful, spite-
5 ful mutt!

[BIFF *breaks from* HAPPY. WILLY, *in fright, starts up the stair.* BIFF *grabs him.*]

BIFF [*at the peak of his fury*]. Pop, I'm nothing! I'm nothing, Pop. Can't you understand
10 that? There's no spite in it any more. I'm just what I am, that's all.

[BIFF'S *fury has spent itself, and he breaks down, sobbing, holding on to* WILLY, *who dumbly fumbles for* BIFF'S *face.*]

15 WILLY [*astonished*]. What're you doing? What're you doing? [*To* LINDA.] Why is he crying?

BIFF [*crying, broken*]. Will you let me go, for Christ's sake? Will you take that phony
20 dream and burn it before something happens? [*Struggling to contain himself, he pulls away and moves to the stairs.*] I'll go in the morning. Put him—put him to bed. [*Exhausted,* BIFF *moves up the stairs to his room.*]

25 WILLY [*after a long pause, astonished, elevated*]. Isn't that—isn't that remarkable? Biff—he likes me!

LINDA. He loves you, Willy!

HAPPY [*deeply moved*]. Always did, Pop.
30 WILLY. Oh, Biff! [*Staring wildly.*] He cried! Cried to me. [*He is choking with his love, and now cries out his promise.*] That boy—that boy is going to be magnificent!

[BEN *appears in the light just outside the*
35 *kitchen.*]

BEN. Yes, outstanding, with twenty thousand behind him.

LINDA [*sensing the racing of his mind, fearfully, carefully*]. Now come to bed, Willy. It's
40 all settled now.

WILLY [*finding it difficult not to rush out of the house*]. Yes, we'll sleep. Come on. Go to sleep, Hap.

BEN. And it does take a great kind of a man
45 to crack the jungle.

[*In accents of dread,* BEN'S *idyllic music starts up.*]

HAPPY [*his arm around* LINDA]. I'm getting married, Pop, don't forget it. I'm changing everything. I'm gonna run that department be-
50 fore the year is up. You'll see, Mom. [*He kisses her.*]

BEN. The jungle is dark but full of diamonds, Willy.

[WILLY *turns, moves, listening to* BEN.]
55 LINDA. Be good. You're both good boys, just act that way, that's all.

HAPPY. 'Night, Pop. [*He goes upstairs.*]

LINDA [*to* WILLY]. Come, dear.

BEN [*with greater force*]. One must go in to
60 fetch a diamond out.

WILLY [*to* LINDA, *as he moves slowly along the edge of the kitchen, toward the door*]. I just want to get settled down, Linda. Let me sit alone for a little.
65 LINDA [*almost uttering her fear*]. I want you upstairs.

WILLY [*taking her in his arms*]. In a few minutes, Linda. I couldn't sleep right now. Go on, you look awful tired. [*He kisses her.*]
70 BEN. Not like an appointment at all. A diamond is rough and hard to the touch.

WILLY. Go on now. I'll be right up.

LINDA. I think this is the only way, Willy.

WILLY. Sure, it's the best thing.
75 BEN. Best thing!

WILLY. The only way. Everything is gonna be—go on, kid, get to bed. You look so tired.

LINDA. Come right up.

WILLY. Two minutes.
80 [LINDA *goes into the living-room, then reappears in her bedroom.* WILLY *moves just outside the kitchen door.*]

WILLY. Loves me. [*Wonderingly.*] Always loved me. Isn't that a remarkable thing? Ben,
85 he'll worship me for it!

BEN [*with promise*]. It's dark there, but full of diamonds.

WILLY. Can you imagine that magnificence with twenty thousand dollars in his pocket?
90 LINDA [*calling from her room*]. Willy! Come up!

WILLY [*calling into the kitchen*]. Yes! Yes. Coming! It's very smart, you realize that, don't you, sweetheart? Even Ben sees it. I gotta go, baby. 'Bye! 'Bye! [*Going over to* BEN, *almost dancing.*] Imagine? When the mail comes he'll be ahead of Bernard again!

5 BEN. A perfect proposition all around.

WILLY. Did you see how he cried to me? Oh, if I could kiss him, Ben!

BEN. Time, William, time!

WILLY. Oh, Ben, I always knew one way or
10 another we were gonna make it, Biff and I!

BEN [*looking at his watch*]. The boat. We'll be late. [*He moves slowly off into the darkness.*]

WILLY [*elegiacally, turning to the house*].
15 Now when you kick off, boy, I want a seventy-yard boot, and get right down the field under the ball, and when you hit, hit low and hit hard, because it's important, boy. [*He swings around and faces the audience.*] There's all
20 kinds of important people in the stands, and the first thing you know . . . . [*Suddenly realizing he is alone.*] Ben! Ben, where do I . . .? [*He makes a sudden movement of search.*] Ben, how do I . . .?

25 LINDA [*calling*]. Willy, you coming up?

WILLY [*uttering a gasp of fear, whirling about as if to quiet her*]. Sh! [*He turns around as if to find his way; sounds, faces, voices, seem to be swarming in upon him and he flicks at
30 them, crying,*] "Sh! Sh!" [*Suddenly music, faint and high, stops him. It rises in intensity, almost to an unbearable scream. He goes up and down on his toes, and rushes off around the house.*] Shhh!

35 LINDA. Willy?

[*There is no answer.* LINDA *waits.* BIFF *gets up off his bed. He is still in his clothes.* HAPPY *sits up.* BIFF *stands listening.*]

LINDA [*with real fear*]. Willy, answer me!
40 Willy!

[*There is the sound of a car starting and moving away at full speed.*]

LINDA. No!

BIFF [*rushing down the stairs*]. Pop!

45 [*As the car speeds off, the music crashes down in a frenzy of sound, which becomes the soft pulsation of a single 'cello string.* BIFF *slowly returns to his bedroom. He and* HAPPY *gravely don their jackets.* LINDA *slowly walks out of her room. The music has developed into
50 a dead march. The leaves of day are appearing over everything.* CHARLEY *and* BERNARD, *somberly dressed, appear and knock on the kitchen door.* BIFF *and* HAPPY *slowly descend the stairs to the kitchen as* CHARLEY *and* BER-
55 NARD *enter. All stop a moment when* LINDA, *in clothes of mourning, bearing a little bunch of roses, comes through the draped doorway into the kitchen. She goes to* CHARLEY *and takes his arm. Now all move toward the aud-
60 ience, through the wall-line of the kitchen. At the limit of the apron,* LINDA *lays down the flowers, kneels, and sits back on her heels. All stare down at the grave.*]

REQUIEM

CHARLEY. It's getting dark, Linda.
65
[LINDA *doesn't react. She stares at the grave.*]

BIFF. How about it, Mom? Better get some rest, heh? They'll be closing the gate soon.

[LINDA *makes no move. Pause.*]
70
HAPPY [*deeply angered*]. He had no right to do that. There was no necessity for it. We would've helped him.

CHARLEY [*grunting*]. Hmmm.

BIFF. Come along, Mom.
75
LINDA. Why didn't anybody come?

CHARLEY. It was a very nice funeral.

LINDA. But where are all the people he knew? Maybe they blame him.

CHARLEY. Naa. It's a rough world, Linda.
80 They wouldn't blame him.

LINDA. I can't understand it. At this time especially. First time in thirty-five years we were just about free and clear. He only needed a little salary. He was even finished with the
85 dentist.

CHARLEY. No man only needs a little salary.

LINDA. I can't understand it.

BIFF. There were a lot of nice days. When he'd come home from a trip; or on Sundays,
90 making the stoop; finishing the cellar; putting

on the new porch; when he built the extra bathroom; and put up the garage. You know something, Charley, there's more of him in that front stoop than in all the sales he ever made.

CHARLEY. Yeah. He was a happy man with a batch of cement.

LINDA. He was so wonderful with his hands.

BIFF. He had the wrong dreams. All, all, wrong.

HAPPY [almost ready to fight BIFF]. Don't say that!

BIFF. He never knew who he was.

CHARLEY [stopping HAPPY's movement and reply. To BIFF]. Nobody dast blame this man. You don't understand; Willy was a salesman. And for a salesman, there is no rock bottom to the life. He don't put a bolt to a nut, he don't tell you the law or give you medicine. He's a man way out there in the blue, riding on a smile and a shoeshine. And when they start not smiling back—that's an earthquake. And then you get yourself a couple of spots on your hat, and you're finished. Nobody dast blame this man. A salesman is got to dream, boy. It comes with the territory.

BIFF. Charley, the man didn't know who he was.

HAPPY [infuriated]. Don't say that!

BIFF. Why don't you come with me, Happy?

HAPPY. I'm not licked that easily. I'm staying right in this city, and I'm gonna beat this racket! [He looks at BIFF, his chin set.] The Loman Brothers!

BIFF. I know who I am, kid.

HAPPY. All right, boy. I'm gonna show you and everybody else that Willy Loman did not die in vain. He had a good dream. It's the only dream you can have—to come out number-one man. He fought it out here, and this is where I'm gonna win it for him.

BIFF [with a hopeless glance at HAPPY, bends toward his mother]. Let's go, Mom.

LINDA. I'll be with you in a minute. Go on, Charley. [He hesitates.] I want to, just for a minute. I never had a chance to say good-bye.

[CHARLEY moves away, followed by HAPPY. BIFF remains a slight distance up and left of LINDA. She sits there, summoning herself. The flute begins, not far away, playing behind her speech.]

LINDA. Forgive me, dear. I can't cry. I don't know what it is, but I can't cry. I don't understand it. Why did you ever do that? Help me, Willy, I can't cry. It seems to me that you're just on another trip. I keep expecting you. Willy, dear, I can't cry. Why did you do it? I search and search and I search, and I can't understand it, Willy. I made the last payment on the house today. Today, dear. And there'll be nobody home. [A sob rises in her throat.] We're free and clear. [Sobbing more fully, released.] We're free. [BIFF comes slowly toward her.] We're free . . . we're free . . .

[BIFF lifts her to her feet and moves out up right with her in his arms. LINDA sobs quietly. BERNARD and CHARLEY come together and follow them, followed by HAPPY. Only the music of the flute is left on the darkening stage as over the house the hard towers of the apartment buildings rise into sharp focus.]

Curtain

Samuel Beckett

1906–

All
That Fall

1957

Act Without
Words I

1957

It is commonly said that Samuel Beckett contemplates the human condition without hope and without faith, representing life as futile and man as impotent. It would be nothing new for a dramatist to ponder how life may be sustained without the support of hope and faith. That vision has entered into the terror and dignity of great tragic drama, whether Sophoclean or Shakespearean. Nor does comedy refuse to recognize some ultimate absurdity in human predicaments. When at the end of *Juno and the Paycock* the two befuddled derelicts judge the whole world to be "in a terrible state o' chassis," the scene mingles the pathetic and the ludicrous.

Beckett's is a special kind of drama that fuses and also reanimates the traditional comic and tragic modes. His perspective embraces contraries. Whatever appears tragic, spiritual, or even merely decorous in human behavior is seen to be toppling into the rankest commonplace; whatever seems grossly physical, or grotesque has a tone of spiritual desolation, a dying echo of tragic suffering. His most characteristic effect is a sudden and ludicrous deflation or exposure of pretentions (an effect properly known as *bathos).* However, he also sometimes reverses the process, investing the most ordinary event or object with comic nobility. No sentiment is too lofty to be shot down, no fact too mean to be oddly significant.

In *All That Fall* Mrs. Rooney's ejaculations inspired by the death of a hen illustrate Beckett's characteristic manner. Her eulogy, mingling the vulgar and the sentimental, is of course ridiculously inflated:

What a death! One minute picking happy at the dung, on the road, in the sun, with now and then a dust bath, and then—bang!— all her troubles over. [*Pause.*] All the laying and the hatching. [*Pause.*] Just one great squawk and then . . . peace. [*Pause.*] They would have slit her weasand in any case. [*Pause.*]

Absurd. Yet in full context Mrs. Rooney's words are neither purely sentimental nor merely vulgar. The theme of the play is a commonplace, that in the midst of life we are in death. Realized most obviously in the accidental death of a child, it reverberates throughout. At the beginning and the end are allusions to Schubert's "Death and the Maiden," a song in which Death whispers amorously to a dying girl. And there are scores of other similar allusions—for example, to hymns and biblical texts conventionally associated with funerals, and to the death of Mrs. Rooney's daughter. The flow of time itself, although spanning literally only an hour of a June day, is toward the fall and winter. Given such orchestration of the theme of death, in every key from inanity to horror, Mrs. Rooney's eulogy on a dead hen contributes its odd hilarious solemnity to the changes rung on the title, *All That Fall*.

That the play was written for radio does not limit its dramatic force. It exploits in addition to verbal meaning the imagined scenes and gestures that sounds powerfully suggest—bird calls, train noises, shuffling feet—and, especially, the pauses, hundreds of momentary silences that feed the imagination. Because its language is both bizarre and exact, punctuated by fertile silences, *All That Fall* possesses an outlandish realism. Because it excites the imagination, the whole conveys not a depressing weight of philosophic despair, but an impression of extraordinary and sometimes outrageous liveliness.

Act Without Words, consisting only of stage directions, as purely represents the visual and gestural elements of drama as *All That Fall* represents the auditory. From one viewpoint the "mime" describes a series of sadistically inflicted frustrations; from another it describes a clown's meticulous parody of self-pity. Characteristically, Beckett excludes neither viewpoint. The combination provokes a double vision achieved with economy and verve. Although without much hope or faith, Beckett brings to the drama a renovation of words and actions through a form and style both traditional and new.

All That Fall

A Play for Radio

BECKETT

CHARACTERS

Mrs. Rooney (Maddy)   *a lady in her seventies*
Christy   *a carter*
Mr. Tyler   *a retired bill-broker*
Mr. Slocum   *Clerk of the Racecourse*
Tommy   *a porter*
Mr. Barrell   *a station-master*
Miss Fitt   *a lady in her thirties*
A Female Voice
Dolly   *a small girl*
Mr. Rooney (Dan)   *husband of* Mrs. Rooney, *blind*
Jerry   *a small boy*

[*Rural sounds. Sheep, bird, cow, cock, severally, then together. Silence.* Mrs. Rooney *advances along country road towards railway station. Sound of her dragging feet. Music faint from house by way. "Death and the Maiden."* 5 *The steps slow down, stop.*]

Mrs. Rooney. Poor woman. All alone in that ruinous old house.

[*Music louder. Silence but for music playing. The steps resume. Music dies.* Mrs. 10 Rooney *murmurs, melody. Her murmur dies. Sound of approaching cartwheels. The cart stops. The steps slow down, stop.*]

Mrs. Rooney. Is that you, Christy?
Christy. It is, Ma'am.   15

MRS. ROONEY. I thought the hinny was familiar. How is your poor wife?

CHRISTY. No better, Ma'am.

MRS. ROONEY. Your daughter then?

CHRISTY. No worse, Ma'am.

[*Silence.*]

MRS. ROONEY. Why do you halt? [*Pause.*] But why do I halt?

[*Silence.*]

CHRISTY. Nice day for the races, Ma'am.

MRS. ROONEY. No doubt it is. [*Pause.*] But will it hold up? [*Pause. With emotion.*] Will it hold up?

[*Silence.*]

CHRISTY. I suppose you wouldn't—

MRS. ROONEY. Hist! [*Pause.*] Surely to goodness that cannot be the up mail I hear already.

[*Silence. The hinny neighs. Silence.*]

CHRISTY. Damn the mail.

MRS. ROONEY. Oh thank God for that! I could have sworn I heard it, thundering up the track in the far distance. [*Pause.*] So hinnies whinny. Well, it is not surprising.

CHRISTY. I suppose you wouldn't be in need of a small load of dung?

MRS. ROONEY. Dung? What class of dung?

CHRISTY. Stydung.

MRS. ROONEY. Stydung . . . I like your frankness, Christy. [*Pause.*] I'll ask the master. [*Pause.*] Christy.

CHRISTY. Yes, Ma'am.

MRS. ROONEY. Do you find anything . . . bizarre about my way of speaking? [*Pause.*] I do not mean the voice. [*Pause.*] No, I mean the words. [*Pause. More to herself.*] I use none but the simplest words, I hope, and yet I sometimes find my way of speaking very . . . bizarre. [*Pause.*] Mercy! What was that?

CHRISTY. Never mind her, Ma'am, she's very fresh in herself today.

[*Silence.*]

MRS. ROONEY. Dung? What would we want with dung, at our time of life? [*Pause.*] Why are you on your feet down on the road? Why do you not climb up on the crest of your manure and let yourself be carried along? Is it that you have no head for heights?

[*Silence.*]

CHRISTY [*to the hinny*]. Yep! [*Pause. Louder.*]

Yep wiyya to hell owwa that!

[*Silence.*]

MRS. ROONEY. She does not move a muscle. [*Pause.*] I too should be getting along, if I do not wish to arrive late at the station. [*Pause.*] But a moment ago she neighed and pawed the ground. And now she refuses to advance. Give her a good welt on the rump. [*Sound of welt. Pause.*] Harder! [*Sound of welt. Pause.*] Well! If someone were to do that for me I should not dally. [*Pause.*] How she gazes at me to be sure, with her great moist cleg-tormented° eyes! Perhaps if I were to move on, down the road, out of her field of vision . . . . [*Sound of welt.*] No, no, enough! Take her by the snaffle and pull her eyes away from me. Oh this is awful! [*She moves on. Sound of her dragging feet.*] What have I done to deserve all this, what, what? [*Dragging feet.*] So long ago . . . . No! No! [*Dragging feet. Quotes.*] "Sigh out a something something tale of things, Done long ago and ill done." [*She halts.*] How can I go on, I cannot. Oh let me just flop down flat on the road like a big fat jelly out of a bowl and never move again! A great big slop thick with grit and dust and flies, they would have to scoop me up with a shovel. [*Pause.*] Heavens, there is that up mail again, what will become of me! [*The dragging steps resume.*] Oh I am just a hysterical old hag, I know, destroyed with sorrow and pining and gentility and church-going and fat and rheumatism and childlessness. [*Pause. Brokenly.*] Minnie! Little Minnie! [*Pause.*] Love, that is all I asked, a little love, daily, twice daily, fifty years of twice daily love like a Paris horse-butcher's regular, what normal woman wants affection? A peck on the jaw at morning, near the ear, and another at evening, peck, peck, till you grow whiskers on you. There is that lovely laburnum again.

[*Dragging feet. Sound of bicycle-bell. It is old MR. TYLER coming up behind her on his bicycle, on his way to the station. Squeak of brakes. He slows down and rides abreast of her.*]

MR. TYLER. Mrs. Rooney! Pardon me if I do

cleg-tormented tormented by horseflies.

not doff my cap, I'd fall off. Divine day for the meeting.

MRS. ROONEY. Oh, Mr. Tyler, you startled the life out of me stealing up behind me like that like a deer-stalker! Oh!

MR. TYLER [*playfully*]. I rang my bell, Mrs. Rooney, the moment I sighted you I started tinkling my bell, now don't you deny it.

MRS. ROONEY. Your bell is one thing, Mr. Tyler, and you are another. What news of your poor daughter?

MR. TYLER. Fair, fair. They removed everything, you know, the whole . . . er . . . bag of tricks. Now I am grandchildless.

[*Dragging feet.*]

MRS. ROONEY. Gracious how you wobble! Dismount, for mercy's sake, or ride on.

MR. TYLER. Perhaps if I were to lay my hand lightly on your shoulder, Mrs. Rooney, how would that be? [*Pause.*] Would you permit that?

MRS. ROONEY. No, Mr. Rooney, Mr. Tyler I mean, I am tired of light old hands on my shoulders and other senseless places, sick and tired of them. Heavens, here comes Connolly's van! [*She halts. Sound of motor-van. It approaches, passes with thunderous rattle, recedes.*] Are you all right, Mr. Tyler? [*Pause.*] Where is he? [*Pause.*] Ah there you are! [*The dragging steps resume.*] That was a narrow squeak.

MR. TYLER. I alit in the nick of time.

MRS. ROONEY. It is suicide to be abroad. But what is it to be at home, Mr. Tyler, what is it to be at home? A lingering dissolution. Now we are white with dust from head to foot. I beg your pardon?

MR. TYLER. Nothing, Mrs. Rooney, nothing, I was merely cursing, under my breath, God and man, under my breath, and the wet Saturday afternoon of my conception. My back tire has gone down again. I pumped it hard as iron before I set out. And now I am on the rim.

MRS. ROONEY. Oh what a shame!

MR. TYLER. Now if it were the front I should not so much mind. But the back. The back! The chain! The oil! The grease! The hub! The brakes! The gear! No! It is too much!

[*Dragging steps.*]

MRS. ROONEY. Are we very late, Mr. Tyler? I have not the courage to look at my watch.

MR. TYLER [*bitterly*]. Late! I on my bicycle as I bowled along was already late. Now therefore we are doubly late, trebly, quadrupedly late. Would I had shot by you, without a word.

[*Dragging feet.*]

MRS. ROONEY. Whom are you meeting, Mr. Tyler?

MR. TYLER. Hardy. [*Pause.*] We used to climb together. [*Pause.*] I saved his life once. [*Pause.*] I have not forgotten it.

[*Dragging feet. They stop.*]

MRS. ROONEY. Let us halt a moment and let this vile dust fall back upon the viler worms.

[*Silence. Rural sounds.*]

MR. TYLER. What sky! What light! Ah in spite of all it is a blessed thing to be alive in such weather, and out of hospital.

MRS. ROONEY. Alive?

MR. TYLER. Well half alive shall we say?

MRS. ROONEY. Speak for yourself, Mr. Tyler. I am not half alive nor anything approaching it. [*Pause.*] What are we standing here for? This dust will not settle in our time. And when it does some great roaring machine will come and whirl it all skyhigh again.

MR. TYLER. Well, shall we be getting along in that case?

MRS. ROONEY. No.

MR. TYLER. Come, Mrs. Rooney—

MRS. ROONEY. Go, Mr. Tyler, go on and leave me, listening to the cooing of the ring-doves. [*Cooing.*] If you see my poor blind Dan tell him I was on my way to meet him when it all came over me again, like a flood. Say to him, Your poor wife, she told me to tell you it all came flooding over her again and . . . [*the voice breaks*] . . . she simply went back home . . . straight back home . . .

MR. TYLER. Come, Mrs. Rooney, come, the mail has not yet gone up, just take my free arm and we'll be there with time and to spare.

MRS. ROONEY [*sobbing*]. What? What's all this now? [*Calmer.*] Can't you see I'm in trouble? [*With anger.*] Have you no respect for misery? [*Sobbing.*] Minnie! Little Minnie!

MR. TYLER. Come, Mrs. Rooney, come, the mail has not yet gone up, just take my free arm and we'll be there with time and to spare.

MRS. ROONEY [*brokenly*]. In her forties now she'd be, I don't know, fifty, girding up her lovely little loins, getting ready for the change . . .

MR. TYLER. Come, Mrs. Rooney, come, the mail—

MRS. ROONEY [*exploding*]. Will you get along with you, Mr. Rooney, Mr. Tyler I mean, will you get along with you now and cease molesting me? What kind of a country is this where a woman can't weep her heart out on the highways and byways without being tormented by retired bill-brokers! [MR. TYLER *prepares to mount his bicycle*.] Heavens you're not going to ride her flat! [MR. TYLER *mounts*.] You'll tear your tube to ribbons! [MR. TYLER *rides off. Receding sound of bumping bicycle. Silence. Cooing*.] Venus birds! Billing in the woods all the long summer long. [*Pause*.] Oh cursed corset! If I could let it out, without indecent exposure. Mr. Tyler! Mr. Tyler! Come back and unlace me behind the hedge! [*She laughs wildly, ceases*.] What's wrong with me, what's wrong with me, never tranquil, seething out of my dirty old pelt, out of my skull, oh to be in atoms, in atoms! [*Frenziedly*.] ATOMS! [*Silence. Cooing. Faintly*.] Jesus! [*Pause*.] Jesus!

[*Sound of car coming up behind her. It slows down and draws up beside her, engine running. It is* MR. SLOCUM, *the Clerk of the Racecourse*.]

MR. SLOCUM. Is anything wrong, Mrs. Rooney? You are bent all double. Have you a pain in the stomach?

[*Silence.* MRS. ROONEY *laughs wildly. Finally*.]

MRS. ROONEY. Well if it isn't my old admirer the Clerk of the Course, in his limousine.

MR. SLOCUM. May I offer you a lift, Mrs. Rooney? Are you going in my direction?

MRS. ROONEY. I am, Mr. Slocum, we all are. [*Pause*.] How is your poor mother?

MR. SLOCUM. Thank you, she is fairly comfortable. We manage to keep her out of pain. That is the great thing, Mrs. Rooney, is it not?

MRS. ROONEY. Yes, indeed, Mr. Slocum, that is the great thing, I don't know how you do it. [*Pause. She slaps her cheek violently*.] Ah these wasps!

MR. SLOCUM [*coolly*]. May I then offer you a seat, Madam?

MRS. ROONEY [*with exaggerated enthusiasm*]. Oh that would be heavenly, Mr. Slocum, just simply heavenly. [*Dubiously*.] But would I ever get in, you look very high off the ground today, these new balloon tires I presume. [*Sound of door opening and* MRS. ROONEY *trying to get in*.] Does this roof never come off? No? [*Efforts of* MRS. ROONEY.] No . . . I'll never do it . . . you'll have to get down, Mr. Slocum, and help me from the rear. [*Pause*.] What was that? [*Pause. Aggrieved*.] This is all your suggestion, Mr. Slocum, not mine. Drive on, Sir, drive on.

MR. SLOCUM [*switching off the engine*]. I'm coming, Mrs. Rooney, I'm coming, give me time, I'm as stiff as yourself.

[*Sound of* MR. SLOCUM *extracting himself from driver's seat*.]

MRS. ROONEY. Stiff! Well I like that! And me heaving all over back and front. [*To herself*.] The dry old reprobate!

MR. SLOCUM [*in position behind her*]. Now, Mrs. Rooney, how shall we do this?

MRS. ROONEY. As if I were a bale, Mr. Slocum, don't be afraid. [*Pause. Sounds of effort*.] That's the way! [*Effort*.] Lower! [*Effort*.] Wait! [*Pause*.] No, don't let go! [*Pause*.] Suppose I do get up, will I ever get down?

MR. SLOCUM [*breathing hard*]. You'll get down, Mrs. Rooney, you'll get down. We may not get you up, but I warrant you we'll get you down.

[*He resumes his efforts. Sound of these*.]

MRS. ROONEY. Oh! . . . Lower! . . . Don't be afraid! . . . We're past the age when . . . There! . . . Now! . . . Get your shoulder under it . . . Oh! . . . [*Giggles*.] Oh glory! . . . Up! Up! . . . Ah! . . . I'm in! [*Panting of* MR. SLOCUM. *He slams the door. In a scream*.] My frock! You've nipped my frock! [MR. SLOCUM *opens the door.* MRS. ROONEY *frees her frock.* MR. SLOCUM slams the door. His violent unintelligible muttering as he walks round to the other door. Tearfully.] My nice frock! Look what you've done to my nice frock! [MR. SLOCUM gets into his seat, slams driver's door, presses starter. The engine does not start. He releases starter.] What will Dan say when he sees me?

MR. SLOCUM. Has he then recovered his sight?

MRS. ROONEY. No, I mean when he knows, what will he say when he feels the hole? [MR. SLOCUM presses starter. As before. Silence.] What are you doing, Mr. Slocum?

MR. SLOCUM. Gazing straight before me, Mrs. Rooney, through the windscreen, into the void.

MRS. ROONEY. Start her up, I beseech you, and let us be off. This is awful!

MR. SLOCUM [dreamily]. All morning she went like a dream and now she is dead. That is what you get for a good deed. [Pause. Hopefully.] Perhaps if I were to choke her. [He does so, presses the starter. The engine roars. Roaring to make himself heard.] She was getting too much air!

[He throttles down, grinds in his first gear, moves off, changes up in a grinding of gears.]

MRS. ROONEY [in anguish]. Mind the hen! [Scream of brakes. Squawk of hen.] Oh, mother, you have squashed her, drive on, drive on! [The car accelerates. Pause.] What a death! One minute picking happy at the dung, on the road, in the sun, with now and then a dust bath, and then—bang!—all her troubles over. [Pause.] All the laying and the hatching. [Pause.] Just one great squawk and then . . . peace. [Pause.] They would have slit her weasand in any case. [Pause.] Here we are, let me down. [The car slows down, stops, engine running. MR. SLOCUM blows his horn. Pause. Louder. Pause.] What are you up to now, Mr. Slocum? We are at a standstill, all danger is past and you blow your horn. Now if instead of blowing it now you had blown it at that unfortunate—

[Horn violently. TOMMY the porter appears at top of station steps.]

MR. SLOCUM [calling]. Will you come down, Tommy, and help this lady out, she's stuck. [TOMMY descends the steps.] Open the door, Tommy, and ease her out.

[TOMMY opens the door.]

TOMMY. Certainly, sir. Nice day for the races, sir. What would you fancy for—

MRS. ROONEY. Don't mind me. Don't take any notice of me. I do not exist. The fact is well known.

MR. SLOCUM. Do as you're asked, Tommy, for the love of God.

TOMMY. Yessir. Now, Mrs. Rooney.

[He starts pulling her out.]

MRS. ROONEY. Wait, Tommy, wait now, don't bustle me, just let me wheel round and get my feet to the ground. [Her efforts to achieve this.] Now.

TOMMY [pulling her out]. Mind your feather, Ma'am. [Sounds of effort.] Easy now, easy.

MRS. ROONEY. Wait, for God's sake, you'll have me beheaded.

TOMMY. Crouch down, Mrs. Rooney, crouch down, and get your head in the open.

MRS. ROONEY. Crouch down! At my time of life! This is lunacy!

TOMMY. Press her down, sir.

[Sounds of combined efforts.]

MRS. ROONEY. Pity!

TOMMY. Now! She's coming! Straighten up, Ma'am! There!

[MR. SLOCUM slams the door.]

MRS. ROONEY. Am I out?

[The voice of MR. BARRELL, the stationmaster, raised in anger.]

MR. BARRELL. Tommy! Tommy! Where the hell is he?

[MR. SLOCUM grinds in his gear.]

TOMMY [hurriedly]. You wouldn't have something for the Ladies Plate, sir. I was given Flash Harry.

MR. SLOCUM [scornfully]. Flash Harry! That carthorse!

MR. BARRELL [at top of steps, roaring]. Tommy! Blast your bleeding bloody— [He sees MRS. ROONEY]. Oh, Mrs. Rooney . . . . [MR. SLOCUM drives away in a grinding of gears.] Who's that crucifying his gearbox, Tommy?

TOMMY. Old Cissy Slocum.

MRS. ROONEY. Cissy Slocum! That's a nice way to refer to your betters. Cissy Slocum! And you an orphan!

MR. BARRELL [*angrily to* TOMMY]. What are you doing stravaging down here on the public road? This is no place for you at all! Nip up there on the platform now and whip out the truck! Won't the twelve-thirty be on top of us before we can turn round?

TOMMY [*bitterly*]. And that's the thanks you get for a Christian act.

MR. BARRELL [*violently*]. Get on with you now before I report you! [*Slow feet of* TOMMY *climbing steps.*] Do you want me to come down to you with the shovel? [*The feet quicken, recede, cease.*] Ah God forgive me, it's a hard life. [*Pause.*] Well, Mrs. Rooney, it's nice to see you up and about again. You were laid up there a long time.

MRS. ROONEY. Not long enough, Mr. Barrell. [*Pause.*] Would I were still in bed, Mr. Barrell. [*Pause.*] Would I were lying stretched out in my comfortable bed, Mr. Barrell, just wasting slowly, painlessly away, keeping up my strength with arrowroot and calves-foot jelly, till in the end you wouldn't see me under the blankets any more than a board. [*Pause.*] Oh no coughing or spitting or bleeding or vomiting, just drifting gently down into the higher life, and remembering, remembering . . . [*the voice breaks*] . . . all the silly unhappiness . . . as though . . . it had never happened . . . What did I do with that handkerchief? [*Sound of handkerchief loudly applied.*] How long have you been master of this station now, Mr. Barrell?

MR. BARRELL. Don't ask me, Mrs. Rooney, don't ask me.

MRS. ROONEY. You stepped into your father's shoes, I believe, when he took them off.

MR. BARRELL. Poor Pappy! [*Reverent pause.*] He didn't live long to enjoy his ease.

MRS. ROONEY. I remember him clearly. A small ferrety purple-faced widower, deaf as a doornail, very testy and snappy. [*Pause.*] I suppose you'll be retiring soon yourself, Mr. Barrell, and growing your roses. [*Pause.*] Did I understand you to say the twelve-thirty would soon be upon us?

MR. BARRELL. Those were my words.

MRS. ROONEY. But according to my watch which is more or less right—or was—by the eight o'clock news the time is now coming up to twelve . . . [*pause as she consults her watch*] . . . thirty-six. [*Pause.*] And yet upon the other hand the up mail has not yet gone through. [*Pause.*] Or has it sped by unbeknown to me? [*Pause.*] For there was a moment there, I remember now, I was so plunged in sorrow I wouldn't have heard a steam roller go over me. [*Pause.* MR. BARRELL *turns to go.*] Don't go, Mr. Barrell! [MR. BARRELL *goes. Loud.*] Mr. Barrell! [*Pause. Louder.*] Mr. Barrell!

[MR. BARRELL *comes back.*]

MR. BARRELL [*testily*]. What is it, Mrs. Rooney, I have my work to do.

[*Silence. Sound of wind.*]

MRS. ROONEY. The wind is getting up. [*Pause. Wind.*] The best of the day is over. [*Pause. Wind. Dreamily.*] Soon the rain will begin to fall and go on falling, all afternoon. [MR. BARRELL *goes.*] Then at evening the clouds will part, the setting sun will shine an instant, then sink, behind the hills. [*She realizes* MR. BARRELL *has gone.*] Mr. Barrell! Mr. Barrell! [*Silence.*] I estrange them all. They come towards me, uninvited, bygones bygones, full of kindness, anxious to help . . . [*the voice breaks*] . . . genuinely pleased . . . to see me again . . . looking so well . . . . [*Handkerchief.*] A few simple words . . . from my heart . . . and I am all alone . . . once more . . . . [*Handkerchief. Vehemently.*] I should not be out at all. I should never leave the grounds! [*Pause.*] Oh there is that Fitt woman, I wonder will she bow to me. [*Sound of* MISS FITT *approaching, humming a hymn. She starts climbing the steps.*] Miss Fitt! [MISS FITT *halts, stops humming.*] Am I then invisible, Miss Fitt? Is this cretonne so becoming to me that I merge into the masonry? [MISS FITT *descends a step.*] That is right, Miss Fitt, look closely and you will finally distinguish a once female shape.

MISS FITT. Mrs. Rooney! I saw you, but I did not know you.

MRS. ROONEY. Last Sunday we worshipped

together. We knelt side by side at the same altar. We drank from the same chalice. Have I so changed since then?

Miss Fitt [*shocked*]. Oh but in church, Mrs. Rooney, in church I am alone with my Maker. Are not you? [*Pause.*] Why even the sexton himself, you know, when he takes up the collection, knows it is useless to pause before me. I simply do not see the plate, or bag, whatever it is they use, how could I? [*Pause.*] Why even when all is over and I go out into the sweet fresh air, why even then for the first furlong or so I stumble in a kind of daze as you might say, oblivious to my co-religionists. And they are very kind I must admit—the vast majority —very kind and understanding. They know me now and take no umbrage. There she goes, they say, there goes the dark Miss Fitt, alone with her Maker, take no notice of her. And they step down off the path to avoid my running into them. [*Pause.*] Ah yes, I am distray, very distray, even on week-days. Ask Mother, if you do not believe me. Hetty, she says, when I start eating my doily instead of the thin bread and butter, Hetty, how can you be so distray? [*Sighs.*] I suppose the truth is I am not there, Mrs. Rooney, just not really there at all. I see, hear, smell, and so on, I go through the usual motions, but my heart is not in it, Mrs. Rooney, but heart is in none of it. Left to myself, with no one to check me, I would soon be flown . . . home. [*Pause.*] So if you think I cut you just now, Mrs. Rooney, you do me an injustice. All I saw was a big pale blur, just another big pale blur. [*Pause.*] Is anything amiss, Mrs. Rooney, you do not look normal somehow. So bowed and bent.

Mrs. Rooney [*ruefully*]. Maddy Rooney, née Dunne, the big pale blur. [*Pause.*] You have piercing sight, Miss Fitt, if you only knew it, literally piercing.

[*Pause.*]

Miss Fitt. Well . . . is there anything I can do, now that I am here?

Mrs. Rooney. If you would help me up the face of this cliff, Miss Fitt, I have little doubt your Maker would requite you, if no one else.

Miss Fitt. Now, now, Mrs. Rooney, don't put your teeth in me. Requite! I make these sacrifices for nothing—or not at all. [*Pause. Sound of her descending steps.*] I take it you want to lean on me, Mrs. Rooney.

Mrs. Rooney. I asked Mr. Barrell to give me his arm, just give me his arm. [*Pause.*] He turned on his heel and strode away.

Miss Fitt. Is it my arm you want then? [*Pause. Impatiently.*] Is it my arm you want, Mrs. Rooney, or what is it?

Mrs. Rooney [*exploding*]. Your arm! Any arm! A helping hand! For five seconds! Christ what a planet!

Miss Fitt. Really. . . . Do you know what it is, Mrs. Rooney, I do not think it is wise of you to be going about at all.

Mrs. Rooney [*violently*]. Come down here, Miss Fitt, and give me your arm, before I scream down the parish!

[*Pause. Wind. Sound of* Miss Fitt *descending last steps.*]

Miss Fitt [*resignedly*]. Well, I suppose it is the Protestant thing to do.

Mrs. Rooney. Pismires do it for one another. [*Pause.*] I have seen slugs do it. [Miss Fitt *proffers her arm.*] No, the other side, my dear, if it's all the same to you, I'm left-handed on top of everything else. [*She takes* Miss Fitt's *right arm.*] Heavens, child, you're just a bag of bones, you need building up. [*Sound of her toiling up steps on* Miss Fitt's *arm.*] This is worse than the Matterhorn, were you ever up the Matterhorn, Miss Fitt, great honeymoon resort. [*Sound of toiling.*] Why don't they have a handrail? [*Panting.*] Wait till I get some air. [*Pause.*] Don't let me go! [Miss Fitt *hums her hymn.° After a moment* Mrs. Rooney *joins in with the words.*] . . . the encircling gloo-oom . . . [Miss Fitt *stops humming*] . . . tum tum me on. [*Forte.*] The night is dark and I am far from ho-ome, tum tum—

Miss Fitt [*hysterically*]. Stop it, Mrs. Rooney, stop it, or I'll drop you!

Mrs. Rooney. Wasn't it that they sung on the *Lusitania*? Or Rock of Ages? Most touching it must have been. Or was it the *Titanic*?

her hymn John Henry Newman's "Lead, Kindly Light"

[*Attracted by the noise a group, including*
MR. TYLER, MR. BARRELL, *and* TOMMY, *gathers
at top of steps.*]

MR. BARRELL. What the—

5 [*Silence.*]

MR. TYLER. Lovely day for the fixture.

[*Loud titter from* TOMMY *cut short by* MR.
BARRELL *with back-handed blow in the
stomach. Appropriate noise from* TOMMY.]

10 FEMALE VOICE [*shrill*]. Oh look, Dolly, look!

DOLLY. What, Mamma?

FEMALE VOICE. They are stuck! [*Cackling
laugh.*] They are stuck!

MRS. ROONEY. Now we are the laughing-

15 stock of the twenty-six counties. Or is it
thirty-six?

MR. TYLER. That is a nice way to treat your
defenseless subordinates, Mr. Barrell, hitting
them without warning in the pit of the

20 stomach.

MISS FITT. Has anybody seen my mother?

MR. BARRELL. Who is that?

TOMMY. The dark Miss Fitt.

MR. BARRELL. Where is her face?

25 MRS. ROONEY. Now, deary, I am ready if
you are. [*They toil up remaining steps.*] Stand
back, you cads!

[*Shuffle of feet.*]

FEMALE VOICE. Mind yourself, Dolly!

30 MRS. ROONEY. Thank you, Miss Fitt, thank
you, that will do, just prop me up against the
wall like a roll of tarpaulin and that will be
all, for the moment. [*Pause.*] I am sorry for
all this ramdam,° Miss Fitt, had I known you

35 were looking for your mother I should not
have importuned you, I know what it is.

MR. TYLER [*in marvelling aside*]. Ramdam!

FEMALE VOICE. Come, Dolly darling, let us
take up our stand before the first class

40 smokers. Give me your hand and hold me tight,
one can be sucked under.

MR. TYLER. You have lost your mother, Miss
Fitt?

MISS FITT. Good morning, Mr. Tyler.

45 MR. TYLER. Good morning, Miss Fitt.

MR. BARRELL. Good morning, Miss Fitt.

MISS FITT. Good morning, Mr. Barrell.

MR. TYLER. You have lost your mother, Miss
Fitt?

MISS FITT. She said she would be on the last   50
train.

MRS. ROONEY. Do not imagine, because I am
silent, that I am not present, and alive, to all
that is going on.

MR. TYLER [*to* MISS FITT]. When you say the   55
last train—

MRS. ROONEY. Do not flatter yourselves for
one moment, because I hold aloof, that my
sufferings have ceased. No. The entire scene,
the hills, the plain, the racecourse with its   60
miles and miles of white rails and three red
stands, the pretty little wayside station, even
you yourselves, yes, I mean it, and over all the
clouding blue, I see it all, I stand here and see
it all with eyes . . . [*the voice breaks*] . . .   65
through eyes . . . oh if you had my eyes . . .
you would understand . . . the things they have
seen . . . and not looked away . . . this is nothing
. . . nothing . . . what did I do with the handkerchief?   70

[*Pause.*]

MR. TYLER [*to* MISS FITT]. When you say
the last train—[MRS. ROONEY *blows her nose
violently and long*]—when you say the last
train, Miss Fitt, I take it you mean the twelve-   75
thirty.

MISS FITT. What else could I mean, Mr.
Tyler, what else could I *conceivably* mean?

MR. TYLER. Then you have no cause for
anxiety, Miss Fitt, for the twelve-thirty has   80
not yet arrived. Look. [MISS FITT *looks*.] No,
up the line. [MISS FITT *looks. Patiently*.] No,
Miss Fitt, follow the direction of my index.
[MISS FITT *looks*.] There. You see now. The
signal. At the bawdy hour of nine. [*In rueful*   85
afterthought.] Or three alas! [MR. BARRELL
stifles a guffaw.] Thank you, Mr. Barrell.

MISS FITT. But the time is now getting on
for—

MR. TYLER [*patiently*]. We all know, Miss   90
Fitt, we all know only too well what the time
is now getting on for, and yet the cruel fact
remains that the twelve-thirty has not yet arrived.

ramdam rumpus or rampage

SAMUEL BECKETT

Miss Fitt. Not an accident, I trust! [*Pause.*] Do not tell me she has left the track! [*Pause.*] Oh darling mother! With the fresh sole for lunch!

5 [*Loud titter from* Tommy, *checked as before by* Mr. Barrell.]

Mr. Barrell. That's enough old guff out of you. Nip up to the box now and see has Mr. Case anything for me.

10 [Tommy *goes.*]

Mrs. Rooney. Poor Dan!

Miss Fitt [*in anguish*]. What terrible thing has happened?

Mr. Tyler. Now now, Miss Fitt, do not—

15 Mrs. Rooney [*with vehement sadness*]. Poor Dan!

Mr. Tyler. Now now, Miss Fitt, do not give way . . . to despair, all will come right . . . in the end. [*Aside to* Mr. Barrell.] What *is* the
20 situation, Mr. Barrell? Not a collision surely?

Mrs. Rooney [*enthusiastically*]. A collision! Oh that would be wonderful!

Miss Fitt [*horrified*]. A collision! I knew it!

Mr. Tyler. Come, Miss Fitt, let us move a
25 little up the platform.

Mrs. Rooney. Yes, let us all do that. [*Pause.*] No? [*Pause.*] You have changed your mind? [*Pause.*] I quite agree, we are better here, in the shadow of the waiting-room.

30 Mr. Barrell. Excuse me a moment.

Mrs. Rooney. Before you slink away, Mr. Barrell, please, a statement of some kind, I insist. Even the slowest train on this brief line is not ten minutes and more behind its
35 scheduled time without good cause, one imagines. [*Pause.*] We all know your station is the best kept of the entire network, but there are times when that is not enough, just not enough. [*Pause.*] Now, Mr. Barrell, leave off
40 chewing your whiskers, we are waiting to hear from you—we the unfortunate ticket-holders' nearest if not dearest.

[*Pause.*]

Mr. Tyler [*reasonably*]. I do think we are
45 owed some kind of explanation, Mr. Barrell, if only to set our minds at rest.

Mr. Barrell. I know nothing. All I know is there has been a hitch. All traffic is retarded.

Mrs. Rooney [*derisively*]. Retarded! A hitch! Ah these celibates! Here we are eating 50 our hearts out with anxiety for our loved ones and he calls that a hitch! Those of us like myself with heart and kidney trouble may collapse at any moment and he calls that a hitch! In our ovens the Saturday roast is burning to a 55 shrivel and he calls that—

Mr. Tyler. Here comes Tommy, running! I am glad I have been spared to see this.

Tommy [*excitedly, in the distance*]. She's coming. [*Pause. Nearer.*] She's at the level-60 crossing!

[*Immediately exaggerated station sounds. Falling signals. Bells. Whistles. Crescendo of train whistle approaching. Sound of train rushing through station.*] 65

Mrs. Rooney [*above rush of train*]. The up mail! The up mail! [*The up mail recedes, the down train approaches, enters the station, pulls up with great hissing of steam and clashing of couplings. Noise of passengers descending,* 70 *doors banging,* Mr. Barrell *shouting "Boghill! Boghill!", etc. Piercingly.*] Dan! . . . Are you all right? . . . Where is he? . . . Dan! . . . Did you see my husband? . . . Dan! . . . [*Noise of station emptying. Guard's whistle. Train* 75 *departing, receding. Silence.*] He isn't on it! The misery I have endured, to get here, and he isn't on it! . . . Mr. Barrell! . . . Was he not on it? [*Pause.*] Is anything the matter, you look as if you had seen a ghost. [*Pause.*] Tommy! 80 . . . Did you see the master?

Tommy. He'll be along, Ma'am, Jerry is minding him.

[Mr. Rooney *suddenly appears on platform, advancing on small boy* Jerry's *arm. He is* 85 *blind, thumps the ground with his stick and pants incessantly.*]

Mrs. Rooney. Oh, Dan! There you are! [*Her dragging feet as she hastens towards him. She reaches him. They halt.*] Where in the 90 world were you?

Mr. Rooney [*coolly*]. Maddy.

Mrs. Rooney. Where were you all this time?

Mr. Rooney. In the men's. 95

Mrs. Rooney. Kiss me!

MR. ROONEY. Kiss you? In public? On the platform? Before the boy? Have you taken leave of your senses?

MRS. ROONEY. Jerry wouldn't mind. Would you, Jerry?

JERRY. No, Ma'am.

MRS. ROONEY. How is your poor father?

JERRY. They took him away, Ma'am.

MRS. ROONEY. Then you are all alone?

JERRY. Yes, Ma'am.

MR. ROONEY. Why are you here? You did not notify me.

MRS. ROONEY. I wanted to give you a surprise. For your birthday.

MR. ROONEY. My birthday?

MRS. ROONEY. Don't you remember? I wished you your happy returns in the bathroom.

MR. ROONEY. I did not hear you.

MRS. ROONEY. But I gave you a tie! You have it on!

[*Pause.*]

MR. ROONEY. How old am I now?

MRS. ROONEY. Now never mind about that. Come.

MR. ROONEY. Why did you not cancel the boy? Now we shall have to give him a penny.

MRS. ROONEY [*miserably*]. I forgot! I had such a time getting here! Such horrid nasty people! [*Pause. Pleading.*] Be nice to me, Dan, be nice to me today!

MR. ROONEY. Give the boy a penny.

MRS. ROONEY. Here are two halfpennies, Jerry. Run along now and buy yourself a nice gobstopper.

JERRY. Yes, Ma'am.

MR. ROONEY. Come for me on Monday, if I am still alive.

JERRY. Yessir.

[*He runs off.*]

MR. ROONEY. We could have saved sixpence. We have saved fivepence. [*Pause.*] But at what cost?

[*They move off along platform arm in arm. Dragging feet, panting, thudding stick.*]

MRS. ROONEY. Are you not well?

[*They halt, on* MR. ROONEY's *initiative.*]

MR. ROONEY. Once and for all, do not ask me to speak and move at the same time. I shall not say this in this life again.

[*They move off. Dragging feet, etc. They halt at top of steps.*]

MRS. ROONEY. Are you not—

MR. ROONEY. Let us get this precipice over.

MRS. ROONEY. Put your arm around me.

MR. ROONEY. Have you been drinking again? [*Pause.*] You are quivering like a blanc-mange. [*Pause.*] Are you in a condition to lead me? [*Pause.*] We shall fall into the ditch.

MRS. ROONEY. Oh, Dan! It will be like old times!

MR. ROONEY. Pull yourself together or I shall send Tommy for the cab. Then instead of having saved sixpence, no, fivepence, we shall have lost . . . [*calculating mumble*] . . . two and three less six one and no plus one one and no plus three one and nine and one ten and three two and one . . . [*normal voice*] two and one, we shall be the poorer to the tune of two and one. [*Pause.*] Curse that sun, it has gone in. What is the day doing?

[*Wind.*]

MRS. ROONEY. Shrouding, shrouding, the best of it is past. [*Pause.*] Soon the first great drops will fall splashing in the dust.

MR. ROONEY. And yet the glass was firm. [*Pause.*] Let us hasten home and sit before the fire. We shall draw the blinds. You will read to me. I think Effie is going to commit adultery with the Major. [*Brief drag of feet.*] Wait! [*Feet cease. Stick tapping at steps.*] I have been up and down these steps five thousand times and still I do not know how many there are. When I think there are six there are four or five or seven or eight and when I remember there are five there are three or four or six or seven and when finally I realize there are seven there are five or six or eight or nine. Sometimes I wonder if they do not change them in the night. [*Pause. Irritably.*] Well? How many do you make them today?

MRS. ROONEY. Do not ask me to count, Dan, not now.

MR. ROONEY. Not count! One of the few satisfactions in life!

MRS. ROONEY. Not steps, Dan, please, I al-

SAMUEL BECKETT

ways get them wrong. Then you might fall on your wound and I would have that on my manure-heap on top of everything else. No, just cling to me and all will be well.

5 [*Confused noise of their descent. Panting, stumbling, ejaculations, curses. Silence.*]

MR. ROONEY. Well! That is what you call well!

MRS. ROONEY. We are down. And little the
10 worse. [*Silence. A donkey brays. Silence.*] That was a true donkey. Its father and mother were donkeys.

[*Silence.*]

MR. ROONEY. Do you know what it is, I
15 think I shall retire.

MRS. ROONEY [*appalled*]. Retire! And live at home? On your grant!

MR. ROONEY. Never tread these cursed steps again. Trudge this hellish road for the last
20 time. Sit at home on the remnants of my bottom counting the hours—till the next meal. [*Pause.*] The very thought puts life in me! Forward, before it dies!

[*They move on. Dragging feet, panting, thud-
25 ding stick.*]

MRS. ROONEY. Now mind, here is the path . . . Up! . . . Well done! Now we are in safety and a straight run home.

MR. ROONEY [*without halting, between
30 gasps*]. A straight . . . run! . . . She calls that . . . a straight . . . run! . . .

MRS. ROONEY. Hush! Do not speak as you go along, you know it is not good for your coronary. [*Dragging steps, etc.*] Just concen-
35 trate on putting one foot before the next or whatever the expression is. [*Dragging feet, etc.*] That is the way, now we are doing nicely. [*Dragging feet, etc. They suddenly halt, on MRS. ROONEY's initiative.*] Heavens! I knew
40 there was something! With all the excitement! I forgot!

MR. ROONEY [*quietly*]. Good God.

MRS. ROONEY. But you must know, Dan, of course, you were on it. Whatever happened?
45 Tell me!

MR. ROONEY. I have never known anything to happen.

MRS. ROONEY. But you must—

MR. ROONEY [*violently*]. All this stopping and starting again is devilish, devilish! I get 50 a little way on me and begin to be carried along when suddenly you stop dead! Two hundred pounds of unhealthy fat! What possessed you to come out at all? Let go of me!

MRS. ROONEY [*in great agitation*]. No, I 55 must know, we won't stir from here till you tell me. Fifteen minutes late! On a thirty-minute run! It's unheard of!

MR. ROONEY. I know nothing. Let go of me before I shake you off. 60

MRS. ROONEY. But you must know! You were on it! Was it at the terminus? Did you leave on time? Or was it on the line? [*Pause.*] Did something happen on the line? [*Pause.*] Dan! [*Brokenly.*] Why won't you tell me! 65

[*Silence. They move off. Dragging feet, etc. They halt. Pause.*]

MR. ROONEY. Poor Maddy! [*Pause. Children's cries.*] What was that?

[*Pause for MRS. ROONEY to ascertain.*] 70

MRS. ROONEY. The Lynch twins jeering at us. [*Cries.*]

MR. ROONEY. Will they pelt us with mud today, do you suppose?

[*Cries.*] 75

MRS. ROONEY. Let us turn and face them. [*Cries. They turn. Silence.*] Threaten them with your stick. [*Silence.*] They have run away.

[*Pause.*] 80

MR. ROONEY. Did you ever wish to kill a child? [*Pause.*] Nip some young doom in the bud. [*Pause.*] Many a time at night, in winter, on the black road home, I nearly attacked the boy. [*Pause.*] Poor Jerry! [*Pause.*] What res- 85 trained me then? [*Pause.*] Not fear of man. [*Pause.*] Shall we go on backwards now a little?

MRS. ROONEY. Backwards?

MR. ROONEY. Yes. Or you forwards and I 90 backwards. The perfect pair. Like Dante's damned, with their faces arsy-versy. Our tears will water our bottoms.

MRS. ROONEY. What is the matter, Dan? Are you not well? 95

MR. ROONEY. Well! Did you ever know me

to be well? The day you met me I should have been in bed. The day you proposed to me the doctors gave me up. You knew that, did you not? The night you married me they came for me with an ambulance. You have not forgotten that, I suppose? [*Pause.*] No, I cannot be said to be well. But I am no worse. Indeed I am better than I was. The loss of my sight was a great fillip. If I could go deaf and dumb I think I might pant on to be a hundred. Or have I done so? [*Pause.*] Was I a hundred today? [*Pause.*] Am I a hundred, Maddy?

[*Silence.*]

MRS. ROONEY. All is still. No living soul in sight. There is no one to ask. The world is feeding. The wind—[*brief wind*]—scarcely stirs the leaves and the birds—[*brief chirp*]—are tired singing. The cows—[*brief moo*]—and sheep—[*brief baa*]—ruminate in silence. The dogs—[*brief bark*]—are hushed and the hens —[*brief cackle*]—sprawl torpid in the dust. We are alone. There is no one to ask.

[*Silence.*]

MR. ROONEY [*clearing his throat, narrative tone*]. We drew out on the tick of time, I can vouch for that. I was—

MRS. ROONEY. How can you vouch for it?

MR. ROONEY [*normal tone, angrily*]. I can vouch for it, I tell you! Do you want my relation or don't you? [*Pause. Narrative tone.*] On the tick of time. I had the compartment to myself, as usual. At least I hope so, for I made no attempt to restrain myself. My mind— [*Normal tone.*] But why do we not sit down somewhere? Are we afraid we should never rise again?

MRS. ROONEY. Sit down on what?

MR. ROONEY. On a bench, for example.

MRS. ROONEY. There is no bench.

MR. ROONEY. Then on a bank, let us sink down upon a bank.

MRS. ROONEY. There is no bank.

MR. ROONEY. Then we cannot. [*Pause.*] I dream of other roads, in other lands. Of another home, another—[*he hesitates*]—another home. [*Pause.*] What was I trying to say?

MRS. ROONEY. Something about your mind.

MR. ROONEY [*startled*]. My mind? Are you sure? [*Pause. Incredulous.*] My mind? . . . [*Pause.*] Ah yes. [*Narrative tone.*] Alone in the compartment my mind began to work, as so often after office hours, on the way home, in the train, to the lilt of the bogeys. Your season-ticket, I said, costs you twelve pounds a year and you earn, on an average, seven and six a day, that is to say barely enough to keep you alive and twitching with the help of food, drink, tobacco and periodicals until you finally reach home and fall into bed. Add to this—or subtract from it—rent, stationery, various subscriptions, tramfares to and fro, light and heat, permits and licences, hairtrims and shaves, tips to escorts, upkeep of premises and appearances, and a thousand unspecifiable sundries, and it is clear that by lying at home in bed, day and night, winter and summer, with a change of pyjamas once a fortnight, you would add very considerably to your income. Business, I said— [*A cry. Pause. Again. Normal tone.*] Did I hear a cry?

MRS. ROONEY. Mrs. Tully I fancy. Her poor husband is in constant pain and beats her unmercifully.

[*Silence.*]

MR. ROONEY. That was a short knock. [*Pause.*] What was I trying to get at?

MRS. ROONEY. Business.

MR. ROONEY. Ah yes, business. [*Narrative tone.*] Business, old man, I said, retire from business, it has retired from you. [*Normal tone.*] One has these moments of lucidity.

MRS. ROONEY. I feel very cold and weak.

MR. ROONEY [*narrative tone*]. On the other hand, I said, there are the horrors of home life, the dusting, sweeping, airing, scrubbing, waxing, waning, washing, mangling, drying, mowing, clipping, raking, rolling, scuffling, shovelling, grinding, tearing, pounding, banging and slamming. And the brats, the happy little healthy little howling neighbour's brats. Of all this and much more the week-end, the Saturday intermission and then the day of rest, have given you some idea. But what must it be like on a working-day? A Wednesday? A Friday! What must it be like on a Friday! And I fell to thinking of my silent, backstreet, basement office, with its obliterated plate, rest-couch and velvet hangings, and what it means to be buried there alive, if only from ten to five, with convenient to the one hand a bottle of light pale ale and to the other a long ice-cold fillet of hake. Nothing, I said, not even fully certified death, can ever take the place of that. It was then I noticed we were at a standstill. [*Pause. Normal tone. Irritably.*] Why are you hanging out of me like that? Have you swooned away?

MRS. ROONEY. I feel very cold and faint. The wind—[*whistling wind*]—is whistling through my summer frock as if I had nothing on over my bloomers. I have had no solid food since my elevenses.°

MR. ROONEY. You have ceased to care. I speak—and you listen to the wind.

MRS. ROONEY. No no, I am agog, tell me all, we shall press on and never pause, never pause, till we come safe to haven.

[*Pause.*]

MR. ROONEY. Never pause . . . safe to haven. . . . Do you know, Maddy, sometimes one would think you were struggling with a dead language.

MRS. ROONEY. Yes indeed, Dan, I know full well what you mean, I often have that feeling, it is unspeakably excruciating.

MR. ROONEY. I confess I have it sometimes myself, when I happen to overhear what I am saying.

MRS. ROONEY. Well, you know, it will be dead in time, just like our own poor dear Gaelic, there is that to be said.

[*Urgent baa.*]

MR. ROONEY [*startled*]. Good God!

MRS. ROONEY. Oh the pretty little woolly lamb, crying to suck its mother! Theirs has not changed, since Arcady.

[*Pause.*]

MR. ROONEY. Where was I in my composition?

MRS. ROONEY. At a standstill.

MR. ROONEY. Ah yes. [*Clears his throat. Narrative tone.*] I concluded naturally that we

elevenses a light midmorning meal

had entered a station and would soon be on our way again, and I sat on, without misgiving. Not a sound. Things are very dull today, I said, nobody getting down, nobody getting on. Then as time flew by and nothing happened I realized my error. We had not entered a station.

MRS. ROONEY. Did you not spring up and poke your head out of the window?

MR. ROONEY. What good would that have done me?

MRS. ROONEY. Why to call out to be told what was amiss.

MR. ROONEY. I did not care what was amiss. No, I just sat on, saying, If this train were never to move again I should not greatly mind. Then gradually a—how shall I say—a growing desire to—er—you know—welled up within me. Nervous probably. In fact now I am sure. You know, the feeling of being confined.

MRS. ROONEY. Yes yes, I have been through that.

MR. ROONEY. If we sit here much longer, I said, I really do not know what I shall do. I got up and paced to and fro between the seats, like a caged beast.

MRS. ROONEY. That is a help sometimes.

MR. ROONEY. After what seemed an eternity we simply moved off. And the next thing was Barrell bawling the abhorred name. I got down and Jerry led me to the men's, or Fir as they call it now, from Vir Viris I suppose, the V becoming F, in accordance with Grimm's Law. [*Pause.*] The rest you know. [*Pause.*] You say nothing? [*Pause.*] Say something, Maddy. Say you believe me.

MRS. ROONEY. I remember once attending a lecture by one of these new mind doctors, I forget what you call them. He spoke—

MR. ROONEY. A lunatic specialist?

MRS. ROONEY. No no, just the troubled mind. I was hoping he might shed a little light on my lifelong preoccupation with horses' buttocks.

MR. ROONEY. A neurologist.

MRS. ROONEY. No no, just mental distress, the name will come back to me in the night. I remember his telling us the story of a little girl, very strange and unhappy in her ways, and how he treated her unsuccessfully over a period of years and was finally obliged to give up the case. He could find nothing wrong with her, he said. The only thing wrong with her as far as he could see was that she was dying. And she did in fact die, shortly after he washed his hands of her.

MR. ROONEY. Well? What is there so wonderful about that?

MRS. ROONEY. No, it was just something he said, and the way he said it, that have haunted me ever since.

MR. ROONEY. You lie awake at night, tossing to and fro and brooding on it.

MRS. ROONEY. On it and other . . . wretchedness. [*Pause.*] When he had done with the little girl he stood there motionless for some time, quite two minutes I should say, looking down at his table. Then he suddenly raised his head and exclaimed, as if he had had a revelation, The trouble with her was she had never been really born! [*Pause.*] He spoke throughout without notes. [*Pause.*] I left before the end.

MR. ROONEY. Nothing about your buttocks? [MRS. ROONEY *weeps. In affectionate remonstrance.*] Maddy!

MRS. ROONEY. There is nothing to be done for those people!

MR. ROONEY. For which is there? [*Pause.*] That does not sound right somehow. [*Pause.*] What way am I facing?

MRS. ROONEY. What?

MR. ROONEY. I have forgotten what way I am facing.

MRS. ROONEY. You have turned aside and are bowed down over the ditch.

MR. ROONEY. There is a dead dog down there.

MRS. ROONEY. No no, just the rotting leaves.

MR. ROONEY. In June? Rotting leaves in June?

MRS. ROONEY. Yes, dear, from last year, and from the year before last, and from the year before that again. [*Silence. Rainy wind. They move on. Dragging steps, etc.*] There is that lovely laburnum again. Poor thing, it is losing all its tassels. [*Dragging steps, etc.*] There are

the first drops. [*Rain. Dragging feet, etc.*] Golden drizzle. [*Dragging steps, etc.*] Do not mind me, dear, I am just talking to myself. [*Rain heavier. Dragging steps, etc.*] Can hinnies procreate, I wonder?

[*They halt.*]

MR. ROONEY. Say that again.

MRS. ROONEY. Come on, dear, don't mind me, we are getting drenched.

MR. ROONEY [*forcibly*]. Can what what?

MRS. ROONEY. Hinnies procreate. [*Silence.*] You know, hinnies, or jinnies, aren't they barren, or sterile, or whatever it is? [*Pause.*] It wasn't an ass's colt° at all, you know, I asked the Regius Professor.

[*Pause.*]

MR. ROONEY. He should know.

MRS. ROONEY. Yes, it was a hinny, he rode into Jerusalem or wherever it was on a hinny. [*Pause.*] That must mean something. [*Pause.*] It's like the sparrows, than many of which we are of more value, they weren't sparrows at all.

MR. ROONEY. Than many of which! . . . You exaggerate, Maddy.

MRS. ROONEY [*with emotion*]. They weren't sparrows at all!

MR. ROONEY. Does that put our price up?

[*Silence. They move on. Wind and rain. Dragging feet, etc. They halt.*]

MRS. ROONEY. Do you want some dung? [*Silence. They move on. Wind and rain, etc. They halt.*] Why do you stop? Do you want to say something?

MR. ROONEY. No.

MRS. ROONEY. Then why do you stop?

MR. ROONEY. It is easier.

MRS. ROONEY. Are you very wet?

MR. ROONEY. To the buff.

MRS. ROONEY. The buff?

MR. ROONEY. The buff. From buffalo.

MRS. ROONEY. We shall hang up all our things in the hot-cupboard and get into our dressing-gowns. [*Pause.*] Put your arm round me. [*Pause.*] Be nice to me! [*Pause. Gratefully.*] Ah, Dan! [*They move on. Wind and

---

an ass's colt on which Jesus rode into Jerusalem on Palm Sunday; see Matthew 21:2–8.

rain. *Dragging feet, etc. Faintly same music as before. They halt. Music clearer. Silence but for music playing. Music dies.*] All day the same old record. All alone in that great empty house. She must be a very old woman now.

MR. ROONEY [*indistinctly*]. Death and the Maiden.

[*Silence.*]

MRS. ROONEY. You are crying. [*Pause.*] Are you crying?

MR. ROONEY [*violently*]. Yes! [*They move on. Wind and rain. Dragging feet, etc. They halt. They move on. Wind and rain. Dragging feet, etc. They halt.*] Who is the preacher to-morrow? The incumbent?

MRS. ROONEY. No.

MR. ROONEY. Thank God for that. Who?

MRS. ROONEY. Hardy.

MR. ROONEY. "How to be Happy though Married"?

MRS. ROONEY. No no, he died, you remember. No connexion.

MR. ROONEY. Has he announced his text?

MRS. ROONEY. "The Lord upholdeth all that fall and raiseth up all those that be bowed down." [*Silence. They join in wild laughter. They move on. Wind and rain. Dragging feet, etc.*] Hold me tighter, Dan! [*Pause.*] Oh yes!

[*They halt.*]

MR. ROONEY. I hear something behind us.

[*Pause.*]

MRS. ROONEY. It looks like Jerry. [*Pause.*] It is Jerry.

[*Sound of* JERRY's *running steps approaching. He halts beside them, panting.*]

JERRY [*panting*]. You dropped—

MRS. ROONEY. Take your time, my little man, you will burst a blood-vessel.

JERRY [*panting*]. You dropped something, sir. Mr. Barrell told me to run after you.

MRS. ROONEY. Show. [*She takes the object.*] What is it? [*She examines it.*] What is this thing, Dan?

MR. ROONEY. Perhaps it is not mine at all.

JERRY. Mr. Barrell said it was, sir.

MRS. ROONEY. It looks like a kind of ball. And yet it is not a ball.

MR. ROONEY. Give it to me.

MRS. ROONEY [*giving it*]. What *is* it, Dan?

MR. ROONEY. It is a thing I carry about with me.

MRS. ROONEY. Yes, but what—

MR. ROONEY [*violently*]. It is a thing I carry about with me!

[*Silence.* MRS. ROONEY *looks for a penny.*]

MRS. ROONEY. I have no small money. Have you?

MR. ROONEY. I have none of any kind.

MRS. ROONEY. We are out of change, Jerry. Remind Mr. Rooney on Monday and he will give you a penny for your pains.

JERRY. Yes, Ma'am.

MR. ROONEY. If I am alive.

JERRY. Yessir.

[JERRY *starts running back towards the station.*]

MRS. ROONEY. Jerry! [JERRY *halts.*] Did you hear what the hitch was? [*Pause.*] Did you hear what kept the train so late?

MR. ROONEY. How would he have heard? Come on.

MRS. ROONEY. What was it, Jerry?

JERRY. It was a—

MR. ROONEY. Leave the boy alone, he knows nothing! Come on!

MRS. ROONEY. What was it, Jerry?

JERRY. It was a little child, Ma'am.

[MR. ROONEY *groans.*]

MRS. ROONEY. What do you mean, it was a little child?

JERRY. It was a little child fell out of the carriage, Ma'am. [*Pause.*] On to the line, Ma'am. [*Pause.*] Under the wheels, Ma'am.

[*Silence.* JERRY *runs off. His steps die away. Tempest of wind and rain. It abates. They move on. Dragging steps, etc. They halt. Tempest of wind and rain.*]

End

Act Without Words I

A Mime for One Player

BECKETT

Translated from the French by the Author

Desert. Dazzling light.

The man is flung backwards on stage from right wing. He falls, gets up immediately, dusts himself, turns aside, reflects.

5   Whistle from right wing.

He reflects, goes out right.

Immediately flung back on stage he falls, gets up immediately, dusts himself, turns aside, reflects.

10   Whistle from left wing.

He reflects, goes out left.

Immediately flung back on stage he falls, gets up immediately dusts himself, turns aside, reflects.

15   Whistle from left wing.

He reflects, goes towards left wing, hesitates, thinks better of it, halts, turns aside, reflects.

A little tree descends from flies, lands. It 20 has a single bough some three yards from ground and at its summit a meager tuft of palms casting at its foot a circle of shadow.

He continues to reflect.

Whistle from above.

25   He turns, sees tree, reflects, goes to it, sits down in its shadow, looks at his hands.

A pair of tailor's scissors descends from flies,

comes to rest before tree, a yard from ground.

He continues to look at his hands.

Whistle from above.   30

He looks up, sees scissors, takes them and starts to trim his nails.

The palms close like a parasol, the shadow disappears.

He drops scissors, reflects.   35

A tiny carafe, to which is attached a huge label inscribed WATER, descends from flies, comes to rest some three yards from ground.

He continues to reflect.

Whistle from above.   40

He looks up, sees carafe, reflects, gets up, goes and stands under it, tries in vain to reach it, renounces, turns aside, reflects.

A big cube descends from flies, lands.

He continues to reflect.   45

Whistle from above.

He turns, sees cube, looks at it, at carafe, reflects, goes to cube, takes it up, carries it over and sets it down under carafe, tests its stability, gets up on it, tries in vain to reach 50 carafe, renounces, gets down, carries cube back to its place, turns aside, reflects.

A second smaller cube descends from flies, lands.

He continues to reflect.   55

Whistle from above.

He turns, sees second cube, looks at it, at carafe, goes to second cube, takes it up, carries it over and sets it down under carafe, tests its stability, gets up on it, tries in vain to reach 60 carafe, renounces, gets down, takes up second cube to carry it back to its place, hesitates, thinks better of it, sets it down, goes to big cube, takes it up, carries it over and puts it on small one, tests their stability, gets up on them, 65 the cubes collapse, he falls, gets up immediately, brushes himself, reflects.

He takes up small cube, puts it on big one, tests their stability, gets up on them and is about to reach carafe when it is pulled up a 70 little way and comes to rest beyond his reach.

He gets down, reflects, carries cubes back to their place, one by one, turns aside, reflects.

A third still smaller cube descends from flies, lands.   75

He continues to reflect.

Whistle from above.

He turns, sees third cube, looks at it, reflects, turns aside, reflects.

5   The third cube is pulled up and disappears in flies.

Beside carafe a rope descends from flies, with knots to facilitate ascent.

He continues to reflect.

10   Whistle from above.

He turns, sees rope, reflects, goes to it, climbs up it and is about to reach carafe when rope is let out and deposits him back on ground.

15   He reflects, looks around for scissors, sees them, goes and picks them up, returns to rope and starts to cut it with scissors.

The rope is pulled up, lifts him off ground, he hangs on, succeeds in cutting rope, falls
20   back on ground, drops scissors, falls, gets up again immediately, brushes himself, reflects.

The rope is pulled up quickly and disappears in flies.

With length of rope in his possession he
25   makes a lasso with which he tries to lasso carafe.

The carafe is pulled up quickly and disappears in flies.

He turns aside, reflects.

30   He goes with lasso in his hand to tree, looks at bough, turns and looks at cubes, looks again at bough, drops lasso, goes to cubes, takes up small one, carries it over and sets it down under bough, goes back for big one,
35   takes it up and carries it over under bough, makes to put it on small one, hesitates, thinks better of it, sets it down, takes up small one and puts it on big one, tests their stability, turns aside and stoops to pick up lasso.

40   The bough folds down against trunk.

He straightens up with lasso in his hand, turns and sees what has happened.

He drops lasso, turns aside, reflects.

He carries back cubes to their place, one by
45   one, goes back for lasso, carries it over to cubes and lays it in a neat coil on small one.

He turns aside, reflects.

Whistle from right wing.

He reflects, goes out right.

Immediately flung back on stage he falls, 50
gets up immediately, brushes himself, turns aside, reflects.

Whistle from left wing.

He does not move.

He looks at his hands, looks around for 55
scissors, sees them, goes and picks them up, starts to trim his nails, stops, reflects, runs his finger along blade of scissors, goes and lays them on small cube, turns aside, opens his collar, frees his neck and fingers it. 60

The small cube is pulled up and disappears in flies, carrying away rope and scissors.

He turns to take scissors, sees what has happened.

He turns aside, reflects. 65

He goes and sits down on big cube.

The big cube is pulled from under him. He falls. The big cube is pulled up and disappears in flies.

He remains lying on his side, his face to- 70
wards auditorium, staring before him.

The carafe descends from flies and comes to rest a few feet from his body.

He does not move.

Whistle from above. 75

He does not move.

The carafe descends further, dangles and plays about his face.

He does not move.

The carafe is pulled up and disappears in 80
flies.

The bough returns to horizontal, the palms open, the shadow returns.

Whistle from above.

He does not move. 85

The tree is pulled up and disappears in flies.

He looks at his hands.

End

Harold Pinter

1930–

The Caretaker

1960

Around discussions of the plays of Harold Pinter recur certain critical terms: Theatre of the Absurd (Martin Esslin's coinage), naturalism, realism, and poetic realism, to name a few of the most common. *The Caretaker* is absurd in that it neither implies nor projects any "feeling that the world makes sense, or can be reduced into an integrated system of values." It is naturalistic both in its lack of concern for any fourth dimension of religion or spirituality—heaven, hell, or hereafter—and in its unavoidance of the low and ugly aspects of humanity. It is realistic in its precise, almost microscopic focus on what lies under the playwright's dramatic lens: three lives of varying degrees of shabbiness entering, leaving, or dwelling in a room the clutter and rubbish of which are catalogued in the opening stage direction. And its realism is poetic, though not at first glance, in its language and structure. The language has been called by Ruby Cohn "the most brilliant and brutal stylization of contemporary cliché on the English stage today" (although there's much more to it than that). The structure is evident, for instance, in curtain lines (or silences) as abruptly forceful as those in Ibsen or Beckett and in the sense of inevitability that stems from the plot's psychological integrity and the play's architectural economy.

The three persons of the play are Aston, the elder brother, Mick, the younger, and Davies (or Jenkins, for he claims both names), the tramp who would seem to be the play's title figure. Years back the gentle Aston underwent shock treatments for some undefined mental disorder. The treatments affected him as might a lobotomy, slowing down his thoughts, numbing his will, making him avoid most human contact. Through much of the play he seeks tools he neither needs nor uses; he fails in his attempts to repair an electric toaster; he collects the drippings from a leak in the roof rather than repairing it; and he impotently yearns to build a workshop for the carpentry he vaguely plans to perform on the house. At the play's start, though, slight but significant change has begun. Like the good Samaritan aiding the man set upon by thieves, Aston has rescued the old tramp from a beating, brought him back to his room, given him tobacco, a few shillings, a bed, and a chance to stay on as caretaker.

Mick, the younger brother, whose business seems to have something to do with interior decorating—although he more talks that occupation than practices it—is his brother's undemonstratively affectionate keeper. He is also something of a bullyboy, who hurts and frightens the old tramp by twisting his arm, then muddles his enfeebled mind with reiterated questionings, plays a childish game of keep-away with the old man's trousers, suddenly befriends him with a shared sandwich and cozy images of a shared future in this old house, then finally heaps insults upon him, culminating thus: "You're a barbarian. And to put the tin lid on it, you stink from arse-hole to breakfast-time."

Mick, like Aston, offers Davies the position of caretaker. And Davies, the tramp, a piece of human flotsam, almost mindless, his memory a thing of shreds and patches, as is his speech—except as resentment rises and his complaints begin to flow—Davies is both arrogant and servile, infinitely vulnerable, and incredibly uncertain about his identity. Where was he born? asks Aston: "I was . . . uh . . . oh, it's a bit hard, like, to set your mind back . . . see what I mean . . . going back . . . a good way . . . lost a bit of track, like . . . you know. . . ." But down in the suburb of Sidcup, he repeatedly avers, a man Davies knows has Davies' papers: "I left them with him. You see? They prove who I am! I can't move without them papers. They tell you who I am. You see! I'm stuck without them." But all that was fifteen years ago. The shoes Aston offers Davies are never good enough, says Davies, for that long trip; yearning for Sidcup as for a lost Eden, Davies never makes a step in its direction.

In the shifting encounters among these three—all needing human companionship, all needing to be needed, all reaching out toward identities never fulfilled—lies the play's plot. Davies attempts to latch first onto Aston, then onto Mick, pitting younger brother against the older in a savagely selfish betrayal of his befriender. The brothers see through him, however—Mick at once, Aston more slowly—and the play comes to its close with that roof leak stopped, with Aston resolute almost to the point of action about beginning the shed, with the brothers bonded more closely than before, with the room about to be rid of Davies' obnoxious presence, and with the old tramp once more, but surely not for the last time, self-defeated, rejected, shambling yet more aimlessly along his life's pointless journey.

The language of the play comes close to music, fractured though its instruments may be: Davies' scraps of talk fading into pauses, his crescendos of complaint, his sudden recapturing of conversational motifs sounded earlier—as of his fear of the Indian neighbors, his pathetic moments of pride, his need of shoes, fear of draughts, dependence on clocks—his brutal jeering at Aston—all these find their counterpoint in Aston's short, simple sentences or his long semi-soliloquy at the end of Act II wherein he relives his mental illness and recuperation. And the speech of both Davies and Aston finds complement and balance in the speech of Mick, which is the most varied of all. His are improvisational passages of exuberant volubility wherein scraps of commercial and contractual jargon slip into street slang without changing pace or losing a syllable. His are ominous repetitions, as in a minor key, then staccato questionings, then the flowing chat of warm bar buddies. And always, with the full value they have in music, Pinter endows the speech of his characters with pauses, rests, silences. Realistic the dialogues and monologues truly are, but it is the realism of poetry, the best words (for their speakers) and the best silences in what is for them the best order . . . and disorder.

The play's economical architecture deserves special recognition. For all the clutter in the room and in the lives of the three men, Pinter provides nothing not relevant—whether it be the leak in the roof, the broken toaster, the battered suitcase, or the plaster Buddha— nothing not contributing to the balanced flaring up of life in the old tramp and to its inevitable guttering down if not out, as in the play's perfect ending. Aston is standing still, his back to Davies, and Davies, voice weakening along with will, half mouths his dying hopes:

"Listen . . . if I . . . got down . . . if I was to . . . get my papers . . . would you . . . would you let . . . would you . . . if I got down . . . and got my . . .

"*Long silence.*

"*Curtain.*"

The Caretaker

PINTER

CHARACTERS

MICK *a man in his late twenties*
ASTON *a man in his early thirties*
DAVIES *an old man*

The action of the play takes place in a house in west London

ACT I. *A night in winter*
ACT II. *A few seconds later*
ACT III. *A fortnight later*

A room. A window in the back wall, the bottom half covered by a sack. An iron bed along the left wall. Above is a small cupboard, paint buckets, boxes containing nuts, screws, etc. More boxes, vases, by the side of the bed. A door, up right. To the right of the window, a mound: a kitchen sink, a step-ladder, a coal bucket, a lawn-mower, a shopping trolley, boxes, sideboard drawers. Under this mound an iron bed. In front of it a gas stove. On the gas stove a statue of Buddha. Down right, a fireplace. Around it a couple of suitcases, a rolled carpet, a blow-lamp,° a wooden chair on its side, boxes, a number of orna- ments, a clothes horse, a few short planks of wood, a small electric fire, and a very old electric toaster. Below this a pile of old newspapers. Under ASTON's bed by the left wall, is an electrolux, which is not seen till used. A bucket hangs from the ceiling.

ACT I

[MICK *is alone in the room, sitting on the bed. He wears a leather jacket.*
Silence.
He slowly looks about the room, looking at each object in turn. He looks up at the ceiling, and stares at the

Blow-lamp blowtorch

*bucket. Ceasing, he sits quite still, expressionless, look-
ing out front.*

Silence for thirty seconds.

A door bangs. Muffled voices are heard.

5 M ICK *turns his head. He stands, moves silently to
the door, goes out, and closes the door quietly.*

Silence.

*Voices are heard again. They draw nearer, and stop.
The door opens,* ASTON *and* DAVIES *enter,* ASTON *first,*
10 DAVIES *following, shambling, breathing heavily.*

ASTON *wears an old tweed overcoat, and under it a
thin shabby dark-blue pinstripe suit, single-breasted, with
a pullover and faded shirt and tie.* DAVIES *wears a worn
brown overcoat, shapeless trousers, a waistcoat, vest,*
15 *no shirt, and sandals.* ASTON *puts the key in his pocket
and closes the door.* DAVIES *looks about the room.]*

ASTON. Sit down.

DAVIES. Thanks. *[Looking about.]* Uuh. . . .

ASTON. Just a minute.

20 *[*ASTON *looks around for a chair, sees one lying on
its side by the rolled carpet at the fireplace, and starts
to get it out.]*

DAVIES. Sit down? Huh . . . I haven't had a good
sit down . . . I haven't had a proper sit down . . .
25 well, I couldn't tell you. . . .

ASTON *[placing the chair].* Here you are.

DAVIES. Ten minutes off for a tea-break in the
middle of the night in that place and I couldn't
find a seat, not one. All them Greeks had it, Poles,
30 Greeks, Blacks, the lot of them, all them aliens had
it. And they had me working there . . . they had
me working. . . .

*[*ASTON *sits on the bed, takes out a tobacco tin and
papers, and begins to roll himself a cigarette.* DAVIES
35 *watches him.]*

All them Blacks had it, Blacks, Greeks, Poles, the
lot of them, that's what, doing me out of a seat,
treating me like dirt. When he come at me tonight
I told him.

40 *[Pause.]*

ASTON. Take a seat.

DAVIES. Yes, but what I got to do first, you see,
what I got to do, I got to loosen myself up, you
see what I mean? I could have got done in down
45 there.

*[*DAVIES *exclaims loudly, punches downward with
closed fist, turns his back to* ASTON *and stares at the
wall. Pause.* ASTON *lights a cigarette.]*

ASTON. You want to roll yourself one of these?

DAVIES *[turning].* What? No, no, I never smoke 50
a cigarette. *[Pause. He comes forward.]* I'll tell you
what, though. I'll have a bit of that tobacco there
for my pipe, if you like.

ASTON *[handing him the tin].* Yes. Go on. Take
some out of that. 55

DAVIES. That's kind of you, mister. Just enough
to fill my pipe, that's all. *[He takes a pipe from his
pocket and fills it.]* I had a tin, only . . . only a while
ago. But it was knocked off.° It was knocked off
on the Great West Road.° *[He holds out the tin.]* 60
Where shall I put it?

ASTON. I'll take it.

DAVIES *[handing the tin.]* When he come at me
tonight I told him. Didn't I? You heard me tell
him, didn't you? 65

ASTON. I saw him have a go at° you.

DAVIES. Go at me? You wouldn't grumble. The
filthy skate, an old man like me, I've had dinner
with the best.

[Pause.] 70

ASTON. Yes, I saw him have a go at you.

DAVIES. All them toe-rags,° mate, got the manners of pigs. I might have been on the road a few
years but you can take it from me I'm clean. I keep
myself up. That's why I left my wife. Fortnight 75
after I married her, no, not so much as that, no
more than a week, I took the lid off a saucepan,
you know what was in it? A pile of her under-
clothing, unwashed. The pan for vegetables, it was.
The vegetable pan. That's when I left her and I 80
haven't seen her since.

*[*DAVIES *turns, shambles across the room, comes face
to face with a statue of Buddha standing on the gas
stove, looks at it and turns.]*

I've eaten my dinner off the best of plates. But I'm 85
not young any more. I remember the days I was
as handy as any of them. They didn't take any
liberties with me. But I haven't been so well lately.
I've had a few attacks.

[Pause.] 90

knocked off   swiped, stolen
Great West Road   the first of a dozen or more names of
    streets, sections, bus or underground stations, and suburbs
    of London, hereafter not annotated
have a go at   pick a fight with, take a poke at
toe-rags   beggars, scum

[*Coming closer.*] Did you see what happened with that one?

ASTON. I only got the end of it.

DAVIES. Comes up to me, parks a bucket of rub-
5 bish at me, tells me to take it out the back. It's not
my job to take out the bucket! They got a boy there
for taking out the bucket. I wasn't engaged to take
out buckets. My job's cleaning the floor, clearing
up the tables, doing a bit of washing-up, nothing
10 to do with taking out buckets!

ASTON. Uh.

[*He crosses down right, to get the electric toaster.*]

DAVIES [*following*]. Yes, well say I had! Even if I
had! Even if I was supposed to take out the bucket,
15 who was this git° to come up and give me orders?
We got the same standing. He's not my boss. He's
nothing superior to me.

ASTON. What was he, a Greek?

DAVIES. Not him, he was a Scotch. He was a
20 Scotchman.

[ASTON *goes back to his bed with the toaster and
starts to unscrew the plug.* DAVIES *follows him.*] You
got an eye of him, did you?

ASTON. Yes.

25 DAVIES. I told him what to do with his bucket.
Didn't I? You heard. Look here, I said, I'm an old
man, I said, where I was brought up we had some
idea how to talk to old people with the proper
respect, we was brought up with the right ideas,
30 if I had a few years off me I'd . . . break you in
half. That was after the guvnor give me the bullet.°
Making too much commotion, he says. Commotion, me! Look here, I said to him, I got my rights.
I told him that. I might have been on the road but
35 nobody's got more rights than I have. Let's have
a bit of fair play, I said. Anyway, he give me the
bullet. [*He sits in the chair.*] That's the sort of place.

[*Pause.*]

If you hadn't come out and stopped that Scotch
40 git I'd be inside the hospital now. I'd have cracked
my head on that pavement if he'd have landed.
I'll get him. One night I'll get him. When I find
myself around that direction.

[ASTON *crosses to the plug box to get another plug.*]
45 I wouldn't mind so much but I left all my belongings in that place, in the back room there.

git guy, bum
guvnor give me the bullet boss fired me

All of them, the lot there was, you see, in this
bag. Every lousy blasted bit of all my bleeding
belongings I left down there now. In the rush of
it, I bet he's having a poke around in it now this 50
very moment.

ASTON. I'll pop down sometime and pick them
up for you.

[ASTON *goes back to his bed and starts to fix the plug
on the toaster.*] 55

DAVIES. Anyway, I'm obliged to you, letting me
. . . letting me have a bit of a rest, like . . . for a
few minutes. [*He looks about.*] This your room?

ASTON. Yes.

DAVIES. You got a good bit of stuff here. 60

ASTON. Yes.

DAVIES. Must be worth a few bob,° this . . . put
it all together.

[*Pause.*]

There's enough of it. 65

ASTON. There's a good bit of it, all right.

DAVIES. You sleep here, do you?

ASTON. Yes.

DAVIES. What, in that?

ASTON. Yes. 70

DAVIES. Yes, well, you'd be well out of the
draught there.

ASTON. You don't get much wind.

DAVIES. You'd be well out of it. It's different when
you're kipping° out. 75

ASTON. Would be.

DAVIES. Nothing but wind then.

[*Pause.*]

ASTON. Yes, when the wind gets up it . . .

[*Pause.*] 80

DAVIES. Yes. . . .

ASTON. Mmnn. . . .

[*Pause.*]

DAVIES. Gets very draughty.

ASTON. Ah. 85

DAVIES. I'm very sensitive to it.

ASTON. Are you?

DAVIES. Always have been.

[*Pause.*]

You got any more rooms then, have you? 90

ASTON. Where?

bob shilling(s)
kipping sleeping

DAVIES. I mean, along the landing here . . . up the landing there.

ASTON. They're out of commission.

DAVIES. Get away.

5 ASTON. They need a lot of doing to.

[Slight pause.]

DAVIES. What about downstairs?

ASTON. That's closed up. Needs seeing to. . . . The floors. . . .

10 [Pause.]

DAVIES. I was lucky you come into that caff.° I might have been done by that Scotch git. I been left for dead more than once.

[Pause.]

15 I noticed that there was someone was living in the house next door.

ASTON. What?

DAVIES [gesturing]. I noticed. . . .

ASTON. Yes. There's people living all along the 20 road.

DAVIES. Yes, I noticed the curtains pulled down there next door as we came along.

ASTON. They're neighbours.

[Pause.]

25 DAVIES. This your house then, is it?

[Pause.]

ASTON. I'm in charge.

DAVIES. You the landlord, are you?

[He puts a pipe in his mouth and puffs without light-30 ing it.]

Yes, I noticed them heavy curtains pulled across next door as we came along. I noticed them heavy big curtains right across the window down there. I thought there must be someone living there.

35 ASTON. Family of Indians live there.

DAVIES. Blacks?

ASTON. I don't see much of them.

DAVIES. Blacks, eh? [DAVIES stands and moves about.] Well you've got some knick-knacks here all right, 40 I'll say that. I don't like a bare room. [ASTON joins DAVIES upstage centre.] I'll tell you what, mate, you haven't got a spare pair of shoes?

ASTON. Shoes?

[ASTON moves downstage right.]

45 DAVIES. Them bastards at the monastery let me down again.

ASTON [going to his bed]. Where?

DAVIES. Down in Luton. Monastery down at Luton. . . . I got a mate at Shepherd's Bush, you see. . . . 50

ASTON [looking under his bed]. I might have a pair.

DAVIES. I got this mate at Shephard's Bush. In the convenience.° Well, he was in the conven-ience. Run about the best convenience they had. [He watches ASTON.] Run about the best one. Al- 55 ways slipped me a bit of soap, any time I went in there. Very good soap. They have to have the best soap. I was never without a piece of soap, when-ever I happened to be knocking about the Shep-herd's Bush area. 60

ASTON [emerging from under the bed with shoes]. Pair of brown.

DAVIES. He's gone now. Went. He was the one who put me on to this monastery. Just the other side of Luton. He'd heard they give away shoes. 65

ASTON. You've got to have a good pair of shoes.

DAVIES. Shoes? It's life and death to me. I had to go all the way to Luton in these.

ASTON. What happened when you got there, then? 70

[Pause.]

DAVIES. I used to know a bootmaker in Acton. He was a good mate to me.

[Pause.]

You know what that bastard monk said to me? 75

[Pause.]

How many more Blacks you got around here then?

ASTON. What?

DAVIES. You got any more Blacks around here?

ASTON [holding out the shoes]. See if these are any 80 good.

DAVIES. You know what that bastard monk said to me? [He looks over to the shoes.] I think those'd be a bit small.

ASTON. Would they? 85

DAVIES. No, don't look the right size.

ASTON. Not bad trim.

DAVIES. Can't wear shoes that don't fit. Nothing worse. I said to this monk, here, I said, look here, mister, he opened the door, big door, he opened 90 it, look here, mister, I said, I come all the way down here, look, I said, I showed him these, I said, you haven't got a pair of shoes, have you, a

---

caff cafeteria

convenience public lavatory

pair of shoes, I said, enough to keep me on my way. Look at these, they're nearly out, I said, they're no good to me. I heard you got a stock of shoes here. Piss off, he said to me. Now look here,
5 I said, I'm an old man, you can't talk to me like that, I don't care who you are. If you don't piss off, he says, I'll kick you all the way to the gate. Now look here, I said, now wait a minute, all I'm asking for is a pair of shoes, you don't want to
10 start taking liberties with me, it's taken me three days to get here, I said to him, three days without a bite, I'm worth a bite to eat, en I? Get out round the corner to the kitchen, he says, get out round the corner, and when you've had your meal, piss
15 off out of it. I went round to this kitchen, see? Meal they give me! A bird, I tell you, a little bird, a little tiny bird, he could have ate it in under two minutes. Right, they said to me, you've had your meal, get off out of it. Meal? I said, what do you
20 think I am, a dog? Nothing better than a dog. What do you think I am, a wild animal? What about them shoes I come all the way here to get I heard you was giving away? I've a good mind to report you to your mother superior. One of them, an
25 Irish hooligan, come at me. I cleared out. I took a short cut to Watford and picked up a pair there. Got onto the North Circular, just past Hendon, the sole come off, right where I was walking. Lucky I had my old ones wrapped up, still carrying them,
30 otherwise I'd have been finished, man. So I've had to stay with these, you see, they're gone, they're no good, all the good's gone out of them.

ASTON. Try these.

[DAVIES *takes the shoes, takes off his sandals and tries*
35 *them on.*]

DAVIES. Not a bad pair of shoes. [*He trudges round the room.*] They're strong, all right. Yes. Not a bad shape of shoe. This leather's hardy, en't? Very hardy. Some bloke tried to flog° me some suede
40 the other day. I wouldn't wear them. Can't beat leather, for wear. Suede goes off, it creases, it stains for life in five minutes. You can't beat leather. Yes. Good shoe this.

ASTON. Good.

45 [DAVIES *waggles his feet.*]

DAVIES. Don't fit though.

ASTON. Oh?

DAVIES. No. I got a very broad foot.

ASTON. Mmnn.

DAVIES. These are too pointed, you see. 50

ASTON. Ah.

DAVIES. They'd cripple me in a week. I mean these ones I got on, they're no good but at least they're comfortable. Not much cop,° but I mean they don't hurt. [*He takes them off and gives them* 55 *back.*] Thanks anyway, mister.

ASTON. I'll see what I can look out for you.

DAVIES. Good luck. I can't go on like this. Can't get from one place to another. And I'll have to be moving about, you see, try to get fixed up. 60

ASTON. Where you going to go?

DAVIES. Oh, I got one or two things in mind. I'm waiting for the weather to break.

[*Pause.*]

ASTON [*attending to the toaster*]. Would . . . would 65 you like to sleep here?

DAVIES. Here?

ASTON. You can sleep here if you like.

DAVIES. Here? Oh, I don't know about that.

[*Pause.*] 70
How long for?

ASTON. Till you . . . get yourself fixed up.

DAVIES [*sitting*]. Ay well, that. . . .

ASTON. Get yourself sorted out. . . .

DAVIES. Oh, I'll be fixed up . . . pretty soon 75 now. . . .

[*Pause.*]
Where would you I sleep?

ASTON. Here. The other rooms would . . . would be no good to you. 80

DAVIES [*rising, looking about*]. Here? Where?

ASTON [*rising, pointing upstage right*]. There's a bed behind all that.

DAVIES. Oh, I see. Well, that's handy. Well, that's . . . I tell you what, I might do that . . . just till I 85 get myself sorted out. You got enough furniture here.

ASTON. I picked it up. Just keeping it here for the time being. Thought it might come in handy.

DAVIES. This gas stove work, do it? 90

ASTON. No.

DAVIES. What do you do for a cup of tea?

flog sell

cop good

ASTON. Nothing.

DAVIES. That's a bit rough. [DAVIES *observes the planks.*] You building something?

ASTON. I might build a shed out the back.

5   DAVIES. Carpenter, eh? [*He turns to the lawnmower.*] Got a lawn.

ASTON. Have a look.

[ASTON *lifts the sack at the window. They look out.*]

DAVIES. Looks a bit thick.

10   ASTON. Overgrown.

DAVIES. What's that, a pond?

ASTON. Yes.

DAVIES. What you got, fish?

ASTON. No. There isn't anything in there.

15   [*Pause.*]

DAVIES. Where you going to put your shed?

ASTON [*turning*]. I'll have to clear the garden first.

DAVIES. You'd need a tractor, man.

ASTON. I'll get it done.

20   DAVIES. Carpentry, eh?

ASTON [*standing still*]. I like . . . working with my hands.

[DAVIES *picks up the statue of Buddha.*]

DAVIES. What's this?

25   ASTON [*taking and studying it*]. That's a Buddha.

DAVIES. Get on.

ASTON. Yes. I quite like it. Picked it up in a . . . in a shop. Looked quite nice to me. Don't know why. What do you think of these Buddhas?

30   DAVIES. Oh, they're . . . they're all right, en't they?

ASTON. Yes, I was pleased when I got hold of this one. It's very well made.

[DAVIES *turns and peers under the sink.*]

35   DAVIES. This the bed here, is it?

ASTON [*moving to the bed*]. We'll get rid of all that. The ladder'll fit under the bed. [*They put the ladder under the bed.*]

DAVIES [*indicating the sink*]. What about this?

40   ASTON. I think that'll fit in under here as well.

DAVIES. I'll give you a hand. [*They lift it.*] It's a ton weight, en't?

ASTON. Under here.

DAVIES. This in use at all, then?

45   ASTON. No. I'll be getting rid of it. Here.

[*They place the sink under the bed.*]

There's a lavatory down the landing. It's got a sink in there. We can put this stuff over there.

[*They begin to move the coal bucket, shopping trolley, lawnmower and sideboard drawers to the right wall.*]

50   DAVIES [*stopping*]. You don't share it, do you?

ASTON. What?

DAVIES. I mean you don't share the toilet with them Blacks, do you?

ASTON. They live next door.

55   DAVIES. They don't come in?

[ASTON *puts a drawer against the wall.*]

Because, you know . . . I mean . . . fair's fair. . . .

[ASTON *goes to the bed, blows dust and shakes a blanket.*]

60   ASTON. You see a blue case?

DAVIES. Blue case? Down here. Look. By the carpet.

[ASTON *goes to the case, opens it, takes out a sheet and pillow and puts them on the bed.*]

65   That's a nice sheet.

ASTON. The blanket'll be a bit dusty.

DAVIES. Don't you worry about that.

[ASTON *stands upright, takes out his tobacco and begins to roll a cigarette. He goes to his bed and sits.*]

70   ASTON. How are you off for money?

DAVIES. Oh well . . . now, mister, if you want the truth . . . I'm a bit short.

[ASTON *takes some coins from his pocket, sorts them, and holds out five shillings.*]

75   ASTON. Here's a few bob.

DAVIES [*taking the coins*]. Thank you, thank you, good luck. I just happen to find myself a bit short. You see, I got nothing for all that week's work I did last week. That's the position, that's what it is.

80   [*Pause.*]

ASTON. I went into a pub the other day. Ordered a Guinness. They gave it to me in a thick mug. I sat down but I couldn't drink it, I can't drink Guinness from a thick mug. I only like it out of a thin

85   glass. I had a few sips but I couldn't finish it.

[ASTON *picks up a screwdriver and plug from the bed and begins to poke the plug.*]

DAVIES [*with great feeling*]. If only the weather would break! Then I'd be able to get down to Sid-

90   cup!

ASTON. Sidcup?

DAVIES. The weather's so blasted bloody awful, how can I get down to Sidcup in these shoes?

ASTON. Why do you want to get down to Sid-

95   cup?

DAVIES. I got my papers there!

[*Pause.*]

ASTON. Your what?

DAVIES. I got my papers there!

5 [*Pause.*]

ASTON. What are they doing at Sidcup?

DAVIES. A man I know has got them. I left them with him. You see? They prove who I am! I can't move without them papers. They tell you who I

10 am. You see! I'm stuck without them.

ASTON. Why's that?

DAVIES. You see, what it is, you see, I changed my name! Years ago. I been going around under an assumed name! That's not my real name.

15 ASTON. What name you been going under?

DAVIES. Jenkins. Bernard Jenkins. That's my name. That's the name I'm known, anyway. But it's no good me going on with that name. I got no rights. I got an insurance card here. [*He takes a card*

20 *from his pocket.*] Under the name of Jenkins, See? Bernard Jenkins. Look. It's got four stamps on it. Four of them. But I can't go along with these. That's not my real name, they'd find out, they'd have me in the nick. Four stamps. I haven't paid out

25 pennies. I've paid out pounds. I've paid out pounds, not pennies. There's been other stamps, plenty, but they haven't put them on, the nigs,° I never had enough time to go into it.

ASTON. They should have stamped your card.

30 DAVIES. It would have done no good! I'd have got nothing anyway. That's not my real name. If I take that card along I go in the nick.

ASTON. What's your real name, then?

DAVIES. Davies. Mac Davies. That was before I

35 changed my name.

[*Pause.*]

ASTON. It looks as though you want to sort all that out.

DAVIES. If only I could get down to Sidcup! I've

40 been waiting for the weather to break. He's got my papers, this man I left them with, it's got it all down there, I could prove everything.

ASTON. How long's he had them?

DAVIES. What?

45 ASTON. How long's he had them?

nick jail
nigs niggards, cheapskates

DAVIES. Oh, must be . . . it was in the war . . . must be . . . about near on fifteen year ago.

[*He suddenly becomes aware of the bucket and looks up.*]

ASTON. Any time you want to . . . get into bed, 50 just get in. Don't worry about me.

DAVIES [*taking off his overcoat*]. Eh, well, I think I will. I'm a bit . . . a bit done in. [*He steps out of his trousers, and holds them out*]. Shall I put these on here? 55

ASTON. Yes.

[DAVIES *puts the coat and trousers on the clothes horse.*]

DAVIES. I see you got a bucket up here.

ASTON. Leak. 60

[DAVIES *looks up.*]

DAVIES. Well, I'll try your bed then. You getting in?

ASTON. I'm mending this plug.

[DAVIES *looks at him and then at the gas stove.*] 65

DAVIES. You . . . you can't move this, eh?

ASTON. Bit heavy.

DAVIES. Yes.

[DAVIES *gets into bed. He tests his weight and length.*] Not bad. Not bad. A fair bed. I think I'll sleep in 70 this.

ASTON. I'll have to fix a proper shade on that bulb. The light's a bit glaring.

DAVIES. Don't you worry about that, mister, don't you worry about that. [*He turns and puts the cover* 75 *up.*]

[ASTON *sits, poking his plug.*

The LIGHTS FADE OUT. *Darkness.*

LIGHTS UP. *Morning.*

ASTON *is fastening his trousers, standing by the bed.* 80 *He straightens his bed. He turns, goes to the centre of the room and looks at* DAVIES. *He turns, puts his jacket on, turns, goes towards* DAVIES *and looks down on him. He coughs.* DAVIES *sits up abruptly.*]

DAVIES. What? What's this? What's this? 85

ASTON. It's all right.

DAVIES [*staring*]. What's this?

ASTON. It's all right.

[DAVIES *looks about.*]

DAVIES. Oh, yes. 90

[ASTON *goes to his bed, picks up the plug and shakes it.*]

ASTON. Sleep well?

DAVIES. Yes. Dead out. Must have been dead out.

[ASTON *goes downstage right, collects the toaster and examines it.*]

5 ASTON. You . . . er. . . .

DAVIES. Eh?

ASTON. Were you dreaming or something?

DAVIES. Dreaming?

ASTON. Yes.

10 DAVIES. I don't dream. I've never dreamed.

ASTON. No, nor have I.

DAVIES. Nor me.

[*Pause.*]

Why you ask me that, then?

15 ASTON. You were making noises.

DAVIES. Who was?

ASTON. You were.

[DAVIES *gets out of bed. He wears long underpants.*]

DAVIES. Now, wait a minute. Wait a minute, what

20 do you mean? What kind of noises?

ASTON. You were making groans. You were jabbering.

DAVIES. Jabbering? Me?

ASTON. Yes.

25 DAVIES. I don't jabber, man. Nobody ever told me that before.

[*Pause.*]

What would I be jabbering about?

ASTON. I don't know.

30 DAVIES. I mean, where's the sense in it?

[*Pause.*]

Nobody ever told me that before.

[*Pause.*]

You got hold of the wrong bloke, mate.

35 ASTON [*crossing to the bed with the toaster*]. No. You woke me up. I thought you might have been dreaming.

DAVIES. I wasn't dreaming. I never had a dream in my life.

40 [*Pause.*]

ASTON. Maybe it was the bed.

DAVIES. Nothing wrong with this bed.

ASTON. Might be a bit unfamiliar.

DAVIES. There's nothing unfamiliar about me with

45 beds. I slept in beds. I don't make noises just because I sleep in a bed. I slept in plenty of beds.

[*Pause.*]

I tell you what, maybe it were them Blacks.

ASTON. What?

DAVIES. Them noises. 50

ASTON. What Blacks?

DAVIES. Them you got. Next door. Maybe it were them Blacks making noises, coming up through the walls.

ASTON. Hmmnn. 55

DAVIES. That's my opinion.

[ASTON *puts down the plug and moves to the door.*] Where you going, you going out?

ASTON. Yes.

DAVIES [*seizing the sandals*]. Wait a minute then, 60 just a minute.

ASTON. What you doing?

DAVIES [*putting on the sandals*]. I better come with you.

ASTON. Why? 65

DAVIES. I mean, I better come out with you, anyway.

ASTON. Why?

DAVIES. Well . . . don't you want me to go out?

ASTON. What for? 70

DAVIES. I mean . . . when you're out. Don't you want me to get out . . . when you're out?

ASTON. You don't have to go out.

DAVIES. You mean . . . I can stay here?

ASTON. Do what you like. You don't have to 75 come out just because I go out.

DAVIES. You don't mind me staying here?

ASTON. I've got a couple of keys. [*He goes to a box by his bed and finds them.*] This door and the front door. [*He hands them to* DAVIES.] 80

DAVIES. Thanks very much, the best of luck.

[*Pause.* ASTON *stands.*]

ASTON. I think I'll take a stroll down the road. A little . . . kind of a shop. Man there'd got a jig saw the other day. I quite liked the look of it. 85

DAVIES. A jig saw, mate?

ASTON. Yes. Could be very useful.

DAVIES. Yes.

[*Slight pause.*]

What's that then, exactly, then? 90

[ASTON *walks up to the window and looks out.*]

ASTON. A jig saw? Well, it comes from the same family as the fret saw. But it's an appliance, you see. You have to fix it on to a portable drill.

DAVIES. Ah, that's right. They're very handy. 95

ASTON. They are, yes.

[*Pause.*]
You know, I was sitting in a café the other day. I happened to be sitting at the same table as this woman. Well, we started to . . . we started to pick
5 up a bit of a conversation. I don't know . . . about her holiday, it was, where she'd been. She'd been down to the south coast. I can't remember where though. Anyway, we were just sitting there, having this bit of a conversation . . . then suddenly she put
10 her hand over to mine . . . and she said, how would you like me to have a look at your body?

DAVIES. Get out of it.

[*Pause.*]

ASTON. Yes. To come out with it just like that,
15 in the middle of this conversation. Struck me as a bit odd.

DAVIES. They've said the same thing to me.

ASTON. Have they?

DAVIES. Women? There's many a time they've
20 come up to me and asked me more or less the same question.

[*Pause.*]

ASTON. What did you say your name was?

DAVIES. Bernard Jenkins is my assumed one.

25 ASTON. No, your other one?

DAVIES. Davies. Mac Davies.

ASTON. Welsh, are you?

DAVIES. Eh?

ASTON. You Welsh?

30 [*Pause.*]

DAVIES. Well, I been around, you know . . . what I mean . . . I been about. . . .

ASTON. Where were you born then?

DAVIES [*darkly*]. What do you mean?

35 ASTON. Where were you born?

DAVIES. I was . . . uh . . . oh, it's a bit hard, like, to set your mind back . . . see what I mean . . . going back . . . a good way . . . lose a bit of track, like . . . you know. . . .

40 ASTON [*going to below the fireplace*]. See this plug? Switch it on here, if you like. This little fire.

DAVIES. Right, mister.

ASTON. Just plug in here.

DAVIES. Right, mister.

45 [ASTON *goes towards the door.*]
[*Anxiously*]. What do I do?

ASTON. Just switch it on, that's all. The fire'll come on.

DAVIES. I tell you what. I won't bother about it.

ASTON. No trouble. 50

DAVIES. No, I don't go in for them things much.

ASTON. Should work. [*Turning.*] Right.

DAVIES. Eh, I was going to ask you, mister, what about this stove? I mean, do you think it's going to be letting out any . . . what do you think? 55

ASTON. It's not connected.

DAVIES. You see, the trouble is, it's right on top of my bed, you see? What I got to watch is nudging . . . one of them gas taps with my elbow when I get up, you get my meaning? 60

[*He goes round to the other side of stove and examines it.*]

ASTON. There's nothing to worry about.

DAVIES. Now look here, don't you worry about it. All I'll do, I'll keep an eye on these taps every 65 now and again, like, you see. See they're switched off. You leave it to me.

ASTON. I don't think. . . .

DAVIES [*coming round*]. Eh, mister, just one thing . . . eh . . . you couldn't slip me a couple of bob, 70 for a cup of tea, just, you know?

ASTON. I gave you a few bob last night.

DAVIES. Eh, so you did. So you did. I forgot. Went clean out of my mind. That's right. Thank you, mister. Listen. You're sure now, you're sure 75 you don't mind me staying here? I mean, I'm not the sort of man who wants to take any liberties.

ASTON. No, that's all right.

DAVIES. I might get down to Wembley later on in the day. 80

ASTON. Uh-uh.

DAVIES. There's a caff down there, you see, might be able to get fixed up there. I was there, see? I know they were a bit short-handed. They might be in the need of a bit of staff. 85

ASTON. When was that?

DAVIES. Eh? Oh, well, that was . . . near on . . . that'll be . . . that'll be a little while ago now. But of course what it is, they can't find the right kind of people in these places. What they want to do, 90 they're trying to do away with these foreigners, you see, in catering. They want an Englishman to pour their tea, that's what they want, that's what they're crying out for. It's only common sense, en't? Oh, I got all that under way . . . that's . . . 95 uh . . . that's . . . what I'll be doing.

[*Pause.*]

If only I could get down there.

ASTON. Mmnn. [ASTON *moves to the door.*] Well, I'll be seeing you then.

5   DAVIES. Yes. Right.

[ASTON *goes out and closes the door.*

DAVIES *stands still. He waits a few seconds, then goes to the door, opens it, looks out, closes it, stands with his back to it, turns swiftly, opens it, looks out, comes*
10 *back, closes the door, finds the keys in his pocket, tries one, tries the other, locks the door. He looks about the room. He then goes quickly to* ASTON's *bed, bends, brings out the pair of shoes and examines them.*]

Not a bad pair of shoes. Bit pointed.

15 [*He puts them back under the bed. He examines the area by* ASTON's *bed, picks up a vase and looks into it, then picks up a box and shakes it.*]

Screws!

[*He sees paint buckets at the top of the bed, goes to*
20 *them, and examines them.*]

Paint. What's he going to paint?

[*He puts the bucket down, comes to the centre of the room, looks up at bucket, and grimaces.*]

I'll have to find out about that. [*He crosses right,*
25 *and picks up a blow-lamp.*] He's got some stuff in here. [*He picks up the Buddha and looks at it.*] Full of stuff. Look at all this. [*His eye falls on the piles of papers.*] What's he got all those papers for? Damn pile of papers.

30 [*He goes to a pile and touches it. The pile wobbles. He steadies it.*]

Hold it, hold it!

[*He holds the pile and pushes the papers back into place. The door opens.*

35 MICK *comes in, puts the key in his pocket, and closes the door silently. He stands at the door and watches* DAVIES.]

What's he got all these papers for? [DAVIES *climbs over the rolled carpet to the blue case.*] Had a sheet
40 and pillow ready in here. [*He opens the case.*] Nothing. [*He shuts the case.*] Still, I had a sleep though. I don't make no noises. [*He looks at the window.*] What's this?

[*He picks up another case and tries to open it.* MICK
45 *moves upstage, silently.*]

Locked. [*He puts it down and moves downstage.*] Must be something in it. [*He picks up a sideboard drawer, rummages in the contents, then puts it down.*]

[MICK *slides across the room.*

DAVIES *half turns,* MICK *seizes his arm and forces it* 50
up his back. DAVIES *screams.*]

Uuuuuuuhhh! Uuuuuuuhhh! What! What! What! Uuuuuuuhhh!

[MICK *swiftly forces him to the floor, with* DAVIES *struggling, grimacing, whimpering and staring.* 55

MICK *holds his arm, puts his other hand to his lips, then puts his hand to* DAVIES' *lips.* DAVIES *quietens.* MICK *lets him go.* DAVIES *writhes.* MICK *holds out a warning finger. He then squats down to regard* DAVIES. *He regards him, then stands looking down on him.* DAVIES 60 *massages his arm, watching* MICK. MICK *turns slowly to look at the room. He goes to* DAVIES' *bed and uncovers it. He turns, goes to the clothes horse and picks up* DAVIES' *trousers.* DAVIES *starts to rise.* MICK *presses him down with his foot and stands over him. Finally,* 65 *he removes his foot. He examines the trousers and throws them back.* DAVIES *remains on the floor, crouched.* MICK *slowly goes to the chair, sits, and watches* DAVIES, *expressionless.*

Silence.] 70

MICK. What's the game?

Curtain.

ACT II

[*A few seconds later*]

[MICK *is seated,* DAVIES *on the floor, half seated, crouched. Silence.*]

MICK. Well? 75

DAVIES. Nothing, nothing. Nothing.

[*A drip sounds in the bucket overhead. They look up.* MICK *looks back to* DAVIES.]

MICK. What's your name?

DAVIES. I don't know you. I don't know who 80 you are.

[*Pause.*]

MICK. Eh?

DAVIES. Jenkins.

MICK. Jenkins? 85

DAVIES. Yes.

MICK. Jen . . . kins.

[*Pause.*]

You sleep here last night?

DAVIES. Yes. 90

MICK. Sleep well?

DAVIES. Yes.

MICK. I'm awfully glad. It's awfully nice to meet you.

[*Pause.*]

What did you say your name was?

5 DAVIES. Jenkins.

MICK. I beg your pardon?

DAVIES. Jenkins!

[*Pause.*]

MICK. Jen . . . kins.

10 [*A drip sounds in the bucket.* DAVIES *looks up.*]
You remind me of my uncle's brother. He was always on the move, that man. Never without his passport. Had an eye for the girls. Very much your build. Bit of an athlete. Long-jump specialist. He

15 had a habit of demonstrating different run-ups in the drawing-room round about Christmas time. Had a penchant for nuts. That's what it was. Nothing else but a penchant. Couldn't eat enough of them. Peanuts, walnuts, Brazil nuts, monkey

20 nuts, wouldn't touch a piece of fruit cake. Had a marvellous stopwatch. Picked it up in Hong Kong. The day after they chucked him out of the Salvation Army. Used to go in number four for Beckenham Reserves.° That was before he got his Gold

25 Medal. Had a funny habit of carrying his fiddle on his back. Like a papoose, I think there was a bit of the Red Indian in him. To be honest, I've never made out how he came to be my uncle's brother. I've often thought that maybe it was the

30 other way round. I mean that my uncle was his brother and he was my uncle. But I never called him uncle. As a matter of fact I called him Sid. My mother called him Sid too. It was a funny business. Your spitting image he was. Married a

35 Chinaman and went to Jamaica.

[*Pause.*]

I hope you slept well last night.

DAVIES. Listen! I don't know who you are!

MICK. What bed you sleep in?

40 DAVIES. Now look here—

MICK. Eh?

DAVIES. That one.

MICK. Not the other one?

DAVIES. No.

45 MICK. Choosy.

[*Pause.*]

How do you like my room?

DAVIES. Your room?

MICK. Yes.

DAVIES. This ain't your room. I don't know who 50
you are. I ain't never seen you before.

MICK. You know, believe it or not, you've got a funny kind of resemblance to a bloke I once knew in Shoreditch. Actually he lived in Aldgate. I was staying with a cousin in Camden Town. This chap, 55
he used to have a pitch° in Finsbury Park, just by the bus depot. When I got to know him I found out he was brougnt up in Putney. That didn't make any difference to me. I know quite a few people who were born in Putney. Even if they weren't 60
born in Putney they were born in Fulham. The only trouble was, he wasn't born in Putney, he was only brought up in Putney. It turned out he was born in the Caledonian Road, just before you get to the Nag's Head. His old mum was still liv- 65
ing at the Angel. All the buses passed right by the door. She could get a 38, 581, 30 or 38A, take her down the Essex Road to Dalston Junction in next to no time. Well, of course, if she got the 30 he'd take her up Upper Street way, round by Highbury 70
Corner and down to St. Paul's Church, but she'd get to Dalston Junction just the same in the end. I used to leave my bike in her garden on my way to work. Yes, it was a curious affair. Dead spit of you he was. Bit bigger round the nose but there 75
was nothing in it.

[*Pause.*]

Did you sleep here last night?

DAVIES. Yes.

MICK. Sleep well? 80

DAVIES. Yes!

MICK. Did you have to get up in the night?

DAVIES. No!

[*Pause.*]

MICK. What's your name? 85

DAVIES [*shifting, about to rise.*] Now look here!

MICK. What?

DAVIES. Jenkins!

MICK. Jen . . . kins.

[DAVIES *makes a sudden move to rise. A violent bel-* 90
low from MICK *sends him back.*]

---

number four for Beckenham Reserves the fourth batsman on Beckenham's second team

pitch set location of a sidewalk vendor

[*A shout.*] Sleep here last night?

DAVIES. Yes. . . .

MICK [*continuing at great pace*]. How'd you sleep?

DAVIES. I slept—

5 MICK. Sleep well?

DAVIES. Now look—

MICK. What bed?

DAVIES. That—

MICK. Not the other?

10 DAVIES. No!

MICK. Choosy.

[*Pause.*]

[*Quietly.*] Choosy.

[*Pause.*]

15 [*Again amiable.*] What sort of sleep did you have in that bed?

DAVIES [*banging on floor*]. All right!

MICK. You weren't uncomfortable?

DAVIES [*groaning*]. All right!

20 [MICK *stands, and moves to him.*]

MICK. You a foreigner?

DAVIES. No.

MICK. Born and bred in the British Isles?

DAVIES. I was!

25 MICK. What did they teach you?

[*Pause.*]

How did you like my bed?

[*Pause.*]

That's my bed. You want to mind you don't catch

30 a draught.

DAVIES. From the bed?

MICK. No, now, up your arse.

[DAVIES *stares warily at* MICK, *who turns.* DAVIES *scrambles to the clothes horse and seizes his trousers.*

35 MICK *turns swiftly and grabs them.* DAVIES *lunges for them.* MICK *holds out a hand warningly.*]

You intending to settle down here?

DAVIES. Give me my trousers then.

MICK. You settling down for a long stay?

40 DAVIES. Give me my bloody trousers!

MICK. Why, where you going?

DAVIES. Give me and I'm going, I'm going to Sidcup!

MICK *flicks the trousers in* DAVIES' *face several times.*

45 DAVIES *retreats.*]

[*Pause.*]

MICK. You know, you remind me of a bloke I bumped into once, just the other side of the Guildford by-pass—

DAVIES. I was brought here! 50

[*Pause.*]

MICK. Pardon?

DAVIES. I was brought here! I was brought here!

MICK. Brought here? Who brought you here?

DAVIES. Man who lives here . . . he. . . . 55

[*Pause.*]

MICK. Fibber.

DAVIES. I was brought here, last night . . . met him in a caff . . . I was working . . . I got the bullet . . . I was working there . . . bloke saved me from 60 a punch up, brought me here, brought me right here.

[*Pause.*]

MICK. I'm afraid you're a born fibber, en't you? You're speaking to the owner. This is my room. 65 You're standing in my house.

DAVIES. It's his . . . he seen me all right . . . he. . . .

MICK [*pointing to* DAVIES' *bed*]. That's my bed.

DAVIES. What about that, then?

MICK. That's my mother's bed. 70

DAVIES. Well she wasn't in it last night!

MICK [*moving to him*]. Now don't get perky, son, don't get perky. Keep your hands off my old mum.

DAVIES. I ain't . . . I haven't. . . .

MICK. Don't get out of your depth, friend, don't 75 start taking liberties with my old mother, let's have a bit of respect.

DAVIES. I got respect, you won't find anyone with more respect.

MICK. Well, stop telling me all these fibs. 80

DAVIES. Now listen to me. I never seen you before, have I?

MICK. Never seen my mother before either, I suppose?

[*Pause.*] 85

I think I'm coming to the conclusion that you're an old rogue. You're nothing but an old scoundrel.

DAVIES. Now wait—

MICK. Listen, son. Listen, sonny. You stink. 90

DAVIES. You ain't got no right to—

MICK. You're stinking the place out. You're an old robber, there's no getting away from it. You're an old skate. You don't belong in a nice place like this. You're an old barbarian. Honest. You got no 95 business wandering about in an unfurnished flat. I could charge seven quid a week for this if I wanted to. Get a taker tomorrow. Three hundred and fifty

a year exclusive. No argument. I mean, if that sort
of money's in your range don't be afraid to say
so. Here you are. Furniture and fittings, I'll take
four hundred or the nearest offer. Rateable° value
5 ninety quid° for the annum. You can reckon water,
heating and lighting at close on fifty. That'll cost
you eight hundred and ninety if you're all that
keen. Say the word and I'll have my solicitors draft
you out a contract. Otherwise, I've got the van
10 outside, I can run you to the police station in five
minutes, have you in for trespassing, loitering with
intent, daylight robbery, filching, thieving and
stinking the place out. What do you say? Unless
you're really keen on a straightforward purchase.
15 Of course, I'll get my brother to decorate it up for
you first. I've got a brother who's a number one
decorator. He'll decorate it up for you. If you want
more space, there's four more rooms along the
landing ready to go. Bathroom, livingroom, bed-
20 room and nursery. You can have this as your study.
This brother I mentioned, he's just about to start
on the other rooms. Yes, just about to start. So
what do you say? Eight hundred odd for this room
or three thousand down for the whole upper sto-
25 rey. On the other hand, if you prefer to approach
it in the long-term way I know an insurance firm
in West Ham'll be pleased to handle the deal for
you. No strings attached, open and above board,
untarnished record; twenty per cent interest, fifty
30 per cent deposit; down payments, back payments,
family allowances, bonus schemes, remission of
term for good behaviour, six months lease, yearly
examination of the relevant archives, tea laid on,°
disposal of shares, benefit extension, compensa-
35 tion on cessation, comprehensive indemnity against
Riot, Civil Commotion, Labour Disturbances,
Storm, Tempest, Thunderbolt, Larceny or Cattle
all subject to a daily check and double check. Of
course we'd need a signed declaration from your
40 personal medical attendant as assurance that you
possess the requisite fitness to carry the can,° won't
we? Who do you bank with?
[*Pause.*]
Who do you bank with?

Rateable assessed
quid pound(s)
laid on provided
carry the can handle the obligation

[*The door opens.* Aston *comes in.* Mick *turns and* 45
drops the trousers. Davies *picks them up and puts them*
on. Aston, *after a glance at the other two, goes to his*
bed, places a bag which he is carrying on it, sits down
and resumes fixing the toaster. Davies *retreats to his*
corner. Mick *sits in the chair.* 50
[*Silence.*
A drip sounds in the bucket. They all look up.
Silence.]
You still got that leak.
Aston. Yes. 55
[*Pause.*]
It's coming from the roof.
Mick. From the roof, eh?
Aston. Yes.
[*Pause.*] 60
I'll have to tar it over.
Mick. You're going to tar it over?
Aston. Yes.
Mick. What?
Aston. The cracks. 65
[*Pause.*]
Mick. You'll be tarring over the cracks on the
roof.
Aston. Yes.
[*Pause.*] 70
Mick. Think that'll do it?
Aston. It'll do it, for the time being.
Mick. Uh.
[*Pause.*]
Davies [*abruptly*]. What do you do—? 75
[*They both look at him.*]
What do you do . . . when that bucket's full?
[*Pause.*]
Aston. Empty it.
[*Pause.*] 80
Mick. I was telling my friend you were about to
start decorating the other rooms.
Aston. Yes.
[*Pause.*]
[*To* Davies.] I got your bag. 85
Davies. Oh. [*Crossing to him and taking it*]. Oh
thanks, mister, thanks. Give it to you, did they?
[Davies *crosses back with the bag.*
Mick *rises and snatches it.*]
Mick. What's this? 90
Davies. Give us it, that's my bag!
Mick [*warding him off*]. I've seen this bag before.
Davies. That's my bag!

MICK [*eluding him*]. This bag's very familiar.
DAVIES. What do you mean?
MICK. Where'd you get it?
ASTON [*rising, to them*]. Scrub it.°
5 DAVIES. That's mine.
MICK. Whose?
DAVIES. It's mine! Tell him it's mine!
MICK. This your bag?
DAVIES. Give me it!
10 ASTON. Give it to him.
MICK. What? Give him what?
DAVIES. That bloody bag!
MICK [*slipping it behind the gas stove*]. What bag?
[*To* DAVIES.] What bag?
15 DAVIES [*moving*]. Look here!
MICK [*facing him*]. Where you going?
DAVIES. I'm going to get . . . my old . . .
MICK. Watch your step, sonny! You're knocking
at the door when no one's at home. Don't push it
20 too hard. You come busting into a private house,
laying your hands on anything you can lay your
hands on. Don't overstep the mark, son.
[ASTON *picks up the bag.*]
DAVIES. You thieving bastard . . . you thieving
25 skate . . . let me get my—
ASTON. Here you are. [ASTON *offers the bag to*
DAVIES.]
[MICK *grabs it.* ASTON *takes it.*
MICK *grabs it.* DAVIES *reaches for it.*
30 ASTON *takes it.* MICK *reaches for it.*
ASTON *gives it to* DAVIES. MICK *grabs it.*]
[*Pause.*]
[ASTON *takes it.* DAVIES *takes it.* MICK *takes it.* DAVIES
reaches for it. ASTON *takes it.*]
35 [*Pause.*]
[ASTON *gives it to* MICK. MICK *gives it to* DAVIES.
DAVIES *grasps it to him.*]
[*Pause.*]
[MICK *looks at* ASTON. DAVIES *moves away with the*
40 *bag. He drops it.*]
[*Pause.*]
[*They watch him. He picks it up. Goes to his bed,*
and sits. ASTON *goes to his bed, sits, and begins to*
roll a cigarette. MICK *stands still.*]
45 [*Pause.*]
[*A drip sounds in the bucket. They all look up.*]

Scrub it stop it, cut it out

[*Pause.*]
How did you get on at Wembley?
DAVIES. Well, I didn't get down there.
[*Pause.*] 50
No. I couldn't make it.
[MICK *goes to the door and exits.*]
ASTON. I had a bit of bad luck with that jig saw.
When I got there it had gone.
[*Pause.*] 55
DAVIES. Who was that feller?
ASTON. He's my brother.
DAVIES. Is he? He's a bit of a joker, en'he?
ASTON. Uh.
DAVIES. Yes . . . he's a real joker. 60
ASTON. He's got a sense of humour.
DAVIES. Yes, I noticed.
[*Pause.*]
He's a real joker, that lad, you can see that.
[*Pause.*] 65
ASTON. Yes, he tends . . . he tends to see the
funny side of things.
DAVIES. Well, he's got a sense of humour, en'he?
ASTON. Yes.
DAVIES. Yes, you could tell that. 70
[*Pause.*]
I could tell the first time I saw him he had his own
way of looking at things.
[ASTON *stands, goes to the sideboard drawer, right,*
picks up the statue of Buddha, and puts it on the gas 75
stove.]
ASTON. I'm supposed to be doing up the upper
part of the house for him.
DAVIES. What . . . you mean . . . you mean it's
his house? 80
ASTON. Yes. I'm supposed to be decorating this
landing for him. Make a flat out of it.
DAVIES. What does he do, then?
ASTON. He's in the building trade. He's got his
own van. 85
DAVIES. He don't live here, do he?
ASTON. Once I get that shed up outside . . . I'll
be able to give a bit more thought to the flat, you
see. Perhaps I can knock up one or two things for
it. [*He walks to the window.*] I can work with my 90
hands, you see. That's one thing I can do. I never
knew I could. But I can do all sorts of things now,
with my hands. You know, manual things. When
I get that shed up out there . . . I'll have a work-

shop, you see. I . . . could do a bit of woodwork. Simple woodwork, to start. Working with . . . good wood.

[*Pause.*]

5 Of course, there's a lot to be done to this place. What I think, though, I think I'll put in a partition . . . in one of the rooms along the landing. I think it'll take it. You know . . . they've got these screens . . . you know . . . Oriental. They break up a room
10 with them. Make it into two parts. I could either do that or I could have a partition. I could knock them up, you see, if I had a workshop.

[*Pause.*]

Anyway, I think I've decided on the partition.
15 [*Pause.*]

DAVIES. Eh, look here, I been thinking. This ain't my bag.

ASTON. Oh. No.

DAVIES. No, this ain't my bag. My bag, it was
20 another kind of bag altogether, you see. I know what they've done. What they done, they kept my bag, and they given you another one altogether.

ASTON. No . . . what happened was, someone had gone off with your bag.

25 DAVIES [*rising*]. That's what I said!

ASTON. Anyway, I picked that bag up somewhere else. It's got a few . . . pieces of clothes in it too. He let me have the whole lot cheap.

DAVIES [*opening the bag*]. Any shoes?

30 [DAVIES *takes two check shirts, bright red and bright green, from the bag. He holds them up.*]
Check.

ASTON. Yes.

DAVIES. Yes . . . well, I know about these sort of
35 shirts, you see. Shirts like these, they don't go far in the wintertime, I mean, that's one thing I know for a fact. No, what I need, is a kind of a shirt with stripes, a good solid shirt, with stripes going down. That's what I want. [*He takes from the bag a*
40 *deep-red velvet smoking-jacket.*] What's this?

ASTON. It's a smoking-jacket.

DAVIES. A smoking-jacket? [*He feels it.*] This ain't a bad piece of cloth. I'll see how it fits.

[*He tries it on.*]

45 You ain't got a mirror here, have you?

ASTON. I don't think I have.

DAVIES. Well, it don't fit too bad. How do you think it looks?

ASTON. Looks all right.

DAVIES. Well, I won't say no to this, then. 50

[ASTON *picks up the plug and examines it.*]
No, I wouldn't say no to this.

[*Pause.*]

ASTON. You could be . . . caretaker here, if you liked. 55

DAVIES. What?

ASTON. You could . . . look after the place, if you liked . . . you know, the stairs and the landing, the front steps, keep an eye on it. Polish the bells. 60

DAVIES. Bells?

ASTON. I'll be fixing a few, down by the front door. Brass.

DAVIES. Caretaking, eh?

ASTON. Yes. 65

DAVIES. Well, I . . . I never done caretaking before, you know . . . I mean to say . . . I never . . . what I mean to say is . . . I never been a caretaker before.

[*Pause.*] 70

ASTON. How do you feel about being one, then?

DAVIES. Well, I reckon . . . Well, I'd have to know . . . you know. . . .

ASTON. What sort of. . . .

DAVIES. Yes, what sort of . . . you know. . . . 75

[*Pause.*]

ASTON. Well, I mean. . . .

DAVIES. I mean, I'd have to . . . I'd have to. . . .

ASTON. Well, I could tell you. . . .

DAVIES. That's . . . that's it . . . you see . . . you 80 get my meaning?

ASTON. When the time comes. . . .

DAVIES. I mean, that's what I'm getting at, you see. . . .

ASTON. More or less exactly what you. . . . 85

DAVIES. You see, what I mean to say . . . what I'm getting at is . . . I mean, what sort of jobs. . . .

[*Pause.*]

ASTON. Well, there's things like the stairs . . . and the . . . the bells. . . . 90

DAVIES. But it'd be a matter . . . wouldn't it . . . it'd be a matter of a broom . . . isn't it?

ASTON. Yes, and of course, you'd need a few brushes.

DAVIES. You'd need implements . . . you see . . . 95 you'd need a good few implements. . . .

[ASTON *takes a white overall from a nail over his bed, and shows it to* DAVIES.]

ASTON. You could wear this, if you liked.

DAVIES. Well . . . that's nice, en't?

5 ASTON. It'd keep the dust off.

DAVIES [*putting it on.*] Yes, this'd keep the dust off, all right. Well off. Thanks very much, mister.

ASTON. You see, what we could do, we could . . . I could fit a bell at the bottom, outside the

10 front door, with "Caretaker" on it. And you could answer any queries.

DAVIES. Oh, I don't know about that.

ASTON. Why not?

DAVIES. Well, I mean, you don't know who might

15 come up them front steps, do you? I got to be a bit careful.

ASTON. Why, someone after you?

DAVIES. After me? Well, I could have that Scotch git coming looking after me, couldn't I? All I'd do,

20 I'd hear the bell, I'd go down there, open the door, who might be there, any Harry might be there. I could be buggered as easy as that, man. They might be there after my card, I mean look at it, here I am, I only got four stamps, on this card, here it

25 is, look, four stamps, that's all I got, I ain't got any more, that's all I got, they ring the bell called Caretaker, they'd have me in, that's what they'd do, I wouldn't stand a chance. Of course I got plenty of other cards lying about, but they don't

30 know that, and I can't tell them, can I, because then they'd find out I was going about under an assumed name. You see, the name I call myself now, that's not my real name. My real name's not the one I'm using, you see. It's different. You see,

35 the name I go under now ain't my real one. It's assumed.

[*Silence.*]

[THE LIGHTS FADE TO BLACKOUT.

THEN UP TO DIM LIGHT THROUGH THE WINDOW.

40 *A door bangs.*

Sound of a key in the door of the room.]

[DAVIES *enters, closes the door, and tries the light switch, on, off, on, off.*]

DAVIES [*muttering*]. What's this? [*He switches on

45 and off.*] What's the matter with this damn light? [*He switches on and off.*] Aaah. Don't tell me the damn light's gone now.

[*Pause.*]

What'll I do? Damn light's gone now. Can't see a thing.   50

[*Pause.*]

What'll I do now? [*He moves, stumbles.*] Ah God, what's that? Give me a light. Wait a minute.

[*He feels for matches in his pocket, takes out a box and lights one. The match goes out. The box falls.*]   55

Aah! Where is it? [*Stooping.*] Where's the bloody box?

[*The box is kicked.*]

What's that? What? Who's that? What's that?

[*Pause. He moves.*]   60

Where's my box? It was down here. Who's this? Who's moving it?

[*Silence.*]

Come on. Who's this? Who's this got my box?

[*Pause.*]   65

Who's in here!

[*Pause.*]

I got a knife here. I'm ready. Come on then, who are you?

[*He moves, stumbles, falls and cries out.*   70

Silence.

A faint whimper from DAVIES. *He gets up.*]

All right!

[*He stands. Heavy breathing.*

Suddenly the electrolux starts to hum. A figure moves   75

with it, guiding it. The nozzle moves along the floor after DAVIES, *who skips, dives away from it and falls, breathlessly.*]

Ah, ah, ah, ah, ah, ah! Get away-y-y-y-y!

[*The electrolux stops. The figure jumps on* ASTON's   80

bed.]

I'm ready for you! I'm . . . I'm . . . I'm here!

[*The figure takes out the electrolux plug from the light socket and fits the bulb. The light goes on.* DAVIES *flattens himself against right wall, knife in hand.* MICK   85

stands on the bed, holding the plug.]

MICK. I was just doing some spring cleaning. [*He gets down.*] There used to be a wall plug for this electrolux. But it doesn't work. I had to fit it in the light socket. [*He puts the electrolux under   90

ASTON's *bed.*] How do you think the place is looking? I gave it a good going over.

[*Pause.*]

We take it in turns, once a fortnight, my brother and me, to give the place a thorough going over.   95

I was working late tonight, I only just got here.

But I thought I better get on with it, as it's my turn.

[*Pause.*]

It's not that I actually live here. I don't. As a matter
5 of fact I live somewhere else. But after all, I'm
responsible for the upkeep of the premises, en' I?
Can't help being house-proud.

[*He moves towards* DAVIES *and indicates the knife.*]
What are you waving that about for?

10 DAVIES. You come near me. . . .

MICK. I'm sorry if I gave you a start. But I had you
in mind too, you know. I mean, my brother's guest.
We got to think of your comfort, en't we? Don't
want the dust to get up your nose. How long you
15 thinking of staying here, by the way? As a matter
of fact, I was going to suggest that we'd lower your
rent, make it just a nominal sum, I mean until you
get fixed up. Just nominal, that's all.

[*Pause.*]

20 Still, if you're going to be spiky,° I'll have to reconsider the whole proposition.

[*Pause.*]

Eh, you're not thinking of doing any violence on
me, are you? You're not the violent sort, are you?

25 DAVIES [*vehemently*]. I keep myself to myself,
mate. But if anyone starts with me though, they
know what they got coming.

MICK. I can believe that.

DAVIES. You do. I been all over, see? You un-
30 derstand my meaning? I don't mind a bit of a joke
now and then, but anyone'll tell you . . . that no
one starts anything with me.

MICK. I get what you mean, yes.

DAVIES. I can be pushed so far . . . but. . . .

35 MICK. No further.

DAVIES. That's it.

[MICK *sits on junk down right.*]
What you doing?

MICK. No, I just want to say that . . . I'm very
40 impressed by that.

DAVIES. Eh?

MICK. I'm very impressed by what you've just
said.

[*Pause.*]

45 Yes, that's impressive, that is.

[*Pause.*]

I'm impressed, anyway.

DAVIES. You know what I'm talking about then?

MICK. Yes, I know. I think we understand one
another. 50

DAVIES. Uh? Well . . . I'll tell you . . . I'd . . . I'd
like to think that. You been playing me about, you
know. I don't know why. I never done you no
harm.

MICK. No, you know what it was? We just got 55
off on the wrong foot. That's all it was.

DAVIES. Ay, we did.

[DAVIES *joins* MICK *in junk.*]

MICK. Like a sandwich?

DAVIES. What? 60

MICK [*taking a sandwich from his pocket*]. Have one
of these.

DAVIES. Don't you pull anything.

MICK. No, you're still not understanding me. I
can't help being interested in any friend of my 65
brother's. I mean, you're my brother's friend, aren't
you?

DAVIES. Well, I . . . I wouldn't put it as far as
that.

MICK. Don't you find him friendly, then? 70

DAVIES. Well, I wouldn't say we was all that
friends. I mean he done me no harm, but I wouldn't
say he was any particular friend of mine. What's
in that sandwich, then?

MICK. Cheese. 75

DAVIES. That'll do me.

MICK. Take one.

DAVIES. Thank you, mister.

MICK. I'm sorry to hear my brother's not very
friendly. 80

DAVIES. He's friendly, he's friendly, I didn't say
he wasn't. . . .

MICK [*taking a salt-cellar from his pocket*]. Salt?

DAVIES. No thanks. [*He munches the sandwich.*] I
just can't exactly . . . make him out. 85

MICK [*feeling in his pocket*]. I forgot the pepper.

DAVIES. Just can't get the hang of him, that's all.

MICK. I had a bit of beetroot° somewhere. Must
have mislaid it.

[*Pause.*] 90

[DAVIES *chews the sandwich.* MICK *watches him eat.
He then rises and strolls downstage.*]

---

spiky   touchy, hard to get along with

beetroot   beet

Uuh . . . listen . . . can I ask your advice? I mean, you're a man of the world. Can I ask your advice about something?

DAVIES. You go right ahead.

5 MICK. Well, what it is, you see, I'm . . . I'm a bit worried about my brother.

DAVIES. Your brother?

MICK. Yes . . . you see, his trouble is. . . .

DAVIES. What?

10 MICK. Well, it's not a very nice thing to say. . . .

DAVIES [rising, coming downstage]. Go on now, you say it.

[MICK looks at him.]

MICK. He doesn't like work.

15 [Pause.]

DAVIES. Go on!

MICK. No, he just doesn't like work, that's his trouble.

DAVIES. Is that a fact?

20 MICK. It's a terrible thing to have to say about your own brother.

DAVIES. Ay.

MICK. He's just shy of it. Very shy of it.

DAVIES. I know that sort.

25 MICK. You know the type?

DAVIES. I've met them.

MICK. I mean, I want to get him going in the world.

DAVIES. Stands to reason, man.

30 MICK. If you got an older brother you want to push him on, you want to see him make his way. Can't have him idle, he's only doing himself harm. That's what I say.

DAVIES. Yes.

35 MICK. But he won't buckle down to the job.

DAVIES. He don't like work.

MICK. Work shy.

DAVIES. Sounds like it to me.

MICK. You've met the type, have you?

40 DAVIES. Me? I know that sort.

MICK. Yes.

DAVIES. I know that sort, I've met them.

MICK. Causing me great anxiety. You see, I'm a working man: I'm a tradesman. I've got my own

45 van.

DAVIES. Is that a fact?

MICK. He's supposed to be doing a little job for me . . . I keep him here to do a little job . . . but I don't know . . . I'm coming to the conclusion he's a slow worker. 50

[Pause.]

What would your advice be?

DAVIES. Well . . . he's a funny bloke, your brother.

MICK. What?

DAVIES. I was saying, he's . . . he's a bit of a 55 funny bloke, your brother.

[MICK stares at him.]

MICK. Funny? Why?

DAVIES. Well . . . he's funny. . . .

MICK. What's funny about him? 60

[Pause.]

DAVIES. Not liking work.

MICK. What's funny about that?

DAVIES. Nothing.

[Pause.] 65

MICK. I don't call it funny.

DAVIES. Nor me.

MICK. You don't want to start getting hypercritical.

DAVIES. No, no, I wasn't that, I wasn't . . . I was 70 only saying. . . .

MICK. Don't get too glib.

DAVIES. Look, all I meant was—

MICK. Cut it! [Briskly.] Look! I got a proposition to make to you. I'm thinking of taking over the 75 running of this place, you see? I think it could be run a bit more efficiently. I got a lot of ideas, a lot of plans. [He eyes DAVIES.] How would you like to stay on here, as caretaker?

DAVIES. What? 80

MICK. I'll be quite open with you. I could rely on a man like you around the place, keeping an eye on things.

DAVIES. Well now . . . wait a minute . . . I . . . I ain't never done no caretaking before, you 85 know. . . .

MICK. Doesn't matter about that. It's just that you look a capable sort of man to me.

DAVIES. I am a capable sort of man. I mean to say, I've had plenty offers in my time, you know, 90 there's no getting away from that.

MICK. Well, I could see before, when you took out that knife, that you wouldn't let anyone mess you about.

DAVIES. No one messes me about, man.

MICK. I mean, you've been in the services, haven't you?

DAVIES. The what?

5 MICK. You been in the services. You can tell by your stance.

DAVIES. Oh . . . yes. Spent half my life there, man. Overseas . . . like . . . serving . . . I was.

MICK. In the colonies, weren't you?

10 DAVIES. I was over there. I was one of the first over there.

MICK. That's it. You're just the man I been looking for.

DAVIES. What for?

15 MICK. Caretaker.

DAVIES. Yes, well . . . look . . . listen . . . who's the landlord here, him or you?

MICK. Me. I am. I got deeds to prove it.

DAVIES. Ah . . . [*Decisively.*] Well listen, I don't

20 mind doing a bit of caretaking, I wouldn't mind looking after the place for you.

MICK. Of course, we'd come to a small financial agreement, mutually beneficial.

DAVIES. I leave you to reckon that out, like.

25 MICK. Thanks. There's only one thing.

DAVIES. What's that?

MICK. Can you give me any references?

DAVIES. Eh?

MICK. Just to satisfy my solicitor.

30 DAVIES. I got plenty of references. All I got to do is to go down to Sidcup tomorrow. I got all the references I want down there.

MICK. Where's that?

DAVIES. Sidcup. He ain't only got my references

35 down there, he got all my papers down there. I know that place like the back of my hand. I'm going down there anyway, see what I mean, I got to get down there, or I'm done.

MICK. So we can always get hold of these ref-

40 erences if we want them.

DAVIES. I'll be down there any day, I tell you. I was going down today, but I'm . . . I'm waiting for the weather to break.

MICK. Ah.

45 DAVIES. Listen. You can't pick me up a pair of good shoes, can you? I got a bad need for a good pair of shoes. I can't get anywhere without a pair of good shoes, see? Do you think there's any chance of you being able to pick me up a pair?

[THE LIGHTS FADE TO BLACKOUT. 50
LIGHTS UP. *Morning.*]

[ASTON *is pulling on his trousers over long underwear. A slight grimace. He looks around at the head of his bed, takes a towel from the rail and waves it about. He pulls it down, goes to* DAVIES *and wakes him.* DA- 55
VIES *sits up abruptly.*]

ASTON. You said you wanted me to get you up.

DAVIES. What for?

ASTON. You said you were thinking of going to Sidcup. 60

DAVIES. Ay, that'd be a good thing, if I got there.

ASTON. Doesn't look much of a day.

DAVIES. Ay, well, that's shot it, en't it?

ASTON. I . . . I didn't have a very good night again. 65

DAVIES. I slept terrible.

[*Pause.*]

ASTON. You were making. . . .

DAVIES. Terrible. Had a bit of rain in the night, didn't it? 70

ASTON. Just a bit.

[*He goes to his bed, picks up a small plank and begins to sandpaper it.*]

DAVIES. Thought so. Come in on my head.

[*Pause.*] 75

Draught's blowing right in on my head, anyway.

[*Pause.*]

Can't you close that window behind that sack?

ASTON. You could.

DAVIES. Well then, what about it, then? The rain's 80
coming right in on my head.

ASTON. Got to have a bit of air.

[DAVIES *gets out of bed. He is wearing his trousers, waistcoat and vest.*]

DAVIES [*putting on his sandals.*] Listen. I've lived 85
all my life in the air, boy. You don't have to tell me about air. What I'm saying is, there's too much air coming in that window when I'm asleep.

ASTON. Gets very stuffy in here without that window open. 90

[ASTON *crosses to the chair, puts the plank on it, and continues sandpapering.*]

DAVIES. Yes, but listen, you don't know what I'm telling you. That bloody rain, man, come right

in on my head. Spoils my sleep. I could catch my death of cold with it, with that draught. That's all I'm saying. Just shut that window and no one's going to catch any colds, that's all I'm saying.

5 [*Pause.*]

ASTON. I couldn't sleep in here without that window open.

DAVIES. Yes, but what about me? What . . . what you got to say about my position?

10 ASTON. Why don't you sleep the other way round?

DAVIES. What do you mean?

ASTON. Sleep with your feet to the window.

DAVIES. What good would that do?

15 ASTON. The rain wouldn't come in on your head.

DAVIES. No, I couldn't do that. I couldn't do that.

[*Pause.*]

I mean, I got used to sleeping this way. It isn't me has to change, it's that window. You see, it's rain-

20 ing now. Look at it. It's coming down now.

[*Pause.*]

ASTON. I think I'll have a walk down to Gold-hawk Road. I got talking to a man there. He had a saw bench. It looked in pretty good condition to

25 me. Don't think it's much good to him.

[*Pause.*]

Have a walk down there, I think.

DAVIES. Listen to that. That's done my trip to Sidcup. Eh, what about closing that window now?

30 It'll be coming in here.

ASTON. Close it for the time being.

[DAVIES *closes the window and looks out.*]

DAVIES. What's all that under that tarpaulin out there?

35 ASTON. Wood.

DAVIES. What for?

ASTON. To build my shed.

[DAVIES *sits on his bed.*]

DAVIES. You haven't come across that pair of

40 shoes you was going to look out for me, have you?

ASTON. Oh. No. I'll see if I can pick some up today.

DAVIES. I can't go out in this with these, can I? I can't even go out and get a cup of tea.

45 ASTON. There's a café just along the road.

DAVIES. There may be, mate.

[*During* ASTON's *speech the room grows darker. By the close of the speech only* ASTON *can be seen*

clearly. DAVIES *and all the other objects are in the shadow. The fadedown of the light must be as gradual, as pro-* 50 *tracted and as unobtrusive as possible.*]

ASTON. I used to go there quite a bit. Oh, years ago now. But I stopped. I used to like that place. Spent quite a bit of time in there. That was before I went away. Just before. I think that . . . place 55 had a lot to do with it. They were all . . . a good bit older than me. But they always used to listen. I thought . . . they understood what I said. I mean I used to talk to them. I talked too much. That was my mistake. The same in the factory. Standing 60 there, or in the breaks, I used to . . . talk about things. And these men, they used to listen, when-ever I . . . had anything to say. It was all right. The trouble was, I used to have kind of hallucina-tions. They weren't hallucinations, they . . . I used 65 to get the feeling I could see things . . . very clearly . . . everything . . . was so clear . . . everything used . . . everything used to get very quiet . . . everything got very quiet . . . all this . . . quiet . . . and . . . this clear sight . . . it was . . . but maybe 70 I was wrong. Anyway, someone must have said something. I didn't know anything about it. And . . . some kind of lie must have got around. And this lie went round. I thought people started being funny. In that café. The factory. I couldn't under- 75 stand it. Then one day they took me to a hospital, right outside London. They . . . got me there. I didn't want to go. Anyway . . . I tried to get out, quite a few times. But . . . it wasn't very easy. They asked me questions, in there. Got me in and 80 asked me all sorts of questions. Well, I told them . . . when they wanted to know . . . what my thoughts were. Hmmnn. Then one day . . . this man . . . doctor, I suppose . . . the head one . . . he was quite a man of . . . distinction . . . although 85 I wasn't so sure about that. He called me in. He said . . . he told me I had something. He said they'd concluded their examination. That's what he said. And he showed me a pile of papers and he said that I'd got something, some complaint. He said 90 . . . he just said that, you see. You've got . . . this thing. That's your complaint. And we've decided, he said, that in your interests there's only one course we can take. He said . . . but I can't . . . exactly remember . . . how he put it . . . he said, 95 we're going to do something to your brain. He

said . . . if we don't, you'll be in here for the rest of your life, but if we do, you stand a chance. You can go out, he said, and live like the others. What do you want to do to my brain, I said to him. But
5 he just repeated what he'd said. Well, I wasn't a fool. I knew I was a minor. I knew he couldn't do anything to me without getting permission. I knew he had to get permission from my mother. So I wrote to her and told her what they were trying
10 to do. But she signed their form, you see, giving them permission. I know that because he showed me her signature when I brought it up. Well, that night I tried to escape, that night. I spent five hours sawing at one of the bars on the window in this
15 ward. Right throughout the dark. They used to shine a torch over the beds every half hour. So I timed it just right. And then it was nearly done, and a man had a . . . he had a fit, right next to me. And they caught me, anyway. About a week
20 later they started to come round and do this thing to the brain. We were all supposed to have it done, in this ward. And they came round and did it one at a time. One a night. I was one of the last. And I could see quite clearly what they did to the others.
25 They used to come round with these . . . I don't know what they were . . . they looked like big pincers, with wires on, the wires were attached to a little machine. It was electric. They used to hold the man down, and this chief . . . the chief doctor,
30 used to fit the pincers, something like earphones, he used to fit them on either side of the man's skull. There was a man holding the machine, you see, and he'd . . . turn it on, and the chief would just press these pincers on either side of the skull
35 and keep them there. Then he'd take them off. They'd cover the man up . . . and they wouldn't touch him again until later on. Some used to put up a fight, but most of them didn't. They just lay there. Well, they were coming round to me, and
40 the night they came I got up and stood against the wall. They told me to get on the bed, and I knew they had to get me on the bed because if they did it while I was standing up they might break my spine. So I stood up and then one or two of them
45 came for me, well, I was younger then, I was much stronger than I am now, I was quite strong then, I laid one of them out and I had another one round the throat, and then suddenly this chief had these

pincers on my skull and I knew he wasn't supposed to do it while I was standing up, that's why 50
I . . . . . anyway, he did it. So I did get out. I got
out of the place . . . but I couldn't walk very well.
I don't think my spine was damaged. That was
perfectly all right. The trouble was . . . my thoughts
. . . had become very slow . . . I couldn't think at 55
all . . . I couldn't . . . get . . . my thoughts . . .
together . . . uuuhh . . . I could . . . never quite
get it . . . together. The trouble was, I couldn't
hear what people were saying. I couldn't look to
the right or the left, I had to look straight in front 60
of me, because if I turned my head round . . . I
couldn't keep . . . upright. And I had these head-
aches. I used to sit in my room. That was when I
lived with my mother. And my brother. He was
younger than me. And I laid everything out, in 65
order, in my room, all the things I knew were
mine, but I didn't die. The thing is, I should have
been dead. I should have died. Anyway, I feel
much better now. But I don't talk to people now.
I steer clear of places like that café. I never go into 70
them now. I don't talk to anyone . . . like that.
I've often thought of going back and trying to find
the man who did that to me. But I want to do
something first. I want to build that shed out in
the garden. 75

Curtain

ACT III

[*Two weeks later.*]

[Mick *is lying on the floor, down left, his head resting on the rolled carpet, looking up at the ceiling.*

Davies *is sitting in the chair, holding his pipe. He
is wearing the smoking jacket. It is afternoon.* 80
Silence.]

Davies. I got a feeling he's done something to
them cracks.

[*Pause.*]

See, there's been plenty of rain in the last week, 85
but it ain't been dripping into the bucket.

[*Pause.*]

He must have tarred it over up there.

[*Pause.*]

There was someone walking about on the roof the 90
other night. It must have been him.

[*Pause.*]

But I got a feeling he's tarred it over on the roof up there. Ain't said a word to me about it. Don't say a word to me.

[*Pause.*]

5 He don't answer me when I talk to him.

[*He lights a match, holds it to his pipe, and blows it.*]

He don't give me no knife!

[*Pause.*]

10 He don't give me no knife to cut my bread.

[*Pause.*]

How can I cut a loaf of bread without no knife?

[*Pause.*]

It's an impossibility.

15 [*Pause.*]

MICK. You've got a knife.

DAVIES. What?

MICK. You've got a knife.

DAVIES. I got a knife, sure I got a knife, but how

20 do you expect me to cut a good loaf of bread with that? That's not a bread-knife. It's nothing to do with cutting bread. I picked it up somewhere. I don't know where it's been, do I? No, what I want—

25 MICK. I know what you want.

[*Pause. DAVIES rises and goes to the gas stove.*]

DAVIES. What about this gas stove? He tells me it's not connected. How do I know it's not connected? Here I am, I'm sleeping right with it, I

30 wake up in the middle of the night, I'm looking right into the oven, man! It's right next to my face, how do I know, I could be lying there in bed, it might blow up, it might do me harm!

[*Pause.*]

35 But he don't seem to take any notice of what I say to him. I told him the other day, see, I told him about them Blacks, about them Blacks coming up from next door, and using the lavatory. I told him, it was all dirty in there, all the banisters were dirty,

40 they were black, all the lavatory was black. But what did he do? He's supposed to be in charge of it here, he had nothing to say, he hadn't got a word to say.

[*Pause.*]

45 Couple of weeks ago . . . he sat there, he give me a long chat . . . about a couple of weeks ago. A long chat he give me. Since then he ain't said hardly a word. He went on talking there . . . I don't know

what he was . . . he wasn't looking at me, he wasn't talking to me, he don't care about me. He was 50 talking to himself! That's all he worries about. I mean, you come up to me, you ask my advice, he wouldn't never do a thing like that. I mean, we don't have any conversation, you see? You can't live in the same room with someone who . . . who 55 don't have any conversation with you.

[*Pause.*]

I just can't get the hang of him.

[*Pause.*]

You and me, we could get this place going. 60

MICK [*ruminatively*]. Yes, you're quite right. Look what I could do with this place.

[*Pause.*]

I could turn this place into a penthouse. For instance . . . this room. This room you could have 65 as the kitchen. Right size, nice window, sun comes in. I'd have . . . I'd have teal-blue, copper and parchment linoleum squares. I'd have those colours re-echoed in the walls. I'd offset the kitchen units with charcoal-grey worktops. Plenty of room 70 for cupboards for the crockery. We'd have a small wall cupboard, a large wall cupboard, a corner wall cupboard with revolving shelves. You wouldn't be short of cupboards. You could put the dining-room across the landing, see? Yes. Venetian blinds on 75 the window, cork floor, cork tiles. You could have an off-white pile linen rug, a table in . . . in afromosia° teak veneer, sideboard with matt° black drawers, curved chairs with cushioned seats, armchairs in oatmeal tweed, a beech frame settee with 80 a woven sea-grass seat, white-topped heat-resistant coffee table, white tile surround. Yes. Then the bedroom. What's a bedroom? It's a retreat. It's a place to go for rest and peace. So you want quiet decoration. The lighting functional. Furniture . . . 85 mahogany and rosewood. Deep azure-blue carpet, unglazed blue and white curtains, a bedspread with a pattern of small blue roses on a white ground, dressing-table with a lift-up top containing a plastic tray, table lamp of white raffia . . . 90 [MICK *sits up.*] it wouldn't be a flat it'd be a palace.

DAVIES. I'd say it would, man.

MICK. A palace.

afromosia i.e., afrormosia, a West African hardwood
matt satin finish

DAVIES. Who would live there?

MICK. I would. My brother and me.

[*Pause.*]

DAVIES. What about me?

5   MICK [*quietly*]. All this junk here, it's no good to anyone. It's just a lot of old iron, that's all. Clobber. You couldn't make a home out of this. There's no way you could arrange it. It's junk. He could never sell it, either, he wouldn't get tuppence for
10 it.

    [*Pause.*]

Junk.

    [*Pause.*]

But he doesn't seem to be interested in what I got
15 in mind, that's the trouble. Why don't you have a chat with him, see if he's interested?

DAVIES. Me?

MICK. Yes. You're a friend of his.

DAVIES. He's no friend of mine.

20   MICK. You're living in the same room with him, en't you?

DAVIES. He's no friend of mine. You don't know where you are with him. I mean, with a bloke like you, you know where you are.

25   [MICK *looks at him.*]

I mean, you got your own ways. I'm not saying you ain't got your own ways, anyone can see that. You may have some funny ways, but that's the same with all of us, but with him it's different,
30 see? I mean at least with you, the thing with you is you're. . . .

MICK. Straightforward.

DAVIES. That's it, you're straightforward.

MICK. Yes.

35   DAVIES. But with him, you don't know what he's up to half the time!

MICK. Uh.

DAVIES. He's got no feelings!

[*Pause.*]

40 See, what I need is a clock! I need a clock to tell the time! How can I tell the time without a clock? I can't do it! I said to him, I said, look here, what about getting in a clock, so's I can tell what time it is? I mean, if you can't tell what time you're at
45 you don't know where you are, you understand my meaning? See, what I got to do now, if I'm walking about outside, I got to get my eye on a clock, and keep the time in my head for when I

come in. But that's no good, I mean I'm not in here five minutes and I forgotten it. I forgotten
50 what time it was!

[DAVIES *walks up and down the room.*]

Look at it this way. If I don't feel well I have a bit of a lay down, then, when I wake up, I don't know what time it is to go and have a cup of tea! You
55 see, it's not so bad when I'm coming in. I can see the clock on the corner, the moment I'm stepping into the house I know what the time is, but when I'm *in*! It's when I'm *in* . . . that I haven't the foggiest idea what time it is!
60

[*Pause.*]

No, what I need is a clock in here, in this room, and then I stand a bit of a chance. But he don't give me one.

[DAVIES *sits in the chair.*]
65

He wakes me up! He wakes me up in the middle of the night! Tells me I'm making noises! I tell you I've half a mind to give him a mouthful one of these days.

MICK. He don't let you sleep?
70

DAVIES. He don't let me sleep! He wakes me up!

MICK. That's terrible.

DAVIES. I been plenty of other places. They always let me sleep. It's the same the whole world over. Except here.
75

MICK. Sleep's essential. I've always said that.

DAVIES. You're right, it's essential. I get up in the morning, I'm worn out! I got business to see to. I got to move myself, I got to sort myself out, I got to get fixed up. But when I wake up in the
80 morning. I ain't got no energy in me. And on top of that I ain't got no clock.

MICK. Yes.

DAVIES [*standing, moving*]. He goes out, I don't know where he goes to, where's he go, he never
85 tells me. We used to have a bit of a chat, not any more. I never see him, he goes out, he comes in late, next thing I know he's shoving me about in the middle of the night.

[*Pause.*]
90

Listen! I wake up in the morning . . . I wake up in the morning and he's smiling at me! He's standing there, looking at me, smiling! I can see him, you see, I can see him through the blanket. He puts on his coat, he turns himself round, he looks
95 down at my bed, there's a smile on his face! What

the hell's he smiling at? What he don't know is
that I'm watching him through that blanket. He
don't know that! He don't know I can see him, he
thinks I'm asleep, but I got my eye on him all the
5 time through the blanket, see? But he don't know
that! He just looks at me and he smiles, but he
don't know that I can see him doing it!

[*Pause.*]

[*Bending, close to* MICK.] No, what you want to
10 do, you want to speak to him, see? I got . . . I got
that worked out. You want to tell him . . . that we
got ideas for this place, we could build it up, we
could get it started. You see, I could decorate it
out for you. I could give you a hand in doing it
15 . . . between us.

[*Pause.*]

Where do you live now, then?

MICK. Me? Oh, I've got a little place. Not bad.
Everything laid on. You must come up and have
20 a drink some time. Listen to some Tchaikovsky.

DAVIES. No, you see, you're the bloke who wants
to talk to him. I mean, you're his brother.

[*Pause.*]

MICK. Yes . . . maybe I will.

25 [*A door bangs.*]

[MICK *rises, goes to the door and exits.*]

DAVIES. Where you going? This is him!

[*Silence.*]

[DAVIES *stands, then goes to the window and looks*
30 *out.*]

[ASTON *enters. He is carrying a paper bag. He takes*
off his overcoat, opens the bag and takes out a pair of
shoes.]

ASTON. Pair of shoes.

35 DAVIES [*turning*]. What?

ASTON. I picked them up. Try them.

DAVIES. Shoes? What sort?

ASTON. They might do you.

[DAVIES *comes down stage, takes off his sandals and*
40 *tries the shoes on. He walks about, waggling his feet,*
bends, and presses the leather.]

DAVIES. No, they're not right.

ASTON. Aren't they?

DAVIES. No, they don't fit.

45 ASTON. Mmnn.

[*Pause.*]

DAVIES. Well, I'll tell you what, they might do
. . . until I get another pair.

[*Pause.*]

Where's the laces? 50

ASTON. No laces.

DAVIES. I can't wear them without laces.

ASTON. I just got the shoes.

DAVIES. Well now, look that puts the lid on it,
don't it? I mean, you couldn't keep these shoes 55
on right without a pair of laces. The only way to
keep a pair of shoes on, if you haven't got no
laces, is to tighten the foot, see? Walk about with
a tight foot, see? Well, that's no good for the foot.
Puts a bad strain on the foot. If you can do the 60
shoes up proper there's less chance of you getting
a strain.

[ASTON *goes round to the top of his bed.*]

ASTON. I might have some somewhere.

DAVIES. You see what I'm getting at? 65

[*Pause.*]

ASTON. Here's some. [*He hands them to* DAVIES.]

DAVIES. These are brown.

ASTON. That's all I got.

DAVIES. These shoes are black. 70

[ASTON *does not answer.*]

Well, they can do, anyway, until I get another
pair.

[DAVIES *sits in the chair and begins to lace his shoes.*]

Maybe they'll get me down to Sidcup tomorrow. 75
If I get down there I'll be able to sort myself out.

[*Pause.*]

I've been offered a good job. Man has offered it
to me, he's . . . he's got plenty of ideas. He's got
a bit of a future. But they want my papers, you 80
see, they want my references. I'd have to get down
to Sidcup before I could get hold of them. That's
where they are, see. Trouble is, getting there. That's
my problem. The weather's dead against it.

[ASTON *quietly exits, unnoticed.*] 85

Don't know as these shoes'll be much good. It's a
hard road, I been down there before. Coming the
other way, like. Last time I left there, it was . . .
last time . . . getting on a while back . . . the road
was bad, the rain was coming down, lucky I didn't 90
die there on the road, but I got here. I kept going,
all along . . . yes . . . I kept going all along. But all
the same, I can't go on like this, what I got to do,
I got to get back there, find this man—

[*He turns and looks about the room.*] 95

Christ! That bastard, he ain't even listening to me!

[BLACKOUT.

DIM LIGHT THROUGH THE WINDOW.

It is night. ASTON *and* DAVIES *are in bed,* DAVIES *groaning.* ASTON *sits up, gets out of bed, switches on* 5 *the light, goes over to* DAVIES *and shakes him.*]

ASTON. Hey, stop it, will you? I can't sleep.

DAVIES. What? What? What's going on?

ASTON. You're making noises.

DAVIES. I'm an old man, what do you expect me 10 to do, stop breathing?

ASTON. You're making noises.

DAVIES. What do you expect me to do, stop breathing?

[ASTON *goes to his bed, and puts on his trousers.*]
15 ASTON. I'll get a bit of air.

DAVIES. What do you expect me to do? I tell you, mate. I'm not surprised they took you in. Waking an old man up in the middle of the night, you must be off your nut! Giving me bad dreams, who's 20 responsible, then, for me having bad dreams? If you wouldn't keep mucking me about I wouldn't make no noises! How do you expect me to sleep peaceful when you keep poking me all the time? What do you want me to do, stop breathing?

25 [*He throws the cover off and gets out of bed, wearing his vest, waistcoat and trousers.*]

It's getting so freezing in here I have to keep my trousers on to go to bed. I never done that before in my life. But that's what I got to do here. Just 30 because you won't put in any bleeding heating! I've had just about enough with you mucking me about. I've seen better days than you have, man. Nobody ever got me inside one of them places, anyway. I'm a sane man! So don't you start muck- 35 ing me about. I'll be all right as long as you keep your place. Just you keep your place, that's all. Because I can tell you, your brother's got his eye on you. He knows all about you. I got a friend there, don't you worry about that. I got a true pal 40 there. Treating me like dirt! Why'd you invite me in here in the first place if you was going to treat me like this? You think you're better than me you got another think coming. I know enough. They had you inside one of them places before, they 45 can have you inside again. Your brother's got his eye on you! They can put the pincers on your head again, man! They can have them on again! Any time. All they got to do is get the word. They'd carry you in there, boy. They'd come here and pick you up and carry you in! They'd keep you 50 fixed! They'd put them pincers on your head, they'd have you fixed! They'd take one look at all this junk I got to sleep with they'd know you were a creamer.° That was the greatest mistake they made, you take my tip, letting you get out of that place. 55 Nobody knows what you're at, you go out you come in, nobody knows what you're at! Well, nobody messes me about for long. You think I'm going to do your dirty work? Haaaaahhhhh! You better think again! You want me to do all the dirty 60 work all up and down them stairs just so I can sleep in this lousy filthy hole every night? Not me, boy. Not for you boy. You don't know what you're doing half the time. You're up the creek! You're half off! You can tell it by looking at you. Who 65 ever saw you slip me a few bob? Treating me like a bloody animal! I never been inside a nuthouse!

[ASTON *makes a slight move towards him.* DAVIES *takes his knife from his back pocket.*]

Don't come° nothing with me, mate. I got this here. 70 I used it. I used it. Don't come it with me.

[*A pause. They stare at each other.*]

Mind what you do now.

[*Pause.*]

Don't you try anything with me. 75

[*Pause.*]

ASTON. I . . . I think it's about time you found somewhere else. I don't think we're hitting it off.

DAVIES. Find somewhere else?

ASTON. Yes. 80

DAVIES. Me? You talking to me? Not me, man! You!

ASTON. What?

DAVIES. You! You better find somewhere else!

ASTON. I live here. You don't. 85

DAVIES. Don't I? Well, I live here. I been offered a job here.

ASTON. Yes . . . well, I don't think you're really suitable.

DAVIES. Not suitable? Well, I can tell you, there's 90 someone here thinks I am suitable. And I'll tell you, I'm staying on here as caretaker! Get it! Your brother, he's told me, see, he's told me the job is

creamer crackpot
come try

mine. Mine! So that's where I am. I'm going to be his caretaker.

ASTON. My brother?

DAVIES. He's staying, he's going to run this place,
5 and I'm staying with him.

ASTON. Look. If I give you . . . a few bob you can get down to Sidcup.

DAVIES. You build your shed first! A few bob! When I can earn a steady wage here! You build
10 your stinking shed first! That's what!

[ASTON *stares at him.*]

ASTON. That's not a stinking shed.

[*Silence.*

ASTON *moves to him.*]
15 It's clean. It's all good wood. I'll get it up. No trouble.

DAVIES. Don't come too near!

ASTON. You've no reason to call that shed stinking.
20 [DAVIES *points the knife.*]
You stink.

DAVIES. What!

ASTON. You've been stinking the place out.

DAVIES. Christ, you say that to me!
25 ASTON. For days. That's one reason I can't sleep.

DAVIES. You call me that! You call me stinking!

ASTON. You better go.

DAVIES. I'LL STINK YOU!

[*He thrusts his arm out, the arm trembling, the knife*
30 *pointing at* ASTON's *stomach.* ASTON *does not move. Silence.* DAVIES' *arm moves no further. They stand.*]
I'll stink you. . . .

[*Pause.*]

ASTON. Get your stuff.
35 [DAVIES *draws the knife in to his chest, breathing heavily.* ASTON *goes to* DAVIES' *bed, collects his bag and puts a few of* DAVIES' *things into it.*

DAVIES. You ain't . . . you ain't got the right . . . Leave that alone, that's mine!
40 [DAVIES *takes the bag and presses the contents down.*] All right . . . I been offered a job here . . . you wait . . . [*He puts on his smoking-jacket.*] . . . you wait . . . your brother . . . he'll sort you out . . . you call me that . . . you call me that . . . no one's ever
45 called me that . . . [*He puts on his overcoat.*] You'll be sorry you called me that . . . you ain't heard the last of this . . . [*He picks up his bag and goes to the door.*] You'll be sorry you called me that. . . .

[*He opens the door,* ASTON *watching him.*]
Now I know who I can trust. 50

[DAVIES *goes out.* ASTON *stands.*

BLACKOUT.

LIGHTS UP. *Early evening.*

Voices on the stairs.

MICK and DAVIES *enter.*] 55

DAVIES. Stink! You hear that! Me! I told you what he said, didn't I? Stink! You hear that? That's what he said to me!

MICK. Tch, tch, tch.

DAVIES. That's what he said to me. 60

MICK. You don't stink.

DAVIES. No, sir!

MICK. If you stank I'd be the first one to tell you.

DAVIES. I told him, I told him he . . . I said to him, you ain't heard the last of this man! I said, 65 don't you forget your brother. I told him you'd be coming along to sort him out. He don't know what he's started, doing that. Doing that to me. I said to him, I said to him, he'll be along, your brother'll be along, he's got sense, not like you— 70

MICK. What do you mean?

DAVIES. Eh?

MICK. You saying my brother hasn't got any sense?

DAVIES. What? What I'm saying is, you got ideas 75 for this place, all this . . . all this decorating, see? I mean, he's got no right to order me about. I take orders from you, I do my caretaking for you, I mean, you look upon me . . . you don't treat me like a lump of dirt . . . we can both . . . we can 80 both see him for what he is.

[*Pause.*]

MICK. What did he say then, when you told him I'd offered you the job as caretaker?

DAVIES. He . . . he said . . . he said . . . some- 85 thing about . . . he lived here.

MICK. Yes, he's got a point, en he?

DAVIES. A point! This is your house, en't? You let him live here!

MICK. I could tell him to go, I suppose. 90

DAVIES. That's what I'm saying.

MICK. Yes. I could tell him to go. I mean, I'm the landlord. On the other hand, he's the sitting tenant. Giving him notice, you see, what it is, it's a technical matter, that's what it is. It depends 95 how you regard this room. I mean it depends

whether you regard this room as furnished or unfurnished. See what I mean?

DAVIES. No, I don't.

MICK. All this furniture, you see, in here, it's all
his, except the beds, of course. So what it is, it's
a fine legal point, that's what it is.

[*Pause.*]

DAVIES. I tell you he should go back where he
come from!

MICK [*turning to look at him*]. Come from?

DAVIES. Yes.

MICK. Where did he come from?

DAVIES. Well . . . he . . . he. . . .

MICK. You get a bit out of your depth sometimes, don't you?

[*Pause.*]

[*Rising, briskly.*] Well, anyway, as things stand,
I don't mind having a go at doing up the place. . . .

DAVIES. That's what I wanted to hear!

MICK. No, I don't mind.

[*He turns to face* DAVIES.]

But you better be as good as you say you are.

DAVIES. What do you mean?

MICK. Well, you say you're an interior decorator, you'd better be a good one.

DAVIES. A what?

MICK. What do you mean, a what? A decorator.
An interior decorator.

DAVIES. Me? What do you mean? I never touched
that. I never been that.

MICK. You've never what?

DAVIES. No, no, not me, man. I'm not an interior
decorator. I been too busy. Too many other things
to do, you see. But I . . . but I could always turn
my hand to most things . . . give me . . . give me
a bit of time to pick it up.

MICK. I don't want you to pick it up. I want a
first-class experienced interior decorator. I thought
you were one.

DAVIES. Me? Now wait a minute—wait a
minute—you got the wrong man.

MICK. How could I have the wrong man? You're
the only man I've spoken to. You're the only man
I've told, about my dreams, about my deepest
wishes, you're the only one I've told, and I only
told you because I understood you were an experienced first-class professional interior and exterior decorator.

DAVIES. Now look here—

MICK. You mean you wouldn't know how to fit
teal-blue, copper and parchment linoleum squares
and have those colours re-echoed in the walls?

DAVIES. Now, look here, where'd you get—?

MICK. You wouldn't be able to decorate out a
table in afromosia teak veneer, an armchair in oatmeal tweed and a beech frame settee with a woven
sea-grass seat?

DAVIES. I never said that!

MICK. Christ! I must have been under a false
impression!

DAVIES. I never said it!

MICK. You're a bloody imposter, mate!

DAVIES. Now you don't want to say that sort of
thing to me. You took me on here as caretaker. I
was going to give you a helping hand, that's all,
for a small . . . for a small wage, I never said nothing about that . . . you start calling me names—

MICK. What is your name?

DAVIES. Don't start that—

MICK. No, what's your real name?

DAVIES. My real name's Davies.

MICK. What's the name you go under?

DAVIES. Jenkins!

MICK. You got two names. What about the rest?
Eh? Now come on, why did you tell me all this
dirt about you being an interior decorator?

DAVIES. I didn't tell you nothing! Won't you listen to what I'm saying?

[*Pause.*]

It was him who told you. It was your brother who
must have told you. He's nutty! He'd tell you anything, out of spite, he's nutty, he's half way gone,
it was him who told you.

[MICK *walks slowly to him.*]

MICK. What did you call my brother?

DAVIES. When?

MICK. He's what?

DAVIES. I . . . now get this straight. . . .

MICK. Nutty? Who's nutty?

[*Pause.*]

Did you call my brother nutty? My brother. That's
a bit of . . . that's a bit of an impertinent thing to
say, isn't it?

DAVIES. But he says so himself!

[MICK *walks slowly round* DAVIES' *figure, regarding
him, once. He circles him, once.*]

MICK. What a strange man you are. Aren't you?
You're really strange. Ever since you come into
this house there's been nothing but trouble. Honest. I can take nothing you say at face value. Every
5 word you speak is open to any number of different
interpretations. Most of what you say is lies. You're
violent, you're erratic, you're just completely un-
predictable. You're nothing else but a wild animal,
when you come down to it. You're a barbarian.
10 And to put the old tin lid on it, you stink from
arse-hole to breakfast time. Look at it. You come
here recommending yourself as an interior decorator, whereupon I take you on, and what happens? You make a long speech about all the ref-
15 erences you've got down at Sidcup, and what
happens? I haven't noticed you go down to Sidcup
to obtain them. It's all most regrettable but it looks
as though I'm compelled to pay you off for your
caretaking work. Here's half a dollar.
20 [He feels in his pocket, takes out a half-crown and
tosses it at DAVIES' feet. DAVIES stands still. MICK walks
to the gas stove and picks up the Buddha.]
DAVIES [slowly]. All right then . . . you do that
. . . you do it . . . if that's what you want. . . .
25 MICK. THAT'S WHAT I WANT!
[He hurls the Buddha against the gas stove. It breaks.]
[Passionately.] Anyone would think this house was
all I got to worry about. I got plenty of other things
I can worry about. I've got other things. I've got
30 plenty of other interests. I've got my own business
to build up, haven't I? I got to think about expanding . . . in all directions. I don't stand still.
I'm moving about, all the time. I'm moving . . . all
the time. I've got to think about the future. I'm
35 not worried about this house. I'm not interested.
My brother can worry about it. He can do it up,
he can decorate it, he can do what he likes with
it. I'm not bothered. I thought I was doing him a
favour, letting him live here. He's got his own
40 ideas. Let him have them. I'm going to chuck it
in.
[Pause.]
DAVIES. What about me?
[Silence. MICK does not look at him.
45 A door bangs.
Silence. They do not move.
ASTON comes in. He closes the door, moves into the
room and faces MICK. They look at each other. Both are
smiling, faintly.]

MICK [beginning to speak to ASTON]. Look . . . 50
uh . . .
[He stops, goes to the door and exits. ASTON leaves
the door open, crosses behind DAVIES, sees the broken
Buddha, and looks at the pieces for a moment. He then
goes to his bed, takes off his overcoat, sits, takes the 55
screwdriver and plug and pokes the plug.]
DAVIES. I just come back for my pipe.
ASTON. Oh yes.
DAVIES. I got out and . . . half way down I . . .
I suddenly . . . found out . . . you see . . . that I 60
hadn't got my pipe. So I come back to get it. . . .
[Pause. He moves to ASTON.]
That ain't the same plug, is it, you been. . . ?
[Pause.]
Still can't get anywhere with it, eh? 65
[Pause.]
Well, if you . . . persevere, in my opinion, you'll
probably. . .
[Pause.]
Listen. . . . 70
[Pause.]
You didn't mean that, did you, about me stinking,
did you?
[Pause.]
Did you? You been a good friend to me. You took 75
me in. You took me in, you didn't ask me no ques-
tions, you give me a bed, you been a mate to me.
Listen. I been thinking, why I made all them noises,
it was because of the draught, see, that draught
was on me as I was sleeping, made me make noises 80
without me knowing it, so I been thinking, what
I mean to say, if you was to give me your bed,
and you have my bed, there's not all that difference between them, they're the same sort of bed,
if I was to have yourn, you sleep, wherever bed 85
you're in, so you have mine, I have yourn, and
that'll be all right, I'll be out of the draught, see,
I mean, you don't mind a bit of wind, you need
a bit of air, I can understand that, you being in
that place that time, with all them doctors and all 90
they done, closed up, I know them places, too
hot, you see, they're always too hot, I had a peep
in one once, nearly suffocated me, so I reckon that'd
be the best way out of it, we swap beds, and then
we could get down to what we was saying, I'd 95
look after the place for you, I'd keep an eye on it
for you, for you, like, not for the other . . . not for
. . . for your brother, you see, not for him, for you,

I'll be your man, you say the word, just say the word. . . .

[*Pause.*]

What do you think of this I'm saying?

5 [*Pause.*]

Aston. No, I like sleeping in this bed.

Davies. But you don't understand my meaning!

Aston. Anyway, that one's my brother's bed.

Davies. Your brother?

10 Aston. Any time he stays here. This is my bed. It's the only bed I can sleep in.

Davies. But your brother's gone! He's gone!

[*Pause.*]

Aston. No. I couldn't change beds.

15 Davies. But you don't understand my meaning!

Aston. Anyway, I'm going to be busy. I've got that shed to get up. If I don't get it up now it'll never go up. Until it's up I can't get started.

Davies. I'll give you a hand to put up your shed,
20 that's what I'll do!

[*Pause.*]

I'll give you a hand! We'll both put up that shed together! See? Get it done in next to no time! Do you see what I'm saying?

25 [*Pause.*]

Aston. No. I can get it up myself.

Davies. But listen. I'm with you, I'll be here, I'll do it for you!

[*Pause.*]

30 We'll do it together!

[*Pause.*]

Christ, we'll change beds!

[Aston *moves to the window and stands with his back to* Davies.]

35 You mean you're throwing me out? You can't do that. Listen man, listen man, I don't mind, you see, I don't mind, I'll stay, I don't mind, I'll tell you what, if you don't want to change beds, we'll keep it as it is, I'll stay in the same bed, maybe if
40 I can get a stronger piece of sacking, like, to go over the window, keep out the draught, that'll do it, what do you say, we'll keep it as it is?

[*Pause.*]

Aston. No.

45 Davies. Why . . . not?

[Aston *turns to look at him.*]

Aston. You make too much noise.

Davies. But . . . but . . . look . . . listen . . . listen here . . . I mean. . . .

[Aston *turns back to the window.*] 50

What am I going to do?

[*Pause.*]

What shall I do?

[*Pause.*]

Where am I going to go? 55

[*Pause.*]

If you want me to go . . . I'll go. You just say the word.

[*Pause.*]

I'll tell you what though . . . them shoes . . . them 60 shoes you give me . . . they're working out all right . . . they're all right. Maybe I could . . . get down. . . .

[Aston *remains still, his back to him, at the window.*] 65

Listen . . . if I . . . got down . . . if I was to . . . get my papers . . . would you . . . would you let . . . would you . . . if I got down . . . and got my. . . .

[*Long silence.*]

Curtain.

Imamu Amiri Baraka

(LeRoi Jones)

1934–

Dutchman

1964

Dutchman is raw, ugly, powerful—repelling and compelling in almost equal measure. Nowhere in the play is there tenderness or affection. There is no sociability, no friendship, nothing remotely reminiscent of love. The sex, which is here in plenty, is animal and predatory. The wit, which keeps breaking its own measure, serves but to hone the edge of hostility. Contempt is merely the mildest of the play's destructive emotions. Anger, hatred, and rage fuse with it in the spasm of the final episode.

Emotion as savage as that in *Dutchman* awes us, frightens us, rivets us to our place. Like Oedipus we may fear what we are to hear, but hear we must. And what we hear haunts us with its burden of obscure meaning. Our setting is "the flying underbelly of the city," "the subway heaped in modern myth." We move through obliquities of mood and eccentricities of emotion. Clay, whose name suggests mortality, cannot fathom the lapses of Lula's attention, her boredoms, her irritations, her hysteria. Lula, who lies, who plays with clichés and rehearses roles, drifts in and out of focus, only intermittently aware of the robot-like part she seems programmed to play. And as the play reaches its catastrophe, its mode nightmarishly modulates from realism to expressionism, Lula's fellow-passengers mechanistically witnessing and participating in her act of ritual violence.

Clay and Lula, it seems to our retrospect, meet in a dance of death, their differences of gender, culture, and race drawing them together no less surely than certain radical similarities. If Lula acts, Clay acts too, his three-button suit and striped tie the costume of the Ivy-league part he plays. If she lies, he lies too, denying by his Uncle Tomism the racial hatred and racial pride of his "pumping black heart." And if Lula suffers from a "novel form of insanity," Clay recognizes that he, too, is "insane," choosing as he does words instead of acts of emancipation.

IMAMU AMIRI BARAKA

For all the obscurities surrounding him, Clay is fairly easy to comprehend. He is a decorous young man who somewhat self-consciously accommodates—to the white man's image of gentility, to the white woman's offer of seduction. When he is ridiculed and humiliated, he erupts in a fury that subsides to cold hatred, expressing in that wave of emotion certain convictions—or myths: that blacks know sex, hence life, as whites cannot; that out of their sex and their hatred, blacks generate jazz; and that ultimately blacks may emancipate themselves by emulating the whites—that is, by coldly, rationally, murdering the other race.

Lula is harder to read. Part of her seems to wish for Clay the freedom that comes from rebelling. Let him cease imitating the white man. Let him do the nasty with the white woman. Let him "scream meaningless shit in these hopeless faces." Is it freedom for Clay that she wants, though, or is it her own escape from the limitations of race and role that she is projecting on him? Further, if part of her seems to seek his freedom, a larger, more abiding part demands, plots, and achieves his destruction. That larger part, so the play seems to suggest, derives from racial psychology, from some kind of genetic need to dominate; but it derives too, and more importantly, from ancient literary tradition. Lula, like Shakespeare's Iago, descends from the vice in the medieval mystery play. She is the stereotyped figure of temptation who preys on the imagination of her victim until the veneer of his civilization is stripped from him and his peace and his life are destroyed.

That Clay and Lula, like the rest of us, are simultaneously individuals and types is clear. What may not be clear is whether they are yet more—representatives or stand-ins for their races. Does "Clay" equal "blacks" and "Lula" equal "whites"? Does the plot of *Dutchman* exhibit the truth of the relations between the races? Does it indict the blacks for their accommodation, the whites for their brutality? Or do such questions take the part for the whole and reduce to precise allegory what is, in fact, only proximate metaphor?

Dutchman°

BARAKA

CHARACTERS

CLAY *twenty-year-old Negro*
LULA *thirty-year-old white woman*
RIDERS OF COACH *white and black*
YOUNG NEGRO
CONDUCTOR

In the flying underbelly of the city. Steaming hot, and summer on top, outside. Underground. The subway heaped in modern myth.

Opening scene is a man sitting in a subway seat, holding a magazine but looking vacantly just above its wilting pages. Occasionally he looks blankly toward the window on his right. Dim lights and darkness whistling by against the glass. (Or paste the lights, as admitted props, right on the subway windows. Have them move, even dim and flicker. But give the sense of speed. Also stations, whether the train is stopped or the glitter and activity of these stations merely flashes by the windows.)

The man is sitting alone. That is, only his seat is visible, though the rest of the car is outfitted as a complete subway car. But only his seat is shown. There might be, for a time, as the play begins, a loud scream of the actual train. And it can recur throughout the play, or continue on a lower key once the dialogue starts.

Dutchman this enigmatic title has been much debated. It may refer to the first slave ship that came to the colonies, a Dutch frigate that landed at Jamestown in 1619 with 20 "negars." Or it may allude to the legend of the Flying Dutchman, the ship doomed to sail forever because of its captain's blasphemy.

The train slows after a time, pulling to a brief stop at one of the stations. The man looks idly up, until he sees a woman's face staring at him through the window; when it realizes that the man has noticed the face, it begins very premeditatedly to smile. The man smiles too, for a moment, without a trace of self-consciousness. Almost an instinctive though undesirable response. Then a kind of awkwardness or embarrassment sets in, and the man makes to look away, is further embarrassed, so he brings back his eyes to where the face was, but by now the train is moving again, and the face would seem to be left behind by the way the man turns his head to look back through the other windows at the slowly fading platform. He smiles then; more comfortably confident, hoping perhaps that his memory of this brief encounter will be pleasant. And then he is idle again.

SCENE I

Train roars. Lights flash outside the windows.

LULA *enters from the rear of the car in bright, skimpy summer clothes and sandals. She carries a net bag full of paper books, fruit, and other anonymous articles. She is wearing sunglasses,* 5 *which she pushes up on her forehead from time to time.* LULA *is a tall, slender, beautiful woman with long red hair hanging straight down her back, wearing only loud lipstick in somebody's good taste. She is eating an apple, very daintily.* 10 *Coming down the car toward* CLAY.

She stops beside CLAY'S *seat and hangs languidly from the strap, still managing to eat the apple. It is apparent that she is going to sit in the seat next to* CLAY, *and that she is only waiting* 15 *for him to notice her before she sits.*

CLAY *sits as before, looking just beyond his magazine, now and again pulling the magazine slowly back and forth in front of his face in a hopeless effort to fan himself. Then he sees the* 20 *woman hanging there beside him and he looks up into her face, smiling quizzically.*

LULA. Hello.
CLAY. Uh, hi're you?
LULA. I'm going to sit down. . . . O.K.? 25

CLAY. Sure.

LULA [*Swings down onto the seat, pushing her legs straight out as if she is very weary*]. Oooof! Too much weight.

5 CLAY. Ha, doesn't look like much to me. [*Leaning back against the window, a little surprised and maybe stiff.*]

LULA. It's so anyway. [*And she moves her toes in the sandals, then pulls her right leg up on* 10 *the left knee, better to inspect the bottoms of the sandals and the back of her heel. She appears for a second not to notice that* CLAY *is sitting next to her or that she has spoken to him just a second before.* CLAY *looks at the magazine, then out the* 15 *black window. As he does this, she turns very quickly toward him.*] Weren't you staring at me through the window?

CLAY [*Wheeling around and very much stiffened*]. What?

20 LULA. Weren't you staring at me through the window? At the last stop?

CLAY. Staring at you? What do you mean?

LULA. Don't you know what staring means?

CLAY. I saw you through the window . . . 25 if that's what it means. I don't know if I was staring. Seems to me you were staring through the window at me.

LULA. I was. But only after I'd turned around and saw you staring through that window 30 down in the vicinity of my ass and legs.

CLAY. Really?

LULA. Really. I guess you were just taking those idle potshots. Nothing else to do. Run your mind over people's flesh.

35 CLAY. Oh boy. Wow, now I admit I was looking in your direction. But the rest of that weight is yours.

LULA. I suppose.

CLAY. Staring through train windows is 40 weird business. Much weirder than staring very sedately at abstract asses.

LULA. That's why I came looking through the window . . . so you'd have more than that to go on. I even smiled at you.

45 CLAY. That's right.

LULA. I even got into this train, going some other way than mine. Walked down the aisle . . . searching you out.

CLAY. Really? That's pretty funny.

LULA. That's pretty funny. . . . God, you're 50 dull.

CLAY. Well, I'm sorry, lady, but I really wasn't prepared for party talk.

LULA. No, you're not. What are you prepared for? [*Wrapping the apple core in a Kleenex and* 55 *dropping it on the floor.*]

CLAY [*Takes her conversation as pure sex talk. He turns to confront her squarely with this idea*]. I'm prepared for anything. How about you? 60

LULA [*Laughing loudly and cutting it off abruptly*]. What do you think you're doing?

CLAY. What?

LULA. You think I want to pick you up, get you to take me somewhere and screw me, 65 huh?

CLAY. Is that the way I look?

LULA. You look like you been trying to grow a beard. That's exactly what you look like. You look like you live in New Jersey with your 70 parents and are trying to grow a beard. That's what. You look like you've been reading Chinese poetry and drinking lukewarm sugarless tea. [*Laughs, uncrossing and recrossing her legs.*] You look like death eating a soda cracker. 75

CLAY [*Cocking his head from one side to the other, embarrassed and trying to make some comeback, but also intrigued by what the woman is saying . . . even the sharp city coarseness of her voice, which is still a kind of gentle sidewalk* 80 *throb*]. Really? I look like all that?

LULA. Not all of it. [*She feints a seriousness to cover an actual somber tone.*] I lie a lot. [*Smiling.*] It helps me control the world.

CLAY [*Relieved and laughing louder than the* 85 *humor*]. Yeah, I bet.

LULA. But it's true, most of it, right? Jersey? Your bumpy neck?

CLAY. How'd you know all that? Huh? Really, I mean about Jersey . . . and even the 90 beard. I met you before? You know Warren Enright?

LULA. You tried to make it with your sister when you were ten. [CLAY *leans back hard against the back of the seat, his eyes opening* 95 *now, still trying to look amused.*] But I succeeded a few weeks ago. [*She starts to laugh again.*]

CLAY. What're you talking about? Warren tell you that? You're a friend of Georgia's?

LULA. I told you I lie. I don't know your
5 sister. I don't know Warren Enright.

CLAY. You mean you're just picking these things out of the air?

LULA. Is Warren Enright a tall skinny black black boy with a phony English accent?
10 CLAY. I figured you knew him.

LULA. But I don't. I just figured you would know somebody like that. [*Laughs.*]

CLAY. Yeah, yeah.

LULA. You're probably on your way to his
15 house now.

CLAY. That's right.

LULA [*Putting her hand on* CLAY's *closest knee, drawing it from the knee up to the thigh's hinge, then removing it, watching his face very
20 closely, and continuing to laugh, perhaps more gently than before*]. Dull, dull, dull. I bet you think I'm exciting.

CLAY. You're O.K.

LULA. Am I exciting you now?
25 CLAY. Right. That's not what's supposed to happen?

LULA. How do I know? [*She returns her hand, without moving it, then takes it away and plunges it in her bag to draw out an apple.*] You want
30 this?

CLAY. Sure.

LULA [*She gets one out of the bag for herself*]. Eating apples together is always the first step. Or walking up uninhabited Seventh Avenue
35 in the twenties on weekends. [*Bites and giggles, glancing at* CLAY *and speaking in loose sing-song.*] Can get you involved . . . boy! Get us involved. Um-huh. [*Mock seriousness.*] Would you like to get involved with me, Mister Man?
40 CLAY [*Trying to be as flippant as Lula, whacking happily at the apple*]. Sure. Why not? A beautiful woman like you. Huh, I'd be a fool not to.

LULA. And I bet you're sure you know what
45 you're talking about. [*Taking him a little roughly by the wrist, so he cannot eat the apple, then shaking the wrist.*] I bet you're sure of almost everything anybody ever asked you

about . . . right? [*Shakes his wrist harder.*] Right? 50

CLAY. Yeah, right. . . . Wow, you're pretty strong, you know? Whatta you, a lady wrestler or something?

LULA. What's wrong with lady wrestlers? And don't answer because you never knew 55 any. Huh. [*Cynically.*] That's for sure. They don't have any lady wrestlers in that part of Jersey. That's for sure.

CLAY. Hey, you still haven't told me how you know so much about me. 60

LULA. I told you I didn't know anything about *you* . . . you're a well-known type.

CLAY. Really?

LULA. Or at least I know the type very well. And your skinny English friend too. 65

CLAY. Anonymously?

LULA [*Settles back in seat, single-mindedly finishing her apple and humming snatches of rhythm and blues song*]. What?

CLAY. Without knowing us specifically? 70

LULA. Oh boy. [*Looking quickly at* CLAY.] What a face. You know, you could be a handsome man.

CLAY. I can't argue with you.

LULA [*Vague, off-center response*]. What? 75

CLAY [*Raising his voice, thinking the train noise has drowned part of his sentence*]. I can't argue with you.

LULA. My hair is turning gray. A gray hair for each year and type I've come through. 80

CLAY. Why do you want to sound so old?

LULA. But it's always gentle when it starts. [*Attention drifting.*] Hugged against tenements, day or night.

CLAY. What? 85

LULA [*Refocusing*]. Hey, why don't you take me to that party you're going to?

CLAY. You must be a friend of Warren's to know about the party.

LULA. Wouldn't you like to take me to the 90 party? [*Imitates clinging vine.*] Oh, come on, ask me to your party.

CLAY. Of course I'll ask you to come with me to the party. And I'll bet you're a friend of Warren's. 95

LULA. Why not be a friend of Warren's?

Why not? [*Taking his arm.*] Have you asked me yet?

CLAY. How can I ask you when I don't know your name?

5 LULA. Are you talking to my name?

CLAY. What is it, a secret?

LULA. I'm Lena the Hyena.

CLAY. The famous woman poet?

LULA. Poetess! The same!

10 CLAY. Well, you know so much about me . . . what's my name?

LULA. Morris the Hyena.

CLAY. The famous woman poet?

LULA. The same. [*Laughing and going into 15 her bag.*] You want another apple?

CLAY. Can't make it, lady. I only have to keep one doctor away a day.

LULA. I bet your name is . . . something like . . . uh, Gerald or Walter. Huh?

20 CLAY. God, no.

LULA. Lloyd, Norman? One of those hopeless colored names creeping out of New Jersey. Leonard? Gag. . . .

CLAY. Like Warren?

25 LULA. Definitely. Just exactly like Warren. Or Everett.

CLAY. Gag. . . .

LULA. Well, for sure, it's not Willie.

CLAY. It's Clay.

30 LULA. Clay? Really? Clay what?

CLAY. Take your pick. Jackson, Johnson, or Williams.

LULA. Oh, really? Good for you. But it's got to be Williams. You're too pretentious to be a 35 Jackson or Johnson.

CLAY. Thass right.

LULA. But Clay's O.K.

CLAY. So's Lena.

LULA. It's Lula.

40 CLAY. Oh?

LULA. Lula the Hyena.

CLAY. Very good.

LULA [*Starts laughing again*]. Now you say to me, "Lula, Lula, why don't you go to this 45 party with me tonight?" It's your turn, and let those be your lines.

CLAY. Lula, why don't you go to this party with me tonight, Huh?

LULA. Say my name twice before you ask, and no huh's. 50

CLAY. Lula, Lula, why don't you go to this party with me tonight?

LULA. I'd like to go, Clay, but how can you ask me to go when you barely know me?

CLAY. That is strange, isn't it? 55

LULA. What kind of reaction is that? You're supposed to say, "Aw, come on, we'll get to know each other better at the party."

CLAY. That's pretty corny.

LULA. What are you into anyway? [*Looking 60 at him half sullenly but still amused.*] What thing are you playing at, Mister? Mister Clay Williams? [*Grabs his thigh, up near the crotch.*] What are *you* thinking about?

CLAY. Watch it now, you're gonna excite 65 me for real.

LULA [*Taking her hand away and throwing her apple core through the window*]. I bet. [*She slumps in the seat and is heavily silent.*]

CLAY. I thought you knew everything about 70 me? What happened? [LULA *looks at him, then looks slowly away, then over where the other aisle would be. Noise of the train. She reaches in her bag and pulls out one of the paper books. She puts it on her leg and thumbs the pages listlessly. 75* CLAY *cocks his head to see the title of the book. Noise of the train.* LULA *flips pages and her eyes drift. Both remain silent.*] Are you going to the party with me, Lula?

LULA [*Bored and not even looking*]. I don't 80 even know you.

CLAY. You said you know my type.

LULA [*Strangely irritated*]. Don't get smart with me, Buster. I know you like the palm of my hand. 85

CLAY. The one you eat the apples with?

LULA. Yeh. And the one I open doors late Saturday evening with. That's my door. Up at the top of the stairs. Five flights. Above a lot of Italians and lying Americans. And scrape 90 carrots with. Also . . . [*looks at him*] the same hand I unbutton my dress with, or let my skirt fall down. Same hand. Lover.

CLAY. Are you angry about anything? Did I say something wrong? 95

LULA. Everything you say is wrong. [*Mock

smile.] That's what makes you so attractive. Ha. In that funnybook jacket with all the buttons. [*More animate, taking hold of his jacket.*] What've you got that jacket and tie on in all this heat for? And why're you wearing a jacket and tie like that? Did your people ever burn witches or start revolutions over the price of tea? Boy, those narrow-shoulder clothes come from a tradition you ought to feel oppressed by. A three-button suit. What right do you have to be wearing a three-button suit and striped tie? Your grandfather was a slave, he didn't go to Harvard.

CLAY. My grandfather was a night watchman.

LULA. And you went to a colored college where everybody thought they were Averell Harriman.

CLAY. All except me.

LULA. And who did you think you were? Who do you think you are now?

CLAY [*Laughs as if to make light of the whole trend of the conversation*]. Well, in college I thought I was Baudelaire.° But I've slowed down since.

LULA. I bet you never once thought you were a black nigger. [*Mock serious, then she howls with laughter. CLAY is stunned but after initial reaction, he quickly tries to appreciate the humor. LULA almost shrieks.*] A black Baudelaire.

CLAY. That's right.

LULA. Boy, are you corny. I take back what I said before. Everything you say is not wrong. It's perfect. You should be on television.

CLAY. You act like you're on television already.

LULA. That's because I'm an actress.

CLAY. I thought so.

LULA. Well, you're wrong. I'm no actress. I told you I always lie. I'm nothing, honey, and don't you ever forget it. [*Lighter.*] Although my mother was a Communist. The only person in my family ever to amount to anything.

Averell Harriman distinguished statesman and public official, Democratic governor of New York, 1955–59
Baudelaire Charles Baudelaire (1821–67), French Symbolist poet and critic, author of *Flowers of Evil*

CLAY. My mother was a Republican.

LULA. And your father voted for the man rather than the party.

CLAY. Right!

LULA. Yea for him. Yea, yea for him.

CLAY. Yea!

LULA. And yea for America where he is free to vote for the mediocrity of his choice! Yea!

CLAY. Yea!

LULA. And yea for both your parents who even though they differ about so crucial a matter as the body politic still forged a union of love and sacrifice that was destined to flower at the birth of the noble Clay . . . what's your middle name?

CLAY. Clay.

LULA. A union of love and sacrifice that was destined to flower at the birth of the noble Clay Clay Williams. Yea! And most of all yea yea for you, Clay Clay. The Black Baudelaire! Yes! [*And with knifelike cynicism.*] My Christ. My Christ.

CLAY. Thank you, ma'am.

LULA. May the people accept you as a ghost of the future. And love you, that you might not kill them when you can.

CLAY. What?

LULA. You're a murderer, Clay, and you know it. [*Her voice darkening with significance.*] You know goddamn well what I mean.

CLAY. I do?

LULA. So we'll pretend the air is light and full of perfume.

CLAY [*Sniffing at her blouse*]. It is.

LULA. And we'll pretend the people cannot see you. That is, the citizens. And that you are free of your own history. And I am free of my history. We'll pretend that we are both anonymous beauties smashing along through the city's entrails. [*She yells as loud as she can.*] GROOVE!

Black

SCENE II

Scene is the same as before, though now there are other seats visible in the car. And throughout the scene other people get on the subway. There are maybe one or two seated in the car as the scene opens, though neither CLAY *nor* LULA *notices them.* CLAY's *tie is open.* LULA *is hugging his arm.*

CLAY. The party!

LULA. I know it'll be something good. You can come in with me, looking casual and significant. I'll be strange, haughty, and silent, and walk with long slow strides.

CLAY. Right.

LULA. When you get drunk, pat me once, very lovingly on the flanks, and I'll look at you cryptically, licking my lips.

CLAY. It sounds like something we can do.

LULA. You'll go around talking to young men about your mind, and to old men about your plans. If you meet a very close friend who is also with someone like me, we can stand together, sipping our drinks and exchanging codes of lust. The atmosphere will be slithering in love and half-love and very open moral decision.

CLAY. Great. Great.

LULA. And everyone will pretend they don't know your name, and then . . . [*she pauses heavily*] later, when they have to, they'll claim a friendship that denies your sterling character.

CLAY [*Kissing her neck and fingers*]. And then what?

LULA. Then? Well, then we'll go down the street, late night, eating apples and winding very deliberately toward my house.

CLAY. Deliberately?

LULA. I mean, we'll look in all the shop-windows, and make fun of the queers. Maybe we'll meet a Jewish Buddhist and flatten his conceits over some very pretentious coffee.

CLAY. In honor of whose God?

LULA. Mine.

CLAY. Who is . . . ?

LULA. Me . . . and you?

CLAY. A corporate Godhead.

LULA. Exactly. Exactly. [*Notices one of the other people entering.*]

CLAY. Go on with the chronicle. Then what happens to us?

LULA [*A mild depression, but she still makes her description triumphant and increasingly direct*]. To my house, of course.

CLAY. Of course.

LULA. And up the narrow steps of the tenement.

CLAY. You live in a tenement?

LULA. Wouldn't live anywhere else. Reminds me specifically of my novel form of insanity.

CLAY. Up the tenement stairs.

LULA. And with my apple-eating hand I push open the door and lead you, my tender big-eyed prey, into my . . . God, what can I call it . . . into my hovel.

CLAY. Then what happens?

LULA. After the dancing and games, after the long drinks and long walks, the real fun begins.

CLAY. Ah, the real fun. [*Embarrassed, in spite of himself.*] Which is . . . ?

LULA [*Laughs at him*]. Real fun in the dark house. Hah! Real fun in the dark house, high up above the street and the ignorant cowboys. I lead you in, holding your wet hand gently in my hand . . .

CLAY. Which is not wet?

LULA. Which is dry as ashes.

CLAY. And cold?

LULA. Don't think you'll get out of your responsibility that way. It's not cold at all. You Fascist! Into my dark living room. Where we'll sit and talk endlessly, endlessly.

CLAY. About what?

LULA. About what? About your manhood, what do you think? What do you think we've been talking about all this time?

CLAY. Well, I didn't know it was that. That's for sure. Every other thing in the world but that. [*Notices another person entering, looks quickly, almost involuntarily up and down the car, seeing the other people in the car.*] Hey, I didn't even notice when those people got on.

LULA. Yeah, I know.

CLAY. Man, this subway is slow.

LULA. Yeah, I know.

CLAY. Well, go on. We were talking about my manhood.

LULA. We still are. All the time.

CLAY. We were in your living room.

LULA. My dark living room. Talking endlessly.

CLAY. About my manhood.

5 LULA. I'll make you a map of it. Just as soon as we get to my house.

CLAY. Well, that's great.

LULA. One of the things we do while we talk. And screw.

10 CLAY [*Trying to make his smile broader and less shaky*]. We finally got there.

LULA. And you'll call my rooms black as a grave. You'll say, "This place is like Juliet's tomb."

15 CLAY [*Laughs*]. I might.

LULA. I know. You've probably said it before.

CLAY. And is that all? The whole grand tour?

20 LULA. Not all. You'll say to me very close to my face, many, many times, you'll say, even whisper, that you love me.

CLAY. Maybe I will.

LULA. And you'll be lying.

25 CLAY. I wouldn't lie about something like that.

LULA. Hah. It's the only kind of thing you will lie about. Especially if you think it'll keep me alive.

30 CLAY. Keep you alive? I don't understand.

LULA [*Bursting out laughing, but too shrilly*]. Don't understand? Well, don't look at me. It's the path I take, that's all. Where both feet take me when I set them down. One in front of the 35 other.

CLAY. Morbid. Morbid. You sure you're not an actress? All that self-aggrandizement.

LULA. Well, I told you I wasn't an actress . . . but I also told you I lie all the time. Draw your 40 own conclusions.

CLAY. Morbid. Morbid. You sure you're not an actress? All scribed? There's no more?

LULA. I've told you all I know. Or almost all.

CLAY. There's no funny parts?

45 LULA. I thought it was all funny.

CLAY. But you mean peculiar, not ha-ha.

LULA. You don't know what I mean.

CLAY. Well, tell me the almost part then. You said almost all. What else? I want the whole 50 story.

LULA [*Searching aimlessly through her bag. She begins to talk breathlessly, with a light and silly tone*]. All stories are whole stories. All of 'em. Our whole story . . . nothing but change. How could things go on like that forever? Huh? 55 [*Slaps him on the shoulder, begins finding things in her bag, taking them out and throwing them over her shoulder into the aisle.*] Except I do go on as I do. Apples and long walks with deathless intelligent lovers. But you mix it up. Look 60 out the window, all the time. Turning pages. Change change change. Till, shit, I don't know you. Wouldn't, for that matter. You're too serious. I bet you're even too serious to be psychoanalyzed. Like all those Jewish poets 65 from Yonkers, who leave their mothers looking for other mothers, or others' mothers, on whose baggy tits they lay their fumbling heads. Their poems are always funny, and all about sex. 70

CLAY. They sound great. Like movies.

LULA. But you change. [*Blankly.*] And things work on you till you hate them. [*More people come into the train. They come closer to the couple, some of them not sitting, but swinging 75 drearily on the straps, staring at the two with uncertain interest.*]

CLAY. Wow. All these people, so suddenly. They must all come from the same place.

LULA. Right. That they do. 80

CLAY. Oh? You know about them too?

LULA. Oh yeah. About them more than I know about you. Do they frighten you?

CLAY. Frighten me? Why should they frighten me? 85

LULA. 'Cause you're an escaped nigger.

CLAY. Yeah?

LULA. 'Cause you crawled through the wire and made tracks to my side.

CLAY. Wire? 90

LULA. Don't they have wire around plantations?

CLAY. You must be Jewish. All you can think about is wire. Plantations didn't have any wire. Plantations were big open whitewashed 95 places like heaven, and everybody on 'em was

grooved to be there. Just strummin' and hum-
min' all day.

LULA. Yes, yes.

CLAY. And that's how the blues was born.

5 LULA. Yes, yes. And that's how the blues
was born. [*Begins to make up a song that becomes quickly hysterical. As she sings she rises
from her seat, still throwing things out of her bag
into the aisle, beginning a rhythmical shudder and*
10 *twistlike wiggle, which she continues up and down
the aisle, bumping into many of the standing
people and tripping over the feet of those sitting.
Each time she runs into a person she lets out a
very vicious piece of profanity, wiggling and*
15 *stepping all the time.*] And that's how the blues
was born. Yes. Yes. Son of a bitch, get out of
the way. Yes. Quack. Yes. Yes. And that's how
the blues was born. Ten little niggers sitting
on a limb, but none of them ever looked like
20 him. [*Points to* CLAY, *returns toward the seat,
with her hands extended for him to rise and
dance with her.*] And that's how blues was
born. Yes. Come on, Clay. Let's do the nasty.
Rub bellies. Rub bellies.

25 CLAY [*Waves his hands to refuse. He is embarrassed, but determined to get a kick out of the
proceedings*]. Hey, what was in those apples?
Mirror, mirror on the wall, who's the fairest
one of all? Snow White, baby, and don't you
30 forget it.

LULA [*Grabbing for his hands, which he draws
away*]. Come on, Clay. Let's rub bellies on the
train. The nasty. The nasty. Do the gritty grind,
like your ol' rag-head mammy. Grind till you
35 lose your mind. Shake it, shake it, shake it,
shake it! OOOOweeee! Come on, Clay. Let's
do the choo-choo train shuffle, the navel
scratcher.

CLAY. Hey, you coming on like the lady who
40 smoked up her grass skirt.

LULA [*Becoming annoyed that he will not
dance, and becoming more animated as if to embarrass him still further*]. Come on, Clay . . .
let's do the thing. Uhh! Uhh! Clay! Clay! You
45 middle-class black bastard. Forget your social-
working mother for a few seconds and let's
knock stomachs. Clay, you liver-lipped white
man. You would-be Christian. You ain't no

nigger, you're just a dirty white man. Get up,
Clay. Dance with me, Clay. 50

CLAY. Lula! Sit down, now. Be cool.

LULA [*Mocking him, in wild dance*]. Be cool.
Be cool. That's all you know . . . shaking that
wildroot cream-oil on your knotty head, jackets
buttoning up to your chin, so full of white 55
man's words. Christ. God. Get up and scream
at these people. Like scream meaningless shit
in these hopeless faces. [*She screams at people
in train, still dancing.*] Red trains cough Jewish
underwear for keeps! Expanding smells of 60
silence. Gravy snot whistling like sea birds.

CLAY. Clay, you got to break out. Don't sit
there dying the way they want you to die.
Get up.

CLAY. Oh, sit the fuck down. [*He moves to 65
restrain her.*] Sit down, goddamn it.

LULA [*Twisting out of his reach*]. Screw
yourself, Uncle Tom. Thomas Woolly-Head.
[*Begins to dance a kind of jig, mocking* CLAY *with
loud forced humor.*] There is Uncle Tom . . . I 70
mean, Uncle Thomas Woolly-Head. With old
white matted mane. He hobbles on his wooden
cane. Old Tom. Old Tom. Let the white man
hump his ol' mama, and he jes' shuffle off in
the woods and hide his gentle gray head. 75
Ol' Thomas Woolly-Head. [*Some of the other
riders are laughing now. A drunk gets up and
joins* LULA *in her dance, singing, as best he can,
her "song." * CLAY *gets up out of his seat and
visibly scans the faces of the other riders.*] 80

CLAY. Lula! Lula! [*She is dancing and turning,
still shouting as loud as she can. The drunk too
is shouting, and waving his hands wildly.*]
Lula . . . you dumb bitch. Why don't you stop
it? [*He rushes half stumbling from his seat, and 85
grabs one of her flailing arms.*]

LULA. Let me go! You black son of a bitch.
[*She struggles against him.*] Let me go! Help!
[CLAY *is dragging her towards her seat, and the
drunk seeks to interfere. He grabs* CLAY *around 90
the shoulders and begins wrestling with him.*
CLAY *clubs the drunk to the floor without releasing* LULA, *who is still screaming.* CLAY *finally gets
her to the seat and throws her into it.*]

CLAY. Now you shut the hell up. [*Grabbing 95
her shoulders.*] Just shut up. You don't know

what you're talking about. You don't know anything. So just keep your stupid mouth closed.

LULA. You're afraid of white people. And your father was. Uncle Tom Big Lip!

CLAY [*Slaps her as hard as he can, across the mouth. LULA's head bangs against the back of the seat. When she raises it again, CLAY slaps her again*]. Now shut up and let me talk. [*He turns toward the other riders, some of whom are sitting on the edge of their seats. The drunk is on one knee, rubbing his head, and singing softly the same song. He shuts up too when he sees CLAY watching him. The others go back to newspapers or stare out the windows.*] Shit, you don't have any sense, Lula, nor feelings either. I could murder you now. Such a tiny ugly throat. I could squeeze it flat, and watch you turn blue, on a humble. For dull kicks. And all these weak-faced ofays° squatting around here, staring over their papers at me. Murder them too. Even if they expected it. That man there . . . [*Points to well-dressed man.*] I could rip that *Times* right out of his hand, as skinny and middle-classed as I am, I could rip that paper out of his hand and just as easily rip out his throat. It takes no great effort. For what? To kill you soft idiots? You don't understand anything but luxury.

LULA. You fool!

CLAY [*Pushing her against the seat*]. I'm not telling you again, Tallulah Bankhead!° Luxury. In your face and your fingers. You telling me what I ought to do. [*Sudden scream frightening the whole coach.*] Well, don't! Don't you tell me anything! If I'm a middle-class fake white man . . . let me be. And let me be in the way I want. [*Through his teeth.*] I'll rip your lousy breasts off! Let me be who I feel like being. Uncle Tom. Thomas. Whoever. It's none of your business. You don't know anything except what's there for you to see. An act. Lies. Device. Not the pure heart, the pumping black heart. You don't ever know that. And I sit here, in this buttoned-up suit, to keep myself from cutting all your throats. I mean wantonly. You great liberated whore! You fuck some black man, and right away you're an expert on black people. What a lotta shit that is. The only thing you know is that you come if he bangs you hard enough. And that's all. The belly rub? You wanted to do the belly rub? Shit, you don't even know how. You don't know how. That ol' dipty-dip shit you do, rolling your ass like an elephant. That's not my kind of belly rub. Belly rub is not Queens.° Belly rub is dark places, with big hats and overcoats held up with one arm. Belly rub hates you. Old bald-headed four-eyed ofays popping their fingers . . . and don't know yet what they're doing. They say, "I love Bessie Smith."° And don't even understand that Bessie Smith is saying, "Kiss my ass, kiss my black unruly ass." Before love, suffering, desire, anything you can explain, she's saying, and very plainly, "Kiss my black ass." And if you don't know that, it's you that's doing the kissing.

Charlie Parker?° Charlie Parker. All the hip white boys scream for Bird. And Bird saying, "Up your ass, feebleminded ofay! Up your ass." And they sit there talking about the tortured genius of Charlie Parker. Bird would've played not a note of music if he just walked up to East Sixty-seventh Street and killed the first ten white people he saw. Not a note! And I'm the great would-be poet. Yes. That's right! Poet. Some kind of bastard literature . . . all it needs is a simple knife thrust. Just let me bleed you, you loud whore, and one poem vanished. A whole people of neurotics, struggling to keep from being sane. And the only thing that would cure the neurosis would be your murder. Simple as that. I mean if I murdered you, then other white people would begin to understand me. You understand? No.

ofays whites (perhaps from "foes" in pig-Latin)
Tallulah Bankhead (1903–68) beautiful, brilliant and uninhibited white actress
Queens a borough of New York, used here to suggest dullness, staidness, middle-class whiteness
Bessie Smith (1898?–1937) "Empress of the Blues"
Charlie Parker "Yardbird" Parker (1920–55), black jazz composer and alto saxophone virtuoso, one of the founders of the bop style

928

IMAMU AMIRI BARAKA | Scene II

I guess not. If Bessie Smith had killed some white people she wouldn't have needed that music. She could have talked very straight and plain about the world. No metaphors. No grunts. No wiggles in the dark of her soul. Just straight two and two are four. Money. Power. Luxury. Like that. All of them. Crazy niggers turning their backs on sanity. When all it needs is that simple act. Murder. Just murder! Would make us all sane. [*Suddenly weary.*] Ahhh. Shit. But who needs it? I'd rather be a fool. Insane. Safe with my words, and no deaths, and clean, hard thoughts, urging me to new conquests. My people's madness. Hah! That's a laugh. My people. They don't need me to claim them. They got legs and arms of their own. Personal insanities. Mirrors. They don't need all those words. They don't need any defense. But listen, though, one more thing. And you tell this to your father, who's probably the kind of man who needs to know at once. So he can plan ahead. Tell him not to preach so much rationalism and cold logic to these niggers. Let them alone. Let them sing curses at you in code and see your filth as simple lack of style. Don't make the mistake, through some irresponsible surge of Christian charity, of talking too much about the advantages of Western rationalism, or the great intellectual legacy of the white man, or maybe they'll begin to listen. And then, maybe one day, you'll find they actually do understand exactly what you are talking about, all these fantasy people. All these blues people. And on that day, as sure as shit, when you really believe you can "accept" them into your fold, as half-white trusties late of the subject peoples. With no more blues, except the very old ones, and not a watermelon in sight, the great missionary heart will have triumphed, and all of those ex-coons will be stand-up Western men, with eyes for clean hard useful lives, sober, pious and sane, and they'll murder you. They'll murder you, and have very rational explanations. Very much like your own. They'll cut your throats, and drag you out to the edge of your cities so the flesh can fall away from your bones, in sanitary isolation.

LULA [*Her voice takes on a different, more businesslike quality*]. I've heard enough.

CLAY [*Reaching for his books*]. I bet you have. I guess I better collect my stuff and get off this train. Looks like we won't be acting out that little pageant you outlined before.

LULA. No. We won't. You're right about that, at least. [*She turns to look quickly around the rest of the car.*] All right! [*The others respond.*]

CLAY [*Bending across the girl to retrieve his belongings*]. Sorry, baby, I don't think we could make it. [*As he is bending over her, the girl brings up a small knife and plunges it into* CLAY's *chest. Twice. He slumps across her knees, his mouth working stupidly.*]

LULA. Sorry is right. [*Turning to the others in the car who have already gotten up from their seats.*] Sorry is the rightest thing you've said. Get this man off me! Hurry, now! [*The others come and drag* CLAY's *body down the aisle.*] Open the door and throw his body out. [*They throw him off.*] And all of you get off at the next stop. [LULA *busies herself straightening her things. Getting everything in order. She takes out a notebook and makes a quick scribbling note. Drops it in her bag. The train apparently stops and all the others get off, leaving her alone in the coach.*

Very soon a young Negro of about twenty comes into the coach, with a couple of books under his arm. He sits a few seats in back of LULA. *When he is seated she turns and gives him a long slow look. He looks up from his book and drops the book on his lap. Then an old Negro conductor comes into the car, doing a sort of restrained soft shoe, and half mumbling the words of some song. He looks at the young man, briefly, with a quick greeting.*]

CONDUCTOR. Hey, brother!

YOUNG MAN. Hey. [*The conductor continues down the aisle with his little dance and the mumbled song.* LULA *turns to stare at him and follows his movements down the aisle. The conductor tips his hat when he reaches her seat, and continues out the car.*]

Curtain

Athol Fugard

1932

John Kani
Winston Ntshona

Sizwe Bansi Is Dead

1972

The ascription of authorship for *Sizwe Bansi Is Dead* deserves comment. It means that Fugard, who is primarily a playwright rather than an actor, presents this work as a collaboration with Kani and Ntshona, who are primarily actors, members of the Serpent Players, a South African theater company with which Fugard was also associated. Furthermore, it stresses the equality of cooperation between Fugard, a white South African, and the two black South Africans. Defying the spirit of official *apartheid,* this fact underscores the significance of this particular play as affirming humane values that are insulted by ethnic and political separatism.

In the collaboration that produced this play, Fugard saw himself as "a scribe," a modest term indicating that he participated less as author than as recorder, drawing from the actors their responses in word and deed to thematic situations and emotions that were by no means remote from the actors' personal experiences. Although the details of the play sprang from a great deal of initial improvisation, "the final dramatic structure," Fugard says, "was [my] responsibility."

In the history of the drama it is not unusual for a playwright to be guided and sustained by the influence of gifted actors and actresses. Shaw, for example, created some characters, in part, to reflect the individuality of Mrs. Patrick Campbell or, in the case of *Saint Joan,* of Sybil Thorndike. They lent something of their own personalities to Shaw's conception of characters whom the actresses in turn portrayed. Similarly, the remarkably subtle ensemble acting style developed at the Moscow Art Theatre enabled Chekhov to experiment with presenting intricately balanced groups of characters whose interactions could be properly projected only through skilled ensemble playing.

The editors regret being unable to provide birthdates for Mr. Kani and Winston Ntshona.

Fugard's connection with the Serpent Players and with the Space Theatre of Cape Town comparably influenced his development. In later plays, such as *A Lesson from Aloes* and *"Master Harold" . . . and the boys,* he has resumed the more independent role of dramatist but has not forgotten what a cohesive company of performers can contribute to the shaping of characters and situations that have not been immutably inscribed in a fixed text. In this regard he is rather unlike Samuel Beckett, to whom he has sometimes been compared, since Beckett appears to adhere to the principle of an unalterable text and, perhaps, to the ideal of a definitive production.

Sizwe Bansi Is Dead was conceived as an "experiment"—Fugard's word—which involves the readiness to risk failure and disappointment in order to explore unusual modes of dramatic realization. Readiness to experiment is, indeed, an identifying trait of modern dramatists, and it affects choice of subject, methods of acting, and stagecraft in all of its variety. One result of widespread experimentation has been to emphasize that a dramatic text is not an end in itself, as the literary study of classic texts might seem to imply, but essentially demands fulfillment in production and performance. The process of working a script up into an actual presentation is integral to drama—which explains why no individual production, no matter how complete, realizes all the potentialities of a script.

One of the experimental aspects of *Sizwe Bansi Is Dead* is the relative absence of realistic staging in a play that nonetheless presents many realistic details of daily life. Some modern plays require a high degree of visual realism, with respect to setting, costume, and lighting—as does *Hedda Gabler,* for example. Fugard displaces attention away from surface realism, however, by effects specifically theatrical—by the use of blackouts, by sudden switches of place and time, by minimal use of scenery and furnishings. The result is that acting itself is highlighted by gesture and vocalization, by mimicry. Individual bits of experience are italicized by setting the play in a photographic studio, where significant moments are captured—disjointedly, vividly.

The subject of this play can be and of course has been conveyed nondramatically, as in news reports, biographical narratives, and documentary films. But Fugard's play does more than transmit a message, and it is not just a technical experiment. The collaboration between playwright and actors on a basis of artistic and social equality, and the use of improvisation to generate energy and insight, result in a play that is itself an example of life metamorphosing toward freedom. Form and substance are fused. Aristotle calls drama "the imitation of an action." In this play the action itself is an imitation of action—that is, of the act of acting out, of inventing characters and situations. The actors and the characters they portray are improvising the shape of their lives. Kani, who is also "Styles" and "Buntu," benevolently runs through a series of roles that assist Ntshona, who is also "Sizwe" and becomes "Zwelinzima," to find a new plane of existence. For Sizwe this change of identity combined with the loss or concealment of his name threatens to uncreate him—which would indeed be a deadly danger if the self consists of nothing but masks and roles. In the end he discovers that playacting is not an end but a means, and he finds the courage to let "Sizwe Bansi" appear to "die," so that the living man can affirmatively carry on his life.

Sizwe Bansi Is Dead

FUGARD, KANI, NTSHONA

CHARACTERS

STYLES
SIZWE BANSI
BUNTU

Styles's Photographic Studio in the African town-ship° of New Brighton, Port Elizabeth. Positioned prominently, the name-board:

> *Styles Photographic Studio. Reference Books; Passports; Weddings; Engagements; Birthday Parties and Parties. Prop.—Styles.*

Underneath this a display of photographs of various sizes. Centre stage, a table and chair. This is obviously used for photographs because a camera on a tripod stands ready a short distance away.

There is also another table, or desk, with odds and ends of photographic equipment and an assortment of 'props' for photographs.

The setting for this and subsequent scenes should be as simple as possible so that the action can be continuous.

STYLES *walks on with a newspaper. A dapper, alert young man wearing a white dustcoat and bowtie. He sits down at the table and starts to read the paper.*

STYLES [*reading the headlines*]. 'Storm buffets Na-

township segregated black area

Sizwe Bansi Is Dead by Athol Fugard, John Kani, and Winston Ntshona, Copyright © 1973, 1974 by Athol Fugard, John Kani, and Winston Ntshona. Reprinted by permission of Viking Penguin, Inc.
    Special thanks to R. Neville Choonoo for assistance with the annotations.

tal. Damage in many areas . . . trees snapped like . . . what? . . . matchsticks. . . .' [*He laughs.*] They're having it, boy! And I'm watching it . . . in the paper.   5

[*Turning the page, another headline.*]
'China: A question-mark on South West Africa.' What's China want there? *Yo!* They better be careful. China gets in there. . . ! [*Laugh.*] I'll tell you what happens. . . .   10

[*Stops abruptly. Looks around as if someone might be eavesdropping on his intimacy with the audience.*] No comment.

[*Back to his paper.*]
What's this? . . . *Ag!* American politics. Nixon and all his votes. Means buggerall° to us.   15

[*Another page, another headline.*]
'Car plant expansion. 1.5 million rand plan.' *Ja.* I'll tell you what *that* means . . . more machines, bigger buildings . . . never any expansion to the pay-packet. Makes me fed-up. I know what I'm talking   20 about. I worked at Ford one time. We used to read in the newspaper . . . big headlines! . . . 'So and so from America or London made a big speech: ". . . going to see to it that the conditions of their   25 non-white workers in Southern Africa were substantially improved." ' The talk ended in the bloody newspaper. Never in the pay-packet.
Another time we read: Mr Henry Ford Junior Number two or whatever the hell he is . . . is vis-   30 iting the Ford Factories in South Africa!

[*Shakes his head ruefully at the memory.*]
Big news for us, man! When a big man like that visited the plant there was usually a few cents more in the pay-packet at the end of the week.   35 *Ja,* a Thursday morning. I walked into the plant . . . 'Hey! What's this?' . . . Everything was quiet! Those big bloody machines that used to make so much noise made my head go around. . . ? Silent! Went to the notice-board and read: Mr Ford's visit   40 today!
The one in charge of us . . . [*laugh*] hey! I remember him. General Foreman Mr 'Baas' Bradley. Good man that one, if you knew how to handle him . . . he called us all together.   45

[*STYLES mimics Mr 'Baas' Bradley. A heavy Afrikaans accent.*]

buggerall not a damn thing

'Listen, boys, don't go to work on the line. There is going to be a General Cleaning first.'

I used to like General Cleaning. Nothing specific, you know, little bit here, little bit there. But that
5   day! Yessus . . . in came the big machines with hot water and brushes—sort of electric mop—and God alone knows what else. We started on the floors. The oil and dirt under the machines was thick, man. All the time the bosses were walking
10 around watching us:

   [*Slapping his hands together as he urges on the 'boys'.*]
'Come on, boys! It's got to be spotless! Big day for the plant!' Even the *big* boss, the one we only used to see lunch-times, walking to the canteen with a
15 big cigar in his mouth and his hands in his pocket . . . that day? Sleeves rolled up, running around us:

   Come on! Spotless, my boys! Over there, John. . . .
I thought: What the hell is happening? It was be-
20 ginning to feel like hard work, man. I'm telling you we cleaned that place—spot-checked after fifteen minutes! . . . like you would have thought it had just been built.

First stage of General Cleaning finished. We started
25 on the second. Mr 'Baas' Bradley came in with paint and brushes. I watched.
W—h—i—t—e l—i—n—e

   [*Mr 'Baas' Bradley paints a long white line on the floor.*]
30 What's this? Been here five years and I never seen a white line before. Then:

   [*Mr 'Baas' Bradley at work with the paint-brush.*]
CAREFUL THIS SIDE. TOW MOTOR IN MOTION.
35   [STYLES *laughs.*]
It was nice, man. Safety-precautions after six years. Then another gallon of paint.
Y—e—l—l—o—w l—i—n—e
NO SMOKING IN THIS AREA. DANGER!
40 Then another gallon:
G—r—e—e—n l—i—n—e
I noticed that that line cut off the roughcasting section, where we worked with the rough engine blocks as we got them from Iscor. Dangerous world
45 that. Bit machines! One mistake there and you're in trouble. I watched them and thought: What's going to happen here? When the green line was finished, down they went on the floor—Mr 'Baas'

Bradley, the lot!—with a big green board, a little brush, and a tin of white paint.   50
EYE PROTECTION AREA. Then my big moment:
'Styles!'
'Yes, sir!'
[*Mr 'Baas' Bradley's heavy Afrikaans accent*] 'What do you say in your language for this? Eye Protection   55
Area.'
It was easy, man!
'*Gqokra Izi Khuselo Zamehlo Kule Ndawo.*'°
Nobody wrote it!
'Don't bloody fool me, Styles!'   60
'No, sir!'
'Then spell it . . . slowly.'
   [STYLES *has a big laugh.*]
Hey! That was my moment, man. Kneeling there on the floor . . . foreman, general foreman, plant   65
supervisor, plant manager . . . and Styles? Standing!

   [*Folds his arms as he acts out his part to the imaginary figures crouched on the floor.*]
'G—q—o—k—r—a' . . . and on I went, with Mr   70
'Baas' Bradley painting and saying as he wiped away the sweat:
'You're not fooling me, hey!'
After that the green board went up. We all stood and admired it. Plant was looking nice, man! Col-   75
ourful!
Into the third phase of General Cleaning.
'Styles!'
'Yes, sir!'
'Tell all the boys they must now go to the bath-   80
room and wash themselves clean.'
We needed it! Into the bathroom, under the showers . . . hot water, soap . . . on a Thursday! Before ten! Yo! What's happening in the plant? The other chaps asked me: What's going on, Styles? I told   85
them: 'Big-shot cunt from America coming to visit you.' When we finished washing they gave us towels . . . [*laugh*].
Three hundred of us, man! We were so clean we felt shy! Stand there like little ladies in front of the   90
mirror. From there to the General Store.
Handed in my dirty overall.
'Throw it on the floor.'

Gqokra . . . Ndawo put on safety glasses here (Fugard's note)

'Yes, sir!'
New overall comes, wrapped in plastic. Brand new,
man! I normally take a thirty-eight but this one
was a forty-two. Then next door to the tool room
5 . . . brand new tool bag, set of spanners, shifting
spanner, torque wrench—all of them brand new—
and because I worked in the dangerous hot test
section I was also given a new asbestos apron and
fire-proof gloves to replace the ones I had lost about
10 a year ago. I'm telling you I walked back heavy to
my spot. Armstrong° on the moon! Inside the plant
it was general meeting again. General Foreman Mr
'Baas' Bradley called me.
'Styles!'
15 'Yes, sir.'
'Come translate.'
'Yes, sir!'
        [STYLES *pulls out a chair. Mr. 'Baas' Bradley speaks
        on one side, Styles translates on the other.*]
20 'Tell the boys in your language, that this is a very
big day in their lives.'
'Gentlemen, this old fool says this is a hell of a
big day in our lives.'
The men laughed.
25 'They are very happy to hear that, sir.'
'Tell the boys that Mr Henry Ford the Second, the
owner of this place, is going to visit us. Tell them
Mr Ford is the big Baas. He owns the plant and
everything in it.'
30 'Gentlemen, old Bradley says this Ford is a big
bastard. He owns everything in this building, which
means you as well.'
A voice came out of the crowd:
'Is he a bigger fool than Bradley?'
35 'They're asking, sir, is he bigger than you?'
'Certainly . . . [*blustering*] . . . certainly. He is a very
big baas. He's a . . . [*groping for words*] . . . he's a
Makulu° Baas.'
I loved that one!
40 'Mr "Baas" Bradley says most certainly Mr Ford
is bigger than him. In fact Mr Ford is the grandmother baas of them all . . . that's what he said to
me.'
'Styles, tell the boys that when Mr Henry Ford

comes into the plant I want them all to look happy. 45
We will slow down the speed of the line so that
they can sing and smile while they are working.'
'Gentlemen, he says that when the door opens
and his grandmother walks in you must see to it
that you are wearing a mask of smiles. Hide your 50
true feelings, brothers. You must sing. The joyous
songs of the days of old before we had fools like
this one next to me to worry about.' [*To Bradley.*]
'Yes, sir!'
'Say to them, Styles, that they must try to impress 55
Mr Henry Ford that they are better than those
monkeys in his own country, those niggers in
Harlem who know nothing but strike, strike.'
Yo! I liked that one too.
'Gentlemen, he says we must remember, when 60
Mr Ford walks in, that we are South African mon-
keys, not American monkeys. South African mon-
keys are much better trained. . . .''
Before I could even finish, a voice was shouting
out of the crowd: 65
'He's talking shit!' I had to be careful!
        [*Servile and full of smiles as he turns back to Brad-
        ley.*]
'No, sir! The men say they are much too happy to
behave like those American monkeys.' 70
Right! Line was switched on nice and slow—and
we started working.
        [*At work on the Assembly Line; singing.*]
'Tshotsholoza . . . Tshotsholoza . . . kulezondawo. . . .'° 75
We had all the time in the world, man! . . . torque
wrench out . . . tighten the cylinder-head nut . . .
wait for the next one. . . . [*Singing*] 'Vyabaleka . . .
vyabaleka . . . kulezondawo. . . .' I kept my eye on
the front office. I could see them—Mr 'Baas' Brad- 80
ley, the line supervisor—through the big glass
window, brushing their hair, straightening the tie.
There was some General Cleaning going on there
too.
        [*He laughs.*] 85
We were watching them. Nobody was watching
us. Even the old Security Guard. The one who
every time he saw a black man walk past with his

Armstrong Neil Armstrong, first man on the moon, July 20,
  1969, wore a bulky space suit.
Makulu grandmother (Fugard's note)

Tshotsholoza . . . kulezondawo opening phrase of an African work-chant; literally, work steady, the train is coming
  (Fugard's note)

hands in his pockets he saw another spark-plug
walk out of the plant. Today? To hell and gone
there on the other side polishing his black shoes.
Then, through the window, I saw three long black
5 Galaxies zoom up. I passed the word down the
line: He's come!
Let me tell you what happened. The big doors
opened; next thing the General Superintendent,
Line Supervisor, General Foreman, Manager,
10 Senior Manager, Managing Director . . . the bloody
lot were there . . . like a pack of puppies!
[*Mimics a lot of fawning men retreating before an
important person.*]
I looked and laughed! 'Yessus, Styles, they're all
15 playing your part today!' They ran, man! In came
a tall man, six foot six, hefty, full of respect and
dignity . . . I marvelled at him! Let me show you
what he did.
[*Three enormous strides*] One . . . two . . . three. . . .
20 [*Cursory look around as he turns and takes the same
three strides back.*]
One . . . two . . . three . . . OUT! Into the Galaxie
and gone! That's all. Didn't talk to me. Mr 'Baas'
Bradley, Line Supervisor, or anybody. He didn't
25 even look at the plant! And what did I see when
those three Galaxies disappeared? The white staff
at the main switchboard.
'Double speed on the line! Make up for production
lost!'
30 It ended up with us working harder that bloody
day than ever before. Just because that big. . . .
[*shakes his head.*] Six years there. Six years a bloody
fool.
[*Back to his newspaper. A few more headlines with
35 appropriate comment, then. . . .*]
[*Reading*] 'The Mass Murderer! Doom!'
[*Smile of recognition.*]
'For fleas . . . Doom. Flies . . . Doom. Bedbugs . . .
Doom. For cockroaches and other household pests.
40 The household insecticide . . . Doom.' Useful stuff.
Remember, Styles? *Ja.*
[*To the audience.*] After all that time at Ford I sat
down one day. I said to myself:
'Styles, you're a bloody monkey, boy!'
45 'What do you mean?'
'You're a monkey, man.'
'Go to hell!'
'Come on, Styles, you're a monkey, man, and you
know it. Run up and down the whole bloody day!'

Your life doesn't belong to you. You've sold it. 50
For what, Styles? Gold wrist-watch in twenty-five
years time when they sign you off because you're
too old for anything any more?'
I was right. I took a good look at my life. What
did I see? A bloody circus monkey! Selling most 55
of his time on this earth to another man. Out of
every twenty-four hours I could only properly call
mine the six when I was sleeping. What the hell
is the use of that?
Think about it, friend. Wake up in the morning, 60
half-past six, out of the pyjamas and into the bathtub, put on your shirt with one hand, socks with
the other, realize you got your shoes on the wrong
bloody feet, and all the time the seconds are passing and if you don't hurry up you'll miss the 65
bus. . . . 'Get the lunch, dear. I'm late. My lunch,
please, darling!' . . . then the children come in . . .
'Daddy, can I have this? Daddy, I want money for
that.' 'Go to your mother. I haven't got time. Look
after the children, please, sweetheart!!' . . . grab 70
your lunch . . . 'Bye Bye!!' and then run like I-
don't-know-what for the bus stop. You call that
living? I went back to myself for another chat:
'Suppose you're right. What then?'
'Try something else.' 75
'Like what?'
Silly question to ask. I knew what I was going to
say. Photographer! It was my hobby in those days.
I used to pick up a few cents on the side taking
cards at parties, weddings, big occasions. But when 80
it came to telling my wife and parents that I wanted
to turn professional. . . !!
My father was the worst.
'You call that work? Click-click with a camera. Are
you mad?' I tried to explain. 'Daddy, if I could 85
stand on my own two feet and not be somebody
else's tool, I'd have some respect for myself. I'd
be a man.'
'What do you mean? Aren't you one already?
You're circumcised, you've got a wife. . . .' 90
Talk about the generation gap!
Anyway I thought: To hell with them. I'm trying
it.
It was the Christmas shutdown, so I had lots of
time to look around for a studio. My friend 95
Dhlamini at the Funeral Parlour told me about a
vacant room next door. He encouraged me. I remember his words. 'Grab your chance, Styles. Grab

it before somebody in my line puts you in a box and closes the lid.' I applied for permission to use the room as a studio. After some time the first letter back:

'Your application has been received and is being considered.' A month later: 'The matter is receiving the serious consideration of the Board.' Another month: 'Your application is now on the director's table.' I nearly gave up, friends. But one day, a knock at the door—the postman—I had to sign for a registered letter. 'We are pleased to inform you. . . .'

[STYLES *has a good laugh.*]

I ran all the way to the Administration Offices, grabbed the key, ran all the way back to Red Location, unlocked the door, and walked in!

What I found sobered me up a little bit. Window panes were all broken; big hole in the roof, cobwebs in the corners. I didn't let that put me off though. Said to myself: 'This is your chance, Styles. Grab it.' Some kids helped me clean it out. The dust! *Yo!* When the broom walked in the Sahara Desert walked out! But at the end of that day it was reasonably clean. I stood here in the middle of the floor, straight! You know what that means? To stand straight in a place of your own? To be your own . . . General Foreman, Mr 'Baas,' Line Supervisor—the lot! I was tall, six foot six and doing my own inspection of the plant.

So I'm standing there—here—feeling big and what do I see on the walls? Cockroaches. *Ja,* cockroaches . . . in *my* place. I don't mean those little things that run all over the place when you pull out the kitchen drawer. I'm talking about the big bastards, the paratroopers as we call them. I didn't like them. I'm not afraid of them but I just don't like them! All over. On the floors, the walls. I heard the one on the wall say: 'What's going on? Who opened the door?' The one on the floor answered: 'Relax. He won't last. This place is condemned.' That's when I thought: Doom.

Out of here and into the Chinaman's shop. 'Good day, sir. I've got a problem. Cockroaches.'

The Chinaman didn't even think, man, he just said: 'Doom!' I said: 'Certainly.' He said: 'Doom, seventy-five cents a tin.' Paid him for two and went back. *Yo!* You should have seen me! Two-tin Charlie!

[*His two tins at the ready, forefingers on the press-buttons,* STYLES *gives us a graphic reenactment of what happened. There is a brief respite to 'reload'—shake the tins—and tie a handkerchief around his nose, after which he returns to the fight.* STYLES *eventually backs through the imaginary door, still firing, and closes it. Spins the tins and puts them into their holsters.*]

I went home to sleep. *I* went to sleep. Not them [*the cockroaches*]. What do you think happened here? General meeting under the floorboards. All the bloody survivors. The old professor addressed them: 'Brothers, we face a problem of serious pollution . . . contamination! The menace appears to be called Doom. I have recommended a general inoculation of the whole community. Everybody in line, please. [*Inoculation proceeds.*] Next . . . next . . . next. . . .' While poor old Styles is smiling in his sleep! Next morning I walked in. . . . [*He stops abruptly.*] . . . What's this? Cockroach walking on the floor? Another one on the ceiling? Not a damn! Doom did it yesterday. Doom does it today. [*Whips out the two tins and goes in fighting. This time, however, it is not long before they peter out.*] Pssssssssss . . . psssssss . . . pssss . . . pss [*a last desperate shake, but he barely manages to get out a squirt*].

Pss.

No bloody good! The old bastard on the floor just waved his feelers in the air as if he was enjoying air-conditioning.

I went next door to Dhlamini and told him about my problem. He laughed. 'Doom? You're wasting your time, Styles. You want to solve your problem, get a cat. What do you think a cat lives on in the township? Milk? If there's any the baby gets it. Meat? When the family sees it only once a week? Mice? The little boys got rid of them years ago. Insects, man, township cats are insect-eaters. Here. . . .'

He gave me a little cat. I'm . . . I'm not too fond of cats normally. This one was called Blackie . . . I wasn't too fond of that name either. But . . . Kitsy! Kitsy! Kitsy . . . little Blackie followed me back to the studio.

The next morning when I walked in what do you think I saw? Wings. I smiled. Because one thing I do know is that no cockroach can take his wings off. He's dead!

[*Proud gesture taking in the whole of his studio.*]

So here it is!

[*To his name-board.*]

'Styles Photographic Studio. Reference Books; Passports; Weddings; Engagements; Birthday Parties and Parties. Proprietor: Styles.'

When you look at this, what do you see? Just an-
5 other photographic studio? Where people come because they've lost their Reference Book and need a photo for the new one? That I sit them down, set up the camera . . . 'No expression, please.' . . . click-click . . . 'Come back tomorrow, please' . . .
10 and then kick them out and wait for the next? No, friend. It's more than just that. This is a strong-room of dreams. The dreamers? My people. The simple people, who you never find mentioned in the history books, who never get statues erected
15 to them, or monuments commemorating their great deeds. People who would be forgotten, and their dreams with them, if it wasn't for Styles. That's what I do, friends. Put down, in my way, on paper the dreams and hopes of my people so that
20 even their children's children will remember a man . . . 'This was our Grandfather' . . . and say his name. Walk into the houses of New Brighton and on the walls you'll find hanging the story of the people the writers of the big books forgot about.
25 [To his display-board.]

This one [a photograph] walked in here one morning. I was just passing the time. Midweek. Business is always slow then. Anyway, a knock at the door. Yes! I must explain something. I get two
30 types of knock here. When I hear . . . [knocks solemnly on the table] . . . I don't even look up, man. 'Funeral parlour is next door.' But when I hear . . . [energetic rap on the table . . . he laughs] . . . that's my sound, and I shout 'Come in!'
35 In walked a chap, full of smiles, little parcel under his arm. I can still see him, man!

[STYLES acts both roles.]

'Mr Styles?'

I said: 'Come in!'
40 'Mr Styles, I've come to take a snap, Mr Styles.'

I said: 'Sit down! Sit down, my friend!'

'No, Mr Styles. I want to take the snap standing. [Barely containing his suppressed excitement and happiness] Mr Styles, take the card, please!'
45 I said: 'Certainly, friend.'

Something you mustn't do is interfere with a man's dream. If he wants to do it standing, let him stand. If he wants to sit, let him sit. Do exactly what they want! Sometimes they come in here, all smart in a suit, then off comes the jacket and shoes and
50 socks . . . [adopts a boxer's stance] . . . 'Take it, Mr Styles. Take it!' And I take it. No questions! Start asking stupid questions and you destroy that dream. Anyway, this chap I'm telling you about . . . [laughing warmly as he remembers] . . . I've seen
55 a lot of smiles in my business, friends, but that one gets first prize. I set up my camera, and just as I was ready to go . . . 'Wait, wait, Mr Styles! I want you to take the card with this.' Out of his parcel came a long piece of white paper . . . looked
60 like some sort of document . . . he held it in front of him. [STYLES demonstrates.] For once I didn't have to say, 'Smile!' Just: 'Hold it!' . . . and, click, . . . finished. I asked him what the document was.

'You see, Mr Styles, I'm forty-eight years old. I
65 work twenty-two years for the municipality and the foreman kept on saying to me if I want promotion to Boss-boy I must try to better my education. I didn't write well, Mr Styles. So I took a course with the Damelin Correspondence College.
70 Seven years, Mr Styles! And at last I made it. Here it is. Standard Six Certificate, School Leaving, Third Class! I made it, Mr Styles. I made it. But I'm not finished. I'm going to take up for the Junior Certificate, then Matric . . . and you watch, Mr Styles.
75 One day I walk out of my house, graduate, self-made! Bye-bye, Mr Styles,' . . . and he walked out of here happy man, self-made.

[Back to his display-board; another photograph.]

My best. Family Card. You know the Family Card?
80 Good for business. Lot of people and they all want copies.

One Saturday morning. Suddenly a hell of a noise outside in the street. I thought: What's going on now? Next thing that door burst open and in they
85 came! First the little ones, then the five- and six-year-olds. . . . I didn't know what was going on, man! Stupid children, coming to mess up my place. I was still trying to chase them out when the bigger boys and girls came through the door. Then
90 it clicked. Family Card!

[Changing his manner abruptly.]

'Come in! Come in!'

[Ushering a crowd of people into his studio.]

. . . now the young men and women were coming
95 in, then the mothers and fathers, uncles and aun-

ties . . . the eldest son, a mature man, and finally. . .

[*Shaking his head with admiration at the memory.*]
the Old Man, the Grandfather! [*The 'old man' walks
5 slowly and with dignity into the studio and sits down
in the chair.*]
I looked at him. His grey hair was a sign of wisdom. His face, weather-beaten and lined with experience. Looking at it was like paging the volume
10 of his history, written by himself. He was a living
symbol of Life, of all it means and does to a man. I
adored him. He sat there—half smiling, half serious—as if he had already seen the end of his road.
The eldest son said to me: 'Mr Styles, this is my
15 father, my mother, my brothers and sisters, their
wives and husbands, our children. Twenty-seven
of us, Mr Styles. We have come to take a card. My
father. . .,' he pointed to the old man, '. . . my
father always wanted it.'
20 I said: 'Certainly. Leave the rest to me.' I went to
work.
[*Another graphic reenactment of the scene as he describes it.*]
The old lady here, the eldest son there. Then the
25 other one, with the other one. On this side I did
something with the daughters, aunties, and one
bachelor brother. Then in front of it all the eight-
to-twelves, standing, in front of them, the four-
to-sevens, kneeling, and finally right on the floor
30 everything that was left, sitting. Jesus, it was hard
work, but finally I had them all sorted out and I
went behind the camera.
[*Behind his camera.*]
Just starting to focus . . .
35 [*Imaginary child in front of the lens;* STYLES *chases
the child back to the family group.*]
'. . . Sit down! Sit down!'
Back to the camera, start to focus again. . . . Not
One Of Them Was Smiling! I tried the old trick.
40 'Say cheese, please.' At first they just looked at
me. 'Come on! Cheese!' The children were the first
to pick it up.
[*Child's voice.*] 'Cheese. Cheese. Cheese.' Then the
ones a little bit bigger—'Cheese'—then the next
45 lot—'Cheese'—the uncles and aunties—'Cheese'—
and finally the old man himself—'Cheese'! I
thought the roof was going off, man! People outside in the street came and looked through the
window. They joined in: 'Cheese.' When I looked
again the mourners from the funeral parlour were 50
there wiping away their tears and saying 'Cheese.'
Pressed my little button and there it was—New
Brighton's smile, twenty-seven variations. Don't
you believe those bloody fools who make out we
don't know how to smile! 55
Anyway, you should have seen me then. Moved
the bachelor this side, sister-in-laws that side. Put
the eldest son behind the old man. Reorganized
the children. . . . [*Back behind his camera.*] 'Once
again, please! Cheese!' Back to work . . . old man 60
and old woman together, daughters behind them,
sons on the side. Those that were kneeling now
standing, those that were standing, now kneeling. . . . Ten times, friends! Each one different!
[*An exhausted* STYLES *collapses in a chair.*] 65
When they walked out finally I almost said Never
Again! A week later the eldest son came back for
the cards. I had them ready. The moment he
walked through that door I could see he was in
trouble. He said to me: 'Mr Styles, we almost didn't 70
make it. My father died two days after the card.
He will never see it.' 'Come on,' I said. 'You're a
man. One day or the other everyone of us must
go home. Here. . . .' I grabbed the cards. 'Here.
Look at your father and thank God for the time 75
he was given on this earth.' We went through them
together. He looked at them in silence. After the
third one, the tear went slowly down his cheek.
But at the same time . . . I was watching him carefully . . . something started to happen as he saw 80
his father there with himself, his brothers and sisters, and all the little grandchildren. He began to
smile. 'That's it, brother,' I said, 'Smile! Smile at
your father. Smile at the world.'
When he left, I thought of him going back to his 85
little house somewhere in New Brighton, filled that
day with the little mothers in black because a man
had died. I saw my cards passing from hand to
hand. I saw hands wipe away tears, and then the
first timid little smiles. 90
You must understand one thing. We own nothing
except ourselves. This world and its laws, allows
us nothing, except ourselves. There is nothing we
can leave behind when we die, except the memory
of ourselves. I know what I'm talking about, 95
friends—I had a father, and he died.

[*To the display-board.*]
Here he is. My father. That's him. Fought in the
war. Second World War. Fought at Tobruk. In
Egypt. He fought in France so that this country
5 and all the others could stay Free. When he came
back they stripped him at the docks—his gun, his
uniform, the dignity they'd allowed him for a few
mad years because the world needed men to fight
and be ready to sacrifice themselves for something
10 called Freedom. In return they let him keep his
scoff-tin° and gave him a bicycle. Size twenty-eight.
I remember, because it was too big for me. When
he died, in a rotten old suitcase amongst some of
his old rags, I found that photograph. That's all.
15 That's all I have from him.
    [*The display-board again.*]
Or this old lady. Mrs Matothlana. Used to stay in
Sangocha Street. You remember! Her husband was
arrested. . . .
20 [*Knock at the door.*]
Tell you about it later. Come in!
    [*A* MAN *walks nervously into the studio. Dressed in
    an ill-fitting new double-breasted suit. He is carrying a
    plastic bag with a hat in it. His manner is hesitant and
25 shy.* STYLES *takes one look at him and breaks into an
    enormous smile.*]
    [*An aside to the audience.*] A Dream!
    [*To the* MAN.] Come in, my friend.
    MAN. Mr Styles?
30 STYLES. That's me. Come in! You have come to
take a card?
    MAN. Snap.
    STYLES. Yes, a card. Have you got a deposit?
    MAN. Yes.
35 STYLES. Good. Let me just take your name down.
You see, you pay deposit now, and when you
come for the card, you pay the rest.
    MAN. Yes.
    STYLES [*to his desk and a black book for names and
40 addresses*]. What is your name? [*The* MAN *hesitates,
    as if not sure of himself.*]
Your name, please?
    [*Pause.*]
Come on, my friend. You must surely have a name.
45 MAN [*pulling himself together, but still very nervous*].
Robert Zwelinzima.
    STYLES [*writing*]. 'Robert Zwelinzima.' Address?

scoff-tin coin bank; small savings

MAN [*swallowing*]. Fifty, Mapija Street.
STYLES [*writes, then pauses*]. 'Fifty, Mapija?'
MAN. Yes.   50
STYLES. You staying with Buntu?
MAN. Buntu.
STYLES. Very good somebody that one. Came here
for his Wedding Card. Always helping people. If
that man was white they'd call him a liberal.   55
    [*Now finished writing. Back to his customer.*]
All right. How many cards do you want?
    MAN. One card.
    STYLES [*disappointed*]. Only one?
    MAN. One.   60
    STYLES. How do you want to take the card?
    [*The* MAN *is not sure of what the question means.*]
You can take the card standing . . .
    [STYLES *strikes a stylish pose next to the table.*]
sitting . . .   65
    [*Another pose . . . this time in the chair.*]
anyhow. How do you want it?
    MAN. Anyhow.
    STYLES. Right. Sit down.
    [ROBERT *hesitates.*]   70
Sit down!
    STYLES *fetches a vase with plastic flowers, dusts them
    off, and places them on the table.* ROBERT *holds up his
    plastic bag.*]
What you got there?   75
    [*Out comes the hat.*]
Aha! Stetson. Put it on, my friend.
    [ROBERT *handles it shyly.*]
You can put it on, Robert.
    [ROBERT *pulls it on.* STYLES *does up one of his jacket* 80
    buttons.]
What a beautiful suit, my friend! Where did you
buy it?
    MAN. Sales House.
    STYLES [*quoting a sales slogan*]. 'Where the Black 85
world buys the best. Six months to pay. Pay as
you wear.'
    [*Nudges* ROBERT.]
. . . and they never repossess!
    [*They share a laugh.*]   90
What are you going to do with this card?
    [*Chatting away as he goes to his camera and sets it
    up for the photo.* ROBERT *watches the preparations ap-
    prehensively.*]
    MAN. Send it to my wife.   95
    STYLES. Your wife!

MAN. Nowetu.

STYLES. Where's your wife?

MAN. King William's Town.

STYLES [*exaggerated admiration*]. At last! The kind
5 of man I like. Not one of those foolish young boys
who come here to find work and then forget their
families back home. A man, with responsibility!
Where do you work?

MAN. Feltex.

10 STYLES. I hear they pay good there.

MAN. Not bad.

[*He is now very tense, staring fixedly at the camera.*
STYLES *straightens up behind it.*]

STYLES. Come on, Robert! You want your wife
15 to get a card with her husband looking like he's
got all the worries in the world on his back? What
will she think? 'My poor husband is in trouble!'
You must smile!

[ROBERT *shamefacedly relaxes a little and starts to*
20 *smile.*]

That's it!

[*He relaxes still more. Beginning to enjoy himself.
Uncertainly produces a very fancy pipe from one of his
pockets.*

25 STYLES *now really warming to the assignment.*]

Look, have you ever walked down the passage to
the office with the big glass door and the board
outside: 'Manager—Bestuurder'. Imagine it, man,
you, Robert Zwelinzima, behind a desk in an of-
30 fice like that! It can happen, Robert. Quick promotion to Chief Messenger. I'll show you what
we do.

[STYLES *produces a Philips' class-room map of the
world, which he hangs behind the table as a backdrop to*
35 *the photo.*]

Look at it, Robert. America, England, Africa, Russia, Asia!

[*Carried away still further by his excitement,* STYLES
finds a cigarette, lights it, and gives it to ROBERT *to*
40 *hold. The latter is now ready for the 'card' . . . pipe in
one hand and cigarette in the other.* STYLES *stands behind his camera and admires his handiwork.*]

Mr Robert Zwelinzima, Chief Messenger at Feltex,
sitting in his office with the world behind him.
45 Smile, Robert, Smile!

[*Studying his subject through the viewfinder of the
camera.*]

Lower your hand, Robert . . . towards the ashtray
. . . more . . . now make a four with your legs. . . .

[*He demonstrates behind the camera.* ROBERT *crosses* 50
his legs.]

Hold it, Robert. . . . Keep on smiling . . . that's
it. . . . [*presses the release button—the shutter clicks.*]
Beautiful! All right, Robert.

[ROBERT *and his smile remain frozen.*] 55

Robert. You can relax now. It's finished!

MAN. Finished?

STYLES. Yes. You just want the one card?

MAN. Yes.

STYLES. What happens if you lose it? Hey? I've 60
heard stories about those postmen, Robert. *Yo!* Sit
on the side of the road and open the letters they
should be delivering! 'Dear wife . . .'—one rand
this side, letter thrown away. 'Dear wife . . .'—
another rand this side, letter thrown away. You 65
want that to happen to you? Come on! What about
a movie, man?

MAN. Movie?

STYLES. Don't you know the movie?

MAN. No. 70

STYLES. Simple! You just walk you see . . .

[STYLES *demonstrates; at a certain point freezes in
mid-stride.*]

. . . and I take the card! Then you can write to
your wife: 'Dear wife, I am coming home at Christ- 75
mas. . . .' Put the card in your letter and post it.
Your wife opens the letter and what does she see?
Her Robert, walking home to her! She shows it to
the children. 'Look, children, your daddy is coming!' The children jump and clap their hands: 80
'Daddy is coming! Daddy is coming!'

MAN [*excited by the picture* STYLES *has conjured up*].
All right!

STYLES. You want a movie?

MAN. I want a movie. 85

STYLES. That's my man! Look at this, Robert.

[STYLES *reverses the map hanging behind the table to
reveal a gaudy painting of a futuristic city.*]

City of the Future! Look at it. Mr. Robert Zwelinzima, man about town, future head of Feltex, 90
walking through the City of the Future!

MAN [*examining the backdrop with admiration. He
recognizes a landmark.*] OK.

STYLES. OK Bazaars . . . [*the other buildings*] . . .
Mutual Building Society, Barclays Bank . . . the lot! 95
What you looking for, Robert?

MAN. Feltex.

STYLES. Yes . . . well, you see, I couldn't fit

everything on, Robert. But if I had had enough
space Feltex would have been here.

[*To his table for props.*]

Walking-stick . . . newspaper. . . .

5   MAN [*diffidently*]. I don't read.

STYLES. That is not important, my friend. You
think all those monkeys carrying newspapers can
read? They look at the pictures.

[*After 'dressing'* ROBERT *with the props he moves*
10 *back to his camera.*]

This is going to be beautiful, Robert. My best card.
I must send one to the magazines.

All right, Robert, now move back. Remember what
I showed you. Just walk towards me and right in
15 front of the City of the Future. I'll take the picture.
Ready? Now come, Robert. . . .

[*Pipe in mouth, walking-stick in hand, newspaper
under the other arm,* ROBERT *takes a jaunty step and
then freezes, as* STYLES *had shown him earlier.*]

20 Come, Robert. . . .

[*Another step.*]

Just one more, Robert. . . .

[*Another step.*]

Stop! Hold it, Robert. Hold it!

25 [*The camera flash goes off; simultaneously a blackout
except for one light on* ROBERT, *frozen in the pose that
will appear in the picture. We are in fact looking at the
photograph. It 'comes to life' and dictates the letter that
will accompany it to Nowetu in King William's Town.*]

30 MAN. Nowetu . . .

[*Correcting himself.*]

Dear Nowetu,

I've got wonderful news for you in this letter. My
troubles are over, I think. You won't believe it,
35 but I must tell you. Sizwe Bansi, in a manner of
speaking, is dead! I'll tell you what I can.

As you know, when I left the Railway Compound
I went to stay with a friend of mine called Zola.
A very good friend that, Nowetu. In fact he was
40 even trying to help me find some job. But that's
not easy, Nowetu, because Port Elizabeth is also
a big place, a very big place with lots of factories
but also lots of people looking for a job like me.
There are so many men, Nowetu, who have left
45 their places because they are dry and have come
here to find work!

After a week with Zola, I was in big trouble.
The headman came around, and after a lot of hap-
penings which I will tell you when I see you, they
put a stamp in my passbook which said I must 50
leave Port Elizabeth at once in three days time. I
was very much unhappy, Nowetu. I couldn't stay
with Zola because if the headman found me there
again my troubles would be even bigger. So Zola
took me to a friend of his called Buntu, and asked 55
him if I could stay with him until I decided what
to do. . . .

[BUNTU's *house in New Brighton. Table and two chairs.*
ROBERT *in a direct continuation of the preceding scene,
is already there, as* BUNTU, *jacket slung over his shoul-* 60
der, walks in. Holds out his hand to ROBERT.]

BUNTU. Hi. Buntu.

[*They shake hands.*]

MAN. Sizwe Bansi.

BUNTU. Sit down.   65

[*They sit.*]

Zola told me you were coming. Didn't have time
to explain anything. Just asked if you could spend
a few nights here. You can perch yourself on that
sofa in the corner. I'm alone at the moment. My 70
wife is a domestic . . . sleep-in at Kabega Park . . .
only comes home weekends. Hot today, hey?

[*In the course of this scene* BUNTU *will busy himself
first by having a wash—basin and jug of water on the
table—and then by changing from his working clothes* 75
preparatory to going out. SIZWE BANSI *stays in his chair.*]
What's your problem, friend?

MAN. I've got no permit to stay in Port Elizabeth.

BUNTU. Where do you have a permit to stay? 80

MAN. King William's Town.

BUNTU. How did they find out?

MAN [*tells his story with the hesitation and uncertainty of the illiterate. When words fail him he tries to
use his hands.*]   85

I was staying with Zola, as you know. I was very
happy there. But one night . . . I was sleeping on
the floor . . . I heard some noises and when I looked
up I saw torches shining in through the window
. . . then there was a loud knocking on the door. 90
When I got up Zola was there in the dark . . . he
was trying to whisper something. I think he was
saying I must hide. So I crawled under the table.
The headman came in and looked around and
found me hiding under the table . . . and dragged 95
me out.

BUNTU. Raid?

MAN. Yes, it was a raid. I was just wearing my pants. My shirt was lying on the other side. I just managed to grab it as they were pushing me

5 out. . . . I finished dressing in the van. They drove straight to the administration office . . . and then from there they drove to the Labour Bureau. I was made to stand in the passage there, with everybody looking at me and shaking their heads like

10 they knew I was in big trouble. Later I was taken into an office and made to stand next to the door. . . . The white man behind the desk had my book and he also looked at me and shook his head. Just then one other white man came in with a

15 card. . . .

BUNTU. A card?

MAN. He was carrying a card.

BUNTU. Pink card?

MAN. Yes, the card was pink.

20 BUNTU. Record card. Your whole bloody life is written down on that. Go on.

MAN. Then the first white man started writing something on the card . . . and just then somebody came in carrying a. . . .

25 [*demonstrates what he means by banging a clenched fist on the table.*]

BUNTU. A stamp?

MAN. Yes, a stamp. [*Repeats the action.*] He was carrying a stamp.

30 BUNTU. And then?

MAN. He put it on my passbook.

BUNTU. Let me see your book?

[SIZWE *produces his passbook from the back-pocket of his trousers.* BUNTU *examines it.*]

35 Shit! You know what this is? [*The stamp.*]

MAN. I can't read.

BUNTU. Listen . . . [*reads*]. 'You are required to report to the Bantu Affairs Commissioner, King William's Town, within three days of the above-

40 mentioned date for the. . . .' You should have been home yesterday! . . . 'for the purpose of repatriation to home district.' Influx Control. You're in trouble, Sizwe.

MAN. I don't want to leave Port Elizabeth.

45 BUNTU. Maybe. But if that book says go, you go.

MAN. Can't I maybe burn this book and get a new one?

BUNTU. Burn that book? Stop kidding yourself, Sizwe! Anyway suppose you do. You must im-

50 mediately go apply for a new one. Right? And until that new one comes, be careful the police don't stop you and ask for your book. Into the Courtroom, brother. Charge: Failing to produce Reference Book on Demand. Five rand or five days.

55 Finally the new book comes. Down to the Labour Bureau for a stamp . . . it's got to be endorsed with permission to be in this area. White man at the Labour Bureau takes the book, looks at it—doesn't look at you!—goes to the big machine and feeds

60 in your number . . .

[BUNTU *goes through the motions of punching out a number on a computer.*]

. . . card jumps out, he reads: 'Sizwe Bansi. Endorsed to King William's Town. . . .' Takes your

65 book, fetches that same stamp, and in it goes again. So you burn that book, or throw it away, and get another one. Same thing happens.

[BUNTU *feeds the computer; the card jumps out.*]

'Sizwe Bansi. Endorsed to King William's

70 Town. . . .' Stamp goes in the third time. . . . But this time it's also into a van and off to the Native Commissioner's Office; card around your neck with your number on it; escort on both sides and back to King William's Town. They make you pay for

75 the train fare too!

MAN. I think I will try to look for some jobs in the garden.

BUNTU. You? Job as a garden-boy? Don't you read the newspapers?

80 MAN. I can't read.

BUNTU. I'll tell you what the little white ladies say: 'Domestic vacancies. I want a garden-boy with good manners and a wide knowledge of seasons and flowers. Book in order.' Yours in order? Any-

85 way what the hell do you know about seasons and flowers? [*After a moment's thought.*] Do you know any white man who's prepared to give you a job?

MAN. No. I don't know any white man.

BUNTU. Pity. We might have been able to work

90 something then. You talk to the white man, you see, and ask him to write a letter saying he's got a job for you. You take that letter from the white man and go back to King William's Town, where you show it to the Native Commissioner there.

95 The Native Commissioner in King William's Town reads that letter from the white man in Port Eliz-

abeth who is ready to give you the job. He then
writes a letter back to the Native Commissioner in
Port Elizabeth. So you come back here with the
two letters. Then the Native Commissioner in Port
5 Elizabeth reads the letter from the Native Commissioner in King William's Town together with
the first letter from the white man who is prepared
to give you a job, and he says when he reads the
letters: Ay yes, this man Sizwe Bansi can get a job.
10 So the Native Commissioner in Port Elizabeth then
writes a letter which you take with the letters from
the Native Commissioner in King William's Town
and the white man in Port Elizabeth, to the Senior
Officer at the Labour Bureau, who reads all the
15 letters. Then he will put the right stamp in your
book and give you another letter from himself
which together with the letters from the white man
and the two Native Affairs Commissioners, you
take to the Administration Office here in New
20 Brighton and make an application for Residence
Permit, so that you don't fall victim of raids again.
Simple.

MAN. Maybe I can start a little business selling
potatoes and. . . .
25 BUNTU. Where do you get the potatoes and . . . ?
MAN. I'll buy them.
BUNTU. With what?
MAN. Borrow some money. . . .
BUNTU. Who is going to lend money to a some-
30 body endorsed to hell and gone out in the bush?
And how you going to buy your potatoes at the
market without a Hawker's Licence? Same story,
Sizwe. You won't get that because of the bloody
stamp in your book.
35 There's no way out, Sizwe. You're not the first
one who has tried to find it. Take my advice and
catch that train back to King William's Town. If
you need work so bad go knock on the door of
the Mines Recruiting Office. Dig gold for the white
40 man. That's the only time they don't worry about
Influx Control.

MAN. I don't want to work on the mines. There
is no money there. And it's dangerous, under the
ground. Many black men get killed when the rocks
45 fall. You can die there.

BUNTU [stopped by the last remark into taking possibly his first real look at SIZWE].
You don't want to die.

MAN. I don't want to die.

BUNTU [stops whatever he is doing to sit down and 50
talk to SIZWE with an intimacy that was not there before.]
You married, Sizwe?

MAN. Yes.

BUNTU. How many children? 55

MAN. I've got four children.

BUNTU. Boys? Girls?

MAN. I've got three boys and one girl.

BUNTU. Schooling?

MAN. Two are schooling. The other two stay at 60
home with their mother.

BUNTU. Your wife is not working.

MAN. The place where we stay is fifteen miles
from town. There is only one shop there. Baas van
Wyk. He has already got a woman working for 65
him. King William's Town is a dry place Mr Buntu
. . . very small and too many people. That is why
I don't want to go back.

BUNTU. Ag, friend . . . I don't know! I'm also
married. One child. 70

MAN. Only one?

BUNTU. Ja, my wife attends this Birth Control
Clinic rubbish. The child is staying with my mother.
[Shaking his head.] Hai, Sizwe! If I had to tell you
the trouble I had before I could get the right stamps 75
in my book, even though I was born in this area!
The trouble I had before I could get a decent job
. . . born in this area! The trouble I had to get this
two-roomed house . . . born in this area!

MAN. Why is there so much trouble, Mr Buntu? 80

BUNTU. Two weeks back I went to a funeral with
a friend of mine. Out in the country. An old relative of his passed away. Usual thing . . . sermons
in the house, sermons in the church, sermons at
the graveside. I thought they were never going to 85
stop talking!
At the graveside service there was one fellow, a
lay preacher . . . short man, neat little moustache,
wearing one of those old-fashioned double-breasted
black suits. . . . Haai! He was wonderful. While he 90
talked he had a gesture with his hands . . . like
this . . . that reminded me of our youth, when we
learnt to fight with kieries.° His text was 'Going

---

kieries fighting sticks carried by young African men (Fugard's note)

Home.' He handled it well, Sizwe. Started by saying that the first man to sign the Death Contract with God, was Adam, when he sinned in Eden. Since that day, wherever Man is, or whatever he
5 does, he is never without his faithful companion, Death. So with Outa Jacob . . . the dead man's name . . . he has at last accepted the terms of his contract with God.

But in his life, friends, he walked the roads of this
10 land. He helped print those footpaths which lead through the bush and over the veld . . . footpaths which his children are now walking. He worked on farms from this district down to the coast and north as far as Pretoria. I knew him. He was a
15 friend. Many people knew Outa Jacob. For a long time he worked for Baas van der Walt. But when the old man died his young son Hendrik said: 'I don't like you. Go!' Outa Jacob picked up his load and put it on his shoulders. His wife followed. He
20 went to the next farm . . . through the fence, up to the house. . . : 'Work, please, Baas.' Baas Potgieter took him. He stayed a long time there too, until one day there was trouble between the Madam and his wife. Jacob and his wife were walking again.
25 The load on his back was heavier, he wasn't so young any more, and there were children behind them now as well. On to the next farm. No work. The next one. No work. Then the next one. A little time there. But the drought was bad and the farmer
30 said: 'Sorry, Jacob. The cattle are dying. I'm moving to the city.' Jacob picked up his load yet again. So it went, friends. On and on . . . until he arrived there. [*The grave at his feet.*] Now at last it's over. No matter how hard-arsed the boer° on this farm
35 wants to be, he cannot move Outa Jacob. He has reached Home.

[*Pause.*]

That's it, brother. The only time we'll find peace is when they dig a hole for us and press our face
40 into the earth.

[*Putting on his coat.*]

Ag, to hell with it. If we go on like this much longer we'll do the digging for them.

[*Changing his tone.*]
45 You know Sky's place, Sizwe?

MAN. No.

BUNTU. Come. Let me give you a treat. I'll do you there.

[*Exit* BUNTU.

Blackout except for a light on SIZWE. *He continues* 50 *his letter to Nowetu.*]

MAN. Sky's place? [*Shakes his head and laughs.*] Hey, Nowetu! When I mention that name again, I get a headache . . . the same headache I had when I woke up in Buntu's place the next morn- 55 ing. You won't believe what it was like. You cannot! It would be like you walking down Pickering Street in King William's Town and going into Koekemoer's Café to buy bread, and what do you see sitting there at the smart table and chairs? Your 60 husband, Sizwe Bansi, being served ice-cream and cool drinks by old Mrs Koekemoer herself. Such would be your surprise if you had seen me at Sky's place. Only they weren't serving cool drinks and ice-cream. No! First-class booze, Nowetu. And it 65 wasn't old Mrs. Koekemoer serving me, but a certain lovely and beautiful lady called Miss Nkonyemi. And it wasn't just your husband Sizwe sitting there with all the most important people of New Brighton, but *Mister* Bansi. 70

[*He starts to laugh.*]

Mister Bansi!

[*As the laugh gets bigger,* SIZWE *rises to his feet.*]

[*The street outside Sky's Shebeen° in New Brighton. Our man is amiably drunk. He addresses the audience.*] 75

MAN. Do you know who I am, friend? Take my hand, friend. Take my hand, I am Mister Bansi, friend. Do you know where I come from? I come from Sky's place, friend. A most wonderful place. I met everybody there, good people. I've been 80 drinking, my friends—brandy, wine, beer. . . . Don't you want to go in there, good people? Let's all go to Sky's place. [*Shouting.*] Mr Buntu! Mr Buntu!

[BUNTU *enters shouting goodbye to friends at the She-* 85 *been. He joins* SIZWE. BUNTU, *though not drunk, is also amiably talkative under the influence of a good few drinks.*]

BUNTU [*discovering the audience*]. Hey, where did you get all these wonderful people? 90

MAN. I just found them here, Mr Buntu.

BUNTU. Wonderful!

---

boer white settler, land-owner

Shebeen an illegal bar

FUGARD | KANI | NTSHONA

MAN. I'm inviting them to Sky's place, Mr Buntu.

BUNTU. You tell them about Sky's?

MAN. I told them about Sky's place, Mr Buntu.

BUNTU [to the audience]. We been having a time
5 there, man!

MAN. They know it. I told them everything.

BUNTU [laughing]. Sizwe! We had our fun there.

MAN. Hey. . . . hey. . . .

BUNTU. Remember that Member of the Advisory
10 Board?

MAN. Hey. . . . Hey . . . Mr Buntu! You know I
respect you, friend. You must call me nice.

BUNTU. What do you mean?

MAN [clumsy dignity]. I'm not just Sizwe no more.
15 He might have walked in, but Mr Bansi walked
out!

BUNTU [playing along]. I am terribly sorry, Mr
Bansi. I apologize for my familiarity. Please don't
be offended.
20 [Handing over one of the two oranges he is carrying.]
Allow me . . . with the compliments of Miss
Nkonyeni.

MAN [taking the orange with a broad but sheepish
grin]. Miss Nkonyeni!
25 BUNTU. Sweet dreams, Mr Bansi.

MAN [tears the orange with his thumbs and starts
eating it messily]. Lovely lady, Mr Buntu.

BUNTU [leaves SIZWE with a laugh. To the audience].
Back there in the Shebeen a Member of the Ad-
30 visory Board hears that he comes from King William's Town. He goes up to Sizwe. 'Tell me, Mr
Bansi, what do you think of Ciskeian° Independence?'

MAN [interrupting]. Ja, I remember that one.
35 Bloody Mister Member of the Advisory Board.
Talking about Ciskeian Independence!

[To the audience.]
I must tell you, friend . . . when a car passes or
the wind blows up the dust, Ciskeian Independ-
40 ence makes you cough. I'm telling you, friend . . .
put a man in a pondok° and call that Independence? My good friend, let me tell you . . . Ciskeian
Independence is shit!

BUNTU. Or that other chap! Old Jolobe. The fat

Ciskeian the Ciskei is a recently organized black "home-
land," a showpiece of official *apartheid*
pondok shack; shanty (Fugard's note)

tycoon man! [to the audience] Comes to me . . . 45
[pompous voice] . . . 'Your friend, Mr Bansi is he on
an official visit to town?' 'No,' I said, 'Mr Bansi is
on an official walkout!' [BUNTU thinks this is a big
joke.]

MAN [stubbornly]. I'm here to stay. 50

BUNTU [looking at his watch]. Hey, Sizwe. . . .

MAN [reproachfully]. Mr Buntu!

BUNTU [correcting himself]. Mr Bansi, it is getting
late. I've got to work tomorrow. Care to lead the
way, Mr Bansi? 55

MAN. You think I can't? You think Mr Bansi is
lost?

BUNTU. I didn't say that.

MAN. You are thinking it, friend. I'll show you.
This is Chinga Street. 60

BUNTU. Very good! But which way do we. . . ?

MAN [setting off]. This way.

BUNTU [pulling him back]. Mistake. You're heading for Site and Service and a lot of trouble with
the Tsotsis.° 65

MAN [the opposite direction]. That way.

BUNTU. Lead on. I'm right behind you.

MAN. Ja, you are right, Mr Buntu. There is Newell High School. Now. . . .

BUNTU. Think carefully! 70

MAN. . . . when we were going to Sky's we had
Newell in front. So when we leave Sky's we put
Newell behind.

BUNTU. Very good!

[An appropriate change in direction. They continue 75
walking, and eventually arrive at a square, with roads
leading off in many directions. SIZWE is lost. He wanders around, uncertain of the direction to take.]

MAN. Haai, Mr Buntu. . . !

BUNTU. Mbizweni Square. 80

MAN. Yo! Cross-roads to hell, wait . . . [Closer
look at landmark.] . . . that building . . . Rio Cinema!
So we must. . . .

BUNTU. Rio Cinema? With a white cross on top,
bell outside, and the big show on Sundays? 85

MAN [sheepishly]. You're right, friend. I've got it,
Mr. Buntu. That way.

[He starts off. BUNTU watches him.]

BUNTU. Goodbye. King William's Town a
hundred and fifty miles. Don't forget to write. 90

Tsotsis street gangs

MAN [*hurried about-turn*]. *Haai . . . haai. . . .*

BUNTU. Okay, Sizwe, I'll take over from here. But just hang on for a second I want to have a piss. Don't move!

5 [BUNTU *disappears into the dark.*]

MAN. *Haai,* Sizwe! You are a country fool! Leading Mr Buntu and Mr Bansi astray. You think you know this place New Brighton? You know nothing!

10 [BUNTU *comes running back.*]

BUNTU [*urgently*]. Let's get out of here.

MAN. Wait, Mr Buntu, I'm telling that fool Sizwe. . . .

BUNTU. Come on! There's trouble there . . .

15 [*pointing in the direction from which he has come*] . . . let's move.

MAN. Wait, Mr Buntu, wait. Let me first tell that Sizwe. . . .

BUNTU. There's a dead man lying there!

20 MAN. Dead man?

BUNTU. I thought I was just pissing on a pile of rubbish, but when I looked carefully I saw it was a man. Dead. Covered in blood. Tsotsis must have got him. Let's get the hell out of here before any-

25 body sees us.

MAN. Buntu . . . Buntu. . . .

BUNTU. Listen to me, Sizwe! The Tsotsis might still be around.

MAN. Buntu. . . .

30 BUNTU. Do you want to join him?

MAN. I don't want to join him.

BUNTU. Then come.

MAN. Wait, Buntu.

BUNTU. Jesus! If Zola had told me how much

35 trouble you were going to be!

MAN. Buntu, . . . we must report that man to the police station.

BUNTU. Police Station! Are you mad? You drunk, passbook not in order . . . 'We've come to report

40 a dead man, Sergeant.' 'Grab them!' Case closed. We killed him.

MAN. Mr Buntu, . . . we can't leave him. . . .

BUNTU. Please, Sizwe!

MAN. Wait. Let's carry him home.

45 BUNTU. Just like that! Walk through New Brighton streets, at this hour, carrying a dead man. Anyway we don't know where he stays. Come.

MAN. Wait, Buntu, . . . listen. . . .

BUNTU. Sizwe!

MAN. Buntu, we can know where he stays. That 50 passbook of his will talk. It talks, friend, like mine. His passbook will tell you.

BUNTU [*after a moment's desperate hesitation*]. You really want to land me in the shit, hey.

[*Disappears into the dark again.*] 55

MAN. It will tell you in good English where he stays. My passbook talks good English too . . . big words that Sizwe can't read and doesn't understand. Sizwe wants to stay here in New Brighton and find a job; passbook says, 'No! Report back.' 60 Sizwe wants to feed his wife and children; passbook says, 'No. Endorsed out.'

Sizwe wants to. . . .

[BUNTU *reappears, a passbook in his hand. Looks around furtively and moves to the light under a lamp-* 65 *post.*]

They never told us it would be like that when they introduced it. They said: Book of Life! Your friend! You'll never get lost! They told us lies.

[*He joins* BUNTU *who is examining the book.*] 70

BUNTU. *Haai!* Look at him [*the photograph in the book, reading*]. 'Robert Zwelinzima. Tribe: Xhosa. Native Identification Number. . . .'

MAN. Where does he stay, Buntu?

BUNTU [*paging through the book*]. Worked at Dor- 75 man Long seven years . . . Kilomet Engineering . . . eighteen months . . . Anderson Hardware two years . . . now unemployed. Hey, look, Sizwe! He's one up on you. He's got a work-seeker's permit.

MAN. Where does he stay, Buntu? 80

BUNTU. Lodger's Permit at 42 Mdala Street. From there to Sangocha Street . . . now at. . . .

[*Pause. Closes the book abruptly.*]

To hell with it I'm not going *there.*

MAN. Where, Buntu? 85

BUNTU. [*emphatically*]. I Am Not Going There!

MAN. Buntu. . . .

BUNTU. You know where he is staying now? Single Men's Quarters! If you think I'm going there this time of the night you got another guess com- 90 ing.

[SIZWE *doesn't understand.*]

Look, Sizwe . . . I stay in a house, there's a street name and a number. Easy to find. Ask anybody . . . Mapija Street? That way. You know what Sin- 95 gle Men's Quarters is? Big bloody concentration

camp with rows of things that look like train carriages. Six doors to each! Twelve people behind each door! You want me to go there now? Knock on the first one: 'Does Robert Zwelinzima live here?'
5 'No!' Next one: 'Does Robert. . . ?' 'Buggeroff, we're trying to sleep!' Next one: 'Does Robert Zwelinzima. . . ?' They'll fuck us up, man! I'm putting this book back and we're going home.

MAN. Buntu!

10 BUNTU [half-way back to the alleyway]. What?

MAN. Would you do that to me, friend? If the Tsotsis had stabbed Sizwe, and left him lying there, would you walk away from him as well?

[The accusation stops BUNTU.]

15 Would you leave me lying there, wet with your piss? I wish I was dead. I wish I was dead because I don't care a damn about anything any more.

[Turning away from BUNTU to the audience.]

What's happening in this world, good people? Who
20 cares for who in this world? Who wants who? Who wants me, friend? What's wrong with me? I'm a man. I've got eyes to see. I've got ears to listen when people talk. I've got a head to think good things. What's wrong with me?

25 [Starts to tear off his clothes.]

Look at me! I'm a man. I've got legs. I can run with a wheelbarrow full of cement! I'm strong! I'm a man. Look! I've got a wife. I've got four children. How many has he made, lady? [The man sitting
30 next to her.] Is he a man? What has he got that I haven't. . . ?

[A thoughtful BUNTU rejoins them, the dead man's reference book still in his hand.]

BUNTU. Let me see your book?

35 [SIZWE doesn't respond.]

Give me your book!

MAN. Are you a policeman now, Buntu?

BUNTU. Give me your bloody book, Sizwe!

MAN [handing it over]. Take it, Buntu. Take this
40 book and read it carefully, friend, and tell me what it says about me. Buntu, does that book tell you I'm a man?

[BUNTU studies the two books. SIZWE turns back to the audience.]

45 That bloody book . . . ! People, do you know? No! Wherever you go . . . it's that bloody book. You go to school, it goes too. Go to work, it goes too. Go to church and pray and sing lovely hymns, it

sits there with you. Go to hospital to die, it lies there too!
50

[BUNTU has collected SIZWE's discarded clothing.]

BUNTU. Come!

[BUNTU's house, as earlier. Table and two chairs. BUNTU pushes SIZWE down into a chair. SIZWE still muttering, starts to struggle back into his clothes. BUNTU
55 opens the two reference books and places them side by side on the table. He produces a pot of glue, then very carefully tears out the photograph in each book. A dab of glue on the back of each and then SIZWE's goes back into ROBERT's book, and ROBERT's into SIZWE's. SIZWE
60 watches this operation, at first uninterestedly, but when he realizes what BUNTU is up to, with growing alarm. When he is finished, BUNTU pushes the two books in front of SIZWE.]

MAN [shaking his head emphatically]. Yo! Haai, haai.°
65 No, Buntu.

BUNTU. It's a chance.

MAN. Haai, haai, haai . . .

BUNTU. It's your only chance!

MAN. No, Buntu! What's it mean? That me, Sizwe
70 Bansi. . . .

BUNTU. Is dead.

MAN. I'm not dead, friend.

BUNTU. We burn this book . . . [SIZWE's original] . . . and Sizwe Bansi disappears off the face of the
75 earth.

MAN. What about the man we left lying in the alleyway?

BUNTU. Tomorrow the Flying Squad passes there and finds him. Check in his pockets . . . no pass-
80 book. Mount Road Mortuary. After three days nobody has identified him. Pauper's Burial. Case closed.

MAN. And then?

BUNTU. Tomorrow I contact my friend Norman
85 at Feltex. He's a boss-boy there. I tell him about another friend, Robert Zwelinzima, book in order, who's looking for a job. You roll up later, hand over the book to the white man. Who does Robert Zwelinzima look like? You! Who gets the pay on
90 Friday? You, man!

MAN. What about all that shit at the Labour Bureau, Buntu?

haai exclamation of surprise (Fugard's note)

BUNTU. You don't have to go there. This chap had a work-seeker's permit, Sizwe. All you do is hand over the book to the white man. *He* checks at the Labour Bureau. They check with their big machine. 'Robert Zwelinzima has the right to be employed and stay in this town.'

MAN. I don't want to lose my name, Buntu.

BUNTU. You mean you don't want to lose your bloody passbook! You love it, hey?

MAN. Buntu. I cannot lose my name.

BUNTU [*leaving the table*]. All right, I was only trying to help. as Robert Zwelinzima you could have stayed and worked in this town. As Sizwe Bansi . . . ? Start walking, friend. King William's Town. Hundred and fifty miles. And don't waste any time! You've got to be there by yesterday. Hope you enjoy it.

MAN. Buntu. . . .

BUNTU. Lots of scenery in a hundred and fifty miles.

MAN. Buntu! . . .

BUNTU. Maybe a better idea is just to wait until they pick you up. Save yourself all that walking. Into the train with the escort! Smart stuff, hey. Hope it's not too crowded though. Hell of a lot of people being kicked out, I hear.

MAN. Buntu! . . .

BUNTU. But once you're back! Sit down on the side of the road next to your pondok with your family . . . the whole Bansi clan on leave . . . for life! Hey, that sounds okay. Watching all the cars passing, and as you say, friend, cough your bloody lungs out with Ciskeian Independence.

MAN [*now really desperate*]. Buntu!!!

BUNTU. What you waiting for? Go!

MAN. Buntu.

BUNTU. What?

MAN. What about my wife, Nowetu?

BUNTU. What about her?

MAN [*maudlin tears*]. Her loving husband, Sizwe Bansi, is dead!

BUNTU. So what! She's going to marry a better man.

MAN [*bridling*]. Who?

BUNTU. You . . . Robert Zwelinzima.

MAN [*thoroughly confused*]. How can I marry my wife, Buntu?

BUNTU. Get her down here and I'll introduce you.

MAN. Don't make jokes, Buntu. Robert . . . Sizwe . . . I'm all mixed up. Who am I?

BUNTU. A fool who is not taking his chance.

MAN. And my children! Their father is Sizwe Bansi! They're registered at school under Bansi. . . .

BUNTU. Are you really worried about your children, friend, or are you just worried about yourself and your bloody name? Wake up, man! Use that book and with your pay on Friday you'll have a real chance to do something for them.

MAN. I'm afraid. How do I get used to Robert? How do I live as another man's ghost!

BUNTU. Wasn't Sizwe Bansi a ghost?

MAN. No!

BUNTU. No? When the white man looked at you at the Labour Bureau what did he see? A man with dignity or a bloody passbook with an N.I. number? Isn't that a ghost? When the white man sees you walk down the street and calls out, 'Hey, John! Come here' . . . to you, *Sizwe Bansi* . . . isn't that a ghost? Or when his little child calls you 'Boy' . . . you a man, circumcised with a wife and four children . . . isn't that a ghost? Stop fooling yourself. All I'm saying is be a real ghost, if that is what they want, what they've turned us into. Spook them into hell, man!

[SIZWE *is silenced.* BUNTU *realizes his words are beginning to reach the other man. He paces quietly, looking for his next move. He finds it.*]

Suppose you try my plan. Friday. Roughcasting section at Feltex. Paytime. Line of men—non-skilled labourers. White man with the big box full of pay-packets.

'John Kani!' 'Yes, sir!' Pay-packet is handed over. 'Thank you, sir.'

Another one. [BUNTU *reads the name on an imaginary pay-packet.*] 'Winston Ntshona!' 'Yes, sir!' Pay-packet over. 'Thank you, sir!' Another one. 'Fats Bhokolane!' *'Hier is ek, my baas!'* Pay-packet over. *'Dankie, my baas!'*

Another one. 'Robert Zwelinzima!'

[*No response from* SIZWE.]

'Robert Zwelinzima!'

MAN. Yes, sir.

BUNTU [*handling him the imaginary pay-packet*]. Open it. Go on. [*Takes back the packet, tears it open, empties its contents on the table, and counts it.*]

Five . . . ten . . . eleven . . . twelve . . . and ninety-nine cents. In *your* pocket!

[B<small>UNTU</small> *again paces quietly, leaving* S<small>IZWE</small> *to think. Eventually. . . .*] Saturday. Man in overalls, twelve rand ninety-nine cents in the back pocket, walking down Main Street looking for Sales House. Finds it and walks in. Salesman comes forward to meet him.

'I've come to buy a suit.' Salesman is very friendly. 'Certainly. Won't you take a seat. I'll get the forms. I'm sure you want to open an account, sir. Six months to pay. But first I'll need all your particulars.'

[B<small>UNTU</small> *has turned the table, with* S<small>IZWE</small> *on the other side, into the imaginary scene at Sales House.*]

B<small>UNTU</small> [*pencil poised, ready to fill in a form*]. Your name, please, sir?

M<small>AN</small> [*playing along uncertainly*]. Robert Zwelinzima.

B<small>UNTU</small> [*writing*]. 'Robert Zwelinzima.' Address?

M<small>AN</small>. Fifty, Mapija Street.

B<small>UNTU</small>. Where do you work?

M<small>AN</small>. Feltex.

B<small>UNTU</small>. And how much do you get paid?

M<small>AN</small>. Twelve . . . twelve rand ninety-nine cents.

B<small>UNTU</small>. N.I. Number, please?

[S<small>IZWE</small> *hesitates.*]

Your Native Identity number please?

[S<small>IZWE</small> *is still uncertain.* B<small>UNTU</small> *abandons the act and picks up Robert Zwelinzima's passbook. He reads out the number.*]

N—I—3—8—1—1—8—6—3.

Burn that into your head, friend. You hear me? It's more important than your name.

N.I. number . . . three. . . .

M<small>AN</small>. Three.

B<small>UNTU</small>. Eight.

M<small>AN</small>. Eight.

B<small>UNTU</small>. One.

M<small>AN</small>. One.

B<small>UNTU</small>. One.

M<small>AN</small>. One.

B<small>UNTU</small>. Eight.

M<small>AN</small>. Eight.

B<small>UNTU</small>. Six.

M<small>AN</small>. Six.

B<small>UNTU</small>. Three

M<small>AN</small>. Three

B<small>UNTU</small>. Again. Three.

M<small>AN</small>. Three.

B<small>UNTU</small>. Eight.

M<small>AN</small>. Eight.

B<small>UNTU</small>. One.

M<small>AN</small>. One.

B<small>UNTU</small>. One.

M<small>AN</small>. One.

B<small>UNTU</small>. Eight.

M<small>AN</small>. Eight.

B<small>UNTU</small>. Six.

M<small>AN</small>. Six.

B<small>UNTU</small>. Three.

M<small>AN</small>. Three.

B<small>UNTU</small> [*picking up his pencil and returning to the role of the salesman*]. N.I. number, please.

M<small>AN</small> [*pausing frequently, using his hands to remember*]. Three . . . eight . . . one . . . one . . . eight . . . six . . . three. . . .

B<small>UNTU</small> [*abandoning the act*]. Good boy.

[*He paces.* S<small>IZWE</small> *sits and waits.*]

Sunday. Man in a Sales House suit, hat on top, going to church. Hymn book and bible under the arm. Sits down in the front pew. Priest in the pulpit.

[B<small>UNTU</small> *jumps on to a chair in his new role.* S<small>IZWE</small> *kneels.*]

The Time has come!

M<small>AN</small>. Amen!

B<small>UNTU</small>. Pray, brothers and sisters. . . . Pray. . . . Now!

M<small>AN</small>. Amen.

B<small>UNTU</small>. The Lord wants to save you. Hand yourself over to him, while there is still time, while Jesus is still prepared to listen to you.

M<small>AN</small> [*carried away by what he is feeling*]. Amen, Jesus!

B<small>UNTU</small>. Be careful, my brothers and sisters. . . .

M<small>AN</small>. Hallelujah!

B<small>UNTU</small>. Be careful lest when the big day comes and the pages of the big book are turned, it is found that your name is missing. Repent before it is too late.

M<small>AN</small>. Hallelujah! Amen.

B<small>UNTU</small>. Will all those who have not yet handed in their names for membership of our burial society please remain behind.

[B<small>UNTU</small> *leaves the pulpit and walks around with a register.*]

Name, please, sir? Number? Thank you.

Good afternoon, sister. Your name, please.
Address? Number? God bless you.

[*He has reached* Sizwe.]

Your name, please, brother?

5 Man. Robert Zwelinzima.

Buntu. Address?

Man. Fifty, Mapija Street.

Buntu. N.I. number.

Man [*again tremendous effort to remember*]. Three
10 . . . eight . . . one . . . one . . . eight . . . six . . .
three. . . .

[*They both relax.*]

Buntu [*after pacing for a few seconds*]. Same man
leaving the church . . . walking down the street.

15 [Buntu *acts out the role while* Sizwe *watches. He
greets other members of the congregation.*]

'God bless you, Brother Bansi. May you always
stay within the Lord's mercy.'

'Greetings, Brother Bansi. We welcome you into
20 the flock of Jesus with happy spirits.'

'God bless you, Brother Bansi. Stay with the Lord,
the Devil is strong.'

Suddenly. . . .

[Buntu *has moved to behind* Sizwe. *He grabs him*
25 *roughly by the shoulder.*]

Police!

Sizwe *stands up frightened.* Buntu *watches him carefully.*]

No, man! Clean your face.

30 [Sizwe *adopts an impassive expression.* Buntu *continues as the policeman.*]

What's your name?

Man. Robert Zwelinzima.

Buntu. Where do you work?

35 Man. Feltex.

Buntu. Book!

[Sizwe *hands over the book and waits while the policeman opens it, looks at the photograph, then* Sizwe,
and finally checks through its stamps and endorsements.
40 *While all this is going on* Sizwe *stands quietly, looking
down at his feet, whistling under his breath. The book
is finally handed back.*]

Okay.

[Sizwe *takes his book and sits down.*]

45 Man [*after a pause*]. I'll try it, Buntu.

Buntu. Of course you must, if you want to stay
alive.

Man. Yes, but Sizwe Bansi is dead.

Buntu. What about Robert Zwelinzima then?

That poor bastard I pissed on out there in the dark. 50
So *he's* alive again. Bloody miracle, man.

Look, if someone was to offer me the things I
wanted most in my life, the things that would make
me, my wife, and my child happy, in exchange
for the name Buntu . . . you think I wouldn't swop? 55

Man. Are you sure, Buntu?

Buntu [*examining the question seriously*]. If there
was just me . . . I mean, if I was alone, if I didn't
have anyone to worry about or look after except
myself . . . maybe then I'd be prepared to pay some 60
sort of price for a little pride. But if I had a wife
and four children wasting away their one and only
life in the dust and poverty of Ciskeian Independence . . . if I had four children waiting for me, their
father, to do something about their lives . . . ag, 65
no, Sizwe. . . .

Man. Robert, Buntu.

Buntu [*angry*]. All right! Robert, John, Athol,
Winston. . . . Shit on names, man! To hell with
them if in exchange you can get a piece of bread 70
for your stomach and a blanket in winter. Understand me, brother, I'm not saying that pride isn't
a way for us. What I'm saying is shit on our pride
if we only bluff ourselves that we are men.
Take your name back, Sizwe Bansi, if it's so im- 75
portant to you. But next time you hear a white
man say 'John' to you, don't say '*Ja, Baas*?' And
next time the bloody white man says to you, a
man, 'Boy, come here,' don't run to him and lick
his arse like we all do. Face him and tell him: 'White 80
man. I'm a Man!' *Ag kak!* We're bluffing ourselves.
It's like my father's hat. Special hat, man! Carefully wrapped in plastic on top of the wardrobe in
his room. God help the child who so much as
touches it! Sunday it goes on his head, and a man, 85
full of dignity, a man I respect, walks down the
street. White man stops him: 'Come here, *kaffir!*'°
What does he do?

[Buntu *whips the imaginary hat off his head and
crumples it in his hands as he adopts a fawning, servile 90
pose in front of the white man.*]

'What is it, Baas?'

If that is what you call pride, then shit on it! Take
mine and give me food for my children.

[*Pause.*] 95

Look, brother, Robert Zwelinzima, that poor bas-

kaffir a black African; a derogatory term

tard out there in the alleyway, if there *are* ghosts,
he is smiling tonight. He is here, with us, and he's
saying: 'Good luck, Sizwe! I hope it works.' He's
a brother, man.

5   MAN. For how long, Buntu?

BUNTU. How long? For as long as you can stay
out of trouble. Trouble will mean police station,
then fingerprints off to Pretoria to check on previous convictions . . . and when they do that . . .

10 Sizwe Bansi will live again and you will have had
it.

MAN. Buntu, you know what you are saying? A
black man stay out of trouble? Impossible, Buntu.
Our skin is trouble.

15 BUNTU [*wearily*]. You said you wanted to try.

MAN. And I will.

BUNTU [*picks up his coat*]. I'm tired, . . . Robert,
Good luck. See you tomorrow.

[*Exit* BUNTU, SIZWE *picks up the passbook, looks at*
20 *it for a long time, then puts it in his back pocket. He*
finds his walking-stick, newspaper, and pipe and moves
downstage into a solitary light. He finishes the letter to
his wife.]

MAN. So Nowetu, for the time being my trou-
25 bles are over. Christmas I come home. In the
meantime Buntu is working a plan to get me a
Lodger's Permit. If I get it, you and the children
can come here and spend some days with me in
Port Elizabeth. Spend the money I am sending
30 you carefully. If all goes well I will send some
more each week.

I do not forget you, my dear wife.

Your loving Husband,
Sizwe Bansi.

35   [*As he finishes the letter,* SIZWE *returns to the pose*
of the photo. Styles Photographic Studio. STYLES *is be-*
hind the camera.]

STYLES. Hold it, Robert. Hold it just like that.
Just one more. Now smile, Robert. . . . Smile. . . .
40 Smile. . . .

Camera flash and blackout.

Peter Shaffer

1926–

Equus

1973

Readers of plays, as distinguished from spectators, cannot escape the task of trying to imagine the play as performed in what Carlyle called "the theater under my own hat." Peter Shaffer goes to unusual lengths to assist the reader in that task. It is remarkable that all productions of *Equus,* until a film version appeared in 1977, were copied in detail from the original London production. That was staged, costumed, lighted, and choreographed to emphasize at all points the playing of a play. It sought not the illusion of reality, rather the reality of illusion.

Commenting on the comparatively realistic film version (which presents live horses rather than actors wearing stylized masks) Vincent Canby of the *New York Times* found something missing, "specifically our need to use our imagination to fill in the visual and emotional gaps in the stories." Because the play is shaped as a psychoanalytic penetration into ever-deepening scenic levels of interior life, the successive disclosures invite the audience to advance imaginatively toward the revelation — and perhaps the solution — of a mystery. Like Williams' Production Notes for *The Glass Menagerie,* Shaffer's prefatory notes and elaborated text afford an opportunity to see a playwright striving to actualize an interpretive performance of his script.

Shaffer's effort to specify and stabilize a nearly ideal production contrasts noticeably with Athol Fugard's insistence on the value of improvisation in the genesis of *Sizwe Bansi Is Dead.* Both attitudes are indicative of cross-currents contending in the modern theater.

Equus

SHAFFER

A Note on the Play

One weekend over two years ago, I was driving with a friend through bleak countryside. We passed a stable. Suddenly he was reminded by it of an alarming crime which he had heard about recently at a dinner party in London. He knew only one horrible detail, and his complete mention of it could barely have lasted a minute—but it was enough to arouse in me an intense fascination.

The act had been committed several years before by a highly disturbed young man. It had deeply shocked a local bench of magistrates. It lacked, finally, any coherent explanation.

A few months later my friend died. I could not verify what he had said, or ask him to expand it. He had given me no name, no place, and no time. I don't think he knew them. All I possessed was his report of a dreadful event, and the feeling it engendered in me. I knew

very strongly that I wanted to interpret it in some entirely personal way. I had to create a mental world in which the deed could be made comprehensible.

Every person and incident in *Equus* is of my own invention, save the crime itself: and even that I modified to accord with what I feel to be acceptable theatrical proportion. I am grateful now that I have never received confirmed details of the real story, since my concern has been more and more with a different kind of exploration.

I have been lucky, in doing final work on the play, to have enjoyed the advice and expert comment of a distinguished child psychiatrist. Through him I have tried to keep things real in a more naturalistic sense. I have also come to perceive that psychiatrists are an immensely varied breed, professing immensely varied methods and techniques. Martin Dysart is simply one doctor in one hospital. I must take responsibility for him, as I do for his patient.

The Set

A square of wood set on a circle of wood.

The square resembles a railed boxing ring. The rail, also of wood, encloses three sides. It is perforated on each side by an opening. Under the rail are a few vertical slats, as if in a fence. On the downstage side there is no rail. The whole square is set on ball bearings, so that by slight pressure from actors standing round it on the circle, it can be made to turn round smoothly by hand.

On the square are set three little plain benches, also of wood. They are placed parallel with the rail, against the slats, but can be moved out by the actors to stand at right angles to them.

Set into the floor of the square, and flush with it, is a thin metal pole, about a yard high. This can be raised out of the floor, to stand upright. It acts as a support for the actor playing Nugget, when he is ridden.

In the area outside the circle stand benches. Two downstage left and right, are curved to accord with the circle. The left one is used by

Dysart as a listening and observing post when he is out of the square, and also by Alan as his hospital bed. The right one is used by Alan's parents, who sit side by side on it. (Viewpoint is from the main body of the audience.)

Further benches stand upstage, and accommodate the other actors. All the cast of *Equus* sits on stage the entire evening. They get up to perform their scenes, and return when they are done to their places around the set. They are witnesses, assistants — and especially a Chorus.

Upstage, forming a backdrop to the whole, are tiers of seats in the fashion of a dissecting theatre, formed into two railed-off blocks, pierced by a central tunnel. In these blocks sit members of the audience. During the play, Dysart addresses them directly from time to time, as he addresses the main body of the theatre. No other actor ever refers to them.

To left and right, downstage, stand two ladders on which are suspended horse masks.

The colour of all benches is olive green.

Above the stage hangs a battery of lights, set in a huge metal ring. Light cues, in this version, will be only of the most general description.

The Horses

The actors wear track-suits of chestnut velvet. On their feet are light strutted hooves, about four inches high, set on metal horse-shoes. On their hands are gloves of the same color. On their heads are tough masks made of alternating bands of silver wire and leather: their eyes are outlined by leather blinkers. The actors' own heads are seen beneath them: no attempt should be made to conceal them.

Any literalism which could suggest the cosy familiarity of a domestic animal — or worse, a pantomime horse — should be avoided. The actors should never crouch on all fours, or even bend forward. They must always — except on the one occasion where Nugget is ridden — stand upright, as if the body of the horse extended invisibly behind them. Animal effect must be created entirely mimetically, through

the use of legs, knees, neck, face, and the turn of the head which can move the mask above it through all the gestures of equine wariness and pride. Great care must also be taken that the masks are put on before the audience with very precise timing — the actors watching each other, so that the masking has an exact and ceremonial effect.

The Chorus

References are made in the text to the Equus Noise. I have in mind a choric effect, made by all the actors sitting round upstage, and composed of humming, thumping, and stamping — though never of neighing or whinnying. This Noise heralds or illustrates the presence of Equus the God.

CHARACTERS

MARTIN DYSART *a psychiatrist*
ALAN STRANG
FRANK STRANG *his father*
DORA STRANG *his mother*
HESTHER SALOMON *a magistrate*
JILL MASON
HARRY DALTON *a stable owner*
A YOUNG HORSEMAN
A NURSE
SIX ACTORS *including the Young Horseman, who also plays Nugget — appear as Horses.*

The main action of the play takes place in Rokeby Psychiatric Hospital in Southern England. The time is the present.

The play is divided into numbered scenes, indicating a change of time or locale or mood. The action, however, is continuous.

ACT ONE

1

Darkness.
Silence.
Dim light up on the square. In a spotlight stands ALAN STRANG, *a lean boy of seventeen, in sweater and jeans. In front of him, the horse* NUGGET. 5

ALAN'S *pose represents a contour of great tenderness: his head is pressed against the shoulder of the horse, his hands stretching up to fondle its head. The horse in turn nuzzles his neck.*

5   *The flame of a cigarette lighter jumps in the dark. Lights come up slowly on the circle. On the left bench, downstage,* MARTIN DYSART, *smoking. A man in his mid-forties.*

DYSART. With one particular horse, called
10 Nugget, he embraces. The animal digs its sweaty brow into his cheek, and they stand in the dark for an hour—like a necking couple. And of all nonsensical things—I keep thinking about the *horse!* Not the boy: the horse, and
15 what it may be trying to do. I keep seeing that huge head kissing him with its chained mouth. Nudging through the metal some desire absolutely irrelevant to filling its belly or propagating its own kind. What desire could
20 that be? Not to stay a horse any longer? Not to remain reined up for ever in those particular genetic strings? Is it possible, at certain moments we cannot imagine, a horse can add its sufferings together—the non-stop jerks and
25 jabs that are its daily life—and turn them into grief? What use is grief to a horse?
  [ALAN *leads* NUGGET *out of the square and they disappear together up the tunnel, the horse's hooves scraping delicately on the wood.*]
30   [DYSART *rises, and addresses both the large audience in the theatre and the smaller one on stage.*]
You see, I'm lost. What use, I should be asking, are questions like these to an overworked psy-
35 chiatrist in a provincial hospital? They're worse than useless: they are, in fact, subversive.
  [*He enters the square. The light grows brighter.*]
The thing is, I'm desperate. You see, I'm wearing that horse's head myself. That's the feeling.
40 All reined up in old language and old assumptions, straining to jump clean-hoofed on to a whole new track of being I only suspect is there. I can't see it, because my educated, average head is being held at the wrong angle.
45 I can't jump because the bit forbids it, and my own basic force—my horsepower, if you like—is too little. The only thing I know for sure is

this: a horse's head is finally unknowable to me. Yet I handle children's heads—which I must presume to be more complicated, at
50 least in the area of my chief concern. . . . In a way, it has nothing to do with this boy. The doubts have been there for years, piling up steadily in this dreary place. It's only the extremity of this case that's made them active.
55 I know that. The *extremity* is the point! All the same, whatever the reason, they are now, these doubts, not just vaguely worrying—but intolerable . . . I'm sorry. I'm not making much sense. Let me start properly: in order. It began
60 one Monday last month, with Hesther's visit.

2

  [*The light gets warmer.*]
  [*He sits.* NURSE *enters the square.*]
NURSE. Mrs Salomon to see you, Doctor.
DYSART. Show her in, please.   65
  [NURSE *leaves and crosses to where* HESTHER *sits.*]
Some days I blame Hesther. She brought him to see me. But of course that's nonsense. What is he but a last straw? a last symbol? If it hadn't 70
been him, it would have been the next patient, or the next. At least, I suppose so.
  [HESTHER *enters the square: a woman in her mid-forties.*]
HESTHER. Hallo, Martin.   75
  [DYSART *rises and kisses her on the cheek.*]
DYSART. Madam Chairman! Welcome to the torture chamber!
HESTHER. It's good of you to see me right away.   80
DYSART. You're a welcome relief. Take a couch.
HESTHER. It's been a day?
DYSART. No—just a fifteen year old schizophrenic, and a girl of eight thrashed into 85
catatonia by her father. Normal, really . . . You're in a state.
HESTHER. Martin, this is the most shocking case I ever tried.
DYSART. So you said on the phone.   90
HESTHER. I mean it. My bench° wanted to

---

my bench other magistrates who heard the case

send the boy to prison. For life, if they could manage it. It took me two hours solid arguing to get him sent to you instead.

DYSART. Me?

5 HESTHER. I mean, to hospital.

DYSART. Now look, Hesther. Before you say anything else, I can take no more patients at the moment. I can't even cope with the ones I have.

10 HESTHER. You must.

DYSART. Why?

HESTHER. Because most people are going to be disgusted by the whole thing. Including doctors.

15 DYSART. May I remind you that I share this room with two highly competent psychiatrists?

HESTHER. Bennett and Thoroughgood. They'll be as shocked as the public.

DYSART. That's an absolutely unwarrantable

20 statement.

HESTHER. Oh, they'll be cool and exact. And underneath they'll be revolted, and immovably English. Just like my bench.

DYSART. Well, what am I? Polynesian?

25 HESTHER. You know exactly what I mean! ... [*pause.*] Please, Martin. It's vital. You're this boy's only chance.

DYSART. Why? What's he done? Dosed some little girl's Pepsi with Spanish Fly?° What

30 could possibly throw your bench into two-hour convulsions?

HESTHER. He blinded six horses with a metal spike.

[*A long pause.*]

35 DYSART. Blinded?

HESTHER. Yes.

DYSART. All at once, or over a period?

HESTHER. All on the same night.

DYSART. Where?

40 HESTHER. In a riding stable near Winchester. He worked there at weekends.

DYSART. How old?

HESTHER. Seventeen.

DYSART. What did he say in Court?

45 HESTHER. Nothing. He just sang.

Spanish Fly a powder made of dried beetles, reputedly an aphrodisiac

DYSART. Sang?

HESTHER. Any time anyone asked him anything.

[*Pause.*]

Please take him, Martin. It's the last favour 50 I'll ever ask you.

DYSART. No, it's not.

HESTHER. No, it's not—and he's probably abominable. All I know is, he needs you badly. Because there really is nobody within a hun- 55 dred miles of your desk who can handle him. And perhaps understand what this is about. Also. . . .

DYSART. What?

HESTHER. There's something very special 60 about him.

DYSART. In what way?

HESTHER. Vibrations.

DYSART. You and your vibrations.

HESTHER. They're quite startling. You'll 65 see.

DYSART. When does he get here?

HESTHER. Tomorrow morning. Luckily there was a bed in Neville Ward. I know this is an awful imposition, Martin. Frankly I didn't 70 know what else to do.

[*Pause.*]

DYSART. Can you come in and see me on Friday?

HESTHER. Bless you! 75

DYSART. If you come after work I can give you a drink. Will 6:30 be all right?

HESTHER. You're a dear. You really are.

DYSART. Famous for it.

HESTHER. Goodbye. 80

DYSART. By the way, what's his name?

HESTHER. Alan Strang.

[*She leaves and returns to her seat.*]

DYSART [*to audience*]. What did I expect of him? Very little, I promise you. One more 85 dented little face. One more adolescent freak. The usual unusual. One great thing about being in the adjustment business: you're never short of customers.

[NURSE *comes down the tunnel, followed by* 90 ALAN. *She enters the square.*]

NURSE. Alan Strang, Doctor.

[*The boy comes in.*]

DYSART. Hallo. My name's Martin Dysart. I'm pleased to meet you.

[*He puts out his hand.* ALAN *does not respond in any way.*]

5 That'll be all, Nurse, thank you.

3

[NURSE *goes out and back to her place.*]

[DYSART *sits, opening a file.*]

So: did you have a good journey? I hope they gave you lunch at least. Not that there's much
10 to choose between a British Rail meal and one here.

[ALAN *stands staring at him.*]

DYSART. Won't you sit down?

[*Pause. He does not.* DYSART *consults his*
15 *file.*]

Is this your full name? Alan Strang?

[*Silence.*]

And you're seventeen. Is that right? Seventeen? . . . Well?

20 ALAN [*singing low*]. Double your pleasure, Double your fun
With Doublemint, Doublemint
Doublemint gum.

DYSART [*unperturbed*]. Now, let's see. You
25 work in an electrical shop during the week. You live with your parents, and your father's a printer. What sort of things does he print?

ALAN [*singing louder*]. Double your pleasure Double your fun
30 With Doublemint, Doublemint
Doublemint gum.

DYSART. I mean does he do leaflets and calendars? Things like that?

[*The boy approaches him, hostile.*]

35 ALAN [*singing*]. Try the taste of Martini The most beautiful drink in the world.
It's the right one—
The bright one—
That's Martini!

40 DYSART. I wish you'd sit down, if you're going to sing. Don't you think you'd be more comfortable?

[*Pause.*]

ALAN [*singing*]. There's only one T in Typhoo!
45 In packets and in teabags too.
Any way you make it, you'll find it's true:

There's only one T in Typhoo!

DYSART [*appreciatively*]. Now that's a good song. I like it better than the other two. Can I hear that one again? 50

[ALAN *starts away from him, and sits on the upstage bench.*]

ALAN [*singing*]. Double your pleasure Double your fun
With Doublemint, Doublemint 55
Doublemint gum.

DYSART [*smiling*]. You know I was wrong. I really do think that one's better. It's got such a catchy tune. Please do that one again.

[*Silence. The boy glares at him.*] 60

I'm going to put you in a private bedroom for a little while. There are one or two available, and they're rather more pleasant than being in a ward. Will you please come and see me tomorrow? . . . [*He rises.*] By the way, which 65
parent is it who won't allow you to watch television? Mother or father? Or is it both? [*calling out of the door.*] Nurse!

[ALAN *stares at him.* NURSE *comes in.*]

NURSE. Yes, Doctor? 70

DYSART. Take Strang here to Number Three, will you? He's moving in there for a while.

NURSE. Very good, Doctor.

DYSART [*to* ALAN]. You'll like that room. It's nice. 75

[*The boy sits staring at* DYSART.]

[DYSART *returns the stare.*]

NURSE. Come along, young man. This way. . . . I said this way, please.

[*Reluctantly* ALAN *rises and goes to* NURSE, 80
passing dangerously close to DYSART, *and out through the left door.* DYSART *looks after him, fascinated.*]

4

[NURSE *and patient move on to the circle, and walk downstage to the bench where the doctor* 85
first sat, which is to serve also as ALAN's *bed.*]

NURSE. Well, now: isn't this nice? You're lucky to be in here, you know, rather than the ward. That ward's a noisy old place.

ALAN [*singing*]. Let's go where you wanna 90
go—Texaco!

NURSE [*contemplating him*]. I hope you're

not going to make a nuisance of yourself. You'll have a much better time of it here, you know, if you behave yourself.

ALAN. Fuck off.

NURSE [*tight*]. That's the bell there. The lav's down the corridor.

[*She leaves him, and goes back to her place.*]
[ALAN *lies down.*]

5

[DYSART *stands in the middle of the square and addresses the audience. He is agitated.*]

DYSART. That night, I had this very explicit dream. In it I'm a chief priest in Homeric Greece. I'm wearing a wide gold mask, all noble and bearded, like the so-called Mask of Agamemnon found at Mycenae. I'm standing by a thick round stone and holding a sharp knife. In fact, I'm officiating at some immensely important ritual sacrifice, on which depends the fate of the crops or of a military expedition. The sacrifice is a herd of children: about five hundred boys and girls. I can see them stretching away in a long queue, right across the plain of Argos. I know it's Argos because of the red soil. On either side of me stand two assistant priests, wearing masks as well: lumpy, pop-eyed masks, such as also were found at Mycenae. They are enormously strong, these other priests, and absolutely tireless. As each child steps forward, they grab it from behind and throw it over the stone. Then, with a surgical skill which amazes even me, I fit in the knife and slice elegantly down to the navel, just like a seamstress following a pattern. I part the flaps, sever the inner tubes, yank them out and throw them hot and steaming on to the floor. The other two then study the pattern they make, as if they were reading hieroglyphics. It's obvious to me that I'm tops as chief priest. It's this unique talent for carving that has got me where I am. The only thing is, unknown to them, I've started to feel distinctly nauseous. And with each victim, it's getting worse. My face is going green behind the mask. Of course, I redouble my efforts to look professional—cutting and snipping for all I'm worth: mainly because I know that if

ever those two assistants so much as glimpse my distress—and the implied doubt that this repetitive and smelly work is doing any social good at all—I will be the next across the stone. And, then, of course—the damn mask begins to slip. The priests both turn and look at it—it slips some more—they see the green sweat running down my face—their gold pop-eyes suddenly fill up with blood—they tear the knife out of my hand . . . and I wake up.

6

[HESTHER *enters the square. Light grows warmer.*]

HESTHER. That's the most indulgent thing I ever heard.

DYSART. You think?

HESTHER. Please don't be ridiculous. You've done the most superb work with children. You must know that.

DYSART. Yes, but do the children?

HESTHER. Really!

DYSART. I'm sorry.

HESTHER. So you should be.

DYSART. I don't know why you listen. It's just professional menopause. Everyone gets it sooner or later. Except you.

HESTHER. Oh, of course. I feel totally fit to be a magistrate all the time.

DYSART. No, you don't—but then that's you feeling unworthy to fill a job. I feel the job is unworthy to fill me.

HESTHER. Do you seriously?

DYSART. More and more. I'd like to spend the next ten years wandering very slowly around the *real* Greece . . . Anyway, all this dream nonsense is your fault.

HESTHER. Mine?

DYSART. It's that lad of yours who started it off. Do you know it's his face I saw on every victim across the stone?

HESTHER. Strang?

DYSART. He has the strangest stare I ever met.

HESTHER. Yes.

DYSART. It's exactly like being accused. Violently accused. But what of? . . . Treating him is going to be unsettling. Especially in my present state. His singing was direct enough. His speech is more so.

HESTHER [*surprised*]. He's talking to you, then?

5 DYSART. Oh yes. It took him two more days of commercials, and then he snapped. Just like that—I suspect it has something to do with his nightmares.

[NURSE *walks briskly round the circle, a blanket*
10 *over her arm, a clipboard of notes in her hand.*]

HESTHER. He has nightmares?

DYSART. Bad ones.

NURSE. We had to give him a sedative or two, Doctor. Last night it was exactly the same.

15 DYSART [*to* NURSE]. What does he do? Call out?

NURSE [*to desk*]. A lot of screaming, Doctor.

DYSART [*to* NURSE]. Screaming?

NURSE. One word in particular.

20 DYSART [*to* NURSE]. You mean a special word?

NURSE. Over and over again. [*Consulting clipboard.*] It sounds like 'Ek.'

HESTHER. Ek?

25 NURSE. Yes, Doctor. Ek. . . . 'Ek!' he goes. 'Ek!'

HESTHER. How weird.

NURSE. When I woke him up he clung to me like he was going to break my arm.

30 [*She stops at* ALAN's *bed. He is sitting up. She puts the blanket over him, and returns to her place.*]

DYSART. And then he burst in—just like that—without knocking or anything. For-
35 tunately, I didn't have a patient with me.

ALAN [*Jumping up*]. *Dad!*

HESTHER. What?

DYSART. The answer to a question I'd asked him two days before. Spat out with the same
40 anger as he sang the commercials.

HESTER. Dad what?

ALAN. Who hates telly.

[*He lies downstage on the circle, as if watching television.*]

45 HESTHER. You mean his dad forbids him to watch?

DYSART. Yes.

ALAN. It's a dangerous drug.

HESTHER. Oh, really!

[FRANK *stands up and enters the scene down-* 50
stage on the circle. A man in his fifties.]

FRANK [*to* ALAN]. It may not look like that, but that's what it is. Absolutely fatal mentally, if you receive my meaning.

[DORA *follows him on. She is also middle-* 55
aged.]

DORA. That's a little extreme, dear, isn't it?

FRANK. You sit in front of that thing long enough, you'll become stupid for life—like most of the population. [*to* ALAN.] The thing 60
is, it's a *swiz.*° It seems to be offering you something, but actually it's taking something away. Your intelligence and your concentration, every minute you watch it. That's a true swiz, do you see? 65

[*Seated on the floor,* ALAN *shrugs.*]

I don't want to sound like a spoilsport, old chum—but there really is no substitute for reading. What's the matter: don't you like it?

ALAN. It's all right. 70

FRANK. I know you think it's none of my beeswax,° but it really is you know . . . Actually, it's a disgrace when you come to think of it. You the son of a printer, and never opening a book! If all the world was like you, 75
I'd be out of a job, if you receive my meaning!

DORA. All the same, times change, Frank.

FRANK [*reasonably*]. They change if you let then change, Dora. Please return that set in the 80
morning.

ALAN [*crying out*]. No!

DORA. Frank! No!

FRANK. I'm sorry, Dora, but I'm not having that thing in the house a moment longer. I 85
told you I didn't want it to begin with.

DORA. But, dear, everyone watches television these days!

FRANK. Yes, and what do they watch? Mindless violence! Mindless jokes! Every five 90
minutes some laughing idiot selling you something you don't want, just to bolster up the economic system. [*to* ALAN.] I'm sorry, old chum.

swiz swindle
beeswax slang, esp. children's; business

[*He leaves the scene and sits again in his place.*]

HESTHER. He's a Communist, then?

DYSART. Old-type Socialist, I'd say. Relentlessly self-improving.

HESTHER. They're *both* older than you'd expect.

DYSART. So I gather.

DORA [*looking after* FRANK]. Really, dear, you are very extreme!

[*She leaves the scene too, and again sits beside her husband.*]

HESTHER. She's an ex-school teacher, isn't she?

DYSART. Yes. The boy's proud of that. We got on to it this afternoon.

ALAN [*belligerently, standing up*]. She knows more than you.

[HESTHER *crosses and sits by* DYSART. *During the following, the boy walks round the circle, speaking to* DYSART *but not looking at him.* DYSART *replies in the same manner.*]

DYSART [*to* ALAN]. Does she?

ALAN. I bet I do too. I bet I know more history than you.

DYSART [*to* ALAN]. Well, I bet you don't.

ALAN. All right: who was the Hammer of the Scots?

DYSART [*to* ALAN]. I don't know: who?

ALAN. King Edward the First.° Who never smiled again?

DYSART [*to* ALAN]. I don't know: who?

ALAN. You don't know anything, do you? It was Henry the First.° I know all the Kings.

DYSART [*to* ALAN]. And who's your favourite?

ALAN. John.°

DYSART [*to* ALAN]. Why?

ALAN. Because he put out the eyes of that smarty little—

[*Pause.*]

King Edward the First (1239–1307), who aggressively invaded Scotland

Henry the First (1068–1135), who is supposed never to have smiled again after the drowning of his only male heir, Prince William

John (1167–1216), who ordered the blinding of his young nephew Prince Arthur, who talked his jailer out of harming him. (See Shakespeare's *King John*, IV, i.)

[*sensing he has said something wrong.*] Well, he didn't really. He was prevented, because the jailer was merciful!

HESTHER. Oh dear.

ALAN. *He was prevented!*

DYSART. Something odder was to follow.

ALAN. Who said 'Religion is the opium of the people'?

HESTHER. Good Lord!

[ALAN *giggles.*]

DYSART. The odd thing was, he said it with a sort of guilty snigger. The sentence is obviously associated with some kind of tension.

HESTHER. What did you say?

DYSART. I gave him the right answer. [*to* ALAN.] Karl Marx.

ALAN. No.

DYSART [*to* ALAN]. Then who?

ALAN. Mind your own beeswax.

DYSART. It's probably his dad. He may say it to provoke his wife.

HESTHER. And you mean she's religious?

DYSART. She could be. I tried to discover— none too successfully.

ALAN. Mind your own beeswax!

[ALAN *goes back to bed and lies down in the dark.*]

DYSART. However, I shall find out on Sunday.

HESTHER. What do you mean?

DYSART [*getting up*]. I want to have a look at his home, so I invited myself over.

HESTHER. Did you?

DYSART. If there's any tension over religion, it should be evident on a Sabbath evening! I'll let you know.

[*He kisses her cheek and they part, both leaving the square.* HESTHER *sits in her place again;* DYSART *walks round the circle, and greets* DORA *who stands waiting for him downstage.*]

7

DYSART [*shaking hands*]. Mrs Strang.

DORA. Mr Strang's still at the Press, I'm afraid. He should be home in a minute.

DYSART. He works Sundays as well?

DORA. Oh, yes. He doesn't set much store by Sundays.

DYSART. Perhaps you and I could have a little talk before he comes in.

DORA. Certainly. Won't you come into the living room?

5 [*She leads the way into the square. She is very nervous.*]

Please. . . .

[*She motions him to sit, then holds her hands tightly together.*]

10 DYSART. Mrs Strang, have you any idea how this thing could have occurred?

DORA. I can't imagine, Doctor. It's all so unbelievable! . . . Alan's always been such a gentle boy. He loves animals! Especially

15 horses.

DYSART. Especially!

DORA. Yes. He even has a photograph of one up in his bedroom. A beautiful white one, looking over a gate. His father gave it to him

20 a few years ago, off a calendar he'd printed — and he's never taken it down . . . And when he was seven or eight, I used to have to read him the same book over and over, all *about* a horse.

DYSART. Really?

25 DORA. Yes: it was called Prince, and no one could ride him.

[ALAN *calls from his bed, not looking at his mother.*]

ALAN [*excited, younger voice*]. Why not? . . .

30 Why not? . . . Say it! In his voice!

DORA. He loved the idea of animals talking.

DYSART. Did he?

ALAN. Say it! Say it! . . . Use his voice!

DORA ['*proud*' *voice*]. 'Because I am faithful!'

35 [ALAN *giggles.*]

My name is Prince, and I'm a Prince among horses! Only my young Master can ride me! Anyone else — I'll *throw off!*'

[ALAN *giggles louder.*]

40 And then I remember I used to tell him a funny thing about falling off horses. Did you know that when Christian cavalry first appeared in the New World, the pagans thought horse and rider was one person?

45 DYSART. Really?

ALAN [*sitting up, amazed*]. One person?

DORA. Actually they thought it must be a god.

ALAN. *A god!*

DORA. It was only when one rider fell off, 50 they realized the truth.

DYSART. That's fascinating. I never heard that before. . . . Can you remember anything else like that you may have told him about horses? 55

DORA. Well, not really. They're in the Bible, of course. 'He saith among the trumpets, Ha, ha.'

DYSART. Ha, ha?

DORA. The Book of Job. Such a noble passage. 60 *You* know — [*quoting.*] 'Hast thou given the horse strength?'

ALAN [*responding*]. 'Hast thou clothed his neck with thunder?'

DORA [*to* ALAN]. 'The glory of his nostrils 65 is terrible!'

ALAN. 'He swallows the ground with fierceness and rage!'

DORA. 'He saith among the trumpets —'

ALAN [*trumpeting*]. 'Ha! Ha!' 70

DORA [*to* DYSART]. Isn't that splendid?

DYSART. It certainly is.

ALAN [*trumpeting*]. Ha! Ha!

DORA. And then, of course, we saw an awful lot of Westerns on the television. He couldn't 75 have enough of those.

DYSART. But surely you don't have a set, do you? I understood Mr Strang doesn't approve.

DORA [*conspiratorially*]. He doesn't . . . I used to let him slip off in the afternoons to a 80 friend next door.

DYSART [*smiling*]. You mean without his father's knowledge?

DORA. What the eye does not see, the heart does not grieve over, does it? Anyway, West- 85 erns are harmless enough, surely?

[FRANK *stands up and enters the square.*]

[ALAN *lies back under the blanket.*]

[*to* FRANK.] Oh, hallo dear. This is Dr Dysart.

FRANK [*shaking hands*]. How d'you do? 90

DYSART. How d'you do?

DORA. I was just telling the Doctor, Alan's always adored horses.

FRANK [*tight*].° We assumed he did.

[tight] warily

DORA. You know he did, dear. Look how he liked that photograph you gave him.

FRANK [*startled*]. What about it?

DORA. Nothing, dear. Just that he pestered
5 you to have it as soon as he saw it. Do you remember? [*to* DYSART.] We've always been a horsey family. At least my side of it has. My grandfather used to ride every morning on the downs behind Brighton, all dressed up in
10 bowler hat and jodhpurs! He used to look splendid. Indulging in equitation, he called it.

[FRANK *moves away from them and sits wearily.*]

ALAN [*trying the word*]. Equitation. . . .
15 DORA. I remember I told him how that came from *equus*, the Latin word for horse. Alan was fascinated by that word, I know. I suppose because he'd never come across one with two U's together before.
20 ALAN [*savouring it*]. Equus!

DORA. I always wanted the boy to ride himself. He'd have so enjoyed it.

DYSART. But surely he did?

DORA. No.
25 DYSART. Never?

DORA. He didn't care for it. He was most definite about not wanting to.

DYSART. But he must have had to at the stables? I mean, it would be part of the job.
30 DORA. You'd have thought so, but no. He absolutely wouldn't, would he, dear?

FRANK [*dryly*]. It seems he was perfectly happy raking out manure.

DYSART. Did he ever give a reason for this?
35 DORA. No. I must say we both thought it most peculiar, but he wouldn't discuss it. I mean, you'd have thought he'd be longing to get out in the air after being cooped up all week in that dreadful shop. Electrical and
40 kitchenware! Isn't *that* an environment for a sensitive boy, Doctor? . . .

FRANK. Dear, have you offered the doctor a cup of tea?

DORA. Oh dear, no, I haven't! . . . And you
45 must be dying for one.

DYSART. That would be nice.

DORA. Of course it would . . . Excuse me . . .

[*She goes out — but lingers on the circle, eaves-dropping near the right door.* ALAN *stretches out under his blanket and sleeps.* FRANK *gets up.*]
50 FRANK. My wife has romantic ideas, if you receive my meaning.

DYSART. About her family?

FRANK. She thinks she married beneath her. I daresay she did. I don't understand these
55 things myself.

DYSART. Mr Strang, I'm fascinated by the fact that Alan wouldn't ride.

FRANK. Yes, well that's him. He's always been a weird lad, I have to be honest. Can you
60 imagine spending your weekends like that — just cleaning out stalls — with all the things that he could have been doing in the way of Further Education?°

DYSART. Except he's hardly a scholar.
65 FRANK. How do we know? He's never really tried. His mother indulged him. She doesn't care if he can hardly write his own name, and she a school teacher that was. Just as long as he's happy, she says . . .
70 [DORA *wrings her hands in anguish.*]

[FRANK *sits again.*]

DYSART. Would you say she was closer to him than you are?

FRANK. They've always been thick as thieves.
75 I can't say I entirely approve — especially when I hear her whispering that Bible to him hour after hour, up there in his room.

DYSART. Your wife is religious?

FRANK. Some might say excessively so. Mind
80 you that's her business. But when it comes to dosing it down the boy's throat — well, frankly, he's my son as well as hers. She doesn't see that. Of course, that's the funny thing about religious people. They always think their
85 susceptibilities are more important than non-religious.

DYSART. And you're non-religious, I take it?

FRANK. I'm an atheist, and I don't mind admitting it. If you want my opinion, it's the
90 Bible that's responsible for all this.

DYSART. Why?

FRANK. Well, look at it yourself. A boy

Further Education state-supported educational programs beyond high school

spends night after night having this stuff read into him: an innocent man tortured to death—thorns driven into his head—nails into his hands—a spear jammed through his ribs. It

5 can mark anyone for life, that kind of thing. I'm not joking. The boy was absolutely fascinated by all that. He was always mooning over religious pictures. I mean real kinky° ones, if you receive my meaning. I had to put a stop to

10 it once or twice! . . . [pause.] Bloody religion —it's our only real problem in this house, but it's insuperable: I don't mind admitting it.

[Unable to stand any more, DORA comes in again.]

15 DORA [pleasantly]. You must excuse my husband, Doctor. This one subject is something of an obsession with him, isn't it, dear? You must admit.

FRANK. Call it what you like. All that stuff to

20 me is just bad sex.

DORA. And what has that got to do with Alan?

FRANK. Everything! . . . [seriously.] Everything, Dora!

25 DORA. I don't understand. What are you saying?

[He turns away from her.]

DYSART [calmingly]. Mr. Strang, exactly how informed do you judge your son to be about

30 sex?

FRANK [tight]. I don't know.

DYSART. You didn't actually instruct him yourself?

FRANK. Not in so many words, no.

35 DYSART. Did you, Mrs Strang?

DORA. Well, I spoke a little, yes. I had to. I've been a teacher, Doctor, and I know what happens if you don't. They find out through magazines and dirty books.

40 DYSART. What sort of thing did you tell him? I'm sorry if this is embarrassing.

DORA. I told him the biological facts. But I also told him what I believed. That sex is not just a biological matter, but spiritual as well.

45 That if God willed, he would fall in love one day. That his task was to prepare himself for

kinky bizarre, sexually perverse

the most important happening of his life. And after that, if he was lucky, he might come to know a higher love still . . . I simply . . . don't understand. . . . Alan! . . . 50

[She breaks down in sobs.]

[Her husband gets up and goes to her.]

FRANK [embarrassed]. There now. There now, Dora. Come on!

DORA [with sudden desperation]. All right— 55 laugh! Laugh, as usual!

FRANK [kindly]. No one's laughing, Dora.

[She glares at him. He puts his arms around her shoulders.]

No one's laughing, are they, Doctor? 60

[Tenderly, he leads his wife out of the square, and they resume their places on the bench.]

[Lights grow much dimmer.]

8

[A strange noise begins. ALAN begins to murmur from his bed. He is having a bad nightmare, 65 moving his hands and body as if frantically straining to tug something back. DYSART leaves the square as the boy's cries increase.]

ALAN. Ek! . . . Ek! . . . Ek! . . .

[Cries of Ek! on tape fill the theatre, from all 70 around. DYSART reaches the foot of ALAN's bed as the boy gives a terrible cry—]

EK!

[—and wakes up. The sounds snap off. ALAN and the DOCTOR stare at each other. Then 75 abruptly DYSART leaves the area and re-enters the square.]

9

[Lights grow brighter.]

[DYSART sits on his bench, left, and opens his file. ALAN gets out of bed, leaves his blanket, and 80 comes in. He looks truculent.]

DYSART. Hallo. How are you this morning? [ALAN stares at him.]

Come on: sit down.

[ALAN crosses the stage and sits on the bench, 85 opposite.]

Sorry if I gave you a start last night. I was collecting some papers from my office, and I thought I'd look in on you. Do you dream often? 90

ALAN. Do *you?*

DYSART. It's my job to ask the questions. Yours to answer them.

ALAN. Says who?

5 DYSART. Says me. Do you dream often?

ALAN. Do you?

DYSART. Look—Alan.

ALAN. I'll answer if you answer. In turns. [*Pause.*]

10 DYSART. Very well. Only we have to speak the truth.

ALAN [*mocking*]. Very well.

DYSART. So. Do you dream often?

ALAN. Yes. Do you?

15 DYSART. Yes. Do you have a special dream?

ALAN. No. Do you?

DYSART. Yes. What was your dream about last night?

ALAN. Can't remember. What's yours about?

20 DYSART. I said the truth.

ALAN. That is the truth. What's yours about? The special one.

DYSART. Carving up children.

[*ALAN smiles.*]

25 My turn!

ALAN. What?

DYSART. What is your first memory of a horse?

ALAN. What d'you mean?

30 DYSART. The first time one entered your life, in any way.

ALAN. Can't remember.

DYSART. Are you sure?

ALAN. Yes.

35 DYSART. You have no recollection of the first time you noticed a horse?

ALAN. I told you. Now it's my turn. Are you married?

DYSART [*controlling himself*]. I am.

40 ALAN. Is she a doctor too?

DYSART. It's my turn.

ALAN. Yes, well what?

DYSART. What is Ek?

[*Pause.*]

45 You shouted it out last night in your sleep. I thought you might like to talk about it.

ALAN [*singing*]. Double your pleasure, Double your fun!

DYSART. Come on, now. You can do better than that. 50

ALAN [*singing louder*]. With Doublemint, Doublemint Doublemint gum!

DYSART. All right. Good morning.

ALAN. What d'you mean?

DYSART. We're finished for today. 55

ALAN. But I've only had ten minutes.

DYSART. Too bad.

[*He picks up a file and studies it.*]

[*ALAN lingers.*]

Didn't you hear me? I said, Good morning. 60

ALAN. That's not fair!

DYSART. No?

ALAN [*savagely*]. The Government pays you twenty quid° an hour to see me. I know. I heard downstairs. 65

DYSART. Well, go back there and hear some more.

ALAN. *That's not fair!*

[*He springs up, clenching his fists in a sudden violent rage.*] 70

You're a—you're a—You're a swiz! . . . Bloody swiz! . . . Fucking swiz!

DYSART. Do I have to call Nurse?

ALAN. She puts a finger on me, I'll bash her!

DYSART. She'll bash you much harder, I can 75 assure you. Now go away.

[*He reads his file.* ALAN *stays where he is, emptily clenching his hands. He turns away.*]

[*A pause.*]

[*A faint hum starts from the* CHORUS.] 80

ALAN [*sullenly*]. On a beach. . . .

10

[*He steps out of the square, upstage, and begins to walk round the circle. Warm light glows on it.*]

DYSART. What? 85

ALAN. Where I saw a horse. Swizzy.

[*Lazily he kicks at the sand, and throws stones at the sea.*]

DYSART. How old were you?

ALAN. How should I know? . . . Six. 90

DYSART. Well, go on. What were you doing there?

twenty quid pounds sterling, about $40.00

ALAN. Digging.

[*He throws himself on the ground, downstage center of the circle, and starts scuffing with his hands.*]

5 DYSART. A sandcastle?

ALAN. Well, what else?

DYSART [*warningly*]. And?

ALAN. Suddenly I heard this noise. Coming up behind me.

10 [*A young* HORSEMAN *issues in* slow motion *out of the tunnel. He carries a riding crop with which he is urging on his invisible horse, down the right side of the circle. The hum increases.*]

DYSART. What noise?

15 ALAN. Hooves. Splashing.

DYSART. Splashing?

ALAN. The tide was out and he was galloping.

DYSART. Who was?

20 ALAN. This fellow. Like a college chap. He was on a big horse — urging him on. I thought he hadn't seen me. I called out: Hey!

[*The* HORSEMAN *goes into* natural time, *charging fast round the downstage corner of the* 25 *square straight at* ALAN.]

and they just swerved in time!

HORSEMAN [*reining back*]. Whoa! . . . Whoa there! *Whoa!* . . . Sorry! I didn't see you! . . . Did I scare you?

30 ALAN. No!

HORSEMAN [*looking down on him*]. That's a terrific castle!

ALAN. What's his name?

HORSEMAN. Trojan. You can stroke him, if 35 you like. He won't mind.

[*Shyly* ALAN *stretches up on tip-toe, and pats an invisible shoulder.*]

[*amused.*] You can hardly reach down there. Would you like to come up?

40 [ALAN *nods, eyes wide.*]

All right. Come round this side. You always mount a horse from the left. I'll give you a lift. O.K.?

[ALAN *goes round on the other side.*]

45 Here we go, now. Just do nothing. Upsadaisy!

[ALAN *sets his foot on the* HORSEMAN's *thigh, and is lifted by him up on his shoulders.*]

[*The hum from the* CHORUS *becomes exultant. Then stops.*]

All right? 50

[ALAN *nods.*]

Good. Now all you do is hold onto his mane.

[*He holds up the crop, and* ALAN *grips on to it.*]

Tight now. And grip with your knees. All 55 right? All set? . . . Come on, then, Trojan. Let's go!

[*The* HORSEMAN *walks slowly upstage round the circle, with* ALAN's *legs tight round his neck.*]

DYSART. How was it? Was it wonderful? 60

[ALAN *rides in silence.*]

Can't you remember?

HORSEMAN. Do you want to go faster?

ALAN. Yes!

HORSEMAN. O.K. All you have to do is say 65 'Come on, Trojan — bear me away!' . . . Say it, then!

ALAN. Bear me away!

[*The* HORSEMAN *starts to run with* ALAN *round the circle.*] 70

DYSART. You went fast?

ALAN. Yes!

DYSART. Weren't you frightened?

ALAN. No!

HORSEMAN. Come on now, Trojan! Bear us 75 away! Hold on! Come on now! . . .

[*He runs faster.* ALAN *begins to laugh. Then suddenly, as they reach again the right downstage corner,* FRANK *and* DORA *stand up in alarm.*]

DORA. Alan! 80

FRANK. Alan!

DORA. Alan, stop!

[FRANK *runs round after them.* DORA *follows behind.*]

FRANK. Hey, you! *You!* . . . 85

HORSEMAN. Whoa, boy! . . . Whoa! . . .

[*He reins the horse round, and wheels to face the parents. This all goes fast.*]

FRANK. What do you imagine you are doing? 90

HORSEMAN [*ironic*]. 'Imagine'?

FRANK. What is my son doing up there?

HORSEMAN. Water-skiing!

[DORA *joins them, breathless.*]

DORA. Is he all right, Frank? . . . He's not 95 hurt?

FRANK. Don't you think you should ask permission before doing a stupid thing like that?

HORSEMAN. What's stupid?

ALAN. It's lovely, dad!

DORA. Alan, come down here!

HORSEMAN. The boy's perfectly safe. Please
5 don't be hysterical.

FRANK. Don't you be la-di-da with me, young
man! Come down here, Alan. You heard what
your mother said.

ALAN. No.

10 FRANK. Come down at once. Right this moment.

ALAN. No . . . NO!

FRANK [*in a fury*]. I said—this moment!

[*He pulls* ALAN *from the* HORSEMAN'S
15 *shoulders. The boy shrieks, and falls to the
ground.*]

HORSEMAN. Watch it!

DORA. Frank!

[*She runs to her son, and kneels. The* HORSE-
20 MAN *skitters.*]

HORSEMAN. Are you mad? D'you want to
terrify the horse?

DORA. He's grazed his knee. Frank—the
boy's hurt!

25 ALAN. I'm not! I'm *not!*

FRANK. What's your name?

HORSEMAN. Jesse James.

DORA. Frank, he's bleeding!

FRANK. I intend to report you to the police
30 for endangering the lives of children.

HORSEMAN. Go right ahead!

DORA. Can you stand, dear!

ALAN. Oh, *stop* it! . . .

FRANK. You're a public menace, d'you know
35 that? How dare you pick up children and put
them on dangerous animals.

HORSEMAN. Dangerous?

FRANK. Of course dangerous. Look at his
eyes. They're rolling.

40 HORSEMAN. So are yours!

FRANK. In my opinion that is a dangerous
animal. In my considered opinion you are
both dangers to the safety of this beach.

HORSEMAN. And in my opinion, you're a
45 stupid fart!

DORA. Frank, leave it!

FRANK. What did you say?

DORA. It's not important, Frank—really!

FRANK. *What did you say?*

HORSEMAN. Oh bugger off! Sorry, chum! 50
Come on, Trojan!

[*He urges his horse straight at them, then
wheels it and gallops off round the right side of
the circle and away up the tunnel, out of sight.
The parents cry out, as they are covered with sand* 55
and water. FRANK *runs after him, and round the
left side of the circle, with his wife following
after.*]

ALAN. Splash, splash, splash! All three of us
got covered with water! Dad got absolutely 60
soaked!

FRANK [*shouting after the* HORSEMAN]. Hooligan! Filthy hooligan!

ALAN. I wanted to laugh!

FRANK. Upper class riff-raff! That's all they 65
are, people who go riding! That's what they
want—trample on ordinary people!

DORA. Don't be absurd, Frank.

FRANK. It's why they do it. It's why they
bloody do it! 70

DORA [*amused*]. Look at you. You're covered!

FRANK. Not as much as you. There's sand all
over your hair!

[*She starts to laugh.*]

[*shouting.*] Hooligan! Bloody hooligan! 75

[*She starts to laugh more. He tries to brush
the sand out of her hair.*]

What are you laughing at? It's not funny.
It's not funny at all, Dora.

[*She goes off, right, still laughing.* ALAN *edges* 80
into the square, still on the ground.]

It's just not funny! . . .

[FRANK *returns to his place on the bench,
sulky.*]

[*Abrupt silence.*] 85

ALAN. And that's all I remember.

DYSART. And a lot, too. Thank you . . . You
know, I've never been on a horse in my life.

ALAN [*not looking at him*]. Nor me.

DYSART. You mean, after that? 90

ALAN. Yes.

DYSART. But you must have done at the
stables?

ALAN. No.

DYSART. Never? 95

ALAN. No.

DYSART. How come?

ALAN. I didn't care to.

DYSART. Did it have anything to do with falling off like that, all those years ago?

ALAN [tight]. I just didn't care to, that's all.

DYSART. Do you think of that scene often?

5 ALAN. I suppose.

DYSART. Why, do you think?

ALAN. 'Cos it's funny.

DYSART. Is that all?

ALAN. What else? My turn. . . . I told you a
10 secret: now you tell me one.

DYSART. All right. I have patients who've got things to tell me, only they're ashamed to say them to my face. What do you think I do about that?

15 ALAN. What?

DYSART. I give them this little tape recorder.

[He takes a small tape recorder and microphone from his pocket.]

They go off to another room, and send me the
20 tape through Nurse. They don't have to listen to it with me.

ALAN. That's stupid.

DYSART. All you do is press this button, and speak into this. It's very simple. Anyway,
25 your time's up for today. I'll see you tomorrow.

ALAN [getting up]. Maybe.

DYSART. Maybe?

ALAN. If I feel like it.

[He is about to go out. Then suddenly he re-
30 turns to DYSART and takes the machine from him.]

It's stupid.

[He leaves the square and goes back to his bed.]

11

DORA [calling out]. Doctor!

[DORA re-enters and comes straight on to the
35 square from the right. She wears an overcoat, and is nervously carrying a shopping bag.]

DYSART. That same evening, his mother appeared.

DORA. Hallo, Doctor.

40 DYSART. Mrs Strang!

DORA. I've been shopping in the neighbour-hood. I thought I might just look in.

DYSART. Did you want to see Alan?

DORA [uncomfortably]. No, no . . . Not just
45 at the moment. Actually, it's more you I wanted to see.

DYSART. Yes?

DORA. You see, there's something Mr Strang and I thought you ought to know. We dis-cussed it, and it might just be important. 50

DYSART. Well, come and sit down.

DORA. I can't stay more than a moment. I'm late as it is. Mr Strang will be wanting his dinner.

DYSART. Ah. [encouragingly.] So, what was 55 it you wanted to tell me?

[She sits on the upstage bench.]

DORA. Well, do you remember that photo-graph I mentioned to you. The one Mr Strang gave Alan to decorate his bedroom a few years 60 ago?

DYSART. Yes. A horse looking over a gate, wasn't it?

DORA. That's right. Well, actually, it took the place of another kind of picture altogether. 65

DYSART. What kind?

DORA. It was a reproduction of Our Lord on his way to Calvary. Alan found it in Reeds Art Shop, and fell absolutely in love with it. He insisted on buying it with his pocket money, 70 and hanging it at the foot of his bed where he could see it last thing at night. My husband was very displeased.

DYSART. Because it was religious?

DORA. In all fairness I must admit it was a 75 little extreme. The Christ was loaded down with chains, and the centurions were really laying on the stripes.° It certainly would not have been my choice, but I don't believe in interfering too much with children, so I said 80 nothing.

DYSART. But Mr Strang did?

DORA. He stood it for a while, but one day we had one of our tiffs about religion, and he went straight upstairs, tore it off the boy's 85 wall and threw it in the dustbin. Alan went quite hysterical. He cried for days without stopping—and he was not a crier, you know.

DYSART. But he recovered when he was given the photograph of the horse in its place? 90

DORA. He certainly seemed to. At least, he

stripes lashes (See Matt. 27:27)

hung it in exactly the same position, and we had no more of that awful weeping.

DYSART. Thank you, Mrs Strang. That *is* interesting . . . Exactly how long ago was
5 that? Can you remember?

DORA. It must be five years ago, Doctor. Alan would have been about twelve. How is he, by the way?

DYSART. Bearing up.
10 [*She rises.*]

DORA. Please give him my love.

DYSART. You can see him any time you want, you know.

DORA. Perhaps if I could come one afternoon
15 without Mr Strang. He and Alan don't exactly get on at the moment, as you can imagine.

DYSART. Whatever you decide, Mrs Strang . . . Oh, one thing.

DORA. Yes?
20 DYSART. Could you describe that photograph of the horse in a little more detail for me? I presume it's still in his bedroom?

DORA. Oh, yes. It's a most remarkable picture, really. You very rarely see a horse taken
25 from that angle—absolutely head on. That's what makes it so interesting.

DYSART. Why? What does it look like?

DORA. Well, it's most extraordinary. It comes out all eyes.
30 DYSART. Staring straight at you?

DORA. Yes, that's right . . .

[*An uncomfortable pause.*]

I'll come and see him one day very soon, Doctor. Good-bye.
35 [*She leaves, and resumes her place by her husband.*]

DYSART [*to audience*]. It was then—that moment—I felt real alarm. What was it? The shadow of a giant head across my desk? . . .
40 At any rate, the feeling got worse with the stable-owner's visit.

12

[DALTON *comes in to the square: heavy-set: mid-fifties.*]

DALTON. Dr Dysart?
45 DYSART. Mr Dalton. It's very good of you to come.

DALTON. It is, actually. In my opinion the boy should be in prison. Not in a hospital at the tax-payers' expense.

DYSART. Please sit down. 50

[DALTON *sits.*]

This must have been a terrible experience for you.

DALTON. Terrible? I don't think I'll ever get over it. Jill's had a nervous breakdown. 55

DYSART. Jill?

DALTON. The girl who worked for me. Of course, she feels responsible in a way. Being the one who introduced him in the first place.

DYSART. He was introduced to the stable by 60 a girl?

DALTON. Jill Mason. He met her somewhere, and asked for a job. She told him to come and see me. I wish to Christ she never had.

DYSART. But when he first appeared he 65 didn't seem in any way peculiar?

DALTON. No, he was bloody good. He'd spend hours with the horses cleaning and grooming them, way over the call of duty. I thought he was a real find. 70

DYSART. Apparently, during the whole time he worked for you, he never actually rode.

DALTON. That's true.

DYSART. Wasn't that peculiar?

DALTON. Very . . . *If* he didn't. 75

DYSART. What do you mean?

[DALTON *rises.*]

DALTON. Because on and off, that whole year, I had the feeling the horses were being taken out at night. 80

DYSART. At night?

DALTON. There were just odd things I noticed. I mean too often one or other of them would be sweaty first thing in the morning, when it wasn't sick. Very sweaty, too. And its 85 stall wouldn't be near as mucky as it should be if it had been in all night. I never paid it much mind at the time. It was only when I realised I'd been hiring a loony, I came to wonder if he hadn't been riding all the time, behind our 90 backs.

DYSART. But wouldn't you have noticed if things had been disturbed?

DALTON. Nothing ever was. Still, he's a neat

worker. That wouldn't prove anything.

DYSART. Aren't the stables locked at night?

DALTON. Yes.

DYSART. And someone sleeps on the prem-
5 ises?

DALTON. Me and my son.

DYSART. Two people?

DALTON. I'm sorry, Doctor. It's obviously
just my fancy. I tell you, this thing has shaken
10 me so bad, I'm liable to believe anything. If
there's nothing else, I'll be going.

DYSART. Look: even if you were right, why
should anyone do that? Why would any boy
prefer to ride by himself at night, when he
15 could go off with others during the day.

DALTON. Are you asking me? He's a loony,
isn't he?

[DALTON *leaves the square and sits again in
his place.* DYSART *watches him go.*]

20 ALAN. It was *sexy.*

DYSART. His tape arrived that evening.

13

[ALAN *is sitting on his bed holding the tape-
recorder.* NURSE *approaches briskly, takes the
machine from him—gives it to* DYSART *in the
25 square—and leaves again, resuming her seat.*
DYSART *switches on the tape.*]

ALAN. That's what you want to know, isn't
it? All right: it was. I'm talking about the
beach. That time when I was a kid. What I
30 told you about. . . .

[*Pause. He is in great emotional difficulty.*]

[DYSART *sits on the left bench listening, file in
hand.* ALAN *rises and stands directly behind him,
but on the circle, as if recording the ensuing
35 speech. He never, of course, looks directly at the
Doctor.*]

I was pushed forward on the horse. There was
sweat on my legs from his neck. The fellow
held me tight, and let me turn the horse which
40 way I wanted. All that power going any way
you wanted . . . His sides were all warm, and
the smell . . . Then suddenly I was on the
ground, where Dad pulled me. I could have
bashed him . . .

45 [*Pause.*]

Something else. When the horse first appeared,
I looked up into his mouth. It was huge. There
was this chain in it. The fellow pulled it, and
cream dripped out. I said 'Does it hurt?' And
he said—the horse said—said—   50

[*He stops, in anguish.* DYSART *makes a note
in his file.*]

[*desperately.*] It was always the same, after
that. Every time I heard one clop by, I had to
run and see. Up a country lane or anywhere.   55
They sort of pulled me. I couldn't take my eyes
off them. Just to watch their skins. The way
their necks twist, and sweat shines in the
folds . . . [*pause*] I can't remember when it
started. Mum reading to me about Prince who   60
no one could ride, except one boy. Or the
white horse in Revelations. 'He that sat upon
him was called Faithful and True. His eyes
were as flames of fire, and he had a name
written that no man knew but himself' . . .   65
Words like reins. Stirrup. Flanks . . . 'Dashing
his spurs against his charger's flanks!' . . .
Even the words made me feel— . . . Years, I
never told anyone. Mum wouldn't understand.
She likes 'Equitation'. Bowler hats and jodh-   70
purs! 'My grandfather dressed for the horse,'
she says. What does that mean? The horse
isn't dressed. It's the most naked thing you
ever saw! More than a dog or a cat or anything.
Even the most broken down old nag has got   75
its *life!* To put a bowler on it is *filthy!* . . . Putting them through their paces! Bloody gymkhanas!° . . . No one understands! . . . Except
cowboys. They do. I wish I was a cowboy.
They're free. They just swing up and then it's   80
miles of grass . . . I bet all cowboys are orphans! . . . I bet they are!

NURSE. Mr Strang to see you, Doctor.

DYSART [*in surprise*]. Mr. Strang? Show him
up, please.   85

ALAN. No one ever says to cowboys 'Receive
my meaning'! They wouldn't dare. Or 'God'
all the time. [*mimicking his mother.*] 'God sees
you, Alan. God's got eyes everywhere—'

[*He stops abruptly.*]   90

I'm not doing any more! . . . I hate this! . . .
You can whistle for anymore. I've had it!

gymkhanas here, horse shows and riding competitions

[*He returns angrily to his bed, throwing the blanket over him.*]

[DYSART *switches off the tape.*]

14

[FRANK STRANG *comes into the square, his hat in his hand. He is nervous and embarrassed.*]

DYSART [*welcoming*]. Hallo, Mr. Strang.

FRANK. I was just passing. I hope it's not too late.

DYSART. Of course not. I'm delighted to see you.

FRANK. My wife doesn't know I'm here. I'd be grateful to you if you didn't enlighten her, if you receive my meaning.

DYSART. Everything that happens in this room is confidential, Mr Strang.

FRANK. I hope so . . . I hope so . . .

DYSART [*gently*]. Do you have something to tell me?

FRANK. As a matter of fact I have. Yes.

DYSART. Your wife told me about the photograph.

FRANK. I know, it's not that! It's *about* that, but it's—worse. . . . I wanted to tell you the other night, but I couldn't in front of Dora. Maybe I should have. It might show her where all that stuff leads to, she drills into the boy behind my back.

DYSART. What kind of thing is it?

FRANK. Something I witnessed.

DYSART. Where?

FRANK. At home. About eighteen months ago.

DYSART. Go on.

FRANK. It was late. I'd gone upstairs to fetch something. The boy had been in bed hours, or so I thought.

DYSART. Go on.

FRANK. As I came along the passage I saw the door of his bedroom was ajar. I'm sure he didn't know it was. From inside I heard the sound of this chanting.

DYSART. Chanting?

FRANK. Like the Bible. One of those lists his mother's always reading to him.

DYSART. What kind of list?

FRANK. Those Begats. So-and-so begat, you know. Genealogy.

DYSART. Can you remember what Alan's list sounded like?

FRANK. Well, the *sort* of thing. I stood there absolutely astonished. The first word I heard was . . .

ALAN [*rising and chanting*]. Prince!

DYSART. Prince?

FRANK. Prince begat Prance. That sort of nonsense.

[ALAN *moves slowly to the center of the circle, downstage.*]

ALAN. And Prance begat Prankus! And Prankus begat Flankus!

FRANK. I looked through the door, and he was standing in the moonlight in his pyjamas, right in front of that big photograph.

DYSART. The horse with the huge eyes?

FRANK. Right.

ALAN. Flankus begat Spankus. And Spankus begat Spunkus the Great, who lived three score years!

FRANK. It was all like that. I can't remember the exact names, of course. Then suddenly he knelt down.

DYSART. In front of the photograph?

FRANK. Yes. Right there at the foot of his bed.

ALAN [*kneeling*]. And Legwus begat Neckwus. And Neckwus begat Fleckwus, the King of Spit. And Fleckwus spoke out of his chinkle-chankle!

[*He bows himself to the ground.*]

DYSART. What?

FRANK. I'm sure that was the word. I've never forgotten it. Chinkle-chankle.

[ALAN *raises his head and extends his hands up in glory.*]

ALAN. And he said 'Behold—I give you Equus, my only begotten son!'

DYSART. Equus?

FRANK. Yes. No doubt of that. He repeated that word several times. 'Equus my only begotten son.'

ALAN [*reverently*]. Ek . . . . wus!

DYSART [*suddenly understanding: almost 'aside'*]. Ek . . . . Ek . . . .

FRANK [*embarrassed*]. And then . . .

DYSART. Yes: what?

FRANK. He took a piece of string out of his pocket. Made up into a noose. And put it in his mouth.

[ALAN *bridles himself with invisible string, and pulls it back.*]

And then with his other hand he picked up a coat hanger. A wooden coat hanger, and — and —

DYSART. Began to beat himself?

[ALAN, *in mime, begins to thrash himself, increasing the strokes in speed and viciousness.*]

[*Pause.*]

FRANK. You see why I couldn't tell his mother. . . . Religion. Religion's at the bottom of all this!

DYSART. What did you do?

FRANK. Nothing. I coughed — and went back downstairs.

[*The boy starts guiltily — tears the string from his mouth — and scrambles back to bed.*]

DYSART. Did you ever speak to him about it later? Even obliquely?

FRANK [*unhappily*]. I can't speak of things like that, Doctor. It's not my nature.

DYSART [*kindly*]. No. I see that.

FRANK. But I thought you ought to know. So I came.

DYSART [*warmly*]. Yes. I'm very grateful to you. Thank you.

[*Pause.*]

FRANK. Well, that's it . . .

DYSART. Is there anything else?

FRANK [*even more embarrassed*]. There is actually. One thing.

DYSART. What's that?

FRANK. On the night that he did it — that awful thing in the stable —

DYSART. Yes?

FRANK. That very night, he was out with a girl.

DYSART. How d'you know that?

FRANK. I just know.

DYSART [*puzzled*]. Did he tell you?

FRANK. I can't say any more.

DYSART. I don't quite understand.

FRANK. Everything said in here is confidential, you said.

DYSART. Absolutely.

FRANK. Then ask him. Ask him about taking a girl out, that very night he did it. . . . [*abruptly*] Goodbye, Doctor.

[*He goes.* DYSART *looks after him.*]

[FRANK *resumes his seat.*]

15

[ALAN *gets up and enters the square.*]

DYSART. Alan! Come in. Sit down. [*pleasantly*] What did you do last night?

ALAN. Watched telly.

DYSART. Any good?

ALAN. All right.

DYSART. Thanks for the tape. It was excellent.

ALAN. I'm not making any more.

DYSART. One thing I didn't quite understand. You began to say something about the horse on the beach talking to you.

ALAN. That's stupid. Horses don't talk.

DYSART. So I believe.

ALAN. I don't know what you mean.

DYSART. Never mind. Tell me something else. Who introduced you to the stable to begin with?

[*Pause.*]

ALAN. Someone I met.

DYSART. Where?

ALAN. Bryson's.

DYSART. The shop where you worked?

ALAN. Yes.

DYSART. That's a funny place for you to be. Whose idea was that?

ALAN. Dad.

DYSART. I'd have thought he'd have wanted you to work with him.

ALAN. I haven't the aptitude. And printing's a failing trade. If you receive my meaning.

DYSART [*amused*]. I see . . . What did your mother think?

ALAN. Shops are common.

DYSART. And you?

ALAN. I loved it.

DYSART. Really?

ALAN [*sarcastic*]. Why not? You get to spend every minute with electrical things. It's fun.

[NURSE, DALTON *and the actors playing horses call out to him as* CUSTOMERS, *seated where they are. Their voices are aggressive and demanding.*]

There is a constant background mumbling, made up of trade names, out of which can clearly be distinguished the italicized words, which are shouted out.]

5   CUSTOMER. *Philco!*

ALAN [*to* DYSART]. Of course it might just drive you off your chump.

CUSTOMER. I want to buy a hot-plate. I'm told the *Philco* is a good make!

10   ALAN. I think it is, madam.

CUSTOMER. Remington ladies' shavers?

ALAN. I'm not sure, madam.

CUSTOMER. *Robex* tableware?

CUSTOMER. *Croydex?*

15   CUSTOMER. *Volex?*

CUSTOMER. *Pifco* automatic toothbrushes?

ALAN. I'll find out, sir.

CUSTOMER. Beautiflor!

CUSTOMER. Windowlene!

20   CUSTOMER. I want a *Philco* transistor radio!

CUSTOMER. This isn't a *Remington!* I wanted a *Remington!*

ALAN. Sorry.

CUSTOMER. Are you a dealer for *Hoover?*

25   ALAN. Sorry.

CUSTOMER. I wanted the heat retaining *Pifco!*

ALAN. *Sorry!*

[JILL *comes into the square; a girl in her early* 30 *twenties, pretty and middle class. She wears a sweater and jeans. The mumbling stops.*]

JILL. Hallo.

ALAN. Hallo.

JILL. Have you any blades for a clipping 35 machine?

ALAN. Clipping?

JILL. To clip horses.

[*Pause. He stares at her, open-mouthed.*] What's the matter?

40   ALAN. You work at Dalton's stables. I've seen you.

[*During the following, he mimes putting away a pile of boxes on a shelf in the shop.*]

JILL. I've seen you too, haven't I? You're the 45 boy who's always staring into the yard around lunch-time.

ALAN. Me?

JILL. You're there most days.

ALAN. Not me.

JILL [*amused*]. Of course it's you. Mr. Dal- 50 ton was only saying the other day: 'Who's that boy keeps staring in at the door?' Are you looking for a job or something?

ALAN [*eagerly*]. Is there one?

JILL. I don't know. 55

ALAN. I can only do weekends.

JILL. That's when most people ride. We can always use extra hands. It'd mainly be mucking out.

ALAN. I don't mind. 60

JILL. Can you ride?

ALAN. No . . . No . . . I don't want to.

[*She looks at him curiously.*]

Please.

JILL. Come up on Saturday. I'll introduce you 65 to Mr Dalton.

[*She leaves the square.*]

DYSART. When was this? About a year ago?

ALAN. I suppose.

DYSART. And she did? 70

ALAN. Yes.

[*Briskly he moves the three benches to form three stalls in the stable.*]

16

[*Rich light falls on the square.*]

[*An exultant humming from the* CHORUS.] 75

[*Tramping is heard. Three actors playing horses rise from their places. Together they unhook three horse masks from the ladders to left and right, put them on with rigid timing, and walk with swaying horse-motion into the square. Their* 80 *metal hooves stamp on the wood. Their masks turn and toss high above their heads — as they will do sporadically throughout all horse scenes — making the steel gleam in the light.*]

[*For a moment they seem to converge on the* 85 *boy as he stands in the middle of the stable, but then they swiftly turn and take up positions as if tethered by the head, with their invisible rumps towards him, one by each bench.* ALAN *is sunk in this glowing world of horses. Lost in wonder,* 90 *he starts almost involuntarily to kneel on the floor in reverence — but is sharply interrupted by the cheery voice of* DALTON, *coming into the stable, followed by* JILL. *The boy straightens up guiltily.*]

DALTON. First thing to learn is drill. Learn it and keep to it. I want this place neat, dry and
5 clean at all times. After you've mucked out, Jill will show you some grooming. What we call strapping a horse.

JILL. I think Trooper's got a stone.

DALTON. Yes? Let's see.

10 [*He crosses to the horse by the left bench, who is balancing one hoof on its tip. He picks up the hoof.*]

You're right. [*to* ALAN.] See this? This V here. It's what's called a frog. Sort of shock-absorber.
15 Once you pierce that, it takes ages to heal—so you want to watch for it. You clean it out with this. What we call a hoof-pick.

[*He takes from his pocket an invisible pick.*]

Mind how you go with it. It's very sharp. Use
20 it like this.

[*He quickly takes the stone out.*]

See?

[ALAN *nods, fascinated.*]

You'll soon get the hang of it. Jill will look after
25 you. What she doesn't know about stables, isn't worth knowing.

JILL [*pleased*]. Oh yes, I'm sure!

DALTON [*handing Alan the pick*]. Careful how you go with that. The main rule is: anything
30 you don't know—ask. Never pretend you know something when you don't. [*smiling.*] Actually, the main rule is: enjoy yourself. All right?

ALAN. Yes, sir.

35 DALTON. Good lad. See you later.

[*He nods to them cheerfully, and leaves the square.* ALAN *clearly puts the invisible hoof-pick on the rail, downstage left.*]

JILL. All right, let's start on some grooming.
40 Why don't we begin with him? He looks as if he needs it.

[*They approach* NUGGET, *who is standing to the right. She pats him.* ALAN *sits and watches her.*]

45 This is Nugget. He's my favorite. He's as gentle as a baby, aren't you? But terribly fast if you want him to be.

[*During the following, she mimes both the*

actions and the objects, which she picks up from the right bench.]

50 Now this is the dandy, and we start with that. Then you move on to the body brush. This is the most important, and you use it with this curry-comb. Now you always groom the same way: from the ears downward. Don't be
55 afraid to do it hard. The harder you do it, the more the horse loves it. Push it right through the coat: like this.

[*The boy watches in fascination as she brushes the invisible body of* NUGGET, *scraping the dirt*
60 *and hair off on to the invisible curry-comb. Now and then the horse mask moves very slightly in pleasure.*]

Down towards the tail and right through the coat. See how he loves it? I'm giving you a
65 lovely massage, boy, aren't I? . . . You try.

[*She hands him the brush. Gingerly he rises and approaches* NUGGET. *Embarrassed and excited, he copies her movements, inexpertly.*]

Keep it nice and easy. Never rush. Down to-
70 wards the tail and right through the coat. That's it. Again. Down towards the tail and right through the coat. . . . Very good. Now you keep that up for fifteen minutes and then do old Trooper. Will you?
75 [ALAN *nods.*]

You've got a feel for it. I can tell. It's going to be nice teaching you. See you later.

[*She leaves the square and resumes her place.*]

[ALAN *is left alone with the horses.*]
80 [*They all stamp. He approaches* NUGGET *again, and touches the horse's shoulder. The mask turns sharply in his direction. The boy pauses, then moves his hand gently over the outline of the neck and back. The mask is re-assured. It stares*
85 *ahead unmoving. Then* ALAN *lifts his palm to his face and smells it deeply, closing his eyes.*]

[DYSART *rises from his bench, and begins to walk slowly upstage round the circle.*]

DYSART. Was that good? Touching them.
90 [ALAN *gives a faint groan.*]

ALAN. Mmm.

DYSART. It must have been marvelous, being near them at last . . . Stroking them . . . Making them fresh and glossy . . . Tell me . . .
95 [*Silence.* ALAN *begins to brush* NUGGET.]

How about the girl? Did you like her?

ALAN [*tight*]. All right.

DYSART. Just all right?

[ALAN *changes his position, moving round*
5 NUGGET'S *rump so that his back is to the audience.
He brushes harder.* DYSART *comes downstage
around the circle, and finally back to his bench.*]
Was she friendly?

ALAN. Yes.

10 DYSART. Or stand-offish?

ALAN. Yes.

DYSART. Well which?

ALAN. What?

DYSART. Which was she?

15 [ALAN *brushes harder.*]
Did you take her out? Come on now: tell me.
Did you have a date with her?

ALAN. What?

DYSART [*sitting*]. Tell me if you did.

20 [*The boy suddenly explodes in one of his rages.*]

ALAN [*yelling*]. TELL ME!

[*All the masks toss at the noise.*]

DYSART. What?

ALAN. *Tell me, tell me, tell me, tell me!*

25 [ALAN *storms out of the square, and downstage
to where* DYSART *sits. He is raging. During the
ensuing, the horses leave by all three openings.*]
On and on, sitting there! Nosey Parker!
That's all you are! Bloody Nosey Parker! Just
30 like Dad. On and on and bloody on! Tell me,
tell me, tell me! . . . Answer this. Answer that.
Never stop!—

[*He marches round the circle and back into the
square.* DYSART *rises and enters it from the other
35 side.*]

17

[*Lights brighten.*]

DYSART. I'm sorry.

[ALAN *slams about what is now the office
again, replacing the benches to their usual
40 position.*]

ALAN. All right, it's my turn now. You tell
me! Answer me!

DYSART. We're not playing that game now.

ALAN. We're playing what I say.

45 DYSART. All right. What do you want to
know?

[*He sits.*]

ALAN. Do *you* have dates?

DYSART. I told you. I'm married.

[ALAN *approaches him, very hostile.*] 50

ALAN. I know. Her name's Margaret. She's
a dentist! You see, I found out! What made
you go with her? Did you used to bite her
hands when she did you in the chair?

[*The boy sits next to him, close.*] 55

DYSART. That's not very funny.

ALAN. Do you have girls behind her back?

DYSART. No.

ALAN. Then what? Do you fuck her?

DYSART. That's enough now. 60

[*He rises and moves away.*]

ALAN. Come on, tell me! Tell me, tell me!

DYSART. I said that's enough now.

[ALAN *rises too and walks around him.*]
I bet you don't. I bet you never touch her. 65
Come on, tell me. You've got no kids, have
you? Is that because you don't fuck?

DYSART [*sharp*]. Go to your room. Go on:
quick march.

[*Pause.* ALAN *moves away from him, insolently* 70
takes up a packet of DYSART'S *cigarettes from the
bench, and extracts one.*]
Give me those cigarettes.

[*The boy puts one in his mouth.*]
[*exploding.*] Alan, give them to me! 75

[*Reluctantly* ALAN *shoves the cigarette back
in the packet, turns and hands it to him.*]
Now go!

[ALAN *bolts out of the square, and back to his
bed.* DYSART, *unnerved, addresses the audience.*] 80
Brilliant! Absolutely brilliant! The boy's on the
run, so he gets defensive. What am I, then? . . .
Wicked little bastard—he knew exactly what
questions to try. He'd actually marched himself round the hospital, making enquiries 85
about my wife. Wicked and—of course, per-
ceptive. Every since I made that crack about
carving up children, he's been aware of me in
an absolutely specific way. Of course, there's
nothing novel in that. Advanced neurotics 90
can be dazzling at that game. They aim un-
swervingly at your area of maximum vulnerability . . . Which I suppose is as good a way
as any of describing Margaret.

[*He sits.* HESTHER *enters the square.*]
[*Light grows warmer.*]

18

HESTHER. Now stop it.

DYSART. Do I embarrass you?

5   HESTHER. I suspect you're about to.
[*Pause.*]

DYSART. My wife doesn't understand me, Your Honour.

HESTHER. Do you understand her?

10   DYSART. No. Obviously I never did.

HESTHER. I'm sorry. I've never liked to ask but I've always imagined you weren't exactly compatible.
[*She moves to sit opposite.*]

15   DYSART. We were. It actually worked for a bit. I mean for both of us. We worked for each other, she actually for me through a kind of briskness. A clear, red-headed, inaccessible briskness which kept me keyed up for months.

20   Mind you, if you're kinky for Northern Hygenic,° as I am, you can't find anything much more compelling than a Scottish Lady Dentist.

HESTHER. It's *you* who are wicked, you know!

25   DYSART. Not at all: She got exactly the same from me. Antiseptic proficiency. I was like that in those days. We suited each other admirably. I see us in our wedding photo: Doctor and Doctor Mac Brisk. We were brisk in our

30   wooing, brisk in our wedding, brisk in our disappointment. We turned from each other briskly into our separate surgeries:° and now there's damn all.

HESTHER. You have no children, have you?

35   DYSART. No, we didn't go in for them. Instead, she sits beside our salmon-pink, glazed brick fireplace, and knits things for orphans in a home she helps with. And I sit opposite, turning the pages of art books on Ancient

40   Greece. Occasionally, I still trail a faint scent of my enthusiasm across her path. I pass her a picture of the sacred acrobats of Crete leaping

through the horns of running bulls — and she'll say: 'Och, Martin. what an *absurred* thing to be doing! The Highland Games, now there's 45 *norrmal sport!*' Or she'll observe, just after I've told her a story from the Iliad: 'You know, when you come to think of it, Agamemnon and that lot were nothing but a bunch of ruffians from the Gorbals,° only with fancy 50 names!' [*He rises*] You get the picture. She's turned into a Shrink. The familiar domestic monster. Margaret Dysart: the Shrink's Shrink.

HESTHER. That's cruel, Martin.

DYSART. Yes. Do you know what it's like for 55 two people to live in the same house as if they were in different parts of the world? Mentally, she's always in some drizzly kirk° of her own inheriting: and I'm in some Doric temple — clouds tearing through pillars — eagles bearing 60 prophecies out of the sky. She finds all that repulsive. All my wife has ever taken from the Mediterranean — from that whole vast intuitive culture — are four bottles of Chianti to make into lamps, and two china condiment donkeys 65 labelled Sally and Peppy.

[*Pause.*]
[*more intimately.*] I wish there was one person in my life I could show. One instinctive, absolutely unbrisk person I could take to Greece, 70 and stand in front of certain shrines and sacred streams and say 'Look! Life is only comprehensible through a thousand local Gods. And not just the old dead ones with names like Zeus — no, but living Geniuses° of Place and 75 Person! And not just Greece but modern England! Spirits of certain trees, certain curves of brick wall, certain chip shops, if you like, and slate roofs — just as of certain frowns in people and slouches . . . I'd say to them — 80 'Worship as many as you can see — and more will appear!' . . . If I had a son, I bet you he'd come out exactly like his mother. Utterly worshipless. Would you like a drink?

HESTHER. No, thanks. Actually, I've got to 85 be going. As usual . . .

Northern Hygenic anyone associated with Scottish health services
surgeries dental and medical offices

the Gorbals a proverbially rowdy district of Glasgow
kirk Scottish Presbyterian church
Geniuses presiding spirits or deities

DYSART. Really?

HESTHER. Really. I've got an Everest of papers to get through before bed.

DYSART. You never stop, do you?

5 HESTHER. Do you?

DYSART. This boy, with his stare. He's trying to save himself through me.

HESTHER. I'd say so.

DYSART. What am I trying to do to him?

10 HESTHER. Restore him, surely?

DYSART. To what?

HESTHER. A normal life.

DYSART. Normal?

HESTHER. It still means something.

15 DYSART. Does it?

HESTHER. Of course.

DYSART. You mean a normal boy has one head: a normal head has two ears?

HESTHER. You know I don't.

20 DYSART. Then what else?

HESTHER [*lightly*]. Oh, stop it.

DYSART. No, what? You tell me.

HESTHER [*rising: smiling*]. I won't be put on the stand like this, Martin. You're really dis-

25 graceful! . . . [*Pause*] You know what I mean by a normal smile in a child's eyes, and one that isn't—even if I can't exactly define it. Don't you?

DYSART. Yes.

30 HESTHER. Then we have a duty to that, surely? Both of us.

DYSART. Touché. . . . I'll talk to you.

HESTHER. Dismissed?

DYSART. You said you had to go.

35 HESTHER. I do . . . [*she kisses his cheek*]. Thank you for what you're doing. . . . You're going through a rotten patch at the moment. I'm sorry . . . I suppose one of the few things one can do is simply hold on to priorities.

40 DYSART. Like what?

HESTHER. Oh—children before grown-ups. Things like that.

[*He contemplates her.*]

DYSART. You're really quite splendid.

45 HESTHER. Famous for it. Goodnight.

[*She leaves him.*]

DYSART [*to himself—or to the audience*]. Normal! . . . Normal!

19

[ALAN *rises and enters the square. He is subdued.*] 50

DYSART. Good afternoon.

ALAN. Afternoon.

DYSART. I'm sorry about our row yesterday.

ALAN. It was stupid.

DYSART. It was. 55

ALAN. What I said, I mean.

DYSART. How are you sleeping?

[ALAN *shrugs.*]

You're not feeling well, are you?

ALAN. All right. 60

DYSART. Would you like to play a game? It could make you feel better.

ALAN. What kind?

DYSART. It's called *Blink*. You have to fix your eyes on something: say, that little stain 65 over there on the wall—and I tap this pen on the desk. The first time I tap it, you close your eyes. The next time you open them. And so on. Close, open, close, open, till I say Stop.

ALAN. How can that make you feel better? 70

DYSART. It relaxes you. You'll feel as though you're talking to me in your sleep.

ALAN. It's stupid.

DYSART. You don't have to do it, if you don't want to. 75

ALAN. I didn't say I didn't want to.

DYSART. Well?

ALAN. I don't mind.

DYSART. Good. Sit down and start watching that stain. Put your hands by your sides, and 80 open your fingers wide.

[*He opens the left bench and* ALAN *sits on the end of it.*]

The thing is to feel comfortable, and relax absolutely . . . Are you looking at the stain? 85

ALAN. Yes.

DYSART. Right. Now try and keep your mind as blank as possible.

ALAN. That's not difficult.

DYSART. Ssh. Stop talking . . . On the first 90 tap, close. On the second, open. Are you ready?

[ALAN *nods.* DYSART *taps his pen on the wooden rail.* ALAN *shuts his eyes.* DYSART *taps again.* ALAN *opens them. The taps are evenly spaced.*

After four of them the sound cuts out, and is
replaced by a louder, metallic sound, on tape.
DYSART *talks through this, to the audience — the*
light changes to cold — while the boy sits in front
5 *of him, staring at the wall, opening and shutting*
his eyes.]
The Normal is the good smile in a child's eyes
— all right. It is also the dead stare in a million
adults. It both sustains and kills — like a God.
10 It is the Ordinary made beautiful: it is also
the Average made lethal. The Normal is the
indispensable, murderous God of Health, and
I am his Priest. My tools are very delicate.
My compassion is honest. I have honestly
15 assisted children in this room. I have talked
away terrors and relieved many agonies. But
also — beyond question — I have cut from them
parts of individuality repugnant to this God,
in both his aspects. Parts sacred to rarer and
20 more wonderful Gods. And at what length . . .
Sacrifices to Zeus took at the most surely,
sixty seconds each. Sacrifices to the Normal
can take as long as sixty months.
[*The natural sound of the pencil resumes.*]
25 [*Light changes back.*]
[*to* ALAN] Now your eyes are feeling heavy.
You want to sleep, don't you? You want a long,
deep sleep. Have it. Your head is heavy. Very
heavy. Your shoulders are heavy. Sleep.
30 [*The pencil stops.* ALAN'S *eyes remain shut*
and his head has sunk on his chest.]
Can you hear me?
ALAN. Mmm.
DYSART. You can speak normally. Say Yes,
35 if you can.
ALAN. Yes.
DYSART. Good boy. Now raise your head,
and open your eyes.
[*He does so.*]
40 Now, Alan, you're going to answer questions
I'm going to ask you. Do you understand?
ALAN. Yes.
DYSART. And when you wake up, you are
going to remember everything you tell me.
45 All right?
ALAN. Yes.
DYSART. Good. Now I want you to think
back in time. You are on that beach you told
me about. The tide has gone out, and you're

making sandcastles. Above you, staring down 50
at you, is that great horse's head, and the cream
dropping from it. Can you see that?
ALAN. Yes.
DYSART. You ask him a question. 'Does the
chain hurt?' 55
ALAN. Yes.
DYSART. Do you ask him aloud?
ALAN. No.
DYSART. And what does the horse say back?
ALAN. 'Yes.' 60
DYSART. Then what do you say?
ALAN. 'I'll take it out for you.'
DYSART. And he says?
ALAN. 'It never comes out. They have me in
chains.' 65
DYSART. Like Jesus?
ALAN. Yes!
DYSART. Only his name isn't Jesus, is it?
ALAN. No.
DYSART. What is it? 70
ALAN. No one knows but him and me.
DYSART. You can tell me, Alan. Name him.
ALAN. Equus.
DYSART. Thank you. Does he live in all
horses or just some? 75
ALAN. All.
DYSART. Good boy. Now: you leave the
beach. You're in your bedroom at home.
You're twelve years old. You're in front of the
picture. You're looking at Equus from the foot 80
of your bed. Would you like to kneel down?
ALAN. Yes.
DYSART [*encouragingly*]. Go on, then.
[ALAN *kneels.*]
Now tell me. Why is Equus in chains? 85
ALAN. For the sins of the world.
DYSART. What does he say to you?
ALAN. 'I see you.' 'I will save you.'
DYSART. How?
ALAN. 'Bear you away. Two shall be one.' 90
DYSART. Horse and rider shall be one beast?
ALAN. One person!
DYSART. Go on.
ALAN. 'And my chinkle-chankle shall be in
thy hand.' 95
DYSART. Chinkle-chankle? That's his mouth
chain?
ALAN. Yes.

DYSART. Good. You can get up . . . Come on.
[ALAN *rises.*]
Now: think of the stable. What is the stable?
His Temple? His Holy of Holies?
5   ALAN. Yes.
DYSART. Where you wash him? Where you
tend him, and brush him with many brushes?
ALAN. Yes.
DYSART. And there he spoke to you, didn't
10   he? He looked at you with his gentle eyes,
and spake unto you?
ALAN. Yes.
DYSART. What did he say? 'Ride me? Mount
me, and ride me forth at night?'
15   ALAN. Yes.
DYSART. And you obeyed?
ALAN. Yes.
DYSART. How did you learn? By watching
others?
20   ALAN. Yes.
DYSART. It must have been difficult. You
bounced about?
ALAN. Yes.
DYSART. But he showed you, didn't he?
25   Equus showed you the way.
ALAN. No!
DYSART. He didn't?
ALAN. He showed me nothing! He's a mean
bugger! Ride—or fall! That's Straw Law.
30   DYSART. Straw Law?
ALAN. He was born in the straw, and this
is his law.
DYSART. But you managed? You mastered
him?
35   ALAN. Had to!
DYSART. And then you rode in secret?
ALAN. Yes.
DYSART. How often?
ALAN. Every three weeks. More, people
40   would notice.
DYSART. On a particular horse?
ALAN. No.
DYSART. How did you get into the stable?
ALAN. Stole a key. Had it copied at Bryson's.
45   DYSART. Clever boy.
[ALAN *smiles.*]
Then you'd slip out of the house?
ALAN. Midnight! On the stroke!
DYSART. How far's the stable?

ALAN. Two miles.   50
[*Pause.*]
DYSART. Let's do it! Let's go riding! . . .
Now!
[*He stands up, and pushes in his bench.*]
You are there now, in front of the stable door. 55
[ALAN *turns upstage.*]
That key's in your hand. Go and open it.

20

[ALAN *moves upstage, and mimes opening the
door.*]
[*Soft light on the circle.*]   60
[*Humming from the* CHORUS: *the Equus noise.*]
[*The horse actors enter, raise high their masks,
and put them on all together. They stand around
the circle—*NUGGET *in the mouth of the tunnel.*]
DYSART. Quietly as possible. Dalton may   65
still be awake. Sssh . . . Quietly . . . Good. Now
go in.
[ALAN *steps secretly out of the square through
the central opening on to the circle, now glowing
with a warm light. He looks about him. The horses 70
stamp uneasily: their masks turn towards him.*]
You are on the inside now. All the horses are
staring at you. Can you see them?
ALAN [*excited*]. Yes!
DYSART. Which one are you going to take? 75
ALAN. Nugget.
[ALAN *reaches up and mimes leading* NUGGET
*carefully round the circle downstage with a
rope, past all the horses on the right.*]
DYSART. What colour is Nugget?   80
ALAN. Chestnut.
[*The horse picks his way with care.* ALAN *halts
him at the corner of the square.*]
DYSART. What do you do, first thing?
ALAN. Put on his sandals.   85
DYSART. Sandals?
[*He kneels, downstage centre.*]
ALAN. Sandals of majesty! . . . Made of sack.
[*He picks up the invisible sandals, and kisses
them devoutly.*]   90
Tie them round his hooves.
[*He taps* NUGGET's *right leg: the horse raises
it and the boy mimes tying the sack round it.*]
DYSART. All four hooves?
ALAN. Yes.   95
DYSART. Then?

ALAN. Chinkle-chankle.

[*He mimes picking up the bridle and bit.*]

He doesn't like it so late, but he takes it for my sake. He bends for me. He stretches forth his neck to it.

[NUGGET *bends his head down.* ALAN *first ritually puts the bit into his own mouth, then crosses, and transfers it into* NUGGET'S. *He reaches up and buckles on the bridle. Then he leads him by the invisible reins, across the front of the stage and up round the left side of the circle.* NUGGET *follows obediently.*]

ALAN. Buckle and lead out.

DYSART. No saddle?

ALAN. Never.

DYSART. Go on.

ALAN. Walk down the path behind. He's quiet. Always is, this bit. Meek and mild legs. At least till the field. Then there's trouble.

[*The horse jerks back. The mask tosses.*]

DYSART. What kind?

ALAN. Won't go in.

DYSART. Why not?

ALAN. It's his place of Ha Ha.

DYSART. What?

ALAN. Ha Ha.

DYSART. Make him go into it.

ALAN [*whispering fiercely*]. Come on! . . . Come on! . . .

[*He drags the horse into the square as* DYSART *steps out of it.*]

21

[NUGGET *comes to a halt staring diagonally down what is now the field. The Equus noise dies away. The boy looks about him.*]

DYSART [*from the circle*]. Is it a big field?

ALAN. Huge!

DYSART. What's it like?

ALAN. Full of mist. Nettles on your feet.

[*He mimes taking off his shoes — and the sting.*]

Ah!

DYSART [*going back to his bench*]. You take your shoes off?

ALAN. Everything.

DYSART. All your clothes?

ALAN. Yes.

[*He mimes undressing completely in front of the horse. When he is finished, and obviously quite naked, he throws out his arms and shows himself fully to his God, bowing his head before* NUGGET.]

DYSART. Where do you leave them?

ALAN. Tree hole near the gate. No one could find them.

[*He walks upstage and crouches by the bench, stuffing the invisible clothes beneath it.* DYSART *sits again on the left bench, downstage beyond the circle.*]

DYSART. How does it feel now?

ALAN [*holds himself*]. Burns.

DYSART. Burns?

ALAN. The mist!

DYSART. Go on. Now what?

ALAN. The Manbit.

[*He reaches again under the bench and draws out an invisible stick.*]

DYSART. Manbit?

ALAN. The stick for my mouth.

DYSART. Your mouth?

ALAN. To bite on.

DYSART. Why? What for?

ALAN. So's it won't happen too quick.

DYSART. Is it always the same stick?

ALAN. Course. Sacred stick. Keep it in the hole. The Ark of the Manbit.

DYSART. And now what? . . . What do you do now?

[*Pause. He rises and approaches* NUGGET.]

ALAN. Touch him!

DYSART. Where?

ALAN [*in wonder*]. All over. Everywhere. Belly. Ribs. His ribs are of ivory. Of great value! . . . His flank is cool. His nostrils open for me. His eyes shine. They can see in the dark . . . *Eyes!* —

[*Suddenly he dashes in distress to the farthest corner of the square.*]

DYSART. *Go on!* . . . Then?

[*Pause.*]

ALAN. Give sugar.

DYSART. A lump of sugar?

[ALAN *returns to* NUGGET.]

ALAN. His Last Supper.

DYSART. Last before what?

ALAN. Ha Ha.

[*He kneels before the horse, palms upward and joined together.*]

DYSART. Do you say anything when you give it to him?

5 ALAN [*offering it*]. Take my sins. Eat them for my sake . . . He always does.

[NUGGET *bows the mask into* ALAN'S *palm, then takes a step back to eat.*]

And then he's ready.

10 DYSART. You can get up on him now?

ALAN. Yes!

DYSART. Do it, then. Mount him.

[ALAN, *lying before* NUGGET, *stretches out on the square. He grasps the top of the thin metal*

15 *pole embedded in the wood. He whispers his God's name ceremonially.*]

ALAN. Equus! . . . Equus! . . . Equus!

[*He pulls the pole upright. The actor playing* NUGGET *leans forward and grabs it. At the same*

20 *instant all the other horses lean forward around the circle, each placing a gloved hand on the rail.* ALAN *rises and walks right back to the upstage corner, left.*]

Take me!

25 [*He runs and jumps high on to* NUGGET'S *back.*] [*crying out*] Ah!

DYSART. What is it?

ALAN. Hurts!

DYSART. Hurts?

30 ALAN. Knives in his skin! Little knives—all inside my legs.

[NUGGET *mimes restiveness.*]

ALAN. Stay, Equus. No one said Go! . . . That's it. He's good. Equus the Godslave,

35 Faithful and True. Into my hands he commends himself—naked in his chinkle-chankle. [*he punches*] Stop it! . . . He wants to go so badly.

DYSART. Go, then. Leave me behind. Ride

40 away now, Alan. Now! . . . Now you are alone with Equus.

[ALAN *stiffens his body.*]

ALAN [*ritually*]. Equus—son of Fleckwus—son of Neckwus—*Walk.*

45 [*A hum from the* CHORUS.]

[*Very slowly the horses standing on the circle begin to turn the square by gently pushing the wooden rail.* ALAN *and his mount start to revolve.*

The effect, immediately, is of a statue being slowly turned round on a plinth. During the ride however 50 *the speed increases, and the light decreases until it is only a fierce spotlight on horse and rider, with the overspill glinting on the other masks leaning in towards them.*]

Here we go. The King rides out on Equus, 55 mightiest of horses. Only I can ride him. He lets me turn him this way and that. His neck comes out of my body. It lifts in the dark. Equus, my Godslave! . . . Now the King commands you. Tonight, we ride against them all. 60

DYSART. Who's all?

ALAN. My foes and His.

DYSART. Who are your foes?

ALAN. The Hosts of Hoover. The Hosts of Philco. The Hosts of Pifco. The House of 65 Remington and all its tribe!

DYSART. Who are His foes?

ALAN. The Hosts of Jodhpur. The Hosts of Bowler and Gymkhana. All those who show him off for their vanity. Tie rosettes on his 70 head for their vanity! Come on, Equus. Let's get them! . . . *Trot!*

[*The speed of the turning square increases.*]

Stead-y! Stead-y! Stead-y! Stead-y! Cowboys are watching! Take off their stetsons. They 75 know who we are. They're admiring us! Bowing low unto us! Come on now—show them! *Canter!* . . . CANTER!

[*He whips* NUGGET.]

And Equus the Mighty rose against All! 80 His enemies scatter, his enemies fall! TURN!

Trample them, trample them, Trample them, trample them, TURN! 85 TURN!! TURN!!!

[*The Equus noise increases in volume.*]

[*shouting*] WEE! . . . WAA! . . . WONDER- FUL! . . . 90

I'm stiff! Stiff in the wind! *My* mane, stiff in the wind! *My* flanks! *My* hooves! Mane on my legs, on my flanks, like whips! Raw! 95 Raw!

I'm raw! Raw!
Feel me on you! *On* you! *On* you! *On* you!
I want to be *in* you!
I want to BE you forever and ever! —
5 *Equus, I love you!*
Now! —
Bear me away!
Make us One Person!
[*He rides* EQUUS *frantically.*]
10 *One Person! One Person! One Person! One*
Person!
[*He rises up on the horse's back, and calls*
like a trumpet.]
Ha-HA! . . . Ha-HA! . . . Ha HA!
15 [*The trumpet turns to great cries.*]
HA-HA! HA-HA! HA-HA! HA-HA! HA! . . .
HA! . . . HAAAAA!
[*He twists like a flame.*]
[*Silence.*]
20 [*The turning square comes to a stop in the*
same position it occupied at the opening of the
Act.]
[*Slowly the boy drops off the horse's back on*
to the ground.]
25 [*He lowers his head and kisses* NUGGET'S
hoof.]
[*Finally he flings back his head and cries up*
to him:]
AMEN!
30 [NUGGET *snorts, once.*]

Blackout

ACT TWO

22

[*Darkness.*]
[*Lights come slowly up on* ALAN *kneeling in*
the night at the hooves of NUGGET. *Slowly he*
35 *gets up, climbing lovingly up the body of the*
horse until he can stand and kiss it. DYSART *sits*
on the downstage bench where he began Act
One.]
DYSART. With one particular horse, called
40 Nugget, he embraces. He showed me how he
stands with it afterwards in the night, one
hand on its chest, one on its neck, like a frozen
tango dancer, inhaling its cold sweet breath.

'Have you noticed,' he said, 'about horses:
how they'll stand one hoof on its end, like   45
those girls in the ballet?'
[ALAN *leads* NUGGET *out of the square.*
DYSART *rises. The horse walks away up the tunnel*
and disappears. The boy comes downstage and
sits on the bench DYSART *has vacated.* DYSART   50
crosses downstage and moves slowly up round
the circle, until he reaches the central entrance
to the square.]
Now he's gone off to rest, leaving me alone
with Equus. I can hear the creature's voice.   55
It's calling me out of the black cave of the
Psyche. I shove in my dim little torch, and
there he stands — waiting for me. He raises his
matted head. He opens his great square teeth,
and says — [*mocking*] 'Why? . . . Why Me? . . .   60
Why — ultimately — Me? . . . Do you really
imagine you can account for Me? Totally, in-
fallibly, inevitably account for Me? . . . Poor
Doctor Dysart!'
[*He enters the square.*]   65
Of course I've stared at such images before.
Or been stared at by them, whichever way you
look at it. And weirdly often now with me the
feeling is that *they* are staring at *us* — that in
some quite palpable way they precede us.   70
Meaningless, but unsettling . . . In either case,
this one is the most alarming yet. It asks
questions I've avoided all my professional
life. [*Pause*] A child is born into a world of
phenomena all equal in their power to enslave.   75
It sniffs — it sucks — it strokes its eyes over the
whole uncountable range. Suddenly one
strikes. Why? Moments snap together like
magnets, forging a chain of shackles. Why?
I can trace them. I can even, with time, pull   80
time apart again. But why at the start they were
ever magnetized at all — just those particular
moments of experience and no others — I don't
know. *And nor does anyone else.* Yet *if* I don't
know — if I can never know that — then what   85
am I doing here? I don't mean clinically doing
or socially doing — I mean *fundamentally!*
These questions, these Whys, are fundamental — yet they have no place in a consulting
room. So then, do I? . . . This is the feeling   90
more and more with me — No Place. Displace-

ment. . . . 'Account for me,' says staring Equus. 'First account for Me! . . .' I fancy this is more than menopause.

[NURSE *rushes in.*]

5 NURSE. Doctor! . . . Doctor! There's a terrible scene with the Strang boy. His mother came to visit him, and I gave her the tray to take in. He threw it at her. She's saying the most dreadful things.

10 [ALAN *springs up, down left.* DORA *springs up, down right. They face each other across the bottom end of the stage. It is observable that at the start of this Act* FRANK *is not sitting beside his wife on their bench. It is hopefully not ob-*
15 *servable that he is placed among the audience upstage, in the gloom, by the central tunnel.*]

DORA. Don't you dare! *Don't you dare!*

DYSART. Is she still there?

NURSE. Yes!

20 [*He quickly leaves the square, followed by the* NURSE. DORA *moves towards her son.*]

DORA. Don't you look at me like that! I'm not a doctor, you know, who'll take anything. Don't you dare give me that stare, young man!

25 [*She slaps his face.* DYSART *joins them.*]

DYSART. Mrs Strang!

DORA. I know your stares. They don't work on me!

DYSART [*to her*]. Leave this room.

30 DORA. What did you say?

DYSART. I tell you to leave here at once.

[DORA *hesitates. Then:*]

DORA. Goodbye, Alan.

[*She walks past her son, and round into the*
35 *square.* DYSART *follows her. Both are very upset.* ALAN *returns to his bench and* NURSE *to her place.*]

23

[*Lights up on the square.*]

DYSART. I must ask you never to come here
40 again.

DORA. Do you think I want to? Do you think I want to?

DYSART. Mrs Strang, what on earth has got into you? Can't you see the boy is highly dis-
45 tressed?

DORA [*ironic*]. Really?

DYSART. Of course! He's at a most delicate stage of treatment. He's totally exposed. Ashamed. Everything you can imagine!

DORA [*exploding*]. And me? What about me? 50 . . . *What do you think I am?* . . . I'm a parent, of course—so it doesn't count. That's a dirty word in here, isn't it, 'parent'?

DYSART. You know that's not true.

DORA. Oh, I know. I know, all right! I've 55 heard it all my life. It's *our* fault. Whatever happens, *we* did it. Alan's just a little victim. He's really done nothing at all! [*savagely*] What do you have to do in this world to get any sympathy—blind animals? 60

DYSART. Sit down, Mrs Strang.

DORA [*ignoring him: more and more urgently*]. Look, Doctor: you don't have to live with this. Alan is one patient to you: one out of many. He's my son. I lie awake every night thinking 65 about it. Frank lies there beside me. I can hear him. Neither of us sleeps all night. You come to us and say Who forbids television? who does what behind whose back?—as if we're criminals. Let me tell you something. We're 70 not criminals. We've done nothing wrong. We loved Alan. We gave him the best love we could. All right, we quarrel sometimes—all parents quarrel—we always make it up. My husband is a good man. He's an upright man, 75 religion or no religion. He cares for his home, for the world, and for his boy. Alan had love and care and treats, and as much fun as any boy in the world. I know about loveless homes: I was a teacher. Our home wasn't loveless. I 80 know about privacy too—not invading a child's privacy. All right, Frank may be at fault there—he digs into him too much—but nothing in excess. He's not a bully . . . [*gravely*] No, doctor. Whatever's happened has hap- 85 pened *because of Alan.* Alan is himself. Every soul is itself. If you added up everything we ever did to him, from his first day on earth to this, you wouldn't find why he did this terrible thing—because that's *him*: not just all of our 90 things added up. Do you understand what I'm saying? I want you to understand, because I lie awake and awake thinking it out, and I want you to know that I deny it absolutely

what he's doing now, staring at me, attacking me for what *he's* done, for what *he* is! [*pause: calmer*] You've got your words, and I've got mine. You call it a complex, I suppose. But if
5 you knew God, Doctor, you would know about the Devil. You'd know the Devil isn't made by what mummy says and daddy says. The Devil's *there*. It's an old-fashioned word, but a true thing . . . I'll go. What I did in there was
10 inexcusable. I only know he was my little Alan, and then the Devil came.

[*She leaves the square, and resumes her place. DYSART watches her go, then leaves himself by the opposite entrance, and approaches ALAN.*]

24

15 [*Seated on his bench, the boy glares at him.*]
DYSART. I thought you liked your mother.
[*Silence.*]
She doesn't know anything, you know. I haven't told her what you told me. You do
20 know that, don't you?
ALAN. It was lies anyway.
DYSART. What?
ALAN. You and your pencil. Just a con trick, that's all.
25 DYSART. What do you mean?
ALAN. Made me say a lot of lies.
DYSART. Did it? . . . Like what?
ALAN. All of it. Everything I said. Lot of lies.
[*Pause.*]
30 DYSART. I see.
ALAN. You ought to be locked up. Your bloody tricks.
DYSART. I thought you liked tricks.
ALAN. It'll be the drug next. I know.
35 [*DYSART turns, sharply.*]
DYSART. What drug?
ALAN. I've heard. I'm not ignorant. I know what you get up to in here. Shove needles in people, pump them full of truth drug, so they
40 can't help saying things. That's next, isn't it?
[*Pause.*]
DYSART. Alan, do you know why you're here?
ALAN. So you can give me truth drugs.
45 [*He glares at him.*]
[*DYSART leaves abruptly, and returns to the square.*]

25

[*HESTHER comes in simultaneously from the other side.*]
DYSART [*agitated*]. He actually thinks they 50 exist! And of course he wants one.
HESTHER. It doesn't sound like that to me.
DYSART. Of course he does. Why mention them otherwise? He wants a way to speak. To finally tell me what happened in that stable. 55 Tape's too isolated, and hypnosis is a trick. At least that's the pretence.
HESTHER. Does he still say that today?
DYSART. I haven't seen him. I cancelled his appointment this morning, and let him stew 60 in his own anxiety. Now I am almost tempted to play a real trick on him.
HESTHER [*sitting*]. Like what?
DYSART. The old placebo.
HESTHER. You mean a harmless pill? 65
DYSART. Full of *alleged* Truth Drug. Probably an aspirin.
HESTHER. But he'd deny it afterwards. Same thing all over.
DYSART. No. Because he's ready to abreact. 70
HESTHER. Abreact?
DYSART. Live it all again. He won't be able to deny it after that, because he'll have shown me. Not just told me—but acted it out in front of me. 75
HESTHER. Can you get him to do that?
DYSART. I think so. He's nearly done it already. Under all that glowering, he trusts me. Do you realise that?
HESTHER [*warmly*]. I'm sure he does. 80
DYSART. Poor bloody fool.
HESTHER. Don't start that again.
[*Pause.*]
DYSART [*quietly*]. Can you think of anything worse one can do to anybody than take away 85 their worship?
HESTHER. Worship?
DYSART. Yes, that word again!
HESTHER. Aren't you being a little extreme?
DYSART. Extremity's the point. 90
HESTHER. Worship isn't destructive, Martin. I know that.
DYSART. I don't. I only know it's the core of his life. What else has he got? Think about him.

He can hardly read. He knows no physics or engineering to make the world real for him. No paintings to show him how others have enjoyed it. No music except television jingles.
5 No history except tales from a desperate mother. No friends. Not one kid to give him a joke, or make him know himself more moderately. He's a modern citizen for whom society doesn't exist. He lives *one hour* every three
10 weeks — howling in a mist. And after the service kneels to a slave who stands over him obviously and unthrowably his master. With my body I thee worship!° . . . Many men have less vital relationships with their wives.

15 [*Pause.*]
HESTHER. All the same, they don't usually blind their wives, do they?
DYSART. Oh, come on!
HESTHER. Well, do they?
20 DYSART [*sarcastically*]. You mean he's dangerous? A violent, dangerous madman who's going to run round the country doing it again and again?
HESTHER. I mean he's in pain, Martin. He's
25 been in pain for most of his life. That much, at least, you *know*.
DYSART. Possibly.
HESTHER. *Possibly?* ! . . . That cut-off little figure you just described must have been in
30 pain for years.
DYSART [*doggedly*]. Possibly.
HESTHER. And you can take it away.
DYSART. Still — possibly.
HESTHER. Then that's enough. That simply
35 has to be enough for you, surely?
DYSART. No!
HESTHER. Why not?
DYSART. Because it's his.
HESTHER. I don't understand.
40 DYSART. His pain. His own. He made it.
[*Pause.*]
[*earnestly.*] Look . . . to go through life and call it yours — *your life* — you first have to get your own pain. Pain that's unique to you. You
45 can't just dip into the common bin and say 'That's enough!' . . . He's done that. All right,

he's sick. He's full of misery and fear. He was dangerous, and could be again, though I doubt it. But that boy has known a passion more ferocious than I have felt in any second of my 50 life. And let me tell you something: I envy it.
HESTHER. You can't.
DYSART [*vehemently*]. Don't you see? That's the Accusation! That's what his stare has been saying to me all the time. '*At least I galloped!* 55 *When did you?*' . . . [*simply*] I'm jealous, Hester. Jealous of Alan Strang.
HESTHER. That's absurd.
DYSART. Is it? . . . I go on about my wife. That smug woman by the fire. Have you 60 thought of the fellow on the other side of it? The finicky, critical husband looking through his art books on mythical Greece. What worship has *he* ever known? Real worship! Without worship you shrink, it's as brutal as that 65 . . . I shrank my *own* life. No one can do it for you. I settled for being pallid and provincial, out of my own eternal timidity. The old story of bluster, and do bugger-all° . . . I imply that we can't have children: but actually, it's only 70 me. I had myself tested behind her back. The lowest sperm count you could find. And I never told her. That's all I need — her sympathy mixed with resentment . . . I tell everyone Margaret's the puritan, I'm the pagan. Some 75 pagan! Such wild returns I make to the womb of civilization. Three weeks a year in the Peloponnese, every bed booked in advance, every meal paid for by vouchers, cautious jaunts in hired Fiats, suitcase crammed with 80 Kao-Pectate!° Such a fantastic surrender to the primitive. And I use that word endlessly: 'primitive'. 'Oh, the primitive world,' I say. 'What instinctual truths were lost with it!' And while I sit there, baiting a poor unimagi- 85 native woman with the word, that freaky boy tries to conjure the reality! I sit looking at pages of centaurs trampling the soil of Argos — and outside my window he is trying to *become one*, in a Hampshire° field! . . . I watch that woman 90

With my body, etc.   a phrase from the Church of England marriage-service

bugger-all   slang; "not a damn thing"
Kao-Pectate   brand name of a medicine for diarrhea
Hampshire   a southern county of England, where Winchester is located

knitting, night after night — a woman I haven't *kissed* in six years — and he stands in the dark for an hour, sucking the sweat off his God's hairy cheek! [*pause*] Then in the morning, I 5 put away my books on the cultural shelf, close up the kodachrome snaps of Mount Olympus, touch my reproduction statue of Dionysus for luck — and go off to hospital to treat him for insanity. Do you see?

10   HESTHER. The boy's in pain, Martin. That's all I see. In the end . . . I'm sorry.

    [*He looks at her. ALAN gets up from his bench and stealthily places an envelope in the left-hand entrance of the square, then goes back and sits 15 with his back to the audience, as if watching television.*]

    [*HESTHER rises.*]

    HESTHER. That stare of his. Have you thought it might not be accusing you at all?

20   DYSART. What then?

    HESTHER. Claiming you.

    DYSART. For what?

    HESTHER [*mischievously*]. A new God.

    [*Pause.*]

25   DYSART. Too conventional, for him. Finding a religion in Psychiatry is really for very ordinary patients.

    [*She laughs.*]

    HESTHER. Maybe he just wants a new Dad. 30 Or is that too conventional too? . . . Since you're questioning your profession anyway, perhaps you ought to try it and see.

    DYSART [*amused*]. I'll talk to you.

    HESTHER. Goodbye.

35   [*She smiles, and leaves him.*]

26

    [*DYSART becomes aware of the letter lying on the floor. He picks it up, opens and reads it.*]

    ALAN [*speaking stiffly, as DYSART reads*]. 'It is all true, what I said after you tapped the 40 pencil. I'm sorry if I said different. Post Scriptum: I know why I'm in here.'

    [*Pause.*]

    DYSART [*calling, joyfully*]. Nurse!

    [*NURSE comes in.*]

45   NURSE. Yes, Doctor?

    DYSART [*trying to conceal his pleasure*]. Good evening!

    NURSE. You're in late tonight.

    DYSART. Yes! . . . Tell me, is the Strang boy in bed yet?   50

    NURSE. Oh, no, Doctor. He's bound to be upstairs looking at television. He always watches to the last possible moment. He doesn't like going to his room at all.

    DYSART. You mean he's still having night- 55 mares?

    NURSE. He had a bad one last night.

    DYSART. Would you ask him to come down here, please?

    NURSE [*faint surprise*]. Now?   60

    DYSART. I'd like a word with him.

    NURSE [*puzzled*]. Very good, Doctor.

    DYSART. If he's not back in his room by lights out, tell Night Nurse not to worry. I'll see he gets back to bed all right. And would you 65 phone my home and tell my wife I may be in late?

    NURSE. Yes, Doctor.

    DYSART. Ask him to come straight away, please.   70

    [*NURSE goes to the bench, taps ALAN on the shoulder, whispers her message in his ear, and returns to her place. ALAN stands up and pauses for a second — then steps into the square.*]

27

    [*He stands in the doorway, depressed.*]   75

    DYSART. Hallo.

    ALAN. Hallo.

    DYSART. I got your letter. Thank you. [*pause*] Also the Post Scriptum.

    ALAN [*defensively*]. That's the right word. 80 My mum told me. It's Latin for 'After-writing'.

    DYSART. How are you feeling?

    ALAN. All right.

    DYSART. I'm sorry I didn't see you today.

    ALAN. You were fed up with me.   85

    DYSART. Yes. [*pause*] Can I make it up to you now?

    ALAN. What'd you mean?

    DYSART. I thought we'd have a session.

    ALAN [*startled*]. Now?   90

    DYSART. Yes! At dead of night! . . . Better

than going to sleep, isn't it?

[*The boy flinches.*]

Alan — look. Everything I say has a trick or a catch. Everything I do is a trick or a catch.
5 That's all I know to do. But they work — and you know that. Trust me.

[*Pause.*]

ALAN. You got another trick, then?

DYSART. Yes.
10 ALAN. A truth drug?

DYSART. If you like.

ALAN. What's it do?

DYSART. Make it easier for you to talk.

ALAN. Like you can't help yourself?
15 DYSART. That's right. Like you have to speak the truth at all costs. And all of it.

[*Pause.*]

ALAN [*slyly*]. Comes in a needle, doesn't it?

DYSART. No.
20 ALAN. Where is it?

DYSART [*indicating his pocket*]. In here.

ALAN. Let's see.

[DYSART *solemnly takes a bottle of pills out of his pocket.*]
25 DYSART. There.

ALAN [*suspicious*]. That really it?

DYSART. It is . . . Do you want to try it?

ALAN. No.

DYSART. I think you do.
30 ALAN. I don't. Not at all.

DYSART. Afterwards you'd sleep. You'd have no bad dreams all night. Probably many nights, from then on . . .

[*Pause.*]
35 ALAN. How long's it take to work?

DYSART. It's instant. Like coffee.

ALAN [*half believing*]. It isn't!

DYSART. I promise you . . . Well?

ALAN. Can I have a fag?
40 DYSART. Pill first. Do you want some water?

ALAN. No.

[DYSART *shakes one out on to his palm.* ALAN *hesitates for a second — then takes it and swallows it.*]
45 DYSART. Then you can chase it down with this. Sit down.

[*He offers him a cigarette, and lights it for him.*]

ALAN [*nervous*]. What happens now?

DYSART. We wait for it to work.   50

ALAN. What'll I feel first?

DYSART. Nothing much. After a minute, about a hundred green snakes should come out of that cupboard singing the Hallelujah Chorus.   55

ALAN [*annoyed*]. *I'm serious!*

DYSART [*earnestly*]. You'll feel nothing. Nothing's going to happen now but what you want to happen. You're not going to say anything to me but what you want to say. Just 60
relax. Lie back and finish your fag.

[ALAN *stares at him. Then accepts the situation, and lies back.*]

DYSART. Good boy.

ALAN. I bet this room's heard some funny 65
things.

DYSART. It certainly has.

ALAN. I like it.

DYSART. This room?

ALAN. Don't you?   70

DYSART. Well, there's not much to like, is there?

ALAN. How long am I going to be in here?

DYSART. It's hard to say. I quite see you want
to leave.   75

ALAN. No.

DYSART. You don't?

ALAN. Where would I go?

DYSART. Home. . . .

[*The boy looks at him.* DYSART *crosses and sits* 80
on the rail upstage, his feet on the bench. A pause.]

Actually, I'd like to leave this room and never see it again in my life.

ALAN [*surprise*]. Why?   85

DYSART. I've been in it too long.

ALAN. Where would you go?

DYSART. Somewhere.

ALAN. Secret?

DYSART. Yes. There's a sea — a great sea — I 90
love . . . It's where the Gods used to go to bathe.

ALAN. What Gods?

DYSART. The old ones. Before they died.

ALAN. Gods don't die.   95

DYSART. Yes, they do.

[*Pause.*]
There's a village I spent one night in, where I'd like to live. It's all white.

5   ALAN. How would you Nosey Parker, though? You wouldn't have a room for it any more.

   DYSART. I wouldn't mind. I don't actually enjoy being a Nosey Parker, you know.

   ALAN. Then why do it?

10   DYSART. Because you're unhappy.

   ALAN. So are you.

[DYSART *looks at him sharply.* ALAN *sits up in alarm.*]
Oooh, I didn't mean that!

15   DYSART. Didn't you?

   ALAN. Here—is that how it works? Things just slip out, not feeling anything?

   DYSART. That's right.

   ALAN. But it's so quick!

20   DYSART. I told you: it's instant.

   ALAN [*delighted*]. It's wicked, isn't it? I mean, you can say anything under it.

   DYSART. Yes.

   ALAN. Ask me a question.

25   DYSART. Tell me about Jill.

[*Pause. The boy turns away.*]

   ALAN. There's nothing to tell.

   DYSART. Nothing?

   ALAN. No.

30   DYSART. Well, for example—is she pretty? You've never described her.

   ALAN. She's all right.

   DYSART. What colour hair?

   ALAN. Dunno.

35   DYSART. Is it long or short?

   ALAN. Dunno.

   DYSART [*lightly*]. You must know that.

   ALAN. I don't remember. *I don't!*

[DYSART *rises and comes down to him. He*
40 *takes the cigarette out of his hand.*]

   DYSART [*firmly*]. Lie back . . . Now listen. You have to do this. And now. You are going to tell me everything that happened with this girl. Any not just *tell* me—*show* me. Act it
45 out, if you like—even more than you did when I tapped the pencil. I want you to feel free to do absolutely anything in this room. The pill will help you. I will help you . . . Now, where does she live?

[*A long pause.*]   50
   ALAN [*tight*]. Near the stables. About a mile.

[DYSART *steps down out of the square as* JILL *enters it. He sits again on the downstage bench.*]

28

[*The light grows warmer.*]
   JILL. It's called The China Pantry.   55

[*She comes down and sits casually on the rail. Her manner is open and lightly provocative. During these scenes* ALAN *acts directly with her, and never looks over at* DYSART *when he replies to him.*]   60
When Daddy disappeared, she was left without a bean. She had to earn her own living. I must say she did jolly well, considering she was never trained in business.

   DYSART. What do you mean, 'disappeared'?   65

   ALAN [*to* DYSART]. He ran off. No one ever saw him again.

   JILL. Just left a note on her dressing table saying 'Sorry. I've had it.' Just like that. She never got over it. It turned her right off men.   70
All my dates have to be sort of secret. I mean, she knows about them, but I can't ever bring anyone back home. She's so rude to them.

   ALAN [*to* DYSART]. She was always looking.

   DYSART. At you?   75

   ALAN [*to* DYSART]. Saying stupid things.

[*She jumps off the bench.*]

   JILL. You've got super eyes.

   ALAN [*to* DYSART]. Anyway, *she* was the one who had them.   80

[*She sits next to him. Embarrassed, the boy tries to move away as far as he can.*]

   JILL. There was an article in the paper last week saying what points about boys fascinate girls. They said Number One is bottoms. I   85
think it's eyes every time . . . They fascinate you too, don't they?

   ALAN. Me?

   JILL [*sly*]. Or is it only horses' eyes?

   ALAN [*startled*]. What'd you mean?   90

   JILL. I saw you staring into Nugget's eyes yesterday for ages. I spied on you through the door!

   ALAN [*hotly*]. There must have been something in it!   95

JILL. You're a real Man of Mystery, aren't you?

ALAN [*to* DYSART]. Sometimes, it was like she knew.

5 DYSART. Did you ever hint?

ALAN [*to* DYSART]. Course not!

JILL. I love horses' eyes. The way you can see yourself in them. D'you find them sexy?

ALAN [*outraged*]. What?!

10 JILL. Horses.

ALAN. Don't be daft!

[*He springs up, and away from her.*]

JILL. Girls do. I mean, they go through a period when they pat them and kiss them a lot.

15 I know *I* did. I suppose it's just a substitute, really.

ALAN [*to* DYSART]. That kind of thing, all the time. Until one night . . .

DYSART. Yes? What?

20 ALAN [*to* DYSART: *defensively*]. She did it! Not me. It was her idea, the whole thing! . . . She got me into it!

DYSART. What are you saying? 'One night': go on from there.

25 [*A pause.*]

ALAN [*to* DYSART]. Saturday night. We were just closing up.

JILL. How would you like to take me out?

ALAN. What?

30 JILL [*coolly*]. How would you like to take me out tonight?

ALAN. I've got to go home.

JILL. What for?

[*He tries to escape upstage.*]

35 ALAN. They expect me.

JILL. Ring up and say you're going out.

ALAN. I can't.

JILL. Why?

ALAN. They expect me.

40 JILL. Look. Either we go out together and have some fun, or you go back to your boring home, *as usual,* and I go back to mine. That's the situation, isn't it?

ALAN. Well . . . where would we go?

45 JILL. The pictures! There's a skinflick over in Winchester! I've never seen one, have you?

ALAN. No.

JILL. Wouldn't you like to? *I* would. All those heavy Swedes, panting at each other! . . .

What d'you say? 50

ALAN [*grinning*]. Yeh! . . .

JILL. Good! . . .

[*He turns away.*]

DYSART. Go on, please.

[*He steps off the square.*] 55

ALAN [*to* DYSART]. I'm tired now!

DYSART. Come on now. You can't stop there.

[*He storms round the circle to* DYSART, *and faces him directly.*]

ALAN. I'm *tired!* I want to go to bed! 60

DYSART [*sharply*]. Well, you can't. I want to hear about the film.

ALAN [*hostile*]. Hear what? . . . *What?* . . . It was bloody awful!

[*The actors playing horses come swiftly on to* 65 *the square, dressed in sports coats or raincoats. They move the benches to be parallel with the audience, and sit on them—staring out front.*]

DYSART. Why?

ALAN. Nosey Parker! 70

DYSART. *Why?*

ALAN. *Because!* . . . Well—we went into the Cinema!

29

[*A burst of Rock music, instantly fading down. Lights darken.*] 75

[ALAN *re-enters the square.* JILL *rises and together they grope their way to the downstage bench, as if in a dark auditorium.*]

ALAN [*to* DYSART]. The whole place was full of men. Jill was the only girl. 80

[*They push by a patron seated at the end, and sit side by side, staring up at the invisible screen, located above the heads of the main audience. A spotlight hits the boy's face.*]

We sat down and the film came on. It was daft. 85 Nothing happened for ages. There was this girl Brita, who was sixteen. She went to stay in this house, where there was an older boy. He kept giving her looks, but she ignored him completely. In the end she took a shower. She 90 went into the bathroom and took off all her clothes. The lot. Very slowly. . . . What she didn't know was the boy was looking through the door all the time. . . . [*he starts to become excited*] It was fantastic! The water fell on her 95 breasts, bouncing down her. . . .

[FRANK *steps into the square furtively from the back, hat in hand, and stands looking about for a place.*]

DYSART. Was that the first time you'd seen a girl naked?

ALAN [*to* DYSART]. Yes! You couldn't see everything, though. . . . [*looking about him*] All round me they were all looking. All the men—staring up like they were in church. Like they were a sort of congregation. And then—[*he sees his father*] Ah!

[*At the same instant* FRANK *sees him.*]

FRANK. Alan!

ALAN. God!

JILL. What is it?

ALAN. *Dad!*

JILL. *Where?*

ALAN. At the back! *He saw me!*

JILL. You sure?

ALAN. Yes!

FRANK [*calling*]. Alan!

ALAN. Oh God!

[*He tries to hide his face in the girl's shoulder. His father comes down the aisle towards him.*]

FRANK. Alan! You can hear me! Don't pretend!

PATRONS. Ssssh!

FRANK [*approaching the row of seats*]. Do I have to come and fetch you out? . . . Do I? . . .

[*Cries of 'Sssh!' and 'Shut up!'*]

Do I, Alan?

ALAN [*through gritted teeth*]. Oh fuck!

[*He gets up as the noise increases.* JILL *gets up too and follows him.*]

DYSART. You went?

ALAN [*to* DYSART]. What else could I do? He kept shouting. Everyone was saying Shut up!

[*They go out, right, through the group of Patrons—who rise protesting as they pass, quickly replace the benches and leave the square.*]

[DYSART *enters it.*]

30

[*Light brightens from the cinema, but remains cold: streets at night.*]

[*The three walk round the circle downstage in a line:* FRANK *leading, wearing his hat. He halts in the middle of the left rail, and stands staring straight ahead of him, rigid with embarrassment.*]

[ALAN *is very agitated.*]

ALAN [*to* DYSART]. We went into the street, all three of us. It was weird. We just stood there by the bus stop—like we were three people in a queue, and we didn't know each other. Dad was all white and sweaty. He didn't look at us at all. It must have gone on for about five minutes. I tried to speak. I said—[*to his father*] I—I—I've never been there before. Honest . . . Never . . . [*to* DYSART] He didn't seem to hear. Jill tried.

JILL. It's true, Mr Strang. It wasn't Alan's idea to go there. It was mine.

ALAN [*to* DYSART]. He just went on staring, straight ahead. It was awful.

JILL. I'm not shocked by films like that. I think they're just silly.

ALAN [*to* DYSART]. The bus wouldn't come. We just stood and stood. . . . Then suddenly he spoke.

[FRANK *takes off his hat.*]

FRANK [*stiffly*]. I'd like you to know something. Both of you. I came here tonight to see the Manager. He asked me to call on him for business purposes. I happen to be a printer, Miss. A picture house needs posters. That's entirely why I'm here. To discuss posters. While I was waiting I happened to glance in, that's all. I can only say I'm going to complain to the council. I had no idea they showed films like this. I'm certainly going to refuse my services.

JILL [*kindly*]. Yes, of course.

FRANK. So long as that's understood.

ALAN [*to* DYSART]. Then the bus came along.

FRANK. Come along now, Alan.

[*He moves away downstage.*]

ALAN. No.

FRANK [*turning*]. No fuss, please. Say Goodnight to the young lady.

ALAN [*timid but firm*]. No. I'm stopping here . . . I've got to see her home . . . It's proper.

[*Pause.*]

FRANK [*as dignified as possible*]. Very well. I'll see you when you choose to return. Very well then . . . Yes . . .

[*He walks back to his original seat, next to his wife. He stares across the square at his son — who stares back at him. Then, slowly, he sits.*]

ALAN [*to* DYSART]. And he got in, and we 5 didn't. He sat down and looked at me through the glass. And I saw . . .

DYSART [*soft*]. What?

ALAN [*to* DYSART]. His face. It was scared.

DYSART. Of you?

10 ALAN [*to* DYSART]. It was terrible. We had to walk home. Four miles. I got the shakes.

DYSART. You were scared too?

ALAN [*to* DYSART]. It was like a hole had been drilled in my tummy. A hole — right here. 15 And the air was getting in!

[*He starts to walk upstage, round the circle.*]

31

[*The girl stays still.*]

JILL [*aware of other people looking*]. Alan . . .

ALAN [*to* DYSART]. People kept turning 20 round in the street to look.

JILL. Alan!

ALAN [*to* DYSART]. I kept seeing him, just as he drove off. Scared of me. . . . And me scared of *him*. . . . I kept thinking — all those airs he 25 put on! . . . 'Receive my meaning. Improve your mind!' . . . All those nights he said he'd be in late. 'Keep my supper hot, Dora!' 'Your poor father: he works so hard!' . . . Bugger! Old bugger! . . . Filthy old bugger!

30 [*He stops, clenching his fists.*]

JILL. Hey! Wait for me!

[*She runs after him. He waits.*]

What are you thinking about?

ALAN. Nothing.

35 JILL. Mind my own beeswax?

[*She laughs.*]

ALAN [*to* DYSART]. And suddenly she began to laugh.

JILL. I'm sorry. But it's pretty funny, when 40 you think of it.

ALAN [*bewildered*]. What?

JILL. Catching him like that! I mean, it's terrible — but it's very funny.

ALAN. Yeh!

45 [*He turns from her.*]

JILL. No, wait! . . . I'm sorry. I know you're upset. But it's not the end of the world, is it? I mean, what was he doing? Only what we were. Watching a silly film. It's a case of like father like son, I'd say! . . . I mean, when that 50 girl was taking a shower, you were pretty interested, weren't you?

[*He turns round and looks at her.*]

We keep saying old people are square. Then when they suddenly aren't — we don't like it! 55

DYSART. What did you think about that?

ALAN [*to* DYSART]. I don't know. I kept looking at all the people in the street. They were mostly men coming out of pubs. I suddenly thought — *they all do it! All of them!* . . . 60 They're not just Dads — they're people with pricks! . . . And Dad — he's just not Dad either. He's a man with a prick too. You know, I'd never thought about it.

[*Pause.*] 65

We went into the country.

[*He walks again.* JILL *follows. They turn the corner and come downstage, right.*]

We kept walking. I just thought about Dad, and how he was nothing special — just a poor 70 old sod on his own.

[*He stops.*]

[*to* JILL: *realising it*] Poor old sod!

JILL. That's right!

ALAN [*grappling with it*]. I mean, what else 75 has he got? . . . He's got mum, of course, but well — she — she — she——

JILL. She doesn't give him anything?

ALAN. That's right. I bet you . . . She doesn't give him anything. That's right . . . That's 80 really right! . . . She likes Ladies and Gentlemen. Do you understand what I mean?

JILL [*mischievously*]. Ladies and gentlemen aren't naked?

ALAN. That's right! Never! . . . *Never!* That 85 would be disgusting! She'd have to put bowler hats on them! . . . Jodhpurs!

[JILL *laughs.*]

DYSART. Was that the first time you ever thought anything like that about your mother? 90 . . . I mean, that she was unfair to your dad?

ALAN [*to* DYSART]. Absolutely!

DYSART. How did you feel?

ALAN [*to* DYSART]. Sorry. I mean for him.

Poor old sod, that's what I felt—he's just like
me! He hates ladies and gents just like me!
Posh things—and la-di-da. He goes off by
himself at night, and does his own secret
5 thing which no one'll know about, just like
me! There's no difference—he's just the same
as me—just the same!—

[*He stops in distress, then bolts back a little
upstage.*]

10 Christ!

DYSART [*sternly*]. Go on.

ALAN [*to* DYSART]. I can't.

DYSART. Of course you can. You're doing
wonderfully.

15 ALAN [*to* DYSART]. No, please. *Don't make
me!*

DYSART [*firm*]. Don't think: just answer. You
were happy at that second, weren't you? When
you realised about your dad. How lots of
20 people have secrets, not just you?

ALAN [*to* DYSART]. Yes.

DYSART. You felt sort of free, didn't you? I
mean, free to do anything?

ALAN [*to* DYSART, *looking at* JILL]. Yes!

25 DYSART. What was she doing?

ALAN [*to* DYSART]. Holding my hand.

DYSART. And that was good?

ALAN [*to* DYSART]. Oh, yes!

DYSART. Remember what you thought. *As
30 if it's happening to you now. This very moment
. . .* What's in your head?

ALAN [*to* DYSART]. Her eyes. *She's* the one
with eyes! . . . I keep looking at them, because
I really want—

35 DYSART. To look at her breasts?

ALAN [*to* DYSART]. Yes.

DYSART. Like in the film.

ALAN [*to* DYSART]. Yes . . . Then she starts
to scratch my hand.

40 JILL. You're really very nice, you know that?

ALAN [*to* DYSART]. Moving her nails on the
back. Her face so warm. Her eyes.

DYSART. You want her very much?

ALAN [*to* DYSART]. Yes . . .

45 JILL. I love your eyes.

[*She kisses him.*]

[*whispering*] Let's go!

ALAN. Where?

JILL. I know a place. It's right near here.

ALAN. Where? 50

JILL. Surprise! . . . Come on!

[*She darts away round the circle, across the
stage and up the left side.*]

Come *on!*

ALAN [*to* DYSART]. She runs ahead. I follow. 55
And then—and then—!

[*He halts.*]

DYSART. What?

ALAN [*to* DYSART]. I see what she means.

DYSART. What? . . . Where are you? . . . 60
Where has she taken you?

ALAN [*to* JILL]. *The Stables?*

JILL. Of course!

32

[CHORUS *makes a warning hum.*]

[*The horse-actors enter, and ceremonially put* 65
*on their masks—first raising them high above
their heads.* NUGGET *stands in the central tunnel.*]

ALAN [*recoiling*]. No!

JILL. Where else? They're perfect!

ALAN. No! 70

[*He turns his head from her.*]

JILL. Or do you want to go home now and
face your dad?

ALAN. No!

JILL. Then come on! 75

[*He edges nervously past the horse standing at
the left, which turns its neck and even moves a
challenging step after him.*]

ALAN. Why not your place?

JILL. I can't. Mother doesn't like me bringing 80
back boys. I told you. . . . Anyway, the barn's
better.

ALAN. No!

JILL. All that straw. It's cosy.

ALAN. No. 85

JILL. *Why not?*

ALAN. Them!

JILL. Dalton will be in bed . . . What's the
matter? . . . Don't you want to?

ALAN [*aching to*]. Yes! 90

JILL. So?

ALAN [*desperate*]. Them! . . . Them! . . .

JILL. Who?

ALAN [*low*]. Horses.

JILL. *Horses?* . . . You're really dotty, aren't you? . . . What do you mean?

[*He starts shaking.*]

Oh, you're freezing . . . Let's get under the
5 straw. You'll be warm there.

ALAN [*pulling away*]. No!

JILL. What on earth's the matter with you? . . .

[*Silence. He won't look at her.*]

10 Look, if the sight of horses offends you, my lord, we can just shut the door. You won't have to see them. All right?

DYSART. What door is that? In the barn?

ALAN [*to* DYSART]. Yes.

15 DYSART. So what do you do? You go in?

ALAN [*to* DYSART]. Yes.

33

[*A rich light falls.*]

[*Furtively* ALAN *enters the square from the top end, and* JILL *follows. The horses on the circle*
20 *retire out of sight on either side.* NUGGET *retreats up the tunnel and stands where he can just be glimpsed in the dimness.*]

DYSART. Into the Temple? The Holy of Holies?

25 ALAN [*to* DYSART: *desperate*]. What else can I do? . . . I can't say! I can't tell her . . . [*to* JILL] Shut it tight.

JILL. All right . . . You're crazy!

ALAN. Lock it.

30 JILL. Lock?

ALAN. Yes.

JILL. It's just an old door. What's the matter with you? They're in their boxes. They can't get out . . . Are you all right?

35 ALAN. Why?

JILL. You look weird.

ALAN. *Lock it!*

JILL. Ssssh! D'you want to wake up Dalton? . . . Stay there, idiot.

40 [*She mimes locking a heavy door, upstage.*]

DYSART. Describe the barn, please.

ALAN [*walking round it: to* DYSART]. Large room. Straw everywhere. Some tools . . . [*as if picking it up off the rail where he left it in Act*
45 *One*] A hoof pick! . . .

[*He 'drops' it hastily, and dashes away from the spot.*]

DYSART. *Go on.*

ALAN [*to* DYSART]. At the end this big door. Behind it— 50

DYSART. Horses.

ALAN [*to* DYSART]. Yes.

DYSART. How many?

ALAN [*to* DYSART]. Six.

DYSART. Jill closes the door so you can't see 55
them?

ALAN [*to* DYSART]. Yes.

DYSART. And then? . . . What happens now? . . . Come on, Alan. Show me.

JILL. See, it's all shut. There's just us . . . 60
Let's sit down. Come on.

[*They sit together on the same bench, left.*]
Hallo.

ALAN [*quickly*]. Hallo.

[*She kisses him lightly. He responds. Suddenly* 65
a faint trampling of hooves, off-stage, makes him jump up.]

JILL. What is it?

[*He turns his head upstage, listening.*]
Relax. There's no one there. Come here. 70

[*She touches his hand. He turns to her again.*]
You're very gentle. I love that . . .

ALAN. So are you . . . I mean . . .

[*He kisses her spontaneously. The hooves trample again, harder. He breaks away from her* 75
abruptly towards the upstage corner.]

JILL [*rising*]. What is it?

ALAN. Nothing!

[*She moves towards him. He turns and moves past her. He is clearly distressed. She contem-* 80
plates him for a moment.]

JILL [*gently*]. Take your sweater off.

ALAN. What?

JILL. I will, if you will.

[*He stares at her. A pause.*] 85

[*She lifts her sweater over head: he watches—then unzips his. They each remove their shoes, their socks, and their jeans. Then they look at each other diagonally across the square, in which the light is gently increasing.*] 90

ALAN. You're . . . You're very . . .

JILL. So are you. . . . [*pause*] Come here.

[*He goes to her. She comes to him. They meet*

in the middle, and hold each other, and embrace.
ALAN [*to* DYSART]. She put her mouth in
mine. It was lovely! *Oh, it was lovely!*
[*They burst into giggles. He lays her gently on*
5 *the floor in the centre of the square, and bends*
over her eagerly. Suddenly the noise of Equus
fills the place. Hooves smash on wood. ALAN
straightens up, rigid. He stares straight ahead of
him over the prone body of the girl.]
10 DYSART. Yes, what happened then, Alan?
ALAN [*to* DYSART: *brutally*]. I put it in her!
DYSART. Yes?
ALAN [*to* DYSART]. I put it in her.
DYSART. You did?
15 ALAN [*to* DYSART]. Yes!
DYSART. Was it easy?
ALAN [*to* DYSART]. Yes.
DYSART. Describe it.
ALAN [*to* DYSART]. I told you.
20 DYSART. More exactly.
ALAN [*to* DYSART]. I put it in her!
DYSART. Did you?
ALAN [*to* DYSART]. All the way!
DYSART. Did you, Alan?
25 ALAN [*to* DYSART]. All the way. I shoved it.
I put it in her all the way.
DYSART. Did you?
ALAN [*to* DYSART]. Yes!
DYSART. Did you?
30 ALAN [*to* DYSART]. Yes! . . . Yes!
DYSART. Give me the TRUTH! . . . Did you?
. . . *Honestly?*
ALAN [*to* DYSART]. Fuck off!
[*He collapses, lying upstage on his face.* JILL
35 *lies on her back motionless, her head downstage,*
her arms extended behind her. A pause.]
DYSART [*gently*]. What was it? You couldn't?
Though you wanted to very much?
ALAN [*to* DYSART]. I couldn't . . . see her.
40 DYSART. What do you mean?
ALAN [*to* DYSART]. Only Him. Every time I
kissed her—*He* was in the way.
DYSART. Who?
[ALAN *turns on his back.*]
45 ALAN [*to* DYSART]. You *know* who! . . . When
I touched her, I felt *Him*. Under me . . . His
side, waiting for my hand . . . His flanks . . . I
refused him. I looked. I looked right at her . . .
and I couldn't do it. When I shut my eyes, I

saw him at once. The streaks on his belly . . . 50
[*with more desperation*] I couldn't feel *her*
flesh at all! I wanted the foam off his neck. His
sweaty hide. Not flesh. *Hide! Horse-hide!* . . .
Then I couldn't even kiss her.
[JILL *sits up.*] 55
JILL. What is it?
ALAN [*dodging her hand*]. No!
[*He scrambles up and crouches in the corner*
against the rails, like a little beast in a cage.]
JILL. Alan! 60
ALAN. Stop it!
[JILL *gets up.*]
JILL. It's all right . . . It's all right . . . Don't
worry about it. It often happens—honest. . . .
There's nothing wrong. I don't mind, you 65
know . . . I don't at all.
[*He dashes past her downstage.*]
Alan, look at me . . . Alan? . . . Alan!
[*He collapses again by the rail.*]
ALAN. Get out! . . . 70
JILL. What?
ALAN [*soft*]. Out!
JILL. There's nothing wrong: believe me! It's
very common.
ALAN. *Get out!* 75
[*He snatches up the invisible pick.*]
GET OUT!
JILL. Put that down!
ALAN. Leave me alone!
JILL. Put that down, Alan. It's very danger- 80
ous. Go on, please—drop it.
[*He 'drops' it, and turns from her.*]
ALAN. You ever tell anyone. Just you tell . . .
JILL. Who do you think I am? . . . I'm your
friend—Alan . . . 85
[*She goes towards him.*]
Listen: you don't have to do anything. Try to
realize that. Nothing at all. Why don't we just
lie here together in the straw. And talk.
ALAN [*low*]. Please . . . 90
JILL. Just talk.
ALAN. *Please!*
JILL. All right, I'm going . . . Let me put my
clothes on first.
[*She dresses, hastily.*] 95
ALAN. You tell anyone! . . . Just tell and
see. . . .
JILL. *Oh, stop it!* . . . I wish you could be-

lieve me. It's not in the least important.
[*Pause.*]
Anyway, I won't say anything. You know that.
You know I won't. . . .
5 [*Pause. He stands with his back to her.*]
Goodnight, then, Alan. . . . I wish—I really
wish—
[*He turns on her, hissing. His face is distorted—
possessed. In horrified alarm she turns—fumbles
10 the door open—leaves the barn—shuts the door
hard behind her, and dashes up the tunnel out of
sight, past the barely visible figure of* NUGGET.]

34

[ALAN *stands alone, and naked.*]
[*A faint humming and drumming. The boy
15 looks about him in growing terror.*]
DYSART. What?
ALAN [*to* DYSART]. He was there. Through
the door. The door was shut, but he was there!
. . . He'd seen everything. I could hear him.
20 He was laughing.
DYSART. Laughing?
ALAN [*to* DYSART]. Mocking! . . . *Mock-
ing!* . . .
[*Standing downstage he stares up towards the
25 tunnel. A great silence weighs on the square.*]
[*To the silence: terrified*] Friend . . . Equus the
Kind . . . The Merciful! . . . Forgive me! . . .
[*Silence.*]
It wasn't me. Not really me. Me! . . . Forgive
30 me! . . . Take me back again! Please! . . .
PLEASE!
[*He kneels on the downstage lip of the square,
still facing the door, huddling in fear.*]
I'll never do it again. I swear . . . I swear! . . .
35 [*Silence.*]
[*in a moan*] Please ! ! ! . . .
DYSART. And He? What does He say?
ALAN [*to* DYSART: *whispering*]. 'Mine! . . .
You're mine! . . . I am yours and you are mine!'
40 . . . Then I see his eyes. They are rolling!
[NUGGET *begins to advance slowly, with re-
lentless hooves, down the central tunnel.*]
'I see you. I see you. Always! Everywhere!
Forever!'
45 DYSART. Kiss anyone and I will see?
ALAN [*to* DYSART]. Yes!
DYSART. Lie with anyone and I will see?

ALAN [*to* DYSART]. Yes!
DYSART. And you will fail! Forever and ever
you will *fail*! You will see ME—and you will 50
FAIL!
[*The boy turns round, hugging himself in pain.
From the sides two more horses converge with*
NUGGET *on the rails. Their hooves stamp angrily.
The Equus noise is heard more terribly.*] 55
The Lord thy God is a Jealous God. He sees
you. He sees you forever and ever, Alan. He
sees you' . . . *He sees you!*
ALAN [*in terror*]. Eyes! . . . White eyes—never
closed! Eyes like flames—coming—coming! . . . 60
God seest! God seest! . . . NO! . . .
[*Pause. He steadies himself. The stage begins to
blacken.*]
[*quieter*] No more. No more, Equus.
[*He gets up. He goes to the bench. He takes* 65
*up the invisible pick. He moves slowly upstage
towards* NUGGET, *concealing the weapon behind
his naked back, in the growing darkness. He
stretches out his hand and fondles* NUGGET's
mask.] 70
[*gently*] Equus . . . Noble Equus . . . Faithful
and True . . . Godslave . . . Thou—God—Seest
—NOTHING!
[*He stabs out* NUGGET's *eyes. The horse stamps
in agony. A great screaming begins to fill the* 75
theatre, growing ever louder. ALAN *dashes at
the other two horses and blinds them too, stabbing
over the rails. Their metal hooves join in the
stamping.*]
[*Relentlessly, as this happens, three more* 80
*horses appear in cones of light: not naturalistic
animals like the first three, but dreadful creatures
out of nightmare. Their eyes flare—their nostrils
flare—their mouths flare. They are archetypal
images—judging, punishing, pitiless. They do* 85
*not halt at the rail, but invade the square. As
they trample at him, the boy leaps desperately at
them, jumping high and naked in the dark,
slashing at their heads with arms upraised. The
screams increase. The other horses follow into* 90
*the square. The whole place is filled with cannon-
ing, blinded horses—and the boy dodging among
them, avoiding their slashing hooves as best he
can. Finally they plunge off into darkness and
away out of sight. The noise dies abruptly, and all* 95
we hear is ALAN *yelling in hysteria as he col-*

lapses on the ground—stabbing at his own eyes with the invisible pick.]

ALAN. Find me! . . . Find me! . . . Find me! . . . KILL ME! . . . KILL ME! . . .

35

5 [*The light changes quickly back to brightness.*]

[DYSART *enters swiftly, hurls a blanket on the left bench, and rushes over to* ALAN. *The boy is having convulsions on the floor.* DYSART *grabs his hands, forces them from his eyes, scoops him*

10 *up in his arms and carries him over to the bench.* ALAN *hurls his arms round* DYSART *and clings to him, gasping and kicking his legs in dreadful frenzy.*]

[DYSART *lays him down and presses his head*

15 *back on the bench. He keeps talking—urgently talking—soothing the agony as he can.*]

DYSART. Here . . . Here . . . Sssssh . . . Sssssh . . . Calm now . . . Lie back. *Just lie back!* Now breathe in deep. Very deep. In . . . Out . . . In

20 . . . Out . . . That's it. . . . In. *Out . . . In . . . Out . . .*

[*The boy's breath is drawn into his body with a harsh rasping sound, which slowly grows less.* DYSART *puts the blanket over him.*]

25 Keep it going . . . That's a good boy . . . Very good boy . . . It's all over now, Alan. It's all over. He'll go away now. You'll never see him again, I promise. You'll have no more bad dreams. No more awful nights. Think of that!

30 . . . You are going to be well. I'm going to make you well, I promise you. . . . You'll be here for a while. but I'll be here too, so it won't be so bad. Just trust me . . .

[*He stands upright. The boy lies still.*]

35 Sleep now. Have a good long sleep. You've earned it . . . Sleep. Just sleep. . . . I'm going to make you well.

[*He steps backwards into the centre of the square. The light brightens some more.*]

40 [*A pause.*]

DYSART. I'm lying to you, Alan. He won't really go that easily. Just clop away from you like a nice old nag. Oh, no! When Equus leaves —if he leaves at all—it will be with your in-

45 testines in his teeth. And I don't stock replace-

ments . . . If you knew anything, you'd get up this minute and run from me fast as you could.

[HESTHER *speaks from her place.*]

HESTHER. The boy's in pain, Martin.

DYSART. Yes.   50

HESTHER. And you can take it away.

DYSART. Yes.

HESTHER. Then that has to be enough for you, surely? . . . In the end!

DYSART [*crying out*]. All right! I'll take it   55
away! He'll be delivered from madness. *What then?* He'll feel himself acceptable! *What then?* Do you think feelings like his can be simply re-attached, like plasters? Stuck on to other objects we select? *Look at him!* . . . My desire   60
might be to make this boy an ardent husband —a caring citizen—a worshipper of abstract and unifying God. My achievement, however, is more likely to make a ghost! . . . Let me tell you exactly what I'm going to do to him!   65

[*He steps out of the square and walks round the upstage end of it, storming at the audience.*]
I'll heal the rash on his body. I'll erase the welts cut into his mind by flying manes. When that's done, I'll set him on a nice mini-scooter and   70
send him puttering off into the Normal world where animals are treated *properly*: made extinct, or put into servitude, or tethered all their lives in dim light, just to feed it! I'll give him the good Normal world where we're   75
tethered beside them—blinking our nights away in a nonstop drench of cathode-ray over our shrivelling heads! I'll take away his Field of Ha Ha, and give him Normal places for his ecstasy—multi-lane highways driven through   80
the guts of cities, extinguishing Place alto-gether, *even the idea of Place!* He'll trot on his metal pony tamely through the concrete evening—and one thing I promise you: he will never touch hide again! With any luck his   85
private parts will come to feel as plastic to him as the products of the factory to which he will almost certainly be sent. Who knows? He may even come to find sex funny. Smirky funny. Bit of grunt funny. Trampled and furtive and   90
entirely in control. Hopefully, he'll feel nothing at his fork but Approved Flesh. *I doubt, how-ever, with much passion!* . . . Passion, you see,

can be destroyed by a doctor. It cannot be
created.

[*He addresses* ALAN *directly, in farewell.*]
You won't gallop any more, Alan. Horses will
5 be quite safe. You'll save your pennies every
week, till you can change that scooter in for a
car, and put the odd fifty p on the gee-gees,°
quite forgetting that they were ever anything
more to you than bearers of little profits and
10 little losses. You will, however, be without
pain. More or less completely without pain.

[*Pause.*]

[*He speaks directly to the theatre, standing by
the motionless body of* ALAN STRANG, *under the*
15 *blanket.*]
And now for me it never stops: that voice of
Equus out of the cave — 'Why Me? . . . Why
Me? . . . Account for Me!' . . . All right — I surrender! I say it . . . In an ultimate sense I can-
20 not know what I do in this place — yet I do
ultimate things. Essentially I cannot know
what I do — yet I do essential things. Irre-
versible, terminal things. I stand in the dark
with a pick in my hand, striking at heads!

25 [*He moves away from* ALAN, *back to the downstage bench, and finally sits.*]
I need — more desperately than my children
need me — a way of seeing in the dark. What
way is this? . . . *What dark is this?* . . . I cannot
30 call it ordained of God: I can't get that far. I
will however pay it so much homage. There
is now, in my mouth, this sharp chain. And
it never comes out.

[*A long pause.*]
35 [DYSART *sits staring.*]

Blackout

---

fifty p on the gee-gees a fifty-pence bet (about $1.00)
on the horses